Holy Bible

This Bible belongs to

_____

_____

_____

Date

_____

—The New—
POSSIBILITY
THINKERS
◇ BIBLE ◇

with

Introduction
Introduction to the Books of the Bible
"Stepping Stones on the Walk of Faith"

by

Paul David Dunn

Robert H. Schuller
Executive Editor

New King James Version

THOMAS NELSON PUBLISHERS
Nashville • Atlanta • London • Vancouver

When faced
with a mountain
I WILL NOT QUIT!
I will keep on striving
until I climb over,
find a pass through,
tunnel underneath—
or simply stay
and turn the mountain
into a gold mine,
with God's help!

Introduction

This is the day which the Lord has made;
We will rejoice and be glad in it (Ps. 118:24).

This is the day to be happy. For you hold in your hand today, God's special message to you! What could make the day happier than a message from your best friend? What greater gift could come to you today than a personal word from the God who created you and put you into this world? This is what you are holding in your hand—the Holy Bible! God's message to you.

How do you introduce the president of the United States to American citizens? How would you introduce the pope to Roman Catholic believers? How would you introduce the North Star to a group of astronomers?

If that would be difficult, then imagine how difficult it is to introduce the Holy Bible to Christian believers. I can only share my personal testimony.

I am immensely pleased and proud to present to you this copy of my favorite Book! It has been my guiding star, my central source of divine inspiration, since I was a little boy. Some children are blessed by being born into a privileged household. Such was my heritage. For no inheritance can match the value and the worth of the heritage of a godly faith in the Holy Book communicated through the life of a father and mother, who believe it and live by it. Every noon and every evening our family would gather around the humble kitchen table on our Iowa farm for a ritual that never varied. We would always pray with bowed heads before we ate the food. This was a prayer for God's blessing. After the food was enjoyed, my father would reach his hand underneath the table where a secret ledge held the family Bible. Then after an entire chapter

from the Scriptures was read, he would offer a closing prayer of thanksgiving to God, "for the food we have now received for the soul as well as the body." Without fail, this happened every noon and every night, seven days a week, throughout my entire childhood!

Through my many years I have heard what critics have said about the Sacred Scriptures. I am reminded, however, of the anvil on my father's farm. Dad would often take pieces of iron, making them red hot, and then he would lift them with tongs to the anvil, hammering and beating the red-hot pieces of steel until they were shaped to form the tool that he had in mind. The hammers wore out in time. The handles broke. The chunks of molten iron changed shape and moved on to find their proper place. But the anvil survived all the blows and all the years. Now as I reach the mature years of my life, I can testify that this Book, like a great old anvil, has survived thousands of years, and has served me better than I could ever have expected from any printed matter.

Yes, it is my favorite Book. I am convinced, beyond a shadow of doubt, that it is God's Book. That alone can explain why it never fails to nourish my faith. I believe in God because I have chosen this faith. I cannot prove that He is alive. If proof is possible, then faith is impossible. That is the way God wants it. He wants our relationship to be built on trust, not on scientific documentation. This is the only kind of interpersonal arrangement that allows for unalloyed affection. Yet, God is obligated to give us a solid basis for our faith. He is morally obligated to let us know that He is alive, what He expects from us, and what we can expect from Him. For conflict within interpersonal relationships is always a result of confused expectations, usually on the nonverbalized level. To clarify expectations in our relationship, God has written this Book. It is a witness to Him—His life, His work, His hopes, and His dreams! Yes, God is the supernatural possibility thinker! He has plans; He has dreams; He has hopes.

In this Book, we read the story of His dreams of creating a place of beauty called the universe, unlimited as far as we know! Here we encounter His dreams of creating persons who could have a mind capable of believing in a God that is invisible to the eye! Here we have the marvelous story of God creating a creature called the human being, who would share the divine qualities of creativity, imagination, and the ability to think of possibilities! We see in this Book, God's dream coming to its grand and glorious opening in the Garden of Eden. We read how the dream fell and was broken. We see how God never gives up! Through prophets and through the centuries He keeps reaching to redeem a dream! Finally, the Father sends His Son into this world in human flesh and gives Him the name Jesus. Here God fulfills His Holy obligation to draw the draperies, lift the curtains, put the lights on Himself, and expose His true self for all of us to behold. We look at Jesus—His life, His work, His death, His Easter resurrection. We know that indeed God is alive. Therefore, the Holy Bible is called the Sacred Scriptures; it is God's Word about Himself. And Christ is the Word incarnate!

The divine inspirational nature of the Bible becomes convincing when we remember that it is a collection of sixty-six books, written by as many as forty authors over a period of approximately sixteen hundred years, I have often been asked, "But how reliable is the text if it is such an ancient writing? It must have been copied and recopied so often through the centuries. Have not many errors crept in?" The most exciting report I can bring is the news that when the latest manuscripts are matched with the oldest manuscripts few discrepancies are reflected, and those are of an extremely minor nature that in no way affect the substance of religious belief. Therefore, the latest findings are a convincing and final justification of trusting the reliability and integrity of the printed message. We can say without risk of error that what is written in the Sacred Scriptures, that you hold in your hand right now, is without a doubt the authentic message that the authors intended to convey.

The enormous span of centuries gives us a beautiful illustration of how God has operated with the human family. Nothing in the Sacred Scripture would lead us to believe that God is impatient. On the contrary, His patience is profound. Slowly, gradually, with a patient progressiveness, He reveals Himself in this Holy Book.

First in the opening chapters, He reveals that He is the creative source of all life. The revelation of Himself is progressive as we move through the story of Abraham where God revealed Himself as an ethical being and a single God. We call this "ethical monotheism." A very remarkable and indistinctive religious concept in the history of religion. But with the founding of the Hebrew faith and its concept that God was one God and a good God, a religion was established that has set faith apart from the practicing of primitive religion that employed a variety of abominations (e.g. human sacrifice and temple prostitution) under the name and authority of religion. Now through Abraham and later through the Ten Commandments, that were given to Moses, God revealed to the human race on planet earth that He expected a high level of human morality. Glimpses into the nature of God, that were perceived by Abraham, Moses, and later by the prophets, revealed Him to be a just and merciful Father in heaven. The psalmists came to understand this, and in poetry the beauty of the Lord reaches crystal- and gem-like insights of flashing glory! Yet even the Old Testament prophets at their best and the psalmists in their most positive writings lack the true knowledge of what the true God is like. It remained for Christ to take on the human form through the Incarnation, walking among the human family.

"If there is a God, then He is morally obligated to reveal Himself in flesh and bones," was the challenging thought that came to me early in my ministry. The answer to that is Christ. He was and is the living appearance of the eternal God to the human flesh. In the Gospel of John He is called the Word. In Him we have the final revelation of what God is really like. Progressive revelation culminated in the character of the incarnated Jesus Christ! An understanding of how people responded to Him and found redemption in Him brings us into the New Testament Epistles. Finally, the Bible closes with the hope that one day life on planet earth will come to an end—and not when the sun runs out of gas, turning this planet earth into a frozen black ball, nor by some human catastrophic thermonuclear war which would destroy all human life. Instead this same God, who gave life to the creatures of the sea, the animals, the birds of the air, and finally His crowning glory—human being, will have His dream come true at last! In that final day, we shall all stand before Christ, the King of Kings and Lord of Lords.

So the Bible becomes a living Book! Not just a Book of dead history, but a Book alive with inspiring faith of the greatest heroes of the human family. For a start, you might want to read Hebrews chapter 11 which highlights faith, hope, and love, the central themes of Scripture. Approach the Sacred Scriptures to look for these coordinating themes—hope, faith, and love! See how God deals with human beings at their best and at their worst, at their sin and at their glory, and how God never gives up on the human race! The principles of possibility thinking are seen so clearly in how God deals with the human family. God simply does not accept ultimate defeat. He will not surrender to those negative emotions that human beings call depression and despair. After the flood, there came the rainbow. One can see a rainbow almost every day throughout the Holy Scriptures.

When you approach a well-decorated room, you will notice a single coordinated color that ties the entire decoration together. Observe the well-dressed man or woman and you will see that there is a central color that forms the unifying theme. Color the Bible with emotional colors of faith, hope, and love. Look for these themes recurring continually. They are the redemptive emotions. Avoid being trapped by the letter of the law. Be under the captured control of the compassionate, living Holy Spirit; breathe from the true stories found in these sacred pages. "The letter kills, but the Spirit gives life" (2 Cor. 3:6). Read it and you will find that God is at the opening of the Book; God is at the middle of it; and God will be at the end of it. God has the first word in Creation, and God will have the last word after human history has been fulfilled under the lordship of Christ.

So let this Book—my favorite Book, God's Book, the Living Book—become your Book! Find in it a picture of yourself. Here you will see a mirror of yourself, at your best, and you will praise God for creating you and for creating me. Here you will see a picture of yourself, at your worst, and you will not be depressed for you know that God loves you, even at your worst. You and I at our worst are still of a greater worth to the Lord than a mountain, a waterfall, or any bird. None of us are ever without some possibilities that can be developed under the miraculous touch of Jesus Christ our Savior!

So approach this Book and do not turn it into a textbook on science. Scientists can tell us much more about geology, genetics, or astronomy, than the Scriptures do. Do not make the mistake of trying to turn it into a chronological account of humanity on planet earth. Look for the deeper truths that transcend such shallow presumptions. The deeper truths are that God loves you—and we should love each other too! To help this living Book become your redeeming guide through life and into heaven, you will find in this special Possibility Thinkers Edition key verses highlighted for your inspiration. Commentary by my companion editor, Paul David Dunn, will help you to look for the positive thinking power that is contained in this—God's very special Book!

In the closing pages of this special edition, you will find some inspirational writings and special prayers that we trust will help you to become the great possibility thinker that God wants you to be. For what is possibility thinking? It is believing in God, then believing in ourselves, then believing in our fellow human beings, to the end that we might create God's kingdom on earth through the power of the Holy Spirit. What is God's kingdom? It is a collection of human beings, who can be redeemed from their sin, insecurity, and shame into a self-esteem instilled with the Holy Spirit. Result? We treat each other as a human family—a redeemed brotherhood and sisterhood!

Draw now from the power of the greatest Book ever written. You will come, through your own experience, to share my testimony that it is the Word of God given to us for our illumination and spiritual truth, showing us the path of salvation! Let your life become a living Bible!

Oh yes, we have retained the most classic of all English translations—the King James Version, with limited new revisions to carry the title the New King James Version. To all the women who read the Sacred Scriptures: We have left the male gender where the original text called for it. Please give yourself a special spiritual treat, substitute the word *woman* for *man* when you read these pages. Together we will feel that the Book was written just for ourselves.

Read the Scriptures the way you would solve a difficult problem. Work one part of it at a time. If there is a part of the problem that defies solution, leave it and come back to it later. The same way with the Sacred Scriptures. If there is a part of it that you find difficult to comprehend, grasp, understand, or accept, have the humility to assume that the truth is there, even if you cannot embrace it, keep reading, and let God continue to speak to you.

With that humble, faithful, believing, positive attitude, God's peace will surely fall upon you from these Holy pages.

Now, may the Lord bless you and keep you; the Lord make His face shine upon you, and be gracious to you; may God grant unto you His peace in your going out and in your coming in, in your lying down and in your rising up, in your labor and in your leisure, in your laughter and in your tears, until you come to stand before Jesus, in that day in which there is no sunset and no dawning. Amen.

Welcome

to *The New Possibility Thinkers Bible*

The first *Possibility Thinkers Bible* was published in 1984. Now, I am pleased to offer you the revised and expanded edition of that wonderful product. *The New Possibility Thinkers Bible* contains brand new maps, expanded book introductions, a thorough index, more than 1500 highlighted possibility verses, and two-color text—all in a fresh new design.

Throughout the Bible you will find "Stepping Stones on the Walk of Faith," a series of positive, inspirational articles that correspond to specific passages of scripture. In the back of the Bible we have included the popular article "The Greatest Possibility Thinker Who Ever Lived" and a section entitled "The Life of the Greatest Possibility Thinker." To help you build a positive prayer life, we have provided "Prayers for Positive Faith." For easy reference, you may use the "Positive Verses for Possibility Thinking" section, which will direct you to over 700 positive verses in a variety of categories.

The Holy Bible is my favorite Book and I believe this edition, *The New Possibility Thinkers Bible,* will be a special blessing to you.

Books of the Old and New Testaments and Their Abbreviations

The Old Testament

	ABBREV.	PAGE		ABBREV.	PAGE
Genesis	Gen.	1	Ecclesiastes	Eccl.	748
Exodus	Ex.	60	Song of Solomon	Song	764
Leviticus	Lev.	107	Isaiah	Is.	772
Numbers	Num.	140	Jeremiah	Jer.	855
Deuteronomy	Deut.	188	Lamentations	Lam.	928
Joshua	Josh.	228	Ezekiel	Ezek.	937
Judges	Judg.	260	Daniel	Dan.	997
Ruth	Ruth	292	Hosea	Hos.	1016
1 Samuel	1 Sam.	299	Joel	Joel	1030
2 Samuel	2 Sam.	341	Amos	Amos	1037
1 Kings	1 Kin.	373	Obadiah	Obad.	1048
2 Kings	2 Kin.	413	Jonah	Jon.	1051
1 Chronicles	1 Chr.	449	Micah	Mic.	1055
2 Chronicles	2 Chr.	481	Nahum	Nah.	1064
Ezra	Ezra	522	Habakkuk	Hab.	1069
Nehemiah	Neh.	535	Zephaniah	Zeph.	1075
Esther	Esth.	555	Haggai	Hag.	1082
Job	Job	565	Zechariah	Zech.	1085
Psalms	Ps.	606	Malachi	Mal.	1100
Proverbs	Prov.	709			

The New Testament

	ABBREV.	PAGE		ABBREV.	PAGE
Matthew	Matt.	1109	1 Timothy	1 Tim.	1429
Mark	Mark	1155	2 Timothy	2 Tim.	1435
Luke	Luke	1185	Titus	Titus	1439
John	John	1239	Philemon	Philem.	1444
Acts	Acts	1281	Hebrews	Heb.	1448
Romans	Rom.	1331	James	James	1463
1 Corinthians	1 Cor.	1353	1 Peter	1 Pet.	1470
2 Corinthians	2 Cor.	1372	2 Peter	2 Pet.	1478
Galatians	Gal.	1385	1 John	1 John	1484
Ephesians	Eph.	1393	2 John	2 John	1492
Philippians	Phil.	1403	3 John	3 John	1494
Colossians	Col.	1411	Jude	Jude	1497
1 Thessalonians	1 Thess.	1419	Revelation	Rev.	1500
2 Thessalonians	2 Thess.	1426			

Contents

Index to

Stepping Stones on the Walk of Faith

Index to

Maps

Preface

to
The New King James Version

Purpose

In the preface to the 1611 edition, the translators of the Authorized Version, known popularly as the King James Bible, state that it was not their purpose "to make a new translation . . . but to make a good one better." Indebted to the earlier work of William Tyndale and others, they saw their best contribution to consist in revising and enhancing the excellence of the English versions which had sprung from the Reformation of the sixteenth century. In harmony with the purpose of the King James scholars, the translators and editors of the present work have not pursued a goal of innovation. They have perceived the Holy Bible, New King James Version, as a continuation of the labors of the earlier translators, thus unlocking for today's readers the spiritual treasures found especially in the Authorized Version of the Holy Scriptures.

A Living Legacy

For nearly four hundred years, and throughout several revisions of its English form, the King James Bible has been deeply revered among the English-speaking peoples of the world. The precision of translation for which it is historically renowned, and its majesty of style, have enabled that monumental version of the Word of God to become the mainspring of the religion, language, and legal foundations of our civilization.

Although the Elizabethan period and our own era share in zeal for technical advance, the former period was more aggressively devoted to classical learning. Along with this awakened concern for the classics came a flourishing companion interest in the Scriptures, an interest that was enlivened by the conviction that the manuscripts were providentially handed down and were a trustworthy record of the inspired Word of God. The King James translators were committed to producing an English Bible that would be a precise translation, and by no means a paraphrase or a broadly approximate rendering. On the one hand, the scholars were almost as familiar with the original languages of the Bible as with their native English. On the other hand, their reverence for the divine Author and His Word assured a translation of the Scriptures in which only a principle of utmost accuracy could be accepted.

In 1786 Catholic scholar Alexander Geddes said of the King James Bible, "If accuracy and strictest attention to the letter of the text be supposed to constitute an excellent version, this is of all versions the most excellent." George Bernard Shaw became a literary legend in our century because of his severe and often humorous criticisms of our most cherished values. Surprisingly, however, Shaw pays the following tribute to the scholars commissioned by King James: "The translation was extraordinarily well done because to the translators what they were translating was not merely a curious collection of ancient books written by different authors in different stages of culture, but the Word of God divinely revealed through His chosen and expressly inspired scribes. In this conviction they carried out their work with boundless reverence and care and achieved a beautifully artistic result." History agrees with these estimates. Therefore, while seeking to unveil the excellent *form* of the traditional English Bible, special care has also been taken in the present edition to preserve the work of *precision* which is the legacy of the 1611 translators.

Complete Equivalence in Translation

Where new translation has been necessary in the New King James Version, the most complete representation of the original has been rendered by considering the history of usage and etymology of words in their contexts. This principle of complete equivalence seeks to preserve *all* of the information in the text, while presenting it in good literary form. Dynamic equivalence, a recent procedure in Bible translation, commonly results in paraphrasing where a more literal rendering is needed to reflect a specific and vital sense. For example, complete equivalence truly renders the original text in expressions such as "lifted her voice and wept" (Gen. 21:16); "I gave you cleanness of teeth" (Amos 4:6); "Jesus met them, saying, 'Rejoice!'" (Matt. 28:9); and "'Woman, what does your concern have to do with Me?'" (John 2:4). Complete equivalence translates fully, in order to provide an English text that is both accurate and readable.

In keeping with the principle of complete equivalence, it is the policy to translate interjections which are commonly omitted in modern language renderings of the Bible. As an example, the interjection *behold*, in the older King James editions, continues to have a place in English usage, especially in dramatically calling attention to a spectacular scene, or an event of profound importance such as the Immanuel prophecy of Isaiah 7:14. Consequently, *behold* is retained for these occasions in the present edition. However, the Hebrew and Greek originals for this word can be translated variously, depending on the circumstances in the passage. Therefore, in addition to *behold*, words such as *indeed, look, see,* and *surely* are also rendered to convey the appropriate sense suggested by the context in each case.

In faithfulness to God and to our readers, it was deemed appropriate that all participating scholars sign a statement affirming their belief in the verbal and plenary inspiration of Scripture, and in the inerrancy of the original autographs.

Devotional Quality

The King James scholars readily appreciated the intrinsic beauty of divine revelation. They accordingly disciplined their talents to render well-chosen English words of their time, as well as a graceful, often musical arrangement of language, which has stirred the hearts of Bible readers through the years. The translators, the committees, and the editors of the present edition, while sensitive to the late-twentieth-century English idiom, and while adhering faithfully to the Hebrew, Aramaic, and Greek texts, have sought to maintain those lyrical and devotional qualities that are so highly regarded in the Authorized Version. This devotional quality is especially apparent in the poetic and prophetic books, although even the relatively plain style of the Gospels and Epistles cannot strictly be likened, as sometimes suggested, to modern newspaper style. The Koine Greek of the New Testament is influenced by the Hebrew background of the writers, for whom even the Gospel narratives were not merely flat utterance, but often song in various degrees of rhythm.

The Style

Students of the Bible applaud the timeless devotional character of our historic Bible. Yet it is also universally understood that our language, like all living languages, has undergone profound change since 1611. Subsequent revisions of the King James Bible have sought to keep abreast of changes in English speech. The present work is a further step toward this objective. Where obsolescence and other reading difficulties exist, present-day vocabulary, punctuation, and grammar have been carefully integrated. Words representing ancient objects, such as *chariot* and *phylactery,* have no modern substitutes and are therefore retained.

A special feature of the New King James Version is its conformity to the thought flow of the 1611 Bible. The reader discovers that the sequence and selection of words, phrases, and clauses of the new edition, while much clearer, are so close to the traditional that there is remarkable ease in listening to the reading of either edition while following with the other.

In the discipline of translating biblical and other ancient languages, a standard method of transliteration, that is, the English spelling of untranslated words, such as names of persons and places, has never been commonly adopted. In keeping with the design of the present work, the King James spelling of untranslated words is retained, although made uniform throughout. For example, instead of the spellings *Isaiah* and *Elijah* in the Old Testament, and *Esaias* and *Elias* in the New Testament, *Isaiah* and *Elijah* now appear in both Testaments.

King James doctrinal and theological terms, for example, *propitiation, justification,* and *sanctification,* are generally familiar to English-speaking peoples. Such terms have been retained except where the original language indicates need for a more precise translation.

Readers of the Authorized Version will immediately be struck by the absence of several pronouns: *thee, thou,* and *ye* are replaced by the simple *you,* while *your* and *yours* are substituted for *thy* and *thine* as applicable. *Thee, thou, thy* and *thine* were once forms of address to express a special relationship to human as well as divine persons. These pronouns are no longer part of our language. However, reverence for God in the present work is preserved by capitalizing pronouns, including *You, Your,* and *Yours,* which refer to Him. Additionally, capitalization of these pronouns benefits the reader by clearly distinguishing divine and human persons referred to in a passage. Without such capitalization the distinction is often obscure, because the antecedent of a pronoun is not always clear in the English translation.

In addition to the pronoun usages of the seventeenth century, the *-eth* and *-est* verb endings, so familiar in the earlier King James editions, are now obsolete. Unless a speaker is schooled in these verb endings, there is common difficulty in selecting the correct form to be used with a given subject of the verb in vocal prayer. That is, should we use *love, loveth,* or *lovest? do, doeth, doest,* or *dost? have, hath,* or *hast?* Because these forms are obsolete, contemporary English usage has been substituted for the previous verb endings.

In older editions of the King James Version, the frequency of the connective *and* far exceeded the limits of present English usage. Also, biblical linguists agree that the Hebrew and Greek original words for this conjunction may commonly be translated otherwise, depending on the immediate context. Therefore, instead of *and,* alternatives such as *also, but, however, now, so, then,* and *thus* are accordingly rendered in the present edition, when the original language permits.

The real character of the Authorized Version does not reside in its archaic pronouns or verbs or other grammatical forms of the seventeenth century, but rather in the care taken by its scholars to impart the letter and spirit of the original text in a majestic and reverent style.

The Format

The format of the New King James Version is designed to enhance the vividness and devotional quality of the Holy Scriptures:

- Words or phrases in *italics* indicate expressions in the original language which require clarification by additional English words, as also done throughout the history of the King James Bible.
- *Oblique type* in the New Testament indicates a quotation from the Old Testament.
- Poetry is structured as contemporary verse to reflect the poetic form and beauty of the passage in the original language.
- The covenant name of God was usually translated from the Hebrew as "LORD" or "GOD" (using capital letters as shown) in the King James Old Testament. This tradition is maintained. In the present edition the name is so capitalized whenever the covenant name is quoted in the New Testament from a passage in the Old Testament.

The Old Testament Text

The Hebrew Bible has come down to us through the scrupulous care of ancient scribes who copied the original text in successive generations. By the sixth century A.D. the scribes were succeeded by a group known as the Masoretes, who continued to preserve the sacred Scriptures for another five hundred years in a form known as the Masoretic Text. Babylonia, Palestine, and Tiberias were the main centers of Masoretic activity; but by the tenth century A.D. the Masoretes of Tiberias, led by the family of ben Asher, gained the ascendancy. Through subsequent editions, the ben Asher text became in the twelfth century the only recognized form of the Hebrew Scriptures.

Daniel Bomberg printed the first Rabbinic Bible in 1516-17; that work was followed in 1524–25 by a second edition prepared by Jacob ben Chayyim and also published by Bomberg. The text of ben Chayyim was adopted in most subsequent Hebrew Bibles, including those used by the King James translators. The ben Chayyim text was also used for the first two editions of Rudolph Kittel's *Biblia Hebraica* of 1906 and 1912. In 1937 Paul Kahle published a third edition of *Biblia Hebraica*. This edition was based on the oldest dated manuscript of the ben Asher text, the Leningrad Manuscript B19a (A.D. 1008), which Kahle regarded as superior to that used by ben Chayyim.

For the New King James Version the text used was the 1967/1977 Stuttgart edition of the *Biblia Hebraica,* with frequent comparisons being made with the Bomberg edition of 1524–25. The Septuagint (Greek) Version of the Old Testament and the Latin Vulgate also were consulted. In addition to referring to a variety of ancient versions of the Hebrew Scriptures, the New King James Version draws on the resources of relevant manuscripts from the Dead Sea caves. In the few places where the Hebrew was so obscure that the 1611 King James was compelled to follow one of the versions, but where information is now available to resolve the problems, the New King James Version follows the Hebrew text. Significant variations are recorded in footnotes.

The New Testament Text

There is more manuscript support for the New Testament than for any other body of ancient literature. Over five thousand Greek, eight thousand Latin, and many more manuscripts in other languages attest the integrity of the New Testament. There is only one basic New Testament used by Protestants, Roman Catholics, and Orthodox, by conservatives and liberals. Minor variations in hand copying have appeared through the centuries, before mechanical printing began about A.D. 1450.

Some variations exist in the spelling of Greek words, in word order, and in similar details. These ordinarily do not show up in translation and do not affect the sense of the text in any way.

Other manuscript differences such as omission or inclusion of a word or a clause, and two paragraphs in the Gospels, should not overshadow the overwhelming degree of *agreement* which exists among the ancient records. Bible readers may be assured that the most important differences in English New Testaments of today are due, not to manuscript divergence, but to the way in which translators view the task of translation: How literally should the text be rendered? How does the translator view the matter of biblical inspiration? Does the translator adopt a paraphrase when a literal rendering would be quite clear and more to the point? The New King James Version follows the historic precedent of the Authorized Version in maintaining a literal approach to translation, except where the idiom of the original language cannot be translated directly into our tongue.

The King James New Testament was based on the traditional text of the Greek-speaking churches, first published in 1516, and later called the Textus Receptus or Received Text. Although based on the relatively few available manuscripts, these were representative of many more which existed at the time but only became known later. In the late nineteenth century, B. Westcott and F. Hort taught that this text had been officially edited by the fourth-century church, but a total lack of historical evidence for this event has forced a revision of the theory. It is now widely held that the Byzantine Text that largely supports the Textus Receptus has as much right as the Alexandrian or any other tradition to be weighed in determining the text of the New Testament. Those readings in the Textus Receptus which have weak support are indicated in the footnotes as being opposed by both Critical and Majority Texts (see "New King James Footnotes").

Since the 1880s most contemporary translations of the New Testament have relied upon a relatively few manuscripts discovered chiefly in the late nineteenth and early twentieth centuries. Such translations depend primarily on two manuscripts, Codex Vaticanus and Codex Sinaiticus, because of their greater age. The Greek text obtained by using these sources and the related papyri (our most ancient manuscripts) is known as the Alexandrian Text. However, some scholars have grounds for doubting the faithfulness of Vaticanus and Sinaiticus, since they often disagree with one another, and Sinaiticus exhibits excessive omission.

A third viewpoint of New Testament scholarship holds that the best text is based on the consensus of the majority of existing Greek manuscripts. This text is called the Majority Text. Most of these manuscripts are in substantial agreement. Even though many are late, and none is earlier than the fifth century, usually their readings are verified by papyri, ancient versions, quotations from the early church fathers, or a combination of these. The Majority Text is similar to the Textus Receptus, but it corrects those readings which have little or no support in the Greek manuscript tradition.

Preface

Today, scholars agree that the science of New Testament textual criticism is in a state of flux. Very few scholars still favor the Textus Receptus as such, and then often for its historical prestige as the text of Luther, Calvin, Tyndale, and the King James Version. For about a century most have followed a Critical Text (so called because it is edited according to specific principles of textual criticism) which depends heavily upon the Alexandrian type of text. Most recently many have abandoned this Critical Text (which is quite similar to the one edited by Westcott and Hort) for one that is more eclectic. Finally, a small but growing number of scholars prefer the Majority Text, which is close to the traditional text except in the Revelation.

In light of these facts, and also because the New King James Version is the fifth revision of a historic document translated from specific Greek texts, the editors decided to retain the traditional text in the body of the New Testament and to indicate major Critical and Majority Text variant readings in the footnotes. Although these variations are duly indicated in the footnotes of the present edition, it is most important to emphasize that fully eighty-five percent of the New Testament text is the same in the Textus Receptus, the Alexandrian Text, and the Majority Text.

Footnotes

Significant textual variations, explanatory notes, alternate translations, and cross-references, as well as New Testament citations of Old Testament passages, are supplied in footnotes.

Important textual variants in the Old Testament are identified in a standard form.

The textual notes in the present edition of the New Testament make no evaluation of readings, but do clearly indicate the manuscript sources of readings. They objectively present the facts without such tendentious remarks as "the best manuscripts omit" or "the most reliable manuscripts read." Such notes are value judgments that differ according to varying viewpoints on the text. By giving a clearly defined set of variants the New King James Version benefits readers of all textual persuasions.

Where significant variations occur in the New Testament Greek manuscripts, textual notes are classified as follows:

1. NU-Text

   These variations from the traditional text generally represent the Alexandrian or Egyptian type of text described previously in "The New Testament Text." They are found in the Critical Text published in the twenty-sixth edition of the Nestle-Aland Greek New Testament (N) and in the United Bible Societies' third edition (U), hence the acronym, "NU-Text."

2. M-Text

   This symbol indicates points of variation in the Majority Text from the traditional text, as also previously discussed in "The New Testament Text." It should be noted that M stands for whatever reading is printed in the first edition of *The Greek New Testament According to the Majority Text*, whether supported by overwhelming, strong, or only a divided majority textual tradition.

The textual notes reflect the scholarship of the past 150 years and will assist the reader to observe the variations between the different manuscript traditions of the New Testament. Such information is generally not available in English translations of the New Testament.

The
Old Testament

Genesis

Overview of Genesis

G enesis is the book of beginnings, of creation, and of an ideal man walking with God in a positive life-giving relationship and environment. God created the heavens and the earth out of absolutely nothing. As the Master Sculptor, He formed the land, carved out the mountains, filled the oceans, cast the first rays of light into the darkness, planted trees, launched the birds in flight, placed the clouds above, and lit the night sky with stars. Then as a crowning triumph, God formed man from the dust of the earth and breathed into him His life-giving spirit, making man in His own image. God gave man a woman to be his helpmate to share their lives together in His creation. God looked around at all He had done—and He pronounced it good!

And it was good—until man failed to trust God and did what was wrong in the eyes of the Lord. Man's position and relationship with God were changed. Man was no longer allowed in the garden. The image of God in man was marred, but not destroyed. You can bomb a cathedral, but it still remains a cathedral. Man can turn from God and sin, but intrinsically he still has within him the image of God to create, bear life, and do good.

Immediately, Genesis records a promise of restoration initiated by God toward man, the promise of a Savior to bring man back to his proper relationship with God. The all-powerful God who created the universe would not abandon His crowning glory. He was there with them when they fell and He promised to lift them up and to restore them to their original position, and even higher. This promise is continued throughout the lives of the patriarchs as recorded in Genesis. Abraham is assured that his generations will be blessed and will be a blessing. Out of this heritage will come the Son of God to redeem all peoples and to restore them to what God intended them to be.

The Book of Genesis tells us that we have intrinsic value and worth to God. We are created in His image. God has given us the creative powers, knowledge, and wisdom to do His will. Genesis reveals that the love of God is with us even in our failures. He has not abandoned us. We are God's project and God never fails! When we place our faith in God all things are possible!

Jesus in Genesis

Genesis moves from the general to the specific in its prophecy of the coming Messiah: Jesus is the Seed of the woman (3:15), from the line of Seth (4:25), the son of Shem (9:27), the descendant of Abraham (12:3), of Isaac (21:12), of Jacob (25:23), and of the tribe of Judah (49:10).

Genesis is a book full of types—Old Testament lessons that foreshadow New Testament realities. Adam, for example, was a type of Christ, "Him who was to come" (Rom. 5:14). Both men entered the world as sinless men through special acts of God. Adam is the head of the old creation. Christ is the Head of the new creation. Abel's acceptable blood offering points to the blood of Jesus later offered for the sin of all people. Melchizedek, the priest, foreshadows Jesus' ministry as our intercessor. Joseph is a type of Christ as the special son of his father, the one rejected and sold for silver, and a man who suffered greatly and then was exalted by God. As you read, look for other types of Christ in the Book of Genesis.

Keys to Genesis

Key Word: Beginnings. Genesis records the origins of almost everything, including the beginning of the universe, life, death, man, marriage, sin, relationships, culture, and redemption.

Key Verse: "And I will put enmity between you and the woman, and between your seed and her Seed; He shall bruise your head, and you shall bruise His heel" (3:15).

Key Chapter: Genesis 15. Central to all of Scripture is the Abrahamic Covenant, which is given in 12:1-3 and ratified in 15:1–21. This covenant gave Israel three specific promises: (1) the promise of a great land "from the river of Egypt to the great river, the River Euphrates" (15:18); (2) the promise of a great nation—"and I will make your descendants as the dust of the earth" (13:16); and (3) the promise of a great blessing—"I will bless you and make your name great; and you shall be a blessing" (12:2).

1 In the beginning God created the heavens and the earth. 2 The earth was without form, and void; and darkness *was*ª on the face of the deep. And the Spirit of God was hovering over the face of the waters.

3 Then God said, "Let there be light"; and there was light. 4 And God saw the light, that *it was* good; and God divided the light from the darkness. 5 God called the light Day, and the darkness He called Night. So the evening and the morning were the first day.

6 Then God said, "Let there be a firmament in the midst of the waters, and let it divide the waters from the waters." 7 Thus God made the firmament, and divided the waters which *were* under the firmament from the waters which *were* above the firmament; and it was so. 8 And God called the firmament Heaven. So the evening and the morning were the second day.

9 Then God said, "Let the waters under the heavens be gathered together into one place, and let the dry *land* appear"; and it was so. 10 And God called the dry *land* Earth, and the gathering together of the waters He called Seas. And God saw that *it was* good.

11 Then God said, "Let the earth bring forth grass, the herb *that* yields seed, *and* the fruit tree *that* yields fruit according to its kind, whose seed *is* in itself, on the earth"; and it was so. 12 And the earth brought forth grass, the herb *that* yields seed according to its kind, and the tree *that* yields fruit, whose seed *is* in itself according to its kind. And God saw that *it was* good. 13 So the evening and the morning were the third day.

14 Then God said, "Let there be lights in the firmament of the heavens to divide the day from the night; and let them be for signs and seasons, and for days and years; 15 and let them be for lights in the firmament of the heavens to give light on the earth"; and it was so. 16 Then God made two great lights:

the greater light to rule the day, and the lesser light to rule the night. *He made* the stars also. 17 God set them in the firmament of the heavens to give light on the earth, 18 and to rule over the day and over the night, and to divide the light from the darkness. And God saw that *it was* good. 19 So the evening and the morning were the fourth day.

20 Then God said, "Let the waters abound with an abundance of living creatures, and let birds fly above the earth across the face of the firmament of the heavens." 21 So God created great sea creatures and every living thing that moves, with which the waters abounded, according to their kind, and every winged bird according to its kind. And God saw that *it was* good. 22 And God blessed them, saying, "Be fruitful and multiply, and fill the waters in the seas, and let birds multiply on the earth." 23 So the evening and the morning were the fifth day.

24 Then God said, "Let the earth bring forth the living creature according to its kind: cattle and creeping thing and beast of the earth, *each* according to its kind"; and it was so. 25 And God made the beast of the earth according to its kind, cattle according to its kind, and everything that creeps on the earth according to its kind. And God saw that *it was* good.

26 Then God said, "Let Us make man in Our image, according to Our likeness; let them have dominion over the fish of the sea, over the birds of the air, and over the cattle, over allª the earth and over every creeping thing that creeps on the earth." 27 So God created man in His *own* image; in the image of God He created him; male and female He created them. 28 Then God blessed them, and God said to them, "Be fruitful and multiply; fill the earth and subdue it; have dominion over the fish of the sea, over the birds of the air, and over every living thing that moves on the earth."

29 And God said, "See, I have given

1:2 ªWords in italic type have been added for clarity. They are not found in the original Hebrew or Aramaic.   1:26 ªSyriac reads *all the wild animals of.*

Decide to Begin

Abraham obeyed God's call to pursue his inheritance (Heb. 11:8–10). Likewise, when God gives you a dream, you must prepare to act on it.

Faith is not daydreaming; it is obedience!

We exercise our faith when we make the toughest decision—the decision to get started.

Procrastination is an exercise of doubt. Postponing tough decisions is, more often than not, the result of a lack of faith.

God does not promise to bless us until we make a commitment to live and walk by faith.

We cannot expect God to bless our profession of faith until we stop doing nothing and start doing something.

> Determine to tackle your biggest enemy—inertia.
> Walk!
> Run!
> Talk!
> Write!
> Launch the project!
> Tell people what you are starting!

In all of these things, trust God to enable you to keep moving once you demonstrate enough faith to get going!

You will succeed, for just beginning is often the very hardest part!

you every herb *that* yields seed which *is* on the face of all the earth, and every tree whose fruit yields seed; to you it shall be for food. 30 Also, to every beast of the earth, to every bird of the air, and to everything that creeps on the earth, in which *there is* life, *I have given* every green herb for food"; and it was so. 31 Then God saw everything that He had made, and indeed *it was* very good. So the evening and the morning were the sixth day.

2 Thus the heavens and the earth, and all the host of them, were finished. 2 And on the seventh day God ended His work which He had done, and He rested on the seventh day from all His work which He had done. 3 Then God blessed the seventh day and sanctified it, because in it He rested from all His work which God had created and made.

4 This *is* the history^a of the heavens and the earth when they were created, in the day that the LORD God made the earth and the heavens, 5 before any plant of the field was in the earth and before any herb of the field had grown. For the LORD God had not caused it to rain on the earth, and *there was* no man to till the ground; 6 but a mist went up from the earth and watered the whole face of the ground.

7 And the LORD God formed man *of* the dust of the ground, and breathed into his nostrils the breath of life; and man became a living being.

8 The LORD God planted a garden eastward in Eden, and there He put the man whom He had formed. 9 And out of the ground the LORD God made every tree grow that is pleasant to the sight and good for food. The tree of life *was* also in the midst of the garden, and the tree of the knowledge of good and evil.

10 Now a river went out of Eden to water the garden, and from there it parted and became four riverheads. 11 The name of the first *is* Pishon; it *is* the one which skirts the whole land of Havilah, where *there is* gold. 12 And the gold of that land *is* good. Bdellium and the onyx stone *are* there. 13 The name of the second river *is* Gihon; it *is* the one which

goes around the whole land of Cush. 14 The name of the third river *is* Hiddekel;^a it *is* the one which goes toward the east of Assyria. The fourth river *is* the Euphrates.

15 Then the LORD God took the man and put him in the garden of Eden to tend and keep it. 16 And the LORD God commanded the man, saying, "Of every tree of the garden you may freely eat; 17 but of the tree of the knowledge of good and evil you shall not eat, for in the day that you eat of it you shall surely die."

18 And the LORD God said, "It is not good that man should be alone; I will make him a helper comparable to him." 19 Out of the ground the LORD God formed every beast of the field and every bird of the air, and brought *them* to Adam to see what he would call them. And whatever Adam called each living creature, that *was* its name. 20 So Adam gave names to all cattle, to the birds of the air, and to every beast of the field. But for Adam there was not found a helper comparable to him.

21 And the LORD God caused a deep sleep to fall on Adam, and he slept; and He took one of his ribs, and closed up the flesh in its place. 22 Then the rib which the LORD God had taken from man He made into a woman, and He brought her to the man.

23 And Adam said:

"This *is* now bone of my bones
And flesh of my flesh;
She shall be called Woman,
Because she was taken out of Man."

24 Therefore a man shall leave his father and mother and be joined to his wife, and they shall become one flesh. 25 And they were both naked, the man and his wife, and were not ashamed.

3 Now the serpent was more cunning than any beast of the field which the LORD God had made. And he said to the woman, "Has God indeed said, 'You shall not eat of every tree of the garden'?" 2 And the woman said to the ser-

The Garden of Eden

The Garden of Eden was the first home of Adam and Eve, the first man and woman (Gen. 2:4; 3:24). Eden is a translation of a Hebrew word which means "Delight," suggesting a "Garden of Delight." The garden contained many beautiful and fruitbearing trees, including the "tree of life" and the "tree of the knowledge of good and evil" (Gen. 2:9).

Identifying the exact location of the Garden of Eden is impossible. The text tells us it was planted "eastward in Eden" (Gen. 2:8). Since the writer was probably writing in Egypt or Palestine, "eastward" from that point would place the garden in the direction of Arabia or Mesopotamia. Two of the rivers issuing from the garden are known to us as the Tigris and Euphrates. The identities of the other two rivers named are unknown, though scholars have considered locations ranging from the Nile River in Africa to the Indus River in India.

pent, "We may eat the fruit of the trees of the garden; 3 but of the fruit of the tree which *is* in the midst of the garden, God has said, 'You shall not eat it, nor shall you touch it, lest you die.' "

4 Then the serpent said to the woman, "You will not surely die. 5 For God knows that in the day you eat of it your eyes will be opened, and you will be like God, knowing good and evil."

6 So when the woman saw that the tree *was* good for food, that it *was* pleasant to the eyes, and a tree desirable to make *one* wise, she took of its fruit and ate. She also gave to her husband with her, and he ate. 7 Then the eyes of both of them were opened, and they knew that they *were* naked; and they sewed fig leaves together and made themselves coverings.

8 And they heard the sound of the Lord God walking in the garden in the cool of the day, and Adam and his wife hid themselves from the presence of the Lord God among the trees of the garden. 9 Then the Lord God called to Adam and said to him, "Where *are* you?"

10 So he said, "I heard Your voice in the garden, and I was afraid because I was naked; and I hid myself."

11 And He said, "Who told you that you *were* naked? Have you eaten from the tree of which I commanded you that you should not eat?"

12 Then the man said, "The woman whom You gave *to be* with me, she gave me of the tree, and I ate."

13 And the Lord God said to the woman, "What *is* this you have done?"

The woman said, "The serpent deceived me, and I ate."

14 So the Lord God said to the serpent:

"Because you have done this,
   You *are* cursed more than all
     cattle,
   And more than every beast of
     the field;
On your belly you shall go,
   And you shall eat dust
   All the days of your life.
15 And I will put enmity
   Between you and the woman,
   And between your seed and her
     Seed;

   He shall bruise your head,
   And you shall bruise His heel."

16 To the woman He said:

"I will greatly multiply your
   sorrow and your conception;
In pain you shall bring forth
   children;
Your desire *shall be* for your
   husband,
And he shall rule over you."

17 Then to Adam He said, "Because you have heeded the voice of your wife, and have eaten from the tree of which I commanded you, saying, 'You shall not eat of it':

"Cursed *is* the ground for your
   sake;
In toil you shall eat *of* it
All the days of your life.
18 Both thorns and thistles it shall
   bring forth for you,
And you shall eat the herb of
   the field.
19 In the sweat of your face you
   shall eat bread
Till you return to the ground,
For out of it you were taken;
For dust you *are,*
And to dust you shall return."

20 And Adam called his wife's name Eve, because she was the mother of all living. 21 Also for Adam and his wife the Lord God made tunics of skin, and clothed them. 22 Then the Lord God said, "Behold, the man has become like one of Us, to know good and evil. And now, lest he put out his hand and take also of the tree of life, and eat, and live forever"— 23 therefore the Lord God sent him out of the garden of Eden to till the ground from which he was taken. 24 So He drove out the man; and He placed cherubim at the east of the garden of Eden, and a flaming sword which turned every way, to guard the way to the tree of life.

4 Now Adam knew Eve his wife, and she conceived and bore Cain, and said, "I have acquired a man from the Lord." 2 Then she bore again, this time his brother Abel. Now Abel was a keeper of sheep, but Cain was a tiller of the ground.

3 And in the process of time it came to pass that Cain brought an offering of the fruit of the ground to the LORD. 4 Abel also brought of the firstborn of his flock and of their fat. And the LORD respected Abel and his offering, 5 but He did not respect Cain and his offering. And Cain was very angry, and his countenance fell.

6 So the LORD said to Cain, "Why are you angry? And why has your countenance fallen? 7 If you do well, will you not be accepted? And if you do not do well, sin lies at the door. And its desire is for you, but you should rule over it."

8 Now Cain talked with Abel his brother;ᵃ and it came to pass, when they were in the field, that Cain rose up against Abel his brother and killed him.

9 Then the LORD said to Cain, "Where is Abel your brother?"

He said, "I do not know. Am I my brother's keeper?"

10 And He said, "What have you done? The voice of your brother's blood cries out to Me from the ground. 11 So now you are cursed from the earth, which has opened its mouth to receive your brother's blood from your hand. 12 When you till the ground, it shall no longer yield its strength to you. A fugitive and a vagabond you shall be on the earth."

13 And Cain said to the LORD, "My punishment is greater than I can bear! 14 Surely You have driven me out this day from the face of the ground; I shall be hidden from Your face; I shall be a fugitive and a vagabond on the earth, and it will happen that anyone who finds me will kill me."

15 And the LORD said to him, "Therefore,ᵃ whoever kills Cain, vengeance shall be taken on him sevenfold." And the LORD set a mark on Cain, lest anyone finding him should kill him.

16 Then Cain went out from the presence of the LORD and dwelt in the land of Nod on the east of Eden. 17 And Cain knew his wife, and she conceived and bore Enoch. And he built a city, and called the name of the city after the name of his son—Enoch. 18 To Enoch was born Irad; and Irad begot Mehujael, and Mehujael begot Methushael, and Methushael begot Lamech.

19 Then Lamech took for himself two wives: the name of one was Adah, and the name of the second was Zillah. 20 And Adah bore Jabal. He was the father of those who dwell in tents and have livestock. 21 His brother's name was Jubal. He was the father of all those who play the harp and flute. 22 And as for Zillah, she also bore Tubal-Cain, an instructor of every craftsman in bronze and iron. And the sister of Tubal-Cain was Naamah.

23 Then Lamech said to his wives:

"Adah and Zillah, hear my voice;
Wives of Lamech, listen to my speech!
For I have killed a man for wounding me,
Even a young man for hurting me.
24 If Cain shall be avenged sevenfold,
Then Lamech seventy-sevenfold."

25 And Adam knew his wife again, and she bore a son and named him Seth, "For God has appointed another seed for me instead of Abel, whom Cain killed." 26 And as for Seth, to him also a son was born; and he named him Enosh.ᵃ Then men began to call on the name of the LORD.

5 This is the book of the genealogy of Adam. In the day that God created man, He made him in the likeness of God. 2 He created them male and female, and blessed them and called them Mankind in the day they were created. 3 And Adam lived one hundred and thirty years, and begot a son in his own likeness, after his image, and named him Seth. 4 After he begot Seth, the days of Adam were eight hundred years; and he had sons and daughters. 5 So all the days that Adam lived were nine hundred and thirty years; and he died.

6 Seth lived one hundred and five years, and begot Enosh. 7 After he

4:8 ᵃSamaritan Pentateuch, Septuagint, Syriac, and Vulgate add "Let us go out to the field."
4:15 ᵃFollowing Masoretic Text and Targum; Septuagint, Syriac, and Vulgate read Not so.
4:26 ᵃGreek Enos

begot Enosh, Seth lived eight hundred and seven years, and had sons and daughters. 8 So all the days of Seth were nine hundred and twelve years; and he died.

9 Enosh lived ninety years, and begot Cainan.ᵃ 10 After he begot Cainan, Enosh lived eight hundred and fifteen years, and had sons and daughters. 11 So all the days of Enosh were nine hundred and five years; and he died.

12 Cainan lived seventy years, and begot Mahalalel. 13 After he begot Mahalalel, Cainan lived eight hundred and forty years, and had sons and daughters. 14 So all the days of Cainan were nine hundred and ten years; and he died.

15 Mahalalel lived sixty-five years, and begot Jared. 16 After he begot Jared, Mahalalel lived eight hundred and thirty years, and had sons and daughters. 17 So all the days of Mahalalel were eight hundred and ninety-five years; and he died.

18 Jared lived one hundred and sixty-two years, and begot Enoch. 19 After he begot Enoch, Jared lived eight hundred years, and had sons and daughters. 20 So all the days of Jared were nine hundred and sixty-two years; and he died.

21 Enoch lived sixty-five years, and begot Methuselah. 22 After he begot Methuselah, Enoch walked with God three hundred years, and had sons and daughters. 23 So all the days of Enoch were three hundred and sixty-five years. 24 And Enoch walked with God; and he was not, for God took him.

25 Methuselah lived one hundred and eighty-seven years, and begot Lamech. 26 After he begot Lamech, Methuselah lived seven hundred and eighty-two years, and had sons and daughters. 27 So all the days of Methuselah were nine hundred and sixty-nine years; and he died.

28 Lamech lived one hundred and eighty-two years, and had a son. 29 And he called his name Noah, saying, "This one will comfort us concerning our work and the toil of our hands, because of the ground which the LORD has cursed." 30 After he begot Noah, Lamech lived five hundred and ninety-five years, and had sons

and daughters. 31 So all the days of Lamech were seven hundred and seventy-seven years; and he died.

32 And Noah was five hundred years old, and Noah begot Shem, Ham, and Japheth.

6 Now it came to pass, when men began to multiply on the face of the earth, and daughters were born to them, 2 that the sons of God saw the daughters of men, that they were beautiful; and they took wives for themselves of all whom they chose.

3 And the LORD said, "My Spirit shall not striveᵃ with man forever, for he is indeed flesh; yet his days shall be one hundred and twenty years."

4 There were giants on the earth in those days, and also afterward, when the sons of God came in to the daughters of men and they bore children to them. Those were the mighty men who were of old, men of renown.

5 Then the LORDᵃ saw that the wickedness of man was great in the earth, and that every intent of the thoughts of his heart was only evil continually. 6 And the LORD was sorry that He had made man on the earth, and He was grieved in His heart. 7 So the LORD said, "I will destroy man whom I have created from the face of the earth, both man and beast, creeping thing and birds of the air, for I am sorry that I have made them." 8 But Noah found grace in the eyes of the LORD.

9 This is the genealogy of Noah. Noah was a just man, perfect in his generations. Noah walked with God. 10 And Noah begot three sons: Shem, Ham, and Japheth.

11 The earth also was corrupt before God, and the earth was filled with violence. 12 So God looked upon the earth, and indeed it was corrupt; for all flesh had corrupted their way on the earth.

13 And God said to Noah, "The end of all flesh has come before Me, for the earth is filled with violence through them; and behold, I will destroy them with the earth. 14 Make yourself an ark of gopherwood; make rooms in the ark, and cover it inside and outside with pitch. 15 And this is how you shall make it: The length of the ark shall be three

5:9 ᵃHebrew Qenan   6:3 ᵃSeptuagint, Syriac, Targum, and Vulgate read abide.   6:5 ᵃFollowing Masoretic Text and Targum; Vulgate reads God; Septuagint reads LORD God.

hundred cubits, its width fifty cubits, and its height thirty cubits. 16 You shall make a window for the ark, and you shall finish it to a cubit from above; and set the door of the ark in its side. You shall make it *with* lower, second, and third *decks.* 17 And behold, I Myself am bringing floodwaters on the earth, to destroy from under heaven all flesh in which *is* the breath of life; everything that *is* on the earth shall die. 18 But I will establish My covenant with you; and you shall go into the ark—you, your sons, your wife, and your sons' wives with you. 19 And of every living thing of all flesh you shall bring two of every *sort* into the ark, to keep *them* alive with you; they shall be male and female. 20 Of the birds after their kind, of animals after their kind, and of every creeping thing of the earth after its kind, two of every *kind* will come to you to keep *them* alive. 21 And you shall take for yourself of all food that is eaten, and you shall gather *it* to yourself; and it shall be food for you and for them."

22 Thus Noah did; according to all that God commanded him, so he did.

7 Then the LORD said to Noah, "Come into the ark, you and all your household, because I have seen *that* you *are* righteous before Me in this generation. 2 You shall take with you seven each of every clean animal, a male and his female; two each of animals that *are* unclean, a male and his female; 3 also seven each of birds of the air, male and female, to keep the species alive on the face of all the earth. 4 For after seven more days I will cause it to rain on the earth forty days and forty nights, and I will destroy from the face of the earth all living things that I have made." 5 And Noah did according to all that the LORD commanded him.
6 Noah *was* six hundred years old when the floodwaters were on the earth.

7 So Noah, with his sons, his wife, and his sons' wives, went into the ark because of the waters of the flood. 8 Of clean animals, of animals that *are* unclean, of birds, and of everything that creeps on the earth, 9 two by two they went into the ark to Noah, male and female, as God had commanded Noah. 10 And it came to pass after seven days that the waters of the flood were on the earth. 11 In the six hundredth year of Noah's life, in the second month, the seventeenth day of the month, on that day all the fountains of the great deep were broken up, and the windows of heaven were opened. 12 And the rain was on the earth forty days and forty nights.

13 On the very same day Noah and Noah's sons, Shem, Ham, and Japheth, and Noah's wife and the three wives of his sons with them, entered the ark— 14 they and every beast after its kind, all cattle after their kind, every creeping thing that creeps on the earth after its kind, and every bird after its kind, every bird of every sort. 15 And they went into the ark to Noah, two by two, of all flesh in which *is* the breath of life. 16 So those that entered, male and female of all flesh, went in as God had commanded him; and the LORD shut him in.

17 Now the flood was on the earth forty days. The waters increased and lifted up the ark, and it rose high above the earth. 18 The waters prevailed and greatly increased on the earth, and the ark moved about on the surface of the waters. 19 And the waters prevailed exceedingly on the earth, and all the high hills under the whole heaven were covered. 20 The waters prevailed fifteen cubits upward, and the mountains were covered. 21 And all flesh died that moved on the earth: birds and cattle and beasts and every creeping thing that creeps on the earth, and every man. 22 All in whose nostrils *was* the breath of the spirit*a* of life, all that *was* on the dry *land,* died. 23 So He destroyed all living things which were on the face of the ground: both man and cattle, creeping thing and bird of the air. They were destroyed from the earth. Only Noah and those who *were* with him in the ark remained *alive.* 24 And the waters prevailed on the earth one hundred and fifty days.

8 Then God remembered Noah, and every living thing, and all the animals that *were* with him in the ark. And God made a wind to pass over

---

7:22 *a*Septuagint and Vulgate omit *of the spirit.*

the earth, and the waters subsided. 2 The fountains of the deep and the windows of heaven were also stopped, and the rain from heaven was restrained. 3 And the waters receded continually from the earth. At the end of the hundred and fifty days the waters decreased. 4 Then the ark rested in the seventh month, the seventeenth day of the month, on the mountains of Ararat. 5 And the waters decreased continually until the tenth month. In the tenth *month,* on the first *day* of the month, the tops of the mountains were seen.

6 So it came to pass, at the end of forty days, that Noah opened the window of the ark which he had made. 7 Then he sent out a raven, which kept going to and fro until the waters had dried up from the earth. 8 He also sent out from himself a dove, to see if the waters had receded from the face of the ground. 9 But the dove found no resting place for the sole of her foot, and she returned into the ark to him, for the waters *were* on the face of the whole earth. So he put out his hand and took her, and drew her into the ark to himself. 10 And he waited yet another seven days, and again he sent the dove out from the ark. 11 Then the dove came to him in the evening, and behold, a freshly plucked olive leaf *was* in her mouth; and Noah knew that the waters had receded from the earth. 12 So he waited yet another seven days and sent out the dove, which did not return again to him anymore.

13 And it came to pass in the six hundred and first year, in the first *month,* the first *day* of the month, that the waters were dried up from the earth; and Noah removed the covering of the ark and looked, and indeed the surface of the ground was dry. 14 And in the second month, on the twenty-seventh day of the month, the earth was dried.

15 Then God spoke to Noah, saying, 16 "Go out of the ark, you and your wife, and your sons and your sons' wives with you. 17 Bring out with you every living thing of all flesh that *is* with you: birds and cattle and every creeping thing that creeps on the earth, so that they may abound on the earth, and be fruitful and multiply on the earth." 18 So Noah went out, and his sons and his wife and his sons' wives with him. 19 Every animal, every creeping thing, every bird, *and* whatever creeps on the earth, according to their families, went out of the ark.

20 Then Noah built an altar to the LORD, and took of every clean animal and of every clean bird, and offered burnt offerings on the altar. 21 And the LORD smelled a soothing aroma. Then the LORD said in His heart, "I will never again curse the ground for man's sake, although the imagination of man's heart *is* evil from his youth; nor will I again destroy every living thing as I have done.

22 "While the earth remains,
　　Seedtime and harvest,
　　Cold and heat,
　　Winter and summer,
　　And day and night
　　Shall not cease."

9 So God blessed Noah and his sons, and said to them: "Be fruitful and multiply, and fill the earth.[a] 2 And the fear of you and the dread of you shall be on every beast of the earth, on every bird of the air, on all that move *on* the earth, and on all the fish of the sea. They are given into your hand. 3 Every moving thing that lives shall be food for you. I have given you all things, even as the green herbs. 4 But you shall not eat flesh with its life, *that is,* its blood. 5 Surely for your lifeblood I will demand *a reckoning;* from the hand of every beast I will require it, and from the hand of man. From the hand of every man's brother I will require the life of man.

6 "Whoever sheds man's blood,
　　By man his blood shall be shed;
　　For in the image of God
　　He made man.
7 And as for you, be fruitful and multiply;
　　Bring forth abundantly in the earth
　　And multiply in it."

8 Then God spoke to Noah and to his sons with him, saying: 9 "And as for Me, behold, I establish My covenant with you and with your descen-

dants[a] after you, 10 and with every living creature that *is* with you: the birds, the cattle, and every beast of the earth with you, of all that go out of the ark, every beast of the earth. 11 Thus I establish My covenant with you: Never again shall all flesh be cut off by the waters of the flood; never again shall there be a flood to destroy the earth."

12 And God said: "This *is* the sign of the covenant which I make between Me and you, and every living creature that *is* with you, for perpetual generations: 13 I set My rainbow in the cloud, and it shall be for the sign of the covenant between Me and the earth. 14 It shall be, when I bring a cloud over the earth, that the rainbow shall be seen in the cloud; 15 and I will remember My covenant which *is* between Me and you and every living creature of all flesh; the waters shall never again become a flood to destroy all flesh. 16 The rainbow shall be in the cloud, and I will look on it to remember the everlasting covenant between God and every living creature of all flesh that *is* on the earth." 17 And God said to Noah, "This *is* the sign of the covenant which I have established between Me and all flesh that *is* on the earth."

18 Now the sons of Noah who went out of the ark were Shem, Ham, and Japheth. And Ham *was* the father of Canaan. 19 These three *were* the sons of Noah, and from these the whole earth was populated.

20 And Noah began *to be* a farmer, and he planted a vineyard. 21 Then he drank of the wine and was drunk, and became uncovered in his tent. 22 And Ham, the father of Canaan, saw the nakedness of his father, and told his two brothers outside. 23 But Shem and Japheth took a garment, laid *it* on both their shoulders, and went backward and covered the nakedness of their father. Their faces *were* turned away, and they did not see their father's nakedness.

24 So Noah awoke from his wine, and knew what his younger son had done to him. 25 Then he said:

"Cursed *be* Canaan;
   A servant of servants
   He shall be to his brethren."

26 And he said:

"Blessed *be* the LORD,
   The God of Shem,
   And may Canaan be his
      servant.
27   May God enlarge Japheth,
   And may he dwell in the tents
      of Shem;
   And may Canaan be his
      servant."

28 And Noah lived after the flood three hundred and fifty years. 29 So all the days of Noah were nine hundred and fifty years; and he died.

10 Now this *is* the genealogy of the sons of Noah: Shem, Ham, and Japheth. And sons were born to them after the flood.

2 The sons of Japheth *were* Gomer, Magog, Madai, Javan, Tubal, Meshech, and Tiras. 3 The sons of Gomer *were* Ashkenaz, Riphath,[a] and Togarmah. 4 The sons of Javan *were* Elishah, Tarshish, Kittim, and Dodanim.[a] 5 From these the coastland *peoples* of the Gentiles were separated into their lands, everyone according to his language, according to their families, into their nations.

6 The sons of Ham *were* Cush, Mizraim, Put,[a] and Canaan. 7 The sons of Cush *were* Seba, Havilah, Sabtah, Raamah, and Sabtechah; and the sons of Raamah *were* Sheba and Dedan.

8 Cush begot Nimrod; he began to be a mighty one on the earth. 9 He was a mighty hunter before the LORD; therefore it is said, "Like Nimrod the mighty hunter before the LORD." 10 And the beginning of his kingdom was Babel, Erech, Accad, and Calneh, in the land of Shinar. 11 From that land he went to Assyria and built Nineveh, Rehoboth Ir, Calah, 12 and Resen between Nineveh and Calah (that *is* the principal city).

13 Mizraim begot Ludim, Anamim, Lehabim, Naphtuhim, 14 Pathrusim, and Casluhim (from whom came the Philistines and Caphtorim).

15 Canaan begot Sidon his firstborn, and Heth; 16 the Jebusite, the Amorite, and the Girgashite; 17 the Hivite, the Arkite, and the Si-

9:9 [a]Literally *seed*   10:3 [a]Spelled *Diphath* in 1 Chronicles 1:6   10:4 [a]Spelled *Rodanim* in Samaritan Pentateuch and 1 Chronicles 1:7   10:6 [a]Or *Phut* nite; 18 the Arvadite, the Zemarite, and the Hamathite. Afterward the families of the Canaanites were dispersed. 19 And the border of the Canaanites was from Sidon as you go toward Gerar, as far as Gaza; then as you go toward Sodom, Gomorrah, Admah, and Zeboiim, as far as Lasha. 20 These *were* the sons of Ham, according to their families, according to their languages, in their lands *and* in their nations.

21 And *children* were born also to Shem, the father of all the children of Eber, the brother of Japheth the elder. 22 The sons of Shem *were* Elam, Asshur, Arphaxad, Lud, and Aram. 23 The sons of Aram *were* Uz, Hul, Gether, and Mash.*ᵃ* 24 Arphaxad begot Salah,*ᵃ* and Salah begot Eber. 25 To Eber were born two sons: the name of one *was* Peleg, for in his days the earth was divided; and his brother's name *was* Joktan. 26 Joktan begot Almodad, Sheleph, Hazarmaveth, Jerah, 27 Hadoram, Uzal, Diklah, 28 Obal,*ᵃ* Abimael, Sheba, 29 Ophir, Havilah, and Jobab. All these *were* the sons of Joktan. 30 And their dwelling place was from Mesha as you go toward Sephar, the mountain of the east. 31 These *were* the sons of Shem, according to their families, according to their languages, in their lands, according to their nations.

32 These *were* the families of the sons of Noah, according to their generations, in their nations; and from these the nations were divided on the earth after the flood.

11 Now the whole earth had one language and one speech. 2 And it came to pass, as they journeyed from the east, that they found a plain in the land of Shinar, and they dwelt there. 3 Then they said to one another, "Come, let us make bricks and bake *them* thoroughly." They had brick for stone, and they had asphalt for mortar. 4 And they said, "Come, let us build ourselves a city, and a tower whose top *is* in the heavens; let us make a name for ourselves, lest we be scattered abroad over the face of the whole earth."

5 But the LORD came down to see the city and the tower which the sons of men had built. 6 And the LORD said, "Indeed the people *are* one and they all have one language, and this is what they begin to do; now nothing that they propose to do will be withheld from them. 7 Come, let Us go down and there confuse their language, that they may not understand one another's speech." 8 So the LORD scattered them abroad from there over the face of all the earth, and they ceased building the city. 9 Therefore its name is called Babel, because there the LORD confused the language of all the earth; and from there the LORD scattered them abroad over the face of all the earth.

10 This *is* the genealogy of Shem: Shem *was* one hundred years old, and begot Arphaxad two years after the flood. 11 After he begot Arphaxad, Shem lived five hundred years, and begot sons and daughters.

12 Arphaxad lived thirty-five years, and begot Salah. 13 After he begot Salah, Arphaxad lived four hundred and three years, and begot sons and daughters.

14 Salah lived thirty years, and begot Eber. 15 After he begot Eber, Salah lived four hundred and three years, and begot sons and daughters.

16 Eber lived thirty-four years, and begot Peleg. 17 After he begot Peleg, Eber lived four hundred and thirty years, and begot sons and daughters.

18 Peleg lived thirty years, and begot Reu. 19 After he begot Reu, Peleg lived two hundred and nine years, and begot sons and daughters.

20 Reu lived thirty-two years, and begot Serug. 21 After he begot Serug, Reu lived two hundred and seven years, and begot sons and daughters.

22 Serug lived thirty years, and begot Nahor. 23 After he begot Nahor, Serug lived two hundred years, and begot sons and daughters.

24 Nahor lived twenty-nine years, and begot Terah. 25 After he begot Terah, Nahor lived one hundred and nineteen years, and begot sons and daughters.

26 Now Terah lived seventy years, and begot Abram, Nahor, and Haran.

27 This *is* the genealogy of Terah: Terah begot Abram, Nahor, and

---

10:23 *ᵃCalled Meshech in Septuagint and 1 Chronicles 1:17* 　　10:24 *ᵃFollowing Masoretic Text, Vulgate, and Targum; Septuagint reads Arphaxad begot Cainan, and Cainan begot Salah (compare Luke 3:35,36).* 　　10:28 *ᵃSpelled Ebal in 1 Chronicles 1:22*

Haran. Haran begot Lot. 28 And Haran died before his father Terah in his native land, in Ur of the Chaldeans. 29 Then Abram and Nahor took wives: the name of Abram's wife *was* Sarai, and the name of Nahor's wife, Milcah, the daughter of Haran the father of Milcah and the father of Iscah. 30 But Sarai was barren; she had no child.

31 And Terah took his son Abram and his grandson Lot, the son of Haran, and his daughter-in-law Sarai, his son Abram's wife, and they went out with them from Ur of the Chaldeans to go to the land of Canaan; and they came to Haran and dwelt there. 32 So the days of Terah were two hundred and five years, and Terah died in Haran.

12 Now the LORD had said to Abram:

    "Get out of your country,
    From your family
    And from your father's house,
    To a land that I will show you.
2   I will make you a great nation;
    I will bless you
    And make your name great;
    And you shall be a blessing.
3   I will bless those who bless you,
    And I will curse him who
       curses you;
    And in you all the families of
       the earth shall be blessed."

4 So Abram departed as the LORD had spoken to him, and Lot went with him. And Abram *was* seventy-five years old when he departed from Haran. 5 Then Abram took Sarai his wife and Lot his brother's son, and all their possessions that they had gathered, and the people whom they had acquired in Haran, and they departed to go to the land of Canaan. So they came to the land of Canaan. 6 Abram passed through the land to the place of Shechem, as far as the terebinth tree of Moreh.*a* And the Canaanites *were* then in the land.

7 Then the LORD appeared to Abram and said, "To your descendants I will give this land." And there he built an altar to the LORD, who had appeared to him. 8 And he moved from there to the mountain east of Bethel, and he pitched his tent *with*

Bethel on the west and Ai on the east; there he built an altar to the LORD and called on the name of the LORD. 9 So Abram journeyed, going on still toward the South.*a*

10 Now there was a famine in the land, and Abram went down to Egypt to dwell there, for the famine *was* severe in the land. 11 And it came to pass, when he was close to entering Egypt, that he said to Sarai his wife, "Indeed I know that you *are* a woman of beautiful countenance. 12 Therefore it will happen, when the Egyptians see you, that they will say, 'This *is* his wife'; and they will kill me, but they will let you live. 13 Please say you *are* my sister, that it may be well with me for your sake, and that I*a* may live because of you."

14 So it was, when Abram came into Egypt, that the Egyptians saw the woman, that she *was* very beautiful. 15 The princes of Pharaoh also saw her and commended her to Pharaoh. And the woman was taken to Pharaoh's house. 16 He treated Abram well for her sake. He had sheep, oxen, male donkeys, male and female servants, female donkeys, and camels.

17 But the LORD plagued Pharaoh and his house with great plagues because of Sarai, Abram's wife. 18 And Pharaoh called Abram and said, "What *is* this you have done to me? Why did you not tell me that she *was* your wife? 19 Why did you say, 'She *is* my sister'? I might have taken her as my wife. Now therefore, here is your wife; take *her* and go your way." 20 So Pharaoh commanded *his* men concerning him; and they sent him away, with his wife and all that he had.

13 Then Abram went up from Egypt, he and his wife and all that he had, and Lot with him, to the South.*a* 2 Abram *was* very rich in livestock, in silver, and in gold. 3 And he went on his journey from the South as far as Bethel, to the place where his tent had been at the beginning, between Bethel and Ai, 4 to the place of the altar which he had made there at first. And there Abram called on the name of the LORD.

5 Lot also, who went with Abram,

12:6 *a*Hebrew *Alon Moreh*   12:9 *a*Hebrew *Negev*   12:13 *a*Literally *my soul*   13:1 *a*Hebrew *Negev*

The Faith of Abraham

Abraham is a great example of possibility thinking faith. No other man has been called by God to attempt such a great task as to father a nation for Him.

Following God's call must not have been an easy task for Abraham. He was a well-to-do citizen of the thriving cosmopolitan city in ancient Mesopotamia, Ur of the Chaldees. Abraham, then called "Abram" or "exalted father," lived in a city whose religious worship focused on the moon god, Nannar. Temple prostitution and human sacrifice were accepted religious practices. From this environment, Abraham was called to venture out to an unknown land (see Heb. 11:8).

As Abraham and his family journeyed out in faith to pursue God's promises, they encountered the obstacles of war, family strife, impatience and fear. This could hardly have seemed like the "promised land."

Even at age one hundred, Abraham and his ninety-year-old wife, Sarah, were without the heir that God had promised (see Gen. 17:17). How could he be the "father of many nations"? But Abraham kept believing and as a sign of His covenant, God changed his name from "Abram" to "Abraham," meaning "father of many nations." And, as God had spoken, Isaac was born.

Abraham faced the greatest challenge to his faith when God tested him saying, "Take now your son, your only *son* Isaac, whom you love, and go to the land of Moriah, and offer him there as a burnt offering on one of the mountains of which I shall tell you" (Gen. 22:2).

Was God's covenant of no avail? Was He the same as the bloodthirsty false gods Abraham had left behind in Ur? Or could God raise Isaac from the dead? Genesis 22:9 explains how Abraham faithfully tied his son on the altar and raised the knife to complete the sacrifice. But God had a different plan. Seizing the hand of Abraham, the Angel of the Lord said to him, "Do not lay your hand on the lad, or do anything to him; for now I know that you fear God, since you have not withheld your son, your only *son* from Me" (Gen. 22:12). And God provided a ram, caught in a thicket, for the sacrifice.

Abraham's faith was not to go unrewarded. For his descendants became as many as the stars of heaven and as innumerable as the sands of the seashore (see Heb. 11:12).

Your life may not be as dramatic as Abraham's, but no matter where you are, God can use you to step out in faith and attempt something great for Him. When God gives you a dream, it may seem impossible. But if you have the faith of Abraham—nothing will be impossible for you!

had flocks and herds and tents. 6 Now the land was not able to support them, that they might dwell together, for their possessions were so great that they could not dwell together. 7 And there was strife between the herdsmen of Abram's livestock and the herdsmen of Lot's livestock. The Canaanites and the Perizzites then dwelt in the land.

8 So Abram said to Lot, "Please let there be no strife between you and me, and between my herdsmen and your herdsmen; for we *are* brethren. 9 *Is* not the whole land before you? Please separate from me. If *you take* the left, then I will go to the right; or, if *you go* to the right, then I will go to the left."

10 And Lot lifted his eyes and saw all the plain of Jordan, that it *was* well watered everywhere (before the LORD destroyed Sodom and Gomorrah) like the garden of the LORD, like the land of Egypt as you go toward Zoar. 11 Then Lot chose for himself all the plain of Jordan, and Lot journeyed east. And they separated from each other. 12 Abram dwelt in the land of Canaan, and Lot dwelt in the cities of the plain and pitched *his* tent even as far as Sodom. 13 But the men of Sodom *were* exceedingly wicked and sinful against the LORD.

14 And the LORD said to Abram, after Lot had separated from him: "Lift your eyes now and look from the place where you are—northward, southward, eastward, and westward; 15 for all the land which you see I give to you and your descendants[a] forever. 16 And I will make your descendants as the dust of the earth; so that if a man could number the dust of the earth, *then* your descendants also could be numbered. 17 Arise, walk in the land through its length and its width, for I give it to you."

18 Then Abram moved *his* tent, and went and dwelt by the terebinth trees of Mamre,[a] which *are* in Hebron, and built an altar there to the LORD.

14 And it came to pass in the days of Amraphel king of Shinar, Arioch king of Ellasar, Chedorlaomer king of Elam, and Tidal king of nations,[a] 2 *that* they made war with Bera king of Sodom, Birsha king of Gomorrah, Shinab king of Admah, Shemeber king of Zeboiim, and the king of Bela (that is, Zoar). 3 All these joined together in the Valley of Siddim (that is, the Salt Sea). 4 Twelve years they served Chedorlaomer, and in the thirteenth year they rebelled.

5 In the fourteenth year Chedorlaomer and the kings that *were* with him came and attacked the Rephaim in Ashteroth Karnaim, the Zuzim in Ham, the Emim in Shaveh Kiriathaim, 6 and the Horites in their mountain of Seir, as far as El Paran, which *is* by the wilderness. 7 Then they turned back and came to En Mishpat (that *is,* Kadesh), and attacked all the country of the Amalekites, and also the Amorites who dwelt in Hazezon Tamar.

8 And the king of Sodom, the king of Gomorrah, the king of Admah, the king of Zeboiim, and the king of Bela (that *is,* Zoar) went out and joined together in battle in the Valley of Siddim 9 against Chedorlaomer king of Elam, Tidal king of nations,[a] Amraphel king of Shinar, and Arioch king of Ellasar—four kings against five. 10 Now the Valley of Siddim *was full of* asphalt pits; and the kings of Sodom and Gomorrah fled; *some* fell there, and the remainder fled to the mountains. 11 Then they took all the goods of Sodom and Gomorrah, and all their provisions, and went their way. 12 They also took Lot, Abram's brother's son who dwelt in Sodom, and his goods, and departed.

13 Then one who had escaped came and told Abram the Hebrew, for he dwelt by the terebinth trees of Mamre[a] the Amorite, brother of Eshcol and brother of Aner; and they *were* allies with Abram. 14 Now when Abram heard that his brother was taken captive, he armed his three hundred and eighteen trained *servants* who were born in his own house, and went in pursuit as far as Dan. 15 He divided his forces against them by night, and he and his servants attacked them and pursued them as far as Hobah, which *is* north of Damascus. 16 So he brought back all the goods, and also brought back his brother Lot and his goods, as well as the women and the people.

13:15 aLiterally *seed,* and so throughout the book   13:18 aHebrew *Alon Mamre*
14:1 aHebrew *goyim*   14:9 aHebrew *goyim*   14:13 aHebrew *Alon Mamre*

17 And the king of Sodom went out to meet him at the Valley of Shaveh (that *is,* the King's Valley), after his return from the defeat of Chedorlaomer and the kings who *were* with him.

18 Then Melchizedek king of Salem brought out bread and wine; he *was* the priest of God Most High. 19 And he blessed him and said:

"Blessed be Abram of God Most High,
Possessor of heaven and earth;
20 And blessed be God Most High,
Who has delivered your
enemies into your hand."

And he gave him a tithe of all.

21 Now the king of Sodom said to Abram, "Give me the persons, and take the goods for yourself."

22 But Abram said to the king of Sodom, "I have raised my hand to the LORD, God Most High, the Possessor of heaven and earth, 23 that I *will take* nothing, from a thread to a sandal strap, and that I will not take anything that *is* yours, lest you should say, 'I have made Abram rich'— 24 except only what the young men have eaten, and the portion of the men who went with me: Aner, Eshcol, and Mamre; let them take their portion."

15 After these things the word of the LORD came to Abram in a vision, saying, "Do not be afraid, Abram. I *am* your shield, your exceedingly great reward."

2 But Abram said, "Lord GOD, what will You give me, seeing I go childless, and the heir of my house *is* Eliezer of Damascus?" 3 Then Abram said, "Look, You have given me no offspring; indeed one born in my house is my heir!"

4 And behold, the word of the LORD *came* to him, saying, "This one shall not be your heir, but one who will come from your own body shall be your heir." 5 Then He brought him outside and said, "Look now toward heaven, and count the stars if you are able to number them." And He said to him, "So shall your descendants be."

6 And he believed in the LORD, and He accounted it to him for righteousness.

7 Then He said to him, "I *am* the LORD, who brought you out of Ur of the Chaldeans, to give you this land to inherit it."

8 And he said, "Lord GOD, how shall I know that I will inherit it?"

9 So He said to him, "Bring Me a three-year-old heifer, a three-year-old female goat, a three-year-old ram, a turtledove, and a young pigeon." 10 Then he brought all these to Him and cut them in two, down the middle, and placed each piece opposite the other; but he did not cut the birds in two. 11 And when the vultures came down on the carcasses, Abram drove them away.

12 Now when the sun was going down, a deep sleep fell upon Abram; and behold, horror *and* great darkness fell upon him. 13 Then He said to Abram: "Know certainly that your descendants will be strangers in a land *that is* not theirs, and will serve them, and they will afflict them four hundred years. 14 And also the nation whom they serve I will judge; afterward they shall come out with great possessions. 15 Now as for you, you shall go to your fathers in peace; you shall be buried at a good old age. 16 But in the fourth generation they shall return here, for the iniquity of the Amorites *is* not yet complete."

17 And it came to pass, when the sun went down and it was dark, that behold, there appeared a smoking oven and a burning torch that passed between those pieces. 18 On the same day the LORD made a covenant with Abram, saying:

"To your descendants I have given this land, from the river of Egypt to the great river, the River Euphrates— 19 the Kenites, the Kenezzites, the Kadmonites, 20 the Hittites, the Perizzites, the Rephaim, 21 the Amorites, the Canaanites, the Girgashites, and the Jebusites."

16 Now Sarai, Abram's wife, had borne him no *children.* And she had an Egyptian maidservant whose name was Hagar. 2 So Sarai said to Abram, "See now, the LORD has restrained me from bearing *children.* Please, go in to my maid; perhaps I shall obtain children by her." And Abram heeded the voice of Sarai. 3 Then Sarai, Abram's wife, took Hagar her maid, the Egyptian, and gave her to her husband Abram to be his wife, after Abram had dwelt ten years in the land of Canaan. 4 So he went in to Hagar, and she conceived. And when she saw that she had conceived, her mistress became despised in her eyes.

5 Then Sarai said to Abram, "My wrong *be* upon you! I gave my maid into your embrace; and when she saw that she had conceived, I became despised in her eyes. The LORD judge between you and me."

6 So Abram said to Sarai, "Indeed your maid *is* in your hand; do to her as you please." And when Sarai dealt harshly with her, she fled from her presence.

7 Now the Angel of the LORD found her by a spring of water in the wilderness, by the spring on the way to Shur. 8 And He said, "Hagar, Sarai's maid, where have you come from, and where are you going?"

She said, "I am fleeing from the presence of my mistress Sarai."

9 The Angel of the LORD said to her, "Return to your mistress, and submit yourself under her hand." 10 Then the Angel of the LORD said to her, "I will multiply your descendants exceedingly, so that they shall not be counted for multitude." 11 And the Angel of the LORD said to her:

"Behold, you *are* with child,
And you shall bear a son.
You shall call his name
   Ishmael,
Because the LORD has heard
   your affliction.
12 He shall be a wild man;
His hand *shall be* against every
   man,
And every man's hand against
   him.
And he shall dwell in the
   presence of all his brethren."

13 Then she called the name of the LORD who spoke to her, You-Are-the-God-Who-Sees; for she said, "Have I also here seen Him who sees me?" 14 Therefore the well was called Beer Lahai Roi;[a] observe, *it is* between Kadesh and Bered.

15 So Hagar bore Abram a son; and Abram named his son, whom Hagar bore, Ishmael. 16 Abram *was* eighty-six years old when Hagar bore Ishmael to Abram.

17 When Abram was ninety-nine years old, the LORD appeared to Abram and said to him, "I *am* Almighty God; walk before Me and be blameless. 2 And I will make My covenant between Me and you, and will multiply you exceedingly." 3 Then Abram fell on his face, and God talked with him, saying: 4 "As for Me, behold, My covenant is with you, and you shall be a father of many nations. 5 No longer shall your name be called Abram, but your name shall be Abraham; for I have made you a father of many nations. 6 I will make you exceedingly fruitful; and I will make nations of you, and kings shall come from you. 7 And I will establish My covenant between Me and you and your descendants after you in their generations, for an everlasting covenant, to be God to you and your descendants after you. 8 Also I give to you and your descendants after you the land in which you are a stranger, all the land of Canaan, as an everlasting possession; and I will be their God."

9 And God said to Abraham: "As for you, you shall keep My covenant, you and your descendants after you throughout their generations. 10 This *is* My covenant which you shall keep, between Me and you and your descendants after you: Every male child among you shall be circumcised; 11 and you shall be circumcised in the flesh of your foreskins, and it shall be a sign of the covenant between Me and you. 12 He who is eight days old among you shall be circumcised, every male child in your generations, he who is born in your house or bought with money from any foreigner who is not your descendant. 13 He who is born in your house and he who is bought with your money must be circumcised, and My covenant shall be in your flesh for an everlasting covenant. 14 And the uncircumcised male child, who is not circumcised in the flesh of his foreskin, that person shall be cut off from his people; he has broken My covenant."

15 Then God said to Abraham, "As for Sarai your wife, you shall not call her name Sarai, but Sarah *shall be* her name. 16 And I will bless her and also give you a son by her; then I will

16:14 [a]Literally *Well of the One Who Lives and Sees Me*

bless her, and she shall be *a mother of* nations; kings of peoples shall be from her."

17 Then Abraham fell on his face and laughed, and said in his heart, "Shall *a child* be born to a man who is one hundred years old? And shall Sarah, who is ninety years old, bear *a child?*" 18 And Abraham said to God, "Oh, that Ishmael might live before You!"

19 Then God said: "No, Sarah your wife shall bear you a son, and you shall call his name Isaac; I will establish My covenant with him for an everlasting covenant, *and* with his descendants after him. 20 And as for Ishmael, I have heard you. Behold, I have blessed him, and will make him fruitful, and will multiply him exceedingly. He shall beget twelve princes, and I will make him a great nation. 21 But My covenant I will establish with Isaac, whom Sarah shall bear to you at this set time next year." 22 Then He finished talking with him, and God went up from Abraham.

23 So Abraham took Ishmael his son, all who were born in his house and all who were bought with his money, every male among the men of Abraham's house, and circumcised the flesh of their foreskins that very same day, as God had said to him. 24 Abraham *was* ninety-nine years old when he was circumcised in the flesh of his foreskin. 25 And Ishmael his son *was* thirteen years old when he was circumcised in the flesh of his foreskin. 26 That very same day Abraham was circumcised, and his son Ishmael; 27 and all the men of his house, born in the house or bought with money from a foreigner, were circumcised with him.

18 Then the LORD appeared to him by the terebinth trees of Mamre,*a* as he was sitting in the tent door in the heat of the day. 2 So he lifted his eyes and looked, and behold, three men were standing by him; and when he saw *them,* he ran from the tent door to meet them, and bowed himself to the ground, 3 and said, "My Lord, if I have now found favor in Your sight, do not pass on by Your servant. 4 Please let a little water be brought, and wash

your feet, and rest yourselves under the tree. 5 And I will bring a morsel of bread, that you may refresh your hearts. After that you may pass by, inasmuch as you have come to your servant."

They said, "Do as you have said."

6 So Abraham hurried into the tent to Sarah and said, "Quickly, make ready three measures of fine meal; knead *it* and make cakes." 7 And Abraham ran to the herd, took a tender and good calf, gave *it* to a young man, and he hastened to prepare it. 8 So he took butter and milk and the calf which he had prepared, and set *it* before them; and he stood by them under the tree as they ate.

9 Then they said to him, "Where *is* Sarah your wife?"

So he said, "Here, in the tent."

10 And He said, "I will certainly return to you according to the time of life, and behold, Sarah your wife shall have a son."

(Sarah was listening in the tent door which *was* behind him.) 11 Now Abraham and Sarah were old, well advanced in age; *and* Sarah had passed the age of childbearing.*a* 12 Therefore Sarah laughed within herself, saying, "After I have grown old, shall I have pleasure, my lord being old also?"

13 And the LORD said to Abraham, "Why did Sarah laugh, saying, 'Shall I surely bear *a child,* since I am old?' 14 Is anything too hard for the LORD? At the appointed time I will return to you, according to the time of life, and Sarah shall have a son."

15 But Sarah denied *it,* saying, "I did not laugh," for she was afraid.

And He said, "No, but you did laugh!"

16 Then the men rose from there and looked toward Sodom, and Abraham went with them to send them on the way. 17 And the LORD said, "Shall I hide from Abraham what I am doing, 18 since Abraham shall surely become a great and mighty nation, and all the nations of the earth shall be blessed in him? 19 For I have known him, in order that he may command his children and his household after him, that they keep the way of the LORD, to do righteousness and justice, that the LORD may bring to Abraham what He

18:1 *a*Hebrew *Alon Mamre*   18:11 *a*Literally *the manner of women had ceased to be with Sarah* has spoken to him." 20 And the LORD said, "Because the outcry against Sodom and Gomorrah is great, and because their sin is very grave, 21 I will go down now and see whether they have done altogether according to the outcry against it that has come to Me; and if not, I will know."

22 Then the men turned away from there and went toward Sodom, but Abraham still stood before the LORD. 23 And Abraham came near and said, "Would You also destroy the righteous with the wicked? 24 Suppose there were fifty righteous within the city; would You also destroy the place and not spare it for the fifty righteous that were in it? 25 Far be it from You to do such a thing as this, to slay the righteous with the wicked, so that the righteous should be as the wicked; far be it from You! Shall not the Judge of all the earth do right?"

26 So the LORD said, "If I find in Sodom fifty righteous within the city, then I will spare all the place for their sakes."

27 Then Abraham answered and said, "Indeed now, I who am but dust and ashes have taken it upon myself to speak to the Lord: 28 Suppose there were five less than the fifty righteous; would You destroy all of the city for lack of five?"

So He said, "If I find there forty-five, I will not destroy it."

29 And he spoke to Him yet again and said, "Suppose there should be forty found there?"

So He said, "I will not do it for the sake of forty."

30 Then he said, "Let not the Lord be angry, and I will speak: Suppose thirty should be found there?"

So He said, "I will not do it if I find thirty there."

31 And he said, "Indeed now, I have taken it upon myself to speak to the Lord: Suppose twenty should be found there?"

So He said, "I will not destroy it for the sake of twenty."

32 Then he said, "Let not the Lord be angry, and I will speak but once more: Suppose ten should be found there?"

And He said, "I will not destroy it for the sake of ten." 33 So the LORD went His way as soon as He had finished speaking with Abraham; and Abraham returned to his place.

19 Now the two angels came to Sodom in the evening, and Lot was sitting in the gate of Sodom. When Lot saw them, he rose to meet them, and he bowed himself with his face toward the ground. 2 And he said, "Here now, my lords, please turn in to your servant's house and spend the night, and wash your feet; then you may rise early and go on your way."

And they said, "No, but we will spend the night in the open square."

3 But he insisted strongly; so they turned in to him and entered his house. Then he made them a feast, and baked unleavened bread, and they ate.

4 Now before they lay down, the men of the city, the men of Sodom, both old and young, all the people from every quarter, surrounded the house. 5 And they called to Lot and said to him, "Where are the men who came to you tonight? Bring them out to us that we may know them carnally."

6 So Lot went out to them through the doorway, shut the door behind him, 7 and said, "Please, my brethren, do not do so wickedly! 8 See now, I have two daughters who have not known a man; please, let me bring them out to you, and you may do to them as you wish; only do nothing to these men, since this is the reason they have come under the shadow of my roof."

9 And they said, "Stand back!" Then they said, "This one came in to stay here, and he keeps acting as a judge; now we will deal worse with you than with them." So they pressed hard against the man Lot, and came near to break down the door. 10 But the men reached out their hands and pulled Lot into the house with them, and shut the door. 11 And they struck the men who were at the doorway of the house with blindness, both small and great, so that they became weary trying to find the door.

12 Then the men said to Lot, "Have you anyone else here? Son-in-law, your sons, your daughters, and whomever you have in the city—take them out of this place! 13 For we will destroy this place, because the outcry against them has grown great before the face of the LORD, and the LORD has sent us to destroy it."

14 So Lot went out and spoke to his sons-in-law, who had married his daughters, and said, "Get up, get out of this place; for the LORD will destroy this city!" But to his sons-in-law he seemed to be joking.

15 When the morning dawned, the angels urged Lot to hurry, saying, "Arise, take your wife and your two daughters who are here, lest you be consumed in the punishment of the city." 16 And while he lingered, the men took hold of his hand, his wife's hand, and the hands of his two daughters, the LORD being merciful to him, and they brought him out and set him outside the city. 17 So it came to pass, when they had brought them outside, that he*a* said, "Escape for your life! Do not look behind you nor stay anywhere in the plain. Escape to the mountains, lest you be destroyed."

18 Then Lot said to them, "Please, no, my lords! 19 Indeed now, your servant has found favor in your sight, and you have increased your mercy which you have shown me by saving my life; but I cannot escape to the mountains, lest some evil overtake me and I die. 20 See now, this city *is* near *enough* to flee to, and it *is* a little one; please let me escape there (*is it* not a little one?) and my soul shall live."

21 And he said to him, "See, I have favored you concerning this thing also, in that I will not overthrow this city for which you have spoken. 22 Hurry, escape there. For I cannot do anything until you arrive there."

Therefore the name of the city was called Zoar.

23 The sun had risen upon the earth when Lot entered Zoar. 24 Then the LORD rained brimstone and fire on Sodom and Gomorrah, from the LORD out of the heavens. 25 So He overthrew those cities, all the plain, all the inhabitants of the cities, and what grew on the ground.

26 But his wife looked back behind him, and she became a pillar of salt.

27 And Abraham went early in the morning to the place where he had stood before the LORD. 28 Then he looked toward Sodom and Gomorrah, and toward all the land of the plain; and he saw, and behold, the smoke of the land which went up like the smoke of a furnace. 29 And it came to pass, when God destroyed the cities of the plain, that God remembered Abraham, and sent Lot out of the midst of the overthrow, when He overthrew the cities in which Lot had dwelt.

30 Then Lot went up out of Zoar and dwelt in the mountains, and his two daughters were with him; for he was afraid to dwell in Zoar. And he and his two daughters dwelt in a cave. 31 Now the firstborn said to the younger, "Our father *is* old, and *there is* no man on the earth to come in to us as is the custom of all the earth. 32 Come, let us make our father drink wine, and we will lie with him, that we may preserve the lineage of our father." 33 So they made their father drink wine that night. And the firstborn went in and lay with her father, and he did not know when she lay down or when she arose.

34 It happened on the next day that the firstborn said to the younger, "Indeed I lay with my father last night; let us make him drink wine tonight also, and you go in *and* lie with him, that we may preserve the lineage of our father." 35 Then they made their father drink wine that night also. And the younger arose and lay with him, and he did not know when she lay down or when she arose.

36 Thus both the daughters of Lot were with child by their father. 37 The firstborn bore a son and called his name Moab; he *is* the father of the Moabites to this day. 38 And the younger, she also bore a son and called his name Ben-Ammi; he *is* the father of the people of Ammon to this day.

20 And Abraham journeyed from there to the South, and dwelt between Kadesh and Shur, and stayed in Gerar. 2 Now Abraham said of Sarah his wife, "She *is* my sister." And Abimelech king of Gerar sent and took Sarah.

3 But God came to Abimelech in a dream by night, and said to him, "Indeed you *are* a dead man because of the woman whom you have taken, for she *is* a man's wife."

4 But Abimelech had not come near her; and he said, "Lord, will You slay

19:17 *a*Septuagint, Syriac, and Vulgate read *they.*

a righteous nation also? 5 Did he not say to me, 'She *is* my sister'? And she, even she herself said, 'He *is* my brother.' In the integrity of my heart and innocence of my hands I have done this."

6 And God said to him in a dream, "Yes, I know that you did this in the integrity of your heart. For I also withheld you from sinning against Me; therefore I did not let you touch her. 7 Now therefore, restore the man's wife; for he *is* a prophet, and he will pray for you and you shall live. But if you do not restore *her,* know that you shall surely die, you and all who *are* yours."

8 So Abimelech rose early in the morning, called all his servants, and told all these things in their hearing; and the men were very much afraid. 9 And Abimelech called Abraham and said to him, "What have you done to us? How have I offended you, that you have brought on me and on my kingdom a great sin? You have done deeds to me that ought not to be done." 10 Then Abimelech said to Abraham, "What did you have in view, that you have done this thing?" 11 And Abraham said, "Because I thought, surely the fear of God *is* not in this place; and they will kill me on account of my wife. 12 But indeed *she is* truly my sister. She *is* the daughter of my father, but not the daughter of my mother; and she became my wife. 13 And it came to pass, when God caused me to wander from my father's house, that I said to her, 'This *is* your kindness that you should do for me: in every place, wherever we go, say of me, "He *is* my brother."'"

14 Then Abimelech took sheep, oxen, and male and female servants, and gave *them* to Abraham; and he restored Sarah his wife to him. 15 And Abimelech said, "See, my land *is* before you; dwell where it pleases you." 16 Then to Sarah he said, "Behold, I have given your brother a thousand *pieces* of silver; indeed this vindicates you*a* before all who *are* with you and before everybody." Thus she was rebuked.

17 So Abraham prayed to God; and God healed Abimelech, his wife, and his female servants. Then they bore *children;* 18 for the LORD had closed up all the wombs of the house of Abimelech because of Sarah, Abraham's wife.

21 And the LORD visited Sarah as He had said, and the LORD did for Sarah as He had spoken. 2 For Sarah conceived and bore Abraham a son in his old age, at the set time of which God had spoken to him. 3 And Abraham called the name of his son who was born to him—whom Sarah bore to him—Isaac. 4 Then Abraham circumcised his son Isaac when he was eight days old, as God had commanded him. 5 Now Abraham was one hundred years old when his son Isaac was born to him. 6 And Sarah said, "God has made me laugh, *and* all who hear will laugh with me." 7 She also said, "Who would have said to Abraham that Sarah would nurse children? For I have borne *him* a son in his old age."

8 So the child grew and was weaned. And Abraham made a great feast on the same day that Isaac was weaned.

9 And Sarah saw the son of Hagar the Egyptian, whom she had borne to Abraham, scoffing. 10 Therefore she said to Abraham, "Cast out this bondwoman and her son; for the son of this bondwoman shall not be heir with my son, *namely* with Isaac." 11 And the matter was very displeasing in Abraham's sight because of his son.

12 But God said to Abraham, "Do not let it be displeasing in your sight because of the lad or because of your bondwoman. Whatever Sarah has said to you, listen to her voice; for in Isaac your seed shall be called. 13 Yet I will also make a nation of the son of the bondwoman, because he *is* your seed."

14 So Abraham rose early in the morning, and took bread and a skin of water; and putting *it* on her shoulder, he gave *it* and the boy to Hagar, and sent her away. Then she departed and wandered in the Wilderness of Beersheba. 15 And the water in the skin was used up, and she placed the boy under one of the shrubs. 16 Then she went and sat down across from *him* at a distance of about a bowshot; for she said to

20:16 *a* Literally *it is a covering of the eyes for you*

herself, "Let me not see the death of the boy." So she sat opposite *him,* and lifted her voice and wept.

17 And God heard the voice of the lad. Then the angel of God called to Hagar out of heaven, and said to her, "What ails you, Hagar? Fear not, for God has heard the voice of the lad where he *is.* 18 Arise, lift up the lad and hold him with your hand, for I will make him a great nation."

19 Then God opened her eyes, and she saw a well of water. And she went and filled the skin with water, and gave the lad a drink. 20 So God was with the lad; and he grew and dwelt in the wilderness, and became an archer. 21 He dwelt in the Wilderness of Paran; and his mother took a wife for him from the land of Egypt.

22 And it came to pass at that time that Abimelech and Phichol, the commander of his army, spoke to Abraham, saying, "God *is* with you in all that you do. 23 Now therefore, swear to me by God that you will not deal falsely with me, with my offspring, or with my posterity; but that according to the kindness that I have done to you, you will do to me and to the land in which you have dwelt."

24 And Abraham said, "I will swear."

25 Then Abraham rebuked Abimelech because of a well of water which Abimelech's servants had seized. 26 And Abimelech said, "I do not know who has done this thing; you did not tell me, nor had I heard *of it* until today." 27 So Abraham took sheep and oxen and gave them to Abimelech, and the two of them made a covenant. 28 And Abraham set seven ewe lambs of the flock by themselves.

29 Then Abimelech asked Abraham, "What *is the meaning of* these seven ewe lambs which you have set by themselves?"

30 And he said, "You will take *these* seven ewe lambs from my hand, that they may be my witness that I have dug this well." 31 Therefore he called that place Beersheba,ᵃ because the two of them swore an oath there.

32 Thus they made a covenant at Beersheba. So Abimelech rose with Phichol, the commander of his army, and they returned to the land of the Philistines. 33 Then *Abraham* planted a tamarisk tree in Beersheba, and there called on the name of the LORD, the Everlasting God. 34 And Abraham stayed in the land of the Philistines many days.

22 Now it came to pass after these things that God tested Abraham, and said to him, "Abraham!"

And he said, "Here I am."

2 Then He said, "Take now your son, your only *son* Isaac, whom you love, and go to the land of Moriah, and offer him there as a burnt offering on one of the mountains of which I shall tell you."

3 So Abraham rose early in the morning and saddled his donkey, and took two of his young men with him, and Isaac his son; and he split the wood for the burnt offering, and arose and went to the place of which God had told him. 4 Then on the third day Abraham lifted his eyes and saw the place afar off. 5 And Abraham said to his young men, "Stay here with the donkey; the ladᵃ and I will go yonder and worship, and we will come back to you."

6 So Abraham took the wood of the burnt offering and laid *it* on Isaac his son; and he took the fire in his hand, and a knife, and the two of them went together. 7 But Isaac spoke to Abraham his father and said, "My father!"

And he said, "Here I am, my son."

Then he said, "Look, the fire and the wood, but where *is* the lamb for a burnt offering?"

8 And Abraham said, "My son, God will provide for Himself the lamb for a burnt offering." So the two of them went together.

9 Then they came to the place of which God had told him. And Abraham built an altar there and placed the wood in order; and he bound Isaac his son and laid him on the altar, upon the wood. 10 And Abraham stretched out his hand and took the knife to slay his son.

11 But the Angel of the LORD called to him from heaven and said, "Abraham, Abraham!"

So he said, "Here I am."

12 And He said, "Do not lay your hand on the lad, or do anything to him; for now I know that you fear God, since you have not withheld

---

21:31 ᵃLiterally *Well of the Oath* or *Well of the Seven*   22:5 ᵃOr *young man* your son, your only *son,* from Me."

13 Then Abraham lifted his eyes and looked, and there behind *him was* a ram caught in a thicket by its horns. So Abraham went and took the ram, and offered it up for a burnt offering instead of his son. 14 And Abraham called the name of the place, The-LORD-Will-Provide;*a* as it is said *to* this day, "In the Mount of the LORD it shall be provided."

15 Then the Angel of the LORD called to Abraham a second time out of heaven, 16 and said: "By Myself I have sworn, says the LORD, because you have done this thing, and have not withheld your son, your only son— 17 blessing I will bless you, and multiplying I will multiply your descendants as the stars of the heaven and as the sand which *is* on the seashore; and your descendants shall possess the gate of their enemies. 18 In your seed all the nations of the earth shall be blessed, because you have obeyed My voice." 19 So Abraham returned to his young men, and they rose and went together to Beersheba; and Abraham dwelt at Beersheba.

20 Now it came to pass after these things that it was told Abraham, saying, "Indeed Milcah also has borne children to your brother Nahor: 21 Huz his firstborn, Buz his brother, Kemuel the father of Aram, 22 Chesed, Hazo, Pildash, Jidlaph, and Bethuel." 23 And Bethuel begot Rebekah.*a* These eight Milcah bore to Nahor, Abraham's brother. 24 His concubine, whose name was Reumah, also bore Tebah, Gaham, Thahash, and Maachah.

23 Sarah lived one hundred and twenty-seven years; *these were* the years of the life of Sarah. 2 So Sarah died in Kirjath Arba (that is, Hebron) in the land of Canaan, and Abraham came to mourn for Sarah and to weep for her.

3 Then Abraham stood up from before his dead, and spoke to the sons of Heth, saying, 4 "I *am* a foreigner and a visitor among you. Give me property for a burial place among you, that I may bury my dead out of my sight."

5 And the sons of Heth answered Abraham, saying to him, 6 "Hear us, my lord: You *are* a mighty prince among us; bury your dead in the choicest of our burial places. None of us will withhold from you his burial place, that you may bury your dead."

7 Then Abraham stood up and bowed himself to the people of the land, the sons of Heth. 8 And he spoke with them, saying, "If it is your wish that I bury my dead out of my sight, hear me, and meet with Ephron the son of Zohar for me, 9 that he may give me the cave of Machpelah which he has, which *is* at the end of his field. Let him give it to me at the full price, as property for a burial place among you."

10 Now Ephron dwelt among the sons of Heth; and Ephron the Hittite answered Abraham in the presence of the sons of Heth, all who entered at the gate of his city, saying, 11 "No, my lord, hear me: I give you the field and the cave that *is* in it; I give it to you in the presence of the sons of my people. I give it to you. Bury your dead!"

12 Then Abraham bowed himself down before the people of the land; 13 and he spoke to Ephron in the hearing of the people of the land, saying, "If you *will give it,* please hear me. I will give you money for the field; take *it* from me and I will bury my dead there."

14 And Ephron answered Abraham, saying to him, 15 "My lord, listen to me; the land *is worth* four hundred shekels of silver. What *is* that between you and me? So bury your dead." 16 And Abraham listened to Ephron; and Abraham weighed out the silver for Ephron which he had named in the hearing of the sons of Heth, four hundred shekels of silver, currency of the merchants.

17 So the field of Ephron which *was* in Machpelah, which *was* before Mamre, the field and the cave which *was* in it, and all the trees that *were* in the field, which *were* within all the surrounding borders, were deeded 18 to Abraham as a possession in the presence of the sons of Heth, before all who went in at the gate of his city.

19 And after this, Abraham buried Sarah his wife in the cave of the field of Machpelah, before Mamre (that *is,* Hebron) in the land of Canaan.

22:14 *a*Hebrew *YHWH Yireh*   22:23 *a*Spelled *Rebecca* in Romans 9:10

20 So the field and the cave that *is* in it were deeded to Abraham by the sons of Heth as property for a burial place.

24 Now Abraham was old, well advanced in age; and the LORD had blessed Abraham in all things. 2 So Abraham said to the oldest servant of his house, who ruled over all that he had, "Please, put your hand under my thigh, 3 and I will make you swear by the LORD, the God of heaven and the God of the earth, that you will not take a wife for my son from the daughters of the Canaanites, among whom I dwell; 4 but you shall go to my country and to my family, and take a wife for my son Isaac."

5 And the servant said to him, "Perhaps the woman will not be willing to follow me to this land. Must I take your son back to the land from which you came?"

6 But Abraham said to him, "Beware that you do not take my son back there. 7 The LORD God of heaven, who took me from my father's house and from the land of my family, and who spoke to me and swore to me, saying, 'To your descendants*a* I give this land,' He will send His angel before you, and you shall take a wife for my son from there. 8 And if the woman is not willing to follow you, then you will be released from this oath; only do not take my son back there." 9 So the servant put his hand under the thigh of Abraham his master, and swore to him concerning this matter.

10 Then the servant took ten of his master's camels and departed, for all his master's goods *were in* his hand. And he arose and went to Mesopotamia, to the city of Nahor. 11 And he made his camels kneel down outside the city by a well of water at evening time, the time when women go out to draw *water.* 12 Then he said, "O LORD God of my master Abraham, please give me success this day, and show kindness to my master Abraham. 13 Behold, *here* I stand by the well of water, and the daughters of the men of the city are coming out to draw water. 14 Now let it be that the young woman to whom I say, 'Please let down your pitcher that I may drink,' and she says, 'Drink, and I will also give your camels a drink'— let her *be the one* You have appointed for Your servant Isaac. And by this I will know that You have shown kindness to my master."

15 And it happened, before he had finished speaking, that behold, Rebekah, who was born to Bethuel, son of Milcah, the wife of Nahor, Abraham's brother, came out with her pitcher on her shoulder. 16 Now the young woman *was* very beautiful to behold, a virgin; no man had known her. And she went down to the well, filled her pitcher, and came up. 17 And the servant ran to meet her and said, "Please let me drink a little water from your pitcher."

18 So she said, "Drink, my lord." Then she quickly let her pitcher down to her hand, and gave him a drink. 19 And when she had finished giving him a drink, she said, "I will draw *water* for your camels also, until they have finished drinking." 20 Then she quickly emptied her pitcher into the trough, ran back to the well to draw *water,* and drew for all his camels. 21 And the man, wondering at her, remained silent so as to know whether the LORD had made his journey prosperous or not.

22 So it was, when the camels had finished drinking, that the man took a golden nose ring weighing half a shekel, and two bracelets for her wrists weighing ten *shekels* of gold, 23 and said, "Whose daughter *are* you? Tell me, please, is there room *in* your father's house for us to lodge?"

24 So she said to him, "I *am* the daughter of Bethuel, Milcah's son, whom she bore to Nahor." 25 Moreover she said to him, "We have both straw and feed enough, and room to lodge."

26 Then the man bowed down his head and worshiped the LORD. 27 And he said, "Blessed *be* the LORD God of my master Abraham, who has not forsaken His mercy and His truth toward my master. As for me, being on the way, the LORD led me to the house of my master's brethren." 28 So the young woman ran and told her mother's household these things.

29 Now Rebekah had a brother whose name *was* Laban, and Laban ran out to the man by the well. 30 So it came to pass, when he saw

24:7 *a*Literally *seed*

the nose ring, and the bracelets on his sister's wrists, and when he heard the words of his sister Rebekah, saying, "Thus the man spoke to me," that he went to the man. And there he stood by the camels at the well. 31 And he said, "Come in, O blessed of the LORD! Why do you stand outside? For I have prepared the house, and a place for the camels."

32 Then the man came to the house. And he unloaded the camels, and provided straw and feed for the camels, and water to wash his feet and the feet of the men who *were* with him. 33 *Food* was set before him to eat, but he said, "I will not eat until I have told about my errand."

And he said, "Speak on."

34 So he said, "I *am* Abraham's servant. 35 The LORD has blessed my master greatly, and he has become great; and He has given him flocks and herds, silver and gold, male and female servants, and camels and donkeys. 36 And Sarah my master's wife bore a son to my master when she was old; and to him he has given all that he has. 37 Now my master made me swear, saying, 'You shall not take a wife for my son from the daughters of the Canaanites, in whose land I dwell; 38 but you shall go to my father's house and to my family, and take a wife for my son.' 39 And I said to my master, 'Perhaps the woman will not follow me.' 40 But he said to me, 'The LORD, before whom I walk, will send His angel with you and prosper your way; and you shall take a wife for my son from my family and from my father's house. 41 You will be clear from this oath when you arrive among my family; for if they will not give *her* to you, then you will be released from my oath.'

42 "And this day I came to the well and said, 'O LORD God of my master Abraham, if You will now prosper the way in which I go, 43 behold, I stand by the well of water; and it shall come to pass that when the virgin comes out to draw *water,* and I say to her, "Please give me a little water from your pitcher to drink," 44 and she says to me, "Drink, and I will draw for your camels also,"—*let* her *be* the woman whom the LORD has appointed for my master's son.'

45 "But before I had finished speaking in my heart, there was Rebekah, coming out with her pitcher on her shoulder; and she went down to the well and drew *water.* And I said to her, 'Please let me drink.' 46 And she made haste and let her pitcher down from her *shoulder,* and said, 'Drink, and I will give your camels a drink also.' So I drank, and she gave the camels a drink also. 47 Then I asked her, and said, 'Whose daughter *are* you?' And she said, 'The daughter of Bethuel, Nahor's son, whom Milcah bore to him.' So I put the nose ring on her nose and the bracelets on her wrists. 48 And I bowed my head and worshiped the LORD, and blessed the LORD God of my master Abraham, who had led me in the way of truth to take the daughter of my master's brother for his son. 49 Now if you will deal kindly and truly with my master, tell me. And if not, tell me, that I may turn to the right hand or to the left."

50 Then Laban and Bethuel answered and said, "The thing comes from the LORD; we cannot speak to you either bad or good. 51 Here *is* Rebekah before you; take *her* and go, and let her be your master's son's wife, as the LORD has spoken."

52 And it came to pass, when Abraham's servant heard their words, that he worshiped the LORD, *bowing himself* to the earth. 53 Then the servant brought out jewelry of silver, jewelry of gold, and clothing, and gave *them* to Rebekah. He also gave precious things to her brother and to her mother.

54 And he and the men who *were* with him ate and drank and stayed all night. Then they arose in the morning, and he said, "Send me away to my master."

55 But her brother and her mother said, "Let the young woman stay with us *a few* days, at least ten; after that she may go."

56 And he said to them, "Do not hinder me, since the LORD has prospered my way; send me away so that I may go to my master."

57 So they said, "We will call the young woman and ask her personally." 58 Then they called Rebekah and said to her, "Will you go with this man?"

And she said, "I will go."

59 So they sent away Rebekah their sister and her nurse, and Abraham's servant and his men. 60 And they blessed Rebekah and said to her:

"Our sister, *may* you *become*
The *mother of* thousands of ten
thousands;
And may your descendants
possess
The gates of those who hate
them."

61 Then Rebekah and her maids
arose, and they rode on the camels
and followed the man. So the servant
took Rebekah and departed.

62 Now Isaac came from the way
of Beer Lahai Roi, for he dwelt in the
South. 63 And Isaac went out to meditate in the field in the evening; and
he lifted his eyes and looked, and
there, the camels *were* coming.
64 Then Rebekah lifted her eyes, and
when she saw Isaac she dismounted
from her camel; 65 for she had said
to the servant, "Who *is* this man
walking in the field to meet us?"
The servant said, "It *is* my master."
So she took a veil and covered herself.

66 And the servant told Isaac all the
things that he had done. 67 Then
Isaac brought her into his mother
Sarah's tent; and he took Rebekah
and she became his wife, and he
loved her. So Isaac was comforted after his mother's *death.*

25 Abraham again took a wife,
and her name *was* Keturah.
2 And she bore him Zimran, Jokshan,
Medan, Midian, Ishbak, and Shuah.
3 Jokshan begot Sheba and Dedan.
And the sons of Dedan were As-
shurim, Letushim, and Leummim.
4 And the sons of Midian *were*
Ephah, Epher, Hanoch, Abidah, and
Eldaah. All these *were* the children
of Keturah.

5 And Abraham gave all that he
had to Isaac. 6 But Abraham gave
gifts to the sons of the concubines
which Abraham had; and while he
was still living he sent them eastward, away from Isaac his son, to the
country of the east.

7 This *is* the sum of the years of
Abraham's life which he lived: one
hundred and seventy-five years.
8 Then Abraham breathed his last
and died in a good old age, an old
man and full *of years,* and was gathered to his people. 9 And his sons
Isaac and Ishmael buried him in the
cave of Machpelah, which *is* before
Mamre, in the field of Ephron the son
of Zohar the Hittite, 10 the field which
Abraham purchased from the sons of
Heth. There Abraham was buried,
and Sarah his wife. 11 And it came
to pass, after the death of Abraham,
that God blessed his son Isaac. And
Isaac dwelt at Beer Lahai Roi.

12 Now this *is* the genealogy of Ishmael, Abraham's son, whom Hagar
the Egyptian, Sarah's maidservant,
bore to Abraham. 13 And these *were*
the names of the sons of Ishmael, by
their names, according to their generations: The firstborn of Ishmael,
Nebajoth; then Kedar, Adbeel, Mibsam, 14 Mishma, Dumah, Massa,
15 Hadar,[a] Tema, Jetur, Naphish, and
Kedemah. 16 These *were* the sons of
Ishmael and these *were* their names,
by their towns and their settlements,
twelve princes according to their nations. 17 These *were* the years of the
life of Ishmael: one hundred and
thirty-seven years; and he breathed
his last and died, and was gathered
to his people. 18 (They dwelt from
Havilah as far as Shur, which *is* east
of Egypt as you go toward Assyria.)
He died in the presence of all his
brethren.

19 This *is* the genealogy of Isaac,
Abraham's son. Abraham begot
Isaac. 20 Isaac was forty years old
when he took Rebekah as wife, the
daughter of Bethuel the Syrian of Padan Aram, the sister of Laban the
Syrian. 21 Now Isaac pleaded with
the LORD for his wife, because she
was barren; and the LORD granted his
plea, and Rebekah his wife conceived. 22 But the children struggled
together within her; and she said, "If
all is well, why *am I like* this?" So
she went to inquire of the LORD.

23 And the LORD said to her:

"Two nations *are* in your womb,
Two peoples shall be separated
from your body;
One people shall be stronger
than the other,
And the older shall serve the
younger."

24 So when her days were fulfilled
for her to give birth, indeed *there
were* twins in her womb. 25 And the
first came out red. *He was* like a

hairy garment all over; so they called his name Esau.*a* 26 Afterward his brother came out, and his hand took hold of Esau's heel; so his name was called Jacob.*a* Isaac *was* sixty years old when she bore them.

27 So the boys grew. And Esau was a skillful hunter, a man of the field; but Jacob was a mild man, dwelling in tents. 28 And Isaac loved Esau because he ate *of his* game, but Rebekah loved Jacob.

29 Now Jacob cooked a stew; and Esau came in from the field, and he *was* weary. 30 And Esau said to Jacob, "Please feed me with that same red *stew,* for I *am* weary." Therefore his name was called Edom.*a*

31 But Jacob said, "Sell me your birthright as of this day."

32 And Esau said, "Look, I *am* about to die; so what *is* this birthright to me?"

33 Then Jacob said, "Swear to me as of this day."

So he swore to him, and sold his birthright to Jacob. 34 And Jacob gave Esau bread and stew of lentils; then he ate and drank, arose, and went his way. Thus Esau despised *his* birthright.

26 There was a famine in the land, besides the first famine that was in the days of Abraham. And Isaac went to Abimelech king of the Philistines, in Gerar.

2 Then the LORD appeared to him and said: "Do not go down to Egypt; live in the land of which I shall tell you. 3 Dwell in this land, and I will be with you and bless you; for to you and your descendants I give all these lands, and I will perform the oath which I swore to Abraham your father. 4 And I will make your descendants multiply as the stars of heaven; I will give to your descendants all these lands; and in your seed all the nations of the earth shall be blessed; 5 because Abraham obeyed My voice and kept My charge, My commandments, My statutes, and My laws."

6 So Isaac dwelt in Gerar. 7 And the men of the place asked about his wife. And he said, "She *is* my sister"; for he was afraid to say, "*She is* my wife," *because he thought,* "lest the men of the place

kill me for Rebekah, because she *is* beautiful to behold." 8 Now it came to pass, when he had been there a long time, that Abimelech king of the Philistines looked through a window, and saw, and there was Isaac, showing endearment to Rebekah his wife. 9 Then Abimelech called Isaac and said, "Quite obviously she *is* your wife; so how could you say, 'She *is* my sister'?"

Isaac said to him, "Because I said, 'Lest I die on account of her.' "

10 And Abimelech said, "What *is* this you have done to us? One of the people might soon have lain with your wife, and you would have brought guilt on us." 11 So Abimelech charged all *his* people, saying, "He who touches this man or his wife shall surely be put to death."

12 Then Isaac sowed in that land, and reaped in the same year a hundredfold; and the LORD blessed him. 13 The man began to prosper, and continued prospering until he became very prosperous; 14 for he had possessions of flocks and possessions of herds and a great number of servants. So the Philistines envied him. 15 Now the Philistines had stopped up all the wells which his father's servants had dug in the days of Abraham his father, and they had filled them with earth. 16 And Abimelech said to Isaac, "Go away from us, for you are much mightier than we."

17 Then Isaac departed from there and pitched his tent in the Valley of Gerar, and dwelt there. 18 And Isaac dug again the wells of water which they had dug in the days of Abraham his father, for the Philistines had stopped them up after the death of Abraham. He called them by the names which his father had called them.

19 Also Isaac's servants dug in the valley, and found a well of running water there. 20 But the herdsmen of Gerar quarreled with Isaac's herdsmen, saying, "The water *is* ours." So he called the name of the well Esek,*a* because they quarreled with him. 21 Then they dug another well, and they quarreled over that *one* also. So he called its name Sitnah.*a* 22 And he moved from there and dug another well, and they did not quarrel over

Streams of Living Water

In the hot, parched summer months when temperatures rise to and above one hundred degrees from Galilee to Jericho, water is a precious commodity for the people of Israel. Even in the winter months, many areas of the land get little or no rainfall.

This element is so vital that the Bible records neighboring tribes disputing over water—sometimes to the point of war. In Genesis 26, Isaac fought with the herdsmen of Gerar over the wells dug by Abraham.

The Bible records three methods of obtaining water: by collecting rainfall runoff in a cistern; by digging a well; and by locating a running stream or river. Both digging a well and hewing out a cistern require considerable human effort. A stream, however, can be considered a gift of grace, freely given by God.

In Old Testament times, spring water was the most sought-after type of water and among ancient peoples, was considered to be "living water." Even in the Hebrew language, the words "running water" and "living water" are the same.

Beyond providing a perennial source of water, streams had a unique purpose for the early Israelites. The Jewish law required one to ritually purify himself with "living water" from a stream before entering the holy temple. In the first century, however, there were no streams at the elevated height of the temple.

To provide running water for the required purification baths at the temple, Herod the Great performed an engineering feat still visible today. He built an aqueduct carrying water ten miles from the pools of Solomon to the temple stairs in Jerusalem. Herod ingeniously accomplished the task of running the water downstream while dropping the aqueduct only ninety feet over its ten-mile course.

In front of these famous purification baths adjacent to the stairway entrance of the temple, Jesus stood on the final day of the Feast of Dedication and cried out: "He who believes in Me . . . out of his heart will flow rivers of living water" (John 7:38).

In one bold statement, Jesus offered living water that could purify and satisfy the heart, mind, and soul. If we have faith in Him, this living water has the power to purify our lives from negative emotions, thoughts, and deeds. Even in the most scorched, dry days of our lives, it is an unending spring of love, joy, and peace.

How do we find this living water? Jesus told the Samaritan woman at the well, "Whoever drinks of this water will thirst again, but whoever drinks of the water that I shall give him will never thirst . . . a fountain of water springing up into everlasting life" (John 4:13, 14).

We find this living water in Jesus Himself and in the life we experience through our faith in Him.

it. So he called its name Rehoboth,^a because he said, "For now the LORD has made room for us, and we shall be fruitful in the land."

23 Then he went up from there to Beersheba. 24 And the LORD appeared to him the same night and said, "I *am* the God of your father Abraham; do not fear, for I *am* with you. I will bless you and multiply your descendants for My servant Abraham's sake." 25 So he built an altar there and called on the name of the LORD, and he pitched his tent there; and there Isaac's servants dug a well.

26 Then Abimelech came to him from Gerar with Ahuzzath, one of his friends, and Phichol the commander of his army. 27 And Isaac said to them, "Why have you come to me, since you hate me and have sent me away from you?"

28 But they said, "We have certainly seen that the LORD is with you. So we said, 'Let there now be an oath between us, between you and us; and let us make a covenant with you, 29 that you will do us no harm, since we have not touched you, and since we have done nothing to you but good and have sent you away in peace. You *are* now the blessed of the LORD.'"

30 So he made them a feast, and they ate and drank. 31 Then they arose early in the morning and swore an oath with one another; and Isaac sent them away, and they departed from him in peace.

32 It came to pass the same day that Isaac's servants came and told him about the well which they had dug, and said to him, "We have found water." 33 So he called it Shebah.^a Therefore the name of the city *is* Beersheba^b to this day.

34 When Esau was forty years old, he took as wives Judith the daughter of Beeri the Hittite, and Basemath the daughter of Elon the Hittite. 35 And they were a grief of mind to Isaac and Rebekah.

27 Now it came to pass, when Isaac was old and his eyes were so dim that he could not see, that he called Esau his older son and said to him, "My son."

And he answered him, "Here I am."

2 Then he said, "Behold now, I am old. I do not know the day of my death. 3 Now therefore, please take your weapons, your quiver and your bow, and go out to the field and hunt game for me. 4 And make me savory food, such as I love, and bring *it* to me that I may eat, that my soul may bless you before I die."

5 Now Rebekah was listening when Isaac spoke to Esau his son. And Esau went to the field to hunt game and to bring *it.* 6 So Rebekah spoke to Jacob her son, saying, "Indeed I heard your father speak to Esau your brother, saying, 7 'Bring me game and make savory food for me, that I may eat it and bless you in the presence of the LORD before my death.' 8 Now therefore, my son, obey my voice according to what I command you. 9 Go now to the flock and bring me from there two choice kids of the goats, and I will make savory food from them for your father, such as he loves. 10 Then you shall take *it* to your father, that he may eat *it,* and that he may bless you before his death."

11 And Jacob said to Rebekah his mother, "Look, Esau my brother *is* a hairy man, and I *am* a smooth-skinned man. 12 Perhaps my father will feel me, and I shall seem to be a deceiver to him; and I shall bring a curse on myself and not a blessing."

13 But his mother said to him, "*Let* your curse *be* on me, my son; only obey my voice, and go, get *them* for me." 14 And he went and got *them* and brought *them* to his mother, and his mother made savory food, such as his father loved. 15 Then Rebekah took the choice clothes of her elder son Esau, which *were* with her in the house, and put them on Jacob her younger son. 16 And she put the skins of the kids of the goats on his hands and on the smooth part of his neck. 17 Then she gave the savory food and the bread, which she had prepared, into the hand of her son Jacob.

18 So he went to his father and said, "My father."

And he said, "Here I am. Who *are* you, my son?"

26:22 ^aLiterally *Spaciousness* 　26:33 ^aLiterally *Oath* or *Seven*　^bLiterally *Well of the Oath* or *Well of the Seven*

19 Jacob said to his father, "I *am* Esau your firstborn; I have done just as you told me; please arise, sit and eat of my game, that your soul may bless me."

20 But Isaac said to his son, "How *is it* that you have found *it* so quickly, my son?"

And he said, "Because the LORD your God brought *it* to me."

21 Then Isaac said to Jacob, "Please come near, that I may feel you, my son, whether you *are* really my son Esau or not." 22 So Jacob went near to Isaac his father, and he felt him and said, "The voice *is* Jacob's voice, but the hands *are* the hands of Esau." 23 And he did not recognize him, because his hands were hairy like his brother Esau's hands; so he blessed him.

24 Then he said, "*Are* you really my son Esau?"

He said, "I *am*."

25 He said, "Bring *it* near to me, and I will eat of my son's game, so that my soul may bless you." So he brought *it* near to him, and he ate; and he brought him wine, and he drank. 26 Then his father Isaac said to him, "Come near now and kiss me, my son." 27 And he came near and kissed him; and he smelled the smell of his clothing, and blessed him and said:

"Surely, the smell of my son
   Is like the smell of a field
   Which the LORD has blessed.
28 Therefore may God give you
   Of the dew of heaven,
   Of the fatness of the earth,
   And plenty of grain and wine.
29 Let peoples serve you,
   And nations bow down to you.
   Be master over your brethren,
   And let your mother's sons bow
     down to you.
   Cursed *be* everyone who curses
     you,
   And blessed *be* those who bless
     you!"

30 Now it happened, as soon as Isaac had finished blessing Jacob, and Jacob had scarcely gone out from the presence of Isaac his father, that Esau his brother came in from his hunting. 31 He also had made savory food, and brought it to his father, and said to his father, "Let my father arise and eat of his son's game, that your soul may bless me."

32 And his father Isaac said to him, "Who *are* you?"

So he said, "I *am* your son, your firstborn, Esau."

33 Then Isaac trembled exceedingly, and said, "Who? Where *is* the one who hunted game and brought *it* to me? I ate all *of it* before you came, and I have blessed him—*and* indeed he shall be blessed."

34 When Esau heard the words of his father, he cried with an exceedingly great and bitter cry, and said to his father, "Bless me—me also, O my father!"

35 But he said, "Your brother came with deceit and has taken away your blessing."

36 And *Esau* said, "Is he not rightly named Jacob? For he has supplanted me these two times. He took away my birthright, and now look, he has taken away my blessing!" And he said, "Have you not reserved a blessing for me?"

37 Then Isaac answered and said to Esau, "Indeed I have made him your master, and all his brethren I have given to him as servants; with grain and wine I have sustained him. What shall I do now for you, my son?"

38 And Esau said to his father, "Have you only one blessing, my father? Bless me—me also, O my father!" And Esau lifted up his voice and wept.

39 Then Isaac his father answered and said to him:

"Behold, your dwelling shall be
   of the fatness of the earth,
   And of the dew of heaven from
     above.
40 By your sword you shall live,
   And you shall serve your
     brother;
   And it shall come to pass, when
     you become restless,
   That you shall break his yoke
     from your neck."

41 So Esau hated Jacob because of the blessing with which his father blessed him, and Esau said in his heart, "The days of mourning for my father are at hand; then I will kill my brother Jacob."

42 And the words of Esau her older son were told to Rebekah. So she

sent and called Jacob her younger son, and said to him, "Surely your brother Esau comforts himself concerning you *by intending* to kill you. 43 Now therefore, my son, obey my voice: arise, flee to my brother Laban in Haran. 44 And stay with him a few days, until your brother's fury turns away, 45 until your brother's anger turns away from you, and he forgets what you have done to him; then I will send and bring you from there. Why should I be bereaved also of you both in one day?"

46 And Rebekah said to Isaac, "I am weary of my life because of the daughters of Heth; if Jacob takes a wife of the daughters of Heth, like these *who are* the daughters of the land, what good will my life be to me?"

28 Then Isaac called Jacob and blessed him, and charged him, and said to him: "You shall not take a wife from the daughters of Canaan. 2 Arise, go to Padan Aram, to the house of Bethuel your mother's father; and take yourself a wife from there of the daughters of Laban your mother's brother.

3   "May God Almighty bless you,
    And make you fruitful and
      multiply you,
    That you may be an assembly
      of peoples;
4   And give you the blessing of
    Abraham,
    To you and your descendants
      with you,
    That you may inherit the land
    In which you are a stranger,
    Which God gave to Abraham."

5 So Isaac sent Jacob away, and he went to Padan Aram, to Laban the son of Bethuel the Syrian, the brother of Rebekah, the mother of Jacob and Esau.

6 Esau saw that Isaac had blessed Jacob and sent him away to Padan Aram to take himself a wife from there, *and that* as he blessed him he gave him a charge, saying, "You shall not take a wife from the daughters of Canaan," 7 and that Jacob had obeyed his father and his mother and had gone to Padan Aram. 8 Also Esau saw that the daughters of Canaan did not please his father Isaac. 9 So Esau went to Ishmael and took Mahalath

the daughter of Ishmael, Abraham's son, the sister of Nebajoth, to be his wife in addition to the wives he had.

10 Now Jacob went out from Beersheba and went toward Haran. 11 So he came to a certain place and stayed there all night, because the sun had set. And he took one of the stones of that place and put it at his head, and he lay down in that place to sleep. 12 Then he dreamed, and behold, a ladder *was* set up on the earth, and its top reached to heaven; and there the angels of God were ascending and descending on it.

13 And behold, the LORD stood above it and said: "I *am* the LORD God of Abraham your father and the God of Isaac; the land on which you lie I will give to you and your descendants. 14 Also your descendants shall be as the dust of the earth; you shall spread abroad to the west and the east, to the north and the south; and in you and in your seed all the families of the earth shall be blessed. 15 Behold, I *am* with you and will keep you wherever you go, and will bring you back to this land; for I will not leave you until I have done what I have spoken to you."

16 Then Jacob awoke from his sleep and said, "Surely the LORD is in this place, and I did not know *it*." 17 And he was afraid and said, "How awesome *is* this place! This *is* none other than the house of God, and this *is* the gate of heaven!"

18 Then Jacob rose early in the morning, and took the stone that he had put at his head, set it up as a pillar, and poured oil on top of it. 19 And he called the name of that place Bethel;[a] but the name of that city had been Luz previously. 20 Then Jacob made a vow, saying, "If God will be with me, and keep me in this way that I am going, and give me bread to eat and clothing to put on, 21 so that I come back to my father's house in peace, then the LORD shall be my God. 22 And this stone which I have set as a pillar shall be God's house, and of all that You give me I will surely give a tenth to You."

29 So Jacob went on his journey and came to the land of the people of the East. 2 And he looked,

28:19 *a*Or *House of God*

and saw a well in the field; and behold, there *were* three flocks of sheep lying by it; for out of that well they watered the flocks. A large stone *was* on the well's mouth. 3 Now all the flocks would be gathered there; and they would roll the stone from the well's mouth, water the sheep, and put the stone back in its place on the well's mouth.

4 And Jacob said to them, "My brethren, where *are* you from?"

And they said, "We *are* from Haran."

5 Then he said to them, "Do you know Laban the son of Nahor?"

And they said, "We know him."

6 So he said to them, "Is he well?"

And they said, "*He is* well. And look, his daughter Rachel is coming with the sheep."

7 Then he said, "Look, *it is* still high day; *it is* not time for the cattle to be gathered together. Water the sheep, and go and feed *them*."

8 But they said, "We cannot until all the flocks are gathered together, and they have rolled the stone from the well's mouth; then we water the sheep."

9 Now while he was still speaking with them, Rachel came with her father's sheep, for she was a shepherdess. 10 And it came to pass, when Jacob saw Rachel the daughter of Laban his mother's brother, and the sheep of Laban his mother's brother, that Jacob went near and rolled the stone from the well's mouth, and watered the flock of Laban his mother's brother. 11 Then Jacob kissed Rachel, and lifted up his voice and wept. 12 And Jacob told Rachel that he *was* her father's relative and that he *was* Rebekah's son. So she ran and told her father.

13 Then it came to pass, when Laban heard the report about Jacob his sister's son, that he ran to meet him, and embraced him and kissed him, and brought him to his house. So he told Laban all these things. 14 And Laban said to him, "Surely you *are* my bone and my flesh." And he stayed with him for a month.

15 Then Laban said to Jacob, "Because you *are* my relative, should you therefore serve me for nothing? Tell me, what *should* your wages be?" 16 Now Laban had two daughters: the name of the elder *was* Leah, and the name of the younger *was* Rachel. 17 Leah's eyes *were* delicate, but Rachel was beautiful of form and appearance.

18 Now Jacob loved Rachel; so he said, "I will serve you seven years for Rachel your younger daughter."

19 And Laban said, "*It is* better that I give her to you than that I should give her to another man. Stay with me." 20 So Jacob served seven years for Rachel, and they seemed *only* a few days to him because of the love he had for her.

21 Then Jacob said to Laban, "Give *me* my wife, for my days are fulfilled, that I may go in to her." 22 And Laban gathered together all the men of the place and made a feast. 23 Now it came to pass in the evening, that he took Leah his daughter and brought her to Jacob; and he went in to her. 24 And Laban gave his maid Zilpah to his daughter Leah *as* a maid. 25 So it came to pass in the morning, that behold, it *was* Leah. And he said to Laban, "What is this you have done to me? Was it not for Rachel that I served you? Why then have you deceived me?"

26 And Laban said, "It must not be done so in our country, to give the younger before the firstborn. 27 Fulfill her week, and we will give you this one also for the service which you will serve with me still another seven years."

28 Then Jacob did so and fulfilled her week. So he gave him his daughter Rachel as wife also. 29 And Laban gave his maid Bilhah to his daughter Rachel as a maid. 30 Then *Jacob* also went in to Rachel, and he also loved Rachel more than Leah. And he served with Laban still another seven years.

31 When the LORD saw that Leah *was* unloved, He opened her womb; but Rachel *was* barren. 32 So Leah conceived and bore a son, and she called his name Reuben;*a* for she said, "The LORD has surely looked on my affliction. Now therefore, my husband will love me." 33 Then she conceived again and bore a son, and said, "Because the LORD has heard that I *am* unloved, He has therefore given me this *son* also." And she called his name Simeon.*a* 34 She con-

29:32 *a*Literally *See, a Son*   29:33 *a*Literally *Heard* ceived again and bore a son, and said, "Now this time my husband will become attached to me, because I have borne him three sons." Therefore his name was called Levi.*a* 35 And she conceived again and bore a son, and said, "Now I will praise the LORD." Therefore she called his name Judah.*a* Then she stopped bearing.

30 Now when Rachel saw that she bore Jacob no children, Rachel envied her sister, and said to Jacob, "Give me children, or else I die!"

2 And Jacob's anger was aroused against Rachel, and he said, "*Am* I in the place of God, who has withheld from you the fruit of the womb?"

3 So she said, "Here is my maid Bilhah; go in to her, and she will bear *a child* on my knees, that I also may have children by her." 4 Then she gave him Bilhah her maid as wife, and Jacob went in to her. 5 And Bilhah conceived and bore Jacob a son. 6 Then Rachel said, "God has judged my case; and He has also heard my voice and given me a son." Therefore she called his name Dan.*a* 7 And Rachel's maid Bilhah conceived again and bore Jacob a second son. 8 Then Rachel said, "With great wrestlings I have wrestled with my sister, *and* indeed I have prevailed." So she called his name Naphtali.*a*

9 When Leah saw that she had stopped bearing, she took Zilpah her maid and gave her to Jacob as wife. 10 And Leah's maid Zilpah bore Jacob a son. 11 Then Leah said, "A troop comes!"*a* So she called his name Gad.*b* 12 And Leah's maid Zilpah bore Jacob a second son. 13 Then Leah said, "I am happy, for the daughters will call me blessed." So she called his name Asher.*a*

14 Now Reuben went in the days of wheat harvest and found mandrakes in the field, and brought them to his mother Leah. Then Rachel said to Leah, "Please give me *some* of your son's mandrakes."

15 But she said to her, "*Is it* a small matter that you have taken away my husband? Would you take away my son's mandrakes also?"

And Rachel said, "Therefore he will lie with you tonight for your son's mandrakes."

16 When Jacob came out of the field in the evening, Leah went out to meet him and said, "You must come in to me, for I have surely hired you with my son's mandrakes." And he lay with her that night.

17 And God listened to Leah, and she conceived and bore Jacob a fifth son. 18 Leah said, "God has given me my wages, because I have given my maid to my husband." So she called his name Issachar.*a* 19 Then Leah conceived again and bore Jacob a sixth son. 20 And Leah said, "God has endowed me *with* a good endowment; now my husband will dwell with me, because I have borne him six sons." So she called his name Zebulun.*a* 21 Afterward she bore a daughter, and called her name Dinah.

22 Then God remembered Rachel, and God listened to her and opened her womb. 23 And she conceived and bore a son, and said, "God has taken away my reproach." 24 So she called his name Joseph,*a* and said, "The LORD shall add to me another son."

25 And it came to pass, when Rachel had borne Joseph, that Jacob said to Laban, "Send me away, that I may go to my own place and to my country. 26 Give *me* my wives and my children for whom I have served you, and let me go; for you know my service which I have done for you."

27 And Laban said to him, "Please stay, if I have found favor in your eyes, *for* I have learned by experience that the LORD has blessed me for your sake." 28 Then he said, "Name me your wages, and I will give *it*."

29 So *Jacob* said to him, "You know how I have served you and how your livestock has been with me. 30 For what you had before I *came* *was* little, and it has increased to a great amount; the LORD has blessed you since my coming. And now, when shall I also provide for my own house?"

29:34 *a*Literally *Attached*   29:35 *a*Literally *Praise*   30:6 *a*Literally *Judge*   30:8 *a*Literally *My Wrestling*   30:11 *a*Following Qere, Syriac, and Targum; Kethib, Septuagint, and Vulgate read *in fortune.* *b*Literally *Troop* or *Fortune*   30:13 *a*Literally *Happy*   30:18 *a*Literally *Wages* 30:20 *a*Literally *Dwelling*   30:24 *a*Literally *He Will Add*

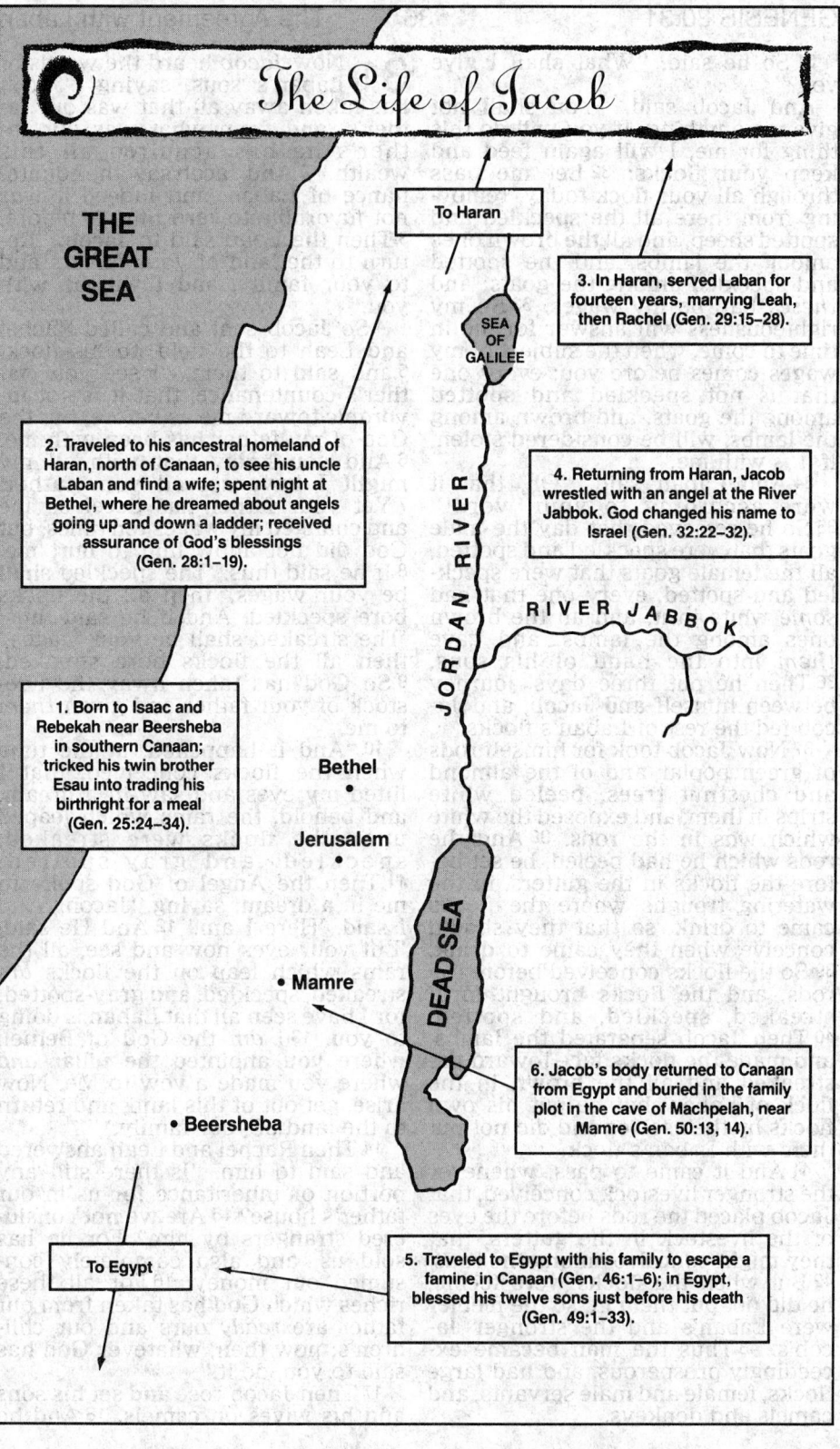

The Life of Jacob

THE GREAT SEA

To Haran

SEA OF GALILEE

JORDAN RIVER

RIVER JABBOK

Bethel

Jerusalem

Mamre

DEAD SEA

Beersheba

To Egypt

3. In Haran, served Laban for fourteen years, marrying Leah, then Rachel (Gen. 29:15–28).

2. Traveled to his ancestral homeland of Haran, north of Canaan, to see his uncle Laban and find a wife; spent night at Bethel, where he dreamed about angels going up and down a ladder; received assurance of God's blessings (Gen. 28:1–19).

4. Returning from Haran, Jacob wrestled with an angel at the River Jabbok. God changed his name to Israel (Gen. 32:22–32).

1. Born to Isaac and Rebekah near Beersheba in southern Canaan; tricked his twin brother Esau into trading his birthright for a meal (Gen. 25:24–34).

6. Jacob's body returned to Canaan from Egypt and buried in the family plot in the cave of Machpelah, near Mamre (Gen. 50:13, 14).

5. Traveled to Egypt with his family to escape a famine in Canaan (Gen. 46:1–6); in Egypt, blessed his twelve sons just before his death (Gen. 49:1–33).

31 So he said, "What shall I give you?"

And Jacob said, "You shall not give me anything. If you will do this thing for me, I will again feed and keep your flocks: 32 Let me pass through all your flock today, removing from there all the speckled and spotted sheep, and all the brown ones among the lambs, and the spotted and speckled among the goats; and *these* shall be my wages. 33 So my righteousness will answer for me in time to come, when the subject of my wages comes before you: every one that *is* not speckled and spotted among the goats, and brown among the lambs, will be considered stolen, if *it is* with me."

34 And Laban said, "Oh, that it were according to your word!" 35 So he removed that day the male goats that were speckled and spotted, all the female goats that were speckled and spotted, every one that had *some* white in it, and all the brown ones among the lambs, and gave *them* into the hand of his sons. 36 Then he put three days' journey between himself and Jacob, and Jacob fed the rest of Laban's flocks.

37 Now Jacob took for himself rods of green poplar and of the almond and chestnut trees, peeled white strips in them, and exposed the white which *was* in the rods. 38 And the rods which he had peeled, he set before the flocks in the gutters, in the watering troughs where the flocks came to drink, so that they should conceive when they came to drink. 39 So the flocks conceived before the rods, and the flocks brought forth streaked, speckled, and spotted. 40 Then Jacob separated the lambs, and made the flocks face toward the streaked and all the brown in the flock of Laban; but he put his own flocks by themselves and did not put them with Laban's flock.

41 And it came to pass, whenever the stronger livestock conceived, that Jacob placed the rods before the eyes of the livestock in the gutters, that they might conceive among the rods. 42 But when the flocks were feeble, he did not put *them* in; so the feebler were Laban's and the stronger Jacob's. 43 Thus the man became exceedingly prosperous, and had large flocks, female and male servants, and camels and donkeys.

31 Now *Jacob* heard the words of Laban's sons, saying, "Jacob has taken away all that was our father's, and from what was our father's he has acquired all this wealth." 2 And Jacob saw the countenance of Laban, and indeed it *was* not *favorable* toward him as before. 3 Then the LORD said to Jacob, "Return to the land of your fathers and to your family, and I will be with you."

4 So Jacob sent and called Rachel and Leah to the field, to his flock, 5 and said to them, "I see your father's countenance, that it *is* not *favorable* toward me as before; but the God of my father has been with me. 6 And you know that with all my might I have served your father. 7 Yet your father has deceived me and changed my wages ten times, but God did not allow him to hurt me. 8 If he said thus: 'The speckled shall be your wages,' then all the flocks bore speckled. And if he said thus: 'The streaked shall be your wages,' then all the flocks bore streaked. 9 So God has taken away the livestock of your father and given *them* to me.

10 "And it happened, at the time when the flocks conceived, that I lifted my eyes and saw in a dream, and behold, the rams which leaped upon the flocks *were* streaked, speckled, and gray-spotted. 11 Then the Angel of God spoke to me in a dream, saying, 'Jacob.' And I said, 'Here I am.' 12 And He said, 'Lift your eyes now and see, all the rams which leap on the flocks *are* streaked, speckled, and gray-spotted; for I have seen all that Laban is doing to you. 13 I *am* the God of Bethel, where you anointed the pillar *and* where you made a vow to Me. Now arise, get out of this land, and return to the land of your family.' "

14 Then Rachel and Leah answered and said to him, "Is there still any portion or inheritance for us in our father's house? 15 Are we not considered strangers by him? For he has sold us, and also completely consumed our money. 16 For all these riches which God has taken from our father are *really* ours and our children's; now then, whatever God has said to you, do it."

17 Then Jacob rose and set his sons and his wives on camels. 18 And he

carried away all his livestock and all his possessions which he had gained, his acquired livestock which he had gained in Padan Aram, to go to his father Isaac in the land of Canaan. 19 Now Laban had gone to shear his sheep, and Rachel had stolen the household idols that were her father's. 20 And Jacob stole away, unknown to Laban the Syrian, in that he did not tell him that he intended to flee. 21 So he fled with all that he had. He arose and crossed the river, and headed toward the mountains of Gilead.

22 And Laban was told on the third day that Jacob had fled. 23 Then he took his brethren with him and pursued him for seven days' journey, and he overtook him in the mountains of Gilead. 24 But God had come to Laban the Syrian in a dream by night, and said to him, "Be careful that you speak to Jacob neither good nor bad."

25 So Laban overtook Jacob. Now Jacob had pitched his tent in the mountains, and Laban with his brethren pitched in the mountains of Gilead.

26 And Laban said to Jacob: "What have you done, that you have stolen away unknown to me, and carried away my daughters like captives taken with the sword? 27 Why did you flee away secretly, and steal away from me, and not tell me; for I might have sent you away with joy and songs, with timbrel and harp? 28 And you did not allow me to kiss my sons and my daughters. Now you have done foolishly in so doing. 29 It is in my power to do you harm, but the God of your father spoke to me last night, saying, 'Be careful that you speak to Jacob neither good nor bad.' 30 And now you have surely gone because you greatly long for your father's house, but why did you steal my gods?"

31 Then Jacob answered and said to Laban, "Because I was afraid, for I said, 'Perhaps you would take your daughters from me by force.' 32 With whomever you find your gods, do not let him live. In the presence of our brethren, identify what I have of yours and take it with you." For Jacob did not know that Rachel had stolen them.

33 And Laban went into Jacob's tent, into Leah's tent, and into the two maids' tents, but he did not find them. Then he went out of Leah's tent and entered Rachel's tent. 34 Now Rachel had taken the household idols, put them in the camel's saddle, and sat on them. And Laban searched all about the tent but did not find them. 35 And she said to her father, "Let it not displease my lord that I cannot rise before you, for the manner of women is with me." And he searched but did not find the household idols.

36 Then Jacob was angry and rebuked Laban, and Jacob answered and said to Laban: "What is my trespass? What is my sin, that you have so hotly pursued me? 37 Although you have searched all my things, what part of your household things have you found? Set it here before my brethren and your brethren, that they may judge between us both! 38 These twenty years I have been with you; your ewes and your female goats have not miscarried their young, and I have not eaten the rams of your flock. 39 That which was torn by beasts I did not bring to you; I bore the loss of it. You required it from my hand, whether stolen by day or stolen by night. 40 There I was! In the day the drought consumed me, and the frost by night, and my sleep departed from my eyes. 41 Thus I have been in your house twenty years; I served you fourteen years for your two daughters, and six years for your flock, and you have changed my wages ten times. 42 Unless the God of my father, the God of Abraham and the Fear of Isaac, had been with me, surely now you would have sent me away empty-handed. God has seen my affliction and the labor of my hands, and rebuked you last night."

43 And Laban answered and said to Jacob, "These daughters are my daughters, and these children are my children, and this flock is my flock; all that you see is mine. But what can I do this day to these my daughters or to their children whom they have borne? 44 Now therefore, come, let us make a covenant, you and I, and let it be a witness between you and me."

45 So Jacob took a stone and set it up as a pillar. 46 Then Jacob said to his brethren, "Gather stones." And they took stones and made a heap, and they ate there on the heap.

47 Laban called it Jegar Sahadutha,ᵃ but Jacob called it Galeed.ᵇ 48 And Laban said, "This heap *is* a witness between you and me this day." Therefore its name was called Galeed, 49 also Mizpah,ᵃ because he said, "May the LORD watch between you and me when we are absent one from another. 50 If you afflict my daughters, or if you take *other* wives besides my daughters, *although* no man *is* with us—see, God *is* witness between you and me!"

51 Then Laban said to Jacob, "Here is this heap and here is *this* pillar, which I have placed between you and me. 52 This heap *is* a witness, and *this* pillar *is* a witness, that I will not pass beyond this heap to you, and you will not pass beyond this heap and this pillar to me, for harm. 53 The God of Abraham, the God of Nahor, and the God of their father judge between us." And Jacob swore by the Fear of his father Isaac. 54 Then Jacob offered a sacrifice on the mountain, and called his brethren to eat bread. And they ate bread and stayed all night on the mountain. 55 And early in the morning Laban arose, and kissed his sons and daughters and blessed them. Then Laban departed and returned to his place.

32 So Jacob went on his way, and the angels of God met him. 2 When Jacob saw them, he said, "This *is* God's camp." And he called the name of that place Mahanaim.ᵃ

3 Then Jacob sent messengers before him to Esau his brother in the land of Seir, the country of Edom. 4 And he commanded them, saying, "Speak thus to my lord Esau, 'Thus your servant Jacob says: "I have dwelt with Laban and stayed there until now. 5 I have oxen, donkeys, flocks, and male and female servants; and I have sent to tell my lord, that I may find favor in your sight." ' "

6 Then the messengers returned to Jacob, saying, "We came to your brother Esau, and he also is coming to meet you, and four hundred men *are* with him." 7 So Jacob was greatly afraid and distressed; and he divided the people that *were* with him, and the flocks and herds and camels, into two companies. 8 And he said, "If Esau comes to the one company and attacks it, then the other company which is left will escape."

9 Then Jacob said, "O God of my father Abraham and God of my father Isaac, the LORD who said to me, 'Return to your country and to your family, and I will deal well with you': 10 I am not worthy of the least of all the mercies and of all the truth which You have shown Your servant; for I crossed over this Jordan with my staff, and now I have become two companies. 11 Deliver me, I pray, from the hand of my brother, from the hand of Esau; for I fear him, lest he come and attack me *and* the mother with the children. 12 For You said, 'I will surely treat you well, and make your descendants as the sand of the sea, which cannot be numbered for multitude.' "

13 So he lodged there that same night, and took what came to his hand as a present for Esau his brother: 14 two hundred female goats and twenty male goats, two hundred ewes and twenty rams, 15 thirty milk camels with their colts, forty cows and ten bulls, twenty female donkeys and ten foals. 16 Then he delivered *them* to the hand of his servants, every drove by itself, and said to his servants, "Pass over before me, and put some distance between successive droves." 17 And he commanded the first one, saying, "When Esau my brother meets you and asks you, saying, 'To whom do you belong, and where are you going? Whose *are* these in front of you?' 18 then you shall say, 'They *are* your servant Jacob's. It *is* a present sent to my lord Esau; and behold, he also *is* behind us.' " 19 So he commanded the second, the third, and all who followed the droves, saying, "In this manner you shall speak to Esau when you find him; 20 and also say, 'Behold, your servant Jacob *is* behind us.' " For he said, "I will appease him with the present that goes before me, and afterward I will see his face; perhaps he will accept me." 21 So the present went on over before him, but he himself lodged that night in the camp.

22 And he arose that night and took his two wives, his two female ser-

31:47 ᵃLiterally, in Aramaic, *Heap of Witness*   ᵇLiterally, in Hebrew, *Heap of Witness*
31:49 ᵃLiterally *Watch*   32:2 ᵃLiterally *Double Camp*

vants, and his eleven sons, and crossed over the ford of Jabbok. 23 He took them, sent them over the brook, and sent over what he had. 24 Then Jacob was left alone; and a Man wrestled with him until the breaking of day. 25 Now when He saw that He did not prevail against him, He touched the socket of his hip; and the socket of Jacob's hip was out of joint as He wrestled with him. 26 And He said, "Let Me go, for the day breaks."

But he said, "I will not let You go unless You bless me!"

27 So He said to him, "What is your name?"

He said, "Jacob."

28 And He said, "Your name shall no longer be called Jacob, but Israel;[a] for you have struggled with God and with men, and have prevailed."

29 Then Jacob asked, saying, "Tell me Your name, I pray."

And He said, "Why is it that you ask about My name?" And He blessed him there.

30 So Jacob called the name of the place Peniel:[a] "For I have seen God face to face, and my life is preserved." 31 Just as he crossed over Penuel[a] the sun rose on him, and he limped on his hip. 32 Therefore to this day the children of Israel do not eat the muscle that shrank, which is on the hip socket, because He touched the socket of Jacob's hip in the muscle that shrank.

33 Now Jacob lifted his eyes and looked, and there, Esau was coming, and with him were four hundred men. So he divided the children among Leah, Rachel, and the two maidservants. 2 And he put the maidservants and their children in front, Leah and her children behind, and Rachel and Joseph last. 3 Then he crossed over before them and bowed himself to the ground seven times, until he came near to his brother.

4 But Esau ran to meet him, and embraced him, and fell on his neck and kissed him, and they wept. 5 And he lifted his eyes and saw the women and children, and said, "Who are these with you?"

So he said, "The children whom God has graciously given your ser-

vant." 6 Then the maidservants came near, they and their children, and bowed down. 7 And Leah also came near with her children, and they bowed down. Afterward Joseph and Rachel came near, and they bowed down.

8 Then Esau said, "What do you mean by all this company which I met?"

And he said, "These are to find favor in the sight of my lord."

9 But Esau said, "I have enough, my brother; keep what you have for yourself."

10 And Jacob said, "No, please, if I have now found favor in your sight, then receive my present from my hand, inasmuch as I have seen your face as though I had seen the face of God, and you were pleased with me. 11 Please, take my blessing that is brought to you, because God has dealt graciously with me, and because I have enough." So he urged him, and he took it.

12 Then Esau said, "Let us take our journey; let us go, and I will go before you."

13 But Jacob said to him, "My lord knows that the children are weak, and the flocks and herds which are nursing are with me. And if the men should drive them hard one day, all the flock will die. 14 Please let my lord go on ahead before his servant. I will lead on slowly at a pace which the livestock that go before me, and the children, are able to endure, until I come to my lord in Seir."

15 And Esau said, "Now let me leave with you some of the people who are with me."

But he said, "What need is there? Let me find favor in the sight of my lord." 16 So Esau returned that day on his way to Seir. 17 And Jacob journeyed to Succoth, built himself a house, and made booths for his livestock. Therefore the name of the place is called Succoth.[a]

18 Then Jacob came safely to the city of Shechem, which is in the land of Canaan, when he came from Padan Aram; and he pitched his tent before the city. 19 And he bought the parcel of land, where he had pitched his tent, from the children of Hamor, Shechem's father, for one hundred

32:28 [a]Literally Prince with God   32:30 [a]Literally Face of God   32:31 [a]Same as Peniel, verse 30
33:17 [a]Literally Booths

pieces of money. 20 Then he erected an altar there and called it El Elohe Israel.a

34 Now Dinah the daughter of Leah, whom she had borne to Jacob, went out to see the daughters of the land. 2 And when Shechem the son of Hamor the Hivite, prince of the country, saw her, he took her and lay with her, and violated her. 3 His soul was strongly attracted to Dinah the daughter of Jacob, and he loved the young woman and spoke kindly to the young woman. 4 So Shechem spoke to his father Hamor, saying, "Get me this young woman as a wife."

5 And Jacob heard that he had defiled Dinah his daughter. Now his sons were with his livestock in the field; so Jacob held his peace until they came. 6 Then Hamor the father of Shechem went out to Jacob to speak with him. 7 And the sons of Jacob came in from the field when they heard it; and the men were grieved and very angry, because he had done a disgraceful thing in Israel by lying with Jacob's daughter, a thing which ought not to be done. 8 But Hamor spoke with them, saying, "The soul of my son Shechem longs for your daughter. Please give her to him as a wife. 9 And make marriages with us; give your daughters to us, and take our daughters to yourselves. 10 So you shall dwell with us, and the land shall be before you. Dwell and trade in it, and acquire possessions for yourselves in it."

11 Then Shechem said to her father and her brothers, "Let me find favor in your eyes, and whatever you say to me I will give. 12 Ask me ever so much dowry and gift, and I will give according to what you say to me; but give me the young woman as a wife."

13 But the sons of Jacob answered Shechem and Hamor his father, and spoke deceitfully, because he had defiled Dinah their sister. 14 And they said to them, "We cannot do this thing, to give our sister to one who is uncircumcised, for that would be a reproach to us. 15 But on this condition we will consent to you: If you will become as we are, if every male of you is circumcised, 16 then we will give our daughters to you, and we will take your daughters to us; and we will dwell with you, and we will become one people. 17 But if you will not heed us and be circumcised, then we will take our daughter and be gone."

18 And their words pleased Hamor and Shechem, Hamor's son. 19 So the young man did not delay to do the thing, because he delighted in Jacob's daughter. He was more honorable than all the household of his father.

20 And Hamor and Shechem his son came to the gate of their city, and spoke with the men of their city, saying: 21 "These men are at peace with us. Therefore let them dwell in the land and trade in it. For indeed the land is large enough for them. Let us take their daughters to us as wives, and let us give them our daughters. 22 Only on this condition will the men consent to dwell with us, to be one people: if every male among us is circumcised as they are circumcised. 23 Will not their livestock, their property, and every animal of theirs be ours? Only let us consent to them, and they will dwell with us." 24 And all who went out of the gate of his city heeded Hamor and Shechem his son; every male was circumcised, all who went out of the gate of his city.

25 Now it came to pass on the third day, when they were in pain, that two of the sons of Jacob, Simeon and Levi, Dinah's brothers, each took his sword and came boldly upon the city and killed all the males. 26 And they killed Hamor and Shechem his son with the edge of the sword, and took Dinah from Shechem's house, and went out. 27 The sons of Jacob came upon the slain, and plundered the city, because their sister had been defiled. 28 They took their sheep, their oxen, and their donkeys, what was in the city and what was in the field, 29 and all their wealth. All their little ones and their wives they took captive; and they plundered even all that was in the houses.

30 Then Jacob said to Simeon and Levi, "You have troubled me by making me obnoxious among the inhabitants of the land, among the Canaanites and the Perizzites; and since I am few in number, they will gather

33:20 aLiterally God, the God of Israel

themselves together against me and kill me. I shall be destroyed, my household and I."

31 But they said, "Should he treat our sister like a harlot?"

35 Then God said to Jacob, "Arise, go up to Bethel and dwell there; and make an altar there to God, who appeared to you when you fled from the face of Esau your brother."

2 And Jacob said to his household and to all who *were* with him, "Put away the foreign gods that *are* among you, purify yourselves, and change your garments. 3 Then let us arise and go up to Bethel; and I will make an altar there to God, who answered me in the day of my distress and has been with me in the way which I have gone." 4 So they gave Jacob all the foreign gods which *were* in their hands, and the earrings which *were* in their ears; and Jacob hid them under the terebinth tree which *was* by Shechem.

5 And they journeyed, and the terror of God was upon the cities that *were* all around them, and they did not pursue the sons of Jacob. 6 So Jacob came to Luz (that *is,* Bethel), which *is* in the land of Canaan, he and all the people who *were* with him. 7 And he built an altar there and called the place El Bethel,*a* because there God appeared to him when he fled from the face of his brother.

8 Now Deborah, Rebekah's nurse, died, and she was buried below Bethel under the terebinth tree. So the name of it was called Allon Bachuth.*a*

9 Then God appeared to Jacob again, when he came from Padan Aram, and blessed him. 10 And God said to him, "Your name *is* Jacob; your name shall not be called Jacob anymore, but Israel shall be your name." So He called his name Israel. 11 Also God said to him: "I *am* God Almighty. Be fruitful and multiply; a nation and a company of nations shall proceed from you, and kings shall come from your body. 12 The land which I gave Abraham and Isaac I give to you; and to your descendants after you I give this land." 13 Then God went up from him

in the place where He talked with him. 14 So Jacob set up a pillar in the place where He talked with him, a pillar of stone; and he poured a drink offering on it, and he poured oil on it. 15 And Jacob called the name of the place where God spoke with him, Bethel.

16 Then they journeyed from Bethel. And when there was but a little distance to go to Ephrath, Rachel labored *in childbirth,* and she had hard labor. 17 Now it came to pass, when she was in hard labor, that the midwife said to her, "Do not fear; you will have this son also." 18 And so it was, as her soul was departing (for she died), that she called his name Ben-Oni;*a* but his father called him Benjamin.*b* 19 So Rachel died and was buried on the way to Ephrath (that *is,* Bethlehem). 20 And Jacob set a pillar on her grave, which *is* the pillar of Rachel's grave to this day.

21 Then Israel journeyed and pitched his tent beyond the tower of Eder. 22 And it happened, when Israel dwelt in that land, that Reuben went and lay with Bilhah his father's concubine; and Israel heard *about it.*

Now the sons of Jacob were twelve: 23 the sons of Leah *were* Reuben, Jacob's firstborn, and Simeon, Levi, Judah, Issachar, and Zebulun; 24 the sons of Rachel *were* Joseph and Benjamin; 25 the sons of Bilhah, Rachel's maidservant, *were* Dan and Naphtali; 26 and the sons of Zilpah, Leah's maidservant, *were* Gad and Asher. These *were* the sons of Jacob who were born to him in Padan Aram.

27 Then Jacob came to his father Isaac at Mamre, or Kirjath Arba*a* (that *is,* Hebron), where Abraham and Isaac had dwelt. 28 Now the days of Isaac were one hundred and eighty years. 29 So Isaac breathed his last and died, and was gathered to his people, *being* old and full of days. And his sons Esau and Jacob buried him.

36 Now this *is* the genealogy of Esau, who is Edom. 2 Esau took his wives from the daughters of Canaan: Adah the daughter of Elon the Hittite; Aholibamah the daughter of

---

35:7 *a*Literally *God of the House of God*   35:8 *a*Literally *Terebinth of Weeping*   35:18 *a*Literally *Son of My Sorrow*   *b*Literally *Son of the Right Hand*   35:27 *a*Literally *Town of Arbah*

Anah, the daughter of Zibeon the Hivite; 3 and Basemath, Ishmael's daughter, sister of Nebajoth. 4 Now Adah bore Eliphaz to Esau, and Basemath bore Reuel. 5 And Aholibamah bore Jeush, Jaalam, and Korah. These *were* the sons of Esau who were born to him in the land of Canaan.

6 Then Esau took his wives, his sons, his daughters, and all the persons of his household, his cattle and all his animals, and all his goods which he had gained in the land of Canaan, and went to a country away from the presence of his brother Jacob. 7 For their possessions were too great for them to dwell together, and the land where they were strangers could not support them because of their livestock. 8 So Esau dwelt in Mount Seir. Esau *is* Edom.

9 And this *is* the genealogy of Esau the father of the Edomites in Mount Seir. 10 These *were* the names of Esau's sons: Eliphaz the son of Adah the wife of Esau, and Reuel the son of Basemath the wife of Esau. 11 And the sons of Eliphaz were Teman, Omar, Zepho,*a* Gatam, and Kenaz.

12 Now Timna was the concubine of Eliphaz, Esau's son, and she bore Amalek to Eliphaz. These *were* the sons of Adah, Esau's wife.

13 These *were* the sons of Reuel: Nahath, Zerah, Shammah, and Mizzah. These were the sons of Basemath, Esau's wife.

14 These were the sons of Aholibamah, Esau's wife, the daughter of Anah, the daughter of Zibeon. And she bore to Esau: Jeush, Jaalam, and Korah.

15 These *were* the chiefs of the sons of Esau. The sons of Eliphaz, the firstborn *son* of Esau, were Chief Teman, Chief Omar, Chief Zepho, Chief Kenaz, 16 Chief Korah,*a* Chief Gatam, *and* Chief Amalek. These *were* the chiefs of Eliphaz in the land of Edom. They *were* the sons of Adah.

17 These *were* the sons of Reuel, Esau's son: Chief Nahath, Chief Zerah, Chief Shammah, and Chief Mizzah. These *were* the chiefs of Reuel in the land of Edom. These

were the sons of Basemath, Esau's wife.

18 And these *were* the sons of Aholibamah, Esau's wife: Chief Jeush, Chief Jaalam, and Chief Korah. These *were* the chiefs *who* descended from Aholibamah, Esau's wife, the daughter of Anah. 19 These *were* the sons of Esau, who is Edom, and these *were* their chiefs.

20 These *were* the sons of Seir the Horite who inhabited the land: Lotan, Shobal, Zibeon, Anah, 21 Dishon, Ezer, and Dishan. These *were* the chiefs of the Horites, the sons of Seir, in the land of Edom.

22 And the sons of Lotan were Hori and Hemam.*a* Lotan's sister *was* Timna.

23 These *were* the sons of Shobal: Alvan,*a* Manahath, Ebal, Shepho,*b* and Onam.

24 These *were* the sons of Zibeon: both Ajah and Anah. This *was the* Anah who found the water*a* in the wilderness as he pastured the donkeys of his father Zibeon. 25 These *were* the children of Anah: Dishon and Aholibamah the daughter of Anah.

26 These *were* the sons of Dishon:*a* Hemdan,*b* Eshban, Ithran, and Cheran. 27 These *were* the sons of Ezer: Bilhan, Zaavan, and Akan.*a* 28 These *were* the sons of Dishan: Uz and Aran.

29 These *were* the chiefs of the Horites: Chief Lotan, Chief Shobal, Chief Zibeon, Chief Anah, 30 Chief Dishon, Chief Ezer, and Chief Dishan. These *were* the chiefs of the Horites, according to their chiefs in the land of Seir.

31 Now these *were* the kings who reigned in the land of Edom before any king reigned over the children of Israel: 32 Bela the son of Beor reigned in Edom, and the name of his city *was* Dinhabah. 33 And when Bela died, Jobab the son of Zerah of Bozrah reigned in his place. 34 When Jobab died, Husham of the land of the Temanites reigned in his place. 35 And when Husham died, Hadad the son of Bedad, who attacked Midian in the field of Moab, reigned in his place. And the name

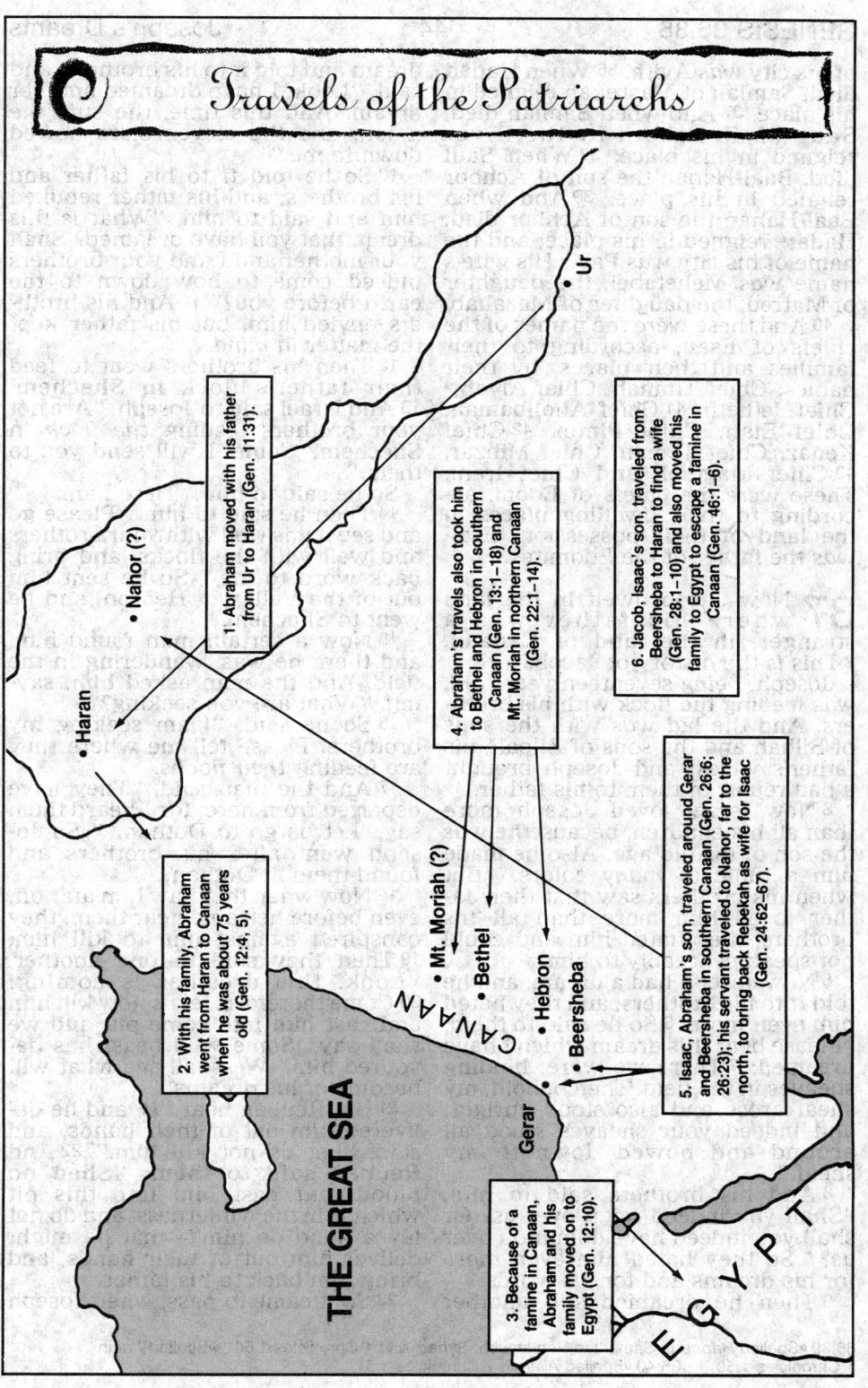

Travels of the Patriarchs

1. Abraham moved with his father from Ur to Haran (Gen. 11:31).

2. With his family, Abraham went from Haran to Canaan when he was about 75 years old (Gen. 12:4, 5).

3. Because of a famine in Canaan, Abraham and his family moved on to Egypt (Gen. 12:10).

4. Abraham's travels also took him to Bethel and Hebron in southern Canaan (Gen. 13:1–18) and Mt. Moriah in northern Canaan (Gen. 22:1–14).

5. Isaac, Abraham's son, traveled around Gerar (Gen. 26:6; 26:23); his servant traveled to Nahor, far to the north, to bring back Rebekah as wife for Isaac (Gen. 24:62–67).

6. Jacob, Isaac's son, traveled from Beersheba to Haran to find a wife (Gen. 28:1–10) and also moved his family to Egypt to escape a famine in Canaan (Gen. 46:1–6).

Ur

Haran

Nahor (?)

Mt. Moriah (?)

Bethel

Hebron

Beersheba

Gerar

CANAAN

THE GREAT SEA

EGYPT

of his city *was* Avith. 36 When Hadad died, Samlah of Masrekah reigned in his place. 37 And when Samlah died, Saul of Rehoboth-*by*-the-River reigned in his place. 38 When Saul died, Baal-Hanan the son of Achbor reigned in his place. 39 And when Baal-Hanan the son of Achbor died, Hadar*ᵃ* reigned in his place; and the name of his city *was* Pau.*ᵇ* His wife's name *was* Mehetabel, the daughter of Matred, the daughter of Mezahab.

40 And these *were* the names of the chiefs of Esau, according to their families and their places, by their names: Chief Timnah, Chief Alvah,*ᵃ* Chief Jetheth, 41 Chief Aholibamah, Chief Elah, Chief Pinon, 42 Chief Kenaz, Chief Teman, Chief Mibzar, 43 Chief Magdiel, and Chief Iram. These *were* the chiefs of Edom, according to their dwelling places in the land of their possession. Esau *was* the father of the Edomites.

37 Now Jacob dwelt in the land where his father was a stranger, in the land of Canaan. 2 This *is* the history of Jacob.

Joseph, *being* seventeen years old, was feeding the flock with his brothers. And the lad *was* with the sons of Bilhah and the sons of Zilpah, his father's wives; and Joseph brought a bad report of them to his father. 3 Now Israel loved Joseph more than all his children, because he *was* the son of his old age. Also he made him a tunic of *many* colors. 4 But when his brothers saw that their father loved him more than all his brothers, they hated him and could not speak peaceably to him.

5 Now Joseph had a dream, and he told *it* to his brothers; and they hated him even more. 6 So he said to them, "Please hear this dream which I have dreamed: 7 There we were, binding sheaves in the field. Then behold, my sheaf arose and also stood upright; and indeed your sheaves stood all around and bowed down to my sheaf."

8 And his brothers said to him, "Shall you indeed reign over us? Or shall you indeed have dominion over us?" So they hated him even more for his dreams and for his words. 9 Then he dreamed still another dream and told it to his brothers, and said, "Look, I have dreamed another dream. And this time, the sun, the moon, and the eleven stars bowed down to me."

10 So he told *it* to his father and his brothers; and his father rebuked him and said to him, "What *is* this dream that you have dreamed? Shall your mother and I and your brothers indeed come to bow down to the earth before you?" 11 And his brothers envied him, but his father kept the matter *in mind*.

12 Then his brothers went to feed their father's flock in Shechem. 13 And Israel said to Joseph, "Are not your brothers feeding *the flock* in Shechem? Come, I will send you to them."

So he said to him, "Here I am."

14 Then he said to him, "Please go and see if it is well with your brothers and well with the flocks, and bring back word to me." So he sent him out of the Valley of Hebron, and he went to Shechem.

15 Now a certain man found him, and there he was, wandering in the field. And the man asked him, saying, "What are you seeking?"

16 So he said, "I am seeking my brothers. Please tell me where they are feeding *their flocks*."

17 And the man said, "They have departed from here, for I heard them say, 'Let us go to Dothan.' " So Joseph went after his brothers and found them in Dothan.

18 Now when they saw him afar off, even before he came near them, they conspired against him to kill him. 19 Then they said to one another, "Look, this dreamer is coming! 20 Come therefore, let us now kill him and cast him into some pit; and we shall say, 'Some wild beast has devoured him.' We shall see what will become of his dreams!"

21 But Reuben heard *it,* and he delivered him out of their hands, and said, "Let us not kill him." 22 And Reuben said to them, "Shed no blood, *but* cast him into this pit which *is* in the wilderness, and do not lay a hand on him"—that he might deliver him out of their hands, and bring him back to his father.

23 So it came to pass, when Joseph

36:39 *ᵃ*Spelled *Hadad* in Samaritan Pentateuch, Syriac, and 1 Chronicles 1:50 *ᵇ*Spelled *Pai* in 1 Chronicles 1:50   36:40 *ᵃ*Spelled *Aliah* in 1 Chronicles 1:51

had come to his brothers, that they stripped Joseph *of* his tunic, the tunic of *many* colors that *was* on him. 24 Then they took him and cast him into a pit. And the pit *was* empty; *there was* no water in it.

25 And they sat down to eat a meal. Then they lifted their eyes and looked, and there was a company of Ishmaelites, coming from Gilead with their camels, bearing spices, balm, and myrrh, on their way to carry *them* down to Egypt. 26 So Judah said to his brothers, "What profit *is there* if we kill our brother and conceal his blood? 27 Come and let us sell him to the Ishmaelites, and let not our hand be upon him, for he *is* our brother *and* our flesh." And his brothers listened. 28 Then Midianite traders passed by; so *the brothers* pulled Joseph up and lifted him out of the pit, and sold him to the Ishmaelites for twenty *shekels* of silver. And they took Joseph to Egypt.

29 Then Reuben returned to the pit, and indeed Joseph *was* not in the pit; and he tore his clothes. 30 And he returned to his brothers and said, "The lad *is no more;* and I, where shall I go?"

31 So they took Joseph's tunic, killed a kid of the goats, and dipped the tunic in the blood. 32 Then they sent the tunic of *many* colors, and they brought *it* to their father and said, "We have found this. Do you know whether it *is* your son's tunic or not?"

33 And he recognized it and said, "*It is* my son's tunic. A wild beast has devoured him. Without doubt Joseph is torn to pieces." 34 Then Jacob tore his clothes, put sackcloth on his waist, and mourned for his son many days. 35 And all his sons and all his daughters arose to comfort him; but he refused to be comforted, and he said, "For I shall go down into the grave to my son in mourning." Thus his father wept for him.

36 Now the Midianites*a* had sold him in Egypt to Potiphar, an officer of Pharaoh *and* captain of the guard.

38 It came to pass at that time that Judah departed from his brothers, and visited a certain Adullamite whose name *was* Hirah. 2 And Judah saw there a daughter of a certain Ca-naanite whose name *was* Shua, and he married her and went in to her. 3 So she conceived and bore a son, and he called his name Er. 4 She conceived again and bore a son, and she called his name Onan. 5 And she conceived yet again and bore a son, and called his name Shelah. He was at Chezib when she bore him.

6 Then Judah took a wife for Er his firstborn, and her name *was* Tamar. 7 But Er, Judah's firstborn, was wicked in the sight of the Lord, and the Lord killed him. 8 And Judah said to Onan, "Go in to your brother's wife and marry her, and raise up an heir to your brother." 9 But Onan knew that the heir would not be his; and it came to pass, when he went in to his brother's wife, that he emitted on the ground, lest he should give an heir to his brother. 10 And the thing which he did displeased the Lord; therefore He killed him also.

11 Then Judah said to Tamar his daughter-in-law, "Remain a widow in your father's house till my son Shelah is grown." For he said, "Lest he also die like his brothers." And Tamar went and dwelt in her father's house.

12 Now in the process of time the daughter of Shua, Judah's wife, died; and Judah was comforted, and went up to his sheepshearers at Timnah, he and his friend Hirah the Adullamite. 13 And it was told Tamar, saying, "Look, your father-in-law is going up to Timnah to shear his sheep." 14 So she took off her widow's garments, covered *herself* with a veil and wrapped herself, and sat in an open place which *was* on the way to Timnah; for she saw that Shelah was grown, and she was not given to him as a wife. 15 When Judah saw her, he thought she *was* a harlot, because she had covered her face. 16 Then he turned to her by the way, and said, "Please let me come in to you"; for he did not know that she *was* his daughter-in-law.

So she said, "What will you give me, that you may come in to me?"

17 And he said, "I will send a young goat from the flock."

So she said, "Will you give *me* a pledge till you send *it*?"

18 Then he said, "What pledge shall I give you?"

So she said, "Your signet and cord, and your staff that *is* in your hand." Then he gave *them* to her, and went in to her, and she conceived by him. 19 So she arose and went away, and laid aside her veil and put on the garments of her widowhood.

20 And Judah sent the young goat by the hand of his friend the Adullamite, to receive *his* pledge from the woman's hand, but he did not find her. 21 Then he asked the men of that place, saying, "Where is the harlot who *was* openly by the roadside?"

And they said, "There was no harlot in this *place*."

22 So he returned to Judah and said, "I cannot find her. Also, the men of the place said there was no harlot in this *place*."

23 Then Judah said, "Let her take *them* for herself, lest we be shamed; for I sent this young goat and you have not found her."

24 And it came to pass, about three months after, that Judah was told, saying, "Tamar your daughter-in-law has played the harlot; furthermore she *is* with child by harlotry."

So Judah said, "Bring her out and let her be burned!"

25 When she *was* brought out, she sent to her father-in-law, saying, "By the man to whom these belong, I *am* with child." And she said, "Please determine whose these *are*—the signet and cord, and staff."

26 So Judah acknowledged *them* and said, "She has been more righteous than I, because I did not give her to Shelah my son." And he never knew her again.

27 Now it came to pass, at the time for giving birth, that behold, twins *were* in her womb. 28 And so it was, when she was giving birth, that *the one* put out *his* hand; and the midwife took a scarlet *thread* and bound it on his hand, saying, "This one came out first." 29 Then it happened, as he drew back his hand, that his brother came out unexpectedly; and she said, "How did you break through? *This* breach *be* upon you!" Therefore his name was called Perez.ᵃ 30 Afterward his brother came out who had the scarlet *thread* on his hand. And his name was called Zerah.

38:29 ᵃLiterally *Breach* or *Breakthrough*

39

Now Joseph had been taken down to Egypt. And Potiphar, an officer of Pharaoh, captain of the guard, an Egyptian, bought him from the Ishmaelites who had taken him down there. 2 The Lord was with Joseph, and he was a successful man; and he was in the house of his master the Egyptian. 3 And his master saw that the Lord *was* with him and that the Lord made all he did to prosper in his hand. 4 So Joseph found favor in his sight, and served him. Then he made him overseer of his house, and all *that* he had he put under his authority. 5 So it was, from the time *that* he had made him overseer of his house and all that he had, that the Lord blessed the Egyptian's house for Joseph's sake; and the blessing of the Lord was on all that he had in the house and in the field. 6 Thus he left all that he had in Joseph's hand, and he did not know what he had except for the bread which he ate.

Now Joseph was handsome in form and appearance.

7 And it came to pass after these things that his master's wife cast longing eyes on Joseph, and she said, "Lie with me."

8 But he refused and said to his master's wife, "Look, my master does not know what *is* with me in the house, and he has committed all that he has to my hand. 9 *There is* no one greater in this house than I, nor has he kept back anything from me but you, because you *are* his wife. How then can I do this great wickedness, and sin against God?"

10 So it was, as she spoke to Joseph day by day, that he did not heed her, to lie with her *or* to be with her.

11 But it happened about this time, when Joseph went into the house to do his work, and none of the men of the house *was* inside, 12 that she caught him by his garment, saying, "Lie with me." But he left his garment in her hand, and fled and ran outside. 13 And so it was, when she saw that he had left his garment in her hand and fled outside, 14 that she called to the men of her house and spoke to them, saying, "See, he has brought in to us a Hebrew to mock us. He came in to me to lie with me, and I cried out with a loud voice.

15 And it happened, when he heard that I lifted my voice and cried out, that he left his garment with me, and fled and went outside."

16 So she kept his garment with her until his master came home. 17 Then she spoke to him with words like these, saying, "The Hebrew servant whom you brought to us came in to me to mock me; 18 so it happened, as I lifted my voice and cried out, that he left his garment with me and fled outside."

19 So it was, when his master heard the words which his wife spoke to him, saying, "Your servant did to me after this manner," that his anger was aroused. 20 Then Joseph's master took him and put him into the prison, a place where the king's prisoners were confined. And he was there in the prison. 21 But the LORD was with Joseph and showed him mercy, and He gave him favor in the sight of the keeper of the prison. 22 And the keeper of the prison committed to Joseph's hand all the prisoners who were in the prison; whatever they did there, it was his doing. 23 The keeper of the prison did not look into anything that was under Joseph's authority,a because the LORD was with him; and whatever he did, the LORD made it prosper.

40 It came to pass after these things that the butler and the baker of the king of Egypt offended their lord, the king of Egypt. 2 And Pharaoh was angry with his two officers, the chief butler and the chief baker. 3 So he put them in custody in the house of the captain of the guard, in the prison, the place where Joseph was confined. 4 And the captain of the guard charged Joseph with them, and he served them; so they were in custody for a while.

5 Then the butler and the baker of the king of Egypt, who were confined in the prison, had a dream, both of them, each man's dream in one night and each man's dream with its own interpretation. 6 And Joseph came in to them in the morning and looked at them, and saw that they were sad. 7 So he asked Pharaoh's officers who were with him in the custody of his lord's house, saying, "Why do you look so sad today?"

8 And they said to him, "We each have had a dream, and there is no interpreter of it."

So Joseph said to them, "Do not interpretations belong to God? Tell them to me, please."

9 Then the chief butler told his dream to Joseph, and said to him, "Behold, in my dream a vine was before me, 10 and in the vine were three branches; it was as though it budded, its blossoms shot forth, and its clusters brought forth ripe grapes. 11 Then Pharaoh's cup was in my hand; and I took the grapes and pressed them into Pharaoh's cup, and placed the cup in Pharaoh's hand."

12 And Joseph said to him, "This is the interpretation of it: The three branches are three days. 13 Now within three days Pharaoh will lift up your head and restore you to your place, and you will put Pharaoh's cup in his hand according to the former manner, when you were his butler. 14 But remember me when it is well with you, and please show kindness to me; make mention of me to Pharaoh, and get me out of this house. 15 For indeed I was stolen away from the land of the Hebrews; and also I have done nothing here that they should put me into the dungeon."

16 When the chief baker saw that the interpretation was good, he said to Joseph, "I also was in my dream, and there were three white baskets on my head. 17 In the uppermost basket were all kinds of baked goods for Pharaoh, and the birds ate them out of the basket on my head."

18 So Joseph answered and said, "This is the interpretation of it: The three baskets are three days. 19 Within three days Pharaoh will lift off your head from you and hang you on a tree; and the birds will eat your flesh from you."

20 Now it came to pass on the third day, which was Pharaoh's birthday, that he made a feast for all his servants; and he lifted up the head of the chief butler and of the chief baker among his servants. 21 Then he restored the chief butler to his butlership again, and he placed the cup in Pharaoh's hand. 22 But he hanged the chief baker, as Joseph had inter-

preted to them. 23 Yet the chief butler did not remember Joseph, but forgot him.

41 Then it came to pass, at the end of two full years, that Pharaoh had a dream; and behold, he stood by the river. 2 Suddenly there came up out of the river seven cows, fine looking and fat; and they fed in the meadow. 3 Then behold, seven other cows came up after them out of the river, ugly and gaunt, and stood by the *other* cows on the bank of the river. 4 And the ugly and gaunt cows ate up the seven fine looking and fat cows. So Pharaoh awoke. 5 He slept and dreamed a second time; and suddenly seven heads of grain came up on one stalk, plump and good. 6 Then behold, seven thin heads, blighted by the east wind, sprang up after them. 7 And the seven thin heads devoured the seven plump and full heads. So Pharaoh awoke, and indeed, *it was* a dream. 8 Now it came to pass in the morning that his spirit was troubled, and he sent and called for all the magicians of Egypt and all its wise men. And Pharaoh told them his dreams, but *there was* no one who could interpret them for Pharaoh.

9 Then the chief butler spoke to Pharaoh, saying: "I remember my faults this day. 10 When Pharaoh was angry with his servants, and put me in custody in the house of the captain of the guard, *both* me and the chief baker, 11 we each had a dream in one night, he and I. Each of us dreamed according to the interpretation of his *own* dream. 12 Now there *was* a young Hebrew man with us there, a servant of the captain of the guard. And we told him, and he interpreted our dreams for us; to each man he interpreted according to his *own* dream. 13 And it came to pass, just as he interpreted for us, so it happened. He restored me to my office, and he hanged him."

14 Then Pharaoh sent and called Joseph, and they brought him quickly out of the dungeon; and he shaved, changed his clothing, and came to Pharaoh. 15 And Pharaoh said to Joseph, "I have had a dream, and *there is* no one who can interpret it. But I have heard it said of you *that* you can understand a dream, to interpret it."

16 So Joseph answered Pharaoh, saying, "*It is* not in me; God will give Pharaoh an answer of peace."

17 Then Pharaoh said to Joseph: "Behold, in my dream I stood on the bank of the river. 18 Suddenly seven cows came up out of the river, fine looking and fat; and they fed in the meadow. 19 Then behold, seven other cows came up after them, poor and very ugly and gaunt, such ugliness as I have never seen in all the land of Egypt. 20 And the gaunt and ugly cows ate up the first seven, the fat cows. 21 When they had eaten them up, no one would have known that they had eaten them, for they *were* just as ugly as at the beginning. So I awoke. 22 Also I saw in my dream, and suddenly seven heads came up on one stalk, full and good. 23 Then behold, seven heads, withered, thin, *and* blighted by the east wind, sprang up after them. 24 And the thin heads devoured the seven good heads. So I told *this* to the magicians, but *there was* no one who could explain *it* to me."

25 Then Joseph said to Pharaoh, "The dreams of Pharaoh *are* one; God has shown Pharaoh what He *is* about to do: 26 The seven good cows *are* seven years, and the seven good heads *are* seven years; the dreams *are* one. 27 And the seven thin and ugly cows which came up after them *are* seven years, and the seven empty heads blighted by the east wind are seven years of famine. 28 This *is* the thing which I have spoken to Pharaoh. God has shown Pharaoh what He *is* about to do. 29 Indeed seven years of great plenty will come throughout all the land of Egypt; 30 but after them seven years of famine will arise, and all the plenty will be forgotten in the land of Egypt; and the famine will deplete the land. 31 So the plenty will not be known in the land because of the famine following, for it *will be* very severe. 32 And the dream was repeated to Pharaoh twice because the thing *is* established by God, and God will shortly bring it to pass.

33 "Now therefore, let Pharaoh select a discerning and wise man, and set him over the land of Egypt. 34 Let Pharaoh do *this,* and let him appoint officers over the land, to collect one-fifth *of the produce* of the land of Egypt in the seven plentiful

years. 35 And let them gather all the food of those good years that are coming, and store up grain under the authority of Pharaoh, and let them keep food in the cities. 36 Then that food shall be as a reserve for the land for the seven years of famine which shall be in the land of Egypt, that the land may not perish during the famine."

37 So the advice was good in the eyes of Pharaoh and in the eyes of all his servants. 38 And Pharaoh said to his servants, "Can we find such a one as this, a man in whom is the Spirit of God?"

39 Then Pharaoh said to Joseph, "Inasmuch as God has shown you all this, there is no one as discerning and wise as you. 40 You shall be over my house, and all my people shall be ruled according to your word; only in regard to the throne will I be greater than you." 41 And Pharaoh said to Joseph, "See, I have set you over all the land of Egypt."

42 Then Pharaoh took his signet ring off his hand and put it on Joseph's hand; and he clothed him in garments of fine linen and put a gold chain around his neck. 43 And he had him ride in the second chariot which he had; and they cried out before him, "Bow the knee!" So he set him over all the land of Egypt. 44 Pharaoh also said to Joseph, "I am Pharaoh, and without your consent no man may lift his hand or foot in all the land of Egypt." 45 And Pharaoh called Joseph's name Zaphnath-Paaneah. And he gave him as a wife Asenath, the daughter of Poti-Pherah priest of On. So Joseph went out over all the land of Egypt.

46 Joseph was thirty years old when he stood before Pharaoh king of Egypt. And Joseph went out from the presence of Pharaoh, and went throughout all the land of Egypt. 47 Now in the seven plentiful years the ground brought forth abundantly. 48 So he gathered up all the food of the seven years which were in the land of Egypt, and laid up the food in the cities; he laid up in every city the food of the fields which surrounded them. 49 Joseph gathered very much grain, as the sand of the sea, until he stopped counting, for it was immeasurable.

50 And to Joseph were born two sons before the years of famine came, whom Asenath, the daughter of Poti-Pherah priest of On, bore to him. 51 Joseph called the name of the firstborn Manasseh:a "For God has made me forget all my toil and all my father's house." 52 And the name of the second he called Ephraim:a "For God has caused me to be fruitful in the land of my affliction."

53 Then the seven years of plenty which were in the land of Egypt ended, 54 and the seven years of famine began to come, as Joseph had said. The famine was in all lands, but in all the land of Egypt there was bread. 55 So when all the land of Egypt was famished, the people cried to Pharaoh for bread. Then Pharaoh said to all the Egyptians, "Go to Joseph; whatever he says to you, do." 56 The famine was over all the face of the earth, and Joseph opened all the storehousesa and sold to the Egyptians. And the famine became severe in the land of Egypt. 57 So all countries came to Joseph in Egypt to buy grain, because the famine was severe in all lands.

42 When Jacob saw that there was grain in Egypt, Jacob said to his sons, "Why do you look at one another?" 2 And he said, "Indeed I have heard that there is grain in Egypt; go down to that place and buy for us there, that we may live and not die."

3 So Joseph's ten brothers went down to buy grain in Egypt. 4 But Jacob did not send Joseph's brother Benjamin with his brothers, for he said, "Lest some calamity befall him." 5 And the sons of Israel went to buy grain among those who journeyed, for the famine was in the land of Canaan.

6 Now Joseph was governor over the land; and it was he who sold to all the people of the land. And Joseph's brothers came and bowed down before him with their faces to the earth. 7 Joseph saw his brothers and recognized them, but he acted as a stranger to them and spoke roughly to them. Then he said to them, "Where do you come from?"

And they said, "From the land of Canaan to buy food."

41:51 aLiterally Making Forgetful   41:52 aLiterally Fruitfulness   41:56 aLiterally all that was in them

8 So Joseph recognized his brothers, but they did not recognize him. 9 Then Joseph remembered the dreams which he had dreamed about them, and said to them, "You *are* spies! You have come to see the nakedness of the land!"

10 And they said to him, "No, my lord, but your servants have come to buy food. 11 We *are* all one man's sons; we *are* honest *men;* your servants are not spies."

12 But he said to them, "No, but you have come to see the nakedness of the land."

13 And they said, "Your servants *are* twelve brothers, the sons of one man in the land of Canaan; and in fact, the youngest *is* with our father today, and one *is* no more."

14 But Joseph said to them, "It *is* as I spoke to you, saying, 'You *are* spies!' 15 In this *manner* you shall be tested: By the life of Pharaoh, you shall not leave this place unless your youngest brother comes here. 16 Send one of you, and let him bring your brother; and you shall be kept in prison, that your words may be tested to see whether *there is* any truth in you; or else, by the life of Pharaoh, surely you *are* spies!" 17 So he put them all together in prison three days.

18 Then Joseph said to them the third day, "Do this and live, *for* I fear God: 19 If you *are* honest *men,* let one of your brothers be confined to your prison house; but you, go and carry grain for the famine of your houses. 20 And bring your youngest brother to me; so your words will be verified, and you shall not die."

And they did so. 21 Then they said to one another, "We *are* truly guilty concerning our brother, for we saw the anguish of his soul when he pleaded with us, and we would not hear; therefore this distress has come upon us."

22 And Reuben answered them, saying, "Did I not speak to you, saying, 'Do not sin against the boy'; and you would not listen? Therefore behold, his blood is now required of us." 23 But they did not know that Joseph understood *them,* for he spoke to them through an interpreter. 24 And he turned himself away from them and wept. Then he returned to them again, and talked with them.

And he took Simeon from them and bound him before their eyes.

25 Then Joseph gave a command to fill their sacks with grain, to restore every man's money to his sack, and to give them provisions for the journey. Thus he did for them. 26 So they loaded their donkeys with the grain and departed from there. 27 But as one *of them* opened his sack to give his donkey feed at the encampment, he saw his money; and there it was, in the mouth of his sack. 28 So he said to his brothers, "My money has been restored, and there it is, in my sack!" Then their hearts failed *them* and they were afraid, saying to one another, "What *is* this *that* God has done to us?"

29 Then they went to Jacob their father in the land of Canaan and told him all that had happened to them, saying: 30 "The man *who is* lord of the land spoke roughly to us, and took us for spies of the country. 31 But we said to him, 'We *are* honest *men;* we are not spies. 32 We *are* twelve brothers, sons of our father; one *is* no *more,* and the youngest *is* with our father this day in the land of Canaan.' 33 Then the man, the lord of the country, said to us, 'By this I will know that you *are* honest *men:* Leave one of your brothers *here* with me, take *food for* the famine of your households, and be gone. 34 And bring your youngest brother to me; so I shall know that you *are* not spies, but *that* you *are* honest *men.* I will grant your brother to you, and you may trade in the land.' "

35 Then it happened as they emptied their sacks, that surprisingly each man's bundle of money *was* in his sack; and when they and their father saw the bundles of money, they were afraid. 36 And Jacob their father said to them, "You have bereaved me: Joseph is no *more,* Simeon is no *more,* and you want to take Benjamin. All these things are against me."

37 Then Reuben spoke to his father, saying, "Kill my two sons if I do not bring him *back* to you; put him in my hands, and I will bring him back to you."

38 But he said, "My son shall not go down with you, for his brother is dead, and he is left alone. If any calamity should befall him along the way in which you go, then you would

bring down my gray hair with sorrow to the grave."

43 Now the famine *was* severe in the land. 2 And it came to pass, when they had eaten up the grain which they had brought from Egypt, that their father said to them, "Go back, buy us a little food."

3 But Judah spoke to him, saying, "The man solemnly warned us, saying, 'You shall not see my face unless your brother *is* with you.' 4 If you send our brother with us, we will go down and buy you food. 5 But if you will not send *him,* we will not go down; for the man said to us, 'You shall not see my face unless your brother *is* with you.' "

6 And Israel said, "Why did you deal *so* wrongfully with me *as* to tell the man whether you had still *another* brother?"

7 But they said, "The man asked us pointedly about ourselves and our family, saying, '*Is* your father still alive? Have you *another* brother?' And we told him according to these words. Could we possibly have known that he would say, 'Bring your brother down'?"

8 Then Judah said to Israel his father, "Send the lad with me, and we will arise and go, that we may live and not die, both we and you *and* also our little ones. 9 I myself will be surety for him; from my hand you shall require him. If I do not bring him *back* to you and set him before you, then let me bear the blame forever. 10 For if we had not lingered, surely by now we would have returned this second time."

11 And their father Israel said to them, "If *it must be* so, then do this: Take some of the best fruits of the land in your vessels and carry down a present for the man—a little balm and a little honey, spices and myrrh, pistachio nuts and almonds. 12 Take double money in your hand, and take back in your hand the money that was returned in the mouth of your sacks; perhaps it was an oversight. 13 Take your brother also, and arise, go back to the man. 14 And may God Almighty give you mercy before the man, that he may release your other brother and Benjamin. If I am bereaved, I am bereaved!"

15 So the men took that present and Benjamin, and they took double money in their hand, and arose and went down to Egypt; and they stood before Joseph. 16 When Joseph saw Benjamin with them, he said to the steward of his house, "Take *these* men to my home, and slaughter an animal and make ready; for *these* men will dine with me at noon." 17 Then the man did as Joseph ordered, and the man brought the men into Joseph's house.

18 Now the men were afraid because they were brought into Joseph's house; and they said, "*It is* because of the money, which was returned in our sacks the first time, that we are brought in, so that he may make a case against us and seize us, to take us as slaves with our donkeys."

19 When they drew near to the steward of Joseph's house, they talked with him at the door of the house, 20 and said, "O sir, we indeed came down the first time to buy food; 21 but it happened, when we came to the encampment, that we opened our sacks, and there, *each* man's money *was* in the mouth of his sack, our money in full weight; so we have brought it back in our hand. 22 And we have brought down other money in our hands to buy food. We do not know who put our money in our sacks."

23 But he said, "Peace *be* with you, do not be afraid. Your God and the God of your father has given you treasure in your sacks; I had your money." Then he brought Simeon out to them.

24 So the man brought the men into Joseph's house and gave *them* water, and they washed their feet; and he gave their donkeys feed. 25 Then they made the present ready for Joseph's coming at noon, for they heard that they would eat bread there.

26 And when Joseph came home, they brought him the present which *was* in their hand into the house, and bowed down before him to the earth. 27 Then he asked them about *their* well-being, and said, "*Is* your father well, the old man of whom you spoke? *Is* he still alive?"

28 And they answered, "Your servant our father *is* in good health; he *is* still alive." And they bowed their heads down and prostrated themselves.

29 Then he lifted his eyes and saw his brother Benjamin, his mother's son, and said, "*Is* this your younger brother of whom you spoke to me?" And he said, "God be gracious to you, my son." 30 Now his heart yearned for his brother; so Joseph made haste and sought *somewhere* to weep. And he went into *his* chamber and wept there. 31 Then he washed his face and came out; and he restrained himself, and said, "Serve the bread."

32 So they set him a place by himself, and them by themselves, and the Egyptians who ate with him by themselves; because the Egyptians could not eat food with the Hebrews, for that *is* an abomination to the Egyptians. 33 And they sat before him, the firstborn according to his birthright and the youngest according to his youth; and the men looked in astonishment at one another. 34 Then he took servings to them from before him, but Benjamin's serving was five times as much as any of theirs. So they drank and were merry with him.

44 And he commanded the steward of his house, saying, "Fill the men's sacks with food, as much as they can carry, and put each man's money in the mouth of his sack. 2 Also put my cup, the silver cup, in the mouth of the sack of the youngest, and his grain money." So he did according to the word that Joseph had spoken. 3 As soon as the morning dawned, the men were sent away, they and their donkeys. 4 When they had gone out of the city, *and* were not *yet* far off, Joseph said to his steward, "Get up, follow the men; and when you overtake them, say to them, 'Why have you repaid evil for good? 5 *Is* not this *the one* from which my lord drinks, and with which he indeed practices divination? You have done evil in so doing.'"

6 So he overtook them, and he spoke to them these same words. 7 And they said to him, "Why does my lord say these words? Far be it from us that your servants should do such a thing. 8 Look, we brought back to you from the land of Canaan the money which we found in the mouth of our sacks. How then could we steal silver or gold from your lord's house? 9 With whomever of your servants it is found, let him die, and we also will be my lord's slaves."

10 And he said, "Now also *let it be* according to your words; he with whom it is found shall be my slave, and you shall be blameless." 11 Then each man speedily let down his sack to the ground, and each opened his sack. 12 So he searched. He began with the oldest and left off with the youngest; and the cup was found in Benjamin's sack. 13 Then they tore their clothes, and each man loaded his donkey and returned to the city.

14 So Judah and his brothers came to Joseph's house, and he *was* still there; and they fell before him on the ground. 15 And Joseph said to them, "What deed *is* this you have done? Did you not know that such a man as I can certainly practice divination?"

16 Then Judah said, "What shall we say to my lord? What shall we speak? Or how shall we clear ourselves? God has found out the iniquity of your servants; here we are, my lord's slaves, both we and *he* also with whom the cup was found."

17 But he said, "Far be it from me that I should do so; the man in whose hand the cup was found, he shall be my slave. And as for you, go up in peace to your father."

18 Then Judah came near to him and said: "O my lord, please let your servant speak a word in my lord's hearing, and do not let your anger burn against your servant; for you *are* even like Pharaoh. 19 My lord asked his servants, saying, 'Have you a father or a brother?' 20 And we said to my lord, 'We have a father, an old man, and a child of *his* old age, *who* is young; his brother is dead, and he alone is left of his mother's children, and his father loves him.' 21 Then you said to your servants, 'Bring him down to me, that I may set my eyes on him.' 22 And we said to my lord, 'The lad cannot leave his father, for *if* he should leave his father, *his father* would die.' 23 But you said to your servants, 'Unless your youngest brother comes down with you, you shall see my face no more.'

24 "So it was, when we went up to your servant my father, that we told him the words of my lord. 25 And our father said, 'Go back *and* buy us a little food.' 26 But we said, 'We can-

not go down; if our youngest brother is with us, then we will go down; for we may not see the man's face unless our youngest brother *is* with us.' 27 Then your servant my father said to us, 'You know that my wife bore me two sons; 28 and the one went out from me, and I said, "Surely he is torn to pieces"; and I have not seen him since. 29 But if you take this one also from me, and calamity befalls him, you shall bring down my gray hair with sorrow to the grave.'

30 "Now therefore, when I come to your servant my father, and the lad *is* not with us, since his life is bound up in the lad's life, 31 it will happen, when he sees that the lad *is* not *with us,* that he will die. So your servants will bring down the gray hair of your servant our father with sorrow to the grave. 32 For your servant became surety for the lad to my father, saying, 'If I do not bring him *back* to you, then I shall bear the blame before my father forever.' 33 Now therefore, please let your servant remain instead of the lad as a slave to my lord, and let the lad go up with his brothers. 34 For how shall I go up to my father if the lad *is* not with me, lest perhaps I see the evil that would come upon my father?"

45 Then Joseph could not restrain himself before all those who stood by him, and he cried out, "Make everyone go out from me!" So no one stood with him while Joseph made himself known to his brothers. 2 And he wept aloud, and the Egyptians and the house of Pharaoh heard *it.*

3 Then Joseph said to his brothers, "I *am* Joseph; does my father still live?" But his brothers could not answer him, for they were dismayed in his presence. 4 And Joseph said to his brothers, "Please come near to me." So they came near. Then he said: "I *am* Joseph your brother, whom you sold into Egypt. 5 But now, do not therefore be grieved or angry with yourselves because you sold me here; for God sent me before you to preserve life. 6 For these two years the famine *has been* in the land, and *there are* still five years in which *there will be* neither plowing nor harvesting. 7 And God sent me before you to preserve a posterity for you in the earth, and to save your lives

by a great deliverance. 8 So now *it was* not you *who* sent me here, but God; and He has made me a father to Pharaoh, and lord of all his house, and a ruler throughout all the land of Egypt.

9 "Hurry and go up to my father, and say to him, 'Thus says your son Joseph: "God has made me lord of all Egypt; come down to me, do not tarry. 10 You shall dwell in the land of Goshen, and you shall be near to me, you and your children, your children's children, your flocks and your herds, and all that you have. 11 There I will provide for you, lest you and your household, and all that you have, come to poverty; for *there are* still five years of famine." '

12 "And behold, your eyes and the eyes of my brother Benjamin see that *it is* my mouth that speaks to you. 13 So you shall tell my father of all my glory in Egypt, and of all that you have seen; and you shall hurry and bring my father down here." 14 Then he fell on his brother Benjamin's neck and wept, and Benjamin wept on his neck. 15 Moreover he kissed all his brothers and wept over them, and after that his brothers talked with him.

16 Now the report of it was heard in Pharaoh's house, saying, "Joseph's brothers have come." So it pleased Pharaoh and his servants well. 17 And Pharaoh said to Joseph, "Say to your brothers, 'Do this: Load your animals and depart; go to the land of Canaan. 18 Bring your father and your households and come to me; I will give you the best of the land of Egypt, and you will eat the fat of the land. 19 Now you are commanded—do this: Take carts out of the land of Egypt for your little ones and your wives; bring your father and come. 20 Also do not be concerned about your goods, for the best of all the land of Egypt *is* yours.' "

21 Then the sons of Israel did so; and Joseph gave them carts, according to the command of Pharaoh, and he gave them provisions for the journey. 22 He gave to all of them, to each man, changes of garments; but to Benjamin he gave three hundred *pieces* of silver and five changes of garments. 23 And he sent to his father these *things:* ten donkeys loaded with the good things of Egypt, and ten female donkeys loaded with

grain, bread, and food for his father for the journey. 24 So he sent his brothers away, and they departed; and he said to them, "See that you do not become troubled along the way."

25 Then they went up out of Egypt, and came to the land of Canaan to Jacob their father. 26 And they told him, saying, "Joseph *is* still alive, and he *is* governor over all the land of Egypt." And Jacob's heart stood still, because he did not believe them. 27 But when they told him all the words which Joseph had said to them, and when he saw the carts which Joseph had sent to carry him, the spirit of Jacob their father revived. 28 Then Israel said, "*It is* enough. Joseph my son *is* still alive. I will go and see him before I die."

46 So Israel took his journey with all that he had, and came to Beersheba, and offered sacrifices to the God of his father Isaac. 2 Then God spoke to Israel in the visions of the night, and said, "Jacob, Jacob!"

And he said, "Here I am."

3 So He said, "I *am* God, the God of your father; do not fear to go down to Egypt, for I will make of you a great nation there. 4 I will go down with you to Egypt, and I will also surely bring you up *again;* and Joseph will put his hand on your eyes."

5 Then Jacob arose from Beersheba; and the sons of Israel carried their father Jacob, their little ones, and their wives, in the carts which Pharaoh had sent to carry him. 6 So they took their livestock and their goods, which they had acquired in the land of Canaan, and went to Egypt, Jacob and all his descendants with him. 7 His sons and his sons' sons, his daughters and his sons' daughters, and all his descendants he brought with him to Egypt.

8 Now these *were* the names of the children of Israel, Jacob and his sons, who went to Egypt: Reuben *was* Jacob's firstborn. 9 The sons of Reuben *were* Hanoch, Pallu, Hezron, and Carmi. 10 The sons of Simeon *were* Jemuel,*a* Jamin, Ohad, Jachin,*b* Zo-

har,*c* and Shaul, the son of a Canaanite woman. 11 The sons of Levi *were* Gershon, Kohath, and Merari. 12 The sons of Judah *were* Er, Onan, Shelah, Perez, and Zerah (but Er and Onan died in the land of Canaan). The sons of Perez were Hezron and Hamul. 13 The sons of Issachar *were* Tola, Puvah,*a* Job,*b* and Shimron. 14 The sons of Zebulun *were* Sered, Elon, and Jahleel. 15 These *were* the sons of Leah, whom she bore to Jacob in Padan Aram, with his daughter Dinah. All the persons, his sons and his daughters, *were* thirty-three.

16 The sons of Gad *were* Ziphion,*a* Haggi, Shuni, Ezbon,*b* Eri, Arodi,*c* and Areli. 17 The sons of Asher *were* Jimnah, Ishuah, Isui, Beriah, and Serah, their sister. And the sons of Beriah *were* Heber and Malchiel. 18 These *were* the sons of Zilpah, whom Laban gave to Leah his daughter; and these she bore to Jacob: sixteen persons.

19 The sons of Rachel, Jacob's wife, *were* Joseph and Benjamin. 20 And to Joseph in the land of Egypt were born Manasseh and Ephraim, whom Asenath, the daughter of Poti-Pherah priest of On, bore to him. 21 The sons of Benjamin *were* Belah, Becher, Ashbel, Gera, Naaman, Ehi, Rosh, Muppim, Huppim,*a* and Ard. 22 These *were* the sons of Rachel, who were born to Jacob: fourteen persons in all.

23 The son of Dan *was* Hushim.*a* 24 The sons of Naphtali *were* Jahzeel,*a* Guni, Jezer, and Shillem.*b* 25 These *were* the sons of Bilhah, whom Laban gave to Rachel his daughter, and she bore these to Jacob: seven persons in all.

26 All the persons who went with Jacob to Egypt, who came from his body, besides Jacob's sons' wives, *were* sixty-six persons in all. 27 And the sons of Joseph who were born to him in Egypt *were* two persons. All the persons of the house of Jacob who went to Egypt were seventy.

28 Then he sent Judah before him to Joseph, to point out before him *the way* to Goshen. And they came to the

---

46:10 *a*Spelled *Nemuel* in 1 Chronicles 4:24　　*b*Called *Jarib* in 1 Chronicles 4:24　　*c*Called *Zerah* in 1 Chronicles 4:24　　46:13 *a*Spelled *Puah* in 1 Chronicles 7:1　　*b*Same as *Jashub* in Numbers 26:24 and 1 Chronicles 7:1　　46:16 *a*Spelled *Zephon* in Samaritan Pentateuch, Septuagint, and Numbers 26:15 *b*Called *Ozni* in Numbers 26:16　　*c*Spelled *Arod* in Numbers 26:17　　46:21 *a*Called *Hupham* in Numbers 26:39　　46:23 *a*Called *Shuham* in Numbers 26:42　　46:24 *a*Spelled *Jahziel* in 1 Chronicles 7:13 *b*Spelled *Shallum* in 1 Chronicles 7:13

land of Goshen. 29 So Joseph made ready his chariot and went up to Goshen to meet his father Israel; and he presented himself to him, and fell on his neck and wept on his neck a good while.

30 And Israel said to Joseph, "Now let me die, since I have seen your face, because you *are* still alive."

31 Then Joseph said to his brothers and to his father's household, "I will go up and tell Pharaoh, and say to him, 'My brothers and those of my father's house, who *were* in the land of Canaan, have come to me. 32 And the men *are* shepherds, for their occupation has been to feed livestock; and they have brought their flocks, their herds, and all that they have.' 33 So it shall be, when Pharaoh calls you and says, 'What is your occupation?' 34 that you shall say, 'Your servants' occupation has been with livestock from our youth even till now, both we *and* also our fathers,' that you may dwell in the land of Goshen; for every shepherd *is* an abomination to the Egyptians."

47 Then Joseph went and told Pharaoh, and said, "My father and my brothers, their flocks and their herds and all that they possess, have come from the land of Canaan; and indeed they *are* in the land of Goshen." 2 And he took five men from among his brothers and presented them to Pharaoh. 3 Then Pharaoh said to his brothers, "What *is* your occupation?"

And they said to Pharaoh, "Your servants *are* shepherds, both we *and* also our fathers." 4 And they said to Pharaoh, "We have come to dwell in the land, because your servants have no pasture for their flocks, for the famine *is* severe in the land of Canaan. Now therefore, please let your servants dwell in the land of Goshen."

5 Then Pharaoh spoke to Joseph, saying, "Your father and your brothers have come to you. 6 The land of Egypt *is* before you. Have your father and brothers dwell in the best of the land; let them dwell in the land of Goshen. And if you know *any* competent men among them, then make them chief herdsmen over my livestock."

7 Then Joseph brought in his father Jacob and set him before Pharaoh; and Jacob blessed Pharaoh. 8 Pharaoh said to Jacob, "How old *are* you?"

9 And Jacob said to Pharaoh, "The days of the years of my pilgrimage *are* one hundred and thirty years; few and evil have been the days of the years of my life, and they have not attained to the days of the years of the life of my fathers in the days of their pilgrimage." 10 So Jacob blessed Pharaoh, and went out from before Pharaoh.

11 And Joseph situated his father and his brothers, and gave them a possession in the land of Egypt, in the best of the land, in the land of Rameses, as Pharaoh had commanded. 12 Then Joseph provided his father, his brothers, and all his father's household with bread, according to the number in *their* families.

13 Now *there was* no bread in all the land; for the famine *was* very severe, so that the land of Egypt and the land of Canaan languished because of the famine. 14 And Joseph gathered up all the money that was found in the land of Egypt and in the land of Canaan, for the grain which they bought; and Joseph brought the money into Pharaoh's house.

15 So when the money failed in the land of Egypt and in the land of Canaan, all the Egyptians came to Joseph and said, "Give us bread, for why should we die in your presence? For the money has failed."

16 Then Joseph said, "Give your livestock, and I will give you *bread* for your livestock, if the money is gone." 17 So they brought their livestock to Joseph, and Joseph gave them bread *in exchange* for the horses, the flocks, the cattle of the herds, and for the donkeys. Thus he fed them with bread *in exchange* for all their livestock that year.

18 When that year had ended, they came to him the next year and said to him, "We will not hide from my lord that our money is gone; my lord also has our herds of livestock. There is nothing left in the sight of my lord but our bodies and our lands. 19 Why should we die before your eyes, both we and our land? Buy us and our land for bread, and we and our land will be servants of Pharaoh; give *us* seed, that we may live and

not die, that the land may not be desolate."

20 Then Joseph bought all the land of Egypt for Pharaoh; for every man of the Egyptians sold his field, because the famine was severe upon them. So the land became Pharaoh's. 21 And as for the people, he moved them into the cities,ᵃ from *one* end of the borders of Egypt to the *other* end. 22 Only the land of the priests he did not buy; for the priests had rations *allotted to them* by Pharaoh, and they ate their rations which Pharaoh gave them; therefore they did not sell their lands.

23 Then Joseph said to the people, "Indeed I have bought you and your land this day for Pharaoh. Look, *here is* seed for you, and you shall sow the land. 24 And it shall come to pass in the harvest that you shall give one-fifth to Pharaoh. Four-fifths shall be your own, as seed for the field and for your food, for those of your households and as food for your little ones."

25 So they said, "You have saved our lives; let us find favor in the sight of my lord, and we will be Pharaoh's servants." 26 And Joseph made it a law over the land of Egypt to this day, *that* Pharaoh should have one-fifth, except for the land of the priests only, *which* did not become Pharaoh's.

27 So Israel dwelt in the land of Egypt, in the country of Goshen; and they had possessions there and grew and multiplied exceedingly. 28 And Jacob lived in the land of Egypt seventeen years. So the length of Jacob's life was one hundred and forty-seven years. 29 When the time drew near that Israel must die, he called his son Joseph and said to him, "Now if I have found favor in your sight, please put your hand under my thigh, and deal kindly and truly with me. Please do not bury me in Egypt, 30 but let me lie with my fathers; you shall carry me out of Egypt and bury me in their burial place."

And he said, "I will do as you have said."

31 Then he said, "Swear to me." And he swore to him. So Israel bowed himself on the head of the bed.

48 Now it came to pass after these things that Joseph was told, "Indeed your father *is* sick"; and he took with him his two sons, Manasseh and Ephraim. 2 And Jacob was told, "Look, your son Joseph is coming to you"; and Israel strengthened himself and sat up on the bed. 3 Then Jacob said to Joseph: "God Almighty appeared to me at Luz in the land of Canaan and blessed me, 4 and said to me, 'Behold, I will make you fruitful and multiply you, and I will make of you a multitude of people, and give this land to your descendants after you *as* an everlasting possession.' 5 And now your two sons, Ephraim and Manasseh, who were born to you in the land of Egypt before I came to you in Egypt, *are* mine; as Reuben and Simeon, they shall be mine. 6 Your offspring whom you beget after them shall be yours; they will be called by the name of their brothers in their inheritance. 7 But as for me, when I came from Padan, Rachel died beside me in the land of Canaan on the way, when *there was* but a little distance to go to Ephrath; and I buried her there on the way to Ephrath (that is, Bethlehem)."

8 Then Israel saw Joseph's sons, and said, "Who *are* these?"

9 Joseph said to his father, "They *are* my sons, whom God has given me in this *place*."

And he said, "Please bring them to me, and I will bless them." 10 Now the eyes of Israel were dim with age, *so that* he could not see. Then Joseph brought them near him, and he kissed them and embraced them. 11 And Israel said to Joseph, "I had not thought to see your face; but in fact, God has also shown me your offspring!"

12 So Joseph brought them from beside his knees, and he bowed down with his face to the earth. 13 And Joseph took them both, Ephraim with his right hand toward Israel's left hand, and Manasseh with his left hand toward Israel's right hand, and brought *them* near him. 14 Then Israel stretched out his right hand and laid *it* on Ephraim's head, who *was* the younger, and his left hand on Manasseh's head, guiding his hands

47:21 ᵃFollowing Masoretic Text and Targum; Samaritan Pentateuch, Septuagint, and Vulgate read *made the people virtual slaves.*

knowingly, for Manasseh *was* the firstborn. 15 And he blessed Joseph, and said:

"God, before whom my fathers
    Abraham and Isaac walked,
The God who has fed me all my
    life long to this day,
16 The Angel who has redeemed
    me from all evil,
Bless the lads;
Let my name be named upon
    them,
And the name of my fathers
    Abraham and Isaac;
And let them grow into a
    multitude in the midst of the
    earth."

17 Now when Joseph saw that his father laid his right hand on the head of Ephraim, it displeased him; so he took hold of his father's hand to remove it from Ephraim's head to Manasseh's head. 18 And Joseph said to his father, "Not so, my father, for this *one is* the firstborn; put your right hand on his head."

19 But his father refused and said, "I know, my son, I know. He also shall become a people, and he also shall be great; but truly his younger brother shall be greater than he, and his descendants shall become a multitude of nations."

20 So he blessed them that day, saying, "By you Israel will bless, saying, 'May God make you as Ephraim and as Manasseh!'" And thus he set Ephraim before Manasseh.

21 Then Israel said to Joseph, "Behold, I am dying, but God will be with you and bring you back to the land of your fathers. 22 Moreover I have given to you one portion above your brothers, which I took from the hand of the Amorite with my sword and my bow."

49

And Jacob called his sons and said, "Gather together, that I may tell you what shall befall you in the last days:

2 "Gather together and hear, you
    sons of Jacob,
And listen to Israel your father.

3 "Reuben, you are my firstborn,
My might and the beginning of
    my strength,

The excellency of dignity and
    the excellency of power.
4 Unstable as water, you shall
    not excel,
Because you went up to your
    father's bed;
Then you defiled *it*—
He went up to my couch.

5 "Simeon and Levi *are* brothers;
Instruments of cruelty *are in*
    their dwelling place.
6 Let not my soul enter their
    council;
Let not my honor be united to
    their assembly;
For in their anger they slew a
    man,
And in their self-will they
    hamstrung an ox.
7 Cursed *be* their anger, for *it is*
    fierce;
And their wrath, for it is cruel!
I will divide them in Jacob
And scatter them in Israel.

8 "Judah, you *are he* whom your
    brothers shall praise;
Your hand *shall be* on the neck
    of your enemies;
Your father's children shall
    bow down before you.
9 Judah *is* a lion's whelp;
From the prey, my son, you
    have gone up.
He bows down, he lies down as
    a lion;
And as a lion, who shall rouse
    him?
10 The scepter shall not depart
    from Judah,
Nor a lawgiver from between
    his feet,
Until Shiloh comes;
And to Him *shall be* the
    obedience of the people.
11 Binding his donkey to the vine,
And his donkey's colt to the
    choice vine,
He washed his garments in
    wine,
And his clothes in the blood of
    grapes.
12 His eyes *are* darker than wine,
And his teeth whiter than milk.

13 "Zebulun shall dwell by the
    haven of the sea;
He *shall become* a haven for
    ships,
And his border shall adjoin
    Sidon.

14 "Issachar is a strong donkey,
    Lying down between two
      burdens;
15 He saw that rest *was* good,
    And that the land *was* pleasant;
    He bowed his shoulder to bear
      a burden,
    And became a band of slaves.

16 "Dan shall judge his people
    As one of the tribes of Israel.
17 Dan shall be a serpent by the
      way,
    A viper by the path,
    That bites the horse's heels
    So that its rider shall fall
      backward.
18 I have waited for your
      salvation, O LORD!

19 "Gad, a troop shall tramp upon
      him,
    But he shall triumph at last.

20 "Bread from Asher *shall be* rich,
    And he shall yield royal
      dainties.

21 "Naphtali *is* a deer let loose;
    He uses beautiful words.

22 "Joseph *is* a fruitful bough,
    A fruitful bough by a well;
    His branches run over the wall.
23 The archers have bitterly
      grieved him,
    Shot *at him* and hated him.
24 But his bow remained in
      strength,
    And the arms of his hands were
      made strong
    By the hands of the Mighty *God*
      of Jacob
    (From there *is* the Shepherd,
      the Stone of Israel),
25 By the God of your father who
      will help you,
    And by the Almighty who will
      bless you
    With blessings of heaven
      above,
    Blessings of the deep that lies
      beneath,
    Blessings of the breasts and of
      the womb.
26 The blessings of your father
    Have excelled the blessings of
      my ancestors,
    Up to the utmost bound of the
      everlasting hills.
    They shall be on the head of
      Joseph,

    And on the crown of the head
      of him who was separate
      from his brothers.

27 "Benjamin is a ravenous wolf;
    In the morning he shall devour
      the prey,
    And at night he shall divide the
      spoil."

28 All these *are* the twelve tribes of Israel, and this *is* what their father spoke to them. And he blessed them; he blessed each one according to his own blessing.
29 Then he charged them and said to them: "I am to be gathered to my people; bury me with my fathers in the cave that *is* in the field of Ephron the Hittite, 30 in the cave that *is* in the field of Machpelah, which *is* before Mamre in the land of Canaan, which Abraham bought with the field of Ephron the Hittite as a possession for a burial place. 31 There they buried Abraham and Sarah his wife, there they buried Isaac and Rebekah his wife, and there I buried Leah. 32 The field and the cave that *is* there *were* purchased from the sons of Heth." 33 And when Jacob had finished commanding his sons, he drew his feet up into the bed and breathed his last, and was gathered to his people.

50 Then Joseph fell on his father's face, and wept over him, and kissed him. 2 And Joseph commanded his servants the physicians to embalm his father. So the physicians embalmed Israel. 3 Forty days were required for him, for such are the days required for those who are embalmed; and the Egyptians mourned for him seventy days.

4 Now when the days of his mourning were past, Joseph spoke to the household of Pharaoh, saying, "If now I have found favor in your eyes, please speak in the hearing of Pharaoh, saying, 5 'My father made me swear, saying, "Behold, I am dying; in my grave which I dug for myself in the land of Canaan, there you shall bury me." Now therefore, please let me go up and bury my father, and I will come back.'"

6 And Pharaoh said, "Go up and bury your father, as he made you swear."

7 So Joseph went up to bury his fa-

ther; and with him went up all the servants of Pharaoh, the elders of his house, and all the elders of the land of Egypt, 8 as well as all the house of Joseph, his brothers, and his father's house. Only their little ones, their flocks, and their herds they left in the land of Goshen. 9 And there went up with him both chariots and horsemen, and it was a very great gathering.

10 Then they came to the threshing floor of Atad, which *is* beyond the Jordan, and they mourned there with a great and very solemn lamentation. He observed seven days of mourning for his father. 11 And when the inhabitants of the land, the Canaanites, saw the mourning at the threshing floor of Atad, they said, "This *is* a deep mourning of the Egyptians." Therefore its name was called Abel Mizraim,*a* which *is* beyond the Jordan.

12 So his sons did for him just as he had commanded them. 13 For his sons carried him to the land of Canaan, and buried him in the cave of the field of Machpelah, before Mamre, which Abraham bought with the field from Ephron the Hittite as property for a burial place. 14 And after he had buried his father, Joseph returned to Egypt, he and his brothers and all who went up with him to bury his father.

15 When Joseph's brothers saw that their father was dead, they said, "Perhaps Joseph will hate us, and may actually repay us for all the evil which we did to him." 16 So they sent *messengers* to Joseph, saying, "Before your father died he commanded, saying, 17 'Thus you shall say to Joseph: "I beg you, please forgive the trespass of your brothers and their sin; for they did evil to you." ' Now, please, forgive the trespass of the servants of the God of your father." And Joseph wept when they spoke to him.

18 Then his brothers also went and fell down before his face, and they said, "Behold, we *are* your servants."

19 Joseph said to them, "Do not be afraid, for *am* I in the place of God? 20 But as for you, you meant evil against me; *but* God meant it for good, in order to bring it about as *it is* this day, to save many people alive. 21 Now therefore, do not be afraid; I will provide for you and your little ones." And he comforted them and spoke kindly to them.

22 So Joseph dwelt in Egypt, he and his father's household. And Joseph lived one hundred and ten years. 23 Joseph saw Ephraim's children to the third *generation*. The children of Machir, the son of Manasseh, were also brought up on Joseph's knees.

24 And Joseph said to his brethren, "I am dying; but God will surely visit you, and bring you out of this land to the land of which He swore to Abraham, to Isaac, and to Jacob." 25 Then Joseph took an oath from the children of Israel, saying, "God will surely visit you, and you shall carry up my bones from here." 26 So Joseph died, *being* one hundred and ten years old; and they embalmed him, and he was put in a coffin in Egypt.

50:11 *a*Literally *Mourning of Egypt*

Exodus

Overview of Exodus

Moses was the right person at the right place at the right time! In the Book of Exodus, we learn how God used this possibility thinker to lead His people.

Written by Moses about 1400 B.C., Exodus opens with the story of the Israelites in exile in Egypt. Moses, an Israelite taken into Pharaoh's court as a baby, was the God-appointed leader to save God's people from their severe sufferings. Moses had God's backing and assurance that "I AM WHO I AM"—the name of the self-existent, all-powerful God—would be with him.

Through a series of plagues, Moses courageously challenged Pharaoh and the false gods of Egypt to let God's people go. The Egyptians worshiped many gods—the Nile River, cattle, locusts, frogs, insects, various animals, the fly-god (Beelzebub), and the sun. The plagues were directed at these false deities to show God's supreme power. Finally, Pharaoh relinquished his grip on the Israelites and let them go.

Moses faced his second greatest challenge outside of Egypt in the wilderness wanderings through Sinai. For forty years the people lived in the wilderness, completely dependent on God and Moses for all their needs. God appeared to Moses, giving him the Ten Commandments to help guide and direct His people. The Israelites often complained about their nomadic life-style. Moses had to keep the dream of the Promised Land alive, helping them to eliminate the negative and focus on the positive. Moses believed, therefore the people believed, God's promise. Their faith would build them up!

Despite all the negative-thinking "experts," those people who quickly advised the Israelites to quit their needless wanderings, Moses held true to the God-given dream. He never let his problems stop him from making the right decision. He made a decision and then solved his problems. Because of Moses' positive, unyielding faith, the Israelites acquired their goal. The Promised Land was theirs!

Jesus in Exodus

Exodus is full of types and portraits of Christ. Perhaps the most significant and familiar type is the sacrifice of the spotless Passover lamb, a shadow of the perfect Lamb of God who would become a sacrifice for all. Other types in the Book of Exodus include the seven feasts, the Exodus, the manna and the water, the tabernacle, and the office of the High Priest.

Keys to Exodus

Key Word: Redemption. The central theme of Exodus is redemption. Israel was redeemed from bondage in Egypt into a covenant relationship with God. From the redemption of baby Moses in the river to God's redeeming presence in the tabernacle, Exodus records God's overwhelming acts of deliverance from bad situations into good ones.

Key Verses: "Therefore say to the children of Israel: 'I *am* the LORD; I will bring you out from under the burdens of the Egyptians, I will rescue you from their bondage, and I will redeem you with an outstretched arm and with great judgments'" (6:6).

"Now therefore, if you will indeed obey My voice and keep My covenant, then you shall be a special treasure to Me above all people; for all the earth *is* Mine" (19:5).

Key Chapters: Exodus 12—14. The climax of the entire Old Testament is in chapters 12—14: the salvation through blood (the Passover) and through power (the parting of the Red Sea). The Exodus is the central event of the Old Testament as the cross is the pivotal point of the New Testament.

1 Now these *are* the names of the children of Israel who came to Egypt; each man and his household came with Jacob: 2 Reuben, Simeon, Levi, and Judah; 3 Issachar, Zebulun, and Benjamin; 4 Dan, Naphtali, Gad, and Asher. 5 All those who were descendants[a] of Jacob were seventy[b]

1:5 [a]Literally *who came from the loins of*   [b]Dead Sea Scrolls and Septuagint read *seventy-five* (compare Acts 7:14).

persons (for Joseph was in Egypt *already*). 6 And Joseph died, all his brothers, and all that generation. 7 But the children of Israel were fruitful and increased abundantly, multiplied and grew exceedingly mighty; and the land was filled with them.

8 Now there arose a new king over Egypt, who did not know Joseph. 9 And he said to his people, "Look, the people of the children of Israel *are* more and mightier than we; 10 come, let us deal shrewdly with them, lest they multiply, and it happen, in the event of war, that they also join our enemies and fight against us, and *so* go up out of the land." 11 Therefore they set taskmasters over them to afflict them with their burdens. And they built for Pharaoh supply cities, Pithom and Raamses. 12 But the more they afflicted them, the more they multiplied and grew. And they were in dread of the children of Israel. 13 So the Egyptians made the children of Israel serve with rigor. 14 And they made their lives bitter with hard bondage—in mortar, in brick, and in all manner of service in the field. All their service in which they made them serve *was* with rigor.

15 Then the king of Egypt spoke to the Hebrew midwives, of whom the name of one *was* Shiphrah and the name of the other Puah; 16 and he said, "When you do the duties of a midwife for the Hebrew women, and see *them* on the birthstools, if it *is* a son, then you shall kill him; but if it *is* a daughter, then she shall live." 17 But the midwives feared God, and did not do as the king of Egypt commanded them, but saved the male children alive. 18 So the king of Egypt called for the midwives and said to them, "Why have you done this thing, and saved the male children alive?"

19 And the midwives said to Pharaoh, "Because the Hebrew women *are* not like the Egyptian women; for they *are* lively and give birth before the midwives come to them."

20 Therefore God dealt well with the midwives, and the people multiplied and grew very mighty. 21 And so it was, because the midwives feared God, that He provided households for them.

22 So Pharaoh commanded all his people, saying, "Every son who is born[a] you shall cast into the river, and every daughter you shall save alive."

2 And a man of the house of Levi went and took *as wife* a daughter of Levi. 2 So the woman conceived and bore a son. And when she saw that he *was* a beautiful *child*, she hid him three months. 3 But when she could no longer hide him, she took an ark of bulrushes for him, daubed it with asphalt and pitch, put the child in it, and laid *it* in the reeds by the river's bank. 4 And his sister stood afar off, to know what would be done to him.

5 Then the daughter of Pharaoh came down to bathe at the river. And her maidens walked along the riverside; and when she saw the ark among the reeds, she sent her maid to get it. 6 And when she opened *it*, she saw the child, and behold, the baby wept. So she had compassion on him, and said, "This is one of the Hebrews' children."

7 Then his sister said to Pharaoh's daughter, "Shall I go and call a nurse for you from the Hebrew women, that she may nurse the child for you?"

8 And Pharaoh's daughter said to her, "Go." So the maiden went and called the child's mother. 9 Then Pharaoh's daughter said to her, "Take this child away and nurse him for me, and I will give *you* your wages." So the woman took the child and nursed him. 10 And the child grew, and she brought him to Pharaoh's daughter, and he became her son. So she called his name Moses,[a] saying, "Because I drew him out of the water."

11 Now it came to pass in those days, when Moses was grown, that he went out to his brethren and looked at their burdens. And he saw an Egyptian beating a Hebrew, one of his brethren. 12 So he looked this way and that way, and when he saw no one, he killed the Egyptian and hid him in the sand. 13 And when he went out the second day, behold, two Hebrew men were fighting, and he said to the one who did the wrong,

1:22 [a]Samaritan Pentateuch, Septuagint, and Targum add *to the Hebrews.*   2:10 [a]Literally *Drawn Out*

"Why are you striking your companion?"

14 Then he said, "Who made you a prince and a judge over us? Do you intend to kill me as you killed the Egyptian?"

So Moses feared and said, "Surely this thing is known!" 15 When Pharaoh heard of this matter, he sought to kill Moses. But Moses fled from the face of Pharaoh and dwelt in the land of Midian; and he sat down by a well.

16 Now the priest of Midian had seven daughters. And they came and drew water, and they filled the troughs to water their father's flock. 17 Then the shepherds came and drove them away; but Moses stood up and helped them, and watered their flock.

18 When they came to Reuel their father, he said, "How is it that you have come so soon today?"

19 And they said, "An Egyptian delivered us from the hand of the shepherds, and he also drew enough water for us and watered the flock."

20 So he said to his daughters, "And where is he? Why is it that you have left the man? Call him, that he may eat bread."

21 Then Moses was content to live with the man, and he gave Zipporah his daughter to Moses. 22 And she bore him a son. He called his name Gershom,ᵃ for he said, "I have been a stranger in a foreign land."

23 Now it happened in the process of time that the king of Egypt died. Then the children of Israel groaned because of the bondage, and they cried out; and their cry came up to God because of the bondage. 24 So God heard their groaning, and God remembered His covenant with Abraham, with Isaac, and with Jacob. 25 And God looked upon the children of Israel, and God acknowledged them.

3 Now Moses was tending the flock of Jethro his father-in-law, the priest of Midian. And he led the flock to the back of the desert, and came to Horeb, the mountain of God. 2 And the Angel of the LORD appeared to him in a flame of fire from the midst of a bush. So he looked, and behold, the bush was burning with fire, but the bush was not consumed. 3 Then Moses said, "I will now turn aside and see this great sight, why the bush does not burn."

4 So when the LORD saw that he turned aside to look, God called to him from the midst of the bush and said, "Moses, Moses!"

And he said, "Here I am."

5 Then He said, "Do not draw near this place. Take your sandals off your feet, for the place where you stand is holy ground." 6 Moreover He said, "I am the God of your father—the God of Abraham, the God of Isaac, and the God of Jacob." And Moses hid his face, for he was afraid to look upon God.

7 And the LORD said: "I have surely seen the oppression of My people who are in Egypt, and have heard their cry because of their taskmasters, for I know their sorrows. 8 So I have come down to deliver them out of the hand of the Egyptians, and to bring them up from that land to a good and large land, to a land flowing with milk and honey, to the place of the Canaanites and the Hittites and the Amorites and the Perizzites and the Hivites and the Jebusites. 9 Now therefore, behold, the cry of the children of Israel has come to Me, and I have also seen the oppression with which the Egyptians oppress them. 10 Come now, therefore, and I will send you to Pharaoh that you may bring My people, the children of Israel, out of Egypt."

11 But Moses said to God, "Who am I that I should go to Pharaoh, and that I should bring the children of Israel out of Egypt?"

12 So He said, "I will certainly be with you. And this shall be a sign to you that I have sent you: When you have brought the people out of Egypt, you shall serve God on this mountain."

13 Then Moses said to God, "Indeed, when I come to the children of Israel and say to them, 'The God of your fathers has sent me to you,' and they say to me, 'What is His name?' what shall I say to them?"

14 And God said to Moses, "I AM WHO I AM." And He said, "Thus you shall say to the children of Israel, 'I AM has sent me to you.'"

15 Moreover God said to Moses,

2:22 ᵃLiterally Stranger There

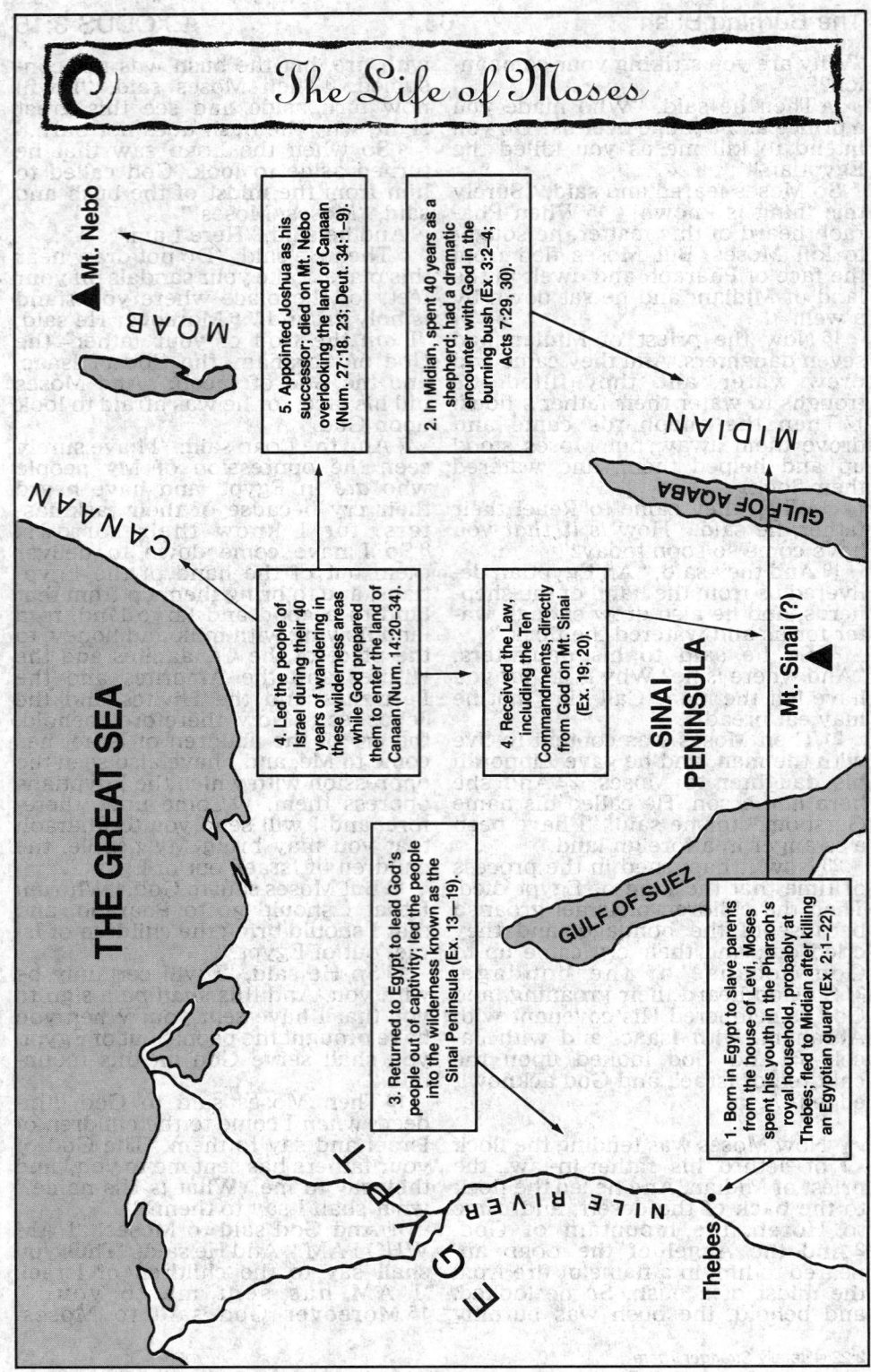

The Life of Moses

5. Appointed Joshua as his successor; died on Mt. Nebo overlooking the land of Canaan (Num. 27:18, 23; Deut. 34:1–9).

2. In Midian, spent 40 years as a shepherd; had a dramatic encounter with God in the burning bush (Ex. 3:2–4; Acts 7:29, 30).

4. Led the people of Israel during their 40 years of wandering in these wilderness areas while God prepared them to enter the land of Canaan (Num. 14:20–34).

4. Received the Law, including the Ten Commandments, directly from God on Mt. Sinai (Ex. 19; 20).

3. Returned to Egypt to lead God's people out of captivity; led the people into the wilderness known as the Sinai Peninsula (Ex. 13—19).

1. Born in Egypt to slave parents from the house of Levi, Moses spent his youth in the Pharaoh's royal household, probably at Thebes; fled to Midian after killing an Egyptian guard (Ex. 2:1–22).

Mt. Nebo

MOAB

MIDIAN

GULF OF AQABA

CANAAN

THE GREAT SEA

Mt. Sinai (?)

SINAI PENINSULA

GULF OF SUEZ

EGYPT

NILE RIVER

Thebes

"Thus you shall say to the children of Israel: 'The LORD God of your fathers, the God of Abraham, the God of Isaac, and the God of Jacob, has sent me to you. This *is* My name forever, and this *is* My memorial to all generations.' 16 Go and gather the elders of Israel together, and say to them, 'The LORD God of your fathers, the God of Abraham, of Isaac, and of Jacob, appeared to me, saying, "I have surely visited you and *seen* what is done to you in Egypt; 17 and I have said I will bring you up out of the affliction of Egypt to the land of the Canaanites and the Hittites and the Amorites and the Perizzites and the Hivites and the Jebusites, to a land flowing with milk and honey." ' 18 Then they will heed your voice; and you shall come, you and the elders of Israel, to the king of Egypt; and you shall say to him, 'The LORD God of the Hebrews has met with us; and now, please, let us go three days' journey into the wilderness, that we may sacrifice to the LORD our God.' 19 But I am sure that the king of Egypt will not let you go, no, not even by a mighty hand. 20 So I will stretch out My hand and strike Egypt with all My wonders which I will do in its midst; and after that he will let you go. 21 And I will give this people favor in the sight of the Egyptians; and it shall be, when you go, that you shall not go empty-handed. 22 But every woman shall ask of her neighbor, namely, of her who dwells near her house, articles of silver, articles of gold, and clothing; and you shall put *them* on your sons and on your daughters. So you shall plunder the Egyptians."

4 Then Moses answered and said, "But suppose they will not believe me or listen to my voice; suppose they say, 'The LORD has not appeared to you.' "

2 So the LORD said to him, "What *is* that in your hand?"

He said, "A rod."

3 And He said, "Cast it on the ground." So he cast it on the ground, and it became a serpent; and Moses fled from it. 4 Then the LORD said to Moses, "Reach out your hand and take *it* by the tail" (and he reached out his hand and caught it, and it be-

came a rod in his hand), 5 "that they may believe that the LORD God of their fathers, the God of Abraham, the God of Isaac, and the God of Jacob, has appeared to you."

6 Furthermore the LORD said to him, "Now put your hand in your bosom." And he put his hand in his bosom, and when he took it out, behold, his hand *was* leprous, like snow. 7 And He said, "Put your hand in your bosom again." So he put his hand in his bosom again, and drew it out of his bosom, and behold, it was restored like his *other* flesh. 8 "Then it will be, if they do not believe you, nor heed the message of the first sign, that they may believe the message of the latter sign. 9 And it shall be, if they do not believe even these two signs, or listen to your voice, that you shall take water from the river*a* and pour *it* on the dry *land*. The water which you take from the river will become blood on the dry *land*."

10 Then Moses said to the LORD, "O my Lord, I *am* not eloquent, neither before nor since You have spoken to Your servant; but I *am* slow of speech and slow of tongue."

11 So the LORD said to him, "Who has made man's mouth? Or who makes the mute, the deaf, the seeing, or the blind? *Have* not I, the LORD? 12 Now therefore, go, and I will be with your mouth and teach you what you shall say."

13 But he said, "O my Lord, please send by the hand of whomever *else* You may send."

14 So the anger of the LORD was kindled against Moses, and He said: "Is not Aaron the Levite your brother? I know that he can speak well. And look, he is also coming out to meet you. When he sees you, he will be glad in his heart. 15 Now you shall speak to him and put the words in his mouth. And I will be with your mouth and with his mouth, and I will teach you what you shall do. 16 So he shall be your spokesman to the people. And he himself shall be as a mouth for you, and you shall be to him as God. 17 And you shall take this rod in your hand, with which you shall do the signs."

18 So Moses went and returned to Jethro his father-in-law, and said to

4:9 *a*That is, the Nile

him, "Please let me go and return to my brethren who *are* in Egypt, and see whether they are still alive."

And Jethro said to Moses, "Go in peace."

19 Now the LORD said to Moses in Midian, "Go, return to Egypt; for all the men who sought your life are dead." 20 Then Moses took his wife and his sons and set them on a donkey, and he returned to the land of Egypt. And Moses took the rod of God in his hand.

21 And the LORD said to Moses, "When you go back to Egypt, see that you do all those wonders before Pharaoh which I have put in your hand. But I will harden his heart, so that he will not let the people go. 22 Then you shall say to Pharaoh, 'Thus says the LORD: "Israel *is* My son, My firstborn. 23 So I say to you, let My son go that he may serve Me. But if you refuse to let him go, indeed I will kill your son, your firstborn." ' "

24 And it came to pass on the way, at the encampment, that the LORD met him and sought to kill him. 25 Then Zipporah took a sharp stone and cut off the foreskin of her son and cast *it* at *Moses'*[a] feet, and said, "Surely you *are* a husband of blood to me!" 26 So He let him go. Then she said, "*You are* a husband of blood!"—because of the circumcision.

27 And the LORD said to Aaron, "Go into the wilderness to meet Moses." So he went and met him on the mountain of God, and kissed him. 28 So Moses told Aaron all the words of the LORD who had sent him, and all the signs which He had commanded him. 29 Then Moses and Aaron went and gathered together all the elders of the children of Israel. 30 And Aaron spoke all the words which the LORD had spoken to Moses. Then he did the signs in the sight of the people. 31 So the people believed; and when they heard that the LORD had visited the children of Israel and that He had looked on their affliction, then they bowed their heads and worshiped.

5 Afterward Moses and Aaron went in and told Pharaoh, "Thus says the LORD God of Israel: 'Let My peo-

ple go, that they may hold a feast to Me in the wilderness.' "

2 And Pharaoh said, "Who *is* the LORD, that I should obey His voice to let Israel go? I do not know the LORD, nor will I let Israel go."

3 So they said, "The God of the Hebrews has met with us. Please, let us go three days' journey into the desert and sacrifice to the LORD our God, lest He fall upon us with pestilence or with the sword."

4 Then the king of Egypt said to them, "Moses and Aaron, why do you take the people from their work? Get *back* to your labor." 5 And Pharaoh said, "Look, the people of the land *are* many now, and you make them rest from their labor!"

6 So the same day Pharaoh commanded the taskmasters of the people and their officers, saying, 7 "You shall no longer give the people straw to make brick as before. Let them go and gather straw for themselves. 8 And you shall lay on them the quota of bricks which they made before. You shall not reduce it. For they are idle; therefore they cry out, saying, 'Let us go *and* sacrifice to our God.' 9 Let more work be laid on the men, that they may labor in it, and let them not regard false words."

10 And the taskmasters of the people and their officers went out and spoke to the people, saying, "Thus says Pharaoh: 'I will not give you straw. 11 Go, get yourselves straw where you can find it; yet none of your work will be reduced.' "
12 So the people were scattered abroad throughout all the land of Egypt to gather stubble instead of straw. 13 And the taskmasters forced *them* to hurry, saying, "Fulfill your work, *your* daily quota, as when there was straw." 14 Also the officers of the children of Israel, whom Pharaoh's taskmasters had set over them, were beaten *and* were asked, "Why have you not fulfilled your task in making brick both yesterday and today, as before?"

15 Then the officers of the children of Israel came and cried out to Pharaoh, saying, "Why are you dealing thus with your servants? 16 There is no straw given to your servants, and they say to us, 'Make brick!' And

4:25 [a]Literally *his*

indeed your servants *are* beaten, but the fault *is* in your *own* people.''

17 But he said, "You *are* idle! Idle! Therefore you say, 'Let us go *and* sacrifice to the LORD.' 18 Therefore go now *and* work; for no straw shall be given you, yet you shall deliver the quota of bricks." 19 And the officers of the children of Israel saw *that* they *were* in trouble after it was said, "You shall not reduce *any* bricks from your daily quota."

20 Then, as they came out from Pharaoh, they met Moses and Aaron who stood there to meet them. 21 And they said to them, "Let the LORD look on you and judge, because you have made us abhorrent in the sight of Pharaoh and in the sight of his servants, to put a sword in their hand to kill us."

22 So Moses returned to the LORD and said, "Lord, why have You brought trouble on this people? Why *is* it You have sent me? 23 For since I came to Pharaoh to speak in Your name, he has done evil to this people; neither have You delivered Your people at all."

6 Then the LORD said to Moses, "Now you shall see what I will do to Pharaoh. For with a strong hand he will let them go, and with a strong hand he will drive them out of his land."

2 And God spoke to Moses and said to him: "I *am* the LORD. 3 I appeared to Abraham, to Isaac, and to Jacob, as God Almighty, but *by* My name LORD*ᵃ* I was not known to them. 4 I have also established My covenant with them, to give them the land of Canaan, the land of their pilgrimage, in which they were strangers. 5 And I have also heard the groaning of the children of Israel whom the Egyptians keep in bondage, and I have remembered My covenant. 6 Therefore say to the children of Israel: 'I *am* the LORD; I will bring you out from under the burdens of the Egyptians, I will rescue you from their bondage, and I will redeem you with an outstretched arm and with great judgments. 7 I will take you as My people, and I will be your God. Then you shall know that I *am* the LORD your God who brings you out from under the burdens of the Egyp-

tians. 8 And I will bring you into the land which I swore to give to Abraham, Isaac, and Jacob; and I will give it to you *as* a heritage: I *am* the LORD.' " 9 So Moses spoke thus to the children of Israel; but they did not heed Moses, because of anguish of spirit and cruel bondage.

10 And the LORD spoke to Moses, saying, 11 "Go in, tell Pharaoh king of Egypt to let the children of Israel go out of his land."

12 And Moses spoke before the LORD, saying, "The children of Israel have not heeded me. How then shall Pharaoh heed me, for I *am* of uncircumcised lips?"

13 Then the LORD spoke to Moses and Aaron, and gave them a command for the children of Israel and for Pharaoh king of Egypt, to bring the children of Israel out of the land of Egypt.

14 These *are* the heads of their fathers' houses: The sons of Reuben, the firstborn of Israel, *were* Hanoch, Pallu, Hezron, and Carmi. These are the families of Reuben. 15 And the sons of Simeon *were* Jemuel,*ᵃ* Jamin, Ohad, Jachin, Zohar, and Shaul the son of a Canaanite woman. These *are* the families of Simeon. 16 These *are* the names of the sons of Levi according to their generations: Gershon, Kohath, and Merari. And the years of the life of Levi *were* one hundred and thirty-seven. 17 The sons of Gershon *were* Libni and Shimi according to their families. 18 And the sons of Kohath *were* Amram, Izhar, Hebron, and Uzziel. And the years of the life of Kohath *were* one hundred and thirty-three. 19 The sons of Merari *were* Mahli and Mushi. These *are* the families of Levi according to their generations.

20 Now Amram took for himself Jochebed, his father's sister, as wife; and she bore him Aaron and Moses. And the years of the life of Amram *were* one hundred and thirty-seven. 21 The sons of Izhar *were* Korah, Nepheg, and Zichri. 22 And the sons of Uzziel *were* Mishael, Elzaphan, and Zithri. 23 Aaron took to himself Elisheba, daughter of Amminadab, sister of Nahshon, as wife; and she bore him Nadab, Abihu, Eleazar, and Ithamar. 24 And the sons of Korah *were* Assir, Elkanah, and Abiasaph.

6:3 *ᵃ*Hebrew *YHWH*, traditionally *Jehovah*   6:15 *ᵃ*Spelled *Nemuel* in Numbers 26:12

These are the families of the Korahites. 25 Eleazar, Aaron's son, took for himself one of the daughters of Putiel as wife; and she bore him Phinehas. These *are* the heads of the fathers' houses of the Levites according to their families.

26 These *are the same* Aaron and Moses to whom the LORD said, "Bring out the children of Israel from the land of Egypt according to their armies." 27 These *are* the ones who spoke to Pharaoh king of Egypt, to bring out the children of Israel from Egypt. These *are the same* Moses and Aaron.

28 And it came to pass, on the day the LORD spoke to Moses in the land of Egypt, 29 that the LORD spoke to Moses, saying, "I *am* the LORD. Speak to Pharaoh king of Egypt all that I say to you."

30 But Moses said before the LORD, "Behold, I *am* of uncircumcised lips, and how shall Pharaoh heed me?"

7 So the LORD said to Moses: "See, I have made you *as* God to Pharaoh, and Aaron your brother shall be your prophet. 2 You shall speak all that I command you. And Aaron your brother shall tell Pharaoh to send the children of Israel out of his land. 3 And I will harden Pharaoh's heart, and multiply My signs and My wonders in the land of Egypt. 4 But Pharaoh will not heed you, so that I may lay My hand on Egypt and bring My armies *and* My people, the children of Israel, out of the land of Egypt by great judgments. 5 And the Egyptians shall know that I *am* the LORD, when I stretch out My hand on Egypt and bring out the children of Israel from among them."

6 Then Moses and Aaron did *so;* just as the LORD commanded them, so they did. 7 And Moses *was* eighty years old and Aaron eighty-three years old when they spoke to Pharaoh.

8 Then the LORD spoke to Moses and Aaron, saying, 9 "When Pharaoh speaks to you, saying, 'Show a miracle for yourselves,' then you shall say to Aaron, 'Take your rod and cast *it* before Pharaoh, *and* let it become a serpent.' " 10 So Moses and Aaron went in to Pharaoh, and they did so, just as the LORD commanded. And Aaron cast down his rod before Pharaoh and before his servants, and it became a serpent.

11 But Pharaoh also called the wise men and the sorcerers; so the magicians of Egypt, they also did in like manner with their enchantments. 12 For every man threw down his rod, and they became serpents. But Aaron's rod swallowed up their rods. 13 And Pharaoh's heart grew hard, and he did not heed them, as the LORD had said.

14 So the LORD said to Moses: "Pharaoh's heart *is* hard; he refuses to let the people go. 15 Go to Pharaoh in the morning, when he goes out to the water, and you shall stand by the river's bank to meet him; and the rod which was turned to a serpent you shall take in your hand. 16 And you shall say to him, 'The LORD God of the Hebrews has sent me to you, saying, "Let My people go, that they may serve Me in the wilderness"; but indeed, until now you would not hear! 17 Thus says the LORD: "By this you shall know that I *am* the LORD. Behold, I will strike the waters which *are* in the river with the rod that *is* in my hand, and they shall be turned to blood. 18 And the fish that *are* in the river shall die, the river shall stink, and the Egyptians will loathe to drink the water of the river." ' "

19 Then the LORD spoke to Moses, "Say to Aaron, 'Take your rod and stretch out your hand over the waters of Egypt, over their streams, over their rivers, over their ponds, and over all their pools of water, that they may become blood. And there shall be blood throughout all the land of Egypt, both in *buckets of* wood and *pitchers of* stone.' " 20 And Moses and Aaron did so, just as the LORD commanded. So he lifted up the rod and struck the waters that *were* in the river, in the sight of Pharaoh and in the sight of his servants. And all the waters that *were* in the river were turned to blood. 21 The fish that *were* in the river died, the river stank, and the Egyptians could not drink the water of the river. So there was blood throughout all the land of Egypt.

22 Then the magicians of Egypt did so with their enchantments; and Pharaoh's heart grew hard, and he did not heed them, as the LORD had said. 23 And Pharaoh turned and went into his house. Neither was his heart moved by this. 24 So all the

Egyptians dug all around the river for water to drink, because they could not drink the water of the river. 25 And seven days passed after the LORD had struck the river.

8 And the LORD spoke to Moses, "Go to Pharaoh and say to him, 'Thus says the LORD: "Let My people go, that they may serve Me. 2 But if you refuse to let *them* go, behold, I will smite all your territory with frogs. 3 So the river shall bring forth frogs abundantly, which shall go up and come into your house, into your bedroom, on your bed, into the houses of your servants, on your people, into your ovens, and into your kneading bowls. 4 And the frogs shall come up on you, on your people, and on all your servants."' "

5 Then the LORD spoke to Moses, "Say to Aaron, 'Stretch out your hand with your rod over the streams, over the rivers, and over the ponds, and cause frogs to come up on the land of Egypt.' " 6 So Aaron stretched out his hand over the waters of Egypt, and the frogs came up and covered the land of Egypt. 7 And the magicians did so with their enchantments, and brought up frogs on the land of Egypt.

8 Then Pharaoh called for Moses and Aaron, and said, "Entreat the LORD that He may take away the frogs from me and from my people; and I will let the people go, that they may sacrifice to the LORD."

9 And Moses said to Pharaoh, "Accept the honor of saying when I shall intercede for you, for your servants, and for your people, to destroy the frogs from you and your houses, *that* they may remain in the river only."

10 So he said, "Tomorrow." And he said, "*Let it be* according to your word, that you may know that *there is* no one like the LORD our God. 11 And the frogs shall depart from you, from your houses, from your servants, and from your people. They shall remain in the river only."

12 Then Moses and Aaron went out from Pharaoh. And Moses cried out to the LORD concerning the frogs which He had brought against Pharaoh. 13 So the LORD did according to the word of Moses. And the frogs died out of the houses, out of the courtyards, and out of the fields. 14 They gathered them together in heaps, and the land stank. 15 But when Pharaoh saw that there was relief, he hardened his heart and did not heed them, as the LORD had said.

16 So the LORD said to Moses, "Say to Aaron, 'Stretch out your rod, and strike the dust of the land, so that it may become lice throughout all the land of Egypt.' " 17 And they did so. For Aaron stretched out his hand with his rod and struck the dust of the earth, and it became lice on man and beast. All the dust of the land became lice throughout all the land of Egypt.

18 Now the magicians so worked with their enchantments to bring forth lice, but they could not. So there were lice on man and beast. 19 Then the magicians said to Pharaoh, "This *is* the finger of God." But Pharaoh's heart grew hard, and he did not heed them, just as the LORD had said.

20 And the LORD said to Moses, "Rise early in the morning and stand before Pharaoh as he comes out to the water. Then say to him, 'Thus says the LORD: "Let My people go, that they may serve Me. 21 Or else, if you will not let My people go, behold, I will send swarms *of flies* on you and your servants, on your people and into your houses. The houses of the Egyptians shall be full of swarms *of flies*, and also the ground on which they *stand*. 22 And in that day I will set apart the land of Goshen, in which My people dwell, that no swarms *of flies* shall be there, in order that you may know that I *am* the LORD in the midst of the land. 23 I will make a difference[a] between My people and your people. Tomorrow this sign shall be."' " 24 And the LORD did so. Thick swarms *of flies* came into the house of Pharaoh, *into* his servants' houses, and into all the land of Egypt. The land was corrupted because of the swarms *of flies*.

25 Then Pharaoh called for Moses and Aaron, and said, "Go, sacrifice to your God in the land."

26 And Moses said, "It is not right to do so, for we would be sacrificing the abomination of the Egyptians to the LORD our God. If we sacrifice the abomination of the Egyptians before

8:23 aLiterally *set a ransom* (compare Exodus 9:4 and 11:7)

Let My People Go

The ancient Israelites had an appreciation for seeing God at work in the everyday events of life. They understood God's use of His creation and natural phenomena to reveal Himself (see Rom. 1:20).

This attitude is often lost in modern society when we test God to reveal Himself in a "supernatural" way. There are times when God does perform signs and wonders, such as raising Lazarus from the dead, Jesus walking on the water, or the resurrection of Christ. When Moses challenged the Egyptian Pharaoh to free the Israelites from slavery and Pharaoh refused, ten plagues fell upon the land of Egypt. These included plagues of frogs, lice, flies, diseased cattle, boils, locusts, and more. Each time a plague fell on the land, the Egyptians were called to worship a god-like image of whatever the plague was.

When God sent the plagues on the Egyptians, He showed His power over false gods. The intensity, severity and timing of the plagues revealed the greatness of the God of the Israelites. Using natural phenomena, God worked miracles for His people.

Later when Moses died and Joshua commanded the Israelites, God used other natural events to reveal His greatness. Upon their crossing the Jordan River, God parted the waters near the towns of Gilgal and Adamah. In our century the Jordan River has often been dammed from mud slides which occur near these ancient towns. Whether God parted the waters for the Israelites supernaturally or through a beautiful illustration of natural phenomena such as the mud slides, timed perfectly, we do not know. But regardless, the Israelites saw God revealed in the miracle.

We must develop an appreciation for God's lordship throughout His creation. His ability to alter natural circumstances to aid us is as prominent as it was for the ancient Israelites. But we also need to recognize God in the common events of life, such as bringing the right people into our lives when we need help and encouragement. All we need to do is look around at the everyday events in our lives. God is revealing Himself to us in many ways.

their eyes, then will they not stone us? 27 We will go three days' journey into the wilderness and sacrifice to the LORD our God as He will command us."

28 So Pharaoh said, "I will let you go, that you may sacrifice to the LORD your God in the wilderness; only you shall not go very far away. Intercede for me."

29 Then Moses said, "Indeed I am going out from you, and I will entreat the LORD, that the swarms *of flies* may depart tomorrow from Pharaoh, from his servants, and from his people. But let Pharaoh not deal deceitfully anymore in not letting the people go to sacrifice to the LORD."

30 So Moses went out from Pharaoh and entreated the LORD. 31 And the LORD did according to the word of Moses; He removed the swarms *of flies* from Pharaoh, from his servants, and from his people. Not one remained. 32 But Pharaoh hardened his heart at this time also; neither would he let the people go.

9 Then the LORD said to Moses, "Go in to Pharaoh and tell him, 'Thus says the LORD God of the Hebrews: "Let My people go, that they may serve Me. 2 For if you refuse to let *them* go, and still hold them, 3 behold, the hand of the LORD will be on your cattle in the field, on the horses, on the donkeys, on the camels, on the oxen, and on the sheep— a very severe pestilence. 4 And the LORD will make a difference between the livestock of Israel and the livestock of Egypt. So nothing shall die of all *that* belongs to the children of Israel." ' " 5 Then the LORD appointed a set time, saying, "Tomorrow the LORD will do this thing in the land."

6 So the LORD did this thing on the next day, and all the livestock of Egypt died; but of the livestock of the children of Israel, not one died. 7 Then Pharaoh sent, and indeed, not even one of the livestock of the Israelites was dead. But the heart of Pharaoh became hard, and he did not let the people go.

8 So the LORD said to Moses and Aaron, "Take for yourselves handfuls of ashes from a furnace, and let Moses scatter it toward the heavens in the sight of Pharaoh. 9 And it will become fine dust in all the land of Egypt, and it will cause boils that break out in sores on man and beast throughout all the land of Egypt." 10 Then they took ashes from the furnace and stood before Pharaoh, and Moses scattered *them* toward heaven. And *they* caused boils that break out in sores on man and beast. 11 And the magicians could not stand before Moses because of the boils, for the boils were on the magicians and on all the Egyptians. 12 But the LORD hardened the heart of Pharaoh; and he did not heed them, just as the LORD had spoken to Moses.

13 Then the LORD said to Moses, "Rise early in the morning and stand before Pharaoh, and say to him, 'Thus says the LORD God of the Hebrews: "Let My people go, that they may serve Me, 14 for at this time I will send all My plagues to your very heart, and on your servants and on your people, that you may know that *there is* none like Me in all the earth. 15 Now if I had stretched out My hand and struck you and your people with pestilence, then you would have been cut off from the earth. 16 But indeed for this *purpose* I have raised you up, that I may show My power *in* you, and that My name may be declared in all the earth. 17 As yet you exalt yourself against My people in that you will not let them go. 18 Behold, tomorrow about this time I will cause very heavy hail to rain down, such as has not been in Egypt since its founding until now. 19 Therefore send now *and* gather your livestock and all that you have in the field, for the hail shall come down on every man and every animal which is found in the field and is not brought home; and they shall die." ' "

20 He who feared the word of the LORD among the servants of Pharaoh made his servants and his livestock flee to the houses. 21 But he who did not regard the word of the LORD left his servants and his livestock in the field.

22 Then the LORD said to Moses, "Stretch out your hand toward heaven, that there may be hail in all the land of Egypt—on man, on beast, and on every herb of the field, throughout the land of Egypt." 23 And Moses stretched out his rod toward heaven; and the LORD sent thunder and hail, and fire darted to the ground. And the LORD rained hail

on the land of Egypt. 24 So there was hail, and fire mingled with the hail, so very heavy that there was none like it in all the land of Egypt since it became a nation. 25 And the hail struck throughout the whole land of Egypt, all that *was* in the field, both man and beast; and the hail struck every herb of the field and broke every tree of the field. 26 Only in the land of Goshen, where the children of Israel *were*, there was no hail.

27 And Pharaoh sent and called for Moses and Aaron, and said to them, "I have sinned this time. The LORD *is* righteous, and my people and I *are* wicked. 28 Entreat the LORD, that there may be no *more* mighty thundering and hail, for *it is* enough. I will let you go, and you shall stay no longer."

29 So Moses said to him, "As soon as I have gone out of the city, I will spread out my hands to the LORD; the thunder will cease, and there will be no more hail, that you may know that the earth *is* the LORD's. 30 But as for you and your servants, I know that you will not yet fear the LORD God."

31 Now the flax and the barley were struck, for the barley *was* in the head and the flax *was* in bud. 32 But the wheat and the spelt were not struck, for they *are* late crops.

33 So Moses went out of the city from Pharaoh and spread out his hands to the LORD; then the thunder and the hail ceased, and the rain was not poured on the earth. 34 And when Pharaoh saw that the rain, the hail, and the thunder had ceased, he sinned yet more; and he hardened his heart, he and his servants. 35 So the heart of Pharaoh was hard; neither would he let the children of Israel go, as the LORD had spoken by Moses.

10 Now the LORD said to Moses, "Go in to Pharaoh; for I have hardened his heart and the hearts of his servants, that I may show these signs of Mine before him, 2 and that you may tell in the hearing of your son and your son's son the mighty things I have done in Egypt, and My signs which I have done among them, that you may know that I *am* the LORD."

3 So Moses and Aaron came in to Pharaoh and said to him, "Thus says the LORD God of the Hebrews: 'How long will you refuse to humble yourself before Me? Let My people go, that they may serve Me. 4 Or else, if you refuse to let My people go, behold, tomorrow I will bring locusts into your territory. 5 And they shall cover the face of the earth, so that no one will be able to see the earth; and they shall eat the residue of what is left, which remains to you from the hail, and they shall eat every tree which grows up for you out of the field. 6 They shall fill your houses, the houses of all your servants, and the houses of all the Egyptians—which neither your fathers nor your fathers' fathers have seen, since the day that they were on the earth to this day.' " And he turned and went out from Pharaoh.

7 Then Pharaoh's servants said to him, "How long shall this man be a snare to us? Let the men go, that they may serve the LORD their God. Do you not yet know that Egypt is destroyed?"

8 So Moses and Aaron were brought again to Pharaoh, and he said to them, "Go, serve the LORD your God. Who *are* the ones that are going?"

9 And Moses said, "We will go with our young and our old; with our sons and our daughters, with our flocks and our herds we will go, for we must hold a feast to the LORD."

10 Then he said to them, "The LORD had better be with you when I let you and your little ones go! Beware, for evil is ahead of you. 11 Not so! Go now, you *who are* men, and serve the LORD, for that is what you desired." And they were driven out from Pharaoh's presence.

12 Then the LORD said to Moses, "Stretch out your hand over the land of Egypt for the locusts, that they may come upon the land of Egypt, and eat every herb of the land—all that the hail has left." 13 So Moses stretched out his rod over the land of Egypt, and the LORD brought an east wind on the land all that day and all *that* night. When it was morning, the east wind brought the locusts. 14 And the locusts went up over all the land of Egypt and rested on all the territory of Egypt. *They were* very severe; previously there had been no such locusts as they, nor shall there be such after them. 15 For they covered the face of the

whole earth, so that the land was darkened; and they ate every herb of the land and all the fruit of the trees which the hail had left. So there remained nothing green on the trees or on the plants of the field throughout all the land of Egypt.

16 Then Pharaoh called for Moses and Aaron in haste, and said, "I have sinned against the LORD your God and against you. 17 Now therefore, please forgive my sin only this once, and entreat the LORD your God, that He may take away from me this death only." 18 So he went out from Pharaoh and entreated the LORD. 19 And the LORD turned a very strong west wind, which took the locusts away and blew them into the Red Sea. There remained not one locust in all the territory of Egypt. 20 But the LORD hardened Pharaoh's heart, and he did not let the children of Israel go.

21 Then the LORD said to Moses, "Stretch out your hand toward heaven, that there may be darkness over the land of Egypt, darkness *which* may even be felt." 22 So Moses stretched out his hand toward heaven, and there was thick darkness in all the land of Egypt three days. 23 They did not see one another; nor did anyone rise from his place for three days. But all the children of Israel had light in their dwellings.

24 Then Pharaoh called to Moses and said, "Go, serve the LORD; only let your flocks and your herds be kept back. Let your little ones also go with you."

25 But Moses said, "You must also give us sacrifices and burnt offerings, that we may sacrifice to the LORD our God. 26 Our livestock also shall go with us; not a hoof shall be left behind. For we must take some of them to serve the LORD our God, and even we do not know with what we must serve the LORD until we arrive there."

27 But the LORD hardened Pharaoh's heart, and he would not let them go. 28 Then Pharaoh said to him, "Get away from me! Take heed to yourself and see my face no more! For in the day you see my face you shall die!"

29 So Moses said, "You have spoken well. I will never see your face again."

11 And the LORD said to Moses, "I will bring one more plague on Pharaoh and on Egypt. Afterward he will let you go from here. When he lets *you* go, he will surely drive you out of here altogether. 2 Speak now in the hearing of the people, and let every man ask from his neighbor and every woman from her neighbor, articles of silver and articles of gold." 3 And the LORD gave the people favor in the sight of the Egyptians. Moreover the man Moses *was* very great in the land of Egypt, in the sight of Pharaoh's servants and in the sight of the people.

4 Then Moses said, "Thus says the LORD: 'About midnight I will go out into the midst of Egypt; 5 and all the firstborn in the land of Egypt shall die, from the firstborn of Pharaoh who sits on his throne, even to the firstborn of the female servant who *is* behind the handmill, and all the firstborn of the animals. 6 Then there shall be a great cry throughout all the land of Egypt, such as was not like it *before*, nor shall be like it again. 7 But against none of the children of Israel shall a dog move its tongue, against man or beast, that you may know that the LORD does make a difference between the Egyptians and Israel.' 8 And all these your servants shall come down to me and bow down to me, saying, 'Get out, and all the people who follow you!' After that I will go out." Then he went out from Pharaoh in great anger.

9 But the LORD said to Moses, "Pharaoh will not heed you, so that My wonders may be multiplied in the land of Egypt." 10 So Moses and Aaron did all these wonders before Pharaoh; and the LORD hardened Pharaoh's heart, and he did not let the children of Israel go out of his land.

12 Now the LORD spoke to Moses and Aaron in the land of Egypt, saying, 2 "This month *shall be* your beginning of months; it *shall be* the first month of the year to you. 3 Speak to all the congregation of Israel, saying: 'On the tenth of this month every man shall take for himself a lamb, according to the house of *his* father, a lamb for a household. 4 And if the household is too small for the lamb, let him and his neighbor next to his house take *it* according to the number of the persons; according to each man's need you shall make your count for the lamb. 5 Your lamb shall be without blemish, a male of the first year. You may take *it* from the sheep or from the goats. 6 Now you shall keep it until the fourteenth day of the same month. Then the whole assembly of the congregation of Israel shall kill it at twilight. 7 And they shall take *some* of the blood and put *it* on the two doorposts and on the lintel of the houses where they eat it. 8 Then they shall eat the flesh on that night; roasted in fire, with unleavened bread *and* with bitter *herbs* they shall eat it. 9 Do not eat it raw, nor boiled at all with water, but roasted in fire— its head with its legs and its entrails. 10 You shall let none of it remain until morning, and what remains of it until morning you shall burn with fire. 11 And thus you shall eat it: *with* a belt on your waist, your sandals on your feet, and your staff in your hand. So you shall eat it in haste. It *is* the LORD's Passover.

12 'For I will pass through the land of Egypt on that night, and will strike all the firstborn in the land of Egypt, both man and beast; and against all the gods of Egypt I will execute judgment: I *am* the LORD. 13 Now the blood shall be a sign for you on the houses where you *are*. And when I see the blood, I will pass over you; and the plague shall not be on you to destroy *you* when I strike the land of Egypt.

14 'So this day shall be to you a memorial; and you shall keep it as a feast to the LORD throughout your generations. You shall keep it as a feast by an everlasting ordinance. 15 Seven days you shall eat unleavened bread. On the first day you shall remove leaven from your houses. For whoever eats leavened bread from the first day until the seventh day, that person shall be cut off from Israel. 16 On the first day *there shall be* a holy convocation, and on the seventh day there shall be a holy convocation for you. No manner of work shall be done on them; but *that* which everyone must eat—that only may be prepared by you. 17 So you shall observe *the Feast of* Unleavened Bread, for on this same day I will have brought your armies out of the land of Egypt. Therefore you shall observe this day throughout your generations as an everlasting ordinance. 18 In the first *month,* on the fourteenth day of the month at evening, you shall eat unleavened bread, until the twenty-first day of the month at evening. 19 For seven days no leaven shall be found in your houses, since whoever eats what is leavened, that same person shall be cut off from the congregation of Israel, whether *he is* a stranger or a native of the land. 20 You shall eat nothing leavened; in all your dwellings you shall eat unleavened bread.' "

21 Then Moses called for all the elders of Israel and said to them, "Pick out and take lambs for yourselves according to your families, and kill the Passover *lamb.* 22 And you shall take a bunch of hyssop, dip *it* in the blood that *is* in the basin, and strike the lintel and the two doorposts with the blood that *is* in the basin. And none of you shall go out of the door of his house until morning. 23 For the LORD will pass through to strike the Egyptians; and when He sees the blood on the lintel and on the two doorposts, the LORD will pass over the door and not allow the destroyer to come into your houses to strike *you.* 24 And you shall observe this thing as an ordinance for you and your sons forever. 25 It will come to pass when you come to the land which the LORD will give you, just as He promised, that you shall keep this service. 26 And it shall be, when your children say to you, 'What do you mean by this service?' 27 that you shall say, 'It *is* the Passover sacrifice of the LORD, who passed over the houses of the children of Israel in Egypt when He struck the Egyptians and delivered our households.' " So the people bowed their heads and worshiped. 28 Then the children of Israel went away and did *so;* just as the LORD had commanded Moses and Aaron, so they did.

29 And it came to pass at midnight that the LORD struck all the firstborn in the land of Egypt, from the firstborn of Pharaoh who sat on his throne to the firstborn of the captive who *was* in the dungeon, and all the firstborn of livestock. 30 So Pharaoh rose in the night, he, all his servants, and all the Egyptians; and there was a great cry in Egypt, for *there was*

God's Covenant—Forgiveness

   In the Bible there are three ways of establishing and sealing a covenant: the word covenant, the salt covenant, and the sharing of a covenant meal. The first and most common covenant is the word covenant. The second method is the salt covenant. This was commonly used between enemies to establish peace. Even in modern times it is still practiced. In 1978 President Anwar Sadat of Egypt and Prime Minister Menachem Begin of Israel sealed the Camp David Peace Accord by taking a pinch of salt and tasting it together. The third, and perhaps the most interesting, method of establishing a covenant was to eat a meal together. This was not only a sign of peace, but a sign of forgiveness.

   In the story of the Prodigal Son, the father ordered a feast to assure the boy of his forgiveness when he returned. The elder son did not participate in the meal because he was unable to forgive his younger brother.

   During the Passover meal, Jesus instituted the Lord's Supper as a reminder of God's forgiveness. When Jesus was arrested and crucified, the disciples fled and abandoned Him. After His resurrection Jesus assured and comforted His disciples that they were forgiven by asking them if they had anything to eat (Luke 24:41). John 21:12 records how Jesus prepared and shared a complete meal with the disciples beside the Sea of Galilee before He ascended.

   Jesus offers us the same comfort and assurance that our sins are forgiven when He says, "Behold, I stand at the door and knock. If anyone hears My voice and opens the door, I will come in to him and dine with him, and he with Me" (Rev. 3:20).

not a house where *there was* not one dead.

31 Then he called for Moses and Aaron by night, and said, "Rise, go out from among my people, both you and the children of Israel. And go, serve the LORD as you have said. 32 Also take your flocks and your herds, as you have said, and be gone; and bless me also."

33 And the Egyptians urged the people, that they might send them out of the land in haste. For they said, "We *shall* all *be* dead." 34 So the people took their dough before it was leavened, having their kneading bowls bound up in their clothes on their shoulders. 35 Now the children of Israel had done according to the word of Moses, and they had asked from the Egyptians articles of silver, articles of gold, and clothing. 36 And the LORD had given the people favor in the sight of the Egyptians, so that they granted them *what they requested*. Thus they plundered the Egyptians.

37 Then the children of Israel journeyed from Rameses to Succoth, about six hundred thousand men on foot, besides children. 38 A mixed multitude went up with them also, and flocks and herds—a great deal of livestock. 39 And they baked unleavened cakes of the dough which they had brought out of Egypt; for it was not leavened, because they were driven out of Egypt and could not wait, nor had they prepared provisions for themselves.

40 Now the sojourn of the children of Israel who lived in Egypt*ᵃ was* four hundred and thirty years. 41 And it came to pass at the end of the four hundred and thirty years—on that very same day—it came to pass that all the armies of the LORD went out from the land of Egypt. 42 It *is* a night of solemn observance to the LORD for bringing them out of the land of Egypt. This *is* that night of the LORD, a solemn observance for all the children of Israel throughout their generations.

43 And the LORD said to Moses and Aaron, "This *is* the ordinance of the Passover: No foreigner shall eat it. 44 But every man's servant who is bought for money, when you have circumcised him, then he may eat it.

45 A sojourner and a hired servant shall not eat it. 46 In one house it shall be eaten; you shall not carry any of the flesh outside the house, nor shall you break one of its bones. 47 All the congregation of Israel shall keep it. 48 And when a stranger dwells with you *and wants* to keep the Passover to the LORD, let all his males be circumcised, and then let him come near and keep it; and he shall be as a native of the land. For no uncircumcised person shall eat it. 49 One law shall be for the native-born and for the stranger who dwells among you."

50 Thus all the children of Israel did; as the LORD commanded Moses and Aaron, so they did. 51 And it came to pass, on that very same day, that the LORD brought the children of Israel out of the land of Egypt according to their armies.

13 Then the LORD spoke to Moses, saying, 2 "Consecrate to Me all the firstborn, whatever opens the womb among the children of Israel, *both* of man and beast; it is Mine."

3 And Moses said to the people: "Remember this day in which you went out of Egypt, out of the house of bondage; for by strength of hand the LORD brought you out of this *place*. No leavened bread shall be eaten. 4 On this day you are going out, in the month Abib. 5 And it shall be, when the LORD brings you into the land of the Canaanites and the Hittites and the Amorites and the Hivites and the Jebusites, which He swore to your fathers to give you, a land flowing with milk and honey, that you shall keep this service in this month. 6 Seven days you shall eat unleavened bread, and on the seventh day *there shall be* a feast to the LORD. 7 Unleavened bread shall be eaten seven days. And no leavened bread shall be seen among you, nor shall leaven be seen among you in all your quarters. 8 And you shall tell your son in that day, saying, 'This is done because of what the LORD did for me when I came up from Egypt.' 9 It shall be as a sign to you on your hand and as a memorial between your eyes, that the LORD's law may be in your mouth; for with a strong hand the LORD has brought you out of Egypt. 10 You shall therefore keep

---

12:40 ᵃSamaritan Pentateuch and Septuagint read *Egypt and Canaan*.

this ordinance in its season from year to year.

11 "And it shall be, when the LORD brings you into the land of the Canaanites, as He swore to you and your fathers, and gives it to you, 12 that you shall set apart to the LORD all that open the womb, that is, every firstborn that comes from an animal which you have; the males *shall be* the LORD's. 13 But every firstborn of a donkey you shall redeem with a lamb; and if you will not redeem *it*, then you shall break its neck. And all the firstborn of man among your sons you shall redeem. 14 So it shall be, when your son asks you in time to come, saying, 'What *is* this?' that you shall say to him, 'By strength of hand the LORD brought us out of Egypt, out of the house of bondage. 15 And it came to pass, when Pharaoh was stubborn about letting us go, that the LORD killed all the firstborn in the land of Egypt, both the firstborn of man and the firstborn of beast. Therefore I sacrifice to the LORD all males that open the womb, but all the firstborn of my sons I redeem.' 16 It shall be as a sign on your hand and as frontlets between your eyes, for by strength of hand the LORD brought us out of Egypt."

17 Then it came to pass, when Pharaoh had let the people go, that God did not lead them *by* way of the land of the Philistines, although that *was* near; for God said, "Lest perhaps the people change their minds when they see war, and return to Egypt." 18 So God led the people around *by* way of the wilderness of the Red Sea. And the children of Israel went up in orderly ranks out of the land of Egypt.

19 And Moses took the bones of Joseph with him, for he had placed the children of Israel under solemn oath, saying, "God will surely visit you, and you shall carry up my bones from here with you."ᵃ

20 So they took their journey from Succoth and camped in Etham at the edge of the wilderness. 21 And the LORD went before them by day in a pillar of cloud to lead the way, and by night in a pillar of fire to give them light, so as to go by day and night. 22 He did not take away the pillar of cloud by day or the pillar of fire by night *from* before the people.

14 Now the LORD spoke to Moses, saying: 2 "Speak to the children of Israel, that they turn and camp before Pi Hahiroth, between Migdol and the sea, opposite Baal Zephon; you shall camp before it by the sea. 3 For Pharaoh will say of the children of Israel, 'They *are* bewildered by the land; the wilderness has closed them in.' 4 Then I will harden Pharaoh's heart, so that he will pursue them; and I will gain honor over Pharaoh and over all his army, that the Egyptians may know that I *am* the LORD." And they did so.

5 Now it was told the king of Egypt that the people had fled, and the heart of Pharaoh and his servants was turned against the people; and they said, "Why have we done this, that we have let Israel go from serving us?" 6 So he made ready his chariot and took his people with him. 7 Also, he took six hundred choice chariots, and all the chariots of Egypt with captains over every one of them. 8 And the LORD hardened the heart of Pharaoh king of Egypt, and he pursued the children of Israel; and the children of Israel went out with boldness. 9 So the Egyptians pursued them, all the horses *and* chariots of Pharaoh, his horsemen and his army, and overtook them camping by the sea beside Pi Hahiroth, before Baal Zephon.

10 And when Pharaoh drew near, the children of Israel lifted their eyes, and behold, the Egyptians marched after them. So they were very afraid, and the children of Israel cried out to the LORD. 11 Then they said to Moses, "Because *there were* no graves in Egypt, have you taken us away to die in the wilderness? Why have you so dealt with us, to bring us up out of Egypt? 12 *Is* this not the word that we told you in Egypt, saying, 'Let us alone that we may serve the Egyptians?' For *it would have been* better for us to serve the Egyptians than that we should die in the wilderness."

13 And Moses said to the people, "Do not be afraid. Stand still, and see the salvation of the LORD, which He will accomplish for you today. For the Egyptians whom you see today,

you shall see again no more forever. 14 The LORD will fight for you, and you shall hold your peace."

15 And the LORD said to Moses, "Why do you cry to Me? Tell the children of Israel to go forward. 16 "But lift up your rod, and stretch out your hand over the sea and divide it. And the children of Israel shall go on dry *ground* through the midst of the sea. 17 And I indeed will harden the hearts of the Egyptians, and they shall follow them. So I will gain honor over Pharaoh and over all his army, his chariots, and his horsemen. 18 Then the Egyptians shall know that I *am* the LORD, when I have gained honor for Myself over Pharaoh, his chariots, and his horsemen."

19 And the Angel of God, who went before the camp of Israel, moved and went behind them; and the pillar of cloud went from before them and stood behind them. 20 So it came between the camp of the Egyptians and the camp of Israel. Thus it was a cloud and darkness *to the one,* and it gave light by night *to the other,* so that the one did not come near the other all that night. 21 Then Moses stretched out his hand over the sea; and the LORD caused the sea to go *back* by a strong east wind all that night, and made the sea into dry *land,* and the waters were divided. 22 So the children of Israel went into the midst of the sea on the dry *ground,* and the waters *were* a wall to them on their right hand and on their left. 23 And the Egyptians pursued and went after them into the midst of the sea, all Pharaoh's horses, his chariots, and his horsemen.

24 Now it came to pass, in the morning watch, that the LORD looked down upon the army of the Egyptians through the pillar of fire and cloud, and He troubled the army of the Egyptians. 25 And He took off[a] their chariot wheels, so that they drove them with difficulty; and the Egyptians said, "Let us flee from the face of Israel, for the LORD fights for them against the Egyptians."

26 Then the LORD said to Moses, "Stretch out your hand over the sea, that the waters may come back upon the Egyptians, on their chariots, and on their horsemen." 27 And Moses stretched out his hand over the sea; and when the morning appeared, the sea returned to its full depth, while the Egyptians were fleeing into it. So the LORD overthrew the Egyptians in the midst of the sea. 28 Then the waters returned and covered the chariots, the horsemen, *and* all the army of Pharaoh that came into the sea after them. Not so much as one of them remained. 29 But the children of Israel had walked on dry *land* in the midst of the sea, and the waters *were* a wall to them on their right hand and on their left.

30 So the LORD saved Israel that day out of the hand of the Egyptians, and Israel saw the Egyptians dead on the seashore. 31 Thus Israel saw the great work which the LORD had done in Egypt; so the people feared the LORD, and believed the LORD and His servant Moses.

15 Then Moses and the children of Israel sang this song to the LORD, and spoke, saying:

"I will sing to the LORD,
　For He has triumphed
　　gloriously!
　The horse and its rider
　He has thrown into the sea!
2　The LORD *is* my strength and
　　song,
　And He has become my
　　salvation;
　He *is* my God, and I will praise
　　Him;
　My father's God, and I will
　　exalt Him.
3　The LORD *is* a man of war;
　The LORD *is* His name.
4　Pharaoh's chariots and his
　　army He has cast into the
　　sea;
　His chosen captains also are
　　drowned in the Red Sea.
5　The depths have covered them;
　They sank to the bottom like a
　　stone.

6　"Your right hand, O LORD, has
　　become glorious in power;
　Your right hand, O LORD, has
　　dashed the enemy in pieces.
7　And in the greatness of Your
　　excellence

14:25 [a]Samaritan Pentateuch, Septuagint, and Syriac read *bound.*

You have overthrown those
who rose against You;
You sent forth Your wrath;
It consumed them like stubble.
8 And with the blast of Your
nostrils
The waters were gathered
together;
The floods stood upright like a
heap;
The depths congealed in the
heart of the sea.
9 The enemy said, 'I will pursue,
I will overtake,
I will divide the spoil;
My desire shall be satisfied on
them.
I will draw my sword,
My hand shall destroy them.'
10 You blew with Your wind,
The sea covered them;
They sank like lead in the
mighty waters.

11 "Who is like You, O LORD,
among the gods?
Who is like You, glorious in
holiness,
Fearful in praises, doing
wonders?
12 You stretched out Your right
hand;
The earth swallowed them.
13 You in Your mercy have led
forth
The people whom You have
redeemed;
You have guided them in Your
strength
To Your holy habitation.

14 "The people will hear and be
afraid;
Sorrow will take hold of the
inhabitants of Philistia.
15 Then the chiefs of Edom will be
dismayed;
The mighty men of Moab,
Trembling will take hold of
them;
All the inhabitants of Canaan
will melt away.
16 Fear and dread will fall on
them;
By the greatness of Your arm
They will be as still as a stone,
Till Your people pass over, O
LORD,
Till the people pass over
Whom You have purchased.

17 You will bring them in and
plant them
In the mountain of Your
inheritance,
In the place, O LORD, which
You have made
For Your own dwelling,
The sanctuary, O LORD, which
Your hands have established.

18 "The LORD shall reign forever
and ever."

19 For the horses of Pharaoh went
with his chariots and his horsemen
into the sea, and the LORD brought
back the waters of the sea upon
them. But the children of Israel went
on dry land in the midst of the sea.
20 Then Miriam the prophetess, the
sister of Aaron, took the timbrel in
her hand; and all the women went
out after her with timbrels and with
dances. 21 And Miriam answered
them:

"Sing to the LORD,
For He has triumphed
gloriously!
The horse and its rider
He has thrown into the sea!"

22 So Moses brought Israel from
the Red Sea; then they went out into
the Wilderness of Shur. And they
went three days in the wilderness
and found no water. 23 Now when
they came to Marah, they could not
drink the waters of Marah, for they
were bitter. Therefore the name of it
was called Marah.a 24 And the people
complained against Moses, saying,
"What shall we drink?" 25 So he
cried out to the LORD, and the LORD
showed him a tree. When he cast it
into the waters, the waters were
made sweet.
There He made a statute and an ordinance for them, and there He tested
them, 26 and said, "If you diligently
heed the voice of the LORD your God
and do what is right in His sight, give
ear to His commandments and keep
all His statutes, I will put none of the
diseases on you which I have brought
on the Egyptians. For I am the LORD
who heals you."
27 Then they came to Elim, where
there were twelve wells of water and

15:23 aLiterally Bitter

seventy palm trees; so they camped there by the waters.

16 And they journeyed from Elim, and all the congregation of the children of Israel came to the Wilderness of Sin, which is between Elim and Sinai, on the fifteenth day of the second month after they departed from the land of Egypt. 2 Then the whole congregation of the children of Israel complained against Moses and Aaron in the wilderness. 3 And the children of Israel said to them, "Oh, that we had died by the hand of the LORD in the land of Egypt, when we sat by the pots of meat *and* when we ate bread to the full! For you have brought us out into this wilderness to kill this whole assembly with hunger."

4 Then the LORD said to Moses, "Behold, I will rain bread from heaven for you. And the people shall go out and gather a certain quota every day, that I may test them, whether they will walk in My law or not. 5 And it shall be on the sixth day that they shall prepare what they bring in, and it shall be twice as much as they gather daily."

6 Then Moses and Aaron said to all the children of Israel, "At evening you shall know that the LORD has brought you out of the land of Egypt. 7 And in the morning you shall see the glory of the LORD; for He hears your complaints against the LORD. But what *are* we, that you complain against us?" 8 Also Moses said, "*This shall be seen* when the LORD gives you meat to eat in the evening, and in the morning bread to the full; for the LORD hears your complaints which you make against Him. And what *are* we? Your complaints *are* not against us but against the LORD."

9 Then Moses spoke to Aaron, "Say to all the congregation of the children of Israel, 'Come near before the LORD, for He has heard your complaints.' " 10 Now it came to pass, as Aaron spoke to the whole congregation of the children of Israel, that they looked toward the wilderness, and behold, the glory of the LORD appeared in the cloud.

11 And the LORD spoke to Moses, saying, 12 "I have heard the complaints of the children of Israel. Speak to them, saying, 'At twilight you shall eat meat, and in the morn-ing you shall be filled with bread. And you shall know that I *am* the LORD your God.' "

13 So it was that quails came up at evening and covered the camp, and in the morning the dew lay all around the camp. 14 And when the layer of dew lifted, there, on the surface of the wilderness, was a small round substance, *as* fine as frost on the ground. 15 So when the children of Israel saw *it*, they said to one another, "What is it?" For they did not know what it *was*.

And Moses said to them, "This *is* the bread which the LORD has given you to eat. 16 This is the thing which the LORD has commanded: 'Let every man gather it according to each one's need, one omer for each person, *according to the* number of persons; let every man take for *those* who *are* in his tent.' "

17 Then the children of Israel did so and gathered, some more, some less. 18 So when they measured *it* by omers, he who gathered much had nothing left over, and he who gathered little had no lack. Every man had gathered according to each one's need. 19 And Moses said, "Let no one leave any of it till morning." 20 Notwithstanding they did not heed Moses. But some of them left part of it until morning, and it bred worms and stank. And Moses was angry with them. 21 So they gathered it every morning, every man according to his need. And when the sun became hot, it melted.

22 And so it was, on the sixth day, *that* they gathered twice as much bread, two omers for each one. And all the rulers of the congregation came and told Moses. 23 Then he said to them, "This *is what* the LORD has said: 'Tomorrow *is* a Sabbath rest, a holy Sabbath to the LORD. Bake what you will bake *today,* and boil what you will boil; and lay up for yourselves all that remains, to be kept until morning.' " 24 So they laid it up till morning, as Moses commanded; and it did not stink, nor were there any worms in it. 25 Then Moses said, "Eat that today, for today *is* a Sabbath to the LORD; today you will not find it in the field. 26 Six days you shall gather it, but on the seventh day, the Sabbath, there will be none."

27 Now it happened *that some* of the people went out on the seventh

day to gather, but they found none. 28 And the LORD said to Moses, "How long do you refuse to keep My commandments and My laws? 29 See! For the LORD has given you the Sabbath; therefore He gives you on the sixth day bread for two days. Let every man remain in his place; let no man go out of his place on the seventh day." 30 So the people rested on the seventh day.

31 And the house of Israel called its name Manna.ª And it *was* like white coriander seed, and the taste of it *was* like wafers *made* with honey.

32 Then Moses said, "This *is* the thing which the LORD has commanded: 'Fill an omer with it, to be kept for your generations, that they may see the bread with which I fed you in the wilderness, when I brought you out of the land of Egypt.' " 33 And Moses said to Aaron, "Take a pot and put an omer of manna in it, and lay it up before the LORD, to be kept for your generations." 34 As the LORD commanded Moses, so Aaron laid it up before the Testimony, to be kept. 35 And the children of Israel ate manna forty years, until they came to an inhabited land; they ate manna until they came to the border of the land of Canaan. 36 Now an omer *is* one-tenth of an ephah.

17 Then all the congregation of the children of Israel set out on their journey from the Wilderness of Sin, according to the commandment of the LORD, and camped in Rephidim; but *there was* no water for the people to drink. 2 Therefore the people contended with Moses, and said, "Give us water, that we may drink."

So Moses said to them, "Why do you contend with me? Why do you tempt the LORD?"

3 And the people thirsted there for water, and the people complained against Moses, and said, "Why *is* it you have brought us up out of Egypt, to kill us and our children and our livestock with thirst?"

4 So Moses cried out to the LORD, saying, "What shall I do with this people? They are almost ready to stone me!"

5 And the LORD said to Moses, "Go on before the people, and take with you some of the elders of Israel. Also take in your hand your rod with which you struck the river, and go. 6 Behold, I will stand before you there on the rock in Horeb; and you shall strike the rock, and water will come out of it, that the people may drink."

And Moses did so in the sight of the elders of Israel. 7 So he called the name of the place Massahª and Meribah,ᵇ because of the contention of the children of Israel, and because they tempted the LORD, saying, "Is the LORD among us or not?"

8 Now Amalek came and fought with Israel in Rephidim. 9 And Moses said to Joshua, "Choose us some men and go out, fight with Amalek. Tomorrow I will stand on the top of the hill with the rod of God in my hand." 10 So Joshua did as Moses said to him, and fought with Amalek. And Moses, Aaron, and Hur went up to the top of the hill. 11 And so it was, when Moses held up his hand, that Israel prevailed; and when he let down his hand, Amalek prevailed. 12 But Moses' hands *became* heavy; so they took a stone and put *it* under him, and he sat on it. And Aaron and Hur supported his hands, one on one side, and the other on the other side; and his hands were steady until the going down of the sun. 13 So Joshua defeated Amalek and his people with the edge of the sword.

14 Then the LORD said to Moses, "Write this *for* a memorial in the book and recount *it* in the hearing of Joshua, that I will utterly blot out the remembrance of Amalek from under heaven." 15 And Moses built an altar and called its name, The-LORD-Is-My-Banner;ª 16 for he said, "Because the LORD has sworn: the LORD *will have* war with Amalek from generation to generation."

18 And Jethro, the priest of Midian, Moses' father-in-law, heard of all that God had done for Moses and for Israel His people—that the LORD had brought Israel out of Egypt. 2 Then Jethro, Moses' father-in-law, took Zipporah, Moses' wife, after he had sent her back, 3 with her

---

16:31 ªLiterally *What?* (compare Exodus 16:15)   17:7 ªLiterally *Tempted*   ᵇLiterally *Contention*
17:15 ªHebrew *YHWH Nissi*

two sons, of whom the name of one *was* Gershom (for he said, "I have been a stranger in a foreign land")*a* 4 and the name of the other *was* Eliezer*a* (for *he said,* "The God of my father *was* my help, and delivered me from the sword of Pharaoh"); 5 and Jethro, Moses' father-in-law, came with his sons and his wife to Moses in the wilderness, where he was encamped at the mountain of God. 6 Now he had said to Moses, "I, your father-in-law Jethro, am coming to you with your wife and her two sons with her."

7 So Moses went out to meet his father-in-law, bowed down, and kissed him. And they asked each other about *their* well-being, and they went into the tent. 8 And Moses told his father-in-law all that the LORD had done to Pharaoh and to the Egyptians for Israel's sake, all the hardship that had come upon them on the way, and *how* the LORD had delivered them. 9 Then Jethro rejoiced for all the good which the LORD had done for Israel, whom He had delivered out of the hand of the Egyptians. 10 And Jethro said, "Blessed *be* the LORD, who has delivered you out of the hand of the Egyptians and out of the hand of Pharaoh, *and* who has delivered the people from under the hand of the Egyptians. 11 Now I know that the LORD *is* greater than all the gods; for in the very thing in which they behaved proudly, *He was* above them." 12 Then Jethro, Moses' father-in-law, took*a* a burnt offering and *other* sacrifices *to offer* to God. And Aaron came with all the elders of Israel to eat bread with Moses' father-in-law before God.

13 And so it was, on the next day, that Moses sat to judge the people; and the people stood before Moses from morning until evening. 14 So when Moses' father-in-law saw all that he did for the people, he said, "What *is* this thing that you are doing for the people? Why do you alone sit, and all the people stand before you from morning until evening?" 15 And Moses said to his father-in-law, "Because the people come to me to inquire of God. 16 When they have a difficulty, they come to me, and I judge between one and another; and

I make known the statutes of God and His laws."

17 So Moses' father-in-law said to him, "The thing that you do *is* not good. 18 Both you and these people who *are* with you will surely wear yourselves out. For this thing *is* too much for you; you are not able to perform it by yourself. 19 Listen now to my voice; I will give you counsel, and God will be with you: Stand before God for the people, so that you may bring the difficulties to God. 20 And you shall teach them the statutes and the laws, and show them the way in which they must walk and the work they must do. 21 Moreover you shall select from all the people able men, such as fear God, men of truth, hating covetousness; and place *such* over them *to be* rulers of thousands, rulers of hundreds, rulers of fifties, and rulers of tens. 22 And let them judge the people at all times. Then it will be *that* every great matter they shall bring to you, but every small matter they themselves shall judge. So it will be easier for you, for they will bear *the burden* with you. 23 If you do this thing, and God *so* commands you, then you will be able to endure, and all this people will also go to their place in peace."

24 So Moses heeded the voice of his father-in-law and did all that he had said. 25 And Moses chose able men out of all Israel, and made them heads over the people: rulers of thousands, rulers of hundreds, rulers of fifties, and rulers of tens. 26 So they judged the people at all times; the hard cases they brought to Moses, but they judged every small case themselves.

27 Then Moses let his father-in-law depart, and he went his way to his own land.

19 In the third month after the children of Israel had gone out of the land of Egypt, on the same day, they came *to* the Wilderness of Sinai. 2 For they had departed from Rephidim, had come *to* the Wilderness of Sinai, and camped in the wilderness. So Israel camped there before the mountain.

3 And Moses went up to God, and the LORD called to him from the

---

18:3 *a*Compare Exodus 2:22   18:4 *a*Literally *My God Is Help*   18:12 *a*Following Masoretic Text and Septuagint; Syriac, Targum, and Vulgate read *offered.*

mountain, saying, "Thus you shall say to the house of Jacob, and tell the children of Israel: 4 'You have seen what I did to the Egyptians, and *how* I bore you on eagles' wings and brought you to Myself. 5 Now therefore, if you will indeed obey My voice and keep My covenant, then you shall be a special treasure to Me above all people; for all the earth *is* Mine. 6 And you shall be to Me a kingdom of priests and a holy nation.' These *are* the words which you shall speak to the children of Israel."

7 So Moses came and called for the elders of the people, and laid before them all these words which the LORD commanded him. 8 Then all the people answered together and said, "All that the LORD has spoken we will do." So Moses brought back the words of the people to the LORD. 9 And the LORD said to Moses, "Behold, I come to you in the thick cloud, that the people may hear when I speak with you, and believe you forever."

So Moses told the words of the people to the LORD.

10 Then the LORD said to Moses, "Go to the people and consecrate them today and tomorrow, and let them wash their clothes. 11 And let them be ready for the third day. For on the third day the LORD will come down upon Mount Sinai in the sight of all the people. 12 You shall set bounds for the people all around, saying, 'Take heed to yourselves *that* you do *not* go up to the mountain or touch its base. Whoever touches the mountain shall surely be put to death. 13 Not a hand shall touch him, but he shall surely be stoned or shot *with an arrow;* whether man or beast, he shall not live.' When the trumpet sounds long, they shall come near the mountain."

14 So Moses went down from the mountain to the people and sanctified the people, and they washed their clothes. 15 And he said to the people, "Be ready for the third day; do not come near *your* wives."

16 Then it came to pass on the third day, in the morning, that there were thunderings and lightnings, and a thick cloud on the mountain; and the sound of the trumpet was very loud, so that all the people who *were* in the camp trembled. 17 And Moses

brought the people out of the camp to meet with God, and they stood at the foot of the mountain. 18 Now Mount Sinai *was* completely in smoke, because the LORD descended upon it in fire. Its smoke ascended like the smoke of a furnace, and the whole mountain*a* quaked greatly. 19 And when the blast of the trumpet sounded long and became louder and louder, Moses spoke, and God answered him by voice. 20 Then the LORD came down upon Mount Sinai, on the top of the mountain. And the LORD called Moses to the top of the mountain, and Moses went up.

21 And the LORD said to Moses, "Go down and warn the people, lest they break through to gaze at the LORD, and many of them perish. 22 Also let the priests who come near the LORD consecrate themselves, lest the LORD break out against them."

23 But Moses said to the LORD, "The people cannot come up to Mount Sinai; for You warned us, saying, 'Set bounds around the mountain and consecrate it.'"

24 Then the LORD said to him, "Away! Get down and then come up, you and Aaron with you. But do not let the priests and the people break through to come up to the LORD, lest He break out against them." 25 So Moses went down to the people and spoke to them.

20 And God spoke all these words, saying:

2 "I *am* the LORD your God, who brought you out of the land of Egypt, out of the house of bondage. 3 You shall have no other gods before Me.

4 "You shall not make for yourself a carved image—any likeness *of anything* that *is* in heaven above, or that *is* in the earth beneath, or that *is* in the water under the earth; 5 you shall not bow down to them nor serve them. For I, the LORD your God, *am* a jealous God, visiting the iniquity of the fathers upon the children to the third and fourth *generations* of those who hate Me, 6 but showing mercy to thousands, to those

19:18 *a*Septuagint reads *all the people.*

who love Me and keep My commandments.

7 "You shall not take the name of the LORD your God in vain, for the LORD will not hold *him* guiltless who takes His name in vain.

8 "Remember the Sabbath day, to keep it holy. 9 Six days you shall labor and do all your work, 10 but the seventh day *is* the Sabbath of the LORD your God. *In it* you shall do no work: you, nor your son, nor your daughter, nor your male servant, nor your female servant, nor your cattle, nor your stranger who *is* within your gates. 11 For *in* six days the LORD made the heavens and the earth, the sea, and all that *is* in them, and rested the seventh day. Therefore the LORD blessed the Sabbath day and hallowed it.

12 "Honor your father and your mother, that your days may be long upon the land which the LORD your God is giving you.

13 "You shall not murder.

14 "You shall not commit adultery.

15 "You shall not steal.

16 "You shall not bear false witness against your neighbor.

17 "You shall not covet your neighbor's house; you shall not covet your neighbor's wife, nor his male servant, nor his female servant, nor his ox, nor his donkey, nor anything that *is* your neighbor's."

18 Now all the people witnessed the thunderings, the lightning flashes, the sound of the trumpet, and the mountain smoking; and when the people saw *it,* they trembled and stood afar off. 19 Then they said to Moses, "You speak with us, and we will hear; but let not God speak with us, lest we die."

20 And Moses said to the people, "Do not fear; for God has come to test you, and that His fear may be before you, so that you may not sin." 21 So the people stood afar off, but Moses drew near the thick darkness where God *was.*

22 Then the LORD said to Moses, "Thus you shall say to the children of Israel: 'You have seen that I have talked with you from heaven. 23 You shall not make *anything to be* with Me—gods of silver or gods of gold you shall not make for yourselves. 24 An altar of earth you shall make for Me, and you shall sacrifice on it your burnt offerings and your peace offerings, your sheep and your oxen. In every place where I record My name I will come to you, and I will bless you. 25 And if you make Me an altar of stone, you shall not build it of hewn stone; for if you use your tool on it, you have profaned it. 26 Nor shall you go up by steps to My altar, that your nakedness may not be exposed on it.'

21 "Now these *are* the judgments which you shall set before them: 2 If you buy a Hebrew servant, he shall serve six years; and in the seventh he shall go out free and pay nothing. 3 If he comes in by himself, he shall go out by himself; if he *comes in* married, then his wife shall go out with him. 4 If his master has given him a wife, and she has borne him sons or daughters, the wife and her children shall be her master's, and he shall go out by himself. 5 But if the servant plainly says, 'I love my master, my wife, and my children; I will not go out free,' 6 then his master shall bring him to the judges. He shall also bring him to the door, or to the doorpost, and his master shall pierce his ear with an awl; and he shall serve him forever.

7 "And if a man sells his daughter to be a female slave, she shall not go out as the male slaves do. 8 If she does not please her master, who has betrothed her to himself, then he shall let her be redeemed. He shall have no right to sell her to a foreign people, since he has dealt deceitfully with her. 9 And if he has betrothed her to his son, he shall deal with her according to the custom of daughters. 10 If he takes another *wife,* he shall not diminish her food, her clothing, and her marriage rights. 11 And if he does not do these three for her, then she shall go out free, without *paying* money.

12 "He who strikes a man so that he dies shall surely be put to death. 13 However, if he did not lie in wait,

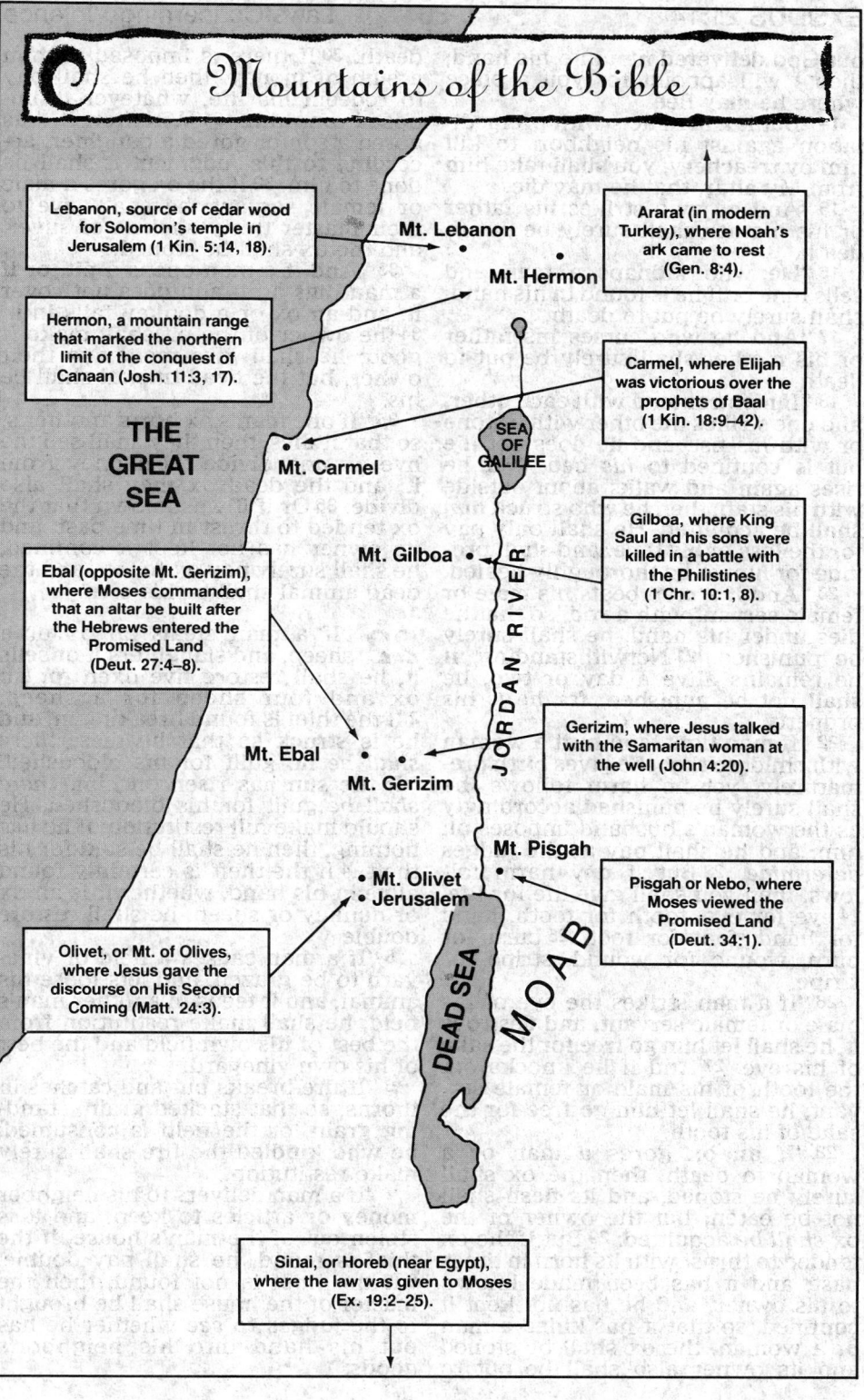

Mountains of the Bible

Lebanon, source of cedar wood for Solomon's temple in Jerusalem (1 Kin. 5:14, 18).

Ararat (in modern Turkey), where Noah's ark came to rest (Gen. 8:4).

Hermon, a mountain range that marked the northern limit of the conquest of Canaan (Josh. 11:3, 17).

Carmel, where Elijah was victorious over the prophets of Baal (1 Kin. 18:9–42).

Gilboa, where King Saul and his sons were killed in a battle with the Philistines (1 Chr. 10:1, 8).

Ebal (opposite Mt. Gerizim), where Moses commanded that an altar be built after the Hebrews entered the Promised Land (Deut. 27:4–8).

Gerizim, where Jesus talked with the Samaritan woman at the well (John 4:20).

Pisgah or Nebo, where Moses viewed the Promised Land (Deut. 34:1).

Olivet, or Mt. of Olives, where Jesus gave the discourse on His Second Coming (Matt. 24:3).

Sinai, or Horeb (near Egypt), where the law was given to Moses (Ex. 19:2–25).

Mt. Lebanon
Mt. Hermon
Mt. Carmel
SEA OF GALILEE
Mt. Gilboa
JORDAN RIVER
Mt. Ebal
Mt. Gerizim
Mt. Pisgah
Mt. Olivet
Jerusalem
THE GREAT SEA
DEAD SEA
MOAB

but God delivered *him* into his hand, then I will appoint for you a place where he may flee.

14 "But if a man acts with premeditation against his neighbor, to kill him by treachery, you shall take him from My altar, that he may die.

15 "And he who strikes his father or his mother shall surely be put to death.

16 "He who kidnaps a man and sells him, or if he is found in his hand, shall surely be put to death.

17 "And he who curses his father or his mother shall surely be put to death.

18 "If men contend with each other, and one strikes the other with a stone or with *his* fist, and he does not die but is confined to *his* bed, 19 if he rises again and walks about outside with his staff, then he who struck *him* shall be acquitted. He shall only pay *for* the loss of his time, and shall provide *for him* to be thoroughly healed.

20 "And if a man beats his male or female servant with a rod, so that he dies under his hand, he shall surely be punished. 21 Notwithstanding, if he remains alive a day or two, he shall not be punished; for he *is* his property.

22 "If men fight, and hurt a woman with child, so that she gives birth prematurely, yet no harm follows, he shall surely be punished accordingly as the woman's husband imposes on him; and he shall pay as the judges *determine*. 23 But if *any* harm follows, then you shall give life for life, 24 eye for eye, tooth for tooth, hand for hand, foot for foot, 25 burn for burn, wound for wound, stripe for stripe.

26 "If a man strikes the eye of his male or female servant, and destroys it, he shall let him go free for the sake of his eye. 27 And if he knocks out the tooth of his male or female servant, he shall let him go free for the sake of his tooth.

28 "If an ox gores a man or a woman to death, then the ox shall surely be stoned, and its flesh shall not be eaten; but the owner of the ox *shall be* acquitted. 29 But if the ox tended to thrust with its horn in times past, and it has been made known to his owner, and he has not kept it confined, so that it has killed a man or a woman, the ox shall be stoned and its owner also shall be put to death. 30 If there is imposed on him a sum of money, then he shall pay to redeem his life, whatever is imposed on him. 31 Whether it has gored a son or gored a daughter, according to this judgment it shall be done to him. 32 If the ox gores a male or female servant, he shall give to their master thirty shekels of silver, and the ox shall be stoned.

33 "And if a man opens a pit, or if a man digs a pit and does not cover it, and an ox or a donkey falls in it, 34 the owner of the pit shall make *it* good; he shall give money to their owner, but the dead *animal* shall be his.

35 "If one man's ox hurts another's, so that it dies, then they shall sell the live ox and divide the money from it; and the dead *ox* they shall also divide. 36 Or if it was known that the ox tended to thrust in time past, and its owner has not kept it confined, he shall surely pay ox for ox, and the dead animal shall be his own.

22 "If a man steals an ox or a sheep, and slaughters it or sells it, he shall restore five oxen for an ox and four sheep for a sheep. 2 If the thief is found breaking in, and he is struck so that he dies, *there shall be* no guilt for his bloodshed. 3 If the sun has risen on him, *there shall be* guilt for his bloodshed. He should make full restitution; if he has nothing, then he shall be sold for his theft. 4 If the theft is certainly found alive in his hand, whether it is an ox or donkey or sheep, he shall restore double.

5 "If a man causes a field or vineyard to be grazed, and lets loose his animal, and it feeds in another man's field, he shall make restitution from the best of his own field and the best of his own vineyard.

6 "If fire breaks out and catches in thorns, so that stacked grain, standing grain, or the field is consumed, he who kindled the fire shall surely make restitution.

7 "If a man delivers to his neighbor money or articles to keep, and it is stolen out of the man's house, if the thief is found, he shall pay double. 8 If the thief is not found, then the master of the house shall be brought to the judges *to see* whether he has put his hand into his neighbor's goods.

9 "For any kind of trespass, *whether it concerns* an ox, a donkey, a sheep, or clothing, *or* for any kind of lost thing which *another* claims to be his, the cause of both parties shall come before the judges; *and* whomever the judges condemn shall pay double to his neighbor. 10 If a man delivers to his neighbor a donkey, an ox, a sheep, or any animal to keep, and it dies, is hurt, or driven away, no one seeing *it,* 11 *then* an oath of the LORD shall be between them both, that he has not put his hand into his neighbor's goods; and the owner of it shall accept *that,* and he shall not make *it* good. 12 But if, in fact, it is stolen from him, he shall make restitution to the owner of it. 13 If it is torn to pieces *by a beast, then* he shall bring it as evidence, *and* he shall not make good what was torn.

14 "And if a man borrows *anything* from his neighbor, and it becomes injured or dies, the owner of it not *being* with it, he shall surely make *it* good. 15 If its owner *was* with it, he shall not make *it* good; if it *was* hired, it came for its hire.

16 "If a man entices a virgin who is not betrothed, and lies with her, he shall surely pay the bride-price for her *to be* his wife. 17 If her father utterly refuses to give her to him, he shall pay money according to the bride-price of virgins.

18 "You shall not permit a sorceress to live.

19 "Whoever lies with an animal shall surely be put to death.

20 "He who sacrifices to *any* god, except to the LORD only, he shall be utterly destroyed.

21 "You shall neither mistreat a stranger nor oppress him, for you were strangers in the land of Egypt.

22 "You shall not afflict any widow or fatherless child. 23 If you afflict them in any way, *and* they cry at all to Me, I will surely hear their cry; 24 and My wrath will become hot, and I will kill you with the sword; your wives shall be widows, and your children fatherless.

25 "If you lend money to *any of* My people *who are* poor among you, you shall not be like a moneylender to him; you shall not charge him interest. 26 If you ever take your neighbor's garment as a pledge, you shall return it to him before the sun goes down. 27 For that *is* his only covering, it *is* his garment for his skin. What will he sleep in? And it will be that when he cries to Me, I will hear, for I *am* gracious.

28 "You shall not revile God, nor curse a ruler of your people.

29 "You shall not delay *to offer* the first of your ripe produce and your juices. The firstborn of your sons you shall give to Me. 30 Likewise you shall do with your oxen *and* your sheep. It shall be with its mother seven days; on the eighth day you shall give it to Me.

31 "And you shall be holy men to Me: you shall not eat meat torn *by beasts* in the field; you shall throw it to the dogs.

23 "You shall not circulate a false report. Do not put your hand with the wicked to be an unrighteous witness. 2 You shall not follow a crowd to do evil; nor shall you testify in a dispute so as to turn aside after many to pervert *justice.* 3 You shall not show partiality to a poor man in his dispute.

4 "If you meet your enemy's ox or his donkey going astray, you shall surely bring it back to him again. 5 If you see the donkey of one who hates you lying under its burden, and you would refrain from helping it, you shall surely help him with it.

6 "You shall not pervert the judgment of your poor in his dispute. 7 Keep yourself far from a false matter; do not kill the innocent and righteous. For I will not justify the wicked. 8 And you shall take no bribe, for a bribe blinds the discerning and perverts the words of the righteous.

9 "Also you shall not oppress a stranger, for you know the heart of a stranger, because you were strangers in the land of Egypt.

10 "Six years you shall sow your land and gather in its produce, 11 but the seventh *year* you shall let it rest and lie fallow, that the poor of your people may eat; and what they leave, the beasts of the field may eat. In like manner you shall do with your vineyard *and* your olive grove. 12 Six days you shall do your work, and on the seventh day you shall rest, that your ox and your donkey may rest, and the son of your female servant and the stranger may be refreshed.

13 "And in all that I have said to you, be circumspect and make no mention of the name of other gods, nor let it be heard from your mouth.
14 "Three times you shall keep a feast to Me in the year: 15 You shall keep the Feast of Unleavened Bread (you shall eat unleavened bread seven days, as I commanded you, at the time appointed in the month of Abib, for in it you came out of Egypt; none shall appear before Me empty); 16 and the Feast of Harvest, the first-fruits of your labors which you have sown in the field; and the Feast of Ingathering at the end of the year, when you have gathered in *the fruit of* your labors from the field.
17 "Three times in the year all your males shall appear before the Lord God.*a*
18 "You shall not offer the blood of My sacrifice with leavened bread; nor shall the fat of My sacrifice remain until morning. 19 The first of the firstfruits of your land you shall bring into the house of the LORD your God. You shall not boil a young goat in its mother's milk.
20 "Behold, I send an Angel before you to keep you in the way and to bring you into the place which I have prepared. 21 Beware of Him and obey His voice; do not provoke Him, for He will not pardon your transgressions; for My name *is* in Him. 22 But if you indeed obey His voice and do all that I speak, then I will be an enemy to your enemies and an adversary to your adversaries. 23 For My Angel will go before you and bring you in to the Amorites and the Hittites and the Perizzites and the Canaanites and the Hivites and the Jebusites; and I will cut them off. 24 You shall not bow down to their gods, nor serve them, nor do according to their works; but you shall utterly overthrow them and completely break down their *sacred* pillars. 25 "So you shall serve the LORD your God, and He will bless your bread and your water. And I will take sickness away from the midst of you. 26 No one shall suffer miscarriage or be barren in your land; I will fulfill the number of your days.
27 "I will send My fear before you, I will cause confusion among all the people to whom you come, and will make all your enemies turn *their* backs to you. 28 And I will send hornets before you, which shall drive out the Hivite, the Canaanite, and the Hittite from before you. 29 I will not drive them out from before you in one year, lest the land become desolate and the beasts of the field become too numerous for you. 30 Little by little I will drive them out from before you, until you have increased, and you inherit the land. 31 And I will set your bounds from the Red Sea to the sea, Philistia, and from the desert to the River.*a* For I will deliver the inhabitants of the land into your hand, and you shall drive them out before you. 32 You shall make no covenant with them, nor with their gods. 33 They shall not dwell in your land, lest they make you sin against Me. For *if* you serve their gods, it will surely be a snare to you."

24 Now He said to Moses, "Come up to the LORD, you and Aaron, Nadab and Abihu, and seventy of the elders of Israel, and worship from afar. 2 And Moses alone shall come near the LORD, but they shall not come near; nor shall the people go up with him."
3 So Moses came and told the people all the words of the LORD and all the judgments. And all the people answered with one voice and said, "All the words which the LORD has said we will do." 4 And Moses wrote all the words of the LORD. And he rose early in the morning, and built an altar at the foot of the mountain, and twelve pillars according to the twelve tribes of Israel. 5 Then he sent young men of the children of Israel, who offered burnt offerings and sacrificed peace offerings of oxen to the LORD. 6 And Moses took half the blood and put *it* in basins, and half the blood he sprinkled on the altar. 7 Then he took the Book of the Covenant and read in the hearing of the people. And they said, "All that the LORD has said we will do, and be obedient." 8 And Moses took the blood, sprinkled *it* on the people, and said, "This is the blood of the covenant which the LORD has made with you according to all these words."
9 Then Moses went up, also Aaron,

23:17 *a*Hebrew *YHWH,* usually translated LORD　　23:31 *a*Hebrew *Nahar,* the Euphrates

Nadab, and Abihu, and seventy of the elders of Israel, 10 and they saw the God of Israel. And *there was* under His feet as it were a paved work of sapphire stone, and it was like the very heavens in *its* clarity. 11 But on the nobles of the children of Israel He did not lay His hand. So they saw God, and they ate and drank.

12 Then the LORD said to Moses, "Come up to Me on the mountain and be there; and I will give you tablets of stone, and the law and commandments which I have written, that you may teach them."

13 So Moses arose with his assistant Joshua, and Moses went up to the mountain of God. 14 And he said to the elders, "Wait here for us until we come back to you. Indeed, Aaron and Hur *are* with you. If any man has a difficulty, let him go to them." 15 Then Moses went up into the mountain, and a cloud covered the mountain.

16 Now the glory of the LORD rested on Mount Sinai, and the cloud covered it six days. And on the seventh day He called to Moses out of the midst of the cloud. 17 The sight of the glory of the LORD *was* like a consuming fire on the top of the mountain in the eyes of the children of Israel. 18 So Moses went into the midst of the cloud and went up into the mountain. And Moses was on the mountain forty days and forty nights.

25 Then the LORD spoke to Moses, saying: 2 "Speak to the children of Israel, that they bring Me an offering. From everyone who gives it willingly with his heart you shall take My offering. 3 And this *is* the offering which you shall take from them: gold, silver, and bronze; 4 blue, purple, and scarlet *thread,* fine linen, and goats' *hair;* 5 ram skins dyed red, badger skins, and acacia wood; 6 oil for the light, and spices for the anointing oil and for the sweet incense; 7 onyx stones, and stones to be set in the ephod and in the breastplate. 8 And let them make Me a sanctuary, that I may dwell among them. 9 According to all that I show you, *that is,* the pattern of the tabernacle and the pattern of all its furnishings, just so you shall make *it.*

10 "And they shall make an ark of acacia wood; two and a half cubits *shall be* its length, a cubit and a half its width, and a cubit and a half its height. 11 And you shall overlay it with pure gold, inside and out you shall overlay it, and shall make on it a molding of gold all around. 12 You shall cast four rings of gold for it, and put *them* in its four corners; two rings *shall be* on one side, and two rings on the other side. 13 And you shall make poles *of* acacia wood, and overlay them with gold. 14 You shall put the poles into the rings on the sides of the ark, that the ark may be carried by them. 15 The poles shall be in the rings of the ark; they shall not be taken from it. 16 And you shall put into the ark the Testimony which I will give you.

17 "You shall make a mercy seat of pure gold; two and a half cubits *shall be* its length and a cubit and a half its width. 18 And you shall make two cherubim of gold; of hammered work you shall make them at the two ends of the mercy seat. 19 Make one cherub at one end, and the other cherub at the other end; you shall make the cherubim at the two ends of it *of one piece* with the mercy seat. 20 And the cherubim shall stretch out *their* wings above, covering the mercy seat with their wings, and they shall face one another; the faces of the cherubim *shall be* toward the mercy seat. 21 You shall put the mercy seat on top of the ark, and in the ark you shall put the Testimony that I will give you. 22 And there I will meet with you, and I will speak with you from above the mercy seat, from between the two cherubim which *are* on the ark of the Testimony, about everything which I will give you in commandment to the children of Israel.

23 "You shall also make a table of acacia wood; two cubits *shall be* its length, a cubit its width, and a cubit and a half its height. 24 And you shall overlay it with pure gold, and make a molding of gold all around. 25 You shall make for it a frame of a handbreadth all around, and you shall make a gold molding for the frame all around. 26 And you shall make for it four rings of gold, and put the rings on the four corners that *are* at its four legs. 27 The rings shall be close to the frame, as holders for the poles to bear the table. 28 And you shall make the poles of acacia

wood, and overlay them with gold, that the table may be carried with them. 29 You shall make its dishes, its pans, its pitchers, and its bowls for pouring. You shall make them of pure gold. 30 And you shall set the showbread on the table before Me always.

31 "You shall also make a lampstand of pure gold; the lampstand shall be of hammered work. Its shaft, its branches, its bowls, its *ornamental* knobs, and flowers shall be *of one piece.* 32 And six branches shall come out of its sides: three branches of the lampstand out of one side, and three branches of the lampstand out of the other side. 33 Three bowls *shall be* made like almond *blossoms* on one branch, *with* an *ornamental* knob and a flower, and three bowls made like almond *blossoms* on the other branch, *with* an *ornamental* knob and a flower—and so for the six branches that come out of the lampstand. 34 On the lampstand itself four bowls *shall be* made like almond *blossoms, each with* its *ornamental* knob and flower. 35 And *there shall be* a knob under the *first* two branches of the same, a knob under the *second* two branches of the same, and a knob under the *third* two branches of the same, according to the six branches that extend from the lampstand. 36 Their knobs and their branches *shall be of one piece;* all of it *shall be* one hammered piece of pure gold. 37 You shall make seven lamps for it, and they shall arrange its lamps so that they give light in front of it. 38 And its wick-trimmers and their trays *shall be* of pure gold. 39 It shall be made of a talent of pure gold, with all these utensils. 40 And see to it that you make *them* according to the pattern which was shown you on the mountain.

26 "Moreover you shall make the tabernacle *with* ten curtains *of* fine woven linen and blue, purple, and scarlet *thread;* with artistic designs of cherubim you shall weave them. 2 The length of each curtain *shall be* twenty-eight cubits, and the width of each curtain four cubits. And every one of the curtains shall have the same measurements. 3 Five curtains shall be coupled to one another, and *the other* five curtains *shall be* coupled to one another.

4 And you shall make loops of blue *yarn* on the edge of the curtain on the selvedge of *one* set, and likewise you shall do on the outer edge of *the other* curtain of the second set. 5 Fifty loops you shall make in the one curtain, and fifty loops you shall make on the edge of the curtain that *is* on the end of the second set, that the loops may be clasped to one another. 6 And you shall make fifty clasps of gold, and couple the curtains together with the clasps, so that it may be one tabernacle.

7 "You shall also make curtains of goats' *hair,* to be a tent over the tabernacle. You shall make eleven curtains. 8 The length of each curtain *shall be* thirty cubits, and the width of each curtain four cubits; and the eleven curtains shall all have the same measurements. 9 And you shall couple five curtains by themselves and six curtains by themselves, and you shall double over the sixth curtain at the forefront of the tent. 10 You shall make fifty loops on the edge of the curtain that is outermost in *one* set, and fifty loops on the edge of the curtain of the second set. 11 And you shall make fifty bronze clasps, put the clasps into the loops, and couple the tent together, that it may be one. 12 The remnant that remains of the curtains of the tent, the half curtain that remains, shall hang over the back of the tabernacle. 13 And a cubit on one side and a cubit on the other side, of what remains of the length of the curtains of the tent, shall hang over the sides of the tabernacle, on this side and on that side, to cover it.

14 "You shall also make a covering of ram skins dyed red for the tent, and a covering of badger skins above that.

15 "And for the tabernacle you shall make the boards of acacia wood, standing upright. 16 Ten cubits *shall be* the length of a board, and a cubit and a half *shall be* the width of each board. 17 Two tenons *shall be* in each board for binding one to another. Thus you shall make for all the boards of the tabernacle. 18 And you shall make the boards for the tabernacle, twenty boards for the south side. 19 You shall make forty sockets of silver under the twenty boards: two sockets under each of the boards for its two tenons. 20 And for the sec-

ond side of the tabernacle, the north side, *there shall be* twenty boards 21 and their forty sockets of silver: two sockets under each of the boards. 22 For the far side of the tabernacle, westward, you shall make six boards. 23 And you shall also make two boards for the two back corners of the tabernacle. 24 They shall be coupled together at the bottom and they shall be coupled together at the top by one ring. Thus it shall be for both of them. They shall be for the two corners. 25 So there shall be eight boards with their sockets of silver—sixteen sockets—two sockets under each of the boards.

26 "And you shall make bars of acacia wood: five for the boards on one side of the tabernacle, 27 five bars for the boards on the other side of the tabernacle, and five bars for the boards of the side of the tabernacle, for the far side westward. 28 The middle bar shall pass through the midst of the boards from end to end. 29 You shall overlay the boards with gold, make their rings of gold *as* holders for the bars, and overlay the bars with gold. 30 And you shall raise up the tabernacle according to its pattern which you were shown on the mountain.

31 "You shall make a veil woven of blue, purple, and scarlet *thread,* and fine woven linen. It shall be woven with an artistic design of cherubim. 32 You shall hang it upon the four pillars of acacia *wood* overlaid with gold. Their hooks *shall be* gold, upon four sockets of silver. 33 And you shall hang the veil from the clasps. Then you shall bring the ark of the Testimony in there, behind the veil. The veil shall be a divider for you between the holy *place* and the Most Holy. 34 You shall put the mercy seat upon the ark of the Testimony in the Most Holy. 35 You shall set the table outside the veil, and the lampstand across from the table on the side of the tabernacle toward the south; and you shall put the table on the north side.

36 "You shall make a screen for the door of the tabernacle, *woven of* blue, purple, and scarlet *thread,* and fine woven linen, made by a weaver. 37 And you shall make for the screen five pillars of acacia *wood,* and overlay them with gold; their hooks *shall*

be gold, and you shall cast five sockets of bronze for them.

27 "You shall make an altar of acacia wood, five cubits long and five cubits wide—the altar shall be square—and its height *shall be* three cubits. 2 You shall make its horns on its four corners; its horns shall be of one piece with it. And you shall overlay it with bronze. 3 Also you shall make its pans to receive its ashes, and its shovels and its basins and its forks and its firepans; you shall make all its utensils of bronze. 4 You shall make a grate for it, a network of bronze; and on the network you shall make four bronze rings at its four corners. 5 You shall put it under the rim of the altar beneath, that the network may be midway up the altar. 6 And you shall make poles for the altar, poles of acacia wood, and overlay them with bronze. 7 The poles shall be put in the rings, and the poles shall be on the two sides of the altar to bear it. 8 You shall make it hollow with boards; as it was shown you on the mountain, so shall they make *it*.

9 "You shall also make the court of the tabernacle. For the south side *there shall be* hangings for the court *made of* fine woven linen, one hundred cubits long for one side. 10 And its twenty pillars and their twenty sockets *shall be* bronze. The hooks of the pillars and their bands *shall be* silver. 11 Likewise along the length of the north side *there shall be* hangings one hundred *cubits* long, with its twenty pillars and their twenty sockets of bronze, and the hooks of the pillars and their bands of silver.

12 "And along the width of the court on the west side *shall be* hangings of fifty cubits, with their ten pillars and their ten sockets. 13 The width of the court on the east side *shall be* fifty cubits. 14 The hangings on *one* side *of the gate shall be* fifteen cubits, *with* their three pillars and their three sockets. 15 And on the other side *shall be* hangings of fifteen *cubits, with* their three pillars and their three sockets.

16 "For the gate of the court *there shall be* a screen twenty cubits long, *woven of* blue, purple, and scarlet *thread,* and fine woven linen, made

by a weaver. It *shall have* four pillars and four sockets. 17 All the pillars around the court shall have bands of silver; their hooks *shall be* of silver and their sockets of bronze. 18 The length of the court *shall be* one hundred cubits, the width fifty throughout, and the height five cubits, *made of* fine woven linen, and its sockets of bronze. 19 All the utensils of the tabernacle for all its service, all its pegs, and all the pegs of the court, *shall be* of bronze.

20 "And you shall command the children of Israel that they bring you pure oil of pressed olives for the light, to cause the lamp to burn continually. 21 In the tabernacle of meeting, outside the veil which *is* before the Testimony, Aaron and his sons shall tend it from evening until morning before the LORD. *It shall be* a statute forever to their generations on behalf of the children of Israel.

28 "Now take Aaron your brother, and his sons with him, from among the children of Israel, that he may minister to Me as priest, Aaron *and* Aaron's sons: Nadab, Abihu, Eleazar, and Ithamar. 2 And you shall make holy garments for Aaron your brother, for glory and for beauty. 3 So you shall speak to all *who are* gifted artisans, whom I have filled with the spirit of wisdom, that they may make Aaron's garments, to consecrate him, that he may minister to Me as priest. 4 And these *are* the garments which they shall make: a breastplate, an ephod,*a* a robe, a skillfully woven tunic, a turban, and a sash. So they shall make holy garments for Aaron your brother and his sons, that he may minister to Me as priest.

5 "They shall take the gold, blue, purple, and scarlet *thread,* and the fine linen, 6 and they shall make the ephod of gold, blue, purple, *and* scarlet *thread,* and fine woven linen, artistically worked. 7 It shall have two shoulder straps joined at its two edges, and *so* it shall be joined together. 8 And the intricately woven band of the ephod, which *is* on it, shall be of the same workmanship, *made of* gold, blue, purple, and scarlet *thread,* and fine woven linen.

9 "Then you shall take two onyx stones and engrave on them the names of the sons of Israel: 10 six of their names on one stone and six names on the other stone, in order of their birth. 11 With the work of an engraver in stone, *like* the engravings of a signet, you shall engrave the two stones with the names of the sons of Israel. You shall set them in settings of gold. 12 And you shall put the two stones on the shoulders of the ephod *as* memorial stones for the sons of Israel. So Aaron shall bear their names before the LORD on his two shoulders as a memorial. 13 You shall also make settings of gold, 14 and you shall make two chains of pure gold like braided cords, and fasten the braided chains to the settings.

15 "You shall make the breastplate of judgment. Artistically woven according to the workmanship of the ephod you shall make it: of gold, blue, purple, and scarlet *thread,* and fine woven linen, you shall make it. 16 It shall be doubled into a square: a span *shall be* its length, and a span *shall be* its width. 17 And you shall put settings of stones in it, four rows of stones: *The first* row *shall be* a sardius, a topaz, and an emerald; *this shall be* the first row; 18 the second row *shall be* a turquoise, a sapphire, and a diamond; 19 the third row, a jacinth, an agate, and an amethyst; 20 and the fourth row, a beryl, an onyx, and a jasper. They shall be set in gold settings. 21 And the stones shall have the names of the sons of Israel, twelve according to their names, *like* the engravings of a signet, each one with its own name; they shall be according to the twelve tribes.

22 "You shall make chains for the breastplate at the end, like braided cords of pure gold. 23 And you shall make two rings of gold for the breastplate, and put the two rings on the two ends of the breastplate. 24 Then you shall put the two braided *chains* of gold in the two rings which are on the ends of the breastplate; 25 and the *other* two ends of the two braided *chains* you shall fasten to the two settings, and put them on the shoulder straps of the ephod in the front.

26 "You shall make two rings of

28:4 *a*That is, an ornamented vest

gold, and put them on the two ends of the breastplate, on the edge of it, which is on the inner side of the ephod. 27 And two *other* rings of gold you shall make, and put them on the two shoulder straps, underneath the ephod toward its front, right at the seam above the intricately woven band of the ephod. 28 They shall bind the breastplate by means of its rings to the rings of the ephod, using a blue cord, so that it is above the intricately woven band of the ephod, and so that the breastplate does not come loose from the ephod.

29 "So Aaron shall bear the names of the sons of Israel on the breastplate of judgment over his heart, when he goes into the holy *place,* as a memorial before the LORD continually. 30 And you shall put in the breastplate of judgment the Urim and the Thummim,*a* and they shall be over Aaron's heart when he goes in before the LORD. So Aaron shall bear the judgment of the children of Israel over his heart before the LORD continually.

31 "You shall make the robe of the ephod all of blue. 32 There shall be an opening for his head in the middle of it; it shall have a woven binding all around its opening, like the opening in a coat of mail, so that it does not tear. 33 And upon its hem you shall make pomegranates of blue, purple, and scarlet, all around its hem, and bells of gold between them all around: 34 a golden bell and a pomegranate, a golden bell and a pomegranate, upon the hem of the robe all around. 35 And it shall be upon Aaron when he ministers, and its sound will be heard when he goes into the holy *place* before the LORD and when he comes out, that he may not die.

36 "You shall also make a plate of pure gold and engrave on it, *like* the engraving of a signet:

HOLINESS TO THE LORD.

37 And you shall put it on a blue cord, that it may be on the turban; it shall be on the front of the turban. 38 So it shall be on Aaron's forehead, that Aaron may bear the iniquity of the holy things which the children of Israel hallow in all their holy gifts;

and it shall always be on his forehead, that they may be accepted before the LORD.

39 "You shall skillfully weave the tunic of fine linen *thread,* you shall make the turban of fine linen, and you shall make the sash of woven work.

40 "For Aaron's sons you shall make tunics, and you shall make sashes for them. And you shall make hats for them, for glory and beauty. 41 So you shall put them on Aaron your brother and on his sons with him. You shall anoint them, consecrate them, and sanctify them, that they may minister to Me as priests. 42 And you shall make for them linen trousers to cover their nakedness; they shall reach from the waist to the thighs. 43 They shall be on Aaron and on his sons when they come into the tabernacle of meeting, or when they come near the altar to minister in the holy *place,* that they do not incur iniquity and die. *It shall be* a statute forever to him and his descendants after him.

29 "And this is what you shall do to them to hallow them for ministering to Me as priests: Take one young bull and two rams without blemish, 2 and unleavened bread, unleavened cakes mixed with oil, and unleavened wafers anointed with oil (you shall make them of wheat flour). 3 You shall put them in one basket and bring them in the basket, with the bull and the two rams.

4 "And Aaron and his sons you shall bring to the door of the tabernacle of meeting, and you shall wash them with water. 5 Then you shall take the garments, put the tunic on Aaron, and the robe of the ephod, the ephod, and the breastplate, and gird him with the intricately woven band of the ephod. 6 You shall put the turban on his head, and put the holy crown on the turban. 7 And you shall take the anointing oil, pour *it* on his head, and anoint him. 8 Then you shall bring his sons and put tunics on them. 9 And you shall gird them with sashes, Aaron and his sons, and put the hats on them. The priesthood shall be theirs for a perpetual statute. So you shall consecrate Aaron and his sons.

28:30 *a*Literally *the Lights and the Perfections* (compare Leviticus 8:8)

10 "You shall also have the bull brought before the tabernacle of meeting, and Aaron and his sons shall put their hands on the head of the bull. 11 Then you shall kill the bull before the LORD, *by* the door of the tabernacle of meeting. 12 You shall take *some* of the blood of the bull and put *it* on the horns of the altar with your finger, and pour all the blood beside the base of the altar. 13 And you shall take all the fat that covers the entrails, the fatty lobe *attached* to the liver, and the two kidneys and the fat that *is* on them, and burn *them* on the altar. 14 But the flesh of the bull, with its skin and its offal, you shall burn with fire outside the camp. It *is* a sin offering.

15 "You shall also take one ram, and Aaron and his sons shall put their hands on the head of the ram; 16 and you shall kill the ram, and you shall take its blood and sprinkle *it* all around on the altar. 17 Then you shall cut the ram in pieces, wash its entrails and its legs, and put *them* with its pieces and with its head. 18 And you shall burn the whole ram on the altar. It *is* a burnt offering to the LORD; it *is* a sweet aroma, an offering made by fire to the LORD.

19 "You shall also take the other ram, and Aaron and his sons shall put their hands on the head of the ram. 20 Then you shall kill the ram, and take some of its blood and put *it* on the tip of the right ear of Aaron and on the tip of the right ear of his sons, on the thumb of their right hand and on the big toe of their right foot, and sprinkle the blood all around on the altar. 21 And you shall take some of the blood that is on the altar, and some of the anointing oil, and sprinkle *it* on Aaron and on his garments, on his sons and on the garments of his sons with him; and he and his garments shall be hallowed, and his sons and his sons' garments with him.

22 "Also you shall take the fat of the ram, the fat tail, the fat that covers the entrails, the fatty lobe *attached to* the liver, the two kidneys and the fat on them, the right thigh (for it *is* a ram of consecration), 23 one loaf of bread, one cake *made with* oil, and one wafer from the basket of the unleavened bread that *is* before the LORD; 24 and you shall put all these in the hands of Aaron and in the hands of his sons, and you shall wave them *as* a wave offering before the LORD. 25 You shall receive them back from their hands and burn *them* on the altar as a burnt offering, as a sweet aroma before the LORD. It *is* an offering made by fire to the LORD.

26 "Then you shall take the breast of the ram of Aaron's consecration and wave it *as* a wave offering before the LORD; and it shall be your portion. 27 And from the ram of the consecration you shall consecrate the breast of the wave offering which is waved, and the thigh of the heave offering which is raised, of *that* which *is* for Aaron and of *that* which is for his sons. 28 It shall be from the children of Israel *for* Aaron and his sons by a statute forever. For it is a heave offering; it shall be a heave offering from the children of Israel from the sacrifices of their peace offerings, *that is,* their heave offering to the LORD.

29 "And the holy garments of Aaron shall be his sons' after him, to be anointed in them and to be consecrated in them. 30 That son who becomes priest in his place shall put them on for seven days, when he enters the tabernacle of meeting to minister in the holy *place*.

31 "And you shall take the ram of the consecration and boil its flesh in the holy place. 32 Then Aaron and his sons shall eat the flesh of the ram, and the bread that *is* in the basket, *by* the door of the tabernacle of meeting. 33 They shall eat those things with which the atonement was made, to consecrate *and* to sanctify them; but an outsider shall not eat *them,* because they *are* holy. 34 And if any of the flesh of the consecration offerings, or of the bread, remains until the morning, then you shall burn the remainder with fire. It shall not be eaten, because it *is* holy.

35 "Thus you shall do to Aaron and his sons, according to all that I have commanded you. Seven days you shall consecrate them. 36 And you shall offer a bull every day *as* a sin offering for atonement. You shall cleanse the altar when you make atonement for it, and you shall anoint it to sanctify it. 37 Seven days you shall make atonement for the altar and sanctify it. And the altar shall

be most holy. Whatever touches the altar must be holy.[a]

38 "Now this *is* what you shall offer on the altar: two lambs of the first year, day by day continually. 39 One lamb you shall offer in the morning, and the other lamb you shall offer at twilight. 40 With the one lamb shall be one-tenth *of an ephah* of flour mixed with one-fourth of a hin of pressed oil, and one-fourth of a hin of wine *as* a drink offering. 41 And the other lamb you shall offer at twilight; and you shall offer with it the grain offering and the drink offering, as in the morning, for a sweet aroma, an offering made by fire to the LORD. 42 *This shall be* a continual burnt offering throughout your generations *at* the door of the tabernacle of meeting before the LORD, where I will meet you to speak with you. 43 And there I will meet with the children of Israel, and *the tabernacle* shall be sanctified by My glory. 44 So I will consecrate the tabernacle of meeting and the altar. I will also consecrate both Aaron and his sons to minister to Me as priests. 45 I will dwell among the children of Israel and will be their God. 46 And they shall know that I *am* the LORD their God, who brought them up out of the land of Egypt, that I may dwell among them. I *am* the LORD their God.

30 "You shall make an altar to burn incense on; you shall make it of acacia wood. 2 A cubit *shall be* its length and a cubit its width—it shall be square—and two cubits *shall be* its height. Its horns *shall be* of one piece with it. 3 And you shall overlay its top, its sides all around, and its horns with pure gold; and you shall make for it a molding of gold all around. 4 Two gold rings you shall make for it, under the molding on both its sides. You shall place *them* on its two sides, and they will be holders for the poles with which to bear it. 5 You shall make the poles of acacia wood, and overlay them with gold. 6 And you shall put it before the veil that *is* before the ark of the Testimony, before the mercy seat that *is* over the Testimony, where I will meet with you.

7 "Aaron shall burn on it sweet incense every morning; when he tends the lamps, he shall burn incense on it. 8 And when Aaron lights the lamps at twilight, he shall burn incense on it, a perpetual incense before the LORD throughout your generations. 9 You shall not offer strange incense on it, or a burnt offering, or a grain offering; nor shall you pour a drink offering on it. 10 And Aaron shall make atonement upon its horns once a year with the blood of the sin offering of atonement; once a year he shall make atonement upon it throughout your generations. It *is* most holy to the LORD."

11 Then the LORD spoke to Moses, saying: 12 "When you take the census of the children of Israel for their number, then every man shall give a ransom for himself to the LORD, when you number them, that there may be no plague among them when *you* number them. 13 This is what everyone among those who are numbered shall give: half a shekel according to the shekel of the sanctuary (a shekel *is* twenty gerahs). The half-shekel *shall be* an offering to the LORD. 14 Everyone included among those who are numbered, from twenty years old and above, shall give an offering to the LORD. 15 The rich shall not give more and the poor shall not give less than half a shekel, when *you* give an offering to the LORD, to make atonement for yourselves. 16 And you shall take the atonement money of the children of Israel, and shall appoint it for the service of the tabernacle of meeting, that it may be a memorial for the children of Israel before the LORD, to make atonement for yourselves."

17 Then the LORD spoke to Moses, saying: 18 "You shall also make a laver of bronze, with its base also of bronze, for washing. You shall put it between the tabernacle of meeting and the altar. And you shall put water in it, 19 for Aaron and his sons shall wash their hands and their feet in water from it. 20 When they go into the tabernacle of meeting, or when they come near the altar to minister, to burn an offering made by fire to the LORD, they shall wash with water, lest they die. 21 So they shall wash

29:37 [a]Compare Numbers 4:15 and Haggai 2:11–13

their hands and their feet, lest they die. And it shall be a statute forever to them—to him and his descendants throughout their generations."

22 Moreover the LORD spoke to Moses, saying: 23 "Also take for yourself quality spices—five hundred *shekels* of liquid myrrh, half as much sweet-smelling cinnamon (two hundred and fifty *shekels*), two hundred and fifty *shekels* of sweet-smelling cane, 24 five hundred *shekels* of cassia, according to the shekel of the sanctuary, and a hin of olive oil. 25 And you shall make from these a holy anointing oil, an ointment compounded according to the art of the perfumer. It shall be a holy anointing oil. 26 With it you shall anoint the tabernacle of meeting and the ark of the Testimony; 27 the table and all its utensils, the lampstand and its utensils, and the altar of incense; 28 the altar of burnt offering with all its utensils, and the laver and its base. 29 You shall consecrate them, that they may be most holy; whatever touches them must be holy.*a* 30 And you shall anoint Aaron and his sons, and consecrate them, that *they* may minister to Me as priests.

31 "And you shall speak to the children of Israel, saying: 'This shall be a holy anointing oil to Me throughout your generations. 32 It shall not be poured on man's flesh; nor shall you make *any other* like it, according to its composition. It *is* holy, *and* it shall be holy to you. 33 Whoever compounds *any* like it, or whoever puts *any* of it on an outsider, shall be cut off from his people.' "

34 And the LORD said to Moses: "Take sweet spices, stacte and onycha and galbanum, and pure frankincense with *these* sweet spices; there shall be equal amounts of each. 35 You shall make of these an incense, a compound according to the art of the perfumer, salted, pure, *and* holy. 36 And you shall beat *some* of it very fine, and put some of it before the Testimony in the tabernacle of meeting where I will meet with you. It shall be most holy to you. 37 But *as for* the incense which you shall make, you shall not make any for yourselves, according to its composition. It shall be to you holy for the LORD. 38 Whoever makes *any* like

it, to smell it, he shall be cut off from his people."

31 Then the LORD spoke to Moses, saying: 2 "See, I have called by name Bezalel the son of Uri, the son of Hur, of the tribe of Judah. 3 And I have filled him with the Spirit of God, in wisdom, in understanding, in knowledge, and in all *manner of* workmanship, 4 to design artistic works, to work in gold, in silver, in bronze, 5 in cutting jewels for setting, in carving wood, and to work in all *manner of* workmanship.

6 "And I, indeed I, have appointed with him Aholiab the son of Ahisamach, of the tribe of Dan; and I have put wisdom in the hearts of all the gifted artisans, that they may make all that I have commanded you: 7 the tabernacle of meeting, the ark of the Testimony and the mercy seat that *is* on it, and all the furniture of the tabernacle— 8 the table and its utensils, the pure *gold* lampstand with all its utensils, the altar of incense, 9 the altar of burnt offering with all its utensils, and the laver and its base— 10 the garments of ministry,*a* the holy garments for Aaron the priest and the garments of his sons, to minister as priests, 11 and the anointing oil and sweet incense for the holy *place.* According to all that I have commanded you they shall do."

12 And the LORD spoke to Moses, saying, 13 "Speak also to the children of Israel, saying: 'Surely My Sabbaths you shall keep, for it *is* a sign between Me and you throughout your generations, that *you* may know that I *am* the LORD who sanctifies you. 14 You shall keep the Sabbath, therefore, for *it is* holy to you. Everyone who profanes it shall surely be put to death; for whoever does *any* work on it, that person shall be cut off from among his people. 15 Work shall be done for six days, but the seventh *is* the Sabbath of rest, holy to the LORD. Whoever does *any* work on the Sabbath day, he shall surely be put to death. 16 Therefore the children of Israel shall keep the Sabbath, to observe the Sabbath throughout their generations *as* a perpetual covenant. 17 It *is* a sign between Me and the children of Israel forever; for in

---

30:29 *a*Compare Numbers 4:15 and Haggai 2:11–13　　　31:10 *a*Or *woven garments* six days the LORD made the heavens and the earth, and on the seventh day He rested and was refreshed.' "

18 And when He had made an end of speaking with him on Mount Sinai, He gave Moses two tablets of the Testimony, tablets of stone, written with the finger of God.

32 Now when the people saw that Moses delayed coming down from the mountain, the people gathered together to Aaron, and said to him, "Come, make us gods that shall go before us; for *as for* this Moses, the man who brought us up out of the land of Egypt, we do not know what has become of him."

2 And Aaron said to them, "Break off the golden earrings which *are* in the ears of your wives, your sons, and your daughters, and bring *them* to me." 3 So all the people broke off the golden earrings which *were* in their ears, and brought *them* to Aaron. 4 And he received *the gold* from their hand, and he fashioned it with an engraving tool, and made a molded calf.

Then they said, "This *is* your god, O Israel, that brought you out of the land of Egypt!"

5 So when Aaron saw *it*, he built an altar before it. And Aaron made a proclamation and said, "Tomorrow *is* a feast to the LORD." 6 Then they rose early on the next day, offered burnt offerings, and brought peace offerings; and the people sat down to eat and drink, and rose up to play.

7 And the LORD said to Moses, "Go, get down! For your people whom you brought out of the land of Egypt have corrupted *themselves*. 8 They have turned aside quickly out of the way which I commanded them. They have made themselves a molded calf, and worshiped it and sacrificed to it, and said, 'This *is* your god, O Israel, that brought you out of the land of Egypt!' " 9 And the LORD said to Moses, "I have seen this people, and indeed it *is* a stiff-necked people! 10 Now therefore, let Me alone, that My wrath may burn hot against them and I may consume them. And I will make of you a great nation."

11 Then Moses pleaded with the LORD his God, and said: "LORD, why does Your wrath burn hot against Your people whom You have

brought out of the land of Egypt with great power and with a mighty hand? 12 Why should the Egyptians speak, and say, 'He brought them out to harm them, to kill them in the mountains, and to consume them from the face of the earth'? Turn from Your fierce wrath, and relent from this harm to Your people. 13 Remember Abraham, Isaac, and Israel, Your servants, to whom You swore by Your own self, and said to them, 'I will multiply your descendants as the stars of heaven; and all this land that I have spoken of I give to your descendants, and they shall inherit *it* forever.' "a 14 So the LORD relented from the harm which He said He would do to His people.

15 And Moses turned and went down from the mountain, and the two tablets of the Testimony *were* in his hand. The tablets *were* written on both sides; on the one *side* and on the other they were written. 16 Now the tablets *were* the work of God, and the writing *was* the writing of God engraved on the tablets.

17 And when Joshua heard the noise of the people as they shouted, he said to Moses, "There *is* a noise of war in the camp."

18 But he said:

"*It is* not the noise of the shout of victory,
Nor the noise of the cry of defeat,
But the sound of singing I hear."

19 So it was, as soon as he came near the camp, that he saw the calf *and* the dancing. So Moses' anger became hot, and he cast the tablets out of his hands and broke them at the foot of the mountain. 20 Then he took the calf which they had made, burned *it* in the fire, and ground *it* to powder; and he scattered *it* on the water and made the children of Israel drink *it*. 21 And Moses said to Aaron, "What did this people do to you that you have brought *so* great a sin upon them?"

22 So Aaron said, "Do not let the anger of my lord become hot. You know the people, that they *are set* on evil. 23 For they said to me, 'Make us gods that shall go before us; *as*

32:13 ªGenesis 13:15 and 22:17

for this Moses, the man who brought us out of the land of Egypt, we do not know what has become of him.' 24 And I said to them, 'Whoever has any gold, let them break *it* off.' So they gave *it* to me, and I cast it into the fire, and this calf came out.''

25 Now when Moses saw that the people *were* unrestrained (for Aaron had not restrained them, to *their* shame among their enemies), 26 then Moses stood in the entrance of the camp, and said, "Whoever *is* on the Lord's side—*come* to me!'' And all the sons of Levi gathered themselves together to him. 27 And he said to them, "Thus says the Lord God of Israel: 'Let every man put his sword on his side, and go in and out from entrance to entrance throughout the camp, and let every man kill his brother, every man his companion, and every man his neighbor.' '' 28 So the sons of Levi did according to the word of Moses. And about three thousand men of the people fell that day. 29 Then Moses said, "Consecrate yourselves today to the Lord, that He may bestow on you a blessing this day, for every man has opposed his son and his brother.''

30 Now it came to pass on the next day that Moses said to the people, "You have committed a great sin. So now I will go up to the Lord; perhaps I can make atonement for your sin.'' 31 Then Moses returned to the Lord and said, "Oh, these people have committed a great sin, and have made for themselves a god of gold! 32 Yet now, if You will forgive their sin—but if not, I pray, blot me out of Your book which You have written.''

33 And the Lord said to Moses, "Whoever has sinned against Me, I will blot him out of My book. 34 Now therefore, go, lead the people to *the place* of which I have spoken to you. Behold, My Angel shall go before you. Nevertheless, in the day when I visit for punishment, I will visit punishment upon them for their sin.''

35 So the Lord plagued the people because of what they did with the calf which Aaron made.

33 Then the Lord said to Moses, "Depart *and* go up from here, you and the people whom you have brought out of the land of Egypt, to the land of which I swore to Abraham, Isaac, and Jacob, saying, 'To your descendants I will give it.' 2 And I will send *My* Angel before you, and I will drive out the Canaanite and the Amorite and the Hittite and the Perizzite and the Hivite and the Jebusite. 3 *Go up* to a land flowing with milk and honey; for I will not go up in your midst, lest I consume you on the way, for you *are* a stiff-necked people.''

4 And when the people heard this bad news, they mourned, and no one put on his ornaments. 5 For the Lord had said to Moses, "Say to the children of Israel, 'You *are* a stiff-necked people. I could come up into your midst in one moment and consume you. Now therefore, take off your ornaments, that I may know what to do to you.' '' 6 So the children of Israel stripped themselves of their ornaments by Mount Horeb.

7 Moses took his tent and pitched it outside the camp, far from the camp, and called it the tabernacle of meeting. And it came to pass *that* everyone who sought the Lord went out to the tabernacle of meeting which *was* outside the camp. 8 So it was, whenever Moses went out to the tabernacle, *that* all the people rose, and each man stood *at* his tent door and watched Moses until he had gone into the tabernacle. 9 And it came to pass, when Moses entered the tabernacle, that the pillar of cloud descended and stood *at* the door of the tabernacle, and *the* Lord talked with Moses. 10 All the people saw the pillar of cloud standing *at* the tabernacle door, and all the people rose and worshiped, each man *in* his tent door. 11 So the Lord spoke to Moses face to face, as a man speaks to his friend. And he would return to the camp, but his servant Joshua the son of Nun, a young man, did not depart from the tabernacle.

12 Then Moses said to the Lord, "See, You say to me, 'Bring up this people.' But You have not let me know whom You will send with me. Yet You have said, 'I know you by name, and you have also found grace in My sight.' 13 Now therefore, I pray, if I have found grace in Your sight, show me now Your way, that I may know You and that I may find grace in Your sight. And consider that this nation *is* Your people.''

14 And He said, "My Presence will go *with you*, and I will give you rest." 15 Then he said to Him, "If Your Presence does not go *with us*, do not bring us up from here. 16 For how then will it be known that Your people and I have found grace in Your sight, except You go with us? So we shall be separate, Your people and I, from all the people who *are* upon the face of the earth." 17 So the LORD said to Moses, "I will also do this thing that you have spoken; for you have found grace in My sight, and I know you by name." 18 And he said, "Please, show me Your glory." 19 Then He said, "I will make all My goodness pass before you, and I will proclaim the name of the LORD before you. I will be gracious to whom I will be gracious, and I will have compassion on whom I will have compassion." 20 But He said, "You cannot see My face; for no man shall see Me, and live." 21 And the LORD said, "Here is a place by Me, and you shall stand on the rock. 22 So it shall be, while My glory passes by, that I will put you in the cleft of the rock, and will cover you with My hand while I pass by. 23 Then I will take away My hand, and you shall see My back; but My face shall not be seen."

34 And the LORD said to Moses, "Cut two tablets of stone like the first *ones*, and I will write on *these* tablets the words that were on the first tablets which you broke. 2 So be ready in the morning, and come up in the morning to Mount Sinai, and present yourself to Me there on the top of the mountain. 3 And no man shall come up with you, and let no man be seen throughout all the mountain; let neither flocks nor herds feed before that mountain." 4 So he cut two tablets of stone like the first *ones*. Then Moses rose early in the morning and went up Mount Sinai, as the LORD had commanded him; and he took in his hand the two tablets of stone. 5 Now the LORD descended in the cloud and stood with him there, and proclaimed the name of the LORD. 6 And the LORD passed before him and proclaimed, "The LORD, the LORD God, merciful and gracious, longsuf-

fering, and abounding in goodness and truth, 7 keeping mercy for thousands, forgiving iniquity and transgression and sin, by no means clearing *the guilty*, visiting the iniquity of the fathers upon the children and the children's children to the third and the fourth generation." 8 So Moses made haste and bowed his head toward the earth, and worshiped. 9 Then he said, "If now I have found grace in Your sight, O Lord, let my Lord, I pray, go among us, even though we *are* a stiff-necked people; and pardon our iniquity and our sin, and take us as Your inheritance."

10 And He said: "Behold, I make a covenant. Before all your people I will do marvels such as have not been done in all the earth, nor in any nation; and all the people among whom you *are* shall see the work of the LORD. For it *is* an awesome thing that I will do with you. 11 Observe what I command you this day. Behold, I am driving out from before you the Amorite and the Canaanite and the Hittite and the Perizzite and the Hivite and the Jebusite. 12 Take heed to yourself, lest you make a covenant with the inhabitants of the land where you are going, lest it be a snare in your midst. 13 But you shall destroy their altars, break their *sacred* pillars, and cut down their wooden images 14 (for you shall worship no other god, for the LORD, whose name *is* Jealous, *is* a jealous God), 15 lest you make a covenant with the inhabitants of the land, and they play the harlot with their gods and make sacrifice to their gods, and *one of them* invites you and you eat of his sacrifice, 16 and you take of his daughters for your sons, and his daughters play the harlot with their gods and make your sons play the harlot with their gods. 17 "You shall make no molded gods for yourselves.
18 "The Feast of Unleavened Bread you shall keep. Seven days you shall eat unleavened bread, as I commanded you, in the appointed time of the month of Abib; for in the month of Abib you came out from Egypt. 19 "All that open the womb *are* Mine, and every male firstborn among your livestock, *whether* ox or sheep. 20 But the firstborn of a don-

key you shall redeem with a lamb.
And if you will not redeem *him*, then
you shall break his neck. All the firstborn of your sons you shall redeem.

"And none shall appear before Me
empty-handed.

21 "Six days you shall work, but on
the seventh day you shall rest; in
plowing time and in harvest you shall
rest.

22 "And you shall observe the Feast
of Weeks, of the firstfruits of wheat
harvest, and the Feast of Ingathering
at the year's end.

23 "Three times in the year all your
men shall appear before the Lord, the
LORD God of Israel. 24 For I will cast
out the nations before you and enlarge your borders; neither will any
man covet your land when you go up
to appear before the LORD your God
three times in the year.

25 "You shall not offer the blood of
My sacrifice with leaven, nor shall
the sacrifice of the Feast of the Passover be left until morning.

26 "The first of the firstfruits of
your land you shall bring to the
house of the LORD your God. You
shall not boil a young goat in its
mother's milk."

27 Then the LORD said to Moses,
"Write these words, for according to
the tenor of these words I have made
a covenant with you and with Israel."
28 So he was there with the LORD
forty days and forty nights; he neither ate bread nor drank water. And
He wrote on the tablets the words of
the covenant, the Ten Commandments.*a*

29 Now it was so, when Moses
came down from Mount Sinai (and
the two tablets of the Testimony *were*
in Moses' hand when he came down
from the mountain), that Moses did
not know that the skin of his face
shone while he talked with Him.
30 So when Aaron and all the children of Israel saw Moses, behold, the
skin of his face shone, and they were
afraid to come near him. 31 Then Moses called to them, and Aaron and
all the rulers of the congregation returned to him; and Moses talked with
them. 32 Afterward all the children of
Israel came near, and he gave them
as commandments all that the LORD
had spoken with him on Mount Sinai.
33 And when Moses had finished
speaking with them, he put a veil on
his face. 34 But whenever Moses went
in before the LORD to speak with Him,
he would take the veil off until he
came out; and he would come out
and speak to the children of Israel
whatever he had been commanded.
35 And whenever the children of Israel saw the face of Moses, that the
skin of Moses' face shone, then Moses would put the veil on his face
again, until he went in to speak with
Him.

35 Then Moses gathered all the
congregation of the children of
Israel together, and said to them,
"These *are* the words which the LORD
has commanded *you* to do: 2 Work
shall be done for six days, but the
seventh day shall be a holy day for
you, a Sabbath of rest to the LORD.
Whoever does any work on it shall
be put to death. 3 You shall kindle no
fire throughout your dwellings on the
Sabbath day."

4 And Moses spoke to all the congregation of the children of Israel,
saying, "This *is* the thing which the
LORD commanded, saying: 5 'Take
from among you an offering to the
LORD. Whoever *is* of a willing heart,
let him bring it as an offering to the
LORD: gold, silver, and bronze;
6 blue, purple, and scarlet *thread,*
fine linen, and goats' *hair;* 7 ram
skins dyed red, badger skins, and
acacia wood; 8 oil for the light, and
spices for the anointing oil and for
the sweet incense; 9 onyx stones, and
stones to be set in the ephod and in
the breastplate.

10 'All *who are* gifted artisans
among you shall come and make all
that the LORD has commanded:
11 the tabernacle, its tent, its covering, its clasps, its boards, its bars, its
pillars, and its sockets; 12 the ark and
its poles, *with* the mercy seat, and
the veil of the covering; 13 the table
and its poles, all its utensils, and the
showbread; 14 also the lampstand for
the light, its utensils, its lamps, and
the oil for the light; 15 the incense altar, its poles, the anointing oil, the
sweet incense, and the screen for the
door at the entrance of the tabernacle; 16 the altar of burnt offering with
its bronze grating, its poles, all its
utensils, *and* the laver and its base;

34:28 *a*Literally *Ten Words*

17 the hangings of the court, its pillars, their sockets, and the screen for the gate of the court; 18 the pegs of the tabernacle, the pegs of the court, and their cords; 19 the garments of ministry,ᵃ for ministering in the holy *place*—the holy garments for Aaron the priest and the garments of his sons, to minister as priests.' "

20 And all the congregation of the children of Israel departed from the presence of Moses. 21 Then everyone came whose heart was stirred, and everyone whose spirit was willing, *and* they brought the LORD's offering for the work of the tabernacle of meeting, for all its service, and for the holy garments. 22 They came, both men and women, as many as had a willing heart, *and* brought earrings and nose rings, rings and necklaces, all jewelry of gold, that is, every man who *made* an offering of gold to the LORD. 23 And every man, with whom was found blue, purple, and scarlet *thread*, fine linen, and goats' *hair*, red skins of rams, and badger skins, brought *them*. 24 Everyone who offered an offering of silver or bronze brought the LORD's offering. And everyone with whom was found acacia wood for any work of the service, brought *it*. 25 All the women *who were* gifted artisans spun yarn with their hands, and brought what they had spun, of blue, purple, *and* scarlet, and fine linen. 26 And all the women whose hearts stirred with wisdom spun yarn of goats' *hair*. 27 The rulers brought onyx stones, and the stones to be set in the ephod and in the breastplate, 28 and spices and oil for the light, for the anointing oil, and for the sweet incense. 29 The children of Israel brought a freewill offering to the LORD, all the men and women whose hearts were willing to bring *material* for all kinds of work which the LORD, by the hand of Moses, had commanded to be done.

30 And Moses said to the children of Israel, "See, the LORD has called by name Bezalel the son of Uri, the son of Hur, of the tribe of Judah; 31 and He has filled him with the Spirit of God, in wisdom and understanding, in knowledge and all manner of workmanship, 32 to design artistic works, to work in gold and silver and bronze, 33 in cutting jewels for setting, in carving wood, and to work in all manner of artistic workmanship.

34 "And He has put in his heart the ability to teach, *in* him and Aholiab the son of Ahisamach, of the tribe of Dan. 35 He has filled them with skill to do all manner of work of the engraver and the designer and the tapestry maker, in blue, purple, and scarlet *thread,* and fine linen, and of the weaver—those who do every work and those who design artistic works.

36 "And Bezalel and Aholiab, and every gifted artisan in whom the LORD has put wisdom and understanding, to know how to do all manner of work for the service of the sanctuary, shall do according to all that the LORD has commanded."

2 Then Moses called Bezalel and Aholiab, and every gifted artisan in whose heart the LORD had put wisdom, everyone whose heart was stirred, to come and do the work. 3 And they received from Moses all the offering which the children of Israel had brought for the work of the service of making the sanctuary. So they continued bringing to him freewill offerings every morning. 4 Then all the craftsmen who were doing all the work of the sanctuary came, each from the work he was doing, 5 and they spoke to Moses, saying, "The people bring much more than enough for the service of the work which the LORD commanded *us* to do."

6 So Moses gave a commandment, and they caused it to be proclaimed throughout the camp, saying, "Let neither man nor woman do any more work for the offering of the sanctuary." And the people were restrained from bringing, 7 for the material they had was sufficient for all the work to be done—indeed too much.

8 Then all the gifted artisans among them who worked on the tabernacle made ten curtains woven of fine linen, and of blue, purple, and scarlet *thread; with* artistic designs of cherubim they made them. 9 The length of each curtain *was* twenty-eight cubits, and the width of

35:19 ᵃOr *woven garments*

each curtain four cubits; the curtains *were* all the same size. 10 And he coupled five curtains to one another, and *the other* five curtains he coupled to one another. 11 He made loops of blue *yarn* on the edge of the curtain on the selvedge of one set; likewise he did on the outer edge of *the other* curtain of the second set. 12 Fifty loops he made on one curtain, and fifty loops he made on the edge of the curtain on the end of the second set; the loops held one *curtain* to another. 13 And he made fifty clasps of gold, and coupled the curtains to one another with the clasps, that it might be one tabernacle.

14 He made curtains of goats' *hair* for the tent over the tabernacle; he made eleven curtains. 15 The length of each curtain *was* thirty cubits, and the width of each curtain four cubits; the eleven curtains *were* the same size. 16 He coupled five curtains by themselves and six curtains by themselves. 17 And he made fifty loops on the edge of the curtain that is outermost in one set, and fifty loops he made on the edge of the curtain of the second set. 18 He also made fifty bronze clasps to couple the tent together, that it might be one. 19 Then he made a covering for the tent of ram skins dyed red, and a covering of badger skins above *that*.

20 For the tabernacle he made boards of acacia wood, standing upright. 21 The length of each board *was* ten cubits, and the width of each board a cubit and a half. 22 Each board had two tenons for binding one to another. Thus he made for all the boards of the tabernacle. 23 And he made boards for the tabernacle, twenty boards for the south side. 24 Forty sockets of silver he made to go under the twenty boards: two sockets under each of the boards for its two tenons. 25 And for the other side of the tabernacle, the north side, he made twenty boards 26 and their forty sockets of silver: two sockets under each of the boards. 27 For the west side of the tabernacle he made six boards. 28 He also made two boards for the two back corners of the tabernacle. 29 And they were coupled at the bottom and coupled together at the top by one ring. Thus he made both of them for the two corners. 30 So there were eight boards and their sockets—sixteen sockets of

silver—two sockets under each of the boards.

31 And he made bars of acacia wood: five for the boards on one side of the tabernacle, 32 five bars for the boards on the other side of the tabernacle, and five bars for the boards of the tabernacle on the far side westward. 33 And he made the middle bar to pass through the boards from one end to the other. 34 He overlaid the boards with gold, made their rings of gold *to be* holders for the bars, and overlaid the bars with gold.

35 And he made a veil of blue, purple, and scarlet *thread,* and fine woven linen; it was worked *with* an artistic design of cherubim. 36 He made for it four pillars of acacia *wood,* and overlaid them with gold, with their hooks of gold; and he cast four sockets of silver for them.

37 He also made a screen for the tabernacle door, of blue, purple, and scarlet *thread,* and fine woven linen, made by a weaver, 38 and its five pillars with their hooks. And he overlaid their capitals and their rings with gold, but their five sockets *were* bronze.

37 Then Bezalel made the ark of acacia wood; two and a half cubits *was* its length, a cubit and a half its width, and a cubit and a half its height. 2 He overlaid it with pure gold inside and outside, and made a molding of gold all around it. 3 And he cast for it four rings of gold *to be set* in its four corners: two rings on one side, and two rings on the other side of it. 4 He made poles of acacia wood, and overlaid them with gold. 5 And he put the poles into the rings at the sides of the ark, to bear the ark. 6 He also made the mercy seat of pure gold; two and a half cubits *was* its length and a cubit and a half its width. 7 He made two cherubim of beaten gold; he made them of one piece at the two ends of the mercy seat: 8 one cherub at one end on this side, and the other cherub at the *other* end on that side. He made the cherubim at the two ends *of one piece* with the mercy seat. 9 The cherubim spread out *their* wings above, *and* covered the mercy seat with their wings. They faced one another; the faces of the cherubim were toward the mercy seat.

10 He made the table of acacia wood; two cubits *was* its length, a cubit its width, and a cubit and a half its height. 11 And he overlaid it with pure gold, and made a molding of gold all around it. 12 Also he made a frame of a handbreadth all around it, and made a molding of gold for the frame all around it. 13 And he cast for it four rings of gold, and put the rings on the four corners that *were* at its four legs. 14 The rings were close to the frame, as holders for the poles to bear the table. 15 And he made the poles of acacia wood to bear the table, and overlaid them with gold. 16 He made of pure gold the utensils which were on the table: its dishes, its cups, its bowls, and its pitchers for pouring.

17 He also made the lampstand of pure gold; of hammered work he made the lampstand. Its shaft, its branches, its bowls, its *ornamental* knobs, and its flowers were of the same piece. 18 And six branches came out of its sides: three branches of the lampstand out of one side, and three branches of the lampstand out of the other side. 19 There were three bowls made like almond *blossoms* on one branch, with an *ornamental* knob and a flower, and three bowls made like almond *blossoms* on the other branch, with an *ornamental* knob and a flower—and so for the six branches coming out of the lampstand. 20 And on the lampstand itself *were* four bowls made like almond *blossoms, each with* its *ornamental* knob and flower. 21 *There was* a knob under the *first* two branches of the same, a knob under the *second* two branches of the same, and a knob under the *third* two branches of the same, according to the six branches extending from it. 22 Their knobs and their branches were of one piece; all of it *was* one hammered piece of pure gold. 23 And he made its seven lamps, its wick-trimmers, and its trays of pure gold. 24 Of a talent of pure gold he made it, with all its utensils.

25 He made the incense altar of acacia wood. Its length *was* a cubit and its width a cubit—*it was* square—and two cubits *was* its height. Its horns were *of one piece* with it. 26 And he overlaid it with pure gold: its top, its sides all around, and its horns. He also made for it a molding of gold all around it. 27 He made two rings of gold for it under its molding, by its two corners on both sides, as holders for the poles with which to bear it. 28 And he made the poles of acacia wood, and overlaid them with gold.

29 He also made the holy anointing oil and the pure incense of sweet spices, according to the work of the perfumer.

38

He made the altar of burnt offering of acacia wood; five cubits *was* its length and five cubits its width—*it was* square—and its height *was* three cubits. 2 He made its horns on its four corners; the horns were *of one piece* with it. And he overlaid it with bronze. 3 He made all the utensils for the altar: the pans, the shovels, the basins, the forks, and the firepans; all its utensils he made of bronze. 4 And he made a grate of bronze network for the altar, under its rim, midway from the bottom. 5 He cast four rings for the four corners of the bronze grating, *as* holders for the poles. 6 And he made the poles of acacia wood, and overlaid them with bronze. 7 Then he put the poles into the rings on the sides of the altar, with which to bear it. He made the altar hollow with boards.

8 He made the laver of bronze and its base of bronze, from the bronze mirrors of the serving women who assembled at the door of the tabernacle of meeting.

9 Then he made the court on the south side; the hangings of the court *were of* fine woven linen, one hundred cubits long. 10 There *were* twenty pillars for them, with twenty bronze sockets. The hooks of the pillars and their bands *were* silver. 11 On the north side *the hangings were* one hundred cubits *long,* with twenty pillars and their twenty bronze sockets. The hooks of the pillars and their bands *were* silver. 12 And on the west side *there were* hangings of fifty cubits, with ten pillars and their ten sockets. The hooks of the pillars and their bands *were* silver. 13 For the east side *the hangings were* fifty cubits. 14 The hangings of one side *of the gate were* fifteen cubits *long, with* their three pillars and their three sockets, 15 and the same for the other side of the court gate; on this side and that

were hangings of fifteen cubits, *with* their three pillars and their three sockets. 16 All the hangings of the court all around *were of* fine woven linen. 17 The sockets for the pillars *were* bronze, the hooks of the pillars and their bands *were* silver, and the overlay of their capitals *was* silver; and all the pillars of the court had bands of silver. 18 The screen for the gate of the court *was* woven of blue, purple, and scarlet *thread,* and of fine woven linen. The length *was* twenty cubits, and the height along its width *was* five cubits, corresponding to the hangings of the court. 19 And *there were* four pillars *with* their four sockets of bronze; their hooks *were* silver, and the overlay of their capitals and their bands *was* silver. 20 All the pegs of the tabernacle, and of the court all around, *were* bronze.

21 This is the inventory of the tabernacle, the tabernacle of the Testimony, which was counted according to the commandment of Moses, for the service of the Levites, by the hand of Ithamar, son of Aaron the priest.

22 Bezalel the son of Uri, the son of Hur, of the tribe of Judah, made all that the LORD had commanded Moses. 23 And with him *was* Aholiab the son of Ahisamach, of the tribe of Dan, an engraver and designer, a weaver of blue, purple, and scarlet *thread,* and of fine linen.

24 All the gold that was used in all the work of the holy *place,* that is, the gold of the offering, was twenty-nine talents and seven hundred and thirty shekels, according to the shekel of the sanctuary. 25 And the silver from those who were numbered of the congregation *was* one hundred talents and one thousand seven hundred and seventy-five shekels, according to the shekel of the sanctuary: 26 a bekah for each man (*that is,* half a shekel, according to the shekel of the sanctuary), for everyone included in the numbering from twenty years old and above, for six hundred and three thousand, five hundred and fifty *men.* 27 And from the hundred talents of silver were cast the sockets of the sanctuary and the bases of the veil: one hundred sockets from the hundred talents, one talent for each socket. 28 Then

from the one thousand seven hundred and seventy-five *shekels* he made hooks for the pillars, overlaid their capitals, and made bands for them.

29 The offering of bronze *was* seventy talents and two thousand four hundred shekels. 30 And with it he made the sockets for the door of the tabernacle of meeting, the bronze altar, the bronze grating for it, and all the utensils for the altar, 31 the sockets for the court all around, the bases for the court gate, all the pegs for the tabernacle, and all the pegs for the court all around.

39 Of the blue, purple, and scarlet *thread* they made garments of ministry,*ᵃ* for ministering in the holy *place,* and made the holy garments for Aaron, as the LORD had commanded Moses.

2 He made the ephod of gold, blue, purple, and scarlet *thread,* and of fine woven linen. 3 And they beat the gold into thin sheets and cut *it into* threads, to work *it in with* the blue, purple, and scarlet *thread,* and the fine linen, *into* artistic designs. 4 They made shoulder straps for it to couple *it* together; it was coupled together at its two edges. 5 And the intricately woven band of his ephod that *was* on it *was* of the same workmanship, *woven of* gold, blue, purple, and scarlet *thread,* and of fine woven linen, as the LORD had commanded Moses.

6 And they set onyx stones, enclosed in settings of gold; they were engraved, as signets are engraved, with the names of the sons of Israel. 7 He put them on the shoulders of the ephod *as* memorial stones for the sons of Israel, as the LORD had commanded Moses.

8 And he made the breastplate, artistically woven like the workmanship of the ephod, of gold, blue, purple, and scarlet *thread,* and of fine woven linen. 9 They made the breastplate square by doubling it; a span *was* its length and a span its width when doubled. 10 And they set in it four rows of stones: a row with a sardius, a topaz, and an emerald *was* the first row; 11 the second row, a turquoise, a sapphire, and a diamond; 12 the third row, a jacinth, an agate,

39:1 ᵃOr *woven garments*

and an amethyst; 13 the fourth row, a beryl, an onyx, and a jasper. *They were* enclosed in settings of gold in their mountings. 14 *There were* twelve stones according to the names of the sons of Israel: according to their names, *engraved like* a signet, each one with its own name according to the twelve tribes. 15 And they made chains for the breastplate at the ends, like braided cords of pure gold. 16 They also made two settings of gold and two gold rings, and put the two rings on the two ends of the breastplate. 17 And they put the two braided *chains* of gold in the two rings on the ends of the breastplate. 18 The two ends of the two braided *chains* they fastened in the two settings, and put them on the shoulder straps of the ephod in the front. 19 And they made two rings of gold and put *them* on the two ends of the breastplate, on the edge of it, which *was* on the inward side of the ephod. 20 They made two *other* gold rings and put them on the two shoulder straps, underneath the ephod toward its front, right at the seam above the intricately woven band of the ephod. 21 And they bound the breastplate by means of its rings to the rings of the ephod with a blue cord, so that it would be above the intricately woven band of the ephod, and that the breastplate would not come loose from the ephod, as the LORD had commanded Moses.

22 He made the robe of the ephod of woven work, all of blue. 23 And *there was* an opening in the middle of the robe, like the opening in a coat of mail, *with* a woven binding all around the opening, so that it would not tear. 24 They made on the hem of the robe pomegranates of blue, purple, and scarlet, and of fine woven *linen.* 25 And they made bells of pure gold, and put the bells between the pomegranates on the hem of the robe all around between the pomegranates: 26 a bell and a pomegranate, a bell and a pomegranate, all around the hem of the robe to minister in, as the LORD had commanded Moses. 27 They made tunics, artistically woven of fine linen, for Aaron and his sons, 28 a turban of fine linen, exquisite hats of fine linen, short trousers of fine woven linen, 29 and a

sash of fine woven linen with blue, purple, and scarlet *thread,* made by a weaver, as the LORD had commanded Moses.

30 Then they made the plate of the holy crown of pure gold, and wrote on it an inscription *like* the engraving of a signet:

HOLINESS TO THE LORD.

31 And they tied to it a blue cord, to fasten *it* above on the turban, as the LORD had commanded Moses.

32 Thus all the work of the tabernacle of the tent of meeting was finished. And the children of Israel did according to all that the LORD had commanded Moses; so they did. 33 And they brought the tabernacle to Moses, the tent and all its furnishings: its clasps, its boards, its bars, its pillars, and its sockets; 34 the covering of ram skins dyed red, the covering of badger skins, and the veil of the covering; 35 the ark of the Testimony with its poles, and the mercy seat; 36 the table, all its utensils, and the showbread; 37 the pure *gold* lampstand with its lamps (the lamps set in order), all its utensils, and the oil for light; 38 the gold altar, the anointing oil, and the sweet incense; the screen for the tabernacle door; 39 the bronze altar, its grate of bronze, its poles, and all its utensils; the laver with its base; 40 the hangings of the court, its pillars and its sockets, the screen for the court gate, its cords, and its pegs; all the utensils for the service of the tabernacle, for the tent of meeting; 41 and the garments of ministry,[a] to minister in the holy *place:* the holy garments for Aaron the priest, and his sons' garments, to minister as priests.

42 According to all that the LORD had commanded Moses, so the children of Israel did all the work. 43 Then Moses looked over all the work, and indeed they had done it; as the LORD had commanded, just so they had done it. And Moses blessed them.

40 Then the LORD spoke to Moses, saying: 2 "On the first day of the first month you shall set up the tabernacle of the tent of meeting.

39:41 *a*Or woven garments

3 You shall put in it the ark of the Testimony, and partition off the ark with the veil. 4 You shall bring in the table and arrange the things that are to be set in order on it; and you shall bring in the lampstand and light its lamps. 5 You shall also set the altar of gold for the incense before the ark of the Testimony, and put up the screen for the door of the tabernacle. 6 Then you shall set the altar of the burnt offering before the door of the tabernacle of the tent of meeting. 7 And you shall set the laver between the tabernacle of meeting and the altar, and put water in it. 8 You shall set up the court all around, and hang up the screen at the court gate.

9 "And you shall take the anointing oil, and anoint the tabernacle and all that *is* in it; and you shall hallow it and all its utensils, and it shall be holy. 10 You shall anoint the altar of the burnt offering and all its utensils, and consecrate the altar. The altar shall be most holy. 11 And you shall anoint the laver and its base, and consecrate it.

12 "Then you shall bring Aaron and his sons to the door of the tabernacle of meeting and wash them with water. 13 You shall put the holy garments on Aaron, and anoint him and consecrate him, that he may minister to Me as priest. 14 And you shall bring his sons and clothe them with tunics. 15 You shall anoint them, as you anointed their father, that they may minister to Me as priests; for their anointing shall surely be an everlasting priesthood throughout their generations."

16 Thus Moses did; according to all that the LORD had commanded him, so he did.

17 And it came to pass in the first month of the second year, on the first *day* of the month, *that* the tabernacle was raised up. 18 So Moses raised up the tabernacle, fastened its sockets, set up its boards, put in its bars, and raised up its pillars. 19 And he spread out the tent over the tabernacle and put the covering of the tent on top of it, as the LORD had commanded Moses. 20 He took the Testimony and put *it* into the ark, inserted the poles through the rings of the ark, and put the mercy seat on top of the ark.

21 And he brought the ark into the tabernacle, hung up the veil of the covering, and partitioned off the ark of the Testimony, as the LORD had commanded Moses.

22 He put the table in the tabernacle of meeting, on the north side of the tabernacle, outside the veil; 23 and he set the bread in order upon it before the LORD, as the LORD had commanded Moses. 24 He put the lampstand in the tabernacle of meeting, across from the table, on the south side of the tabernacle; 25 and he lit the lamps before the LORD, as the LORD had commanded Moses. 26 He put the gold altar in the tabernacle of meeting in front of the veil; 27 and he burned sweet incense on it, as the LORD had commanded Moses. 28 He hung up the screen *at* the door of the tabernacle. 29 And he put the altar of burnt offering *before* the door of the tabernacle of the tent of meeting, and offered upon it the burnt offering and the grain offering, as the LORD had commanded Moses. 30 He set the laver between the tabernacle of meeting and the altar, and put water there for washing; 31 and Moses, Aaron, and his sons would wash their hands and their feet *with water* from it. 32 Whenever they went into the tabernacle of meeting, and when they came near the altar, they washed, as the LORD had commanded Moses. 33 And he raised up the court all around the tabernacle and the altar, and hung up the screen of the court gate. So Moses finished the work.

34 Then the cloud covered the tabernacle of meeting, and the glory of the LORD filled the tabernacle. 35 And Moses was not able to enter the tabernacle of meeting, because the cloud rested above it, and the glory of the LORD filled the tabernacle. 36 Whenever the cloud was taken up from above the tabernacle, the children of Israel would go onward in all their journeys. 37 But if the cloud was not taken up, then they did not journey till the day that it was taken up. 38 For the cloud of the LORD *was* above the tabernacle by day, and fire was over it by night, in the sight of all the house of Israel, throughout all their journeys.

Leviticus

Overview of Leviticus

Leviticus is the third book of the Pentateuch—the first five books of the Bible written by Moses about 1400 B.C. Leviticus falls between the end of Exodus and the beginning of Numbers, a period of one month. The book picks up the story of Israel after the completion of the tabernacle and takes place entirely at the base of Mount Sinai.

Leviticus is the record of God's presence in the midst of His people during their wanderings. It contains laws by which the people could properly worship and serve God and live positively in their community.

God promised to dwell with the people in the tabernacle, assuring them that He would be there during difficult times and arduous wanderings. He would not leave them alone. Elsewhere in Moses' recounting of their life in the wilderness, we know that God led the children of Israel with a "pillar of cloud by day and in a pillar of fire by night" (Num. 14:14).

The laws that God gave them were to give positive direction to their lives and aspirations. The instructions would enable them to live healthy, positive lives, coupled with pledges that they would inherit the land promised to them.

Leviticus was God's way to the good life for the Israelites! The psalmist David surely was reflecting on these words when he wrote Psalm 19.

> The law of the LORD is *perfect, converting the*
> *soul;*
> The testimony of the LORD is *sure, making wise*
> *the simple;*
> The statutes of the LORD are *right, rejoicing the*
> *heart;*
> The commandment of the LORD is *pure,*
> *enlightening the eyes;*
> The fear of the LORD is *clean, enduring forever;*
> The judgments of the LORD are *true* and *righteous*
> *altogether.*

More to be desired are they *than gold,*
Yea, than much fine gold;
Sweeter also than honey and the honeycomb.
Moreover by them Your servant is warned,
And *in keeping them* there is *great reward.*

(Ps. 19:7–11)

Jesus in Leviticus

Like many Old Testament books, Leviticus is replete with types and shadows of Jesus Christ, most notably in the sacrificial system. Some of the types of Christ include the five offerings (burnt, meal, peace, sin, trespass) which Jesus offered once and for all; the office of the High Priest, which Jesus fills as our intercessor; and the seven feasts (Passover, Unleavened Bread, Firstfruits, Pentecost, Trumpets, the Day of Atonement, and Tabernacles).

Keys to Leviticus

Key Word: Holiness. Leviticus helps us to see the holiness of God and how an unholy people can approach Him, be acceptable to Him, and remain in fellowship with Him. The only way to God is through blood sacrifice and the only way to continue walking with Him is through obedience to His laws.

Key Verses: "For the life of the flesh *is* in the blood, and I have given it to you upon the altar to make atonement for your souls; for it *is* the blood *that* makes atonement for the soul" (17:11).

"Consecrate yourselves therefore, and be holy, for I *am* the LORD your God. And you shall keep My statutes, and perform them: I *am* the LORD who sanctifies you" (20:7, 8).

Key Chapter: Leviticus 16—The Day of Atonement (Yom Kippur) was the most important single day in the Hebrew calendar as it was the only day on which the High Priest entered into the Most Holy Place to "make atonement for you, to cleanse you, *that* you may be clean from all your sins before the LORD" (16:30).

1 Now the LORD called to Moses, and spoke to him from the tabernacle of meeting, saying, 2 "Speak to the children of Israel, and say to them: 'When any one of you brings an offering to the LORD, you shall bring your offering of the livestock—of the herd and of the flock.

3 'If his offering *is* a burnt sacrifice of the herd, let him offer a male without blemish; he shall offer it of his own free will at the door of the tabernacle of meeting before the LORD. 4 Then he shall put his hand on the head of the burnt offering, and it will be accepted on his behalf to make atonement for him. 5 He shall kill the bull before the LORD; and the priests, Aaron's sons, shall bring the blood and sprinkle the blood all around on the altar that *is by* the door of the tabernacle of meeting. 6 And he shall skin the burnt offering and cut it into its pieces. 7 The sons of Aaron the priest shall put fire on the altar, and lay the wood in order on the fire. 8 Then the priests, Aaron's sons, shall lay the parts, the head, and the fat in order on the wood that *is* on the fire upon the altar; 9 but he shall wash its entrails and its legs with water. And the priest shall burn all on the altar as a burnt sacrifice, an offering made by fire, a sweet aroma to the LORD.

10 'If his offering *is* of the flocks—of the sheep or of the goats—as a burnt sacrifice, he shall bring a male without blemish. 11 He shall kill it on the north side of the altar before the LORD; and the priests, Aaron's sons, shall sprinkle its blood all around on the altar. 12 And he shall cut it into its pieces, with its head and its fat; and the priest shall lay them in order on the wood that *is* on the fire upon the altar; 13 but he shall wash the entrails and the legs with water. Then the priest shall bring *it* all and burn *it* on the altar; it *is* a burnt sacrifice, an offering made by fire, a sweet aroma to the LORD.

14 'And if the burnt sacrifice of his offering to the LORD *is* of birds, then he shall bring his offering of turtledoves or young pigeons. 15 The priest shall bring it to the altar, wring off its head, and burn *it* on the altar; its blood shall be drained out at the side of the altar. 16 And he shall remove its crop with its feathers and cast it beside the altar on the east side, into the place for ashes. 17 Then he shall split it at its wings, *but* shall not divide *it* completely; and the priest shall burn it on the altar, on the wood that *is* on the fire. It *is* a burnt sacrifice, an offering made by fire, a sweet aroma to the LORD.

2 'When anyone offers a grain offering to the LORD, his offering shall be *of* fine flour. And he shall pour oil on it, and put frankincense on it. 2 He shall bring it to Aaron's sons, the priests, one of whom shall take from it his handful of fine flour and oil with all the frankincense. And the priest shall burn *it as* a memorial on the altar, an offering made by fire, a sweet aroma to the LORD. 3 The rest of the grain offering *shall be* Aaron's and his sons'. *It is* most holy of the offerings to the LORD made by fire.

4 'And if you bring as an offering a grain offering baked in the oven, *it shall be* unleavened cakes of fine flour mixed with oil, or unleavened wafers anointed with oil. 5 But if your offering *is* a grain offering *baked* in a pan, *it shall be of* fine flour, unleavened, mixed with oil. 6 You shall break it in pieces and pour oil on it; it *is* a grain offering.

7 'If your offering *is* a grain offering *baked* in a covered pan, it shall be made *of* fine flour with oil. 8 You shall bring the grain offering that is made of these things to the LORD. And when it is presented to the priest, he shall bring it to the altar. 9 Then the priest shall take from the grain offering a memorial portion, and burn *it* on the altar. *It is* an offering made by fire, a sweet aroma to the LORD. 10 And what is left of the grain offering *shall be* Aaron's and his sons'. *It is* most holy of the offerings to the LORD made by fire.

11 'No grain offering which you bring to the LORD shall be made with leaven, for you shall burn no leaven nor any honey in any offering to the LORD made by fire. 12 As for the offering of the firstfruits, you shall offer

them to the LORD, but they shall not be burned on the altar for a sweet aroma. 13 And every offering of your grain offering you shall season with salt; you shall not allow the salt of the covenant of your God to be lacking from your grain offering. With all your offerings you shall offer salt.

14 'If you offer a grain offering of your firstfruits to the LORD, you shall offer for the grain offering of your firstfruits green heads of grain roasted on the fire, grain beaten from full heads. 15 And you shall put oil on it, and lay frankincense on it. It is a grain offering. 16 Then the priest shall burn the memorial portion: part of its beaten grain and part of its oil, with all the frankincense, as an offering made by fire to the LORD.

3 'When his offering is a sacrifice of a peace offering, if he offers it of the herd, whether male or female, he shall offer it without blemish before the LORD. 2 And he shall lay his hand on the head of his offering, and kill it at the door of the tabernacle of meeting; and Aaron's sons, the priests, shall sprinkle the blood all around on the altar. 3 Then he shall offer from the sacrifice of the peace offering an offering made by fire to the LORD. The fat that covers the entrails and all the fat that is on the entrails, 4 the two kidneys and the fat that is on them by the flanks, and the fatty lobe attached to the liver above the kidneys, he shall remove; 5 and Aaron's sons shall burn it on the altar upon the burnt sacrifice, which is on the wood that is on the fire, as an offering made by fire, a sweet aroma to the LORD.

6 'If his offering as a sacrifice of a peace offering to the LORD is of the flock, whether male or female, he shall offer it without blemish. 7 If he offers a lamb as his offering, then he shall offer it before the LORD. 8 And he shall lay his hand on the head of his offering, and kill it before the tabernacle of meeting; and Aaron's sons shall sprinkle its blood all around on the altar.

9 'Then he shall offer from the sacrifice of the peace offering, as an offering made by fire to the LORD, its fat and the whole fat tail which he shall remove close to the backbone. And the fat that covers the entrails and all the fat that is on the entrails,

10 the two kidneys and the fat that is on them by the flanks, and the fatty lobe attached to the liver above the kidneys, he shall remove; 11 and the priest shall burn them on the altar as food, an offering made by fire to the LORD.

12 'And if his offering is a goat, then he shall offer it before the LORD. 13 He shall lay his hand on its head and kill it before the tabernacle of meeting; and the sons of Aaron shall sprinkle its blood all around on the altar. 14 Then he shall offer from it his offering, as an offering made by fire to the LORD. The fat that covers the entrails and all the fat that is on the entrails, 15 the two kidneys and the fat that is on them by the flanks, and the fatty lobe attached to the liver above the kidneys, he shall remove; 16 and the priest shall burn them on the altar as food, an offering made by fire for a sweet aroma; all the fat is the LORD's.

17 'This shall be a perpetual statute throughout your generations in all your dwellings: you shall eat neither fat nor blood.' "

4 Now the LORD spoke to Moses, saying, 2 "Speak to the children of Israel, saying: 'If a person sins unintentionally against any of the commandments of the LORD in anything which ought not to be done, and does any of them, 3 if the anointed priest sins, bringing guilt on the people, then let him offer to the LORD for his sin which he has sinned a young bull without blemish as a sin offering. 4 He shall bring the bull to the door of the tabernacle of meeting before the LORD, lay his hand on the bull's head, and kill the bull before the LORD. 5 Then the anointed priest shall take some of the bull's blood and bring it to the tabernacle of meeting. 6 The priest shall dip his finger in the blood and sprinkle some of the blood seven times before the LORD, in front of the veil of the sanctuary. 7 And the priest shall put some of the blood on the horns of the altar of sweet incense before the LORD, which is in the tabernacle of meeting; and he shall pour the remaining blood of the bull at the base of the altar of the burnt offering, which is at the door of the tabernacle of meeting. 8 He shall take from it all the fat of the bull as the sin offering. The fat

that covers the entrails and all the fat which *is* on the entrails, 9 the two kidneys and the fat that *is* on them by the flanks, and the fatty lobe *attached* to the liver above the kidneys, he shall remove, 10 as it was taken from the bull of the sacrifice of the peace offering; and the priest shall burn them on the altar of the burnt offering. 11 But the bull's hide and all its flesh, with its head and legs, its entrails and offal— 12 the whole bull he shall carry outside the camp to a clean place, where the ashes are poured out, and burn it on wood with fire; where the ashes are poured out it shall be burned.

13 'Now if the whole congregation of Israel sins unintentionally, and the thing is hidden from the eyes of the assembly, and they have done *something against* any of the commandments of the LORD *in anything* which should not be done, and are guilty; 14 when the sin which they have committed becomes known, then the assembly shall offer a young bull for the sin, and bring it before the tabernacle of meeting. 15 And the elders of the congregation shall lay their hands on the head of the bull before the LORD. Then the bull shall be killed before the LORD. 16 The anointed priest shall bring some of the bull's blood to the tabernacle of meeting. 17 Then the priest shall dip his finger in the blood and sprinkle *it* seven times before the LORD, in front of the veil. 18 And he shall put *some* of the blood on the horns of the altar which *is* before the LORD, which *is* in the tabernacle of meeting; and he shall pour the remaining blood at the base of the altar of burnt offering, which *is* at the door of the tabernacle of meeting. 19 He shall take all the fat from it and burn *it* on the altar. 20 And he shall do with the bull as he did with the bull as a sin offering; thus he shall do with it. So the priest shall make atonement for them, and it shall be forgiven them. 21 Then he shall carry the bull outside the camp, and burn it as he burned the first bull. It *is* a sin offering for the assembly.

22 'When a ruler has sinned, and done *something* unintentionally *against* any of the commandments of the LORD his God *in anything* which should not be done, and is guilty, 23 or if his sin which he has committed comes to his knowledge, he shall bring as his offering a kid of the goats, a male without blemish. 24 And he shall lay his hand on the head of the goat, and kill it at the place where they kill the burnt offering before the LORD. It *is* a sin offering. 25 The priest shall take some of the blood of the sin offering with his finger, put *it* on the horns of the altar of burnt offering, and pour its blood at the base of the altar of burnt offering. 26 And he shall burn all its fat on the altar, like the fat of the sacrifice of the peace offering. So the priest shall make atonement for him concerning his sin, and it shall be forgiven him.

27 'If anyone of the common people sins unintentionally by doing *something against* any of the commandments of the LORD *in anything* which ought not to be done, and is guilty, 28 or if his sin which he has committed comes to his knowledge, then he shall bring as his offering a kid of the goats, a female without blemish, for his sin which he has committed. 29 And he shall lay his hand on the head of the sin offering, and kill the sin offering at the place of the burnt offering. 30 Then the priest shall take *some* of its blood with his finger, put *it* on the horns of the altar of burnt offering, and pour all *the remaining* blood at the base of the altar. 31 He shall remove all its fat, as fat is removed from the sacrifice of the peace offering; and the priest shall burn it on the altar for a sweet aroma to the LORD. So the priest shall make atonement for him, and it shall be forgiven him.

32 'If he brings a lamb as his sin offering, he shall bring a female without blemish. 33 Then he shall lay his hand on the head of the sin offering, and kill it as a sin offering at the place where they kill the burnt offering. 34 The priest shall take *some* of the blood of the sin offering with his finger, put *it* on the horns of the altar of burnt offering, and pour all *the remaining* blood at the base of the altar. 35 He shall remove all its fat, as the fat of the lamb is removed from the sacrifice of the peace offering. Then the priest shall burn it on the altar, according to the offerings made by fire to the LORD. So the priest shall make atonement for his sin that he has committed, and it shall be forgiven him.

5 'If a person sins in hearing the utterance of an oath, and *is* a witness, whether he has seen or known *of the matter*—if he does not tell *it*, he bears guilt.

2 'Or if a person touches any unclean thing, whether *it is* the carcass of an unclean beast, or the carcass of unclean livestock, or the carcass of unclean creeping things, and he is unaware of it, he also shall be unclean and guilty. 3 Or if he touches human uncleanness—whatever uncleanness with which a man may be defiled, and he is unaware of it— when he realizes *it*, then he shall be guilty.

4 'Or if a person swears, speaking thoughtlessly with *his* lips to do evil or to do good, whatever *it is* that a man may pronounce by an oath, and he is unaware of it—when he realizes *it*, then he shall be guilty in any of these *matters*.

5 'And it shall be, when he is guilty in any of these *matters*, that he shall confess that he has sinned in that *thing;* 6 and he shall bring his trespass offering to the LORD for his sin which he has committed, a female from the flock, a lamb or a kid of the goats as a sin offering. So the priest shall make atonement for him concerning his sin.

7 'If he is not able to bring a lamb, then he shall bring to the LORD, for his trespass which he has committed, two turtledoves or two young pigeons: one as a sin offering and the other as a burnt offering. 8 And he shall bring them to the priest, who shall offer *that* which *is* for the sin offering first, and wring off its head from its neck, but shall not divide *it* completely. 9 Then he shall sprinkle *some* of the blood of the sin offering on the side of the altar, and the rest of the blood shall be drained out at the base of the altar. It *is* a sin offering. 10 And he shall offer the second *as* a burnt offering according to the prescribed manner. So the priest shall make atonement on his behalf for his sin which he has committed, and it shall be forgiven him.

11 'But if he is not able to bring two turtledoves or two young pigeons, then he who sinned shall bring for his offering one-tenth of an ephah of fine flour as a sin offering. He shall put no oil on it, nor shall he put frankincense on it, for it *is* a sin offering. 12 Then he shall bring it to the priest, and the priest shall take his handful of it as a memorial portion, and burn *it* on the altar according to the offerings made by fire to the LORD. It *is* a sin offering. 13 The priest shall make atonement for him, for his sin that he has committed in any of these matters; and it shall be forgiven him. *The rest* shall be the priest's as a grain offering.' "

14 Then the LORD spoke to Moses, saying: 15 "If a person commits a trespass, and sins unintentionally in regard to the holy things of the LORD, then he shall bring to the LORD as his trespass offering a ram without blemish from the flocks, with your valuation in shekels of silver according to the shekel of the sanctuary, as a trespass offering. 16 And he shall make restitution for the harm that he has done in regard to the holy thing, and shall add one-fifth to it and give it to the priest. So the priest shall make atonement for him with the ram of the trespass offering, and it shall be forgiven him.

17 "If a person sins, and commits any of these things which are forbidden to be done by the commandments of the LORD, though he does not know *it*, yet he is guilty and shall bear his iniquity. 18 And he shall bring to the priest a ram without blemish from the flock, with your valuation, as a trespass offering. So the priest shall make atonement for him regarding his ignorance in which he erred and did not know *it*, and it shall be forgiven him. 19 It is a trespass offering; he has certainly trespassed against the LORD."

6 And the LORD spoke to Moses, saying: 2 "If a person sins and commits a trespass against the LORD by lying to his neighbor about what was delivered to him for safekeeping, or about a pledge, or about a robbery, or if he has extorted from his neighbor, 3 or if he has found what was lost and lies concerning it, and swears falsely—in any one of these things that a man may do in which he sins: 4 then it shall be, because he has sinned and is guilty, that he shall restore what he has stolen, or the thing which he has extorted, or what was delivered to him for safekeeping, or the lost thing which he found, 5 or all that about which he has sworn falsely. He shall restore its full value, add one-fifth more to it, *and* give it to whomever it belongs, on the day of his trespass offering. 6 And he shall bring his trespass offering to the LORD, a ram without blemish from the flock, with your valuation, as a trespass offering, to the priest. 7 So the priest shall make atonement for him before the LORD, and he shall be forgiven for any one of these things that he may have done in which he trespasses."

8 Then the LORD spoke to Moses, saying, 9 "Command Aaron and his sons, saying, 'This *is* the law of the burnt offering: The burnt offering *shall be* on the hearth upon the altar all night until morning, and the fire of the altar shall be kept burning on it. 10 And the priest shall put on his linen garment, and his linen trousers he shall put on his body, and take up the ashes of the burnt offering which the fire has consumed on the altar, and he shall put them beside the altar. 11 Then he shall take off his garments, put on other garments, and carry the ashes outside the camp to a clean place. 12 And the fire on the altar shall be kept burning on it; it shall not be put out. And the priest shall burn wood on it every morning, and lay the burnt offering in order on it; and he shall burn on it the fat of the peace offerings. 13 A fire shall always be burning on the altar; it shall never go out.

14 'This *is* the law of the grain offering: The sons of Aaron shall offer it on the altar before the LORD. 15 He shall take from it his handful of the fine flour of the grain offering, with its oil, and all the frankincense which *is* on the grain offering, and shall burn *it* on the altar *for* a sweet aroma, as a memorial to the LORD. 16 And the remainder of it Aaron and his sons shall eat; with unleavened bread it shall be eaten in a holy place; in the court of the tabernacle of meeting they shall eat it. 17 It shall not be baked with leaven. I have given it *as* their portion of My offerings made by fire; it *is* most holy, like the sin offering and the trespass offering. 18 All the males among the children of Aaron may eat it. *It shall be* a statute forever in your generations con-

cerning the offerings made by fire to the LORD. Everyone who touches them must be holy.' "[a]

19 And the LORD spoke to Moses, saying, 20 "This *is* the offering of Aaron and his sons, which they shall offer to the LORD, *beginning* on the day when he is anointed: one-tenth of an ephah of fine flour as a daily grain offering, half of it in the morning and half of it at night. 21 It shall be made in a pan with oil. *When it is* mixed, you shall bring it in. The baked pieces of the grain offering you shall offer *for* a sweet aroma to the LORD. 22 The priest from among his sons, who is anointed in his place, shall offer it. *It is* a statute forever to the LORD. It shall be wholly burned. 23 For every grain offering for the priest shall be wholly burned. It shall not be eaten."

24 Also the LORD spoke to Moses, saying, 25 "Speak to Aaron and to his sons, saying, 'This *is* the law of the sin offering: In the place where the burnt offering is killed, the sin offering shall be killed before the LORD. It *is* most holy. 26 The priest who offers it for sin shall eat it. In a holy place it shall be eaten, in the court of the tabernacle of meeting. 27 Everyone who touches its flesh must be holy.[a] And when its blood is sprinkled on any garment, you shall wash that on which it was sprinkled, in a holy place. 28 But the earthen vessel in which it is boiled shall be broken. And if it is boiled in a bronze pot, it shall be both scoured and rinsed in water. 29 All the males among the priests may eat it. It *is* most holy. 30 But no sin offering from which *any* of the blood is brought into the tabernacle of meeting, to make atonement in the holy *place,*[a] shall be eaten. It shall be burned in the fire.

7 'Likewise this *is* the law of the trespass offering (it *is* most holy): 2 In the place where they kill the burnt offering they shall kill the trespass offering. And its blood he shall sprinkle all around on the altar. 3 And he shall offer from it all its fat. The fat tail and the fat that covers the entrails, 4 the two kidneys and the fat that *is* on them by the flanks,

6:18 aCompare Numbers 4:15 and Haggai 2:11–13   6:27 aCompare Numbers 4:15 and Haggai 2:11–13   6:30 aThe Most Holy Place when capitalized and the fatty lobe *attached* to the liver above the kidneys, he shall remove; 5 and the priest shall burn them on the altar *as* an offering made by fire to the LORD. It *is* a trespass offering. 6 Every male among the priests may eat it. It shall be eaten in a holy place. It *is* most holy. 7 The trespass offering *is* like the sin offering; *there is* one law for them both: the priest who makes atonement with it shall have *it*. 8 And the priest who offers anyone's burnt offering, that priest shall have for himself the skin of the burnt offering which he has offered. 9 Also every grain offering that is baked in the oven and all that is prepared in the covered pan, or in a pan, shall be the priest's who offers it. 10 Every grain offering, *whether* mixed with oil or dry, shall belong to all the sons of Aaron, to one *as much* as the other.

11 'This *is* the law of the sacrifice of peace offerings which he shall offer to the LORD: 12 If he offers it for a thanksgiving, then he shall offer, with the sacrifice of thanksgiving, unleavened cakes mixed with oil, unleavened wafers anointed with oil, or cakes of blended flour mixed with oil. 13 Besides the cakes, *as* his offering he shall offer leavened bread with the sacrifice of thanksgiving of his peace offering. 14 And from it he shall offer one cake from each offering *as* a heave offering to the LORD. It shall belong to the priest who sprinkles the blood of the peace offering.

15 'The flesh of the sacrifice of his peace offering for thanksgiving shall be eaten the same day it is offered. He shall not leave any of it until morning. 16 But if the sacrifice of his offering *is* a vow or a voluntary offering, it shall be eaten the same day that he offers his sacrifice; but on the next day the remainder of it also may be eaten; 17 the remainder of the flesh of the sacrifice on the third day must be burned with fire. 18 And if *any* of the flesh of the sacrifice of his peace offering is eaten at all on the third day, it shall not be accepted, nor shall it be imputed to him; it shall be an abomination *to* him who offers it, and the person who eats of it shall bear guilt.

19 'The flesh that touches any un-clean thing shall not be eaten. It shall be burned with fire. And as for the *clean* flesh, all who are clean may eat of it. 20 But the person who eats the flesh of the sacrifice of the peace offering that *belongs* to the LORD, while he is unclean, that person shall be cut off from his people. 21 Moreover the person who touches any unclean thing, *such as* human uncleanness, *an* unclean animal, or any abominable unclean thing,[a] and who eats the flesh of the sacrifice of the peace offering that *belongs* to the LORD, that person shall be cut off from his people.' "

22 And the LORD spoke to Moses, saying, 23 "Speak to the children of Israel, saying: 'You shall not eat any fat, of ox or sheep or goat. 24 And the fat of an animal that dies *naturally*, and the fat of what is torn by wild beasts, may be used in any other way; but you shall by no means eat it. 25 For whoever eats the fat of the animal of which men offer an offering made by fire to the LORD, the person who eats *it* shall be cut off from his people. 26 Moreover you shall not eat any blood in any of your dwellings, *whether* of bird or beast. 27 Whoever eats any blood, that person shall be cut off from his people.' "

28 Then the LORD spoke to Moses, saying, 29 "Speak to the children of Israel, saying: 'He who offers the sacrifice of his peace offering to the LORD shall bring his offering to the LORD from the sacrifice of his peace offering. 30 His own hands shall bring the offerings made by fire to the LORD. The fat with the breast he shall bring, that the breast may be waved *as* a wave offering before the LORD. 31 And the priest shall burn the fat on the altar, but the breast shall be Aaron's and his sons'. 32 Also the right thigh you shall give to the priest *as* a heave offering from the sacrifices of your peace offerings. 33 He among the sons of Aaron, who offers the blood of the peace offering and the fat, shall have the right thigh for *his* part. 34 For the breast of the wave offering and the thigh of the heave offering I have taken from the children of Israel, from the sacrifices of their peace offerings, and I have given them to Aaron the priest and

7:21 aFollowing Masoretic Text, Septuagint, and Vulgate; Samaritan Pentateuch, Syriac, and Targum read *swarming thing* (compare 5:2).

to his sons from the children of Israel by a statute forever.'"

35 This *is* the consecrated portion for Aaron and his sons, from the offerings made by fire to the LORD, on the day when *Moses* presented them to minister to the LORD as priests. 36 The LORD commanded this to be given to them by the children of Israel, on the day that He anointed them, *by* a statute forever throughout their generations.

37 This *is* the law of the burnt offering, the grain offering, the sin offering, the trespass offering, the consecrations, and the sacrifice of the peace offering, 38 which the LORD commanded Moses on Mount Sinai, on the day when He commanded the children of Israel to offer their offerings to the LORD in the Wilderness of Sinai.

8 And the LORD spoke to Moses, saying: 2 "Take Aaron and his sons with him, and the garments, the anointing oil, a bull as the sin offering, two rams, and a basket of unleavened bread; 3 and gather all the congregation together at the door of the tabernacle of meeting."

4 So Moses did as the LORD commanded him. And the congregation was gathered together at the door of the tabernacle of meeting. 5 And Moses said to the congregation, "This *is* what the LORD commanded to be done."

6 Then Moses brought Aaron and his sons and washed them with water. 7 And he put the tunic on him, girded him with the sash, clothed him with the robe, and put the ephod on him; and he girded him with the intricately woven band of the ephod, and with it tied *the ephod* on him. 8 Then he put the breastplate on him, and he put the Urim and the Thummim[a] in the breastplate. 9 And he put the turban on his head. Also on the turban, on its front, he put the golden plate, the holy crown, as the LORD had commanded Moses.

10 Also Moses took the anointing oil, and anointed the tabernacle and all that *was* in it, and consecrated them. 11 He sprinkled some of it on the altar seven times, anointed the altar and all its utensils, and the laver and its base, to consecrate them.

12 And he poured some of the anointing oil on Aaron's head and anointed him, to consecrate him.

13 Then Moses brought Aaron's sons and put tunics on them, girded them with sashes, and put hats on them, as the LORD had commanded Moses.

14 And he brought the bull for the sin offering. Then Aaron and his sons laid their hands on the head of the bull for the sin offering, 15 and Moses killed *it*. Then he took the blood, and put *some* on the horns of the altar all around with his finger, and purified the altar. And he poured the blood at the base of the altar, and consecrated it, to make atonement for it. 16 Then he took all the fat that *was* on the entrails, the fatty lobe *attached to* the liver, and the two kidneys with their fat, and Moses burned *them* on the altar. 17 But the bull, its hide, its flesh, and its offal, he burned with fire outside the camp, as the LORD had commanded Moses.

18 Then he brought the ram as the burnt offering. And Aaron and his sons laid their hands on the head of the ram, 19 and Moses killed *it*. Then he sprinkled the blood all around on the altar. 20 And he cut the ram into pieces; and Moses burned the head, the pieces, and the fat. 21 Then he washed the entrails and the legs in water. And Moses burned the whole ram on the altar. It *was* a burnt sacrifice for a sweet aroma, an offering made by fire to the LORD, as the LORD had commanded Moses.

22 And he brought the second ram, the ram of consecration. Then Aaron and his sons laid their hands on the head of the ram, 23 and Moses killed *it*. Also he took *some* of its blood and put it on the tip of Aaron's right ear, on the thumb of his right hand, and on the big toe of his right foot. 24 Then he brought Aaron's sons. And Moses put *some* of the blood on the tips of their right ears, on the thumbs of their right hands, and on the big toes of their right feet. And Moses sprinkled the blood all around on the altar. 25 Then he took the fat and the fat tail, all the fat that *was* on the entrails, the fatty lobe *attached to* the liver, the two kidneys and their fat, and the right thigh; 26 and from the basket of unleavened bread that was before the LORD he

---

8:8 [a]Literally *the Lights and the Perfections* (compare Exodus 28:30)

took one unleavened cake, a cake of bread *anointed with* oil, and one wafer, and put *them* on the fat and on the right thigh; 27 and he put all *these* in Aaron's hands and in his sons' hands, and waved them *as* a wave offering before the LORD. 28 Then Moses took them from their hands and burned *them* on the altar, on the burnt offering. They *were* consecration offerings for a sweet aroma. That *was* an offering made by fire to the LORD. 29 And Moses took the breast and waved it *as* a wave offering before the LORD. It was Moses' part of the ram of consecration, as the LORD had commanded Moses.

30 Then Moses took some of the anointing oil and some of the blood which *was* on the altar, and sprinkled *it* on Aaron, on his garments, on his sons, and on the garments of his sons with him; and he consecrated Aaron, his garments, his sons, and the garments of his sons with him.

31 And Moses said to Aaron and his sons, "Boil the flesh *at* the door of the tabernacle of meeting, and eat it there with the bread that *is* in the basket of consecration offerings, as I commanded, saying, 'Aaron and his sons shall eat it.' 32 What remains of the flesh and of the bread you shall burn with fire. 33 And you shall not go outside the door of the tabernacle of meeting *for* seven days, until the days of your consecration are ended. For seven days he shall consecrate you. 34 As he has done this day, *so* the LORD has commanded to do, to make atonement for you. 35 Therefore you shall stay *at* the door of the tabernacle of meeting day and night for seven days, and keep the charge of the LORD, so that you may not die; for so I have been commanded." 36 So Aaron and his sons did all the things that the LORD had commanded by the hand of Moses.

9 It came to pass on the eighth day that Moses called Aaron and his sons and the elders of Israel. 2 And he said to Aaron, "Take for yourself a young bull as a sin offering and a ram as a burnt offering, without blemish, and offer *them* before the LORD. 3 And to the children of Israel you shall speak, saying, 'Take a kid of the goats as a sin offering, and a calf and a lamb, *both* of the first year, without blemish, as a burnt of-

fering, 4 also a bull and a ram as peace offerings, to sacrifice before the LORD, and a grain offering mixed with oil; for today the LORD will appear to you.'"

5 So they brought what Moses commanded before the tabernacle of meeting. And all the congregation drew near and stood before the LORD. 6 Then Moses said, "This *is* the thing which the LORD commanded you to do, and the glory of the LORD will appear to you." 7 And Moses said to Aaron, "Go to the altar, offer your sin offering and your burnt offering, and make atonement for yourself and for the people. Offer the offering of the people, and make atonement for them, as the LORD commanded."

8 Aaron therefore went to the altar and killed the calf of the sin offering, which *was* for himself. 9 Then the sons of Aaron brought the blood to him. And he dipped his finger in the blood, put *it* on the horns of the altar, and poured the blood at the base of the altar. 10 But the fat, the kidneys, and the fatty lobe from the liver of the sin offering he burned on the altar, as the LORD had commanded Moses. 11 The flesh and the hide he burned with fire outside the camp.

12 And he killed the burnt offering; and Aaron's sons presented to him the blood, which he sprinkled all around on the altar. 13 Then they presented the burnt offering to him, with its pieces and head, and he burned *them* on the altar. 14 And he washed the entrails and the legs, and burned *them* with the burnt offering on the altar.

15 Then he brought the people's offering, and took the goat, which *was* the sin offering for the people, and killed it and offered it for sin, like the first one. 16 And he brought the burnt offering and offered it according to the prescribed manner. 17 Then he brought the grain offering, took a handful of it, and burned *it* on the altar, besides the burnt sacrifice of the morning.

18 He also killed the bull and the ram *as* sacrifices of peace offerings, which *were* for the people. And Aaron's sons presented to him the blood, which he sprinkled all around on the altar, 19 and the fat from the bull and the ram—the fatty tail, what covers *the entrails* and the kidneys, and the fatty lobe *attached to* the liver;

20 and they put the fat on the breasts. Then he burned the fat on the altar; 21 but the breasts and the right thigh Aaron waved *as* a wave offering before the LORD, as Moses had commanded.

22 Then Aaron lifted his hand toward the people, blessed them, and came down from offering the sin offering, the burnt offering, and peace offerings. 23 And Moses and Aaron went into the tabernacle of meeting, and came out and blessed the people. Then the glory of the LORD appeared to all the people, 24 and fire came out from before the LORD and consumed the burnt offering and the fat on the altar. When all the people saw *it,* they shouted and fell on their faces.

10 Then Nadab and Abihu, the sons of Aaron, each took his censer and put fire in it, put incense on it, and offered profane fire before the LORD, which He had not commanded them. 2 So fire went out from the LORD and devoured them, and they died before the LORD. 3 And Moses said to Aaron, "This is what the LORD spoke, saying:

'By those who come near Me
I must be regarded as holy;
And before all the people
I must be glorified.' "

So Aaron held his peace.

4 Then Moses called Mishael and Elzaphan, the sons of Uzziel the uncle of Aaron, and said to them, "Come near, carry your brethren from before the sanctuary out of the camp." 5 So they went near and carried them by their tunics out of the camp, as Moses had said.

6 And Moses said to Aaron, and to Eleazar and Ithamar, his sons, "Do not uncover your heads nor tear your clothes, lest you die, and wrath come upon all the people. But let your brethren, the whole house of Israel, bewail the burning which the LORD has kindled. 7 You shall not go out from the door of the tabernacle of meeting, lest you die, for the anointing oil of the LORD *is* upon you." And they did according to the word of Moses.

8 Then the LORD spoke to Aaron, saying: 9 "Do not drink wine or intoxicating drink, you, nor your sons with you, when you go into the tabernacle of meeting, lest you die. *It shall be* a statute forever throughout your generations, 10 that you may distinguish between holy and unholy, and between unclean and clean, 11 and that you may teach the children of Israel all the statutes which the LORD has spoken to them by the hand of Moses."

12 And Moses spoke to Aaron, and to Eleazar and Ithamar, his sons who were left: "Take the grain offering that remains of the offerings made by fire to the LORD, and eat it without leaven beside the altar; for it *is* most holy. 13 You shall eat it in a holy place, because it *is* your due and your sons' due, of the sacrifices made by fire to the LORD; for so I have been commanded. 14 The breast of the wave offering and the thigh of the heave offering you shall eat in a clean place, you, your sons, and your daughters with you; for *they are* your due and your sons' due, *which* are given from the sacrifices of peace offerings of the children of Israel. 15 The thigh of the heave offering and the breast of the wave offering they shall bring with the offerings of fat made by fire, to offer *as* a wave offering before the LORD. And it shall be yours and your sons' with you, by a statute forever, as the LORD has commanded."

16 Then Moses made careful inquiry about the goat of the sin offering, and there it was—burned up. And he was angry with Eleazar and Ithamar, the sons of Aaron *who were* left, saying, 17 "Why have you not eaten the sin offering in a holy place, since it *is* most holy, and *God* has given it to you to bear the guilt of the congregation, to make atonement for them before the LORD? 18 See! Its blood was not brought inside the holy *place;*[a] indeed you should have eaten it in a holy *place,* as I commanded."

19 And Aaron said to Moses, "Look, this day they have offered their sin offering and their burnt offering before the LORD, and such things have befallen me! *If* I had eaten the sin offering today, would it have been accepted in the sight of the LORD?" 20 So when Moses heard *that,* he was content.

10:18 [a]The Most Holy Place when capitalized

11 Now the LORD spoke to Moses and Aaron, saying to them, 2 "Speak to the children of Israel, saying, 'These *are* the animals which you may eat among all the animals that *are* on the earth: 3 Among the animals, whatever divides the hoof, having cloven hooves *and* chewing the cud—that you may eat. 4 Nevertheless these you shall not eat among those that chew the cud or those that have cloven hooves: the camel, because it chews the cud but does not have cloven hooves, is unclean to you; 5 the rock hyrax, because it chews the cud but does not have cloven hooves, *is* unclean to you; 6 the hare, because it chews the cud but does not have cloven hooves, *is* unclean to you; 7 and the swine, though it divides the hoof, having cloven hooves, yet does not chew the cud, *is* unclean to you. 8 Their flesh you shall not eat, and their carcasses you shall not touch. They *are* unclean to you.

9 'These you may eat of all that *are* in the water: whatever in the water has fins and scales, whether in the seas or in the rivers—that you may eat. 10 But all in the seas or in the rivers that do not have fins and scales, all that move in the water or any living thing which *is* in the water, they *are* an abomination to you. 11 They shall be an abomination to you; you shall not eat their flesh, but you shall regard their carcasses as an abomination. 12 Whatever in the water does not have fins or scales— that *shall be* an abomination to you.

13 'And these you shall regard as an abomination among the birds; they shall not be eaten, they *are* an abomination: the eagle, the vulture, the buzzard, 14 the kite, and the falcon after its kind; 15 every raven after its kind, 16 the ostrich, the short-eared owl, the seagull, and the hawk after its kind; 17 the little owl, the fisher owl, and the screech owl; 18 the white owl, the jackdaw, and the carrion vulture; 19 the stork, the heron after its kind, the hoopoe, and the bat.

20 'All flying insects that creep on *all* fours *shall be* an abomination to you. 21 Yet these you may eat of every flying insect that creeps on *all* fours: those which have jointed legs above their feet with which to leap on the earth. 22 These you may eat:

the locust after its kind, the destroying locust after its kind, the cricket after its kind, and the grasshopper after its kind. 23 But all *other* flying insects which have four feet *shall be* an abomination to you.

24 'By these you shall become unclean; whoever touches the carcass of any of them shall be unclean until evening; 25 whoever carries part of the carcass of any of them shall wash his clothes and be unclean until evening: 26 *The carcass* of any animal which divides the foot, but is not cloven-hoofed or does not chew the cud, *is* unclean to you. Everyone who touches it shall be unclean. 27 And whatever goes on its paws, among all kinds of animals that go on *all* fours, those *are* unclean to you. Whoever touches any such carcass shall be unclean until evening. 28 Whoever carries *any such* carcass shall wash his clothes and be unclean until evening. It *is* unclean to you.

29 'These also *shall be* unclean to you among the creeping things that creep on the earth: the mole, the mouse, and the large lizard after its kind; 30 the gecko, the monitor lizard, the sand reptile, the sand lizard, and the chameleon. 31 These *are* unclean to you among all that creep. Whoever touches them when they are dead shall be unclean until evening. 32 Anything on which *any* of them falls, when they are dead shall be unclean, whether *it is* any item of wood or clothing or skin or sack, whatever item *it is*, in which *any* work is done, it must be put in water. And it shall be unclean until evening; then it shall be clean. 33 Any earthen vessel into which *any* of them falls you shall break; and whatever *is* in it shall be unclean: 34 in such a vessel, any edible food upon which water falls becomes unclean, and any drink that may be drunk from it becomes unclean. 35 And everything on which *a part* of *any such* carcass falls shall be unclean; *whether it is* an oven or cooking stove, it shall be broken down; *for* they *are* unclean, and shall be unclean to you. 36 Nevertheless a spring or a cistern, *in which there is* plenty of water, shall be clean, but whatever touches any such carcass becomes unclean. 37 And if a part of *any such* carcass falls on any planting seed which is to be sown, it *remains* clean. 38 But if water is put on

the seed, and if *a part* of *any such* carcass falls on it, it *becomes* unclean to you.

39 'And if any animal which you may eat dies, he who touches its carcass shall be unclean until evening. 40 He who eats of its carcass shall wash his clothes and be unclean until evening. He also who carries its carcass shall wash his clothes and be unclean until evening.

41 'And every creeping thing that creeps on the earth *shall be* an abomination. It shall not be eaten. 42 Whatever crawls on its belly, whatever goes on *all* fours, or whatever has many feet among all creeping things that creep on the earth—these you shall not eat, for they *are* an abomination. 43 You shall not make yourselves abominable with any creeping thing that creeps; nor shall you make yourselves unclean with them, lest you be defiled by them. 44 For I *am* the LORD your God. You shall therefore consecrate yourselves, and you shall be holy; for I *am* holy. Neither shall you defile yourselves with any creeping thing that creeps on the earth. 45 For I *am* the LORD who brings you up out of the land of Egypt, to be your God. You shall therefore be holy, for I *am* holy.

46 'This *is* the law of the animals and the birds and every living creature that moves in the waters, and of every creature that creeps on the earth, 47 to distinguish between the unclean and the clean, and between the animal that may be eaten and the animal that may not be eaten.' "

12 Then the LORD spoke to Moses, saying, 2 "Speak to the children of Israel, saying: 'If a woman has conceived, and borne a male child, then she shall be unclean seven days; as in the days of her customary impurity she shall be unclean. 3 And on the eighth day the flesh of his foreskin shall be circumcised. 4 She shall then continue in the blood of *her* purification thirty-three days. She shall not touch any hallowed thing, nor come into the sanctuary until the days of her purification are fulfilled.

5 'But if she bears a female child, then she shall be unclean two weeks, as in her customary impurity, and she shall continue in the blood of *her* purification sixty-six days.

6 'When the days of her purification are fulfilled, whether for a son or a daughter, she shall bring to the priest a lamb of the first year as a burnt offering, and a young pigeon or a turtledove as a sin offering, to the door of the tabernacle of meeting. 7 Then he shall offer it before the LORD, and make atonement for her. And she shall be clean from the flow of her blood. This *is* the law for her who has borne a male or a female.

8 'And if she is not able to bring a lamb, then she may bring two turtledoves or two young pigeons—one as a burnt offering and the other as a sin offering. So the priest shall make atonement for her, and she will be clean.' "

13 And the LORD spoke to Moses and Aaron, saying: 2 "When a man has on the skin of his body a swelling, a scab, or a bright spot, and it becomes on the skin of his body *like* a leprous[a] sore, then he shall be brought to Aaron the priest or to one of his sons the priests. 3 The priest shall examine the sore on the skin of the body; and if the hair on the sore has turned white, and the sore appears *to be* deeper than the skin of his body, it *is* a leprous sore. Then the priest shall examine him, and pronounce him unclean. 4 But if the bright spot *is* white on the skin of his body, and does not appear *to be* deeper than the skin, and its hair has not turned white, then the priest shall isolate *the one who has* the sore seven days. 5 And the priest shall examine him on the seventh day; and indeed *if* the sore appears to be as it was, *and* the sore has not spread on the skin, then the priest shall isolate him another seven days. 6 Then the priest shall examine him again on the seventh day; and indeed *if* the sore has faded, *and* the sore has not spread on the skin, then the priest shall pronounce him clean; it *is only* a scab, and he shall wash his clothes and be clean. 7 But if the scab should at all spread over the skin, after he has been seen by the priest for his cleansing, he shall be seen by the priest again. 8 And *if* the priest sees

13:2 aHebrew *saraath,* disfiguring skin diseases, including leprosy, and so in verses 2–46 and 14:1–32 that the scab has indeed spread on the skin, then the priest shall pronounce him unclean. It *is* leprosy.

9 "When the leprous sore is on a person, then he shall be brought to the priest. 10 And the priest shall examine *him;* and indeed *if* the swelling on the skin *is* white, and it has turned the hair white, and *there is* a spot of raw flesh in the swelling, 11 it *is* an old leprosy on the skin of his body. The priest shall pronounce him unclean, and shall not isolate him, for he *is* unclean.

12 "And if leprosy breaks out all over the skin, and the leprosy covers all the skin of *the one who has* the sore, from his head to his foot, wherever the priest looks, 13 then the priest shall consider; and indeed *if* the leprosy has covered all his body, he shall pronounce *him* clean *who has* the sore. It has all turned white. He *is* clean. 14 But when raw flesh appears on him, he shall be unclean. 15 And the priest shall examine the raw flesh and pronounce him to be unclean; *for* the raw flesh *is* unclean. It *is* leprosy. 16 Or if the raw flesh changes and turns white again, he shall come to the priest. 17 And the priest shall examine him; and indeed *if* the sore has turned white, then the priest shall pronounce *him* clean *who has* the sore. He *is* clean.

18 "If the body develops a boil in the skin, and it is healed, 19 and in the place of the boil there comes a white swelling or a bright spot, reddish-white, then it shall be shown to the priest; 20 and *if,* when the priest sees it, it indeed *appears* deeper than the skin, and its hair has turned white, the priest shall pronounce him unclean. It *is* a leprous sore which has broken out of the boil. 21 But if the priest examines it, and indeed *there are* no white hairs in it, and it *is* not deeper than the skin, but has faded, then the priest shall isolate him seven days; 22 and if it should at all spread over the skin, then the priest shall pronounce him unclean. It *is* a leprous sore. 23 But if the bright spot stays in one place, *and* has not spread, it *is* the scar of the boil; and the priest shall pronounce him clean.

24 "Or if the body receives a burn on its skin by fire, and the raw *flesh* of the burn becomes a bright spot, reddish-white or white, 25 then the priest shall examine it; and indeed *if* the hair of the bright spot has turned white, and it appears deeper than the skin, it *is* leprosy broken out in the burn. Therefore the priest shall pronounce him unclean. It *is* a leprous sore. 26 But if the priest examines it, and indeed *there are* no white hairs in the bright spot, and it *is* not deeper than the skin, but has faded, then the priest shall isolate him seven days. 27 And the priest shall examine him on the seventh day. If it has at all spread over the skin, then the priest shall pronounce him unclean. It *is* a leprous sore. 28 But if the bright spot stays in one place, *and* has not spread on the skin, but has faded, it *is* a swelling from the burn. The priest shall pronounce him clean, for it *is* the scar from the burn.

29 "If a man or woman has a sore on the head or the beard, 30 then the priest shall examine the sore; and indeed if it appears deeper than the skin, *and there is* in it thin yellow hair, then the priest shall pronounce him unclean. It *is* a scaly leprosy of the head or beard. 31 But if the priest examines the scaly sore, and indeed it does not appear deeper than the skin, and *there is* no black hair in it, then the priest shall isolate *the one who has* the scale seven days. 32 And on the seventh day the priest shall examine the sore; and indeed *if* the scale has not spread, and there is no yellow hair in it, and the scale does not appear deeper than the skin, 33 he shall shave himself, but the scale he shall not shave. And the priest shall isolate *the one who has* the scale another seven days. 34 On the seventh day the priest shall examine the scale; and indeed *if* the scale has not spread over the skin, and does not appear deeper than the skin, then the priest shall pronounce him clean. He shall wash his clothes and be clean. 35 But if the scale should at all spread over the skin after his cleansing, 36 then the priest shall examine him; and indeed *if* the scale has spread over the skin, the priest need not seek for yellow hair. He *is* unclean. 37 But if the scale appears to be at a standstill, and there is black hair grown up in it, the scale has healed. He *is* clean, and the priest shall pronounce him clean.

38 "If a man or a woman has bright spots on the skin of the body, *specifically* white bright spots, 39 then the

priest shall look; and indeed *if* the bright spots on the skin of the body *are* dull white, it *is* a white spot *that* grows on the skin. He *is* clean.

40 "As for the man whose hair has fallen from his head, he *is* bald, *but* he *is* clean. 41 He whose hair has fallen from his forehead, he *is* bald on the forehead, *but* he *is* clean. 42 And if there is on the bald head or bald forehead a reddish-white sore, it *is* leprosy breaking out on his bald head or his bald forehead. 43 Then the priest shall examine it; and indeed *if* the swelling of the sore *is* reddish-white on his bald head or on his bald forehead, as the appearance of leprosy on the skin of the body, 44 he is a leprous man. He *is* unclean. The priest shall surely pronounce him unclean; his sore *is* on his head.

45 "Now the leper on whom the sore is, his clothes shall be torn and his head bare; and he shall cover his mustache, and cry, 'Unclean! Unclean!' 46 He shall be unclean. All the days he has the sore he shall be unclean. He *is* unclean, and he shall dwell alone; his dwelling *shall be* outside the camp.

47 "Also, if a garment has a leprous plague*a* in it, *whether it is* a woolen garment or a linen garment, 48 whether *it is* in the warp or woof of linen or wool, whether in leather or in anything made of leather, 49 and if the plague is greenish or reddish in the garment or in the leather, whether in the warp or in the woof, or in anything made of leather, it *is* a leprous plague and shall be shown to the priest. 50 The priest shall examine the plague and isolate *that which has* the plague seven days. 51 And he shall examine the plague on the seventh day. If the plague has spread in the garment, either in the warp or in the woof, in the leather *or* in anything made of leather, the plague *is* an active leprosy. It *is* unclean. 52 He shall therefore burn that garment in which is the plague, whether warp or woof, in wool or in linen, or anything of leather, for it *is* an active leprosy; *the garment* shall be burned in the fire.

53 "But if the priest examines *it,* and indeed the plague has not spread in the garment, either in the warp or in the woof, or in anything made of leather, 54 then the priest shall command that they wash *the thing* in which *is* the plague; and he shall isolate it another seven days. 55 Then the priest shall examine the plague after it has been washed; and indeed *if* the plague has not changed its color, though the plague has not spread, it *is* unclean, and you shall burn in the fire; it continues eating away, *whether* the damage *is* outside or inside. 56 If the priest examines *it,* and indeed the plague has faded after washing it, then he shall tear it out of the garment, whether out of the warp or out of the woof, or out of the leather. 57 But if it appears again in the garment, either in the warp or in the woof, or in anything made of leather, it *is* a spreading *plague;* you shall burn with fire that in which is the plague. 58 And if you wash the garment, either warp or woof, or whatever is made of leather, if the plague has disappeared from it, then it shall be washed a second time, and shall be clean.

59 "This *is* the law of the leprous plague in a garment of wool or linen, either in the warp or woof, or in anything made of leather, to pronounce it clean or to pronounce it unclean."

14 Then the LORD spoke to Moses, saying, 2 "This shall be the law of the leper for the day of his cleansing: He shall be brought to the priest. 3 And the priest shall go out of the camp, and the priest shall examine *him;* and indeed, *if* the leprosy is healed in the leper, 4 then the priest shall command to take for him who is to be cleansed two living *and* clean birds, cedar wood, scarlet, and hyssop. 5 And the priest shall command that one of the birds be killed in an earthen vessel over running water. 6 As for the living bird, he shall take it, the cedar wood and the scarlet and the hyssop, and dip them and the living bird in the blood of the bird *that was* killed over the running water. 7 And he shall sprinkle it seven times on him who is to be cleansed from the leprosy, and shall pronounce him clean, and shall let the living bird loose in the open field. 8 He who is to be cleansed shall wash his clothes, shave off all his hair, and wash him-

13:47 *a*A mold, fungus, or similar infestation, and so in verses 47–59 self in water, that he may be clean. After that he shall come into the camp, and shall stay outside his tent seven days. 9 But on the seventh day he shall shave all the hair off his head and his beard and his eyebrows—all his hair he shall shave off. He shall wash his clothes and wash his body in water, and he shall be clean.

10 "And on the eighth day he shall take two male lambs without blemish, one ewe lamb of the first year without blemish, three-tenths *of an ephah* of fine flour mixed with oil as a grain offering, and one log of oil. 11 Then the priest who makes *him* clean shall present the man who is to be made clean, and those things, before the LORD, *at* the door of the tabernacle of meeting. 12 And the priest shall take one male lamb and offer it as a trespass offering, and the log of oil, and wave them *as* a wave offering before the LORD. 13 Then he shall kill the lamb in the place where he kills the sin offering and the burnt offering, in a holy place; for as the sin offering *is* the priest's, so *is* the trespass offering. It *is* most holy. 14 The priest shall take *some* of the blood of the trespass offering, and the priest shall put *it* on the tip of the right ear of him who is to be cleansed, on the thumb of his right hand, and on the big toe of his right foot. 15 And the priest shall take *some* of the log of oil, and pour *it* into the palm of his own left hand. 16 Then the priest shall dip his right finger in the oil that *is* in his left hand, and shall sprinkle some of the oil with his finger seven times before the LORD. 17 And of the rest of the oil in his hand, the priest shall put *some* on the tip of the right ear of him who is to be cleansed, on the thumb of his right hand, and on the big toe of his right foot, on the blood of the trespass offering. 18 The rest of the oil that *is* in the priest's hand he shall put on the head of him who is to be cleansed. So the priest shall make atonement for him before the LORD.

19 "Then the priest shall offer the sin offering, and make atonement for him who is to be cleansed from his uncleanness. Afterward he shall kill the burnt offering. 20 And the priest shall offer the burnt offering and the grain offering on the altar. So the priest shall make atonement for him, and he shall be clean.

21 "But if he *is* poor and cannot afford it, then he shall take one male lamb *as* a trespass offering to be waved, to make atonement for him, one-tenth *of an ephah* of fine flour mixed with oil as a grain offering, a log of oil, 22 and two turtledoves or two young pigeons, such as he is able to afford: one shall be a sin offering and the other a burnt offering. 23 He shall bring them to the priest on the eighth day for his cleansing, to the door of the tabernacle of meeting, before the LORD. 24 And the priest shall take the lamb of the trespass offering and the log of oil, and the priest shall wave them *as* a wave offering before the LORD. 25 Then he shall kill the lamb of the trespass offering, and the priest shall take *some* of the blood of the trespass offering and put *it* on the tip of the right ear of him who is to be cleansed, on the thumb of his right hand, and on the big toe of his right foot. 26 And the priest shall pour some of the oil into the palm of his own left hand. 27 Then the priest shall sprinkle with his right finger *some* of the oil that *is* in his left hand seven times before the LORD. 28 And the priest shall put *some* of the oil that *is* in his hand on the tip of the right ear of him who is to be cleansed, on the thumb of the right hand, and on the big toe of his right foot, on the place of the blood of the trespass offering. 29 The rest of the oil that *is* in the priest's hand he shall put on the head of him who is to be cleansed, to make atonement for him before the LORD. 30 And he shall offer one of the turtledoves or young pigeons, such as he can afford— 31 such as he is able to afford, the one *as* a sin offering and the other *as* a burnt offering, with the grain offering. So the priest shall make atonement for him who is to be cleansed before the LORD. 32 This *is* the law for *one* who had a leprous sore, who cannot afford the usual cleansing."

33 And the LORD spoke to Moses and Aaron, saying: 34 "When you have come into the land of Canaan, which I give you as a possession, and I put the leprous plague[a] in a house in the land of your possession,

14:34 [a]Decomposition by mildew, mold, dry rot, etc., and so in verses 34–53

35 and he who owns the house comes and tells the priest, saying, 'It seems to me that *there is* some plague in the house,' 36 then the priest shall command that they empty the house, before the priest goes *into it* to examine the plague, that all that *is* in the house may not be made unclean; and afterward the priest shall go in to examine the house. 37 And he shall examine the plague; and indeed *if* the plague *is* on the walls of the house with ingrained streaks, greenish or reddish, which appear to be deep in the wall, 38 then the priest shall go out of the house, to the door of the house, and shut up the house seven days. 39 And the priest shall come again on the seventh day and look; and indeed *if* the plague has spread on the walls of the house, 40 then the priest shall command that they take away the stones in which *is* the plague, and they shall cast them into an unclean place outside the city. 41 And he shall cause the house to be scraped inside, all around, and the dust that they scrape off they shall pour out in an unclean place outside the city. 42 Then they shall take other stones and put *them* in the place of *those* stones, and he shall take other mortar and plaster the house.

43 "Now if the plague comes back and breaks out in the house, after he has taken away the stones, after he has scraped the house, and after it is plastered, 44 then the priest shall come and look; and indeed *if* the plague has spread in the house, it *is* an active leprosy in the house. It *is* unclean. 45 And he shall break down the house, its stones, its timber, and all the plaster of the house, and he shall carry *them* outside the city to an unclean place. 46 Moreover he who goes into the house at all while it is shut up shall be unclean until evening. 47 And he who lies down in the house shall wash his clothes, and he who eats in the house shall wash his clothes.

48 "But if the priest comes in and examines *it,* and indeed the plague has not spread in the house after the house was plastered, then the priest shall pronounce the house clean, because the plague is healed. 49 And he shall take, to cleanse the house, two birds, cedar wood, scarlet, and hyssop. 50 Then he shall kill one of the birds in an earthen vessel over run-

ning water; 51 and he shall take the cedar wood, the hyssop, the scarlet, and the living bird, and dip them in the blood of the slain bird and in the running water, and sprinkle the house seven times. 52 And he shall cleanse the house with the blood of the bird and the running water and the living bird, with the cedar wood, the hyssop, and the scarlet. 53 Then he shall let the living bird loose outside the city in the open field, and make atonement for the house, and it shall be clean.

54 "This *is* the law for any leprous sore and scale, 55 for the leprosy of a garment and of a house, 56 for a swelling and a scab and a bright spot, 57 to teach when *it is* unclean and when *it is* clean. This *is* the law of leprosy."

15 And the LORD spoke to Moses and Aaron, saying, 2 "Speak to the children of Israel, and say to them: 'When any man has a discharge from his body, his discharge *is* unclean. 3 And this shall be his uncleanness in regard to his discharge—whether his body runs with his discharge, or his body is stopped up by his discharge, it *is* his uncleanness. 4 Every bed is unclean on which he who has the discharge lies, and everything on which he sits shall be unclean. 5 And whoever touches his bed shall wash his clothes and bathe in water, and be unclean until evening. 6 He who sits on anything on which he who has the discharge sat shall wash his clothes and bathe in water, and be unclean until evening. 7 And he who touches the body of him who has the discharge shall wash his clothes and bathe in water, and be unclean until evening. 8 If he who has the discharge spits on him who is clean, then he shall wash his clothes and bathe in water, and be unclean until evening. 9 Any saddle on which he who has the discharge rides shall be unclean. 10 Whoever touches anything that was under him shall be unclean until evening. He who carries *any of* those things shall wash his clothes and bathe in water, and be unclean until evening. 11 And whomever the one who has the discharge touches, and has not rinsed his hands in water, he shall wash his clothes and bathe in water, and be unclean until evening.

12 The vessel of earth that he who has the discharge touches shall be broken, and every vessel of wood shall be rinsed in water.

13 'And when he who has a discharge is cleansed of his discharge, then he shall count for himself seven days for his cleansing, wash his clothes, and bathe his body in running water; then he shall be clean. 14 On the eighth day he shall take for himself two turtledoves or two young pigeons, and come before the LORD, to the door of the tabernacle of meeting, and give them to the priest. 15 Then the priest shall offer them, the one *as* a sin offering and the other *as* a burnt offering. So the priest shall make atonement for him before the LORD because of his discharge.

16 'If any man has an emission of semen, then he shall wash all his body in water, and be unclean until evening. 17 And any garment and any leather on which there is semen, it shall be washed with water, and be unclean until evening. 18 Also, when a woman lies with a man, and *there is* an emission of semen, they shall bathe in water, and be unclean until evening.

19 'If a woman has a discharge, *and* the discharge from her body is blood, she shall be set apart seven days; and whoever touches her shall be unclean until evening. 20 Everything that she lies on during her impurity shall be unclean; also everything that she sits on shall be unclean. 21 Whoever touches her bed shall wash his clothes and bathe in water, and be unclean until evening. 22 And whoever touches anything that she sat on shall wash his clothes and bathe in water, and be unclean until evening. 23 If *anything* is on *her* bed or on anything on which she sits, when he touches it, he shall be unclean until evening. 24 And if any man lies with her at all, so that her impurity is on him, he shall be unclean seven days; and every bed on which he lies shall be unclean.

25 'If a woman has a discharge of blood for many days, other than at the time of her *customary* impurity, or if it runs beyond her *usual time of* impurity, all the days of her unclean discharge shall be as the days of her *customary* impurity. She *shall be* unclean. 26 Every bed on which she lies all the days of her discharge shall be to her as the bed of her impurity; and whatever she sits on shall be unclean, as the uncleanness of her impurity. 27 Whoever touches those things shall be unclean; he shall wash his clothes and bathe in water, and be unclean until evening.

28 'But if she is cleansed of her discharge, then she shall count for herself seven days, and after that she shall be clean. 29 And on the eighth day she shall take for herself two turtledoves or two young pigeons, and bring them to the priest, to the door of the tabernacle of meeting. 30 Then the priest shall offer the one *as* a sin offering and the other *as* a burnt offering, and the priest shall make atonement for her before the LORD for the discharge of her uncleanness.

31 'Thus you shall separate the children of Israel from their uncleanness, lest they die in their uncleanness when they defile My tabernacle that *is* among them. 32 This *is* the law for one who has a discharge, and *for him* who emits semen and is unclean thereby, 33 and for her who is indisposed because of her *customary* impurity, and for one who has a discharge, either man or woman, and for him who lies with her who is unclean.' "

16 Now the LORD spoke to Moses after the death of the two sons of Aaron, when they offered *profane fire* before the LORD, and died; 2 and the LORD said to Moses: "Tell Aaron your brother not to come at *just* any time into the Holy *Place* inside the veil, before the mercy seat which *is* on the ark, lest he die; for I will appear in the cloud above the mercy seat.

3 "Thus Aaron shall come into the Holy *Place*: with *the blood of* a young bull as a sin offering, and *of* a ram as a burnt offering. 4 He shall put the holy linen tunic and the linen trousers on his body; he shall be girded with a linen sash, and with the linen turban he shall be attired. These *are* holy garments. Therefore he shall wash his body in water, and put them on. 5 And he shall take from the congregation of the children of Israel two kids of the goats as a sin offering, and one ram as a burnt offering.

6 "Aaron shall offer the bull as a sin offering, which *is* for himself, and make atonement for himself and for his house. 7 He shall take the two goats and present them before the LORD *at* the door of the tabernacle of meeting. 8 Then Aaron shall cast lots for the two goats: one lot for the LORD and the other lot for the scapegoat. 9 And Aaron shall bring the goat on which the LORD's lot fell, and offer it *as* a sin offering. 10 But the goat on which the lot fell to be the scapegoat shall be presented alive before the LORD, to make atonement upon it, *and* to let it go as the scapegoat into the wilderness.

11 "And Aaron shall bring the bull of the sin offering, which is for himself, and make atonement for himself and for his house, and shall kill the bull as the sin offering which *is* for himself. 12 Then he shall take a censer full of burning coals of fire from the altar before the LORD, with his hands full of sweet incense beaten fine, and bring *it* inside the veil. 13 And he shall put the incense on the fire before the LORD, that the cloud of incense may cover the mercy seat that *is* on the Testimony, lest he die. 14 He shall take some of the blood of the bull and sprinkle *it* with his finger on the mercy seat on the east *side;* and before the mercy seat he shall sprinkle some of the blood with his finger seven times.

15 "Then he shall kill the goat of the sin offering, which *is* for the people, bring its blood inside the veil, do with that blood as he did with the blood of the bull, and sprinkle it on the mercy seat and before the mercy seat. 16 So he shall make atonement for the Holy *Place,* because of the uncleanness of the children of Israel, and because of their transgressions, for all their sins; and so he shall do for the tabernacle of meeting which remains among them in the midst of their uncleanness. 17 There shall be no man in the tabernacle of meeting when he goes in to make atonement in the Holy *Place,* until he comes out, that he may make atonement for himself, for his household, and for all the assembly of Israel. 18 And he shall go out to the altar that *is* before the LORD, and make atonement for it, and shall take some of the blood of the bull and some of the blood of the goat, and put it on the horns of the altar all around. 19 Then he shall sprinkle some of the blood on it with his finger seven times, cleanse it, and consecrate it from the uncleanness of the children of Israel.

20 "And when he has made an end of atoning for the Holy *Place,* the tabernacle of meeting, and the altar, he shall bring the live goat. 21 Aaron shall lay both his hands on the head of the live goat, confess over it all the iniquities of the children of Israel, and all their transgressions, concerning all their sins, putting them on the head of the goat, and shall send *it* away into the wilderness by the hand of a suitable man. 22 The goat shall bear on itself all their iniquities to an uninhabited land; and he shall release the goat in the wilderness.

23 "Then Aaron shall come into the tabernacle of meeting, shall take off the linen garments which he put on when he went into the Holy *Place,* and shall leave them there. 24 And he shall wash his body with water in a holy place, put on his garments, come out and offer his burnt offering and the burnt offering of the people, and make atonement for himself and for the people. 25 The fat of the sin offering he shall burn on the altar. 26 And he who released the goat as the scapegoat shall wash his clothes and bathe his body in water, and afterward he may come into the camp. 27 The bull *for* the sin offering and the goat *for* the sin offering, whose blood was brought in to make atonement in the Holy *Place,* shall be carried outside the camp. And they shall burn in the fire their skins, their flesh, and their offal. 28 Then he who burns them shall wash his clothes and bathe his body in water, and afterward he may come into the camp.

29 "*This* shall be a statute forever for you: In the seventh month, on the tenth *day* of the month, you shall afflict your souls, and do no work at all, *whether* a native of your own country or a stranger who dwells among you. 30 For on that day *the priest* shall make atonement for you, to cleanse you, *that* you may be clean from all your sins before the LORD. 31 It *is* a sabbath of solemn rest for you, and you shall afflict your souls. *It is* a statute forever. 32 And the priest, who is anointed and consecrated to minister as priest in his father's place, shall make atonement,

and put on the linen clothes, the holy garments; 33 then he shall make atonement for the Holy Sanctuary,[a] and he shall make atonement for the tabernacle of meeting and for the altar, and he shall make atonement for the priests and for all the people of the assembly. 34 This shall be an everlasting statute for you, to make atonement for the children of Israel, for all their sins, once a year." And he did as the LORD commanded Moses.

17 And the LORD spoke to Moses, saying, 2 "Speak to Aaron, to his sons, and to all the children of Israel, and say to them, 'This is the thing which the LORD has commanded, saying: 3 "Whatever man of the house of Israel who kills an ox or lamb or goat in the camp, or who kills it outside the camp, 4 and does not bring it to the door of the tabernacle of meeting to offer an offering to the LORD before the tabernacle of the LORD, the guilt of bloodshed shall be imputed to that man. He has shed blood; and that man shall be cut off from among his people, 5 to the end that the children of Israel may bring their sacrifices which they offer in the open field, that they may bring them to the LORD at the door of the tabernacle of meeting, to the priest, and offer them as peace offerings to the LORD. 6 And the priest shall sprinkle the blood on the altar of the LORD at the door of the tabernacle of meeting, and burn the fat for a sweet aroma to the LORD. 7 They shall no more offer their sacrifices to demons, after whom they have played the harlot. This shall be a statute forever for them throughout their generations." '

8 "Also you shall say to them: 'Whatever man of the house of Israel, or of the strangers who dwell among you, who offers a burnt offering or sacrifice, 9 and does not bring it to the door of the tabernacle of meeting, to offer it to the LORD, that man shall be cut off from among his people.

10 'And whatever man of the house of Israel, or of the strangers who dwell among you, who eats any blood, I will set My face against that person who eats blood, and will cut him off from among his people. 11 For the life of the flesh is in the blood, and I have given it to you upon the altar to make atonement for your souls; for it is the blood that makes atonement for the soul.' 12 Therefore I said to the children of Israel, 'No one among you shall eat blood, nor shall any stranger who dwells among you eat blood.'

13 "Whatever man of the children of Israel, or of the strangers who dwell among you, who hunts and catches any animal or bird that may be eaten, he shall pour out its blood and cover it with dust; 14 for it is the life of all flesh. Its blood sustains its life. Therefore I said to the children of Israel, 'You shall not eat the blood of any flesh, for the life of all flesh is its blood. Whoever eats it shall be cut off.'

15 "And every person who eats what died naturally or what was torn by beasts, whether he is a native of your own country or a stranger, he shall both wash his clothes and bathe in water, and be unclean until evening. Then he shall be clean. 16 But if he does not wash them or bathe his body, then he shall bear his guilt."

18 Then the LORD spoke to Moses, saying, 2 "Speak to the children of Israel, and say to them: 'I am the LORD your God. 3 According to the doings of the land of Egypt, where you dwelt, you shall not do; and according to the doings of the land of Canaan, where I am bringing you, you shall not do; nor shall you walk in their ordinances. 4 You shall observe My judgments and keep My ordinances, to walk in them: I am the LORD your God. 5 You shall therefore keep My statutes and My judgments, which if a man does, he shall live by them: I am the LORD.

6 'None of you shall approach anyone who is near of kin to him, to uncover his nakedness: I am the LORD. 7 The nakedness of your father or the nakedness of your mother you shall not uncover. She is your mother; you shall not uncover her nakedness. 8 The nakedness of your father's wife you shall not uncover; it is your father's nakedness. 9 The nakedness of your sister, the daughter of your father, or the daughter of your mother, whether born at home or elsewhere, their nakedness you shall not un-

16:33 [a]That is, the Most Holy Place

cover. 10 The nakedness of your son's daughter or your daughter's daughter, their nakedness you shall not uncover; for theirs *is* your own nakedness. 11 The nakedness of your father's wife's daughter, begotten by your father—she *is* your sister—you shall not uncover her nakedness. 12 You shall not uncover the nakedness of your father's sister; she *is* near of kin to your father. 13 You shall not uncover the nakedness of your mother's sister, for she *is* near of kin to your mother. 14 You shall not uncover the nakedness of your father's brother. You shall not approach his wife; she *is* your aunt. 15 You shall not uncover the nakedness of your daughter-in-law—she *is* your son's wife—you shall not uncover her nakedness. 16 You shall not uncover the nakedness of your brother's wife; it *is* your brother's nakedness. 17 You shall not uncover the nakedness of a woman and her daughter, nor shall you take her son's daughter or her daughter's daughter, to uncover her nakedness. They *are* near of kin to her. It *is* wickedness. 18 Nor shall you take a woman as a rival to her sister, to uncover her nakedness while the other is alive.

19 'Also you shall not approach a woman to uncover her nakedness as long as she is in her *customary* impurity. 20 Moreover you shall not lie carnally with your neighbor's wife, to defile yourself with her. 21 And you shall not let any of your descendants pass through *the fire* to Molech, nor shall you profane the name of your God: I *am* the LORD. 22 You shall not lie with a male as with a woman. It *is* an abomination. 23 Nor shall you mate with any animal, to defile yourself with it. Nor shall any woman stand before an animal to mate with it. It *is* perversion.

24 'Do not defile yourselves with any of these things; for by all these the nations are defiled, which I am casting out before you. 25 For the land is defiled; therefore I visit the punishment of its iniquity upon it, and the land vomits out its inhabitants. 26 You shall therefore keep My statutes and My judgments, and shall not commit *any* of these abominations, *either* any of your own nation or any stranger who dwells among you 27 (for all these abominations the

men of the land have done, who *were* before you, and thus the land is defiled), 28 lest the land vomit you out also when you defile it, as it vomited out the nations that *were* before you. 29 For whoever commits any of these abominations, the persons who commit *them* shall be cut off from among their people.

30 'Therefore you shall keep My ordinance, so that *you* do not commit *any* of these abominable customs which were committed before you, and that you do not defile yourselves by them: I *am* the LORD your God.' "

19 And the LORD spoke to Moses, saying, 2 "Speak to all the congregation of the children of Israel, and say to them: 'You shall be holy, for I the LORD your God *am* holy.

3 'Every one of you shall revere his mother and his father, and keep My Sabbaths: I *am* the LORD your God.

4 'Do not turn to idols, nor make for yourselves molded gods: I *am* the LORD your God.

5 'And if you offer a sacrifice of a peace offering to the LORD, you shall offer it of your own free will. 6 It shall be eaten the same day you offer *it,* and on the next day. And if any remains until the third day, it shall be burned in the fire. 7 And if it is eaten at all on the third day, it *is* an abomination. It shall not be accepted. 8 Therefore *everyone* who eats it shall bear his iniquity, because he has profaned the hallowed *offering* of the LORD; and that person shall be cut off from his people.

9 'When you reap the harvest of your land, you shall not wholly reap the corners of your field, nor shall you gather the gleanings of your harvest. 10 And you shall not glean your vineyard, nor shall you gather *every* grape of your vineyard; you shall leave them for the poor and the stranger: I *am* the LORD your God.

11 'You shall not steal, nor deal falsely, nor lie to one another. 12 And you shall not swear by My name falsely, nor shall you profane the name of your God: I *am* the LORD.

13 'You shall not cheat your neighbor, nor rob *him.* The wages of him who is hired shall not remain with you all night until morning. 14 You shall not curse the deaf, nor put a stumblingblock before the blind, but shall fear your God: I *am* the LORD.

15 'You shall do no injustice in judgment. You shall not be partial to the poor, nor honor the person of the mighty. In righteousness you shall judge your neighbor. 16 You shall not go about *as* a talebearer among your people; nor shall you take a stand against the life of your neighbor: I *am* the LORD.

17 'You shall not hate your brother in your heart. You shall surely rebuke your neighbor, and not bear sin because of him. 18 You shall not take vengeance, nor bear any grudge against the children of your people, but you shall love your neighbor as yourself: I *am* the LORD.

19 'You shall keep My statutes. You shall not let your livestock breed with another kind. You shall not sow your field with mixed seed. Nor shall a garment of mixed linen and wool come upon you.

20 'Whoever lies carnally with a woman who *is* betrothed to a man as a concubine, and who has not at all been redeemed nor given her freedom, for this there shall be scourging; *but* they shall not be put to death, because she was not free. 21 And he shall bring his trespass offering to the LORD, to the door of the tabernacle of meeting, a ram as a trespass offering. 22 The priest shall make atonement for him with the ram of the trespass offering before the LORD for his sin which he has committed. And the sin which he has committed shall be forgiven him.

23 'When you come into the land, and have planted all kinds of trees for food, then you shall count their fruit as uncircumcised. Three years it shall be as uncircumcised to you. *It* shall not be eaten. 24 But in the fourth year all its fruit shall be holy, a praise to the LORD. 25 And in the fifth year you may eat its fruit, that it may yield to you its increase: I *am* the LORD your God.

26 'You shall not eat *anything* with the blood, nor shall you practice divination or soothsaying. 27 You shall not shave around the sides of your head, nor shall you disfigure the edges of your beard. 28 You shall not make any cuttings in your flesh for the dead, nor tattoo any marks on you: I *am* the LORD.

29 'Do not prostitute your daughter, to cause her to be a harlot, lest the land fall into harlotry, and the land become full of wickedness.

30 'You shall keep My Sabbaths and reverence My sanctuary: I *am* the LORD.

31 'Give no regard to mediums and familiar spirits; do not seek after them, to be defiled by them: I *am* the LORD your God.

32 'You shall rise before the gray headed and honor the presence of an old man, and fear your God: I *am* the LORD.

33 'And if a stranger dwells with you in your land, you shall not mistreat him. 34 The stranger who dwells among you shall be to you as one born among you, and you shall love him as yourself; for you were strangers in the land of Egypt: I *am* the LORD your God.

35 'You shall do no injustice in judgment, in measurement of length, weight, or volume. 36 You shall have honest scales, honest weights, an honest ephah, and an honest hin: I *am* the LORD your God, who brought you out of the land of Egypt.

37 'Therefore you shall observe all My statutes and all My judgments, and perform them: I *am* the LORD.' "

20 Then the LORD spoke to Moses, saying, 2 "Again, you shall say to the children of Israel: 'Whoever of the children of Israel, or of the strangers who dwell in Israel, who gives *any* of his descendants to Molech, he shall surely be put to death. The people of the land shall stone him with stones. 3 I will set My face against that man, and will cut him off from his people, because he has given *some* of his descendants to Molech, to defile My sanctuary and profane My holy name. 4 And if the people of the land should in any way hide their eyes from the man, when he gives *some* of his descendants to Molech, and they do not kill him, 5 then I will set My face against that man and against his family; and I will cut him off from his people, and all who prostitute themselves with him to commit harlotry with Molech.

6 'And the person who turns to mediums and familiar spirits, to prostitute himself with them, I will set My face against that person and cut him off from his people. 7 Consecrate yourselves therefore, and be holy, for

I *am* the LORD your God. 8 And you shall keep My statutes, and perform them: I *am* the LORD who sanctifies you.

9 'For everyone who curses his father or his mother shall surely be put to death. He has cursed his father or his mother. His blood *shall be* upon him.

10 'The man who commits adultery with *another* man's wife, *he* who commits adultery with his neighbor's wife, the adulterer and the adulteress, shall surely be put to death. 11 The man who lies with his father's wife has uncovered his father's nakedness; both of them shall surely be put to death. Their blood *shall be* upon them. 12 If a man lies with his daughter-in-law, both of them shall surely be put to death. They have committed perversion. Their blood *shall be* upon them. 13 If a man lies with a male as he lies with a woman, both of them have committed an abomination. They shall surely be put to death. Their blood *shall be* upon them. 14 If a man marries a woman and her mother, it *is* wickedness. They shall be burned with fire, both he and they, that there may be no wickedness among you. 15 If a man mates with an animal, he shall surely be put to death, and you shall kill the animal. 16 If a woman approaches any animal and mates with it, you shall kill the woman and the animal. They shall surely be put to death. Their blood *is* upon them.

17 'If a man takes his sister, his father's daughter or his mother's daughter, and sees her nakedness and she sees his nakedness, it *is* a wicked thing. And they shall be cut off in the sight of their people. He has uncovered his sister's nakedness. He shall bear his guilt. 18 If a man lies with a woman during her sickness and uncovers her nakedness, he has exposed her flow, and she has uncovered the flow of her blood. Both of them shall be cut off from their people.

19 'You shall not uncover the nakedness of your mother's sister nor of your father's sister, for that would uncover his near of kin. They shall bear their guilt. 20 If a man lies with his uncle's wife, he has uncovered his uncle's nakedness. They shall bear their sin; they shall die childless. 21 If a man takes his brother's wife, it *is* an unclean thing. He has uncovered his brother's nakedness. They shall be childless.

22 'You shall therefore keep all My statutes and all My judgments, and perform them, that the land where I am bringing you to dwell may not vomit you out. 23 And you shall not walk in the statutes of the nation which I am casting out before you; for they commit all these things, and therefore I abhor them. 24 But I have said to you, "You shall inherit their land, and I will give it to you to possess, a land flowing with milk and honey." I *am* the LORD your God, who has separated you from the peoples. 25 You shall therefore distinguish between clean animals and unclean, between unclean birds and clean, and you shall not make yourselves abominable by beast or by bird, or by any kind of living thing that creeps on the ground, which I have separated from you as unclean. 26 And you shall be holy to Me, for I the LORD *am* holy, and have separated you from the peoples, that you should be Mine.

27 'A man or a woman who is a medium, or who has familiar spirits, shall surely be put to death; they shall stone them with stones. Their blood *shall be* upon them.' "

21 And the LORD said to Moses, "Speak to the priests, the sons of Aaron, and say to them: 'None shall defile himself for the dead among his people, 2 except for his relatives who are nearest to him: his mother, his father, his son, his daughter, and his brother; 3 also his virgin sister who is near to him, who has had no husband, for her he may defile himself. 4 *Otherwise* he shall not defile himself, *being* a chief man among his people, to profane himself.

5 'They shall not make any bald *place* on their heads, nor shall they shave the edges of their beards nor make any cuttings in their flesh. 6 They shall be holy to their God and not profane the name of their God, for they offer the offerings of the LORD made by fire, *and* the bread of their God; therefore they shall be holy. 7 They shall not take a wife *who is* a harlot or a defiled woman, nor shall they take a woman divorced

from her husband; for *the priest*[a] is holy to his God. 8 Therefore you shall consecrate him, for he offers the bread of your God. He shall be holy to you, for I the LORD, who sanctify you, *am* holy. 9 The daughter of any priest, if she profanes herself by playing the harlot, she profanes her father. She shall be burned with fire.

10 '*He who is* the high priest among his brethren, on whose head the anointing oil was poured and who is consecrated to wear the garments, shall not uncover his head nor tear his clothes; 11 nor shall he go near any dead body, nor defile himself for his father or his mother; 12 nor shall he go out of the sanctuary, nor profane the sanctuary of his God; for the consecration of the anointing oil of his God *is* upon him: I *am* the LORD. 13 And he shall take a wife in her virginity. 14 A widow or a divorced woman or a defiled woman *or* a harlot—these he shall not marry; but he shall take a virgin of his own people as wife. 15 Nor shall he profane his posterity among his people, for I the LORD sanctify him.' "

16 And the LORD spoke to Moses, saying, 17 "Speak to Aaron, saying: 'No man of your descendants in *succeeding* generations, who has *any* defect, may approach to offer the bread of his God. 18 For any man who has a defect shall not approach: a man blind or lame, who has a marred *face* or any *limb* too long, 19 a man who has a broken foot or broken hand, 20 or is a hunchback or a dwarf, or *a man* who has a defect in his eye, or eczema or scab, or is a eunuch. 21 No man of the descendants of Aaron the priest, who has a defect, shall come near to offer the offerings made by fire to the LORD. He has a defect; he shall not come near to offer the bread of his God. 22 He may eat the bread of his God, *both* the most holy and the holy; 23 only he shall not go near the veil or approach the altar, because he has a defect, lest he profane My sanctuaries; for I the LORD sanctify them.' "

24 And Moses told *it* to Aaron and his sons, and to all the children of Israel.

22 Then the LORD spoke to Moses, saying, 2 "Speak to Aaron and his sons, that they separate themselves from the holy things of the children of Israel, and that they do not profane My holy name *by* what they dedicate to Me: I *am* the LORD. 3 Say to them: 'Whoever of all your descendants throughout your generations, who goes near the holy things which the children of Israel dedicate to the LORD, while he has uncleanness upon him, that person shall be cut off from My presence: I *am* the LORD.

4 'Whatever man of the descendants of Aaron, who *is* a leper or has a discharge, shall not eat the holy offerings until he is clean. And whoever touches anything made unclean by a corpse, or a man who has had an emission of semen, 5 or whoever touches any creeping thing by which he would be made unclean, or any person by whom he would become unclean, whatever his uncleanness may be— 6 the person who has touched any such thing shall be unclean until evening, and shall not eat the holy *offerings* unless he washes his body with water. 7 And when the sun goes down he shall be clean; and afterward he may eat the holy *offerings*, because it *is* his food. 8 Whatever dies *naturally* or is torn *by beasts* he shall not eat, to defile himself with it: I *am* the LORD.

9 'They shall therefore keep My ordinance, lest they bear sin for it and die thereby, if they profane it: I the LORD sanctify them.

10 'No outsider shall eat the holy *offering*; one who dwells with the priest, or a hired servant, shall not eat the holy thing. 11 But if the priest buys a person with his money, he may eat it; and one who is born in his house may eat his food. 12 If the priest's daughter is married to an outsider, she may not eat of the holy offerings. 13 But if the priest's daughter is a widow or divorced, and has no child, and has returned to her father's house as in her youth, she may eat her father's food; but no outsider shall eat it.

14 'And if a man eats the holy *offering* unintentionally, then he shall restore a holy *offering* to the priest, and add one-fifth to it. 15 They shall not profane the holy *offerings* of the children of Israel, which they offer to the

21:7 [a]Literally *he*

LORD, 16 or allow them to bear the guilt of trespass when they eat their holy *offerings;* for I the LORD sanctify them.' "

17 And the LORD spoke to Moses, saying, 18 "Speak to Aaron and his sons, and to all the children of Israel, and say to them: 'Whatever man of the house of Israel, or of the strangers in Israel, who offers his sacrifice for any of his vows or for any of his freewill offerings, which they offer to the LORD as a burnt offering— 19 *you shall offer* of your own free will a male without blemish from the cattle, from the sheep, or from the goats. 20 Whatever has a defect, you shall not offer, for it shall not be acceptable on your behalf. 21 And whoever offers a sacrifice of a peace offering to the LORD, to fulfill *his* vow, or a freewill offering from the cattle or the sheep, it must be perfect to be accepted; there shall be no defect in it. 22 Those *that are* blind or broken or maimed, or have an ulcer or eczema or scabs, you shall not offer to the LORD, nor make an offering by fire of them on the altar to the LORD. 23 Either a bull or a lamb that has any limb too long or too short you may offer *as* a freewill offering, but for a vow it shall not be accepted.

24 'You shall not offer to the LORD what is bruised or crushed, or torn or cut; nor shall you make *any offering of them* in your land. 25 Nor from a foreigner's hand shall you offer any of these as the bread of your God, because their corruption *is* in them, *and* defects *are* in them. They shall not be accepted on your behalf.' "

26 And the LORD spoke to Moses, saying: 27 "When a bull or a sheep or a goat is born, it shall be seven days with its mother; and from the eighth day and thereafter it shall be accepted as an offering made by fire to the LORD. 28 *Whether it is* a cow or ewe, do not kill both her and her young on the same day. 29 And when you offer a sacrifice of thanksgiving to the LORD, offer *it* of your own free will. 30 On the same day it shall be eaten; you shall leave none of it until morning: I *am* the LORD.

31 "Therefore you shall keep My commandments, and perform them: I *am* the LORD. 32 You shall not profane My holy name, but I will be hallowed among the children of Israel. I *am* the LORD who sanctifies you,

33 who brought you out of the land of Egypt, to be your God: I *am* the LORD."

23 And the LORD spoke to Moses, saying, 2 "Speak to the children of Israel, and say to them: 'The feasts of the LORD, which you shall proclaim *to be* holy convocations, these *are* My feasts.

3 'Six days shall work be done, but the seventh day *is* a Sabbath of solemn rest, a holy convocation. You shall do no work *on it;* it *is* the Sabbath of the LORD in all your dwellings.

4 'These *are* the feasts of the LORD, holy convocations which you shall proclaim at their appointed times. 5 On the fourteenth *day* of the first month at twilight *is* the LORD's Passover. 6 And on the fifteenth day of the same month *is* the Feast of Unleavened Bread to the LORD; seven days you must eat unleavened bread. 7 On the first day you shall have a holy convocation; you shall do no customary work on it. 8 But you shall offer an offering made by fire to the LORD for seven days. The seventh day *shall be* a holy convocation; you shall do no customary work *on it.*' "

9 And the LORD spoke to Moses, saying, 10 "Speak to the children of Israel, and say to them: 'When you come into the land which I give to you, and reap its harvest, then you shall bring a sheaf of the firstfruits of your harvest to the priest. 11 He shall wave the sheaf before the LORD, to be accepted on your behalf; on the day after the Sabbath the priest shall wave it. 12 And you shall offer on that day, when you wave the sheaf, a male lamb of the first year, without blemish, as a burnt offering to the LORD. 13 Its grain offering *shall be* two-tenths *of an ephah* of fine flour mixed with oil, an offering made by fire to the LORD, for a sweet aroma; and its drink offering *shall be* of wine, one-fourth of a hin. 14 You shall eat neither bread nor parched grain nor fresh grain until the same day that you have brought an offering to your God; *it shall be* a statute forever throughout your generations in all your dwellings.

15 'And you shall count for yourselves from the day after the Sabbath, from the day that you brought the sheaf of the wave offering: seven

Sabbaths shall be completed. 16 Count fifty days to the day after the seventh Sabbath; then you shall offer a new grain offering to the LORD. 17 You shall bring from your dwellings two wave *loaves* of two-tenths *of an ephah.* They shall be of fine flour; they shall be baked with leaven. *They are* the firstfruits to the LORD. 18 And you shall offer with the bread seven lambs of the first year, without blemish, one young bull, and two rams. They shall be *as* a burnt offering to the LORD, with their grain offering and their drink offerings, an offering made by fire for a sweet aroma to the LORD. 19 Then you shall sacrifice one kid of the goats as a sin offering, and two male lambs of the first year as a sacrifice of a peace offering. 20 The priest shall wave them with the bread of the firstfruits *as* a wave offering before the LORD, with the two lambs. They shall be holy to the LORD for the priest. 21 And you shall proclaim on the same day *that* it is a holy convocation to you. You shall do no customary work *on it. It shall be* a statute forever in all your dwellings throughout your generations.

22 'When you reap the harvest of your land, you shall not wholly reap the corners of your field when you reap, nor shall you gather any gleaning from your harvest. You shall leave them for the poor and for the stranger: I *am* the LORD your God.' "

23 Then the LORD spoke to Moses, saying, 24 "Speak to the children of Israel, saying: 'In the seventh month, on the first *day* of the month, you shall have a sabbath-*rest*, a memorial of blowing of trumpets, a holy convocation. 25 You shall do no customary work *on it;* and you shall offer an offering made by fire to the LORD.' "

26 And the LORD spoke to Moses, saying: 27 "Also the tenth *day* of this seventh month *shall be* the Day of Atonement. It shall be a holy convocation for you; you shall afflict your souls, and offer an offering made by fire to the LORD. 28 And you shall do no work on that same day, for it *is* the Day of Atonement, to make atonement for you before the LORD your God. 29 For any person who is not afflicted *in soul* on that same day shall be cut off from his people. 30 And any person who does any

work on that same day, that person I will destroy from among his people. 31 You shall do no manner of work; *it shall be* a statute forever throughout your generations in all your dwellings. 32 It *shall be* to you a sabbath of *solemn* rest, and you shall afflict your souls; on the ninth *day* of the month at evening, from evening to evening, you shall celebrate your sabbath."

33 Then the LORD spoke to Moses, saying, 34 "Speak to the children of Israel, saying: 'The fifteenth day of this seventh month *shall be* the Feast of Tabernacles *for* seven days to the LORD. 35 On the first day *there shall be* a holy convocation. You shall do no customary work *on it.* 36 *For* seven days you shall offer an offering made by fire to the LORD. On the eighth day you shall have a holy convocation, and you shall offer an offering made by fire to the LORD. It *is* a sacred assembly, *and* you shall do no customary work *on it.*

37 'These *are* the feasts of the LORD which you shall proclaim *to be* holy convocations, to offer an offering made by fire to the LORD, a burnt offering and a grain offering, a sacrifice and drink offerings, everything on its day— 38 besides the Sabbaths of the LORD, besides your gifts, besides all your vows, and besides all your freewill offerings which you give to the LORD.

39 'Also on the fifteenth day of the seventh month, when you have gathered in the fruit of the land, you shall keep the feast of the LORD *for* seven days; on the first day *there shall be* a sabbath-*rest*, and on the eighth day a sabbath-*rest*. 40 And you shall take for yourselves on the first day the fruit of beautiful trees, branches of palm trees, the boughs of leafy trees, and willows of the brook; and you shall rejoice before the LORD your God for seven days. 41 You shall keep it as a feast to the LORD for seven days in the year. *It shall be* a statute forever in your generations. You shall celebrate it in the seventh month. 42 You shall dwell in booths for seven days. All who are native Israelites shall dwell in booths, 43 that your generations may know that I made the children of Israel dwell in booths when I brought them out of the land of Egypt: I *am* the LORD your God.' "

44 So Moses declared to the children of Israel the feasts of the Lord.

24 Then the Lord spoke to Moses, saying: 2 "Command the children of Israel that they bring to you pure oil of pressed olives for the light, to make the lamps burn continually. 3 Outside the veil of the Testimony, in the tabernacle of meeting, Aaron shall be in charge of it from evening until morning before the Lord continually; *it shall be* a statute forever in your generations. 4 He shall be in charge of the lamps on the pure *gold* lampstand before the Lord continually.

5 "And you shall take fine flour and bake twelve cakes with it. Two-tenths *of an ephah* shall be in each cake. 6 You shall set them in two rows, six in a row, on the pure *gold* table before the Lord. 7 And you shall put pure frankincense on *each* row, that it may be on the bread for a memorial, an offering made by fire to the Lord. 8 Every Sabbath he shall set it in order before the Lord continually, *being taken* from the children of Israel by an everlasting covenant. 9 And it shall be for Aaron and his sons, and they shall eat it in a holy place; for it *is* most holy to him from the offerings of the Lord made by fire, by a perpetual statute."

10 Now the son of an Israelite woman, whose father *was* an Egyptian, went out among the children of Israel; and this Israelite *woman's* son and a man of Israel fought each other in the camp. 11 And the Israelite woman's son blasphemed the name *of the* Lord and cursed; and so they brought him to Moses. (His mother's name *was* Shelomith the daughter of Dibri, of the tribe of Dan.) 12 Then they put him in custody, that the mind of the Lord might be shown to them.

13 And the Lord spoke to Moses, saying, 14 "Take outside the camp him who has cursed; then let all who heard *him* lay their hands on his head, and let all the congregation stone him. 15 "Then you shall speak to the children of Israel, saying: 'Whoever curses his God shall bear his sin. 16 And whoever blasphemes the name of the Lord shall surely be put to death. All the congregation shall certainly stone him, the stranger as well as him who is born in the land. When he blasphemes the name *of the* Lord, he shall be put to death. 17 'Whoever kills any man shall surely be put to death. 18 Whoever kills an animal shall make it good, animal for animal.

19 'If a man causes disfigurement of his neighbor, as he has done, so shall it be done to him— 20 fracture for fracture, eye for eye, tooth for tooth; as he has caused disfigurement of a man, so shall it be done to him. 21 And whoever kills an animal shall restore it; but whoever kills a man shall be put to death. 22 You shall have the same law for the stranger and for one from your own country; for I *am* the Lord your God.'"

23 Then Moses spoke to the children of Israel; and they took outside the camp him who had cursed, and stoned him with stones. So the children of Israel did as the Lord commanded Moses.

25 And the Lord spoke to Moses on Mount Sinai, saying, 2 "Speak to the children of Israel, and say to them: 'When you come into the land which I give you, then the land shall keep a sabbath to the Lord. 3 Six years you shall sow your field, and six years you shall prune your vineyard, and gather its fruit; 4 but in the seventh year there shall be a sabbath of solemn rest for the land, a sabbath to the Lord. You shall neither sow your field nor prune your vineyard. 5 What grows of its own accord of your harvest you shall not reap, nor gather the grapes of your untended vine, *for* it is a year of rest for the land. 6 And the sabbath *produce* of the land shall be food for you: for you, your male and female servants, your hired man, and the stranger who dwells with you, 7 for your livestock and the beasts that *are* in your land—all its produce shall be for food.

8 'And you shall count seven sabbaths of years for yourself, seven times seven years; and the time of the seven sabbaths of years shall be to you forty-nine years. 9 Then you shall cause the trumpet of the Jubilee to sound on the tenth *day* of the seventh month; on the Day of Atonement you shall make the trumpet to

sound throughout all your land.
10 And you shall consecrate the fiftieth year, and proclaim liberty throughout *all* the land to all its inhabitants. It shall be a Jubilee for you; and each of you shall return to his possession, and each of you shall return to his family. 11 That fiftieth year shall be a Jubilee to you; in it you shall neither sow nor reap what grows of its own accord, nor gather *the grapes* of your untended vine. 12 For it *is* the Jubilee; it shall be holy to you; you shall eat its produce from the field.

13 'In this Year of Jubilee, each of you shall return to his possession. 14 And if you sell anything to your neighbor or buy from your neighbor's hand, you shall not oppress one another. 15 According to the number of years after the Jubilee you shall buy from your neighbor, and according to the number of years of crops he shall sell to you. 16 According to the multitude of years you shall increase its price, and according to the fewer number of years you shall diminish its price; for he sells to you *according* to the number *of the years* of the crops. 17 Therefore you shall not oppress one another, but you shall fear your God; for I *am* the LORD your God.

18 'So you shall observe My statutes and keep My judgments, and perform them; and you will dwell in the land in safety. 19 Then the land will yield its fruit, and you will eat your fill, and dwell there in safety. 20 'And if you say, "What shall we eat in the seventh year, since we shall not sow nor gather in our produce?" 21 Then I will command My blessing on you in the sixth year, and it will bring forth produce enough for three years. 22 And you shall sow in the eighth year, and eat old produce until the ninth year; until its produce comes in, you shall eat *of* the old *harvest.*

23 'The land shall not be sold permanently, for the land *is* Mine; for you *are* strangers and sojourners with Me. 24 And in all the land of your possession you shall grant redemption of the land.

25 'If one of your brethren becomes poor, and has sold *some* of his possession, and if his redeeming relative comes to redeem it, then he may redeem what his brother sold.

26 Or if the man has no one to redeem it, but he himself becomes able to redeem it, 27 then let him count the years since its sale, and restore the remainder to the man to whom he sold it, that he may return to his possession. 28 But if he is not able to have *it* restored to himself, then what was sold shall remain in the hand of him who bought it until the Year of Jubilee; and in the Jubilee it shall be released, and he shall return to his possession.

29 'If a man sells a house in a walled city, then he may redeem it within a whole year after it is sold; *within* a full year he may redeem it. 30 But if it is not redeemed within the space of a full year, then the house in the walled city shall belong permanently to him who bought it, throughout his generations. It shall not be released in the Jubilee. 31 However the houses of villages which have no wall around them shall be counted as the fields of the country. They may be redeemed, and they shall be released in the Jubilee. 32 Nevertheless the cities of the Levites, *and* the houses in the cities of their possession, the Levites may redeem at any time. 33 And if a man purchases a house from the Levites, then the house that was sold in the city of his possession shall be released in the Jubilee; for the houses in the cities of the Levites *are* their possession among the children of Israel. 34 But the field of the common-land of their cities may not be sold, for it *is* their perpetual possession.

35 'If one of your brethren becomes poor, and falls into poverty among you, then you shall help him, like a stranger or a sojourner, that he may live with you. 36 Take no usury or interest from him; but fear your God, that your brother may live with you. 37 You shall not lend him your money for usury, nor lend him your food at a profit. 38 I *am* the LORD your God, who brought you out of the land of Egypt, to give you the land of Canaan *and* to be your God.

39 'And if *one of* your brethren *who dwells* by you becomes poor, and sells himself to you, you shall not compel him to serve as a slave. 40 As a hired servant *and* a sojourner he shall be with you, *and* shall serve you until the Year of Jubilee. 41 And *then* he shall depart from

Peace: It's All in the Word

When God gives His word, we know He will keep it (see Luke 21:33). His word is in fact a work already accomplished. It is known that in biblical times, the spoken word carried with it the same credibility as a legal written contract. Verbal oaths were binding agreements between two parties. In the speaking of the word, the work was literally accomplished.

This is still evident in the Middle East today. The common greeting, "Peace be with you," and "Peace be with you, also," is exchanged primarily among friends. For the speaking of the word, peace actually establishes peace.

In fact, should a disagreement break out between friends, or even new acquaintances, it is not uncommon for either party to ask for his "peace" back. The other person must return the peace with the phrase, "I give your peace back to you."

Unlike the peace of men, God has given us eternal peace in Jesus Christ (see Matt. 28:20). "Let not your heart be troubled; you believe in God, believe also in Me" (John 14:1).

What is peace? Peace is the inner knowledge that your relationship with God is secure. It is the assurance that your sins are forgiven. Your life is clean and new through the shed blood of Jesus.

Peace—it's all in the word. And the Living Word is the person and work of Jesus Christ. Look to Him for peace with God and peace with others. He will never take His peace from us for He said, "My peace I give to you; not as the world gives" (John 14:27). God's eternal peace will bring us into a loving, lasting relationship with Him forever.

you—he and his children with him—and shall return to his own family. He shall return to the possession of his fathers. 42 For they *are* My servants, whom I brought out of the land of Egypt; they shall not be sold as slaves. 43 You shall not rule over him with rigor, but you shall fear your God. 44 And as for your male and female slaves whom you may have—from the nations that are around you, from them you may buy male and female slaves. 45 Moreover you may buy the children of the strangers who dwell among you, and their families who are with you, which they beget in your land; and they shall become your property. 46 And you may take them as an inheritance for your children after you, to inherit *them as* a possession; they shall be your permanent slaves. But regarding your brethren, the children of Israel, you shall not rule over one another with rigor.

47 'Now if a sojourner or stranger close to you becomes rich, and *one of* your brethren *who dwells* by him becomes poor, and sells himself to the stranger *or* sojourner close to you, or to a member of the stranger's family, 48 after he is sold he may be redeemed again. One of his brothers may redeem him; 49 or his uncle or his uncle's son may redeem him; or *anyone* who is near of kin to him in his family may redeem him; or if he is able he may redeem himself. 50 Thus he shall reckon with him who bought him: The price of his release shall be according to the number of years, from the year that he was sold to him until the Year of Jubilee; *it shall be* according to the time of a hired servant for him. 51 If *there are* still many years *remaining,* according to them he shall repay the price of his redemption from the money with which he was bought. 52 And if there remain but a few years until the Year of Jubilee, then he shall reckon with him, *and* according to his years he shall repay him the price of his redemption. 53 He shall be with him as a yearly hired servant, and he shall not rule with rigor over him in your sight. 54 And if he is not redeemed in these *years,* then he shall be released in the Year of Jubilee—he and his children with him. 55 For the children of Israel *are* servants to Me; they *are* My servants

whom I brought out of the land of Egypt: I *am* the LORD your God.

26 'You shall not make idols for yourselves;
neither a carved image nor a *sacred* pillar shall you rear up for yourselves;
nor shall you set up an engraved stone in your land, to bow down to it;
for I *am* the LORD your God.

2   You shall keep My Sabbaths and reverence My sanctuary: I *am* the LORD.

3   'If you walk in My statutes and keep My commandments, and perform them,
4   then I will give you rain in its season, the land shall yield its produce, and the trees of the field shall yield their fruit.
5   Your threshing shall last till the time of vintage, and the vintage shall last till the time of sowing;
you shall eat your bread to the full, and dwell in your land safely.
6   I will give peace in the land, and you shall lie down, and none will make *you* afraid;
I will rid the land of evil beasts, and the sword will not go through your land.
7   You will chase your enemies, and they shall fall by the sword before you.
8   Five of you shall chase a hundred, and a hundred of you shall put ten thousand to flight;
your enemies shall fall by the sword before you.

9   'For I will look on you favorably and make you fruitful, multiply you and confirm My covenant with you.
10 You shall eat the old harvest, and clear out the old because of the new.
11 I will set My tabernacle among you, and My soul shall not abhor you.
12 I will walk among you and be your God, and you shall be My people.
13 I *am* the LORD your God, who

brought you out of the land
of Egypt, that *you* should not
be their slaves;
I have broken the bands of your
yoke and made you walk
upright.

14 'But if you do not obey Me, and
do not observe all these
commandments,
15 and if you despise My statutes,
or if your soul abhors My
judgments, so that you do not
perform all My
commandments, *but* break
My covenant,
16 I also will do this to you:
I will even appoint terror over
you, wasting disease and
fever which shall consume
the eyes and cause sorrow of
heart.
And you shall sow your seed
in vain, for your enemies
shall eat it.
17 I will set My face against you,
and you shall be defeated by
your enemies.
Those who hate you shall reign
over you, and you shall flee
when no one pursues you.

18 'And after all this, if you do not
obey Me, then I will punish
you seven times more for
your sins.
19 I will break the pride of your
power;
I will make your heavens like
iron and your earth like
bronze.
20 And your strength shall be
spent in vain;
for your land shall not yield its
produce, nor shall the trees
of the land yield their fruit.
21 'Then, if you walk contrary to
Me, and are not willing to
obey Me, I will bring on you
seven times more plagues,
according to your sins.
22 I will also send wild beasts
among you, which shall rob
you of your children, destroy
your livestock, and make you
few in number;
and your highways shall be
desolate.

23 'And if by these things you are
not reformed by Me, but walk
contrary to Me,

24 then I also will walk contrary
to you, and I will punish you
yet seven times for your sins.
25 And I will bring a sword
against you that will execute
the vengeance of the
covenant;
when you are gathered
together within your cities I
will send pestilence among
you;
and you shall be delivered into
the hand of the enemy.
26 When I have cut off your
supply of bread, ten women
shall bake your bread in one
oven, and they shall bring
back your bread by weight,
and you shall eat and not be
satisfied.

27 'And after all this, if you do not
obey Me, but walk contrary
to Me,
28 then I also will walk contrary
to you in fury;
and I, even I, will chastise you
seven times for your sins.
29 You shall eat the flesh of your
sons, and you shall eat the
flesh of your daughters.
30 I will destroy your high places,
cut down your incense altars,
and cast your carcasses on
the lifeless forms of your
idols;
and My soul shall abhor you.
31 I will lay your cities waste and
bring your sanctuaries to
desolation, and I will not
smell the fragrance of your
sweet aromas.
32 I will bring the land to
desolation, and your enemies
who dwell in it shall be
astonished at it.
33 I will scatter you among the
nations and draw out a sword
after you;
your land shall be desolate and
your cities waste.
34 Then the land shall enjoy its
sabbaths as long as it lies
desolate and you *are* in your
enemies' land;
then the land shall rest and
enjoy its sabbaths.
35 As long as *it* lies desolate it
shall rest—
for the time it did not rest on
your sabbaths when you
dwelt in it.

36 'And as for those of you who are
left, I will send faintness into
their hearts in the lands of
their enemies;
the sound of a shaken leaf shall
cause them to flee;
they shall flee as though fleeing
from a sword, and they shall
fall when no one pursues.
37 They shall stumble over one
another, as it were before a
sword, when no one pursues;
and you shall have no *power*
to stand before your enemies.
38 You shall perish among the
nations, and the land of your
enemies shall eat you up.
39 And those of you who are left
shall waste away in their
iniquity in your enemies'
lands;
also in their fathers' iniquities,
which are with them, they
shall waste away.

40 'But if they confess their
iniquity and the iniquity of
their fathers, with their
unfaithfulness in which they
were unfaithful to Me, and
that they also have walked
contrary to Me,
41 and *that* I also have walked
contrary to them and have
brought them into the land of
their enemies;
if their uncircumcised hearts
are humbled, and they accept
their guilt—
42 then I will remember My
covenant with Jacob, and My
covenant with Isaac and My
covenant with Abraham I
will remember;
I will remember the land.
43 The land also shall be left
empty by them, and will
enjoy its sabbaths while it
lies desolate without them;
they will accept their guilt,
because they despised My
judgments and because their
soul abhorred My statutes.
44 Yet for all that, when they are
in the land of their enemies,
I will not cast them away, nor
shall I abhor them, to utterly
destroy them and break My
covenant with them;
for I *am* the LORD their God.
45 But for their sake I will
remember the covenant of
their ancestors, whom I
brought out of the land of
Egypt in the sight of the
nations, that I might be their
God:
I *am* the LORD.' "

46 These *are* the statutes and judgments and laws which the LORD made
between Himself and the children of
Israel on Mount Sinai by the hand
of Moses.

27 Now the LORD spoke to Moses,
saying, 2 "Speak to the children of Israel, and say to them:
'When a man consecrates by a vow
certain persons to the LORD, according to your valuation, 3 if your valuation is of a male from twenty years
old up to sixty years old, then your
valuation shall be fifty shekels of silver, according to the shekel of the
sanctuary. 4 If it *is* a female, then
your valuation shall be thirty shekels; 5 and if from five years old up
to twenty years old, then your valuation for a male shall be twenty shekels, and for a female ten shekels;
6 and if from a month old up to five
years old, then your valuation for a
male shall be five shekels of silver,
and for a female your valuation shall
be three shekels of silver; 7 and if
from sixty years old and above, if *it
is* a male, then your valuation shall
be fifteen shekels, and for a female
ten shekels.
8 'But if he is too poor to pay your
valuation, then he shall present himself before the priest, and the priest
shall set a value for him; according
to the ability of him who vowed, the
priest shall value him.
9 'If *it is* an animal that men may
bring as an offering to the LORD, all
that *anyone* gives to the LORD shall
be holy. 10 He shall not substitute it
or exchange it, good for bad or bad
for good; and if he at all exchanges
animal for animal, then both it and
the one exchanged for it shall be
holy. 11 If *it is* an unclean animal
which they do not offer as a sacrifice
to the LORD, then he shall present the
animal before the priest; 12 and the
priest shall set a value for it, whether
it is good or bad; as you, the priest,
value it, so it shall be. 13 But if he
wants at all *to* redeem it, then he
must add one-fifth to your valuation.
14 'And when a man dedicates his

house *to be* holy to the LORD, then the priest shall set a value for it, whether it is good or bad; as the priest values it, so it shall stand. 15 If he who dedicated it *wants to* redeem his house, then he must add one-fifth of the money of your valuation to it, and it shall be his.

16 'If a man dedicates to the LORD *part* of a field of his possession, then your valuation shall be according to the seed for it. A homer of barley seed *shall be valued* at fifty shekels of silver. 17 If he dedicates his field from the Year of Jubilee, according to your valuation it shall stand. 18 But if he dedicates his field after the Jubilee, then the priest shall reckon to him the money due according to the years that remain till the Year of Jubilee, and it shall be deducted from your valuation. 19 And if he who dedicates the field ever wishes to redeem it, then he must add one-fifth of the money of your valuation to it, and it shall belong to him. 20 But if he does not want to redeem the field, or if he has sold the field to another man, it shall not be redeemed anymore; 21 but the field, when it is released in the Jubilee, shall be holy to the LORD, as a devoted field; it shall be the possession of the priest.

22 'And if a man dedicates to the LORD a field which he has bought, which is not the field of his possession, 23 then the priest shall reckon to him the worth of your valuation, up to the Year of Jubilee, and he shall give your valuation on that day *as a* holy *offering* to the LORD. 24 In the Year of Jubilee the field shall return to him from whom it was bought, to the one who *owned* the land as a possession. 25 And all your valuations shall be according to the shekel of the sanctuary: twenty gerahs to the shekel.

26 'But the firstborn of the animals, which should be the LORD's firstborn, no man shall dedicate; whether *it is* an ox or sheep, it *is* the LORD's. 27 And if *it is* an unclean animal, then he shall redeem *it* according to your valuation, and shall add one-fifth to it; or if it is not redeemed, then it shall be sold according to your valuation.

28 'Nevertheless no devoted *offering* that a man may devote to the LORD of all that he has, *both* man and beast, or the field of his possession, shall be sold or redeemed; every devoted *offering is* most holy to the LORD. 29 No person under the ban, who may become doomed to destruction among men, shall be redeemed, *but* shall surely be put to death. 30 And all the tithe of the land, *whether* of the seed of the land *or* of the fruit of the tree, *is* the LORD's. It *is* holy to the LORD. 31 If a man wants at all to redeem *any* of his tithes, he shall add one-fifth to it. 32 And concerning the tithe of the herd or the flock, of whatever passes under the rod, the tenth one shall be holy to the LORD. 33 He shall not inquire whether it is good or bad, nor shall he exchange it; and if he exchanges it at all, then both it and the one exchanged for it shall be holy; it shall not be redeemed.' "

34 These *are* the commandments which the LORD commanded Moses for the children of Israel on Mount Sinai.

Numbers

Overview of Numbers

Numbers is Moses' fourth book about the journey through the desert wilderness. Written around 1400 B.C., this book concerns events just prior to the people's entrance into the Promised Land. It records the service and worship of the people before God. Two "numberings" are listed which outline specific functions of worship and service of the people. The first numbering took place during the second year of the Israelites' wanderings in the wilderness, recording the generation of God's people who left the bondage of Egypt. The second was thirty-eight years later, recording the next generation just prior to their conquest of Canaan.

Numbers also records the successful conquest of Transjordan. From the lofty heights of their newly conquered territory, Moses and the people looked down over the land of Canaan. They had a "peak" experience that enabled them to have a "peek" into their future homeland. With their dream within reach, the people took the time to number themselves and rededicate their lives to God. They also organized and planned their life in the new land, allotting territories and assigning leaders to each tribe. They planned their future, for they knew they had to live there!

They believed their dream was already a reality! In their minds, they believed it before they achieved it! Faith is adventuring into new territories. The Israelites looked out over the land with anticipation, unafraid with God as their guide. They knew God would always be with them. They could not travel beyond His care and keeping.

Numbers is a great example of what a "peak" to "peek" experience can do in your life. When God gives you a beautiful success, then you can go out with confidence to do even more for Him!

Jesus in Numbers

Perhaps the clearest portrait of Christ in Numbers is the bronze serpent on the stake that Moses lifted up as a means of healing for those who had been snake-bitten, just as Jesus was lifted up on the cross as God's healing provision for our sin. The rock that provided water to quench the people's thirst and the daily manna from heaven also provide pictures of Jesus. And Balaam prophesies the Messiah's rule in Numbers 24:17.

Keys to Numbers

Key Word: Wanderings. Numbers records Israel's wandering in the wilderness for forty years before they finally were ready to enter into the land God had promised them.

Key Verses: "Because all these men who have seen My glory and the signs which I did in Egypt and in the wilderness, and have put Me to the test now these ten times, and have not heeded My voice, they certainly shall not see the land of which I swore to their fathers, nor shall any of those who rejected Me see it" (14:22, 23).

"Then the LORD spoke to Moses and Aaron, 'Because you did not believe Me, to hallow Me in the eyes of the children of Israel, therefore you shall not bring this assembly into the land which I have given them'" (20:12).

Key Chapter: Numbers 14. The critical turning point of Numbers occurs in chapter 14 when Israel chooses a negative path by rejecting God and refusing to go up and conquer the Promised Land.

1 Now the LORD spoke to Moses in the Wilderness of Sinai, in the tabernacle of meeting, on the first *day* of the second month, in the second year after they had come out of the land of Egypt, saying: 2 "Take a census of all the congregation of the children of Israel, by their families, by their fathers' houses, according to the number of names, every male individually, 3 from twenty years old and above—all who *are able to* go to war in Israel. You and Aaron shall number them by their armies. 4 And with you there shall be a man from every tribe, each one the head of his father's house.

5 "These are the names of the men who shall stand with you: from Reuben, Elizur the son of Shedeur; 6 from Simeon, Shelumiel the son of Zurishaddai; 7 from Judah, Nahshon the son of Amminadab; 8 from Issachar, Nethanel the son of Zuar; 9 from Zebulun, Eliab the son of Helon; 10 from the sons of Joseph: from Ephraim, Elishama the son of Ammihud; from Manasseh, Gamaliel the son of Pedahzur; 11 from Benjamin, Abidan the son of Gideoni; 12 from Dan, Ahiezer the son of Ammishaddai; 13 from Asher, Pagiel the son of Ocran; 14 from Gad, Eliasaph the son of Deuel;*a* 15 from Naphtali, Ahira the son of Enan." 16 These were chosen from the congregation, leaders of their fathers' tribes, heads of the divisions in Israel.

17 Then Moses and Aaron took these men who had been mentioned by name, 18 and they assembled all the congregation together on the first *day* of the second month; and they recited their ancestry by families, by their fathers' houses, according to the number of names, from twenty years old and above, each one individually. 19 As the LORD commanded Moses, so he numbered them in the Wilderness of Sinai.

20 Now the children of Reuben, Israel's oldest son, their genealogies by their families, by their fathers' house, according to the number of names, every male individually, from twenty years old and above, all who *were able to* go to war: 21 those who were numbered of the tribe of Reuben *were* forty-six thousand five hundred.

22 From the children of Simeon, their genealogies by their families, by their fathers' house, of those who were numbered, according to the number of names, every male individually, from twenty years old and above, all who *were able to* go to war: 23 those who were numbered of the tribe of Simeon *were* fifty-nine thousand three hundred.

24 From the children of Gad, their genealogies by their families, by

their fathers' house, according to the number of names, from twenty years old and above, all who *were able to* go to war: 25 those who were numbered of the tribe of Gad *were* forty-five thousand six hundred and fifty.

26 From the children of Judah, their genealogies by their families, by their fathers' house, according to the number of names, from twenty years old and above, all who *were able to* go to war: 27 those who were numbered of the tribe of Judah *were* seventy-four thousand six hundred.

28 From the children of Issachar, their genealogies by their families, by their fathers' house, according to the number of names, from twenty years old and above, all who *were able to* go to war: 29 those who were numbered of the tribe of Issachar *were* fifty-four thousand four hundred.

30 From the children of Zebulun, their genealogies by their families, by their fathers' house, according to the number of names, from twenty years old and above, all who *were able to* go to war: 31 those who were numbered of the tribe of Zebulun *were* fifty-seven thousand four hundred.

32 From the sons of Joseph, the children of Ephraim, their genealogies by their families, by their fathers' house, according to the number of names, from twenty years old and above, all who *were able to* go to war: 33 those who were numbered of the tribe of Ephraim *were* forty thousand five hundred.

34 From the children of Manasseh, their genealogies by their families, by their fathers' house, according to the number of names, from twenty years old and above, all who *were able to* go to war: 35 those who were numbered of the tribe of Manasseh *were* thirty-two thousand two hundred.

36 From the children of Benjamin, their genealogies by their families, by their fathers' house, according to the number of names, from twenty years old and above, all who *were able to* go to war: 37 those who were numbered of the tribe of Benjamin *were* thirty-five thousand four hundred.

38 From the children of Dan, their

1:14 *a*Spelled *Reuel* in 2:14

genealogies by their families, by their fathers' house, according to the number of names, from twenty years old and above, all who *were able to* go to war: 39 those who were numbered of the tribe of Dan *were* sixty-two thousand seven hundred.

40 From the children of Asher, their genealogies by their families, by their fathers' house, according to the number of names, from twenty years old and above, all who *were able to* go to war: 41 those who were numbered of the tribe of Asher *were* forty-one thousand five hundred.

42 From the children of Naphtali, their genealogies by their families, by their fathers' house, according to the number of names, from twenty years old and above, all who *were able to* go to war: 43 those who were numbered of the tribe of Naphtali *were* fifty-three thousand four hundred.

44 These are the ones who were numbered, whom Moses and Aaron numbered, with the leaders of Israel, twelve men, each one representing his father's house. 45 So all who were numbered of the children of Israel, by their fathers' houses, from twenty years old and above, all who *were able to* go to war in Israel— 46 all who were numbered were six hundred and three thousand five hundred and fifty.

47 But the Levites were not numbered among them by their fathers' tribe; 48 for the LORD had spoken to Moses, saying: 49 "Only the tribe of Levi you shall not number, nor take a census of them among the children of Israel; 50 but you shall appoint the Levites over the tabernacle of the Testimony, over all its furnishings, and over all things that belong to it; they shall carry the tabernacle and all its furnishings; they shall attend to it and camp around the tabernacle. 51 And when the tabernacle is to go forward, the Levites shall take it down; and when the tabernacle is to be set up, the Levites shall set it up. The outsider who comes near shall be put to death. 52 The children of Israel shall pitch their tents, everyone by his own camp, everyone by his own standard, according to their armies; 53 but the Levites shall camp around the tabernacle of the Testi-

mony, that there may be no wrath on the congregation of the children of Israel; and the Levites shall keep charge of the tabernacle of the Testimony."

54 Thus the children of Israel did; according to all that the LORD commanded Moses, so they did.

2 And the LORD spoke to Moses and Aaron, saying: 2 "Everyone of the children of Israel shall camp by his own standard, beside the emblems of his father's house; they shall camp some distance from the tabernacle of meeting. 3 On the east side, toward the rising of the sun, those of the standard of the forces with Judah shall camp according to their armies; and Nahshon the son of Amminadab *shall be* the leader of the children of Judah." 4 And his army was numbered at seventy-four thousand six-hundred.

5 "Those who camp next to him *shall be* the tribe of Issachar, and Nethanel the son of Zuar *shall be* the leader of the children of Issachar." 6 And his army was numbered at fifty-four thousand four hundred.

7 "Then *comes* the tribe of Zebulun, and Eliab the son of Helon *shall be* the leader of the children of Zebulun." 8 And his army was numbered at fifty-seven thousand four hundred. 9 "All who were numbered according to their armies of the forces with Judah, one hundred and eighty-six thousand four hundred—these shall break camp first.

10 "On the south side *shall be* the standard of the forces with Reuben according to their armies, and the leader of the children of Reuben *shall be* Elizur the son of Shedeur." 11 And his army was numbered at forty-six thousand five hundred.

12 "Those who camp next to him *shall be* the tribe of Simeon, and the leader of the children of Simeon *shall be* Shelumiel the son of Zurishaddai." 13 And his army was numbered at fifty-nine thousand three hundred.

14 "Then *comes* the tribe of Gad, and the leader of the children of Gad *shall be* Eliasaph the son of Reuel."[a] 15 And his army was numbered at forty-five thousand six hundred and fifty. 16 "All who were numbered according to their armies of the forces

2:14 [a]Spelled *Deuel* in 1:14 and 7:42

with Reuben, one hundred and fifty-one thousand four hundred and fifty—they shall be the second to break camp.

17 "And the tabernacle of meeting shall move out with the camp of the Levites in the middle of the camps; as they camp, so they shall move out, everyone in his place, by their standards.

18 "On the west side *shall be* the standard of the forces with Ephraim according to their armies, and the leader of the children of Ephraim *shall be* Elishama the son of Ammihud." 19 And his army was numbered at forty thousand five hundred.

20 "Next to him *comes* the tribe of Manasseh, and the leader of the children of Manasseh *shall be* Gamaliel the son of Pedahzur." 21 And his army was numbered at thirty-two thousand two hundred.

22 "Then *comes* the tribe of Benjamin, and the leader of the children of Benjamin *shall be* Abidan the son of Gideoni." 23 And his army was numbered at thirty-five thousand four hundred. 24 "All who were numbered according to their armies of the forces with Ephraim, one hundred and eight thousand one hundred—they shall be the third to break camp.

25 "The standard of the forces with Dan *shall be* on the north side according to their armies, and the leader of the children of Dan *shall be* Ahiezer the son of Ammishaddai." 26 And his army was numbered at sixty-two thousand seven hundred.

27 "Those who camp next to him *shall be* the tribe of Asher, and the leader of the children of Asher *shall be* Pagiel the son of Ocran." 28 And his army was numbered at forty-one thousand five hundred.

29 "Then *comes* the tribe of Naphtali, and the leader of the children of Naphtali *shall be* Ahira the son of Enan." 30 And his army was numbered at fifty-three thousand four hundred. 31 "All who were numbered of the forces with Dan, one hundred and fifty-seven thousand six hundred—they shall break camp last, with their standards."

32 These *are* the ones who were numbered of the children of Israel by their fathers' houses. All who were numbered according to their armies of the forces *were* six hundred and three thousand five hundred and fifty. 33 But the Levites were not numbered among the children of Israel, just as the LORD commanded Moses.

34 Thus the children of Israel did according to all that the LORD commanded Moses; so they camped by their standards and so they broke camp, each one by his family, according to their fathers' houses.

3 Now these *are* the records of Aaron and Moses when the LORD spoke with Moses on Mount Sinai. 2 And these *are* the names of the sons of Aaron: Nadab, the firstborn, and Abihu, Eleazar, and Ithamar. 3 These *are* the names of the sons of Aaron, the anointed priests, whom he consecrated to minister as priests. 4 Nadab and Abihu had died before the LORD when they offered profane fire before the LORD in the Wilderness of Sinai; and they had no children. So Eleazar and Ithamar ministered as priests in the presence of Aaron their father.

5 And the LORD spoke to Moses, saying: 6 "Bring the tribe of Levi near, and present them before Aaron the priest, that they may serve him. 7 And they shall attend to his needs and the needs of the whole congregation before the tabernacle of meeting, to do the work of the tabernacle. 8 Also they shall attend to all the furnishings of the tabernacle of meeting, and to the needs of the children of Israel, to do the work of the tabernacle. 9 And you shall give the Levites to Aaron and his sons; they *are* given entirely to him[a] from among the children of Israel. 10 So you shall appoint Aaron and his sons, and they shall attend to their priesthood; but the outsider who comes near shall be put to death."

11 Then the LORD spoke to Moses, saying: 12 "Now behold, I Myself have taken the Levites from among the children of Israel instead of every firstborn who opens the womb among the children of Israel. Therefore the Levites shall be Mine, 13 because all the firstborn *are* Mine. On the day that I struck all the firstborn in the land of Egypt, I sanctified to Myself all the firstborn in Israel,

3:9 [a]Samaritan Pentateuch and Septuagint read *Me*.

both man and beast. They shall be Mine: I *am* the LORD."

14 Then the LORD spoke to Moses in the Wilderness of Sinai, saying: 15 "Number the children of Levi by their fathers' houses, by their families; you shall number every male from a month old and above."

16 So Moses numbered them according to the word of the LORD, as he was commanded. 17 These were the sons of Levi by their names: Gershon, Kohath, and Merari. 18 And these *are* the names of the sons of Gershon by their families: Libni and Shimei. 19 And the sons of Kohath by their families: Amram, Izehar, Hebron, and Uzziel. 20 And the sons of Merari by their families: Mahli and Mushi. These *are* the families of the Levites by their fathers' houses.

21 From Gershon *came* the family of the Libnites and the family of the Shimites; these *were* the families of the Gershonites. 22 Those who were numbered, according to the number of all the males from a month old and above—of those who were numbered *there were* seven thousand five hundred. 23 The families of the Gershonites were to camp behind the tabernacle westward. 24 And the leader of the father's house of the Gershonites *was* Eliasaph the son of Lael. 25 The duties of the children of Gershon in the tabernacle of meeting *included* the tabernacle, the tent with its covering, the screen for the door of the tabernacle of meeting, 26 the screen for the door of the court, the hangings of the court which *are* around the tabernacle and the altar, and their cords, according to all the work relating to them.

27 From Kohath *came* the family of the Amramites, the family of the Izharites, the family of the Hebronites, and the family of the Uzzielites; these *were* the families of the Kohathites. 28 According to the number of all the males, from a month old and above, *there were* eight thousand six[a] hundred keeping charge of the sanctuary. 29 The families of the children of Kohath were to camp on the south side of the tabernacle. 30 And the leader of the fathers' house of the families of the Kohathites *was* Elizaphan the son of Uzziel. 31 Their duty *included* the ark, the ta-

ble, the lampstand, the altars, the utensils of the sanctuary with which they ministered, the screen, and all the work relating to them.

32 And Eleazar the son of Aaron the priest *was to be* chief over the leaders of the Levites, *with* oversight of those who kept charge of the sanctuary.

33 From Merari *came* the family of the Mahlites and the family of the Mushites; these *were* the families of Merari. 34 And those who were numbered, according to the number of all the males from a month old and above, *were* six thousand two hundred. 35 The leader of the fathers' house of the families of Merari *was* Zuriel the son of Abihail. These *were* to camp on the north side of the tabernacle. 36 And the appointed duty of the children of Merari *included* the boards of the tabernacle, its bars, its pillars, its sockets, its utensils, all the work relating to them, 37 and the pillars of the court all around, with their sockets, their pegs, and their cords.

38 Moreover those who were to camp before the tabernacle on the east, before the tabernacle of meeting, *were* Moses, Aaron, and his sons, keeping charge of the sanctuary, to meet the needs of the children of Israel; but the outsider who came near was to be put to death. 39 All who were numbered of the Levites, whom Moses and Aaron numbered at the commandment of the LORD, by their families, all the males from a month old and above, *were* twenty-two thousand.

40 Then the LORD said to Moses: "Number all the firstborn males of the children of Israel from a month old and above, and take the number of their names. 41 And you shall take the Levites for Me—I *am* the LORD— instead of all the firstborn among the children of Israel, and the livestock of the Levites instead of all the firstborn among the livestock of the children of Israel." 42 So Moses numbered all the firstborn among the children of Israel, as the LORD commanded him. 43 And all the firstborn males, according to the number of names from a month old and above, of those who were numbered of them, were twenty-two thousand two hundred and seventy-three.

3:28 [a]Some manuscripts of the Septuagint read *three*.

44 Then the LORD spoke to Moses, saying: 45 "Take the Levites instead of all the firstborn among the children of Israel, and the livestock of the Levites instead of their livestock. The Levites shall be Mine: I *am* the LORD. 46 And for the redemption of the two hundred and seventy-three of the firstborn of the children of Israel, who are more than the number of the Levites, 47 you shall take five shekels for each one individually; you shall take *them* in the currency of the shekel of the sanctuary, the shekel of twenty gerahs. 48 And you shall give the money, with which the excess number of them is redeemed, to Aaron and his sons."

49 So Moses took the redemption money from those who were over and above those who were redeemed by the Levites. 50 From the firstborn of the children of Israel he took the money, one thousand three hundred and sixty-five *shekels,* according to the shekel of the sanctuary. 51 And Moses gave their redemption money to Aaron and his sons, according to the word of the LORD, as the LORD commanded Moses.

4 Then the LORD spoke to Moses and Aaron, saying: 2 "Take a census of the sons of Kohath from among the children of Levi, by their families, by their fathers' house, 3 from thirty years old and above, even to fifty years old, all who enter the service to do the work in the tabernacle of meeting.

4 "This *is* the service of the sons of Kohath in the tabernacle of meeting, *relating to* the most holy things: 5 When the camp prepares to journey, Aaron and his sons shall come, and they shall take down the covering veil and cover the ark of the Testimony with it. 6 Then they shall put on it a covering of badger skins, and spread over *that* a cloth entirely of blue; and they shall insert its poles.

7 "On the table of showbread they shall spread a blue cloth, and put on it the dishes, the pans, the bowls, and the pitchers for pouring; and the showbread[a] shall be on it. 8 They shall spread over them a scarlet cloth, and cover the same with a covering of badger skins; and they shall insert its poles. 9 And they shall take a blue cloth and cover the lampstand of the light, with its lamps, its wick-trimmers, its trays, and all its oil vessels, with which they service it. 10 Then they shall put it with all its utensils in a covering of badger skins, and put *it* on a carrying beam.

11 "Over the golden altar they shall spread a blue cloth, and cover it with a covering of badger skins; and they shall insert its poles. 12 Then they shall take all the utensils of service with which they minister in the sanctuary, put *them* in a blue cloth, cover them with a covering of badger skins, and put *them* on a carrying beam. 13 Also they shall take away the ashes from the altar, and spread a purple cloth over it. 14 They shall put on it all its implements with which they minister there—the firepans, the forks, the shovels, the basins, and all the utensils of the altar—and they shall spread on it a covering of badger skins, and insert its poles. 15 And when Aaron and his sons have finished covering the sanctuary and all the furnishings of the sanctuary, when the camp is set to go, then the sons of Kohath shall come to carry *them;* but they shall not touch any holy thing, lest they die.

"These *are* the things in the tabernacle of meeting which the sons of Kohath are to carry.

16 "The appointed duty of Eleazar the son of Aaron the priest *is* the oil for the light, the sweet incense, the daily grain offering, the anointing oil, the oversight of all the tabernacle, of all that *is* in it, with the sanctuary and its furnishings."

17 Then the LORD spoke to Moses and Aaron, saying: 18 "Do not cut off the tribe of the families of the Kohathites from among the Levites; 19 but do this in regard to them, that they may live and not die when they approach the most holy things: Aaron and his sons shall go in and appoint each of them to his service and his task. 20 But they shall not go in to watch while the holy things are being covered, lest they die."

21 Then the LORD spoke to Moses, saying: 22 "Also take a census of the sons of Gershon, by their fathers' house, by their families. 23 From thirty years old and above, even to fifty years old, you shall number

4:7 aLiterally *the continual bread*

them, all who enter to perform the service, to do the work in the tabernacle of meeting. 24 This *is* the service of the families of the Gershonites, in serving and carrying: 25 They shall carry the curtains of the tabernacle and the tabernacle of meeting *with* its covering, the covering of badger skins that *is* on it, the screen for the door of the tabernacle of meeting, 26 the screen for the door of the gate of the court, the hangings of the court which *are* around the tabernacle and altar, and their cords, all the furnishings for their service and all that is made for these things: so shall they serve.

27 "Aaron and his sons shall assign all the service of the sons of the Gershonites, all their tasks and all their service. And you shall appoint to them all their tasks as their duty. 28 This *is* the service of the families of the sons of Gershon in the tabernacle of meeting. And their duties *shall be* under the authority[a] of Ithamar the son of Aaron the priest.

29 "*As for* the sons of Merari, you shall number them by their families and by their fathers' house. 30 From thirty years old and above, even to fifty years old, you shall number them, everyone who enters the service to do the work of the tabernacle of meeting. 31 And this *is* what they must carry as all their service for the tabernacle of meeting: the boards of the tabernacle, its bars, its pillars, its sockets, 32 and the pillars around the court with their sockets, pegs, and cords, with all their furnishings and all their service; and you shall assign *to each man* by name the items he must carry. 33 This *is* the service of the families of the sons of Merari, as all their service for the tabernacle of meeting, under the authority[a] of Ithamar the son of Aaron the priest."

34 And Moses, Aaron, and the leaders of the congregation numbered the sons of the Kohathites by their families and by their fathers' house, 35 from thirty years old and above, even to fifty years old, everyone who entered the service for work in the tabernacle of meeting; 36 and those who were numbered by their families were two thousand seven hundred and fifty. 37 These *were* the ones who

were numbered of the families of the Kohathites, all who might serve in the tabernacle of meeting, whom Moses and Aaron numbered according to the commandment of the LORD by the hand of Moses.

38 And those who were numbered of the sons of Gershon, by their families and by their fathers' house, 39 from thirty years old and above, even to fifty years old, everyone who entered the service for work in the tabernacle of meeting— 40 those who were numbered by their families, by their fathers' house, were two thousand six hundred and thirty. 41 These *are* the ones who were numbered of the families of the sons of Gershon, of all who might serve in the tabernacle of meeting, whom Moses and Aaron numbered according to the commandment of the LORD.

42 Those of the families of the sons of Merari who were numbered, by their families, by their fathers' house, 43 from thirty years old and above, even to fifty years old, everyone who entered the service for work in the tabernacle of meeting— 44 those who were numbered by their families were three thousand two hundred. 45 These *are* the ones who were numbered of the families of the sons of Merari, whom Moses and Aaron numbered according to the word of the LORD by the hand of Moses.

46 All who were numbered of the Levites, whom Moses, Aaron, and the leaders of Israel numbered, by their families and by their fathers' houses, 47 from thirty years old and above, even to fifty years old, everyone who came to do the work of service and the work of bearing burdens in the tabernacle of meeting— 48 those who were numbered were eight thousand five hundred and eighty. 49 According to the commandment of the LORD they were numbered by the hand of Moses, each according to his service and according to his task; thus were they numbered by him, as the LORD commanded Moses.

5 And the LORD spoke to Moses, saying: 2 "Command the children of Israel that they put out of the camp every leper, everyone who has a discharge, and whoever becomes de-

4:28 aLiterally *hand*   4:33 aLiterally *hand*

filed by a corpse. 3 You shall put out both male and female; you shall put them outside the camp, that they may not defile their camps in the midst of which I dwell." 4 And the children of Israel did so, and put them outside the camp; as the LORD spoke to Moses, so the children of Israel did.

5 Then the LORD spoke to Moses, saying, 6 "Speak to the children of Israel: 'When a man or woman commits any sin that men commit in unfaithfulness against the LORD, and that person is guilty, 7 then he shall confess the sin which he has committed. He shall make restitution for his trespass in full, plus one-fifth of it, and give it to the one he has wronged. 8 But if the man has no relative to whom restitution may be made for the wrong, the restitution for the wrong must go to the LORD for the priest, in addition to the ram of the atonement with which atonement is made for him. 9 Every offering of all the holy things of the children of Israel, which they bring to the priest, shall be his. 10 And every man's holy things shall be his; whatever any man gives the priest shall be his.' "

11 And the LORD spoke to Moses, saying, 12 "Speak to the children of Israel, and say to them: 'If any man's wife goes astray and behaves unfaithfully toward him, 13 and a man lies with her carnally, and it is hidden from the eyes of her husband, and it is concealed that she has defiled herself, and there was no witness against her, nor was she caught— 14 if the spirit of jealousy comes upon him and he becomes jealous of his wife, who has defiled herself; or if the spirit of jealousy comes upon him and he becomes jealous of his wife, although she has not defiled herself— 15 then the man shall bring his wife to the priest. He shall bring the offering required for her, one-tenth of an ephah of barley meal; he shall pour no oil on it and put no frankincense on it, because it is a grain offering of jealousy, an offering for remembering, for bringing iniquity to remembrance.

16 'And the priest shall bring her near, and set her before the LORD. 17 The priest shall take holy water in an earthen vessel, and take some of the dust that is on the floor of the tabernacle and put it into the water.

18 Then the priest shall stand the woman before the LORD, uncover the woman's head, and put the offering for remembering in her hands, which is the grain offering of jealousy. And the priest shall have in his hand the bitter water that brings a curse. 19 And the priest shall put her under oath, and say to the woman, "If no man has lain with you, and if you have not gone astray to uncleanness while under your husband's authority, be free from this bitter water that brings a curse. 20 But if you have gone astray while under your husband's authority, and if you have defiled yourself and some man other than your husband has lain with you"— 21 then the priest shall put the woman under the oath of the curse, and he shall say to the woman—"the LORD make you a curse and an oath among your people, when the LORD makes your thigh rot and your belly swell; 22 and may this water that causes the curse go into your stomach, and make your belly swell and your thigh rot."

'Then the woman shall say, "Amen, so be it."

23 'Then the priest shall write these curses in a book, and he shall scrape them off into the bitter water. 24 And he shall make the woman drink the bitter water that brings a curse, and the water that brings the curse shall enter her to become bitter. 25 Then the priest shall take the grain offering of jealousy from the woman's hand, shall wave the offering before the LORD, and bring it to the altar; 26 and the priest shall take a handful of the offering, as its memorial portion, burn it on the altar, and afterward make the woman drink the water. 27 When he has made her drink the water, then it shall be, if she has defiled herself and behaved unfaithfully toward her husband, that the water that brings a curse will enter her and become bitter, and her belly will swell, her thigh will rot, and the woman will become a curse among her people. 28 But if the woman has not defiled herself, and is clean, then she shall be free and may conceive children.

29 'This is the law of jealousy, when a wife, while under her husband's authority, goes astray and defiles herself, 30 or when the spirit of jealousy comes upon a man, and he becomes

jealous of his wife; then he shall stand the woman before the LORD, and the priest shall execute all this law upon her. 31 Then the man shall be free from iniquity, but that woman shall bear her guilt.' "

6 Then the LORD spoke to Moses, saying, 2 "Speak to the children of Israel, and say to them: 'When either a man or woman consecrates an offering to take the vow of a Nazirite, to separate himself to the LORD, 3 he shall separate himself from wine and *similar* drink; he shall drink neither vinegar made from wine nor vinegar made from *similar* drink; neither shall he drink any grape juice, nor eat fresh grapes or raisins. 4 All the days of his separation he shall eat nothing that is produced by the grapevine, from seed to skin.

5 'All the days of the vow of his separation no razor shall come upon his head; until the days are fulfilled for which he separated himself to the LORD, he shall be holy. *Then* he shall let the locks of the hair of his head grow. 6 All the days that he separates himself to the LORD he shall not go near a dead body. 7 He shall not make himself unclean even for his father or his mother, for his brother or his sister, when they die, because his separation to God *is* on his head. 8 All the days of his separation he shall be holy to the LORD.

9 'And if anyone dies very suddenly beside him, and he defiles his consecrated head, then he shall shave his head on the day of his cleansing; on the seventh day he shall shave it. 10 Then on the eighth day he shall bring two turtledoves or two young pigeons to the priest, to the door of the tabernacle of meeting; 11 and the priest shall offer one as a sin offering and *the* other as a burnt offering, and make atonement for him, because he sinned in regard to the corpse; and he shall sanctify his head that same day. 12 He shall consecrate to the LORD the days of his separation, and bring a male lamb in its first year as a trespass offering; but the former days shall be lost, because his separation was defiled.

13 'Now this *is* the law of the Nazirite: When the days of his separation are fulfilled, he shall be brought to the door of the tabernacle of meeting. 14 And he shall present his offering to the LORD: one male lamb in its first year without blemish as a burnt offering, one ewe lamb in its first year without blemish as a sin offering, one ram without blemish as a peace offering, 15 a basket of unleavened bread, cakes of fine flour mixed with oil, unleavened wafers anointed with oil, and their grain offering with their drink offerings.

16 'Then the priest shall bring *them* before the LORD and offer his sin offering and his burnt offering; 17 and he shall offer the ram as a sacrifice of a peace offering to the LORD, with the basket of unleavened bread; the priest shall also offer its grain offering and its drink offering. 18 Then the Nazirite shall shave his consecrated head *at* the door of the tabernacle of meeting, and shall take the hair from his consecrated head and put *it* on the fire which is under the sacrifice of the peace offering.

19 'And the priest shall take the boiled shoulder of the ram, one unleavened cake from the basket, and one unleavened wafer, and put *them* upon the hands of the Nazirite after he has shaved his consecrated *hair*, 20 and the priest shall wave them as a wave offering before the LORD; they *are* holy for the priest, together with the breast of the wave offering and the thigh of the heave offering. After that the Nazirite may drink wine.'

21 "This is the law of the Nazirite who vows to the LORD the offering for his separation, and besides that, whatever else his hand is able to provide; according to the vow which he takes, so he must do according to the law of his separation.' "

22 And the LORD spoke to Moses, saying: 23 "Speak to Aaron and his sons, saying, 'This is the way you shall bless the children of Israel. Say to them:

24 "The LORD bless you and keep you;
25 The LORD make His face shine upon you,
And be gracious to you;
26 The LORD lift up His countenance upon you,
And give you peace.' ' "

27 "So they shall put My name on the children of Israel, and I will bless them.''

7 Now it came to pass, when Moses had finished setting up the tabernacle, that he anointed it and consecrated it and all its furnishings, and the altar and all its utensils; so he anointed them and consecrated them. 2 Then the leaders of Israel, the heads of their fathers' houses, who *were* the leaders of the tribes and over those who were numbered, made an offering. 3 And they brought their offering before the LORD, six covered carts and twelve oxen, a cart for *every* two of the leaders, and for each one an ox; and they presented them before the tabernacle.

4 Then the LORD spoke to Moses, saying, 5 "Accept *these* from them, that they may be used in doing the work of the tabernacle of meeting; and you shall give them to the Levites, *to* every man according to his service." 6 So Moses took the carts and the oxen, and gave them to the Levites. 7 Two carts and four oxen he gave to the sons of Gershon, according to their service; 8 and four carts and eight oxen he gave to the sons of Merari, according to their service, under the authority[a] of Ithamar the son of Aaron the priest. 9 But to the sons of Kohath he gave none, because theirs *was* the service of the holy things, *which* they carried on their shoulders.

10 Now the leaders offered the dedication *offering* for the altar when it was anointed; so the leaders offered their offering before the altar. 11 For the LORD said to Moses, "They shall offer their offering, one leader each day, for the dedication of the altar."

12 And the one who offered his offering on the first day *was* Nahshon the son of Amminadab, from the tribe of Judah. 13 His offering *was* one silver platter, the weight of which *was* one hundred and thirty *shekels,* and one silver bowl of seventy shekels, according to the shekel of the sanctuary, both of them full of fine flour mixed with oil as a grain offering; 14 one gold pan of ten *shekels,* full of incense; 15 one young bull, one ram, and one male lamb in its first year, as a burnt offering; 16 one kid of the goats as a sin offering; 17 and for the sacrifice of peace offerings: two oxen, five rams, five male goats, and five male lambs in their first year. This *was* the offering of Nahshon the son of Amminadab.

18 On the second day Nethanel the son of Zuar, leader of Issachar, presented *an offering.* 19 *For* his offering he offered one silver platter, the weight of which *was* one hundred and thirty *shekels,* and one silver bowl of seventy shekels, according to the shekel of the sanctuary, both of them full of fine flour mixed with oil as a grain offering; 20 one gold pan of ten *shekels,* full of incense; 21 one young bull, one ram, and one male lamb in its first year, as a burnt offering; 22 one kid of the goats as a sin offering; 23 and as the sacrifice of peace offerings: two oxen, five rams, five male goats, and five male lambs in their first year. This *was* the offering of Nethanel the son of Zuar.

24 On the third day Eliab the son of Helon, leader of the children of Zebulun, *presented an offering.* 25 His offering *was* one silver platter, the weight of which *was* one hundred and thirty *shekels,* and one silver bowl of seventy shekels, according to the shekel of the sanctuary, both of them full of fine flour mixed with oil as a grain offering; 26 one gold pan of ten *shekels,* full of incense; 27 one young bull, one ram, and one male lamb in its first year, as a burnt offering; 28 one kid of the goats as a sin offering; 29 and for the sacrifice of peace offerings: two oxen, five rams, five male goats, and five male lambs in their first year. This *was* the offering of Eliab the son of Helon.

30 On the fourth day Elizur the son of Shedeur, leader of the children of Reuben, *presented an offering.* 31 His offering *was* one silver platter, the weight of which *was* one hundred and thirty *shekels,* and one silver bowl of seventy shekels, according to the shekel of the sanctuary, both of them full of fine flour mixed with oil as a grain offering; 32 one gold pan of ten *shekels,* full of incense; 33 one young bull, one ram, and one male lamb in its first year, as a burnt offering; 34 one kid of the goats as a sin offering; 35 and as the sacrifice of peace offerings: two oxen, five rams, five male goats, and five male lambs in their first year. This *was* the offering of Elizur the son of Shedeur.

7:8 *a*Literally *hand*

36 On the fifth day Shelumiel the son of Zurishaddai, leader of the children of Simeon, *presented an offering.* 37 His offering *was* one silver platter, the weight of which *was* one hundred and thirty *shekels,* and one silver bowl of seventy shekels, according to the shekel of the sanctuary, both of them full of fine flour mixed with oil as a grain offering; 38 one gold pan of ten *shekels,* full of incense; 39 one young bull, one ram, and one male lamb in its first year, as a burnt offering; 40 one kid of the goats as a sin offering; 41 and as the sacrifice of peace offerings: two oxen, five rams, five male goats, and five male lambs in their first year. This *was* the offering of Shelumiel the son of Zurishaddai.

42 On the sixth day Eliasaph the son of Deuel,*a* leader of the children of Gad, *presented an offering.* 43 His offering *was* one silver platter, the weight of which *was* one hundred and thirty *shekels,* and one silver bowl of seventy shekels, according to the shekel of the sanctuary, both of them full of fine flour mixed with oil as a grain offering; 44 one gold pan of ten *shekels,* full of incense; 45 one young bull, one ram, and one male lamb in its first year, as a burnt offering; 46 one kid of the goats as a sin offering; 47 and as the sacrifice of peace offerings: two oxen, five rams, five male goats, and five male lambs in their first year. This *was* the offering of Eliasaph the son of Deuel.

48 On the seventh day Elishama the son of Ammihud, leader of the children of Ephraim, *presented an offering.* 49 His offering *was* one silver platter, the weight of which *was* one hundred and thirty *shekels,* and one silver bowl of seventy shekels, according to the shekel of the sanctuary, both of them full of fine flour mixed with oil as a grain offering; 50 one gold pan of ten *shekels,* full of incense; 51 one young bull, one ram, and one male lamb in its first year, as a burnt offering; 52 one kid of the goats as a sin offering; 53 and as the sacrifice of peace offerings: two oxen, five rams, five male goats, and five male lambs in their first year. This *was* the offering of Elishama the son of Ammihud.

54 On the eighth day Gamaliel the son of Pedahzur, leader of the children of Manasseh, *presented an offering.* 55 His offering *was* one silver platter, the weight of which *was* one hundred and thirty *shekels,* and one silver bowl of seventy shekels, according to the shekel of the sanctuary, both of them full of fine flour mixed with oil as a grain offering; 56 one gold pan of ten *shekels,* full of incense; 57 one young bull, one ram, and one male lamb in its first year, as a burnt offering; 58 one kid of the goats as a sin offering; 59 and as the sacrifice of peace offerings: two oxen, five rams, five male goats, and five male lambs in their first year. This *was* the offering of Gamaliel the son of Pedahzur.

60 On the ninth day Abidan the son of Gideoni, leader of the children of Benjamin, *presented an offering.* 61 His offering *was* one silver platter, the weight of which *was* one hundred and thirty *shekels,* and one silver bowl of seventy shekels, according to the shekel of the sanctuary, both of them full of fine flour mixed with oil as a grain offering; 62 one gold pan of ten *shekels,* full of incense; 63 one young bull, one ram, and one male lamb in its first year, as a burnt offering; 64 one kid of the goats as a sin offering; 65 and as the sacrifice of peace offerings: two oxen, five rams, five male goats, and five male lambs in their first year. This *was* the offering of Abidan the son of Gideoni.

66 On the tenth day Ahiezer the son of Ammishaddai, leader of the children of Dan, *presented an offering.* 67 His offering *was* one silver platter, the weight of which *was* one hundred and thirty *shekels,* and one silver bowl of seventy shekels, according to the shekel of the sanctuary, both of them full of fine flour mixed with oil as a grain offering; 68 one gold pan of ten *shekels,* full of incense; 69 one young bull, one ram, and one male lamb in its first year, as a burnt offering; 70 one kid of the goats as a sin offering; 71 and as the sacrifice of peace offerings: two oxen, five rams, five male goats, and five male lambs in their first year. This *was* the offering of Ahiezer the son of Ammishaddai.

72 On the eleventh day Pagiel the son of Ocran, leader of the children

7:42 *a* Spelled *Reuel* in 2:14

of Asher, *presented an offering.*
73 His offering *was* one silver platter,
the weight of which *was* one hundred
and thirty *shekels,* and one silver
bowl of seventy shekels, according
to the shekel of the sanctuary, both
of them full of fine flour mixed with
oil as a grain offering; 74 one gold
pan of ten *shekels,* full of incense;
75 one young bull, one ram, and one
male lamb in its first year, as a burnt
offering; 76 one kid of the goats as a
sin offering; 77 and as the sacrifice of
peace offerings: two oxen, five rams,
five male goats, and five male lambs
in their first year. This *was* the offering of Pagiel the son of Ocran.

78 On the twelfth day Ahira the son
of Enan, leader of the children of
Naphtali, *presented an offering.*
79 His offering *was* one silver platter,
the weight of which *was* one hundred
and thirty *shekels,* and one silver
bowl of seventy shekels, according
to the shekel of the sanctuary, both
of them full of fine flour mixed with
oil as a grain offering; 80 one gold
pan of ten *shekels,* full of incense;
81 one young bull, one ram, and one
male lamb in its first year, as a burnt
offering; 82 one kid of the goats as a
sin offering; 83 and as the sacrifice of
peace offerings: two oxen, five rams,
five male goats, and five male lambs
in their first year. This *was* the offering of Ahira the son of Enan.

84 This *was* the dedication *offering*
for the altar from the leaders of Israel, when it was anointed: twelve
silver platters, twelve silver bowls,
and twelve gold pans. 85 Each silver
platter *weighed* one hundred and
thirty *shekels* and each bowl seventy
shekels. All the silver of the vessels
weighed two thousand four hundred
shekels, according to the shekel of
the sanctuary. 86 The twelve gold
pans full of incense *weighed* ten
shekels apiece, according to the
shekel of the sanctuary; all the gold
of the pans *weighed* one hundred and
twenty *shekels.* 87 All the oxen for
the burnt offering *were* twelve young
bulls, the rams twelve, the male
lambs in their first year twelve, with
their grain offering, and the kids of
the goats as a sin offering twelve.
88 And all the oxen for the sacrifice
of peace offerings were twenty-four
bulls, the rams sixty, the male goats
sixty, and the lambs in their first year
sixty. This *was* the dedication *offer-*

ing for the altar after it was anointed.

89 Now when Moses went into the
tabernacle of meeting to speak with
Him, he heard the voice of One
speaking to him from above the
mercy seat that *was* on the ark of the
Testimony, from between the two
cherubim; thus He spoke to him.

8 And the LORD spoke to Moses,
saying: 2 "Speak to Aaron, and
say to him, 'When you arrange the
lamps, the seven lamps shall give
light in front of the lampstand.'"
3 And Aaron did so; he arranged the
lamps to face toward the front of the
lampstand, as the LORD commanded
Moses. 4 Now this workmanship of
the lampstand *was* hammered gold;
from its shaft to its flowers it *was*
hammered work. According to the
pattern which the LORD had shown
Moses, so he made the lampstand.

5 Then the LORD spoke to Moses,
saying: 6 "Take the Levites from
among the children of Israel and
cleanse them *ceremonially.* 7 Thus
you shall do to them to cleanse them:
Sprinkle water of purification on
them, and let them shave all their
body, and let them wash their
clothes, and *so* make themselves
clean. 8 Then let them take a young
bull with its grain offering of fine
flour mixed with oil, and you shall
take another young bull as a sin offering. 9 And you shall bring the Levites before the tabernacle of meeting, and you shall gather together the
whole congregation of the children
of Israel. 10 So you shall bring the
Levites before the LORD, and the children of Israel shall lay their hands
on the Levites; 11 and Aaron shall offer the Levites before the LORD *like*
a wave offering from the children of
Israel, that they may perform the
work of the LORD. 12 Then the Levites
shall lay their hands on the heads of
the young bulls, and you shall offer
one as a sin offering and the other
as a burnt offering to the LORD, to
make atonement for the Levites.

13 "And you shall stand the Levites
before Aaron and his sons, and then
offer them *like* a wave offering to the
LORD. 14 Thus you shall separate the
Levites from among the children of
Israel, and the Levites shall be Mine.
15 After that the Levites shall go in
to service the tabernacle of meeting.
So you shall cleanse them and offer

them *like* a wave offering. 16 For they *are* wholly given to Me from among the children of Israel; I have taken them for Myself instead of all who open the womb, the firstborn of all the children of Israel. 17 For all the firstborn among the children of Israel *are* Mine, *both* man and beast; on the day that I struck all the firstborn in the land of Egypt I sanctified them to Myself. 18 I have taken the Levites instead of all the firstborn of the children of Israel. 19 And I have given the Levites as a gift to Aaron and his sons from among the children of Israel, to do the work for the children of Israel in the tabernacle of meeting, and to make atonement for the children of Israel, that there be no plague among the children of Israel when the children of Israel come near the sanctuary."

20 Thus Moses and Aaron and all the congregation of the children of Israel did to the Levites; according to all that the LORD commanded Moses concerning the Levites, so the children of Israel did to them. 21 And the Levites purified themselves and washed their clothes; then Aaron presented them *like* a wave offering before the LORD, and Aaron made atonement for them to cleanse them. 22 After that the Levites went in to do their work in the tabernacle of meeting before Aaron and his sons; as the LORD commanded Moses concerning the Levites, so they did to them.

23 Then the LORD spoke to Moses, saying, 24 "This *is* what *pertains* to the Levites: From twenty-five years old and above one may enter to perform service in the work of the tabernacle of meeting; 25 and at the age of fifty years they must cease performing this work, and shall work no more. 26 They may minister with their brethren in the tabernacle of meeting, to attend to needs, but they *themselves* shall do no work. Thus you shall do to the Levites regarding their duties."

9 Now the LORD spoke to Moses in the Wilderness of Sinai, in the first month of the second year after they had come out of the land of Egypt, saying: 2 "Let the children of Israel keep the Passover at its appointed time. 3 On the fourteenth day of this month, at twilight, you shall keep it at its appointed time. According to all its rites and ceremonies you shall keep it." 4 So Moses told the children of Israel that they should keep the Passover. 5 And they kept the Passover on the fourteenth day of the first month, at twilight, in the Wilderness of Sinai; according to all that the LORD commanded Moses, so the children of Israel did.

6 Now there were *certain* men who were defiled by a human corpse, so that they could not keep the Passover on that day; and they came before Moses and Aaron that day. 7 And those men said to him, "We *became* defiled by a human corpse. Why are we kept from presenting the offering of the LORD at its appointed time among the children of Israel?"

8 And Moses said to them, "Stand still, that I may hear what the LORD will command concerning you."

9 Then the LORD spoke to Moses, saying, 10 "Speak to the children of Israel, saying: 'If anyone of you or your posterity is unclean because of a corpse, or *is* far away on a journey, he may still keep the LORD's Passover. 11 On the fourteenth day of the second month, at twilight, they may keep it. They shall eat it with unleavened bread and bitter herbs. 12 They shall leave none of it until morning, nor break one of its bones. According to all the ordinances of the Passover they shall keep it. 13 But the man who *is* clean and is not on a journey, and ceases to keep the Passover, that same person shall be cut off from among his people, because he did not bring the offering of the LORD at its appointed time; that man shall bear his sin.

14 'And if a stranger dwells among you, and would keep the LORD's Passover, he must do so according to the rite of the Passover and according to its ceremony; you shall have one ordinance, both for the stranger and the native of the land.'"

15 Now on the day that the tabernacle was raised up, the cloud covered the tabernacle, the tent of the Testimony; from evening until morning it was above the tabernacle like the appearance of fire. 16 So it was always: the cloud covered it *by day*, and the appearance of fire by night. 17 Whenever the cloud was taken up from above the tabernacle, after that the children of Israel would journey;

and in the place where the cloud settled, there the children of Israel would pitch their tents. 18 At the command of the LORD the children of Israel would journey, and at the command of the LORD they would camp; as long as the cloud stayed above the tabernacle they remained encamped. 19 Even when the cloud continued long, many days above the tabernacle, the children of Israel kept the charge of the LORD and did not journey. 20 So it was, when the cloud was above the tabernacle a few days: according to the command of the LORD they would remain encamped, and according to the command of the LORD they would journey. 21 So it was, when the cloud remained only from evening until morning: when the cloud was taken up in the morning, then they would journey; whether by day or by night, whenever the cloud was taken up, they would journey. 22 *Whether it was* two days, a month, or a year that the cloud remained above the tabernacle, the children of Israel would remain encamped and not journey; but when it was taken up, they would journey. 23 At the command of the LORD they remained encamped, and at the command of the LORD they journeyed; they kept the charge of the LORD, at the command of the LORD by the hand of Moses.

10 And the LORD spoke to Moses, saying: 2 "Make two silver trumpets for yourself; you shall make them of hammered work; you shall use them for calling the congregation and for directing the movement of the camps. 3 When they blow both of them, all the congregation shall gather before you at the door of the tabernacle of meeting. 4 But if they blow *only* one, then the leaders, the heads of the divisions of Israel, shall gather to you. 5 When you sound the advance, the camps that lie on the east side shall then begin their journey. 6 When you sound the advance the second time, then the camps that lie on the south side shall begin their journey; they shall sound the call for them to begin their journeys. 7 And when the assembly is to be gathered together, you shall blow, but not sound the advance. 8 The sons of Aaron, the priests, shall blow the trumpets; and these shall be to you as an ordinance forever throughout your generations.

9 "When you go to war in your land against the enemy who oppresses you, then you shall sound an alarm with the trumpets, and you will be remembered before the LORD your God, and you will be saved from your enemies. 10 Also in the day of your gladness, in your appointed feasts, and at the beginning of your months, you shall blow the trumpets over your burnt offerings and over the sacrifices of your peace offerings; and they shall be a memorial for you before your God: I *am* the LORD your God."

11 Now it came to pass on the twentieth *day* of the second month, in the second year, that the cloud was taken up from above the tabernacle of the Testimony. 12 And the children of Israel set out from the Wilderness of Sinai on their journeys; then the cloud settled down in the Wilderness of Paran. 13 So they started out for the first time according to the command of the LORD by the hand of Moses.

14 The standard of the camp of the children of Judah set out first according to their armies; over their army was Nahshon the son of Amminadab. 15 Over the army of the tribe of the children of Issachar *was* Nethanel the son of Zuar. 16 And over the army of the tribe of the children of Zebulun *was* Eliab the son of Helon.

17 Then the tabernacle was taken down; and the sons of Gershon and the sons of Merari set out, carrying the tabernacle.

18 And the standard of the camp of Reuben set out according to their armies; over their army *was* Elizur the son of Shedeur. 19 Over the army of the tribe of the children of Simeon *was* Shelumiel the son of Zurishaddai. 20 And over the army of the tribe of the children of Gad *was* Eliasaph the son of Deuel.

21 Then the Kohathites set out, carrying the holy things. (The tabernacle would be prepared for their arrival.)

22 And the standard of the camp of the children of Ephraim set out according to their armies; over their army *was* Elishama the son of Ammihud. 23 Over the army of the tribe of the children of Manasseh *was* Gamaliel the son of Pedahzur.

24 And over the army of the tribe of the children of Benjamin *was* Abidan the son of Gideoni.
25 Then the standard of the camp of the children of Dan (the rear guard of all the camps) set out according to their armies; over their army *was* Ahiezer the son of Ammishaddai.
26 Over the army of the tribe of the children of Asher *was* Pagiel the son of Ocran. 27 And over the army of the tribe of the children of Naphtali *was* Ahira the son of Enan.
28 Thus *was* the order of march of the children of Israel, according to their armies, when they began their journey.
29 Now Moses said to Hobab the son of Reuel[a] the Midianite, Moses' father-in-law, "We are setting out for the place of which the LORD said, 'I will give it to you.' Come with us, and we will treat you well; for the LORD has promised good things to Israel."
30 And he said to him, "I will not go, but I will depart to my *own* land and to my relatives."
31 So *Moses* said, "Please do not leave, inasmuch as you know how we are to camp in the wilderness, and you can be our eyes. 32 And it shall be, if you go with us—indeed it shall be—that whatever good the LORD will do to us, the same we will do to you."
33 So they departed from the mountain of the LORD on a journey of three days; and the ark of the covenant of the LORD went before them for the three days' journey, to search out a resting place for them. 34 And the cloud of the LORD *was* above them by day when they went out from the camp.
35 So it was, whenever the ark set out, that Moses said:

"Rise up, O LORD!
Let Your enemies be scattered,
And let those who hate You flee
before You."

36 And when it rested, he said:

"Return, O LORD,
To the many thousands of
Israel."

11 Now *when* the people complained, it displeased the LORD; for the LORD heard *it,* and His anger

was aroused. So the fire of the LORD burned among them, and consumed *some* in the outskirts of the camp. 2 Then the people cried out to Moses, and when Moses prayed to the LORD, the fire was quenched. 3 So he called the name of the place Taberah,[a] because the fire of the LORD had burned among them.
4 Now the mixed multitude who were among them yielded to intense craving; so the children of Israel also wept again and said: "Who will give us meat to eat? 5 We remember the fish which we ate freely in Egypt, the cucumbers, the melons, the leeks, the onions, and the garlic; 6 but now our whole being *is* dried up; *there is* nothing at all except this manna *before* our eyes!"
7 Now the manna *was* like coriander seed, and its color like the color of bdellium. 8 The people went about and gathered *it,* ground *it* on millstones or beat *it* in the mortar, cooked *it* in pans, and made cakes of it; and its taste was like the taste of pastry prepared with oil. 9 And when the dew fell on the camp in the night, the manna fell on it.
10 Then Moses heard the people weeping throughout their families, everyone at the door of his tent; and the anger of the LORD was greatly aroused; Moses also was displeased. 11 So Moses said to the LORD, "Why have You afflicted Your servant? And why have I not found favor in Your sight, that You have laid the burden of all these people on me? 12 Did I conceive all these people? Did I beget them, that You should say to me, 'Carry them in your bosom, as a guardian carries a nursing child,' to the land which You swore to their fathers? 13 Where am I to get meat to give to all these people? For they weep all over me, saying, 'Give us meat, that we may eat.' 14 I am not able to bear all these people alone, because the burden *is* too heavy for me. 15 If You treat me like this, please kill me here and now—if I have found favor in Your sight—and do not let me see my wretchedness!"
16 So the LORD said to Moses: "Gather to Me seventy men of the elders of Israel, whom you know to be the elders of the people and officers over them; bring them to the tab-

ernacle of meeting, that they may stand there with you. 17 Then I will come down and talk with you there. I will take of the Spirit that *is* upon you and will put *the same* upon them; and they shall bear the burden of the people with you, that you may not bear *it* yourself alone. 18 Then you shall say to the people, 'Consecrate yourselves for tomorrow, and you shall eat meat; for you have wept in the hearing of the LORD, saying, "Who will give us meat to eat? For *it was* well with us in Egypt." Therefore the LORD will give you meat, and you shall eat. 19 You shall eat, not one day, nor two days, nor five days, nor ten days, nor twenty days, 20 but *for* a whole month, until it comes out of your nostrils and becomes loathsome to you, because you have despised the LORD who is among you, and have wept before Him, saying, "Why did we ever come up out of Egypt?" ' "

21 And Moses said, "The people whom I *am* among *are* six hundred thousand men on foot; yet You have said, 'I will give them meat, that they may eat *for* a whole month.' 22 Shall flocks and herds be slaughtered for them, to provide enough for them? Or shall all the fish of the sea be gathered together for them, to provide enough for them?"

23 And the LORD said to Moses, "Has the LORD's arm been shortened? Now you shall see whether what I say will happen to you or not."

24 So Moses went out and told the people the words of the LORD, and he gathered the seventy men of the elders of the people and placed them around the tabernacle. 25 Then the LORD came down in the cloud, and spoke to him, and took of the Spirit that *was* upon him, and placed *the same* upon the seventy elders; and it happened, when the Spirit rested upon them, that they prophesied, although they never did *so* again.*a*

26 But two men had remained in the camp: the name of one *was* Eldad, and the name of the other Medad. And the Spirit rested upon them. Now they *were* among those listed, but who had not gone out to the tabernacle; yet they prophesied in the camp. 27 And a young man ran and told Moses, and said, "Eldad and Me-

dad are prophesying in the camp."

28 So Joshua the son of Nun, Moses' assistant, *one* of his choice men, answered and said, "Moses my lord, forbid them!"

29 Then Moses said to him, "Are you zealous for my sake? Oh, that all the LORD's people were prophets *and* that the LORD would put His Spirit upon them!" 30 And Moses returned to the camp, he and the elders of Israel.

31 Now a wind went out from the LORD, and it brought quail from the sea and left *them* fluttering near the camp, about a day's journey on this side and about a day's journey on the other side, all around the camp, and about two cubits above the surface of the ground. 32 And the people stayed up all that day, all night, and all the next day, and gathered the quail (he who gathered least gathered ten homers); and they spread *them* out for themselves all around the camp. 33 But while the meat *was* still between their teeth, before it was chewed, the wrath of the LORD was aroused against the people, and the LORD struck the people with a very great plague. 34 So he called the name of that place Kibroth Hattaavah,*a* because there they buried the people who had yielded to craving.

35 From Kibroth Hattaavah the people moved to Hazeroth, and camped at Hazeroth.

12 Then Miriam and Aaron spoke against Moses because of the Ethiopian woman whom he had married; for he had married an Ethiopian woman. 2 So they said, "Has the LORD indeed spoken only through Moses? Has He not spoken through us also?" And the LORD heard *it*. 3 (Now the man Moses *was* very humble, more than all men who *were* on the face of the earth.)

4 Suddenly the LORD said to Moses, Aaron, and Miriam, "Come out, you three, to the tabernacle of meeting!" So the three came out. 5 Then the LORD came down in the pillar of cloud and stood *in* the door of the tabernacle, and called Aaron and Miriam. And they both went forward. 6 Then He said, "Hear now My words:

11:25 *a*Targum and Vulgate read *did not cease.*   11:34 *a*Literally *Graves of Craving*

"If there is a prophet among you,
  I, the LORD, make Myself
    known to him in a vision;
  I speak to him in a dream.
7 Not so with My servant Moses;
  He *is* faithful in all My house.
8 I speak with him face to face,
  Even plainly, and not in dark
    sayings;
  And he sees the form of the
    LORD.
  Why then were you not afraid
  To speak against My servant
    Moses?"

9 So the anger of the LORD was aroused against them, and He departed. 10 And when the cloud departed from above the tabernacle, suddenly Miriam *became* leprous, as *white as* snow. Then Aaron turned toward Miriam, and there she was, a leper. 11 So Aaron said to Moses, "Oh, my lord! Please do not lay *this* sin on us, in which we have done foolishly and in which we have sinned. 12 "Please do not let her be as one dead, whose flesh is half consumed when he comes out of his mother's womb!"

13 So Moses cried out to the LORD, saying, "Please heal her, O God, I pray!"

14 Then the LORD said to Moses, "If her father had but spit in her face, would she not be shamed seven days? Let her be shut out of the camp seven days, and afterward she may be received *again*." 15 So Miriam was shut out of the camp seven days, and the people did not journey till Miriam was brought in *again*. 16 And afterward the people moved from Hazeroth and camped in the Wilderness of Paran.

13 And the LORD spoke to Moses, saying, 2 "Send men to spy out the land of Canaan, which I am giving to the children of Israel; from each tribe of their fathers you shall send a man, every one a leader among them."

3 So Moses sent them from the Wilderness of Paran according to the command of the LORD, all of them men who *were* heads of the children of Israel. 4 Now these *were* their names: from the tribe of Reuben,

Shammua the son of Zaccur; 5 from the tribe of Simeon, Shaphat the son of Hori; 6 from the tribe of Judah, Caleb the son of Jephunneh; 7 from the tribe of Issachar, Igal the son of Joseph; 8 from the tribe of Ephraim, Hoshea[a] the son of Nun; 9 from the tribe of Benjamin, Palti the son of Raphu; 10 from the tribe of Zebulun, Gaddiel the son of Sodi; 11 from the tribe of Joseph, *that is,* from the tribe of Manasseh, Gaddi the son of Susi; 12 from the tribe of Dan, Ammiel the son of Gemalli; 13 from the tribe of Asher, Sethur the son of Michael; 14 from the tribe of Naphtali, Nahbi the son of Vophsi; 15 from the tribe of Gad, Geuel the son of Machi.

16 These *are* the names of the men whom Moses sent to spy out the land. And Moses called Hoshea[a] the son of Nun, Joshua.

17 Then Moses sent them to spy out the land of Canaan, and said to them, "Go up this *way* into the South, and go up to the mountains, 18 and see what the land is like: whether the people who dwell in it *are* strong or weak, few or many; 19 whether the land they dwell in *is* good or bad; whether the cities they inhabit *are* like camps or strongholds; 20 whether the land *is* rich or poor; and whether there are forests there or not. Be of good courage. And bring some of the fruit of the land." Now the time *was* the season of the first ripe grapes.

21 So they went up and spied out the land from the Wilderness of Zin as far as Rehob, near the entrance of Hamath. 22 And they went up through the South and came to Hebron; Ahiman, Sheshai, and Talmai, the descendants of Anak, *were* there. (Now Hebron was built seven years before Zoan in Egypt.) 23 Then they came to the Valley of Eshcol, and there cut down a branch with one cluster of grapes; they carried it between two of them on a pole. *They* also *brought* some of the pomegranates and figs. 24 The place was called the Valley of Eshcol,[a] because of the cluster which the men of Israel cut down there. 25 And they returned from spying out the land after forty days.

13:8 [a]Septuagint and Vulgate read *Oshea*.   13:16 [a]Septuagint and Vulgate read *Oshea*.
13:24 [a]Literally *Cluster*

26 Now they departed and came back to Moses and Aaron and all the congregation of the children of Israel in the Wilderness of Paran, at Kadesh; they brought back word to them and to all the congregation, and showed them the fruit of the land. 27 Then they told him, and said: "We went to the land where you sent us. It truly flows with milk and honey, and this is its fruit. 28 Nevertheless the people who dwell in the land are strong; the cities are fortified and very large; moreover we saw the descendants of Anak there. 29 The Amalekites dwell in the land of the South; the Hittites, the Jebusites, and the Amorites dwell in the mountains; and the Canaanites dwell by the sea and along the banks of the Jordan."

30 Then Caleb quieted the people before Moses, and said, "Let us go up at once and take possession, for we are well able to overcome it."

31 But the men who had gone up with him said, "We are not able to go up against the people, for they are stronger than we." 32 And they gave the children of Israel a bad report of the land which they had spied out, saying, "The land through which we have gone as spies is a land that devours its inhabitants, and all the people whom we saw in it are men of great stature. 33 There we saw the giants[a] (the descendants of Anak came from the giants); and we were like grasshoppers in our own sight, and so we were in their sight."

14 So all the congregation lifted up their voices and cried, and the people wept that night. 2 And all the children of Israel complained against Moses and Aaron, and the whole congregation said to them, "If only we had died in the land of Egypt! Or if only we had died in this wilderness! 3 Why has the LORD brought us to this land to fall by the sword, that our wives and children should become victims? Would it not be better for us to return to Egypt?" 4 So they said to one another, "Let us select a leader and return to Egypt."

5 Then Moses and Aaron fell on their faces before all the assembly of the congregation of the children of Israel.

6 But Joshua the son of Nun and Caleb the son of Jephunneh, who were among those who had spied out the land, tore their clothes; 7 and they spoke to all the congregation of the children of Israel, saying: "The land we passed through to spy out is an exceedingly good land. 8 If the LORD delights in us, then He will bring us into this land and give it to us, 'a land which flows with milk and honey.'[a] 9 Only do not rebel against the LORD, nor fear the people of the land, for they are our bread; their protection has departed from them, and the LORD is with us. Do not fear them."

10 And all the congregation said to stone them with stones. Now the glory of the LORD appeared in the tabernacle of meeting before all the children of Israel.

11 Then the LORD said to Moses: "How long will these people reject Me? And how long will they not believe Me, with all the signs which I have performed among them? 12 I will strike them with the pestilence and disinherit them, and I will make of you a nation greater and mightier than they."

13 And Moses said to the LORD: "Then the Egyptians will hear it, for by Your might You brought these people up from among them, 14 and they will tell it to the inhabitants of this land. They have heard that You, LORD, are among these people; that You, LORD, are seen face to face and Your cloud stands above them, and You go before them in a pillar of cloud by day and in a pillar of fire by night. 15 Now if You kill these people as one man, then the nations which have heard of Your fame will speak, saying, 16 'Because the LORD was not able to bring this people to the land which He swore to give them, therefore He killed them in the wilderness.' 17 And now, I pray, let the power of my Lord be great, just as You have spoken, saying, 18 'The LORD is longsuffering and abundant in mercy, forgiving iniquity and transgression; but He by no means clears the guilty, visiting the iniquity of the fathers on the children to the third and fourth generation.'[a] 19 Pardon the iniquity of this people, I pray, according to the great-

Two Spies

Moses and the Israelites arrived at the borders of the long-awaited Promised Land, Canaan. Unsure of what lay before them, Moses sent twelve spies into the country to spy out its condition and bring back a report to the Israelites.

Of the twelve spies, ten returned with a gloomy, despondent picture. The country was dominated by giants who were unconquerable and unwilling to give up their land. The advice of the ten spies was to remain in the desert.

Two spies, however, returned with a completely different picture. Joshua and Caleb reported seeing a land filled with milk and honey. Compared to the desert, the land was beautiful. It was filled with green rolling hills, freshwater springs, and lush fruit trees. Their advice was to move ahead.

These two possibility thinkers looked at the opportunities, not the obstacles. Their only mention of the existing people and armies that needed to be conquered was, "They *are* our bread; their protection has departed from them" (Num. 14:9). Their vision of the new land was greater than any problem that needed to be solved. In contrast, the other ten spies never mentioned the bounty of the country. They were too blinded by fear to see the good things God had prepared for them.

After the Israelites' forty years of wandering in the inhospitable wilderness because of their unbelief, Joshua and Caleb led the Israelites to conquer the land with a superb military strategy. Their reward was worth the effort.

In our lives, we must guard against missing beautiful opportunities because of seemingly insurmountable obstacles. We need to take on the attitude of the two spies and realize the possibilities before us. Once our eyes are set on the Lord, problems become minuscule and are easily solved. Then we truly can move ahead in faith. This is possibility thinking!

ness of Your mercy, just as You have forgiven this people, from Egypt even until now."

20 Then the LORD said: "I have pardoned, according to your word; 21 but truly, as I live, all the earth shall be filled with the glory of the LORD— 22 because all these men who have seen My glory and the signs which I did in Egypt and in the wilderness, and have put Me to the test now these ten times, and have not heeded My voice, 23 they certainly shall not see the land of which I swore to their fathers, nor shall any of those who rejected Me see it. 24 But My servant Caleb, because he has a different spirit in him and has followed Me fully, I will bring into the land where he went, and his descendants shall inherit it. 25 Now the Amalekites and the Canaanites dwell in the valley; tomorrow turn and move out into the wilderness by the Way of the Red Sea."

26 And the LORD spoke to Moses and Aaron, saying, 27 "How long shall I bear with this evil congregation who complain against Me? I have heard the complaints which the children of Israel make against Me. 28 Say to them, 'As I live,' says the LORD, 'just as you have spoken in My hearing, so I will do to you: 29 The carcasses of you who have complained against Me shall fall in this wilderness, all of you who were numbered, according to your entire number, from twenty years old and above. 30 Except for Caleb the son of Jephunneh and Joshua the son of Nun, you shall by no means enter the land which I swore I would make you dwell in. 31 But your little ones, whom you said would be victims, I will bring in, and they shall know the land which you have despised. 32 But as for you, your carcasses shall fall in this wilderness. 33 And your sons shall be shepherds in the wilderness forty years, and bear the brunt of your infidelity, until your carcasses are consumed in the wilderness. 34 According to the number of the days in which you spied out the land, forty days, for each day you shall bear your guilt one year, namely forty years, and you shall know My rejection. 35 I the LORD have spoken this. I will surely do so to all this evil congregation who are gathered together against Me. In this wilderness they shall be consumed, and there they shall die.' "

36 Now the men whom Moses sent to spy out the land, who returned and made all the congregation complain against him by bringing a bad report of the land, 37 those very men who brought the evil report about the land, died by the plague before the LORD. 38 But Joshua the son of Nun and Caleb the son of Jephunneh remained alive, of the men who went to spy out the land.

39 Then Moses told these words to all the children of Israel, and the people mourned greatly. 40 And they rose early in the morning and went up to the top of the mountain, saying, "Here we are, and we will go up to the place which the LORD has promised, for we have sinned!"

41 And Moses said, "Now why do you transgress the command of the LORD? For this will not succeed. 42 Do not go up, lest you be defeated by your enemies, for the LORD is not among you. 43 For the Amalekites and the Canaanites are there before you, and you shall fall by the sword; because you have turned away from the LORD, the LORD will not be with you."

44 But they presumed to go up to the mountaintop. Nevertheless, neither the ark of the covenant of the LORD nor Moses departed from the camp. 45 Then the Amalekites and the Canaanites who dwelt in that mountain came down and attacked them, and drove them back as far as Hormah.

15 And the LORD spoke to Moses, saying, 2 "Speak to the children of Israel, and say to them: 'When you have come into the land you are to inhabit, which I am giving to you, 3 and you make an offering by fire to the LORD, a burnt offering or a sacrifice, to fulfill a vow or as a freewill offering or in your appointed feasts, to make a sweet aroma to the LORD, from the herd or the flock, 4 then he who presents his offering to the LORD shall bring a grain offering of one-tenth of an ephah of fine flour mixed with one-fourth of a hin of oil; 5 and one-fourth of a hin of wine as a drink offering you shall prepare with the burnt offering or the sacrifice, for each lamb. 6 Or for a ram you shall prepare as a grain of-

fering two-tenths *of an ephah* of fine flour mixed with one-third of a hin of oil; 7 and as a drink offering you shall offer one-third of a hin of wine as a sweet aroma to the LORD. 8 And when you prepare a young bull as a burnt offering, or as a sacrifice to fulfill a vow, or as a peace offering to the LORD, 9 then shall be offered with the young bull a grain offering of three-tenths *of an ephah* of fine flour mixed with half a hin of oil; 10 and you shall bring as the drink offering half a hin of wine as an offering made by fire, a sweet aroma to the LORD.

11 'Thus it shall be done for each young bull, for each ram, or for each lamb or young goat. 12 According to the number that you prepare, so you shall do with everyone according to their number. 13 All who are native-born shall do these things in this manner, in presenting an offering made by fire, a sweet aroma to the LORD. 14 And if a stranger dwells with you, or whoever *is* among you throughout your generations, and would present an offering made by fire, a sweet aroma to the LORD, just as you do, so shall he do. 15 One ordinance *shall be* for you of the assembly and for the stranger who dwells *with you,* an ordinance forever throughout your generations; as you are, so shall the stranger be before the LORD. 16 One law and one custom shall be for you and for the stranger who dwells with you.' "[a]

17 Again the LORD spoke to Moses, saying, 18 "Speak to the children of Israel, and say to them: 'When you come into the land to which I bring you, 19 then it will be, when you eat of the bread of the land, that you shall offer up a heave offering to the LORD. 20 You shall offer up a cake of the first of your ground meal *as* a heave offering; as a heave offering of the threshing floor, so shall you offer it up. 21 Of the first of your ground meal you shall give to the LORD a heave offering throughout your generations.

22 'If you sin unintentionally, and do not observe all these commandments which the LORD has spoken to Moses— 23 all that the LORD has commanded you by the hand of Moses, from the day the LORD gave commandment and onward throughout your generations— 24 then it will be, if it is unintentionally committed, without the knowledge of the congregation, that the whole congregation shall offer one young bull as a burnt offering, as a sweet aroma to the LORD, with its grain offering and its drink offering, according to the ordinance, and one kid of the goats as a sin offering. 25 So the priest shall make atonement for the whole congregation of the children of Israel, and it shall be forgiven them, for it was unintentional; they shall bring their offering, an offering made by fire to the LORD, and their sin offering before the LORD, for their unintended sin. 26 It shall be forgiven the whole congregation of the children of Israel and the stranger who dwells among them, because all the people *did it* unintentionally.

27 'And if a person sins unintentionally, then he shall bring a female goat in its first year as a sin offering. 28 So the priest shall make atonement for the person who sins unintentionally, when he sins unintentionally before the LORD, to make atonement for him; and it shall be forgiven him. 29 You shall have one law for him who sins unintentionally, *for* him who is native-born among the children of Israel and for the stranger who dwells among them.

30 'But the person who does *anything* presumptuously, *whether he is* native-born or a stranger, that one brings reproach on the LORD, and he shall be cut off from among his people. 31 Because he has despised the word of the LORD, and has broken His commandment, that person shall be completely cut off; his guilt *shall be* upon him.' "

32 Now while the children of Israel were in the wilderness, they found a man gathering sticks on the Sabbath day. 33 And those who found him gathering sticks brought him to Moses and Aaron, and to all the congregation. 34 They put him under guard, because it had not been explained what should be done to him.

35 Then the LORD said to Moses, "The man must surely be put to death; all the congregation shall stone him with stones outside the camp." 36 So, as the LORD com-

15:16 aCompare Exodus 12:49

manded Moses, all the congregation brought him outside the camp and stoned him with stones, and he died.

37 Again the LORD spoke to Moses, saying, 38 "Speak to the children of Israel: Tell them to make tassels on the corners of their garments throughout their generations, and to put a blue thread in the tassels of the corners. 39 And you shall have the tassel, that you may look upon it and remember all the commandments of the LORD and do them, and that you *may* not follow the harlotry to which your own heart and your own eyes are inclined, 40 and that you may remember and do all My commandments, and be holy for your God. 41 I *am* the LORD your God, who brought you out of the land of Egypt, to be your God: I *am* the LORD your God."

16 Now Korah the son of Izhar, the son of Kohath, the son of Levi, with Dathan and Abiram the sons of Eliab, and On the son of Peleth, sons of Reuben, took *men;* 2 and they rose up before Moses with some of the children of Israel, two hundred and fifty leaders of the congregation, representatives of the congregation, men of renown. 3 They gathered together against Moses and Aaron, and said to them, "*You take* too much upon yourselves, for all the congregation *is* holy, every one of them, and the LORD *is* among them. Why then do you exalt yourselves above the assembly of the LORD?"

4 So when Moses heard *it,* he fell on his face; 5 and he spoke to Korah and all his company, saying, "Tomorrow morning the LORD will show who *is* His and *who is* holy, and will cause *him* to come near to Him. That one whom He chooses He will cause to come near to Him. 6 Do this: Take censers, Korah and all your company; 7 put fire in them and put incense in them before the LORD tomorrow, and it shall be *that* the man whom the LORD chooses *is* the holy one. *You take* too much upon yourselves, you sons of Levi!"

8 Then Moses said to Korah, "Hear now, you sons of Levi: 9 *Is it* a small thing to you that the God of Israel has separated you from the congregation of Israel, to bring you near to Himself, to do the work of the tabernacle of the LORD, and to stand before

the congregation to serve them; 10 and that He has brought you near *to Himself,* you and all your brethren, the sons of Levi, with you? And are you seeking the priesthood also? 11 Therefore you and all your company *are* gathered together against the LORD. And what *is* Aaron that you complain against him?"

12 And Moses sent to call Dathan and Abiram the sons of Eliab, but they said, "We will not come up! 13 *Is it* a small thing that you have brought us up out of a land flowing with milk and honey, to kill us in the wilderness, that you should keep acting like a prince over us? 14 Moreover you have not brought us into a land flowing with milk and honey, nor given us inheritance of fields and vineyards. Will you put out the eyes of these men? We will not come up!"

15 Then Moses was very angry, and said to the LORD, "Do not respect their offering. I have not taken one donkey from them, nor have I hurt one of them."

16 And Moses said to Korah, "Tomorrow, you and all your company be present before the LORD—you and they, as well as Aaron. 17 Let each take his censer and put incense in it, and each of you bring his censer before the LORD, two hundred and fifty censers; both you and Aaron, each *with* his censer." 18 So every man took his censer, put fire in it, laid incense on it, and stood at the door of the tabernacle of meeting with Moses and Aaron. 19 And Korah gathered all the congregation against them at the door of the tabernacle of meeting. Then the glory of the LORD appeared to all the congregation.

20 And the LORD spoke to Moses and Aaron, saying, 21 "Separate yourselves from among this congregation, that I may consume them in a moment."

22 Then they fell on their faces, and said, "O God, the God of the spirits of all flesh, shall one man sin, and You be angry with all the congregation?"

23 So the LORD spoke to Moses, saying, 24 "Speak to the congregation, saying, 'Get away from the tents of Korah, Dathan, and Abiram.' "

25 Then Moses rose and went to Dathan and Abiram, and the elders of Israel followed him. 26 And he spoke to the congregation, saying,

"Depart now from the tents of these wicked men! Touch nothing of theirs, lest you be consumed in all their sins." 27 So they got away from around the tents of Korah, Dathan, and Abiram; and Dathan and Abiram came out and stood at the door of their tents, with their wives, their sons, and their little children.

28 And Moses said: "By this you shall know that the LORD has sent me to do all these works, for *I have* not *done them* of my own will. 29 If these men die naturally like all men, or if they are visited by the common fate of all men, *then* the LORD has not sent me. 30 But if the LORD creates a new thing, and the earth opens its mouth and swallows them up with all that belongs to them, and they go down alive into the pit, then you will understand that these men have rejected the LORD."

31 Now it came to pass, as he finished speaking all these words, that the ground split apart under them, 32 and the earth opened its mouth and swallowed them up, with their households and all the men with Korah, with all *their* goods. 33 So they and all those with them went down alive into the pit; the earth closed over them, and they perished from among the assembly. 34 Then all Israel who *were* around them fled at their cry, for they said, "Lest the earth swallow us up *also!*"

35 And a fire came out from the LORD and consumed the two hundred and fifty men who were offering incense.

36 Then the LORD spoke to Moses, saying: 37 "Tell Eleazar, the son of Aaron the priest, to pick up the censers out of the blaze, for they are holy, and scatter the fire some distance away. 38 The censers of these men who sinned against their own souls, let them be made into hammered plates as a covering for the altar. Because they presented them before the LORD, therefore they are holy; and they shall be a sign to the children of Israel." 39 So Eleazar the priest took the bronze censers, which those who were burned up had presented, and they were hammered out as a covering on the altar, 40 *to be* a memorial to the children of Israel that no outsider, who *is* not a descendant of Aaron, should come near to offer incense before the LORD, that he might not become like Korah and his companions, just as the LORD had said to him through Moses.

41 On the next day all the congregation of the children of Israel complained against Moses and Aaron, saying, "You have killed the people of the LORD." 42 Now it happened, when the congregation had gathered against Moses and Aaron, that they turned toward the tabernacle of meeting; and suddenly the cloud covered it, and the glory of the LORD appeared. 43 Then Moses and Aaron came before the tabernacle of meeting.

44 And the LORD spoke to Moses, saying, 45 "Get away from among this congregation, that I may consume them in a moment."

And they fell on their faces.

46 So Moses said to Aaron, "Take a censer and put fire in it from the altar, put incense *on it*, and take it quickly to the congregation and make atonement for them; for wrath has gone out from the LORD. The plague has begun." 47 Then Aaron took *it* as Moses commanded, and ran into the midst of the assembly; and already the plague had begun among the people. So he put in the incense and made atonement for the people. 48 And he stood between the dead and the living; so the plague was stopped. 49 Now those who died in the plague were fourteen thousand seven hundred, besides those who died in the Korah incident. 50 So Aaron returned to Moses at the door of the tabernacle of meeting, for the plague had stopped.

17 And the LORD spoke to Moses, saying: 2 "Speak to the children of Israel, and get from them a rod from each father's house, all their leaders according to their fathers' houses—twelve rods. Write each man's name on his rod. 3 And you shall write Aaron's name on the rod of Levi. For there shall be one rod for the head of *each* father's house. 4 Then you shall place them in the tabernacle of meeting before the Testimony, where I meet with you. 5 And it shall be *that* the rod of the man whom I choose will blossom; thus I will rid Myself of the complaints of the children of Israel, which they make against you."

6 So Moses spoke to the children

of Israel, and each of their leaders gave him a rod apiece, for each leader according to their fathers' houses, twelve rods; and the rod of Aaron *was* among their rods. 7 And Moses placed the rods before the LORD in the tabernacle of witness.

8 Now it came to pass on the next day that Moses went into the tabernacle of witness, and behold, the rod of Aaron, of the house of Levi, had sprouted and put forth buds, had produced blossoms and yielded ripe almonds. 9 Then Moses brought out all the rods from before the LORD to all the children of Israel; and they looked, and each man took his rod. 10 And the LORD said to Moses, "Bring Aaron's rod back before the Testimony, to be kept as a sign against the rebels, that you may put their complaints away from Me, lest they die." 11 Thus did Moses; just as the LORD had commanded him, so he did.

12 So the children of Israel spoke to Moses, saying, "Surely we die, we perish, we all perish! 13 Whoever even comes near the tabernacle of the LORD must die. Shall we all utterly die?"

18 Then the LORD said to Aaron: "You and your sons and your father's house with you shall bear the iniquity *related to* the sanctuary, and you and your sons with you shall bear the iniquity *associated with* your priesthood. 2 Also bring with you your brethren of the tribe of Levi, the tribe of your father, that they may be joined with you and serve you while you and your sons *are* with you before the tabernacle of witness. 3 They shall attend to your needs and all the needs of the tabernacle; but they shall not come near the articles of the sanctuary and the altar, lest they die—they and you also. 4 They shall be joined with you and attend to the needs of the tabernacle of meeting, for all the work of the tabernacle; but an outsider shall not come near you. 5 And you shall attend to the duties of the sanctuary and the duties of the altar, that there *may* be no more wrath on the children of Israel. 6 Behold, I Myself have taken your brethren the Levites from among the children of Israel; *they are* a gift to you, given by the LORD, to do the work of the tabernacle of

meeting. 7 Therefore you and your sons with you shall attend to your priesthood for everything at the altar and behind the veil; and you shall serve. I give your priesthood *to you* as a gift for service, but the outsider who comes near shall be put to death."

8 And the LORD spoke to Aaron: "Here, I Myself have also given you charge of My heave offerings, all the holy gifts of the children of Israel; I have given them as a portion to you and your sons, as an ordinance forever. 9 This shall be yours of the most holy things *reserved* from the fire: every offering of theirs, every grain offering and every sin offering and every trespass offering which they render to Me, *shall be* most holy for you and your sons. 10 In a most holy *place* you shall eat it; every male shall eat it. It shall be holy to you.

11 This also *is* yours: the heave offering of their gift, with all the wave offerings of the children of Israel; I have given them to you, and your sons and daughters with you, as an ordinance forever. Everyone who is clean in your house may eat it.

12 "All the best of the oil, all the best of the new wine and the grain, their firstfruits which they offer to the LORD, I have given them to you. 13 Whatever first ripe fruit is in their land, which they bring to the LORD, shall be yours. Everyone who is clean in your house may eat it.

14 "Every devoted thing in Israel shall be yours.

15 "Everything that first opens the womb of all flesh, which they bring to the LORD, whether man or beast, shall be yours; nevertheless the firstborn of man you shall surely redeem, and the firstborn of unclean animals you shall redeem. 16 And those redeemed of the devoted things you shall redeem when one month old, according to your valuation, for five shekels of silver, according to the shekel of the sanctuary, which *is* twenty gerahs. 17 But the firstborn of a cow, the firstborn of a sheep, or the firstborn of a goat you shall not redeem; they *are* holy. You shall sprinkle their blood on the altar, and burn their fat *as* an offering made by fire for a sweet aroma to the LORD. 18 And their flesh shall be yours, just as the wave breast and the right thigh are yours.

19 "All the heave offerings of the holy things, which the children of Israel offer to the LORD, I have given to you and your sons and daughters with you as an ordinance forever; it *is* a covenant of salt forever before the LORD with you and your descendants with you."

20 Then the LORD said to Aaron: "You shall have no inheritance in their land, nor shall you have any portion among them; I *am* your portion and your inheritance among the children of Israel.

21 "Behold, I have given the children of Levi all the tithes in Israel as an inheritance in return for the work which they perform, the work of the tabernacle of meeting. 22 Hereafter the children of Israel shall not come near the tabernacle of meeting, lest they bear sin and die. 23 But the Levites shall perform the work of the tabernacle of meeting, and they shall bear their iniquity; *it shall be* a statute forever, throughout your generations, that among the children of Israel they shall have no inheritance. 24 For the tithes of the children of Israel, which they offer up *as* a heave offering to the LORD, I have given to the Levites as an inheritance; therefore I have said to them, 'Among the children of Israel they shall have no inheritance.' "

25 Then the LORD spoke to Moses, saying, 26 "Speak thus to the Levites, and say to them: 'When you take from the children of Israel the tithes which I have given you from them as your inheritance, then you shall offer up a heave offering of it to the LORD, a tenth of the tithe. 27 And your heave offering shall be reckoned to you as though *it were* the grain of the threshing floor and as the fullness of the winepress. 28 Thus you shall also offer a heave offering to the LORD from all your tithes which you receive from the children of Israel, and you shall give the LORD's heave offering from it to Aaron the priest. 29 Of all your gifts you shall offer up every heave offering due to the LORD, from all the best of them, the consecrated part of them.' 30 Therefore you shall say to them: 'When you have lifted up the best of it, then *the rest* shall be accounted to the Levites as the produce of the threshing floor and as the produce of the winepress. 31 You may eat it in any place, you and your households, for it *is* your reward for your work in the tabernacle of meeting. 32 And you shall bear no sin because of it, when you have lifted up the best of it. But you shall not profane the holy gifts of the children of Israel, lest you die.' "

19 Now the LORD spoke to Moses and Aaron, saying, 2 "This *is* the ordinance of the law which the LORD has commanded, saying: 'Speak to the children of Israel, that they bring you a red heifer without blemish, in which there *is* no defect *and* on which a yoke has never come. 3 You shall give it to Eleazar the priest, that he may take it outside the camp, and it shall be slaughtered before him; 4 and Eleazar the priest shall take some of its blood with his finger, and sprinkle some of its blood seven times directly in front of the tabernacle of meeting. 5 Then the heifer shall be burned in his sight: its hide, its flesh, its blood, and its offal shall be burned. 6 And the priest shall take cedar wood and hyssop and scarlet, and cast *them* into the midst of the fire burning the heifer. 7 Then the priest shall wash his clothes, he shall bathe in water, and afterward he shall come into the camp; the priest shall be unclean until evening. 8 And the one who burns it shall wash his clothes in water, bathe in water, and shall be unclean until evening. 9 Then a man *who is* clean shall gather up the ashes of the heifer, and store *them* outside the camp in a clean place; and they shall be kept for the congregation of the children of Israel for the water of purification;*a* it *is* for purifying from sin. 10 And the one who gathers the ashes of the heifer shall wash his clothes, and be unclean until evening. It shall be a statute forever to the children of Israel and to the stranger who dwells among them.

11 'He who touches the dead body of anyone shall be unclean seven days. 12 He shall purify himself with the water on the third day and on the seventh day; *then* he will be clean. But if he does not purify himself on the third day and on the seventh day,

19:9 *a*Literally *impurity*

he will not be clean. 13 Whoever touches the body of anyone who has died, and does not purify himself, defiles the tabernacle of the LORD. That person shall be cut off from Israel. He shall be unclean, because the water of purification was not sprinkled on him; his uncleanness *is* still on him.

14 'This *is* the law when a man dies in a tent: All who come into the tent and all who *are* in the tent shall be unclean seven days; 15 and every open vessel, which has no cover fastened on it, *is* unclean. 16 Whoever in the open field touches one who is slain by a sword or who has died, or a bone of a man, or a grave, shall be unclean seven days.

17 'And for an unclean *person* they shall take some of the ashes of the heifer burnt for purification from sin, and running water shall be put on them in a vessel. 18 A clean person shall take hyssop and dip *it* in the water, sprinkle *it* on the tent, on all the vessels, on the persons who were there, or on the one who touched a bone, the slain, the dead, or a grave. 19 The clean *person* shall sprinkle the unclean on the third day and on the seventh day; and on the seventh day he shall purify himself, wash his clothes, and bathe in water; and at evening he shall be clean.

20 'But the man who is unclean and does not purify himself, that person shall be cut off from among the assembly, because he has defiled the sanctuary of the LORD. The water of purification has not been sprinkled on him; he *is* unclean. 21 It shall be a perpetual statute for them. He who sprinkles the water of purification shall wash his clothes; and he who touches the water of purification shall be unclean until evening. 22 Whatever the unclean *person* touches shall be unclean; and the person who touches *it* shall be unclean until evening.'"

20 Then the children of Israel, the whole congregation, came into the Wilderness of Zin in the first month, and the people stayed in Kadesh; and Miriam died there and was buried there.

2 Now there was no water for the congregation; so they gathered together against Moses and Aaron. 3 And the people contended with Moses and spoke, saying: "If only we had died when our brethren died before the LORD! 4 Why have you brought up the assembly of the LORD into this wilderness, that we and our animals should die here? 5 And why have you made us come up out of Egypt, to bring us to this evil place? It *is* not a place of grain or figs or vines or pomegranates; nor *is* there any water to drink." 6 So Moses and Aaron went from the presence of the assembly to the door of the tabernacle of meeting, and they fell on their faces. And the glory of the LORD appeared to them.

7 Then the LORD spoke to Moses, saying, 8 "Take the rod; you and your brother Aaron gather the congregation together. Speak to the rock before their eyes, and it will yield its water; thus you shall bring water for them out of the rock, and give drink to the congregation and their animals." 9 So Moses took the rod from before the LORD as He commanded him.

10 And Moses and Aaron gathered the assembly together before the rock; and he said to them, "Hear now, you rebels! Must we bring water for you out of this rock?" 11 Then Moses lifted his hand and struck the rock twice with his rod; and water came out abundantly, and the congregation and their animals drank.

12 Then the LORD spoke to Moses and Aaron, "Because you did not believe Me, to hallow Me in the eyes of the children of Israel, therefore you shall not bring this assembly into the land which I have given them."

13 This *was* the water of Meribah,[a] because the children of Israel contended with the LORD, and He was hallowed among them.

14 Now Moses sent messengers from Kadesh to the king of Edom. "Thus says your brother Israel: 'You know all the hardship that has befallen us, 15 how our fathers went down to Egypt, and we dwelt in Egypt a long time, and the Egyptians afflicted us and our fathers. 16 When we cried out to the LORD, He heard our voice and sent the Angel and brought us up out of Egypt; now

20:13 aLiterally *Contention*

Water from a Rock

There is no hopeless situation until you become a hopeless person. From Moses, we learn a powerful lesson about believing in God's unlimited ability!

With God's help, Moses faced the mighty Pharaoh to lead the children of Israel out of Egypt. Even through forty years in the desert of Sinai, he stood fast in his faithfulness. In the vast, harsh wilderness, Moses looked to God to provide for the needs of his people. He learned the ancient survival secrets still practiced by the nomadic Bedouin shepherds who live in the Sinai desert today. A constant problem for Moses then and the Bedouins today is the scarcity of food and water. But to those who know its secrets, the desert holds many life-giving resources.

Every year thousands of quail migrate south from modern-day Turkey across the Mediterranean to the coast of Sinai and North Africa. Exhausted from their trans-Mediterranean flight, the quail fall to the desert sand of the Sinai coast. It was a simple task for Moses and the children of Israel to gather the quail, but the timing and large number of quail demonstrates God's supernatural power as "the Provider." "Now a wind went out from the LORD, and it brought quail from the sea and left *them* fluttering near the camp" (Num. 11:31). Today, as a variation of this practice, the Bedouin set up nets to entrap the tired quail for their meals.

The desert also provides water for the experienced traveler. The large, black granite mountains, rising sharply from the desert floor, hide reservoirs of water within their walls. Rainfall seeps into the mountain crevices and is trapped in the porous limestone veins woven throughout the granite cliffs. One sharp blow of a staff to the limestone brings forth a gushing stream of water.

Moses knew of this common practice. Yet God asked Moses to perform the uncommon. He told Moses to go and speak to the rock. Moses, accustomed to hitting the rock, failed to recognize God's unlimited abilities. Moses was so skilled in the ordinary that he did not see God's power at work. He expected God to provide the water for that vast number of people in the ordinary way. God wanted to do something extraordinary.

God's plan for our lives may include extraordinary opportunities. Be open to the possibility of His doing the impossible in your life. Believe in God's unlimited ability!

here we are in Kadesh, a city on the edge of your border. 17 Please let us pass through your country. We will not pass through fields or vineyards, nor will we drink water from wells; we will go along the King's Highway; we will not turn aside to the right hand or to the left until we have passed through your territory.' "

18 Then Edom said to him, "You shall not pass through my *land,* lest I come out against you with the sword."

19 So the children of Israel said to him, "We will go by the Highway, and if I or my livestock drink any of your water, then I will pay for it; let me only pass through on foot, nothing *more.*"

20 Then he said, "You shall not pass through." So Edom came out against them with many men and with a strong hand. 21 Thus Edom refused to give Israel passage through his territory; so Israel turned away from him.

22 Now the children of Israel, the whole congregation, journeyed from Kadesh and came to Mount Hor. 23 And the LORD spoke to Moses and Aaron in Mount Hor by the border of the land of Edom, saying: 24 "Aaron shall be gathered to his people, for he shall not enter the land which I have given to the children of Israel, because you rebelled against My word at the water of Meribah. 25 Take Aaron and Eleazar his son, and bring them up to Mount Hor; 26 and strip Aaron of his garments and put them on Eleazar his son; for Aaron shall be gathered *to his people* and die there." 27 So Moses did just as the LORD commanded, and they went up to Mount Hor in the sight of all the congregation. 28 Moses stripped Aaron of his garments and put them on Eleazar his son; and Aaron died there on the top of the mountain. Then Moses and Eleazar came down from the mountain. 29 Now when all the congregation saw that Aaron was dead, all the house of Israel mourned for Aaron thirty days.

21 The king of Arad, the Canaanite, who dwelt in the South, heard that Israel was coming on the road to Atharim. Then he fought against Israel and took *some* of them prisoners. 2 So Israel made a vow to the LORD, and said, "If You will indeed deliver this people into my hand, then I will utterly destroy their cities." 3 And the LORD listened to the voice of Israel and delivered up the Canaanites, and they utterly destroyed them and their cities. So the name of that place was called Hormah.*a*

4 Then they journeyed from Mount Hor by the Way of the Red Sea, to go around the land of Edom; and the soul of the people became very discouraged on the way. 5 And the people spoke against God and against Moses: "Why have you brought us up out of Egypt to die in the wilderness? For *there is* no food and no water, and our soul loathes this worthless bread." 6 So the LORD sent fiery serpents among the people, and they bit the people; and many of the people of Israel died.

7 Therefore the people came to Moses, and said, "We have sinned, for we have spoken against the LORD and against you; pray to the LORD that He take away the serpents from us." So Moses prayed for the people.

8 Then the LORD said to Moses, "Make a fiery *serpent,* and set it on a pole; and it shall be that everyone who is bitten, when he looks at it, shall live." 9 So Moses made a bronze serpent, and put it on a pole; and so it was, if a serpent had bitten anyone, when he looked at the bronze serpent, he lived.

10 Now the children of Israel moved on and camped in Oboth. 11 And they journeyed from Oboth and camped at Ije Abarim, in the wilderness which *is* east of Moab, toward the sunrise. 12 From there they moved and camped in the Valley of Zered. 13 From there they moved and camped on the other side of the Arnon, which *is* in the wilderness that extends from the border of the Amorites; for the Arnon *is* the border of Moab, between Moab and the Amorites. 14 Therefore it is said in the Book of the Wars of the LORD:

"Waheb in Suphah,*a*
    The brooks of the Arnon,

21:3 *a*Literally *Utter Destruction*   21:14 *a*Ancient unknown places; Vulgate reads *what He did in the Red Sea.*

Allow God

A little-understood scripture is Jesus' statement, "As Moses lifted up the serpent in the wilderness, even so must the Son of Man be lifted up" (John 3:14).

During the Israelite wanderings in Sinai, the people were bitten by snakes. God asked Moses to make an image of a bronze serpent and lift it up for all the people of Israel to see. Then when they were bitten by snakes, they needed only look at the bronze serpent to be healed.

We know from the Book of Exodus that Moses' father-in-law was a priest in the land of Midian. Moses spent many years tending flocks in this country. Undoubtedly, he was exposed to the Midianite practice of worshiping snakes.

A recent archaeological discovery in Sinai verifies that Midianites worshiped snakes. A Midianite temple, with various cultic vessels, was discovered with a bronze serpent lying across the central altar.

When the Israelites were bitten by snakes, God used something that Moses considered a negative from his past to produce a life-giving healing result for the people of Israel. Jesus' reference to this event, in association with His coming death and resurrection is quite clear now. God can use any negative event in the history of His people or in the life of His only Son to reinterpret it and turn it into a positive life-giving result. The cross of Jesus Christ is perhaps the most cruel, vicious act imposed on any innocent person in history. But God used it as history's most positive life-giving event, the resurrection of Jesus Christ.

Do not limit God. Allow Him to take anything He wants from your life and turn it into a blessing for you and others. Allow God to take an old negative event in your life, and put it into a positive light. Remember, allow God!

15 And the slope of the brooks
That reaches to the dwelling of
Ar,
And lies on the border of
Moab.''

16 From there *they went* to Beer,
which *is* the well where the LORD said
to Moses, "Gather the people together, and I will give them water.''
17 Then Israel sang this song:

"Spring up, O well!
All of you sing to it—
18 The well the leaders sank,
Dug by the nation's nobles,
By the lawgiver, with their
staves.''

And from the wilderness *they went*
to Mattanah, 19 from Mattanah to Nahaliel, from Nahaliel to Bamoth,
20 and from Bamoth, *in* the valley
that *is* in the country of Moab, to the
top of Pisgah which looks down on
the wasteland.*ª*
21 Then Israel sent messengers to
Sihon king of the Amorites, saying,
22 "Let me pass through your land.
We will not turn aside into fields or
vineyards; we will not drink water
from wells. We will go by the King's
Highway until we have passed
through your territory." 23 But Sihon
would not allow Israel to pass
through his territory. So Sihon gathered all his people together and went
out against Israel in the wilderness,
and he came to Jahaz and fought
against Israel. 24 Then Israel defeated him with the edge of the
sword, and took possession of his
land from the Arnon to the Jabbok,
as far as the people of Ammon; for
the border of the people of Ammon
was fortified. 25 So Israel took all
these cities, and Israel dwelt in all the
cities of the Amorites, in Heshbon
and in all its villages. 26 For Heshbon
was the city of Sihon king of the Amorites, who had fought against the
former king of Moab, and had taken
all his land from his hand as far as
the Arnon. 27 Therefore those who
speak in proverbs say:

"Come to Heshbon, let it be
built;
Let the city of Sihon be
repaired.

28 "For fire went out from
Heshbon,
A flame from the city of Sihon;
It consumed Ar of Moab,
The lords of the heights of the
Arnon.
29 Woe to you, Moab!
You have perished, O people of
Chemosh!
He has given his sons as
fugitives,
And his daughters into
captivity,
To Sihon king of the Amorites.

30 "But we have shot at them;
Heshbon has perished as far as
Dibon.
Then we laid waste as far as
Nophah,
Which *reaches* to Medeba."

31 Thus Israel dwelt in the land of
the Amorites. 32 Then Moses sent to
spy out Jazer; and they took its villages and drove out the Amorites
who *were* there.
33 And they turned and went up by
the way to Bashan. So Og king of
Bashan went out against them, he
and all his people, to battle at Edrei.
34 Then the LORD said to Moses, "Do
not fear him, for I have delivered him
into your hand, with all his people
and his land; and you shall do to him
as you did to Sihon king of the Amorites, who dwelt at Heshbon."
35 So they defeated him, his sons, and
all his people, until there was no survivor left him; and they took possession of his land.

22 Then the children of Israel
moved, and camped in the
plains of Moab on the side of the Jordan *across from* Jericho.
2 Now Balak the son of Zippor saw
all that Israel had done to the Amorites. 3 And Moab was exceedingly
afraid of the people because they
were many, and Moab was sick with
dread because of the children of Israel. 4 So Moab said to the elders of
Midian, "Now this company will lick
up everything around us, as an ox
licks up the grass of the field." And
Balak the son of Zippor *was* king of
the Moabites at that time. 5 Then he
sent messengers to Balaam the son
of Beor at Pethor, which *is* near the

21:20 ªHebrew *Jeshimon*

River[a] in the land of the sons of his people,[b] to call him, saying: "Look, a people has come from Egypt. See, they cover the face of the earth, and are settling next to me! 6 Therefore please come at once, curse this people for me, for they *are* too mighty for me. Perhaps I shall be able to defeat them and drive them out of the land, for I know that he whom you bless *is* blessed, and he whom you curse is cursed."

7 So the elders of Moab and the elders of Midian departed with the diviner's fee in their hand, and they came to Balaam and spoke to him the words of Balak. 8 And he said to them, "Lodge here tonight, and I will bring back word to you, as the LORD speaks to me." So the princes of Moab stayed with Balaam.

9 Then God came to Balaam and said, "Who *are* these men with you?"

10 So Balaam said to God, "Balak the son of Zippor, king of Moab, has sent to me, *saying,* 11 'Look, a people has come out of Egypt, and they cover the face of the earth. Come now, curse them for me; perhaps I shall be able to overpower them and drive them out.' "

12 And God said to Balaam, "You shall not go with them; you shall not curse the people, for they *are* blessed."

13 So Balaam rose in the morning and said to the princes of Balak, "Go back to your land, for the LORD has refused to give me permission to go with you."

14 And the princes of Moab rose and went to Balak, and said, "Balaam refuses to come with us."

15 Then Balak again sent princes, more numerous and more honorable than they. 16 And they came to Balaam and said to him, "Thus says Balak the son of Zippor: 'Please let nothing hinder you from coming to me; 17 for I will certainly honor you greatly, and I will do whatever you say to me. Therefore please come, curse this people for me.' "

18 Then Balaam answered and said to the servants of Balak, "Though Balak were to give me his house full of silver and gold, I could not go beyond the word of the LORD my God, to do less or more. 19 Now therefore, please, you also stay here tonight, that I may know what more the LORD will say to me."

20 And God came to Balaam at night and said to him, "If the men come to call you, rise *and* go with them; but only the word which I speak to you—that you shall do."

21 So Balaam rose in the morning, saddled his donkey, and went with the princes of Moab.

22 Then God's anger was aroused because he went, and the Angel of the LORD took His stand in the way as an adversary against him. And he was riding on his donkey, and his two servants *were* with him. 23 Now the donkey saw the Angel of the LORD standing in the way with His drawn sword in His hand, and the donkey turned aside out of the way and went into the field. So Balaam struck the donkey to turn her back onto the road. 24 Then the Angel of the LORD stood in a narrow path between the vineyards, *with* a wall on this side and a wall on that side. 25 And when the donkey saw the Angel of the LORD, she pushed herself against the wall and crushed Balaam's foot against the wall; so he struck her again. 26 Then the Angel of the LORD went further, and stood in a narrow place where there *was* no way to turn either to the right hand or to the left. 27 And when the donkey saw the Angel of the LORD, she lay down under Balaam; so Balaam's anger was aroused, and he struck the donkey with his staff.

28 Then the LORD opened the mouth of the donkey, and she said to Balaam, "What have I done to you, that you have struck me these three times?"

29 And Balaam said to the donkey, "Because you have abused me. I wish there were a sword in my hand, for now I would kill you!"

30 So the donkey said to Balaam, "*Am* I not your donkey on which you have ridden, ever since *I* became yours, to this day? Was I ever disposed to do this to you?"

And he said, "No."

31 Then the LORD opened Balaam's eyes, and he saw the Angel of the LORD standing in the way with His drawn sword in His hand; and he bowed his head and fell flat on his face. 32 And the Angel of the LORD

22:5 [a]That is, the Euphrates   [b]Or *the people of Amau*

said to him, "Why have you struck your donkey these three times? Behold, I have come out to stand against you, because *your* way is perverse before Me. 33 The donkey saw Me and turned aside from Me these three times. If she had not turned aside from Me, surely I would also have killed you by now, and let her live."

34 And Balaam said to the Angel of the LORD, "I have sinned, for I did not know You stood in the way against me. Now therefore, if it displeases You, I will turn back."

35 Then the Angel of the LORD said to Balaam, "Go with the men, but only the word that I speak to you, that you shall speak." So Balaam went with the princes of Balak.

36 Now when Balak heard that Balaam was coming, he went out to meet him at the city of Moab, which *is* on the border at the Arnon, the boundary of the territory. 37 Then Balak said to Balaam, "Did I not earnestly send to you, calling for you? Why did you not come to me? Am I not able to honor you?"

38 And Balaam said to Balak, "Look, I have come to you! Now, have I any power at all to say anything? The word that God puts in my mouth, that I must speak." 39 So Balaam went with Balak, and they came to Kirjath Huzoth. 40 Then Balak offered oxen and sheep, and he sent *some* to Balaam and to the princes who *were* with him.

41 So it was, the next day, that Balak took Balaam and brought him up to the high places of Baal, that from there he might observe the extent of the people.

23 Then Balaam said to Balak, "Build seven altars for me here, and prepare for me here seven bulls and seven rams."

2 And Balak did just as Balaam had spoken, and Balak and Balaam offered a bull and a ram on *each* altar. 3 Then Balaam said to Balak, "Stand by your burnt offering, and I will go; perhaps the LORD will come to meet me, and whatever He shows me I will tell you." So he went to a desolate height. 4 And God met Balaam, and he said to Him, "I have prepared the

seven altars, and I have offered on *each* altar a bull and a ram."

5 Then the LORD put a word in Balaam's mouth, and said, "Return to Balak, and thus you shall speak." 6 So he returned to him, and there he was, standing by his burnt offering, he and all the princes of Moab.

7 And he took up his oracle and said:

> "Balak the king of Moab has
>   brought me from Aram,
> From the mountains of the east.
> 'Come, curse Jacob for me,
> And come, denounce Israel!'
>
> 8 "How shall I curse whom God
>   has not cursed?
> And how shall I denounce
>   *whom* the LORD has not
>   denounced?
> 9 For from the top of the rocks I
>   see him,
> And from the hills I behold
>   him;
> There! A people dwelling
>   alone,
> Not reckoning itself among the
>   nations.
>
> 10 "Who can count the dust[a] of
>   Jacob,
> Or number one-fourth of
>   Israel?
> Let me die the death of the
>   righteous,
> And let my end be like his!"

11 Then Balak said to Balaam, "What have you done to me? I took you to curse my enemies, and look, you have blessed *them* bountifully!" 12 So he answered and said, "Must I not take heed to speak what the LORD has put in my mouth?" 13 Then Balak said to him, "Please come with me to another place from which you may see them; you shall see only the outer part of them, and shall not see them all; curse them for me from there." 14 So he brought him to the field of Zophim, to the top of Pisgah, and built seven altars, and offered a bull and a ram on *each* altar.

15 And he said to Balak, "Stand here by your burnt offering while I meet[a] *the* LORD over there."

16 Then the LORD met Balaam, and put a word in his mouth, and said,

23:10 [a]Or *dust cloud*   23:15 [a]Following Masoretic Text, Targum, and Vulgate; Syriac reads *call*; Septuagint reads *go and ask God*.

"Go back to Balak, and thus you shall speak." 17 So he came to him, and there he was, standing by his burnt offering, and the princes of Moab were with him. And Balak said to him, "What has the LORD spoken?"

18 Then he took up his oracle and said:

> "Rise up, Balak, and hear!
> Listen to me, son of Zippor!
>
> 19 "God *is* not a man, that He
>   should lie,
>   Nor a son of man, that He
>   should repent.
>   Has He said, and will He not
>   do?
>   Or has He spoken, and will He
>   not make it good?
> 20 Behold, I have received *a
>   command* to bless;
>   He has blessed, and I cannot
>   reverse it.
>
> 21 "He has not observed iniquity in
>   Jacob,
>   Nor has He seen wickedness in
>   Israel.
>   The LORD his God *is* with him,
>   And the shout of a King *is*
>   among them.
> 22 God brings them out of Egypt;
>   He has strength like a wild ox.
>
> 23 "For *there is* no sorcery against
>   Jacob,
>   Nor any divination against
>   Israel.
>   It now must be said of Jacob
>   And of Israel, 'Oh, what God
>   has done!'
> 24 Look, a people rises like a
>   lioness,
>   And lifts itself up like a lion;
>   It shall not lie down until it
>   devours the prey,
>   And drinks the blood of the
>   slain."

25 Then Balak said to Balaam, "Neither curse them at all, nor bless them at all!"

26 So Balaam answered and said to Balak, "Did I not tell you, saying, 'All that the LORD speaks, that I must do'?"

27 Then Balak said to Balaam, "Please come, I will take you to another place; perhaps it will please God that you may curse them for me

from there." 28 So Balak took Balaam to the top of Peor, that overlooks the wasteland.ᵃ 29 Then Balaam said to Balak, "Build for me here seven altars, and prepare for me here seven bulls and seven rams." 30 And Balak did as Balaam had said, and offered a bull and a ram on *every* altar.

24 Now when Balaam saw that it pleased the LORD to bless Israel, he did not go as at other times, to seek to use sorcery, but he set his face toward the wilderness. 2 And Balaam raised his eyes, and saw Israel encamped according to their tribes; and the Spirit of God came upon him.

3 Then he took up his oracle and said:

> "The utterance of Balaam the
>   son of Beor,
>   The utterance of the man
>   whose eyes are opened,
> 4   The utterance of him who hears
>   the words of God,
>   Who sees the vision of the
>   Almighty,
>   Who falls down, with eyes wide
>   open:
>
> 5 "How lovely are your tents, O
>   Jacob!
>   Your dwellings, O Israel!
> 6   Like valleys that stretch out,
>   Like gardens by the riverside,
>   Like aloes planted by the LORD,
>   Like cedars beside the waters.
> 7   He shall pour water from his
>   buckets,
>   And his seed *shall be* in many
>   waters.
>
>   "His king shall be higher than
>   Agag,
>   And his kingdom shall be
>   exalted.
>
> 8 "God brings him out of Egypt;
>   He has strength like a wild ox;
>   He shall consume the nations,
>   his enemies;
>   He shall break their bones
>   And pierce *them* with his
>   arrows.
> 9   'He bows down, he lies down as
>   a lion;
>   And as a lion, who shall rouse
>   him?'ᵃ

23:28 ᵃHebrew *Jeshimon*   24:9 ᵃGenesis 49:9

"Blessed *is* he who blesses you,
And cursed *is* he who curses
you."

10 Then Balak's anger was aroused against Balaam, and he struck his hands together; and Balak said to Balaam, "I called you to curse my enemies, and look, you have bountifully blessed *them* these three times! 11 Now therefore, flee to your place. I said I would greatly honor you, but in fact, the LORD has kept you back from honor."

12 So Balaam said to Balak, "Did I not also speak to your messengers whom you sent to me, saying, 13 'If Balak were to give me his house full of silver and gold, I could not go beyond the word of the LORD, to do good or bad of my own will. What the LORD says, that I must speak'? 14 And now, indeed, I am going to my people. Come, I will advise you what this people will do to your people in the latter days."

15 So he took up his oracle and said:

"The utterance of Balaam the
son of Beor,
And the utterance of the man
whose eyes are opened;
16   The utterance of him who hears
the words of God,
And has the knowledge of the
Most High,
Who sees the vision of the
Almighty,
Who falls down, with eyes wide
open:

17 "I see Him, but not now;
I behold Him, but not near;
A Star shall come out of Jacob;
A Scepter shall rise out of
Israel,
And batter the brow of Moab,
And destroy all the sons of
tumult.*a*

18 "And Edom shall be a
possession;
Seir also, his enemies, shall be
a possession,
While Israel does valiantly.
19   Out of Jacob One shall have
dominion,

And destroy the remains of the
city."

20 Then he looked on Amalek, and he took up his oracle and said:

"Amalek *was* first among the
nations,
But *shall be* last until he
perishes."

21 Then he looked on the Kenites, and he took up his oracle and said:

"Firm is your dwelling place,
And your nest is set in the rock;
22   Nevertheless Kain shall be
burned.
How long until Asshur carries
you away captive?"

23 Then he took up his oracle and said:

"Alas! Who shall live when God
does this?
24   But ships *shall come* from the
coasts of Cyprus,*a*
And they shall afflict Asshur
and afflict Eber,
And so shall *Amalek,b* until he
perishes."

25 So Balaam rose and departed and returned to his place; Balak also went his way.

25 Now Israel remained in Acacia Grove,*a* and the people began to commit harlotry with the women of Moab. 2 They invited the people to the sacrifices of their gods, and the people ate and bowed down to their gods. 3 So Israel was joined to Baal of Peor, and the anger of the LORD was aroused against Israel.

4 Then the LORD said to Moses, "Take all the leaders of the people and hang the offenders before the LORD, out in the sun, that the fierce anger of the LORD may turn away from Israel."

5 So Moses said to the judges of Israel, "Every one of you kill his men who were joined to Baal of Peor."

6 And indeed, one of the children of Israel came and presented to his brethren a Midianite woman in the sight of Moses and in the sight of all

24:17 *a*Hebrew *Sheth* (compare Jeremiah 48:45)
25:1 *a*Hebrew *Shittim*

24:24 *a*Hebrew *Kittim*   *b*Literally *he* or *that one*

the congregation of the children of Israel, who *were* weeping at the door of the tabernacle of meeting. 7 Now when Phinehas the son of Eleazar, the son of Aaron the priest, saw *it,* he rose from among the congregation and took a javelin in his hand; 8 and he went after the man of Israel into the tent and thrust both of them through, the man of Israel, and the woman through her body. So the plague was stopped among the children of Israel. 9 And those who died in the plague were twenty-four thousand.

10 Then the LORD spoke to Moses, saying: 11 "Phinehas the son of Eleazar, the son of Aaron the priest, has turned back My wrath from the children of Israel, because he was zealous with My zeal among them, so that I did not consume the children of Israel in My zeal. 12 Therefore say, 'Behold, I give to him My covenant of peace; 13 and it shall be to him and his descendants after him a covenant of an everlasting priesthood, because he was zealous for his God, and made atonement for the children of Israel.' "

14 Now the name of the Israelite who was killed, who was killed with the Midianite woman, *was* Zimri the son of Salu, a leader of a father's house among the Simeonites. 15 And the name of the Midianite woman who was killed *was* Cozbi the daughter of Zur; he *was* head of the people of a father's house in Midian.

16 Then the LORD spoke to Moses, saying: 17 "Harass the Midianites, and attack them; 18 for they harassed you with their schemes by which they seduced you in the matter of Peor and in the matter of Cozbi, the daughter of a leader of Midian, their sister, who was killed in the day of the plague because of Peor."

26 And it came to pass, after the plague, that the LORD spoke to Moses and Eleazar the son of Aaron the priest, saying: 2 "Take a census of all the congregation of the children of Israel from twenty years old and above, by their fathers' houses, all who are able to go to war in Israel."

3 So Moses and Eleazar the priest spoke with them in the plains of Moab by the Jordan, *across from* Jericho, saying: 4 "*Take a census of the people* from twenty years old and above, just as the LORD commanded Moses and the children of Israel who came out of the land of Egypt."

5 Reuben *was* the firstborn of Israel. The children of Reuben *were:* of Hanoch, the family of the Hanochites; *of* Pallu, the family of the Palluites; 6 *of* Hezron, the family of the Hezronites; *of* Carmi, the family of the Carmites. 7 These *are* the families of the Reubenites: those who were numbered of them were forty-three thousand seven hundred and thirty. 8 And the son of Pallu *was* Eliab. 9 The sons of Eliab *were* Nemuel, Dathan, and Abiram. These *are* the Dathan and Abiram, representatives of the congregation, who contended against Moses and Aaron in the company of Korah, when they contended against the LORD; 10 and the earth opened its mouth and swallowed them up together with Korah when that company died, when the fire devoured two hundred and fifty men; and they became a sign. 11 Nevertheless the children of Korah did not die.

12 The sons of Simeon according to their families *were:* of Nemuel,[a] the family of the Nemuelites; *of* Jamin, the family of the Jaminites; *of* Jachin,[b] the family of the Jachinites; 13 *of* Zerah,[a] the family of the Zarhites; *of* Shaul, the family of the Shaulites. 14 These *are* the families of the Simeonites: twenty-two thousand two hundred.

15 The sons of Gad according to their families *were:* of Zephon,[a] the family of the Zephonites; *of* Haggi, the family of the Haggites; *of* Shuni, the family of the Shunites; 16 *of* Ozni,[a] the family of the Oznites; *of* Eri, the family of the Erites; 17 *of* Arod,[a] the family of the Arodites; *of* Areli, the family of the Arelites. 18 These *are* the families of the sons of Gad according to those who were numbered of them: forty thousand five hundred.

19 The sons of Judah *were* Er and Onan; and Er and Onan died in the land of Canaan. 20 And the sons of

26:12 [a]Spelled *Jemuel* in Genesis 46:10 and Exodus 6:15 [b]Called *Jarib* in 1 Chronicles 4:24
26:13 [a]Called *Zohar* in Genesis 46:10 26:15 [a]Called *Ziphion* in Genesis 46:16 26:16 [a]Called *Ezbon* in Genesis 46:16 26:17 [a]Spelled *Arodi* in Samaritan Pentateuch, Syriac, and Genesis 46:16

Judah according to their families were: *of* Shelah, the family of the Shelanites; *of* Perez, the family of the Parzites; *of* Zerah, the family of the Zarhites. 21 And the sons of Perez were: *of* Hezron, the family of the Hezronites; *of* Hamul, the family of the Hamulites. 22 These *are* the families of Judah according to those who were numbered of them: seventy-six thousand five hundred.

23 The sons of Issachar according to their families *were: of* Tola, the family of the Tolaites; of Puah,[a] the family of the Punites;[b] 24 of Jashub, the family of the Jashubites; of Shimron, the family of the Shimronites. 25 These *are* the families of Issachar according to those who were numbered of them: sixty-four thousand three hundred.

26 The sons of Zebulun according to their families *were:* of Sered, the family of the Sardites; of Elon, the family of the Elonites; of Jahleel, the family of the Jahleelites. 27 These *are* the families of the Zebulunites according to those who were numbered of them: sixty thousand five hundred.

28 The sons of Joseph according to their families, by Manasseh and Ephraim, *were:* 29 The sons of Manasseh: of Machir, the family of the Machirites; and Machir begot Gilead; of Gilead, the family of the Gileadites. 30 These *are* the sons of Gilead: *of* Jeezer,[a] the family of the Jeezerites; of Helek, the family of the Helekites; 31 *of* Asriel, the family of the Asrielites; *of* Shechem, the family of the Shechemites; 32 *of* Shemida, the family of the Shemidaites; *of* Hepher, the family of the Hepherites. 33 Now Zelophehad the son of Hepher had no sons, but daughters; and the names of the daughters of Zelophehad *were* Mahlah, Noah, Hoglah, Milcah, and Tirzah. 34 These *are* the families of Manasseh; and those who were numbered of them *were* fifty-two thousand seven hundred.

35 These *are* the sons of Ephraim according to their families: of Shuthelah, the family of the Shuthalhites; of Becher,[a] the family of the Bachrites; of Tahan, the family of the Tahanites. 36 And these *are* the sons of Shuthelah: of Eran, the family of the Eranites. 37 These *are* the families of the sons of Ephraim according to those who were numbered of them: thirty-two thousand five hundred.

These *are* the sons of Joseph according to their families.

38 The sons of Benjamin according to their families were: of Bela, the family of the Belaites; of Ashbel, the family of the Ashbelites; of Ahiram, the family of the Ahiramites; 39 of Shupham,[a] the family of the Shuphamites; of Hupham,[b] the family of the Huphamites. 40 And the sons of Bela were Ard[a] and Naaman: *of Ard,* the family of the Ardites; of Naaman, the family of the Naamites. 41 These *are* the sons of Benjamin according to their families; and those who were numbered of them *were* forty-five thousand six hundred.

42 These *are* the sons of Dan according to their families: of Shuham,[a] the family of the Shuhamites. These *are* the families of Dan according to their families. 43 All the families of the Shuhamites, according to those who were numbered of them, *were* sixty-four thousand four hundred.

44 The sons of Asher according to their families *were:* of Jimna, the family of the Jimnites; of Jesui, the family of the Jesuites; of Beriah, the family of the Beriites. 45 Of the sons of Beriah: of Heber, the family of the Heberites; of Malchiel, the family of the Malchielites. 46 And the name of the daughter of Asher *was* Serah. 47 These *are* the families of the sons of Asher according to those who were numbered of them: fifty-three thousand four hundred.

48 The sons of Naphtali according to their families *were:* of Jahzeel,[a] the family of the Jahzeelites; of Guni, the family of the Gunites; 49 of Jezer, the family of the Jezerites; of Shillem, the family of the Shillemites. 50 These *are* the families of Naphtali according to their families; and those who were numbered of them *were* forty-five thousand four hundred.

51 These *are* those who were num-

26:23 [a]Hebrew *Puvah* (compare Genesis 46:13 and 1 Chronicles 7:1); Samaritan Pentateuch, Septuagint, Syriac, and Vulgate read *Puah.*   [b]Samaritan Pentateuch, Septuagint, Syriac, and Vulgate read *Puaites.*
26:30 [a]Called *Abiezer* in Joshua 17:2   26:35 [a]Called *Bered* in 1 Chronicles 7:20   26:39 [a]Masoretic Text reads *Shephupham,* spelled *Shephuphan* in 1 Chronicles 8:5.   [b]Called *Huppim* in Genesis 46:21
26:40 [a]Called *Addar* in 1 Chronicles 8:3   26:42 [a]Called *Hushim* in Genesis 46:23   26:48 [a]Spelled *Jahziel* in 1 Chronicles 7:13

bered of the children of Israel: six hundred and one thousand seven hundred and thirty.

52 Then the LORD spoke to Moses, saying: 53 "To these the land shall be divided as an inheritance, according to the number of names. 54 To a large *tribe* you shall give a larger inheritance, and to a small *tribe* you shall give a smaller inheritance. Each shall be given its inheritance according to those who were numbered of them. 55 But the land shall be divided by lot; they shall inherit according to the names of the tribes of their fathers. 56 According to the lot their inheritance shall be divided between the larger and the smaller."

57 And these *are* those who were numbered of the Levites according to their families: of Gershon, the family of the Gershonites; of Kohath, the family of the Kohathites; of Merari, the family of the Merarites. 58 These *are* the families of the Levites: the family of the Libnites, the family of the Hebronites, the family of the Mahlites, the family of the Mushites, and the family of the Korathites. And Kohath begot Amram. 59 The name of Amram's wife *was* Jochebed the daughter of Levi, who was born to Levi in Egypt; and to Amram she bore Aaron and Moses and their sister Miriam. 60 To Aaron were born Nadab and Abihu, Eleazar and Ithamar. 61 And Nadab and Abihu died when they offered profane fire before the LORD.

62 Now those who were numbered of them were twenty-three thousand, every male from a month old and above; for they were not numbered among the other children of Israel, because there was no inheritance given to them among the children of Israel.

63 These *are* those who were numbered by Moses and Eleazar the priest, who numbered the children of Israel in the plains of Moab by the Jordan, *across from* Jericho. 64 But among these there was not a man of those who were numbered by Moses and Aaron the priest when they numbered the children of Israel in the Wilderness of Sinai. 65 For the LORD had said of them, "They shall surely die in the wilderness." So there was not left a man of them, except Caleb the son of Jephunneh and Joshua the son of Nun.

27 Then came the daughters of Zelophehad the son of Hepher, the son of Gilead, the son of Machir, the son of Manasseh, from the families of Manasseh the son of Joseph; and these *were* the names of his daughters: Mahlah, Noah, Hoglah, Milcah, and Tirzah. 2 And they stood before Moses, before Eleazar the priest, and before the leaders and all the congregation, *by* the doorway of the tabernacle of meeting, saying: 3 "Our father died in the wilderness; but he was not in the company of those who gathered together against the LORD, in company with Korah, but he died in his own sin; and he had no sons. 4 Why should the name of our father be removed from among his family because he had no son? Give us a possession among our father's brothers."

5 So Moses brought their case before the LORD.

6 And the LORD spoke to Moses, saying: 7 "The daughters of Zelophehad speak *what is* right; you shall surely give them a possession of inheritance among their father's brothers, and cause the inheritance of their father to pass to them. 8 And you shall speak to the children of Israel, saying: 'If a man dies and has no son, then you shall cause his inheritance to pass to his daughter. 9 If he has no daughter, then you shall give his inheritance to his brothers. 10 If he has no brothers, then you shall give his inheritance to his father's brothers. 11 And if his father has no brothers, then you shall give his inheritance to the relative closest to him in his family, and he shall possess it.' " And it shall be to the children of Israel a statute of judgment, just as the LORD commanded Moses.

12 Now the LORD said to Moses: "Go up into this Mount Abarim, and see the land which I have given to the children of Israel. 13 And when you have seen it, you also shall be gathered to your people, as Aaron your brother was gathered. 14 For in the Wilderness of Zin, during the strife of the congregation, you rebelled against My command to hallow Me at the waters before their eyes." (These *are* the waters of Meribah, at Kadesh in the Wilderness of Zin.)

15 Then Moses spoke to the LORD, saying: 16 "Let the LORD, the God of

the spirits of all flesh, set a man over the congregation, 17 who may go out before them and go in before them, who may lead them out and bring them in, that the congregation of the LORD may not be like sheep which have no shepherd."

18 And the LORD said to Moses: "Take Joshua the son of Nun with you, a man in whom *is* the Spirit, and lay your hand on him; 19 set him before Eleazar the priest and before all the congregation, and inaugurate him in their sight. 20 And you shall give *some* of your authority to him, that all the congregation of the children of Israel may be obedient. 21 He shall stand before Eleazar the priest, who shall inquire before the LORD for him by the judgment of the Urim. At his word they shall go out, and at his word they shall come in, he and all the children of Israel with him—all the congregation."

22 So Moses did as the LORD commanded him. He took Joshua and set him before Eleazar the priest and before all the congregation. 23 And he laid his hands on him and inaugurated him, just as the LORD commanded by the hand of Moses.

28 Now the LORD spoke to Moses, saying, 2 "Command the children of Israel, and say to them, 'My offering, My food for My offerings made by fire as a sweet aroma to Me, you shall be careful to offer to Me at their appointed time.'

3 "And you shall say to them, 'This *is* the offering made by fire which you shall offer to the LORD: two male lambs in their first year without blemish, day by day, as a regular burnt offering. 4 The one lamb you shall offer in the morning, the other lamb you shall offer in the evening, 5 and one-tenth of an ephah of fine flour as a grain offering mixed with one-fourth of a hin of pressed oil. 6 *It is* a regular burnt offering which was ordained at Mount Sinai for a sweet aroma, an offering made by fire to the LORD. 7 And its drink offering *shall be* one-fourth of a hin for each lamb; in a holy *place* you shall pour out the drink to the LORD as an offering. 8 The other lamb you shall offer in the evening; as the morning grain offering and its drink offering, you shall offer *it* as an offering made by fire, a sweet aroma to the LORD.

9 'And on the Sabbath day two lambs in their first year, without blemish, and two-tenths *of an ephah* of fine flour as a grain offering, mixed with oil, with its drink offering— 10 *this is* the burnt offering for every Sabbath, besides the regular burnt offering with its drink offering.

11 'At the beginnings of your months you shall present a burnt offering to the LORD: two young bulls, one ram, and seven lambs in their first year, without blemish; 12 three-tenths *of an ephah* of fine flour as a grain offering, mixed with oil, for each bull; two-tenths *of an ephah* of fine flour as a grain offering, mixed with oil, for the one ram; 13 and one-tenth *of an ephah* of fine flour, mixed with oil, as a grain offering for each lamb, as a burnt offering of sweet aroma, an offering made by fire to the LORD. 14 Their drink offering shall be half a hin of wine for a bull, one-third of a hin for a ram, and one-fourth of a hin for a lamb; this *is* the burnt offering for each month throughout the months of the year. 15 Also one kid of the goats as a sin offering to the LORD shall be offered, besides the regular burnt offering and its drink offering.

16 'On the fourteenth day of the first month *is* the Passover of the LORD. 17 And on the fifteenth day of this month *is* the feast; unleavened bread shall be eaten for seven days. 18 On the first day *you shall have* a holy convocation. You shall do no customary work. 19 And you shall present an offering made by fire as a burnt offering to the LORD: two young bulls, one ram, and seven lambs in their first year. Be sure they are without blemish. 20 Their grain offering shall be of fine flour mixed with oil: three-tenths *of an ephah* you shall offer for a bull, and two-tenths for a ram; 21 you shall offer one-tenth *of an ephah* for each of the seven lambs; 22 also one goat *as* a sin offering, to make atonement for you. 23 You shall offer these besides the burnt offering of the morning, which *is* for a regular burnt offering. 24 In this manner you shall offer the food of the offering made by fire daily for seven days, as a sweet aroma to the LORD; it shall be offered besides the regular burnt offering and its drink offering. 25 And on the seventh day you shall have a holy

convocation. You shall do no customary work.

26 'Also on the day of the firstfruits, when you bring a new grain offering to the LORD at your *Feast of* Weeks, you shall have a holy convocation. You shall do no customary work. 27 You shall present a burnt offering as a sweet aroma to the LORD: two young bulls, one ram, and seven lambs in their first year, 28 with their grain offering of fine flour mixed with oil: three-tenths *of an ephah* for each bull, two-tenths for the one ram, 29 and one-tenth for each of the seven lambs; 30 *also* one kid of the goats, to make atonement for you. 31 Be sure they are without blemish. You shall present *them* with their drink offerings, besides the regular burnt offering with its grain offering.

29 'And in the seventh month, on the first *day* of the month, you shall have a holy convocation. You shall do no customary work. For you it is a day of blowing the trumpets. 2 You shall offer a burnt offering as a sweet aroma to the LORD: one young bull, one ram, *and* seven lambs in their first year, without blemish. 3 Their grain offering *shall be* fine flour mixed with oil: three-tenths *of an ephah* for the bull, two-tenths for the ram, 4 and one-tenth for each of the seven lambs; 5 also one kid of the goats *as* a sin offering, to make atonement for you; 6 besides the burnt offering with its grain offering for the New Moon, the regular burnt offering with its grain offering, and their drink offerings, according to their ordinance, as a sweet aroma, an offering made by fire to the LORD.

7 'On the tenth *day* of this seventh month you shall have a holy convocation. You shall afflict your souls; you shall not do any work. 8 You shall present a burnt offering to the LORD *as* a sweet aroma: one young bull, one ram, *and* seven lambs in their first year. Be sure they are without blemish. 9 Their grain offering *shall be of* fine flour mixed with oil: three-tenths *of an ephah* for the bull, two-tenths for the one ram, 10 and one-tenth for each of the seven lambs; 11 also one kid of the goats *as* a sin offering, besides the sin offering for atonement, the regular

burnt offering with its grain offering, and their drink offerings.

12 'On the fifteenth day of the seventh month you shall have a holy convocation. You shall do no customary work, and you shall keep a feast to the LORD seven days. 13 You shall present a burnt offering, an offering made by fire as a sweet aroma to the LORD: thirteen young bulls, two rams, *and* fourteen lambs in their first year. They shall be without blemish. 14 Their grain offering *shall be of* fine flour mixed with oil: three-tenths *of an ephah* for each of the thirteen bulls, two-tenths for each of the two rams, 15 and one-tenth for each of the fourteen lambs; 16 also one kid of the goats *as* a sin offering, besides the regular burnt offering, its grain offering, and its drink offering.

17 'On the second day *present* twelve young bulls, two rams, fourteen lambs in their first year without blemish, 18 and their grain offering and their drink offerings for the bulls, for the rams, and for the lambs, by their number, according to the ordinance; 19 also one kid of the goats *as* a sin offering, besides the regular burnt offering with its grain offering, and their drink offerings.

20 'On the third day *present* eleven bulls, two rams, fourteen lambs in their first year without blemish, 21 and their grain offering and their drink offerings for the bulls, for the rams, and for the lambs, by their number, according to the ordinance; 22 also one goat *as* a sin offering, besides the regular burnt offering, its grain offering, and its drink offering.

23 'On the fourth day *present* ten bulls, two rams, *and* fourteen lambs in their first year, without blemish, 24 and their grain offering and their drink offerings for the bulls, for the rams, and for the lambs, by their number, according to the ordinance; 25 also one kid of the goats *as* a sin offering, besides the regular burnt offering, its grain offering, and its drink offering.

26 'On the fifth day *present* nine bulls, two rams, *and* fourteen lambs in their first year without blemish, 27 and their grain offering and their drink offerings for the bulls, for the rams, and for the lambs, by their number, according to the ordinance; 28 also one goat *as* a sin offering, besides the regular burnt offering, its

grain offering, and its drink offering.

29 'On the sixth day *present* eight bulls, two rams, *and* fourteen lambs in their first year without blemish, 30 and their grain offering and their drink offerings for the bulls, for the rams, and for the lambs, by their number, according to the ordinance; 31 also one goat *as* a sin offering, besides the regular burnt offering, its grain offering, and its drink offering.

32 'On the seventh day *present* seven bulls, two rams, *and* fourteen lambs in their first year without blemish, 33 and their grain offering and their drink offerings for the bulls, for the rams, and for the lambs, by their number, according to the ordinance; 34 also one goat *as* a sin offering, besides the regular burnt offering, its grain offering, and its drink offering.

35 'On the eighth day you shall have a sacred assembly. You shall do no customary work. 36 You shall present a burnt offering, an offering made by fire as a sweet aroma to the LORD: one bull, one ram, seven lambs in their first year without blemish, 37 and their grain offering and their drink offerings for the bull, for the ram, and for the lambs, by their number, according to the ordinance; 38 also one goat *as* a sin offering, besides the regular burnt offering, its grain offering, and its drink offering.

39 'These you shall present to the LORD at your appointed feasts (besides your vowed offerings and your freewill offerings) as your burnt offerings and your grain offerings, as your drink offerings and your peace offerings.' "

40 So Moses told the children of Israel everything, just as the LORD commanded Moses.

30 Then Moses spoke to the heads of the tribes concerning the children of Israel, saying, "This *is* the thing which the LORD has commanded: 2 If a man makes a vow to the LORD, or swears an oath to bind himself by some agreement, he shall not break his word; he shall do according to all that proceeds out of his mouth.

3 "Or if a woman makes a vow to the LORD, and binds *herself* by some agreement while in her father's house in her youth, 4 and her father hears her vow and the agreement by which she has bound herself, and her father holds his peace, then all her vows shall stand, and every agreement with which she has bound herself shall stand. 5 But if her father overrules her on the day that he hears, then none of her vows nor her agreements by which she has bound herself shall stand; and the LORD will release her, because her father overruled her.

6 "If indeed she takes a husband, while bound by her vows or by a rash utterance from her lips by which she bound herself, 7 and her husband hears *it,* and makes no response to her on the day that he hears, then her vows shall stand, and her agreements by which she bound herself shall stand. 8 But if her husband overrules her on the day that he hears *it,* he shall make void her vow which she took and what she uttered with her lips, by which she bound herself, and the LORD will release her.

9 "Also any vow of a widow or a divorced woman, by which she has bound herself, shall stand against her.

10 "If she vowed in her husband's house, or bound herself by an agreement with an oath, 11 and her husband heard *it,* and made no response to her *and* did not overrule her, then all her vows shall stand, and every agreement by which she bound herself shall stand. 12 But if her husband truly made them void on the day he heard *them,* then whatever proceeded from her lips concerning her vows or concerning the agreement binding her, it shall not stand; her husband has made them void, and the LORD will release her. 13 Every vow and every binding oath to afflict her soul, her husband may confirm it, or her husband may make it void. 14 Now if her husband makes no response whatever to her from day to day, then he confirms all her vows or all the agreements that bind her; he confirms them, because he made no response to her on the day that he heard *them.* 15 But if he does make them void after he has heard *them,* then he shall bear her guilt."

16 These *are* the statutes which the LORD commanded Moses, between a man and his wife, and between a fa-

ther and his daughter in her youth in her father's house.

31 And the LORD spoke to Moses, saying: 2 "Take vengeance on the Midianites for the children of Israel. Afterward you shall be gathered to your people."
3 So Moses spoke to the people, saying, "Arm some of yourselves for war, and let them go against the Midianites to take vengeance for the LORD on Midian. 4 A thousand from each tribe of all the tribes of Israel you shall send to the war."
5 So there were recruited from the divisions of Israel one thousand from *each* tribe, twelve thousand armed for war. 6 Then Moses sent them to the war, one thousand from *each* tribe; he sent them to the war with Phinehas the son of Eleazar the priest, with the holy articles and the signal trumpets in his hand. 7 And they warred against the Midianites, just as the LORD commanded Moses, and they killed all the males. 8 They killed the kings of Midian with *the rest of* those who were killed—Evi, Rekem, Zur, Hur, and Reba, the five kings of Midian. Balaam the son of Beor they also killed with the sword.
9 And the children of Israel took the women of Midian captive, with their little ones, and took as spoil all their cattle, all their flocks, and all their goods. 10 They also burned with fire all the cities where they dwelt, and all their forts. 11 And they took all the spoil and all the booty—of man and beast.
12 Then they brought the captives, the booty, and the spoil to Moses, to Eleazar the priest, and to the congregation of the children of Israel, to the camp in the plains of Moab by the Jordan, *across from* Jericho. 13 And Moses, Eleazar the priest, and all the leaders of the congregation, went to meet them outside the camp. 14 But Moses was angry with the officers of the army, *with* the captains over thousands and captains over hundreds, who had come from the battle.
15 And Moses said to them: "Have you kept all the women alive? 16 Look, these *women* caused the children of Israel, through the counsel of Balaam, to trespass against the LORD in the incident of Peor, and

there was a plague among the congregation of the LORD. 17 Now therefore, kill every male among the little ones, and kill every woman who has known a man intimately. 18 But keep alive for yourselves all the young girls who have not known a man intimately. 19 And as for you, remain outside the camp seven days; whoever has killed any person, and whoever has touched any slain, purify yourselves and your captives on the third day and on the seventh day. 20 Purify every garment, everything made of leather, everything woven of goats' *hair,* and everything made of wood."
21 Then Eleazar the priest said to the men of war who had gone to the battle, "This *is* the ordinance of the law which the LORD commanded Moses: 22 "Only the gold, the silver, the bronze, the iron, the tin, and the lead, 23 everything that can endure fire, you shall put through the fire, and it shall be clean; and it shall be purified with the water of purification. But all that cannot endure fire you shall put through water. 24 And you shall wash your clothes on the seventh day and be clean, and afterward you may come into the camp."
25 Now the LORD spoke to Moses, saying: 26 "Count up the plunder that was taken—of man and beast—you and Eleazar the priest and the chief fathers of the congregation; 27 and divide the plunder into two parts, between those who took part in the war, who went out to battle, and all the congregation. 28 And levy a tribute for the LORD on the men of war who went out to battle: one of every five hundred of the persons, the cattle, the donkeys, and the sheep; 29 take *it* from their half, and give *it* to Eleazar the priest as a heave offering to the LORD. 30 And from the children of Israel's half you shall take one of every fifty, drawn from the persons, the cattle, the donkeys, and the sheep, from all the livestock, and give them to the Levites who keep charge of the tabernacle of the LORD." 31 So Moses and Eleazar the priest did as the LORD commanded Moses.
32 The booty remaining from the plunder, which the men of war had taken, was six hundred and seventy-five thousand sheep, 33 seventy-two thousand cattle, 34 sixty-one thou-

sand donkeys, 35 and thirty-two thousand persons in all, of women who had not known a man intimately. 36 And the half, the portion for those who had gone out to war, was in number three hundred and thirty-seven thousand five hundred sheep; 37 and the LORD's tribute of the sheep was six hundred and seventy-five. 38 The cattle *were* thirty-six thousand, of which the LORD's tribute *was* seventy-two. 39 The donkeys *were* thirty thousand five hundred, of which the LORD's tribute *was* sixty-one. 40 The persons *were* sixteen thousand, of which the LORD's tribute *was* thirty-two persons. 41 So Moses gave the tribute *which was* the LORD's heave offering to Eleazar the priest, as the LORD commanded Moses.

42 And from the children of Israel's half, which Moses separated from the men who fought— 43 now the half belonging to the congregation was three hundred and thirty-seven thousand five hundred sheep, 44 thirty-six thousand cattle, 45 thirty thousand five hundred donkeys, 46 and sixteen thousand persons— 47 and from the children of Israel's half Moses took one of every fifty, drawn from man and beast, and gave them to the Levites, who kept charge of the tabernacle of the LORD, as the LORD commanded Moses.

48 Then the officers who *were* over thousands of the army, the captains of thousands and captains of hundreds, came near to Moses; 49 and they said to Moses, "Your servants have taken a count of the men of war who *are* under our command, and not a man of us is missing. 50 Therefore we have brought an offering for the LORD, what every man found of ornaments of gold: armlets and bracelets and signet rings and earrings and necklaces, to make atonement for ourselves before the LORD." 51 So Moses and Eleazar the priest received the gold from them, all the fashioned ornaments. 52 And all the gold of the offering that they offered to the LORD, from the captains of thousands and captains of hundreds, was sixteen thousand seven hundred and fifty shekels. 53 (The men of war had taken spoil, every man for himself.) 54 And Moses and Eleazar the priest received the gold from the captains of thousands and of hundreds, and brought it into the tabernacle of meeting as a memorial for the children of Israel before the LORD.

32 Now the children of Reuben and the children of Gad had a very great multitude of livestock; and when they saw the land of Jazer and the land of Gilead, that indeed the region *was* a place for livestock, 2 the children of Gad and the children of Reuben came and spoke to Moses, to Eleazar the priest, and to the leaders of the congregation, saying, 3 "Ataroth, Dibon, Jazer, Nimrah, Heshbon, Elealeh, Shebam, Nebo, and Beon, 4 the country which the LORD defeated before the congregation of Israel, *is* a land for livestock, and your servants have livestock." 5 Therefore they said, "If we have found favor in your sight, let this land be given to your servants as a possession. Do not take us over the Jordan."

6 And Moses said to the children of Gad and to the children of Reuben: "Shall your brethren go to war while you sit here? 7 Now why will you discourage the heart of the children of Israel from going over into the land which the LORD has given them? 8 Thus your fathers did when I sent them away from Kadesh Barnea to see the land. 9 For when they went up to the Valley of Eshcol and saw the land, they discouraged the heart of the children of Israel, so that they did not go into the land which the LORD had given them. 10 So the LORD's anger was aroused on that day, and He swore an oath, saying, 11 'Surely none of the men who came up from Egypt, from twenty years old and above, shall see the land of which I swore to Abraham, Isaac, and Jacob, because they have not wholly followed Me, 12 except Caleb the son of Jephunneh, the Kenizzite, and Joshua the son of Nun, for they have wholly followed the LORD.' 13 So the LORD's anger was aroused against Israel, and He made them wander in the wilderness forty years, until all the generation that had done evil in the sight of the LORD was gone. 14 And look! You have risen in your fathers' place, a brood of sinful men, to increase still more the fierce anger of the LORD against Israel. 15 For if you turn away from following Him,

He will once again leave them in the wilderness, and you will destroy all these people."

16 Then they came near to him and said: "We will build sheepfolds here for our livestock, and cities for our little ones, 17 but we ourselves will be armed, ready *to go* before the children of Israel until we have brought them to their place; and our little ones will dwell in the fortified cities because of the inhabitants of the land. 18 We will not return to our homes until every one of the children of Israel has received his inheritance. 19 For we will not inherit with them on the other side of the Jordan and beyond, because our inheritance has fallen to us on this eastern side of the Jordan."

20 Then Moses said to them: "If you do this thing, if you arm yourselves before the LORD for the war, 21 and all your armed men cross over the Jordan before the LORD until He has driven out His enemies from before Him, 22 and the land is subdued before the LORD, then afterward you may return and be blameless before the LORD and before Israel; and this land shall be your possession before the LORD. 23 But if you do not do so, then take note, you have sinned against the LORD; and be sure your sin will find you out. 24 Build cities for your little ones and folds for your sheep, and do what has proceeded out of your mouth."

25 And the children of Gad and the children of Reuben spoke to Moses, saying: "Your servants will do as my lord commands. 26 Our little ones, our wives, our flocks, and all our livestock will be there in the cities of Gilead; 27 but your servants will cross over, every man armed for war, before the LORD to battle, just as my lord says."

28 So Moses gave command concerning them to Eleazar the priest, to Joshua the son of Nun, and to the chief fathers of the tribes of the children of Israel. 29 And Moses said to them: "If the children of Gad and the children of Reuben cross over the Jordan with you, every man armed for battle before the LORD, and the land is subdued before you, then you shall give them the land of Gilead as a possession. 30 But if they do not

cross over armed with you, they shall have possessions among you in the land of Canaan."

31 Then the children of Gad and the children of Reuben answered, saying: "As the LORD has said to your servants, so we will do. 32 We will cross over armed before the LORD into the land of Canaan, but the possession of our inheritance *shall remain* with us on this side of the Jordan."

33 So Moses gave to the children of Gad, to the children of Reuben, and to half the tribe of Manasseh the son of Joseph, the kingdom of Sihon king of the Amorites and the kingdom of Og king of Bashan, the land with its cities within the borders, the cities of the surrounding country. 34 And the children of Gad built Dibon and Ataroth and Aroer, 35 Atroth and Shophan and Jazer and Jogbehah, 36 Beth Nimrah and Beth Haran, fortified cities, and folds for sheep. 37 And the children of Reuben built Heshbon and Elealeh and Kirjathaim, 38 Nebo and Baal Meon (*their* names being changed) and Shibmah; and they gave *other* names to the cities which they built.

39 And the children of Machir the son of Manasseh went to Gilead and took it, and dispossessed the Amorites who *were* in it. 40 So Moses gave Gilead to Machir the son of Manasseh, and he dwelt in it. 41 Also Jair the son of Manasseh went and took its small towns, and called them Havoth Jair.ᵃ 42 Then Nobah went and took Kenath and its villages, and he called it Nobah, after his own name.

33 These *are* the journeys of the children of Israel, who went out of the land of Egypt by their armies under the hand of Moses and Aaron. 2 Now Moses wrote down the starting points of their journeys at the command of the LORD. And these *are* their journeys according to their starting points:

3 They departed from Rameses in the first month, on the fifteenth day of the first month; on the day after the Passover the children of Israel went out with boldness in the sight of all the Egyptians. 4 For the Egyptians were burying all *their* firstborn, whom the LORD had killed among

32:41 ᵃLiterally *Towns of Jair*

them. Also on their gods the LORD had executed judgments.

5 Then the children of Israel moved from Rameses and camped at Succoth. 6 They departed from Succoth and camped at Etham, which *is* on the edge of the wilderness. 7 They moved from Etham and turned back to Pi Hahiroth, which *is* east of Baal Zephon; and they camped near Migdol. 8 They departed from before Hahiroth[a] and passed through the midst of the sea into the wilderness, went three days' journey in the Wilderness of Etham, and camped at Marah. 9 They moved from Marah and came to Elim. At Elim *were* twelve springs of water and seventy palm trees; so they camped there.

10 They moved from Elim and camped by the Red Sea. 11 They moved from the Red Sea and camped in the Wilderness of Sin. 12 They journeyed from the Wilderness of Sin and camped at Dophkah. 13 They departed from Dophkah and camped at Alush. 14 They moved from Alush and camped at Rephidim, where there was no water for the people to drink.

15 They departed from Rephidim and camped in the Wilderness of Sinai. 16 They moved from the Wilderness of Sinai and camped at Kibroth Hattaavah. 17 They departed from Kibroth Hattaavah and camped at Hazeroth. 18 They departed from Hazeroth and camped at Rithmah. 19 They departed from Rithmah and camped at Rimmon Perez. 20 They departed from Rimmon Perez and camped at Libnah. 21 They moved from Libnah and camped at Rissah. 22 They journeyed from Rissah and camped at Kehelathah. 23 They went from Kehelathah and camped at Mount Shepher. 24 They moved from Mount Shepher and camped at Haradah. 25 They moved from Haradah and camped at Makheloth. 26 They moved from Makheloth and camped at Tahath. 27 They departed from Tahath and camped at Terah. 28 They moved from Terah and camped at Mithkah. 29 They went from Mithkah and camped at Hashmonah. 30 They departed from Hashmonah and camped at Moseroth. 31 They departed from Moseroth and camped at Bene Jaakan. 32 They moved from Bene Jaakan and camped at Hor Hagidgad. 33 They went from Hor Hagidgad and camped at Jotbathah. 34 They moved from Jotbathah and camped at Abronah. 35 They departed from Abronah and camped at Ezion Geber. 36 They moved from Ezion Geber and camped in the Wilderness of Zin, which *is* Kadesh. 37 They moved from Kadesh and camped at Mount Hor, on the boundary of the land of Edom.

38 Then Aaron the priest went up to Mount Hor at the command of the LORD, and died there in the fortieth year after the children of Israel had come out of the land of Egypt, on the first *day* of the fifth month. 39 Aaron *was* one hundred and twenty-three years old when he died on Mount Hor.

40 Now the king of Arad, the Canaanite, who dwelt in the South in the land of Canaan, heard of the coming of the children of Israel.

41 So they departed from Mount Hor and camped at Zalmonah. 42 They departed from Zalmonah and camped at Punon. 43 They departed from Punon and camped at Oboth. 44 They departed from Oboth and camped at Ije Abarim, at the border of Moab. 45 They departed from Ijim[a] and camped at Dibon Gad. 46 They moved from Dibon Gad and camped at Almon Diblathaim. 47 They moved from Almon Diblathaim and camped in the mountains of Abarim, before Nebo. 48 They departed from the mountains of Abarim and camped in the plains of Moab by the Jordan, *across from* Jericho. 49 They camped by the Jordan, from Beth Jesimoth as far as the Abel Acacia Grove[a] in the plains of Moab.

50 Now the LORD spoke to Moses in the plains of Moab by the Jordan, *across from* Jericho, saying, 51 "Speak to the children of Israel, and say to them: 'When you have crossed the Jordan into the land of Canaan, 52 then you shall drive out all the inhabitants of the land from before you, destroy all their engraved stones, destroy all their molded images, and demolish all their high places; 53 you shall dispossess *the inhabitants of* the land and dwell in it, for I have given you the land to pos-

---

33:8 [a]Many Hebrew manuscripts, Samaritan Pentateuch, Syriac, Targum, and Vulgate read *from Pi Hahiroth* (compare verse 7).   33:45 [a]Same as *Ije Abarim*, verse 44   33:49 [a]Hebrew *Abel Shittim* sess. 54 And you shall divide the land by lot as an inheritance among your families; to the larger you shall give a larger inheritance, and to the smaller you shall give a smaller inheritance; there everyone's *inheritance* shall be whatever falls to him by lot. You shall inherit according to the tribes of your fathers. 55 But if you do not drive out the inhabitants of the land from before you, then it shall be that those whom you let remain *shall be* irritants in your eyes and thorns in your sides, and they shall harass you in the land where you dwell. 56 Moreover it shall be *that* I will do to you as I thought to do to them.' "

34 Then the LORD spoke to Moses, saying, 2 "Command the children of Israel, and say to them: 'When you come into the land of Canaan, this *is* the land that shall fall to you as an inheritance—the land of Canaan to its boundaries. 3 Your southern border shall be from the Wilderness of Zin along the border of Edom; then your southern border shall extend eastward to the end of the Salt Sea; 4 your border shall turn from the southern side of the Ascent of Akrabbim, continue to Zin, and be on the south of Kadesh Barnea; then it shall go on to Hazar Addar, and continue to Azmon; 5 the border shall turn from Azmon to the Brook of Egypt, and it shall end at the Sea.

6 'As for the western border, you shall have the Great Sea for a border; this shall be your western border.

7 'And this shall be your northern border: From the Great Sea you shall mark out your *border* line to Mount Hor; 8 from Mount Hor you shall mark out *your border* to the entrance of Hamath; then the direction of the border shall be toward Zedad; 9 the border shall proceed to Ziphron, and it shall end at Hazar Enan. This shall be your northern border.

10 'You shall mark out your eastern border from Hazar Enan to Shepham; 11 the border shall go down from Shepham to Riblah on the east side of Ain; the border shall go down and reach to the eastern side of the Sea of Chinnereth; 12 the border shall go down along the Jordan, and it shall end at the Salt Sea. This shall be your land with its surrounding boundaries.' "

13 Then Moses commanded the children of Israel, saying: "This *is* the land which you shall inherit by lot, which the LORD has commanded to give to the nine tribes and to the half-tribe. 14 For the tribe of the children of Reuben according to the house of their fathers, and the tribe of the children of Gad according to the house of their fathers, have received *their inheritance;* and the half-tribe of Manasseh has received its inheritance. 15 The two tribes and the half-tribe have received their inheritance on this side of the Jordan, *across from* Jericho eastward, toward the sunrise."

16 And the LORD spoke to Moses, saying, 17 "These *are* the names of the men who shall divide the land among you as an inheritance: Eleazar the priest and Joshua the son of Nun. 18 And you shall take one leader of every tribe to divide the land for the inheritance. 19 These *are* the names of the men: from the tribe of Judah, Caleb the son of Jephunneh; 20 from the tribe of the children of Simeon, Shemuel the son of Ammihud; 21 from the tribe of Benjamin, Elidad the son of Chislon; 22 a leader from the tribe of the children of Dan, Bukki the son of Jogli; 23 from the sons of Joseph: a leader from the tribe of the children of Manasseh, Hanniel the son of Ephod, 24 and a leader from the tribe of the children of Ephraim, Kemuel the son of Shiphtan; 25 a leader from the tribe of the children of Zebulun, Elizaphan the son of Parnach; 26 a leader from the tribe of the children of Issachar, Paltiel the son of Azzan; 27 a leader from the tribe of the children of Asher, Ahihud the son of Shelomi; 28 and a leader from the tribe of the children of Naphtali, Pedahel the son of Ammihud."

29 These *are* the ones the LORD commanded to divide the inheritance among the children of Israel in the land of Canaan.

35 And the LORD spoke to Moses in the plains of Moab by the Jordan *across from* Jericho, saying: 2 "Command the children of Israel that they give the Levites cities to dwell in from the inheritance of their possession, and you shall *also* give the Levites common-land around the cities. 3 They shall have the cities to dwell in; and their common-land shall be for their cattle, for their herds, and for all their animals. 4 The common-land of the cities which you will give the Levites *shall extend* from the wall of the city outward a thousand cubits all around. 5 And you shall measure outside the city on the east side two thousand cubits, on the south side two thousand cubits, on the west side two thousand cubits, and on the north side two thousand cubits. The city *shall be* in the middle. This shall belong to them as common-land for the cities.

6 "Now among the cities which you will give to the Levites *you shall appoint* six cities of refuge, to which a manslayer may flee. And to these you shall add forty-two cities. 7 So all the cities you will give to the Levites *shall be* forty-eight; these *you shall give* with their common-land. 8 And the cities which you will give *shall be* from the possession of the children of Israel; from the larger *tribe* you shall give many, from the smaller you shall give few. Each shall give some of its cities to the Levites, in proportion to the inheritance that each receives."

9 Then the LORD spoke to Moses, saying, 10 "Speak to the children of Israel, and say to them: 'When you cross the Jordan into the land of Canaan, 11 then you shall appoint cities to be cities of refuge for you, that the manslayer who kills any person accidentally may flee there. 12 They shall be cities of refuge for you from the avenger, that the manslayer may not die until he stands before the congregation in judgment. 13 And of the cities which you give, you shall have six cities of refuge. 14 You shall appoint three cities on this side of the Jordan, and three cities you shall appoint in the land of Canaan, *which* will be cities of refuge. 15 These six cities shall be for refuge for the children of Israel, for the stranger, and for the sojourner among them, that anyone who kills a person accidentally may flee there.

16 But if he strikes him with an iron implement, so that he dies, he *is* a murderer; the murderer shall surely be put to death. 17 And if he strikes him with a stone in the hand, by which one could die, and he does die, he *is* a murderer; the murderer shall surely be put to death. 18 Or *if* he strikes him with a wooden hand weapon, by which one could die, and he does die, he *is* a murderer; the murderer shall surely be put to death. 19 The avenger of blood himself shall put the murderer to death; when he meets him, he shall put him to death. 20 If he pushes him out of hatred or, while lying in wait, hurls something at him so that he dies, 21 or in enmity he strikes him with his hand so that he dies, the one who struck *him* shall surely be put to death. He *is* a murderer. The avenger of blood shall put the murderer to death when he meets him.

22 However, if he pushes him suddenly without enmity, or throws anything at him without lying in wait, 23 or uses a stone, by which a man could die, throwing *it* at him without seeing *him*, so that he dies, while he was not his enemy or seeking his harm, 24 then the congregation shall judge between the manslayer and the avenger of blood according to these judgments. 25 So the congregation shall deliver the manslayer from the hand of the avenger of blood, and the congregation shall return him to the city of refuge where he had fled, and he shall remain there until the death of the high priest who was anointed with the holy oil. 26 But if the manslayer at any time goes outside the limits of the city of refuge where he fled, 27 and the avenger of blood finds him outside the limits of his city of refuge, and the avenger of blood kills the manslayer, he shall not be guilty of blood, 28 because he should have remained in his city of refuge until the death of the high priest. But after the death of the high priest the manslayer may return to the land of his possession.

29 'And these *things* shall be a statute of judgment to you throughout your generations in all your dwellings. 30 Whoever kills a person, the murderer shall be put to death on the testimony of witnesses; but one witness is not *sufficient* testimony against a person for the death *penalty*. 31 Moreover you shall take no ransom for the life of a murderer who *is* guilty of death, but he shall surely be put to death. 32 And you shall take no ransom for him who has fled to his city of refuge, that he may return to dwell in the land before the death of the priest. 33 So you shall not pol-

lute the land where you *are;* for blood defiles the land, and no atonement can be made for the land, for the blood that is shed on it, except by the blood of him who shed it. 34 Therefore do not defile the land which you inhabit, in the midst of which I dwell; for I the LORD dwell among the children of Israel.' "

36 Now the chief fathers of the families of the children of Gilead the son of Machir, the son of Manasseh, of the families of the sons of Joseph, came near and spoke before Moses and before the leaders, the chief fathers of the children of Israel. 2 And they said: "The LORD commanded my lord *Moses* to give the land as an inheritance by lot to the children of Israel, and my lord was commanded by the LORD to give the inheritance of our brother Zelophehad to his daughters. 3 Now if they are married to any of the sons of the *other* tribes of the children of Israel, then their inheritance will be taken from the inheritance of our fathers, and it will be added to the inheritance of the tribe into which they marry; so it will be taken from the lot of our inheritance. 4 And when the Jubilee of the children of Israel comes, then their inheritance will be added to the inheritance of the tribe into which they marry; so their inheritance will be taken away from the inheritance of the tribe of our fathers."

5 Then Moses commanded the children of Israel according to the word of the LORD, saying: "What the tribe of the sons of Joseph speaks is right. 6 This *is* what the LORD commands concerning the daughters of Zelophehad, saying, 'Let them marry whom they think best, but they may marry only within the family of their father's tribe.' 7 So the inheritance of the children of Israel shall not change hands from tribe to tribe, for every one of the children of Israel shall keep the inheritance of the tribe of his fathers. 8 And every daughter who possesses an inheritance in any tribe of the children of Israel shall be the wife of one of the family of her father's tribe, so that the children of Israel each may possess the inheritance of his fathers. 9 Thus no inheritance shall change hands from *one* tribe to another, but every tribe of the children of Israel shall keep its own inheritance."

10 Just as the LORD commanded Moses, so did the daughters of Zelophehad; 11 for Mahlah, Tirzah, Hoglah, Milcah, and Noah, the daughters of Zelophehad, were married to the sons of their father's brothers. 12 They were married into the families of the children of Manasseh the son of Joseph, and their inheritance remained in the tribe of their father's family.

13 These *are* the commandments and the judgments which the LORD commanded the children of Israel by the hand of Moses in the plains of Moab by the Jordan, *across from* Jericho.

Deuteronomy

Overview of Deuteronomy

Deuteronomy is an inspiring account of the children of Israel's preparation to enter the Promised Land. Their dream was about to become a reality!

Written by Moses about 1400 B.C., Deuteronomy summarizes the forty years of hard wilderness wandering and God's faithfulness throughout their time of need. Moses reiterates the Ten Commandments to the people as God's way to the good life. He also gives them new laws to help guard their minds and thoughts upon entering the new land with its foreign customs, cultures, and false gods.

Although Moses knew he would not enter the land which he had led the people to, he was not bitter or negative. Rather, he recounted for his countrymen the blessings of God, His care and comfort of His people, and their blessings upon reaching the Promised Land. He also spoke a special blessing for each tribe and prayed for their continued success.

Moses also appointed Joshua as the new leader of the people and encouraged him with the promise, "Be strong and of good courage, for you must go with this people to the land which the LORD has sworn to their fathers to give them, and you shall cause them to inherit it. And the LORD, He *is* the One who goes before you. He will be with you, He will not leave you nor forsake you; do not fear nor be dismayed" (Deut. 31:7, 8).

When the Israelites were on the threshold of realizing their dream, Moses reminded them to "love the LORD your God with all your heart, with all your soul, and with all your strength" (Deut. 6:5). Moses wanted to ensure that the Israelites would make a careful assessment of their lives. They needed to map out not only their future plans, but their personal relationships with God as well. Their dream would come true when they tapped into God's power!

Jesus in Deuteronomy

Moses himself is a type of Christ, filling for Israel the three offices of prophet, priest, and king. Both Moses and Jesus are in danger during childhood; both are saviors and intercessors for their people; and both are rejected by their brethren. Moses prophesies about Jesus' coming in Deuteronomy 18:15, telling Israel that God will raise up a Prophet among them and "Him you shall hear."

Keys to Deuteronomy

Key Word: Covenant. The primary theme of the entire Book of Deuteronomy is the renewal of the covenant. Originally established at Mount Sinai, the covenant is enlarged and renewed on the plains of Moab.

Key Verses: "And now, Israel, what does the LORD your God require of you, but to fear the LORD your God, to walk in all His ways and to love Him, to serve the LORD your God with all your heart and with all your soul, *and* to keep the commandments of the LORD and His statutes which I command you today for your good?" (10:12, 13).

"I call heaven and earth as witnesses today against you, *that* I have set before you life and death, blessing and cursing; therefore choose life, that both you and your descendants may live; that you may love the LORD your God, that you may obey His voice, and that you may cling to Him, for He *is* your life and the length of your days; and that you may dwell in the land which the LORD swore to your fathers, to Abraham, Isaac, and Jacob, to give them" (30:19, 20).

Key Chapter: Deuteronomy 27. The formal ratification of the covenant occurs in chapter 27 as Moses and the priests declare, "This day you have become the people of the LORD your God" (27:9).

1 These *are* the words which Moses spoke to all Israel on this side of the Jordan in the wilderness, in the plain*a* opposite Suph,*b* between Paran, Tophel, Laban, Hazeroth, and Dizahab. 2 *It is* eleven days' *journey* from Horeb by way of Mount Seir to Kadesh Barnea. 3 Now it came to pass in the fortieth year, in the eleventh month, on the first *day* of the month, *that* Moses spoke to the children of Israel according to all that the LORD had given him as commandments to them, 4 after he had killed Sihon king of the Amorites, who dwelt in Heshbon, and Og king of Bashan, who dwelt at Ashtaroth in*a* Edrei.

5 On this side of the Jordan in the land of Moab, Moses began to ex-

1:1 *a*Hebrew *arabah*   *b*One manuscript of the Septuagint, also Targum and Vulgate, read *Red Sea.*
1:4 *a*Septuagint, Syriac, and Vulgate read *and* (compare Joshua 12:4).

plain this law, saying, 6 "The LORD our God spoke to us in Horeb, saying: 'You have dwelt long enough at this mountain. 7 Turn and take your journey, and go to the mountains of the Amorites, to all the neighboring *places* in the plain,*a* in the mountains and in the lowland, in the South and on the seacoast, to the land of the Canaanites and to Lebanon, as far as the great river, the River Euphrates. 8 See, I have set the land before you; go in and possess the land which the LORD swore to your fathers—to Abraham, Isaac, and Jacob—to give to them and their descendants after them.'

9 "And I spoke to you at that time, saying: 'I alone am not able to bear you. 10 The LORD your God has multiplied you, and here you *are* today, as the stars of heaven in multitude. 11 May the LORD God of your fathers make you a thousand times more numerous than you are, and bless you as He has promised you! 12 How can I alone bear your problems and your burdens and your complaints? 13 Choose wise, understanding, and knowledgeable men from among your tribes, and I will make them heads over you.' 14 And you answered me and said, 'The thing which you have told *us* to do *is* good.' 15 So I took the heads of your tribes, wise and knowledgeable men, and made them heads over you, leaders of thousands, leaders of hundreds, leaders of fifties, leaders of tens, and officers for your tribes.

16 "Then I commanded your judges at that time, saying, 'Hear *the cases* between your brethren, and judge righteously between a man and his brother or the stranger who is with him. 17 You shall not show partiality in judgment; you shall hear the small as well as the great; you shall not be afraid in any man's presence, for the judgment *is* God's. The case that is too hard for you, bring to me, and I will hear it.' 18 And I commanded you at that time all the things which you should do.

19 "So we departed from Horeb, and went through all that great and terrible wilderness which you saw on the way to the mountains of the Amorites, as the LORD our God had commanded us. Then we came to Kadesh Barnea. 20 And I said to you, 'You have come to the mountains of the Amorites, which the LORD our God is giving us. 21 Look, the LORD your God has set the land before you; go up *and* possess *it*, as the LORD God of your fathers has spoken to you; do not fear or be discouraged.'

22 "And every one of you came near to me and said, 'Let us send men before us, and let them search out the land for us, and bring back word to us of the way by which we should go up, and of the cities into which we shall come.'

23 "The plan pleased me well; so I took twelve of your men, one man from *each* tribe. 24 And they departed and went up into the mountains, and came to the Valley of Eshcol, and spied it out. 25 They also took *some* of the fruit of the land in their hands and brought *it* down to us; and they brought back word to us, saying, '*It is* a good land which the LORD our God is giving us.'

26 "Nevertheless you would not go up, but rebelled against the command of the LORD your God; 27 and you complained in your tents, and said, 'Because the LORD hates us, He has brought us out of the land of Egypt to deliver us into the hand of the Amorites, to destroy us. 28 Where can we go up? Our brethren have discouraged our hearts, saying, "The people *are* greater and taller than we; the cities *are* great and fortified up to heaven; moreover we have seen the sons of the Anakim there." '

29 "Then I said to you, 'Do not be terrified, or afraid of them. 30 The LORD your God, who goes before you, He will fight for you, according to all He did for you in Egypt before your eyes, 31 and in the wilderness where you saw how the LORD your God carried you, as a man carries his son, in all the way that you went until you came to this place.' 32 Yet, for all that, you did not believe the LORD your God, 33 who went in the way before you to search out a place for you to pitch your tents, to show you the way you should go, in the fire by night and in the cloud by day.

34 "And the LORD heard the sound of your words, and was angry, and took an oath, saying, 35 'Surely not one of these men of this evil genera-

1:7 *a*Hebrew *arabah*

tion shall see that good land of which I swore to give to your fathers, 36 except Caleb the son of Jephunneh; he shall see it, and to him and his children I am giving the land on which he walked, because he wholly followed the Lord.' 37 The Lord was also angry with me for your sakes, saying, 'Even you shall not go in there. 38 Joshua the son of Nun, who stands before you, he shall go in there. Encourage him, for he shall cause Israel to inherit it.

39 'Moreover your little ones and your children, who you say will be victims, who today have no knowledge of good and evil, they shall go in there; to them I will give it, and they shall possess it. 40 But *as for* you, turn and take your journey into the wilderness by the Way of the Red Sea.'

41 "Then you answered and said to me, 'We have sinned against the Lord; we will go up and fight, just as the Lord our God commanded us.' And when everyone of you had girded on his weapons of war, you were ready to go up into the mountain.

42 "And the Lord said to me, 'Tell them, "Do not go up nor fight, for I *am* not among you; lest you be defeated before your enemies."'

43 So I spoke to you; yet you would not listen, but rebelled against the command of the Lord, and presumptuously went up into the mountain. 44 And the Amorites who dwelt in that mountain came out against you and chased you as bees do, and drove you back from Seir to Hormah. 45 Then you returned and wept before the Lord, but the Lord would not listen to your voice nor give ear to you.

46 "So you remained in Kadesh many days, according to the days that you spent *there*.

2 "Then we turned and journeyed into the wilderness of the Way of the Red Sea, as the Lord spoke to me, and we skirted Mount Seir for many days.

2 "And the Lord spoke to me, saying: 3 'You have skirted this mountain long enough; turn northward. 4 And command the people, saying, "You *are about to* pass through the territory of your brethren, the descendants of Esau, who live in Seir; and they will be afraid of you. Therefore watch yourselves carefully. 5 Do not meddle with them, for I will not give you *any* of their land, no, not so much as one footstep, because I have given Mount Seir to Esau *as* a possession. 6 You shall buy food from them with money, that you may eat; and you shall also buy water from them with money, that you may drink.

7 "For the Lord your God has blessed you in all the work of your hand. He knows your trudging through this great wilderness. These forty years the Lord your God *has been* with you; you have lacked nothing."'

8 "And when we passed beyond our brethren, the descendants of Esau who dwell in Seir, away from the road of the plain, away from Elath and Ezion Geber, we turned and passed by way of the Wilderness of Moab. 9 Then the Lord said to me, 'Do not harass Moab, nor contend with them in battle, for I will not give you *any* of their land *as* a possession, because I have given Ar to the descendants of Lot *as* a possession.' "

10 (The Emim had dwelt there in times past, a people as great and numerous and tall as the Anakim. 11 They were also regarded as giants,*a* like the Anakim, but the Moabites call them Emim. 12 The Horites formerly dwelt in Seir, but the descendants of Esau dispossessed them and destroyed them from before them, and dwelt in their place, just as Israel did to the land of their possession which the Lord gave them.)

13 " 'Now rise and cross over the Valley of the Zered.' So we crossed over the Valley of the Zered. 14 And the time we took to come from Kadesh Barnea until we crossed over the Valley of the Zered *was* thirty-eight years, until all the generation of the men of war was consumed from the midst of the camp, just as the Lord had sworn to them. 15 For indeed the hand of the Lord was against them, to destroy them from the midst of the camp until they were consumed.

16 "So it was, when all the men of war had finally perished from among the people, 17 that the Lord spoke to

2:11 *a*Hebrew *rephaim*

me, saying: 18 'This day you are to cross over at Ar, the boundary of Moab. 19 And *when* you come near the people of Ammon, do not harass them or meddle with them, for I will not give you *any* of the land of the people of Ammon *as* a possession, because I have given it to the descendants of Lot *as* a possession.' "

20 (That was also regarded as a land of giants;[a] giants formerly dwelt there. But the Ammonites call them Zamzummim, 21 a people as great and numerous and tall as the Anakim. But the LORD destroyed them before them, and they dispossessed them and dwelt in their place, 22 just as He had done for the descendants of Esau, who dwelt in Seir, when He destroyed the Horites from before them. They dispossessed them and dwelt in their place, even to this day. 23 And the Avim, who dwelt in villages as far as Gaza—the Caphtorim, who came from Caphtor, destroyed them and dwelt in their place.)

24 " 'Rise, take your journey, and cross over the River Arnon. Look, I have given into your hand Sihon the Amorite, king of Heshbon, and his land. Begin to possess *it*, and engage him in battle. 25 This day I will begin to put the dread and fear of you upon the nations under the whole heaven, who shall hear the report of you, and shall tremble and be in anguish because of you.'

26 "And I sent messengers from the Wilderness of Kedemoth to Sihon king of Heshbon, with words of peace, saying, 27 'Let me pass through your land; I will keep strictly to the road, and I will turn neither to the right nor to the left. 28 You shall sell me food for money, that I may eat, and give me water for money, that I may drink; only let me pass through on foot, 29 just as the descendants of Esau who dwell in Seir and the Moabites who dwell in Ar did for me, until I cross the Jordan to the land which the LORD our God is giving us.'

30 "But Sihon king of Heshbon would not let us pass through, for the LORD your God hardened his spirit and made his heart obstinate, that He might deliver him into your hand, as *it is* this day.

31 "And the LORD said to me, 'See, I have begun to give Sihon and his land over to you. Begin to possess *it*, that you may inherit his land.' 32 Then Sihon and all his people came out against us to fight at Jahaz. 33 And the LORD our God delivered him over to us; so we defeated him, his sons, and all his people. 34 We took all his cities at that time, and we utterly destroyed the men, women, and little ones of every city; we left none remaining. 35 We took only the livestock as plunder for ourselves, with the spoil of the cities which we took. 36 From Aroer, which *is* on the bank of the River Arnon, and *from* the city that *is* in the ravine, as far as Gilead, there was not one city too strong for us; the LORD our God delivered all to us. 37 Only you did not go near the land of the people of Ammon—anywhere along the River Jabbok, or to the cities of the mountains, or wherever the LORD our God had forbidden us.

3 "Then we turned and went up the road to Bashan; and Og king of Bashan came out against us, he and all his people, to battle at Edrei. 2 And the LORD said to me, 'Do not fear him, for I have delivered him and all his people and his land into your hand; you shall do to him as you did to Sihon king of the Amorites, who dwelt at Heshbon.'

3 "So the LORD our God also delivered into our hands Og king of Bashan, with all his people, and we attacked him until he had no survivors remaining. 4 And we took all his cities at that time; there was not a city which we did not take from them: sixty cities, all the region of Argob, the kingdom of Og in Bashan. 5 All these cities *were* fortified with high walls, gates, and bars, besides a great many rural towns. 6 And we utterly destroyed them, as we did to Sihon king of Heshbon, utterly destroying the men, women, and children of every city. 7 But all the livestock and the spoil of the cities we took as booty for ourselves.

8 "And at that time we took the land from the hand of the two kings of the Amorites who *were* on this side of the Jordan, from the River Arnon to Mount Hermon 9 (the Sidonians

2:20 [a]Hebrew *rephaim*

Alive and Flowing

The Jordan Rift Valley is one of the most interesting geological structures in the world, stretching from Lake Homs in Syria, all the way down to Lake Victoria in Africa.

This 1,500-mile-long earthquake fault passes through a variety of terrains, ranging from the snow-capped panoramic mountains of northern Syria to the barren desert landscape of Sinai. The Rift Valley encompasses two landlocked bodies of water: the Sea of Galilee, located 700 feet below sea level, and the Dead Sea, located 1,300 feet below sea level.

Both seas are located in the same valley, fed by the same Jordan River. Yet, they are completely different in nature. The Sea of Galilee is a freshwater lake teeming with fish, while the Dead Sea is thirty-three percent salt in which no living thing can exist.

The difference between the two lakes is that the northern Sea of Galilee has a southern exit through which it can give out the water it takes in. The Dead Sea does not. The water that enters the Dead Sea is not allowed to circulate. It has no exit, so it stagnates, dries up, and crystallizes, until it forms large blocks of salt around the shores of the sea.

We must be like the northern Sea of Galilee and allow dreams and creative ideas to flow into our lives and circulate with our time, talents, abilities, energies, and education. As we share our gifts with others, Ephesians 4:15, 16 says we will enrich the lives of others and cause "the growth of the body for the [building up] of itself in love."

If we can be service-minded, then we can be used by God and give life to those around us!

call Hermon Sirion, and the Amorites call it Senir), 10 all the cities of the plain, all Gilead, and all Bashan, as far as Salcah and Edrei, cities of the kingdom of Og in Bashan.

11 "For only Og king of Bashan remained of the remnant of the giants.[a] Indeed his bedstead *was* an iron bedstead. (*Is* it not in Rabbah of the people of Ammon?) Nine cubits *is* its length and four cubits its width, according to the standard cubit.

12 And this land, *which* we possessed at that time, from Aroer, which *is* by the River Arnon, and half the mountains of Gilead and its cities, I gave to the Reubenites and the Gadites. 13 The rest of Gilead, and all Bashan, the kingdom of Og, I gave to half the tribe of Manasseh. (All the region of Argob, with all Bashan, was called the land of the giants.[a] 14 Jair the son of Manasseh took all the region of Argob, as far as the border of the Geshurites and the Maachathites, and called Bashan after his own name, Havoth Jair,[a] to this day.)

15 "Also I gave Gilead to Machir. 16 And to the Reubenites and the Gadites I gave from Gilead as far as the River Arnon, the middle of the river as *the* border, as far as the River Jabbok, the border of the people of Ammon; 17 the plain also, with the Jordan as *the* border, from Chinnereth as far as the east side of the Sea of the Arabah (the Salt Sea), below the slopes of Pisgah.

18 "Then I commanded you at that time, saying: 'The Lord your God has given you this land to possess. All you men of valor shall cross over armed before your brethren, the children of Israel. 19 But your wives, your little ones, and your livestock (I know that you have much livestock) shall stay in your cities which I have given you, 20 until the Lord has given rest to your brethren as to you, and they also possess the land which the Lord your God is giving them beyond the Jordan. Then each of you may return to his possession which I have given you.'

21 And I commanded Joshua at that time, saying, 'Your eyes have seen all that the Lord your God has done to these two kings; so will the Lord do to all the kingdoms through which you pass. 22 You must not fear them, for the Lord your God Himself fights for you.'

23 "Then I pleaded with the Lord at that time, saying: 24 'O Lord God, You have begun to show Your servant Your greatness and Your mighty hand, for what god *is there* in heaven or on earth who can do *anything* like Your works and Your mighty *deeds?* 25 I pray, let me cross over and see the good land beyond the Jordan, those pleasant mountains, and Lebanon.'

26 "But the Lord was angry with me on your account, and would not listen to me. So the Lord said to me: 'Enough of that! Speak no more to Me of this matter. 27 Go up to the top of Pisgah, and lift your eyes toward the west, the north, the south, and the east; behold *it* with your eyes, for you shall not cross over this Jordan. 28 But command Joshua, and encourage him and strengthen him; for he shall go over before this people, and he shall cause them to inherit the land which you will see.'

29 "So we stayed in the valley opposite Beth Peor.

4 "Now, O Israel, listen to the statutes and the judgments which I teach you to observe, that you may live, and go in and possess the land which the Lord God of your fathers is giving you. 2 You shall not add to the word which I command you, nor take from it, that you may keep the commandments of the Lord your God which I command you. 3 Your eyes have seen what the Lord did at Baal Peor; for the Lord your God has destroyed from among you all the men who followed Baal of Peor. 4 But you who held fast to the Lord your God *are* alive today, every one of you.

5 "Surely I have taught you statutes and judgments, just as the Lord my God commanded me, that you should act according *to them* in the land which you go to possess. 6 Therefore be careful to observe *them;* for this *is* your wisdom and your understanding in the sight of the peoples who will hear all these statutes, and say, 'Surely this great nation *is* a wise and understanding people.'

7 "For what great nation *is there*

3:11 ᵃHebrew *rephaim*   3:13 ᵃHebrew *rephaim*   3:14 ᵃLiterally *Towns of Jair* that has God *so* near to it, as the LORD our God *is* to us, for whatever *reason* we may call upon Him? 8 And what great nation *is there* that has *such* statutes and righteous judgments as are in all this law which I set before you this day? 9 Only take heed to yourself, and diligently keep yourself, lest you forget the things your eyes have seen, and lest they depart from your heart all the days of your life. And teach them to your children and your grandchildren, 10 *especially concerning* the day you stood before the LORD your God in Horeb, when the LORD said to me, 'Gather the people to Me, and I will let them hear My words, that they may learn to fear Me all the days they live on the earth, and *that* they may teach their children.'

11 "Then you came near and stood at the foot of the mountain, and the mountain burned with fire to the midst of heaven, with darkness, cloud, and thick darkness. 12 And the LORD spoke to you out of the midst of the fire. You heard the sound of the words, but saw no form; *you* only *heard* a voice. 13 So He declared to you His covenant which He commanded you to perform, the Ten Commandments; and He wrote them on two tablets of stone. 14 And the LORD commanded me at that time to teach you statutes and judgments, that you might observe them in the land which you cross over to possess.

15 "Take careful heed to yourselves, for you saw no form when the LORD spoke to you at Horeb out of the midst of the fire, 16 lest you act corruptly and make for yourselves a carved image in the form of any figure: the likeness of male or female, 17 the likeness of any animal that *is* on the earth or the likeness of any winged bird that flies in the air, 18 the likeness of anything that creeps on the ground or the likeness of any fish that *is* in the water beneath the earth. 19 And *take heed,* lest you lift your eyes to heaven, and *when* you see the sun, and the moon, and the stars, all the host of heaven, you feel driven to worship them and serve them, which the LORD your God has given to all the peoples under the whole heaven as a heritage. 20 But the LORD has taken you and brought you out of the iron furnace, out of Egypt, to be His people, an in-

heritance, as you are this day. 21 Furthermore the LORD was angry with me for your sakes, and swore that I would not cross over the Jordan, and that I would not enter the good land which the LORD your God is giving you as an inheritance. 22 But I must die in this land, I must not cross over the Jordan; but you shall cross over and possess that good land. 23 Take heed to yourselves, lest you forget the covenant of the LORD your God which He made with you, and make for yourselves a carved image in the form of anything which the LORD your God has forbidden you. 24 For the LORD your God *is* a consuming fire, a jealous God.

25 "When you beget children and grandchildren and have grown old in the land, and act corruptly and make a carved image in the form of anything, and do evil in the sight of the LORD your God to provoke Him to anger, 26 I call heaven and earth to witness against you this day, that you will soon utterly perish from the land which you cross over the Jordan to possess; you will not prolong *your* days in it, but will be utterly destroyed. 27 And the LORD will scatter you among the peoples, and you will be left few in number among the nations where the LORD will drive you. 28 And there you will serve gods, the work of men's hands, wood and stone, which neither see nor hear nor eat nor smell. 29 But from there you will seek the LORD your God, and you will find *Him* if you seek Him with all your heart and with all your soul. 30 When you are in distress, and all these things come upon you in the latter days, when you turn to the LORD your God and obey His voice 31 (for the LORD your God *is* a merciful God), He will not forsake you nor destroy you, nor forget the covenant of your fathers which He swore to them.

32 "For ask now concerning the days that are past, which were before you, since the day that God created man on the earth, and *ask* from one end of heaven to the other, whether *any* great *thing* like this has happened, or *anything* like it has been heard. 33 Did *any* people *ever* hear the voice of God speaking out of the midst of the fire, as you have heard, and live? 34 Or did God *ever* try to go *and* take for Himself a nation from

the midst of *another* nation, by trials, by signs, by wonders, by war, by a mighty hand and an outstretched arm, and by great terrors, according to all that the LORD your God did for you in Egypt before your eyes? 35 To you it was shown, that you might know that the LORD Himself *is* God; *there is* none other besides Him. 36 Out of heaven He let you hear His voice, that He might instruct you; on earth He showed you His great fire, and you heard His words out of the midst of the fire. 37 And because He loved your fathers, therefore He chose their descendants after them; and He brought you out of Egypt with His Presence, with His mighty power, 38 driving out from before you nations greater and mightier than you, to bring you in, to give you their land *as* an inheritance, as *it is* this day. 39 Therefore know this day, and consider *it* in your heart, that the LORD Himself *is* God in heaven above and on the earth beneath; *there is* no other. 40 You shall therefore keep His statutes and His commandments which I command you today, that it may go well with you and with your children after you, and that you may prolong *your* days in the land which the LORD your God is giving you for all time."

41 Then Moses set apart three cities on this side of the Jordan, toward the rising of the sun, 42 that the manslayer might flee there, who kills his neighbor unintentionally, without having hated him in time past, and that by fleeing to one of these cities he might live: 43 Bezer in the wilderness on the plateau for the Reubenites, Ramoth in Gilead for the Gadites, and Golan in Bashan for the Manassites.

44 Now this *is* the law which Moses set before the children of Israel. 45 These *are* the testimonies, the statutes, and the judgments which Moses spoke to the children of Israel after they came out of Egypt, 46 on this side of the Jordan, in the valley opposite Beth Peor, in the land of Sihon king of the Amorites, who dwelt at Heshbon, whom Moses and the children of Israel defeated after they came out of Egypt. 47 And they took possession of his land and the land of Og king of Bashan, two kings of the Amorites, who *were* on this side of the Jordan, toward the rising of the sun, 48 from Aroer, which *is* on the bank of the River Arnon, even to Mount Sion[a] (that is, Hermon), 49 and all the plain on the east side of the Jordan as far as the Sea of the Arabah, below the slopes of Pisgah.

5 And Moses called all Israel, and said to them: "Hear, O Israel, the statutes and judgments which I speak in your hearing today, that you may learn them and be careful to observe them. 2 The LORD our God made a covenant with us in Horeb. 3 The LORD did not make this covenant with our fathers, but with us, those who *are* here today, all of us who *are* alive. 4 The LORD talked with you face to face on the mountain from the midst of the fire. 5 I stood between the LORD and you at that time, to declare to you the word of the LORD; for you were afraid because of the fire, and you did not go up the mountain. '*He* said:

6   'I *am* the LORD your God who brought you out of the land of Egypt, out of the house of bondage.

7   'You shall have no other gods before Me.

8   'You shall not make for yourself a carved image—any likeness *of anything* that *is* in heaven above, or that *is* in the earth beneath, or that *is* in the water under the earth; 9 you shall not bow down to them nor serve them. For I, the LORD your God, *am* a jealous God, visiting the iniquity of the fathers upon the children to the third and fourth *generations* of those who hate Me, 10 but showing mercy to thousands, to those who love Me and keep My commandments.

11   'You shall not take the name of the LORD your God in vain, for the LORD will not hold *him* guiltless who takes His name in vain.

12   'Observe the Sabbath day, to keep it holy, as the LORD your God commanded you.

13   Six days you shall labor

and do all your work,
14 but the seventh day *is* the Sabbath of the LORD your God. *In it* you shall do no work: you, nor your son, nor your daughter, nor your male servant, nor your female servant, nor your ox, nor your donkey, nor any of your cattle, nor your stranger who *is* within your gates, that your male servant and your female servant may rest as well as you. 15 And remember that you were a slave in the land of Egypt, and the LORD your God brought you out from there by a mighty hand and by an outstretched arm; therefore the LORD your God commanded you to keep the Sabbath day.

16 'Honor your father and your mother, as the LORD your God has commanded you, that your days may be long, and that it may be well with you in the land which the LORD your God is giving you.
17 'You shall not murder.
18 'You shall not commit adultery.
19 'You shall not steal.
20 'You shall not bear false witness against your neighbor.
21 'You shall not covet your neighbor's wife; and you shall not desire your neighbor's house, his field, his male servant, his female servant, his ox, his donkey, or anything that *is* your neighbor's.'

22 "These words the LORD spoke to all your assembly, in the mountain from the midst of the fire, the cloud, and the thick darkness, with a loud voice; and He added no more. And He wrote them on two tablets of stone and gave them to me.
23 "So it was, when you heard the voice from the midst of the darkness, while the mountain was burning with fire, that you came near to me, all the heads of your tribes and your elders. 24 And you said: 'Surely the LORD our God has shown us His glory and His greatness, and we have heard His voice from the midst of the fire. We have seen this day that God

speaks with man; yet he *still* lives. 25 Now therefore, why should we die? For this great fire will consume us; if we hear the voice of the LORD our God anymore, then we shall die. 26 For who *is there* of all flesh who has heard the voice of the living God speaking from the midst of the fire, as we *have*, and lived? 27 You go near and hear all that the LORD our God may say, and tell us all that the LORD our God says to you, and we will hear and do *it*.'

28 "Then the LORD heard the voice of your words when you spoke to me, and the LORD said to me: 'I have heard the voice of the words of this people which they have spoken to you. They are right *in* all that they have spoken. 29 Oh, that they had such a heart in them that they would fear Me and always keep all My commandments, that it might be well with them and with their children forever! 30 Go and say to them, "Return to your tents." 31 But as for you, stand here by Me, and I will speak to you all the commandments, the statutes, and the judgments which you shall teach them, that they may observe *them* in the land which I am giving them to possess.'
32 "Therefore you shall be careful to do as the LORD your God has commanded you; you shall not turn aside to the right hand or to the left. 33 You shall walk in all the ways which the LORD your God has commanded you, that you may live and *that it may be* well with you, and *that* you may prolong *your* days in the land which you shall possess.

6 "Now this *is* the commandment, *and these are* the statutes and judgments which the LORD your God has commanded to teach you, that you may observe *them* in the land which you are crossing over to possess, 2 that you may fear the LORD your God, to keep all His statutes and His commandments which I command you, you and your son and your grandson, all the days of your life, and that your days may be prolonged. 3 Therefore hear, O Israel, and be careful to observe *it*, that it may be well with you, and that you may multiply greatly as the LORD God of your fathers has promised

you—'a land flowing with milk and honey.'*a*

4 "Hear, O Israel: The LORD our God, the LORD *is* one!*a* 5 You shall love the LORD your God with all your heart, with all your soul, and with all your strength.

6 "And these words which I command you today shall be in your heart. 7 You shall teach them diligently to your children, and shall talk of them when you sit in your house, when you walk by the way, when you lie down, and when you rise up. 8 You shall bind them as a sign on your hand, and they shall be as frontlets between your eyes. 9 You shall write them on the doorposts of your house and on your gates.

10 "So it shall be, when the LORD your God brings you into the land of which He swore to your fathers, to Abraham, Isaac, and Jacob, to give you large and beautiful cities which you did not build, 11 houses full of all good things, which you did not fill, hewn-out wells which you did not dig, vineyards and olive trees which you did not plant—when you have eaten and are full— 12 *then* beware, lest you forget the LORD who brought you out of the land of Egypt, from the house of bondage. 13 You shall fear the LORD your God and serve Him, and shall take oaths in His name. 14 You shall not go after other gods, the gods of the peoples who *are* all around you 15 (for the LORD your God *is* a jealous God among you), lest the anger of the LORD your God be aroused against you and destroy you from the face of the earth.

16 "You shall not tempt the LORD your God as you tempted *Him* in Massah. 17 You shall diligently keep the commandments of the LORD your God, His testimonies, and His statutes which He has commanded you. 18 And you shall do *what is* right and good in the sight of the LORD, that it may be well with you, and that you may go in and possess the good land of which the LORD swore to your fathers, 19 to cast out all your enemies from before you, as the LORD has spoken.

20 "When your son asks you in time to come, saying, 'What *is the* meaning *of* the testimonies, the stat-

utes, and the judgments which the LORD our God has commanded you?' 21 then you shall say to your son: 'We were slaves of Pharaoh in Egypt, and the LORD brought us out of Egypt with a mighty hand; 22 and the LORD showed signs and wonders before our eyes, great and severe, against Egypt, Pharaoh, and all his household. 23 Then He brought us out from there, that He might bring us in, to give us the land of which He swore to our fathers. 24 And the LORD commanded us to observe all these statutes, to fear the LORD our God, for our good always, that He might preserve us alive, as *it is* this day. 25 Then it will be righteousness for us, if we are careful to observe all these commandments before the LORD our God, as He has commanded us.'

7 "When the LORD your God brings you into the land which you go to possess, and has cast out many nations before you, the Hittites and the Girgashites and the Amorites and the Canaanites and the Perizzites and the Hivites and the Jebusites, seven nations greater and mightier than you, 2 and when the LORD your God delivers them over to you, you shall conquer them *and* utterly destroy them. You shall make no covenant with them nor show mercy to them. 3 Nor shall you make marriages with them. You shall not give your daughter to their son, nor take their daughter for your son. 4 For they will turn your sons away from following Me, to serve other gods; so the anger of the LORD will be aroused against you and destroy you suddenly. 5 But thus you shall deal with them: you shall destroy their altars, and break down their *sacred* pillars, and cut down their wooden images,*a* and burn their carved images with fire.

6 "For you *are* a holy people to the LORD your God; the LORD your God has chosen you to be a people for Himself, a special treasure above all the peoples on the face of the earth. 7 The LORD did not set His love on you nor choose you because you were more in number than any other people, for you were the least of all peoples; 8 but because the LORD loves

6:3 *a*Exodus 3:8   6:4 *a*Or *The* LORD *is our God, the* LORD *alone* (that is, the only one)   7:5 *a*Hebrew *Asherim,* Canaanite deities you, and because He would keep the oath which He swore to your fathers, the LORD has brought you out with a mighty hand, and redeemed you from the house of bondage, from the hand of Pharaoh king of Egypt.

9 "Therefore know that the LORD your God, He *is* God, the faithful God who keeps covenant and mercy for a thousand generations with those who love Him and keep His commandments; 10 and He repays those who hate Him to their face, to destroy them. He will not be slack with him who hates Him; He will repay him to his face. 11 Therefore you shall keep the commandment, the statutes, and the judgments which I command you today, to observe them.

12 "Then it shall come to pass, because you listen to these judgments, and keep and do them, that the LORD your God will keep with you the covenant and the mercy which He swore to your fathers. 13 And He will love you and bless you and multiply you; He will also bless the fruit of your womb and the fruit of your land, your grain and your new wine and your oil, the increase of your cattle and the offspring of your flock, in the land of which He swore to your fathers to give you. 14 You shall be blessed above all peoples; there shall not be a male or female barren among you or among your livestock. 15 And the LORD will take away from you all sickness, and will afflict you with none of the terrible diseases of Egypt which you have known, but will lay *them* on all those who hate you. 16 Also you shall destroy all the peoples whom the LORD your God delivers over to you; your eye shall have no pity on them; nor shall you serve their gods, for that *will be* a snare to you.

17 "If you should say in your heart, 'These nations are greater than I; how can I dispossess them?'— 18 you shall not be afraid of them, *but* you shall remember well what the LORD your God did to Pharaoh and to all Egypt: 19 the great trials which your eyes saw, the signs and the wonders, the mighty hand and the outstretched arm, by which the LORD your God brought you out. So shall the LORD your God do to all the peoples of whom you are afraid. 20 Moreover the LORD your God will send the hornet among them until those who are left, who hide themselves from you, are destroyed. 21 You shall not be terrified of them; for the LORD your God, the great and awesome God, *is* among you. 22 And the LORD your God will drive out those nations before you little by little; you will be unable to destroy them at once, lest the beasts of the field become *too* numerous for you. 23 But the LORD your God will deliver them over to you, and will inflict defeat upon them until they are destroyed. 24 And He will deliver their kings into your hand, and you will destroy their name from under heaven; no one shall be able to stand against you until you have destroyed them. 25 You shall burn the carved images of their gods with fire; you shall not covet the silver or gold *that is* on them, nor take *it* for yourselves, lest you be snared by it; for it *is* an abomination to the LORD your God. 26 Nor shall you bring an abomination into your house, lest you be doomed to destruction like it. You shall utterly detest it and utterly abhor it, for it *is* an accursed thing.

8 "Every commandment which I command you today you must be careful to observe, that you may live and multiply, and go in and possess the land of which the LORD swore to your fathers. 2 And you shall remember that the LORD your God led you all the way these forty years in the wilderness, to humble you *and* test you, to know what *was* in your heart, whether you would keep His commandments or not. 3 So He humbled you, allowed you to hunger, and fed you with manna which you did not know nor did your fathers know, that He might make you know that man shall not live by bread alone; but man lives by every *word* that proceeds from the mouth of the LORD. 4 Your garments did not wear out on you, nor did your foot swell these forty years. 5 You should know in your heart that as a man chastens his son, *so* the LORD your God chastens you.

6 "Therefore you shall keep the commandments of the LORD your God, to walk in His ways and to fear Him. 7 For the LORD your God is bringing you into a good land, a land of brooks of water, of fountains and springs, that flow out of valleys and

hills; 8 a land of wheat and barley, of vines and fig trees and pomegranates, a land of olive oil and honey; 9 a land in which you will eat bread without scarcity, in which you will lack nothing; a land whose stones are iron and out of whose hills you can dig copper. 10 When you have eaten and are full, then you shall bless the LORD your God for the good land which He has given you.

11 "Beware that you do not forget the LORD your God by not keeping His commandments, His judgments, and His statutes which I command you today, 12 lest—when you have eaten and are full, and have built beautiful houses and dwell in them; 13 and when your herds and your flocks multiply, and your silver and your gold are multiplied, and all that you have is multiplied; 14 when your heart is lifted up, and you forget the LORD your God who brought you out of the land of Egypt, from the house of bondage; 15 who led you through that great and terrible wilderness, in which were fiery serpents and scorpions and thirsty land where there was no water; who brought water for you out of the flinty rock; 16 who fed you in the wilderness with manna, which your fathers did not know, that He might humble you and that He might test you, to do you good in the end— 17 then you say in your heart, 'My power and the might of my hand have gained me this wealth.'

18 "And you shall remember the LORD your God, for it is He who gives you power to get wealth, that He may establish His covenant which He swore to your fathers, as it is this day. 19 Then it shall be, if you by any means forget the LORD your God, and follow other gods, and serve them and worship them, I testify against you this day that you shall surely perish. 20 As the nations which the LORD destroys before you, so you shall perish, because you would not be obedient to the voice of the LORD your God.

9 "Hear, O Israel: You are to cross over the Jordan today, and go in to dispossess nations greater and mightier than yourself, cities great and fortified up to heaven, 2 a people great and tall, the descendants of the Anakim, whom you know, and of whom you heard it said, 'Who can stand before the descendants of Anak?' 3 Therefore understand today that the LORD your God is He who goes over before you as a consuming fire. He will destroy them and bring them down before you; so you shall drive them out and destroy them quickly, as the LORD has said to you.

4 "Do not think in your heart, after the LORD your God has cast them out before you, saying, 'Because of my righteousness the LORD has brought me in to possess this land'; but it is because of the wickedness of these nations that the LORD is driving them out from before you. 5 It is not because of your righteousness or the uprightness of your heart that you go in to possess their land, but because of the wickedness of these nations that the LORD your God drives them out from before you, and that He may fulfill the word which the LORD swore to your fathers, to Abraham, Isaac, and Jacob. 6 Therefore understand that the LORD your God is not giving you this good land to possess because of your righteousness, for you are a stiff-necked people.

7 "Remember! Do not forget how you provoked the LORD your God to wrath in the wilderness. From the day that you departed from the land of Egypt until you came to this place, you have been rebellious against the LORD. 8 Also in Horeb you provoked the LORD to wrath, so that the LORD was angry enough with you to have destroyed you. 9 When I went up into the mountain to receive the tablets of stone, the tablets of the covenant which the LORD made with you, then I stayed on the mountain forty days and forty nights. I neither ate bread nor drank water. 10 Then the LORD delivered to me two tablets of stone written with the finger of God, and on them were all the words which the LORD had spoken to you on the mountain from the midst of the fire in the day of the assembly. 11 And it came to pass, at the end of forty days and forty nights, that the LORD gave me the two tablets of stone, the tablets of the covenant.

12 "Then the LORD said to me, 'Arise, go down quickly from here, for your people whom you brought out of Egypt have acted corruptly; they have quickly turned aside from the way which I commanded them;

they have made themselves a molded image.'

13 "Furthermore the LORD spoke to me, saying, 'I have seen this people, and indeed they are a stiff-necked people. 14 Let Me alone, that I may destroy them and blot out their name from under heaven; and I will make of you a nation mightier and greater than they.'

15 "So I turned and came down from the mountain, and the mountain burned with fire; and the two tablets of the covenant *were* in my two hands. 16 And I looked, and behold, you had sinned against the LORD your God—had made for yourselves a molded calf! You had turned aside quickly from the way which the LORD had commanded you. 17 Then I took the two tablets and threw them out of my two hands and broke them before your eyes. 18 And I fell down before the LORD, as at the first, forty days and forty nights; I neither ate bread nor drank water, because of all your sin which you committed in doing wickedly in the sight of the LORD, to provoke Him to anger. 19 For I was afraid of the anger and hot displeasure with which the LORD was angry with you, to destroy you. But the LORD listened to me at that time also. 20 And the LORD was very angry with Aaron *and* would have destroyed him; so I prayed for Aaron also at the same time. 21 Then I took your sin, the calf which you had made, and burned it with fire and crushed it *and* ground *it* very small, until it was as fine as dust; and I threw its dust into the brook that descended from the mountain.

22 "Also at Taberah and Massah and Kibroth Hattaavah you provoked the LORD to wrath. 23 Likewise, when the LORD sent you from Kadesh Barnea, saying, 'Go up and possess the land which I have given you,' then you rebelled against the commandment of the LORD your God, and you did not believe Him nor obey His voice. 24 You have been rebellious against the LORD from the day that I knew you.

25 "Thus I prostrated myself before the LORD; forty days and forty nights I kept prostrating myself, because the LORD had said He would destroy you. 26 Therefore I prayed to the LORD, and said: 'O Lord GOD, do not destroy Your people and Your inheritance whom You have redeemed through Your greatness, whom You have brought out of Egypt with a mighty hand. 27 Remember Your servants, Abraham, Isaac, and Jacob; do not look on the stubbornness of this people, or on their wickedness or their sin, 28 lest the land from which You brought us should say, "Because the LORD was not able to bring them to the land which He promised them, and because He hated them, He has brought them out to kill them in the wilderness." 29 Yet they *are* Your people and Your inheritance, whom You brought out by Your mighty power and by Your outstretched arm.'

10 "At that time the LORD said to me, 'Hew for yourself two tablets of stone like the first, and come up to Me on the mountain and make yourself an ark of wood. 2 And I will write on the tablets the words that were on the first tablets, which you broke; and you shall put them in the ark.'

3 "So I made an ark of acacia wood, hewed two tablets of stone like the first, and went up the mountain, having the two tablets in my hand. 4 And He wrote on the tablets according to the first writing, the Ten Commandments, which the LORD had spoken to you in the mountain from the midst of the fire in the day of the assembly; and the LORD gave them to me. 5 Then I turned and came down from the mountain, and put the tablets in the ark which I had made; and there they are, just as the LORD commanded me."

6 (Now the children of Israel journeyed from the wells of Bene Jaakan to Moserah, where Aaron died, and where he was buried; and Eleazar his son ministered as priest in his stead. 7 From there they journeyed to Gudgodah, and from Gudgodah to Jotbathah, a land of rivers of water. 8 At that time the LORD separated the tribe of Levi to bear the ark of the covenant of the LORD, to stand before the LORD to minister to Him and to bless in His name, to this day. 9 Therefore Levi has no portion nor inheritance with his brethren; the LORD *is* his inheritance, just as the LORD your God promised him.)

10 "As at the first time, I stayed in the mountain forty days and forty

nights; the Lord also heard me at that time, *and* the Lord chose not to destroy you. 11 Then the Lord said to me, 'Arise, begin *your* journey before the people, that they may go in and possess the land which I swore to their fathers to give them.'

12 "And now, Israel, what does the Lord your God require of you, but to fear the Lord your God, to walk in all His ways and to love Him, to serve the Lord your God with all your heart and with all your soul, 13 *and* to keep the commandments of the Lord and His statutes which I command you today for your good? 14 Indeed heaven and the highest heavens belong to the Lord your God, *also* the earth with all that *is* in it. 15 The Lord delighted only in your fathers, to love them; and He chose their descendants after them, you above all peoples, as *it is* this day. 16 Therefore circumcise the foreskin of your heart, and be stiffnecked no longer. 17 For the Lord your God *is* God of gods and Lord of lords, the great God, mighty and awesome, who shows no partiality nor takes a bribe. 18 He administers justice for the fatherless and the widow, and loves the stranger, giving him food and clothing. 19 Therefore love the stranger, for you were strangers in the land of Egypt. 20 You shall fear the Lord your God; you shall serve Him, and to Him you shall hold fast, and take oaths in His name. 21 He *is* your praise, and He *is* your God, who has done for you these great and awesome things which your eyes have seen. 22 Your fathers went down to Egypt with seventy persons, and now the Lord your God has made you as the stars of heaven in multitude.

11 "Therefore you shall love the Lord your God, and keep His charge, His statutes, His judgments, and His commandments always. 2 Know today that *I do* not *speak* with your children, who have not known and who have not seen the chastening of the Lord your God, His greatness and His mighty hand and His outstretched arm— 3 His signs and His acts which He did in the midst of Egypt, to Pharaoh king of Egypt, and to all his land; 4 what He did to the army of Egypt, to their horses and their chariots: how He made the waters of the Red Sea overflow them as they pursued you, and *how* the Lord has destroyed them to this day; 5 what He did for you in the wilderness until you came to this place; 6 and what He did to Dathan and Abiram the sons of Eliab, the son of Reuben: how the earth opened its mouth and swallowed them up, their households, their tents, and all the substance that *was* in their possession, in the midst of all Israel— 7 but your eyes have seen every great act of the Lord which He did.

8 "Therefore you shall keep every commandment which I command you today, that you may be strong, and go in and possess the land which you cross over to possess, 9 and that you may prolong *your* days in the land which the Lord swore to give your fathers, to them and their descendants, 'a land flowing with milk and honey.'*ª* 10 For the land which you go to possess *is* not like the land of Egypt from which you have come, where you sowed your seed and watered *it* by foot, as a vegetable garden; 11 but the land which you cross over to possess *is* a land of hills and valleys, which drinks water from the rain of heaven, 12 a land for which the Lord your God cares; the eyes of the Lord your God *are* always on it, from the beginning of the year to the very end of the year.

13 'And it shall be that if you earnestly obey My commandments which I command you today, to love the Lord your God and serve Him with all your heart and with all your soul, 14 then I*ª* will give *you* the rain for your land in its season, the early rain and the latter rain, that you may gather in your grain, your new wine, and your oil. 15 And I will send grass in your fields for your livestock, that you may eat and be filled.' 16 Take heed to yourselves, lest your heart be deceived, and you turn aside and serve other gods and worship them, 17 lest the Lord's anger be aroused against you, and He shut up the heavens so that there be no rain, and the land yield no produce, and you per-

11:9 ªExodus 3:8   11:14 ªFollowing Masoretic Text and Targum; Samaritan Pentateuch, Septuagint, and Vulgate read *He.*

ish quickly from the good land which the LORD is giving you.

18 "Therefore you shall lay up these words of mine in your heart and in your soul, and bind them as a sign on your hand, and they shall be as frontlets between your eyes. 19 You shall teach them to your children, speaking of them when you sit in your house, when you walk by the way, when you lie down, and when you rise up. 20 And you shall write them on the doorposts of your house and on your gates, 21 that your days and the days of your children may be multiplied in the land of which the LORD swore to your fathers to give them, like the days of the heavens above the earth.

22 "For if you carefully keep all these commandments which I command you to do—to love the LORD your God, to walk in all His ways, and to hold fast to Him— 23 then the LORD will drive out all these nations from before you, and you will dispossess greater and mightier nations than yourselves. 24 Every place on which the sole of your foot treads shall be yours: from the wilderness and Lebanon, from the river, the River Euphrates, even to the Western Sea,[a] shall be your territory. 25 No man shall be able to stand against you; the LORD your God will put the dread of you and the fear of you upon all the land where you tread, just as He has said to you.

26 "Behold, I set before you today a blessing and a curse: 27 the blessing, if you obey the commandments of the LORD your God which I command you today; 28 and the curse, if you do not obey the commandments of the LORD your God, but turn aside from the way which I command you today, to go after other gods which you have not known. 29 Now it shall be, when the LORD your God has brought you into the land which you go to possess, that you shall put the blessing on Mount Gerizim and the curse on Mount Ebal. 30 Are they not on the other side of the Jordan, toward the setting sun, in the land of the Canaanites who dwell in the plain opposite Gilgal, beside the terebinth trees of Moreh? 31 For you will cross over the Jordan and go in to possess the land which the LORD your God is giving you, and you will possess it and dwell in it. 32 And you shall be careful to observe all the statutes and judgments which I set before you today.

12 "These *are* the statutes and judgments which you shall be careful to observe in the land which the LORD God of your fathers is giving you to possess, all the days that you live on the earth. 2 You shall utterly destroy all the places where the nations which you shall dispossess served their gods, on the high mountains and on the hills and under every green tree. 3 And you shall destroy their altars, break their *sacred* pillars, and burn their wooden images with fire; you shall cut down the carved images of their gods and destroy their names from that place. 4 You shall not worship the LORD your God *with* such *things.*

5 "But you shall seek the place where the LORD your God chooses, out of all your tribes, to put His name for His dwelling place; and there you shall go. 6 There you shall take your burnt offerings, your sacrifices, your tithes, the heave offerings of your hand, your vowed offerings, your freewill offerings, and the firstborn of your herds and flocks. 7 And there you shall eat before the LORD your God, and you shall rejoice in all to which you have put your hand, you and your households, in which the LORD your God has blessed you.

8 "You shall not at all do as we are doing here today—every man doing whatever *is* right in his own eyes— 9 for as yet you have not come to the rest and the inheritance which the LORD your God is giving you. 10 But *when* you cross over the Jordan and dwell in the land which the LORD your God is giving you to inherit, and He gives you rest from all your enemies round about, so that you dwell in safety, 11 then there will be the place where the LORD your God chooses to make His name abide. There you shall bring all that I command you: your burnt offerings, your sacrifices, your tithes, the heave offerings of your hand, and all your choice offerings which you vow to the LORD. 12 And you shall rejoice before the LORD your God, you and your

11:24 [a] That is, the Mediterranean

sons and your daughters, your male and female servants, and the Levite who *is* within your gates, since he has no portion nor inheritance with you. 13 Take heed to yourself that you do not offer your burnt offerings in every place that you see; 14 but in the place which the LORD chooses, in one of your tribes, there you shall offer your burnt offerings, and there you shall do all that I command you.

15 "However, you may slaughter and eat meat within all your gates, whatever your heart desires, according to the blessing of the LORD your God which He has given you; the unclean and the clean may eat of it, of the gazelle and the deer alike. 16 Only you shall not eat the blood; you shall pour it on the earth like water. 17 You may not eat within your gates the tithe of your grain or your new wine or your oil, of the firstborn of your herd or your flock, of any of your offerings which you vow, of your freewill offerings, or of the heave offering of your hand. 18 But you must eat them before the LORD your God in the place which the LORD your God chooses, you and your son and your daughter, your male servant and your female servant, and the Levite who *is* within your gates; and you shall rejoice before the LORD your God in all to which you put your hands. 19 Take heed to yourself that you do not forsake the Levite as long as you live in your land.

20 "When the LORD your God enlarges your border as He has promised you, and you say, 'Let me eat meat,' because you long to eat meat, you may eat as much meat as your heart desires. 21 If the place where the LORD your God chooses to put His name is too far from you, then you may slaughter from your herd and from your flock which the LORD has given you, just as I have commanded you, and you may eat within your gates as much as your heart desires. 22 Just as the gazelle and the deer are eaten, so you may eat them; the unclean and the clean alike may eat them. 23 Only be sure that you do not eat the blood, for the blood *is* the life; you may not eat the life with the meat. 24 You shall not eat it; you shall pour it on the earth like water. 25 You shall not eat it, that it may go

well with you and your children after you, when you do *what is* right in the sight of the LORD. 26 Only the holy things which you have, and your vowed offerings, you shall take and go to the place which the LORD chooses. 27 And you shall offer your burnt offerings, the meat and the blood, on the altar of the LORD your God; and the blood of your sacrifices shall be poured out on the altar of the LORD your God, and you shall eat the meat. 28 Observe and obey all these words which I command you, that it may go well with you and your children after you forever, when you do *what is* good and right in the sight of the LORD your God.

29 "When the LORD your God cuts off from before you the nations which you go to dispossess, and you displace them and dwell in their land, 30 take heed to yourself that you are not ensnared to follow them, after they are destroyed from before you, and that you do not inquire after their gods, saying, 'How did these nations serve their gods? I also will do likewise.' 31 You shall not worship the LORD your God in that way; for every abomination to the LORD which He hates they have done to their gods; for they burn even their sons and daughters in the fire to their gods.

32 "Whatever I command you, be careful to observe it; you shall not add to it nor take away from it.

13 "If there arises among you a prophet or a dreamer of dreams, and he gives you a sign or a wonder, 2 and the sign or the wonder comes to pass, of which he spoke to you, saying, 'Let us go after other gods'—which you have not known— 'and let us serve them,' 3 you shall not listen to the words of that prophet or that dreamer of dreams, for the LORD your God is testing you to know whether you love the LORD your God with all your heart and with all your soul. 4 You shall walk after the LORD your God and fear Him, and keep His commandments and obey His voice; you shall serve Him and hold fast to Him. 5 But that prophet or that dreamer of dreams shall be put to death, because he has spoken in order to turn *you* away from the LORD your God, who brought you out of the land of Egypt and redeemed you from the house of bondage, to entice

you from the way in which the LORD your God commanded you to walk. So you shall put away the evil from your midst.

6 "If your brother, the son of your mother, your son or your daughter, the wife of your bosom, or your friend who is as your own soul, secretly entices you, saying, 'Let us go and serve other gods,' which you have not known, neither you nor your fathers, 7 of the gods of the people which *are* all around you, near to you or far off from you, from *one* end of the earth to the *other* end of the earth, 8 you shall not consent to him or listen to him, nor shall your eye pity him, nor shall you spare him or conceal him; 9 but you shall surely kill him; your hand shall be first against him to put him to death, and afterward the hand of all the people. 10 And you shall stone him with stones until he dies, because he sought to entice you away from the LORD your God, who brought you out of the land of Egypt, from the house of bondage. 11 So all Israel shall hear and fear, and not again do such wickedness as this among you.

12 "If you hear someone in one of your cities, which the LORD your God gives you to dwell in, saying, 13 'Corrupt men have gone out from among you and enticed the inhabitants of their city, saying, "Let us go and serve other gods"'—which you have not known— 14 then you shall inquire, search out, and ask diligently. And *if it is* indeed true *and* certain *that* such an abomination was committed among you, 15 you shall surely strike the inhabitants of that city with the edge of the sword, utterly destroying it, all that is in it and its livestock—with the edge of the sword. 16 And you shall gather all its plunder into the middle of the street, and completely burn with fire the city and all its plunder, for the LORD your God. It shall be a heap forever; it shall not be built again. 17 So none of the accursed things shall remain in your hand, that the LORD may turn from the fierceness of His anger and show you mercy, have compassion on you and multiply you, just as He swore to your fathers, 18 because you have listened to the voice of the LORD your

God, to keep all His commandments which I command you today, to do *what is* right in the eyes of the LORD your God.

14 "You *are* the children of the LORD your God; you shall not cut yourselves nor shave the front of your head for the dead. 2 For you *are* a holy people to the LORD your God, and the LORD has chosen you to be a people for Himself, a special treasure above all the peoples who *are* on the face of the earth.

3 "You shall not eat any detestable thing. 4 These *are* the animals which you may eat: the ox, the sheep, the goat, 5 the deer, the gazelle, the roe deer, the wild goat, the mountain goat,[a] the antelope, and the mountain sheep. 6 And you may eat every animal with cloven hooves, having the hoof split into two parts, *and that* chews the cud, among the animals. 7 Nevertheless, of those that chew the cud or have cloven hooves, you shall not eat, *such as* these: the camel, the hare, and the rock hyrax; for they chew the cud but do not have cloven hooves; they *are* unclean for you. 8 Also the swine is unclean for you, because it has cloven hooves, yet *does* not *chew* the cud; you shall not eat their flesh or touch their dead carcasses.

9 "These you may eat of all that *are* in the waters: you may eat all that have fins and scales. 10 And whatever does not have fins and scales you shall not eat; it *is* unclean for you.

11 "All clean birds you may eat. 12 But these you shall not eat: the eagle, the vulture, the buzzard, 13 the red kite, the falcon, and the kite after their kinds; 14 every raven after its kind; 15 the ostrich, the short-eared owl, the seagull, and the hawk after their kinds; 16 the little owl, the screech owl, the white owl, 17 the jackdaw, the carrion vulture, the fisher owl, 18 the stork, the heron after its kind, and the hoopoe and the bat.

19 "Also every creeping thing that flies is unclean for you; they shall not be eaten.

20 "You may eat all clean birds.

21 "You shall not eat anything that dies *of itself;* you may give it to the

14:5 *a*Or *addax*

alien who *is* within your gates, that he may eat it, or you may sell it to a foreigner; for you *are* a holy people to the Lord your God.

"You shall not boil a young goat in its mother's milk.

22 "You shall truly tithe all the increase of your grain that the field produces year by year. 23 And you shall eat before the Lord your God, in the place where He chooses to make His name abide, the tithe of your grain and your new wine and your oil, of the firstborn of your herds and your flocks, that you may learn to fear the Lord your God always. 24 But if the journey is too long for you, so that you are not able to carry *the tithe, or* if the place where the Lord your God chooses to put His name is too far from you, when the Lord your God has blessed you, 25 then you shall exchange *it* for money, take the money in your hand, and go to the place which the Lord your God chooses. 26 And you shall spend that money for whatever your heart desires: for oxen or sheep, for wine or similar drink, for whatever your heart desires; you shall eat there before the Lord your God, and you shall rejoice, you and your household. 27 You shall not forsake the Levite who *is* within your gates, for he has no part nor inheritance with you.

28 "At the end of *every* third year you shall bring out the tithe of your produce of that year and store *it* up within your gates. 29 And the Levite, because he has no portion nor inheritance with you, and the stranger and the fatherless and the widow who *are* within your gates, may come and eat and be satisfied, that the Lord your God may bless you in all the work of your hand which you do.

15 "At the end of *every* seven years you shall grant a release *of debts.* 2 And this *is* the form of the release: Every creditor who has lent *anything* to his neighbor shall release *it;* he shall not require *it* of his neighbor or his brother, because it is called the Lord's release. 3 Of a foreigner you may require *it;* but you shall give up your claim to what is owed by your brother, 4 except when there may be no poor among you; for the Lord will greatly bless you in the land which the Lord

your God is giving you to possess *as* an inheritance— 5 only if you carefully obey the voice of the Lord your God, to observe with care all these commandments which I command you today. 6 For the Lord your God will bless you just as He promised you; you shall lend to many nations, but you shall not borrow; you shall reign over many nations, but they shall not reign over you.

7 "If there is among you a poor man of your brethren, within any of the gates in your land which the Lord your God is giving you, you shall not harden your heart nor shut your hand from your poor brother, 8 but you shall open your hand wide to him and willingly lend him sufficient for his need, whatever he needs. 9 Beware lest there be a wicked thought in your heart, saying, 'The seventh year, the year of release, is at hand,' and your eye be evil against your poor brother and you give him nothing, and he cry out to the Lord against you, and it become sin among you. 10 You shall surely give to him, and your heart should not be grieved when you give to him, because for this thing the Lord your God will bless you in all your works and in all to which you put your hand. 11 For the poor will never cease from the land; therefore I command you, saying, 'You shall open your hand wide to your brother, to your poor and your needy, in your land.'

12 "If your brother, a Hebrew man, or a Hebrew woman, is sold to you and serves you six years, then in the seventh year you shall let him go free from you. 13 And when you send him away free from you, you shall not let him go away empty-handed; 14 you shall supply him liberally from your flock, from your threshing floor, and from your winepress. *From what* the Lord has blessed you with, you shall give to him. 15 You shall remember that you were a slave in the land of Egypt, and the Lord your God redeemed you; therefore I command you this thing today. 16 And if it happens that he says to you, 'I will not go away from you,' because he loves you and your house, since he prospers with you, 17 then you shall take an awl and thrust *it* through his ear to the door, and he shall be your servant forever. Also to your female servant you shall do likewise. 18 It shall

not seem hard to you when you send him away free from you; for he has been worth a double hired servant in serving you six years. Then the LORD your God will bless you in all that you do.

19 "All the firstborn males that come from your herd and your flock you shall sanctify to the LORD your God; you shall do no work with the firstborn of your herd, nor shear the firstborn of your flock. 20 You and your household shall eat it before the LORD your God year by year in the place which the LORD chooses. 21 But if there is a defect in it, if it is lame or blind or has any serious defect, you shall not sacrifice it to the LORD your God. 22 You may eat it within your gates; the unclean and the clean person alike may eat it, as if it were a gazelle or a deer. 23 Only you shall not eat its blood; you shall pour it on the ground like water.

16 "Observe the month of Abib, and keep the Passover to the LORD your God, for in the month of Abib the LORD your God brought you out of Egypt by night. 2 Therefore you shall sacrifice the Passover to the LORD your God, from the flock and the herd, in the place where the LORD chooses to put His name. 3 You shall eat no leavened bread with it; seven days you shall eat unleavened bread with it, that is, the bread of affliction (for you came out of the land of Egypt in haste), that you may remember the day in which you came out of the land of Egypt all the days of your life. 4 And no leaven shall be seen among you in all your territory for seven days, nor shall any of the meat which you sacrifice the first day at twilight remain overnight until morning.

5 "You may not sacrifice the Passover within any of your gates which the LORD your God gives you; 6 but at the place where the LORD your God chooses to make His name abide, there you shall sacrifice the Passover at twilight, at the going down of the sun, at the time you came out of Egypt. 7 And you shall roast and eat it in the place which the LORD your God chooses, and in the morning you shall turn and go to your tents. 8 Six days you shall eat unleavened bread, and on the seventh day there shall be a sacred assembly to the LORD your God. You shall do no work on it.

9 "You shall count seven weeks for yourself; begin to count the seven weeks from the time you begin to put the sickle to the grain. 10 Then you shall keep the Feast of Weeks to the LORD your God with the tribute of a freewill offering from your hand, which you shall give as the LORD your God blesses you. 11 You shall rejoice before the LORD your God, you and your son and your daughter, your male servant and your female servant, the Levite who is within your gates, the stranger and the fatherless and the widow who are among you, at the place where the LORD your God chooses to make His name abide. 12 And you shall remember that you were a slave in Egypt, and you shall be careful to observe these statutes.

13 "You shall observe the Feast of Tabernacles seven days, when you have gathered from your threshing floor and from your winepress. 14 And you shall rejoice in your feast, you and your son and your daughter, your male servant and your female servant and the Levite, the stranger and the fatherless and the widow, who are within your gates. 15 Seven days you shall keep a sacred feast to the LORD your God in the place which the LORD chooses, because the LORD your God will bless you in all your produce and in all the work of your hands, so that you surely rejoice.

16 "Three times a year all your males shall appear before the LORD your God in the place which He chooses: at the Feast of Unleavened Bread, at the Feast of Weeks, and at the Feast of Tabernacles; and they shall not appear before the LORD empty-handed. 17 Every man shall give as he is able, according to the blessing of the LORD your God which He has given you.

18 "You shall appoint judges and officers in all your gates, which the LORD your God gives you, according to your tribes, and they shall judge the people with just judgment. 19 You shall not pervert justice; you shall not show partiality, nor take a bribe, for a bribe blinds the eyes of the wise and twists the words of the righteous. 20 You shall follow what is altogether just, that you may live

and inherit the land which the LORD your God is giving you.

21 "You shall not plant for yourself any tree, as a wooden image, near the altar which you build for yourself to the LORD your God. 22 You shall not set up a sacred pillar, which the LORD your God hates.

17 "You shall not sacrifice to the LORD your God a bull or sheep which has any blemish or defect, for that is an abomination to the LORD your God.

2 "If there is found among you, within any of your gates which the LORD your God gives you, a man or a woman who has been wicked in the sight of the LORD your God, in transgressing His covenant, 3 who has gone and served other gods and worshiped them, either the sun or moon or any of the host of heaven, which I have not commanded, 4 and it is told you, and you hear of it, then you shall inquire diligently. And if it is indeed true and certain that such an abomination has been committed in Israel, 5 then you shall bring out to your gates that man or woman who has committed that wicked thing, and shall stone to death that man or woman with stones. 6 Whoever is deserving of death shall be put to death on the testimony of two or three witnesses; he shall not be put to death on the testimony of one witness. 7 The hands of the witnesses shall be the first against him to put him to death, and afterward the hands of all the people. So you shall put away the evil from among you.

8 "If a matter arises which is too hard for you to judge, between degrees of guilt for bloodshed, between one judgment or another, or between one punishment or another, matters of controversy within your gates, then you shall arise and go up to the place which the LORD your God chooses. 9 And you shall come to the priests, the Levites, and to the judge there in those days, and inquire of them; they shall pronounce upon you the sentence of judgment. 10 You shall do according to the sentence which they pronounce upon you in that place which the LORD chooses. And you shall be careful to do according to all that they order you. 11 According to the sentence of the law in which they instruct you, ac-

cording to the judgment which they tell you, you shall do; you shall not turn aside to the right hand or to the left from the sentence which they pronounce upon you. 12 Now the man who acts presumptuously and will not heed the priest who stands to minister there before the LORD your God, or the judge, that man shall die. So you shall put away the evil from Israel. 13 And all the people shall hear and fear, and no longer act presumptuously.

14 "When you come to the land which the LORD your God is giving you, and possess it and dwell in it, and say, 'I will set a king over me like all the nations that are around me,' 15 you shall surely set a king over you whom the LORD your God chooses; one from among your brethren you shall set as king over you; you may not set a foreigner over you, who is not your brother. 16 But he shall not multiply horses for himself, nor cause the people to return to Egypt to multiply horses, for the LORD has said to you, 'You shall not return that way again.' 17 Neither shall he multiply wives for himself, lest his heart turn away; nor shall he greatly multiply silver and gold for himself.

18 "Also it shall be, when he sits on the throne of his kingdom, that he shall write for himself a copy of this law in a book, from the one before the priests, the Levites. 19 And it shall be with him, and he shall read it all the days of his life, that he may learn to fear the LORD his God and be careful to observe all the words of this law and these statutes, 20 that his heart may not be lifted above his brethren, that he may not turn aside from the commandment to the right hand or to the left, and that he may prolong his days in his kingdom, he and his children in the midst of Israel.

18 "The priests, the Levites—all the tribe of Levi—shall have no part nor inheritance with Israel; they shall eat the offerings of the LORD made by fire, and His portion. 2 Therefore they shall have no inheritance among their brethren; the LORD is their inheritance, as He said to them.

3 "And this shall be the priest's due from the people, from those who of-

fer a sacrifice, whether *it is* bull or sheep: they shall give to the priest the shoulder, the cheeks, and the stomach. 4 The firstfruits of your grain and your new wine and your oil, and the first of the fleece of your sheep, you shall give him. 5 For the LORD your God has chosen him out of all your tribes to stand to minister in the name of the LORD, him and his sons forever.

6 "So if a Levite comes from any of your gates, from where he dwells among all Israel, and comes with all the desire of his mind to the place which the LORD chooses, 7 then he may serve in the name of the LORD his God as all his brethren the Levites *do*, who stand there before the LORD. 8 They shall have equal portions to eat, besides what comes from the sale of his inheritance.

9 "When you come into the land which the LORD your God is giving you, you shall not learn to follow the abominations of those nations. 10 There shall not be found among you *anyone* who makes his son or his daughter pass through the fire, *or one* who practices witchcraft, *or* a soothsayer, or one who interprets omens, or a sorcerer, 11 or one who conjures spells, or a medium, or a spiritist, or one who calls up the dead. 12 For all who do these things *are* an abomination to the LORD, and because of these abominations the LORD your God drives them out from before you. 13 You shall be blameless before the LORD your God. 14 For these nations which you will dispossess listened to soothsayers and diviners; but as for you, the LORD your God has not appointed such for you.

15 "The LORD your God will raise up for you a Prophet like me from your midst, from your brethren. Him you shall hear, 16 according to all you desired of the LORD your God in Horeb in the day of the assembly, saying, 'Let me not hear again the voice of the LORD my God, nor let me see this great fire anymore, lest I die.' 17 "And the LORD said to me: 'What they have spoken is good. 18 I will raise up for them a Prophet like you from among their brethren, and will put My words in His mouth, and He shall speak to them all that I command Him. 19 And it shall be *that* whoever will not hear My words, which He speaks in My name, I will

require *it* of him. 20 But the prophet who presumes to speak a word in My name, which I have not commanded him to speak, or who speaks in the name of other gods, that prophet shall die.' 21 And if you say in your heart, 'How shall we know the word which the LORD has not spoken?'— 22 when a prophet speaks in the name of the LORD, if the thing does not happen or come to pass, that *is* the thing which the LORD has not spoken; the prophet has spoken it presumptuously; you shall not be afraid of him.

19 "When the LORD your God has cut off the nations whose land the LORD your God is giving you, and you dispossess them and dwell in their cities and in their houses, 2 you shall separate three cities for yourself in the midst of your land which the LORD your God is giving you to possess. 3 You shall prepare roads for yourself, and divide into three parts the territory of your land which the LORD your God is giving you to inherit, that any manslayer may flee there.

4 "And this *is* the case of the manslayer who flees there, that he may live: Whoever kills his neighbor unintentionally, not having hated him in time past— 5 as when *a man* goes to the woods with his neighbor to cut timber, and his hand swings a stroke with the ax to cut down the tree, and the head slips from the handle and strikes his neighbor so that he dies— he shall flee to one of these cities and live; 6 lest the avenger of blood, while his anger is hot, pursue the manslayer and overtake him, because the way is long, and kill him, though he *was* not deserving of death, since he had not hated the victim in time past. 7 Therefore I command you, saying, 'You shall separate three cities for yourself.'

8 "Now if the LORD your God enlarges your territory, as He swore to your fathers, and gives you the land which He promised to give to your fathers, 9 and if you keep all these commandments and do them, which I command you today, to love the LORD your God and to walk always in His ways, then you shall add three more cities for yourself besides these three, 10 lest innocent blood be shed in the midst of your land which the

LORD your God is giving you *as* an inheritance, and *thus* guilt of bloodshed be upon you.

11 "But if anyone hates his neighbor, lies in wait for him, rises against him and strikes him mortally, so that he dies, and he flees to one of these cities, 12 then the elders of his city shall send and bring him from there, and deliver him over to the hand of the avenger of blood, that he may die. 13 Your eye shall not pity him, but you shall put away *the guilt of* innocent blood from Israel, that it may go well with you.

14 "You shall not remove your neighbor's landmark, which the men of old have set, in your inheritance which you will inherit in the land that the LORD your God is giving you to possess.

15 "One witness shall not rise against a man concerning any iniquity or any sin that he commits; by the mouth of two or three witnesses the matter shall be established. 16 If a false witness rises against any man to testify against him of wrongdoing, 17 then both men in the controversy shall stand before the LORD, before the priests and the judges who serve in those days. 18 And the judges shall make careful inquiry, and indeed, *if* the witness *is* a false witness, who has testified falsely against his brother, 19 then you shall do to him as he thought to have done to his brother; so you shall put away the evil from among you. 20 And those who remain shall hear and fear, and hereafter they shall not again commit such evil among you. 21 Your eye shall not pity: life *shall be* for life, eye for eye, tooth for tooth, hand for hand, foot for foot.

20 "When you go out to battle against your enemies, and see horses and chariots *and* people more numerous than you, do not be afraid of them; for the LORD your God *is* with you, who brought you up from the land of Egypt. 2 So it shall be, when you are on the verge of battle, that the priest shall approach and speak to the people. 3 And he shall say to them, 'Hear, O Israel: Today you are on the verge of battle with your enemies. Do not let your heart faint, do not be afraid, and do not tremble or be terrified because of them; 4 for the LORD your God *is* He who goes with you, to fight for you against your enemies, to save you.'

5 "Then the officers shall speak to the people, saying: 'What man *is there* who has built a new house and has not dedicated it? Let him go and return to his house, lest he die in the battle and another man dedicate it. 6 Also what man *is there* who has planted a vineyard and has not eaten of it? Let him go and return to his house, lest he die in the battle and another man eat of it. 7 And what man *is there* who is betrothed to a woman and has not married her? Let him go and return to his house, lest he die in the battle and another man marry her.'

8 "The officers shall speak further to the people, and say, 'What man *is there who is* fearful and fainthearted? Let him go and return to his house, lest the heart of his brethren faint[a] like his heart.' 9 And so it shall be, when the officers have finished speaking to the people, that they shall make captains of the armies to lead the people.

10 "When you go near a city to fight against it, then proclaim an offer of peace to it. 11 And it shall be that if they accept your offer of peace, and open to you, then all the people *who are* found in it shall be placed under tribute to you, and serve you. 12 Now if *the city* will not make peace with you, but war against you, then you shall besiege it. 13 And when the LORD your God delivers it into your hands, you shall strike every male in it with the edge of the sword. 14 But the women, the little ones, the livestock, and all that is in the city, all its spoil, you shall plunder for yourself; and you shall eat the enemies' plunder which the LORD your God gives you. 15 Thus you shall do to all the cities *which are* very far from you, which *are* not of the cities of these nations.

16 "But of the cities of these peoples which the LORD your God gives you *as* an inheritance, you shall let nothing that breathes remain alive, 17 but you shall utterly destroy them:

20:8 [a]Following Masoretic Text and Targum; Samaritan Pentateuch, Septuagint, Syriac, and Vulgate read *lest he make his brother's heart faint.*

the Hittite and the Amorite and the Canaanite and the Perizzite and the Hivite and the Jebusite, just as the LORD your God has commanded you, 18 lest they teach you to do according to all their abominations which they have done for their gods, and you sin against the LORD your God.

19 "When you besiege a city for a long time, while making war against it to take it, you shall not destroy its trees by wielding an ax against them; if you can eat of them, do not cut them down to use in the siege, for the tree of the field *is* man's food. 20 Only the trees which you know *are* not trees for food you may destroy and cut down, to build siegeworks against the city that makes war with you, until it is subdued.

21 "If *anyone* is found slain, lying in the field in the land which the LORD your God is giving you to possess, *and* it is not known who killed him, 2 then your elders and your judges shall go out and measure *the distance* from the slain man to the surrounding cities. 3 And it shall be *that* the elders of the city nearest to the slain man will take a heifer which has not been worked *and* which has not pulled with a yoke. 4 The elders of that city shall bring the heifer down to a valley with flowing water, which is neither plowed nor sown, and they shall break the heifer's neck there in the valley. 5 Then the priests, the sons of Levi, shall come near, for the LORD your God has chosen them to minister to Him and to bless in the name of the LORD; by their word every controversy and every assault shall be *settled*. 6 And all the elders of that city nearest to the slain *man* shall wash their hands over the heifer whose neck was broken in the valley. 7 Then they shall answer and say, 'Our hands have not shed this blood, nor have our eyes seen *it*. 8 Provide atonement, O LORD, for Your people Israel, whom You have redeemed, and do not lay innocent blood to the charge of Your people Israel.' And atonement shall be provided on their behalf for the blood. 9 So you shall put away the *guilt of* innocent blood from among you when you do *what is* right in the sight of the LORD.

10 "When you go out to war against your enemies, and the LORD your God delivers them into your hand, and you take them captive, 11 and you see among the captives a beautiful woman, and desire her and would take her for your wife, 12 then you shall bring her home to your house, and she shall shave her head and trim her nails. 13 She shall put off the clothes of her captivity, remain in your house, and mourn her father and her mother a full month; after that you may go in to her and be her husband, and she shall be your wife. 14 And it shall be, if you have no delight in her, then you shall set her free, but *you* certainly shall not sell her for money; you shall not treat her brutally, because you have humbled her.

15 "If a man has two wives, one loved and the other unloved, and they have borne him children, *both* the loved and the unloved, and *if* the firstborn son is of her who is unloved, 16 then it shall be, on the day he bequeaths his possessions to his sons, *that* he must not bestow firstborn status on the son of the loved wife in preference to the son of the unloved, the *true* firstborn. 17 But he shall acknowledge the son of the unloved wife *as* the firstborn by giving him a double portion of all that he has, for he *is* the beginning of his strength; the right of the firstborn *is* his.

18 "If a man has a stubborn and rebellious son who will not obey the voice of his father or the voice of his mother, and, *who*, when they have chastened him, will not heed them, 19 then his father and his mother shall take hold of him and bring him out to the elders of his city, to the gate of his city. 20 And they shall say to the elders of his city, 'This son of ours is stubborn and rebellious; he will not obey our voice; he is a glutton and a drunkard.' 21 Then all the men of his city shall stone him to death with stones; so you shall put away the evil from among you, and all Israel shall hear and fear.

22 "If a man has committed a sin deserving of death, and he is put to death, and you hang him on a tree, 23 his body shall not remain overnight on the tree, but you shall surely bury him that day, so that you do not defile the land which the LORD your God is giving you *as* an inheritance;

for he who is hanged *is* accursed of God.

22 "You shall not see your brother's ox or his sheep going astray, and hide yourself from them; you shall certainly bring them back to your brother. 2 And if your brother *is* not near you, or if you do not know him, then you shall bring it to your own house, and it shall remain with you until your brother seeks it; then you shall restore it to him. 3 You shall do the same with his donkey, and so shall you do with his garment; with any lost thing of your brother's, which he has lost and you have found, you shall do likewise; you must not hide yourself.

4 "You shall not see your brother's donkey or his ox fall down along the road, and hide yourself from them; you shall surely help him lift *them* up again.

5 "A woman shall not wear anything that pertains to a man, nor shall a man put on a woman's garment, for all who do so *are* an abomination to the LORD your God.

6 "If a bird's nest happens to be before you along the way, in any tree or on the ground, with young ones or eggs, with the mother sitting on the young or on the eggs, you shall not take the mother with the young; 7 you shall surely let the mother go, and take the young for yourself, that it may be well with you and *that* you may prolong *your* days.

8 "When you build a new house, then you shall make a parapet for your roof, that you may not bring guilt of bloodshed on your household if anyone falls from it.

9 "You shall not sow your vineyard with different kinds of seed, lest the yield of the seed which you have sown and the fruit of your vineyard be defiled.

10 "You shall not plow with an ox and a donkey together.

11 "You shall not wear a garment of different sorts, *such as* wool and linen mixed together.

12 "You shall make tassels on the four corners of the clothing with which you cover *yourself.*

13 "If any man takes a wife, and goes in to her, and detests her, 14 and charges her with shameful conduct, and brings a bad name on her, and says, 'I took this woman, and when I came to her I found she *was* not a virgin,' 15 then the father and mother of the young woman shall take and bring out *the evidence of* the young woman's virginity to the elders of the city at the gate. 16 And the young woman's father shall say to the elders, 'I gave my daughter to this man as wife, and he detests her. 17 Now he has charged her with shameful conduct, saying, "I found your daughter *was* not a virgin," and yet these *are the evidences of* my daughter's virginity.' And they shall spread the cloth before the elders of the city. 18 Then the elders of that city shall take that man and punish him; 19 and they shall fine him one hundred *shekels* of silver and give *them* to the father of the young woman, because he has brought a bad name on a virgin of Israel. And she shall be his wife; he cannot divorce her all his days.

20 "But if the thing is true, *and evidences of* virginity are not found for the young woman, 21 then they shall bring out the young woman to the door of her father's house, and the men of her city shall stone her to death with stones, because she has done a disgraceful thing in Israel, to play the harlot in her father's house. So you shall put away the evil from among you.

22 "If a man is found lying with a woman married to a husband, then both of them shall die—the man that lay with the woman, and the woman; so you shall put away the evil from Israel.

23 "If a young woman *who is* a virgin is betrothed to a husband, and a man finds her in the city and lies with her, 24 then you shall bring them both out to the gate of that city, and you shall stone them to death with stones, the young woman because she did not cry out in the city, and the man because he humbled his neighbor's wife; so you shall put away the evil from among you.

25 "But if a man finds a betrothed young woman in the countryside, and the man forces her and lies with her, then only the man who lay with her shall die. 26 But you shall do nothing to the young woman; *there is* in the young woman no sin *deserving* of death, for just as when a man rises against his neighbor and kills him, even so *is* this matter. 27 For he

found her in the countryside, *and* the betrothed young woman cried out, but *there was* no one to save her.

28 "If a man finds a young woman *who is* a virgin, who is not betrothed, and he seizes her and lies with her, and they are found out, 29 then the man who lay with her shall give to the young woman's father fifty *shekels* of silver, and she shall be his wife because he has humbled her; he shall not be permitted to divorce her all his days.

30 "A man shall not take his father's wife, nor uncover his father's bed.

23 "He who is emasculated by crushing or mutilation shall not enter the assembly of the LORD.

2 "One of illegitimate birth shall not enter the assembly of the LORD; even to the tenth generation none of his *descendants* shall enter the assembly of the LORD.

3 "An Ammonite or Moabite shall not enter the assembly of the LORD; even to the tenth generation none of his *descendants* shall enter the assembly of the LORD forever, 4 because they did not meet you with bread and water on the road when you came out of Egypt, and because they hired against you Balaam the son of Beor from Pethor of Mesopotamia,*a* to curse you. 5 Nevertheless the LORD your God would not listen to Balaam, but the LORD your God turned the curse into a blessing for you, because the LORD your God loves you. 6 You shall not seek their peace nor their prosperity all your days forever.

7 "You shall not abhor an Edomite, for he *is* your brother. You shall not abhor an Egyptian, because you were an alien in his land. 8 The children of the third generation born to them may enter the assembly of the LORD.

9 "When the army goes out against your enemies, then keep yourself from every wicked thing. 10 If there is any man among you who be comes unclean by some occurrence in the night, then he shall go outside the camp; he shall not come inside the camp. 11 But it shall be, when evening comes, that he shall wash with water; and when the sun

sets, he may come into the camp. 12 "Also you shall have a place outside the camp, where you may go out; 13 and you shall have an implement among your equipment, and when you sit down outside, you shall dig with it and turn and cover your refuse. 14 For the LORD your God walks in the midst of your camp, to deliver you and give your enemies over to you; therefore your camp shall be holy, that He may see no unclean thing among you, and turn away from you.

15 "You shall not give back to his master the slave who has escaped from his master to you. 16 He may dwell with you in your midst, in the place which he chooses within one of your gates, where it seems best to him; you shall not oppress him.

17 "There shall be no *ritual* harlot*a* of the daughters of Israel, or a perverted*b* one of the sons of Israel. 18 You shall not bring the wages of a harlot or the price of a dog to the house of the LORD your God for any vowed offering, for both of these *are* an abomination to the LORD your God.

19 "You shall not charge interest to your brother—interest on money *or* food *or* anything that is lent out at interest. 20 To a foreigner you may charge interest, but to your brother you shall not charge interest, that the LORD your God may bless you in all to which you set your hand in the land which you are entering to possess.

21 "When you make a vow to the LORD your God, you shall not delay to pay it; for the LORD your God will surely require it of you, and it would be sin to you. 22 But if you abstain from vowing, it shall not be sin to you. 23 That which has gone from your lips you shall keep and perform, for you voluntarily vowed to the LORD your God what you have promised with your mouth.

24 "When you come into your neighbor's vineyard, you may eat your fill of grapes at your pleasure, but you shall not put *any* in your container. 25 When you come into your neighbor's standing grain, you may pluck the heads with your hand, but you shall not use a sickle on your neighbor's standing grain.

23:4 *a*Hebrew *Aram Naharaim*   23:17 *a*Hebrew *qedeshah*, feminine of *qadesh* (see note b)   *b*Hebrew *qadesh*, that is, one practicing sodomy and prostitution in religious rituals

24 "When a man takes a wife and marries her, and it happens that she finds no favor in his eyes because he has found some uncleanness in her, and he writes her a certificate of divorce, puts *it* in her hand, and sends her out of his house, 2 when she has departed from his house, and goes and becomes another man's *wife,* 3 *if* the latter husband detests her and writes her a certificate of divorce, puts *it* in her hand, and sends her out of his house, or if the latter husband dies who took her as his wife, 4 *then* her former husband who divorced her must not take her back to be his wife after she has been defiled; for that *is* an abomination before the LORD, and you shall not bring sin on the land which the LORD your God is giving you *as* an inheritance.

5 "When a man has taken a new wife, he shall not go out to war or be charged with any business; he shall be free at home one year, and bring happiness to his wife whom he has taken.

6 "No man shall take the lower or the upper millstone in pledge, for he takes *one's* living in pledge.

7 "If a man is found kidnapping any of his brethren of the children of Israel, and mistreats him or sells him, then that kidnapper shall die; and you shall put away the evil from among you.

8 "Take heed in an outbreak of leprosy, that you carefully observe and do according to all that the priests, the Levites, shall teach you; just as I commanded them, *so* you shall be careful to do. 9 Remember what the LORD your God did to Miriam on the way when you came out of Egypt!

10 "When you lend your brother anything, you shall not go into his house to get his pledge. 11 You shall stand outside, and the man to whom you lend shall bring the pledge out to you. 12 And if the man *is* poor, you shall not keep his pledge overnight. 13 You shall in any case return the pledge to him again when the sun goes down, that he may sleep in his own garment and bless you; and it shall be righteousness to you before the LORD your God.

14 "You shall not oppress a hired servant *who is* poor and needy, *whether* one of your brethren or one of the aliens who *is* in your land within your gates. 15 Each day you shall give *him* his wages, and not let the sun go down on it, for he *is* poor and has set his heart on it; lest he cry out against you to the LORD, and it be sin to you.

16 "Fathers shall not be put to death for *their* children, nor shall children be put to death for *their* fathers; a person shall be put to death for his own sin.

17 "You shall not pervert justice due the stranger or the fatherless, nor take a widow's garment as a pledge. 18 But you shall remember that you were a slave in Egypt, and the LORD your God redeemed you from there; therefore I command you to do this thing.

19 "When you reap your harvest in your field, and forget a sheaf in the field, you shall not go back to get it; it shall be for the stranger, the fatherless, and the widow, that the LORD your God may bless you in all the work of your hands. 20 When you beat your olive trees, you shall not go over the boughs again; it shall be for the stranger, the fatherless, and the widow. 21 When you gather the grapes of your vineyard, you shall not glean *it* afterward; it shall be for the stranger, the fatherless, and the widow. 22 And you shall remember that you were a slave in the land of Egypt; therefore I command you to do this thing.

25 "If there is a dispute between men, and they come to court, that *the judges* may judge them, and they justify the righteous and condemn the wicked, 2 then it shall be, if the wicked man deserves to be beaten, that the judge will cause him to lie down and be beaten in his presence, according to his guilt, with a certain number of blows. 3 Forty blows he may give him *and* no more, lest he should exceed this and beat him with many blows above these, and your brother be humiliated in your sight.

4 "You shall not muzzle an ox while it treads out *the grain.*

5 "If brothers dwell together, and one of them dies and has no son, the widow of the dead man shall not be *married* to a stranger outside *the family;* her husband's brother shall go in to her, take her as his wife, and perform the duty of a husband's

brother to her. 6 And it shall be *that* the firstborn son which she bears will succeed to the name of his dead brother, that his name may not be blotted out of Israel. 7 But if the man does not want to take his brother's wife, then let his brother's wife go up to the gate to the elders, and say, 'My husband's brother refuses to raise up a name to his brother in Israel; he will not perform the duty of my husband's brother.' 8 Then the elders of his city shall call him and speak to him. But *if* he stands firm and says, 'I do not want to take her,' 9 then his brother's wife shall come to him in the presence of the elders, remove his sandal from his foot, spit in his face, and answer and say, 'So shall it be done to the man who will not build up his brother's house.' 10 And his name shall be called in Israel, 'The house of him who had his sandal removed.'

11 "If *two* men fight together, and the wife of one draws near to rescue her husband from the hand of the one attacking him, and puts out her hand and seizes him by the genitals, 12 then you shall cut off her hand; your eye shall not pity *her.*

13 "You shall not have in your bag differing weights, a heavy and a light. 14 You shall not have in your house differing measures, a large and a small. 15 You shall have a perfect and just weight, a perfect and just measure, that your days may be lengthened in the land which the LORD your God is giving you. 16 For all who do such things, all who behave unrighteously, *are* an abomination to the LORD your God.

17 "Remember what Amalek did to you on the way as you were coming out of Egypt, 18 how he met you on the way and attacked your rear ranks, all the stragglers at your rear, when you *were* tired and weary; and he did not fear God. 19 Therefore it shall be, when the LORD your God has given you rest from your enemies all around, in the land which the LORD your God is giving you to possess *as* an inheritance, *that* you will blot out the remembrance of Amalek from under heaven. You shall not forget.

26 "And it shall be, when you come into the land which the LORD your God is giving you *as* an inheritance, and you possess it and dwell in it, 2 that you shall take some of the first of all the produce of the ground, which you shall bring from your land that the LORD your God is giving you, and put *it* in a basket and go to the place where the LORD your God chooses to make His name abide. 3 And you shall go to the one who is priest in those days, and say to him, 'I declare today to the LORD your[a] God that I have come to the country which the LORD swore to our fathers to give us.'

4 "Then the priest shall take the basket out of your hand and set it down before the altar of the LORD your God. 5 And you shall answer and say before the LORD your God: 'My father *was* a Syrian,[a] about to perish, and he went down to Egypt and dwelt there, few in number; and there he became a nation, great, mighty, and populous. 6 But the Egyptians mistreated us, afflicted us, and laid hard bondage on us. 7 Then we cried out to the LORD God of our fathers, and the LORD heard our voice and looked on our affliction and our labor and our oppression. 8 So the LORD brought us out of Egypt with a mighty hand and with an outstretched arm, with great terror and with signs and wonders. 9 He has brought us to this place and has given us this land, "a land flowing with milk and honey";[a] 10 and now, behold, I have brought the firstfruits of the land which you, O LORD, have given me.'

"Then you shall set it before the LORD your God, and worship before the LORD your God. 11 So you shall rejoice in every good *thing* which the LORD your God has given to you and your house, you and the Levite and the stranger who *is* among you.

12 "When you have finished laying aside all the tithe of your increase in the third year—the year of tithing—and have given *it* to the Levite, the stranger, the fatherless, and the widow, so that they may eat within your gates and be filled, 13 then you shall say before the LORD your God: 'I have removed the holy *tithe* from *my* house, and also have given them to the Levite, the stranger, the fatherless, and the widow, according to all

---

26:3 [a]Septuagint reads *my.*   26:5 [a]Or *Aramean*   26:9 [a]Exodus 3:8

Your commandments which You have commanded me; I have not transgressed Your commandments, nor have I forgotten *them.* 14 I have not eaten any of it when in mourning, nor have I removed *any* of it for an unclean *use,* nor given *any* of it for the dead. I have obeyed the voice of the LORD my God, and have done according to all that You have commanded me. 15 Look down from Your holy habitation, from heaven, and bless Your people Israel and the land which You have given us, just as You swore to our fathers, "a land flowing with milk and honey." '*a*

16 "This day the LORD your God commands you to observe these statutes and judgments; therefore you shall be careful to observe them with all your heart and with all your soul. 17 Today you have proclaimed the LORD to be your God, and that you will walk in His ways and keep His statutes, His commandments, and His judgments, and that you will obey His voice. 18 Also today the LORD has proclaimed you to be His special people, just as He promised you, that *you* should keep all His commandments, 19 and that He will set you high above all nations which He has made, in praise, in name, and in honor, and that you may be a holy people to the LORD your God, just as He has spoken."

27 Now Moses, with the elders of Israel, commanded the people, saying: "Keep all the commandments which I command you today. 2 And it shall be, on the day when you cross over the Jordan to the land which the LORD your God is giving you, that you shall set up for yourselves large stones, and whitewash them with lime. 3 You shall write on them all the words of this law, when you have crossed over, that you may enter the land which the LORD your God is giving you, 'a land flowing with milk and honey,'*a* just as the LORD God of your fathers promised you. 4 Therefore it shall be, when you have crossed over the Jordan, *that* on Mount Ebal you shall set up these stones, which I command you today, and you shall whitewash them with lime. 5 And there you shall build an altar to the LORD your God, an altar of stones; you shall not use an iron *tool* on them. 6 You shall build with whole stones the altar of the LORD your God, and offer burnt offerings on it to the LORD your God. 7 You shall offer peace offerings, and shall eat there, and rejoice before the LORD your God. 8 And you shall write very plainly on the stones all the words of this law."

9 Then Moses and the priests, the Levites, spoke to all Israel, saying, "Take heed and listen, O Israel: This day you have become the people of the LORD your God. 10 Therefore you shall obey the voice of the LORD your God, and observe His commandments and His statutes which I command you today."

11 And Moses commanded the people on the same day, saying, 12 "These shall stand on Mount Gerizim to bless the people, when you have crossed over the Jordan: Simeon, Levi, Judah, Issachar, Joseph, and Benjamin; 13 and these shall stand on Mount Ebal to curse: Reuben, Gad, Asher, Zebulun, Dan, and Naphtali.

14 "And the Levites shall speak with a loud voice and say to all the men of Israel: 15 'Cursed *is* the one who makes a carved or molded image, an abomination to the LORD, the work of the hands of the craftsman, and sets *it* up in secret.'

"And all the people shall answer and say, 'Amen!'

16 'Cursed *is* the one who treats his father or his mother with contempt.'

"And all the people shall say, 'Amen!'

17 'Cursed *is* the one who moves his neighbor's landmark.'

"And all the people shall say, 'Amen!'

18 'Cursed *is* the one who makes the blind to wander off the road.'

"And all the people shall say, 'Amen!'

19 'Cursed *is* the one who perverts the justice due the stranger, the fatherless, and widow.'

"And all the people shall say, 'Amen!'

20 'Cursed *is* the one who lies with his father's wife, because he has uncovered his father's bed.'

"And all the people shall say, 'Amen!'

26:15 *a*Exodus 3:8　　　27:3 *a*Exodus 3:8

21 'Cursed *is* the one who lies with any kind of animal.'

"And all the people shall say, 'Amen!'

22 'Cursed *is* the one who lies with his sister, the daughter of his father or the daughter of his mother.'

"And all the people shall say, 'Amen!'

23 'Cursed *is* the one who lies with his mother-in-law.'

"And all the people shall say, 'Amen!'

24 'Cursed *is* the one who attacks his neighbor secretly.'

"And all the people shall say, 'Amen!'

25 'Cursed *is* the one who takes a bribe to slay an innocent person.'

"And all the people shall say, 'Amen!'

26 'Cursed *is* the one who does not confirm *all* the words of this law.'

"And all the people shall say, 'Amen!'"

28 "Now it shall come to pass, if you diligently obey the voice of the LORD your God, to observe carefully all His commandments which I command you today, that the LORD your God will set you high above all nations of the earth. 2 And all these blessings shall come upon you and overtake you, because you obey the voice of the LORD your God:

3 "Blessed *shall* you *be* in the city, and blessed *shall* you *be* in the country.

4 "Blessed *shall be* the fruit of your body, the produce of your ground and the increase of your herds, the increase of your cattle and the off-spring of your flocks.

5 "Blessed *shall be* your basket and your kneading bowl.

6 "Blessed *shall* you *be* when you come in, and blessed *shall* you *be* when you go out.

7 "The LORD will cause your enemies who rise against you to be defeated before your face; they shall come out against you one way and flee before you seven ways.

8 "The LORD will command the blessing on you in your storehouses and in all to which you set your hand, and He will bless you in the land which the LORD your God is giving you.

9 "The LORD will establish you as a holy people to Himself, just as He has sworn to you, if you keep the commandments of the LORD your God and walk in His ways. 10 Then all peoples of the earth shall see that you are called by the name of the LORD, and they shall be afraid of you. 11 And the LORD will grant you plenty of goods, in the fruit of your body, in the increase of your livestock, and in the produce of your ground, in the land of which the LORD swore to your fathers to give you. 12 The LORD will open to you His good treasure, the heavens, to give the rain to your land in its season, and to bless all the work of your hand. You shall lend to many nations, but you shall not borrow. 13 And the LORD will make you the head and not the tail; you shall be above only, and not be beneath, if you heed the commandments of the LORD your God, which I command you today, and are careful to observe *them.* 14 So you shall not turn aside from any of the words which I command you this day, *to* the right or the left, to go after other gods to serve them.

15 "But it shall come to pass, if you do not obey the voice of the LORD your God, to observe carefully all His commandments and His statutes which I command you today, that all these curses will come upon you and overtake you:

16 "Cursed *shall* you *be* in the city, and cursed *shall* you *be* in the country.

17 "Cursed *shall be* your basket and your kneading bowl.

18 "Cursed *shall be* the fruit of your body and the produce of your land, the increase of your cattle and the offspring of your flocks.

19 "Cursed *shall* you *be* when you come in, and cursed *shall* you *be* when you go out.

20 "The LORD will send on you cursing, confusion, and rebuke in all that you set your hand to do, until you are destroyed and until you perish quickly, because of the wickedness of your doings in which you have forsaken Me. 21 The LORD will make the plague cling to you until He has consumed you from the land which you are going to possess. 22 The LORD will strike you with consumption, with fever, with inflammation, with severe burning fever, with the sword, with scorching, and with mildew; they shall pursue you until you perish.

23 And your heavens which *are* over your head shall be bronze, and the earth which is under you *shall be* iron. 24 The LORD will change the rain of your land to powder and dust; from the heaven it shall come down on you until you are destroyed.

25 "The LORD will cause you to be defeated before your enemies; you shall go out one way against them and flee seven ways before them; and you shall become troublesome to all the kingdoms of the earth. 26 Your carcasses shall be food for all the birds of the air and the beasts of the earth, and no one shall frighten *them* away. 27 The LORD will strike you with the boils of Egypt, with tumors, with the scab, and with the itch, from which you cannot be healed. 28 The LORD will strike you with madness and blindness and confusion of heart. 29 And you shall grope at noonday, as a blind man gropes in darkness; you shall not prosper in your ways; you shall be only oppressed and plundered continually, and no one shall save *you*.

30 "You shall betroth a wife, but another man shall lie with her; you shall build a house, but you shall not dwell in it; you shall plant a vineyard, but shall not gather its grapes. 31 Your ox *shall be* slaughtered before your eyes, but you shall not eat of it; your donkey *shall be* violently taken away from before you, and shall not be restored to you; your sheep *shall be* given to your enemies, and you shall have no one to rescue *them*. 32 Your sons and your daughters *shall be* given to another people, and your eyes shall look and fail *with longing* for them all day long; and *there shall be* no strength in your hand. 33 A nation whom you have not known shall eat the fruit of your land and the produce of your labor, and you shall be only oppressed and crushed continually. 34 So you shall be driven mad because of the sight which your eyes see. 35 The LORD will strike you in the knees and on the legs with severe boils which cannot be healed, and from the sole of your foot to the top of your head.

36 "The LORD will bring you and the king whom you set over you to a nation which neither you nor your fathers have known, and there you shall serve other gods—wood and stone. 37 And you shall become an astonishment, a proverb, and a byword among all nations where the LORD will drive you.

38 "You shall carry much seed out to the field but gather little in, for the locust shall consume it. 39 You shall plant vineyards and tend *them*, but you shall neither drink *of* the wine nor gather the *grapes;* for the worms shall eat them. 40 You shall have olive trees throughout all your territory, but you shall not anoint *yourself* with the oil; for your olives shall drop off. 41 You shall beget sons and daughters, but they shall not be yours; for they shall go into captivity. 42 Locusts shall consume all your trees and the produce of your land.

43 "The alien who *is* among you shall rise higher and higher above you, and you shall come down lower and lower. 44 He shall lend to you, but you shall not lend to him; he shall be the head, and you shall be the tail.

45 "Moreover all these curses shall come upon you and pursue and overtake you, until you are destroyed, because you did not obey the voice of the LORD your God, to keep His commandments and His statutes which He commanded you. 46 And they shall be upon you for a sign and a wonder, and on your descendants forever.

47 "Because you did not serve the LORD your God with joy and gladness of heart, for the abundance of everything, 48 therefore you shall serve your enemies, whom the LORD will send against you, in hunger, in thirst, in nakedness, and in need of everything; and He will put a yoke of iron on your neck until He has destroyed you. 49 The LORD will bring a nation against you from afar, from the end of the earth, *as swift* as the eagle flies, a nation whose language you will not understand, 50 a nation of fierce countenance, which does not respect the elderly nor show favor to the young. 51 And they shall eat the increase of your livestock and the produce of your land, until you are destroyed; they shall not leave you grain or new wine or oil, *or* the increase of your cattle or the offspring of your flocks, until they have destroyed you.

52 "They shall besiege you at all your gates until your high and fortified walls, in which you trust, come down throughout all your land; and

they shall besiege you at all your gates throughout all your land which the LORD your God has given you. 53 You shall eat the fruit of your own body, the flesh of your sons and your daughters whom the LORD your God has given you, in the siege and desperate straits in which your enemy shall distress you. 54 The sensitive and very refined man among you will be hostile toward his brother, toward the wife of his bosom, and toward the rest of his children whom he leaves behind, 55 so that he will not give any of them the flesh of his children whom he will eat, because he has nothing left in the siege and desperate straits in which your enemy shall distress you at all your gates. 56 The tender and delicate woman among you, who would not venture to set the sole of her foot on the ground because of her delicateness and sensitivity, will refuse,*a* to the husband of her bosom, and to her son and her daughter, 57 her placenta which comes out from between her feet and her children whom she bears; for she will eat them secretly for lack of everything in the siege and desperate straits in which your enemy shall distress you at all your gates.

58 "If you do not carefully observe all the words of this law that are written in this book, that you may fear this glorious and awesome name, THE LORD YOUR GOD, 59 then the LORD will bring upon you and your descendants extraordinary plagues—great and prolonged plagues—and serious and prolonged sicknesses. 60 Moreover He will bring back on you all the diseases of Egypt, of which you were afraid, and they shall cling to you. 61 Also every sickness and every plague, which *is* not written in this Book of the Law, will the LORD bring upon you until you are destroyed. 62 You shall be left few in number, whereas you were as the stars of heaven in multitude, because you would not obey the voice of the LORD your God. 63 And it shall be, *that* just as the LORD rejoiced over you to do you good and multiply you, so the LORD will rejoice over you to destroy you and bring you to nothing; and you shall be plucked from off the land which you go to possess.

64 "Then the LORD will scatter you among all peoples, from one end of the earth to the other, and there you shall serve other gods, which neither you nor your fathers have known—wood and stone. 65 And among those nations you shall find no rest, nor shall the sole of your foot have a resting place; but there the LORD will give you a trembling heart, failing eyes, and anguish of soul. 66 Your life shall hang in doubt before you; you shall fear day and night, and have no assurance of life. 67 In the morning you shall say, 'Oh, that it were evening!' And at evening you shall say, 'Oh, that it were morning!' because of the fear which terrifies your heart, and because of the sight which your eyes see.

68 "And the LORD will take you back to Egypt in ships, by the way of which I said to you, 'You shall never see it again.' And there you shall be offered for sale to your enemies as male and female slaves, but no one will buy *you*."

29 These *are* the words of the covenant which the LORD commanded Moses to make with the children of Israel in the land of Moab, besides the covenant which He made with them in Horeb.

2 Now Moses called all Israel and said to them: "You have seen all that the LORD did before your eyes in the land of Egypt, to Pharaoh and to all his servants and to all his land— 3 the great trials which your eyes have seen, the signs, and those great wonders. 4 Yet the LORD has not given you a heart to perceive and eyes to see and ears to hear, to this *very* day. 5 And I have led you forty years in the wilderness. Your clothes have not worn out on you, and your sandals have not worn out on your feet. 6 You have not eaten bread, nor have you drunk wine or *similar* drink, that you may know that I *am* the LORD your God. 7 And when you came to this place, Sihon king of Heshbon and Og king of Bashan came out against us to battle, and we conquered them. 8 We took their land and gave it as an inheritance to the Reubenites, to the Gadites, and to half the tribe of Manasseh. 9 Therefore keep the words of this

28:56 *a*Literally *her eye shall be evil toward*

covenant, and do them, that you may prosper in all that you do.

10 "All of you stand today before the LORD your God: your leaders and your tribes and your elders and your officers, all the men of Israel, 11 your little ones and your wives— also the stranger who is in your camp, from the one who cuts your wood to the one who draws your water— 12 that you may enter into covenant with the LORD your God, and into His oath, which the LORD your God makes with you today, 13 that He may establish you today as a people for Himself, and that He may be God to you, just as He has spoken to you, and just as He has sworn to your fathers, to Abraham, Isaac, and Jacob.

14 "I make this covenant and this oath, not with you alone, 15 but with him who stands here with us today before the LORD our God, as well as with him who is not here with us to-day 16 (for you know that we dwelt in the land of Egypt and that we came through the nations which you passed by, 17 and you saw their abominations and their idols which were among them—wood and stone and silver and gold); 18 so that there may not be among you man or woman or family or tribe, whose heart turns away today from the LORD our God, to go and serve the gods of these nations, and that there may not be among you a root bearing bitterness or wormwood; 19 and so it may not happen, when he hears the words of this curse, that he blesses himself in his heart, saying, 'I shall have peace, even though I follow the dictates[a] of my heart'—as though the drunkard could be included with the sober.

20 "The LORD would not spare him; for then the anger of the LORD and His jealousy would burn against that man, and every curse that is written in this book would settle on him, and the LORD would blot out his name from under heaven. 21 And the LORD would separate him from all the tribes of Israel for adversity, accord-ing to all the curses of the covenant that are written in this Book of the Law, 22 so that the coming genera-tion of your children who rise up af-ter you, and the foreigner who comes from a far land, would say, when they see the plagues of that land and the sicknesses which the LORD has laid on it:

23 'The whole land is brimstone, salt, and burning; it is not sown, nor does it bear, nor does any grass grow there, like the overthrow of Sodom and Gomorrah, Admah, and Ze-boiim, which the LORD overthrew in His anger and His wrath.' 24 All na-tions would say, 'Why has the LORD done so to this land? What does the heat of this great anger mean?' 25 Then people would say: 'Because they have forsaken the covenant of the LORD God of their fathers, which He made with them when He brought them out of the land of Egypt; 26 for they went and served other gods and worshiped them, gods that they did not know and that He had not given to them. 27 Then the anger of the LORD was aroused against this land, to bring on it every curse that is written in this book. 28 And the LORD uprooted them from their land in anger, in wrath, and in great indig-nation, and cast them into another land, as it is this day.'

29 "The secret things belong to the LORD our God, but those things which are revealed belong to us and to our children forever, that we may do all the words of this law.

30 "Now it shall come to pass, when all these things come upon you, the blessing and the curse which I have set before you, and you call them to mind among all the na-tions where the LORD your God drives you, 2 and you return to the LORD your God and obey His voice, according to all that I command you today, you and your children, with all your heart and with all your soul, 3 that the LORD your God will bring you back from captivity, and have compassion on you, and gather you again from all the nations where the LORD your God has scattered you. 4 If any of you are driven out to the farthest parts under heaven, from there the LORD your God will gather you, and from there He will bring you. 5 Then the LORD your God will bring you to the land which your fa-thers possessed, and you shall pos-sess it. He will prosper you and

29:19 [a]Or stubbornness

Dare to Decide

Success never happens until you make it happen. And you make good things happen when you make decisions that cause a movement to begin. You can be sure that you are walking the walk of faith so long as you make those decisions. Read Deuteronomy 30, which records Moses' challenge to the Israelites. He urged them to return to the Lord, to commit their way to Him, and in this way to "choose life."

How can you make a decision when there is risk involved?

How can you make a decision when dangers may follow?

Do you refuse to make decisions because problems and perils might result? Do you want to play it safe? When you play it safe, you can be sure you will face the dangers that inevitably come: boredom; lack of growth; stagnation; emotional death! The zest that comes from decisions will be gone. What is left is a shriveling and shrinking spirit with false promises of security.

Of all the cruel illusions there is none more insidious or disastrous than the alluring call of safety and shelter when you retreat from taking a risk!

The truth is, if you continue to make daring decisions, you will succeed—at least you will succeed in filling each day with excitement!

The promise from the God of life, abundant and eternal, is only offered to those who dare to walk the walk of faith.

Keep walking that path by daring to make the decision you have already postponed too long!

Success is no accident. Success is a commitment—not a coincidence! Decide today where you want to be five, ten, twenty years from today.

multiply you more than your fathers. 6 And the LORD your God will circumcise your heart and the heart of your descendants, to love the LORD your God with all your heart and with all your soul, that you may live.

7 "Also the LORD your God will put all these curses on your enemies and on those who hate you, who persecuted you. 8 And you will again obey the voice of the LORD and do all His commandments which I command you today. 9 The LORD your God will make you abound in all the work of your hand, in the fruit of your body, in the increase of your livestock, and in the produce of your land for good. For the LORD will again rejoice over you for good as He rejoiced over your fathers, 10 if you obey the voice of the LORD your God, to keep His commandments and His statutes which are written in this Book of the Law, *and* if you turn to the LORD your God with all your heart and with all your soul.

11 "For this commandment which I command you today *is* not *too* mysterious for you, nor *is* it far off. 12 It *is* not in heaven, that you should say, 'Who will ascend into heaven for us and bring it to us, that we may hear it and do it?' 13 Nor *is* it beyond the sea, that you should say, 'Who will go over the sea for us and bring it to us, that we may hear it and do it?' 14 But the word *is* very near you, in your mouth and in your heart, that you may do it.

15 "See, I have set before you today life and good, death and evil, 16 in that I command you today to love the LORD your God, to walk in His ways, and to keep His commandments, His statutes, and His judgments, that you may live and multiply; and the LORD your God will bless you in the land which you go to possess. 17 But if your heart turns away so that you do not hear, and are drawn away, and worship other gods and serve them, 18 I announce to you today that you shall surely perish; you shall not prolong *your* days in the land which you cross over the Jordan to go in and possess. 19 I call heaven and earth as witnesses today against you, *that* I have set before you life and death, blessing and cursing; therefore choose life, that both you and your descendants may live; 20 that you may love

the LORD your God, that you may obey His voice, and that you may cling to Him, for He *is* your life and the length of your days; and that you may dwell in the land which the LORD swore to your fathers, to Abraham, Isaac, and Jacob, to give them."

31 Then Moses went and spoke these words to all Israel. 2 And he said to them: "I *am* one hundred and twenty years old today. I can no longer go out and come in. Also the LORD has said to me, 'You shall not cross over this Jordan.' 3 The LORD your God Himself crosses over before you; He will destroy these nations from before you, and you shall dispossess them. Joshua himself crosses over before you, just as the LORD has said. 4 And the LORD will do to them as He did to Sihon and Og, the kings of the Amorites and their land, when He destroyed them. 5 The LORD will give them over to you, that you may do to them according to every commandment which I have commanded you. 6 Be strong and of good courage, do not fear nor be afraid of them; for the LORD your God, He *is* the One who goes with you. He will not leave you nor forsake you."

7 Then Moses called Joshua and said to him in the sight of all Israel, "Be strong and of good courage, for you must go with this people to the land which the LORD has sworn to their fathers to give them, and you shall cause them to inherit it. 8 And the LORD, He *is* the One who goes before you. He will be with you, He will not leave you nor forsake you; do not fear nor be dismayed."

9 So Moses wrote this law and delivered it to the priests, the sons of Levi, who bore the ark of the covenant of the LORD, and to all the elders of Israel. 10 And Moses commanded them, saying: "At the end of *every* seven years, at the appointed time in the year of release, at the Feast of Tabernacles, 11 when all Israel comes to appear before the LORD your God in the place which He chooses, you shall read this law before all Israel in their hearing. 12 Gather the people together, men and women and little ones, and the stranger who *is* within your gates, that they may hear and that they may learn to fear the LORD your God and carefully observe all

the words of this law, 13 and *that* their children, who have not known it, may hear and learn to fear the LORD your God as long as you live in the land which you cross the Jordan to possess."

14 Then the LORD said to Moses, "Behold, the days approach when you must die; call Joshua, and present yourselves in the tabernacle of meeting, that I may inaugurate him."

So Moses and Joshua went and presented themselves in the tabernacle of meeting. 15 Now the LORD appeared at the tabernacle in a pillar of cloud, and the pillar of cloud stood above the door of the tabernacle.

16 And the LORD said to Moses: "Behold, you will rest with your fathers; and this people will rise and play the harlot with the gods of the foreigners of the land, where they go *to be* among them, and they will forsake Me and break My covenant which I have made with them. 17 Then My anger shall be aroused against them in that day, and I will forsake them, and I will hide My face from them, and they shall be devoured. And many evils and troubles shall befall them, so that they will say in that day, 'Have not these evils come upon us because our God *is* not among us?' 18 And I will surely hide My face in that day because of all the evil which they have done, in that they have turned to other gods.

19 "Now therefore, write down this song for yourselves, and teach it to the children of Israel; put it in their mouths, that this song may be a witness for Me against the children of Israel. 20 When I have brought them to the land flowing with milk and honey, of which I swore to their fathers, and they have eaten and filled themselves and grown fat, then they will turn to other gods and serve them; and they will provoke Me and break My covenant. 21 Then it shall be, when many evils and troubles have come upon them, that this song will testify against them as a witness; for it will not be forgotten in the mouths of their descendants, for I know the inclination of their behavior today, even before I have brought them to the land of which I swore *to give them*."

22 Therefore Moses wrote this song the same day, and taught it to the children of Israel. 23 Then He inaugurated Joshua the son of Nun, and said, "Be strong and of good courage; for you shall bring the children of Israel into the land of which I swore to them, and I will be with you."

24 So it was, when Moses had completed writing the words of this law in a book, when they were finished, 25 that Moses commanded the Levites, who bore the ark of the covenant of the LORD, saying: 26 "Take this Book of the Law, and put it beside the ark of the covenant of the LORD your God, that it may be there as a witness against you; 27 for I know your rebellion and your stiff neck. *If* today, while I am yet alive with you, you have been rebellious against the LORD, then how much more after my death? 28 Gather to me all the elders of your tribes, and your officers, that I may speak these words in their hearing and call heaven and earth to witness against them. 29 For I know that after my death you will become utterly corrupt, and turn aside from the way which I have commanded you. And evil will befall you in the latter days, because you will do evil in the sight of the LORD, to provoke Him to anger through the work of your hands."

30 Then Moses spoke in the hearing of all the assembly of Israel the words of this song until they were ended:

32 "Give ear, O heavens, and I will speak;
And hear, O earth, the words of my mouth.
2 Let my teaching drop as the rain,
My speech distill as the dew,
As raindrops on the tender herb,
And as showers on the grass.
3 For I proclaim the name of the LORD:
Ascribe greatness to our God.
4 *He is* the Rock, His work *is* perfect;
For all His ways *are* justice,
A God of truth and without injustice;
Righteous and upright *is* He.

5 "They have corrupted themselves;
They are not His children,
Because of their blemish:

A perverse and crooked
generation.

6 Do you thus deal with the LORD,
O foolish and unwise people?
Is He not your Father, *who*
bought you?
Has He not made you and
established you?

7 "Remember the days of old,
Consider the years of many
generations.
Ask your father, and he will
show you;
Your elders, and they will tell
you:

8 When the Most High divided
their inheritance to the
nations,
When He separated the sons of
Adam,
He set the boundaries of the
peoples
According to the number of the
children of Israel.

9 For the LORD's portion *is* His
people;
Jacob *is* the place of His
inheritance.

10 "He found him in a desert land
And in the wasteland, a
howling wilderness;
He encircled him, He instructed
him,
He kept him as the apple of His
eye.

11 As an eagle stirs up its nest,
Hovers over its young,
Spreading out its wings, taking
them up,
Carrying them on its wings,

12 *So* the LORD alone led him,
And *there was* no foreign god
with him.

13 "He made him ride in the
heights of the earth,
That he might eat the produce
of the fields;
He made him draw honey from
the rock,
And oil from the flinty rock;

14 Curds from the cattle, and milk
of the flock,
With fat of lambs;
And rams of the breed of
Bashan, and goats,
With the choicest wheat;
And you drank wine, the blood
of the grapes.

15 "But Jeshurun grew fat and
kicked;
You grew fat, you grew thick,
You are obese!
Then he forsook God *who*
made him,
And scornfully esteemed the
Rock of his salvation.

16 They provoked Him to jealousy
with foreign *gods;*
With abominations they
provoked Him to anger.

17 They sacrificed to demons, not
to God,
To gods they did not know,
To new *gods,* new arrivals
That your fathers did not fear.

18 Of the Rock *who* begot you,
you are unmindful,
And have forgotten the God
who fathered you.

19 "And when the LORD saw *it,* He
spurned *them,*
Because of the provocation of
His sons and His daughters.

20 And He said: 'I will hide My
face from them,
I will see what their end *will be,*
For they *are* a perverse
generation,
Children in whom *is* no faith.

21 They have provoked Me to
jealousy by *what* is not God;
They have moved Me to anger
by their foolish idols.
But I will provoke them to
jealousy by *those who are*
not a nation;
I will move them to anger by a
foolish nation.

22 For a fire is kindled in My
anger,
And shall burn to the lowest
hell;
It shall consume the earth with
her increase,
And set on fire the foundations
of the mountains.

23 'I will heap disasters on them;
I will spend My arrows on
them.

24 *They shall be* wasted with
hunger,
Devoured by pestilence and
bitter destruction;
I will also send against them
the teeth of beasts,
With the poison of serpents of
the dust.

25 The sword shall destroy
    outside;
There shall be terror within
For the young man and virgin,
The nursing child with the man
    of gray hairs.
26 I would have said, "I will dash
    them in pieces,
I will make the memory of them
    to cease from among men,"
27 Had I not feared the wrath of
    the enemy,
Lest their adversaries should
    misunderstand,
Lest they should say, "Our
    hand *is* high;
And it is not the LORD who has
    done all this."'

28 "For they *are* a nation void of
    counsel,
Nor *is there any* understanding
    in them.
29 Oh, that they were wise, *that*
    they understood this,
That they would consider their
    latter end!
30 How could one chase a
    thousand,
And two put ten thousand to
    flight,
Unless their Rock had sold
    them,
And the LORD had surrendered
    them?
31 For their rock *is* not like our
    Rock,
Even our enemies themselves
    being judges.
32 For their vine *is* of the vine of
    Sodom
And of the fields of Gomorrah;
Their grapes *are* grapes of gall,
Their clusters *are* bitter.
33 Their wine *is* the poison of
    serpents,
And the cruel venom of cobras.

34 'Is this not laid up in store with
    Me,
Sealed up among My
    treasures?
35 Vengeance is Mine, and
    recompense;
Their foot shall slip in *due* time;
For the day of their calamity *is*
    at hand,
And the things to come hasten
    upon them.'

36 "For the LORD will judge His
    people
And have compassion on His
    servants,
When He sees that *their* power
    is gone,
And *there is* no one *remaining*,
    bond or free.
37 He will say: 'Where *are* their
    gods,
The rock in which they sought
    refuge?
38 Who ate the fat of their
    sacrifices,
And drank the wine of their
    drink offering?
Let them rise and help you,
And be your refuge.

39 'Now see that I, *even* I, *am* He,
And *there is* no God besides
    Me;
I kill and I make alive;
I wound and I heal;
Nor *is there any* who can
    deliver from My hand.
40 For I raise My hand to heaven,
And say, "*As* I live forever,
41 If I whet My glittering sword,
And My hand takes hold on
    judgment,
I will render vengeance to My
    enemies,
And repay those who hate Me.
42 I will make My arrows drunk
    with blood,
And My sword shall devour
    flesh,
With the blood of the slain and
    the captives,
From the heads of the leaders
    of the enemy."'

43 "Rejoice, O Gentiles, *with* His
    people;^a
For He will avenge the blood
    of His servants,
And render vengeance to His
    adversaries;
He will provide atonement for
    His land *and* His people."

44 So Moses came with Joshua^a the
son of Nun and spoke all the words
of this song in the hearing of the people. 45 Moses finished speaking all
these words to all Israel, 46 and he
said to them: "Set your hearts on all
the words which I testify among you

today, which you shall command your children to be careful to observe—all the words of this law. 47 For it *is* not a futile thing for you, because it *is* your life, and by this word you shall prolong *your* days in the land which you cross over the Jordan to possess."

48 Then the LORD spoke to Moses that very same day, saying: 49 "Go up this mountain of the Abarim, Mount Nebo, which *is* in the land of Moab, across from Jericho; view the land of Canaan, which I give to the children of Israel as a possession; 50 and die on the mountain which you ascend, and be gathered to your people, just as Aaron your brother died on Mount Hor and was gathered to his people; 51 because you trespassed against Me among the children of Israel at the waters of Meribah Kadesh, in the Wilderness of Zin, because you did not hallow Me in the midst of the children of Israel. 52 Yet you shall see the land before *you*, though you shall not go there, into the land which I am giving to the children of Israel."

33 Now this *is* the blessing with which Moses the man of God blessed the children of Israel before his death. 2 And he said:

"The LORD came from Sinai,
    And dawned on them from
        Seir;
    He shone forth from Mount
        Paran,
    And He came with ten
        thousands of saints;
    From His right hand
    Came a fiery law for them.
3   Yes, He loves the people;
    All His saints *are* in Your hand;
    They sit down at Your feet;
    Everyone receives Your words.
4   Moses commanded a law for
        us,
    A heritage of the congregation
        of Jacob.
5   And He was King in Jeshurun,
    When the leaders of the people
        were gathered,
    All the tribes of Israel together.

6   "Let Reuben live, and not die,
    Nor let his men be few."

7 And this he said of Judah:

"Hear, LORD, the voice of Judah,
    And bring him to his people;
    Let his hands be sufficient for
        him,
    And may You be a help against
        his enemies."

8 And of Levi he said:

"*Let* Your Thummim and Your
        Urim *be* with Your holy one,
    Whom You tested at Massah,
    And with whom You contended
        at the waters of Meribah,
9   Who says of his father and
        mother,
    'I have not seen them';
    Nor did he acknowledge his
        brothers,
    Or know his own children;
    For they have observed Your
        word
    And kept Your covenant.
10   They shall teach Jacob Your
        judgments,
    And Israel Your law.
    They shall put incense before
        You,
    And a whole burnt sacrifice on
        Your altar.
11   Bless his substance, LORD,
    And accept the work of his
        hands;
    Strike the loins of those who
        rise against him,
    And of those who hate him,
        that they rise not again."

12 Of Benjamin he said:

"The beloved of the LORD shall
        dwell in safety by Him,
    Who shelters him all the day
        long;
    And he shall dwell between His
        shoulders."

13 And of Joseph he said:

"Blessed of the LORD *is* his land,
    With the precious things of
        heaven, with the dew,
    And the deep lying beneath,
14   With the precious fruits of the
        sun,
    With the precious produce of
        the months,
15   With the best things of the
        ancient mountains,
    With the precious things of the
        everlasting hills,
16   With the precious things of the

earth and its fullness,
And the favor of Him who
dwelt in the bush.
Let *the blessing* come 'on the
head of Joseph,
And on the crown of the head
of him *who was* separate
from his brothers.'*a*
17 His glory *is like* a firstborn bull,
And his horns *like* the horns of
the wild ox;
Together with them
He shall push the peoples
To the ends of the earth;
They *are* the ten thousands of
Ephraim,
And they *are* the thousands of
Manasseh."

18 And of Zebulun he said:

"Rejoice, Zebulun, in your going
out,
And Issachar in your tents!
19 They shall call the peoples *to*
the mountain;
There they shall offer sacrifices
of righteousness;
For they shall partake *of* the
abundance of the seas
And *of* treasures hidden in the
sand."

20 And of Gad he said:

"Blessed *is* he who enlarges
Gad;
He dwells as a lion,
And tears the arm and the
crown of his head.
21 He provided the first *part* for
himself,
Because a lawgiver's portion
was reserved there.
He came *with* the heads of the
people;
He administered the justice of
the LORD,
And His judgments with
Israel."

22 And of Dan he said:

"Dan *is* a lion's whelp;
He shall leap from Bashan."

23 And of Naphtali he said:

"O Naphtali, satisfied with
favor,

And full of he [...]
LORD,
Possess the wes[...]
south."

24 And of Asher he s[...]

"Asher *is* most ble[...]
Let him be favore[...]
brothers,
And let him dip his [...]
25 Your sandals *shall* [...]
bronze;
As your days, *so sh[...]
strength *be.*

26 "*There is* no one like t[...]
Jeshurun,
Who rides the heaven[...]
you,
And in His excellency o[...]
clouds.
27 The eternal God *is your* refug[...]
And underneath *are* the
everlasting arms;
He will thrust out the enemy
from before you,
And will say, 'Destroy!'
28 Then Israel shall dwell in
safety,
The fountain of Jacob alone,
In a land of grain and new
wine;
His heavens shall also drop
dew.
29 Happy *are* you, O Israel!
Who *is* like you, a people saved
by the LORD,
The shield of your help
And the sword of your majesty!
Your enemies shall submit to
you,
And you shall tread down their
high places."

34 Then Moses went up from the
plains of Moab to Mount Nebo,
to the top of Pisgah, which is across
from Jericho. And the LORD showed
him all the land of Gilead as far as
Dan, 2 all Naphtali and the land of
Ephraim and Manasseh, all the land
of Judah as far as the Western Sea,*a*
3 the South, and the plain of the Valley of Jericho, the city of palm trees,
as far as Zoar. 4 Then the LORD said
to him, "This *is* the land of which I
swore to give Abraham, Isaac, and
Jacob, saying, 'I will give it to your

33:16 *a*Genesis 49:26   34:2 *a*That is, the Mediterranean

DEUTERON...

I have caused you to ... our eyes, but you shall see ... there."

descen... ...es the servant of the LORD ... in the land of Moab, ac-... the word of the LORD.

...e buried him in a valley in ... of Moab, opposite Beth Peor; ...one knows his grave to this ... Moses *was* one hundred and ...ty years old when he died. His ... were not dim nor his natural ...or diminished. 8 And the children ...Israel wept for Moses in the plains ...f Moab thirty days. So the days of weeping *and* mourning for Moses ...ended.

9 Now Joshua the son of Nun was full of the spirit of wisdom, for Moses had laid his hands on him; so the children of Israel heeded him, and did as the LORD had commanded Moses.

10 But since then there has not arisen in Israel a prophet like Moses, whom the LORD knew face to face, 11 in all the signs and wonders which the LORD sent him to do in the land of Egypt, before Pharaoh, before all his servants, and in all his land, 12 and by all that mighty power and all the great terror which Moses performed in the sight of all Israel.

Joshua

Overview of Joshua

Joshua dared to believe in conquest when others predicted catastrophe. He marched forth with faith and courage, dedicated to conquering the land God had promised the Israelites.

Joshua wrote this fascinating account sometime during the fourteenth or fifteenth century B.C. It vividly depicts brilliant military strategy and God's miraculous intervention in the conquest of Canaan.

Joshua ordered his armies into a two-pronged attack. One began at Jericho, the pantry of the wilderness, from which he could supply food and water to his troops. The other struck north at Hazor, which controlled the major highway above the Sea of Galilee.

Joshua quickly secured the Judean ridge and high mountains of northern Galilee, from which he launched guerilla-like warfare tactics into the surrounding areas.

Employing this battle plan, Joshua was able to cut his problem in half. He knew that his greatest asset was not in numerical superiority or military might, but in a deep-rooted faith in God's ability to conquer any problem. Joshua had an inspiring and committed faith. "Choose for yourselves this day whom you will serve . . . But as for me and my house, we will serve the LORD" (Josh. 24:15).

Life is a collection of decisions. Joshua knew the value of right choices. As a great possibility thinker, Joshua chose to look at his prospects, not his problems; his resources, not his reservations; and his opportunities, not his obstacles.

With this faith, Joshua's military campaign of the Promised Land resulted in conquest, not catastrophe. He knew they could inhabit the land if they were not inhibited. He knew that with God all things are possible.

Jesus in Joshua

Joshua is clearly a type of Christ. His name is the Hebrew equivalent of Jesus, and it means "Yahweh Is Salvation." Triumphantly leading his people into the Promised Land, Joshua foreshadows the One who will bring many people into their inheritance of the likeness of Jesus. As Joshua succeeds Moses and attains the victory that Moses did not, Jesus will succeed the Mosaic Law and win the victory unreachable by the Law.

Keys to Joshua

Key Word: Conquest. The entire Book of Joshua describes the entering, conquering, and occupying of the land of Canaan. The book begins with a statement of the promise of conquest (Josh. 1:2, 3) and ends with the completion of conquest (23:14).

Key Verses: "This Book of the Law shall not depart from your mouth, but you shall meditate in it day and night, that you may observe to do according to all that is written in it. For then you will make your way prosperous, and then you will have good success" (1:8).

"So Joshua took the whole land, according to all that the LORD had said to Moses; and Joshua gave it as an inheritance to Israel according to their divisions by their tribes. Then the land from war" (11:23).

Key Chapter: Joshua 24. Some of the most critical periods in Israel's history are transitions of leadership. Before his death and in preparation for a major change from leadership by one man (Joshua) to leadership by many (the judges), Joshua reviews for the people God's fulfillment of His promises and then challenges them to review their commitment to the covenant, which is the foundation of successful national life.

1 After the death of Moses the servant of the LORD, it came to pass that the LORD spoke to Joshua the son of Nun, Moses' assistant, saying: 2 "Moses My servant is dead. Now therefore, arise, go over this Jordan, you and all this people, to the land which I am giving to them—the children of Israel. 3 Every place that the sole of your foot will tread upon I have given you, as I said to Moses. 4 From the wilderness and this Lebanon as far as the great river, the River Euphrates, all the land of the Hittites, and to the Great Sea toward the going down of the sun, shall be your territory. 5 No man shall *be able to* stand before you all the days of your life; as I was with Moses, *so* I will be with you. I will not leave you nor forsake you. 6 Be strong and of good courage, for to this people you shall divide as an inheritance the land which I swore to their fathers to give them. 7 Only be strong and very courageous, that you may observe to do according to all the law which Moses My servant commanded you; do not turn from it to the right hand or to the left, that you may prosper wherever you go. 8 This Book of the Law shall not depart from your mouth, but you shall meditate in it day and night, that you may observe to do according to all that is written in it. For then you will make your way prosperous, and then you will have good success. 9 Have I not commanded you? Be strong and of good courage; do not be afraid, nor be dismayed, for the LORD your God *is* with you wherever you go."

10 Then Joshua commanded the officers of the people, saying, 11 "Pass through the camp and command the people, saying, 'Prepare provisions for yourselves, for within three days you will cross over this Jordan, to go in to possess the land which the LORD your God is giving you to possess.'"

12 And to the Reubenites, the Gadites, and half the tribe of Manasseh Joshua spoke, saying, 13 "Remember the word which Moses the servant of the LORD commanded you, saying, 'The LORD your God is giving you rest and is giving you this land.' 14 Your wives, your little ones, and your livestock shall remain in the land which Moses gave you on this side of the Jordan. But you shall pass before your brethren armed, all your

No One Is Too Far from God's Love

When Joshua and the Israelites conquered the city of Jericho, they were aided by a most unusual woman—a prostitute named Rahab. Hearing of the Israelites' faith in the one true God, Rahab took it upon herself to hide two of Joshua's top espionage agents who were scouting the land.

Jericho was the pantry of the wilderness—the only city with supplies for the desert. The spring of Jericho pumped three thousand gallons of water a minute.

Joshua's strategy was to secure Jericho before moving into the hill country and continuing his conquest of Canaan. In Joshua 2:1, two spies were commissioned to "go, view the land, especially Jericho." When the two spies entered Rahab's house, word of their coming had already reached Jericho's king. Defying the king's request to send out the spies, Rahab welcomed the pure God-fearing worship of the Israelites, saying, "The LORD your God, He *is* God in heaven above and on earth beneath" (Josh. 2:11).

In return for hiding the spies in her house, Rahab asked the Israelites to spare her and her family when they conquered Jericho. In exchange for her assistance, the Israelites welcomed her into their community. God acknowledged her faith by honoring her in history. Rahab became a respected citizen of the Israelite community and married the son of Caleb, one of the two spies. As a result of her faith, Rahab was included as an ancestor in the genealogy of Christ.

God's redemption of Rahab and His using her to accomplish His work shows clearly that no one is too far from His love. No one is too small for God's work. Like Rahab, recognize the one true God. Then do your part for the advancement of His kingdom. Believe in God—believe in His plan—and then believe in yourself!

mighty men of valor, and help them, 15 until the LORD has given your brethren rest, as He *gave* you, and they also have taken possession of the land which the LORD your God is giving them. Then you shall return to the land of your possession and enjoy it, which Moses the LORD's servant gave you on this side of the Jordan toward the sunrise."

16 So they answered Joshua, saying, "All that you command us we will do, and wherever you send us we will go. 17 Just as we heeded Moses in all things, so we will heed you. Only the LORD your God be with you, as He was with Moses. 18 Whoever rebels against your command and does not heed your words, in all that you command him, shall be put to death. Only be strong and of good courage."

2 Now Joshua the son of Nun sent out two men from Acacia Grove*a* to spy secretly, saying, "Go, view the land, especially Jericho."

So they went, and came to the house of a harlot named Rahab, and lodged there. 2 And it was told the king of Jericho, saying, "Behold, men have come here tonight from the children of Israel to search out the country."

3 So the king of Jericho sent to Rahab, saying, "Bring out the men who have come to you, who have entered your house, for they have come to search out all the country."

4 Then the woman took the two men and hid them. So she said, "Yes, the men came to me, but I did not know where they *were* from. 5 And it happened as the gate was being shut, when it was dark, that the men went out. Where the men went I do not know; pursue them quickly, for you may overtake them." 6 (But she had brought them up to the roof and hidden them with the stalks of flax, which she had laid in order on the roof.) 7 Then the men pursued them by the road to the Jordan, to the fords. And as soon as those who pursued them had gone out, they shut the gate.

8 Now before they lay down, she came up to them on the roof, 9 and said to the men: "I know that the LORD has given you the land, that the terror of you has fallen on us, and that all the inhabitants of the land are fainthearted because of you. 10 For we have heard how the LORD dried up the water of the Red Sea for you when you came out of Egypt, and what you did to the two kings of the Amorites who *were* on the other side of the Jordan, Sihon and Og, whom you utterly destroyed. 11 And as soon as we heard *these things,* our hearts melted; neither did there remain any more courage in anyone because of you, for the LORD your God, He *is* God in heaven above and on earth beneath. 12 Now therefore, I beg you, swear to me by the LORD, since I have shown you kindness, that you also will show kindness to my father's house, and give me a true token, 13 and spare my father, my mother, my brothers, my sisters, and all that they have, and deliver our lives from death."

14 So the men answered her, "Our lives for yours, if none of you tell this business of ours. And it shall be, when the LORD has given us the land, that we will deal kindly and truly with you."

15 Then she let them down by a rope through the window, for her house *was* on the city wall; she dwelt on the wall. 16 And she said to them, "Get to the mountain, lest the pursuers meet you. Hide there three days, until the pursuers have returned. Afterward you may go your way."

17 So the men said to her: "We *will be* blameless of this oath of yours which you have made us swear, 18 unless, *when* we come into the land, you bind this line of scarlet cord in the window through which you let us down, and unless you bring your father, your mother, your brothers, and all your father's household to your own home. 19 So it shall be *that* whoever goes outside the doors of your house into the street, his blood *shall be* on his own head, and we *will be* guiltless. And whoever is with you in the house, his blood *shall be* on our head if a hand is laid on him. 20 And if you tell this business of ours, then we will be free from your oath which you made us swear."

21 Then she said, "According to your words, so *be* it." And she sent

2:1 *a* Hebrew *Shittim*

From Egypt to Canaan

The precise route taken by the Israelites from Egypt to Mt. Sinai is uncertain. Scholars have proposed both northern and southern routes, with the southern path most likely. The journey to Sinai took approximately two months, after which the Israelites camped for roughly ten months during the period of divine revelation. It was on Mt. Sinai that Moses received the Ten Commandments. Thirty-nine years later he appointed Joshua as his successor and died on Mt. Nebo, overlooking Canaan. Under Joshua's skillful leadership, the Israelites were able to conquer the land of Canaan and eventually settle in the Promised Land.

On the journey from Egypt to Sinai, three important Hebrew traditions were instituted: the Passover (Ex. 12:27, 43–49); the Feast of Unleavened Bread (Ex. 13:3–10); and the consecration of every first-born male to the Lord (Ex. 13:2).

During the time between the Exodus and the giving of the Law at Sinai, the Israelites often grumbled and complained to God and to Moses. Frequently, their murmurings concerned difficult living conditions and scarcity of food in the desert. Miraculously, God answered every need with perfect provision.

On their way from Egypt to Canaan, the Lord turned the seeming impossibilities of desert travel into great opportunities for His power in the lives of the children of Israel.

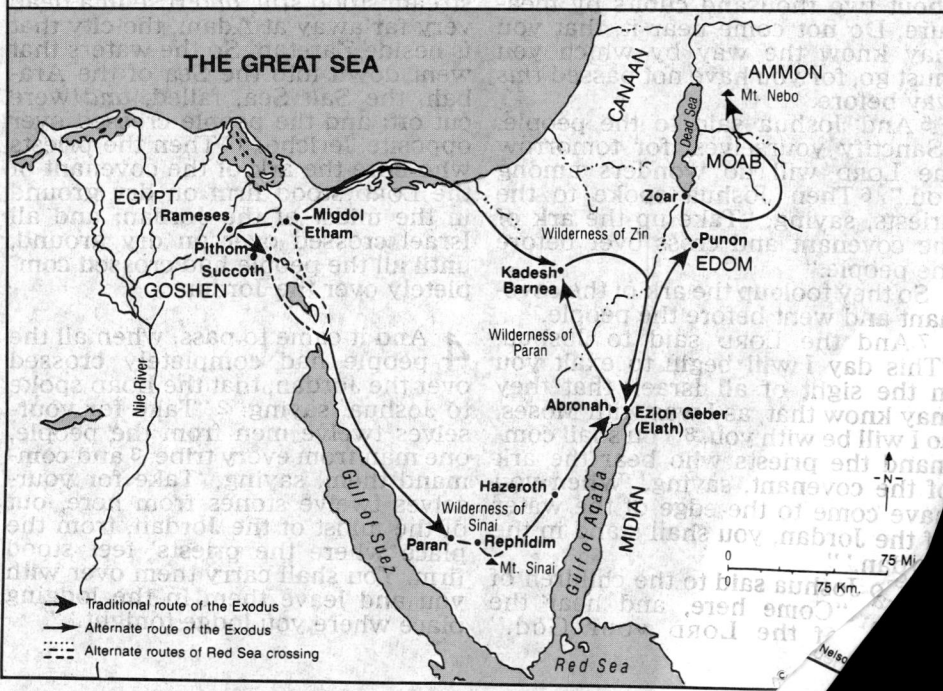

them away, and they departed. And she bound the scarlet cord in the window.

22 They departed and went to the mountain, and stayed there three days until the pursuers returned. The pursuers sought *them* all along the way, but did not find *them*. 23 So the two men returned, descended from the mountain, and crossed over; and they came to Joshua the son of Nun, and told him all that had befallen them. 24 And they said to Joshua, "Truly the LORD has delivered all the land into our hands, for indeed all the inhabitants of the country are fainthearted because of us."

3 Then Joshua rose early in the morning; and they set out from Acacia Grove*a* and came to the Jordan, he and all the children of Israel, and lodged there before they crossed over. 2 So it was, after three days, that the officers went through the camp; 3 and they commanded the people, saying, "When you see the ark of the covenant of the LORD your God, and the priests, the Levites, bearing it, then you shall set out from your place and go after it. 4 Yet there shall be a space between you and it, about two thousand cubits by measure. Do not come near it, that you may know the way by which you must go, for you have not passed *this* way before."

5 And Joshua said to the people, "Sanctify yourselves, for tomorrow the LORD will do wonders among you." 6 Then Joshua spoke to the priests, saying, "Take up the ark of the covenant and cross over before the people."

So they took up the ark of the cove-
and went before the people.
the LORD said to Joshua,
I will begin to exalt you
of all Israel, that they
at, as I was with Moses,
h you. 8 You shall com-
ts who bear the ark
saying, 'When you
edge of the water
shall stand in the

the children of
and hear the
your God."

10 And Joshua said, "By this you shall know that the living God *is* among you, and *that* He will without fail drive out from before you the Canaanites and the Hittites and the Hivites and the Perizzites and the Girgashites and the Amorites and the Jebusites: 11 Behold, the ark of the covenant of the Lord of all the earth is crossing over before you into the Jordan. 12 Now therefore, take for yourselves twelve men from the tribes of Israel, one man from every tribe. 13 And it shall come to pass, as soon as the soles of the feet of the priests who bear the ark of the LORD, the Lord of all the earth, shall rest in the waters of the Jordan, *that* the waters of the Jordan shall be cut off, the waters that come down from upstream, and they shall stand as a heap."

14 So it was, when the people set out from their camp to cross over the Jordan, with the priests bearing the ark of the covenant before the people, 15 and as those who bore the ark came to the Jordan, and the feet of the priests who bore the ark dipped in the edge of the water (for the Jordan overflows all its banks during the whole time of harvest), 16 that the waters which came down from upstream stood *still, and* rose in a heap very far away at Adam, the city that *is* beside Zaretan. So the waters that went down into the Sea of the Arabah, the Salt Sea, failed, *and* were cut off; and the people crossed over opposite Jericho. 17 Then the priests who bore the ark of the covenant of the LORD stood firm on dry ground in the midst of the Jordan; and all Israel crossed over on dry ground, until all the people had crossed completely over the Jordan.

4 And it came to pass, when all the people had completely crossed over the Jordan, that the LORD spoke to Joshua, saying: 2 "Take for yourselves twelve men from the people, one man from every tribe, 3 and command them, saying, 'Take for yourselves twelve stones from here, out of the midst of the Jordan, from the place where the priests' feet stood firm. You shall carry them over with you and leave them in the lodging place where you lodge tonight.'"

4 Then Joshua called the twelve men whom he had appointed from the children of Israel, one man from every tribe; 5 and Joshua said to them: "Cross over before the ark of the LORD your God into the midst of the Jordan, and each one of you take up a stone on his shoulder, according to the number of the tribes of the children of Israel, 6 that this may be a sign among you when your children ask in time to come, saying, 'What do these stones *mean* to you?' 7 Then you shall answer them that the waters of the Jordan were cut off before the ark of the covenant of the LORD; when it crossed over the Jordan, the waters of the Jordan were cut off. And these stones shall be for a memorial to the children of Israel forever."

8 And the children of Israel did so, just as Joshua commanded, and took up twelve stones from the midst of the Jordan, as the LORD had spoken to Joshua, according to the number of the tribes of the children of Israel, and carried them over with them to the place where they lodged, and laid them down there. 9 Then Joshua set up twelve stones in the midst of the Jordan, in the place where the feet of the priests who bore the ark of the covenant stood; and they are there to this day.

10 So the priests who bore the ark stood in the midst of the Jordan until everything was finished that the LORD had commanded Joshua to speak to the people, according to all that Moses had commanded Joshua; and the people hurried and crossed over. 11 Then it came to pass, when all the people had completely crossed over, that the ark of the LORD and the priests crossed over in the presence of the people. 12 And the men of Reuben, the men of Gad, and half the tribe of Manasseh crossed over armed before the children of Israel, as Moses had spoken to them. 13 About forty thousand prepared for war crossed over before the LORD for battle, to the plains of Jericho. 14 On that day the LORD exalted Joshua in the sight of all Israel; and they feared him, as they had feared Moses, all the days of his life.

15 Then the LORD spoke to Joshua, saying, 16 "Command the priests who bear the ark of the Testimony to come up from the Jordan." 17 Joshua therefore commanded the priests, saying, "Come up from the Jordan." 18 And it came to pass, when the priests who bore the ark of the covenant of the LORD had come from the midst of the Jordan, *and* the soles of the priests' feet touched the dry land, that the waters of the Jordan returned to their place and overflowed all its banks as before.

19 Now the people came up from the Jordan on the tenth *day* of the first month, and they camped in Gilgal on the east border of Jericho. 20 And those twelve stones which they took out of the Jordan, Joshua set up in Gilgal. 21 Then he spoke to the children of Israel, saying: "When your children ask their fathers in time to come, saying, 'What *are* these stones?' 22 then you shall let your children know, saying, 'Israel crossed over this Jordan on dry land'; 23 for the LORD your God dried up the waters of the Jordan before you until you had crossed over, as the LORD your God did to the Red Sea, which He dried up before us until we had crossed over, 24 that all the peoples of the earth may know the hand of the LORD, that it *is* mighty, that you may fear the LORD your God forever."

5 So it was, when all the kings of the Amorites who *were* on the west side of the Jordan, and all the kings of the Canaanites who *were* by the sea, heard that the LORD had dried up the waters of the Jordan from before the children of Israel until we[a] had crossed over, that their heart melted; and there was no spirit in them any longer because of the children of Israel.

2 At that time the LORD said to Joshua, "Make flint knives for yourself, and circumcise the sons of Israel again the second time." 3 So Joshua made flint knives for himself, and circumcised the sons of Israel at the hill of the foreskins.[a] 4 And this *is* the reason why Joshua circumcised them: All the people who came out of Egypt *who were* males, all the men of war, had died in the wilderness on

5:1 ᵃFollowing Kethib; Qere, some Hebrew manuscripts and editions, Septuagint, Syriac, Targum, and Vulgate read *they*.   5:3 ᵃHebrew *Gibeath Haaraloth* the way, after they had come out of Egypt. 5 For all the people who came out had been circumcised, but all the people born in the wilderness, on the way as they came out of Egypt, had not been circumcised. 6 For the children of Israel walked forty years in the wilderness, till all the people *who were* men of war, who came out of Egypt, were consumed, because they did not obey the voice of the LORD—to whom the LORD swore that He would not show them the land which the LORD had sworn to their fathers that He would give us, "a land flowing with milk and honey."*a* 7 Then Joshua circumcised their sons *whom* He raised up in their place; for they were uncircumcised, because they had not been circumcised on the way.

8 So it was, when they had finished circumcising all the people, that they stayed in their places in the camp till they were healed. 9 Then the LORD said to Joshua, "This day I have rolled away the reproach of Egypt from you." Therefore the name of the place is called Gilgal*a* to this day.

10 Now the children of Israel camped in Gilgal, and kept the Passover on the fourteenth day of the month at twilight on the plains of Jericho. 11 And they ate of the produce of the land on the day after the Passover, unleavened bread and parched grain, on the very same day. 12 Then the manna ceased on the day after they had eaten the produce of the land; and the children of Israel no longer had manna, but they ate the food of the land of Canaan that year.

13 And it came to pass, when Joshua was by Jericho, that he lifted his eyes and looked, and behold, a Man stood opposite him with His sword drawn in His hand. And Joshua went to Him and said to Him, "*Are* You for us or for our adversaries?"

14 So He said, "No, but *as* Commander of the army of the LORD I have now come."

And Joshua fell on his face to the earth and worshiped, and said to Him, "What does my Lord say to His servant?"

15 Then the Commander of the LORD's army said to Joshua, "Take your sandal off your foot, for the place where you stand *is* holy." And Joshua did so.

6 Now Jericho was securely shut up because of the children of Israel; none went out, and none came in. 2 And the LORD said to Joshua: "See! I have given Jericho into your hand, its king, *and* the mighty men of valor. 3 You shall march around the city, all *you* men of war; you shall go all around the city once. This you shall do six days. 4 And seven priests shall bear seven trumpets of rams' horns before the ark. But the seventh day you shall march around the city seven times, and the priests shall blow the trumpets. 5 It shall come to pass, when they make a long *blast* with the ram's horn, *and* when you hear the sound of the trumpet, that all the people shall shout with a great shout; then the wall of the city will fall down flat. And the people shall go up every man straight before him."

6 Then Joshua the son of Nun called the priests and said to them, "Take up the ark of the covenant, and let seven priests bear seven trumpets of rams' horns before the ark of the LORD." 7 And he said to the people, "Proceed, and march around the city, and let him who is armed advance before the ark of the LORD."

8 So it was, when Joshua had spoken to the people, that the seven priests bearing the seven trumpets of rams' horns before the LORD advanced and blew the trumpets, and the ark of the covenant of the LORD followed them. 9 The armed men went before the priests who blew trumpets, and the rear guard came after the ark, while *the priests* continued blowing the trumpets. 10 Now Joshua had commanded the people, saying, "You shall not shout or make any noise with your voice, nor shall a word proceed out of your mouth, until the day I say to you, 'Shout!' Then you shall shout." 11 So he had the ark of the LORD circle the city, going around *it* once. Then they came into the camp and lodged in the camp.

12 And Joshua rose early in the morning, and the priests took up the ark of the LORD. 13 Then seven priests

5:6 *a*Exodus 3:8   5:9 *a*Literally *Rolling*

bearing seven trumpets of rams' horns before the ark of the LORD went on continually and blew with the trumpets. And the armed men went before them. But the rear guard came after the ark of the LORD, while *the priests* continued blowing the trumpets. 14 And the second day they marched around the city once and returned to the camp. So they did six days.

15 But it came to pass on the seventh day that they rose early, about the dawning of the day, and marched around the city seven times in the same manner. On that day only they marched around the city seven times. 16 And the seventh time it happened, when the priests blew the trumpets, that Joshua said to the people: "Shout, for the LORD has given you the city! 17 Now the city shall be doomed by the LORD to destruction, it and all who *are* in it. Only Rahab the harlot shall live, she and all who *are* with her in the house, because she hid the messengers that we sent. 18 And you, by all means abstain from the accursed things, lest you become accursed when you take of the accursed things, and make the camp of Israel a curse, and trouble it. 19 But all the silver and gold, and vessels of bronze and iron, *are* consecrated to the LORD; they shall come into the treasury of the LORD."

20 So the people shouted when *the priests* blew the trumpets. And it happened when the people heard the sound of the trumpet, and the people shouted with a great shout, that the wall fell down flat. Then the people went up into the city, every man straight before him, and they took the city. 21 And they utterly destroyed all that *was* in the city, both man and woman, young and old, ox and sheep and donkey, with the edge of the sword.

22 But Joshua had said to the two men who had spied out the country, "Go into the harlot's house, and from there bring out the woman and all that she has, as you swore to her." 23 And the young men who had been spies went in and brought out Rahab, her father, her mother, her brothers, and all that she had. So they brought out all her relatives and left them outside the camp of Israel. 24 But they burned the city and all that *was* in it with fire. Only the silver and gold, and the vessels of bronze and iron, they put into the treasury of the house of the LORD. 25 And Joshua spared Rahab the harlot, her father's household, and all that she had. So she dwells in Israel to this day, because she hid the messengers whom Joshua sent to spy out Jericho.

26 Then Joshua charged *them* at that time, saying, "Cursed *be* the man before the LORD who rises up and builds this city Jericho; he shall lay its foundation with his firstborn, and with his youngest he shall set up its gates."

27 So the LORD was with Joshua, and his fame spread throughout all the country.

7 But the children of Israel committed a trespass regarding the accursed things, for Achan the son of Carmi, the son of Zabdi,[a] the son of Zerah, of the tribe of Judah, took of the accursed things; so the anger of the LORD burned against the children of Israel.

2 Now Joshua sent men from Jericho to Ai, which *is* beside Beth Aven, on the east side of Bethel, and spoke to them, saying, "Go up and spy out the country." So the men went up and spied out Ai. 3 And they returned to Joshua and said to him, "Do not let all the people go up, but let about two or three thousand men go up and attack Ai. Do not weary all the people there, for *the people of Ai are* few." 4 So about three thousand men went up there from the people, but they fled before the men of Ai. 5 And the men of Ai struck down about thirty-six men, for they chased them *from* before the gate as far as Shebarim, and struck them down on the descent; therefore the hearts of the people melted and became like water.

6 Then Joshua tore his clothes, and fell to the earth on his face before the ark of the LORD until evening, he and the elders of Israel; and they put dust on their heads. 7 And Joshua said, "Alas, Lord GOD, why have You brought this people over the Jordan at all—to deliver us into the hand of the Amorites, to destroy us? Oh, that we had been content, and dwelt on

7:1 aCalled *Zimri* in 1 Chronicles 2:6

the other side of the Jordan! 8 O Lord, what shall I say when Israel turns its back before its enemies? 9 For the Canaanites and all the inhabitants of the land will hear *it*, and surround us, and cut off our name from the earth. Then what will You do for Your great name?"

10 So the LORD said to Joshua: "Get up! Why do you lie thus on your face? 11 Israel has sinned, and they have also transgressed My covenant which I commanded them. For they have even taken some of the accursed things, and have both stolen and deceived; and they have also put *it* among their own stuff. 12 Therefore the children of Israel could not stand before their enemies, *but* turned *their* backs before their enemies, because they have become doomed to destruction. Neither will I be with you anymore, unless you destroy the accursed from among you. 13 Get up, sanctify the people, and say, 'Sanctify yourselves for tomorrow, because thus says the LORD God of Israel: "*There is* an accursed thing in your midst, O Israel; you cannot stand before your enemies until you take away the accursed thing from among you." 14 In the morning therefore you shall be brought according to your tribes. And it shall be *that* the tribe which the LORD takes shall come according to families; and the family which the LORD takes shall come by households; and the household which the LORD takes shall come man by man. 15 Then it shall be *that* he who is taken with the accursed thing shall be burned with fire, he and all that he has, because he has transgressed the covenant of the LORD, and because he has done a disgraceful thing in Israel.'"

16 So Joshua rose early in the morning and brought Israel by their tribes, and the tribe of Judah was taken. 17 He brought the clan of Judah, and he took the family of the Zarhites; and he brought the family of the Zarhites man by man, and Zabdi was taken. 18 Then he brought his household man by man, and Achan the son of Carmi, the son of Zabdi, the son of Zerah, of the tribe of Judah, was taken.

19 Now Joshua said to Achan, "My son, I beg you, give glory to the LORD God of Israel, and make confession to Him, and tell me now what you have done; do not hide *it* from me."

20 And Achan answered Joshua and said, "Indeed I have sinned against the LORD God of Israel, and this is what I have done: 21 When I saw among the spoils a beautiful Babylonian garment, two hundred shekels of silver, and a wedge of gold weighing fifty shekels, I coveted them and took them. And there they are, hidden in the earth in the midst of my tent, with the silver under it."

22 So Joshua sent messengers, and they ran to the tent; and there it was, hidden in his tent, with the silver under it. 23 And they took them from the midst of the tent, brought them to Joshua and to all the children of Israel, and laid them out before the LORD. 24 Then Joshua, and all Israel with him, took Achan the son of Zerah, the silver, the garment, the wedge of gold, his sons, his daughters, his oxen, his donkeys, his sheep, his tent, and all that he had, and they brought them to the Valley of Achor. 25 And Joshua said, "Why have you troubled us? The LORD will trouble you this day." So all Israel stoned him with stones; and they burned them with fire after they had stoned them with stones.

26 Then they raised over him a great heap of stones, still there to this day. So the LORD turned from the fierceness of His anger. Therefore the name of that place has been called the Valley of Achor[a] to this day.

8 Now the LORD said to Joshua: "Do not be afraid, nor be dismayed; take all the people of war with you, and arise, go up to Ai. See, I have given into your hand the king of Ai, his people, his city, and his land. 2 And you shall do to Ai and its king as you did to Jericho and its king. Only its spoil and its cattle you shall take as booty for yourselves. Lay an ambush for the city behind it."

3 So Joshua arose, and all the people of war, to go up against Ai; and Joshua chose thirty thousand mighty men of valor and sent them away by night. 4 And he commanded them, saying: "Behold, you shall lie in ambush against the city, behind the city.

7:26 aLiterally *Trouble*

Do not go very far from the city, but all of you be ready. 5 Then I and all the people who *are* with me will approach the city; and it will come about, when they come out against us as at the first, that we shall flee before them. 6 For they will come out after us till we have drawn them from the city, for they will say, 'They *are* fleeing before us as at the first.' Therefore we will flee before them. 7 Then you shall rise from the ambush and seize the city, for the LORD your God will deliver it into your hand. 8 And it will be, when you have taken the city, *that* you shall set the city on fire. According to the commandment of the LORD you shall do. See, I have commanded you."

9 Joshua therefore sent them out; and they went to lie in ambush, and stayed between Bethel and Ai, on the west side of Ai; but Joshua lodged that night among the people. 10 Then Joshua rose up early in the morning and mustered the people, and went up, he and the elders of Israel, before the people to Ai. 11 And all the people of war who *were* with him went up and drew near; and they came before the city and camped on the north side of Ai. Now a valley *lay* between them and Ai. 12 So he took about five thousand men and set them in ambush between Bethel and Ai, on the west side of the city. 13 And when they had set the people, all the army that *was* on the north of the city, and its rear guard on the west of the city, Joshua went that night into the midst of the valley.

14 Now it happened, when the king of Ai saw *it*, that the men of the city hurried and rose early and went out against Israel to battle, he and all his people, at an appointed place before the plain. But he did not know that *there was* an ambush against him behind the city. 15 And Joshua and all Israel made as if they were beaten before them, and fled by the way of the wilderness. 16 So all the people who *were* in Ai were called together to pursue them. And they pursued Joshua and were drawn away from the city. 17 There was not a man left in Ai or Bethel who did not go out after Israel. So they left the city open and pursued Israel.

18 Then the LORD said to Joshua, "Stretch out the spear that *is* in your hand toward Ai, for I will give it into your hand." And Joshua stretched out the spear that *was* in his hand toward the city. 19 So *those in* ambush arose quickly out of their place; they ran as soon as he had stretched out his hand, and they entered the city and took it, and hurried to set the city on fire. 20 And when the men of Ai looked behind them, they saw, and behold, the smoke of the city ascended to heaven. So they had no power to flee this way or that way, and the people who had fled to the wilderness turned back on the pursuers.

21 Now when Joshua and all Israel saw that the ambush had taken the city and that the smoke of the city ascended, they turned back and struck down the men of Ai. 22 Then the others came out of the city against them; so they were *caught* in the midst of Israel, some on this side and some on that side. And they struck them down, so that they let none of them remain or escape. 23 But the king of Ai they took alive, and brought him to Joshua.

24 And it came to pass when Israel had made an end of slaying all the inhabitants of Ai in the field, in the wilderness where they pursued them, and when they all had fallen by the edge of the sword until they were consumed, that all the Israelites returned to Ai and struck it with the edge of the sword. 25 So it was *that* all who fell that day, both men and women, *were* twelve thousand—all the people of Ai. 26 For Joshua did not draw back his hand, with which he stretched out the spear, until he had utterly destroyed all the inhabitants of Ai. 27 Only the livestock and the spoil of that city Israel took as booty for themselves, according to the word of the LORD which He had commanded Joshua. 28 So Joshua burned Ai and made it a heap forever, a desolation to this day. 29 And the king of Ai he hanged on a tree until evening. And as soon as the sun was down, Joshua commanded that they should take his corpse down from the tree, cast it at the entrance of the gate of the city, and raise over it a great heap of stones *that remains* to this day.

30 Now Joshua built an altar to the LORD God of Israel in Mount Ebal, 31 as Moses the servant of the LORD

had commanded the children of Israel, as it is written in the Book of the Law of Moses: "an altar of whole stones over which no man has wielded an iron *tool.*"*a* And they offered on it burnt offerings to the LORD, and sacrificed peace offerings. 32 And there, in the presence of the children of Israel, he wrote on the stones a copy of the law of Moses, which he had written. 33 Then all Israel, with their elders and officers and judges, stood on either side of the ark before the priests, the Levites, who bore the ark of the covenant of the LORD, the stranger as well as he who was born among them. Half of them *were* in front of Mount Gerizim and half of them in front of Mount Ebal, as Moses the servant of the LORD had commanded before, that they should bless the people of Israel. 34 And afterward he read all the words of the law, the blessings and the cursings, according to all that is written in the Book of the Law. 35 There was not a word of all that Moses had commanded which Joshua did not read before all the assembly of Israel, with the women, the little ones, and the strangers who were living among them.

9 And it came to pass when all the kings who *were* on this side of the Jordan, in the hills and in the lowland and in all the coasts of the Great Sea toward Lebanon—the Hittite, the Amorite, the Canaanite, the Perizzite, the Hivite, and the Jebusite— heard *about it,* 2 that they gathered together to fight with Joshua and Israel with one accord.

3 But when the inhabitants of Gibeon heard what Joshua had done to Jericho and Ai, 4 they worked craftily, and went and pretended to be ambassadors. And they took old sacks on their donkeys, old wineskins torn and mended, 5 old and patched sandals on their feet, and old garments on themselves; and all the bread of their provision was dry *and* moldy. 6 And they went to Joshua, to the camp at Gilgal, and said to him and to the men of Israel, "We have come from a far country; now therefore, make a covenant with us."

7 Then the men of Israel said to the Hivites, "Perhaps you dwell among us; so how can we make a covenant with you?"

8 But they said to Joshua, "We *are* your servants."

And Joshua said to them, "Who *are* you, and where do you come from?"

9 So they said to him: "From a very far country your servants have come, because of the name of the LORD your God; for we have heard of His fame, and all that He did in Egypt, 10 and all that He did to the two kings of the Amorites who *were* beyond the Jordan—to Sihon king of Heshbon, and Og king of Bashan, who was at Ashtaroth. 11 Therefore our elders and all the inhabitants of our country spoke to us, saying, 'Take provisions with you for the journey, and go to meet them, and say to them, "We *are* your servants; now therefore, make a covenant with us." ' 12 This bread of ours we took hot *for* our provision from our houses on the day we departed to come to you. But now look, it is dry and moldy. 13 And these wineskins which we filled *were* new, and see, they are torn; and these our garments and our sandals have become old because of the very long journey."

14 Then the men of Israel took some of their provisions; but they did not ask counsel of the LORD. 15 So Joshua made peace with them, and made a covenant with them to let them live; and the rulers of the congregation swore to them.

16 And it happened at the end of three days, after they had made a covenant with them, that they heard that they *were* their neighbors who dwelt near them. 17 Then the children of Israel journeyed and came to their cities on the third day. Now their cities *were* Gibeon, Chephirah, Beeroth, and Kirjath Jearim. 18 But the children of Israel did not attack them, because the rulers of the congregation had sworn to them by the LORD God of Israel. And all the congregation complained against the rulers.

19 Then all the rulers said to all the congregation, "We have sworn to them by the LORD God of Israel; now therefore, we may not touch them. 20 This we will do to them: We will let them live, lest wrath be upon us because of the oath which we swore to them." 21 And the rulers said to

them, "Let them live, but let them be woodcutters and water carriers for all the congregation, as the rulers had promised them."

22 Then Joshua called for them, and he spoke to them, saying, "Why have you deceived us, saying, 'We *are* very far from you,' when you dwell near us? 23 Now therefore, you *are* cursed, and none of you shall be freed from being slaves—woodcutters and water carriers for the house of my God."

24 So they answered Joshua and said, "Because your servants were clearly told that the LORD your God commanded His servant Moses to give you all the land, and to destroy all the inhabitants of the land from before you; therefore we were very much afraid for our lives because of you, and have done this thing. 25 And now, here we are, in your hands; do with us as it seems good and right to do to us." 26 So he did to them, and delivered them out of the hand of the children of Israel, so that they did not kill them. 27 And that day Joshua made them woodcutters and water carriers for the congregation and for the altar of the LORD, in the place which He would choose, even to this day.

10 Now it came to pass when Adoni-Zedek king of Jerusalem heard how Joshua had taken Ai and had utterly destroyed it—as he had done to Jericho and its king, so he had done to Ai and its king—and how the inhabitants of Gibeon had made peace with Israel and were among them, 2 that they feared greatly, because Gibeon *was* a great city, like one of the royal cities, and because it *was* greater than Ai, and all its men *were* mighty. 3 Therefore Adoni-Zedek king of Jerusalem sent to Hoham king of Hebron, Piram king of Jarmuth, Japhia king of Lachish, and Debir king of Eglon, saying, 4 "Come up to me and help me, that we may attack Gibeon, for it has made peace with Joshua and with the children of Israel." 5 Therefore the five kings of the Amorites, the king of Jerusalem, the king of Hebron, the king of Jarmuth, the king of Lachish, *and* the king of Eglon, gathered together and went up, they and all their armies, and

camped before Gibeon and made war against it.

6 And the men of Gibeon sent to Joshua at the camp at Gilgal, saying, "Do not forsake your servants; come up to us quickly, save us and help us, for all the kings of the Amorites who dwell in the mountains have gathered together against us."

7 So Joshua ascended from Gilgal, he and all the people of war with him, and all the mighty men of valor. 8 And the LORD said to Joshua, "Do not fear them, for I have delivered them into your hand; not a man of them shall stand before you." 9 Joshua therefore came upon them suddenly, having marched all night from Gilgal. 10 So the LORD routed them before Israel, killed them with a great slaughter at Gibeon, chased them along the road that goes to Beth Horon, and struck them down as far as Azekah and Makkedah. 11 And it happened, as they fled before Israel *and* were on the descent of Beth Horon, that the LORD cast down large hailstones from heaven on them as far as Azekah, and they died. *There were* more who died from the hailstones than the children of Israel killed with the sword.

12 Then Joshua spoke to the LORD in the day when the LORD delivered up the Amorites before the children of Israel, and he said in the sight of Israel:

"Sun, stand still over Gibeon;
And Moon, in the Valley of Aijalon."
13 So the sun stood still,
And the moon stopped,
Till the people had revenge
Upon their enemies.

Is this not written in the Book of Jasher? So the sun stood still in the midst of heaven, and did not hasten to go *down* for about a whole day. 14 And there has been no day like that, before it or after it, that the LORD heeded the voice of a man; for the LORD fought for Israel.

15 Then Joshua returned, and all Israel with him, to the camp at Gilgal.

16 But these five kings had fled and hidden themselves in a cave at Makkedah. 17 And it was told Joshua, saying, "The five kings have been found hidden in the cave at Makkedah."

A Peak to Peek Experience

When Joshua and the Israelites first conquered the land of Canaan, they literally had a "peak to peek" experience. Following the conquest of Jericho, Joshua and his army led a campaign against the cities located on the Judean ridge. Joshua's strategy was to gain a foothold on these mountain peaks from which the Israelites could carry out lightning-like guerrilla raids into the surrounding country to broaden their base.

Because the Israelite army "did not ask counsel of the LORD" (Josh. 9:14), they were tricked into an alliance with the local Gibeonites who pretended to be foreigners. When the Gibeonites were attacked by five armies from the south, Joshua kept his promise and came to their defense. Marching from 1,300 feet below sea level to 3,000 feet above sea level, Joshua's men journeyed twenty-six miles under cover of darkness. When the sun was rising in the eyes of the five southerly kings and their armies, Joshua commanded the sun to stand still while Israel attacked and quickly gained victory (see Josh. 10:12).

The battle was hard but quick. Upon reaching the peak of the ridge, Joshua heard that the five kings and their armies were hidden in caves in the valley below. He got a glimpse, a peek, of a greater victory. Joshua prayed for strength and God's aid to completely eliminate the enemy. God sent a hailstorm to assist the Israelites in their conquest. By nightfall they gained victory over the Canaanite kings.

Joshua's "peak to peek" experience was not unlike one you have probably had in your own life. A peak is a victory, a special accomplishment you have which enables you to get a "peek"—a look at an even greater possibility. Every success in your life does this for you. Success is never final. It is always transcended! Just when you think you have reached the peak of your efforts, the top of success, you discover another opportunity.

Look back at the peak experiences of your life. You will know God was there to help you. And as you peek into the view of new mountains to climb, you know He will be there again. Joshua had more to conquer, and so do you!

18 So Joshua said, "Roll large stones against the mouth of the cave, and set men by it to guard them. 19 And do not stay *there* yourselves, *but* pursue your enemies, and attack their rear *guard*. Do not allow them to enter their cities, for the LORD your God has delivered them into your hand." 20 Then it happened, while Joshua and the children of Israel made an end of slaying them with a very great slaughter, till they had finished, that those who escaped entered fortified cities, 21 And all the people returned to the camp, to Joshua at Makkedah, in peace.

No one moved his tongue against any of the children of Israel.

22 Then Joshua said, "Open the mouth of the cave, and bring out those five kings to me from the cave." 23 And they did so, and brought out those five kings to him from the cave: the king of Jerusalem, the king of Hebron, the king of Jarmuth, the king of Lachish, *and* the king of Eglon.

24 So it was, when they brought out those kings to Joshua, that Joshua called for all the men of Israel, and said to the captains of the men of war who went with him, "Come near, put your feet on the necks of these kings." And they drew near and put their feet on their necks. 25 Then Joshua said to them, "Do not be afraid, nor be dismayed; be strong and of good courage, for thus the LORD will do to all your enemies against whom you fight." 26 And afterward Joshua struck them and killed them, and hanged them on five trees; and they were hanging on the trees until evening. 27 So it was at the time of the going down of the sun *that* Joshua commanded, and they took them down from the trees, cast them into the cave where they had been hidden, and laid large stones against the cave's mouth, *which remain* until this very day.

28 On that day Joshua took Makkedah, and struck it and its king with the edge of the sword. He utterly destroyed them[a]—all the people who *were* in it. He let none remain. He also did to the king of Makkedah as he had done to the king of Jericho.

29 Then Joshua passed from Makkedah, and all Israel with him, to Libnah; and they fought against Libnah. 30 And the LORD also delivered it and its king into the hand of Israel; he struck it and all the people who *were* in it with the edge of the sword. He let none remain in it, but did to its king as he had done to the king of Jericho.

31 Then Joshua passed from Libnah, and all Israel with him, to Lachish; and they encamped against it and fought against it. 32 And the LORD delivered Lachish into the hand of Israel, who took it on the second day, and struck it and all the people who *were* in it with the edge of the sword, according to all that he had done to Libnah. 33 Then Horam king of Gezer came up to help Lachish; and Joshua struck him and his people, until he left him none remaining.

34 From Lachish Joshua passed to Eglon, and all Israel with him; and they encamped against it and fought against it. 35 They took it on that day and struck it with the edge of the sword; all the people who *were* in it he utterly destroyed that day, according to all that he had done to Lachish.

36 So Joshua went up from Eglon, and all Israel with him, to Hebron; and they fought against it. 37 And they took it and struck it with the edge of the sword—its king, all its cities, and all the people who *were* in it; he left none remaining, according to all that he had done to Eglon, but utterly destroyed it and all the people who *were* in it.

38 Then Joshua returned, and all Israel with him, to Debir; and they fought against it. 39 And he took it and its king and all its cities; they struck them with the edge of the sword and utterly destroyed all the people who *were* in it. He left none remaining; as he had done to Hebron, so he did to Debir and its king, as he had done also to Libnah and its king.

40 So Joshua conquered all the land: the mountain country and the South[a] and the lowland and the wilderness slopes, and all their kings; he left none remaining, but utterly destroyed all that breathed, as the LORD God of Israel had commanded.

10:28 [a]Following Masoretic Text and most authorities; many Hebrew manuscripts, some manuscripts of the Septuagint, and some manuscripts of the Targum read *it*.   10:40 [a]Hebrew *Negev,* and so throughout this book

41 And Joshua conquered them from Kadesh Barnea as far as Gaza, and all the country of Goshen, even as far as Gibeon. 42 All these kings and their land Joshua took at one time, because the LORD God of Israel fought for Israel. 43 Then Joshua returned, and all Israel with him, to the camp at Gilgal.

11 And it came to pass, when Jabin king of Hazor heard *these things*, that he sent to Jobab king of Madon, to the king of Shimron, to the king of Achshaph, 2 and to the kings who *were* from the north, in the mountains, in the plain south of Chinneroth, in the lowland, and in the heights of Dor on the west, 3 to the Canaanites in the east and in the west, the Amorite, the Hittite, the Perizzite, the Jebusite in the mountains, and the Hivite below Hermon in the land of Mizpah. 4 So they went out, they and all their armies with them, *as* many people *as* the sand that *is* on the seashore in multitude, with very many horses and chariots. 5 And when all these kings had met together, they came and camped together at the waters of Merom to fight against Israel.

6 But the LORD said to Joshua, "Do not be afraid because of them, for tomorrow about this time I will deliver all of them slain before Israel. You shall hamstring their horses and burn their chariots with fire." 7 So Joshua and all the people of war with him came against them suddenly by the waters of Merom, and they attacked them. 8 And the LORD delivered them into the hand of Israel, who defeated them and chased them to Greater Sidon, to the Brook Misrephoth,*ª* and to the Valley of Mizpah eastward; they attacked them until they left none of them remaining. 9 So Joshua did to them as the LORD had told him: he hamstrung their horses and burned their chariots with fire.

10 Joshua turned back at that time and took Hazor, and struck its king with the sword; for Hazor was formerly the head of all those kingdoms. 11 And they struck all the people who *were* in it with the edge of the sword, utterly destroying *them*. There was none left breathing. Then he burned Hazor with fire.

12 So all the cities of those kings, and all their kings, Joshua took and struck with the edge of the sword. He utterly destroyed them, as Moses the servant of the LORD had commanded. 13 But *as for* the cities that stood on their mounds,*ª* Israel burned none of them, except Hazor only, *which* Joshua burned. 14 And all the spoil of these cities and the livestock, the children of Israel took as booty for themselves; but they struck every man with the edge of the sword until they had destroyed them, and they left none breathing. 15 As the LORD had commanded Moses his servant, so Moses commanded Joshua, and so Joshua did. He left nothing undone of all that the LORD had commanded Moses.

16 Thus Joshua took all this land: the mountain country, all the South, all the land of Goshen, the lowland, and the Jordan plain*ª*—the mountains of Israel and its lowlands, 17 from Mount Halak and the ascent to Seir, even as far as Baal Gad in the Valley of Lebanon below Mount Hermon. He captured all their kings, and struck them down and killed them. 18 Joshua made war a long time with all those kings. 19 There was not a city that made peace with the children of Israel, except the Hivites, the inhabitants of Gibeon. All *the others* they took in battle. 20 For it was of the LORD to harden their hearts, that they should come against Israel in battle, that He might utterly destroy them, *and* that they might receive no mercy, but that He might destroy them, as the LORD had commanded Moses.

21 And at that time Joshua came and cut off the Anakim from the mountains: from Hebron, from Debir, from Anab, from all the mountains of Judah, and from all the mountains of Israel; Joshua utterly destroyed them with their cities. 22 None of the Anakim were left in the land of the children of Israel; they remained only in Gaza, in Gath, and in Ashdod.

23 So Joshua took the whole land, according to all that the LORD had said to Moses; and Joshua gave it as

---

11:8 *ª*Hebrew *Misrephoth Maim*   11:13 *ª*Hebrew *tel*, a heap of successive city ruins
11:16 *ª*Hebrew *arabah*

an inheritance to Israel according to their divisions by their tribes. Then the land rested from war.

12 These *are* the kings of the land whom the children of Israel defeated, and whose land they possessed on the other side of the Jordan toward the rising of the sun, from the River Arnon to Mount Hermon, and all the eastern Jordan plain: 2 *One king was* Sihon king of the Amorites, who dwelt in Heshbon *and* ruled half of Gilead, from Aroer, which is on the bank of the River Arnon, from the middle of that river, even as far as the River Jabbok, *which is* the border of the Ammonites, 3 and the eastern Jordan plain from the Sea of Chinneroth as far as the Sea of the Arabah (the Salt Sea), the road to Beth Jeshimoth, and southward below the slopes of Pisgah. 4 *The other king was* Og king of Bashan and his territory, *who was* of the remnant of the giants, who dwelt at Ashtaroth and at Edrei, 5 and reigned over Mount Hermon, over Salcah, over all Bashan, as far as the border of the Geshurites and the Maachathites, and over half of Gilead *to* the border of Sihon king of Heshbon.

6 These Moses the servant of the LORD and the children of Israel had conquered; and Moses the servant of the LORD had given it *as* a possession to the Reubenites, the Gadites, and half the tribe of Manasseh.

7 And these *are* the kings of the country which Joshua and the children of Israel conquered on this side of the Jordan, on the west, from Baal Gad in the Valley of Lebanon as far as Mount Halak and the ascent to Seir, which Joshua gave to the tribes of Israel *as* a possession according to their divisions, 8 in the mountain country, in the lowlands, in the *Jordan* plain, in the slopes, in the wilderness, and in the South—the Hittites, the Amorites, the Canaanites, the Perizzites, the Hivites, and the Jebusites: 9 the king of Jericho, one; the king of Ai, which *is* beside Bethel, one; 10 the king of Jerusalem, one; the king of Hebron, one; 11 the king of Jarmuth, one; the king of Lachish, one; 12 the king of Eglon, one; the king of Gezer, one; 13 the king of De-

bir, one; the king of Geder, one; 14 the king of Hormah, one; the king of Arad, one; 15 the king of Libnah, one; the king of Adullam, one; 16 the king of Makkedah, one; the king of Bethel, one; 17 the king of Tappuah, one; the king of Hepher, one; 18 the king of Aphek, one; the king of Lasharon, one; 19 the king of Madon, one; the king of Hazor, one; 20 the king of Shimron Meron, one; the king of Achshaph, one; 21 the king of Taanach, one; the king of Megiddo, one; 22 the king of Kedesh, one; the king of Jokneam in Carmel, one; 23 the king of Dor in the heights of Dor, one; the king of the people of Gilgal, one; 24 the king of Tirzah, one—all the kings, thirty-one.

13 Now Joshua was old, advanced in years. And the LORD said to him: "You are old, advanced in years, and there remains very much land yet to be possessed. 2 This is the land that yet remains: all the territory of the Philistines and all *that* of the Geshurites, 3 from Sihor, which *is* east of Egypt, as far as the border of Ekron northward (*which* is counted as Canaanite); the five lords of the Philistines—the Gazites, the Ashdodites, the Ashkelonites, the Gittites, and the Ekronites; also the Avites; 4 from the south, all the land of the Canaanites, and Mearah that belongs to the Sidonians as far as Aphek, to the border of the Amorites; 5 the land of the Gebalites,*a* and all Lebanon, toward the sunrise, from Baal Gad below Mount Hermon as far as the entrance to Hamath; 6 all the inhabitants of the mountains from Lebanon as far as the Brook Misrephoth,*a* *and* all the Sidonians— them I will drive out from before the children of Israel; only divide it by lot to Israel as an inheritance, as I have commanded you. 7 Now therefore, divide this land as an inheritance to the nine tribes and half the tribe of Manasseh."

8 With the other half tribe the Reubenites and the Gadites received their inheritance, which Moses had given them, beyond the Jordan eastward, as Moses the servant of the LORD had given them: 9 from Aroer which *is* on the bank of the River Arnon, and the town that *is* in the midst

13:5 *a* Or *Giblites*   13:6 *a* Hebrew *Misrephoth Maim*

of the ravine, and all the plain of Medeba as far as Dibon; 10 all the cities of Sihon king of the Amorites, who reigned in Heshbon, as far as the border of the children of Ammon; 11 Gilead, and the border of the Geshurites and Maachathites, all Mount Hermon, and all Bashan as far as Salcah; 12 all the kingdom of Og in Bashan, who reigned in Ashtaroth and Edrei, who remained of the remnant of the giants; for Moses had defeated and cast out these.

13 Nevertheless the children of Israel did not drive out the Geshurites or the Maachathites, but the Geshurites and the Maachathites dwell among the Israelites until this day.

14 Only to the tribe of Levi he had given no inheritance; the sacrifices of the LORD God of Israel made by fire *are* their inheritance, as He said to them.

15 And Moses had given to the tribe of the children of Reuben *an inheritance* according to their families. 16 Their territory was from Aroer, which *is* on the bank of the River Arnon, and the city that *is* in the midst of the ravine, and all the plain by Medeba; 17 Heshbon and all its cities that *are* in the plain: Dibon, Bamoth Baal, Beth Baal Meon, 18 Jahaza, Kedemoth, Mephaath, 19 Kirjathaim, Sibmah, Zereth Shahar on the mountain of the valley, 20 Beth Peor, the slopes of Pisgah, and Beth Jeshimoth— 21 all the cities of the plain and all the kingdom of Sihon king of the Amorites, who reigned in Heshbon, whom Moses had struck with the princes of Midian: Evi, Rekem, Zur, Hur, and Reba, who *were* princes of Sihon dwelling in the country. 22 The children of Israel also killed with the sword Balaam the son of Beor, the soothsayer, among those who were killed by them. 23 And the border of the children of Reuben was the bank of the Jordan. This *was* the inheritance of the children of Reuben according to their families, the cities and their villages.

24 Moses also had given *an inheritance* to the tribe of Gad, to the children of Gad according to their families. 25 Their territory was Jazer, and all the cities of Gilead, and half the land of the Ammonites as far as Aroer, which *is* before Rabbah, 26 and from Heshbon to Ramath Mizpah and Betonim, and from Ma-

hanaim to the border of Debir, 27 and in the valley Beth Haram, Beth Nimrah, Succoth, and Zaphon, the rest of the kingdom of Sihon king of Heshbon, with the Jordan as *its* border, as far as the edge of the Sea of Chinnereth, on the other side of the Jordan eastward. 28 This *is* the inheritance of the children of Gad according to their families, the cities and their villages.

29 Moses also had given *an inheritance* to half the tribe of Manasseh; it was for half the tribe of the children of Manasseh according to their families: 30 Their territory was from Mahanaim, all Bashan, all the kingdom of Og king of Bashan, and all the towns of Jair which are in Bashan, sixty cities; 31 half of Gilead, and Ashtaroth and Edrei, cities of the kingdom of Og in Bashan, *were* for the children of Machir the son of Manasseh, for half of the children of Machir according to their families.

32 These *are the areas* which Moses had distributed as an inheritance in the plains of Moab on the other side of the Jordan, by Jericho eastward. 33 But to the tribe of Levi Moses had given no inheritance; the LORD God of Israel *was* their inheritance, as He had said to them.

14 These *are the areas* which the children of Israel inherited in the land of Canaan, which Eleazar the priest, Joshua the son of Nun, and the heads of the fathers of the tribes of the children of Israel distributed as an inheritance to them. 2 Their inheritance *was* by lot, as the LORD had commanded by the hand of Moses, for the nine tribes and the half-tribe. 3 For Moses had given the inheritance of the two tribes and the half-tribe on the other side of the Jordan; but to the Levites he had given no inheritance among them. 4 For the children of Joseph were two tribes: Manasseh and Ephraim. And they gave no part to the Levites in the land, except cities to dwell *in,* with their common-lands for their livestock and their property. 5 As the LORD had commanded Moses, so the children of Israel did; and they divided the land.

6 Then the children of Judah came to Joshua in Gilgal. And Caleb the son of Jephunneh the Kenizzite said to him: "You know the word which

the Lord said to Moses the man of God concerning you and me in Kadesh Barnea. 7 I was forty years old when Moses the servant of the Lord sent me from Kadesh Barnea to spy out the land, and I brought back word to him as it was in my heart. 8 Nevertheless my brethren who went up with me made the heart of the people melt, but I wholly followed the Lord my God. 9 So Moses swore on that day, saying, 'Surely the land where your foot has trodden shall be your inheritance and your children's forever, because you have wholly followed the Lord my God.' 10 And now, behold, the Lord has kept me alive, as He said, these forty-five years, ever since the Lord spoke this word to Moses while Israel wandered in the wilderness; and now, here I am this day, eighty-five years old. 11 As yet I am as strong this day as on the day that Moses sent me; just as my strength was then, so now is my strength for war, both for going out and for coming in. 12 Now therefore, give me this mountain of which the Lord spoke in that day; for you heard in that day how the Anakim were there, and that the cities were great and fortified. It may be that the Lord will be with me, and I shall be able to drive them out as the Lord said."

13 And Joshua blessed him, and gave Hebron to Caleb the son of Jephunneh as an inheritance. 14 Hebron therefore became the inheritance of Caleb the son of Jephunneh the Kenizzite to this day, because he wholly followed the Lord God of Israel. 15 And the name of Hebron formerly was Kirjath Arba (Arba was the greatest man among the Anakim).

Then the land had rest from war.

15 So this was the lot of the tribe of the children of Judah according to their families:

The border of Edom at the Wilderness of Zin southward was the extreme southern boundary. 2 And their southern border began at the shore of the Salt Sea, from the bay that faces southward. 3 Then it went out to the southern side of the Ascent of Akrabbim, passed along to Zin, ascended on the south side of Kadesh Barnea, passed along to Hezron, went up to Adar, and went around to Karkaa. 4 From there it passed toward Azmon and went out to the Brook of Egypt; and the border ended at the sea. This shall be your southern border.

5 The east border was the Salt Sea as far as the mouth of the Jordan.

And the border on the northern quarter began at the bay of the sea at the mouth of the Jordan. 6 The border went up to Beth Hoglah and passed north of Beth Arabah; and the border went up to the stone of Bohan the son of Reuben. 7 Then the border went up toward Debir from the Valley of Achor, and it turned northward toward Gilgal, which is before the Ascent of Adummim, which is on the south side of the valley. The border continued toward the waters of En Shemesh and ended at En Rogel. 8 And the border went up by the Valley of the Son of Hinnom to the southern slope of the Jebusite city (which is Jerusalem). The border went up to the top of the mountain that lies before the Valley of Hinnom westward, which is at the end of the Valley of Rephaim[a] northward. 9 Then the border went around from the top of the hill to the fountain of the water of Nephtoah, and extended to the cities of Mount Ephron. And the border went around to Baalah (which is Kirjath Jearim). 10 Then the border turned westward from Baalah to Mount Seir, passed along to the side of Mount Jearim on the north (which is Chesalon), went down to Beth Shemesh, and passed on to Timnah. 11 And the border went out to the side of Ekron northward. Then the border went around to Shicron, passed along to Mount Baalah, and extended to Jabneel; and the border ended at the sea.

12 The west border was the coastline of the Great Sea. This is the boundary of the children of Judah all around according to their families.

13 Now to Caleb the son of Jephunneh he gave a share among the children of Judah, according to the commandment of the Lord to Joshua, namely, Kirjath Arba, which is Hebron (Arba was the father of Anak). 14 Caleb drove out the three sons of Anak from there: Sheshai, Ahiman,

and Talmai, the children of Anak. 15 Then he went up from there to the inhabitants of Debir (formerly the name of Debir *was* Kirjath Sepher).

16 And Caleb said, "He who attacks Kirjath Sepher and takes it, to him I will give Achsah my daughter as wife." 17 So Othniel the son of Kenaz, the brother of Caleb, took it; and he gave him Achsah his daughter as wife. 18 Now it was so, when she came *to him,* that she persuaded him to ask her father for a field. So she dismounted from *her* donkey, and Caleb said to her, "What do you wish?" 19 She answered, "Give me a blessing; since you have given me land in the South, give me also springs of water." So he gave her the upper springs and the lower springs.

20 This *was* the inheritance of the tribe of the children of Judah according to their families:

21 The cities at the limits of the tribe of the children of Judah, toward the border of Edom in the South, were Kabzeel, Eder, Jagur, 22 Kinah, Dimonah, Adadah, 23 Kedesh, Hazor, Ithnan, 24 Ziph, Telem, Bealoth, 25 Hazor, Hadattah, Kerioth, Hezron (which *is* Hazor), 26 Amam, Shema, Moladah, 27 Hazar Gaddah, Heshmon, Beth Pelet, 28 Hazar Shual, Beersheba, Bizjothjah, 29 Baalah, Ijim, Ezem, 30 Eltolad, Chesil, Hormah, 31 Ziklag, Madmannah, Sansannah, 32 Lebaoth, Shilhim, Ain, and Rimmon: all the cities *are* twenty-nine, with their villages.

33 In the lowland: Eshtaol, Zorah, Ashnah, 34 Zanoah, En Gannim, Tappuah, Enam, 35 Jarmuth, Adullam, Socoh, Azekah, 36 Sharaim, Adithaim, Gederah, and Gederothaim: fourteen cities with their villages; 37 Zenan, Hadashah, Migdal Gad, 38 Dilean, Mizpah, Joktheel, 39 Lachish, Bozkath, Eglon, 40 Cabbon, Lahmas,*a* Kithlish, 41 Gederoth, Beth Dagon, Naamah, and Makkedah: sixteen cities with their villages; 42 Libnah, Ether, Ashan, 43 Jiphtah, Ashnah, Nezib, 44 Keilah, Achzib, and Mareshah: nine cities with their villages; 45 Ekron, with its towns and villages; 46 from Ekron to the sea, all that *lay* near Ashdod, with their villages; 47 Ashdod with its towns and villages, Gaza with its towns and villages—as far as the Brook of Egypt and the Great Sea with *its* coastline.

48 And in the mountain country: Shamir, Jattir, Sochoh, 49 Dannah, Kirjath Sannah (which *is* Debir), 50 Anab, Eshtemoh, Anim, 51 Goshen, Holon, and Giloh: eleven cities with their villages; 52 Arab, Dumah, Eshean, 53 Janum, Beth Tappuah, Aphekah, 54 Humtah, Kirjath Arba (which *is* Hebron), and Zior: nine cities with their villages; 55 Maon, Carmel, Ziph, Juttah, 56 Jezreel, Jokdeam, Zanoah, 57 Kain, Gibeah, and Timnah: ten cities with their villages; 58 Halhul, Beth Zur, Gedor, 59 Maarath, Beth Anoth, and Eltekon: six cities with their villages; 60 Kirjath Baal (which *is* Kirjath Jearim) and Rabbah: two cities with their villages.

61 In the wilderness: Beth Arabah, Middin, Secacah, 62 Nibshan, the City of Salt, and En Gedi: six cities with their villages.

63 As for the Jebusites, the inhabitants of Jerusalem, the children of Judah could not drive them out; but the Jebusites dwell with the children of Judah at Jerusalem to this day.

16 The lot fell to the children of Joseph from the Jordan, by Jericho, to the waters of Jericho on the east, to the wilderness that goes up from Jericho through the mountains to Bethel, 2 then went out from Bethel to Luz,*a* passed along to the border of the Archites at Ataroth, 3 and went down westward to the boundary of the Japhletites, as far as the boundary of Lower Beth Horon to Gezer; and it ended at the sea.

4 So the children of Joseph, Manasseh and Ephraim, took their inheritance.

5 The border of the children of Ephraim, according to their families, was *thus:* The border of their inheritance on the east side was Ataroth Addar as far as Upper Beth Horon.

6 And the border went out toward the sea on the north side of Michmethath; then the border went around eastward to Taanath Shiloh, and passed by it on the east of Janohah. 7 Then it went down from Janohah to Ataroth and Naarah,*a* reached

Settlement of the Tribes

After the conquest of the Promised Land under Joshua, the land formerly occupied by the Canaanites was assigned to the descendants of the sons of Jacob (Josh. 13—21). In a restricted sense, the land stretched from the Jordan River on the east to the Great Sea (Mediterranean) on the west. Reuben, Gad, and Manasseh eventually inhabited land east of the Jordan. From north to south, it covered the territory between the Sinai peninsula and the ancient coastal nation of Phoenicia. Land was allotted to the descendants of all Jacob's sons except Levi (Josh. 13:33). Levi's portion went to the two sons of Joseph—Manasseh and Ephraim (Josh. 14:3, 4). The Levites were set apart for priestly service: their portion was to be God Himself (Num. 18:20). However God provided 48 cities throughout Palestine for use of the Levites (Josh. 21:1–42). This map shows the approximate locations of the tribal settlements, based on the boundaries mentioned in the Book of Joshua.

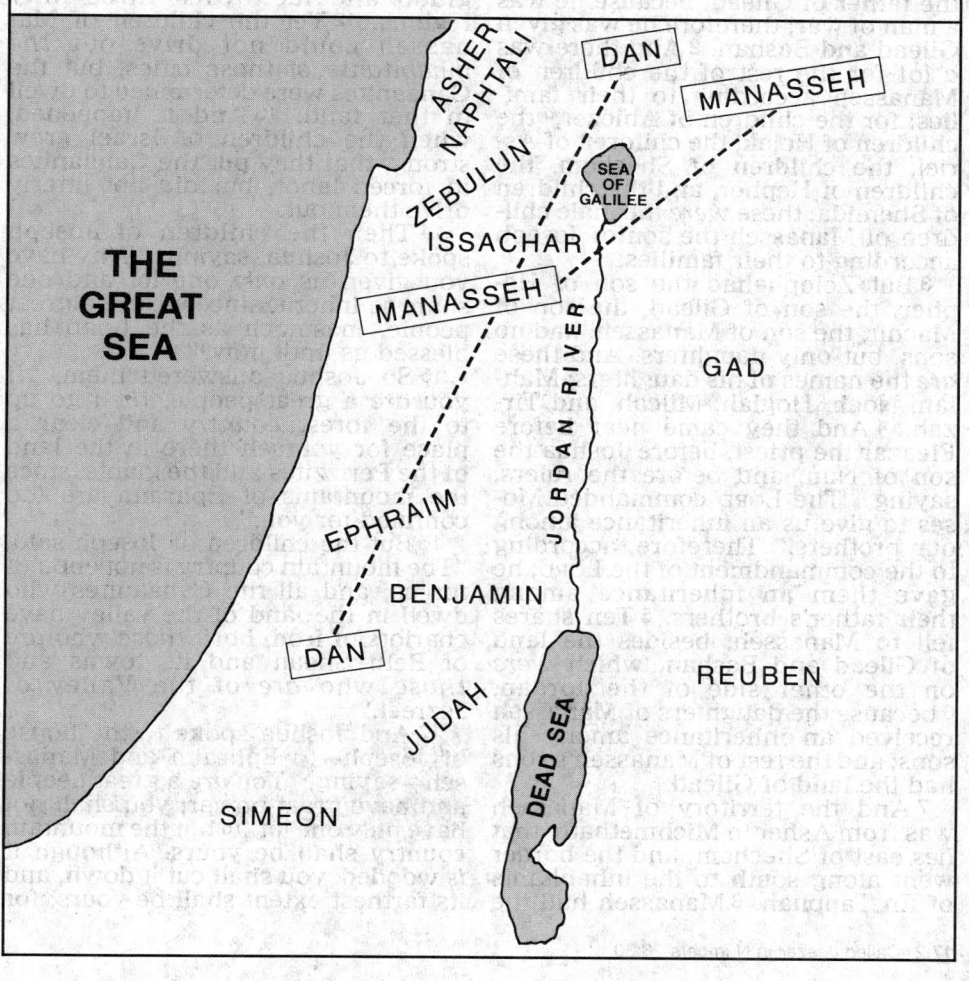

to Jericho, and came out at the Jordan.

8 The border went out from Tappuah westward to the Brook Kanah, and it ended at the sea. This *was* the inheritance of the tribe of the children of Ephraim according to their families. 9 The separate cities for the children of Ephraim *were* among the inheritance of the children of Manasseh, all the cities with their villages.

10 And they did not drive out the Canaanites who dwelt in Gezer; but the Canaanites dwell among the Ephraimites to this day and have become forced laborers.

17 There was also a lot for the tribe of Manasseh, for he *was* the firstborn of Joseph: *namely* for Machir the firstborn of Manasseh, the father of Gilead, because he was a man of war; therefore he was given Gilead and Bashan. 2 And there was *a lot* for the rest of the children of Manasseh according to their families: for the children of Abiezer,[a] the children of Helek, the children of Asriel, the children of Shechem, the children of Hepher, and the children of Shemida; these *were* the male children of Manasseh the son of Joseph according to their families.

3 But Zelophehad the son of Hepher, the son of Gilead, the son of Machir, the son of Manasseh, had no sons, but only daughters. And these *are* the names of his daughters: Mahlah, Noah, Hoglah, Milcah, and Tirzah. 4 And they came near before Eleazar the priest, before Joshua the son of Nun, and before the rulers, saying, "The LORD commanded Moses to give us an inheritance among our brothers." Therefore, according to the commandment of the LORD, he gave them an inheritance among their father's brothers. 5 Ten shares fell to Manasseh, besides the land of Gilead and Bashan, which *were* on the other side of the Jordan, 6 because the daughters of Manasseh received an inheritance among his sons; and the rest of Manasseh's sons had the land of Gilead.

7 And the territory of Manasseh was from Asher to Michmethath, that *lies* east of Shechem; and the border went along south to the inhabitants of En Tappuah. 8 Manasseh had the land of Tappuah, but Tappuah on the border of Manasseh *belonged* to the children of Ephraim. 9 And the border descended to the Brook Kanah, southward to the brook. These cities of Ephraim *are* among the cities of Manasseh. The border of Manasseh *was* on the north side of the brook; and it ended at the sea.

10 Southward *it was* Ephraim's, northward *it was* Manasseh's, and the sea was its border. Manasseh's territory was adjoining Asher on the north and Issachar on the east. 11 And in Issachar and in Asher, Manasseh had Beth Shean and its towns, Ibleam and its towns, the inhabitants of Dor and its towns, the inhabitants of En Dor and its towns, the inhabitants of Taanach and its towns, and the inhabitants of Megiddo and its towns—three hilly regions. 12 Yet the children of Manasseh could not drive out *the inhabitants of* those cities, but the Canaanites were determined to dwell in that land. 13 And it happened, when the children of Israel grew strong, that they put the Canaanites to forced labor, but did not utterly drive them out.

14 Then the children of Joseph spoke to Joshua, saying, "Why have you given us *only* one lot and one share to inherit, since we *are* a great people, inasmuch as the LORD has blessed us until now?"

15 So Joshua answered them, "If you *are* a great people, *then* go up to the forest *country* and clear a place for yourself there in the land of the Perizzites and the giants, since the mountains of Ephraim are too confined for you."

16 But the children of Joseph said, "The mountain country is not enough for us; and all the Canaanites who dwell in the land of the valley have chariots of iron, *both those* who *are* of Beth Shean and its towns and *those* who *are* of the Valley of Jezreel."

17 And Joshua spoke to the house of Joseph—to Ephraim and Manasseh—saying, "You *are* a great people and have great power; you shall not have *only* one lot, 18 but the mountain country shall be yours. Although it *is* wooded, you shall cut it down, and its farthest extent shall be yours; for

17:2 aCalled *Jeezer* in Numbers 26:30

you shall drive out the Canaanites, though they have iron chariots *and* are strong."

18 Now the whole congregation of the children of Israel assembled together at Shiloh, and set up the tabernacle of meeting there. And the land was subdued before them. 2 But there remained among the children of Israel seven tribes which had not yet received their inheritance.

3 Then Joshua said to the children of Israel: "How long will you neglect to go and possess the land which the LORD God of your fathers has given you? 4 Pick out from among you three men for *each* tribe, and I will send them; they shall rise and go through the land, survey it according to their inheritance, and come *back* to me. 5 And they shall divide it into seven parts. Judah shall remain in their territory on the south, and the house of Joseph shall remain in their territory on the north. 6 You shall therefore survey the land in seven parts and bring *the survey* here to me, that I may cast lots for you here before the LORD our God. 7 But the Levites have no part among you, for the priesthood of the LORD *is* their inheritance. And Gad, Reuben, and half the tribe of Manasseh have received their inheritance beyond the Jordan on the east, which Moses the servant of the LORD gave them."

8 Then the men arose to go away; and Joshua charged those who went to survey the land, saying, "Go, walk through the land, survey it, and come back to me, that I may cast lots for you here before the LORD in Shiloh." 9 So the men went, passed through the land, and wrote the survey in a book in seven parts by cities; and they came to Joshua at the camp in Shiloh. 10 Then Joshua cast lots for them in Shiloh before the LORD, and there Joshua divided the land to the children of Israel according to their divisions.

11 Now the lot of the tribe of the children of Benjamin came up according to their families, and the territory of their lot came out between the children of Judah and the children of Joseph. 12 Their border on the north side began at the Jordan, and the border went up to the side

of Jericho on the north, and went up through the mountains westward; it ended at the Wilderness of Beth Aven. 13 The border went over from there toward Luz, to the side of Luz (which *is* Bethel) southward; and the border descended to Ataroth Addar, near the hill that *lies* on the south side of Lower Beth Horon.

14 Then the border extended around the west side to the south, from the hill that *lies* before Beth Horon southward; and it ended at Kirjath Baal (which *is* Kirjath Jearim), a city of the children of Judah. This *was* the west side.

15 The south side *began* at the end of Kirjath Jearim, and the border extended on the west and went out to the spring of the waters of Nephtoah. 16 Then the border came down to the end of the mountain that *lies* before the Valley of the Son of Hinnom, which *is* in the Valley of the Rephaim[a] on the north, descended to the Valley of Hinnom, to the side of the Jebusite *city* on the south, and descended to En Rogel. 17 And it went around from the north, went out to En Shemesh, and extended toward Geliloth, which is before the Ascent of Adummim, and descended to the stone of Bohan the son of Reuben. 18 Then it passed along toward the north side of Arabah,[a] and went down to Arabah. 19 And the border passed along to the north side of Beth Hoglah; then the border ended at the north bay at the Salt Sea, at the south end of the Jordan. This *was* the southern boundary.

20 The Jordan was its border on the east side. This *was* the inheritance of the children of Benjamin, according to its boundaries all around, according to their families.

21 Now the cities of the tribe of the children of Benjamin, according to their families, were Jericho, Beth Hoglah, Emek Keziz, 22 Beth Arabah, Zemaraim, Bethel, 23 Avim, Parah, Ophrah, 24 Chephar Haammoni, Ophni, and Gaba: twelve cities with their villages; 25 Gibeon, Ramah, Beeroth, 26 Mizpah, Chephirah, Mozah, 27 Rekem, Irpeel, Taralah, 28 Zelah, Eleph, Jebus (which *is* Jerusalem), Gibeath, *and* Kirjath: fourteen cities with their villages. This was the inheritance of the children

18:16 [a]Literally *Giants*   18:18 [a]Or *Beth Arabah* (compare 15:6 and 18:22)

of Benjamin according to their families.

19 The second lot came out for Simeon, for the tribe of the children of Simeon according to their families. And their inheritance was within the inheritance of the children of Judah. 2 They had in their inheritance Beersheba (Sheba), Moladah, 3 Hazar Shual, Balah, Ezem, 4 Eltolad, Bethul, Hormah, 5 Ziklag, Beth Marcaboth, Hazar Susah, 6 Beth Lebaoth, and Sharuhen: thirteen cities and their villages; 7 Ain, Rimmon, Ether, and Ashan: four cities and their villages; 8 and all the villages that *were* all around these cities as far as Baalath Beer, Ramah of the South. This *was* the inheritance of the tribe of the children of Simeon according to their families.

9 The inheritance of the children of Simeon *was included* in the share of the children of Judah, for the share of the children of Judah was too much for them. Therefore the children of Simeon had *their* inheritance within the inheritance of that people.

10 The third lot came out for the children of Zebulun according to their families, and the border of their inheritance was as far as Sarid. 11 Their border went toward the west and to Maralah, went to Dabbasheth, and extended along the brook that is east of Jokneam. 12 Then from Sarid it went eastward toward the sunrise along the border of Chisloth Tabor, and went out toward Daberath, bypassing Japhia. 13 And from there it passed along on the east of Gath Hepher, toward Eth Kazin, and extended to Rimmon, which borders on Neah. 14 Then the border went around it on the north side of Hannathon, and it ended in the Valley of Jiphthah El. 15 Included were Kattath, Nahallal, Shimron, Idalah, and Bethlehem: twelve cities with their villages. 16 This *was* the inheritance of the children of Zebulun according to their families, these cities with their villages.

17 The fourth lot came out to Issachar, for the children of Issachar according to their families. 18 And their territory went to Jezreel, and *included* Chesulloth, Shunem, 19 Haphraim, Shion, Anaharath, 20 Rabbith, Kishion, Abez, 21 Remeth, En Gannim, En Haddah, and Beth Pazzez. 22 And the border reached to Tabor, Shahazimah, and Beth Shemesh; their border ended at the Jordan: sixteen cities with their villages. 23 This *was* the inheritance of the tribe of the children of Issachar according to their families, the cities and their villages.

24 The fifth lot came out for the tribe of the children of Asher according to their families. 25 And their territory included Helkath, Hali, Beten, Achshaph, 26 Alammelech, Amad, and Mishal; it reached to Mount Carmel westward, along *the Brook* Shihor Libnath. 27 It turned toward the sunrise to Beth Dagon; and it reached to Zebulun and to the Valley of Jiphthah El, then northward beyond Beth Emek and Neiel, bypassing Cabul *which was* on the left, 28 including Ebron,*ª* Rehob, Hammon, and Kanah, as far as Greater Sidon. 29 And the border turned to Ramah and to the fortified city of Tyre; then the border turned to Hosah, and ended at the sea by the region of Achzib. 30 Also Ummah, Aphek, and Rehob *were included*: twenty-two cities with their villages. 31 This *was* the inheritance of the tribe of the children of Asher according to their families, these cities with their villages.

32 The sixth lot came out to the children of Naphtali, for the children of Naphtali according to their families. 33 And their border began at Heleph, enclosing the territory from the terebinth tree in Zaanannim, Adami Nekeb, and Jabneel, as far as Lakkum; it ended at the Jordan. 34 From Heleph the border extended westward to Aznoth Tabor, and went out from there toward Hukkok; it adjoined Zebulun on the south side and Asher on the west side, and ended at Judah by the Jordan toward the sunrise. 35 And the fortified cities *are* Ziddim, Zer, Hammath, Rakkath, Chinnereth, 36 Adamah, Ramah, Hazor, 37 Kedesh, Edrei, En Hazor, 38 Iron, Migdal El, Horem, Beth Anath, and Beth Shemesh: nineteen cities with their villages. 39 This *was*

19:28 ªFollowing Masoretic Text, Targum, and Vulgate; a few Hebrew manuscripts read *Abdon* (compare 21:30 and 1 Chronicles 6:74).

Cities of Refuge

Six cities of refuge were designated throughout Israel in Old Testament times to provide a haven for people who killed other persons by accident. Protection like this was necessary because of the "avenger of blood," the relative who considered it his duty to slay the killer. Eligibility for refuge was determined by a judge. For convenience, three of the cities were located on either side of the Jordon River.

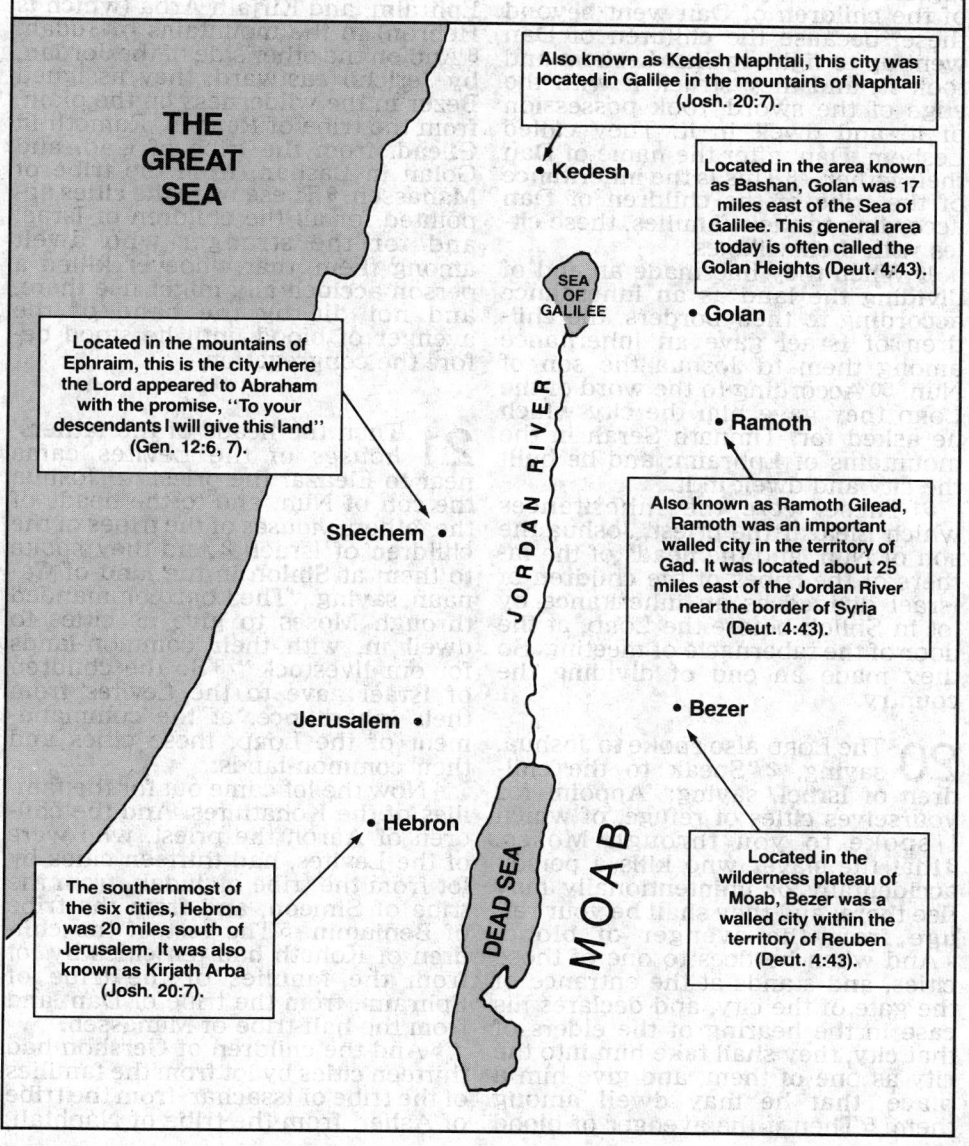

THE GREAT SEA

Also known as Kedesh Naphtali, this city was located in Galilee in the mountains of Naphtali (Josh. 20:7).

• Kedesh

Located in the area known as Bashan, Golan was 17 miles east of the Sea of Galilee. This general area today is often called the Golan Heights (Deut. 4:43).

SEA OF GALILEE

• Golan

Located in the mountains of Ephraim, this is the city where the Lord appeared to Abraham with the promise, "To your descendants I will give this land" (Gen. 12:6, 7).

JORDAN RIVER

• Ramoth

Shechem •

Also known as Ramoth Gilead, Ramoth was an important walled city in the territory of Gad. It was located about 25 miles east of the Jordan River near the border of Syria (Deut. 4:43).

• Bezer

Jerusalem •

• Hebron

DEAD SEA

MOAB

The southernmost of the six cities, Hebron was 20 miles south of Jerusalem. It was also known as Kirjath Arba (Josh. 20:7).

Located in the wilderness plateau of Moab, Bezer was a walled city within the territory of Reuben (Deut. 4:43).

the inheritance of the tribe of the children of Naphtali according to their families, the cities and their villages.

40 The seventh lot came out for the tribe of the children of Dan according to their families. 41 And the territory of their inheritance was Zorah, Eshtaol, Ir Shemesh, 42 Shaalabbin, Aijalon, Jethlah, 43 Elon, Timnah, Ekron, 44 Eltekeh, Gibbethon, Baalath, 45 Jehud, Bene Berak, Gath Rimmon, 46 Me Jarkon, and Rakkon, with the region near Joppa. 47 And the border of the children of Dan went beyond these, because the children of Dan went up to fight against Leshem and took it; and they struck it with the edge of the sword, took possession of it, and dwelt in it. They called Leshem, Dan, after the name of Dan their father. 48 This is the inheritance of the tribe of the children of Dan according to their families, these cities with their villages.

49 When they had made an end of dividing the land as an inheritance according to their borders, the children of Israel gave an inheritance among them to Joshua the son of Nun. 50 According to the word of the LORD they gave him the city which he asked for, Timnath Serah in the mountains of Ephraim; and he built the city and dwelt in it.

51 These were the inheritances which Eleazar the priest, Joshua the son of Nun, and the heads of the fathers of the tribes of the children of Israel divided as an inheritance by lot in Shiloh before the LORD, at the door of the tabernacle of meeting. So they made an end of dividing the country.

20 The LORD also spoke to Joshua, saying, 2 "Speak to the children of Israel, saying: 'Appoint for yourselves cities of refuge, of which I spoke to you through Moses, 3 that the slayer who kills a person accidentally or unintentionally may flee there; and they shall be your refuge from the avenger of blood. 4 And when he flees to one of those cities, and stands at the entrance of the gate of the city, and declares his case in the hearing of the elders of that city, they shall take him into the city as one of them, and give him a place, that he may dwell among them. 5 Then if the avenger of blood

pursues him, they shall not deliver the slayer into his hand, because he struck his neighbor unintentionally, but did not hate him beforehand. 6 And he shall dwell in that city until he stands before the congregation for judgment, and until the death of the one who is high priest in those days. Then the slayer may return and come to his own city and his own house, to the city from which he fled.' "

7 So they appointed Kedesh in Galilee, in the mountains of Naphtali, Shechem in the mountains of Ephraim, and Kirjath Arba (which is Hebron) in the mountains of Judah. 8 And on the other side of the Jordan, by Jericho eastward, they assigned Bezer in the wilderness on the plain, from the tribe of Reuben, Ramoth in Gilead, from the tribe of Gad, and Golan in Bashan, from the tribe of Manasseh. 9 These were the cities appointed for all the children of Israel and for the stranger who dwelt among them, that whoever killed a person accidentally might flee there, and not die by the hand of the avenger of blood until he stood before the congregation.

21 Then the heads of the fathers' houses of the Levites came near to Eleazar the priest, to Joshua the son of Nun, and to the heads of the fathers' houses of the tribes of the children of Israel. 2 And they spoke to them at Shiloh in the land of Canaan, saying, "The LORD commanded through Moses to give us cities to dwell in, with their common-lands for our livestock." 3 So the children of Israel gave to the Levites from their inheritance, at the commandment of the LORD, these cities and their common-lands:

4 Now the lot came out for the families of the Kohathites. And the children of Aaron the priest, who were of the Levites, had thirteen cities by lot from the tribe of Judah, from the tribe of Simeon, and from the tribe of Benjamin. 5 The rest of the children of Kohath had ten cities by lot from the families of the tribe of Ephraim, from the tribe of Dan, and from the half-tribe of Manasseh.

6 And the children of Gershon had thirteen cities by lot from the families of the tribe of Issachar, from the tribe of Asher, from the tribe of Naphtali,

and from the half-tribe of Manasseh in Bashan.

7 The children of Merari according to their families had twelve cities from the tribe of Reuben, from the tribe of Gad, and from the tribe of Zebulun.

8 And the children of Israel gave these cities with their common-lands by lot to the Levites, as the LORD had commanded by the hand of Moses.

9 So they gave from the tribe of the children of Judah and from the tribe of the children of Simeon these cities which are designated by name, 10 which were for the children of Aaron, one of the families of the Kohathites, *who were* of the children of Levi; for the lot was theirs first. 11 And they gave them Kirjath Arba (*Arba was* the father of Anak), which *is* Hebron, in the mountains of Judah, with the common-land surrounding it. 12 But the fields of the city and its villages they gave to Caleb the son of Jephunneh as his possession.

13 Thus to the children of Aaron the priest they gave Hebron with its common-land (a city of refuge for the slayer), Libnah with its common-land, 14 Jattir with its common-land, Eshtemoa with its common-land, 15 Holon with its common-land, Debir with its common-land, 16 Ain with its common-land, Juttah with its common-land, and Beth Shemesh with its common-land: nine cities from those two tribes; 17 and from the tribe of Benjamin, Gibeon with its common-land, Geba with its common-land, 18 Anathoth with its common-land, and Almon with its common-land: four cities. 19 All the cities of the children of Aaron, the priests, *were* thirteen cities with their common-lands.

20 And the families of the children of Kohath, the Levites, the rest of the children of Kohath, even they had the cities of their lot from the tribe of Ephraim. 21 For they gave them Shechem with its common-land in the mountains of Ephraim (a city of refuge for the slayer), Gezer with its common-land, 22 Kibzaim with its common-land, and Beth Horon with its common-land: four cities; 23 and from the tribe of Dan, Eltekeh with its common-land, Gibbethon

with its common-land, 24 Aijalon with its common-land, *and* Gath Rimmon with its common-land: four cities; 25 and from the half-tribe of Manasseh, Tanach with its common-land and Gath Rimmon with its common-land: two cities. 26 All the ten cities with their common-lands were for the rest of the families of the children of Kohath.

27 Also to the children of Gershon, of the families of the Levites, from the *other* half-tribe of Manasseh, *they gave* Golan in Bashan with its common-land (a city of refuge for the slayer), and Be Eshterah with its common-land: two cities; 28 and from the tribe of Issachar, Kishion with its common-land, Daberath with its common-land, 29 Jarmuth with its common-land, *and* En Gannim with its common-land: four cities; 30 and from the tribe of Asher, Mishal with its common-land, Abdon with its common-land, 31 Helkath with its common-land, and Rehob with its common-land: four cities; 32 and from the tribe of Naphtali, Kedesh in Galilee with its common-land (a city of refuge for the slayer), Hammoth Dor with its common-land, and Kartan with its common-land: three cities. 33 All the cities of the Gershonites according to their families *were* thirteen cities with their common-lands.

34 And to the families of the children of Merari, the rest of the Levites, from the tribe of Zebulun, Jokneam with its common-land, Kartah with its common-land, 35 Dimnah with its common-land, *and* Nahalal with its common-land: four cities; 36 and from the tribe of Reuben, Bezer with its common-land, Jahaz with its common-land, 37 Kedemoth with its common-land, and Mephaath with its common-land: four cities;[a] 38 and from the tribe of Gad, Ramoth in Gilead with its common-land (a city of refuge for the slayer), Mahanaim with its common-land, 39 Heshbon with its common-land, *and* Jazer with its common-land: four cities in all. 40 So all the cities for the children of Merari according to their families, the rest of the families of the Levites, were *by* their lot twelve cities.

41 All the cities of the Levites

21:37 [a]Following Septuagint and Vulgate (compare 1 Chronicles 6:78, 79); Masoretic Text, Bomberg, and Targum omit verses 36 and 37.

within the possession of the children of Israel *were* forty-eight cities with their common-lands. 42 Every one of these cities had its common-land surrounding it; thus *were* all these cities.

43 So the LORD gave to Israel all the land of which He had sworn to give to their fathers, and they took possession of it and dwelt in it. 44 The LORD gave them rest all around, according to all that He had sworn to their fathers. And not a man of all their enemies stood against them; the LORD delivered all their enemies into their hand. 45 Not a word failed of any good thing which the LORD had spoken to the house of Israel. All came to pass.

22 Then Joshua called the Reubenites, the Gadites, and half the tribe of Manasseh, 2 and said to them: "You have kept all that Moses the servant of the LORD commanded you, and have obeyed my voice in all that I commanded you. 3 You have not left your brethren these many days, up to this day, but have kept the charge of the commandment of the LORD your God. 4 And now the LORD your God has given rest to your brethren, as He promised them; now therefore, return and go to your tents *and* to the land of your possession, which Moses the servant of the LORD gave you on the other side of the Jordan. 5 But take careful heed to do the commandment and the law which Moses the servant of the LORD commanded you, to love the LORD your God, to walk in all His ways, to keep His commandments, to hold fast to Him, and to serve Him with all your heart and with all your soul." 6 So Joshua blessed them and sent them away, and they went to their tents.

7 Now to half the tribe of Manasseh Moses had given a possession in Bashan, but to the *other* half of it Joshua gave *a possession* among their brethren on this side of the Jordan, westward. And indeed, when Joshua sent them away to their tents, he blessed them, 8 and spoke to them, saying, "Return with much riches to your tents, with very much livestock, with silver, with gold, with bronze, with iron, and with very much cloth-ing. Divide the spoil of your enemies with your brethren."

9 So the children of Reuben, the children of Gad, and half the tribe of Manasseh returned, and departed from the children of Israel at Shiloh, which *is* in the land of Canaan, to go to the country of Gilead, to the land of their possession, which they had obtained according to the word of the LORD by the hand of Moses.

10 And when they came to the region of the Jordan which *is* in the land of Canaan, the children of Reuben, the children of Gad, and half the tribe of Manasseh built an altar there by the Jordan—a great, impressive altar. 11 Now the children of Israel heard *someone* say, "Behold, the children of Reuben, the children of Gad, and half the tribe of Manasseh have built an altar on the frontier of the land of Canaan, in the region of the Jordan—on the children of Israel's side." 12 And when the children of Israel heard *of it*, the whole congregation of the children of Israel gathered together at Shiloh to go to war against them.

13 Then the children of Israel sent Phinehas the son of Eleazar the priest to the children of Reuben, to the children of Gad, and to half the tribe of Manasseh, into the land of Gilead, 14 and with him ten rulers, one ruler each from the chief house of every tribe of Israel; and each one *was* the head of the house of his father among the divisions[a] of Israel. 15 Then they came to the children of Reuben, to the children of Gad, and to half the tribe of Manasseh, to the land of Gilead, and they spoke with them, saying, 16 "Thus says the whole congregation of the LORD: 'What treachery *is* this that you have committed against the God of Israel, to turn away this day from following the LORD, in that you have built for yourselves an altar, that you might rebel this day against the LORD? 17 *Is* the iniquity of Peor not enough for us, from which we are not cleansed till this day, although there was a plague in the congregation of the LORD, 18 but that you must turn away this day from following the LORD? And it shall be, if you rebel today against the LORD, that tomorrow He will be angry with the

22:14 aLiterally *thousands*

whole congregation of Israel. 19 Nevertheless, if the land of your possession *is* unclean, *then* cross over to the land of the possession of the LORD, where the LORD's tabernacle stands, and take possession among us; but do not rebel against the LORD, nor rebel against us, by building yourselves an altar besides the altar of the LORD our God. 20 Did not Achan the son of Zerah commit a trespass in the accursed thing, and wrath fell on all the congregation of Israel? And that man did not perish alone in his iniquity.' "

21 Then the children of Reuben, the children of Gad, and half the tribe of Manasseh answered and said to the heads of the divisions*a* of Israel: 22 "The LORD God of gods, the LORD God of gods, He knows, and let Israel itself know—if *it is* in rebellion, or if in treachery against the LORD, do not save us this day. 23 If we have built ourselves an altar to turn from following the LORD, or if to offer on it burnt offerings or grain offerings, or if to offer peace offerings on it, let the LORD Himself require *an account.* 24 But in fact we have done it for fear, for a reason, saying, 'In time to come your descendants may speak to our descendants, saying, "What have you to do with the LORD God of Israel? 25 For the LORD has made the Jordan a border between you and us, *you* children of Reuben and children of Gad. You have no part in the LORD." So your descendants would make our descendants cease fearing the LORD.' 26 Therefore we said, 'Let us now prepare to build ourselves an altar, not for burnt offering nor for sacrifice, 27 but *that it may be* a witness between you and us and our generations after us, that we may perform the service of the LORD before Him with our burnt offerings, with our sacrifices, and with our peace offerings; that your descendants may not say to our descendants in time to come, "You have no part in the LORD." ' 28 Therefore we said that it will be, when they say *this* to us or to our generations in time to come, that we may say, 'Here is the replica of the altar of the LORD which our fathers made, though not for burnt offerings nor for sacrifices; but

it *is* a witness between you and us.' 29 Far be it from us that we should rebel against the LORD, and turn from following the LORD this day, to build an altar for burnt offerings, for grain offerings, or for sacrifices, besides the altar of the LORD our God which *is* before His tabernacle."

30 Now when Phinehas the priest and the rulers of the congregation, the heads of the divisions*a* of Israel who *were* with him, heard the words that the children of Reuben, the children of Gad, and the children of Manasseh spoke, it pleased them. 31 Then Phinehas the son of Eleazar the priest said to the children of Reuben, the children of Gad, and the children of Manasseh, "This day we perceive that the LORD *is* among us, because you have not committed this treachery against the LORD. Now you have delivered the children of Israel out of the hand of the LORD."

32 And Phinehas the son of Eleazar the priest, and the rulers, returned from the children of Reuben and the children of Gad, from the land of Gilead to the land of Canaan, to the children of Israel, and brought back word to them. 33 So the thing pleased the children of Israel, and the children of Israel blessed God; they spoke no more of going against them in battle, to destroy the land where the children of Reuben and Gad dwelt.

34 The children of Reuben and the children of Gad*a* called the altar, *Witness,* "For *it is* a witness between us that the LORD *is* God."

23 Now it came to pass, a long time after the LORD had given rest to Israel from all their enemies round about, that Joshua was old, advanced in age. 2 And Joshua called for all Israel, for their elders, for their heads, for their judges, and for their officers, and said to them:

"I am old, advanced in age. 3 You have seen all that the LORD your God has done to all these nations because of you, for the LORD your God *is* He who has fought for you. 4 See, I have divided to you by lot these nations that remain, to be an inheritance for your tribes, from the Jordan, with all the nations that

---

22:21 *a*Literally *thousands*   22:30 *a*Literally *thousands*   22:34 *a*Septuagint adds *and half the tribe of Manasseh*

I have cut off, as far as the Great Sea westward. 5 And the LORD your God will expel them from before you and drive them out of your sight. So you shall possess their land, as the LORD your God promised you. 6 Therefore be very courageous to keep and to do all that is written in the Book of the Law of Moses, lest you turn aside from it to the right hand or to the left, 7 *and* lest you go among these nations, these who remain among you. You shall not make mention of the name of their gods, nor cause *anyone* to swear *by them;* you shall not serve them nor bow down to them, 8 but you shall hold fast to the LORD your God, as you have done to this day. 9 For the LORD has driven out from before you great and strong nations; but *as for* you, no one has been able to stand against you to this day. 10 One man of you shall chase a thousand, for the LORD your God *is* He who fights for you, as He promised you. 11 Therefore take careful heed to yourselves, that you love the LORD your God. 12 Or else, if indeed you do go back, and cling to the remnant of these nations—these that remain among you—and make marriages with them, and go in to them and they to you, 13 know for certain that the LORD your God will no longer drive out these nations from before you. But they shall be snares and traps to you, and scourges on your sides and thorns in your eyes, until you perish from this good land which the LORD your God has given you.

14 "Behold, this day I *am* going the way of all the earth. And you know in all your hearts and in all your souls that not one thing has failed of all the good things which the LORD your God spoke concerning you. All have come to pass for you; not one word of them has failed. 15 Therefore it shall come to pass, that as all the good things have come upon you which the LORD your God promised you, so the LORD will bring upon you all harmful things, until He has destroyed you from this good land which the LORD your God has given you. 16 When you have transgressed the covenant of the LORD your God, which He commanded you, and have gone and served other gods, and bowed down to them, then the anger of the LORD will burn against you, and you shall perish quickly from the good land which He has given you."

24 Then Joshua gathered all the tribes of Israel to Shechem and called for the elders of Israel, for their heads, for their judges, and for their officers; and they presented themselves before God. 2 And Joshua said to all the people, "Thus says the LORD God of Israel: 'Your fathers, *including* Terah, the father of Abraham and the father of Nahor, dwelt on the other side of the River[a] in old times; and they served other gods. 3 Then I took your father Abraham from the other side of the River, led him throughout all the land of Canaan, and multiplied his descendants and gave him Isaac. 4 To Isaac I gave Jacob and Esau. To Esau I gave the mountains of Seir to possess, but Jacob and his children went down to Egypt. 5 Also I sent Moses and Aaron, and I plagued Egypt, according to what I did among them. Afterward I brought you out.

6 'Then I brought your fathers out of Egypt, and you came to the sea; and the Egyptians pursued your fathers with chariots and horsemen to the Red Sea. 7 So they cried out to the LORD; and He put darkness between you and the Egyptians, brought the sea upon them, and covered them. And your eyes saw what I did in Egypt. Then you dwelt in the wilderness a long time. 8 And I brought you into the land of the Amorites, who dwelt on the other side of the Jordan, and they fought with you. But I gave them into your hand, that you might possess their land, and I destroyed them from before you. 9 Then Balak the son of Zippor, king of Moab, arose to make war against Israel, and sent and called Balaam the son of Beor to curse you. 10 But I would not listen to Balaam; therefore he continued to bless you. So I delivered you out of his hand. 11 Then you went over the Jordan and came to Jericho. And the men of Jericho fought against you—*also* the Amorites, the Perizzites, the Canaanites, the Hittites, the Girgashites, the Hivites, and the Jebusites. But I delivered them into your hand. 12 I sent the hornet before you which

24:2 [a]Hebrew *Nahar,* the Euphrates, and so in verses 3, 14, and 15 drove them out from before you, *also* the two kings of the Amorites, *but* not with your sword or with your bow. 13 I have given you a land for which you did not labor, and cities which you did not build, and you dwell in them; you eat of the vineyards and olive groves which you did not plant.'

14 "Now therefore, fear the LORD, serve Him in sincerity and in truth, and put away the gods which your fathers served on the other side of the River and in Egypt. Serve the LORD! 15 And if it seems evil to you to serve the LORD, choose for yourselves this day whom you will serve, whether the gods which your fathers served that *were* on the other side of the River, or the gods of the Amorites, in whose land you dwell. But as for me and my house, we will serve the LORD."

16 So the people answered and said: "Far be it from us that we should forsake the LORD to serve other gods; 17 for the LORD our God *is* He who brought us and our fathers up out of the land of Egypt, from the house of bondage, who did those great signs in our sight, and preserved us in all the way that we went and among all the people through whom we passed. 18 And the LORD drove out from before us all the people, including the Amorites who dwelt in the land. We also will serve the LORD, for He *is* our God."

19 But Joshua said to the people, "You cannot serve the LORD, for He *is* a holy God. He *is* a jealous God; He will not forgive your transgressions nor your sins. 20 If you forsake the LORD and serve foreign gods, then He will turn and do you harm and consume you, after He has done you good."

21 And the people said to Joshua, "No, but we will serve the LORD!"

22 So Joshua said to the people, "You *are* witnesses against yourselves that you have chosen the LORD for yourselves, to serve Him."

And they said, "*We are* witnesses!"

23 "Now therefore," *he said,* "put away the foreign gods which *are* among you, and incline your heart to the LORD God of Israel."

24 And the people said to Joshua, "The LORD our God we will serve, and His voice we will obey!"

25 So Joshua made a covenant with the people that day, and made for them a statute and an ordinance in Shechem.

26 Then Joshua wrote these words in the Book of the Law of God. And he took a large stone, and set it up there under the oak that *was* by the sanctuary of the LORD. 27 And Joshua said to all the people, "Behold, this stone shall be a witness to us, for it has heard all the words of the LORD which He spoke to us. It shall therefore be a witness to you, lest you deny your God." 28 So Joshua let the people depart, each to his own inheritance.

29 Now it came to pass after these things that Joshua the son of Nun, the servant of the LORD, died, *being* one hundred and ten years old. 30 And they buried him within the border of his inheritance at Timnath Serah, which *is* in the mountains of Ephraim, on the north side of Mount Gaash.

31 Israel served the LORD all the days of Joshua, and all the days of the elders who outlived Joshua, who had known all the works of the LORD which He had done for Israel.

32 The bones of Joseph, which the children of Israel had brought up out of Egypt, they buried at Shechem, in the plot of ground which Jacob had bought from the sons of Hamor the father of Shechem for one hundred pieces of silver, and which had become an inheritance of the children of Joseph.

33 And Eleazar the son of Aaron died. They buried him in a hill *belonging to* Phinehas his son, which was given to him in the mountains of Ephraim.

Judges

Overview of Judges

The Book of Judges shows God's faithfulness in raising up positive leaders for His people during times of adversity and trouble. The Israelites, faced with the negative influences of the Canaanite societies, often adopted their neighbors' sinful ways. God raised up judges to lead the people out of this ungodly situation.

Judges was written between 1043 and 1004 B.C., probably by Samuel. The book records seven distinct instances when the people of Israel turned from God and needed divine leadership through His appointed judges to bring them back to Him.

Judges tells the stories of some of the most fascinating possibility thinkers of the Bible. Each judge stood alone in the nation to present a positive message of return to God. When faced with insurmountable odds, they did not allow their problems to dictate their course of action. Deborah and Samson are two of the more familiar judges. Long before any women's movement, Deborah proved to be a successful leader of her people. Courageous, intelligent, and committed to her God, she defeated the warring Canaanite army. Deborah's famous song in chapter five suggests her leadership abilities.

> When leaders lead in Israel,
> When the people willingly offer themselves,
> Bless the LORD!
>
> Hear, O kings! Give ear, O princes!
> I, even I, will sing to the LORD;
> I will sing praise to the LORD God of
> Israel.

(Judg. 5:2, 3)

Samson is another example of one whose strength and leadership were used for God. The story of Samson reads like an ancient drama, depicting the strengths and weaknesses of a human being struggling to lead his people, yet torn by his human desire. Samson's dramatic defeat of the Philistines following his final prayer to God reveals his deepest loyalty.

The Book of Judges clearly indicates that everyone needs leadership. Without strong leaders, we can easily be distracted by the negative influences around us. This book demonstrates that the overall leadership in our work and deeds must be God, our Master, Lord, and Judge.

Jesus in Judges

Each judge is a savior and a ruler, a spiritual and political deliverer, just as Jesus is the Savior and King of His people. The seventeen judges (including Samuel, whose story is told in the Book of First Samuel) include warrior-rulers (Othniel and Gideon), a priest (Eli), and a prophet (Samuel). Together they offer a cumulative picture of the three roles of Jesus as Prophet, Priest, and King.

Keys to Judges

Key Word: Cycles. Because the Book of Judges is written primarily on a thematic, rather than a chronological basis, chapters 16 through 21 actually precede chapters 3 through 15. The stories of the various judges recount Israel's cycles in her relationship to God: sin, servitude, supplication, salvation, and silence.

Key Verses: "Nevertheless the LORD raised up judges who delivered them out of the hand of those who plundered them. And when the LORD raised up judges for them, the LORD was with the judge and delivered them out of the hand of their enemies all the days of the judge; for the LORD was moved to pity by their groaning because of those who oppressed them and harassed them" (2:16, 18).

Key Chapter: Judges 2. The second chapter of Judges is a miniature of the whole book as it records the transition of the godly to the ungodly generation, the format of the cycles, and the purpose of God in not destroying the Canaanites.

1 Now after the death of Joshua it came to pass that the children of Israel asked the LORD, saying, "Who shall be first to go up for us against the Canaanites to fight against them?"

2 And the LORD said, "Judah shall go up. Indeed I have delivered the land into his hand."

3 So Judah said to Simeon his brother, "Come up with me to my allotted territory, that we may fight against the Canaanites; and I will likewise go with you to your allotted territory." And Simeon went with him. 4 Then Judah went up, and the LORD delivered the Canaanites and the Perizzites into their hand; and they killed ten thousand men at Bezek. 5 And they found Adoni-Bezek in Bezek, and fought against him; and they defeated the Canaanites and the Perizzites. 6 Then Adoni-Bezek fled, and they pursued him and caught him and cut off his thumbs and big toes. 7 And Adoni-Bezek said, "Seventy kings with their thumbs and big toes cut off used to gather *scraps* under my table; as I have done, so God has repaid me." Then they brought him to Jerusalem, and there he died.

8 Now the children of Judah fought against Jerusalem and took it; they struck it with the edge of the sword and set the city on fire. 9 And afterward the children of Judah went down to fight against the Canaanites who dwelt in the mountains, in the South,[a] and in the lowland. 10 Then Judah went against the Canaanites who dwelt in Hebron. (Now the name of Hebron *was* formerly Kirjath Arba.) And they killed Sheshai, Ahiman, and Talmai.

11 From there they went against the inhabitants of Debir. (The name of Debir *was* formerly Kirjath Sepher.) 12 Then Caleb said, "Whoever attacks Kirjath Sepher and takes it, to him I will give my daughter Achsah as wife." 13 And Othniel the son of Kenaz, Caleb's younger brother, took it; so he gave him his daughter Achsah as wife. 14 Now it happened, when she came *to him,* that she

urged him[a] to ask her father for a field. And she dismounted from *her* donkey, and Caleb said to her, "What do you wish?" 15 So she said to him, "Give me a blessing; since you have given me land in the South, give me also springs of water."

And Caleb gave her the upper springs and the lower springs.

16 Now the children of the Kenite, Moses' father-in-law, went up from the City of Palms with the children of Judah into the Wilderness of Judah, which *lies* in the South *near* Arad; and they went and dwelt among the people. 17 And Judah went with his brother Simeon, and they attacked the Canaanites who inhabited Zephath, and utterly destroyed it. So the name of the city was called Hormah. 18 Also Judah took Gaza with its territory, Ashkelon with its territory, and Ekron with its territory. 19 So the LORD was with Judah. And they drove out the mountaineers, but they could not drive out the inhabitants of the lowland, because they had chariots of iron. 20 And they gave Hebron to Caleb, as Moses had said. Then he expelled from there the three sons of Anak. 21 But the children of Benjamin did not drive out the Jebusites who inhabited Jerusalem; so the Jebusites dwell with the children of Benjamin in Jerusalem to this day.

22 And the house of Joseph also went up against Bethel, and the LORD *was* with them. 23 So the house of Joseph sent men to spy out Bethel. (The name of the city *was* formerly Luz.) 24 And when the spies saw a man coming out of the city, they said to him, "Please show us the entrance to the city, and we will show you mercy." 25 So he showed them the entrance to the city, and they struck the city with the edge of the sword; but they let the man and all his family go. 26 And the man went to the land of the Hittites, built a city, and called its name Luz, which *is* its name to this day.

27 However, Manasseh did not drive out *the inhabitants of* Beth Shean and its villages, or Taanach

1:9 aHebrew *Negev,* and so throughout this book   1:14 aSeptuagint and Vulgate read *he urged her.*

and its villages, or the inhabitants of Dor and its villages, or the inhabitants of Ibleam and its villages, or the inhabitants of Megiddo and its villages; for the Canaanites were determined to dwell in that land. 28 And it came to pass, when Israel was strong, that they put the Canaanites under tribute, but did not completely drive them out.

29 Nor did Ephraim drive out the Canaanites who dwelt in Gezer; so the Canaanites dwelt in Gezer among them.

30 Nor did Zebulun drive out the inhabitants of Kitron or the inhabitants of Nahalol; so the Canaanites dwelt among them, and were put under tribute.

31 Nor did Asher drive out the inhabitants of Acco or the inhabitants of Sidon, or of Ahlab, Achzib, Helbah, Aphik, or Rehob. 32 So the Asherites dwelt among the Canaanites, the inhabitants of the land; for they did not drive them out.

33 Nor did Naphtali drive out the inhabitants of Beth Shemesh or the inhabitants of Beth Anath; but they dwelt among the Canaanites, the inhabitants of the land. Nevertheless the inhabitants of Beth Shemesh and Beth Anath were put under tribute to them.

34 And the Amorites forced the children of Dan into the mountains, for they would not allow them to come down to the valley; 35 and the Amorites were determined to dwell in Mount Heres, in Aijalon, and in Shaalbim;a yet when the strength of the house of Joseph became greater, they were put under tribute.

36 Now the boundary of the Amorites was from the Ascent of Akrabbim, from Sela, and upward.

2 Then the Angel of the LORD came up from Gilgal to Bochim, and said: "I led you up from Egypt and brought you to the land of which I swore to your fathers; and I said, 'I will never break My covenant with you. 2 And you shall make no covenant with the inhabitants of this land; you shall tear down their altars.' But you have not obeyed My voice. Why have you done this? 3 Therefore I also said, 'I will not drive them out

before you; but they shall be *thorns* in your side,a and their gods shall be a snare to you.'" 4 So it was, when the Angel of the LORD spoke these words to all the children of Israel, that the people lifted up their voices and wept.

5 Then they called the name of that place Bochim;a and they sacrificed there to the LORD. 6 And when Joshua had dismissed the people, the children of Israel went each to his own inheritance to possess the land.

7 So the people served the LORD all the days of Joshua, and all the days of the elders who outlived Joshua, who had seen all the great works of the LORD which He had done for Israel. 8 Now Joshua the son of Nun, the servant of the LORD, died *when he was* one hundred and ten years old. 9 And they buried him within the border of his inheritance at Timnath Heres, in the mountains of Ephraim, on the north side of Mount Gaash. 10 When all that generation had been gathered to their fathers, another generation arose after them who did not know the LORD nor the work which He had done for Israel.

11 Then the children of Israel did evil in the sight of the LORD, and served the Baals; 12 and they forsook the LORD God of their fathers, who had brought them out of the land of Egypt; and they followed other gods from *among* the gods of the people who *were* all around them, and they bowed down to them; and they provoked the LORD to anger. 13 They forsook the LORD and served Baal and the Ashtoreths.a 14 And the anger of the LORD was hot against Israel. So He delivered them into the hands of plunderers who despoiled them; and He sold them into the hands of their enemies all around, so that they could no longer stand before their enemies. 15 Wherever they went out, the hand of the LORD was against them for calamity, as the LORD had said, and as the LORD had sworn to them. And they were greatly distressed.

16 Nevertheless, the LORD raised up judges who delivered them out of the hand of those who plundered them. 17 Yet they would not listen to their judges, but they played the harlot

1:35 aSpelled *Shaalabbin* in Joshua 19:42   2:3 aSeptuagint, Targum, and Vulgate read *enemies to you*.   2:5 aLiterally *Weeping*   2:13 aCanaanite goddesses with other gods, and bowed down to them. They turned quickly from the way in which their fathers walked, in obeying the commandments of the LORD; they did not do so. 18 And when the LORD raised up judges for them, the LORD was with the judge and delivered them out of the hand of their enemies all the days of the judge; for the LORD was moved to pity by their groaning because of those who oppressed them and harassed them. 19 And it came to pass, when the judge was dead, that they reverted and behaved more corruptly than their fathers, by following other gods, to serve them and bow down to them. They did not cease from their own doings nor from their stubborn way.

20 Then the anger of the LORD was hot against Israel; and He said, "Because this nation has transgressed My covenant which I commanded their fathers, and has not heeded My voice, 21 I also will no longer drive out before them any of the nations which Joshua left when he died, 22 so that through them I may test Israel, whether they will keep the ways of the LORD, to walk in them as their fathers kept *them*, or not." 23 Therefore the LORD left those nations, without driving them out immediately; nor did He deliver them into the hand of Joshua.

3 Now these *are* the nations which the LORD left, that He might test Israel by them, *that is,* all who had not known any of the wars in Canaan 2 (*this was* only so that the generations of the children of Israel might be taught to know war, at least those who had not formerly known it), 3 *namely,* five lords of the Philistines, all the Canaanites, the Sidonians, and the Hivites who dwelt in Mount Lebanon, from Mount Baal Hermon to the entrance of Hamath. 4 And they were *left, that He might* test Israel by them, to know whether they would obey the commandments of the LORD, which He had commanded their fathers by the hand of Moses. 5 Thus the children of Israel dwelt among the Canaanites, the Hittites, the Amorites, the Perizzites, the Hivites, and the Jebusites. 6 And they took their daughters to be their wives, and gave their daughters to their sons; and they served their gods.

7 So the children of Israel did evil in the sight of the LORD. They forgot the LORD their God, and served the Baals and Asherahs.ᵃ 8 Therefore the anger of the LORD was hot against Israel, and He sold them into the hand of Cushan-Rishathaim king of Mesopotamia; and the children of Israel served Cushan-Rishathaim eight years. 9 When the children of Israel cried out to the LORD, the LORD raised up a deliverer for the children of Israel, who delivered them: Othniel the son of Kenaz, Caleb's younger brother. 10 The Spirit of the LORD came upon him, and he judged Israel. He went out to war, and the LORD delivered Cushan-Rishathaim king of Mesopotamia into his hand; and his hand prevailed over Cushan-Rishathaim. 11 So the land had rest for forty years. Then Othniel the son of Kenaz died.

12 And the children of Israel again did evil in the sight of the LORD. So the LORD strengthened Eglon king of Moab against Israel, because they had done evil in the sight of the LORD. 13 Then he gathered to himself the people of Ammon and Amalek, went and defeated Israel, and took possession of the City of Palms. 14 So the children of Israel served Eglon king of Moab eighteen years.

15 But when the children of Israel cried out to the LORD, the LORD raised up a deliverer for them: Ehud the son of Gera, the Benjamite, a left-handed man. By him the children of Israel sent tribute to Eglon king of Moab. 16 Now Ehud made himself a dagger (it was double-edged and a cubit in length) and fastened it under his clothes on his right thigh. 17 So he brought the tribute to Eglon king of Moab. (Now Eglon *was* a very fat man.) 18 And when he had finished presenting the tribute, he sent away the people who had carried the tribute. 19 But he himself turned back from the stone images that *were* at Gilgal, and said, "I have a secret message for you, O king."

He said, "Keep silence!" And all who attended him went out from him.

20 So Ehud came to him (now he

3:7 ᵃName or symbol for Canaanite goddesses

was sitting upstairs in his cool private chamber). Then Ehud said, "I have a message from God for you." So he arose from *his* seat. 21 Then Ehud reached with his left hand, took the dagger from his right thigh, and thrust it into his belly. 22 Even the hilt went in after the blade, and the fat closed over the blade, for he did not draw the dagger out of his belly; and his entrails came out. 23 Then Ehud went out through the porch and shut the doors of the upper room behind him and locked them.

24 When he had gone out, *Eglon's*[a] servants came to look, and *to their* surprise, the doors of the upper room were locked. So they said, "He is probably attending to his needs in the cool chamber." 25 So they waited till they were embarrassed, and still he had not opened the doors of the upper room. Therefore they took the key and opened *them*. And there was their master, fallen dead on the floor.

26 But Ehud had escaped while they delayed, and passed beyond the stone images and escaped to Seirah. 27 And it happened, when he arrived, that he blew the trumpet in the mountains of Ephraim, and the children of Israel went down with him from the mountains; and he led them. 28 Then he said to them, "Follow *me*, for the LORD has delivered your enemies the Moabites into your hand." So they went down after him, seized the fords of the Jordan leading to Moab, and did not allow anyone to cross over. 29 And at that time they killed about ten thousand men of Moab, all stout men of valor; not a man escaped. 30 So Moab was subdued that day under the hand of Israel. And the land had rest for eighty years.

31 After him was Shamgar the son of Anath, who killed six hundred men of the Philistines with an ox goad; and he also delivered Israel.

4 When Ehud was dead, the children of Israel again did evil in the sight of the LORD. 2 So the LORD sold them into the hand of Jabin king of Canaan, who reigned in Hazor. The commander of his army *was* Sisera, who dwelt in Harosheth Hagoyim. 3 And the children of Israel cried out to the LORD; for Jabin had nine hundred chariots of iron, and for twenty years he had harshly oppressed the children of Israel.

4 Now Deborah, a prophetess, the wife of Lapidoth, was judging Israel at that time. 5 And she would sit under the palm tree of Deborah between Ramah and Bethel in the mountains of Ephraim. And the children of Israel came up to her for judgment. 6 Then she sent and called for Barak the son of Abinoam from Kedesh in Naphtali, and said to him, "Has not the LORD God of Israel commanded, 'Go and deploy *troops* at Mount Tabor; take with you ten thousand men of the sons of Naphtali and of the sons of Zebulun; 7 and against you I will deploy Sisera, the commander of Jabin's army, with his chariots and his multitude at the River Kishon; and I will deliver him into your hand'?"

8 And Barak said to her, "If you will go with me, then I will go; but if you will not go with me, I will not go!"

9 So she said, "I will surely go with you; nevertheless there will be no glory for you in the journey you are taking, for the LORD will sell Sisera into the hand of a woman." Then Deborah arose and went with Barak to Kedesh. 10 And Barak called Zebulun and Naphtali to Kedesh; he went up with ten thousand men under his command,[a] and Deborah went up with him.

11 Now Heber the Kenite, of the children of Hobab the father-in-law of Moses, had separated himself from the Kenites and pitched his tent near the terebinth tree at Zaanaim, which *is* beside Kedesh.

12 And they reported to Sisera that Barak the son of Abinoam had gone up to Mount Tabor. 13 So Sisera gathered together all his chariots, nine hundred chariots of iron, and all the people who *were* with him, from Harosheth Hagoyim to the River Kishon. 14 Then Deborah said to Barak, "Up! For this *is* the day in which the LORD has delivered Sisera into your hand. Has not the LORD gone out before you?" So Barak went down from Mount Tabor with ten thousand men following him. 15 And the LORD routed Sisera and all *his* chariots and all *his* army with the edge of the

3:24 aLiterally *his*   4:10 aLiterally *at his feet*

Women of Positive Faith

The Old Testament is filled with stories of women of positive faith. They were women much like the women of today—career women, mothers, wives, and friends. Long before any women's movement, the Old Testament women held roles of leadership and influence. Like all great people of faith, they had successes and failures that God used to help shape the course of their lives and their societies.

Sarah is the classic example of the wife of a prominent leader who was respected by his people. With Abraham, Sarah left her comfortable surroundings to journey hundreds of miles into unknown territory. She was supportive and uncomplaining as they traveled in tents, and she willingly accepted the God of Israel. God promised a blessed generation to Abraham. Yet after years of believing, Sarah remained childless and barren. When her faith in God's promise wavered, she reacted by offering her maid-servant, Hagar, to her husband.

But God had greater plans for Sarah. When she was ninety, He made Sarah's barren womb alive with new life. Sarah's lack of patience tripped her, but she did not fall. She praised God for her new son, Isaac, and raised him up for a life of service.

The judge and prophetess, Deborah, was raised to a position of leading the entire nation of Israel (see Judges 4, 5). During uncertain times, Deborah stood fast in her commitment to God. Because she completely trusted His ability, she was able to unite and lead the people of Israel in a successful revolt against Sisera, the leader of the chariot-drawn Canaanites. Like an ancient prime minister or president, Deborah was not afraid to assume the responsibilities thrust upon her by Barak, who knew that God spoke through her. In her famous song, Deborah's faith, determination, and courage as a woman of God are expressed. As a result of her leadership, Israel lived in peace for forty years (see Judges 5:31).

Throughout the Old Testament women of positive faith speak out. Eve, Sarah, Rebekah, Deborah, Leah, Rachel, Miriam, Rahab, Ruth, and Hannah are all excellent examples of God's work in the lives of women. They were not perfect saints who never lacked in belief, but they had a positive and a decisive faith. They faced the future unafraid and ventured into new territories. They stood up for their convictions and won a place in history by believing God.

The woman of faith in the Old Testament knew what today's woman of positive faith knows—that God can do great things through ordinary people!

sword before Barak; and Sisera alighted from *his* chariot and fled away on foot. 16 But Barak pursued the chariots and the army as far as Harosheth Hagoyim, and all the army of Sisera fell by the edge of the sword; not a man was left.

17 However, Sisera had fled away on foot to the tent of Jael, the wife of Heber the Kenite; for *there was* peace between Jabin king of Hazor and the house of Heber the Kenite. 18 And Jael went out to meet Sisera, and said to him, "Turn aside, my lord, turn aside to me; do not fear." And when he had turned aside with her into the tent, she covered him with a blanket.

19 Then he said to her, "Please give me a little water to drink, for I am thirsty." So she opened a jug of milk, gave him a drink, and covered him. 20 And he said to her, "Stand at the door of the tent, and if any man comes and inquires of you, and says, 'Is there any man here?' you shall say, 'No.'"

21 Then Jael, Heber's wife, took a tent peg and took a hammer in her hand, and went softly to him and drove the peg into his temple, and it went down into the ground; for he was fast asleep and weary. So he died. 22 And then, as Barak pursued Sisera, Jael came out to meet him, and said to him, "Come, I will show you the man whom you seek." And when he went into her *tent*, there lay Sisera, dead with the peg in his temple.

23 So on that day God subdued Jabin king of Canaan in the presence of the children of Israel. 24 And the hand of the children of Israel grew stronger and stronger against Jabin king of Canaan, until they had destroyed Jabin king of Canaan.

5 Then Deborah and Barak the son of Abinoam sang on that day, saying:

2 "When leaders lead in Israel,
When the people willingly offer themselves,
Bless the LORD!

3 "Hear, O kings! Give ear, O princes!
I, *even* I, will sing to the LORD;
I will sing praise to the LORD God of Israel.

4 "LORD, when You went out from Seir,
When You marched from the field of Edom,
The earth trembled and the heavens poured,
The clouds also poured water;

5 The mountains gushed before the LORD,
This Sinai, before the LORD God of Israel.

6 "In the days of Shamgar, son of Anath,
In the days of Jael,
The highways were deserted,
And the travelers walked along the byways.

7 Village life ceased, it ceased in Israel,
Until I, Deborah, arose,
Arose a mother in Israel.

8 They chose new gods;
Then *there was* war in the gates;
Not a shield or spear was seen among forty thousand in Israel.

9 My heart *is* with the rulers of Israel
Who offered themselves willingly with the people.
Bless the LORD!

10 "Speak, you who ride on white donkeys,
Who sit in judges' attire,
And who walk along the road.

11 Far from the noise of the archers, among the watering places,
There they shall recount the righteous acts of the LORD,
The righteous acts *for* His villagers in Israel;
Then the people of the LORD shall go down to the gates.

12 "Awake, awake, Deborah!
Awake, awake, sing a song!
Arise, Barak, and lead your captives away,
O son of Abinoam!

13 "Then the survivors came down, the people against the nobles;
The LORD came down for me against the mighty.

14 From Ephraim *were* those whose roots were in Amalek.

After you, Benjamin, with your
  peoples,
From Machir rulers came
  down,
And from Zebulun those who
  bear the recruiter's staff.
15 And the princes of Issachar[a]
  were with Deborah;
As Issachar, so *was* Barak
Sent into the valley under his
  command;[b]
Among the divisions of Reuben
There were great resolves of
  heart.
16 Why did you sit among the
  sheepfolds,
To hear the pipings for the
  flocks?
The divisions of Reuben have
  great searchings of heart.
17 Gilead stayed beyond the
  Jordan,
And why did Dan remain on
  ships?[a]
Asher continued at the
  seashore,
And stayed by his inlets.
18 Zebulun *is* a people *who*
  jeopardized their lives to the
  point of death,
Naphtali also, on the heights of
  the battlefield.

19 "The kings came *and* fought,
Then the kings of Canaan
  fought
In Taanach, by the waters of
  Megiddo;
They took no spoils of silver.
20 They fought from the heavens;
The stars from their courses
  fought against Sisera.
21 The torrent of Kishon swept
  them away,
That ancient torrent, the
  torrent of Kishon.
O my soul, march on in
  strength!
22 Then the horses' hooves
  pounded,
The galloping, galloping of his
  steeds.
23 'Curse Meroz,' said the angel[a]
  of the LORD,
'Curse its inhabitants bitterly,
Because they did not come to
  the help of the LORD,
To the help of the LORD against
  the mighty.'

24 "Most blessed among women is
  Jael,
The wife of Heber the Kenite;
Blessed is she among women
  in tents.
25 He asked for water, she gave
  milk;
She brought out cream in a
  lordly bowl.
26 She stretched her hand to the
  tent peg,
Her right hand to the
  workmen's hammer;
She pounded Sisera, she
  pierced his head,
She split and struck through
  his temple.
27 At her feet he sank, he fell, he
  lay still;
At her feet he sank, he fell;
Where he sank, there he fell
  dead.

28 "The mother of Sisera looked
  through the window,
And cried out through the
  lattice,
'Why is his chariot *so* long in
  coming?
Why tarries the clatter of his
  chariots?'
29 Her wisest ladies answered her,
Yes, she answered herself,
30 'Are they not finding and
  dividing the spoil:
To every man a girl *or* two;
For Sisera, plunder of dyed
  garments,
Plunder of garments
  embroidered and dyed,
Two pieces of dyed embroidery
  for the neck of the looter?'

31 "Thus let all Your enemies
  perish, O LORD!
But *let* those who love Him *be*
  like the sun
When it comes out in full
  strength."

So the land had rest for forty years.

6 Then the children of Israel did evil in the sight of the LORD. So the LORD delivered them into the hand of Midian for seven years, 2 and the hand of Midian prevailed

---

5:15 [a]Following Septuagint, Syriac, Targum, and Vulgate; Masoretic Text reads *And my prince in Issachar.* [b]Literally *at his feet*   5:17 [a]Or *at ease*   5:23 [a]Or *Angel*

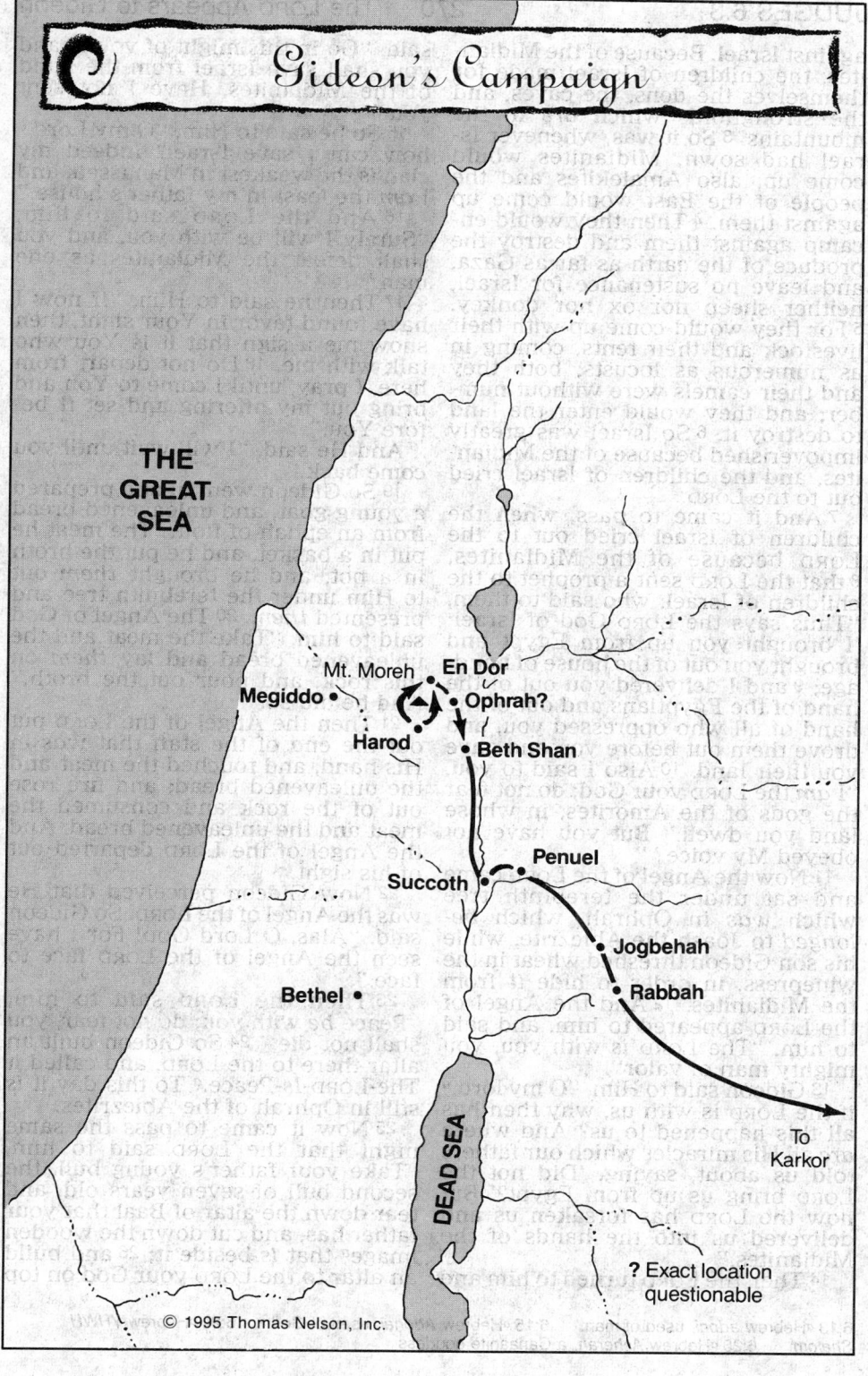

Gideon's Campaign

THE GREAT SEA

Megiddo •

Mt. Moreh   En Dor
             Ophrah?
Harod   Beth Shan

                    Penuel
Succoth

                    Jogbehah
Bethel •   Rabbah

DEAD SEA

To Karkor

? Exact location
questionable

against Israel. Because of the Midianites, the children of Israel made for themselves the dens, the caves, and the strongholds which *are* in the mountains. 3 So it was, whenever Israel had sown, Midianites would come up; also Amalekites and the people of the East would come up against them. 4 Then they would encamp against them and destroy the produce of the earth as far as Gaza, and leave no sustenance for Israel, neither sheep nor ox nor donkey. 5 For they would come up with their livestock and their tents, coming in as numerous as locusts; both they and their camels were without number; and they would enter the land to destroy it. 6 So Israel was greatly impoverished because of the Midianites, and the children of Israel cried out to the LORD.

7 And it came to pass, when the children of Israel cried out to the LORD because of the Midianites, 8 that the LORD sent a prophet to the children of Israel, who said to them, "Thus says the LORD God of Israel: 'I brought you up from Egypt and brought you out of the house of bondage; 9 and I delivered you out of the hand of the Egyptians and out of the hand of all who oppressed you, and drove them out before you and gave you their land. 10 Also I said to you, "I *am* the LORD your God; do not fear the gods of the Amorites, in whose land you dwell." But you have not obeyed My voice.' "

11 Now the Angel of the LORD came and sat under the terebinth tree which *was* in Ophrah, which *belonged* to Joash the Abiezrite, while his son Gideon threshed wheat in the winepress, in order to hide *it* from the Midianites. 12 And the Angel of the LORD appeared to him, and said to him, "The LORD *is* with you, you mighty man of valor!"

13 Gideon said to Him, "O my lord,[a] if the LORD is with us, why then has all this happened to us? And where *are* all His miracles which our fathers told us about, saying, 'Did not the LORD bring us up from Egypt?' But now the LORD has forsaken us and delivered us into the hands of the Midianites."

14 Then the LORD turned to him and said, "Go in this might of yours, and you shall save Israel from the hand of the Midianites. Have I not sent you?"

15 So he said to Him, "O my Lord,[a] how can I save Israel? Indeed my clan *is* the weakest in Manasseh, and I *am* the least in my father's house."

16 And the LORD said to him, "Surely I will be with you, and you shall defeat the Midianites as one man."

17 Then he said to Him, "If now I have found favor in Your sight, then show me a sign that it is You who talk with me. 18 Do not depart from here, I pray, until I come to You and bring out my offering and set *it* before You."

And He said, "I will wait until you come back."

19 So Gideon went in and prepared a young goat, and unleavened bread from an ephah of flour. The meat he put in a basket, and he put the broth in a pot; and he brought *them* out to Him under the terebinth tree and presented *them*. 20 The Angel of God said to him, "Take the meat and the unleavened bread and lay *them* on this rock, and pour out the broth." And he did so.

21 Then the Angel of the LORD put out the end of the staff that *was* in His hand, and touched the meat and the unleavened bread; and fire rose out of the rock and consumed the meat and the unleavened bread. And the Angel of the LORD departed out of his sight.

22 Now Gideon perceived that He *was* the Angel of the LORD. So Gideon said, "Alas, O Lord GOD! For I have seen the Angel of the LORD face to face."

23 Then the LORD said to him, "Peace *be* with you; do not fear, you shall not die." 24 So Gideon built an altar there to the LORD, and called it The-LORD-*Is*-Peace.[a] To this day it *is* still in Ophrah of the Abiezrites.

25 Now it came to pass the same night that the LORD said to him, "Take your father's young bull, the second bull of seven years old, and tear down the altar of Baal that your father has, and cut down the wooden image[a] that *is* beside it; 26 and build an altar to the LORD your God on top

---

6:13 [a]Hebrew *adoni*, used of man   6:15 [a]Hebrew *Adonai*, used of God   6:24 [a]Hebrew *YHWH* Shalom   6:25 [a]Hebrew *Asherah*, a Canaanite goddess

There is Power in Faith

What triumphant power there is in faith! Look what a tough-minded faith you have!

1. Faith provides *shielding power*. Shield your mind from the negative thoughts by affirming:
   - I have broken free from the tyranny of past mistakes, sins, and errors.
   - I no longer react to great ideas with the "impossibility complex."
   - I am in love with life, with the Lord, with other human beings, and with myself.
   - I find that this perfect love casts out all fear.

2. Faith provides *fielding power*. Now use this faith-power to field the opportunities around you. Affirm:
   - I gather the opportunities. When I was a child, I had dreams of finding lots of nickles and dimes on the ground or in the grass. That childhood dream has become a reality!
   - I search for opportunities to grow, to study, to develop possibilities all around me!

3. Faith provides *wielding power*. Wow! How wonderful this possibility-thinking faith works! You are *shielded* from the negative thoughts that tell you it won't work. Immediately you begin to *field* the opportunities, and now you *wield leadership*.
   - Take command!
   - Set goals!

4. Faith provides *yielding power*. Faith gives you the freedom to take control. Affirm:
   - I will *not yield* to any negative persons the right to make the decisions that affect my future.
   - I *yield* my life to the lordship of Jesus Christ, the greatest Possibility Thinker of all time!

of this rock in the proper arrangement, and take the second bull and offer a burnt sacrifice with the wood of the image which you shall cut down." 27 So Gideon took ten men from among his servants and did as the LORD had said to him. But because he feared his father's household and the men of the city too much to do it by day, he did it by night.

28 And when the men of the city arose early in the morning, there was the altar of Baal, torn down; and the wooden image that was beside it was cut down, and the second bull was being offered on the altar which had been built. 29 So they said to one another, "Who has done this thing?" And when they had inquired and asked, they said, "Gideon the son of Joash has done this thing." 30 Then the men of the city said to Joash, "Bring out your son, that he may die, because he has torn down the altar of Baal, and because he has cut down the wooden image that was beside it."

31 But Joash said to all who stood against him, "Would you plead for Baal? Would you save him? Let the one who would plead for him be put to death by morning! If he is a god, let him plead for himself, because his altar has been torn down!" 32 Therefore on that day he called him Jerubbaal,ᵃ saying, "Let Baal plead against him, because he has torn down his altar."

33 Then all the Midianites and Amalekites, the people of the East, gathered together; and they crossed over and encamped in the Valley of Jezreel. 34 But the Spirit of the LORD came upon Gideon; then he blew the trumpet, and the Abiezrites gathered behind him. 35 And he sent messengers throughout all Manasseh, who also gathered behind him. He also sent messengers to Asher, Zebulun, and Naphtali; and they came up to meet them.

36 So Gideon said to God, "If You will save Israel by my hand as You have said— 37 look, I shall put a fleece of wool on the threshing floor; if there is dew on the fleece only, and it is dry on all the ground, then I shall know that You will save Israel by my hand, as You have said." 38 And it was so. When he rose early the next morning and squeezed the fleece together, he wrung the dew out of the fleece, a bowlful of water. 39 Then Gideon said to God, "Do not be angry with me, but let me speak just once more: Let me test, I pray, just once more with the fleece; let it now be dry only on the fleece, but on all the ground let there be dew." 40 And God did so that night. It was dry on the fleece only, but there was dew on all the ground.

7 Then Jerubbaal (that is, Gideon) and all the people who were with him rose early and encamped beside the well of Harod, so that the camp of the Midianites was on the north side of them by the hill of Moreh in the valley.

2 And the LORD said to Gideon, "The people who are with you are too many for Me to give the Midianites into their hands, lest Israel claim glory for itself against Me, saying, 'My own hand has saved me.' 3 Now therefore, proclaim in the hearing of the people, saying, 'Whoever is fearful and afraid, let him turn and depart at once from Mount Gilead.'" And twenty-two thousand of the people returned, and ten thousand remained.

4 But the LORD said to Gideon, "The people are still too many; bring them down to the water, and I will test them for you there. Then it will be, that of whom I say to you, 'This one shall go with you,' the same shall go with you; and of whomever I say to you, 'This one shall not go with you,' the same shall not go." 5 So he brought the people down to the water. And the LORD said to Gideon, "Everyone who laps from the water with his tongue, as a dog laps, you shall set apart by himself; likewise everyone who gets down on his knees to drink." 6 And the number of those who lapped, putting their hand to their mouth, was three hundred men; but all the rest of the people got down on their knees to drink water. 7 Then the LORD said to Gideon, "By the three hundred men who lapped I will save you, and deliver the Midianites into your hand. Let all the other people go, every man to his place." 8 So the people took provisions and their trumpets in their

6:32 ᵃLiterally Let Baal Plead

Gideon and the Midianites

When you think you have exhausted all the possibilities, remember, you have not.

During the period of the judges, the Midianite army, aided by the Amalekites and the Ammonites, poured into Israel (see Judg. 3:13). They destroyed the countryside from Jezreel to the Gaza Strip. The terrified Israelites fled their towns, homes, and villages and hid in mountain caves.

There was one man, the timid Gideon, who cried out that God would deliver his people. Gideon never lost faith or hope. After much prayer and with the reassurance of God's answers, he dared to believe that God would raise up a mighty army to crush the Midianites and return the people to their land.

God asked Gideon to gather all of the able-bodied military men in the Valley of Jezreel at the hill of Moreh to organize an army to attack the Midianites. Gideon persuaded 22,000 men to join him at his camp (see Judg. 7:3).

However, God wanted Gideon to believe that anything was possible, so he asked Gideon to multiply his resources by trimming down his forces. God ordered Gideon to get rid of 21,700 men. With only 300 men, Gideon was told he could defeat hundreds of thousands of Midianites.

Gideon dared to believe God. At nightfall, Gideon assembled his troops on the slopes of the hill of Moreh. On his command, they were to light torches, smash empty water pitchers, and shout at the top of their lungs while attacking the Midianite army. At night this looked like a tremendous swarm of soldiers coming down on the Midianite army. The Midianites turned and fled in fear.

In the darkness of the evening, the Midianite soldiers began to attack each other. Hundreds of thousands of soldiers fell on the slopes of the hills around the Jordan and Jezreel valleys. Inspired by Gideon's great courage, the Israelites from all over the land came and aided in the battle. Finally, the Midianites were completely defeated.

Be like Gideon: when you think you have exhausted all the possibilities, remember—you have not. Pray, think, ask God for an idea and a solution. Be clever and bold. Go after your problem; trick your problem! Multiply your resources by stripping away unneeded excess. When the call came for Gideon to fight, he was gathering wheat; he was not sitting around doing nothing.

What is holding you back? Are you waiting for conditions to be perfect? Move ahead with faith and possibility thinking!

hands. And he sent away all *the rest of* Israel, every man to his tent, and retained those three hundred men. Now the camp of Midian was below him in the valley.

9 It happened on the same night that the LORD said to him, "Arise, go down against the camp, for I have delivered it into your hand. 10 But if you are afraid to go down, go down to the camp with Purah your servant, 11 and you shall hear what they say; and afterward your hands shall be strengthened to go down against the camp." Then he went down with Purah his servant to the outpost of the armed men who *were* in the camp. 12 Now the Midianites and Amalekites, all the people of the East, were lying in the valley as numerous as locusts; and their camels *were* without number, as the sand by the seashore in multitude.

13 And when Gideon had come, there was a man telling a dream to his companion. He said, "I have had a dream: *To my* surprise, a loaf of barley bread tumbled into the camp of Midian; it came to a tent and struck it so that it fell and overturned, and the tent collapsed."

14 Then his companion answered and said, "This *is* nothing else but the sword of Gideon the son of Joash, a man of Israel! Into his hand God has delivered Midian and the whole camp."

15 And so it was, when Gideon heard the telling of the dream and its interpretation, that he worshiped. He returned to the camp of Israel, and said, "Arise, for the LORD has delivered the camp of Midian into your hand." 16 Then he divided the three hundred men *into* three companies, and he put a trumpet into every man's hand, with empty pitchers, and torches inside the pitchers. 17 And he said to them, "Look at me and do likewise; watch, and when I come to the edge of the camp you shall do as I do: 18 When I blow the trumpet, I and all who *are* with me, then you also blow the trumpets on every side of the whole camp, and say, 'The sword *of* the LORD and of Gideon!'"

19 So Gideon and the hundred men who *were* with him came to the outpost of the camp at the beginning of the middle watch, just as they had posted the watch; and they blew the trumpets and broke the pitchers that *were* in their hands. 20 Then the three companies blew the trumpets and broke the pitchers—they held the torches in their left hands and the trumpets in their right hands for blowing—and they cried, "The sword of the LORD and of Gideon!" 21 And every man stood in his place all around the camp; and the whole army ran and cried out and fled. 22 When the three hundred blew the trumpets, the LORD set every man's sword against his companion throughout the whole camp; and the army fled to Beth Acacia,[a] toward Zererah, as far as the border of Abel Meholah, by Tabbath.

23 And the men of Israel gathered together from Naphtali, Asher, and all Manasseh, and pursued the Midianites.

24 Then Gideon sent messengers throughout all the mountains of Ephraim, saying, "Come down against the Midianites, and seize from them the watering places as far as Beth Barah and the Jordan." Then all the men of Ephraim gathered together and seized the watering places as far as Beth Barah and the Jordan. 25 And they captured two princes of the Midianites, Oreb and Zeeb. They killed Oreb at the rock of Oreb, and Zeeb they killed at the winepress of Zeeb. They pursued Midian and brought the heads of Oreb and Zeeb to Gideon on the other side of the Jordan.

8 Now the men of Ephraim said to him, "Why have you done this to us by not calling us when you went to fight with the Midianites?" And they reprimanded him sharply.

2 So he said to them, "What have I done now in comparison with you? *Is* not the gleaning *of the grapes* of Ephraim better than the vintage of Abiezer? 3 God has delivered into your hands the princes of Midian, Oreb and Zeeb. And what was I able to do in comparison with you?" Then their anger toward him subsided when he said that.

4 When Gideon came to the Jordan, he and the three hundred men who *were* with him crossed over, ex-

7:22 aHebrew *Beth Shittah*

hausted but still in pursuit. 5 Then he said to the men of Succoth, "Please give loaves of bread to the people who follow me, for they are exhausted, and I am pursuing Zebah and Zalmunna, kings of Midian."

6 And the leaders of Succoth said, "Are the hands of Zebah and Zalmunna now in your hand, that we should give bread to your army?"

7 So Gideon said, "For this cause, when the LORD has delivered Zebah and Zalmunna into my hand, then I will tear your flesh with the thorns of the wilderness and with briers!" 8 Then he went up from there to Penuel and spoke to them in the same way. And the men of Penuel answered him as the men of Succoth had answered. 9 So he also spoke to the men of Penuel, saying, "When I come back in peace, I will tear down this tower!"

10 Now Zebah and Zalmunna were at Karkor, and their armies with them, about fifteen thousand, all who were left of all the army of the people of the East; for one hundred and twenty thousand men who drew the sword had fallen. 11 Then Gideon went up by the road of those who dwell in tents on the east of Nobah and Jogbehah; and he attacked the army while the camp felt secure. 12 When Zebah and Zalmunna fled, he pursued them; and he took the two kings of Midian, Zebah and Zalmunna, and routed the whole army.

13 Then Gideon the son of Joash returned from battle, from the Ascent of Heres. 14 And he caught a young man of the men of Succoth and interrogated him; and he wrote down for him the leaders of Succoth and its elders, seventy-seven men. 15 Then he came to the men of Succoth and said, "Here are Zebah and Zalmunna, about whom you ridiculed me, saying, 'Are the hands of Zebah and Zalmunna now in your hand, that we should give bread to your weary men?' " 16 And he took the elders of the city, and thorns of the wilderness and briers, and with them he taught the men of Succoth. 17 Then he tore down the tower of Penuel and killed the men of the city.

18 And he said to Zebah and Zalmunna, "What kind of men were they whom you killed at Tabor?"

So they answered, "As you are, so were they; each one resembled the son of a king."

19 Then he said, "They were my brothers, the sons of my mother. As the LORD lives, if you had let them live, I would not kill you." 20 And he said to Jether his firstborn, "Rise, kill them!" But the youth would not draw his sword; for he was afraid, because he was still a youth.

21 So Zebah and Zalmunna said, "Rise yourself, and kill us; for as a man is, so is his strength." So Gideon arose and killed Zebah and Zalmunna, and took the crescent ornaments that were on their camels' necks.

22 Then the men of Israel said to Gideon, "Rule over us, both you and your son, and your grandson also; for you have delivered us from the hand of Midian."

23 But Gideon said to them, "I will not rule over you, nor shall my son rule over you; the LORD shall rule over you." 24 Then Gideon said to them, "I would like to make a request of you, that each of you would give me the earrings from his plunder." For they had golden earrings, because they were Ishmaelites.

25 So they answered, "We will gladly give them." And they spread out a garment, and each man threw into it the earrings from his plunder. 26 Now the weight of the gold earrings that he requested was one thousand seven hundred shekels of gold, besides the crescent ornaments, pendants, and purple robes which were on the kings of Midian, and besides the chains that were around their camels' necks. 27 Then Gideon made it into an ephod and set it up in his city, Ophrah. And all Israel played the harlot with it there. It became a snare to Gideon and to his house.

28 Thus Midian was subdued before the children of Israel, so that they lifted their heads no more. And the country was quiet for forty years in the days of Gideon.

29 Then Jerubbaal the son of Joash went and dwelt in his own house. 30 Gideon had seventy sons who were his own offspring, for he had many wives. 31 And his concubine who was in Shechem also bore him a son, whose name he called Abimelech. 32 Now Gideon the son of Joash died at a good old age, and was bur-

ied in the tomb of Joash his father, in Ophrah of the Abiezrites.

33 So it was, as soon as Gideon was dead, that the children of Israel again played the harlot with the Baals, and made Baal-Berith their god. 34 Thus the children of Israel did not remember the LORD their God, who had delivered them from the hands of all their enemies on every side; 35 nor did they show kindness to the house of Jerubbaal (Gideon) in accordance with the good he had done for Israel.

9 Then Abimelech the son of Jerubbaal went to Shechem, to his mother's brothers, and spoke with them and with all the family of the house of his mother's father, saying, 2 "Please speak in the hearing of all the men of Shechem: 'Which is better for you, that all seventy of the sons of Jerubbaal reign over you, or that one reign over you?' Remember that I *am* your own flesh and bone."

3 And his mother's brothers spoke all these words concerning him in the hearing of all the men of Shechem; and their heart was inclined to follow Abimelech, for they said, "He is our brother." 4 So they gave him seventy *shekels* of silver from the temple of Baal-Berith, with which Abimelech hired worthless and reckless men; and they followed him. 5 Then he went to his father's house at Ophrah and killed his brothers, the seventy sons of Jerubbaal, on one stone. But Jotham the youngest son of Jerubbaal was left, because he hid himself. 6 And all the men of Shechem gathered together, all of Beth Millo, and they went and made Abimelech king beside the terebinth tree at the pillar that *was* in Shechem.

7 Now when they told Jotham, he went and stood on top of Mount Gerizim, and lifted his voice and cried out. And he said to them:

"Listen to me, you men of
        Shechem,
That God may listen to you!

8 "The trees once went forth to
        anoint a king over them.
    And they said to the olive tree,
    'Reign over us!'
9   But the olive tree said to them,
    'Should I cease giving my oil,

With which they honor God
        and men,
    And go to sway over trees?'

10 "Then the trees said to the fig
        tree,
    'You come *and* reign over us!'
11   But the fig tree said to them,
    'Should I cease my sweetness
        and my good fruit,
    And go to sway over trees?'

12 "Then the trees said to the vine,
    'You come *and* reign over us!'
13   But the vine said to them,
    'Should I cease my new wine,
    Which cheers *both* God and
        men,
    And go to sway over trees?'

14 "Then all the trees said to the
        bramble,
    'You come *and* reign over us!'
15   And the bramble said to the
        trees,
    'If in truth you anoint me as
        king over you,
    Then come *and* take shelter in
        my shade;
    But if not, let fire come out of
        the bramble
    And devour the cedars of
        Lebanon!'

16 "Now therefore, if you have acted in truth and sincerity in making Abimelech king, and if you have dealt well with Jerubbaal and his house, and have done to him as he deserves— 17 for my father fought for you, risked his life, and delivered you out of the hand of Midian; 18 but you have risen up against my father's house this day, and killed his seventy sons on one stone, and made Abimelech, the son of his female servant, king over the men of Shechem, because he is your brother— 19 if then you have acted in truth and sincerity with Jerubbaal and with his house this day, *then* rejoice in Abimelech, and let him also rejoice in you. 20 But if not, let fire come from Abimelech and devour the men of Shechem and Beth Millo; and let fire come from the men of Shechem and from Beth Millo and devour Abimelech!" 21 And Jotham ran away and fled; and he went to Beer and dwelt there, for fear of Abimelech his brother.

22 After Abimelech had reigned over Israel three years, 23 God sent

a spirit of ill will between Abimelech and the men of Shechem; and the men of Shechem dealt treacherously with Abimelech, 24 that the crime *done* to the seventy sons of Jerubbaal might be settled and their blood be laid on Abimelech their brother, who killed them, and on the men of Shechem, who aided him in the killing of his brothers. 25 And the men of Shechem set men in ambush against him on the tops of the mountains, and they robbed all who passed by them along that way; and it was told Abimelech.

26 Now Gaal the son of Ebed came with his brothers and went over to Shechem; and the men of Shechem put their confidence in him. 27 So they went out into the fields, and gathered *grapes* from their vineyards and trod *them*, and made merry. And they went into the house of their god, and ate and drank, and cursed Abimelech. 28 Then Gaal the son of Ebed said, "Who *is* Abimelech, and who *is* Shechem, that we should serve him? *Is he* not the son of Jerubbaal, and *is not* Zebul his officer? Serve the men of Hamor the father of Shechem; but why should we serve him? 29 If only this people were under my authority!*a* Then I would remove Abimelech." So he*b* said to Abimelech, "Increase your army and come out!"

30 When Zebul, the ruler of the city, heard the words of Gaal the son of Ebed, his anger was aroused. 31 And he sent messengers to Abimelech secretly, saying, "Take note! Gaal the son of Ebed and his brothers have come to Shechem; and here they are, fortifying the city against you. 32 Now therefore, get up by night, you and the people who *are* with you, and lie in wait in the field. 33 And it shall be, as soon as the sun is up in the morning, *that* you shall rise early and rush upon the city; and *when* he and the people who are with him come out against you, you may then do to them as you find opportunity."

34 So Abimelech and all the people who *were* with him rose by night, and lay in wait against Shechem in four companies. 35 When Gaal the son of Ebed went out and stood in the entrance to the city gate, Abimelech and the people who *were* with him rose from lying in wait. 36 And when Gaal saw the people, he said to Zebul, "Look, people are coming down from the tops of the mountains!"

But Zebul said to him, "You see the shadows of the mountains as *if they were* men."

37 So Gaal spoke again and said, "See, people are coming down from the center of the land, and another company is coming from the Diviners'*a* Terebinth Tree."

38 Then Zebul said to him, "Where indeed *is* your mouth now, with which you said, 'Who is Abimelech, that we should serve him?' *Are* not these the people whom you despised? Go out, if you will, and fight with them now."

39 So Gaal went out, leading the men of Shechem, and fought with Abimelech. 40 And Abimelech chased him, and he fled from him; and many fell wounded, to the *very* entrance of the gate. 41 Then Abimelech dwelt at Arumah, and Zebul drove out Gaal and his brothers, so that they would not dwell in Shechem.

42 And it came about on the next day that the people went out into the field, and they told Abimelech. 43 So he took his people, divided them into three companies, and lay in wait in the field. And he looked, and there were the people, coming out of the city; and he rose against them and attacked them. 44 Then Abimelech and the company that *was* with him rushed forward and stood at the entrance of the gate of the city; and the *other* two companies rushed upon all who *were* in the fields and killed them. 45 So Abimelech fought against the city all that day; he took the city and killed the people who *were* in it; and he demolished the city and sowed it with salt.

46 Now when all the men of the tower of Shechem had heard *that*, they entered the stronghold of the temple of the god Berith. 47 And it was told Abimelech that all the men of the tower of Shechem were gathered together. 48 Then Abimelech went up to Mount Zalmon, he and all the people who *were* with him.

9:29 *a*Literally *hand*   *b*Following Masoretic Text and Targum; Dead Sea Scrolls read *they;* Septuagint reads *I.*   9:37 *a*Hebrew *Meonenim*

And Abimelech took an ax in his hand and cut down a bough from the trees, and took it and laid *it* on his shoulder; then he said to the people who were with him, "What you have seen me do, make haste *and* do as I *have done.*" 49 So each of the people likewise cut down his own bough and followed Abimelech, put *them* against the stronghold, and set the stronghold on fire above them, so that all the people of the tower of Shechem died, about a thousand men and women.

50 Then Abimelech went to Thebez, and he encamped against Thebez and took it. 51 But there was a strong tower in the city, and all the men and women—all the people of the city— fled there and shut themselves in; then they went up to the top of the tower. 52 So Abimelech came as far as the tower and fought against it; and he drew near the door of the tower to burn it with fire. 53 But a certain woman dropped an upper millstone on Abimelech's head and crushed his skull. 54 Then he called quickly to the young man, his armor-bearer, and said to him, "Draw your sword and kill me, lest men say of me, 'A woman killed him.'" So his young man thrust him through, and he died. 55 And when the men of Israel saw that Abimelech was dead, they departed, every man to his place.

56 Thus God repaid the wickedness of Abimelech, which he had done to his father by killing his seventy brothers. 57 And all the evil of the men of Shechem God returned on their own heads, and on them came the curse of Jotham the son of Jerubbaal.

10 After Abimelech there arose to save Israel Tola the son of Puah, the son of Dodo, a man of Issachar; and he dwelt in Shamir in the mountains of Ephraim. 2 He judged Israel twenty-three years; and he died and was buried in Shamir.

3 After him arose Jair, a Gileadite; and he judged Israel twenty-two years. 4 Now he had thirty sons who rode on thirty donkeys; they also had thirty towns, which are called "Havoth Jair"*ᵃ* to this day, which *are* in the land of Gilead. 5 And Jair died and was buried in Camon.

6 Then the children of Israel again did evil in the sight of the LORD, and served the Baals and the Ashtoreths, the gods of Syria, the gods of Sidon, the gods of Moab, the gods of the people of Ammon, and the gods of the Philistines; and they forsook the LORD and did not serve Him. 7 So the anger of the LORD was hot against Israel; and He sold them into the hands of the Philistines and into the hands of the people of Ammon. 8 From that year they harassed and oppressed the children of Israel for eighteen years—all the children of Israel who *were* on the other side of the Jordan in the land of the Amorites, in Gilead. 9 Moreover the people of Ammon crossed over the Jordan to fight against Judah also, against Benjamin, and against the house of Ephraim, so that Israel was severely distressed.

10 And the children of Israel cried out to the LORD, saying, "We have sinned against You, because we have both forsaken our God and served the Baals!"

11 So the LORD said to the children of Israel, "*Did I* not *deliver you* from the Egyptians and from the Amorites and from the people of Ammon and from the Philistines? 12 Also the Sidonians and Amalekites and Maonites*ᵃ* oppressed you; and you cried out to Me, and I delivered you from their hand. 13 Yet you have forsaken Me and served other gods. Therefore I will deliver you no more. 14 Go and cry out to the gods which you have chosen; let them deliver you in your time of distress."

15 And the children of Israel said to the LORD, "We have sinned! Do to us whatever seems best to You; only deliver us this day, we pray." 16 So they put away the foreign gods from among them and served the LORD. And His soul could no longer endure the misery of Israel.

17 Then the people of Ammon gathered together and encamped in Gilead. And the children of Israel assembled together and encamped in Mizpah. 18 And the people, the leaders of Gilead, said to one another, "Who *is* the man who will begin the

---

10:4 ᵃLiterally *Towns of Jair* (compare Numbers 32:41 and Deuteronomy 3:14)   10:12 ᵃSome Septuagint manuscripts read *Midianites.*

Israel's Judges

After the death of Joshua, the nation of Israel was ruled by judges, or heroic military deliverers, for about 300 years until the united monarchy was established under King Saul. The era of the judges was a time of instability and moral depravity, a dark period when "every man did *that which was* right in his own eyes" (Judg. 17:6). The judges tried to rally the people against their enemies, but many of the judges were morally weak and the people often turned to idolatry. Along with the well-known judges portrayed on this map, there were several minor judges whose battles are not recorded in the Bible: Abimelech, Tola, Jair, Ibzan, Elon, and Abdon.

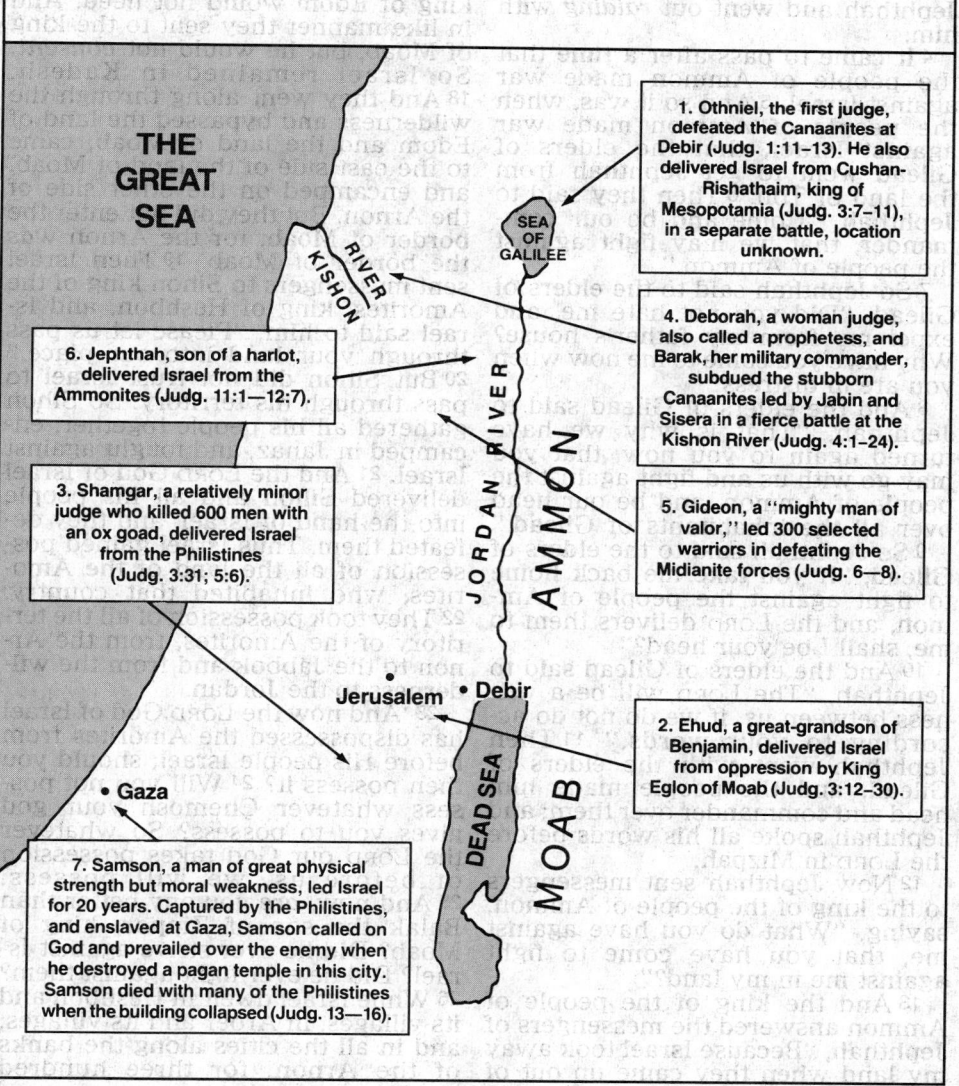

THE GREAT SEA

1. Othniel, the first judge, defeated the Canaanites at Debir (Judg. 1:11–13). He also delivered Israel from Cushan-Rishathaim, king of Mesopotamia (Judg. 3:7–11), in a separate battle, location unknown.

4. Deborah, a woman judge, also called a prophetess, and Barak, her military commander, subdued the stubborn Canaanites led by Jabin and Sisera in a fierce battle at the Kishon River (Judg. 4:1–24).

6. Jephthah, son of a harlot, delivered Israel from the Ammonites (Judg. 11:1–12:7).

3. Shamgar, a relatively minor judge who killed 600 men with an ox goad, delivered Israel from the Philistines (Judg. 3:31; 5:6).

5. Gideon, a "mighty man of valor," led 300 selected warriors in defeating the Midianite forces (Judg. 6—8).

2. Ehud, a great-grandson of Benjamin, delivered Israel from oppression by King Eglon of Moab (Judg. 3:12–30).

7. Samson, a man of great physical strength but moral weakness, led Israel for 20 years. Captured by the Philistines, and enslaved at Gaza, Samson called on God and prevailed over the enemy when he destroyed a pagan temple in this city. Samson died with many of the Philistines when the building collapsed (Judg. 13—16).

KISHON RIVER

SEA OF GALILEE

JORDAN RIVER

AMMON

Jerusalem • Debir

• Gaza

DEAD SEA

MOAB

fight against the people of Ammon? He shall be head over all the inhabitants of Gilead."

11 Now Jephthah the Gileadite was a mighty man of valor, but he *was* the son of a harlot; and Gilead begot Jephthah. 2 Gilead's wife bore sons; and when his wife's sons grew up, they drove Jephthah out, and said to him, "You shall have no inheritance in our father's house, for you *are* the son of another woman." 3 Then Jephthah fled from his brothers and dwelt in the land of Tob; and worthless men banded together with Jephthah and went out *raiding* with him.

4 It came to pass after a time that the people of Ammon made war against Israel. 5 And so it was, when the people of Ammon made war against Israel, that the elders of Gilead went to get Jephthah from the land of Tob. 6 Then they said to Jephthah, "Come and be our commander, that we may fight against the people of Ammon."

7 So Jephthah said to the elders of Gilead, "Did you not hate me, and expel me from my father's house? Why have you come to me now when you are in distress?"

8 And the elders of Gilead said to Jephthah, "That is why we have turned again to you now, that you may go with us and fight against the people of Ammon, and be our head over all the inhabitants of Gilead."

9 So Jephthah said to the elders of Gilead, "If you take me back home to fight against the people of Ammon, and the LORD delivers them to me, shall I be your head?"

10 And the elders of Gilead said to Jephthah, "The LORD will be a witness between us, if we do not do according to your words." 11 Then Jephthah went with the elders of Gilead, and the people made him head and commander over them; and Jephthah spoke all his words before the LORD in Mizpah.

12 Now Jephthah sent messengers to the king of the people of Ammon, saying, "What do you have against me, that you have come to fight against me in my land?"

13 And the king of the people of Ammon answered the messengers of Jephthah, "Because Israel took away my land when they came up out of Egypt, from the Arnon as far as the Jabbok, and to the Jordan. Now therefore, restore those *lands* peaceably."

14 So Jephthah again sent messengers to the king of the people of Ammon, 15 and said to him, "Thus says Jephthah: 'Israel did not take away the land of Moab, nor the land of the people of Ammon; 16 for when Israel came up from Egypt, they walked through the wilderness as far as the Red Sea and came to Kadesh. 17 Then Israel sent messengers to the king of Edom, saying, "Please let me pass through your land." But the king of Edom would not heed. And in like manner they sent to the king of Moab, but he would not *consent*. So Israel remained in Kadesh. 18 And they went along through the wilderness and bypassed the land of Edom and the land of Moab, came to the east side of the land of Moab, and encamped on the other side of the Arnon. But they did not enter the border of Moab, for the Arnon *was* the border of Moab. 19 Then Israel sent messengers to Sihon king of the Amorites, king of Heshbon; and Israel said to him, "Please let us pass through your land into our place." 20 But Sihon did not trust Israel to pass through his territory. So Sihon gathered all his people together, encamped in Jahaz, and fought against Israel. 21 And the LORD God of Israel delivered Sihon and all his people into the hand of Israel, and they defeated them. Thus Israel gained possession of all the land of the Amorites, who inhabited that country. 22 They took possession of all the territory of the Amorites, from the Arnon to the Jabbok and from the wilderness to the Jordan.

23 'And now the LORD God of Israel has dispossessed the Amorites from before His people Israel; should you then possess it? 24 Will you not possess whatever Chemosh your god gives you to possess? So whatever the LORD our God takes possession of before us, we will possess. 25 And now, *are* you any better than Balak the son of Zippor, king of Moab? Did he ever strive against Israel? Did he ever fight against them? 26 While Israel dwelt in Heshbon and its villages, in Aroer and its villages, and in all the cities along the banks of the Arnon, for three hundred

years, why did you not recover *them* within that time? 27 Therefore I have not sinned against you, but you wronged me by fighting against me. May the LORD, the Judge, render judgment this day between the children of Israel and the people of Ammon.'" 28 However, the king of the people of Ammon did not heed the words which Jephthah sent him.

29 Then the Spirit of the LORD came upon Jephthah, and he passed through Gilead and Manasseh, and passed through Mizpah of Gilead; and from Mizpah of Gilead he advanced *toward* the people of Ammon. 30 And Jephthah made a vow to the LORD, and said, "If You will indeed deliver the people of Ammon into my hands, 31 then it will be that whatever comes out of the doors of my house to meet me, when I return in peace from the people of Ammon, shall surely be the LORD's, and I will offer it up as a burnt offering."

32 So Jephthah advanced toward the people of Ammon to fight against them, and the LORD delivered them into his hands. 33 And he defeated them from Aroer as far as Minnith—twenty cities—and to Abel Keramim,[a] with a very great slaughter. Thus the people of Ammon were subdued before the children of Israel.

34 When Jephthah came to his house at Mizpah, there was his daughter, coming out to meet him with timbrels and dancing; and she *was his* only child. Besides her he had neither son nor daughter. 35 And it came to pass, when he saw her, that he tore his clothes, and said, "Alas, my daughter! You have brought me very low! You are among those who trouble me! For I have given my word to the LORD, and I cannot go back on it."

36 So she said to him, "My father, *if* you have given your word to the LORD, do to me according to what has gone out of your mouth, because the LORD has avenged you of your enemies, the people of Ammon."
37 Then she said to her father, "Let this thing be done for me: let me alone for two months, that I may go and wander on the mountains and bewail my virginity, my friends and I."
38 So he said, "Go." And he sent her away *for* two months; and she went with her friends, and bewailed her virginity on the mountains. 39 And it was so at the end of two months that she returned to her father, and he carried out his vow with her which he had vowed. She knew no man.

And it became a custom in Israel 40 *that* the daughters of Israel went four days each year to lament the daughter of Jephthah the Gileadite.

12 Then the men of Ephraim gathered together, crossed over toward Zaphon, and said to Jephthah, "Why did you cross over to fight against the people of Ammon, and did not call us to go with you? We will burn your house down on you with fire!"

2 And Jephthah said to them, "My people and I were in a great struggle with the people of Ammon; and when I called you, you did not deliver me out of their hands. 3 So when I saw that you would not deliver *me,* I took my life in my hands and crossed over against the people of Ammon; and the LORD delivered them into my hand. Why then have you come up to me this day to fight against me?"
4 Now Jephthah gathered together all the men of Gilead and fought against Ephraim. And the men of Gilead defeated Ephraim, because they said, "You Gileadites *are* fugitives of Ephraim among the Ephraimites *and* among the Manassites." 5 The Gileadites seized the fords of the Jordan before the Ephraimites *arrived.* And when *any* Ephraimite who escaped said, "Let me cross over," the men of Gilead would say to him, "*Are* you an Ephraimite?" If he said, "No," 6 then they would say to him, "Then say, 'Shibboleth'!" And he would say, "Sibboleth," for he could not pronounce *it* right. Then they would take him and kill him at the fords of the Jordan. There fell at that time forty-two thousand Ephraimites.

7 And Jephthah judged Israel six years. Then Jephthah the Gileadite died and was buried among the cities of Gilead.

8 After him, Ibzan of Bethlehem judged Israel. 9 He had thirty sons. And he gave away thirty daughters in marriage, and brought in thirty

11:33 ªLiterally *Plain of Vineyards*

daughters from elsewhere for his sons. He judged Israel seven years. 10 Then Ibzan died and was buried at Bethlehem.

11 After him, Elon the Zebulunite judged Israel. He judged Israel ten years. 12 And Elon the Zebulunite died and was buried at Aijalon in the country of Zebulun.

13 After him, Abdon the son of Hillel the Pirathonite judged Israel. 14 He had forty sons and thirty grandsons, who rode on seventy young donkeys. He judged Israel eight years. 15 Then Abdon the son of Hillel the Pirathonite died and was buried in Pirathon in the land of Ephraim, in the mountains of the Amalekites.

13

Again the children of Israel did evil in the sight of the LORD, and the LORD delivered them into the hand of the Philistines for forty years.

2 Now there was a certain man from Zorah, of the family of the Danites, whose name was Manoah; and his wife was barren and had no children. 3 And the Angel of the LORD appeared to the woman and said to her, "Indeed now, you are barren and have borne no children, but you shall conceive and bear a son. 4 Now therefore, please be careful not to drink wine or similar drink, and not to eat anything unclean. 5 For behold, you shall conceive and bear a son. And no razor shall come upon his head, for the child shall be a Nazirite to God from the womb; and he shall begin to deliver Israel out of the hand of the Philistines."

6 So the woman came and told her husband, saying, "A Man of God came to me, and His countenance was like the countenance of the Angel of God, very awesome; but I did not ask Him where He was from, and He did not tell me His name. 7 And He said to me, 'Behold, you shall conceive and bear a son. Now drink no wine or similar drink, nor eat anything unclean, for the child shall be a Nazirite to God from the womb to the day of his death.' "

8 Then Manoah prayed to the LORD, and said, "O my Lord, please let the Man of God whom You sent come to us again and teach us what we shall do for the child who will be born."

9 And God listened to the voice of Manoah, and the Angel of God came to the woman again as she was sitting in the field; but Manoah her husband was not with her. 10 Then the woman ran in haste and told her husband, and said to him, "Look, the Man who came to me the other day has just now appeared to me!"

11 So Manoah arose and followed his wife. When he came to the Man, he said to Him, "Are You the Man who spoke to this woman?"

And He said, "I am."

12 Manoah said, "Now let Your words come to pass! What will be the boy's rule of life, and his work?"

13 So the Angel of the LORD said to Manoah, "Of all that I said to the woman let her be careful. 14 She may not eat anything that comes from the vine, nor may she drink wine or similar drink, nor eat anything unclean. All that I commanded her let her observe."

15 Then Manoah said to the Angel of the LORD, "Please let us detain You, and we will prepare a young goat for You."

16 And the Angel of the LORD said to Manoah, "Though you detain Me, I will not eat your food. But if you offer a burnt offering, you must offer it to the LORD." (For Manoah did not know He was the Angel of the LORD.)

17 Then Manoah said to the Angel of the LORD, "What is Your name, that when Your words come to pass we may honor You?"

18 And the Angel of the LORD said to him, "Why do you ask My name, seeing it is wonderful?"

19 So Manoah took the young goat with the grain offering, and offered it upon the rock to the LORD. And He did a wondrous thing while Manoah and his wife looked on— 20 it happened as the flame went up toward heaven from the altar—the Angel of the LORD ascended in the flame of the altar! When Manoah and his wife saw this, they fell on their faces to the ground. 21 When the Angel of the LORD appeared no more to Manoah and his wife, then Manoah knew that He was the Angel of the LORD.

22 And Manoah said to his wife, "We shall surely die, because we have seen God!"

23 But his wife said to him, "If the LORD had desired to kill us, He would not have accepted a burnt offering

and a grain offering from our hands, nor would He have shown us all these *things,* nor would He have told us *such things* as these at this time."

24 So the woman bore a son and called his name Samson; and the child grew, and the LORD blessed him. 25 And the Spirit of the LORD began to move upon him at Mahaneh Dan[a] between Zorah and Eshtaol.

14 Now Samson went down to Timnah, and saw a woman in Timnah of the daughters of the Philistines. 2 So he went up and told his father and mother, saying, "I have seen a woman in Timnah of the daughters of the Philistines; now therefore, get her for me as a wife."

3 Then his father and mother said to him, "*Is there* no woman among the daughters of your brethren, or among all my people, that you must go and get a wife from the uncircumcised Philistines?"

And Samson said to his father, "Get her for me, for she pleases me well."

4 But his father and mother did not know that it was of the LORD—that He was seeking an occasion to move against the Philistines. For at that time the Philistines had dominion over Israel.

5 So Samson went down to Timnah with his father and mother, and came to the vineyards of Timnah.

Now *to his* surprise, a young lion *came* roaring against him. 6 And the Spirit of the LORD came mightily upon him, and he tore the lion apart as one would have torn apart a young goat, though *he had* nothing in his hand. But he did not tell his father or his mother what he had done.

7 Then he went down and talked with the woman; and she pleased Samson well. 8 After some time, when he returned to get her, he turned aside to see the carcass of the lion. And behold, a swarm of bees and honey *were* in the carcass of the lion. 9 He took some of it in his hands and went along, eating. When he came to his father and mother, he gave *some* to them, and they also ate. But he did not tell them that he had taken the honey out of the carcass of the lion.

10 So his father went down to the woman. And Samson gave a feast there, for young men used to do so. 11 And it happened, when they saw him, that they brought thirty companions to be with him.

12 Then Samson said to them, "Let me pose a riddle to you. If you can correctly solve and explain it to me within the seven days of the feast, then I will give you thirty linen garments and thirty changes of clothing. 13 But if you cannot explain *it* to me, then you shall give me thirty linen garments and thirty changes of clothing."

And they said to him, "Pose your riddle, that we may hear it."

14 So he said to them:

"Out of the eater came
    something to eat,
And out of the strong came
    something sweet."

Now for three days they could not explain the riddle.

15 But it came to pass on the seventh[a] day that they said to Samson's wife, "Entice your husband, that he may explain the riddle to us, or else we will burn you and your father's house with fire. Have you invited us in order to take what is ours? *Is that not so?*"

16 Then Samson's wife wept on him, and said, "You only hate me! You do not love me! You have posed a riddle to the sons of my people, but you have not explained *it* to me."

And he said to her, "Look, I have not explained *it* to my father or my mother; so should I explain *it* to you?" 17 Now she had wept on him the seven days while their feast lasted. And it happened on the seventh day that he told her, because she pressed him so much. Then she explained the riddle to the sons of her people. 18 So the men of the city said to him on the seventh day before the sun went down:

"What *is* sweeter than honey?
    And what *is* stronger than a
    lion?"

13:25 [a]Literally *Camp of Dan* (compare 18:12)   14:15 [a]Following Masoretic Text, Targum, and Vulgate; Septuagint and Syriac read *fourth.*

And he said to them:

> "If you had not plowed with my
>   heifer,
>   You would not have solved my
>   riddle!"

19 Then the Spirit of the LORD came upon him mightily, and he went down to Ashkelon and killed thirty of their men, took their apparel, and gave the changes *of clothing* to those who had explained the riddle. So his anger was aroused, and he went back up to his father's house. 20 And Samson's wife was *given* to his companion, who had been his best man.

15 After a while, in the time of wheat harvest, it happened that Samson visited his wife with a young goat. And he said, "Let me go in to my wife, into *her* room." But her father would not permit him to go in.
2 Her father said, "I really thought that you thoroughly hated her; therefore I gave her to your companion. *Is* not her younger sister better than she? Please, take her instead."
3 And Samson said to them, "This time I shall be blameless regarding the Philistines if I harm them!" 4 Then Samson went and caught three hundred foxes; and he took torches, turned *the foxes* tail to tail, and put a torch between each pair of tails. 5 When he had set the torches on fire, he let *the foxes* go into the standing grain of the Philistines, and burned up both the shocks and the standing grain, as well as the vineyards *and* olive groves.
6 Then the Philistines said, "Who has done this?"
And they answered, "Samson, the son-in-law of the Timnite, because he has taken his wife and given her to his companion." So the Philistines came up and burned her and her father with fire.
7 Samson said to them, "Since you would do a thing like this, I will surely take revenge on you, and after that I will cease." 8 So he attacked them hip and thigh with a great slaughter; then he went down and dwelt in the cleft of the rock of Etam.
9 Now the Philistines went up, encamped in Judah, and deployed themselves against Lehi. 10 And the men of Judah said, "Why have you come up against us?"
So they answered, "We have come up to arrest Samson, to do to him as he has done to us."
11 Then three thousand men of Judah went down to the cleft of the rock of Etam, and said to Samson, "Do you not know that the Philistines rule over us? What *is* this you have done to us?"
And he said to them, "As they did to me, so I have done to them."
12 But they said to him, "We have come down to arrest you, that we may deliver you into the hand of the Philistines."
Then Samson said to them, "Swear to me that you will not kill me yourselves."
13 So they spoke to him, saying, "No, but we will tie you securely and deliver you into their hand; but we will surely not kill you." And they bound him with two new ropes and brought him up from the rock.
14 When he came to Lehi, the Philistines came shouting against him. Then the Spirit of the LORD came mightily upon him; and the ropes that *were* on his arms became like flax that is burned with fire, and his bonds broke loose from his hands. 15 He found a fresh jawbone of a donkey, reached out his hand and took it, and killed a thousand men with it. 16 Then Samson said:

> "With the jawbone of a donkey,
>   Heaps upon heaps,
>   With the jawbone of a donkey
>   I have slain a thousand men!"

17 And so it was, when he had finished speaking, that he threw the jawbone from his hand, and called that place Ramath Lehi.[a]
18 Then he became very thirsty; so he cried out to the LORD and said, "You have given this great deliverance by the hand of Your servant; and now shall I die of thirst and fall into the hand of the uncircumcised?" 19 So God split the hollow place that *is* in Lehi,[a] and water came out, and he drank; and his spirit returned, and he revived. Therefore he called its name En Hakkore,[b] which is in Lehi

15:17 [a]Literally *Jawbone Height*   15:19 [a]Literally *Jawbone* (compare verse 14)   [b]Literally *Spring of the Caller* to this day. 20 And he judged Israel twenty years in the days of the Philistines.

16 Now Samson went to Gaza and saw a harlot there, and went in to her. 2 *When* the Gazites *were told,* "Samson has come here!" they surrounded *the place* and lay in wait for him all night at the gate of the city. They were quiet all night, saying, "In the morning, when it is daylight, we will kill him." 3 And Samson lay *low* till midnight; then he arose at midnight, took hold of the doors of the gate of the city and the two gateposts, pulled them up, bar and all, put *them* on his shoulders, and carried them to the top of the hill that faces Hebron.

4 Afterward it happened that he loved a woman in the Valley of Sorek, whose name *was* Delilah. 5 And the lords of the Philistines came up to her and said to her, "Entice him, and find out where his great strength *lies,* and by what *means* we may overpower him, that we may bind him to afflict him; and every one of us will give you eleven hundred *pieces* of silver."

6 So Delilah said to Samson, "Please tell me where your great strength *lies,* and with what you may be bound to afflict you."

7 And Samson said to her, "If they bind me with seven fresh bowstrings, not yet dried, then I shall become weak, and be like any *other* man."

8 So the lords of the Philistines brought up to her seven fresh bowstrings, not yet dried, and she bound him with them. 9 Now *men were* lying in wait, staying with her in the room. And she said to him, "The Philistines *are* upon you, Samson!" But he broke the bowstrings as a strand of yarn breaks when it touches fire. So the secret of his strength was not known.

10 Then Delilah said to Samson, "Look, you have mocked me and told me lies. Now, please tell me what you may be bound with."

11 So he said to her, "If they bind me securely with new ropes that have never been used, then I shall become weak, and be like any *other* man."

12 Therefore Delilah took new ropes and bound him with them, and said to him, "The Philistines *are* upon you, Samson!" And *men were* lying in wait, staying in the room. But he broke them off his arms like a thread.

13 Delilah said to Samson, "Until now you have mocked me and told me lies. Tell me what you may be bound with."

And he said to her, "If you weave the seven locks of my head into the web of the loom"—

14 So she wove *it* tightly with the batten of the loom, and said to him, "The Philistines *are* upon you, Samson!" But he awoke from his sleep, and pulled out the batten and the web from the loom.

15 Then she said to him, "How can you say, 'I love you,' when your heart *is* not with me? You have mocked me these three times, and have not told me where your great strength *lies.*" 16 And it came to pass, when she pestered him daily with her words and pressed him, *so* that his soul was vexed to death, 17 that he told her all his heart, and said to her, "No razor has ever come upon my head, for I *have been* a Nazirite to God from my mother's womb. If I am shaven, then my strength will leave me, and I shall become weak, and be like any *other* man."

18 When Delilah saw that he had told her all his heart, she sent and called for the lords of the Philistines, saying, "Come up once more, for he has told me all his heart." So the lords of the Philistines came up to her and brought the money in their hand. 19 Then she lulled him to sleep on her knees, and called for a man and had him shave off the seven locks of his head. Then she began to torment him,^a and his strength left him. 20 And she said, "The Philistines *are* upon you, Samson!" So he awoke from his sleep, and said, "I will go out as before, at other times, and shake myself free!" But he did not know that the LORD had departed from him.

21 Then the Philistines took him and put out his eyes, and brought him down to Gaza. They bound him with bronze fetters, and he became a grinder in the prison. 22 However, the hair of his head began to grow again after it had been shaven.

16:19 ^aFollowing Masoretic Text, Targum, and Vulgate; Septuagint reads *he began to be weak.*

23 Now the lords of the Philistines gathered together to offer a great sacrifice to Dagon their god, and to rejoice. And they said:

"Our god has delivered into our
    hands
Samson our enemy!"

24 When the people saw him, they praised their god; for they said:

"Our god has delivered into our
    hands our enemy,
The destroyer of our land,
And the one who multiplied our
    dead."

25 So it happened, when their hearts were merry, that they said, "Call for Samson, that he may perform for us." So they called for Samson from the prison, and he performed for them. And they stationed him between the pillars. 26 Then Samson said to the lad who held him by the hand, "Let me feel the pillars which support the temple, so that I can lean on them." 27 Now the temple was full of men and women. All the lords of the Philistines *were* there—about three thousand men and women on the roof watching while Samson performed.

28 Then Samson called to the LORD, saying, "O Lord GOD, remember me, I pray! Strengthen me, I pray, just this once, O God, that I may with one *blow* take vengeance on the Philistines for my two eyes!" 29 And Samson took hold of the two middle pillars which supported the temple, and he braced himself against them, one on his right and the other on his left. 30 Then Samson said, "Let me die with the Philistines!" And he pushed with *all his* might, and the temple fell on the lords and all the people who *were* in it. So the dead that he killed at his death were more than he had killed in his life.

31 And his brothers and all his father's household came down and took him, and brought *him* up and buried him between Zorah and Eshtaol in the tomb of his father Manoah. He had judged Israel twenty years.

17 Now there was a man from the mountains of Ephraim, whose name *was* Micah. 2 And he said to his mother, "The eleven hundred *shekels* of silver that were taken from you, and on which you put a curse, even saying it in my ears—here *is* the silver with me; I took it."

And his mother said, "*May you be* blessed by the LORD, my son!" 3 So when he had returned the eleven hundred *shekels* of silver to his mother, his mother said, "I had wholly dedicated the silver from my hand to the LORD for my son, to make a carved image and a molded image; now therefore, I will return it to you." 4 Thus he returned the silver to his mother. Then his mother took two hundred *shekels* of silver and gave them to the silversmith, and he made it into a carved image and a molded image; and they were in the house of Micah.

5 The man Micah had a shrine, and made an ephod and household idols;*a* and he consecrated one of his sons, who became his priest. 6 In those days *there was* no king in Israel; everyone did *what was* right in his own eyes.

7 Now there was a young man from Bethlehem in Judah, of the family of Judah; he *was* a Levite, and was staying there. 8 The man departed from the city of Bethlehem in Judah to stay wherever he could find *a place*. Then he came to the mountains of Ephraim, to the house of Micah, as he journeyed. 9 And Micah said to him, "Where do you come from?"

So he said to him, "I *am* a Levite from Bethlehem in Judah, and I am on my way to find *a place* to stay."

10 Micah said to him, "Dwell with me, and be a father and a priest to me, and I will give you ten *shekels* of silver per year, a suit of clothes, and your sustenance." So the Levite went in. 11 Then the Levite was content to dwell with the man; and the young man became like one of his sons to him. 12 So Micah consecrated the Levite, and the young man became his priest, and lived in the house of Micah. 13 Then Micah said, "Now I know that the LORD will be good to me, since I have a Levite as priest!"

18 In those days *there was* no king in Israel. And in those days the

17:5 *a*Hebrew teraphim

tribe of the Danites was seeking an inheritance for itself to dwell in; for until that day *their* inheritance among the tribes of Israel had not fallen to them. 2 So the children of Dan sent five men of their family from their territory, men of valor from Zorah and Eshtaol, to spy out the land and search it. They said to them, "Go, search the land." So they went to the mountains of Ephraim, to the house of Micah, and lodged there. 3 While they *were* at the house of Micah, they recognized the voice of the young Levite. They turned aside and said to him, "Who brought you here? What are you doing in this *place*? What do you have here?"

4 He said to them, "Thus and so Micah did for me. He has hired me, and I have become his priest."

5 So they said to him, "Please inquire of God, that we may know whether the journey on which we go will be prosperous."

6 And the priest said to them, "Go in peace. The presence of the LORD *be* with you on your way."

7 So the five men departed and went to Laish. They saw the people who *were* there, how they dwelt safely, in the manner of the Sidonians, quiet and secure. *There were* no rulers in the land who might put *them* to shame for anything. They *were* far from the Sidonians, and they had no ties with anyone.*ᵃ*

8 Then *the spies* came back to their brethren at Zorah and Eshtaol, and their brethren said to them, "What *is* your *report*?"

9 So they said, "Arise, let us go up against them. For we have seen the land, and indeed it *is* very good. *Would* you *do* nothing? Do not hesitate to go, *and* enter to possess the land. 10 When you go, you will come to a secure people and a large land. For God has given it into your hands, a place where *there is* no lack of anything that *is* on the earth."

11 And six hundred men of the family of the Danites went from there, from Zorah and Eshtaol, armed with weapons of war. 12 Then they went up and encamped in Kirjath Jearim in Judah. (Therefore they call that place Mahaneh Dan*ᵃ* to this day. There *it is*, west of Kirjath Jearim.)

13 And they passed from there to the mountains of Ephraim, and came to the house of Micah.

14 Then the five men who had gone to spy out the country of Laish answered and said to their brethren, "Do you know that there are in these houses an ephod, household idols, a carved image, and a molded image? Now therefore, consider what you should do." 15 So they turned aside there, and came to the house of the young Levite man—to the house of Micah—and greeted him. 16 The six hundred men armed with their weapons of war, who *were* of the children of Dan, stood by the entrance of the gate. 17 Then the five men who had gone to spy out the land went up. Entering there, they took the carved image, the ephod, the household idols, and the molded image. The priest stood at the entrance of the gate with the six hundred men *who were* armed with weapons of war.

18 When these went into Micah's house and took the carved image, the ephod, the household idols, and the molded image, the priest said to them, "What are you doing?"

19 And they said to him, "Be quiet, put your hand over your mouth, and come with us; be a father and a priest to us. *Is it* better for you to be a priest to the household of one man, or that you be a priest to a tribe and a family in Israel?" 20 So the priest's heart was glad; and he took the ephod, the household idols, and the carved image, and took his place among the people.

21 Then they turned and departed, and put the little ones, the livestock, and the goods in front of them. 22 When they were a good way from the house of Micah, the men who *were* in the houses near Micah's house gathered together and overtook the children of Dan. 23 And they called out to the children of Dan. So they turned around and said to Micah, "What ails you, that you have gathered such a company?"

24 So he said, "You have taken away my gods which I made, and the priest, and you have gone away. Now what more do I have? How can you say to me, 'What ails you?'"

25 And the children of Dan said to

18:7 *ᵃ*Following Masoretic Text, Targum, and Vulgate; Septuagint reads *with Syria.*   18:12 *ᵃ*Literally *Camp of Dan* him, "Do not let your voice be heard among us, lest angry men fall upon you, and you lose your life, with the lives of your household!" 26 Then the children of Dan went their way. And when Micah saw that they *were* too strong for him, he turned and went back to his house.

27 So they took *the things* Micah had made, and the priest who had belonged to him, and went to Laish, to a people quiet and secure; and they struck them with the edge of the sword and burned the city with fire. 28 *There was* no deliverer, because it *was* far from Sidon, and they had no ties with anyone. It was in the valley that belongs to Beth Rehob. So they rebuilt the city and dwelt there. 29 And they called the name of the city Dan, after the name of Dan their father, who was born to Israel. However, the name of the city formerly *was* Laish.

30 Then the children of Dan set up for themselves the carved image; and Jonathan the son of Gershom, the son of Manasseh,*a* and his sons were priests to the tribe of Dan until the day of the captivity of the land. 31 So they set up for themselves Micah's carved image which he made, all the time that the house of God was in Shiloh.

19 And it came to pass in those days, when *there was* no king in Israel, that there was a certain Levite staying in the remote mountains of Ephraim. He took for himself a concubine from Bethlehem in Judah. 2 But his concubine played the harlot against him, and went away from him to her father's house at Bethlehem in Judah, and was there four whole months. 3 Then her husband arose and went after her, to speak kindly to her *and* bring her back, having his servant and a couple of donkeys with him. So she brought him into her father's house; and when the father of the young woman saw him, he was glad to meet him. 4 Now his father-in-law, the young woman's father, detained him; and he stayed with him three days. So they ate and drank and lodged there.

5 Then it came to pass on the fourth day that they arose early in the morning, and he stood to depart; but the young woman's father said to his son-in-law, "Refresh your heart with a morsel of bread, and afterward go your way."

6 So they sat down, and the two of them ate and drank together. Then the young woman's father said to the man, "Please be content to stay all night, and let your heart be merry." 7 And when the man stood to depart, his father-in-law urged him; so he lodged there again. 8 Then he arose early in the morning on the fifth day to depart, but the young woman's father said, "Please refresh your heart." So they delayed until afternoon; and both of them ate.

9 And when the man stood to depart—he and his concubine and his servant—his father-in-law, the young woman's father, said to him, "Look, the day is now drawing toward evening; please spend the night. See, the day is coming to an end; lodge here, that your heart may be merry. Tomorrow go your way early, so that you may get home."

10 However, the man was not willing to spend that night; so he rose and departed, and came to opposite Jebus (that *is,* Jerusalem). With him were the two saddled donkeys; his concubine *was* also with him. 11 They *were* near Jebus, and the day was far spent; and the servant said to his master, "Come, please, and let us turn aside into this city of the Jebusites and lodge in it."

12 But his master said to him, "We will not turn aside here into a city of foreigners, who *are* not of the children of Israel; we will go on to Gibeah." 13 So he said to his servant, "Come, let us draw near to one of these places, and spend the night in Gibeah or in Ramah." 14 And they passed by and went their way; and the sun went down on them near Gibeah, which belongs to Benjamin. 15 They turned aside there to go in to lodge in Gibeah. And when he went in, he sat down in the open square of the city, for no one would take them into *his* house to spend the night.

16 Just then an old man came in from his work in the field at evening, who also *was* from the mountains of Ephraim; he was staying in Gibeah, whereas the men of the place *were*

18:30 *a*Septuagint and Vulgate read *Moses.*

Benjamites. 17 And when he raised his eyes, he saw the traveler in the open square of the city; and the old man said, "Where are you going, and where do you come from?"

18 So he said to him, "We *are* passing from Bethlehem in Judah toward the remote mountains of Ephraim; I *am* from there. I went to Bethlehem in Judah; *now* I am going to the house of the LORD. But there *is* no one who will take me into his house, 19 although we have both straw and fodder for our donkeys, and bread and wine for myself, for your female servant, and for the young man *who is* with your servant; *there is* no lack of anything."

20 And the old man said, "Peace *be* with you! However, *let* all your needs *be* my responsibility; only do not spend the night in the open square." 21 So he brought him into his house, and gave fodder to the donkeys. And they washed their feet, and ate and drank.

22 As they were enjoying themselves, suddenly certain men of the city, perverted men,ᵃ surrounded the house *and* beat on the door. They spoke to the master of the house, the old man, saying, "Bring out the man who came to your house, that we may know him *carnally!*"

23 But the man, the master of the house, went out to them and said to them, "No, my brethren! I beg you, do not act *so* wickedly! Seeing this man has come into my house, do not commit this outrage. 24 Look, *here is* my virgin daughter and *the man's*ᵃ concubine; let me bring them out now. Humble them, and do with them as you please; but to this man do not do such a vile thing!" 25 But the men would not heed him. So the man took his concubine and brought *her* out to them. And they knew her and abused her all night until morning; and when the day began to break, they let her go.

26 Then the woman came as the day was dawning, and fell down at the door of the man's house where her master *was*, till it was light.

27 When her master arose in the morning, and opened the doors of the house and went out to go his way, there was his concubine, fallen *at* the door of the house with her hands on the threshold. 28 And he said to her, "Get up and let us be going." But there was no answer. So the man lifted her onto the donkey; and the man got up and went to his place.

29 When he entered his house he took a knife, laid hold of his concubine, and divided her into twelve pieces, limb by limb,ᵃ and sent her throughout all the territory of Israel. 30 And so it was that all who saw it said, "No such deed has been done or seen from the day that the children of Israel came up from the land of Egypt until this day. Consider it, confer, and speak up!"

20 So all the children of Israel came out, from Dan to Beersheba, as well as from the land of Gilead, and the congregation gathered together as one man before the LORD at Mizpah. 2 And the leaders of all the people, all the tribes of Israel, presented themselves in the assembly of the people of God, four hundred thousand foot soldiers who drew the sword. 3 (Now the children of Benjamin heard that the children of Israel had gone up to Mizpah.)

Then the children of Israel said, "Tell *us*, how did this wicked deed happen?"

4 So the Levite, the husband of the woman who was murdered, answered and said, "My concubine and I went into Gibeah, which belongs to Benjamin, to spend the night. 5 And the men of Gibeah rose against me, and surrounded the house at night because of me. They intended to kill me, but instead they ravished my concubine so that she died. 6 So I took hold of my concubine, cut her in pieces, and sent her throughout all the territory of the inheritance of Israel, because they committed lewdness and outrage in Israel. 7 "Look! All of you *are* children of Israel; give your advice and counsel here and now!"

8 So all the people arose as one man, saying, "None *of us* will go to his tent, nor will any turn back to his house; 9 but now this *is* the thing which we will do to Gibeah: *We will go up* against it by lot. 10 We will take ten men out of *every* hundred throughout all the tribes of Israel, a

19:22 ᵃLiterally *sons of Belial*   19:24 ᵃLiterally *his*   19:29 ᵃLiterally *with her bones* hundred out of *every* thousand, and a thousand out of *every* ten thousand, to make provisions for the people, that when they come to Gibeah in Benjamin, they may repay all the vileness that they have done in Israel." 11 So all the men of Israel were gathered against the city, united together as one man.

12 Then the tribes of Israel sent men through all the tribe of Benjamin, saying, "What *is* this wickedness that has occurred among you? 13 Now therefore, deliver up the men, the perverted men^a who *are* in Gibeah, that we may put them to death and remove the evil from Israel!" But the children of Benjamin would not listen to the voice of their brethren, the children of Israel. 14 Instead, the children of Benjamin gathered together from their cities to Gibeah, to go to battle against the children of Israel. 15 And from their cities at that time the children of Benjamin numbered twenty-six thousand men who drew the sword, besides the inhabitants of Gibeah, who numbered seven hundred select men. 16 Among all this people *were* seven hundred select men *who were* left-handed; every one could sling a stone at a hair's *breadth* and not miss. 17 Now besides Benjamin, the men of Israel numbered four hundred thousand men who drew the sword; all of these *were* men of war.

18 Then the children of Israel arose and went up to the house of God^a to inquire of God. They said, "Which of us shall go up first to battle against the children of Benjamin?"

The LORD said, "Judah first!"

19 So the children of Israel rose in the morning and encamped against Gibeah. 20 And the men of Israel went out to battle against Benjamin, and the men of Israel put themselves in battle array to fight against them at Gibeah. 21 Then the children of Benjamin came out of Gibeah, and on that day cut down to the ground twenty-two thousand men of the Israelites. 22 And the people, that is, the men of Israel, encouraged themselves and again formed the battle line at the place where they had put themselves in array on the first day. 23 Then the children of Israel went up and wept before the LORD until eve-

ning, and asked counsel of the LORD, saying, "Shall I again draw near for battle against the children of my brother Benjamin?"

And the LORD said, "Go up against him."

24 So the children of Israel approached the children of Benjamin on the second day. 25 And Benjamin went out against them from Gibeah on the second day, and cut down to the ground eighteen thousand more of the children of Israel; all these drew the sword.

26 Then all the children of Israel, that is, all the people, went up and came to the house of God^a and wept. They sat there before the LORD and fasted that day until evening; and they offered burnt offerings and peace offerings before the LORD. 27 So the children of Israel inquired of the LORD (the ark of the covenant of God *was* there in those days, 28 and Phinehas the son of Eleazar, the son of Aaron, stood before it in those days), saying, "Shall I yet again go out to battle against the children of my brother Benjamin, or shall I cease?"

And the LORD said, "Go up, for tomorrow I will deliver them into your hand."

29 Then Israel set men in ambush all around Gibeah. 30 And the children of Israel went up against the children of Benjamin on the third day, and put themselves in battle array against Gibeah as at the other times. 31 So the children of Benjamin went out against the people, *and* were drawn away from the city. They began to strike down *and* kill some of the people, as at the other times, in the highways (one of which goes up to Bethel and the other to Gibeah) and in the field, about thirty men of Israel. 32 And the children of Benjamin said, "They *are* defeated before us, as at first."

But the children of Israel said, "Let us flee and draw them away from the city to the highways." 33 So all the men of Israel rose from their place and put themselves in battle array at Baal Tamar. Then Israel's men in ambush burst forth from their position in the plain of Geba. 34 And ten thousand select men from all Israel came against Gibeah, and the battle was

20:13 ^aLiterally *sons of Belial*   20:18 ^aHebrew *Bethel*   20:26 ^aHebrew *Bethel* fierce. But *the Benjamites*[a] did not know that disaster *was* upon them. 35 The LORD defeated Benjamin before Israel. And the children of Israel destroyed that day twenty-five thousand one hundred Benjamites; all these drew the sword.

36 So the children of Benjamin saw that they were defeated. The men of Israel had given ground to the Benjamites, because they relied on the men in ambush whom they had set against Gibeah. 37 And the men in ambush quickly rushed upon Gibeah; the men in ambush spread out and struck the whole city with the edge of the sword. 38 Now the appointed signal between the men of Israel and the men in ambush was that they would make a great cloud of smoke rise up from the city, 39 whereupon the men of Israel would turn in battle. Now Benjamin had begun to strike *and* kill about thirty of the men of Israel. For they said, "Surely they are defeated before us, as *in* the first battle." 40 But when the cloud began to rise from the city in a column of smoke, the Benjamites looked behind them, and there was the whole city going up *in smoke* to heaven. 41 And when the men of Israel turned back, the men of Benjamin panicked, for they saw that disaster had come upon them. 42 Therefore they turned *their backs* before the men of Israel in the direction of the wilderness; but the battle overtook them, and whoever *came* out of the cities they destroyed in their midst. 43 They surrounded the Benjamites, chased them, *and* easily trampled them down as far as the front of Gibeah toward the east. 44 And eighteen thousand men of Benjamin fell; all these *were* men of valor. 45 Then they[a] turned and fled toward the wilderness to the rock of Rimmon; and they cut down five thousand of them on the highways. Then they pursued them relentlessly up to Gidom, and killed two thousand of them. 46 So all who fell of Benjamin that day were twenty-five thousand men who drew the sword; all these *were* men of valor.

47 But six hundred men turned and fled toward the wilderness to the rock of Rimmon, and they stayed at the rock of Rimmon for four months.

48 And the men of Israel turned back against the children of Benjamin, and struck them down with the edge of the sword—from *every* city, men and beasts, all who were found. They also set fire to all the cities they came to.

21 Now the men of Israel had sworn an oath at Mizpah, saying, "None of us shall give his daughter to Benjamin as a wife." 2 Then the people came to the house of God,[a] and remained there before God till evening. They lifted up their voices and wept bitterly, 3 and said, "O LORD God of Israel, why has this come to pass in Israel, that today there should be one tribe *missing* in Israel?"

4 So it was, on the next morning, that the people rose early and built an altar there, and offered burnt offerings and peace offerings. 5 The children of Israel said, "Who *is there* among all the tribes of Israel who did not come up with the assembly to the LORD?" For they had made a great oath concerning anyone who had not come up to the LORD at Mizpah, saying, "He shall surely be put to death." 6 And the children of Israel grieved for Benjamin their brother, and said, "One tribe is cut off from Israel today. 7 What shall we do for wives for those who remain, seeing we have sworn by the LORD that we will not give them our daughters as wives?"

8 And they said, "What one *is there* from the tribes of Israel who did not come up to Mizpah to the LORD?" And, in fact, no one had come to the camp from Jabesh Gilead to the assembly. 9 For when the people were counted, indeed, not one of the inhabitants of Jabesh Gilead *was* there. 10 So the congregation sent out there twelve thousand of their most valiant men, and commanded them, saying, "Go and strike the inhabitants of Jabesh Gilead with the edge of the sword, including the women and children. 11 And this *is* the thing that you shall do: You shall utterly destroy every male, and every woman who has known a man intimately." 12 So they found among the inhabitants of Jabesh Gilead four hundred young virgins who had not known a man intimately; and they brought

20:34 aLiterally *they*   20:45 aSeptuagint reads *the rest.*   21:2 aHebrew *Bethel* them to the camp at Shiloh, which is in the land of Canaan.

13 Then the whole congregation sent *word* to the children of Benjamin who *were* at the rock of Rimmon, and announced peace to them. 14 So Benjamin came back at that time, and they gave them the women whom they had saved alive of the women of Jabesh Gilead; and yet they had not found enough for them.

15 And the people grieved for Benjamin, because the LORD had made a void in the tribes of Israel.

16 Then the elders of the congregation said, "What shall we do for wives for those who remain, since the women of Benjamin have been destroyed?" 17 And they said, "*There must be* an inheritance for the survivors of Benjamin, that a tribe may not be destroyed from Israel. 18 However, we cannot give them wives from our daughters, for the children of Israel have sworn an oath, saying, 'Cursed *be* the one who gives a wife to Benjamin.'" 19 Then they said, "In fact, *there is* a yearly feast of the LORD in Shiloh, which *is* north of Bethel, on the east side of the highway that goes up from Bethel to Shechem, and south of Lebonah."

20 Therefore they instructed the children of Benjamin, saying, "Go, lie in wait in the vineyards, 21 and watch; and just when the daughters of Shiloh come out to perform their dances, then come out from the vineyards, and every man catch a wife for himself from the daughters of Shiloh; then go to the land of Benjamin. 22 Then it shall be, when their fathers or their brothers come to us to complain, that we will say to them, 'Be kind to them for our sakes, because we did not take a wife for any of them in the war; for *it is* not *as though* you have given the *women* to them at this time, making yourselves guilty of your oath.'"

23 And the children of Benjamin did so; they took enough wives for their number from those who danced, whom they caught. Then they went and returned to their inheritance, and they rebuilt the cities and dwelt in them. 24 So the children of Israel departed from there at that time, every man to his tribe and family; they went out from there, every man to his inheritance.

25 In those days *there was* no king in Israel; everyone did *what was* right in his own eyes.

Ruth

Overview of Ruth

R uth is the story of an exceptionally positive woman committed to trusting in God. Ruth means "friend," and she was dedicated to a rare friendship with her mother-in-law, Naomi.

Robbed by death of her husband of ten years, Ruth was left childless and in poverty. Yet nowhere in the book is there any record of self-pity. Rather, she exuded a positive, unselfish devotion to Naomi as she left her homeland of Moab and journeyed to the foreign land of Israel. Having become a worshiper of the true God of her Hebrew husband, Ruth avoided the temptation of yielding to her comfortable surroundings and returning to the worship of false gods. Knowing that God sees the end from the beginning, Ruth calmly submitted herself to God's will in a foreign setting.

> *Entreat me not to leave you,*
> *Or to turn back from following after you;*
> *For wherever you go, I will go;*
> *And wherever you lodge, I will lodge;*
> *Your people* shall be *my people,*
> *And your God, my God.*
> *Where you die, I will die,*
> *And there will I be buried.*
> *The LORD do so to me, and more also,*
> *If* anything but *death parts you and me.*
>   (Ruth 1: 16, 17)

The widowed, self-reliant Ruth faced her new circumstances by doing what she could, where she was, with what she had. Daily she gleaned in the fields of the wealthy landowner, Boaz. She stood out as a positive person who joyfully did her work unashamedly.

Boaz noticed Ruth among all others and was impressed with her diligence and beauty. In a beautiful love story, Boaz married Ruth, lifting her out of obscurity, replacing her rags with riches, and elevating her from poverty to plenty.

Ruth, a woman who withstood hard times with faith, received the blessings that she trusted God would provide. She even became the great-grandmother of King David and was in the lineage of the Messiah (Matt. 1:5).

Jesus in Ruth

Boaz, as Ruth's kinsman-redeemer, offers an important portrayal of the work of Jesus. The redeemer must be related by blood to those he saves; he must be able to pay the price of redemption; he must be willing to redeem; and he must be free himself. Jesus was the ultimate fulfillment of these qualities of the kinsman-redeemer.

Keys to Ruth

Key Word: Kinsman-Redeemer. The Hebrew word for kinsman appears thirteen times in Ruth and basically means "one who redeems." By buying back the land of Naomi, as well as marrying Ruth and fathering a son to keep the family line alive, Boaz acts as a redeemer.

Key Verses: "But Ruth said: 'Entreat me not to leave you, *Or to* turn back from following after you; For wherever you go, I will go; And wherever you lodge, I will lodge; Your people shall be my people, And your God my God. Where you die, I will die, And there will I be buried. The LORD do so to me, and more also, If *anything but* death parts you and me'" (1:16, 17).

"And now, my daughter, do not fear. I will do for you all that you request, for all the people of my town know that you *are* a virtuous woman" (3:11).

Key Chapter: Ruth 4. In twenty-two short verses, Ruth moves from widowhood and poverty to marriage and wealth. In exercising the law regulating the redemption of property and the law concerning a brother's duty to raise up children in the name of the deceased, Boaz brings a Moabite woman into the family line of David.

1 Now it came to pass, in the days when the judges ruled, that there was a famine in the land. And a certain man of Bethlehem, Judah, went to dwell in the country of Moab, he and his wife and his two sons. 2 The name of the man *was* Elimelech, the name of his wife *was* Naomi, and the names of his two sons *were* Mahlon and Chilion— Ephrathites of Bethlehem, Judah. And they went to the country of Moab and remained there. 3 Then Elimelech, Naomi's husband, died; and she was left, and her two sons. 4 Now they took wives of the women of Moab: the name of the one *was* Orpah, and the name of the other Ruth. And they dwelt there about ten years. 5 Then both Mahlon and Chilion also died; so the woman survived her two sons and her husband.

6 Then she arose with her daughters-in-law that she might return from the country of Moab, for she had heard in the country of Moab that the LORD had visited His people by giving them bread. 7 Therefore she went out from the place where she was, and her two daughters-in-law with her; and they went on the way to return to the land of Judah. 8 And Naomi said to her two daughters-in-law, "Go, return each to her

The Great Sea

The Mediterranean Sea is a large body of water in the Middle East bordered by many important nations, including Israel, Greece, Lebanon, and Italy. Its southern coastline stretches 2,200 miles from the coast of Palestine to the Straits of Gibraltar off the coast of Spain. The sea is 80 miles wide at its narrowest point between Sicily and North Africa. Many ancient civilizations grew up around this sea, using it for transportation and commerce (see map).

While the Israelites were wandering in the Wilderness, they received instructions from God about the future boundaries of the land that God had promised to Abraham and his descendants. The Mediterranean Sea was established as the western boundary of their territory (Num. 34:6).

In the Bible, the Mediterranean is also referred to as "the great sea" (Josh. 1:4), "the uttermost sea" (Deut. 11:24), and simply "the sea" (Josh. 16:8). The Romans called it *Mare Nostrum*, or "Our Sea," because of its importance to their empire in trade and commerce. In the time of Jesus and Paul, the Mediterranean was controlled by the Romans, who also used it to transport soldiers to the East to keep order in the provinces.

Perhaps the first people to exploit the trading advantages offered by the Mediterranean Sea were the Phoenicians. Through their fine port cities of Tyre and Sidon, they imported and exported goods from many nations of the ancient world. But the Israelites were never a seafaring people. Even Solomon, with all his wealth, formed an alliance with the Phoenicians under which they conducted import and export services for the Israelites (1 Kin. 9:27).

The Philistines also loved the sea. Some scholars believe they migrated to Palestine from their original home on the island of Crete, or Caphtor, in the Mediterranean. The Mediterranean is called "the sea of the Philistines" in Exodus 23:31.

The Mediterranean also played a key role in the early expansion of Christianity. Paul crossed the Mediterranean during his missionary journeys and set sail from many of its ports, including Caesarea (Acts 9:30), Seleucia (Acts 13:4), and Cenchrea (Acts 18:18). He was shipwrecked on the Mediterranean while sailing to Rome in late autumn (Acts 27).

mother's house. The LORD deal kindly with you, as you have dealt with the dead and with me. 9 The LORD grant that you may find rest, each in the house of her husband."

So she kissed them, and they lifted up their voices and wept. 10 And they said to her, "Surely we will return with you to your people."

11 But Naomi said, "Turn back, my daughters; why will you go with me? *Are* there still sons in my womb, that they may be your husbands? 12 Turn back, my daughters, go—for I am too old to have a husband. If I should say I have hope, *if* I should have a husband tonight and should also bear sons, 13 would you wait for them till they were grown? Would you restrain yourselves from having husbands? No, my daughters; for it grieves me very much for your sakes that the hand of the LORD has gone out against me!"

14 Then they lifted up their voices and wept again; and Orpah kissed her mother-in-law, but Ruth clung to her.

15 And she said, "Look, your sister-in-law has gone back to her people and to her gods; return after your sister-in-law."

16 But Ruth said:

"Entreat me not to leave you,
 Or to turn back from following
  after you;
For wherever you go, I will go;
And wherever you lodge, I will
  lodge;
Your people *shall be* my
  people,
And your God, my God.
17 Where you die, I will die,
  And there will I be buried.
  The LORD do so to me, and
   more also,
  If *anything but* death parts you
   and me."

18 When she saw that she was determined to go with her, she stopped speaking to her.

19 Now the two of them went until they came to Bethlehem. And it happened, when they had come to Bethlehem, that all the city was excited because of them; and the women said, "*Is* this Naomi?"

20 But she said to them, "Do not call me Naomi;[a] call me Mara,[b] for the Almighty has dealt very bitterly with me. 21 I went out full, and the LORD has brought me home again empty. Why do you call me Naomi, since the LORD has testified against me, and the Almighty has afflicted me?"

22 So Naomi returned, and Ruth the Moabitess her daughter-in-law with her, who returned from the country of Moab. Now they came to Bethlehem at the beginning of barley harvest.

2 There was a relative of Naomi's husband, a man of great wealth, of the family of Elimelech. His name *was* Boaz. 2 So Ruth the Moabitess said to Naomi, "Please let me go to the field, and glean heads of grain after *him* in whose sight I may find favor."

And she said to her, "Go, my daughter."

3 Then she left, and went and gleaned in the field after the reapers. And she happened to come to the part of the field *belonging* to Boaz, who *was* of the family of Elimelech.

4 Now behold, Boaz came from Bethlehem, and said to the reapers, "The LORD *be* with you!"

And they answered him, "The LORD bless you!"

5 Then Boaz said to his servant who was in charge of the reapers, "Whose young woman *is* this?"

6 So the servant who was in charge of the reapers answered and said, "It *is* the young Moabite woman who came back with Naomi from the country of Moab. 7 And she said, 'Please let me glean and gather after the reapers among the sheaves.' So she came and has continued from morning until now, though she rested a little in the house."

8 Then Boaz said to Ruth, "You will listen, my daughter, will you not? Do not go to glean in another field, nor go from here, but stay close by my young women. 9 *Let* your eyes *be* on the field which they reap, and go after them. Have I not commanded the young men not to touch you? And when you are thirsty, go to the vessels and drink from what the young men have drawn."

1:20 aLiterally *Pleasant* bLiterally *Bitter*

10 So she fell on her face, bowed down to the ground, and said to him, "Why have I found favor in your eyes, that you should take notice of me, since I *am* a foreigner?"

11 And Boaz answered and said to her, "It has been fully reported to me, all that you have done for your mother-in-law since the death of your husband, and *how* you have left your father and your mother and the land of your birth, and have come to a people whom you did not know before. 12 The LORD repay your work, and a full reward be given you by the LORD God of Israel, under whose wings you have come for refuge."

13 Then she said, "Let me find favor in your sight, my lord; for you have comforted me, and have spoken kindly to your maidservant, though I am not like one of your maidservants."

14 Now Boaz said to her at mealtime, "Come here, and eat of the bread, and dip your piece of bread in the vinegar." So she sat beside the reapers, and he passed parched *grain* to her; and she ate and was satisfied, and kept some back. 15 And when she rose up to glean, Boaz commanded his young men, saying, "Let her glean even among the sheaves, and do not reproach her. 16 Also let *grain* from the bundles fall purposely for her; leave *it* that she may glean, and do not rebuke her."

17 So she gleaned in the field until evening, and beat out what she had gleaned, and it was about an ephah of barley. 18 Then she took *it* up and went into the city, and her mother-in-law saw what she had gleaned. So she brought out and gave to her what she had kept back after she had been satisfied.

19 And her mother-in-law said to her, "Where have you gleaned today? And where did you work? Blessed be the one who took notice of you."

So she told her mother-in-law with whom she had worked, and said, "The man's name with whom I worked today *is* Boaz."

20 Then Naomi said to her daughter-in-law, "Blessed *be* he of the LORD, who has not forsaken His kindness to the living and the dead!" And Naomi said to her, "This man *is* a re-

lation of ours, one of our close relatives."

21 Ruth the Moabitess said, "He also said to me, 'You shall stay close by my young men until they have finished all my harvest.'"

22 And Naomi said to Ruth her daughter-in-law, "*It is* good, my daughter, that you go out with his young women, and that people do not meet you in any other field."

23 So she stayed close by the young women of Boaz, to glean until the end of barley harvest and wheat harvest; and she dwelt with her mother-in-law.

3 Then Naomi her mother-in-law said to her, "My daughter, shall I not seek security for you, that it may be well with you? 2 Now Boaz, whose young women you were with, *is he* not our relative? In fact, he is winnowing barley tonight at the threshing floor. 3 Therefore wash yourself and anoint yourself, put on your *best* garment and go down to the threshing floor; *but* do not make yourself known to the man until he has finished eating and drinking. 4 Then it shall be, when he lies down, that you shall notice the place where he lies; and you shall go in, uncover his feet, and lie down; and he will tell you what you should do."

5 And she said to her, "All that you say to me I will do."

6 So she went down to the threshing floor and did according to all that her mother-in-law instructed her. 7 And after Boaz had eaten and drunk, and his heart was cheerful, he went to lie down at the end of the heap of grain; and she came softly, uncovered his feet, and lay down.

8 Now it happened at midnight that the man was startled, and turned himself; and there, a woman was lying at his feet. 9 And he said, "Who *are* you?"

So she answered, "I *am* Ruth, your maidservant. Take your maidservant under your wing,*a* for you are a close relative."

10 Then he said, "Blessed *are* you of the LORD, my daughter! For you have shown more kindness at the end than at the beginning, in that you did not go after young men, whether poor or rich. 11 And now, my daugh-

3:9 *a*Or *Spread the corner of your garment over your maidservant* ter, do not fear. I will do for you all that you request, for all the people of my town know that you *are* a virtuous woman. 12 Now it is true that I *am* a close relative; however, there is a relative closer than I. 13 Stay this night, and in the morning it shall be *that* if he will perform the duty of a close relative for you—good; let him do it. But if he does not want to perform the duty for you, then I will perform the duty for you, *as* the LORD lives! Lie down until morning."

14 So she lay at his feet until morning, and she arose before one could recognize another. Then he said, "Do not let it be known that the woman came to the threshing floor." 15 Also he said, "Bring the shawl that *is* on you and hold it." And when she held it, he measured six *ephahs* of barley, and laid *it* on her. Then she*a* went into the city.

16 When she came to her mother-in-law, she said, "*Is* that you, my daughter?"

Then she told her all that the man had done for her. 17 And she said, "These six *ephahs* of barley he gave me; for he said to me, 'Do not go empty-handed to your mother-in-law.'"

18 Then she said, "Sit still, my daughter, until you know how the matter will turn out; for the man will not rest until he has concluded the matter this day."

4 Now Boaz went up to the gate and sat down there; and behold, the close relative of whom Boaz had spoken came by. So Boaz said, "Come aside, friend,*a* sit down here." So he came aside and sat down. 2 And he took ten men of the elders of the city, and said, "Sit down here." So they sat down. 3 Then he said to the close relative, "Naomi, who has come back from the country of Moab, sold the piece of land which *belonged* to our brother Elimelech. 4 And I thought to inform you, saying, 'Buy *it* back in the presence of the inhabitants and the elders of my people. If you will redeem *it*, redeem *it*; but if you*a* will not redeem *it*, *then* tell me, that I may know; for *there is* no one but you to redeem *it*, and I *am* next after you.'"

And he said, "I will redeem *it*."

5 Then Boaz said, "On the day you buy the field from the hand of Naomi, you must also buy *it* from Ruth the Moabitess, the wife of the dead, to perpetuate*a* the name of the dead through his inheritance."

6 And the close relative said, "I cannot redeem *it* for myself, lest I ruin my own inheritance. You redeem my right of redemption for yourself, for I cannot redeem *it*."

7 Now this *was the custom* in former times in Israel concerning redeeming and exchanging, to confirm anything: one man took off his sandal and gave *it* to the other, and this *was* a confirmation in Israel.

8 Therefore the close relative said to Boaz, "Buy *it* for yourself." So he took off his sandal. 9 And Boaz said to the elders and all the people, "You *are* witnesses this day that I have bought all that was Elimelech's, and all that *was* Chilion's and Mahlon's, from the hand of Naomi. 10 Moreover, Ruth the Moabitess, the widow of Mahlon, I have acquired as my wife, to perpetuate the name of the dead through his inheritance, that the name of the dead may not be cut off from among his brethren and from his position at the gate.*a* You *are* witnesses this day."

11 And all the people who *were* at the gate, and the elders, said, "*We are* witnesses. The LORD make the woman who is coming to your house like Rachel and Leah, the two who built the house of Israel; and may you prosper in Ephrathah and be famous in Bethlehem. 12 May your house be like the house of Perez, whom Tamar bore to Judah, because of the offspring which the LORD will give you from this young woman."

13 So Boaz took Ruth and she became his wife; and when he went in to her, the LORD gave her conception, and she bore a son. 14 Then the women said to Naomi, "Blessed *be* the LORD, who has not left you this day without a close relative; and may his name be famous in Israel! 15 And may he be to you a restorer of life and a nourisher of your old age; for your daughter-in-law, who loves you, who is better to you than

3:15 *a*Many Hebrew manuscripts, Syriac, and Vulgate read *she;* Masoretic Text, Septuagint, and Targum read *he.*   4:1 *a*Hebrew *peloni almoni;* literally *so and so*   4:4 *a*Following many Hebrew manuscripts, Septuagint, Syriac, Targum, and Vulgate; Masoretic Text reads *he.*   4:5 *a*Literally *raise up*
4:10 *a*Probably his civic office

seven sons, has borne him." 16 Then Naomi took the child and laid him on her bosom, and became a nurse to him. 17 Also the neighbor women gave him a name, saying, "There is a son born to Naomi." And they called his name Obed. He *is* the father of Jesse, the father of David.

18 Now this *is* the genealogy of Perez: Perez begot Hezron; 19 Hezron begot Ram, and Ram begot Amminadab; 20 Amminadab begot Nahshon, and Nahshon begot Salmon;[a] 21 Salmon begot Boaz, and Boaz begot Obed; 22 Obed begot Jesse, and Jesse begot David.

4:20 aHebrew *Salmah*

First Samuel

Overview of First Samuel

irst and Second Samuel record the reigns of the first two kings of Israel—Saul and David. This period in Israel's history saw a major change in the leadership of the nation from a theocracy under Moses, Joshua, and the judges, to a monarchy of God's appointed men. Written by Samuel, David, Nathan, and Gad between 1150 and 950 B.C., First Samuel may have been put in its final form at a later date. The book tells of Samuel's life and leadership, Saul's reign, and God's choice of David to succeed Saul as king.

Through the life of David we see the outstanding positive qualities that made him a great leader chosen by God to rule the people. David was a young boy tending his father's flocks near Bethlehem when the prophet Samuel announced boldly that this lad was God's anointed. Immediately David rose to the task and challenged the Philistine giant, Goliath. His faith told him that God was bigger than this challenge. When Saul became jealous of David's great victory and tried to kill him, the young man believed God was in control, and so he would not fight King Saul.

David was committed to Saul's son, Jonathan, and won his allegiance. Refusing to strike back at Saul, David demonstrated great control over his emotions. When Saul died, David was sorrowful at the loss of Israel's first king.

From David's reactions in times of crises, we gain great insight into his character. David was loving, forgiving, brave, bold, intelligent, godly, and sacrificing. He put his life on the line for others. But most of all, David was a possibility thinker. He took chances and took charge!

The source of David's strength and courage is probably best revealed in one of his many psalms:

> The LORD is *my light and my salvation;*
> *Whom shall I fear?*
> The LORD is *the strength of my life;*
> *Of whom shall I be afraid?*
> *One* thing *I have desired of the* LORD,
> *That will I seek:*
> *That I may dwell in the house of the* LORD
> *All the days of my life.*
>
> (Ps. 27:1, 4)

Jesus in First Samuel

David is one of the primary Old Testament portrayals of the person of Jesus. He is born in Bethlehem, works as a shepherd, and rules as king of Israel. He is the anointed king, the forerunner of the messianic King. His messianic psalms are born of his years of rejection and danger, particularly Psalm 22.

Keys to First Samuel

Key Word: Transition. First Samuel records the transition in Israel from the rule of God through the judges to His rule through the kings. The transition goes through three stages: Eli to Samuel, Samuel to Saul, and Saul to David.

Key Verses: "But now your kingdom shall not continue. The LORD has sought for Himself a man after His own heart, and the LORD has commanded him *to be* commander over His people, because you have not kept what the LORD commanded you" (13:14, 15).

"So Samuel said, 'Has the LORD *as great* delight in burnt offerings and sacrifices, As in obeying the voice of the LORD? Behold, to obey is better than sacrifice, *And* to heed than the fat of rams" (15:22).

1 Now there was a certain man of Ramathaim Zophim, of the mountains of Ephraim, and his name *was* Elkanah the son of Jeroham, the son of Elihu,*a* the son of Tohu,*b* the son of Zuph, an Ephraimite. 2 And he had two wives: the name of one *was* Hannah, and the name of the other Peninnah. Peninnah had children, but Hannah had no children. 3 This man went up from his city yearly to worship and sacrifice to the LORD of hosts in Shiloh. Also the two sons of Eli, Hophni and Phinehas, the priests of the LORD, *were* there. 4 And whenever the time came for Elkanah to make an offering, he would give portions to Peninnah his wife and to all her sons and daughters. 5 But to Hannah he would give a double portion, for he loved Hannah, although the LORD had closed her womb. 6 And her rival also provoked her severely, to make her miserable, because the LORD had closed her womb. 7 So it was, year by year, when she went up to the house of the LORD, that she provoked her; therefore she wept and did not eat.

8 Then Elkanah her husband said to her, "Hannah, why do you weep? Why do you not eat? And why is your heart grieved? *Am* I not better to you than ten sons?"

9 So Hannah arose after they had finished eating and drinking in Shiloh. Now Eli the priest was sitting on the seat by the doorpost of the tabernacle*a* of the LORD. 10 And she *was* in bitterness of soul, and prayed to the LORD and wept in anguish. 11 Then she made a vow and said, "O LORD of hosts, if You will indeed look on the affliction of Your maidservant and remember me, and not forget Your maidservant, but will give Your maidservant a male child, then I will give him to the LORD all the days of his life, and no razor shall come upon his head."

12 And it happened, as she continued praying before the LORD, that Eli watched her mouth. 13 Now Hannah spoke in her heart; only her lips moved, but her voice was not heard. Therefore Eli thought she was drunk. 14 So Eli said to her, "How long will you be drunk? Put your wine away from you!"

15 But Hannah answered and said, "No, my lord, I *am* a woman of sorrowful spirit. I have drunk neither wine nor intoxicating drink, but have poured out my soul before the LORD. 16 Do not consider your maidservant a wicked woman,*a* for out of the abundance of my complaint and grief I have spoken until now."

17 Then Eli answered and said, "Go in peace, and the God of Israel grant your petition which you have asked of Him."

18 And she said, "Let your maidservant find favor in your sight." So the woman went her way and ate, and her face was no longer *sad.*

19 Then they rose early in the morning and worshiped before the

1:1 *a*Spelled *Eliel* in 1 Chronicles 6:34   *b*Spelled *Toah* in 1 Chronicles 6:34   1:9 *a*Hebrew *heykal,* palace or temple   1:16 *a*Literally *daughter of Belial*

LORD, and returned and came to their house at Ramah. And Elkanah knew Hannah his wife, and the LORD remembered her. 20 So it came to pass in the process of time that Hannah conceived and bore a son, and called his name Samuel,ᵃ saying, "Because I have asked for him from the LORD."

21 Now the man Elkanah and all his house went up to offer to the LORD the yearly sacrifice and his vow. 22 But Hannah did not go up, for she said to her husband, "Not until the child is weaned; then I will take him, that he may appear before the LORD and remain there forever."

23 So Elkanah her husband said to her, "Do what seems best to you; wait until you have weaned him. Only let the LORD establish Hisᵃ word." Then the woman stayed and nursed her son until she had weaned him.

24 Now when she had weaned him, she took him up with her, with three bulls,ᵃ one ephah of flour, and a skin of wine, and brought him to the house of the LORD in Shiloh. And the child was young. 25 Then they slaughtered a bull, and brought the child to Eli. 26 And she said, "O my lord! As your soul lives, my lord, I am the woman who stood by you here, praying to the LORD. 27 For this child I prayed, and the LORD has granted me my petition which I asked of Him. 28 Therefore I also have lent him to the LORD; as long as he lives he shall be lent to the LORD." So they worshiped the LORD there.

2 And Hannah prayed and said:

"My heart rejoices in the LORD;
My hornᵃ is exalted in the
  LORD.
I smile at my enemies,
Because I rejoice in Your
  salvation.

2 "No one is holy like the LORD,
For there is none besides You,
Nor is there any rock like our
  God.

3 "Talk no more so very proudly;
Let no arrogance come from
  your mouth,

For the LORD is the God of
  knowledge;
And by Him actions are
  weighed.

4 "The bows of the mighty men
  are broken,
And those who stumbled are
  girded with strength.
5 Those who were full have hired
  themselves out for bread,
And the hungry have ceased to
  hunger.
Even the barren has borne
  seven,
And she who has many
  children has become feeble.

6 "The LORD kills and makes alive;
He brings down to the grave
  and brings up.
7 The LORD makes poor and
  makes rich;
He brings low and lifts up.
8 He raises the poor from the
  dust
And lifts the beggar from the
  ash heap,
To set them among princes
And make them inherit the
  throne of glory.
"For the pillars of the earth are
  the LORD's,
And He has set the world upon
  them.
9 He will guard the feet of His
  saints,
But the wicked shall be silent
  in darkness.

"For by strength no man shall
  prevail.
10 The adversaries of the LORD
  shall be broken in pieces;
From heaven He will thunder
  against them.
The LORD will judge the ends
  of the earth.
"He will give strength to His
  king,
And exalt the horn of His
  anointed."

11 Then Elkanah went to his house at Ramah. But the child ministered to the LORD before Eli the priest. 12 Now the sons of Eli were corrupt;ᵃ they did not know the LORD.

1:20 ᵃLiterally Heard by God   1:23 ᵃFollowing Masoretic Text, Targum, and Vulgate; Dead Sea Scrolls, Septuagint, and Syriac read your.   1:24 ᵃDead Sea Scrolls, Septuagint, and Syriac read a three-year-old bull.   2:1 ᵃThat is, strength   2:12 ᵃLiterally sons of Belial

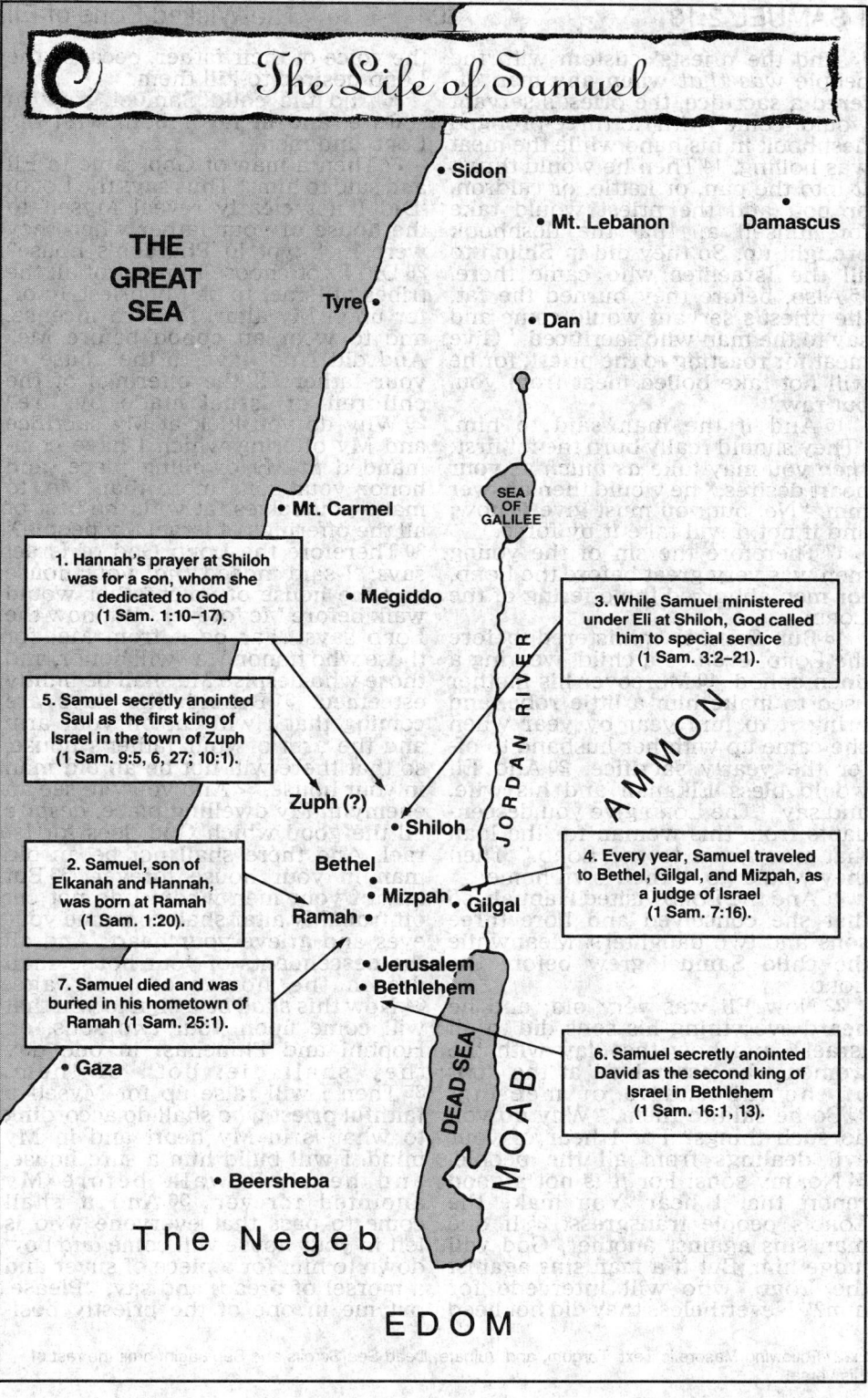

The Life of Samuel

- Sidon
- Mt. Lebanon   Damascus
- Tyre
- Dan

THE GREAT SEA

- Mt. Carmel

SEA OF GALILEE

- Megiddo

1. Hannah's prayer at Shiloh was for a son, whom she dedicated to God (1 Sam. 1:10–17).

3. While Samuel ministered under Eli at Shiloh, God called him to special service (1 Sam. 3:2–21).

5. Samuel secretly anointed Saul as the first king of Israel in the town of Zuph (1 Sam. 9:5, 6, 27; 10:1).

JORDAN RIVER

AMMON

Zuph (?)
- Shiloh

2. Samuel, son of Elkanah and Hannah, was born at Ramah (1 Sam. 1:20).

Bethel
- Mizpah
Ramah - Gilgal

4. Every year, Samuel traveled to Bethel, Gilgal, and Mizpah, as a judge of Israel (1 Sam. 7:16).

7. Samuel died and was buried in his hometown of Ramah (1 Sam. 25:1).

- Jerusalem
- Bethlehem

6. Samuel secretly anointed David as the second king of Israel in Bethlehem (1 Sam. 16:1, 13).

- Gaza

DEAD SEA

MOAB

- Beersheba

The Negeb

EDOM

13 And the priests' custom with the people *was that* when any man offered a sacrifice, the priest's servant would come with a three-pronged fleshhook in his hand while the meat was boiling. 14 Then he would thrust *it* into the pan, or kettle, or caldron, or pot; and the priest would take for himself all that the fleshhook brought up. So they did in Shiloh to all the Israelites who came there. 15 Also, before they burned the fat, the priest's servant would come and say to the man who sacrificed, "Give meat for roasting to the priest, for he will not take boiled meat from you, but raw."

16 And *if* the man said to him, "They should really burn the fat first; *then* you may take *as much* as your heart desires," he would then answer him, "*No,* but you must give *it* now; and if not, I will take *it* by force."

17 Therefore the sin of the young men was very great before the LORD, for men abhorred the offering of the LORD.

18 But Samuel ministered before the LORD, *even as* a child, wearing a linen ephod. 19 Moreover his mother used to make him a little robe, and bring *it* to him year by year when she came up with her husband to offer the yearly sacrifice. 20 And Eli would bless Elkanah and his wife, and say, "The LORD give you descendants from this woman for the loan that was given to the LORD." Then they would go to their own home.

21 And the LORD visited Hannah, so that she conceived and bore three sons and two daughters. Meanwhile the child Samuel grew before the LORD.

22 Now Eli was very old; and he heard everything his sons did to all Israel,*a* and how they lay with the women who assembled at the door of the tabernacle of meeting. 23 So he said to them, "Why do you do such things? For I hear of your evil dealings from all the people. 24 No, my sons! For *it is* not a good report that I hear. You make the LORD's people transgress. 25 If one man sins against another, God will judge him. But if a man sins against the LORD, who will intercede for him?" Nevertheless they did not heed the voice of their father, because the LORD desired to kill them.

26 And the child Samuel grew in stature, and in favor both with the LORD and men.

27 Then a man of God came to Eli and said to him, "Thus says the LORD: 'Did I not clearly reveal Myself to the house of your father when they were in Egypt in Pharaoh's house? 28 Did I not choose him out of all the tribes of Israel *to be* My priest, to offer upon My altar, to burn incense, and to wear an ephod before Me? And did I not give to the house of your father all the offerings of the children of Israel made by fire? 29 Why do you kick at My sacrifice and My offering which I have commanded *in My* dwelling place, and honor your sons more than Me, to make yourselves fat with the best of all the offerings of Israel My people?' 30 Therefore the LORD God of Israel says: 'I said indeed *that* your house and the house of your father would walk before Me forever.' But now the LORD says: 'Far be it from Me; for those who honor Me I will honor, and those who despise Me shall be lightly esteemed. 31 Behold, the days are coming that I will cut off your arm and the arm of your father's house, so that there will not be an old man in your house. 32 And you will see an enemy *in My* dwelling place, *despite* all the good which God does for Israel. And there shall not be an old man in your house forever. 33 But any of your men *whom* I do not cut off from My altar shall consume your eyes and grieve your heart. And all the descendants of your house shall die in the flower of their age. 34 Now this *shall be* a sign to you that will come upon your two sons, on Hophni and Phinehas: in one day they shall die, both of them. 35 Then I will raise up for Myself a faithful priest *who* shall do according to what *is* in My heart and in My mind. I will build him a sure house, and he shall walk before My anointed forever. 36 And it shall come to pass that everyone who is left in your house will come *and* bow down to him for a piece of silver and a morsel of bread, and say, "Please, put me in one of the priestly posi-

2:22 *a*Following Masoretic Text, Targum, and Vulgate; Dead Sea Scrolls and Septuagint omit the rest of this verse.

Listen for God's Voice

Faith is a two-sided power. On one side is the activity of rejecting negative inputs. On the opposite side is the activity of following God's voice.

Even an electric cord has both a negative and a positive wire. So even as you reject the destructive negative stimuli that enter your brain, also accept and listen to the positive emotions and incentives that whisper in the back of your mind.

Seek out friends, acquaintances, literature, books, television programs, and movies that will entertain, amuse, inspire, uplift, educate, motivate, and challenge you to become a better and more productive person.

I know of no positive voice of any living person that is more helpful to me on a moment-to-moment basis than that of my closest Friend, Jesus Christ!

How can you follow the positive voice of God?

Constantly ask God questions and wait for His answer in the hidden corner of your brain. Read what He said, what He did, and how He lived in the Bible. Seek His advice and expect Him to answer. The still, small voice will come into the silence of the holy chamber of your subconscious. It is the voice of your Friend, Jesus Christ.

He nudges you forward. He affirms you can be forgiven of all sins. He instills new passion to do His good work. He is speaking to you through this moment of meditation. Simply listen, then follow. That means you will take action.

tions, that I may eat a piece of bread.' ' "

3 Now the boy Samuel ministered to the LORD before Eli. And the word of the LORD was rare in those days; *there was* no widespread revelation. 2 And it came to pass at that time, while Eli *was* lying down in his place, and when his eyes had begun to grow so dim that he could not see, 3 and before the lamp of God went out in the tabernacle[a] of the LORD where the ark of God *was,* and while Samuel was lying down, 4 that the LORD called Samuel. And he answered, "Here I am!" 5 So he ran to Eli and said, "Here I am, for you called me."

And he said, "I did not call; lie down again." And he went and lay down.

6 Then the LORD called yet again, "Samuel!"

So Samuel arose and went to Eli, and said, "Here I am, for you called me." He answered, "I did not call, my son; lie down again." 7 (Now Samuel did not yet know the LORD, nor was the word of the LORD yet revealed to him.)

8 And the LORD called Samuel again the third time. So he arose and went to Eli, and said, "Here I am, for you did call me."

Then Eli perceived that the LORD had called the boy. 9 Therefore Eli said to Samuel, "Go, lie down; and it shall be, if He calls you, that you must say, 'Speak, LORD, for Your servant hears.' " So Samuel went and lay down in his place.

10 Now the LORD came and stood and called as at other times, "Samuel! Samuel!"

And Samuel answered, "Speak, for Your servant hears."

11 Then the LORD said to Samuel: "Behold, I will do something in Israel at which both ears of everyone who hears it will tingle. 12 In that day I will perform against Eli all that I have spoken concerning his house, from beginning to end. 13 For I have told him that I will judge his house forever for the iniquity which he knows, because his sons made themselves vile, and he did not restrain

them. 14 And therefore I have sworn to the house of Eli that the iniquity of Eli's house shall not be atoned for by sacrifice or offering forever."

15 So Samuel lay down until morning,[a] and opened the doors of the house of the LORD. And Samuel was afraid to tell Eli the vision. 16 Then Eli called Samuel and said, "Samuel, my son!"

He answered, "Here I am."

17 And he said, "What *is* the word that *the* LORD spoke to you? Please do not hide *it* from me. God do so to you, and more also, if you hide anything from me of all the things that He said to you." 18 Then Samuel told him everything, and hid nothing from him. And he said, "It *is* the LORD. Let Him do what seems good to Him."

19 So Samuel grew, and the LORD was with him and let none of his words fall to the ground. 20 And all Israel from Dan to Beersheba knew that Samuel *had been* established as a prophet of the LORD. 21 Then the LORD appeared again in Shiloh. For the LORD revealed Himself to Samuel in Shiloh by the word of the LORD.

4 And the word of Samuel came to all Israel.[a]

Now Israel went out to battle against the Philistines, and encamped beside Ebenezer; and the Philistines encamped in Aphek. 2 Then the Philistines put themselves in battle array against Israel. And when they joined battle, Israel was defeated by the Philistines, who killed about four thousand men of the army in the field. 3 And when the people had come into the camp, the elders of Israel said, "Why has the LORD defeated us today before the Philistines? Let us bring the ark of the covenant of the LORD from Shiloh to us, that when it comes among us it may save us from the hand of our enemies." 4 So the people sent to Shiloh, that they might bring from there the ark of the covenant of the LORD of hosts, who dwells *between* the cherubim. And the two sons of Eli, Hophni and Phinehas, *were* there with the ark of the covenant of God. 5 And when the ark of the covenant

---

3:3 [a]Hebrew *heykal,* palace or temple   3:15 [a]Following Masoretic Text, Targum, and Vulgate; Septuagint adds *and he arose in the morning.*   4:1 [a]Following Masoretic Text and Targum; Septuagint and Vulgate add *And it came to pass in those days that the Philistines gathered themselves together to fight;* Septuagint adds further *against Israel.*

of the LORD came into the camp, all Israel shouted so loudly that the earth shook. 6 Now when the Philistines heard the noise of the shout, they said, "What *does* the sound of this great shout in the camp of the Hebrews *mean*?" Then they understood that the ark of the LORD had come into the camp. 7 So the Philistines were afraid, for they said, "God has come into the camp!" And they said, "Woe to us! For such a thing has never happened before. 8 Woe to us! Who will deliver us from the hand of these mighty gods? These *are* the gods who struck the Egyptians with all the plagues in the wilderness. 9 Be strong and conduct yourselves like men, you Philistines, that you do not become servants of the Hebrews, as they have been to you. Conduct yourselves like men, and fight!"

10 So the Philistines fought, and Israel was defeated, and every man fled to his tent. There was a very great slaughter, and there fell of Israel thirty thousand foot soldiers. 11 Also the ark of God was captured; and the two sons of Eli, Hophni and Phinehas, died.

12 Then a man of Benjamin ran from the battle line the same day, and came to Shiloh with his clothes torn and dirt on his head. 13 Now when he came, there was Eli, sitting on a seat by the wayside watching,*a* for his heart trembled for the ark of God. And when the man came into the city and told *it*, all the city cried out. 14 When Eli heard the noise of the outcry, he said, "What *does* the sound of this tumult *mean*?" And the man came quickly and told Eli. 15 Eli was ninety-eight years old, and his eyes were so dim that he could not see.

16 Then the man said to Eli, "I *am* he who came from the battle. And I fled today from the battle line."

And he said, "What happened, my son?"

17 So the messenger answered and said, "Israel has fled before the Philistines, and there has been a great slaughter among the people. Also your two sons, Hophni and Phinehas, are dead; and the ark of God has been captured."

18 Then it happened, when he made mention of the ark of God, that Eli fell off the seat backward by the side of the gate; and his neck was broken and he died, for the man was old and heavy. And he had judged Israel forty years.

19 Now his daughter-in-law, Phinehas' wife, was with child, *due* to be delivered; and when she heard the news that the ark of God was captured, and that her father-in-law and her husband were dead, she bowed herself and gave birth, for her labor pains came upon her. 20 And about the time of her death the women who stood by her said to her, "Do not fear, for you have borne a son." But she did not answer, nor did she regard *it*. 21 Then she named the child Ichabod,*a* saying, "The glory has departed from Israel!" because the ark of God had been captured and because of her father-in-law and her husband. 22 And she said, "The glory has departed from Israel, for the ark of God has been captured."

5 Then the Philistines took the ark of God and brought it from Ebenezer to Ashdod. 2 When the Philistines took the ark of God, they brought it into the house of Dagon*a* and set it by Dagon. 3 And when the people of Ashdod arose early in the morning, there was Dagon, fallen on its face to the earth before the ark of the LORD. So they took Dagon and set it in its place again. 4 And when they arose early the next morning, there was Dagon, fallen on its face to the ground before the ark of the LORD. The head of Dagon and both the palms of its hands *were* broken off on the threshold; only Dagon's torso*a* was left of it. 5 Therefore neither the priests of Dagon nor any who come into Dagon's house tread on the threshold of Dagon in Ashdod to this day.

6 But the hand of the LORD was heavy on the people of Ashdod, and He ravaged them and struck them with tumors,*a* both Ashdod and its territory. 7 And when the men of

---

4:13 *a*Following Masoretic Text and Vulgate; Septuagint reads *beside the gate watching the road.*
4:21 *a*Literally *Inglorious* 5:2 *a*A Philistine idol 5:4 *a*Following Septuagint, Syriac, Targum, and Vulgate; Masoretic Text reads *Dagon.* 5:6 *a*Probably bubonic plague. Septuagint and Vulgate add here *And in the midst of their land rats sprang up, and there was a great death panic in the city.*

Ashdod saw how *it was*, they said, "The ark of the God of Israel must not remain with us, for His hand is harsh toward us and Dagon our god." 8 Therefore they sent and gathered to themselves all the lords of the Philistines, and said, "What shall we do with the ark of the God of Israel?"

And they answered, "Let the ark of the God of Israel be carried away to Gath." So they carried the ark of the God of Israel away. 9 So it was, after they had carried it away, that the hand of the Lord was against the city with a very great destruction; and He struck the men of the city, both small and great, and tumors broke out on them.

10 Therefore they sent the ark of God to Ekron. So it was, as the ark of God came to Ekron, that the Ekronites cried out, saying, "They have brought the ark of the God of Israel to us, to kill us and our people!" 11 So they sent and gathered together all the lords of the Philistines, and said, "Send away the ark of the God of Israel, and let it go back to its own place, so that it does not kill us and our people." For there was a deadly destruction throughout all the city; the hand of God was very heavy there. 12 And the men who did not die were stricken with the tumors, and the cry of the city went up to heaven.

6 Now the ark of the Lord was in the country of the Philistines seven months. 2 And the Philistines called for the priests and the diviners, saying, "What shall we do with the ark of the Lord? Tell us how we should send it to its place."

3 So they said, "If you send away the ark of the God of Israel, do not send it empty; but by all means return *it* to Him *with* a trespass offering. Then you will be healed, and it will be known to you why His hand is not removed from you."

4 Then they said, "What *is* the trespass offering which we shall return to Him?"

They answered, "Five golden tumors and five golden rats, *according to* the number of the lords of the Philistines. For the same plague *was* on all of you and on your lords. 5 Therefore you shall make images of your tumors and images of your rats that ravage the land, and you shall

give glory to the God of Israel; perhaps He will lighten His hand from you, from your gods, and from your land. 6 Why then do you harden your hearts as the Egyptians and Pharaoh hardened their hearts? When He did mighty things among them, did they not let the people go, that they might depart? 7 Now therefore, make a new cart, take two milk cows which have never been yoked, and hitch the cows to the cart; and take their calves home, away from them. 8 Then take the ark of the Lord and set it on the cart; and put the articles of gold which you are returning to Him *as a* trespass offering in a chest by its side. Then send it away, and let it go. 9 And watch: if it goes up the road to its own territory, to Beth Shemesh, *then* He has done us this great evil. But if not, then we shall know that *it is* not His hand *that* struck us—it happened to us by chance."

10 Then the men did so; they took two milk cows and hitched them to the cart, and shut up their calves at home. 11 And they set the ark of the Lord on the cart, and the chest with the gold rats and the images of their tumors. 12 Then the cows headed straight for the road to Beth Shemesh, *and* went along the highway, lowing as they went, and did not turn aside to the right hand or the left. And the lords of the Philistines went after them to the border of Beth Shemesh.

13 Now *the people of* Beth Shemesh *were* reaping their wheat harvest in the valley; and they lifted their eyes and saw the ark, and rejoiced to see *it*. 14 Then the cart came into the field of Joshua of Beth Shemesh, and stood there; a large stone *was* there. So they split the wood of the cart and offered the cows as a burnt offering to the Lord. 15 The Levites took down the ark of the Lord and the chest that *was* with it, in which *were* the articles of gold, and put *them* on the large stone. Then the men of Beth Shemesh offered burnt offerings and made sacrifices the same day to the Lord. 16 So when the five lords of the Philistines had seen *it*, they returned to Ekron the same day.

17 These *are* the golden tumors which the Philistines returned *as* a trespass offering to the Lord: one for Ashdod, one for Gaza, one for Ash-

The Capture of the Ark

The ark of the covenant, a sacred portable chest, was the most sacred object in the tabernacle and the temple. It symbolized God's presence and His covenant with Israel. Believing the ark would protect them in battle, the army of Israel carried the sacred chest into conflict with the Philistines. The Philistines captured the ark but were eager to return it when they were visited by a series of plagues.

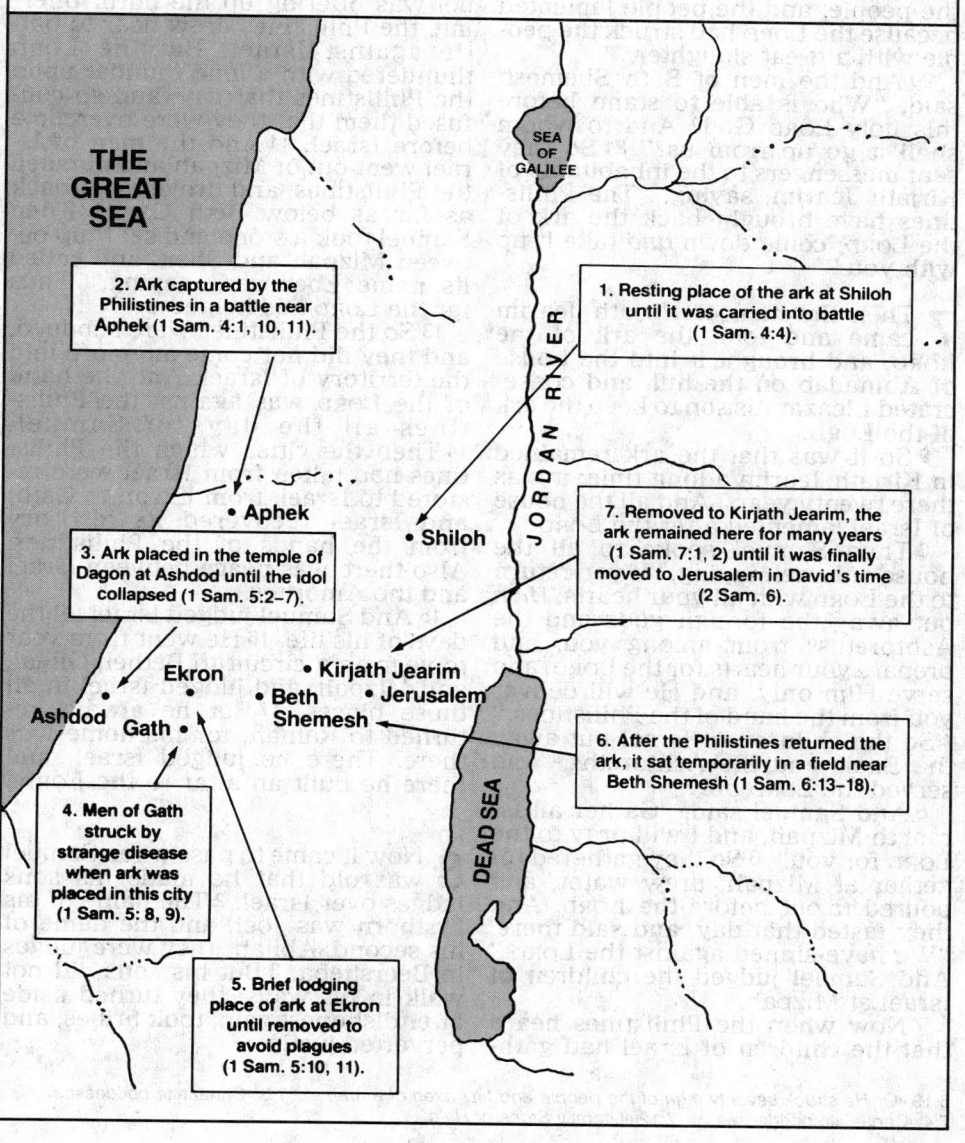

THE GREAT SEA

SEA OF GALILEE

JORDAN RIVER

DEAD SEA

2. Ark captured by the Philistines in a battle near Aphek (1 Sam. 4:1, 10, 11).

1. Resting place of the ark at Shiloh until it was carried into battle (1 Sam. 4:4).

• Aphek

• Shiloh

3. Ark placed in the temple of Dagon at Ashdod until the idol collapsed (1 Sam. 5:2–7).

7. Removed to Kirjath Jearim, the ark remained here for many years (1 Sam. 7:1, 2) until it was finally moved to Jerusalem in David's time (2 Sam. 6).

Ekron • Kirjath Jearim
• Beth   • Jerusalem
Ashdod • Shemesh
Gath •

6. After the Philistines returned the ark, it sat temporarily in a field near Beth Shemesh (1 Sam. 6:13–18).

4. Men of Gath struck by strange disease when ark was placed in this city (1 Sam. 5: 8, 9).

5. Brief lodging place of ark at Ekron until removed to avoid plagues (1 Sam. 5:10, 11).

kelon, one for Gath, one for Ekron; 18 and the golden rats, *according to* the number of all the cities of the Philistines *belonging* to the five lords, *both* fortified cities and country villages, even as far as the large *stone of* Abel on which they set the ark of the LORD, *which stone remains* to this day in the field of Joshua of Beth Shemesh.

19 Then He struck the men of Beth Shemesh, because they had looked into the ark of the LORD. He struck fifty thousand and seventy men[a] of the people, and the people lamented because the LORD had struck the people with a great slaughter.

20 And the men of Beth Shemesh said, "Who is able to stand before this holy LORD God? And to whom shall it go up from us?" 21 So they sent messengers to the inhabitants of Kirjath Jearim, saying, "The Philistines have brought back the ark of the LORD; come down *and* take it up with you."

7 Then the men of Kirjath Jearim came and took the ark of the LORD, and brought it into the house of Abinadab on the hill, and consecrated Eleazar his son to keep the ark of the LORD.

2 So it was that the ark remained in Kirjath Jearim a long time; it was there twenty years. And all the house of Israel lamented after the LORD.

3 Then Samuel spoke to all the house of Israel, saying, "If you return to the LORD with all your hearts, *then* put away the foreign gods and the Ashtoreths[a] from among you, and prepare your hearts for the LORD, and serve Him only; and He will deliver you from the hand of the Philistines."

4 So the children of Israel put away the Baals and the Ashtoreths,[a] and served the LORD only.

5 And Samuel said, "Gather all Israel to Mizpah, and I will pray to the LORD for you." 6 So they gathered together at Mizpah, drew water, and poured *it* out before the LORD. And they fasted that day, and said there, "We have sinned against the LORD." And Samuel judged the children of Israel at Mizpah.

7 Now when the Philistines heard that the children of Israel had gathered together at Mizpah, the lords of the Philistines went up against Israel. And when the children of Israel heard *of it,* they were afraid of the Philistines. 8 So the children of Israel said to Samuel, "Do not cease to cry out to the LORD our God for us, that He may save us from the hand of the Philistines."

9 And Samuel took a suckling lamb and offered *it as* a whole burnt offering to the LORD. Then Samuel cried out to the LORD for Israel, and the LORD answered him. 10 Now as Samuel was offering up the burnt offering, the Philistines drew near to battle against Israel. But the LORD thundered with a loud thunder upon the Philistines that day, and so confused them that they were overcome before Israel. 11 And the men of Israel went out of Mizpah and pursued the Philistines, and drove them back as far as below Beth Car. 12 Then Samuel took a stone and set *it* up between Mizpah and Shen, and called its name Ebenezer,[a] saying, "Thus far the LORD has helped us."

13 So the Philistines were subdued, and they did not come anymore into the territory of Israel. And the hand of the LORD was against the Philistines all the days of Samuel. 14 Then the cities which the Philistines had taken from Israel were restored to Israel, from Ekron to Gath; and Israel recovered its territory from the hands of the Philistines. Also there was peace between Israel and the Amorites.

15 And Samuel judged Israel all the days of his life. 16 He went from year to year on a circuit to Bethel, Gilgal, and Mizpah, and judged Israel in all those places. 17 But he always returned to Ramah, for his home *was* there. There he judged Israel, and there he built an altar to the LORD.

8 Now it came to pass when Samuel was old that he made his sons judges over Israel. 2 The name of his firstborn was Joel, and the name of his second, Abijah; *they were* judges in Beersheba. 3 But his sons did not walk in his ways; they turned aside after dishonest gain, took bribes, and perverted justice.

6:19 [a]Or *He struck seventy men of the people and fifty oxen of a man*   7:3 [a]Canaanite goddesses
7:4 [a]Canaanite goddesses   7:12 [a]Literally *Stone of Help*

4 Then all the elders of Israel gathered together and came to Samuel at Ramah, 5 and said to him, "Look, you are old, and your sons do not walk in your ways. Now make us a king to judge us like all the nations."

6 But the thing displeased Samuel when they said, "Give us a king to judge us." So Samuel prayed to the LORD. 7 And the LORD said to Samuel, "Heed the voice of the people in all that they say to you; for they have not rejected you, but they have rejected Me, that I should not reign over them. 8 According to all the works which they have done since the day that I brought them up out of Egypt, even to this day—with which they have forsaken Me and served other gods—so they are doing to you also. 9 Now therefore, heed their voice. However, you shall solemnly forewarn them, and show them the behavior of the king who will reign over them."

10 So Samuel told all the words of the LORD to the people who asked him for a king. 11 And he said, "This will be the behavior of the king who will reign over you: He will take your sons and appoint *them* for his own chariots and *to be* his horsemen, and *some* will run before his chariots. 12 He will appoint captains over his thousands and captains over his fifties, *will set some* to plow his ground and reap his harvest, and *some* to make his weapons of war and equipment for his chariots. 13 He will take your daughters *to be* perfumers, cooks, and bakers. 14 And he will take the best of your fields, your vineyards, and your olive groves, and give *them* to his servants. 15 He will take a tenth of your grain and your vintage, and give it to his officers and servants. 16 And he will take your male servants, your female servants, your finest young men,*ᵃ* and your donkeys, and put *them* to his work. 17 He will take a tenth of your sheep. And you will be his servants. 18 And you will cry out in that day because of your king whom you have chosen for yourselves, and the LORD will not hear you in that day."

19 Nevertheless the people refused to obey the voice of Samuel; and they said, "No, but we will have a king over us, 20 that we also may be like all the nations, and that our king may judge us and go out before us and fight our battles."

21 And Samuel heard all the words of the people, and he repeated them in the hearing of the LORD. 22 So the LORD said to Samuel, "Heed their voice, and make them a king."

And Samuel said to the men of Israel, "Every man go to his city."

9 There was a man of Benjamin whose name *was* Kish the son of Abiel, the son of Zeror, the son of Bechorath, the son of Aphiah, a Benjamite, a mighty man of power. 2 And he had a choice and handsome son whose name *was* Saul. *There was* not a more handsome person than he among the children of Israel. From his shoulders upward *he was* taller than any of the people.

3 Now the donkeys of Kish, Saul's father, were lost. And Kish said to his son Saul, "Please take one of the servants with you, and arise, go and look for the donkeys." 4 So he passed through the mountains of Ephraim and through the land of Shalisha, but they did not find *them*. Then they passed through the land of Shaalim, and *they were* not *there*. Then he passed through the land of the Benjamites, but they did not find *them*.

5 When they had come to the land of Zuph, Saul said to his servant who *was* with him, "Come, let us return, lest my father cease *caring* about the donkeys and become worried about us."

6 And he said to him, "Look now, *there is* in this city a man of God, and *he is* an honorable man; all that he says surely comes to pass. So let us go there; perhaps he can show us the way that we should go."

7 Then Saul said to his servant, "But look, *if* we go, what shall we bring the man? For the bread in our vessels is all gone, and *there is* no present to bring to the man of God. What do we have?"

8 And the servant answered Saul again and said, "Look, I have here at hand one-fourth of a shekel of silver. I will give *that* to the man of God, to tell us our way." 9 (Formerly in Israel, when a man went to inquire of God, he spoke thus: "Come, let us go to the seer"; for *he who is* now

8:16 ᵃSeptuagint reads *cattle*.

called a prophet was formerly called a seer.)

10 Then Saul said to his servant, "Well said; come, let us go." So they went to the city where the man of God *was*.

11 As they went up the hill to the city, they met some young women going out to draw water, and said to them, "Is the seer here?"

12 And they answered them and said, "Yes, there he is, just ahead of you. Hurry now; for today he came to this city, because there is a sacrifice of the people today on the high place. 13 As soon as you come into the city, you will surely find him before he goes up to the high place to eat. For the people will not eat until he comes, because he must bless the sacrifice; afterward those who are invited will eat. Now therefore, go up, for about this time you will find him."

14 So they went up to the city. As they were coming into the city, there was Samuel, coming out toward them on his way up to the high place.

15 Now the LORD had told Samuel in his ear the day before Saul came, saying, 16 "Tomorrow about this time I will send you a man from the land of Benjamin, and you shall anoint him commander over My people Israel, that he may save My people from the hand of the Philistines; for I have looked upon My people, because their cry has come to Me."

17 So when Samuel saw Saul, the LORD said to him, "There he is, the man of whom I spoke to you. This one shall reign over My people."

18 Then Saul drew near to Samuel in the gate, and said, "Please tell me, where *is* the seer's house?"

19 Samuel answered Saul and said, "I *am* the seer. Go up before me to the high place, for you shall eat with me today; and tomorrow I will let you go and will tell you all that *is* in your heart. 20 But as for your donkeys that were lost three days ago, do not be anxious about them, for they have been found. And on whom *is* all the desire of Israel? *Is it* not on you and on all your father's house?"

21 And Saul answered and said, "*Am* I not a Benjamite, of the smallest of the tribes of Israel, and my family the least of all the families of the tribe*ᵃ* of Benjamin? Why then do you speak like this to me?"

22 Now Samuel took Saul and his servant and brought them into the hall, and had them sit in the place of honor among those who were invited; there *were* about thirty persons. 23 And Samuel said to the cook, "Bring the portion which I gave you, of which I said to you, 'Set it apart.' " 24 So the cook took up the thigh with its upper part and set *it* before Saul. And *Samuel* said, "Here it is, what was kept back. *It* was set apart for you. Eat; for until this time it has been kept for you, since I said I invited the people." So Saul ate with Samuel that day.

25 When they had come down from the high place into the city, *Samuel* spoke with Saul on the top of the house.*ᵃ* 26 They arose early; and it was about the dawning of the day that Samuel called to Saul on the top of the house, saying, "Get up, that I may send you on your way." And Saul arose, and both of them went outside, he and Samuel.

27 As they were going down to the outskirts of the city, Samuel said to Saul, "Tell the servant to go on ahead of us." And he went on. "But you stand here awhile, that I may announce to you the word of God."

10 Then Samuel took a flask of oil and poured *it* on his head, and kissed him and said: "*Is it* not because the LORD has anointed you commander over His inheritance?*ᵃ* 2 When you have departed from me today, you will find two men by Rachel's tomb in the territory of Benjamin at Zelzah; and they will say to you, 'The donkeys which you went to look for have been found. And now your father has ceased caring about the donkeys and is worrying about you, saying, "What shall I do about my son?" ' 3 Then you shall go on forward from there and come to the terebinth tree of Tabor. There three men going up to God at Bethel

---

9:21 ᵃLiterally *tribes*   9:25 ᵃFollowing Masoretic Text and Targum; Septuagint omits *He spoke with Saul on top of the house;* Septuagint and Vulgate add *And he prepared a bed for Saul on top of the house, and he slept.*   10:1 ᵃFollowing Masoretic Text, Targum, and Vulgate; Septuagint reads *His people Israel; and you shall rule the people of the Lord;* Septuagint and Vulgate add *And you shall deliver His people from the hands of their enemies all around them. And this shall be a sign to you, that God has anointed you to be prince.*

will meet you, one carrying three young goats, another carrying three loaves of bread, and another carrying a skin of wine. 4 And they will greet you and give you two *loaves* of bread, which you shall receive from their hands. 5 After that you shall come to the hill of God where the Philistine garrison *is.* And it will happen, when you have come there to the city, that you will meet a group of prophets coming down from the high place with a stringed instrument, a tambourine, a flute, and a harp before them; and they will be prophesying. 6 Then the Spirit of the LORD will come upon you, and you will prophesy with them and be turned into another man. 7 And let it be, when these signs come to you, *that* you do as the occasion demands; for God *is* with you. 8 You shall go down before me to Gilgal; and surely I will come down to you to offer burnt offerings *and* make sacrifices of peace offerings. Seven days you shall wait, till I come to you and show you what you should do."

9 So it was, when he had turned his back to go from Samuel, that God gave him another heart; and all those signs came to pass that day. 10 When they came there to the hill, there was a group of prophets to meet him; then the Spirit of God came upon him, and he prophesied among them. 11 And it happened, when all who knew him formerly saw that he indeed prophesied among the prophets, that the people said to one another, "What *is* this *that* has come upon the son of Kish? *Is* Saul also among the prophets?" 12 Then a man from there answered and said, "But who *is* their father?" Therefore it became a proverb: "*Is* Saul also among the prophets?" 13 And when he had finished prophesying, he went to the high place.

14 Then Saul's uncle said to him and his servant, "Where did you go?"

So he said, "To look for the donkeys. When we saw that *they were* nowhere *to be found,* we went to Samuel."

15 And Saul's uncle said, "Tell me, please, what Samuel said to you."

16 So Saul said to his uncle, "He told us plainly that the donkeys had been found." But about the matter of the kingdom, he did not tell him what Samuel had said.

17 Then Samuel called the people together to the LORD at Mizpah, 18 and said to the children of Israel, "Thus says the LORD God of Israel: 'I brought up Israel out of Egypt, and delivered you from the hand of the Egyptians *and* from the hand of all kingdoms and from those who oppressed you.' 19 But you have today rejected your God, who Himself saved you from all your adversities and your tribulations; and you have said to Him, 'No, set a king over us!' Now therefore, present yourselves before the LORD by your tribes and by your clans."*a*

20 And when Samuel had caused all the tribes of Israel to come near, the tribe of Benjamin was chosen. 21 When he had caused the tribe of Benjamin to come near by their families, the family of Matri was chosen. And Saul the son of Kish was chosen. But when they sought him, he could not be found. 22 Therefore they inquired of the LORD further, "Has the man come here yet?"

And the LORD answered, "There he is, hidden among the equipment."

23 So they ran and brought him from there; and when he stood among the people, he was taller than any of the people from his shoulders upward. 24 And Samuel said to all the people, "Do you see him whom the LORD has chosen, that *there is* no one like him among all the people?"

So all the people shouted and said, "Long live the king!"

25 Then Samuel explained to the people the behavior of royalty, and wrote *it* in a book and laid *it* up before the LORD. And Samuel sent all the people away, every man to his house. 26 And Saul also went home to Gibeah; and valiant *men* went with him, whose hearts God had touched. 27 But some rebels said, "How can this man save us?" So they despised him, and brought him no presents. But he held his peace.

11 Then Nahash the Ammonite came up and encamped against Jabesh Gilead; and all the men of Jabesh said to Nahash, "Make a covenant with us, and we will serve you."

2 And Nahash the Ammonite an-

swered them, "On this *condition* I will make *a covenant* with you, that I may put out all your right eyes, and bring reproach on all Israel."

3 Then the elders of Jabesh said to him, "Hold off for seven days, that we may send messengers to all the territory of Israel. And then, if *there is* no one to save us, we will come out to you."

4 So the messengers came to Gibeah of Saul and told the news in the hearing of the people. And all the people lifted up their voices and wept. 5 Now there was Saul, coming behind the herd from the field; and Saul said, "What *troubles* the people, that they weep?" And they told him the words of the men of Jabesh. 6 Then the Spirit of God came upon Saul when he heard this news, and his anger was greatly aroused. 7 So he took a yoke of oxen and cut them in pieces, and sent *them* throughout all the territory of Israel by the hands of messengers, saying, "Whoever does not go out with Saul and Samuel to battle, so it shall be done to his oxen."

And the fear of the LORD fell on the people, and they came out with one consent. 8 When he numbered them in Bezek, the children of Israel were three hundred thousand, and the men of Judah thirty thousand. 9 And they said to the messengers who came, "Thus you shall say to the men of Jabesh Gilead: 'Tomorrow, by *the time* the sun is hot, you shall have help.'" Then the messengers came and reported *it* to the men of Jabesh, and they were glad. 10 Therefore the men of Jabesh said, "Tomorrow we will come out to you, and you may do with us whatever seems good to you."

11 So it was, on the next day, that Saul put the people in three companies; and they came into the midst of the camp in the morning watch, and killed Ammonites until the heat of the day. And it happened that those who survived were scattered, so that no two of them were left together.

12 Then the people said to Samuel, "Who *is* he who said, 'Shall Saul reign over us?' Bring the men, that we may put them to death."

13 But Saul said, "Not a man shall be put to death this day, for today the LORD has accomplished salvation in Israel."

14 Then Samuel said to the people, "Come, let us go to Gilgal and renew the kingdom there." 15 So all the people went to Gilgal, and there they made Saul king before the LORD in Gilgal. There they made sacrifices of peace offerings before the LORD, and there Saul and all the men of Israel rejoiced greatly.

12 Now Samuel said to all Israel: "Indeed I have heeded your voice in all that you said to me, and have made a king over you. 2 And now here is the king, walking before you; and I am old and grayheaded, and look, my sons *are* with you. I have walked before you from my childhood to this day. 3 Here I am. Witness against me before the LORD and before His anointed: Whose ox have I taken, or whose donkey have I taken, or whom have I cheated? Whom have I oppressed, or from whose hand have I received *any* bribe with which to blind my eyes? I will restore *it* to you."

4 And they said, "You have not cheated us or oppressed us, nor have you taken anything from any man's hand."

5 Then he said to them, "The LORD is witness against you, and His anointed *is* witness this day, that you have not found anything in my hand."

And they answered, "*He is* witness."

6 Then Samuel said to the people, "*It is* the LORD who raised up Moses and Aaron, and who brought your fathers up from the land of Egypt. 7 Now therefore, stand still, that I may reason with you before the LORD concerning all the righteous acts of the LORD which He did to you and your fathers: 8 When Jacob had gone into Egypt,*a* and your fathers cried out to the LORD, then the LORD sent Moses and Aaron, who brought your fathers out of Egypt and made them dwell in this place. 9 And when they forgot the LORD their God, He sold them into the hand of Sisera, commander of the army of Hazor, into the hand of the Philistines, and into the hand of the king of Moab; and

12:8 *a*Following Masoretic Text, Targum, and Vulgate; Septuagint adds *and the Egyptians afflicted them*.

they fought against them. 10 Then they cried out to the LORD, and said, 'We have sinned, because we have forsaken the LORD and served the Baals and Ashtoreths;ᵃ but now deliver us from the hand of our enemies, and we will serve You.' 11 And the LORD sent Jerubbaal,ᵃ Bedan,ᵇ Jephthah, and Samuel,ᶜ and delivered you out of the hand of your enemies on every side; and you dwelt in safety. 12 And when you saw that Nahash king of the Ammonites came against you, you said to me, 'No, but a king shall reign over us,' when the LORD your God *was* your king.

13 "Now therefore, here is the king whom you have chosen *and* whom you have desired. And take note, the LORD has set a king over you. 14 If you fear the LORD and serve Him and obey His voice, and do not rebel against the commandment of the LORD, then both you and the king who reigns over you will continue following the LORD your God. 15 However, if you do not obey the voice of the LORD, but rebel against the commandment of the LORD, then the hand of the LORD will be against you, as *it was* against your fathers.

16 "Now therefore, stand and see this great thing which the LORD will do before your eyes: 17 *Is* today not the wheat harvest? I will call to the LORD, and He will send thunder and rain, that you may perceive and see that your wickedness *is* great, which you have done in the sight of the LORD, in asking a king for yourselves."

18 So Samuel called to the LORD, and the LORD sent thunder and rain that day; and all the people greatly feared the LORD and Samuel.

19 And all the people said to Samuel, "Pray for your servants to the LORD your God, that we may not die; for we have added to all our sins the evil of asking a king for ourselves."

20 Then Samuel said to the people, "Do not fear. You have done all this wickedness; yet do not turn aside from following the LORD, but serve the LORD with all your heart. 21 And do not turn aside; for *then you would go* after empty things which

cannot profit or deliver, for they *are* nothing. 22 For the LORD will not forsake His people, for His great name's sake, because it has pleased the LORD to make you His people. 23 Moreover, as for me, far be it from me that I should sin against the LORD in ceasing to pray for you; but I will teach you the good and the right way. 24 Only fear the LORD, and serve Him in truth with all your heart; for consider what great things He has done for you. 25 But if you still do wickedly, you shall be swept away, both you and your king."

13 Saul reigned one year; and when he had reigned two years over Israel,ᵃ 2 Saul chose for himself three thousand *men* of Israel. Two thousand were with Saul in Michmash and in the mountains of Bethel, and a thousand were with Jonathan in Gibeah of Benjamin. The rest of the people he sent away, every man to his tent.

3 And Jonathan attacked the garrison of the Philistines that *was* in Geba, and the Philistines heard *of it*. Then Saul blew the trumpet throughout all the land, saying, "Let the Hebrews hear!" 4 Now all Israel heard it said *that* Saul had attacked a garrison of the Philistines, and *that* Israel had also become an abomination to the Philistines. And the people were called together to Saul at Gilgal.

5 Then the Philistines gathered together to fight with Israel, thirtyᵃ thousand chariots and six thousand horsemen, and people as the sand which *is* on the seashore in multitude. And they came up and encamped in Michmash, to the east of Beth Aven. 6 When the men of Israel saw that they were in danger (for the people were distressed), then the people hid in caves, in thickets, in rocks, in holes, and in pits. 7 And *some of* the Hebrews crossed over the Jordan to the land of Gad and Gilead.

As for Saul, he *was* still in Gilgal, and all the people followed him trembling. 8 Then he waited seven days, according to the time set by Samuel. But Samuel did not come to Gilgal;

12:10 ᵃCanaanite goddesses   12:11 ᵃSyriac reads *Deborah*; Targum reads *Gideon*.   ᵇSeptuagint and Syriac read *Barak;* Targum reads *Simson*.   ᶜSyriac reads *Simson*.   13:1 ᵃThe Hebrew is difficult (compare 2 Samuel 5:4; 2 Kings 14:2; see also 2 Samuel 2:10; Acts 13:21).   13:5 ᵃFollowing Masoretic Text, Septuagint, Targum, and Vulgate; Syriac and some manuscripts of the Septuagint read *three*.

Saul's Military Campaigns

As the first king of the united kingdom of Israel, Saul's major task was to subdue the nation's enemies. At first, he won several decisive battles. But his campaigns bogged down when he turned his attention to David, attempting to wipe out what he perceived as a threat to his power. Saul and his sons were eventually killed by the Philistines.

THE GREAT SEA

SEA OF GALILEE

4. Saul committed suicide at Mt. Gilboa after suffering mortal wounds in a humiliating defeat by the Philistines (1 Sam. 31).

Mt. Gilboa

JORDAN RIVER

AMMON

2. Saul also waged successful campaigns against the Moabites, Ammonites, and Edomites (1 Sam. 14:47).

1. In his first campaign, Saul defeated a garrison of Philistines at Geba (1 Sam. 13; 14).

• Geba

• Jerusalem

3. Saul defeated the Amalekites, apparently in southern Palestine, but he disobeyed God by sparing the life of King Agag and failing to destroy some of the choice spoils of war (1 Sam. 15:1–9).

DEAD SEA

M O A B

E D O M

and the people were scattered from him. 9 So Saul said, "Bring a burnt offering and peace offerings here to me." And he offered the burnt offering. 10 Now it happened, as soon as he had finished presenting the burnt offering, that Samuel came; and Saul went out to meet him, that he might greet him.

11 And Samuel said, "What have you done?"

Saul said, "When I saw that the people were scattered from me, and *that* you did not come within the days appointed, and *that* the Philistines gathered together at Michmash, 12 then I said, 'The Philistines will now come down on me at Gilgal, and I have not made supplication to the LORD.' Therefore I felt compelled, and offered a burnt offering."

13 And Samuel said to Saul, "You have done foolishly. You have not kept the commandment of the LORD your God, which He commanded you. For now the LORD would have established your kingdom over Israel forever. 14 But now your kingdom shall not continue. The LORD has sought for Himself a man after His own heart, and the LORD has commanded him *to be* commander over His people, because you have not kept what the LORD commanded you."

15 Then Samuel arose and went up from Gilgal to Gibeah of Benjamin.[a] And Saul numbered the people present with him, about six hundred men.

16 Saul, Jonathan his son, and the people present with them remained in Gibeah of Benjamin. But the Philistines encamped in Michmash. 17 Then raiders came out of the camp of the Philistines in three companies. One company turned onto the road to Ophrah, to the land of Shual, 18 another company turned to the road *to* Beth Horon, and another company turned *to* the road of the border that overlooks the Valley of Zeboim toward the wilderness.

19 Now there was no blacksmith to be found throughout all the land of Israel, for the Philistines said, "Lest the Hebrews make swords or spears." 20 But all the Israelites would go down to the Philistines to sharpen each man's plowshare, his mattock, his ax, and his sickle; 21 and the charge for a sharpening was a pim[a] for the plowshares, the mattocks, the forks, and the axes, and to set the points of the goads. 22 So it came about, on the day of battle, that there was neither sword nor spear found in the hand of any of the people who *were* with Saul and Jonathan. But they were found with Saul and Jonathan his son.

23 And the garrison of the Philistines went out to the pass of Michmash.

14 Now it happened one day that Jonathan the son of Saul said to the young man who bore his armor, "Come, let us go over to the Philistines' garrison that *is* on the other side." But he did not tell his father. 2 And Saul was sitting in the outskirts of Gibeah under a pomegranate tree which *is* in Migron. The people who *were* with him *were* about six hundred men. 3 Ahijah the son of Ahitub, Ichabod's brother, the son of Phinehas, the son of Eli, the LORD's priest in Shiloh, was wearing an ephod. But the people did not know that Jonathan had gone.

4 Between the passes, by which Jonathan sought to go over to the Philistines' garrison, *there was* a sharp rock on one side and a sharp rock on the other side. And the name of one *was* Bozez, and the name of the other Seneh. 5 The front of one faced northward opposite Michmash, and the other southward opposite Gibeah.

6 Then Jonathan said to the young man who bore his armor, "Come, let us go over to the garrison of these uncircumcised; it may be that the LORD will work for us. For nothing restrains the LORD from saving by many or by few."

7 So his armorbearer said to him, "Do all that is in your heart. Go then; here I am with you, according to your heart."

8 Then Jonathan said, "Very well, let us cross over to *these* men, and we will show ourselves to them. 9 If they say thus to us, 'Wait until we come to you,' then we will stand

13:15 aFollowing Masoretic Text and Targum; Septuagint and Vulgate add *And the rest of the people went up after Saul to meet the people who fought against them, going from Gilgal to Gibeah in the hill of Benjamin.*   13:21 aAbout two-thirds shekel weight still in our place and not go up to them. 10 But if they say thus, 'Come up to us,' then we will go up. For the LORD has delivered them into our hand, and this *will be* a sign to us."

11 So both of them showed themselves to the garrison of the Philistines. And the Philistines said, "Look, the Hebrews are coming out of the holes where they have hidden." 12 Then the men of the garrison called to Jonathan and his armorbearer, and said, "Come up to us, and we will show you something."

Jonathan said to his armorbearer, "Come up after me, for the LORD has delivered them into the hand of Israel." 13 And Jonathan climbed up on his hands and knees with his armorbearer after him; and they fell before Jonathan. And as he came after him, his armorbearer killed them. 14 That first slaughter which Jonathan and his armorbearer made was about twenty men within about half an acre of land.*a*

15 And there was trembling in the camp, in the field, and among all the people. The garrison and the raiders also trembled; and the earth quaked, so that it was a very great trembling. 16 Now the watchmen of Saul in Gibeah of Benjamin looked, and *there* was the multitude, melting away; and they went here and there. 17 Then Saul said to the people who *were* with him, "Now call the roll and see who has gone from us." And when they had called the roll, surprisingly, Jonathan and his armorbearer *were* not *there.* 18 And Saul said to Ahijah, "Bring the ark*a* of God here" (for at that time the ark*b* of God was with the children of Israel). 19 Now it happened, while Saul talked to the priest, that the noise which *was* in the camp of the Philistines continued to increase; so Saul said to the priest, "Withdraw your hand." 20 Then Saul and all the people who *were* with him assembled, and they went to the battle; and indeed every man's sword was against his neighbor, *and there was* very great confusion. 21 Moreover the Hebrews *who* were with the Philistines before that time, who went up with them into the camp *from the* sur-

rounding *country,* they also joined the Israelites who *were* with Saul and Jonathan. 22 Likewise all the men of Israel who had hidden in the mountains of Ephraim, *when* they heard that the Philistines fled, they also followed hard after them in the battle. 23 So the LORD saved Israel that day, and the battle shifted to Beth Aven.

24 And the men of Israel were distressed that day, for Saul had placed the people under oath, saying, "Cursed *is* the man who eats *any* food until evening, before I have taken vengeance on my enemies." So none of the people tasted food. 25 Now all *the people* of the land came to a forest; and there was honey on the ground. 26 And when the people had come into the woods, there was the honey, dripping; but no one put his hand to his mouth, for the people feared the oath. 27 But Jonathan had not heard his father charge the people with the oath; therefore he stretched out the end of the rod that *was* in his hand and dipped it in a honeycomb, and put his hand to his mouth; and his countenance brightened. 28 Then one of the people said, "Your father strictly charged the people with an oath, saying, 'Cursed *is* the man who eats food this day.'" And the people were faint.

29 But Jonathan said, "My father has troubled the land. Look now, how my countenance has brightened because I tasted a little of this honey. 30 How much better if the people had eaten freely today of the spoil of their enemies which they found! For now would there not have been a much greater slaughter among the Philistines?"

31 Now they had driven back the Philistines that day from Michmash to Aijalon. So the people were very faint. 32 And the people rushed on the spoil, and took sheep, oxen, and calves, and slaughtered *them* on the ground; and the people ate *them* with the blood. 33 Then they told Saul, saying, "Look, the people are sinning against the LORD by eating with the blood!"

So he said, "You have dealt treacherously; roll a large stone to me this

---

14:14 *a*Literally *half the area plowed by a yoke* (of oxen in a day)   14:18 *a*Following Masoretic Text, Targum, and Vulgate; Septuagint reads *ephod.*   *b*Following Masoretic Text, Targum, and Vulgate; Septuagint reads *ephod.*

day." 34 Then Saul said, "Disperse yourselves among the people, and say to them, 'Bring me here every man's ox and every man's sheep, slaughter *them* here, and eat; and do not sin against the LORD by eating with the blood.' " So every one of the people brought his ox with him that night, and slaughtered *it* there. 35 Then Saul built an altar to the LORD. This was the first altar that he built to the LORD.

36 Now Saul said, "Let us go down after the Philistines by night, and plunder them until the morning light; and let us not leave a man of them."

And they said, "Do whatever seems good to you."

Then the priest said, "Let us draw near to God here."

37 So Saul asked counsel of God, "Shall I go down after the Philistines? Will You deliver them into the hand of Israel?" But He did not answer him that day. 38 And Saul said, "Come over here, all you chiefs of the people, and know and see what this sin was today. 39 For *as* the LORD lives, who saves Israel, though it be in Jonathan my son, he shall surely die." But not a man among all the people answered him. 40 Then he said to all Israel, "You be on one side, and my son Jonathan and I will be on the other side."

And the people said to Saul, "Do what seems good to you."

41 Therefore Saul said to the LORD God of Israel, "Give a perfect *lot.*"*a* So Saul and Jonathan were taken, but the people escaped. 42 And Saul said, "Cast *lots* between my son Jonathan and me." So Jonathan was taken. 43 Then Saul said to Jonathan, "Tell me what you have done."

And Jonathan told him, and said, "I only tasted a little honey with the end of the rod that *was* in my hand. So now I must die!"

44 Saul answered, "God do so and more also; for you shall surely die, Jonathan."

45 But the people said to Saul, "Shall Jonathan die, who has accomplished this great deliverance in Israel? Certainly not! *As* the LORD lives, not one hair of his head shall

fall to the ground, for he has worked with God this day." So the people rescued Jonathan, and he did not die.

46 Then Saul returned from pursuing the Philistines, and the Philistines went to their own place.

47 So Saul established his sovereignty over Israel, and fought against all his enemies on every side, against Moab, against the people of Ammon, against Edom, against the kings of Zobah, and against the Philistines. Wherever he turned, he harassed *them.*ª 48 And he gathered an army and attacked the Amalekites, and delivered Israel from the hands of those who plundered them.

49 The sons of Saul were Jonathan, Jishui,ª and Malchishua. And the names of his two daughters *were these:* the name of the firstborn Merab, and the name of the younger Michal. 50 The name of Saul's wife *was* Ahinoam the daughter of Ahimaaz. And the name of the commander of his army *was* Abner the son of Ner, Saul's uncle. 51 Kish *was* the father of Saul, and Ner the father of Abner *was* the son of Abiel.

52 Now there was fierce war with the Philistines all the days of Saul. And when Saul saw any strong man or any valiant man, he took him for himself.

15 Samuel also said to Saul, "The LORD sent me to anoint you king over His people, over Israel. Now therefore, heed the voice of the words of the LORD. 2 Thus says the LORD of hosts: 'I will punish Amalek *for* what he did to Israel, how he ambushed him on the way when he came up from Egypt. 3 Now go and attack Amalek, and utterly destroy all that they have, and do not spare them. But kill both man and woman, infant and nursing child, ox and sheep, camel and donkey.' "

4 So Saul gathered the people together and numbered them in Telaim, two hundred thousand foot soldiers and ten thousand men of Judah. 5 And Saul came to a city of Amalek, and lay in wait in the valley.

6 Then Saul said to the Kenites, "Go, depart, get down from among

---

14:41 ªFollowing Masoretic Text and Targum; Septuagint and Vulgate read *Why do You not answer Your servant today? If the injustice is with me or Jonathan my son, O LORD God of Israel, give proof; and if You say it is with Your people Israel, give holiness.*   14:47 ªSeptuagint and Vulgate read *prospered.*
14:49 ªCalled *Abinadab* in 1 Chronicles 8:33 and 9:39

the Amalekites, lest I destroy you with them. For you showed kindness to all the children of Israel when they came up out of Egypt." So the Kenites departed from among the Amalekites. 7 And Saul attacked the Amalekites, from Havilah all the way to Shur, which is east of Egypt. 8 He also took Agag king of the Amalekites alive, and utterly destroyed all the people with the edge of the sword. 9 But Saul and the people spared Agag and the best of the sheep, the oxen, the fatlings, the lambs, and all *that was* good, and were unwilling to utterly destroy them. But everything despised and worthless, that they utterly destroyed.

10 Now the word of the LORD came to Samuel, saying, 11 "I greatly regret that I have set up Saul *as* king, for he has turned back from following Me, and has not performed My commandments." And it grieved Samuel, and he cried out to the LORD all night. 12 So when Samuel rose early in the morning to meet Saul, it was told Samuel, saying, "Saul went to Carmel, and indeed, he set up a monument for himself; and he has gone on around, passed by, and gone down to Gilgal." 13 Then Samuel went to Saul, and Saul said to him, "Blessed *are* you of the LORD! I have performed the commandment of the LORD."

14 But Samuel said, "What then *is* this bleating of the sheep in my ears, and the lowing of the oxen which I hear?"

15 And Saul said, "They have brought them from the Amalekites; for the people spared the best of the sheep and the oxen, to sacrifice to the LORD your God; and the rest we have utterly destroyed."

16 Then Samuel said to Saul, "Be quiet! And I will tell you what the LORD said to me last night."

And he said to him, "Speak on."

17 So Samuel said, "When you *were* little in your own eyes, *were* you not head of the tribes of Israel? And did not the LORD anoint you king over Israel? 18 Now the LORD sent you on a mission, and said, 'Go, and utterly destroy the sinners, the Amalekites, and fight against them until they are consumed.' 19 Why then did you not obey the voice of the LORD? Why did you swoop down on the spoil, and do evil in the sight of the LORD?"

20 And Saul said to Samuel, "But I have obeyed the voice of the LORD, and gone on the mission on which the LORD sent me, and brought back Agag king of Amalek; I have utterly destroyed the Amalekites. 21 But the people took of the plunder, sheep and oxen, the best of the things which should have been utterly destroyed, to sacrifice to the LORD your God in Gilgal."

22 So Samuel said:

"Has the LORD *as great* delight
   in burnt offerings and
   sacrifices,
As in obeying the voice of the
   LORD?
Behold, to obey is better than
   sacrifice,
And to heed than the fat of
   rams.
23 For rebellion *is as* the sin of
   witchcraft,
And stubbornness *is as* iniquity
   and idolatry.
Because you have rejected the
   word of the LORD,
He also has rejected you from
   being king."

24 Then Saul said to Samuel, "I have sinned, for I have transgressed the commandment of the LORD and your words, because I feared the people and obeyed their voice. 25 Now therefore, please pardon my sin, and return with me, that I may worship the LORD."

26 But Samuel said to Saul, "I will not return with you, for you have rejected the word of the LORD, and the LORD has rejected you from being king over Israel."

27 And as Samuel turned around to go away, *Saul* seized the edge of his robe, and it tore. 28 So Samuel said to him, "The LORD has torn the kingdom of Israel from you today, and has given it to a neighbor of yours, *who is* better than you. 29 And also the Strength of Israel will not lie nor relent. For He *is* not a man, that He should relent."

30 Then he said, "I have sinned; *yet* honor me now, please, before the elders of my people and before Israel, and return with me, that I may worship the LORD your God." 31 So Samuel turned back after Saul, and Saul worshiped the LORD.

32 Then Samuel said, "Bring Agag king of the Amalekites here to me." So Agag came to him cautiously.

And Agag said, "Surely the bitterness of death is past."

33 But Samuel said, "As your sword has made women childless, so shall your mother be childless among women." And Samuel hacked Agag in pieces before the LORD in Gilgal.

34 Then Samuel went to Ramah, and Saul went up to his house at Gibeah of Saul. 35 And Samuel went no more to see Saul until the day of his death. Nevertheless Samuel mourned for Saul, and the LORD regretted that He had made Saul king over Israel.

16 Now the LORD said to Samuel, "How long will you mourn for Saul, seeing I have rejected him from reigning over Israel? Fill your horn with oil, and go; I am sending you to Jesse the Bethlehemite. For I have provided Myself a king among his sons."

2 And Samuel said, "How can I go? If Saul hears it, he will kill me."

But the LORD said, "Take a heifer with you, and say, 'I have come to sacrifice to the LORD.' 3 Then invite Jesse to the sacrifice, and I will show you what you shall do; you shall anoint for Me the one I name to you."

4 So Samuel did what the LORD said, and went to Bethlehem. And the elders of the town trembled at his coming, and said, "Do you come peaceably?"

5 And he said, "Peaceably; I have come to sacrifice to the LORD. Sanctify yourselves, and come with me to the sacrifice." Then he consecrated Jesse and his sons, and invited them to the sacrifice.

6 So it was, when they came, that he looked at Eliab and said, "Surely the LORD's anointed is before Him!"

7 But the LORD said to Samuel, "Do not look at his appearance or at his physical stature, because I have refused him. For the LORD does not see as man sees;ᵃ for man looks at the outward appearance, but the LORD looks at the heart."

8 So Jesse called Abinadab, and made him pass before Samuel. And he said, "Neither has the LORD chosen this one." 9 Then Jesse made Shammah pass by. And he said, "Neither has the LORD chosen this one." 10 Thus Jesse made seven of his sons pass before Samuel. And Samuel said to Jesse, "The LORD has not chosen these." 11 And Samuel said to Jesse, "Are all the young men here?" Then he said, "There remains yet the youngest, and there he is, keeping the sheep."

And Samuel said to Jesse, "Send and bring him. For we will not sit downᵃ till he comes here." 12 So he sent and brought him in. Now he was ruddy, with bright eyes, and good-looking. And the LORD said, "Arise, anoint him; for this is the one!"

13 Then Samuel took the horn of oil and anointed him in the midst of his brothers; and the Spirit of the LORD came upon David from that day forward. So Samuel arose and went to Ramah.

14 But the Spirit of the LORD departed from Saul, and a distressing spirit from the LORD troubled him. 15 And Saul's servants said to him, "Surely, a distressing spirit from God is troubling you. 16 Let our master now command your servants, who are before you, to seek out a man who is a skillful player on the harp. And it shall be that he will play it with his hand when the distressing spirit from God is upon you, and you shall be well."

17 So Saul said to his servants, "Provide me now a man who can play well, and bring him to me."

18 Then one of the servants answered and said, "Look, I have seen a son of Jesse the Bethlehemite, who is skillful in playing, a mighty man of valor, a man of war, prudent in speech, and a handsome person; and the LORD is with him."

19 Therefore Saul sent messengers to Jesse, and said, "Send me your son David, who is with the sheep." 20 And Jesse took a donkey loaded with bread, a skin of wine, and a young goat, and sent them by his son David to Saul. 21 So David came to Saul and stood before him. And he loved him greatly, and he became his armorbearer. 22 Then Saul sent to Jesse, saying, "Please let David stand before me, for he has found favor in

16:7 ᵃSeptuagint reads *For God does not see as man sees*; Targum reads *It is not by the appearance of a man*; Vulgate reads *Nor do I judge according to the looks of a man.*   16:11 ᵃFollowing Septuagint and Vulgate; Masoretic Text reads *turn around*; Targum and Syriac read *turn away.*

my sight." 23 And so it was, whenever the spirit from God was upon Saul, that David would take a harp and play *it* with his hand. Then Saul would become refreshed and well, and the distressing spirit would depart from him.

17 Now the Philistines gathered their armies together to battle, and were gathered at Sochoh, which *belongs* to Judah; they encamped between Sochoh and Azekah, in Ephes Dammim. 2 And Saul and the men of Israel were gathered together, and they encamped in the Valley of Elah, and drew up in battle array against the Philistines. 3 The Philistines stood on a mountain on one side, and Israel stood on a mountain on the other side, with a valley between them.

4 And a champion went out from the camp of the Philistines, named Goliath, from Gath, whose height *was* six cubits and a span. 5 *He had* a bronze helmet on his head, and he *was* armed with a coat of mail, and the weight of the coat *was* five thousand shekels of bronze. 6 And *he had* bronze armor on his legs and a bronze javelin between his shoulders. 7 Now the staff of his spear *was* like a weaver's beam, and his iron spearhead *weighed* six hundred shekels; and a shield-bearer went before him. 8 Then he stood and cried out to the armies of Israel, and said to them, "Why have you come out to line up for battle? *Am* I not a Philistine, and you the servants of Saul? Choose a man for yourselves, and let him come down to me. 9 If he is able to fight with me and kill me, then we will be your servants. But if I prevail against him and kill him, then you shall be our servants and serve us." 10 And the Philistine said, "I defy the armies of Israel this day; give me a man, that we may fight together." 11 When Saul and all Israel heard these words of the Philistine, they were dismayed and greatly afraid.

12 Now David *was* the son of that Ephrathite of Bethlehem Judah, whose name *was* Jesse, and who had eight sons. And the man was old, advanced *in years,* in the days of Saul. 13 The three oldest sons of Jesse had gone to follow Saul to the battle. The names of his three sons who went to the battle *were* Eliab the firstborn,

next to him Abinadab, and the third Shammah. 14 David *was* the youngest. And the three oldest followed Saul. 15 But David occasionally went and returned from Saul to feed his father's sheep at Bethlehem.

16 And the Philistine drew near and presented himself forty days, morning and evening.

17 Then Jesse said to his son David, "Take now for your brothers an ephah of this dried *grain* and these ten loaves, and run to your brothers at the camp. 18 And carry these ten cheeses to the captain of *their* thousand, and see how your brothers fare, and bring back news of them." 19 Now Saul and they and all the men of Israel *were* in the Valley of Elah, fighting with the Philistines.

20 So David rose early in the morning, left the sheep with a keeper, and took *the things* and went as Jesse had commanded him. And he came to the camp as the army was going out to the fight and shouting for the battle. 21 For Israel and the Philistines had drawn up in battle array, army against army. 22 And David left his supplies in the hand of the supply keeper, ran to the army, and came and greeted his brothers. 23 Then as he talked with them, there was the champion, the Philistine of Gath, Goliath by name, coming up from the armies of the Philistines; and he spoke according to the same words. So David heard *them.* 24 And all the men of Israel, when they saw the man, fled from him and were dreadfully afraid. 25 So the men of Israel said, "Have you seen this man who has come up? Surely he has come up to defy Israel; and it shall be *that* the man who kills him the king will enrich with great riches, will give him his daughter, and give his father's house exemption *from taxes* in Israel."

26 Then David spoke to the men who stood by him, saying, "What shall be done for the man who kills this Philistine and takes away the reproach from Israel? For who *is* this uncircumcised Philistine, that he should defy the armies of the living God?"

27 And the people answered him in this manner, saying, "So shall it be done for the man who kills him."

28 Now Eliab his oldest brother heard when he spoke to the men; and

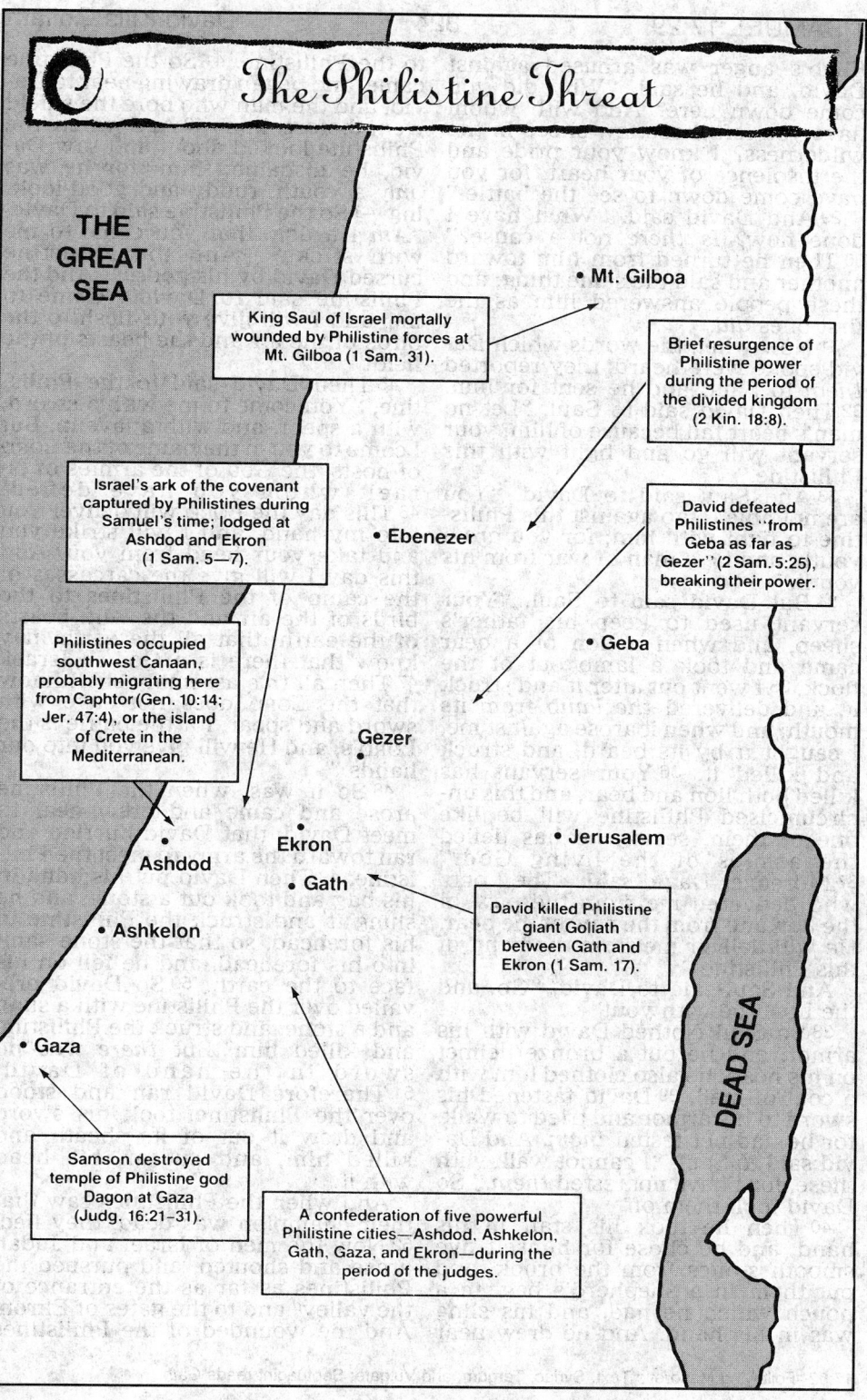

The Philistine Threat

THE GREAT SEA

King Saul of Israel mortally wounded by Philistine forces at Mt. Gilboa (1 Sam. 31).

Brief resurgence of Philistine power during the period of the divided kingdom (2 Kin. 18:8).

Israel's ark of the covenant captured by Philistines during Samuel's time; lodged at Ashdod and Ekron (1 Sam. 5—7).

David defeated Philistines "from Geba as far as Gezer" (2 Sam. 5:25), breaking their power.

Philistines occupied southwest Canaan, probably migrating here from Caphtor (Gen. 10:14; Jer. 47:4), or the island of Crete in the Mediterranean.

David killed Philistine giant Goliath between Gath and Ekron (1 Sam. 17).

Samson destroyed temple of Philistine god Dagon at Gaza (Judg. 16:21–31).

A confederation of five powerful Philistine cities—Ashdod, Ashkelon, Gath, Gaza, and Ekron—during the period of the judges.

- Mt. Gilboa
- Ebenezer
- Geba
- Gezer
- Ekron
- Gath
- Jerusalem
- Ashdod
- Ashkelon
- Gaza

DEAD SEA

Eliab's anger was aroused against David, and he said, "Why did you come down here? And with whom have you left those few sheep in the wilderness? I know your pride and the insolence of your heart, for you have come down to see the battle."

29 And David said, "What have I done now? *Is there* not a cause?" 30 Then he turned from him toward another and said the same thing; and these people answered him as the first ones *did*.

31 Now when the words which David spoke were heard, they reported *them* to Saul; and he sent for him. 32 Then David said to Saul, "Let no man's heart fail because of him; your servant will go and fight with this Philistine."

33 And Saul said to David, "You are not able to go against this Philistine to fight with him; for you *are* a youth, and he a man of war from his youth."

34 But David said to Saul, "Your servant used to keep his father's sheep, and when a lion or a bear came and took a lamb out of the flock, 35 I went out after it and struck it, and delivered *the lamb* from its mouth; and when it arose against me, I caught *it* by its beard, and struck and killed it. 36 Your servant has killed both lion and bear; and this uncircumcised Philistine will be like one of them, seeing he has defied the armies of the living God." 37 Moreover David said, "The LORD, who delivered me from the paw of the lion and from the paw of the bear, He will deliver me from the hand of this Philistine."

And Saul said to David, "Go, and the LORD be with you!"

38 So Saul clothed David with his armor, and he put a bronze helmet on his head; he also clothed him with a coat of mail. 39 David fastened his sword to his armor and tried to walk, for he had not tested *them*. And David said to Saul, "I cannot walk with these, for I have not tested *them*." So David took them off.

40 Then he took his staff in his hand; and he chose for himself five smooth stones from the brook, and put them in a shepherd's bag, in a pouch which he had, and his sling was in his hand. And he drew near to the Philistine. 41 So the Philistine came, and began drawing near to David, and the man who bore the shield *went* before him. 42 And when the Philistine looked about and saw David, he disdained him; for he was *only* a youth, ruddy and good-looking. 43 So the Philistine said to David, "*Am* I a dog, that you come to me with sticks?" And the Philistine cursed David by his gods. 44 And the Philistine said to David, "Come to me, and I will give your flesh to the birds of the air and the beasts of the field!"

45 Then David said to the Philistine, "You come to me with a sword, with a spear, and with a javelin. But I come to you in the name of the LORD of hosts, the God of the armies of Israel, whom you have defied. 46 This day the LORD will deliver you into my hand, and I will strike you and take your head from you. And this day I will give the carcasses of the camp of the Philistines to the birds of the air and the wild beasts of the earth, that all the earth may know that there is a God in Israel. 47 Then all this assembly shall know that the LORD does not save with sword and spear; for the battle *is* the LORD's, and He will give you into our hands."

48 So it was, when the Philistine arose and came and drew near to meet David, that David hurried and ran toward the army to meet the Philistine. 49 Then David put his hand in his bag and took out a stone; and he slung *it* and struck the Philistine in his forehead, so that the stone sank into his forehead, and he fell on his face to the earth. 50 So David prevailed over the Philistine with a sling and a stone, and struck the Philistine and killed him. But *there was* no sword in the hand of David. 51 Therefore David ran and stood over the Philistine, took his sword and drew it out of its sheath and killed him, and cut off his head with it.

And when the Philistines saw that their champion was dead, they fled. 52 Now the men of Israel and Judah arose and shouted, and pursued the Philistines as far as the entrance of the valley[a] and to the gates of Ekron. And the wounded of the Philistines

---

17:52 [a]Following Masoretic Text, Syriac, Targum, and Vulgate; Septuagint reads *Gath*.

David and Goliath

The Bible tells us that the Israelites were often in insurmountable situations when they faced their enemies. Perhaps one of the most dramatic events occurred when King Saul reigned over the land. The Philistine army from the coast threatened to advance up the low-lying hilly passes to Jerusalem. Determined to defend their country, the Israelites boldly went forth to fight. But upon seeing the Philistine army, the Israelites shrank in fear, for the invading army had giants. One soldier in particular was awesome—that was the mighty Goliath.

Recent archaeological excavations near the Valley of Elah have revealed Philistine burial sites. Many Philistine skeletons have been measured as large as six to seven feet tall. Although there is no way of knowing Goliath's exact height, estimates place him between seven and nine feet.

Every day the Israelites and Philistines lined up for battle, Goliath stepped forward. He issued a challenge to fight, one on one, with any Israelite brave enough to face him. No one, not even the king's mightiest warriors, dared to step out.

No one, that is, until a small shepherd boy heard the giant's mockery of the living God. David, son of Jesse, was out in the hills of Bethlehem tending his father's flock when he was ordered to bring food to his brothers fighting in the army. Upon completing the twenty-mile hike to the Israelite camp, David was present for Goliath's daily challenge.

When David heard Goliath's taunts, his tremendous love for God stirred him to action. David knew that no problem was too big for God. And in total faith, this small boy refused the king's armor and marched straight down to face the armor-clad giant. With only a tiny stone from the brook of Elah and his slingshot, David defeated the invincible Goliath in the name of the Lord.

David's act of faith encouraged the entire Israelite army. Attacking the Philistines with full force, they drove back and destroyed the advancing army, all the way to the gates of their coastal cities. David was fearless because he knew God was on Israel's side. He faced the enemy with God's ability, not with his own strength. David knew that God's plans would work only if he were available.

With God's ability, we too can conquer our seemingly impossible problems. Like giants that would mock God and frighten us, these problems are not as insurmountable. For God is larger and stronger than our problems. In John 16:33, Jesus puts it this way: "In the world you have tribulation, but take courage: I have overcome the world."

fell along the road to Shaaraim, even as far as Gath and Ekron. 53 Then the children of Israel returned from chasing the Philistines, and they plundered their tents. 54 And David took the head of the Philistine and brought it to Jerusalem, but he put his armor in his tent.

55 When Saul saw David going out against the Philistine, he said to Abner, the commander of the army, "Abner, whose son *is* this youth?"

And Abner said, "As your soul lives, O king, I do not know."

56 So the king said, "Inquire whose son this young man *is.*"

57 Then, as David returned from the slaughter of the Philistine, Abner took him and brought him before Saul with the head of the Philistine in his hand. 58 And Saul said to him, "Whose son *are* you, young man?"

So David answered, "*I am* the son of your servant Jesse the Bethlehemite."

18 Now when he had finished speaking to Saul, the soul of Jonathan was knit to the soul of David, and Jonathan loved him as his own soul. 2 Saul took him that day, and would not let him go home to his father's house anymore. 3 Then Jonathan and David made a covenant, because he loved him as his own soul. 4 And Jonathan took off the robe that *was* on him and gave it to David, with his armor, even to his sword and his bow and his belt.

5 So David went out wherever Saul sent him, *and* behaved wisely. And Saul set him over the men of war, and he was accepted in the sight of all the people and also in the sight of Saul's servants. 6 Now it had happened as they were coming *home,* when David was returning from the slaughter of the Philistine, that the women had come out of all the cities of Israel, singing and dancing, to meet King Saul, with tambourines, with joy, and with musical instruments. 7 So the women sang as they danced, and said:

"Saul has slain his thousands,
And David his ten thousands."

8 Then Saul was very angry, and the saying displeased him; and he said,

"They have ascribed to David ten thousands, and to me they have ascribed *only* thousands. Now *what* more can he have but the kingdom?" 9 So Saul eyed David from that day forward.

10 And it happened on the next day that the distressing spirit from God came upon Saul, and he prophesied inside the house. So David played *music* with his hand, as at other times; but *there was* a spear in Saul's hand. 11 And Saul cast the spear, for he said, "I will pin David to the wall!" But David escaped his presence twice.

12 Now Saul was afraid of David, because the Lord was with him, but had departed from Saul. 13 Therefore Saul removed him from his presence, and made him his captain over a thousand; and he went out and came in before the people. 14 And David behaved wisely in all his ways, and the Lord *was* with him. 15 Therefore, when Saul saw that he behaved very wisely, he was afraid of him. 16 But all Israel and Judah loved David, because he went out and came in before them.

17 Then Saul said to David, "Here is my older daughter Merab; I will give her to you as a wife. Only be valiant for me, and fight the Lord's battles." For Saul thought, "Let my hand not be against him, but let the hand of the Philistines be against him."

18 So David said to Saul, "Who *am* I, and what *is* my life *or* my father's family in Israel, that I should be son-in-law to the king?" 19 But it happened at the time when Merab, Saul's daughter, should have been given to David, that she was given to Adriel the Meholathite as a wife.

20 Now Michal, Saul's daughter, loved David. And they told Saul, and the thing pleased him. 21 So Saul said, "I will give her to him, that she may be a snare to him, and that the hand of the Philistines may be against him." Therefore Saul said to David a second time, "You shall be my son-in-law today."

22 And Saul commanded his servants, "Communicate with David secretly, and say, 'Look, the king has delight in you, and all his servants love you. Now therefore, become the king's son-in-law.'"

23 So Saul's servants spoke those

words in the hearing of David. And David said, "Does it seem to you *a* light *thing* to be a king's son-in-law, seeing I *am* a poor and lightly esteemed man?" 24 And the servants of Saul told him, saying, "In this manner David spoke."

25 Then Saul said, "Thus you shall say to David: 'The king does not desire any dowry but one hundred foreskins of the Philistines, to take vengeance on the king's enemies.' " But Saul thought to make David fall by the hand of the Philistines. 26 So when his servants told David these words, it pleased David well to become the king's son-in-law. Now the days had not expired; 27 therefore David arose and went, he and his men, and killed two hundred men of the Philistines. And David brought their foreskins, and they gave them in full count to the king, that he might become the king's son-in-law. Then Saul gave him Michal his daughter as a wife.

28 Thus Saul saw and knew that the LORD *was* with David, and *that* Michal, Saul's daughter, loved him; 29 and Saul was still more afraid of David. So Saul became David's enemy continually. 30 Then the princes of the Philistines went out *to war.* And so it was, whenever they went out, *that* David behaved more wisely than all the servants of Saul, so that his name became highly esteemed.

19 Now Saul spoke to Jonathan his son and to all his servants, that they should kill David; but Jonathan, Saul's son, delighted greatly in David. 2 So Jonathan told David, saying, "My father Saul seeks to kill you. Therefore please be on your guard until morning, and stay in a secret *place* and hide. 3 And I will go out and stand beside my father in the field where you *are,* and I will speak with my father about you. Then what I observe, I will tell you."

4 Thus Jonathan spoke well of David to Saul his father, and said to him, "Let not the king sin against his servant, against David, because he has not sinned against you, and because his works *have been* very good toward you. 5 For he took his life in his hands and killed the Philistine, and the LORD brought about a great deliverance for all Israel. You saw *it* and rejoiced. Why then will you sin

against innocent blood, to kill David without a cause?"

6 So Saul heeded the voice of Jonathan, and Saul swore, "As the LORD lives, he shall not be killed." 7 Then Jonathan called David, and Jonathan told him all these things. So Jonathan brought David to Saul, and he was in his presence as in times past.

8 And there was war again; and David went out and fought with the Philistines, and struck them with a mighty blow, and they fled from him.

9 Now the distressing spirit from the LORD came upon Saul as he sat in his house with his spear in his hand. And David was playing *music* with *his* hand. 10 Then Saul sought to pin David to the wall with the spear, but he slipped away from Saul's presence; and he drove the spear into the wall. So David fled and escaped that night.

11 Saul also sent messengers to David's house to watch him and to kill him in the morning. And Michal, David's wife, told him, saying, "If you do not save your life tonight, tomorrow you will be killed." 12 So Michal let David down through a window. And he went and fled and escaped. 13 And Michal took an image and laid *it* in the bed, put a cover of goats' *hair* for his head, and covered *it* with clothes. 14 So when Saul sent messengers to take David, she said, "He is sick."

15 Then Saul sent the messengers *back* to see David, saying, "Bring him up to me in the bed, that I may kill him." 16 And when the messengers had come in, there was the image in the bed, with a cover of goats' *hair* for his head. 17 Then Saul said to Michal, "Why have you deceived me like this, and sent my enemy away, so that he has escaped?"

And Michal answered Saul, "He said to me, 'Let me go! Why should I kill you?' "

18 So David fled and escaped, and went to Samuel at Ramah, and told him all that Saul had done to him. And he and Samuel went and stayed in Naioth. 19 Now it was told Saul, saying, "Take note, David *is* at Naioth in Ramah!" 20 Then Saul sent messengers to take David. And when they saw the group of prophets prophesying, and Samuel standing *as* leader over them, the Spirit of God

came upon the messengers of Saul, and they also prophesied. 21 And when Saul was told, he sent other messengers, and they prophesied likewise. Then Saul sent messengers again the third time, and they prophesied also. 22 Then he also went to Ramah, and came to the great well that *is* at Sechu. So he asked, and said, "Where *are* Samuel and David?"

And *someone* said, "Indeed *they are* at Naioth in Ramah." 23 So he went there to Naioth in Ramah. Then the Spirit of God was upon him also, and he went on and prophesied until he came to Naioth in Ramah. 24 And he also stripped off his clothes and prophesied before Samuel in like manner, and lay down naked all that day and all that night. Therefore they say, "*Is* Saul also among the prophets?"*a*

20 Then David fled from Naioth in Ramah, and went and said to Jonathan, "What have I done? What *is* my iniquity, and what *is* my sin before your father, that he seeks my life?"

2 So Jonathan said to him, "By no means! You shall not die! Indeed, my father will do nothing either great or small without first telling me. And why should my father hide this thing from me? It *is* not *so!*"

3 Then David took an oath again, and said, "Your father certainly knows that I have found favor in your eyes, and he has said, 'Do not let Jonathan know this, lest he be grieved.' But truly, *as* the LORD lives and *as* your soul lives, *there is* but a step between me and death."

4 So Jonathan said to David, "Whatever you yourself desire, I will do *it* for you."

5 And David said to Jonathan, "Indeed tomorrow *is* the New Moon, and I should not fail to sit with the king to eat. But let me go, that I may hide in the field until the third *day* at evening. 6 If your father misses me at all, then say, 'David earnestly asked *permission* of me that he might run over to Bethlehem, his city, for *there is* a yearly sacrifice there for all the family.' 7 If he says thus: 'It *is* well,' your servant will be safe. But if he is very angry, be sure that evil is determined

by him. 8 Therefore you shall deal kindly with your servant, for you have brought your servant into a covenant of the LORD with you. Nevertheless, if there is iniquity in me, kill me yourself, for why should you bring me to your father?"

9 But Jonathan said, "Far be it from you! For if I knew certainly that evil was determined by my father to come upon you, then would I not tell you?"

10 Then David said to Jonathan, "Who will tell me, or what *if* your father answers you roughly?"

11 And Jonathan said to David, "Come, let us go out into the field." So both of them went out into the field. 12 Then Jonathan said to David: "The LORD God of Israel *is witness!* When I have sounded out my father sometime tomorrow, *or* the third *day*, and indeed *there is* good toward David, and I do not send to you and tell you, 13 may the LORD do so and much more to Jonathan. But if it pleases my father *to do* you evil, then I will report it to you and send you away, that you may go in safety. And the LORD be with you as He has been with my father. 14 And you shall not only show me the kindness of the LORD while I still live, that I may not die; 15 but you shall not cut off your kindness from my house forever, no, not when the LORD has cut off every one of the enemies of David from the face of the earth." 16 So Jonathan made *a covenant* with the house of David, *saying*, "Let the LORD require *it* at the hand of David's enemies."

17 Now Jonathan again caused David to vow, because he loved him; for he loved him as he loved his own soul. 18 Then Jonathan said to David, "Tomorrow *is* the New Moon; and you will be missed, because your seat will be empty. 19 And *when* you have stayed three days, go down quickly and come to the place where you hid on the day of the deed; and remain by the stone Ezel. 20 Then I will shoot three arrows to the side, as though I shot at a target; 21 and there I will send a lad, *saying*, 'Go, find the arrows.' If I expressly say to the lad, 'Look, the arrows *are* on this side of you; get them and come'—then, as the LORD lives, *there is* safety for you and no harm. 22 But if I say thus to

the young man, 'Look, the arrows *are* beyond you'—go your way, for the LORD has sent you away. 23 And as for the matter which you and I have spoken of, indeed the LORD *be* between you and me forever."

24 Then David hid in the field. And when the New Moon had come, the king sat down to eat the feast. 25 Now the king sat on his seat, as at other times, on a seat by the wall. And Jonathan arose,*ᵃ* and Abner sat by Saul's side, but David's place was empty. 26 Nevertheless Saul did not say anything that day, for he thought, "Something has happened to him; he *is* unclean, surely he *is* unclean." 27 And it happened the next day, the second *day* of the month, that David's place was empty. And Saul said to Jonathan his son, "Why has the son of Jesse not come to eat, either yesterday or today?"

28 So Jonathan answered Saul, "David earnestly asked *permission* of me *to go* to Bethlehem. 29 And he said, 'Please let me go, for our family has a sacrifice in the city, and my brother has commanded me *to be there*. And now, if I have found favor in your eyes, please let me get away and see my brothers.' Therefore he has not come to the king's table."

30 Then Saul's anger was aroused against Jonathan, and he said to him, "You son of a perverse, rebellious *woman!* Do I not know that you have chosen the son of Jesse to your own shame and to the shame of your mother's nakedness? 31 For as long as the son of Jesse lives on the earth, you shall not be established, nor your kingdom. Now therefore, send and bring him to me, for he shall surely die."

32 And Jonathan answered Saul his father, and said to him, "Why should he be killed? What has he done?" 33 Then Saul cast a spear at him to kill him, by which Jonathan knew that it was determined by his father to kill David.

34 So Jonathan arose from the table in fierce anger, and ate no food the second day of the month, for he was grieved for David, because his father had treated him shamefully.

35 And so it was, in the morning, that Jonathan went out into the field at the time appointed with David, and a little lad *was* with him. 36 Then he said to his lad, "Now run, find the arrows which I shoot." As the lad ran, he shot an arrow beyond him. 37 When the lad had come to the place where the arrow was which Jonathan had shot, Jonathan cried out after the lad and said, "*Is* not the arrow beyond you?" 38 And Jonathan cried out after the lad, "Make haste, hurry, do not delay!" So Jonathan's lad gathered up the arrows and came back to his master. 39 But the lad did not know anything. Only Jonathan and David knew of the matter. 40 Then Jonathan gave his weapons to his lad, and said to him, "Go, carry *them* to the city."

41 As soon as the lad had gone, David arose from *a place* toward the south, fell on his face to the ground, and bowed down three times. And they kissed one another; and they wept together, but David more so. 42 Then Jonathan said to David, "Go in peace, since we have both sworn in the name of the LORD, saying, 'May the LORD be between you and me, and between your descendants and my descendants, forever.'" So he arose and departed, and Jonathan went into the city.

21 Now David came to Nob, to Ahimelech the priest. And Ahimelech was afraid when he met David, and said to him, "Why *are* you alone, and no one is with you?"

2 So David said to Ahimelech the priest, "The king has ordered me on some business, and said to me, 'Do not let anyone know anything about the business on which I send you, or what I have commanded you.' And I have directed *my* young men to such and such a place. 3 Now therefore, what have you on hand? Give *me* five *loaves of* bread in my hand, or whatever can be found."

4 And the priest answered David and said, "*There is* no common bread on hand; but there is holy bread, if the young men have at least kept themselves from women."

5 Then David answered the priest, and said to him, "Truly, women *have been* kept from us about three days since I came out. And the vessels of

20:25 *ᵃ*Following Masoretic Text, Syriac, Targum, and Vulgate; Septuagint reads *he sat across from Jonathan*.

the young men are holy, and *the bread is* in effect common, even though it was consecrated in the vessel this day."

6 So the priest gave him holy *bread;* for there was no bread there but the showbread which had been taken from before the LORD, in order to put hot bread *in its place* on the day when it was taken away.

7 Now a certain man of the servants of Saul *was* there that day, detained before the LORD. And his name *was* Doeg, an Edomite, the chief of the herdsmen who *belonged* to Saul.

8 And David said to Ahimelech, "Is there not here on hand a spear or a sword? For I have brought neither my sword nor my weapons with me, because the king's business required haste."

9 So the priest said, "The sword of Goliath the Philistine, whom you killed in the Valley of Elah, there it is, wrapped in a cloth behind the ephod. If you will take that, take *it.* For *there is* no other except that one here."

And David said, "*There is* none like it; give it to me."

10 Then David arose and fled that day from before Saul, and went to Achish the king of Gath. 11 And the servants of Achish said to him, "*Is* this not David the king of the land? Did they not sing of him to one another in dances, saying:

    'Saul has slain his thousands,
    And David his ten
       thousands'?"[a]

12 Now David took these words to heart, and was very much afraid of Achish the king of Gath. 13 So he changed his behavior before them, pretended madness in their hands, scratched on the doors of the gate, and let his saliva fall down on his beard. 14 Then Achish said to his servants, "Look, you see the man is insane. Why have you brought him to me? 15 Have I need of madmen, that you have brought this *fellow* to play the madman in my presence? Shall this *fellow* come into my house?"

22 David therefore departed from there and escaped to the cave of Adullam. So when his brothers and all his father's house heard *it,* they went down there to him. 2 And everyone *who was* in distress, everyone who *was* in debt, and everyone *who was* discontented gathered to him. So he became captain over them. And there were about four hundred men with him.

3 Then David went from there to Mizpah of Moab; and he said to the king of Moab, "Please let my father and mother come here with you, till I know what God will do for me." 4 So he brought them before the king of Moab, and they dwelt with him all the time that David was in the stronghold.

5 Now the prophet Gad said to David, "Do not stay in the stronghold; depart, and go to the land of Judah." So David departed and went into the forest of Hereth.

6 When Saul heard that David and the men who *were* with him had been discovered—now Saul was staying in Gibeah under a tamarisk tree in Ramah, with his spear in his hand, and all his servants standing about him— 7 then Saul said to his servants who stood about him, "Hear now, you Benjamites! Will the son of Jesse give every one of you fields and vineyards, *and* make you all captains of thousands and captains of hundreds? 8 All of you have conspired against me, and *there is* no one who reveals to me that my son has made a covenant with the son of Jesse; and *there is* not one of you who is sorry for me or reveals to me that my son has stirred up my servant against me, to lie in wait, as *it is* this day."

9 Then answered Doeg the Edomite, who was set over the servants of Saul, and said, "I saw the son of Jesse going to Nob, to Ahimelech the son of Ahitub. 10 And he inquired of the LORD for him, gave him provisions, and gave him the sword of Goliath the Philistine."

11 So the king sent to call Ahimelech the priest, the son of Ahitub, and all his father's house, the priests who *were* in Nob. And they all came to the king. 12 And Saul said, "Hear now, son of Ahitub!"

He answered, "Here I am, my lord."

13 Then Saul said to him, "Why

have you conspired against me, you and the son of Jesse, in that you have given him bread and a sword, and have inquired of God for him, that he should rise against me, to lie in wait, as it is this day?"

14 So Ahimelech answered the king and said, "And who among all your servants *is as* faithful as David, who is the king's son-in-law, who goes at your bidding, and is honorable in your house? 15 Did I then begin to inquire of God for him? Far be it from me! Let not the king impute anything to his servant, *or* to any in the house of my father. For your servant knew nothing of all this, little or much."

16 And the king said, "You shall surely die, Ahimelech, you and all your father's house!" 17 Then the king said to the guards who stood about him, "Turn and kill the priests of the LORD, because their hand also *is* with David, and because they knew when he fled and did not tell it to me." But the servants of the king would not lift their hands to strike the priests of the LORD. 18 And the king said to Doeg, "You turn and kill the priests!" So Doeg the Edomite turned and struck the priests, and killed on that day eighty-five men who wore a linen ephod. 19 Also Nob, the city of the priests, he struck with the edge of the sword, both men and women, children and nursing infants, oxen and donkeys and sheep—with the edge of the sword.

20 Now one of the sons of Ahimelech the son of Ahitub, named Abiathar, escaped and fled after David. 21 And Abiathar told David that Saul had killed the LORD's priests. 22 So David said to Abiathar, "I knew that day, when Doeg the Edomite *was* there, that he would surely tell Saul. I have caused *the death* of all the persons of your father's house. 23 Stay with me; do not fear. For he who seeks my life seeks your life, but with me you *shall be* safe."

23 Then they told David, saying, "Look, the Philistines are fighting against Keilah, and they are robbing the threshing floors."

2 Therefore David inquired of the LORD, saying, "Shall I go and attack these Philistines?"

And the LORD said to David, "Go and attack the Philistines, and save Keilah."

3 But David's men said to him, "Look, we are afraid here in Judah. How much more then if we go to Keilah against the armies of the Philistines?" 4 Then David inquired of the LORD once again.

And the LORD answered him and said, "Arise, go down to Keilah. For I will deliver the Philistines into your hand." 5 And David and his men went to Keilah and fought with the Philistines, struck them with a mighty blow, and took away their livestock. So David saved the inhabitants of Keilah.

6 Now it happened, when Abiathar the son of Ahimelech fled to David at Keilah, *that* he went down *with* an ephod in his hand.

7 And Saul was told that David had gone to Keilah. So Saul said, "God has delivered him into my hand, for he has shut himself in by entering a town that has gates and bars." 8 Then Saul called all the people together for war, to go down to Keilah to besiege David and his men.

9 When David knew that Saul plotted evil against him, he said to Abiathar the priest, "Bring the ephod here." 10 Then David said, "O LORD God of Israel, Your servant has certainly heard that Saul seeks to come to Keilah to destroy the city for my sake. 11 Will the men of Keilah deliver me into his hand? Will Saul come down, as Your servant has heard? O LORD God of Israel, I pray, tell Your servant."

And the LORD said, "He will come down."

12 Then David said, "Will the men of Keilah deliver me and my men into the hand of Saul?"

And the LORD said, "They will deliver *you*."

13 So David and his men, about six hundred, arose and departed from Keilah and went wherever they could go. Then it was told Saul that David had escaped from Keilah; so he halted the expedition.

14 And David stayed in strongholds in the wilderness, and remained in the mountains in the Wilderness of Ziph. Saul sought him every day, but God did not deliver him into his hand. 15 So David saw that Saul had come out to seek his life. And David

was in the Wilderness of Ziph in a forest.*a* 16 Then Jonathan, Saul's son, arose and went to David in the woods and strengthened his hand in God. 17 And he said to him, "Do not fear, for the hand of Saul my father shall not find you. You shall be king over Israel, and I shall be next to you. Even my father Saul knows that." 18 So the two of them made a covenant before the LORD. And David stayed in the woods, and Jonathan went to his own house.

19 Then the Ziphites came up to Saul at Gibeah, saying, "Is David not hiding with us in strongholds in the woods, in the hill of Hachilah, which *is* on the south of Jeshimon? 20 Now therefore, O king, come down according to all the desire of your soul to come down; and our part *shall be* to deliver him into the king's hand."

21 And Saul said, "Blessed *are* you of the LORD, for you have compassion on me. 22 Please go and find out for sure, and see the place where his hideout is, *and* who has seen him there. For I am told he is very crafty. 23 See therefore, and take knowledge of all the lurking places where he hides; and come back to me with certainty, and I will go with you. And it shall be, if he is in the land, that I will search for him throughout all the clans*a* of Judah."

24 So they arose and went to Ziph before Saul. But David and his men *were* in the Wilderness of Maon, in the plain on the south of Jeshimon. 25 When Saul and his men went to seek *him,* they told David. Therefore he went down to the rock, and stayed in the Wilderness of Maon. And when Saul heard *that,* he pursued David in the Wilderness of Maon. 26 Then Saul went on one side of the mountain, and David and his men on the other side of the mountain. So David made haste to get away from Saul, for Saul and his men were encircling David and his men to take them.

27 But a messenger came to Saul, saying, "Hurry and come, for the Philistines have invaded the land!" 28 Therefore Saul returned from pursuing David, and went against the Philistines; so they called that place the Rock of Escape.*a* 29 Then David

went up from there and dwelt in strongholds at En Gedi.

24 Now it happened, when Saul had returned from following the Philistines, that it was told him, saying, "Take note! David *is* in the Wilderness of En Gedi." 2 Then Saul took three thousand chosen men from all Israel, and went to seek David and his men on the Rocks of the Wild Goats. 3 So he came to the sheepfolds by the road, where there *was* a cave; and Saul went in to attend to his needs. (David and his men were staying in the recesses of the cave.) 4 Then the men of David said to him, "This is the day of which the LORD said to you, 'Behold, I will deliver your enemy into your hand, that you may do to him as it seems good to you.'" And David arose and secretly cut off a corner of Saul's robe. 5 Now it happened afterward that David's heart troubled him because he had cut Saul's *robe.* 6 And he said to his men, "The LORD forbid that I should do this thing to my master, the LORD's anointed, to stretch out my hand against him, seeing he *is* the anointed of the LORD." 7 So David restrained his servants with *these* words, and did not allow them to rise against Saul. And Saul got up from the cave and went on *his* way.

8 David also arose afterward, went out of the cave, and called out to Saul, saying, "My lord the king!" And when Saul looked behind him, David stooped with his face to the earth, and bowed down. 9 And David said to Saul: "Why do you listen to the words of men who say, 'Indeed David seeks your harm'? 10 Look, this day your eyes have seen that the LORD delivered you today into my hand in the cave, and *someone* urged *me* to kill you. But *my eye* spared you, and I said, 'I will not stretch out my hand against my lord, for he *is* the LORD's anointed.' 11 Moreover, my father, see! Yes, see the corner of your robe in my hand! For in that I cut off the corner of your robe, and did not kill you, know and see that *there is* neither evil nor rebellion in my hand, and I have not sinned against you. Yet you hunt my life to take it. 12 Let the LORD judge between

23:15 *a*Or *in Horesh*   23:23 *a*Literally *thousands*   23:28 *a*Hebrew *Sela Hammahlekoth* you and me, and let the LORD avenge me on you. But my hand shall not be against you. 13 As the proverb of the ancients says, 'Wickedness proceeds from the wicked.' But my hand shall not be against you. 14 After whom has the king of Israel come out? Whom do you pursue? A dead dog? A flea? 15 Therefore let the LORD be judge, and judge between you and me, and see and plead my case, and deliver me out of your hand."

16 So it was, when David had finished speaking these words to Saul, that Saul said, "Is this your voice, my son David?" And Saul lifted up his voice and wept. 17 Then he said to David: "You are more righteous than I; for you have rewarded me with good, whereas I have rewarded you with evil. 18 And you have shown this day how you have dealt well with me; for when the LORD delivered me into your hand, you did not kill me. 19 For if a man finds his enemy, will he let him get away safely? Therefore may the LORD reward you with good for what you have done to me this day. 20 And now I know indeed that you shall surely be king, and that the kingdom of Israel shall be established in your hand. 21 Therefore swear now to me by the LORD that you will not cut off my descendants after me, and that you will not destroy my name from my father's house."

22 So David swore to Saul. And Saul went home, but David and his men went up to the stronghold.

25 Then Samuel died; and the Israelites gathered together and lamented for him, and buried him at his home in Ramah. And David arose and went down to the Wilderness of Paran.[a]

2 Now there was a man in Maon whose business was in Carmel, and the man was very rich. He had three thousand sheep and a thousand goats. And he was shearing his sheep in Carmel. 3 The name of the man was Nabal, and the name of his wife Abigail. And she was a woman of good understanding and beautiful appearance; but the man was harsh and evil in his doings. He was of the house of Caleb.

4 When David heard in the wilderness that Nabal was shearing his sheep, 5 David sent ten young men; and David said to the young men, "Go up to Carmel, go to Nabal, and greet him in my name. 6 And thus you shall say to him who lives in prosperity: 'Peace be to you, peace to your house, and peace to all that you have! 7 Now I have heard that you have shearers. Your shepherds were with us, and we did not hurt them, nor was there anything missing from them all the while they were in Carmel. 8 Ask your young men, and they will tell you. Therefore let my young men find favor in your eyes, for we come on a feast day. Please give whatever comes to your hand to your servants and to your son David.' "

9 So when David's young men came, they spoke to Nabal according to all these words in the name of David, and waited.

10 Then Nabal answered David's servants, and said, "Who is David, and who is the son of Jesse? There are many servants nowadays who break away each one from his master. 11 Shall I then take my bread and my water and my meat that I have killed for my shearers, and give it to men when I do not know where they are from?"

12 So David's young men turned on their heels and went back; and they came and told him all these words. 13 Then David said to his men, "Every man gird on his sword." So every man girded on his sword, and David also girded on his sword. And about four hundred men went with David, and two hundred stayed with the supplies.

14 Now one of the young men told Abigail, Nabal's wife, saying, "Look, David sent messengers from the wilderness to greet our master; and he reviled them. 15 But the men were very good to us, and we were not hurt, nor did we miss anything as long as we accompanied them, when we were in the fields. 16 They were a wall to us both by night and day, all the time we were with them keeping the sheep. 17 Now therefore, know and consider what you will do, for harm is determined against our master and against all his household.

25:1 [a]Following Masoretic Text, Syriac, Targum, and Vulgate; Septuagint reads Maon.

For he *is such* a scoundrel[a] that *one* cannot speak to him."

18 Then Abigail made haste and took two hundred *loaves* of bread, two skins of wine, five sheep already dressed, five seahs of roasted *grain,* one hundred clusters of raisins, and two hundred cakes of figs, and loaded *them* on donkeys. 19 And she said to her servants, "Go on before me; see, I am coming after you." But she did not tell her husband Nabal.

20 So it was, *as* she rode on the donkey, that she went down under cover of the hill; and there were David and his men, coming down toward her, and she met them. 21 Now David had said, "Surely in vain I have protected all that this *fellow* has in the wilderness, so that nothing was missed of all that *belongs* to him. And he has repaid me evil for good. 22 May God do so, and more also, to the enemies of David, if I leave one male of all who *belong* to him by morning light."

23 Now when Abigail saw David, she dismounted quickly from the donkey, fell on her face before David, and bowed down to the ground. 24 So she fell at his feet and said: "On me, my lord, *on* me *let* this iniquity *be!* And please let your maidservant speak in your ears, and hear the words of your maidservant. 25 Please, let not my lord regard this scoundrel Nabal. For as his name *is,* so *is* he: Nabal[a] *is* his name, and folly *is* with him! But I, your maidservant, did not see the young men of my lord whom you sent. 26 Now therefore, my lord, *as* the LORD lives and *as* your soul lives, since the LORD has held you back from coming to bloodshed and from avenging yourself with your own hand, now then, let your enemies and those who seek harm for my lord be as Nabal. 27 And now this present which your maidservant has brought to my lord, let it be given to the young men who follow my lord. 28 Please forgive the trespass of your maidservant. For the LORD will certainly make for my lord an enduring house, because my lord fights the battles of the LORD, and evil is not found in you throughout your days. 29 Yet a man has risen to pursue you and seek your life, but the life of my lord shall be bound in the bundle of the living with the LORD your God; and the lives of your enemies He shall sling out, *as from* the pocket of a sling. 30 And it shall come to pass, when the LORD has done for my lord according to all the good that He has spoken concerning you, and has appointed you ruler over Israel, 31 that this will be no grief to you, nor offense of heart to my lord, either that you have shed blood without cause, or that my lord has avenged himself. But when the LORD has dealt well with my lord, then remember your maidservant."

32 Then David said to Abigail: "Blessed *is* the LORD God of Israel, who sent you this day to meet me! 33 And blessed *is* your advice and blessed *are* you, because you have kept me this day from coming to bloodshed and from avenging myself with my own hand. 34 For indeed, *as* the LORD God of Israel lives, who has kept me back from hurting you, unless you had hurried and come to meet me, surely by morning light no males would have been left to Nabal!" 35 So David received from her hand what she had brought him, and said to her, "Go up in peace to your house. See, I have heeded your voice and respected your person."

36 Now Abigail went to Nabal, and there he was, holding a feast in his house, like the feast of a king. And Nabal's heart *was* merry within him, for he *was* very drunk; therefore she told him nothing, little or much, until morning light. 37 So it was, in the morning, when the wine had gone from Nabal, and his wife had told him these things, that his heart died within him, and he became *like* a stone. 38 Then it happened, *after* about ten days, that the LORD struck Nabal, and he died.

39 So when David heard that Nabal was dead, he said, "Blessed *be* the LORD, who has pleaded the cause of my reproach from the hand of Nabal, and has kept His servant from evil! For the LORD has returned the wickedness of Nabal on his own head."

And David sent and proposed to Abigail, to take her as his wife. 40 When the servants of David had come to Abigail at Carmel, they spoke to her saying, "David sent us to you, to ask you to become his wife."

41 Then she arose, bowed her face to the earth, and said, "Here is your maidservant, a servant to wash the feet of the servants of my lord." 42 So Abigail rose in haste and rode on a donkey, attended by five of her maidens; and she followed the messengers of David, and became his wife. 43 David also took Ahinoam of Jezreel, and so both of them were his wives.

44 But Saul had given Michal his daughter, David's wife, to Palti[a] the son of Laish, who *was* from Gallim.

26 Now the Ziphites came to Saul at Gibeah, saying, "Is David not hiding in the hill of Hachilah, opposite Jeshimon?" 2 Then Saul arose and went down to the Wilderness of Ziph, having three thousand chosen men of Israel with him, to seek David in the Wilderness of Ziph. 3 And Saul encamped in the hill of Hachilah, which *is* opposite Jeshimon, by the road. But David stayed in the wilderness, and he saw that Saul came after him into the wilderness. 4 David therefore sent out spies, and understood that Saul had indeed come.

5 So David arose and came to the place where Saul had encamped. And David saw the place where Saul lay, and Abner the son of Ner, the commander of his army. Now Saul lay within the camp, with the people encamped all around him. 6 Then David answered, and said to Ahimelech the Hittite and to Abishai the son of Zeruiah, brother of Joab, saying, "Who will go down with me to Saul in the camp?"

And Abishai said, "I will go down with you."

7 So David and Abishai came to the people by night; and there Saul lay sleeping within the camp, with his spear stuck in the ground by his head. And Abner and the people lay all around him. 8 Then Abishai said to David, "God has delivered your enemy into your hand this day. Now therefore, please, let me strike him at once with the spear, right to the earth; and I will not *have to strike* him a second time!"

9 But David said to Abishai, "Do not destroy him; for who can stretch out his hand against the LORD's anointed, and be guiltless?" 10 David said furthermore, "As the LORD lives, the LORD shall strike him, or his day shall come to die, or he shall go out to battle and perish. 11 The LORD forbid that I should stretch out my hand against the LORD's anointed. But please, take now the spear and the jug of water that *are* by his head, and let us go." 12 So David took the spear and the jug of water *by* Saul's head, and they got away; and no man saw or knew *it* or awoke. For they *were* all asleep, because a deep sleep from the LORD had fallen on them.

13 Now David went over to the other side, and stood on the top of a hill afar off, a great distance *being* between them. 14 And David called out to the people and to Abner the son of Ner, saying, "Do you not answer, Abner?"

Then Abner answered and said, "Who *are* you, calling out to the king?"

15 So David said to Abner, "*Are* you not a man? And who *is* like you in Israel? Why then have you not guarded your lord the king? For one of the people came in to destroy your lord the king. 16 This thing that you have done *is* not good. *As* the LORD lives, you deserve to die, because you have not guarded your master, the LORD's anointed. And now see where the king's spear *is*, and the jug of water that *was* by his head."

17 Then Saul knew David's voice, and said, "*Is* that your voice, my son David?"

David said, "*It is* my voice, my lord, O king." 18 And he said, "Why does my lord thus pursue his servant? For what have I done, or what evil *is* in my hand? 19 Now therefore, please, let my lord the king hear the words of his servant: If the LORD has stirred you up against me, let Him accept an offering. But if *it is* the children of men, *may* they *be* cursed before the LORD, for they have driven me out this day from sharing in the inheritance of the LORD, saying, 'Go, serve other gods.' 20 So now, do not let my blood fall to the earth before the face of the LORD. For the king of Israel has come out to seek a flea,

25:44 [a]Spelled *Paltiel* in 2 Samuel 3:15

as when one hunts a partridge in the mountains."

21 Then Saul said, "I have sinned. Return, my son David. For I will harm you no more, because my life was precious in your eyes this day. Indeed I have played the fool and erred exceedingly."

22 And David answered and said, "Here is the king's spear. Let one of the young men come over and get it. 23 May the LORD repay every man *for* his righteousness and his faithfulness; for the LORD delivered you into *my* hand today, but I would not stretch out my hand against the LORD's anointed. 24 And indeed, as your life was valued much this day in my eyes, so let my life be valued much in the eyes of the LORD, and let Him deliver me out of all tribulation."

25 Then Saul said to David, "*May* you *be* blessed, my son David! You shall both do great things and also still prevail."

So David went on his way, and Saul returned to his place.

27 And David said in his heart, "Now I shall perish someday by the hand of Saul. *There is* nothing better for me than that I should speedily escape to the land of the Philistines; and Saul will despair of me, to seek me anymore in any part of Israel. So I shall escape out of his hand." 2 Then David arose and went over with the six hundred men who *were* with him to Achish the son of Maoch, king of Gath. 3 So David dwelt with Achish at Gath, he and his men, each man with his household, *and* David with his two wives, Ahinoam the Jezreelitess, and Abigail the Carmelitess, Nabal's widow. 4 And it was told Saul that David had fled to Gath; so he sought him no more.

5 Then David said to Achish, "If I have now found favor in your eyes, let them give me a place in some town in the country, that I may dwell there. For why should your servant dwell in the royal city with you?" 6 So Achish gave him Ziklag that day. Therefore Ziklag has belonged to the kings of Judah to this day. 7 Now the time that David dwelt in

the country of the Philistines was one full year and four months.

8 And David and his men went up and raided the Geshurites, the Girzites,*a* and the Amalekites. For those nations were the inhabitants of the land from of old, as you go to Shur, even as far as the land of Egypt. 9 Whenever David attacked the land, he left neither man nor woman alive, but took away the sheep, the oxen, the donkeys, the camels, and the apparel, and returned and came to Achish. 10 Then Achish would say, "Where have you made a raid today?" And David would say, "Against the southern *area* of Judah, or against the southern *area* of the Jerahmeelites, or against the southern *area* of the Kenites." 11 David would save neither man nor woman alive, to bring *news* to Gath, saying, "Lest they should inform on us, saying, 'Thus David did.' " And thus *was* his behavior all the time he dwelt in the country of the Philistines. 12 So Achish believed David, saying, "He has made his people Israel utterly abhor him; therefore he will be my servant forever."

28 Now it happened in those days that the Philistines gathered their armies together for war, to fight with Israel. And Achish said to David, "You assuredly know that you will go out with me to battle, you and your men."

2 So David said to Achish, "Surely you know what your servant can do."

And Achish said to David, "Therefore I will make you one of my chief guardians forever."

3 Now Samuel had died, and all Israel had lamented for him and buried him in Ramah, in his own city. And Saul had put the mediums and the spiritists out of the land.

4 Then the Philistines gathered together, and came and encamped at Shunem. So Saul gathered all Israel together, and they encamped at Gilboa. 5 When Saul saw the army of the Philistines, he was afraid, and his heart trembled greatly. 6 And when Saul inquired of the LORD, the LORD did not answer him, either by dreams or by Urim or by the prophets.

7 Then Saul said to his servants, "Find me a woman who is a medium,

Making Peace with Your Enemies

One of the qualities that made David a great leader was his ability to overcome any obstacle that lay in his path. When faced with a difficult situation he believed in exhausting all possibilities!

Following his victory over the Philistine giant, Goliath, young David spent years fleeing from the jealous King Saul. Many times David had the opportunity to strike back at Saul, but he refused to harm God's anointed king. David believed God could deliver him in any and all circumstances.

Perhaps one of the most difficult situations David encountered was during a narrow escape from King Saul in the lower hill country near the dangerous Philistine coastal territory. David continually fled from Saul in the eastern wilderness areas, only to be flushed out by the king's army. This left him with only one avenue of escape—directly through Philistine territory and the royal city of Gath. David knew that within the city was one of his most vengeful adversaries, Achish, king of Gath, a ruler who had every reason to kill him.

Achish ruled Gath, one of five royal Philistine cities which also included Ashdod, Ashkelon, Ekron, and Gaza. He was a member of the royal family and most likely a relative (and possibly the brother) of Goliath. Achish knew of David's wars against the Philistines and would have remembered David's slaying of not only Goliath but also of the giant's sons and brothers (1 Chr. 20:4–8). There seemed to be no reasonable way that King Achish would protect David from Saul, but David believed that the same God who delivered him from the bear and the lion would turn the heart of Achish. He knew that with God all things are possible. With the same indomitable spirit David displayed before Goliath, he now approached Achish, king of Gath, and requested his protection.

God honored David's attempt to make peace with his enemy. Impressed by his bravery, Achish not only welcomed David but appointed him as ruler over the city of Ziklag, an important Philistine defense post (see 1 Sam. 27, 28). David knew that if he believed God, no situation was hopeless. Making peace with an enemy becomes a possibility with faith in God! "You prepare a table before me in the presence of my enemies" (Ps. 23:5).

that I may go to her and inquire of her."

And his servants said to him, "In fact, *there is* a woman who is a medium at En Dor."

8 So Saul disguised himself and put on other clothes, and he went, and two men with him; and they came to the woman by night. And he said, "Please conduct a séance for me, and bring up for me the one I shall name to you."

9 Then the woman said to him, "Look, you know what Saul has done, how he has cut off the mediums and the spiritists from the land. Why then do you lay a snare for my life, to cause me to die?"

10 And Saul swore to her by the LORD, saying, "*As* the LORD lives, no punishment shall come upon you for this thing."

11 Then the woman said, "Whom shall I bring up for you?"

And he said, "Bring up Samuel for me."

12 When the woman saw Samuel, she cried out with a loud voice. And the woman spoke to Saul, saying, "Why have you deceived me? For you *are* Saul!"

13 And the king said to her, "Do not be afraid. What did you see?"

And the woman said to Saul, "I saw a spirit*a* ascending out of the earth."

14 So he said to her, "What *is* his form?"

And she said, "An old man is coming up, and he *is* covered with a mantle." And Saul perceived that it *was* Samuel, and he stooped with *his* face to the ground and bowed down.

15 Now Samuel said to Saul, "Why have you disturbed me by bringing me up?"

And Saul answered, "I am deeply distressed; for the Philistines make war against me, and God has departed from me and does not answer me anymore, neither by prophets nor by dreams. Therefore I have called you, that you may reveal to me what I should do."

16 Then Samuel said: "So why do you ask me, seeing the LORD has departed from you and has become your enemy? 17 And the LORD has done for Himself*a* as He spoke by me. For the LORD has torn the kingdom

out of your hand and given it to your neighbor, David. 18 Because you did not obey the voice of the LORD nor execute His fierce wrath upon Amalek, therefore the LORD has done this thing to you this day. 19 Moreover the LORD will also deliver Israel with you into the hand of the Philistines. And tomorrow you and your sons *will be* with me. The LORD will also deliver the army of Israel into the hand of the Philistines."

20 Immediately Saul fell full length on the ground, and was dreadfully afraid because of the words of Samuel. And there was no strength in him, for he had eaten no food all day or all night.

21 And the woman came to Saul and saw that he was severely troubled, and said to him, "Look, your maidservant has obeyed your voice, and I have put my life in my hands and heeded the words which you spoke to me. 22 Now therefore, please, heed also the voice of your maidservant, and let me set a piece of bread before you; and eat, that you may have strength when you go on *your* way."

23 But he refused and said, "I will not eat."

So his servants, together with the woman, urged him; and he heeded their voice. Then he arose from the ground and sat on the bed. 24 Now the woman had a fatted calf in the house, and she hastened to kill it. And she took flour and kneaded *it,* and baked unleavened bread from it. 25 So she brought *it* before Saul and his servants, and they ate. Then they rose and went away that night.

29 Then the Philistines gathered together all their armies at Aphek, and the Israelites encamped by a fountain which *is* in Jezreel. 2 And the lords of the Philistines passed in review by hundreds and by thousands, but David and his men passed in review at the rear with Achish. 3 Then the princes of the Philistines said, "What *are* these Hebrews *doing here?*"

And Achish said to the princes of the Philistines, "*Is* this not David, the servant of Saul king of Israel, who has been with me these days, or these years? And to this day I have found

28:13 *a*Hebrew *elohim*   28:17 *a*Or *him,* that is, David no fault in him since he defected *to me.*"

4 But the princes of the Philistines were angry with him; so the princes of the Philistines said to him, "Make this fellow return, that he may go back to the place which you have appointed for him, and do not let him go down with us to battle, lest in the battle he become our adversary. For with what could he reconcile himself to his master, if not with the heads of these men? 5 *Is* this not David, of whom they sang to one another in dances, saying:

'Saul has slain his thousands,
And David his ten
thousands'?"*a*

6 Then Achish called David and said to him, "Surely, *as* the LORD lives, you have been upright, and your going out and your coming in with me in the army *is* good in my sight. For to this day I have not found evil in you since the day of your coming to me. Nevertheless the lords do not favor you. 7 Therefore return now, and go in peace, that you may not displease the lords of the Philistines."

8 So David said to Achish, "But what have I done? And to this day what have you found in your servant as long as I have been with you, that I may not go and fight against the enemies of my lord the king?"

9 Then Achish answered and said to David, "I know that you *are* as good in my sight as an angel of God; nevertheless the princes of the Philistines have said, 'He shall not go up with us to the battle.' 10 Now therefore, rise early in the morning with your master's servants who have come with you.*a* And as soon as you are up early in the morning and have light, depart."

11 So David and his men rose early to depart in the morning, to return to the land of the Philistines. And the Philistines went up to Jezreel.

30 Now it happened, when David and his men came to Ziklag, on the third day, that the Amalekites had invaded the South and Ziklag,

attacked Ziklag and burned it with fire, 2 and had taken captive the women and those who *were* there, from small to great; they did not kill anyone, but carried *them* away and went their way. 3 So David and his men came to the city, and there it was, burned with fire; and their wives, their sons, and their daughters had been taken captive. 4 Then David and the people who *were* with him lifted up their voices and wept, until they had no more power to weep. 5 And David's two wives, Ahinoam the Jezreelitess, and Abigail the widow of Nabal the Carmelite, had been taken captive. 6 Now David was greatly distressed, for the people spoke of stoning him, because the soul of all the people was grieved, every man for his sons and his daughters. But David strengthened himself in the LORD his God.

7 Then David said to Abiathar the priest, Ahimelech's son, "Please bring the ephod here to me." And Abiathar brought the ephod to David. 8 So David inquired of the LORD, saying, "Shall I pursue this troop? Shall I overtake them?"

And He answered him, "Pursue, for you shall surely overtake *them* and without fail recover *all.*"

9 So David went, he and the six hundred men who *were* with him, and came to the Brook Besor, where those stayed who were left behind. 10 But David pursued, he and four hundred men; for two hundred stayed *behind,* who were so weary that they could not cross the Brook Besor.

11 Then they found an Egyptian in the field, and brought him to David; and they gave him bread and he ate, and they let him drink water. 12 And they gave him a piece of a cake of figs and two clusters of raisins. So when he had eaten, his strength came back to him; for he had eaten no bread nor drunk water for three days and three nights. 13 Then David said to him, "To whom do you *belong,* and where *are* you from?"

And he said, "I *am* a young man from Egypt, servant of an Amalekite; and my master left me behind, be-

---

29:5 *a*Compare 1 Samuel 18:7   29:10 *a*Following Masoretic Text, Targum, and Vulgate; Septuagint adds *and go to the place which I have selected for you there; and set no bothersome word in your heart, for you are good before me. And rise on your way.*

cause three days ago I fell sick. 14 We made an invasion of the southern *area* of the Cherethites, in the *territory* which *belongs* to Judah, and of the southern *area* of Caleb; and we burned Ziklag with fire."

15 And David said to him, "Can you take me down to this troop?"

So he said, "Swear to me by God that you will neither kill me nor deliver me into the hands of my master, and I will take you down to this troop."

16 And when he had brought him down, there they were, spread out over all the land, eating and drinking and dancing, because of all the great spoil which they had taken from the land of the Philistines and from the land of Judah. 17 Then David attacked them from twilight until the evening of the next day. Not a man of them escaped, except four hundred young men who rode on camels and fled. 18 So David recovered all that the Amalekites had carried away, and David rescued his two wives. 19 And nothing of theirs was lacking, either small or great, sons or daughters, spoil or anything which they had taken from them; David recovered all. 20 Then David took all the flocks and herds they had driven before those *other* livestock, and said, "This *is* David's spoil."

21 Now David came to the two hundred men who had been so weary that they could not follow David, whom they also had made to stay at the Brook Besor. So they went out to meet David and to meet the people who *were* with him. And when David came near the people, he greeted them. 22 Then all the wicked and worthless men*a* of those who went with David answered and said, "Because they did not go with us, we will not give them *any* of the spoil that we have recovered, except for every man's wife and children, that they may lead *them* away and depart."

23 But David said, "My brethren, you shall not do so with what the LORD has given us, who has preserved us and delivered into our hand the troop that came against us. 24 For who will heed you in this matter? But as his part *is* who goes down to the battle, so *shall* his part *be* who stays by the supplies; they shall share alike." 25 So it was, from that day forward; he made it a statute and an ordinance for Israel to this day.

26 Now when David came to Ziklag, he sent *some* of the spoil to the elders of Judah, to his friends, saying, "Here is a present for you from the spoil of the enemies of the LORD"— 27 to *those* who *were* in Bethel, *those* who *were* in Ramoth of the South, *those* who *were* in Jattir, 28 *those* who *were* in Aroer, *those* who *were* in Siphmoth, *those* who *were* in Eshtemoa, 29 *those* who *were* in Rachal, *those* who *were* in the cities of the Jerahmeelites, *those* who *were* in the cities of the Kenites, 30 *those* who *were* in Hormah, *those* who *were* in Chorashan,*a* *those* who *were* in Athach, 31 *those* who *were* in Hebron, and to all the places where David himself and his men were accustomed to rove.

31 Now the Philistines fought against Israel; and the men of Israel fled from before the Philistines, and fell slain on Mount Gilboa. 2 Then the Philistines followed hard after Saul and his sons. And the Philistines killed Jonathan, Abinadab, and Malchishua, Saul's sons. 3 The battle became fierce against Saul. The archers hit him, and he was severely wounded by the archers.

4 Then Saul said to his armorbearer, "Draw your sword, and thrust me through with it, lest these uncircumcised men come and thrust me through and abuse me."

But his armorbearer would not, for he was greatly afraid. Therefore Saul took a sword and fell on it. 5 And when his armorbearer saw that Saul was dead, he also fell on his sword, and died with him. 6 So Saul, his three sons, his armorbearer, and all his men died together that same day.

7 And when the men of Israel who *were* on the other side of the valley, and *those* who *were* on the other side of the Jordan, saw that the men of Israel had fled and that Saul and his sons were dead, they forsook the cities and fled; and the Philistines came and dwelt in them. 8 So it happened the next day, when the Philistines came to strip the slain, that they found Saul and his three sons fallen

---

30:22 *a*Literally *men of Belial*   30:30 *a*Or *Borashan* on Mount Gilboa. 9 And they cut off his head and stripped off his armor, and sent *word* throughout the land of the Philistines, to proclaim *it in* the temple of their idols and among the people. 10 Then they put his armor in the temple of the Ashtoreths, and they fastened his body to the wall of Beth Shan.*a*

11 Now when the inhabitants of Ja-besh Gilead heard what the Philistines had done to Saul, 12 all the valiant men arose and traveled all night, and took the body of Saul and the bodies of his sons from the wall of Beth Shan; and they came to Jabesh and burned them there. 13 Then they took their bones and buried *them* under the tamarisk tree at Jabesh, and fasted seven days.

31:10 *a*Spelled *Beth Shean* in Joshua 17:11 and elsewhere

Second Samuel

Overview of Second Samuel

S econd Samuel was compiled from the writings of Samuel, David, Nathan, and Gad between 1150–950 B.C. It tells the story of David's life as king of Israel. The book opens with the ascension of King David to Israel's throne following Saul's death. Second Samuel records David's strength as a leader in difficult times. Israel fought ten wars in forty years, and David's early years as king were filled with the task of suppressing civil war. Chapter five describes the heroic capture of Jerusalem by David and his commanding officers.

David's rule as king was not to be void of family and personal problems. Though a great leader in Israel's history, David faced failure and sin that could have ruined his life. In an incident with the wife of one of his commanding officers, David committed adultery and then tried to cover up his sin by murder. He married Bathsheba, the widowed wife of the commander Uriah, whom David had ordered into the front lines and certain death.

Rebuked for his sins by the prophet Nathan, David anguished over his failure, fearful that God could not forgive him. But God did forgive him, and later Bathsheba gave birth to Solomon, who was to become successor to the throne and was included in the genealogy of Jesus Christ. David and Bathsheba experienced firsthand God's ability to turn their scar into a star! This forgiveness is evident in many of David's psalms:

> *Blessed* is he whose *transgression* is *forgiven,*
> Whose *sin* is *covered.*
> *Blessed* is *the man to whom the Lord does not impute iniquity,*
> *And in whose spirit* there is *no deceit.*
>
>   (Ps. 32:2, 3)

David was a king who turned impossibilities into possibilities, problems into opportunities, and scars into stars—with God's help!

Jesus in Second Samuel

David is one of the most important types of Jesus in the Old Testament. His rule is characterized by justice, wisdom, integrity, and compassion. Having conquered Jerusalem, he sits upon the throne of Melchizedek, the "God Most High" (Gen 14:18). The closest way in which David foreshadows the coming King is in the important covenant God makes with him. David wants to build a house for God; instead, God makes a house for David. The three promises of an eternal kingdom, throne, and seed are later given to Jesus.

Keys to Second Samuel

Key Word: David. The central character of Second Samuel is David, around whom the entire book is written. The key truth illustrated is the same as the theme of Deuteronomy: obedience brings blessing and disobedience brings judgment.

Key Verses: "When your days are fulfilled and you rest with your fathers, I will set up your seed after you, who will come from your body, and I will establish his kingdom. He shall build a house for My name, and I will establish the throne of his kingdom forever" (7:12, 13).

"The LORD rewarded me according to my righteousness; According to the cleanness of my hands He has recompensed me" (22:21).

Key Chapter: Second Samuel 11. The eleventh chapter is pivotal for the entire book. This chapter records the tragic sins of David regarding Bathsheba and her husband Uriah. All of the widespread blessings on David's family and his kingdom are quickly removed as God chastises His anointed one.

1 Now it came to pass after the death of Saul, when David had returned from the slaughter of the Amalekites, and David had stayed two days in Ziklag, 2 on the third day, behold, it happened that a man came from Saul's camp with his clothes torn and dust on his head. So it was, when he came to David, that he fell to the ground and prostrated himself.

3 And David said to him, "Where have you come from?"

So he said to him, "I have escaped from the camp of Israel."

4 Then David said to him, "How did the matter go? Please tell me."

And he answered, "The people have fled from the battle, many of the people are fallen and dead, and Saul and Jonathan his son are dead also."

5 So David said to the young man who told him, "How do you know that Saul and Jonathan his son are dead?"

6 Then the young man who told him said, "As I happened by chance *to be* on Mount Gilboa, there was Saul, leaning on his spear; and indeed the chariots and horsemen followed hard after him. 7 Now when he looked behind him, he saw me and called to me. And I answered, 'Here I am.' 8 And he said to me, 'Who *are* you?' So I answered him, 'I *am* an Amalekite.' 9 He said to me again, 'Please stand over me and kill me, for anguish has come upon me, but my life still *remains* in me.' 10 So I stood over him and killed him, because I was sure that he could not live after he had fallen. And I took the crown that *was* on his head and the bracelet that *was* on his arm, and have brought them here to my lord."

11 Therefore David took hold of his own clothes and tore them, and *so did* all the men who *were* with him. 12 And they mourned and wept and fasted until evening for Saul and for Jonathan his son, for the people of the LORD and for the house of Israel, because they had fallen by the sword.

13 Then David said to the young man who told him, "Where *are* you from?"

And he answered, "I *am* the son of an alien, an Amalekite."

14 So David said to him, "How was it you were not afraid to put forth your hand to destroy the LORD's anointed?" 15 Then David called one of the young men and said, "Go near, *and* execute him!" And he struck him so that he died. 16 So David said to him, "Your blood *is* on your own head, for your own mouth has testified against you, saying, 'I have killed the LORD's anointed.'"

17 Then David lamented with this lamentation over Saul and over Jonathan his son, 18 and he told *them* to teach the children of Judah *the Song of* the Bow; indeed *it is* written in the Book of Jasher:

19 "The beauty of Israel is slain on
    your high places!
How the mighty have fallen!

20 Tell *it* not in Gath,
     Proclaim *it* not in the streets of
       Ashkelon—
     Lest the daughters of the
       Philistines rejoice,
     Lest the daughters of the
       uncircumcised triumph.

21 "O mountains of Gilboa,
     Let there be no dew nor rain
       upon you,
     Nor fields of offerings.
     For the shield of the mighty is
       cast away there!
     The shield of Saul, not anointed
       with oil.
22 From the blood of the slain,
     From the fat of the mighty,
     The bow of Jonathan did not
       turn back,
     And the sword of Saul did not
       return empty.

23 "Saul and Jonathan *were*
       beloved and pleasant in their
       lives,
     And in their death they were
       not divided;
     They were swifter than eagles,
     They were stronger than lions.

24 "O daughters of Israel, weep
       over Saul,
     Who clothed you in scarlet,
       with luxury;
     Who put ornaments of gold on
       your apparel.

25 "How the mighty have fallen in
       the midst of the battle!
     Jonathan *was* slain in your
       high places.
26 I am distressed for you, my
       brother Jonathan;
     You have been very pleasant to
       me;
     Your love to me was
       wonderful,
     Surpassing the love of women.

27 "How the mighty have fallen,
     And the weapons of war
       perished!"

2 It happened after this that David
  inquired of the LORD, saying,
"Shall I go up to any of the cities of
Judah?"
   And the LORD said to him, "Go up."

David said, "Where shall I go up?"
And He said, "To Hebron."
   2 So David went up there, and his
two wives also, Ahinoam the Jezreelitess, and Abigail the widow of Nabal
the Carmelite. 3 And David brought
up the men who *were* with him, every
man with his household. So they
dwelt in the cities of Hebron.
   4 Then the men of Judah came, and
there they anointed David king over
the house of Judah. And they told
David, saying, "The men of Jabesh
Gilead *were the ones* who buried
Saul." 5 So David sent messengers to
the men of Jabesh Gilead, and said
to them, "You *are* blessed of the
LORD, for you have shown this kindness to your lord, to Saul, and have
buried him. 6 And now may the LORD
show kindness and truth to you. I
also will repay you this kindness, because you have done this thing.
7 Now therefore, let your hands be
strengthened, and be valiant; for
your master Saul is dead, and also
the house of Judah has anointed me
king over them."
   8 But Abner the son of Ner, commander of Saul's army, took Ishbosheth*ᵃ* the son of Saul and brought
him over to Mahanaim; 9 and he
made him king over Gilead, over the
Ashurites, over Jezreel, over Ephraim, over Benjamin, and over all Israel. 10 Ishbosheth, Saul's son, *was*
forty years old when he began to
reign over Israel, and he reigned two
years. Only the house of Judah followed David. 11 And the time that
David was king in Hebron over the
house of Judah was seven years and
six months.
   12 Now Abner the son of Ner, and
the servants of Ishbosheth the son of
Saul, went out from Mahanaim to
Gibeon. 13 And Joab the son of Zeruiah, and the servants of David, went
out and met them by the pool of
Gibeon. So they sat down, one on one
side of the pool and the other on the
other side of the pool. 14 Then Abner
said to Joab, "Let the young men
now arise and compete before us."
   And Joab said, "Let them arise."
   15 So they arose and went over by
number, twelve from Benjamin, *followers* of Ishbosheth the son of Saul,
and twelve from the servants of David. 16 And each one grasped his op-

2:8 ᵃCalled *Esh-Baal* in 1 Chronicles 8:33 and 9:39

ponent by the head and *thrust* his sword in his opponent's side; so they fell down together. Therefore that place was called the Field of Sharp Swords,[a] which *is* in Gibeon. 17 So there was a very fierce battle that day, and Abner and the men of Israel were beaten before the servants of David.

18 Now the three sons of Zeruiah were there: Joab and Abishai and Asahel. And Asahel *was as* fleet of foot as a wild gazelle. 19 So Asahel pursued Abner, and in going he did not turn to the right hand or to the left from following Abner.

20 Then Abner looked behind him and said, "*Are* you Asahel?"

He answered, "I *am.*"

21 And Abner said to him, "Turn aside to your right hand or to your left, and lay hold on one of the young men and take his armor for yourself." But Asahel would not turn aside from following him. 22 So Abner said again to Asahel, "Turn aside from following me. Why should I strike you to the ground? How then could I face your brother Joab?" 23 However, he refused to turn aside. Therefore Abner struck him in the stomach with the blunt end of the spear, so that the spear came out of his back; and he fell down there and died on the spot. So it was *that* as many as came to the place where Asahel fell down and died, stood still.

24 Joab and Abishai also pursued Abner. And the sun was going down when they came to the hill of Ammah, which *is* before Giah by the road to the Wilderness of Gibeon. 25 Now the children of Benjamin gathered together behind Abner and became a unit, and took their stand on top of a hill. 26 Then Abner called to Joab and said, "Shall the sword devour forever? Do you not know that it will be bitter in the latter end? How long will it be then until you tell the people to return from pursuing their brethren?"

27 And Joab said, "*As* God lives, unless you had spoken, surely then by morning all the people would have given up pursuing their brethren." 28 So Joab blew a trumpet; and all the people stood still and did not pursue Israel anymore, nor did they fight anymore. 29 Then Abner and his men went on all that night through the plain, crossed over the Jordan, and went through all Bithron; and they came to Mahanaim.

30 So Joab returned from pursuing Abner. And when he had gathered all the people together, there were missing of David's servants nineteen men and Asahel. 31 But the servants of David had struck down, of Benjamin and Abner's men, three hundred and sixty men who died. 32 Then they took up Asahel and buried him in his father's tomb, which *was in* Bethlehem. And Joab and his men went all night, and they came to Hebron at daybreak.

3 Now there was a long war between the house of Saul and the house of David. But David grew stronger and stronger, and the house of Saul grew weaker and weaker.

2 Sons were born to David in Hebron: His firstborn was Amnon by Ahinoam the Jezreelitess; 3 his second, Chileab, by Abigail the widow of Nabal the Carmelite; the third, Absalom the son of Maacah, the daughter of Talmai, king of Geshur; 4 the fourth, Adonijah the son of Haggith; the fifth, Shephatiah the son of Abital; 5 and the sixth, Ithream, by David's wife Eglah. These were born to David in Hebron.

6 Now it was so, while there was war between the house of Saul and the house of David, that Abner was strengthening *his hold* on the house of Saul.

7 And Saul had a concubine, whose name *was* Rizpah, the daughter of Aiah. So *Ishbosheth* said to Abner, "Why have you gone in to my father's concubine?"

8 Then Abner became very angry at the words of Ishbosheth, and said, "*Am* I a dog's head that belongs to Judah? Today I show loyalty to the house of Saul your father, to his brothers, and to his friends, and have not delivered you into the hand of David; and you charge me today with a fault concerning this woman? 9 May God do so to Abner, and more also, if I do not do for David as the Lord has sworn to him— 10 to transfer the kingdom from the house of Saul, and set up the throne of David over Israel and over Judah, from Dan

2:16 [a]Hebrew *Helkath Hazzurim*

to Beersheba." 11 And he could not answer Abner another word, because he feared him.

12 Then Abner sent messengers on his behalf to David, saying, "Whose *is* the land?" saying *also,* "Make your covenant with me, and indeed my hand *shall be* with you to bring all Israel to you."

13 And *David* said, "Good, I will make a covenant with you. But one thing I require of you: you shall not see my face unless you first bring Michal, Saul's daughter, when you come to see my face." 14 So David sent messengers to Ishbosheth, Saul's son, saying, "Give *me* my wife Michal, whom I betrothed to myself for a hundred foreskins of the Philistines." 15 And Ishbosheth sent and took her from *her* husband, from Paltiel[a] the son of Laish. 16 Then her husband went along with her to Bahurim, weeping behind her. So Abner said to him, "Go, return!" And he returned.

17 Now Abner had communicated with the elders of Israel, saying, "In time past you were seeking for David *to be* king over you. 18 Now then, do *it!* For the LORD has spoken of David, saying, 'By the hand of My servant David, I[a] will save My people Israel from the hand of the Philistines and the hand of all their enemies.' " 19 And Abner also spoke in the hearing of Benjamin. Then Abner also went to speak in the hearing of David in Hebron all that seemed good to Israel and the whole house of Benjamin.

20 So Abner and twenty men with him came to David at Hebron. And David made a feast for Abner and the men who *were* with him. 21 Then Abner said to David, "I will arise and go, and gather all Israel to my lord the king, that they may make a covenant with you, and that you may reign over all that your heart desires." So David sent Abner away, and he went in peace.

22 At that moment the servants of David and Joab came from a raid and brought much spoil with them. But Abner *was* not with David in Hebron, for he had sent him away, and he had gone in peace. 23 When Joab and all the troops that *were* with him had

come, they told Joab, saying, "Abner the son of Ner came to the king, and he sent him away, and he has gone in peace." 24 Then Joab came to the king and said, "What have you done? Look, Abner came to you; why *is* it *that* you sent him away, and he has already gone? 25 Surely you realize that Abner the son of Ner came to deceive you, to know your going out and your coming in, and to know all that you are doing."

26 And when Joab had gone from David's presence, he sent messengers after Abner, who brought him back from the well of Sirah. But David did not know *it.* 27 Now when Abner had returned to Hebron, Joab took him aside in the gate to speak with him privately, and there stabbed him in the stomach, so that he died for the blood of Asahel his brother.

28 Afterward, when David heard *it,* he said, "My kingdom and I *are* guiltless before the LORD forever of the blood of Abner the son of Ner. 29 Let it rest on the head of Joab and on all his father's house; and let there never fail to be in the house of Joab one who has a discharge or is a leper, who leans on a staff or falls by the sword, or who lacks bread." 30 So Joab and Abishai his brother killed Abner, because he had killed their brother Asahel at Gibeon in the battle.

31 Then David said to Joab and to all the people who were with him, "Tear your clothes, gird yourselves with sackcloth, and mourn for Abner." And King David followed the coffin. 32 So they buried Abner in Hebron; and the king lifted up his voice and wept at the grave of Abner, and all the people wept. 33 And the king sang *a lament* over Abner and said:

"Should Abner die as a fool dies?
34   Your hands were not bound
    Nor your feet put into fetters;
    As a man falls before wicked
     men, *so* you fell."

Then all the people wept over him again.

35 And when all the people came to persuade David to eat food while it was still day, David took an oath,

---

3:15 [a]Spelled *Palti* in 1 Samuel 25:44   3:18 [a]Following many Hebrew manuscripts, Septuagint, Syriac, and Targum; Masoretic Text reads *he.*

saying, "God do so to me, and more also, if I taste bread or anything else till the sun goes down!" 36 Now all the people took note *of it*, and it pleased them, since whatever the king did pleased all the people. 37 For all the people and all Israel understood that day that it had not been the king's *intent* to kill Abner the son of Ner. 38 Then the king said to his servants, "Do you not know that a prince and a great man has fallen this day in Israel? 39 And I *am* weak today, though anointed king; and these men, the sons of Zeruiah, *are* too harsh for me. The LORD shall repay the evildoer according to his wickedness."

4 When Saul's son[a] heard that Abner had died in Hebron, he lost heart, and all Israel was troubled. 2 Now Saul's son *had* two men *who were* captains of troops. The name of one *was* Baanah and the name of the other Rechab, the sons of Rimmon the Beerothite, of the children of Benjamin. (For Beeroth also was *part* of Benjamin, 3 because the Beerothites fled to Gittaim and have been sojourners there until this day.)

4 Jonathan, Saul's son, had a son *who was* lame in *his* feet. He was five years old when the news about Saul and Jonathan came from Jezreel; and his nurse took him up and fled. And it happened, as she made haste to flee, that he fell and became lame. His name *was* Mephibosheth.[a]

5 Then the sons of Rimmon the Beerothite, Rechab and Baanah, set out and came at about the heat of the day to the house of Ishbosheth, who was lying on his bed at noon. 6 And they came there, all the way into the house, *as though* to get wheat, and they stabbed him in the stomach. Then Rechab and Baanah his brother escaped. 7 For when they came into the house, he was lying on his bed in his bedroom; then they struck him and killed him, beheaded him and took his head, and were all night escaping through the plain. 8 And they brought the head of Ishbosheth to David at Hebron, and said to the king, "Here is the head of Ishbosheth, the son of Saul your enemy, who sought your life; and the LORD

has avenged my lord the king this day of Saul and his descendants."

9 But David answered Rechab and Baanah his brother, the sons of Rimmon the Beerothite, and said to them, "*As* the LORD lives, who has redeemed my life from all adversity, 10 when someone told me, saying, 'Look, Saul is dead,' thinking to have brought good news, I arrested him and had him executed in Ziklag—the one who *thought* I would give him a reward for *his* news. 11 How much more, when wicked men have killed a righteous person in his own house on his bed? Therefore, shall I not now require his blood at your hand and remove you from the earth?" 12 So David commanded his young men, and they executed them, cut off their hands and feet, and hanged *them* by the pool in Hebron. But they took the head of Ishbosheth and buried *it* in the tomb of Abner in Hebron.

5 Then all the tribes of Israel came to David at Hebron and spoke, saying, "Indeed we *are* your bone and your flesh. 2 Also, in time past, when Saul was king over us, you were the one who led Israel out and brought them in; and the LORD said to you, 'You shall shepherd My people Israel, and be ruler over Israel.'" 3 Therefore all the elders of Israel came to the king at Hebron, and King David made a covenant with them at Hebron before the LORD. And they anointed David king over Israel. 4 David *was* thirty years old when he began to reign, *and* he reigned forty years. 5 In Hebron he reigned over Judah seven years and six months, and in Jerusalem he reigned thirty-three years over all Israel and Judah.

6 And the king and his men went to Jerusalem against the Jebusites, the inhabitants of the land, who spoke to David, saying, "You shall not come in here; but the blind and the lame will repel you," thinking, "David cannot come in here." 7 Nevertheless David took the stronghold of Zion (that *is*, the City of David). 8 Now David said on that day, "Whoever climbs up by way of the water shaft and defeats the Jebusites (the lame and the blind, *who are* hated by David's soul), he shall be

4:1 *a*That is, Ishbosheth   4:4 *a*Called *Merib-Baal* in 1 Chronicles 8:34 and 9:40

Find a Pass Through

The city of Jerusalem did not always belong to the Israelites. For over two hundred years, the once powerful city-state (then called Jebus) was controlled by the Jebusites. God had promised the city to the Israelites, but how were they to get it?

David, the God-appointed leader, and his mighty, valiant Israelite warriors were no match for the large Jebusite army. Their city was impregnable with thirty-foot-wide fortress walls punctuated by ninety-foot-high towers from which soldiers easily defended the city. The Bible records that the Jebusites were so confident in their ability to defend Jerusalem that they mocked David and his army saying, "The blind and lame will repel you" (2 Sam. 5:6).

The Jebusite stronghold was built high on a mountain. The only water source was outside the city walls at the base of the hill, where the Jebusites obtained their water to withstand siege. David surmised that there was a secret water source coming from outside the city. David was determined to capture the city God had promised to them. The mountainous task seemed impossible, yet the leader David determined a way—through an underground water shaft. Perhaps one man could get inside the walls to open the city gates, thus allowing his troops to storm the city. Perhaps a shaft or tunnel, sunk deep beneath the earth, brought water from an underground spring.

David challenged his men. Whoever could climb the shaft and let their army into the city would be made chief over the troops. Joab, one of David's finest soldiers, undertook the dangerous mission of climbing the shaft.

This water shaft is still visible in Jerusalem today and has been climbed by only a few skilled climbers. It has no footholds nor handholds. Anyone attempting to climb the shaft must brace himself with his back against one wall and his feet extended to the opposite wall. Slowly, he must inch his way upward.

Joab was successful in his climb, entered the city, and allowed David and his men to defeat the Jebusites. Their victory was dependent on David's belief that they could find a pass through. When faced with a mountain, they did not quit! They found a pass through!

When you face a mountainous problem, remember, do not quit. Climb over, tunnel underneath, find a pass through, or simply speak to your mountain with mountain-moving faith, and nothing will be impossible for you (see Mt. 19:26).

chief and captain."[a] Therefore they say, "The blind and the lame shall not come into the house."

9 Then David dwelt in the stronghold, and called it the City of David. And David built all around from the Millo[a] and inward. 10 So David went on and became great, and the LORD God of hosts was with him.

11 Then Hiram king of Tyre sent messengers to David, and cedar trees, and carpenters and masons. And they built David a house. 12 So David knew that the LORD had established him as king over Israel, and that He had exalted His kingdom for the sake of His people Israel.

13 And David took more concubines and wives from Jerusalem, after he had come from Hebron. Also more sons and daughters were born to David. 14 Now these are the names of those who were born to him in Jerusalem: Shammua,[a] Shobab, Nathan, Solomon, 15 Ibhar, Elishua,[a] Nepheg, Japhia, 16 Elishama, Eliada, and Eliphelet.

17 Now when the Philistines heard that they had anointed David king over Israel, all the Philistines went up to search for David. And David heard of it and went down to the stronghold. 18 The Philistines also went and deployed themselves in the Valley of Rephaim. 19 So David inquired of the LORD, saying, "Shall I go up against the Philistines? Will You deliver them into my hand?"

And the LORD said to David, "Go up, for I will doubtless deliver the Philistines into your hand."

20 So David went to Baal Perazim, and David defeated them there; and he said, "The LORD has broken through my enemies before me, like a breakthrough of water." Therefore he called the name of that place Baal Perazim.[a] 21 And they left their images there, and David and his men carried them away.

22 Then the Philistines went up once again and deployed themselves in the Valley of Rephaim. 23 Therefore David inquired of the LORD, and He said, "You shall not go up; circle around behind them, and come upon them in front of the mulberry trees. 24 And it shall be, when you hear the sound of marching in the tops of the mulberry trees, then you shall advance quickly. For then the LORD will go out before you to strike the camp of the Philistines." 25 And David did so, as the LORD commanded him; and he drove back the Philistines from Geba[a] as far as Gezer.

6 Again David gathered all the choice men of Israel, thirty thousand. 2 And David arose and went with all the people who were with him from Baale Judah to bring up from there the ark of God, whose name is called by the Name,[a] the LORD of Hosts, who dwells between the cherubim. 3 So they set the ark of God on a new cart, and brought it out of the house of Abinadab, which was on the hill; and Uzzah and Ahio, the sons of Abinadab, drove the new cart.[a] 4 And they brought it out of the house of Abinadab, which was on the hill, accompanying the ark of God; and Ahio went before the ark. 5 Then David and all the house of Israel played music before the LORD on all kinds of instruments of fir wood, on harps, on stringed instruments, on tambourines, on sistrums, and on cymbals.

6 And when they came to Nachon's threshing floor, Uzzah put out his hand to the ark of God and took hold of it, for the oxen stumbled. 7 Then the anger of the LORD was aroused against Uzzah, and God struck him there for his error; and he died there by the ark of God. 8 And David became angry because of the LORD's outbreak against Uzzah; and he called the name of the place Perez Uzzah[a] to this day.

9 David was afraid of the LORD that day; and he said, "How can the ark of the LORD come to me?" 10 So David would not move the ark of the LORD with him into the City of David; but David took it aside into the house of Obed-Edom the Gittite. 11 The ark of the LORD remained in the house of Obed-Edom the Gittite three months.

5:8 [a]Compare 1 Chronicles 11:6   5:9 [a]Literally The Landfill   5:14 [a]Spelled Shimea in 1 Chronicles 3:5   5:15 [a]Spelled Elishama in 1 Chronicles 3:6   5:20 [a]Literally Master of Breakthroughs   5:25 [a]Following Masoretic Text, Targum, and Vulgate; Septuagint reads Gibeon.   6:2 [a]Septuagint, Targum, and Vulgate omit by the Name; many Hebrew manuscripts and Syriac read there.   6:3 [a]Septuagint adds with the ark.   6:8 [a]Literally Outburst Against Uzzah

And the LORD blessed Obed-Edom and all his household.

12 Now it was told King David, saying, "The LORD has blessed the house of Obed-Edom and all that *belongs* to him, because of the ark of God." So David went and brought up the ark of God from the house of Obed-Edom to the City of David with gladness. 13 And so it was, when those bearing the ark of the LORD had gone six paces, that he sacrificed oxen and fatted sheep. 14 Then David danced before the LORD with all *his* might; and David *was* wearing a linen ephod. 15 So David and all the house of Israel brought up the ark of the LORD with shouting and with the sound of the trumpet.

16 Now as the ark of the LORD came into the City of David, Michal, Saul's daughter, looked through a window and saw King David leaping and whirling before the LORD; and she despised him in her heart. 17 So they brought the ark of the LORD, and set it in its place in the midst of the tabernacle that David had erected for it. Then David offered burnt offerings and peace offerings before the LORD. 18 And when David had finished offering burnt offerings and peace offerings, he blessed the people in the name of the LORD of hosts. 19 Then he distributed among all the people, among the whole multitude of Israel, both the women and the men, to everyone a loaf of bread, a piece *of meat*, and a cake of raisins. So all the people departed, everyone to his house.

20 Then David returned to bless his household. And Michal the daughter of Saul came out to meet David, and said, "How glorious was the king of Israel today, uncovering himself today in the eyes of the maids of his servants, as one of the base fellows shamelessly uncovers himself!"

21 So David said to Michal, "*It was* before the LORD, who chose me instead of your father and all his house, to appoint me ruler over the people of the LORD, over Israel. Therefore I will play *music* before the LORD. 22 And I will be even more undignified than this, and will be humble in my own sight. But as for the maidservants of whom you have spoken, by them I will be held in honor."

23 Therefore Michal the daughter of Saul had no children to the day of her death.

7 Now it came to pass when the king was dwelling in his house, and the LORD had given him rest from all his enemies all around, 2 that the king said to Nathan the prophet, "See now, I dwell in a house of cedar, but the ark of God dwells inside tent curtains."

3 Then Nathan said to the king, "Go, do all that *is* in your heart, for the LORD *is* with you."

4 But it happened that night that the word of the LORD came to Nathan, saying, 5 "Go and tell My servant David, 'Thus says the LORD: "Would you build a house for Me to dwell in? 6 For I have not dwelt in a house since the time that I brought the children of Israel up from Egypt, even to this day, but have moved about in a tent and in a tabernacle. 7 Wherever I have moved about with all the children of Israel, have I ever spoken a word to anyone from the tribes of Israel, whom I commanded to shepherd My people Israel, saying, 'Why have you not built Me a house of cedar?' " ' 8 Now therefore, thus shall you say to My servant David, 'Thus says the LORD of hosts: "I took you from the sheepfold, from following the sheep, to be ruler over My people, over Israel. 9 And I have been with you wherever you have gone, and have cut off all your enemies from before you, and have made you a great name, like the name of the great men who *are* on the earth. 10 Moreover I will appoint a place for My people Israel, and will plant them, that they may dwell in a place of their own and move no more; nor shall the sons of wickedness oppress them anymore, as previously, 11 since the time that I commanded judges *to be* over My people Israel, and have caused you to rest from all your enemies. Also the LORD tells you that He will make you a house.[a]

12 "When your days are fulfilled and you rest with your fathers, I will set up your seed after you, who will come from your body, and I will establish his kingdom. 13 He shall build a house for My name, and I will establish the throne of his kingdom for-

7:11 [a]That is, a royal dynasty

ever. 14 I will be his Father, and he shall be My son. If he commits iniquity, I will chasten him with the rod of men and with the blows of the sons of men. 15 But My mercy shall not depart from him, as I took *it* from Saul, whom I removed from before you. 16 And your house and your kingdom shall be established forever before you.*a* Your throne shall be established forever." ' "

17 According to all these words and according to all this vision, so Nathan spoke to David.

18 Then King David went in and sat before the LORD; and he said: "Who *am* I, O Lord GOD? And what is my house, that You have brought me this far? 19 And yet this was a small thing in Your sight, O Lord GOD; and You have also spoken of Your servant's house for a great while to come. *Is* this the manner of man, O Lord GOD? 20 Now what more can David say to You? For You, Lord GOD, know Your servant. 21 For Your word's sake, and according to Your own heart, You have done all these great things, to make Your servant know *them.* 22 Therefore You are great, O Lord GOD.*a* For *there is* none like You, nor *is there any* God besides You, according to all that we have heard with our ears. 23 And who *is* like Your people, like Israel, the one nation on the earth whom God went to redeem for Himself as a people, to make for Himself a name—and to do for Yourself great and awesome deeds for Your land—before Your people whom You redeemed for Yourself from Egypt, the nations, and their gods? 24 For You have made Your people Israel Your very own people forever; and You, LORD, have become their God.

25 "Now, O LORD God, the word which You have spoken concerning Your servant and concerning his house, establish *it* forever and do as You have said. 26 So let Your name be magnified forever, saying, 'The LORD of hosts *is* the God over Israel.' And let the house of Your servant David be established before You. 27 For You, O LORD of hosts, God of Israel, have revealed *this* to Your servant, saying, 'I will build you a

house.' Therefore Your servant has found it in his heart to pray this prayer to You.

28 "And now, O Lord GOD, You are God, and Your words are true, and You have promised this goodness to Your servant. 29 Now therefore, let it please You to bless the house of Your servant, that it may continue before You forever; for You, O Lord GOD, have spoken *it,* and with Your blessing let the house of Your servant be blessed forever."

8 After this it came to pass that David attacked the Philistines and subdued them. And David took Metheg Ammah from the hand of the Philistines.

2 Then he defeated Moab. Forcing them down to the ground, he measured them off with a line. With two lines he measured off those to be put to death, and with one full line those to be kept alive. So the Moabites became David's servants, *and* brought tribute.

3 David also defeated Hadadezer the son of Rehob, king of Zobah, as he went to recover his territory at the River Euphrates. 4 David took from him one thousand *chariots,* seven hundred*a* horsemen, and twenty thousand foot soldiers. Also David hamstrung all the chariot horses, except that he spared *enough* of them for one hundred chariots.

5 When the Syrians of Damascus came to help Hadadezer king of Zobah, David killed twenty-two thousand of the Syrians. 6 Then David put garrisons in Syria of Damascus; and the Syrians became David's servants, *and* brought tribute. So the LORD preserved David wherever he went. 7 And David took the shields of gold that had belonged to the servants of Hadadezer, and brought them to Jerusalem. 8 Also from Betah*a* and from Berothai, cities of Hadadezer, King David took a large amount of bronze.

9 When Toi*a* king of Hamath heard that David had defeated all the army of Hadadezer, 10 then Toi sent Joram*a* his son to King David, to greet him and bless him, because he had fought against Hadadezer and de-

7:16 *a*Septuagint reads *Me.*   7:22 *a*Targum and Syriac read O LORD God.   8:4 *a*Or *seven thousand* (compare 1 Chronicles 18:4)   8:8 *a*Spelled *Tibhath* in 1 Chronicles 18:8   8:9 *a*Spelled *Tou* in 1 Chronicles 18:9   8:10 *a*Spelled *Hadoram* in 1 Chronicles 18:10

feated him (for Hadadezer had been at war with Toi); and *Joram* brought with him articles of silver, articles of gold, and articles of bronze. 11 King David also dedicated these to the LORD, along with the silver and gold that he had dedicated from all the nations which he had subdued— 12 from Syria,*a* from Moab, from the people of Ammon, from the Philistines, from Amalek, and from the spoil of Hadadezer the son of Rehob, king of Zobah.

13 And David made *himself* a name when he returned from killing eighteen thousand Syrians*a* in the Valley of Salt. 14 He also put garrisons in Edom; throughout all Edom he put garrisons, and all the Edomites became David's servants. And the LORD preserved David wherever he went.

15 So David reigned over all Israel; and David administered judgment and justice to all his people. 16 Joab the son of Zeruiah *was* over the army; Jehoshaphat the son of Ahilud *was* recorder; 17 Zadok the son of Ahitub and Ahimelech the son of Abiathar *were* the priests; Seraiah*a* *was* the scribe; 18 Benaiah the son of Jehoiada *was over* both the Cherethites and the Pelethites; and David's sons were chief ministers.

9 Now David said, "Is there still anyone who is left of the house of Saul, that I may show him kindness for Jonathan's sake?"

2 And *there was* a servant of the house of Saul whose name *was* Ziba. So when they had called him to David, the king said to him, "*Are* you Ziba?"

He said, "At your service!"

3 Then the king said, "*Is* there not still someone of the house of Saul, to whom I may show the kindness of God?"

And Ziba said to the king, "There is still a son of Jonathan *who is* lame in *his* feet."

4 So the king said to him, "Where *is* he?"

And Ziba said to the king, "Indeed he *is* in the house of Machir the son of Ammiel, in Lo Debar."

5 Then King David sent and brought him out of the house of Ma-

chir the son of Ammiel, from Lo Debar.

6 Now when Mephibosheth the son of Jonathan, the son of Saul, had come to David, he fell on his face and prostrated himself. Then David said, "Mephibosheth?"

And he answered, "Here is your servant!"

7 So David said to him, "Do not fear, for I will surely show you kindness for Jonathan your father's sake, and will restore to you all the land of Saul your grandfather; and you shall eat bread at my table continually."

8 Then he bowed himself, and said, "What *is* your servant, that you should look upon such a dead dog as I?"

9 And the king called to Ziba, Saul's servant, and said to him, "I have given to your master's son all that belonged to Saul and to all his house. 10 You therefore, and your sons and your servants, shall work the land for him, and you shall bring in *the harvest,* that your master's son may have food to eat. But Mephibosheth your master's son shall eat bread at my table always." Now Ziba had fifteen sons and twenty servants.

11 Then Ziba said to the king, "According to all that my lord the king has commanded his servant, so will your servant do."

"As for Mephibosheth," *said the king,* "he shall eat at my table*a* like one of the king's sons." 12 Mephibosheth had a young son whose name *was* Micha. And all who dwelt in the house of Ziba *were* servants of Mephibosheth. 13 So Mephibosheth dwelt in Jerusalem, for he ate continually at the king's table. And he was lame in both his feet.

10 It happened after this that the king of the people of Ammon died, and Hanun his son reigned in his place. 2 Then David said, "I will show kindness to Hanun the son of Nahash, as his father showed kindness to me."

So David sent by the hand of his servants to comfort him concerning his father. And David's servants

8:12 *a*Septuagint, Syriac, and some Hebrew manuscripts read *Edom.*   8:13 *a*Septuagint, Syriac, and some Hebrew manuscripts read *Edomites* (compare 1 Chronicles 18:12).   8:17 *a*Spelled *Shavsha* in 1 Chronicles 18:16   9:11 *a*Septuagint reads *David's table.*

came into the land of the people of Ammon. 3 And the princes of the people of Ammon said to Hanun their lord, "Do you think that David really honors your father because he has sent comforters to you? Has David not *rather* sent his servants to you to search the city, to spy it out, and to overthrow it?"

4 Therefore Hanun took David's servants, shaved off half of their beards, cut off their garments in the middle, at their buttocks, and sent them away. 5 When they told David, he sent to meet them, because the men were greatly ashamed. And the king said, "Wait at Jericho until your beards have grown, and *then* return."

6 When the people of Ammon saw that they had made themselves repulsive to David, the people of Ammon sent and hired the Syrians of Beth Rehob and the Syrians of Zoba, twenty thousand foot soldiers; and from the king of Maacah one thousand men, and from Ish-Tob twelve thousand men. 7 Now when David heard *of it,* he sent Joab and all the army of the mighty men. 8 Then the people of Ammon came out and put themselves in battle array at the entrance of the gate. And the Syrians of Zoba, Beth Rehob, Ish-Tob, and Maacah *were* by themselves in the field.

9 When Joab saw that the battle line was against him before and behind, he chose some of Israel's best and put *them* in battle array against the Syrians. 10 And the rest of the people he put under the command of Abishai his brother, that he might set *them* in battle array against the people of Ammon. 11 Then he said, "If the Syrians are too strong for me, then you shall help me; but if the people of Ammon are too strong for you, then I will come and help you. 12 Be of good courage, and let us be strong for our people and for the cities of our God. And may the LORD do *what is* good in His sight."

13 So Joab and the people who *were* with him drew near for the battle against the Syrians, and they fled before him. 14 When the people of Ammon saw that the Syrians were fleeing, they also fled before Abishai, and entered the city. So Joab re-

turned from the people of Ammon and went to Jerusalem.

15 When the Syrians saw that they had been defeated by Israel, they gathered together. 16 Then Hadadezer[a] sent and brought out the Syrians who *were* beyond the River,[b] and they came to Helam. And Shobach the commander of Hadadezer's army *went* before them. 17 When it was told David, he gathered all Israel, crossed over the Jordan, and came to Helam. And the Syrians set themselves in battle array against David and fought with him. 18 Then the Syrians fled before Israel; and David killed seven hundred charioteers and forty thousand horsemen of the Syrians, and struck Shobach the commander of their army, who died there. 19 And when all the kings *who were* servants to Hadadezer[a] saw that they were defeated by Israel, they made peace with Israel and served them. So the Syrians were afraid to help the people of Ammon anymore.

11 It happened in the spring of the year, at the time when kings go out *to battle,* that David sent Joab and his servants with him, and all Israel; and they destroyed the people of Ammon and besieged Rabbah. But David remained at Jerusalem.

2 Then it happened one evening that David arose from his bed and walked on the roof of the king's house. And from the roof he saw a woman bathing, and the woman *was* very beautiful to behold. 3 So David sent and inquired about the woman. And *someone* said, "*Is* this not Bathsheba, the daughter of Eliam, the wife of Uriah the Hittite?" 4 Then David sent messengers, and took her; and she came to him, and he lay with her, for she was cleansed from her impurity; and she returned to her house. 5 And the woman conceived; so she sent and told David, and said, "I *am* with child."

6 Then David sent to Joab, *saying,* "Send me Uriah the Hittite." And Joab sent Uriah to David. 7 When Uriah had come to him, David asked how Joab was doing, and how the people were doing, and how the war prospered. 8 And David said to Uriah, "Go down to your house and

10:16 *a*Hebrew *Hadarezer*   *b*That is, the Euphrates   10:19 *a*Hebrew *Hadarezer* wash your feet." So Uriah departed from the king's house, and a gift *of food* from the king followed him. 9 But Uriah slept at the door of the king's house with all the servants of his lord, and did not go down to his house. 10 So when they told David, saying, "Uriah did not go down to his house," David said to Uriah, "Did you not come from a journey? Why did you not go down to your house?"

11 And Uriah said to David, "The ark and Israel and Judah are dwelling in tents, and my lord Joab and the servants of my lord are encamped in the open fields. Shall I then go to my house to eat and drink, and to lie with my wife? *As* you live, and *as* your soul lives, I will not do this thing."

12 Then David said to Uriah, "Wait here today also, and tomorrow I will let you depart." So Uriah remained in Jerusalem that day and the next. 13 Now when David called him, he ate and drank before him; and he made him drunk. And at evening he went out to lie on his bed with the servants of his lord, but he did not go down to his house.

14 In the morning it happened that David wrote a letter to Joab and sent *it* by the hand of Uriah. 15 And he wrote in the letter, saying, "Set Uriah in the forefront of the hottest battle, and retreat from him, that he may be struck down and die." 16 So it was, while Joab besieged the city, that he assigned Uriah to a place where he knew there *were* valiant men. 17 Then the men of the city came out and fought with Joab. And *some* of the people of the servants of David fell; and Uriah the Hittite died also.

18 Then Joab sent and told David all the things concerning the war, 19 and charged the messenger, saying, "When you have finished telling the matters of the war to the king, 20 if it happens that the king's wrath rises, and he says to you: 'Why did you approach so near to the city when you fought? Did you not know that they would shoot from the wall? 21 Who struck Abimelech the son of Jerubbesheth?ᵃ Was it not a woman who cast a piece of a millstone on him from the wall, so that he died in Thebez? Why did you go near the wall?'—then you shall say, 'Your ser-

vant Uriah the Hittite is dead also.'"

22 So the messenger went, and came and told David all that Joab had sent by him. 23 And the messenger said to David, "Surely the men prevailed against us and came out to us in the field; then we drove them back as far as the entrance of the gate. 24 The archers shot from the wall at your servants; and *some* of the king's servants are dead, and your servant Uriah the Hittite is dead also."

25 Then David said to the messenger, "Thus you shall say to Joab: 'Do not let this thing displease you, for the sword devours one as well as another. Strengthen your attack against the city, and overthrow it.' So encourage him."

26 When the wife of Uriah heard that Uriah her husband was dead, she mourned for her husband. 27 And when her mourning was over, David sent and brought her to his house, and she became his wife and bore him a son. But the thing that David had done displeased the LORD.

12 Then the LORD sent Nathan to David. And he came to him, and said to him: "There were two men in one city, one rich and the other poor. 2 The rich *man* had exceedingly many flocks and herds. 3 But the poor *man* had nothing, except one little ewe lamb which he had bought and nourished; and it grew up together with him and with his children. It ate of his own food and drank from his own cup and lay in his bosom; and it was like a daughter to him. 4 And a traveler came to the rich man, who refused to take from his own flock and from his own herd to prepare one for the wayfaring man who had come to him; but he took the poor man's lamb and prepared it for the man who had come to him."

5 So David's anger was greatly aroused against the man, and he said to Nathan, "*As* the LORD lives, the man who has done this shall surely die! 6 And he shall restore fourfold for the lamb, because he did this thing and because he had no pity."

7 Then Nathan said to David, "You *are* the man! Thus says the LORD God of Israel: 'I anointed you king over Israel, and I delivered you from the

11:21 ᵃSame as *Jerubbaal* (Gideon), Judges 6:32ff

hand of Saul. 8 I gave you your master's house and your master's wives into your keeping, and gave you the house of Israel and Judah. And if *that had been* too little, I also would have given you much more! 9 Why have you despised the commandment of the LORD, to do evil in His sight? You have killed Uriah the Hittite with the sword; you have taken his wife *to be* your wife, and have killed him with the sword of the people of Ammon. 10 Now therefore, the sword shall never depart from your house, because you have despised Me, and have taken the wife of Uriah the Hittite to be your wife.' 11 Thus says the LORD: 'Behold, I will raise up adversity against you from your own house; and I will take your wives before your eyes and give *them* to your neighbor, and he shall lie with your wives in the sight of this sun. 12 For you did *it* secretly, but I will do this thing before all Israel, before the sun.' "

13 So David said to Nathan, "I have sinned against the LORD."

And Nathan said to David, "The LORD also has put away your sin; you shall not die. 14 However, because by this deed you have given great occasion to the enemies of the LORD to blaspheme, the child also *who is* born to you shall surely die." 15 Then Nathan departed to his house.

And the LORD struck the child that Uriah's wife bore to David, and it became ill. 16 David therefore pleaded with God for the child, and David fasted and went in and lay all night on the ground. 17 So the elders of his house arose *and went* to him, to raise him up from the ground. But he would not, nor did he eat food with them. 18 Then on the seventh day it came to pass that the child died. And the servants of David were afraid to tell him that the child was dead. For they said, "Indeed, while the child was alive, we spoke to him, and he would not heed our voice. How can we tell him that the child is dead? He may do some harm!"

19 When David saw that his servants were whispering, David perceived that the child was dead. Therefore David said to his servants, "Is the child dead?"

And they said, "He is dead."

20 So David arose from the ground, washed and anointed himself, and changed his clothes; and he went into the house of the LORD and worshiped. Then he went to his own house; and when he requested, they set food before him, and he ate. 21 Then his servants said to him, "What *is* this that you have done? You fasted and wept for the child *while he was* alive, but when the child died, you arose and ate food."

22 And he said, "While the child was alive, I fasted and wept; for I said, 'Who can tell *whether* the LORD[a] will be gracious to me, that the child may live?' 23 But now he is dead; why should I fast? Can I bring him back again? I shall go to him, but he shall not return to me."

24 Then David comforted Bathsheba his wife, and went in to her and lay with her. So she bore a son, and he[a] called his name Solomon. Now the LORD loved him, 25 and He sent *word* by the hand of Nathan the prophet: So he[a] called his name Jedidiah,[b] because of the LORD.

26 Now Joab fought against Rabbah of the people of Ammon, and took the royal city. 27 And Joab sent messengers to David, and said, "I have fought against Rabbah, and I have taken the city's water *supply*. 28 Now therefore, gather the rest of the people together and encamp against the city and take it, lest I take the city and it be called after my name." 29 So David gathered all the people together and went to Rabbah, fought against it, and took it. 30 Then he took their king's crown from his head. Its weight *was* a talent of gold, with precious stones. And it was *set* on David's head. Also he brought out the spoil of the city in great abundance. 31 And he brought out the people who *were* in it, and put *them to work* with saws and iron picks and iron axes, and made them cross over to the brick works. So he did to all the cities of the people of Ammon. Then David and all the people returned to Jerusalem.

13

After this Absalom the son of David had a lovely sister, whose name *was* Tamar; and Amnon

---

12:22 [a]A few Hebrew manuscripts and Syriac read *God.*   12:24 [a]Following Kethib, Septuagint, and Vulgate; Qere, a few Hebrew manuscripts, Syriac, and Targum read *she.*   12:25 [a]Qere, some Hebrew manuscripts, Syriac, and Targum read *she.*   [b]Literally *Beloved of the* LORD the son of David loved her. 2 Amnon was so distressed over his sister Tamar that he became sick; for she *was* a virgin. And it was improper for Amnon to do anything to her. 3 But Amnon had a friend whose name *was* Jonadab the son of Shimeah, David's brother. Now Jonadab *was* a very crafty man. 4 And he said to him, "Why *are* you, the king's son, becoming thinner day after day? Will you not tell me?"

Amnon said to him, "I love Tamar, my brother Absalom's sister."

5 So Jonadab said to him, "Lie down on your bed and pretend to be ill. And when your father comes to see you, say to him, 'Please let my sister Tamar come and give me food, and prepare the food in my sight, that I may see *it* and eat it from her hand.'" 6 Then Amnon lay down and pretended to be ill; and when the king came to see him, Amnon said to the king, "Please let Tamar my sister come and make a couple of cakes for me in my sight, that I may eat from her hand."

7 And David sent home to Tamar, saying, "Now go to your brother Amnon's house, and prepare food for him." 8 So Tamar went to her brother Amnon's house; and he was lying down. Then she took flour and kneaded *it,* made cakes in his sight, and baked the cakes. 9 And she took the pan and placed *them* out before him, but he refused to eat. Then Amnon said, "Have everyone go out from me." And they all went out from him. 10 Then Amnon said to Tamar, "Bring the food into the bedroom, that I may eat from your hand." And Tamar took the cakes which she had made, and brought *them* to Amnon her brother in the bedroom. 11 Now when she had brought *them* to him to eat, he took hold of her and said to her, "Come, lie with me, my sister."

12 But she answered him, "No, my brother, do not force me, for no such thing should be done in Israel. Do not do this disgraceful thing! 13 And I, where could I take my shame? And as for you, you would be like one of the fools in Israel. Now therefore, please speak to the king; for he will not withhold me from you." 14 However, he would not heed her voice; and being stronger than she, he forced her and lay with her.

15 Then Amnon hated her exceedingly, so that the hatred with which he hated her *was* greater than the love with which he had loved her. And Amnon said to her, "Arise, be gone!"

16 So she said to him, "No, indeed! This evil of sending me away *is* worse than the other that you did to me."

But he would not listen to her. 17 Then he called his servant who attended him, and said, "Here! Put this *woman* out, away from me, and bolt the door behind her." 18 Now she had on a robe of many colors, for the king's virgin daughters wore such apparel. And his servant put her out and bolted the door behind her.

19 Then Tamar put ashes on her head, and tore her robe of many colors that *was* on her, and laid her hand on her head and went away crying bitterly. 20 And Absalom her brother said to her, "Has Amnon your brother been with you? But now hold your peace, my sister. He *is* your brother; do not take this thing to heart." So Tamar remained desolate in her brother Absalom's house.

21 But when King David heard of all these things, he was very angry. 22 And Absalom spoke to his brother Amnon neither good nor bad. For Absalom hated Amnon, because he had forced his sister Tamar.

23 And it came to pass, after two full years, that Absalom had sheepshearers in Baal Hazor, which *is* near Ephraim; so Absalom invited all the king's sons. 24 Then Absalom came to the king and said, "Kindly note, your servant has sheepshearers; please, let the king and his servants go with your servant."

25 But the king said to Absalom, "No, my son, let us not all go now, lest we be a burden to you." Then he urged him, but he would not go; and he blessed him.

26 Then Absalom said, "If not, please let my brother Amnon go with us."

And the king said to him, "Why should he go with you?" 27 But Absalom urged him; so he let Amnon and all the king's sons go with him.

28 Now Absalom had commanded his servants, saying, "Watch now, when Amnon's heart is merry with wine, and when I say to you, 'Strike Amnon!' then kill him. Do not be

afraid. Have I not commanded you? Be courageous and valiant."
29 So the servants of Absalom did to Amnon as Absalom had commanded. Then all the king's sons arose, and each one got on his mule and fled.

30 And it came to pass, while they were on the way, that news came to David, saying, "Absalom has killed all the king's sons, and not one of them is left!" 31 So the king arose and tore his garments and lay on the ground, and all his servants stood by with their clothes torn. 32 Then Jonadab the son of Shimeah, David's brother, answered and said, "Let not my lord suppose they have killed all the young men, the king's sons, for only Amnon is dead. For by the command of Absalom this has been determined from the day that he forced his sister Tamar. 33 Now therefore, let not my lord the king take the thing to his heart, to think that all the king's sons are dead. For only Amnon is dead."

34 Then Absalom fled. And the young man who was keeping watch lifted his eyes and looked, and there, many people were coming from the road on the hillside behind him.*a* 35 And Jonadab said to the king, "Look, the king's sons are coming; as your servant said, so it is." 36 So it was, as soon as he had finished speaking, that the king's sons indeed came, and they lifted up their voice and wept. Also the king and all his servants wept very bitterly.

37 But Absalom fled and went to Talmai the son of Ammihud, king of Geshur. And *David* mourned for his son every day. 38 So Absalom fled and went to Geshur, and was there three years. 39 And King David*a* longed to go to*b* Absalom. For he had been comforted concerning Amnon, because he was dead.

14 So Joab the son of Zeruiah perceived that the king's heart *was* concerned about Absalom. 2 And Joab sent to Tekoa and brought from there a wise woman, and said to her, "Please pretend to be a mourner, and put on mourning apparel; do not anoint yourself with oil, but act like a woman who has been mourning a long time for the dead. 3 Go to the king and speak to him in this manner." So Joab put the words in her mouth.

4 And when the woman of Tekoa spoke*a* to the king, she fell on her face to the ground and prostrated herself, and said, "Help, O king!"

5 Then the king said to her, "What troubles you?"

And she answered, "Indeed I *am* a widow, my husband is dead. 6 Now your maidservant had two sons; and the two fought with each other in the field, and *there was* no one to part them, but the one struck the other and killed him. 7 And now the whole family has risen up against your maidservant, and they said, 'Deliver him who struck his brother, that we may execute him for the life of his brother whom he killed; and we will destroy the heir also.' So they would extinguish my ember that is left, and leave to my husband *neither* name nor remnant on the earth."

8 Then the king said to the woman, "Go to your house, and I will give orders concerning you."

9 And the woman of Tekoa said to the king, "My lord, O king, *let* the iniquity *be* on me and on my father's house, and the king and his throne *be* guiltless."

10 So the king said, "Whoever says *anything* to you, bring him to me, and he shall not touch you anymore."

11 Then she said, "Please let the king remember the LORD your God, and do not permit the avenger of blood to destroy anymore, lest they destroy my son."

And he said, "*As* the LORD lives, not one hair of your son shall fall to the ground."

12 Therefore the woman said, "Please, let your maidservant speak *another* word to my lord the king."

And he said, "Say on."

13 So the woman said: "Why then have you schemed such a thing against the people of God? For the king speaks this thing as one who is

---

13:34 *a*Septuagint adds *And the watchman went and told the king, and said, "I see men from the way of Horonaim, from the regions of the mountains."* 13:39 *a*Following Masoretic Text, Syriac, and Vulgate; Septuagint reads *the spirit of the king;* Targum reads *the soul of King David.* *b*Following Masoretic Text and Targum; Septuagint and Vulgate read *ceased to pursue after.* 14:4 *a*Many Hebrew manuscripts, Septuagint, Syriac, and Vulgate read *came.*

guilty, *in that* the king does not bring his banished one home again. 14 For we will surely die and *become* like water spilled on the ground, which cannot be gathered up again. Yet God does not take away a life; but He devises means, so that His banished ones are not expelled from Him. 15 Now therefore, I have come to speak of this thing to my lord the king because the people have made me afraid. And your maidservant said, 'I will now speak to the king; it may be that the king will perform the request of his maidservant. 16 For the king will hear and deliver his maidservant from the hand of the man *who would* destroy me and my son together from the inheritance of God.' 17 Your maidservant said, 'The word of my lord the king will now be comforting; for as the angel of God, so *is* my lord the king in discerning good and evil. And may the LORD your God be with you.' "

18 Then the king answered and said to the woman, "Please do not hide from me anything that I ask you."

And the woman said, "Please, let my lord the king speak."

19 So the king said, "*Is* the hand of Joab with you in all this?" And the woman answered and said, "As you live, my lord the king, no one can turn to the right hand or to the left from anything that my lord the king has spoken. For your servant Joab commanded me, and he put all these words in the mouth of your maidservant. 20 To bring about this change of affairs your servant Joab has done this thing; but my lord *is* wise, according to the wisdom of the angel of God, to know everything that *is* in the earth."

21 And the king said to Joab, "All right, I have granted this thing. Go therefore, bring back the young man Absalom."

22 Then Joab fell to the ground on his face and bowed himself, and thanked the king. And Joab said, "Today your servant knows that I have found favor in your sight, my lord, O king, in that the king has fulfilled the request of his servant." 23 So Joab arose and went to Geshur, and brought Absalom to Jerusalem. 24 And the king said, "Let him return to his own house, but do not let him see my face." So Absalom returned to his own house, but did not see the king's face.

25 Now in all Israel there was no one who was praised as much as Absalom for his good looks. From the sole of his foot to the crown of his head there was no blemish in him. 26 And when he cut the hair of his head—at the end of every year he cut *it* because it was heavy on him—when he cut it, he weighed the hair of his head at two hundred shekels according to the king's standard. 27 To Absalom were born three sons, and one daughter whose name *was* Tamar. She was a woman of beautiful appearance.

28 And Absalom dwelt two full years in Jerusalem, but did not see the king's face. 29 Therefore Absalom sent for Joab, to send him to the king, but he would not come to him. And when he sent again the second time, he would not come. 30 So he said to his servants, "See, Joab's field is near mine, and he has barley there; go and set it on fire." And Absalom's servants set the field on fire.

31 Then Joab arose and came to Absalom's house, and said to him, "Why have your servants set my field on fire?"

32 And Absalom answered Joab, "Look, I sent to you, saying, 'Come here, so that I may send you to the king, to say, "Why have I come from Geshur? *It would be* better for me to *be* there still." ' Now therefore, let me see the king's face; but if there is iniquity in me, let him execute me."

33 So Joab went to the king and told him. And when he had called for Absalom, he came to the king and bowed himself on his face to the ground before the king. Then the king kissed Absalom.

15 After this it happened that Absalom provided himself with chariots and horses, and fifty men to run before him. 2 Now Absalom would rise early and stand beside the way to the gate. *So* it was, whenever anyone who had a lawsuit came to the king for a decision, that Absalom would call to him and say, "What city *are* you from?" And he would say, "Your servant *is* from such and such a tribe of Israel." 3 Then Absalom would say to him, "Look, your case *is* good and right; but *there is* no deputy of the king to hear you."

4 Moreover Absalom would say, "Oh, that I were made judge in the land, and everyone who has any suit or cause would come to me; then I would give him justice." 5 And *so* it was, whenever anyone came near to bow down to him, that he would put out his hand and take him and kiss him. 6 In this manner Absalom acted toward all Israel who came to the king for judgment. So Absalom stole the hearts of the men of Israel.

7 Now it came to pass after forty[a] years that Absalom said to the king, "Please, let me go to Hebron and pay the vow which I made to the LORD. 8 For your servant took a vow while I dwelt at Geshur in Syria, saying, 'If the LORD indeed brings me back to Jerusalem, then I will serve the LORD.' "

9 And the king said to him, "Go in peace." So he arose and went to Hebron.

10 Then Absalom sent spies throughout all the tribes of Israel, saying, "As soon as you hear the sound of the trumpet, then you shall say, 'Absalom reigns in Hebron!'" 11 And with Absalom went two hundred men invited from Jerusalem, and they went along innocently and did not know anything. 12 Then Absalom sent for Ahithophel the Gilonite, David's counselor, from his city—from Giloh—while he offered sacrifices. And the conspiracy grew strong, for the people with Absalom continually increased in number.

13 Now a messenger came to David, saying, "The hearts of the men of Israel are with Absalom."

14 So David said to all his servants who *were* with him at Jerusalem, "Arise, and let us flee, or we shall not escape from Absalom. Make haste to depart, lest he overtake us suddenly and bring disaster upon us, and strike the city with the edge of the sword."

15 And the king's servants said to the king, "We *are* your servants, *ready to do* whatever my lord the king commands." 16 Then the king went out with all his household after him. But the king left ten women, concubines, to keep the house. 17 And the king went out with all the people after him, and stopped at the outskirts. 18 Then all his servants passed before him; and all the Cherethites, all the Pelethites, and all the Gittites, six hundred men who had followed him from Gath, passed before the king.

19 Then the king said to Ittai the Gittite, "Why are you also going with us? Return and remain with the king. For you *are* a foreigner and also an exile from your own place. 20 In fact, you came *only* yesterday. Should I make you wander up and down with us today, since I go I know not where? Return, and take your brethren back. Mercy and truth *be* with you."

21 But Ittai answered the king and said, "As the LORD lives, and *as* my lord the king lives, surely in whatever place my lord the king shall be, whether in death or life, even there also your servant will be."

22 So David said to Ittai, "Go, and cross over." Then Ittai the Gittite and all his men and all the little ones who *were* with him crossed over. 23 And all the country wept with a loud voice, and all the people crossed over. The king himself also crossed over the Brook Kidron, and all the people crossed over toward the way of the wilderness.

24 There was Zadok also, and all the Levites with him, bearing the ark of the covenant of God. And they set down the ark of God, and Abiathar went up until all the people had finished crossing over from the city. 25 Then the king said to Zadok, "Carry the ark of God back into the city. If I find favor in the eyes of the LORD, He will bring me back and show me *both* it and His dwelling place. 26 But if He says thus: 'I have no delight in you,' here I am, let Him do to me as seems good to Him." 27 The king also said to Zadok the priest, "*Are* you *not* a seer? Return to the city in peace, and your two sons with you, Ahimaaz your son, and Jonathan the son of Abiathar. 28 See, I will wait in the plains of the wilderness until word comes from you to inform me." 29 Therefore Zadok and Abiathar carried the ark of God back to Jerusalem. And they remained there.

30 So David went up by the Ascent of the *Mount of* Olives, and wept as he went up; and he had his head cov-

15:7 [a]Septuagint manuscripts, Syriac, and Josephus read *four*.

ered and went barefoot. And all the people who *were* with him covered their heads and went up, weeping as they went up. 31 Then *someone* told David, saying, "Ahithophel *is* among the conspirators with Absalom." And David said, "O Lord, I pray, turn the counsel of Ahithophel into foolishness!"

32 Now it happened when David had come to the top *of the mountain,* where he worshiped God—there was Hushai the Archite coming to meet him with his robe torn and dust on his head. 33 David said to him, "If you go on with me, then you will become a burden to me. 34 But if you return to the city, and say to Absalom, 'I will be your servant, O king; *as I was* your father's servant previously, so I *will* now also *be* your servant,' then you may defeat the counsel of Ahithophel for me. 35 And *do* you not *have* Zadok and Abiathar the priests with you there? Therefore it will be *that* whatever you hear from the king's house, you shall tell to Zadok and Abiathar the priests. 36 Indeed *they have* there with them their two sons, Ahimaaz, Zadok's *son,* and Jonathan, Abiathar's *son;* and by them you shall send me everything you hear."

37 So Hushai, David's friend, went into the city. And Absalom came into Jerusalem.

16 When David was a little past the top *of the mountain,* there was Ziba the servant of Mephibosheth, who met him with a couple of saddled donkeys, and on them two hundred *loaves* of bread, one hundred clusters of raisins, one hundred summer fruits, and a skin of wine. 2 And the king said to Ziba, "What do you mean to do with these?"

So Ziba said, "The donkeys *are* for the king's household to ride on, the bread and summer fruit for the young men to eat, and the wine for those who are faint in the wilderness to drink."

3 Then the king said, "And where *is* your master's son?"

And Ziba said to the king, "Indeed he is staying in Jerusalem, for he said, 'Today the house of Israel will restore the kingdom of my father to me.'"

4 So the king said to Ziba, "Here, all that *belongs* to Mephibosheth *is* yours."

And Ziba said, "I humbly bow before you, *that* I may find favor in your sight, my lord, O king!"

5 Now when King David came to Bahurim, there was a man from the family of the house of Saul, whose name *was* Shimei the son of Gera, coming from there. He came out, cursing continuously as he came. 6 And he threw stones at David and at all the servants of King David. And all the people and all the mighty men *were* on his right hand and on his left. 7 Also Shimei said thus when he cursed: "Come out! Come out! You bloodthirsty man, you rogue! 8 The Lord has brought upon you all the blood of the house of Saul, in whose place you have reigned; and the Lord has delivered the kingdom into the hand of Absalom your son. So now you *are caught* in your own evil, because you are a bloodthirsty man!"

9 Then Abishai the son of Zeruiah said to the king, "Why should this dead dog curse my lord the king? Please, let me go over and take off his head!"

10 But the king said, "What have I to do with you, you sons of Zeruiah? So let him curse, because the Lord has said to him, 'Curse David.' Who then shall say, 'Why have you done so?'"

11 And David said to Abishai and all his servants, "See how my son who came from my own body seeks my life. How much more now *may this* Benjamite? Let him alone, and let him curse; for so the Lord has ordered him. 12 It may be that the Lord will look on my affliction,[a] and that the Lord will repay me with good for his cursing this day." 13 And as David and his men went along the road, Shimei went along the hillside opposite him and cursed as he went, threw stones at him and kicked up dust. 14 Now the king and all the people who *were* with him became weary; so they refreshed themselves there.

15 Meanwhile Absalom and all the people, the men of Israel, came to Je-

16:12 [a]Following Kethib, Septuagint, Syriac, and Vulgate; Qere reads *my eyes;* Targum reads *tears of my eyes*.

rusalem; and Ahithophel *was* with him. 16 And so it was, when Hushai the Archite, David's friend, came to Absalom, that Hushai said to Absalom, "*Long* live the king! *Long* live the king!"

17 So Absalom said to Hushai, "*Is* this your loyalty to your friend? Why did you not go with your friend?"

18 And Hushai said to Absalom, "No, but whom the LORD and this people and all the men of Israel choose, his I will be, and with him I will remain. 19 "Furthermore, whom should I serve? *Should* I not *serve* in the presence of his son? As I have served in your father's presence, so will I be in your presence."

20 Then Absalom said to Ahithophel, "Give advice as to what we should do."

21 And Ahithophel said to Absalom, "Go in to your father's concubines, whom he has left to keep the house; and all Israel will hear that you are abhorred by your father. Then the hands of all who are with you will be strong." 22 So they pitched a tent for Absalom on the top of the house, and Absalom went in to his father's concubines in the sight of all Israel.

23 Now the advice of Ahithophel, which he gave in those days, *was* as if one had inquired at the oracle of God. So *was* all the advice of Ahithophel both with David and with Absalom.

17 Moreover Ahithophel said to Absalom, "Now let me choose twelve thousand men, and I will arise and pursue David tonight. 2 I will come upon him while he *is* weary and weak, and make him afraid. And all the people who *are* with him will flee, and I will strike only the king. 3 Then I will bring back all the people to you. When all return except the man whom you seek, all the people will be at peace." 4 And the saying pleased Absalom and all the elders of Israel.

5 Then Absalom said, "Now call Hushai the Archite also, and let us hear what he says too." 6 And when Hushai came to Absalom, Absalom spoke to him, saying, "Ahithophel has spoken in this manner. Shall we do as he says? If not, speak up."

7 So Hushai said to Absalom: "The advice that Ahithophel has given *is* not good at this time. 8 For," said Hushai, "you know your father and his men, that they *are* mighty men, and they *are* enraged in their minds, like a bear robbed of her cubs in the field; and your father *is* a man of war, and will not camp with the people. 9 Surely by now he is hidden in some pit, or in some *other* place. And it will be, when some of them are overthrown at the first, that whoever hears *it* will say, 'There is a slaughter among the people who follow Absalom.' 10 And even he *who is* valiant, whose heart *is* like the heart of a lion, will melt completely. For all Israel knows that your father *is* a mighty man, and *those* who *are* with him *are* valiant men. 11 Therefore I advise that all Israel be fully gathered to you, from Dan to Beersheba, like the sand that *is* by the sea for multitude, and that you go to battle in person. 12 So we will come upon him in some place where he may be found, and we will fall on him as the dew falls on the ground. And of him and all the men who *are* with him there shall not be left so much as one. 13 Moreover, if he has withdrawn into a city, then all Israel shall bring ropes to that city; and we will pull it into the river, until there is not one small stone found there."

14 So Absalom and all the men of Israel said, "The advice of Hushai the Archite *is* better than the advice of Ahithophel." For the LORD had purposed to defeat the good advice of Ahithophel, to the intent that the LORD might bring disaster on Absalom.

15 Then Hushai said to Zadok and Abiathar the priests, "Thus and so Ahithophel advised Absalom and the elders of Israel, and thus and so I have advised. 16 Now therefore, send quickly and tell David, saying, 'Do not spend this night in the plains of the wilderness, but speedily cross over, lest the king and all the people who *are* with him be swallowed up.' "

17 Now Jonathan and Ahimaaz stayed at En Rogel, for they dared not be seen coming into the city; so a female servant would come and tell them, and they would go and tell King David. 18 Nevertheless a lad saw them, and told Absalom. But both of them went away quickly and came to a man's house in Bahurim, who had a well in his court; and they

went down into it. 19 Then the woman took and spread a covering over the well's mouth, and spread ground grain on it; and the thing was not known. 20 And when Absalom's servants came to the woman at the house, they said, "Where *are* Ahimaaz and Jonathan?"

So the woman said to them, "They have gone over the water brook."

And when they had searched and could not find *them,* they returned to Jerusalem. 21 Now it came to pass, after they had departed, that they came up out of the well and went and told King David, and said to David, "Arise and cross over the water quickly. For thus has Ahithophel advised against you." 22 So David and all the people who *were* with him arose and crossed over the Jordan. By morning light not one of them was left who had not gone over the Jordan.

23 Now when Ahithophel saw that his advice was not followed, he saddled a donkey, and arose and went home to his house, to his city. Then he put his household in order, and hanged himself, and died; and he was buried in his father's tomb.

24 Then David went to Mahanaim. And Absalom crossed over the Jordan, he and all the men of Israel with him. 25 And Absalom made Amasa captain of the army instead of Joab. This Amasa *was* the son of a man whose name *was* Jithra,[a] an Israelite,[b] who had gone in to Abigail the daughter of Nahash, sister of Zeruiah, Joab's mother. 26 So Israel and Absalom encamped in the land of Gilead.

27 Now it happened, when David had come to Mahanaim, that Shobi the son of Nahash from Rabbah of the people of Ammon, Machir the son of Ammiel from Lo Debar, and Barzillai the Gileadite from Rogelim, 28 brought beds and basins, earthen vessels and wheat, barley and flour, parched *grain* and beans, lentils and parched *seeds,* 29 honey and curds, sheep and cheese of the herd, for David and the people who *were* with him to eat. For they said, "The people are hungry and weary and thirsty in the wilderness."

18 And David numbered the people who *were* with him, and set captains of thousands and captains of hundreds over them. 2 Then David sent out one third of the people under the hand of Joab, one third under the hand of Abishai the son of Zeruiah, Joab's brother, and one third under the hand of Ittai the Gittite. And the king said to the people, "I also will surely go out with you myself."

3 But the people answered, "You shall not go out! For if we flee away, they will not care about us; nor if half of us die, will they care about us. But *you are* worth ten thousand of us now. For you are now more help to us in the city."

4 Then the king said to them, "Whatever seems best to you I will do." So the king stood beside the gate, and all the people went out by hundreds and by thousands. 5 Now the king had commanded Joab, Abishai, and Ittai, saying, "*Deal* gently for my sake with the young man Absalom." And all the people heard when the king gave all the captains orders concerning Absalom.

6 So the people went out into the field of battle against Israel. And the battle was in the woods of Ephraim. 7 The people of Israel were overthrown there before the servants of David, and a great slaughter of twenty thousand took place there that day. 8 For the battle there was scattered over the face of the whole countryside, and the woods devoured more people that day than the sword devoured.

9 Then Absalom met the servants of David. Absalom rode on a mule. The mule went under the thick boughs of a great terebinth tree, and his head caught in the terebinth; so he was left hanging between heaven and earth. And the mule which *was* under him went on. 10 Now a certain man saw *it* and told Joab, and said, "I just saw Absalom hanging in a terebinth tree!"

11 So Joab said to the man who told him, "You just saw *him!* And why did you not strike him there to the ground? I would have given you ten *shekels* of silver and a belt."

17:25 [a]Spelled *Jether* in 1 Chronicles 2:17 and elsewhere [b]Following Masoretic Text, some manuscripts of the Septuagint, and Targum; some manuscripts of the Septuagint read *Ishmaelite* (compare 1 Chronicles 2:17); Vulgate reads *of Jezreal.*

12 But the man said to Joab, "Though I were to receive a thousand *shekels* of silver in my hand, I would not raise my hand against the king's son. For in our hearing the king commanded you and Abishai and Ittai, saying, 'Beware lest anyone *touch* the young man Absalom!'*ᵃ* 13 Otherwise I would have dealt falsely against my own life. For there is nothing hidden from the king, and you yourself would have set yourself against *me*."

14 Then Joab said, "I cannot linger with you." And he took three spears in his hand and thrust them through Absalom's heart, while he was *still* alive in the midst of the terebinth tree. 15 And ten young men who bore Joab's armor surrounded Absalom, and struck and killed him.

16 So Joab blew the trumpet, and the people returned from pursuing Israel. For Joab held back the people. 17 And they took Absalom and cast him into a large pit in the woods, and laid a very large heap of stones over him. Then all Israel fled, everyone to his tent.

18 Now Absalom in his lifetime had taken and set up a pillar for himself, which *is* in the King's Valley. For he said, "I have no son to keep my name in remembrance." He called the pillar after his own name. And to this day it is called Absalom's Monument.

19 Then Ahimaaz the son of Zadok said, "Let me run now and take the news to the king, how the Lord has avenged him of his enemies."

20 And Joab said to him, "You shall not take the news this day, for you shall take the news another day. But today you shall take no news, because the king's son is dead."

21 Then Joab said to the Cushite, "Go, tell the king what you have seen." So the Cushite bowed himself to Joab and ran.

22 And Ahimaaz the son of Zadok said again to Joab, "But whatever happens, please let me also run after the Cushite."

So Joab said, "Why will you run, my son, since you have no news ready?"

23 "But whatever happens," *he said,* "let me run."

So he said to him, "Run." Then Ahimaaz ran by way of the plain, and outran the Cushite.

24 Now David was sitting between the two gates. And the watchman went up to the roof over the gate, to the wall, lifted his eyes and looked, and there was a man, running alone. 25 Then the watchman cried out and told the king. And the king said, "If he *is* alone, *there is* news in his mouth." And he came rapidly and drew near.

26 Then the watchman saw *another* man running, and the watchman called to the gatekeeper and said, "There is *another* man, running alone!"

And the king said, "He also brings news."

27 So the watchman said, "I think the running of the first is like the running of Ahimaaz the son of Zadok."

And the king said, "He *is* a good man, and comes with good news."

28 So Ahimaaz called out and said to the king, "All is well!" Then he bowed down with his face to the earth before the king, and said, "Blessed *be* the Lord your God, who has delivered up the men who raised their hand against my lord the king!"

29 The king said, "Is the young man Absalom safe?"

Ahimaaz answered, "When Joab sent the king's servant and *me* your servant, I saw a great tumult, but I did not know what *it was about*."

30 And the king said, "Turn aside *and* stand here." So he turned aside and stood still.

31 Just then the Cushite came, and the Cushite said, "There is good news, my lord the king! For the Lord has avenged you this day of all those who rose against you."

32 And the king said to the Cushite, "Is the young man Absalom safe?"

So the Cushite answered, "May the enemies of my lord the king, and all who rise against you to do harm, be like *that* young man!"

33 Then the king was deeply moved, and went up to the chamber over the gate, and wept. And as he went, he said thus: "O my son Absalom—my son, my son Absalom—if only I had died in your place! O Absalom my son, my son!"

18:12 ᵃThe ancient versions read *'Protect the young man Absalom for me!'*

19 And Joab was told, "Behold, the king is weeping and mourning for Absalom." 2 So the victory that day was *turned* into mourning for all the people. For the people heard it said that day, "The king is grieved for his son." 3 And the people stole back into the city that day, as people who are ashamed steal away when they flee in battle. 4 But the king covered his face, and the king cried out with a loud voice, "O my son Absalom! O Absalom, my son, my son!"

5 Then Joab came into the house to the king, and said, "Today you have disgraced all your servants who today have saved your life, the lives of your sons and daughters, the lives of your wives and the lives of your concubines, 6 in that you love your enemies and hate your friends. For you have declared today that you regard neither princes nor servants; for today I perceive that if Absalom had lived and all of us had died today, then it would have pleased you well. 7 Now therefore, arise, go out and speak comfort to your servants. For I swear by the LORD, if you do not go out, not one will stay with you this night. And that will be worse for you than all the evil that has befallen you from your youth until now." 8 Then the king arose and sat in the gate. And they told all the people, saying, "There is the king, sitting in the gate." So all the people came before the king.

For everyone of Israel had fled to his tent.

9 Now all the people were in a dispute throughout all the tribes of Israel, saying, "The king saved us from the hand of our enemies, he delivered us from the hand of the Philistines, and now he has fled from the land because of Absalom. 10 But Absalom, whom we anointed over us, has died in battle. Now therefore, why do you say nothing about bringing back the king?"

11 So King David sent to Zadok and Abiathar the priests, saying, "Speak to the elders of Judah, saying, 'Why are you the last to bring the king back to his house, since the words of all Israel have come to the king, to his *very* house? 12 You *are* my brethren, you *are* my bone and my flesh. Why then are you the last to bring back the king?' 13 And say to Amasa, 'Are you not my bone and my flesh? God do so to me, and more also, if you are not commander of the army before me continually in place of Joab.' " 14 So he swayed the hearts of all the men of Judah, just as *the heart of* one man, so that they sent *this word* to the king: "Return, you and all your servants!"

15 Then the king returned and came to the Jordan. And Judah came to Gilgal, to go to meet the king, to escort the king across the Jordan. 16 And Shimei the son of Gera, a Benjamite, who *was* from Bahurim, hurried and came down with the men of Judah to meet King David. 17 *There were* a thousand men of Benjamin with him, and Ziba the servant of the house of Saul, and his fifteen sons and his twenty servants with him; and they went over the Jordan before the king. 18 Then a ferryboat went across to carry over the king's household, and to do what he thought good.

Now Shimei the son of Gera fell down before the king when he had crossed the Jordan. 19 Then he said to the king, "Do not let my lord impute iniquity to me, or remember what wrong your servant did on the day that my lord the king left Jerusalem, that the king should take *it* to heart. 20 For I, your servant, know that I have sinned. Therefore here I am, the first to come today of all the house of Joseph to go down to meet my lord the king."

21 But Abishai the son of Zeruiah answered and said, "Shall not Shimei be put to death for this, because he cursed the LORD's anointed?"

22 And David said, "What have I to do with you, you sons of Zeruiah, that you should be adversaries to me today? Shall any man be put to death today in Israel? For do I not know that today I *am* king over Israel?" 23 Therefore the king said to Shimei, "You shall not die." And the king swore to him.

24 Now Mephibosheth the son of Saul came down to meet the king. And he had not cared for his feet, nor trimmed his mustache, nor washed his clothes, from the day the king departed until the day he returned in peace. 25 So it was, when he had come to Jerusalem to meet the king, that the king said to him, "Why did you not go with me, Mephibosheth?"

26 And he answered, "My lord, O king, my servant deceived me. For your servant said, 'I will saddle a donkey for myself, that I may ride on it and go to the king,' because your servant *is* lame. 27 And he has slandered your servant to my lord the king, but my lord the king *is* like the angel of God. Therefore do *what is* good in your eyes. 28 For all my father's house were but dead men before my lord the king. Yet you set your servant among those who eat at your own table. Therefore what right have I still to cry out anymore to the king?"

29 So the king said to him, "Why do you speak anymore of your matters? I have said, 'You and Ziba divide the land.'"

30 Then Mephibosheth said to the king, "Rather, let him take it all, inasmuch as my lord the king has come back in peace to his own house."

31 And Barzillai the Gileadite came down from Rogelim and went across the Jordan with the king, to escort him across the Jordan. 32 Now Barzillai was a very aged man, eighty years old. And he had provided the king with supplies while he stayed at Mahanaim, for he *was* a very rich man. 33 And the king said to Barzillai, "Come across with me, and I will provide for you while you are with me in Jerusalem."

34 But Barzillai said to the king, "How long have I to live, that I should go up with the king to Jerusalem? 35 I *am* today eighty years old. Can I discern between the good and bad? Can your servant taste what I eat or what I drink? Can I hear any longer the voice of singing men and singing women? Why then should your servant be a further burden to my lord the king? 36 Your servant will go a little way across the Jordan with the king. And why should the king repay me *with* such a reward? 37 Please let your servant turn back again, that I may die in my own city, near the grave of my father and mother. But here is your servant Chimham; let him cross over with my lord the king, and do for him what seems good to you."

38 And the king answered, "Chimham shall cross over with me, and I will do for him what seems good to

you. Now whatever you request of me, I will do for you." 39 Then all the people went over the Jordan. And when the king had crossed over, the king kissed Barzillai and blessed him, and he returned to his own place.

40 Now the king went on to Gilgal, and Chimham[a] went on with him. And all the people of Judah escorted the king, and also half the people of Israel. 41 Just then all the men of Israel came to the king, and said to the king, "Why have our brethren, the men of Judah, stolen you away and brought the king, his household, and all David's men with him across the Jordan?"

42 So all the men of Judah answered the men of Israel, "Because the king *is* a close relative of ours. Why then are you angry over this matter? Have we ever eaten at the king's *expense?* Or has he given us any gift?"

43 And the men of Israel answered the men of Judah, and said, "We have ten shares in the king; therefore we also have more *right* to David than you. Why then do you despise us—were we not the first to advise bringing back our king?" Yet the words of the men of Judah were fiercer than the words of the men of Israel.

20

And there happened to be there a rebel,[a] whose name *was* Sheba the son of Bichri, a Benjamite. And he blew a trumpet, and said:

"We have no share in David,
  Nor do we have inheritance in
    the son of Jesse;
  Every man to his tents, O
    Israel!"

2 So every man of Israel deserted David, *and* followed Sheba the son of Bichri. But the men of Judah, from the Jordan as far as Jerusalem, remained loyal to their king.

3 Now David came to his house at Jerusalem. And the king took the ten women, his concubines whom he had left to keep the house, and put them in seclusion and supported them, but did not go in to them. So they were shut up to the day of their death, living in widowhood.

19:40 [a]Masoretic Text reads *Chimhan.*   20:1 [a]Literally *man of Belial*

4 And the king said to Amasa, "Assemble the men of Judah for me within three days, and be present here yourself." 5 So Amasa went to assemble *the men of* Judah. But he delayed longer than the set time which David had appointed him. 6 And David said to Abishai, "Now Sheba the son of Bichri will do us more harm than Absalom. Take your lord's servants and pursue him, lest he find for himself fortified cities, and escape us." 7 So Joab's men, with the Cherethites, the Pelethites, and all the mighty men, went out after him. And they went out of Jerusalem to pursue Sheba the son of Bichri. 8 When they *were* at the large stone which *is* in Gibeon, Amasa came before them. Now Joab was dressed in battle armor; on it was a belt *with* a sword fastened in its sheath at his hips; and as he was going forward, it fell out. 9 Then Joab said to Amasa, "*Are* you in health, my brother?" And Joab took Amasa by the beard with his right hand to kiss him. 10 But Amasa did not notice the sword that *was* in Joab's hand. And he struck him with it in the stomach, and his entrails poured out on the ground; and he did not *strike* him again. Thus he died.

Then Joab and Abishai his brother pursued Sheba the son of Bichri. 11 Meanwhile one of Joab's men stood near Amasa, and said, "Whoever favors Joab and whoever *is* for David—follow Joab!" 12 But Amasa wallowed in *his* blood in the middle of the highway. And when the man saw that all the people stood still, he moved Amasa from the highway to the field and threw a garment over him, when he saw that everyone who came upon him halted. 13 When he was removed from the highway, all the people went on after Joab to pursue Sheba the son of Bichri.

14 And he went through all the tribes of Israel to Abel and Beth Maachah and all the Berites. So they were gathered together and also went after Sheba.ᵃ 15 Then they came and besieged him in Abel of Beth Maachah; and they cast up a siege mound against the city, and it stood by the rampart. And all the people who *were* with Joab battered the wall to throw it down.

16 Then a wise woman cried out from the city, "Hear, hear! Please say to Joab, 'Come nearby, that I may speak with you.' " 17 When he had come near to her, the woman said, "*Are* you Joab?"

He answered, "I *am*."

Then she said to him, "Hear the words of your maidservant."

And he answered, "I am listening."

18 So she spoke, saying, "They used to talk in former times, saying, 'They shall surely seek *guidance* at Abel,' and so they would end *disputes*. 19 I *am among the* peaceable *and* faithful in Israel. You seek to destroy a city and a mother in Israel. Why would you swallow up the inheritance of the LORD?"

20 And Joab answered and said, "Far be it, far be it from me, that I should swallow up or destroy! 21 That *is* not so. But a man from the mountains of Ephraim, Sheba the son of Bichri by name, has raised his hand against the king, against David. Deliver him only, and I will depart from the city."

So the woman said to Joab, "Watch, his head will be thrown to you over the wall." 22 Then the woman in her wisdom went to all the people. And they cut off the head of Sheba the son of Bichri, and threw *it* out to Joab. Then he blew a trumpet, and they withdrew from the city, every man to his tent. So Joab returned to the king at Jerusalem.

23 And Joab *was* over all the army of Israel; Benaiah the son of Jehoiada *was* over the Cherethites and the Pelethites; 24 Adoram *was* in charge of revenue; Jehoshaphat the son of Ahilud *was* recorder; 25 Sheva *was* scribe; Zadok and Abiathar *were* the priests; 26 and Ira the Jairite was a chief minister under David.

21 Now there was a famine in the days of David for three years, year after year; and David inquired of the LORD. And the LORD answered, "*It is* because of Saul and *his* bloodthirsty house, because he killed the Gibeonites." 2 So the king called the Gibeonites and spoke to them. Now the Gibeonites *were* not of the children of Israel, but of the remnant of the Amorites; the children of Israel had sworn protection to them, but

20:14 ᵃLiterally *him*

Saul had sought to kill them in his zeal for the children of Israel and Judah.

3 Therefore David said to the Gibeonites, "What shall I do for you? And with what shall I make atonement, that you may bless the inheritance of the LORD?"

4 And the Gibeonites said to him, "We will have no silver or gold from Saul or from his house, nor shall you kill any man in Israel for us."

So he said, "Whatever you say, I will do for you."

5 Then they answered the king, "As for the man who consumed us and plotted against us, *that* we should be destroyed from remaining in any of the territories of Israel, 6 let seven men of his descendants be delivered to us, and we will hang them before the LORD in Gibeah of Saul, *whom* the LORD chose."

And the king said, "I will give *them*."

7 But the king spared Mephibosheth the son of Jonathan, the son of Saul, because of the LORD's oath that *was* between them, between David and Jonathan the son of Saul. 8 So the king took Armoni and Mephibosheth, the two sons of Rizpah the daughter of Aiah, whom she bore to Saul, and the five sons of Michal[a] the daughter of Saul, whom she brought up for Adriel the son of Barzillai the Meholathite; 9 and he delivered them into the hands of the Gibeonites, and they hanged them on the hill before the LORD. So they fell, *all* seven together, and were put to death in the days of harvest, in the first *days*, in the beginning of barley harvest.

10 Now Rizpah the daughter of Aiah took sackcloth and spread it for herself on the rock, from the beginning of harvest until the late rains poured on them from heaven. And she did not allow the birds of the air to rest on them by day nor the beasts of the field by night.

11 And David was told what Rizpah the daughter of Aiah, the concubine of Saul, had done. 12 Then David went and took the bones of Saul, and the bones of Jonathan his son, from the men of Jabesh Gilead who had stolen them from the street of Beth Shan,[a] where the Philistines had hung them up, after the Philistines had struck down Saul in Gilboa. 13 So he brought up the bones of Saul and the bones of Jonathan his son from there; and they gathered the bones of those who had been hanged. 14 They buried the bones of Saul and Jonathan his son in the country of Benjamin in Zelah, in the tomb of Kish his father. So they performed all that the king commanded. And after that God heeded the prayer for the land.

15 When the Philistines were at war again with Israel, David and his servants with him went down and fought against the Philistines; and David grew faint. 16 Then Ishbi-Benob, who *was* one of the sons of the giant, the weight of whose bronze spear *was* three hundred *shekels,* who was bearing a new *sword,* thought he could kill David. 17 But Abishai the son of Zeruiah came to his aid, and struck the Philistine and killed him. Then the men of David swore to him, saying, "You shall go out no more with us to battle, lest you quench the lamp of Israel."

18 Now it happened afterward that there was again a battle with the Philistines at Gob. Then Sibbechai the Hushathite killed Saph,[a] who *was* one of the sons of the giant. 19 Again there was war at Gob with the Philistines, where Elhanan the son of Jaare-Oregim[a] the Bethlehemite killed *the brother of* Goliath the Gittite, the shaft of whose spear *was* like a weaver's beam.

20 Yet again there was war at Gath, where there was a man of *great* stature, who had six fingers on each hand and six toes on each foot, twenty-four in number; and he also was born to the giant. 21 So when he defied Israel, Jonathan the son of Shimea,[a] David's brother, killed him.

22 These four were born to the giant in Gath, and fell by the hand of David and by the hand of his servants.

22 Then David spoke to the LORD the words of this song, on the day when the LORD had delivered

---

21:8 [a]Or *Merab* (compare 1 Samuel 18:19 and 25:44; 2 Samuel 3:14 and 6:23)   21:12 [a]Spelled *Beth Shan* in Joshua 17:11 and elsewhere   21:18 [a]Spelled *Sippai* in 1 Chronicles 20:4   21:19 [a]Spelled *Jair* in 1 Chronicles 20:5   21:21 [a]Spelled *Shammah* in 1 Samuel 16:9 and elsewhere him from the hand of all his enemies, and from the hand of Saul. 2 And he said:[a]

"The LORD *is* my rock and my fortress and my deliverer;
3   The God of my strength, in whom I will trust;
My shield and the horn of my salvation,
My stronghold and my refuge;
My Savior, You save me from violence.
4   I will call upon the LORD, *who is worthy* to be praised;
So shall I be saved from my enemies.

5   "When the waves of death surrounded me,
The floods of ungodliness made me afraid.
6   The sorrows of Sheol surrounded me;
The snares of death confronted me.
7   In my distress I called upon the LORD,
And cried out to my God;
He heard my voice from His temple,
And my cry *entered* His ears.

8   "Then the earth shook and trembled;
The foundations of heaven[a] quaked and were shaken,
Because He was angry.
9   Smoke went up from His nostrils,
And devouring fire from His mouth;
Coals were kindled by it.
10   He bowed the heavens also, and came down
With darkness under His feet.
11   He rode upon a cherub, and flew;
And He was seen[a] upon the wings of the wind.
12   He made darkness canopies around Him,
Dark waters *and* thick clouds of the skies.
13   From the brightness before Him
Coals of fire were kindled.

14   "The LORD thundered from heaven,
And the Most High uttered His voice.
15   He sent out arrows and scattered them;
Lightning bolts, and He vanquished them.
16   Then the channels of the sea were seen,
The foundations of the world were uncovered,
At the rebuke of the LORD,
At the blast of the breath of His nostrils.

17   "He sent from above, He took me,
He drew me out of many waters.
18   He delivered me from my strong enemy,
From those who hated me;
For they were too strong for me.
19   They confronted me in the day of my calamity,
But the LORD was my support.
20   He also brought me out into a broad place;
He delivered me because He delighted in me.

21   "The LORD rewarded me according to my righteousness;
According to the cleanness of my hands
He has recompensed me.
22   For I have kept the ways of the LORD,
And have not wickedly departed from my God.
23   For all His judgments *were* before me;
And *as for* His statutes, I did not depart from them.
24   I was also blameless before Him,
And I kept myself from my iniquity.
25   Therefore the LORD has recompensed me according to my righteousness,
According to my cleanness in His eyes.[a]

22:2 [a]Compare Psalm 18   22:8 [a]Following Masoretic Text, Septuagint, and Targum; Syriac and Vulgate read *hills* (compare Psalm 18:7).   22:11 [a]Following Masoretic Text and Septuagint; many Hebrew manuscripts, Syriac, and Vulgate read *He flew* (compare Psalm 18:10); Targum reads *He spoke with power*.   22:25 [a]Septuagint, Syriac, and Vulgate read *the cleanness of my hands in His sight* (compare Psalm 18:24); Targum reads *my cleanness before His word*.

26 "With the merciful You will
show Yourself merciful;
With a blameless man You will
show Yourself blameless;
27 With the pure You will show
Yourself pure;
And with the devious You will
show Yourself shrewd.
28 You will save the humble
people;
But Your eyes *are* on the
haughty, *that* You may bring
them down.

29 "For You *are* my lamp, O Lord;
The Lord shall enlighten my
darkness.
30 For by You I can run against a
troop;
By my God I can leap over a
wall.
31 *As for* God, His way *is* perfect;
The word of the Lord *is* proven;
He *is* a shield to all who trust
in Him.

32 "For who *is* God, except the
Lord?
And who *is* a rock, except our
God?
33 God *is* my strength *and* power,*a*
And He makes my*b* way
perfect.
34 He makes my*a* feet like the *feet*
of deer,
And sets me on my high places.
35 He teaches my hands to make
war,
So that my arms can bend a
bow of bronze.

36 "You have also given me the
shield of Your salvation;
Your gentleness has made me
great.
37 You enlarged my path under
me;
So my feet did not slip.

38 "I have pursued my enemies and
destroyed them;
Neither did I turn back again
till they were destroyed.
39 And I have destroyed them and
wounded them,
So that they could not rise;

They have fallen under my feet.
40 For You have armed me with
strength for the battle;
You have subdued under me
those who rose against me.
41 You have also given me the
necks of my enemies,
So that I destroyed those who
hated me.
42 They looked, but *there was*
none to save;
Even to the Lord, but He did
not answer them.
43 Then I beat them as fine as the
dust of the earth;
I trod them like dirt in the
streets,
And I spread them out.

44 "You have also delivered me
from the strivings of my
people;
You have kept me as the head
of the nations.
A people I have not known
shall serve me.
45 The foreigners submit to me;
As soon as they hear, they obey
me.
46 The foreigners fade away,
And come frightened*a* from
their hideouts.

47 "The Lord lives!
Blessed *be* my Rock!
Let God be exalted,
The Rock of my salvation!
48 *It is* God who avenges me,
And subdues the peoples under
me;
49 He delivers me from my
enemies.
You also lift me up above those
who rise against me;
You have delivered me from
the violent man.
50 Therefore I will give thanks to
You, O Lord, among the
Gentiles,
And sing praises to Your name.

51 *He is* the tower of salvation to
His king,
And shows mercy to His
anointed,
To David and his descendants
forevermore."

22:33 *a*Dead Sea Scrolls, Septuagint, Syriac, and Vulgate read *It is God who arms me with strength* (compare
Psalm 18:32); Targum reads *It is God who sustains me with strength.*   *b*Following Qere, Septuagint, Syriac,
Targum, and Vulgate (compare Psalm 18:32); Kethib reads *His.*   22:34 *a*Following Qere, Septuagint,
Syriac, Targum, and Vulgate (compare Psalm 18:33); Kethib reads *His.*   22:46 *a*Following Septuagint,
Targum, and Vulgate (compare Psalm 18:45); Masoretic Text reads *gird themselves.*

23

Now these *are* the last words of David.

Thus says David the son of
   Jesse;
Thus says the man raised up on
   high,
The anointed of the God of
   Jacob,
And the sweet psalmist of
   Israel:

2 "The Spirit of the LORD spoke by
   me,
And His word *was* on my
   tongue.
3 The God of Israel said,
The Rock of Israel spoke to me:
'He who rules over men *must*
   be just,
Ruling in the fear of God.
4 And *he shall be* like the light
   of the morning *when* the sun
   rises,
A morning without clouds,
Like the tender grass *springing*
   out of the earth,
By clear shining after rain.'

5 "Although my house *is* not so
   with God,
Yet He has made with me an
   everlasting covenant,
Ordered in all *things* and
   secure.
For *this is* all my salvation and
   all *my* desire;
Will He not make *it* increase?
6 But *the sons* of rebellion *shall*
   all *be* as thorns thrust away,
Because they cannot be taken
   with hands.
7 But the man *who* touches them
Must be armed with iron and
   the shaft of a spear,
And they shall be utterly
   burned with fire in *their*
   place."

8 These *are* the names of the
mighty men whom David had:
Josheb-Basshebeth[a] the Tachmonite,
chief among the captains.[b] He was
called Adino the Eznite, because he
had killed eight hundred men at one
time. 9 And after him *was* Eleazar the
son of Dodo,[a] the Ahohite, *one* of the
three mighty men with David when
they defied the Philistines *who*
were gathered there for battle, and
the men of Israel had retreated.
10 He arose and attacked the Philistines until his hand was weary, and
his hand stuck to the sword. The
LORD brought about a great victory
that day; and the people returned after him only to plunder. 11 And after
him *was* Shammah the son of Agee
the Hararite. The Philistines had
gathered together into a troop where
there was a piece of ground full of
lentils. So the people fled from the
Philistines. 12 But he stationed himself in the middle of the field, defended it, and killed the Philistines.
So the LORD brought about a great
victory.

13 Then three of the thirty chief
men went down at harvest time and
came to David at the cave of Adullam. And the troop of Philistines encamped in the Valley of Rephaim.
14 David *was* then in the stronghold,
and the garrison of the Philistines
was then *in* Bethlehem. 15 And David
said with longing, "Oh, that someone
would give me a drink of the water
from the well of Bethlehem, which
is by the gate!" 16 So the three mighty
men broke through the camp of the
Philistines, drew water from the well
of Bethlehem that *was* by the gate,
and took it and brought *it* to David.
Nevertheless he would not drink it,
but poured it out to the LORD.
17 And he said, "Far be it from me,
O LORD, that I should do this! Is *this*
not the blood of the men who went
in *jeopardy of* their lives?" Therefore
he would not drink it.

These things were done by the
three mighty men.
18 Now Abishai the brother of
Joab, the son of Zeruiah, was chief
of *another* three.[a] He lifted his spear
against three hundred *men,* killed
them, and won a name among *these*
three. 19 Was he not the most honored of three? Therefore he became
their captain. However, he did not attain to the *first* three.
20 Benaiah *was* the son of Jehoiada, the son of a valiant man from
Kabzeel, who had done many deeds.
He had killed two lion-like heroes of

23:8 [a]Literally *One Who Sits in the Seat* (compare 1 Chronicles 11:11)   [b]Following Masoretic Text and
Targum; Septuagint and Vulgate read *the three.*   23:9 [a]Spelled *Dodai* in 1 Chronicles 27:4
23:18 [a]Following Masoretic Text, Septuagint, and Vulgate; some Hebrew manuscripts and Syriac read *thirty;*
Targum reads *the mighty men.*

On the High Places

The strong, determined ibex (wild goat) scales the steepest cliffs with speed and agility, nimbly leaping up the sheer face of the rocks. Found throughout the wilderness, the ibex symbolized beauty to the people of ancient times.

It is not uncommon to see herds of graceful ibex scale and descend more than twenty mountains a day. The ibex can use only a small crack in the sheerest cliff as a foothold to leap two or three yards.

Usually traveling in herds of thirty or more, the ibex feed on the leaves of small bushes and trees scantily dotting the mountaintops. Upon the approach of an enemy or intruding predator, the ibex will leap quickly up the side of the cliff to higher ground.

The writer of 2 Samuel 22:33, 34 draws from the agility of the ibex to describe the power of God: "God *is* my strength *and* power, and He makes my way perfect. He makes my *feet* like the feet of [ibex], and sets me on my high places."

God makes us like the ibex. When faced with a mountainous problem, we can climb over it. Straight up with grace and agility, we can leap over our problems even with the smallest footholds. Then we can stand on the high places.

When faced with a mountain, remember the ibex. Do not quit! Climb over!

Moab. He also had gone down and killed a lion in the midst of a pit on a snowy day. 21 And he killed an Egyptian, a spectacular man. The Egyptian *had* a spear in his hand; so he went down to him with a staff, wrested the spear out of the Egyptian's hand, and killed him with his own spear. 22 These *things* Benaiah the son of Jehoiada did, and won a name among three mighty men. 23 He was more honored than the thirty, but he did not attain to the *first* three. And David appointed him over his guard.

24 Asahel the brother of Joab *was* one of the thirty; Elhanan the son of Dodo of Bethlehem, 25 Shammah the Harodite, Elika the Harodite, 26 Helez the Paltite, Ira the son of Ikkesh the Tekoite, 27 Abiezer the Anathothite, Mebunnai the Hushathite, 28 Zalmon the Ahohite, Maharai the Netophathite, 29 Heleb the son of Baanah (the Netophathite), Ittai the son of Ribai from Gibeah of the children of Benjamin, 30 Benaiah a Pirathonite, Hiddai from the brooks of Gaash, 31 Abi-Albon the Arbathite, Azmaveth the Barhumite, 32 Eliahba the Shaalbonite (of the sons of Jashen), Jonathan, 33 Shammah the Hararite, Ahiam the son of Sharar the Hararite, 34 Eliphelet the son of Ahasbai, the son of the Maachathite, Eliam the son of Ahithophel the Gilonite, 35 Hezrai*ᵃ* the Carmelite, Paarai the Arbite, 36 Igal the son of Nathan of Zobah, Bani the Gadite, 37 Zelek the Ammonite, Naharai the Beerothite (armorbearer of Joab the son of Zeruiah), 38 Ira the Ithrite, Gareb the Ithrite, 39 *and* Uriah the Hittite: thirty-seven in all.

24 Again the anger of the LORD was aroused against Israel, and He moved David against them to say, "Go, number Israel and Judah."

2 So the king said to Joab the commander of the army who *was* with him, "Now go throughout all the tribes of Israel, from Dan to Beersheba, and count the people, that I may know the number of the people."

3 And Joab said to the king, "Now may the LORD your God add to the people a hundred times more than

there are, and may the eyes of my lord the king see *it*. But why does my lord the king desire this thing?" 4 Nevertheless the king's word prevailed against Joab and against the captains of the army. Therefore Joab and the captains of the army went out from the presence of the king to count the people of Israel.

5 And they crossed over the Jordan and camped in Aroer, on the right side of the town which *is* in the midst of the ravine of Gad, and toward Jazer. 6 Then they came to Gilead and to the land of Tahtim Hodshi; they came to Dan Jaan and around to Sidon; 7 and they came to the stronghold of Tyre and to all the cities of the Hivites and the Canaanites. Then they went out to South Judah *as far as* Beersheba. 8 So when they had gone through all the land, they came to Jerusalem at the end of nine months and twenty days. 9 Then Joab gave the sum of the number of the people to the king. And there were in Israel eight hundred thousand valiant men who drew the sword, and the men of Judah were five hundred thousand men.

10 And David's heart condemned him after he had numbered the people. So David said to the LORD, "I have sinned greatly in what I have done; but now, I pray, O LORD, take away the iniquity of Your servant, for I have done very foolishly."

11 Now when David arose in the morning, the word of the LORD came to the prophet Gad, David's seer, saying, 12 "Go and tell David, 'Thus says the LORD: "I offer you three *things*; choose one of them for yourself, that I may do *it* to you." ' " 13 So Gad came to David and told him; and he said to him, "Shall seven*ᵃ* years of famine come to you in your land? Or shall you flee three months before your enemies, while they pursue you? Or shall there be three days' plague in your land? Now consider and see what answer I should take back to Him who sent me."

14 And David said to Gad, "I am in great distress. Please let us fall into the hand of the LORD, for His mercies *are* great; but do not let me fall into the hand of man."

15 So the LORD sent a plague upon

23:35 *ᵃ*Spelled *Hezro* in 1 Chronicles 11:37   24:13 *ᵃ*Following Masoretic Text, Syriac, Targum, and Vulgate; Septuagint reads *three* (compare 1 Chronicles 21:12).

Israel from the morning till the appointed time. From Dan to Beersheba seventy thousand men of the people died. 16 And when the angel[a] stretched out His hand over Jerusalem to destroy it, the LORD relented from the destruction, and said to the angel who was destroying the people, "It is enough; now restrain your hand." And the angel of the LORD was by the threshing floor of Araunah[b] the Jebusite.

17 Then David spoke to the LORD when he saw the angel who was striking the people, and said, "Surely I have sinned, and I have done wickedly; but these sheep, what have they done? Let Your hand, I pray, be against me and against my father's house."

18 And Gad came that day to David and said to him, "Go up, erect an altar to the LORD on the threshing floor of Araunah the Jebusite." 19 So David, according to the word of Gad, went up as the LORD commanded. 20 Now Araunah looked, and saw the king and his servants coming toward him. So Araunah went out and bowed before the king with his face to the ground.

21 Then Araunah said, "Why has my lord the king come to his servant?"

And David said, "To buy the threshing floor from you, to build an altar to the LORD, that the plague may be withdrawn from the people."

22 Now Araunah said to David, "Let my lord the king take and offer up whatever *seems* good to him. Look, *here are* oxen for burnt sacrifice, and threshing implements and the yokes of the oxen for wood. 23 All these, O king, Araunah has given to the king."

And Araunah said to the king, "May the LORD your God accept you."

24 Then the king said to Araunah, "No, but I will surely buy *it* from you for a price; nor will I offer burnt offerings to the LORD my God with that which costs me nothing." So David bought the threshing floor and the oxen for fifty shekels of silver. 25 And David built there an altar to the LORD, and offered burnt offerings and peace offerings. So the LORD heeded the prayers for the land, and the plague was withdrawn from Israel.

24:16 [a]Or *Angel*   [b]Spelled *Ornan* in 1 Chronicles 21:15

First Kings

Overview of First Kings

First Kings dramatically illustrates the importance of positive leadership as it records the history of the kings of Israel and Judah from the time of King Solomon through King Ahaziah. This book was written by scribes and prophets whose duty it was to record the history of Israel between approximately 1000 and 600 B.C.

The rule of Solomon highlights the Book of First Kings. Crowned by David before the monarch's death, Solomon was one of the greatest kings in Israel's history. His dedication and faith led the people for over forty years. Upon his coronation, Solomon asked of God one gift to help him rule the people—wisdom and understanding. Solomon's goal was not riches or power, but the discerning wisdom to help other people with their problems. He knew that true leadership was willingness to make other people's problems his problems. God not only granted his request by making his wisdom known throughout many lands, but He granted him riches and power as well.

Solomon's writings, including his famous proverbs, are a living memorial to his divinely-given wisdom.

> Trust in the LORD with all your heart,
> And lean not on your own understanding;
> Do not withhold good from those to whom it is due,
> When it is in the power of your hand to do so.
> The fear of the LORD is the beginning of wisdom,
> And the knowledge of the Holy One is understanding.
> (Prov. 3:5, 27; 9:10)

Solomon was also a great visionary who dreamed of building a great temple for God of which the people could be proud. He instilled this vision into the people who readily gave their time, talents, and energy to the completion of this project.

Solomon truly was one of the greatest positive leaders of Israel, teaching his people the main principles of possibility thinking: Attempt great things for God and expect great things from God!

Jesus in First Kings

Solomon portrays Jesus in a number of ways. His renowned wisdom points ahead to Jesus, who embodied God's wisdom. Solomon's fame, glory, wealth, and honor foreshadow all that will come to the Son of God when He sits on the throne of His kingdom.

Keys to First Kings

Key Word: Divisions of the Kingdom. The theme of First Kings centers on the fact that the welfare of Israel and Judah depends on the faithfulness of the people and their king to the covenant with God. The book provides an evaluation of the spiritual and moral causes that led to the political and economic demise of the two kingdoms. The lives of these kings are used to teach that observance of God's law produces blessing, but apostasy is rewarded by judgment.

Key Verses: "Now if you walk before Me as your father David walked, in integrity of heart and in uprightness, to do according to all that I have commanded you, *and* if you keep My statutes and My judgments, then I will establish the throne of your kingdom over Israel forever, as I promised David your father, saying, 'You shall not fail to have a man on the throne of Israel'" (9:4, 5).

"Therefore the LORD said to Solomon, 'Because you have done this, and have not kept My covenant and My statutes, which I have commanded you, I will surely tear the kingdom away from you and give it to your servant'" (11:11).

Key Chapter: First Kings 12. The critical turning point in First Kings occurs in chapter 12 when the united kingdom becomes the divided kingdom. Solomon dies, and his son Rehoboam becomes king and unwisely leads the nation into two separate, and at times conflicting, nations. Instead of unity, God's people now have two kings, two capitals, and two religions.

1 Now King David was old, advanced in years; and they put covers on him, but he could not get warm. 2 Therefore his servants said to him, "Let a young woman, a virgin, be sought for our lord the king, and let her stand before the king, and let her care for him; and let her lie in your bosom, that our lord the king may be warm." 3 So they sought for a lovely young woman throughout all the territory of Israel, and found Abishag the Shunammite, and brought her to the king. 4 The young woman *was* very lovely; and she cared for the king, and served him; but the king did not know her.

5 Then Adonijah the son of Haggith exalted himself, saying, "I will be king"; and he prepared for himself chariots and horsemen, and fifty men to run before him. 6 (And his father had not rebuked him at any time by saying, "Why have you done so?" He *was* also very good-looking. *His mother* had borne him after Absalom.) 7 Then he conferred with Joab the son of Zeruiah and with Abiathar the priest, and they followed and helped Adonijah. 8 But Zadok the

priest, Benaiah the son of Jehoiada, Nathan the prophet, Shimei, Rei, and the mighty men who *belonged* to David were not with Adonijah.

9 And Adonijah sacrificed sheep and oxen and fattened cattle by the stone of Zoheleth, which *is* by En Rogel; he also invited all his brothers, the king's sons, and all the men of Judah, the king's servants. 10 But he did not invite Nathan the prophet, Benaiah, the mighty men, or Solomon his brother.

11 So Nathan spoke to Bathsheba the mother of Solomon, saying, "Have you not heard that Adonijah the son of Haggith has become king, and David our lord does not know *it*? 12 Come, please, let me now give you advice, that you may save your own life and the life of your son Solomon. 13 Go immediately to King David and say to him, 'Did you not, my lord, O king, swear to your maidservant, saying, "Assuredly your son Solomon shall reign after me, and he shall sit on my throne"? Why then has Adonijah become king?' 14 Then, while you are still talking there with the king, I also will come in after you and confirm your words."

15 So Bathsheba went into the chamber to the king. (Now the king was very old, and Abishag the Shunammite was serving the king.) 16 And Bathsheba bowed and did homage to the king. Then the king said, "What is your wish?"

17 Then she said to him, "My lord, you swore by the LORD your God to your maidservant, *saying,* 'Assuredly Solomon your son shall reign after me, and he shall sit on my throne.' 18 So now, look! Adonijah has become king; and now, my lord the king, you do not know about *it.* 19 He has sacrificed oxen and fattened cattle and sheep in abundance, and has invited all the sons of the king, Abiathar the priest, and Joab the commander of the army; but Solomon your servant he has not invited. 20 And as for you, my lord, O king, the eyes of all Israel *are* on you, that you should tell them who will sit on the throne of my lord the king after him. 21 Otherwise it will happen, when my lord the king rests with his fathers, that I and my son Solomon will be counted as offenders."

22 And just then, while she was still talking with the king, Nathan the prophet also came in. 23 So they told the king, saying, "Here is Nathan the prophet." And when he came in before the king, he bowed down before the king with his face to the ground. 24 And Nathan said, "My lord, O king, have you said, 'Adonijah shall reign after me, and he shall sit on my throne'? 25 For he has gone down today, and has sacrificed oxen and fattened cattle and sheep in abundance, and has invited all the king's sons, and the commanders of the army, and Abiathar the priest; and look! They are eating and drinking before him; and they say, '*Long* live King Adonijah!' 26 But he has not invited me—me your servant—nor Zadok the priest, nor Benaiah the son of Jehoiada, nor your servant Solomon. 27 Has this thing been done by my lord the king, and you have not told your servant who should sit on the throne of my lord the king after him?"

28 Then King David answered and said, "Call Bathsheba to me." So she came into the king's presence and stood before the king. 29 And the king took an oath and said, "*As* the LORD lives, who has redeemed my life from every distress, 30 just as I swore to you by the LORD God of Israel, saying, 'Assuredly Solomon your son shall be king after me, and he shall sit on my throne in my place,' so I certainly will do this day."

31 Then Bathsheba bowed with *her* face to the earth, and paid homage to the king, and said, "Let my lord King David live forever!"

32 And King David said, "Call to me Zadok the priest, Nathan the prophet, and Benaiah the son of Jehoiada." So they came before the king. 33 The king also said to them, "Take with you the servants of your lord, and have Solomon my son ride on my own mule, and take him down to Gihon. 34 There let Zadok the priest and Nathan the prophet anoint him king over Israel; and blow the horn, and say, '*Long* live King Solomon!' 35 Then you shall come up after him, and he shall come and sit on my throne, and he shall be king in my place. For I have appointed him to be ruler over Israel and Judah."

36 Benaiah the son of Jehoiada answered the king and said, "Amen!

May the LORD God of my lord the king say so *too.* 37 As the LORD has been with my lord the king, even so may He be with Solomon, and make his throne greater than the throne of my lord King David."

38 So Zadok the priest, Nathan the prophet, Benaiah the son of Jehoiada, the Cherethites, and the Pelethites went down and had Solomon ride on King David's mule, and took him to Gihon. 39 Then Zadok the priest took a horn of oil from the tabernacle and anointed Solomon. And they blew the horn, and all the people said, "*Long* live King Solomon!" 40 And all the people went up after him; and the people played the flutes and rejoiced with great joy, so that the earth *seemed to* split with their sound.

41 Now Adonijah and all the guests who *were* with him heard *it* as they finished eating. And when Joab heard the sound of the horn, he said, "Why *is* the city in such a noisy uproar?" 42 While he was still speaking, there came Jonathan, the son of Abiathar the priest. And Adonijah said to him, "Come in, for you *are* a prominent man, and bring good news."

43 Then Jonathan answered and said to Adonijah, "No! Our lord King David has made Solomon king. 44 The king has sent with him Zadok the priest, Nathan the prophet, Benaiah the son of Jehoiada, the Cherethites, and the Pelethites; and they have made him ride on the king's mule. 45 So Zadok the priest and Nathan the prophet have anointed him king at Gihon; and they have gone up from there rejoicing, so that the city is in an uproar. This *is* the noise that you have heard. 46 Also Solomon sits on the throne of the kingdom. 47 And moreover the king's servants have gone to bless our lord King David, saying, 'May God make the name of Solomon better than your name, and may He make his throne greater than your throne.' Then the king bowed himself on the bed. 48 Also the king said thus, 'Blessed *be* the LORD God of Israel, who has given *one* to sit on my throne this day, while my eyes see *it!* ' "

49 So all the guests who were with Adonijah were afraid, and arose, and each one went his way.

50 Now Adonijah was afraid of Solomon; so he arose, and went and took hold of the horns of the altar. 51 And it was told Solomon, saying, "Indeed Adonijah is afraid of King Solomon; for look, he has taken hold of the horns of the altar, saying, 'Let King Solomon swear to me today that he will not put his servant to death with the sword.' "

52 Then Solomon said, "If he proves himself a worthy man, not one hair of him shall fall to the earth; but if wickedness is found in him, he shall die." 53 So King Solomon sent them to bring him down from the altar. And he came and fell down before King Solomon; and Solomon said to him, "Go to your house."

2 Now the days of David drew near that he should die, and he charged Solomon his son, saying: 2 "I go the way of all the earth; be strong, therefore, and prove yourself a man. 3 And keep the charge of the LORD your God: to walk in His ways, to keep His statutes, His commandments, His judgments, and His testimonies, as it is written in the Law of Moses, that you may prosper in all that you do and wherever you turn; 4 that the LORD may fulfill His word which He spoke concerning me, saying, 'If your sons take heed to their way, to walk before Me in truth with all their heart and with all their soul,' He said, 'you shall not lack a man on the throne of Israel.'

5 "Moreover you know also what Joab the son of Zeruiah did to me, *and* what he did to the two commanders of the armies of Israel, to Abner the son of Ner and Amasa the son of Jether, whom he killed. And he shed the blood of war in peacetime, and put the blood of war on his belt that *was* around his waist, and on his sandals that *were* on his feet. 6 Therefore do according to your wisdom, and do not let his gray hair go down to the grave in peace.

7 "But show kindness to the sons of Barzillai the Gileadite, and let them be among those who eat at your table, for so they came to me when I fled from Absalom your brother.

8 "And see, *you have* with you Shimei the son of Gera, a Benjamite from Bahurim, who cursed me with a malicious curse in the day when I went to Mahanaim. But he came down to meet me at the Jordan, and I swore to him by the LORD, saying,

'I will not put you to death with the sword.' 9 Now therefore, do not hold him guiltless, for you *are* a wise man and know what you ought to do to him; but bring his gray hair down to the grave with blood.'

10 So David rested with his fathers, and was buried in the City of David. 11 The period that David reigned over Israel *was* forty years; seven years he reigned in Hebron, and in Jerusalem he reigned thirty-three years. 12 Then Solomon sat on the throne of his father David; and his kingdom was firmly established.

13 Now Adonijah the son of Haggith came to Bathsheba the mother of Solomon. So she said, "Do you come peaceably?"

And he said, "Peaceably." 14 Moreover he said, "I have something *to say* to you."

And she said, "Say it."

15 Then he said, "You know that the kingdom was mine, and all Israel had set their expectations on me, that I should reign. However, the kingdom has been turned over, and has become my brother's; for it was his from the LORD. 16 Now I ask one petition of you; do not deny me."

And she said to him, "Say it."

17 Then he said, "Please speak to King Solomon, for he will not refuse you, that he may give me Abishag the Shunammite as wife."

18 So Bathsheba said, "Very well, I will speak for you to the king."

19 Bathsheba therefore went to King Solomon, to speak to him for Adonijah. And the king rose up to meet her and bowed down to her, and sat down on his throne and had a throne set for the king's mother; so she sat at his right hand. 20 Then she said, "I desire one small petition of you; do not refuse me."

And the king said to her, "Ask it, my mother, for I will not refuse you."

21 So she said, "Let Abishag the Shunammite be given to Adonijah your brother as wife."

22 And King Solomon answered and said to his mother, "Now why do you ask Abishag the Shunammite for Adonijah? Ask for him the kingdom also—for he *is* my older brother—for him, and for Abiathar the priest, and for Joab the son of Zeruiah." 23 Then King Solomon

swore by the LORD, saying, "May God do so to me, and more also, if Adonijah has not spoken this word against his own life! 24 Now therefore, *as* the LORD lives, who has confirmed me and set me on the throne of David my father, and who has established a house[a] for me, as He promised, Adonijah shall be put to death today!"

25 So King Solomon sent by the hand of Benaiah the son of Jehoiada; and he struck him down, and he died.

26 And to Abiathar the priest the king said, "Go to Anathoth, to your own fields, for you *are* deserving of death; but I will not put you to death at this time, because you carried the ark of the Lord GOD before my father David, and because you were afflicted every time my father was afflicted." 27 So Solomon removed Abiathar from being priest to the LORD, that he might fulfill the word of the LORD which He spoke concerning the house of Eli at Shiloh.

28 Then news came to Joab, for Joab had defected to Adonijah, though he had not defected to Absalom. So Joab fled to the tabernacle of the LORD, and took hold of the horns of the altar. 29 And King Solomon was told, "Joab has fled to the tabernacle of the LORD; there *he is*, by the altar." Then Solomon sent Benaiah the son of Jehoiada, saying, "Go, strike him down." 30 So Benaiah went to the tabernacle of the LORD, and said to him, "Thus says the king, 'Come out!' "

And he said, "No, but I will die here." And Benaiah brought back word to the king, saying, "Thus said Joab, and thus he answered me."

31 Then the king said to him, "Do as he has said, and strike him down and bury him, that you may take away from me and from the house of my father the innocent blood which Joab shed. 32 So the LORD will return his blood on his head, because he struck down two men more righteous and better than he, and killed them with the sword—Abner the son of Ner, the commander of the army of Israel, and Amasa the son of Jether, the commander of the army of Judah—though my father David did not know *it*. 33 Their blood shall

2:24 aThat is, a royal dynasty

therefore return upon the head of Joab and upon the head of his descendants forever. But upon David and his descendants, upon his house and his throne, there shall be peace forever from the LORD."

34 So Benaiah the son of Jehoiada went up and struck and killed him; and he was buried in his own house in the wilderness. 35 The king put Benaiah the son of Jehoiada in his place over the army, and the king put Zadok the priest in the place of Abiathar.

36 Then the king sent and called for Shimei, and said to him, "Build yourself a house in Jerusalem and dwell there, and do not go out from there anywhere. 37 For it shall be, on the day you go out and cross the Brook Kidron, know for certain you shall surely die; your blood shall be on your own head."

38 And Shimei said to the king, "The saying is good. As my lord the king has said, so your servant will do." So Shimei dwelt in Jerusalem many days.

39 Now it happened at the end of three years, that two slaves of Shimei ran away to Achish the son of Maachah, king of Gath. And they told Shimei, saying, "Look, your slaves are in Gath!" 40 So Shimei arose, saddled his donkey, and went to Achish at Gath to seek his slaves. And Shimei went and brought his slaves from Gath. 41 And Solomon was told that Shimei had gone from Jerusalem to Gath and had come back. 42 Then the king sent and called for Shimei, and said to him, "Did I not make you swear by the LORD, and warn you, saying, 'Know for certain that on the day you go out and travel anywhere, you shall surely die'? And you said to me, 'The word I have heard is good.' 43 Why then have you not kept the oath of the LORD and the commandment that I gave you?" 44 The king said moreover to Shimei, "You know, as your heart acknowledges, all the wickedness that you did to my father David; therefore the LORD will return your wickedness on your own head. 45 But King Solomon shall be blessed, and the throne of David shall be established before the LORD forever."

46 So the king commanded Benaiah the son of Jehoiada; and he went out and struck him down, and he died. Thus the kingdom was established in the hand of Solomon.

3 Now Solomon made a treaty with Pharaoh king of Egypt, and married Pharaoh's daughter; then he brought her to the City of David until he had finished building his own house, and the house of the LORD, and the wall all around Jerusalem. 2 Meanwhile the people sacrificed at the high places, because there was no house built for the name of the LORD until those days. 3 And Solomon loved the LORD, walking in the statutes of his father David, except that he sacrificed and burned incense at the high places.

4 Now the king went to Gibeon to sacrifice there, for that was the great high place: Solomon offered a thousand burnt offerings on that altar. 5 At Gibeon the LORD appeared to Solomon in a dream by night; and God said, "Ask! What shall I give you?"

6 And Solomon said: "You have shown great mercy to Your servant David my father, because he walked before You in truth, in righteousness, and in uprightness of heart with You; You have continued this great kindness for him, and You have given him a son to sit on his throne, as it is this day. 7 Now, O LORD my God, You have made Your servant king instead of my father David, but I am a little child; I do not know how to go out or come in. 8 And Your servant is in the midst of Your people whom You have chosen, a great people, too numerous to be numbered or counted. 9 Therefore give to Your servant an understanding heart to judge Your people, that I may discern between good and evil. For who is able to judge this great people of Yours?"

10 The speech pleased the LORD, that Solomon had asked this thing. 11 Then God said to him: "Because you have asked this thing, and have not asked long life for yourself, nor have asked riches for yourself, nor have asked the life of your enemies, but have asked for yourself understanding to discern justice, 12 behold, I have done according to your words; see, I have given you a wise and understanding heart, so that there has not been anyone like you before you, nor shall any like you arise after you.

13 And I have also given you what you have not asked: both riches and honor, so that there shall not be anyone like you among the kings all your days. 14 So if you walk in My ways, to keep My statutes and My commandments, as your father David walked, then I will lengthen your days."

15 Then Solomon awoke; and indeed it had been a dream. And he came to Jerusalem and stood before the ark of the covenant of the LORD, offered up burnt offerings, offered peace offerings, and made a feast for all his servants.

16 Now two women *who were* harlots came to the king, and stood before him. 17 And one woman said, "O my lord, this woman and I dwell in the same house; and I gave birth while she *was* in the house. 18 Then it happened, the third day after I had given birth, that this woman also gave birth. And we *were* together; no one *was* with us in the house, except the two of us in the house. 19 And this woman's son died in the night, because she lay on him. 20 So she arose in the middle of the night and took my son from my side, while your maidservant slept, and laid him in her bosom, and laid her dead child in my bosom. 21 And when I rose in the morning to nurse my son, there he was, dead. But when I had examined him in the morning, indeed, he was not my son whom I had borne."

22 Then the other woman said, "No! But the living one *is* my son, and the dead one *is* your son."

And the first woman said, "No! But the dead one *is* your son, and the living one *is* my son."

Thus they spoke before the king.

23 And the king said, "The one says, 'This *is* my son, who lives, and your son *is* the dead one'; and the other says, 'No! But your son *is* the dead one, and my son *is* the living one.' " 24 Then the king said, "Bring me a sword." So they brought a sword before the king. 25 And the king said, "Divide the living child in two, and give half to one, and half to the other."

26 Then the woman whose son *was* living spoke to the king, for she yearned with compassion for her son; and she said, "O my lord, give her the living child, and by no means kill him!"

But the other said, "Let him be neither mine nor yours, *but* divide *him*."

27 So the king answered and said, "Give the first woman the living child, and by no means kill him; she *is* his mother."

28 And all Israel heard of the judgment which the king had rendered; and they feared the king, for they saw that the wisdom of God *was* in him to administer justice.

4 So King Solomon was king over all Israel. 2 And these *were* his officials: Azariah the son of Zadok, the priest; 3 Elihoreph and Ahijah, the sons of Shisha, scribes; Jehoshaphat the son of Ahilud, the recorder; 4 Benaiah the son of Jehoiada, over the army; Zadok and Abiathar, the priests; 5 Azariah the son of Nathan, over the officers; Zabud the son of Nathan, a priest *and* the king's friend; 6 Ahishar, over the household; and Adoniram the son of Abda, over the labor force.

7 And Solomon had twelve governors over all Israel, who provided food for the king and his household; each one made provision for one month of the year. 8 These *are* their names: Ben-Hur,*a* in the mountains of Ephraim; 9 Ben-Deker,*a* in Makaz, Shaalbim, Beth Shemesh, and Elon Beth Hanan; 10 Ben-Hesed,*a* in Aruboth; to him *belonged* Sochoh and all the land of Hepher; 11 Ben-Abinadab,*a in* all the regions of Dor; he had Taphath the daughter of Solomon as wife; 12 Baana the son of Ahilud, *in* Taanach, Megiddo, and all Beth Shean, which *is* beside Zaretan below Jezreel, from Beth Shean to Abel Meholah, as far as the other side of Jokneam; 13 Ben-Geber,*a* in Ramoth Gilead; to him *belonged* the towns of Jair the son of Manasseh, in Gilead; to him *also belonged* the region of Argob in Bashan—sixty large cities with walls and bronze gate-bars; 14 Ahinadab the son of Iddo, *in* Mahanaim; 15 Ahimaaz, in Naphtali; he also took Basemath the daughter of Solomon as wife; 16 Baanah the son of Hushai, in Asher and Aloth;

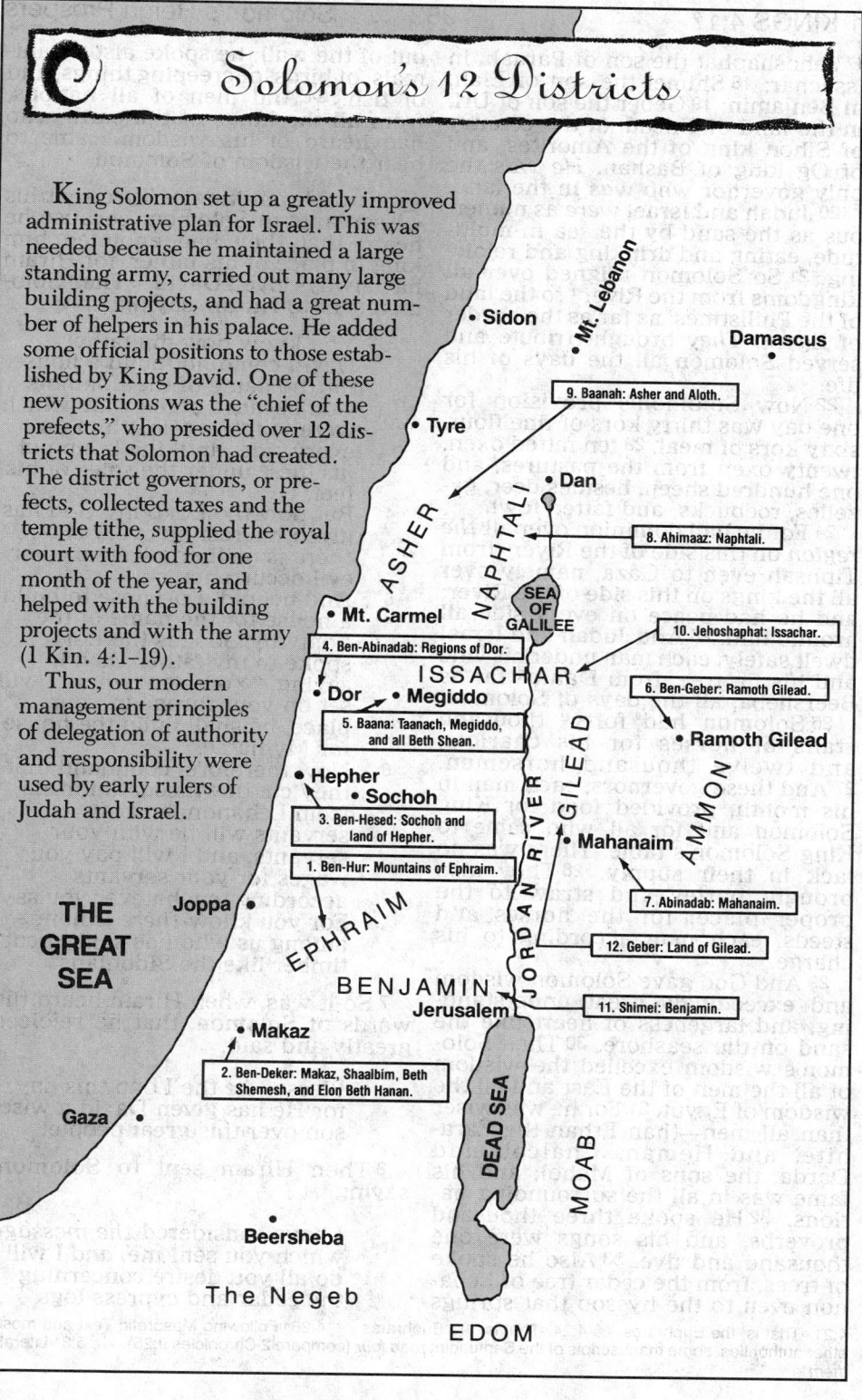

Solomon's 12 Districts

King Solomon set up a greatly improved administrative plan for Israel. This was needed because he maintained a large standing army, carried out many large building projects, and had a great number of helpers in his palace. He added some official positions to those established by King David. One of these new positions was the "chief of the prefects," who presided over 12 districts that Solomon had created. The district governors, or prefects, collected taxes and the temple tithe, supplied the royal court with food for one month of the year, and helped with the building projects and with the army (1 Kin. 4:1–19).

Thus, our modern management principles of delegation of authority and responsibility were used by early rulers of Judah and Israel.

• Sidon

Mt. Lebanon

Damascus

• Tyre

9. Baanah: Asher and Aloth.

• Dan

ASHER

NAPHTALI

SEA OF GALILEE

8. Ahimaaz: Naphtali.

• Mt. Carmel

4. Ben-Abinadab: Regions of Dor.

ISSACHAR

10. Jehoshaphat: Issachar.

• Dor • Megiddo

6. Ben-Geber: Ramoth Gilead.

5. Baana: Taanach, Megiddo, and all Beth Shean.

GILEAD

• Ramoth Gilead

AMMON

• Hepher
  • Sochoh

3. Ben-Hesed: Sochoh and land of Hepher.

1. Ben-Hur: Mountains of Ephraim.

• Mahanaim

7. Abinadab: Mahanaim.

JORDAN RIVER

THE GREAT SEA

Joppa •

EPHRAIM

12. Geber: Land of Gilead.

BENJAMIN

Jerusalem

11. Shimei: Benjamin.

• Makaz

2. Ben-Deker: Makaz, Shaalbim, Beth Shemesh, and Elon Beth Hanan.

DEAD SEA

MOAB

Gaza •

• Beersheba

The Negeb

EDOM

17 Jehoshaphat the son of Paruah, in Issachar; 18 Shimei the son of Elah, in Benjamin; 19 Geber the son of Uri, in the land of Gilead, *in* the country of Sihon king of the Amorites, and of Og king of Bashan. *He was* the only governor who *was* in the land.

20 Judah and Israel *were* as numerous as the sand by the sea in multitude, eating and drinking and rejoicing. 21 So Solomon reigned over all kingdoms from the River*a to* the land of the Philistines, as far as the border of Egypt. *They* brought tribute and served Solomon all the days of his life.

22 Now Solomon's provision for one day was thirty kors of fine flour, sixty kors of meal, 23 ten fatted oxen, twenty oxen from the pastures, and one hundred sheep, besides deer, gazelles, roebucks, and fatted fowl. 24 For he had dominion over all *the region* on this side of the River*a* from Tiphsah even to Gaza, namely over all the kings on this side of the River; and he had peace on every side all around him. 25 And Judah and Israel dwelt safely, each man under his vine and his fig tree, from Dan as far as Beersheba, all the days of Solomon. 26 Solomon had forty*a* thousand stalls of horses for his chariots, and twelve thousand horsemen. 27 And these governors, each man in his month, provided food for King Solomon and for all who came to King Solomon's table. There was no lack in their supply. 28 They also brought barley and straw to the proper place, for the horses and steeds, each man according to his charge.

29 And God gave Solomon wisdom and exceedingly great understanding, and largeness of heart like the sand on the seashore. 30 Thus Solomon's wisdom excelled the wisdom of all the men of the East and all the wisdom of Egypt. 31 For he was wiser than all men—than Ethan the Ezrahite, and Heman, Chalcol, and Darda, the sons of Mahol; and his fame was in all the surrounding nations. 32 He spoke three thousand proverbs, and his songs were one thousand and five. 33 Also he spoke of trees, from the cedar tree of Lebanon even to the hyssop that springs out of the wall; he spoke also of animals, of birds, of creeping things, and of fish. 34 And men of all nations, from all the kings of the earth who had heard of his wisdom, came to hear the wisdom of Solomon.

5 Now Hiram king of Tyre sent his servants to Solomon, because he heard that they had anointed him king in place of his father, for Hiram had always loved David. 2 Then Solomon sent to Hiram, saying:

3   You know how my father David could not build a house for the name of the LORD his God because of the wars which were fought against him on every side, until the LORD put *his foes*a* under the soles of his feet.

4   But now the LORD my God has given me rest on every side; *there is* neither adversary nor evil occurrence.

5   And behold, I propose to build a house for the name of the LORD my God, as the LORD spoke to my father David, saying, "Your son, whom I will set on your throne in your place, he shall build the house for My name."

6   Now therefore, command that they cut down cedars for me from Lebanon; and my servants will be with your servants, and I will pay you wages for your servants according to whatever you say. For you know *there is* none among us who has skill to cut timber like the Sidonians.

7 So it was, when Hiram heard the words of Solomon, that he rejoiced greatly and said,

Blessed *be* the LORD this day, for He has given David a wise son over this great people!

8 Then Hiram sent to Solomon, saying:

I have considered *the message* which you sent me, *and* I will do all you desire concerning the cedar and cypress logs.

4:21 *a*That is, the Euphrates   4:24 *a*That is, the Euphrates   4:26 *a*Following Masoretic Text and most other authorities; some manuscripts of the Septuagint read *four* (compare 2 Chronicles 9:25).   5:3 *a*Literally *them*

9 My servants shall bring *them* down from Lebanon to the sea; I will float them in rafts by sea to the place you indicate to me, and will have them broken apart there; then you can take *them* away. And you shall fulfill my desire by giving food for my household.

10 Then Hiram gave Solomon cedar and cypress logs *according to* all his desire. 11 And Solomon gave Hiram twenty thousand kors of wheat *as* food for his household, and twenty[a] kors of pressed oil. Thus Solomon gave to Hiram year by year.

12 So the LORD gave Solomon wisdom, as He had promised him; and there was peace between Hiram and Solomon, and the two of them made a treaty together.

13 Then King Solomon raised up a labor force out of all Israel; and the labor force was thirty thousand men. 14 And he sent them to Lebanon, ten thousand a month in shifts: they were one month in Lebanon *and* two months at home; Adoniram *was* in charge of the labor force. 15 Solomon had seventy thousand who carried burdens, and eighty thousand who quarried *stone* in the mountains, 16 besides three thousand three hundred[a] from the chiefs of Solomon's deputies, who supervised the people who labored in the work. 17 And the king commanded them to quarry large stones, costly stones, *and* hewn stones, to lay the foundation of the temple.[a] 18 So Solomon's builders, Hiram's builders, and the Gebalites quarried *them;* and they prepared timber and stones to build the temple.

6 And it came to pass in the four hundred and eightieth[a] year after the children of Israel had come out of the land of Egypt, in the fourth year of Solomon's reign over Israel, in the month of Ziv, which *is* the second month, that he began to build the house of the LORD. 2 Now the house which King Solomon built for the

LORD, its length *was* sixty cubits, its width twenty, and its height thirty cubits. 3 The vestibule in front of the sanctuary[a] of the house *was* twenty cubits long across the width of the house, *and* the width of *the vestibule*[b] extended ten cubits from the front of the house. 4 And he made for the house windows with beveled frames.

5 Against the wall of the temple he built chambers all around, *against* the walls of the temple, all around the sanctuary and the inner sanctuary.[a] Thus he made side chambers all around it. 6 The lowest chamber *was* five cubits wide, the middle *was* six cubits wide, and the third *was* seven cubits wide; for he made narrow ledges around the outside of the temple, so that *the support beams* would not be fastened into the walls of the temple. 7 And the temple, when it was being built, was built with stone finished at the quarry, so that no hammer or chisel *or* any iron tool was heard in the temple while it was being built. 8 The doorway for the middle story[a] *was* on the right side of the temple. They went up by stairs to the middle *story,* and from the middle to the third.

9 So he built the temple and finished it, and he paneled the temple with beams and boards of cedar. 10 And he built side chambers against the entire temple, each five cubits high; they were attached to the temple with cedar beams.

11 Then the word of the LORD came to Solomon, saying: 12 "Concerning this temple which you are building, if you walk in My statutes, execute My judgments, keep all My commandments, and walk in them, then I will perform My word with you, which I spoke to your father David. 13 And I will dwell among the children of Israel, and will not forsake My people Israel."

14 So Solomon built the temple and finished it. 15 And he built the inside walls of the temple with cedar boards; from the floor of the temple to the ceiling he paneled the inside

5:11 aFollowing Masoretic Text, Targum, and Vulgate; Septuagint and Syriac read *twenty thousand.*
5:16 aFollowing Masoretic Text, Targum, and Vulgate; Septuagint reads *three thousand six hundred.*
5:17 aLiterally *house,* and so frequently throughout this book   6:1 aFollowing Masoretic Text, Targum, and Vulgate; Septuagint reads *fortieth.*   6:3 aHebrew *heykal;* here the main room of the temple, elsewhere called the holy place (compare Exodus 26:33 and Ezekiel 41:1)   bLiterally *it*   6:5 aHebrew *debir;* here the inner room of the temple, elsewhere called the Most Holy Place (compare verse 16)   6:8 aFollowing Masoretic Text and Vulgate; Septuagint reads *upper story;* Targum reads *ground story.*

with wood; and he covered the floor of the temple with planks of cypress. 16 Then he built the twenty-cubit room at the rear of the temple, from floor to ceiling, with cedar boards; he built *it* inside as the inner sanctuary, as the Most Holy *Place.* 17 And in front of it the temple sanctuary was forty cubits *long.* 18 The inside of the temple was cedar, carved with ornamental buds and open flowers. All *was* cedar; there was no stone *to be* seen.

19 And he prepared the inner sanctuary inside the temple, to set the ark of the covenant of the LORD there. 20 The inner sanctuary *was* twenty cubits long, twenty cubits wide, and twenty cubits high. He overlaid it with pure gold, and overlaid the altar of cedar. 21 So Solomon overlaid the inside of the temple with pure gold. He stretched gold chains across the front of the inner sanctuary, and overlaid it with gold. 22 The whole temple he overlaid with gold, until he had finished all the temple; also he overlaid with gold the entire altar that *was* by the inner sanctuary.

23 Inside the inner sanctuary he made two cherubim *of* olive wood, *each* ten cubits high. 24 One wing of the cherub *was* five cubits, and the other wing of the cherub five cubits: ten cubits from the tip of one wing to the tip of the other. 25 And the other cherub *was* ten cubits; both cherubim *were* of the same size and shape. 26 The height of one cherub *was* ten cubits, and so *was* the other cherub. 27 Then he set the cherubim inside the inner room;*a* and they stretched out the wings of the cherubim so that the wing of the one touched *one* wall, and the wing of the other cherub touched the other wall. And their wings touched each other in the middle of the room. 28 Also he overlaid the cherubim with gold.

29 Then he carved all the walls of the temple all around, both the inner and outer *sanctuaries,* with carved figures of cherubim, palm trees, and open flowers. 30 And the floor of the temple he overlaid with gold, both the inner and outer *sanctuaries.*

31 For the entrance of the inner sanctuary he made doors *of* olive wood; the lintel *and* doorposts *were* one-fifth *of the wall.* 32 The two doors

were of olive wood; and he carved on them figures of cherubim, palm trees, and open flowers, and overlaid *them* with gold; and he spread gold on the cherubim and on the palm trees. 33 So for the door of the sanctuary he also made doorposts *of* olive wood, one-fourth *of the wall.* 34 And the two doors *were of* cypress wood; two panels *comprised* one folding door, and two panels *comprised* the other folding door. 35 Then he carved cherubim, palm trees, and open flowers *on them,* and overlaid *them* with gold applied evenly on the carved work.

36 And he built the inner court with three rows of hewn stone and a row of cedar beams.

37 In the fourth year the foundation of the house of the LORD was laid, in the month of Ziv. 38 And in the eleventh year, in the month of Bul, which is the eighth month, the house was finished in all its details and according to all its plans. So he was seven years in building it.

7 But Solomon took thirteen years to build his own house; so he finished all his house.

2 He also built the House of the Forest of Lebanon; its length *was* one hundred cubits; its width fifty cubits, and its height thirty cubits, with four rows of cedar pillars, and cedar beams on the pillars. 3 And *it was* paneled with cedar above the beams that *were* on forty-five pillars, fifteen *to* a row. 4 *There were* windows *with* beveled *frames in* three rows, and window *was* opposite window *in* three tiers. 5 And all the doorways and doorposts *had* rectangular frames; and window *was* opposite window *in* three tiers.

6 He also made the Hall of Pillars: its length *was* fifty cubits, and its width thirty cubits; and in front of them *was* a portico with pillars, and a canopy *was* in front of them.

7 Then he made a hall for the throne, the Hall of Judgment, where he might judge; and *it was* paneled with cedar from floor to ceiling.*a*

8 And the house where he dwelt *had* another court inside the hall, of like workmanship. Solomon also made a house like this hall for Pha-

6:27 aLiterally *house*   7:7 aLiterally *floor,* that is, of the upper level raoh's daughter, whom he had taken *as wife.*

9 All these *were of* costly stones cut to size, trimmed with saws, inside and out, from the foundation to the eaves, and also on the outside to the great court. 10 The foundation *was of* costly stones, large stones, some ten cubits and some eight cubits. 11 And above *were* costly stones, hewn to size, and cedar wood. 12 The great court *was* enclosed with three rows of hewn stones and a row of cedar beams. So were the inner court of the house of the LORD and the vestibule of the temple.

13 Now King Solomon sent and brought Huram[a] from Tyre. 14 He *was* the son of a widow from the tribe of Naphtali, and his father *was* a man of Tyre, a bronze worker; he was filled with wisdom and understanding and skill in working with all kinds of bronze work. So he came to King Solomon and did all his work.

15 And he cast two pillars of bronze, each one eighteen cubits high, and a line of twelve cubits measured the circumference of each. 16 Then he made two capitals *of* cast bronze, to set on the tops of the pillars. The height of one capital *was* five cubits, and the height of the other capital *was* five cubits. 17 *He made* a lattice network, with wreaths of chainwork, for the capitals which *were* on top of the pillars: seven chains for one capital and seven for the other capital. 18 So he made the pillars, and two rows of pomegranates above the network all around to cover the capitals that *were* on top; and thus he did for the other capital.

19 The capitals which *were* on top of the pillars in the hall *were* in the shape of lilies, four cubits. 20 The capitals on the two pillars also *had* pomegranates above, by the convex surface which *was* next to the network; and there *were* two hundred such pomegranates in rows on each of the capitals all around.

21 Then he set up the pillars by the vestibule of the temple; he set up the pillar on the right and called its name Jachin, and he set up the pillar on the left and called its name Boaz.

22 The tops of the pillars were in the shape of lilies. So the work of the pillars was finished.

23 And he made the Sea of cast bronze, ten cubits from one brim to the other; *it was* completely round. Its height *was* five cubits, and a line of thirty cubits measured its circumference.

24 Below its brim *were* ornamental buds encircling it all around, ten to a cubit, all the way around the Sea. The ornamental buds *were* cast in two rows when it was cast. 25 It stood on twelve oxen: three looking toward the north, three looking toward the west, three looking toward the south, and three looking toward the east; the Sea *was set* upon them, and all their back parts *pointed* inward. 26 It *was* a handbreadth thick; and its brim was shaped like the brim of a cup, *like* a lily blossom. It contained two thousand[a] baths.

27 He also made ten carts of bronze; four cubits *was* the length of each cart, four cubits its width, and three cubits its height. 28 And this *was* the design of the carts: They had panels, and the panels *were* between frames; 29 on the panels that *were* between the frames *were* lions, oxen, and cherubim. And on the frames *was* a pedestal on top. Below the lions and oxen *were* wreaths of plaited work. 30 Every cart had four bronze wheels and axles of bronze, and its four feet had supports. Under the laver *were* supports of cast *bronze* beside each wreath. 31 Its opening inside the crown at the top *was* one cubit in diameter; and the opening *was* round, shaped *like* a pedestal, one and a half cubits in outside diameter; and also on the opening *were* engravings, but the panels were square, not round. 32 Under the panels *were* the four wheels, and the axles of the wheels *were joined* to the cart. The height of a wheel *was* one and a half cubits. 33 The workmanship of the wheels *was* like the workmanship of a chariot wheel; their axle pins, their rims, their spokes, and their hubs *were* all of cast *bronze.* 34 And *there were* four supports at the four corners of each cart; its supports *were* part of the cart itself. 35 On the top of the

---

7:13 [a]Hebrew *Hiram* (compare 2 Chronicles 2:13, 14) 4:5)

7:26 [a]Or *three thousand* (compare 2 Chronicles

cart, at the height of half a cubit, *it was* perfectly round. And on the top of the cart, its flanges and its panels *were* of the same casting. 36 On the plates of its flanges and on its panels he engraved cherubim, lions, and palm trees, wherever there was a clear space on each, with wreaths all around. 37 Thus he made the ten carts. All of them were of the same mold, one measure, *and* one shape.

38 Then he made ten lavers of bronze; each laver contained forty baths, *and* each laver *was* four cubits. On each of the ten carts *was* a laver. 39 And he put five carts on the right side of the house, and five on the left side of the house. He set the Sea on the right side of the house, toward the southeast.

40 Huram*a* made the lavers and the shovels and the bowls. So Huram finished doing all the work that he was to do for King Solomon *for* the house of the LORD: 41 the two pillars, the *two* bowl-shaped capitals that *were* on top of the two pillars; the two networks covering the two bowl-shaped capitals which *were* on top of the pillars; 42 four hundred pomegranates for the two networks (two rows of pomegranates for each network, to cover the two bowl-shaped capitals that *were* on top of the pillars); 43 the ten carts, and ten lavers on the carts; 44 one Sea, and twelve oxen under the Sea; 45 the pots, the shovels, and the bowls.

All these articles which Huram*a* made for King Solomon *for* the house of the LORD *were of* burnished bronze. 46 In the plain of Jordan the king had them cast in clay molds, between Succoth and Zaretan. 47 And Solomon did not weigh all the articles, because *there were* so many; the weight of the bronze was not determined.

48 Thus Solomon had all the furnishings made for the house of the LORD: the altar of gold, and the table of gold on which *was* the showbread; 49 the lampstands of pure gold, five on the right *side* and five on the left in front of the inner sanctuary, with the flowers and the lamps and the wick-trimmers of gold; 50 the basins, the trimmers, the bowls, the ladles, and the censers of pure gold; and the hinges of gold, *both* for the doors of the inner room (the Most Holy *Place*) *and* for the doors of the main hall of the temple.

51 So all the work that King Solomon had done for the house of the LORD was finished; and Solomon brought in the things which his father David had dedicated: the silver and the gold and the furnishings. He put them in the treasuries of the house of the LORD.

8 Now Solomon assembled the elders of Israel and all the heads of the tribes, the chief fathers of the children of Israel, to King Solomon in Jerusalem, that they might bring up the ark of the covenant of the LORD from the City of David, which *is* Zion. 2 Therefore all the men of Israel assembled with King Solomon at the feast in the month of Ethanim, which *is* the seventh month. 3 So all the elders of Israel came, and the priests took up the ark. 4 Then they brought up the ark of the LORD, the tabernacle of meeting, and all the holy furnishings that *were* in the tabernacle. The priests and the Levites brought them up. 5 Also King Solomon, and all the congregation of Israel who were assembled with him, *were* with him before the ark, sacrificing sheep and oxen that could not be counted or numbered for multitude. 6 Then the priests brought in the ark of the covenant of the LORD to its place, into the inner sanctuary of the temple, to the Most Holy *Place*, under the wings of the cherubim. 7 For the cherubim spread *their* two wings over the place of the ark, and the cherubim overshadowed the ark and its poles. 8 The poles extended so that the ends of the poles could be seen from the holy *place*, in front of the inner sanctuary; but they could not be seen from outside. And they are there to this day. 9 Nothing *was* in the ark except the two tablets of stone which Moses put there at Horeb, when the LORD made *a* covenant with the children of Israel, when they came out of the land of Egypt.

10 And it came to pass, when the priests came out of the holy *place*, that the cloud filled the house of the LORD, 11 so that the priests could not

---

7:40 *a*Hebrew *Hiram* (compare 2 Chronicles 2:13, 14)   7:45 *a*Hebrew *Hiram* (compare 2 Chronicles 2:13, 14)

continue ministering because of the cloud; for the glory of the LORD filled the house of the LORD.

12 Then Solomon spoke:

"The LORD said He would dwell in the dark cloud.
13 I have surely built You an exalted house,
And a place for You to dwell in forever."

14 Then the king turned around and blessed the whole assembly of Israel, while all the assembly of Israel was standing. 15 And he said: "Blessed *be* the LORD God of Israel, who spoke with His mouth to my father David, and with His hand has fulfilled *it*, saying, 16 'Since the day that I brought My people Israel out of Egypt, I have chosen no city from any tribe of Israel *in which* to build a house, that My name might be there; but I chose David to be over My people Israel.' 17 Now it was in the heart of my father David to build a temple*ᵃ* for the name of the LORD God of Israel. 18 But the LORD said to my father David, 'Whereas it was in your heart to build a temple for My name, you did well that it was in your heart. 19 Nevertheless you shall not build the temple, but your son who will come from your body, he shall build the temple for My name.' 20 So the LORD has fulfilled His word which He spoke; and I have filled the position of my father David, and sit on the throne of Israel, as the LORD promised; and I have built a temple for the name of the LORD God of Israel. 21 And there I have made a place for the ark, in which *is* the covenant of the LORD which He made with our fathers, when He brought them out of the land of Egypt."

22 Then Solomon stood before the altar of the LORD in the presence of all the assembly of Israel, and spread out his hands toward heaven; 23 and he said: "LORD God of Israel, *there is* no God in heaven above or on earth below like You, who keep *Your* covenant and mercy with Your servants who walk before You with all their hearts. 24 You have kept what You promised Your servant David my father; You have both spoken with Your mouth and fulfilled *it* with

Your hand, as *it is* this day. 25 Therefore, LORD God of Israel, now keep what You promised Your servant David my father, saying, 'You shall not fail to have a man sit before Me on the throne of Israel, only if your sons take heed to their way, that they walk before Me as you have walked before Me.' 26 And now I pray, O God of Israel, let Your word come true, which You have spoken to Your servant David my father.

27 "But will God indeed dwell on the earth? Behold, heaven and the heaven of heavens cannot contain You. How much less this temple which I have built! 28 Yet regard the prayer of Your servant and his supplication, O LORD my God, and listen to the cry and the prayer which Your servant is praying before You today: 29 that Your eyes may be open toward this temple night and day, toward the place of which You said, 'My name shall be there,' that You may hear the prayer which Your servant makes toward this place. 30 And may You hear the supplication of Your servant and of Your people Israel, when they pray toward this place. Hear in heaven Your dwelling place; and when You hear, forgive.

31 "When anyone sins against his neighbor, and is forced to take an oath, and comes *and* takes an oath before Your altar in this temple, 32 then hear in heaven, and act, and judge Your servants, condemning the wicked, bringing his way on his head, and justifying the righteous by giving him according to his righteousness.

33 "When Your people Israel are defeated before an enemy because they have sinned against You, and when they turn back to You and confess Your name, and pray and make supplication to You in this temple, 34 then hear in heaven, and forgive the sin of Your people Israel, and bring them back to the land which You gave to their fathers.

35 "When the heavens are shut up and there is no rain because they have sinned against You, when they pray toward this place and confess Your name, and turn from their sin because You afflict them, 36 then hear in heaven, and forgive the sin

8:17 *ᵃ*Literally *house*, and so in verses 18–20

Jerusalem

There are infinite possibilities in little beginnings if God is in them. One beautiful example of this is the city of Jerusalem. Once a small village located by a tiny stream, Jerusalem had a population of less than five hundred people prior to the time of Abraham. Yet by the New Testament period, she would grow to a city of two million inhabitants during the Passover Feast.

All the great cities of the ancient world were aided by natural resources in their growth. Athens had a seaport and an easy travel route connecting it with Asia Minor and Europe. Alexandria and Memphis in North Africa had the famous Egyptian Nile which provided food and water for the region. Babylon in Mesopotamia was near the great Euphrates River, and Rome sat on seven major hills around the Tiber River. All of these cities possessed tokens of civic promise.

Jerusalem had none of the conditions of a great city. No heavily traveled highway passed by her doors. She had no harbor from which to launch her ships for trade with her neighbors. Her back door was the wilderness of Judea, one of the most devastated and desolate areas in the region. There were no fertile fields to develop the city's agriculture. Security for the town's defenses was precarious. The city's water sources were barely large enough to supply the needs of a few thousand people.

What was the success behind Jerusalem? Perhaps it is found in her name, meaning "Possession of Peace." The real character and strength of Jerusalem was not in her natural resources, but in her people's faith in God. In Micah 4:2, God's purpose for Jerusalem is clear—"Many nations shall come and say, 'Come and let us go up to the mountain of the Lord, to the house of the God of Jacob; He will teach us His ways, and we shall walk in His paths. For out of Zion the law shall go forth and the word of the Lord from Jerusalem.'" Throughout Jerusalem's history, God lifted her above the limiting conditions and resources. With faith, she became an influential power center of the world.

Like the city of Jerusalem, our lives are often limited by what we may consider to be a lack of important resources—talent, money, education, or contacts. We may look at successful people and feel that they have more resources than we have. Yet as Christians, we have a greater resource. With a committed faith in God, we are assured that He will make up the difference between what we have and what we need (see Phil 4:9).

Allow God to turn your little beginnings into infinite possibilities! Put your faith in Him. He is the unending resource for the accomplishment of your dreams.

of Your servants, Your people Israel, that You may teach them the good way in which they should walk; and send rain on Your land which You have given to Your people as an inheritance.

37 "When there is famine in the land, pestilence or blight or mildew, locusts or grasshoppers; when their enemy besieges them in the land of their cities; whatever plague or whatever sickness there is; 38 whatever prayer, whatever supplication is made by anyone, or by all Your people Israel, when each one knows the plague of his own heart, and spreads out his hands toward this temple: 39 then hear in heaven Your dwelling place, and forgive, and act, and give to everyone according to all his ways, whose heart You know (for You alone know the hearts of all the sons of men), 40 that they may fear You all the days that they live in the land which You gave to our fathers.

41 "Moreover, concerning a foreigner, who is not of Your people Israel, but has come from a far country for Your name's sake 42 (for they will hear of Your great name and Your strong hand and Your outstretched arm), when he comes and prays toward this temple, 43 hear in heaven Your dwelling place, and do according to all for which the foreigner calls to You, that all peoples of the earth may know Your name and fear You, as do Your people Israel, and that they may know that this temple which I have built is called by Your name.

44 "When Your people go out to battle against their enemy, wherever You send them, and when they pray to the LORD toward the city which You have chosen and the temple which I have built for Your name, 45 then hear in heaven their prayer and their supplication, and maintain their cause.

46 "When they sin against You (for there is no one who does not sin), and You become angry with them and deliver them to the enemy, and they take them captive to the land of the enemy, far or near; 47 yet when they come to themselves in the land where they were carried captive, and repent, and make supplication to You in the land of those who took them captive, saying, 'We have sinned and done wrong, we have committed wickedness'; 48 and when they return to You with all their heart and with all their soul in the land of their enemies who led them away captive, and pray to You toward their land which You gave to their fathers, the city which You have chosen and the temple which I have built for Your name: 49 then hear in heaven Your dwelling place their prayer and their supplication, and maintain their cause, 50 and forgive Your people who have sinned against You, and all their transgressions which they have transgressed against You; and grant them compassion before those who took them captive, that they may have compassion on them 51 (for they are Your people and Your inheritance, whom You brought out of Egypt, out of the iron furnace), 52 that Your eyes may be open to the supplication of Your servant and the supplication of Your people Israel, to listen to them whenever they call to You. 53 For You separated them from among all the peoples of the earth to be Your inheritance, as You spoke by Your servant Moses, when You brought our fathers out of Egypt, O Lord GOD."

54 And so it was, when Solomon had finished praying all this prayer and supplication to the LORD, that he arose from before the altar of the LORD, from kneeling on his knees with his hands spread up to heaven. 55 Then he stood and blessed all the assembly of Israel with a loud voice, saying: 56 "Blessed be the LORD, who has given rest to His people Israel, according to all that He promised. There has not failed one word of all His good promise, which He promised through His servant Moses. 57 May the LORD our God be with us, as He was with our fathers. May He not leave us nor forsake us, 58 that He may incline our hearts to Himself, to walk in all His ways, and to keep His commandments and His statutes and His judgments, which He commanded our fathers. 59 And may these words of mine, with which I have made supplication before the LORD, be near the LORD our God day and night, that He may maintain the cause of His servant and the cause of His people Israel, as each day may require, 60 that all the peoples of the earth may know that the LORD is God; there is no

other. 61 Let your heart therefore be loyal to the LORD our God, to walk in His statutes and keep His commandments, as at this day."

62 Then the king and all Israel with him offered sacrifices before the LORD. 63 And Solomon offered a sacrifice of peace offerings, which he offered to the LORD, twenty-two thousand bulls and one hundred and twenty thousand sheep. So the king and all the children of Israel dedicated the house of the LORD. 64 On the same day the king consecrated the middle of the court that *was* in front of the house of the LORD; for there he offered burnt offerings, grain offerings, and the fat of the peace offerings, because the bronze altar that *was* before the LORD *was* too small to receive the burnt offerings, the grain offerings, and the fat of the peace offerings.

65 At that time Solomon held a feast, and all Israel with him, a great assembly from the entrance of Hamath to the Brook of Egypt, before the LORD our God, seven days and seven *more* days—fourteen days. 66 On the eighth day he sent the people away; and they blessed the king, and went to their tents joyful and glad of heart for all the good that the LORD had done for His servant David, and for Israel His people.

9 And it came to pass, when Solomon had finished building the house of the LORD and the king's house, and all Solomon's desire which he wanted to do, 2 that the LORD appeared to Solomon the second time, as He had appeared to him at Gibeon. 3 And the LORD said to him: "I have heard your prayer and your supplication that you have made before Me; I have consecrated this house which you have built to put My name there forever, and My eyes and My heart will be there perpetually. 4 Now if you walk before Me as your father David walked, in integrity of heart and in uprightness, to do according to all that I have commanded you, *and* if you keep My statutes and My judgments, 5 then I will establish the throne of your kingdom over Israel forever, as I promised David your father, saying, 'You shall not fail to have a man on the throne of Israel.' 6 *But* if you or your sons at all turn from following Me, and do not keep My commandments *and* My statutes which I have set before you, but go and serve other gods and worship them, 7 then I will cut off Israel from the land which I have given them; and this house which I have consecrated for My name I will cast out of My sight. Israel will be a proverb and a byword among all peoples. 8 And as for this house, *which* is exalted, everyone who passes by it will be astonished and will hiss, and say, 'Why has the LORD done thus to this land and to this house?' 9 Then they will answer, 'Because they forsook the LORD their God, who brought their fathers out of the land of Egypt, and have embraced other gods, and worshiped them and served them; therefore the LORD has brought all this calamity on them.' "

10 Now it happened at the end of twenty years, when Solomon had built the two houses, the house of the LORD and the king's house 11 (Hiram the king of Tyre had supplied Solomon with cedar and cypress and gold, as much as he desired), *that* King Solomon then gave Hiram twenty cities in the land of Galilee. 12 Then Hiram went from Tyre to see the cities which Solomon had given him, but they did not please him. 13 So he said, "What *kind of* cities *are* these which you have given me, my brother?" And he called them the land of Cabul,*a* as they are to this day. 14 Then Hiram sent the king one hundred and twenty talents of gold.

15 And this *is* the reason for the labor force which King Solomon raised: to build the house of the LORD, his own house, the Millo,*a* the wall of Jerusalem, Hazor, Megiddo, and Gezer. 16 (Pharaoh king of Egypt had gone up and taken Gezer and burned it with fire, had killed the Canaanites who dwelt in the city, and had given it *as* a dowry to his daughter, Solomon's wife.) 17 And Solomon built Gezer, Lower Beth Horon, 18 Baalath, and Tadmor in the wilderness, in the land of *Judah*, 19 all the storage cities that Solomon had, cities for his chariots and cities for his cavalry, and whatever Solomon desired to build in Jerusalem, in Leba-

9:13 *a*Literally *Good for Nothing*   9:15 *a*Literally *The Landfill*

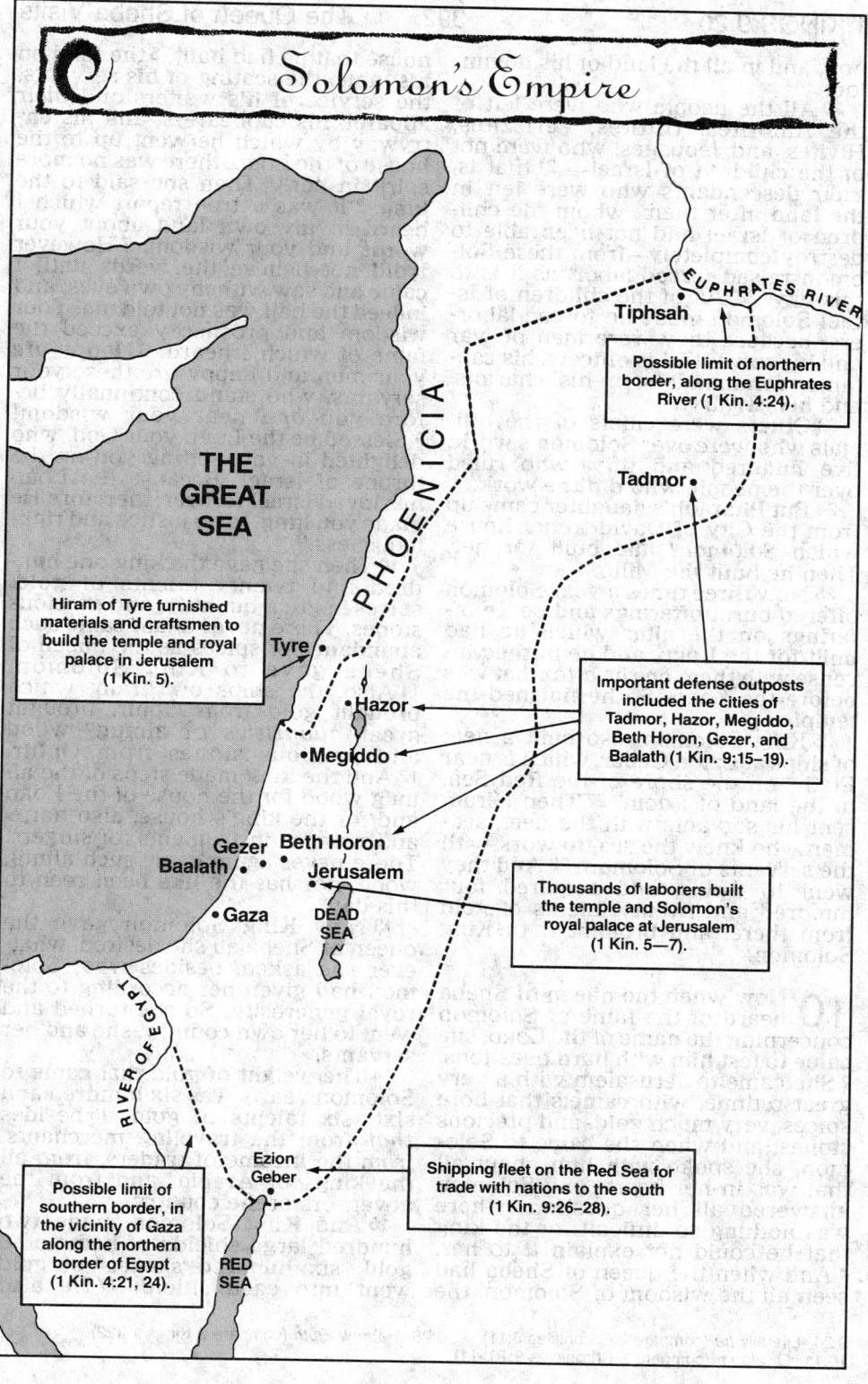

Solomon's Empire

THE GREAT SEA

PHOENICIA

EUPHRATES RIVER

Tiphsah

Possible limit of northern border, along the Euphrates River (1 Kin. 4:24).

Tadmor

Hiram of Tyre furnished materials and craftsmen to build the temple and royal palace in Jerusalem (1 Kin. 5).

Tyre

Hazor

Important defense outposts included the cities of Tadmor, Hazor, Megiddo, Beth Horon, Gezer, and Baalath (1 Kin. 9:15–19).

Megiddo

Gezer   Beth Horon

Baalath

Jerusalem

Gaza

DEAD SEA

Thousands of laborers built the temple and Solomon's royal palace at Jerusalem (1 Kin. 5—7).

RIVER OF EGYPT

Ezion Geber

Shipping fleet on the Red Sea for trade with nations to the south (1 Kin. 9:26–28).

Possible limit of southern border, in the vicinity of Gaza along the northern border of Egypt (1 Kin. 4:21, 24).

RED SEA

non, and in all the land of his dominion.

20 All the people *who were* left of the Amorites, Hittites, Perizzites, Hivites, and Jebusites, who *were* not of the children of Israel— 21 that is, their descendants who were left in the land after them, whom the children of Israel had not been able to destroy completely—from these Solomon raised forced labor, as it is to this day. 22 But of the children of Israel Solomon made no forced laborers, because they *were* men of war and his servants: his officers, his captains, commanders of his chariots, and his cavalry.

23 Others *were* chiefs of the officials who *were* over Solomon's work: five hundred and fifty, who ruled over the people who did the work.

24 But Pharaoh's daughter came up from the City of David to her house which *Solomon*[a] had built for her. Then he built the Millo.

25 Now three times a year Solomon offered burnt offerings and peace offerings on the altar which he had built for the LORD, and he burned incense with them *on the altar* that *was* before the LORD. So he finished the temple.

26 King Solomon also built a fleet of ships at Ezion Geber, which *is* near Elath[a] on the shore of the Red Sea, in the land of Edom. 27 Then Hiram sent his servants with the fleet, seamen who knew the sea, to work with the servants of Solomon. 28 And they went to Ophir, and acquired four hundred and twenty talents of gold from there, and brought *it* to King Solomon.

10 Now when the queen of Sheba heard of the fame of Solomon concerning the name of the LORD, she came to test him with hard questions. 2 She came to Jerusalem with a very great retinue, with camels that bore spices, very much gold, and precious stones; and when she came to Solomon, she spoke with him about all that was in her heart. 3 So Solomon answered all her questions; there was nothing so difficult for the king that he could not explain *it* to her. 4 And when the queen of Sheba had seen all the wisdom of Solomon, the

house that he had built, 5 the food on his table, the seating of his servants, the service of his waiters and their apparel, his cupbearers, and his entryway by which he went up to the house of the LORD, there was no more spirit in her. 6 Then she said to the king: "It was a true report which I heard in my own land about your words and your wisdom. 7 However I did not believe the words until I came and saw with my own eyes; and indeed the half was not told me. Your wisdom and prosperity exceed the fame of which I heard. 8 Happy *are* your men and happy *are* these your servants, who stand continually before you *and* hear your wisdom! 9 Blessed be the LORD your God, who delighted in you, setting you on the throne of Israel! Because the LORD has loved Israel forever, therefore He made you king, to do justice and righteousness."

10 Then she gave the king one hundred and twenty talents of gold, spices in great quantity, and precious stones. There never again came such abundance of spices as the queen of Sheba gave to King Solomon. 11 Also, the ships of Hiram, which brought gold from Ophir, brought great *quantities* of almug[a] wood and precious stones from Ophir. 12 And the king made steps of the almug wood for the house of the LORD and for the king's house, also harps and stringed instruments for singers. There never again came such almug wood, nor has the like been seen to this day.

13 Now King Solomon gave the queen of Sheba all she desired, whatever she asked, besides what Solomon had given her according to the royal generosity. So she turned and went to her own country, she and her servants.

14 The weight of gold that came to Solomon yearly was six hundred and sixty-six talents of gold, 15 besides *that* from the traveling merchants, from the income of traders, from all the kings of Arabia, and from the governors of the country.

16 And King Solomon made two hundred large shields *of* hammered gold; six hundred *shekels* of gold went into each shield. 17 He also

9:24 aLiterally *he* (compare 2 Chronicles 8:11)   9:26 aHebrew *Eloth* (compare 2 Kings 14:22)
10:11 aOr *algum* (compare 2 Chronicles 9:10, 11)

made three hundred shields *of* hammered gold; three minas of gold went into each shield. The king put them in the House of the Forest of Lebanon.

18 Moreover the king made a great throne of ivory, and overlaid it with pure gold. 19 The throne had six steps, and the top of the throne *was* round at the back; *there were* armrests on either side of the place of the seat, and two lions stood beside the armrests. 20 Twelve lions stood there, one on each side of the six steps; nothing like *this* had been made for any *other* kingdom.

21 All King Solomon's drinking vessels *were* gold, and all the vessels of the House of the Forest of Lebanon *were* pure gold. Not *one was* silver, for this was accounted as nothing in the days of Solomon. 22 For the king had merchant ships*ª* at sea with the fleet of Hiram. Once every three years the merchant ships came bringing gold, silver, ivory, apes, and monkeys.*b* 23 So King Solomon surpassed all the kings of the earth in riches and wisdom.

24 Now all the earth sought the presence of Solomon to hear his wisdom, which God had put in his heart. 25 Each man brought his present: articles of silver and gold, garments, armor, spices, horses, and mules, at a set rate year by year.

26 And Solomon gathered chariots and horsemen; he had one thousand four hundred chariots and twelve thousand horsemen, whom he stationed*ª* in the chariot cities and with the king at Jerusalem. 27 The king made silver *as common* in Jerusalem as stones, and he made cedar trees as abundant as the sycamores which *are* in the lowland.

28 Also Solomon had horses imported from Egypt and Keveh; the king's merchants bought them in Keveh at the *current* price. 29 Now a chariot that was imported from Egypt cost six hundred *shekels* of silver, and a horse one hundred and fifty; and thus, through their agents,*ª* they exported *them* to all the kings of the Hittites and the kings of Syria.

11 But King Solomon loved many foreign women, as well as the daughter of Pharaoh: women of the Moabites, Ammonites, Edomites, Sidonians, *and* Hittites— 2 from the nations of whom the Lord had said to the children of Israel, "You shall not intermarry with them, nor they with you. Surely they will turn away your hearts after their gods." Solomon clung to these in love. 3 And he had seven hundred wives, princesses, and three hundred concubines; and his wives turned away his heart. 4 For it was so, when Solomon was old, that his wives turned his heart after other gods; and his heart was not loyal to the Lord his God, as *was* the heart of his father David. 5 For Solomon went after Ashtoreth the goddess of the Sidonians, and after Milcom the abomination of the Ammonites. 6 Solomon did evil in the sight of the Lord, and did not fully follow the Lord, as *did* his father David. 7 Then Solomon built a high place for Chemosh the abomination of Moab, on the hill that *is* east of Jerusalem, and for Molech the abomination of the people of Ammon. 8 And he did likewise for all his foreign wives, who burned incense and sacrificed to their gods.

9 So the Lord became angry with Solomon, because his heart had turned from the Lord God of Israel, who had appeared to him twice, 10 and had commanded him concerning this thing, that he should not go after other gods; but he did not keep what the Lord had commanded. 11 Therefore the Lord said to Solomon, "Because you have done this, and have not kept My covenant and My statutes, which I have commanded you, I will surely tear the kingdom away from you and give it to your servant. 12 Nevertheless I will not do it in your days, for the sake of your father David; I will tear it out of the hand of your son. 13 However I will not tear away the whole kingdom; I will give one tribe to your son for the sake of my servant David, and for the sake of Jerusalem which I have chosen."

14 Now the Lord raised up an adversary against Solomon, Hadad the Edomite; he *was* a descendant of the king in Edom. 15 For it happened, when David was in Edom, and Joab

---

10:22 *ª*Literally *ships of Tarshish,* deep-sea vessels   *b*Or *peacocks*   10:26 *ª*Following Septuagint, Syriac, Targum, and Vulgate (compare 2 Chronicles 9:25); Masoretic Text reads *led.*   10:29 *ª*Literally *by their hands* the commander of the army had gone up to bury the slain, after he had killed every male in Edom 16 (because for six months Joab remained there with all Israel, until he had cut down every male in Edom), 17 that Hadad fled to go to Egypt, he and certain Edomites of his father's servants with him. Hadad *was* still a little child. 18 Then they arose from Midian and came to Paran; and they took men with them from Paran and came to Egypt, to Pharaoh king of Egypt, who gave him a house, apportioned food for him, and gave him land. 19 And Hadad found great favor in the sight of Pharaoh, so that he gave him as wife the sister of his own wife, that is, the sister of Queen Tahpenes. 20 Then the sister of Tahpenes bore him Genubath his son, whom Tahpenes weaned in Pharaoh's house. And Genubath was in Pharaoh's household among the sons of Pharaoh.

21 So when Hadad heard in Egypt that David rested with his fathers, and that Joab the commander of the army was dead, Hadad said to Pharaoh, "Let me depart, that I may go to my own country."

22 Then Pharaoh said to him, "But what have you lacked with me, that suddenly you seek to go to your own country?"

So he answered, "Nothing, but do let me go anyway."

23 And God raised up *another* adversary against him, Rezon the son of Eliadah, who had fled from his lord, Hadadezer king of Zobah. 24 So he gathered men to him and became captain over a band *of raiders,* when David killed those *of Zobah.* And they went to Damascus and dwelt there, and reigned in Damascus. 25 He was an adversary of Israel all the days of Solomon (besides the trouble that Hadad *caused*); and he abhorred Israel, and reigned over Syria.

26 Then Solomon's servant, Jeroboam the son of Nebat, an Ephraimite from Zereda, whose mother's name *was* Zeruah, a widow, also rebelled against the king. 27 And this *is* what caused him to rebel against the king: Solomon had built the Millo *and* repaired the damages to the City of David his father.

28 The man Jeroboam *was* a mighty man of valor; and Solomon, seeing that the young man was industrious, made him the officer over all the labor force of the house of Joseph.

29 Now it happened at that time, when Jeroboam went out of Jerusalem, that the prophet Ahijah the Shilonite met him on the way; and he had clothed himself with a new garment, and the two *were* alone in the field. 30 Then Ahijah took hold of the new garment that *was* on him, and tore it *into* twelve pieces. 31 And he said to Jeroboam, "Take for yourself ten pieces, for thus says the LORD, the God of Israel: 'Behold, I will tear the kingdom out of the hand of Solomon and will give ten tribes to you 32 (but he shall have one tribe for the sake of My servant David, and for the sake of Jerusalem, the city which I have chosen out of all the tribes of Israel), 33 because they have*a* forsaken Me, and worshiped Ashtoreth the goddess of the Sidonians, Chemosh the god of the Moabites, and Milcom the god of the people of Ammon, and have not walked in My ways to do *what is* right in My eyes and *keep* My statutes and My judgments, as *did* his father David. 34 However I will not take the whole kingdom out of his hand, because I have made him ruler all the days of his life for the sake of My servant David, whom I chose because he kept My commandments and My statutes. 35 But I will take the kingdom out of his son's hand and give it to you— ten tribes. 36 And to his son I will give one tribe, that My servant David may always have a lamp before Me in Jerusalem, the city which I have chosen for Myself, to put My name there. 37 So I will take you, and you shall reign over all your heart desires, and you shall be king over Israel. 38 Then it shall be, if you heed all that I command you, walk in My ways, and do *what is* right in My sight, to keep My statutes and My commandments, as My servant David did, then I will be with you and build for you an enduring house, as I built for David, and will give Israel to you. 39 And I will afflict the descendants of David because of this, but not forever.' "

40 Solomon therefore sought to kill

11:33 *a*Following Masoretic Text and Targum; Septuagint, Syriac, and Vulgate read *he has.*

Jeroboam. But Jeroboam arose and fled to Egypt, to Shishak king of Egypt, and was in Egypt until the death of Solomon.

41 Now the rest of the acts of Solomon, all that he did, and his wisdom, *are* they not written in the book of the acts of Solomon? 42 And the period that Solomon reigned in Jerusalem over all Israel *was* forty years. 43 Then Solomon rested with his fathers, and was buried in the City of David his father. And Rehoboam his son reigned in his place.

12 And Rehoboam went to Shechem, for all Israel had gone to Shechem to make him king. 2 So it happened, when Jeroboam the son of Nebat heard *it* (he was still in Egypt, for he had fled from the presence of King Solomon and had been dwelling in Egypt), 3 that they sent and called him. Then Jeroboam and the whole assembly of Israel came and spoke to Rehoboam, saying, 4 "Your father made our yoke heavy; now therefore, lighten the burdensome service of your father, and his heavy yoke which he put on us, and we will serve you."

5 So he said to them, "Depart *for* three days, then come back to me." And the people departed.

6 Then King Rehoboam consulted the elders who stood before his father Solomon while he still lived, and he said, "How do you advise *me* to answer these people?"

7 And they spoke to him, saying, "If you will be a servant to these people today, and serve them, and answer them, and speak good words to them, then they will be your servants forever."

8 But he rejected the advice which the elders had given him, and consulted the young men who had grown up with him, who stood before him. 9 And he said to them, "What advice do you give? How should we answer this people who have spoken to me, saying, 'Lighten the yoke which your father put on us'?"

10 Then the young men who had grown up with him spoke to him, saying, "Thus you should speak to this people who have spoken to you, saying, 'Your father made our yoke heavy, but you make *it* lighter on us'—thus you shall say to them: 'My little *finger* shall be thicker than my father's waist! 11 And now, whereas my father put a heavy yoke on you, I will add to your yoke; my father chastised you with whips, but I will chastise you with scourges!' "[a]

12 So Jeroboam and all the people came to Rehoboam the third day, as the king had directed, saying, "Come back to me the third day." 13 Then the king answered the people roughly, and rejected the advice which the elders had given him; 14 and he spoke to them according to the advice of the young men, saying, "My father made your yoke heavy, but I will add to your yoke; my father chastised you with whips, but I will chastise you with scourges!"[a] 15 So the king did not listen to the people; for the turn *of events* was from the LORD, that He might fulfill His word, which the LORD had spoken by Ahijah the Shilonite to Jeroboam the son of Nebat.

16 Now when all Israel saw that the king did not listen to them, the people answered the king, saying:

"What share have we in David?
We have no inheritance in the
 son of Jesse.
To your tents, O Israel!
Now, see to your own house,
 O David!"

So Israel departed to their tents. 17 But Rehoboam reigned over the children of Israel who dwelt in the cities of Judah.

18 Then King Rehoboam sent Adoram, who *was* in charge of the revenue; but all Israel stoned him with stones, and he died. Therefore King Rehoboam mounted his chariot in haste to flee to Jerusalem. 19 So Israel has been in rebellion against the house of David to this day.

20 Now it came to pass when all Israel heard that Jeroboam had come back, they sent for him and called him to the congregation, and made him king over all Israel. There was none who followed the house of David, but the tribe of Judah only.

21 And when Rehoboam came to Jerusalem, he assembled all the house of Judah with the tribe of Benjamin, one hundred and eighty thou-

12:11 [a]Literally *scorpions*   12:14 [a]Literally *scorpions* sand chosen *men* who were warriors, to fight against the house of Israel, that he might restore the kingdom to Rehoboam the son of Solomon. 22 But the word of God came to Shemaiah the man of God, saying, 23 "Speak to Rehoboam the son of Solomon, king of Judah, to all the house of Judah and Benjamin, and to the rest of the people, saying, 24 'Thus says the LORD: "You shall not go up nor fight against your brethren the children of Israel. Let every man return to his house, for this thing is from Me." ' " Therefore they obeyed the word of the LORD, and turned back, according to the word of the LORD.

25 Then Jeroboam built Shechem in the mountains of Ephraim, and dwelt there. Also he went out from there and built Penuel. 26 And Jeroboam said in his heart, "Now the kingdom may return to the house of David: 27 If these people go up to offer sacrifices in the house of the LORD at Jerusalem, then the heart of this people will turn back to their lord, Rehoboam king of Judah, and they will kill me and go back to Rehoboam king of Judah."

28 Therefore the king asked advice, made two calves of gold, and said to the people, "It is too much for you to go up to Jerusalem. Here are your gods, O Israel, which brought you up from the land of Egypt!" 29 And he set up one in Bethel, and the other he put in Dan. 30 Now this thing became a sin, for the people went *to worship* before the one as far as Dan. 31 He made shrines*a* on the high places, and made priests from every class of people, who were not of the sons of Levi.

32 Jeroboam ordained a feast on the fifteenth day of the eighth month, like the feast that *was* in Judah, and offered sacrifices on the altar. So he did at Bethel, sacrificing to the calves that he had made. And at Bethel he installed the priests of the high places which he had made. 33 So he made offerings on the altar which he had made at Bethel on the fifteenth day of the eighth month, in the month which he had devised in his own heart. And he ordained a feast for the children of Israel, and offered sacrifices on the altar and burned incense.

13 And behold, a man of God went from Judah to Bethel by the word of the LORD, and Jeroboam stood by the altar to burn incense. 2 Then he cried out against the altar by the word of the LORD, and said, "O altar, altar! Thus says the LORD: 'Behold, a child, Josiah by name, shall be born to the house of David; and on you he shall sacrifice the priests of the high places who burn incense on you, and men's bones shall be burned on you.' " 3 And he gave a sign the same day, saying, "This *is* the sign which the LORD has spoken: Surely the altar shall split apart, and the ashes on it shall be poured out."

4 So it came to pass when King Jeroboam heard the saying of the man of God, who cried out against the altar in Bethel, that he stretched out his hand from the altar, saying, "Arrest him!" Then his hand, which he stretched out toward him, withered, so that he could not pull it back to himself. 5 The altar also was split apart, and the ashes poured out from the altar, according to the sign which the man of God had given by the word of the LORD. 6 Then the king answered and said to the man of God, "Please entreat the favor of the LORD your God, and pray for me, that my hand may be restored to me." So the man of God entreated the LORD, and the king's hand was restored to him, and became as before. 7 Then the king said to the man of God, "Come home with me and refresh yourself, and I will give you a reward."

8 But the man of God said to the king, "If you were to give me half your house, I would not go in with you; nor would I eat bread nor drink water in this place. 9 For so it was commanded me by the word of the LORD, saying, 'You shall not eat bread, nor drink water, nor return by the same way you came.' " 10 So he went another way and did not return by the way he came to Bethel.

11 Now an old prophet dwelt in Bethel, and his sons came and told him all the works that the man of God had done that day in Bethel; they also told their father the words which he had spoken to the king. 12 And their father said to them,

12:31 *a*Literally *a house*

"Which way did he go?" For his sons had seen[a] which way the man of God went who came from Judah. 13 Then he said to his sons, "Saddle the donkey for me." So they saddled the donkey for him; and he rode on it, 14 and went after the man of God, and found him sitting under an oak. Then he said to him, *"Are* you the man of God who came from Judah?"

And he said, "I *am.*"

15 Then he said to him, "Come home with me and eat bread."

16 And he said, "I cannot return with you nor go in with you; neither can I eat bread nor drink water with you in this place. 17 For I have been told by the word of the LORD, 'You shall not eat bread nor drink water there, nor return by going the way you came.'"

18 He said to him, "I too *am* a prophet as you *are,* and an angel spoke to me by the word of the LORD, saying, 'Bring him back with you to your house, that he may eat bread and drink water.'" (He was lying to him.)

19 So he went back with him, and ate bread in his house, and drank water.

20 Now it happened, as they sat at the table, that the word of the LORD came to the prophet who had brought him back; 21 and he cried out to the man of God who came from Judah, saying, "Thus says the LORD: 'Because you have disobeyed the word of the LORD, and have not kept the commandment which the LORD your God commanded you, 22 but you came back, ate bread, and drank water in the place of which *the* LORD said to you, "Eat no bread and drink no water," your corpse shall not come to the tomb of your fathers.'"

23 So it was, after he had eaten bread and after he had drunk, that he saddled the donkey for him, the prophet whom he had brought back. 24 When he was gone, a lion met him on the road and killed him. And his corpse was thrown on the road, and the donkey stood by it. The lion also stood by the corpse. 25 And there, men passed by and saw the corpse thrown on the road, and the lion standing by the corpse. Then they went and told *it* in the city where the old prophet dwelt.

26 Now when the prophet who had brought him back from the way heard *it,* he said, "It *is* the man of God who was disobedient to the word of the LORD. Therefore the LORD has delivered him to the lion, which has torn him and killed him, according to the word of the LORD which He spoke to him." 27 And he spoke to his sons, saying, "Saddle the donkey for me." So they saddled *it.* 28 Then he went and found his corpse thrown on the road, and the donkey and the lion standing by the corpse. The lion had not eaten the corpse nor torn the donkey. 29 And the prophet took up the corpse of the man of God, laid it on the donkey, and brought it back. So the old prophet came to the city to mourn, and to bury him. 30 Then he laid the corpse in his own tomb; and they mourned over him, *saying,* "Alas, my brother!" 31 So it was, after he had buried him, that he spoke to his sons, saying, "When I am dead, then bury me in the tomb where the man of God *is* buried; lay my bones beside his bones. 32 For the saying which he cried out by the word of the LORD against the altar in Bethel, and against all the shrines[a] on the high places which *are* in the cities of Samaria, will surely come to pass."

33 After this event Jeroboam did not turn from his evil way, but again he made priests from every class of people for the high places; whoever wished, he consecrated him, and he became *one* of the priests of the high places. 34 And this thing was the sin of the house of Jeroboam, so as to exterminate and destroy *it* from the face of the earth.

14 At that time Abijah the son of Jeroboam became sick. 2 And Jeroboam said to his wife, "Please arise, and disguise yourself, that they may not recognize you as the wife of Jeroboam, and go to Shiloh. Indeed, Ahijah the prophet *is* there, who told me that *I would be* king over this people. 3 Also take with you ten loaves, *some* cakes, and a jar of honey, and go to him; he will tell you what will become of the

---

13:12 [a]Septuagint, Syriac, Targum, and Vulgate read *showed him.*   13:32 [a]Literally *houses* child." 4 And Jeroboam's wife did so; she arose and went to Shiloh, and came to the house of Ahijah. But Ahijah could not see, for his eyes were glazed by reason of his age.

5 Now the LORD had said to Ahijah, "Here is the wife of Jeroboam, coming to ask you something about her son, for he *is* sick. Thus and thus you shall say to her; for it will be, when she comes in, that she will pretend *to be* another *woman.*"

6 And so it was, when Ahijah heard the sound of her footsteps as she came through the door, he said, "Come in, wife of Jeroboam. Why do you pretend *to be* another *person?* For I *have been* sent to you *with* bad *news.* 7 Go, tell Jeroboam, 'Thus says the LORD God of Israel: "Because I exalted you from among the people, and made you ruler over My people Israel, 8 and tore the kingdom away from the house of David, and gave it to you; and *yet* you have not been as My servant David, who kept My commandments and who followed Me with all his heart, to do only *what was* right in My eyes; 9 but you have done more evil than all who were before you, for you have gone and made for yourself other gods and molded images to provoke Me to anger, and have cast Me behind your back— 10 therefore behold! I will bring disaster on the house of Jeroboam, and will cut off from Jeroboam every male in Israel, bond and free; I will take away the remnant of the house of Jeroboam, as one takes away refuse until it is all gone. 11 The dogs shall eat whoever belongs to Jeroboam and dies in the city, and the birds of the air shall eat whoever dies in the field; for the LORD has spoken!" ' 12 Arise therefore, go to your own house. When your feet enter the city, the child shall die. 13 And all Israel shall mourn for him and bury him, for he is the only one of Jeroboam who shall come to the grave, because in him there is found something good toward the LORD God of Israel in the house of Jeroboam.

14 "Moreover the LORD will raise up for Himself a king over Israel who shall cut off the house of Jeroboam; this is the day. What? Even now!

15 For the LORD will strike Israel, as a reed is shaken in the water. He will uproot Israel from this good land which He gave to their fathers, and will scatter them beyond the River,[a] because they have made their wooden images,[b] provoking the LORD to anger. 16 And He will give Israel up because of the sins of Jeroboam, who sinned and who made Israel sin."

17 Then Jeroboam's wife arose and departed, and came to Tirzah. When she came to the threshold of the house, the child died. 18 And they buried him; and all Israel mourned for him, according to the word of the LORD which He spoke through His servant Ahijah the prophet.

19 Now the rest of the acts of Jeroboam, how he made war and how he reigned, indeed they *are* written in the book of the chronicles of the kings of Israel. 20 The period that Jeroboam reigned *was* twenty-two years. So he rested with his fathers. Then Nadab his son reigned in his place.

21 And Rehoboam the son of Solomon reigned in Judah. Rehoboam *was* forty-one years old when he became king. He reigned seventeen years in Jerusalem, the city which the LORD had chosen out of all the tribes of Israel, to put His name there. His mother's name *was* Naamah, an Ammonitess. 22 Now Judah did evil in the sight of the LORD, and they provoked Him to jealousy with their sins which they committed, more than all that their fathers had done. 23 For they also built for themselves high places, *sacred* pillars, and wooden images on every high hill and under every green tree. 24 And there were also perverted persons[a] in the land. They did according to all the abominations of the nations which the LORD had cast out before the children of Israel.

25 It happened in the fifth year of King Rehoboam *that* Shishak king of Egypt came up against Jerusalem. 26 And he took away the treasures of the house of the LORD and the treasures of the king's house; he took away everything. He also took away all the gold shields which Solomon had made. 27 Then King Rehoboam

---

14:15 [a]That is, the Euphrates   [b]Hebrew *Asherim*, Canaanite deities   14:24 [a]Hebrew *qadesh*, that is, one practicing sodomy and prostitution in religious rituals made bronze shields in their place, and committed *them* to the hands of the captains of the guard, who guarded the doorway of the king's house. 28 And whenever the king entered the house of the LORD, the guards carried them, then brought them back into the guardroom.

29 Now the rest of the acts of Rehoboam, and all that he did, *are* they not written in the book of the chronicles of the kings of Judah? 30 And there was war between Rehoboam and Jeroboam all *their* days. 31 So Rehoboam rested with his fathers, and was buried with his fathers in the City of David. His mother's name *was* Naamah, an Ammonitess. Then Abijam*a* his son reigned in his place.

15 In the eighteenth year of King Jeroboam the son of Nebat, Abijam became king over Judah. 2 He reigned three years in Jerusalem. His mother's name *was* Maachah the granddaughter of Abishalom. 3 And he walked in all the sins of his father, which he had done before him; his heart was not loyal to the LORD his God, as was the heart of his father David. 4 Nevertheless for David's sake the LORD his God gave him a lamp in Jerusalem, by setting up his son after him and by establishing Jerusalem; 5 because David did *what was* right in the eyes of the LORD, and had not turned aside from anything that He commanded him all the days of his life, except in the matter of Uriah the Hittite. 6 And there was war between Rehoboam*a* and Jeroboam all the days of his life. 7 Now the rest of the acts of Abijam, and all that he did, *are* they not written in the book of the chronicles of the kings of Judah? And there was war between Abijam and Jeroboam.

8 So Abijam rested with his fathers, and they buried him in the City of David. Then Asa his son reigned in his place.

9 In the twentieth year of Jeroboam king of Israel, Asa became king over Judah. 10 And he reigned forty-one years in Jerusalem. His grandmother's name *was* Maachah the grand-

daughter of Abishalom. 11 Asa did *what was* right in the eyes of the LORD, as *did* his father David. 12 And he banished the perverted persons*a* from the land, and removed all the idols that his fathers had made. 13 Also he removed Maachah his grandmother from *being* queen mother, because she had made an obscene image of Asherah.*a* And Asa cut down her obscene image and burned *it* by the Brook Kidron. 14 But the high places were not removed. Nevertheless Asa's heart was loyal to the LORD all his days. 15 He also brought into the house of the LORD the things which his father had dedicated, and the things which he himself had dedicated: silver and gold and utensils.

16 Now there was war between Asa and Baasha king of Israel all their days. 17 And Baasha king of Israel came up against Judah, and built Ramah, that he might let none go out or come in to Asa king of Judah. 18 Then Asa took all the silver and gold *that was* left in the treasuries of the house of the LORD and the treasuries of the king's house, and delivered them into the hand of his servants. And King Asa sent them to Ben-Hadad the son of Tabrimmon, the son of Hezion, king of Syria, who dwelt in Damascus, saying, 19 "*Let there be* a treaty between you and me, as there was between my father and your father. See, I have sent you a present of silver and gold. Come and break your treaty with Baasha king of Israel, so that he will withdraw from me."

20 So Ben-Hadad heeded King Asa, and sent the captains of his armies against the cities of Israel. He attacked Ijon, Dan, Abel Beth Maachah, and all Chinneroth, with all the land of Naphtali. 21 Now it happened, when Baasha heard *it*, that he stopped building Ramah, and remained in Tirzah.

22 Then King Asa made a proclamation throughout all Judah; none *was* exempted. And they took away the stones and timber of Ramah, which Baasha had used for building; and with them King Asa built Geba of Benjamin, and Mizpah.

14:31 *a*Spelled *Abijah* in 2 Chronicles 12:16ff   15:6 *a*Following Masoretic Text, Septuagint, Targum, and Vulgate; some Hebrew manuscripts and Syriac read *Abijam*.   15:12 *a*Hebrew *qedeshim*, that is, those practicing sodomy and prostitution in religious rituals   15:13 *a*A Canaanite goddess

23 The rest of all the acts of Asa, all his might, all that he did, and the cities which he built, *are* they not written in the book of the chronicles of the kings of Judah? But in the time of his old age he was diseased in his feet. 24 So Asa rested with his fathers, and was buried with his fathers in the City of David his father. Then Jehoshaphat his son reigned in his place.

25 Now Nadab the son of Jeroboam became king over Israel in the second year of Asa king of Judah, and he reigned over Israel two years. 26 And he did evil in the sight of the LORD, and walked in the way of his father, and in his sin by which he had made Israel sin.

27 Then Baasha the son of Ahijah, of the house of Issachar, conspired against him. And Baasha killed him at Gibbethon, which *belonged* to the Philistines, while Nadab and all Israel laid siege to Gibbethon. 28 Baasha killed him in the third year of Asa king of Judah, and reigned in his place. 29 And it was so, when he became king, *that* he killed all the house of Jeroboam. He did not leave to Jeroboam anyone that breathed, until he had destroyed him, according to the word of the LORD which He had spoken by His servant Ahijah the Shilonite, 30 because of the sins of Jeroboam, which he had sinned and by which he had made Israel sin, because of his provocation with which he had provoked the LORD God of Israel to anger.

31 Now the rest of the acts of Nadab, and all that he did, *are* they not written in the book of the chronicles of the kings of Israel? 32 And there was war between Asa and Baasha king of Israel all their days.

33 In the third year of Asa king of Judah, Baasha the son of Ahijah became king over all Israel in Tirzah, and *reigned* twenty-four years. 34 He did evil in the sight of the LORD, and walked in the way of Jeroboam, and in his sin by which he had made Israel sin.

16 Then the word of the LORD came to Jehu the son of Hanani, against Baasha, saying: 2 "Inasmuch as I lifted you out of the dust and made you ruler over My people Israel, and you have walked in the way of Jeroboam, and have

made My people Israel sin, to provoke Me to anger with their sins, 3 surely I will take away the posterity of Baasha and the posterity of his house, and I will make your house like the house of Jeroboam the son of Nebat. 4 The dogs shall eat whoever belongs to Baasha and dies in the city, and the birds of the air shall eat whoever dies in the fields."

5 Now the rest of the acts of Baasha, what he did, and his might, *are* they not written in the book of the chronicles of the kings of Israel? 6 So Baasha rested with his fathers and was buried in Tirzah. Then Elah his son reigned in his place.

7 And also the word of the LORD came by the prophet Jehu the son of Hanani against Baasha and his house, because of all the evil that he did in the sight of the LORD in provoking Him to anger with the work of his hands, in being like the house of Jeroboam, and because he killed them.

8 In the twenty-sixth year of Asa king of Judah, Elah the son of Baasha became king over Israel, *and reigned* two years in Tirzah. 9 Now his servant Zimri, commander of half *his* chariots, conspired against him as he was in Tirzah drinking himself drunk in the house of Arza, steward of *his* house in Tirzah. 10 And Zimri went in and struck him and killed him in the twenty-seventh year of Asa king of Judah, and reigned in his place.

11 Then it came to pass, when he began to reign, as soon as he was seated on his throne, *that* he killed all the household of Baasha; he did not leave him one male, neither of his relatives nor of his friends. 12 Thus Zimri destroyed all the household of Baasha, according to the word of the LORD, which He spoke against Baasha by Jehu the prophet, 13 for all the sins of Baasha and the sins of Elah his son, by which they had sinned and by which they had made Israel sin, in provoking the LORD God of Israel to anger with their idols.

14 Now the rest of the acts of Elah, and all that he did, *are* they not written in the book of the chronicles of the kings of Israel?

15 In the twenty-seventh year of Asa king of Judah, Zimri had reigned in Tirzah seven days. And the people *were* encamped against Gibbethon,

Put Your Trust in a Stranger

Is it really possible to trust a stranger?

Well, that's what happens when two people marry, for you really don't know your mate until you live together through years of happiness and tears.

Even then, do you ever really know each other? For you are constantly changing and growing, aren't you?

I've been happily married to my wife for thirty-three years, yet I'm constantly amazed at how I have guessed her wrong many times. It is these surprises that keep our relationship from growing stale.

When you walk the walk of faith, you need to trust others. When you trust someone, you bring out the best in him or her. Even the worst person will manifest good qualities when another person trusts him or her.

But what happens when you try to trust people only to have them let you down? Guard yourself against the cynical reaction of the negative thinker: "I'll never trust anybody again." Such a decision is an invitation to a haunting hollowness and devastating loneliness.

Instead, place your trust in Jesus Christ. Trust Him—even though you may not understand who He is, where He is, or what He can do for you. Trust Him—even though He may yet be a holy Stranger to you. Trust Him. He will draw greatness out of you that you never knew was there.

Dear Lord, there is so much I don't know about You. But I do believe You are the reflection of the eternal God and so I trust You to be my Friend. I ask You to be my closest Companion as I walk the walk of faith.

which *belonged* to the Philistines.
16 Now the people *who were* encamped heard it said, "Zimri has
conspired and also has killed the
king." So all Israel made Omri, the
commander of the army, king over
Israel that day in the camp.
17 Then Omri and all Israel with him
went up from Gibbethon, and they
besieged Tirzah. 18 And it happened,
when Zimri saw that the city was
taken, that he went into the citadel
of the king's house and burned the
king's house down upon himself with
fire, and died, 19 because of the sins
which he had committed in doing evil
in the sight of the LORD, in walking
in the way of Jeroboam, and in his
sin which he had committed to make
Israel sin.

20 Now the rest of the acts of Zimri,
and the treason he committed, *are*
they not written in the book of the
chronicles of the kings of Israel?

21 Then the people of Israel were
divided into two parts: half of the
people followed Tibni the son of Ginath, to make him king, and half followed Omri. 22 But the people who
followed Omri prevailed over the
people who followed Tibni the son
of Ginath. So Tibni died and Omri
reigned. 23 In the thirty-first year of
Asa king of Judah, Omri became
king over Israel, *and reigned* twelve
years. Six years he reigned in Tirzah.
24 And he bought the hill of Samaria
from Shemer for two talents of silver;
then he built on the hill, and called
the name of the city which he built,
Samaria, after the name of Shemer,
owner of the hill. 25 Omri did evil in
the eyes of the LORD, and did worse
than all who *were* before him.
26 For he walked in all the ways of
Jeroboam the son of Nebat, and in
his sin by which he had made Israel
sin, provoking the LORD God of Israel
to anger with their idols.

27 Now the rest of the acts of Omri
which he did, and the might that he
showed, *are* they not written in the
book of the chronicles of the kings
of Israel?

28 So Omri rested with his fathers
and was buried in Samaria. Then
Ahab his son reigned in his place.

29 In the thirty-eighth year of Asa
king of Judah, Ahab the son of Omri
became king over Israel; and Ahab
the son of Omri reigned over Israel
in Samaria twenty-two years.
30 Now Ahab the son of Omri did evil
in the sight of the LORD, more than
all who *were* before him. 31 And it
came to pass, as though it had been
a trivial thing for him to walk in the
sins of Jeroboam the son of Nebat,
that he took as wife Jezebel the
daughter of Ethbaal, king of the Sidonians; and he went and served Baal
and worshiped him. 32 Then he set up
an altar for Baal in the temple of
Baal, which he had built in Samaria.
33 And Ahab made a wooden image.*ᵃ*
Ahab did more to provoke the LORD
God of Israel to anger than all the
kings of Israel who were before him.
34 In his days Hiel of Bethel built Jericho. He laid its foundation with Abiram his firstborn, and with his
youngest *son* Segub he set up its
gates, according to the word of the
LORD, which He had spoken through
Joshua the son of Nun.*ᵃ*

17 And Elijah the Tishbite, of the
inhabitants of Gilead, said to
Ahab, "As the LORD God of Israel
lives, before whom I stand, there
shall not be dew nor rain these years,
except at my word."

2 Then the word of the LORD came
to him, saying, 3 "Get away from
here and turn eastward, and hide by
the Brook Cherith, which flows into
the Jordan. 4 And it will be *that* you
shall drink from the brook, and I
have commanded the ravens to feed
you there."

5 So he went and did according to
the word of the LORD, for he went and
stayed by the Brook Cherith, which
flows into the Jordan. 6 The ravens
brought him bread and meat in the
morning, and bread and meat in the
evening; and he drank from the
brook. 7 And it happened after a
while that the brook dried up, because there had been no rain in the
land.

8 Then the word of the LORD came
to him, saying, 9 "Arise, go to Zarephath, which *belongs* to Sidon, and
dwell there. See, I have commanded
a widow there to provide for you."
10 So he arose and went to Zarephath. And when he came to the gate
of the city, indeed a widow *was* there
gathering sticks. And he called to her

16:33 ᵃHebrew *Asherah*, a Canaanite goddess   16:34 ᵃCompare Joshua 6:26

and said, "Please bring me a little water in a cup, that I may drink." 11 And as she was going to get *it*, he called to her and said, "Please bring me a morsel of bread in your hand."

12 So she said, "As the LORD your God lives, I do not have bread, only a handful of flour in a bin, and a little oil in a jar; and see, I *am* gathering a couple of sticks that I may go in and prepare it for myself and my son, that we may eat it, and die."

13 And Elijah said to her, "Do not fear; go *and* do as you have said, but make me a small cake from it first, and bring *it* to me; and afterward make *some* for yourself and your son. 14 For thus says the LORD God of Israel: 'The bin of flour shall not be used up, nor shall the jar of oil run dry, until the day the LORD sends rain on the earth.' "

15 So she went away and did according to the word of Elijah; and she and he and her household ate for *many* days. 16 The bin of flour was not used up, nor did the jar of oil run dry, according to the word of the LORD which He spoke by Elijah.

17 Now it happened after these things *that* the son of the woman who owned the house became sick. And his sickness was so serious that there was no breath left in him. 18 So she said to Elijah, "What have I to do with you, O man of God? Have you come to me to bring my sin to remembrance, and to kill my son?"

19 And he said to her, "Give me your son." So he took him out of her arms and carried him to the upper room where he was staying, and laid him on his own bed. 20 Then he cried out to the LORD and said, "O LORD my God, have You also brought tragedy on the widow with whom I lodge, by killing her son?" 21 And he stretched himself out on the child three times, and cried out to the LORD and said, "O LORD my God, I pray, let this child's soul come back to him." 22 Then the LORD heard the voice of Elijah; and the soul of the child came back to him, and he revived.

23 And Elijah took the child and brought him down from the upper room into the house, and gave him to his mother. And Elijah said, "See, your son lives!"

24 Then the woman said to Elijah, "Now by this I know that you *are* a man of God, *and* that the word of the LORD in your mouth *is* the truth."

18 And it came to pass *after* many days that the word of the LORD came to Elijah, in the third year, saying, "Go, present yourself to Ahab, and I will send rain on the earth."

2 So Elijah went to present himself to Ahab; and *there was* a severe famine in Samaria. 3 And Ahab had called Obadiah, who *was* in charge of *his* house. (Now Obadiah feared the LORD greatly. 4 For so it was, while Jezebel massacred the prophets of the LORD, that Obadiah had taken one hundred prophets and hidden them, fifty to a cave, and had fed them with bread and water.) 5 And Ahab had said to Obadiah, "Go into the land to all the springs of water and to all the brooks; perhaps we may find grass to keep the horses and mules alive, so that we will not have to kill any livestock." 6 So they divided the land between them to explore it; Ahab went one way by himself, and Obadiah went another way by himself.

7 Now as Obadiah was on his way, suddenly Elijah met him; and he recognized him, and fell on his face, and said, "Is that you, my lord Elijah?"

8 And he answered him, "It is I. Go, tell your master, 'Elijah *is here.*' "

9 So he said, "How have I sinned, that you are delivering your servant into the hand of Ahab, to kill me? 10 As the LORD your God lives, there is no nation or kingdom where my master has not sent someone to hunt for you; and when they said, 'He is not *here*,' he took an oath from the kingdom or nation that they could not find you. 11 And now you say, 'Go, tell your master, "Elijah *is here"* '! 12 And it shall come to pass, as soon as I am gone from you, that the Spirit of the LORD will carry you to a place I do not know; so when I go and tell Ahab, and he cannot find you, he will kill me. But I your servant have feared the LORD from my youth. 13 Was it not reported to my lord what I did when Jezebel killed the prophets of the LORD, how I hid one hundred men of the LORD's prophets, fifty to a cave, and fed them with bread and water? 14 And now you say, 'Go, tell your master, "Elijah *is here.*" ' He will kill me!"

15 Then Elijah said, "As the LORD

of hosts lives, before whom I stand, I will surely present myself to him today."

16 So Obadiah went to meet Ahab, and told him; and Ahab went to meet Elijah.

17 Then it happened, when Ahab saw Elijah, that Ahab said to him, "*Is that* you, O troubler of Israel?"

18 And he answered, "I have not troubled Israel, but you and your father's house *have,* in that you have forsaken the commandments of the LORD and have followed the Baals. 19 Now therefore, send *and* gather all Israel to me on Mount Carmel, the four hundred and fifty prophets of Baal, and the four hundred prophets of Asherah,*ᵃ* who eat at Jezebel's table."

20 So Ahab sent for all the children of Israel, and gathered the prophets together on Mount Carmel. 21 And Elijah came to all the people, and said, "How long will you falter between two opinions? If the LORD *is* God, follow Him; but if Baal, follow him." But the people answered him not a word. 22 Then Elijah said to the people, "I alone am left a prophet of the LORD; but Baal's prophets *are* four hundred and fifty men. 23 Therefore let them give us two bulls; and let them choose one bull for themselves, cut it in pieces, and lay *it* on the wood, but put no fire *under it;* and I will prepare the other bull, and lay *it* on the wood, but put no fire *under it.* 24 Then you call on the name of your gods, and I will call on the name of the LORD; and the God who answers by fire, He is God."

So all the people answered and said, "It is well spoken."

25 Now Elijah said to the prophets of Baal, "Choose one bull for yourselves and prepare *it* first, for you *are* many; and call on the name of your god, but put no fire *under it.*"

26 So they took the bull which was given them, and they prepared *it,* and called on the name of Baal from morning even till noon, saying, "O Baal, hear us!" But *there was* no voice; no one answered. Then they leaped about the altar which they had made.

27 And so it was, at noon, that Elijah mocked them and said, "Cry aloud, for he *is* a god; either he is

meditating, or he is busy, or he is on a journey, *or* perhaps he is sleeping and must be awakened." 28 So they cried aloud, and cut themselves, as was their custom, with knives and lances, until the blood gushed out on them. 29 And when midday was past, they prophesied until the *time* of the offering of the *evening* sacrifice. But *there was* no voice; no one answered, no one paid attention.

30 Then Elijah said to all the people, "Come near to me." So all the people came near to him. And he repaired the altar of the LORD *that was* broken down. 31 And Elijah took twelve stones, according to the number of the tribes of the sons of Jacob, to whom the word of the LORD had come, saying, "Israel shall be your name."*ᵃ* 32 Then with the stones he built an altar in the name of the LORD; and he made a trench around the altar large enough to hold two seahs of seed. 33 And he put the wood in order, cut the bull in pieces, and laid *it* on the wood, and said, "Fill four waterpots with water, and pour *it* on the burnt sacrifice and on the wood." 34 Then he said, "Do *it* a second time," and they did *it* a second time; and he said, "Do *it* a third time," and they did *it* a third time. 35 So the water ran all around the altar; and he also filled the trench with water.

36 And it came to pass, at *the time* of the offering of the *evening* sacrifice, that Elijah the prophet came near and said, "LORD God of Abraham, Isaac, and Israel, let it be known this day that You *are* God in Israel and I *am* Your servant, and *that* I have done all these things at your word. 37 Hear me, O LORD, hear me, that this people may know that You *are* the LORD God, and *that* You have turned their hearts back *to You* again."

38 Then the fire of the LORD fell and consumed the burnt sacrifice, and the wood and the stones and the dust, and it licked up the water that *was* in the trench. 39 Now when all the people saw *it,* they fell on their faces; and they said, "The LORD, He *is* God! The LORD, He *is* God!"

40 And Elijah said to them, "Seize the prophets of Baal! Do not let one of them escape!" So they seized

18:19 ᵃA Canaanite goddess   18:31 ᵃGenesis 32:28

The Life of Elijah

4. Worked miracles for a needy widow at Zarephath (1 Kin. 17:8–24).

5. Victorious over the prophets of Baal on Mt. Carmel (1 Kin. 18:20–40).

1. Apparently from the village of Tishbe, south of the Sea of Galilee, since he was known as "Elijah the Tishbite" (1 Kin. 17:1).

• Zarephath

THE GREAT SEA

SEA OF GALILEE

BROOK CHERITH

• Mt. Carmel

PLAIN OF JEZREEL

Tishbe

• Abel Meholah

3. Miraculous feeding by ravens while in hiding around the Brook Cherith (1 Kin. 17:1–7).

JORDAN RIVER

2. Predicted drought as God's punishment; prophesied against kings Ahab and Ahaziah of Israel at capital city of Samaria in ninth century B.C.

• Samaria

7. Elisha selected as Elijah's successor at Abel Meholah (1 Kin. 19:16–21).

• Bethel

• Gilgal

8. Elijah taken up into heaven in the vicinity of Bethel and Gilgal (2 Kin. 2:1–12).

• Jerusalem

DEAD SEA

6. Fled to Beersheba and Mt. Horeb to escape the wrath of Queen Jezebel (1 Kin. 19:1–18).

• Beersheba

To Mt. Horeb

them; and Elijah brought them down to the Brook Kishon and executed them there.

41 Then Elijah said to Ahab, "Go up, eat and drink; for *there is* the sound of abundance of rain." 42 So Ahab went up to eat and drink. And Elijah went up to the top of Carmel; then he bowed down on the ground, and put his face between his knees, 43 and said to his servant, "Go up now, look toward the sea."

So he went up and looked, and said, "*There is* nothing." And seven times he said, "Go again."

44 Then it came to pass the seventh *time,* that he said, "There is a cloud, as small as a man's hand, rising out of the sea!" So he said, "Go up, say to Ahab, 'Prepare *your chariot,* and go down before the rain stops you.'"

45 Now it happened in the meantime that the sky became black with clouds and wind, and there was a heavy rain. So Ahab rode away and went to Jezreel. 46 Then the hand of the LORD came upon Elijah; and he girded up his loins and ran ahead of Ahab to the entrance of Jezreel.

19 And Ahab told Jezebel all that Elijah had done, also how he had executed all the prophets with the sword. 2 Then Jezebel sent a messenger to Elijah, saying, "So let the gods do *to me,* and more also, if I do not make your life as the life of one of them by tomorrow about this time." 3 And when he saw *that,* he arose and ran for his life, and went to Beersheba, which *belongs* to Judah, and left his servant there.

4 But he himself went a day's journey into the wilderness, and came and sat down under a broom tree. And he prayed that he might die, and said, "It is enough! Now, LORD, take my life, for I *am* no better than my fathers!"

5 Then as he lay and slept under a broom tree, suddenly an angel[a] touched him, and said to him, "Arise *and* eat." 6 Then he looked, and there by his head *was* a cake baked on coals, and a jar of water. So he ate and drank, and lay down again. 7 And the angel[a] of the LORD came back the second time, and touched him, and said, "Arise *and* eat, because the journey *is* too great for

you." 8 So he arose, and ate and drank; and he went in the strength of that food forty days and forty nights as far as Horeb, the mountain of God.

9 And there he went into a cave, and spent the night in that place; and behold, the word of the LORD *came* to him, and He said to him, "What are you doing here, Elijah?"

10 So he said, "I have been very zealous for the LORD God of hosts; for the children of Israel have forsaken Your covenant, torn down Your altars, and killed Your prophets with the sword. I alone am left; and they seek to take my life."

11 Then He said, "Go out, and stand on the mountain before the LORD." And behold, the LORD passed by, and a great and strong wind tore into the mountains and broke the rocks in pieces before the LORD, *but* the LORD *was* not in the wind; and after the wind an earthquake, *but* the LORD *was* not in the earthquake; 12 and after the earthquake a fire, *but* the LORD *was* not in the fire; and after the fire a still small voice.

13 So it was, when Elijah heard *it,* that he wrapped his face in his mantle and went out and stood in the entrance of the cave. Suddenly a voice *came* to him, and said, "What are you doing here, Elijah?"

14 And he said, "I have been very zealous for the LORD God of hosts; because the children of Israel have forsaken Your covenant, torn down Your altars, and killed Your prophets with the sword. I alone am left; and they seek to take my life."

15 Then the LORD said to him: "Go, return on your way to the Wilderness of Damascus; and when you arrive, anoint Hazael *as* king over Syria. 16 Also you shall anoint Jehu the son of Nimshi *as* king over Israel. And Elisha the son of Shaphat of Abel Meholah you shall anoint *as* prophet in your place. 17 It shall be *that* whoever escapes the sword of Hazael, Jehu will kill; and whoever escapes the sword of Jehu, Elisha will kill. 18 Yet I have reserved seven thousand in Israel, all whose knees have not bowed to Baal, and every mouth that has not kissed him."

19 So he departed from there, and found Elisha the son of Shaphat, who

19:5 aOr Angel   19:7 aOr Angel

Elijah's Triumph

Have you ever known someone who, just when he seemed to succeed, fell flat on his face? Such a man was the Old Testament prophet, Elijah. But he did not quit. He moved forward in faith and went on to have tremendous victories for God.

During the reign of King Ahab, the people of Israel turned to the pagan worship of Baal. Fashioned in the image of a calf, Baal was a nature god. The people thought that during a lightning storm, Baal was throwing his spear of fire from heaven and that during a thunder storm, he was clapping his hands to produce rain. In those days, there was a desperate need for rain because God's prophet, Elijah, had proclaimed that there would be no rain, "except at my word" (1 Kin. 17:1).

Following three years of drought, God called Elijah to end the drought by directly challenging this false god, Baal. He called together the prophets of Baal in a contest to determine the one true God. Two bulls would be placed on two altars atop Mount Carmel. The true God would consume the sacrifice by answering with fire, Elijah said. Despite Baal's prophets' screaming, yelling, and cutting themselves for hours before their god, their altar and sacrifice remained untouched. Then, Elijah, determined to glorify God, rebuilt the altar of the Lord and twice threw water over his sacrifice before sending up his prayers. Immediately God sent fire upon the altar to consume the sacrifice.

The contest of the sacrifice took place sometime between 3 and 6 P.M. After God consumed the sacrifice, Elijah called on God to send rain and sent Ahab to ride to the city of Jezreel before the storm. Elijah was then anointed by God and, on foot, he too set out for Jezreel. Elijah was victorious and reached the city gates early in the morning.

News soon came to Elijah that Queen Jezebel (whose name means "princess of Baal") wanted to kill him. Being spiritually, emotionally, and physically exhausted after running so far, he fled 167 miles to Beersheba. There, he wondered why God had failed him. Elijah's hopes for national repentance were gone. King Ahab and Jezebel's power seemed invincible. Elijah's self-respect was at its lowest point. He wanted to die.

Alone in the wilderness, God met Elijah's needs. First, God fed and strengthened him, then inspired him by promising Elijah that He would be with him always. God spoke to Elijah in a still, small voice at the opening of a cave, "What are you doing here?" Elijah answered, "I alone am left; and they seek to take my life" (1 Kin. 19:13, 14). God assured him that he was not alone, for over seven thousand men in Israel had not bowed down to Baal. No matter what problem arose, Elijah and God were strong enough to overcome. Encouraged and strengthened by this time alone with God, Elijah returned to complete his ministry.

There are times in all our lives when, like Elijah, we are so fatigued that we make a decision that does not reflect our faith in God. Yet, like Elijah, when we find time alone with God we will be strengthened and nourished. We must see God in famine and feast, in success and failure. Failure does not mean that God has abandoned us. It means He has a better idea.

In times of stress and turmoil, remember to be quiet before God. Listen to His still, small voice. His power will strengthen you to go out and, like Elijah, with God's help defeat any problem!

was plowing *with* twelve yoke *of oxen* before him, and he was with the twelfth. Then Elijah passed by him and threw his mantle on him. 20 And he left the oxen and ran after Elijah, and said, "Please let me kiss my father and my mother, and *then* I will follow you."

And he said to him, "Go back again, for what have I done to you?"

21 So *Elisha* turned back from him, and took a yoke of oxen and slaughtered them and boiled their flesh, using the oxen's equipment, and gave it to the people, and they ate. Then he arose and followed Elijah, and became his servant.

20 Now Ben-Hadad the king of Syria gathered all his forces together; thirty-two kings *were* with him, with horses and chariots. And he went up and besieged Samaria, and made war against it. 2 Then he sent messengers into the city to Ahab king of Israel, and said to him, "Thus says Ben-Hadad: 3 'Your silver and your gold *are* mine; your loveliest wives and children are mine.' "

4 And the king of Israel answered and said, "My lord, O king, just as you say, I and all that I have *are* yours."

5 Then the messengers came back and said, "Thus speaks Ben-Hadad, saying, 'Indeed I have sent to you, saying, "You shall deliver to me your silver and your gold, your wives and your children"; 6 but I will send my servants to you tomorrow about this time, and they shall search your house and the houses of your servants. And it shall be, *that* whatever is pleasant in your eyes, they will put *it* in their hands and take *it*.' "

7 So the king of Israel called all the elders of the land, and said, "Notice, please, and see how this *man* seeks trouble, for he sent to me for my wives, my children, my silver, and my gold; and I did not deny him."

8 And all the elders and all the people said to him, "Do not listen or consent."

9 Therefore he said to the messengers of Ben-Hadad, "Tell my lord the king, 'All that you sent for to your servant the first time I will do, but this thing I cannot do.' "

And the messengers departed and brought back word to him.

10 Then Ben-Hadad sent to him and said, "The gods do so to me, and more also, if enough dust is left of Samaria for a handful for each of the people who follow me."

11 So the king of Israel answered and said, "Tell *him,* 'Let not the one who puts on *his armor* boast like the one who takes *it off.*' "

12 And it happened when *Ben-Hadad* heard this message, as he and the kings *were* drinking at the command post, that he said to his servants, "Get ready." And they got ready to attack the city.

13 Suddenly a prophet approached Ahab king of Israel, saying, "Thus says the LORD: 'Have you seen all this great multitude? Behold, I will deliver it into your hand today, and you shall know that I *am* the LORD.' "

14 So Ahab said, "By whom?"

And he said, "Thus says the LORD: 'By the young leaders of the provinces.' "

Then he said, "Who will set the battle in order?"

And he answered, "You."

15 Then he mustered the young leaders of the provinces, and there were two hundred and thirty-two; and after them he mustered all the people, all the children of Israel— seven thousand.

16 So they went out at noon. Meanwhile Ben-Hadad and the thirty-two kings helping him were getting drunk at the command post. 17 The young leaders of the provinces went out first. And Ben-Hadad sent out *a patrol,* and they told him, saying, "Men are coming out of Samaria!" 18 So he said, "If they have come out for peace, take them alive; and if they have come out for war, take them alive."

19 Then these young leaders of the provinces went out of the city with the army which followed them. 20 And each one killed his man; so the Syrians fled, and Israel pursued them; and Ben-Hadad the king of Syria escaped on a horse with the cavalry. 21 Then the king of Israel went out and attacked the horses and chariots, and killed the Syrians with a great slaughter.

22 And the prophet came to the king of Israel and said to him, "Go, strengthen yourself; take note, and see what you should do, for in the spring of the year the king of Syria will come up against you."

23 Then the servants of the king of Syria said to him, "Their gods *are* gods of the hills. Therefore they were stronger than we; but if we fight against them in the plain, surely we will be stronger than they. 24 So do this thing: Dismiss the kings, each from his position, and put captains in their places; 25 and you shall muster an army like the army that you have lost, horse for horse and chariot for chariot. Then we will fight against them in the plain; surely we will be stronger than they."

And he listened to their voice and did so.

26 So it was, in the spring of the year, that Ben-Hadad mustered the Syrians and went up to Aphek to fight against Israel. 27 And the children of Israel were mustered and given provisions, and they went against them. Now the children of Israel encamped before them like two little flocks of goats, while the Syrians filled the countryside.

28 Then a man of God came and spoke to the king of Israel, and said, "Thus says the LORD: 'Because the Syrians have said, "The LORD *is* God of the hills, but He *is* not God of the valleys," therefore I will deliver all this great multitude into your hand, and you shall know that I *am* the LORD.' " 29 And they encamped opposite each other for seven days. So it was that on the seventh day the battle was joined; and the children of Israel killed one hundred thousand foot soldiers *of* the Syrians in one day. 30 But the rest fled to Aphek, into the city; then a wall fell on twenty-seven thousand of the men *who were* left.

And Ben-Hadad fled and went into the city, into an inner chamber.

31 Then his servants said to him, "Look now, we have heard that the kings of the house of Israel *are* merciful kings. Please, let us put sackcloth around our waists and ropes around our heads, and go out to the king of Israel; perhaps he will spare your life." 32 So they wore sackcloth around their waists and *put* ropes around their heads, and came to the king of Israel and said, "Your servant Ben-Hadad says, 'Please let me live.' "

And he said, "*Is* he still alive? He *is* my brother."

33 Now the men were watching closely to see whether *any sign of mercy would come* from him; and they quickly grasped *at this word* and said, "Your brother Ben-Hadad."

So he said, "Go, bring him." Then Ben-Hadad came out to him; and he had him come up into the chariot.

34 So *Ben-Hadad* said to him, "The cities which my father took from your father I will restore; and you may set up marketplaces for yourself in Damascus, as my father did in Samaria."

Then *Ahab said,* "I will send you away with this treaty." So he made a treaty with him and sent him away.

35 Now a certain man of the sons of the prophets said to his neighbor by the word of the LORD, "Strike me, please." And the man refused to strike him. 36 Then he said to him, "Because you have not obeyed the voice of the LORD, surely, as soon as you depart from me, a lion shall kill you." And as soon as he left him, a lion found him and killed him.

37 And he found another man, and said, "Strike me, please." So the man struck him, inflicting a wound. 38 Then the prophet departed and waited for the king by the road, and disguised himself with a bandage over his eyes. 39 Now as the king passed by, he cried out to the king and said, "Your servant went out into the midst of the battle; and there, a man came over and brought a man to me, and said, 'Guard this man; if by any means he is missing, your life shall be for his life, or else you shall pay a talent of silver.' 40 While your servant was busy here and there, he was gone."

Then the king of Israel said to him, "So *shall* your judgment *be;* you yourself have decided *it.*"

41 And he hastened to take the bandage away from his eyes; and the king of Israel recognized him as one of the prophets. 42 Then he said to him, "Thus says the LORD: 'Because you have let slip out of *your* hand a man whom I appointed to utter destruction, therefore your life shall go for his life, and your people for his people.' "

43 So the king of Israel went to his house sullen and displeased, and came to Samaria.

21 And it came to pass after these things *that* Naboth the Jezreelite had a vineyard which *was* in Jezreel, next to the palace of Ahab king of Samaria. 2 So Ahab spoke to Naboth, saying, "Give me your vineyard, that I may have it for a vegetable garden, because it *is* near, next to my house; and for it I will give you a vineyard better than it. *Or,* if it seems good to you, I will give you its worth in money."

3 But Naboth said to Ahab, "The LORD forbid that I should give the inheritance of my fathers to you!"

4 So Ahab went into his house sullen and displeased because of the word which Naboth the Jezreelite had spoken to him; for he had said, "I will not give you the inheritance of my fathers." And he lay down on his bed, and turned away his face, and would eat no food. 5 But Jezebel his wife came to him, and said to him, "Why is your spirit so sullen that you eat no food?"

6 He said to her, "Because I spoke to Naboth the Jezreelite, and said to him, 'Give me your vineyard for money; or else, if it pleases you, I will give you *another* vineyard for it.' And he answered, 'I will not give you my vineyard.'"

7 Then Jezebel his wife said to him, "You now exercise authority over Israel! Arise, eat food, and let your heart be cheerful; I will give you the vineyard of Naboth the Jezreelite." 8 And she wrote letters in Ahab's name, sealed *them* with his seal, and sent the letters to the elders and the nobles who *were* dwelling in the city with Naboth. 9 She wrote in the letters, saying,

Proclaim a fast, and seat Naboth with high honor among the people; 10 and seat two men, scoundrels, before him to bear witness against him, saying, "You have blasphemed God and the king." *Then* take him out, and stone him, that he may die.

11 So the men of his city, the elders and nobles who were inhabitants of his city, did as Jezebel had sent to them, as it *was* written in the letters which she had sent to them. 12 They proclaimed a fast, and seated Naboth with high honor among the people. 13 And two men, scoundrels, came in and sat before him; and the scoundrels witnessed against him, against Naboth, in the presence of the people, saying, "Naboth has blasphemed God and the king!" Then they took him outside the city and stoned him with stones, so that he died. 14 Then they sent to Jezebel, saying, "Naboth has been stoned and is dead."

15 And it came to pass, when Jezebel heard that Naboth had been stoned and was dead, that Jezebel said to Ahab, "Arise, take possession of the vineyard of Naboth the Jezreelite, which he refused to give you for money; for Naboth is not alive, but dead." 16 So it was, when Ahab heard that Naboth was dead, that Ahab got up and went down to take possession of the vineyard of Naboth the Jezreelite.

17 Then the word of the LORD came to Elijah the Tishbite, saying, 18 "Arise, go down to meet Ahab king of Israel, who *lives* in Samaria. There *he is,* in the vineyard of Naboth, where he has gone down to take possession of it. 19 You shall speak to him, saying, 'Thus says the LORD: "Have you murdered and also taken possession?"' And you shall speak to him, saying, 'Thus says the LORD: "In the place where dogs licked the blood of Naboth, dogs shall lick your blood, even yours."'"

20 So Ahab said to Elijah, "Have you found me, O my enemy?"

And he answered, "I have found *you,* because you have sold yourself to do evil in the sight of the LORD: 21 'Behold, I will bring calamity on you. I will take away your posterity, and will cut off from Ahab every male in Israel, both bond and free. 22 I will make your house like the house of Jeroboam the son of Nebat, and like the house of Baasha the son of Ahijah, because of the provocation with which you have provoked *Me* to anger, and made Israel sin.' 23 And concerning Jezebel the LORD also spoke, saying, 'The dogs shall eat Jezebel by the wall[a] of Jezreel.' 24 The dogs shall eat whoever belongs to Ahab and dies in the city, and the birds of the air

21:23 [a]Following Masoretic Text and Septuagint; some Hebrew manuscripts, Syriac, Targum, and Vulgate read *plot of ground* (compare 2 Kings 9:36).

shall eat whoever dies in the field."

25 But there was no one like Ahab who sold himself to do wickedness in the sight of the LORD, because Jezebel his wife stirred him up. 26 And he behaved very abominably in following idols, according to all *that* the Amorites had done, whom the LORD had cast out before the children of Israel.

27 So it was, when Ahab heard those words, that he tore his clothes and put sackcloth on his body, and fasted and lay in sackcloth, and went about mourning.

28 And the word of the LORD came to Elijah the Tishbite, saying, 29 "See how Ahab has humbled himself before Me? Because he has humbled himself before Me, I will not bring the calamity in his days. In the days of his son I will bring the calamity on his house."

22 Now three years passed without war between Syria and Israel. 2 Then it came to pass, in the third year, that Jehoshaphat the king of Judah went down to *visit* the king of Israel.

3 And the king of Israel said to his servants, "Do you know that Ramoth in Gilead *is* ours, but we hesitate to take it out of the hand of the king of Syria?" 4 So he said to Jehoshaphat, "Will you go with me to fight at Ramoth Gilead?"

Jehoshaphat said to the king of Israel, "I *am* as you *are,* my people as your people, my horses as your horses." 5 Also Jehoshaphat said to the king of Israel, "Please inquire for the word of the LORD today."

6 Then the king of Israel gathered the prophets together, about four hundred men, and said to them, "Shall I go against Ramoth Gilead to fight, or shall I refrain?"

So they said, "Go up, for the Lord will deliver *it* into the hand of the king."

7 And Jehoshaphat said, "*Is there* not still a prophet of the LORD here, that we may inquire of Him?"[a]

8 So the king of Israel said to Jehoshaphat, "*There is* still one man, Micaiah the son of Imlah, by whom we may inquire of the LORD; but I hate him, because he does not prophesy good concerning me, but evil."

And Jehoshaphat said, "Let not the king say such things!"

9 Then the king of Israel called an officer and said, "Bring Micaiah the son of Imlah quickly!"

10 The king of Israel and Jehoshaphat the king of Judah, having put on *their* robes, sat each on his throne, at a threshing floor at the entrance of the gate of Samaria; and all the prophets prophesied before them. 11 Now Zedekiah the son of Chenaanah had made horns of iron for himself; and he said, "Thus says the LORD: 'With these you shall gore the Syrians until they are destroyed.' " 12 And all the prophets prophesied so, saying, "Go up to Ramoth Gilead and prosper, for the LORD will deliver *it* into the king's hand."

13 Then the messenger who had gone to call Micaiah spoke to him, saying, "Now listen, the words of the prophets with one accord encourage the king. Please, let your word be like the word of one of them, and speak encouragement."

14 And Micaiah said, "*As* the LORD lives, whatever the LORD says to me, that I will speak."

15 Then he came to the king; and the king said to him, "Micaiah, shall we go to war against Ramoth Gilead, or shall we refrain?"

And he answered him, "Go and prosper, for the LORD will deliver *it* into the hand of the king!"

16 So the king said to him, "How many times shall I make you swear that you tell me nothing but the truth in the name of the LORD?"

17 Then he said, "I saw all Israel scattered on the mountains, as sheep that have no shepherd. And the LORD said, 'These have no master. Let each return to his house in peace.' "

18 And the king of Israel said to Jehoshaphat, "Did I not tell you he would not prophesy good concerning me, but evil?"

19 Then *Micaiah* said, "Therefore hear the word of the LORD: I saw the LORD sitting on His throne, and all the host of heaven standing by, on His right hand and on His left. 20 And the LORD said, 'Who will persuade Ahab to go up, that he may fall at Ramoth Gilead?' So one spoke in this manner, and another spoke in that manner. 21 Then a spirit came

forward and stood before the LORD, and said, 'I will persuade him.' 22 The LORD said to him, 'In what way?' So he said, 'I will go out and be a lying spirit in the mouth of all his prophets.' And the LORD said, 'You shall persuade *him,* and also prevail. Go out and do so.' 23 Therefore look! The LORD has put a lying spirit in the mouth of all these prophets of yours, and the LORD has declared disaster against you."

24 Now Zedekiah the son of Chenaanah went near and struck Micaiah on the cheek, and said, "Which way did the spirit from the LORD go from me to speak to you?"

25 And Micaiah said, "Indeed, you shall see on that day when you go into an inner chamber to hide!"

26 So the king of Israel said, "Take Micaiah, and return him to Amon the governor of the city and to Joash the king's son; 27 and say, 'Thus says the king: "Put this *fellow* in prison, and feed him with bread of affliction and water of affliction, until I come in peace."' "

28 But Micaiah said, "If you ever return in peace, the LORD has not spoken by me." And he said, "Take heed, all you people!"

29 So the king of Israel and Jehoshaphat the king of Judah went up to Ramoth Gilead. 30 And the king of Israel said to Jehoshaphat, "I will disguise myself and go into battle; but you put on your robes." So the king of Israel disguised himself and went into battle.

31 Now the king of Syria had commanded the thirty-two captains of his chariots, saying, "Fight with no one small or great, but only with the king of Israel." 32 So it was, when the captains of the chariots saw Jehoshaphat, that they said, "Surely it *is* the king of Israel!" Therefore they turned aside to fight against him, and Jehoshaphat cried out. 33 And it happened, when the captains of the chariots saw that it *was* not the king of Israel, that they turned back from pursuing him. 34 Now a *certain* man drew a bow at random, and struck the king of Israel between the joints of his armor. So he said to the driver of his chariot, "Turn around and take me out of the battle, for I am wounded."

35 The battle increased that day; and the king was propped up in his chariot, facing the Syrians, and died at evening. The blood ran out from the wound onto the floor of the chariot. 36 Then, as the sun was going down, a shout went throughout the army, saying, "Every man to his city, and every man to his own country!"

37 So the king died, and was brought to Samaria. And they buried the king in Samaria. 38 Then *someone* washed the chariot at a pool in Samaria, and the dogs licked up his blood while the harlots bathed,[a] according to the word of the LORD which He had spoken.

39 Now the rest of the acts of Ahab, and all that he did, the ivory house which he built and all the cities that he built, *are* they not written in the book of the chronicles of the kings of Israel? 40 So Ahab rested with his fathers. Then Ahaziah his son reigned in his place.

41 Jehoshaphat the son of Asa had become king over Judah in the fourth year of Ahab king of Israel. 42 Jehoshaphat *was* thirty-five years old when he became king, and he reigned twenty-five years in Jerusalem. His mother's name *was* Azubah the daughter of Shilhi. 43 And he walked in all the ways of his father Asa. He did not turn aside from them, doing *what was* right in the eyes of the LORD. Nevertheless the high places were not taken away, *for* the people offered sacrifices and burned incense on the high places. 44 Also Jehoshaphat made peace with the king of Israel.

45 Now the rest of the acts of Jehoshaphat, the might that he showed, and how he made war, *are* they not written in the book of the chronicles of the kings of Judah? 46 And the rest of the perverted persons,[a] who remained in the days of his father Asa, he banished from the land. 47 *There was* then no king in Edom, only a deputy of the king.

48 Jehoshaphat made merchant ships[a] to go to Ophir for gold; but they never sailed, for the ships were wrecked at Ezion Geber. 49 Then Ahaziah the son of Ahab said to Jehoshaphat, "Let my servants go with

your servants in the ships." But Jehoshaphat would not.

50 And Jehoshaphat rested with his fathers, and was buried with his fathers in the City of David his father. Then Jehoram his son reigned in his place.

51 Ahaziah the son of Ahab became king over Israel in Samaria in the seventeenth year of Jehoshaphat king of Judah, and reigned two years over Israel. 52 He did evil in the sight of the LORD, and walked in the way of his father and in the way of his mother and in the way of Jeroboam the son of Nebat, who had made Israel sin; 53 for he served Baal and worshiped him, and provoked the LORD God of Israel to anger, according to all that his father had done.

Second Kings

Overview of Second Kings

During the period of history recorded in Second Kings, God's people lived in a world of constant change. Uncertainty and insecurity dominated their lives. No sooner would one invading army pour over the land than another neighboring kingdom would ravage their cities. The two nations of the divided monarchy, Judah and Israel, warred against each other and against other nations. One God-fearing ruler would shortly be followed with a godless king who would turn the hearts of the people to the worship of false gods, bringing upon them the negative results.

But God would not give up on His people. He provided many leaders to keep His light shining. Prophets like Elijah and Elisha encouraged the people to remain committed to their faith in God and to turn from foreign, pagan influences.

Then the king stood by a pillar and made a covenant before the LORD, to follow the LORD and to keep His commandments and His testimonies and His statutes, with all his heart and all his soul, to perform the words of this covenant

that were written in this book. And all the people took a
stand for the covenant.

(2 Kin. 23:3)

Second Kings reveals that life is a series of choices. It is
also the confidence that God is able to turn negatives into
positives, rebellion into reform, and captivity into freedom!
Even at the close of the book with the people in captivity in
Babylon, God placed the ruler of Israel in a position of
prominence, preparing the way for the people's freedom.
Second Kings is a book of confidence that God will never
leave or forsake His people.

Jesus in Second Kings

Unlike the nine different dynasties in the northern kingdom, the kings of Judah reign as one continuous dynasty.
God remains faithful to His covenant with David by preserving his lineage. Jesus is David's direct descendant.
Elisha, in contrast to Elijah, provides a picture of Jesus,
living among the people and emphasizing grace, life, and
hope.

Keys to Second Kings

Key Word: The Duty of the King. The prophets of God
play a prominent role in First and Second Kings as He uses
them to remind the kings of their covenant responsibilities
as His administrators. When the king keeps the covenant,
he and the nation are richly blessed. But judgment consistently falls upon those who refuse to obey God's law. Un-
happily, the people are concerned more with their own
plans, and their rejection of God's rule leads to exile at the
hands of the Assyrians and Babylonians.

Key Verses: "And he [Josiah] did *what was* right in the
sight of the LORD, and walked in all the ways of his father
David; he did not turn aside to the right hand or to the left"
(22:2).

"And the LORD said, 'I will also remove Judah from My
sight, as I have removed Israel, and will cast off this city
Jerusalem which I have chosen, and the house of which I
said, "My name shall be there"'" (23:27).

Key Chapter: Second Kings 25. The last chapter of the
book records the utter destruction of the city of Jerusalem
and its glorious temple. Only the poor of Israel are left, and

even some of them flee for their lives to Egypt. Hope is still alive, however, with the remnant in Babylonian captivity as Evil-Merodach frees Jehoiachin from prison and treats him kindly.

1 Moab rebelled against Israel after the death of Ahab.

2 Now Ahaziah fell through the lattice of his upper room in Samaria, and was injured; so he sent messengers and said to them, "Go, inquire of Baal-Zebub, the god of Ekron, whether I shall recover from this injury." 3 But the angel*a* of the LORD said to Elijah the Tishbite, "Arise, go up to meet the messengers of the king of Samaria, and say to them, '*Is it* because *there is* no God in Israel *that* you are going to inquire of Baal-Zebub, the god of Ekron?' 4 Now therefore, thus says the LORD: 'You shall not come down from the bed to which you have gone up, but you shall surely die.'" So Elijah departed.

5 And when the messengers returned to him, he said to them, "Why have you come back?"

6 So they said to him, "A man came up to meet us, and said to us, 'Go, return to the king who sent you, and say to him, "Thus says the LORD: '*Is it* because *there is* no God in Israel *that* you are sending to inquire of Baal-Zebub, the god of Ekron? Therefore you shall not come down from the bed to which you have gone up, but you shall surely die.'"'"

7 Then he said to them, "What kind of man *was it* who came up to meet you and told you these words?"

8 So they answered him, "A hairy man wearing a leather belt around his waist."

And he said, "It *is* Elijah the Tishbite."

9 Then the king sent to him a captain of fifty with his fifty men. So he went up to him; and there he was, sitting on the top of a hill. And he spoke to him: "Man of God, the king has said, 'Come down!'"

10 So Elijah answered and said to the captain of fifty, "If I *am* a man of God, then let fire come down from heaven and consume you and your fifty men." And fire came down from heaven and consumed him and his fifty. 11 Then he sent to him another captain of fifty with his fifty men.

And he answered and said to him: "Man of God, thus has the king said, 'Come down quickly!'"

12 So Elijah answered and said to them, "If I *am* a man of God, let fire come down from heaven and consume you and your fifty men." And the fire of God came down from heaven and consumed him and his fifty.

13 Again, he sent a third captain of fifty with his fifty men. And the third captain of fifty went up, and came and fell on his knees before Elijah, and pleaded with him, and said to him: "Man of God, please let my life and the life of these fifty servants of yours be precious in your sight. 14 Look, fire has come down from heaven and burned up the first two captains of fifties with their fifties. But let my life now be precious in your sight."

1:3 *a*Or *Angel*

15 And the angel[a] of the LORD said to Elijah, "Go down with him; do not be afraid of him." So he arose and went down with him to the king. 16 Then he said to him, "Thus says the LORD: 'Because you have sent messengers to inquire of Baal-Zebub, the god of Ekron, *is it* because *there is* no God in Israel to inquire of His word? Therefore you shall not come down from the bed to which you have gone up, but you shall surely die.'"

17 So *Ahaziah* died according to the word of the LORD which Elijah had spoken. Because he had no son, Jehoram[a] became king in his place, in the second year of Jehoram the son of Jehoshaphat, king of Judah.

18 Now the rest of the acts of Ahaziah which he did, *are* they not written in the book of the chronicles of the kings of Israel?

2 And it came to pass, when the LORD was about to take up Elijah into heaven by a whirlwind, that Elijah went with Elisha from Gilgal. 2 Then Elijah said to Elisha, "Stay here, please, for the LORD has sent me on to Bethel."

But Elisha said, "*As* the LORD lives, and *as* your soul lives, I will not leave you!" So they went down to Bethel.

3 Now the sons of the prophets who *were* at Bethel came out to Elisha, and said to him, "Do you know that the LORD will take away your master from over you today?"

And he said, "Yes, I know; keep silent!"

4 Then Elijah said to him, "Elisha, stay here, please, for the LORD has sent me on to Jericho."

But he said, "*As* the LORD lives, and *as* your soul lives, I will not leave you!" So they came to Jericho.

5 Now the sons of the prophets who *were* at Jericho came to Elisha and said to him, "Do you know that the LORD will take away your master from over you today?"

So he answered, "Yes, I know; keep silent!"

6 Then Elijah said to him, "Stay here, please, for the LORD has sent me on to the Jordan."

But he said, "*As* the LORD lives, and *as* your soul lives, I will not leave you!" So the two of them went on.

7 And fifty men of the sons of the prophets went and stood facing *them* at a distance, while the two of them stood by the Jordan. 8 Now Elijah took his mantle, rolled *it* up, and struck the water; and it was divided this way and that, so that the two of them crossed over on dry ground.

9 And so it was, when they had crossed over, that Elijah said to Elisha, "Ask! What may I do for you, before I am taken away from you?"

Elisha said, "Please let a double portion of your spirit be upon me."

10 So he said, "You have asked a hard thing. *Nevertheless*, if you see me *when I am* taken from you, it shall be so for you; but if not, it shall not be *so*." 11 Then it happened, as they continued on and talked, that suddenly a chariot of fire *appeared* with horses of fire, and separated the two of them; and Elijah went up by a whirlwind into heaven.

12 And Elisha saw *it*, and he cried out, "My father, my father, the chariot of Israel and its horsemen!" So he saw him no more. And he took hold of his own clothes and tore them into two pieces. 13 He also took up the mantle of Elijah that had fallen from him, and went back and stood by the bank of the Jordan. 14 Then he took the mantle of Elijah that had fallen from him, and struck the water, and said, "Where *is* the LORD God of Elijah?" And when he also had struck the water, it was divided this way and that; and Elisha crossed over.

15 Now when the sons of the prophets who *were* from Jericho saw him, they said, "The spirit of Elijah rests on Elisha." And they came to meet him, and bowed to the ground before him. 16 Then they said to him, "Look now, there are fifty strong men with your servants. Please let them go and search for your master, lest perhaps the Spirit of the LORD has taken him up and cast him upon some mountain or into some valley."

And he said, "You shall not send anyone."

17 But when they urged him till he was ashamed, he said, "Send *them!*" Therefore they sent fifty men, and they searched for three days but did not find him. 18 And when they came back to him, for he had stayed in Jeri-

---

1:15 [a]Or *Angel*   1:17 [a]The son of Ahab king of Israel (compare 3:1) cho, he said to them, "Did I not say to you, 'Do not go'?"

19 Then the men of the city said to Elisha, "Please notice, the situation of this city is pleasant, as my lord sees; but the water is bad, and the ground barren."

20 And he said, "Bring me a new bowl, and put salt in it." So they brought it to him. 21 Then he went out to the source of the water, and cast in the salt there, and said, "Thus says the LORD: 'I have healed this water; from it there shall be no more death or barrenness.'" 22 So the water remains healed to this day, according to the word of Elisha which he spoke.

23 Then he went up from there to Bethel; and as he was going up the road, some youths came from the city and mocked him, and said to him, "Go up, you baldhead! Go up, you baldhead!"

24 So he turned around and looked at them, and pronounced a curse on them in the name of the LORD. And two female bears came out of the woods and mauled forty-two of the youths.

25 Then he went from there to Mount Carmel, and from there he returned to Samaria.

3 Now Jehoram the son of Ahab became king over Israel at Samaria in the eighteenth year of Jehoshaphat king of Judah, and reigned twelve years. 2 And he did evil in the sight of the LORD, but not like his father and mother; for he put away the sacred pillar of Baal that his father had made. 3 Nevertheless he persisted in the sins of Jeroboam the son of Nebat, who had made Israel sin; he did not depart from them.

4 Now Mesha king of Moab was a sheepbreeder, and he regularly paid the king of Israel one hundred thousand lambs and the wool of one hundred thousand rams. 5 But it happened, when Ahab died, that the king of Moab rebelled against the king of Israel.

6 So King Jehoram went out of Samaria at that time and mustered all Israel. 7 Then he went and sent to Jehoshaphat king of Judah, saying, "The king of Moab has rebelled against me. Will you go with me to fight against Moab?"

And he said, "I will go up; I am as you are, my people as your people, my horses as your horses." 8 Then he said, "Which way shall we go up?"

And he answered, "By way of the Wilderness of Edom."

9 So the king of Israel went with the king of Judah and the king of Edom, and they marched on that roundabout route seven days; and there was no water for the army, nor for the animals that followed them. 10 And the king of Israel said, "Alas! For the LORD has called these three kings together to deliver them into the hand of Moab."

11 But Jehoshaphat said, "Is there no prophet of the LORD here, that we may inquire of the LORD by him?"

So one of the servants of the king of Israel answered and said, "Elisha the son of Shaphat is here, who poured water on the hands of Elijah."

12 And Jehoshaphat said, "The word of the LORD is with him." So the king of Israel and Jehoshaphat and the king of Edom went down to him.

13 Then Elisha said to the king of Israel, "What have I to do with you? Go to the prophets of your father and the prophets of your mother."

But the king of Israel said to him, "No, for the LORD has called these three kings together to deliver them into the hand of Moab."

14 And Elisha said, "As the LORD of hosts lives, before whom I stand, surely were it not that I regard the presence of Jehoshaphat king of Judah, I would not look at you, nor see you. 15 But now bring me a musician."

Then it happened, when the musician played, that the hand of the LORD came upon him. 16 And he said, "Thus says the LORD: 'Make this valley full of ditches.' 17 For thus says the LORD: 'You shall not see wind, nor shall you see rain; yet that valley shall be filled with water, so that you, your cattle, and your animals may drink.' 18 And this is a simple matter in the sight of the LORD; He will also deliver the Moabites into your hand. 19 Also you shall attack every fortified city and every choice city, and shall cut down every good tree, and stop up every spring of water, and ruin every good piece of land with stones."

20 Now it happened in the morning,

when the grain offering was offered, that suddenly water came by way of Edom, and the land was filled with water.

21 And when all the Moabites heard that the kings had come up to fight against them, all who were able to bear arms and older were gathered; and they stood at the border. 22 Then they rose up early in the morning, and the sun was shining on the water; and the Moabites saw the water on the other side *as* red as blood. 23 And they said, "This is blood; the kings have surely struck swords and have killed one another; now therefore, Moab, to the spoil!"

24 So when they came to the camp of Israel, Israel rose up and attacked the Moabites, so that they fled before them; and they entered *their* land, killing the Moabites. 25 Then they destroyed the cities, and each man threw a stone on every good piece of land and filled it; and they stopped up all the springs of water and cut down all the good trees. But they left the stones of Kir Haraseth *intact*. However the slingers surrounded and attacked it.

26 And when the king of Moab saw that the battle was too fierce for him, he took with him seven hundred men who drew swords, to break through to the king of Edom, but they could not. 27 Then he took his eldest son who would have reigned in his place, and offered him *as* a burnt offering upon the wall; and there was great indignation against Israel. So they departed from him and returned to *their own* land.

4 A certain woman of the wives of the sons of the prophets cried out to Elisha, saying, "Your servant my husband is dead, and you know that your servant feared the LORD. And the creditor is coming to take my two sons to be his slaves."

2 So Elisha said to her, "What shall I do for you? Tell me, what do you have in the house?" And she said, "Your maidservant has nothing in the house but a jar of oil."

3 Then he said, "Go, borrow vessels from everywhere, from all your neighbors—empty vessels; do not gather just a few. 4 And when you have come in, you shall shut the door behind you and your sons; then pour it into all those vessels, and set aside the full ones."

5 So she went from him and shut the door behind her and her sons, who brought *the vessels* to her; and she poured *it* out. 6 Now it came to pass, when the vessels were full, that she said to her son, "Bring me another vessel."

And he said to her, "*There is* not another vessel." So the oil ceased. 7 Then she came and told the man of God. And he said, "Go, sell the oil and pay your debt; and you *and your* sons live on the rest."

8 Now it happened one day that Elisha went to Shunem, where there *was* a notable woman, and she persuaded him to eat some food. So it was, as often as he passed by, he would turn in there to eat some food. 9 And she said to her husband, "Look now, I know that this *is* a holy man of God, who passes by us regularly. 10 Please, let us make a small upper room on the wall; and let us put a bed for him there, and a table and a chair and a lampstand; so it will be, whenever he comes to us, he can turn in there."

11 And it happened one day that he came there, and he turned in to the upper room and lay down there. 12 Then he said to Gehazi his servant, "Call this Shunammite woman." When he had called her, she stood before him. 13 And he said to him, "Say now to her, 'Look, you have been concerned for us with all this care. What *can I* do for you? Do you want me to speak on your behalf to the king or to the commander of the army?'"

She answered, "I dwell among my own people."

14 So he said, "What then *is* to be done for her?"

And Gehazi answered, "Actually, she has no son, and her husband is old."

15 So he said, "Call her." When he had called her, she stood in the doorway. 16 Then he said, "About this time next year you shall embrace a son."

And she said, "No, my lord. Man of God, do not lie to your maidservant!"

17 But the woman conceived, and bore a son when the appointed time had come, of which Elisha had told her.

I Say to You, "Arise"

At the base of Mount Moreh in the Jezreel Valley is the ancient city of Nain. Due to its location overlooking the fertile valley with springs, the city's name means "pleasant."

One day, as Jesus approached the city's gate, a large funeral procession was in progress. The burial was for the only son of a widow. Jesus moved through the mourning crowd toward the coffin and stopped the pallbearers. Turning to the widow, who had no chance for another son, Jesus comforted her, saying, "Do not weep." Then Jesus touched the coffin and said, "Young man, I say to you, arise" (Luke 7:14). Immediately, the son sat up and began to speak.

Astonished, the crowd ran throughout the countryside exclaiming that a prophet had raised the boy from the dead. Most certainly, the New Testament inhabitants of Nain recalled a similar event which took place hundreds of years earlier on the other side of Mount Moreh in the village of Shunem, only one mile from Nain. The great prophet Elisha had entered the house of the Shunammite woman whose son was also dead (see 2 Kin. 4:20–37). Under God's command, Elisha breathed life back into her son, raising him from the dead. Perhaps, the amazed New Testament crowd considered Jesus to be the prophet Elisha.

What a beautiful parallel of God's power over death! Of course Jesus was much more than the prophet. He was the fulfillment of the prophet's messages. Even today, Jesus is fulfilling the promises He gave when He said, "Whoever lives and believes in Me shall never die" (John 11:26).

Jesus promises to raise us from the dead, not only physically but spiritually and emotionally. When we are depressed and have given up hope, Jesus brings new life to our dreams. In our most desperate time of need, Jesus says to us, "Do not weep."

His promise of eternal life is our assurance that we have been given the ultimate victory over death. Allow Jesus to do the impossible in your life. Heed His call when He says, "I say to you, arise!"

18 And the child grew. Now it happened one day that he went out to his father, to the reapers. 19 And he said to his father, "My head, my head!"

So he said to a servant, "Carry him to his mother." 20 When he had taken him and brought him to his mother, he sat on her knees till noon, and *then* died. 21 And she went up and laid him on the bed of the man of God, shut *the door* upon him, and went out. 22 Then she called to her husband, and said, "Please send me one of the young men and one of the donkeys, that I may run to the man of God and come back."

23 So he said, "Why are you going to him today? *It is* neither the New Moon nor the Sabbath."

And she said, "*It is* well." 24 Then she saddled a donkey, and said to her servant, "Drive, and go forward; do not slacken the pace for me unless I tell you." 25 And so she departed, and went to the man of God at Mount Carmel.

So it was, when the man of God saw her afar off, that he said to his servant Gehazi, "Look, the Shunammite woman! 26 Please run now to meet her, and say to her, '*Is it* well with you? *Is it* well with your husband? *Is it* well with the child?' "

And she answered, "*It is* well." 27 Now when she came to the man of God at the hill, she caught him by the feet, but Gehazi came near to push her away. But the man of God said, "Let her alone; for her soul *is* in deep distress, and the LORD has hidden *it* from me, and has not told me."

28 So she said, "Did I ask a son of my lord? Did I not say, 'Do not deceive me'?"

29 Then he said to Gehazi, "Get yourself ready, and take my staff in your hand, and be on your way. If you meet anyone, do not greet him; and if anyone greets you, do not answer him; but lay my staff on the face of the child."

30 And the mother of the child said, "*As* the LORD lives, and *as* your soul lives, I will not leave you." So he arose and followed her. 31 Now Gehazi went on ahead of them, and laid the staff on the face of the child; but *there was* neither voice nor hearing. Therefore he went back to meet him,

and told him, saying, "The child has not awakened."

32 When Elisha came into the house, there was the child, lying dead on his bed. 33 He went in therefore, shut the door behind the two of them, and prayed to the LORD. 34 And he went up and lay on the child, and put his mouth on his mouth, his eyes on his eyes, and his hands on his hands; and he stretched himself out on the child, and the flesh of the child became warm. 35 He returned and walked back and forth in the house, and again went up and stretched himself out on him; then the child sneezed seven times, and the child opened his eyes. 36 And he called Gehazi and said, "Call this Shunammite woman." So he called her. And when she came in to him, he said, "Pick up your son." 37 So she went in, fell at his feet, and bowed to the ground; then she picked up her son and went out.

38 And Elisha returned to Gilgal, and *there was* a famine in the land. Now the sons of the prophets *were* sitting before him; and he said to his servant, "Put on the large pot, and boil stew for the sons of the prophets." 39 So one went out into the field to gather herbs, and found a wild vine, and gathered from it a lapful of wild gourds, and came and sliced *them* into the pot of stew, though they did not know *what they were.* 40 Then they served it to the men to eat. Now it happened, as they were eating the stew, that they cried out and said, "Man of God, *there is* death in the pot!" And they could not eat *it.*

41 So he said, "Then bring some flour." And he put *it* into the pot, and said, "Serve *it* to the people, that they may eat." And there was nothing harmful in the pot.

42 Then a man came from Baal Shalisha, and brought the man of God bread of the firstfruits, twenty loaves of barley bread, and newly ripened grain in his knapsack. And he said, "Give *it* to the people, that they may eat."

43 But his servant said, "What? Shall I set this before one hundred men?"

He said again, "Give it to the people, that they may eat; for thus says the LORD: 'They shall eat and have *some* left over.' " 44 So he set *it* before them; and they ate and had *some* left over, according to the word of the LORD.

5 Now Naaman, commander of the army of the king of Syria, was a great and honorable man in the eyes of his master, because by him the LORD had given victory to Syria. He was also a mighty man of valor, *but* a leper. 2 And the Syrians had gone out on raids, and had brought back captive a young girl from the land of Israel. She waited on Naaman's wife. 3 Then she said to her mistress, "If only my master *were* with the prophet who *is* in Samaria! For he would heal him of his leprosy." 4 And *Naaman* went in and told his master, saying, "Thus and thus said the girl who *is* from the land of Israel."

5 Then the king of Syria said, "Go now, and I will send a letter to the king of Israel."

So he departed and took with him ten talents of silver, six thousand *shekels* of gold, and ten changes of clothing. 6 Then he brought the letter to the king of Israel, which said,

> Now be advised, when this letter comes to you, that I have sent Naaman my servant to you, that you may heal him of his leprosy.

7 And it happened, when the king of Israel read the letter, that he tore his clothes and said, "*Am* I God, to kill and make alive, that this man sends a man to me to heal him of his leprosy? Therefore please consider, and see how he seeks a quarrel with me."

8 So it was, when Elisha the man of God heard that the king of Israel had torn his clothes, that he sent to the king, saying, "Why have you torn your clothes? Please let him come to me, and he shall know that there is a prophet in Israel."

9 Then Naaman went with his horses and chariot, and he stood at the door of Elisha's house. 10 And Elisha sent a messenger to him, saying, "Go and wash in the Jordan seven times, and your flesh shall be restored to you, and *you shall* be clean." 11 But Naaman became furious, and went away and said, "In-

deed, I said to myself, 'He will surely come out *to me*, and stand and call on the name of the LORD his God, and wave his hand over the place, and heal the leprosy.' 12 *Are* not the Abanah[a] and the Pharpar, the rivers of Damascus, better than all the waters of Israel? Could I not wash in them and be clean?" So he turned and went away in a rage. 13 And his servants came near and spoke to him, and said, "My father, *if* the prophet had told you *to do* something great, would you not have done *it*? How much more then, when he says to you, 'Wash, and be clean'?" 14 So he went down and dipped seven times in the Jordan, according to the saying of the man of God; and his flesh was restored like the flesh of a little child, and he was clean.

15 And he returned to the man of God, he and all his aides, and came and stood before him; and he said, "Indeed, now I know that *there is* no God in all the earth, except in Israel; now therefore, please take a gift from your servant."

16 But he said, "*As* the LORD lives, before whom I stand, I will receive nothing." And he urged him to take *it*, but he refused.

17 So Naaman said, "Then, if not, please let your servant be given two mule-loads of earth; for your servant will no longer offer either burnt offering or sacrifice to other gods, but to the LORD. 18 Yet in this thing may the LORD pardon your servant: when my master goes into the temple of Rimmon to worship there, and he leans on my hand, and I bow down in the temple of Rimmon—when I bow down in the temple of Rimmon, may the LORD please pardon your servant in this thing."

19 Then he said to him, "Go in peace." So he departed from him a short distance.

20 But Gehazi, the servant of Elisha the man of God, said, "Look, my master has spared Naaman this Syrian, while not receiving from his hands what he brought; but *as* the LORD lives, I will run after him and take something from him." 21 So Gehazi pursued Naaman. When Naaman saw *him* running after him, he got down from the chariot to meet him, and said, "*Is* all well?"

5:12 aFollowing Kethib, Septuagint, and Vulgate; Qere, Syriac, and Targum read *Amanah*.

22 And he said, "All *is* well. My master has sent me, saying, 'Indeed, just now two young men of the sons of the prophets have come to me from the mountains of Ephraim. Please give them a talent of silver and two changes of garments.' "

23 So Naaman said, "Please, take two talents." And he urged him, and bound two talents of silver in two bags, with two changes of garments, and handed *them* to two of his servants; and they carried *them* on ahead of him. 24 When he came to the citadel, he took *them* from their hand, and stored *them* away in the house; then he let the men go, and they departed. 25 Now he went in and stood before his master. Elisha said to him, "Where *did you go*, Gehazi?"

And he said, "Your servant did not go anywhere."

26 Then he said to him, "Did not my heart go *with you* when the man turned back from his chariot to meet you? *Is it* time to receive money and to receive clothing, olive groves and vineyards, sheep and oxen, male and female servants? 27 Therefore the leprosy of Naaman shall cling to you and your descendants forever." And he went out from his presence leprous, *as white* as snow.

6 And the sons of the prophets said to Elisha, "See now, the place where we dwell with you is too small for us. 2 Please, let us go to the Jordan, and let every man take a beam from there, and let us make there a place where we may dwell."

So he answered, "Go."

3 Then one said, "Please consent to go with your servants."

And he answered, "I will go." 4 So he went with them. And when they came to the Jordan, they cut down trees. 5 But as one was cutting down a tree, the iron *ax head* fell into the water; and he cried out and said, "Alas, master! For it was borrowed."

6 So the man of God said, "Where did it fall?" And he showed him the place. So he cut off a stick, and threw *it* in there; and he made the iron float. 7 Therefore he said, "Pick *it* up for yourself." So he reached out his hand and took it.

8 Now the king of Syria was making war against Israel; and he consulted with his servants, saying, "My camp *will be* in such and such a place." 9 And the man of God sent to the king of Israel, saying, "Beware that you do not pass this place, for the Syrians are coming down there." 10 Then the king of Israel sent *someone* to the place of which the man of God had told him. Thus he warned him, and he was watchful there, not just once or twice.

11 Therefore the heart of the king of Syria was greatly troubled by this thing; and he called his servants and said to them, "Will you not show me which of us *is* for the king of Israel?"

12 And one of his servants said, "None, my lord, O king; but Elisha, the prophet who *is* in Israel, tells the king of Israel the words that you speak in your bedroom."

13 So he said, "Go and see where he *is*, that I may send and get him."

And it was told him, saying, "Surely *he is* in Dothan."

14 Therefore he sent horses and chariots and a great army there, and they came by night and surrounded the city. 15 And when the servant of the man of God arose early and went out, there was an army, surrounding the city with horses and chariots. And his servant said to him, "Alas, my master! What shall we do?"

16 So he answered, "Do not fear, for those who *are* with us *are* more than those who *are* with them."

17 And Elisha prayed, and said, "LORD, I pray, open his eyes that he may see." Then the LORD opened the eyes of the young man, and he saw. And behold, the mountain *was* full of horses and chariots of fire all around Elisha. 18 So when *the Syrians* came down to him, Elisha prayed to the LORD, and said, "Strike this people, I pray, with blindness." And He struck them with blindness according to the word of Elisha.

19 Now Elisha said to them, "This *is* not the way, nor *is* this the city. Follow me, and I will bring you to the man whom you seek." But he led them to Samaria.

20 So it was, when they had come to Samaria, that Elisha said, "LORD, open the eyes of these *men*, that they may see." And the LORD opened their eyes, and they saw; and there *they were*, inside Samaria!

21 Now when the king of Israel saw them, he said to Elisha, "My father, shall I kill *them*? Shall I kill *them*?"

22 But he answered, "You shall not

Elisha's Ministry

SYRIA

At Shunem, Elisha brought a widow's son back to life (2 Kin. 4:8–37).

Damascus

At Damascus, Elisha predicted that the wicked Hazael would succeed Ben-Hadad as king of Syria (2 Kin. 8:7–15).

THE GREAT SEA

Elisha protected the cities of Dothan and Samaria through chariots of fire and by bringing blindness upon the Syrian army (2 Kin. 6:13–23).

SEA OF GALILEE

• Shunem

JORDAN RIVER

• Dothan

• Samaria

• Jerusalem

The prophet Elisha continued Elijah's work (1 Kin. 19:16–21) in the northern kingdom of Israel, from Syria in the north to Edom in the south.

DEAD SEA

EDOM

kill *them*. Would you kill those whom you have taken captive with your sword and your bow? Set food and water before them, that they may eat and drink and go to their master." 23 Then he prepared a great feast for them; and after they ate and drank, he sent them away and they went to their master. So the bands of Syrian *raiders* came no more into the land of Israel.

24 And it happened after this that Ben-Hadad king of Syria gathered all his army, and went up and besieged Samaria. 25 And there was a great famine in Samaria; and indeed they besieged it until a donkey's head was *sold* for eighty *shekels* of silver, and one-fourth of a kab of dove droppings for five *shekels* of silver.

26 Then, as the king of Israel was passing by on the wall, a woman cried out to him, saying, "Help, my lord, O king!"

27 And he said, "If the LORD does not help you, where can I find help for you? From the threshing floor or from the winepress?" 28 Then the king said to her, "What is troubling you?"

And she answered, "This woman said to me, 'Give your son, that we may eat him today, and we will eat my son tomorrow.' 29 So we boiled my son, and ate him. And I said to her on the next day, 'Give your son, that we may eat him'; but she has hidden her son."

30 Now it happened, when the king heard the words of the woman, that he tore his clothes; and as he passed by on the wall, the people looked, and there underneath *he had* sackcloth on his body. 31 Then he said, "God do so to me and more also, if the head of Elisha the son of Shaphat remains on him today!"

32 But Elisha was sitting in his house, and the elders were sitting with him. And *the king* sent a man ahead of him, but before the messenger came to him, he said to the elders, "Do you see how this son of a murderer has sent someone to take away my head? Look, when the messenger comes, shut the door, and hold him fast at the door. *Is* not the sound of his master's feet behind him?" 33 And while he was still talking with them, there was the messenger, coming down to him; and then *the king* said, "Surely this calamity *is* from the LORD; why should I wait for the LORD any longer?"

7 Then Elisha said, "Hear the word of the LORD. Thus says the LORD: 'Tomorrow about this time a seah of fine flour *shall be sold* for a shekel, and two seahs of barley for a shekel, at the gate of Samaria.'"

2 So an officer on whose hand the king leaned answered the man of God and said, "Look, *if* the LORD would make windows in heaven, could this thing be?"

And he said, "In fact, you shall see *it* with your eyes, but you shall not eat of it."

3 Now there were four leprous men at the entrance of the gate; and they said to one another, "Why are we sitting here until we die? 4 If we say, 'We will enter the city,' the famine *is* in the city, and we shall die there. And if we sit here, we die also. Now therefore, come, let us surrender to the army of the Syrians. If they keep us alive, we shall live; and if they kill us, we shall only die." 5 And they rose at twilight to go to the camp of the Syrians; and when they had come to the outskirts of the Syrian camp, to their surprise no one *was* there. 6 For the LORD had caused the army of the Syrians to hear the noise of chariots and the noise of horses—the noise of a great army; so they said to one another, "Look, the king of Israel has hired against us the kings of the Hittites and the kings of the Egyptians to attack us!" 7 Therefore they arose and fled at twilight, and left the camp intact—their tents, their horses, and their donkeys—and they fled for their lives. 8 And when these lepers came to the outskirts of the camp, they went into one tent and ate and drank, and carried from it silver and gold and clothing, and went and hid *them;* then they came back and entered another tent, and carried *some* from there *also*, and went and hid *it*.

9 Then they said to one another, "We are not doing right. This day *is* a day of good news, and we remain silent. If we wait until morning light, some punishment will come upon us. Now therefore, come, let us go and tell the king's household." 10 So they went and called to the gatekeepers of the city, and told them, saying,

"We went to the Syrian camp, and surprisingly no one *was* there, not a human sound—only horses and donkeys tied, and the tents intact." 11 And the gatekeeperscalled out, and they told *it* to the king's household inside.

12 So the king arose in the night and said to his servants, "Let me now tell you what the Syrians have done to us. They know that we *are* hungry; therefore they have gone out of the camp to hide themselves in the field, saying, 'When they come out of the city, we shall catch them alive, and get into the city.'"

13 And one of his servants answered and said, "Please, let several *men* take five of the remaining horses which are left in the city. Look, they *may either become* like all the multitude of Israel that are left in it; or indeed, *I say*, they *may become* like all the multitude of Israel left from those who are consumed; so let us send them and see."
14 Therefore they took two chariots with horses; and the king sent them in the direction of the Syrian army, saying, "Go and see." 15 And they went after them to the Jordan; and indeed all the road *was* full of garments and weapons which the Syrians had thrown away in their haste. So the messengers returned and told the king. 16 Then the people went out and plundered the tents of the Syrians. So a seah of fine flour was *sold* for a shekel, and two seahs of barley for a shekel, according to the word of the LORD.

17 Now the king had appointed the officer on whose hand he leaned to have charge of the gate. But the people trampled him in the gate, and he died, just as the man of God had said, who spoke when the king came down to him. 18 So it happened just as the man of God had spoken to the king, saying, "Two seahs of barley for a shekel, and a seah of fine flour for a shekel, shall be *sold* tomorrow about this time in the gate of Samaria."
19 Then that officer had answered the man of God, and said, "Now look, *if* the LORD would make windows in heaven, could such a thing be?"

And he had said, "In fact, you shall see *it* with your eyes, but you shall not eat of it." 20 And so it happened to him, for the people trampled him in the gate, and he died.

8 Then Elisha spoke to the woman whose son he had restored to life, saying, "Arise and go, you and your household, and stay wherever you can; for the LORD has called for a famine, and furthermore, it will come upon the land for seven years." 2 So the woman arose and did according to the saying of the man of God, and she went with her household and dwelt in the land of the Philistines seven years.

3 It came to pass, at the end of seven years, that the woman returned from the land of the Philistines; and she went to make an appealto the king for her house and for her land. 4 Then the king talked with Gehazi, the servant of theman of God, saying, "Tell me, please, all the great things Elisha has done." 5 Now it happened, as he was telling the king how he had restored the dead to life, that there was the woman whose son he had restored to life, appealing to the king for her house and for her land. And Gehazi said, "My lord, O king, this *is* the woman, and this *is* her son whom Elisha restored to life." 6 And when the king asked the woman, she told him.

So the king appointed a certain officer for her, saying, "Restore all that *was* hers, and all the proceeds of the field from the day that she left the land until now."

7 Then Elisha went to Damascus, and Ben-Hadad king of Syria was sick; and it was told him, saying, "The man of God has come here." 8 And the king said to Hazael, "Take a present in your hand, and go to meet the man of God, and inquire of the LORD by him, saying, 'Shall I recover from this disease?'" 9 So Hazael went to meet him and took a present with him, of every good thing of Damascus, forty camel-loads; and he came and stood before him, and said, "Your son Ben-Hadad king of Syria has sent me to you, saying, 'Shall I recover from this disease?'"

10 And Elisha said to him, "Go, say to him, 'You shall certainly recover.' However the LORD has shown me that he will really die." 11 Then he set his countenance in a stare until he was ashamed; and the man of God wept. 12 And Hazael said, "Why is my lord weeping?"

He answered, "Because I know the evil that you will do to the children of Israel: Their strongholds you will set on fire, and their young men you will kill with the sword; and you will dash their children, and rip open their women with child."

13 So Hazael said, "But what *is* your servant—a dog, that he should do this gross thing?"

And Elisha answered, "The LORD has shown me that you *will become* king over Syria."

14 Then he departed from Elisha, and came to his master, who said to him, "What did Elisha say to you?" And he answered, "He told me you would surely recover." 15 But it happened on the next day that he took a thick cloth and dipped *it* in water, and spread *it* over his face so that he died; and Hazael reigned in his place.

16 Now in the fifth year of Joram the son of Ahab, king of Israel, Jehoshaphat *having been* king of Judah, Jehoram the son of Jehoshaphat began to reign as king of Judah. 17 He was thirty-two years old when he became king, and he reigned eight years in Jerusalem. 18 And he walked in the way of the kings of Israel, just as the house of Ahab had done, for the daughter of Ahab was his wife; and he did evil in the sight of the LORD. 19 Yet the LORD would not destroy Judah, for the sake of his servant David, as He promised him to give a lamp to him *and* his sons forever.

20 In his days Edom revolted against Judah's authority, and made a king over themselves. 21 So Joram*ᵃ* went to Zair, and all his chariots with him. Then he rose by night and attacked the Edomites who had surrounded him and the captains of the chariots; and the troops fled to their tents. 22 Thus Edom has been in revolt against Judah's authority to this day. And Libnah revolted at that time.

23 Now the rest of the acts of Joram, and all that he did, *are* they not written in the book of the chronicles of the kings of Judah? 24 So Joram rested with his fathers, and was buried with his fathers in the City of David. Then Ahaziah his son reigned in his place.

25 In the twelfth year of Joram the son of Ahab, king of Israel, Ahaziah the son of Jehoram, king of Judah, began to reign. 26 Ahaziah *was* twenty-two years old when he became king, and he reigned one year in Jerusalem. His mother's name *was* Athaliah the granddaughter of Omri, king of Israel. 27 And he walked in the way of the house of Ahab, and did evil in the sight of the LORD, like the house of Ahab, for he *was* the son-in-law of the house of Ahab.

28 Now he went with Joram the son of Ahab to war against Hazael king of Syria at Ramoth Gilead; and the Syrians wounded Joram. 29 Then King Joram went back to Jezreel to recover from the wounds which the Syrians had inflicted on him at Ramah, when he fought against Hazael king of Syria. And Ahaziah the son of Jehoram, king of Judah, went down to see Joram the son of Ahab in Jezreel, because he was sick.

9 And Elisha the prophet called one of the sons of the prophets, and said to him, "Get yourself ready, take this flask of oil in your hand, and go to Ramoth Gilead. 2 Now when you arrive at that place, look there for Jehu the son of Jehoshaphat, the son of Nimshi, and go in and make him rise up from among his associates, and take him to an inner room. 3 Then take the flask of oil, and pour *it* on his head, and say, 'Thus says the LORD: "I have anointed you king over Israel." ' Then open the door and flee, and do not delay."

4 So the young man, the servant of the prophet, went to Ramoth Gilead. 5 And when he arrived, there *were* the captains of the army sitting; and he said, "I have a message for you, Commander."

Jehu said, "For which *one* of us?"

And he said, "For you, Commander." 6 Then he arose and went into the house. And he poured the oil on his head, and said to him, "Thus says the LORD God of Israel: 'I have anointed you king over the people of the LORD, over Israel. 7 You shall strike down the house of Ahab your master, that I may avenge the blood of My servants the prophets, and the blood of all the servants of the LORD, at the hand of Jezebel. 8 For the whole house of Ahab shall perish; and I will cut off from Ahab all the

8:21 ᵃSpelled *Jehoram* in verse 16

males in Israel, both bond and free. 9 So I will make the house of Ahab like the house of Jeroboam the son of Nebat, and like the house of Baasha the son of Ahijah. 10 The dogs shall eat Jezebel on the plot *of ground* at Jezreel, and *there shall be none to bury her.*' " And he opened the door and fled.

11 Then Jehu came out to the servants of his master, and *one* said to him, "*Is* all well? Why did this madman come to you?"

And he said to them, "You know the man and his babble."

12 And they said, "A lie! Tell us now."

So he said, "Thus and thus he spoke to me, saying, 'Thus says the LORD: "I have anointed you king over Israel." ' "

13 Then each man hastened to take his garment and put *it* under him on the top of the steps; and they blew trumpets, saying, "Jehu is king!"

14 So Jehu the son of Jehoshaphat, the son of Nimshi, conspired against Joram. (Now Joram had been defending Ramoth Gilead, he and all Israel, against Hazael king of Syria. 15 But King Joram had returned to Jezreel to recover from the wounds which the Syrians had inflicted on him when he fought with Hazael king of Syria.) And Jehu said, "If you are so minded, let no one leave *or* escape from the city to go and tell *it* in Jezreel." 16 So Jehu rode in a chariot and went to Jezreel, for Joram was laid up there; and Ahaziah king of Judah had come down to see Joram.

17 Now a watchman stood on the tower in Jezreel, and he saw the company of Jehu as he came, and said, "I see a company of men."

And Joram said, "Get a horseman and send him to meet them, and let him say, '*Is it* peace?' "

18 So the horseman went to meet him, and said, "Thus says the king: '*Is it* peace?' "

And Jehu said, "What have you to do with peace? Turn around and follow me."

So the watchman reported, saying, "The messenger went to them, but is not coming back."

19 Then he sent out a second horseman who came to them, and said, "Thus says the king: '*Is it* peace?' "

And Jehu answered, "What have you to do with peace? Turn around and follow me."

20 So the watchman reported, saying, "He went up to them and is not coming back; and the driving *is* like the driving of Jehu the son of Nimshi, for he drives furiously!"

21 Then Joram said, "Make ready." And his chariot was made ready. Then Joram king of Israel and Ahaziah king of Judah went out, each in his chariot; and they went out to meet Jehu, and met him on the property of Naboth the Jezreelite. 22 Now it happened, when Joram saw Jehu, that he said, "*Is it* peace, Jehu?"

So he answered, "What peace, as long as the harlotries of your mother Jezebel and her witchcraft *are* so many?"

23 Then Joram turned around and fled, and said to Ahaziah, "Treachery, Ahaziah!" 24 Now Jehu drew his bow with full strength and shot Jehoram between his arms; and the arrow came out at his heart, and he sank down in his chariot. 25 Then *Jehu* said to Bidkar his captain, "Pick *him* up, *and* throw him into the tract of the field of Naboth the Jezreelite; for remember, when you and I were riding together behind Ahab his father, that the LORD laid this burden upon him: 26 'Surely I saw yesterday the blood of Naboth and the blood of his sons,' says the LORD, 'and I will repay you in this plot,' says the LORD. Now therefore, take *and* throw him on the plot *of ground,* according to the word of the LORD."

27 But when Ahaziah king of Judah saw *this,* he fled by the road to Beth Haggan.ᵃ So Jehu pursued him, and said, "Shoot him also in the chariot." *And they shot him* at the Ascent of Gur, which is by Ibleam. Then he fled to Megiddo, and died there. 28 And his servants carried him in the chariot to Jerusalem, and buried him in his tomb with his fathers in the City of David. 29 In the eleventh year of Joram the son of Ahab, Ahaziah had become king over Judah.

30 Now when Jehu had come to Jezreel, Jezebel heard *of it;* and she put paint on her eyes and adorned her head, and looked through a window. 31 Then, as Jehu entered at the

9:27 ᵃLiterally *The Garden House*

gate, she said, "Is it peace, Zimri, murderer of your master?"

32 And he looked up at the window, and said, "Who is on my side? Who?" So two or three eunuchs looked out at him. 33 Then he said, "Throw her down." So they threw her down, and some of her blood spattered on the wall and on the horses; and he trampled her underfoot. 34 And when he had gone in, he ate and drank. Then he said, "Go now, see to this accursed woman, and bury her, for she was a king's daughter." 35 So they went to bury her, but they found no more of her than the skull and the feet and the palms of her hands. 36 Therefore they came back and told him. And he said, "This is the word of the LORD, which He spoke by His servant Elijah the Tishbite, saying, 'On the plot of ground at Jezreel dogs shall eat the flesh of Jezebel;[a] 37 and the corpse of Jezebel shall be as refuse on the surface of the field, in the plot at Jezreel, so that they shall not say, "Here lies Jezebel." ' "

10 Now Ahab had seventy sons in Samaria. And Jehu wrote and sent letters to Samaria, to the rulers of Jezreel,[a] to the elders, and to those who reared Ahab's sons, saying:

2　Now as soon as this letter comes to you, since your master's sons are with you, and you have chariots and horses, a fortified city also, and weapons, 3 choose the best qualified of your master's sons, set him on his father's throne, and fight for your master's house.

4 But they were exceedingly afraid, and said, "Look, two kings could not stand up to him; how then can we stand?" 5 And he who was in charge of the house, and he who was in charge of the city, the elders also, and those who reared the sons, sent to Jehu, saying, "We are your servants, we will do all you tell us; but we will not make anyone king. Do what is good in your sight." 6 Then he wrote a second letter to them, saying:

If you are for me and will obey my voice, take the heads of the men, your master's sons, and come to me at Jezreel by this time tomorrow.

Now the king's sons, seventy persons, were with the great men of the city, who were rearing them. 7 So it was, when the letter came to them, that they took the king's sons and slaughtered seventy persons, put their heads in baskets and sent them to him at Jezreel.

8 Then a messenger came and told him, saying, "They have brought the heads of the king's sons."

And he said, "Lay them in two heaps at the entrance of the gate until morning."

9 So it was, in the morning, that he went out and stood, and said to all the people, "You are righteous. Indeed I conspired against my master and killed him; but who killed all these? 10 Know now that nothing shall fall to the earth of the word of the LORD which the LORD spoke concerning the house of Ahab; for the LORD has done what He spoke by His servant Elijah." 11 So Jehu killed all who remained of the house of Ahab in Jezreel, and all his great men and his close acquaintances and his priests, until he left him none remaining.

12 And he arose and departed and went to Samaria. On the way, at Beth Eked[a] of the Shepherds, 13 Jehu met with the brothers of Ahaziah king of Judah, and said, "Who are you?"

So they answered, "We are the brothers of Ahaziah; we have come down to greet the sons of the king and the sons of the queen mother."

14 And he said, "Take them alive!" So they took them alive, and killed them at the well of Beth Eked, forty-two men; and he left none of them.

15 Now when he departed from there, he met Jehonadab the son of Rechab, coming to meet him; and he greeted him and said to him, "Is your heart right, as my heart is toward your heart?"

And Jehonadab answered, "It is."

Jehu said, "If it is, give me your hand." So he gave him his hand, and he took him up to him into the char-

9:36 ª1 Kings 21:23　　10:1 ªFollowing Masoretic Text, Syriac, and Targum; Septuagint reads Samaria; Vulgate reads city.　　10:12 ªOr The Shearing House iot. 16 Then he said, "Come with me, and see my zeal for the LORD." So they had him ride in his chariot. 17 And when he came to Samaria, he killed all who remained to Ahab in Samaria, till he had destroyed them, according to the word of the LORD which He spoke to Elijah.

18 Then Jehu gathered all the people together, and said to them, "Ahab served Baal a little, Jehu will serve him much. 19 Now therefore, call to me all the prophets of Baal, all his servants, and all his priests. Let no one be missing, for I have a great sacrifice for Baal. Whoever is missing shall not live." But Jehu acted deceptively, with the intent of destroying the worshipers of Baal. 20 And Jehu said, "Proclaim a solemn assembly for Baal." So they proclaimed it. 21 Then Jehu sent throughout all Israel; and all the worshipers of Baal came, so that there was not a man left who did not come. So they came into the temple*a* of Baal, and the temple of Baal was full from one end to the other. 22 And he said to the one in charge of the wardrobe, "Bring out vestments for all the worshipers of Baal." So he brought out vestments for them. 23 Then Jehu and Jehonadab the son of Rechab went into the temple of Baal, and said to the worshipers of Baal, "Search and see that no servants of the LORD are here with you, but only the worshipers of Baal." 24 So they went in to offer sacrifices and burnt offerings. Now Jehu had appointed for himself eighty men on the outside, and had said, "*If* any of the men whom I have brought into your hands escapes, *whoever lets him escape, it shall be* his life for the life of the other."

25 Now it happened, as soon as he had made an end of offering the burnt offering, that Jehu said to the guard and to the captains, "Go in *and* kill them; let no one come out!" And they killed them with the edge of the sword; then the guards and the officers threw *them* out, and went into the inner room of the temple of Baal. 26 And they brought the *sacred* pillars out of the temple of Baal and burned them. 27 Then they broke down the *sacred* pillar of Baal, and tore down the temple of Baal and made it a refuse dump to this day.

28 Thus Jehu destroyed Baal from Israel.

29 However Jehu did not turn away from the sins of Jeroboam the son of Nebat, who had made Israel sin, *that is,* from the golden calves that *were* at Bethel and Dan. 30 And the LORD said to Jehu, "Because you have done well in doing *what is* right in My sight, *and* have done to the house of Ahab all that *was* in My heart, your sons shall sit on the throne of Israel to the fourth *generation.*" 31 But Jehu took no heed to walk in the law of the LORD God of Israel with all his heart; for he did not depart from the sins of Jeroboam, who had made Israel sin.

32 In those days the LORD began to cut off *parts* of Israel; and Hazael conquered them in all the territory of Israel 33 from the Jordan eastward: all the land of Gilead—Gad, Reuben, and Manasseh—from Aroer, which *is* by the River Arnon, including Gilead and Bashan.

34 Now the rest of the acts of Jehu, all that he did, and all his might, *are* they not written in the book of the chronicles of the kings of Israel? 35 So Jehu rested with his fathers, and they buried him in Samaria. Then Jehoahaz his son reigned in his place. 36 And the period that Jehu reigned over Israel in Samaria *was* twenty-eight years.

11 When Athaliah the mother of Ahaziah saw that her son was dead, she arose and destroyed all the royal heirs. 2 But Jehosheba, the daughter of King Joram, sister of Ahaziah, took Joash the son of Ahaziah, and stole him away from among the king's sons *who were* being murdered; and they hid him and his nurse in the bedroom, from Athaliah, so that he was not killed. 3 So he was hidden with her in the house of the LORD for six years, while Athaliah reigned over the land.

4 In the seventh year Jehoiada sent and brought the captains of hundreds—of the bodyguards and the escorts—and brought them into the house of the LORD to him. And he made a covenant with them and took an oath from them in the house of the LORD, and showed them the king's son. 5 Then he commanded

them, saying, "This *is* what you shall do: One-third of you who come on duty on the Sabbath shall be keeping watch over the king's house, 6 one-third *shall be* at the gate of Sur, and one-third at the gate behind the escorts. You shall keep the watch of the house, lest it be broken down. 7 The two contingents of you who go off duty on the Sabbath shall keep the watch of the house of the LORD for the king. 8 But you shall surround the king on all sides, every man with his weapons in his hand; and whoever comes within range, let him be put to death. You are to be with the king as he goes out and as he comes in."

9 So the captains of the hundreds did according to all that Jehoiada the priest commanded. Each of them took his men who were to be on duty on the Sabbath, with those who were going off duty on the Sabbath, and came to Jehoiada the priest. 10 And the priest gave the captains of hundreds the spears and shields which *had belonged* to King David, that were in the temple of the LORD. 11 Then the escorts stood, every man with his weapons in his hand, all around the king, from the right side of the temple to the left side of the temple, by the altar and the house. 12 And he brought out the king's son, put the crown on him, and *gave him* the Testimony;^a they made him king and anointed him, and they clapped their hands and said, "Long live the king!"

13 Now when Athaliah heard the noise of the escorts *and* the people, she came to the people *in* the temple of the LORD. 14 When she looked, there was the king standing by a pillar according to custom; and the leaders and the trumpeters were by the king. All the people of the land were rejoicing and blowing trumpets. So Athaliah tore her clothes and cried out, "Treason! Treason!"

15 And Jehoiada the priest commanded the captains of the hundreds, the officers of the army, and said to them, "Take her outside under guard, and slay with the sword whoever follows her." For the priest had said, "Do not let her be killed in the house of the LORD." 16 So they seized her; and she went by way of the horses' entrance *into* the king's house, and there she was killed.

17 Then Jehoiada made a covenant between the LORD, the king, and the people, that they should be the LORD's people, and *also* between the king and the people. 18 And all the people of the land went to the temple of Baal, and tore it down. They thoroughly broke in pieces its altars and images, and killed Mattan the priest of Baal before the altars. And the priest appointed officers over the house of the LORD. 19 Then he took the captains of hundreds, the bodyguards, the escorts, and all the people of the land; and they brought the king down from the house of the LORD, and went by way of the gate of the escorts to the king's house. Then he sat on the throne of the kings. 20 So all the people of the land rejoiced; and the city was quiet, for they had slain Athaliah with the sword *in* the king's house. 21 Jehoash *was* seven years old when he became king.

12 In the seventh year of Jehu, Jehoash^a became king, and he reigned forty years in Jerusalem. His mother's name *was* Zibiah of Beersheba. 2 Jehoash did *what was* right in the sight of the LORD all the days in which Jehoiada the priest instructed him. 3 But the high places were not taken away; the people still sacrificed and burned incense on high places.

4 And Jehoash said to the priests, "All the money of the dedicated gifts that are brought into the house of the LORD—each man's census money, each man's assessment money^a—*and* all the money that a man purposes in his heart to bring into the house of the LORD, 5 let the priests take *it* themselves, each from his constituency; and let them repair the damages of the temple, wherever any dilapidation is found."

6 Now it was so, by the twenty-third year of King Jehoash, *that* the priests had not repaired the damages of the temple. 7 So King Jehoash called Jehoiada the priest and the *other* priests, and said to them, "Why have you not repaired the damages

---

11:12 ^aThat is, the Law (compare Exodus 25:16, 21 and Deuteronomy 31:9)   12:1 ^aSpelled *Joash* in 11:2ff   12:4 ^aCompare Leviticus 27:2ff of the temple? Now therefore, do not take *more* money from your constituency, but deliver it for repairing the damages of the temple." 8 And the priests agreed that they would neither receive *more* money from the people, nor repair the damages of the temple.

9 Then Jehoiada the priest took a chest, bored a hole in its lid, and set it beside the altar, on the right side as one comes into the house of the LORD; and the priests who kept the door put there all the money brought into the house of the LORD. 10 So it was, whenever they saw that *there was* much money in the chest, that the king's scribe and the high priest came up and put it in bags, and counted the money that was found in the house of the LORD. 11 Then they gave the money, which had been apportioned, into the hands of those who did the work, who had the oversight of the house of the LORD; and they paid it out to the carpenters and builders who worked on the house of the LORD, 12 and to masons and stonecutters, and for buying timber and hewn stone, to repair the damage of the house of the LORD, and for all that was paid out to repair the temple. 13 However there were not made for the house of the LORD basins of silver, trimmers, sprinkling-bowls, trumpets, any articles of gold or articles of silver, from the money brought into the house of the LORD. 14 But they gave that to the workmen, and they repaired the house of the LORD with it. 15 Moreover they did not require an account from the men into whose hand they delivered the money to be paid to workmen, for they dealt faithfully. 16 The money from the trespass offerings and the money from the sin offerings was not brought into the house of the LORD. It belonged to the priests.

17 Hazael king of Syria went up and fought against Gath, and took it; then Hazael set his face to go up to Jerusalem. 18 And Jehoash king of Judah took all the sacred things that his fathers, Jehoshaphat and Jehoram and Ahaziah, kings of Judah, had dedicated, and his own sacred things, and all the gold found in the treasuries of the house of the LORD and in the king's house, and sent *them* to Hazael king of Syria. Then he went away from Jerusalem.

19 Now the rest of the acts of Joash,*a* and all that he did, *are* they not written in the book of the chronicles of the kings of Judah?

20 And his servants arose and formed a conspiracy, and killed Joash in the house of the Millo,*a* which goes down to Silla. 21 For Jozachar*a* the son of Shimeath and Jehozabad the son of Shomer,*b* his servants, struck him. So he died, and they buried him with his fathers in the City of David. Then Amaziah his son reigned in his place.

13 In the twenty-third year of Joash*a* the son of Ahaziah, king of Judah, Jehoahaz the son of Jehu became king over Israel in Samaria, *and reigned* seventeen years. 2 And he did evil in the sight of the LORD, and followed the sins of Jeroboam the son of Nebat, who had made Israel sin. He did not depart from them.

3 Then the anger of the LORD was aroused against Israel, and He delivered them into the hand of Hazael king of Syria, and into the hand of Ben-Hadad the son of Hazael, all *their* days. 4 So Jehoahaz pleaded with the LORD, and the LORD listened to him; for He saw the oppression of Israel, because the king of Syria oppressed them. 5 Then the LORD gave Israel a deliverer, so that they escaped from under the hand of the Syrians; and the children of Israel dwelt in their tents as before. 6 Nevertheless they did not depart from the sins of the house of Jeroboam, who had made Israel sin, *but* walked in them; and the wooden image*a* also remained in Samaria. 7 For He left of the army of Jehoahaz only fifty horsemen, ten chariots, and ten thousand foot soldiers; for the king of Syria had destroyed them and made them like the dust at threshing.

8 Now the rest of the acts of Jehoahaz, all that he did, and his might, *are* they not written in the book of the chronicles of the kings of Israel?

12:19 aSpelled *Jehoash* in 12:1ff   12:20 aLiterally *The Landfill*   12:21 aCalled *Zabad* in 2 Chronicles 24:26   bCalled *Shimrith* in 2 Chronicles 24:26   13:1 aSpelled *Jehoash* in 12:1ff   13:6 aHebrew *Asherah*, a Canaanite goddess

9 So Jehoahaz rested with his fathers, and they buried him in Samaria. Then Joash his son reigned in his place.

10 In the thirty-seventh year of Joash king of Judah, Jehoash[a] the son of Jehoahaz became king over Israel in Samaria, *and reigned* sixteen years. 11 And he did evil in the sight of the LORD. He did not depart from all the sins of Jeroboam the son of Nebat, who made Israel sin, *but* walked in them.

12 Now the rest of the acts of Joash, all that he did, and his might with which he fought against Amaziah king of Judah, *are* they not written in the book of the chronicles of the kings of Israel? 13 So Joash rested with his fathers. Then Jeroboam sat on his throne. And Joash was buried in Samaria with the kings of Israel.

14 Elisha had become sick with the illness of which he would die. Then Joash the king of Israel came down to him, and wept over his face, and said, "O my father, my father, the chariots of Israel and their horsemen!"

15 And Elisha said to him, "Take a bow and some arrows." So he took himself a bow and some arrows. 16 Then he said to the king of Israel, "Put your hand on the bow." So he put his hand *on it*, and Elisha put his hands on the king's hands. 17 And he said, "Open the east window"; and he opened *it*. Then Elisha said, "Shoot"; and he shot. And he said, "The arrow of the LORD's deliverance and the arrow of deliverance from Syria; for you must strike the Syrians at Aphek till you have destroyed *them*." 18 Then he said, "Take the arrows"; so he took *them*. And he said to the king of Israel, "Strike the ground"; so he struck three times, and stopped. 19 And the man of God was angry with him, and said, "You should have struck five or six times; then you would have struck Syria till you had destroyed *it!* But now you will strike Syria *only* three times."

20 Then Elisha died, and they buried him. And the *raiding* bands from Moab invaded the land in the spring of the year. 21 So it was, as they were burying a man, that suddenly they spied a band *of raiders;* and they put the man in the tomb of Elisha; and when the man was let down and touched the bones of Elisha, he revived and stood on his feet.

22 And Hazael king of Syria oppressed Israel all the days of Jehoahaz. 23 But the LORD was gracious to them, had compassion on them, and regarded them, because of His covenant with Abraham, Isaac, and Jacob, and would not yet destroy them or cast them from His presence.

24 Now Hazael king of Syria died. Then Ben-Hadad his son reigned in his place. 25 And Jehoash[a] the son of Jehoahaz recaptured from the hand of Ben-Hadad, the son of Hazael, the cities which he had taken out of the hand of Jehoahaz his father by war. Three times Joash defeated him and recaptured the cities of Israel.

14 In the second year of Joash the son of Jehoahaz, king of Israel, Amaziah the son of Joash, king of Judah, became king. 2 He was twenty-five years old when he became king, and he reigned twenty-nine years in Jerusalem. His mother's name was Jehoaddan of Jerusalem. 3 And he did *what was* right in the sight of the LORD, yet not like his father David; he did everything as his father Joash had done. 4 However the high places were not taken away, and the people still sacrificed and burned incense on the high places.

5 Now it happened, as soon as the kingdom was established in his hand, that he executed his servants who had murdered his father the king. 6 But the children of the murderers he did not execute, according to what is written in the Book of the Law of Moses, in which the LORD commanded, saying, "Fathers shall not be put to death for their children, nor shall children be put to death for their fathers; but a person shall be put to death for his own sin."[a]

7 He killed ten thousand Edomites in the Valley of Salt, and took Sela by war, and called its name Joktheel to this day.

8 Then Amaziah sent messengers to Jehoash[a] the son of Jehoahaz, the son of Jehu, king of Israel, saying, "Come, let us face one another *in battle.*" 9 And Jehoash king of Israel

13:10 aSpelled *Joash* in verse 9   13:25 aSpelled *Joash* in verses 12–14, 25   14:6 aDeuteronomy 24:16   14:8 aSpelled *Joash* in 13:12ff and 2 Chronicles 25:17ff sent to Amaziah king of Judah, saying, "The thistle that *was* in Lebanon sent to the cedar that *was* in Lebanon, saying, 'Give your daughter to my son as wife'; and a wild beast that *was* in Lebanon passed by and trampled the thistle. 10 You have indeed defeated Edom, and your heart has lifted you up. Glory *in that,* and stay at home; for why should you meddle with trouble so that you fall—you and Judah with you?"

11 But Amaziah would not heed. Therefore Jehoash king of Israel went out; so he and Amaziah king of Judah faced one another at Beth Shemesh, which *belongs* to Judah. 12 And Judah was defeated by Israel, and every man fled to his tent. 13 Then Jehoash king of Israel captured Amaziah king of Judah, the son of Jehoash, the son of Ahaziah, at Beth Shemesh; and he went to Jerusalem, and broke down the wall of Jerusalem from the Gate of Ephraim to the Corner Gate—four hundred cubits. 14 And he took all the gold and silver, all the articles that were found in the house of the LORD and in the treasuries of the king's house, and hostages, and returned to Samaria.

15 Now the rest of the acts of Jehoash which he did—his might, and how he fought with Amaziah king of Judah—*are* they not written in the book of the chronicles of the kings of Israel? 16 So Jehoash rested with his fathers, and was buried in Samaria with the kings of Israel. Then Jeroboam his son reigned in his place.

17 Amaziah the son of Joash, king of Judah, lived fifteen years after the death of Jehoash the son of Jehoahaz, king of Israel. 18 Now the rest of the acts of Amaziah, *are* they not written in the book of the chronicles of the kings of Judah? 19 And they formed a conspiracy against him in Jerusalem, and he fled to Lachish; but they sent after him to Lachish and killed him there. 20 Then they brought him on horses, and he was buried at Jerusalem with his fathers in the City of David.

21 And all the people of Judah took Azariah,[a] who *was* sixteen years old, and made him king instead of his father Amaziah. 22 He built Elath and restored it to Judah, after the king rested with his fathers.

23 In the fifteenth year of Amaziah the son of Joash, king of Judah, Jeroboam the son of Joash, king of Israel, became king in Samaria, *and reigned* forty-one years. 24 And he did evil in the sight of the LORD; he did not depart from all the sins of Jeroboam the son of Nebat, who had made Israel sin. 25 He restored the territory of Israel from the entrance of Hamath to the Sea of the Arabah, according to the word of the LORD God of Israel, which He had spoken through His servant Jonah the son of Amittai, the prophet who *was* from Gath Hepher. 26 For the LORD saw *that* the affliction of Israel *was* very bitter; and whether bond or free, there was no helper for Israel. 27 And the LORD did not say that He would blot out the name of Israel from under heaven; but He saved them by the hand of Jeroboam the son of Joash.

28 Now the rest of the acts of Jeroboam, and all that he did—his might, how he made war, and how he recaptured for Israel, from Damascus and Hamath, *what had belonged* to Judah—*are* they not written in the book of the chronicles of the kings of Israel? 29 So Jeroboam rested with his fathers, the kings of Israel. Then Zechariah his son reigned in his place.

15 In the twenty-seventh year of Jeroboam king of Israel, Azariah the son of Amaziah, king of Judah, became king. 2 He was sixteen years old when he became king, and he reigned fifty-two years in Jerusalem. His mother's name *was* Jecholiah of Jerusalem. 3 And he did *what was* right in the sight of the LORD, according to all that his father Amaziah had done, 4 except that the high places were not removed; the people still sacrificed and burned incense on the high places. 5 Then the LORD struck the king, so that he was a leper until the day of his death; so he dwelt in an isolated house. And Jotham the king's son *was* over the *royal* house, judging the people of the land.

6 Now the rest of the acts of Azariah, and all that he did, *are* they not written in the book of the chronicles

14:21 ªCalled *Uzziah* in 2 Chronicles 26:1ff, Isaiah 6:1, and elsewhere of the kings of Judah? 7 So Azariah rested with his fathers, and they buried him with his fathers in the City of David. Then Jotham his son reigned in his place.

8 In the thirty-eighth year of Azariah king of Judah, Zechariah the son of Jeroboam reigned over Israel in Samaria six months. 9 And he did evil in the sight of the LORD, as his fathers had done; he did not depart from the sins of Jeroboam the son of Nebat, who had made Israel sin. 10 Then Shallum the son of Jabesh conspired against him, and struck and killed him in front of the people; and he reigned in his place.

11 Now the rest of the acts of Zechariah, indeed they *are* written in the book of the chronicles of the kings of Israel.

12 This *was* the word of the LORD which He spoke to Jehu, saying, "Your sons shall sit on the throne of Israel to the fourth *generation.*"*a* And so it was.

13 Shallum the son of Jabesh became king in the thirty-ninth year of Uzziah*a* king of Judah; and he reigned a full month in Samaria. 14 For Menahem the son of Gadi went up from Tirzah, came to Samaria, and struck Shallum the son of Jabesh in Samaria and killed him; and he reigned in his place.

15 Now the rest of the acts of Shallum, and the conspiracy which he led, indeed they *are* written in the book of the chronicles of the kings of Israel. 16 Then from Tirzah, Menahem attacked Tiphsah, all who *were* there, and its territory. Because they did not surrender, therefore he attacked *it*. All the women there who were with child he ripped open.

17 In the thirty-ninth year of Azariah king of Judah, Menahem the son of Gadi became king over Israel, *and reigned* ten years in Samaria. 18 And he did evil in the sight of the LORD; he did not depart all his days from the sins of Jeroboam the son of Nebat, who had made Israel sin. 19 Pul*a* king of Assyria came against the land; and Menahem gave Pul a thousand talents of silver, that his hand might be with him to strengthen the kingdom under his control. 20 And Menahem exacted the money from Israel, from all the very wealthy, from each man fifty shekels of silver, to give to the king of Assyria. So the king of Assyria turned back, and did not stay there in the land.

21 Now the rest of the acts of Menahem, and all that he did, *are* they not written in the book of the chronicles of the kings of Israel? 22 So Menahem rested with his fathers. Then Pekahiah his son reigned in his place.

23 In the fiftieth year of Azariah king of Judah, Pekahiah the son of Menahem became king over Israel in Samaria, *and reigned* two years. 24 And he did evil in the sight of the LORD; he did not depart from the sins of Jeroboam the son of Nebat, who had made Israel sin. 25 Then Pekah the son of Remaliah, an officer of his, conspired against him and killed him in Samaria, in the citadel of the king's house, along with Argob and Arieh; and with him were fifty men of Gilead. He killed him and reigned in his place.

26 Now the rest of the acts of Pekahiah, and all that he did, indeed they *are* written in the book of the chronicles of the kings of Israel.

27 In the fifty-second year of Azariah king of Judah, Pekah the son of Remaliah became king over Israel in Samaria, *and reigned* twenty years. 28 And he did evil in the sight of the LORD; he did not depart from the sins of Jeroboam the son of Nebat, who had made Israel sin. 29 In the days of Pekah king of Israel, Tiglath-Pileser king of Assyria came and took Ijon, Abel Beth Maachah, Janoah, Kedesh, Hazor, Gilead, and Galilee, all the land of Naphtali; and he carried them captive to Assyria. 30 Then Hoshea the son of Elah led a conspiracy against Pekah the son of Remaliah, and struck and killed him; so he reigned in his place in the twentieth year of Jotham the son of Uzziah.

31 Now the rest of the acts of Pekah, and all that he did, indeed they *are* written in the book of the chronicles of the kings of Israel.

32 In the second year of Pekah the son of Remaliah, king of Israel, Jotham the son of Uzziah, king of Judah, began to reign. 33 He was

15:12 *a*2 Kings 10:30   15:13 *a*Called *Azariah* in 14:21ff and 15:1ff   15:19 *a*That is, Tiglath-Pileser III (compare verse 29)

twenty-five years old when he became king, and he reigned sixteen years in Jerusalem. His mother's name *was* Jerusha[a] the daughter of Zadok. 34 And he did *what was* right in the sight of the LORD; he did according to all that his father Uzziah had done. 35 However the high places were not removed; the people still sacrificed and burned incense on the high places. He built the Upper Gate of the house of the LORD.

36 Now the rest of the acts of Jotham, and all that he did, *are* they not written in the book of the chronicles of the kings of Judah? 37 In those days the LORD began to send Rezin king of Syria and Pekah the son of Remaliah against Judah. 38 So Jotham rested with his fathers, and was buried with his fathers in the City of David his father. Then Ahaz his son reigned in his place.

16 In the seventeenth year of Pekah the son of Remaliah, Ahaz the son of Jotham, king of Judah, began to reign. 2 Ahaz *was* twenty years old when he became king, and he reigned sixteen years in Jerusalem; and he did not do *what was* right in the sight of the LORD his God, as his father David *had* done. 3 But he walked in the way of the kings of Israel; indeed he made his son pass through the fire, according to the abominations of the nations whom the LORD had cast out from before the children of Israel. 4 And he sacrificed and burned incense on the high places, on the hills, and under every green tree.

5 Then Rezin king of Syria and Pekah the son of Remaliah, king of Israel, came up to Jerusalem to *make* war; and they besieged Ahaz but could not overcome *him.* 6 At that time Rezin king of Syria captured Elath for Syria, and drove the men of Judah from Elath. Then the Edomites[a] went to Elath, and dwell there to this day.

7 So Ahaz sent messengers to Tiglath-Pileser king of Assyria, saying, "I *am* your servant and your son. Come up and save me from the hand of the king of Syria and from the hand of the king of Israel, who rise up against me." 8 And Ahaz took the silver and gold that was found in the house of the LORD, and in the treasuries of the king's house, and sent *it* as a present to the king of Assyria. 9 So the king of Assyria heeded him; for the king of Assyria went up against Damascus and took it, carried *its people* captive to Kir, and killed Rezin.

10 Now King Ahaz went to Damascus to meet Tiglath-Pileser king of Assyria, and saw an altar that *was* at Damascus; and King Ahaz sent to Urijah the priest the design of the altar and its pattern, according to all its workmanship. 11 Then Urijah the priest built an altar according to all that King Ahaz had sent from Damascus. So Urijah the priest made *it* before King Ahaz came back from Damascus. 12 And when the king came back from Damascus, the king saw the altar; and the king approached the altar and made offerings on it. 13 So he burned his burnt offering and his grain offering; and he poured his drink offering and sprinkled the blood of his peace offerings on the altar. 14 He also brought the bronze altar which *was* before the LORD, from the front of the temple—from between the *new* altar and the house of the LORD—and put it on the north side of the *new* altar. 15 Then King Ahaz commanded Urijah the priest, saying, "On the great *new* altar burn the morning burnt offering, the evening grain offering, the king's burnt sacrifice, and his grain offering, with the burnt offering of all the people of the land, their grain offering, and their drink offerings; and sprinkle on it all the blood of the burnt offering and all the blood of the sacrifice. And the bronze altar shall be for me to inquire *by.*" 16 Thus did Urijah the priest, according to all that King Ahaz commanded.

17 And King Ahaz cut off the panels of the carts, and removed the lavers from them; and he took down the Sea from the bronze oxen that *were* under it, and put it on a pavement of stones. 18 Also he removed the Sabbath pavilion which they had built in the temple, and he removed the king's outer entrance from the house of the LORD, on account of the king of Assyria.

19 Now the rest of the acts of Ahaz

15:33 [a]Spelled *Jerushah* in 2 Chronicles 27:1   16:6 [a]Some ancient authorities read *Syrians.*

which he did, *are* they not written in the book of the chronicles of the kings of Judah? 20 So Ahaz rested with his fathers, and was buried with his fathers in the City of David. Then Hezekiah his son reigned in his place.

17 In the twelfth year of Ahaz king of Judah, Hoshea the son of Elah became king of Israel in Samaria, *and he reigned* nine years. 2 And he did evil in the sight of the LORD, but not as the kings of Israel who were before him. 3 Shalmaneser king of Assyria came up against him; and Hoshea became his vassal, and paid him tribute money. 4 And the king of Assyria uncovered a conspiracy by Hoshea; for he had sent messengers to So, king of Egypt, and brought no tribute to the king of Assyria, as *he had done* year by year. Therefore the king of Assyria shut him up, and bound him in prison.

5 Now the king of Assyria went throughout all the land, and went up to Samaria and besieged it for three years. 6 In the ninth year of Hoshea, the king of Assyria took Samaria and carried Israel away to Assyria, and placed them in Halah and by the Habor, the River of Gozan, and in the cities of the Medes.

7 For so it was that the children of Israel had sinned against the LORD their God, who had brought them up out of the land of Egypt, from under the hand of Pharaoh king of Egypt; and they had feared other gods, 8 and had walked in the statutes of the nations whom the LORD had cast out from before the children of Israel, and of the kings of Israel, which they had made. 9 Also the children of Israel secretly did against the LORD their God things that *were* not right, and they built for themselves high places in all their cities, from watchtower to fortified city. 10 They set up for themselves *sacred* pillars and wooden images[a] on every high hill and under every green tree. 11 There they burned incense on all the high places, like the nations whom the LORD had carried away before them; and they did wicked things to provoke the LORD to anger, 12 for they served idols, of which the LORD had said to them, "You shall not do this thing."

13 Yet the LORD testified against Israel and against Judah, by all of His prophets, every seer, saying, "Turn from your evil ways, and keep My commandments *and* My statutes, according to all the law which I commanded your fathers, and which I sent to you by My servants the prophets." 14 Nevertheless they would not hear, but stiffened their necks, like the necks of their fathers, who did not believe in the LORD their God. 15 And they rejected His statutes and His covenant that He had made with their fathers, and His testimonies which He had testified against them; they followed idols, became idolaters, and *went* after the nations who *were* all around them, *concerning* whom the LORD had charged them that they should not do like them. 16 So they left all the commandments of the LORD their God, made for themselves a molded image *and* two calves, made a wooden image and worshiped all the host of heaven, and served Baal. 17 And they caused their sons and daughters to pass through the fire, practiced witchcraft and soothsaying, and sold themselves to do evil in the sight of the LORD, to provoke Him to anger. 18 Therefore the LORD was very angry with Israel, and removed them from His sight; there was none left but the tribe of Judah alone.

19 Also Judah did not keep the commandments of the LORD their God, but walked in the statutes of Israel which they made. 20 And the LORD rejected all the descendants of Israel, afflicted them, and delivered them into the hand of plunderers, until He had cast them from His sight. 21 For He tore Israel from the house of David, and they made Jeroboam the son of Nebat king. Then Jeroboam drove Israel from following the LORD, and made them commit a great sin. 22 For the children of Israel walked in all the sins of Jeroboam which he did; they did not depart from them, 23 until the LORD removed Israel out of His sight, as He had said by all His servants the prophets. So Israel was carried away from their own land to Assyria, *as it is* to this day.

17:10 aHebrew *Asherim,* Canaanite deities

24 Then the king of Assyria brought *people* from Babylon, Cuthah, Ava, Hamath, and from Sepharvaim, and placed *them* in the cities of Samaria instead of the children of Israel; and they took possession of Samaria and dwelt in its cities. 25 And it was so, at the beginning of their dwelling there, *that* they did not fear the LORD; therefore the LORD sent lions among them, which killed *some* of them. 26 So they spoke to the king of Assyria, saying, "The nations whom you have removed and placed in the cities of Samaria do not know the rituals of the God of the land; therefore He has sent lions among them, and indeed, they are killing them because they do not know the rituals of the God of the land." 27 Then the king of Assyria commanded, saying, "Send there one of the priests whom you brought from there; let him go and dwell there, and let him teach them the rituals of the God of the land." 28 Then one of the priests whom they had carried away from Samaria came and dwelt in Bethel, and taught them how they should fear the LORD.

29 However every nation continued to make gods of its own, and put *them* in the shrines on the high places which the Samaritans had made, *every* nation in the cities where they dwelt. 30 The men of Babylon made Succoth Benoth, the men of Cuth made Nergal, the men of Hamath made Ashima, 31 and the Avites made Nibhaz and Tartak; and the Sepharvites burned their children in fire to Adrammelech and Anammelech, the gods of Sepharvaim. 32 So they feared the LORD, and from every class they appointed for themselves priests of the high places, who sacrificed for them in the shrines of the high places. 33 They feared the LORD, yet served their own gods—according to the rituals of the nations from among whom they were carried away.

34 To this day they continue practicing the former rituals; they do not fear the LORD, nor do they follow their statutes or their ordinances, or the law and commandment which the LORD had commanded the children of Jacob, whom He named Israel, 35 with whom the LORD had made a covenant and charged them, saying: "You shall not fear other gods, nor bow down to them nor serve them nor sacrifice to them; 36 but the LORD, who brought you up from the land of Egypt with great power and an outstretched arm, Him you shall fear, Him you shall worship, and to Him you shall offer sacrifice. 37 And the statutes, the ordinances, the law, and the commandment which He wrote for you, you shall be careful to observe forever; you shall not fear other gods. 38 And the covenant that I have made with you, you shall not forget, nor shall you fear other gods. 39 But the LORD your God you shall fear; and He will deliver you from the hand of all your enemies." 40 However they did not obey, but they followed their former rituals. 41 So these nations feared the LORD, yet served their carved images; also their children and their children's children have continued doing as their fathers did, even to this day.

18 Now it came to pass in the third year of Hoshea the son of Elah, king of Israel, *that* Hezekiah the son of Ahaz, king of Judah, began to reign. 2 He was twenty-five years old when he became king, and he reigned twenty-nine years in Jerusalem. His mother's name *was* Abi*a* the daughter of Zechariah. 3 And he did *what was* right in the sight of the LORD, according to all that his father David had done.

4 He removed the high places and broke the *sacred* pillars, cut down the wooden image*a* and broke in pieces the bronze serpent that Moses had made; for until those days the children of Israel burned incense to it, and called it Nehushtan.*b* 5 He trusted in the LORD God of Israel, so that after him was none like him among all the kings of Judah, nor who were before him. 6 For he held fast to the LORD; he did not depart from following Him, but kept His commandments, which the LORD had commanded Moses. 7 The LORD was with him; he prospered wherever he went. And he rebelled against the king of Assyria and did not serve him. 8 He subdued the Philistines, as

18:2 *a*Called *Abijah* in 2 Chronicles 29:1ff   18:4 *a*Hebrew *Asherah*, a Canaanite goddess   *b*Literally *Bronze Thing* far as Gaza and its territory, from watchtower to fortified city.

9 Now it came to pass in the fourth year of King Hezekiah, which *was* the seventh year of Hoshea the son of Elah, king of Israel, *that* Shalmaneser king of Assyria came up against Samaria and besieged it. 10 And at the end of three years they took it. In the sixth year of Hezekiah, that *is,* the ninth year of Hoshea king of Israel, Samaria was taken. 11 Then the king of Assyria carried Israel away captive to Assyria, and put them in Halah and by the Habor, the River of Gozan, and in the cities of the Medes, 12 because they did not obey the voice of the LORD their God, but transgressed His covenant *and* all that Moses the servant of the LORD had commanded; and they would neither hear nor do *them.*

13 And in the fourteenth year of King Hezekiah, Sennacherib king of Assyria came up against all the fortified cities of Judah and took them. 14 Then Hezekiah king of Judah sent to the king of Assyria at Lachish, saying, "I have done wrong; turn away from me; whatever you impose on me I will pay." And the king of Assyria assessed Hezekiah king of Judah three hundred talents of silver and thirty talents of gold. 15 So Hezekiah gave *him* all the silver that was found in the house of the LORD and in the treasuries of the king's house. 16 At that time Hezekiah stripped *the gold from* the doors of the temple of the LORD, and *from* the pillars which Hezekiah king of Judah had overlaid, and gave it to the king of Assyria.

17 Then the king of Assyria sent *the* Tartan,[a] *the* Rabsaris,[b] and *the* Rabshakeh[c] from Lachish, with a great army against Jerusalem, to King Hezekiah. And they went up and came to Jerusalem. When they had come up, they went and stood by the aqueduct from the upper pool, which *was* on the highway to the Fuller's Field. 18 And when they had called to the king, Eliakim the son of Hilkiah, who *was* over the household, Shebna the scribe, and Joah the son of Asaph, the recorder, came out to them. 19 Then *the* Rabshakeh said to them, "Say now to Hezekiah, 'Thus

says the great king, the king of Assyria: "What confidence *is* this in which you trust? 20 You speak of *having* plans and power for war; but *they are* mere words. And in whom do you trust, that you rebel against me? 21 Now look! You are trusting in the staff of this broken reed, Egypt, on which if a man leans, it will go into his hand and pierce it. So *is* Pharaoh king of Egypt to all who trust in him. 22 But if you say to me, 'We trust in the LORD our God,' *is* it not He whose high places and whose altars Hezekiah has taken away, and said to Judah and Jerusalem, 'You shall worship before this altar in Jerusalem'?" ' 23 Now therefore, I urge you, give a pledge to my master the king of Assyria, and I will give you two thousand horses—if you are able on your part to put riders on them! 24 How then will you repel one captain of the least of my master's servants, and put your trust in Egypt for chariots and horsemen? 25 Have I now come up without the LORD against this place to destroy it? The LORD said to me, 'Go up against this land, and destroy it.' "

26 Then Eliakim the son of Hilkiah, Shebna, and Joah said to *the* Rabshakeh, "Please speak to your servants in Aramaic, for we understand *it;* and do not speak to us in Hebrew[a] in the hearing of the people who *are* on the wall."

27 But *the* Rabshakeh said to them, "Has my master sent me to your master and to you to speak these words, and not to the men who sit on the wall, who will eat and drink their own waste with you?"

28 Then *the* Rabshakeh stood and called out with a loud voice in Hebrew, and spoke, saying, "Hear the word of the great king, the king of Assyria! 29 Thus says the king: 'Do not let Hezekiah deceive you, for he shall not be able to deliver you from his hand; 30 nor let Hezekiah make you trust in the LORD, saying, "The LORD will surely deliver us; this city shall not be given into the hand of the king of Assyria." ' 31 Do not listen to Hezekiah; for thus says the king of Assyria: 'Make *peace* with me by a present and come out to me; and every one of you eat from his own

---

18:17 aA title, probably *Commander in Chief*   bA title, probably *Chief Officer*   cA title, probably *Chief of Staff* or *Governor*   18:26 aLiterally *Judean* vine and every one from his own fig tree, and every one of you drink the waters of his own cistern; 32 until I come and take you away to a land like your own land, a land of grain and new wine, a land of bread and vineyards, a land of olive groves and honey, that you may live and not die. But do not listen to Hezekiah, lest he persuade you, saying, "The LORD will deliver us." 33 Has any of the gods of the nations at all delivered its land from the hand of the king of Assyria? 34 Where *are* the gods of Hamath and Arpad? Where *are* the gods of Sepharvaim and Hena and Ivah? Indeed, have they delivered Samaria from my hand? 35 Who among all the gods of the lands have delivered their countries from my hand, that the LORD should deliver Jerusalem from my hand?' "

36 But the people held their peace and answered him not a word; for the king's commandment was, "Do not answer him." 37 Then Eliakim the son of Hilkiah, who *was* over the household, Shebna the scribe, and Joah the son of Asaph, the recorder, came to Hezekiah with *their* clothes torn, and told him the words of *the* Rabshakeh.

19 And so it was, when King Hezekiah heard *it*, that he tore his clothes, covered himself with sackcloth, and went into the house of the LORD. 2 Then he sent Eliakim, who *was* over the household, Shebna the scribe, and the elders of the priests, covered with sackcloth, to Isaiah the prophet, the son of Amoz. 3 And they said to him, "Thus says Hezekiah: 'This day *is* a day of trouble, and rebuke, and blasphemy; for the children have come to birth, but *there is* no strength to bring them forth. 4 It may be that the LORD your God will hear all the words of *the* Rabshakeh, whom his master the king of Assyria has sent to reproach the living God, and will rebuke the words which the LORD your God has heard. Therefore lift up *your* prayer for the remnant that is left.' "

5 So the servants of King Hezekiah came to Isaiah. 6 And Isaiah said to them, "Thus you shall say to your master, 'Thus says the LORD: "Do not be afraid of the words which you have heard, with which the servants

of the king of Assyria have blasphemed Me. 7 Surely I will send a spirit upon him, and he shall hear a rumor and return to his own land; and I will cause him to fall by the sword in his own land." ' "

8 Then *the* Rabshakeh returned and found the king of Assyria warring against Libnah, for he heard that he had departed from Lachish. 9 And the king heard concerning Tirhakah king of Ethiopia, "Look, he has come out to make war with you." So he again sent messengers to Hezekiah, saying, 10 "Thus you shall speak to Hezekiah king of Judah, saying: 'Do not let your God in whom you trust deceive you, saying, "Jerusalem shall not be given into the hand of the king of Assyria." 11 Look! You have heard what the kings of Assyria have done to all lands by utterly destroying them; and shall you be delivered? 12 Have the gods of the nations delivered those whom my fathers have destroyed, Gozan and Haran and Rezeph, and the people of Eden who *were* in Telassar? 13 Where *is* the king of Hamath, the king of Arpad, and the king of the city of Sepharvaim, Hena, and Ivah?' "

14 And Hezekiah received the letter from the hand of the messengers, and read it; and Hezekiah went up to the house of the LORD, and spread it before the LORD. 15 Then Hezekiah prayed before the LORD, and said: "O LORD God of Israel, *the One* who dwells *between* the cherubim, You are God, You alone, of all the kingdoms of the earth. You have made heaven and earth. 16 Incline Your ear, O LORD, and hear; open Your eyes, O LORD, and see; and hear the words of Sennacherib, which he has sent to reproach the living God. 17 Truly, LORD, the kings of Assyria have laid waste the nations and their lands, 18 and have cast their gods into the fire; for they *were* not gods, but the work of men's hands—wood and stone. Therefore they destroyed them. 19 Now therefore, O LORD our God, I pray, save us from his hand, that all the kingdoms of the earth may know that You *are* the LORD God, You alone."

20 Then Isaiah the son of Amoz sent to Hezekiah, saying, "Thus says the LORD God of Israel: 'Because you have prayed to Me against Sen-

nacherib king of Assyria, I have heard.' 21 This *is* the word which the LORD has spoken concerning him:

> 'The virgin, the daughter of
>   Zion,
> Has despised you, laughed you
>   to scorn;
> The daughter of Jerusalem
> Has shaken *her* head behind
>   your back!

22 'Whom have you reproached
>   and blasphemed?
> Against whom have you raised
>   *your* voice,
> And lifted up your eyes on
>   high?
> Against the Holy *One* of Israel.
23 By your messengers you have
>   reproached the Lord,
> And said: "By the multitude of
>   my chariots
> I have come up to the height
>   of the mountains,
> To the limits of Lebanon;
> I will cut down its tall cedars
> *And* its choice cypress trees;
> I will enter the extremity of its
>   borders,
> *To* its fruitful forest.
24 I have dug and drunk strange
>   water,
> And with the soles of my feet I
>   have dried up
> All the brooks of defense."

25 'Did you not hear long ago
> *How* I made it,
> From ancient times that I
>   formed it?
> Now I have brought it to pass,
> That you should be
> For crushing fortified cities *into*
>   heaps of ruins.
26 Therefore their inhabitants had
>   little power;
> They were dismayed and
>   confounded;
> They were *as* the grass of the
>   field
> And the green herb,
> *As* the grass on the housetops
> And *grain* blighted before it is
>   grown.

27 'But I know your dwelling place,
> Your going out and your
>   coming in,
> And your rage against Me.
28 Because your rage against Me
>   and your tumult
> Have come up to My ears,
> Therefore I will put My hook
>   in your nose
> And My bridle in your lips,
> And I will turn you back
> By the way which you came.

29 'This *shall be* a sign to you:

> You shall eat this year such as
>   grows of itself,
> And in the second year what
>   springs from the same;
> Also in the third year sow and
>   reap,
> Plant vineyards and eat the
>   fruit of them.
30 And the remnant who have
>   escaped of the house of
>   Judah
> Shall again take root
>   downward,
> And bear fruit upward.
31 For out of Jerusalem shall go
>   a remnant,
> And those who escape from
>   Mount Zion.
> The zeal of the LORD of hosts[a]
>   will do this.'

32 "Therefore thus says the LORD concerning the king of Assyria:

> 'He shall not come into this city,
> Nor shoot an arrow there,
> Nor come before it with shield,
> Nor build a siege mound
>   against it.
33 By the way that he came,
> By the same shall he return;
> And he shall not come into this
>   city,'
> Says the LORD.
34 'For I will defend this city, to
>   save it
> For My own sake and for My
>   servant David's sake.' "

35 And it came to pass on a certain night that the angel[a] of the LORD went out, and killed in the camp of the Assyrians one hundred and eighty-five thousand; and when *people* arose early in the morning, there were the corpses—all dead. 36 So Sennacherib king of Assyria

---

19:31 [a]Following many Hebrew manuscripts and ancient versions (compare Isaiah 37:32); Masoretic Text omits *of hosts*.   19:35 [a]Or *Angel*

When Faced with a Mountain —Tunnel Underneath

In 721 B.C. the mighty Assyrian empire came marching down on the kingdom of Israel. The Assyrian king, Sennacherib, led his soldiers on a lightning-quick campaign against the fortified cities of Judah. His military strategy was to conquer Galilee and the coastal plains. Once these were controlled, Sennacherib could march on Jerusalem, knowing that all escape routes from the city would be cut off.

When King Hezekiah, the monarch of Jerusalem, saw that Sennacherib was headed toward Jerusalem, he took action. He knew Jerusalem was next. To decide how to defend Jerusalem against this powerful foe, he "took counsel with his leaders and commanders" to preserve the water supply (2 Chr. 32:3).

Second, he fortified the city wall and made an abundance of weapons. Then he set military captains over his people and gave them encouragement of God's presence and support.

Third, God gave him an "impossible" solution to his greatest problem of all—protecting Jerusalem's water source. The only spring providing water for Jerusalem was located outside the city wall at the bottom of a hill. If the Assyrian army cut off the water supply, Jerusalem would fall within a few days.

As the Assyrian army approached, King Hezekiah ordered a tunnel to be dug which would bring water inside the city from outside the wall. One work crew would not have enough time to accomplish this before Sennacherib and his army arrived. To solve this, Hezekiah conceived the impossible: two work crews, one outside and one inside the city walls, would tunnel toward each other. Day and night they worked, cutting through the mountain of solid rock. Winding and twisting, the tunnel became a 1,700-foot-long maze.

Finally, early one morning, just before the Assyrian army crested the hill overlooking Jerusalem, one of the work crews, deep in the bowels of the earth, heard the sounds of the other's pick axes. Miraculously, they had met less than one foot from each other. They had saved the city. Jerusalem withstood the siege and the Assyrian army returned home.

No known mathematical or engineering formula could have accomplished this. The world's greatest archaeologists are still puzzled by this feat.

When faced with a mountain, King Hezekiah prayed and sought counsel and did not quit—he tunneled underneath. Always remember that God can give you, too, creative and unexpected solutions to your obstacles.

departed and went away, returned *home*, and remained at Nineveh. 37 Now it came to pass, as he was worshiping in the temple of Nisroch his god, that his sons Adrammelech and Sharezer struck him down with the sword; and they escaped into the land of Ararat. Then Esarhaddon his son reigned in his place.

20 In those days Hezekiah was sick and near death. And Isaiah the prophet, the son of Amoz, went to him and said to him, "Thus says the LORD: 'Set your house in order, for you shall die, and not live.' "

2 Then he turned his face toward the wall, and prayed to the LORD, saying, 3 "Remember now, O LORD, I pray, how I have walked before You in truth and with a loyal heart, and have done *what was* good in Your sight." And Hezekiah wept bitterly.

4 And it happened, before Isaiah had gone out into the middle court, that the word of the LORD came to him, saying, 5 "Return and tell Hezekiah the leader of My people, 'Thus says the LORD, the God of David your father: "I have heard your prayer, I have seen your tears; surely I will heal you. On the third day you shall go up to the house of the LORD. 6 And I will add to your days fifteen years. I will deliver you and this city from the hand of the king of Assyria; and I will defend this city for My own sake, and for the sake of My servant David." ' "

7 Then Isaiah said, "Take a lump of figs." So they took and laid *it* on the boil, and he recovered.

8 And Hezekiah said to Isaiah, "What *is* the sign that the LORD will heal me, and that I shall go up to the house of the LORD the third day?"

9 Then Isaiah said, "This is the sign to you from the LORD, that the LORD will do the thing which He has spoken: *shall* the shadow go forward ten degrees or go backward ten degrees?"

10 And Hezekiah answered, "It is an easy thing for the shadow to go down ten degrees; no, but let the shadow go backward ten degrees."

11 So Isaiah the prophet cried out to the LORD, and He brought the shadow ten degrees backward, by which it had gone down on the sundial of Ahaz.

12 At that time Berodach-Baladan[a] the son of Baladan, king of Babylon, sent letters and a present to Hezekiah, for he heard that Hezekiah had been sick. 13 And Hezekiah was attentive to them, and showed them all the house of his treasures—the silver and gold, the spices and precious ointment, and all[a] his armory—all that was found among his treasures. There was nothing in his house or in all his dominion that Hezekiah did not show them.

14 Then Isaiah the prophet went to King Hezekiah, and said to him, "What did these men say, and from where did they come to you?"

So Hezekiah said, "They came from a far country, from Babylon."

15 And he said, "What have they seen in your house?"

So Hezekiah answered, "They have seen all that *is* in my house; there is nothing among my treasures that I have not shown them."

16 Then Isaiah said to Hezekiah, "Hear the word of the LORD: 17 'Behold, the days are coming when all that *is* in your house, and what your fathers have accumulated until this day, shall be carried to Babylon; nothing shall be left,' says the LORD. 18 'And they shall take away some of your sons who will descend from you, whom you will beget; and they shall be eunuchs in the palace of the king of Babylon.' "

19 So Hezekiah said to Isaiah, "The word of the LORD which you have spoken *is* good!" For he said, "Will there not be peace and truth at least in my days?"

20 Now the rest of the acts of Hezekiah—all his might, and how he made a pool and a tunnel and brought water into the city—*are* they not written in the book of the chronicles of the kings of Judah? 21 So Hezekiah rested with his fathers. Then Manasseh his son reigned in his place.

21 Manasseh *was* twelve years old when he became king, and he reigned fifty-five years in Jerusalem. His mother's name *was* Hephzibah. 2 And he did evil in the sight of the

---

20:12 [a]Spelled *Merodach-Baladan* in Isaiah 39:1 and Targum; Masoretic Text omits *all*.   20:13 [a]Following many Hebrew manuscripts, Syriac,

LORD, according to the abominations of the nations whom the LORD had cast out before the children of Israel. 3 For he rebuilt the high places which Hezekiah his father had destroyed; he raised up altars for Baal, and made a wooden image,[a] as Ahab king of Israel had done; and he worshiped all the host of heaven[b] and served them. 4 He also built altars in the house of the LORD, of which the LORD had said, "In Jerusalem I will put My name." 5 And he built altars for all the host of heaven in the two courts of the house of the LORD. 6 Also he made his son pass through the fire, practiced soothsaying, used witchcraft, and consulted spiritists and mediums. He did much evil in the sight of the LORD, to provoke *Him* to anger. 7 He even set a carved image of Asherah[a] that he had made, in the house of which the LORD had said to David and to Solomon his son, "In this house and in Jerusalem, which I have chosen out of all the tribes of Israel, I will put My name forever; 8 and I will not make the feet of Israel wander anymore from the land which I gave their fathers—only if they are careful to do according to all that I have commanded them, and according to all the law that My servant Moses commanded them." 9 But they paid no attention, and Manasseh seduced them to do more evil than the nations whom the LORD had destroyed before the children of Israel.

10 And the LORD spoke by His servants the prophets, saying, 11 "Because Manasseh king of Judah has done these abominations (he has acted more wickedly than all the Amorites who *were* before him, and has also made Judah sin with his idols), 12 therefore thus says the LORD God of Israel: 'Behold, *I* am bringing *such* calamity upon Jerusalem and Judah, that whoever hears of it, both his ears will tingle. 13 And I will stretch over Jerusalem the measuring line of Samaria and the plummet of the house of Ahab; I will wipe Jerusalem as *one* wipes a dish, wiping *it* and turning *it* upside down. 14 So I will forsake the remnant of My inheritance and deliver them into the hand of their enemies; and they shall become victims of plunder to all their enemies, 15 because they have done evil in My sight, and have provoked Me to anger since the day their fathers came out of Egypt, even to this day.' "

16 Moreover Manasseh shed very much innocent blood, till he had filled Jerusalem from one end to another, besides his sin by which he made Judah sin, in doing evil in the sight of the LORD.

17 Now the rest of the acts of Manasseh—all that he did, and the sin that he committed—*are* they not written in the book of the chronicles of the kings of Judah? 18 So Manasseh rested with his fathers, and was buried in the garden of his own house, in the garden of Uzza. Then his son Amon reigned in his place.

19 Amon *was* twenty-two years old when he became king, and he reigned two years in Jerusalem. His mother's name *was* Meshullemeth the daughter of Haruz of Jotbah. 20 And he did evil in the sight of the LORD, as his father Manasseh had done. 21 So he walked in all the ways that his father had walked; and he served the idols that his father had served, and worshiped them. 22 He forsook the LORD God of his fathers, and did not walk in the way of the LORD.

23 Then the servants of Amon conspired against him, and killed the king in his own house. 24 But the people of the land executed all those who had conspired against King Amon. Then the people of the land made his son Josiah king in his place.

25 Now the rest of the acts of Amon which he did, *are* they not written in the book of the chronicles of the kings of Judah? 26 And he was buried in his tomb in the garden of Uzza. Then Josiah his son reigned in his place.

22 Josiah *was* eight years old when he became king, and he reigned thirty-one years in Jerusalem. His mother's name *was* Jedidah the daughter of Adaiah of Bozkath. 2 And he did *what was* right in the sight of the LORD, and walked in all the ways of his father David; he did not turn aside to the right hand or to the left.

21:3 [a]Hebrew *Asherah*, a Canaanite goddess   [b]The gods of the Assyrians   21:7 [a]A Canaanite goddess

3 Now it came to pass, in the eighteenth year of King Josiah, *that* the king sent Shaphan the scribe, the son of Azaliah, the son of Meshullam, to the house of the LORD, saying: 4 "Go up to Hilkiah the high priest, that he may count the money which has been brought into the house of the LORD, which the doorkeepers have gathered from the people. 5 And let them deliver it into the hand of those doing the work, who are the overseers in the house of the LORD; let them give it to those who *are* in the house of the LORD doing the work, to repair the damages of the house— 6 to carpenters and builders and masons—and to buy timber and hewn stone to repair the house. 7 However there need be no accounting made with them of the money delivered into their hand, because they deal faithfully."

8 Then Hilkiah the high priest said to Shaphan the scribe, "I have found the Book of the Law in the house of the LORD." And Hilkiah gave the book to Shaphan, and he read it. 9 So Shaphan the scribe went to the king, bringing the king word, saying, "Your servants have gathered the money that was found in the house, and have delivered it into the hand of those who do the work, who oversee the house of the LORD." 10 Then Shaphan the scribe showed the king, saying, "Hilkiah the priest has given me a book." And Shaphan read it before the king.

11 Now it happened, when the king heard the words of the Book of the Law, that he tore his clothes. 12 Then the king commanded Hilkiah the priest, Ahikam the son of Shaphan, Achbor[a] the son of Michaiah, Shaphan the scribe, and Asaiah a servant of the king, saying, 13 "Go, inquire of the LORD for me, for the people and for all Judah, concerning the words of this book that has been found; for great *is* the wrath of the LORD that is aroused against us, because our fathers have not obeyed the words of this book, to do according to all that is written concerning us."

14 So Hilkiah the priest, Ahikam, Achbor, Shaphan, and Asaiah went to Huldah the prophetess, the wife of Shallum the son of Tikvah, the son of Harhas, keeper of the wardrobe. (She dwelt in Jerusalem in the Second Quarter.) And they spoke with her. 15 Then she said to them, "Thus says the LORD God of Israel, 'Tell the man who sent you to Me, 16 "Thus says the LORD: 'Behold, I will bring calamity on this place and on its inhabitants—all the words of the book which the king of Judah has read— 17 because they have forsaken Me and burned incense to other gods, that they might provoke Me to anger with all the works of their hands. Therefore My wrath shall be aroused against this place and shall not be quenched.' " ' 18 But as for the king of Judah, who sent you to inquire of the LORD, in this manner you shall speak to him, 'Thus says the LORD God of Israel: "*Concerning* the words which you have heard— 19 because your heart was tender, and you humbled yourself before the LORD when you heard what I spoke against this place and against its inhabitants, that they would become a desolation and a curse, and you tore your clothes and wept before Me, I also have heard *you*," says the LORD. 20 Surely, therefore, I will gather you to your fathers, and you shall be gathered to your grave in peace; and your eyes shall not see all the calamity which I will bring on this place." ' " So they brought back word to the king.

23 Now the king sent them to gather all the elders of Judah and Jerusalem to him. 2 The king went up to the house of the LORD with all the men of Judah, and with him all the inhabitants of Jerusalem—the priests and the prophets and all the people, both small and great. And he read in their hearing all the words of the Book of the Covenant which had been found in the house of the LORD.

3 Then the king stood by a pillar and made a covenant before the LORD, to follow the LORD and to keep His commandments and His testimonies and His statutes, with all *his* heart and all *his* soul, to perform the words of this covenant that were written in this book. And all the people took a stand for the covenant. 4 And the king commanded Hilkiah the high priest, the priests of the sec-

22:12 *a*Abdon the son of Micah in 2 Chronicles 34:20

ond order, and the doorkeepers, to bring out of the temple of the LORD all the articles that were made for Baal, for Asherah,[a] and for all the host of heaven;[b] and he burned them outside Jerusalem in the fields of Kidron, and carried their ashes to Bethel. 5 Then he removed the idolatrous priests whom the kings of Judah had ordained to burn incense on the high places in the cities of Judah and in the places all around Jerusalem, and those who burned incense to Baal, to the sun, to the moon, to the constellations, and to all the host of heaven. 6 And he brought out the wooden image[a] from the house of the LORD, to the Brook Kidron outside Jerusalem, burned it at the Brook Kidron and ground it to ashes, and threw its ashes on the graves of the common people. 7 Then he tore down the ritual booths of the perverted persons[a] that were in the house of the LORD, where the women wove hangings for the wooden image. 8 And he brought all the priests from the cities of Judah, and defiled the high places where the priests had burned incense, from Geba to Beersheba; also he broke down the high places at the gates which were at the entrance of the Gate of Joshua the governor of the city, which were to the left of the city gate. 9 Nevertheless the priests of the high places did not come up to the altar of the LORD in Jerusalem, but they ate unleavened bread among their brethren.

10 And he defiled Topheth, which is in the Valley of the Son[a] of Hinnom, that no man might make his son or his daughter pass through the fire to Molech. 11 Then he removed the horses that the kings of Judah had dedicated to the sun, at the entrance to the house of the LORD, by the chamber of Nathan-Melech, the officer who was in the court; and he burned the chariots of the sun with fire. 12 The altars that were on the roof, the upper chamber of Ahaz, which the kings of Judah had made, and the altars which Manasseh had made in the two courts of the house of the LORD, the king broke down and pulverized there, and threw

their dust into the Brook Kidron. 13 Then the king defiled the high places that were east of Jerusalem, which were on the south of the Mount of Corruption, which Solomon king of Israel had built for Ashtoreth the abomination of the Sidonians, for Chemosh the abomination of the Moabites, and for Milcom the abomination of the people of Ammon. 14 And he broke in pieces the sacred pillars and cut down the wooden images, and filled their places with the bones of men.

15 Moreover the altar that was at Bethel, and the high place which Jeroboam the son of Nebat, who made Israel sin, had made, both that altar and the high place he broke down; and he burned the high place and crushed it to powder, and burned the wooden image. 16 As Josiah turned, he saw the tombs that were there on the mountain. And he sent and took the bones out of the tombs and burned them on the altar, and defiled it according to the word of the LORD which the man of God proclaimed, who proclaimed these words. 17 Then he said, "What gravestone is this that I see?"

So the men of the city told him, "It is the tomb of the man of God who came from Judah and proclaimed these things which you have done against the altar of Bethel."

18 And he said, "Let him alone; let no one move his bones." So they let his bones alone, with the bones of the prophet who came from Samaria.

19 Now Josiah also took away all the shrines of the high places that were in the cities of Samaria, which the kings of Israel had made to provoke the LORD[a] to anger; and he did to them according to all the deeds he had done in Bethel. 20 He executed all the priests of the high places who were there, on the altars, and burned men's bones on them; and he returned to Jerusalem.

21 Then the king commanded all the people, saying, "Keep the Passover to the LORD your God, as it is written in this Book of the Covenant." 22 Such a Passover surely had never been held since the days of the judges who judged Israel, nor in all

23:4 [a]A Canaanite goddess [b]The gods of the Assyrians   23:6 [a]Hebrew Asherah, a Canaanite goddess   23:7 [a]Hebrew qedeshim, that is, those practicing sodomy and prostitution in religious rituals   23:10 [a]Kethib reads Sons.   23:19 [a]Following Septuagint, Syriac, and Vulgate; Masoretic Text and Targum omit the LORD.

the days of the kings of Israel and the kings of Judah. 23 But in the eighteenth year of King Josiah this Passover was held before the LORD in Jerusalem. 24 Moreover Josiah put away those who consulted mediums and spiritists, the household gods and idols, all the abominations that were seen in the land of Judah and in Jerusalem, that he might perform the words of the law which were written in the book that Hilkiah the priest found in the house of the LORD. 25 Now before him there was no king like him, who turned to the LORD with all his heart, with all his soul, and with all his might, according to all the Law of Moses; nor after him did *any* arise like him.

26 Nevertheless the LORD did not turn from the fierceness of His great wrath, with which His anger was aroused against Judah, because of all the provocations with which Manasseh had provoked Him. 27 And the LORD said, "I will also remove Judah from My sight, as I have removed Israel, and will cast off this city Jerusalem which I have chosen, and the house of which I said, 'My name shall be there.' "[a]

28 Now the rest of the acts of Josiah, and all that he did, *are* they not written in the book of the chronicles of the kings of Judah? 29 In his days Pharaoh Necho king of Egypt went to the aid of the king of Assyria, to the River Euphrates; and King Josiah went against him. And *Pharaoh Necho* killed him at Megiddo when he confronted him. 30 Then his servants moved his body in a chariot from Megiddo, brought him to Jerusalem, and buried him in his own tomb. And the people of the land took Jehoahaz the son of Josiah, anointed him, and made him king in his father's place.

31 Jehoahaz *was* twenty-three years old when he became king, and he reigned three months in Jerusalem. His mother's name *was* Hamutal the daughter of Jeremiah of Libnah. 32 And he did evil in the sight of the LORD, according to all that his fathers had done. 33 Now Pharaoh Necho put him in prison at Riblah in the land of Hamath, that he might not reign in Jerusalem; and he imposed on the land a tribute of one hundred talents of silver and a talent of gold.

34 Then Pharaoh Necho made Eliakim the son of Josiah king in place of his father Josiah, and changed his name to Jehoiakim. And *Pharaoh* took Jehoahaz and went to Egypt, and he[a] died there.

35 So Jehoiakim gave the silver and gold to Pharaoh; but he taxed the land to give money according to the command of Pharaoh; he exacted the silver and gold from the people of the land, from every one according to his assessment, to give *it* to Pharaoh Necho. 36 Jehoiakim *was* twenty-five years old when he became king, and he reigned eleven years in Jerusalem. His mother's name *was* Zebudah the daughter of Pedaiah of Rumah. 37 And he did evil in the sight of the LORD, according to all that his fathers had done.

24 In his days Nebuchadnezzar king of Babylon came up, and Jehoiakim became his vassal *for* three years. Then he turned and rebelled against him. 2 And the LORD sent against him *raiding* bands of Chaldeans, bands of Syrians, bands of Moabites, and bands of the people of Ammon; He sent them against Judah to destroy it, according to the word of the LORD which He had spoken by His servants the prophets. 3 Surely at the commandment of the LORD *this* came upon Judah, to remove *them* from His sight because of the sins of Manasseh, according to all that he had done, 4 and also because of the innocent blood that he had shed; for he had filled Jerusalem with innocent blood, which the LORD would not pardon.

5 Now the rest of the acts of Jehoiakim, and all that he did, *are* they not written in the book of the chronicles of the kings of Judah? 6 So Jehoiakim rested with his fathers. Then Jehoiachin his son reigned in his place.

7 And the king of Egypt did not come out of his land anymore, for the king of Babylon had taken all that belonged to the king of Egypt from the Brook of Egypt to the River Euphrates.

8 Jehoiachin *was* eighteen years old when he became king, and he reigned in Jerusalem three months. His mother's name *was* Nehushta the

daughter of Elnathan of Jerusalem. 9 And he did evil in the sight of the LORD, according to all that his father had done.

10 At that time the servants of Nebuchadnezzar king of Babylon came up against Jerusalem, and the city was besieged. 11 And Nebuchadnezzar king of Babylon came against the city, as his servants were besieging it. 12 Then Jehoiachin king of Judah, his mother, his servants, his princes, and his officers went out to the king of Babylon; and the king of Babylon, in the eighth year of his reign, took him prisoner.

13 And he carried out from there all the treasures of the house of the LORD and the treasures of the king's house, and he cut in pieces all the articles of gold which Solomon king of Israel had made in the temple of the LORD, as the LORD had said. 14 Also he carried into captivity all Jerusalem: all the captains and all the mighty men of valor, ten thousand captives, and all the craftsmen and smiths. None remained except the poorest people of the land. 15 And he carried Jehoiachin captive to Babylon. The king's mother, the king's wives, his officers, and the mighty of the land he carried into captivity from Jerusalem to Babylon. 16 All the valiant men, seven thousand, and craftsmen and smiths, one thousand, all who were strong and fit for war, these the king of Babylon brought captive to Babylon.

17 Then the king of Babylon made Mattaniah, Jehoiachin's^a uncle, king in his place, and changed his name to Zedekiah.

18 Zedekiah was twenty-one years old when he became king, and he reigned eleven years in Jerusalem. His mother's name was Hamutal the daughter of Jeremiah of Libnah. 19 He also did evil in the sight of the LORD, according to all that Jehoiakim had done. 20 For because of the anger of the LORD this happened in Jerusalem and Judah, that He finally cast them out from His presence. Then Zedekiah rebelled against the king of Babylon.

25 Now it came to pass in the ninth year of his reign, in the tenth month, on the tenth day of the month, that Nebuchadnezzar king of Babylon and all his army came against Jerusalem and encamped against it; and they built a siege wall against it all around. 2 So the city was besieged until the eleventh year of King Zedekiah. 3 By the ninth day of the fourth month the famine had become so severe in the city that there was no food for the people of the land.

4 Then the city wall was broken through, and all the men of war fled at night by way of the gate between two walls, which was by the king's garden, even though the Chaldeans were still encamped all around against the city. And the king^a went by way of the plain.^b 5 But the army of the Chaldeans pursued the king, and they overtook him in the plains of Jericho. All his army was scattered from him. 6 So they took the king and brought him up to the king of Babylon at Riblah, and they pronounced judgment on him. 7 Then they killed the sons of Zedekiah before his eyes, put out the eyes of Zedekiah, bound him with bronze fetters, and took him to Babylon.

8 And in the fifth month, on the seventh day of the month (which was the nineteenth year of King Nebuchadnezzar king of Babylon), Nebuzaradan the captain of the guard, a servant of the king of Babylon, came to Jerusalem. 9 He burned the house of the LORD and the king's house; all the houses of Jerusalem, that is, all the houses of the great, he burned with fire. 10 And all the army of the Chaldeans who were with the captain of the guard broke down the walls of Jerusalem all around.

11 Then Nebuzaradan the captain of the guard carried away captive the rest of the people who remained in the city and the defectors who had deserted to the king of Babylon, with the rest of the multitude. 12 But the captain of the guard left some of the poor of the land as vinedressers and farmers. 13 The bronze pillars that were in the house of the LORD, and the carts and the bronze Sea that were in the house of the LORD, the Chaldeans broke in pieces, and carried their bronze to Babylon. 14 They also took away the pots, the

shovels, the trimmers, the spoons, and all the bronze utensils with which the priests ministered. 15 The firepans and the basins, the things of solid gold and solid silver, the captain of the guard took away. 16 The two pillars, one Sea, and the carts, which Solomon had made for the house of the LORD, the bronze of all these articles was beyond measure. 17 The height of one pillar *was* eighteen cubits, and the capital on it *was* of bronze. The height of the capital was three cubits, and the network and pomegranates all around the capital were all of bronze. The second pillar was the same, with a network.

18 And the captain of the guard took Seraiah the chief priest, Zephaniah the second priest, and the three doorkeepers. 19 He also took out of the city an officer who had charge of the men of war, five men of the king's close associates who were found in the city, the chief recruiting officer of the army, who mustered the people of the land, and sixty men of the people of the land *who were* found in the city. 20 So Nebuzaradan, captain of the guard, took these and brought them to the king of Babylon at Riblah. 21 Then the king of Babylon struck them and put them to death at Riblah in the land of Hamath. Thus Judah was carried away captive from its own land.

22 Then he made Gedaliah the son of Ahikam, the son of Shaphan, governor over the people who remained in the land of Judah, whom Nebuchadnezzar king of Babylon had left. 23 Now when all the captains of the armies, they and *their* men, heard that the king of Babylon had made Gedaliah governor, they came to Gedaliah at Mizpah—Ishmael the son of Nethaniah, Johanan the son of Careah, Seraiah the son of Tanhumeth the Netophathite, and Jaazaniah[a] the son of a Maachathite, they and their men. 24 And Gedaliah took an oath before them and their men, and said to them, "Do not be afraid of the servants of the Chaldeans. Dwell in the land and serve the king of Babylon, and it shall be well with you."

25 But it happened in the seventh month that Ishmael the son of Nethaniah, the son of Elishama, of the royal family, came with ten men and struck and killed Gedaliah, the Jews, as well as the Chaldeans who were with him at Mizpah. 26 And all the people, small and great, and the captains of the armies, arose and went to Egypt; for they were afraid of the Chaldeans.

27 Now it came to pass in the thirty-seventh year of the captivity of Jehoiachin king of Judah, in the twelfth month, on the twenty-seventh *day* of the month, *that* Evil-Merodach[a] king of Babylon, in the year that he began to reign, released Jehoiachin king of Judah from prison. 28 He spoke kindly to him, and gave him a more prominent seat than those of the kings who *were* with him in Babylon. 29 So Jehoiachin changed from his prison garments, and he ate bread regularly before the king all the days of his life. 30 And as for his provisions, *there was* a regular ration given him by the king, a portion for each day, all the days of his life.

25:23 aSpelled *Jezaniah* in Jeremiah 40:8   25:27 aLiterally *Man of Marduk*

First Chronicles

Overview of First Chronicles

The Book of First Chronicles is a companion volume to the Books of First and Second Samuel and First and Second Kings. It was most likely compiled by Ezra using public records of the scribes and prophets through the centuries between 1000 and 500 B.C.

Containing a multitude of genealogies, First Chronicles lists the family background of Israel's leaders. Focusing on Saul and David, Chronicles records their rule as Israel's first two kings.

Highlighting the Book of First Chronicles is the reign of King David, who was a just and godly king who fought many wars, gaining victory over the Syrians, Ammonites, and Philistines. David was a powerful personality who instilled courage in his men to fight against insurmountable odds. These soldiers were known as "the mighty men."

David understood the nature of worship. In praising God he said, "O LORD, there is none like You, nor is there any God besides You . . ." (1 Chr. 17:20). He brought the ark of the covenant, which had been removed from its rightful place, back to the tabernacle in Jerusalem. David also organized a large choir and put his beautiful psalms to music.

O LORD, our Lord,
How excellent is Your name in all the earth,
Who have set Your glory above the heavens!
When I consider Your heavens, the work of Your fingers,
The moon and the stars, which You have ordained,
What is man that You are mindful of him,
And the son of man that You visit him?
For You have made him a little lower than the angels,
And You have crowned him with glory and honor.
O LORD, our Lord,
How excellent is Your name in all the earth!

(Ps. 8:1, 3–5, 9)

Finally, although David was not to build the temple, he prepared the hearts of the people for the task. Having accomplished much, David was able to say at the end of his life that he had a dream. He instilled godly motivation and positive thoughts in the people that would last beyond his lifetime! David shared a dream to build a future!

Jesus in First Chronicles

King David is a type of Christ (see the introductions to First and Second Samuel). The covenant that God made with David, first given in Second Samuel, appears again in First Chronicles. Solomon fulfilled the covenant in part, but the everlasting nature of David's throne can only point to the coming of Jesus the Messiah.

Keys to First Chronicles

Key Verses: "And it shall be, when your days are fulfilled, when you must go *to be* with your fathers, that I will set up your seed after you, who will be of your sons; and I will establish his kingdom. He shall build Me a house, and I will establish his throne forever. I will be his Father, and he shall be My son; and I will not take My mercy away from him, as I took *it* from *him* who was before you. And I will establish him in My house and in My kingdom forever; and his throne shall be established forever" (17:11–14).

"Yours, O LORD, *is* the greatness, the power and the glory, the victory and the majesty; for all *that is* in heaven and in earth *is Yours;* Yours is the kingdom, O LORD, and You are exalted as head over all" (29:11).

Key Chapter: First Chronicles 17. Pivotal for this book as well as for the rest of the Scriptures is God's covenant with David. God promises him that his descendant, referring to Jesus, will reign forever.

1 Adam, Seth, Enosh, 2 Cainan,^a Mahalalel, Jared, 3 Enoch, Methuselah, Lamech, 4 Noah,^a Shem, Ham, and Japheth.

5 The sons of Japheth *were* Gomer, Magog, Madai, Javan, Tubal, Meshech, and Tiras. 6 The sons of Gomer *were* Ashkenaz, Diphath,^a and Togarmah. 7 The sons of Javan *were* Elishah, Tarshishah,^a Kittim, and Rodanim.^b

8 The sons of Ham *were* Cush, Mizraim, Put, and Canaan. 9 The sons of Cush *were* Seba, Havilah, Sabta,^a Raama,^b and Sabtecha. The sons of Raama *were* Sheba and Dedan. 10 Cush begot Nimrod; he began to be a mighty one on the earth. 11 Mizraim begot Ludim, Anamim, Lehabim, Naphtuhim, 12 Pathrusim, Casluhim (from whom came the Philistines and the Caphtorim). 13 Canaan begot Sidon, his firstborn, and Heth; 14 the Jebusite, the Amorite, and the Girgashite; 15 the Hivite, the Arkite, and the Sinite; 16 the Arvadite, the Zemarite, and the Hamathite.

17 The sons of Shem *were* Elam, Asshur, Arphaxad, Lud, Aram, Uz, Hul, Gether, and Meshech.^a 18 Arphaxad begot Shelah, and Shelah begot Eber. 19 To Eber were born two sons: the name of one *was* Peleg,^a for in his days the earth was divided; and his brother's name *was* Joktan. 20 Joktan begot Almodad, Sheleph, Hazarmaveth, Jerah, 21 Hadoram, Uzal, Diklah, 22 Ebal,^a Abimael, Sheba, 23 Ophir, Havilah, and Jobab. All these *were* the sons of Joktan.

24 Shem, Arphaxad, Shelah, 25 Eber, Peleg, Reu, 26 Serug, Nahor, Terah, 27 and Abram, who *is* Abraham. 28 The sons of Abraham *were* Isaac and Ishmael.

29 These *are* their genealogies: The firstborn of Ishmael *was* Nebajoth; then Kedar, Adbeel, Mibsam, 30 Mishma, Dumah, Massa, Hadad,^a Tema, 31 Jetur, Naphish, and Kedemah. These *were* the sons of Ishmael.

32 Now the sons born to Keturah, Abraham's concubine, *were* Zimran, Jokshan, Medan, Midian, Ishbak, and Shuah. The sons of Jokshan *were* Sheba and Dedan. 33 The sons of Midian *were* Ephah, Epher, Hanoch, Abida, and Eldaah. All these were the children of Keturah.

34 And Abraham begot Isaac. The sons of Isaac *were* Esau and Israel. 35 The sons of Esau *were* Eliphaz, Reuel, Jeush, Jaalam, and Korah. 36 And the sons of Eliphaz *were* Teman, Omar, Zephi,^a Gatam, *and* Kenaz; and *by* Timna,^b Amalek. 37 The sons of Reuel *were* Nahath, Zerah, Shammah, and Mizzah.

38 The sons of Seir *were* Lotan, Shobal, Zibeon, Anah, Dishon, Ezer, and Dishan. 39 And the sons of Lotan *were* Hori and Homam; Lotan's sister *was* Timna. 40 The sons of Shobal *were* Alian,^a Manahath, Ebal, Shephi,^b and Onam. The sons of Zibeon *were* Ajah and Anah. 41 The son of Anah *was* Dishon. The sons of Dishon *were* Hamran,^a Eshban, Ithran, and Cheran. 42 The sons of Ezer *were* Bilhan, Zaavan, *and* Jaakan.^a The sons of Dishan *were* Uz and Aran.

43 Now these *were* the kings who reigned in the land of Edom before a king reigned over the children of Israel: Bela the son of Beor, and the name of his city was Dinhabah. 44 And when Bela died, Jobab the son of Zerah of Bozrah reigned in his place. 45 When Jobab died, Husham of the land of the Temanites reigned in his place. 46 And when Husham died, Hadad the son of Bedad, who attacked Midian in the field of Moab, reigned in his place. The name of his city *was* Avith. 47 When Hadad died, Samlah of Masrekah reigned in his place. 48 And when Samlah died,

---

1:2 ^aHebrew *Qenan*   1:4 ^aFollowing Masoretic Text and Vulgate; Septuagint adds *the sons of Noah.*
1:6 ^aSpelled *Riphath* in Genesis 10:3   1:7 ^aSpelled *Tarshish* in Genesis 10:4   ^bSpelled *Dodanim* in
Genesis 10:4   1:9 ^aSpelled *Sabtah* in Genesis 10:7   ^bSpelled *Raamah* in Genesis 10:7   1:17 ^aSpelled
Mash in Genesis 10:23   1:19 ^aLiterally *Division*   1:22 ^aSpelled *Obal* in Genesis 10:28   1:30 ^aSpelled
Hadar in Genesis 25:15   1:36 ^aSpelled *Zepho* in Genesis 36:11   ^bCompare Genesis 36:12
1:40 ^aSpelled *Alvan* in Genesis 36:23   ^bSpelled *Shepho* in Genesis 36:23   1:41 ^aSpelled *Hemdan* in
Genesis 36:26   1:42 ^aSpelled *Akan* in Genesis 36:27

Saul of Rehoboth-by-the-River reigned in his place. 49 When Saul died, Baal-Hanan the son of Achbor reigned in his place. 50 And when Baal-Hanan died, Hadad*a* reigned in his place; and the name of his city was Pai.*b* His wife's name was Mehetabel the daughter of Matred, the daughter of Mezahab. 51 Hadad died also. And the chiefs of Edom were Chief Timnah, Chief Aliah,*a* Chief Jetheth, 52 Chief Aholibamah, Chief Elah, Chief Pinon, 53 Chief Kenaz, Chief Teman, Chief Mibzar, 54 Chief Magdiel, and Chief Iram. These *were* the chiefs of Edom.

2 These *were* the sons of Israel: Reuben, Simeon, Levi, Judah, Issachar, Zebulun, 2 Dan, Joseph, Benjamin, Naphtali, Gad, and Asher.

3 The sons of Judah *were* Er, Onan, and Shelah. *These* three were born to him by the daughter of Shua, the Canaanitess. Er, the firstborn of Judah, was wicked in the sight of the LORD; so He killed him. 4 And Tamar, his daughter-in-law, bore him Perez and Zerah. All the sons of Judah *were* five.

5 The sons of Perez *were* Hezron and Hamul. 6 The sons of Zerah *were* Zimri, Ethan, Heman, Calcol, and Dara—five of them in all.

7 The son of Carmi *was* Achar,*a* the troubler of Israel, who transgressed in the accursed thing.

8 The son of Ethan *was* Azariah.

9 Also the sons of Hezron who were born to him *were* Jerahmeel, Ram, and Chelubai.*a* 10 Ram begot Amminadab, and Amminadab begot Nahshon, leader of the children of Judah; 11 Nahshon begot Salma,*a* and Salma begot Boaz; 12 Boaz begot Obed, and Obed begot Jesse; 13 Jesse begot Eliab his firstborn, Abinadab the second, Shimea*a* the third, 14 Nethanel the fourth, Raddai the fifth, 15 Ozem the sixth, *and* David the seventh.

16 Now their sisters *were* Zeruiah and Abigail. And the sons of Zeruiah *were* Abishai, Joab, and Asahel— three. 17 Abigail bore Amasa; and the father of Amasa *was* Jether the Ishmaelite.*a*

18 Caleb the son of Hezron had children by Azubah, *his* wife, and by Jerioth. Now these were her sons: Jesher, Shobab, and Ardon. 19 When Azubah died, Caleb took Ephrath*a* as his wife, who bore him Hur. 20 And Hur begot Uri, and Uri begot Bezalel.

21 Now afterward Hezron went in to the daughter of Machir the father of Gilead, whom he married when he *was* sixty years old; and she bore him Segub. 22 Segub begot Jair, who had twenty-three cities in the land of Gilead. 23 (Geshur and Syria took from them the towns of Jair, with Kenath and its towns—sixty towns.) All these *belonged to* the sons of Machir the father of Gilead. 24 After Hezron died in Caleb Ephrathah, Hezron's wife Abijah bore him Ashhur the father of Tekoa.

25 The sons of Jerahmeel, the firstborn of Hezron, *were* Ram, the firstborn, and Bunah, Oren, Ozem, *and* Ahijah. 26 Jerahmeel had another wife, whose name was Atarah; she was the mother of Onam. 27 The sons of Ram, the firstborn of Jerahmeel, were Maaz, Jamin, and Eker. 28 The sons of Onam were Shammai and Jada. The sons of Shammai *were* Nadab and Abishur.

29 And the name of the wife of Abishur *was* Abihail, and she bore him Ahban and Molid. 30 The sons of Nadab *were* Seled and Appaim; Seled died without children. 31 The son of Appaim *was* Ishi, the son of Ishi *was* Sheshan, and Sheshan's son *was* Ahlai. 32 The sons of Jada, the brother of Shammai, *were* Jether and Jonathan; Jether died without children. 33 The sons of Jonathan *were* Peleth and Zaza. These were the sons of Jerahmeel.

34 Now Sheshan had no sons, only daughters. And Sheshan had an Egyptian servant whose name *was* Jarha. 35 Sheshan gave his daughter to Jarha his servant as wife, and she bore him Attai. 36 Attai begot Nathan, and Nathan begot Zabad; 37 Zabad begot Ephlal, and Ephlal begot Obed; 38 Obed begot Jehu, and Jehu begot Azariah; 39 Azariah begot Helez, and Helez begot Eleasah;

1:50 *a*Spelled *Hadar* in Genesis 36:39   *b*Spelled *Pau* in Genesis 36:39   1:51 *a*Spelled *Alvah* in Genesis 36:40   2:7 *a*Spelled *Achan* in Joshua 7:1 and elsewhere   2:9 *a*Spelled *Caleb* in 2:18, 42
2:11 *a*Spelled *Salmon* in Ruth 4:21 and Luke 3:32   2:13 *a*Spelled *Shammah* in 1 Samuel 16:9 and elsewhere   2:17 *a*Compare 2 Samuel 17:25   2:19 *a*Spelled *Ephrathah* elsewhere

40 Eleasah begot Sismai, and Sismai begot Shallum; 41 Shallum begot Jekamiah, and Jekamiah begot Elishama.

42 The descendants of Caleb the brother of Jerahmeel were Mesha, his firstborn, who was the father of Ziph, and the sons of Mareshah the father of Hebron. 43 The sons of Hebron were Korah, Tappuah, Rekem, and Shema. 44 Shema begot Raham the father of Jorkoam, and Rekem begot Shammai. 45 And the son of Shammai was Maon, and Maon was the father of Beth Zur.

46 Ephah, Caleb's concubine, bore Haran, Moza, and Gazez; and Haran begot Gazez. 47 And the sons of Jahdai were Regem, Jotham, Geshan, Pelet, Ephah, and Shaaph.

48 Maachah, Caleb's concubine, bore Sheber and Tirhanah. 49 She also bore Shaaph the father of Madmannah, Sheva the father of Machbenah and the father of Gibea. And the daughter of Caleb was Achsah.

50 These were the descendants of Caleb: The sons of Hur, the firstborn of Ephrathah, were Shobal the father of Kirjath Jearim, 51 Salma the father of Bethlehem, and Hareph the father of Beth Gader.

52 And Shobal the father of Kirjath Jearim had descendants: Haroeh, and half of the families of Manuhoth.ª 53 The families of Kirjath Jearim were the Ithrites, the Puthites, the Shumathites, and the Mishraites. From these came the Zorathites and the Eshtaolites.

54 The sons of Salma were Bethlehem, the Netophathites, Atroth Beth Joab, half of the Manahethites, and the Zorites.

55 And the families of the scribes who dwelt at Jabez were the Tirathites, the Shimeathites, and the Suchathites. These were the Kenites who came from Hammath, the father of the house of Rechab.

3 Now these were the sons of David who were born to him in Hebron: The firstborn was Amnon, by Ahinoam the Jezreelitess; the second, Daniel,ª by Abigail the Carmelitess; 2 the third, Absalom the son of Maacah, the daughter of Talmai, king of Geshur; the fourth, Adonijah the son of Haggith; 3 the fifth, Shephatiah, by Abital; the sixth, Ithream, by his wife Eglah.

4 These six were born to him in Hebron. There he reigned seven years and six months, and in Jerusalem he reigned thirty-three years. 5 And these were born to him in Jerusalem: Shimea,ª Shobab, Nathan, and Solomon—four by Bathshuab the daughter of Ammiel.c 6 Also there were Ibhar, Elishama,ª Eliphelet,b 7 Nogah, Nepheg, Japhia, 8 Elishama, Eliada,ª and Eliphelet—nine in all. 9 These were all the sons of David, besides the sons of the concubines, and Tamar their sister.

10 Solomon's son was Rehoboam; Abijahª was his son, Asa his son, Jehoshaphat his son, 11 Joramª his son, Ahaziah his son, Joashb his son, 12 Amaziah his son, Azariahª his son, Jotham his son, 13 Ahaz his son, Hezekiah his son, Manasseh his son, 14 Amon his son, and Josiah his son. 15 The sons of Josiah were Johanan the firstborn, the second Jehoiakim, the third Zedekiah, and the fourth Shallum.ª 16 The sons of Jehoiakim were Jeconiah his son and Zedekiahª his son.

17 And the sons of Jeconiahª were Assir,b Shealtiel his son, 18 and Malchiram, Pedaiah, Shenazzar, Jecamiah, Hoshama, and Nedabiah. 19 The sons of Pedaiah were Zerubbabel and Shimei. The sons of Zerubbabel were Meshullam, Hananiah, Shelomith their sister, 20 and Hashubah, Ohel, Berechiah, Hasadiah, and Jushab-Hesed—five in all.

21 The sons of Hananiah were Pelatiah and Jeshaiah, the sons of Rephaiah, the sons of Arnan, the sons of Obadiah, and the sons of Shechaniah. 22 The son of Shechaniah was Shemaiah. The sons of Shemaiah were Hattush, Igal, Bariah, Neariah, and Shaphat—six in all. 23 The sons of Neariah were Elioenai, Hezekiah,

---

2:52 ªSame as the Manahethites, verse 54   3:1 ªCalled Chileab in 2 Samuel 3:3   3:5 ªSpelled Shammua in 14:4 and 2 Samuel 5:14   bSpelled Bathsheba in 2 Samuel 11:3   cCalled Eliam in 2 Samuel 11:3   3:6 ªSpelled Elishua in 14:5 and 2 Samuel 5:15   bSpelled Elpelet in 14:5   3:8 ªSpelled Beeliada in 14:7   3:10 ªSpelled Abijam in 1 Kings 15:1   3:11 ªSpelled Jehoram in 2 Kings 1:17 and 8:16   bSpelled Jehoash in 2 Kings 12:1   3:12 ªCalled Uzziah in Isaiah 6:1   3:15 ªCalled Jehoahaz in 2 Kings 23:31   3:16 ªCompare 2 Kings 24:17   3:17 ªAlso called Coniah in Jeremiah 22:24 and Jehoiachin in 2 Kings 24:8   bOr the captive were and Azrikam—three *in all.* 24 The sons of Elioenai *were* Hodaviah, Eliashib, Pelaiah, Akkub, Johanan, Delaiah, and Anani—seven *in all.*

4 The sons of Judah *were* Perez, Hezron, Carmi, Hur, and Shobal. 2 And Reaiah the son of Shobal begot Jahath, and Jahath begot Ahumai and Lahad. These *were* the families of the Zorathites. 3 These *were* the sons of *the father* of Etam: Jezreel, Ishma, and Idbash; and the name of their sister *was* Hazelelponi; 4 and Penuel *was* the father of Gedor, and Ezer *was the* father of Hushah.

These *were* the sons of Hur, the firstborn of Ephrathah the father of Bethlehem.

5 And Ashhur the father of Tekoa had two wives, Helah and Naarah. 6 Naarah bore him Ahuzzam, Hepher, Temeni, and Haahashtari. These *were* the sons of Naarah. 7 The sons of Helah *were* Zereth, Zohar, and Ethnan; 8 and Koz begot Anub, Zobebah, and the families of Aharhel the son of Harum.

9 Now Jabez was more honorable than his brothers, and his mother called his name Jabez,[a] saying, "Because I bore *him* in pain." 10 And Jabez called on the God of Israel saying, "Oh, that You would bless me indeed, and enlarge my territory, that Your hand would be with me, and that You would keep *me* from evil, that I may not cause pain!" So God granted him what he requested.

11 Chelub the brother of Shuhah begot Mehir, who *was* the father of Eshton. 12 And Eshton begot Beth-Rapha, Paseah, and Tehinnah the father of Ir-Nahash. These *were* the men of Rechah.

13 The sons of Kenaz *were* Othniel and Seraiah. The sons of Othniel *were* Hathath,[a] 14 and Meonothai who begot Ophrah. Seraiah begot Joab the father of Ge Harashim,[a] for they were craftsmen. 15 The sons of Caleb the son of Jephunneh *were* Iru, Elah, and Naam. The son of Elah *was* Kenaz. 16 The sons of Jehallelel *were* Ziph, Ziphah, Tiria, and Asarel. 17 The sons of Ezrah *were* Jether, Mered, Epher, and Jalon. And

Mered's wife[a] bore Miriam, Shammai, and Ishbah the father of Eshtemoa. 18 (His wife Jehudijah[a] bore Jered the father of Gedor, Heber the father of Sochoh, and Jekuthiel the father of Zanoah.) And these were the sons of Bithiah the daughter of Pharaoh, whom Mered took.

19 The sons of Hodiah's wife, the sister of Naham, *were* the fathers of Keilah the Garmite and of Eshtemoa the Maachathite. 20 And the sons of Shimon *were* Amnon, Rinnah, Ben-Hanan, and Tilon. And the sons of Ishi *were* Zoheth and Ben-Zoheth.

21 The sons of Shelah the son of Judah *were* Er the father of Lecah, Laadah the father of Mareshah, and the families of the house of the linen workers of the house of Ashbea; 22 also Jokim, the men of Chozeba, and Joash; Saraph, who ruled in Moab, and Jashubi-Lehem. Now the records are ancient. 23 These *were* the potters and those who dwell at Netaim[a] and Gederah;[b] there they dwelt with the king for his work.

24 The sons of Simeon *were* Nemuel, Jamin, Jarib,[a] Zerah,[b] *and* Shaul, 25 Shallum his son, Mibsam his son, and Mishma his son. 26 And the sons of Mishma *were* Hamuel his son, Zacchur his son, and Shimei his son. 27 Shimei had sixteen sons and six daughters; but his brothers did not have many children, nor did any of their families multiply as much as the children of Judah.

28 They dwelt at Beersheba, Moladah, Hazar Shual, 29 Bilhah, Ezem, Tolad, 30 Bethuel, Hormah, Ziklag, 31 Beth Marcaboth, Hazar Susim, Beth Biri, and at Shaaraim. These *were* their cities until the reign of David. 32 And their villages *were* Etam, Ain, Rimmon, Tochen, and Ashan— five cities— 33 and all the villages that *were* around these cities as far as Baal.[a] These *were* their dwelling places, and they maintained their genealogy: 34 Meshobab, Jamlech, and Joshah the son of Amaziah; 35 Joel, and Jehu the son of Joshibiah, the son of Seraiah, the son of Asiel; 36 Elioenai, Jaakobah, Jeshohaiah, Asaiah, Adiel, Jesimiel, and Benaiah; 37 Ziza the son of Shiphi,

---

4:9 [a]Literally *He Will Cause Pain*   4:13 [a]Septuagint and Vulgate add *and Meonothai.*   4:14 [a]Literally *Valley of Craftsmen*   4:17 [a]Literally *she*   4:18 [a]Or *His Judean wife*   4:23 [a]Literally *Plants*   [b]Literally *Hedges*   4:24 [a]Called *Jachin* in Genesis 46:10   [b]Called *Zohar* in Genesis 46:10   4:33 [a]Or *Baalath Beer* (compare Joshua 19:8) the son of Allon, the son of Jedaiah, the son of Shimri, the son of Shemaiah— 38 these mentioned by name *were* leaders in their families, and their father's house increased greatly.

39 So they went to the entrance of Gedor, as far as the east side of the valley, to seek pasture for their flocks. 40 And they found rich, good pasture, and the land *was* broad, quiet, and peaceful; for some Hamites formerly lived there.

41 These recorded by name came in the days of Hezekiah king of Judah; and they attacked their tents and the Meunites who were found there, and utterly destroyed them, as it is to this day. So they dwelt in their place, because *there was* pasture for their flocks there. 42 Now *some* of them, five hundred men of the sons of Simeon, went to Mount Seir, having as their captains Pelatiah, Neariah, Rephaiah, and Uzziel, the sons of Ishi. 43 And they defeated the rest of the Amalekites who had escaped. They have dwelt there to this day.

5 Now the sons of Reuben the firstborn of Israel—he *was* indeed the firstborn, but because he defiled his father's bed, his birthright was given to the sons of Joseph, the son of Israel, so that the genealogy is not listed according to the birthright; 2 yet Judah prevailed over his brothers, and from him *came* a ruler, although the birthright was Joseph's— 3 the sons of Reuben the firstborn of Israel were Hanoch, Pallu, Hezron, and Carmi.

4 The sons of Joel *were* Shemaiah his son, Gog his son, Shimei his son, 5 Micah his son, Reaiah his son, Baal his son, 6 and Beerah his son, whom Tiglath-Pileser[a] king of Assyria carried into captivity. He *was* leader of the Reubenites. 7 And his brethren by their families, when the genealogy of their generations was registered: the chief, Jeiel, and Zechariah, 8 and Bela the son of Azaz, the son of Shema, the son of Joel, who dwelt in Aroer, as far as Nebo and Baal Meon. 9 Eastward they settled as far as the entrance of the wilderness this side of the River Euphrates, because their cattle had multiplied in the land of Gilead.

10 Now in the days of Saul they made war with the Hagrites, who fell by their hand; and they dwelt in their tents throughout the entire *area* east of Gilead.

11 And the children of Gad dwelt next to them in the land of Bashan as far as Salcah: 12 Joel *was* the chief, Shapham the next, then Jaanai and Shaphat in Bashan, 13 and their brethren of their father's house: Michael, Meshullam, Sheba, Jorai, Jachan, Zia, and Eber—seven *in all.* 14 These *were* the children of Abihail the son of Huri, the son of Jaroah, the son of Gilead, the son of Michael, the son of Jeshishai, the son of Jahdo, the son of Buz; 15 Ahi the son of Abdiel, the son of Guni, *was* chief of their father's house. 16 And *the Gadites* dwelt in Gilead, in Bashan and in its villages, and in all the common-lands of Sharon within their borders. 17 All these were registered by genealogies in the days of Jotham king of Judah, and in the days of Jeroboam king of Israel.

18 The sons of Reuben, the Gadites, and half the tribe of Manasseh *had* forty-four thousand seven hundred and sixty valiant men, men able to bear shield and sword, to shoot with the bow, and skillful in war, who went to war. 19 They made war with the Hagrites, Jetur, Naphish, and Nodab. 20 And they were helped against them, and the Hagrites were delivered into their hand, and all who *were* with them, for they cried out to God in the battle. He heeded their prayer, because they put their trust in Him. 21 Then they took away their livestock—fifty thousand of their camels, two hundred and fifty thousand of their sheep, and two thousand of their donkeys—also one hundred thousand of their men; 22 for many fell dead, because the war *was* God's. And they dwelt in their place until the captivity.

23 So the children of the half-tribe of Manasseh dwelt in the land. Their *numbers* increased from Bashan to Baal Hermon, that is, to Senir, or Mount Hermon. 24 These *were* the heads of their fathers' houses: Epher, Ishi, Eliel, Azriel, Jeremiah, Hodaviah, and Jahdiel. They were mighty men of valor, famous men, *and* heads of their fathers' houses.

5:6 [a]Hebrew *Tilgath-Pilneser*

25 And they were unfaithful to the God of their fathers, and played the harlot after the gods of the peoples of the land, whom God had destroyed before them. 26 So the God of Israel stirred up the spirit of Pul king of Assyria, that is, Tiglath-Pileser[a] king of Assyria. He carried the Reubenites, the Gadites, and the half-tribe of Manasseh into captivity. He took them to Halah, Habor, Hara, and the river of Gozan to this day.

6 The sons of Levi were Gershon, Kohath, and Merari. 2 The sons of Kohath were Amram, Izhar, Hebron, and Uzziel. 3 The children of Amram were Aaron, Moses, and Miriam. And the sons of Aaron were Nadab, Abihu, Eleazar, and Ithamar. 4 Eleazar begot Phinehas, and Phinehas begot Abishua; 5 Abishua begot Bukki, and Bukki begot Uzzi; 6 Uzzi begot Zerahiah, and Zerahiah begot Meraioth; 7 Meraioth begot Amariah, and Amariah begot Ahitub; 8 Ahitub begot Zadok, and Zadok begot Ahimaaz; 9 Ahimaaz begot Azariah, and Azariah begot Johanan; 10 Johanan begot Azariah (it was he who ministered as priest in the temple that Solomon built in Jerusalem); 11 Azariah begot Amariah, and Amariah begot Ahitub; 12 Ahitub begot Zadok, and Zadok begot Shallum; 13 Shallum begot Hilkiah, and Hilkiah begot Azariah; 14 Azariah begot Seraiah, and Seraiah begot Jehozadak. 15 Jehozadak went into captivity when the LORD carried Judah and Jerusalem into captivity by the hand of Nebuchadnezzar.

16 The sons of Levi were Gershon,[a] Kohath, and Merari. 17 These are the names of the sons of Gershon: Libni and Shimei. 18 The sons of Kohath were Amram, Izhar, Hebron, and Uzziel. 19 The sons of Merari were Mahli and Mushi. Now these are the families of the Levites according to their fathers: 20 Of Gershon were Libni his son, Jahath his son, Zimmah his son, 21 Joah his son, Iddo his son, Zerah his son, and Jeatherai his son. 22 The sons of Kohath were Amminadab his son, Korah his son,

Assir his son, 23 Elkanah his son, Ebiasaph his son, Assir his son, 24 Tahath his son, Uriel his son, Uzziah his son, and Shaul his son. 25 The sons of Elkanah were Amasai and Ahimoth. 26 As for Elkanah,[a] the sons of Elkanah were Zophai[b] his son, Nahath[c] his son, 27 Eliab[a] his son, Jeroham his son, and Elkanah his son. 28 The sons of Samuel were Joel[a] the firstborn, and Abijah the second.[b] 29 The sons of Merari were Mahli, Libni his son, Shimei his son, Uzzah his son, 30 Shimea his son, Haggiah his son, and Asaiah his son.

31 Now these are the men whom David appointed over the service of song in the house of the LORD, after the ark came to rest. 32 They were ministering with music before the dwelling place of the tabernacle of meeting, until Solomon had built the house of the LORD in Jerusalem, and they served in their office according to their order.

33 And these are the ones who ministered with their sons: Of the sons of the Kohathites were Heman the singer, the son of Joel, the son of Samuel, 34 the son of Elkanah, the son of Jeroham, the son of Eliel,[a] the son of Toah,[b] 35 the son of Zuph, the son of Elkanah, the son of Mahath, the son of Amasai, 36 the son of Elkanah, the son of Joel, the son of Azariah, the son of Zephaniah, 37 the son of Tahath, the son of Assir, the son of Ebiasaph, the son of Korah, 38 the son of Izhar, the son of Kohath, the son of Levi, the son of Israel. 39 And his brother Asaph, who stood at his right hand, was Asaph the son of Berachiah, the son of Shimea, 40 the son of Michael, the son of Baaseiah, the son of Malchijah, 41 the son of Ethni, the son of Zerah, the son of Adaiah, 42 the son of Ethan, the son of Zimmah, the son of Shimei, 43 the son of Jahath, the son of Gershon, the son of Levi.

44 Their brethren, the sons of Merari, on the left hand, were Ethan the son of Kishi, the son of Abdi, the son of Malluch, 45 the son of Hashabiah, the son of Amaziah, the son of Hilkiah, 46 the son of Amzi, the son of

---

5:26 [a]Hebrew *Tilgath-Pilneser*   6:16 [a]Hebrew *Gershom* (alternate spelling of *Gershon*, as in verses 1, 17, 20, 43, 62, and 71)   6:26 [a]Compare verse 35   [b]Spelled *Zuph* in verse 35 and 1 Samuel 1:1   [c]Compare verse 34   6:27 [a]Compare verse 34   6:28 [a]Following Septuagint, Syriac, and Arabic (compare verse 33 and 1 Samuel 8:2)   [b]Hebrew *Vasheni*   6:34 [a]Spelled *Elihu* in 1 Samuel 1:1   [b]Spelled *Tohu* in 1 Samuel 1:1

Bani, the son of Shamer, 47 the son of Mahli, the son of Mushi, the son of Merari, the son of Levi.

48 And their brethren, the Levites, *were* appointed to every kind of service of the tabernacle of the house of God.

49 But Aaron and his sons offered sacrifices on the altar of burnt offering and on the altar of incense, for all the work of the Most Holy *Place,* and to make atonement for Israel, according to all that Moses the servant of God had commanded. 50 Now these *are* the sons of Aaron: Eleazar his son, Phinehas his son, Abishua his son, 51 Bukki his son, Uzzi his son, Zerahiah his son, 52 Meraioth his son, Amariah his son, Ahitub his son, 53 Zadok his son, *and* Ahimaaz his son.

54 Now these *are* their dwelling places throughout their settlements in their territory, for they were *given* by lot to the sons of Aaron, of the family of the Kohathites: 55 They gave them Hebron in the land of Judah, with its surrounding commonlands. 56 But the fields of the city and its villages they gave to Caleb the son of Jephunneh. 57 And to the sons of Aaron they gave *one of* the cities of refuge, Hebron; also Libnah with its common-lands, Jattir, Eshtemoa with its common-lands, 58 Hilen*ᵃ* with its common-lands, Debir with its common-lands, 59 Ashan*ᵃ* with its common-lands, and Beth Shemesh with its common-lands. 60 And from the tribe of Benjamin: Geba with its common-lands, Alemeth*ᵃ* with its common-lands, and Anathoth with its common-lands. All their cities among their families *were* thirteen.

61 To the rest of the family of the tribe of the Kohathites *they gave* by lot ten cities from half the tribe of Manasseh. 62 And to the sons of Gershon, throughout their families, *they gave* thirteen cities from the tribe of Issachar, from the tribe of Asher, from the tribe of Naphtali, and from the tribe of Manasseh in Bashan. 63 To the sons of Merari, throughout their families, *they gave* twelve cities from the tribe of Reuben, from the tribe of Gad, and from the tribe of Zebulun. 64 So the children of Israel gave *these* cities with their common-lands to the Levites. 65 And they gave by lot from the tribe of the children of Judah, from the tribe of the children of Simeon, and from the tribe of the children of Benjamin these cities which are called by *their* names.

66 Now some of the families of the sons of Kohath *were given* cities as their territory from the tribe of Ephraim. 67 And they gave them *one of* the cities of refuge, Shechem with its common-lands, in the mountains of Ephraim, also Gezer with its common-lands, 68 Jokmeam with its common-lands, Beth Horon with its common-lands, 69 Aijalon with its common-lands, and Gath Rimmon with its common-lands. 70 And from the half-tribe of Manasseh: Aner with its common-lands and Bileam with its common-lands, for the rest of the family of the sons of Kohath.

71 From the family of the half-tribe of Manasseh the sons of Gershon *were given* Golan in Bashan with its common-lands and Ashtaroth with its common-lands. 72 And from the tribe of Issachar: Kedesh with its common-lands, Daberath with its common-lands, 73 Ramoth with its common-lands, and Anem with its common-lands. 74 And from the tribe of Asher: Mashal with its common-lands, Abdon with its common-lands, 75 Hukok with its common-lands, and Rehob with its common-lands. 76 And from the tribe of Naphtali: Kedesh in Galilee with its common-lands, Hammon with its common-lands, and Kirjathaim with its common-lands.

77 From the tribe of Zebulun the rest of the children of Merari *were given* Rimmon*ᵃ* with its common-lands and Tabor with its common-lands. 78 And on the other side of the Jordan, across from Jericho, on the east side of the Jordan, *they were given* from the tribe of Reuben: Bezer in the wilderness with its common-lands, Jahzah with its common-lands, 79 Kedemoth with its common-lands, and Mephaath with its common-lands. 80 And from the tribe of Gad: Ramoth in Gilead with its common-lands, Mahanaim with its common-lands, 81 Heshbon with its common-lands, and Jazer with its common-lands.

6:58 ᵃSpelled *Holon* in Joshua 21:15   6:59 ᵃSpelled *Ain* in Joshua 21:16   6:60 ᵃSpelied *Almon* in Joshua 21:18   6:77 ᵃHebrew *Rimmono,* alternate spelling of *Rimmon;* see 4:32

7 The sons of Issachar *were* Tola, Puah,[a] Jashub, and Shimron— four *in all*. 2 The sons of Tola *were* Uzzi, Rephaiah, Jeriel, Jahmai, Jibsam, and Shemuel, heads of their father's house. *The sons* of Tola *were* mighty men of valor in their generations; their number in the days of David *was* twenty-two thousand six hundred. 3 The son of Uzzi *was* Izrahiah, and the sons of Izrahiah *were* Michael, Obadiah, Joel, and Ishiah. All five of them *were* chief men. 4 And with them, by their generations, according to their fathers' houses, *were* thirty-six thousand troops ready for war; for they had many wives and sons.

5 Now their brethren among all the families of Issachar *were* mighty men of valor, listed by their genealogies, eighty-seven thousand in all.

6 *The sons* of Benjamin *were* Bela, Becher, and Jediael—three *in all*. 7 The sons of Bela were Ezbon, Uzzi, Uzziel, Jerimoth, and Iri—five *in all*. They *were* heads of *their* fathers' houses, and they were listed by their genealogies, twenty-two thousand and thirty-four mighty men of valor.

8 The sons of Becher *were* Zemirah, Joash, Eliezer, Elioenai, Omri, Jerimoth, Abijah, Anathoth, and Alemeth. All these *are* the sons of Becher. 9 And they were recorded by genealogy according to their generations, heads of their fathers' houses, twenty thousand two hundred mighty men of valor. 10 The son of Jediael *was* Bilhan, and the sons of Bilhan *were* Jeush, Benjamin, Ehud, Chenaanah, Zethan, Tharshish, and Ahishahar.

11 All these sons of Jediael *were* heads of their fathers' houses; *there were* seventeen thousand two hundred mighty men of valor fit to go out for war *and* battle. 12 Shuppim and Huppim[a] *were* the sons of Ir, *and* Hushim *was* the son of Aher.

13 The sons of Naphtali *were* Jahziel,[a] Guni, Jezer, and Shallum,[b] the sons of Bilhah.

14 The descendants of Manasseh: his Syrian concubine bore him Machir the father of Gilead, the father of Asriel.[a] 15 Machir took as his wife *the sister* of Huppim and Shuppim,[a] whose name *was* Maachah. The name of *Gilead's* grandson[b] *was* Zelophehad,[c] but Zelophehad begot only daughters. 16 (Maachah the wife of Machir bore a son, and she called his name Peresh. The name of his brother *was* Sheresh, and his sons *were* Ulam and Rakem. 17 The son of Ulam *was* Bedan.) These *were* the descendants of Gilead the son of Machir, the son of Manasseh.

18 His sister Hammoleketh bore Ishhod, Abiezer, and Mahlah.

19 And the sons of Shemida *were* Ahian, Shechem, Likhi, and Aniam.

20 The sons of Ephraim *were* Shuthelah, Bered his son, Tahath his son, Eladah his son, Tahath his son, 21 Zabad his son, Shuthelah his son, and Ezer and Elead. The men of Gath who were born in *that* land killed *them* because they came down to take away their cattle. 22 Then Ephraim their father mourned many days, and his brethren came to comfort him.

23 And when he went in to his wife, she conceived and bore a son; and he called his name Beriah,[a] because tragedy had come upon his house. 24 Now his daughter *was* Sheerah, who built Lower and Upper Beth Horon and Uzzen Sheerah; 25 and Rephah *was* his son, *as well as* Resheph, and Telah his son, Tahan his son, 26 Laadan his son, Ammihud his son, Elishama his son, 27 Nun[a] his son, and Joshua his son.

28 Now their possessions and dwelling places *were* Bethel and its towns: to the east Naaran, to the west Gezer and its towns, and Shechem and its towns, as far as Ayyah[a] and its towns; 29 and by the borders of the children of Manasseh *were* Beth Shean and its towns, Taanach and its towns, Megiddo and its towns, Dor and its towns. In these dwelt the children of Joseph, the son of Israel.

30 The sons of Asher *were* Imnah, Ishvah, Ishvi, Beriah, and their sister Serah. 31 The sons of Beriah *were* Heber and Malchiel, who was the father of Birzaith.[a] 32 And Heber begot

7:1 [a]Spelled *Puvah* in Genesis 46:13   7:12 [a]Called *Hupham* in Numbers 26:39   7:13 [a]Spelled *Jahzeel* in Genesis 46:24   [b]Spelled *Shillem* in Genesis 46:24   7:14 [a]The son of Gilead (compare Numbers 26:30, 31)   7:15 [a]Compare verse 12   [b]Literally *the second*   [c]Compare Numbers 26:30–33   7:23 [a]Literally *In Tragedy*   7:27 [a]Hebrew *Non*   7:28 [a]Many Hebrew manuscripts, Bomberg, Septuagint, Targum, and Vulgate read *Gazza*.   7:31 [a]Or *Birzavith* or *Birzoth*

Japhlet, Shomer,*a* Hotham,*b* and their sister Shua. 33 The sons of Japhlet *were* Pasach, Bimhal, and Ashvath. These *were* the children of Japhlet. 34 The sons of Shemer *were* Ahi, Rohgah, Jehubbah, and Aram. 35 And the sons of his brother Helem *were* Zophah, Imna, Shelesh, and Amal. 36 The sons of Zophah *were* Suah, Harnepher, Shual, Beri, Imrah, 37 Bezer, Hod, Shamma, Shilshah, Jithran,*a* and Beera. 38 The sons of Jether *were* Jephunneh, Pispah, and Ara. 39 The sons of Ulla *were* Arah, Haniel, and Rizia.

40 All these *were* the children of Asher, heads of *their* fathers' houses, choice men, mighty men of valor, chief leaders. And they were recorded by genealogies among the army fit for battle; their number *was* twenty-six thousand.

8 Now Benjamin begot Bela his firstborn, Ashbel the second, Aharah*a* the third, 2 Nohah the fourth, and Rapha the fifth. 3 The sons of Bela *were* Addar,*a* Gera, Abihud, 4 Abishua, Naaman, Ahoah, 5 Gera, Shephuphan, and Huram.

6 These *are* the sons of Ehud, who were the heads of the fathers' *houses* of the inhabitants of Geba, and who forced them to move to Manahath: 7 Naaman, Ahijah, and Gera who forced them to move. He begot Uzza and Ahihud.

8 Also Shaharaim had children in the country of Moab, after he had sent away Hushim and Baara his wives. 9 By Hodesh his wife he begot Jobab, Zibia, Mesha, Malcam, 10 Jeuz, Sachiah, and Mirmah. These *were* his sons, heads of their fathers' *houses.*

11 And by Hushim he begot Abitub and Elpaal. 12 The sons of Elpaal *were* Eber, Misham, and Shemed, who built Ono and Lod with its towns; 13 and Beriah and Shema, who *were* heads of their fathers' *houses* of the inhabitants of Aijalon, who drove out the inhabitants of Gath. 14 Ahio, Shashak, Jeremoth, 15 Zebadiah, Arad, Eder, 16 Michael, Ispah, and Joha *were* the sons of Be-

riah. 17 Zebadiah, Meshullam, Hizki, Heber, 18 Ishmerai, Jizliah, and Jobab *were* the sons of Elpaal. 19 Jakim, Zichri, Zabdi, 20 Elienai, Zillethai, Eliel, 21 Adaiah, Beraiah, and Shimrath *were* the sons of Shimei. 22 Ishpan, Eber, Eliel, 23 Abdon, Zichri, Hanan, 24 Hananiah, Elam, Antothijah, 25 Iphdeiah, and Penuel *were* the sons of Shashak. 26 Shamsherai, Shehariah, Athaliah, 27 Jaareshiah, Elijah, and Zichri *were* the sons of Jeroham.

28 These *were* heads of the fathers' *houses* by their generations, chief men. These dwelt in Jerusalem.

29 Now the father of Gibeon, whose wife's name *was* Maacah, dwelt at Gibeon. 30 And his firstborn son *was* Abdon, then Zur, Kish, Baal, Nadab, 31 Gedor, Ahio, Zecher, 32 and Mikloth, *who* begot Shimeah.*a* They also dwelt alongside their relatives in Jerusalem, with their brethren. 33 Ner*a* begot Kish, Kish begot Saul, and Saul begot Jonathan, Malchishua, Abinadab,*b* and Esh-Baal.*c* 34 The son of Jonathan *was* Merib-Baal,*a* and Merib-Baal begot Micah. 35 The sons of Micah *were* Pithon, Melech, Tarea, and Ahaz. 36 And Ahaz begot Jehoaddah;*a* Jehoaddah begot Alemeth, Azmaveth, and Zimri; and Zimri begot Moza. 37 Moza begot Binea, Raphah*a* his son, Eleasah his son, *and* Azel his son.

38 Azel had six sons whose names *were* these: Azrikam, Bocheru, Ishmael, Sheariah, Obadiah, and Hanan. All these *were* the sons of Azel. 39 And the sons of Eshek his brother *were* Ulam his firstborn, Jeush the second, and Eliphelet the third.

40 The sons of Ulam were mighty men of valor—archers. *They* had many sons and grandsons, one hundred and fifty *in all.* These *were* all sons of Benjamin.

9 So all Israel was recorded by genealogies, and, indeed, they *were* inscribed in the book of the kings of Israel. But Judah was carried away captive to Babylon because of their

---

7:32 *a*Spelled *Shemer* in verse 34   *b*Spelled *Helem* in verse 35   7:37 *a*Spelled *Jether* in verse 38
8:1 *a*Spelled *Ahiram* in Numbers 26:38   8:3 *a*Called *Ard* in Numbers 26:40   8:32 *a*Spelled *Shimeam*
in 9:38   8:33 *a*Also the son of Gibeon (compare 9:36, 39)   *b*Called *Jishui* in 1 Samuel 14:49   *c*Called
Ishbosheth in 2 Samuel 2:8 and elsewhere   8:34 *a*Called *Mephibosheth* in 2 Samuel 4:4   8:36 *a*Spelled
Jarah in 9:42   8:37 *a*Spelled *Rephaiah* in 9:43

unfaithfulness. 2 And the first inhabitants who *dwelt* in their possessions in their cities *were* Israelites, priests, Levites, and the Nethinim.

3 Now in Jerusalem the children of Judah dwelt, and some of the children of Benjamin, and of the children of Ephraim and Manasseh: 4 Uthai the son of Ammihud, the son of Omri, the son of Imri, the son of Bani, of the descendants of Perez, the son of Judah. 5 Of the Shilonites: Asaiah the firstborn and his sons. 6 Of the sons of Zerah: Jeuel, and their brethren—six hundred and ninety. 7 Of the sons of Benjamin: Sallu the son of Meshullam, the son of Hodaviah, the son of Hassenuah; 8 Ibneiah the son of Jeroham; Elah the son of Uzzi, the son of Michri; Meshullam the son of Shephatiah, the son of Reuel, the son of Ibnijah; 9 and their brethren, according to their generations—nine hundred and fifty-six. All these men *were* heads of a father's *house* in their fathers' houses.

10 Of the priests: Jedaiah, Jehoiarib, and Jachin; 11 Azariah the son of Hilkiah, the son of Meshullam, the son of Zadok, the son of Meraioth, the son of Ahitub, the officer over the house of God; 12 Adaiah the son of Jeroham, the son of Pashur, the son of Malchijah; Maasai the son of Adiel, the son of Jahzerah, the son of Meshullam, the son of Meshillemith, the son of Immer; 13 and their brethren, heads of their fathers' *houses*—one thousand seven hundred and sixty. *They were* very able men for the work of the service of the house of God.

14 Of the Levites: Shemaiah the son of Hasshub, the son of Azrikam, the son of Hashabiah, of the sons of Merari; 15 Bakbakkar, Heresh, Galal, and Mattaniah the son of Micah, the son of Zichri, the son of Asaph; 16 Obadiah the son of Shemaiah, the son of Galal, the son of Jeduthun; and Berechiah the son of Asa, the son of Elkanah, who lived in the villages of the Netophathites.

17 And the gatekeepers *were* Shallum, Akkub, Talmon, Ahiman, and their brethren. Shallum *was* the chief. 18 Until then *they had been* gatekeepers for the camps of the children of Levi at the King's Gate on the east.

19 Shallum the son of Kore, the son of Ebiasaph, the son of Korah, and his brethren, from his father's house, the Korahites, *were* in charge of the work of the service, gatekeepers of the tabernacle. Their fathers had been keepers of the entrance to the camp of the LORD. 20 And Phinehas the son of Eleazar had been the officer over them in time past; the LORD *was* with him. 21 Zechariah the son of Meshelemiah *was* keeper of the door of the tabernacle of meeting.

22 All those chosen as gatekeepers *were* two hundred and twelve. They were recorded by their genealogy, in their villages. David and Samuel the seer had appointed them to their trusted office. 23 So they and their children *were* in charge of the gates of the house of the LORD, the house of the tabernacle, by assignment. 24 The gatekeepers were assigned to the four directions: the east, west, north, and south. 25 And their brethren in their villages *had* to come with them from time to time for seven days. 26 For in this trusted office *were* four chief gatekeepers; they were Levites. And they had charge over the chambers and treasuries of the house of God. 27 And they lodged *all* around the house of God because they *had* the responsibility, and they *were* in charge of opening *it* every morning.

28 Now *some* of them were in charge of the serving vessels, for they brought them in and took them out by count. 29 *Some* of them *were* appointed over the furnishings and over all the implements of the sanctuary, and over the fine flour and the wine and the oil and the incense and the spices. 30 And *some* of the sons of the priests made the ointment of the spices.

31 Mattithiah of the Levites, the firstborn of Shallum the Korahite, had the trusted office over the things that were baked in the pans. 32 And some of their brethren of the sons of the Kohathites *were* in charge of preparing the showbread for every Sabbath.

33 These are the singers, heads of the fathers' *houses* of the Levites, who *lodged* in the chambers, and *were* free *from other duties;* for they were employed in *that* work day and night. 34 These heads of the fathers' *houses* of the Levites *were* heads throughout their generations. They dwelt at Jerusalem.

35 Jeiel the father of Gibeon, whose wife's name *was* Maacah, dwelt at Gibeon. 36 His firstborn son *was* Abdon, then Zur, Kish, Baal, Ner, Nadab, 37 Gedor, Ahio, Zechariah,[a] and Mikloth. 38 And Mikloth begot Shimeam.[a] They also dwelt alongside their relatives in Jerusalem, with their brethren. 39 Ner begot Kish, Kish begot Saul, and Saul begot Jonathan, Malchishua, Abinadab, and Esh-Baal. 40 The son of Jonathan *was* Merib-Baal, and Merib-Baal begot Micah. 41 The sons of Micah *were* Pithon, Melech, Tahrea,[a] and Ahaz.[b] 42 And Ahaz begot Jarah;[a] Jarah begot Alemeth, Azmaveth, and Zimri; and Zimri begot Moza; 43 Moza begot Binea, Rephaiah[a] his son, Eleasah his son, and Azel his son.

44 And Azel had six sons whose names *were* these: Azrikam, Bocheru, Ishmael, Sheariah, Obadiah, and Hanan; these *were* the sons of Azel.

10 Now the Philistines fought against Israel; and the men of Israel fled from before the Philistines, and fell slain on Mount Gilboa. 2 Then the Philistines followed hard after Saul and his sons. And the Philistines killed Jonathan, Abinadab, and Malchishua, Saul's sons. 3 The battle became fierce against Saul. The archers hit him, and he was wounded by the archers. 4 Then Saul said to his armorbearer, "Draw your sword, and thrust me through with it, lest these uncircumcised men come and abuse me." But his armorbearer would not, for he was greatly afraid. Therefore Saul took a sword and fell on it. 5 And when his armorbearer saw that Saul was dead, he also fell on his sword and died. 6 So Saul and his three sons died, and all his house died together. 7 And when all the men of Israel who *were* in the valley saw that they had fled and that Saul and his sons were dead, they forsook their cities and fled; then the Philistines came and dwelt in them.

8 So it happened the next day, when the Philistines came to strip the slain, that they found Saul and his sons fallen on Mount Gilboa.

9 And they stripped him and took his head and his armor, and sent word *throughout* the land of the Philistines to proclaim the news *in the temple* of their idols and among the people. 10 Then they put his armor in the temple of their gods, and fastened his head in the temple of Dagon.

11 And when all Jabesh Gilead heard all that the Philistines had done to Saul, 12 all the valiant men arose and took the body of Saul and the bodies of his sons; and they brought them to Jabesh, and buried their bones under the tamarisk tree at Jabesh, and fasted seven days.

13 So Saul died for his unfaithfulness which he had committed against the LORD, because he did not keep the word of the LORD, and also because he consulted a medium for guidance. 14 But *he* did not inquire of the LORD; therefore He killed him, and turned the kingdom over to David the son of Jesse.

11 Then all Israel came together to David at Hebron, saying, "Indeed we *are* your bone and your flesh. 2 Also, in time past, even when Saul was king, you *were* the one who led Israel out and brought them in; and the LORD your God said to you, 'You shall shepherd My people Israel, and be ruler over My people Israel.' " 3 Therefore all the elders of Israel came to the king at Hebron, and David made a covenant with them at Hebron before the LORD. And they anointed David king over Israel, according to the word of the LORD by Samuel.

4 And David and all Israel went to Jerusalem, which is Jebus, where the Jebusites *were,* the inhabitants of the land. 5 But the inhabitants of Jebus said to David, "You shall not come in here!" Nevertheless David took the stronghold of Zion (that is, the City of David). 6 Now David said, "Whoever attacks the Jebusites first shall be chief and captain." And Joab the son of Zeruiah went up first, and became chief. 7 Then David dwelt in the stronghold; therefore they called it the City of David. 8 And he built the city around it, from the Millo[a] to the surrounding area. Joab repaired

---

9:37 [a]Called *Zecher* in 8:31   9:38 [a]Spelled *Shimeah* in 8:32   9:41 [a]Spelled *Tarea* in 8:35   [b]Following Arabic, Syriac, Targum, and Vulgate (compare 8:35); Masoretic Text and Septuagint omit *and Ahaz*. 9:42 [a]Spelled *Jehoaddah* in 8:36   9:43 [a]Spelled *Raphah* in 8:37   11:8 [a]Literally *The Landfill* the rest of the city. 9 So David went on and became great, and the LORD of hosts *was* with him.

10 Now these *were* the heads of the mighty men whom David had, who strengthened themselves with him in his kingdom, with all Israel, to make him king, according to the word of the LORD concerning Israel.

11 And this *is* the number of the mighty men whom David had: Jashobeam the son of a Hachmonite, chief of the captains;[a] he had lifted up his spear against three hundred, killed *by him* at one time.

12 After him *was* Eleazar the son of Dodo, the Ahohite, who *was one* of the three mighty men. 13 He was with David at Pasdammim. Now there the Philistines were gathered for battle, and there was a piece of ground full of barley. So the people fled from the Philistines. 14 But they stationed themselves in the middle of *that* field, defended it, and killed the Philistines. So the LORD brought about a great victory.

15 Now three of the thirty chief men went down to the rock to David, into the cave of Adullam; and the army of the Philistines encamped in the Valley of Rephaim. 16 David *was* then in the stronghold, and the garrison of the Philistines *was* then in Bethlehem. 17 And David said with longing, "Oh, that someone would give me a drink of water from the well of Bethlehem, which is by the gate!" 18 So the three broke through the camp of the Philistines, drew water from the well of Bethlehem that *was* by the gate, and took *it* and brought *it* to David. Nevertheless David would not drink it, but poured it out to the LORD. 19 And he said, "Far be it from me, O my God, that I should do this! Shall I drink the blood of these men *who have put* their lives *in jeopardy?* For at the risk of their lives they brought it." Therefore he would not drink it. These things were done by the three mighty men.

20 Abishai the brother of Joab was chief of *another* three.[a] He had lifted up his spear against three hundred *men*, killed *them*, and won a name among *these* three. 21 Of the three he was more honored than the other two men. Therefore he became their captain. However he did not attain to the *first* three.

22 Benaiah was the son of Jehoiada, the son of a valiant man from Kabzeel, who had done many deeds. He had killed two lion-like heroes of Moab. He also had gone down and killed a lion in the midst of a pit on a snowy day. 23 And he killed an Egyptian, a man of *great* height, five cubits tall. In the Egyptian's hand *there was* a spear like a weaver's beam; and he went down to him with a staff, wrested the spear out of the Egyptian's hand, and killed him with his own spear. 24 These *things* Benaiah the son of Jehoiada did, and won a name among three mighty men. 25 Indeed he was more honored than the thirty, but he did not attain to the *first* three. And David appointed him over his guard.

26 Also the mighty warriors *were* Asahel the brother of Joab, Elhanan the son of Dodo of Bethlehem, 27 Shammoth the Harorite,[a] Helez the Pelonite,[b] 28 Ira the son of Ikkesh the Tekoite, Abiezer the Anathothite, 29 Sibbechai the Hushathite, Ilai the Ahohite, 30 Maharai the Netophathite, Heled[a] the son of Baanah the Netophathite, 31 Ithai[a] the son of Ribai of Gibeah, of the sons of Benjamin, Benaiah the Pirathonite, 32 Hurai[a] of the brooks of Gaash, Abiel[b] the Arbathite, 33 Azmaveth the Baharumite,[a] Eliahba the Shaalbonite, 34 the sons of Hashem the Gizonite, Jonathan the son of Shageh the Hararite, 35 Ahiam the son of Sacar the Hararite, Eliphal the son of Ur, 36 Hepher the Mecherathite, Ahijah the Pelonite, 37 Hezro the Carmelite, Naarai the son of Ezbai, 38 Joel the brother of Nathan, Mibhar the son of Hagri, 39 Zelek the Ammonite, Naharai the Berothite[a] (the armorbearer of Joab the son of Zeruiah), 40 Ira the Ithrite, Gareb the Ithrite, 41 Uriah the Hittite, Zabad the son of Ahlai, 42 Adina the son of Shiza the Reubenite (a chief of the Reubenites) and thirty with

---

11:11 [a]Following Qere; Kethib, Septuagint, and Vulgate read *the thirty* (compare 2 Samuel 23:8).
11:20 [a]Following Masoretic Text, Septuagint, and Vulgate; Syriac reads *thirty*.   11:27 [a]Spelled *Harodite* in 2 Samuel 23:25   [b]Called *Paltite* in 2 Samuel 23:26   11:30 [a]Spelled *Heleb* in 2 Samuel 23:29 and *Heldai* in 1 Chronicles 27:15   11:31 [a]Spelled *Ittai* in 2 Samuel 23:29   11:32 [a]Spelled *Hiddai* in 2 Samuel 23:30   [b]Spelled *Abi-Albon* in 2 Samuel 23:31   11:33 [a]Spelled *Barhumite* in 2 Samuel 23:31
11:39 [a]Spelled *Beerothite* in 2 Samuel 23:37

him, 43 Hanan the son of Maachah, Joshaphat the Mithnite, 44 Uzzia the Ashterathite, Shama and Jeiel the sons of Hotham the Aroerite, 45 Jediael the son of Shimri, and Joha his brother, the Tizite, 46 Eliel the Mahavite, Jeribai and Joshaviah the sons of Elnaam, Ithmah the Moabite, 47 Eliel, Obed, and Jaasiel the Mezobaite.

12 Now these *were* the men who came to David at Ziklag while he was still a fugitive from Saul the son of Kish; and they *were* among the mighty men, helpers in the war, 2 armed with bows, using both the right hand and the left in *hurling* stones and *shooting* arrows with the bow. *They were* of Benjamin, Saul's brethren.

3 The chief *was* Ahiezer, then Joash, the sons of Shemaah the Gibeathite; Jeziel and Pelet the sons of Azmaveth; Berachah, and Jehu the Anathothite; 4 Ishmaiah the Gibeonite, a mighty man among the thirty, and over the thirty; Jeremiah, Jahaziel, Johanan, and Jozabad the Gederathite; 5 Eluzai, Jerimoth, Bealiah, Shemariah, and Shephatiah the Haruphite; 6 Elkanah, Jisshiah, Azarel, Joezer, and Jashobeam, the Korahites; 7 and Joelah and Zebadiah the sons of Jeroham of Gedor.

8 *Some* Gadites joined David at the stronghold in the wilderness, mighty men of valor, men trained for battle, who could handle shield and spear, whose faces *were like* the faces of lions, and *were* as swift as gazelles on the mountains: 9 Ezer the first, Obadiah the second, Eliab the third, 10 Mishmannah the fourth, Jeremiah the fifth, 11 Attai the sixth, Eliel the seventh, 12 Johanan the eighth, Elzabad the ninth, 13 Jeremiah the tenth, and Machbanai the eleventh. 14 These *were* from the sons of Gad, captains of the army; the least was over a hundred, and the greatest was over a thousand. 15 These *are* the ones who crossed the Jordan in the first month, when it had overflowed all its banks; and they put to flight all *those* in the valleys, to the east and to the west.

16 Then some of the sons of Benjamin and Judah came to David at the stronghold. 17 And David went out to meet them, and answered and said to them, "If you have come peaceably to me to help me, my heart will be united with you; but if to betray me to my enemies, since *there is* no wrong in my hands, may the God of our fathers look and bring judgment." 18 Then the Spirit came upon Amasai, chief of the captains, *and he said:*

"*We are* yours, O David;
We *are* on your side, O son of Jesse!
Peace, peace to you,
And peace to your helpers!
For your God helps you."

So David received them, and made them captains of the troop.

19 And *some* from Manasseh defected to David when he was going with the Philistines to battle against Saul; but they did not help them, for the lords of the Philistines sent him away by agreement, saying, "He may defect to his master Saul *and endanger* our heads." 20 When he went to Ziklag, those of Manasseh who defected to him were Adnah, Jozabad, Jediael, Michael, Jozabad, Elihu, and Zillethai, captains of the thousands who *were* from Manasseh. 21 And they helped David against the bands *of raiders,* for they *were* all mighty men of valor, and they were captains in the army. 22 For at *that* time they came to David day by day to help him, until *it was* a great army, like the army of God.

23 Now these *were* the numbers of the divisions *that were* equipped for war, *and* came to David at Hebron to turn *over* the kingdom of Saul to him, according to the word of the LORD: 24 of the sons of Judah bearing shield and spear, six thousand eight hundred armed for war; 25 of the sons of Simeon, mighty men of valor fit for war, seven thousand one hundred; 26 of the sons of Levi four thousand six hundred; 27 Jehoiada, the leader of the Aaronites, and with him three thousand seven hundred; 28 Zadok, a young man, a valiant warrior, and from his father's house twenty-two captains; 29 of the sons of Benjamin, relatives of Saul, three thousand (until then the greatest part of them had remained loyal to the house of Saul); 30 of the sons of Ephraim twenty thousand eight hundred, mighty men of valor, famous men throughout their father's house;

31 of the half-tribe of Manasseh eighteen thousand, who were designated by name to come and make David king; 32 of the sons of Issachar who had understanding of the times, to know what Israel ought to do, their chiefs were two hundred; and all their brethren were at their command; 33 of Zebulun there were fifty thousand who went out to battle, expert in war with all weapons of war, stouthearted men who could keep ranks; 34 of Naphtali one thousand captains, and with them thirty-seven thousand with shield and spear; 35 of the Danites who could keep battle formation, twenty-eight thousand six hundred; 36 of Asher, those who could go out to war, able to keep battle formation, forty thousand; 37 of the Reubenites and the Gadites and the half-tribe of Manasseh, from the other side of the Jordan, one hundred and twenty thousand armed for battle with every *kind* of weapon of war.

38 All these men of war, who could keep ranks, came to Hebron with a loyal heart, to make David king over all Israel; and all the rest of Israel *were* of one mind to make David king. 39 And they were there with David three days, eating and drinking, for their brethren had prepared for them. 40 Moreover those who were near to them, from as far away as Issachar and Zebulun and Naphtali, were bringing food on donkeys and camels, on mules and oxen—provisions of flour and cakes of figs and cakes of raisins, wine and oil and oxen and sheep abundantly, for *there was* joy in Israel.

13 Then David consulted with the captains of thousands and hundreds, *and* with every leader. 2 And David said to all the assembly of Israel, "If *it seems* good to you, and if it is of the LORD our God, let us send out to our brethren everywhere *who are* left in all the land of Israel, and with them to the priests and Levites *who are* in their cities *and* their common-lands, that they may gather together to us; 3 and let us bring the ark of our God back to us, for we have not inquired at it since the days of Saul." 4 Then all the

assembly said that they would do so, for the thing was right in the eyes of all the people.

5 So David gathered all Israel together, from Shihor in Egypt to as far as the entrance of Hamath, to bring the ark of God from Kirjath Jearim. 6 And David and all Israel went up to Baalah,*a* to Kirjath Jearim, which belonged to Judah, to bring up from there the ark of God the LORD, who dwells *between* the cherubim, where *His* name is proclaimed. 7 So they carried the ark of God on a new cart from the house of Abinadab, and Uzza and Ahio drove the cart. 8 Then David and all Israel played *music* before God with all *their* might, with singing, on harps, on stringed instruments, on tambourines, on cymbals, and with trumpets.

9 And when they came to Chidon's*a* threshing floor, Uzza put out his hand to hold the ark, for the oxen stumbled. 10 Then the anger of the LORD was aroused against Uzza, and He struck him because he put his hand to the ark; and he died there before God. 11 And David became angry because of the LORD's outbreak against Uzza; therefore that place is called Perez Uzza*a* to this day. 12 David was afraid of God that day, saying, "How can I bring the ark of God to me?"

13 So David would not move the ark with him into the City of David, but took it aside into the house of Obed-Edom the Gittite. 14 The ark of God remained with the family of Obed-Edom in his house three months. And the LORD blessed the house of Obed-Edom and all that he had.

14 Now Hiram king of Tyre sent messengers to David, and cedar trees, with masons and carpenters, to build him a house. 2 So David knew that the LORD had established him as king over Israel, for his kingdom was highly exalted for the sake of His people Israel.

3 Then David took more wives in Jerusalem, and David begot more sons and daughters. 4 And these are the names of his children whom he had in Jerusalem: Shammua,*a* Sho-

13:6 *a*Called *Baale Judah* in 2 Samuel 6:2   13:9 *a*Called *Nachon* in 2 Samuel 6:6   13:11 *a*Literally *Outburst Against Uzza*   14:4 *a*Spelled *Shimea* in 3:5

bab, Nathan, Solomon, 5 Ibhar, Eli-shua,*a* Elpelet,*b* 6 Nogah, Nepheg, Japhia, 7 Elishama, Beeliada,*a* and Eliphelet.

8 Now when the Philistines heard that David had been anointed king over all Israel, all the Philistines went up to search for David. And David heard *of it* and went out against them. 9 Then the Philistines went and made a raid on the Valley of Rephaim. 10 And David inquired of God, saying, "Shall I go up against the Philistines? Will You deliver them into my hand?"

The LORD said to him, "Go up, for I will deliver them into your hand."

11 So they went up to Baal Perazim, and David defeated them there. Then David said, "God has broken through my enemies by my hand like a break-through of water." Therefore they called the name of that place Baal Perazim.*a* 12 And when they left their gods there, David gave a command-ment, and they were burned with fire.

13 Then the Philistines once again made a raid on the valley.

14 Therefore David inquired again of God, and God said to him, "You shall not go up after them; circle around them, and come upon them in front of the mulberry trees. 15 And it shall be, when you hear a sound of march-ing in the tops of the mulberry trees, then you shall go out to battle, for God has gone out before you to strike the camp of the Philistines."

16 So David did as God commanded him, and they drove back the army of the Philistines from Gibeon as far as Gezer. 17 Then the fame of David went out into all lands, and the LORD brought the fear of him upon all nations.

15 *David* built houses for himself in the City of David; and he prepared a place for the ark of God, and pitched a tent for it. 2 Then David said, "No one may carry the ark of God but the Levites, for the LORD has chosen them to carry the ark of God and to minister before Him forever." 3 And David gathered all Israel to-gether at Jerusalem, to bring up the ark of the LORD to its place, which he had prepared for it. 4 Then David assembled the children of Aaron and

the Levites: 5 of the sons of Kohath, Uriel the chief, and one hundred and twenty of his brethren; 6 of the sons of Merari, Asaiah the chief, and two hundred and twenty of his brethren; 7 of the sons of Gershom, Joel the chief, and one hundred and thirty of his brethren; 8 of the sons of Eliza-phan, Shemaiah the chief, and two hundred of his brethren; 9 of the sons of Hebron, Eliel the chief, and eighty of his brethren; 10 of the sons of Uz-ziel, Amminadab the chief, and one hundred and twelve of his brethren.

11 And David called for Zadok and Abiathar the priests, and for the Levites: for Uriel, Asaiah, Joel, Shemaiah, Eliel, and Amminadab. 12 He said to them, "You *are* the heads of the fathers' *houses* of the Levites; sanctify yourselves, you and your brethren, that you may bring up the ark of the LORD God of Israel to *the place* I have prepared for it. 13 For because you *did* not *do it* the first *time*, the LORD our God broke out against us, because we did not consult Him about the proper order."

14 So the priests and the Levites sanctified themselves to bring up the ark of the LORD God of Israel. 15 And the children of the Levites bore the ark of God on their shoul-ders, by its poles, as Moses had com-manded according to the word of the LORD.

16 Then David spoke to the leaders of the Levites to appoint their breth-ren *to be* the singers accompanied by instruments of music, stringed in-struments, harps, and cymbals, by raising the voice with resounding joy. 17 So the Levites appointed He-man the son of Joel; and of his breth-ren, Asaph the son of Berechiah; and of their brethren, the sons of Me-rari, Ethan the son of Kushaiah; 18 and with them their brethren of the second *rank*: Zechariah, Ben,*a* Jaa-ziel, Shemiramoth, Jehiel, Unni, Eliab, Benaiah, Maaseiah, Matti-thiah, Elipheleh, Mikneiah, Obed-Edom, and Jeiel, the gatekeepers; 19 the singers, Heman, Asaph, and Ethan, *were* to sound the cymbals of bronze; 20 Zechariah, Aziel, Shemi-ramoth, Jehiel, Unni, Eliab, Maas-eiah, and Benaiah, with strings ac-cording to Alamoth; 21 Mattithiah, Elipheleh, Mikneiah, Obed-Edom,

---

14:5 *a*Spelled *Elishama* in 3:6   *b*Spelled *Eliphelet* in 3:6   14:7 *a*Spelled *Eliada* in 3:8   14:11 *a*Literally *Master of Breakthroughs*   15:18 *a*Following Masoretic Text and Vulgate; Septuagint omits *Ben*.

Jeiel, and Azaziah, to direct with harps on the Sheminith; 22 Chenaniah, leader of the Levites, was instructor *in charge of* the music, because he *was* skillful; 23 Berechiah and Elkanah *were* doorkeepers for the ark; 24 Shebaniah, Joshaphat, Nethanel, Amasai, Zechariah, Benaiah, and Eliezer, the priests, were to blow the trumpets before the ark of God; and Obed-Edom and Jehiah, doorkeepers for the ark.

25 So David, the elders of Israel, and the captains over thousands went to bring up the ark of the covenant of the LORD from the house of Obed-Edom with joy. 26 And so it was, when God helped the Levites who bore the ark of the covenant of the LORD, that they offered seven bulls and seven rams. 27 David was clothed with a robe of fine linen, as were all the Levites who bore the ark, the singers, and Chenaniah the music master *with* the singers. David also wore a linen ephod. 28 Thus all Israel brought up the ark of the covenant of the LORD with shouting and with the sound of the horn, with trumpets and with cymbals, making music with stringed instruments and harps.

29 And it happened, *as* the ark of the covenant of the LORD came to the City of David, that Michal, Saul's daughter, looked through a window and saw King David whirling and playing music; and she despised him in her heart.

16 So they brought the ark of God, and set it in the midst of the tabernacle that David had erected for it. Then they offered burnt offerings and peace offerings before God. 2 And when David had finished offering the burnt offerings and the peace offerings, he blessed the people in the name of the LORD. 3 Then he distributed to everyone of Israel, both man and woman, to everyone a loaf of bread, a piece *of meat,* and a cake of raisins.

4 And he appointed some of the Levites to minister before the ark of the LORD, to commemorate, to thank, and to praise the LORD God of Israel: 5 Asaph the chief, and next to him Zechariah, *then* Jeiel, Shemiramoth, Jehiel, Mattithiah, Eliab, Benaiah, and Obed-Edom: Jeiel with stringed instruments and harps, but Asaph made music with cymbals; 6 Benaiah

and Jahaziel the priests regularly *blew* the trumpets before the ark of the covenant of God.

7 On that day David first delivered *this psalm* into the hand of Asaph and his brethren, to thank the LORD:

8 Oh, give thanks to the LORD!
   Call upon His name;
   Make known His deeds among
      the peoples!
9 Sing to Him, sing psalms to
      Him;
   Talk of all His wondrous
      works!
10 Glory in His holy name;
   Let the hearts of those rejoice
      who seek the LORD!
11 Seek the LORD and His
      strength;
   Seek His face evermore!
12 Remember His marvelous
      works which He has done,
   His wonders, and the
      judgments of His mouth,
13 O seed of Israel His servant,
   You children of Jacob, His
      chosen ones!

14 He *is* the LORD our God;
   His judgments *are* in all the
      earth.
15 Remember His covenant
      forever,
   The word which He
      commanded, for a thousand
      generations,
16 *The covenant which* He made
      with Abraham,
   And His oath to Isaac,
17 And confirmed it to Jacob for
      a statute,
   To Israel *for* an everlasting
      covenant,
18 Saying, "To you I will give the
      land of Canaan
   As the allotment of your
      inheritance,"
19 When you were few in number,
   Indeed very few, and strangers
      in it.
20 When they went from one
      nation to another,
   And from *one* kingdom to
      another people,
21 He permitted no man to do
      them wrong;
   Yes, He rebuked kings for their
      sakes,
22 *Saying,* "Do not touch My
      anointed ones,

And do My prophets no
    harm."[a]

23 Sing to the LORD, all the earth;
    Proclaim the good news of His
        salvation from day to day.
24 Declare His glory among the
        nations,
    His wonders among all
        peoples.
25 For the LORD is great and
        greatly to be praised;
    He is also to be feared above
        all gods.
26 For all the gods of the peoples
        are idols,
    But the LORD made the
        heavens.
27 Honor and majesty are before
        Him;
    Strength and gladness are in
        His place.

28 Give to the LORD, O families of
        the peoples,
    Give to the LORD glory and
        strength.
29 Give to the LORD the glory due
        His name;
    Bring an offering, and come
        before Him.
    Oh, worship the LORD in the
        beauty of holiness!
30 Tremble before Him, all the
        earth.
    The world also is firmly
        established,
    It shall not be moved.

31 Let the heavens rejoice, and let
        the earth be glad;
    And let them say among the
        nations, "The LORD reigns."
32 Let the sea roar, and all its
        fullness;
    Let the field rejoice, and all that
        is in it.
33 Then the trees of the woods
        shall rejoice before the LORD,
    For He is coming to judge the
        earth.[a]

34 Oh, give thanks to the LORD, for
        He is good!
    For His mercy endures
        forever.[a]
35 And say, "Save us, O God of
        our salvation;

Gather us together, and deliver
        us from the Gentiles,
    To give thanks to Your holy
        name,
    To triumph in Your praise."

36 Blessed be the LORD God of
        Israel
    From everlasting to
        everlasting![a]

And all the people said, "Amen!" and
praised the LORD.

37 So he left Asaph and his brothers there before the ark of the covenant of the LORD to minister before
the ark regularly, as every day's
work required; 38 and Obed-Edom
with his sixty-eight brethren, including Obed-Edom the son of Jeduthun,
and Hosah, to be gatekeepers;
39 and Zadok the priest and his brethren the priests, before the tabernacle
of the LORD at the high place that was
at Gibeon, 40 to offer burnt offerings
to the LORD on the altar of burnt offering regularly morning and evening, and to do according to all that
is written in the Law of the LORD
which He commanded Israel;
41 and with them Heman and Jeduthun and the rest who were chosen,
who were designated by name, to
give thanks to the LORD, because His
mercy endures forever; 42 and with
them Heman and Jeduthun, to sound
aloud with trumpets and cymbals
and the musical instruments of God.
Now the sons of Jeduthun were
gatekeepers.

43 Then all the people departed, every man to his house; and David returned to bless his house.

17 Now it came to pass, when David was dwelling in his house,
that David said to Nathan the
prophet, "See now, I dwell in a house
of cedar, but the ark of the covenant
of the LORD is under tent curtains."
2 Then Nathan said to David, "Do
all that is in your heart, for God is
with you."
3 But it happened that night that
the word of God came to Nathan,
saying, 4 "Go and tell My servant David, 'Thus says the LORD: "You shall
not build Me a house to dwell in.

16:22 aCompare verses 8–22 with Psalm 105:1–15   16:33 aCompare verses 23–33 with Psalm
95:1–13   16:34 aCompare verse 34 with Psalm 106:1   16:36 aCompare verses 35, 36 with Psalm
106:47, 48

5 For I have not dwelt in a house since the time that I brought up Israel, even to this day, but have gone from tent to tent, and from *one* tabernacle *to another*. 6 Wherever I have moved about with all Israel, have I ever spoken a word to any of the judges of Israel, whom I commanded to shepherd My people, saying, 'Why have you not built Me a house of cedar?' " ' 7 Now therefore, thus shall you say to My servant David, 'Thus says the LORD of hosts: "I took you from the sheepfold, from following the sheep, to be ruler over My people Israel. 8 And I have been with you wherever you have gone, and have cut off all your enemies from before you, and have made you a name like the name of the great men who *are* on the earth. 9 Moreover I will appoint a place for My people Israel, and will plant them, that they may dwell in a place of their own and move no more; nor shall the sons of wickedness oppress them anymore, as previously, 10 since the time that I commanded judges *to be* over My people Israel. Also I will subdue all your enemies. Furthermore I tell you that the LORD will build you a house.ᵃ 11 And it shall be, when your days are fulfilled, when you must go *to be* with your fathers, that I will set up your seed after you, who will be of your sons; and I will establish his kingdom. 12 He shall build Me a house, and I will establish his throne forever. 13 I will be his Father, and he shall be My son; and I will not take My mercy away from him, as I took *it* from *him* who was before you. 14 And I will establish him in My house and in My kingdom forever; and his throne shall be established forever." ' "

15 According to all these words and according to all this vision, so Nathan spoke to David.

16 Then King David went in and sat before the LORD; and he said: "Who *am* I, O LORD God? And what is my house, that You have brought me this far? 17 And *yet* this was a small thing in Your sight, O God; and You have *also* spoken of Your servant's house for a great while to come, and have regarded me according to the rank of a man of high degree, O LORD God.

18 What more can David *say* to You for the honor of Your servant? For You know Your servant. 19 O LORD, for Your servant's sake, and according to Your own heart, You have done all this greatness, in making known all these great things. 20 O LORD, *there is* none like You, nor *is there any* God besides You, according to all that we have heard with our ears. 21 And who *is* like Your people Israel, the one nation on the earth whom God went to redeem for Himself *as* a people—to make for Yourself a name by great and awesome deeds, by driving out nations from before Your people whom You redeemed from Egypt? 22 For You have made Your people Israel Your very own people forever; and You, LORD, have become their God.

23 "And now, O LORD, the word which You have spoken concerning Your servant and concerning his house, *let it* be established forever, and do as You have said. 24 So let it be established, that Your name may be magnified forever, saying, 'The LORD of hosts, the God of Israel, *is* Israel's God.' And let the house of Your servant David be established before You. 25 For You, O my God, have revealed to Your servant that You will build him a house. Therefore Your servant has found it *in his heart* to pray before You. 26 And now, LORD, You are God, and have promised this goodness to Your servant. 27 Now You have been pleased to bless the house of Your servant, that it may continue before You forever; for You have blessed it, O LORD, and *it shall be* blessed forever."

18 After this it came to pass that David attacked the Philistines, subdued them, and took Gath and its towns from the hand of the Philistines. 2 Then he defeated Moab, and the Moabites became David's servants, *and* brought tribute.

3 And David defeated Hadadezerᵃ king of Zobah *as far as* Hamath, as he went to establish his power by the River Euphrates. 4 David took from him one thousand chariots, seven thousandᵃ horsemen, and twenty thousand foot soldiers. Also David hamstrung all the chariot *horses,* ex-

17:10 ᵃThat is, a royal dynasty   18:3 ᵃHebrew *Hadarezer,* and so throughout chapters 18 and 19
18:4 ᵃOr *seven hundred* (compare 2 Samuel 8:4)

The Life of David

THE GREAT SEA

Sidon

Mt. Lebanon

Damascus

Tyre

• Dan

3. David, who served as a soldier in Saul's army, killed Goliath in the Valley of Elah (1 Sam. 17:19, 45–50).

2. David was a harpist in King Saul's court at the capital city of Gibeah (1 Sam. 16:23).

• Mt. Carmel

SEA OF GALILEE

Megiddo

4. Saul became angry at David, even though he was a friend of Saul's son Jonathan. David hid in Nob, Gath, Keilah, and other places (1 Sam. 19—23).

1. David, youngest son of Jesse, was born in Bethlehem and tended his father's sheep there (1 Sam. 17:12, 15).

JORDAN RIVER

AMMON

Joppa

Elah

Gibeah • • Nob

7. As king of all Israel, David reigned at Jerusalem (2 Sam. 5:1–5).

• Jerusalem

• Gath • • Bethlehem

PHILISTINES

• Keilah

• Hebron

Gaza

DEAD SEA

MOAB

6. Among David's conquests were Edom, Moab, the Ammonites, the Amalekites, and the Philistines (2 Sam. 8:11, 12).

• Beersheba

The Negeb

E D O M

5. David became king of Judah, with his capital at Hebron (2 Sam. 2:1–4).

cept that he spared enough of them for one hundred chariots.

5 When the Syrians of Damascus came to help Hadadezer king of Zobah, David killed twenty-two thousand of the Syrians. 6 Then David put *garrisons* in Syria of Damascus; and the Syrians became David's servants, *and* brought tribute. So the LORD preserved David wherever he went. 7 And David took the shields of gold that were on the servants of Hadadezer, and brought them to Jerusalem. 8 Also from Tibhath[a] and from Chun, cities of Hadadezer, David brought a large amount of bronze, with which Solomon made the bronze Sea, the pillars, and the articles of bronze.

9 Now when Tou[a] king of Hamath heard that David had defeated all the army of Hadadezer king of Zobah, 10 he sent Hadoram[a] his son to King David, to greet him and bless him, because he had fought against Hadadezer and defeated him (for Hadadezer had been at war with Tou); and *Hadoram brought with him* all kinds of articles of gold, silver, and bronze. 11 King David also dedicated these to the LORD, along with the silver and gold that he had brought from all *these* nations—from Edom, from Moab, from the people of Ammon, from the Philistines, and from Amalek.

12 Moreover Abishai the son of Zeruiah killed eighteen thousand Edomites[a] in the Valley of Salt. 13 He also put garrisons in Edom, and all the Edomites became David's servants. And the LORD preserved David wherever he went.

14 So David reigned over all Israel, and administered judgment and justice to all his people. 15 Joab the son of Zeruiah *was* over the army; Jehoshaphat the son of Ahilud *was* recorder; 16 Zadok the son of Ahitub and Abimelech the son of Abiathar *were* the priests; Shavsha[a] *was* the scribe; 17 Benaiah the son of Jehoiada *was* over the Cherethites and the Pelethites; and David's sons *were* chief ministers at the king's side.

19 It happened after this that Nahash the king of the people of Ammon died, and his son reigned in his place. 2 Then David said, "I will show kindness to Hanun the son of Nahash, because his father showed kindness to me." So David sent messengers to comfort him concerning his father. And David's servants came to Hanun in the land of the people of Ammon to comfort him.

3 And the princes of the people of Ammon said to Hanun, "Do you think that David really honors your father because he has sent comforters to you? Did his servants not come to you to search and to overthrow and to spy out the land?"

4 Therefore Hanun took David's servants, shaved them, and cut off their garments in the middle, at their buttocks, and sent them away. 5 Then *some* went and told David about the men; and he sent to meet them, because the men were greatly ashamed. And the king said, "Wait at Jericho until your beards have grown, and *then* return."

6 When the people of Ammon saw that they had made themselves repulsive to David, Hanun and the people of Ammon sent a thousand talents of silver to hire for themselves chariots and horsemen from Mesopotamia,[a] from Syrian Maacah, and from Zobah.[b] 7 So they hired for themselves thirty-two thousand chariots, with the king of Maacah and his people, who came and encamped before Medeba. Also the people of Ammon gathered together from their cities, and came to battle.

8 Now when David heard *of it,* he sent Joab and all the army of the mighty men. 9 Then the people of Ammon came out and put themselves in battle array before the gate of the city, and the kings who had come *were* by themselves in the field.

10 When Joab saw that the battle line was against him before and behind, he chose some of Israel's best and put *them* in battle array against the Syrians. 11 And the rest of the people he put under the command of Abishai his brother, and they set *themselves* in battle array against the people of Ammon. 12 Then he said, "If the Syrians are too strong for me, then you shall help me; but if the peo-

---

18:8 [a]Spelled *Betah* in 2 Samuel 8:8   18:9 [a]Spelled *Toi* in 2 Samuel 8:9, 10   18:10 [a]Spelled *Joram* in 2 Samuel 8:10   18:12 [a]Or *Syrians* (compare 2 Samuel 8:13)   18:16 [a]Spelled *Seraiah* in 2 Samuel 8:17   19:6 [a]Hebrew *Aram Naharaim*   [b]Spelled *Zoba* in 2 Samuel 10:6

ple of Ammon are too strong for you, then I will help you. 13 Be of good courage, and let us be strong for our people and for the cities of our God. And may the LORD do *what is* good in His sight."

14 So Joab and the people who *were* with him drew near for the battle against the Syrians, and they fled before him. 15 When the people of Ammon saw that the Syrians were fleeing, they also fled before Abishai his brother, and entered the city. So Joab went to Jerusalem.

16 Now when the Syrians saw that they had been defeated by Israel, they sent messengers and brought the Syrians who were beyond the River,*a* and Shophach*b* the commander of Hadadezer's army *went* before them. 17 When it was told David, he gathered all Israel, crossed over the Jordan and came upon them, and set up in battle array against them. So when David had set up in *battle* array against the Syrians, they fought with him. 18 Then the Syrians fled before Israel; and David killed seven thousand*a* charioteers and forty thousand foot soldiers*b* of the Syrians, and killed Shophach the commander of the army. 19 And when the servants of Hadadezer saw that they were defeated by Israel, they made peace with David and became his servants. So the Syrians were not willing to help the people of Ammon anymore.

20 It happened in the spring of the year, at the time kings go out *to battle*, that Joab led out the armed forces and ravaged the country of the people of Ammon, and came and besieged Rabbah. But David stayed at Jerusalem. And Joab defeated Rabbah and overthrew it. 2 Then David took their king's crown from his head, and found it to weigh a talent of gold, and *there were* precious stones in it. And it was set on David's head. Also he brought out the spoil of the city in great abundance. 3 And he brought out the people who *were* in it, and put *them* to work*a* with saws, with iron picks, and with axes. So David did to all the cities

of the people of Ammon. Then David and all the people returned *to* Jerusalem.

4 Now it happened afterward that war broke out at Gezer with the Philistines, at which time Sibbechai the Hushathite killed Sippai,*a who was* one of the sons of the giant. And they were subdued.

5 Again there was war with the Philistines, and Elhanan the son of Jair*a* killed Lahmi the brother of Goliath the Gittite, the shaft of whose spear *was* like a weaver's beam.

6 Yet again there was war at Gath, where there was a man of *great* stature, with twenty-four fingers and toes, six *on each hand* and six *on each foot;* and he also was born to the giant. 7 So when he defied Israel, Jonathan the son of Shimea,*a* David's brother, killed him.

8 These were born to the giant in Gath, and they fell by the hand of David and by the hand of his servants.

21 Now Satan stood up against Israel, and moved David to number Israel. 2 So David said to Joab and to the leaders of the people, "Go, number Israel from Beersheba to Dan, and bring the number of them to me that I may know *it*."

3 And Joab answered, "May the LORD make His people a hundred times more than they are. But, my lord the king, *are* they not all my lord's servants? Why then does my lord require this thing? Why should he be a cause of guilt in Israel?"

4 Nevertheless the king's word prevailed against Joab. Therefore Joab departed and went throughout all Israel and came to Jerusalem. 5 Then Joab gave the sum of the number of the people to David. All Israel *had* one million one hundred thousand men who drew the sword, and Judah *had* four hundred and seventy thousand men who drew the sword. 6 But he did not count Levi and Benjamin among them, for the king's word was abominable to Joab.

7 And God was displeased with this thing; therefore He struck Israel. 8 So David said to God, "I have

19:16 *a*That is, the Euphrates   *b*Spelled *Shobach* in 2 Samuel 10:16   19:18 *a*Or *seven hundred* (compare 2 Samuel 10:18)   *b*Or *horsemen* (compare 2 Samuel 10:18)   20:3 *a*Septuagint reads *cut them.* 20:4 *a*Spelled *Saph* in 2 Samuel 21:18   20:5 *a*Spelled *Jaare-Oregim* in 2 Samuel 21:19   20:7 *a*Spelled *Shimeah* in 2 Samuel 21:21 and *Shammah* in 1 Samuel 16:9

sinned greatly, because I have done this thing; but now, I pray, take away the iniquity of Your servant, for I have done very foolishly."

9 Then the LORD spoke to Gad, David's seer, saying, 10 "Go and tell David, saying, 'Thus says the LORD: "I offer you three *things;* choose one of them for yourself, that I may do *it* to you." ' "

11 So Gad came to David and said to him, "Thus says the LORD: 'Choose for yourself, 12 either three[a] years of famine, or three months to be defeated by your foes with the sword of your enemies overtaking *you,* or else for three days the sword of the LORD—the plague in the land, with the angel[b] of the LORD destroying throughout all the territory of Israel.' Now consider what answer I should take back to Him who sent me."

13 And David said to Gad, "I am in great distress. Please let me fall into the hand of the LORD, for His mercies *are* very great; but do not let me fall into the hand of man."

14 So the LORD sent a plague upon Israel, and seventy thousand men of Israel fell. 15 And God sent an angel to Jerusalem to destroy it. As he[a] was destroying, the LORD looked and relented of the disaster, and said to the angel who was destroying, "It is enough; now restrain your[b] hand." And the angel of the LORD stood by the threshing floor of Ornan[c] the Jebusite.

16 Then David lifted his eyes and saw the angel of the LORD standing between earth and heaven, having in his hand a drawn sword stretched out over Jerusalem. So David and the elders, clothed in sackcloth, fell on their faces. 17 And David said to God, "Was it not I who commanded the people to be numbered? I am the one who has sinned and done evil indeed; but these sheep, what have they done? Let Your hand, I pray, O LORD my God, be against me and my father's house, but not against Your people that they should be plagued."

18 Therefore, the angel of the LORD commanded Gad to say to David that David should go and erect an altar to the LORD on the threshing floor of Ornan the Jebusite. 19 So David went up at the word of Gad, which he had spoken in the name of the LORD. 20 Now Ornan turned and saw the angel; and his four sons *who were* with him hid themselves, but Ornan continued threshing wheat. 21 So David came to Ornan, and Ornan looked and saw David. And he went out from the threshing floor, and bowed before David with *his* face to the ground. 22 Then David said to Ornan, "Grant me the place of *this* threshing floor, that I may build an altar on it to the LORD. You shall grant it to me at the full price, that the plague may be withdrawn from the people."

23 But Ornan said to David, "Take *it* to yourself, and let my lord the king do *what is* good in his eyes. Look, I *also* give *you* the oxen for burnt offerings, the threshing implements for wood, and the wheat for the grain offering; I give *it* all."

24 Then King David said to Ornan, "No, but I will surely buy *it* for the full price, for I will not take what is yours for the LORD, nor offer burnt offerings with *that which* costs *me* nothing." 25 So David gave Ornan six hundred shekels of gold by weight for the place. 26 And David built there an altar to the LORD, and offered burnt offerings and peace offerings, and called on the LORD; and He answered him from heaven by fire on the altar of burnt offering.

27 So the LORD commanded the angel, and he returned his sword to its sheath.

28 At that time, when David saw that the LORD had answered him on the threshing floor of Ornan the Jebusite, he sacrificed there. 29 For the tabernacle of the LORD and the altar of the burnt offering, which Moses had made in the wilderness, *were* at that time at the high place in Gibeon. 30 But David could not go before it to inquire of God, for he was afraid of the sword of the angel of the LORD.

22 Then David said, "This *is* the house of the LORD God, and this *is* the altar of burnt offering for Israel." 2 So David commanded to gather the aliens who *were* in the land of Israel; and he appointed masons to cut hewn stones to build the house of God. 3 And David prepared

---

21:12 [a]Or *seven* (compare 2 Samuel 24:13)   [b]Or *Angel,* and so elsewhere in this chapter   21:15 [a]Or *He*   [b]Or *Your*   [c]Spelled *Araunah* in 2 Samuel 24:16

iron in abundance for the nails of the doors of the gates and for the joints, and bronze in abundance beyond measure, 4 and cedar trees in abundance; for the Sidonians and those from Tyre brought much cedar wood to David.

5 Now David said, "Solomon my son *is* young and inexperienced, and the house to be built for the LORD *must be* exceedingly magnificent, famous and glorious throughout all countries. I will now make preparation for it." So David made abundant preparations before his death.

6 Then he called for his son Solomon, and charged him to build a house for the LORD God of Israel. 7 And David said to Solomon: "My son, as for me, it was in my mind to build a house to the name of the LORD my God; 8 but the word of the LORD came to me, saying, 'You have shed much blood and have made great wars; you shall not build a house for My name, because you have shed much blood on the earth in My sight. 9 Behold, a son shall be born to you, who shall be a man of rest; and I will give him rest from all his enemies all around. His name shall be Solomon,*a* for I will give peace and quietness to Israel in his days. 10 He shall build a house for My name, and he shall be My son, and I *will be* his Father; and I will establish the throne of his kingdom over Israel forever.' 11 Now, my son, may the LORD be with you; and may you prosper, and build the house of the LORD your God, as He has said to you. 12 Only may the LORD give you wisdom and understanding, and give you charge concerning Israel, that you may keep the law of the LORD your God. 13 Then you will prosper, if you take care to fulfill the statutes and judgments with which the LORD charged Moses concerning Israel. Be strong and of good courage; do not fear nor be dismayed. 14 Indeed I have taken much trouble to prepare for the house of the LORD one hundred thousand talents of gold and one million talents of silver, and bronze and iron beyond measure, for it is so abundant. I have prepared timber and stone also, and you may add to them. 15 Moreover *there are* workmen with

you in abundance: woodsmen and stonecutters, and all types of skillful men for every kind of work. 16 Of gold and silver and bronze and iron *there is* no limit. Arise and begin working, and the LORD be with you."

17 David also commanded all the leaders of Israel to help Solomon his son, *saying,* 18 "*Is* not the LORD your God with you? And has He *not* given you rest on every side? For He has given the inhabitants of the land into my hand, and the land is subdued before the LORD and before His people. 19 Now set your heart and your soul to seek the LORD your God. Therefore arise and build the sanctuary of the LORD God, to bring the ark of the covenant of the LORD and the holy articles of God into the house that is to be built for the name of the LORD."

23 So when David was old and full of days, he made his son Solomon king over Israel.

2 And he gathered together all the leaders of Israel, with the priests and the Levites. 3 Now the Levites were numbered from the age of thirty years and above; and the number of individual males was thirty-eight thousand. 4 Of these, twenty-four thousand *were* to look after the work of the house of the LORD, six thousand *were* officers and judges, 5 four thousand *were* gatekeepers, and four thousand praised the LORD with *musical* instruments, "which I made," *said David,* "for giving praise."

6 Also David separated them into divisions among the sons of Levi: Gershon, Kohath, and Merari.

7 Of the Gershonites: Laadan*a* and Shimei. 8 The sons of Laadan: the first Jehiel, then Zetham and Joel— three *in all.* 9 The sons of Shimei: Shelomith, Haziel, and Haran—three *in all.* These were the heads of the fathers' *houses* of Laadan. 10 And the sons of Shimei: Jahath, Zina,*a* Jeush, and Beriah. These *were* the four sons of Shimei. 11 Jahath was the first and Zizah the second. But Jeush and Beriah did not have many sons; therefore they were assigned as one father's house.

12 The sons of Kohath: Amram, Izhar, Hebron, and Uzziel—four *in*

22:9 *a*Literally *Peaceful*   23:7 *a*Spelled *Libni* in Exodus 6:17   23:10 *a*Septuagint and Vulgate read *Zizah*
(compare verse 11).

all. 13 The sons of Amram: Aaron and Moses; and Aaron was set apart, he and his sons forever, that he should sanctify the most holy things, to burn incense before the LORD, to minister to Him, and to give the blessing in His name forever. 14 Now the sons of Moses the man of God were reckoned to the tribe of Levi. 15 The sons of Moses *were* Gershon[a] and Eliezer. 16 Of the sons of Gershon, Shebuel[a] *was* the first. 17 Of the descendants of Eliezer, Rehabiah was the first. And Eliezer had no other sons, but the sons of Rehabiah were very many. 18 Of the sons of Izhar, Shelomith *was* the first. 19 Of the sons of Hebron, Jeriah *was* the first, Amariah the second, Jahaziel the third, and Jekameam the fourth. 20 Of the sons of Uzziel, Michah *was* the first and Jesshiah the second.

21 The sons of Merari *were* Mahli and Mushi. The sons of Mahli *were* Eleazar and Kish. 22 And Eleazar died, and had no sons, but only daughters; and their brethren, the sons of Kish, took them *as* wives. 23 The sons of Mushi *were* Mahli, Eder, and Jeremoth—three *in all.*

24 These *were* the sons of Levi by their fathers' houses—the heads of the fathers' *houses* as they were counted individually by the number of their names, who did the work for the service of the house of the LORD, from the age of twenty years and above.

25 For David said, "The LORD God of Israel has given rest to His people, that they may dwell in Jerusalem forever"; 26 and also to the Levites, "They shall no longer carry the tabernacle, or any of the articles for its service." 27 For by the last words of David the Levites *were* numbered from twenty years old and above; 28 because their duty *was* to help the sons of Aaron in the service of the house of the LORD, in the courts and in the chambers, in the purifying of all holy things and the work of the service of the house of God, 29 both with the showbread and the fine flour for the grain offering, with the unleavened cakes and *what is baked in* the pan, with what is mixed and with all kinds of measures and sizes; 30 to stand every morning to thank and praise the LORD, and likewise at evening; 31 and at every presentation of a burnt offering to the LORD on the Sabbaths and on the New Moons and on the set feasts, by number according to the ordinance governing them, regularly before the LORD; 32 and that they should attend to the needs of the tabernacle of meeting, the needs of the holy *place,* and the needs of the sons of Aaron their brethren in the work of the house of the LORD.

24 Now *these are* the divisions of the sons of Aaron. The sons of Aaron *were* Nadab, Abihu, Eleazar, and Ithamar. 2 And Nadab and Abihu died before their father, and had no children; therefore Eleazar and Ithamar ministered as priests. 3 Then David with Zadok of the sons of Eleazar, and Ahimelech of the sons of Ithamar, divided them according to the schedule of their service.

4 There were more leaders found of the sons of Eleazar than of the sons of Ithamar, and *thus* they were divided. Among the sons of Eleazar *were* sixteen heads of *their* fathers' houses, and eight heads of their fathers' houses among the sons of Ithamar. 5 Thus they were divided by lot, one group as another, for there were officials of the sanctuary and officials *of the house* of God, from the sons of Eleazar and from the sons of Ithamar. 6 And the scribe, Shemaiah the son of Nethanel, *one of* the Levites, wrote them down before the king, the leaders, Zadok the priest, Ahimelech the son of Abiathar, and the heads of the fathers' *houses* of the priests and Levites, one father's house taken for Eleazar and *one* for Ithamar.

7 Now the first lot fell to Jehoiarib, the second to Jedaiah, 8 the third to Harim, the fourth to Seorim, 9 the fifth to Malchijah, the sixth to Mijamin, 10 the seventh to Hakkoz, the eighth to Abijah, 11 the ninth to Jeshua, the tenth to Shecaniah, 12 the eleventh to Eliashib, the twelfth to Jakim, 13 the thirteenth to Huppah, the fourteenth to Jeshebeab, 14 the fifteenth to Bilgah, the sixteenth to Immer, 15 the seventeenth to Hezir, the eighteenth to Happizzez,[a] 16 the nineteenth to Pethahiah,

---

23:15 [a]Hebrew *Gershom* (compare 6:16)   23:16 [a]Spelled *Shubael* in 24:20   24:15 [a]Septuagint and Vulgate read *Aphses.*

the twentieth to Jehezekel,[a] 17 the twenty-first to Jachin, the twenty-second to Gamul, 18 the twenty-third to Delaiah, the twenty-fourth to Maaziah.

19 This *was* the schedule of their service for coming into the house of the LORD according to their ordinance by the hand of Aaron their father, as the LORD God of Israel had commanded him.

20 And the rest of the sons of Levi: of the sons of Amram, Shubael;[a] of the sons of Shubael, Jehdeiah. 21 Concerning Rehabiah, of the sons of Rehabiah, the first *was* Isshiah. 22 Of the Izharites, Shelomoth;[a] of the sons of Shelomoth, Jahath. 23 Of the sons *of Hebron,*[a] Jeriah *was the first,*[b] Amariah the second, Jahaziel the third, *and* Jekameam the fourth. 24 *Of* the sons of Uzziel, Michah; of the sons of Michah, Shamir. 25 The brother of Michah, Isshiah; of the sons of Isshiah, Zechariah. 26 The sons of Merari *were* Mahli and Mushi; the son of Jaaziah, Beno. 27 The sons of Merari by Jaaziah *were* Beno, Shoham, Zaccur, and Ibri. 28 Of Mahli: Eleazar, who had no sons. 29 Of Kish: the son of Kish, Jerahmeel.

30 Also the sons of Mushi *were* Mahli, Eder, and Jerimoth. These *were* the sons of the Levites according to their fathers' houses.

31 These also cast lots just as their brothers the sons of Aaron did, in the presence of King David, Zadok, Ahimelech, and the heads of the fathers' *houses* of the priests and Levites. The chief fathers *did* just as their younger brethren.

25

Moreover David and the captains of the army separated for the service *some* of the sons of Asaph, of Heman, and of Jeduthun, who *should* prophesy with harps, stringed instruments, and cymbals. And the number of the skilled men performing their service was: 2 Of the sons of Asaph: Zaccur, Joseph, Nethaniah, and Asharelah;[a] the sons of Asaph *were* under the direction of Asaph, who prophesied according to the order of the king. 3 Of Jeduthun, the sons of Jeduthun: Gedaliah, Zeri,[a] Jeshaiah, Shimei, Hashabiah, and Mattithiah, six,[b] under the direction of their father Jeduthun, who prophesied with a harp to give thanks and to praise the LORD. 4 Of Heman, the sons of Heman: Bukkiah, Mattaniah, Uzziel,[a] Shebuel,[b] Jerimoth,[c] Hananiah, Hanani, Eliathah, Giddalti, Romamti-Ezer, Joshbekashah, Mallothi, Hothir, *and* Mahazioth. 5 All these *were* the sons of Heman the king's seer in the words of God, to exalt his horn.[a] For God gave Heman fourteen sons and three daughters.

6 All these *were* under the direction of their father for the music *in* the house of the LORD, with cymbals, stringed instruments, and harps, for the service of the house of God. Asaph, Jeduthun, and Heman *were* under the authority of the king. 7 So the number of them, with their brethren who were instructed in the songs of the LORD, all who were skillful, *was* two hundred and eighty-eight.

8 And they cast lots for their duty, the small as well as the great, the teacher with the student.

9 Now the first lot for Asaph came out for Joseph; the second for Gedaliah, him with his brethren and sons, twelve; 10 the third for Zaccur, his sons and his brethren, twelve; 11 the fourth for Jizri,[a] his sons and his brethren, twelve; 12 the fifth for Nethaniah, his sons and his brethren, twelve; 13 the sixth for Bukkiah, his sons and his brethren, twelve; 14 the seventh for Jesharelah,[a] his sons and his brethren, twelve; 15 the eighth for Jeshaiah, his sons and his brethren, twelve; 16 the ninth for Mattaniah, his sons and his brethren, twelve; 17 the tenth for Shimei, his sons and his brethren, twelve; 18 the eleventh for Azarel,[a] his sons and his brethren, twelve; 19 the

24:16 [a]Masoretic Text reads *Jehezkel.*   24:20 [a]Spelled *Shebuel* in 23:16   24:22 [a]Spelled *Shelomith* in 23:18   24:23 [a]Supplied from 23:19 (following some Hebrew manuscripts and Septuagint manuscripts) [b]Supplied from 23:19 (following some Hebrew manuscripts and Septuagint manuscripts)   25:2 [a]Spelled *Jesharelah* in verse 14   25:3 [a]Spelled *Jizri* in verse 11   [b]*Shimei,* appearing in one Hebrew and several Septuagint manuscripts, completes the total of six sons (compare verse 17).   25:4 [a]Spelled *Azarel* in verse 18   [b]Spelled *Shubael* in verse 20   [c]Spelled *Jeremoth* in verse 22   25:5 [a]That is, to increase his power or influence   25:11 [a]Spelled *Zeri* in verse 3   25:14 [a]Spelled *Asharelah* in verse 2   25:18 [a]Spelled *Uzziel* in verse 4 twelfth for Hashabiah, his sons and his brethren, twelve; 20 the thirteenth for Shubael,*a* his sons and his brethren, twelve; 21 the fourteenth for Mattithiah, his sons and his brethren, twelve; 22 the fifteenth for Jeremoth,*a* his sons and his brethren, twelve; 23 the sixteenth for Hananiah, his sons and his brethren, twelve; 24 the seventeenth for Joshbekashah, his sons and his brethren, twelve; 25 the eighteenth for Hanani, his sons and his brethren, twelve; 26 the nineteenth for Mallothi, his sons and his brethren, twelve; 27 the twentieth for Eliathah, his sons and his brethren, twelve; 28 the twenty-first for Hothir, his sons and his brethren, twelve; 29 the twenty-second for Giddalti, his sons and his brethren, twelve; 30 the twenty-third for Mahazioth, his sons and his brethren, twelve; 31 the twenty-fourth for Romamti-Ezer, his sons and his brethren, twelve.

26 Concerning the divisions of the gatekeepers: of the Korahites, Meshelemiah the son of Kore, of the sons of Asaph. 2 And the sons of Meshelemiah *were* Zechariah the firstborn, Jediael the second, Zebadiah the third, Jathniel the fourth, 3 Elam the fifth, Jehohanan the sixth, Eliehoenai the seventh.

4 Moreover the sons of Obed-Edom *were* Shemaiah the firstborn, Jehozabad the second, Joah the third, Sacar the fourth, Nethanel the fifth, 5 Ammiel the sixth, Issachar the seventh, Peulthai the eighth; for God blessed him.

6 Also to Shemaiah his son were sons born who governed their fathers' houses, because they *were* men of great ability. 7 The sons of Shemaiah *were* Othni, Rephael, Obed, and Elzabad, whose brothers Elihu and Semachiah *were* able men.

8 All these *were* of the sons of Obed-Edom, they and their sons and their brethren, able men with strength for the work: sixty-two of Obed-Edom.

9 And Meshelemiah had sons and brethren, eighteen able men.

10 Also Hosah, of the children of Merari, had sons: Shimri the first (for *though* he was not the firstborn, his father made him the first), 11 Hilkiah the second, Tebaliah the third, Zechariah the fourth; all the sons and brethren of Hosah *were* thirteen.

12 Among these *were* the divisions of the gatekeepers, among the chief men, *having* duties just like their brethren, to serve in the house of the LORD. 13 And they cast lots for each gate, the small as well as the great, according to their father's house. 14 The lot for the East *Gate* fell to Shelemiah. Then they cast lots *for* his son Zechariah, a wise counselor, and his lot came out for the North Gate; 15 to Obed-Edom the South Gate, and to his sons the storehouse.*a* 16 To Shuppim and Hosah *the lot came out* for the West Gate, with the Shallecheth Gate on the ascending highway—watchman opposite watchman. 17 On the east were *six* Levites, on the north four each day, on the south four each day, and for the storehouse*a* two by two. 18 As for the Parbar*a* on the west, *there* were four on the highway *and* two at the Parbar. 19 These were the divisions of the gatekeepers among the sons of Korah and among the sons of Merari.

20 Of the Levites, Ahijah *was* over the treasuries of the house of God and over the treasuries of the dedicated things. 21 The sons of Laadan, the descendants of the Gershonites of Laadan, heads of their fathers' *houses,* of Laadan the Gershonite: Jehieli. 22 The sons of Jehieli, Zetham and Joel his brother, *were* over the treasuries of the house of the LORD. 23 Of the Amramites, the Izharites, the Hebronites, and the Uzzielites: 24 Shebuel the son of Gershom, the son of Moses, *was* overseer of the treasuries. 25 And his brethren by Eliezer *were* Rehabiah his son, Jeshaiah his son, Joram his son, Zichri his son, and Shelomith his son.

26 This Shelomith and his brethren *were* over all the treasuries of the dedicated things which King David and the heads of fathers' *houses,* the captains over thousands and hundreds, and the captains of the army, had dedicated. 27 Some of the spoils won in battles they dedicated to maintain the house of the LORD.

25:20 *a*Spelled *Shebuel* in verse 4　　25:22 *a*Spelled *Jerimoth* in verse 4　　26:15 *a*Hebrew *asuppim*
26:17 *a*Hebrew *asuppim*　　26:18 *a*Probably a court or colonnade extending west of the temple

28 And all that Samuel the seer, Saul the son of Kish, Abner the son of Ner, and Joab the son of Zeruiah had dedicated, every dedicated *thing*, was under the hand of Shelomith and his brethren.

29 Of the Izharites, Chenaniah and his sons *performed* duties as officials and judges over Israel outside Jerusalem.

30 Of the Hebronites, Hashabiah and his brethren, one thousand seven hundred able men, had the oversight of Israel on the west side of the Jordan for all the business of the LORD, and in the service of the king. 31 Among the Hebronites, Jerijah *was* head of the Hebronites according to his genealogy of the fathers. In the fortieth year of the reign of David they were sought, and there were found among them capable men at Jazer of Gilead. 32 And his brethren *were* two thousand seven hundred able men, heads of fathers' *houses,* whom King David made officials over the Reubenites, the Gadites, and the half-tribe of Manasseh, for every matter pertaining to God and the affairs of the king.

27 And the children of Israel, according to their number, the heads of fathers' *houses*, the captains of thousands and hundreds and their officers, served the king in every matter of the *military* divisions. *These divisions* came in and went out month by month throughout all the months of the year, each division *having* twenty-four thousand.

2 Over the first division for the first month *was* Jashobeam the son of Zabdiel, and in his division *were* twenty-four thousand; 3 he *was* of the children of Perez, and the chief of all the captains of the army for the first month. 4 Over the division of the second month *was* Dodai[a] an Ahohite, and of his division Mikloth also *was* the leader; in his division *were* twenty-four thousand. 5 The third captain of the army for the third month *was* Benaiah, the son of Jehoiada the priest, who was chief; in his division *were* twenty-four thousand. 6 This was the Benaiah *who was* mighty *among* the thirty, and was over the thirty; in his division *was*

Ammizabad his son. 7 The fourth *captain* for the fourth month *was* Asahel the brother of Joab, and Zebadiah his son after him; in his division *were* twenty-four thousand. 8 The fifth *captain* for the fifth month *was* Shamhuth[a] the Izrahite; in his division were twenty-four thousand. 9 The sixth *captain* for the sixth month *was* Ira the son of Ikkesh the Tekoite; in his division *were* twenty-four thousand. 10 The seventh *captain* for the seventh month *was* Helez the Pelonite, of the children of Ephraim; in his division *were* twenty-four thousand. 11 The eighth *captain* for the eighth month *was* Sibbechai the Hushathite, of the Zarhites; in his division *were* twenty-four thousand. 12 The ninth *captain* for the ninth month *was* Abiezer the Anathothite, of the Benjamites; in his division *were* twenty-four thousand. 13 The tenth *captain* for the tenth month *was* Maharai the Netophathite, of the Zarhites; in his division *were* twenty-four thousand. 14 The eleventh *captain* for the eleventh month *was* Benaiah the Pirathonite, of the children of Ephraim; in his division *were* twenty-four thousand. 15 The twelfth *captain* for the twelfth month *was* Heldai[a] the Netophathite, of Othniel; in his division *were* twenty-four thousand.

16 Furthermore, over the tribes of Israel: the officer over the Reubenites *was* Eliezer the son of Zichri; over the Simeonites, Shephatiah the son of Maachah; 17 over the Levites, Hashabiah the son of Kemuel; over the Aaronites, Zadok; 18 over Judah, Elihu, *one* of David's brothers; *over* Issachar, Omri the son of Michael; 19 over Zebulun, Ishmaiah the son of Obadiah; *over* Naphtali, Jerimoth the son of Azriel; 20 over the children of Ephraim, Hoshea the son of Azaziah; *over* the half-tribe of Manasseh, Joel the son of Pedaiah; 21 over the half-*tribe* of Manasseh in Gilead, Iddo the son of Zechariah; *over* Benjamin, Jaasiel the son of Abner; 22 over Dan, Azarel the son of Jeroham. These *were* the leaders of the tribes of Israel.

23 But David did not take the number of those twenty years old and under, because the LORD had said He

---

27:4 [a]Hebrew *Dodai,* usually spelled *Dodo* (compare 2 Samuel 23:9)   27:8 [a]Spelled *Shammoth* in 11:27 and *Shammah* in 2 Samuel 23:11   27:15 [a]Spelled *Heled* in 11:30 and *Heleb* in 2 Samuel 23:29

would multiply Israel like the stars of the heavens. 24 Joab the son of Zeruiah began a census, but he did not finish, for wrath came upon Israel because of this census; nor was the number recorded in the account of the chronicles of King David.

25 And Azmaveth the son of Adiel was over the king's treasuries; and Jehonathan the son of Uzziah was over the storehouses in the field, in the cities, in the villages, and in the fortresses. 26 Ezri the son of Chelub was over those who did the work of the field for tilling the ground. 27 And Shimei the Ramathite was over the vineyards, and Zabdi the Shiphmite was over the produce of the vineyards for the supply of wine. 28 Baal-Hanan the Gederite was over the olive trees and the sycamore trees that were in the lowlands, and Joash was over the store of oil. 29 And Shitrai the Sharonite was over the herds that fed in Sharon, and Shaphat the son of Adlai was over the herds that were in the valleys. 30 Obil the Ishmaelite was over the camels, Jehdeiah the Meronothite was over the donkeys, 31 and Jaziz the Hagrite was over the flocks. All these were the officials over King David's property.

32 Also Jehonathan, David's uncle, was a counselor, a wise man, and a scribe; and Jehiel the son of Hachmoni was with the king's sons. 33 Ahithophel was the king's counselor, and Hushai the Archite was the king's companion. 34 After Ahithophel was Jehoiada the son of Benaiah, then Abiathar. And the general of the king's army was Joab.

28 Now David assembled at Jerusalem all the leaders of Israel: the officers of the tribes and the captains of the divisions who served the king, the captains over thousands and captains over hundreds, and the stewards over all the substance and possessions of the king and of his sons, with the officials, the valiant men, and all the mighty men of valor. 2 Then King David rose to his feet and said, "Hear me, my brethren and my people: I had it in my heart to build a house of rest for the ark of the covenant of the LORD, and for the footstool of our God, and had made preparations to build it. 3 But God said to me, 'You shall not build a

house for My name, because you have been a man of war and have shed blood.' 4 However the LORD God of Israel chose me above all the house of my father to be king over Israel forever, for He has chosen Judah to be the ruler. And of the house of Judah, the house of my father, and among the sons of my father, He was pleased with me to make me king over all Israel. 5 And of all my sons (for the LORD has given me many sons) He has chosen my son Solomon to sit on the throne of the kingdom of the LORD over Israel. 6 Now He said to me, 'It is your son Solomon who shall build My house and My courts; for I have chosen him to be My son, and I will be his Father. 7 Moreover I will establish his kingdom forever, if he is steadfast to observe My commandments and My judgments, as it is this day.' 8 Now therefore, in the sight of all Israel, the assembly of the LORD, and in the hearing of our God, be careful to seek out all the commandments of the LORD your God, that you may possess this good land, and leave it as an inheritance for your children after you forever.

9 "As for you, my son Solomon, know the God of your father, and serve Him with a loyal heart and with a willing mind; for the LORD searches all hearts and understands all the intent of the thoughts. If you seek Him, He will be found by you; but if you forsake Him, He will cast you off forever. 10 Consider now, for the LORD has chosen you to build a house for the sanctuary; be strong, and do it."

11 Then David gave his son Solomon the plans for the vestibule, its houses, its treasuries, its upper chambers, its inner chambers, and the place of the mercy seat; 12 and the plans for all that he had by the Spirit, of the courts of the house of the LORD, of all the chambers all around, of the treasuries of the house of God, and of the treasuries for the dedicated things; 13 also for the division of the priests and the Levites, for all the work of the service of the house of the LORD, and for all the articles of service in the house of the LORD. 14 He gave gold by weight for things of gold, for all articles used in every kind of service; also silver for all articles of silver by weight, for all articles used in

every kind of service; 15 the weight for the lampstands of gold, and their lamps of gold, by weight for each lampstand and its lamps; for the lampstands of silver by weight, for the lampstand and its lamps, according to the use of each lampstand. 16 And by weight *he gave* gold for the tables of the showbread, for each table, and silver for the tables of silver; 17 also pure gold for the forks, the basins, the pitchers of pure gold, and the golden bowls—*he gave gold* by weight for every bowl; and for the silver bowls, *silver* by weight for every bowl; 18 and refined gold by weight for the altar of incense, and for the construction of the chariot, that is, the gold cherubim that spread *their wings* and overshadowed the ark of the covenant of the LORD. 19 "All *this*," *said David*, "the LORD made me understand in writing, by *His* hand upon me, all the works of these plans."

20 And David said to his son Solomon, "Be strong and of good courage, and do *it*; do not fear nor be dismayed, for the LORD God—my God—*will be* with you. He will not leave you nor forsake you, until you have finished all the work for the service of the house of the LORD. 21 *Here are* the divisions of the priests and the Levites for all the service of the house of God; and every willing craftsman *will be* with you for all manner of workmanship, for every kind of service; also the leaders and all the people *will be* completely at your command."

29 Furthermore King David said to all the assembly: "My son Solomon, whom alone God has chosen, *is* young and inexperienced; and the work *is* great, because the temple*ᵃ* is not for man but for the LORD God. 2 Now for the house of my God I have prepared with all my might: gold for *things to be made of* gold, silver for *things of* silver, bronze for *things of* bronze, iron for *things of* iron, wood for *things of* wood, onyx stones, *stones* to be set, glistening stones of various colors, all kinds of precious stones, and marble slabs in abundance. 3 Moreover, because I have set my affection on the house of my God, I have given to the house

of my God, over and above all that I have prepared for the holy house, my own special treasure of gold and silver: 4 three thousand talents of gold, of the gold of Ophir, and seven thousand talents of refined silver, to overlay the walls of the houses; 5 the gold for *things of* gold and the silver for *things of* silver, and for all kinds of work *to be done* by the hands of craftsmen. Who *then* is willing to consecrate himself this day to the LORD?"

6 Then the leaders of the fathers' *houses,* leaders of the tribes of Israel, the captains of thousands and of hundreds, with the officers over the king's work, offered willingly. 7 They gave for the work of the house of God five thousand talents and ten thousand darics of gold, ten thousand talents of silver, eighteen thousand talents of bronze, and one hundred thousand talents of iron. 8 And whoever had *precious* stones gave *them* to the treasury of the house of the LORD, into the hand of Jehiel*ᵃ* the Gershonite. 9 Then the people rejoiced, for they had offered willingly, because with a loyal heart they had offered willingly to the LORD; and King David also rejoiced greatly.

10 Therefore David blessed the LORD before all the assembly; and David said:

> "Blessed are You, LORD God of
>   Israel, our Father, forever
>   and ever.
> 11 Yours, O LORD, *is* the greatness,
>   The power and the glory,
>   The victory and the majesty;
>   For all *that is* in heaven and
>   in earth *is Yours;*
>   Yours *is* the kingdom, O LORD,
>   And You are exalted as head
>   over all.
> 12 Both riches and honor *come*
>   from You,
>   And You reign over all.
>   In Your hand *is* power and
>   might;
>   In Your hand *it is* to make great
>   And to give strength to all.

13 "Now therefore, our God,
    We thank You
    And praise Your glorious
        name.

29:1 *ᵃ*Literally *palace*   29:8 *ᵃ*Possibly the same as *Jehieli* (compare 26:21, 22)

14 But who *am* I, and who *are* my
    people,
   That we should be able to offer
    so willingly as this?
   For all things *come* from You,
   And of Your own we have
    given You.
15 For we *are* aliens and pilgrims
    before You,
   As *were* all our fathers;
   Our days on earth *are* as a
    shadow,
   And without hope.

16 "O LORD our God, all this abundance that we have prepared to build
You a house for Your holy name is
from Your hand, and *is* all Your own.
17 I know also, my God, that You test
the heart and have pleasure in uprightness. As for me, in the uprightness of my heart I have willingly offered all these *things;* and now with
joy I have seen Your people, who are
present here to offer willingly to You.
18 O LORD God of Abraham, Isaac,
and Israel, our fathers, keep this forever in the intent of the thoughts of
the heart of Your people, and fix their
heart toward You. 19 And give my
son Solomon a loyal heart to keep
Your commandments and Your testimonies and Your statutes, to do all
these things, and to build the temple[a]
for which I have made provision."
20 Then David said to all the assembly, "Now bless the LORD your God."
So all the assembly blessed the LORD
God of their fathers, and bowed their
heads and prostrated themselves before the LORD and the king.

29:19 [a]Literally *palace*

21 And they made sacrifices to the
LORD and offered burnt offerings to
the LORD on the next day: a thousand
bulls, a thousand rams, a thousand
lambs, with their drink offerings, and
sacrifices in abundance for all Israel.
22 So they ate and drank before the
LORD with great gladness on that day.
And they made Solomon the son of
David king the second time, and
anointed *him* before the LORD *to be*
the leader, and Zadok *to be* priest.
23 Then Solomon sat on the throne
of the LORD as king instead of David
his father, and prospered; and all Israel obeyed him. 24 All the leaders
and the mighty men, and also all the
sons of King David, submitted themselves to King Solomon. 25 So the
LORD exalted Solomon exceedingly
in the sight of all Israel, and bestowed on him *such* royal majesty as
had not been on any king before him
in Israel.
26 Thus David the son of Jesse
reigned over all Israel. 27 And the period that he reigned over Israel *was*
forty years; seven years he reigned
in Hebron, and thirty-three *years* he
reigned in Jerusalem. 28 So he died
in a good old age, full of days and
riches and honor; and Solomon his
son reigned in his place. 29 Now the
acts of King David, first and last, indeed they *are* written in the book of
Samuel the seer, in the book of Nathan the prophet, and in the book of
Gad the seer, 30 with all his reign and
his might, and the events that happened to him, to Israel, and to all the
kingdoms of the lands.

Second Chronicles

Overview of Second Chronicles

Second Chronicles covers the period from the reign of Solomon through the Babylonian captivity. With First Chronicles it forms a companion volume to First and Second Samuel and First and Second Kings. It was probably compiled by Ezra about 450 B.C.

The focal point of the book is a moving account of the completion of a vision. One of King David's dreams that outlived him was to build a beautiful temple to the glory of God. Solomon, David's successor, shared his father's dream and made it a reality. The people rallied around Solomon's leadership and committed themselves to the completion of this task. The building project took approximately twenty years and required the complete dedication of the nation. People from far-off lands participated by sending cedar and fir trees, silver, brass, iron, and gold. Solomon put together a core task force of 200,000 men to oversee the project. Solomon taught the nation that it takes two to complete a project—God and man. By giving them a vision, Solomon directed the people's hearts to God. God was to dwell in this temple and they knew that they had to make their plans big enough for God to fit in.

Then Solomon spoke:
"The LORD said He would dwell in the dark cloud.
I have surely built You an exalted house,
And a place for You to dwell in forever."

"But will God indeed dwell with men on the earth? Behold, heaven and the heaven of heavens cannot contain You. How much less this temple which I have built! Yet regard the prayer of Your servant . . . that Your eyes may be open toward this temple day and night, toward the place where You said You would put Your name, that You may hear the prayer which Your servant makes toward this place."

When Solomon had finished praying, fire came down from heaven and consumed the burnt offering and the sacri-

fices; and the glory of the LORD filled the temple.

(2 Chr. 6:1, 2, 18–20; 7:1)

Solomon and the people preferred to attempt something great for God and risk failure than to do nothing and succeed. For if they attempted great things for God, they could expect great things from God!

Jesus in Second Chronicles

The temple built by Solomon prefigures Jesus. In John 2:19, Jesus likens His body to the temple. John also prophesies in Revelation that Jesus will replace the temple: "But I saw no temple in it, for the Lord God Almighty and the Lamb are its temple" (21:22).

Keys to Second Chronicles

Key Word: Priestly View of Judah. The temple symbolizes God's presence among His people and reminds them of their high calling. It provides the spiritual link between their past and future. Thus, Ezra wrote this historical account to encourage the people to accept the new raised on the site of the old and to remind them of their true calling and God's faithfulness despite their low circumstances. The Davidic line, temple, and priesthood are still theirs.

Key Verses: "If My people who are called by My name will humble themselves, and pray and seek My face, and turn from their wicked ways, then I will hear from heaven, and will forgive their sin and heal their land" (7:14).

"For the eyes of the LORD run to and fro throughout the whole earth, to show Himself strong on behalf of *those* whose heart *is* loyal to Him. In this you have done foolishly; therefore from now on you shall have wars" (16:9).

Key Chapter: Second Chronicles 34. Second Chronicles records the reforms and revivals under such kings as Asa, Jehoshaphat, Joash, Hezekiah, and Josiah. Chapter 34 traces the dramatic revival that takes place under Josiah when the "Book of the Law" is found, read, and obeyed.

1 Now Solomon the son of David was strengthened in his kingdom, and the LORD his God *was* with him and exalted him exceedingly.

2 And Solomon spoke to all Israel, to the captains of thousands and of hundreds, to the judges, and to every leader in all Israel, the heads of the fathers' *houses*. 3 Then Solomon, and all the assembly with him, went to the high place that *was* at Gibeon; for the tabernacle of meeting with God was there, which Moses the servant of the LORD had made in the wil-

derness. 4 But David had brought up the ark of God from Kirjath Jearim to *the place* David had prepared for it, for he had pitched a tent for it at Jerusalem. 5 Now the bronze altar that Bezalel the son of Uri, the son of Hur, had made, he put*a* before the tabernacle of the LORD; Solomon and the assembly sought Him *there*. 6 And Solomon went up there to the bronze altar before the LORD, which *was* at the tabernacle of meeting, and offered a thousand burnt offerings on it.

7 On that night God appeared to Solomon, and said to him, "Ask! What shall I give you?"

8 And Solomon said to God: "You have shown great mercy to David my father, and have made me king in his place. 9 Now, O LORD God, let Your promise to David my father be established, for You have made me king over a people like the dust of the earth in multitude. 10 Now give me wisdom and knowledge, that I may go out and come in before this people; for who can judge this great people of Yours?"

11 Then God said to Solomon: "Because this was in your heart, and you have not asked riches or wealth or honor or the life of your enemies, nor have you asked long life—but have asked wisdom and knowledge for yourself, that you may judge My people over whom I have made you king— 12 wisdom and knowledge *are* granted to you; and I will give you riches and wealth and honor, such as none of the kings have had who *were* before you, nor shall any after you have the like."

13 So Solomon came to Jerusalem from the high place that *was* at Gibeon, from before the tabernacle of meeting, and reigned over Israel. 14 And Solomon gathered chariots and horsemen; he had one thousand four hundred chariots and twelve thousand horsemen, whom he stationed in the chariot cities and with the king in Jerusalem. 15 Also the king made silver and gold as common in Jerusalem as stones, and he made cedars as abundant as the sycamores which *are* in the lowland. 16 And Solomon had horses imported from Egypt and Keveh; the king's

merchants bought them in Keveh at the *current* price. 17 They also acquired and imported from Egypt a chariot for six hundred *shekels* of silver, and a horse for one hundred and fifty; thus, through their agents,*a* they exported them to all the kings of the Hittites and the kings of Syria.

2 Then Solomon determined to build a temple for the name of the LORD, and a royal house for himself. 2 Solomon selected seventy thousand men to bear burdens, eighty thousand to quarry *stone* in the mountains, and three thousand six hundred to oversee them.

3 Then Solomon sent to Hiram*a* king of Tyre, saying:

As you have dealt with David my father, and sent him cedars to build himself a house to dwell in, *so deal with me.* 4 Behold, I am building a temple for the name of the LORD my God, to dedicate *it* to Him, to burn before Him sweet incense, for the continual showbread, for the burnt offerings morning and evening, on the Sabbaths, on the New Moons, and on the set feasts of the LORD our God. This *is an ordinance* forever to Israel.

5   And the temple which I build *will be* great, for our God is greater than all gods. 6 But who is able to build Him a temple, since heaven and the heaven of heavens cannot contain Him? Who *am* I then, that I should build Him a temple, except to burn sacrifice before Him?

7   Therefore send me at once a man skillful to work in gold and silver, in bronze and iron, in purple and crimson and blue, who has skill to engrave with the skillful men who are with me in Judah and Jerusalem, whom David my father provided. 8 Also send me cedar and cypress and algum logs from Lebanon, for I know that your servants have skill to cut timber in Lebanon; and indeed

---

1:5 *a*Some authorities read *it was there.*   1:17 *a*Literally *by their hands*   2:3 *a*Hebrew *Huram* (compare 1 Kings 5:1)

my servants *will be* with your servants, 9 to prepare timber for me in abundance, for the temple which I am about to build *shall be* great and wonderful.

10　And indeed I will give to your servants, the woodsmen who cut timber, twenty thousand kors of ground wheat, twenty thousand kors of barley, twenty thousand baths of wine, and twenty thousand baths of oil.

11 Then Hiram king of Tyre answered in writing, which he sent to Solomon:

Because the LORD loves His people, He has made you king over them.

12 Hiram*a* also said:

Blessed *be* the LORD God of Israel, who made heaven and earth, for He has given King David a wise son, endowed with prudence and understanding, who will build a temple for the LORD and a royal house for himself!

13　And now I have sent a skillful man, endowed with understanding, Huram*a* my master*b* *craftsman* 14 (the son of a woman of the daughters of Dan, and his father was a man of Tyre), skilled to work in gold and silver, bronze and iron, stone and wood, purple and blue, fine linen and crimson, and to make any engraving and to accomplish any plan which may be given to him, with your skillful men and with the skillful men of my lord David your father.

15　Now therefore, the wheat, the barley, the oil, and the wine which my lord has spoken of, let him send to his servants. 16 And we will cut wood from

Lebanon, as much as you need; we will bring it to you in rafts by sea to Joppa, and you will carry it up to Jerusalem.

17 Then Solomon numbered all the aliens who *were* in the land of Israel, after the census in which David his father had numbered them; and there were found to be one hundred and fifty-three thousand six hundred. 18 And he made seventy thousand of them bearers of burdens, eighty thousand stonecutters in the mountain, and three thousand six hundred overseers to make the people work.

3 Now Solomon began to build the house of the LORD at Jerusalem on Mount Moriah, where *the LORD*[a] had appeared to his father David, at the place that David had prepared on the threshing floor of Ornan[b] the Jebusite. 2 And he began to build on the second *day* of the second month in the fourth year of his reign. 3 This is the foundation which Solomon laid for building the house of God: The length *was* sixty cubits (by cubits according to the former measure) and the width twenty cubits. 4 And the vestibule that *was* in front of *the sanctuary*[a] was twenty cubits long across the width of the house, and the height *was* one hundred and[b] twenty. He overlaid the inside with pure gold. 5 The larger room[a] he paneled with cypress which he overlaid with fine gold, and he carved palm trees and chainwork on it. 6 And he decorated the house with precious stones for beauty, and the gold *was* gold from Parvaim. 7 He also overlaid the house—the beams and doorposts, its walls and doors—with gold; and he carved cherubim on the walls.

8 And he made the Most Holy Place. Its length was according to the width of the house, twenty cubits, and its width twenty cubits. He overlaid it with six hundred talents of fine gold. 9 The weight of the nails *was* fifty shekels of gold; and he overlaid the upper area with gold. 10 In the Most Holy Place he made two cherubim, fashioned by carving, and over-

2:12 *a*Hebrew *Huram* (compare 1 Kings 5:1)　　2:13 *a*Spelled *Hiram* in 1 Kings 7:13　*b*Literally *father* (compare 1 Kings 7:13, 14)　　3:1 *a*Literally *He,* following Masoretic Text and Vulgate; Septuagint reads *the LORD;* Targum reads *the Angel of the LORD.*　*b*Spelled *Araunah* in 2 Samuel 24:16ff　　3:4 *a*The main room of the temple; elsewhere called the holy place (compare 1 Kings 6:3)　*b*Following Masoretic Text, Septuagint, and Vulgate; Arabic, some manuscripts of the Septuagint, and Syriac omit *one hundred and.*　3:5 *a*Literally *house* laid them with gold. 11 The wings of the cherubim *were* twenty cubits in *overall* length: one wing *of the one cherub was* five cubits, touching the wall of the room, and the other wing *was* five cubits, touching the wing of the other cherub; 12 *one* wing of the other cherub *was* five cubits, touching the wall of the room, and the other wing *also was* five cubits, touching the wing of the other cherub. 13 The wings of these cherubim spanned twenty cubits overall. They stood on their feet, and they faced inward. 14 And he made the veil of blue, purple, crimson, and fine linen, and wove cherubim into it.

15 Also he made in front of the temple*a* two pillars thirty-five*b* cubits high, and the capital that *was* on the top of each of *them* was five cubits. 16 He made wreaths of chainwork, as in the inner sanctuary, and put *them* on top of the pillars; and he made one hundred pomegranates, and put *them* on the wreaths of chainwork. 17 Then he set up the pillars before the temple, one on the right hand and the other on the left; he called the name of the one on the right hand Jachin, and the name of the one on the left Boaz.

4 Moreover he made a bronze altar: twenty cubits was its length, twenty cubits its width, and ten cubits its height.
2 Then he made the Sea of cast *bronze*, ten cubits from one brim to the other; *it was* completely round. Its height *was* five cubits, and a line of thirty cubits measured its circumference. 3 And under it *was* the likeness of oxen encircling it all around, ten to a cubit, all the way around the Sea. The oxen *were* cast in two rows, when it was cast. 4 It stood on twelve oxen: three looking toward the north, three looking toward the west, three looking toward the south, and three looking toward the east; the Sea *was* set upon them, and all their back parts *pointed* inward. 5 It *was* a handbreadth thick; and its brim was shaped like the brim of a cup, *like* a lily blossom. It contained three thousand*a* baths.
6 He also made ten lavers, and put five on the right side and five on the left, to wash in them; such things as they offered for the burnt offering they would wash in them, but the Sea *was* for the priests to wash in. 7 And he made ten lampstands of gold according to their design, and set *them* in the temple, five on the right side and five on the left. 8 He also made ten tables, and placed *them* in the temple, five on the right side and five on the left. And he made one hundred bowls of gold.

9 Furthermore he made the court of the priests, and the great court and doors for the court; and he overlaid these doors with bronze. 10 He set the Sea on the right side, toward the southeast.

11 Then Huram made the pots and the shovels and the bowls. So Huram finished doing the work that he was to do for King Solomon for the house of God: 12 the two pillars and the bowl-shaped capitals *that were* on top of the two pillars; the two networks covering the two bowl-shaped capitals which *were* on top of the pillars; 13 four hundred pomegranates for the two networks (two rows of pomegranates for each network, to cover the two bowl-shaped capitals that *were* on the pillars); 14 he also made carts and the lavers on the carts; 15 one Sea and twelve oxen under it; 16 also the pots, the shovels, the forks—and all their articles Huram his master*a* *craftsman* made of burnished bronze for King Solomon for the house of the LORD.
17 In the plain of Jordan the king had them cast in clay molds, between Succoth and Zeredah.*a* 18 And Solomon had all these articles made in such great abundance that the weight of the bronze was not determined.
19 Thus Solomon had all the furnishings made for the house of God: the altar of gold and the tables on which *was* the showbread; 20 the lampstands with their lamps of pure gold, to burn in the prescribed manner in front of the inner sanctuary, 21 with the flowers and the lamps and the wick-trimmers of gold, of purest gold; 22 the trimmers, the bowls, the ladles, and the censers of pure gold. As for the entry of the sanctuary, its inner doors to the Most Holy *Place*,

3:15 *a*Literally *house*   *b*Or *eighteen* (compare 1 Kings 7:15; 2 Kings 25:17; and Jeremiah 52:21)
4:5 *a*Or *two thousand* (compare 1 Kings 7:26)   4:16 *a*Literally *father*   4:17 *a*Spelled *Zaretan* in 1 Kings 7:46

and the doors of the main hall of the temple, *were* gold.

5 So all the work that Solomon had done for the house of the LORD was finished; and Solomon brought in the things which his father David had dedicated: the silver and the gold and all the furnishings. And he put *them* in the treasuries of the house of God.

2 Now Solomon assembled the elders of Israel and all the heads of the tribes, the chief fathers of the children of Israel, in Jerusalem, that they might bring the ark of the covenant of the LORD up from the City of David, which *is* Zion. 3 Therefore all the men of Israel assembled with the king at the feast, which *was* in the seventh month. 4 So all the elders of Israel came, and the Levites took up the ark. 5 Then they brought up the ark, the tabernacle of meeting, and all the holy furnishings that *were* in the tabernacle. The priests and the Levites brought them up. 6 Also King Solomon, and all the congregation of Israel who were assembled with him before the ark, were sacrificing sheep and oxen that could not be counted or numbered for multitude. 7 Then the priests brought in the ark of the covenant of the LORD to its place, into the inner sanctuary of the temple,*a* to the Most Holy *Place,* under the wings of the cherubim. 8 For the cherubim spread *their* wings over the place of the ark, and the cherubim overshadowed the ark and its poles. 9 The poles extended so that the ends of the poles of the ark could be seen from *the holy place,* in front of the inner sanctuary; but they could not be seen from outside. And they are there to this day. 10 Nothing was in the ark except the two tablets which Moses put *there* at Horeb, when the LORD made *a* covenant with the children of Israel, when they had come out of Egypt.

11 And it came to pass when the priests came out of the *Most* Holy *Place* (for all the priests who *were* present had sanctified themselves, without keeping to their divisions), 12 and the Levites *who were* the singers, all those of Asaph and Heman and Jeduthun, with their sons and their brethren, stood at the east end of the altar, clothed in white linen, having cymbals, stringed instruments and harps, and with them one hundred and twenty priests sounding with trumpets— 13 indeed it came to pass, when the trumpeters and singers *were* as one, to make one sound to be heard in praising and thanking the LORD, and when they lifted up their voice with the trumpets and cymbals and instruments of music, and praised the LORD, *saying:*

"*For He is* good,
For His mercy *endures*
forever,"*a*

that the house, the house of the LORD, was filled with a cloud, 14 so that the priests could not continue ministering because of the cloud; for the glory of the LORD filled the house of God.

6 Then Solomon spoke:

"The LORD said He would dwell in the dark cloud.
2 I have surely built You an exalted house,
And a place for You to dwell in forever."

3 Then the king turned around and blessed the whole assembly of Israel, while all the assembly of Israel was standing. 4 And he said: "Blessed *be* the LORD God of Israel, who has fulfilled with His hands *what* He spoke with His mouth to my father David, saying, 5 'Since the day that I brought My people out of the land of Egypt, I have chosen no city from any tribe of Israel *in which* to build a house, that My name might be there, nor did I choose any man to be a ruler over My people Israel. 6 Yet I have chosen Jerusalem, that My name may be there, and I have chosen David to be over My people Israel.' 7 Now it was in the heart of my father David to build a temple*a* for the name of the LORD God of Israel. 8 But the LORD said to my father David, 'Whereas it was in your heart to build a temple for My name, you did well in that it was in your heart. 9 Nevertheless you shall not build the temple, but your son who will come from your body, he shall build the temple for My

5:7 *a*Literally *house*   5:13 *a*Compare Psalm 106:1   6:7 *a*Literally *house,* and so in verses 8–10 name.' 10 So the LORD has fulfilled His word which He spoke, and I have filled the position of my father David, and sit on the throne of Israel, as the LORD promised; and I have built the temple for the name of the LORD God of Israel. 11 And there I have put the ark, in which *is* the covenant of the LORD which He made with the children of Israel."

12 Then *Solomon*[a] stood before the altar of the LORD in the presence of all the assembly of Israel, and spread out his hands 13 (for Solomon had made a bronze platform five cubits long, five cubits wide, and three cubits high, and had set it in the midst of the court; and he stood on it, knelt down on his knees before all the assembly of Israel, and spread out his hands toward heaven); 14 and he said: "LORD God of Israel, *there is* no God in heaven or on earth like You, who keep *Your* covenant and mercy with Your servants who walk before You with all their hearts. 15 You have kept what You promised Your servant David my father; You have both spoken with Your mouth and fulfilled *it* with Your hand, as *it is* this day. 16 Therefore, LORD God of Israel, now keep what You promised Your servant David my father, saying, 'You shall not fail to have a man sit before Me on the throne of Israel, only if your sons take heed to their way, that they walk in My law as you have walked before Me.' 17 And now, O LORD God of Israel, let Your word come true, which You have spoken to Your servant David.

18 "But will God indeed dwell with men on the earth? Behold, heaven and the heaven of heavens cannot contain You. How much less this temple[a] which I have built! 19 Yet regard the prayer of Your servant and his supplication, O LORD my God, and listen to the cry and the prayer which Your servant is praying before You: 20 that Your eyes may be open toward this temple day and night, toward the place where *You* said *You would* put Your name, that You may hear the prayer which Your servant makes toward this place. 21 And may You hear the supplications of Your servant and of Your people Israel, when they pray toward this place. Hear from heaven Your dwelling place, and when You hear, forgive.

22 "If anyone sins against his neighbor, and is forced to take an oath, and comes *and* takes an oath before Your altar in this temple, 23 then hear from heaven, and act, and judge Your servants, bringing retribution on the wicked by bringing his way on his own head, and justifying the righteous by giving him according to his righteousness.

24 "Or if Your people Israel are defeated before an enemy because they have sinned against You, and return and confess Your name, and pray and make supplication before You in this temple, 25 then hear from heaven and forgive the sin of Your people Israel, and bring them back to the land which You gave to them and their fathers.

26 "When the heavens are shut up and there is no rain because they have sinned against You, when they pray toward this place and confess Your name, and turn from their sin because You afflict them, 27 then hear *in* heaven, and forgive the sin of Your servants, Your people Israel, that You may teach them the good way in which they should walk; and send rain on Your land which You have given to Your people as an inheritance.

28 "When there is famine in the land, pestilence or blight or mildew, locusts or grasshoppers; when their enemies besiege them in the land of their cities; whatever plague or whatever sickness *there is;* 29 whatever prayer, whatever supplication is *made* by anyone, or by all Your people Israel, when each one knows his own burden and his own grief, and spreads out his hands to this temple: 30 then hear from heaven Your dwelling place, and forgive, and give to everyone according to all his ways, whose heart You know (for You alone know the hearts of the sons of men), 31 that they may fear You, to walk in Your ways as long as they live in the land which You gave to our fathers.

32 "Moreover, concerning a foreigner, who is not of Your people Israel, but has come from a far country for the sake of Your great name and Your mighty hand and Your outstretched arm, when they come and

6:12 *a*Literally *he* (compare 1 Kings 8:22)   6:18 *a*Literally *house* pray in this temple; 33 then hear from heaven Your dwelling place, and do according to all for which the foreigner calls to You, that all peoples of the earth may know Your name and fear You, as *do* Your people Israel, and that they may know that this temple which I have built is called by Your name.

34 "When Your people go out to battle against their enemies, wherever You send them, and when they pray to You toward this city which You have chosen and the temple which I have built for Your name, 35 then hear from heaven their prayer and their supplication, and maintain their cause.

36 "When they sin against You (for *there is* no one who does not sin), and You become angry with them and deliver them to the enemy, and they take them captive to a land far or near; 37 *yet* when they come to themselves in the land where they were carried captive, and repent, and make supplication to You in the land of their captivity, saying, 'We have sinned, we have done wrong, and have committed wickedness'; 38 and *when* they return to You with all their heart and with all their soul in the land of their captivity, where they have been carried captive, and pray toward their land which You gave to their fathers, the city which You have chosen, and toward the temple which I have built for Your name: 39 then hear from heaven Your dwelling place their prayer and their supplications, and maintain their cause, and forgive Your people who have sinned against You. 40 Now, my God, I pray, let Your eyes be open and *let* Your ears *be* attentive to the prayer *made* in this place.

41 "Now therefore,
Arise, O Lord God, to Your
   resting place,
You and the ark of Your
   strength.
Let Your priests, O Lord God,
   be clothed with salvation,
And let Your saints rejoice in
   goodness.

42 "O Lord God, do not turn away
the face of Your Anointed;

Remember the mercies of Your servant David."[a]

7

When Solomon had finished praying, fire came down from heaven and consumed the burnt offering and the sacrifices; and the glory of the Lord filled the temple.[a] 2 And the priests could not enter the house of the Lord, because the glory of the Lord had filled the Lord's house. 3 When all the children of Israel saw how the fire came down, and the glory of the Lord on the temple, they bowed their faces to the ground on the pavement, and worshiped and praised the Lord, *saying:*

"For *He is* good,
For His mercy *endures*
   forever."[a]

4 Then the king and all the people offered sacrifices before the Lord. 5 King Solomon offered a sacrifice of twenty-two thousand bulls and one hundred and twenty thousand sheep. So the king and all the people dedicated the house of God. 6 And the priests attended to their services; the Levites also with instruments of the music of the Lord, which King David had made to praise the Lord, saying, "For His mercy *endures* forever,"[a] whenever David offered praise by their ministry. The priests sounded trumpets opposite them, while all Israel stood.

7 Furthermore Solomon consecrated the middle of the court that *was* in front of the house of the Lord; for there he offered burnt offerings and the fat of the peace offerings, because the bronze altar which Solomon had made was not able to receive the burnt offerings, the grain offerings, and the fat.

8 At that time Solomon kept the feast seven days, and all Israel with him, a very great assembly from the entrance of Hamath to the Brook of Egypt.[a] 9 And on the eighth day they held a sacred assembly, for they observed the dedication of the altar seven days, and the feast seven days. 10 On the twenty-third day of the seventh month he sent the people away to their tents, joyful and glad of heart

6:42 aCompare Psalm 132:8–10   7:1 aLiterally *house*   7:3 aCompare Psalm 106:1   7:6 aCompare Psalm 106:1   7:8 aThat is, the Shihor (compare 1 Chronicles 13:5)

for the good that the LORD had done for David, for Solomon, and for His people Israel. 11 Thus Solomon finished the house of the LORD and the king's house; and Solomon successfully accomplished all that came into his heart to make in the house of the LORD and in his own house.

12 Then the LORD appeared to Solomon by night, and said to him: "I have heard your prayer, and have chosen this place for Myself as a house of sacrifice. 13 When I shut up heaven and there is no rain, or command the locusts to devour the land, or send pestilence among My people, 14 if My people who are called by My name will humble themselves, and pray and seek My face, and turn from their wicked ways, then I will hear from heaven, and will forgive their sin and heal their land. 15 Now My eyes will be open and My ears attentive to prayer *made* in this place. 16 For now I have chosen and sanctified this house, that My name may be there forever; and My eyes and My heart will be there perpetually. 17 As for you, if you walk before Me as your father David walked, and do according to all that I have commanded you, and if you keep My statutes and My judgments, 18 then I will establish the throne of your kingdom, as I covenanted with David your father, saying, 'You shall not fail *to have* a man as ruler in Israel.'

19 "But if you turn away and forsake My statutes and My commandments which I have set before you, and go and serve other gods, and worship them, 20 then I will uproot them from My land which I have given them; and this house which I have sanctified for My name I will cast out of My sight, and will make it a proverb and a byword among all peoples.

21 "And *as for* this house, which is exalted, everyone who passes by it will be astonished and say, 'Why has the LORD done thus to this land and this house?' 22 Then they will answer, 'Because they forsook the LORD God of their fathers, who brought them out of the land of Egypt, and embraced other gods, and worshiped them and served them; therefore He has brought all this calamity on them.' "

8 It came to pass at the end of twenty years, when Solomon had built the house of the LORD and his own house, 2 that the cities which Hiram[a] had given to Solomon, Solomon built them; and he settled the children of Israel there. 3 And Solomon went to Hamath Zobah and seized it. 4 He also built Tadmor in the wilderness, and all the storage cities which he built in Hamath. 5 He built Upper Beth Horon and Lower Beth Horon, fortified cities *with* walls, gates, and bars, 6 also Baalath and all the storage cities that Solomon had, and all the chariot cities and the cities of the cavalry, and all that Solomon desired to build in Jerusalem, in Lebanon, and in all the land of his dominion.

7 All the people *who were* left of the Hittites, Amorites, Perizzites, Hivites, and Jebusites, who *were* not of Israel— 8 that is, their descendants who were left in the land after them, whom the children of Israel did not destroy—from these Solomon raised forced labor, as it is to this day. 9 But Solomon did not make the children of Israel servants for his work. Some *were* men of war, captains of his officers, captains of his chariots, and his cavalry. 10 And others *were* chiefs of the officials of King Solomon: two hundred and fifty, who ruled over the people.

11 Now Solomon brought the daughter of Pharaoh up from the City of David to the house he had built for her, for he said, "My wife shall not dwell in the house of David king of Israel, because *the places* to which the ark of the LORD has come are holy."

12 Then Solomon offered burnt offerings to the LORD on the altar of the LORD which he had built before the vestibule, 13 according to the daily rate, offering according to the commandment of Moses, for the Sabbaths, the New Moons, and the three appointed yearly feasts—the Feast of Unleavened Bread, the Feast of Weeks, and the Feast of Tabernacles. 14 And, according to the order of David his father, he appointed the divisions of the priests for their service, the Levites for their duties (to praise and serve before the priests) as the duty of each day required, and the gatekeepers by their divisions at

8:2 [a]Hebrew *Huram* (compare 2 Chronicles 2:3)

each gate; for so David the man of God had commanded. 15 They did not depart from the command of the king to the priests and Levites concerning any matter or concerning the treasuries.

16 Now all the work of Solomon was well-ordered from[a] the day of the foundation of the house of the LORD until it was finished. So the house of the LORD was completed.

17 Then Solomon went to Ezion Geber and Elath[a] on the seacoast, in the land of Edom. 18 And Hiram sent him ships by the hand of his servants, and servants who knew the sea. They went with the servants of Solomon to Ophir, and acquired four hundred and fifty talents of gold from there, and brought it to King Solomon.

9 Now when the queen of Sheba heard of the fame of Solomon, she came to Jerusalem to test Solomon with hard questions, *having* a very great retinue, camels that bore spices, gold in abundance, and precious stones; and when she came to Solomon, she spoke with him about all that was in her heart. 2 So Solomon answered all her questions; there was nothing so difficult for Solomon that he could not explain it to her. 3 And when the queen of Sheba had seen the wisdom of Solomon, the house that he had built, 4 the food on his table, the seating of his servants, the service of his waiters and their apparel, his cupbearers and their apparel, and his entryway by which he went up to the house of the LORD, there was no more spirit in her.

5 Then she said to the king: "*It was* a true report which I heard in my own land about your words and your wisdom. 6 However I did not believe their words until I came and saw with my own eyes; and indeed the half of the greatness of your wisdom was not told me. You exceed the fame of which I heard. 7 Happy *are* your men and happy *are* these your servants, who stand continually before you and hear your wisdom! 8 Blessed be the LORD your God, who delighted in you, setting you on His throne *to be* king for the LORD your God! Because your God has loved Israel, to establish them forever, therefore He made you king over them, to do justice and righteousness."

9 And she gave the king one hundred and twenty talents of gold, spices in great abundance, and precious stones; there never were any spices such as those the queen of Sheba gave to King Solomon.

10 Also, the servants of Hiram and the servants of Solomon, who brought gold from Ophir, brought algum[a] wood and precious stones. 11 And the king made walkways *of* the algum[a] wood for the house of the LORD and for the king's house, also harps and stringed instruments for singers; and there were none such *as these* seen before in the land of Judah.

12 Now King Solomon gave to the queen of Sheba all she desired, whatever she asked, *much more* than she had brought to the king. So she turned and went to her own country, she and her servants.

13 The weight of gold that came to Solomon yearly was six hundred and sixty-six talents of gold, 14 besides *what* the traveling merchants and traders brought. And all the kings of Arabia and governors of the country brought gold and silver to Solomon. 15 And King Solomon made two hundred large shields of hammered gold; six hundred *shekels* of hammered gold went into each shield. 16 *He* also *made* three hundred shields of hammered gold; three hundred *shekels*[a] of gold went into each shield. The king put them in the House of the Forest of Lebanon.

17 Moreover the king made a great throne of ivory, and overlaid it with pure gold. 18 The throne *had* six steps, with a footstool of gold, *which were* fastened to the throne; there were armrests on either side of the place of the seat, and two lions stood beside the armrests. 19 Twelve lions stood there, one on each side of the six steps; nothing like *this* had been made for any *other* kingdom.

20 All King Solomon's drinking vessels *were* gold, and all the vessels of the House of the Forest of Lebanon *were* pure gold. Not *one was* silver, for this was accounted as nothing in the days of Solomon. 21 For the

8:16 aFollowing Septuagint, Syriac, and Vulgate; Masoretic Text reads *as far as*.   8:17 aHebrew *Eloth* (compare 2 Kings 14:22)   9:10 aOr *almug* (compare 1 Kings 10:11, 12)   9:11 aOr *almug* (compare 1 Kings 10:11, 12)   9:16 aOr *three minas* (compare 1 Kings 10:17)

A Kingdom Divided

Following King Solomon's death in 922 B.C., the united kingdom of Israel was divided into the 2 kingdoms—the Kingdom of Israel and the Kingdom of Judah. Most scholars agree that the split occurred because of a policy maintained by Solomon's son and successor, Rehoboam. Solomon had imposed heavy taxes and forced labor upon the people of Israel in order to accommodate his luxurious habits. After his death, the people asked Rehoboam to relieve some of their duties. When he refused, the ten northern tribes declared their independence from the two southern tribes.

The Kingdom of Judah, in the south, included the tribe of Judah and part of Benjamin. The tribe of Simeon may have joined them later. Its boundaries stretched from just north of Mizpah (in the north) to the desert region called Negeb (in the south) and from the Great Sea east to the Jordan River. Jerusalem was the capital city.

Israel, the Northern Kingdom, had its northern boundary near the city of Dan and extended south to Bethel. The Great Sea and the city of Rabbah, respectively, formed the western and eastern boundaries. The Northern Kingdom had three capital cities—first Shechem, then Tirzah, and finally, Samaria.

king's ships went to Tarshish with the servants of Hiram.[a] Once every three years the merchant ships[b] came, bringing gold, silver, ivory, apes, and monkeys.[c]

22 So King Solomon surpassed all the kings of the earth in riches and wisdom. 23 And all the kings of the earth sought the presence of Solomon to hear his wisdom, which God had put in his heart. 24 Each man brought his present: articles of silver and gold, garments, armor, spices, horses, and mules, at a set rate year by year.

25 Solomon had four thousand stalls for horses and chariots, and twelve thousand horsemen whom he stationed in the chariot cities and with the king at Jerusalem.

26 So he reigned over all the kings from the River[a] to the land of the Philistines, as far as the border of Egypt. 27 The king made silver *as common* in Jerusalem as stones, and he made cedar trees as abundant as the sycamores which *are* in the lowland. 28 And they brought horses to Solomon from Egypt and from all lands.

29 Now the rest of the acts of Solomon, first and last, *are* they not written in the book of Nathan the prophet, in the prophecy of Ahijah the Shilonite, and in the visions of Iddo the seer concerning Jeroboam the son of Nebat? 30 Solomon reigned in Jerusalem over all Israel forty years. 31 Then Solomon rested with his fathers, and was buried in the City of David his father. And Rehoboam his son reigned in his place.

10 And Rehoboam went to Shechem, for all Israel had gone to Shechem to make him king. 2 So it happened, when Jeroboam the son of Nebat heard *it* (he was in Egypt, where he had fled from the presence of King Solomon), that Jeroboam returned from Egypt. 3 Then they sent for him and called him. And Jeroboam and all Israel came and spoke to Rehoboam, saying, 4 "Your father made our yoke heavy; now therefore, lighten the burdensome service of your father and his heavy yoke which he

put on us, and we will serve you."

5 So he said to them, "Come back to me after three days." And the people departed.

6 Then King Rehoboam consulted the elders who stood before his father Solomon while he still lived, saying, "How do you advise *me* to answer these people?"

7 And they spoke to him, saying, "If you are kind to these people, and please them, and speak good words to them, they will be your servants forever."

8 But he rejected the advice which the elders had given him, and consulted the young men who had grown up with him, who stood before him. 9 And he said to them, "What advice do you give? How should we answer this people who have spoken to me, saying, 'Lighten the yoke which your father put on us'?"

10 Then the young men who had grown up with him spoke to him, saying, "Thus you should speak to the people who have spoken to you, saying, 'Your father made our yoke heavy, but you make *it* lighter on us'—thus you shall say to them: 'My little *finger* shall be thicker than my father's waist! 11 And now, whereas my father put a heavy yoke on you, I will add to your yoke; my father chastised you with whips, but I *will chastise you* with scourges!' "[a]

12 So Jeroboam and all the people came to Rehoboam on the third day, as the king had directed, saying, "Come back to me the third day." 13 Then the king answered them roughly. King Rehoboam rejected the advice of the elders, 14 and he spoke to them according to the advice of the young men, saying, "My father[a] made your yoke heavy, but I will add to it; my father chastised you with whips, but I *will chastise you* with scourges!"[b] 15 So the king did not listen to the people; for the turn of *events* was from God, that the LORD might fulfill His word, which He had spoken by the hand of Ahijah the Shilonite to Jeroboam the son of Nebat.

16 Now when all Israel *saw* that the king did not listen to them, the people answered the king, saying:

9:21 [a]Hebrew *Huram* (compare 1 Kings 10:22)   [b]Literally *ships of Tarshish* (deep-sea vessels)   [c]Or *peacocks*   9:26 [a]That is, the Euphrates   10:11 [a]Literally *scorpions*   10:14 [a]Following many Hebrew manuscripts, Septuagint, Syriac, and Vulgate (compare verse 10 and 1 Kings 12:14); Masoretic Text reads *I.*   [b]Literally *scorpions*

"What share have we in David?
We have no inheritance in the
son of Jesse.
Every man to your tents, O
Israel!
Now see to your own house, O
David!"

So all Israel departed to their tents.
17 But Rehoboam reigned over the
children of Israel who dwelt in the
cities of Judah.

18 Then King Rehoboam sent Hadoram, who *was* in charge of revenue; but the children of Israel stoned
him with stones, and he died. Therefore King Rehoboam mounted *his*
chariot in haste to flee to Jerusalem.
19 So Israel has been in rebellion
against the house of David to this
day.

11 Now when Rehoboam came to
Jerusalem, he assembled from
the house of Judah and Benjamin one
hundred and eighty thousand chosen
men who were warriors, to fight
against Israel, that he might restore
the kingdom to Rehoboam.
2 But the word of the LORD came
to Shemaiah the man of God, saying,
3 "Speak to Rehoboam the son of
Solomon, king of Judah, and to all
Israel in Judah and Benjamin, saying, 4 'Thus says the LORD: "You shall
not go up or fight against your brethren! Let every man return to his
house, for this thing is from Me." ' "
Therefore they obeyed the words of
the LORD, and turned back from attacking Jeroboam.
5 So Rehoboam dwelt in Jerusalem, and built cities for defense in Judah. 6 And he built Bethlehem, Etam,
Tekoa, 7 Beth Zur, Sochoh, Adullam,
8 Gath, Mareshah, Ziph, 9 Adoraim,
Lachish, Azekah, 10 Zorah, Aijalon,
and Hebron, which are in Judah and
Benjamin, fortified cities. 11 And he
fortified the strongholds, and put
captains in them, and stores of food,
oil, and wine. 12 Also in every city *he
put* shields and spears, and made
them very strong, having Judah and
Benjamin on his side.
13 And from all their territories the
priests and the Levites who *were* in
all Israel took their stand with him.
14 For the Levites left their common-

lands and their possessions and came
to Judah and Jerusalem, for Jeroboam and his sons had rejected them
from serving as priests to the LORD.
15 Then he appointed for himself
priests for the high places, for the demons, and the calf idols which he had
made. 16 And after *the Levites left,*[a]
those from all the tribes of Israel,
such as set their heart to seek the
LORD God of Israel, came to Jerusalem to sacrifice to the LORD God of
their fathers. 17 So they strengthened
the kingdom of Judah, and made Rehoboam the son of Solomon strong
for three years, because they walked
in the way of David and Solomon for
three years.
18 Then Rehoboam took for himself as wife Mahalath the daughter
of Jerimoth the son of David, *and of*
Abihail the daughter of Eliah the son
of Jesse. 19 And she bore him children: Jeush, Shamariah, and Zaham.
20 After her he took Maachah the
granddaughter[a] of Absalom; and she
bore him Abijah, Attai, Ziza, and
Shelomith. 21 Now Rehoboam loved
Maachah the granddaughter of Absalom more than all his wives and
his concubines; for he took eighteen
wives and sixty concubines, and begot twenty-eight sons and sixty
daughters. 22 And Rehoboam appointed Abijah the son of Maachah
as chief, *to be* leader among his
brothers; for he *intended* to make
him king. 23 He dealt wisely, and dispersed some of his sons throughout
all the territories of Judah and Benjamin, to every fortified city; and he
gave them provisions in abundance.
He also sought many wives *for them.*

12 Now it came to pass, when Rehoboam had established the
kingdom and had strengthened himself, that he forsook the law of the
LORD, and all Israel along with him.
2 And it happened in the fifth year
of King Rehoboam *that* Shishak king
of Egypt came up against Jerusalem,
because they had transgressed
against the LORD, 3 with twelve hundred chariots, sixty thousand horsemen, and people without number
who came with him out of Egypt—
the Lubim and the Sukkiim and the
Ethiopians. 4 And he took the forti-

11:16 *a*Literally *after them*   11:20 *a*Literally *daughter,* but in the broader sense of granddaughter (compare
2 Chronicles 13:2)

fied cities of Judah and came to Jerusalem.

5 Then Shemaiah the prophet came to Rehoboam and the leaders of Judah, who were gathered together in Jerusalem because of Shishak, and said to them, "Thus says the LORD: 'You have forsaken Me, and therefore I also have left you in the hand of Shishak.' "

6 So the leaders of Israel and the king humbled themselves; and they said, "The LORD *is* righteous."

7 Now when the LORD saw that they humbled themselves, the word of the LORD came to Shemaiah, saying, "They have humbled themselves; *therefore* I will not destroy them, but I will grant them some deliverance. My wrath shall not be poured out on Jerusalem by the hand of Shishak. 8 Nevertheless they will be his servants, that they may distinguish My service from the service of the kingdoms of the nations."

9 So Shishak king of Egypt came up against Jerusalem, and took away the treasures of the house of the LORD and the treasures of the king's house; he took everything. He also carried away the gold shields which Solomon had made. 10 Then King Rehoboam made bronze shields in their place, and committed *them* to the hands of the captains of the guard, who guarded the doorway of the king's house. 11 And whenever the king entered the house of the LORD, the guard would go and bring them out; then they would take them back into the guardroom. 12 When he humbled himself, the wrath of the LORD turned from him, so as not to destroy *him* completely; and things also went well in Judah.

13 Thus King Rehoboam strengthened himself in Jerusalem and reigned. Now Rehoboam *was* forty-one years old when he became king; and he reigned seventeen years in Jerusalem, the city which the LORD had chosen out of all the tribes of Israel, to put His name there. His mother's name *was* Naamah, an Ammonitess. 14 And he did evil, because he did not prepare his heart to seek the LORD.

15 The acts of Rehoboam, first and last, *are* they not written in the book of Shemaiah the prophet, and of Iddo the seer concerning genealogies?

And *there were* wars between Rehoboam and Jeroboam all their days. 16 So Rehoboam rested with his fathers, and was buried in the City of David. Then Abijah*ᵃ* his son reigned in his place.

13 In the eighteenth year of King Jeroboam, Abijah became king over Judah. 2 He reigned three years in Jerusalem. His mother's name *was* Michaiah*ᵃ* the daughter of Uriel of Gibeah.

And there was war between Abijah and Jeroboam. 3 Abijah set the battle in order with an army of valiant warriors, four hundred thousand choice men. Jeroboam also drew up in battle formation against him with eight hundred thousand choice men, mighty men of valor.

4 Then Abijah stood on Mount Zemaraim, which *is* in the mountains of Ephraim, and said, "Hear me, Jeroboam and all Israel: 5 Should you not know that the LORD God of Israel gave the dominion over Israel to David forever, to him and his sons, by a covenant of salt? 6 Yet Jeroboam the son of Nebat, the servant of Solomon the son of David, rose up and rebelled against his lord. 7 Then worthless rogues gathered to him, and strengthened themselves against Rehoboam the son of Solomon, when Rehoboam was young and inexperienced and could not withstand them. 8 And now you think to withstand the kingdom of the LORD, which is in the hand of the sons of David; and you *are* a great multitude, and with you are the gold calves which Jeroboam made for you as gods. 9 Have you not cast out the priests of the LORD, the sons of Aaron, and the Levites, and made for yourselves priests, like the peoples of *other* lands, so that whoever comes to consecrate himself with a young bull and seven rams may be a priest of *things that are* not gods? 10 But as for us, the LORD *is* our God, and we have not forsaken Him; and the priests who minister to the LORD *are* the sons of Aaron, and the Levites *attend* to *their* duties. 11 And they burn to the LORD every morning and every evening burnt sacrifices and sweet incense; *they* also *set* the showbread *in order on* the pure *gold* table, and the lampstand of gold with

12:16 *ᵃ*Spelled *Abijam* in 1 Kings 14:31   13:2 *ᵃ*Spelled *Maachah* in 11:20, 21 and 1 Kings 15:2

its lamps to burn every evening; for we keep the command of the LORD our God, but you have forsaken Him. 12 Now look, God Himself is with us as *our* head, and His priests with sounding trumpets to sound the alarm against you. O children of Israel, do not fight against the LORD God of your fathers, for you shall not prosper!"

13 But Jeroboam caused an ambush to go around behind them; so they were in front of Judah, and the ambush *was* behind them. 14 And when Judah looked around, to their surprise the battle line *was* at both front and rear; and they cried out to the LORD, and the priests sounded the trumpets. 15 Then the men of Judah gave a shout; and as the men of Judah shouted, it happened that God struck Jeroboam and all Israel before Abijah and Judah. 16 And the children of Israel fled before Judah, and God delivered them into their hand. 17 Then Abijah and his people struck them with a great slaughter; so five hundred thousand choice men of Israel fell slain. 18 Thus the children of Israel were subdued at that time; and the children of Judah prevailed, because they relied on the LORD God of their fathers.

19 And Abijah pursued Jeroboam and took cities from him: Bethel with its villages, Jeshanah with its villages, and Ephrain*a* with its villages. 20 So Jeroboam did not recover strength again in the days of Abijah; and the LORD struck him, and he died.

21 But Abijah grew mighty, married fourteen wives, and begot twenty-two sons and sixteen daughters. 22 Now the rest of the acts of Abijah, his ways, and his sayings *are* written in the annals of the prophet Iddo.

14 So Abijah rested with his fathers, and they buried him in the City of David. Then Asa his son reigned in his place. In his days the land was quiet for ten years.

2 Asa did *what was* good and right in the eyes of the LORD his God, 3 for he removed the altars of the foreign *gods* and the high places, and broke down the *sacred* pillars and cut down the wooden images. 4 He commanded Judah to seek the LORD

God of their fathers, and to observe the law and the commandment. 5 He also removed the high places and the incense altars from all the cities of Judah, and the kingdom was quiet under him. 6 And he built fortified cities in Judah, for the land had rest; he had no war in those years, because the LORD had given him rest. 7 Therefore he said to Judah, "Let us build these cities and make walls around *them*, and towers, gates, and bars, *while* the land *is* yet before us, because we have sought the LORD our God; we have sought *Him*, and He has given us rest on every side." So they built and prospered. 8 And Asa had an army of three hundred thousand from Judah who carried shields and spears, and from Benjamin two hundred and eighty thousand men who carried shields and drew bows; all these *were* mighty men of valor.

9 Then Zerah the Ethiopian came out against them with an army of a million men and three hundred chariots, and he came to Mareshah. 10 So Asa went out against him, and they set the troops in battle array in the Valley of Zephathah at Mareshah. 11 And Asa cried out to the LORD his God, and said, "LORD, *it is* nothing for You to help, whether with many or with those who have no power; help us, O LORD our God, for we rest on You, and in Your name we go against this multitude. O LORD, You *are* our God; do not let man prevail against You!"

12 So the LORD struck the Ethiopians before Asa and Judah, and the Ethiopians fled. 13 And Asa and the people who *were* with him pursued them to Gerar. So the Ethiopians were overthrown, and they could not recover, for they were broken before the LORD and His army. And they carried away very much spoil. 14 Then they defeated all the cities around Gerar, for the fear of the LORD came upon them; and they plundered all the cities, for there was exceedingly much spoil in them. 15 They also attacked the livestock enclosures, and carried off sheep and camels in abundance, and returned to Jerusalem.

15 Now the Spirit of God came upon Azariah the son of Oded. 2 And he went out to meet Asa, and

The Pinnacle of the Temple

Archaeologists have recently unearthed an interesting inscription in Jerusalem which sheds new light on one of the major events in Jesus' life. This inscription is at the base of the southern-most point of the temple mount. It reads, "to the place of the blowing of the shofar."

Every Sabbath in ancient Jerusalem, the new day was announced with the blowing of the shofar—a ram's horn. The ancient historian Josephus records that the ram's horn was always blown from the pinnacle of the temple.

During Jesus' temptation, He was taken to the pinnacle of the temple. There He was told that if He truly was the Son of God, he should throw Himself off and God would send angels to bear Him up, so that not even His foot should strike the stones (see Matt. 4:6).

For years, scholars thought that the pinnacle of the temple was an isolated area at the far-eastern corner of the temple mount. They interpreted Jesus' temptation as merely testing God's faithfulness to Him. But this recent archaeological discovery reveals that it meant much more than that.

The pinnacle was in fact at the opposite side of the temple. It overlooked the marketplace of the nations. Here merchants and businessmen from all corners of the Roman Empire gathered to trade goods and exchange stories of far-off lands. Jesus had a perfect opportunity to show representatives of the then-known world that He was the Son of God, simply by jumping off and letting God's angels protect Him. But He chose to keep to His divine calling. Rather than seek glory from men, Jesus honored God by fulfilling His purpose on earth (see John 8:54).

There are many times when we are seduced to do the spectacular simply to receive recognition, honor, and praise from others. Sometimes this recognition is deserved and ordained by God. But when it comes in direct conflict with God's will for our lives, then we must follow Christ's example. We must stay single-minded in our purpose and accept God's divine calling for our lives. The reward for doing so cannot compare with any passing praise on earth.

said to him: "Hear me, Asa, and all Judah and Benjamin. The LORD *is* with you while you are with Him. If you seek Him, He will be found by you; but if you forsake Him, He will forsake you. 3 For a long time Israel *has been* without the true God, without a teaching priest, and without law; 4 but when in their trouble they turned to the LORD God of Israel, and sought Him, He was found by them. 5 And in those times *there was* no peace to the one who went out, nor to the one who came in, but great turmoil *was* on all the inhabitants of the lands. 6 So nation was destroyed by nation, and city by city, for God troubled them with every adversity. 7 But you, be strong and do not let your hands be weak, for your work shall be rewarded!"

8 And when Asa heard these words and the prophecy of Oded[a] the prophet, he took courage, and removed the abominable idols from all the land of Judah and Benjamin and from the cities which he had taken in the mountains of Ephraim; and he restored the altar of the LORD that *was* before the vestibule of the LORD. 9 Then he gathered all Judah and Benjamin, and those who dwelt with them from Ephraim, Manasseh, and Simeon, for they came over to him in great numbers from Israel when they saw that the LORD his God was with him.

10 So they gathered together at Jerusalem in the third month, in the fifteenth year of the reign of Asa. 11 And they offered to the LORD at that time seven hundred bulls and seven thousand sheep from the spoil they had brought. 12 Then they entered into a covenant to seek the LORD God of their fathers with all their heart and with all their soul; 13 and whoever would not seek the LORD God of Israel was to be put to death, whether small or great, whether man or woman. 14 Then they took an oath before the LORD with a loud voice, with shouting and trumpets and rams' horns. 15 And all Judah rejoiced at the oath, for they had sworn with all their heart and sought Him with all their soul; and He was found by them, and the LORD gave them rest all around.

16 Also he removed Maachah, the mother of Asa the king, from *being* queen mother, because she had made an obscene image of Asherah;[a] and Asa cut down her obscene image, then crushed and burned *it* by the Brook Kidron. 17 But the high places were not removed from Israel. Nevertheless the heart of Asa was loyal all his days.

18 He also brought into the house of God the things that his father had dedicated and that he himself had dedicated: silver and gold and utensils. 19 And there was no war until the thirty-fifth year of the reign of Asa.

16 In the thirty-sixth year of the reign of Asa, Baasha king of Israel came up against Judah and built Ramah, that he might let none go out or come in to Asa king of Judah. 2 Then Asa brought silver and gold from the treasuries of the house of the LORD and of the king's house, and sent to Ben-Hadad king of Syria, who dwelt in Damascus, saying, 3 "*Let there be* a treaty between you and me, as there was between my father and your father. See, I have sent you silver and gold; come, break your treaty with Baasha king of Israel, so that he will withdraw from me."

4 So Ben-Hadad heeded King Asa, and sent the captains of his armies against the cities of Israel. They attacked Ijon, Dan, Abel Maim, and all the storage cities of Naphtali. 5 Now it happened, when Baasha heard *it*, that he stopped building Ramah and ceased his work. 6 Then King Asa took all Judah, and they carried away the stones and timber of Ramah, which Baasha had used for building; and with them he built Geba and Mizpah.

7 And at that time Hanani the seer came to Asa king of Judah, and said to him: "Because you have relied on the king of Syria, and have not relied on the LORD your God, therefore the army of the king of Syria has escaped from your hand. 8 Were the Ethiopians and the Lubim not a huge army with very many chariots and horsemen? Yet, because you relied on the LORD, He delivered them into your

15:8 [a]Following Masoretic Text and Septuagint; Syriac and Vulgate read *Azariah the son of Oded* (compare verse 1).   15:16 [a]A Canaanite deity hand. 9 For the eyes of the LORD run to and fro throughout the whole earth, to show Himself strong on behalf of *those* whose heart *is* loyal to Him. In this you have done foolishly; therefore from now on you shall have wars." 10 Then Asa was angry with the seer, and put him in prison, for *he was* enraged at him because of this. And Asa oppressed *some* of the people at that time.

11 Note that the acts of Asa, first and last, are indeed written in the book of the kings of Judah and Israel. 12 And in the thirty-ninth year of his reign, Asa became diseased in his feet, and his malady was severe; yet in his disease he did not seek the LORD, but the physicians.

13 So Asa rested with his fathers; he died in the forty-first year of his reign. 14 They buried him in his own tomb, which he had made for himself in the City of David; and they laid him in the bed which was filled with spices and various ingredients prepared in a mixture of ointments. They made a very great burning for him.

17 Then Jehoshaphat his son reigned in his place, and strengthened himself against Israel. 2 And he placed troops in all the fortified cities of Judah, and set garrisons in the land of Judah and in the cities of Ephraim which Asa his father had taken. 3 Now the LORD was with Jehoshaphat, because he walked in the former ways of his father David; he did not seek the Baals, 4 but sought the God*ᵃ* of his father, and walked in His commandments and not according to the acts of Israel. 5 Therefore the LORD established the kingdom in his hand; and all Judah gave presents to Jehoshaphat, and he had riches and honor in abundance. 6 And his heart took delight in the ways of the LORD; moreover he removed the high places and wooden images from Judah.

7 Also in the third year of his reign he sent his leaders, Ben-Hail, Obadiah, Zechariah, Nethanel, and Michaiah, to teach in the cities of Judah. 8 And with them *he sent* Levites: Shemaiah, Nethaniah, Zebadiah, Asahel, Shemiramoth, Jehonathan,

Adonijah, Tobijah, and Tobadonijah—the Levites; and with them Elishama and Jehoram, the priests. 9 So they taught in Judah, and *had* the Book of the Law of the LORD with them; they went throughout all the cities of Judah and taught the people.

10 And the fear of the LORD fell on all the kingdoms of the lands that *were* around Judah, so that they did not make war against Jehoshaphat. 11 Also *some* of the Philistines brought Jehoshaphat presents and silver as tribute; and the Arabians brought him flocks, seven thousand seven hundred rams and seven thousand seven hundred male goats.

12 So Jehoshaphat became increasingly powerful, and he built fortresses and storage cities in Judah. 13 He had much property in the cities of Judah; and the men of war, mighty men of valor, *were* in Jerusalem.

14 These *are* their numbers, according to their fathers' houses. Of Judah, the captains of thousands: Adnah the captain, and with him three hundred thousand mighty men of valor; 15 and next to him *was* Jehohanan the captain, and with him two hundred and eighty thousand; 16 and next to him *was* Amasiah the son of Zichri, who willingly offered himself to the LORD, and with him two hundred thousand mighty men of valor. 17 Of Benjamin: Eliada a mighty man of valor, and with him two hundred thousand men armed with bow and shield; 18 and next to him *was* Jehozabad, and with him one hundred and eighty thousand prepared for war. 19 These served the king, besides those the king put in the fortified cities throughout all Judah.

18 Jehoshaphat had riches and honor in abundance; and by marriage he allied himself with Ahab. 2 After some years he went down to *visit* Ahab in Samaria; and Ahab killed sheep and oxen in abundance for him and the people who were with him, and persuaded him to go up *with him* to Ramoth Gilead. 3 So Ahab king of Israel said to Jehoshaphat king of Judah, "Will you go with me *against* Ramoth Gilead?"

And he answered him, "I *am* as you *are*, and my people as your peo-

---

17:4 ᵃSeptuagint reads LORD God.

ple; *we will be* with you in the war."

4 Also Jehoshaphat said to the king of Israel, "Please inquire for the word of the LORD today."

5 Then the king of Israel gathered the prophets together, four hundred men, and said to them, "Shall we go to war against Ramoth Gilead, or shall I refrain?"

So they said, "Go up, for God will deliver it into the king's hand."

6 But Jehoshaphat said, "*Is there* not still a prophet of the LORD here, that we may inquire of Him?"*a*

7 So the king of Israel said to Jehoshaphat, "*There is* still one man by whom we may inquire of the LORD; but I hate him, because he never prophesies good concerning me, but always evil. He *is* Micaiah the son of Imla."

And Jehoshaphat said, "Let not the king say such things!"

8 Then the king of Israel called one of *his* officers and said, "Bring Micaiah the son of Imla quickly!"

9 The king of Israel and Jehoshaphat king of Judah, clothed in *their* robes, sat each on his throne; and they sat at a threshing floor at the entrance of the gate of Samaria; and all the prophets prophesied before them. 10 Now Zedekiah the son of Chenaanah had made horns of iron for himself; and he said, "Thus says the LORD: 'With these you shall gore the Syrians until they are destroyed.'"

11 And all the prophets prophesied so, saying, "Go up to Ramoth Gilead and prosper, for the LORD will deliver *it* into the king's hand."

12 Then the messenger who had gone to call Micaiah spoke to him, saying, "Now listen, the words of the prophets with one accord encourage the king. Therefore please let your word be like *the word of* one of them, and speak encouragement."

13 And Micaiah said, "*As* the LORD lives, whatever my God says, that I will speak."

14 Then he came to the king; and the king said to him, "Micaiah, shall we go to war against Ramoth Gilead, or shall I refrain?"

And he said, "Go and prosper, and they shall be delivered into your hand!"

15 So the king said to him, "How

many times shall I make you swear that you tell me nothing but the truth in the name of the LORD?"

16 Then he said, "I saw all Israel scattered on the mountains, as sheep that have no shepherd. And the LORD said, 'These have no master. Let each return to his house in peace.'"

17 And the king of Israel said to Jehoshaphat, "Did I not tell you he would not prophesy good concerning me, but evil?"

18 Then *Micaiah* said, "Therefore hear the word of the LORD: I saw the LORD sitting on His throne, and all the host of heaven standing on His right hand and His left. 19 And the LORD said, 'Who will persuade Ahab king of Israel to go up, that he may fall at Ramoth Gilead?' So one spoke in this manner, and another spoke in that manner. 20 Then a spirit came forward and stood before the LORD, and said, 'I will persuade him.' The LORD said to him, 'In what way?' 21 So he said, 'I will go out and be a lying spirit in the mouth of all his prophets.' And *the* LORD said, 'You shall persuade *him* and also prevail; go out and do so.' 22 Therefore look! The LORD has put a lying spirit in the mouth of these prophets of yours, and the LORD has declared disaster against you."

23 Then Zedekiah the son of Chenaanah went near and struck Micaiah on the cheek, and said, "Which way did the spirit from the LORD go from me to speak to you?"

24 And Micaiah said, "Indeed you shall see on that day when you go into an inner chamber to hide!"

25 Then the king of Israel said, "Take Micaiah, and return him to Amon the governor of the city and to Joash the king's son; 26 and say, 'Thus says the king: "Put this *fellow* in prison, and feed him with bread of affliction and water of affliction, until I return in peace."'"

27 But Micaiah said, "If you ever return in peace, the LORD has not spoken by me." And he said, "Take heed, all you people!"

28 So the king of Israel and Jehoshaphat the king of Judah went up to Ramoth Gilead. 29 And the king of Israel said to Jehoshaphat, "I will disguise myself and go into battle; but you put on your robes." So the king

18:6 *a*Or *him*

of Israel disguised himself, and they went into battle.

30 Now the king of Syria had commanded the captains of the chariots who *were* with him, saying, "Fight with no one small or great, but only with the king of Israel."

31 So it was, when the captains of the chariots saw Jehoshaphat, that they said, "It *is* the king of Israel!" Therefore they surrounded him to attack; but Jehoshaphat cried out, and the LORD helped him, and God diverted them from him. 32 For so it was, when the captains of the chariots saw that it was not the king of Israel, that they turned back from pursuing him. 33 Now a certain man drew a bow at random, and struck the king of Israel between the joints of his armor. So he said to the driver of his chariot, "Turn around and take me out of the battle, for I am wounded." 34 The battle increased that day, and the king of Israel propped *himself* up in *his* chariot facing the Syrians until evening; and about the time of sunset he died.

19 Then Jehoshaphat the king of Judah returned safely to his house in Jerusalem. 2 And Jehu the son of Hanani the seer went out to meet him, and said to King Jehoshaphat, "Should you help the wicked and love those who hate the LORD? Therefore the wrath of the LORD *is* upon you. 3 Nevertheless good things are found in you, in that you have removed the wooden images from the land, and have prepared your heart to seek God."

4 So Jehoshaphat dwelt at Jerusalem; and he went out again among the people from Beersheba to the mountains of Ephraim, and brought them back to the LORD God of their fathers. 5 Then he set judges in the land throughout all the fortified cities of Judah, city by city, 6 and said to the judges, "Take heed to what you are doing, for you do not judge for man but for the LORD, who *is* with you in the judgment. 7 Now therefore, let the fear of the LORD be upon you; take care and do *it*, for *there is* no iniquity with the LORD our God, no partiality, nor taking of bribes."

8 Moreover in Jerusalem, for the judgment of the LORD and for controversies, Jehoshaphat appointed some of the Levites and priests, and some of the chief fathers of Israel, when they returned to Jerusalem.ª 9 And he commanded them, saying, "Thus you shall act in the fear of the LORD, faithfully and with a loyal heart: 10 Whatever case comes to you from your brethren who dwell in their cities, whether of bloodshed or offenses against law or commandment, against statutes or ordinances, you shall warn them, lest they trespass against the LORD and wrath come upon you and your brethren. Do this, and you will not be guilty. 11 And take notice: Amariah the chief priest *is* over you in all matters of the LORD; and Zebadiah the son of Ishmael, the ruler of the house of Judah, for all the king's matters; also the Levites *will be* officials before you. Behave courageously, and the LORD will be with the good."

20 It happened after this *that* the people of Moab with the people of Ammon, and *others* with them besides the Ammonites,ª came to battle against Jehoshaphat. 2 Then some came and told Jehoshaphat, saying, "A great multitude is coming against you from beyond the sea, from Syria;ª and they are in Hazazon Tamar" (which *is* En Gedi). 3 And Jehoshaphat feared, and set himself to seek the LORD, and proclaimed a fast throughout all Judah. 4 So Judah gathered together to ask *help* from the LORD; and from all the cities of Judah they came to seek the LORD.

5 Then Jehoshaphat stood in the assembly of Judah and Jerusalem, in the house of the LORD, before the new court, 6 and said: "O LORD God of our fathers, *are* You not God in heaven, and do You *not* rule over all the kingdoms of the nations, and in Your hand *is there not* power and might, so that no one is able to withstand You? 7 *Are* You not our God, *who* drove out the inhabitants of this land before Your people Israel, and gave it to the descendants of Abraham Your friend forever? 8 And they dwell in it, and have built You a sanc-

19:8 ªSeptuagint and Vulgate read *for the inhabitants of Jerusalem*.   20:1 ªFollowing Masoretic Text and Vulgate; Septuagint reads *Meunites* (compare 26:7).   20:2 ªFollowing Masoretic Text, Septuagint, and Vulgate; some Hebrew manuscripts and Old Latin read *Edom*.

tuary in it for Your name, saying, 9 'If disaster comes upon us—sword, judgment, pestilence, or famine—we will stand before this temple and in Your presence (for Your name *is* in this temple), and cry out to You in our affliction, and You will hear and save.' 10 And now, here are the people of Ammon, Moab, and Mount Seir—whom You would not let Israel invade when they came out of the land of Egypt, but they turned from them and did not destroy them— 11 here they are, rewarding us by coming to throw us out of Your possession which You have given us to inherit. 12 O our God, will You not judge them? For we have no power against this great multitude that is coming against us; nor do we know what to do, but our eyes *are* upon You."

13 Now all Judah, with their little ones, their wives, and their children, stood before the LORD.

14 Then the Spirit of the LORD came upon Jahaziel the son of Zechariah, the son of Benaiah, the son of Jeiel, the son of Mattaniah, a Levite of the sons of Asaph, in the midst of the assembly. 15 And he said, "Listen, all you of Judah and you inhabitants of Jerusalem, and you, King Jehoshaphat! Thus says the LORD to you: 'Do not be afraid nor dismayed because of this great multitude, for the battle *is* not yours, but God's. 16 Tomorrow go down against them. They will surely come up by the Ascent of Ziz, and you will find them at the end of the brook before the Wilderness of Jeruel. 17 You will not *need* to fight in this *battle*. Position yourselves, stand still and see the salvation of the LORD, who is with you, O Judah and Jerusalem!' Do not fear or be dismayed; tomorrow go out against them, for the LORD *is* with you."

18 And Jehoshaphat bowed his head with *his* face to the ground, and all Judah and the inhabitants of Jerusalem bowed before the LORD, worshiping the LORD. 19 Then the Levites of the children of the Kohathites and of the children of the Korahites stood up to praise the LORD God of Israel with voices loud and high.

20 So they rose early in the morning and went out into the Wilderness of Tekoa; and as they went out, Jehoshaphat stood and said, "Hear me, O Judah and you inhabitants of Jerusalem: Believe in the LORD your God, and you shall be established; believe His prophets, and you shall prosper." 21 And when he had consulted with the people, he appointed those who should sing to the LORD, and who should praise the beauty of holiness, as they went out before the army and were saying:

"Praise the LORD,
For His mercy *endures*
forever."*a*

22 Now when they began to sing and to praise, the LORD set ambushes against the people of Ammon, Moab, and Mount Seir, who had come against Judah; and they were defeated. 23 For the people of Ammon and Moab stood up against the inhabitants of Mount Seir to utterly kill and destroy *them*. And when they had made an end of the inhabitants of Seir, they helped to destroy one another.

24 So when Judah came to a place overlooking the wilderness, they looked toward the multitude; and there *were* their dead bodies, fallen on the earth. No one had escaped. 25 When Jehoshaphat and his people came to take away their spoil, they found among them an abundance of valuables on the dead bodies,*a* and precious jewelry, which they stripped off for themselves, more than they could carry away; and they were three days gathering the spoil because there was so much. 26 And on the fourth day they assembled in the Valley of Berachah, for there they blessed the LORD; therefore the name of that place was called The Valley of Berachah*a* until this day. 27 Then they returned, every man of Judah and Jerusalem, with Jehoshaphat in front of them, to go back to Jerusalem with joy, for the LORD had made them rejoice over their enemies. 28 So they came to Jerusalem, with stringed instruments and harps and trumpets, to the house of the LORD. 29 And the fear of God was on all the kingdoms of *those* countries when they heard that the

20:21 *a*Compare Psalm 106:1   20:25 *a*A few Hebrew manuscripts, Old Latin, and Vulgate read *garments;* Septuagint reads *armor.*   20:26 *a*Literally *Blessing*

Our Greatest Enemy

Do positive-thinking people deny the reality of evil? Not at all. We recognize that there is an opposite to everything; when we declare our faith in positive thinking we automatically acknowledge the alternative—negative thinking.

So we can expect to encounter enemies as we walk the path of faith. However, we also know that God can give us victory over our enemies (2 Chr. 20:27).

What enemies have you encountered, so far, on the walk of faith?

In the walk of faith we describe an enemy as anybody who diminishes your faith in yourself, in your neighbors, and in almighty God!

Therefore, our strongest enemies are the negative thoughts that come into our minds.

Who then is your greatest enemy? You may lament the fact that those closest to you do not give the encouragement you think they should. But nobody puts you down more than you do yourself. Nobody has rejected more of your best ideas than you have!

How many good ideas have come into your mind only to be discarded by you?

Feed your positive thoughts with faith. Fill your mind with beautiful affirmations and powerful promises that are abundant throughout the Bible. As a result, your walk of faith will be productive, joyous, and worthwhile!

Lord had fought against the enemies of Israel. 30 Then the realm of Jehoshaphat was quiet, for his God gave him rest all around.

31 So Jehoshaphat was king over Judah. *He was* thirty-five years old when he became king, and he reigned twenty-five years in Jerusalem. His mother's name *was* Azubah the daughter of Shilhi. 32 And he walked in the way of his father Asa, and did not turn aside from it, doing *what was* right in the sight of the Lord. 33 Nevertheless the high places were not taken away, for as yet the people had not directed their hearts to the God of their fathers.

34 Now the rest of the acts of Jehoshaphat, first and last, indeed they *are* written in the book of Jehu the son of Hanani, which *is* mentioned in the book of the kings of Israel.

35 After this Jehoshaphat king of Judah allied himself with Ahaziah king of Israel, who acted very wickedly. 36 And he allied himself with him to make ships to go to Tarshish, and they made the ships in Ezion Geber. 37 But Eliezer the son of Dodavah of Mareshah prophesied against Jehoshaphat, saying, "Because you have allied yourself with Ahaziah, the Lord has destroyed your works." Then the ships were wrecked, so that they were not able to go to Tarshish.

21 And Jehoshaphat rested with his fathers, and was buried with his fathers in the City of David. Then Jehoram his son reigned in his place. 2 He had brothers, the sons of Jehoshaphat: Azariah, Jehiel, Zechariah, Azaryahu, Michael, and Shephatiah; all these *were* the sons of Jehoshaphat king of Israel. 3 Their father gave them great gifts of silver and gold and precious things, with fortified cities in Judah; but he gave the kingdom to Jehoram, because he *was* the firstborn.

4 Now when Jehoram was established over the kingdom of his father, he strengthened himself and killed all his brothers with the sword, and also *others* of the princes of Israel. 5 Jehoram *was* thirty-two years old when he became king, and he reigned eight years in Jerusalem. 6 And he walked in the way of the kings of Israel, just as the house of Ahab had done, for he had the daughter of Ahab as a wife; and he did evil in the sight of the Lord. 7 Yet the Lord would not destroy the house of David, because of the covenant that He had made with David, and since He had promised to give a lamp to him and to his sons forever.

8 In his days Edom revolted against Judah's authority, and made a king over themselves. 9 So Jehoram went out with his officers, and all his chariots with him. And he rose by night and attacked the Edomites who had surrounded him and the captains of the chariots. 10 Thus Edom has been in revolt against Judah's authority to this day. At that time Libnah revolted against his rule, because he had forsaken the Lord God of his fathers. 11 Moreover he made high places in the mountains of Judah, and caused the inhabitants of Jerusalem to commit harlotry, and led Judah astray.

12 And a letter came to him from Elijah the prophet, saying,

Thus says the Lord God of your father David:
Because you have not walked in the ways of Jehoshaphat your father, or in the ways of Asa king of Judah, 13 but have walked in the way of the kings of Israel, and have made Judah and the inhabitants of Jerusalem to play the harlot like the harlotry of the house of Ahab, and also have killed your brothers, those of your father's household, *who were* better than yourself, 14 behold, the Lord will strike your people with a serious affliction—your children, your wives, and all your possessions; 15 and you *will become* very sick with a disease of your intestines, until your intestines come out by reason of the sickness, day by day.

16 Moreover the Lord stirred up against Jehoram the spirit of the Philistines and the Arabians who *were* near the Ethiopians. 17 And they came up into Judah and invaded it, and carried away all the possessions that were found in the king's house, and also his sons and his wives, so that there was not a son left to him

except Jehoahaz,ᵃ the youngest of his sons.

18 After all this the LORD struck him in his intestines with an incurable disease. 19 Then it happened in the course of time, after the end of two years, that his intestines came out because of his sickness; so he died in severe pain. And his people made no burning for him, like the burning for his fathers.

20 He was thirty-two years old when he became king. He reigned in Jerusalem eight years and, to no one's sorrow, departed. However they buried him in the City of David, but not in the tombs of the kings.

22 Then the inhabitants of Jerusalem made Ahaziah his youngest son king in his place, for the raiders who came with the Arabians into the camp had killed all the older *sons*. So Ahaziah the son of Jehoram, king of Judah, reigned. 2 Ahaziah *was* forty-twoᵃ years old when he became king, and he reigned one year in Jerusalem. His mother's name *was* Athaliah the granddaughter of Omri. 3 He also walked in the ways of the house of Ahab, for his mother advised him to do wickedly. 4 Therefore he did evil in the sight of the LORD, like the house of Ahab; for they were his counselors after the death of his father, to his destruction. 5 He also followed their advice, and went with Jehoramᵃ the son of Ahab king of Israel to war against Hazael king of Syria at Ramoth Gilead; and the Syrians wounded Joram. 6 Then he returned to Jezreel to recover from the wounds which he had received at Ramah, when he fought against Hazael king of Syria. And Azariahᵃ the son of Jehoram, king of Judah, went down to see Jehoram the son of Ahab in Jezreel, because he was sick.

7 His going to Joram was God's occasion for Ahaziah's downfall; for when he arrived, he went out with Jehoram against Jehu the son of Nimshi, whom the LORD had anointed to cut off the house of Ahab. 8 And it happened, when Jehu was executing judgment on the house of Ahab, and found the princes of Judah and the sons of Ahaziah's brothers who served Ahaziah, that he killed them. 9 Then he searched for Ahaziah; and they caught him (he was hiding in Samaria), and brought him to Jehu. When they had killed him, they buried him, "because," they said, "he is the son of Jehoshaphat, who sought the LORD with all his heart."

So the house of Ahaziah had no one to assume power over the kingdom.

10 Now when Athaliah the mother of Ahaziah saw that her son was dead, she arose and destroyed all the royal heirs of the house of Judah. 11 But Jehoshabeath,ᵃ the daughter of the king, took Joash the son of Ahaziah, and stole him away from among the king's sons who were being murdered, and put him and his nurse in a bedroom. So Jehoshabeath, the daughter of King Jehoram, the wife of Jehoiada the priest (for she was the sister of Ahaziah), hid him from Athaliah so that she did not kill him. 12 And he was hidden with them in the house of God for six years, while Athaliah reigned over the land.

23 In the seventh year Jehoiada strengthened himself, *and made a* covenant with the captains of hundreds: Azariah the son of Jeroham, Ishmael the son of Jehohanan, Azariah the son of Obed, Maaseiah the son of Adaiah, and Elishaphat the son of Zichri. 2 And they went throughout Judah and gathered the Levites from all the cities of Judah, and the chief fathers of Israel, and they came to Jerusalem.

3 Then all the assembly made a covenant with the king in the house of God. And he said to them, "Behold, the king's son shall reign, as the LORD has said of the sons of David. 4 This *is* what you shall do: One-third of you entering on the Sabbath, of the priests and the Levites, *shall be* keeping watch over the doors; 5 one-third *shall be* at the king's house; and one-third at the Gate of the Foundation. All the people *shall be* in the courts of the house of the LORD. 6 But let no one come into the house of the LORD except the priests

and those of the Levites who serve. They may go in, for they *are* holy; but all the people shall keep the watch of the LORD. 7 And the Levites shall surround the king on all sides, every man with his weapons in his hand; and whoever comes into the house, let him be put to death. You are to be with the king when he comes in and when he goes out."

8 So the Levites and all Judah did according to all that Jehoiada the priest commanded. And each man took his men who were to be on duty on the Sabbath, with those who were going *off duty* on the Sabbath; for Jehoiada the priest had not dismissed the divisions. 9 And Jehoiada the priest gave to the captains of hundreds the spears and the large and small shields which *had belonged* to King David, that *were* in the temple of God. 10 Then he set all the people, every man with his weapon in his hand, from the right side of the temple to the left side of the temple, along by the altar and by the temple, all around the king. 11 And they brought out the king's son, put the crown on him, *gave him* the Testimony,*a* and made him king. Then Jehoiada and his sons anointed him, and said, "*Long* live the king!"

12 Now when Athaliah heard the noise of the people running and praising the king, she came to the people *in* the temple of the LORD. 13 *When* she looked, there was the king standing by his pillar at the entrance; and the leaders and the trumpeters *were* by the king. All the people of the land were rejoicing and blowing trumpets, also the singers with musical instruments, and those who led in praise. So Athaliah tore her clothes and said, "Treason! Treason!"

14 And Jehoiada the priest brought out the captains of hundreds who were set over the army, and said to them, "Take her outside under guard, and slay with the sword whoever follows her." For the priest had said, "Do not kill her in the house of the LORD."

15 So they seized her; and she went by way of the entrance of the Horse Gate *into* the king's house, and they killed her there.

16 Then Jehoiada made a covenant between himself, the people, and the king, that they should be the LORD's people. 17 And all the people went to the temple*a* of Baal, and tore it down. They broke in pieces its altars and images, and killed Mattan the priest of Baal before the altars. 18 Also Jehoiada appointed the oversight of the house of the LORD to the hand of the priests, the Levites, whom David had assigned in the house of the LORD, to offer the burnt offerings of the LORD, as *it is* written in the Law of Moses, with rejoicing and with singing, *as it was established* by David. 19 And he set the gatekeepers at the gates of the house of the LORD, so that no one *who was* in any way unclean should enter.

20 Then he took the captains of hundreds, the nobles, the governors of the people, and all the people of the land, and brought the king down from the house of the LORD; and they went through the Upper Gate to the king's house, and set the king on the throne of the kingdom. 21 So all the people of the land rejoiced; and the city was quiet, for they had slain Athaliah with the sword.

24 Joash *was* seven years old when he became king, and he reigned forty years in Jerusalem. His mother's name *was* Zibiah of Beersheba. 2 Joash did *what was* right in the sight of the LORD all the days of Jehoiada the priest. 3 And Jehoiada took two wives for him, and he had sons and daughters.

4 Now it happened after this *that* Joash set his heart on repairing the house of the LORD. 5 Then he gathered the priests and the Levites, and said to them, "Go out to the cities of Judah, and gather from all Israel money to repair the house of your God from year to year, and see that you do it quickly."

However the Levites did not do it quickly. 6 So the king called Jehoiada the chief *priest,* and said to him, "Why have you not required the Levites to bring in from Judah and from Jerusalem the collection, *according to the commandment* of Moses the servant of the LORD and of the assembly of Israel, for the tabernacle of witness?" 7 For the sons of Athaliah, that wicked woman, had broken into the house of God, and had also presented all the dedicated things of the house of the LORD to the Baals.

8 Then at the king's command they made a chest, and set it outside at the gate of the house of the LORD. 9 And they made a proclamation throughout Judah and Jerusalem to bring to the LORD the collection *that* Moses the servant of God *had imposed* on Israel in the wilderness. 10 Then all the leaders and all the people rejoiced, brought their contributions, and put *them* into the chest until all had given. 11 So it was, at that time, when the chest was brought to the king's official by the hand of the Levites, and when they saw that *there was* much money, that the king's scribe and the high priest's officer came and emptied the chest, and took it and returned it to its place. Thus they did day by day, and gathered money in abundance.

12 The king and Jehoiada gave it to those who did the work of the service of the house of the LORD; and they hired masons and carpenters to repair the house of the LORD, and also those who worked in iron and bronze to restore the house of the LORD. 13 So the workmen labored, and the work was completed by them; they restored the house of God to its original condition and reinforced it. 14 When they had finished, they brought the rest of the money before the king and Jehoiada; they made from it articles for the house of the LORD, articles for serving and offering, spoons and vessels of gold and silver. And they offered burnt offerings in the house of the LORD continually all the days of Jehoiada.

15 But Jehoiada grew old and was full of days, and he died; *he was* one hundred and thirty years old when he died. 16 And they buried him in the City of David among the kings, because he had done good in Israel, both toward God and His house.

17 Now after the death of Jehoiada the leaders of Judah came and bowed down to the king. And the king listened to them. 18 Therefore they left the house of the LORD God of their fathers, and served wooden images and idols; and wrath came upon Judah and Jerusalem because of their

trespass. 19 Yet He sent prophets to them, to bring them back to the LORD; and they testified against them, but they would not listen.

20 Then the Spirit of God came upon Zechariah the son of Jehoiada the priest, who stood above the people, and said to them, "Thus says God: 'Why do you transgress the commandments of the LORD, so that you cannot prosper? Because you have forsaken the LORD, He also has forsaken you.' " 21 So they conspired against him, and at the command of the king they stoned him with stones in the court of the house of the LORD. 22 Thus Joash the king did not remember the kindness which Jehoiada his father had done to him, but killed his son; and as he died, he said, "The LORD look on *it*, and repay!"

23 So it happened in the spring of the year *that* the army of Syria came up against him; and they came to Judah and Jerusalem, and destroyed all the leaders of the people from among the people, and sent all their spoil to the king of Damascus. 24 For the army of the Syrians came with a small company of men; but the LORD delivered a very great army into their hand, because they had forsaken the LORD God of their fathers. So they executed judgment against Joash. 25 And when they had withdrawn from him (for they left him severely wounded), his own servants conspired against him because of the blood of the sons[a] of Jehoiada the priest, and killed him on his bed. So he died. And they buried him in the City of David, but they did not bury him in the tombs of the kings.

26 These are the ones who conspired against him: Zabad[a] the son of Shimeath the Ammonitess, and Jehozabad the son of Shimrith[b] the Moabitess. 27 Now *concerning* his sons, and the many oracles about him, and the repairing of the house of God, indeed they *are* written in the annals of the book of the kings. Then Amaziah his son reigned in his place.

25 Amaziah *was* twenty-five years old *when* he became king, and he reigned twenty-nine years in Jerusalem. His mother's name *was* Jehoaddan of Jerusalem. 2 And he did

24:25 [a]Septuagint and Vulgate read *son* (compare verses 20–22).　　24:26 [a]Or *Jozachar* (compare 2 Kings 12:21)　　[b]Or *Shomer* (compare 2 Kings 12:21)

what was right in the sight of the LORD, but not with a loyal heart.

3 Now it happened, as soon as the kingdom was established for him, that he executed his servants who had murdered his father the king. 4 However he did not execute their children, but *did* as *it is* written in the Law in the Book of Moses, where the LORD commanded, saying, "The fathers shall not be put to death for their children, nor shall the children be put to death for their fathers; but a person shall die for his own sin."[a]

5 Moreover Amaziah gathered Judah together and set over them captains of thousands and captains of hundreds, according to *their* fathers' houses, throughout all Judah and Benjamin; and he numbered them from twenty years old and above, and found them to be three hundred thousand choice *men, able* to go to war, who could handle spear and shield. 6 He also hired one hundred thousand mighty men of valor from Israel for one hundred talents of silver. 7 But a man of God came to him, saying, "O king, do not let the army of Israel go with you, for the LORD *is* not with Israel—*not with* any of the children of Ephraim. 8 But if you go, be gone! Be strong in battle! *Even so,* God shall make you fall before the enemy; for God has power to help and to overthrow."

9 Then Amaziah said to the man of God, "But what *shall we* do about the hundred talents which I have given to the troops of Israel?"

And the man of God answered, "The LORD is able to give you much more than this." 10 So Amaziah discharged the troops that had come to him from Ephraim, to go back home. Therefore their anger was greatly aroused against Judah, and they returned home in great anger.

11 Then Amaziah strengthened himself, and leading his people, he went to the Valley of Salt and killed ten thousand of the people of Seir. 12 Also the children of Judah took captive ten thousand alive, brought them to the top of the rock, and cast them down from the top of the rock, so that they all were dashed in pieces.

13 But as for the soldiers of the army which Amaziah had dis-charged, so that they would not go with him to battle, they raided the cities of Judah from Samaria to Beth Horon, killed three thousand in them, and took much spoil.

14 Now it was so, after Amaziah came from the slaughter of the Edomites, that he brought the gods of the people of Seir, set them up *to be* his gods, and bowed down before them and burned incense to them. 15 Therefore the anger of the LORD was aroused against Amaziah, and He sent him a prophet who said to him, "Why have you sought the gods of the people, which could not rescue their own people from your hand?"

16 So it was, as he talked with him, that *the king* said to him, "Have we made you the king's counselor? Cease! Why should you be killed?"

Then the prophet ceased, and said, "I know that God has determined to destroy you, because you have done this and have not heeded my advice."

17 Now Amaziah king of Judah asked advice and sent to Joash[a] the son of Jehoahaz, the son of Jehu, king of Israel, saying, "Come, let us face one another *in battle.*"

18 And Joash king of Israel sent to Amaziah king of Judah, saying, "The thistle that *was* in Lebanon sent to the cedar that was in Lebanon, saying, 'Give your daughter to my son as wife'; and a wild beast that *was* in Lebanon passed by and trampled the thistle. 19 Indeed you say that you have defeated the Edomites, and your heart is lifted up to boast. Stay at home now; why should you meddle with trouble, that you should fall—you and Judah with you?"

20 But Amaziah would not heed, for it *came* from God, that He might give them into the hand *of their enemies,* because they sought the gods of Edom. 21 So Joash king of Israel went out; and he and Amaziah king of Judah faced one another at Beth Shemesh, which *belongs* to Judah. 22 And Judah was defeated by Israel, and every man fled to his tent. 23 Then Joash the king of Israel captured Amaziah king of Judah, the son of Joash, the son of Jehoahaz, at Beth Shemesh; and he brought him to Jerusalem, and broke down the wall of Jerusalem from the Gate of Ephraim to the Corner Gate—four hundred cu-

25:4 [a]Deuteronomy 24:16   25:17 [a]Spelled *Jehoash* in 2 Kings 14:8ff bits. 24 And *he took* all the gold and silver, all the articles that were found in the house of God with Obed-Edom, the treasures of the king's house, and hostages, and returned to Samaria.

25 Amaziah the son of Joash, king of Judah, lived fifteen years after the death of Joash the son of Jehoahaz, king of Israel. 26 Now the rest of the acts of Amaziah, from first to last, indeed *are* they not written in the book of the kings of Judah and Israel? 27 After the time that Amaziah turned away from following the LORD, they made a conspiracy against him in Jerusalem, and he fled to Lachish; but they sent after him to Lachish and killed him there. 28 Then they brought him on horses and buried him with his fathers in the City of Judah.

26 Now all the people of Judah took Uzziah,*ᵃ* who *was* sixteen years old, and made him king instead of his father Amaziah. 2 He built Elath*ᵃ* and restored it to Judah, after the king rested with his fathers.

3 Uzziah *was* sixteen years old when he became king, and he reigned fifty-two years in Jerusalem. His mother's name was Jecholiah of Jerusalem. 4 And he did *what was* right in the sight of the LORD, according to all that his father Amaziah had done. 5 He sought God in the days of Zechariah, who had understanding in the visions*ᵃ* of God; and as long as he sought the LORD, God made him prosper.

6 Now he went out and made war against the Philistines, and broke down the wall of Gath, the wall of Jabneh, and the wall of Ashdod; and he built cities *around* Ashdod and among the Philistines. 7 God helped him against the Philistines, against the Arabians who lived in Gur Baal, and against the Meunites. 8 Also the Ammonites brought tribute to Uzziah. His fame spread as far as the entrance of Egypt, for he became exceedingly strong.

9 And Uzziah built towers in Jerusalem at the Corner Gate, at the Valley Gate, and at the corner buttress of the wall; then he fortified them. 10 Also he built towers in the desert. He dug many wells, for he had much livestock, both in the lowlands and in the plains; *he also had* farmers and vinedressers in the mountains and in Carmel, for he loved the soil.

11 Moreover Uzziah had an army of fighting men who went out to war by companies, according to the number on their roll as prepared by Jeiel the scribe and Maaseiah the officer, under the hand of Hananiah, *one* of the king's captains. 12 The total number of chief officers*ᵃ* of the mighty men of valor *was* two thousand six hundred. 13 And under their authority *was* an army of three hundred and seven thousand five hundred, that made war with mighty power, to help the king against the enemy. 14 Then Uzziah prepared for them, for the entire army, shields, spears, helmets, body armor, bows, and slings *to cast* stones. 15 And he made devices in Jerusalem, invented by skillful men, to be on the towers and the corners, to shoot arrows and large stones. So his fame spread far and wide, for he was marvelously helped till he became strong.

16 But when he was strong his heart was lifted up, to *his* destruction, for he transgressed against the LORD his God by entering the temple of the LORD to burn incense on the altar of incense. 17 So Azariah the priest went in after him, and with him were eighty priests of the LORD—valiant men. 18 And they withstood King Uzziah, and said to him, "*It is* not for you, Uzziah, to burn incense to the LORD, but for the priests, the sons of Aaron, who are consecrated to burn incense. Get out of the sanctuary, for you have trespassed! You *shall have* no honor from the LORD God."

19 Then Uzziah became furious; and he *had* a censer in his hand to burn incense. And while he was angry with the priests, leprosy broke out on his forehead, before the priests in the house of the LORD, beside the incense altar. 20 And Azariah the chief priest and all the priests looked at him, and there, on his forehead, he *was* leprous; so they thrust him out of that place. Indeed he also hurried to get out, because the LORD had struck him.

21 King Uzziah was a leper until the day of his death. He dwelt in an

isolated house, because he was a leper; for he was cut off from the house of the LORD. Then Jotham his son *was* over the king's house, judging the people of the land.

22 Now the rest of the acts of Uzziah, from first to last, the prophet Isaiah the son of Amoz wrote. 23 So Uzziah rested with his fathers, and they buried him with his fathers in the field of burial which *belonged* to the kings, for they said, "He is a leper." Then Jotham his son reigned in his place.

27 Jotham *was* twenty-five years old when he became king, and he reigned sixteen years in Jerusalem. His mother's name *was* Jerushah[a] the daughter of Zadok. 2 And he did *what was* right in the sight of the LORD, according to all that his father Uzziah had done (although he did not enter the temple of the LORD). But still the people acted corruptly.

3 He built the Upper Gate of the house of the LORD, and he built extensively on the wall of Ophel. 4 Moreover he built cities in the mountains of Judah, and in the forests he built fortresses and towers. 5 He also fought with the king of the Ammonites and defeated them. And the people of Ammon gave him in that year one hundred talents of silver, ten thousand kors of wheat, and ten thousand of barley. The people of Ammon paid this to him in the second and third years also. 6 So Jotham became mighty, because he prepared his ways before the LORD his God.

7 Now the rest of the acts of Jotham, and all his wars and his ways, indeed they *are* written in the book of the kings of Israel and Judah. 8 He was twenty-five years old when he became king, and he reigned sixteen years in Jerusalem. 9 So Jotham rested with his fathers, and they buried him in the City of David. Then Ahaz his son reigned in his place.

28 Ahaz *was* twenty years old when he became king, and he reigned sixteen years in Jerusalem; and he did not do *what was* right in the sight of the LORD, as his father David *had done.* 2 For he walked in the ways of the kings of Israel, and made molded images for the Baals. 3 He burned incense in the Valley of the Son of Hinnom, and burned his children in the fire, according to the abominations of the nations whom the LORD had cast out before the children of Israel. 4 And he sacrificed and burned incense on the high places, on the hills, and under every green tree.

5 Therefore the LORD his God delivered him into the hand of the king of Syria. They defeated him, and carried away a great multitude of them as captives, and brought *them* to Damascus. Then he was also delivered into the hand of the king of Israel, who defeated him with a great slaughter. 6 For Pekah the son of Remaliah killed one hundred and twenty thousand in Judah in one day, all valiant men, because they had forsaken the LORD God of their fathers. 7 Zichri, a mighty man of Ephraim, killed Maaseiah the king's son, Azrikam the officer over the house, and Elkanah *who was* second to the king. 8 And the children of Israel carried away captive of their brethren two hundred thousand women, sons, and daughters; and they also took away much spoil from them, and brought the spoil to Samaria.

9 But a prophet of the LORD was there, whose name *was* Oded; and he went out before the army that came to Samaria, and said to them: "Look, because the LORD God of your fathers was angry with Judah, He has delivered them into your hand; but you have killed them in a rage *that* reaches up to heaven. 10 And now you propose to force the children of Judah and Jerusalem to be your male and female slaves; *but are* you not also guilty before the LORD your God? 11 Now hear me, therefore, and return the captives, whom you have taken captive from your brethren, for the fierce wrath of the LORD *is* upon you."

12 Then some of the heads of the children of Ephraim, Azariah the son of Johanan, Berechiah the son of Meshillemoth, Jehizkiah the son of Shallum, and Amasa the son of Hadlai, stood up against those who came from the war, 13 and said to them, "You shall not bring the captives here, for we *already* have offended

the LORD. You intend to add to our sins and to our guilt; for our guilt is great, and *there is* fierce wrath against Israel." 14 So the armed men left the captives and the spoil before the leaders and all the assembly. 15 Then the men who were designated by name rose up and took the captives, and from the spoil they clothed all who were naked among them, dressed them and gave them sandals, gave them food and drink, and anointed them; and they let all the feeble ones ride on donkeys. So they brought them to their brethren at Jericho, the city of palm trees. Then they returned to Samaria.

16 At the same time King Ahaz sent to the kings*a* of Assyria to help him. 17 For again the Edomites had come, attacked Judah, and carried away captives. 18 The Philistines also had invaded the cities of the lowland and of the South of Judah, and had taken Beth Shemesh, Aijalon, Gederoth, Sochoh with its villages, Timnah with its villages, and Gimzo with its villages; and they dwelt there. 19 For the LORD brought Judah low because of Ahaz king of Israel, for he had encouraged moral decline in Judah and had been continually unfaithful to the LORD. 20 Also Tiglath-Pileser*a* king of Assyria came to him and distressed him, and did not assist him. 21 For Ahaz took part *of the treasures* from the house of the LORD, from the house of the king, and from the leaders, and he gave *it* to the king of Assyria; but he did not help him.

22 Now in the time of his distress King Ahaz became increasingly unfaithful to the LORD. This *is that* King Ahaz. 23 For he sacrificed to the gods of Damascus which had defeated him, saying, "Because the gods of the kings of Syria help them, I will sacrifice to them that they may help me." But they were the ruin of him and of all Israel. 24 So Ahaz gathered the articles of the house of God, cut in pieces the articles of the house of God, shut up the doors of the house of the LORD, and made for himself altars in every corner of Jerusalem. 25 And in every single city of Judah he made high places to burn incense to other gods, and provoked to anger the LORD God of his fathers.

26 Now the rest of his acts and all his ways, from first to last, indeed they *are* written in the book of the kings of Judah and Israel. 27 So Ahaz rested with his fathers, and they buried him in the city, in Jerusalem; but they did not bring him into the tombs of the kings of Israel. Then Hezekiah his son reigned in his place.

29 Hezekiah became king *when he was* twenty-five years old, and he reigned twenty-nine years in Jerusalem. His mother's name *was* Abijah*a* the daughter of Zechariah. 2 And he did *what was* right in the sight of the LORD, according to all that his father David had done.

3 In the first year of his reign, in the first month, he opened the doors of the house of the LORD and repaired them. 4 Then he brought in the priests and the Levites, and gathered them in the East Square, 5 and said to them: "Hear me, Levites! Now sanctify yourselves, sanctify the house of the LORD God of your fathers, and carry out the rubbish from the holy *place*. 6 For our fathers have trespassed and done evil in the eyes of the LORD our God; they have forsaken Him, have turned their faces away from the dwelling place of the LORD, and turned *their* backs *on Him*. 7 They have also shut up the doors of the vestibule, put out the lamps, and have not burned incense or offered burnt offerings in the holy *place* to the God of Israel. 8 Therefore the wrath of the LORD fell upon Judah and Jerusalem, and He has given them up to trouble, to desolation, and to jeering, as you see with your eyes. 9 For indeed, because of this our fathers have fallen by the sword; and our sons, our daughters, and our wives *are* in captivity.

10 "Now *it is* in my heart to make a covenant with the LORD God of Israel, that His fierce wrath may turn away from us. 11 My sons, do not be negligent now, for the LORD has chosen you to stand before Him, to serve Him, and that you should minister to Him and burn incense."

12 Then these Levites arose: Mahath the son of Amasai and Joel the son of Azariah, of the sons of the Kohathites; of the sons of Merari, Kish

28:16 *a*Septuagint, Syriac, and Vulgate read *king* (compare verse 20).   28:20 *a*Hebrew *Tilgath-Pilneser*   29:1 *a*Spelled *Abi* in 2 Kings 18:2

the son of Abdi and Azariah the son of Jehallelel; of the Gershonites, Joah the son of Zimmah and Eden the son of Joah; 13 of the sons of Elizaphan, Shimri and Jeiel; of the sons of Asaph, Zechariah and Mattaniah; 14 of the sons of Heman, Jehiel and Shimei; and of the sons of Jeduthun, Shemaiah and Uzziel.

15 And they gathered their brethren, sanctified themselves, and went according to the commandment of the king, at the words of the LORD, to cleanse the house of the LORD. 16 Then the priests went into the inner part of the house of the LORD to cleanse *it*, and brought out all the debris that they found in the temple of the LORD to the court of the house of the LORD. And the Levites took *it* out and carried *it* to the Brook Kidron.

17 Now they began to sanctify on the first *day* of the first month, and on the eighth day of the month they came to the vestibule of the LORD. So they sanctified the house of the LORD in eight days, and on the sixteenth day of the first month they finished.

18 Then they went in to King Hezekiah and said, "We have cleansed all the house of the LORD, the altar of burnt offerings with all its articles, and the table of the showbread with all its articles. 19 Moreover all the articles which King Ahaz in his reign had cast aside in his transgression we have prepared and sanctified; and there they *are*, before the altar of the LORD."

20 Then King Hezekiah rose early, gathered the rulers of the city, and went up to the house of the LORD. 21 And they brought seven bulls, seven rams, seven lambs, and seven male goats for a sin offering for the kingdom, for the sanctuary, and for Judah. Then he commanded the priests, the sons of Aaron, to offer *them* on the altar of the LORD. 22 So they killed the bulls, and the priests received the blood and sprinkled *it* on the altar. Likewise they killed the rams and sprinkled the blood on the altar. They also killed the lambs and sprinkled the blood on the altar. 23 Then they brought out the male goats *for* the sin offering before the king and the assembly, and they laid their hands on them. 24 And the priests killed them; and they presented their blood on the al-

tar as a sin offering to make an atonement for all Israel, for the king commanded *that* the burnt offering and the sin offering *be made* for all Israel.

25 And he stationed the Levites in the house of the LORD with cymbals, with stringed instruments, and with harps, according to the commandment of David, of Gad the king's seer, and of Nathan the prophet; for thus *was* the commandment of the LORD by his prophets. 26 The Levites stood with the instruments of David, and the priests with the trumpets. 27 Then Hezekiah commanded *them* to offer the burnt offering on the altar. And when the burnt offering began, the song of the LORD *also* began, with the trumpets and with the instruments of David king of Israel. 28 So all the assembly worshiped, the singers sang, and the trumpeters sounded; all *this continued* until the burnt offering was finished. 29 And when they had finished offering, the king and all who were present with him bowed and worshiped. 30 Moreover King Hezekiah and the leaders commanded the Levites to sing praise to the LORD with the words of David and of Asaph the seer. So they sang praises with gladness, and they bowed their heads and worshiped.

31 Then Hezekiah answered and said, "Now *that* you have consecrated yourselves to the LORD, come near, and bring sacrifices and thank offerings into the house of the LORD." So the assembly brought in sacrifices and thank offerings, and as many as were of a willing heart *brought* burnt offerings. 32 And the number of the burnt offerings which the assembly brought was seventy bulls, one hundred rams, *and* two hundred lambs; all these *were* for a burnt offering to the LORD. 33 The consecrated things *were* six hundred bulls and three thousand sheep. 34 But the priests were too few, so that they could not skin all the burnt offerings; therefore their brethren the Levites helped them until the work was ended and until the *other* priests had sanctified themselves, for the Levites were more diligent in sanctifying themselves than the priests. 35 Also the burnt offerings *were* in abundance, with the fat of the peace offerings and *with* the drink offerings for *every* burnt offering.

So the service of the house of the LORD was set in order. 36 Then Hezekiah and all the people rejoiced that God had prepared the people, since the events took place so suddenly.

30 And Hezekiah sent to all Israel and Judah, and also wrote letters to Ephraim and Manasseh, that they should come to the house of the LORD at Jerusalem, to keep the Passover to the LORD God of Israel. 2 For the king and his leaders and all the assembly in Jerusalem had agreed to keep the Passover in the second month. 3 For they could not keep it at the regular time,*a* because a sufficient number of priests had not consecrated themselves, nor had the people gathered together at Jerusalem. 4 And the matter pleased the king and all the assembly. 5 So they resolved to make a proclamation throughout all Israel, from Beersheba to Dan, that they should come to keep the Passover to the LORD God of Israel at Jerusalem, since they had not done *it* for a long *time* in the *prescribed* manner.

6 Then the runners went throughout all Israel and Judah with the letters from the king and his leaders, and spoke according to the command of the king: "Children of Israel, return to the LORD God of Abraham, Isaac, and Israel; then He will return to the remnant of you who have escaped from the hand of the kings of Assyria. 7 And do not be like your fathers and your brethren, who trespassed against the LORD God of their fathers, so that He gave them up to desolation, as you see. 8 Now do not be stiff-necked, as your fathers *were*, *but* yield yourselves to the LORD; and enter His sanctuary, which He has sanctified forever, and serve the LORD your God, that the fierceness of His wrath may turn away from you. 9 For if you return to the LORD, your brethren and your children *will be treated* with compassion by those who lead them captive, so that they may come back to this land; for the LORD your God *is* gracious and merciful, and will not turn *His* face from you if you return to Him."

10 So the runners passed from city to city through the country of Ephraim and Manasseh, as far as Zebulun; but they laughed at them and mocked them. 11 Nevertheless some from Asher, Manasseh, and Zebulun humbled themselves and came to Jerusalem. 12 Also the hand of God was on Judah to give them singleness of heart to obey the command of the king and the leaders, at the word of the LORD.

13 Now many people, a very great assembly, gathered at Jerusalem to keep the Feast of Unleavened Bread in the second month. 14 They arose and took away the altars that *were* in Jerusalem, and they took away all the incense altars and cast *them* into the Brook Kidron. 15 Then they slaughtered the Passover *lambs* on the fourteenth *day* of the second month. The priests and the Levites were ashamed, and sanctified themselves, and brought the burnt offerings to the house of the LORD. 16 They stood in their place according to their custom, according to the Law of Moses the man of God; the priests sprinkled the blood *received* from the hand of the Levites. 17 For *there were* many in the assembly who had not sanctified themselves; therefore the Levites had charge of the slaughter of the Passover *lambs* for everyone *who was* not clean, to sanctify *them* to the LORD. 18 For a multitude of the people, many from Ephraim, Manasseh, Issachar, and Zebulun, had not cleansed themselves, yet they ate the Passover contrary to what was written. But Hezekiah prayed for them, saying, "May the good LORD provide atonement for everyone 19 *who* prepares his heart to seek God, the LORD God of his fathers, though *he is* not *cleansed* according to the purification of the sanctuary." 20 And the LORD listened to Hezekiah and healed the people.

21 So the children of Israel who were present at Jerusalem kept the Feast of Unleavened Bread seven days with great gladness; and the Levites and the priests praised the LORD day by day, *singing* to the LORD, accompanied by loud instruments. 22 And Hezekiah gave encouragement to all the Levites who taught the good knowledge of the LORD; and they ate throughout the feast seven days, offering peace offerings and

30:3 *a*That is, the first month (compare Leviticus 23:5); literally *at that time* making confession to the LORD God of their fathers.

23 Then the whole assembly agreed to keep *the feast* another seven days, and they kept it *another* seven days with gladness. 24 For Hezekiah king of Judah gave to the assembly a thousand bulls and seven thousand sheep, and the leaders gave to the assembly a thousand bulls and ten thousand sheep; and a great number of priests sanctified themselves. 25 The whole assembly of Judah rejoiced, also the priests and Levites, all the assembly that came from Israel, the sojourners who came from the land of Israel, and those who dwelt in Judah. 26 So there was great joy in Jerusalem, for since the time of Solomon the son of David, king of Israel, *there had* been nothing like this in Jerusalem. 27 Then the priests, the Levites, arose and blessed the people, and their voice was heard; and their prayer came *up* to His holy dwelling place, to heaven.

31 Now when all this was finished, all Israel who were present went out to the cities of Judah and broke the sacred pillars in pieces, cut down the wooden images, and threw down the high places and the altars—from all Judah, Benjamin, Ephraim, and Manasseh—until they had utterly destroyed them all. Then all the children of Israel returned to their own cities, every man to his possession.

2 And Hezekiah appointed the divisions of the priests and the Levites according to their divisions, each man according to his service, the priests and Levites for burnt offerings and peace offerings, to serve, to give thanks, and to praise in the gates of the camp*ᵃ* of the LORD. 3 The king also *appointed* a portion of his possessions for the burnt offerings: for the morning and evening burnt offerings, the burnt offerings for the Sabbaths and the New Moons and the set feasts, as *it is* written in the Law of the LORD.

4 Moreover he commanded the people who dwelt in Jerusalem to contribute support for the priests and the Levites, that they might devote themselves to the Law of the LORD. 5 As soon as the commandment was circulated, the children of Israel brought in abundance the firstfruits of grain and wine, oil and honey, and of all the produce of the field; and they brought in abundantly the tithe of everything. 6 And the children of Israel and Judah, who dwelt in the cities of Judah, brought the tithe of oxen and sheep; also the tithe of holy things which were consecrated to the LORD their God they laid in heaps.

7 In the third month they began laying them in heaps, and they finished in the seventh month. 8 And when Hezekiah and the leaders came and saw the heaps, they blessed the LORD and His people Israel. 9 Then Hezekiah questioned the priests and the Levites concerning the heaps. 10 And Azariah the chief priest, from the house of Zadok, answered him and said, "Since *the people* began to bring the offerings into the house of the LORD, we have had enough to eat and have plenty left, for the LORD has blessed His people; and what is left *is* this great abundance."

11 Now Hezekiah commanded *them* to prepare rooms in the house of the LORD, and they prepared them. 12 Then they faithfully brought in the offerings, the tithes, and the dedicated things; Cononiah the Levite had charge of them, and Shimei his brother *was* the next. 13 Jehiel, Azaziah, Nahath, Asahel, Jerimoth, Jozabad, Eliel, Ismachiah, Mahath, and Benaiah *were* overseers under the hand of Cononiah and Shimei his brother, at the commandment of Hezekiah the king and Azariah the ruler of the house of God. 14 Kore the son of Imnah the Levite, the keeper of the East Gate, *was* over the freewill offerings to God, to distribute the offerings of the LORD and the most holy things. 15 And under him *were* Eden, Miniamin, Jeshua, Shemaiah, Amariah, and Shecaniah, *his* faithful assistants in the cities of the priests, to distribute allotments to their brethren by divisions, to the great as well as the small.

16 Besides those males from three years old and up who were written in the genealogy, they distributed to everyone who entered the house of the LORD his daily portion for the work of his service, by his division,

31:2 *ᵃ*That is, the temple

17 and to the priests who were written in the genealogy according to their father's house, and to the Levites from twenty years old and up according to their work, by their divisions, 18 and to all who were written in the genealogy—their little ones and their wives, their sons and daughters, the whole company of them—for in their faithfulness they sanctified themselves in holiness.

19 Also for the sons of Aaron the priests, *who were* in the fields of the common-lands of their cities, in every single city, *there were* men who were designated by name to distribute portions to all the males among the priests and to all who were listed by genealogies among the Levites.

20 Thus Hezekiah did throughout all Judah, and he did what *was* good and right and true before the LORD his God. 21 And in every work that he began in the service of the house of God, in the law and in the commandment, to seek his God, he did *it* with all his heart. So he prospered.

32 After these deeds of faithfulness, Sennacherib king of Assyria came and entered Judah; he encamped against the fortified cities, thinking to win them over to himself. 2 And when Hezekiah saw that Sennacherib had come, and that his purpose was to make war against Jerusalem, 3 he consulted with his leaders and commanders[a] to stop the water from the springs which *were* outside the city; and they helped him. 4 Thus many people gathered together who stopped all the springs and the brook that ran through the land, saying, "Why should the kings[a] of Assyria come and find much water?" 5 And he strengthened himself, built up all the wall that was broken, raised *it* up to the towers, and *built* another wall outside; also he repaired the Millo[a] *in* the City of David, and made weapons and shields in abundance. 6 Then he set military captains over the people, gathered them together to him in the open square of the city gate, and gave them encouragement, saying, 7 "Be strong and courageous; do not be afraid nor dismayed before the king of Assyria, nor before all the

multitude that *is* with him; for *there are* more with us than with him. 8 With him *is* an arm of flesh; but with us *is* the LORD our God, to help us and to fight our battles." And the people were strengthened by the words of Hezekiah king of Judah.

9 After this Sennacherib king of Assyria sent his servants to Jerusalem (but he and all the forces with him *laid siege* against Lachish), to Hezekiah king of Judah, and to all Judah who *were* in Jerusalem, saying, 10 "Thus says Sennacherib king of Assyria: 'In what do you trust, that you remain under siege in Jerusalem? 11 Does not Hezekiah persuade you to give yourselves over to die by famine and by thirst, saying, "The LORD our God will deliver us from the hand of the king of Assyria"? 12 Has not the same Hezekiah taken away His high places and His altars, and commanded Judah and Jerusalem, saying, "You shall worship before one altar and burn incense on it"? 13 Do you not know what I and my fathers have done to all the peoples of *other* lands? Were the gods of the nations of those lands in any way able to deliver their lands out of my hand? 14 Who *was there* among all the gods of those nations that my fathers utterly destroyed that could deliver his people from my hand, that your God should be able to deliver you from my hand? 15 Now therefore, do not let Hezekiah deceive you or persuade you like this, and do not believe him; for no god of any nation or kingdom was able to deliver his people from my hand or the hand of my fathers. How much less will your God deliver you from my hand?' "

16 Furthermore, his servants spoke against the LORD God and against His servant Hezekiah.

17 He also wrote letters to revile the LORD God of Israel, and to speak against Him, saying, "As the gods of the nations of *other* lands have not delivered their people from my hand, so the God of Hezekiah will not deliver His people from my hand." 18 Then they called out with a loud voice in Hebrew[a] to the people of Jerusalem who *were* on the wall, to frighten them and trouble them, that

32:3 [a]Literally *mighty men*　32:4 [a]Following Masoretic Text and Vulgate; Arabic, Septuagint, and Syriac read *king*.　32:5 [a]Literally *The Landfill*　32:18 [a]Literally *Judean* they might take the city. 19 And they spoke against the God of Jerusalem, as against the gods of the people of the earth—the work of men's hands.

20 Now because of this King Hezekiah and the prophet Isaiah, the son of Amoz, prayed and cried out to heaven. 21 Then the LORD sent an angel who cut down every mighty man of valor, leader, and captain in the camp of the king of Assyria. So he returned shamefaced to his own land. And when he had gone into the temple of his god, some of his own offspring struck him down with the sword there.

22 Thus the LORD saved Hezekiah and the inhabitants of Jerusalem from the hand of Sennacherib the king of Assyria, and from the hand of all *others*, and guided them[a] on every side. 23 And many brought gifts to the LORD at Jerusalem, and presents to Hezekiah king of Judah, so that he was exalted in the sight of all nations thereafter.

24 In those days Hezekiah was sick and near death, and he prayed to the LORD; and He spoke to him and gave him a sign. 25 But Hezekiah did not repay according to the favor *shown* him, for his heart was lifted up; therefore wrath was looming over him and over Judah and Jerusalem. 26 Then Hezekiah humbled himself for the pride of his heart, he and the inhabitants of Jerusalem, so that the wrath of the LORD did not come upon them in the days of Hezekiah.

27 Hezekiah had very great riches and honor. And he made himself treasuries for silver, for gold, for precious stones, for spices, for shields, and for all kinds of desirable items; 28 storehouses for the harvest of grain, wine, and oil; and stalls for all kinds of livestock, and folds for flocks.[a] 29 Moreover he provided cities for himself, and possessions of flocks and herds in abundance; for God had given him very much property. 30 This same Hezekiah also stopped the water outlet of Upper Gihon, and brought the water by tunnel[a] to the west side of the City of David. Hezekiah prospered in all his works.

31 However, *regarding* the ambassadors of the princes of Babylon, whom they sent to him to inquire about the wonder that was *done* in the land, God withdrew from him, in order to test him, that He might know all *that was* in his heart.

32 Now the rest of the acts of Hezekiah, and his goodness, indeed they *are* written in the vision of Isaiah the prophet, the son of Amoz, *and* in the book of the kings of Judah and Israel. 33 So Hezekiah rested with his fathers, and they buried him in the upper tombs of the sons of David; and all Judah and the inhabitants of Jerusalem honored him at his death. Then Manasseh his son reigned in his place.

33 Manasseh *was* twelve years old when he became king, and he reigned fifty-five years in Jerusalem. 2 But he did evil in the sight of the LORD, according to the abominations of the nations whom the LORD had cast out before the children of Israel. 3 For he rebuilt the high places which Hezekiah his father had broken down; he raised up altars for the Baals, and made wooden images; and he worshiped all the host of heaven[a] and served them. 4 He also built altars in the house of the LORD, of which the LORD had said, "In Jerusalem shall My name be forever." 5 And he built altars for all the host of heaven in the two courts of the house of the LORD. 6 Also he caused his sons to pass through the fire in the Valley of the Son of Hinnom; he practiced soothsaying, used witchcraft and sorcery, and consulted mediums and spiritists. He did much evil in the sight of the LORD, to provoke Him to anger. 7 He even set a carved image, the idol which he had made, in the house of God, of which God had said to David and to Solomon his son, "In this house and in Jerusalem, which I have chosen out of all the tribes of Israel, I will put My name forever; 8 and I will not again remove the foot of Israel from the land which I have appointed for your fathers—only if they are careful to do all that I have commanded them, according to the whole law and the statutes and the ordinances by the hand

---

32:22 [a]Septuagint reads *gave them rest;* Vulgate reads *gave them treasures.*   32:28 [a]Following Septuagint and Vulgate; Arabic and Syriac omit *folds for flocks;* Masoretic Text reads *flocks for sheepfolds.*   32:30 [a]Literally *brought it straight* (compare 2 Kings 20:20)   33:3 [a]The gods of the Assyrians of Moses." 9 So Manasseh seduced Judah and the inhabitants of Jerusalem to do more evil than the nations whom the LORD had destroyed before the children of Israel.

10 And the LORD spoke to Manasseh and his people, but they would not listen. 11 Therefore the LORD brought upon them the captains of the army of the king of Assyria, who took Manasseh with hooks,ᵃ bound him with bronze *fetters*, and carried him off to Babylon. 12 Now when he was in affliction, he implored the LORD his God, and humbled himself greatly before the God of his fathers, 13 and prayed to Him; and He received his entreaty, heard his supplication, and brought him back to Jerusalem into his kingdom. Then Manasseh knew that the LORD *was* God.

14 After this he built a wall outside the City of David on the west side of Gihon, in the valley, as far as the entrance of the Fish Gate; and *it* enclosed Ophel, and he raised it to a very great height. Then he put military captains in all the fortified cities of Judah. 15 He took away the foreign gods and the idol from the house of the LORD, and all the altars that he had built in the mount of the house of the LORD and in Jerusalem; and he cast *them* out of the city. 16 He also repaired the altar of the LORD, sacrificed peace offerings and thank offerings on it, and commanded Judah to serve the LORD God of Israel. 17 Nevertheless the people still sacrificed on the high places, *but* only to the LORD their God.

18 Now the rest of the acts of Manasseh, his prayer to his God, and the words of the seers who spoke to him in the name of the LORD God of Israel, indeed they *are written* in the bookᵃ of the kings of Israel. 19 Also his prayer and how God received his entreaty, and all his sin and trespass, and the sites where he built high places and set up wooden images and carved images, before he was humbled, indeed they *are* written among the sayings of Hozai.ᵃ 20 So Manasseh rested with his fathers, and they buried him in his own house. Then his son Amon reigned in his place.

21 Amon *was* twenty-two years old when he became king, and he reigned two years in Jerusalem. 22 But he did evil in the sight of the LORD, as his father Manasseh had done; for Amon sacrificed to all the carved images which his father Manasseh had made, and served them. 23 And he did not humble himself before the LORD, as his father Manasseh had humbled himself; but Amon trespassed more and more.

24 Then his servants conspired against him, and killed him in his own house. 25 But the people of the land executed all those who had conspired against King Amon. Then the people of the land made his son Josiah king in his place.

34 Josiah *was* eight years old when he became king, and he reigned thirty-one years in Jerusalem. 2 And he did *what was* right in the sight of the LORD, and walked in the ways of his father David; *he* did *not* turn aside to the right hand or to the left.

3 For in the eighth year of his reign, while he was still young, he began to seek the God of his father David; and in the twelfth year he began to purge Judah and Jerusalem of the high places, the wooden images, the carved images, and the molded images. 4 They broke down the altars of the Baals in his presence, and the incense altars which *were* above them he cut down; and the wooden images, the carved images, and the molded images he broke in pieces, and made dust of them and scattered *it* on the graves of those who had sacrificed to them. 5 He also burned the bones of the priests on their altars, and cleansed Judah and Jerusalem. 6 And so he did in the cities of Manasseh, Ephraim, and Simeon, as far as Naphtali and all around, with axes.ᵃ 7 When he had broken down the altars and the wooden images, had beaten the carved images into powder, and cut down all the incense altars throughout all the land of Israel, he returned to Jerusalem.

8 In the eighteenth year of his reign, when he had purged the land and the temple,ᵃ he sent Shaphan the son of Azaliah, Maaseiah the gover-

---

33:11 ᵃThat is, nose hooks (compare 2 Kings 19:28) *the seers.*   34:6 ᵃLiterally *swords*   34:8 ᵃLiterally *house*   33:18 ᵃLiterally *words*   33:19 ᵃSeptuagint reads nor of the city, and Joah the son of Joahaz the recorder, to repair the house of the LORD his God. 9 When they came to Hilkiah the high priest, they delivered the money that was brought into the house of God, which the Levites who kept the doors had gathered from the hand of Manasseh and Ephraim, from all the remnant of Israel, from all Judah and Benjamin, and *which* they had brought back to Jerusalem. 10 Then they put *it* in the hand of the foremen who had the oversight of the house of the LORD; and they gave it to the workmen who worked in the house of the LORD, to repair and restore the house. 11 They gave *it* to the craftsmen and builders to buy hewn stone and timber for beams, and to floor the houses which the kings of Judah had destroyed. 12 And the men did the work faithfully. Their overseers *were* Jahath and Obadiah the Levites, of the sons of Merari, and Zechariah and Meshullam, of the sons of the Kohathites, to supervise. *Others of* the Levites, all of whom were skillful with instruments of music, 13 *were* over the burden bearers and *were* overseers of all who did work in any kind of service. And *some* of the Levites *were* scribes, officers, and gatekeepers.

14 Now when they brought out the money that was brought into the house of the LORD, Hilkiah the priest found the Book of the Law of the LORD *given* by Moses. 15 Then Hilkiah answered and said to Shaphan the scribe, "I have found the Book of the Law in the house of the LORD." And Hilkiah gave the book to Shaphan. 16 So Shaphan carried the book to the king, bringing the king word, saying, "All that was committed to your servants they are doing. 17 And they have gathered the money that was found in the house of the LORD, and have delivered it into the hand of the overseers and the workmen." 18 Then Shaphan the scribe told the king, saying, "Hilkiah the priest has given me a book." And Shaphan read it before the king.

19 Thus it happened, when the king heard the words of the Law, that he tore his clothes. 20 Then the king commanded Hilkiah, Ahikam the son of Shaphan, Abdon[a] the son of Micah, Shaphan the scribe, and Asaiah a servant of the king, saying, 21 "Go, inquire of the LORD for me, and for those who are left in Israel and Judah, concerning the words of the book that is found; for great *is* the wrath of the LORD that is poured out on us, because our fathers have not kept the word of the LORD, to do according to all that is written in this book."

22 So Hilkiah and those the king *had appointed* went to Huldah the prophetess, the wife of Shallum the son of Tokhath,[a] the son of Hasrah,[b] keeper of the wardrobe. (She dwelt in Jerusalem in the Second Quarter.) And they spoke to her to that *effect*.

23 Then she answered them, "Thus says the LORD God of Israel, 'Tell the man who sent you to Me, 24 Thus says the LORD: 'Behold, I will bring calamity on this place and on its inhabitants, all the curses that are written in the book which they have read before the king of Judah, 25 because they have forsaken Me and burned incense to other gods, that they might provoke Me to anger with all the works of their hands. Therefore My wrath will be poured out on this place, and not be quenched.''' 26 But as for the king of Judah, who sent you to inquire of the LORD, in this manner you shall speak to him, 'Thus says the LORD God of Israel: "Concerning the words which you have heard— 27 because your heart was tender, and you humbled yourself before God when you heard His words against this place and against its inhabitants, and you humbled yourself before Me, and you tore your clothes and wept before Me, I also have heard *you*," says the LORD. 28 Surely I will gather you to your fathers, and you shall be gathered to your grave in peace; and your eyes shall not see all the calamity which I will bring on this place and its inhabitants."'" So they brought back word to the king.

29 Then the king sent and gathered all the elders of Judah and Jerusalem. 30 The king went up to the house of the LORD, with all the men of Judah and the inhabitants of Jerusalem— the priests and the Levites, and all

34:20 *a*Achbor the son of Michaiah in 2 Kings 22:12 Harhas in 2 Kings 22:14

34:22 *a*Spelled *Tikvah* in 2 Kings 22:14 *b*Spelled

the people, great and small. And he read in their hearing all the words of the Book of the Covenant which had been found in the house of the LORD. 31 Then the king stood in his place and made a covenant before the LORD, to follow the LORD, and to keep His commandments and His testimonies and His statutes with all his heart and all his soul, to perform the words of the covenant that were written in this book. 32 And he made all who were present in Jerusalem and Benjamin take a stand. So the inhabitants of Jerusalem did according to the covenant of God, the God of their fathers. 33 Thus Josiah removed all the abominations from all the country that *belonged* to the children of Israel, and made all who were present in Israel diligently serve the LORD their God. All his days they did not depart from following the LORD God of their fathers.

35 Now Josiah kept a Passover to the LORD in Jerusalem, and they slaughtered the Passover *lambs* on the fourteenth *day* of the first month. 2 And he set the priests in their duties and encouraged them for the service of the house of the LORD. 3 Then he said to the Levites who taught all Israel, who were holy to the LORD: "Put the holy ark in the house which Solomon the son of David, king of Israel, built. *It shall* no longer *be* a burden on *your* shoulders. Now serve the LORD your God and His people Israel. 4 Prepare *yourselves* according to your fathers' houses, according to your divisions, following the written instruction of David king of Israel and the written instruction of Solomon his son. 5 And stand in the holy *place* according to the divisions of the fathers' houses of your brethren the *lay* people, and *according to* the division of the father's house of the Levites. 6 So slaughter the Passover *offerings*, consecrate yourselves, and prepare *them* for your brethren, that *they* may do according to the word of the LORD by the hand of Moses."

7 Then Josiah gave the *lay* people lambs and young goats from the flock, all for Passover *offerings* for all who were present, to the number of thirty thousand, as well as three thousand cattle; these *were* from the king's possessions. 8 And his leaders

gave willingly to the people, to the priests, and to the Levites. Hilkiah, Zechariah, and Jehiel, rulers of the house of God, gave to the priests for the Passover *offerings* two thousand six hundred *from the flock,* and three hundred cattle. 9 Also Conaniah, his brothers Shemaiah and Nethanel, and Hashabiah and Jeiel and Jozabad, chief of the Levites, gave to the Levites for Passover *offerings* five thousand *from the flock* and five hundred cattle.

10 So the service was prepared, and the priests stood in their places, and the Levites in their divisions, according to the king's command. 11 And they slaughtered the Passover *offerings;* and the priests sprinkled *the blood* with their hands, while the Levites skinned *the animals*. 12 Then they removed the burnt offerings that *they* might give them to the divisions of the fathers' houses of the *lay* people, to offer to the LORD, as *it is* written in the Book of Moses. And so *they did* with the cattle. 13 Also they roasted the Passover *offerings* with fire according to the ordinance; but the *other* holy *offerings* they boiled in pots, in caldrons, and in pans, and divided *them* quickly among all the *lay* people. 14 Then afterward they prepared portions for themselves and for the priests, because the priests, the sons of Aaron, *were busy* in offering burnt offerings and fat until night; therefore the Levites prepared portions for themselves and for the priests, the sons of Aaron. 15 And the singers, the sons of Asaph, *were* in their places, according to the command of David, Asaph, Heman, and Jeduthun the king's seer. Also the gatekeepers were at each gate; they did not have to leave their position, because their brethren the Levites prepared portions for them.

16 So all the service of the LORD was prepared the same day, to keep the Passover and to offer burnt offerings on the altar of the LORD, according to the command of King Josiah. 17 And the children of Israel who were present kept the Passover at that time, and the Feast of Unleavened Bread for seven days. 18 There had been no Passover kept in Israel like that since the days of Samuel the prophet; and none of the kings of Israel had kept such a Passover as Jo-

Freedom to Stand Before God

As Christians, we experience great freedom in worship before God. In light of the ancient Jewish worship of God, we can gain greater appreciation of our access to our Lord.

Recent archaeological excavations of the Jerusalem temple unearthed two stone plaques bearing the inscription, "Gentiles and nations prohibited beyond this point." Dated to the time of Christ, these inscriptions were affixed to the outer court area of the temple. Anyone of a nation other than Israel was forbidden to enter the temple's inner court.

The temple consisted of the outer court, the inner courts, and the innermost court, the Most Holy Place. At Passover, the priest symbolically made atonement for the sins of the entire nation by placing blood from a sacrificial lamb on the mercy seat of the altar in this holiest of places. Only the priest could enter the Most Holy Place. Great restrictions were placed on access to the presence of God, even for the Jews.

Because of the sacrificial death and resurrection of Jesus Christ, no one is separated from God any longer. Instead, we can all enter the Most Holy Place and experience the presence of God. The Book of Hebrews confirms that once and for all individuals can approach God directly. Hebrews 4:16 tells us to "Come boldly before the throne of grace that we may obtain mercy and find grace to help in time of need."

Matthew, Mark, and Luke all record that when Jesus was crucified and died, the temple veil covering the Most Holy Place was torn in two. Ancient Jewish literature also records an unusual occurrence at the temple one Passover. The Most Holy Place curtain was torn in two during the reign of Pontius Pilate, the governor under which Jesus was crucified. Could this be a reference to the same event as recorded in the Bible? It is quite possible.

Through Jesus' death and resurrection, we have the confidence to draw near to God in full assurance. We have the freedom to stand before God knowing He will meet our needs. We are not bound like those unable to enter the temple's inner courts. Nor are we like those who could not enter the Most Holy Place. Rather, we have the blessings of a beautiful relationship with God, free to boldly walk into His presence.

siah kept, with the priests and the Levites, all Judah and Israel who were present, and the inhabitants of Jerusalem. 19 In the eighteenth year of the reign of Josiah this Passover was kept.

20 After all this, when Josiah had prepared the temple, Necho king of Egypt came up to fight against Carchemish by the Euphrates; and Josiah went out against him. 21 But he sent messengers to him, saying, "What have I to do with you, king of Judah? *I have* not *come* against you this day, but against the house with which I have war; for God commanded me to make haste. Refrain *from meddling with God, who is* with me, lest He destroy you." 22 Nevertheless Josiah would not turn his face from him, but disguised himself so that he might fight with him, and did not heed the words of Necho from the mouth of God. So he came to fight in the Valley of Megiddo.

23 And the archers shot King Josiah; and the king said to his servants, "Take me away, for I am severely wounded." 24 His servants therefore took him out of that chariot and put him in the second chariot that he had, and they brought him to Jerusalem. So he died, and was buried in *one of* the tombs of his fathers. And all Judah and Jerusalem mourned for Josiah.

25 Jeremiah also lamented for Josiah. And to this day all the singing men and the singing women speak of Josiah in their lamentations. They made it a custom in Israel; and indeed they *are* written in the Laments.

26 Now the rest of the acts of Josiah and his goodness, according to *what was* written in the Law of the LORD, 27 and his deeds from first to last, indeed they *are* written in the book of the kings of Israel and Judah.

36 Then the people of the land took Jehoahaz the son of Josiah, and made him king in his father's place in Jerusalem. 2 Jehoahaz[a] *was* twenty-three years old when he became king, and he reigned three months in Jerusalem. 3 Now the king of Egypt deposed him at Jerusalem; and he imposed on the land a tribute of one hundred talents of silver and a talent of gold. 4 Then the king of Egypt made *Jehoahaz's*[a] brother Eliakim king over Judah and Jerusalem, and changed his name to Jehoiakim. And Necho took Jehoahaz[b] his brother and carried him off to Egypt.

5 Jehoiakim *was* twenty-five years old when he became king, and he reigned eleven years in Jerusalem. And he did evil in the sight of the LORD his God. 6 Nebuchadnezzar king of Babylon came up against him, and bound him in bronze *fetters* to carry him off to Babylon. 7 Nebuchadnezzar also carried off *some* of the articles from the house of the LORD to Babylon, and put them in his temple at Babylon. 8 Now the rest of the acts of Jehoiakim, the abominations which he did, and what was found against him, indeed they *are* written in the book of the kings of Israel and Judah. Then Jehoiachin his son reigned in his place.

9 Jehoiachin *was* eight[a] years old when he became king, and he reigned in Jerusalem three months and ten days. And he did evil in the sight of the LORD. 10 At the turn of the year King Nebuchadnezzar summoned *him* and took him to Babylon, with the costly articles from the house of the LORD, and made Zedekiah, *Jehoiakim's*[a] brother, king over Judah and Jerusalem.

11 Zedekiah *was* twenty-one years old when he became king, and he reigned eleven years in Jerusalem. 12 He did evil in the sight of the LORD his God, *and* did not humble himself before Jeremiah the prophet, *who* spoke from the mouth of the LORD. 13 And he also rebelled against King Nebuchadnezzar, who had made him swear *an oath* by God; but he stiffened his neck and hardened his heart against turning to the LORD God of Israel. 14 Moreover all the leaders of the priests and the people transgressed more and more, *according* to all the abominations of the nations, and defiled the house of the LORD which He had consecrated in Jerusalem.

36:2 [a]Masoretic Text reads *Joahaz.*   36:4 [a]Literally *his*   [b]Masoretic Text reads *Joahaz.*   36:9 [a]Some Hebrew manuscripts, Septuagint, Syriac, and 2 Kings 24:8 read *eighteen.*   36:10 [a]Literally *his* (compare 2 Kings 24:17)

Important Capital Cities

NINEVEH: Capital of Assyria; ancient walled city was scene of the prophet Jonah's reluctant preaching mission (Jon. 3:1–3).

BABYLON: Capital city of the Babylonian Empire in the land of the Chaldeans (Jer. 24:5); city to which citizens of Judah were carried after the fall of Jerusalem (2 Chr. 36:18, 20).

ACHMETHA: Also known as Ecbatana, Achmetha was capital of the Median Empire (Ezra 6:2); served as the summer residence of Persian kings.

SHUSHAN: Also known as Susa, Shushan was capital of ancient Elam and later capital of the Persian Empire; most events in the Book of Esther occurred in this city (Esth. 1:2–5).

UR: Capital of ancient Sumer on the Euphrates River; Abraham lived here before moving to Haran (Gen. 11:31).

SHECHEM: First capital of the northern kingdom following Solomon's reign; located in the hill country of Ephraim (Gen. 12:6).

JERUSALEM: Made capital of the United Kingdom by David (2 Sam. 5:6, 7); location of Solomon's temple, known as the Holy City and Zion by the Jewish people.

DAMASCUS: Capital of Syria and important trade center; oldest continually inhabited city in the world (Gen. 14:15).

SAMARIA: Permanent capital of the northern kingdom; built by Omri, sixth king of Israel, in 880 B.C. (1 Kin. 16:23, 24).

HEBRON: David's capital as he ruled Judah (2 Sam. 2:1–4). Abraham's home after his return from Egypt (Gen. 13:18).

NO: Also known as Thebes, No was capital of Egypt and center of pagan worship on banks of the Nile River (Ezek. 30:13.–16).

PERSIAN GULF

ARABIAN DESERT

THE GREAT SEA

RED SEA

EGYPT

Achmetha

Shushan

Nineveh

Babylon

Ur

Damascus

Samaria

Shechem

Jerusalem

Hebron

No (Thebes)

15 And the LORD God of their fathers sent *warnings* to them by His messengers, rising up early and sending *them,* because He had compassion on His people and on His dwelling place. 16 But they mocked the messengers of God, despised His words, and scoffed at His prophets, until the wrath of the LORD arose against His people, till *there was* no remedy.

17 Therefore He brought against them the king of the Chaldeans, who killed their young men with the sword in the house of their sanctuary, and had no compassion on young man or virgin, on the aged or the weak; He gave *them* all into his hand. 18 And all the articles from the house of God, great and small, the treasures of the house of the LORD, and the treasures of the king and of his leaders, all *these* he took to Babylon. 19 Then they burned the house of God, broke down the wall of Jerusalem, burned all its palaces with fire, and destroyed all its precious possessions. 20 And those who escaped from the sword he carried away to Babylon, where they became servants to him and his sons until the rule of the kingdom of Persia, 21 to fulfill the word of the LORD by the mouth of Jeremiah, until the land had enjoyed her Sabbaths. As long as she lay desolate she kept Sabbath, to fulfill seventy years.

22 Now in the first year of Cyrus king of Persia, that the word of the LORD by the mouth of Jeremiah might be fulfilled, the LORD stirred up the spirit of Cyrus king of Persia, so that he made a proclamation throughout all his kingdom, and also *put it* in writing, saying,

23   Thus says Cyrus king of Persia: All the kingdoms of the earth the LORD God of heaven has given me. And He has commanded me to build Him a house at Jerusalem which is in Judah. Who *is* among you of all His people? May the LORD his God *be* with him, and let him go up!

Ezra

Overview of Ezra

The Book of Ezra teaches that even if you have good reason to be sorrowful you can still be resourceful and ultimately successful!

Written by the scribe Ezra between 457 and 444 B.C., the book records two major exoduses of the Jewish people from Babylon.

Ezra chronicles the events concerning the rebuilding of the temple. Instilled with a dream, the people began the task of rebuilding their place of worship. Slowly they saw their dream rise from the rubble and ashes of the destruction wrought by Nebuchadnezzar on the ancient city of Jerusalem. Ezra told the people that now was the time to build a sanctuary of worship for their God.

Who is among you of all His people? May his God be with him, and let him go up to Jerusalem, which is in Judah, and build the house of the LORD God of Israel (He is God), which is in Jerusalem. And whoever is left in any place where he dwells, let the man of his place help him with silver and gold, with goods and livestock, besides the freewill offerings for the house of God which is in Jerusalem.

(Ezra 1:3, 4)

He encouraged them to look not at the ruins but toward the results. They faced many obstacles—lack of money, lack of manpower, and pressure from local military authorities who opposed the project. There were many reasons the temple should not have been built. But Ezra looked toward his goal. He made his decisions, and then he solved his problems. He never let his problems stop him from completing his God-ordained dream.

Ezra set out to find solutions to the obstacles in his way. Because of his faith and leadership, the dream of the temple became a reality!

Jesus in Ezra

Ezra reveals God's continued fulfillment of His promise to keep David's descendants alive. Zerubbabel himself is part of the messianic line. There is a note of hope in Ezra and Nehemiah because the remnant returned to the land of promise, where the promises of the Messiah will be fulfilled, in cities such as Bethlehem and Jerusalem.

The Book of Ezra as a whole also typifies Jesus' work of forgiveness and restoration.

Keys to Ezra

Key Word: Temple. The basic theme of Ezra is the restoration of the temple and the spiritual, moral, and social restoration of the returned remnant in Jerusalem under the leadership of Zerubbabel and Ezra. Israel's worship is revitalized and the people are purified. God's faithfulness is seen in the way He sovereignly protects His people while they are in captivity. They prosper in exile, and God raises up pagan kings who are sympathetic to their cause and encourage them to rebuild their homeland. God also provides zealous and capable spiritual leaders who direct the return and the rebuilding.

Key Verses: "Who *is* among you of all His people? May his God be with him, and let him go up to Jerusalem, which *is* in Judah, and build the house of the LORD God of Israel (He *is* God), which *is* in Jerusalem. And whoever is left in any place where he dwells, let the men of his place help him with silver and gold, with goods and livestock, besides the freewill offerings for the house of God which *is* in Jerusalem" (1:3, 4).

"For Ezra had prepared his heart to seek the Law of the LORD, and to do it, and to teach statutes and ordinances in Israel" (7:10).

Key Chapter: Ezra 6. Ezra 6 records the completion and dedication of the temple which stimulates the obedience of the remnant to keep the Passover and separate themselves from the "filth of the nations of the land" (6:21).

1 Now in the first year of Cyrus king of Persia, that the word of the LORD by the mouth of Jeremiah might be fulfilled, the LORD stirred up the spirit of Cyrus king of Persia, so that he made a proclamation throughout all his kingdom, and also *put it* in writing, saying,

2 Thus says Cyrus king of Persia: All the kingdoms of the earth the LORD God of heaven has given me. And He has commanded me to build Him a house at Jerusalem which *is* in Judah. 3 Who *is* among you of all His people? May his God be with him, and let him go up to Jerusalem which *is* in Judah, and build the house of the LORD God of Israel (He *is* God), which *is* in Jerusalem.

4 And whoever is left in any place where he dwells, let the men of his place help him with silver and gold, with goods and livestock, besides the freewill offerings for the house of God which *is* in Jerusalem.

5 Then the heads of the fathers' *houses* of Judah and Benjamin, and the priests and the Levites, with all whose spirits God had moved, arose to go up and build the house of the LORD which *is* in Jerusalem. 6 And all those who *were* around them encouraged them with articles of silver and gold, with goods and livestock, and with precious things, besides all *that* was willingly offered. 7 King Cyrus also brought out the articles of the house of the LORD, which Nebuchadnezzar had taken

from Jerusalem and put in the temple of his gods; 8 and Cyrus king of Persia brought them out by the hand of Mithredath the treasurer, and counted them out to Sheshbazzar the prince of Judah. 9 This *is* the number of them: thirty gold platters, one thousand silver platters, twenty-nine knives, 10 thirty gold basins, four hundred and ten silver basins of a similar *kind, and* one thousand other articles. 11 All the articles of gold and silver *were* five thousand four hundred. All *these* Sheshbazzar took with the captives who were brought from Babylon to Jerusalem.

2 Now*a* these *are* the people of the province who came back from the captivity, of those who had been carried away, whom Nebuchadnezzar the king of Babylon had carried away to Babylon, and who returned to Jerusalem and Judah, everyone to his *own* city.

2 *Those* who came with Zerubbabel *were* Jeshua, Nehemiah, Seraiah, Reelaiah, Mordecai, Bilshan, Mispar,*a* Bigvai, Rehum,*b and* Baanah. The number of the men of the people of Israel: 3 the people of Parosh, two thousand one hundred and seventy-two; 4 the people of Shephatiah, three hundred and seventy-two; 5 the people of Arah, seven hundred and seventy-five; 6 the people of Pahath-Moab, of the people of Jeshua *and* Joab, two thousand eight hundred and twelve; 7 the people of Elam, one thousand two hundred and fifty-four; 8 the people of Zattu, nine hundred and forty-five; 9 the people of Zaccai, seven hundred and sixty; 10 the people of Bani,*a* six hundred and forty-two; 11 the people of Bebai, six hundred and twenty-three; 12 the people of Azgad, one thousand two hundred and twenty-two; 13 the people of Adonikam, six hundred and sixty-six; 14 the people of Bigvai, two thousand and fifty-six; 15 the people of Adin, four hundred and fifty-four; 16 the people of Ater of Hezekiah, ninety-eight; 17 the people of Bezai, three hundred and

twenty-three; 18 the people of Jorah,*a* one hundred and twelve; 19 the people of Hashum, two hundred and twenty-three; 20 the people of Gibbar,*a* ninety-five; 21 the people of Bethlehem, one hundred and twenty-three; 22 the men of Netophah, fifty-six; 23 the men of Anathoth, one hundred and twenty-eight; 24 the people of Azmaveth,*a* forty-two; 25 the people of Kirjath Arim,*a* Chephirah, and Beeroth, seven hundred and forty-three; 26 the people of Ramah and Geba, six hundred and twenty-one; 27 the men of Michmas, one hundred and twenty-two; 28 the men of Bethel and Ai, two hundred and twenty-three; 29 the people of Nebo, fifty-two; 30 the people of Magbish, one hundred and fifty-six; 31 the people of the other Elam, one thousand two hundred and fifty-four; 32 the people of Harim, three hundred and twenty; 33 the people of Lod, Hadid, and Ono, seven hundred and twenty-five; 34 the people of Jericho, three hundred and forty-five; 35 the people of Senaah, three thousand six hundred and thirty.

36 The priests: the sons of Jedaiah, of the house of Jeshua, nine hundred and seventy-three; 37 the sons of Immer, one thousand and fifty-two; 38 the sons of Pashhur, one thousand two hundred and forty-seven; 39 the sons of Harim, one thousand and seventeen.

40 The Levites: the sons of Jeshua and Kadmiel, of the sons of Hodaviah,*a* seventy-four.

41 The singers: the sons of Asaph, one hundred and twenty-eight.

42 The sons of the gatekeepers: the sons of Shallum, the sons of Ater, the sons of Talmon, the sons of Akkub, the sons of Hatita, and the sons of Shobai, one hundred and thirty-nine *in* all.

43 The Nethinim: the sons of Ziha, the sons of Hasupha, the sons of Tabbaoth, 44 the sons of Keros, the sons of Siaha,*a* the sons of Padon, 45 the sons of Lebanah, the sons of Hagabah, the sons of Akkub, 46 the sons of Hagab, the sons of Shalmai, the sons of Hanan, 47 the sons

2:1 *a*Compare this chapter with Nehemiah 7:6–73.   2:2 *a*Spelled *Mispereth* in Nehemiah 7:7   *b*Spelled *Nehum* in Nehemiah 7:7   2:10 *a*Spelled *Binnui* in Nehemiah 7:15   2:18 *a*Called *Hariph* in Nehemiah 7:24   2:20 *a*Called *Gibeon* in Nehemiah 7:25   2:24 *a*Called *Beth Azmaveth* in Nehemiah 7:28   2:25 *a*Called *Kirjath Jearim* in Nehemiah 7:29   2:40 *a*Spelled *Hodevah* in Nehemiah 7:43   2:44 *a*Spelled *Sia* in Nehemiah 7:47

of Giddel, the sons of Gahar, the sons of Reaiah, 48 the sons of Rezin, the sons of Nekoda, the sons of Gazzam, 49 the sons of Uzza, the sons of Paseah, the sons of Besai, 50 the sons of Asnah, the sons of Meunim, the sons of Nephusim,[a] 51 the sons of Bakbuk, the sons of Hakupha, the sons of Harhur, 52 the sons of Bazluth,[a] the sons of Mehida, the sons of Harsha, 53 the sons of Barkos, the sons of Sisera, the sons of Tamah, 54 the sons of Neziah, and the sons of Hatipha.

55 The sons of Solomon's servants: the sons of Sotai, the sons of Sophereth, the sons of Peruda,[a] 56 the sons of Jaala, the sons of Darkon, the sons of Giddel, 57 the sons of Shephatiah, the sons of Hattil, the sons of Pochereth of Zebaim, and the sons of Ami.[a] 58 All the Nethinim and the children of Solomon's servants were three hundred and ninety-two.

59 And these were the ones who came up from Tel Melah, Tel Harsha, Cherub, Addan,[a] and Immer; but they could not identify their father's house or their genealogy,[b] whether they were of Israel: 60 the sons of Delaiah, the sons of Tobiah, and the sons of Nekoda, six hundred and fifty-two; 61 and of the sons of the priests: the sons of Habaiah, the sons of Koz,[a] and the sons of Barzillai, who took a wife of the daughters of Barzillai the Gileadite, and was called by their name. 62 These sought their listing among those who were registered by genealogy, but they were not found; therefore they were excluded from the priesthood as defiled. 63 And the governor[a] said to them that they should not eat of the most holy things till a priest could consult with the Urim and Thummim.

64 The whole assembly together was forty-two thousand three hundred and sixty, 65 besides their male and female servants, of whom there were seven thousand three hundred and thirty-seven; and they had two hundred men and women singers. 66 Their horses were seven hundred and thirty-six, their mules two hundred and forty-five, 67 their camels four hundred and thirty-five, and

their donkeys six thousand seven hundred and twenty.

68 Some of the heads of the fathers' houses, when they came to the house of the LORD which is in Jerusalem, offered freely for the house of God, to erect it in its place: 69 According to their ability, they gave to the treasury for the work sixty-one thousand gold drachmas, five thousand minas of silver, and one hundred priestly garments.

70 So the priests and the Levites, some of the people, the singers, the gatekeepers, and the Nethinim, dwelt in their cities, and all Israel in their cities.

3 And when the seventh month had come, and the children of Israel were in the cities, the people gathered together as one man to Jerusalem. 2 Then Jeshua the son of Jozadak[a] and his brethren the priests, and Zerubbabel the son of Shealtiel and his brethren, arose and built the altar of the God of Israel, to offer burnt offerings on it, as it is written in the Law of Moses the man of God. 3 Though fear had come upon them because of the people of those countries, they set the altar on its bases; and they offered burnt offerings on it to the LORD, both the morning and evening burnt offerings. 4 They also kept the Feast of Tabernacles, as it is written, and offered the daily burnt offerings in the number required by ordinance for each day. 5 Afterwards they offered the regular burnt offering, and those for New Moons and for all the appointed feasts of the LORD that were consecrated, and those of everyone who willingly offered a freewill offering to the LORD. 6 From the first day of the seventh month they began to offer burnt offerings to the LORD, although the foundation of the temple of the LORD had not been laid. 7 They also gave money to the masons and the carpenters, and food, drink, and oil to the people of Sidon and Tyre to bring cedar logs from Lebanon to the sea, to Joppa, according to the permission which they had from Cyrus king of Persia.

2:50 [a]Spelled Nephishesim in Nehemiah 7:52   2:52 [a]Spelled Bazlith in Nehemiah 7:54   2:55 [a]Spelled Perida in Nehemiah 7:57   2:57 [a]Spelled Amon in Nehemiah 7:59   2:59 [a]Spelled Addon in Nehemiah 7:61   [b]Literally seed   2:61 [a]Or Hakkoz   2:63 [a]Hebrew Tirshatha   3:2 [a]Spelled Jehozadak in 1 Chronicles 6:14

8 Now in the second month of the second year of their coming to the house of God at Jerusalem, Zerubbabel the son of Shealtiel, Jeshua the son of Jozadak,*a* and the rest of their brethren the priests and the Levites, and all those who had come out of the captivity to Jerusalem, began *work* and appointed the Levites from twenty years old and above to oversee the work of the house of the LORD. 9 Then Jeshua *with* his sons and brothers, Kadmiel *with* his sons, and the sons of Judah,*a* arose as one to oversee those working on the house of God: the sons of Henadad *with* their sons and their brethren the Levites.

10 When the builders laid the foundation of the temple of the LORD, the priests stood*a* in their apparel with trumpets, and the Levites, the sons of Asaph, with cymbals, to praise the LORD, according to the ordinance of David king of Israel. 11 And they sang responsively, praising and giving thanks to the LORD:

> "For *He is* good,
>   For His mercy *endures* forever
>   toward Israel."*a*

Then all the people shouted with a great shout, when they praised the LORD, because the foundation of the house of the LORD was laid. 12 But many of the priests and Levites and heads of the fathers' *houses,* old men who had seen the first temple, wept with a loud voice when the foundation of this temple was laid before their eyes. Yet many shouted aloud for joy, 13 so that the people could not discern the noise of the shout of joy from the noise of the weeping of the people, for the people shouted with a loud shout, and the sound was heard afar off.

4 Now when the adversaries of Judah and Benjamin heard that the descendants of the captivity were building the temple of the LORD God of Israel, 2 they came to Zerubbabel and the heads of the fathers' *houses,* and said to them, "Let us build with you, for we seek your God as you *do;*

and we have sacrificed to Him since the days of Esarhaddon king of Assyria, who brought us here." 3 But Zerubbabel and Jeshua and the rest of the heads of the fathers' *houses* of Israel said to them, "You may do nothing with us to build a house for our God; but we alone will build to the LORD God of Israel, as King Cyrus the king of Persia has commanded us." 4 Then the people of the land tried to discourage the people of Judah. They troubled them in building, 5 and hired counselors against them to frustrate their purpose all the days of Cyrus king of Persia, even until the reign of Darius king of Persia.

6 In the reign of Ahasuerus, in the beginning of his reign, they wrote an accusation against the inhabitants of Judah and Jerusalem.

7 In the days of Artaxerxes also, Bishlam, Mithredath, Tabel, and the rest of their companions wrote to Artaxerxes king of Persia; and the letter *was* written in Aramaic script, and translated into the Aramaic language. 8 Rehum*a* the commander and Shimshai the scribe wrote a letter against Jerusalem to King Artaxerxes in this fashion:

9   From*a* Rehum the commander, Shimshai the scribe, and the rest of their companions— *representatives* of the Dinaites, the Apharsathchites, the Tarpelites, the people of Persia and Erech and Babylon and Shushan,*b* the Dehavites, the Elamites, 10 and the rest of the nations whom the great and noble Osnapper took captive and settled in the cities of Samaria and the remainder beyond the River*a*—and so forth.*b*

11 (This *is* a copy of the letter that they sent him)

To King Artaxerxes from your servants, the men *of the region* beyond the River, and so forth:*a*

12   Let it be known to the king that the Jews who came up from you have come to us at

---

3:8 *a*Spelled *Jehozadak* in 1 Chronicles 6:14   3:9 *a*Or *Hodaviah* (compare 2:40)   3:10 *a*Following Septuagint, Syriac, and Vulgate; Masoretic Text reads *they stationed the priests.*   3:11 *a*Compare Psalm 136:1   4:8 *a*The original language of Ezra 4:8 through 6:18 is Aramaic.   4:9 *a*Literally *Then* *b*Or *Susa*   4:10 *a*That is, the Euphrates   *b*Literally *and now*   4:11 *a*Literally *and now*

Jerusalem, and are building the rebellious and evil city, and are finishing *its* walls and repairing the foundations. 13 Let it now be known to the king that, if this city is built and the walls completed, they will not pay tax, tribute, or custom, and the king's treasury will be diminished. 14 Now because we receive support from the palace, it was not proper for us to see the king's dishonor; therefore we have sent and informed the king, 15 that search may be made in the book of the records of your fathers. And you will find in the book of the records and know that this city *is* a rebellious city, harmful to kings and provinces, and that they have incited sedition within the city in former times, for which cause this city was destroyed.

16 We inform the king that if this city is rebuilt and its walls are completed, the result will be that you will have no dominion beyond the River.

17 The king sent an answer:

To Rehum the commander, *to* Shimshai the scribe, *to* the rest of their companions who dwell in Samaria, and *to* the remainder beyond the River:

Peace, and so forth.ᵃ

18 The letter which you sent to us has been clearly read before me. 19 And I gave the command, and a search has been made, and it was found that this city in former times has revolted against kings, and rebellion and sedition have been fostered in it. 20 There have also been mighty kings over Jerusalem, who have ruled over all *the region* beyond the River; and tax, tribute, and custom were paid to them. 21 Now give the command to make these men cease, that this city may not be built until the command is given by me.

22 Take heed now that you do not fail to do this. Why should damage increase to the hurt of the kings?

23 Now when the copy of King Artaxerxes' letter *was* read before Rehum, Shimshai the scribe, and their companions, they went up in haste to Jerusalem against the Jews, and by force of arms made them cease. 24 Thus the work of the house of God which *is* at Jerusalem ceased, and it was discontinued until the second year of the reign of Darius king of Persia.

5 Then the prophet Haggai and Zechariah the son of Iddo, prophets, prophesied to the Jews who *were* in Judah and Jerusalem, in the name of the God of Israel, *who was* over them. 2 So Zerubbabel the son of Shealtiel and Jeshua the son of Jozadakᵃ rose up and began to build the house of God which *is* in Jerusalem; and the prophets of God *were* with them, helping them.

3 At the same time Tattenai the governor of *the region* beyond the Riverᵃ and Shethar-Boznai and their companions came to them and spoke thus to them: "Who has commanded you to build this temple and finish this wall?" 4 Then, accordingly, we told them the names of the men who were constructing this building. 5 But the eye of their God was upon the elders of the Jews, so that they could not make them cease till a report could go to Darius. Then a written answer was returned concerning this *matter.* 6 This is a copy of the letter that Tattenai sent:

The governor of *the region* beyond the River, and Shethar-Boznai, and his companions, the Persians who *were in the region* beyond the River, to Darius the king.

7 (They sent a letter to him, in which was written thus)

To Darius the king:

All peace.

8 Let it be known to the king that we went into the province of

Judea, to the temple of the great God, which is being built with heavy stones, and timber is being laid in the walls; and this work goes on diligently and prospers in their hands.

9 Then we asked those elders, *and* spoke thus to them: "Who commanded you to build this temple and to finish these walls?" 10 We also asked them their names to inform you, that we might write the names of the men who *were* chief among them.

11 And thus they returned us an answer, saying: "We are the servants of the God of heaven and earth, and we are rebuilding the temple that was built many years ago, which a great king of Israel built and completed. 12 But because our fathers provoked the God of heaven to wrath, He gave them into the hand of Nebuchadnezzar king of Babylon, the Chaldean, *who* destroyed this temple and carried the people away to Babylon. 13 However, in the first year of Cyrus king of Babylon, King Cyrus issued a decree to build this house of God. 14 Also, the gold and silver articles of the house of God, which Nebuchadnezzar had taken from the temple that *was* in Jerusalem and carried into the temple of Babylon— those King Cyrus took from the temple of Babylon, and they were given to one named Sheshbazzar, whom he had made governor. 15 And he said to him, 'Take these articles; go, carry them to the temple *site* that *is* in Jerusalem, and let the house of God be rebuilt on its former site.' 16 Then the same Sheshbazzar came *and* laid the foundation of the house of God which *is* in Jerusalem; but from that time even until now it has been under construction, and it is not finished."

17 Now therefore, if *it seems* good to the king, let a search be made in the king's treasure house, which *is* there in Babylon, whether it is *so* that a decree was issued by King Cyrus to build this house of God at Jerusalem, and let the king send us his pleasure concerning this *matter.*

6 Then King Darius issued a decree, and a search was made in the archives,[a] where the treasures were stored in Babylon. 2 And at Achmetha,[a] in the palace that *is* in the province of Media, a scroll was found, and in it a record *was* written thus:

3 In the first year of King Cyrus, King Cyrus issued a decree *concerning* the house of God at Jerusalem: "Let the house be rebuilt, the place where they offered sacrifices; and let the foundations of it be firmly laid, its height sixty cubits *and* its width sixty cubits, 4 *with* three rows of heavy stones and one row of new timber. Let the expenses be paid from the king's treasury. 5 Also let the gold and silver articles of the house of God, which Nebuchadnezzar took from the temple which *is* in Jerusalem and brought to Babylon, be restored and taken back to the temple which *is* in Jerusalem, *each* to its place; and deposit *them* in the house of God"—

6 Now *therefore*, Tattenai, governor of *the region* beyond the River, and Shethar-Boznai, and your companions the Persians who *are* beyond the River, keep yourselves far from there. 7 Let the work of this house of God alone; let the governor of the Jews and the elders of the Jews build this house of God on its site.

8 Moreover I issue a decree *as to* what you shall do for the elders of these Jews, for the building of this house of God: Let the cost be paid at the king's expense from taxes on the

6:1 [a]Literally *house of the scrolls*   6:2 [a]Probably *Ecbatana*, the ancient capital of Media *region* beyond the River; this is to be given immediately to these men, so that they are not hindered. 9 And whatever they need—young bulls, rams, and lambs for the burnt offerings of the God of heaven, wheat, salt, wine, and oil, according to the request of the priests who *are* in Jerusalem—let it be given them day by day without fail, 10 that they may offer sacrifices of sweet aroma to the God of heaven, and pray for the life of the king and his sons.

11 Also I issue a decree that whoever alters this edict, let a timber be pulled from his house and erected, and let him be hanged on it; and let his house be made a refuse heap because of this. 12 And may the God who causes His name to dwell there destroy any king or people who put their hand to alter it, or to destroy this house of God which is in Jerusalem. I Darius issue a decree; let it be done diligently.

13 Then Tattenai, governor of *the region* beyond the River, Shethar-Boznai, and their companions diligently did according to what King Darius had sent. 14 So the elders of the Jews built, and they prospered through the prophesying of Haggai the prophet and Zechariah the son of Iddo. And they built and finished *it*, according to the commandment of the God of Israel, and according to the command of Cyrus, Darius, and Artaxerxes king of Persia. 15 Now the temple was finished on the third day of the month of Adar, which was in the sixth year of the reign of King Darius. 16 Then the children of Israel, the priests and the Levites and the rest of the descendants of the captivity, celebrated the dedication of this house of God with joy. 17 And they offered sacrifices at the dedication of this house of God, one hundred bulls, two hundred rams, four hundred lambs, and as a sin offering for all Israel twelve male goats, according to the number of the tribes of Israel. 18 They assigned the priests to their divisions and the Levites to their divisions, over the service of God in Jeru-

salem, as it is written in the Book of Moses.
19 And the descendants of the captivity kept the Passover on the fourteenth *day* of the first month. 20 For the priests and the Levites had purified themselves; all of them *were ritually* clean. And they slaughtered the Passover *lambs* for all the descendants of the captivity, for their brethren the priests, and for themselves. 21 Then the children of Israel who had returned from the captivity ate together with all who had separated themselves from the filth of the nations of the land in order to seek the LORD God of Israel. 22 And they kept the Feast of Unleavened Bread seven days with joy; for the LORD made them joyful, and turned the heart of the king of Assyria toward them, to strengthen their hands in the work of the house of God, the God of Israel.

7 Now after these things, in the reign of Artaxerxes king of Persia, Ezra the son of Seraiah, the son of Azariah, the son of Hilkiah, 2 the son of Shallum, the son of Zadok, the son of Ahitub, 3 the son of Amariah, the son of Azariah, the son of Meraioth, 4 the son of Zerahiah, the son of Uzzi, the son of Bukki, 5 the son of Abishua, the son of Phinehas, the son of Eleazar, the son of Aaron the chief priest— 6 this Ezra came up from Babylon; and he *was* a skilled scribe in the Law of Moses, which the LORD God of Israel had given. The king granted him all his request, according to the hand of the LORD his God upon him. 7 *Some* of the children of Israel, the priests, the Levites, the singers, the gatekeepers, and the Nethinim came up to Jerusalem in the seventh year of King Artaxerxes. 8 And Ezra came to Jerusalem in the fifth month, which *was* in the seventh year of the king. 9 On the first *day* of the first month he began *his* journey from Babylon, and on the first *day* of the fifth month he came to Jerusalem, according to the good hand of his God upon him. 10 For Ezra had prepared his heart to seek the Law of the LORD, and to do *it*, and to teach statutes and ordinances in Israel.
11 This *is* a copy of the letter that King Artaxerxes gave Ezra the priest, the scribe, expert in the words

of the commandments of the LORD, and of His statutes to Israel:

12 Artaxerxes,[a] king of kings,

To Ezra the priest, a scribe of the Law of the God of heaven:

Perfect *peace*, and so forth.[b]

13 I issue a decree that all those of the people of Israel and the priests and Levites in my realm, who volunteer to go up to Jerusalem, may go with you. 14 And whereas you are being sent by the king and his seven counselors to inquire concerning Judah and Jerusalem, with regard to the Law of your God which *is* in your hand; 15 and *whereas you are* to carry the silver and gold which the king and his counselors have freely offered to the God of Israel, whose dwelling *is* in Jerusalem; 16 and *whereas* all the silver and gold that you may find in all the province of Babylon, along with the freewill offering of the people and the priests, *are to be* freely offered for the house of their God in Jerusalem— 17 now therefore, be careful to buy with this money bulls, rams, and lambs, with their grain offerings and their drink offerings, and offer them on the altar of the house of your God in Jerusalem.

18 And whatever seems good to you and your brethren to do with the rest of the silver and the gold, do it according to the will of your God. 19 Also the articles that are given to you for the service of the house of your God, deliver in full before the God of Jerusalem. 20 And whatever more may be needed for the house of your God, which you may have occasion to provide, pay *for it* from the king's treasury.

21 And I, *even* I, Artaxerxes the king, issue a decree to all the treasurers who *are* in the *region* beyond the River, that whatever Ezra the priest, the scribe of the Law of the God of heaven, may require of you, let it be done diligently, 22 up to one hundred talents of silver, one hundred kors of wheat, one hundred baths of wine, one hundred baths of oil, and salt without prescribed limit. 23 Whatever is commanded by the God of heaven, let it diligently be done for the house of the God of heaven. For why should there be wrath against the realm of the king and his sons?

24 Also we inform you that it shall not be lawful to impose tax, tribute, or custom *on* any of the priests, Levites, singers, gatekeepers, Nethinim, or servants of this house of God. 25 And you, Ezra, according to your God-given wisdom, set magistrates and judges who may judge all the people who *are in the region* beyond the River, all such as know the laws of your God; and teach those who do not know *them*. 26 Whoever will not observe the law of your God and the law of the king, let judgment be executed speedily on him, whether *it be* death, or banishment, or confiscation of goods, or imprisonment.

27 Blessed *be* the LORD God of our fathers, who has put *such a thing* as this in the king's heart, to beautify the house of the LORD which *is* in Jerusalem, 28 and has extended mercy to me before the king and his counselors, and before all the king's mighty princes.

So I was encouraged, as the hand of the LORD my God *was* upon me; and I gathered leading men of Israel to go up with me.

8 These *are* the heads of their fathers' *houses*, and *this is* the genealogy of those who went up with me from Babylon, in the reign of King Artaxerxes: 2 of the sons of

7:12 [a]The original language of Ezra 7:12–26 is Aramaic. [b]Literally *and now*

Phinehas, Gershom; of the sons of Ithamar, Daniel; of the sons of David, Hattush; 3 of the sons of Shecaniah, of the sons of Parosh, Zechariah; and registered with him *were* one hundred and fifty males; 4 of the sons of Pahath-Moab, Eliehoenai the son of Zerahiah, and with him two hundred males; 5 of the sons of Shechaniah,*a* Ben-Jahaziel, and with him three hundred males; 6 of the sons of Adin, Ebed the son of Jonathan, and with him fifty males; 7 of the sons of Elam, Jeshaiah the son of Athaliah, and with him seventy males; 8 of the sons of Shephatiah, Zebadiah the son of Michael, and with him eighty males; 9 of the sons of Joab, Obadiah the son of Jehiel, and with him two hundred and eighteen males; 10 of the sons of Shelomith,*a* Ben-Josiphiah, and with him one hundred and sixty males; 11 of the sons of Bebai, Zechariah the son of Bebai, and with him twenty-eight males; 12 of the sons of Azgad, Johanan the son of Hakkatan, and with him one hundred and ten males; 13 of the last sons of Adonikam, whose names *are* these—Eliphelet, Jeiel, and Shemaiah—and with them sixty males; 14 also of the sons of Bigvai, Uthai and Zabbud, and with them seventy males.

15 Now I gathered them by the river that flows to Ahava, and we camped there three days. And I looked among the people and the priests, and found none of the sons of Levi there. 16 Then I sent for Eliezer, Ariel, Shemaiah, Elnathan, Jarib, Elnathan, Nathan, Zechariah, and Meshullam, leaders; also for Joiarib and Elnathan, men of understanding. 17 And I gave them a command for Iddo the chief man at the place Casiphia, and I told them what they should say to Iddo *and* his brethren*a* the Nethinim at the place Casiphia—that they should bring us servants for the house of our God. 18 Then, by the good hand of our God upon us, they brought us a man of understanding, of the sons of Mahli the son of Levi, the son of Israel, namely Sherebiah, with his sons and brothers, eighteen men; 19 and Hashabiah, and with him Jeshaiah of the sons of Merari, his brothers and

their sons, twenty men; 20 also of the Nethinim, whom David and the leaders had appointed for the service of the Levites, two hundred and twenty Nethinim. All of them were designated by name.

21 Then I proclaimed a fast there at the river of Ahava, that we might humble ourselves before our God, to seek from Him the right way for us and our little ones and all our possessions. 22 For I was ashamed to request of the king an escort of soldiers and horsemen to help us against the enemy on the road, because we had spoken to the king, saying, "The hand of our God *is* upon all those for good who seek Him, but His power and His wrath *are* against all those who forsake Him." 23 So we fasted and entreated our God for this, and He answered our prayer.

24 And I separated twelve of the leaders of the priests—Sherebiah, Hashabiah, and ten of their brethren with them— 25 and weighed out to them the silver, the gold, and the articles, the offering for the house of our God which the king and his counselors and his princes, and all Israel *who were* present, had offered. 26 I weighed into their hand six hundred and fifty talents of silver, silver articles *weighing* one hundred talents, one hundred talents of gold, 27 twenty gold basins *worth* a thousand drachmas, and two vessels of fine polished bronze, precious as gold. 28 And I said to them, "You *are* holy to the LORD; the articles *are* holy also; and the silver and the gold *are* a freewill offering to the LORD God of your fathers. 29 Watch and keep *them* until you weigh *them* before the leaders of the priests and the Levites and heads of the fathers' *houses* of Israel in Jerusalem, *in* the chambers of the house of the LORD." 30 So the priests and the Levites received the silver and the gold and the articles by weight, to bring *them* to Jerusalem to the house of our God.

31 Then we departed from the river of Ahava on the twelfth *day* of the first month, to go to Jerusalem. And the hand of our God was upon us, and He delivered us from the hand of the enemy and from ambush along

8:5 *a*Following Masoretic Text and Vulgate; Septuagint reads *the sons of Zatho, Shechaniah.*
8:10 *a*Following Masoretic Text and Vulgate; Septuagint reads *the sons of Banni, Shelomith.*
8:17 *a*Following Vulgate; Masoretic Text reads *to Iddo his brother;* Septuagint reads *to their brethren.*

the road. 32 So we came to Jerusalem, and stayed there three days.

33 Now on the fourth day the silver and the gold and the articles were weighed in the house of our God by the hand of Meremoth the son of Uriah the priest, and with him *was* Eleazar the son of Phinehas; with them *were* the Levites, Jozabad the son of Jeshua and Noadiah the son of Binnui, 34 with the number *and* weight of everything. All the weight was written down at that time.

35 The children of those who had been carried away captive, who had come from the captivity, offered burnt offerings to the God of Israel: twelve bulls for all Israel, ninety-six rams, seventy-seven lambs, and twelve male goats *as* a sin offering. All *this was* a burnt offering to the LORD.

36 And they delivered the king's orders to the king's satraps and the governors *in the region* beyond the River. So they gave support to the people and the house of God.

9 When these things were done, the leaders came to me, saying, "The people of Israel and the priests and the Levites have not separated themselves from the peoples of the lands, with respect to the abominations of the Canaanites, the Hittites, the Perizzites, the Jebusites, the Ammonites, the Moabites, the Egyptians, and the Amorites. 2 For they have taken some of their daughters *as wives* for themselves and their sons, so that the holy seed is mixed with the peoples of *those* lands. Indeed, the hand of the leaders and rulers has been foremost in this trespass." 3 So when I heard this thing, I tore my garment and my robe, and plucked out some of the hair of my head and beard, and sat down astonished. 4 Then everyone who trembled at the words of the God of Israel assembled to me, because of the transgression of those who had been carried away captive, and I sat astonished until the evening sacrifice.

5 At the evening sacrifice I arose from my fasting; and having torn my garment and my robe, I fell on my knees and spread out my hands to the LORD my God. 6 And I said: "O my God, I am too ashamed and humiliated to lift up my face to You, my God; for our iniquities have risen higher than *our* heads, and our guilt has grown up to the heavens. 7 Since the days of our fathers to this day we *have been* very guilty, and for our iniquities we, our kings, *and* our priests have been delivered into the hand of the kings of the lands, to the sword, to captivity, to plunder, and to humiliation, as *it is* this day. 8 And now for a little while grace has been *shown* from the LORD our God, to leave us a remnant to escape, and to give us a peg in His holy place, that our God may enlighten our eyes and give us a measure of revival in our bondage. 9 For we *were* slaves. Yet our God did not forsake us in our bondage; but He extended mercy to us in the sight of the kings of Persia, to revive us, to repair the house of our God, to rebuild its ruins, and to give us a wall in Judah and Jerusalem. 10 And now, O our God, what shall we say after this? For we have forsaken Your commandments, 11 which You commanded by Your servants the prophets, saying, 'The land which you are entering to possess is an unclean land, with the uncleanness of the peoples of the lands, with their abominations which have filled it from one end to another with their impurity. 12 Now therefore, do not give your daughters as wives for their sons, nor take their daughters to your sons; and never seek their peace or prosperity, that you may be strong and eat the good of the land, and leave *it* as an inheritance to your children forever.' 13 And after all that has come upon us for our evil deeds and for our great guilt, since You our God have punished us less than our iniquities *deserve*, and have given us *such* deliverance as this, 14 should we again break Your commandments, and join in marriage with the people *committing* these abominations? Would You not be angry with us until You had consumed *us*, so that *there would be* no remnant or survivor? 15 O LORD God of Israel, You *are* righteous, for we are left as a remnant, as *it is* this day. Here we *are* before You, in our guilt, though no one can stand before You because of this!"

10 Now while Ezra was praying, and while he was confessing, weeping, and bowing down before the house of God, a very large assembly of men, women, and children

gathered to him from Israel; for the people wept very bitterly. 2 And Shechaniah the son of Jehiel, *one* of the sons of Elam, spoke up and said to Ezra, "We have trespassed against our God, and have taken pagan wives from the peoples of the land; yet now there is hope in Israel in spite of this. 3 Now therefore, let us make a covenant with our God to put away all these wives and those who have been born to them, according to the advice of my master and of those who tremble at the commandment of our God; and let it be done according to the law. 4 Arise, for *this* matter *is* your *responsibility.* We also *are* with you. Be of good courage, and do *it.*"

5 Then Ezra arose, and made the leaders of the priests, the Levites, and all Israel swear an oath that they would do according to this word. So they swore an oath. 6 Then Ezra rose up from before the house of God, and went into the chamber of Jehohanan the son of Eliashib; and *when* he came there, he ate no bread and drank no water, for he mourned because of the guilt of those from the captivity.

7 And they issued a proclamation throughout Judah and Jerusalem to all the descendants of the captivity, that they must gather at Jerusalem, 8 and that whoever would not come within three days, according to the instructions of the leaders and elders, all his property would be confiscated, and he himself would be separated from the assembly of those from the captivity.

9 So all the men of Judah and Benjamin gathered at Jerusalem within three days. It *was* the ninth month, on the twentieth of the month; and all the people sat in the open square of the house of God, trembling because of *this* matter and because of heavy rain. 10 Then Ezra the priest stood up and said to them, "You have transgressed and have taken pagan wives, adding to the guilt of Israel. 11 Now therefore, make confession to the LORD God of your fathers, and do His will; separate yourselves from the peoples of the land, and from the pagan wives."

12 Then all the assembly answered and said with a loud voice, "Yes! As you have said, so we must do.

13 But *there are* many people; *it is* the season for heavy rain, and we are not able to stand outside. Nor *is this* the work of one or two days, for *there are* many of us who have transgressed in this matter. 14 Please, let the leaders of our entire assembly stand; and let all those in our cities who have taken pagan wives come at appointed times, together with the elders and judges of their cities, until the fierce wrath of our God is turned away from us in this matter." 15 Only Jonathan the son of Asahel and Jahaziah the son of Tikvah opposed this, and Meshullam and Shabbethai the Levite gave them support.

16 Then the descendants of the captivity did so. And Ezra the priest, *with* certain heads of the fathers' *households,* were set apart by the fathers' *households,* each of them by name; and they sat down on the first day of the tenth month to examine the matter. 17 By the first day of the first month they finished *questioning* all the men who had taken pagan wives.

18 And among the sons of the priests who had taken pagan wives *the following* were found of the sons of Jeshua the son of Jozadak,[a] and his brothers: Maaseiah, Eliezer, Jarib, and Gedaliah. 19 And they gave their promise that they would put away their wives; and *being* guilty, *they presented* a ram of the flock as their trespass offering.

20 Also of the sons of Immer: Hanani and Zebadiah; 21 of the sons of Harim: Maaseiah, Elijah, Shemaiah, Jehiel, and Uzziah; 22 of the sons of Pashhur: Elioenai, Maaseiah, Ishmael, Nethanel, Jozabad, and Elasah.

23 Also of the Levites: Jozabad, Shimei, Kelaiah (the same *is* Kelita), Pethahiah, Judah, and Eliezer.

24 Also of the singers: Eliashib; and of the gatekeepers: Shallum, Telem, and Uri.

25 And others of Israel: of the sons of Parosh: Ramiah, Jeziah, Malchiah, Mijamin, Eleazar, Malchijah, and Benaiah; 26 of the sons of Elam: Mattaniah, Zechariah, Jehiel, Abdi, Jeremoth, and Eliah; 27 of the sons of Zattu: Elioenai, Eliashib, Mattaniah, Jeremoth, Zabad, and Aziza;

10:18 aSpelled *Jehozadak* in 1 Chronicles 6:14

28 of the sons of Bebai: Jehohanan, Hananiah, Zabbai, *and* Athlai; 29 of the sons of Bani: Meshullam, Malluch, Adaiah, Jashub, Sheal, *and* Ramoth;*a* 30 of the sons of Pahath-Moab: Adna, Chelal, Benaiah, Maaseiah, Mattaniah, Bezalel, Binnui, and Manasseh; 31 *of* the sons of Harim: Eliezer, Ishijah, Malchijah, Shemaiah, Shimeon, 32 Benjamin, Malluch, *and* Shemariah; 33 of the sons of Hashum: Mattenai, Mattattah, Zabad, Eliphelet, Jeremai, Manasseh, *and* Shimei; 34 of the sons of Bani: Maadai, Amram, Uel, 35 Benaiah, Bedeiah, Cheluh,*a* 36 Vaniah, Meremoth, Eliashib, 37 Mattaniah, Mattenai, Jaasai,*a* 38 Bani, Binnui, Shimei, 39 Shelemiah, Nathan, Adaiah, 40 Machnadebai, Shashai, Sharai, 41 Azarel, Shelemiah, Shemariah, 42 Shallum, Amariah, *and* Joseph; 43 of the sons of Nebo: Jeiel, Mattithiah, Zabad, Zebina, Jaddai,*a* Joel, *and* Benaiah.

44 All these had taken pagan wives, and *some* of them had wives *by whom* they had children.

10:29 *a*Or *Jeremoth*   10:35 *a*Or *Cheluhi,* or *Cheluhu*   10:37 *a*Or *Jaasu*   10:43 *a*Or *Jaddu*

Nehemiah

Overview of Nehemiah

The Book of Nehemiah relates the story of common people committed to a great and uncommon goal—the rebuilding of God's temple!

The name Nehemiah means "the comfort of Yahweh." This book was written approximately 445 B.C., following the return of the Jewish people from exile in Babylon. Nehemiah faced the task of motivating the returning Jews to rebuild the temple and the walls of Jerusalem, which had fallen into disrepair during the destruction wrought by Nebuchadnezzar in 587–586 B.C.

Nehemiah and the leaders asked the people of Jerusalem to tithe toward the rebuilding of the temple and city walls. Elsewhere in Levitical law a tenth and sometimes a quarter of all one's possessions and income was the normal amount given back to God. This time, Nehemiah asked not for a percentage, but requested the people to give what they could and commit themselves to the rebuilding of the temple and city walls. Because of this approach, the people of Jerusalem became united in their efforts to complete the projects. As a result, they brought an overabundance of offerings. Nehemiah had to ask the people to cease bringing their gifts. They had more than they could use!

When people get together and believe in the completion of a dream, their giving will be endless and they can accomplish anything they choose!

Praise ye the Lord, the Almighty, the King of Creation!
O my soul praise Him, for He is thy health and salvation!
All ye who hear, now to His temple draw near;
Join me in glad adoration!

Jesus in Nehemiah

Like Ezra, Nehemiah portrays Jesus in His ministry of restoration. Nehemiah illustrates Christ in that he gives up a high position in order to identify with the plight of his people; he comes with a specific mission and fulfills it; and his life is characterized by prayerful dependence upon God.

Keys to Nehemiah

Key Word: Jerusalem Walls. While Ezra deals with the religious restoration of Judah, Nehemiah is primarily concerned with Judah's political and geographical restoration. The first seven chapters are devoted to the rebuilding of Jerusalem's walls, because Jerusalem was the spiritual and political center of Judah. Without walls, Jerusalem could hardly be considered a city at all. As governor, Nehemiah also establishes firm civil authority. Ezra and Nehemiah work together to build the people spiritually and morally so that the restoration will be complete.

Key Verses: "So the wall was finished on the twenty-fifth *day* of Elul, in fifty-two days. And it happened, when all our enemies heard *of it,* and all the nations around us saw *these things,* that they were very disheartened in their own eyes; for they perceived that this work was done by our God" (6:15, 16).

"So they read distinctly from the book, in the Law of God; and they gave the sense, and helped *them* to understand the reading" (8:8).

Key Chapter: Nehemiah 9. The key to the Old Testament is the covenant, which is its theme and unifying factor. Israel's history can be divided according to the nation's obedience or disobedience to God's conditional covenant: blessings from obedience and destruction from disobedience. Nehemiah 9 records that upon completion of the Jerusalem wall the nation reaffirmed its loyalty to the covenant.

1 The words of Nehemiah the son of Hachaliah.

It came to pass in the month of Chislev, *in* the twentieth year, as I was in Shushan[a] the citadel, 2 that Hanani one of my brethren came with men from Judah; and I asked them concerning the Jews who had escaped, who had survived the captivity, and concerning Jerusalem. 3 And they said to me, "The survivors who are left from the captivity in the province *are* there in great distress and reproach. The wall of Jerusalem *is* also broken down, and its gates *are* burned with fire."

4 So it was, when I heard these words, that I sat down and wept, and mourned *for many* days; I was fasting and praying before the God of heaven.

5 And I said: "I pray, LORD God of heaven, O great and awesome God, *You* who keep *Your* covenant and mercy with those who love You[a] and observe Your[b] commandments, 6 please let Your ear be attentive and Your eyes open, that You may hear the prayer of Your servant which I pray before You now, day and night, for the children of Israel Your servants, and confess the sins of the children of Israel which we have sinned against You. Both my father's house and I have sinned. 7 We have acted very corruptly against You, and have not kept the commandments, the statutes, nor the ordinances which You commanded Your servant Moses. 8 Remember, I pray, the word that You commanded Your servant Moses, saying, '*If* you are unfaithful, I will scatter you among the nations;[a] 9 but *if* you return to Me, and keep My commandments and do them, though some of you were cast out to the farthest part of the heavens, *yet* I will gather them from there, and bring them to the place which I have chosen as a dwelling for My name.'[a] 10 Now these *are* Your servants and Your people, whom You have redeemed by Your great power, and by Your strong hand. 11 O Lord, I pray, please let Your ear be attentive to the prayer of Your servant, and to the prayer of Your servants who desire to fear Your name; and let Your servant prosper this day, I pray, and grant him mercy in the sight of this man."

For I was the king's cupbearer.

2 And it came to pass in the month of Nisan, in the twentieth year of King Artaxerxes, *when* wine *was* before him, that I took the wine and gave it to the king. Now I had never been sad in his presence before. 2 Therefore the king said to me, "Why *is* your face sad, since you *are* not sick? This *is* nothing but sorrow of heart."

So I became dreadfully afraid, 3 and said to the king, "May the king live forever! Why should my face not be sad, when the city, the place of my fathers' tombs, *lies* waste, and its gates are burned with fire?"

4 Then the king said to me, "What do you request?"

So I prayed to the God of heaven. 5 And I said to the king, "If it pleases the king, and if your servant has found favor in your sight, I ask that you send me to Judah, to the city of my fathers' tombs, that I may rebuild it."

6 Then the king said to me (the queen also sitting beside him), "How long will your journey be? And when will you return?" So it pleased the king to send me; and I set him a time.

7 Furthermore I said to the king, "If it pleases the king, let letters be given to me for the governors *of the region* beyond the River,*ª* that they must permit me to pass through till I come to Judah, 8 and a letter to Asaph the keeper of the king's forest, that he must give me timber to make beams for the gates of the citadel which *pertains* to the temple,*ª* for the city wall, and for the house that I will occupy." And the king granted *them* to me according to the good hand of my God upon me.

9 Then I went to the governors *in the region* beyond the River, and gave them the king's letters. Now the king had sent captains of the army and horsemen with me. 10 When Sanballat the Horonite and Tobiah the Ammonite official*ª* heard *of it,* they were deeply disturbed that a man had come to seek the well-being of the children of Israel.

11 So I came to Jerusalem and was there three days. 12 Then I arose in the night, I and a few men with me; I told no one what my God had put in my heart to do at Jerusalem; nor

was there any animal with me, except the one on which I rode. 13 And I went out by night through the Valley Gate to the Serpent Well and the Refuse Gate, and viewed the walls of Jerusalem which were broken down and its gates which were burned with fire. 14 Then I went on to the Fountain Gate and to the King's Pool, but *there was* no room for the animal under me to pass. 15 So I went up in the night by the valley, and viewed the wall; then I turned back and entered by the Valley Gate, and so returned. 16 And the officials did not know where I had gone or what I had done; I had not yet told the Jews, the priests, the nobles, the officials, or the others who did the work.

17 Then I said to them, "You see the distress that we *are* in, how Jerusalem *lies* waste, and its gates are burned with fire. Come and let us build the wall of Jerusalem, that we may no longer be a reproach." 18 And I told them of the hand of my God which had been good upon me, and also of the king's words that he had spoken to me.

So they said, "Let us rise up and build." Then they set their hands to *this* good *work.*

19 But when Sanballat the Horonite, Tobiah the Ammonite official, and Geshem the Arab heard *of it,* they laughed at us and despised us, and said, "What *is* this thing that you are doing? Will you rebel against the king?"

20 So I answered them, and said to them, "The God of heaven Himself will prosper us; therefore we His servants will arise and build, but you have no heritage or right or memorial in Jerusalem."

3 Then Eliashib the high priest rose up with his brethren the priests and built the Sheep Gate; they consecrated it and hung its doors. They built as far as the Tower of the Hundred,*ª and* consecrated it, then as far as the Tower of Hananel. 2 Next to *Eliashib*ª the men of Jericho built. And next to them Zaccur the son of Imri built.

3 Also the sons of Hassenaah built the Fish Gate; they laid its beams and

---

2:7 ªThat is, the Euphrates, and so elsewhere in this book   2:8 ªLiterally *house*   2:10 ªLiterally *servant,* and so elsewhere in this book   3:1 ªHebrew *Hammeah,* also at 12:39   3:2 ªLiterally *On his hand*

hung its doors with its bolts and bars.
⁴ And next to them Meremoth the son of Urijah, the son of Koz,ᵃ made repairs. Next to them Meshullam the son of Berechiah, the son of Meshezabel, made repairs. Next to them Zadok the son of Baana made repairs. ⁵ Next to them the Tekoites made repairs; but their nobles did not put their shouldersᵃ to the work of their Lord.

⁶ Moreover Jehoiada the son of Paseah and Meshullam the son of Besodeiah repaired the Old Gate; they laid its beams and hung its doors, with its bolts and bars. ⁷ And next to them Melatiah the Gibeonite, Jadon the Meronothite, the men of Gibeon and Mizpah, repaired the residenceᵃ of the governor of the region beyond the River. ⁸ Next to him Uzziel the son of Harhaiah, one of the goldsmiths, made repairs. Also next to him Hananiah, oneᵃ of the perfumers, made repairs; and they fortified Jerusalem as far as the Broad Wall. ⁹ And next to them Rephaiah the son of Hur, leader of half the district of Jerusalem, made repairs. ¹⁰ Next to them Jedaiah the son of Harumaph made repairs in front of his house. And next to him Hattush the son of Hashabniah made repairs.

¹¹ Malchijah the son of Harim and Hashub the son of Pahath-Moab repaired another section, as well as the Tower of the Ovens. ¹² And next to him was Shallum the son of Hallohesh, leader of half the district of Jerusalem; he and his daughters made repairs.

¹³ Hanun and the inhabitants of Zanoah repaired the Valley Gate. They built it, hung its doors with its bolts and bars, and repaired a thousand cubits of the wall as far as the Refuse Gate.

¹⁴ Malchijah the son of Rechab, leader of the district of Beth Haccerem, repaired the Refuse Gate; he built it and hung its doors with its bolts and bars.

¹⁵ Shallun the son of Col-Hozeh, leader of the district of Mizpah, repaired the Fountain Gate; he built it, covered it, hung its doors with its

bolts and bars, and repaired the wall of the Pool of Shelah by the King's Garden, as far as the stairs that go down from the City of David. ¹⁶ After him Nehemiah the son of Azbuk, leader of half the district of Beth Zur, made repairs as far as the place in front of the tombsᵃ of David, to the man-made pool, and as far as the House of the Mighty.

¹⁷ After him the Levites, under Rehum the son of Bani, made repairs. Next to him Hashabiah, leader of half the district of Keilah, made repairs for his district. ¹⁸ After him their brethren, under Bavaiᵃ the son of Henadad, leader of the other half of the district of Keilah, made repairs. ¹⁹ And next to him Ezer the son of Jeshua, the leader of Mizpah, repaired another section in front of the Ascent to the Armory at the buttress. ²⁰ After him Baruch the son of Zabbaiᵃ carefully repaired the other section, from the buttress to the door of the house of Eliashib the high priest. ²¹ After him Meremoth the son of Urijah, the son of Koz,ᵃ repaired another section, from the door of the house of Eliashib to the end of the house of Eliashib.

²² And after him the priests, the men of the plain, made repairs. ²³ After him Benjamin and Hasshub made repairs opposite their house. After them Azariah the son of Maaseiah, the son of Ananiah, made repairs by his house. ²⁴ After him Binnui the son of Henadad repaired another section, from the house of Azariah to the buttress, even as far as the corner. ²⁵ Palal the son of Uzai made repairs opposite the buttress, and on the tower which projects from the king's upper house that was by the court of the prison. After him Pedaiah the son of Parosh made repairs.

²⁶ Moreover the Nethinim who dwelt in Ophel made repairs as far as the place in front of the Water Gate toward the east, and on the projecting tower. ²⁷ After them the Tekoites repaired another section, next to the great projecting tower, and as far as the wall of Ophel.

²⁸ Beyond the Horse Gate the

3:4 ᵃOr Hakkoz   3:5 ᵃLiterally necks   3:7 ᵃLiterally throne   3:8 ᵃLiterally the son
3:16 ᵃSeptuagint, Syriac, and Vulgate read tomb.   3:18 ᵃFollowing Masoretic Text and Vulgate; some Hebrew manuscripts, Septuagint, and Syriac read Binnui (compare verse 24).   3:20 ᵃA few Hebrew manuscripts, Syriac, and Vulgate read Zaccai.   3:21 ᵃOr Hakkoz

priests made repairs, each in front of his *own* house. 29 After them Zadok the son of Immer made repairs in front of his *own* house. After him Shemaiah the son of Shechaniah, the keeper of the East Gate, made repairs. 30 After him Hananiah the son of Shelemiah, and Hanun, the sixth son of Zalaph, repaired another section. After him Meshullam the son of Berechiah made repairs in front of his dwelling. 31 After him Malchijah, one of the goldsmiths, made repairs as far as the house of the Nethinim and of the merchants, in front of the Miphkad[a] Gate, and as far as the upper room at the corner. 32 And between the upper room at the corner, as far as the Sheep Gate, the goldsmiths and the merchants made repairs.

4 But it so happened, when Sanballat heard that we were rebuilding the wall, that he was furious and very indignant, and mocked the Jews. 2 And he spoke before his brethren and the army of Samaria, and said, "What are these feeble Jews doing? Will they fortify themselves? Will they offer sacrifices? Will they complete it in a day? Will they revive the stones from the heaps of rubbish— *stones* that are burned?"

3 Now Tobiah the Ammonite *was* beside him, and he said, "Whatever they build, if even a fox goes up *on it,* he will break down their stone wall."

4 Hear, O our God, for we are despised; turn their reproach on their own heads, and give them as plunder to a land of captivity! 5 Do not cover their iniquity, and do not let their sin be blotted out from before You; for they have provoked *You* to anger before the builders.

6 So we built the wall, and the entire wall was joined together up to half its *height,* for the people had a mind to work.

7 Now it happened, when Sanballat, Tobiah, the Arabs, the Ammonites, and the Ashdodites heard that the walls of Jerusalem were being restored and the gaps were beginning to be closed, that they became very angry, 8 and all of them conspired together to come *and* attack Jerusalem and create confusion. 9 Nevertheless

we made our prayer to our God, and because of them we set a watch against them day and night.

10 Then Judah said, "The strength of the laborers is failing, and *there is* so much rubbish that we are not able to build the wall."

11 And our adversaries said, "They will neither know nor see anything, till we come into their midst and kill them and cause the work to cease."

12 So it was, when the Jews who dwelt near them came, that they told us ten times, "From whatever place you turn, *they will be* upon us."

13 Therefore I positioned *men* behind the lower parts of the wall, at the openings; and I set the people according to their families, with their swords, their spears, and their bows. 14 And I looked, and arose and said to the nobles, to the leaders, and to the rest of the people, "Do not be afraid of them. Remember the Lord, great and awesome, and fight for your brethren, your sons, your daughters, your wives, and your houses."

15 And it happened, when our enemies heard that it was known to us, and *that* God had brought their plot to nothing, that all of us returned to the wall, everyone to his work. 16 So it was, from that time on, *that* half of my servants worked at construction, while the other half held the spears, the shields, the bows, and *wore* armor; and the leaders *were* behind all the house of Judah. 17 Those who built on the wall, and those who carried burdens, loaded themselves so that with one hand they worked at construction, and with the other held a weapon. 18 Every one of the builders had his sword girded at his side as he built. And the one who sounded the trumpet *was* beside me.

19 Then I said to the nobles, the rulers, and the rest of the people, "The work *is* great and extensive, and we are separated far from one another on the wall. 20 Wherever you hear the sound of the trumpet, rally to us there. Our God will fight for us."

21 So we labored in the work, and half of *the men*[a] held the spears from daybreak until the stars appeared. 22 At the same time I also said to the people, "Let each man and his ser-

3:31 [a]Literally *Inspection* or *Recruiting*   4:21 [a]Literally *them* vant stay at night in Jerusalem, that they may be our guard by night and a working party by day." 23 So neither I, my brethren, my servants, nor the men of the guard who followed me took off our clothes, *except* that everyone took them off for washing.

5 And there was a great outcry of the people and their wives against their Jewish brethren. 2 For there were those who said, "We, our sons, and our daughters *are* many; therefore let us get grain, that we may eat and live."

3 There were also *some* who said, "We have mortgaged our lands and vineyards and houses, that we might buy grain because of the famine."

4 There were also those who said, "We have borrowed money for the king's tax *on* our lands and vineyards. 5 Yet now our flesh *is* as the flesh of our brethren, our children as their children; and indeed we are forcing our sons and our daughters to be slaves, and *some* of our daughters have been brought into slavery. *It is* not in our power *to redeem them,* for other men have our lands and vineyards."

6 And I became very angry when I heard their outcry and these words. 7 After serious thought, I rebuked the nobles and rulers, and said to them, "Each of you is exacting usury from his brother." So I called a great assembly against them. 8 And I said to them, "According to our ability we have redeemed our Jewish brethren who were sold to the nations. Now indeed, will you even sell your brethren? Or should they be sold to us?" Then they were silenced and found nothing *to say.* 9 Then I said, "What you are doing *is* not good. Should you not walk in the fear of our God because of the reproach of the nations, our enemies? 10 I also, *with* my brethren and my servants, am lending them money and grain. Please, let us stop this usury! 11 Restore now to them, even this day, their lands, their vineyards, their olive groves, and their houses, also a hundredth of the money and the grain, the new wine and the oil, that you have charged them."

12 So they said, "We will restore *it,*

and will require nothing from them; we will do as you say."

Then I called the priests, and required an oath from them that they would do according to this promise. 13 Then I shook out the fold of my garment*a* and said, "So may God shake out each man from his house, and from his property, who does not perform this promise. Even thus may he be shaken out and emptied."

And all the assembly said, "Amen!" and praised the LORD. Then the people did according to this promise.

14 Moreover, from the time that I was appointed to be their governor in the land of Judah, from the twentieth year until the thirty-second year of King Artaxerxes, twelve years, neither I nor my brothers ate the governor's provisions. 15 But the former governors who *were* before me laid burdens on the people, and took from them bread and wine, besides forty shekels of silver. Yes, even their servants bore rule over the people, but I did not do so, because of the fear of God. 16 Indeed, I also continued the work on this wall, and we*a* did not buy any land. All my servants *were* gathered there for the work.

17 And at my table *were* one hundred and fifty Jews and rulers, besides those who came to us from the nations around us. 18 Now *that* which was prepared daily *was* one ox *and* six choice sheep. Also fowl were prepared for me, and once every ten days an abundance of all kinds of wine. Yet in spite of this I did not demand the governor's provisions, because the bondage was heavy on this people.

19 Remember me, my God, for good, *according to* all that I have done for this people.

6 Now it happened when Sanballat, Tobiah, Geshem the Arab, and the rest of our enemies heard that I had rebuilt the wall, and *that* there were no breaks left in it (though at that time I had not hung the doors in the gates), 2 that Sanballat and Geshem sent to me, saying, "Come, let us meet together among the villages in the plain of Ono." But they thought to do me harm.

3 So I sent messengers to them,

5:13 *a*Literally *my lap*   5:16 *a*Following Masoretic Text; Septuagint, Syriac, and Vulgate read *I.*

saying, "I *am* doing a great work, so that I cannot come down. Why should the work cease while I leave it and go down to you?"

4 But they sent me this message four times, and I answered them in the same manner.

5 Then Sanballat sent his servant to me as before, the fifth time, with an open letter in his hand. 6 In it *was* written:

It is reported among the nations, and Geshem[a] says, *that* you and the Jews plan to rebel; therefore, according to these rumors, you are rebuilding the wall, that you may be their king. 7 And you have also appointed prophets to proclaim concerning you at Jerusalem, saying, "*There is* a king in Judah!" Now these matters will be reported to the king. So come, therefore, and let us consult together.

8 Then I sent to him, saying, "No such things as you say are being done, but you invent them in your own heart."

9 For they all *were trying to* make us afraid, saying, "Their hands will be weakened in the work, and it will not be done."

Now therefore, O God, strengthen my hands.

10 Afterward I came to the house of Shemaiah the son of Delaiah, the son of Mehetabel, who *was* a secret informer; and he said, "Let us meet together in the house of God, within the temple, and let us close the doors of the temple, for they are coming to kill you; indeed, at night they will come to kill you."

11 And I said, "Should such a man as I flee? And who *is there* such as I who would go into the temple to save his life? I will not go in!" 12 Then I perceived that God had not sent him at all, but that he pronounced *this* prophecy against me because Tobiah and Sanballat had hired him. 13 For this reason he *was* hired, that I should be afraid and act that way and sin, so *that* they might have *cause* for an evil report, that they might reproach me.

14 My God, remember Tobiah and Sanballat, according to these their works, and the prophetess Noadiah and the rest of the prophets who would have made me afraid.

15 So the wall was finished on the twenty-fifth *day* of Elul, in fifty-two days. 16 And it happened, when all our enemies heard *of it*, and all the nations around us saw *these things*, that they were very disheartened in their own eyes; for they perceived that this work was done by our God.

17 Also in those days the nobles of Judah sent many letters to Tobiah, and *the letters of* Tobiah came to them. 18 For many in Judah were pledged to him, because he was the son-in-law of Shechaniah the son of Arah, and his son Jehohanan had married the daughter of Meshullam the son of Berechiah. 19 Also they reported his good deeds before me, and reported my words to him. Tobiah sent letters to frighten me.

7 Then it was, when the wall was built and I had hung the doors, when the gatekeepers, the singers, and the Levites had been appointed, 2 that I gave the charge of Jerusalem to my brother Hanani, and Hananiah the leader of the citadel, for he *was* a faithful man and feared God more than many.

3 And I said to them, "Do not let the gates of Jerusalem be opened until the sun is hot; and while they stand *guard*, let them shut and bar the doors; and appoint guards from among the inhabitants of Jerusalem, one at his watch station and another in front of his own house."

4 Now the city *was* large and spacious, but the people in it *were* few, and the houses *were* not rebuilt. 5 Then my God put it into my heart to gather the nobles, the rulers, and the people, that they might be registered by genealogy. And I found a register of the genealogy of those who had come up in the first *return*, and found written in it:

6 These[a] *are* the people of the province who came back from the captivity, of those who had been carried away, whom Nebuchadnezzar the king of Babylon had carried away, and

The Exiles Return

After the city of Jerusalem was destroyed by the Babylonians about 586 B.C., the leading citizens of Judah were carried away as captives and resettled in the pagan city of Babylon. When the Babylonians were overthrown by the Persians about seventy years later, the stage was set for God's people to return to their beloved homeland.

There were actually three separate groups of Jewish citizens who made the return from Babylon and Persia to Jerusalem. Each of these groups had a specific task to accomplish.

1. The first group under Zerubbabel returned about 525 B.C. to rebuild the temple. Completed about 515 B.C., the temple was dedicated with great celebration and rejoicing by the Jewish people (Ezra 6:15–22).

2. The second group of Jewish exiles, under the leadership of Ezra the priest, returned to Jerusalem about 458 B.C. Ezra's task was to reestablish the Law as the basis of Jewish life. In a special assembly in the city of Jerusalem, Ezra read from the Law and challenged the people to follow the Lord's teachings (Neh. 8:1–12).

3. The third group under Nehemiah returned about 444 B.C. Nehemiah led the people to rebuild the wall around Jerusalem. In spite of opposition from their enemies, Nehemiah rallied and encouraged the people so effectively that the entire project was completed in fifty-two days (Neh. 6:15).

Three prophets of the Old Testament—Haggai, Zechariah, and Malachi—lived and ministered in Jerusalem during this time known as the postexilic period. Haggai and Zechariah encouraged the people to complete the task of building the temple, while Malachi rebuked the returned captives for their sin, idolatry, and shallow worship practices.

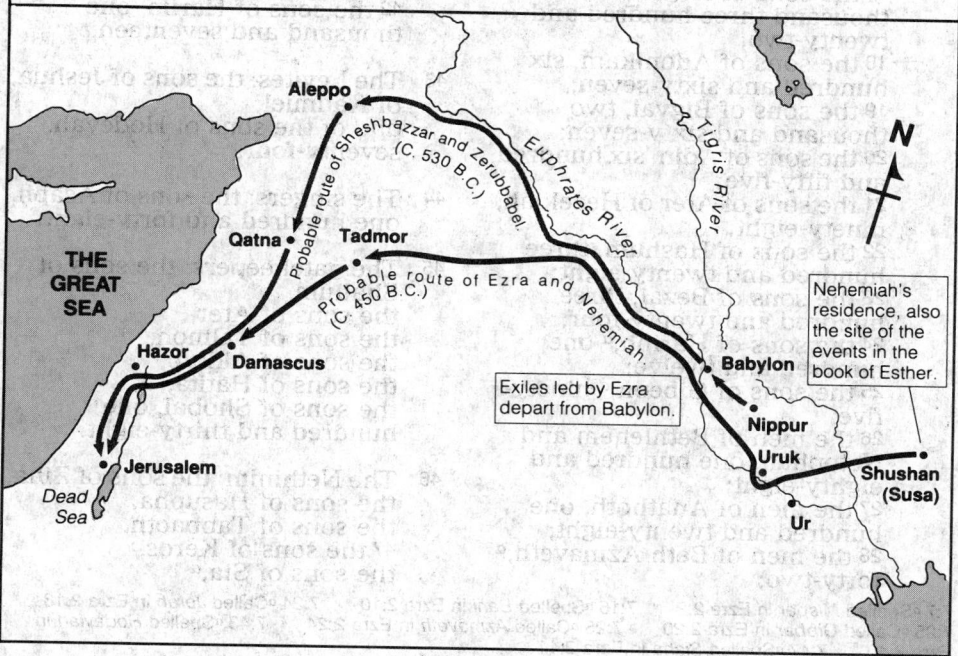

who returned to Jerusalem and Judah, everyone to his city.

7 Those who came with Zerubbabel *were* Jeshua, Nehemiah, Azariah, Raamiah, Nahamani, Mordecai, Bilshan, Mispereth,[a] Bigvai, Nehum, and Baanah.

The number of the men of the people of Israel: 8 the sons of Parosh, two thousand one hundred and seventy-two;
9 the sons of Shephatiah, three hundred and seventy-two;
10 the sons of Arah, six hundred and fifty-two;
11 the sons of Pahath-Moab, of the sons of Jeshua and Joab, two thousand eight hundred and eighteen;
12 the sons of Elam, one thousand two hundred and fifty-four;
13 the sons of Zattu, eight hundred and forty-five;
14 the sons of Zaccai, seven hundred and sixty;
15 the sons of Binnui,[a] six hundred and forty-eight;
16 the sons of Bebai, six hundred and twenty-eight;
17 the sons of Azgad, two thousand three hundred and twenty-two;
18 the sons of Adonikam, six hundred and sixty-seven;
19 the sons of Bigvai, two thousand and sixty-seven;
20 the sons of Adin, six hundred and fifty-five;
21 the sons of Ater of Hezekiah, ninety-eight;
22 the sons of Hashum, three hundred and twenty-eight;
23 the sons of Bezai, three hundred and twenty-four;
24 the sons of Hariph,[a] one hundred and twelve;
25 the sons of Gibeon,[a] ninety-five;
26 the men of Bethlehem and Netophah, one hundred and eighty-eight;
27 the men of Anathoth, one hundred and twenty-eight;
28 the men of Beth Azmaveth,[a] forty-two;

29 the men of Kirjath Jearim, Chephirah, and Beeroth, seven hundred and forty-three;
30 the men of Ramah and Geba, six hundred and twenty-one;
31 the men of Michmas, one hundred and twenty-two;
32 the men of Bethel and Ai, one hundred and twenty-three;
33 the men of the other Nebo, fifty-two;
34 the sons of the other Elam, one thousand two hundred and fifty-four;
35 the sons of Harim, three hundred and twenty;
36 the sons of Jericho, three hundred and forty-five;
37 the sons of Lod, Hadid, and Ono, seven hundred and twenty-one;
38 the sons of Senaah, three thousand nine hundred and thirty.

39 The priests: the sons of Jedaiah, of the house of Jeshua, nine hundred and seventy-three;
40 the sons of Immer, one thousand and fifty-two;
41 the sons of Pashhur, one thousand two hundred and forty-seven;
42 the sons of Harim, one thousand and seventeen.

43 The Levites: the sons of Jeshua, of Kadmiel,
and of the sons of Hodevah,[a] seventy-four.

44 The singers: the sons of Asaph, one hundred and forty-eight.

45 The gatekeepers: the sons of Shallum,
the sons of Ater,
the sons of Talmon,
the sons of Akkub,
the sons of Hatita,
the sons of Shobai, one hundred and thirty-eight.

46 The Nethinim: the sons of Ziha,
the sons of Hasupha,
the sons of Tabbaoth,
47 the sons of Keros,
the sons of Sia,[a]

the sons of Padon,
48 the sons of Lebana,[a]
the sons of Hagaba,[b]
the sons of Salmai,[c]
49 the sons of Hanan,
the sons of Giddel,
the sons of Gahar,
50 the sons of Reaiah,
the sons of Rezin,
the sons of Nekoda,
51 the sons of Gazzam,
the sons of Uzza,
the sons of Paseah,
52 the sons of Besai,
the sons of Meunim,
the sons of Nephishesim,[a]
53 the sons of Bakbuk,
the sons of Hakupha,
the sons of Harhur,
54 the sons of Bazlith,[a]
the sons of Mehida,
the sons of Harsha,
55 the sons of Barkos,
the sons of Sisera,
the sons of Tamah,
56 the sons of Neziah,
and the sons of Hatipha.

57 The sons of Solomon's
servants: the sons of Sotai,
the sons of Sophereth,
the sons of Perida,[a]
58 the sons of Jaala,
the sons of Darkon,
the sons of Giddel,
59 the sons of Shephatiah,
the sons of Hattil,
the sons of Pochereth of
Zebaim,
and the sons of Amon.[a]
60 All the Nethinim, and the
sons of Solomon's servants,
were three hundred and ninety-
two.

61 And these *were* the ones who
came up from Tel Melah, Tel
Harsha, Cherub, Addon,[a] and
Immer, but they could not
identify their father's house nor
their lineage, whether they
were of Israel: 62 the sons of
Delaiah,
the sons of Tobiah,
the sons of Nekoda, six
hundred and forty-two;
63 and of the priests: the sons
of Habaiah,

the sons of Koz,[a]
the sons of Barzillai, who took
a wife of the daughters of
Barzillai the Gileadite, and was
called by their name.
64 These sought their listing
among those who were
registered by genealogy, but it
was not found; therefore they
were excluded from the
priesthood as defiled. 65 And
the governor[a] said to them that
they should not eat of the most
holy things till a priest could
consult with the Urim and
Thummim.

66 Altogether the whole assembly
was forty-two thousand three
hundred and sixty, 67 besides
their male and female servants,
of whom *there were* seven
thousand three hundred and
thirty-seven; and they had two
hundred and forty-five men
and women singers. 68 Their
horses were seven hundred and
thirty-six, their mules two
hundred and forty-five,
69 *their* camels four hundred
and thirty-five, *and* donkeys six
thousand seven hundred and
twenty.

70 And some of the heads of the
fathers' houses gave to the
work. The governor[a] gave to
the treasury one thousand gold
drachmas, fifty basins, and five
hundred and thirty priestly
garments. 71 Some of the heads
of the fathers' *houses* gave to
the treasury of the work twenty
thousand gold drachmas, and
two thousand two hundred
silver minas. 72 And that which
the rest of the people gave *was*
twenty thousand gold
drachmas, two thousand silver
minas, and sixty-seven priestly
garments.

73 So the priests, the Levites, the
gatekeepers, the singers, *some* of the
people, the Nethinim, and all Israel
dwelt in their cities.
When the seventh month came, the
children of Israel *were* in their cities.

7:48 [a]Masoretic Text reads *Lebanah*.   [b]Masoretic Text reads *Hogabah*.   [c]Or *Shalmai*, or *Shamlai*
7:52 [a]Spelled *Nephusim* in Ezra 2:50   7:54 [a]Spelled *Bazluth* in Ezra 2:52   7:57 [a]Spelled *Peruda* in
Ezra 2:55   7:59 [a]Spelled *Ami* in Ezra 2:57   7:61 [a]Spelled *Addan* in Ezra 2:59   7:63 [a]Or *Hakkoz*
7:65 [a]Hebrew *Tirshatha*   7:70 [a]Hebrew *Tirshatha*

8 Now all the people gathered together as one man in the open square that *was* in front of the Water Gate; and they told Ezra the scribe to bring the Book of the Law of Moses, which the LORD had commanded Israel. 2 So Ezra the priest brought the Law before the assembly of men and women and all who *could* hear with understanding on the first day of the seventh month. 3 Then he read from it in the open square that *was* in front of the Water Gate from morning until midday, before the men and women and those who could understand; and the ears of all the people *were attentive* to the Book of the Law.

4 So Ezra the scribe stood on a platform of wood which they had made for the purpose; and beside him, at his right hand, stood Mattithiah, Shema, Anaiah, Urijah, Hilkiah, and Maaseiah; and at his left hand Pedaiah, Mishael, Malchijah, Hashum, Hashbadana, Zechariah, *and* Meshullam. 5 And Ezra opened the book in the sight of all the people, for he was *standing* above all the people; and when he opened it, all the people stood up. 6 And Ezra blessed the LORD, the great God.

Then all the people answered, "Amen, Amen!" while lifting up their hands. And they bowed their heads and worshiped the LORD with *their* faces to the ground.

7 Also Jeshua, Bani, Sherebiah, Jamin, Akkub, Shabbethai, Hodijah, Maaseiah, Kelita, Azariah, Jozabad, Hanan, Pelaiah, and the Levites, helped the people to understand the Law; and the people *stood* in their place. 8 So they read distinctly from the book, in the Law of God; and they gave the sense, and helped *them* to understand the reading.

9 And Nehemiah, who *was* the governor,[a] Ezra the priest *and* scribe, and the Levites who taught the people said to all the people, "This day *is* holy to the LORD your God; do not mourn nor weep." For all the people wept, when they heard the words of the Law.

10 Then he said to them, "Go your way, eat the fat, drink the sweet, and send portions to those for whom nothing is prepared; for *this* day *is* holy to our LORD. Do not sorrow, for the joy of the LORD is your strength."

11 So the Levites quieted all the people, saying, "Be still, for the day *is* holy; do not be grieved." 12 And all the people went their way to eat and drink, to send portions and rejoice greatly, because they understood the words that were declared to them.

13 Now on the second day the heads of the fathers' *houses* of all the people, with the priests and Levites, were gathered to Ezra the scribe, in order to understand the words of the Law. 14 And they found written in the Law, which the LORD had commanded by Moses, that the children of Israel should dwell in booths during the feast of the seventh month, 15 and that they should announce and proclaim in all their cities and in Jerusalem, saying, "Go out to the mountain, and bring olive branches, branches of oil trees, myrtle branches, palm branches, and branches of leafy trees, to make booths, as *it is* written."

16 Then the people went out and brought *them* and made themselves booths, each one on the roof of his house, or in their courtyards or the courts of the house of God, and in the open square of the Water Gate and in the open square of the Gate of Ephraim. 17 So the whole assembly of those who had returned from the captivity made booths and sat under the booths; for since the days of Joshua the son of Nun until that day the children of Israel had not done so. And there was very great gladness. 18 Also day by day, from the first day until the last day, he read from the Book of the Law of God. And they kept the feast seven days; and on the eighth day *there was* a sacred assembly, according to the *prescribed* manner.

9 Now on the twenty-fourth day of this month the children of Israel were assembled with fasting, in sackcloth, and with dust on their heads.[a] 2 Then those of Israelite lineage separated themselves from all foreigners; and they stood and confessed their sins and the iniquities of their fathers. 3 And they stood up in their place and read from the Book of the Law of the LORD their God *for one-*

Dare to Wade Deeper

Miracles happen when you practice the faith of deep water.

Your first acts of faith were like approaching the water on the beach with a timid toe, suspecting an unpleasant chill. You continued to move cautiously, deeper and deeper into the water. Soon the water reached your waist, then your chest. Then your arms reached out to fan and skim the surface. Finally, leaving the solid bottom, by faith you swam to the deeper waters.

Faith always calls you forward. It never allows you to settle back and be satisfied. Faith compels you to wade deeper—to go the extra distance. The people of Israel exercised such faith at the Red Sea, stepping forth into the path God had made for them in the midst of the water (Neh. 9:11). Faith keeps you from giving up. Faith calls you again, echoing and reechoing that solitary word, "More!"

It takes faith to wade into deep waters—especially when you don't know where the bottom is. You do not know what the future holds, but you know who holds the future.

God is your Captain, and He knows the waters well. He keeps calling you onward and forward. God is committed to leading us always onward to new life. God knows that something dies within us when we are so safe and secure we no longer need daring and courageous faith. He is not satisfied if He sees you become stagnant. For stagnation quickly leads to swamps.

Join in praying this prayer: *God, give me the courage to swim in the strong stream, to wade into the deeper water, to move into an area where it will be impossible to succeed without Your help! Only then will I know I live by faith. Thank You, Lord. Amen.*

fourth of the day; and *for another* fourth they confessed and worshiped the LORD their God.

4 Then Jeshua, Bani, Kadmiel, Shebaniah, Bunni, Sherebiah, Bani, *and* Chenani stood on the stairs of the Levites and cried out with a loud voice to the LORD their God. 5 And the Levites, Jeshua, Kadmiel, Bani, Hashabniah, Sherebiah, Hodijah, Shebaniah, *and* Pethahiah, said:

"Stand up *and* bless the LORD your God
Forever and ever!

"Blessed be Your glorious name,
Which is exalted above all blessing and praise!
6 You alone *are* the LORD;
You have made heaven,
The heaven of heavens, with all their host,
The earth and everything on it,
The seas and all that is in them,
And You preserve them all.
The host of heaven worships You.

7 "You *are* the LORD God,
Who chose Abram,
And brought him out of Ur of the Chaldeans,
And gave him the name Abraham;
8 You found his heart faithful before You,
And made a covenant with him
To give the land of the Canaanites,
The Hittites, the Amorites,
The Perizzites, the Jebusites,
And the Girgashites—
To give *it* to his descendants.
You have performed Your words,
For You *are* righteous.

9 "You saw the affliction of our fathers in Egypt,
And heard their cry by the Red Sea.
10 You showed signs and wonders against Pharaoh,
Against all his servants,
And against all the people of his land.
For You knew that they acted proudly against them.
So You made a name for Yourself, as *it is* this day.

11 And You divided the sea before them,
So that they went through the midst of the sea on the dry land;
And their persecutors You threw into the deep,
As a stone into the mighty waters.
12 Moreover You led them by day with a cloudy pillar,
And by night with a pillar of fire,
To give them light on the road
Which they should travel.

13 "You came down also on Mount Sinai,
And spoke with them from heaven,
And gave them just ordinances and true laws,
Good statutes and commandments.
14 You made known to them Your holy Sabbath,
And commanded them precepts, statutes and laws,
By the hand of Moses Your servant.
15 You gave them bread from heaven for their hunger,
And brought them water out of the rock for their thirst,
And told them to go in to possess the land
Which You had sworn to give them.

16 "But they and our fathers acted proudly,
Hardened their necks,
And did not heed Your commandments.
17 They refused to obey,
And they were not mindful of Your wonders
That You did among them.
But they hardened their necks,
And in their rebellion[a]
They appointed a leader
To return to their bondage.
But You *are* God,
Ready to pardon,
Gracious and merciful,
Slow to anger,
Abundant in kindness,
And did not forsake them.

9:17 [a]Following Masoretic Text and Vulgate; Septuagint reads *in Egypt.*

18 "Even when they made a
    molded calf for themselves,
And said, 'This *is* your god
That brought you up out of
    Egypt,'
And worked great
    provocations,
19 Yet in Your manifold mercies
You did not forsake them in the
    wilderness.
The pillar of the cloud did not
    depart from them by day,
To lead them on the road;
Nor the pillar of fire by night,
To show them light,
And the way they should go.
20 You also gave Your good Spirit
    to instruct them,
And did not withhold Your
    manna from their mouth,
And gave them water for their
    thirst.
21 Forty years You sustained
    them in the wilderness;
They lacked nothing;
Their clothes did not wear out[a]
And their feet did not swell.

22 "Moreover You gave them
    kingdoms and nations,
And divided them into
    districts.[a]
So they took possession of the
    land of Sihon,
The land of[b] the king of
    Heshbon,
And the land of Og king of
    Bashan.
23 You also multiplied their
    children as the stars of
    heaven,
And brought them into the land
Which You had told their
    fathers
To go in and possess.
24 So the people went in
And possessed the land;
You subdued before them the
    inhabitants of the land,
The Canaanites,
And gave them into their
    hands,
With their kings
And the people of the land,
That they might do with them
    as they wished.
25 And they took strong cities and
    a rich land,
And possessed houses full of all
    goods,

Cisterns *already* dug,
    vineyards, olive groves,
And fruit trees in abundance.
So they ate and were filled and
    grew fat,
And delighted themselves in
    Your great goodness.

26 "Nevertheless they were
    disobedient
And rebelled against You,
Cast Your law behind their
    backs
And killed Your prophets, who
    testified against them
To turn them to Yourself;
And they worked great
    provocations.
27 Therefore You delivered them
    into the hand of their
    enemies,
Who oppressed them;
And in the time of their trouble,
When they cried to You,
You heard from heaven;
And according to Your
    abundant mercies
You gave them deliverers who
    saved them
From the hand of their
    enemies.

28 "But after they had rest,
They again did evil before You.
Therefore You left them in the
    hand of their enemies,
So that they had dominion over
    them;
Yet when they returned and
    cried out to You,
You heard from heaven;
And many times You delivered
    them according to Your
    mercies,
29 And testified against them,
That You might bring them
    back to Your law.
Yet they acted proudly,
And did not heed Your
    commandments,
But sinned against Your
    judgments,
'Which if a man does, he shall
    live by them.'[a]
And they shrugged their
    shoulders,
Stiffened their necks,
And would not hear.
30 Yet for many years You had
    patience with them,

9:21 [a]Compare Deuteronomy 29:5   9:22 [a]Literally *corners* [b]Following Masoretic Text and Vulgate;
Septuagint omits *The land of*.   9:29 [a]Leviticus 18:5

And testified against them by
Your Spirit in Your prophets.
Yet they would not listen;
Therefore You gave them into
the hand of the peoples of the
lands.
31 Nevertheless in Your great
mercy
You did not utterly consume
them nor forsake them;
For You *are* God, gracious and
merciful.

32 "Now therefore, our God,
The great, the mighty, and
awesome God,
Who keeps covenant and
mercy:
Do not let all the trouble seem
small before You
That has come upon us,
Our kings and our princes,
Our priests and our prophets,
Our fathers and on all Your
people,
From the days of the kings of
Assyria until this day.
33 However You *are* just in all that
has befallen us;
For You have dealt faithfully,
But we have done wickedly.
34 Neither our kings nor our
princes,
Our priests nor our fathers,
Have kept Your law,
Nor heeded Your
commandments and Your
testimonies,
With which You testified
against them.
35 For they have not served You
in their kingdom,
Or in the many good *things* that
You gave them,
Or in the large and rich land
which You set before them;
Nor did they turn from their
wicked works.

36 "Here we *are*, servants today!
And the land that You gave to
our fathers,
To eat its fruit and its bounty,
Here we *are*, servants in it!
37 And it yields much increase to
the kings
You have set over us,
Because of our sins;
Also they have dominion over
our bodies and our cattle
At their pleasure;
And we *are* in great distress.

38 "And because of all this,
We make a sure *covenant* and
write *it;*
Our leaders, our Levites, *and*
our priests seal *it.*"

10 Now those who placed *their*
seal on *the document were:*

Nehemiah the governor, the
son of Hacaliah, and Zedekiah,
2 Seraiah, Azariah, Jeremiah,
3 Pashhur, Amariah,
Malchijah, 4 Hattush,
Shebaniah, Malluch,
5 Harim, Meremoth, Obadiah,
6 Daniel, Ginnethon, Baruch,
7 Meshullam, Abijah, Mijamin,
8 Maaziah, Bilgai, *and*
Shemaiah. These *were* the
priests.

9 The Levites: Jeshua the son of
Azaniah, Binnui of the sons of
Henadad, *and* Kadmiel.

10 Their brethren: Shebaniah,
Hodijah, Kelita, Pelaiah,
Hanan, 11 Micha, Rehob,
Hashabiah, 12 Zaccur,
Sherebiah, Shebaniah,
13 Hodijah, Bani, *and* Beninu.

14 The leaders of the people:
Parosh, Pahath-Moab, Elam,
Zattu, Bani, 15 Bunni, Azgad,
Bebai, 16 Adonijah, Bigvai,
Adin, 17 Ater, Hezekiah, Azzur,
18 Hodijah, Hashum, Bezai,
19 Hariph, Anathoth, Nebai,
20 Magpiash, Meshullam,
Hezir, 21 Meshezabel, Zadok,
Jaddua, 22 Pelatiah, Hanan,
Anaiah, 23 Hoshea, Hananiah,
Hasshub, 24 Hallohesh, Pilha,
Shobek, 25 Rehum, Hashabnah,
Maaseiah, 26 Ahijah, Hanan,
Anan, 27 Malluch, Harim, *and*
Baanah.

28 Now the rest of the people—the
priests, the Levites, the gatekeepers,
the singers, the Nethinim, and all
those who had separated themselves
from the peoples of the lands to the
Law of God, their wives, their sons,
and their daughters, everyone who
had knowledge and understanding—
29 these joined with their brethren,
their nobles, and entered into a curse
and an oath to walk in God's Law,
which was given by Moses the ser-

vant of God, and to observe and do all the commandments of the LORD our Lord, and His ordinances and His statutes: 30 We would not give our daughters as wives to the peoples of the land, nor take their daughters for our sons; 31 *if* the peoples of the land brought wares or any grain to sell on the Sabbath day, we would not buy it from them on the Sabbath, or on a holy day; and we would forego the seventh year's *produce* and the exacting of every debt.

32 Also we made ordinances for ourselves, to exact from ourselves yearly one-third of a shekel for the service of the house of our God: 33 for the showbread, for the regular grain offering, for the regular burnt offering of the Sabbaths, the New Moons, and the set feasts; for the holy things, for the sin offerings to make atonement for Israel, and all the work of the house of our God. 34 We cast lots among the priests, the Levites, and the people, for *bringing* the wood offering into the house of our God, according to our fathers' houses, at the appointed times year by year, to burn on the altar of the LORD our God as *it is* written in the Law.

35 And *we made ordinances* to bring the firstfruits of our ground and the firstfruits of all fruit of all trees, year by year, to the house of the LORD; 36 to bring the firstborn of our sons and our cattle, as *it is* written in the Law, and the firstborn of our herds and our flocks, to the house of our God, to the priests who minister in the house of our God; 37 to bring the firstfruits of our dough, our offerings, the fruit from all kinds of trees, *the* new wine and oil, to the priests, to the storerooms of the house of our God; and to bring the tithes of our land to the Levites, for the Levites should receive the tithes in all our farming communities. 38 And the priest, the descendant of Aaron, shall be with the Levites when the Levites receive tithes; and the Levites shall bring up a tenth of the tithes to the house of our God, to the rooms of the storehouse.

39 For the children of Israel and the children of Levi shall bring the offering of the grain, of the new wine and the oil, to the storerooms where the articles of the sanctuary *are, where* the priests who minister and the gatekeepers and the singers *are;* and we will not neglect the house of our God.

11 Now the leaders of the people dwelt at Jerusalem; the rest of the people cast lots to bring one out of ten to dwell in Jerusalem, the holy city, and nine-tenths *were to dwell* in *other* cities. 2 And the people blessed all the men who willingly offered themselves to dwell at Jerusalem.

3 These *are* the heads of the province who dwelt in Jerusalem. (But in the cities of Judah everyone dwelt in his own possession in their cities—Israelites, priests, Levites, Nethinim, and descendants of Solomon's servants.) 4 Also in Jerusalem dwelt *some* of the children of Judah and of the children of Benjamin.

The children of Judah: Athaiah the son of Uzziah, the son of Zechariah, the son of Amariah, the son of Shephatiah, the son of Mahalalel, of the children of Perez; 5 and Maaseiah the son of Baruch, the son of Col-Hozeh, the son of Hazaiah, the son of Adaiah, the son of Joiarib, the son of Zechariah, the son of Shiloni. 6 All the sons of Perez who dwelt at Jerusalem *were* four hundred and sixty-eight valiant men.

7 And these are the sons of Benjamin: Sallu the son of Meshullam, the son of Joed, the son of Pedaiah, the son of Kolaiah, the son of Maaseiah, the son of Ithiel, the son of Jeshaiah; 8 and after him Gabbai *and* Sallai, nine hundred and twenty-eight. 9 Joel the son of Zichri *was* their overseer, and Judah the son of Senuah[a] *was* second over the city.

10 Of the priests: Jedaiah the son of Joiarib, and Jachin; 11 Seraiah the son of Hilkiah, the son of Meshullam, the son of Zadok, the son of Meraioth, the son of Ahitub, *was* the leader of the house of God. 12 Their brethren who did the work of the house *were* eight hundred and twenty-two; and Adaiah the son of Jeroham, the son of Pelaliah, the son of Amzi, the son of Zechariah, the son of Pashhur, the son of Malchijah, 13 and his brethren, heads of the fathers' *houses, were* two hundred and

11:9 *a*Or *Hassenuah*

forty-two; and Amashai the son of Azarel, the son of Ahzai, the son of Meshillemoth, the son of Immer, 14 and their brethren, mighty men of valor, *were* one hundred and twenty-eight. Their overseer *was* Zabdiel the son of *one* of the great men.*a*

15 Also of the Levites: Shemaiah the son of Hasshub, the son of Azrikam, the son of Hashabiah, the son of Bunni; 16 Shabbethai and Jozabad, of the heads of the Levites, *had* the oversight of the business outside of the house of God; 17 Mattaniah the son of Micha,*a* the son of Zabdi, the son of Asaph, the leader *who* began the thanksgiving with prayer; Bakbukiah, the second among his brethren; and Abda the son of Shammua, the son of Galal, the son of Jeduthun. 18 All the Levites in the holy city *were* two hundred and eighty-four.

19 Moreover the gatekeepers, Akkub, Talmon, and their brethren who kept the gates, *were* one hundred and seventy-two.

20 And the rest of Israel, of the priests *and* Levites, *were* in all the cities of Judah, everyone in his inheritance. 21 But the Nethinim dwelt in Ophel. And Ziha and Gishpa *were* over the Nethinim.

22 Also the overseer of the Levites at Jerusalem *was* Uzzi the son of Bani, the son of Hashabiah, the son of Mattaniah, the son of Micha, of the sons of Asaph, the singers in charge of the service of the house of God. 23 For *it was* the king's command concerning them that a certain portion should be for the singers, a quota day by day. 24 Pethahiah the son of Meshezabel, of the children of Zerah the son of Judah, *was* the king's deputy*a* in all matters concerning the people.

25 And as for the villages with their fields, *some* of the children of Judah dwelt in Kirjath Arba and its villages, Dibon and its villages, Jekabzeel and its villages; 26 in Jeshua, Moladah, Beth Pelet, 27 Hazar Shual, and Beersheba and its villages; 28 in Ziklag and Meconah and its villages; 29 in En Rimmon, Zorah, Jarmuth, 30 Zanoah, Adullam, and their villages; in Lachish and its fields; in Azekah and its villages. They dwelt from Beersheba to the Valley of Hinnom.

31 Also the children of Benjamin from Geba *dwelt* in Michmash, Aija, and Bethel, and their villages; 32 in Anathoth, Nob, Ananiah; 33 in Hazor, Ramah, Gittaim; 34 in Hadid, Zeboim, Neballat; 35 in Lod, Ono, *and* the Valley of Craftsmen. 36 Some of the Judean divisions of Levites *were* in Benjamin.

12 Now these *are* the priests and the Levites who came up with Zerubbabel the son of Shealtiel, and Jeshua: Seraiah, Jeremiah, Ezra, 2 Amariah, Malluch, Hattush, 3 Shechaniah, Rehum, Meremoth, 4 Iddo, Ginnethoi,*a* Abijah, 5 Mijamin, Maadiah, Bilgah, 6 Shemaiah, Joiarib, Jedaiah, 7 Sallu, Amok, Hilkiah, *and* Jedaiah.

These *were* the heads of the priests and their brethren in the days of Jeshua.

8 Moreover the Levites *were* Jeshua, Binnui, Kadmiel, Sherebiah, Judah, *and* Mattaniah *who* led the thanksgiving *psalms,* he and his brethren. 9 Also Bakbukiah and Unni, their brethren, *stood* across from them in *their* duties.

10 Jeshua begot Joiakim, Joiakim begot Eliashib, Eliashib begot Joiada, 11 Joiada begot Jonathan, and Jonathan begot Jaddua.

12 Now in the days of Joiakim, the priests, the heads of the fathers' *houses were:* of Seraiah, Meraiah; of Jeremiah, Hananiah; 13 of Ezra, Meshullam; of Amariah, Jehohanan; 14 of Melichu,*a* Jonathan; of Shebaniah,*b* Joseph; 15 of Harim,*a* Adna; of Meraioth,*b* Helkai; 16 of Iddo, Zechariah; of Ginnethon, Meshullam; 17 of Abijah, Zichri; *the son of* Minjamin;*a* of Moadiah,*b* Piltai; 18 of Bilgah, Shammua; of Shemaiah, Jehonathan; 19 of Joiarib, Mattenai; of Jedaiah, Uzzi; 20 of Sallai,*a* Kallai; of Amok, Eber; 21 of Hilkiah, Hashabiah; *and* of Jedaiah, Nethanel.

22 During the reign of Darius the Persian, a record *was also kept* of the Levites and priests *who had been* heads of their fathers' *houses* in the

---

11:14 *aOr the son of Haggedolim*   11:17 *aOr Michah*   11:24 *aLiterally at the king's hand*   12:4 *aOr Ginnethon* (compare verse 16)   12:14 *aOr Malluch* (compare verse 2)   *bOr Shechaniah* (compare verse 3)   12:15 *aOr Rehum* (compare verse 3)   *bOr Meremoth* (compare verse 3)   12:17 *aOr Mijamin* (compare verse 5)   *bOr Maadiah* (compare verse 5)   12:20 *aOr Sallu* (compare verse 7) days of Eliashib, Joiada, Johanan, and Jaddua. 23 The sons of Levi, the heads of the fathers' *houses* until the days of Johanan the son of Eliashib, *were* written in the book of the chronicles.

24 And the heads of the Levites *were* Hashabiah, Sherebiah, and Jeshua the son of Kadmiel, with their brothers across from them, to praise *and* give thanks, group alternating with group, according to the command of David the man of God. 25 Mattaniah, Bakbukiah, Obadiah, Meshullam, Talmon, and Akkub *were* gatekeepers keeping the watch at the storerooms of the gates. 26 These *lived* in the days of Joiakim the son of Jeshua, the son of Jozadak,[a] and in the days of Nehemiah the governor, and of Ezra the priest, the scribe.

27 Now at the dedication of the wall of Jerusalem they sought out the Levites in all their places, to bring them to Jerusalem to celebrate the dedication with gladness, both with thanksgivings and singing, *with* cymbals and stringed instruments and harps. 28 And the sons of the singers gathered together from the countryside around Jerusalem, from the villages of the Netophathites, 29 from the house of Gilgal, and from the fields of Geba and Azmaveth; for the singers had built themselves villages all around Jerusalem. 30 Then the priests and Levites purified themselves, and purified the people, the gates, and the wall.

31 So I brought the leaders of Judah up on the wall, and appointed two large thanksgiving choirs. *One* went to the right hand on the wall toward the Refuse Gate. 32 After them went Hoshaiah and half of the leaders of Judah, 33 and Azariah, Ezra, Meshullam, 34 Judah, Benjamin, Shemaiah, Jeremiah, 35 and some of the priests' sons with trumpets—Zechariah the son of Jonathan, the son of Shemaiah, the son of Mattaniah, the son of Michaiah, the son of Zaccur, the son of Asaph, 36 and his brethren, Shemaiah, Azarel, Milalai, Gilalai, Maai, Nethanel, Judah, *and* Hanani, with the musical instruments of David the man of God. And Ezra the scribe *went* before them. 37 By the Fountain Gate, in front of them, they went up the stairs of the City of David, on the stairway of the wall, beyond the house of David, as far as the Water Gate eastward.

38 The other thanksgiving choir went the opposite *way*, and I *was* behind them with half of the people on the wall, going past the Tower of the Ovens as far as the Broad Wall, 39 and above the Gate of Ephraim, above the Old Gate, above the Fish Gate, the Tower of Hananel, the Tower of the Hundred, as far as the Sheep Gate; and they stopped by the Gate of the Prison.

40 So the two thanksgiving choirs stood in the house of God, likewise I and the half of the rulers with me; 41 and the priests, Eliakim, Maaseiah, Minjamin,[a] Michaiah, Elioenai, Zechariah, *and* Hananiah, with trumpets; 42 also Maaseiah, Shemaiah, Eleazar, Uzzi, Jehohanan, Malchijah, Elam, and Ezer. The singers sang loudly with Jezrahiah the director.

43 Also that day they offered great sacrifices, and rejoiced, for God had made them rejoice with great joy; the women and the children also rejoiced, so that the joy of Jerusalem was heard afar off.

44 And at the same time some were appointed over the rooms of the storehouse for the offerings, the firstfruits, and the tithes, to gather into them from the fields of the cities the portions specified by the Law for the priests and Levites; for Judah rejoiced over the priests and Levites who ministered. 45 Both the singers and the gatekeepers kept the charge of their God and the charge of the purification, according to the command of David *and* Solomon his son. 46 For in the days of David and Asaph of old *there were* chiefs of the singers, and songs of praise and thanksgiving to God. 47 In the days of Zerubbabel and in the days of Nehemiah all Israel gave the portions for the singers and the gatekeepers, a portion for each day. They also consecrated *holy things* for the Levites, and the Levites consecrated *them* for the children of Aaron.

13

On that day they read from the Book of Moses in the hearing of the people, and in it was found

---

12:26 [a] Spelled *Jehozadak* in 1 Chronicles 6:14   12:41 [a] Or *Mijamin* (compare verse 5)

written that no Ammonite or Moabite should ever come into the assembly of God, 2 because they had not met the children of Israel with bread and water, but hired Balaam against them to curse them. However, our God turned the curse into a blessing. 3 So it was, when they had heard the Law, that they separated all the mixed multitude from Israel.

4 Now before this, Eliashib the priest, having authority over the storerooms of the house of our God, *was* allied with Tobiah. 5 And he had prepared for him a large room, where previously they had stored the grain offerings, the frankincense, the articles, the tithes of grain, the new wine and oil, which were commanded *to be given* to the Levites and singers and gatekeepers, and the offerings for the priests. 6 But during all this I was not in Jerusalem, for in the thirty-second year of Artaxerxes king of Babylon I had returned to the king. Then after certain days I obtained leave from the king, 7 and I came to Jerusalem and discovered the evil that Eliashib had done for Tobiah, in preparing a room for him in the courts of the house of God. 8 And it grieved me bitterly; therefore I threw all the household goods of Tobiah out of the room. 9 Then I commanded them to cleanse the rooms; and I brought back into them the articles of the house of God, with the grain offering and the frankincense.

10 I also realized that the portions for the Levites had not been given *them;* for each of the Levites and the singers who did the work had gone back to his field. 11 So I contended with the rulers, and said, "Why is the house of God forsaken?" And I gathered them together and set them in their place. 12 Then all Judah brought the tithe of the grain and the new wine and the oil to the storehouse. 13 And I appointed as treasurers over the storehouse Shelemiah the priest and Zadok the scribe, and of the Levites, Pedaiah; and next to them *was* Hanan the son of Zaccur, the son of Mattaniah; for they were considered faithful, and their task *was* to distribute to their brethren.

14 Remember me, O my God, concerning this, and do not wipe out my good deeds that I have done for the house of my God, and for its services!

15 In those days I saw *people* in Judah treading wine presses on the Sabbath, and bringing in sheaves, and loading donkeys with wine, grapes, figs, and all *kinds of* burdens, which they brought into Jerusalem on the Sabbath day. And I warned *them* about the day on which they were selling provisions. 16 Men of Tyre dwelt there also, who brought in fish and all kinds of goods, and sold *them* on the Sabbath to the children of Judah, and in Jerusalem.

17 Then I contended with the nobles of Judah, and said to them, "What evil thing *is* this that you do, by which you profane the Sabbath day? 18 Did not your fathers do thus, and did not our God bring all this disaster on us and on this city? Yet you bring added wrath on Israel by profaning the Sabbath."

19 So it was, at the gates of Jerusalem, as it began to be dark before the Sabbath, that I commanded the gates to be shut, and charged that they must not be opened till after the Sabbath. Then I posted *some* of my servants at the gates, *so that* no burdens would be brought in on the Sabbath day. 20 Now the merchants and sellers of all kinds of wares lodged outside Jerusalem once or twice.

21 Then I warned them, and said to them, "Why do you spend the night around the wall? If you do *so* again, I will lay hands on you!" From that time on they came no *more* on the Sabbath. 22 And I commanded the Levites that they should cleanse themselves, and that they should go and guard the gates, to sanctify the Sabbath day.

Remember me, O my God, *concerning* this also, and spare me according to the greatness of Your mercy!

23 In those days I also saw Jews *who* had married women of Ashdod, Ammon, *and* Moab. 24 And half of their children spoke the language of Ashdod, and could not speak the language of Judah, but spoke according to the language of one or the other people.

25 So I contended with them and cursed them, struck some of them and pulled out their hair, and made them swear by God, *saying,* "You shall not give your daughters as wives to their sons, nor take their

daughters for your sons or yourselves. 26 Did not Solomon king of Israel sin by these things? Yet among many nations there was no king like him, who was beloved of his God; and God made him king over all Israel. Nevertheless pagan women caused even him to sin. 27 Should we then hear of your doing all this great evil, transgressing against our God by marrying pagan women?"

28 And *one* of the sons of Joiada, the son of Eliashib the high priest, *was* a son-in-law of Sanballat the Horonite; therefore I drove him from me.

29 Remember them, O my God, because they have defiled the priesthood and the covenant of the priesthood and the Levites.

30 Thus I cleansed them of everything pagan. I also assigned duties to the priests and the Levites, each to his service, 31 and *to bringing* the wood offering and the firstfruits at appointed times.

Remember me, O my God, for good!

Overview of Esther

The Book of Esther is a fascinating account of God's ability to send the right person to the right place at the right time.

The exact date and author of this book are unknown. Most scholars, however, attribute it to a Jewish writer living in the Persian period (539—332 B.C.). The king of this book is generally thought to be Xerxes, king of Persia, whose domain spanned from the Indus River in India, north to the Black Sea, west through Asia Minor and to the shores of North Africa, from 485 to 464 B.C.

The empire of Xerxes was not only powerful, but full of wealth, as is evident from the description of Xerxes' palace in the summer capital of Susa (Esth. 1:4—7). Into this power center walked Esther—a young Jewish virgin—called by God to a mighty position.

Her role as queen was not secure, for even she was subject to the whims of the king. Yet her ascent to royalty held an incredible purpose—to save the Jewish people from destruction; she was the only person who could persuade the king to spare her people.

Esther was beautiful in person and character. But more importantly, she was courageous and wise. Haman, a great enemy of the Jews, had gained Xerxes' approval to put to death all the Jews of the land. Esther felt powerless to help her people. She conquered her fear of the king through prayer and fasting. Then by exercising her charm and womanly gifts, she went before Xerxes. She knew that if he accepted her, her life would be spared, but if he rejected her presence before him, she would be put to death. "And so I will go to the king, which is against the law; and if I perish, I perish!" (Esth. 4:16).

Jesus in Esther

Esther, like Jesus, puts herself in the place of death for her people but receives the approval of the king. She also portrays Jesus' work as Advocate on our behalf. This book reveals another satanic threat to destroy the Jewish people and thus, the messianic line. God continues to preserve His people in spite of opposition and danger, and nothing can prevent the coming of the Messiah.

Keys to Esther

Key Word: Providence. The Book of Esther was written to show how the Jewish people were protected and preserved by the gracious hand of God from the threat of annihilation. Although God disciplines His covenant people, He never abandons them. The God of Israel is the sovereign controller of history, and His providential care can be seen in every detail of Esther's story.

Key Verses: "For if you remain completely silent at this time, relief and deliverance will arise for the Jews from another place, but you and your father's house will perish. Yet who knows whether you have come to the kingdom for *such* a time as this?" (4:14).

"And in every province and city, wherever the king's command and decree came, the Jews had joy and gladness, a feast and a holiday. Then many of the people of the land became Jews, because fear of the Jews fell upon them" (8:17).

Key Chapter: Esther 8. According to the Book of Esther, the salvation of the Jews is accomplished through the second decree of King Ahasuerus, allowing the Jews to defend themselves against their enemies. Chapter 8 records this pivotal event with the accompanying result that many people in the kingdom became Jews.

1 Now it came to pass in the days of Ahasuerus[a] (this *was* the Ahasuerus who reigned over one hundred and twenty-seven provinces, from India to Ethiopia), 2 in those days when King Ahasuerus sat on the throne of his kingdom, which *was* in Shushan[a] the citadel, 3 *that* in the third year of his reign he made a feast for all his officials and servants—the powers of Persia and Media, the nobles, and the princes of the provinces *being* before him— 4 when he showed the riches of his glorious kingdom and the splendor of his excellent majesty for many days, one hundred and eighty days *in all*.

5 And when these days were completed, the king made a feast lasting seven days for all the people who were present in Shushan the citadel, from great to small, in the court of the garden of the king's palace. 6 *There were* white and blue linen *curtains* fastened with cords of fine linen and purple on silver rods and marble pillars; *and the* couches *were* of gold and silver on a *mosaic* pavement of alabaster, turquoise, and white and black marble. 7 And they served drinks in golden vessels, each vessel being different from the other, with royal wine in abundance, ac-

cording to the generosity of the king. 8 In accordance with the law, the drinking was not compulsory; for so the king had ordered all the officers of his household, that they should do according to each man's pleasure.

9 Queen Vashti also made a feast for the women *in* the royal palace which *belonged* to King Ahasuerus.

10 On the seventh day, when the heart of the king was merry with wine, he commanded Mehuman, Biztha, Harbona, Bigtha, Abagtha, Zethar, and Carcas, seven eunuchs who served in the presence of King Ahasuerus, 11 to bring Queen Vashti before the king, *wearing* her royal crown, in order to show her beauty to the people and the officials, for she *was* beautiful to behold. 12 But Queen Vashti refused to come at the king's command *brought* by *his* eunuchs; therefore the king was furious, and his anger burned within him.

13 Then the king said to the wise men who understood the times (for this *was* the king's manner toward all who knew law and justice, 14 those closest to him *being* Carshena, Shethar, Admatha, Tarshish, Meres, Marsena, and Memucan, the seven princes of Persia and Media, who had access to the king's presence, *and* who ranked highest in

the kingdom): 15 "What *shall we* do to Queen Vashti, according to law, because she did not obey the command of King Ahasuerus *brought to her* by the eunuchs?"

16 And Memucan answered before the king and the princes: "Queen Vashti has not only wronged the king, but also all the princes, and all the people who *are* in all the provinces of King Ahasuerus. 17 For the queen's behavior will become known to all women, so that they will despise their husbands in their eyes, when they report, 'King Ahasuerus commanded Queen Vashti to be brought in before him, but she did not come.' 18 This very day the *noble* ladies of Persia and Media will say to all the king's officials that they have heard of the behavior of the queen. Thus *there will be* excessive contempt and wrath. 19 If it pleases the king, let a royal decree go out from him, and let it be recorded in the laws of the Persians and the Medes, so that it will not be altered, that Vashti shall come no more before King Ahasuerus; and let the king give her royal position to another who is better than she. 20 When the king's decree which he will make is proclaimed throughout all his empire (for it is great), all wives will honor their husbands, both great and small."

21 And the reply pleased the king and the princes, and the king did according to the word of Memucan. 22 Then he sent letters to all the king's provinces, to each province in its own script, and to every people in their own language, that each man should be master in his own house, and speak in the language of his own people.

2 After these things, when the wrath of King Ahasuerus subsided, he remembered Vashti, what she had done, and what had been decreed against her. 2 Then the king's servants who attended him said: "Let beautiful young virgins be sought for the king; 3 and let the king appoint officers in all the provinces of his kingdom, that they may gather all the beautiful young virgins to Shushan the citadel, into the women's quarters, under the custody of Hegai[a] the

king's eunuch, custodian of the women. And let beauty preparations be given *them*. 4 Then let the young woman who pleases the king be queen instead of Vashti."

This thing pleased the king, and he did so.

5 In Shushan the citadel there was a certain Jew whose name *was* Mordecai the son of Jair, the son of Shimei, the son of Kish, a Benjamite. 6 *Kish*[a] had been carried away from Jerusalem with the captives who had been captured with Jeconiah[b] king of Judah, whom Nebuchadnezzar the king of Babylon had carried away. 7 And *Mordecai* had brought up Hadassah, that *is*, Esther, his uncle's daughter, for she had neither father nor mother. The young woman *was* lovely and beautiful. When her father and mother died, Mordecai took her as his own daughter.

8 So it was, when the king's command and decree were heard, and when many young women were gathered at Shushan the citadel, *under* the custody of Hegai, that Esther also was taken to the king's palace, into the care of Hegai the custodian of the women. 9 Now the young woman pleased him, and she obtained his favor; so he readily gave beauty preparations to her, besides her allowance. Then seven choice maidservants were provided for her from the king's palace, and he moved her and her maidservants to the best *place* in the house of the women.

10 Esther had not revealed her people or family, for Mordecai had charged her not to reveal *it*. 11 And every day Mordecai paced in front of the court of the women's quarters, to learn of Esther's welfare and what was happening to her.

12 Each young woman's turn came to go in to King Ahasuerus after she had completed twelve months' preparation, according to the regulations for the women, for thus were the days of their preparation apportioned: six months with oil of myrrh, and six months with perfumes and preparations for beautifying women. 13 Thus *prepared, each* young woman went to the king, and she was given whatever she desired to take with her from the women's quarters to the king's palace. 14 In the evening

she went, and in the morning she returned to the second house of the women, to the custody of Shaashgaz, the king's eunuch who kept the concubines. She would not go in to the king again unless the king delighted in her and called for her by name.

15 Now when the turn came for Esther the daughter of Abihail the uncle of Mordecai, who had taken her as his daughter, to go in to the king, she requested nothing but what Hegai the king's eunuch, the custodian of the women, advised. And Esther obtained favor in the sight of all who saw her. 16 So Esther was taken to King Ahasuerus, into his royal palace, in the tenth month, which is the month of Tebeth, in the seventh year of his reign. 17 The king loved Esther more than all the other women, and she obtained grace and favor in his sight more than all the virgins; so he set the royal crown upon her head and made her queen instead of Vashti. 18 Then the king made a great feast, the Feast of Esther, for all his officials and servants; and he proclaimed a holiday in the provinces and gave gifts according to the generosity of a king.

19 When virgins were gathered together a second time, Mordecai sat within the king's gate. 20 Now Esther had not revealed her family and her people, just as Mordecai had charged her, for Esther obeyed the command of Mordecai as when she was brought up by him.

21 In those days, while Mordecai sat within the king's gate, two of the king's eunuchs, Bigthan and Teresh, doorkeepers, became furious and sought to lay hands on King Ahasuerus. 22 So the matter became known to Mordecai, who told Queen Esther, and Esther informed the king in Mordecai's name. 23 And when an inquiry was made into the matter, it was confirmed, and both were hanged on a gallows; and it was written in the book of the chronicles in the presence of the king.

3 After these things King Ahasuerus promoted Haman, the son of Hammedatha the Agagite, and advanced him and set his seat above all the princes who were with him. 2 And all the king's servants who were within the king's gate bowed and paid homage to Haman, for so the king had commanded concerning him. But Mordecai would not bow or pay homage. 3 Then the king's servants who were within the king's gate said to Mordecai, "Why do you transgress the king's command?" 4 Now it happened, when they spoke to him daily and he would not listen to them, that they told it to Haman, to see whether Mordecai's words would stand; for Mordecai had told them that he was a Jew. 5 When Haman saw that Mordecai did not bow or pay him homage, Haman was filled with wrath. 6 But he disdained to lay hands on Mordecai alone, for they had told him of the people of Mordecai. Instead, Haman sought to destroy all the Jews who were throughout the whole kingdom of Ahasuerus—the people of Mordecai.

7 In the first month, which is the month of Nisan, in the twelfth year of King Ahasuerus, they cast Pur (that is, the lot), before Haman to determine the day and the month,a until it fell on the twelfth month,b which is the month of Adar.

8 Then Haman said to King Ahasuerus, "There is a certain people scattered and dispersed among the people in all the provinces of your kingdom; their laws are different from all other people's, and they do not keep the king's laws. Therefore it is not fitting for the king to let them remain. 9 If it pleases the king, let a decree be written that they be destroyed, and I will pay ten thousand talents of silver into the hands of those who do the work, to bring it into the king's treasuries."

10 So the king took his signet ring from his hand and gave it to Haman, the son of Hammedatha the Agagite, the enemy of the Jews. 11 And the king said to Haman, "The money and the people are given to you, to do with them as seems good to you."

12 Then the king's scribes were called on the thirteenth day of the first month, and a decree was written according to all that Haman commanded—to the king's satraps, to the

governors who *were* over each province, to the officials of all people, to every province according to its script, and to every people in their language. In the name of King Ahasuerus it was written, and sealed with the king's signet ring. 13 And the letters were sent by couriers into all the king's provinces, to kill, to destroy, and to annihilate all the Jews, both young and old, little children and women, in one day, on the thirteenth *day* of the twelfth *month,* which *is* the month of Adar, and to plunder their possessions.ᵃ 14 A copy of the document was to be issued as law in every province, being published for all people, that they should be ready for that day. 15 The couriers went out, hastened by the king's command; and the decree was proclaimed in Shushan the citadel. So the king and Haman sat down to drink, but the city of Shushan was perplexed.

4 When Mordecai learned all that had happened, he tore his clothes and put on sackcloth and ashes, and went out into the midst of the city. He cried out with a loud and bitter cry. 2 He went as far as the front of the king's gate, for no one *might* enter the king's gate clothed with sackcloth. 3 And in every province where the king's command and decree arrived, *there was* great mourning among the Jews, with fasting, weeping, and wailing; and many lay in sackcloth and ashes.

4 So Esther's maids and eunuchs came and told her, and the queen was deeply distressed. Then she sent garments to clothe Mordecai and take his sackcloth away from him, but he would not accept *them.* 5 Then Esther called Hathach, *one* of the king's eunuchs whom he had appointed to attend her, and she gave him a command concerning Mordecai, to learn what and why this *was.* 6 So Hathach went out to Mordecai in the city square that *was* in front of the king's gate. 7 And Mordecai told him all that had happened to him, and the sum of money that Haman had promised to pay into the king's treasuries to destroy the Jews. 8 He also gave him a copy of the written decree for their destruction, which was given at Shushan, that he might show it to Esther and explain it to her, and that he might command her to go in to the king to make supplication to him and plead before him for her people. 9 So Hathach returned and told Esther the words of Mordecai.

10 Then Esther spoke to Hathach, and gave him a command for Mordecai: 11 "All the king's servants and the people of the king's provinces know that any man or woman who goes into the inner court to the king, who has not been called, *he has* but one law: put *all* to death, except the one to whom the king holds out the golden scepter, that he may live. Yet I myself have not been called to go in to the king these thirty days." 12 So they told Mordecai Esther's words.

13 And Mordecai told *them* to answer Esther: "Do not think in your heart that you will escape in the king's palace any more than all the other Jews. 14 For if you remain completely silent at this time, relief and deliverance will arise for the Jews from another place, but you and your father's house will perish. Yet who knows whether you have come to the kingdom for *such* a time as this?"

15 Then Esther told *them* to reply to Mordecai: 16 "Go, gather all the Jews who are present in Shushan, and fast for me; neither eat nor drink for three days, night or day. My maids and I will fast likewise. And so I will go to the king, which *is* against the law; and if I perish, I perish!"

17 So Mordecai went his way and did according to all that Esther commanded him.ᵃ

5 Now it happened on the third day that Esther put on *her* royal *robes* and stood in the inner court of the king's palace, across from the king's house, while the king sat on his royal throne in the royal house, facing the entrance of the house.ᵃ 2 So it was, when the king saw Queen Esther standing in the court, *that* she found favor in his sight, and the king held out to Esther the golden scepter that *was* in his hand. Then Esther went

---

3:13 ᵃSeptuagint adds the text of the letter here.   4:17 ᵃSeptuagint adds a prayer of Mordecai here.
5:1 ᵃSeptuagint adds many extra details in verses 1 and 2.

near and touched the top of the scepter.

3 And the king said to her, "What do you wish, Queen Esther? What *is* your request? It shall be given to you—up to half the kingdom!"

4 So Esther answered, "If it pleases the king, let the king and Haman come today to the banquet that I have prepared for him."

5 Then the king said, "Bring Haman quickly, that he may do as Esther has said." So the king and Haman went to the banquet that Esther had prepared.

6 At the banquet of wine the king said to Esther, "What *is* your petition? It shall be granted you. What *is* your request, up to half the kingdom? It shall be done!"

7 Then Esther answered and said, "My petition and request *is this:* 8 If I have found favor in the sight of the king, and if it pleases the king to grant my petition and fulfill my request, then let the king and Haman come to the banquet which I will prepare for them, and tomorrow I will do as the king has said."

9 So Haman went out that day joyful and with a glad heart; but when Haman saw Mordecai in the king's gate, and that he did not stand or tremble before him, he was filled with indignation against Mordecai. 10 Nevertheless Haman restrained himself and went home, and he sent and called for his friends and his wife Zeresh. 11 Then Haman told them of his great riches, the multitude of his children, everything in which the king had promoted him, and how he had advanced him above the officials and servants of the king.

12 Moreover Haman said, "Besides, Queen Esther invited no one but me to come in with the king to the banquet that she prepared; and tomorrow I am again invited by her, along with the king. 13 Yet all this avails me nothing, so long as I see Mordecai the Jew sitting at the king's gate."

14 Then his wife Zeresh and all his friends said to him, "Let a gallows be made, fifty cubits high, and in the morning suggest to the king that Mordecai be hanged on it; then go merrily with the king to the banquet." And the thing pleased Haman; so he had the gallows made.

6 That night the king could not sleep. So one was commanded to bring the book of the records of the chronicles; and they were read before the king. 2 And it was found written that Mordecai had told of Bigthana and Teresh, two of the king's eunuchs, the doorkeepers who had sought to lay hands on King Ahasuerus. 3 Then the king said, "What honor or dignity has been bestowed on Mordecai for this?"

And the king's servants who attended him said, "Nothing has been done for him."

4 So the king said, "Who *is* in the court?" Now Haman had *just* entered the outer court of the king's palace to suggest that the king hang Mordecai on the gallows that he had prepared for him.

5 The king's servants said to him, "Haman is there, standing in the court."

And the king said, "Let him come in."

6 So Haman came in, and the king asked him, "What shall be done for the man whom the king delights to honor?"

Now Haman thought in his heart, "Whom would the king delight to honor more than me?" 7 And Haman answered the king, "*For* the man whom the king delights to honor, 8 let a royal robe be brought which the king has worn, and a horse on which the king has ridden, which has a royal crest placed on its head. 9 Then let this robe and horse be delivered to the hand of one of the king's most noble princes, that he may array the man whom the king delights to honor. Then parade him on horseback through the city square, and proclaim before him: 'Thus shall it be done to the man whom the king delights to honor!' "

10 Then the king said to Haman, "Hurry, take the robe and the horse, as you have suggested, and do so for Mordecai the Jew who sits within the king's gate! Leave nothing undone of all that you have spoken."

11 So Haman took the robe and the horse, arrayed Mordecai and led him on horseback through the city square, and proclaimed before him, "Thus shall it be done to the man whom the king delights to honor!"

12 Afterward Mordecai went back to the king's gate. But Haman hurried

to his house, mourning and with his head covered. 13 When Haman told his wife Zeresh and all his friends everything that had happened to him, his wise men and his wife Zeresh said to him, "If Mordecai, before whom you have begun to fall, is of Jewish descent, you will not prevail against him but will surely fall before him."

14 While they *were* still talking with him, the king's eunuchs came, and hastened to bring Haman to the banquet which Esther had prepared.

7 So the king and Haman went to dine with Queen Esther. 2 And on the second day, at the banquet of wine, the king again said to Esther, "What *is* your petition, Queen Esther? It shall be granted you. And what *is* your request, up to half the kingdom? It shall be done!"

3 Then Queen Esther answered and said, "If I have found favor in your sight, O king, and if it pleases the king, let my life be given me at my petition, and my people at my request. 4 For we have been sold, my people and I, to be destroyed, to be killed, and to be annihilated. Had we been sold as male and female slaves, I would have held my tongue, although the enemy could never compensate for the king's loss."

5 So King Ahasuerus answered and said to Queen Esther, "Who is he, and where is he, who would dare presume in his heart to do such a thing?"

6 And Esther said, "The adversary and enemy *is* this wicked Haman!"

So Haman was terrified before the king and queen.

7 Then the king arose in his wrath from the banquet of wine *and went* into the palace garden; but Haman stood before Queen Esther, pleading for his life, for he saw that evil was determined against him by the king. 8 When the king returned from the palace garden to the place of the banquet of wine, Haman had fallen across the couch where Esther *was*. Then the king said, "Will he also assault the queen while I *am* in the house?"

As the word left the king's mouth, they covered Haman's face. 9 Now Harbonah, one of the eunuchs, said to the king, "Look! The gallows, fifty cubits high, which Haman made for Mordecai, who spoke good on the king's behalf, is standing at the house of Haman."

Then the king said, "Hang him on it!"

10 So they hanged Haman on the gallows that he had prepared for Mordecai. Then the king's wrath subsided.

8 On that day King Ahasuerus gave Queen Esther the house of Haman, the enemy of the Jews. And Mordecai came before the king, for Esther had told how he *was related* to her. 2 So the king took off his signet ring, which he had taken from Haman, and gave it to Mordecai; and Esther appointed Mordecai over the house of Haman.

3 Now Esther spoke again to the king, fell down at his feet, and implored him with tears to counteract the evil of Haman the Agagite, and the scheme which he had devised against the Jews. 4 And the king held out the golden scepter toward Esther. So Esther arose and stood before the king, 5 and said, "If it pleases the king, and if I have found favor in his sight and the thing *seems* right to the king and I am pleasing in his eyes, let it be written to revoke the letters devised by Haman, the son of Hammedatha the Agagite, which he wrote to annihilate the Jews who *are* in all the king's provinces. 6 For how can I endure to see the evil that will come to my people? Or how can I endure to see the destruction of my countrymen?"

7 Then King Ahasuerus said to Queen Esther and Mordecai the Jew, "Indeed, I have given Esther the house of Haman, and they have hanged him on the gallows because he *tried to* lay his hand on the Jews. 8 You yourselves write *a decree* concerning the Jews, as you please, in the king's name, and seal *it* with the king's signet ring; for whatever is written in the king's name and sealed with the king's signet ring no one can revoke."

9 So the king's scribes were called at that time, in the third month, which *is* the month of Sivan, on the twenty-third *day;* and it was written, according to all that Mordecai commanded, to the Jews, the satraps, the governors, and the princes of the provinces from India to Ethiopia, one hundred and twenty-seven provinces

in all, to every province in its own script, to every people in their own language, and to the Jews in their own script and language. 10 And he wrote in the name of King Ahasuerus, sealed *it* with the king's signet ring, and sent letters by couriers on horseback, riding on royal horses bred from swift steeds.*a*

11 By these letters the king permitted the Jews who *were* in every city to gather together and protect their lives—to destroy, kill, and annihilate all the forces of any people or province that would assault them, *both* little children and women, and to plunder their possessions, 12 on one day in all the provinces of King Ahasuerus, on the thirteenth *day* of the twelfth month, which *is* the month of Adar.*a* 13 A copy of the document was to be issued as a decree in every province and published for all people, so that the Jews would be ready on that day to avenge themselves on their enemies. 14 The couriers who rode on royal horses went out, hastened and pressed on by the king's command. And the decree was issued in Shushan the citadel.

15 So Mordecai went out from the presence of the king in royal apparel of blue and white, with a great crown of gold and a garment of fine linen and purple; and the city of Shushan rejoiced and was glad. 16 The Jews had light and gladness, joy and honor. 17 And in every province and city, wherever the king's command and decree came, the Jews had joy and gladness, a feast and a holiday. Then many of the people of the land became Jews, because fear of the Jews fell upon them.

9 Now in the twelfth month, that *is,* the month of Adar, on the thirteenth day, *the time* came for the king's command and his decree to be executed. On the day that the enemies of the Jews had hoped to overpower them, the opposite occurred, in that the Jews themselves overpowered those who hated them. 2 The Jews gathered together in their cities throughout all the provinces of King Ahasuerus to lay hands on those who sought their harm. And no one could withstand them, because fear of them fell upon all people.

3 And all the officials of the provinces, the satraps, the governors, and all those doing the king's work, helped the Jews, because the fear of Mordecai fell upon them. 4 For Mordecai *was* great in the king's palace, and his fame spread throughout all the provinces; for this man Mordecai became increasingly prominent. 5 Thus the Jews defeated all their enemies with the stroke of the sword, with slaughter and destruction, and did what they pleased with those who hated them.

6 And in Shushan the citadel the Jews killed and destroyed five hundred men. 7 Also Parshandatha, Dalphon, Aspatha, 8 Poratha, Adalia, Aridatha, 9 Parmashta, Arisai, Aridai, and Vajezatha— 10 the ten sons of Haman the son of Hammedatha, the enemy of the Jews—they killed; but they did not lay a hand on the plunder.

11 On that day the number of those who were killed in Shushan the citadel was brought to the king. 12 And the king said to Queen Esther, "The Jews have killed and destroyed five hundred men in Shushan the citadel, and the ten sons of Haman. What have they done in the rest of the king's provinces? Now what *is* your petition? It shall be granted to you. Or what *is* your further request? It shall be done."

13 Then Esther said, "If it pleases the king, let it be granted to the Jews who *are* in Shushan to do again tomorrow according to today's decree, and let Haman's ten sons be hanged on the gallows."

14 So the king commanded this to be done; the decree was issued in Shushan, and they hanged Haman's ten sons.

15 And the Jews who *were* in Shushan gathered together again on the fourteenth day of the month of Adar and killed three hundred men at Shushan; but they did not lay a hand on the plunder.

16 The remainder of the Jews in the king's provinces gathered together and protected their lives, had rest from their enemies, and killed seventy-five thousand of their enemies; but they did not lay a hand on the plunder. 17 *This was* on the thirteenth day of the month of Adar. And on

8:10 *a*Literally *sons of the swift horses*   8:12 *a*Septuagint adds the text of the letter here.

the fourteenth of *the month*[a] they rested and made it a day of feasting and gladness.

18 But the Jews who *were* at Shushan assembled together on the thirteenth *day,* as well as on the fourteenth; and on the fifteenth of *the month*[a] they rested, and made it a day of feasting and gladness. 19 Therefore the Jews of the villages who dwelt in the unwalled towns celebrated the fourteenth day of the month of Adar *with* gladness and feasting, as a holiday, and for sending presents to one another.

20 And Mordecai wrote these things and sent letters to all the Jews, near and far, who *were* in all the provinces of King Ahasuerus, 21 to establish among them that they should celebrate yearly the fourteenth and fifteenth days of the month of Adar, 22 as the days on which the Jews had rest from their enemies, as the month which was turned from sorrow to joy for them, and from mourning to a holiday; that they should make them days of feasting and joy, of sending presents to one another and gifts to the poor. 23 So the Jews accepted the custom which they had begun, as Mordecai had written to them, 24 because Haman, the son of Hammedatha the Agagite, the enemy of all the Jews, had plotted against the Jews to annihilate them, and had cast Pur (that *is,* the lot), to consume them and destroy them; 25 but when *Esther*[a] came before the king, he commanded by letter that this[b] wicked plot which *Haman* had devised against the Jews should return on his own head, and that he and his sons should be hanged on the gallows.

26 So they called these days Purim, after the name Pur. Therefore, because of all the words of this letter, what they had seen concerning this matter, and what had happened to them, 27 the Jews established and imposed it upon themselves and their descendants and all who would join them, that without fail they should celebrate these two days every year, according to the written *instructions* and according to the *prescribed* time, 28 *that* these days *should be* remembered and kept throughout every generation, every family, every province, and every city, that these days of Purim should not fail *to be observed* among the Jews, and *that* the memory of them should not perish among their descendants.

29 Then Queen Esther, the daughter of Abihail, with Mordecai the Jew, wrote with full authority to confirm this second letter about Purim. 30 And *Mordecai* sent letters to all the Jews, to the one hundred and twenty-seven provinces of the kingdom of Ahasuerus, *with* words of peace and truth, 31 to confirm these days of Purim at their *appointed* time, as Mordecai the Jew and Queen Esther had prescribed for them, and as they had decreed for themselves and their descendants concerning matters of their fasting and lamenting. 32 So the decree of Esther confirmed these matters of Purim, and it was written in the book.

10 And King Ahasuerus imposed tribute on the land and *on* the islands of the sea. 2 Now all the acts of his power and his might, and the account of the greatness of Mordecai, to which the king advanced him, *are* they not written in the book of the chronicles of the kings of Media and Persia? 3 For Mordecai the Jew *was* second to King Ahasuerus, and was great among the Jews and well received by the multitude of his brethren, seeking the good of his people and speaking peace to all his countrymen.[a]

9:17 [a]Literally *it*   9:18 [a]Literally *it*   9:25 [a]Literally *she* or *it*   [b]Literally *his*   10:3 [a]Literally *seed.*
Septuagint and Vulgate add a dream of Mordecai here; Vulgate adds six more chapters.

Job

Overview of Job

"Though He slay me, yet will I trust Him." This theme dominates the Book of Job, presenting Job as both doubting and trusting God's ultimate providential blessings.

Considered by many the oldest book of the Bible, Job may have been written between 2100 and 1900 B.C. It is the story of one of the world's wealthiest, most prosperous men, whose faith in God was tested. He lost everything he had, including children, land, camels, oxen, donkeys, sheep, and money—*everything*. Then Job was afflicted with a severe and loathsome disease.

This ancient literary masterpiece presents insight into human suffering found nowhere else. Job asks the tough questions concerning life's hardships. Throughout its pages are profound truths that can be revealed only by a person such as Job, who experienced terrible suffering. Job's initial response to his loss was one of obvious grief, yet he displayed an unyielding faith in God's care. As even greater trouble beset him and he found himself criticized by friends, pressured from all sides, and abandoned on a garbage pit, Job's faith turned to doubt.

Job challenged God's love for him and asked, "Why me? Why have you left me?" and "How could you do these things to me?"

In a series of dialogues with Job, God revealed His ultimate power and deity, finally making it clear that, as God, He was worthy of Job's praise regardless of the situation. God wanted Job to quit focusing on the unfathomable, mysterious questions of life and to live in a positive joyful state of praise. Although it is difficult to praise God in tough times, God is to be praised.

Job ultimately responded with praise and was rewarded with twice as many possessions as he had owned before.

Jesus in Job

Job acknowledges a redeemer and cries out for a mediator. Job's story confronts problems and raises questions which are answered perfectly in Jesus, who identifies with our sufferings. Jesus is the believer's Life, Redeemer, Mediator, and Advocate.

Keys to Job

Key Word: Sovereignty. The basic question of the Book of Job is, "Why do the righteous suffer if God is loving and all-powerful?" Suffering itself is not the central theme; rather, the focus is on what Job *learns* from his suffering— the sovereignty of God over all creation. After thirty-five chapters of debate, the conclusion at the whirlwind is that God is sovereign and worthy of worship in *whatever* He chooses to do. Job must learn to trust in the goodness and power of God in adversity by enlarging his concept of God.

Key Verses: "Though He slay me, yet will I trust Him. Even so, I will defend my own ways before Him" (13:15).

"*As for* the Almighty, we cannot find Him; *He is* excellent in power, *in* judgment and abundant justice; He does not oppress. Therefore men fear Him; He shows no partiality to any *who are* wise of heart" (37:23, 24).

Key Chapter: Job 42. The last chapter of the book records the climax of the long and difficult struggle Job has with himself, his wife, his friends, and even his God. Upon Job's full recognition of the utter majesty and sovereignty of the Lord, he repents and no longer demands an answer as to the reason for his plight.

1 There was a man in the land of Uz, whose name *was* Job; and that man was blameless and upright, and one who feared God and shunned evil. 2 And seven sons and three daughters were born to him. 3 Also, his possessions were seven thousand sheep, three thousand camels, five hundred yoke of oxen, five hundred female donkeys, and a very large household, so that this man was the greatest of all the people of the East.

4 And his sons would go and feast *in their* houses, each on his *appointed* day, and would send and invite their three sisters to eat and drink with them. 5 So it was, when the days of feasting had run their course, that Job would send and sanctify them, and he would rise early in the morning and offer burnt offerings *according to* the number of them all. For Job said, "It may be that my sons have sinned and cursed[a] God in their hearts." Thus Job did regularly.

6 Now there was a day when the sons of God came to present themselves before the LORD, and Satan[a] also came among them. 7 And the LORD said to Satan, "From where do you come?"

So Satan answered the LORD and said, "From going to and fro on the earth, and from walking back and forth on it."

8 Then the LORD said to Satan, "Have you considered My servant Job, that *there is* none like him on the earth, a blameless and upright man, one who fears God and shuns evil?"

9 So Satan answered the LORD and said, "Does Job fear God for nothing? 10 Have You not made a hedge around him, around his household, and around all that he has on every side? You have blessed the work of his hands, and his possessions have increased in the land. 11 But now, stretch out Your hand and touch all that he has, and he will surely curse You to Your face!"

12 And the LORD said to Satan, "Behold, all that he has *is* in your power; only do not lay a hand on his *person*."

So Satan went out from the presence of the LORD.

13 Now there was a day when his sons and daughters *were* eating and drinking wine in their oldest brother's house; 14 and a messenger came to Job and said, "The oxen were plowing and the donkeys feeding beside them, 15 when the Sabeans[a] raided *them* and took them away—indeed they have killed the servants with the edge of the sword; and I alone have escaped to tell you!"

16 While he *was* still speaking, another also came and said, "The fire of God fell from heaven and burned up the sheep and the servants, and consumed them; and I alone have escaped to tell you!"

17 While he *was* still speaking, another also came and said, "The Chaldeans formed three bands, raided the camels and took them away, yes, and killed the servants with the edge of the sword; and I alone have escaped to tell you!"

18 While he *was* still speaking, another also came and said, "Your sons and daughters *were* eating and drinking wine in their oldest brother's house, 19 and suddenly a great wind came from across[a] the wilderness and struck the four corners of the house, and it fell on the young people, and they are dead; and I alone have escaped to tell you!"

20 Then Job arose, tore his robe, and shaved his head; and he fell to the ground and worshiped. 21 And he said:

"Naked I came from my
    mother's womb,
And naked shall I return there.
The LORD gave, and the LORD
    has taken away;
Blessed be the name of the
    LORD."

22 In all this Job did not sin nor charge God with wrong.

1:5 [a]Literally *blessed,* but used here in the evil sense, and so in verse 11 and 2:5, 9   1:6 [a]Literally *the Adversary,* and so throughout this book   1:15 [a]Literally *Sheba* (compare 6:19)   1:19 [a]Septuagint omits *across.*

2 Again there was a day when the sons of God came to present themselves before the LORD, and Satan came also among them to present himself before the LORD. 2 And the LORD said to Satan, "From where do you come?"

Satan answered the LORD and said, "From going to and fro on the earth, and from walking back and forth on it."

3 Then the LORD said to Satan, "Have you considered My servant Job, that there is none like him on the earth, a blameless and upright man, one who fears God and shuns evil? And still he holds fast to his integrity, although you incited Me against him, to destroy him without cause."

4 So Satan answered the LORD and said, "Skin for skin! Yes, all that a man has he will give for his life. 5 But stretch out Your hand now, and touch his bone and his flesh, and he will surely curse You to Your face!"

6 And the LORD said to Satan, "Behold, he is in your hand, but spare his life."

7 So Satan went out from the presence of the LORD, and struck Job with painful boils from the sole of his foot to the crown of his head. 8 And he took for himself a potsherd with which to scrape himself while he sat in the midst of the ashes.

9 Then his wife said to him, "Do you still hold fast to your integrity? Curse God and die!"

10 But he said to her, "You speak as one of the foolish women speaks. Shall we indeed accept good from God, and shall we not accept adversity?" In all this Job did not sin with his lips.

11 Now when Job's three friends heard of all this adversity that had come upon him, each one came from his own place—Eliphaz the Temanite, Bildad the Shuhite, and Zophar the Naamathite. For they had made an appointment together to come and mourn with him, and to comfort him. 12 And when they raised their eyes from afar, and did not recognize him, they lifted their voices and wept; and each one tore his robe and sprinkled dust on his head toward heaven. 13 So they sat down with him on the ground seven days and seven nights,

and no one spoke a word to him, for they saw that his grief was very great.

3 After this Job opened his mouth and cursed the day of his birth. 2 And Job spoke, and said:

3 "May the day perish on which I
      was born,
   And the night in which it was
      said,
   'A male child is conceived.'
4 May that day be darkness;
   May God above not seek it,
   Nor the light shine upon it.
5 May darkness and the shadow
      of death claim it;
   May a cloud settle on it;
   May the blackness of the day
      terrify it.
6 As for that night, may darkness
      seize it;
   May it not rejoice[a] among the
      days of the year,
   May it not come into the
      number of the months.
7 Oh, may that night be barren!
   May no joyful shout come into
      it!
8 May those curse it who curse
      the day,
   Those who are ready to arouse
      Leviathan.
9 May the stars of its morning be
      dark;
   May it look for light, but have
      none,
   And not see the dawning of the
      day;
10 Because it did not shut up the
      doors of my mother's womb,
   Nor hide sorrow from my eyes.

11 "Why did I not die at birth?
   Why did I not perish when I
      came from the womb?
12 Why did the knees receive me?
   Or why the breasts, that I
      should nurse?
13 For now I would have lain still
      and been quiet,
   I would have been asleep;
   Then I would have been at rest
14 With kings and counselors of
      the earth,
   Who built ruins for themselves,
15 Or with princes who had gold,
   Who filled their houses with
      silver;

3:6 aSeptuagint, Syriac, Targum, and Vulgate read be joined.

16 Or *why* was I not hidden like
   a stillborn child,
   Like infants who never saw
   light?
17 There the wicked cease *from*
   troubling,
   And there the weary are at rest.
18 *There* the prisoners rest
   together;
   They do not hear the voice of
   the oppressor.
19 The small and great are there,
   And the servant *is* free from his
   master.

20 "Why is light given to him who
   is in misery,
   And life to the bitter of soul,
21 Who long for death, but it does
   not *come,*
   And search for it more than
   hidden treasures;
22 Who rejoice exceedingly,
   And are glad when they can
   find the grave?
23 *Why is light given* to a man
   whose way is hidden,
   And whom God has hedged in?
24 For my sighing comes before I
   eat,[a]
   And my groanings pour out
   like water.
25 For the thing I greatly feared
   has come upon me,
   And what I dreaded has
   happened to me.
26 I am not at ease, nor am I quiet;
   I have no rest, for trouble
   comes."

4 Then Eliphaz the Temanite answered and said:

2 "If one attempts a word with
   you, will you become weary?
   But who can withhold himself
   from speaking?
3 Surely you have instructed
   many,
   And you have strengthened
   weak hands.
4 Your words have upheld him
   who was stumbling,
   And you have strengthened the
   feeble knees;
5 But now it comes upon you,
   and you are weary;
   It touches you, and you are
   troubled.

6 *Is* not your reverence your
   confidence?
   And the integrity of your ways
   your hope?

7 "Remember now, who *ever*
   perished being innocent?
   Or where were the upright *ever*
   cut off?
8 Even as I have seen,
   Those who plow iniquity
   And sow trouble reap the same.
9 By the blast of God they perish,
   And by the breath of His anger
   they are consumed.
10 The roaring of the lion,
   The voice of the fierce lion,
   And the teeth of the young
   lions are broken.
11 The old lion perishes for lack
   of prey,
   And the cubs of the lioness are
   scattered.

12 "Now a word was secretly
   brought to me,
   And my ear received a whisper
   of it.
13 In disquieting thoughts from
   the visions of the night,
   When deep sleep falls on men,
14 Fear came upon me, and
   trembling,
   Which made all my bones
   shake.
15 Then a spirit passed before my
   face;
   The hair on my body stood up.
16 It stood still,
   But I could not discern its
   appearance.
   A form *was* before my eyes;
   There was silence;
   Then I heard a voice *saying:*
17 'Can a mortal be more righteous
   than God?
   Can a man be more pure than
   his Maker?
18 If He puts no trust in His
   servants,
   If He charges His angels with
   error,
19 How much more those who
   dwell in houses of clay,
   Whose foundation is in the
   dust,
   Who are crushed before a
   moth?
20 They are broken in pieces from
   morning till evening;

3:24 [a]Literally *my bread*

They perish forever, with no
    one regarding.
21 Does not their own excellence
    go away?
    They die, even without
    wisdom.'

5 "Call out now;
    Is there anyone who will
      answer you?
    And to which of the holy ones
      will you turn?
2 For wrath kills a foolish man,
    And envy slays a simple one.
3 I have seen the foolish taking
    root,
    But suddenly I cursed his
      dwelling place.
4 His sons are far from safety,
    They are crushed in the gate,
    And *there is* no deliverer.
5 Because the hungry eat up his
    harvest,
    Taking it even from the
      thorns,*a*
    And a snare snatches their
      substance.*b*
6 For affliction does not come
    from the dust,
    Nor does trouble spring from
      the ground;
7 Yet man is born to trouble,
    As the sparks fly upward.

8 "But as for me, I would seek
    God,
    And to God I would commit my
      cause—
9 Who does great things, and
    unsearchable,
    Marvelous things without
      number.
10 He gives rain on the earth,
    And sends waters on the fields.
11 He sets on high those who are
    lowly,
    And those who mourn are lifted
      to safety.
12 He frustrates the devices of the
    crafty,
    So that their hands cannot
      carry out their plans.
13 He catches the wise in their
    own craftiness,
    And the counsel of the cunning
      comes quickly upon them.
14 They meet with darkness in the
    daytime,

And grope at noontime as in
    the night.
15 But He saves the needy from
    the sword,
    From the mouth of the mighty,
    And from their hand.
16 So the poor have hope,
    And injustice shuts her mouth.

17 "Behold, happy *is* the man
    whom God corrects;
    Therefore do not despise the
      chastening of the Almighty.
18 For He bruises, but He binds
    up;
    He wounds, but His hands
      make whole.
19 He shall deliver you in six
    troubles,
    Yes, in seven no evil shall touch
      you.
20 In famine He shall redeem you
    from death,
    And in war from the power of
      the sword.
21 You shall be hidden from the
    scourge of the tongue,
    And you shall not be afraid of
      destruction when it comes.
22 You shall laugh at destruction
    and famine,
    And you shall not be afraid of
      the beasts of the earth.
23 For you shall have a covenant
    with the stones of the field,
    And the beasts of the field shall
      be at peace with you.
24 You shall know that your tent
    is in peace;
    You shall visit your dwelling
      and find nothing amiss.
25 You shall also know that your
    descendants *shall be* many,
    And your offspring like the
      grass of the earth.
26 You shall come to the grave at
    a full age,
    As a sheaf of grain ripens in its
      season.
27 Behold, this we have searched
    out;
    It *is* true.
    Hear it, and know for
      yourself."

6 Then Job answered and said:
2 "Oh, that my grief were fully
    weighed,

5:5 *a*Septuagint reads *They shall not be taken from evil men;* Vulgate reads *And the armed man shall take him by violence.* *b*Septuagint reads *The might shall draw them off;* Vulgate reads *And the thirsty shall drink up their riches.*

And my calamity laid with it on the scales!

3 For then it would be heavier than the sand of the sea— Therefore my words have been rash.

4 For the arrows of the Almighty *are* within me; My spirit drinks in their poison; The terrors of God are arrayed against me.

5 Does the wild donkey bray when it has grass, Or does the ox low over its fodder?

6 Can flavorless food be eaten without salt? Or is there *any* taste in the white of an egg?

7 My soul refuses to touch them; They *are* as loathsome food to me.

8 "Oh, that I might have my request, That God would grant *me* the thing that I long for!

9 That it would please God to crush me, That He would loose His hand and cut me off!

10 Then I would still have comfort; Though in anguish I would exult, He will not spare; For I have not concealed the words of the Holy One.

11 "What strength do I have, that I should hope? And what *is* my end, that I should prolong my life?

12 *Is* my strength the strength of stones? Or is my flesh bronze?

13 *Is* my help not within me? And is success driven from me?

14 "To him who is afflicted, kindness *should be shown* by his friend, Even though he forsakes the fear of the Almighty.

15 My brothers have dealt deceitfully like a brook, Like the streams of the brooks that pass away,

16 Which are dark because of the ice, *And* into which the snow vanishes.

17 When it is warm, they cease to flow; When it is hot, they vanish from their place.

18 The paths of their way turn aside, They go nowhere and perish.

19 The caravans of Tema look, The travelers of Sheba hope for them.

20 They are disappointed because they were confident; They come there and are confused.

21 For now you are nothing, You see terror and are afraid.

22 Did I ever say, 'Bring *something* to me'? Or, 'Offer a bribe for me from your wealth'?

23 Or, 'Deliver me from the enemy's hand'? Or, 'Redeem me from the hand of oppressors'?

24 "Teach me, and I will hold my tongue; Cause me to understand wherein I have erred.

25 How forceful are right words! But what does your arguing prove?

26 Do you intend to rebuke *my* words, And the speeches of a desperate one, *which are* as wind?

27 Yes, you overwhelm the fatherless, And you undermine your friend.

28 Now therefore, be pleased to look at me; For I would never lie to your face.

29 Yield now, let there be no injustice! Yes, concede, my righteousness still stands!

30 Is there injustice on my tongue? Cannot my taste discern the unsavory?

7 "*Is there* not a time of hard service for man on earth? *Are not* his days also like the days of a hired man?

2 Like a servant who earnestly desires the shade, And like a hired man who eagerly looks for his wages,

3 So I have been allotted months
of futility,
And wearisome nights have
been appointed to me.
4 When I lie down, I say, 'When
shall I arise,
And the night be ended?'
For I have had my fill of tossing
till dawn.
5 My flesh is caked with worms
and dust,
My skin is cracked and breaks
out afresh.

6 "My days are swifter than a
weaver's shuttle,
And are spent without hope.
7 Oh, remember that my life *is* a
breath!
My eye will never again see
good.
8 The eye of him who sees me
will see me no *more;*
While your *eyes* are upon me,
I shall no longer *be.*
9 *As* the cloud disappears and
vanishes away,
So he who goes down to the
grave does not come up.
10 He shall never return to his
house,
Nor shall his place know him
anymore.

11 "Therefore I will not restrain my
mouth;
I will speak in the anguish of
my spirit;
I will complain in the bitterness
of my soul.
12 *Am* I a sea, or a sea serpent,
That You set a guard over me?
13 When I say, 'My bed will
comfort me,
My couch will ease my
complaint,'
14 Then You scare me with
dreams
And terrify me with visions,
15 So that my soul chooses
strangling
And death rather than my
body.*a*
16 I loathe *my life;*
I would not live forever.
Let me alone,
For my days *are but* a breath.

17 "What *is* man, that You should
exalt him,

That You should set Your heart
on him,
18 That You should visit him
every morning,
And test him every moment?
19 How long?
Will You not look away from
me,
And let me alone till I swallow
my saliva?
20 Have I sinned?
What have I done to You, O
watcher of men?
Why have You set me as Your
target,
So that I am a burden to
myself?*a*
21 Why then do You not pardon
my transgression,
And take away my iniquity?
For now I will lie down in the
dust,
And You will seek me
diligently,
But I *will* no longer *be.*"

8 Then Bildad the Shuhite answered and said:

2 "How long will you speak these
things,
And the words of your mouth
be like a strong wind?
3 Does God subvert judgment?
Or does the Almighty pervert
justice?
4 If your sons have sinned
against Him,
He has cast them away for their
transgression.
5 If you would earnestly seek
God
And make your supplication to
the Almighty,
6 If you *were* pure and upright,
Surely now He would awake
for you,
And prosper your rightful
dwelling place.
7 Though your beginning was
small,
Yet your latter end would
increase abundantly.

8 "For inquire, please, of the
former age,
And consider the things
discovered by their fathers;

7:15 *a*Literally *my bones*   7:20 *a*Following Masoretic Text, Targum, and Vulgate; Septuagint and Jewish
tradition read *to You.*

9 For we *were born* yesterday,
   and know nothing,
   Because our days on earth *are*
   a shadow.
10 Will they not teach you and tell
   you,
   And utter words from their
   heart?
11 "Can the papyrus grow up
   without a marsh?
   Can the reeds flourish without
   water?
12 While it *is* yet green *and* not cut
   down,
   It withers before any *other*
   plant.
13 So *are* the paths of all who
   forget God;
   And the hope of the hypocrite
   shall perish,
14 Whose confidence shall be cut
   off,
   And whose trust *is* a spider's
   web.
15 He leans on his house, but it
   does not stand.
   He holds it fast, but it does not
   endure.
16 He grows green in the sun,
   And his branches spread out in
   his garden.
17 His roots wrap around the rock
   heap,
   And look for a place in the
   stones.
18 If he is destroyed from his
   place,
   Then *it* will deny him, *saying,*
   'I have not seen you.'
19 "Behold, this is the joy of His
   way,
   And out of the earth others will
   grow.
20 Behold, God will not cast away
   the blameless,
   Nor will He uphold the
   evildoers.
21 He will yet fill your mouth with
   laughing,
   And your lips with rejoicing.
22 Those who hate you will be
   clothed with shame,
   And the dwelling place of the
   wicked will come to
   nothing."*a*

9 Then Job answered and said:

2 "Truly I know *it is* so,

   But how can a man be
   righteous before God?
3 If one wished to contend with
   Him,
   He could not answer Him one
   time out of a thousand.
4 *God is* wise in heart and mighty
   in strength.
   Who has hardened *himself*
   against Him and prospered?
5 He removes the mountains, and
   they do not know
   When He overturns them in His
   anger;
6 He shakes the earth out of its
   place,
   And its pillars tremble;
7 He commands the sun, and it
   does not rise;
   He seals off the stars;
8 He alone spreads out the
   heavens,
   And treads on the waves of the
   sea;
9 He made the Bear, Orion, and
   the Pleiades,
   And the chambers of the south;
10 He does great things past
   finding out,
   Yes, wonders without number.
11 If He goes by me, I do not see
   Him;
   If He moves past, I do not
   perceive Him;
12 If He takes away, who can
   hinder Him?
   Who can say to Him, 'What are
   You doing?'
13 God will not withdraw His
   anger,
   The allies of the proud*a* lie
   prostrate beneath Him.

14 "How then can I answer Him,
   And choose my words *to*
   reason with Him?
15 For though I were righteous, I
   could not answer Him;
   I would beg mercy of my Judge.
16 If I called and He answered me,
   I would not believe that He was
   listening to my voice.
17 For He crushes me with a
   tempest,
   And multiplies my wounds
   without cause.
18 He will not allow me to catch
   my breath,
   But fills me with bitterness.

8:22 *a*Literally *will not be*   9:13 *a*Hebrew *rahab*

Swallow Your Hurts

Job 9:27 suggests a way we sometimes try to handle the rejections, defeats, or failures we experience—by pretending to be okay even though we are really very frightened by the things we can't understand. You may have collected enough hurts to keep you from wanting to press forward. Setbacks can take the joy out of faith if you don't watch out! Even success—steady, solid, and exceptional—can make you the target of criticism from colleagues who are jealous of your achievement.

Careful! Hidden hurts in the heart can nurture and nourish negative thinking. Often the most painful wounds are not the scars that are outwardly seen but the hidden wounds deep in the heart. Because they are hidden they are often the most dangerous.

Swallow your hurts and stimulate a new spirit and spurt of growth! If, in fact, your drive to grow has lost its passionate power, if the flush of enthusiasm has mysteriously diminished, then check the accumulation of negative emotions that have attached themselves to you, much like barnacles that attach to whales.

Along the shoreline in California it is a common sight to see whales stopping alongside rocks to scrape off barnacles as they migrate from Alaska to Mexico. In the walk of faith we, too, will pick up a collection of personal hurts that will attach themselves to our souls like parasites sapping the life and vitality out of us! Ultimately, Job found restoration not in hiding behind a false face of well-being, but in recognizing and acknowledging the greatness of God (Job 42), and so can we.

By faith, learn to swallow hard, and make this prayer your own: *Lord, I acknowledge Your greatness, and I trust You with the things I cannot understand. With Your help, I will swallow the hurts that seek to overwhelm me; and they will pass on and out of my life. Thank You for hearing my prayer. Amen.*

19 If *it is a matter* of strength,
   indeed *He is* strong;
   And if of justice, who will
   appoint my day *in court?*
20 Though I were righteous, my
   own mouth would condemn
   me;
   Though I *were* blameless, it
   would prove me perverse.

21 "I am blameless, yet I do not
   know myself;
   I despise my life.
22 It *is* all one *thing;*
   Therefore I say, 'He destroys
   the blameless and the
   wicked.'
23 If the scourge slays suddenly,
   He laughs at the plight of the
   innocent.
24 The earth is given into the hand
   of the wicked.
   He covers the faces of its
   judges.
   If it is not *He,* who else could
   it be?

25 "Now my days are swifter than
   a runner;
   They flee away, they see no
   good.
26 They pass by like swift ships,
   Like an eagle swooping on its
   prey.
27 If I say, 'I will forget my
   complaint,
   I will put off my sad face and
   wear a smile,'
28 I am afraid of all my sufferings;
   I know that You will not hold
   me innocent.
29 *If* I am condemned,
   Why then do I labor in vain?
30 If I wash myself with snow
   water,
   And cleanse my hands with
   soap,
31 Yet You will plunge me into the
   pit,
   And my own clothes will abhor
   me.

32 "For *He is* not a man, as I *am,*
   That I may answer Him,
   And that we should go to court
   together.
33 Nor is there any mediator
   between us,
   Who may lay his hand on us
   both.
34 Let Him take His rod away
   from me,

And do not let dread of Him
   terrify me.
35 *Then* I would speak and not
   fear Him,
   But it is not so with me.

10 "My soul loathes my life;
   I will give free course to my
   complaint,
   I will speak in the bitterness of
   my soul.
2 I will say to God, 'Do not
   condemn me;
   Show me why You contend
   with me.
3 *Does it* seem good to You that
   You should oppress,
   That You should despise the
   work of Your hands,
   And smile on the counsel of the
   wicked?
4 Do You have eyes of flesh?
   Or do You see as man sees?
5 *Are* Your days like the days of
   a mortal man?
   Are Your years like the days of
   a mighty man,
6 That You should seek for my
   iniquity
   And search out my sin,
7 Although You know that I am
   not wicked,
   And *there is* no one who can
   deliver from Your hand?

8 'Your hands have made me and
   fashioned me,
   An intricate unity;
   Yet You would destroy me.
9 Remember, I pray, that You
   have made me like clay.
   And will You turn me into dust
   again?
10 Did You not pour me out like
   milk,
   And curdle me like cheese,
11 Clothe me with skin and flesh,
   And knit me together with
   bones and sinews?
12 You have granted me life and
   favor,
   And Your care has preserved
   my spirit.

13 'And these *things* You have
   hidden in Your heart;
   I know that this *was* with You:
14 If I sin, then You mark me,
   And will not acquit me of my
   iniquity.
15 If I am wicked, woe to me;

Even *if* I am righteous, I cannot
    lift up my head.
I am full of disgrace;
    See my misery!
16 If *my head* is exalted,
    You hunt me like a fierce lion,
    And again You show Yourself
        awesome against me.
17 You renew Your witnesses
        against me,
    And increase Your indignation
        toward me;
    Changes and war are *ever* with
        me.

18 'Why then have You brought
        me out of the womb?
    Oh, that I had perished and no
        eye had seen me!
19 I would have been as though I
        had not been.
    I would have been carried from
        the womb to the grave.
20 Are not my days few?
    Cease! Leave me alone, that I
        may take a little comfort,
21 Before I go *to the place from
        which* I shall not return,
    To the land of darkness and the
        shadow of death,
22 A land as dark as darkness
        itself,
    As the shadow of death,
        without any order,
    Where even the light *is* like
        darkness.' "

11 Then Zophar the Naamathite
    answered and said:

2 "Should not the multitude of
        words be answered?
    And should a man full of talk
        be vindicated?
3 Should your empty talk make
        men hold their peace?
    And when you mock, should no
        one rebuke you?
4 For you have said,
    'My doctrine *is* pure,
    And I am clean in your eyes.'
5 But oh, that God would speak,
    And open His lips against you,
6 That He would show you the
        secrets of wisdom!
    For *they would* double *your*
        prudence.
    Know therefore that God
        exacts from you
    Less than your iniquity
        deserves.

7 "Can you search out the deep
        things of God?
    Can you find out the limits of
        the Almighty?
8 *They are* higher than heaven—
        what can you do?
    Deeper than Sheol—what can
        you know?
9 Their measure *is* longer than
        the earth
    And broader than the sea.

10 "If He passes by, imprisons, and
        gathers *to judgment,*
    Then who can hinder Him?
11 For He knows deceitful men;
    He sees wickedness also.
    Will He not then consider *it?*
12 For an empty-headed man will
        be wise,
    When a wild donkey's colt is
        born a man.

13 "If you would prepare your
        heart,
    And stretch out your hands
        toward Him;
14 If iniquity *were* in your hand,
        and you put it far away,
    And would not let wickedness
        dwell in your tents;
15 Then surely you could lift up
        your face without spot;
    Yes, you could be steadfast,
        and not fear;
16 Because you would forget *your*
        misery,
    And remember *it* as waters
        that have passed away,
17 And *your* life would be brighter
        than noonday.
    Though you were dark, you
        would be like the morning.
18 And you would be secure,
        because there is hope;
    Yes, you would dig *around you,*
        and take your rest in safety.
19 You would also lie down, and
        no one would make *you*
        afraid;
    Yes, many would court your
        favor.
20 But the eyes of the wicked will
        fail,
    And they shall not escape,
    And their hope—loss of life!"

12 Then Job answered and said:

2 "No doubt you *are* the people,
    And wisdom will die with you!

3 But I have understanding as
   well as you;
   I *am* not inferior to you.
   Indeed, who does not *know*
   such things as these?

4 "I am one mocked by his friends,
   Who called on God, and He
   answered him,
   The just and blameless *who is*
   ridiculed.
5 A lamp*ᵃ* is despised in the
   thought of one who is at ease;
   It is made ready for those
   whose feet slip.
6 The tents of robbers prosper,
   And those who provoke God
   are secure—
   In what God provides by His
   hand.

7 "But now ask the beasts, and
   they will teach you;
   And the birds of the air, and
   they will tell you;
8 Or speak to the earth, and it
   will teach you;
   And the fish of the sea will
   explain to you.
9 Who among all these does not
   know
   That the hand of the LORD has
   done this,
10 In whose hand *is* the life of
   every living thing,
   And the breath of all mankind?
11 Does not the ear test words
   And the mouth taste its food?
12 Wisdom *is* with aged men,
   And with length of days,
   understanding.

13 "With Him *are* wisdom and
   strength,
   He has counsel and
   understanding.
14 If He breaks *a thing* down, it
   cannot be rebuilt;
   If He imprisons a man, there
   can be no release.
15 If He withholds the waters,
   they dry up;
   If He sends them out, they
   overwhelm the earth.
16 With Him *are* strength and
   prudence.
   The deceived and the deceiver
   are His.
17 He leads counselors away
   plundered,

And makes fools of the judges.
18 He loosens the bonds of kings,
   And binds their waist with a
   belt.
19 He leads princes*ᵃ* away
   plundered,
   And overthrows the mighty.
20 He deprives the trusted ones of
   speech,
   And takes away the
   discernment of the elders.
21 He pours contempt on princes,
   And disarms the mighty.
22 He uncovers deep things out of
   darkness,
   And brings the shadow of
   death to light.
23 He makes nations great, and
   destroys them;
   He enlarges nations, and
   guides them.
24 He takes away the
   understanding*ᵃ* of the chiefs
   of the people of the earth,
   And makes them wander in a
   pathless wilderness.
25 They grope in the dark without
   light,
   And He makes them stagger
   like a drunken *man.*

13 "Behold, my eye has seen all
   this,
   My ear has heard and
   understood it.
2 What you know, I also know;
   I *am* not inferior to you.
3 But I would speak to the
   Almighty,
   And I desire to reason with
   God.
4 But you forgers of lies,
   You *are* all worthless
   physicians.
5 Oh, that you would be silent,
   And it would be your wisdom!
6 Now hear my reasoning,
   And heed the pleadings of my
   lips.
7 Will you speak wickedly for
   God,
   And talk deceitfully for Him?
8 Will you show partiality for
   Him?
   Will you contend for God?
9 Will it be well when He
   searches you out?
   Or can you mock Him as one
   mocks a man?
10 He will surely rebuke you

12:5 *ᵃ*Or *disaster*   12:19 *ᵃ*Literally *priests*, but not in the technical sense   12:24 *ᵃ*Literally *heart*

If you secretly show partiality.
11 Will not His excellence make
    you afraid,
    And the dread of Him fall upon
    you?
12 Your platitudes *are* proverbs of
    ashes,
    Your defenses are defenses of
    clay.

13 "Hold your peace with me, and
    let me speak,
    Then let come on me what *may!*
14 Why do I take my flesh in my
    teeth,
    And put my life in my hands?
15 Though He slay me, yet will I
    trust Him.
    Even so, I will defend my own
    ways before Him.
16 He also *shall* be my salvation,
    For a hypocrite could not come
    before Him.
17 Listen carefully to my speech,
    And to my declaration with
    your ears.
18 See now, I have prepared *my*
    case,
    I know that I shall be
    vindicated.
19 Who *is* he *who* will contend
    with me?
    If now I hold my tongue, I
    perish.
20 "Only two *things* do not do to
    me,
    Then I will not hide myself
    from You:
21 Withdraw Your hand far from
    me,
    And let not the dread of You
    make me afraid.
22 Then call, and I will answer;
    Or let me speak, then You
    respond to me.
23 How many *are* my iniquities
    and sins?
    Make me know my
    transgression and my sin.
24 Why do You hide Your face,
    And regard me as Your enemy?
25 Will You frighten a leaf driven
    to and fro?
    And will You pursue dry
    stubble?
26 For You write bitter things
    against me,
    And make me inherit the
    iniquities of my youth.
27 You put my feet in the stocks,

And watch closely all my paths.
You set a limit[a] for the soles of
my feet.

28 "Man[a] decays like a rotten thing,
    Like a garment that is moth-
    eaten.

14 "Man *who is* born of woman
    Is of few days and full of
    trouble.
2   He comes forth like a flower
    and fades away;
    He flees like a shadow and does
    not continue.
3   And do You open Your eyes on
    such a one,
    And bring me[a] to judgment
    with Yourself?
4   Who can bring a clean *thing*
    out of an unclean?
    No one!
5   Since his days *are* determined,
    The number of his months *is*
    with You;
    You have appointed his limits,
    so that he cannot pass.
6   Look away from him that he
    may rest,
    Till like a hired man he finishes
    his day.

7   "For there is hope for a tree,
    If it is cut down, that it will
    sprout again,
    And that its tender shoots will
    not cease.
8   Though its root may grow old
    in the earth,
    And its stump may die in the
    ground,
9   *Yet* at the scent of water it will
    bud
    And bring forth branches like
    a plant.
10 But man dies and is laid away;
    Indeed he breathes his last
    And where *is* he?
11 *As* water disappears from the
    sea,
    And a river becomes parched
    and dries up,
12 So man lies down and does not
    rise.
    Till the heavens *are* no more,
    They will not awake
    Nor be roused from their sleep.

13 "Oh, that You would hide me in
    the grave,

13:27 ᵃLiterally *inscribe a print*   13:28 ᵃLiterally *He*   14:3 ᵃSeptuagint, Syriac, and Vulgate read *him*.

That You would conceal me
    until Your wrath is past,
That You would appoint me a
    set time, and remember me!
14 If a man dies, shall he live
    again?
    All the days of my hard service
      I will wait,
    Till my change comes.
15 You shall call, and I will
    answer You;
    You shall desire the work of
      Your hands.
16 For now You number my steps,
    But do not watch over my sin.
17 My transgression *is* sealed up
    in a bag,
    And You cover*ᵃ* my iniquity.

18 "But *as* a mountain falls *and*
    crumbles away,
    And *as* a rock is moved from
      its place;
19 *As* water wears away stones,
    And as torrents wash away the
      soil of the earth;
    So You destroy the hope of
      man.
20 You prevail forever against
    him, and he passes on;
    You change his countenance
    and send him away.
21 His sons come to honor, and he
    does not know *it;*
    They are brought low, and he
    does not perceive *it.*
22 But his flesh will be in pain
    over it,
    And his soul will mourn over
    it."

15
Then Eliphaz the Temanite answered and said:

2 "Should a wise man answer with
    empty knowledge,
    And fill himself with the east
    wind?
3 Should he reason with
    unprofitable talk,
    Or by speeches with which he
    can do no good?
4 Yes, you cast off fear,
    And restrain prayer before
    God.
5 For your iniquity teaches your
    mouth,
    And you choose the tongue of
    the crafty.

6 Your own mouth condemns
    you, and not I;
    Yes, your own lips testify
    against you.

7 "*Are* you the first man *who* was
    born?
    Or were you made before the
    hills?
8 Have you heard the counsel of
    God?
    Do you limit wisdom to
    yourself?
9 What do you know that we do
    not know?
    What do you understand that
    is not in us?
10 Both the gray-haired and the
    aged *are* among us,
    Much older than your father.
11 *Are* the consolations of God too
    small for you,
    And the word *spoken* gently*ᵃ*
    with you?
12 Why does your heart carry you
    away,
    And what do your eyes wink
    at,
13 That you turn your spirit
    against God,
    And let *such* words go out of
    your mouth?

14 "What *is* man, that he could be
    pure?
    And *he who is* born of a
    woman, that he could be
    righteous?
15 If *God* puts no trust in His
    saints,
    And the heavens are not pure
    in His sight,
16 How much less man, *who is*
    abominable and filthy,
    Who drinks iniquity like water!

17 "I will tell you, hear me;
    What I have seen I will declare,
18 What wise men have told,
    Not hiding *anything received*
    from their fathers,
19 To whom alone the land was
    given,
    And no alien passed among
    them:
20 The wicked man writhes with
    pain all *his* days,
    And the number of years is
    hidden from the oppressor.

14:17 *ᵃ*Literally *plaster over*   15:11 *ᵃ*Septuagint reads *a secret thing.*

21 Dreadful sounds *are* in his ears;
In prosperity the destroyer
comes upon him.
22 He does not believe that he will
return from darkness,
For a sword is waiting for him.
23 He wanders about for bread,
saying, 'Where *is it?*'
He knows that a day of
darkness is ready at his
hand.
24 Trouble and anguish make him
afraid;
They overpower him, like a
king ready for battle.
25 For he stretches out his hand
against God,
And acts defiantly against the
Almighty,
26 Running stubbornly against
Him
With his strong, embossed
shield.
27 "Though he has covered his face
with his fatness,
And made *his* waist heavy with
fat,
28 He dwells in desolate cities,
In houses which no one
inhabits,
Which are destined to become
ruins.
29 He will not be rich,
Nor will his wealth continue,
Nor will his possessions
overspread the earth.
30 He will not depart from
darkness;
The flame will dry out his
branches,
And by the breath of His mouth
he will go away.
31 Let him not trust in futile
things, deceiving himself,
For futility will be his reward.
32 It will be accomplished before
his time,
And his branch will not be
green.
33 He will shake off his unripe
grape like a vine,
And cast off his blossom like
an olive tree.
34 For the company of hypocrites
will be barren,
And fire will consume the tents
of bribery.
35 They conceive trouble and
bring forth futility;
Their womb prepares deceit."

16 Then Job answered and said:

2 "I have heard many such things;
Miserable comforters *are* you
all!
3 Shall words of wind have an
end?
Or what provokes you that you
answer?
4 I also could speak as you *do,*
If your soul were in my soul's
place.
I could heap up words against
you,
And shake my head at you;
5 *But* I would strengthen you
with my mouth,
And the comfort of my lips
would relieve *your grief.*

6 "Though I speak, my grief is not
relieved;
And *if* I remain silent, how am
I eased?
7 But now He has worn me out;
You have made desolate all my
company.
8 You have shriveled me up,
And it is a witness *against
me;*
My leanness rises up against
me
And bears witness to my face.
9 He tears *me* in His wrath, and
hates me;
He gnashes at me with His
teeth;
My adversary sharpens His
gaze on me.
10 They gape at me with their
mouth,
They strike me reproachfully
on the cheek,
They gather together against
me.
11 God has delivered me to the
ungodly,
And turned me over to the
hands of the wicked.
12 I was at ease, but He has
shattered me;
He also has taken *me* by my
neck, and shaken me to
pieces;
He has set me up for His target,
13 His archers surround me.
He pierces my heart[a] and does
not pity;
He pours out my gall on the
ground.

16:13 aLiterally *kidneys*

14 He breaks me with wound upon
   wound;
   He runs at me like a warrior.ᵃ

15 "I have sewn sackcloth over my
   skin,
   And laid my headᵃ in the dust.

16 My face is flushed from
   weeping,
   And on my eyelids is the
   shadow of death;

17 Although no violence is in my
   hands,
   And my prayer is pure.

18 "O earth, do not cover my blood,
   And let my cry have no resting
   place!

19 Surely even now my witness is
   in heaven,
   And my evidence is on high.

20 My friends scorn me;
   My eyes pour out tears to God.

21 Oh, that one might plead for a
   man with God,
   As a man pleads for his
   neighbor!

22 For when a few years are
   finished,
   I shall go the way of no return.

17 "My spirit is broken,
   My days are extinguished,
   The grave is ready for me.

2 Are not mockers with me?
   And does not my eye dwell on
   their provocation?

3 "Now put down a pledge for me
   with Yourself.
   Who is he who will shake
   hands with me?

4 For You have hidden their
   heart from understanding;
   Therefore You will not exalt
   them.

5 He who speaks flattery to his
   friends,
   Even the eyes of his children
   will fail.

6 "But He has made me a byword
   of the people,
   And I have become one in
   whose face men spit.

7 My eye has also grown dim
   because of sorrow,
   And all my members are like
   shadows.

8 Upright men are astonished at
   this,
   And the innocent stirs himself
   up against the hypocrite.

9 Yet the righteous will hold to
   his way,
   And he who has clean hands
   will be stronger and stronger.

10 "But please, come back again,
   all of you,ᵃ
   For I shall not find one wise
   man among you.

11 My days are past,
   My purposes are broken off,
   Even the thoughts of my heart.

12 They change the night into day;
   'The light is near,' they say, in
   the face of darkness.

13 If I wait for the grave as my
   house,
   If I make my bed in the
   darkness,

14 If I say to corruption, 'You are
   my father,'
   And to the worm, 'You are my
   mother and my sister,'

15 Where then is my hope?
   As for my hope, who can see
   it?

16 Will they go down to the gates
   of Sheol?
   Shall we have rest together in
   the dust?"

18 Then Bildad the Shuhite answered and said:

2 "How long till you put an end
   to words?
   Gain understanding, and
   afterward we will speak.

3 Why are we counted as beasts,
   And regarded as stupid in your
   sight?

4 You who tear yourself in anger,
   Shall the earth be forsaken for
   you?
   Or shall the rock be removed
   from its place?

5 "The light of the wicked indeed
   goes out,
   And the flame of his fire does
   not shine.

6 The light is dark in his tent,
   And his lamp beside him is put
   out.

16:14 ᵃVulgate reads *giant.*   16:15 ᵃLiterally *horn*   17:10 ᵃFollowing some Hebrew manuscripts,
Septuagint, Syriac, and Vulgate; Masoretic Text and Targum read *all of them.*

7 The steps of his strength are
shortened,
And his own counsel casts him
down.
8 For he is cast into a net by his
own feet,
And he walks into a snare.
9 The net takes *him* by the heel,
And a snare lays hold of him.
10 A noose *is* hidden for him on
the ground,
And a trap for him in the road.
11 Terrors frighten him on every
side,
And drive him to his feet.
12 His strength is starved,
And destruction *is* ready at his
side.
13 It devours patches of his skin;
The firstborn of death devours
his limbs.
14 He is uprooted from the shelter
of his tent,
And they parade him before the
king of terrors.
15 They dwell in his tent *who are*
none of his;
Brimstone is scattered on his
dwelling.
16 His roots are dried out below,
And his branch withers above.
17 The memory of him perishes
from the earth,
And he has no name among the
renowned.[a]
18 He is driven from light into
darkness,
And chased out of the world.
19 He has neither son nor
posterity among his people,
Nor any remaining in his
dwellings.
20 Those in the west are
astonished at his day,
As those in the east are
frightened.
21 Surely such *are* the dwellings
of the wicked,
And this *is* the place *of him* who
does not know God."

19

Then Job answered and said:

2 "How long will you torment my
soul,
And break me in pieces with
words?
3 These ten times you have
reproached me;

You are not ashamed *that* you
have wronged me.[a]
4 And if indeed I have erred,
My error remains with me.
5 If indeed you exalt *yourselves*
against me,
And plead my disgrace against
me,
6 Know then that God has
wronged me,
And has surrounded me with
His net.

7 "If I cry out concerning wrong,
I am not heard.
If I cry aloud, *there is* no
justice.
8 He has fenced up my way, so
that I cannot pass;
And He has set darkness in my
paths.
9 He has stripped me of my glory,
And taken the crown *from* my
head.
10 He breaks me down on every
side,
And I am gone;
My hope He has uprooted like
a tree.
11 He has also kindled His wrath
against me,
And He counts me as *one of* His
enemies.
12 His troops come together
And build up their road against
me;
They encamp all around my
tent.

13 "He has removed my brothers
far from me,
And my acquaintances are
completely estranged from
me.
14 My relatives have failed,
And my close friends have
forgotten me.
15 Those who dwell in my house,
and my maidservants,
Count me as a stranger;
I am an alien in their sight.
16 I call my servant, but he gives
no answer;
I beg him with my mouth.
17 My breath is offensive to my
wife,
And I am repulsive to the
children of my own body.
18 Even young children despise
me;

18:17 [a]Literally *before the outside*, meaning distinguished, famous   19:3 [a]A Jewish tradition reads *make
yourselves strange to me.*

I arise, and they speak against me.

19 All my close friends abhor me,
And those whom I love have turned against me.
20 My bone clings to my skin and to my flesh,
And I have escaped by the skin of my teeth.

21 "Have pity on me, have pity on me, O you my friends,
For the hand of God has struck me!
22 Why do you persecute me as God does,
And are not satisfied with my flesh?

23 "Oh, that my words were written!
Oh, that they were inscribed in a book!
24 That they were engraved on a rock
With an iron pen and lead, forever!
25 For I know that my Redeemer lives,
And He shall stand at last on the earth;
26 And after my skin is destroyed, this I know,
That in my flesh I shall see God,
27 Whom I shall see for myself,
And my eyes shall behold, and not another.
How my heart yearns within me!
28 If you should say, 'How shall we persecute him?'—
Since the root of the matter is found in me,
29 Be afraid of the sword for yourselves;
For wrath brings the punishment of the sword,
That you may know there is a judgment."

20 Then Zophar the Naamathite answered and said:

2 "Therefore my anxious thoughts make me answer,
Because of the turmoil within me.
3 I have heard the rebuke that reproaches me,
And the spirit of my understanding causes me to answer.

4 "Do you not know this of old,
Since man was placed on earth,
5 That the triumphing of the wicked is short,
And the joy of the hypocrite is but for a moment?
6 Though his haughtiness mounts up to the heavens,
And his head reaches to the clouds,
7 Yet he will perish forever like his own refuse;
Those who have seen him will say, 'Where is he?'
8 He will fly away like a dream, and not be found;
Yes, he will be chased away like a vision of the night.
9 The eye that saw him will see him no more,
Nor will his place behold him anymore.
10 His children will seek the favor of the poor,
And his hands will restore his wealth.
11 His bones are full of his youthful vigor,
But it will lie down with him in the dust.

12 "Though evil is sweet in his mouth,
And he hides it under his tongue,
13 Though he spares it and does not forsake it,
But still keeps it in his mouth,
14 Yet his food in his stomach turns sour;
It becomes cobra venom within him.
15 He swallows down riches
And vomits them up again;
God casts them out of his belly.
16 He will suck the poison of cobras;
The viper's tongue will slay him.
17 He will not see the streams,
The rivers flowing with honey and cream.
18 He will restore that for which he labored,
And will not swallow it down;
From the proceeds of business He will get no enjoyment.
19 For he has oppressed and forsaken the poor,
He has violently seized a house which he did not build.

20 "Because he knows no quietness
in his heart,ᵃ
He will not save anything he
desires.

21 Nothing is left for him to eat;
Therefore his well-being will
not last.

22 In his self-sufficiency he will be
in distress;
Every hand of misery will come
against him.

23 *When* he is about to fill his
stomach,
God will cast on him the fury
of His wrath,
And will rain *it* on him while
he is eating.

24 He will flee from the iron
weapon;
A bronze bow will pierce him
through.

25 It is drawn, and comes out of
the body;
Yes, the glittering *point comes*
out of his gall.
Terrors *come* upon him;

26 Total darkness *is* reserved for
his treasures.
An unfanned fire will consume
him;
It shall go ill with him who is
left in his tent.

27 The heavens will reveal his
iniquity,
And the earth will rise up
against him.

28 The increase of his house will
depart,
And his goods will flow away
in the day of His wrath.

29 This *is* the portion from God for
a wicked man,
The heritage appointed to him
by God."

21 Then Job answered and said:

2 "Listen carefully to my speech,
And let this be your
consolation.

3 Bear with me that I may speak,
And after I have spoken, keep
mocking.

4 "As for me, *is* my complaint
against man?
And if *it were,* why should I not
be impatient?

5 Look at me and be astonished;
Put *your* hand over *your* mouth.

6 Even when I remember I am
terrified,
And trembling takes hold of my
flesh.

7 Why do the wicked live *and*
become old,
Yes, become mighty in power?

8 Their descendants are
established with them in
their sight,
And their offspring before their
eyes.

9 Their houses *are* safe from fear,
Neither *is* the rod of God upon
them.

10 Their bull breeds without
failure;
Their cow calves without
miscarriage.

11 They send forth their little ones
like a flock,
And their children dance.

12 They sing to the tambourine
and harp,
And rejoice to the sound of the
flute.

13 They spend their days in
wealth,
And in a moment go down to
the grave.ᵃ

14 Yet they say to God, 'Depart
from us,
For we do not desire the
knowledge of Your ways.

15 Who *is* the Almighty, that we
should serve Him?
And what profit do we have if
we pray to Him?'

16 Indeed their prosperity *is* not in
their hand;
The counsel of the wicked is far
from me.

17 "How often is the lamp of the
wicked put out?
How often does their
destruction come upon them,
The sorrows *God* distributes in
His anger?

18 They are like straw before the
wind,
And like chaff that a storm
carries away.

19 *They say,* 'God lays up one'sᵃ
iniquity for his children';
Let Him recompense him, that
he may know *it.*

20 Let his eyes see his destruction,
And let him drink of the wrath
of the Almighty.

21 For what does he care about his
household after him,
When the number of his
months is cut in half?

22 "Can *anyone* teach God
knowledge,
Since He judges those on high?

23 One dies in his full strength,
Being wholly at ease and
secure;

24 His pails[a] are full of milk,
And the marrow of his bones
is moist.

25 Another man dies in the
bitterness of his soul,
Never having eaten with
pleasure.

26 They lie down alike in the dust,
And worms cover them.

27 "Look, I know your thoughts,
And the schemes *with which*
you would wrong me.

28 For you say,
'Where *is* the house of the
prince?
And where *is* the tent,[a]
The dwelling place of the
wicked?'

29 Have you not asked those who
travel the road?
And do you not know their
signs?

30 For the wicked are reserved for
the day of doom;
They shall be brought out on
the day of wrath.

31 Who condemns his way to his
face?
And who repays him *for what*
he has done?

32 Yet he shall be brought to the
grave,
And a vigil kept over the tomb.

33 The clods of the valley shall be
sweet to him;
Everyone shall follow him,
As countless *have gone* before
him.

34 How then can you comfort me
with empty words,
Since falsehood remains in
your answers?"

22 Then Eliphaz the Temanite answered and said:

2 "Can a man be profitable to God,

Though he who is wise may be
profitable to himself?

3 *Is it* any pleasure to the
Almighty that you are
righteous?
Or *is it* gain *to Him* that you
make your ways blameless?

4 "Is it because of your fear of Him
that He corrects you,
And enters into judgment with
you?

5 *Is* not your wickedness great,
And your iniquity without
end?

6 For you have taken pledges
from your brother for no
reason,
And stripped the naked of their
clothing.

7 You have not given the weary
water to drink,
And you have withheld bread
from the hungry.

8 But the mighty man possessed
the land,
And the honorable man dwelt
in it.

9 You have sent widows away
empty,
And the strength of the
fatherless was crushed.

10 Therefore snares *are* all around
you,
And sudden fear troubles you,

11 Or darkness *so that* you cannot
see;
And an abundance of water
covers you.

12 "Is not God in the height of
heaven?
And see the highest stars, how
lofty they are!

13 And you say, 'What does God
know?
Can He judge through the deep
darkness?

14 Thick clouds cover Him, so that
He cannot see,
And He walks above the circle
of heaven.'

15 Will you keep to the old way
Which wicked men have trod,

16 Who were cut down before
their time,
Whose foundations were swept
away by a flood?

21:24 [a]Septuagint and Vulgate read *bowels*; Syriac reads *sides*; Targum reads *breasts*. 21:28 [a]Vulgate
omits *the tent*.

17 They said to God, 'Depart from us!
What can the Almighty do to them?'[a]
18 Yet He filled their houses with good *things;*
But the counsel of the wicked is far from me.

19 "The righteous see *it* and are glad,
And the innocent laugh at them:
20 'Surely our adversaries[a] are cut down,
And the fire consumes their remnant.'

21 "Now acquaint yourself with Him, and be at peace;
Thereby good will come to you.
22 Receive, please, instruction from His mouth,
And lay up His words in your heart.
23 If you return to the Almighty, you will be built up;
You will remove iniquity far from your tents.
24 Then you will lay your gold in the dust,
And the *gold* of Ophir among the stones of the brooks.
25 Yes, the Almighty will be your gold[a]
And your precious silver;
26 For then you will have your delight in the Almighty,
And lift up your face to God.
27 You will make your prayer to Him,
He will hear you,
And you will pay your vows.
28 You will also declare a thing,
And it will be established for you;
So light will shine on your ways.
29 When they cast *you* down, and you say, 'Exaltation *will come!*'
Then He will save the humble *person.*
30 He will *even* deliver one who is not innocent;
Yes, he will be delivered by the purity of your hands."

23 Then Job answered and said:

2 "Even today my complaint is bitter;
My[a] hand is listless because of my groaning.
3 Oh, that I knew where I might find Him,
That I might come to His seat!
4 I would present *my* case before Him,
And fill my mouth with arguments.
5 I would know the words *which* He would answer me,
And understand what He would say to me.
6 Would He contend with me in His great power?
No! But He would take *note* of me.
7 There the upright could reason with Him,
And I would be delivered forever from my Judge.

8 "Look, I go forward, but He is not *there,*
And backward, but I cannot perceive Him;
9 When He works on the left hand, I cannot behold *Him;*
When He turns to the right hand, I cannot see *Him.*
10 But He knows the way that I take;
When He has tested me, I shall come forth as gold.
11 My foot has held fast to His steps;
I have kept His way and not turned aside.
12 I have not departed from the commandment of His lips;
I have treasured the words of His mouth
More than my necessary *food.*

13 "But He *is* unique, and who can make Him change?
And *whatever* His soul desires, *that* He does.
14 For He performs *what is* appointed for me,
And many such *things are* with Him.
15 Therefore I am terrified at His presence;

22:17 [a]Septuagint and Syriac read *us.*   22:20 [a]Septuagint reads *substance.*   22:25 [a]The ancient versions suggest *defense;* Hebrew reads *gold* as in verse 24.   23:2 [a]Following Masoretic Text, Targum, and Vulgate; Septuagint and Syriac read *His.*

When I consider *this*, I am
    afraid of Him.
16 For God made my heart weak,
    And the Almighty terrifies me;
17 Because I was not cut off from
    the presence of darkness,
    And He did *not* hide deep
    darkness from my face.

24 "*Since* times are not hidden
    from the Almighty,
    Why do those who know Him
    see not His days?

2 "*Some* remove landmarks;
    They seize flocks violently and
    feed *on them*;
3 They drive away the donkey of
    the fatherless;
    They take the widow's ox as a
    pledge.
4 They push the needy off the
    road;
    All the poor of the land are
    forced to hide.
5 Indeed, *like* wild donkeys in the
    desert,
    They go out to their work,
    searching for food.
    The wilderness *yields* food for
    them *and* for *their* children.
6 They gather their fodder in the
    field
    And glean in the vineyard of
    the wicked.
7 They spend the night naked,
    without clothing,
    And have no covering in the
    cold.
8 They are wet with the showers
    of the mountains,
    And huddle around the rock for
    want of shelter.

9 "*Some* snatch the fatherless
    from the breast,
    And take a pledge from the
    poor.
10 They cause *the poor* to go
    naked, without clothing;
    And they take away the
    sheaves from the hungry.
11 They press out oil within their
    walls,
    And tread winepresses, yet
    suffer thirst.
12 The dying groan in the city,
    And the souls of the wounded
    cry out;

Yet God does not charge *them*
    with wrong.

13 "There are those who rebel
    against the light;
    They do not know its ways
    Nor abide in its paths.
14 The murderer rises with the
    light;
    He kills the poor and needy;
    And in the night he is like a
    thief.
15 The eye of the adulterer waits
    for the twilight,
    Saying, 'No eye will see me';
    And he disguises *his* face.
16 In the dark they break into
    houses
    Which they marked for
    themselves in the daytime;
    They do not know the light.
17 For the morning is the same to
    them as the shadow of death;
    If *someone* recognizes *them*,
    They are in the terrors of the
    shadow of death.

18 "They *should be* swift on the
    face of the waters,
    Their portion *should be* cursed
    in the earth,
    So that no one *would* turn into
    the way of their vineyards.
19 As drought and heat consume
    the snow waters,
    So the grave*a consumes those
    who* have sinned.
20 The womb *should* forget him,
    The worm *should* feed sweetly
    on him;
    He *should* be remembered no
    more,
    And wickedness *should* be
    broken like a tree.
21 For he preys on the barren *who*
    do not bear,
    And does no good for the
    widow.

22 "But *God* draws the mighty
    away with His power;
    He rises up, but no *man* is sure
    of life.
23 He gives them security, and
    they rely *on it*;
    Yet His eyes *are* on their ways.
24 They are exalted for a little
    while,
    Then they are gone.
    They are brought low;

24:19 *Or *Sheol*

They are taken out of the way
like all *others;*
They dry out like the heads of
grain.

25 "Now if *it is* not *so,* who will
prove me a liar,
And make my speech worth
nothing?"

25 Then Bildad the Shuhite answered and said:

2 "Dominion and fear *belong* to
Him;
He makes peace in His high
places.
3 Is there any number to His
armies?
Upon whom does His light not
rise?
4 How then can man be righteous
before God?
Or how can he be pure *who is*
born of a woman?
5 If even the moon does not
shine,
And the stars are not pure in
His sight,
6 How much less man, *who is* a
maggot,
And a son of man, *who is* a
worm?"

26 But Job answered and said:

2 "How have you helped *him who
is* without power?
How have you saved the arm
that has no strength?
3 How have you counseled *one
who has* no wisdom?
And *how* have you declared
sound advice to many?
4 To whom have you uttered
words?
And whose spirit came from
you?

5 "The dead tremble,
Those under the waters and
those inhabiting them.
6 Sheol *is* naked before Him,
And Destruction has no
covering.
7 He stretches out the north over
empty space;
He hangs the earth on nothing.
8 He binds up the water in His
thick clouds,
Yet the clouds are not broken
under it.

9 He covers the face of *His*
throne,
And spreads His cloud over
it.
10 He drew a circular horizon on
the face of the waters,
At the boundary of light and
darkness.
11 The pillars of heaven tremble,
And are astonished at His
rebuke.
12 He stirs up the sea with His
power,
And by His understanding He
breaks up the storm.
13 By His Spirit He adorned the
heavens;
His hand pierced the fleeing
serpent.
14 Indeed these *are* the mere
edges of His ways,
And how small a whisper we
hear of Him!
But the thunder of His power
who can understand?"

27 Moreover Job continued his
discourse, and said:

2 "As God lives, *who* has taken
away my justice,
And the Almighty, *who* has
made my soul bitter,
3 As long as my breath *is* in
me,
And the breath of God in my
nostrils,
4 My lips will not speak
wickedness,
Nor my tongue utter deceit.
5 Far be it from me
That I should say you are right;
Till I die I will not put away my
integrity from me.
6 My righteousness I hold fast,
and will not let it go;
My heart shall not reproach *me*
as long as I live.

7 "May my enemy be like the
wicked,
And he who rises up against me
like the unrighteous.
8 For what is the hope of the
hypocrite,
Though he may gain *much,*
If God takes away his life?
9 Will God hear his cry
When trouble comes upon him?
10 Will he delight himself in the
Almighty?
Will he always call on God?

11 "I will teach you about the hand
    of God;
    What *is* with the Almighty I
      will not conceal.
12 Surely all of you have seen *it;*
    Why then do you behave with
      complete nonsense?

13 "This is the portion of a wicked
    man with God,
    And the heritage of oppressors,
      received from the Almighty:
14 If his children are multiplied, *it
    is* for the sword;
    And his offspring shall not be
      satisfied with bread.
15 Those who survive him shall be
    buried in death,
    And their*a* widows shall not
      weep,
16 Though he heaps up silver like
    dust,
    And piles up clothing like
      clay—
17 He may pile *it* up, but the just
    will wear *it,*
    And the innocent will divide
      the silver.
18 He builds his house like a
    moth,*a*
    Like a booth *which* a
      watchman makes.
19 The rich man will lie down,
    But not be gathered *up;a*
    He opens his eyes,
    And he *is* no more.
20 Terrors overtake him like a
    flood;
    A tempest steals him away in
      the night.
21 The east wind carries him
    away, and he is gone;
    It sweeps him out of his place.
22 It hurls against him and does
    not spare;
    He flees desperately from its
      power.
23 *Men* shall clap their hands at
    him,
    And shall hiss him out of his
      place.

28 "Surely there is a mine for
    silver,
    And a place *where* gold is
      refined.
2 Iron is taken from the earth,

And copper *is* smelted *from*
    ore.
3 *Man* puts an end to darkness,
    And searches every recess
    For ore in the darkness and the
      shadow of death.
4 He breaks open a shaft away
    from people;
    In places forgotten by feet
    They hang far away from men;
    They swing to and fro.
5 *As for* the earth, from it comes
    bread,
    But underneath it is turned up
      as by fire;
6 Its stones *are* the source of
    sapphires,
    And it contains gold dust.
7 *That* path no bird knows,
    Nor has the falcon's eye seen
      it.
8 The proud lions*a* have not
    trodden it,
    Nor has the fierce lion passed
      over it.
9 He puts his hand on the flint;
    He overturns the mountains at
      the roots.
10 He cuts out channels in the
    rocks,
    And his eye sees every precious
      thing.
11 He dams up the streams from
    trickling;
    What is hidden he brings forth
      to light.

12 "But where can wisdom be
    found?
    And where *is* the place of
      understanding?
13 Man does not know its value,
    Nor is it found in the land of
      the living.
14 The deep says, 'It *is* not in me';
    And the sea says, '*It is* not with
      me.'
15 It cannot be purchased for gold,
    Nor can silver be weighed *for*
      its price.
16 It cannot be valued in the gold
    of Ophir,
    In precious onyx or sapphire.
17 Neither gold nor crystal can
    equal it,
    Nor can it be exchanged for
      jewelry of fine gold.

Climb Out of Your Rut

Job, too, had to learn that it takes the power of God to release us from negative, locked-in thinking (Job 29).

Is it possible you are in a negative-thinking rut?

Aeronautical engineers in the 1920s said it was impossible to fly faster than the speed of sound, but they were wrong. Is it possible you might be placing your faith on some negative precept? What ideas are limiting your growth? What opinions are restricting you?

Ruts have a way of becoming security blankets in your second childhood. Most little children have their favorite blanket. Many of your negative, deeply ingrained opinions and well-entrenched conclusions become emotional security blankets, holding you back from

- daring to go out in business for yourself,
- or daring to go back to college,
- or daring to tackle a physical fitness program,
- or daring to learn another language.

It takes a lot of courage to make a major career change in mid-life!

It takes a lot of faith to pack up and move to a new city, state, or country.

What ruts are you in? You're free to leave that rut. A rut, you know, is a grave-- with the ends knocked out.

Come alive. Climb out of it. Tackle some exciting new possibilities today! Just make sure you are guided by God Almighty and His holy Word. Psalm 119:105 says that God's "word *is* a lamp to [your] feet and a light to [your] path"! Follow it. Get started today by accepting His challenge.

18 No mention shall be made of
   coral or quartz,
   For the price of wisdom *is*
   above rubies.
19 The topaz of Ethiopia cannot
   equal it,
   Nor can it be valued in pure
   gold.

20 "From where then does wisdom
   come?
   And where *is* the place of
   understanding?
21 It is hidden from the eyes of all
   living,
   And concealed from the birds
   of the air.
22 Destruction and Death say,
   'We have heard a report about
   it with our ears.'
23 God understands its way,
   And He knows its place.
24 For He looks to the ends of the
   earth,
   And sees under the whole
   heavens,
25 To establish a weight for the
   wind,
   And apportion the waters by
   measure.
26 When He made a law for the
   rain,
   And a path for the thunderbolt,
27 Then He saw *wisdom*[a] and
   declared it;
   He prepared it, indeed, He
   searched it out.
28 And to man He said,
   'Behold, the fear of the Lord,
   that *is* wisdom,
   And to depart from evil *is*
   understanding.' "

29 Job further continued his discourse, and said:

2 "Oh, that I were as *in* months
   past,
   As *in* the days *when* God
   watched over me;
3 When His lamp shone upon my
   head,
   And when by His light I walked
   through darkness;
4 Just as I was in the days of my
   prime,
   When the friendly counsel of
   God *was* over my tent;
5 When the Almighty *was* yet
   with me,

When my children *were* around
   me;
6 When my steps were bathed
   with cream,[a]
   And the rock poured out rivers
   of oil for me!

7 "When I went out to the gate by
   the city,
   When I took my seat in the
   open square,
8 The young men saw me and
   hid,
   And the aged arose *and* stood;
9 The princes refrained from
   talking,
   And put *their* hand on their
   mouth;
10 The voice of nobles was
   hushed,
   And their tongue stuck to the
   roof of their mouth.
11 When the ear heard, then it
   blessed me,
   And when the eye saw, then it
   approved me;
12 Because I delivered the poor
   who cried out,
   The fatherless and *the one who*
   had no helper.
13 The blessing of a perishing
   man came upon me,
   And I caused the widow's heart
   to sing for joy.
14 I put on righteousness, and it
   clothed me;
   My justice *was* like a robe and
   a turban.
15 I *was* eyes to the blind,
   And I *was* feet to the lame.
16 I *was* a father to the poor,
   And I searched out the case
   that I did not know.
17 I broke the fangs of the
   wicked,
   And plucked the victim from
   his teeth.

18 "Then I said, 'I shall die in my
   nest,
   And multiply *my* days as the
   sand.
19 My root *is* spread out to the
   waters,
   And the dew lies all night on
   my branch.
20 My glory *is* fresh within me,
   And my bow is renewed in my
   hand.'

28:27 aLiterally *it*   29:6 aMasoretic Text reads *wrath;* ancient versions and some Hebrew manuscripts
read *cream* (compare 20:17).

21 "*Men* listened to me and waited,
And kept silence for my
counsel.
22 After my words they did not
speak again,
And my speech settled on them
as dew.
23 They waited for me *as* for the
rain,
And they opened their mouth
wide *as* for the spring rain.
24 *If* I mocked at them, they did
not believe *it*,
And the light of my
countenance they did not
cast down.
25 I chose the way for them, and
sat as chief;
So I dwelt as a king in the
army,
As one *who* comforts
mourners.

30 "But now they mock at me,
men younger than I,
Whose fathers I disdained to
put with the dogs of my flock.
2 Indeed, what *profit* is the
strength of their hands to
me?
Their vigor has perished.
3 *They are* gaunt from want and
famine,
Fleeing late to the wilderness,
desolate and waste,
4 Who pluck mallow by the
bushes,
And broom tree roots *for* their
food.
5 They were driven out from
among *men*,
They shouted at them as *at* a
thief.
6 *They had* to live in the clefts of
the valleys,
In caves of the earth and the
rocks.
7 Among the bushes they brayed,
Under the nettles they nestled.
8 *They were* sons of fools,
Yes, sons of vile men;
They were scourged from the
land.

9 "And now I am their taunting
song;
Yes, I am their byword.
10 They abhor me, they keep far
from me;

They do not hesitate to spit in
my face.
11 Because He has loosed my[a]
bowstring and afflicted me,
They have cast off restraint
before me.
12 At *my* right *hand* the rabble
arises;
They push away my feet,
And they raise against me their
ways of destruction.
13 They break up my path,
They promote my calamity;
They have no helper.
14 They come as broad breakers;
Under the ruinous storm they
roll along.
15 Terrors are turned upon me;
They pursue my honor as the
wind,
And my prosperity has passed
like a cloud.

16 "And now my soul is poured out
because of my *plight*;
The days of affliction take hold
of me.
17 My bones are pierced in me at
night,
And my gnawing pains take no
rest.
18 By great force my garment is
disfigured;
It binds me about as the collar
of my coat.
19 He has cast me into the mire,
And I have become like dust
and ashes.

20 "I cry out to You, but You do
not answer me;
I stand up, and You regard me.
21 *But* You have become cruel to
me;
With the strength of Your hand
You oppose me.
22 You lift me up to the wind and
cause me to ride *on it*;
You spoil my success.
23 For I know *that* You will bring
me *to* death,
And *to* the house appointed for
all living.

24 "Surely He would not stretch out
His hand against a heap of
ruins,
If they cry out when He
destroys *it*.

30:11 aFollowing Masoretic Text, Syriac, and Targum; Septuagint and Vulgate read *His*.

25 Have I not wept for him who
      was in trouble?
    Has *not* my soul grieved for the
      poor?
26 But when I looked for good,
      evil came *to me;*
    And when I waited for light,
      then came darkness.
27 My heart is in turmoil and
      cannot rest;
    Days of affliction confront me.
28 I go about mourning, but not
      in the sun;
    I stand up in the assembly *and*
      cry out for help.
29 I am a brother of jackals,
    And a companion of ostriches.
30 My skin grows black and falls
      from me;
    My bones burn with fever.
31 My harp is *turned* to mourning,
    And my flute to the voice of
      those who weep.

31 "I have made a covenant with
      my eyes;
    Why then should I look upon
      a young woman?
2   For what *is* the allotment of
      God from above,
    And the inheritance of the
      Almighty from on high?
3   *Is* it not destruction for the
      wicked,
    And disaster for the workers of
      iniquity?
4   Does He not see my ways,
    And count all my steps?

5   "If I have walked with
      falsehood,
    Or if my foot has hastened to
      deceit,
6   Let me be weighed on honest
      scales,
    That God may know my
      integrity.
7   If my step has turned from the
      way,
    Or my heart walked after my
      eyes,
    Or if any spot adheres to my
      hands,
8   *Then* let me sow, and another
      eat;
    Yes, let my harvest be rooted
      out.

9   "If my heart has been enticed by
      a woman,

    Or *if* I have lurked at my
      neighbor's door,
10   *Then* let my wife grind for
      another,
    And let others bow down over
      her.
11   For that *would be* wickedness;
    Yes, it *would be* iniquity
      deserving of judgment.
12   For that *would be* a fire *that*
      consumes to destruction,
    And would root out all my
      increase.

13 "If I have despised the cause of
      my male or female servant
    When they complained against
      me,
14   What then shall I do when God
      rises up?
    When He punishes, how shall
      I answer Him?
15   Did not He who made me in the
      womb make them?
    Did not the same One fashion
      us in the womb?

16 "If I have kept the poor from
      their desire,
    Or caused the eyes of the
      widow to fail,
17   Or eaten my morsel by myself,
    So that the fatherless could not
      eat of it
18   (But from my youth I reared
      him as a father,
    And from my mother's womb
      I guided *the widow*[a]);
19   If I have seen anyone perish for
      lack of clothing,
    Or any poor *man* without
      covering;
20   If his heart[a] has not blessed
      me,
    And *if* he was *not* warmed with
      the fleece of my sheep;
21   If I have raised my hand
      against the fatherless,
    When I saw I had help in the
      gate;
22   *Then* let my arm fall from my
      shoulder,
    Let my arm be torn from the
      socket.
23   For destruction *from* God *is* a
      terror to me,
    And because of His
      magnificence I cannot
      endure.

31:18 [a]Literally *her* (compare verse 16)   31:20 [a]Literally *loins*

24 "If I have made gold my hope,
     Or said to fine gold, 'You are
          my confidence';
25 If I have rejoiced because my
          wealth was great,
     And because my hand had
          gained much;
26 If I have observed the sun[a]
          when it shines,
     Or the moon moving in
          brightness,
27 So that my heart has been
          secretly enticed,
     And my mouth has kissed my
          hand;
28 This also would be an iniquity
          deserving of judgment,
     For I would have denied God
          who is above.

29 "If I have rejoiced at the
          destruction of him who hated
          me,
     Or lifted myself up when evil
          found him
30 (Indeed I have not allowed my
          mouth to sin
     By asking for a curse on his
          soul);
31 If the men of my tent have not
          said,
     'Who is there that has not been
          satisfied with his meat?'
32 (But no sojourner had to lodge
          in the street,
     For I have opened my doors to
          the traveler[a]);
33 If I have covered my
          transgressions as Adam,
     By hiding my iniquity in my
          bosom,
34 Because I feared the great
          multitude,
     And dreaded the contempt of
          families,
     So that I kept silence
     And did not go out of the
          door—
35 Oh, that I had one to hear me!
     Here is my mark.
     Oh, that the Almighty would
          answer me,
     That my Prosecutor had
          written a book!
36 Surely I would carry it on my
          shoulder,
     And bind it on me like a crown;
37 I would declare to Him the
          number of my steps;

Like a prince I would approach
     Him.

38 "If my land cries out against me,
     And its furrows weep together;
39 If I have eaten its fruit[a] without
          money,
     Or caused its owners to lose
          their lives;
40 Then let thistles grow instead
          of wheat,
     And weeds instead of barley."

The words of Job are ended.

32 So these three men ceased answering Job, because he was
righteous in his own eyes. 2 Then the
wrath of Elihu, the son of Barachel
the Buzite, of the family of Ram, was
aroused against Job; his wrath was
aroused because he justified himself
rather than God. 3 Also against his
three friends his wrath was aroused,
because they had found no answer,
and yet had condemned Job.
4 Now because they were years
older than he, Elihu had waited to
speak to Job.[a] 5 When Elihu saw that
there was no answer in the mouth
of these three men, his wrath was
aroused.
6 So Elihu, the son of Barachel the
Buzite, answered and said:

     "I am young in years, and you
          are very old;
     Therefore I was afraid,
     And dared not declare my
          opinion to you.
7 I said, 'Age[a] should speak,
     And multitude of years should
          teach wisdom.'
8 But there is a spirit in man,
     And the breath of the Almighty
          gives him understanding.
9 Great men[a] are not always
          wise,
     Nor do the aged always
          understand justice.

10 "Therefore I say, 'Listen to me,
     I also will declare my opinion.'
11 Indeed I waited for your words,
     I listened to your reasonings,
          while you searched out what
          to say.
12 I paid close attention to you;

31:26 [a]Literally light   31:32 [a]Following Septuagint, Syriac, Targum, and Vulgate; Masoretic Text reads
road.   31:39 [a]Literally its strength   32:4 [a]Vulgate reads till Job had spoken.   32:7 [a]Literally Days,
that is, years   32:9 [a]Or Men of many years

And surely not one of you
   convinced Job,
Or answered his words—
13 Lest you say,
   'We have found wisdom';
   God will vanquish him, not
   man.
14 Now he has not directed *his*
   words against me;
   So I will not answer him with
   your words.

15 "They are dismayed and answer
   no more;
   Words escape them.
16 And I have waited, because
   they did not speak,
   Because they stood still *and*
   answered no more.
17 I also will answer my part,
   I too will declare my opinion.
18 For I am full of words;
   The spirit within me compels
   me.
19 Indeed my belly *is* like wine
   that has no vent;
   It is ready to burst like new
   wineskins.
20 I will speak, that I may find
   relief;
   I must open my lips and
   answer.
21 Let me not, I pray, show
   partiality to anyone;
   Nor let me flatter any man.
22 For I do not know how to
   flatter,
   Else my Maker would soon
   take me away.

33 "But please, Job, hear my
   speech,
   And listen to all my words.
2 Now, I open my mouth;
   My tongue speaks in my
   mouth.
3 My words *come* from my
   upright heart;
   My lips utter pure knowledge.
4 The Spirit of God has made me,
   And the breath of the Almighty
   gives me life.
5 If you can answer me,
   Set *your words* in order before
   me;
   Take your stand.
6 Truly I *am* as your spokesman[a]
   before God;
   I also have been formed out of
   clay.

7 Surely no fear of me will terrify
   you,
   Nor will my hand be heavy on
   you.

8 "Surely you have spoken in my
   hearing,
   And I have heard the sound of
   your words, *saying,*
9 'I *am* pure, without
   transgression;
   I *am* innocent, and *there is* no
   iniquity in me.
10 Yet He finds occasions against
   me,
   He counts me as His enemy;
11 He puts my feet in the stocks,
   He watches all my paths.'

12 "Look, *in* this you are not
   righteous.
   I will answer you,
   For God is greater than man.
13 Why do you contend with Him?
   For He does not give an
   accounting of any of His
   words.
14 For God may speak in one way,
   or in another,
   Yet man does not perceive it.
15 In a dream, in a vision of the
   night,
   When deep sleep falls upon
   men,
   While slumbering on their
   beds,
16 Then He opens the ears of men,
   And seals their instruction.
17 In order to turn man *from his*
   deed,
   And conceal pride from man,
18 He keeps back his soul from the
   Pit,
   And his life from perishing by
   the sword.

19 "*Man* is also chastened with
   pain on his bed,
   And with strong *pain* in many
   of his bones,
20 So that his life abhors bread,
   And his soul succulent food.
21 His flesh wastes away from
   sight,
   And his bones stick out *which
   once* were not seen.
22 Yes, his soul draws near the
   Pit,
   And his life to the executioners.

33:6 [a]Literally *as your mouth*

23 "If there is a messenger for him,
 A mediator, one among a
  thousand,
 To show man His uprightness,
24 Then He is gracious to him, and
  says,
 'Deliver him from going down
  to the Pit;
 I have found a ransom';
25 His flesh shall be young like a
  child's,
 He shall return to the days of
  his youth.
26 He shall pray to God, and He
  will delight in him,
 He shall see His face with joy,
 For He restores to man His
  righteousness.
27 Then he looks at men and says,
 'I have sinned, and perverted
  what was right,
 And it did not profit me.'
28 He will redeem his^a soul from
  going down to the Pit,
 And his^b life shall see the light.

29 "Behold, God works all these
  things,
 Twice, in fact, three times with
  a man,
30 To bring back his soul from the
  Pit,
 That he may be enlightened
  with the light of life.

31 "Give ear, Job, listen to me;
 Hold your peace, and I will
  speak.
32 If you have anything to say,
  answer me;
 Speak, for I desire to justify
  you.
33 If not, listen to me;
 Hold your peace, and I will
  teach you wisdom."

34 Elihu further answered and
  said:

2 "Hear my words, you wise men;
 Give ear to me, you who have
  knowledge.
3 For the ear tests words
 As the palate tastes food.
4 Let us choose justice for
  ourselves;
 Let us know among ourselves
  what is good.

5 "For Job has said, 'I am
  righteous,

But God has taken away my
 justice;
6 Should I lie concerning my
  right?
 My wound is incurable, though
  I am without transgression.'
7 What man is like Job,
 Who drinks scorn like water,
8 Who goes in company with the
  workers of iniquity,
 And walks with wicked men?
9 For he has said, 'It profits a
  man nothing
 That he should delight in God.'

10 "Therefore listen to me, you men
  of understanding:
 Far be it from God to do
  wickedness,
 And from the Almighty to
  commit iniquity.
11 For He repays man according
  to his work,
 And makes man to find a
  reward according to his way.
12 Surely God will never do
  wickedly,
 Nor will the Almighty pervert
  justice.
13 Who gave Him charge over the
  earth?
 Or who appointed Him over the
  whole world?
14 If He should set His heart on
  it,
 If He should gather to Himself
  His Spirit and His breath,
15 All flesh would perish together,
 And man would return to dust.

16 "If you have understanding,
  hear this;
 Listen to the sound of my
  words:
17 Should one who hates justice
  govern?
 Will you condemn Him who is
  most just?
18 Is it fitting to say to a king,
  'You are worthless,'
 And to nobles, 'You are
  wicked'?
19 Yet He is not partial to princes,
 Nor does He regard the rich
  more than the poor;
 For they are all the work of His
  hands.
20 In a moment they die, in the
  middle of the night;

33:28 ^aOr my (Kethib)   ^bOr my (Kethib)

The people are shaken and
    pass away;
The mighty are taken away
    without a hand.

21 "For His eyes *are* on the ways
    of man,
And He sees all his steps.
22 There is no darkness nor
    shadow of death
Where the workers of iniquity
    may hide themselves.
23 For He need not further
    consider a man,
That he should go before God
    in judgment.
24 He breaks in pieces mighty
    men without inquiry,
And sets others in their place.
25 Therefore He knows their
    works;
He overthrows *them* in the
    night,
And they are crushed.
26 He strikes them as wicked *men*
In the open sight of others,
27 Because they turned back from
    Him,
And would not consider any of
    His ways,
28 So that they caused the cry of
    the poor to come to Him;
For He hears the cry of the
    afflicted.
29 When He gives quietness, who
    then can make trouble?
And when He hides *His* face,
    who then can see Him,
Whether *it is* against a nation
    or a man alone?—
30 That the hypocrite should not
    reign,
Lest the people be ensnared.

31 "For has *anyone* said to God,
    'I have borne *chastening*;
I will offend no more;
32 Teach me *what* I do not see;
If I have done iniquity, I will
    do no more'?
33 Should He repay *it* according
    to your *terms*,
Just because you disavow it?
You must choose, and not I;
Therefore speak what you
    know.

34 "Men of understanding say to
    me,
Wise men who listen to me:
35 'Job speaks without knowledge,
His words *are* without wisdom.'

36 Oh, that Job were tried to the
    utmost,
Because *his* answers *are like*
    those of wicked men!
37 For he adds rebellion to his sin;
He claps *his hands* among us,
And multiplies his words
    against God."

35 Moreover Elihu answered and
    said:

2 "Do you think this is right?
Do you say,
    'My righteousness is more than
        God's'?
3 For you say,
    'What advantage will it be to
        You?
What profit shall I have, more
    than *if* I had sinned?'

4 "I will answer you,
And your companions with
    you.
5 Look to the heavens and see;
And behold the clouds—
They are higher than you.
6 If you sin, what do you
    accomplish against Him?
Or, *if* your transgressions are
    multiplied, what do you do to
        Him?
7 If you are righteous, what do
    you give Him?
Or what does He receive from
    your hand?
8 Your wickedness affects a man
    such as you,
And your righteousness a son
    of man.

9 "Because of the multitude of
    oppressions they cry out;
They cry out for help because
    of the arm of the mighty.
10 But no one says, 'Where *is* God
    my Maker,
Who gives songs in the night,
11 Who teaches us more than the
    beasts of the earth,
And makes us wiser than the
    birds of heaven?'
12 There they cry out, but He does
    not answer,
Because of the pride of evil
    men.
13 Surely God will not listen to
    empty *talk*,
Nor will the Almighty regard it.
14 Although you say you do not
    see Him,

Yet justice *is* before Him, and
you must wait for Him.
15 And now, because He has not
punished in His anger,
Nor taken much notice of folly,
16 Therefore Job opens his mouth
in vain;
He multiplies words without
knowledge."

36

Elihu also proceeded and said:

2 "Bear with me a little, and I will
show you
That *there are* yet words to
speak on God's behalf.
3 I will fetch my knowledge from
afar;
I will ascribe righteousness to
my Maker.
4 For truly my words *are* not
false;
One who is perfect in
knowledge *is* with you.

5 "Behold, God *is* mighty, but
despises *no one*;
He *is* mighty in strength of
understanding.
6 He does not preserve the life of
the wicked,
But gives justice to the
oppressed.
7 He does not withdraw His eyes
from the righteous;
But *they are* on the throne with
kings,
For He has seated them
forever,
And they are exalted.
8 And if *they are* bound in
fetters,
Held in the cords of affliction,
9 Then He tells them their work
and their transgressions—
That they have acted defiantly.
10 He also opens their ear to
instruction,
And commands that they turn
from iniquity.
11 If they obey and serve *Him*,
They shall spend their days in
prosperity,
And their years in pleasures.
12 But if they do not obey,
They shall perish by the sword,
And they shall die without
knowledge.[a]

13 "But the hypocrites in heart
store up wrath;
They do not cry for help when
He binds them.
14 They die in youth,
And their life *ends* among the
perverted persons.[a]
15 He delivers the poor in their
affliction,
And opens their ears in
oppression.

16 "Indeed He would have brought
you out of dire distress,
Into a broad place where *there
is* no restraint;
And what is set on your table
would be full of richness.
17 But you are filled with the
judgment due the wicked;
Judgment and justice take hold
of you.
18 Because *there is* wrath, *beware*
lest He take you away with
one blow;
For a large ransom would not
help you avoid *it*.
19 Will your riches,
Or all the mighty forces,
Keep you from distress?
20 Do not desire the night,
When people are cut off in their
place.
21 Take heed, do not turn to
iniquity,
For you have chosen this rather
than affliction.

22 "Behold, God is exalted by His
power;
Who teaches like Him?
23 Who has assigned Him His
way,
Or who has said, 'You have
done wrong'?

24 "Remember to magnify His
work,
Of which men have sung.
25 Everyone has seen it;
Man looks on *it* from afar.

26 "Behold, God *is* great, and we
do not know *Him*;
Nor can the number of His
years *be* discovered.
27 For He draws up drops of
water,

36:12 [a]Masoretic Text reads *as one without knowledge.*
practicing sodomy and prostitution in religious rituals   36:14 [a]Hebrew *qedeshim*, that is, those

Which distill as rain from the mist,
28 Which the clouds drop down
   And pour abundantly on man.
29 Indeed, can *anyone* understand
   the spreading of clouds,
   The thunder from His canopy?
30 Look, He scatters His light
   upon it,
   And covers the depths of the
   sea.
31 For by these He judges the
   peoples;
   He gives food in abundance.
32 He covers *His* hands with
   lightning,
   And commands it to strike.
33 His thunder declares it,
   The cattle also, concerning the
   rising *storm.*

37 "At this also my heart trembles,
   And leaps from its place.
2 Hear attentively the thunder of
   His voice,
   And the rumbling *that* comes
   from His mouth.
3 He sends it forth under the
   whole heaven,
   His lightning to the ends of the
   earth.
4 After it a voice roars;
   He thunders with His majestic
   voice,
   And He does not restrain them
   when His voice is heard.
5 God thunders marvelously with
   His voice;
   He does great things which we
   cannot comprehend.
6 For He says to the snow, 'Fall
   on the earth';
   Likewise to the gentle rain and
   the heavy rain of His
   strength.
7 He seals the hand of every man,
   That all men may know His
   work.
8 The beasts go into dens,
   And remain in their lairs.
9 From the chamber *of the south*
   comes the whirlwind,
   And cold from the scattering
   winds *of the north.*
10 By the breath of God ice is
   given,
   And the broad waters are
   frozen.
11 Also with moisture He
   saturates the thick clouds;

He scatters His bright clouds.
12 And they swirl about, being
   turned by His guidance,
   That they may do whatever He
   commands them
   On the face of the whole earth.[a]
13 He causes it to come,
   Whether for correction,
   Or for His land,
   Or for mercy.
14 "Listen to this, O Job;
   Stand still and consider the
   wondrous works of God.
15 Do you know when God
   dispatches them,
   And causes the light of His
   cloud to shine?
16 Do you know how the clouds
   are balanced,
   Those wondrous works of Him
   who is perfect in knowledge?
17 Why *are* your garments hot,
   When He quiets the earth by
   the south *wind?*
18 With Him, have you spread out
   the skies,
   Strong as a cast metal mirror?
19 "Teach us what we should say
   to Him,
   For we can prepare nothing
   because of the darkness.
20 Should He be told that I *wish*
   to speak?
   If a man were to speak, surely
   he would be swallowed up.
21 Even now *men* cannot look at
   the light *when it is* bright in
   the skies,
   When the wind has passed and
   cleared them.
22 He comes from the north *as*
   golden *splendor;*
   With God *is* awesome majesty.
23 *As for* the Almighty, we cannot
   find Him;
   He is excellent in power,
   In judgment and abundant
   justice;
   He does not oppress.
24 Therefore men fear Him;
   He shows no partiality to any
   who are wise of heart."

38 Then the Lord answered Job
   out of the whirlwind, and said:

2 "Who *is* this who darkens
   counsel

37:12 [a]Literally *the world of the earth*

By words without knowledge?
3 Now prepare yourself like a
    man;
    I will question you, and you
    shall answer Me.

4 "Where were you when I laid the
    foundations of the earth?
    Tell *Me*, if you have
    understanding.
5 Who determined its
    measurements?
    Surely you know!
    Or who stretched the line upon
    it?
6 To what were its foundations
    fastened?
    Or who laid its cornerstone,
7 When the morning stars sang
    together,
    And all the sons of God shouted
    for joy?

8 "Or *who* shut in the sea with
    doors,
    When it burst forth *and* issued
    from the womb;
9 When I made the clouds its
    garment,
    And thick darkness its
    swaddling band;
10 When I fixed My limit for it,
    And set bars and doors;
11 When I said,
    'This far you may come, but no
    farther,
    And here your proud waves
    must stop!'

12 "Have you commanded the
    morning since your days
    began,
    And caused the dawn to know
    its place,
13 That it might take hold of the
    ends of the earth,
    And the wicked be shaken out
    of it?
14 It takes on form like clay *under*
    a seal,
    And stands out like a garment.
15 From the wicked their light is
    withheld,
    And the upraised arm is
    broken.

16 "Have you entered the springs
    of the sea?
    Or have you walked in search
    of the depths?

17 Have the gates of death been
    revealed to you?
    Or have you seen the doors of
    the shadow of death?
18 Have you comprehended the
    breadth of the earth?
    Tell *Me*, if you know all this.

19 "Where *is* the way *to* the
    dwelling of light?
    And darkness, where *is* its
    place,
20 That you may take it to its
    territory,
    That you may know the paths
    to its home?
21 Do you know *it*, because you
    were born then,
    Or *because* the number of your
    days *is* great?

22 "Have you entered the treasury
    of snow,
    Or have you seen the treasury
    of hail,
23 Which I have reserved for the
    time of trouble,
    For the day of battle and war?
24 By what way is light diffused,
    Or the east wind scattered over
    the earth?

25 "Who has divided a channel for
    the overflowing *water,*
    Or a path for the thunderbolt,
26 To cause it to rain on a land
    where there is no one,
    A wilderness in which *there is*
    no man;
27 To satisfy the desolate waste,
    And cause to spring forth the
    growth of tender grass?
28 Has the rain a father?
    Or who has begotten the drops
    of dew?
29 From whose womb comes the
    ice?
    And the frost of heaven, who
    gives it birth?
30 The waters harden like stone,
    And the surface of the deep is
    frozen.

31 "Can you bind the cluster of the
    Pleiades,
    Or loose the belt of Orion?
32 Can you bring out Mazzaroth[a]
    in its season?
    Or can you guide the Great
    Bear with its cubs?

38:32 aLiterally *Constellations*

33 Do you know the ordinances of
    the heavens?
    Can you set their dominion
    over the earth?

34 "Can you lift up your voice to
    the clouds,
    That an abundance of water
    may cover you?
35 Can you send out lightnings,
    that they may go,
    And say to you, 'Here we *are!*'?
36 Who has put wisdom in the
    mind?[a]
    Or who has given
    understanding to the heart?
37 Who can number the clouds by
    wisdom?
    Or who can pour out the bottles
    of heaven,
38 When the dust hardens in
    clumps,
    And the clods cling together?

39 "Can you hunt the prey for the
    lion,
    Or satisfy the appetite of the
    young lions,
40 When they crouch in *their*
    dens,
    Or lurk in their lairs to lie in
    wait?
41 Who provides food for the
    raven,
    When its young ones cry to
    God,
    And wander about for lack of
    food?

39 "Do you know the time when the
    wild mountain goats bear
    young?
    Or can you mark when the deer
    gives birth?
2 Can you number the months
    that they fulfill?
    Or do you know the time when
    they bear young?
3 They bow down,
    They bring forth their young,
    They deliver their offspring.[a]
4 Their young ones are healthy,
    They grow strong with grain;
    They depart and do not return
    to them.

5 "Who set the wild donkey free?
    Who loosed the bonds of the
    onager,
6 Whose home I have made the
    wilderness,

    And the barren land his
    dwelling?
7 He scorns the tumult of the city;
    He does not heed the shouts of
    the driver.
8 The range of the mountains *is*
    his pasture,
    And he searches after every
    green thing.

9 "Will the wild ox be willing to
    serve you?
    Will he bed by your manger?
10 Can you bind the wild ox in the
    furrow with ropes?
    Or will he plow the valleys
    behind you?
11 Will you trust him because his
    strength *is* great?
    Or will you leave your labor to
    him?
12 Will you trust him to bring
    home your grain,
    And gather it to your threshing
    floor?

13 "The wings of the ostrich wave
    proudly,
    But are her wings and pinions
    like the kindly stork's?
14 For she leaves her eggs on the
    ground,
    And warms them in the dust;
15 She forgets that a foot may
    crush them,
    Or that a wild beast may break
    them.
16 She treats her young harshly,
    as though *they were* not hers;
    Her labor is in vain, without
    concern,
17 Because God deprived her of
    wisdom,
    And did not endow her with
    understanding.
18 When she lifts herself on high,
    She scorns the horse and its
    rider.

19 "Have you given the horse
    strength?
    Have you clothed his neck with
    thunder?[a]
20 Can you frighten him like a
    locust?
    His majestic snorting strikes
    terror.
21 He paws in the valley, and
    rejoices in *his* strength;

38:36 [a]Literally *inward parts*   39:3 [a]Literally *pangs,* figurative of offspring   39:19 [a]Or *a mane*

He gallops into the clash of
arms.
22 He mocks at fear, and is not
frightened;
Nor does he turn back from the
sword.
23 The quiver rattles against him,
The glittering spear and
javelin.
24 He devours the distance with
fierceness and rage;
Nor does he come to a halt
because the trumpet *has*
sounded.
25 At *the blast of* the trumpet he
says, 'Aha!'
He smells the battle from afar,
The thunder of captains and
shouting.

26 "Does the hawk fly by your
wisdom,
And spread its wings toward
the south?
27 Does the eagle mount up at
your command,
And make its nest on high?
28 On the rock it dwells and
resides,
On the crag of the rock and the
stronghold.
29 From there it spies out the prey;
Its eyes observe from afar.
30 Its young ones suck up blood;
And where the slain *are,* there
it *is.*"

40 Moreover the LORD answered
Job, and said:

2 "Shall the one who contends
with the Almighty correct
Him?
He who rebukes God, let him
answer it."

3 Then Job answered the LORD and
said:

4 "Behold, I am vile;
What shall I answer You?
I lay my hand over my mouth.
5 Once I have spoken, but I will
not answer;
Yes, twice, but I will proceed
no further."

6 Then the LORD answered Job out
of the whirlwind, and said:

7 "Now prepare yourself like a
man;
I will question you, and you
shall answer Me:

8 "Would you indeed annul My
judgment?
Would you condemn Me that
you may be justified?
9 Have you an arm like God?
Or can you thunder with a
voice like His?
10 Then adorn yourself *with*
majesty and splendor,
And array yourself with glory
and beauty.
11 Disperse the rage of your
wrath;
Look on everyone *who is*
proud, and humble him.
12 Look on everyone *who is*
proud, *and* bring him low;
Tread down the wicked in their
place.
13 Hide them in the dust together,
Bind their faces in hidden
darkness.
14 Then I will also confess to you
That your own right hand can
save you.

15 "Look now at the behemoth,[a]
which I made *along* with you;
He eats grass like an ox.
16 See now, his strength *is* in his
hips,
And his power *is* in his stomach
muscles.
17 He moves his tail like a cedar;
The sinews of his thighs are
tightly knit.
18 His bones *are like* beams of
bronze,
His ribs like bars of iron.
19 He *is* the first of the ways of
God;
Only He who made him can
bring near His sword.
20 Surely the mountains yield
food for him,
And all the beasts of the field
play there.
21 He lies under the lotus trees,
In a covert of reeds and marsh.
22 The lotus trees cover him *with*
their shade;
The willows by the brook
surround him.
23 Indeed the river may rage,
Yet he is not disturbed;

40:15 [a]A large animal, exact identity unknown

He is confident, though the
   Jordan gushes into his
   mouth.
24 *Though* he takes it in his eyes,
   Or one pierces *his* nose with a
   snare.

41 "Can you draw out Leviathan[a]
   with a hook,
   Or *snare* his tongue with a line
   which you lower?
2 Can you put a reed through his
   nose,
   Or pierce his jaw with a hook?
3 Will he make many
   supplications to you?
   Will he speak softly to you?
4 Will he make a covenant with
   you?
   Will you take him as a servant
   forever?
5 Will you play with him as *with*
   a bird,
   Or will you leash him for your
   maidens?
6 Will *your* companions make a
   banquet[a] of him?
   Will they apportion him among
   the merchants?
7 Can you fill his skin with
   harpoons,
   Or his head with fishing
   spears?
8 Lay your hand on him;
   Remember the battle—
   Never do it again!
9 Indeed, *any* hope of
   overcoming him is false;
   Shall *one not* be overwhelmed
   at the sight of him?
10 No one *is so* fierce that he
   would dare stir him up.
   Who then is able to stand
   against Me?
11 Who has preceded Me, that I
   should pay *him*?
   Everything under heaven is
   Mine.

12 "I will not conceal[a] his limbs,
   His mighty power, or his
   graceful proportions.
13 Who can remove his outer
   coat?
   Who can approach *him* with a
   double bridle?
14 Who can open the doors of his
   face,
   With his terrible teeth all
   around?

15 *His* rows of scales are *his* pride,
   Shut up tightly *as with* a seal;
16 One is so near another
   That no air can come between
   them;
17 They are joined one to another,
   They stick together and cannot
   be parted.
18 His sneezings flash forth light,
   And his eyes *are* like the
   eyelids of the morning.
19 Out of his mouth go burning
   lights;
   Sparks of fire shoot out.
20 Smoke goes out of his nostrils,
   As *from* a boiling pot and
   burning rushes.
21 His breath kindles coals,
   And a flame goes out of his
   mouth.
22 Strength dwells in his neck,
   And sorrow dances before him.
23 The folds of his flesh are joined
   together;
   They are firm on him and
   cannot be moved.
24 His heart is as hard as stone,
   Even as hard as the lower
   millstone.
25 When he raises himself up, the
   mighty are afraid;
   Because of his crashings they
   are beside[a] themselves.
26 *Though* the sword reaches him,
   it cannot avail;
   Nor does spear, dart, or javelin.
27 He regards iron as straw,
   And bronze as rotten wood.
28 The arrow cannot make him
   flee;
   Slingstones become like
   stubble to him.
29 Darts are regarded as straw;
   He laughs at the threat of
   javelins.
30 His undersides *are* like sharp
   potsherds;
   He spreads pointed *marks* in
   the mire.
31 He makes the deep boil like a
   pot;
   He makes the sea like a pot of
   ointment.
32 He leaves a shining wake
   behind him;
   One would think the deep had
   white hair.
33 On earth there is nothing like
   him,

41:1 [a]A large sea creature, exact identity unknown
silent about   41:25 [a]Or *purify themselves*   41:6 [a]Or *bargain over him*   41:12 [a]Literally *keep*

You Can Rise from the Ashes

There are seasons of the soul, as Job could well attest. Just as winter is not the time to cut a tree because a tree that looks dead may have more life in it than you think, a dark time in your life is not the right time to make a decision.

Never set your goals when you are at a low ebb. Believe that springtime will come, and be encouraged by the words of Job 42.

Remember that this depressing season will pass and that positive feelings will return to you. You will come back again.

Yes, your faith will pluck you from the ashes and new life will come from the places that felt dead. Your youthful enthusiasm will return.

Burned out? Take a break. Refuel. Seek a retreat. Find renewal. Replenish. Rest. You can go on again!

Never make a move from weakness. Always move from strength.

And the spring will turn to summer and the summer to harvest time!

You will reap simply because you didn't give up!

Which is made without fear.
34 He beholds every high *thing;*
He *is* king over all the children
of pride."

42 Then Job answered the LORD and said:

2 "I know that You can do
everything,
And that no purpose *of Yours*
can be withheld from You.
3 *You asked,* 'Who *is* this who
hides counsel without
knowledge?'
Therefore I have uttered what
I did not understand,
Things too wonderful for me,
which I did not know.
4 Listen, please, and let me
speak;
You said, 'I will question you,
and you shall answer Me.'

5 "I have heard of You by the
hearing of the ear,
But now my eye sees You.
6 Therefore I abhor *myself,*
And repent in dust and ashes."

7 And so it was, after the LORD had
spoken these words to Job, that the
LORD said to Eliphaz the Temanite,
"My wrath is aroused against you
and your two friends, for you have
not spoken of Me *what is* right, as
My servant Job *has.* 8 Now therefore,
take for yourselves seven bulls and
seven rams, go to My servant Job,
and offer up for yourselves a burnt
offering; and My servant Job shall
pray for you. For I will accept him,
lest I deal with you *according to your*
folly; because you have not spoken
of Me *what is* right, as My servant
Job *has.*"
9 So Eliphaz the Temanite and Bildad the Shuhite *and* Zophar the
Naamathite went and did as the LORD
commanded them; for the LORD had
accepted Job. 10 And the LORD restored Job's losses[a] when he prayed
for his friends. Indeed the LORD gave
Job twice as much as he had before.
11 Then all his brothers, all his sisters, and all those who had been his
acquaintances before, came to him
and ate food with him in his house;
and they consoled him and comforted him for all the adversity that
the LORD had brought upon him.
Each one gave him a piece of silver
and each a ring of gold.
12 Now the LORD blessed the latter
days of Job more than his beginning;
for he had fourteen thousand sheep,
six thousand camels, one thousand
yoke of oxen, and one thousand female donkeys. 13 He also had seven
sons and three daughters. 14 And he
called the name of the first Jemimah,
the name of the second Keziah, and
the name of the third Keren-Hap-
puch. 15 In all the land were found
no women *so* beautiful as the daughters of Job; and their father gave
them an inheritance among their
brothers.
16 After this Job lived one hundred
and forty years, and saw his children
and grandchildren *for* four generations. 17 So Job died, old and full of
days.

42:10 aLiterally *Job's captivity,* that is, what was captured from Job

Psalms

Overview of Psalms

*P*raise! The very word invokes worship and thanksgiving to God. This is the purpose and response of the psalms, for the Hebrew title of the book means "praise."

Most of the psalms of praise were written by David, Moses, and other Israelite leaders between 1450 and 400 B.C. They are the heartfelt prayers of the nation's most devoted and committed men. The psalms reflect all aspects of life, extolling God for His creation, praising Him for His blessings, and enlisting His help in times of turmoil and distress. Many of these psalms were originally to be accompanied by the trumpet, harp, or flute.

David and the other authors were able to look around them and find reasons to praise God despite their circumstances. They saw God at work during times of feasting in Israel, as well as during the captivity in Babylon. Whether in prosperity or in need, the psalmist focused his eyes on God, not on his situation.

It is believed that David wrote many of the psalms at a small spring in the wilderness adjacent to the Dead Sea known as En Gedi. Here, near the beautiful waterfalls and lush gardens, David compared God's care for His people to the life-giving spring in the wilderness.

When fleeing from his enemies, David wrote that God made his feet like those of an antelope-like deer, who scaled cliffs with ease.

> *He makes my feet like the* feet *of deer,*
> *And sets me on my high places.*
> (Ps. 18:33)

God sheltered the psalmist from his problems by hiding him under the rocky overhangs. David wrote:

> If *I take the wings of the morning,*
> *And dwell in the uttermost parts of the sea,*
> *Even there Your hand shall lead me,*

And Your right hand shall hold me.
(Ps. 139:9, 10)

These words of praise can be our own as we worship and reflect on what God has done in our lives. How appropriate it is that the final recorded psalm is one of continual praise. When we face stress and tough times, let us praise God anyway!

Jesus in Psalms

Many of the psalms specifically anticipated the life and ministry of Jesus, the One who came centuries later as the promised Messiah ("Anointed One"). There are five different types of messianic psalms: *typical messianic,* in which the subject of the psalm is in some respects a type of Jesus; *typical prophetic,* in which the psalmist describes his present experience in language which points beyond his own life to the life of Jesus; *indirectly messianic,* in which the psalmist refers to a king or to the house of David in general, but the words are ultimately fulfilled in Jesus; *purely prophetic,* which refer only to Jesus and not to any other son of David; and *enthronement,* in which the psalmist anticipates the coming of Yahweh and the consummation of His kingdom, which will be fulfilled in Jesus.

Keys to Psalms

Key Word: Worship. The central theme of the Book of Psalms is worship—God is worthy of all praise because of who He is, what He has done, and what He will do. His goodness extends through all time and eternity. The psalms present personal responses to God as they reflect on His program for His people. Many of the psalms survey the Word of God and the attributes of God, especially during difficult times. This kind of faith produces confidence in His power in spite of circumstances.

Key Verses: "Let the words of my mouth and the meditation of my heart be acceptable in Your sight, O LORD, my strength and my Redeemer" (19:14).

"My mouth shall speak the praise of the LORD, and all flesh shall bless His holy name forever and ever" (145:21).

Key Chapter: Psalm 100. So many of the favorite chapters of the Bible are contained in the Book of Psalms that it is difficult to select the key chapter among them. The two central themes of worship and praise, however, are beautifully wed in Psalm 100.

Book One   Psalms 1–41

PSALM 1

1 Blessed *is* the man
Who walks not in the counsel of
the ungodly,
Nor stands in the path of
sinners,
Nor sits in the seat of the
scornful;
2 But his delight *is* in the law of
the LORD,
And in His law he meditates
day and night.
3 He shall be like a tree
Planted by the rivers of water,
That brings forth its fruit in its
season,
Whose leaf also shall not
wither;
And whatever he does shall
prosper.

4 The ungodly *are* not so,
But *are* like the chaff which the
wind drives away.
5 Therefore the ungodly shall not
stand in the judgment,
Nor sinners in the congregation
of the righteous.

6 For the LORD knows the way of
the righteous,
But the way of the ungodly shall
perish.

PSALM 2

1 Why do the nations rage,
And the people plot a vain thing?
2 The kings of the earth set
themselves,
And the rulers take counsel
together,
Against the LORD and against His
Anointed, *saying,*
3 "Let us break Their bonds in
pieces
And cast away Their cords from
us."

4 He who sits in the heavens shall
laugh;

The LORD shall hold them in
derision.
5 Then He shall speak to them in
His wrath,
And distress them in His deep
displeasure:
6 "Yet I have set My King
On My holy hill of Zion."

7 "I will declare the decree:
The LORD has said to Me,
'You *are* My Son,
Today I have begotten You.
8 Ask of Me, and I will give *You*
The nations *for* Your inheritance,
And the ends of the earth *for*
Your possession.
9 You shall break*a* them with a rod
of iron;
You shall dash them to pieces
like a potter's vessel.' "

10 Now therefore, be wise, O kings;
Be instructed, you judges of the
earth.
11 Serve the LORD with fear,
And rejoice with trembling.
12 Kiss the Son,*a* lest He*b* be angry,
And you perish *in* the way,
When His wrath is kindled but a
little.
Blessed *are* all those who put
their trust in Him.

PSALM 3

A Psalm of David when he fled from Absalom
his son.

1 LORD, how they have increased
who trouble me!
Many *are* they who rise up
against me.
2 Many *are* they who say of me,
"There is no help for him in God."
Selah

3 But You, O LORD, *are* a shield for
me,
My glory and the One who lifts
up my head.
4 I cried to the LORD with my voice,
And He heard me from His holy
hill.   Selah

2:9 *a*Following Masoretic Text and Targum; Septuagint, Syriac, and Vulgate read *rule* (compare Revelation
2:27).   2:12 *a*Septuagint and Vulgate read *Embrace discipline;* Targum reads *Receive instruction.*
*b*Septuagint reads *the LORD.*

5 I lay down and slept;
   I awoke, for the LORD sustained
   me.
6 I will not be afraid of ten
   thousands of people
   Who have set *themselves* against
   me all around.

7 Arise, O LORD;
   Save me, O my God!
   For You have struck all my
   enemies on the cheekbone;
   You have broken the teeth of the
   ungodly.
8 Salvation *belongs* to the LORD.
   Your blessing *is* upon Your
   people.   Selah

PSALM 4

To the Chief Musician. With stringed
instruments. A Psalm of David.

1 Hear me when I call, O God of
   my righteousness!
   You have relieved me in *my*
   distress;
   Have mercy on me, and hear my
   prayer.

2 How long, O you sons of men,
   Will you turn my glory to shame?
   How long will you love
   worthlessness
   And seek falsehood?   Selah
3 But know that the LORD has set
   apart*a* for Himself him who is
   godly;
   The LORD will hear when I call
   to Him.

4 Be angry, and do not sin.
   Meditate within your heart on
   your bed, and be still.   Selah
5 Offer the sacrifices of
   righteousness,
   And put your trust in the LORD.

6 *There are* many who say,
   "Who will show us *any* good?"
   LORD, lift up the light of Your
   countenance upon us.
7 You have put gladness in my
   heart,
   More than in the season that their
   grain and wine increased.
8 I will both lie down in peace, and
   sleep;
   For You alone, O LORD, make me
   dwell in safety.

PSALM 5

To the Chief Musician. With flutes.*a* A Psalm of
David.

1 Give ear to my words, O LORD,
   Consider my meditation.
2 Give heed to the voice of my cry,
   My King and my God,
   For to You I will pray.
3 My voice You shall hear in the
   morning, O LORD;
   In the morning I will direct *it* to
   You,
   And I will look up.

4 For You *are* not a God who takes
   pleasure in wickedness,
   Nor shall evil dwell with You.
5 The boastful shall not stand in
   Your sight;
   You hate all workers of iniquity.
6 You shall destroy those who
   speak falsehood;
   The LORD abhors the bloodthirsty
   and deceitful man.

7 But as for me, I will come into
   Your house in the multitude of
   Your mercy;
   In fear of You I will worship
   toward Your holy temple.
8 Lead me, O LORD, in Your
   righteousness because of my
   enemies;
   Make Your way straight before
   my face.

9 For *there is* no faithfulness in
   their mouth;
   Their inward part *is* destruction;
   Their throat *is* an open tomb;
   They flatter with their tongue.
10 Pronounce them guilty, O God!
   Let them fall by their own
   counsels;
   Cast them out in the multitude of
   their transgressions,
   For they have rebelled against
   You.

11 But let all those rejoice who put
   their trust in You;
   Let them ever shout for joy,
   because You defend them;
   Let those also who love Your
   name
   Be joyful in You.
12 For You, O LORD, will bless the
   righteous;

4:3 *a*Many Hebrew manuscripts, Septuagint, Targum, and Vulgate read *made wonderful.*   5:title *a*Hebrew
nehiloth

With favor You will surround
him as *with* a shield.

PSALM 6

To the Chief Musician. With stringed
instruments. On an eight-stringed harp.*a* A
Psalm of David.

1 O LORD, do not rebuke me in
Your anger,
Nor chasten me in Your hot
displeasure.
2 Have mercy on me, O LORD, for
I *am* weak;
O LORD, heal me, for my bones
are troubled.
3 My soul also is greatly troubled;
But You, O LORD—how long?

4 Return, O LORD, deliver me!
Oh, save me for Your mercies'
sake!
5 For in death *there is* no
remembrance of You;
In the grave who will give You
thanks?

6 I am weary with my groaning;
All night I make my bed swim;
I drench my couch with my tears.
7 My eye wastes away because of
grief;
It grows old because of all my
enemies.

8 Depart from me, all you workers
of iniquity;
For the LORD has heard the voice
of my weeping.
9 The LORD has heard my
supplication;
The LORD will receive my prayer.
10 Let all my enemies be ashamed
and greatly troubled;
Let them turn back *and* be
ashamed suddenly.

PSALM 7

A Meditation*a* of David, which he sang to the
LORD concerning the words of Cush, a
Benjamite.

1 O LORD my God, in You I put my
trust;
Save me from all those who
persecute me;
And deliver me,
2 Lest they tear me like a lion,
Rending *me* in pieces, while
there is none to deliver.

3 O LORD my God, if I have done
this:
If there is iniquity in my hands,
4 If I have repaid evil to him who
was at peace with me,
Or have plundered my enemy
without cause,
5 Let the enemy pursue me and
overtake *me;*
Yes, let him trample my life to
the earth,
And lay my honor in the dust.
Selah

6 Arise, O LORD, in Your anger;
Lift Yourself up because of the
rage of my enemies;
Rise up for me*a* to the judgment
You have commanded!
7 So the congregation of the
peoples shall surround You;
For their sakes, therefore, return
on high.
8 The LORD shall judge the peoples;
Judge me, O LORD, according to
my righteousness,
And according to my integrity
within me.

9 Oh, let the wickedness of the
wicked come to an end,
But establish the just;
For the righteous God tests the
hearts and minds.
10 My defense *is* of God,
Who saves the upright in heart.

11 God *is* a just judge,
And God is angry *with the
wicked* every day.
12 If he does not turn back,
He will sharpen His sword;
He bends His bow and makes it
ready.
13 He also prepares for Himself
instruments of death;
He makes His arrows into fiery
shafts.

14 Behold, *the wicked* brings forth
iniquity;
Yes, he conceives trouble and
brings forth falsehood.
15 He made a pit and dug it out,
And has fallen into the ditch
which he made.
16 His trouble shall return upon his
own head,

6:title *a*Hebrew *sheminith*   7:title *a*Hebrew *Shiggaion*   7:6 *a*Following Masoretic Text, Targum, and
Vulgate; Septuagint reads O LORD *my God.*

And his violent dealing shall
come down on his own crown.

17 I will praise the LORD according
to His righteousness,
And will sing praise to the name
of the LORD Most High.

PSALM 8

To the Chief Musician. On the instrument of
Gath.[a] A Psalm of David.

1 O LORD, our Lord,
How excellent *is* Your name in
all the earth,
Who have set Your glory above
the heavens!

2 Out of the mouth of babes and
nursing infants
You have ordained strength,
Because of Your enemies,
That You may silence the enemy
and the avenger.

3 When I consider Your heavens,
the work of Your fingers,
The moon and the stars, which
You have ordained,
4 What is man that You are
mindful of him,
And the son of man that You visit
him?
5 For You have made him a little
lower than the angels,[a]
And You have crowned him with
glory and honor.

6 You have made him to have
dominion over the works of
Your hands;
You have put all *things* under his
feet,
7 All sheep and oxen—
Even the beasts of the field,
8 The birds of the air,
And the fish of the sea
That pass through the paths of
the seas.

9 O LORD, our Lord,
How excellent *is* Your name in
all the earth!

PSALM 9

To the Chief Musician. To *the tune of* "Death
of the Son."[a] A Psalm of David.

1 I will praise *You*, O LORD, with
my whole heart;

I will tell of all Your marvelous
works.
2 I will be glad and rejoice in You;
I will sing praise to Your name,
O Most High.

3 When my enemies turn back,
They shall fall and perish at Your
presence.
4 For You have maintained my
right and my cause;
You sat on the throne judging in
righteousness.
5 You have rebuked the nations,
You have destroyed the wicked;
You have blotted out their name
forever and ever.

6 O enemy, destructions are
finished forever!
And you have destroyed cities;
Even their memory has perished.
7 But the LORD shall endure
forever;
He has prepared His throne for
judgment.
8 He shall judge the world in
righteousness,
And He shall administer
judgment for the peoples in
uprightness.

9 The LORD also will be a refuge for
the oppressed,
A refuge in times of trouble.
10 And those who know Your name
will put their trust in You;
For You, LORD, have not forsaken
those who seek You.

11 Sing praises to the LORD, who
dwells in Zion!
Declare His deeds among the
people.
12 When He avenges blood, He
remembers them;
He does not forget the cry of the
humble.

13 Have mercy on me, O LORD!
Consider my trouble from those
who hate me,
You who lift me up from the gates
of death,
14 That I may tell of all Your praise
In the gates of the daughter of
Zion.
I will rejoice in Your salvation.

8:title [a]Hebrew *Al Gittith*   8:5 [a]Hebrew *Elohim, God;* Septuagint, Syriac, Targum, and Jewish tradition
translate as *angels.*   9:title [a]Hebrew *Muth Labben*

15 The nations have sunk down in
   the pit *which* they made;
   In the net which they hid, their
   own foot is caught.
16 The Lord is known *by* the
   judgment He executes;
   The wicked is snared in the work
   of his own hands.
                Meditation.*a*   Selah

17 The wicked shall be turned into
   hell,
   And all the nations that forget
   God.
18 For the needy shall not always be
   forgotten;
   The expectation of the poor shall
   not perish forever.

19 Arise, O Lord,
   Do not let man prevail;
   Let the nations be judged in Your
   sight.
20 Put them in fear, O Lord,
   That the nations may know
   themselves *to be but* men.
                            Selah

PSALM 10

1 Why do You stand afar off, O
  Lord?
  Why do You hide in times of
  trouble?
2 The wicked in *his* pride
  persecutes the poor;
  Let them be caught in the plots
  which they have devised.

3 For the wicked boasts of his
  heart's desire;
  He blesses the greedy *and*
  renounces the Lord.
4 The wicked in his proud
  countenance does not seek
  God;
  God *is* in none of his thoughts.

5 His ways are always prospering;
  Your judgments *are* far above,
  out of his sight;
  As for all his enemies, he sneers
  at them.
6 He has said in his heart, "I shall
  not be moved;
  I shall never be in adversity."
7 His mouth is full of cursing and
  deceit and oppression;
  Under his tongue *is* trouble and
  iniquity.

8 He sits in the lurking places of
  the villages;
  In the secret places he murders
  the innocent;
  His eyes are secretly fixed on the
  helpless.
9 He lies in wait secretly, as a lion
  in his den;
  He lies in wait to catch the poor;
  He catches the poor when he
  draws him into his net.
10 So he crouches, he lies low,
   That the helpless may fall by his
   strength.
11 He has said in his heart,
   "God has forgotten;
   He hides His face;
   He will never see."

12 Arise, O Lord!
   O God, lift up Your hand!
   Do not forget the humble.
13 Why do the wicked renounce
   God?
   He has said in his heart,
   "You will not require an *account*."

14 But You have seen, for You
   observe trouble and grief,
   To repay *it* by Your hand.
   The helpless commits himself to
   You;
   You are the helper of the
   fatherless.
15 Break the arm of the wicked and
   the evil *man*;
   Seek out his wickedness *until*
   You find none.

16 The Lord *is* King forever and
   ever;
   The nations have perished out of
   His land.
17 Lord, You have heard the desire
   of the humble;
   You will prepare their heart;
   You will cause Your ear to hear,
18 To do justice to the fatherless and
   the oppressed,
   That the man of the earth may
   oppress no more.

PSALM 11

To the Chief Musician. A Psalm of David.

1 In the Lord I put my trust;
  How can you say to my soul,
  "Flee *as* a bird to your mountain"?
2 For look! The wicked bend *their*
  bow,

9:16 *a*Hebrew *Higgaion*

They make ready their arrow on
the string,
That they may shoot secretly at
the upright in heart.
3 If the foundations are destroyed,
What can the righteous do?

4 The LORD *is* in His holy temple,
The LORD's throne *is* in heaven;
His eyes behold,
His eyelids test the sons of men.
5 The LORD tests the righteous,
But the wicked and the one who
loves violence His soul hates.
6 Upon the wicked He will rain
coals;
Fire and brimstone and a burning
wind
Shall be the portion of their cup.

7 For the LORD *is* righteous,
He loves righteousness;
His countenance beholds the
upright.*a*

PSALM 12

To the Chief Musician. On an eight-stringed
harp.*a* A Psalm of David.
1 Help, LORD, for the godly man
ceases!
For the faithful disappear from
among the sons of men.
2 They speak idly everyone with
his neighbor;
With flattering lips *and* a double
heart they speak.

3 May the LORD cut off all flattering
lips,
And the tongue that speaks proud
things,
4 Who have said,
"With our tongue we will prevail;
Our lips *are* our own;
Who *is* lord over us?"

5 "For the oppression of the poor,
for the sighing of the needy,
Now I will arise," says the LORD;
"I will set *him* in the safety for
which he yearns."

6 The words of the LORD *are* pure
words,
Like silver tried in a furnace of
earth,
Purified seven times.
7 You shall keep them, O LORD,
You shall preserve them from
this generation forever.

8 The wicked prowl on every side,
When vileness is exalted among
the sons of men.

PSALM 13

To the Chief Musician. A Psalm of David.
1 How long, O LORD? Will You
forget me forever?
How long will You hide Your
face from me?
2 How long shall I take counsel in
my soul,
Having sorrow in my heart daily?
How long will my enemy be
exalted over me?

3 Consider *and* hear me, O LORD
my God;
Enlighten my eyes,
Lest I sleep the *sleep of* death;
4 Lest my enemy say,
"I have prevailed against him";
Lest those who trouble me
rejoice when I am moved.

5 But I have trusted in Your mercy;
My heart shall rejoice in Your
salvation.
6 I will sing to the LORD,
Because He has dealt bountifully
with me.

PSALM 14

To the Chief Musician. A Psalm of David.
1 The fool has said in his heart,
"*There is* no God."
They are corrupt,
They have done abominable
works,
There is none who does good.

2 The LORD looks down from
heaven upon the children of
men,
To see if there are any who
understand, who seek God.
3 They have all turned aside,
They have together become
corrupt;
There is none who does good,
No, not one.

4 Have all the workers of iniquity
no knowledge,
Who eat up my people *as* they
eat bread,
And do not call on the LORD?
5 There they are in great fear,

11:7 *a*Or *The upright beholds His countenance*   12:title *a*Hebrew *sheminith*

For God *is* with the generation of
  the righteous.
6 You shame the counsel of the
  poor,
But the LORD *is* his refuge.

7 Oh, that the salvation of Israel
  would come out of Zion!
When the LORD brings back the
  captivity of His people,
Let Jacob rejoice *and* Israel be
  glad.

PSALM 15

A Psalm of David.

1 LORD, who may abide in Your
  tabernacle?
Who may dwell in Your holy hill?

2 He who walks uprightly,
  And works righteousness,
  And speaks the truth in his
    heart;
3 He *who* does not backbite with
  his tongue,
  Nor does evil to his neighbor,
  Nor does he take up a reproach
    against his friend;
4 In whose eyes a vile person is
  despised,
  But he honors those who fear
    the LORD;
  He *who* swears to his own hurt
    and does not change;
5 He *who* does not put out his
  money at usury,
  Nor does he take a bribe
    against the innocent.

He who does these *things* shall
  never be moved.

PSALM 16

A Michtam of David.

1 Preserve me, O God, for in You
  I put my trust.

2 *O my soul,* you have said to the
  LORD,
"You *are* my Lord,
  My goodness is nothing apart
    from You."
3 As for the saints who *are* on the
  earth,
"They are the excellent ones, in
  whom is all my delight."

4 Their sorrows shall be multiplied
  who hasten *after* another *god;*

Their drink offerings of blood I
  will not offer,
Nor take up their names on my
  lips.

5 O LORD, *You are* the portion of
  my inheritance and my cup;
You maintain my lot.
6 The lines have fallen to me in
  pleasant *places;*
Yes, I have a good inheritance.

7 I will bless the LORD who has
  given me counsel;
My heart also instructs me in the
  night seasons.
8 I have set the LORD always before
  me;
Because *He is* at my right hand I
  shall not be moved.

9 Therefore my heart is glad, and
  my glory rejoices;
My flesh also will rest in hope.
10 For You will not leave my soul
  in Sheol,
Nor will You allow Your Holy
  One to see corruption.
11 You will show me the path of life;
In Your presence *is* fullness of
  joy;
At Your right hand *are* pleasures
  forevermore.

PSALM 17

A Prayer of David.

1 Hear a just cause, O LORD,
Attend to my cry;
Give ear to my prayer *which is*
  not from deceitful lips.
2 Let my vindication come from
  Your presence;
Let Your eyes look on the things
  that are upright.

3 You have tested my heart;
You have visited *me* in the night;
You have tried me and have
  found nothing;
I have purposed that my mouth
  shall not transgress.
4 Concerning the works of men,
By the word of Your lips,
I have kept away from the paths
  of the destroyer.
5 Uphold my steps in Your paths,
That my footsteps may not slip.

6 I have called upon You, for You
  will hear me, O God;

Incline Your ear to me, *and* hear
my speech.
7 Show Your marvelous
lovingkindness by Your right
hand,
O You who save those who trust
in You
From those who rise up *against
them.*
8 Keep me as the apple of Your
eye;
Hide me under the shadow of
Your wings,
9 From the wicked who oppress
me,
From my deadly enemies who
surround me.

10 They have closed up their fat
hearts;
With their mouths they speak
proudly.
11 They have now surrounded us in
our steps;
They have set their eyes,
crouching down to the earth,
12 As a lion is eager to tear his prey,
And like a young lion lurking in
secret places.

13 Arise, O LORD,
Confront him, cast him down;
Deliver my life from the wicked
with Your sword,
14 With Your hand from men, O
LORD,
From men of the world *who have*
their portion in *this* life,
And whose belly You fill with
Your hidden treasure.
They are satisfied with children,
And leave the rest of their
possession for their babes.

15 As for me, I will see Your face
in righteousness;
I shall be satisfied when I awake
in Your likeness.

PSALM 18

To the Chief Musician. A Psalm of David the
servant of the LORD, who spoke to the LORD the
words of this song on the day that the LORD
delivered him from the hand of all his enemies
and from the hand of Saul. And he said:

1 I will love You, O LORD, my
strength.
2 The LORD is my rock and my
fortress and my deliverer;

My God, my strength, in whom I
will trust;
My shield and the horn of my
salvation, my stronghold.
3 I will call upon the LORD, *who is
worthy* to be praised;
So shall I be saved from my
enemies.

4 The pangs of death surrounded
me,
And the floods of ungodliness
made me afraid.
5 The sorrows of Sheol surrounded
me;
The snares of death confronted
me.
6 In my distress I called upon the
LORD,
And cried out to my God;
He heard my voice from His
temple,
And my cry came before Him,
even to His ears.

7 Then the earth shook and
trembled;
The foundations of the hills also
quaked and were shaken,
Because He was angry.
8 Smoke went up from His nostrils,
And devouring fire from His
mouth;
Coals were kindled by it.
9 He bowed the heavens also, and
came down
With darkness under His feet.
10 And He rode upon a cherub, and
flew;
He flew upon the wings of the
wind.
11 He made darkness His secret
place;
His canopy around Him *was* dark
waters
And thick clouds of the skies.
12 From the brightness before Him,
His thick clouds passed with
hailstones and coals of fire.

13 The LORD thundered from
heaven,
And the Most High uttered His
voice,
Hailstones and coals of fire.ᵃ
14 He sent out His arrows and
scattered the foe,
Lightnings in abundance, and He
vanquished them.

18:13 ᵃFollowing Masoretic Text, Targum, and Vulgate; a few Hebrew manuscripts and Septuagint omit
Hailstones and coals of fire.

15 Then the channels of the sea
    were seen,
    The foundations of the world
    were uncovered
    At Your rebuke, O Lord,
    At the blast of the breath of Your
    nostrils.

16 He sent from above, He took me;
    He drew me out of many waters.
17 He delivered me from my strong
    enemy,
    From those who hated me,
    For they were too strong for me.
18 They confronted me in the day
    of my calamity,
    But the Lord was my support.
19 He also brought me out into a
    broad place;
    He delivered me because He
    delighted in me.

20 The Lord rewarded me
    according to my righteousness;
    According to the cleanness of my
    hands
    He has recompensed me.
21 For I have kept the ways of the
    Lord,
    And have not wickedly departed
    from my God.
22 For all His judgments were
    before me,
    And I did not put away His
    statutes from me.
23 I was also blameless before Him,
    And I kept myself from my
    iniquity.
24 Therefore the Lord has
    recompensed me according to
    my righteousness,
    According to the cleanness of my
    hands in His sight.

25 With the merciful You will show
    Yourself merciful;
    With a blameless man You will
    show Yourself blameless;
26 With the pure You will show
    Yourself pure;
    And with the devious You will
    show Yourself shrewd.
27 For You will save the humble
    people,
    But will bring down haughty
    looks.

28 For You will light my lamp;
    The Lord my God will enlighten
    my darkness.
29 For by You I can run against a
    troop,

By my God I can leap over a wall.
30 As for God, His way is perfect;
    The word of the Lord is proven;
    He is a shield to all who trust in
    Him.

31 For who is God, except the Lord?
    And who is a rock, except our
    God?
32 It is God who arms me with
    strength,
    And makes my way perfect.
33 He makes my feet like the feet
    of deer,
    And sets me on my high places.
34 He teaches my hands to make
    war,
    So that my arms can bend a bow
    of bronze.

35 You have also given me the
    shield of Your salvation;
    Your right hand has held me up,
    Your gentleness has made me
    great.
36 You enlarged my path under me,
    So my feet did not slip.

37 I have pursued my enemies and
    overtaken them;
    Neither did I turn back again till
    they were destroyed.
38 I have wounded them,
    So that they could not rise;
    They have fallen under my feet.
39 For You have armed me with
    strength for the battle;
    You have subdued under me
    those who rose up against me.
40 You have also given me
    the necks of my enemies,
    So that I destroyed those who
    hated me.
41 They cried out, but there was
    none to save;
    Even to the Lord, but He did not
    answer them.
42 Then I beat them as fine as the
    dust before the wind;
    I cast them out like dirt in the
    streets.

43 You have delivered me from the
    strivings of the people;
    You have made me the head of
    the nations;
    A people I have not known shall
    serve me.
44 As soon as they hear of me they
    obey me;
    The foreigners submit to me.
45 The foreigners fade away,

And come frightened from their
hideouts.

46 The LORD lives!
Blessed *be* my Rock!
Let the God of my salvation be
exalted.
47 *It is* God who avenges me,
And subdues the peoples under
me;
48 He delivers me from my enemies.
You also lift me up above those
who rise against me;
You have delivered me from the
violent man.
49 Therefore I will give thanks to
You, O LORD, among the
Gentiles,
And sing praises to Your name.

50 Great deliverance He gives to His
king,
And shows mercy to His
anointed,
To David and his descendants
forevermore.

PSALM 19

To the Chief Musician. A Psalm of David.

1 The heavens declare the glory of
God;
And the firmament shows His
handiwork.
2 Day unto day utters speech,
And night unto night reveals
knowledge.
3 *There is* no speech nor language
Where their voice is not heard.
4 Their line*a* has gone out through
all the earth,
And their words to the end of the
world.

In them He has set a tabernacle
for the sun,
5 Which *is* like a bridegroom
coming out of his chamber,
And rejoices like a strong man to
run its race.
6 Its rising *is* from one end of
heaven,
And its circuit to the other end;
And there is nothing hidden from
its heat.

7 The law of the LORD *is* perfect,
converting the soul;
The testimony of the LORD *is* sure,
making wise the simple;

8 The statutes of the LORD *are* right,
rejoicing the heart;
The commandment of the LORD
is pure, enlightening the eyes;
9 The fear of the LORD *is* clean,
enduring forever;
The judgments of the LORD *are*
true *and* righteous altogether.
10 More to be desired *are they* than
gold,
Yea, than much fine gold;
Sweeter also than honey and the
honeycomb.
11 Moreover by them Your servant
is warned,
And in keeping them *there is*
great reward.

12 Who can understand *his* errors?
Cleanse me from secret *faults.*
13 Keep back Your servant also
from presumptuous *sins;*
Let them not have dominion over
me.
Then I shall be blameless,
And I shall be innocent of great
transgression.

14 Let the words of my mouth and
the meditation of my heart
Be acceptable in Your sight,
O LORD, my strength and my
Redeemer.

PSALM 20

To the Chief Musician. A Psalm of David.

1 May the LORD answer you in the
day of trouble;
May the name of the God of
Jacob defend you;
2 May He send you help from the
sanctuary,
And strengthen you out of Zion;
3 May He remember all your
offerings,
And accept your burnt sacrifice.
Selah

4 May He grant you according to
your heart's *desire,*
And fulfill all your purpose.
5 We will rejoice in your salvation,
And in the name of our God we
will set up *our* banners!
May the LORD fulfill all your
petitions.

6 Now I know that the LORD saves
His anointed;

19:4 *a*Septuagint, Syriac, and Vulgate read *sound;* Targum reads *business.*

He will answer him from His holy
heaven
With the saving strength of His
right hand.

7 Some *trust* in chariots, and some
in horses;
But we will remember the name
of the LORD our God.
8 They have bowed down and
fallen;
But we have risen and stand
upright.

9 Save, LORD!
May the King answer us when we
call.

PSALM 21

To the Chief Musician. A Psalm of David.

1 The king shall have joy in Your
strength, O LORD;
And in Your salvation how
greatly shall he rejoice!
2 You have given him his heart's
desire,
And have not withheld the
request of his lips.   Selah

3 For You meet him with the
blessings of goodness;
You set a crown of pure gold
upon his head.
4 He asked life from You, *and* You
gave *it* to him—
Length of days forever and ever.
5 His glory *is* great in Your
salvation;
Honor and majesty You have
placed upon him.
6 For You have made him most
blessed forever;
You have made him exceedingly
glad with Your presence.
7 For the king trusts in the LORD,
And through the mercy of the
Most High he shall not be
moved.

8 Your hand will find all Your
enemies;
Your right hand will find those
who hate You.
9 You shall make them as a fiery
oven in the time of Your anger;
The LORD shall swallow them up
in His wrath,
And the fire shall devour them.

10 Their offspring You shall destroy
from the earth,
And their descendants from
among the sons of men.
11 For they intended evil against
You;
They devised a plot *which* they
are not able *to perform.*
12 Therefore You will make them
turn their back;
You will make ready *Your
arrows* on Your string toward
their faces.

13 Be exalted, O LORD, in Your own
strength!
We will sing and praise Your
power.

PSALM 22

To the Chief Musician. Set to "The Deer of the
Dawn."ᵃ A Psalm of David.

1 My God, My God, why have You
forsaken Me?
Why are You so far from helping
Me,
And from the words of My
groaning?
2 O My God, I cry in the daytime,
but You do not hear;
And in the night season, and am
not silent.

3 But You *are* holy,
Enthroned in the praises of
Israel.
4 Our fathers trusted in You;
They trusted, and You delivered
them.
5 They cried to You, and were
delivered;
They trusted in You, and were
not ashamed.

6 But I *am* a worm, and no man;
A reproach of men, and despised
by the people.
7 All those who see Me ridicule Me;
They shoot out the lip, they shake
the head, *saying,*
8 "He trustedᵃ in the LORD; let Him
rescue Him;
Let Him deliver Him, since He
delights in Him!"

9 But You *are* He who took Me out
of the womb;

22:title ᵃHebrew *Aijeleth Hashahar*   22:8 ᵃSeptuagint, Syriac, and Vulgate read *hoped;* Targum reads *praised.*

The Lord Is My Shepherd

Psalm 23 beautifully reflects both David's early life as a shepherd boy in the hills surrounding Bethlehem and his adult reign as king of Israel.

The youngest child of Jesse, David was responsible for caring for his father's sheep. He was a small lad, yet he was strong and skilled in his work. Daily he guided the flock through the desert wilderness of Judah.

"The Lord is my shepherd; I shall not want" (Ps. 23:1). David's knowledge of shepherding was unsurpassed. He was very familiar with the demands placed on a shepherd to locate food and water for his flock, both of which were scarce in the parched land.

"He makes me to lie down in green pastures; He leads me beside the still waters. He restores my soul; He leads me in the paths of righteousness for His name's sake" (Ps. 23:2, 3).

David the shepherd knew of the few underground springs hidden in the rocky crevices of the wilderness. He carefully led his sheep to the pools of fresh water where they could drink and be restored.

It was not uncommon to spend the night with the flock out in the hills. At dusk, just when the sun sat low in the afternoon sky, the chalky wilderness suddenly became a row of hills and valleys with long dark shadows crisscrossing the land. The high mountain cliffs totally blocked the sunlight, causing dark black ravines where the shepherd and his flock would be found. David recalls these frightful moments when he and his flock were easy prey for wild leopards, lions, and bears. "Yea, though I walk through the valley of the shadow of death, I will fear no evil; for You are with me; Your rod and Your staff, they comfort me" (Ps. 23:4). David's reference to his childhood fear adds an even greater spiritual meaning to his psalm of praise.

As king of Israel, David draws from his kingly experience to further illustrate God's goodness. "You prepare a table before me in the presence of my enemies; You anoint my head with oil; my cup runs over" (Ps. 23:5).

A noted practice of David's day was to break bread—or eat a meal together as a covenant of peace, security, and forgiveness. Here David acknowledges that God makes peace with His enemies. God anoints his head with oil as a sign of His blessing. And his cup running over signifies the success and prosperity God bestowed upon him.

The psalm reflects a beautiful relationship between David and his Lord, for David saw God at work in the ordinary activities of daily life. His psalm of praise can also be ours as we realize God's gifts of security, peace, and prosperity in our lives. Then we can also say with David, "Surely goodness and mercy shall follow me all the days of my life; and I will dwell in the house of the Lord forever" (Ps. 23:6).

You made Me trust *while* on My
mother's breasts.

10 I was cast upon You from birth.
From My mother's womb
You *have been* My God.

11 Be not far from Me,
For trouble *is* near;
For *there is* none to help.

12 Many bulls have surrounded Me;
Strong *bulls* of Bashan have
encircled Me.

13 They gape at Me *with* their
mouths,
Like a raging and roaring lion.

14 I am poured out like water,
And all My bones are out of joint;
My heart is like wax;
It has melted within Me.

15 My strength is dried up like a
potsherd,
And My tongue clings to My
jaws;
You have brought Me to the dust
of death.

16 For dogs have surrounded Me;
The congregation of the wicked
has enclosed Me.
They pierced[a] My hands and My
feet;

17 I can count all My bones.
They look *and* stare at Me.

18 They divide My garments among
them,
And for My clothing they cast
lots.

19 But You, O Lord, do not be far
from Me;
O My Strength, hasten to help
Me!

20 Deliver Me from the sword,
My precious *life* from the power
of the dog.

21 Save Me from the lion's mouth
And from the horns of the wild
oxen!

You have answered Me.

22 I will declare Your name to My
brethren;
In the midst of the assembly I will
praise You.

23 You who fear the Lord, praise
Him!
All you descendants of Jacob,
glorify Him,

And fear Him, all you offspring
of Israel!

24 For He has not despised nor
abhorred the affliction of the
afflicted;
Nor has He hidden His face from
Him;
But when He cried to Him, He
heard.

25 My praise *shall be* of You in the
great assembly;
I will pay My vows before those
who fear Him.

26 The poor shall eat and be
satisfied;
Those who seek Him will praise
the Lord.
Let your heart live forever!

27 All the ends of the world
Shall remember and turn to the
Lord,
And all the families of the nations
Shall worship before You.[a]

28 For the kingdom *is* the Lord's,
And He rules over the nations.

29 All the prosperous of the earth
Shall eat and worship;
All those who go down to the dust
Shall bow before Him,
Even he who cannot keep himself
alive.

30 A posterity shall serve Him.
It will be recounted of the Lord
to the *next* generation.

31 They will come and declare His
righteousness to a people who
will be born,
That He has done *this.*

PSALM 23

A Psalm of David.

1 The Lord *is* my shepherd;
I shall not want.

2 He makes me to lie down in green
pastures;
He leads me beside the still
waters.

3 He restores my soul;
He leads me in the paths of
righteousness
For His name's sake.

4 Yea, though I walk through the
valley of the shadow of death,

22:16 [a]Following some Hebrew manuscripts, Septuagint, Syriac, Vulgate; Masoretic Text reads *Like a
lion.*   22:27 [a]Following Masoretic Text, Septuagint, and Targum; Arabic, Syriac, and Vulgate read *Him.*

Guide Me, Lord

The psalmist David wrote: "Show me Your ways, O Lord; teach me Your paths" (Ps. 25:4). The walk of faith is an adventure in a holy partnership. You are a human being with a mortal starting point at birth and a mortal terminal point at death. The span between your birth and death is your earthly life. Your purpose is to fit into a holy scheme and become a participant with God. He created the world and all of us human beings for the purpose of creatively achieving His holy and happy purposes.

You are walking the walk of faith when you dream God's dreams and seek God's guidance. Therefore, faith is not merely a super-aggressive activity into which you plunge with a gung-ho attitude, to achieve the first impulse that bursts into your mind. Rather, faith is a steady, stable, and steadfast process of opening your conscious and subconscious mind through prayer to the Holy Spirit. The eternal God will shape your will and direct your way! God has promised He will give you guidance.

In the depths of your heart, you know with certainty the course of action your life must take. God Himself answers your prayers for guidance, giving you a strong and powerful will to proceed along the determined pathway. In all your ways, remain open to His leading.

I will fear no evil;
For You *are* with me;
Your rod and Your staff, they
  comfort me.

5 You prepare a table before me in
  the presence of my enemies;
You anoint my head with oil;
My cup runs over.
6 Surely goodness and mercy shall
  follow me
All the days of my life;
And I will dwell[a] in the house of
  the LORD
Forever.

PSALM 24

A Psalm of David.

1 The earth *is* the LORD's, and all
  its fullness,
The world and those who dwell
  therein.
2 For He has founded it upon the
  seas,
And established it upon the
  waters.

3 Who may ascend into the hill of
  the LORD?
Or who may stand in His holy
  place?
4 He who has clean hands and a
  pure heart,
Who has not lifted up his soul to
  an idol,
Nor sworn deceitfully.
5 He shall receive blessing from
  the LORD,
And righteousness from the God
  of his salvation.
6 This *is* Jacob, the generation of
  those who seek Him,
Who seek Your face.   Selah

7 Lift up your heads, O you gates!
And be lifted up, you everlasting
  doors!
And the King of glory shall come
  in.
8 Who *is* this King of glory?
The LORD strong and mighty,
The LORD mighty in battle.
9 Lift up your heads, O you gates!
Lift up, you everlasting doors!
And the King of glory shall come
  in.
10 Who is this King of glory?
The LORD of hosts,

He *is* the King of glory.
                    Selah

PSALM 25

A Psalm of David.

1 To You, O LORD, I lift up my soul.
2 O my God, I trust in You;
Let me not be ashamed;
Let not my enemies triumph over
  me.
3 Indeed, let no one who waits on
  You be ashamed;
Let those be ashamed who deal
  treacherously without cause.

4 Show me Your ways, O LORD;
Teach me Your paths.
5 Lead me in Your truth and teach
  me,
For You *are* the God of my
  salvation;
On You I wait all the day.

6 Remember, O LORD, Your tender
  mercies and Your
  lovingkindnesses,
For they *are* from of old.
7 Do not remember the sins of my
  youth, nor my transgressions;
According to Your mercy
  remember me,
For Your goodness' sake, O LORD.

8 Good and upright *is* the LORD;
Therefore He teaches sinners in
  the way.
9 The humble He guides in justice,
And the humble He teaches His
  way.
10 All the paths of the LORD *are*
  mercy and truth,
To such as keep His covenant
  and His testimonies.
11 For Your name's sake, O LORD,
Pardon my iniquity, for it *is* great.

12 Who *is* the man that fears the
  LORD?
Him shall He[a] teach in the way
  He[a] chooses.

13 He himself shall dwell in
  prosperity,
And his descendants shall inherit
  the earth.
14 The secret of the LORD *is* with
  those who fear Him,

23:6 [a]Following Septuagint, Syriac, Targum, and Vulgate; Masoretic Text reads *return.*   25:12 [a]Or *he*

And He will show them His
covenant.
15 My eyes *are* ever toward the
Lord,
For He shall pluck my feet out of
the net.

16 Turn Yourself to me, and have
mercy on me,
For I *am* desolate and afflicted.
17 The troubles of my heart have
enlarged;
Bring me out of my distresses!
18 Look on my affliction and my
pain,
And forgive all my sins.
19 Consider my enemies, for they
are many;
And they hate me with cruel
hatred.
20 Keep my soul, and deliver me;
Let me not be ashamed, for I put
my trust in You.
21 Let integrity and uprightness
preserve me,
For I wait for You.

22 Redeem Israel, O God,
Out of all their troubles!

PSALM 26

A Psalm of David.
1 Vindicate me, O Lord,
For I have walked in my integrity.
I have also trusted in the Lord;
I shall not slip.
2 Examine me, O Lord, and prove
me;
Try my mind and my heart.
3 For Your lovingkindness *is*
before my eyes,
And I have walked in Your truth.
4 I have not sat with idolatrous
mortals,
Nor will I go in with hypocrites.
5 I have hated the assembly of
evildoers,
And will not sit with the wicked.

6 I will wash my hands in
innocence;
So I will go about Your altar, O
Lord,
7 That I may proclaim with the
voice of thanksgiving,
And tell of all Your wondrous
works.
8 Lord, I have loved the habitation
of Your house,
And the place where Your glory
dwells.

9 Do not gather my soul with
sinners,
Nor my life with bloodthirsty
men,
10 In whose hands *is* a sinister
scheme,
And whose right hand is full of
bribes.

11 But as for me, I will walk in my
integrity;
Redeem me and be merciful to
me.
12 My foot stands in an even place;
In the congregations I will bless
the Lord.

PSALM 27

A Psalm of David.
1 The Lord *is* my light and my
salvation;
Whom shall I fear?
The Lord *is* the strength of my
life;
Of whom shall I be afraid?
2 When the wicked came against
me
To eat up my flesh,
My enemies and foes,
They stumbled and fell.
3 Though an army may encamp
against me,
My heart shall not fear;
Though war may rise against me,
In this I *will be* confident.

4 One *thing* I have desired of the
Lord,
That will I seek:
That I may dwell in the house of
the Lord
All the days of my life,
To behold the beauty of the Lord,
And to inquire in His temple.
5 For in the time of trouble
He shall hide me in His pavilion;
In the secret place of His
tabernacle
He shall hide me;
He shall set me high upon a rock.

6 And now my head shall be lifted
up above my enemies all
around me;
Therefore I will offer sacrifices of
joy in His tabernacle;
I will sing, yes, I will sing praises
to the Lord.

7 Hear, O Lord, *when* I cry with
my voice!

Have mercy also upon me, and
answer me.
8 *When You said,* "Seek My face,"
My heart said to You, "Your face,
Lord, I will seek."
9 Do not hide Your face from me;
Do not turn Your servant away
in anger;
You have been my help;
Do not leave me nor forsake me,
O God of my salvation.
10 When my father and my mother
forsake me,
Then the Lord will take care of
me.

11 Teach me Your way, O Lord,
And lead me in a smooth path,
because of my enemies.
12 Do not deliver me to the will of
my adversaries;
For false witnesses have risen
against me,
And such as breathe out violence.
13 *I would have lost heart,* unless I
had believed
That I would see the goodness of
the Lord
In the land of the living.

14 Wait on the Lord;
Be of good courage,
And He shall strengthen your
heart;
Wait, I say, on the Lord!

PSALM 28

A Psalm of David.
1 To You I will cry, O Lord my
Rock:
Do not be silent to me,
Lest, if You *are* silent to me,
I become like those who go down
to the pit.
2 Hear the voice of my
supplications
When I cry to You,
When I lift up my hands toward
Your holy sanctuary.

3 Do not take me away with the
wicked
And with the workers of iniquity,
Who speak peace to their
neighbors,
But evil *is* in their hearts.
4 Give them according to their
deeds,

And according to the wickedness
of their endeavors;
Give them according to the work
of their hands;
Render to them what they
deserve.
5 Because they do not regard the
works of the Lord,
Nor the operation of His hands,
He shall destroy them
And not build them up.

6 Blessed *be* the Lord,
Because He has heard the voice
of my supplications!
7 The Lord *is* my strength and my
shield;
My heart trusted in Him, and I
am helped;
Therefore my heart greatly
rejoices,
And with my song I will praise
Him.

8 The Lord *is* their strength,[a]
And He *is* the saving refuge of
His anointed.
9 Save Your people,
And bless Your inheritance;
Shepherd them also,
And bear them up forever.

PSALM 29

A Psalm of David.
1 Give unto the Lord, O you mighty
ones,
Give unto the Lord glory and
strength.
2 Give unto the Lord the glory due
to His name;
Worship the Lord in the beauty
of holiness.

3 The voice of the Lord *is* over the
waters;
The God of glory thunders;
The Lord *is* over many waters.
4 The voice of the Lord *is*
powerful;
The voice of the Lord *is* full of
majesty.

5 The voice of the Lord breaks the
cedars,
Yes, the Lord splinters the cedars
of Lebanon.
6 He makes them also skip like a
calf,

28:8 [a]Following Masoretic Text and Targum; Septuagint, Syriac, and Vulgate read *the strength of His people.*

Lebanon and Sirion like a young
wild ox.
7 The voice of the Lord divides the
flames of fire.

8 The voice of the Lord shakes the
wilderness;
The Lord shakes the Wilderness
of Kadesh.
9 The voice of the Lord makes the
deer give birth,
And strips the forests bare;
And in His temple everyone says,
"Glory!"

10 The Lord sat *enthroned* at the
Flood,
And the Lord sits as King
forever.
11 The Lord will give strength to His
people;
The Lord will bless His people
with peace.

PSALM 30

A Psalm. A Song at the dedication of the house
of David.

1 I will extol You, O Lord, for You
have lifted me up,
And have not let my foes rejoice
over me.
2 O Lord my God, I cried out to
You,
And You healed me.
3 O Lord, You brought my soul up
from the grave;
You have kept me alive, that I
should not go down to the pit.*a*

4 Sing praise to the Lord, you
saints of His,
And give thanks at the
remembrance of His holy
name.*a*
5 For His anger *is but for* a
moment,
His favor *is for* life;
Weeping may endure for a night,
But joy *comes* in the morning.

6 Now in my prosperity I said,
"I shall never be moved."
7 Lord, by Your favor You have
made my mountain stand
strong;
You hid Your face, *and* I was
troubled.

8 I cried out to You, O Lord;
And to the Lord I made
supplication:
9 "What profit *is there* in my blood,
When I go down to the pit?
Will the dust praise You?
Will it declare Your truth?
10 Hear, O Lord, and have mercy on
me;
Lord, be my helper!"

11 You have turned for me my
mourning into dancing;
You have put off my sackcloth
and clothed me with gladness,
12 To the end that *my* glory may
sing praise to You and not be
silent.
O Lord my God, I will give
thanks to You forever.

PSALM 31

To the Chief Musician. A Psalm of David.

1 In You, O Lord, I put my trust;
Let me never be ashamed;
Deliver me in Your
righteousness.
2 Bow down Your ear to me,
Deliver me speedily;
Be my rock of refuge,
A fortress of defense to save me.

3 For You *are* my rock and my
fortress;
Therefore, for Your name's sake,
Lead me and guide me.
4 Pull me out of the net which they
have secretly laid for me,
For You *are* my strength.
5 Into Your hand I commit my
spirit;
You have redeemed me, O Lord
God of truth.

6 I have hated those who regard
useless idols;
But I trust in the Lord.
7 I will be glad and rejoice in Your
mercy,
For You have considered my
trouble;
You have known my soul in
adversities,
8 And have not shut me up into the
hand of the enemy;
You have set my feet in a wide
place.

30:3 *a*Following Qere and Targum; Kethib, Septuagint, Syriac, and Vulgate read *from those who descend
to the pit.*   30:4 *a*Or *His holiness*

9 Have mercy on me, O LORD, for
   I am in trouble;
   My eye wastes away with grief,
   Yes, my soul and my body!
10 For my life is spent with grief,
   And my years with sighing;
   My strength fails because of my
   iniquity,
   And my bones waste away.
11 I am a reproach among all my
   enemies,
   But especially among my
   neighbors,
   And *am* repulsive to my
   acquaintances;
   Those who see me outside flee
   from me.
12 I am forgotten like a dead man,
   out of mind;
   I am like a broken vessel.
13 For I hear the slander of many;
   Fear *is* on every side;
   While they take counsel together
   against me,
   They scheme to take away my
   life.

14 But as for me, I trust in You, O
   LORD;
   I say, "You *are* my God."
15 My times *are* in Your hand;
   Deliver me from the hand of my
   enemies,
   And from those who persecute
   me.
16 Make Your face shine upon Your
   servant;
   Save me for Your mercies' sake.
17 Do not let me be ashamed, O
   LORD, for I have called upon
   You;
   Let the wicked be ashamed;
   Let them be silent in the grave.
18 Let the lying lips be put to
   silence,
   Which speak insolent things
   proudly and contemptuously
   against the righteous.

19 Oh, how great *is* Your goodness,
   Which You have laid up for those
   who fear You,
   Which You have prepared for
   those who trust in You
   In the presence of the sons of
   men!
20 You shall hide them in the secret
   place of Your presence
   From the plots of man;

You shall keep them secretly in
   a pavilion
   From the strife of tongues.
21 Blessed *be* the LORD,
   For He has shown me His
   marvelous kindness in a strong
   city!
22 For I said in my haste,
   "I am cut off from before Your
   eyes";
   Nevertheless You heard the voice
   of my supplications
   When I cried out to You.

23 Oh, love the LORD, all you His
   saints!
   For the LORD preserves the
   faithful,
   And fully repays the proud
   person.
24 Be of good courage,
   And He shall strengthen your
   heart,
   All you who hope in the LORD.

PSALM 32

A Psalm of David. A Contemplation.[a]
1 Blessed *is he whose*
   transgression *is* forgiven,
   Whose sin *is* covered.
2 Blessed *is* the man to whom the
   LORD does not impute iniquity,
   And in whose spirit *there is* no
   deceit.

3 When I kept silent, my bones
   grew old
   Through my groaning all the day
   long.
4 For day and night Your hand was
   heavy upon me;
   My vitality was turned into the
   drought of summer.   Selah
5 I acknowledged my sin to You,
   And my iniquity I have not
   hidden.
   I said, "I will confess my
   transgressions to the LORD,"
   And You forgave the iniquity of
   my sin.   Selah

6 For this cause everyone who is
   godly shall pray to You
   In a time when You may be
   found;
   Surely in a flood of great waters
   They shall not come near him.
7 You *are* my hiding place;

You shall preserve me from
   trouble;
You shall surround me with
   songs of deliverance.   Selah

8 I will instruct you and teach you
   in the way you should go;
I will guide you with My eye.
9 Do not be like the horse *or* like
   the mule,
Which have no understanding,
Which must be harnessed with
   bit and bridle,
Else they will not come near you.

10 Many sorrows *shall be* to the
   wicked;
But he who trusts in the LORD,
   mercy shall surround him.
11 Be glad in the LORD and rejoice,
   you righteous;
And shout for joy, all *you* upright
   in heart!

PSALM 33

1 Rejoice in the LORD, O you
   righteous!
For praise from the upright is
   beautiful.
2 Praise the LORD with the harp;
Make melody to Him with an
   instrument of ten strings.
3 Sing to Him a new song;
Play skillfully with a shout of joy.

4 For the word of the LORD *is* right,
And all His work *is done* in truth.
5 He loves righteousness and
   justice;
The earth is full of the goodness
   of the LORD.

6 By the word of the LORD the
   heavens were made,
And all the host of them by the
   breath of His mouth.
7 He gathers the waters of the sea
   together as a heap;[a]
He lays up the deep in
   storehouses.

8 Let all the earth fear the LORD;
Let all the inhabitants of the
   world stand in awe of Him.
9 For He spoke, and it was *done;*
He commanded, and it stood fast.

10 The LORD brings the counsel of
   the nations to nothing;

He makes the plans of the
   peoples of no effect.
11 The counsel of the LORD stands
   forever,
The plans of His heart to all
   generations.
12 Blessed *is* the nation whose God
   is the LORD,
The people He has chosen as His
   own inheritance.

13 The LORD looks from heaven;
He sees all the sons of men.
14 From the place of His dwelling
   He looks
On all the inhabitants of the
   earth;
15 He fashions their hearts
   individually;
He considers all their works.

16 No king *is* saved by the multitude
   of an army;
A mighty man is not delivered by
   great strength.
17 A horse *is* a vain hope for safety;
Neither shall it deliver *any* by its
   great strength.

18 Behold, the eye of the LORD *is* on
   those who fear Him,
On those who hope in His mercy,
19 To deliver their soul from death,
And to keep them alive in famine.

20 Our soul waits for the LORD;
He *is* our help and our shield.
21 For our heart shall rejoice in Him,
Because we have trusted in His
   holy name.
22 Let Your mercy, O LORD, be upon
   us,
Just as we hope in You.

PSALM 34

A Psalm of David when he pretended madness
before Abimelech, who drove him away, and he
departed.

1 I will bless the LORD at all times;
His praise *shall* continually *be* in
   my mouth.
2 My soul shall make its boast in
   the LORD;
The humble shall hear *of it* and
   be glad.
3 Oh, magnify the LORD with me,
And let us exalt His name
   together.

4 I sought the LORD, and He heard
   me,

33:7 [a]Septuagint, Targum, and Vulgate read *in a vessel*.

And delivered me from all my
fears.
5 They looked to Him and were
radiant,
And their faces were not
ashamed.
6 This poor man cried out, and the
LORD heard *him,*
And saved him out of all his
troubles.
7 The angel*ᵃ* of the LORD encamps
all around those who fear Him,
And delivers them.

8 Oh, taste and see that the LORD
is good;
Blessed *is* the man *who* trusts in
Him!
9 Oh, fear the LORD, you His saints!
There is no want to those who
fear Him.
10 The young lions lack and suffer
hunger;
But those who seek the LORD
shall not lack any good *thing.*

11 Come, you children, listen to me;
I will teach you the fear of the
LORD.
12 Who *is* the man *who* desires life,
And loves *many* days, that he
may see good?
13 Keep your tongue from evil,
And your lips from speaking
deceit.
14 Depart from evil and do good;
Seek peace and pursue it.

15 The eyes of the LORD *are* on the
righteous,
And His ears *are open* to their
cry.
16 The face of the LORD *is* against
those who do evil,
To cut off the remembrance of
them from the earth.

17 *The righteous* cry out, and the
LORD hears,
And delivers them out of all their
troubles.
18 The LORD *is* near to those who
have a broken heart,
And saves such as have a contrite
spirit.

19 Many *are* the afflictions of the
righteous,
But the LORD delivers him out of
them all.

20 He guards all his bones;
Not one of them is broken.
21 Evil shall slay the wicked,
And those who hate the righteous
shall be condemned.
22 The LORD redeems the soul of His
servants,
And none of those who trust in
Him shall be condemned.

PSALM 35

A Psalm of David.

1 Plead *my cause,* O LORD, with
those who strive with me;
Fight against those who fight
against me.
2 Take hold of shield and buckler,
And stand up for my help.
3 Also draw out the spear,
And stop those who pursue me.
Say to my soul,
"*I am* your salvation."

4 Let those be put to shame and
brought to dishonor
Who seek after my life;
Let those be turned back and
brought to confusion
Who plot my hurt.
5 Let them be like chaff before the
wind,
And let the angel*ᵃ* of the LORD
chase *them.*
6 Let their way be dark and
slippery,
And let the angel of the LORD
pursue them.
7 For without cause they have
hidden their net for me *in* a pit,
Which they have dug without
cause for my life.
8 Let destruction come upon him
unexpectedly,
And let his net that he has hidden
catch himself;
Into that very destruction let him
fall.

9 And my soul shall be joyful in the
LORD;
It shall rejoice in His salvation.
10 All my bones shall say,
"LORD, who *is* like You,
Delivering the poor from him
who is too strong for him,
Yes, the poor and the needy from
him who plunders him?"

34:7 ᵃOr *Angel*   35:5 ᵃOr *Angel*

11 Fierce witnesses rise up;
They ask me *things* that I do not
know.
12 They reward me evil for good,
To the sorrow of my soul.
13 But as for me, when they were
sick,
My clothing *was* sackcloth;
I humbled myself with fasting;
And my prayer would return to
my own heart.
14 I paced about as though *he were*
my friend *or* brother;
I bowed down heavily, as one
who mourns *for his* mother.

15 But in my adversity they rejoiced
And gathered together;
Attackers gathered against me,
And I did not know *it;*
They tore *at me* and did not
cease;
16 With ungodly mockers at feasts
They gnashed at me with their
teeth.

17 Lord, how long will You look on?
Rescue me from their
destructions,
My precious *life* from the lions.
18 I will give You thanks in the great
assembly;
I will praise You among many
people.

19 Let them not rejoice over me who
are wrongfully my enemies;
Nor let them wink with the eye
who hate me without a cause.
20 For they do not speak peace,
But they devise deceitful matters
Against *the* quiet ones in the
land.
21 They also opened their mouth
wide against me,
And said, "Aha, aha!
Our eyes have seen *it.*"

22 *This* You have seen, O LORD;
Do not keep silence.
O Lord, do not be far from me.
23 Stir up Yourself, and awake to
my vindication,
To my cause, my God and my
Lord.
24 Vindicate me, O LORD my God,
according to Your
righteousness;
And let them not rejoice over me.
25 Let them not say in their hearts,
"Ah, so we would have it!"
Let them not say, "We have
swallowed him up."

26 Let them be ashamed and
brought to mutual confusion
Who rejoice at my hurt;
Let them be clothed with shame
and dishonor
Who exalt themselves against
me.

27 Let them shout for joy and be
glad,
Who favor my righteous cause;
And let them say continually,
"Let the LORD be magnified,
Who has pleasure in the
prosperity of His servant."
28 And my tongue shall speak of
Your righteousness
And of Your praise all the day
long.

PSALM 36

To the Chief Musician. A Psalm of David the
servant of the LORD.

1 An oracle within my heart
concerning the transgression
of the wicked:
There is no fear of God before his
eyes.
2 For he flatters himself in his own
eyes,
When he finds out his iniquity
and when he hates.
3 The words of his mouth *are*
wickedness and deceit;
He has ceased to be wise *and* to
do good.
4 He devises wickedness on his
bed;
He sets himself in a way *that is*
not good;
He does not abhor evil.

5 Your mercy, O LORD, *is* in the
heavens;
Your faithfulness *reaches* to the
clouds.
6 Your righteousness *is* like the
great mountains;
Your judgments *are* a great deep;
O LORD, You preserve man and
beast.

7 How precious *is* Your
lovingkindness, O God!
Therefore the children of men put
their trust under the shadow of
Your wings.
8 They are abundantly satisfied
with the fullness of Your house,
And You give them drink from
the river of Your pleasures.

Make a Commitment

Miracles involve believing, but quite often they also involve acting on belief. Read carefully in the Gospels the words of Jesus, and notice the verbs. *Follow, go, seek, ask, knock.* The walk of faith is not merely the serene, silent, spiritual, unspeaking stroll of a holy man in the stillness of the sunrise or the secret silence of the sunset. Faith is the mental activity that draws God into our minds and imaginations until a passion begins to inflame our wills, motivating us to action! Psalm 37:5 challenges: "Commit your way to the LORD, trust also in Him, and He shall bring *it* to pass."

It is then that the commitment is made. And what is a commitment? It is entering into an honorable contract, pledging oneself before the problems are solved. If we waited until we saw solutions to all problems before we made a commitment, we would obviously not be walking the walk of faith! It is for that reason that commitment—

in marriage,

in religion,

in interpersonal relationships,

in devotion and dedication to your career goal

or the fulfillment of a project—

becomes self-inspiring.

Walk the walk of faith today. Make a fresh commitment to God, praying: *God, I'm ready to take the plunge. Give me the push that I need, and I'm trusting that with Your help we'll tackle every problem at every turn of the road with a positive mental attitude! And together we'll succeed joyously! Amen.*

9 For with You *is* the fountain of
life;
In Your light we see light.

10 Oh, continue Your
lovingkindness to those who
know You,
And Your righteousness to the
upright in heart.

11 Let not the foot of pride come
against me,
And let not the hand of the
wicked drive me away.

12 There the workers of iniquity
have fallen;
They have been cast down and
are not able to rise.

PSALM 37

A Psalm of David.

1 Do not fret because of evildoers,
Nor be envious of the workers of
iniquity.

2 For they shall soon be cut down
like the grass,
And wither as the green herb.

3 Trust in the LORD, and do good;
Dwell in the land, and feed on His
faithfulness.

4 Delight yourself also in the LORD,
And He shall give you the desires
of your heart.

5 Commit your way to the LORD,
Trust also in Him,
And He shall bring *it* to pass.

6 He shall bring forth your
righteousness as the light,
And your justice as the noonday.

7 Rest in the LORD, and wait
patiently for Him;
Do not fret because of him who
prospers in his way,
Because of the man who brings
wicked schemes to pass.

8 Cease from anger, and forsake
wrath;
Do not fret—*it* only *causes* harm.

9 For evildoers shall be cut off;
But those who wait on the LORD,
They shall inherit the earth.

10 For yet a little while and the
wicked *shall be* no *more*;
Indeed, you will look carefully
for his place,
But it *shall be* no *more*.

11 But the meek shall inherit the
earth,

And shall delight themselves in
the abundance of peace.

12 The wicked plots against the just,
And gnashes at him with his
teeth.

13 The Lord laughs at him,
For He sees that his day is
coming.

14 The wicked have drawn the
sword
And have bent their bow,
To cast down the poor and needy,
To slay those who are of upright
conduct.

15 Their sword shall enter their own
heart,
And their bows shall be broken.

16 A little that a righteous man has
Is better than the riches of many
wicked.

17 For the arms of the wicked shall
be broken,
But the LORD upholds the
righteous.

18 The LORD knows the days of the
upright,
And their inheritance shall be
forever.

19 They shall not be ashamed in the
evil time,
And in the days of famine they
shall be satisfied.

20 But the wicked shall perish;
And the enemies of the LORD,
Like the splendor of the
meadows, shall vanish.
Into smoke they shall vanish
away.

21 The wicked borrows and does not
repay,
But the righteous shows mercy
and gives.

22 For *those* blessed by Him shall
inherit the earth,
But *those* cursed by Him shall be
cut off.

23 The steps of a *good* man are
ordered by the LORD,
And He delights in his way.

24 Though he fall, he shall not be
utterly cast down;
For the LORD upholds *him with*
His hand.

25 I have been young, and *now* am
old;

Yet I have not seen the righteous
   forsaken,
Nor his descendants begging
   bread.
26 *He is* ever merciful, and lends;
   And his descendants *are* blessed.

27 Depart from evil, and do good;
   And dwell forevermore.
28 For the Lord loves justice,
   And does not forsake His saints;
   They are preserved forever,
   But the descendants of the
      wicked shall be cut off.
29 The righteous shall inherit the
      land,
   And dwell in it forever.

30 The mouth of the righteous
      speaks wisdom,
   And his tongue talks of justice.
31 The law of his God *is* in his heart;
   None of his steps shall slide.

32 The wicked watches the
      righteous,
   And seeks to slay him.
33 The Lord will not leave him in
      his hand,
   Nor condemn him when he is
      judged.

34 Wait on the Lord,
   And keep His way,
   And He shall exalt you to inherit
      the land;
   When the wicked are cut off, you
      shall see *it.*
35 I have seen the wicked in great
      power,
   And spreading himself like a
      native green tree.
36 Yet he passed away,*a* and behold,
      he *was* no *more;*
   Indeed I sought him, but he could
      not be found.

37 Mark the blameless *man,* and
      observe the upright;
   For the future of *that* man *is*
      peace.
38 But the transgressors shall be
      destroyed together;
   The future of the wicked shall be
      cut off.

39 But the salvation of the righteous
      is from the Lord;
   He *is* their strength in the time
      of trouble.

40 And the Lord shall help them and
      deliver them;
   He shall deliver them from the
      wicked,
   And save them,
   Because they trust in Him.

PSALM 38

A Psalm of David. To bring to remembrance.

1 O Lord, do not rebuke me in
      Your wrath,
   Nor chasten me in Your hot
      displeasure!
2 For Your arrows pierce me
      deeply,
   And Your hand presses me down.

3 *There is* no soundness in my flesh
   Because of Your anger,
   Nor *any* health in my bones
   Because of my sin.
4 For my iniquities have gone over
      my head;
   Like a heavy burden they are too
      heavy for me.
5 My wounds are foul *and* festering
   Because of my foolishness.

6 I am troubled, I am bowed down
      greatly;
   I go mourning all the day long.
7 For my loins are full of
      inflammation,
   And *there is* no soundness in my
      flesh.
8 I am feeble and severely broken;
   I groan because of the turmoil of
      my heart.

9 Lord, all my desire *is* before You;
   And my sighing is not hidden
      from You.
10 My heart pants, my strength fails
      me;
   As for the light of my eyes, it also
      has gone from me.

11 My loved ones and my friends
      stand aloof from my plague,
   And my relatives stand afar off.
12 Those also who seek my life lay
      snares *for me;*
   Those who seek my hurt speak
      of destruction,
   And plan deception all the day
      long.

13 But I, like a deaf *man,* do not
      hear;

37:36 *a*Following Masoretic Text, Septuagint, and Targum; Syriac and Vulgate read *I passed by.*

And *I am* like a mute *who* does not open his mouth.
14 Thus I am like a man who does not hear,
And in whose mouth *is* no response.

15 For in You, O LORD, I hope;
You will hear, O Lord my God.
16 For I said, *"Hear me,* lest they rejoice over me,
Lest, when my foot slips, they exalt *themselves* against me."

17 For I *am* ready to fall,
And my sorrow *is* continually before me.
18 For I will declare my iniquity;
I will be in anguish over my sin.
19 But my enemies *are* vigorous,
and they are strong;
And those who hate me wrongfully have multiplied.
20 Those also who render evil for good,
They are my adversaries,
because I follow *what is* good.

21 Do not forsake me, O LORD;
O my God, be not far from me!
22 Make haste to help me,
O Lord, my salvation!

PSALM 39

To the Chief Musician. To Jeduthun. A Psalm of David.

1 I said, "I will guard my ways,
Lest I sin with my tongue;
I will restrain my mouth with a muzzle,
While the wicked are before me."
2 I was mute with silence,
I held my peace *even* from good;
And my sorrow was stirred up.
3 My heart was hot within me;
While I was musing, the fire burned.
Then I spoke with my tongue:

4 "LORD, make me to know my end,
And what *is* the measure of my days,
That I may know how frail I *am.*
5 Indeed, You have made my days *as* handbreadths,
And my age *is* as nothing before You;
Certainly every man at his best state *is* but vapor.   Selah
6 Surely every man walks about like a shadow;

Surely they busy themselves in vain;
He heaps up *riches,*
And does not know who will gather them.

7 "And now, Lord, what do I wait for?
My hope *is* in You.
8 Deliver me from all my transgressions;
Do not make me the reproach of the foolish.
9 I was mute, I did not open my mouth,
Because it was You who did *it.*
10 Remove Your plague from me;
I am consumed by the blow of Your hand.
11 When with rebukes You correct man for iniquity,
You make his beauty melt away like a moth;
Surely every man *is* vapor.
Selah

12 "Hear my prayer, O LORD,
And give ear to my cry;
Do not be silent at my tears;
For I *am* a stranger with You,
A sojourner, as all my fathers *were.*
13 Remove Your gaze from me, that I may regain strength,
Before I go away and am no more."

PSALM 40

To the Chief Musician. A Psalm of David.

1 I waited patiently for the LORD;
And He inclined to me,
And heard my cry.
2 He also brought me up out of a horrible pit,
Out of the miry clay,
And set my feet upon a rock,
And established my steps.
3 He has put a new song in my mouth—
Praise to our God;
Many will see *it* and fear,
And will trust in the LORD.

4 Blessed *is* that man who makes the LORD his trust,
And does not respect the proud, nor such as turn aside to lies.
5 Many, O LORD my God, *are* Your wonderful works
Which You have done;
And Your thoughts toward us

Cannot be recounted to You in
　　order;
If I would declare and speak *of
　　them,*
They are more than can be
　　numbered.

6　Sacrifice and offering You did
　　not desire;
My ears You have opened.
Burnt offering and sin offering
　　You did not require.

7　Then I said, "Behold, I come;
In the scroll of the book *it is*
　　written of me.

8　I delight to do Your will, O my
　　God,
And Your law *is* within my
　　heart."

9　I have proclaimed the good news
　　of righteousness
In the great assembly;
Indeed, I do not restrain my lips,
O Lord, You Yourself know.

10　I have not hidden Your
　　righteousness within my heart;
I have declared Your faithfulness
　　and Your salvation;
I have not concealed Your
　　lovingkindness and Your truth
From the great assembly.

11　Do not withhold Your tender
　　mercies from me, O Lord;
Let Your lovingkindness and
　　Your truth continually
　　preserve me.

12　For innumerable evils have
　　surrounded me;
My iniquities have overtaken me,
　　so that I am not able to look
　　up;
They are more than the hairs of
　　my head;
Therefore my heart fails me.

13　Be pleased, O Lord, to deliver
　　me;
O Lord, make haste to help me!

14　Let them be ashamed and
　　brought to mutual confusion
Who seek to destroy my life;
Let them be driven backward and
　　brought to dishonor
Who wish me evil.

15　Let them be confounded because
　　of their shame,
Who say to me, "Aha, aha!"

16　Let all those who seek You
　　rejoice and be glad in You;

Let such as love Your salvation
　　say continually,
"The Lord be magnified!"

17　But I *am* poor and needy;
Yet the Lord thinks upon me.
You *are* my help and my
　　deliverer;
Do not delay, O my God.

PSALM 41

To the Chief Musician. A Psalm of David.

1　Blessed *is* he who considers the
　　poor;
The Lord will deliver him in time
　　of trouble.

2　The Lord will preserve him and
　　keep him alive,
And he will be blessed on the
　　earth;
You will not deliver him to the
　　will of his enemies.

3　The Lord will strengthen him on
　　his bed of illness;
You will sustain him on his
　　sickbed.

4　I said, "Lord, be merciful to me;
Heal my soul, for I have sinned
　　against You."

5　My enemies speak evil of me:
"When will he die, and his name
　　perish?"

6　And if he comes to see *me,* he
　　speaks lies;
His heart gathers iniquity to
　　itself;
When he goes out, he tells *it.*

7　All who hate me whisper
　　together against me;
Against me they devise my hurt.

8　"An evil disease," *they say,*
　　"clings to him.
And *now* that he lies down, he
　　will rise up no more."

9　Even my own familiar friend in
　　whom I trusted,
Who ate my bread,
Has lifted up *his* heel against me.

10　But You, O Lord, be merciful to
　　me, and raise me up,
That I may repay them.

11　By this I know that You are well
　　pleased with me,
Because my enemy does not
　　triumph over me.

12　As for me, You uphold me in my
　　integrity,
And set me before Your face
　　forever.

The Remote Places

Throughout Jesus' ministry, our Lord took time to be alone with His Father in prayer. After long days of ministering to the people in Galilee, Jesus often withdrew to deserted places around the sea.

In Christ's day, Galilee was one of the most fertile agricultural areas in all of Palestine. It bustled with life and was a major cosmopolitan center. The region's population was in the millions, with more than twenty-five cities surrounding the lake and another ninety cities within walking distance.

Somehow, Jesus found time and space to be alone with God. The desert places can actually be translated "the remote places" of Galilee. These remote places are the high mountain ranges with beautiful panoramic views of the lake and the surrounding Decapolis mountains. They are the still valleys and the quiet fields covered with beautiful red anemones.

Jesus realized the importance and value of withdrawing to beautiful serene places to commune with God before spending Himself in ministry. We must do the same and draw our serenity and strength from quiet moments alone with God.

If you live in a bustling cosmopolitan center, seize the opportunity to share your faith with the people around you. But remember to make time to retreat to the remote places where you can commune with God. If you live near the ocean, take a moment to walk in the waves and let them lap around your feet. If you are near the mountains, walk with God through the quiet woods and tall majestic trees. If you are in the heart of the city, go to the top of your apartment building and catch the first rays of sunrise as it illuminates the sky above you. If you are in a hospital, close your eyes and remember the beautiful sunsets and sunrises that you have seen throughout your life.

No matter where you are, you can find a remote place to spend time with God. The remote places can become oases. There you commune with God so you can go into your busy world renewed with strength and faith. Whatever you do, remember, do it with God!

13 Blessed *be* the L<small>ORD</small> God of Israel
   From everlasting to everlasting!
   Amen and Amen.

Book Two   Psalms 42–72

PSALM 42

To the Chief Musician. A Contemplation*a* of the
sons of Korah.

1 As the deer pants for the water
      brooks,
   So pants my soul for You, O
      God.
2 My soul thirsts for God, for the
      living God.
   When shall I come and appear
      before God?*a*
3 My tears have been my food day
      and night,
   While they continually say to me,
"Where *is* your God?"

4 When I remember these *things,*
   I pour out my soul within me.
   For I used to go with the
      multitude;
   I went with them to the house of
      God,
   With the voice of joy and praise,
   With a multitude that kept a
      pilgrim feast.

5 Why are you cast down, O my
      soul?
   And *why* are you disquieted
      within me?
   Hope in God, for I shall yet praise
      Him
   For the help of His countenance.*a*

6 O my God,*a* my soul is cast down
      within me;
   Therefore I will remember You
      from the land of the Jordan,
   And from the heights of Hermon,
   From the Hill Mizar.
7 Deep calls unto deep at the noise
      of Your waterfalls;
   All Your waves and billows have
      gone over me.
8 The L<small>ORD</small> will command His
      lovingkindness in the daytime,
   And in the night His song *shall
      be* with me—
   A prayer to the God of my life.

9 I will say to God my Rock,
   "Why have You forgotten me?
   Why do I go mourning because
      of the oppression of the
      enemy?"
10 *As* with a breaking of my bones,
   My enemies reproach me,
   While they say to me all day
      long,
   "Where *is* your God?"

11 Why are you cast down, O my
      soul?
   And why are you disquieted
      within me?
   Hope in God;
   For I shall yet praise Him,
   The help of my countenance and
      my God.

PSALM 43

1 Vindicate me, O God,
   And plead my cause against an
      ungodly nation;
   Oh, deliver me from the deceitful
      and unjust man!
2 For You *are* the God of my
      strength;
   Why do You cast me off?
   Why do I go mourning because
      of the oppression of the
      enemy?

3 Oh, send out Your light and Your
      truth!
   Let them lead me;
   Let them bring me to Your holy
      hill
   And to Your tabernacle.
4 Then I will go to the altar of
      God,
   To God my exceeding joy;
   And on the harp I will praise
      You,
   O God, my God.

5 Why are you cast down, O my
      soul?
   And why are you disquieted
      within me?
   Hope in God;
   For I shall yet praise Him,
   The help of my countenance and
      my God.

42:title *a*Hebrew *Maschil*   42:2 *a*Following Masoretic Text and Vulgate; some Hebrew manuscripts,
Septuagint, Syriac, Targum read *I see the face of God.*   42:5 *a*Following Masoretic Text and Targum; a
few Hebrew manuscripts, Septuagint, Syriac, and Vulgate read *The help of my countenance, my God.*
42:6 *a*Following Masoretic Text and Targum; a few Hebrew manuscripts, Septuagint, Syriac, and Vulgate
put *my God* at the end of verse 5.

PSALM 44

To the Chief Musician. A Contemplation[a] of the sons of Korah.

1   We have heard with our ears, O God,
    Our fathers have told us,
    The deeds You did in their days,
    In days of old:
2   You drove out the nations with Your hand,
    But them You planted;
    You afflicted the peoples, and cast them out.
3   For they did not gain possession of the land by their own sword,
    Nor did their own arm save them;
    But it was Your right hand, Your arm, and the light of Your countenance,
    Because You favored them.

4   You are my King, O God;[a]
    Command[b] victories for Jacob.
5   Through You we will push down our enemies;
    Through Your name we will trample those who rise up against us.
6   For I will not trust in my bow,
    Nor shall my sword save me.
7   But You have saved us from our enemies,
    And have put to shame those who hated us.
8   In God we boast all day long,
    And praise Your name forever.
                              Selah

9   But You have cast us off and put us to shame,
    And You do not go out with our armies.
10 You make us turn back from the enemy,
    And those who hate us have taken spoil for themselves.
11 You have given us up like sheep intended for food,
    And have scattered us among the nations.
12 You sell Your people for next to nothing,
    And are not enriched by selling them.

13 You make us a reproach to our neighbors,
    A scorn and a derision to those all around us.
14 You make us a byword among the nations,
    A shaking of the head among the peoples.
15 My dishonor is continually before me,
    And the shame of my face has covered me,
16 Because of the voice of him who reproaches and reviles,
    Because of the enemy and the avenger.

17 All this has come upon us;
    But we have not forgotten You,
    Nor have we dealt falsely with Your covenant.
18 Our heart has not turned back,
    Nor have our steps departed from Your way;
19 But You have severely broken us in the place of jackals,
    And covered us with the shadow of death.

20 If we had forgotten the name of our God,
    Or stretched out our hands to a foreign god,
21 Would not God search this out?
    For He knows the secrets of the heart.
22 Yet for Your sake we are killed all day long;
    We are accounted as sheep for the slaughter.
23 Awake! Why do You sleep, O Lord?
    Arise! Do not cast us off forever.
24 Why do You hide Your face,
    And forget our affliction and our oppression?
25 For our soul is bowed down to the dust;
    Our body clings to the ground.
26 Arise for our help,
    And redeem us for Your mercies' sake.

PSALM 45

To the Chief Musician. Set to "The Lilies."[a] A Contemplation[b] of the sons of Korah. A Song of Love.

1   My heart is overflowing with a good theme;
    I recite my composition concerning the King;

44:title [a]Hebrew *Maschil*   44:4 [a]Following Masoretic Text and Targum; Septuagint and Vulgate read *and my God*.   [b]Following Masoretic Text and Targum; Septuagint, Syriac, and Vulgate read *who commands*.
45:title [a]Hebrew *Shoshannim*   [b]Hebrew *Maschil*

My tongue *is* the pen of a ready writer.

2 You are fairer than the sons of men;
Grace is poured upon Your lips;
Therefore God has blessed You forever.

3 Gird Your sword upon *Your* thigh, O Mighty One,
With Your glory and Your majesty.

4 And in Your majesty ride prosperously because of truth, humility, *and* righteousness;
And Your right hand shall teach You awesome things.

5 Your arrows *are* sharp in the heart of the King's enemies;
The peoples fall under You.

6 Your throne, O God, *is* forever and ever;
A scepter of righteousness *is* the scepter of Your kingdom.

7 You love righteousness and hate wickedness;
Therefore God, Your God, has anointed You
With the oil of gladness more than Your companions.

8 All Your garments are scented with myrrh and aloes *and* cassia,
Out of the ivory palaces, by which they have made You glad.

9 Kings' daughters *are* among Your honorable women;
At Your right hand stands the queen in gold from Ophir.

10 Listen, O daughter,
Consider and incline your ear;
Forget your own people also, and your father's house;

11 So the King will greatly desire your beauty;
Because He *is* your Lord, worship Him.

12 And the daughter of Tyre *will come* with a gift;
The rich among the people will seek your favor.

13 The royal daughter *is* all glorious within *the palace;*
Her clothing *is* woven with gold.

14 She shall be brought to the King in robes of many colors;
The virgins, her companions who follow her, shall be brought to You.

15 With gladness and rejoicing they shall be brought;
They shall enter the King's palace.

16 Instead of Your fathers shall be Your sons,
Whom You shall make princes in all the earth.

17 I will make Your name to be remembered in all generations;
Therefore the people shall praise You forever and ever.

PSALM 46

To the Chief Musician. A Psalm of the sons of Korah. A Song for Alamoth.

1 God *is* our refuge and strength,
A very present help in trouble.

2 Therefore we will not fear,
Even though the earth be removed,
And though the mountains be carried into the midst of the sea;

3 *Though* its waters roar *and* be troubled,
Though the mountains shake with its swelling.   Selah

4 *There is* a river whose streams shall make glad the city of God,
The holy *place* of the tabernacle of the Most High.

5 God *is* in the midst of her, she shall not be moved;
God shall help her, just at the break of dawn.

6 The nations raged, the kingdoms were moved;
He uttered His voice, the earth melted.

7 The LORD of hosts *is* with us;
The God of Jacob *is* our refuge.   Selah

8 Come, behold the works of the LORD,
Who has made desolations in the earth.

9 He makes wars cease to the end of the earth;
He breaks the bow and cuts the spear in two;
He burns the chariot in the fire.

10 Be still, and know that I *am* God;
I will be exalted among the nations,
I will be exalted in the earth!

Put God on Your North

Beautiful in elevation,
The joy of the whole earth,
Is Mount Zion *on* the sides of the north,
The city of the great King.

(Ps. 48:2)

The city in the psalmist's mind is Jerusalem—the city of God's presence and peace. Jerusalem is set above the surrounding countryside of Judea on an oval-shaped hill. Steep valleys on three sides of the city magnify its impenetrable position. To the east is the Mount of Olives and the Kidron Valley, and to the south and west are the Hinnom and Tyropean Valleys. Only from the north is the city vulnerable.

In biblical times, this easy northern access was the main approach route to Jerusalem. Even today it remains a major travel route. However, it also posed a real threat to the people of the city. For only from the north could an enemy attack the city successfully.

It was here at Jerusalem's unprotected point that the mighty temple was built with its high walls and impregnable fortress. The temple was all that stood between the people of the city and the approaching armies.

The psalmist may have often sat on the Mount of Olives overlooking Jerusalem with her temple, "Mount Zion," reflecting on her geographical position and observing the strong northern walls of God's temple which protected the city. He knew how dependent Jerusalem was on God's protection from her potential problems and enemies. His psalm of praise so appropriately reflects this prayer: "The joy of the whole earth, is Mount Zion on the sides of the north, the city of the great King."

God's presence in His temple, both physically and spiritually, was able to fortify the city where it was vulnerable. Only He can strengthen you where you are weak. Let Him be the fortress between you and the negative influences which would destroy you. Let God be the "Mount Zion" in your life. Put God on your north!

11 The LORD of hosts *is* with us;
    The God of Jacob *is* our refuge.
                                    Selah

PSALM 47

To the Chief Musician. A Psalm of the sons of Korah.

1 Oh, clap your hands, all you
       peoples!
    Shout to God with the voice of
       triumph!
2 For the LORD Most High *is*
       awesome;
    He is a great King over all the
       earth.
3 He will subdue the peoples under
       us,
    And the nations under our feet.
4 He will choose our inheritance
       for us,
    The excellence of Jacob whom
       He loves.   Selah

5 God has gone up with a shout,
    The LORD with the sound of a
       trumpet.
6 Sing praises to God, sing
       praises!
    Sing praises to our King, sing
       praises!
7 For God *is* the King of all the
       earth;
    Sing praises with understanding.

8 God reigns over the nations;
    God sits on His holy throne.
9 The princes of the people have
       gathered together,
    The people of the God of
       Abraham.
    For the shields of the earth
       belong to God;
    He is greatly exalted.

PSALM 48

A Song. A Psalm of the sons of Korah.

1 Great *is* the LORD, and greatly to
       be praised
    In the city of our God,
    In His holy mountain.
2 Beautiful in elevation,
    The joy of the whole earth,
    Is Mount Zion *on* the sides of the
       north,
    The city of the great King.
3 God *is* in her palaces;
    He is known as her refuge.

4 For behold, the kings assembled,
    They passed by together.
5 They saw *it, and* so they
       marveled;
    They were troubled, they
       hastened away.
6 Fear took hold of them there,
    And pain, as of a woman in birth
       pangs,
7 *As when* You break the ships of
       Tarshish
    With an east wind.

8 As we have heard,
    So we have seen
    In the city of the LORD of hosts,
    In the city of our God:
    God will establish it forever.
                                    Selah

9 We have thought, O God, on
       Your lovingkindness,
    In the midst of Your temple.
10 According to Your name, O God,
    So *is* Your praise to the ends of
       the earth;
    Your right hand is full of
       righteousness.
11 Let Mount Zion rejoice,
    Let the daughters of Judah be
       glad,
    Because of Your judgments.

12 Walk about Zion,
    And go all around her.
    Count her towers;
13 Mark well her bulwarks;
    Consider her palaces;
    That you may tell *it* to the
       generation following.
14 For this *is* God,
    Our God forever and ever;
    He will be our guide
    Even to death.[a]

PSALM 49

To the Chief Musician. A Psalm of the sons of Korah.

1 Hear this, all peoples;
    Give ear, all inhabitants of the
       world,
2 Both low and high,
    Rich and poor together.
3 My mouth shall speak wisdom,
    And the meditation of my heart
       shall give understanding.
4 I will incline my ear to a proverb;
    I will disclose my dark saying on
       the harp.

48:14 [a]Following Masoretic Text and Syriac; Septuagint and Vulgate read *Forever*.

5 Why should I fear in the days of evil,
  When the iniquity at my heels surrounds me?
6 Those who trust in their wealth
  And boast in the multitude of their riches,
7 None *of them* can by any means redeem *his* brother,
  Nor give to God a ransom for him—
8 For the redemption of their souls *is* costly,
  And it shall cease forever—
9 That he should continue to live eternally,
  And not see the Pit.

10 For he sees wise men die;
  Likewise the fool and the senseless person perish,
  And leave their wealth to others.
11 Their inner thought *is that* their houses *will last* forever,[a]
  Their dwelling places to all generations;
  They call *their* lands after their own names.
12 Nevertheless man, *though* in honor, does not remain;[a]
  He is like the beasts *that* perish.

13 This is the way of those who *are* foolish,
  And of their posterity who approve their sayings.   Selah
14 Like sheep they are laid in the grave;
  Death shall feed on them;
  The upright shall have dominion over them in the morning;
  And their beauty shall be consumed in the grave, far from their dwelling.
15 But God will redeem my soul from the power of the grave,
  For He shall receive me.
                            Selah

16 Do not be afraid when one becomes rich,
  When the glory of his house is increased;
17 For when he dies he shall carry nothing away;
  His glory shall not descend after him.

18 Though while he lives he blesses himself
  (For *men* will praise you when you do well for yourself),
19 He shall go to the generation of his fathers;
  They shall never see light.
20 A man *who is* in honor, yet does not understand,
  Is like the beasts *that* perish.

PSALM 50

A Psalm of Asaph.

1 The Mighty One, God the LORD,
  Has spoken and called the earth
  From the rising of the sun to its going down.
2 Out of Zion, the perfection of beauty,
  God will shine forth.
3 Our God shall come, and shall not keep silent;
  A fire shall devour before Him,
  And it shall be very tempestuous all around Him.

4 He shall call to the heavens from above,
  And to the earth, that He may judge His people:
5 "Gather My saints together to Me,
  Those who have made a covenant with Me by sacrifice."
6 Let the heavens declare His righteousness,
  For God Himself *is* Judge.
                            Selah

7 "Hear, O My people, and I will speak,
  O Israel, and I will testify against you;
  I *am* God, your God!
8 I will not rebuke you for your sacrifices
  Or your burnt offerings,
  Which are continually before Me.
9 I will not take a bull from your house,
  Nor goats out of your folds.
10 For every beast of the forest *is* Mine,
  And the cattle on a thousand hills.
11 I know all the birds of the mountains,

49:11 [a]Septuagint, Syriac, Targum, and Vulgate read *Their graves shall be their houses forever.*
49:12 [a]Following Masoretic Text and Targum; Septuagint, Syriac, and Vulgate read *understand* (compare verse 20).

And the wild beasts of the field
are Mine.

12 "If I were hungry, I would not tell
you;
For the world *is* Mine, and all its
fullness.
13 Will I eat the flesh of bulls,
Or drink the blood of goats?
14 Offer to God thanksgiving,
And pay your vows to the Most
High.
15 Call upon Me in the day of
trouble;
I will deliver you, and you shall
glorify Me."

16 But to the wicked God says:
"What *right* have you to declare
My statutes,
Or take My covenant in your
mouth,
17 Seeing you hate instruction
And cast My words behind you?
18 When you saw a thief, you
consented[a] with him,
And have been a partaker with
adulterers.
19 You give your mouth to evil,
And your tongue frames deceit.
20 You sit *and* speak against your
brother;
You slander your own mother's
son.
21 These *things* you have done, and
I kept silent;
You thought that I was altogether
like you;
But I will rebuke you,
And set *them* in order before
your eyes.

22 "Now consider this, you who
forget God,
Lest I tear *you* in pieces,
And *there be* none to deliver:
23 Whoever offers praise glorifies
Me;
And to him who orders *his*
conduct *aright*
I will show the salvation of God."

PSALM 51

To the Chief Musician. A Psalm of David when
Nathan the prophet went to him, after he had
gone in to Bathsheba.

1 Have mercy upon me, O God,
According to Your
lovingkindness;

According to the multitude of
Your tender mercies,
Blot out my transgressions.
2 Wash me thoroughly from my
iniquity,
And cleanse me from my sin.

3 For I acknowledge my
transgressions,
And my sin *is* always before me.
4 Against You, You only, have I
sinned,
And done *this* evil in Your
sight—
That You may be found just when
You speak,[a]
And blameless when You judge.

5 Behold, I was brought forth in
iniquity,
And in sin my mother conceived
me.
6 Behold, You desire truth in the
inward parts,
And in the hidden *part* You will
make me to know wisdom.

7 Purge me with hyssop, and I shall
be clean;
Wash me, and I shall be whiter
than snow.
8 Make me hear joy and gladness,
That the bones You have broken
may rejoice.
9 Hide Your face from my sins,
And blot out all my iniquities.

10 Create in me a clean heart, O
God,
And renew a steadfast spirit
within me.
11 Do not cast me away from Your
presence,
And do not take Your Holy Spirit
from me.

12 Restore to me the joy of Your
salvation,
And uphold me *by Your* generous
Spirit.
13 *Then* I will teach transgressors
Your ways,
And sinners shall be converted to
You.

14 Deliver me from the guilt of
bloodshed, O God,
The God of my salvation,

50:18 [a]Septuagint, Syriac, Targum, and Vulgate read *run.*
in Your words.
51:4 [a]Septuagint, Targum, and Vulgate read

And my tongue shall sing aloud
of Your righteousness.
15 O Lord, open my lips,
And my mouth shall show forth
Your praise.
16 For You do not desire sacrifice,
or else I would give *it;*
You do not delight in burnt
offering.
17 The sacrifices of God *are* a
broken spirit,
A broken and a contrite heart—
These, O God, You will not
despise.

18 Do good in Your good pleasure
to Zion;
Build the walls of Jerusalem.
19 Then You shall be pleased with
the sacrifices of righteousness,
With burnt offering and whole
burnt offering;
Then they shall offer bulls on
Your altar.

PSALM 52

To the Chief Musician. A Contemplation*a* of
David when Doeg the Edomite went and told
Saul, and said to him, "David has gone to the
house of Ahimelech."
1 Why do you boast in evil, O
mighty man?
The goodness of God *endures*
continually.
2 Your tongue devises destruction,
Like a sharp razor, working
deceitfully.
3 You love evil more than good,
Lying rather than speaking
righteousness.   Selah
4 You love all devouring words,
You deceitful tongue.

5 God shall likewise destroy you
forever;
He shall take you away, and
pluck you out of *your* dwelling
place,
And uproot you from the land of
the living.   Selah
6 The righteous also shall see and
fear,
And shall laugh at him, *saying,*
7 "Here is the man *who* did not
make God his strength,
But trusted in the abundance of
his riches,
And strengthened himself in his
wickedness."

8 But I *am* like a green olive tree
in the house of God;
I trust in the mercy of God
forever and ever.
9 I will praise You forever,
Because You have done *it;*
And in the presence of Your
saints
I will wait on Your name, for *it
is* good.

PSALM 53

To the Chief Musician. Set to "Mahalath." A
Contemplation*a* of David.
1 The fool has said in his heart,
"There is no God."
They are corrupt, and have done
abominable iniquity;
There is none who does good.

2 God looks down from heaven
upon the children of men,
To see if there are *any* who
understand, who seek God.
3 Every one of them has turned
aside;
They have together become
corrupt;
There is none who does good,
No, not one.

4 Have the workers of iniquity no
knowledge,
Who eat up my people *as* they
eat bread,
And do not call upon God?
5 There they are in great fear
Where no fear was,
For God has scattered the bones
of him who encamps against
you;
You have put *them* to shame,
Because God has despised them.

6 Oh, that the salvation of Israel
would come out of Zion!
When God brings back the
captivity of His people,
Let Jacob rejoice *and* Israel be
glad.

PSALM 54

To the Chief Musician. With stringed
instruments.*a* A Contemplation*b* of David when
the Ziphites went and said to Saul, "Is David
not hiding with us?"
1 Save me, O God, by Your name,
And vindicate me by Your
strength.

52:title *a*Hebrew *Maschil*   53:title *a*Hebrew *Maschil*   54:title *a*Hebrew *neginoth*   *b*Hebrew *Maschil*

Give God Your Burdens

Faith is trusting that God will settle the accounts with those who have been unjust and unfair with you. The psalmist David wrote: "Cast your burden on the LORD, and He shall sustain you; He shall never permit the righteous to be moved" (Ps. 55:22). No one travels the road of life without being affected by injustice at one time or another.

But the worst thing that can happen to you is to develop *victimitis*.

Victimitis is carrying your grudge and nursing the hurts. This only produces a whole new batch of emotional demons to torment your soul! Resentment, anger, self-pity, and even vengeance become a mixed-up recipe for messed-up feelings.

If you walk the walk of faith, there will be times when you'll be treated unfairly. At such times, you can be assured that God can handle the injustice a lot better than you can.

You have the faith that He'll settle the score in a way that will be helpful and not hurtful to everyone concerned. So don't *carry* the grudge; *bury* it.

You can be positive about one thing. God knows the ins and outs of the entire upsetting situation a lot better than you do. God knows how to pull weeds without killing the flowers!

He understands your opponents, adversaries, and enemies a lot better than you do. God knows how to turn an enemy into a friend, too!

Take time to pray: *Dear God, with Your help, I promise to drop all resentments, all injustices, into the deepest sea of Your power and mercy and love. I trust You to settle the matter in the best way!*

Thank You, God, for taking over this problem before it does untold damage to my spirit! Amen.

2 Hear my prayer, O God;
   Give ear to the words of my
     mouth.
3 For strangers have risen up
     against me,
   And oppressors have sought
     after my life;
   They have not set God before
     them.   Selah

4 Behold, God *is* my helper;
   The Lord *is* with those who
     uphold my life.
5 He will repay my enemies for
     their evil.
   Cut them off in Your truth.

6 I will freely sacrifice to You;
   I will praise Your name, O LORD,
     for *it is* good.
7 For He has delivered me out of
     all trouble;
   And my eye has seen *its desire*
     upon my enemies.

PSALM 55

To the Chief Musician. With stringed
instruments.*a* A Contemplation*b* of David.

1 Give ear to my prayer, O God,
   And do not hide Yourself from
     my supplication.
2 Attend to me, and hear me;
   I am restless in my complaint,
     and moan noisily,
3 Because of the voice of the
     enemy,
   Because of the oppression of the
     wicked;
   For they bring down trouble upon
     me,
   And in wrath they hate me.

4 My heart is severely pained
     within me,
   And the terrors of death have
     fallen upon me.
5 Fearfulness and trembling have
     come upon me,
   And horror has overwhelmed
     me.
6 So I said, "Oh, that I had wings
     like a dove!
   I would fly away and be at rest.
7 Indeed, I would wander far off,
   And remain in the wilderness.
                                Selah
8 I would hasten my escape
   From the windy storm *and*
     tempest."

9 Destroy, O Lord, *and* divide their
     tongues,
   For I have seen violence and
     strife in the city.
10 Day and night they go around it
     on its walls;
   Iniquity and trouble *are* also in
     the midst of it.
11 Destruction *is* in its midst;
   Oppression and deceit do not
     depart from its streets.

12 For *it is* not an enemy *who*
     reproaches me;
   Then I could bear *it.*
   Nor *is it* one *who* hates me who
     has exalted *himself* against me;
   Then I could hide from him.
13 But *it was* you, a man my equal,
   My companion and my
     acquaintance.
14 We took sweet counsel together,
   And walked to the house of God
     in the throng.

15 Let death seize them;
   Let them go down alive into hell,
   For wickedness *is* in their
     dwellings *and* among them.

16 As for me, I will call upon God,
   And the LORD shall save me.
17 Evening and morning and at
     noon
   I will pray, and cry aloud,
   And He shall hear my voice.
18 He has redeemed my soul in
     peace from the battle *that was*
     against me,
   For there were many against me.
19 God will hear, and afflict them,
   Even He who abides from of old.
                                Selah
   Because they do not change,
   Therefore they do not fear God.

20 He has put forth his hands
     against those who were at
     peace with him;
   He has broken his covenant.
21 *The words* of his mouth were
     smoother than butter,
   But war *was* in his heart;
   His words were softer than oil,
   Yet they *were* drawn swords.

22 Cast your burden on the LORD,
   And He shall sustain you;
   He shall never permit the
     righteous to be moved.

55:title *a*Hebrew *neginoth*   *b*Hebrew *Maschil*

23 But You, O God, shall bring them
    down to the pit of destruction;
    Bloodthirsty and deceitful men
    shall not live out half their
    days;
    But I will trust in You.

PSALM 56

To the Chief Musician. Set to "The Silent Dove
in Distant Lands."ᵃ A Michtam of David when
the Philistines captured him in Gath.

1 Be merciful to me, O God, for
    man would swallow me up;
    Fighting all day he oppresses me.
2 My enemies would hound *me* all
    day,
    For *there are* many who fight
    against me, O Most High.

3 Whenever I am afraid,
    I will trust in You.
4 In God (I will praise His word),
    In God I have put my trust;
    I will not fear.
    What can flesh do to me?

5 All day they twist my words;
    All their thoughts *are* against me
    for evil.
6 They gather together,
    They hide, they mark my steps,
    When they lie in wait for my life.
7 Shall they escape by iniquity?
    In anger cast down the peoples,
    O God!

8 You number my wanderings;
    Put my tears into Your bottle;
    Are they not in Your book?
9 When I cry out *to You,*
    Then my enemies will turn back;
    This I know, because God *is* for
    me.
10 In God (I will praise *His* word),
    In the LORD (I will praise *His*
    word),
11 In God I have put my trust;
    I will not be afraid.
    What can man do to me?

12 Vows *made* to You *are binding*
    upon me, O God;
    I will render praises to You,
13 For You have delivered my soul
    from death.
    Have You not *kept* my feet from
    falling,
    That I may walk before God
    In the light of the living?

PSALM 57

To the Chief Musician. Set to "Do Not Destroy."ᵃ
A Michtam of David when he fled from Saul into
the cave.

1 Be merciful to me, O God, be
    merciful to me!
    For my soul trusts in You;
    And in the shadow of Your wings
    I will make my refuge,
    Until *these* calamities have
    passed by.

2 I will cry out to God Most High,
    To God who performs *all things*
    for me.
3 He shall send from heaven and
    save me;
    He reproaches the one who
    would swallow me up.   Selah
    God shall send forth His mercy
    and His truth.

4 My soul *is* among lions;
    I lie *among* the sons of men
    Who are set on fire,
    Whose teeth *are* spears and
    arrows,
    And their tongue a sharp sword.
5 Be exalted, O God, above the
    heavens;
    Let Your glory *be* above all the
    earth.

6 They have prepared a net for my
    steps;
    My soul is bowed down;
    They have dug a pit before me;
    Into the midst of it they
    themselves have fallen.
                            Selah

7 My heart is steadfast, O God, my
    heart is steadfast;
    I will sing and give praise.
8 Awake, my glory!
    Awake, lute and harp!
    I will awaken the dawn.

9 I will praise You, O Lord, among
    the peoples;
    I will sing to You among the
    nations.
10 For Your mercy reaches unto the
    heavens,
    And Your truth unto the clouds.

11 Be exalted, O God, above the
    heavens;

Let Your glory *be* above all the earth.

PSALM 58

To the Chief Musician. Set to "Do Not Destroy."*a*
A Michtam of David.

1 Do you indeed speak
  righteousness, you silent ones?
  Do you judge uprightly, you sons
  of men?
2 No, in heart you work
  wickedness;
  You weigh out the violence of
  your hands in the earth.

3 The wicked are estranged from
  the womb;
  They go astray as soon as they
  are born, speaking lies.
4 Their poison *is* like the poison of
  a serpent;
  They are like the deaf cobra *that*
  stops its ear,
5 Which will not heed the voice of
  charmers,
  Charming ever so skillfully.

6 Break their teeth in their mouth,
  O God!
  Break out the fangs of the young
  lions, O LORD!
7 Let them flow away as waters
  which run continually;
  When he bends *his* bow,
  Let his arrows be as if cut in
  pieces.
8 *Let them be* like a snail which
  melts away as it goes,
  Like a stillborn child of a woman,
  that they may not see the sun.

9 Before your pots can feel *the
  burning* thorns,
  He shall take them away as with
  a whirlwind,
  As in His living and burning
  wrath.
10 The righteous shall rejoice when
  he sees the vengeance;
  He shall wash his feet in the
  blood of the wicked,
11 So that men will say,
  "Surely *there is* a reward for the
  righteous;
  Surely He is God who judges in
  the earth."

PSALM 59

To the Chief Musician. Set to "Do Not Destroy."*a*
A Michtam of David when Saul sent men, and
they watched the house in order to kill him.

1 Deliver me from my enemies, O
  my God;
  Defend me from those who rise
  up against me.
2 Deliver me from the workers of
  iniquity,
  And save me from bloodthirsty
  men.

3 For look, they lie in wait for my
  life;
  The mighty gather against me,
  Not *for* my transgression nor *for*
  my sin, O LORD.
4 They run and prepare themselves
  through no fault *of mine.*

  Awake to help me, and behold!
5 You therefore, O LORD God of
  hosts, the God of Israel,
  Awake to punish all the nations;
  Do not be merciful to any wicked
  transgressors.   Selah

6 At evening they return,
  They growl like a dog,
  And go all around the city.
7 Indeed, they belch with their
  mouth;
  Swords *are* in their lips;
  For *they say,* "Who hears?"

8 But You, O LORD, shall laugh at
  them;
  You shall have all the nations in
  derision.
9 I will wait for You,
  O You his Strength;*a*
  For God *is* my defense.
10 My God of mercy*a* shall come to
  meet me;
  God shall let me see *my desire*
  on my enemies.

11 Do not slay them, lest my people
  forget;
  Scatter them by Your power,
  And bring them down,
  O Lord our shield.
12 *For* the sin of their mouth *and* the
  words of their lips,

58:title *a*Hebrew *Al Tashcheth*   59:title *a*Hebrew *Al Tashcheth*   59:9 *a*Following Masoretic Text and Syriac; some Hebrew manuscripts, Septuagint, Targum, and Vulgate read *my Strength.*   59:10 *a*Following Qere; some Hebrew manuscripts, Septuagint, and Vulgate read *My God, His mercy;* Kethib, some Hebrew manuscripts and Targum read *O God, my mercy;* Syriac reads *O God, Your mercy.*

Let them even be taken in their
  pride,
And for the cursing and lying
  which they speak.
13 Consume *them* in wrath,
  consume *them,*
That they *may* not *be;*
And let them know that God rules
  in Jacob
To the ends of the earth.
                Selah

14 And at evening they return,
They growl like a dog,
And go all around the city.
15 They wander up and down for
  food,
And howl[a] if they are not
  satisfied.

16 But I will sing of Your power;
Yes, I will sing aloud of Your
  mercy in the morning;
For You have been my defense
And refuge in the day of my
  trouble.
17 To You, O my Strength, I will
  sing praises;
For God *is* my defense,
My God of mercy.

PSALM 60

To the Chief Musician. Set to "Lily of the
Testimony."[a] A Michtam of David. For teaching.
When he fought against Mesopotamia and Syria
of Zobah, and Joab returned and killed twelve
thousand Edomites in the Valley of Salt.

1 O God, You have cast us off;
You have broken us down;
You have been displeased;
Oh, restore us again!
2 You have made the earth
  tremble;
You have broken it;
Heal its breaches, for it is
  shaking.
3 You have shown Your people
  hard things;
You have made us drink the wine
  of confusion.
4 You have given a banner to those
  who fear You,
That it may be displayed because
  of the truth.   Selah
5 That Your beloved may be
  delivered,
Save *with* Your right hand, and
  hear me.

6 God has spoken in His holiness:
"I will rejoice;
I will divide Shechem
And measure out the Valley of
  Succoth.
7 Gilead *is* Mine, and Manasseh *is*
  Mine;
Ephraim also *is* the helmet for
  My head;
Judah *is* My lawgiver.
8 Moab *is* My washpot;
Over Edom I will cast My shoe;
Philistia, shout in triumph
  because of Me."

9 Who will bring me *to* the strong
  city?
Who will lead me to Edom?
10 *Is it* not You, O God, *who* cast
  us off?
And You, O God, *who* did not go
  out with our armies?
11 Give us help from trouble,
For the help of man *is* useless.
12 Through God we will do
  valiantly,
For *it is* He *who* shall tread down
  our enemies.[a]

PSALM 61

To the Chief Musician. On a stringed
instrument.[a] A Psalm of David.

1 Hear my cry, O God;
Attend to my prayer.
2 From the end of the earth I will
  cry to You,
When my heart is overwhelmed;
Lead me to the rock that is higher
  than I.

3 For You have been a shelter for
  me,
A strong tower from the enemy.
4 I will abide in Your tabernacle
  forever;
I will trust in the shelter of Your
  wings.   Selah

5 For You, O God, have heard my
  vows;
You have given *me* the heritage
  of those who fear Your name.
6 You will prolong the king's life,
His years as many generations.
7 He shall abide before God
  forever.
Oh, prepare mercy and truth,
  which may preserve him!

59:15 [a]Following Septuagint and Vulgate; Masoretic Text, Syriac, and Targum read *spend the night.*
60:title [a]Hebrew *Shushan Eduth*   60:12 [a]Compare verses 5–12 with 108:6–13   61:title [a]Hebrew *neginah*

8 So I will sing praise to Your name
    forever,
    That I may daily perform my
    vows.

PSALM 62

To the Chief Musician. To Jeduthun. A Psalm
of David.

1 Truly my soul silently *waits* for
    God;
    From Him *comes* my salvation.
2 He only *is* my rock and my
    salvation;
    He is my defense;
    I shall not be greatly moved.

3 How long will you attack a man?
    You shall be slain, all of you,
    Like a leaning wall and a
    tottering fence.
4 They only consult to cast *him*
    down from his high position;
    They delight in lies;
    They bless with their mouth,
    But they curse inwardly.   Selah

5 My soul, wait silently for God
    alone,
    For my expectation *is* from Him.
6 He only *is* my rock and my
    salvation;
    He is my defense;
    I shall not be moved.
7 In God *is* my salvation and my
    glory;
    The rock of my strength,
    And my refuge, *is* in God.

8 Trust in Him at all times, you
    people;
    Pour out your heart before Him;
    God *is* a refuge for us.   Selah

9 Surely men of low degree *are* a
    vapor,
    Men of high degree *are* a lie;
    If they are weighed on the scales,
    They *are* altogether *lighter* than
    vapor.
10 Do not trust in oppression,
    Nor vainly hope in robbery;
    If riches increase,
    Do not set *your* heart *on them.*

11 God has spoken once,
    Twice I have heard this:
    That power *belongs* to God.
12 Also to You, O Lord, *belongs*
    mercy;
    For You render to each one
    according to his work.

PSALM 63

A Psalm of David when he was in the wilderness
of Judah.

1 O God, You *are* my God;
    Early will I seek You;
    My soul thirsts for You;
    My flesh longs for You
    In a dry and thirsty land
    Where there is no water.
2 So I have looked for You in the
    sanctuary,
    To see Your power and Your
    glory.

3 Because Your lovingkindness *is*
    better than life,
    My lips shall praise You.
4 Thus I will bless You while I live;
    I will lift up my hands in Your
    name.
5 My soul shall be satisfied as with
    marrow and fatness,
    And my mouth shall praise You
    with joyful lips.

6 When I remember You on my
    bed,
    I meditate on You in the *night*
    watches.
7 Because You have been my help,
    Therefore in the shadow of Your
    wings I will rejoice.
8 My soul follows close behind
    You;
    Your right hand upholds me.

9 But those *who* seek my life, to
    destroy *it,*
    Shall go into the lower parts of
    the earth.
10 They shall fall by the sword;
    They shall be a portion for
    jackals.

11 But the king shall rejoice in God;
    Everyone who swears by Him
    shall glory;
    But the mouth of those who
    speak lies shall be stopped.

PSALM 64

To the Chief Musician. A Psalm of David.

1 Hear my voice, O God, in my
    meditation;
    Preserve my life from fear of the
    enemy.
2 Hide me from the secret plots of
    the wicked,
    From the rebellion of the workers
    of iniquity,

3 Who sharpen their tongue like a
     sword,
   And bend *their bows to shoot*
     their arrows—bitter words,
4 That they may shoot in secret at
     the blameless;
   Suddenly they shoot at him and
     do not fear.

5 They encourage themselves *in* an
     evil matter;
   They talk of laying snares
     secretly;
   They say, "Who will see them?"
6 They devise iniquities:
   "We have perfected a shrewd
     scheme."
   Both the inward thought and the
     heart of man are deep.

7 But God shall shoot at them *with*
     an arrow;
   Suddenly they shall be wounded.
8 So He will make them stumble
     over their own tongue;
   All who see them shall flee away.
9 All men shall fear,
   And shall declare the work of
     God;
   For they shall wisely consider His
     doing.

10 The righteous shall be glad in the
     LORD, and trust in Him.
   And all the upright in heart shall
     glory.

PSALM 65

To the Chief Musician. A Psalm of David. A
Song.

1 Praise is awaiting You, O God,
     in Zion;
   And to You the vow shall be
     performed.
2 O You who hear prayer,
   To You all flesh will come.
3 Iniquities prevail against me;
   As for our transgressions,
   You will provide atonement for
     them.

4 Blessed *is the man* You choose,
   And cause to approach *You,*
   That he may dwell in Your
     courts.
   We shall be satisfied with the
     goodness of Your house,
   Of Your holy temple.

5 By awesome deeds in
     righteousness You will answer
     us,

O God of our salvation,
You who are the confidence of all
   the ends of the earth,
And of the far-off seas;
6 Who established the mountains
   by His strength,
Being clothed with power;
7 You who still the noise of the
   seas,
The noise of their waves,
And the tumult of the peoples.
8 They also who dwell in the
   farthest parts are afraid of
   Your signs;
You make the outgoings of the
   morning and evening rejoice.

9 You visit the earth and water it,
You greatly enrich it;
The river of God is full of water;
You provide their grain,
For so You have prepared it.
10 You water its ridges abundantly,
You settle its furrows;
You make it soft with showers,
You bless its growth.

11 You crown the year with Your
   goodness,
And Your paths drip *with*
   abundance.
12 They drop *on* the pastures of the
   wilderness,
And the little hills rejoice on
   every side.
13 The pastures are clothed with
   flocks;
The valleys also are covered with
   grain;
They shout for joy, they also sing.

PSALM 66

To the Chief Musician. A Song. A Psalm.

1 Make a joyful shout to God, all
   the earth!
2 Sing out the honor of His name;
   Make His praise glorious.
3 Say to God,
"How awesome are Your works!
Through the greatness of Your
   power
Your enemies shall submit
   themselves to You.
4 All the earth shall worship You
And sing praises to You;
They shall sing praises *to* Your
   name."   Selah

5 Come and see the works of God;
He is awesome *in His* doing
   toward the sons of men.

6 He turned the sea into dry *land;*
 They went through the river on
  foot.
 There we will rejoice in Him.
7 He rules by His power forever;
 His eyes observe the nations;
 Do not let the rebellious exalt
  themselves.   Selah

8 Oh, bless our God, you peoples!
 And make the voice of His praise
  to be heard,
9 Who keeps our soul among the
  living,
 And does not allow our feet to be
  moved.
10 For You, O God, have tested us;
 You have refined us as silver is
  refined.
11 You brought us into the net;
 You laid affliction on our backs.
12 You have caused men to ride
  over our heads;
 We went through fire and
  through water;
 But You brought us out to rich
  fulfillment.

13 I will go into Your house with
  burnt offerings;
 I will pay You my vows,
14 Which my lips have uttered
 And my mouth has spoken when
  I was in trouble.
15 I will offer You burnt sacrifices
  of fat animals,
 With the sweet aroma of rams;
 I will offer bulls with goats.
                           Selah

16 Come *and* hear, all you who fear
  God,
 And I will declare what He has
  done for my soul.
17 I cried to Him with my mouth,
 And He was extolled with my
  tongue.
18 If I regard iniquity in my heart,
 The Lord will not hear.
19 *But* certainly God has heard
  me;
 He has attended to the voice of
  my prayer.

20 Blessed *be* God,
 Who has not turned away my
  prayer,
 Nor His mercy from me!

PSALM 67

To the Chief Musician. On stringed instruments.*a*
A Psalm. A Song.

1 God be merciful to us and bless
  us,
 And cause His face to shine upon
  us,   Selah
2 That Your way may be known on
  earth,
 Your salvation among all
  nations.

3 Let the peoples praise You, O
  God;
 Let all the peoples praise You.
4 Oh, let the nations be glad and
  sing for joy!
 For You shall judge the people
  righteously,
 And govern the nations on earth.
                           Selah

5 Let the peoples praise You, O
  God;
 Let all the peoples praise You.
6 *Then* the earth shall yield her
  increase;
 God, our own God, shall bless
  us.
7 God shall bless us,
 And all the ends of the earth shall
  fear Him.

PSALM 68

To the Chief Musician. A Psalm of David. A
Song.

1 Let God arise,
 Let His enemies be scattered;
 Let those also who hate Him flee
  before Him.
2 As smoke is driven away,
 So drive *them* away;
 As wax melts before the fire,
 So let the wicked perish at the
  presence of God.
3 But let the righteous be glad;
 Let them rejoice before God;
 Yes, let them rejoice exceedingly.

4 Sing to God, sing praises to His
  name;
 Extol Him who rides on the
  clouds,*a*
 By His name YAH,
 And rejoice before Him.

67:title *a*Hebrew *neginoth*   68:4 *a*Masoretic Text reads *deserts;* Targum reads *heavens* (compare verse
34 and Isaiah 19:1).

5 A father of the fatherless, a
       defender of widows,
   Is God in His holy habitation.
6 God sets the solitary in families;
   He brings out those who are
       bound into prosperity;
   But the rebellious dwell in a dry
       land.

7 O God, when You went out
       before Your people,
   When You marched through the
       wilderness,   Selah
8 The earth shook;
   The heavens also dropped *rain* at
       the presence of God;
   Sinai itself *was moved* at the
       presence of God, the God of
       Israel.
9 You, O God, sent a plentiful rain,
   Whereby You confirmed Your
       inheritance,
   When it was weary.
10 Your congregation dwelt in it;
   You, O God, provided from Your
       goodness for the poor.

11 The Lord gave the word;
   Great *was* the company of those
       who proclaimed *it:*
12 "Kings of armies flee, they flee,
   And she who remains at home
       divides the spoil.
13 Though you lie down among the
       sheepfolds,
   You will be like the wings of a
       dove covered with silver,
   And her feathers with yellow
       gold."
14 When the Almighty scattered
       kings in it,
   It was *white* as snow in Zalmon.

15 A mountain of God *is* the
       mountain of Bashan;
   A mountain *of many* peaks *is* the
       mountain of Bashan.
16 Why do you fume with envy, you
       mountains *of many* peaks?
   This is the mountain *which* God
       desires to dwell in;
   Yes, the Lord will dwell *in it*
       forever.

17 The chariots of God *are* twenty
       thousand,
   Even thousands of thousands;
   The Lord is among them *as in*
       Sinai, in the Holy *Place.*

18 You have ascended on high,
   You have led captivity captive;
   You have received gifts among
       men,
   Even *from* the rebellious,
   That the Lord God might dwell
       there.

19 Blessed *be* the Lord,
   Who daily loads us *with benefits,*
   The God of our salvation!
                            Selah
20 Our God *is* the God of salvation;
   And to God the Lord *belong*
       escapes from death.

21 But God will wound the head of
       His enemies,
   The hairy scalp of the one who
       still goes on in his trespasses.
22 The Lord said, "I will bring back
       from Bashan,
   I will bring *them* back from the
       depths of the sea,
23 That your foot may crush *them*[a]
       in blood,
   And the tongues of your dogs
       may have their portion from
       your enemies."

24 They have seen Your procession,
       O God,
   The procession of my God, my
       King, into the sanctuary.
25 The singers went before, the
       players on instruments
       followed after;
   Among *them were* the maidens
       playing timbrels.
26 Bless God in the congregations,
   The Lord, from the fountain of
       Israel.
27 There *is* little Benjamin, their
       leader,
   The princes of Judah *and* their
       company,
   The princes of Zebulun *and* the
       princes of Naphtali.

28 Your God has commanded[a] your
       strength;
   Strengthen, O God, what You
       have done for us.
29 Because of Your temple at
       Jerusalem,
   Kings will bring presents to You.
30 Rebuke the beasts of the reeds,
   The herd of bulls with the calves
       of the peoples,

68:23 [a]Septuagint, [Syriac], Targum, and Vulgate read *you may dip your foot.*   68:28 [a]Septuagint, [Syriac],
Targum, and Vulgate read *Command, O God.*

Till everyone submits himself
with pieces of silver.
Scatter the peoples *who* delight
in war.

31 Envoys will come out of Egypt;
Ethiopia will quickly stretch out
her hands to God.

32 Sing to God, you kingdoms of the
earth;
Oh, sing praises to the Lord,
Selah

33 To Him who rides on the heaven
of heavens, *which were* of old!
Indeed, He sends out His voice,
a mighty voice.

34 Ascribe strength to God;
His excellence *is* over Israel,
And His strength *is* in the clouds.

35 O God, *You are* more awesome
than Your holy places.
The God of Israel *is* He who gives
strength and power to *His*
people.

Blessed *be* God!

PSALM 69

To the Chief Musician. Set to "The Lilies."[a] A
Psalm of David.

1 Save me, O God!
For the waters have come up to
my neck.

2 I sink in deep mire,
Where *there is* no standing;
I have come into deep waters,
Where the floods overflow me.

3 I am weary with my crying;
My throat is dry;
My eyes fail while I wait for my
God.

4 Those who hate me without a
cause
Are more than the hairs of my
head;
They are mighty who would
destroy me,
Being my enemies wrongfully;
Though I have stolen nothing,
I *still* must restore *it.*

5 O God, You know my
foolishness;
And my sins are not hidden from
You.

6 Let not those who wait for You,
O Lord GOD of hosts, be
ashamed because of me;

Let not those who seek You be
confounded because of me, O
God of Israel.

7 Because for Your sake I have
borne reproach;
Shame has covered my face.

8 I have become a stranger to my
brothers,
And an alien to my mother's
children;

9 Because zeal for Your house has
eaten me up,
And the reproaches of those who
reproach You have fallen on
me.

10 When I wept *and chastened* my
soul with fasting,
That became my reproach.

11 I also made sackcloth my
garment;
I became a byword to them.

12 Those who sit in the gate speak
against me,
And I *am* the song of the
drunkards.

13 But as for me, my prayer *is* to
You,
O LORD, *in* the acceptable time;
O God, in the multitude of Your
mercy,
Hear me in the truth of Your
salvation.

14 Deliver me out of the mire,
And let me not sink;
Let me be delivered from those
who hate me,
And out of the deep waters.

15 Let not the floodwater overflow
me,
Nor let the deep swallow me up;
And let not the pit shut its mouth
on me.

16 Hear me, O LORD, for Your
lovingkindness *is* good;
Turn to me according to the
multitude of Your tender
mercies.

17 And do not hide Your face from
Your servant,
For I am in trouble;
Hear me speedily.

18 Draw near to my soul, *and*
redeem it;
Deliver me because of my
enemies.

19 You know my reproach, my
shame, and my dishonor;

My adversaries *are* all before
You.

20 Reproach has broken my heart,
And I am full of heaviness;
I looked *for someone* to take pity,
but *there was* none;
And for comforters, but I found
none.

21 They also gave me gall for my
food,
And for my thirst they gave me
vinegar to drink.

22 Let their table become a snare
before them,
And their well-being a trap.

23 Let their eyes be darkened, so
that they do not see;
And make their loins shake
continually.

24 Pour out Your indignation upon
them,
And let Your wrathful anger take
hold of them.

25 Let their dwelling place be
desolate;
Let no one live in their tents.

26 For they persecute the *ones* You
have struck,
And talk of the grief of those You
have wounded.

27 Add iniquity to their iniquity,
And let them not come into Your
righteousness.

28 Let them be blotted out of the
book of the living,
And not be written with the
righteous.

29 But I *am* poor and sorrowful;
Let Your salvation, O God, set me
up on high.

30 I will praise the name of God with
a song,
And will magnify Him with
thanksgiving.

31 *This* also shall please the LORD
better than an ox *or* bull,
Which has horns and hooves.

32 The humble shall see *this and* be
glad;
And you who seek God, your
hearts shall live.

33 For the LORD hears the poor,
And does not despise His
prisoners.

34 Let heaven and earth praise Him,
The seas and everything that
moves in them.

35 For God will save Zion
And build the cities of Judah,
That they may dwell there and
possess it.

36 Also, the descendants of His
servants shall inherit it,
And those who love His name
shall dwell in it.

PSALM 70

To the Chief Musician. *A Psalm* of David. To
bring to remembrance.

1 Make *haste*, O God, to deliver
me!
Make haste to help me, O LORD!

2 Let them be ashamed and
confounded
Who seek my life;
Let them be turned back[a] and
confused
Who desire my hurt.

3 Let them be turned back because
of their shame,
Who say, "Aha, aha!"

4 Let all those who seek You
rejoice and be glad in You;
And let those who love Your
salvation say continually,
"Let God be magnified!"

5 But I *am* poor and needy;
Make haste to me, O God!
You *are* my help and my
deliverer;
O LORD, do not delay.

PSALM 71

1 In You, O LORD, I put my trust;
Let me never be put to shame.

2 Deliver me in Your
righteousness, and cause me to
escape;
Incline Your ear to me, and save
me.

3 Be my strong refuge,
To which I may resort
continually;
You have given the
commandment to save me,
For You *are* my rock and my
fortress.

4 Deliver me, O my God, out of the
hand of the wicked,
Out of the hand of the
unrighteous and cruel man.

70:2 [a]Following Masoretic Text, Septuagint, Targum, and Vulgate; some Hebrew manuscripts and Syriac
read *be appalled* (compare 40:15).

5 For You are my hope, O Lord
  GOD;
  You are my trust from my youth.
6 By You I have been upheld from
  birth;
  You are He who took me out of
  my mother's womb.
  My praise *shall be* continually of
  You.

7 I have become as a wonder to
  many,
  But You *are* my strong refuge.
8 Let my mouth be filled *with* Your
  praise
  And with Your glory all the day.

9 Do not cast me off in the time of
  old age;
  Do not forsake me when my
  strength fails.
10 For my enemies speak against
  me;
  And those who lie in wait for my
  life take counsel together,
11 Saying, "God has forsaken him;
  Pursue and take him, for *there is*
  none to deliver *him.*"

12 O God, do not be far from me;
  O my God, make haste to help
  me!
13 Let them be confounded *and*
  consumed
  Who are adversaries of my life;
  Let them be covered *with*
  reproach and dishonor
  Who seek my hurt.

14 But I will hope continually,
  And will praise You yet more and
  more.
15 My mouth shall tell of Your
  righteousness
  And Your salvation all the day,
  For I do not know *their* limits.
16 I will go in the strength of the
  Lord GOD;
  I will make mention of Your
  righteousness, of Yours only.

17 O God, You have taught me from
  my youth;
  And to this *day* I declare Your
  wondrous works.
18 Now also when *I am* old and
  grayheaded,
  O God, do not forsake me,
  Until I declare Your strength to
  this generation,

Your power to everyone *who* is
  to come.

19 Also Your righteousness, O God,
  is very high,
  You who have done great things;
  O God, who *is* like You?
20 *You,* who have shown me great
  and severe troubles,
  Shall revive me again,
  And bring me up again from the
  depths of the earth.
21 You shall increase my greatness,
  And comfort me on every side.

22 Also with the lute I will praise
  You—
  And Your faithfulness, O my
  God!
  To You I will sing with the harp,
  O Holy One of Israel.
23 My lips shall greatly rejoice when
  I sing to You,
  And my soul, which You have
  redeemed.
24 My tongue also shall talk of Your
  righteousness all the day long;
  For they are confounded,
  For they are brought to shame
  Who seek my hurt.

PSALM 72

A Psalm of Solomon.

1 Give the king Your judgments, O
  God,
  And Your righteousness to the
  king's Son.
2 He will judge Your people with
  righteousness,
  And Your poor with justice.
3 The mountains will bring peace
  to the people,
  And the little hills, by
  righteousness.
4 He will bring justice to the poor
  of the people;
  He will save the children of the
  needy,
  And will break in pieces the
  oppressor.

5 They shall fear You[a]
  As long as the sun and moon
  endure,
  Throughout all generations.
6 He shall come down like rain
  upon the grass before mowing,
  Like showers *that* water the
  earth.

72:5 [a]Following Masoretic Text and Targum; Septuagint and Vulgate read *They shall continue.*

7 In His days the righteous shall
    flourish,
And abundance of peace,
Until the moon is no more.

8 He shall have dominion also from
    sea to sea,
And from the River to the ends
    of the earth.
9 Those who dwell in the
    wilderness will bow before
    Him,
And His enemies will lick the
    dust.
10 The kings of Tarshish and of the
    isles
Will bring presents;
The kings of Sheba and Seba
    Will offer gifts.
11 Yes, all kings shall fall down
    before Him;
All nations shall serve Him.

12 For He will deliver the needy
    when he cries,
The poor also, and *him* who has
    no helper.
13 He will spare the poor and needy,
And will save the souls of the
    needy.
14 He will redeem their life from
    oppression and violence;
And precious shall be their blood
    in His sight.

15 And He shall live;
And the gold of Sheba will be
    given to Him;
Prayer also will be made for Him
    continually,
And daily He shall be praised.

16 There will be an abundance of
    grain in the earth,
On the top of the mountains;
Its fruit shall wave like Lebanon;
And *those* of the city shall
    flourish like grass of the earth.

17 His name shall endure forever;
His name shall continue as long
    as the sun.
And *men* shall be blessed in Him;
All nations shall call Him
    blessed.

18 Blessed *be* the LORD God, the God
    of Israel,
Who only does wondrous things!

19 And blessed *be* His glorious
    name forever!
And let the whole earth be filled
    with His glory.
Amen and Amen.

20 The prayers of David the son of
    Jesse are ended.

Book Three   Psalms 73–89

PSALM 73

A Psalm of Asaph.

1 Truly God *is* good to Israel,
To such as are pure in heart.
2 But as for me, my feet had almost
    stumbled;
My steps had nearly slipped.
3 For I *was* envious of the boastful,
When I saw the prosperity of the
    wicked.

4 For *there are* no pangs in their
    death,
But their strength *is* firm.
5 They *are* not in trouble *as other*
    men,
Nor are they plagued like *other*
    men.
6 Therefore pride serves as their
    necklace;
Violence covers them *like* a
    garment.
7 Their eyes bulge[a] with
    abundance;
They have more than heart could
    wish.
8 They scoff and speak wickedly
    concerning oppression;
They speak loftily.
9 They set their mouth against the
    heavens,
And their tongue walks through
    the earth.

10 Therefore his people return here,
And waters of a full *cup* are
    drained by them.
11 And they say, "How does God
    know?
And is there knowledge in the
    Most High?"
12 Behold, these *are* the ungodly,
Who are always at ease;
They increase *in* riches.
13 Surely I have cleansed my heart
    in vain,

73:7 ^aTargum reads *face bulges;* Septuagint, Syriac, and Vulgate read *iniquity bulges.*

And washed my hands in
innocence.
14 For all day long I have been
plagued,
And chastened every morning.

15 If I had said, "I will speak thus,"
Behold, I would have been untrue
to the generation of Your
children.
16 When I thought *how* to
understand this,
It *was* too painful for me—
17 Until I went into the sanctuary of
God;
Then I understood their end.

18 Surely You set them in slippery
places;
You cast them down to
destruction.
19 Oh, how they are *brought* to
desolation, as in a moment!
They are utterly consumed with
terrors.
20 As a dream when *one* awakes,
So, Lord, when You awake,
You shall despise their image.

21 Thus my heart was grieved,
And I was vexed in my mind.
22 I *was* so foolish and ignorant;
I was *like* a beast before You.
23 Nevertheless I *am* continually
with You;
You hold *me* by my right hand.
24 You will guide me with Your
counsel,
And afterward receive me *to*
glory.

25 Whom have I in heaven *but* You?
And *there is* none upon earth
that I desire besides You.
26 My flesh and my heart fail;
But God *is* the strength of my
heart and my portion forever.

27 For indeed, those who are far
from You shall perish;
You have destroyed all those who
desert You for harlotry.
28 But *it is* good for me to draw near
to God;
I have put my trust in the Lord
GOD,
That I may declare all Your
works.

PSALM 74

A Contemplation[a] of Asaph.

1 O God, why have You cast *us* off
forever?
Why does Your anger smoke
against the sheep of Your
pasture?
2 Remember Your congregation,
which You have purchased of
old,
The tribe of Your inheritance,
which You have redeemed—
This Mount Zion where You have
dwelt.
3 Lift up Your feet to the perpetual
desolations.
The enemy has damaged
everything in the sanctuary.
4 Your enemies roar in the midst
of Your meeting place;
They set up their banners *for*
signs.
5 They seem like men who lift up
Axes among the thick trees.
6 And now they break down its
carved work, all at once,
With axes and hammers.
7 They have set fire to Your
sanctuary;
They have defiled the dwelling
place of Your name to the
ground.
8 They said in their hearts,
"Let us destroy them altogether."
They have burned up all the
meeting places of God in the
land.

9 We do not see our signs;
There is no longer any prophet;
Nor *is there* any among us who
knows how long.
10 O God, how long will the
adversary reproach?
Will the enemy blaspheme Your
name forever?
11 Why do You withdraw Your
hand, even Your right hand?
Take it out of Your bosom and
destroy *them.*
12 For God *is* my King from of old,
Working salvation in the midst of
the earth.
13 You divided the sea by Your
strength;
You broke the heads of the sea
serpents in the waters.
14 You broke the heads of
Leviathan in pieces,

74:title aHebrew *Maschil*

And gave him *as* food to the
   people inhabiting the
   wilderness.
15 You broke open the fountain and
   the flood;
   You dried up mighty rivers.
16 The day *is* Yours, the night also
   is Yours;
   You have prepared the light and
   the sun.
17 You have set all the borders of
   the earth;
   You have made summer and
   winter.

18 Remember this, *that* the enemy
   has reproached, O LORD,
   And *that* a foolish people has
   blasphemed Your name.
19 Oh, do not deliver the life of Your
   turtledove to the wild beast!
   Do not forget the life of Your
   poor forever.
20 Have respect to the covenant;
   For the dark places of the earth
   are full of the haunts of cruelty.
21 Oh, do not let the oppressed
   return ashamed!
   Let the poor and needy praise
   Your name.

22 Arise, O God, plead Your own
   cause;
   Remember how the foolish man
   reproaches You daily.
23 Do not forget the voice of Your
   enemies;
   The tumult of those who rise up
   against You increases
   continually.

PSALM 75

To the Chief Musician. Set to "Do Not Destroy."*a*
A Psalm of Asaph. A Song.

1 We give thanks to You, O God,
   we give thanks!
   For Your wondrous works
   declare *that* Your name is
   near.

2 "When I choose the proper time,
   I will judge uprightly.
3 The earth and all its inhabitants
   are dissolved;
   I set up its pillars firmly.
                              Selah

4 "I said to the boastful, 'Do not deal
   boastfully,'

And to the wicked, 'Do not lift up
   the horn.
5 Do not lift up your horn on high;
   Do *not* speak with a stiff neck.'"

6 For exaltation *comes* neither
   from the east
   Nor from the west nor from the
   south.
7 But God *is* the Judge:
   He puts down one,
   And exalts another.
8 For in the hand of the LORD *there
   is* a cup,
   And the wine is red;
   It is fully mixed, and He pours it
   out;
   Surely its dregs shall all the
   wicked of the earth
   Drain *and* drink down.

9 But I will declare forever,
   I will sing praises to the God of
   Jacob.

10 "All the horns of the wicked I will
   also cut off,
   But the horns of the righteous
   shall be exalted."

PSALM 76

To the Chief Musician. On stringed instruments.*a*
A Psalm of Asaph. A Song.

1 In Judah God *is* known;
   His name *is* great in Israel.
2 In Salem*a* also is His tabernacle,
   And His dwelling place in Zion.
3 There He broke the arrows of the
   bow,
   The shield and sword of battle.
                              Selah

4 You *are* more glorious and
   excellent
   Than the mountains of prey.
5 The stouthearted were
   plundered;
   They have sunk into their sleep;
   And none of the mighty men
   have found the use of their
   hands.
6 At Your rebuke, O God of Jacob,
   Both the chariot and horse were
   cast into a dead sleep.

7 You, Yourself, *are* to be feared;
   And who may stand in Your
   presence
   When once You are angry?

75:title *a*Hebrew *Al Tashcheth*   76:title *a*Hebrew *neginoth*   76:2 *a*That is, Jerusalem

8 You caused judgment to be heard
   from heaven;
   The earth feared and was still,
9 When God arose to judgment,
   To deliver all the oppressed of the
   earth.   Selah

10 Surely the wrath of man shall
   praise You;
   With the remainder of wrath You
   shall gird Yourself.

11 Make vows to the LORD your God,
   and pay them;
   Let all who are around Him bring
   presents to Him who ought to
   be feared.
12 He shall cut off the spirit of
   princes;
   He is awesome to the kings of the
   earth.

PSALM 77

To the Chief Musician. To Jeduthun. A Psalm
of Asaph.

1 I cried out to God with my
   voice—
   To God with my voice;
   And He gave ear to me.
2 In the day of my trouble I sought
   the Lord;
   My hand was stretched out in the
   night without ceasing;
   My soul refused to be comforted.
3 I remembered God, and was
   troubled;
   I complained, and my spirit was
   overwhelmed.   Selah

4 You hold my eyelids open;
   I am so troubled that I cannot
   speak.
5 I have considered the days of old,
   The years of ancient times.
6 I call to remembrance my song
   in the night;
   I meditate within my heart,
   And my spirit makes diligent
   search.

7 Will the Lord cast off forever?
   And will He be favorable no
   more?
8 Has His mercy ceased forever?
   Has His promise failed
   forevermore?
9 Has God forgotten to be
   gracious?

Has He in anger shut up His
   tender mercies?   Selah

10 And I said, "This is my anguish;
   But I will remember the years of
   the right hand of the Most
   High."
11 I will remember the works of the
   LORD;
   Surely I will remember Your
   wonders of old.
12 I will also meditate on all Your
   work,
   And talk of Your deeds.
13 Your way, O God, is in the
   sanctuary;
   Who is so great a God as our
   God?
14 You are the God who does
   wonders;
   You have declared Your strength
   among the peoples.
15 You have with Your arm
   redeemed Your people,
   The sons of Jacob and Joseph.
                              Selah

16 The waters saw You, O God;
   The waters saw You, they were
   afraid;
   The depths also trembled.
17 The clouds poured out water;
   The skies sent out a sound;
   Your arrows also flashed about.
18 The voice of Your thunder was
   in the whirlwind;
   The lightnings lit up the world;
   The earth trembled and shook.
19 Your way was in the sea,
   Your path in the great waters,
   And Your footsteps were not
   known.
20 You led Your people like a flock
   By the hand of Moses and Aaron.

PSALM 78

A Contemplation[a] of Asaph.

1 Give ear, O my people, to my law;
   Incline your ears to the words of
   my mouth.
2 I will open my mouth in a
   parable;
   I will utter dark sayings of old,
3 Which we have heard and
   known,
   And our fathers have told us.
4 We will not hide them from their
   children,

78:title aHebrew Maschil

Telling to the generation to come
the praises of the LORD,
And His strength and His
wonderful works that He has
done.

5 For He established a testimony in
Jacob,
And appointed a law in Israel,
Which He commanded our
fathers,
That they should make them
known to their children;
6 That the generation to come
might know *them,*
The children *who* would be born,
That they may arise and declare
them to their children,
7 That they may set their hope in
God,
And not forget the works of
God,
But keep His commandments;
8 And may not be like their fathers,
A stubborn and rebellious
generation,
A generation *that* did not set its
heart aright,
And whose spirit was not faithful
to God.

9 The children of Ephraim, *being*
armed *and* carrying bows,
Turned back in the day of battle.
10 They did not keep the covenant
of God;
They refused to walk in His law,
11 And forgot His works
And His wonders that He had
shown them.

12 Marvelous things He did in the
sight of their fathers,
In the land of Egypt, *in* the field
of Zoan.
13 He divided the sea and caused
them to pass through;
And He made the waters stand
up like a heap.
14 In the daytime also He led them
with the cloud,
And all the night with a light of
fire.
15 He split the rocks in the
wilderness,
And gave *them* drink in
abundance like the depths.
16 He also brought streams out of
the rock,
And caused waters to run down
like rivers.

17 But they sinned even more
against Him
By rebelling against the Most
High in the wilderness.
18 And they tested God in their
heart
By asking for the food of their
fancy.
19 Yes, they spoke against God:
They said, "Can God prepare a
table in the wilderness?
20 Behold, He struck the rock,
So that the waters gushed out,
And the streams overflowed.
Can He give bread also?
Can He provide meat for His
people?"

21 Therefore the LORD heard *this*
and was furious;
So a fire was kindled against
Jacob,
And anger also came up against
Israel,
22 Because they did not believe in
God,
And did not trust in His salvation.
23 Yet He had commanded the
clouds above,
And opened the doors of
heaven,
24 Had rained down manna on them
to eat,
And given them of the bread of
heaven.
25 Men ate angels' food;
He sent them food to the full.

26 He caused an east wind to blow
in the heavens;
And by His power He brought in
the south wind.
27 He also rained meat on them like
the dust,
Feathered fowl like the sand of
the seas;
28 And He let *them* fall in the midst
of their camp,
All around their dwellings.
29 So they ate and were well filled,
For He gave them their own
desire.
30 They were not deprived of their
craving;
But while their food *was* still in
their mouths,
31 The wrath of God came against
them,
And slew the stoutest of them,
And struck down the choice *men*
of Israel.

32 In spite of this they still sinned,
And did not believe in His
wondrous works.
33 Therefore their days He
consumed in futility,
And their years in fear.

34 When He slew them, then they
sought Him;
And they returned and sought
earnestly for God.
35 Then they remembered that God
was their rock,
And the Most High God their
Redeemer.
36 Nevertheless they flattered Him
with their mouth,
And they lied to Him with their
tongue;
37 For their heart was not steadfast
with Him,
Nor were they faithful in His
covenant.
38 But He, *being* full of compassion,
forgave *their* iniquity,
And did not destroy *them.*
Yes, many a time He turned His
anger away,
And did not stir up all His wrath;
39 For He remembered that they
were but flesh,
A breath that passes away and
does not come again.

40 How often they provoked Him in
the wilderness,
And grieved Him in the desert!
41 Yes, again and again they
tempted God,
And limited the Holy One of
Israel.
42 They did not remember His
power:
The day when He redeemed them
from the enemy,
43 When He worked His signs in
Egypt,
And His wonders in the field of
Zoan;
44 Turned their rivers into blood,
And their streams, that they
could not drink.
45 He sent swarms of flies among
them, which devoured them,
And frogs, which destroyed
them.
46 He also gave their crops to the
caterpillar,
And their labor to the locust.
47 He destroyed their vines with
hail,

And their sycamore trees with
frost.
48 He also gave up their cattle to the
hail,
And their flocks to fiery
lightning.
49 He cast on them the fierceness of
His anger,
Wrath, indignation, and trouble,
By sending angels of destruction
among them.
50 He made a path for His anger;
He did not spare their soul from
death,
But gave their life over to the
plague,
51 And destroyed all the firstborn in
Egypt,
The first of *their* strength in the
tents of Ham.
52 But He made His own people go
forth like sheep,
And guided them in the
wilderness like a flock;
53 And He led them on safely, so
that they did not fear;
But the sea overwhelmed their
enemies.
54 And He brought them to His holy
border,
This mountain *which* His right
hand had acquired.
55 He also drove out the nations
before them,
Allotted them an inheritance by
survey,
And made the tribes of Israel
dwell in their tents.

56 Yet they tested and provoked the
Most High God,
And did not keep His testimonies,
57 But turned back and acted
unfaithfully like their fathers;
They were turned aside like a
deceitful bow.
58 For they provoked Him to anger
with their high places,
And moved Him to jealousy with
their carved images.
59 When God heard *this,* He was
furious,
And greatly abhorred Israel,
60 So that He forsook the tabernacle
of Shiloh,
The tent He had placed among
men,
61 And delivered His strength into
captivity,
And His glory into the enemy's
hand.

62 He also gave His people over to
the sword,
And was furious with His
inheritance.
63 The fire consumed their young
men,
And their maidens were not
given in marriage.
64 Their priests fell by the sword,
And their widows made no
lamentation.

65 Then the Lord awoke as *from*
sleep,
Like a mighty man who shouts
because of wine.
66 And He beat back His enemies;
He put them to a perpetual
reproach.

67 Moreover He rejected the tent of
Joseph,
And did not choose the tribe of
Ephraim,
68 But chose the tribe of Judah,
Mount Zion which He loved.
69 And He built His sanctuary like
the heights,
Like the earth which He has
established forever.
70 He also chose David His servant,
And took him from the
sheepfolds;
71 From following the ewes that had
young He brought him,
To shepherd Jacob His people,
And Israel His inheritance.
72 So he shepherded them
according to the integrity of his
heart,
And guided them by the
skillfulness of his hands.

PSALM 79

A Psalm of Asaph.

1 O God, the nations have come
into Your inheritance;
Your holy temple they have
defiled;
They have laid Jerusalem in
heaps.
2 The dead bodies of Your servants
They have given *as* food for the
birds of the heavens,
The flesh of Your saints to the
beasts of the earth.
3 Their blood they have shed like
water all around Jerusalem,

And *there was* no one to bury
them.
4 We have become a reproach to
our neighbors,
A scorn and derision to those
who are around us.

5 How long, LORD?
Will You be angry forever?
Will Your jealousy burn like fire?
6 Pour out Your wrath on the
nations that do not know You,
And on the kingdoms that do not
call on Your name.
7 For they have devoured Jacob,
And laid waste his dwelling
place.

8 Oh, do not remember former
iniquities against us!
Let Your tender mercies come
speedily to meet us,
For we have been brought very
low.
9 Help us, O God of our salvation,
For the glory of Your name;
And deliver us, and provide
atonement for our sins,
For Your name's sake!
10 Why should the nations say,
"*Where is* their God?"
Let there be known among the
nations in our sight
The avenging of the blood of
Your servants *which has been*
shed.

11 Let the groaning of the prisoner
come before You;
According to the greatness of
Your power
Preserve those who are
appointed to die;
12 And return to our neighbors
sevenfold into their bosom
Their reproach with which they
have reproached You, O Lord.

13 So we, Your people and sheep of
Your pasture,
Will give You thanks forever;
We will show forth Your praise
to all generations.

PSALM 80

To the Chief Musician. Set to "The Lilies."[a] A
Testimony[b] of Asaph. A Psalm.

1 Give ear, O Shepherd of Israel,
You who lead Joseph like a flock;

80:title [a]Hebrew *Shoshannim*   [b]Hebrew *Eduth*

You who dwell *between* the cherubim, shine forth!
2 Before Ephraim, Benjamin, and Manasseh,
Stir up Your strength,
And come *and* save us!

3 Restore us, O God;
Cause Your face to shine,
And we shall be saved!

4 O LORD God of hosts,
How long will You be angry
Against the prayer of Your people?
5 You have fed them with the bread of tears,
And given them tears to drink in great measure.
6 You have made us a strife to our neighbors,
And our enemies laugh among themselves.

7 Restore us, O God of hosts;
Cause Your face to shine,
And we shall be saved!

8 You have brought a vine out of Egypt;
You have cast out the nations, and planted it.
9 You prepared *room* for it,
And caused it to take deep root,
And it filled the land.
10 The hills were covered with its shadow,
And the mighty cedars with its boughs.
11 She sent out her boughs to the Sea,*a*
And her branches to the River.*b*

12 Why have You broken down her hedges,
So that all who pass by the way pluck her *fruit?*
13 The boar out of the woods uproots it,
And the wild beast of the field devours it.

14 Return, we beseech You, O God of hosts;
Look down from heaven and see,
And visit this vine
15 And the vineyard which Your right hand has planted,
And the branch *that* You made strong for Yourself.

16 *It is* burned with fire, *it is* cut down;
They perish at the rebuke of Your countenance.
17 Let Your hand be upon the man of Your right hand,
Upon the son of man *whom* You made strong for Yourself.
18 Then we will not turn back from You;
Revive us, and we will call upon Your name.

19 Restore us, O LORD God of hosts;
Cause Your face to shine,
And we shall be saved!

PSALM 81

To the Chief Musician. On an instrument of Gath.*a* A Psalm of Asaph.

1 Sing aloud to God our strength;
Make a joyful shout to the God of Jacob.
2 Raise a song and strike the timbrel,
The pleasant harp with the lute.

3 Blow the trumpet at the time of the New Moon,
At the full moon, on our solemn feast day.
4 For this *is* a statute for Israel,
A law of the God of Jacob.
5 This He established in Joseph *as* a testimony,
When He went throughout the land of Egypt,
Where I heard a language I did not understand.

6 "I removed his shoulder from the burden;
His hands were freed from the baskets.
7 You called in trouble, and I delivered you;
I answered you in the secret place of thunder;
I tested you at the waters of Meribah.   Selah

8 "Hear, O My people, and I will admonish you!
O Israel, if you will listen to Me!
9 There shall be no foreign god among you;
Nor shall you worship any foreign god.
10 I *am* the LORD your God,

Who brought you out of the land
    of Egypt;
Open your mouth wide, and I will
    fill it.

11 "But My people would not heed
    My voice,
    And Israel would *have* none of
    Me.
12 So I gave them over to their own
    stubborn heart,
    To walk in their own counsels.

13 "Oh, that My people would listen
    to Me,
    That Israel would walk in My
    ways!
14 I would soon subdue their
    enemies,
    And turn My hand against their
    adversaries.
15 The haters of the LORD would
    pretend submission to Him,
    But their fate would endure
    forever.
16 He would have fed them also
    with the finest of wheat;
    And with honey from the rock I
    would have satisfied you."

PSALM 82

A Psalm of Asaph.

1 God stands in the congregation
    of the mighty;
    He judges among the gods.*a*
2 How long will you judge unjustly,
    And show partiality to the
    wicked?   Selah
3 Defend the poor and fatherless;
    Do justice to the afflicted and
    needy.
4 Deliver the poor and needy;
    Free *them* from the hand of the
    wicked.

5 They do not know, nor do they
    understand;
    They walk about in darkness;
    All the foundations of the earth
    are unstable.

6 I said, "You *are* gods,*a*
    And all of you *are* children of the
    Most High.
7 But you shall die like men,
    And fall like one of the princes."

8 Arise, O God, judge the earth;
    For You shall inherit all nations.

PSALM 83

A Song. A Psalm of Asaph.

1 Do not keep silent, O God!
    Do not hold Your peace,
    And do not be still, O God!
2 For behold, Your enemies make
    a tumult;
    And those who hate You have
    lifted up their head.
3 They have taken crafty counsel
    against Your people,
    And consulted together against
    Your sheltered ones.
4 They have said, "Come, and let
    us cut them off from *being* a
    nation,
    That the name of Israel may be
    remembered no more."

5 For they have consulted together
    with one consent;
    They form a confederacy against
    You:
6 The tents of Edom and the
    Ishmaelites;
    Moab and the Hagrites;
7 Gebal, Ammon, and Amalek;
    Philistia with the inhabitants of
    Tyre;
8 Assyria also has joined with
    them;
    They have helped the children of
    Lot.   Selah

9 Deal with them as *with* Midian,
    As *with* Sisera,
    As *with* Jabin at the Brook
    Kishon,
10 Who perished at En Dor,
    Who became *as* refuse on the
    earth.
11 Make their nobles like Oreb and
    like Zeeb,
    Yes, all their princes like Zebah
    and Zalmunna,
12 Who said, "Let us take for
    ourselves
    The pastures of God for a
    possession."

13 O my God, make them like the
    whirling dust,
    Like the chaff before the wind!
14 As the fire burns the woods,
    And as the flame sets the
    mountains on fire,
15 So pursue them with Your
    tempest,

82:1 *a*Hebrew *elohim, mighty ones;* that is, the judges
judges

82:6 *a*Hebrew *elohim, mighty ones;* that is, the

And frighten them with Your storm.

16 Fill their faces with shame,
That they may seek Your name,
O LORD.

17 Let them be confounded and dismayed forever;
Yes, let them be put to shame and perish,

18 That they may know that You,
whose name alone is the LORD,
Are the Most High over all the earth.

PSALM 84

To the Chief Musician. On an instrument of Gath.a A Psalm of the sons of Korah.

1 How lovely is Your tabernacle,
O LORD of hosts!

2 My soul longs, yes, even faints
For the courts of the LORD;
My heart and my flesh cry out for the living God.

3 Even the sparrow has found a home,
And the swallow a nest for herself,
Where she may lay her young—
Even Your altars, O LORD of hosts,
My King and my God.

4 Blessed are those who dwell in Your house;
They will still be praising You.
Selah

5 Blessed is the man whose strength is in You,
Whose heart is set on pilgrimage.

6 As they pass through the Valley of Baca,
They make it a spring;
The rain also covers it with pools.

7 They go from strength to strength;
Each one appears before God in Zion.a

8 O LORD God of hosts, hear my prayer;
Give ear, O God of Jacob!
Selah

9 O God, behold our shield,
And look upon the face of Your anointed.

10 For a day in Your courts is better than a thousand.

I would rather be a doorkeeper
in the house of my God
Than dwell in the tents of wickedness.

11 For the LORD God is a sun and shield;
The LORD will give grace and glory;
No good thing will He withhold
From those who walk uprightly.

12 O LORD of hosts,
Blessed is the man who trusts in You!

PSALM 85

To the Chief Musician. A Psalm of the sons of Korah.

1 LORD, You have been favorable to Your land;
You have brought back the captivity of Jacob.

2 You have forgiven the iniquity of Your people;
You have covered all their sin.
Selah

3 You have taken away all Your wrath;
You have turned from the fierceness of Your anger.

4 Restore us, O God of our salvation,
And cause Your anger toward us to cease.

5 Will You be angry with us forever?
Will You prolong Your anger to all generations?

6 Will You not revive us again,
That Your people may rejoice in You?

7 Show us Your mercy, LORD,
And grant us Your salvation.

8 I will hear what God the LORD will speak,
For He will speak peace
To His people and to His saints;
But let them not turn back to folly.

9 Surely His salvation is near to those who fear Him,
That glory may dwell in our land.

10 Mercy and truth have met together;

84:title aHebrew Al Gittith   84:7 aSeptuagint, Syriac, and Vulgate read The God of gods shall be seen.

Righteousness and peace have
kissed.
11 Truth shall spring out of the
earth,
And righteousness shall look
down from heaven.
12 Yes, the LORD will give *what is*
good;
And our land will yield its
increase.
13 Righteousness will go before
Him,
And shall make His footsteps *our*
pathway.

PSALM 86

A Prayer of David.

1 Bow down Your ear, O LORD,
hear me;
For I *am* poor and needy.
2 Preserve my life, for I *am* holy;
You are my God;
Save Your servant who trusts in
You!
3 Be merciful to me, O Lord,
For I cry to You all day long.
4 Rejoice the soul of Your servant,
For to You, O Lord, I lift up my
soul.
5 For You, Lord, *are* good, and
ready to forgive,
And abundant in mercy to all
those who call upon You.

6 Give ear, O LORD, to my prayer;
And attend to the voice of my
supplications.
7 In the day of my trouble I will
call upon You,
For You will answer me.

8 Among the gods *there is* none
like You, O Lord;
Nor *are there any works* like
Your works.
9 All nations whom You have
made
Shall come and worship before
You, O Lord,
And shall glorify Your name.
10 For You *are* great, and do
wondrous things;
You alone *are* God.

11 Teach me Your way, O LORD;
I will walk in Your truth;
Unite my heart to fear Your
name.
12 I will praise You, O Lord my God,
with all my heart,

And I will glorify Your name
forevermore.
13 For great *is* Your mercy toward
me,
And You have delivered my soul
from the depths of Sheol.

14 O God, the proud have risen
against me,
And a mob of violent *men* have
sought my life,
And have not set You before
them.
15 But You, O Lord, *are* a God full
of compassion, and gracious,
Longsuffering and abundant in
mercy and truth.

16 Oh, turn to me, and have mercy
on me!
Give Your strength to Your
servant,
And save the son of Your
maidservant.
17 Show me a sign for good,
That those who hate me may see
it and be ashamed,
Because You, LORD, have helped
me and comforted me.

PSALM 87

A Psalm of the sons of Korah. A Song.

1 His foundation *is* in the holy
mountains.
2 The LORD loves the gates of Zion
More than all the dwellings of
Jacob.
3 Glorious things are spoken of
you,
O city of God!   Selah

4 "I will make mention of Rahab
and Babylon to those who
know Me;
Behold, O Philistia and Tyre,
with Ethiopia:
'This *one* was born there.'"

5 And of Zion it will be said,
"*This one* and that *one* were born
in her;
And the Most High Himself shall
establish her."
6 The LORD will record,
When He registers the peoples:
"This *one* was born there."
                              Selah

7 Both the singers and the players
on instruments *say*,
"All my springs *are* in you."

PSALM 88

A Song. A Psalm of the sons of Korah. To the Chief Musician. Set to "Mahalath Leannoth." A Contemplation[a] of Heman the Ezrahite.

1 O LORD, God of my salvation,
   I have cried out day and night
   before You.
2 Let my prayer come before You;
   Incline Your ear to my cry.

3 For my soul is full of troubles,
   And my life draws near to the
   grave.
4 I am counted with those who go
   down to the pit;
   I am like a man *who has* no
   strength,
5 Adrift among the dead,
   Like the slain who lie in the
   grave,
   Whom You remember no more,
   And who are cut off from Your
   hand.

6 You have laid me in the lowest
   pit,
   In darkness, in the depths.
7 Your wrath lies heavy upon me,
   And You have afflicted *me* with
   all Your waves.   Selah
8 You have put away my
   acquaintances far from me;
   You have made me an
   abomination to them;
   I am shut up, and I cannot get
   out;
9 My eye wastes away because of
   affliction.

   LORD, I have called daily upon
   You;
   I have stretched out my hands to
   You.
10 Will You work wonders for the
   dead?
   Shall the dead arise *and* praise
   You?   Selah
11 Shall Your lovingkindness be
   declared in the grave?
   Or Your faithfulness in the place
   of destruction?
12 Shall Your wonders be known in
   the dark?
   And Your righteousness in the
   land of forgetfulness?

13 But to You I have cried out, O
   LORD,
   And in the morning my prayer
   comes before You.

14 LORD, why do You cast off my
   soul?
   Why do You hide Your face from
   me?
15 I *have been* afflicted and ready
   to die from *my* youth;
   I suffer Your terrors;
   I am distraught.
16 Your fierce wrath has gone over
   me;
   Your terrors have cut me off.
17 They came around me all day
   long like water;
   They engulfed me altogether.
18 Loved one and friend You have
   put far from me,
   And my acquaintances into
   darkness.

PSALM 89

A Contemplation[a] of Ethan the Ezrahite.

1 I will sing of the mercies of the
   LORD forever;
   With my mouth will I make
   known Your faithfulness to all
   generations.
2 For I have said, "Mercy shall be
   built up forever;
   Your faithfulness You shall
   establish in the very heavens."

3 "I have made a covenant with My
   chosen,
   I have sworn to My servant
   David:
4 'Your seed I will establish forever,
   And build up your throne to all
   generations.'"   Selah

5 And the heavens will praise Your
   wonders, O LORD;
   Your faithfulness also in the
   assembly of the saints.
6 For who in the heavens can be
   compared to the LORD?
   Who among the sons of the
   mighty can be likened to the
   LORD?
7 God is greatly to be feared in the
   assembly of the saints,
   And to be held in reverence by
   all *those* around Him.
8 O LORD God of hosts,
   Who *is* mighty like You, O LORD?
   Your faithfulness also surrounds
   You.
9 You rule the raging of the sea;
   When its waves rise, You still
   them.

88:title [a]Hebrew *Maschil*   89:title [a]Hebrew *Maschil*

10   You have broken Rahab in
    pieces, as one who is slain;
    You have scattered Your enemies
    with Your mighty arm.

11   The heavens *are* Yours, the earth
    also *is* Yours;
    The world and all its fullness,
    You have founded them.
12   The north and the south, You
    have created them;
    Tabor and Hermon rejoice in
    Your name.
13   You have a mighty arm;
    Strong is Your hand, *and* high is
    Your right hand.
14   Righteousness and justice *are* the
    foundation of Your throne;
    Mercy and truth go before Your
    face.
15   Blessed *are* the people who know
    the joyful sound!
    They walk, O LORD, in the light
    of Your countenance.
16   In Your name they rejoice all day
    long,
    And in Your righteousness they
    are exalted.
17   For You *are* the glory of their
    strength,
    And in Your favor our horn is
    exalted.
18   For our shield *belongs* to the
    LORD,
    And our king to the Holy One of
    Israel.

19   Then You spoke in a vision to
    Your holy one,[a]
    And said: "I have given help to
    one who is mighty;
    I have exalted one chosen from
    the people.
20   I have found My servant David;
    With My holy oil I have anointed
    him,
21   With whom My hand shall be
    established;
    Also My arm shall strengthen
    him.
22   The enemy shall not outwit him,
    Nor the son of wickedness afflict
    him.
23   I will beat down his foes before
    his face,
    And plague those who hate him.

24   "But My faithfulness and My
    mercy *shall be* with him,

    And in My name his horn shall
    be exalted.
25   Also I will set his hand over the
    sea,
    And his right hand over the
    rivers.
26   He shall cry to Me, 'You *are* my
    Father,
    My God, and the rock of my
    salvation.'
27   Also I will make him My
    firstborn,
    The highest of the kings of the
    earth.
28   My mercy I will keep for him
    forever,
    And My covenant shall stand
    firm with him.
29   His seed also I will make *to*
    endure forever,
    And his throne as the days of
    heaven.

30   "If his sons forsake My law
    And do not walk in My
    judgments,
31   If they break My statutes
    And do not keep My
    commandments,
32   Then I will punish their
    transgression with the rod,
    And their iniquity with stripes.
33   Nevertheless My lovingkindness
    I will not utterly take from him,
    Nor allow My faithfulness to fail.
34   My covenant I will not break,
    Nor alter the word that has gone
    out of My lips.
35   Once I have sworn by My
    holiness;
    I will not lie to David:
36   His seed shall endure forever,
    And his throne as the sun before
    Me;
37   It shall be established forever like
    the moon,
    Even *like* the faithful witness in
    the sky."   Selah

38   But You have cast off and
    abhorred,
    You have been furious with Your
    anointed.
39   You have renounced the
    covenant of Your servant;
    You have profaned his crown *by*
    casting it to the ground.
40   You have broken down all his
    hedges;

89:19 [a]Following many Hebrew manuscripts; Masoretic Text, Septuagint, Targum, and Vulgate read *holy ones*.

You have brought his
strongholds to ruin.
41 All who pass by the way plunder
him;
He is a reproach to his neighbors.
42 You have exalted the right hand
of his adversaries;
You have made all his enemies
rejoice.
43 You have also turned back the
edge of his sword,
And have not sustained him in
the battle.
44 You have made his glory cease,
And cast his throne down to the
ground.
45 The days of his youth You have
shortened;
You have covered him with
shame.   Selah

46 How long, LORD?
Will You hide Yourself forever?
Will Your wrath burn like fire?
47 Remember how short my time is;
For what futility have You
created all the children of men?
48 What man can live and not see
death?
Can he deliver his life from the
power of the grave?   Selah

49 Lord, where *are* Your former
lovingkindnesses,
Which You swore to David in
Your truth?
50 Remember, Lord, the reproach of
Your servants—
How I bear in my bosom *the
reproach of* all the many
peoples,
51 With which Your enemies have
reproached, O LORD,
With which they have
reproached the footsteps of
Your anointed.

52 Blessed *be* the LORD forevermore!
Amen and Amen.

Book Four   Psalms 90–106

PSALM 90

A Prayer of Moses the man of God.

1 LORD, You have been our
dwelling place*a* in all
generations.
2 Before the mountains were
brought forth,

Or ever You had formed the earth
and the world,
Even from everlasting to
everlasting, You *are* God.

3 You turn man to destruction,
And say, "Return, O children of
men."
4 For a thousand years in Your
sight
Are like yesterday when it is past,
And *like* a watch in the night.
5 You carry them away *like* a flood;
They are like a sleep.
In the morning they are like grass
which grows up:
6 In the morning it flourishes and
grows up;
In the evening it is cut down and
withers.

7 For we have been consumed by
Your anger,
And by Your wrath we are
terrified.
8 You have set our iniquities before
You,
Our secret *sins* in the light of
Your countenance.
9 For all our days have passed
away in Your wrath;
We finish our years like a sigh.
10 The days of our lives *are* seventy
years;
And if by reason of strength *they
are* eighty years,
Yet their boast *is* only labor and
sorrow;
For it is soon cut off, and we fly
away.
11 Who knows the power of Your
anger?
For as the fear of You, *so is* Your
wrath.
12 So teach *us* to number our days,
That we may gain a heart of
wisdom.

13 Return, O LORD!
How long?
And have compassion on Your
servants.
14 Oh, satisfy us early with Your
mercy,
That we may rejoice and be glad
all our days!
15 Make us glad according to the
days *in which* You have
afflicted us,

90:1 *a*Septuagint, Targum, and Vulgate read *refuge*.

The years *in which* we have seen evil.
16 Let Your work appear to Your servants,
And Your glory to their children.
17 And let the beauty of the LORD our God be upon us,
And establish the work of our hands for us;
Yes, establish the work of our hands.

PSALM 91

1 He who dwells in the secret place of the Most High
Shall abide under the shadow of the Almighty.
2 I will say of the LORD, "*He is* my refuge and my fortress;
My God, in Him I will trust."

3 Surely He shall deliver you from the snare of the fowler[a]
And from the perilous pestilence.
4 He shall cover you with His feathers,
And under His wings you shall take refuge;
His truth *shall be your* shield and buckler.
5 You shall not be afraid of the terror by night,
Nor of the arrow *that* flies by day,
6 *Nor* of the pestilence *that* walks in darkness,
Nor of the destruction *that* lays waste at noonday.

7 A thousand may fall at your side,
And ten thousand at your right hand;
But it shall not come near you.
8 Only with your eyes shall you look,
And see the reward of the wicked.

9 Because you have made the LORD, *who is* my refuge,
Even the Most High, your dwelling place,
10 No evil shall befall you,
Nor shall any plague come near your dwelling;
11 For He shall give His angels charge over you,
To keep you in all your ways.

12 In *their* hands they shall bear you up,
Lest you dash your foot against a stone.
13 You shall tread upon the lion and the cobra,
The young lion and the serpent you shall trample underfoot.

14 "Because he has set his love upon Me, therefore I will deliver him;
I will set him on high, because he has known My name.
15 He shall call upon Me, and I will answer him;
I *will be* with him in trouble;
I will deliver him and honor him.
16 With long life I will satisfy him,
And show him My salvation."

PSALM 92

A Psalm. A Song for the Sabbath day.

1 *It is* good to give thanks to the LORD,
And to sing praises to Your name, O Most High;
2 To declare Your lovingkindness in the morning,
And Your faithfulness every night,
3 On an instrument of ten strings,
On the lute,
And on the harp,
With harmonious sound.
4 For You, LORD, have made me glad through Your work;
I will triumph in the works of Your hands.

5 O LORD, how great are Your works!
Your thoughts are very deep.
6 A senseless man does not know,
Nor does a fool understand this.
7 When the wicked spring up like grass,
And when all the workers of iniquity flourish,
It is that they may be destroyed forever.

8 But You, LORD, *are* on high forevermore.
9 For behold, Your enemies, O LORD,
For behold, Your enemies shall perish;
All the workers of iniquity shall be scattered.

91:3 *a*That is, one who catches birds in a trap or snare

10 But my horn You have exalted
     like a wild ox;
   I have been anointed with fresh
     oil.
11 My eye also has seen *my desire*
     on my enemies;
   My ears hear *my desire* on the
     wicked
   Who rise up against me.

12 The righteous shall flourish like
     a palm tree,
   He shall grow like a cedar in
     Lebanon.
13 Those who are planted in the
     house of the LORD
   Shall flourish in the courts of our
     God.
14 They shall still bear fruit in old
     age;
   They shall be fresh and
     flourishing,
15 To declare that the LORD is
     upright;
   He is my rock, and *there is* no
     unrighteousness in Him.

PSALM 93

1 The LORD reigns, He is clothed
     with majesty;
   The LORD is clothed,
   He has girded Himself with
     strength.
   Surely the world is established,
     so that it cannot be moved.
2 Your throne *is* established from
     of old;
   You *are* from everlasting.

3 The floods have lifted up, O LORD,
   The floods have lifted up their
     voice;
   The floods lift up their waves.
4 The LORD on high *is* mightier
   Than the noise of many waters,
   Than the mighty waves of the
     sea.

5 Your testimonies are very sure;
   Holiness adorns Your house,
   O LORD, forever.

PSALM 94

1 O LORD God, to whom vengeance
     belongs—
   O God, to whom vengeance
     belongs, shine forth!
2 Rise up, O Judge of the earth;
   Render punishment to the proud.
3 LORD, how long will the wicked,

How long will the wicked
  triumph?
4 They utter speech, *and* speak
     insolent things;
   All the workers of iniquity boast
     in themselves.
5 They break in pieces Your
     people, O LORD,
   And afflict Your heritage.
6 They slay the widow and the
     stranger,
   And murder the fatherless.
7 Yet they say, "The LORD does not
     see,
   Nor does the God of Jacob
     understand."

8 Understand, you senseless
     among the people;
   And *you* fools, when will you be
     wise?
9 He who planted the ear, shall He
     not hear?
   He who formed the eye, shall He
     not see?
10 He who instructs the nations,
     shall He not correct,
   He who teaches man knowledge?
11 The LORD knows the thoughts of
     man,
   That they *are* futile.

12 Blessed *is* the man whom You
     instruct, O LORD,
   And teach out of Your law,
13 That You may give him rest from
     the days of adversity,
   Until the pit is dug for the wicked.
14 For the LORD will not cast off His
     people,
   Nor will He forsake His
     inheritance.
15 But judgment will return to
     righteousness,
   And all the upright in heart will
     follow it.

16 Who will rise up for me against
     the evildoers?
   Who will stand up for me against
     the workers of iniquity?
17 Unless the LORD *had been* my
     help,
   My soul would soon have settled
     in silence.
18 If I say, "My foot slips,"
   Your mercy, O LORD, will hold me
     up.
19 In the multitude of my anxieties
     within me,
   Your comforts delight my soul.

Start Singing

We are blessed to be able to come before God with many different kinds of prayer:

Prayers of *petition*—prayers in which we ask God for help.
Prayers of *intercession*—prayers on behalf of others who need God's help.
Prayers of *praise*—revering God for all that He is—for His greatness and majesty.
Prayers of *thanksgiving*—acknowledging the many blessings God has given for our enjoyment.

"Two-way" prayers—prayers in which we ask God questions and then let Him answer: *"Dear God, is there anything that I should praise You for today? Is there any reason why I should be thankful?"* Now *listen!* Listen for God's answer: *"Yes, be thankful that I am here. Be thankful that you are alive and can talk to Me!"*

One of the most wonderful prayers we can pray is one of praise. Psalm 96 begins this way: "Oh, sing to the LORD a new song! Sing to the LORD, all the earth." You can choose today to sing a song in discordant melodies of gloom and doom. That's an old song; it's a worn-out record.

Try singing a new song! God is alive. Sing a song of praise to Him. He has spared you from more problems, pains, and perils than you will ever know! Start singing as you pray: *Dear God, I am a believer. I'm going to sing a new song today. My mood is changing. That's a miracle! It's going to be a great day, Lord! Thank You for turning me around. Amen.*

20 Shall the throne of iniquity,
   which devises evil by law,
   Have fellowship with You?
21 They gather together against the
   life of the righteous,
   And condemn innocent blood.
22 But the LORD has been my
   defense,
   And my God the rock of my
   refuge.
23 He has brought on them their
   own iniquity,
   And shall cut them off in their
   own wickedness;
   The LORD our God shall cut them
   off.

PSALM 95

1 Oh come, let us sing to the LORD!
   Let us shout joyfully to the Rock
   of our salvation.
2 Let us come before His presence
   with thanksgiving;
   Let us shout joyfully to Him with
   psalms.
3 For the LORD is the great God,
   And the great King above all
   gods.
4 In His hand are the deep places
   of the earth;
   The heights of the hills are His
   also.
5 The sea is His, for He made it;
   And His hands formed the dry
   land.

6 Oh come, let us worship and bow
   down;
   Let us kneel before the LORD our
   Maker.
7 For He is our God,
   And we are the people of His
   pasture,
   And the sheep of His hand.

   Today, if you will hear His voice:
8 "Do not harden your hearts, as in
   the rebellion,*a*
   As in the day of trial*b* in the
   wilderness,
9 When your fathers tested Me;
   They tried Me, though they saw
   My work.
10 For forty years I was grieved with
   that generation,
   And said, 'It is a people who go
   astray in their hearts,
   And they do not know My ways.'

11 So I swore in My wrath,
   'They shall not enter My rest.' "

PSALM 96

1 Oh, sing to the LORD a new song!
   Sing to the LORD, all the earth.
2 Sing to the LORD, bless His name;
   Proclaim the good news of His
   salvation from day to day.
3 Declare His glory among the
   nations,
   His wonders among all peoples.

4 For the LORD is great and greatly
   to be praised;
   He is to be feared above all gods.
5 For all the gods of the peoples are
   idols,
   But the LORD made the heavens.
6 Honor and majesty are before
   Him;
   Strength and beauty are in His
   sanctuary.

7 Give to the LORD, O families of
   the peoples,
   Give to the LORD glory and
   strength.
8 Give to the LORD the glory due
   His name;
   Bring an offering, and come into
   His courts.
9 Oh, worship the LORD in the
   beauty of holiness!
   Tremble before Him, all the
   earth.

10 Say among the nations, "The
   LORD reigns;
   The world also is firmly
   established,
   It shall not be moved;
   He shall judge the peoples
   righteously."

11 Let the heavens rejoice, and let
   the earth be glad;
   Let the sea roar, and all its
   fullness;
12 Let the field be joyful, and all that
   is in it.
   Then all the trees of the woods
   will rejoice before the LORD.
13 For He is coming, for He is
   coming to judge the earth.
   He shall judge the world with
   righteousness,
   And the peoples with His truth.

95:8 *a*Hebrew *Meribah*   *b*Hebrew *Massah*

God's Shepherds in the Wilderness

A shepherd's life in Palestine is much the same today as it was in biblical times—a constant vigil of tending to his flock. He can be seen roaming the inhospitable countryside locating food and water for his sheep while guarding against wild animals and thieves.

The shepherd's workplace is the Judean wilderness. In the Old Testament the area is called "Heshimon," a Hebrew name meaning "devastation." The wilderness of Judea, east of the Mount of Olives, does not offer the pleasant green pastures often associated with shepherding. There are no fertile plains such as those located on the coast of Palestine. The chocolate-brown soil, red poppies, and fragrant orange blossoms of Galilee are missing here. Instead, the wilderness is known for its scorching heat, chalky yellow sand, and deep limestone gorges. The prevailing life of the shepherd is silent, lonely, and exhausting.

In biblical days, the wilderness was the only place available for the shepherd and his flocks. The great nations of the Philistines and Phoenicians possessed the coastal plains. Galilee was overrun by other mighty kingdoms. Israel was never able to completely drive out these nations and was left with the difficult task of developing a country on the border of a vast wilderness.

From this countryside emerge many biblical images of the shepherd. His life, customs, and habits are used throughout the Bible to illustrate and communicate God's truths. Many of God's great leaders lived the hard life of leading the sheep, before being called to shepherd the people of Israel. The patriarchs Abraham, Isaac, Jacob, Joseph, Moses, and David were all shepherds. At the forefront of Israel's history was the common shepherd.

The psalmist David drew often from his shepherding experiences. In Psalms 23:1 and 100:3 God is referred to as "the shepherd" who cared for "His people and the sheep of His pasture."

In this harsh wilderness the shepherd cares for his flock even to the point of laying down his life for his sheep. In this wasteland Jesus Christ Himself declared, "I am the good shepherd. The good shepherd gives His life for the sheep" (John 10:11).

PSALM 97

1 The LORD reigns;
Let the earth rejoice;
Let the multitude of isles be glad!

2 Clouds and darkness surround
Him;
Righteousness and justice *are* the
foundation of His throne.

3 A fire goes before Him,
And burns up His enemies round
about.

4 His lightnings light the world;
The earth sees and trembles.

5 The mountains melt like wax at
the presence of the LORD,
At the presence of the Lord of the
whole earth.

6 The heavens declare His
righteousness,
And all the peoples see His glory.

7 Let all be put to shame who serve
carved images,
Who boast of idols.
Worship Him, all *you* gods.

8 Zion hears and is glad,
And the daughters of Judah
rejoice
Because of Your judgments, O
LORD.

9 For You, LORD, *are* most high
above all the earth;
You are exalted far above all
gods.

10 You who love the LORD, hate evil!
He preserves the souls of His
saints;
He delivers them out of the hand
of the wicked.

11 Light is sown for the righteous,
And gladness for the upright in
heart.

12 Rejoice in the LORD, you
righteous,
And give thanks at the
remembrance of His holy
name.[a]

PSALM 98

A Psalm.

1 Oh, sing to the LORD a new song!
For He has done marvelous
things;
His right hand and His holy arm
have gained Him the victory.

2 The LORD has made known His
salvation;

His righteousness He has
revealed in the sight of the
nations.

3 He has remembered His mercy
and His faithfulness to the
house of Israel;
All the ends of the earth have
seen the salvation of our God.

4 Shout joyfully to the LORD, all the
earth;
Break forth in song, rejoice, and
sing praises.

5 Sing to the LORD with the harp,
With the harp and the sound of
a psalm,

6 With trumpets and the sound of
a horn;
Shout joyfully before the LORD,
the King.

7 Let the sea roar, and all its
fullness,
The world and those who dwell
in it;

8 Let the rivers clap *their* hands;
Let the hills be joyful together
before the LORD,

9 For He is coming to judge the
earth.
With righteousness He shall
judge the world,
And the peoples with equity.

PSALM 99

1 The LORD reigns;
Let the peoples tremble!
He dwells *between* the cherubim;
Let the earth be moved!

2 The LORD *is* great in Zion,
And He *is* high above all the
peoples.

3 Let them praise Your great and
awesome name—
He *is* holy.

4 The King's strength also loves
justice;
You have established equity;
You have executed justice and
righteousness in Jacob.

5 Exalt the LORD our God,
And worship at His footstool—
He *is* holy.

6 Moses and Aaron *were* among
His priests,
And Samuel *was* among those
who called upon His name;

97:12 [a]Or *His holiness*

They called upon the LORD, and
He answered them.
7 He spoke to them in the cloudy
pillar;
They kept His testimonies and
the ordinance He gave them.

8 You answered them, O LORD our
God;
You were to them God-Who-
Forgives,
Though You took vengeance on
their deeds.
9 Exalt the LORD our God,
And worship at His holy hill;
For the LORD our God is holy.

PSALM 100

A Psalm of Thanksgiving.

1 Make a joyful shout to the LORD,
all you lands!
2 Serve the LORD with gladness;
Come before His presence with
singing.
3 Know that the LORD, He is God;
It is He who has made us, and
not we ourselves;a
We are His people and the sheep
of His pasture.

4 Enter into His gates with
thanksgiving,
And into His courts with praise.
Be thankful to Him, and bless His
name.
5 For the LORD is good;
His mercy is everlasting,
And His truth endures to all
generations.

PSALM 101

A Psalm of David.

1 I will sing of mercy and justice;
To You, O LORD, I will sing
praises.

2 I will behave wisely in a perfect
way.
Oh, when will You come to me?
I will walk within my house with
a perfect heart.

3 I will set nothing wicked before
my eyes;
I hate the work of those who fall
away;
It shall not cling to me.

4 A perverse heart shall depart
from me;
I will not know wickedness.

5 Whoever secretly slanders his
neighbor,
Him I will destroy;
The one who has a haughty look
and a proud heart,
Him I will not endure.

6 My eyes shall be on the faithful
of the land,
That they may dwell with me;
He who walks in a perfect way,
He shall serve me.
7 He who works deceit shall not
dwell within my house;
He who tells lies shall not
continue in my presence.
8 Early I will destroy all the wicked
of the land,
That I may cut off all the
evildoers from the city of the
LORD.

PSALM 102

A Prayer of the afflicted, when he is
overwhelmed and pours out his complaint before
the LORD.

1 Hear my prayer, O LORD,
And let my cry come to You.
2 Do not hide Your face from me
in the day of my trouble;
Incline Your ear to me;
In the day that I call, answer me
speedily.

3 For my days are consumed like
smoke,
And my bones are burned like a
hearth.
4 My heart is stricken and withered
like grass,
So that I forget to eat my bread.
5 Because of the sound of my
groaning
My bones cling to my skin.
6 I am like a pelican of the
wilderness;
I am like an owl of the desert.
7 I lie awake,
And am like a sparrow alone on
the housetop.

8 My enemies reproach me all day
long;
Those who deride me swear an
oath against me.

100:3 aFollowing Kethib, Septuagint, and Vulgate; Qere, many Hebrew manuscripts, and Targum read we
are His.

9 For I have eaten ashes like bread,
And mingled my drink with
weeping,
10 Because of Your indignation and
Your wrath;
For You have lifted me up and
cast me away.
11 My days *are* like a shadow that
lengthens,
And I wither away like grass.

12 But You, O LORD, shall endure
forever,
And the remembrance of Your
name to all generations.
13 You will arise *and* have mercy on
Zion;
For the time to favor her,
Yes, the set time, has come.
14 For Your servants take pleasure
in her stones,
And show favor to her dust.
15 So the nations shall fear the
name of the LORD,
And all the kings of the earth
Your glory.
16 For the LORD shall build up Zion;
He shall appear in His glory.
17 He shall regard the prayer of the
destitute,
And shall not despise their
prayer.

18 This will be written for the
generation to come,
That a people yet to be created
may praise the LORD.
19 For He looked down from the
height of His sanctuary;
From heaven the LORD viewed
the earth,
20 To hear the groaning of the
prisoner,
To release those appointed to
death,
21 To declare the name of the LORD
in Zion,
And His praise in Jerusalem,
22 When the peoples are gathered
together,
And the kingdoms, to serve the
LORD.

23 He weakened my strength in the
way;
He shortened my days.
24 I said, "O my God,
Do not take me away in the midst
of my days;
Your years *are* throughout all
generations.

25 Of old You laid the foundation of
the earth,
And the heavens *are* the work of
Your hands.
26 They will perish, but You will
endure;
Yes, they will all grow old like a
garment;
Like a cloak You will change
them,
And they will be changed.
27 But You *are* the same,
And Your years will have no end.
28 The children of Your servants
will continue,
And their descendants will be
established before You."

PSALM 103

A Psalm of David.

1 Bless the LORD, O my soul;
And all that is within me, *bless*
His holy name!
2 Bless the LORD, O my soul,
And forget not all His benefits:
3 Who forgives all your iniquities,
Who heals all your diseases,
4 Who redeems your life from
destruction,
Who crowns you with
lovingkindness and tender
mercies,
5 Who satisfies your mouth with
good *things*,
So that your youth is renewed
like the eagle's.

6 The LORD executes righteousness
And justice for all who are
oppressed.
7 He made known His ways to
Moses,
His acts to the children of Israel.
8 The LORD *is* merciful and
gracious,
Slow to anger, and abounding in
mercy.
9 He will not always strive *with us*,
Nor will He keep *His anger*
forever.
10 He has not dealt with us
according to our sins,
Nor punished us according to our
iniquities.

11 For as the heavens are high
above the earth,
So great is His mercy toward
those who fear Him;
12 As far as the east is from the
west,

So far has He removed our
transgressions from us.

13 As a father pities *his* children,
So the LORD pities those who fear
Him.

14 For He knows our frame;
He remembers that we *are* dust.

15 *As for* man, his days *are* like
grass;
As a flower of the field, so he
flourishes.

16 For the wind passes over it, and
it is gone,
And its place remembers it no
more.*ª*

17 But the mercy of the LORD *is* from
everlasting to everlasting
On those who fear Him,
And His righteousness to
children's children,

18 To such as keep His covenant,
And to those who remember His
commandments to do them.

19 The LORD has established His
throne in heaven,
And His kingdom rules over all.

20 Bless the LORD, you His angels,
Who excel in strength, who do
His word,
Heeding the voice of His word.

21 Bless the LORD, all you His hosts,
You ministers of His, who do His
pleasure.

22 Bless the LORD, all His works,
In all places of His dominion.

Bless the LORD, O my soul!

PSALM 104

1 Bless the LORD, O my soul!

O LORD my God, You are very
great:
You are clothed with honor and
majesty,

2 Who cover *Yourself* with light as
with a garment,
Who stretch out the heavens like
a curtain.

3 He lays the beams of His upper
chambers in the waters,
Who makes the clouds His
chariot,
Who walks on the wings of the
wind,

4 Who makes His angels spirits,
His ministers a flame of fire.

5 *You who* laid the foundations of
the earth,
So *that* it should not be moved
forever,

6 You covered it with the deep as
with a garment;
The waters stood above the
mountains.

7 At Your rebuke they fled;
At the voice of Your thunder they
hastened away.

8 They went up over the
mountains;
They went down into the valleys,
To the place which You founded
for them.

9 You have set a boundary that
they may not pass over,
That they may not return to cover
the earth.

10 He sends the springs into the
valleys;
They flow among the hills.

11 They give drink to every beast of
the field;
The wild donkeys quench their
thirst.

12 By them the birds of the heavens
have their home;
They sing among the branches.

13 He waters the hills from His
upper chambers;
The earth is satisfied with the
fruit of Your works.

14 He causes the grass to grow for
the cattle,
And vegetation for the service of
man,
That he may bring forth food
from the earth,

15 And wine *that* makes glad the
heart of man,
Oil to make *his* face shine,
And bread *which* strengthens
man's heart.

16 The trees of the LORD are full *of*
sap,
The cedars of Lebanon which He
planted,

17 Where the birds make their
nests;
The stork has her home in the fir
trees.

18 The high hills *are* for the wild
goats;

The cliffs are a refuge for the
rock badgers.[a]
19 He appointed the moon for
seasons;
The sun knows its going down.
20 You make darkness, and it is
night,
In which all the beasts of the
forest creep about.
21 The young lions roar after their
prey,
And seek their food from God.
22 *When* the sun rises, they gather
together
And lie down in their dens.
23 Man goes out to his work
And to his labor until the
evening.

24 O LORD, how manifold are Your
works!
In wisdom You have made them
all.
The earth is full of Your
possessions—
25 This great and wide sea,
In which *are* innumerable
teeming things,
Living things both small and
great.
26 There the ships sail about;
There is that Leviathan
Which You have made to play
there.

27 These all wait for You,
That You may give *them* their
food in due season.
28 *What* You give them they gather
in;
You open Your hand, they are
filled with good.
29 You hide Your face, they are
troubled;
You take away their breath, they
die and return to their dust.
30 You send forth Your Spirit, they
are created;
And You renew the face of the
earth.

31 May the glory of the LORD endure
forever;
May the LORD rejoice in His
works.
32 He looks on the earth, and it
trembles;
He touches the hills, and they
smoke.

33 I will sing to the LORD as long as
I live;
I will sing praise to my God while
I have my being.
34 May my meditation be sweet to
Him;
I will be glad in the LORD.
35 May sinners be consumed from
the earth,
And the wicked be no more.

Bless the LORD, O my soul!
Praise the LORD!

PSALM 105

1 Oh, give thanks to the LORD!
Call upon His name;
Make known His deeds among
the peoples!
2 Sing to Him, sing psalms to Him;
Talk of all His wondrous works!
3 Glory in His holy name;
Let the hearts of those rejoice
who seek the LORD!
4 Seek the LORD and His strength;
Seek His face evermore!
5 Remember His marvelous works
which He has done,
His wonders, and the judgments
of His mouth,
6 O seed of Abraham His servant,
You children of Jacob, His
chosen ones!

7 He *is* the LORD our God;
His judgments *are* in all the earth.
8 He remembers His covenant
forever,
The word *which* He commanded,
for a thousand generations,
9 *The covenant* which He made
with Abraham,
And His oath to Isaac,
10 And confirmed it to Jacob for a
statute,
To Israel *as* an everlasting
covenant,
11 Saying, "To you I will give the
land of Canaan
As the allotment of your
inheritance,"
12 When they were few in number,
Indeed very few, and strangers in
it.

13 When they went from one nation
to another,
From *one* kingdom to another
people,

104:18 [a]Or *rock hyrax* (compare Leviticus 11:5)

14 He permitted no one to do them
    wrong;
    Yes, He rebuked kings for their
    sakes,
15 *Saying,* "Do not touch My
    anointed ones,
    And do My prophets no harm."

16 Moreover He called for a famine
    in the land;
    He destroyed all the provision of
    bread.
17 He sent a man before them—
    Joseph—*who* was sold as a slave.
18 They hurt his feet with fetters,
    He was laid in irons.
19 Until the time that his word came
    to pass,
    The word of the LORD tested
    him.
20 The king sent and released him,
    The ruler of the people let him
    go free.
21 He made him lord of his house,
    And ruler of all his possessions,
22 To bind his princes at his
    pleasure,
    And teach his elders wisdom.

23 Israel also came into Egypt,
    And Jacob dwelt in the land of
    Ham.
24 He increased His people greatly,
    And made them stronger than
    their enemies.
25 He turned their heart to hate His
    people,
    To deal craftily with His servants.

26 He sent Moses His servant,
    And Aaron whom He had chosen.
27 They performed His signs among
    them,
    And wonders in the land of Ham.
28 He sent darkness, and made *it*
    dark;
    And they did not rebel against
    His word.
29 He turned their waters into
    blood,
    And killed their fish.
30 Their land abounded with frogs,
    Even in the chambers of their
    kings.
31 He spoke, and there came
    swarms of flies,
    And lice in all their territory.
32 He gave them hail for rain,
    And flaming fire in their land.
33 He struck their vines also, and
    their fig trees,

And splintered the trees of their
    territory.
34 He spoke, and locusts came,
    Young locusts without number,
35 And ate up all the vegetation in
    their land,
    And devoured the fruit of their
    ground.
36 He also destroyed all the
    firstborn in their land,
    The first of all their strength.

37 He also brought them out with
    silver and gold,
    And *there was* none feeble
    among His tribes.
38 Egypt was glad when they
    departed,
    For the fear of them had fallen
    upon them.
39 He spread a cloud for a covering,
    And fire to give light in the night.
40 *The people* asked, and He
    brought quail,
    And satisfied them with the
    bread of heaven.
41 He opened the rock, and water
    gushed out;
    It ran in the dry places *like* a
    river.

42 For He remembered His holy
    promise,
    And Abraham His servant.
43 He brought out His people with
    joy,
    His chosen ones with gladness.
44 He gave them the lands of the
    Gentiles,
    And they inherited the labor of
    the nations,
45 That they might observe His
    statutes
    And keep His laws.

Praise the LORD!

PSALM 106

1 Praise the LORD!

Oh, give thanks to the LORD, for
    He is good!
    For His mercy *endures* forever.

2 Who can utter the mighty acts of
    the LORD?
    Who can declare all His praise?
3 Blessed *are* those who keep
    justice,

And he who does[a] righteousness
at all times!

4 Remember me, O LORD, with the
favor *You have toward* Your
people.
Oh, visit me with Your salvation,

5 That I may see the benefit of
Your chosen ones,
That I may rejoice in the gladness
of Your nation,
That I may glory with Your
inheritance.

6 We have sinned with our fathers,
We have committed iniquity,
We have done wickedly.

7 Our fathers in Egypt did not
understand Your wonders;
They did not remember the
multitude of Your mercies,
But rebelled by the sea—the Red
Sea.

8 Nevertheless He saved them for
His name's sake,
That He might make His mighty
power known.

9 He rebuked the Red Sea also, and
it dried up;
So He led them through the
depths,
As through the wilderness.

10 He saved them from the hand of
him who hated *them*,
And redeemed them from the
hand of the enemy.

11 The waters covered their
enemies;
There was not one of them left.

12 Then they believed His words;
They sang His praise.

13 They soon forgot His works;
They did not wait for His counsel,

14 But lusted exceedingly in the
wilderness,
And tested God in the desert.

15 And He gave them their request,
But sent leanness into their soul.

16 When they envied Moses in the
camp,
And Aaron the saint of the LORD,

17 The earth opened up and
swallowed Dathan,
And covered the faction of
Abiram.

18 A fire was kindled in their
company;
The flame burned up the wicked.

19 They made a calf in Horeb,
And worshiped the molded
image.

20 Thus they changed their glory
Into the image of an ox that eats
grass.

21 They forgot God their Savior,
Who had done great things in
Egypt,

22 Wondrous works in the land of
Ham,
Awesome things by the Red Sea.

23 Therefore He said that He would
destroy them,
Had not Moses His chosen one
stood before Him in the breach,
To turn away His wrath, lest He
destroy *them*.

24 Then they despised the pleasant
land;
They did not believe His word,

25 But complained in their tents,
And did not heed the voice of the
LORD.

26 Therefore He raised His hand *in
an oath* against them,
To overthrow them in the
wilderness,

27 To overthrow their descendants
among the nations,
And to scatter them in the lands.

28 They joined themselves also to
Baal of Peor,
And ate sacrifices made to the
dead.

29 Thus they provoked *Him* to anger
with their deeds,
And the plague broke out among
them.

30 Then Phinehas stood up and
intervened,
And the plague was stopped.

31 And that was accounted to him
for righteousness
To all generations forevermore.

32 They angered *Him* also at the
waters of strife,[a]
So that it went ill with Moses on
account of them;

33 Because they rebelled against His
Spirit,
So that he spoke rashly with his
lips.

34 They did not destroy the peoples,
Concerning whom the LORD had
commanded them,

106:3 [a]Septuagint, Syriac, Targum, and Vulgate read *those who do.* 106:32 [a]Or *Meribah*

35 But they mingled with the
     Gentiles
   And learned their works;
36 They served their idols,
   Which became a snare to them.
37 They even sacrificed their sons
   And their daughters to demons,
38 And shed innocent blood,
   The blood of their sons and
     daughters,
   Whom they sacrificed to the idols
     of Canaan;
   And the land was polluted with
     blood.
39 Thus they were defiled by their
     own works,
   And played the harlot by their
     own deeds.

40 Therefore the wrath of the Lord
     was kindled against His
     people,
   So that He abhorred His own
     inheritance.
41 And He gave them into the hand
     of the Gentiles,
   And those who hated them ruled
     over them.
42 Their enemies also oppressed
     them,
   And they were brought into
     subjection under their hand.
43 Many times He delivered them;
   But they rebelled in their counsel,
   And were brought low for their
     iniquity.

44 Nevertheless He regarded their
     affliction,
   When He heard their cry;
45 And for their sake He
     remembered His covenant,
   And relented according to the
     multitude of His mercies.
46 He also made them to be pitied
   By all those who carried them
     away captive.

47 Save us, O Lord our God,
   And gather us from among the
     Gentiles,
   To give thanks to Your holy
     name,
   To triumph in Your praise.

48 Blessed be the Lord God of
     Israel
   From everlasting to everlasting!
   And let all the people say,
     "Amen!"

   Praise the Lord!

Book Five   Psalms 107–150

PSALM 107

1 Oh, give thanks to the Lord, for
     He is good!
   For His mercy endures forever.
2 Let the redeemed of the Lord say
     so,
   Whom He has redeemed from the
     hand of the enemy,
3 And gathered out of the lands,
   From the east and from the west,
   From the north and from the
     south.

4 They wandered in the wilderness
     in a desolate way;
   They found no city to dwell in.
5 Hungry and thirsty,
   Their soul fainted in them.
6 Then they cried out to the Lord
     in their trouble,
   And He delivered them out of
     their distresses.
7 And He led them forth by the
     right way,
   That they might go to a city for
     a dwelling place.
8 Oh, that men would give thanks
     to the Lord for His goodness,
   And for His wonderful works to
     the children of men!
9 For He satisfies the longing soul,
   And fills the hungry soul with
     goodness.

10 Those who sat in darkness and
     in the shadow of death,
   Bound in affliction and irons—
11 Because they rebelled against the
     words of God,
   And despised the counsel of the
     Most High,
12 Therefore He brought down their
     heart with labor;
   They fell down, and there was
     none to help.
13 Then they cried out to the Lord
     in their trouble,
   And He saved them out of their
     distresses.
14 He brought them out of darkness
     and the shadow of death,
   And broke their chains in
     pieces.
15 Oh, that men would give thanks
     to the Lord for His goodness,
   And for His wonderful works to
     the children of men!
16 For He has broken the gates of
     bronze,
   And cut the bars of iron in two.

17 Fools, because of their
      transgression,
   And because of their iniquities,
      were afflicted.
18 Their soul abhorred all manner
      of food,
   And they drew near to the gates
      of death.
19 Then they cried out to the LORD
      in their trouble,
   And He saved them out of their
      distresses.
20 He sent His word and healed
      them,
   And delivered *them* from their
      destructions.
21 Oh, that *men* would give thanks
      to the LORD *for* His goodness,
   And *for* His wonderful works to
      the children of men!
22 Let them sacrifice the sacrifices
      of thanksgiving,
   And declare His works with
      rejoicing.

23 Those who go down to the sea
      in ships,
   Who do business on great
      waters,
24 They see the works of the
      LORD,
   And His wonders in the deep.
25 For He commands and raises the
      stormy wind,
   Which lifts up the waves of the
      sea.
26 They mount up to the heavens,
   They go down again to the
      depths;
   Their soul melts because of
      trouble.
27 They reel to and fro, and stagger
      like a drunken man,
   And are at their wits' end.
28 Then they cry out to the LORD in
      their trouble,
   And He brings them out of their
      distresses.
29 He calms the storm,
   So that its waves are still.
30 Then they are glad because they
      are quiet;
   So He guides them to their
      desired haven.
31 Oh, that *men* would give thanks
      to the LORD *for* His goodness,
   And *for* His wonderful works to
      the children of men!
32 Let them exalt Him also in the
      assembly of the people,
   And praise Him in the company
      of the elders.

33 He turns rivers into a wilderness,
   And the watersprings into dry
      ground;
34 A fruitful land into barrenness,
   For the wickedness of those who
      dwell in it.
35 He turns a wilderness into pools
      of water,
   And dry land into watersprings.
36 There He makes the hungry
      dwell,
   That they may establish a city for
      a dwelling place,
37 And sow fields and plant
      vineyards,
   That they may yield a fruitful
      harvest.
38 He also blesses them, and they
      multiply greatly;
   And He does not let their cattle
      decrease.

39 When they are diminished and
      brought low
   Through oppression, affliction
      and sorrow,
40 He pours contempt on princes,
   And causes them to wander in
      the wilderness *where there is*
      no way;
41 Yet He sets the poor on high, far
      from affliction,
   And makes *their* families like a
      flock.
42 The righteous see *it* and rejoice,
   And all iniquity stops its
      mouth.

43 Whoever *is* wise will observe
      these *things,*
   And they will understand the
      lovingkindness of the LORD.

PSALM 108

A Song. A Psalm of David.
1 O God, my heart is steadfast;
   I will sing and give praise, even
      with my glory.
2 Awake, lute and harp!
   I will awaken the dawn.
3 I will praise You, O LORD, among
      the peoples,
   And I will sing praises to You
      among the nations.
4 For Your mercy *is* great above
      the heavens,
   And Your truth *reaches* to the
      clouds.

5 Be exalted, O God, above the
      heavens,

And Your glory above all the
    earth;
6 That Your beloved may be
    delivered,
    Save *with* Your right hand, and
    hear me.

7 God has spoken in His holiness:
    "I will rejoice;
    I will divide Shechem
    And measure out the Valley of
      Succoth.
8 Gilead *is* Mine; Manasseh *is*
    Mine;
    Ephraim also *is* the helmet for
      My head;
    Judah *is* My lawgiver.
9 Moab *is* My washpot;
    Over Edom I will cast My shoe;
    Over Philistia I will triumph."

10 Who will bring me *into* the strong
    city?
    Who will lead me to Edom?
11 *Is it* not *You,* O God, *who* cast
    us off?
    And *You,* O God, *who* did not go
      out with our armies?
12 Give us help from trouble,
    For the help of man is useless.
13 Through God we will do
    valiantly,
    For *it is* He *who* shall tread down
      our enemies.*a*

PSALM 109

To the Chief Musician. A Psalm of David.

1 Do not keep silent,
    O God of my praise!
2 For the mouth of the wicked and
    the mouth of the deceitful
    Have opened against me;
    They have spoken against me
      with a lying tongue.
3 They have also surrounded me
    with words of hatred,
    And fought against me without a
    cause.
4 In return for my love they are my
    accusers,
    But I *give myself to* prayer.
5 Thus they have rewarded me evil
    for good,
    And hatred for my love.

6 Set a wicked man over him,
    And let an accuser*a* stand at his
    right hand.

7 When he is judged, let him be
    found guilty,
    And let his prayer become sin.
8 Let his days be few,
    And let another take his office.
9 Let his children be fatherless,
    And his wife a widow.
10 Let his children continually be
    vagabonds, and beg;
    Let them seek *their bread*a also
      from their desolate places.
11 Let the creditor seize all that he
    has,
    And let strangers plunder his
    labor.
12 Let there be none to extend
    mercy to him,
    Nor let there be any to favor his
    fatherless children.
13 Let his posterity be cut off,
    And in the generation following
    let their name be blotted out.
14 Let the iniquity of his fathers be
    remembered before the LORD,
    And let not the sin of his mother
    be blotted out.
15 Let them be continually before
    the LORD,
    That He may cut off the memory
    of them from the earth;
16 Because he did not remember to
    show mercy,
    But persecuted the poor and
    needy man,
    That he might even slay the
    broken in heart.
17 As he loved cursing, so let it come
    to him;
    As he did not delight in blessing,
    so let it be far from him.
18 As he clothed himself with
    cursing as with his garment,
    So let it enter his body like water,
    And like oil into his bones.
19 Let it be to him like the garment
    which covers him,
    And for a belt with which he
    girds himself continually.
20 *Let* this *be* the LORD's reward to
    my accusers,
    And to those who speak evil
    against my person.

21 But You, O GOD the Lord,
    Deal with me for Your name's
    sake;
    Because Your mercy *is* good,
    deliver me.

108:13 *a*Compare verses 6–13 with 60:5–12   109:6 *a*Hebrew *satan*   109:10 *a*Following Masoretic Text and Targum; Septuagint and Vulgate read *be cast out.*

22 For I *am* poor and needy,
And my heart is wounded within me.
23 I am gone like a shadow when it lengthens;
I am shaken off like a locust.
24 My knees are weak through fasting,
And my flesh is feeble from lack of fatness.
25 I also have become a reproach to them;
When they look at me, they shake their heads.

26 Help me, O LORD my God!
Oh, save me according to Your mercy,
27 That they may know that this *is* Your hand—
That You, LORD, have done it!
28 Let them curse, but You bless;
When they arise, let them be ashamed,
But let Your servant rejoice.
29 Let my accusers be clothed with shame,
And let them cover themselves with their own disgrace as with a mantle.

30 I will greatly praise the LORD with my mouth;
Yes, I will praise Him among the multitude.
31 For He shall stand at the right hand of the poor,
To save *him* from those who condemn him.

PSALM 110

A Psalm of David.

1 The LORD said to my Lord,
"Sit at My right hand,
Till I make Your enemies Your footstool."
2 The LORD shall send the rod of Your strength out of Zion.
Rule in the midst of Your enemies!

3 Your people *shall be* volunteers
In the day of Your power;
In the beauties of holiness, from the womb of the morning,
You have the dew of Your youth.
4 The LORD has sworn
And will not relent,
"You *are* a priest forever
According to the order of Melchizedek."

5 The Lord *is* at Your right hand;
He shall execute kings in the day of His wrath.
6 He shall judge among the nations,
He shall fill *the places* with dead bodies,
He shall execute the heads of many countries.
7 He shall drink of the brook by the wayside;
Therefore He shall lift up the head.

PSALM 111

1 Praise the LORD!

I will praise the LORD with *my* whole heart,
In the assembly of the upright and *in* the congregation.

2 The works of the LORD *are* great,
Studied by all who have pleasure in them.
3 His work *is* honorable and glorious,
And His righteousness endures forever.
4 He has made His wonderful works to be remembered;
The LORD *is* gracious and full of compassion.
5 He has given food to those who fear Him;
He will ever be mindful of His covenant.
6 He has declared to His people the power of His works,
In giving them the heritage of the nations.

7 The works of His hands *are* verity and justice;
All His precepts *are* sure.
8 They stand fast forever and ever,
And are done in truth and uprightness.
9 He has sent redemption to His people;
He has commanded His covenant forever:
Holy and awesome *is* His name.

10 The fear of the LORD *is* the beginning of wisdom;
A good understanding have all those who do *His* commandments.
His praise endures forever.

PSALM 112

1 Praise the Lord!

Blessed *is* the man *who* fears the
    Lord,
Who delights greatly in His
    commandments.

2 His descendants will be mighty
    on earth;
The generation of the upright will
    be blessed.
3 Wealth and riches *will be* in his
    house,
And his righteousness endures
    forever.
4 Unto the upright there arises
    light in the darkness;
He is gracious, and full of
    compassion, and righteous.
5 A good man deals graciously and
    lends;
He will guide his affairs with
    discretion.
6 Surely he will never be shaken;
The righteous will be in
    everlasting remembrance.
7 He will not be afraid of evil
    tidings;
His heart is steadfast, trusting in
    the Lord.
8 His heart *is* established;
He will not be afraid,
Until he sees *his desire* upon his
    enemies.

9 He has dispersed abroad,
He has given to the poor;
His righteousness endures
    forever;
His horn will be exalted with
    honor.
10 The wicked will see *it* and be
    grieved;
He will gnash his teeth and melt
    away;
The desire of the wicked shall
    perish.

PSALM 113

1 Praise the Lord!

Praise, O servants of the Lord,
Praise the name of the Lord!
2 Blessed be the name of the Lord
From this time forth and
    forevermore!
3 From the rising of the sun to its
    going down
The Lord's name *is* to be praised.

4 The Lord *is* high above all
    nations,
His glory above the heavens.
5 Who *is* like the Lord our God,
Who dwells on high,
6 Who humbles Himself to behold
The things that are in the
    heavens and in the earth?

7 He raises the poor out of the dust,
And lifts the needy out of the ash
    heap,
8 That He may seat *him* with
    princes—
With the princes of His people.
9 He grants the barren woman a
    home,
Like a joyful mother of children.

Praise the Lord!

PSALM 114

1 When Israel went out of Egypt,
The house of Jacob from a people
    of strange language,
2 Judah became His sanctuary,
And Israel His dominion.

3 The sea saw *it* and fled;
Jordan turned back.
4 The mountains skipped like
    rams,
The little hills like lambs.
5 What ails you, O sea, that you
    fled?
O Jordan, *that* you turned back?
6 O mountains, *that* you skipped
    like rams?
O little hills, like lambs?

7 Tremble, O earth, at the presence
    of the Lord,
At the presence of the God of
    Jacob,
8 Who turned the rock *into* a pool
    of water,
The flint into a fountain of
    waters.

PSALM 115

1 Not unto us, O Lord, not unto us,
But to Your name give glory,
Because of Your mercy,
Because of Your truth.
2 Why should the Gentiles say,
"So where *is* their God?"

3 But our God *is* in heaven;
He does whatever He pleases.

And They Went Out Singing

The first-century celebration of Passover ended with the singing of Psalms 116 and 118. These are known as the Hallel songs or the Egyptian Hallel.

The Gospel of Matthew records that when Jesus and the disciples finished the Passover meal they left the upper city of Jerusalem singing as they went to the Garden of Gethsemane. It is revealing to take a look at some of the verses that Jesus sang as He went to pray in the garden.

> I love the Lord, because He has heard
> My voice and my supplications (Ps. 116:2).
> Therefore I will call upon Him as long as I live (Ps. 116:2).
> For You have delivered my soul from death,
> My eyes from tears,
> And my feet from falling (Ps. 116:8).
> I will walk before the Lord
> In the land of the living (Ps. 116:9).
> Precious in the sight of the Lord
> Is the death of His saints (Ps. 116:15).
> The Lord is on my side; I will not fear.
> What can man do to me? (Ps. 118:6).
> The Lord is for me among those who help me (Ps. 118:7).
> You pushed me violently, that I might fall,
> But the Lord helped me (Ps. 118:13).
> The Lord is my strength and song,
> And He has become my salvation (Ps. 118:14).
> I shall not die, but live,
> And declare the works of the Lord (Ps. 118:17).
> The stone which the builders rejected
> Has become the chief cornerstone (Ps. 118:22).
> This was the Lord's doing;
> It is marvelous in our eyes (Ps. 118:23).
> This is the day which the Lord has made;
> We will rejoice and be glad in it (Ps. 118:24).

We humans will never fully understand the stress, turmoil, and pressure that Jesus experienced in the garden. But perhaps by knowing the songs He sang, we can gain a deeper appreciation of God's love and forgiveness for us.

If Jesus was able to sing in His most difficult moment, "This is the day the Lord has made; we will rejoice and be glad in it," how much more can we look at our negative circumstances and trust God to turn them into positive, life-giving hope!

God turned death for Jesus Christ into life so that His words about our death could be more fully understood. Jesus said, "I am the resurrection and the life. He who believes in Me, though he may die, he shall live" (John 11:25).

4 Their idols *are* silver and gold,
  The work of men's hands.
5 They have mouths, but they do
    not speak;
  Eyes they have, but they do not
    see;
6 They have ears, but they do not
    hear;
  Noses they have, but they do not
    smell;
7 They have hands, but they do not
    handle;
  Feet they have, but they do not
    walk;
  Nor do they mutter through their
    throat.
8 Those who make them are like
    them;
  So is everyone who trusts in
    them.

9 O Israel, trust in the LORD;
  He *is* their help and their shield.
10 O house of Aaron, trust in the
    LORD;
  He *is* their help and their shield.
11 You who fear the LORD, trust in
    the LORD;
  He *is* their help and their shield.

12 The LORD has been mindful of *us*;
  He will bless us;
  He will bless the house of Israel;
  He will bless the house of Aaron.
13 He will bless those who fear the
    LORD,
  Both small and great.

14 May the LORD give you increase
    more and more,
  You and your children.
15 *May* you *be* blessed by the LORD,
  Who made heaven and earth.

16 The heaven, *even* the heavens,
    are the LORD's;
  But the earth He has given to the
    children of men.
17 The dead do not praise the LORD,
  Nor any who go down into
    silence.
18 But we will bless the LORD
  From this time forth and
    forevermore.

Praise the LORD!

PSALM 116

1 I love the LORD, because He has
    heard
  My voice *and* my supplications.

2 Because He has inclined His ear
    to me,
  Therefore I will call *upon Him* as
    long as I live.

3 The pains of death surrounded
    me,
  And the pangs of Sheol laid hold
    of me;
  I found trouble and sorrow.
4 Then I called upon the name of
    the LORD:
  "O LORD, I implore You, deliver
    my soul!"

5 Gracious *is* the LORD, and
    righteous;
  Yes, our God *is* merciful.
6 The LORD preserves the simple;
  I was brought low, and He saved
    me.
7 Return to your rest, O my soul,
  For the LORD has dealt
    bountifully with you.

8 For You have delivered my soul
    from death,
  My eyes from tears,
  And my feet from falling.
9 I will walk before the LORD
  In the land of the living.
10 I believed, therefore I spoke,
  "I am greatly afflicted."
11 I said in my haste,
  "All men *are* liars."

12 What shall I render to the LORD
  For all His benefits toward me?
13 I will take up the cup of salvation,
  And call upon the name of the
    LORD.
14 I will pay my vows to the LORD
  Now in the presence of all His
    people.

15 Precious in the sight of the LORD
  Is the death of His saints.

16 O LORD, truly I *am* Your servant;
  I *am* Your servant, the son of
    Your maidservant;
  You have loosed my bonds.
17 I will offer to You the sacrifice
    of thanksgiving,
  And will call upon the name of
    the LORD.
18 I will pay my vows to the LORD
  Now in the presence of all His
    people,
19 In the courts of the LORD's house,
  In the midst of you, O Jerusalem.

Praise the LORD!

PSALM 117

1 Praise the LORD, all you Gentiles!
Laud Him, all you peoples!
2 For His merciful kindness is great
toward us,
And the truth of the LORD *endures*
forever.

Praise the LORD!

PSALM 118

1 Oh, give thanks to the LORD, for
He is good!
For His mercy *endures* forever.

2 Let Israel now say,
"His mercy *endures* forever."
3 Let the house of Aaron now say,
"His mercy *endures* forever."
4 Let those who fear the LORD now
say,
"His mercy *endures* forever."

5 I called on the LORD in distress;
The LORD answered me *and set
me* in a broad place.
6 The LORD *is* on my side;
I will not fear.
What can man do to me?
7 The LORD is for me among those
who help me;
Therefore I shall see *my desire* on
those who hate me.
8 *It is* better to trust in the LORD
Than to put confidence in man.
9 *It is* better to trust in the LORD
Than to put confidence in
princes.

10 All nations surrounded me,
But in the name of the LORD I will
destroy them.
11 They surrounded me,
Yes, they surrounded me;
But in the name of the LORD I will
destroy them.
12 They surrounded me like bees;
They were quenched like a fire
of thorns;
For in the name of the LORD I will
destroy them.
13 You pushed me violently, that I
might fall,
But the LORD helped me.
14 The LORD *is* my strength and
song,

And He has become my
salvation.[a]

15 The voice of rejoicing and
salvation
Is in the tents of the righteous;
The right hand of the LORD does
valiantly.
16 The right hand of the LORD is
exalted;
The right hand of the LORD does
valiantly.
17 I shall not die, but live,
And declare the works of the
LORD.
18 The LORD has chastened me
severely,
But He has not given me over to
death.

19 Open to me the gates of
righteousness;
I will go through them,
And I will praise the LORD.
20 This is the gate of the LORD,
Through which the righteous
shall enter.

21 I will praise You,
For You have answered me,
And have become my salvation.

22 The stone *which* the builders
rejected
Has become the chief
cornerstone.
23 This was the LORD's doing;
It *is* marvelous in our eyes.
24 This *is* the day the LORD has
made;
We will rejoice and be glad in it.

25 Save now, I pray, O LORD;
O LORD, I pray, send now
prosperity.
26 Blessed *is* he who comes in the
name of the LORD!
We have blessed you from the
house of the LORD.
27 God *is* the LORD,
And He has given us light;
Bind the sacrifice with cords to
the horns of the altar.
28 You *are* my God, and I will praise
You;
You are my God, I will exalt You.

29 Oh, give thanks to the LORD, for
He is good!
For His mercy *endures* forever.

118:14 aCompare Exodus 15:2

PSALM 119

א   ALEPH

1 Blessed *are* the undefiled in the way,
Who walk in the law of the LORD!
2 Blessed *are* those who keep His testimonies,
Who seek Him with the whole heart!
3 They also do no iniquity;
They walk in His ways.
4 You have commanded *us*
To keep Your precepts diligently.
5 Oh, that my ways were directed
To keep Your statutes!
6 Then I would not be ashamed,
When I look into all Your commandments.
7 I will praise You with uprightness of heart,
When I learn Your righteous judgments.
8 I will keep Your statutes;
Oh, do not forsake me utterly!

ב   BETH

9 How can a young man cleanse his way?
By taking heed according to Your word.
10 With my whole heart I have sought You;
Oh, let me not wander from Your commandments!
11 Your word I have hidden in my heart,
That I might not sin against You.
12 Blessed *are* You, O LORD!
Teach me Your statutes.
13 With my lips I have declared
All the judgments of Your mouth.
14 I have rejoiced in the way of Your testimonies,
As *much as* in all riches.
15 I will meditate on Your precepts,
And contemplate Your ways.
16 I will delight myself in Your statutes;
I will not forget Your word.

ג   GIMEL

17 Deal bountifully with Your servant,
That I may live and keep Your word.
18 Open my eyes, that I may see
Wondrous things from Your law.
19 I *am* a stranger in the earth;
Do not hide Your commandments from me.

20 My soul breaks with longing
For Your judgments at all times.
21 You rebuke the proud—the cursed,
Who stray from Your commandments.
22 Remove from me reproach and contempt,
For I have kept Your testimonies.
23 Princes also sit *and* speak against me,
But Your servant meditates on Your statutes.
24 Your testimonies also *are* my delight
And my counselors.

ד   DALETH

25 My soul clings to the dust;
Revive me according to Your word.
26 I have declared my ways, and You answered me;
Teach me Your statutes.
27 Make me understand the way of Your precepts;
So shall I meditate on Your wonderful works.
28 My soul melts from heaviness;
Strengthen me according to Your word.
29 Remove from me the way of lying,
And grant me Your law graciously.
30 I have chosen the way of truth;
Your judgments I have laid *before me.*
31 I cling to Your testimonies;
O LORD, do not put me to shame!
32 I will run the course of Your commandments,
For You shall enlarge my heart.

ה   HE

33 Teach me, O LORD, the way of Your statutes,
And I shall keep it *to* the end.
34 Give me understanding, and I shall keep Your law;
Indeed, I shall observe it with *my* whole heart.
35 Make me walk in the path of Your commandments,
For I delight in it.
36 Incline my heart to Your testimonies,
And not to covetousness.
37 Turn away my eyes from looking at worthless things,

Be a Dreamer

Who is normal, the cynic or the believer? The positive thinker or the negative thinker? The believer in God or the atheist? The despairing pessimist or the hopeful optimist? Read Psalm 119:41-80 for the profile of a whole, healthy individual.

Unbelief is a sickness, and skepticism is dangerous. It gives birth to a multitude of spiritual demons that can destroy your mental health and spread an epidemic of despair wherever you go. As soon as you surrender yourself to negative thoughts, you become host to an infectious spiritual disease and become the carrier of another epidemic of gloom and doom.

It is normal for a child to dance and laugh and play. It is not normal for a child to be downcast, morbid, withdrawn, and sulking in isolation. It is normal to be a happy believer.

Who is crazy? The realist or the idealist?

The answer is obvious. The Beautiful Dreamer, with His exalted visions of glorious possibilities, is the Uplifting Force in society! He comes bringing solutions. He then becomes the Great Physician, the Healing Source, the Hopeful Friend. We can follow Him.

His name? Jesus, the Lord. Our Savior. Our Friend.

And revive me in Your way.[a]

38 Establish Your word to Your
servant,
Who *is devoted* to fearing You.

39 Turn away my reproach which I
dread,
For Your judgments *are* good.

40 Behold, I long for Your precepts;
Revive me in Your righteousness.

ו WAW

41 Let Your mercies come also to
me, O LORD—
Your salvation according to Your
word.

42 So shall I have an answer for him
who reproaches me,
For I trust in Your word.

43 And take not the word of truth
utterly out of my mouth,
For I have hoped in Your
ordinances.

44 So shall I keep Your law
continually,
Forever and ever.

45 And I will walk at liberty,
For I seek Your precepts.

46 I will speak of Your testimonies
also before kings,
And will not be ashamed.

47 And I will delight myself in Your
commandments,
Which I love.

48 My hands also I will lift up to
Your commandments,
Which I love,
And I will meditate on Your
statutes.

ז ZAYIN

49 Remember the word to Your
servant,
Upon which You have caused me
to hope.

50 This *is* my comfort in my
affliction,
For Your word has given me life.

51 The proud have me in great
derision,
Yet I do not turn aside from Your
law.

52 I remembered Your judgments of
old, O LORD,
And have comforted myself.

53 Indignation has taken hold of me
Because of the wicked, who
forsake Your law.

54 Your statutes have been my
songs
In the house of my pilgrimage.

55 I remember Your name in the
night, O LORD,
And I keep Your law.

56 This has become mine,
Because I kept Your precepts.

ח HETH

57 *You are* my portion, O LORD;
I have said that I would keep
Your words.

58 I entreated Your favor with *my*
whole heart;
Be merciful to me according to
Your word.

59 I thought about my ways,
And turned my feet to Your
testimonies.

60 I made haste, and did not delay
To keep Your commandments.

61 The cords of the wicked have
bound me,
But I have not forgotten Your
law.

62 At midnight I will rise to give
thanks to You,
Because of Your righteous
judgments.

63 I *am* a companion of all who fear
You,
And of those who keep Your
precepts.

64 The earth, O LORD, is full of Your
mercy;
Teach me Your statutes.

ט TETH

65 You have dealt well with Your
servant,
O LORD, according to Your word.

66 Teach me good judgment and
knowledge,
For I believe Your
commandments.

67 Before I was afflicted I went
astray,
But now I keep Your word.

68 You *are* good, and do good;
Teach me Your statutes.

69 The proud have forged a lie
against me,
But I will keep Your precepts
with *my* whole heart.

70 Their heart is as fat as grease,
But I delight in Your law.

71 *It is* good for me that I have been
afflicted,
That I may learn Your statutes.

72 The law of Your mouth *is* better
to me
Than thousands of *coins of* gold
and silver.

119:37 [a]Following Masoretic Text, Septuagint, and Vulgate; Targum reads *Your words*.

י YOD

73 Your hands have made me and
    fashioned me;
    Give me understanding, that I
      may learn Your
      commandments.
74 Those who fear You will be glad
    when they see me,
    Because I have hoped in Your
      word.
75 I know, O Lord, that Your
    judgments *are* right,
    And *that* in faithfulness You
      have afflicted me.
76 Let, I pray, Your merciful
    kindness be for my comfort,
    According to Your word to Your
      servant.
77 Let Your tender mercies come to
    me, that I may live;
    For Your law *is* my delight.
78 Let the proud be ashamed,
    For they treated me wrongfully
      with falsehood;
    But I will meditate on Your
      precepts.
79 Let those who fear You turn to
    me,
    Those who know Your
      testimonies.
80 Let my heart be blameless
    regarding Your statutes,
    That I may not be ashamed.

כ KAPH

81 My soul faints for Your salvation,
    But I hope in Your word.
82 My eyes fail *from searching* Your
    word,
    Saying, "When will You comfort
      me?"
83 For I have become like a
    wineskin in smoke,
    Yet I do not forget Your statutes.
84 How many *are* the days of Your
    servant?
    When will You execute judgment
      on those who persecute me?
85 The proud have dug pits for
    me,
    Which *is* not according to Your
      law.
86 All Your commandments *are*
    faithful;
    They persecute me wrongfully;
    Help me!
87 They almost made an end of me
    on earth,
    But I did not forsake Your
      precepts.
88 Revive me according to Your
    lovingkindness,

So that I may keep the testimony
    of Your mouth.

ל LAMED

89 Forever, O Lord,
    Your word is settled in heaven.
90 Your faithfulness *endures* to all
    generations;
    You established the earth, and it
      abides.
91 They continue this day according
    to Your ordinances,
    For all *are* Your servants.
92 Unless Your law *had been* my
    delight,
    I would then have perished in my
      affliction.
93 I will never forget Your precepts,
    For by them You have given me
      life.
94 I *am* Yours, save me;
    For I have sought Your precepts.
95 The wicked wait for me to
    destroy me,
    But I will consider Your
      testimonies.
96 I have seen the consummation of
    all perfection,
    But Your commandment *is*
      exceedingly broad.

מ MEM

97 Oh, how I love Your law!
    It *is* my meditation all the day.
98 You, through Your
    commandments, make me
    wiser than my enemies;
    For they *are* ever with me.
99 I have more understanding than
    all my teachers,
    For Your testimonies *are* my
      meditation.
100 I understand more than the
    ancients,
    Because I keep Your precepts.
101 I have restrained my feet from
    every evil way,
    That I may keep Your word.
102 I have not departed from Your
    judgments,
    For You Yourself have taught
      me.
103 How sweet are Your words to my
    taste,
    Sweeter than honey to my
      mouth!
104 Through Your precepts I get
    understanding;
    Therefore I hate every false way.

נ NUN

105 Your word *is* a lamp to my feet
    And a light to my path.

106 I have sworn and confirmed
That I will keep Your righteous
judgments.
107 I am afflicted very much;
Revive me, O Lord, according to
Your word.
108 Accept, I pray, the freewill
offerings of my mouth, O Lord,
And teach me Your judgments.
109 My life *is* continually in my hand,
Yet I do not forget Your law.
110 The wicked have laid a snare for
me,
Yet I have not strayed from Your
precepts.
111 Your testimonies I have taken as
a heritage forever,
For they *are* the rejoicing of my
heart.
112 I have inclined my heart to
perform Your statutes
Forever, to the very end.

ס SAMEK
113 I hate the double-minded,
But I love Your law.
114 You *are* my hiding place and my
shield;
I hope in Your word.
115 Depart from me, you evildoers,
For I will keep the
commandments of my God!
116 Uphold me according to Your
word, that I may live;
And do not let me be ashamed
of my hope.
117 Hold me up, and I shall be safe,
And I shall observe Your statutes
continually.
118 You reject all those who stray
from Your statutes,
For their deceit *is* falsehood.
119 You put away all the wicked of
the earth *like* dross;
Therefore I love Your
testimonies.
120 My flesh trembles for fear of You,
And I am afraid of Your
judgments.

ע AYIN
121 I have done justice and
righteousness;
Do not leave me to my
oppressors.
122 Be surety for Your servant for
good;
Do not let the proud oppress me.
123 My eyes fail *from seeking* Your
salvation
And Your righteous word.

124 Deal with Your servant
according to Your mercy,
And teach me Your statutes.
125 I *am* Your servant;
Give me understanding,
That I may know Your
testimonies.
126 *It is* time for *You* to act, O Lord,
For they have regarded Your law
as void.
127 Therefore I love Your
commandments
More than gold, yes, than fine
gold!
128 Therefore all *Your* precepts
concerning all *things*
I consider *to be* right;
I hate every false way.

פ PE
129 Your testimonies are wonderful;
Therefore my soul keeps them.
130 The entrance of Your words
gives light;
It gives understanding to the
simple.
131 I opened my mouth and panted,
For I longed for Your
commandments.
132 Look upon me and be merciful
to me,
As Your custom *is* toward those
who love Your name.
133 Direct my steps by Your word,
And let no iniquity have
dominion over me.
134 Redeem me from the oppression
of man,
That I may keep Your precepts.
135 Make Your face shine upon Your
servant,
And teach me Your statutes.
136 Rivers of water run down from
my eyes,
Because *men* do not keep Your
law.

צ TSADDE
137 Righteous *are* You, O Lord,
And upright *are* Your judgments.
138 Your testimonies, *which* You
have commanded,
Are righteous and very faithful.
139 My zeal has consumed me,
Because my enemies have
forgotten Your words.
140 Your word *is* very pure;
Therefore Your servant loves it.
141 I *am* small and despised,
Yet I do not forget Your precepts.
142 Your righteousness *is* an
everlasting righteousness,

And Your law *is* truth.
143 Trouble and anguish have
overtaken me,
Yet Your commandments *are* my
delights.
144 The righteousness of Your
testimonies *is* everlasting;
Give me understanding, and I
shall live.

ק QOPH
145 I cry out with *my* whole heart;
Hear me, O LORD!
I will keep Your statutes.
146 I cry out to You;
Save me, and I will keep Your
testimonies.
147 I rise before the dawning of the
morning,
And cry for help;
I hope in Your word.
148 My eyes are awake through the
night watches,
That I may meditate on Your
word.
149 Hear my voice according to Your
lovingkindness;
O LORD, revive me according to
Your justice.
150 They draw near who follow after
wickedness;
They are far from Your law.
151 You *are* near, O LORD,
And all Your commandments *are*
truth.
152 Concerning Your testimonies,
I have known of old that You
have founded them forever.

ר RESH
153 Consider my affliction and
deliver me,
For I do not forget Your law.
154 Plead my cause and redeem me;
Revive me according to Your
word.
155 Salvation *is* far from the wicked,
For they do not seek Your
statutes.
156 Great *are* Your tender mercies, O
LORD;
Revive me according to Your
judgments.
157 Many *are* my persecutors and my
enemies,
Yet I do not turn from Your
testimonies.
158 I see the treacherous, and am
disgusted,
Because they do not keep Your
word.

159 Consider how I love Your
precepts;
Revive me, O LORD, according to
Your lovingkindness.
160 The entirety of Your word *is*
truth,
And every one of Your righteous
judgments *endures* forever.

ש SHIN
161 Princes persecute me without a
cause,
But my heart stands in awe of
Your word.
162 I rejoice at Your word
As one who finds great treasure.
163 I hate and abhor lying,
But I love Your law.
164 Seven times a day I praise You,
Because of Your righteous
judgments.
165 Great peace have those who love
Your law,
And nothing causes them to
stumble.
166 LORD, I hope for Your salvation,
And I do Your commandments.
167 My soul keeps Your testimonies,
And I love them exceedingly.
168 I keep Your precepts and Your
testimonies,
For all my ways *are* before You.

ת TAU
169 Let my cry come before You, O
LORD;
Give me understanding
according to Your word.
170 Let my supplication come before
You;
Deliver me according to Your
word.
171 My lips shall utter praise,
For You teach me Your statutes.
172 My tongue shall speak of Your
word,
For all Your commandments *are*
righteousness.
173 Let Your hand become my help,
For I have chosen Your precepts.
174 I long for Your salvation, O LORD,
And Your law *is* my delight.
175 Let my soul live, and it shall
praise You;
And let Your judgments help
me.
176 I have gone astray like a lost
sheep;
Seek Your servant,
For I do not forget Your
commandments.

PSALM 120

A Song of Ascents.

1 In my distress I cried to the LORD,
   And He heard me.
2 Deliver my soul, O LORD, from
   lying lips
   And from a deceitful tongue.

3 What shall be given to you,
   Or what shall be done to you,
   You false tongue?
4 Sharp arrows of the warrior,
   With coals of the broom tree!

5 Woe is me, that I dwell in
   Meshech,
   That I dwell among the tents of
   Kedar!
6 My soul has dwelt too long
   With one who hates peace.
7 I *am for* peace;
   But when I speak, they *are* for
   war.

PSALM 121

A Song of Ascents.

1 I will lift up my eyes to the hills—
   From whence comes my help?
2 My help *comes* from the LORD,
   Who made heaven and earth.

3 He will not allow your foot to be
   moved;
   He who keeps you will not
   slumber.
4 Behold, He who keeps Israel
   Shall neither slumber nor sleep.

5 The LORD *is* your keeper;
   The LORD *is* your shade at your
   right hand.
6 The sun shall not strike you by
   day,
   Nor the moon by night.

7 The LORD shall preserve you from
   all evil;
   He shall preserve your soul.
8 The LORD shall preserve your
   going out and your coming in
   From this time forth, and even
   forevermore.

PSALM 122

A Song of Ascents. Of David.

1 I was glad when they said to me,
   "Let us go into the house of the
   LORD."
2 Our feet have been standing
   Within your gates, O Jerusalem!

3 Jerusalem is built
   As a city that is compact
   together,
4 Where the tribes go up,
   The tribes of the LORD,
   To the Testimony of Israel,
   To give thanks to the name of the
   LORD.
5 For thrones are set there for
   judgment,
   The thrones of the house of
   David.

6 Pray for the peace of Jerusalem:
   "May they prosper who love you.
7 Peace be within your walls,
   Prosperity within your palaces."
8 For the sake of my brethren and
   companions,
   I will now say, "Peace *be* within
   you."
9 Because of the house of the LORD
   our God
   I will seek your good.

PSALM 123

A Song of Ascents.

1 Unto You I lift up my eyes,
   O You who dwell in the heavens.
2 Behold, as the eyes of servants
   look to the hand of their
   masters,
   As the eyes of a maid to the hand
   of her mistress,
   So our eyes *look* to the LORD our
   God,
   Until He has mercy on us.

3 Have mercy on us, O LORD, have
   mercy on us!
   For we are exceedingly filled
   with contempt.
4 Our soul is exceedingly filled
   With the scorn of those who are
   at ease,
   With the contempt of the proud.

PSALM 124

A Song of Ascents. Of David.

1 "If it had not been the LORD who
   was on our side,"
   Let Israel now say—
2 "If it had not been the LORD who
   was on our side,
   When men rose up against us,
3 Then they would have swallowed
   us alive,
   When their wrath was kindled
   against us;

The Mountains Surround Jerusalem

"Those who trust in the LORD *are* like Mount Zion, which cannot be moved, *but* abides forever. As the mountains surround Jerusalem, so the LORD surrounds His people from this time forth and forever" (Ps. 125:1, 2).

The city of Jerusalem, located twenty-nine hundred feet above sea level on the crest of the Judean ridge, is surrounded by hills and steep valleys. The psalmist uses the city's geographical location to paint a vivid picture of God's love toward His people. He compares the permanence of the rocky limestone mountains to the enduring quality of God's love toward us.

Certainly the elevation of the mountains was in the psalmist's mind as he looked north of Jerusalem to the high mountains which acted as sentinels protecting the city from its most vulnerable approach route. God's protection is like the steep mountains west of Jerusalem with their narrow passes easily defended by the city's inhabitants. South and east of Jerusalem lay the barren wilderness that was inhospitable to any advancing army, with scorching hot summers and flash floods in the winter.

The ancient Israelites had a constant reminder that their security came from God. Their natural environment encouraged them in their faith. The mountains surrounding Jerusalem became to them a symbol of God's love, power, and care.

We too can realize the security of God's power in our lives as we trust in God and are assured that we will live forever. Problems that come into our lives cannot move us. God's love is permanent. It elevates us and protects us from life's problems. His love surrounds us, as the psalmist assures, "from this time forth and forever."

4 Then the waters would have
    overwhelmed us,
  The stream would have gone
    over our soul;
5 Then the swollen waters
  Would have gone over our soul."

6 Blessed *be* the LORD,
  Who has not given us *as* prey to
    their teeth.
7 Our soul has escaped as a bird
    from the snare of the fowlers;*a*
  The snare is broken, and we have
    escaped.
8 Our help *is* in the name of the
    LORD,
  Who made heaven and earth.

PSALM 125

A Song of Ascents.
1 Those who trust in the LORD
  Are like Mount Zion,
  Which cannot be moved, *but*
    abides forever.
2 As the mountains surround
    Jerusalem,
  So the LORD surrounds His
    people
  From this time forth and forever.

3 For the scepter of wickedness
    shall not rest
  On the land allotted to the
    righteous,
  Lest the righteous reach out their
    hands to iniquity.

4 Do good, O LORD, to *those who
    are* good,
  And to *those who are* upright in
    their hearts.

5 As for such as turn aside to their
    crooked ways,
  The LORD shall lead them away
  With the workers of iniquity.

  Peace *be* upon Israel!

PSALM 126

A Song of Ascents.
1 When the LORD brought back the
    captivity of Zion,
  We were like those who dream.
2 Then our mouth was filled with
    laughter,
  And our tongue with singing.

  Then they said among the
    nations,
  "The LORD has done great things
    for them."
3 The LORD has done great things
    for us,
  And we are glad.

4 Bring back our captivity, O LORD,
  As the streams in the South.

5 Those who sow in tears
  Shall reap in joy.
6 He who continually goes forth
    weeping,
  Bearing seed for sowing,
  Shall doubtless come again with
    rejoicing,
  Bringing his sheaves *with him.*

PSALM 127

A Song of Ascents. Of Solomon.
1 Unless the LORD builds the house,
  They labor in vain who build it;
  Unless the LORD guards the city,
  The watchman stays awake in
    vain.
2 *It is* vain for you to rise up early,
  To sit up late,
  To eat the bread of sorrows;
  For so He gives His beloved
    sleep.

3 Behold, children *are* a heritage
    from the LORD,
  The fruit of the womb *is* a reward.
4 Like arrows in the hand of a
    warrior,
  So *are* the children of one's
    youth.
5 Happy *is* the man who has his
    quiver full of them;
  They shall not be ashamed,
  But shall speak with their
    enemies in the gate.

PSALM 128

A Song of Ascents.
1 Blessed *is* every one who fears
    the LORD,
  Who walks in His ways.

2 When you eat the labor of your
    hands,
  You *shall be* happy, and *it shall
    be* well with you.
3 Your wife *shall be* like a fruitful
    vine

124:7 *a*That is, persons who catch birds in a trap or snare

In the very heart of your house,
Your children like olive plants
All around your table.
4 Behold, thus shall the man be
blessed
Who fears the LORD.

5 The LORD bless you out of Zion,
And may you see the good of
Jerusalem
All the days of your life.
6 Yes, may you see your children's
children.

Peace be upon Israel!

PSALM 129

A Song of Ascents.

1 "Many a time they have afflicted
me from my youth,"
Let Israel now say—
2 "Many a time they have afflicted
me from my youth;
Yet they have not prevailed
against me.
3 The plowers plowed on my back;
They made their furrows long."
4 The LORD is righteous;
He has cut in pieces the cords of
the wicked.

5 Let all those who hate Zion
Be put to shame and turned back.
6 Let them be as the grass on the
housetops,
Which withers before it grows
up,
7 With which the reaper does not
fill his hand,
Nor he who binds sheaves, his
arms.
8 Neither let those who pass by
them say,
"The blessing of the LORD be upon
you;
We bless you in the name of the
LORD!"

PSALM 130

A Song of Ascents.

1 Out of the depths I have cried to
You, O LORD;
2 Lord, hear my voice!
Let Your ears be attentive
To the voice of my supplications.

3 If You, LORD, should mark
iniquities,
O Lord, who could stand?

4 But there is forgiveness with
You,
That You may be feared.

5 I wait for the LORD, my soul waits,
And in His word I do hope.
6 My soul waits for the Lord
More than those who watch for
the morning—
Yes, more than those who watch
for the morning.

7 O Israel, hope in the LORD;
For with the LORD there is mercy,
And with Him is abundant
redemption.
8 And He shall redeem Israel
From all his iniquities.

PSALM 131

A Song of Ascents. Of David.

1 LORD, my heart is not haughty,
Nor my eyes lofty.
Neither do I concern myself with
great matters,
Nor with things too profound for
me.

2 Surely I have calmed and quieted
my soul,
Like a weaned child with his
mother;
Like a weaned child is my soul
within me.

3 O Israel, hope in the LORD
From this time forth and forever.

PSALM 132

A Song of Ascents.

1 LORD, remember David
And all his afflictions;
2 How he swore to the LORD,
And vowed to the Mighty One of
Jacob:
3 "Surely I will not go into the
chamber of my house,
Or go up to the comfort of my
bed;
4 I will not give sleep to my eyes
Or slumber to my eyelids,
5 Until I find a place for the LORD,
A dwelling place for the Mighty
One of Jacob."

6 Behold, we heard of it in
Ephrathah;
We found it in the fields of the
woods.a

132:6 aHebrew Jaar

7 Let us go into His tabernacle;
　Let us worship at His footstool.
8 Arise, O LORD, to Your resting
　　place,
　You and the ark of Your strength.
9 Let Your priests be clothed with
　　righteousness,
　And let Your saints shout for joy.

10 For Your servant David's sake,
　Do not turn away the face of
　　Your Anointed.

11 The LORD has sworn *in* truth to
　　David;
　He will not turn from it:
　"I will set upon your throne the
　　fruit of your body.
12 If your sons will keep My
　　covenant
　And My testimony which I shall
　　teach them,
　Their sons also shall sit upon
　　your throne forevermore."

13 For the LORD has chosen Zion;
　He has desired *it* for His dwelling
　　place:
14 "This *is* My resting place forever;
　Here I will dwell, for I have
　　desired it.
15 I will abundantly bless her
　　provision;
　I will satisfy her poor with bread.
16 I will also clothe her priests with
　　salvation,
　And her saints shall shout aloud
　　for joy.
17 There I will make the horn of
　　David grow;
　I will prepare a lamp for My
　　Anointed.
18 His enemies I will clothe with
　　shame,
　But upon Himself His crown shall
　　flourish."

PSALM 133

A Song of Ascents. Of David.

1 Behold, how good and how
　　pleasant *it is*
　For brethren to dwell together in
　　unity!

2 *It is* like the precious oil upon the
　　head,
　Running down on the beard,
　The beard of Aaron,
　Running down on the edge of his
　　garments.
3 *It is* like the dew of Hermon,

Descending upon the mountains
　of Zion;
For there the LORD commanded
　the blessing—
Life forevermore.

PSALM 134

A Song of Ascents.

1 Behold, bless the LORD,
　All *you* servants of the LORD,
　Who by night stand in the house
　　of the LORD!
2 Lift up your hands *in* the
　　sanctuary,
　And bless the LORD.

3 The LORD who made heaven and
　　earth
　Bless you from Zion!

PSALM 135

1 Praise the LORD!

　Praise the name of the LORD;
　Praise *Him,* O you servants of the
　　LORD!
2 You who stand in the house of
　　the LORD,
　In the courts of the house of our
　　God,
3 Praise the LORD, for the LORD *is*
　　good;
　Sing praises to His name, for *it
　　is* pleasant.
4 For the LORD has chosen Jacob
　　for Himself,
　Israel for His special treasure.

5 For I know that the LORD *is* great,
　And our Lord *is* above all gods.
6 Whatever the LORD pleases He
　　does,
　In heaven and in earth,
　In the seas and in all deep places.
7 He causes the vapors to ascend
　　from the ends of the earth;
　He makes lightning for the rain;
　He brings the wind out of His
　　treasuries.

8 He destroyed the firstborn of
　　Egypt,
　Both of man and beast.
9 He sent signs and wonders into
　　the midst of you, O Egypt,
　Upon Pharaoh and all his
　　servants.
10 He defeated many nations
　And slew mighty kings—
11 Sihon king of the Amorites,

Og king of Bashan,
And all the kingdoms of
Canaan—
12 And gave their land *as* a heritage,
A heritage to Israel His people.

13 Your name, O LORD, *endures*
forever,
Your fame, O LORD, throughout
all generations.
14 For the LORD will judge His
people,
And He will have compassion on
His servants.

15 The idols of the nations *are* silver
and gold,
The work of men's hands.
16 They have mouths, but they do
not speak;
Eyes they have, but they do not
see;
17 They have ears, but they do not
hear;
Nor is there *any* breath in their
mouths.
18 Those who make them are like
them;
So is everyone who trusts in
them.

19 Bless the LORD, O house of Israel!
Bless the LORD, O house of
Aaron!
20 Bless the LORD, O house of Levi!
You who fear the LORD, bless the
LORD!
21 Blessed be the LORD out of Zion,
Who dwells in Jerusalem!

Praise the LORD!

PSALM 136

1 Oh, give thanks to the LORD, for
He is good!
For His mercy *endures* forever.
2 Oh, give thanks to the God of
gods!
For His mercy *endures* forever.
3 Oh, give thanks to the Lord of
lords!
For His mercy *endures* forever:

4 To Him who alone does great
wonders,
For His mercy *endures* forever;
5 To Him who by wisdom made the
heavens,
For His mercy *endures* forever;

6 To Him who laid out the earth
above the waters,
For His mercy *endures* forever;
7 To Him who made great lights,
For His mercy *endures*
forever—
8 The sun to rule by day,
For His mercy *endures* forever;
9 The moon and stars to rule by
night,
For His mercy *endures* forever.

10 To Him who struck Egypt in their
firstborn,
For His mercy *endures* forever;
11 And brought out Israel from
among them,
For His mercy *endures* forever;
12 With a strong hand, and with an
outstretched arm,
For His mercy *endures* forever;
13 To Him who divided the Red Sea
in two,
For His mercy *endures* forever;
14 And made Israel pass through the
midst of it,
For His mercy *endures* forever;
15 But overthrew Pharaoh and his
army in the Red Sea,
For His mercy *endures* forever;
16 To Him who led His people
through the wilderness,
For His mercy *endures* forever;
17 To Him who struck down great
kings,
For His mercy *endures* forever;
18 And slew famous kings,
For His mercy *endures*
forever—
19 Sihon king of the Amorites,
For His mercy *endures* forever;
20 And Og king of Bashan,
For His mercy *endures*
forever—
21 And gave their land as a heritage,
For His mercy *endures* forever;
22 A heritage to Israel His servant,
For His mercy *endures* forever.

23 Who remembered us in our lowly
state,
For His mercy *endures* forever;
24 And rescued us from our
enemies,
For His mercy *endures* forever;
25 Who gives food to all flesh,
For His mercy *endures* forever.

26 Oh, give thanks to the God of
heaven!
For His mercy *endures* forever.

PSALM 137

1 By the rivers of Babylon,
   There we sat down, yea, we wept
   When we remembered Zion.
2 We hung our harps
   Upon the willows in the midst of
   it.
3 For there those who carried us
   away captive asked of us a
   song,
   And those who plundered us
   requested mirth,
   Saying, "Sing us *one* of the songs
   of Zion!"

4 How shall we sing the LORD's
   song
   In a foreign land?
5 If I forget you, O Jerusalem,
   Let my right hand forget *its skill!*
6 If I do not remember you,
   Let my tongue cling to the roof
   of my mouth—
   If I do not exalt Jerusalem
   Above my chief joy.

7 Remember, O LORD, against the
   sons of Edom
   The day of Jerusalem,
   Who said, "Raze *it,* raze *it,*
   To its very foundation!"

8 O daughter of Babylon, who are
   to be destroyed,
   Happy the one who repays you
   as you have served us!
9 Happy the one who takes and
   dashes
   Your little ones against the rock!

PSALM 138

A Psalm of David.

1 I will praise You with my whole
   heart;
   Before the gods I will sing praises
   to You.
2 I will worship toward Your holy
   temple,
   And praise Your name
   For Your lovingkindness and
   Your truth;
   For You have magnified Your
   word above all Your name.
3 In the day when I cried out, You
   answered me,
   And made me bold *with* strength
   in my soul.

4 All the kings of the earth shall
   praise You, O LORD,
   When they hear the words of
   Your mouth.
5 Yes, they shall sing of the ways
   of the LORD,
   For great *is* the glory of the LORD.
6 Though the LORD *is* on high,
   Yet He regards the lowly;
   But the proud He knows from
   afar.

7 Though I walk in the midst of
   trouble, You will revive me;
   You will stretch out Your hand
   Against the wrath of my enemies,
   And Your right hand will save
   me.
8 The LORD will perfect *that which*
   concerns me;
   Your mercy, O LORD, *endures*
   forever;
   Do not forsake the works of Your
   hands.

PSALM 139

For the Chief Musician. A Psalm of David.

1 O LORD, You have searched me
   and known *me.*
2 You know my sitting down and
   my rising up;
   You understand my thought afar
   off.
3 You comprehend my path and
   my lying down,
   And are acquainted with all my
   ways.
4 For *there is* not a word on my
   tongue,
   But behold, O LORD, You know
   it altogether.
5 You have hedged me behind and
   before,
   And laid Your hand upon me.
6 *Such* knowledge *is* too wonderful
   for me;
   It is high, I cannot *attain* it.

7 Where can I go from Your Spirit?
   Or where can I flee from Your
   presence?
8 If I ascend into heaven, You *are*
   there;
   If I make my bed in hell, behold,
   You *are there.*
9 *If* I take the wings of the morning,
   And dwell in the uttermost parts
   of the sea,
10 Even there Your hand shall lead
   me,
   And Your right hand shall hold
   me.

11 If I say, "Surely the darkness
   shall fall[a] on me,"
   Even the night shall be light
   about me;
12 Indeed, the darkness shall not
   hide from You,
   But the night shines as the day;
   The darkness and the light are
   both alike to You.

13 For You formed my inward parts;
   You covered me in my mother's
   womb.
14 I will praise You, for I am
   fearfully and wonderfully
   made;[a]
   Marvelous are Your works,
   And that my soul knows very
   well.
15 My frame was not hidden from
   You,
   When I was made in secret,
   And skillfully wrought in the
   lowest parts of the earth.
16 Your eyes saw my substance,
   being yet unformed.
   And in Your book they all were
   written,
   The days fashioned for me,
   When as yet there were none of
   them.

17 How precious also are Your
   thoughts to me, O God!
   How great is the sum of them!
18 If I should count them, they
   would be more in number than
   the sand;
   When I awake, I am still with
   You.

19 Oh, that You would slay the
   wicked, O God!
   Depart from me, therefore, you
   bloodthirsty men.
20 For they speak against You
   wickedly;
   Your enemies take Your name in
   vain.[a]
21 Do I not hate them, O LORD, who
   hate You?
   And do I not loathe those who
   rise up against You?
22 I hate them with perfect hatred;
   I count them my enemies.

23 Search me, O God, and know my
   heart;

24 Try me, and know my anxieties;
   And see if there is any wicked
   way in me,
   And lead me in the way
   everlasting.

PSALM 140

To the Chief Musician. A Psalm of David.

1 Deliver me, O LORD, from evil
  men;
  Preserve me from violent men,
2 Who plan evil things in their
  hearts;
  They continually gather together
  for war.
3 They sharpen their tongues like
  a serpent;
  The poison of asps is under their
  lips.   Selah

4 Keep me, O LORD, from the hands
  of the wicked;
  Preserve me from violent men,
  Who have purposed to make my
  steps stumble.
5 The proud have hidden a snare
  for me, and cords;
  They have spread a net by the
  wayside;
  They have set traps for me.
                           Selah

6 I said to the LORD: "You are my
  God;
  Hear the voice of my
  supplications, O LORD.
7 O GOD the Lord, the strength of
  my salvation,
  You have covered my head in the
  day of battle.
8 Do not grant, O LORD, the desires
  of the wicked;
  Do not further his wicked
  scheme,
  Lest they be exalted.   Selah

9 "As for the head of those who
  surround me,
  Let the evil of their lips cover
  them;
10 Let burning coals fall upon them;
   Let them be cast into the fire,
   Into deep pits, that they rise not
   up again.
11 Let not a slanderer be established
   in the earth;

139:11 [a]Vulgate and Symmachus read cover. 139:14 [a]Following Masoretic Text and Targum; Septuagint,
Syriac, and Vulgate read You are fearfully wonderful. 139:20 [a]Septuagint and Vulgate read They take
your cities in vain.

Let evil hunt the violent man to
overthrow *him*."

12 I know that the LORD will
maintain
The cause of the afflicted,
And justice for the poor.
13 Surely the righteous shall give
thanks to Your name;
The upright shall dwell in Your
presence.

PSALM 141

A Psalm of David.

1 LORD, I cry out to You;
Make haste to me!
Give ear to my voice when I cry
out to You.
2 Let my prayer be set before You
as incense,
The lifting up of my hands *as* the
evening sacrifice.

3 Set a guard, O LORD, over my
mouth;
Keep watch over the door of my
lips.
4 Do not incline my heart to any
evil thing,
To practice wicked works
With men who work iniquity;
And do not let me eat of their
delicacies.

5 Let the righteous strike me;
It shall be a kindness.
And let him rebuke me;
It shall be as excellent oil;
Let my head not refuse it.

For still my prayer *is* against the
deeds of the wicked.
6 Their judges are overthrown by
the sides of the cliff,
And they hear my words, for they
are sweet.
7 Our bones are scattered at the
mouth of the grave,
As when one plows and breaks
up the earth.

8 But my eyes *are* upon You, O GOD
the Lord;
In You I take refuge;
Do not leave my soul destitute.
9 Keep me from the snares they
have laid for me,
And from the traps of the
workers of iniquity.

10 Let the wicked fall into their own
nets,
While I escape safely.

PSALM 142

A Contemplation[a] of David. A Prayer when he
was in the cave.

1 I cry out to the LORD with my
voice;
With my voice to the LORD I make
my supplication.
2 I pour out my complaint before
Him;
I declare before Him my trouble.

3 When my spirit was
overwhelmed within me,
Then You knew my path.
In the way in which I walk
They have secretly set a snare for
me.
4 Look on *my* right hand and see,
For *there is* no one who
acknowledges me;
Refuge has failed me;
No one cares for my soul.

5 I cried out to You, O LORD:
I said, "You *are* my refuge,
My portion in the land of the
living.
6 Attend to my cry,
For I am brought very low;
Deliver me from my persecutors,
For they are stronger than I.
7 Bring my soul out of prison,
That I may praise Your name;
The righteous shall surround me,
For You shall deal bountifully
with me."

PSALM 143

A Psalm of David.

1 Hear my prayer, O LORD,
Give ear to my supplications!
In Your faithfulness answer me,
And in Your righteousness.
2 Do not enter into judgment with
Your servant,
For in Your sight no one living
is righteous.

3 For the enemy has persecuted my
soul;
He has crushed my life to the
ground;
He has made me dwell in
darkness,

142:title [a]Hebrew *Maschil*

Like those who have long been
dead.
4 Therefore my spirit is
overwhelmed within me;
My heart within me is distressed.

5 I remember the days of old;
I meditate on all Your works;
I muse on the work of Your
hands.
6 I spread out my hands to You;
My soul *longs* for You like a
thirsty land.   Selah

7 Answer me speedily, O LORD;
My spirit fails!
Do not hide Your face from me,
Lest I be like those who go down
into the pit.
8 Cause me to hear Your
lovingkindness in the morning,
For in You do I trust;
Cause me to know the way in
which I should walk,
For I lift up my soul to You.

9 Deliver me, O LORD, from my
enemies;
In You I take shelter.*a*
10 Teach me to do Your will,
For You *are* my God;
Your Spirit *is* good.
Lead me in the land of
uprightness.

11 Revive me, O LORD, for Your
name's sake!
For Your righteousness' sake
bring my soul out of trouble.
12 In Your mercy cut off my
enemies,
And destroy all those who afflict
my soul;
For I *am* Your servant.

PSALM 144

A Psalm of David.
1 Blessed *be* the LORD my Rock,
Who trains my hands for war,
And my fingers for battle—
2 My lovingkindness and my
fortress,
My high tower and my deliverer,
My shield and *the One* in whom
I take refuge,
Who subdues my people*a* under
me.

3 LORD, what *is* man, that You take
knowledge of him?
Or the son of man, that You are
mindful of him?
4 Man is like a breath;
His days *are* like a passing
shadow.

5 Bow down Your heavens, O
LORD, and come down;
Touch the mountains, and they
shall smoke.
6 Flash forth lightning and scatter
them;
Shoot out Your arrows and
destroy them.
7 Stretch out Your hand from
above;
Rescue me and deliver me out of
great waters,
From the hand of foreigners,
8 Whose mouth speaks lying
words,
And whose right hand *is* a right
hand of falsehood.

9 I will sing a new song to You, O
God;
On a harp of ten strings I will sing
praises to You,
10 *The One* who gives salvation to
kings,
Who delivers David His servant
From the deadly sword.

11 Rescue me and deliver me from
the hand of foreigners,
Whose mouth speaks lying
words,
And whose right hand *is* a right
hand of falsehood—
12 That our sons *may be* as plants
grown up in their youth;
That our daughters *may be* as
pillars,
Sculptured in palace style;
13 *That* our barns *may be* full,
Supplying all kinds of produce;
That our sheep may bring forth
thousands
And ten thousands in our fields;
14 *That* our oxen *may be* well-laden;
That there be no breaking in or
going out;
That there be no outcry in our
streets.
15 Happy *are* the people who are in
such a state;

143:9 *a*Septuagint and Vulgate read *To You I flee.*   144:2 *a*Following Masoretic Text, Septuagint, and
Vulgate; Syriac and Targum read *the peoples* (compare 18:47).

Happy *are* the people whose God *is* the LORD!

PSALM 145

A Praise of David.

1 I will extol You, my God, O King;
And I will bless Your name
forever and ever.
2 Every day I will bless You,
And I will praise Your name
forever and ever.
3 Great *is* the LORD, and greatly to
be praised;
And His greatness *is*
unsearchable.

4 One generation shall praise Your
works to another,
And shall declare Your mighty
acts.
5 I*a* will meditate on the glorious
splendor of Your majesty,
And on Your wondrous works.*b*
6 *Men* shall speak of the might of
Your awesome acts,
And I will declare Your
greatness.
7 They shall utter the memory of
Your great goodness,
And shall sing of Your
righteousness.

8 The LORD *is* gracious and full of
compassion,
Slow to anger and great in mercy.
9 The LORD *is* good to all,
And His tender mercies *are* over
all His works.

10 All Your works shall praise You,
O LORD,
And Your saints shall bless You.
11 They shall speak of the glory of
Your kingdom,
And talk of Your power,
12 To make known to the sons of
men His mighty acts,
And the glorious majesty of His
kingdom.
13 Your kingdom *is* an everlasting
kingdom,
And Your dominion *endures*
throughout all generations.*a*

14 The LORD upholds all who fall,
And raises up all *who are* bowed
down.

15 The eyes of all look expectantly
to You,
And You give them their food in
due season.
16 You open Your hand
And satisfy the desire of every
living thing.

17 The LORD *is* righteous in all His
ways,
Gracious in all His works.
18 The LORD *is* near to all who call
upon Him,
To all who call upon Him in truth.
19 He will fulfill the desire of those
who fear Him;
He also will hear their cry and
save them.
20 The LORD preserves all who love
Him,
But all the wicked He will
destroy.
21 My mouth shall speak the praise
of the LORD,
And all flesh shall bless His holy
name
Forever and ever.

PSALM 146

1 Praise the LORD!

Praise the LORD, O my soul!
2 While I live I will praise the LORD;
I will sing praises to my God
while I have my being.

3 Do not put your trust in princes,
Nor in a son of man, in whom
there is no help.
4 His spirit departs, he returns to
his earth;
In that very day his plans perish.

5 Happy *is he* who *has* the God of
Jacob for his help,
Whose hope *is* in the LORD his
God,
6 Who made heaven and earth,
The sea, and all that *is* in them;
Who keeps truth forever,
7 Who executes justice for the
oppressed,
Who gives food to the hungry.
The LORD gives freedom to the
prisoners.

145:5 *a*Following Masoretic Text and Targum; Dead Sea Scrolls, Septuagint, Syriac, and Vulgate read
They. *b*Literally *on the words of Your wondrous works* 145:13 *a*Following Masoretic Text and Targum;
Dead Sea Scrolls, Septuagint, Syriac, and Vulgate add *The LORD is faithful in all His words, and holy in all
His works.*

8 The LORD opens *the eyes of* the
   blind;
   The LORD raises those who are
   bowed down;
   The LORD loves the righteous.
9 The LORD watches over the
   strangers;
   He relieves the fatherless and
   widow;
   But the way of the wicked He
   turns upside down.

10 The LORD shall reign forever—
   Your God, O Zion, to all
   generations.

   Praise the LORD!

PSALM 147

1 Praise the LORD!
   For *it is* good to sing praises to
   our God;
   For *it is* pleasant, *and* praise is
   beautiful.

2 The LORD builds up Jerusalem;
   He gathers together the outcasts
   of Israel.
3 He heals the brokenhearted
   And binds up their wounds.
4 He counts the number of the
   stars;
   He calls them all by name.
5 Great *is* our Lord, and mighty in
   power;
   His understanding *is* infinite.
6 The LORD lifts up the humble;
   He casts the wicked down to the
   ground.

7 Sing to the LORD with
   thanksgiving;
   Sing praises on the harp to our
   God,
8 Who covers the heavens with
   clouds,
   Who prepares rain for the earth,
   Who makes grass to grow on the
   mountains.
9 He gives to the beast its food,
   And to the young ravens that cry.

10 He does not delight in the
   strength of the horse;
   He takes no pleasure in the legs
   of a man.
11 The LORD takes pleasure in those
   who fear Him,
   In those who hope in His mercy.

12 Praise the LORD, O Jerusalem!
   Praise your God, O Zion!
13 For He has strengthened the bars
   of your gates;
   He has blessed your children
   within you.
14 He makes peace *in* your borders,
   And fills you with the finest
   wheat.

15 He sends out His command *to the*
   earth;
   His word runs very swiftly.
16 He gives snow like wool;
   He scatters the frost like ashes;
17 He casts out His hail like morsels;
   Who can stand before His cold?
18 He sends out His word and melts
   them;
   He causes His wind to blow, *and*
   the waters flow.

19 He declares His word to Jacob,
   His statutes and His judgments to
   Israel.
20 He has not dealt thus with any
   nation;
   And *as for His* judgments, they
   have not known them.

   Praise the LORD!

PSALM 148

1 Praise the LORD!

   Praise the LORD from the
   heavens;
   Praise Him in the heights!
2 Praise Him, all His angels;
   Praise Him, all His hosts!
3 Praise Him, sun and moon;
   Praise Him, all you stars of light!
4 Praise Him, you heavens of
   heavens,
   And you waters above the
   heavens!

5 Let them praise the name of the
   LORD,
   For He commanded and they
   were created.
6 He also established them forever
   and ever;
   He made a decree which shall not
   pass away.

7 Praise the LORD from the earth,
   You great sea creatures and all
   the depths;
8 Fire and hail, snow and clouds;
   Stormy wind, fulfilling His word;

9 Mountains and all hills;
  Fruitful trees and all cedars;
10 Beasts and all cattle;
  Creeping things and flying fowl;
11 Kings of the earth and all
    peoples;
  Princes and all judges of the
    earth;
12 Both young men and maidens;
  Old men and children.

13 Let them praise the name of the
    LORD,
  For His name alone is exalted;
  His glory *is* above the earth and
    heaven.
14 And He has exalted the horn of
    His people,
  The praise of all His saints—
  Of the children of Israel,
  A people near to Him.

      Praise the LORD!

PSALM 149

1 Praise the LORD!

  Sing to the LORD a new song,
  And His praise in the assembly
    of saints.

2 Let Israel rejoice in their Maker;
  Let the children of Zion be joyful
    in their King.
3 Let them praise His name with
    the dance;
  Let them sing praises to Him with
    the timbrel and harp.
4 For the LORD takes pleasure in
    His people;
  He will beautify the humble with
    salvation.

5 Let the saints be joyful in glory;

  Let them sing aloud on their
    beds.
6 *Let* the high praises of God *be*
    in their mouth,
  And a two-edged sword in their
    hand,
7 To execute vengeance on the
    nations,
  And punishments on the peoples;
8 To bind their kings with chains,
  And their nobles with fetters of
    iron;
9 To execute on them the written
    judgment—
  This honor have all His saints.

      Praise the LORD!

PSALM 150

1 Praise the LORD!

  Praise God in His sanctuary;
  Praise Him in His mighty
    firmament!

2 Praise Him for His mighty acts;
  Praise Him according to His
    excellent greatness!

3 Praise Him with the sound of the
    trumpet;
  Praise Him with the lute and
    harp!
4 Praise Him with the timbrel and
    dance;
  Praise Him with stringed
    instruments and flutes!
5 Praise Him with loud cymbals;
  Praise Him with clashing
    cymbals!

6 Let everything that has breath
    praise the LORD.

      Praise the LORD!

Proverbs

Overview of Proverbs

*T*he Book of Proverbs is one of the most practical, positive, life-guiding sources ever written. Written largely by King Solomon about 1000 B.C., these proverbs are treasures of wisdom commenting on life.

Solomon was one of the wisest men of all time. This book records that he was renowned for over three thousand proverbs. Five hundred and sixty of those wise sayings are recorded here. While Solomon is known to have written the first twenty-nine chapters, chapters 30 and 31 are attributed to Agur, the son of Jakeh (Prov. 30:1), and King Lemuel (Prov. 31:1); neither are mentioned elsewhere in Scripture.

Each proverb is like a beautiful diamond, shining gloriously on its own. But put together with the other verses, the effect is dazzling, like a glorious shimmering necklace.

Trust in the LORD with all your heart,
And lean not on your own understanding;
In all your ways acknowledge Him,
And He shall direct your paths . . .
Do not withhold good from those to whom it is due,
When it is in the power of your hand to do so *. . . .*
Wisdom is *the principal thing;*
Therefore get wisdom.
And in all your getting, get understanding . . .
Commit your works to the LORD,
And your thoughts will be established . . .
Train up a child in the way he should go,
And when he is old he will not depart from it.
(Prov. 3:5, 6, 27; 4:7; 16:3; 22:6)

The proverbs are sensitively presented as if from a grandfather giving advice to his grandchildren. Rich in God's wisdom, they act as signs on a road, giving us a glimpse of what is around the next bend. They aim to keep us from detouring from our faith in God.

If you live by these words of faith, you will come to the end of your life with love around you, peace within you, and hope before you!

Jesus in Proverbs

In Proverbs 8, wisdom is personified and seen in its perfection. It is divine. It is the source of biological and spiritual life. It is righteous and moral; and it is available to all who will receive it. This wisdom became incarnate in Jesus, "in whom are hidden all the treasures of wisdom and knowledge" (Col. 2:3).

Keys to Proverbs

Key Word: Wisdom. Proverbs deals with the most fundamental element of wisdom there is: practical righteousness before God in every area of life. This requires knowledge, experience, and a willingness to put God first. Proverbs as a whole is designed both to prevent and to remedy ungodly lifestyles. The book served as a manual to impart the legacy of wisdom, prudence, understanding, discretion, knowledge, guidance, competence, correction, counsel, and truth—from generation to generation.

Key Verses: "A wise *man* will hear and increase learning, and a man of understanding will attain wise counsel, to understand a proverb and an enigma, the words of the wise and their riddles. The fear of the LORD *is* the beginning of knowledge, *but* fools despise wisdom and instruction" (1:5–7).

"Trust in the LORD with all your heart, and lean not on your own understanding; in all your ways acknowledge Him, and He shall direct your paths" (3:5, 6).

Key Chapter: Proverbs 31. The last chapter of Proverbs is unique in ancient literature, as it reveals a very high and noble view of women. The woman in these verses is a good woman, a good mother, a good wife, and a good neighbor. Her conduct, concern, speech, and life stand in sharp contrast to the woman pictured in Proverbs 7.

1 The proverbs of Solomon the son of David, king of Israel:

2 To know wisdom and instruction,
To perceive the words of understanding,

3 To receive the instruction of wisdom,
Justice, judgment, and equity;

4 To give prudence to the
   simple,
   To the young man knowledge
   and discretion—
5 A wise *man* will hear and
   increase learning,
   And a man of understanding
   will attain wise counsel,
6 To understand a proverb and
   an enigma,
   The words of the wise and their
   riddles.

7 The fear of the LORD *is* the
   beginning of knowledge,
   But fools despise wisdom and
   instruction.

8 My son, hear the instruction of
   your father,
   And do not forsake the law of
   your mother;
9 For they *will be* a graceful
   ornament on your head,
   And chains about your neck.

10 My son, if sinners entice you,
   Do not consent.
11 If they say, "Come with us,
   Let us lie in wait to *shed* blood;
   Let us lurk secretly for the
   innocent without cause;
12 Let us swallow them alive like
   Sheol,ª
   And whole, like those who go
   down to the Pit;
13 We shall find all *kinds* of
   precious possessions,
   We shall fill our houses with
   spoil;
14 Cast in your lot among us,
   Let us all have one purse"—
15 My son, do not walk in the way
   with them,
   Keep your foot from their
   path;
16 For their feet run to evil,
   And they make haste to shed
   blood.
17 Surely, in vain the net is spread
   In the sight of any bird;
18 But they lie in wait for their
   own blood,
   They lurk secretly for their *own*
   lives.
19 So *are* the ways of everyone
   who is greedy for gain;
   It takes away the life of its
   owners.

20 Wisdom calls aloud outside;
   She raises her voice in the open
   squares.
21 She cries out in the chief
   concourses,ª
   At the openings of the gates in
   the city
   She speaks her words:
22 "How long, you simple ones, will
   you love simplicity?
   For scorners delight in their
   scorning,
   And fools hate knowledge.
23 Turn at my rebuke;
   Surely I will pour out my spirit
   on you;
   I will make my words known
   to you.
24 Because I have called and you
   refused,
   I have stretched out my hand
   and no one regarded,
25 Because you disdained all my
   counsel,
   And would have none of my
   rebuke,
26 I also will laugh at your
   calamity;
   I will mock when your terror
   comes,
27 When your terror comes like a
   storm,
   And your destruction comes
   like a whirlwind,
   When distress and anguish
   come upon you.

28 "Then they will call on me, but
   I will not answer;
   They will seek me diligently,
   but they will not find me.
29 Because they hated knowledge
   And did not choose the fear of
   the LORD,
30 They would have none of my
   counsel
   And despised my every rebuke.
31 Therefore they shall eat the
   fruit of their own way,
   And be filled to the full with
   their own fancies.
32 For the turning away of the
   simple will slay them,
   And the complacency of fools
   will destroy them;
33 But whoever listens to me will
   dwell safely,
   And will be secure, without
   fear of evil."

1:12 ªOr *the grave*   1:21 ªSeptuagint, Syriac, and Targum read *top of the walls;* Vulgate reads *the head of multitudes*.

2 My son, if you receive my words,
And treasure my commands within you,

2 So that you incline your ear to wisdom,
And apply your heart to understanding;

3 Yes, if you cry out for discernment,
And lift up your voice for understanding,

4 If you seek her as silver,
And search for her as *for* hidden treasures;

5 Then you will understand the fear of the LORD,
And find the knowledge of God.

6 For the LORD gives wisdom;
From His mouth *come* knowledge and understanding;

7 He stores up sound wisdom for the upright;
He is a shield to those who walk uprightly;

8 He guards the paths of justice,
And preserves the way of His saints.

9 Then you will understand righteousness and justice,
Equity *and* every good path.

10 When wisdom enters your heart,
And knowledge is pleasant to your soul,

11 Discretion will preserve you;
Understanding will keep you,

12 To deliver you from the way of evil,
From the man who speaks perverse things,

13 From those who leave the paths of uprightness
To walk in the ways of darkness;

14 Who rejoice in doing evil,
And delight in the perversity of the wicked;

15 Whose ways *are* crooked,
And *who are* devious in their paths;

16 To deliver you from the immoral woman,
From the seductress *who* flatters with her words,

17 Who forsakes the companion of her youth,
And forgets the covenant of her God.

18 For her house leads down to death,
And her paths to the dead;

19 None who go to her return,
Nor do they regain the paths of life—

20 So you may walk in the way of goodness,
And keep *to* the paths of righteousness.

21 For the upright will dwell in the land,
And the blameless will remain in it;

22 But the wicked will be cut off from the earth,
And the unfaithful will be uprooted from it.

3 My son, do not forget my law,
But let your heart keep my commands;

2 For length of days and long life
And peace they will add to you.

3 Let not mercy and truth forsake you;
Bind them around your neck,
Write them on the tablet of your heart,

4 *And* so find favor and high esteem
In the sight of God and man.

5 Trust in the LORD with all your heart,
And lean not on your own understanding;

6 In all your ways acknowledge Him,
And He shall direct[a] your paths.

7 Do not be wise in your own eyes;
Fear the LORD and depart from evil.

8 It will be health to your flesh,[a]
And strength[b] to your bones.

9 Honor the LORD with your possessions,
And with the firstfruits of all your increase;

3:6 [a]Or *make smooth* or *straight*   3:8 [a]Literally *navel*, figurative of the body   [b]Literally *drink* or *refreshment*

10 So your barns will be filled with
plenty,
And your vats will overflow
with new wine.

11 My son, do not despise the
chastening of the LORD,
Nor detest His correction;
12 For whom the LORD loves He
corrects,
Just as a father the son *in
whom* he delights.

13 Happy *is* the man *who* finds
wisdom,
And the man *who* gains
understanding;
14 For her proceeds *are* better
than the profits of silver,
And her gain than fine gold.
15 She *is* more precious than
rubies,
And all the things you may
desire cannot compare with
her.
16 Length of days *is* in her right
hand,
In her left hand riches and
honor.
17 Her ways *are* ways of
pleasantness,
And all her paths *are* peace.
18 She *is* a tree of life to those who
take hold of her,
And happy *are* all who retain
her.

19 The LORD by wisdom founded
the earth;
By understanding He
established the heavens;
20 By His knowledge the depths
were broken up,
And clouds drop down the dew.

21 My son, let them not depart
from your eyes—
Keep sound wisdom and
discretion;
22 So they will be life to your soul
And grace to your neck.
23 Then you will walk safely in
your way,
And your foot will not stumble.
24 When you lie down, you will
not be afraid;
Yes, you will lie down and your
sleep will be sweet.
25 Do not be afraid of sudden
terror,
Nor of trouble from the wicked
when it comes;

26 For the LORD will be your
confidence,
And will keep your foot from
being caught.

27 Do not withhold good from
those to whom it is due,
When it is in the power of your
hand to do *so.*
28 Do not say to your neighbor,
"Go, and come back,
And tomorrow I will give *it,*"
When *you have* it with you.
29 Do not devise evil against your
neighbor,
For he dwells by you for
safety's sake.
30 Do not strive with a man
without cause,
If he has done you no harm.

31 Do not envy the oppressor,
And choose none of his ways;
32 For the perverse *person is* an
abomination to the LORD,
But His secret counsel *is* with
the upright.
33 The curse of the LORD *is* on the
house of the wicked,
But He blesses the home of the
just.
34 Surely He scorns the scornful,
But gives grace to the
humble.
35 The wise shall inherit glory,
But shame shall be the legacy
of fools.

4 Hear, *my* children, the
instruction of a father,
And give attention to know
understanding;
2 For I give you good doctrine:
Do not forsake my law.
3 When I was my father's son,
Tender and the only one in the
sight of my mother,
4 He also taught me, and said to
me:
"Let your heart retain my
words;
Keep my commands, and live.
5 Get wisdom! Get
understanding!
Do not forget, nor turn away
from the words of my mouth.
6 Do not forsake her, and she will
preserve you;
Love her, and she will keep
you.
7 Wisdom *is* the principal thing;
Therefore get wisdom.

And in all your getting, get
understanding.
8 Exalt her, and she will promote
you;
She will bring you honor, when
you embrace her.
9 She will place on your head an
ornament of grace;
A crown of glory she will
deliver to you."

10 Hear, my son, and receive my
sayings,
And the years of your life will
be many.
11 I have taught you in the way
of wisdom;
I have led you in right paths.
12 When you walk, your steps will
not be hindered,
And when you run, you will not
stumble.
13 Take firm hold of instruction,
do not let go;
Keep her, for she is your life.

14 Do not enter the path of the
wicked,
And do not walk in the way of
evil.
15 Avoid it, do not travel on it;
Turn away from it and pass on.
16 For they do not sleep unless
they have done evil;
And their sleep is taken away
unless they make someone
fall.
17 For they eat the bread of
wickedness,
And drink the wine of violence.

18 But the path of the just is like
the shining sun,[a]
That shines ever brighter unto
the perfect day.
19 The way of the wicked is like
darkness;
They do not know what makes
them stumble.

20 My son, give attention to my
words;
Incline your ear to my sayings.
21 Do not let them depart from
your eyes;
Keep them in the midst of your
heart;
22 For they are life to those who
find them,
And health to all their flesh.

23 Keep your heart with all
diligence,
For out of it spring the issues
of life.
24 Put away from you a deceitful
mouth,
And put perverse lips far from
you.
25 Let your eyes look straight
ahead,
And your eyelids look right
before you.
26 Ponder the path of your feet,
And let all your ways be
established.
27 Do not turn to the right or the
left;
Remove your foot from evil.

5 My son, pay attention to my
wisdom;
Lend your ear to my
understanding,
2 That you may preserve
discretion,
And your lips may keep
knowledge.
3 For the lips of an immoral
woman drip honey,
And her mouth is smoother
than oil;
4 But in the end she is bitter as
wormwood,
Sharp as a two-edged sword.
5 Her feet go down to death,
Her steps lay hold of hell.[a]
6 Lest you ponder her path of
life—
Her ways are unstable;
You do not know them.

7 Therefore hear me now, my
children,
And do not depart from the
words of my mouth.
8 Remove your way far from
her,
And do not go near the door
of her house,
9 Lest you give your honor to
others,
And your years to the cruel
one;
10 Lest aliens be filled with your
wealth,
And your labors go to the
house of a foreigner;
11 And you mourn at last,
When your flesh and your body
are consumed,

4:18 aLiterally light   5:5 aOr Sheol

12 And say:
"How I have hated instruction,
And my heart despised
correction!
13 I have not obeyed the voice of
my teachers,
Nor inclined my ear to those
who instructed me!
14 I was on the verge of total ruin,
In the midst of the assembly
and congregation."

15 Drink water from your own
cistern,
And running water from your
own well.
16 Should your fountains be
dispersed abroad,
Streams of water in the streets?
17 Let them be only your own,
And not for strangers with you.
18 Let your fountain be blessed,
And rejoice with the wife of
your youth.
19 As a loving deer and a graceful
doe,
Let her breasts satisfy you at
all times;
And always be enraptured with
her love.
20 For why should you, my son,
be enraptured by an immoral
woman,
And be embraced in the arms
of a seductress?

21 For the ways of man are before
the eyes of the LORD,
And He ponders all his paths.
22 His own iniquities entrap the
wicked man,
And he is caught in the cords
of his sin.
23 He shall die for lack of
instruction,
And in the greatness of his folly
he shall go astray.

6 My son, if you become surety
for your friend,
If you have shaken hands in
pledge for a stranger,
2 You are snared by the words
of your mouth;
You are taken by the words of
your mouth.
3 So do this, my son, and deliver
yourself;
For you have come into the
hand of your friend:

Go and humble yourself;
Plead with your friend.
4 Give no sleep to your eyes,
Nor slumber to your eyelids.
5 Deliver yourself like a gazelle
from the hand of the hunter,
And like a bird from the hand
of the fowler.[a]

6 Go to the ant, you sluggard!
Consider her ways and be wise,
7 Which, having no captain,
Overseer or ruler,
8 Provides her supplies in the
summer,
And gathers her food in the
harvest.
9 How long will you slumber, O
sluggard?
When will you rise from your
sleep?
10 A little sleep, a little slumber,
A little folding of the hands to
sleep—
11 So shall your poverty come on
you like a prowler,
And your need like an armed
man.

12 A worthless person, a wicked
man,
Walks with a perverse mouth;
13 He winks with his eyes,
He shuffles his feet,
He points with his fingers;
14 Perversity is in his heart,
He devises evil continually,
He sows discord.
15 Therefore his calamity shall
come suddenly;
Suddenly he shall be broken
without remedy.

16 These six things the LORD
hates,
Yes, seven are an abomination
to Him:
17 A proud look,
A lying tongue,
Hands that shed innocent
blood,
18 A heart that devises wicked
plans,
Feet that are swift in running
to evil,
19 A false witness who speaks
lies,
And one who sows discord
among brethren.

6:5 [a]That is, one who catches birds in a trap or snare

20 My son, keep your father's command,
And do not forsake the law of your mother.
21 Bind them continually upon your heart;
Tie them around your neck.
22 When you roam, they[a] will lead you;
When you sleep, they will keep you;
And *when* you awake, they will speak with you.
23 For the commandment *is* a lamp,
And the law a light;
Reproofs of instruction *are* the way of life,
24 To keep you from the evil woman,
From the flattering tongue of a seductress.
25 Do not lust after her beauty in your heart,
Nor let her allure you with her eyelids.
26 For by means of a harlot
A man is reduced to a crust of bread;
And an adulteress[a] will prey upon his precious life.
27 Can a man take fire to his bosom,
And his clothes not be burned?
28 Can one walk on hot coals,
And his feet not be seared?
29 So *is* he who goes in to his neighbor's wife;
Whoever touches her shall not be innocent.

30 *People* do not despise a thief
If he steals to satisfy himself when he is starving.
31 Yet *when* he is found, he must restore sevenfold;
He may have to give up all the substance of his house.
32 Whoever commits adultery with a woman lacks understanding;
He *who* does so destroys his own soul.
33 Wounds and dishonor he will get,
And his reproach will not be wiped away.
34 For jealousy *is* a husband's fury;

Therefore he will not spare in the day of vengeance.
35 He will accept no recompense,
Nor will he be appeased though you give many gifts.

7 My son, keep my words,
And treasure my commands within you.
2 Keep my commands and live,
And my law as the apple of your eye.
3 Bind them on your fingers;
Write them on the tablet of your heart.
4 Say to wisdom, "You *are* my sister,"
And call understanding *your* nearest kin,
5 That they may keep you from the immoral woman,
From the seductress *who* flatters with her words.

6 For at the window of my house
I looked through my lattice,
7 And saw among the simple,
I perceived among the youths,
A young man devoid of understanding,
8 Passing along the street near her corner;
And he took the path to her house
9 In the twilight, in the evening,
In the black and dark night.
10 And there a woman met him,
With the attire of a harlot, and a crafty heart.
11 She *was* loud and rebellious,
Her feet would not stay at home.
12 At times *she was* outside, at times in the open square,
Lurking at every corner.
13 So she caught him and kissed him;
With an impudent face she said to him:
14 "*I have* peace offerings with me;
Today I have paid my vows.
15 So I came out to meet you,
Diligently to seek your face,
And I have found you.
16 I have spread my bed with tapestry,
Colored coverings of Egyptian linen.
17 I have perfumed my bed

With myrrh, aloes, and
cinnamon.
18 Come, let us take our fill of love
until morning;
Let us delight ourselves with
love.
19 For my husband *is* not at home;
He has gone on a long journey;
20 He has taken a bag of money
with him,
And will come home on the
appointed day."

21 With her enticing speech she
caused him to yield,
With her flattering lips she
seduced him.
22 Immediately he went after her,
as an ox goes to the
slaughter,
Or as a fool to the correction
of the stocks,*a*
23 Till an arrow struck his liver.
As a bird hastens to the snare,
He did not know it *would cost*
his life.

24 Now therefore, listen to me, *my*
children;
Pay attention to the words of
my mouth:
25 Do not let your heart turn aside
to her ways,
Do not stray into her paths;
26 For she has cast down many
wounded,
And all who were slain by her
were strong *men.*
27 Her house *is* the way to hell,*a*
Descending to the chambers of
death.

8 Does not wisdom cry out,
And understanding lift up her
voice?
2 She takes her stand on the top
of the high hill,
Beside the way, where the
paths meet.
3 She cries out by the gates, at
the entry of the city,
At the entrance of the doors:
4 "To you, O men, I call,
And my voice *is* to the sons of
men.
5 O you simple ones, understand
prudence,
And you fools, be of an
understanding heart.

6 Listen, for I will speak of
excellent things,
And from the opening of my
lips *will come* right things;
7 For my mouth will speak truth;
Wickedness *is* an abomination
to my lips.
8 All the words of my mouth *are*
with righteousness;
Nothing crooked or perverse *is*
in them.
9 They *are* all plain to him who
understands,
And right to those who find
knowledge.
10 Receive my instruction, and not
silver,
And knowledge rather than
choice gold;
11 For wisdom *is* better than
rubies,
And all the things one may
desire cannot be compared
with her.

12 "I, wisdom, dwell with
prudence,
And find out knowledge *and*
discretion.
13 The fear of the LORD *is* to hate
evil;
Pride and arrogance and the
evil way
And the perverse mouth I hate.
14 Counsel *is* mine, and sound
wisdom;
I *am* understanding, I have
strength.
15 By me kings reign,
And rulers decree justice.
16 By me princes rule, and nobles,
All the judges of the earth.*a*
17 I love those who love me,
And those who seek me
diligently will find me.
18 Riches and honor *are* with me,
Enduring riches and
righteousness.
19 My fruit *is* better than gold, yes,
than fine gold,
And my revenue than choice
silver.
20 I traverse the way of
righteousness,
In the midst of the paths of
justice,
21 That I may cause those who
love me to inherit wealth,
That I may fill their treasuries.

7:22 *a*Septuagint, Syriac, and Targum read *as a dog to bonds;* Vulgate reads *as a lamb . . . to bonds.*
7:27 *a*Or *Sheol* 8:16 *a*Masoretic Text, Syriac, Targum, and Vulgate read *righteousness;* Bomberg,
Septuagint, and some manuscripts and editions read *earth.*

22 "The LORD possessed me at the beginning of His way,
Before His works of old.
23 I have been established from everlasting,
From the beginning, before there was ever an earth.
24 When *there were* no depths I was brought forth,
When *there were* no fountains abounding with water.
25 Before the mountains were settled,
Before the hills, I was brought forth;
26 While as yet He had not made the earth or the fields,
Or the primal dust of the world.
27 When He prepared the heavens, I *was* there,
When He drew a circle on the face of the deep,
28 When He established the clouds above,
When He strengthened the fountains of the deep,
29 When He assigned to the sea its limit,
So that the waters would not transgress His command,
When He marked out the foundations of the earth,
30 Then I was beside Him *as* a master craftsman;[a]
And I was daily *His* delight,
Rejoicing always before Him,
31 Rejoicing in His inhabited world,
And my delight *was* with the sons of men.

32 "Now therefore, listen to me, *my* children,
For blessed *are those who* keep my ways.
33 Hear instruction and be wise, And do not disdain *it*.
34 Blessed is the man who listens to me,
Watching daily at my gates,
Waiting at the posts of my doors.
35 For whoever finds me finds life,
And obtains favor from the LORD;
36 But he who sins against me wrongs his own soul;
All those who hate me love death."

9 Wisdom has built her house,
She has hewn out her seven pillars;
2 She has slaughtered her meat,
She has mixed her wine,
She has also furnished her table.
3 She has sent out her maidens,
She cries out from the highest places of the city,
4 "Whoever *is* simple, let him turn in here!"
As for him who lacks understanding, she says to him,
5 "Come, eat of my bread And drink of the wine I have mixed.
6 Forsake foolishness and live,
And go in the way of understanding.

7 "He who corrects a scoffer gets shame for himself,
And he who rebukes a wicked *man only* harms himself.
8 Do not correct a scoffer, lest he hate you;
Rebuke a wise *man*, and he will love you.
9 Give *instruction* to a wise *man*, and he will be still wiser;
Teach a just *man*, and he will increase in learning.

10 "The fear of the LORD *is* the beginning of wisdom,
And the knowledge of the Holy One *is* understanding.
11 For by me your days will be multiplied,
And years of life will be added to you.
12 If you are wise, you are wise for yourself,
And *if* you scoff, you will bear *it* alone."

13 A foolish woman is clamorous;
She is simple, and knows nothing.
14 For she sits at the door of her house,
On a seat *by* the highest places of the city,
15 To call to those who pass by,
Who go straight on their way:
16 "Whoever *is* simple, let him turn in here";
And *as for* him who lacks

8:30 [a]A Jewish tradition reads *one brought up.*

understanding, she says to
him,
17 "Stolen water is sweet,
And bread *eaten* in secret is
pleasant."
18 But he does not know that the
dead *are* there,
That her guests *are* in the
depths of hell.*a*

10

The proverbs of Solomon:

A wise son makes a glad father,
But a foolish son *is* the grief of
his mother.
2 Treasures of wickedness profit
nothing,
But righteousness delivers
from death.
3 The LORD will not allow the
righteous soul to famish,
But He casts away the desire
of the wicked.
4 He who has a slack hand
becomes poor,
But the hand of the diligent
makes rich.
5 He who gathers in summer *is*
a wise son;
He who sleeps in harvest *is* a
son who causes shame.

6 Blessings *are* on the head of the
righteous,
But violence covers the mouth
of the wicked.
7 The memory of the righteous *is*
blessed,
But the name of the wicked will
rot.

8 The wise in heart will receive
commands,
But a prating fool will fall.

9 He who walks with integrity
walks securely,
But he who perverts his ways
will become known.

10 He who winks with the eye
causes trouble,
But a prating fool will fall.

11 The mouth of the righteous *is*
a well of life,
But violence covers the mouth
of the wicked.

12 Hatred stirs up strife,
But love covers all sins.

13 Wisdom is found on the lips of
him who has understanding,
But a rod *is* for the back of him
who is devoid of
understanding.

14 Wise *people* store up
knowledge,
But the mouth of the foolish *is*
near destruction.

15 The rich man's wealth *is* his
strong city;
The destruction of the poor *is*
their poverty.

16 The labor of the righteous *leads*
to life,
The wages of the wicked to sin.

17 He who keeps instruction *is in*
the way of life,
But he who refuses correction
goes astray.

18 Whoever hides hatred *has*
lying lips,
And whoever spreads slander
is a fool.

19 In the multitude of words sin
is not lacking,
But he who restrains his lips *is*
wise.
20 The tongue of the righteous *is*
choice silver;
The heart of the wicked *is*
worth little.
21 The lips of the righteous feed
many,
But fools die for lack of
wisdom.*a*

22 The blessing of the LORD makes
one rich,
And He adds no sorrow with
it.

23 To do evil *is* like sport to a fool,
But a man of understanding
has wisdom.
24 The fear of the wicked will
come upon him,
And the desire of the righteous
will be granted.
25 When the whirlwind passes by,
the wicked *is* no *more,*

9:18 *a*Or *Sheol*   10:21 *a*Literally *heart*

But the righteous *has an* everlasting foundation.

26 As vinegar to the teeth and smoke to the eyes,
So *is* the lazy *man* to those who send him.

27 The fear of the LORD prolongs days,
But the years of the wicked will be shortened.

28 The hope of the righteous *will be* gladness,
But the expectation of the wicked will perish.

29 The way of the LORD *is* strength for the upright,
But destruction *will come* to the workers of iniquity.

30 The righteous will never be removed,
But the wicked will not inhabit the earth.

31 The mouth of the righteous brings forth wisdom,
But the perverse tongue will be cut out.

32 The lips of the righteous know what is acceptable,
But the mouth of the wicked *what is* perverse.

11 Dishonest scales *are* an abomination to the LORD,
But a just weight *is* His delight.

2 When pride comes, then comes shame;
But with the humble *is* wisdom.

3 The integrity of the upright will guide them,
But the perversity of the unfaithful will destroy them.

4 Riches do not profit in the day of wrath,
But righteousness delivers from death.

5 The righteousness of the blameless will direct[a] his way aright,
But the wicked will fall by his own wickedness.

6 The righteousness of the upright will deliver them,
But the unfaithful will be caught by *their* lust.

7 When a wicked man dies, *his* expectation will perish,
And the hope of the unjust perishes.

8 The righteous is delivered from trouble,
And it comes to the wicked instead.

9 The hypocrite with *his* mouth destroys his neighbor,
But through knowledge the righteous will be delivered.

10 When it goes well with the righteous, the city rejoices;
And when the wicked perish, *there is* jubilation.

11 By the blessing of the upright the city is exalted,
But it is overthrown by the mouth of the wicked.

12 He who is devoid of wisdom despises his neighbor,
But a man of understanding holds his peace.

13 A talebearer reveals secrets,
But he who is of a faithful spirit conceals a matter.

14 Where *there is* no counsel, the people fall;
But in the multitude of counselors *there is* safety.

15 He who is surety for a stranger will suffer,
But one who hates being surety is secure.

16 A gracious woman retains honor,
But ruthless *men* retain riches.

17 The merciful man does good for his own soul,
But *he who is* cruel troubles his own flesh.

18 The wicked *man* does deceptive work,
But he who sows righteousness *will have* a sure reward.

19 As righteousness *leads* to life,
So he who pursues evil *pursues it* to his own death.

20 Those who are of a perverse heart *are* an abomination to the LORD,
But *the* blameless in their ways *are* His delight.

11:5 *a*Or *make smooth* or *straight*

21 *Though they join* forces,[a] the
 wicked will not go
 unpunished;
 But the posterity of the
 righteous will be delivered.

22 *As* a ring of gold in a swine's
 snout,
 So is a lovely woman who lacks
 discretion.

23 The desire of the righteous *is*
 only good,
 But the expectation of the
 wicked *is* wrath.

24 There is *one* who scatters, yet
 increases more;
 And there is *one* who withholds
 more than is right,
 But it *leads* to poverty.

25 The generous soul will be made
 rich,
 And he who waters will also be
 watered himself.

26 The people will curse him who
 withholds grain,
 But blessing *will be* on the head
 of him who sells *it.*

27 He who earnestly seeks good
 finds favor,
 But trouble will come to him
 who seeks *evil.*

28 He who trusts in his riches will
 fall,
 But the righteous will flourish
 like foliage.

29 He who troubles his own house
 will inherit the wind,
 And the fool *will be* servant to
 the wise of heart.

30 The fruit of the righteous *is a*
 tree of life,
 And he who wins souls *is* wise.

31 If the righteous will be
 recompensed on the earth,
 How much more the ungodly
 and the sinner.

12 Whoever loves instruction
 loves knowledge,
 But he who hates correction *is*
 stupid.

2 A good *man* obtains favor from
 the LORD,

But a man of wicked intentions
 He will condemn.

3 A man is not established by
 wickedness,
 But the root of the righteous
 cannot be moved.

4 An excellent[a] wife *is* the crown
 of her husband,
 But she who causes shame *is*
 like rottenness in his bones.

5 The thoughts of the righteous
 are right,
 But the counsels of the wicked
 are deceitful.

6 The words of the wicked *are,*
 "Lie in wait for blood,"
 But the mouth of the upright
 will deliver them.

7 The wicked are overthrown
 and *are* no more,
 But the house of the righteous
 will stand.

8 A man will be commended
 according to his wisdom,
 But he who is of a perverse
 heart will be despised.

9 Better *is the one* who is slighted
 but has a servant,
 Than he who honors himself
 but lacks bread.

10 A righteous *man* regards the
 life of his animal,
 But the tender mercies of the
 wicked *are* cruel.

11 He who tills his land will be
 satisfied with bread,
 But he who follows frivolity *is*
 devoid of understanding.[a]

12 The wicked covet the catch of
 evil *men,*
 But the root of the righteous
 yields *fruit.*

13 The wicked is ensnared by the
 transgression of *his* lips,
 But the righteous will come
 through trouble.

14 A man will be satisfied with
 good by the fruit of *his*
 mouth,
 And the recompense of a man's

11:21 [a]Literally *hand in hand*   12:4 [a]Literally *A wife of valor*   12:11 [a]Literally *heart* hands will be rendered to him.

15 The way of a fool *is* right in his own eyes,
But he who heeds counsel *is* wise.
16 A fool's wrath is known at once,
But a prudent *man* covers shame.
17 He *who* speaks truth declares righteousness,
But a false witness, deceit.
18 There is one who speaks like the piercings of a sword,
But the tongue of the wise *promotes* health.
19 The truthful lip shall be established forever,
But a lying tongue *is* but for a moment.
20 Deceit is in the heart of those who devise evil,
But counselors of peace have joy.
21 No grave trouble will overtake the righteous,
But the wicked shall be filled with evil.
22 Lying lips *are* an abomination to the LORD,
But those who deal truthfully *are* His delight.

23 A prudent man conceals knowledge,
But the heart of fools proclaims foolishness.

24 The hand of the diligent will rule,
But the lazy *man* will be put to forced labor.

25 Anxiety in the heart of man causes depression,
But a good word makes it glad.

26 The righteous should choose his friends carefully,
For the way of the wicked leads them astray.

27 The lazy *man* does not roast what he took in hunting,
But diligence *is* man's precious possession.

28 In the way of righteousness *is* life,

And in *its* pathway *there is* no death.

13 A wise son *heeds* his father's instruction,
But a scoffer does not listen to rebuke.
2 A man shall eat well by the fruit of *his* mouth,
But the soul of the unfaithful feeds on violence.
3 He who guards his mouth preserves his life,
But he who opens wide his lips shall have destruction.

4 The soul of a lazy *man* desires, and *has* nothing;
But the soul of the diligent shall be made rich.

5 A righteous *man* hates lying,
But a wicked *man* is loathsome and comes to shame.
6 Righteousness guards *him whose* way is blameless,
But wickedness overthrows the sinner.

7 There is one who makes himself rich, yet *has* nothing;
And one who makes himself poor, yet *has* great riches.

8 The ransom of a man's life *is* his riches,
But the poor does not hear rebuke.

9 The light of the righteous rejoices,
But the lamp of the wicked will be put out.

10 By pride comes nothing but strife,
But with the well-advised *is* wisdom.

11 Wealth *gained by* dishonesty will be diminished,
But he who gathers by labor will increase.

12 Hope deferred makes the heart sick,
But *when* the desire comes, *it is* a tree of life.

13 He who despises the word will be destroyed,
But he who fears the

commandment will be
rewarded.

14 The law of the wise *is* a
fountain of life,
To turn *one* away from the
snares of death.

15 Good understanding gains
favor,
But the way of the unfaithful
is hard.

16 Every prudent *man* acts with
knowledge,
But a fool lays open *his* folly.

17 A wicked messenger falls into
trouble,
But a faithful ambassador
brings health.

18 Poverty and shame *will come*
to him who disdains
correction,
But he who regards a rebuke
will be honored.

19 A desire accomplished is sweet
to the soul,
But *it is* an abomination to
fools to depart from evil.

20 He who walks with wise *men*
will be wise,
But the companion of fools will
be destroyed.

21 Evil pursues sinners,
But to the righteous, good shall
be repaid.

22 A good *man* leaves an
inheritance to his children's
children,
But the wealth of the sinner is
stored up for the righteous.

23 Much food *is in* the fallow
ground of the poor,
And for lack of justice there is
waste.[a]

24 He who spares his rod hates his
son,
But he who loves him
disciplines him promptly.

25 The righteous eats to the
satisfying of his soul,
But the stomach of the wicked
shall be in want.

14 The wise woman builds her
house,
But the foolish pulls it down
with her hands.

2 He who walks in his
uprightness fears the LORD,
But *he who is* perverse in his
ways despises Him.

3 In the mouth of a fool *is* a rod
of pride,
But the lips of the wise will
preserve them.

4 Where no oxen *are,* the trough
is clean;
But much increase *comes* by
the strength of an ox.

5 A faithful witness does not lie,
But a false witness will utter
lies.

6 A scoffer seeks wisdom and
does not *find it,*
But knowledge *is* easy to him
who understands.

7 Go from the presence of a
foolish man,
When you do not perceive *in*
him the lips of knowledge.

8 The wisdom of the prudent *is*
to understand his way,
But the folly of fools *is* deceit.

9 Fools mock at sin,
But among the upright *there is*
favor.

10 The heart knows its own
bitterness,
And a stranger does not share
its joy.

11 The house of the wicked will be
overthrown,
But the tent of the upright will
flourish.

12 There is a way *that seems* right
to a man,
But its end *is* the way of death.

13 Even in laughter the heart may
sorrow,
And the end of mirth *may be*
grief.

13:23 [a]Literally *what is swept away*

Chart the Course

You are walking the walk of faith, thinking God's thoughts, seeking God's guidance, and setting good and godly goals.

Now, how can you possibly succeed when your goals are beyond your grasp? Did you go overboard? Are you thinking too big? Should you scale down your dreams? How can you possibly pull off what seems to be an impossibility?

What you must do is think, plan, and chart your course through the uncharted waters before you. Solomon wrote: "The prudent *man* considers well his steps" (Prov. 14:15).

You cannot expect God's ideas to evolve automatically as actualized achievements. You must assume responsibility to make success happen. You must develop a strategy and a scheme that will allow you to succeed.

Trust God to give you wisdom to chart your course as carefully as a captain who looks at a map, chooses his route, and calculates the time and resources needed to finish the journey.

Determine to reach the destination and see God's dream for your life accomplished. Plan to make it possible.

Be confident that
• if there's a will, there's a way.
• if it's God's will, He will show the way.
• if you keep the faith, He will show you how! Take time to thank God for giving you the motivation to run the race. Thank Him for the wisdom to chart the course that fulfills His successful plan for your life!

14 The backslider in heart will be
filled with his own ways,
But a good man *will be satisfied*
from above.[a]

15 The simple believes every
word,
But the prudent considers well
his steps.

16 A wise *man* fears and departs
from evil,
But a fool rages and is self-
confident.

17 A quick-tempered *man* acts
foolishly,
And a man of wicked
intentions is hated.

18 The simple inherit folly,
But the prudent are crowned
with knowledge.

19 The evil will bow before the
good,
And the wicked at the gates of
the righteous.

20 The poor *man* is hated even by
his own neighbor,
But the rich *has* many friends.

21 He who despises his neighbor
sins;
But he who has mercy on the
poor, happy *is* he.

22 Do they not go astray who
devise evil?
But mercy and truth *belong* to
those who devise good.

23 In all labor there is profit,
But idle chatter[a] *leads* only to
poverty.

24 The crown of the wise is their
riches,
But the foolishness of fools *is*
folly.

25 A true witness delivers souls,
But a deceitful *witness* speaks
lies.

26 In the fear of the LORD *there is*
strong confidence,
And His children will have a
place of refuge.

27 The fear of the LORD *is* a
fountain of life,
To turn *one* away from the
snares of death.

28 In a multitude of people *is* a
king's honor,
But in the lack of people *is* the
downfall of a prince.

29 *He who is* slow to wrath has
great understanding,
But *he who is* impulsive[a] exalts
folly.

30 A sound heart *is* life to the
body,
But envy *is* rottenness to the
bones.

31 He who oppresses the poor
reproaches his Maker,
But he who honors Him has
mercy on the needy.

32 The wicked is banished in his
wickedness,
But the righteous has a refuge
in his death.

33 Wisdom rests in the heart of
him who has understanding,
But *what is* in the heart of fools
is made known.

34 Righteousness exalts a nation,
But sin *is* a reproach to *any*
people.

35 The king's favor *is* toward a
wise servant,
But his wrath *is against* him
who causes shame.

15 A soft answer turns away
wrath,
But a harsh word stirs up
anger.

2 The tongue of the wise uses
knowledge rightly,
But the mouth of fools pours
forth foolishness.

3 The eyes of the LORD *are* in
every place,
Keeping watch on the evil and
the good.

4 A wholesome tongue *is* a tree
of life,
But perverseness in it breaks
the spirit.

5 A fool despises his father's
instruction,

14:14 [a]Literally *from above himself*   14:23 [a]Literally *talk of the lips*   14:29 [a]Literally *short of spirit*

Positive Censorship

In Proverbs 15:26 Solomon wrote that "the thoughts of the wicked *are* an abomination to the LORD, but *the words* of the pure *are* pleasant." Possibility thinking includes the process of positive censoring. It involves sifting out the good from the bad.

Faith asks the question: Does this idea deserve my attention or the trademark of my name? Maintaining a constructive critical overview is a constant process.

Faith is not afraid to censor. It stands guard at the portals of your mind, checking the ethical and moral credentials of the ideas that could disrupt, disturb, and possibly destroy your attitude of faith.

So firm up your willpower.

Assign responsibility to the spiritual laws that manage your thoughts. Without guidelines, controls, and censorship, life is like an airplane with a drunken pilot. A crash landing is always looming.

You need Jesus Christ to guide your thinking. He stands at the door of your mind and heart waiting to help you if you will only ask Him to by praying: *Lord Jesus, my mind was designed to be a mansion with many rooms. Will You come and be the Doorkeeper at the main entrance, admitting only those guests who would bring honor to the household? Please dismiss the unworthy from my doorstep and welcome those visitors who would flood my mind with hope and health and happiness.*

Thank You, Lord. Amen.

But he who receives correction
is prudent.

6 *In* the house of the righteous
there is much treasure,
But in the revenue of the
wicked is trouble.

7 The lips of the wise disperse
knowledge,
But the heart of the fool *does*
not *do* so.

8 The sacrifice of the wicked *is*
an abomination to the LORD,
But the prayer of the upright *is*
His delight.

9 The way of the wicked *is* an
abomination to the LORD,
But He loves him who follows
righteousness.

10 Harsh discipline *is* for him who
forsakes the way,
And he who hates correction
will die.

11 Hell[a] and Destruction[b] *are*
before the LORD;
So how much more the hearts
of the sons of men.

12 A scoffer does not love one who
corrects him,
Nor will he go to the wise.

13 A merry heart makes a cheerful
countenance,
But by sorrow of the heart the
spirit is broken.

14 The heart of him who has
understanding seeks
knowledge,
But the mouth of fools feeds on
foolishness.

15 All the days of the afflicted *are*
evil,
But he who is of a merry heart
has a continual feast.

16 Better *is* a little with the fear
of the LORD,
Than great treasure with
trouble.

17 Better *is* a dinner of herbs[a]
where love is,
Than a fatted calf with hatred.

18 A wrathful man stirs up strife,
But *he who is* slow to anger
allays contention.

19 The way of the lazy *man is* like
a hedge of thorns,
But the way of the upright *is* a
highway.

20 A wise son makes a father glad,
But a foolish man despises his
mother.

21 Folly *is* joy *to him who is*
destitute of discernment,
But a man of understanding
walks uprightly.

22 Without counsel, plans go
awry,
But in the multitude of
counselors they are
established.

23 A man has joy by the answer
of his mouth,
And a word *spoken* in due
season, how good *it is!*

24 The way of life *winds* upward
for the wise,
That he may turn away from
hell[a] below.

25 The LORD will destroy the
house of the proud,
But He will establish the
boundary of the widow.

26 The thoughts of the wicked *are*
an abomination to the LORD,
But *the words* of the pure *are*
pleasant.

27 He who is greedy for gain
troubles his own house,
But he who hates bribes will
live.

28 The heart of the righteous
studies how to answer,
But the mouth of the wicked
pours forth evil.

29 The LORD *is* far from the
wicked,
But He hears the prayer of the
righteous.

30 The light of the eyes rejoices
the heart,

15:11 [a]Or *Sheol* [b]Hebrew *Abaddon* 15:17 [a]Or *vegetables* 15:24 [a]Or *Sheol*

Faith Scans the Horizon

We define *horizon* as the place where heaven meets earth. But it is also where today's state-of-the-art ends and tomorrow's new developments move in. It is where "the old self" dies and "the new self" breathes its first breath. It is where our new life in Christ finds a springboard for breaking out of old habits and shattered hopes.

Faith refuses to surrender control to negative doubts of yesterday, surrendering instead to the Lord's leading (Prov. 16:9). Doubt adds up all of the bungled debts, fruitless research, foiled efforts, and shattered dreams of our old nature.

Doubt finds its life by digging in the cemeteries of buried hopes. Faith finds its life by scanning the horizon, knowing there will be a sunrise tomorrow. Each new day is a fresh beginning. What medical breakthroughs will be made before the sun sets today? What new technological achievements will be possible by the end of this year, or this decade? What new dreams will you dream now that, as a new creature in Christ, you are open to His gentle nudge?

Faith is belief in the future. It is scanning the horizon for new ships that will sail into view, carrying treasured cargo of new discoveries. Faith expects and predicts headlines of new cures and breakthroughs that will be announced in the next 365 days.

Today cultivate a mental attitude that expects progress. Steadfastly scan the heavens!

Through positive prayer, look forward, expectantly and excitedly, thanking God for what He is planning to do in your future.

And a good report makes the bones healthy.[a]

31 The ear that hears the rebukes of life
Will abide among the wise.

32 He who disdains instruction despises his own soul,
But he who heeds rebuke gets understanding.

33 The fear of the LORD is the instruction of wisdom,
And before honor is humility.

16 The preparations of the heart belong to man,
But the answer of the tongue is from the LORD.

2 All the ways of a man are pure in his own eyes,
But the LORD weighs the spirits.

3 Commit your works to the LORD,
And your thoughts will be established.

4 The LORD has made all for Himself,
Yes, even the wicked for the day of doom.

5 Everyone proud in heart is an abomination to the LORD;
Though they join forces,[a] none will go unpunished.

6 In mercy and truth
Atonement is provided for iniquity;
And by the fear of the LORD one departs from evil.

7 When a man's ways please the LORD,
He makes even his enemies to be at peace with him.

8 Better is a little with righteousness,
Than vast revenues without justice.

9 A man's heart plans his way,
But the LORD directs his steps.

10 Divination is on the lips of the king;

His mouth must not transgress in judgment.

11 Honest weights and scales are the LORD'S;
All the weights in the bag are His work.

12 It is an abomination for kings to commit wickedness,
For a throne is established by righteousness.

13 Righteous lips are the delight of kings,
And they love him who speaks what is right.

14 As messengers of death is the king's wrath,
But a wise man will appease it.

15 In the light of the king's face is life,
And his favor is like a cloud of the latter rain.

16 How much better to get wisdom than gold!
And to get understanding is to be chosen rather than silver.

17 The highway of the upright is to depart from evil;
He who keeps his way preserves his soul.

18 Pride goes before destruction,
And a haughty spirit before a fall.

19 Better to be of a humble spirit with the lowly,
Than to divide the spoil with the proud.

20 He who heeds the word wisely will find good,
And whoever trusts in the LORD, happy is he.

21 The wise in heart will be called prudent,
And sweetness of the lips increases learning.

22 Understanding is a wellspring of life to him who has it.
But the correction of fools is folly.

23 The heart of the wise teaches his mouth,
And adds learning to his lips.

15:30 [a]Literally fat   16:5 [a]Literally hand in hand

24 Pleasant words *are like* a
honeycomb,
Sweetness to the soul and
health to the bones.

25 There is a way *that seems* right
to a man,
But its end *is* the way of death.

26 The person who labors, labors
for himself,
For his *hungry* mouth drives
him *on.*

27 An ungodly man digs up evil,
And *it is* on his lips like a
burning fire.

28 A perverse man sows strife,
And a whisperer separates the
best of friends.

29 A violent man entices his
neighbor,
And leads him in a way *that
is* not good.

30 He winks his eye to devise
perverse things;
He purses his lips *and* brings
about evil.

31 The silver-haired head *is* a
crown of glory,
If it is found in the way of
righteousness.

32 *He who is* slow to anger *is*
better than the mighty,
And he who rules his spirit
than he who takes a city.

33 The lot is cast into the lap,
But its every decision *is* from
the LORD.

17

Better *is* a dry morsel with
quietness,
Than a house full of feasting[a]
with strife.

2 A wise servant will rule over a
son who causes shame,
And will share an inheritance
among the brothers.

3 The refining pot *is* for silver
and the furnace for gold,
But the LORD tests the hearts.

4 An evildoer gives heed to false
lips;
A liar listens eagerly to a
spiteful tongue.

5 He who mocks the poor
reproaches his Maker;
He who is glad at calamity will
not go unpunished.

6 Children's children *are* the
crown of old men,
And the glory of children *is*
their father.

7 Excellent speech is not
becoming to a fool,
Much less lying lips to a prince.

8 A present *is* a precious stone
in the eyes of its possessor;
Wherever he turns, he
prospers.

9 He who covers a transgression
seeks love,
But he who repeats a matter
separates friends.

10 Rebuke is more effective for a
wise *man*
Than a hundred blows on a
fool.

11 An evil *man* seeks only
rebellion;
Therefore a cruel messenger
will be sent against him.

12 Let a man meet a bear robbed
of her cubs,
Rather than a fool in his folly.

13 Whoever rewards evil for good,
Evil will not depart from his
house.

14 The beginning of strife *is like*
releasing water;
Therefore stop contention
before a quarrel starts.

15 He who justifies the wicked,
and he who condemns the
just,
Both of them alike *are* an
abomination to the LORD.

16 Why *is there* in the hand of a
fool the purchase price of
wisdom,
Since *he* has no heart *for it?*

17 A friend loves at all times,
And a brother is born for
adversity.

17:1 *aOr sacrificial meals*

18 A man devoid of understanding
shakes hands in a pledge,
And becomes surety for his
friend.

19 He who loves transgression
loves strife,
And he who exalts his gate
seeks destruction.

20 He who has a deceitful heart
finds no good,
And he who has a perverse
tongue falls into evil.

21 He who begets a scoffer *does
so* to his sorrow,
And the father of a fool has no
joy.

22 A merry heart does good, *like*
medicine,[a]
But a broken spirit dries the
bones.

23 A wicked *man* accepts a bribe
behind the back[a]
To pervert the ways of justice.

24 Wisdom *is* in the sight of him
who has understanding,
But the eyes of a fool *are* on
the ends of the earth.

25 A foolish son *is* a grief to his
father,
And bitterness to her who bore
him.

26 Also, to punish the righteous *is*
not good,
Nor to strike princes for *their*
uprightness.

27 He who has knowledge spares
his words,
And a man of understanding is
of a calm spirit.

28 Even a fool is counted wise
when he holds his peace;
When he shuts his lips, *he is
considered* perceptive.

18 A man who isolates himself
seeks his own desire;
He rages against all wise
judgment.

2 A fool has no delight in
understanding,
But in expressing his own
heart.

3 When the wicked comes,
contempt comes also;
And with dishonor *comes*
reproach.

4 The words of a man's mouth
are deep waters;
The wellspring of wisdom *is* a
flowing brook.

5 *It is* not good to show partiality
to the wicked,
Or to overthrow the righteous
in judgment.

6 A fool's lips enter into
contention,
And his mouth calls for blows.

7 A fool's mouth *is* his
destruction,
And his lips *are* the snare of his
soul.

8 The words of a talebearer *are*
like tasty trifles,[a]
And they go down into the
inmost body.

9 He who is slothful in his work
Is a brother to him who is a
great destroyer.

10 The name of the LORD *is* a
strong tower;
The righteous run to it and are
safe.

11 The rich man's wealth *is* his
strong city,
And like a high wall in his own
esteem.

12 Before destruction the heart of
a man is haughty,
And before honor *is* humility.

13 He who answers a matter
before he hears *it,*
It *is* folly and shame to him.

14 The spirit of a man will sustain
him in sickness,
But who can bear a broken
spirit?

15 The heart of the prudent
acquires knowledge,
And the ear of the wise seeks
knowledge.

17:22 [a]Or *makes medicine even better
wounds.* 17:23 [a]Literally *from the bosom* 18:8 [a]A Jewish tradition reads

16 A man's gift makes room for
him,
And brings him before great
men.

17 The first *one* to plead his cause
seems right,
Until his neighbor comes and
examines him.

18 Casting lots causes contentions
to cease,
And keeps the mighty apart.

19 A brother offended *is harder to
win* than a strong city,
And contentions *are* like the
bars of a castle.

20 A man's stomach shall be
satisfied from the fruit of his
mouth;
From the produce of his lips he
shall be filled.

21 Death and life *are* in the power
of the tongue,
And those who love it will eat
its fruit.

22 *He who* finds a wife finds a
good *thing*,
And obtains favor from the
LORD.

23 The poor *man* uses entreaties,
But the rich answers roughly.

24 A man *who has* friends must
himself be friendly,[a]
But there is a friend *who* sticks
closer than a brother.

19 Better *is* the poor who walks in
his integrity
Than *one who is* perverse in his
lips, and is a fool.

2 Also it is not good *for* a soul
to be without knowledge,
And he sins who hastens with
his feet.

3 The foolishness of a man twists
his way,
And his heart frets against the
LORD.

4 Wealth makes many friends,
But the poor is separated from
his friend.

5 A false witness will not go
unpunished,
And *he who* speaks lies will not
escape.

6 Many entreat the favor of the
nobility,
And every man *is* a friend to
one who gives gifts.

7 All the brothers of the poor
hate him;
How much more do his friends
go far from him!
He may pursue *them with*
words, *yet* they abandon
him.

8 He who gets wisdom loves his
own soul;
He who keeps understanding
will find good.

9 A false witness will not go
unpunished,
And *he who* speaks lies shall
perish.

10 Luxury is not fitting for a fool,
Much less for a servant to rule
over princes.

11 The discretion of a man makes
him slow to anger,
And his glory *is* to overlook a
transgression.

12 The king's wrath *is* like the
roaring of a lion,
But his favor *is* like dew on the
grass.

13 A foolish son *is* the ruin of his
father,
And the contentions of a wife
are a continual dripping.

14 Houses and riches *are* an
inheritance from fathers,
But a prudent wife *is* from the
LORD.

15 Laziness casts *one* into a deep
sleep,
And an idle person will suffer
hunger.

16 He who keeps the
commandment keeps his
soul,

18:24 [a]Following Greek manuscripts, Targum, Syriac, and Vulgate; Masoretic Text reads *may come to ruin*

But he who is careless[a] of his
ways will die.

17 He who has pity on the poor
lends to the LORD,
And He will pay back what he
has given.

18 Chasten your son while there
is hope,
And do not set your heart on
his destruction.[a]

19 *A man of* great wrath will
suffer punishment;
For if you rescue *him,* you will
have to do it again.

20 Listen to counsel and receive
instruction,
That you may be wise in your
latter days.

21 There are many plans in a
man's heart,
Nevertheless the LORD's
counsel—that will stand.

22 What is desired in a man is
kindness,
And a poor man is better than
a liar.

23 The fear of the LORD *leads* to
life,
And *he who has it* will abide
in satisfaction;
He will not be visited with evil.

24 A lazy *man* buries his hand in
the bowl,[a]
And will not so much as bring
it to his mouth again.

25 Strike a scoffer, and the simple
will become wary;
Rebuke one who has
understanding, *and* he will
discern knowledge.

26 He who mistreats *his* father *and*
chases away *his* mother
Is a son who causes shame and
brings reproach.

27 Cease listening to instruction,
my son,
And you will stray from the
words of knowledge.

28 A disreputable witness scorns
justice,
And the mouth of the wicked
devours iniquity.

29 Judgments are prepared for
scoffers,
And beatings for the backs of
fools.

20 Wine *is* a mocker,
Strong drink *is* a brawler,
And whoever is led astray by
it is not wise.

2 The wrath[a] of a king *is* like the
roaring of a lion;
Whoever provokes him to
anger sins *against* his own
life.

3 *It is* honorable for a man to
stop striving,
Since any fool can start a
quarrel.

4 The lazy *man* will not plow
because of winter;
He will beg during harvest and
have nothing.

5 Counsel in the heart of man *is*
like deep water,
But a man of understanding
will draw it out.

6 Most men will proclaim each
his own goodness,
But who can find a faithful
man?

7 The righteous *man* walks in his
integrity;
His children *are* blessed after
him.

8 A king who sits on the throne
of judgment
Scatters all evil with his eyes.

9 Who can say, "I have made my
heart clean,
I am pure from my sin"?

10 Diverse weights *and* diverse
measures,
They *are* both alike, an
abomination to the LORD.

19:16 [a]Literally *despises,* figurative of recklessness or carelessness   19:18 [a]Literally *to put him to death;*
a Jewish tradition reads *his crying.*   19:24 [a]Septuagint and Syriac read *bosom;* Targum and Vulgate
read *armpit.*   20:2 [a]Literally *fear* or *terror* which is produced by the king's wrath

11 Even a child is known by his
     deeds,
     Whether what he does *is* pure
       and right.

12 The hearing ear and the seeing
     eye,
     The LORD has made them both.

13 Do not love sleep, lest you
     come to poverty;
     Open your eyes, *and* you will
       be satisfied with bread.

14 "*It is* good for nothing,"*a* cries
     the buyer;
     But when he has gone his way,
       then he boasts.

15 There is gold and a multitude
     of rubies,
     But the lips of knowledge *are*
       a precious jewel.

16 Take the garment of one who
     is surety *for* a stranger,
     And hold it as a pledge *when
     it* is for a seductress.

17 Bread gained by deceit *is* sweet
     to a man,
     But afterward his mouth will be
       filled with gravel.

18 Plans are established by
     counsel;
     By wise counsel wage war.

19 He who goes about *as* a
     talebearer reveals secrets;
     Therefore do not associate with
       one who flatters with his lips.

20 Whoever curses his father or
     his mother,
     His lamp will be put out in deep
       darkness.

21 An inheritance gained hastily
     at the beginning
     Will not be blessed at the end.

22 Do not say, "I will recompense
     evil";
     Wait for the LORD, and He will
       save you.

23 Diverse weights *are* an
     abomination to the LORD,

And dishonest scales *are* not
     good.

24 A man's steps *are* of the LORD;
     How then can a man
       understand his own way?

25 *It is* a snare for a man to devote
     rashly *something as* holy,
     And afterward to reconsider
       his vows.

26 A wise king sifts out the
     wicked,
     And brings the threshing wheel
       over them.

27 The spirit of a man *is* the lamp
     of the LORD,
     Searching all the inner depths
       of his heart.*a*

28 Mercy and truth preserve the
     king,
     And by lovingkindness he
       upholds his throne.

29 The glory of young men *is* their
     strength,
     And the splendor of old men *is*
       their gray head.

30 Blows that hurt cleanse away
     evil,
     As *do* stripes the inner depths
       of the heart.*a*

21 The king's heart *is* in the hand
     of the LORD,
     Like the rivers of water; He
       turns it wherever He wishes.

2 Every way of a man *is* right in
     his own eyes,
     But the LORD weighs the hearts.

3 To do righteousness and justice
     Is more acceptable to the LORD
       than sacrifice.

4 A haughty look, a proud heart,
     And the plowing*a* of the wicked
       are sin.

5 The plans of the diligent *lead*
     surely to plenty,
     But *those of* everyone *who is*
       hasty, surely to poverty.

20:14 *a*Literally *evil, evil
belly*   20:27 *a*Literally *the rooms of the belly*   20:30 *a*Literally *the rooms of the*
     21:4 *a*Or *lamp*

6 Getting treasures by a lying
      tongue
   Is the fleeting fantasy of those
      who seek death.[a]

7 The violence of the wicked will
      destroy them,[a]
   Because they refuse to do
      justice.

8 The way of a guilty man *is*
      perverse;[a]
   But *as for* the pure, his work
      is right.

9 Better to dwell in a corner of a
      housetop,
   Than in a house shared with a
      contentious woman.

10 The soul of the wicked desires
      evil;
   His neighbor finds no favor in
      his eyes.

11 When the scoffer is punished,
      the simple is made wise;
   But when the wise is instructed,
      he receives knowledge.

12 The righteous *God* wisely
      considers the house of the
      wicked,
   Overthrowing the wicked for
      their wickedness.

13 Whoever shuts his ears to the
      cry of the poor
   Will also cry himself and not
      be heard.

14 A gift in secret pacifies anger,
   And a bribe behind the back,[a]
      strong wrath.

15 *It is* a joy for the just to do
      justice,
   But destruction *will come* to the
      workers of iniquity.

16 A man who wanders from the
      way of understanding
   Will rest in the assembly of the
      dead.

17 He who loves pleasure *will be*
      a poor man;

He who loves wine and oil will
   not be rich.

18 The wicked *shall be* a ransom
      for the righteous,
   And the unfaithful for the
      upright.

19 Better to dwell in the
      wilderness,
   Than with a contentious and
      angry woman.

20 *There is* desirable treasure,
   And oil in the dwelling of the
      wise,
   But a foolish man squanders it.

21 He who follows righteousness
      and mercy
   Finds life, righteousness and
      honor.

22 A wise *man* scales the city of
      the mighty,
   And brings down the trusted
      stronghold.

23 Whoever guards his mouth and
      tongue
   Keeps his soul from troubles.

24 A proud *and* haughty *man*—
      "Scoffer" *is* his name;
   He acts with arrogant pride.

25 The desire of the lazy *man* kills
      him,
   For his hands refuse to labor.
26 He covets greedily all day long,
   But the righteous gives and
      does not spare.

27 The sacrifice of the wicked *is*
      an abomination;
   How much more *when* he
      brings it with wicked intent!

28 A false witness shall perish,
   But the man who hears *him* will
      speak endlessly.

29 A wicked man hardens his
      face,
   But *as for* the upright, he
      establishes[a] his way.

21:6 [a]Septuagint reads *Pursue vanity on the snares of death;* Vulgate reads *Is vain and foolish, and shall stumble on the snares of death;* Targum reads *They shall be destroyed, and they shall fall who seek death.*   21:7 [a]Literally *drag them away*   21:8 [a]Or *The way of a man is perverse and strange*   21:14 [a]Literally *in the bosom*   21:29 [a]Qere and Septuagint read *understands.*

30 *There is* no wisdom or
    understanding
    Or counsel against the Lord.

31 The horse *is* prepared for the
    day of battle,
    But deliverance *is* of the Lord.

22 A *good* name is to be chosen
    rather than great riches,
    Loving favor rather than silver
    and gold.

2 The rich and the poor have this
    in common,
    The Lord *is* the maker of them
    all.

3 A prudent *man* foresees evil
    and hides himself,
    But the simple pass on and are
    punished.

4 By humility *and* the fear of the
    Lord
    Are riches and honor and life.

5 Thorns *and* snares *are* in the
    way of the perverse;
    He who guards his soul will be
    far from them.

6 Train up a child in the way he
    should go,
    And when he is old he will not
    depart from it.

7 The rich rules over the poor,
    And the borrower *is* servant to
    the lender.

8 He who sows iniquity will reap
    sorrow,
    And the rod of his anger will
    fail.

9 He who has a generous eye will
    be blessed,
    For he gives of his bread to the
    poor.

10 Cast out the scoffer, and
    contention will leave;
    Yes, strife and reproach will
    cease.

11 He who loves purity of heart
    And has grace on his lips,
    The king *will be* his friend.

12 The eyes of the Lord preserve
    knowledge,

But He overthrows the words
    of the faithless.

13 The lazy *man* says, "There is
    a lion outside!
    I shall be slain in the streets!"

14 The mouth of an immoral
    woman *is* a deep pit;
    He who is abhorred by the
    Lord will fall there.

15 Foolishness *is* bound up in the
    heart of a child;
    The rod of correction will drive
    it far from him.

16 He who oppresses the poor to
    increase his *riches,*
    And he who gives to the rich,
    will surely *come* to poverty.

17 Incline your ear and hear the
    words of the wise,
    And apply your heart to my
    knowledge;

18 For *it is* a pleasant thing if you
    keep them within you;
    Let them all be fixed upon your
    lips,

19 So that your trust may be in the
    Lord;
    I have instructed you today,
    even you.

20 Have I not written to you
    excellent things
    Of counsels and knowledge,

21 That I may make you know the
    certainty of the words of
    truth,
    That you may answer words of
    truth
    To those who send to you?

22 Do not rob the poor because he
    is poor,
    Nor oppress the afflicted at the
    gate;

23 For the Lord will plead their
    cause,
    And plunder the soul of those
    who plunder them.

24 Make no friendship with an
    angry man,
    And with a furious man do not
    go,

25 Lest you learn his ways
    And set a snare for your soul.

26 Do not be one of those who
    shakes hands in a pledge,

One of those who is surety for debts;

27 If you have nothing *with which* to pay,
Why should he take away your bed from under you?

28 Do not remove the ancient landmark
Which your fathers have set.

29 Do you see a man *who* excels in his work?
He will stand before kings;
He will not stand before unknown *men.*

23 When you sit down to eat with a ruler,
Consider carefully what *is* before you;

2 And put a knife to your throat
If you *are* a man given to appetite.

3 Do not desire his delicacies,
For they *are* deceptive food.

4 Do not overwork to be rich;
Because of your own understanding, cease!

5 Will you set your eyes on that which is not?
For *riches* certainly make themselves wings;
They fly away like an eagle *toward* heaven.

6 Do not eat the bread of a miser,[a]
Nor desire his delicacies;

7 For as he thinks in his heart, so *is* he.
"Eat and drink!" he says to you,
But his heart is not with you.

8 The morsel you have eaten, you will vomit up,
And waste your pleasant words.

9 Do not speak in the hearing of a fool,
For he will despise the wisdom of your words.

10 Do not remove the ancient landmark,
Nor enter the fields of the fatherless;

11 For their Redeemer *is* mighty;

He will plead their cause against you.

12 Apply your heart to instruction,
And your ears to words of knowledge.

13 Do not withhold correction from a child,
For *if* you beat him with a rod, he will not die.

14 You shall beat him with a rod,
And deliver his soul from hell.[a]

15 My son, if your heart is wise,
My heart will rejoice—indeed, I myself;

16 Yes, my inmost being will rejoice
When your lips speak right things.

17 Do not let your heart envy sinners,
But *be zealous* for the fear of the LORD all the day;

18 For surely there is a hereafter,
And your hope will not be cut off.

19 Hear, my son, and be wise;
And guide your heart in the way.

20 Do not mix with winebibbers,
Or with gluttonous eaters of meat;

21 For the drunkard and the glutton will come to poverty,
And drowsiness will clothe *a man* with rags.

22 Listen to your father who begot you,
And do not despise your mother when she is old.

23 Buy the truth, and do not sell *it,*
Also wisdom and instruction and understanding.

24 The father of the righteous will greatly rejoice,
And he who begets a wise *child* will delight in him.

25 Let your father and your mother be glad,
And let her who bore you rejoice.

23:6 [a]Literally *one who has an evil eye*   23:14 [a]Or *Sheol*

26 My son, give me your heart,
And let your eyes observe my
ways.
27 For a harlot *is* a deep pit,
And a seductress *is* a narrow
well.
28 She also lies in wait as *for a*
victim,
And increases the unfaithful
among men.

29 Who has woe?
Who has sorrow?
Who has contentions?
Who has complaints?
Who has wounds without
cause?
Who has redness of eyes?
30 Those who linger long at the
wine,
Those who go in search of
mixed wine.
31 Do not look on the wine when
it is red,
When it sparkles in the cup,
When it swirls around
smoothly;
32 At the last it bites like a
serpent,
And stings like a viper.
33 Your eyes will see strange
things,
And your heart will utter
perverse things.
34 Yes, you will be like one who
lies down in the midst of the
sea,
Or like one who lies at the top
of the mast, *saying:*
35 "They have struck me, *but* I was
not hurt;
They have beaten me, but I did
not feel *it.*
When shall I awake, that I may
seek another *drink?*"

24 Do not be envious of evil men,
Nor desire to be with them;
2 For their heart devises
violence,
And their lips talk of
troublemaking.

3 Through wisdom a house is
built,
And by understanding it is
established;
4 By knowledge the rooms are
filled
With all precious and pleasant
riches.

5 A wise man *is* strong,
Yes, a man of knowledge
increases strength;
6 For by wise counsel you will
wage your own war,
And in a multitude of
counselors *there is* safety.
7 Wisdom *is* too lofty for a fool;
He does not open his mouth in
the gate.

8 He who plots to do evil
Will be called a schemer.
9 The devising of foolishness *is*
sin,
And the scoffer *is* an
abomination to men.

10 *If* you faint in the day of
adversity,
Your strength *is* small.

11 Deliver *those who* are drawn
toward death,
And hold back *those* stumbling
to the slaughter.
12 If you say, "Surely we did not
know this,"
Does not He who weighs the
hearts consider *it?*
He who keeps your soul, does
He *not* know *it?*
And will He *not* render to *each*
man according to his deeds?

13 My son, eat honey because *it
is* good,
And the honeycomb *which is*
sweet to your taste;
14 So *shall* the knowledge of
wisdom *be* to your soul;
If you have found *it,* there is a
prospect,
And your hope will not be cut
off.

15 Do not lie in wait, O wicked
man, against the dwelling of
the righteous;
Do not plunder his resting
place;
16 For a righteous *man* may fall
seven times
And rise again,
But the wicked shall fall by
calamity.

17 Do not rejoice when your
enemy falls,
And do not let your heart be
glad when he stumbles;

18 Lest the LORD see *it*, and it
displease Him,
And He turn away His wrath
from him.

19 Do not fret because of
evildoers,
Nor be envious of the wicked;
20 For there will be no prospect
for the evil *man;*
The lamp of the wicked will be
put out.

21 My son, fear the LORD and the
king;
Do not associate with those
given to change;
22 For their calamity will rise
suddenly,
And who knows the ruin those
two can bring?

23 These *things* also *belong* to the
wise:

It is not good to show partiality
in judgment.
24 He who says to the wicked,
"You *are* righteous,"
Him the people will curse;
Nations will abhor him.
25 But those who rebuke *the
wicked* will have delight,
And a good blessing will come
upon them.

26 He who gives a right answer
kisses the lips.

27 Prepare your outside work,
Make it fit for yourself in the
field;
And afterward build your
house.

28 Do not be a witness against
your neighbor without cause,
For would you deceive[a] with
your lips?
29 Do not say, "I will do to him
just as he has done to me;
I will render to the man
according to his work."

30 I went by the field of the lazy
man,
And by the vineyard of the man
devoid of understanding;
31 And there it was, all overgrown
with thorns;

Its surface was covered with
nettles;
Its stone wall was broken
down.
32 When I saw *it,* I considered *it*
well;
I looked on *it and* received
instruction:
33 A little sleep, a little slumber,
A little folding of the hands to
rest;
34 So shall your poverty come *like*
a prowler,
And your need like an armed
man.

25 These also *are* proverbs of Solomon which the men of Hezekiah king of Judah copied:

2 *It is* the glory of God to conceal
a matter,
But the glory of kings *is* to
search out a matter.

3 *As* the heavens for height and
the earth for depth,
So the heart of kings *is*
unsearchable.

4 Take away the dross from
silver,
And it will go to the silversmith
for jewelry.
5 Take away the wicked from
before the king,
And his throne will be
established in righteousness.

6 Do not exalt yourself in the
presence of the king,
And do not stand in the place
of the great;
7 For *it is* better that he say to
you,
"Come up here,"
Than that you should be put
lower in the presence of the
prince,
Whom your eyes have seen.

8 Do not go hastily to court;
For what will you do in the end,
When your neighbor has put
you to shame?
9 Debate your case with your
neighbor,
And do not disclose the secret
to another;

24:28 [a]Septuagint and Vulgate read *Do not deceive.*

Disciplined or Disqualified

Faith is focusing all of your conscious and subconscious thoughts and your natural and supernatural powers to create a spiritual cable more powerful than any steel cable. Faith, through this cable, moves mountains. This cable is *discipline!*

The words *discipline* and *disciple* come from the same root. Early Christians were called disciples. That means they became persons so totally and completely committed to the Christian cause that they were willing to die for it. That, essentially, is the spirit that makes up the word *discipline*.

Solomon wrote: "Whoever *has* no rule over his own spirit *is like* a city broken down, without walls" (Prov. 25:28). The person who disciplines his body practices faith, whether it's through controlling appetite for food or drink, or any other natural physical appetite.

There are mysterious, intricate, and complex connections of body, brain, and soul. Persons who discipline their eating, drinking, and sexual appetites often experience a mysterious upsurge of creativity and a rebirth of spirituality. In contrast, the undisciplined person who "lets himself go" and doesn't care about proper exercise, physical fitness, or dietary disciplines finds his faith becoming "flabby." *Undisciplined* is another word for *disqualified*.

Today determine to qualify as a disciple of Jesus Christ.

Pledge to discipline your eyes, your ears, your mouth, your stomach, your hands, and your sexual desires.

With God's help, bring your body under control.

Become a spiritual athlete!

Now take a moment to pray: *Help me, O God, to succeed in this colossal challenge. Let my life give evidence, O Lord, of being a disciplined disciple! Amen.*

10 Lest he who hears *it* expose
   your shame,
   And your reputation be ruined.

11 A word fitly spoken *is like*
   apples of gold
   In settings of silver.
12 *Like* an earring of gold and an
   ornament of fine gold
   Is a wise rebuker to an obedient
   ear.

13 Like the cold of snow in time
   of harvest
   Is a faithful messenger to those
   who send him,
   For he refreshes the soul of his
   masters.

14 Whoever falsely boasts of
   giving
   Is like clouds and wind without
   rain.

15 By long forbearance a ruler is
   persuaded,
   And a gentle tongue breaks a
   bone.

16 Have you found honey?
   Eat only as much as you need,
   Lest you be filled with it and
   vomit.

17 Seldom set foot in your
   neighbor's house,
   Lest he become weary of you
   and hate you.

18 A man who bears false witness
   against his neighbor
   Is like a club, a sword, and a
   sharp arrow.

19 Confidence in an unfaithful
   man in time of trouble
   Is like a bad tooth and a foot
   out of joint.

20 *Like* one who takes away a
   garment in cold weather,
   And like vinegar on soda,
   Is one who sings songs to a
   heavy heart.

21 If your enemy is hungry, give
   him bread to eat;
   And if he is thirsty, give him
   water to drink;
22 For *so* you will heap coals of
   fire on his head,
   And the LORD will reward you.

23 The north wind brings forth
   rain,
   And a backbiting tongue an
   angry countenance.

24 *It is* better to dwell in a corner
   of a housetop,
   Than in a house shared with a
   contentious woman.

25 *As* cold water to a weary soul,
   So *is* good news from a far
   country.

26 A righteous *man* who falters
   before the wicked
   Is like a murky spring and a
   polluted well.

27 *It is* not good to eat much
   honey;
   So to seek one's own glory *is
   not* glory.

28 Whoever *has* no rule over his
   own spirit
   Is like a city broken down,
   without walls.

26 As snow in summer and rain
   in harvest,
   So honor is not fitting for a fool.

2 Like a flitting sparrow, like a
   flying swallow,
   So a curse without cause shall
   not alight.

3 A whip for the horse,
   A bridle for the donkey,
   And a rod for the fool's back.
4 Do not answer a fool according
   to his folly,
   Lest you also be like him.
5 Answer a fool according to his
   folly,
   Lest he be wise in his own eyes.
6 He who sends a message by the
   hand of a fool
   Cuts off *his own* feet *and* drinks
   violence.
7 *Like* the legs of the lame that
   hang limp
   Is a proverb in the mouth of
   fools.
8 Like one who binds a stone in
   a sling
   Is he who gives honor to a fool.
9 *Like* a thorn *that* goes into the
   hand of a drunkard
   Is a proverb in the mouth of
   fools.

10 The great *God* who formed
   everything
   Gives the fool *his* hire and the
   transgressor *his* wages.[a]
11 As a dog returns to his own
   vomit,
   So a fool repeats his folly.
12 Do you see a man wise in his
   own eyes?
   There is more hope for a fool
   than for him.

13 The lazy *man* says, "*There is*
   a lion in the road!
   A fierce lion *is* in the streets!"
14 *As* a door turns on its hinges,
   So *does* the lazy *man* on his
   bed.
15 The lazy *man* buries his hand
   in the bowl;[a]
   It wearies him to bring it back
   to his mouth.
16 The lazy *man is* wiser in his
   own eyes
   Than seven men who can
   answer sensibly.

17 He who passes by *and* meddles
   in a quarrel not his own
   Is like one who takes a dog by
   the ears.
18 Like a madman who throws
   firebrands, arrows, and
   death,
19 *Is* the man *who* deceives his
   neighbor,
   And says, "I was only joking!"

20 Where *there is* no wood, the
   fire goes out;
   And where *there is* no
   talebearer, strife ceases.
21 *As* charcoal *is* to burning coals,
   and wood to fire,
   So *is* a contentious man to
   kindle strife.
22 The words of a talebearer *are*
   like tasty trifles,
   And they go down into the
   inmost body.

23 Fervent lips with a wicked
   heart
   Are like earthenware covered
   with silver dross.
24 He who hates, disguises *it* with
   his lips,
   And lays up deceit within
   himself;

25 When he speaks kindly, do not
   believe him,
   For *there are* seven
   abominations in his heart;
26 *Though his* hatred is covered
   by deceit,
   His wickedness will be
   revealed before the
   assembly.

27 Whoever digs a pit will fall into
   it,
   And he who rolls a stone will
   have it roll back on him.

28 A lying tongue hates *those who
   are* crushed by it,
   And a flattering mouth works
   ruin.

27 Do not boast about tomorrow,
   For you do not know what a
   day may bring forth.

2 Let another man praise you,
   and not your own mouth;
   A stranger, and not your own
   lips.

3 A stone *is* heavy and sand *is*
   weighty,
   But a fool's wrath *is* heavier
   than both of them.

4 Wrath *is* cruel and anger a
   torrent,
   But who *is* able to stand before
   jealousy?

5 Open rebuke *is* better
   Than love carefully concealed.

6 Faithful *are* the wounds of a
   friend,
   But the kisses of an enemy *are*
   deceitful.

7 A satisfied soul loathes the
   honeycomb,
   But to a hungry soul every
   bitter thing *is* sweet.

8 Like a bird that wanders from
   its nest
   Is a man who wanders from his
   place.

9 Ointment and perfume delight
   the heart,
   And the sweetness of a man's

26:10 [a]The Hebrew is difficult; ancient and modern translators differ greatly.   26:15 [a]Compare 19:24

friend *gives delight* by hearty counsel.

10 Do not forsake your own friend
or your father's friend,
Nor go to your brother's house
in the day of your calamity;
Better *is* a neighbor nearby
than a brother far away.

11 My son, be wise, and make my
heart glad,
That I may answer him who
reproaches me.

12 A prudent *man* foresees evil
and hides himself;
The simple pass on *and* are
punished.

13 Take the garment of him who
is surety for a stranger,
And hold it in pledge *when* he
is surety for a seductress.

14 He who blesses his friend with
a loud voice, rising early in
the morning,
It will be counted a curse to
him.

15 A continual dripping on a very
rainy day
And a contentious woman are
alike;

16 Whoever restrains her
restrains the wind,
And grasps oil with his right
hand.

17 *As* iron sharpens iron,
So a man sharpens the
countenance of his friend.

18 Whoever keeps the fig tree will
eat its fruit;
So he who waits on his master
will be honored.

19 As in water face *reflects* face,
So a man's heart *reveals* the
man.

20 Hell[a] and Destruction[b] are
never full;
So the eyes of man are never
satisfied.

21 The refining pot *is* for silver
and the furnace for gold,

And a man *is valued* by what
others say of him.

22 Though you grind a fool in a
mortar with a pestle along
with crushed grain,
Yet his foolishness will not
depart from him.

23 Be diligent to know the state of
your flocks,
And attend to your herds;

24 For riches *are* not forever,
Nor does a crown *endure* to all
generations.

25 *When* the hay is removed, and
the tender grass shows itself,
And the herbs of the mountains
are gathered in,

26 The lambs *will provide* your
clothing,
And the goats the price of a
field;

27 *You shall have* enough goats'
milk for your food,
For the food of your household,
And the nourishment of your
maidservants.

28

The wicked flee when no one
pursues,
But the righteous are bold as a
lion.

2 Because of the transgression of
a land, many *are* its princes;
But by a man of understanding
and knowledge
Right will be prolonged.

3 A poor man who oppresses the
poor
Is like a driving rain which
leaves no food.

4 Those who forsake the law
praise the wicked,
But such as keep the law
contend with them.

5 Evil men do not understand
justice,
But those who seek the LORD
understand all.

6 Better *is* the poor who walks in
his integrity
Than one perverse *in his* ways,
though he *be* rich.

27:20 [a]Or *Sheol*   [b]Hebrew *Abaddon*

7 Whoever keeps the law *is a*
discerning son,
But a companion of gluttons
shames his father.

8 One who increases his
possessions by usury and
extortion
Gathers it for him who will pity
the poor.

9 One who turns away his ear
from hearing the law,
Even his prayer *is* an
abomination.

10 Whoever causes the upright to
go astray in an evil way,
He himself will fall into his own
pit;
But the blameless will inherit
good.

11 The rich man *is* wise in his own
eyes,
But the poor who has
understanding searches him
out.

12 When the righteous rejoice,
there is great glory;
But when the wicked arise,
men hide themselves.

13 He who covers his sins will not
prosper,
But whoever confesses and
forsakes *them* will have
mercy.

14 Happy *is* the man who is
always reverent,
But he who hardens his heart
will fall into calamity.

15 *Like* a roaring lion and a
charging bear
Is a wicked ruler over poor
people.

16 A ruler who lacks
understanding *is* a great
oppressor,
But he who hates covetousness
will prolong *his* days.

17 A man burdened with
bloodshed will flee into a pit;
Let no one help him.

18 Whoever walks blamelessly
will be saved,

But *he who is* perverse *in his*
ways will suddenly fall.

19 He who tills his land will have
plenty of bread,
But he who follows frivolity
will have poverty enough!

20 A faithful man will abound
with blessings,
But he who hastens to be rich
will not go unpunished.

21 To show partiality *is* not good,
Because for a piece of bread a
man will transgress.

22 A man with an evil eye hastens
after riches,
And does not consider that
poverty will come upon him.

23 He who rebukes a man will find
more favor afterward
Than he who flatters with the
tongue.

24 Whoever robs his father or his
mother,
And says, "*It is* no
transgression,"
The same *is* companion to a
destroyer.

25 He who is of a proud heart stirs
up strife,
But he who trusts in the LORD
will be prospered.

26 He who trusts in his own heart
is a fool,
But whoever walks wisely will
be delivered.

27 He who gives to the poor will
not lack,
But he who hides his eyes will
have many curses.

28 When the wicked arise, men
hide themselves;
But when they perish, the
righteous increase.

29 He who is often rebuked, *and*
hardens *his* neck,
Will suddenly be destroyed,
and that without remedy.

2 When the righteous are in
authority, the people rejoice;

But when a wicked *man* rules,
the people groan.

3 Whoever loves wisdom makes
his father rejoice,
But a companion of harlots
wastes *his* wealth.

4 The king establishes the land
by justice,
But he who receives bribes
overthrows it.

5 A man who flatters his
neighbor
Spreads a net for his feet.

6 By transgression an evil man is
snared,
But the righteous sings and
rejoices.

7 The righteous considers the
cause of the poor,
But the wicked does not
understand *such* knowledge.

8 Scoffers set a city aflame,
But wise *men* turn away wrath.

9 *If* a wise man contends with a
foolish man,
Whether *the fool* rages or
laughs, *there is* no peace.

10 The bloodthirsty hate the
blameless,
But the upright seek his well-
being.*a*

11 A fool vents all his feelings,*a*
But a wise *man* holds them
back.

12 If a ruler pays attention to lies,
All his servants *become*
wicked.

13 The poor *man* and the
oppressor have this in
common:
The LORD gives light to the eyes
of both.

14 The king who judges the poor
with truth,
His throne will be established
forever.

15 The rod and rebuke give
wisdom,
But a child left *to himself*
brings shame to his mother.

16 When the wicked are
multiplied, transgression
increases;
But the righteous will see their
fall.

17 Correct your son, and he will
give you rest;
Yes, he will give delight to your
soul.

18 Where *there is* no revelation,*a*
the people cast off restraint;
But happy *is* he who keeps the
law.

19 A servant will not be corrected
by mere words;
For though he understands, he
will not respond.

20 Do you see a man hasty in his
words?
There is more hope for a fool
than for him.

21 He who pampers his servant
from childhood
Will have him as a son in the
end.

22 An angry man stirs up strife,
And a furious man abounds in
transgression.

23 A man's pride will bring him
low,
But the humble in spirit will
retain honor.

24 Whoever is a partner with a
thief hates his own life;
He swears to tell the truth,*a* but
reveals nothing.

25 The fear of man brings a snare,
But whoever trusts in the LORD
shall be safe.

26 Many seek the ruler's favor,
But justice for man *comes* from
the LORD.

29:10 *a*Literally *soul*   29:11 *a*Literally *spirit*   29:18 *a*Or *prophetic vision*   29:24 *a*Literally *hears the
adjuration*

27 An unjust man *is* an
abomination to the righteous,
And *he who is* upright in the
way *is* an abomination to the
wicked.

30 The words of Agur the son of
Jakeh, *his* utterance. This man
declared to Ithiel—to Ithiel and Ucal:

2 Surely I *am* more stupid than
any man,
And do not have the
understanding of a man.
3 I neither learned wisdom
Nor have knowledge of the
Holy One.

4 Who has ascended into heaven,
or descended?
Who has gathered the wind in
His fists?
Who has bound the waters in
a garment?
Who has established all the
ends of the earth?
What *is* His name, and what *is*
His Son's name,
If you know?

5 Every word of God *is* pure;
He *is* a shield to those who put
their trust in Him.
6 Do not add to His words,
Lest He rebuke you, and you
be found a liar.

7 Two *things* I request of You
(Deprive me not before I die):
8 Remove falsehood and lies far
from me;
Give me neither poverty nor
riches—
Feed me with the food allotted
to me;
9 Lest I be full and deny *You,*
And say, "Who *is* the LORD?"
Or lest I be poor and steal,
And profane the name of my
God.

10 Do not malign a servant to his
master,
Lest he curse you, and you be
found guilty.

11 *There is* a generation *that*
curses its father,
And does not bless its mother.

12 *There is* a generation *that is*
pure in its own eyes,
Yet is not washed from its
filthiness.
13 *There is* a generation—oh, how
lofty are their eyes!
And their eyelids are lifted up.
14 *There is* a generation whose
teeth *are like* swords,
And whose fangs *are like*
knives,
To devour the poor from off the
earth,
And the needy from *among*
men.

15 The leech has two daughters—
Give *and* Give!

There are three *things that* are
never satisfied,
Four never say, "Enough!":
16 The grave,[a]
The barren womb,
The earth *that* is not satisfied
with water—
And the fire never says,
"Enough!"

17 The eye *that* mocks *his* father,
And scorns obedience to *his*
mother,
The ravens of the valley will
pick it out,
And the young eagles will eat
it.

18 There are three *things which*
are too wonderful for me,
Yes, four *which* I do not
understand:
19 The way of an eagle in the air,
The way of a serpent on a rock,
The way of a ship in the midst
of the sea,
And the way of a man with a
virgin.

20 This *is* the way of an adulterous
woman:
She eats and wipes her mouth,
And says, "I have done no
wickedness."

21 For three *things* the earth is
perturbed,
Yes, for four it cannot bear up:
22 For a servant when he reigns,
A fool when he is filled with
food,

30:16 [a]Or *Sheol*

23 A hateful *woman* when she is
    married,
And a maidservant who
    succeeds her mistress.

24 There are four *things which* are
    little on the earth,
But they *are* exceedingly wise:
25 The ants *are* a people not
    strong,
Yet they prepare their food in
    the summer;
26 The rock badgers*a* are a feeble
    folk,
Yet they make their homes in
    the crags;
27 The locusts have no king,
Yet they all advance in ranks;
28 The spider*a* skillfully grasps
    with its hands,
And it is in kings' palaces.

29 There are three *things which*
    are majestic in pace,
Yes, four *which* are stately in
    walk:
30 A lion, *which is* mighty among
    beasts
And does not turn away from
    any;
31 A greyhound,*a*
A male goat also,
And a king *whose* troops *are*
    with him.*b*

32 If you have been foolish in
    exalting yourself,
Or if you have devised evil, *put*
    your hand on *your* mouth.
33 For *as* the churning of milk
    produces butter,
And wringing the nose
    produces blood,
So the forcing of wrath
    produces strife.

31 The words of King Lemuel, the
utterance which his mother
taught him:

2 What, my son?
And what, son of my womb?
And what, son of my vows?
3 Do not give your strength to
    women,
Nor your ways to that which
    destroys kings.

4 *It is* not for kings, O Lemuel,
It is not for kings to drink wine,
Nor for princes intoxicating
    drink;
5 Lest they drink and forget the
    law,
And pervert the justice of all
    the afflicted.
6 Give strong drink to him who
    is perishing,
And wine to those who are
    bitter of heart.
7 Let him drink and forget his
    poverty,
And remember his misery no
    more.

8 Open your mouth for the
    speechless,
In the cause of all *who are*
    appointed to die.*a*
9 Open your mouth, judge
    righteously,
And plead the cause of the poor
    and needy.
10 Who*a* can find a virtuous*b* wife?
For her worth *is* far above
    rubies.
11 The heart of her husband safely
    trusts her;
So he will have no lack of gain.
12 She does him good and not evil
All the days of her life.
13 She seeks wool and flax,
And willingly works with her
    hands.
14 She is like the merchant ships,
She brings her food from afar.
15 She also rises while it is yet
    night,
And provides food for her
    household,
And a portion for her
    maidservants.
16 She considers a field and buys
    it;
From her profits she plants a
    vineyard.
17 She girds herself with strength,
And strengthens her arms.
18 She perceives that her
    merchandise *is* good,
And her lamp does not go out
    by night.
19 She stretches out her hands to
    the distaff,
And her hand holds the
    spindle.

30:26 *a*Or hyraxes   30:28 *a*Or lizard   30:31 *a*Exact identity unknown   *b*A Jewish tradition reads *a king*
against whom there is no uprising.   31:8 *a*Literally *sons of passing away*   31:10 *a*Verses 10 through
31 are an alphabetic acrostic in Hebrew (compare Psalm 119).   *b*Literally *a wife of valor,* in the sense of
all forms of excellence

20 She extends her hand to the poor,
Yes, she reaches out her hands to the needy.
21 She is not afraid of snow for her household,
For all her household *is* clothed with scarlet.
22 She makes tapestry for herself;
Her clothing *is* fine linen and purple.
23 Her husband is known in the gates,
When he sits among the elders of the land.
24 She makes linen garments and sells *them,*
And supplies sashes for the merchants.
25 Strength and honor *are* her clothing;
She shall rejoice in time to come.

26 She opens her mouth with wisdom,
And on her tongue *is* the law of kindness.
27 She watches over the ways of her household,
And does not eat the bread of idleness.
28 Her children rise up and call her blessed;
Her husband *also,* and he praises her:
29 "Many daughters have done well,
But you excel them all."
30 Charm *is* deceitful and beauty *is* passing,
But a woman *who* fears the LORD, she shall be praised.
31 Give her of the fruit of her hands,
And let her own works praise her in the gates.

Ecclesiastes

Overview of Ecclesiastes

When Solomon was anointed king over Israel he requested one special gift—the insight of wisdom. God granted his request, as is evident from Solomon's literary contributions to the Bible—Proverbs, Song of Solomon, Ecclesiastes, and two of the psalms. Written by King Solomon about 940 B.C., Ecclesiastes shares the mature wisdom of one who, near the end of his life, looks back to realize that only a life lived for God is a life fulfilled.

Ecclesiastes presents an exciting message of renewed joy and enthusiasm. Its words of wisdom are an excellent guide for a prosperous and abundant life. Ecclesiastes tackles life's tough questions. Throughout its pages God answers that we can only know all things when we know the One who created us in His image. When we know God, then life's secrets are revealed.

Ecclesiastes begins by exploring a multitude of life's experiences, concluding that a person's relationship to God is the ultimate positive value. In Solomon's words, "all is vanity"—all else falls short of the joy and beauty of knowing God. Solomon did appreciate life, but knew that a person must have a positive relationship with God to fully enjoy its blessings. Finally, Solomon relates the need of God to all work and achievement.

> Cast your bread upon the waters,
> For you will find it after many days . . .
> He who observes the wind will not sow,
> And he who regards the clouds will not reap.
> As you do not know what is the way of the wind,
> Or how the bones grow in the womb of her who is
>   with child,
> So you do not know the works of God who makes
>   everything.
> In the morning sow your seed,
> And in the evening do not withhold your hand;
> For you do not know which will prosper,
> Either this or that,
> Or whether both alike will be good.
>   (Eccl. 11:1, 4–6)

Ecclesiastes truly shows God's way to the good life.

Jesus in Ecclesiastes

Ecclesiastes convincingly portrays the emptiness and perplexity of life without a relationship with God. It also reminds us that there are seasons in God, just as there are seasons in each natural year. Whatever your season in Him, know that He is working for your good and that positive results are coming. Each person has eternity in his heart, and only Jesus can provide ultimate satisfaction, joy, and wisdom. Man's highest good is found in the One who offers abundant life.

Keys to Ecclesiastes

Key Word: Vanity. Ecclesiastes reports the results of a diligent quest for purpose, meaning, and satisfaction in human life. The Preacher poignantly sees the emptiness and futility of power, popularity, prestige, and pleasure apart from God. He also sees that life lived with God will be full, fruitful, and blessed. He encourages readers to pursue positive relationships with God.

Key Verses: "Nothing *is* better for a man *than* that he should eat and drink, and *that* his soul should enjoy good in his labor. This also, I saw, was from the hand of God" (2:24).

"Let us hear the conclusion of the whole matter: Fear God and keep His commandments, for this is man's all. For God will bring every work into judgment, including every secret thing, whether good or evil" (12:13, 14).

Key Chapter: Ecclesiastes 12. The Preacher offers a long list of his personal pursuits in life. No amount of activities or possessions has satisfied the craving of his heart. Every earthly prescription for happiness has left the same bitter aftertaste. Chapter 12 resolves the book's questions about the meaning of life with the single conclusion, "Fear God and keep His commandments, for this is man's all" (12:13). This is the secret of a faith-filled life!

1 The words of the Preacher, the son of David, king in Jerusalem.

2 "Vanity[a] of vanities," says the Preacher;
"Vanity of vanities, all *is* vanity."

3 What profit has a man from all his labor
In which he toils under the sun?

4 *One* generation passes away, and *another* generation comes;
But the earth abides forever.

5 The sun also rises, and the sun goes down,
And hastens to the place where it arose.

6 The wind goes toward the south,
And turns around to the north;
The wind whirls about continually,
And comes again on its circuit.

7 All the rivers run into the sea,
Yet the sea *is* not full;

To the place from which the rivers come,
There they return again.

8 All things *are* full of labor;
Man cannot express *it*.
The eye is not satisfied with seeing,
Nor the ear filled with hearing.

9 That which has been *is* what will be,
That which *is* done is what will be done,
And *there is* nothing new under the sun.

10 Is there anything of which it may be said,
"See, this *is* new"?
It has already been in ancient times before us.

11 *There is* no remembrance of former *things*,
Nor will there be any remembrance of *things* that are to come
By *those* who will come after.

1:2 [a]Or *Absurdity, Frustration, Futility, Nonsense;* and so throughout this book

12 I, the Preacher, was king over Israel in Jerusalem. 13 And I set my heart to seek and search out by wisdom concerning all that is done under heaven; this burdensome task God has given to the sons of man, by which they may be exercised. 14 I have seen all the works that are done under the sun; and indeed, all *is* vanity and grasping for the wind.

15   *What is* crooked cannot be
          made straight,
      And what is lacking cannot be
          numbered.

16 I communed with my heart, saying, "Look, I have attained greatness, and have gained more wisdom than all who were before me in Jerusalem. My heart has understood great wisdom and knowledge." 17 And I set my heart to know wisdom and to know madness and folly. I perceived that this also is grasping for the wind.

18   For in much wisdom *is* much
          grief,
      And he who increases
          knowledge increases sorrow.

2 I said in my heart, "Come now, I will test you with mirth; therefore enjoy pleasure"; but surely, this also *was* vanity. 2 I said of laughter— "Madness!"; and of mirth, "What does it accomplish?" 3 I searched in my heart *how* to gratify my flesh with wine, while guiding my heart with wisdom, and how to lay hold on folly, till I might see what *was* good for the sons of men to do under heaven all the days of their lives.

4 I made my works great, I built myself houses, and planted myself vineyards. 5 I made myself gardens and orchards, and I planted all *kinds* of fruit trees in them. 6 I made myself water pools from which to water the growing trees of the grove. 7 I acquired male and female servants, and had servants born in my house. Yes, I had greater possessions of herds and flocks than all who were in Jerusalem before me. 8 I also gathered for myself silver and gold and the special treasures of kings and of the provinces. I acquired male and female singers, the delights of the sons of men, *and* musical instruments[a] of all kinds.

9 So I became great and excelled more than all who were before me in Jerusalem. Also my wisdom remained with me.

10   Whatever my eyes desired I did
          not keep from them.
      I did not withhold my heart
          from any pleasure,
      For my heart rejoiced in all my
          labor;
      And this was my reward from
          all my labor.
11   Then I looked on all the works
          that my hands had done
      And on the labor in which I had
          toiled;
      And indeed all *was* vanity and
          grasping for the wind.
      There was no profit under the
          sun.
12   Then I turned myself to
          consider wisdom and
          madness and folly;
      For what *can* the man *do* who
          succeeds the king?—
      Only what he has already done.
13   Then I saw that wisdom excels
          folly
      As light excels darkness.
14   The wise man's eyes *are* in his
          head,
      But the fool walks in darkness.
      Yet I myself perceived
      That the same event happens
          to them all.

15   So I said in my heart,
      "As it happens to the fool,
      It also happens to me,
      And why was I then more
          wise?"
      Then I said in my heart,
      "This also *is* vanity."
16   For *there is* no more
          remembrance of the wise
          than of the fool forever,
      Since all that now *is* will be
          forgotten in the days to come.
      And how does a wise *man* die?
      As the fool!

17 Therefore I hated life because the work that was done under the sun *was* distressing to me, for all *is* vanity and grasping for the wind. 18 Then I hated all my labor in which I had toiled under the sun, be-

2:8 aExact meaning unknown

Let Go and Let God

In the biblical tradition, a vinedresser is the keeper of the vineyard or the watchman over the field. His responsibilities seem to fall only during spring and harvest when he can be seen pruning the vines, planting seeds for new vines or reaping the crops. The remaining part of the year, the vinedresser will busy himself clearing a neighbor's rocky field or helping to build a new house in the village. The vinedresser could worry about pestilence, droughts, famine, or the scorching hot east winds, but he knows that God controls those events.

Does this mean that in the off season the vinedresser does not care for his field? No. He has learned the secret of patience. He has done his task; now the power of God, through nature, will bring the crops to fruition. The vinedresser realizes the invaluable secret "to let go and let God."

Jesus taught that we should be like the patient vinedresser. We should not be negative, worrying about events and circumstances beyond our control. Jesus encouraged us to understand that God sees the end from the beginning. The vinedresser's trust in The Vinedresser is rewarded at harvest. Jesus described a similar reward in the parable of the soils—"some a hundredfold, some sixty, some thirty" (Matt. 13:8).

May God grant us the wisdom to know when to plant and when to sow; when to hold on and when to let go; when to undertake new tasks and how to let God bring them to completion; and the knowledge to make the right decisions with dignity!

cause I must leave it to the man who will come after me. 19 And who knows whether he will be wise or a fool? Yet he will rule over all my labor in which I toiled and in which I have shown myself wise under the sun. This also *is* vanity. 20 Therefore I turned my heart and despaired of all the labor in which I had toiled under the sun. 21 For there is a man whose labor *is* with wisdom, knowledge, and skill; yet he must leave his heritage to a man who has not labored for it. This also *is* vanity and a great evil. 22 For what has man for all his labor, and for the striving of his heart with which he has toiled under the sun? 23 For all his days *are* sorrowful, and his work burdensome; even in the night his heart takes no rest. This also is vanity.

24 Nothing *is* better for a man *than* that he should eat and drink, and *that* his soul should enjoy good in his labor. This also, I saw, was from the hand of God. 25 For who can eat, or who can have enjoyment, more than I?[a] 26 For *God* gives wisdom and knowledge and joy to a man who *is* good in His sight; but to the sinner He gives the work of gathering and collecting, that he may give to *him who is* good before God. This also *is* vanity and grasping for the wind.

3 To everything *there is* a season,
A time for every purpose under heaven:

2 A time to be born,
And a time to die;
A time to plant,
And a time to pluck *what is* planted;
3 A time to kill,
And a time to heal;
A time to break down,
And a time to build up;
4 A time to weep,
And a time to laugh;
A time to mourn,
And a time to dance;
5 A time to cast away stones,
And a time to gather stones;
A time to embrace,
And a time to refrain from embracing;
6 A time to gain,
And a time to lose;

A time to keep,
And a time to throw away;
7 A time to tear,
And a time to sew;
A time to keep silence,
And a time to speak;
8 A time to love,
And a time to hate;
A time of war,
And a time of peace.

9 What profit has the worker from that in which he labors? 10 I have seen the God-given task with which the sons of men are to be occupied. 11 He has made everything beautiful in its time. Also He has put eternity in their hearts, except that no one can find out the work that God does from beginning to end.

12 I know that nothing *is* better for them than to rejoice, and to do good in their lives, 13 and also that every man should eat and drink and enjoy the good of all his labor—it *is* the gift of God.

14 I know that whatever God does,
It shall be forever.
Nothing can be added to it,
And nothing taken from it.
God does *it,* that men should fear before Him.
15 That which is has already been,
And what is to be has already been;
And God requires an account of what is past.

16 Moreover I saw under the sun:

In the place of judgment,
Wickedness *was* there;
And *in* the place of righteousness,
Iniquity *was* there.

17 I said in my heart,

"God shall judge the righteous and the wicked,
For *there is* a time there for every purpose and for every work."

18 I said in my heart, "Concerning the condition of the sons of men, God tests them, that they may see that they themselves are *like* animals."

2:25 [a]Following Masoretic Text, Targum, and Vulgate; some Hebrew manuscripts, Septuagint, and Syriac read *without Him.*

19 For what happens to the sons of men also happens to animals; one thing befalls them: as one dies, so dies the other. Surely, they all have one breath; man has no advantage over animals, for all is vanity. 20 All go to one place: all are from the dust, and all return to dust. 21 Who knows the spirit of the sons of men, which goes upward, and the spirit of the animal, which goes down to the earth?[a] 22 So I perceived that nothing is better than that a man should rejoice in his own works, for that is his heritage. For who can bring him to see what will happen after him?

4 Then I returned and considered all the oppression that is done under the sun:

> And look! The tears of the oppressed,
> But they have no comforter—
> On the side of their oppressors there is power,
> But they have no comforter.
> 2 Therefore I praised the dead who were already dead,
> More than the living who are still alive.
> 3 Yet, better than both is he who has never existed,
> Who has not seen the evil work that is done under the sun.

4 Again, I saw that for all toil and every skillful work a man is envied by his neighbor. This also is vanity and grasping for the wind.

> 5 The fool folds his hands
> And consumes his own flesh.
> 6 Better a handful with quietness
> Than both hands full, together with toil and grasping for the wind.

7 Then I returned, and I saw vanity under the sun:

> 8 There is one alone, without companion:
> He has neither son nor brother.
> Yet there is no end to all his labors,
> Nor is his eye satisfied with riches.

> But he never asks,
> "For whom do I toil and deprive myself of good?"
> This also is vanity and a grave misfortune.

> 9 Two are better than one,
> Because they have a good reward for their labor.
> 10 For if they fall, one will lift up his companion.
> But woe to him who is alone when he falls,
> For he has no one to help him up.
> 11 Again, if two lie down together, they will keep warm;
> But how can one be warm alone?
> 12 Though one may be overpowered by another, two can withstand him.
> And a threefold cord is not quickly broken.

> 13 Better a poor and wise youth
> Than an old and foolish king who will be admonished no more.
> 14 For he comes out of prison to be king,
> Although he was born poor in his kingdom.
> 15 I saw all the living who walk under the sun;
> They were with the second youth who stands in his place.
> 16 There was no end of all the people over whom he was made king;
> Yet those who come afterward will not rejoice in him.
> Surely this also is vanity and grasping for the wind.

5 Walk prudently when you go to the house of God; and draw near to hear rather than to give the sacrifice of fools, for they do not know that they do evil.

> 2 Do not be rash with your mouth,
> And let not your heart utter anything hastily before God.
> For God is in heaven, and you on earth;

3:21 [a]Septuagint, Syriac, Targum, and Vulgate read Who knows whether the spirit . . . goes upward, and whether . . . goes downward to the earth?

Therefore let your words be
few.

3 For a dream comes through
  much activity,
  And a fool's voice *is known* by
  his many words.

4 When you make a vow to God,
  do not delay to pay it;
  For *He has* no pleasure in fools.
  Pay what you have vowed—
5 Better not to vow than to vow
  and not pay.

6 Do not let your mouth cause your flesh to sin, nor say before the messenger *of God* that it *was* an error. Why should God be angry at your excuse[a] and destroy the work of your hands? 7 For in the multitude of dreams and many words *there is* also vanity. But fear God.

8 If you see the oppression of the poor, and the violent perversion of justice and righteousness in a province, do not marvel at the matter; for high official watches over high official, and higher officials *are* over them.

9 Moreover the profit of the land is for all; *even* the king is served from the field.

10 He who loves silver will not be
   satisfied with silver;
   Nor he who loves abundance,
   with increase.
   This also *is* vanity.

11 When goods increase,
   They increase who eat them;
   So what profit have the owners
   Except to see *them* with their
   eyes?

12 The sleep of a laboring man *is*
   sweet,
   Whether he eats little or much;
   But the abundance of the rich
   will not permit him to sleep.

13 There is a severe evil *which* I
   have seen under the sun:
   Riches kept for their owner to
   his hurt.
14 But those riches perish through
   misfortune;
   When he begets a son, *there is*
   nothing in his hand.

15 As he came from his mother's
   womb, naked shall he return,
   To go as he came;
   And he shall take nothing from
   his labor
   Which he may carry away in
   his hand.

16 And this also *is* a severe evil—
   Just exactly as he came, so
   shall he go.
   And what profit has he who has
   labored for the wind?
17 All his days he also eats in
   darkness,
   And *he has* much sorrow and
   sickness and anger.

18 Here is what I have seen: *It is* good and fitting *for one* to eat and drink, and to enjoy the good of all his labor in which he toils under the sun all the days of his life which God gives him; for it *is* his heritage. 19 As for every man to whom God has given riches and wealth, and given him power to eat of it, to receive his heritage and rejoice in his labor—this *is* the gift of God. 20 For he will not dwell unduly on the days of his life, because God keeps *him* busy with the joy of his heart.

6 There is an evil which I have seen under the sun, and it *is* common among men: 2 A man to whom God has given riches and wealth and honor, so that he lacks nothing for himself of all he desires; yet God does not give him power to eat of it, but a foreigner consumes it. This *is* vanity, and it *is* an evil affliction.

3 If a man begets a hundred *children* and lives many years, so that the days of his years are many, but his soul is not satisfied with goodness, or indeed he has no burial, I say *that* a stillborn child *is* better than he— 4 for it comes in vanity and departs in darkness, and its name is covered with darkness. 5 Though it has not seen the sun or known *anything*, this has more rest than that man, 6 even if he lives a thousand years twice—but has not seen goodness. Do not all go to one place?

7 All the labor of man *is* for his
  mouth,
  And yet the soul is not satisfied.

5:6 [a]Literally *voice*

8 For what more has the wise
    man than the fool?
  What does the poor man have,
  Who knows *how* to walk before
    the living?
9 Better *is* the sight of the eyes
    than the wandering of desire.
  This also *is* vanity and grasping
    for the wind.

10 Whatever one is, he has been
    named already,
  For it is known that he *is* man;
  And he cannot contend with
    Him who is mightier than he.
11 Since there are many things
    that increase vanity,
  How *is* man the better?

12 For who knows what *is* good for
man in life, all the days of his vain
life which he passes like a shadow?
Who can tell a man what will happen
after him under the sun?

7 A good name *is* better than
    precious ointment,
  And the day of death than the
    day of one's birth;
2 Better to go to the house of
    mourning
  Than to go to the house of
    feasting,
  For that *is* the end of all men;
  And the living will take *it* to
    heart.
3 Sorrow *is* better than laughter,
  For by a sad countenance the
    heart is made better.
4 The heart of the wise *is* in the
    house of mourning,
  But the heart of fools *is* in the
    house of mirth.
5 *It is* better to hear the rebuke
    of the wise
  Than for a man to hear the
    song of fools.
6 For like the crackling of thorns
    under a pot,
  So *is* the laughter of the fool.
  This also is vanity.
7 Surely oppression destroys a
    wise *man's* reason,
  And a bribe debases the heart.

8 The end of a thing *is* better than
    its beginning;
  The patient in spirit *is* better
    than the proud in spirit.
9 Do not hasten in your spirit to
    be angry,

For anger rests in the bosom of
    fools.
10 Do not say,
  "Why were the former days
    better than these?"
  For you do not inquire wisely
    concerning this.
11 Wisdom *is* good with an
    inheritance,
  And profitable to those who see
    the sun.
12 For wisdom *is* a defense *as*
    money *is* a defense,
  But the excellence of
    knowledge *is that* wisdom
    gives life to those who have
    it.

13 Consider the work of God;
  For who can make straight
    what He has made crooked?
14 In the day of prosperity be
    joyful,
  But in the day of adversity
    consider:
  Surely God has appointed the
    one as well as the other,
  So that man can find out
    nothing *that will come* after
    him.

15 I have seen everything in my
days of vanity:

  There is a just *man* who
    perishes in his righteousness,
  And there is a wicked *man* who
    prolongs *life* in his
    wickedness.

16 Do not be overly righteous,
  Nor be overly wise:
  Why should you destroy
    yourself?
17 Do not be overly wicked,
  Nor be foolish:
  Why should you die before
    your time?
18 *It is* good that you grasp this,
  And also not remove your hand
    from the other;
  For he who fears God will
    escape them all.

19 Wisdom strengthens the wise
  More than ten rulers of the city.

20 For *there is* not a just man on
    earth who does good
  And does not sin.

Seasons of Faith

     Doesn't the walk of faith appear to be inflicted with contradictions or paradoxes? Doesn't it seem like a juggling act in a possibility-thinking game? Then remember this: Faith is an art—not a science. Faith advances for a season, then retreats the next. You are ambitious for a season, then relaxed; aggressive, then passive; giving, then taking. Consider Solomon's wise words in Ecclesiastes 8:5: "He who keeps [the king's] command will experience nothing harmful; and a wise man's heart discerns both time and judgment."

     As positive and negative wires generate the power of electricity, so in faith, negatives are used with positives to create mountain-moving energy for the believer.

     Faith is pacing your progress. The challenges come in knowing: when to push forward, when to hold back; when to dig in; when to yield; when to hold on, when to let go; when to plan alone, when to form a partnership.

     Faith paces your progress through life with a rhythmic steadiness regulated by the all-wise Timekeeper, God Almighty. When you walk the walk of faith, you are assured of the divine guidance to make the right move, in the right way, at the right time.

     When you kneel before the throne of the almighty God in respectful humility and cry out, "I need the wisdom of heaven to walk this walk of faith," you reach the level of faith where contradictions become constructive; paradoxes become truth.

     So keep trusting God to give you His sense of timing. Pace yourself. Now you wait. Now you move. Now you race! Now you rest. Now you leap! Now you walk slowly. Possibility thinkers don't quit--they change their pace to win the race.

     Thank God for the exhilaration we experience in the ebb and flow of faith's pilgrimage.

21 Also do not take to heart
    everything people say,
    Lest you hear your servant
    cursing you.
22 For many times, also, your own
    heart has known
    That even you have cursed
    others.

23 All this I have proved by
    wisdom.
    I said, "I will be wise";
    But it *was* far from me.
24 As for that which is far off and
    exceedingly deep,
    Who can find it out?
25 I applied my heart to know,
    To search and seek out wisdom
    and the reason *of things,*
    To know the wickedness of
    folly,
    Even of foolishness *and*
    madness.
26 And I find more bitter than
    death
    The woman whose heart *is*
    snares and nets,
    Whose hands *are* fetters.
    He who pleases God shall
    escape from her,
    But the sinner shall be trapped
    by her.

27 "Here is what I have found,"
    says the Preacher,
    "*Adding* one thing to the other
    to find out the reason,
28 Which my soul still seeks but I
    cannot find:
    One man among a thousand I
    have found,
    But a woman among all these
    I have not found.
29 Truly, this only I have found:
    That God made man upright,
    But they have sought out many
    schemes."

8 Who *is* like a wise *man?*
    And who knows the
    interpretation of a thing?
    A man's wisdom makes his
    face shine,
    And the sternness of his face
    is changed.

2 I *say,* "Keep the king's commandment for the sake of your oath to
God. 3 Do not be hasty to go from
his presence. Do not take your stand

for an evil thing, for he does whatever pleases him."

4 Where the word of a king *is,*
    there is power;
    And who may say to him,
    "What are you doing?"
5 He who keeps his command
    will experience nothing
    harmful;
    And a wise man's heart
    discerns both time and
    judgment,
6 Because for every matter there
    is a time and judgment,
    Though the misery of man
    increases greatly.
7 For he does not know what will
    happen;
    So who can tell him when it will
    occur?
8 No one has power over the
    spirit to retain the spirit,
    And no one has power in the
    day of death.
    There is no release from that
    war,
    And wickedness will not
    deliver those who are given
    to it.

9 All this I have seen, and applied
my heart to every work that is done
under the sun: *There is* a time in
which one man rules over another to
his own hurt.
10 Then I saw the wicked buried,
who had come and gone from the
place of holiness, and they were forgotten[a] in the city where they had so
done. This also *is* vanity. 11 Because
the sentence against an evil work is
not executed speedily, therefore the
heart of the sons of men is fully set
in them to do evil. 12 Though a sinner
does evil a hundred *times,* and his
days are prolonged, yet I surely know
that it will be well with those who
fear God, who fear before Him.
13 But it will not be well with the
wicked; nor will he prolong *his* days,
which are as a shadow, because he
does not fear before God.
14 There is a vanity which occurs
on earth, that there are just *men* to
whom it happens according to the
work of the wicked; again, there are
wicked *men* to whom it happens according to the work of the righteous.
I said that this also *is* vanity.

8:10 [a]Some Hebrew manuscripts, Septuagint, and Vulgate read *praised.*

Reach for the Stars

Once you've achieved success, it takes a lot of faith to believe you can upstage your own accomplishment!

It takes faith for a C student to believe that he can earn B's or A's!

It takes faith for a straight-A student to believe that she can do an A+ job in the career world.

Whether you are a low, medium, or high achiever, it takes a lot of faith to believe that you can do a lot better!

Striving for excellence is an act of faith. God is not honored or glorified by mediocrity. In His Word we read: "Whatever your hand finds to do, do *it* with your might; for *there is* no work or device or knowledge or wisdom in the grave where you are going" (Eccl. 9:10).

How can you motivate yourself or others to strive for excellence? If striving for excellence *is* faith, then today's prescription is aimed at building up your confidence so that you will not fail!

What excellent, superlative, outstanding goals would you go for if you knew you'd make it?

The strong assurance of a genuine possibility of success remains a major motivating force for excellence.

Motivate yourself today by voicing these assurances:

I can do it!

I can become a champion if I set my heart on it!

I feel obligated to perform at my best before the Almighty! Yes, that's what drives me to excellence.

An attitude for opportunity stirs me to noble effort.

Be thankful you're alive! As an expression of your gratitude, give the Lord the best that you have. In so doing, your work will be your worship! Your outstanding effort will be your faith in action, praising God for His goodness.

15 So I commended enjoyment, because a man has nothing better under the sun than to eat, drink, and be merry; for this will remain with him in his labor *all* the days of his life which God gives him under the sun.

16 When I applied my heart to know wisdom and to see the business that is done on earth, even though one sees no sleep day or night, 17 then I saw all the work of God, that a man cannot find out the work that is done under the sun. For though a man labors to discover *it,* yet he will not find *it;* moreover, though a wise *man* attempts to know *it,* he will not be able to find *it.*

9 For I considered all this in my heart, so that I could declare it all: that the righteous and the wise and their works *are* in the hand of God. People know neither love nor hatred *by* anything *they see* before them. 2 All things *come* alike to all:

> One event *happens* to the
>   righteous and the wicked;
> To the good,^a the clean, and the
>   unclean;
> To him who sacrifices and him
>   who does not sacrifice.
> As is the good, so *is* the sinner;
> He who takes an oath as *he*
>   who fears an oath.

3 This *is* an evil in all that is done under the sun: that one thing *happens* to all. Truly the hearts of the sons of men are full of evil; madness *is* in their hearts while they live, and after that *they go* to the dead. 4 But for him who is joined to all the living there is hope, for a living dog is better than a dead lion.

> 5   For the living know that they
>   will die;
>   But the dead know nothing,
>   And they have no more reward,
>   For the memory of them is
>   forgotten.
> 6   Also their love, their hatred,
>   and their envy have now
>   perished;
>   Nevermore will they have a
>   share
>   In anything done under the
>   sun.

> 7   Go, eat your bread with joy,
>   And drink your wine with a
>   merry heart;
>   For God has already accepted
>   your works.
> 8   Let your garments always be
>   white,
>   And let your head lack no oil.

9 Live joyfully with the wife whom you love all the days of your vain life which He has given you under the sun, all your days of vanity; for that *is* your portion in life, and in the labor which you perform under the sun.

10 Whatever your hand finds to do, do *it* with your might; for *there is* no work or device or knowledge or wisdom in the grave where you are going.

11 I returned and saw under the sun that—

> The race *is* not to the swift,
> Nor the battle to the strong,
> Nor bread to the wise,
> Nor riches to men of
>   understanding,
> Nor favor to men of skill;
> But time and chance happen to
>   them all.
> 12   For man also does not know his
>   time:
>   Like fish taken in a cruel net,
>   Like birds caught in a snare,
>   So the sons of men *are* snared
>   in an evil time,
>   When it falls suddenly upon
>   them.

13 This wisdom I have also seen under the sun, and it *seemed* great to me: 14 *There was* a little city with few men in it; and a great king came against it, besieged it, and built great snares^a around it. 15 Now there was found in it a poor wise man, and he by his wisdom delivered the city. Yet no one remembered that same poor man.

16 Then I said:

> "Wisdom *is* better than strength.
> Nevertheless the poor man's
>   wisdom *is* despised,
> And his words are not heard.
> 17   Words of the wise, *spoken*
>   quietly, *should be* heard

9:2 ^aSeptuagint, Syriac, and Vulgate read *good and bad.* bulwarks.   9:14 ^aSeptuagint, Syriac, and Vulgate read

Rather than the shout of a ruler
of fools.

18 Wisdom *is* better than weapons
of war;
But one sinner destroys much
good."

10 Dead flies putrefy[a] the
perfumer's ointment,
And cause it to give off a foul
odor;
So does a little folly to one
respected for wisdom *and*
honor.

2 A wise man's heart *is* at his
right hand,
But a fool's heart at his left.

3 Even when a fool walks along
the way,
He lacks wisdom,
And he shows everyone *that* he
is a fool.

4 If the spirit of the ruler rises
against you,
Do not leave your post;
For conciliation pacifies great
offenses.

5 There is an evil I have seen
under the sun,
As an error proceeding from
the ruler:

6 Folly is set in great dignity,
While the rich sit in a lowly
place.

7 I have seen servants on horses,
While princes walk on the
ground like servants.

8 He who digs a pit will fall into
it,
And whoever breaks through a
wall will be bitten by a
serpent.

9 He who quarries stones may be
hurt by them,
And he who splits wood may
be endangered by it.

10 If the ax is dull,
And one does not sharpen the
edge,
Then he must use more
strength;
But wisdom brings success.

11 A serpent may bite when *it is*
not charmed;
The babbler is no different.

12 The words of a wise man's
mouth *are* gracious,

But the lips of a fool shall
swallow him up;

13 The words of his mouth begin
with foolishness,
And the end of his talk *is* raving
madness.

14 A fool also multiplies words.
No man knows what is to be;
Who can tell him what will be
after him?

15 The labor of fools wearies
them,
For they do not even know how
to go to the city!

16 Woe to you, O land, when your
king *is* a child,
And your princes feast in the
morning!

17 Blessed *are* you, O land, when
your king *is* the son of
nobles,
And your princes feast at the
proper time—
For strength and not for
drunkenness!

18 Because of laziness the
building decays,
And through idleness of hands
the house leaks.

19 A feast is made for laughter,
And wine makes merry;
But money answers everything.

20 Do not curse the king, even in
your thought;
Do not curse the rich, even in
your bedroom;
For a bird of the air may carry
your voice,
And a bird in flight may tell the
matter.

11 Cast your bread upon the
waters,
For you will find it after many
days.

2 Give a serving to seven, and
also to eight,
For you do not know what evil
will be on the earth.

3 If the clouds are full of rain,
They empty *themselves* upon
the earth;
And if a tree falls to the south
or the north,
In the place where the tree
falls, there it shall lie.

10:1 [a]Targum and Vulgate omit *putrefy*.

Sow the Seed of Faith

Throughout the Old and New Testaments there are references to the land—specifically to tilling the soil and planting the seed. For example, in Ecclesiastes 11:6 we read: "In the morning sow your seed, and in the evening do not withhold your hand; for you do not know which will prosper, either this or that, or whether both alike *will be* good."

Ask any farmer what faith is and he will tell you it is planting seeds. In an act of faith a farmer throws seed away in the hope that they will come back multiplied!

Most of us today are not farmers of the field; but we can become farmers of ideas when, as possibility thinkers, we treat ideas as seeds. *Any fool can count the seeds in an apple, but only God can count the apples in one seed.*

Take an idea and treat it like a newborn child. Feed it, nourish it, protect it, and clothe it, for that seed might sprout and become a full-fledged project for the good of our human family and for the glory of God.

The farmer runs the risk that the seed may rot in the soil. We run the risk that our ideas may never materialize as we hoped.

But the person who is unconditionally committed to a lifetime pilgrimage on the path of faith will inevitably come out far ahead of the person who chooses to surrender to doubt and despair.

Have an idea? Do you believe it is from God?

Plant it!

Nothing happens until you do something to start to make something happen!

Plant the seed of faith today in your home, your place of work, your community. Speak a positive word—only a sentence—about your faith in God to someone.

4 He who observes the wind will
  not sow,
  And he who regards the clouds
  will not reap.

5 As you do not know what *is the*
  way of the wind,[a]
  Or how the bones *grow* in the
  womb of her who is with
  child,
  So you do not know the works
  of God who makes
  everything.

6 In the morning sow your seed,
  And in the evening do not
  withhold your hand;
  For you do not know which will
  prosper,
  Either this or that,
  Or whether both alike *will be*
  good.

7 Truly the light is sweet,
  And *it is* pleasant for the eyes
  to behold the sun;

8 But if a man lives many years
  And rejoices in them all,
  Yet let him remember the days
  of darkness,
  For they will be many.
  All that is coming *is* vanity.

9 Rejoice, O young man, in your
  youth,
  And let your heart cheer you
  in the days of your youth;
  Walk in the ways of your heart,
  And in the sight of your eyes;
  But know that for all these
  God will bring you into
  judgment.

10 Therefore remove sorrow from
   your heart,
   And put away evil from your
   flesh,
   For childhood and youth *are*
   vanity.

12 Remember now your Creator
     in the days of your youth,
   Before the difficult days come,
   And the years draw near when
   you say,
   "I have no pleasure in them":

2 While the sun and the light,
  The moon and the stars,
  Are not darkened,
  And the clouds do not return
  after the rain;

3 In the day when the keepers of
  the house tremble,
  And the strong men bow
  down;
  When the grinders cease
  because they are few,
  And those that look through
  the windows grow dim;

4 When the doors are shut in the
  streets,
  And the sound of grinding is
  low;
  When one rises up at the sound
  of a bird,
  And all the daughters of music
  are brought low.

5 Also they are afraid of
  height,
  And of terrors in the way;
  When the almond tree
  blossoms,
  The grasshopper is a burden,
  And desire fails.
  For man goes to his eternal
  home,
  And the mourners go about the
  streets.

6 *Remember your Creator* before
  the silver cord is loosed,[a]
  Or the golden bowl is broken,
  Or the pitcher shattered at the
  fountain,
  Or the wheel broken at the
  well.

7 Then the dust will return to the
  earth as it was,
  And the spirit will return to
  God who gave it.

8 "Vanity of vanities," says the
  Preacher,
  "All *is* vanity."

9 And moreover, because the
Preacher was wise, he still taught the
people knowledge; yes, he pondered
and sought out *and* set in order many
proverbs. 10 The Preacher sought to
find acceptable words; and *what was*
written *was* upright—words of truth.
11 The words of the wise are like
goads, and the words of scholars[a] are
like well-driven nails, given by one
Shepherd. 12 And further, my son, be
admonished by these. Of making
many books *there is* no end, and
much study *is* wearisome to the flesh.

11:5 [a]Or *spirit*   12:6 [a]Following Qere and Targum; Kethib reads *removed*; Septuagint and Vulgate read
broken.   12:11 [a]Literally *masters of assemblies*

13 Let us hear the conclusion of the whole matter:

> Fear God and keep His commandments,

For this is man's all.
14 For God will bring every work into judgment,
Including every secret thing,
Whether good or evil.

Song of Solomon

Overview of Song of Solomon

The Song of Solomon is a glorious celebration of the love between a man and a woman. Written by King Solomon about 960 B.C., this book is the correspondence between himself and a young shepherd girl.

In a beautiful courting dialogue, love's greatest attributes are highlighted. Although physical beauty is a powerful attractive force, love's deeper qualities are also extolled.

There is no lack of words to describe their love. Their dialogue overflows with references to the land and all its glory in springtime. Like the spring, love is a new birth, a finding, a uniting, a bursting forth after the captivity of a cold lonely winter.

At first glance, it may seem awkward to compare a lover to vineyards, a watchtower, lamb's wool, and pomegranates. But on closer examination, these analogies reveal the mind-set of the ancient lovers. Love's value is measured in function as well as appearance. True love is giving, unselfish, supportive, honest, and unconditional. By calling his beloved the rose of Sharon, Solomon brings to mind the symbol of God's blessing which was represented by the blossoming of this flower.

In the Song of Solomon, love is depicted in all its beauty and glory:

For lo, the winter is past,
The rain is over and gone.
The flowers appear on the earth;
The time of singing has come,
And the voice of the turtledove
Is heard in our land.

(Song 2:11, 12)

Jesus in Song of Solomon

In the Old Testament, Israel is regarded as the bride of Yahweh. In the New Testament, the Church is seen as the bride of Christ. The Song of Solomon illustrates the former and anticipates the latter. It shows us Jesus' tender thoughts and great love for His people.

Keys to Song of Solomon

Key Word: Love in Marriage. Interpreted as the poetic record of Solomon's actual romance with a Shulamite woman, the Song is a bold and positive endorsement by God of marital love in all its physical and emotional beauty. This historical interpretation does not mean that the book has no spiritual illustrations and applications. It certainly illustrates God's love for His covenant people, Israel, and anticipates Jesus' love for His bride, the Church.

Key Verses: "I *am* my beloved's, and his desire *is* toward me" (7:10).

"Many waters cannot quench love, nor can the floods drown it. If a man would give for love all the wealth of his house, it would be utterly despised" (8:7).

Key Chapter: Since the whole book is actually one unit, there is no key chapter; rather, all eight chapters beautifully depict the love of a married couple, and symbolically, Jesus' love for us.

1 The song of songs, which *is* Solomon's.

2 Let him kiss me with the kisses
  of his mouth—
For your[a] love *is* better than
  wine.
3 Because of the fragrance of
  your good ointments,
Your name *is* ointment poured
  forth;
Therefore the virgins love you.
4 Draw me away!

We will run after you.[a]

The king has brought me into
  his chambers.

We will be glad and rejoice in
  you.[b]

We will remember your[c] love
  more than wine.

Rightly do they love you.[d]

5 I *am* dark, but lovely,
  O daughters of Jerusalem,
Like the tents of Kedar,
Like the curtains of Solomon.
6 Do not look upon me, because
  I *am* dark,
Because the sun has tanned me.
My mother's sons were angry
  with me;
They made me the keeper of
  the vineyards,
But my own vineyard I have
  not kept.

7 Tell me, O you whom I love,
Where you feed *your flock*,
Where you make *it* rest at
  noon.
For why should I be as one who
  veils herself[a]
By the flocks of your
  companions?

8 If you do not know, O fairest
  among women,
Follow in the footsteps of the
  flock,
And feed your little goats
Beside the shepherds' tents.
9 I have compared you, my love,
To my filly among Pharaoh's
  chariots.
10 Your cheeks are lovely with
  ornaments,
Your neck with chains *of gold*.

11 We will make you[a] ornaments
  of gold
With studs of silver.

12 While the king *is* at his table,
My spikenard sends forth its
  fragrance.
13 A bundle of myrrh *is* my
  beloved to me,
That lies all night between my
  breasts.
14 My beloved *is* to me a cluster
  of henna *blooms*
In the vineyards of En Gedi.

15 Behold, you *are* fair, my love!
Behold, you *are* fair!
You *have* dove's eyes.

---

16 Behold, you *are* handsome, my
beloved!
Yes, pleasant!
Also our bed *is* green.
17 The beams of our houses *are*
cedar,
And our rafters of fir.

2 I *am* the rose of Sharon,
And the lily of the valleys.

2 Like a lily among thorns,
So is my love among the
daughters.

3 Like an apple tree among the
trees of the woods,
So *is* my beloved among the
sons.
I sat down in his shade with
great delight,
And his fruit *was* sweet to my
taste.

4 He brought me to the
banqueting house,
And his banner over me *was*
love.
5 Sustain me with cakes of
raisins,
Refresh me with apples,
For I *am* lovesick.

6 His left hand *is* under my
head,
And his right hand embraces
me.
7 I charge you, O daughters of
Jerusalem,
By the gazelles or by the does
of the field,
Do not stir up nor awaken love
Until it pleases.

8 The voice of my beloved!
Behold, he comes
Leaping upon the mountains,
Skipping upon the hills.
9 My beloved is like a gazelle or
a young stag.
Behold, he stands behind our
wall;
He is looking through the
windows,
Gazing through the lattice.

10 My beloved spoke, and said to
me:
"Rise up, my love, my fair one,
And come away.

11 For lo, the winter is past,
The rain is over *and* gone.
12 The flowers appear on the
earth;
The time of singing has come,
And the voice of the turtledove
Is heard in our land.
13 The fig tree puts forth her green
figs,
And the vines *with* the tender
grapes
Give a good smell.
Rise up, my love, my fair one,
And come away!

14 "O my dove, in the clefts of the
rock,
In the secret *places* of the cliff,
Let me see your face,
Let me hear your voice;
For your voice *is* sweet,
And your face *is* lovely."

15 Catch us the foxes,
The little foxes that spoil the
vines,
For our vines *have* tender
grapes.

16 My beloved *is* mine, and I *am*
his.
He feeds *his flock* among the
lilies.

17 Until the day breaks
And the shadows flee away,
Turn, my beloved,
And be like a gazelle
Or a young stag
Upon the mountains of Bether.[a]

3 By night on my bed I sought
the one I love;
I sought him, but I did not find
him.
2 "I will rise now," *I said,*
"And go about the city;
In the streets and in the squares
I will seek the one I love."
I sought him, but I did not find
him.
3 The watchmen who go about
the city found me;
I said,
"Have you seen the one I love?"
4 Scarcely had I passed by them,
When I found the one I love.
I held him and would not let
him go,

2:17 [a]Literally *Separation*

Until I had brought him to the
house of my mother,
And into the chamber of her
who conceived me.

5 I charge you, O daughters of
Jerusalem,
By the gazelles or by the does
of the field,
Do not stir up nor awaken love
Until it pleases.

6 Who *is* this coming out of the
wilderness
Like pillars of smoke,
Perfumed with myrrh and
frankincense,
With all the merchant's
fragrant powders?

7 Behold, it *is* Solomon's couch,
With sixty valiant men around
it,
Of the valiant of Israel.

8 They all hold swords,
Being expert in war.
Every man *has* his sword on his
thigh
Because of fear in the night.

9 Of the wood of Lebanon
Solomon the King
Made himself a palanquin:*a*

10 He made its pillars *of* silver,
Its support *of* gold,
Its seat *of* purple,
Its interior paved *with* love
By the daughters of Jerusalem.

11 Go forth, O daughters of Zion,
And see King Solomon with the
crown
With which his mother
crowned him
On the day of his wedding,
The day of the gladness of his
heart.

4 Behold, you *are* fair, my love!
Behold, you *are* fair!
You *have* dove's eyes behind
your veil.
Your hair *is* like a flock of
goats,
Going down from Mount
Gilead.

2 Your teeth *are* like a flock of
shorn *sheep*
Which have come up from the
washing,
Every one of which bears
twins,

And none *is* barren among
them.

3 Your lips *are* like a strand of
scarlet,
And your mouth is lovely.
Your temples behind your veil
Are like a piece of
pomegranate.

4 Your neck *is* like the tower of
David,
Built for an armory,
On which hang a thousand
bucklers,
All shields of mighty men.

5 Your two breasts *are* like two
fawns,
Twins of a gazelle,
Which feed among the lilies.

6 Until the day breaks
And the shadows flee away,
I will go my way to the
mountain of myrrh
And to the hill of frankincense.

7 You *are* all fair, my love,
And *there is* no spot in you.

8 Come with me from Lebanon,
my spouse,
With me from Lebanon.
Look from the top of Amana,
From the top of Senir and
Hermon,
From the lions' dens,
From the mountains of the
leopards.

9 You have ravished my heart,
My sister, *my* spouse;
You have ravished my heart
With one *look* of your eyes,
With one *link* of your necklace.

10 How fair is your love,
My sister, *my* spouse!
How much better than wine is
your love,
And the scent of your perfumes
Than all spices!

11 Your lips, O *my* spouse,
Drip as the honeycomb;
Honey and milk *are* under your
tongue;
And the fragrance of your
garments
Is like the fragrance of
Lebanon.

12 A garden enclosed
Is my sister, *my* spouse,

3:9 *a*A portable enclosed chair

A spring shut up,
A fountain sealed.
13 Your plants *are* an orchard of
    pomegranates
With pleasant fruits,
Fragrant henna with
    spikenard,
14 Spikenard and saffron,
Calamus and cinnamon,
With all trees of frankincense,
Myrrh and aloes,
With all the chief spices—
15 A fountain of gardens,
A well of living waters,
And streams from Lebanon.

16 Awake, O north *wind,*
And come, O south!
Blow upon my garden,
That its spices may flow out.
Let my beloved come to his
    garden
And eat its pleasant fruits.

5 I have come to my garden, my
    sister, *my* spouse;
I have gathered my myrrh with
    my spice;
I have eaten my honeycomb
    with my honey;
I have drunk my wine with my
    milk.

Eat, O friends!
Drink, yes, drink deeply,
O beloved ones!

2 I sleep, but my heart is
    awake;
It is the voice of my beloved!
He knocks, *saying,*
"Open for me, my sister, my
    love,
My dove, my perfect one;
For my head is covered with
    dew,
My locks with the drops of the
    night."

3 I have taken off my robe;
How can I put it on *again?*
I have washed my feet;
How can I defile them?
4 My beloved put his hand
By the latch *of the door,*
And my heart yearned for
    him.
5 I arose to open for my beloved,
And my hands dripped *with*
    myrrh,
My fingers with liquid myrrh,
On the handles of the lock.

6 I opened for my beloved,
But my beloved had turned
    away *and* was gone.
My heart leaped up when he
    spoke.
I sought him, but I could not
    find him;
I called him, but he gave me no
    answer.
7 The watchmen who went about
    the city found me.
They struck me, they wounded
    me;
The keepers of the walls
Took my veil away from me.
8 I charge you, O daughters of
    Jerusalem,
If you find my beloved,
That you tell him I *am* lovesick!

9 What *is* your beloved
More than *another* beloved,
O fairest among women?
What *is* your beloved
More than *another* beloved,
That you so charge us?

10 My beloved *is* white and ruddy,
Chief among ten thousand.
11 His head *is like* the finest
    gold;
His locks *are* wavy,
And black as a raven.
12 His eyes *are* like doves
By the rivers of waters,
Washed with milk,
And fitly set.
13 His cheeks *are* like a bed of
    spices,
Banks of scented herbs.
His lips *are* lilies,
Dripping liquid myrrh.

14 His hands *are* rods of gold
Set with beryl.
His body *is* carved ivory
Inlaid *with* sapphires.
15 His legs *are* pillars of marble
Set on bases of fine gold.
His countenance *is* like
    Lebanon,
Excellent as the cedars.
16 His mouth *is* most sweet,
Yes, he *is* altogether lovely.
This *is* my beloved,
And this *is* my friend,
O daughters of Jerusalem!

6 Where has your beloved gone,
O fairest among women?
Where has your beloved turned
    aside,

That we may seek him with
you?

2 My beloved has gone to his
garden,
To the beds of spices,
To feed *his flock* in the gardens,
And to gather lilies.
3 I *am* my beloved's,
And my beloved *is* mine.
He feeds *his flock* among the
lilies.

4 O my love, you *are as* beautiful
as Tirzah,
Lovely as Jerusalem,
Awesome as *an army* with
banners!
5 Turn your eyes away from me,
For they have overcome me.
Your hair *is* like a flock of goats
Going down from Gilead.
6 Your teeth *are* like a flock of
sheep
Which have come up from the
washing;
Every one bears twins,
And none *is* barren among
them.
7 Like a piece of pomegranate
Are your temples behind your
veil.

8 There are sixty queens
And eighty concubines,
And virgins without number.
9 My dove, my perfect one,
Is the only one,
The only one of her mother,
The favorite of the one who
bore her.
The daughters saw her
And called her blessed,
The queens and the
concubines,
And they praised her.

10 Who is she who looks forth as
the morning,
Fair as the moon,
Clear as the sun,
Awesome as *an army* with
banners?

11 I went down to the garden of
nuts
To see the verdure of the valley,
To see whether the vine had
budded

And the pomegranates had
bloomed.
12 Before I was even aware,
My soul had made me
As the chariots of my noble
people.*a*

13 Return, return, O Shulamite;
Return, return, that we may
look upon you!

What would you see in the
Shulamite—
As it were, the dance of the two
camps?*a*

7 How beautiful are your feet in
sandals,
O prince's daughter!
The curves of your thighs *are*
like jewels,
The work of the hands of a
skillful workman.
2 Your navel *is* a rounded
goblet;
It lacks no blended beverage.
Your waist *is* a heap of wheat
Set about with lilies.
3 Your two breasts *are* like two
fawns,
Twins of a gazelle.
4 Your neck *is* like an ivory
tower,
Your eyes *like* the pools in
Heshbon
By the gate of Bath Rabbim.
Your nose *is* like the tower of
Lebanon
Which looks toward
Damascus.
5 Your head *crowns* you like
Mount Carmel,
And the hair of your head *is*
like purple;
A king *is* held captive by *your*
tresses.

6 How fair and how pleasant you
are,
O love, with your delights!
7 This stature of yours is like a
palm tree,
And your breasts *like* its
clusters.
8 I said, "I will go up to the palm
tree,
I will take hold of its branches."
Let now your breasts be like
clusters of the vine,

The fragrance of your breath
like apples,
9 And the roof of your mouth like
the best wine.

The wine goes *down* smoothly
for my beloved,
Moving gently the lips of
sleepers.[a]
10 I *am* my beloved's,
And his desire *is* toward me.

11 Come, my beloved,
Let us go forth to the field;
Let us lodge in the villages.
12 Let us get up early to the
vineyards;
Let us see if the vine has
budded,
Whether the grape blossoms
are open,
And the pomegranates are in
bloom.
There I will give you my love.
13 The mandrakes give off a
fragrance,
And at our gates *are* pleasant
fruits,
All manner, new and old,
Which I have laid up for you,
my beloved.

8 Oh, that you were like my
brother,
Who nursed at my mother's
breasts!
If I should find you outside,
I would kiss you;
I would not be despised.
2 I would lead you *and* bring you
Into the house of my mother,
She *who* used to instruct me.
I would cause you to drink of
spiced wine,
Of the juice of my
pomegranate.

3 His left hand *is* under my head,
And his right hand embraces
me.
4 I charge you, O daughters of
Jerusalem,
Do not stir up nor awaken love
Until it pleases.

5 Who *is* this coming up from the
wilderness,
Leaning upon her beloved?
I awakened you under the
apple tree.

There your mother brought you
forth;
There she *who* bore you
brought *you* forth.

6 Set me as a seal upon your
heart,
As a seal upon your arm;
For love *is as* strong as death,
Jealousy *as* cruel as the grave;[a]
Its flames *are* flames of fire,
A most vehement[b] flame.

7 Many waters cannot quench
love,
Nor can the floods drown it.
If a man would give for love
All the wealth of his house,
It would be utterly despised.

8 We have a little sister,
And she has no breasts.
What shall we do for our sister
In the day when she is spoken
for?
9 If she *is* a wall,
We will build upon her
A battlement of silver;
And if she *is* a door,
We will enclose her
With boards of cedar.

10 I *am* a wall,
And my breasts like towers;
Then I became in his eyes
As one who found peace.
11 Solomon had a vineyard at
Baal Hamon;
He leased the vineyard to
keepers;
Everyone was to bring for its
fruit
A thousand silver coins.

12 My own vineyard *is* before me.
You, O Solomon, *may have* a
thousand,
And those who tend its fruit
two hundred.

13 You who dwell in the gardens,
The companions listen for your
voice—
Let me hear it!

14 Make haste, my beloved,
And be like a gazelle
Or a young stag
On the mountains of spices.

7:9 [a]Septuagint, Syriac, and Vulgate read *lips and teeth.*   8:6 [a]Or *Sheol* [b]Literally *A flame of YAH* (a
poetic form of *YHWH, the* LORD)

Isaiah

Overview of Isaiah

The Book of Isaiah is a beautiful example of God's strength and of the promises He gave to the people when they needed them most. In this instance, God sent the prophet Isaiah to forewarn and prepare the people of Israel for the problems that were to beset them. Like a novelist foretelling his readers of future tragedies and events, God sent the prophet to announce the coming captivity by warring nations and the destruction of Jerusalem. Throughout the historical narrative of these happenings is interwoven the thread of hope—the coming of the Messiah.

> *Therefore the Lord Himself will give you a sign: Behold, the virgin shall conceive and bear a Son, and shall call His name Immanuel.*
>
> (Is. 7:14)

Isaiah promises the people that the coming Messiah will bring them into a loving relationship with God (see Chapter 53). If they look to God and cling to the hope of the Savior, they will be able to handle any circumstance that surrounds them. Despite the coming captivity, Isaiah encourages the people to look beyond their problems. "Those who wait on the LORD shall renew their strength; they shall mount up with wings like eagles, they shall run and not be weary, they shall walk and not faint" (Is. 40:31).

In comparing their lives to the desolate wilderness area, Isaiah promises that:

> *Every valley shall be exalted*
> *And every mountain and hill brought low;*
> *The crooked places shall be made straight,*
> *And the rough places smooth.*
>
> (Is. 40:4)

God promises that even the most desolate and unfortunate life will become successful and productive with His power. When problems would hold us captive, we can hold on to the same hope Isaiah promised—that Jesus will come again. We can look to God for strength, for we know that the ultimate outcome is in His hands. Even the end of the world will be a new beginning. "Behold, I make all things new" (Rev. 21:5).

Jesus in Isaiah

When he speaks of Jesus, Isaiah sounds more like a New Testament writer than an Old Testament prophet. His messianic prophecies are clearer and more explicit than those in any other Old Testament book. They describe many aspects of the person and work of Jesus in His first and second advents, and often blend the two together.

Isaiah 52:13—53:12 is an important passage. Its five stanzas present five different aspects of the saving work of Jesus: His wholehearted sacrifice; His perfect character; the atonement He offers that brings peace with God; His payment for our sins; and His death for the effects of sin.

Keys to Isaiah

Key Word: Salvation Is of the Lord. The basic theme of this book is found in Isaiah's name: "Salvation Is of the Lord." Chapters 1—39 portray man's great need for salvation, and chapters 40—66 reveal God's great provision of salvation. Salvation is of God, not man; and He is seen as the supreme Ruler, the sovereign Lord of history, and the only Savior.

Key Verses: "For unto us a Child is born, unto us a Son is given; and the government will be upon His shoulder. And His name will be called Wonderful, Counselor, Mighty God, Everlasting Father, Prince of Peace. Of the increase of *His* government and peace *there will be* no end, upon the throne of David and over His kingdom, to order it and establish it with judgment and justice from that time forward, even forever. The zeal of the LORD of hosts will perform this" (9:6, 7).

"All we like sheep have gone astray; we have turned, every one, to his own way; and the LORD has laid on Him the iniquity of us all" (53:6).

Key Chapter: Isaiah 53. Along with Psalm 22, Isaiah 53 lists the most remarkable and specific prophecies of the atonement of the Messiah.

1 The vision of Isaiah the son of Amoz, which he saw concerning Judah and Jerusalem in the days of Uzziah, Jotham, Ahaz, *and* Hezekiah, kings of Judah.

2   Hear, O heavens, and give ear, O earth!
For the LORD has spoken:
"I have nourished and brought up children,
And they have rebelled against Me;
3   The ox knows its owner
And the donkey its master's crib;
But Israel does not know,
My people do not consider."

4   Alas, sinful nation,
A people laden with iniquity,
A brood of evildoers,
Children who are corrupters!
They have forsaken the LORD,
They have provoked to anger
The Holy One of Israel,
They have turned away backward.

5   Why should you be stricken again?
You will revolt more and more.
The whole head is sick,
And the whole heart faints.
6   From the sole of the foot even to the head,
There is no soundness in it,
But wounds and bruises and putrefying sores;
They have not been closed or bound up,
Or soothed with ointment.

7   Your country *is* desolate,
Your cities *are* burned with fire;
Strangers devour your land in your presence;
And *it is* desolate, as overthrown by strangers.
8   So the daughter of Zion is left as a booth in a vineyard,
As a hut in a garden of cucumbers,
As a besieged city.
9   Unless the LORD of hosts

Had left to us a very small remnant,
We would have become like Sodom,
We would have been made like Gomorrah.

10   Hear the word of the LORD,
You rulers of Sodom;
Give ear to the law of our God,
You people of Gomorrah:
11   "To what purpose *is* the multitude of your sacrifices to Me?"
Says the LORD.
"I have had enough of burnt offerings of rams
And the fat of fed cattle.
I do not delight in the blood of bulls,
Or of lambs or goats.

12   When you come to appear before Me,
Who has required this from your hand,
To trample My courts?
13   Bring no more futile sacrifices;
Incense is an abomination to Me.
The New Moons, the Sabbaths, and the calling of assemblies—
I cannot endure iniquity and the sacred meeting.
14   Your New Moons and your appointed feasts
My soul hates;
They are a trouble to Me,
I am weary of bearing *them*.
15   When you spread out your hands,
I will hide My eyes from you;
Even though you make many prayers,
I will not hear.
Your hands are full of blood.

16   "Wash yourselves, make yourselves clean;
Put away the evil of your doings from before My eyes.
Cease to do evil,
17   Learn to do good;
Seek justice,
Rebuke the oppressor;[a]

1:17 [a]Some ancient versions read *the oppressed.*

Defend the fatherless,
Plead for the widow.

18 "Come now, and let us reason
    together,"
Says the LORD,
"Though your sins are like
    scarlet,
They shall be as white as
    snow;
Though they are red like
    crimson,
They shall be as wool.
19 If you are willing and obedient,
You shall eat the good of the
    land;
20 But if you refuse and rebel,
You shall be devoured by the
    sword";
For the mouth of the LORD has
    spoken.

21 How the faithful city has
    become a harlot!
It was full of justice;
Righteousness lodged in it,
But now murderers.
22 Your silver has become dross,
Your wine mixed with water.
23 Your princes are rebellious,
And companions of thieves;
Everyone loves bribes,
And follows after rewards.
They do not defend the
    fatherless,
Nor does the cause of the
    widow come before them.

24 Therefore the Lord says,
The LORD of hosts, the Mighty
    One of Israel,
"Ah, I will rid Myself of My
    adversaries,
And take vengeance on My
    enemies.
25 I will turn My hand against
    you,
And thoroughly purge away
    your dross,
And take away all your alloy.
26 I will restore your judges as at
    the first,
And your counselors as at the
    beginning.
Afterward you shall be called
    the city of righteousness, the
    faithful city."

27 Zion shall be redeemed with
    justice,

And her penitents with
    righteousness.
28 The destruction of
    transgressors and of sinners
    shall be together,
And those who forsake the
    LORD shall be consumed.
29 For they[a] shall be ashamed of
    the terebinth trees
Which you have desired;
And you shall be embarrassed
    because of the gardens
Which you have chosen.
30 For you shall be as a terebinth
    whose leaf fades,
And as a garden that has no
    water.
31 The strong shall be as tinder,
And the work of it as a spark;
Both will burn together,
And no one shall quench
    them.

2 The word that Isaiah the son of
Amoz saw concerning Judah and
Jerusalem.

2 Now it shall come to pass in the
    latter days
That the mountain of the
    LORD's house
Shall be established on the top
    of the mountains,
And shall be exalted above the
    hills;
And all nations shall flow to it.
3 Many people shall come and
    say,
"Come, and let us go up to the
    mountain of the LORD,
To the house of the God of
    Jacob;
He will teach us His ways,
And we shall walk in His
    paths."
For out of Zion shall go forth
    the law,
And the word of the LORD from
    Jerusalem.
4 He shall judge between the
    nations,
And rebuke many people;
They shall beat their swords
    into plowshares,
And their spears into pruning
    hooks;
Nation shall not lift up sword
    against nation,
Neither shall they learn war
    anymore.

1:29 aFollowing Masoretic Text, Septuagint, and Vulgate; some Hebrew manuscripts and Targum read you.

5   O house of Jacob, come and let
us walk
In the light of the LORD.

6   For You have forsaken Your
people, the house of Jacob,
Because they are filled with
eastern ways;
They *are* soothsayers like the
Philistines,
And they are pleased with the
children of foreigners.
7   Their land is also full of silver
and gold,
And there is no end to their
treasures;
Their land is also full of horses,
And there is no end to their
chariots.
8   Their land is also full of idols;
They worship the work of their
own hands,
That which their own fingers
have made.
9   People bow down,
And each man humbles
himself;
Therefore do not forgive them.

10   Enter into the rock, and hide in
the dust,
From the terror of the LORD
And the glory of His majesty.
11   The lofty looks of man shall be
humbled,
The haughtiness of men shall
be bowed down,
And the LORD alone shall be
exalted in that day.

12   For the day of the LORD of hosts
Shall come upon everything
proud and lofty,
Upon everything lifted up—
And it shall be brought low—
13   Upon all the cedars of Lebanon
that are high and lifted up,
And upon all the oaks of
Bashan;
14   Upon all the high mountains,
And upon all the hills *that are*
lifted up;
15   Upon every high tower,
And upon every fortified wall;
16   Upon all the ships of Tarshish,
And upon all the beautiful
sloops.
17   The loftiness of man shall be
bowed down,
And the haughtiness of men
shall be brought low;

The LORD alone will be exalted
in that day,
18   But the idols He shall utterly
abolish.

19   They shall go into the holes of
the rocks,
And into the caves of the earth,
From the terror of the LORD
And the glory of His majesty,
When He arises to shake the
earth mightily.
20   In that day a man will cast
away his idols of silver
And his idols of gold,
Which they made, *each* for
himself to worship,
To the moles and bats,
21   To go into the clefts of the
rocks,
And into the crags of the
rugged rocks,
From the terror of the LORD
And the glory of His majesty,
When He arises to shake the
earth mightily.

22   Sever yourselves from such a
man,
Whose breath *is* in his nostrils;
For of what account is he?

3   For behold, the Lord, the LORD
of hosts,
Takes away from Jerusalem
and from Judah
The stock and the store,
The whole supply of bread and
the whole supply of water;
2   The mighty man and the man
of war,
The judge and the prophet,
And the diviner and the elder;
3   The captain of fifty and the
honorable man,
The counselor and the skillful
artisan,
And the expert enchanter.

4   "I will give children *to be* their
princes,
And babes shall rule over them.
5   The people will be oppressed,
Every one by another and
every one by his neighbor;
The child will be insolent
toward the elder,
And the base toward the
honorable."

6   When a man takes hold of his
brother

In the house of his father,
saying,
"You have clothing;
You be our ruler,
And *let* these ruins *be* under
your power,"*a*
7 In that day he will protest,
saying,
"I cannot cure *your* ills,
For in my house *is* neither food
nor clothing;
Do not make me a ruler of the
people."

8 For Jerusalem stumbled,
And Judah is fallen,
Because their tongue and their
doings
Are against the LORD,
To provoke the eyes of His
glory.
9 The look on their countenance
witnesses against them,
And they declare their sin as
Sodom;
They do not hide *it.*
Woe to their soul!
For they have brought evil
upon themselves.

10 "Say to the righteous that *it shall
be* well *with them,*
For they shall eat the fruit of
their doings.
11 Woe to the wicked! *It shall be*
ill *with him,*
For the reward of his hands
shall be given him.
12 *As for* My people, children *are*
their oppressors,
And women rule over them.
O My people! Those who
lead you cause *you* to
err,
And destroy the way of your
paths."

13 The LORD stands up to plead,
And stands to judge the
people.
14 The LORD will enter into
judgment
With the elders of His people
And His princes:
"For you have eaten up the
vineyard;
The plunder of the poor *is* in
your houses.
15 What do you mean by crushing
My people

And grinding the faces of the
poor?"
Says the Lord GOD of hosts.

16 Moreover the LORD says:

"Because the daughters of Zion
are haughty,
And walk with outstretched
necks
And wanton eyes,
Walking and mincing *as* they
go,
Making a jingling with their
feet,
17 Therefore the Lord will strike
with a scab
The crown of the head of the
daughters of Zion,
And the LORD will uncover
their secret parts."

18 In that day the Lord will take
away the finery:
The jingling anklets, the
scarves, and the crescents;
19 The pendants, the bracelets,
and the veils;
20 The headdresses, the leg
ornaments, and the
headbands;
The perfume boxes, the
charms,
21 and the rings;
The nose jewels,
22 the festal apparel, and the
mantles;
The outer garments, the purses,
23 and the mirrors;
The fine linen, the turbans, and
the robes.

24 And so it shall be:

Instead of a sweet smell there
will be a stench;
Instead of a sash, a rope;
Instead of well-set hair,
baldness;
Instead of a rich robe, a girding
of sackcloth;
And branding instead of
beauty.
25 Your men shall fall by the
sword,
And your mighty in the war.

26 Her gates shall lament and
mourn,
And she *being* desolate shall sit
on the ground.

3:6 *a*Literally *hand*

4 And in that day seven women
shall take hold of one man,
saying,
"We will eat our own food and
wear our own apparel;
Only let us be called by your
name,
To take away our reproach."
2 In that day the Branch of the
LORD shall be beautiful and
glorious;
And the fruit of the earth *shall
be* excellent and appealing
For those of Israel who have
escaped.

3 And it shall come to pass that *he
who is* left in Zion and remains in
Jerusalem will be called holy—everyone who is recorded among the living
in Jerusalem. 4 When the Lord has
washed away the filth of the daughters of Zion, and purged the blood
of Jerusalem from her midst, by the
spirit of judgment and by the spirit
of burning, 5 then the LORD will create above every dwelling place of
Mount Zion, and above her assemblies, a cloud and smoke by day and
the shining of a flaming fire by night.
For over all the glory there *will be* a
covering. 6 And there will be a tabernacle for shade in the daytime from
the heat, for a place of refuge, and
for a shelter from storm and rain.

5 Now let me sing to my Well-
beloved
A song of my Beloved
regarding His vineyard:

My Well-beloved has a
vineyard
On a very fruitful hill.
2 He dug it up and cleared out
its stones,
And planted it with the choicest
vine.
He built a tower in its midst,
And also made a winepress in
it;
So He expected *it* to bring forth
good grapes,
But it brought forth wild
grapes.

3 "And now, O inhabitants of
Jerusalem and men of Judah,
Judge, please, between Me and
My vineyard.
4 What more could have been
done to My vineyard

That I have not done in it?
Why then, when I expected *it*
to bring forth *good* grapes,
Did it bring forth wild grapes?
5 And now, please let Me tell you
what I will do to My
vineyard:
I will take away its hedge, and
it shall be burned;
And break down its wall, and
it shall be trampled down.
6 I will lay it waste;
It shall not be pruned or dug,
But there shall come up briers
and thorns.
I will also command the clouds
That they rain no rain on it."

7 For the vineyard of the LORD of
hosts *is* the house of Israel,
And the men of Judah are His
pleasant plant.
He looked for justice, but
behold, oppression;
For righteousness, but behold,
a cry *for help.*

8 Woe to those who join house
to house;
They add field to field,
Till *there is* no place
Where they may dwell alone in
the midst of the land!
9 In my hearing the LORD of hosts
said,
"Truly, many houses shall be
desolate,
Great and beautiful ones,
without inhabitant.
10 For ten acres of vineyard shall
yield one bath,
And a homer of seed shall yield
one ephah."

11 Woe to those who rise early in
the morning,
That they may follow
intoxicating drink;
Who continue until night, *till*
wine inflames them!
12 The harp and the strings,
The tambourine and flute,
And wine are in their feasts;
But they do not regard the
work of the LORD,
Nor consider the operation of
His hands.

13 Therefore my people have gone
into captivity,

Because *they have* no
    knowledge;
Their honorable men *are*
    famished,
And their multitude dried up
    with thirst.

14 Therefore Sheol has enlarged
    itself
And opened its mouth beyond
    measure;
Their glory and their multitude
    and their pomp,
And he who is jubilant, shall
    descend into it.

15 People shall be brought down,
Each man shall be humbled,
And the eyes of the lofty shall
    be humbled.

16 But the LORD of hosts shall be
    exalted in judgment,
And God who is holy shall be
    hallowed in righteousness.

17 Then the lambs shall feed in
    their pasture,
And in the waste places of the
    fat ones strangers shall eat.

18 Woe to those who draw
    iniquity with cords of vanity,
And sin as if with a cart rope;

19 That say, "Let Him make speed
    and hasten His work,
That we may see *it;*
And let the counsel of the Holy
    One of Israel draw near and
    come,
That we may know *it.*"

20 Woe to those who call evil
    good, and good evil;
Who put darkness for light, and
    light for darkness;
Who put bitter for sweet, and
    sweet for bitter!

21 Woe to *those who are* wise in
    their own eyes,
And prudent in their own sight!

22 Woe to men mighty at drinking
    wine,
Woe to men valiant for mixing
    intoxicating drink,

23 Who justify the wicked for a
    bribe,
And take away justice from the
    righteous man!

24 Therefore, as the fire devours
    the stubble,
And the flame consumes the
    chaff,

So their root will be as
    rottenness,
And their blossom will ascend
    like dust;
Because they have rejected the
    law of the LORD of hosts,
And despised the word of the
    Holy One of Israel.

25 Therefore the anger of the
    LORD is aroused against His
    people;
He has stretched out His hand
    against them
And stricken them,
And the hills trembled.
Their carcasses *were* as refuse
    in the midst of the streets.

For all this His anger is not
    turned away,
But His hand *is* stretched out
    still.

26 He will lift up a banner to the
    nations from afar,
And will whistle to them from
    the end of the earth;
Surely they shall come with
    speed, swiftly.

27 No one will be weary or
    stumble among them,
No one will slumber or sleep;
Nor will the belt on their loins
    be loosed,
Nor the strap of their sandals
    be broken;

28 Whose arrows *are* sharp,
And all their bows bent;
Their horses' hooves will seem
    like flint,
And their wheels like a
    whirlwind.

29 Their roaring *will be* like a lion,
They will roar like young lions;
Yes, they will roar
And lay hold of the prey;
They will carry *it* away safely,
And no one will deliver.

30 In that day they will roar
    against them
Like the roaring of the sea.
And if *one* looks to the land,
Behold, darkness *and* sorrow;
And the light is darkened by
    the clouds.

6 In the year that King Uzziah died,
I saw the Lord sitting on a throne,
high and lifted up, and the train of
His *robe* filled the temple. 2 Above it
stood seraphim; each one had six
wings: with two he covered his face,

Lord, Send Us

Deep in the stone chambers beneath the Church of the Holy Sepulchre in Jerusalem is an inscription bearing silent witness to the early church. Etched upon the walls are the words, "Lord, we went . . ." Next to the inscription is a picture of a fishing boat rowing away from Palestine toward other lands of the Roman empire.

Jesus gave His disciples the commission, "As the Father has sent Me, I also send you" (John 20:21). It took great faith on the part of the disciples and the early Christians to realize that they were entrusted with the task of carrying the good news of Jesus Christ's death, burial, and resurrection to a lost and dying world.

Most of the early Jewish Christians had never left the hill country of Judea. The Jews of that period had a tremendous fear of the sea. That was where Leviathan and other sea creatures lived. Through the centuries Israel had warred with people from the coastal areas.

Jesus instilled a revolutionary-type outlook of the world in the disciples. He enabled them to release old suspicions and fears and to trust Him fully. We have the same comfort and assurance that Jesus gave to the early Christians. "But the Helper, the Holy Spirit, whom the Father will send in My name, He will teach you all things, and bring to your remembrance all things that I said to you" (John 14:26).

The disciples of the early church went forth in the knowledge that they were given Christ's peace and assurance. They could accomplish anything that they attempted to do—even convert the mighty Roman empire.

Etched in the wall opposite the inscription, "Lord, we went . . ." is the symbol of the mighty tenth and twelfth Roman legions from whose ranks came the soldiers who crucified Christ. The early Christians knew and understood the totality of Jesus' message of forgiveness. They put aside their prejudices against the Romans and took the good news of Jesus' love and forgiveness to lands and peoples whom they had suffered under.

May we be like the early disciples, and leave an inscription of love, peace, joy, and forgiveness on the hearts and minds of those around us for coming generations to read—"Lord, we went."

with two he covered his feet, and with two he flew. 3 And one cried to another and said:

> "Holy, holy, holy *is* the LORD of hosts;
> The whole earth *is* full of His glory!"

4 And the posts of the door were shaken by the voice of him who cried out, and the house was filled with smoke.

5 So I said:

> "Woe *is* me, for I am undone!
> Because I *am* a man of unclean lips,
> And I dwell in the midst of a people of unclean lips;
> For my eyes have seen the King,
> The LORD of hosts."

6 Then one of the seraphim flew to me, having in his hand a live coal *which* he had taken with the tongs from the altar. 7 And he touched my mouth *with it,* and said:

> "Behold, this has touched your lips;
> Your iniquity is taken away,
> And your sin purged."

8 Also I heard the voice of the Lord, saying:

> "Whom shall I send,
> And who will go for Us?"

Then I said, "Here *am* I! Send me."

9 And He said, "Go, and tell this people:

> 'Keep on hearing, but do not understand;
> Keep on seeing, but do not perceive.'

10 "Make the heart of this people dull,
> And their ears heavy,
> And shut their eyes;
> Lest they see with their eyes,
> And hear with their ears,
> And understand with their heart,
> And return and be healed."

11 Then I said, "Lord, how long?"
And He answered:

> "Until the cities are laid waste and without inhabitant,
> The houses are without a man,
> The land is utterly desolate,
12 The LORD has removed men far away,
> And the forsaken places *are* many in the midst of the land.
13 But yet a tenth *will be* in it,
> And will return and be for consuming,
> As a terebinth tree or as an oak,
> Whose stump *remains* when it is cut down.
> So the holy seed *shall be* its stump."

7 Now it came to pass in the days of Ahaz the son of Jotham, the son of Uzziah, king of Judah, *that* Rezin king of Syria and Pekah the son of Remaliah, king of Israel, went up to Jerusalem to *make* war against it, but could not prevail against it. 2 And it was told to the house of David, saying, "Syria's forces are deployed in Ephraim." So his heart and the heart of his people were moved as the trees of the woods are moved with the wind.

3 Then the LORD said to Isaiah, "Go out now to meet Ahaz, you and Shear-Jashub[a] your son, at the end of the aqueduct from the upper pool, on the highway to the Fuller's Field, 4 and say to him: 'Take heed, and be quiet; do not fear or be fainthearted for these two stubs of smoking firebrands, for the fierce anger of Rezin and Syria, and the son of Remaliah. 5 Because Syria, Ephraim, and the son of Remaliah have plotted evil against you, saying, 6 "Let us go up against Judah and trouble it, and let us make a gap in its wall for ourselves, and set a king over them, the son of Tabel"— 7 thus says the Lord GOD:

> "It shall not stand,
> Nor shall it come to pass.
8 For the head of Syria *is* Damascus,
> And the head of Damascus *is* Rezin.
> Within sixty-five years
> Ephraim will be broken,

7:3 [a]Literally *A Remnant Shall Return*

So that it will not *be* a people.

9 The head of Ephraim *is*
Samaria,
And the head of Samaria *is*
Remaliah's son.
If you will not believe,
Surely you shall not be
established." ' "

10 Moreover the LORD spoke again to Ahaz, saying, 11 "Ask a sign for yourself from the LORD your God; ask it either in the depth or in the height above."
12 But Ahaz said, "I will not ask, nor will I test the LORD!"
13 Then he said, "Hear now, O house of David! *Is it* a small thing for you to weary men, but will you weary my God also? 14 Therefore the Lord Himself will give you a sign: Behold, the virgin shall conceive and bear a Son, and shall call His name Immanuel.*a* 15 Curds and honey He shall eat, that He may know to refuse the evil and choose the good. 16 For before the Child shall know to refuse the evil and choose the good, the land that you dread will be forsaken by both her kings. 17 The LORD will bring the king of Assyria upon you and your people and your father's house—days that have not come since the day that Ephraim departed from Judah."

18 And it shall come to pass in that day
That the LORD will whistle for the fly
That *is* in the farthest part of the rivers of Egypt,
And for the bee that *is* in the land of Assyria.
19 They will come, and all of them will rest
In the desolate valleys and in the clefts of the rocks,
And on all thorns and in all pastures.

20 In the same day the Lord will shave with a hired razor,
With those from beyond the River,*a* with the king of Assyria,
The head and the hair of the legs,
And will also remove the beard.

21 It shall be in that day
That a man will keep alive a young cow and two sheep;
22 So it shall be, from the abundance of milk they give,
That he will eat curds;
For curds and honey everyone will eat who is left in the land.

23 It shall happen in that day,
That wherever there could be a thousand vines
Worth a thousand *shekels* of silver,
It will be for briers and thorns.
24 With arrows and bows men will come there,
Because all the land will become briers and thorns.

25 And to any hill which could be dug with the hoe,
You will not go there for fear of briers and thorns;
But it will become a range for oxen
And a place for sheep to roam.

8 Moreover the LORD said to me, "Take a large scroll, and write on it with a man's pen concerning Maher-Shalal-Hash-Baz.*a* 2 And I will take for Myself faithful witnesses to record, Uriah the priest and Zechariah the son of Jeberechiah."
3 Then I went to the prophetess, and she conceived and bore a son. Then the LORD said to me, "Call his name Maher-Shalal-Hash-Baz; 4 for before the child shall have knowledge to cry 'My father' and 'My mother,' the riches of Damascus and the spoil of Samaria will be taken away before the king of Assyria."
5 The LORD also spoke to me again, saying:

6 "Inasmuch as these people refused
The waters of Shiloah that flow softly,
And rejoice in Rezin and in Remaliah's son;
7 Now therefore, behold, the Lord brings up over them

7:14 *a*Literally *God-With-Us*   7:20 *a*That is, the Euphrates   8:1 *a*Literally *Speed the Spoil, Hasten the Booty*

Light in a Land of Darkness

The land of Zebulun and the land of Naphtali . . .
Those who dwelt in the land of the shadow of death,
Upon them a light has shined.

(Is. 9:1, 2)

From the dawn of recorded history, the inhabitants of Zebulun and Naphtali on the northwest shores of the Sea of Galilee have been trampled beneath the heels of invading armies. Their home was located on the famous Via Maris—"the way of the sea," which connected the empires of the ancient world. Assyria, Babylon, Mesopotamia, Rome, and Greece all sought to control this road to further expand their kingdoms.

The Via Maris was the important land bridge linking the three continents of Europe, Africa, and Asia. Stretching from Egypt and North Africa, this strategic highway ran along the coast of Palestine. In the area of Mount Carmel the Via Maris turned inland through the famous town of Megiddo, across the Jezreel Valley. It continued north through a narrow pass along the Sea of Galilee, and on to Damascus.

The people of Galilee benefited from the commerce and trade provided by the merchant caravans that traveled along this road. But they also suffered greatly under the constant wave of warring armies, who in their quest for power destroyed villages, killed men, raped women, enslaved children, and pillaged the land.

Nation after nation mounted their campaigns along this thoroughfare. Egypt's Thutmose III, Amenhotep II, Ramses II, Seti I; Assyria's Sennacherib; Babylon's Nebuchadnezzar; Macedonia's Alexander the Great; Egypt's Cleopatra; and Rome's Mark Antony, Vespasian, Titus, and many others marched on this highway.

Along the Via Maris, Jesus first began His ministry, and it was here that Jesus appeared after His resurrection to declare the final victory over sin and death. To an area that was overrun by nations trying by force to build their kingdoms, Jesus brought the healing kingdom of God. Where empires had carried on campaigns of violence, destruction, and death, Jesus carried His campaign of peace, hope, and life. To a region that had seen great darkness, Jesus brought light!

The waters of the River,[a] strong
and mighty—
The king of Assyria and all his
glory;
He will go up over all his
channels
And go over all his banks.
8 He will pass through Judah,
He will overflow and pass over,
He will reach up to the neck;
And the stretching out of his
wings
Will fill the breadth of Your
land, O Immanuel.[a]

9 "Be shattered, O you peoples,
and be broken in pieces!
Give ear, all you from far
countries.
Gird yourselves, but be broken
in pieces;
Gird yourselves, but be broken
in pieces.
10 Take counsel together, but it
will come to nothing;
Speak the word, but it will not
stand,
For God is with us."[a]

11 For the LORD spoke thus to me
with a strong hand, and instructed
me that I should not walk in the way
of this people, saying:

12 "Do not say, 'A conspiracy,'
Concerning all that this people
call a conspiracy,
Nor be afraid of their threats,
nor be troubled.
13 The LORD of hosts, Him you
shall hallow;
Let Him be your fear,
And let Him be your dread.
14 He will be as a sanctuary,
But a stone of stumbling and a
rock of offense
To both the houses of Israel,
As a trap and a snare to the
inhabitants of Jerusalem.
15 And many among them shall
stumble;
They shall fall and be broken,
Be snared and taken."

16 Bind up the testimony,
Seal the law among my
disciples.
17 And I will wait on the LORD,

Who hides His face from the
house of Jacob;
And I will hope in Him.
18 Here am I and the children
whom the LORD has given
me!
We are for signs and wonders
in Israel
From the LORD of hosts,
Who dwells in Mount Zion.

19 And when they say to you,
"Seek those who are mediums and
wizards, who whisper and mutter,"
should not a people seek their God?
Should they seek the dead on behalf
of the living? 20 To the law and to the
testimony! If they do not speak according to this word, it is because
there is no light in them.
21 They will pass through it hard
pressed and hungry; and it shall happen, when they are hungry, that they
will be enraged and curse their king
and their God, and look upward.
22 Then they will look to the earth,
and see trouble and darkness, gloom
of anguish; and they will be driven
into darkness.

9 Nevertheless the gloom will
not be upon her who is
distressed,
As when at first He lightly
esteemed
The land of Zebulun and the
land of Naphtali,
And afterward more heavily
oppressed her,
By the way of the sea, beyond
the Jordan,
In Galilee of the Gentiles.
2 The people who walked in
darkness
Have seen a great light;
Those who dwelt in the land of
the shadow of death,
Upon them a light has shined.
3 You have multiplied the nation
And increased its joy;[a]
They rejoice before You
According to the joy of harvest,
As men rejoice when they
divide the spoil.
4 For You have broken the yoke
of his burden
And the staff of his shoulder,

The rod of his oppressor,
As in the day of Midian.
5 For every warrior's sandal
from the noisy battle,
And garments rolled in blood,
Will be used for burning *and*
fuel of fire.

6 For unto us a Child is born,
Unto us a Son is given;
And the government will be
upon His shoulder.
And His name will be called
Wonderful, Counselor, Mighty
God,
Everlasting Father, Prince of
Peace.
7 Of the increase of *His*
government and peace
There will be no end,
Upon the throne of David and
over His kingdom,
To order it and establish it with
judgment and justice
From that time forward, even
forever.
The zeal of the LORD of hosts
will perform this.

8 The LORD sent a word against
Jacob,
And it has fallen on Israel.
9 All the people will know—
Ephraim and the inhabitant of
Samaria—
Who say in pride and
arrogance of heart:
10 "The bricks have fallen down,
But we will rebuild with hewn
stones;
The sycamores are cut down,
But we will replace *them* with
cedars."
11 Therefore the LORD shall set up
The adversaries of Rezin
against him,
And spur his enemies on,
12 The Syrians before and the
Philistines behind;
And they shall devour Israel
with an open mouth.

For all this His anger is not
turned away,
But His hand *is* stretched out
still.

13 For the people do not turn to
Him who strikes them,
Nor do they seek the LORD of
hosts.

14 Therefore the LORD will cut off
head and tail from Israel,
Palm branch and bulrush in
one day.
15 The elder and honorable, he *is*
the head;
The prophet who teaches lies,
he *is* the tail.
16 For the leaders of this people
cause *them* to err,
And *those who are* led by them
are destroyed.
17 Therefore the LORD will have
no joy in their young men,
Nor have mercy on their
fatherless and widows;
For everyone *is* a hypocrite and
an evildoer,
And every mouth speaks folly.

For all this His anger is not
turned away,
But His hand *is* stretched out
still.

18 For wickedness burns as the
fire;
It shall devour the briers and
thorns,
And kindle in the thickets of
the forest;
They shall mount up *like* rising
smoke.
19 Through the wrath of the LORD
of hosts
The land is burned up,
And the people shall be as fuel
for the fire;
No man shall spare his brother.
20 And he shall snatch on the
right hand
And be hungry;
He shall devour on the left
hand
And not be satisfied;
Every man shall eat the flesh
of his own arm.
21 Manasseh *shall devour*
Ephraim, and Ephraim
Manasseh;
Together they *shall be* against
Judah.

For all this His anger is not
turned away,
But His hand *is* stretched out
still.

10 "Woe to those who decree
unrighteous decrees,
Who write misfortune,
Which they have prescribed
2 To rob the needy of justice,

And to take what is right from
the poor of My people,
That widows may be their prey,
And *that* they may rob the
fatherless.

3 What will you do in the day of
punishment,
And in the desolation *which*
will come from afar?
To whom will you flee for help?
And where will you leave your
glory?

4 Without Me they shall bow
down among the prisoners,
And they shall fall among the
slain."

For all this His anger is not
turned away,
But His hand *is* stretched out
still.

5 "Woe to Assyria, the rod of My
anger
And the staff in whose hand is
My indignation.

6 I will send him against an
ungodly nation,
And against the people of My
wrath
I will give him charge,
To seize the spoil, to take the
prey,
And to tread them down like
the mire of the streets.

7 Yet he does not mean so,
Nor does his heart think so;
But *it is* in his heart to destroy,
And cut off not a few nations.

8 For he says,
'*Are* not my princes altogether
kings?

9 *Is* not Calno like Carchemish?
Is not Hamath like Arpad?
Is not Samaria like Damascus?

10 As my hand has found the
kingdoms of the idols,
Whose carved images excelled
those of Jerusalem and
Samaria,

11 As I have done to Samaria and
her idols,
Shall I not do also to Jerusalem
and her idols?'"

12 Therefore it shall come to pass,
when the LORD has performed all His
work on Mount Zion and on Jerusalem, *that He will say*, "I will punish
the fruit of the arrogant heart of the
king of Assyria, and the glory of his
haughty looks."

13 For he says:

"By the strength of my hand I
have done *it*,
And by my wisdom, for I am
prudent;
Also I have removed the
boundaries of the people,
And have robbed their
treasuries;
So I have put down the
inhabitants like a valiant
man.

14 My hand has found like a nest
the riches of the people,
And as one gathers eggs *that
are* left,
I have gathered all the earth;
And there was no one who
moved *his* wing,
Nor opened *his* mouth with
even a peep."

15 Shall the ax boast itself against
him who chops with it?
Or shall the saw exalt itself
against him who saws with
it?
As if a rod could wield *itself*
against those who lift it up,
Or as if a staff could lift up, *as
if it were* not wood!

16 Therefore the Lord, the Lord[a]
of hosts,
Will send leanness among his
fat ones;
And under his glory
He will kindle a burning
Like the burning of a fire.

17 So the Light of Israel will be
for a fire,
And his Holy One for a flame;
It will burn and devour
His thorns and his briers in one
day.

18 And it will consume the glory
of his forest and of his fruitful
field,
Both soul and body;
And they will be as when a sick
man wastes away.

19 Then the rest of the trees of his
forest
Will be so few in number
That a child may write them.

20 And it shall come to pass in that
day
That the remnant of Israel,

10:16 [a]Following Bomberg; Masoretic Text and Dead Sea Scrolls read YHWH (LORD).

And such as have escaped of
the house of Jacob,
Will never again depend on
him who defeated them,
But will depend on the LORD,
the Holy One of Israel, in
truth.
21 The remnant will return, the
remnant of Jacob,
To the Mighty God.
22 For though your people, O
Israel, be as the sand of the
sea,
A remnant of them will return;
The destruction decreed shall
overflow with righteousness.
23 For the Lord GOD of hosts
Will make a determined end
In the midst of all the land.

24 Therefore thus says the Lord
GOD of hosts: "O My people, who
dwell in Zion, do not be afraid of the
Assyrian. He shall strike you with a
rod and lift up his staff against you,
in the manner of Egypt. 25 For yet a
very little while and the indignation
will cease, as will My anger in their
destruction." 26 And the LORD of
hosts will stir up a scourge for him
like the slaughter of Midian at the
rock of Oreb; as His rod was on the
sea, so will He lift it up in the manner
of Egypt.

27 It shall come to pass in that
day
That his burden will be taken
away from your shoulder,
And his yoke from your neck,
And the yoke will be destroyed
because of the anointing oil.

28 He has come to Aiath,
He has passed Migron;
At Michmash he has attended
to his equipment.
29 They have gone along the
ridge,
They have taken up lodging at
Geba.
Ramah is afraid,
Gibeah of Saul has fled.
30 Lift up your voice,
O daughter of Gallim!
Cause it to be heard as far as
Laish—
O poor Anathoth![a]
31 Madmenah has fled,

The inhabitants of Gebim seek
refuge.
32 As yet he will remain at Nob
that day;
He will shake his fist at the
mount of the daughter of
Zion,
The hill of Jerusalem.

33 Behold, the Lord,
The LORD of hosts,
Will lop off the bough with
terror;
Those of high stature will be
hewn down,
And the haughty will be
humbled.
34 He will cut down the thickets
of the forest with iron,
And Lebanon will fall by the
Mighty One.

11 There shall come forth a Rod
from the stem of Jesse,
And a Branch shall grow out
of his roots.
2 The Spirit of the LORD shall rest
upon Him,
The Spirit of wisdom and
understanding,
The Spirit of counsel and
might,
The Spirit of knowledge and of
the fear of the LORD.

3 His delight is in the fear of the
LORD,
And He shall not judge by the
sight of His eyes,
Nor decide by the hearing of
His ears;
4 But with righteousness He shall
judge the poor,
And decide with equity for the
meek of the earth;
He shall strike the earth with
the rod of His mouth,
And with the breath of His
lips He shall slay the
wicked.
5 Righteousness shall be the belt
of His loins,
And faithfulness the belt of His
waist.

6 "The wolf also shall dwell with
the lamb,
The leopard shall lie down with
the young goat,

10:30 [a]Following Masoretic Text, Targum, and Vulgate; Septuagint and Syriac read *Listen to her, O Anathoth*.

The calf and the young lion and
  the fatling together;
And a little child shall lead
  them.
7 The cow and the bear shall
  graze;
Their young ones shall lie
  down together;
And the lion shall eat straw like
  the ox.
8 The nursing child shall play by
  the cobra's hole,
And the weaned child shall put
  his hand in the viper's den.
9 They shall not hurt nor destroy
  in all My holy mountain,
For the earth shall be full of the
  knowledge of the LORD
As the waters cover the sea.

10 "And in that day there shall be
  a Root of Jesse,
Who shall stand as a banner to
  the people;
For the Gentiles shall seek Him,
And His resting place shall be
  glorious."

11 It shall come to pass in that day
That the LORD shall set His
  hand again the second time
To recover the remnant of His
  people who are left,
From Assyria and Egypt,
From Pathros and Cush,
From Elam and Shinar,
From Hamath and the islands
  of the sea.

12 He will set up a banner for the
  nations,
And will assemble the outcasts
  of Israel,
And gather together the
  dispersed of Judah
From the four corners of the
  earth.
13 Also the envy of Ephraim shall
  depart,
And the adversaries of Judah
  shall be cut off;
Ephraim shall not envy Judah,
And Judah shall not harass
  Ephraim.
14 But they shall fly down upon
  the shoulder of the
  Philistines toward the west;
Together they shall plunder the
  people of the East;

They shall lay their hand on
  Edom and Moab;
And the people of Ammon shall
  obey them.
15 The LORD will utterly destroy*a*
  the tongue of the Sea of
  Egypt;
With His mighty wind He will
  shake His fist over the River,*b*
And strike it in the seven
  streams,
And make *men* cross over
  dry-shod.
16 There will be a highway for the
  remnant of His people
Who will be left from Assyria,
As it was for Israel
In the day that he came up from
  the land of Egypt.

12 And in that day you will say:

"O LORD, I will praise You;
  Though You were angry with
    me,
  Your anger is turned away, and
    You comfort me.
2 Behold, God *is* my salvation,
  I will trust and not be afraid;
'For YAH, the LORD, *is* my
    strength and song;
  He also has become
    salvation.' "*a*

3 Therefore with joy you will
  draw water
From the wells of salvation.

4 And in that day you will say:

"Praise the LORD, call upon His
    name;
  Declare His deeds among the
    peoples,
  Make mention that His name is
    exalted.
5 Sing to the LORD,
  For He has done excellent
    things;
  This *is* known in all the earth.
6 Cry out and shout, O inhabitant
    of Zion,
  For great *is* the Holy One of
    Israel in your midst!"

13 The burden against Babylon
  which Isaiah the son of Amoz
saw.

11:15 *a*Following Masoretic Text and Vulgate; Septuagint, Syriac, and Targum read *dry up.*   *b*That is, the
Euphrates   12:2 *a*Exodus 15:2

2 "Lift up a banner on the high
    mountain,
Raise your voice to them;
Wave your hand, that they may
    enter the gates of the nobles.
3 I have commanded My
    sanctified ones;
I have also called My mighty
    ones for My anger—
Those who rejoice in My
    exaltation."

4 The noise of a multitude in the
    mountains,
Like that of many people!
A tumultuous noise of the
    kingdoms of nations
    gathered together!
The LORD of hosts musters
    The army for battle.
5 They come from a far country,
From the end of heaven—
The LORD and His weapons of
    indignation,
To destroy the whole land.

6 Wail, for the day of the LORD
    is at hand!
It will come as destruction from
    the Almighty.
7 Therefore all hands will be
    limp,
Every man's heart will melt,
8 And they will be afraid.
Pangs and sorrows will take
    hold of *them;*
They will be in pain as a
    woman in childbirth;
They will be amazed at one
    another;
Their faces *will be like* flames.

9 Behold, the day of the LORD
    comes,
Cruel, with both wrath and
    fierce anger,
To lay the land desolate;
And He will destroy its sinners
    from it.
10 For the stars of heaven and
    their constellations
Will not give their light;
The sun will be darkened in its
    going forth,
And the moon will not cause its
    light to shine.

11 "I will punish the world for *its*
    evil,
And the wicked for their
    iniquity;

I will halt the arrogance of the
    proud,
And will lay low the
    haughtiness of the terrible.
12 I will make a mortal more rare
    than fine gold,
A man more than the golden
    wedge of Ophir.
13 Therefore I will shake the
    heavens,
And the earth will move out of
    her place,
In the wrath of the LORD of
    hosts
And in the day of His fierce
    anger.
14 It shall be as the hunted
    gazelle,
And as a sheep that no man
    takes up;
Every man will turn to his own
    people,
And everyone will flee to his
    own land.
15 Everyone who is found will be
    thrust through,
And everyone who is captured
    will fall by the sword.
16 Their children also will be
    dashed to pieces before their
    eyes;
Their houses will be plundered
And their wives ravished.

17 "Behold, I will stir up the Medes
    against them,
Who will not regard silver;
And *as for* gold, they will not
    delight in it.
18 Also *their* bows will dash the
    young men to pieces,
And they will have no pity on
    the fruit of the womb;
Their eye will not spare
    children.
19 And Babylon, the glory of
    kingdoms,
The beauty of the Chaldeans'
    pride,
Will be as when God overthrew
    Sodom and Gomorrah.
20 It will never be inhabited,
Nor will it be settled from
    generation to generation;
Nor will the Arabian pitch tents
    there,
Nor will the shepherds make
    their sheepfolds there.
21 But wild beasts of the desert
    will lie there,
And their houses will be full of
    owls;

Ostriches will dwell there,
And wild goats will caper there.
22 The hyenas will howl in their
citadels,
And jackals in their pleasant
palaces.
Her time *is* near to come,
And her days will not be
prolonged."

14 For the LORD will have mercy
on Jacob, and will still choose
Israel, and settle them in their own
land. The strangers will be joined
with them, and they will cling to the
house of Jacob. 2 Then people will
take them and bring them to their
place, and the house of Israel will
possess them for servants and maids
in the land of the LORD; they will take
them captive whose captives they
were, and rule over their oppressors.
3 It shall come to pass in the day
the LORD gives you rest from your
sorrow, and from your fear and the
hard bondage in which you were
made to serve, 4 that you will take
up this proverb against the king of
Babylon, and say:

"How the oppressor has ceased,
The golden*ª* city ceased!
5 The LORD has broken the staff
of the wicked,
The scepter of the rulers;
6 He who struck the people in
wrath with a continual
stroke,
He who ruled the nations in
anger,
Is persecuted *and* no one
hinders.
7 The whole earth is at rest *and*
quiet;
They break forth into singing.
8 Indeed the cypress trees rejoice
over you,
And the cedars of Lebanon,
Saying, 'Since you were cut
down,
No woodsman has come up
against us.'
9 "Hell from beneath is excited
about you,
To meet *you* at your coming;
It stirs up the dead for you,
All the chief ones of the earth;
It has raised up from their
thrones
All the kings of the nations.

10 They all shall speak and say to
you:
'Have you also become as weak
as we?
Have you become like us?
11 Your pomp is brought down to
Sheol,
And the sound of your stringed
instruments;
The maggot is spread under
you,
And worms cover you.'

12 "How you are fallen from
heaven,
O Lucifer,*ª* son of the morning!
How you are cut down to the
ground,
You who weakened the
nations!
13 For you have said in your heart:
'I will ascend into heaven,
I will exalt my throne above the
stars of God;
I will also sit on the mount of
the congregation
On the farthest sides of the
north;
14 I will ascend above the heights
of the clouds,
I will be like the Most High.'
15 Yet you shall be brought down
to Sheol,
To the lowest depths of the Pit.

16 "Those who see you will gaze at
you,
And consider you, *saying:*
'*Is* this the man who made the
earth tremble,
Who shook kingdoms,
17 Who made the world as a
wilderness
And destroyed its cities,
Who did not open the house of
his prisoners?'
18 "All the kings of the nations,
All of them, sleep in glory,
Everyone in his own house;
19 But you are cast out of your
grave
Like an abominable branch,
Like the garment of those who
are slain,
Thrust through with a sword,
Who go down to the stones of
the pit,
Like a corpse trodden
underfoot.

14:4 *ª*Or *insolent*   14:12 *ª*Literally *Day Star*

20 You will not be joined with
    them in burial,
    Because you have destroyed
       your land
    And slain your people.
    The brood of evildoers shall
       never be named.
21 Prepare slaughter for his
    children
    Because of the iniquity of their
       fathers,
    Lest they rise up and possess
       the land,
    And fill the face of the world
       with cities."

22 "For I will rise up against
    them," says the LORD of
    hosts,
   "And cut off from Babylon the
       name and remnant,
    And offspring and posterity,"
    says the LORD.
23 "I will also make it a possession
    for the porcupine,
    And marshes of muddy water;
    I will sweep it with the broom
       of destruction," says the
    LORD of hosts.

24 The LORD of hosts has sworn,
    saying,
   "Surely, as I have thought, so it
       shall come to pass,
    And as I have purposed, *so it*
       shall stand:
25 That I will break the Assyrian
    in My land,
    And on My mountains tread
       him underfoot.
    Then his yoke shall be removed
       from them,
    And his burden removed from
       their shoulders.
26 This *is* the purpose that is
    purposed against the whole
    earth,
    And this *is* the hand that is
       stretched out over all the
       nations.
27 For the LORD of hosts has
    purposed,
    And who will annul *it?*
    His hand *is* stretched out,
    And who will turn it back?"

28 This is the burden which came
in the year that King Ahaz died.

29 "Do not rejoice, all you of
    Philistia,
    Because the rod that struck you
       is broken;
    For out of the serpent's roots
       will come forth a viper,
    And its offspring *will be* a fiery
       flying serpent.
30 The firstborn of the poor will
    feed,
    And the needy will lie down in
       safety;
    I will kill your roots with
       famine,
    And it will slay your remnant.
31 Wail, O gate! Cry, O city!
    All you of Philistia *are*
       dissolved;
    For smoke will come from the
       north,
    And no one *will be* alone in his
       appointed times."

32 What will they answer the
    messengers of the nation?
    That the LORD has founded
       Zion,
    And the poor of His people
       shall take refuge in it.

15

The burden against Moab.

Because in the night Ar of
    Moab is laid waste
    And destroyed,
    Because in the night Kir of
       Moab is laid waste
    And destroyed,
2 He has gone up to the temple[a]
    and Dibon,
    To the high places to weep.
    Moab will wail over Nebo and
       over Medeba;
    On all their heads *will be*
       baldness,
    And every beard cut off.
3 In their streets they will
    clothe themselves with
    sackcloth;
    On the tops of their houses
    And in their streets
    Everyone will wail, weeping
       bitterly.
4 Heshbon and Elealeh will cry
    out,
    Their voice shall be heard as
       far as Jahaz;
    Therefore the armed soldiers[a]
    of Moab will cry out;

15:2 [a]Hebrew *bayith* (*house*)   15:4 [a]Following Masoretic Text, Targum, and Vulgate; Septuagint and Syriac read *loins.*

His life will be burdensome to
him.

5 "My heart will cry out for Moab;
His fugitives *shall flee* to Zoar,
Like a three-year-old heifer.[a]
For by the Ascent of Luhith
They will go up with weeping;
For in the way of Horonaim
They will raise up a cry of
destruction,

6 For the waters of Nimrim will
be desolate,
For the green grass has
withered away;
The grass fails, there is nothing
green.

7 Therefore the abundance they
have gained,
And what they have laid up,
They will carry away to the
Brook of the Willows.

8 For the cry has gone all around
the borders of Moab,
Its wailing to Eglaim
And its wailing to Beer Elim.

9 For the waters of Dimon[a] will
be full of blood;
Because I will bring more upon
Dimon,[b]
Lions upon him who escapes
from Moab,
And on the remnant of the
land."

16 Send the lamb to the ruler of
the land,
From Sela to the wilderness,
To the mount of the daughter
of Zion.

2 For it shall be as a wandering
bird thrown out of the nest;
So shall be the daughters of
Moab at the fords of the
Arnon.

3 "Take counsel, execute
judgment;
Make your shadow like the
night in the middle of the
day;
Hide the outcasts,
Do not betray him who
escapes.

4 Let My outcasts dwell with you,
O Moab;
Be a shelter to them from the
face of the spoiler.
For the extortioner is at an end,

Devastation ceases,
The oppressors are consumed
out of the land.

5 In mercy the throne will be
established;
And One will sit on it in truth,
in the tabernacle of David,
Judging and seeking justice
and hastening
righteousness."

6 We have heard of the pride of
Moab—
He is very proud—
Of his haughtiness and his
pride and his wrath;
But his lies *shall* not *be* so.

7 Therefore Moab shall wail for
Moab;
Everyone shall wail.
For the foundations of Kir
Hareseth you shall mourn;
Surely *they are* stricken.

8 For the fields of Heshbon
languish,
And the vine of Sibmah;
The lords of the nations have
broken down its choice
plants,
Which have reached to Jazer
And wandered through the
wilderness.
Her branches are stretched out,
They are gone over the sea.

9 Therefore I will bewail the vine
of Sibmah,
With the weeping of Jazer;
I will drench you with my tears,
O Heshbon and Elealeh;
For battle cries have fallen
Over your summer fruits and
your harvest.

10 Gladness is taken away,
And joy from the plentiful field;
In the vineyards there will be
no singing,
Nor will there be shouting;
No treaders will tread out wine
in the presses;
I have made their shouting
cease.

11 Therefore my heart shall
resound like a harp for Moab,
And my inner being for Kir
Heres.

15:5 [a]Or *The Third Eglath,* an unknown city (compare Jeremiah 48:34)   15:9 [a]Following Masoretic Text
and Targum; Dead Sea Scrolls and Vulgate read *Dibon;* Septuagint reads *Rimon.*   [b]Following Masoretic
Text and Targum; Dead Sea Scrolls and Vulgate read *Dibon;* Septuagint reads *Rimon.*

12 And it shall come to pass,
 When it is seen that Moab is
  weary on the high place,
 That he will come to his
  sanctuary to pray;
 But he will not prevail.

13 This *is* the word which the LORD
has spoken concerning Moab since
that time. 14 But now the LORD has
spoken, saying, "Within three years,
as the years of a hired man, the glory
of Moab will be despised with all that
great multitude, and the remnant *will
be* very small *and* feeble."

17 The burden against Damascus.

 "Behold, Damascus will cease
  from *being* a city,
 And it will be a ruinous heap.
2 The cities of Aroer *are*
  forsaken;*a*
 They will be for flocks
 Which lie down, and no one
  will make *them* afraid.
3 The fortress also will cease
  from Ephraim,
 The kingdom from Damascus,
 And the remnant of Syria;
 They will be as the glory of the
  children of Israel,"
 Says the LORD of hosts.

4 "In that day it shall come to pass
 That the glory of Jacob will
  wane,
 And the fatness of his flesh
  grow lean.
5 It shall be as when the
  harvester gathers the grain,
 And reaps the heads with his
  arm;
 It shall be as he who gathers
  heads of grain
 In the Valley of Rephaim.
6 Yet gleaning grapes will be left
  in it,
 Like the shaking of an olive
  tree,
 Two *or* three olives at the top
  of the uppermost bough,
 Four *or* five in its most fruitful
  branches,"
 Says the LORD God of Israel.

7 In that day a man will look to
  his Maker,
 And his eyes will have respect
  for the Holy One of Israel.
8 He will not look to the altars,
 The work of his hands;
 He will not respect what his
  fingers have made,
 Nor the wooden images*a* nor
  the incense altars.

9 In that day his strong cities will
  be as a forsaken bough*a*
 And an uppermost branch,*b*
 Which they left because of the
  children of Israel;
 And there will be desolation.

10 Because you have forgotten the
  God of your salvation,
 And have not been mindful of
  the Rock of your stronghold,
 Therefore you will plant
  pleasant plants
 And set out foreign seedlings;
11 In the day you will make your
  plant to grow,
 And in the morning you will
  make your seed to flourish;
 But the harvest *will be* a heap
  of ruins
 In the day of grief and
  desperate sorrow.

12 Woe to the multitude of many
  people
 Who make a noise like the roar
  of the seas,
 And to the rushing of nations
 That make a rushing like
  the rushing of mighty
  waters!
13 The nations will rush like the
  rushing of many waters;
 But *God* will rebuke them and
  they will flee far away,
 And be chased like the chaff of
  the mountains before the
  wind,
 Like a rolling thing before the
  whirlwind.
14 Then behold, at eventide,
  trouble!
 And before the morning, he *is*
  no more.
 This *is* the portion of those who
  plunder us,
 And the lot of those who rob
  us.

17:2 *a*Following Masoretic Text and Vulgate; Septuagint reads *It shall be forsaken forever;* Targum reads *Its cities shall be forsaken and desolate.*   17:8 *a*Hebrew *Asherah,* a Canaanite goddess
17:9 *a*Septuagint reads *Hivites;* Targum reads *laid waste;* Vulgate reads *as the ploughs.*   *b*Septuagint reads *Amorites;* Targum reads *in ruins;* Vulgate reads *corn.*

18 Woe to the land shadowed with
buzzing wings,
Which *is* beyond the rivers of
Ethiopia,
2 Which sends ambassadors by
sea,
Even in vessels of reed on the
waters, *saying,*
"Go, swift messengers, to a
nation tall and smooth *of
skin,*
To a people terrible from their
beginning onward,
A nation powerful and treading
down,
Whose land the rivers divide."

3 All inhabitants of the world
and dwellers on the
earth:
When he lifts up a banner
on the mountains, you see
it;
And when he blows a trumpet,
you hear *it.*

4 For so the LORD said to me,
"I will take My rest,
And I will look from My
dwelling place
Like clear heat in sunshine,
Like a cloud of dew in the heat
of harvest."
5 For before the harvest, when
the bud is perfect
And the sour grape is ripening
in the flower,
He will both cut off the sprigs
with pruning hooks
And take away *and* cut down
the branches.
6 They will be left together for
the mountain birds of prey
And for the beasts of the earth;
The birds of prey will summer
on them,
And all the beasts of the earth
will winter on them.

7 In that time a present will be
brought to the LORD of hosts
From[a] a people tall and smooth
of skin,
And from a people terrible
from their beginning onward,
A nation powerful and treading
down,
Whose land the rivers divide—

To the place of the name of the
LORD of hosts,
To Mount Zion.

19 The burden against Egypt.

Behold, the LORD rides on a
swift cloud,
And will come into Egypt;
The idols of Egypt will totter at
His presence,
And the heart of Egypt will
melt in its midst.

2 "I will set Egyptians against
Egyptians;
Everyone will fight against his
brother,
And everyone against his
neighbor,
City against city, kingdom
against kingdom.
3 The spirit of Egypt will fail in
its midst;
I will destroy their counsel,
And they will consult the idols
and the charmers,
The mediums and the
sorcerers.
4 And the Egyptians I will give
Into the hand of a cruel master,
And a fierce king will rule over
them,"
Says the Lord, the LORD of
hosts.

5 The waters will fail from the
sea,
And the river will be wasted
and dried up.
6 The rivers will turn foul;
The brooks of defense will be
emptied and dried up;
The reeds and rushes will
wither.
7 The papyrus reeds by the
River,[a] by the mouth of the
River,
And everything sown by the
River,
Will wither, be driven away,
and be no more.
8 The fishermen also will mourn;
All those will lament who cast
hooks into the River,
And they will languish who
spread nets on the waters.
9 Moreover those who work in
fine flax

18:7 [a]Following Dead Sea Scrolls, Septuagint, and Vulgate; Masoretic Text omits *From;* Targum reads
To.   19:7 [a]That is, the Nile

And those who weave fine
fabric will be ashamed;
10 And its foundations will be
broken.
All who make wages *will be*
troubled of soul.

11 Surely the princes of Zoan *are*
fools;
Pharaoh's wise counselors give
foolish counsel.
How do you say to Pharaoh, "I
am the son of the wise,
The son of ancient kings?"
12 Where *are* they?
Where are your wise men?
Let them tell you now,
And let them know what the
LORD of hosts has purposed
against Egypt.
13 The princes of Zoan have
become fools;
The princes of Noph[a] are
deceived;
They have also deluded Egypt,
Those who are the mainstay of
its tribes.
14 The LORD has mingled a
perverse spirit in her midst;
And they have caused Egypt to
err in all her work,
As a drunken man staggers in
his vomit.
15 Neither will there be *any* work
for Egypt,
Which the head or tail,
Palm branch or bulrush, may
do.[a]

16 In that day Egypt will be like
women, and will be afraid and fear
because of the waving of the hand
of the LORD of hosts, which He waves
over it. 17 And the land of Judah will
be a terror to Egypt; everyone who
makes mention of it will be afraid in
himself, because of the counsel of the
LORD of hosts which He has determined against it.
18 In that day five cities in the land
of Egypt will speak the language of
Canaan and swear by the LORD of
hosts; one will be called the City of
Destruction.[a]
19 In that day there will be an altar
to the LORD in the midst of the land
of Egypt, and a pillar to the LORD at
its border. 20 And it will be for a sign

and for a witness to the LORD of hosts
in the land of Egypt; for they will cry
to the LORD because of the oppressors, and He will send them a Savior
and a Mighty One, and He will deliver them. 21 Then the LORD will be
known to Egypt, and the Egyptians
will know the LORD in that day, and
will make sacrifice and offering; yes,
they will make a vow to the LORD and
perform *it*. 22 And the LORD will
strike Egypt, He will strike and heal
it; they will return to the LORD, and
He will be entreated by them and
heal them.
23 In that day there will be a highway from Egypt to Assyria, and the
Assyrian will come into Egypt and
the Egyptian into Assyria, and the
Egyptians will serve with the Assyrians.
24 In that day Israel will be one of
three with Egypt and Assyria—a
blessing in the midst of the land,
25 whom the LORD of hosts shall
bless, saying, "Blessed *is* Egypt My
people, and Assyria the work of My
hands, and Israel My inheritance."

20 In the year that Tartan[a] came
to Ashdod, when Sargon the
king of Assyria sent him, and he
fought against Ashdod and took it,
2 at the same time the LORD spoke by
Isaiah the son of Amoz, saying, "Go,
and remove the sackcloth from your
body, and take your sandals off your
feet." And he did so, walking naked
and barefoot.
3 Then the LORD said, "Just as My
servant Isaiah has walked naked and
barefoot three years *for* a sign and a
wonder against Egypt and Ethiopia,
4 so shall the king of Assyria lead
away the Egyptians as prisoners and
the Ethiopians as captives, young
and old, naked and barefoot, with
their buttocks uncovered, to the
shame of Egypt. 5 Then they shall be
afraid and ashamed of Ethiopia their
expectation and Egypt their glory.
6 And the inhabitant of this territory
will say in that day, 'Surely such *is*
our expectation, wherever we flee for
help to be delivered from the king of
Assyria; and how shall we escape?'"

21 The burden against the Wilderness of the Sea.

19:13 [a]That is, ancient Memphis   19:15 [a]Compare Isaiah 9:14–16   19:18 [a]Some Hebrew manuscripts,
Arabic, Dead Sea Scrolls, Targum, and Vulgate read *Sun;* Septuagint reads *Asedek* (literally
Righteousness).   20:1 [a]Or *the Commander in Chief*

As whirlwinds in the South
　　pass through,
So it comes from the desert,
　　from a terrible land.
2　A distressing vision is declared
　　to me;
The treacherous dealer deals
　　treacherously,
And the plunderer plunders.
Go up, O Elam!
Besiege, O Media!
All its sighing I have made to
　　cease.

3　Therefore my loins are filled
　　with pain;
Pangs have taken hold of me,
　　like the pangs of a woman in
　　labor.
I was distressed when *I* heard
　　it;
I was dismayed when *I* saw
　　it.
4　My heart wavered, fearfulness
　　frightened me;
The night for which I longed He
　　turned into fear for me.
5　Prepare the table,
Set a watchman in the tower,
Eat and drink.
Arise, you princes,
Anoint the shield!

6　For thus has the Lord said to
　　me:
"Go, set a watchman,
Let him declare what he sees."
7　And he saw a chariot *with* a
　　pair of horsemen,
A chariot of donkeys, *and* a
　　chariot of camels,
And he listened earnestly with
　　great care.
8　Then he cried, "A lion,[a] my
　　Lord!
I stand continually on the
　　watchtower in the daytime;
I have sat at my post every
　　night.
9　And look, here comes a chariot
　　of men *with* a pair of
　　horsemen!"
Then he answered and said,
"Babylon is fallen, is fallen!
And all the carved images of
　　her gods
He has broken to the ground."

10　Oh, my threshing and the grain
　　of my floor!

That which I have heard from
　　the Lord of hosts,
The God of Israel,
I have declared to you.

11　The burden against Dumah.

He calls to me out of Seir,
"Watchman, what of the night?
Watchman, what of the
　　night?"
12　The watchman said,
"The morning comes, and also
　　the night.
If you will inquire, inquire;
Return! Come back!"

13　The burden against Arabia.

In the forest in Arabia you will
　　lodge,
O you traveling companies of
　　Dedanites.
14　O inhabitants of the land of
　　Tema,
Bring water to him who is
　　thirsty;
With their bread they met him
　　who fled.
15　For they fled from the swords,
　　from the drawn sword,
From the bent bow, and from
　　the distress of war.

16　For thus the Lord has said to me:
"Within a year, according to the year
of a hired man, all the glory of Kedar
will fail; 17 and the remainder of the
number of archers, the mighty men
of the people of Kedar, will be diminished; for the Lord God of Israel has
spoken *it.*"

22 The burden against the Valley of Vision.

What ails you now, that you
　　have all gone up to the
　　housetops,
2　You who are full of noise,
A tumultuous city, a joyous
　　city?
Your slain *men are* not slain
　　with the sword,
Nor dead in battle.
3　All your rulers have fled
　　together;
They are captured by the
　　archers.
All who are found in you are
　　bound together;

21:8 [a]Dead Sea Scrolls read *Then the observer cried.*

They have fled from afar.
4 Therefore I said, "Look away from me,
I will weep bitterly;
Do not labor to comfort me
Because of the plundering of
the daughter of my people."

5 For *it is* a day of trouble and
treading down and
perplexity
By the Lord GOD of hosts
In the Valley of Vision—
Breaking down the walls
And of crying to the mountain.
6 Elam bore the quiver
With chariots of men *and*
horsemen,
And Kir uncovered the shield.
7 It shall come to pass *that* your
choicest valleys
Shall be full of chariots,
And the horsemen shall set
themselves in array at the
gate.

8 He removed the protection of
Judah.
You looked in that day to the
armor of the House of the
Forest;
9 You also saw the damage to the
city of David,
That it was great;
And you gathered together the
waters of the lower pool.
10 You numbered the houses of
Jerusalem,
And the houses you broke
down
To fortify the wall.
11 You also made a reservoir
between the two walls
For the water of the old pool.
But you did not look to its
Maker,
Nor did you have respect for
Him who fashioned it long
ago.

12 And in that day the Lord GOD
of hosts
Called for weeping and for
mourning,
For baldness and for girding
with sackcloth.
13 But instead, joy and gladness,
Slaying oxen and killing sheep,
Eating meat and drinking wine:

"Let us eat and drink, for
tomorrow we die!"

14 Then it was revealed in my
hearing by the LORD of hosts,
"Surely for this iniquity there
will be no atonement for you,
Even to your death," says the
Lord GOD of hosts.

15 Thus says the Lord GOD of hosts:

"Go, proceed to this steward,
To Shebna, who *is* over the
house, *and say:*
16 'What have you here, and whom
have you here,
That you have hewn a
sepulcher here,
As he who hews himself a
sepulcher on high,
Who carves a tomb for himself
in a rock?
17 Indeed, the LORD will throw
you away violently,
O mighty man,
And will surely seize you.
18 He will surely turn violently
and toss you like a ball
Into a large country;
There you shall die, and there
your glorious chariots
Shall be the shame of your
master's house.
19 So I will drive you out of your
office,
And from your position he will
pull you down.[a]

20 'Then it shall be in that day,
That I will call My servant
Eliakim the son of Hilkiah;
21 I will clothe him with your robe
And strengthen him with your
belt;
I will commit your
responsibility into his hand.
He shall be a father to the
inhabitants of Jerusalem
And to the house of Judah.
22 The key of the house of David
I will lay on his shoulder;
So he shall open, and no one
shall shut;
And he shall shut, and no one
shall open.
23 I will fasten him *as* a peg in a
secure place,
And he will become a glorious
throne to his father's house.

22:19 aSeptuagint omits *he will pull you down;* Syriac, Targum, and Vulgate read *I will pull you down.*

24 'They will hang on him all the glory of his father's house, the offspring and the posterity, all vessels of small quantity, from the cups to all the pitchers. 25 In that day,' says the LORD of hosts, 'the peg that is fastened in the secure place will be removed and be cut down and fall, and the burden that *was* on it will be cut off; for the LORD has spoken.' "

23

The burden against Tyre.

Wail, you ships of Tarshish!
For it is laid waste,
So that there is no house, no
 harbor;
From the land of Cyprus[a] it is
 revealed to them.

2 Be still, you inhabitants of the
  coastland,
 You merchants of Sidon,
 Whom those who cross the sea
  have filled.[a]
3 And on great waters the grain
  of Shihor,
 The harvest of the River,[a] *is* her
  revenue;
 And she is a marketplace for
  the nations.

4 Be ashamed, O Sidon;
 For the sea has spoken,
 The strength of the sea, saying,
 "I do not labor, nor bring forth
  children;
 Neither do I rear young men,
 Nor bring up virgins."
5 When the report *reaches*
  Egypt,
 They also will be in agony at
  the report of Tyre.

6 Cross over to Tarshish;
 Wail, you inhabitants of the
  coastland!
7 *Is* this your joyous *city,*
 Whose antiquity *is* from
  ancient days,
 Whose feet carried her far off
  to dwell?
8 Who has taken this counsel
  against Tyre, the crowning
  city,
 Whose merchants *are* princes,
 Whose traders *are* the
  honorable of the earth?

9 The LORD of hosts has purposed
  it,
 To bring to dishonor the pride
  of all glory,
 To bring into contempt all the
  honorable of the earth.

10 Overflow through your land
  like the River,[a]
 O daughter of Tarshish;
 There is no more strength.
11 He stretched out His hand over
  the sea,
 He shook the kingdoms;
 The LORD has given a
  commandment against
  Canaan
 To destroy its strongholds.
12 And He said, "You will rejoice
  no more,
 O you oppressed virgin
  daughter of Sidon.
 Arise, cross over to Cyprus;
 There also you will have no
  rest."

13 Behold, the land of the
  Chaldeans,
 This people *which* was not;
 Assyria founded it for wild
  beasts of the desert.
 They set up its towers,
 They raised up its palaces,
 And brought it to ruin.

14 Wail, you ships of Tarshish!
 For your strength is laid waste.

15 Now it shall come to pass in that day that Tyre will be forgotten seventy years, according to the days of one king. At the end of seventy years it will happen to Tyre as *in* the song of the harlot:

16 "Take a harp, go about the city,
 You forgotten harlot;
 Make sweet melody, sing many
  songs,
 That you may be remembered."

17 And it shall be, at the end of seventy years, that the LORD will deal with Tyre. She will return to her hire, and commit fornication with all the kingdoms of the world on the face of the earth. 18 Her gain and her pay will be set apart for the LORD; it will not be treasured nor laid up, for her

---

23:1 [a]Hebrew *Kittim,* western lands, especially Cyprus 23:2 [a]Following Masoretic Text and Vulgate; Septuagint and Targum read *passing over the water;* Dead Sea Scrolls read *your messengers passing over the sea.* 23:3 [a]That is, the Nile 23:10 [a]That is, the Nile gain will be for those who dwell before the LORD, to eat sufficiently, and for fine clothing.

24 Behold, the LORD makes the earth empty and makes it waste,
Distorts its surface
And scatters abroad its inhabitants.

2 And it shall be:
As with the people, so with the priest;
As with the servant, so with his master;
As with the maid, so with her mistress;
As with the buyer, so with the seller;
As with the lender, so with the borrower;
As with the creditor, so with the debtor.

3 The land shall be entirely emptied and utterly plundered,
For the LORD has spoken this word.

4 The earth mourns *and* fades away,
The world languishes *and* fades away;
The haughty people of the earth languish.

5 The earth is also defiled under its inhabitants,
Because they have transgressed the laws,
Changed the ordinance,
Broken the everlasting covenant.

6 Therefore the curse has devoured the earth,
And those who dwell in it are desolate.
Therefore the inhabitants of the earth are burned,
And few men *are* left.

7 The new wine fails, the vine languishes,
All the merry-hearted sigh.

8 The mirth of the tambourine ceases,
The noise of the jubilant ends,
The joy of the harp ceases.

9 They shall not drink wine with a song;
Strong drink is bitter to those who drink it.

10 The city of confusion is broken down;
Every house is shut up, so that none may go in.

11 *There is* a cry for wine in the streets,
All joy is darkened,
The mirth of the land is gone.

12 In the city desolation is left,
And the gate is stricken with destruction.

13 When it shall be thus in the midst of the land among the people,
It shall be like the shaking of an olive tree,
Like the gleaning of grapes when the vintage is done.

14 They shall lift up their voice, they shall sing;
For the majesty of the LORD
They shall cry aloud from the sea.

15 Therefore glorify the LORD in the dawning light,
The name of the LORD God of Israel in the coastlands of the sea.

16 From the ends of the earth we have heard songs:
"Glory to the righteous!"
But I said, "I am ruined, ruined!
Woe to me!
The treacherous dealers have dealt treacherously,
Indeed, the treacherous dealers have dealt very treacherously."

17 Fear and the pit and the snare
Are upon you, O inhabitant of the earth.

18 And it shall be
That he who flees from the noise of the fear
Shall fall into the pit,
And he who comes up from the midst of the pit
Shall be caught in the snare;
For the windows from on high are open,
And the foundations of the earth are shaken.

19 The earth is violently broken,
The earth is split open,
The earth is shaken exceedingly.

20 The earth shall reel to and fro like a drunkard,

And shall totter like a hut;
Its transgression shall be heavy
upon it,
And it will fall, and not rise
again.

21 It shall come to pass in that day
That the LORD will punish on
high the host of exalted ones,
And on the earth the kings of
the earth.

22 They will be gathered together,
As prisoners are gathered in
the pit,
And will be shut up in the
prison;
After many days they will be
punished.

23 Then the moon will be
disgraced
And the sun ashamed;
For the LORD of hosts will reign
On Mount Zion and in
Jerusalem
And before His elders,
gloriously.

25 O LORD, You *are* my God.
I will exalt You,
I will praise Your name,
For You have done wonderful
things;
Your counsels of old *are*
faithfulness *and* truth.

2 For You have made a city a
ruin,
A fortified city a ruin,
A palace of foreigners to be a
city no more;
It will never be rebuilt.

3 Therefore the strong people
will glorify You;
The city of the terrible nations
will fear You.

4 For You have been a strength
to the poor,
A strength to the needy in his
distress,
A refuge from the storm,
A shade from the heat;
For the blast of the terrible ones
is as a storm *against* the wall.

5 You will reduce the noise of
aliens,
As heat in a dry place;
As heat in the shadow of a
cloud,
The song of the terrible ones
will be diminished.

6 And in this mountain
The LORD of hosts will make for
all people

A feast of choice pieces,
A feast of wines on the lees,
Of fat things full of marrow,
Of well-refined wines on the
lees.

7 And He will destroy on this
mountain
The surface of the covering cast
over all people,
And the veil that is spread over
all nations.

8 He will swallow up death
forever,
And the Lord GOD will wipe
away tears from all faces;
The rebuke of His people
He will take away from all the
earth;
For the LORD has spoken.

9 And it will be said in that day:
"Behold, this *is* our God;
We have waited for Him, and
He will save us.
This *is* the LORD;
We have waited for Him;
We will be glad and rejoice in
His salvation."

10 For on this mountain the hand
of the LORD will rest,
And Moab shall be trampled
down under Him,
As straw is trampled down for
the refuse heap.

11 And He will spread out His
hands in their midst
As a swimmer reaches out to
swim,
And He will bring down their
pride
Together with the trickery of
their hands.

12 The fortress of the high fort of
your walls
He will bring down, lay low,
And bring to the ground, down
to the dust.

26 In that day this song will be
sung in the land of Judah:

"We have a strong city;
God will appoint salvation *for*
walls and bulwarks.

2 Open the gates,
That the righteous nation
which keeps the truth may
enter in.

3 You will keep *him* in perfect
peace,
Whose mind *is* stayed *on You,*

Because he trusts in You.
4 Trust in the LORD forever,
For in YAH, the LORD, *is*
everlasting strength.[a]
5 For He brings down those who
dwell on high,
The lofty city;
He lays it low,
He lays it low to the ground,
He brings it down to the
dust.
6 The foot shall tread it down—
The feet of the poor
And the steps of the needy."

7 The way of the just *is*
uprightness;
O Most Upright,
You weigh the path of the
just.
8 Yes, in the way of Your
judgments,
O LORD, we have waited for
You;
The desire of *our* soul *is* for
Your name
And for the remembrance of
You.
9 With my soul I have desired
You in the night,
Yes, by my spirit within me I
will seek You early;
For when Your judgments *are*
in the earth,
The inhabitants of the world
will learn righteousness.

10 Let grace be shown to the
wicked,
Yet he will not learn
righteousness;
In the land of uprightness he
will deal unjustly,
And will not behold the
majesty of the LORD.
11 LORD, *when* Your hand is lifted
up, they will not see.
But they will see and be
ashamed
For *their* envy of people;
Yes, the fire of Your enemies
shall devour them.

12 LORD, You will establish peace
for us,
For You have also done all our
works in us.
13 O LORD our God, masters
besides You
Have had dominion over us;

But by You only we make
mention of Your name.
14 *They are* dead, they will not
live;
They are deceased, they will
not rise.
Therefore You have punished
and destroyed them,
And made all their memory to
perish.
15 You have increased the nation,
O LORD,
You have increased the nation;
You are glorified;
You have expanded all the
borders of the land.

16 LORD, in trouble they have
visited You,
They poured out a prayer *when*
Your chastening *was* upon
them.
17 As a woman with child
Is in pain and cries out in her
pangs,
When she draws near the time
of her delivery,
So have we been in Your sight,
O LORD.
18 We have been with child, we
have been in pain;
We have, as it were, brought
forth wind;
We have not accomplished any
deliverance in the earth,
Nor have the inhabitants of the
world fallen.

19 Your dead shall live;
Together with my dead body[a]
they shall arise.
Awake and sing, you who
dwell in dust;
For your dew *is like* the dew of
herbs,
And the earth shall cast out the
dead.

20 Come, my people, enter your
chambers,
And shut your doors behind
you;
Hide yourself, as it were, for a
little moment,
Until the indignation is past.
21 For behold, the LORD comes out
of His place
To punish the inhabitants of
the earth for their iniquity;

26:4 [a]Or *Rock of Ages*   26:19 [a]Following Masoretic Text and Vulgate; Syriac and Targum read *their
dead bodies;* Septuagint reads *those in the tombs.*

The earth will also disclose her
  blood,
And will no more cover her
  slain.

27 In that day the LORD with His
  severe sword, great and
  strong,
Will punish Leviathan the
  fleeing serpent,
Leviathan that twisted serpent;
And He will slay the reptile that
  is in the sea.

2 In that day sing to her,
  "A vineyard of red wine!*a*
3 I, the LORD, keep it,
I water it every moment;
Lest any hurt it,
I keep it night and day.
4 Fury *is* not in Me.
Who would set briers *and*
  thorns
Against Me in battle?
I would go through them,
I would burn them together.
5 Or let him take hold of My
  strength,
That he may make peace with
  Me;
And he shall make peace with
  Me."

6 Those who come He shall cause
  to take root in Jacob;
Israel shall blossom and bud,
And fill the face of the world
  with fruit.

7 Has He struck Israel as He
  struck those who struck
  him?
Or has He been slain according
  to the slaughter of those who
  were slain by Him?
8 In measure, by sending it away,
You contended with it.
He removes *it* by His rough
  wind
In the day of the east wind.
9 Therefore by this the iniquity
  of Jacob will be covered;
And this *is* all the fruit of taking
  away his sin:
When he makes all the stones
  of the altar
Like chalkstones that are
  beaten to dust,

Wooden images*a* and incense
  altars shall not stand.
10 Yet the fortified city *will be*
  desolate,
The habitation forsaken and
  left like a wilderness;
There the calf will feed, and
  there it will lie down
And consume its branches.
11 When its boughs are withered,
  they will be broken off;
The women come *and* set them
  on fire.
For it *is* a people of no
  understanding;
Therefore He who made them
  will not have mercy on
  them,
And He who formed them will
  show them no favor.

12 And it shall come to pass in that
  day
That the LORD will thresh,
From the channel of the River*a*
  to the Brook of Egypt;
And you will be gathered one
  by one,
O you children of Israel.

13 So it shall be in that day:
The great trumpet will be
  blown;
They will come, who are about
  to perish in the land of
  Assyria,
And they who are outcasts in
  the land of Egypt,
And shall worship the LORD in
  the holy mount at Jerusalem.

28 Woe to the crown of pride, to
  the drunkards of Ephraim,
Whose glorious beauty *is* a
  fading flower
Which *is* at the head of the
  verdant valleys,
To those who are overcome
  with wine!
2 Behold, the Lord has a mighty
  and strong one,
Like a tempest of hail and a
  destroying storm,
Like a flood of mighty waters
  overflowing,
Who will bring *them* down to
  the earth with *His* hand.

27:2 *a*Following Masoretic Text (Kittel's *Biblia Hebraica*), Bomberg, and Vulgate; Masoretic Text (*Biblia Hebraica Stuttgartensia*), some Hebrew manuscripts, and Septuagint read *delight;* Targum reads *choice vineyard.*   27:9 *a*Hebrew *Asherim*, Canaanite deities   27:12 *a*That is, the Euphrates

3 The crown of pride, the
   drunkards of Ephraim,
   Will be trampled underfoot;
4 And the glorious beauty is a
   fading flower
   Which *is* at the head of the
   verdant valley,
   Like the first fruit before the
   summer,
   Which an observer sees;
   He eats it up while it is still in
   his hand.

5 In that day the LORD of hosts
   will be
   For a crown of glory and a
   diadem of beauty
   To the remnant of His people,
6 For a spirit of justice to him
   who sits in judgment,
   And for strength to those who
   turn back the battle at the
   gate.

7 But they also have erred
   through wine,
   And through intoxicating drink
   are out of the way;
   The priest and the prophet
   have erred through
   intoxicating drink,
   They are swallowed up by
   wine,
   They are out of the way
   through intoxicating drink;
   They err in vision, they stumble
   in judgment.
8 For all tables are full of vomit
   and filth;
   No place *is clean.*

9 "Whom will he teach
   knowledge?
   And whom will he make to
   understand the message?
   Those *just* weaned from milk?
   Those *just* drawn from the
   breasts?
10 For precept *must be* upon
   precept, precept upon
   precept,
   Line upon line, line upon line,
   Here a little, there a little."

11 For with stammering lips and
   another tongue
   He will speak to this people,
12 To whom He said, "This *is* the
   rest *with which*
   You may cause the weary to
   rest,"

And, "This *is* the refreshing";
Yet they would not hear.
13 But the word of the LORD was
   to them,
   "Precept upon precept, precept
   upon precept,
   Line upon line, line upon line,
   Here a little, there a little,"
   That they might go and fall
   backward, and be broken
   And snared and caught.

14 Therefore hear the word of the
   LORD, you scornful men,
   Who rule this people who *are*
   in Jerusalem,
15 Because you have said, "We
   have made a covenant with
   death,
   And with Sheol we are in
   agreement.
   When the overflowing scourge
   passes through,
   It will not come to us,
   For we have made lies our
   refuge,
   And under falsehood we have
   hidden ourselves."

16 Therefore thus says the Lord
GOD:

   "Behold, I lay in Zion a stone for
   a foundation,
   A tried stone, a precious
   cornerstone, a sure
   foundation;
   Whoever believes will not act
   hastily.
17 Also I will make justice the
   measuring line,
   And righteousness the
   plummet;
   The hail will sweep away the
   refuge of lies,
   And the waters will overflow
   the hiding place.
18 Your covenant with death will
   be annulled,
   And your agreement with
   Sheol will not stand;
   When the overflowing scourge
   passes through,
   Then you will be trampled
   down by it.
19 As often as it goes out it will
   take you;
   For morning by morning it will
   pass over,
   And by day and by night;
   It will be a terror just to
   understand the report."

20 For the bed is too short to
stretch out *on*,
And the covering so narrow
that one cannot wrap himself
in it.
21 For the LORD will rise up as *at*
Mount Perazim,
He will be angry as in the
Valley of Gibeon—
That He may do His work, His
awesome work,
And bring to pass His act, His
unusual act.
22 Now therefore, do not be
mockers,
Lest your bonds be made
strong;
For I have heard from the Lord
GOD of hosts,
A destruction determined even
upon the whole earth.

23 Give ear and hear my voice,
Listen and hear my speech.
24 Does the plowman keep
plowing all day to sow?
Does he keep turning his soil
and breaking the clods?
25 When he has leveled its
surface,
Does he not sow the black
cummin
And scatter the cummin,
Plant the wheat in rows,
The barley in the appointed
place,
And the spelt in its place?
26 For He instructs him in right
judgment,
His God teaches him.

27 For the black cummin is not
threshed with a threshing
sledge,
Nor is a cartwheel rolled over
the cummin;
But the black cummin is beaten
out with a stick,
And the cummin with a rod.
28 Bread *flour* must be ground;
Therefore he does not thresh it
forever,
Break *it with* his cartwheel,
Or crush *it with* his horsemen.
29 This also comes from the LORD
of hosts,
Who is wonderful in counsel
and excellent in guidance.

29 "Woe to Ariel,[a] to Ariel, the city
where David dwelt!

29:1 [a]That is, Jerusalem

Add year to year;
Let feasts come around.
2 Yet I will distress Ariel;
There shall be heaviness and
sorrow,
And it shall be to Me as Ariel.
3 I will encamp against you all
around,
I will lay siege against you with
a mound,
And I will raise siegeworks
against you.
4 You shall be brought down,
You shall speak out of the
ground;
Your speech shall be low, out
of the dust;
Your voice shall be like a
medium's, out of the
ground;
And your speech shall whisper
out of the dust.

5 "Moreover the multitude of your
foes
Shall be like fine dust,
And the multitude of the
terrible ones
Like chaff that passes away;
Yes, it shall be in an instant,
suddenly.
6 You will be punished by the
LORD of hosts
With thunder and earthquake
and great noise,
With storm and tempest
And the flame of devouring
fire.
7 The multitude of all the nations
who fight against Ariel,
Even all who fight against her
and her fortress,
And distress her,
Shall be as a dream of a night
vision.
8 It shall even be as when a
hungry man dreams,
And look—he eats;
But he awakes, and his soul is
still empty;
Or as when a thirsty man
dreams,
And look—he drinks;
But he awakes, and indeed *he
is* faint,
And his soul still craves:
So the multitude of all the
nations shall be,
Who fight against Mount
Zion."

9 Pause and wonder!
  Blind yourselves and be blind!
  They are drunk, but not with
    wine;
  They stagger, but not with
    intoxicating drink.
10 For the LORD has poured out on
    you
  The spirit of deep sleep,
  And has closed your eyes,
    namely, the prophets;
  And He has covered your
    heads, *namely*, the seers.

11 The whole vision has become to
you like the words of a book that
is sealed, which *men* deliver to one
who is literate, saying, "Read this,
please."
  And he says, "I cannot, for it *is*
sealed."
12 Then the book is delivered to
one who is illiterate, saying, "Read
this, please."
  And he says, "I am not literate."
13 Therefore the LORD said:

  "Inasmuch as these people draw
    near with their mouths
  And honor Me with their lips,
  But have removed their hearts
    far from Me,
  And their fear toward Me is
    taught by the commandment
    of men,
14 Therefore, behold, I will again
    do a marvelous work
  Among this people,
  A marvelous work and a
    wonder;
  For the wisdom of their wise
    men shall perish,
  And the understanding of their
    prudent *men* shall be
    hidden."

15 Woe to those who seek deep to
    hide their counsel far from
    the LORD,
  And their works are in the
    dark;
  They say, "Who sees us?" and,
  "Who knows us?"
16 Surely you have things turned
    around!
  Shall the potter be esteemed as
    the clay;
  For shall the thing made say of
    him who made it,
  "He did not make me"?
  Or shall the thing formed say
    of him who formed it,
  "He has no understanding"?

17 *Is* it not yet a very little while
    Till Lebanon shall be turned
    into a fruitful field,
  And the fruitful field be
    esteemed as a forest?
18 In that day the deaf shall hear
    the words of the book,
  And the eyes of the blind shall
    see out of obscurity and out
    of darkness.
19 The humble also shall increase
    their joy in the LORD,
  And the poor among men shall
    rejoice
  In the Holy One of Israel.
20 For the terrible one is brought
    to nothing,
  The scornful one is consumed,
  And all who watch for iniquity
    are cut off—
21 Who make a man an offender
    by a word,
  And lay a snare for him who
    reproves in the gate,
  And turn aside the just by
    empty words.

22 Therefore thus says the LORD,
who redeemed Abraham, concerning
the house of Jacob:

  "Jacob shall not now be
    ashamed,
  Nor shall his face now grow
    pale;
23 But when he sees his children,
  The work of My hands, in his
    midst,
  They will hallow My name,
  And hallow the Holy One of
    Jacob,
  And fear the God of Israel.
24 These also who erred in spirit
    will come to understanding,
  And those who complained will
    learn doctrine."

30 "Woe to the rebellious
    children," says the LORD,
  "Who take counsel, but not of
    Me,
  And who devise plans, but not
    of My Spirit,
  That they may add sin to sin;
2 Who walk to go down to Egypt,
  And have not asked My advice,
  To strengthen themselves in
    the strength of Pharaoh,
  And to trust in the shadow of
    Egypt!
3 Therefore the strength of
    Pharaoh

Shall be your shame,
And trust in the shadow of
    Egypt
Shall be *your* humiliation.
4 For his princes were at Zoan,
    And his ambassadors came to
        Hanes.
5 They were all ashamed of a
    people *who* could not benefit
    them,
    Or be help or benefit,
    But a shame and also a
        reproach."

6 The burden against the beasts of
the South.

Through a land of trouble and
    anguish,
From which *came* the lioness
    and lion,
The viper and fiery flying
    serpent,
They will carry their riches on
    the backs of young donkeys,
And their treasures on the
    humps of camels,
To a people *who* shall not
    profit;
7 For the Egyptians shall help in
    vain and to no purpose.
    Therefore I have called her
    Rahab-Hem-Shebeth.[a]

8 Now go, write it before them on
    a tablet,
    And note it on a scroll,
    That it may be for time to come,
    Forever and ever:
9 That this *is* a rebellious people,
    Lying children,
    Children *who* will not hear the
        law of the LORD;
10 Who say to the seers, "Do not
    see,"
    And to the prophets, "Do not
        prophesy to us right things;
    Speak to us smooth things,
        prophesy deceits.
11 Get out of the way,
    Turn aside from the path,
    Cause the Holy One of Israel
    To cease from before us."

12 Therefore thus says the Holy
One of Israel:

"Because you despise this word,
    And trust in oppression and
        perversity,
    And rely on them,

13 Therefore this iniquity shall be
    to you
    Like a breach ready to fall,
    A bulge in a high wall,
    Whose breaking comes
        suddenly, in an instant.
14 And He shall break it like the
    breaking of the potter's
    vessel,
    Which is broken in pieces;
    He shall not spare.
    So there shall not be found
        among its fragments
    A shard to take fire from the
        hearth,
    Or to take water from the
        cistern."

15 For thus says the Lord GOD, the
Holy One of Israel:

"In returning and rest you shall
    be saved;
In quietness and confidence
    shall be your strength."
    But you would not,
16 And you said, "No, for we will
    flee on horses"—
    Therefore you shall flee!
    And, "We will ride on swift
        horses"—
    Therefore those who pursue
        you shall be swift!

17 One thousand *shall flee* at the
    threat of one,
    At the threat of five you shall
        flee,
    Till you are left as a pole on
        top of a mountain
    And as a banner on a hill.
18 Therefore the LORD will wait,
    that He may be gracious to
    you;
    And therefore He will be
        exalted, that He may have
        mercy on you.
    For the LORD *is* a God of justice;
    Blessed *are* all those who wait
        for Him.

19 For the people shall dwell in
    Zion at Jerusalem;
    You shall weep no more.
    He will be very gracious to you
        at the sound of your cry;
    When He hears it, He will
        answer you.
20 And *though* the Lord gives you

30:7 aLiterally *Rahab Sits Idle*

The bread of adversity and the
water of affliction,
Yet your teachers will not be
moved into a corner
anymore,
But your eyes shall see your
teachers.

21 Your ears shall hear a word
behind you, saying,
"This *is* the way, walk in it,"
Whenever you turn to the right
hand
Or whenever you turn to the
left.

22 You will also defile the
covering of your images of
silver,
And the ornament of your
molded images of gold.
You will throw them away as
an unclean thing;
You will say to them, "Get
away!"

23 Then He will give the rain for
your seed
With which you sow the
ground,
And bread of the increase of
the earth;
It will be fat and plentiful.
In that day your cattle will feed
In large pastures.

24 Likewise the oxen and the
young donkeys that work the
ground
Will eat cured fodder,
Which has been winnowed
with the shovel and fan.

25 There will be on every high
mountain
And on every high hill
Rivers *and* streams of waters,
In the day of the great
slaughter,
When the towers fall.

26 Moreover the light of the moon
will be as the light of the
sun,
And the light of the sun will be
sevenfold,
As the light of seven days,
In the day that the Lord binds
up the bruise of His people
And heals the stroke of their
wound.

27 Behold, the name of the Lord
comes from afar,
Burning *with* His anger,
And *His* burden *is* heavy;
His lips are full of indignation,

And His tongue like a
devouring fire.

28 His breath is like an
overflowing stream,
Which reaches up to the neck,
To sift the nations with the
sieve of futility;
And *there shall be* a bridle in
the jaws of the people,
Causing *them* to err.

29 You shall have a song
As in the night *when* a holy
festival is kept,
And gladness of heart as when
one goes with a flute,
To come into the mountain of
the Lord,
To the Mighty One of Israel.

30 The Lord will cause His
glorious voice to be heard,
And show the descent of His
arm,
With the indignation of *His*
anger
And the flame of a devouring
fire,
With scattering, tempest, and
hailstones.

31 For through the voice of the
Lord
Assyria will be beaten down,
As He strikes with the rod.

32 And *in* every place where the
staff of punishment passes,
Which the Lord lays on him,
It will be with tambourines and
harps;
And in battles of brandishing
He will fight with it.

33 For Tophet *was* established of
old,
Yes, for the king it is prepared.
He has made *it* deep and large;
Its pyre *is* fire with much
wood;
The breath of the Lord, like a
stream of brimstone,
Kindles it.

31 Woe to those who go down to
Egypt for help,
And rely on horses,
Who trust in chariots because
they are many,
And in horsemen because they
are very strong,
But who do not look to the Holy
One of Israel,
Nor seek the Lord!

2 Yet He also *is* wise and will
bring disaster,

And will not call back His
words,
But will arise against the house
of evildoers,
And against the help of those
who work iniquity.
3 Now the Egyptians *are* men,
and not God;
And their horses are flesh, and
not spirit.
When the LORD stretches out
His hand,
Both he who helps will fall,
And he who is helped will fall
down;
They all will perish together.

4 For thus the LORD has spoken to
me:

"As a lion roars,
And a young lion over his prey
(When a multitude of
shepherds is summoned
against him,
He will not be afraid of their
voice
Nor be disturbed by their
noise),
So the LORD of hosts will come
down
To fight for Mount Zion and for
its hill.
5 Like birds flying about,
So will the LORD of hosts
defend Jerusalem.
Defending, He will also deliver
it;
Passing over, He will preserve
it."

6 Return *to Him* against whom the
children of Israel have deeply revolted. 7 For in that day every man
shall throw away his idols of silver
and his idols of gold—sin, which your
own hands have made for yourselves.

8 "Then Assyria shall fall by a
sword not of man,
And a sword not of mankind
shall devour him.
But he shall flee from the
sword,
And his young men shall
become forced labor.
9 He shall cross over to his
stronghold for fear,
And his princes shall be afraid
of the banner,"
Says the LORD,

Whose fire *is* in Zion
And whose furnace *is* in
Jerusalem.

32 Behold, a king will reign in
righteousness,
And princes will rule with
justice.
2 A man will be as a hiding place
from the wind,
And a cover from the tempest,
As rivers of water in a dry
place,
As the shadow of a great rock
in a weary land.
3 The eyes of those who see will
not be dim,
And the ears of those who hear
will listen.
4 Also the heart of the rash will
understand knowledge,
And the tongue of the
stammerers will be ready to
speak plainly.
5 The foolish person will no
longer be called generous,
Nor the miser said *to be*
bountiful;
6 For the foolish person will
speak foolishness,
And his heart will work
iniquity:
To practice ungodliness,
To utter error against the LORD,
To keep the hungry unsatisfied,
And he will cause the drink of
the thirsty to fail.
7 Also the schemes of the
schemer *are* evil;
He devises wicked plans
To destroy the poor with lying
words,
Even when the needy speaks
justice.
8 But a generous man devises
generous things,
And by generosity he shall
stand.
9 Rise up, you women who are
at ease,
Hear my voice;
You complacent daughters,
Give ear to my speech.
10 In a year and *some* days
You will be troubled, you
complacent women;
For the vintage will fail,
The gathering will not come.
11 Tremble, you *women* who are
at ease;

Be troubled, you complacent
  ones;
Strip yourselves, make
  yourselves bare,
And gird *sackcloth* on *your*
  waists.

12 People shall mourn upon their
     breasts
   For the pleasant fields, for the
     fruitful vine.
13 On the land of my people will
     come up thorns *and* briers,
   Yes, on all the happy homes *in*
     the joyous city;
14 Because the palaces will be
     forsaken,
   The bustling city will be
     deserted.
   The forts and towers will
     become lairs forever,
   A joy of wild donkeys, a
     pasture of flocks—
15 Until the Spirit is poured upon
     us from on high,
   And the wilderness becomes a
     fruitful field,
   And the fruitful field is counted
     as a forest.
16 Then justice will dwell in the
     wilderness,
   And righteousness remain in
     the fruitful field.
17 The work of righteousness will
     be peace,
   And the effect of righteousness,
     quietness and assurance
     forever.
18 My people will dwell in a
     peaceful habitation,
   In secure dwellings, and in
     quiet resting places,
19 Though hail comes down on
     the forest,
   And the city is brought low in
     humiliation.
20 Blessed *are* you who sow
     beside all waters,
   Who send out freely the feet of
     the ox and the donkey.

33 Woe to you who plunder,
     though you *have* not *been*
     plundered;
   And you who deal
     treacherously, though they
     have not dealt treacherously
     with you!

When you cease plundering,
  You will be plundered;
When you make an end of
  dealing treacherously,
They will deal treacherously
  with you.

2 O LORD, be gracious to us;
  We have waited for You.
  Be their[a] arm every morning,
  Our salvation also in the time
    of trouble.
3 At the noise of the tumult the
    people shall flee;
  When You lift Yourself up, the
    nations shall be scattered;
4 And Your plunder shall be
    gathered
  Like the gathering of the
    caterpillar;
  As the running to and fro of
    locusts,
  He shall run upon them.

5 The LORD is exalted, for He
    dwells on high;
  He has filled Zion with justice
    and righteousness.
6 Wisdom and knowledge will be
    the stability of your times,
  And the strength of salvation;
  The fear of the LORD *is* His
    treasure.

7 Surely their valiant ones shall
    cry outside,
  The ambassadors of peace
    shall weep bitterly.
8 The highways lie waste,
  The traveling man ceases.
  He has broken the covenant,
  He has despised the cities,[a]
  He regards no man.
9 The earth mourns *and*
    languishes,
  Lebanon is shamed *and*
    shriveled;
  Sharon is like a wilderness,
  And Bashan and Carmel shake
    off *their fruits.*

10 "Now I will rise," says the LORD;
   "Now I will be exalted,
   Now I will lift Myself up.
11 You shall conceive chaff,
   You shall bring forth stubble;
   Your breath, *as* fire, shall
     devour you.

33:2 [a]Septuagint omits *their*; Syriac, Targum, and Vulgate read *our.*   33:8 [a]Following Masoretic Text and Vulgate; Dead Sea Scrolls read *witnesses*; Septuagint omits *cities*; Targum reads *They have been removed from their cities.*

12 And the people shall be *like* the
burnings of lime;
Like thorns cut up they shall be
burned in the fire.
13 Hear, you *who are* afar off,
what I have done;
And you *who are* near,
acknowledge My might."

14 The sinners in Zion are afraid;
Fearfulness has seized the
hypocrites:
"Who among us shall dwell with
the devouring fire?
Who among us shall dwell with
everlasting burnings?"
15 He who walks righteously and
speaks uprightly,
He who despises the gain of
oppressions,
Who gestures with his hands,
refusing bribes,
Who stops his ears from
hearing of bloodshed,
And shuts his eyes from seeing
evil:
16 He will dwell on high;
His place of defense *will be* the
fortress of rocks;
Bread will be given him,
His water *will be* sure.

17 Your eyes will see the King in
His beauty;
They will see the land that is
very far off.
18 Your heart will meditate on
terror:
"Where *is* the scribe?
Where *is* he who weighs?
Where *is* he who counts the
towers?"
19 You will not see a fierce people,
A people of obscure speech,
beyond perception,
Of a stammering tongue *that*
you cannot understand.

20 Look upon Zion, the city of our
appointed feasts;
Your eyes will see Jerusalem,
a quiet home,
A tabernacle *that* will not be
taken down;
Not one of its stakes will ever
be removed,
Nor will any of its cords be
broken.
21 But there the majestic LORD *will*
be for us
A place of broad rivers *and*
streams,

In which no galley with oars
will sail,
Nor majestic ships pass by
22 (For the LORD *is* our Judge,
The LORD *is* our Lawgiver,
The LORD *is* our King;
He will save us);
23 Your tackle is loosed,
They could not strengthen their
mast,
They could not spread the sail.

Then the prey of great plunder
is divided;
The lame take the prey.
24 And the inhabitant will not say,
"I am sick";
The people who dwell in it *will*
be forgiven *their* iniquity.

34 Come near, you nations, to
hear;
And heed, you people!
Let the earth hear, and all that
is in it,
The world and all things that
come forth from it.
2 For the indignation of the LORD
is against all nations,
And *His* fury against all their
armies;
He has utterly destroyed them,
He has given them over to the
slaughter.
3 Also their slain shall be thrown
out;
Their stench shall rise from
their corpses,
And the mountains shall be
melted with their blood.
4 All the host of heaven shall be
dissolved,
And the heavens shall be rolled
up like a scroll;
All their host shall fall down
As the leaf falls from the vine,
And as *fruit* falling from a fig
tree.

5 "For My sword shall be bathed
in heaven;
Indeed it shall come down on
Edom,
And on the people of My curse,
for judgment.
6 The sword of the LORD is filled
with blood,
It is made overflowing with
fatness,
With the blood of lambs and
goats,

The Desert—A Garden

"The grass withers, the flower fades, but the word of our God stands forever" (Is. 40:8).

Springtime in Israel is adorned with bright red poppies, yellow mustard plants, and green rolling hills. Yet, within one week the land can be scorched into a dry, colorless dust bowl. The *hamsins*, desert winds from the east, come without warning in April. Like fire, they parch the land of its new growth. Throughout the Old Testament, the psalmist and the prophets note this sudden disaster. Yet it is always followed with a promise; God will make the desert bloom. He will turn wasteland into glory.

Like the *hamsins*, problems and tragedies can come into our lives without warning. Just when a business begins to grow, a project starts to develop, or a relationship begins to flourish, an unforeseen circumstance can change the landscape of our lives. This is when we must not lose hope. We must cling to the promises. God will make the deserts in our lives bloom with new growth. Patience, perseverance, and understanding are all required to let God work. We must give God time to heal our hurts. We must offer Him the chance to reseed and restore our dreams.

Then the problem will become an opportunity! The scar—a star! The desert—a living garden! "The wilderness and the wasteland shall be glad for them, and the desert shall rejoice and blossom as the rose" (Is. 35:1).

With the fat of the kidneys of
　　rams.
For the LORD has a sacrifice in
　　Bozrah,
And a great slaughter in the
　　land of Edom.

7　The wild oxen shall come down
　　with them,
And the young bulls with the
　　mighty bulls;
Their land shall be soaked with
　　blood,
And their dust saturated with
　　fatness."

8　For *it is* the day of the LORD's
　　vengeance,
The year of recompense for the
　　cause of Zion.

9　Its streams shall be turned into
　　pitch,
And its dust into brimstone;
Its land shall become burning
　　pitch.

10　It shall not be quenched night
　　or day;
Its smoke shall ascend forever.
From generation to generation
　　it shall lie waste;
No one shall pass through it
　　forever and ever.

11　But the pelican and the
　　porcupine shall possess it,
Also the owl and the raven
　　shall dwell in it.
And He shall stretch out over
　　it
The line of confusion and the
　　stones of emptiness.

12　They shall call its nobles to the
　　kingdom,
But none *shall be* there, and all
　　its princes shall be nothing.

13　And thorns shall come up in its
　　palaces,
Nettles and brambles in its
　　fortresses;
It shall be a habitation of
　　jackals,
A courtyard for ostriches.

14　The wild beasts of the desert
　　shall also meet with the
　　jackals,
And the wild goat shall bleat
　　to its companion;
Also the night creature shall
　　rest there,
And find for herself a place of
　　rest.

15　There the arrow snake shall
　　make her nest and lay *eggs*
And hatch, and gather *them*
　　under her shadow;
There also shall the hawks be
　　gathered,
Every one with her mate.

16　"Search from the book of the
　　LORD, and read:
Not one of these shall fail;
Not one shall lack her mate.
For My mouth has commanded
　　it, and His Spirit has
　　gathered them.

17　He has cast the lot for them,
And His hand has divided it
　　among them with a
　　measuring line.
They shall possess it forever;
From generation to generation
　　they shall dwell in it."

35　The wilderness and the
　　wasteland shall be glad for
　　them,
And the desert shall rejoice and
　　blossom as the rose;

2　It shall blossom abundantly
　　and rejoice,
Even with joy and singing.
The glory of Lebanon shall be
　　given to it,
The excellence of Carmel and
　　Sharon.
They shall see the glory of the
　　LORD,
The excellency of our God.

3　Strengthen the weak hands,
And make firm the feeble
　　knees.

4　Say to those *who are* fearful-
　　hearted,

"Be strong, do not fear!
Behold, your God will come
　　with vengeance,
With the recompense of God;
He will come and save you."

5　Then the eyes of the blind shall
　　be opened,
And the ears of the deaf shall
　　be unstopped.

6　Then the lame shall leap like a
　　deer,
And the tongue of the dumb
　　sing.
For waters shall burst forth in
　　the wilderness,
And streams in the desert.

7　The parched ground shall
　　become a pool,

Roads of Palestine

The prophet Isaiah spoke symbolically of a "Highway of Holiness" over which "the unclean shall not pass" (Is. 35:8). But the Bible makes few references to the actual physical roads that connected the cities of Palestine and surrounding regions in Bible times. Scholars do know that two major north-to-south trade routes passed through the nation. The first, called "The Way of the Sea," connected the ancient Phoenician seaports of Tyre and Sidon with other cities along the Mediterranean. This road may have stretched as far south as the northern reaches of Egypt.

The second major north-south route across Palestine was the King's Highway, which connected Ezion Geber, or Elath, in the south with the city of Damascus, Syria, in the north.

While Israel was a relatively small nation, other nations often passed through it because of its strategic location as a land bridge between Egypt in the south and the nations of Syria, Assyria, Persia, and Babylon to the north and northeast.

And the thirsty land springs of
water;
In the habitation of jackals,
where each lay,
There shall be grass with reeds
and rushes.

8 A highway shall be there, and
a road,
And it shall be called the
Highway of Holiness.
The unclean shall not pass over
it,
But it *shall be* for others.
Whoever walks the road,
although a fool,
Shall not go astray.
9 No lion shall be there,
Nor shall *any* ravenous beast
go up on it;
It shall not be found there.
But the redeemed shall walk
there,
10 And the ransomed of the LORD
shall return,
And come to Zion with singing,
With everlasting joy on their
heads.
They shall obtain joy and
gladness,
And sorrow and sighing shall
flee away.

36 Now it came to pass in the fourteenth year of King Hezekiah
that Sennacherib king of Assyria
came up against all the fortified cities
of Judah and took them. 2 Then the
king of Assyria sent *the* Rabshakeh[a]
with a great army from Lachish to
King Hezekiah at Jerusalem. And he
stood by the aqueduct from the upper
pool, on the highway to the Fuller's
Field. 3 And Eliakim the son of Hilkiah, who was over the household,
Shebna the scribe, and Joah the son
of Asaph, the recorder, came out to
him.
4 Then *the* Rabshakeh said to
them, "Say now to Hezekiah, 'Thus
says the great king, the king of Assyria: "What confidence is this in
which you trust? 5 I say you speak
of having plans and power for war;
but *they are* mere words. Now in
whom do you trust, that you rebel
against me? 6 Look! You are trusting
in the staff of this broken reed, Egypt,
on which if a man leans, it will go
into his hand and pierce it. So *is*

Pharaoh king of Egypt to all who
trust in him.
7 "But if you say to me, 'We trust
in the LORD our God,' *is it* not He
whose high places and whose altars Hezekiah has taken away, and
said to Judah and Jerusalem, 'You
shall worship before this altar'?"'
8 Now therefore, I urge you, give a
pledge to my master the king of Assyria, and I will give you two thousand horses—if you are able on your
part to put riders on them! 9 How
then will you repel one captain of the
least of my master's servants, and
put your trust in Egypt for chariots
and horsemen? 10 Have I now come
up without the LORD against this land
to destroy it? The LORD said to me,
'Go up against this land, and destroy
it.' "
11 Then Eliakim, Shebna, and Joah
said to *the* Rabshakeh, "Please speak
to your servants in Aramaic, for we
understand *it;* and do not speak to
us in Hebrew[a] in the hearing of the
people who *are* on the wall."
12 But *the* Rabshakeh said, "Has
my master sent me to your master
and to you to speak these words, and
not to the men who sit on the wall,
who will eat and drink their own
waste with you?"
13 Then *the* Rabshakeh stood and
called out with a loud voice in Hebrew, and said, "Hear the words of
the great king, the king of Assyria!
14 Thus says the king: 'Do not let
Hezekiah deceive you, for he will not
be able to deliver you; 15 nor let
Hezekiah make you trust in the LORD,
saying, "The LORD will surely deliver
us; this city will not be given into the
hand of the king of Assyria."'
16 Do not listen to Hezekiah; for thus
says the king of Assyria: 'Make
peace with me *by a* present and come
out to me; and every one of you eat
from his own vine and every one
from his own fig tree, and every one
of you drink the waters of his own
cistern; 17 until I come and take you
away to a land like your own land,
a land of grain and new wine, a land
of bread and vineyards. 18 *Beware*
lest Hezekiah persuade you, saying,
"The LORD will deliver us." Has any
one of the gods of the nations delivered its land from the hand of the
king of Assyria? 19 Where *are* the

36:2 ᵃA title, probably *Chief of Staff* or *Governor*   36:11 ᵃLiterally *Judean* gods of Hamath and Arpad? Where *are* the gods of Sepharvaim? Indeed, have they delivered Samaria from my hand? 20 Who among all the gods of these lands have delivered their countries from my hand, that the LORD should deliver Jerusalem from my hand?' ''

21 But they held their peace and answered him not a word; for the king's commandment was, "Do not answer him." 22 Then Eliakim the son of Hilkiah, who *was* over the household, Shebna the scribe, and Joah the son of Asaph, the recorder, came to Hezekiah with *their* clothes torn, and told him the words of *the* Rabshakeh.

37 And so it was, when King Hezekiah heard *it*, that he tore his clothes, covered himself with sackcloth, and went into the house of the LORD. 2 Then he sent Eliakim, who *was* over the household, Shebna the scribe, and the elders of the priests, covered with sackcloth, to Isaiah the prophet, the son of Amoz. 3 And they said to him, "Thus says Hezekiah: 'This day *is* a day of trouble and rebuke and blasphemy; for the children have come to birth, but *there is* no strength to bring them forth. 4 It may be that the LORD your God will hear the words of *the* Rabshakeh, whom his master the king of Assyria has sent to reproach the living God, and will rebuke the words which the LORD your God has heard. Therefore lift up *your* prayer for the remnant that is left.' ''

5 So the servants of King Hezekiah came to Isaiah. 6 And Isaiah said to them, "Thus you shall say to your master, 'Thus says the LORD: "Do not be afraid of the words which you have heard, with which the servants of the king of Assyria have blasphemed Me. 7 Surely I will send a spirit upon him, and he shall hear a rumor and return to his own land; and I will cause him to fall by the sword in his own land." ' ''

8 Then *the* Rabshakeh returned, and found the king of Assyria warring against Libnah, for he heard that he had departed from Lachish. 9 And the king heard concerning Tirhakah king of Ethiopia, "He has come out to make war with you." So when he heard *it*, he sent messengers to Hezekiah, saying, 10 "Thus you

shall speak to Hezekiah king of Judah, saying: 'Do not let your God in whom you trust deceive you, saying, "Jerusalem shall not be given into the hand of the king of Assyria." 11 Look! You have heard what the kings of Assyria have done to all lands by utterly destroying them; and shall you be delivered? 12 Have the gods of the nations delivered those whom my fathers have destroyed, Gozan and Haran and Rezeph, and the people of Eden who *were* in Telassar? 13 Where *is* the king of Hamath, the king of Arpad, and the king of the city of Sepharvaim, Hena, and Ivah?' ''

14 And Hezekiah received the letter from the hand of the messengers, and read it; and Hezekiah went up to the house of the LORD, and spread it before the LORD. 15 Then Hezekiah prayed to the LORD, saying: 16 "O LORD of hosts, God of Israel, *the One* who dwells *between* the cherubim, You *are* God, You alone, of all the kingdoms of the earth. You have made heaven and earth. 17 Incline Your ear, O LORD, and hear; open Your eyes, O LORD, and see; and hear all the words of Sennacherib, which he has sent to reproach the living God. 18 Truly, LORD, the kings of Assyria have laid waste all the nations and their lands, 19 and have cast their gods into the fire; for they *were* not gods, but the work of men's hands—wood and stone. Therefore they destroyed them. 20 Now therefore, O LORD our God, save us from his hand, that all the kingdoms of the earth may know that You *are* the LORD, You alone."

21 Then Isaiah the son of Amoz sent to Hezekiah, saying, "Thus says the LORD God of Israel, 'Because you have prayed to Me against Sennacherib king of Assyria, 22 this *is* the word which the LORD has spoken concerning him:

"The virgin, the daughter of Zion,
    Has despised you, laughed you to scorn;
    The daughter of Jerusalem
    Has shaken *her* head behind your back!

23 "Whom have you reproached and blasphemed?
    Against whom have you raised *your* voice,

Face Reality with Hope

The inch-by-inch principle is building your faith. The little things you do today for someone else will add up to a lifetime of joy!

You can be genuinely optimistic about the prospect of enjoying life.

You have faith today to be able to accomplish the incredible by using the inch-by-inch principle.

Faith is answering the telephone, it is balancing the checkbook, and it is stepping on the scale!

Faith is confronting reality, not running away from it. If a telephone call brings bad news, have the faith to deal with it inch by inch. If finances are depleted—inch by inch, turn the problem around. If the scale says you're overweight, have the faith to tackle your problem slowly and surely—inch by inch!

Faith is not a contradiction of reality, but the courage to face reality with hope. Many people have found that gradually—over the years—extra pounds creep up on them. "Step on the scale every day" is excellent advice! When they do that, and write down the results, they find themselves succeeding in taking off those unwanted pounds!

Whether your problem is big or small, don't run from it. Instead, face it and give it back to God. Hezekiah himself cried out to God in his illness, and God blessed him with renewed health (Is. 38:3–5).

Today face reality with hope, and begin to turn your life around. Remember, with God all things are possible!

And lifted up your eyes on
  high?
Against the Holy One of Israel.
24 By your servants you have
  reproached the Lord,
And said, 'By the multitude of
  my chariots
I have come up to the height
  of the mountains,
To the limits of Lebanon;
I will cut down its tall cedars
And its choice cypress trees;
I will enter its farthest height,
To its fruitful forest.
25 I have dug and drunk water,
And with the soles of my feet I
  have dried up
All the brooks of defense.'

26 "Did you not hear long ago
How I made it,
From ancient times that I
  formed it?
Now I have brought it to pass,
That you should be
For crushing fortified cities *into*
  heaps of ruins.
27 Therefore their inhabitants *had*
  little power;
They were dismayed and
  confounded;
They were *as* the grass of the
  field
And the green herb,
As the grass on the housetops
And grain blighted before it is
  grown.

28 "But I know your dwelling place,
Your going out and your
  coming in,
And your rage against Me.
29 Because your rage against Me
  and your tumult
Have come up to My ears,
Therefore I will put My hook
  in your nose
And My bridle in your lips,
And I will turn you back
By the way which you came." '

30 "This *shall be* a sign to you:

You shall eat this year such as
  grows of itself,
And the second year what
  springs from the same;
Also in the third year sow and
  reap,

Plant vineyards and eat the
  fruit of them.
31 And the remnant who have
  escaped of the house of
  Judah
Shall again take root
  downward,
And bear fruit upward.
32 For out of Jerusalem shall go
  a remnant,
And those who escape from
  Mount Zion.
The zeal of the LORD of hosts
  will do this.

33 "Therefore thus says the LORD
concerning the king of Assyria:

'He shall not come into this city,
Nor shoot an arrow there,
Nor come before it with shield,
Nor build a siege mound
  against it.
34 By the way that he came,
By the same shall he return;
And he shall not come into this
  city,'
Says the LORD.
35 'For I will defend this city, to
  save it
For My own sake and for My
  servant David's sake.' "

36 Then the angel[a] of the LORD went
out, and killed in the camp of the Assyrians one hundred and eighty-five
thousand; and when *people* arose
early in the morning, there were the
corpses—all dead. 37 So Sennacherib
king of Assyria departed and went
away, returned *home,* and remained
at Nineveh. 38 Now it came to pass,
as he was worshiping in the house
of Nisroch his god, that his sons
Adrammelech and Sharezer struck
him down with the sword; and they
escaped into the land of Ararat. Then
Esarhaddon his son reigned in his
place.

38 In those days Hezekiah was
sick and near death. And Isaiah
the prophet, the son of Amoz, went
to him and said to him, "Thus says
the LORD: 'Set your house in order,
for you shall die and not live.' "
2 Then Hezekiah turned his face toward the wall, and prayed to the
LORD, 3 and said, "Remember now, O
LORD, I pray, how I have walked before You in truth and with a loyal

heart, and have done *what is* good in Your sight." And Hezekiah wept bitterly.

4 And the word of the LORD came to Isaiah, saying, 5 "Go and tell Hezekiah, 'Thus says the LORD, the God of David your father: "I have heard your prayer, I have seen your tears; surely I will add to your days fifteen years. 6 I will deliver you and this city from the hand of the king of Assyria, and I will defend this city." ' 7 And this *is* the sign to you from the LORD, that the LORD will do this thing which He has spoken: 8 Behold, I will bring the shadow on the sundial, which has gone down with the sun on the sundial of Ahaz, ten degrees backward." So the sun returned ten degrees on the dial by which it had gone down.

9 This is the writing of Hezekiah king of Judah, when he had been sick and had recovered from his sickness:

10 I said,

"In the prime of my life
   I shall go to the gates of
     Sheol;
I am deprived of the remainder
   of my years."

11 I said,

"I shall not see YAH,
   The LORD*ᵃ* in the land of the
     living;
I shall observe man no more
   among the inhabitants of the
     world.*ᵇ*

12 My life span is gone,
   Taken from me like a
     shepherd's tent;
I have cut off my life like a
     weaver.
He cuts me off from the loom;
From day until night You make
   an end of me.

13 I have considered until
     morning—
Like a lion,
So He breaks all my bones;
From day until night You make
   an end of me.

14 Like a crane *or* a swallow, so I
     chattered;
I mourned like a dove;

My eyes fail *from looking*
   upward.
O LORD,*ᵃ* I am oppressed;
Undertake for me!

15 "What shall I say?
He has both spoken to me,*ᵃ*
And He Himself has done *it.*
I shall walk carefully all my
     years
In the bitterness of my soul.

16 O LORD, by these *things men*
   live;
And in all these *things is* the
   life of my spirit;
So You will restore me and
   make me live.

17 Indeed *it was for my own* peace
   That I had great bitterness;
But You have lovingly
   delivered my soul from the
   pit of corruption,
For You have cast all my sins
   behind Your back.

18 For Sheol cannot thank You,
Death cannot praise You;
Those who go down to the pit
   cannot hope for Your truth.

19 The living, the living man, he
   shall praise You,
As I *do* this day;
The father shall make known
   Your truth to the children.

20 "The LORD *was ready* to save
   me;
Therefore we will sing my
   songs with stringed
     instruments
All the days of our life, in the
   house of the LORD."

21 Now Isaiah had said, "Let them take a lump of figs, and apply *it* as a poultice on the boil, and he shall recover."

22 And Hezekiah had said, "What *is* the sign that I shall go up to the house of the LORD?"

39 At that time Merodach-Baladan*ᵃ* the son of Baladan, king of Babylon, sent letters and a present to Hezekiah, for he heard that he had been sick and had recovered.

2 And Hezekiah was pleased with

38:11 *ᵃ*Hebrew YAH, YAH   *ᵇ*Following some Hebrew manuscripts; Masoretic Text and Vulgate read *rest;* Septuagint omits *among the inhabitants of the world;* Targum reads *land.*   38:14 *ᵃ*Following Bomberg; Masoretic Text and Dead Sea Scrolls read *Lord.*   38:15 *ᵃ*Following Masoretic Text and Vulgate; Dead Sea Scrolls and Targum read *And shall I say to Him;* Septuagint omits first half of this verse.   39:1 *ᵃ*Spelled *Berodach-Baladan* in 2 Kings 20:12

The Crooked Made Straight

The Judean wilderness is a foreboding and desolate area. Due to its precarious location on one of the earth's greatest geological faults, it has suffered violent earthquakes since the dawn of time. The earth strata normally found deep beneath the surface have been pushed up in this place, forming twisted riverbeds and steep canyons. The wilderness itself plummets to the depths of 1,300 feet below sea level, rising again to 3,000 feet above sea level.

This wilderness was a symbol to Israel's prophets of the power of God to change people's lives. Isaiah foretold that "every valley shall be exalted and every mountain and hill brought low; the crooked places shall be made straight and the rough places smooth; the glory of the LORD shall be revealed" (Is. 40:4, 5).

It was customary in ancient times for kings and princes to send out messengers before them. These scouts made sure the paths were clear to travel. They removed rocks, bushes, and thorns, forded rivers and built bridges, widened narrow passes in the road, and sought out threatening thieves or robbers. John the Baptist was the "scout" for the Lord Jesus Christ. He prepared the hearts of listeners for the message of the Lord.

Jesus fulfilled the prophecy of Isaiah. In His ministry He made the valleys high, the mountains low, and the way straight in the lives of all who believed in Him. Today, Jesus Christ has the power to overcome the valleys of despair and depression in our lives. He makes our mountainous problems into plains. He takes the crooked, twisted, confused aspects of life and makes them a straight highway to move ahead. And He smoothes the rough spots along the way.

Nothing is too great for God's power! Let the glory of the Lord be revealed in your life today!

them, and showed them the house of his treasures—the silver and gold, the spices and precious ointment, and all his armory—all that was found among his treasures. There was nothing in his house or in all his dominion that Hezekiah did not show them.

3 Then Isaiah the prophet went to King Hezekiah, and said to him, "What did these men say, and from where did they come to you?"

So Hezekiah said, "They came to me from a far country, from Babylon."

4 And he said, "What have they seen in your house?"

So Hezekiah answered, "They have seen all that *is* in my house; there is nothing among my treasures that I have not shown them."

5 Then Isaiah said to Hezekiah, "Hear the word of the LORD of hosts: 6 'Behold, the days are coming when all that *is* in your house, and what your fathers have accumulated until this day, shall be carried to Babylon; nothing shall be left,' says the LORD. 7 'And they shall take away *some* of your sons who will descend from you, whom you will beget; and they shall be eunuchs in the palace of the king of Babylon.' "

8 So Hezekiah said to Isaiah, "The word of the LORD which you have spoken *is* good!" For he said, "At least there will be peace and truth in my days."

40 "Comfort, yes, comfort My people!"
Says your God.
2 "Speak comfort to Jerusalem,
and cry out to her,
That her warfare is ended,
That her iniquity is pardoned;
For she has received from the
LORD's hand
Double for all her sins."

3 The voice of one crying in the
wilderness:
"Prepare the way of the LORD;
Make straight in the desert[a]
A highway for our God.
4 Every valley shall be exalted
And every mountain and hill
brought low;

The crooked places shall be
made straight
And the rough places smooth;
5 The glory of the LORD shall be
revealed,
And all flesh shall see *it*
together;
For the mouth of the LORD has
spoken."

6 The voice said, "Cry out!"
And he[a] said, "What shall I
cry?"

"All flesh *is* grass,
And all its loveliness *is* like the
flower of the field.
7 The grass withers, the flower
fades,
Because the breath of the LORD
blows upon it;
Surely the people *are* grass.
8 The grass withers, the flower
fades,
But the word of our God stands
forever."

9 O Zion,
You who bring good tidings,
Get up into the high mountain;
O Jerusalem,
You who bring good tidings,
Lift up your voice with
strength,
Lift *it* up, be not afraid;
Say to the cities of Judah,
"Behold your God!"

10 Behold, the Lord GOD shall
come with a strong *hand*,
And His arm shall rule for Him;
Behold, His reward *is* with
Him,
And His work before Him.
11 He will feed His flock like a
shepherd;
He will gather the lambs with
His arm,
And carry *them* in His bosom,
And gently lead those who are
with young.

12 Who has measured the waters[a]
in the hollow of His hand,
Measured heaven with a span
And calculated the dust of the
earth in a measure?

40:3 [a]Following Masoretic Text, Targum, and Vulgate; Septuagint omits *in the desert.*   40:6 [a]Following Masoretic Text and Targum; Dead Sea Scrolls, Septuagint, and Vulgate read *I.*   40:12 [a]Following Masoretic Text, Septuagint, and Vulgate; Dead Sea Scrolls read *waters of the sea;* Targum reads *waters of the world.*

On Wings of Eagles

From the 9,000-foot-high snow-capped mountains of Lebanon to the jagged peaks of the Sinai wilderness, the majestic golden eagle can be seen floating effortlessly in the wind. He soars, circles, and dives down to the rocks below in search of his prey. The sole monarch of the sky, the eagle has long been a symbol to biblical writers.

After forty years of aimless wandering in the harsh wilderness of Sinai, the Israelites must have looked up into the sky to see these great birds soaring overhead. With uplifted spirits they believed that God would bear them "on eagles' wings" (Ex. 19:4). Swift in flight, eagles can reach a speed of eighty miles per hour. Likewise, the Israelites would be swift and mighty in the conquest of the Promised Land.

God's care and comfort for His people is often likened to the eagle's care for her young. Set on a high ledge, the eagle's nest is secure and virtually inaccessible to predators. Any mountain climber who has been near an eagle's nest knows all too well the fury of the mother eagle protecting her home. With wingspans from nine to ten feet, the bird encompasses her young to shelter them from harm. The psalmist compares God's care for His people to the eagle's wings. "Hide me under the shadow of Your wings" (Ps. 17:8).

Looking to the strong, muscular eagle, the biblical writer described his all-powerful God. "But those who wait on the LORD shall renew *their* strength; they shall mount up with wings like eagles, they shall run and not be weary, they shall walk and not faint" (Is. 40:31).

Like the ancient Israelites, look to God for an eagle-powered faith. Prepare yourself by waiting patiently for your dreams. And when the Almighty God gives them to you, let them soar to new heights of reality. Attempt to do something great for God, even though you might fail, rather than do nothing and succeed.

Weighed the mountains in
scales
And the hills in a balance?
13 Who has directed the Spirit of
the LORD,
Or *as* His counselor has taught
Him?
14 With whom did He take
counsel, and *who* instructed
Him,
And taught Him in the path of
justice?
Who taught Him knowledge,
And showed Him the way of
understanding?

15 Behold, the nations *are* as a
drop in a bucket,
And are counted as the small
dust on the scales;
Look, He lifts up the isles as a
very little thing.
16 And Lebanon *is* not sufficient
to burn,
Nor its beasts sufficient for a
burnt offering.
17 All nations before Him *are* as
nothing,
And they are counted by Him
less than nothing and
worthless.

18 To whom then will you liken
God?
Or what likeness will you
compare to Him?
19 The workman molds an image,
The goldsmith overspreads it
with gold,
And the silversmith casts silver
chains.
20 Whoever *is* too impoverished
for *such* a contribution
Chooses a tree *that* will not rot;
He seeks for himself a skillful
workman
To prepare a carved image *that*
will not totter.

21 Have you not known?
Have you not heard?
Has it not been told you from
the beginning?
Have you not understood from
the foundations of the earth?
22 *It is* He who sits above the
circle of the earth,
And its inhabitants *are* like
grasshoppers,
Who stretches out the heavens
like a curtain,

And spreads them out like a
tent to dwell in.
23 He brings the princes to
nothing;
He makes the judges of the
earth useless.

24 Scarcely shall they be planted,
Scarcely shall they be sown,
Scarcely shall their stock take
root in the earth,
When He will also blow on
them,
And they will wither,
And the whirlwind will take
them away like stubble.

25 "To whom then will you liken
Me,
Or *to whom* shall I be equal?"
says the Holy One.
26 Lift up your eyes on high,
And see who has created these
things,
Who brings out their host by
number;
He calls them all by name,
By the greatness of His might
And the strength of *His* power;
Not one is missing.

27 Why do you say, O Jacob,
And speak, O Israel:
"My way is hidden from the
LORD,
And my just claim is passed
over by my God"?
28 Have you not known?
Have you not heard?
The everlasting God, the LORD,
The Creator of the ends of the
earth,
Neither faints nor is weary.
His understanding is
unsearchable.
29 He gives power to the weak,
And to *those who have* no
might He increases strength.
30 Even the youths shall faint and
be weary,
And the young men shall
utterly fall,
31 But those who wait on the LORD
Shall renew *their* strength;
They shall mount up with
wings like eagles,
They shall run and not be
weary,
They shall walk and not faint.

41 "Keep silence before Me, O
coastlands,

And let the people renew *their*
  strength!
Let them come near, then let
  them speak;
Let us come near together for
  judgment.

2 "Who raised up one from the
    east?
Who in righteousness called
  him to His feet?
Who gave the nations before
  him,
And made *him* rule over kings?
Who gave *them* as the dust *to*
  his sword,
As driven stubble to his bow?
3 Who pursued them, *and* passed
    safely
By the way *that* he had not
  gone with his feet?
4 Who has performed and done
  it,
Calling the generations from
  the beginning?
'I, the LORD, am the first;
And with the last I *am* He.' "

5 The coastlands saw *it* and
    feared,
The ends of the earth were
  afraid;
They drew near and came.
6 Everyone helped his neighbor,
And said to his brother,
  Be of good courage!"
7 So the craftsman encouraged
  the goldsmith;
He who smooths *with* the
  hammer *inspired* him who
  strikes the anvil,
Saying, "It *is* ready for the
  soldering";
Then he fastened it with pegs,
That it might not totter.

8 "But you, Israel, *are* My servant,
Jacob whom I have chosen,
The descendants of Abraham
  My friend.
9 *You* whom I have taken from
  the ends of the earth,
And called from its farthest
  regions,
And said to you,
  'You *are* My servant,
I have chosen you and have not
  cast you away:
10 Fear not, for I *am* with you;
Be not dismayed, for I *am* your
  God.
I will strengthen you,

Yes, I will help you,
I will uphold you with My
  righteous right hand.'

11 "Behold, all those who were
  incensed against you
Shall be ashamed and
  disgraced;
They shall be as nothing,
And those who strive with you
  shall perish.
12 You shall seek them and not
  find them—
Those who contended with
  you.
Those who war against you
Shall be as nothing,
As a nonexistent thing.
13 For I, the LORD your God, will
  hold your right hand,
Saying to you, 'Fear not, I will
  help you.'

14 "Fear not, you worm Jacob,
You men of Israel!
I will help you," says the LORD
And your Redeemer, the Holy
  One of Israel.
15 "Behold, I will make you into a
  new threshing sledge with
  sharp teeth;
You shall thresh the mountains
  and beat *them* small,
And make the hills like chaff.
16 You shall winnow them, the
  wind shall carry them away,
And the whirlwind shall scatter
  them;
You shall rejoice in the LORD,
And glory in the Holy One of
  Israel.

17 "The poor and needy seek
  water, but *there is* none,
Their tongues fail for thirst.
I, the LORD, will hear them;
I, the God of Israel, will not
  forsake them.
18 I will open rivers in desolate
  heights,
And fountains in the midst of
  the valleys;
I will make the wilderness a
  pool of water,
And the dry land springs of
  water.
19 I will plant in the wilderness
  the cedar and the acacia tree,
The myrtle and the oil tree;
I will set in the desert the
  cypress tree *and* the pine
And the box tree together,

20 That they may see and know,
   And consider and understand
      together,
   That the hand of the LORD has
      done this,
   And the Holy One of Israel has
      created it.

21 "Present your case," says the
      LORD.
   "Bring forth your strong
      reasons," says the King of
      Jacob.
22 "Let them bring forth and show
      us what will happen;
   Let them show the former
      things, what they *were,*
   That we may consider them,
   And know the latter end of
      them;
   Or declare to us things to
      come.
23 Show the things that are to
      come hereafter,
   That we may know that you *are*
      gods;
   Yes, do good or do evil,
   That we may be dismayed and
      see *it* together.
24 Indeed you *are* nothing,
   And your work *is* nothing;
   He who chooses you *is* an
      abomination.

25 "I have raised up one from the
      north,
   And he shall come;
   From the rising of the sun he
      shall call on My name;
   And he shall come against
      princes as *though* mortar,
   As the potter treads clay.
26 Who has declared from the
      beginning, that we may
      know?
   And former times, that we may
      say, '*He is* righteous'?
   Surely *there is* no one who
      shows,
   Surely *there is* no one who
      declares,
   Surely *there is* no one who
      hears your words.
27 The first time *I said* to Zion,
   'Look, there they are!'
   And I will give to Jerusalem
      one who brings good tidings.
28 For I looked, and *there was* no
      man;

I looked among them, but *there
      was* no counselor,
   Who, when I asked of them,
      could answer a word.
29 Indeed they *are* all worthless;[a]
   Their works *are* nothing;
   Their molded images *are* wind
      and confusion.

42 "Behold! My Servant whom I
      uphold,
   My Elect One *in whom* My soul
      delights!
   I have put My Spirit upon
      Him;
   He will bring forth justice to the
      Gentiles.
2 He will not cry out, nor raise
      His voice,
   Nor cause His voice to be heard
      in the street.
3 A bruised reed He will not
      break,
   And smoking flax He will not
      quench;
   He will bring forth justice for
      truth.
4 He will not fail nor be
      discouraged,
   Till He has established justice
      in the earth;
   And the coastlands shall wait
      for His law."

5 Thus says God the LORD,
   Who created the heavens and
      stretched them out,
   Who spread forth the earth and
      that which comes from it,
   Who gives breath to the people
      on it,
   And spirit to those who walk
      on it:
6 "I, the LORD, have called You in
      righteousness,
   And will hold Your hand;
   I will keep You and give You
      as a covenant to the people,
   As a light to the Gentiles,
7 To open blind eyes,
   To bring out prisoners from the
      prison,
   Those who sit in darkness from
      the prison house.
8 I *am* the LORD, that *is* My name;
   And My glory I will not give to
      another,
   Nor My praise to carved
      images.

41:29 ªFollowing Masoretic Text and Vulgate; Dead Sea Scrolls, Syriac, and Targum read *nothing;* Septuagint
omits the first line.

9 Behold, the former things have
   come to pass,
   And new things I declare;
   Before they spring forth I tell
   you of them."

10 Sing to the LORD a new song,
   And His praise from the ends
   of the earth,
   You who go down to the sea,
   and all that is in it,
   You coastlands and you
   inhabitants of them!
11 Let the wilderness and its cities
   lift up *their voice,*
   The villages *that* Kedar
   inhabits.
   Let the inhabitants of Sela
   sing,
   Let them shout from the top of
   the mountains.
12 Let them give glory to the
   LORD,
   And declare His praise in the
   coastlands.
13 The LORD shall go forth like a
   mighty man;
   He shall stir up *His* zeal like a
   man of war.
   He shall cry out, yes, shout
   aloud;
   He shall prevail against His
   enemies.

14 "I have held My peace a long
   time,
   I have been still and restrained
   Myself.
   Now I will cry like a woman in
   labor,
   I will pant and gasp at once.
15 I will lay waste the mountains
   and hills,
   And dry up all their vegetation;
   I will make the rivers
   coastlands,
   And I will dry up the pools.
16 I will bring the blind by a way
   they did not know;
   I will lead them in paths they
   have not known.
   I will make darkness light
   before them,
   And crooked places straight.
   These things I will do for
   them,
   And not forsake them.
17 They shall be turned back,
   They shall be greatly ashamed,
   Who trust in carved images,
   Who say to the molded images,
   'You *are* our gods.'

18 "Hear, you deaf;
   And look, you blind, that you
   may see.
19 Who *is* blind but My servant,
   Or deaf as My messenger
   whom I send?
   Who *is* blind as *he who is*
   perfect,
   And blind as the LORD's
   servant?
20 Seeing many things, but you do
   not observe;
   Opening the ears, but he does
   not hear."

21 The LORD is well pleased for
   His righteousness' sake;
   He will exalt the law and make
   it honorable.
22 But this *is* a people robbed and
   plundered;
   All of them are snared in holes,
   And they are hidden in prison
   houses;
   They are for prey, and no one
   delivers;
   For plunder, and no one says,
   "Restore!"

23 Who among you will give ear
   to this?
   Who will listen and hear for the
   time to come?
24 Who gave Jacob for plunder,
   and Israel to the robbers?
   Was it not the LORD,
   He against whom we have
   sinned?
   For they would not walk in His
   ways,
   Nor were they obedient to His
   law.
25 Therefore He has poured on
   him the fury of His anger
   And the strength of battle;
   It has set him on fire all around,
   Yet he did not know;
   And it burned him,
   Yet he did not take *it* to heart.

43 But now, thus says the LORD,
   who created you, O Jacob,
   And He who formed you, O
   Israel:
   "Fear not, for I have redeemed
   you;
   I have called *you* by your name;
   You *are* Mine.
2 When you pass through the
   waters, I *will be* with you;
   And through the rivers, they
   shall not overflow you.

When you walk through the
    fire, you shall not be burned,
Nor shall the flame scorch you.
3   For I *am* the LORD your God,
The Holy One of Israel, your
    Savior;
I gave Egypt for your ransom,
Ethiopia and Seba in your
    place.
4   Since you were precious in My
    sight,
You have been honored,
And I have loved you;
Therefore I will give men for
    you,
And people for your life.
5   Fear not, for I *am* with you;
I will bring your descendants
    from the east,
And gather you from the west;
6   I will say to the north, 'Give
    them up!'
And to the south, 'Do not keep
    them back!'
Bring My sons from afar,
And My daughters from the
    ends of the earth—
7   Everyone who is called by My
    name,
Whom I have created for My
    glory;
I have formed him, yes, I have
    made him."

8   Bring out the blind people who
    have eyes,
And the deaf who have ears.
9   Let all the nations be gathered
    together,
And let the people be
    assembled.
Who among them can declare
    this,
And show us former things?
Let them bring out their
    witnesses, that they may be
    justified;
Or let them hear and say, "It
    is truth."
10 "You *are* My witnesses," says
    the LORD,
"And My servant whom I have
    chosen,
That you may know and
    believe Me,
And understand that I *am* He.
Before Me there was no God
    formed,
Nor shall there be after Me.
11 I, *even* I, *am* the LORD,
And besides Me *there is* no
    savior.

12 I have declared and saved,
I have proclaimed,
And *there was* no foreign *god*
    among you;
Therefore you *are* My
    witnesses,"
Says the LORD, "that I *am* God.
13 Indeed before the day *was,* I *am*
    He;
And *there is* no one who can
    deliver out of My hand;
I work, and who will reverse
    it?"

14 Thus says the LORD, your
    Redeemer,
The Holy One of Israel:
"For your sake I will send to
    Babylon,
And bring them all down as
    fugitives—
The Chaldeans, who rejoice in
    their ships.
15 I *am* the LORD, your Holy One,
The Creator of Israel, your
    King."

16 Thus says the LORD, who
    makes a way in the sea
And a path through the mighty
    waters,
17 Who brings forth the chariot
    and horse,
The army and the power
(They shall lie down together,
    they shall not rise;
They are extinguished, they are
    quenched like a wick):
18 "Do not remember the former
    things,
Nor consider the things of
    old.
19 Behold, I will do a new thing,
Now it shall spring forth;
Shall you not know it?
I will even make a road in the
    wilderness
And rivers in the desert.
20 The beast of the field will honor
    Me,
The jackals and the ostriches,
Because I give waters in the
    wilderness
And rivers in the desert,
To give drink to My people, My
    chosen.
21 This people I have formed for
    Myself;
They shall declare My praise.

22 "But you have not called upon
    Me, O Jacob;

And you have been weary of
Me, O Israel.
23 You have not brought Me the
sheep for your burnt
offerings,
Nor have you honored Me with
your sacrifices.
I have not caused you to serve
with grain offerings,
Nor wearied you with incense.
24 You have bought Me no sweet
cane with money,
Nor have you satisfied Me with
the fat of your sacrifices;
But you have burdened Me
with your sins,
You have wearied Me with
your iniquities.

25 "I, *even* I, *am* He who blots out
your transgressions for My
own sake;
And I will not remember your
sins.
26 Put Me in remembrance;
Let us contend together;
State your *case*, that you may
be acquitted.
27 Your first father sinned,
And your mediators have
transgressed against Me.
28 Therefore I will profane the
princes of the sanctuary;
I will give Jacob to the curse,
And Israel to reproaches.

44 "Yet hear now, O Jacob My
servant,
And Israel whom I have
chosen.
2 Thus says the LORD who made
you
And formed you from the
womb, *who* will help you:
'Fear not, O Jacob My servant;
And you, Jeshurun, whom I
have chosen.
3 For I will pour water on him
who is thirsty,
And floods on the dry ground;
I will pour My Spirit on your
descendants,
And My blessing on your
offspring;
4 They will spring up among the
grass
Like willows by the
watercourses.'
5 One will say, 'I *am* the LORD's';
Another will call *himself* by the
name of Jacob;

Another will write *with* his
hand, 'The LORD's,'
And name *himself* by the name
of Israel.

6 "Thus says the LORD, the King
of Israel,
And his Redeemer, the LORD of
hosts:
'I *am* the First and I *am* the Last;
Besides Me *there is* no God.
7 And who can proclaim as I do?
Then let him declare it and set
it in order for Me,
Since I appointed the ancient
people.
And the things that are coming
and shall come,
Let them show these to them.
8 Do not fear, nor be afraid;
Have I not told you from that
time, and declared *it*?
You *are* My witnesses.
Is there a God besides Me?
Indeed *there is* no other Rock;
I know not *one*.' "

9 Those who make an image, all
of them *are* useless,
And their precious things shall
not profit;
They *are* their own witnesses;
They neither see nor know, that
they may be ashamed.
10 Who would form a god or mold
an image
That profits him nothing?
11 Surely all his companions
would be ashamed;
And the workmen, they *are*
mere men.
Let them all be gathered
together,
Let them stand up;
Yet they shall fear,
They shall be ashamed
together.

12 The blacksmith with the tongs
works one in the coals,
Fashions it with hammers,
And works it with the strength
of his arms.
Even so, he is hungry, and his
strength fails;
He drinks no water and is faint.

13 The craftsman stretches out *his*
rule,
He marks one out with chalk;
He fashions it with a plane,

He marks it out with the
    compass,
And makes it like the figure of
    a man,
According to the beauty of a
    man, that it may remain in
    the house.

14 He cuts down cedars for
    himself,
And takes the cypress and the
    oak;
He secures *it* for himself
    among the trees of the
    forest.
He plants a pine, and the rain
    nourishes *it*.

15 Then it shall be for a man to
    burn,
For he will take some of it and
    warm himself;
Yes, he kindles *it* and bakes
    bread;
Indeed he makes a god and
    worships *it;*
He makes it a carved image,
    and falls down to it.

16 He burns half of it in the fire;
With this half he eats meat;
He roasts a roast, and is
    satisfied.
He even warms *himself* and
    says,
"Ah! I am warm,
I have seen the fire."

17 And the rest of it he makes into
    a god,
His carved image.
He falls down before it and
    worships *it,*
Prays to it and says,
"Deliver me, for you *are* my
    god!"

18 They do not know nor
    understand;
For He has shut their eyes, so
    that they cannot see,
And their hearts, so that they
    cannot understand.

19 And no one considers in his
    heart,
Nor *is there* knowledge nor
    understanding to say,
"I have burned half of it in the
    fire,
Yes, I have also baked bread
    on its coals;
I have roasted meat and eaten
    it;
And shall I make the rest of it
    an abomination?

Shall I fall down before a block
    of wood?"

20 He feeds on ashes;
A deceived heart has turned
    him aside;
And he cannot deliver his soul,
Nor say, "*Is there* not a lie in
    my right hand?"

21 "Remember these, O Jacob,
And Israel, for you *are* My
    servant;
I have formed you, you *are* My
    servant;
O Israel, you will not be
    forgotten by Me!

22 I have blotted out, like a thick
    cloud, your transgressions,
And like a cloud, your sins.
Return to Me, for I have
    redeemed you."

23 Sing, O heavens, for the LORD
    has done *it!*
Shout, you lower parts of the
    earth;
Break forth into singing, you
    mountains,
O forest, and every tree in it!
For the LORD has redeemed
    Jacob,
And glorified Himself in Israel.

24 Thus says the LORD, your
    Redeemer,
And He who formed you from
    the womb:
"I *am* the LORD, who makes all
    things,
Who stretches out the heavens
    all alone,
Who spreads abroad the earth
    by Myself;

25 Who frustrates the signs of the
    babblers,
And drives diviners mad;
Who turns wise men backward,
And makes their knowledge
    foolishness;

26 Who confirms the word of His
    servant,
And performs the counsel of
    His messengers;
Who says to Jerusalem, 'You
    shall be inhabited,'
To the cities of Judah, 'You
    shall be built,'
And I will raise up her waste
    places;

27 Who says to the deep, 'Be
    dry!
And I will dry up your rivers';

28 Who says of Cyrus, 'He is My
  shepherd,
And he shall perform all My
  pleasure,
Saying to Jerusalem, "You
  shall be built,"
And to the temple, "Your
  foundation shall be laid." '

45 "Thus says the LORD to His
  anointed,
To Cyrus, whose right hand I
  have held—
To subdue nations before him
And loose the armor of kings,
To open before him the double
  doors,
So that the gates will not be
  shut:

2 'I will go before you
And make the crooked places[a]
  straight;
I will break in pieces the gates
  of bronze
And cut the bars of iron.
3 I will give you the treasures of
  darkness
And hidden riches of secret
  places,
That you may know that I, the
  LORD,
Who call you by your name,
Am the God of Israel.
4 For Jacob My servant's sake,
And Israel My elect,
I have even called you by your
  name;
I have named you, though you
  have not known Me.
5 I am the LORD, and there is no
  other;
There is no God besides Me.
I will gird you, though you have
  not known Me,
6 That they may know from the
  rising of the sun to its setting
That there is none besides Me.
I am the LORD, and there is no
  other;
7 I form the light and create
  darkness,
I make peace and create
  calamity;
I, the LORD, do all these things.'

8 "Rain down, you heavens, from
  above,
And let the skies pour down
  righteousness;

Let the earth open, let them
  bring forth salvation,
And let righteousness spring
  up together.
I, the LORD, have created it.

9 "Woe to him who strives with
  his Maker!
Let the potsherd strive with the
  potsherds of the earth!
Shall the clay say to him who
  forms it, 'What are you
  making?'
Or shall your handiwork say,
  'He has no hands'?
10 Woe to him who says to his
  father, 'What are you
  begetting?'
Or to the woman, 'What have
  you brought forth?' "

11 Thus says the LORD,
The Holy One of Israel, and his
  Maker:
"Ask Me of things to come
  concerning My sons;
And concerning the work of
  My hands, you command Me.
12 I have made the earth,
And created man on it.
I—My hands—stretched out the
  heavens,
And all their host I have
  commanded.
13 I have raised him up in
  righteousness,
And I will direct all his ways;
He shall build My city
And let My exiles go free,
Not for price nor reward,"
Says the LORD of hosts.

14 Thus says the LORD:

"The labor of Egypt and
  merchandise of Cush
And of the Sabeans, men of
  stature,
Shall come over to you, and
  they shall be yours;
They shall walk behind you,
They shall come over in chains;
And they shall bow down to
  you.
They will make supplication to
  you, saying, 'Surely God is in
  you,
And there is no other;
There is no other God.' "

45:2 [a]Dead Sea Scrolls and Septuagint read mountains; Targum reads I will trample down the walls; Vulgate
reads I will humble the great ones of the earth.

15 Truly You *are* God, who hide
   Yourself,
   O God of Israel, the Savior!
16 They shall be ashamed
   And also disgraced, all of
   them;
   They shall go in confusion
   together,
   Who are makers of idols.
17 *But* Israel shall be saved by the
   LORD
   With an everlasting salvation;
   You shall not be ashamed or
   disgraced
   Forever and ever.

18 For thus says the LORD,
   Who created the heavens,
   Who is God,
   Who formed the earth and
   made it,
   Who has established it,
   Who did not create it in vain,
   Who formed it to be inhabited:
   "I *am* the LORD, and *there is* no
   other.
19 I have not spoken in secret,
   In a dark place of the earth;
   I did not say to the seed of
   Jacob,
   'Seek Me in vain';
   I, the LORD, speak
   righteousness,
   I declare things that are right.

20 "Assemble yourselves and
   come;
   Draw near together,
   You *who have* escaped from
   the nations.
   They have no knowledge,
   Who carry the wood of their
   carved image,
   And pray to a god *that* cannot
   save.
21 Tell and bring forth *your case;*
   Yes, let them take counsel
   together.
   Who has declared this from
   ancient time?
   Who has told it from that
   time?
   Have not I, the LORD?
   And *there is* no other God
   besides Me,
   A just God and a Savior;
   There is none besides Me.

22 "Look to Me, and be saved,
   All you ends of the earth!
   For I *am* God, and *there is* no
   other.

23 I have sworn by Myself;
   The word has gone out of My
   mouth *in* righteousness,
   And shall not return,
   That to Me every knee shall
   bow,
   Every tongue shall take an
   oath.
24 He shall say,
   'Surely in the LORD I have
   righteousness and strength.
   To Him *men* shall come,
   And all shall be ashamed
   Who are incensed against Him.
25 In the LORD all the descendants
   of Israel
   Shall be justified, and shall
   glory.' "

46 Bel bows down, Nebo stoops;
   Their idols were on the beasts
   and on the cattle.
   Your carriages *were* heavily
   loaded,
   A burden to the weary *beast.*
2 They stoop, they bow down
   together;
   They could not deliver the
   burden,
   But have themselves gone into
   captivity.

3 "Listen to Me, O house of Jacob,
   And all the remnant of the
   house of Israel,
   Who have been upheld *by Me*
   from birth,
   Who have been carried from
   the womb:
4 Even to *your* old age, I *am* He,
   And *even* to gray hairs I will
   carry *you!*
   I have made, and I will bear;
   Even I will carry, and will
   deliver *you.*

5 "To whom will you liken Me,
   and make *Me* equal
   And compare Me, that we
   should be alike?
6 They lavish gold out of the
   bag,
   And weigh silver on the scales;
   They hire a goldsmith, and he
   makes it a god;
   They prostrate themselves, yes,
   they worship.
7 They bear it on the shoulder,
   they carry it
   And set it in its place, and it
   stands;
   From its place it shall not move.

Though *one* cries out to it, yet
 it cannot answer
Nor save him out of his trouble.

8 "Remember this, and show
 yourselves men;
Recall to mind, O you
 transgressors.
9 Remember the former things of
 old,
For I *am* God, and *there is* no
 other;
I am God, and *there is* none like
 Me,
10 Declaring the end from the
 beginning,
And from ancient times *things*
 that are not *yet* done,
Saying, 'My counsel shall
 stand,
And I will do all My pleasure,'
11 Calling a bird of prey from the
 east,
The man who executes My
 counsel, from a far country.
Indeed I have spoken *it;*
I will also bring it to pass.
I have purposed *it;*
I will also do it.

12 "Listen to Me, you stubborn-
 hearted,
Who *are* far from
 righteousness:
13 I bring My righteousness near,
 it shall not be far off;
My salvation shall not linger.
And I will place salvation in
 Zion,
For Israel My glory.

47 "Come down and sit in the
 dust,
O virgin daughter of Babylon;
Sit on the ground without a
 throne,
O daughter of the Chaldeans!
For you shall no more be
 called
Tender and delicate.
2 Take the millstones and grind
 meal.
Remove your veil,
Take off the skirt,
Uncover the thigh,
Pass through the rivers.
3 Your nakedness shall be
 uncovered,
Yes, your shame will be seen;
I will take vengeance,
And I will not arbitrate with a
 man."

4 *As for* our Redeemer, the LORD
 of hosts *is* His name,
The Holy One of Israel.

5 "Sit in silence, and go into
 darkness,
O daughter of the Chaldeans;
For you shall no longer be
 called
The Lady of Kingdoms.
6 I was angry with My people;
I have profaned My
 inheritance,
And given them into your hand.
You showed them no mercy;
On the elderly you laid your
 yoke very heavily.
7 And you said, 'I shall be a lady
 forever,'
So that you did not take these
 things to heart,
Nor remember the latter end of
 them.

8 "Therefore hear this now, *you*
 who are given to pleasures,
Who dwell securely,
Who say in your heart,
'I *am*, and *there is* no one else
 besides me;
I shall not sit *as* a widow,
Nor shall I know the loss of
 children';
9 But these two *things* shall come
 to you
In a moment, in one day:
The loss of children, and
 widowhood.
They shall come upon you in
 their fullness
Because of the multitude of
 your sorceries,
For the great abundance of
 your enchantments.

10 "For you have trusted in your
 wickedness;
You have said, 'No one sees
 me';
Your wisdom and your
 knowledge have warped you;
And you have said in your
 heart,
'I *am*, and *there is* no one else
 besides me.'
11 Therefore evil shall come upon
 you;
You shall not know from where
 it arises.
And trouble shall fall upon you;
You will not be able to put it
 off.

Welcome the Adventure

The prophet Isaiah wrote: "You have heard; see all this. And will you *not* declare *it?* I have made you hear new things from this time, even hidden things, and you did not know them" (Is. 48:6). God keeps so many secrets to Himself. Slowly, patiently, He releases new insights and allows each new generation the joy of making its own contributions! When science is on the verge of a new frontier, there are always negative, fearful eyes that see only the potential dangers. It seems contradictory that some people who are known as "people of faith" suddenly lose their faith when it comes to moving into uncharted scientific realms. God created the genes and the potential for life forms to be successfully created through gene splicing. God ultimately holds the final judgment and course of life in His hands.

Christians who walk the walk of faith look positively at the constructive possibilities in scientific discoveries, such as gene splicing. Possibility thinking sees dangers and potential difficulties in every forward move that we might make. But we do not reject an idea of vast positive potential because some incredible dangers might be unleashed. Rather, we take the discovery and try to identify the potential negatives.

We eliminate, isolate, insulate, or sublimate the negative! That's walking the walk of faith. Faith is splicing the gene! It's welcoming the adventure God reserved for a time like ours!

And desolation shall come
upon you suddenly,
Which you shall not know.

12 "Stand now with your
enchantments
And the multitude of your
sorceries,
In which you have labored
from your youth—
Perhaps you will be able to
profit,
Perhaps you will prevail.
13 You are wearied in the
multitude of your counsels;
Let now the astrologers, the
stargazers,
And the monthly
prognosticators
Stand up and save you
From what shall come upon
you.
14 Behold, they shall be as
stubble,
The fire shall burn them;
They shall not deliver
themselves
From the power of the flame;
It shall not *be* a coal to be
warmed by,
Nor a fire to sit before!
15 Thus shall they be to you
With whom you have labored,
Your merchants from your
youth;
They shall wander each one to
his quarter.
No one shall save you.

48 "Hear this, O house of Jacob,
Who are called by the name of
Israel,
And have come forth from the
wellsprings of Judah;
Who swear by the name of the
LORD,
And make mention of the God
of Israel,
But not in truth or in
righteousness;
2 For they call themselves after
the holy city,
And lean on the God of Israel;
The LORD of hosts *is* His name:

3 "I have declared the former
things from the beginning;
They went forth from My
mouth, and I caused them to
hear it.
Suddenly I did *them,* and they
came to pass.

4 Because I knew that you *were*
obstinate,
And your neck *was* an iron
sinew,
And your brow bronze,
5 Even from the beginning I have
declared *it* to you;
Before it came to pass I
proclaimed *it* to you,
Lest you should say, 'My idol
has done them,
And my carved image and my
molded image
Have commanded them.'

6 "You have heard;
See all this.
And will you not declare *it?*
I have made you hear new
things from this time,
Even hidden things, and you
did not know them.
7 They are created now and not
from the beginning;
And before this day you have
not heard them,
Lest you should say, 'Of course
I knew them.'
8 Surely you did not hear,
Surely you did not know;
Surely from long ago your ear
was not opened.
For I knew that you would deal
very treacherously,
And were called a transgressor
from the womb.

9 "For My name's sake I will defer
My anger,
And *for* My praise I will
restrain it from you,
So that I do not cut you off.
10 Behold, I have refined you, but
not as silver;
I have tested you in the furnace
of affliction.
11 For My own sake, for My own
sake, I will do *it;*
For how should *My name* be
profaned?
And I will not give My glory to
another.

12 "Listen to Me, O Jacob,
And Israel, My called:
I *am* He, I *am* the First,
I *am* also the Last.
13 Indeed My hand has laid the
foundation of the earth,
And My right hand has
stretched out the heavens;
When I call to them,
They stand up together.

14 "All of you, assemble
  yourselves, and hear!
Who among them has declared
  these *things*?
The LORD loves him;
He shall do His pleasure on
  Babylon,
And His arm *shall be against*
  the Chaldeans.
15 I, *even* I, have spoken;
Yes, I have called him,
I have brought him, and his
  way will prosper.

16 "Come near to Me, hear this:
I have not spoken in secret
  from the beginning;
From the time that it was, I *was*
  there.
And now the Lord GOD and His
  Spirit
Have[a] sent Me."

17 Thus says the LORD, your
  Redeemer,
The Holy One of Israel:
"I *am* the LORD your God,
Who teaches you to profit,
Who leads you by the way you
  should go.
18 Oh, that you had heeded My
  commandments!
Then your peace would have
  been like a river,
And your righteousness like
  the waves of the sea.
19 Your descendants also would
  have been like the sand,
And the offspring of your body
  like the grains of sand;
His name would not have been
  cut off
Nor destroyed from before
  Me."

20 Go forth from Babylon!
Flee from the Chaldeans!
With a voice of singing,
Declare, proclaim this,
Utter it to the end of the earth;
Say, "The LORD has redeemed
His servant Jacob!"
21 And they did not thirst
When He led them through the
  deserts;
He caused the waters to flow
  from the rock for them;
He also split the rock, and the
  waters gushed out.

22 "*There is* no peace," says the
  LORD, "for the wicked."

49 "Listen, O coastlands, to Me,
And take heed, you peoples
  from afar!
The LORD has called Me from
  the womb;
From the matrix of My mother
He has made mention of My
  name.
2 And He has made My mouth
  like a sharp sword;
In the shadow of His hand He
  has hidden Me,
And made Me a polished shaft;
In His quiver He has hidden
  Me."

3 "And He said to me,
'You *are* My servant, O Israel,
In whom I will be glorified.'
4 Then I said, 'I have labored in
  vain,
I have spent my strength for
  nothing and in vain;
Yet surely my just reward *is*
  with the LORD,
And my work with my God.' "

5 "And now the LORD says,
Who formed Me from the
  womb *to be* His Servant,
To bring Jacob back to Him,
So that Israel is gathered to
  Him[a]
(For I shall be glorious in the
  eyes of the LORD,
And My God shall be My
  strength),
6 Indeed He says,
'It is too small a thing that You
  should be My Servant
To raise up the tribes of Jacob,
And to restore the preserved
  ones of Israel;
I will also give You as a light
  to the Gentiles,
That You should be My
  salvation to the ends of the
  earth.' "

7 Thus says the LORD,
The Redeemer of Israel, their
  Holy One,
To Him whom man despises,
To Him whom the nation
  abhors,
To the Servant of rulers:

48:16 [a]The Hebrew verb is singular.　　49:5 [a]Qere, Dead Sea Scrolls, and Septuagint read *is gathered to Him*; Kethib reads *not gathered*.

"Kings shall see and arise,
Princes also shall worship,
Because of the LORD who is
faithful,
The Holy One of Israel;
And He has chosen You."

8 Thus says the LORD:

"In an acceptable time I have
heard You,
And in the day of salvation I
have helped You;
I will preserve You and give
You
As a covenant to the people,
To restore the earth,
To cause them to inherit the
desolate heritages;
9 That You may say to the
prisoners, 'Go forth,'
To those who are in darkness,
'Show yourselves.'

"They shall feed along the
roads,
And their pastures shall be on
all desolate heights.
10 They shall neither hunger nor
thirst,
Neither heat nor sun shall
strike them;
For He who has mercy on them
will lead them,
Even by the springs of water
He will guide them.
11 I will make each of My
mountains a road,
And My highways shall be
elevated.
12 Surely these shall come from
afar;
Look! Those from the north
and the west,
And these from the land of
Sinim."

13 Sing, O heavens!
Be joyful, O earth!
And break out in singing, O
mountains!
For the LORD has comforted His
people,
And will have mercy on His
afflicted.

14 But Zion said, "The LORD has
forsaken me,
And my Lord has forgotten
me."

15 "Can a woman forget her
nursing child,
And not have compassion on
the son of her womb?
Surely they may forget,
Yet I will not forget you.
16 See, I have inscribed you on the
palms of My hands;
Your walls are continually
before Me.
17 Your sons[a] shall make haste;
Your destroyers and those who
laid you waste
Shall go away from you.
18 Lift up your eyes, look around
and see;
All these gather together and
come to you.
As I live," says the LORD,
"You shall surely clothe
yourselves with them all as
an ornament,
And bind them on you as a
bride does.

19 "For your waste and desolate
places,
And the land of your
destruction,
Will even now be too small for
the inhabitants;
And those who swallowed you
up will be far away.
20 The children you will have,
After you have lost the others,
Will say again in your ears,
'The place is too small for me;
Give me a place where I may
dwell.'
21 Then you will say in your heart,
'Who has begotten these for me,
Since I have lost my children
and am desolate,
A captive, and wandering to
and fro?
And who has brought these up?
There I was, left alone;
But these, where were they?' "

22 Thus says the Lord GOD:

"Behold, I will lift My hand in
an oath to the nations,
And set up My standard for the
peoples;
They shall bring your sons in
their arms,
And your daughters shall be
carried on their shoulders;
23 Kings shall be your foster
fathers,

49:17 [a]Dead Sea Scrolls, Septuagint, Targum, and Vulgate read builders.

And their queens your nursing
    mothers;
They shall bow down to you
    with *their* faces to the earth,
And lick up the dust of your
    feet.
Then you will know that I *am*
    the LORD,
For they shall not be ashamed
    who wait for Me."

24 Shall the prey be taken from
    the mighty,
Or the captives of the
    righteous*a* be delivered?

25 But thus says the LORD:

"Even the captives of the mighty
    shall be taken away,
And the prey of the terrible be
    delivered;
For I will contend with him who
    contends with you,
And I will save your children.
26 I will feed those who oppress
    you with their own flesh,
And they shall be drunk with
    their own blood as with
    sweet wine.
All flesh shall know
That I, the LORD, *am* your
    Savior,
And your Redeemer, the
    Mighty One of Jacob."

50

Thus says the LORD:

"Where *is* the certificate of your
    mother's divorce,
Whom I have put away?
Or which of My creditors *is it*
    to whom I have sold you?
For your iniquities you have
    sold yourselves,
And for your transgressions
    your mother has been put
    away.
2 Why, when I came, *was there*
    no man?
Why, when I called, *was there*
    none to answer?
Is My hand shortened at all that
    it cannot redeem?
Or have I no power to deliver?
Indeed with My rebuke I dry up
    the sea,
I make the rivers a wilderness;

Their fish stink because *there
    is* no water,
And die of thirst.
3 I clothe the heavens with
    blackness,
And I make sackcloth their
    covering."

4 "The Lord GOD has given Me
The tongue of the learned,
That I should know how to
    speak
A word in season to *him who
    is* weary.
He awakens Me morning by
    morning,
He awakens My ear
To hear as the learned.
5 The Lord GOD has opened My
    ear;
And I was not rebellious,
Nor did I turn away.
6 I gave My back to those who
    struck *Me,*
And My cheeks to those who
    plucked out the beard;
I did not hide My face from
    shame and spitting.

7 "For the Lord GOD will help Me;
Therefore I will not be
    disgraced;
Therefore I have set My face
    like a flint,
And I know that I will not be
    ashamed.
8 *He is* near who justifies Me;
Who will contend with Me?
Let us stand together.
Who *is* My adversary?
Let him come near Me.
9 Surely the Lord GOD will help
    Me;
Who *is* he *who* will condemn
    Me?
Indeed they will all grow old
    like a garment;
The moth will eat them up.

10 "Who among you fears the
    LORD?
Who obeys the voice of His
    Servant?
Who walks in darkness
And has no light?
Let him trust in the name of the
    LORD
And rely upon his God.
11 Look, all you who kindle a fire,

49:24 *a*Following Masoretic Text and Targum; Dead Sea Scrolls, Syriac, and Vulgate read *the mighty;*
Septuagint reads *unjustly.*

Who encircle *yourselves* with
sparks:
Walk in the light of your fire
and in the sparks you have
kindled—
This you shall have from My
hand:
You shall lie down in torment.

51 "Listen to Me, you who follow
after righteousness,
You who seek the LORD:
Look to the rock *from which*
you were hewn,
And to the hole of the pit *from
which* you were dug.
2 Look to Abraham your father,
And to Sarah *who* bore you;
For I called him alone,
And blessed him and increased
him."

3 For the LORD will comfort Zion,
He will comfort all her waste
places;
He will make her wilderness
like Eden,
And her desert like the garden
of the LORD;
Joy and gladness will be found
in it,
Thanksgiving and the voice of
melody.

4 "Listen to Me, My people;
And give ear to Me, O My
nation:
For law will proceed from Me,
And I will make My justice
rest
As a light of the peoples.
5 My righteousness *is* near,
My salvation has gone forth,
And My arms will judge the
peoples;
The coastlands will wait upon
Me,
And on My arm they will trust.
6 Lift up your eyes to the
heavens,
And look on the earth beneath.
For the heavens will vanish
away like smoke,
The earth will grow old like a
garment,
And those who dwell in it will
die in like manner;
But My salvation will be
forever,
And My righteousness will not
be abolished.

7 "Listen to Me, you who know
righteousness,
You people in whose heart *is*
My law:
Do not fear the reproach of
men,
Nor be afraid of their insults.
8 For the moth will eat them up
like a garment,
And the worm will eat them
like wool;
But My righteousness will be
forever,
And My salvation from
generation to generation."

9 Awake, awake, put on strength,
O arm of the LORD!
Awake as in the ancient days,
In the generations of old.
Are You not *the arm* that cut
Rahab apart,
And wounded the serpent?

10 *Are* You not *the One* who dried
up the sea,
The waters of the great deep;
That made the depths of the sea
a road
For the redeemed to cross over?
11 So the ransomed of the LORD
shall return,
And come to Zion with singing,
With everlasting joy on their
heads.
They shall obtain joy and
gladness;
Sorrow and sighing shall flee
away.

12 "I, *even* I, *am* He who comforts
you.
Who *are* you that you should
be afraid
Of a man *who* will die,
And of the son of a man *who*
will be made like grass?
13 And you forget the LORD your
Maker,
Who stretched out the heavens
And laid the foundations of the
earth;
You have feared continually
every day
Because of the fury of the
oppressor,
When *he has* prepared to
destroy.
And where *is* the fury of the
oppressor?
14 The captive exile hastens, that
he may be loosed,

That he should not die in the
    pit,
And that his bread should not
    fail.
15 But I *am* the LORD your
    God,
Who divided the sea whose
    waves roared—
The LORD of hosts *is* His
    name.
16 And I have put My words in
    your mouth;
I have covered you with the
    shadow of My hand,
That I may plant the heavens,
Lay the foundations of the
    earth,
And say to Zion, 'You *are* My
    people.' "
17 Awake, awake!
Stand up, O Jerusalem,
You who have drunk at the
    hand of the LORD
The cup of His fury;
You have drunk the dregs of
    the cup of trembling,
And drained *it* out.
18 *There is* no one to guide her
Among all the sons she has
    brought forth;
Nor *is there any* who takes her
    by the hand
Among all the sons she has
    brought up.
19 These two *things* have come to
    you;
Who will be sorry for you?—
Desolation and destruction,
    famine and sword—
By whom will I comfort you?
20 Your sons have fainted,
They lie at the head of all the
    streets,
Like an antelope in a net;
They are full of the fury of the
    LORD,
The rebuke of your God.

21 Therefore please hear this, you
    afflicted,
And drunk but not with
    wine.
22 Thus says your Lord,
The LORD and your God,
Who pleads the cause of His
    people:
"See, I have taken out of your
    hand
The cup of trembling,

The dregs of the cup of My
    fury;
You shall no longer drink it.
23 But I will put it into the hand
    of those who afflict you,
Who have said to you,[a]
'Lie down, that we may walk
    over you.'
And you have laid your body
    like the ground,
And as the street, for those who
    walk over."

52 Awake, awake!
Put on your strength, O Zion;
Put on your beautiful garments,
O Jerusalem, the holy city!
For the uncircumcised and the
    unclean
Shall no longer come to you.
2 Shake yourself from the dust,
    arise;
Sit down, O Jerusalem!
Loose yourself from the bonds
    of your neck,
O captive daughter of Zion!

3 For thus says the LORD:

"You have sold yourselves for
    nothing,
And you shall be redeemed
    without money."

4 For thus says the Lord GOD:

"My people went down at first
Into Egypt to dwell there;
Then the Assyrian oppressed
    them without cause.
5 Now therefore, what have I
    here," says the LORD,
"That My people are taken away
    for nothing?
Those who rule over them
Make them wail,"[a] says the
    LORD,
"And My name *is* blasphemed
    continually every day.
6 Therefore My people shall
    know My name;
Therefore *they shall know* in
    that day
That I *am* He who speaks:
'Behold, *it is* I.' "

7 How beautiful upon the
    mountains

51:23 [a]Literally *your soul*   52:5 [a]Dead Sea Scrolls read *Mock*; Septuagint reads *Marvel and wail*; Targum
reads *Boast themselves*; Vulgate reads *Treat them unjustly*.

Are the feet of him who brings
good news,
Who proclaims peace,
Who brings glad tidings of
good *things,*
Who proclaims salvation,
Who says to Zion,
"Your God reigns!"

8 Your watchmen shall lift up
their voices;
With their voices they shall
sing together;
For they shall see eye to eye
When the LORD brings back
Zion.

9 Break forth into joy, sing
together,
You waste places of Jerusalem!
For the LORD has comforted His
people,
He has redeemed Jerusalem.

10 The LORD has made bare His
holy arm
In the eyes of all the nations;
And all the ends of the earth
shall see
The salvation of our God.

11 Depart! Depart! Go out from
there,
Touch no unclean *thing;*
Go out from the midst of her,
Be clean,
You who bear the vessels of the
LORD.

12 For you shall not go out with
haste,
Nor go by flight;
For the LORD will go before
you,
And the God of Israel *will be*
your rear guard.

13 Behold, My Servant shall deal
prudently;
He shall be exalted and
extolled and be very high.

14 Just as many were astonished
at you,
So His visage was marred more
than any man,
And His form more than the
sons of men;

15 So shall He sprinkle[a] many
nations.
Kings shall shut their mouths
at Him;
For what had not been told
them they shall see,
And what they had not heard
they shall consider.

53 Who has believed our report?
And to whom has the arm of
the LORD been revealed?

2 For He shall grow up before
Him as a tender plant,
And as a root out of dry
ground.
He has no form or comeliness;
And when we see Him,
There is no beauty that we
should desire Him.

3 He is despised and rejected by
men,
A Man of sorrows and
acquainted with grief.
And we hid, as it were, *our*
faces from Him;
He was despised, and we did
not esteem Him.

4 Surely He has borne our griefs
And carried our sorrows;
Yet we esteemed Him stricken,
Smitten by God, and afflicted.

5 But He *was* wounded for our
transgressions,
He was bruised for our
iniquities;
The chastisement for our peace
was upon Him,
And by His stripes we are
healed.

6 All we like sheep have gone
astray;
We have turned, every one, to
his own way;
And the LORD has laid on Him
the iniquity of us all.

7 He was oppressed and He was
afflicted,
Yet He opened not His mouth;
He was led as a lamb to the
slaughter,
And as a sheep before its
shearers is silent,
So He opened not His mouth.

8 He was taken from prison and
from judgment,
And who will declare His
generation?
For He was cut off from the
land of the living;
For the transgressions of My
people He was stricken.

9 And they[a] made His grave with
the wicked—
But with the rich at His death,
Because He had done no
violence,

52:15 [a]Or *startle*   53:9 [a]Literally *he* or *He*

Nor *was any* deceit in His
   mouth.

10 Yet it pleased the LORD to
      bruise Him;
   He has put *Him* to grief.
   When You make His soul an
      offering for sin,
   He shall see *His* seed, He shall
      prolong *His* days,
   And the pleasure of the LORD
      shall prosper in His hand.
11 He shall see the labor of His
      soul,[a] *and* be satisfied.
   By His knowledge My
      righteous Servant shall
      justify many,
   For He shall bear their
      iniquities.
12 Therefore I will divide Him a
      portion with the great,
   And He shall divide the spoil
      with the strong,
   Because He poured out His soul
      unto death,
   And He was numbered with the
      transgressors,
   And He bore the sin of many,
   And made intercession for the
      transgressors.

54 "Sing, O barren,
   You *who* have not borne!
   Break forth into singing, and
      cry aloud,
   You *who* have not labored with
      child!
   For more *are* the children of the
      desolate
   Than the children of the
      married woman," says the
      LORD.
2 "Enlarge the place of your tent,
   And let them stretch out the
      curtains of your dwellings;
   Do not spare;
   Lengthen your cords,
   And strengthen your stakes.
3 For you shall expand to the
      right and to the left,
   And your descendants will
      inherit the nations,
   And make the desolate cities
      inhabited.

4 "Do not fear, for you will not be
      ashamed;
   Neither be disgraced, for you
      will not be put to shame;

For you will forget the shame
   of your youth,
And will not remember the
   reproach of your widowhood
   anymore.
5 For your Maker *is* your
      husband,
   The LORD of hosts *is* His name;
   And your Redeemer *is* the Holy
      One of Israel;
   He is called the God of the
      whole earth.
6 For the LORD has called you
   Like a woman forsaken and
      grieved in spirit,
   Like a youthful wife when you
      were refused,"
   Says your God.
7 "For a mere moment I have
      forsaken you,
   But with great mercies I will
      gather you.
8 With a little wrath I hid My face
      from you for a moment;
   But with everlasting kindness
      I will have mercy on you,"
   Says the LORD, your Redeemer.

9 "For this *is* like the waters of
      Noah to Me;
   For as I have sworn
   That the waters of Noah would
      no longer cover the earth,
   So have I sworn
   That I would not be angry with
      you, nor rebuke you.
10 For the mountains shall depart
   And the hills be removed,
   But My kindness shall not
      depart from you,
   Nor shall My covenant of peace
      be removed,"
   Says the LORD, who has mercy
      on you.

11 "O you afflicted one,
   Tossed with tempest, *and* not
      comforted,
   Behold, I will lay your stones
      with colorful gems,
   And lay your foundations with
      sapphires.
12 I will make your pinnacles of
      rubies,
   Your gates of crystal,
   And all your walls of precious
      stones.
13 All your children *shall be*
      taught by the LORD,

53:11 [a]Following Masoretic Text, Targum, and Vulgate; Dead Sea Scrolls and Septuagint read *from the
labor of His soul He shall see light.*

God's Word—
A Foundation for Faith

The accuracy and reliability of the Bible you hold in your hand is unsurpassed by any other literature from the ancient world. Recent archaeological discoveries further confirm and support this claim.

There are literally thousands of manuscripts from both the Old and New Testaments which, with the exception of minor textual variations, parallel each other perfectly.

Prior to the discovery of the Dead Sea Scrolls, the oldest complete manuscript of the Old Testament was from A.D. 1000. At that time there was reason to doubt whether or not the Bible had been transmitted accurately through the centuries. Or was there? The people who copied the Old Testament text were known as Masoretes. They lived a life of seclusion and discipline, committed to copying every single Old Testament manuscript they could find. Once they copied a manuscript, they destroyed the original, for they believed the new copy was equally or more accurate than the manuscript they had copied from.

The Masoretes recorded the words of every book of the Old Testament verbatim. Each line on a page had the same number of letters, with an assigned numerical value to each letter. They totalled the numbers from each line and recorded it in the left-hand column. When they added the entire column from top to bottom, they had a cumulative number which had to match the number on the original manuscript.

Any reasonable doubt as to the accuracy of the Scriptures was removed by the discovery of the Dead Sea Scrolls. A complete manuscript of the entire Book of Isaiah was discovered in 1947. With the exception of seventeen letters, the Dead Sea Scroll was identical to Isaiah of the Masoretic text. Written no later than 150 B.C., the Dead Sea Scroll predated the Masoretic text by almost 1200 years.

During the middle of the nineteenth century a discovery shocked the world of archaeology. Professor Constantin von Tischendorf of the University of Leipzig was visiting the monastery of St. Catherine on Mount Sinai. One evening he noticed that the monks were about to use what looked like papyrus leaves as kindling for their fire. On closer examination Professor Tischendorf discovered the monks had been using ancient manuscripts of the Septuagint version of the Old Testament to light their fires. He quickly salvaged as many as possible, then brought them back to Europe where they were deciphered and compared with existing manuscripts. On a later trip to the same monastery Tischendorf discovered a copy of most of the Septuagint and the entire New Testament, dating back to the fourth century A.D.

Sources for some New Testament books were written within a few years of Christ's death, burial, and resurrection. The Bible you hold in your hand is a firm foundation for belief. As you read the Bible, you can be confident that God has preserved His truths to inspire, motivate, and enable you to serve Him, to reach your dreams, and to become the person He wants you to be. His Word truly is a rock solid foundation for your faith!

And great *shall be* the peace of
your children.
14 In righteousness you shall be
established;
You shall be far from
oppression, for you shall not
fear;
And from terror, for it shall not
come near you.
15 Indeed they shall surely
assemble, *but* not because of
Me.
Whoever assembles against
you shall fall for your sake.

16 "Behold, I have created the
blacksmith
Who blows the coals in the fire,
Who brings forth an
instrument for his work;
And I have created the spoiler
to destroy.
17 No weapon formed against you
shall prosper,
And every tongue *which* rises
against you in judgment
You shall condemn.
This *is* the heritage of the
servants of the LORD,
And their righteousness *is* from
Me,"
Says the LORD.

55 "Ho! Everyone who thirsts,
Come to the waters;
And you who have no money,
Come, buy and eat.
Yes, come, buy wine and milk
Without money and without
price.
2 Why do you spend money for
what is not bread,
And your wages for *what* does
not satisfy?
Listen carefully to Me, and eat
what is good,
And let your soul delight itself
in abundance.
3 Incline your ear, and come to
Me.
Hear, and your soul shall live;
And I will make an everlasting
covenant with you—
The sure mercies of David.
4 Indeed I have given him *as* a
witness to the people,
A leader and commander for
the people.
5 Surely you shall call a nation
you do not know,
And nations *who* do not know
you shall run to you,

Because of the LORD your God,
And the Holy One of Israel;
For He has glorified you."

6 Seek the LORD while He may
be found,
Call upon Him while He is
near.
7 Let the wicked forsake his
way,
And the unrighteous man his
thoughts;
Let him return to the LORD,
And He will have mercy on
him;
And to our God,
For He will abundantly pardon.

8 "For My thoughts *are* not your
thoughts,
Nor *are* your ways My ways,"
says the LORD.
9 "For *as* the heavens are higher
than the earth,
So are My ways higher than
your ways,
And My thoughts than your
thoughts.

10 "For as the rain comes down,
and the snow from heaven,
And do not return there,
But water the earth,
And make it bring forth and
bud,
That it may give seed to the
sower
And bread to the eater,
11 So shall My word be that goes
forth from My mouth;
It shall not return to Me void,
But it shall accomplish what I
please,
And it shall prosper *in the
thing* for which I sent it.

12 "For you shall go out with joy,
And be led out with peace;
The mountains and the hills
Shall break forth into singing
before you,
And all the trees of the field
shall clap *their* hands.
13 Instead of the thorn shall come
up the cypress tree,
And instead of the brier shall
come up the myrtle tree;
And it shall be to the LORD for
a name,
For an everlasting sign *that*
shall not be cut off."

56

Thus says the LORD:

"Keep justice, and do
  righteousness,
For My salvation *is* about to
  come,
And My righteousness to be
  revealed.
2 Blessed *is* the man *who* does
  this,
And the son of man *who* lays
  hold on it;
Who keeps from defiling the
  Sabbath,
And keeps his hand from doing
  any evil."

3 Do not let the son of the
  foreigner
Who has joined himself to the
  LORD
Speak, saying,
"The LORD has utterly separated
  me from His people";
Nor let the eunuch say,
"Here I am, a dry tree."
4 For thus says the LORD:
"To the eunuchs who keep My
  Sabbaths,
And choose what pleases
  Me,
And hold fast My covenant,
5 Even to them I will give in My
  house
And within My walls a place
  and a name
Better than that of sons and
  daughters;
I will give them[a] an everlasting
  name
That shall not be cut off.

6 "Also the sons of the foreigner
Who join themselves to the
  LORD, to serve Him,
And to love the name of the
  LORD, to be His servants—
Everyone who keeps from
  defiling the Sabbath,
And holds fast My covenant—
7 Even them I will bring to My
  holy mountain,
And make them joyful in My
  house of prayer.
Their burnt offerings and their
  sacrifices
Will be accepted on My altar;
For My house shall be called a
  house of prayer for all
  nations."

8   The Lord GOD, who gathers the
      outcasts of Israel, says,
    "Yet I will gather to him
      Others besides those who are
      gathered to him."

9   All you beasts of the field, come
      to devour,
    All you beasts in the forest.
10   His watchmen *are* blind,
    They are all ignorant;
    They *are* all dumb dogs,
    They cannot bark;
    Sleeping, lying down, loving to
      slumber.
11   Yes, *they are* greedy dogs
    Which never have enough.
    And they *are* shepherds
    Who cannot understand;
    They all look to their own way,
    Every one for his own gain,
    From his *own* territory.
12 "Come," *one says,* "I will bring
      wine,
    And we will fill ourselves with
      intoxicating drink;
    Tomorrow will be as today,
    And much more abundant."

57

The righteous perishes,
And no man takes *it* to heart;
Merciful men *are* taken away,
While no one considers
That the righteous is taken
  away from evil.
2 He shall enter into peace;
They shall rest in their beds,
Each one walking *in* his
  uprightness.

3 "But come here,
You sons of the sorceress,
You offspring of the adulterer
  and the harlot!
4 Whom do you ridicule?
Against whom do you make a
  wide mouth
And stick out the tongue?
Are you not children of
  transgression,
Offspring of falsehood,
5 Inflaming yourselves with gods
  under every green tree,
Slaying the children in the
  valleys,
Under the clefts of the rocks?
6 Among the smooth *stones* of
  the stream
Is your portion;
They, they, *are* your lot!

56:5 [a]Literally *him*

Even to them you have poured
  a drink offering,
You have offered a grain
  offering.
Should I receive comfort in
  these?

7 "On a lofty and high mountain
  You have set your bed;
  Even there you went up
  To offer sacrifice.
8 Also behind the doors and their
  posts
  You have set up your
  remembrance;
  For you have uncovered
  yourself *to those other* than
  Me,
  And have gone up to them;
  You have enlarged your bed
  And made *a covenant* with
  them;
  You have loved their bed,
  Where you saw *their* nudity.*a*
9 You went to the king with
  ointment,
  And increased your perfumes;
  You sent your messengers far
  off,
  And *even* descended to
  Sheol.
10 You are wearied in the length
  of your way;
  Yet you did not say, 'There is
  no hope.'
  You have found the life of your
  hand;
  Therefore you were not
  grieved.

11 "And of whom have you been
  afraid, or feared,
  That you have lied
  And not remembered Me,
  Nor taken *it* to your heart?
  Is it not because I have held My
  peace from of old
  That you do not fear Me?
12 I will declare your
  righteousness
  And your works,
  For they will not profit you.
13 When you cry out,
  Let your collection *of idols*
  deliver you.
  But the wind will carry them all
  away,
  A breath will take *them.*
  But he who puts his trust in Me
  shall possess the land,

And shall inherit My holy
  mountain."

14 And one shall say,
  "Heap it up! Heap it up!
  Prepare the way,
  Take the stumbling block out
  of the way of My people."

15 For thus says the High and
  Lofty One
  Who inhabits eternity, whose
  name *is* Holy:
  "I dwell in the high and holy
  place,
  With him *who* has a contrite
  and humble spirit,
  To revive the spirit of the
  humble,
  And to revive the heart of the
  contrite ones.
16 For I will not contend forever,
  Nor will I always be angry;
  For the spirit would fail before
  Me,
  And the souls *which* I have
  made.
17 For the iniquity of his
  covetousness
  I was angry and struck him;
  I hid and was angry,
  And he went on backsliding in
  the way of his heart.
18 I have seen his ways, and will
  heal him;
  I will also lead him,
  And restore comforts to him
  And to his mourners.
19 "I create the fruit of the lips:
  Peace, peace to *him who is* far
  off and to *him who is* near,"
  Says the LORD,
  "And I will heal him."
20 But the wicked *are* like the
  troubled sea,
  When it cannot rest,
  Whose waters cast up mire and
  dirt.

21 "*There is* no peace,"
  Says my God, "for the wicked."

58 "Cry aloud, spare not;
  Lift up your voice like a
  trumpet;
  Tell My people their
  transgression,
  And the house of Jacob their
  sins.
2 Yet they seek Me daily,

57:8 *a*Literally *hand,* a euphemism

And delight to know My ways,
As a nation that did
   righteousness,
And did not forsake the
   ordinance of their God.
They ask of Me the ordinances
   of justice;
They take delight in
   approaching God.

3 'Why have we fasted,' *they say,*
   'and You have not seen?
Why have we afflicted our
   souls, and You take no
   notice?'

  "In fact, in the day of your fast
   you find pleasure,
And exploit all your laborers.
4 Indeed you fast for strife and
   debate,
And to strike with the fist of
   wickedness.
You will not fast as *you do* this
   day,
To make your voice heard on
   high.
5 Is it a fast that I have chosen,
   A day for a man to afflict his
   soul?
Is it to bow down his head like
   a bulrush,
And to spread out sackcloth
   and ashes?
Would you call this a fast,
And an acceptable day to the
   LORD?

6 "Is this not the fast that I have
   chosen:
To loose the bonds of
   wickedness,
To undo the heavy burdens,
To let the oppressed go free,
And that you break every
   yoke?
7 *Is it* not to share your bread
   with the hungry,
And that you bring to your
   house the poor who are cast
   out;
When you see the naked, that
   you cover him,
And not hide yourself from
   your own flesh?
8 Then your light shall break
   forth like the morning,
Your healing shall spring forth
   speedily,
And your righteousness shall
   go before you;
The glory of the LORD shall be
   your rear guard.

9 Then you shall call, and the
   LORD will answer;
You shall cry, and He will say,
   'Here I *am.*'

  "If you take away the yoke from
   your midst,
The pointing of the finger, and
   speaking wickedness,
10 If you extend your soul to the
   hungry
And satisfy the afflicted soul,
Then your light shall dawn in
   the darkness,
And your darkness shall *be* as
   the noonday.
11 The LORD will guide you
   continually,
And satisfy your soul in
   drought,
And strengthen your bones;
You shall be like a watered
   garden,
And like a spring of water,
   whose waters do not fail.
12 Those from among you
Shall build the old waste
   places;
You shall raise up the
   foundations of many
   generations;
And you shall be called the
   Repairer of the Breach,
The Restorer of Streets to
   Dwell In.

13 "If you turn away your foot from
   the Sabbath,
From doing your pleasure on
   My holy day,
And call the Sabbath a delight,
The holy *day* of the LORD
   honorable,
And shall honor Him, not doing
   your own ways,
Nor finding your own pleasure,
Nor speaking *your own* words,
14 Then you shall delight yourself
   in the LORD;
And I will cause you to ride on
   the high hills of the earth,
And feed you with the heritage
   of Jacob your father.
The mouth of the LORD has
   spoken."

59 Behold, the LORD's hand is not
   shortened,
That it cannot save;
Nor His ear heavy,
That it cannot hear.

2 But your iniquities have
    separated you from your
    God;
And your sins have hidden *His*
    face from you,
So that He will not hear.
3 For your hands are defiled with
    blood,
And your fingers with iniquity;
Your lips have spoken lies,
Your tongue has muttered
    perversity.

4 No one calls for justice,
Nor does *any* plead for truth.
They trust in empty words and
    speak lies;
They conceive evil and bring
    forth iniquity.
5 They hatch vipers' eggs and
    weave the spider's web;
He who eats of their eggs dies,
And *from* that which is crushed
    a viper breaks out.

6 Their webs will not become
    garments,
Nor will they cover themselves
    with their works;
Their works *are* works of
    iniquity,
And the act of violence *is* in
    their hands.
7 Their feet run to evil,
And they make haste to shed
    innocent blood;
Their thoughts *are* thoughts of
    iniquity;
Wasting and destruction *are* in
    their paths.
8 The way of peace they have not
    known,
And *there is* no justice in their
    ways;
They have made themselves
    crooked paths;
Whoever takes that way shall
    not know peace.

9 Therefore justice is far from us,
Nor does righteousness
    overtake us;
We look for light, but there is
    darkness!
For brightness, *but* we walk in
    blackness!
10 We grope for the wall like the
    blind,
And we grope as if *we had* no
    eyes;
We stumble at noonday as at
    twilight;

We are as dead *men* in desolate
    places.
11 We all growl like bears,
And moan sadly like doves;
We look for justice, but *there
    is* none;
For salvation, *but* it is far from
    us.
12 For our transgressions are
    multiplied before You,
And our sins testify against us;
For our transgressions *are* with
    us,
And *as for* our iniquities, we
    know them:
13 In transgressing and lying
    against the LORD,
And departing from our God,
Speaking oppression and
    revolt,
Conceiving and uttering from
    the heart words of falsehood.
14 Justice is turned back,
And righteousness stands afar
    off;
For truth is fallen in the street,
And equity cannot enter.
15 So truth fails,
And he *who* departs from evil
    makes himself a prey.

Then the LORD saw *it,* and it
    displeased Him
That *there was* no justice.
16 He saw that *there was* no man,
And wondered that *there was*
    no intercessor;
Therefore His own arm
    brought salvation for Him;
And His own righteousness, it
    sustained Him.
17 For He put on righteousness as
    a breastplate,
And a helmet of salvation on
    His head;
He put on the garments of
    vengeance for clothing,
And was clad with zeal as a
    cloak.
18 According to *their* deeds,
    accordingly He will repay,
Fury to His adversaries,
Recompense to His enemies;
The coastlands He will fully
    repay.
19 So shall they fear
The name of the LORD from the
    west,
And His glory from the rising
    of the sun;
When the enemy comes in like
    a flood,

The Spirit of the LORD will lift
up a standard against him.

20 "The Redeemer will come to
Zion,
And to those who turn from
transgression in Jacob,"
Says the LORD.

21 "As for Me," says the LORD, "this
is My covenant with them: My Spirit
who is upon you, and My words
which I have put in your mouth, shall
not depart from your mouth, nor
from the mouth of your descendants,
nor from the mouth of your descendants' descendants," says the LORD,
"from this time and forevermore."

60 Arise, shine;
For your light has come!
And the glory of the LORD is
risen upon you.
2 For behold, the darkness shall
cover the earth,
And deep darkness the
people;
But the LORD will arise over
you,
And His glory will be seen
upon you.
3 The Gentiles shall come to your
light,
And kings to the brightness of
your rising.

4 "Lift up your eyes all around,
and see:
They all gather together, they
come to you;
Your sons shall come from
afar,
And your daughters shall be
nursed at your side.
5 Then you shall see and become
radiant,
And your heart shall swell with
joy;
Because the abundance of the
sea shall be turned to you,
The wealth of the Gentiles shall
come to you.
6 The multitude of camels shall
cover your land,
The dromedaries of Midian and
Ephah;
All those from Sheba shall
come;
They shall bring gold and
incense,
And they shall proclaim the
praises of the LORD.

7 All the flocks of Kedar shall be
gathered together to you,
The rams of Nebaioth shall
minister to you;
They shall ascend with
acceptance on My altar,
And I will glorify the house of
My glory.

8 "Who are these who fly like a
cloud,
And like doves to their roosts?
9 Surely the coastlands shall wait
for Me;
And the ships of Tarshish will
come first,
To bring your sons from afar,
Their silver and their gold with
them,
To the name of the LORD your
God,
And to the Holy One of Israel,
Because He has glorified you.

10 "The sons of foreigners shall
build up your walls,
And their kings shall minister
to you;
For in My wrath I struck
you,
But in My favor I have had
mercy on you.
11 Therefore your gates shall be
open continually;
They shall not be shut day or
night,
That men may bring to you the
wealth of the Gentiles,
And their kings in procession.
12 For the nation and kingdom
which will not serve you shall
perish,
And those nations shall be
utterly ruined.

13 "The glory of Lebanon shall
come to you,
The cypress, the pine, and the
box tree together,
To beautify the place of My
sanctuary;
And I will make the place of My
feet glorious.
14 Also the sons of those who
afflicted you
Shall come bowing to you,
And all those who despised you
shall fall prostrate at the
soles of your feet;
And they shall call you The
City of the LORD,
Zion of the Holy One of Israel.

15 "Whereas you have been
     forsaken and hated,
     So that no one went through
        you,
     I will make you an eternal
        excellence,
     A joy of many generations.
16   You shall drink the milk of the
        Gentiles,
     And milk the breast of kings;
     You shall know that I, the
        LORD, *am* your Savior
     And your Redeemer, the
        Mighty One of Jacob.

17 "Instead of bronze I will bring
        gold,
     Instead of iron I will bring
        silver,
     Instead of wood, bronze,
     And instead of stones, iron.
     I will also make your officers
        peace,
     And your magistrates
        righteousness.
18   Violence shall no longer be
        heard in your land,
     Neither wasting nor
        destruction within your
        borders;
     But you shall call your walls
        Salvation,
     And your gates Praise.

19 "The sun shall no longer be your
        light by day,
     Nor for brightness shall the
        moon give light to you;
     But the LORD will be to you an
        everlasting light,
     And your God your glory.
20   Your sun shall no longer go
        down,
     Nor shall your moon withdraw
        itself;
     For the LORD will be your
        everlasting light,
     And the days of your mourning
        shall be ended.
21   Also your people *shall* all *be*
        righteous;
     They shall inherit the land
        forever,
     The branch of My planting,
     The work of My hands,
     That I may be glorified.
22   A little one shall become a
        thousand,
     And a small one a strong
        nation.
     I, the LORD, will hasten it in its
        time."

61 "The Spirit of the Lord GOD *is*
        upon Me,
     Because the LORD has anointed
        Me
     To preach good tidings to the
        poor;
     He has sent Me to heal the
        brokenhearted,
     To proclaim liberty to the
        captives,
     And the opening of the prison
        to *those who are* bound;
2   To proclaim the acceptable
        year of the LORD,
     And the day of vengeance of
        our God;
     To comfort all who mourn,
3   To console those who mourn in
        Zion,
     To give them beauty for ashes,
     The oil of joy for mourning,
     The garment of praise for the
        spirit of heaviness;
     That they may be called trees
        of righteousness,
     The planting of the LORD, that
        He may be glorified."

4   And they shall rebuild the old
        ruins,
     They shall raise up the former
        desolations,
     And they shall repair the
        ruined cities,
     The desolations of many
        generations.
5   Strangers shall stand and feed
        your flocks,
     And the sons of the foreigner
        Shall be your plowmen and
        your vinedressers.
6   But you shall be named the
        priests of the LORD,
     They shall call you the servants
        of our God.
     You shall eat the riches of the
        Gentiles,
     And in their glory you shall
        boast.
7   Instead of your shame *you shall
        have* double *honor,*
     And *instead of* confusion they
        shall rejoice in their portion.
     Therefore in their land they
        shall possess double;
     Everlasting joy shall be theirs.

8 "For I, the LORD, love justice;
     I hate robbery for burnt
        offering;
     I will direct their work in
        truth,

And will make with them an
everlasting covenant.
9 Their descendants shall be
known among the Gentiles,
And their offspring among the
people.
All who see them shall
acknowledge them,
That they *are* the posterity
whom the LORD has blessed."

10 I will greatly rejoice in the
LORD,
My soul shall be joyful in my
God;
For He has clothed me with the
garments of salvation,
He has covered me with the
robe of righteousness,
As a bridegroom decks *himself*
with ornaments,
And as a bride adorns *herself*
with her jewels.
11 For as the earth brings forth its
bud,
As the garden causes the things
that are sown in it to spring
forth,
So the Lord GOD will cause
righteousness and praise to
spring forth before all the
nations.

62 For Zion's sake I will not hold
My peace,
And for Jerusalem's sake I will
not rest,
Until her righteousness goes
forth as brightness,
And her salvation as a lamp
that burns.
2 The Gentiles shall see your
righteousness,
And all kings your glory.
You shall be called by a new
name,
Which the mouth of the LORD
will name.
3 You shall also be a crown of
glory
In the hand of the LORD,
And a royal diadem
In the hand of your God.
4 You shall no longer be termed
Forsaken,
Nor shall your land any more
be termed Desolate;
But you shall be called
Hephzibah,[a] and your land
Beulah;[b]

For the LORD delights in you,
And your land shall be
married.
5 For *as* a young man marries a
virgin,
So shall your sons marry you;
And *as* the bridegroom rejoices
over the bride,
So shall your God rejoice over
you.
6 I have set watchmen on your
walls, O Jerusalem;
They shall never hold their
peace day or night.
You who make mention of the
LORD, do not keep silent,
7 And give Him no rest till He
establishes
And till He makes Jerusalem a
praise in the earth.
8 The LORD has sworn by His
right hand
And by the arm of His strength:
"Surely I will no longer give
your grain
As food for your enemies;
And the sons of the foreigner
shall not drink your new
wine,
For which you have labored.
9 But those who have gathered it
shall eat it,
And praise the LORD;
Those who have brought it
together shall drink it in My
holy courts."
10 Go through,
Go through the gates!
Prepare the way for the people;
Build up,
Build up the highway!
Take out the stones,
Lift up a banner for the
peoples!
11 Indeed the LORD has
proclaimed
To the end of the world:
"Say to the daughter of Zion,
'Surely your salvation is
coming;
Behold, His reward *is* with
Him,
And His work before Him.' "
12 And they shall call them The
Holy People,
The Redeemed of the LORD;

62:4 [a]Literally *My Delight Is in Her* [b]Literally *Married*

And you shall be called Sought
    Out,
A City Not Forsaken.

63 Who *is* this who comes from
    Edom,
With dyed garments from
    Bozrah,
This *One who is* glorious in His
    apparel,
Traveling in the greatness of
    His strength?—

"I who speak in righteousness,
    mighty to save."

2 Why *is* Your apparel red,
And Your garments like one
    who treads in the winepress?

3 "I have trodden the winepress
    alone,
And from the peoples no one
    was with Me.
For I have trodden them in My
    anger,
And trampled them in My fury;
Their blood is sprinkled upon
    My garments,
And I have stained all My
    robes.
4 For the day of vengeance *is* in
    My heart,
And the year of My redeemed
    has come.
5 I looked, but *there was* no one
    to help,
And I wondered
That *there was* no one to
    uphold;
Therefore My own arm brought
    salvation for Me;
And My own fury, it sustained
    Me.
6 I have trodden down the
    peoples in My anger,
Made them drunk in My fury,
And brought down their
    strength to the earth."

7 I will mention the
    lovingkindnesses of the LORD
And the praises of the LORD,
According to all that the LORD
    has bestowed on us,
And the great goodness toward
    the house of Israel,
Which He has bestowed on
    them according to His
    mercies,
According to the multitude of
    His lovingkindnesses.

8 For He said, "Surely they *are*
    My people,
Children *who* will not lie."
So He became their Savior.
9 In all their affliction He was
    afflicted,
And the Angel of His Presence
    saved them;
In His love and in His pity He
    redeemed them;
And He bore them and carried
    them
All the days of old.
10 But they rebelled and grieved
    His Holy Spirit;
So He turned Himself against
    them as an enemy,
And He fought against them.

11 Then he remembered the days
    of old,
Moses *and* his people, *saying:*
"Where *is* He who brought them
    up out of the sea
With the shepherd of His flock?
Where *is* He who put His Holy
    Spirit within them,
12 Who led *them* by the right
    hand of Moses,
With His glorious arm,
Dividing the water before them
To make for Himself an
    everlasting name,
13 Who led them through the
    deep,
As a horse in the wilderness,
That they might not stumble?"

14 As a beast goes down into the
    valley,
And the Spirit of the LORD
    causes him to rest,
So You lead Your people,
To make Yourself a glorious
    name.

15 Look down from heaven,
And see from Your habitation,
    holy and glorious.
Where *are* Your zeal and Your
    strength,
The yearning of Your heart and
    Your mercies toward me?
Are they restrained?
16 Doubtless You *are* our Father,
Though Abraham was ignorant
    of us,
And Israel does not
    acknowledge us.
You, O LORD, *are* our Father;
Our Redeemer from
    Everlasting *is* Your name.

17 O LORD, why have You made
   us stray from Your ways,
And hardened our heart from
   Your fear?
Return for Your servants' sake,
The tribes of Your inheritance.
18 Your holy people have
   possessed *it* but a little
   while;
Our adversaries have trodden
   down Your sanctuary.
19 We have become *like* those of
   old, over whom You never
   ruled,
Those who were never called
   by Your name.

64 Oh, that You would rend the
   heavens!
That You would come down!
That the mountains might
   shake at Your presence—
2 As fire burns brushwood,
As fire causes water to boil—
To make Your name known to
   Your adversaries,
That the nations may tremble
   at Your presence!
3 When You did awesome things
   for which we did not look,
You came down,
The mountains shook at Your
   presence.
4 For since the beginning of the
   world
Men have not heard nor
   perceived by the ear,
Nor has the eye seen any God
   besides You,
Who acts for the one who waits
   for Him.
5 You meet him who rejoices and
   does righteousness,
Who remembers You in Your
   ways.
You are indeed angry, for we
   have sinned—
In these ways we continue;
And we need to be saved.

6 But we are all like an unclean
   thing,
And all our righteousnesses *are*
   like filthy rags;
We all fade as a leaf,
And our iniquities, like the
   wind,
Have taken us away.
7 And *there is* no one who calls
   on Your name,
Who stirs himself up to take
   hold of You;

For You have hidden Your face
   from us,
And have consumed us
   because of our iniquities.

8 But now, O LORD,
You *are* our Father;
We *are* the clay, and You our
   potter;
And all we *are* the work of
   Your hand.
9 Do not be furious, O LORD,
Nor remember iniquity forever;
Indeed, please look—we all *are*
   Your people!
10 Your holy cities are a
   wilderness,
Zion is a wilderness,
Jerusalem a desolation.
11 Our holy and beautiful temple,
Where our fathers praised
   You,
Is burned up with fire;
And all our pleasant things are
   laid waste.
12 Will You restrain Yourself
   because of these *things,* O
   LORD?
Will You hold Your peace, and
   afflict us very severely?

65 "I was sought by *those who* did
   not ask *for Me;*
I was found by *those who* did
   not seek Me.
I said, 'Here I am, here I am,'
To a nation *that* was not called
   by My name.
2 I have stretched out My hands
   all day long to a rebellious
   people,
Who walk in a way *that is* not
   good,
According to their own
   thoughts;
3 A people who provoke Me to
   anger continually to My
   face;
Who sacrifice in gardens,
And burn incense on altars of
   brick;
4 Who sit among the graves,
And spend the night in the
   tombs;
Who eat swine's flesh,
And the broth of abominable
   things is *in* their vessels;
5 Who say, 'Keep to yourself,
Do not come near me,
For I am holier than you!'
These *are* smoke in My nostrils,
A fire that burns all the day.

6 "Behold, *it is* written before Me:
I will not keep silence, but will
repay—
Even repay into their bosom—
7 Your iniquities and the
iniquities of your fathers
together,"
Says the LORD,
"Who have burned incense on
the mountains
And blasphemed Me on the
hills;
Therefore I will measure their
former work into their
bosom."

8 Thus says the LORD:

"As the new wine is found in the
cluster,
And *one* says, 'Do not destroy
it,
For a blessing *is* in it,'
So will I do for My servants'
sake,
That I may not destroy them
all.
9 I will bring forth descendants
from Jacob,
And from Judah an heir of My
mountains;
My elect shall inherit it,
And My servants shall dwell
there.
10 Sharon shall be a fold of flocks,
And the Valley of Achor a place
for herds to lie down,
For My people who have
sought Me.

11 "But you *are* those who forsake
the LORD,
Who forget My holy mountain,
Who prepare a table for Gad,*a*
And who furnish a drink
offering for Meni.*b*
12 Therefore I will number you for
the sword,
And you shall all bow down to
the slaughter;
Because, when I called, you did
not answer;
When I spoke, you did not hear,
But did evil before My eyes,
And chose *that* in which I do
not delight."

13 Therefore thus says the Lord
GOD:

"Behold, My servants shall eat,
But you shall be hungry;
Behold, My servants shall
drink,
But you shall be thirsty;
Behold, My servants shall
rejoice,
But you shall be ashamed;
14 Behold, My servants shall sing
for joy of heart,
But you shall cry for sorrow of
heart,
And wail for grief of spirit.
15 You shall leave your name as
a curse to My chosen;
For the Lord GOD will slay
you,
And call His servants by
another name;
16 So that he who blesses himself
in the earth
Shall bless himself in the God
of truth;
And he who swears in the earth
Shall swear by the God of
truth;
Because the former troubles
are forgotten,
And because they are hidden
from My eyes.

17 "For behold, I create new
heavens and a new earth;
And the former shall not be
remembered or come to
mind.
18 But be glad and rejoice forever
in what I create;
For behold, I create Jerusalem
as a rejoicing,
And her people a joy.
19 I will rejoice in Jerusalem,
And joy in My people;
The voice of weeping shall no
longer be heard in her,
Nor the voice of crying.

20 "No more shall an infant from
there *live but a few* days,
Nor an old man who has not
fulfilled his days;
For the child shall die one
hundred years old,
But the sinner *being* one
hundred years old shall be
accursed.
21 They shall build houses and
inhabit *them;*
They shall plant vineyards and
eat their fruit.

65:11 *a*Literally *Troop* or *Fortune*, a pagan deity   *b*Literally *Number* or *Destiny*, a pagan deity

22 They shall not build and
    another inhabit;
    They shall not plant and
    another eat;
    For as the days of a tree, *so
    shall be* the days of My
    people,
    And My elect shall long enjoy
    the work of their hands.
23 They shall not labor in vain,
    Nor bring forth children for
    trouble;
    For they *shall be* the
    descendants of the blessed of
    the LORD,
    And their offspring with them.
24 "It shall come to pass
    That before they call, I will
    answer;
    And while they are still
    speaking, I will hear.
25 The wolf and the lamb shall
    feed together,
    The lion shall eat straw like the
    ox,
    And dust *shall be* the serpent's
    food.
    They shall not hurt nor destroy
    in all My holy mountain,"
    Says the LORD.

66

Thus says the LORD:

"Heaven *is* My throne,
And earth *is* My footstool.
Where *is* the house that you
    will build Me?
And where *is* the place of My
    rest?
2 For all those *things* My hand
    has made,
    And all those *things* exist,"
    Says the LORD.
    "But on this *one* will I look:
    On *him who is* poor and of a
    contrite spirit,
    And who trembles at My word.

3 "He who kills a bull *is as if* he
    slays a man;
    He who sacrifices a lamb, *as if*
    he breaks a dog's neck;
    He who offers a grain offering,
    as if he offers swine's blood;
    He who burns incense, *as if* he
    blesses an idol.
    Just as they have chosen their
    own ways,
    And their soul delights in their
    abominations,

4 So will I choose their delusions,
    And bring their fears on them;
    Because, when I called, no one
    answered,
    When I spoke they did not
    hear;
    But they did evil before My
    eyes,
    And chose *that* in which I do
    not delight."

5 Hear the word of the LORD,
    You who tremble at His word:
    "Your brethren who hated you,
    Who cast you out for My
    name's sake, said,
    'Let the LORD be glorified,
    That we may see your joy.'
    But they shall be ashamed."

6 The sound of noise from the
    city!
    A voice from the temple!
    The voice of the LORD,
    Who fully repays His enemies!

7 "Before she was in labor, she
    gave birth;
    Before her pain came,
    She delivered a male child.
8 Who has heard such a thing?
    Who has seen such things?
    Shall the earth be made to give
    birth in one day?
    Or shall a nation be born at
    once?
    For as soon as Zion was in
    labor,
    She gave birth to her children.
9 Shall I bring to the time of
    birth, and not cause
    delivery?" says the LORD.
    "Shall I who cause delivery shut
    up *the womb?*" says your
    God.
10 "Rejoice with Jerusalem,
    And be glad with her, all you
    who love her;
    Rejoice for joy with her, all you
    who mourn for her;
11 That you may feed and be
    satisfied
    With the consolation of her
    bosom,
    That you may drink deeply and
    be delighted
    With the abundance of her
    glory."

12 For thus says the LORD:

"Behold, I will extend peace to
    her like a river,

And the glory of the Gentiles
    like a flowing stream.
Then you shall feed;
On *her* sides shall you be
    carried,
And be dandled on *her*
    knees.

13 As one whom his mother
    comforts,
So I will comfort you;
And you shall be comforted in
    Jerusalem."

14 When you see *this,* your heart
    shall rejoice,
And your bones shall flourish
    like grass;
The hand of the LORD shall be
    known to His servants,
And *His* indignation to His
    enemies.

15 For behold, the LORD will come
    with fire
And with His chariots, like a
    whirlwind,
To render His anger with
    fury,
And His rebuke with flames of
    fire.

16 For by fire and by His sword
The LORD will judge all flesh;
And the slain of the LORD shall
    be many.

17 "Those who sanctify themselves
    and purify themselves,
To go to the gardens
After an *idol* in the midst,
Eating swine's flesh and
    the abomination and the
    mouse,
Shall be consumed together,"
    says the LORD.

18 "For I *know* their works and
their thoughts. It shall be that I will
gather all nations and tongues; and
they shall come and see My glory.
19 I will set a sign among them; and
those among them who escape I will
send to the nations: *to* Tarshish and
Pul[a] and Lud, who draw the bow, and
Tubal and Javan, *to* the coastlands
afar off who have not heard My fame
nor seen My glory. And they shall
declare My glory among the Gentiles.
20 Then they shall bring all your
brethren for an offering to the LORD
out of all nations, on horses and in
chariots and in litters, on mules and
on camels, to My holy mountain Jerusalem," says the LORD, "as the children of Israel bring an offering in a
clean vessel into the house of the
LORD. 21 And I will also take some of
them for priests *and* Levites," says
the LORD.

22 "For as the new heavens and the
    new earth
Which I will make shall remain
    before Me," says the LORD,
"So shall your descendants and
    your name remain.

23 And it shall come to pass
That from one New Moon to
    another,
And from one Sabbath to
    another,
All flesh shall come to worship
    before Me," says the LORD.

24 "And they shall go forth and
    look
Upon the corpses of the men
Who have transgressed against
    Me.
For their worm does not die,
And their fire is not quenched.
They shall be an abhorrence to
    all flesh."

66:19 [a]Following Masoretic Text and Targum; Septuagint reads *Put* (compare Jeremiah 46:9).

Jeremiah

Overview of Jeremiah

The Book of Jeremiah is a dramatic adventure of the call of a young man by God to boldly proclaim His truth to a nation that had turned away from Him. The book was written by Jeremiah, aided by his scribe, Baruch, about 627–580 B.C.

Initially, the remarkable young man hesitated to follow God's call, citing his young age as an excuse. "Ah, Lord God! Behold, I cannot speak, for I *am* a youth" (Jer. 1:6). But God's reassurance that He would be with Jeremiah gave him hope and strength to carry out his appointed task.

Jeremiah's responsibility was to forewarn the people of Judah of coming destruction if they failed to turn their hearts back to God. The people had adopted the pagan practices from the surrounding nations and sought to please false gods through such depraved acts as infant sacrifice. Temples and high places to false gods were built throughout the land, while the rightful temple of God was neglected.

Jeremiah's message was not a popular one, but with boldness and confidence he went out to proclaim it. He faced tremendous suffering, including imprisonment, excommunication from the temple, and beatings. Jeremiah was brave enough to accept the responsibility to take positive actions in negative times. It is hard to find someone willing to stand up against the crowd. But Jeremiah obeyed God in the face of obstacles.

Interwoven throughout Jeremiah's warnings to the people are beautiful promises of God. Despite destruction, God's ultimate commitment to His people guaranteed their success and future. "For I know the thoughts that I think toward you, says the Lord, thoughts of peace and not of evil, to give you a future and a hope" (Jer. 29:11).

Jesus in Jeremiah

Jesus the Messiah is clearly seen in 23:1–8 as the coming Shepherd and righteous Branch who "shall reign and prosper, and execute judgment and righteousness in the earth. In His days Judah will be saved, and Israel will dwell safely; now this *is* His name by which He will be called: THE LORD OUR RIGHTEOUSNESS" (23:5, 6). He will bring in the new covenant (31:31–34), which will fulfill God's covenants with Abraham (Gen. 12:1–3; 17:1–8), Moses and the people (Deut. 28—30), and David (2 Sam. 7:1–17).

Keys to Jeremiah

Key Word: Judah's Last Hour. The God of Jeremiah is patient and holy. He withholds His judgment, pleading with His people to repent before it is too late. We learn from the lesson at the potter's house that a ruined vessel can be repaired while still wet (18:1–4); but once dried, a marred pot is mere trash. God's graciousness is clear: He gives Judah more time and encouragement to repent. Because they defy God's words and refuse to repent, the Babylonian captivity is inevitable. Jeremiah proclaims God's gracious promise of hope and restoration.

Key Verses: "For I know the thoughts that I think toward you, says the LORD, thoughts of peace and not of evil, to give you a future and a hope. Then you will call upon Me and go and pray to Me, and I will listen to you. And you will seek Me and find *Me*, when you search for Me with all your heart" (29:11–13).

Key Chapter: Jeremiah 31. Jeremiah proclaims the wonderful promises of God in the midst of judgment. Even though Judah had broken the covenants of God, He would make a new covenant, which would be established by Jesus' death and resurrection.

1 The words of Jeremiah the son of Hilkiah, of the priests who *were* in Anathoth in the land of Benjamin, 2 to whom the word of the LORD came in the days of Josiah the son of Amon, king of Judah, in the thirteenth year of his reign. 3 It came also in the days of Jehoiakim the son of

Josiah, king of Judah, until the end of the eleventh year of Zedekiah the son of Josiah, king of Judah, until the carrying away of Jerusalem captive in the fifth month.

4 Then the word of the LORD came to me, saying:

> 5 "Before I formed you in the
>   womb I knew you;
> Before you were born I
>   sanctified you;
> I ordained you a prophet to the
>   nations."

6 Then said I:

> "Ah, Lord GOD!
> Behold, I cannot speak, for I *am*
>   a youth."

7 But the LORD said to me:

> "Do not say, 'I *am* a youth,'
> For you shall go to all to whom
>   I send you,
> And whatever I command you,
>   you shall speak.
> 8   Do not be afraid of their faces,
> For I *am* with you to deliver
>   you," says the LORD.

9 Then the LORD put forth His hand and touched my mouth, and the LORD said to me:

> "Behold, I have put My words
>   in your mouth.
> 10   See, I have this day set you
>   over the nations and over the
>   kingdoms,
> To root out and to pull down,
> To destroy and to throw down,
> To build and to plant."

11 Moreover the word of the LORD came to me, saying, "Jeremiah, what do you see?"

And I said, "I see a branch of an almond tree."

12 Then the LORD said to me, "You have seen well, for I am ready to perform My word."

13 And the word of the LORD came to me the second time, saying, "What do you see?"

And I said, "I see a boiling pot, and it is facing away from the north."

14 Then the LORD said to me:

> "Out of the north calamity shall
>   break forth

> On all the inhabitants of the
>   land.
> 15 For behold, I am calling
> All the families of the
>   kingdoms of the north," says
>   the LORD;
> "They shall come and each one
>   set his throne
> At the entrance of the gates of
>   Jerusalem,
> Against all its walls all around,
> And against all the cities of
>   Judah.
> 16 I will utter My judgments
> Against them concerning all
>   their wickedness,
> Because they have forsaken
>   Me,
> Burned incense to other gods,
> And worshiped the works of
>   their own hands.

> 17 "Therefore prepare yourself and
>   arise,
> And speak to them all that I
>   command you.
> Do not be dismayed before
>   their faces,
> Lest I dismay you before them.
> 18 For behold, I have made you
>   this day
> A fortified city and an iron
>   pillar,
> And bronze walls against the
>   whole land—
> Against the kings of Judah,
> Against its princes,
> Against its priests,
> And against the people of the
>   land.
> 19 They will fight against you,
> But they shall not prevail
>   against you.
> For I *am* with you," says the
>   LORD, "to deliver you."

2 Moreover the word of the LORD came to me, saying, 2 "Go and cry in the hearing of Jerusalem, saying, 'Thus says the LORD:

> "I remember you,
> The kindness of your youth,
> The love of your betrothal,
> When you went after Me in the
>   wilderness,
> In a land not sown.
> 3   Israel *was* holiness to the LORD,
> The firstfruits of His increase.
> All that devour him will offend;
> Disaster will come upon them,"
>   says the LORD.' "

4 Hear the word of the LORD, O house of Jacob and all the families of the house of Israel. 5 Thus says the LORD:

> "What injustice have your
> fathers found in Me,
> That they have gone far from
> Me,
> Have followed idols,
> And have become idolaters?
> 6 Neither did they say, 'Where *is*
> the LORD,
> Who brought us up out of the
> land of Egypt,
> Who led us through the
> wilderness,
> Through a land of deserts and
> pits,
> Through a land of drought and
> the shadow of death,
> Through a land that no one
> crossed
> And where no one dwelt?'
> 7 I brought you into a bountiful
> country,
> To eat its fruit and its goodness.
> But when you entered, you
> defiled My land
> And made My heritage an
> abomination.
> 8 The priests did not say, 'Where
> *is* the LORD?'
> And those who handle the law
> did not know Me;
> The rulers also transgressed
> against Me;
> The prophets prophesied by
> Baal,
> And walked after *things that*
> do not profit.

> 9 "Therefore I will yet bring
> charges against you," says
> the LORD,
> "And against your children's
> children I will bring
> charges.
> 10 For pass beyond the coasts of
> Cyprus*a* and see,
> Send to Kedar*b* and consider
> diligently,
> And see if there has been such
> *a* thing.
> 11 Has a nation changed *its* gods,
> Which *are* not gods?
> But My people have changed
> their Glory
> For *what* does not profit.

> 12 Be astonished, O heavens, at
> this,
> And be horribly afraid;
> Be very desolate," says the
> LORD.
> 13 "For My people have committed
> two evils:
> They have forsaken Me, the
> fountain of living waters,
> *And* hewn themselves
> cisterns—broken cisterns
> that can hold no water.

> 14 "*Is* Israel a servant?
> *Is* he a homeborn *slave*?
> Why is he plundered?
> 15 The young lions roared at him,
> *and* growled;
> They made his land waste;
> His cities are burned, without
> inhabitant.
> 16 Also the people of Noph*a* and
> Tahpanhes
> Have broken the crown of your
> head.
> 17 Have you not brought this on
> yourself,
> In that you have forsaken the
> LORD your God
> When He led you in the way?
> 18 And now why take the road to
> Egypt,
> To drink the waters of Sihor?
> Or why take the road to
> Assyria,
> To drink the waters of the
> River?*a*
> 19 Your own wickedness will
> correct you,
> And your backslidings will
> rebuke you.
> Know therefore and see that *it*
> is an evil and bitter *thing*
> That you have forsaken the
> LORD your God,
> And the fear of Me *is* not in
> you,"
> Says the Lord GOD of hosts.

> 20 "For of old I have broken your
> yoke *and* burst your
> bonds;
> And you said, 'I will not
> transgress,'
> When on every high hill and
> under every green tree
> You lay down, playing the
> harlot.
> 21 Yet I had planted you a noble

2:10 *a*Hebrew *Kittim*, western lands, especially Cyprus   *b*In the northern Arabian desert, representative of the eastern cultures   2:16 *a*That is, Memphis in ancient Egypt   2:18 *a*That is, the Euphrates

vine, a seed of highest
quality.
How then have you turned
before Me
Into the degenerate plant of an
alien vine?
22 For though you wash yourself
with lye, and use much
soap,
Yet your iniquity is marked
before Me," says the Lord
GOD.

23 "How can you say, 'I am not
polluted,
I have not gone after the
Baals'?
See your way in the valley;
Know what you have done:
You are a swift dromedary
breaking loose in her ways,
24 A wild donkey used to the
wilderness,
That sniffs at the wind in her
desire;
In her time of mating, who can
turn her away?
All those who seek her will not
weary themselves;
In her month they will find her.
25 Withhold your foot from being
unshod, and your throat from
thirst.
But you said, 'There is no hope.
No! For I have loved aliens, and
after them I will go.'

26 "As the thief is ashamed when
he is found out,
So is the house of Israel
ashamed;
They and their kings and their
princes, and their priests and
their prophets,
27 Saying to a tree, 'You *are* my
father,'
And to a stone, 'You gave birth
to me.'
For they have turned *their* back
to Me, and not *their* face.
But in the time of their trouble
They will say, 'Arise and save
us.'
28 But where *are* your gods that
you have made for
yourselves?
Let them arise,
If they can save you in the time
of your trouble;
For *according to* the number of
your cities
Are your gods, O Judah.

29 "Why will you plead with Me?
You all have transgressed
against Me," says the LORD.
30 "In vain I have chastened your
children;
They received no correction.
Your sword has devoured your
prophets
Like a destroying lion.

31 "O generation, see the word of
the LORD!
Have I been a wilderness to
Israel,
Or a land of darkness?
Why do My people say, 'We are
lords;
We will come no more to You'?
32 Can a virgin forget her
ornaments,
Or a bride her attire?
Yet My people have forgotten
Me days without number.

33 "Why do you beautify your way
to seek love?
Therefore you have also taught
The wicked women your ways.
34 Also on your skirts is found
The blood of the lives of the
poor innocents.
I have not found it by secret
search,
But plainly on all these things.
35 Yet you say, 'Because I am
innocent,
Surely His anger shall turn
from me.'
Behold, I will plead My case
against you,
Because you say, 'I have not
sinned.'
36 Why do you gad about so much
to change your way?
Also you shall be ashamed of
Egypt as you were ashamed
of Assyria.
37 Indeed you will go forth from
him
With your hands on your head;
For the LORD has rejected your
trusted allies,
And you will not prosper by
them.

3 "They say, 'If a man divorces his
wife,
And she goes from him
And becomes another man's,
May he return to her again?'
Would not that land be greatly
polluted?

But you have played the harlot
  with many lovers;
Yet return to Me," says the
  LORD.

2 "Lift up your eyes to the
  desolate heights and see:
Where have you not lain *with
  men?*
By the road you have sat for
  them
Like an Arabian in the
  wilderness;
And you have polluted the land
With your harlotries and your
  wickedness.
3 Therefore the showers have
  been withheld,
And there has been no latter
  rain.
You have had a harlot's
  forehead;
You refuse to be ashamed.
4 Will you not from this time cry
  to Me,
'My Father, You *are* the guide
  of my youth?
5 Will He remain angry forever?
Will He keep it to the end?'
Behold, you have spoken and
  done evil things,
As you were able."

6 The LORD said also to me in the days of Josiah the king: "Have you seen what backsliding Israel has done? She has gone up on every high mountain and under every green tree, and there played the harlot. 7 And I said, after she had done all these *things,* 'Return to Me.' But she did not return. And her treacherous sister Judah saw it. 8 Then I saw that for all the causes for which backsliding Israel had committed adultery, I had put her away and given her a certificate of divorce; yet her treacherous sister Judah did not fear, but went and played the harlot also. 9 So it came to pass, through her casual harlotry, that she defiled the land and committed adultery with stones and trees. 10 And yet for all this her treacherous sister Judah has not turned to Me with her whole heart, but in pretense," says the LORD.

11 Then the LORD said to me, "Backsliding Israel has shown herself more righteous than treacherous Judah. 12 Go and proclaim these words toward the north, and say:

'Return, backsliding Israel,'
  says the LORD;
'I will not cause My anger to fall
  on you.
For I *am* merciful,' says the
  LORD;
'I will not remain angry forever.
13 Only acknowledge your
  iniquity,
That you have transgressed
  against the LORD your God,
And have scattered your
  charms
To alien deities under every
  green tree,
And you have not obeyed My
  voice,' says the LORD.

14 "Return, O backsliding children," says the LORD; "for I am married to you. I will take you, one from a city and two from a family, and I will bring you to Zion. 15 And I will give you shepherds according to My heart, who will feed you with knowledge and understanding.

16 Then it shall come to pass, when you are multiplied and increased in the land in those days," says the LORD, "that they will say no more, 'The ark of the covenant of the LORD.' It shall not come to mind, nor shall they remember it, nor shall they visit *it,* nor shall it be made anymore.

17 "At that time Jerusalem shall be called The Throne of the LORD, and all the nations shall be gathered to it, to the name of the LORD, to Jerusalem. No more shall they follow the dictates of their evil hearts.

18 "In those days the house of Judah shall walk with the house of Israel, and they shall come together out of the land of the north to the land that I have given as an inheritance to your fathers.

19 "But I said:

'How can I put you among the
  children
And give you a pleasant land,
A beautiful heritage of the
  hosts of nations?'

"And I said:

'You shall call Me, "My Father,"
And not turn away from Me.'
20 Surely, *as* a wife treacherously
  departs from her husband,
So have you dealt
  treacherously with Me,

O house of Israel," says the
LORD.

21 A voice was heard on the
desolate heights,
Weeping *and* supplications of
the children of Israel.
For they have perverted their
way;
They have forgotten the LORD
their God.
22 "Return, you backsliding
children,
And I will heal your
backslidings."

"Indeed we do come to You,
For You are the LORD our God.
23 Truly, in vain *is salvation
hoped for* from the hills,
And from the multitude of
mountains;
Truly, in the LORD our God
Is the salvation of Israel.
24 For shame has devoured
The labor of our fathers from
our youth—
Their flocks and their herds,
Their sons and their daughters.
25 We lie down in our shame,
And our reproach covers us.
For we have sinned against the
LORD our God,
We and our fathers,
From our youth even to this
day,
And have not obeyed the voice
of the LORD our God."

4 "If you will return, O Israel,"
says the LORD,
"Return to Me;
And if you will put away your
abominations out of My
sight,
Then you shall not be moved.
2 And you shall swear, 'The LORD
lives,'
In truth, in judgment, and in
righteousness;
The nations shall bless
themselves in Him,
And in Him they shall glory."

3 For thus says the LORD to the men
of Judah and Jerusalem:

"Break up your fallow ground,
And do not sow among thorns.
4 Circumcise yourselves to the
LORD,

And take away the foreskins of
your hearts,
You men of Judah and
inhabitants of Jerusalem,
Lest My fury come forth like
fire,
And burn so that no one can
quench *it*,
Because of the evil of your
doings."

5 Declare in Judah and proclaim in
Jerusalem, and say:

"Blow the trumpet in the land;
Cry, 'Gather together,'
And say, 'Assemble yourselves,
And let us go into the fortified
cities.'
6 Set up the standard toward
Zion.
Take refuge! Do not delay!
For I will bring disaster from
the north,
And great destruction."

7 The lion has come up from his
thicket,
And the destroyer of nations is
on his way.
He has gone forth from his
place
To make your land desolate.
Your cities will be laid waste,
Without inhabitant.
8 For this, clothe yourself with
sackcloth,
Lament and wail.
For the fierce anger of the
LORD
Has not turned back from us.

9 "And it shall come to pass in that
day," says the LORD,
"*That* the heart of the king shall
perish,
And the heart of the princes;
The priests shall be astonished,
And the prophets shall
wonder."

10 Then I said, "Ah, Lord GOD!
Surely You have greatly
deceived this people and
Jerusalem,
Saying, 'You shall have peace,'
Whereas the sword reaches to
the heart."

11 At that time it will be said
To this people and to
Jerusalem,

"A dry wind of the desolate
heights *blows* in the
wilderness
Toward the daughter of My
people—
Not to fan or to cleanse—
12 A wind too strong for these will
come for Me;
Now I will also speak judgment
against them."

13 "Behold, he shall come up like
clouds,
And his chariots like a
whirlwind.
His horses are swifter than
eagles.
Woe to us, for we are
plundered!"

14 O Jerusalem, wash your heart
from wickedness,
That you may be saved.
How long shall your evil
thoughts lodge within you?
15 For a voice declares from Dan
And proclaims affliction from
Mount Ephraim:
16 "Make mention to the nations,
Yes, proclaim against
Jerusalem,
That watchers come from a far
country
And raise their voice against
the cities of Judah.
17 Like keepers of a field they are
against her all around,
Because she has been
rebellious against Me," says
the LORD.
18 "Your ways and your doings
Have procured these *things* for
you.
This *is* your wickedness,
Because it is bitter,
Because it reaches to your
heart."

19 O my soul, my soul!
I am pained in my very heart!
My heart makes a noise in
me;
I cannot hold my peace,
Because you have heard, O my
soul,
The sound of the trumpet,
The alarm of war.
20 Destruction upon destruction is
cried,
For the whole land is
plundered.

Suddenly my tents are
plundered,
And my curtains in a moment.
21 How long will I see the
standard,
And hear the sound of the
trumpet?

22 "For My people *are* foolish,
They have not known Me.
They *are* silly children,
And they have no
understanding.
They *are* wise to do evil,
But to do good they have no
knowledge."

23 I beheld the earth, and indeed
it was without form, and
void;
And the heavens, they *had* no
light.
24 I beheld the mountains, and
indeed they trembled,
And all the hills moved back
and forth.
25 I beheld, and indeed *there was*
no man,
And all the birds of the heavens
had fled.
26 I beheld, and indeed the fruitful
land *was* a wilderness,
And all its cities were broken
down
At the presence of the LORD,
By His fierce anger.

27 For thus says the LORD:

"The whole land shall be
desolate;
Yet I will not make a full end.
28 For this shall the earth mourn,
And the heavens above be
black,
Because I have spoken.
I have purposed and will not
relent,
Nor will I turn back from it.
29 The whole city shall flee from
the noise of the horsemen
and bowmen.
They shall go into thickets and
climb up on the rocks.
Every city *shall be* forsaken,
And not a man shall dwell in
it.

30 "And *when* you *are* plundered,
What will you do?
Though you clothe yourself
with crimson,

Though you adorn *yourself*
with ornaments of gold,
Though you enlarge your eyes
with paint,
In vain you will make yourself
fair;
Your lovers will despise you;
They will seek your life.

31 "For I have heard a voice as of
a woman in labor,
The anguish as of her who
brings forth her first child,
The voice of the daughter of
Zion bewailing herself;
She spreads her hands, *saying*,
'Woe *is* me now, for my soul is
weary
Because of murderers!'

5 "Run to and fro through the
streets of Jerusalem;
See now and know;
And seek in her open places
If you can find a man,
If there is *anyone* who executes
judgment,
Who seeks the truth,
And I will pardon her.
2 Though they say, 'As the LORD
lives,'
Surely they swear falsely."

3 O LORD, *are* not Your eyes on
the truth?
You have stricken them,
But they have not grieved;
You have consumed them,
But they have refused to
receive correction.
They have made their faces
harder than rock;
They have refused to return.

4 Therefore I said, "Surely these
are poor.
They are foolish;
For they do not know the way
of the LORD,
The judgment of their God.
5 I will go to the great men and
speak to them,
For they have known the way
of the LORD,
The judgment of their God."

But these have altogether
broken the yoke
And burst the bonds.
6 Therefore a lion from the forest
shall slay them,

A wolf of the deserts shall
destroy them;
A leopard will watch over their
cities.
Everyone who goes out from
there shall be torn in pieces,
Because their transgressions
are many;
Their backslidings have
increased.

7 "How shall I pardon you for
this?
Your children have forsaken
Me
And sworn by *those that are*
not gods.
When I had fed them to the full,
Then they committed adultery
And assembled themselves by
troops in the harlots' houses.
8 They were *like* well-fed lusty
stallions;
Every one neighed after his
neighbor's wife.
9 Shall I not punish *them* for
these *things*?" says the LORD.
"And shall I not avenge Myself
on such a nation as this?

10 "Go up on her walls and destroy,
But do not make a complete
end.
Take away her branches,
For they *are* not the LORD's.
11 For the house of Israel and the
house of Judah
Have dealt very treacherously
with Me," says the LORD.

12 They have lied about the LORD,
And said, "*It is* not He.
Neither will evil come upon us,
Nor shall we see sword or
famine.
13 And the prophets become
wind,
For the word *is* not in them.
Thus shall it be done to them."

14 Therefore thus says the LORD
God of hosts:

"Because you speak this word,
Behold, I will make My words
in your mouth fire,
And this people wood,
And it shall devour them.
15 Behold, I will bring a nation
against you from afar,
O house of Israel," says the
LORD.

"It *is* a mighty nation,
It *is* an ancient nation,
A nation whose language you do not know,
Nor can you understand what they say.
16 Their quiver *is* like an open tomb;
They *are* all mighty men.
17 And they shall eat up your harvest and your bread,
Which your sons and daughters should eat.
They shall eat up your flocks and your herds;
They shall eat up your vines and your fig trees;
They shall destroy your fortified cities,
In which you trust, with the sword.

18 "Nevertheless in those days," says the LORD, "I will not make a complete end of you. 19 And it will be when you say, 'Why does the LORD our God do all these *things* to us?' then you shall answer them, 'Just as you have forsaken Me and served foreign gods in your land, so you shall serve aliens in a land *that is* not yours.'

20 "Declare this in the house of Jacob
And proclaim it in Judah, saying,
21 'Hear this now, O foolish people,
Without understanding,
Who have eyes and see not,
And who have ears and hear not:
22 Do you not fear Me?' says the LORD.
'Will you not tremble at My presence,
Who have placed the sand as the bound of the sea,
By a perpetual decree, that it cannot pass beyond it?
And though its waves toss to and fro,
Yet they cannot prevail;
Though they roar, yet they cannot pass over it.
23 But this people has a defiant and rebellious heart;
They have revolted and departed.
24 They do not say in their heart,

"Let us now fear the LORD our God,
Who gives rain, both the former and the latter, in its season.
He reserves for us the appointed weeks of the harvest."
25 Your iniquities have turned these *things* away,
And your sins have withheld good from you.

26 'For among My people are found wicked *men;*
They lie in wait as one who sets snares;
They set a trap;
They catch men.
27 As a cage is full of birds,
So their houses *are* full of deceit.
Therefore they have become great and grown rich.
28 They have grown fat, they are sleek;
Yes, they surpass the deeds of the wicked;
They do not plead the cause,
The cause of the fatherless;
Yet they prosper,
And the right of the needy they do not defend.
29 Shall I not punish *them* for these *things?*' says the LORD.
'Shall I not avenge Myself on such a nation as this?'

30 "An astonishing and horrible thing
Has been committed in the land:
31 The prophets prophesy falsely,
And the priests rule by their *own* power;
And My people love *to have it* so.
But what will you do in the end?

6 "O you children of Benjamin,
Gather yourselves to flee from the midst of Jerusalem!
Blow the trumpet in Tekoa,
And set up a signal-fire in Beth Haccerem;
For disaster appears out of the north,
And great destruction.
2 I have likened the daughter of Zion

To a lovely and delicate
   woman.
3 The shepherds with their flocks
   shall come to her.
They shall pitch *their* tents
   against her all around.
Each one shall pasture in his
   own place."

4 "Prepare war against her;
Arise, and let us go up at noon.
Woe to us, for the day goes
   away,
For the shadows of the evening
   are lengthening.
5 Arise, and let us go by night,
And let us destroy her
   palaces."

6 For thus has the LORD of hosts
said:

"Cut down trees,
And build a mound against
   Jerusalem.
This *is* the city to be punished.
She *is* full of oppression in her
   midst.
7 As a fountain wells up with
   water,
So she wells up with her
   wickedness.
Violence and plundering are
   heard in her.
Before Me continually *are* grief
   and wounds.
8 Be instructed, O Jerusalem,
Lest My soul depart from you;
Lest I make you desolate,
A land not inhabited."

9 Thus says the LORD of hosts:

"They shall thoroughly glean as
   a vine the remnant of Israel;
As a grape-gatherer, put your
   hand back into the
   branches."

10 To whom shall I speak and give
   warning,
That they may hear?
Indeed their ear *is*
   uncircumcised,
And they cannot give heed.
Behold, the word of the LORD
   is a reproach to them;
They have no delight in it.
11 Therefore I am full of the fury
   of the LORD.
I am weary of holding *it* in.

"I will pour it out on the children
   outside,
And on the assembly of young
   men together;
For even the husband shall be
   taken with the wife,
The aged with *him who is* full
   of days.
12 And their houses shall be
   turned over to others,
Fields and wives together;
For I will stretch out My
   hand
Against the inhabitants of the
   land," says the LORD.
13 "Because from the least of them
   even to the greatest of
   them,
Everyone *is* given to
   covetousness;
And from the prophet even to
   the priest,
Everyone deals falsely.
14 They have also healed the hurt
   of My people slightly,
Saying, 'Peace, peace!'
When *there is* no peace.
15 Were they ashamed when they
   had committed abomination?
No! They were not at all
   ashamed;
Nor did they know how to
   blush.
Therefore they shall fall among
   those who fall;
At the time I punish them,
They shall be cast down," says
   the LORD.

16 Thus says the LORD:

"Stand in the ways and see,
And ask for the old paths,
   where the good way *is*,
And walk in it;
Then you will find rest for your
   souls.
But they said, 'We will not walk
   in it.'
17 Also, I set watchmen over you,
   saying,
'Listen to the sound of the
   trumpet!'
But they said, 'We will not
   listen.'
18 Therefore hear, you nations,
And know, O congregation,
   what *is* among them.
19 Hear, O earth!
Behold, I will certainly bring
   calamity on this people—
The fruit of their thoughts,

Because they have not heeded
My words
Nor My law, but rejected it.
20 For what purpose to Me
Comes frankincense from
Sheba,
And sweet cane from a far
country?
Your burnt offerings *are* not
acceptable,
Nor your sacrifices sweet to
Me."

21 Therefore thus says the LORD:

"Behold, I will lay stumbling
blocks before this people,
And the fathers and the sons
together shall fall on them.
The neighbor and his friend
shall perish."

22 Thus says the LORD:

"Behold, a people comes from
the north country,
And a great nation will be
raised from the farthest parts
of the earth.
23 They will lay hold on bow and
spear;
They *are* cruel and have no
mercy;
Their voice roars like the sea;
And they ride on horses,
As men of war set in array
against you, O daughter of
Zion."

24 We have heard the report of it;
Our hands grow feeble.
Anguish has taken hold of us,
Pain as of a woman in labor.
25 Do not go out into the field,
Nor walk by the way.
Because of the sword of the
enemy,
Fear *is* on every side.
26 O daughter of my people,
Dress in sackcloth
And roll about in ashes!
Make mourning *as for* an only
son, most bitter lamentation;
For the plunderer will suddenly
come upon us.

27 "I have set you *as* an assayer
and a fortress among My
people,
That you may know and test
their way.

28 They *are* all stubborn rebels,
walking as slanderers.
They are bronze and iron,
They *are* all corrupters;
29 The bellows blow fiercely,
The lead is consumed by the
fire;
The smelter refines in vain,
For the wicked are not drawn
off.
30 *People* will call them rejected
silver,
Because the LORD has rejected
them."

7 The word that came to Jeremiah
from the LORD, saying, 2 "Stand
in the gate of the LORD's house, and
proclaim there this word, and say,
'Hear the word of the LORD, all *you*
of Judah who enter in at these gates
to worship the LORD!' " 3 Thus says
the LORD of hosts, the God of Israel:
"Amend your ways and your doings,
and I will cause you to dwell in this
place. 4 Do not trust in these lying
words, saying, 'The temple of the
LORD, the temple of the LORD, the
temple of the LORD *are* these.'
5 "For if you thoroughly amend
your ways and your doings, if you
thoroughly execute judgment between a man and his neighbor,
6 *if* you do not oppress the stranger,
the fatherless, and the widow, and do
not shed innocent blood in this place,
or walk after other gods to your hurt,
7 then I will cause you to dwell in this
place, in the land that I gave to your
fathers forever and ever.
8 "Behold, you trust in lying words
that cannot profit. 9 Will you steal,
murder, commit adultery, swear
falsely, burn incense to Baal, and
walk after other gods whom you do
not know, 10 and *then* come and
stand before Me in this house which
is called by My name, and say, 'We
are delivered to do all these abominations'? 11 Has this house, which is
called by My name, become a den of
thieves in your eyes? Behold, I, even
I, have seen *it*," says the LORD.
12 "But go now to My place which
was in Shiloh, where I set My name
at the first, and see what I did to it
because of the wickedness of My
people Israel. 13 And now, because
you have done all these works," says
the LORD, "and I spoke to you, rising
up early and speaking, but you did
not hear, and I called you, but you

did not answer, 14 therefore I will do to the house which is called by My name, in which you trust, and to this place which I gave to you and your fathers, as I have done to Shiloh. 15 And I will cast you out of My sight, as I have cast out all your brethren— the whole posterity of Ephraim.

16 "Therefore do not pray for this people, nor lift up a cry or prayer for them, nor make intercession to Me; for I will not hear you. 17 Do you not see what they do in the cities of Judah and in the streets of Jerusalem? 18 The children gather wood, the fathers kindle the fire, and the women knead dough, to make cakes for the queen of heaven; and *they* pour out drink offerings to other gods, that they may provoke Me to anger. 19 Do they provoke Me to anger?" says the LORD. "*Do they* not *provoke* themselves, to the shame of their own faces?"

20 Therefore thus says the Lord GOD: "Behold, My anger and My fury will be poured out on this place—on man and on beast, on the trees of the field and on the fruit of the ground. And it will burn and not be quenched."

21 Thus says the LORD of hosts, the God of Israel: "Add your burnt offerings to your sacrifices and eat meat. 22 For I did not speak to your fathers, or command them in the day that I brought them out of the land of Egypt, concerning burnt offerings or sacrifices. 23 But this is what I commanded them, saying, 'Obey My voice, and I will be your God, and you shall be My people. And walk in all the ways that I have commanded you, that it may be well with you.' 24 Yet they did not obey or incline their ear, but followed the counsels *and* the dictates of their evil hearts, and went backward and not forward. 25 Since the day that your fathers came out of the land of Egypt until this day, I have even sent to you all My servants the prophets, daily rising up early and sending *them*. 26 Yet they did not obey Me or incline their ear, but stiffened their neck. They did worse than their fathers.

27 "Therefore you shall speak all these words to them, but they will not obey you. You shall also call to them, but they will not answer you. 28 "So you shall say to them, 'This *is* a nation that does not obey the voice of the LORD their God nor receive correction. Truth has perished and has been cut off from their mouth. 29 Cut off your hair and cast *it* away, and take up a lamentation on the desolate heights; for the LORD has rejected and forsaken the generation of His wrath.' 30 For the children of Judah have done evil in My sight," says the LORD. "They have set their abominations in the house which is called by My name, to pollute it. 31 And they have built the high places of Tophet, which *is* in the Valley of the Son of Hinnom, to burn their sons and their daughters in the fire, which I did not command, nor did it come into My heart.

32 "Therefore behold, the days are coming," says the LORD, "when it will no more be called Tophet, or the Valley of the Son of Hinnom, but the Valley of Slaughter; for they will bury in Tophet until there is no room. 33 The corpses of this people will be food for the birds of the heaven and for the beasts of the earth. And no one will frighten *them away*. 34 Then I will cause to cease from the cities of Judah and from the streets of Jerusalem the voice of mirth and the voice of gladness, the voice of the bridegroom and the voice of the bride. For the land shall be desolate.

8 "At that time," says the LORD, "they shall bring out the bones of the kings of Judah, and the bones of its princes, and the bones of the priests, and the bones of the prophets, and the bones of the inhabitants of Jerusalem, out of their graves. 2 They shall spread them before the sun and the moon and all the host of heaven, which they have loved and which they have served and after which they have walked, which they have sought and which they have worshiped. They shall not be gathered nor buried; they shall be like refuse on the face of the earth. 3 Then death shall be chosen rather than life by all the residue of those who remain of this evil family, who remain in all the places where I have driven them," says the LORD of hosts.

4 "Moreover you shall say to them, 'Thus says the LORD:

"Will they fall and not rise?
Will one turn away and not
    return?

5   Why has this people slidden
     back,
     Jerusalem, in a perpetual
     backsliding?
     They hold fast to deceit,
     They refuse to return.
6   I listened and heard,
     But they do not speak aright.
     No man repented of his
     wickedness,
     Saying, 'What have I done?'
     Everyone turned to his own
     course,
     As the horse rushes into the
     battle.

7   "Even the stork in the heavens
     Knows her appointed times;
     And the turtledove, the swift,
     and the swallow
     Observe the time of their
     coming.
     But My people do not know the
     judgment of the LORD.

8   "How can you say, 'We *are* wise,
     And the law of the LORD *is* with
     us'?
     Look, the false pen of the scribe
     certainly works falsehood.
9   The wise men are ashamed,
     They are dismayed and taken.
     Behold, they have rejected the
     word of the LORD;
     So what wisdom do they have?
10   Therefore I will give their wives
     to others,
     And their fields to those who
     will inherit *them;*
     Because from the least even to
     the greatest
     Everyone is given to
     covetousness;
     From the prophet even to the
     priest
     Everyone deals falsely.
11   For they have healed the hurt
     of the daughter of My people
     slightly,
     Saying, 'Peace, peace!'
     When *there is* no peace.
12   Were they ashamed when they
     had committed abomination?
     No! They were not at all
     ashamed,
     Nor did they know how to
     blush.
     Therefore they shall fall among
     those who fall;
     In the time of their punishment
     They shall be cast down," says
     the LORD.

13   "I will surely consume them,"
     says the LORD.
     "No grapes *shall be* on the vine,
     Nor figs on the fig tree,
     And the leaf shall fade;
     And *the things* I have given
     them shall pass away from
     them." ' "

14   "Why do we sit still?
     Assemble yourselves,
     And let us enter the fortified
     cities,
     And let us be silent there.
     For the LORD our God has put
     us to silence
     And given us water of gall to
     drink,
     Because we have sinned
     against the LORD.

15   *We* looked for peace, but no
     good *came;*
     And for a time of health, and
     there was trouble!
16   The snorting of His horses was
     heard from Dan.
     The whole land trembled at the
     sound of the neighing of His
     strong ones;
     For they have come and
     devoured the land and all
     that is in it,
     The city and those who dwell
     in it."

17   "For behold, I will send serpents
     among you,
     Vipers which cannot be
     charmed,
     And they shall bite you," says
     the LORD.

18   I would comfort myself in
     sorrow;
     My heart *is* faint in me.
19   Listen! The voice,
     The cry of the daughter of my
     people
     From a far country:
     "*Is* not the LORD in Zion?
     Is not her King in her?"

     "Why have they provoked Me to
     anger
     With their carved images—
     With foreign idols?"

20   "The harvest is past,
     The summer is ended,
     And we are not saved!"

21   For the hurt of the daughter of
     my people I am hurt.

I am mourning;
Astonishment has taken hold
of me.
22 *Is there* no balm in Gilead,
Is there no physician there?
Why then is there no recovery
For the health of the daughter
of my people?

9
Oh, that my head were waters,
And my eyes a fountain of
tears,
That I might weep day and
night
For the slain of the daughter of
my people!
2 Oh, that I had in the wilderness
A lodging place for travelers;
That I might leave my people,
And go from them!
For they *are* all adulterers,
An assembly of treacherous
men.

3 "And *like* their bow they have
bent their tongues *for* lies.
They are not valiant for the
truth on the earth.
For they proceed from evil to
evil,
And they do not know Me,"
says the LORD.
4 "Everyone take heed to his
neighbor,
And do not trust any brother;
For every brother will utterly
supplant,
And every neighbor will walk
with slanderers.
5 Everyone will deceive his
neighbor,
And will not speak the truth;
They have taught their tongue
to speak lies;
They weary themselves to
commit iniquity.
6 Your dwelling place *is* in the
midst of deceit;
Through deceit they refuse to
know Me," says the LORD.

7 Therefore thus says the LORD of
hosts:

"Behold, I will refine them and
try them;
For how shall I deal with the
daughter of My people?
8 Their tongue *is* an arrow shot
out;
It speaks deceit;

One speaks peaceably to his
neighbor with his mouth,
But in his heart he lies in wait.
9 Shall I not punish them for
these *things*?" says the LORD.
"Shall I not avenge Myself on
such a nation as this?"

10 I will take up a weeping and
wailing for the mountains,
And for the dwelling places of
the wilderness a lamentation,
Because they are burned up,
So that no one can pass
through;
Nor can *men* hear the voice of
the cattle.
Both the birds of the heavens
and the beasts have fled;
They are gone.

11 "I will make Jerusalem a heap
of ruins, a den of jackals.
I will make the cities of Judah
desolate, without an
inhabitant."

12 Who *is* the wise man who may
understand this? And *who is he* to
whom the mouth of the LORD has spoken, that he may declare it? Why
does the land perish *and* burn up like
a wilderness, so that no one can pass
through?
13 And the LORD said, "Because
they have forsaken My law which I
set before them, and have not obeyed
My voice, nor walked according to
it, 14 but they have walked according
to the dictates of their own hearts
and after the Baals, which their fathers taught them," 15 therefore thus
says the LORD of hosts, the God of
Israel: "Behold, I will feed them, this
people, with wormwood, and give
them water of gall to drink.
16 I will scatter them also among the
Gentiles, whom neither they nor their
fathers have known. And I will send
a sword after them until I have consumed them."
17 Thus says the LORD of hosts:

"Consider and call for the
mourning women,
That they may come;
And send for skillful wailing
women,
That they may come.
18 Let them make haste
And take up a wailing for us,

That our eyes may run with
     tears,
And our eyelids gush with
     water.
19 For a voice of wailing is heard
     from Zion:
'How we are plundered!
We are greatly ashamed,
Because we have forsaken the
     land,
Because we have been cast out
     of our dwellings.' "

20 Yet hear the word of the LORD,
     O women,
And let your ear receive the
     word of His mouth;
Teach your daughters wailing,
And everyone her neighbor a
     lamentation.
21 For death has come through
     our windows,
Has entered our palaces,
To kill off the children—*no
     longer to be* outside!
And the young men—*no longer*
     on the streets!

22 Speak, "Thus says the LORD:

'Even the carcasses of men shall
     fall as refuse on the open
     field,
Like cuttings after the
     harvester,
And no one shall gather
     them.' "

23 Thus says the LORD:

"Let not the wise *man* glory in
     his wisdom,
Let not the mighty *man* glory
     in his might,
Nor let the rich *man* glory in
     his riches;
24 But let him who glories glory
     in this,
That he understands and
     knows Me,
That I *am* the LORD, exercising
     lovingkindness, judgment,
     and righteousness in the
     earth.
For in these I delight," says the
     LORD.

25 "Behold, the days are coming,"
says the LORD, "that I will punish all
who are circumcised with the uncircumcised— 26 Egypt, Judah, Edom,
the people of Ammon, Moab, and all

who are in the farthest corners, who
dwell in the wilderness. For all *these*
nations *are* uncircumcised, and all
the house of Israel *are* uncircumcised
in the heart."

10 Hear the word which the LORD
     speaks to you, O house of Is-
rael.
2 Thus says the LORD:

"Do not learn the way of the
     Gentiles;
Do not be dismayed at the signs
     of heaven,
For the Gentiles are dismayed
     at them.
3 For the customs of the peoples
     are futile;
For *one* cuts a tree from the
     forest,
The work of the hands of the
     workman, with the ax.
4 They decorate it with silver and
     gold;
They fasten it with nails and
     hammers
So that it will not topple.
5 They *are* upright, like a palm
     tree,
And they cannot speak;
They must be carried,
Because they cannot go *by*
     themselves.
Do not be afraid of them,
For they cannot do evil,
Nor can they do any good."

6 Inasmuch as *there is* none like
     You, O LORD
(You *are* great, and Your name
     is great in might),
7 Who would not fear You, O
     King of the nations?
For this is Your rightful due.
For among all the wise *men* of
     the nations,
And in all their kingdoms,
There is none like You.
8 But they are altogether dull-
     hearted and foolish;
A wooden idol *is* a worthless
     doctrine.
9 Silver is beaten into plates;
It is brought from Tarshish,
And gold from Uphaz,
The work of the craftsman
And of the hands of the
     metalsmith;
Blue and purple *are* their
     clothing;

They *are* all the work of skillful
men.

10 But the LORD *is* the true God;
He *is* the living God and the
everlasting King.
At His wrath the earth will
tremble,
And the nations will not be able
to endure His indignation.

11 Thus you shall say to them: "The
gods that have not made the heavens
and the earth shall perish from the
earth and from under these heavens."

12 He has made the earth by His
power,
He has established the world
by His wisdom,
And has stretched out the
heavens at His discretion.
13 When He utters His voice,
There is a multitude of waters
in the heavens:
"And He causes the vapors to
ascend from the ends of the
earth.
He makes lightning for the
rain,
He brings the wind out of His
treasuries."*a*

14 Everyone is dull-hearted,
without knowledge;
Every metalsmith is put to
shame by an image;
For his molded image *is*
falsehood,
And *there is* no breath in them.
15 They *are* futile, a work of
errors;
In the time of their punishment
they shall perish.
16 The Portion of Jacob *is* not like
them,
For He *is* the Maker of all
things,
And Israel *is* the tribe of His
inheritance;
The LORD of hosts *is* His name.
17 Gather up your wares from the
land,
O inhabitant of the fortress!

18 For thus says the LORD:

"Behold, I will throw out at this
time
The inhabitants of the land,

And will distress them,
That they may find *it* so."

19 Woe is me for my hurt!
My wound is severe.
But I say, "Truly this *is* an
infirmity,
And I must bear it."
20 My tent is plundered,
And all my cords are broken;
My children have gone from
me,
And they *are* no more.
There is no one to pitch my tent
anymore,
Or set up my curtains.
21 For the shepherds have become
dull-hearted,
And have not sought the LORD;
Therefore they shall not
prosper,
And all their flocks shall be
scattered.
22 Behold, the noise of the report
has come,
And a great commotion out of
the north country,
To make the cities of Judah
desolate, a den of jackals.
23 O LORD, I know the way of man
is not in himself;
It is not in man who walks to
direct his own steps.
24 O LORD, correct me, but with
justice;
Not in Your anger, lest You
bring me to nothing.
25 Pour out Your fury on the
Gentiles, who do not know
You,
And on the families who do not
call on Your name;
For they have eaten up Jacob,
Devoured him and consumed
him,
And made his dwelling place
desolate.

11

The word that came to Jeremiah from the LORD, saying,
2 "Hear the words of this covenant,
and speak to the men of Judah and
to the inhabitants of Jerusalem;
3 and say to them, 'Thus says the
LORD God of Israel: "Cursed *is* the
man who does not obey the words
of this covenant 4 which I commanded your fathers in the day I
brought them out of the land of
Egypt, from the iron furnace, saying,

10:13 *a*Psalm 135:7

'Obey My voice, and do according to all that I command you; so shall you be My people, and I will be your God,' 5 that I may establish the oath which I have sworn to your fathers, to give them 'a land flowing with milk and honey,'ª as *it is* this day." ' "

And I answered and said, "So be it, LORD."

6 Then the LORD said to me, "Proclaim all these words in the cities of Judah and in the streets of Jerusalem, saying: 'Hear the words of this covenant and do them. 7 For I earnestly exhorted your fathers in the day I brought them up out of the land of Egypt, until this day, rising early and exhorting, saying, "Obey My voice." 8 Yet they did not obey or incline their ear, but everyone followed the dictates of his evil heart; therefore I will bring upon them all the words of this covenant, which I commanded *them* to do, but *which* they have not done.' "

9 And the LORD said to me, "A conspiracy has been found among the men of Judah and among the inhabitants of Jerusalem. 10 They have turned back to the iniquities of their forefathers who refused to hear My words, and they have gone after other gods to serve them; the house of Israel and the house of Judah have broken My covenant which I made with their fathers."

11 Therefore thus says the LORD: "Behold, I will surely bring calamity on them which they will not be able to escape; and though they cry out to Me, I will not listen to them. 12 Then the cities of Judah and the inhabitants of Jerusalem will go and cry out to the gods to whom they offer incense, but they will not save them at all in the time of their trouble. 13 For *according to* the number of your cities were your gods, O Judah; and *according to* the number of the streets of Jerusalem you have set up altars to *that* shameful thing, altars to burn incense to Baal.

14 "So do not pray for this people, or lift up a cry or prayer for them; for I will not hear *them* in the time that they cry out to Me because of their trouble.

15 "What has My beloved to do in My house,

Having done lewd deeds with many?
And the holy flesh has passed from you.
When you do evil, then you rejoice.
16 The LORD called your name,
Green Olive Tree, Lovely *and* of Good Fruit.
With the noise of a great tumult He has kindled fire on it,
And its branches are broken.

17 "For the LORD of hosts, who planted you, has pronounced doom against you for the evil of the house of Israel and of the house of Judah, which they have done against themselves to provoke Me to anger in offering incense to Baal."

18 Now the LORD gave me knowledge *of it*, and I know *it*; for You showed me their doings. 19 But I *was* like a docile lamb brought to the slaughter; and I did not know that they had devised schemes against me, *saying*, "Let us destroy the tree with its fruit, and let us cut him off from the land of the living, that his name may be remembered no more."

20 But, O LORD of hosts,
You who judge righteously,
Testing the mind and the heart,
Let me see Your vengeance on them,
For to You I have revealed my cause.

21 "Therefore thus says the LORD concerning the men of Anathoth who seek your life, saying, 'Do not prophesy in the name of the LORD, lest you die by our hand'— 22 therefore thus says the LORD of hosts: 'Behold, I will punish them. The young men shall die by the sword, their sons and their daughters shall die by famine; 23 and there shall be no remnant of them, for I will bring catastrophe on the men of Anathoth, *even* the year of their punishment.' "

12 Righteous *are* You, O LORD,
when I plead with You;
Yet let me talk with You about *Your* judgments.
Why does the way of the wicked prosper?

Why are those happy who deal
    so treacherously?
2 You have planted them, yes,
    they have taken root;
They grow, yes, they bear fruit.
You *are* near in their mouth
But far from their mind.

3 But You, O LORD, know me;
You have seen me,
And You have tested my heart
    toward You.
Pull them out like sheep for the
    slaughter,
And prepare them for the day
    of slaughter.
4 How long will the land mourn,
And the herbs of every field
    wither?
The beasts and birds are
    consumed,
For the wickedness of those
    who dwell there,
Because they said, "He will not
    see our final end."

5 "If you have run with the
    footmen, and they have
    wearied you,
Then how can you contend
    with horses?
And *if* in the land of peace,
In which you trusted, *they*
    wearied you,
Then how will you do in the
    floodplain[a] of the Jordan?
6 For even your brothers, the
    house of your father,
Even they have dealt
    treacherously with you;
Yes, they have called a
    multitude after you.
Do not believe them,
Even though they speak
    smooth words to you.

7 "I have forsaken My house, I
    have left My heritage;
I have given the dearly beloved
    of My soul into the hand of
    her enemies.
8 My heritage is to Me like a lion
    in the forest;
It cries out against Me;
Therefore I have hated it.
9 My heritage *is* to Me *like* a
    speckled vulture;
The vultures all around *are*
    against her.

Come, assemble all the beasts
    of the field,
Bring them to devour!
10 "Many rulers[a] have destroyed
    My vineyard,
They have trodden My portion
    underfoot;
They have made My pleasant
    portion a desolate
    wilderness.
11 They have made it desolate;
Desolate, it mourns to Me;
The whole land is made
    desolate,
Because no one takes *it* to
    heart.
12 The plunderers have come
On all the desolate heights in
    the wilderness,
For the sword of the LORD shall
    devour
From *one* end of the land to the
    other end of the land;
No flesh shall have peace.
13 They have sown wheat but
    reaped thorns;
They have put themselves to
    pain *but* do not profit.
But be ashamed of your harvest
Because of the fierce anger of
    the LORD."

14 Thus says the LORD: "Against all
My evil neighbors who touch the inheritance which I have caused My
people Israel to inherit—behold, I
will pluck them out of their land and
pluck out the house of Judah from
among them. 15 Then it shall be, after
I have plucked them out, that I will
return and have compassion on them
and bring them back, everyone to his
heritage and everyone to his land.
16 And it shall be, if they will learn
carefully the ways of My people, to
swear by My name, 'As the LORD
lives,' as they taught My people to
swear by Baal, then they shall be established in the midst of My people.
17 But if they do not obey, I will utterly pluck up and destroy that nation," says the LORD.

13 Thus the LORD said to me: "Go
and get yourself a linen sash,
and put it around your waist, but do
not put it in water." 2 So I got a sash
according to the word of the LORD,
and put *it* around my waist.

3 And the word of the LORD came
to me the second time, saying,

4 "Take the sash that you acquired, which *is* around your waist, and arise, go to the Euphrates,[a] and hide it there in a hole in the rock."
5 So I went and hid it by the Euphrates, as the LORD commanded me.

6 Now it came to pass after many days that the LORD said to me, "Arise, go to the Euphrates, and take from there the sash which I commanded you to hide there." 7 Then I went to the Euphrates and dug, and I took the sash from the place where I had hidden it; and there was the sash, ruined. It was profitable for nothing.

8 Then the word of the LORD came to me, saying, 9 "Thus says the LORD: 'In this manner I will ruin the pride of Judah and the great pride of Jerusalem. 10 This evil people, who refuse to hear My words, who follow the dictates of their hearts, and walk after other gods to serve them and worship them, shall be just like this sash which is profitable for nothing. 11 For as the sash clings to the waist of a man, so I have caused the whole house of Israel and the whole house of Judah to cling to Me,' says the LORD, 'that they may become My people, for renown, for praise, and for glory; but they would not hear.'

12 "Therefore you shall speak to them this word: 'Thus says the LORD God of Israel: "Every bottle shall be filled with wine." '

"And they will say to you, 'Do we not certainly know that every bottle will be filled with wine?'

13 "Then you shall say to them, 'Thus says the LORD: "Behold, I will fill all the inhabitants of this land—even the kings who sit on David's throne, the priests, the prophets, and all the inhabitants of Jerusalem—with drunkenness! 14 And I will dash them one against another, even the fathers and the sons together," says the LORD. "I will not pity nor spare nor have mercy, but will destroy them." ' "

15 Hear and give ear:
    Do not be proud,
    For the LORD has spoken.
16 Give glory to the LORD your
      God
    Before He causes darkness,
    And before your feet stumble
    On the dark mountains,

    And while you are looking for
      light,
    He turns it into the shadow of
      death
    And makes *it* dense darkness.
17 But if you will not hear it,
    My soul will weep in secret for
      your pride;
    My eyes will weep bitterly
    And run down with tears,
    Because the LORD's flock has
      been taken captive.

18 Say to the king and to the
      queen mother,
  "Humble yourselves;
    Sit down,
    For your rule shall collapse, the
      crown of your glory."
19 The cities of the South shall be
      shut up,
    And no one shall open *them;*
    Judah shall be carried away
      captive, all of it;
    It shall be wholly carried away
      captive.

20 Lift up your eyes and see
    Those who come from the
      north.
    Where *is* the flock *that* was
      given to you,
    Your beautiful sheep?
21 What will you say when He
      punishes you?
    For you have taught them
    To be chieftains, to be head
      over you.
    Will not pangs seize you,
    Like a woman in labor?
22 And if you say in your heart,
    "Why have these things come
      upon me?"
    For the greatness of your
      iniquity
    Your skirts have been
      uncovered,
    Your heels made bare.
23 Can the Ethiopian change his
      skin or the leopard its spots?
    Then may you also do good
      who are accustomed to do
      evil.

24 "Therefore I will scatter them
      like stubble
    That passes away by the wind
      of the wilderness.
25 This is your lot,

The portion of your measures
from Me," says the LORD,
"Because you have forgotten Me
And trusted in falsehood.

26 Therefore I will uncover your
skirts over your face,
That your shame may appear.

27 I have seen your adulteries
And your *lustful* neighings,
The lewdness of your harlotry,
Your abominations on the hills
in the fields.
Woe to you, O Jerusalem!
Will you still not be made
clean?"

14 The word of the LORD that
came to Jeremiah concerning
the droughts.

2 "Judah mourns,
And her gates languish;
They mourn for the land,
And the cry of Jerusalem has
gone up.

3 Their nobles have sent their
lads for water;
They went to the cisterns *and*
found no water.
They returned with their
vessels empty;
They were ashamed and
confounded
And covered their heads.

4 Because the ground is parched,
For there was no rain in the
land,
The plowmen were ashamed;
They covered their heads.

5 Yes, the deer also gave birth in
the field,
But left because there was no
grass.

6 And the wild donkeys stood in
the desolate heights;
They sniffed at the wind like
jackals;
Their eyes failed because *there
was* no grass."

7 O LORD, though our iniquities
testify against us,
Do it for Your name's sake;
For our backslidings are many,
We have sinned against You.

8 O the Hope of Israel, his Savior
in time of trouble,
Why should You be like a
stranger in the land,
And like a traveler *who* turns
aside to tarry for a night?

9 Why should You be like a man
astonished,
Like a mighty one *who* cannot
save?
Yet You, O LORD, *are* in our
midst,
And we are called by Your
name;
Do not leave us!

10 Thus says the LORD to this people:

"Thus they have loved to
wander;
They have not restrained their
feet.
Therefore the LORD does not
accept them;
He will remember their iniquity
now,
And punish their sins."

11 Then the LORD said to me, "Do
not pray for this people, for *their*
good. 12 When they fast, I will not
hear their cry; and when they offer
burnt offering and grain offering, I
will not accept them. But I will consume them by the sword, by the famine, and by the pestilence."

13 Then I said, "Ah, Lord GOD! Behold, the prophets say to them, 'You
shall not see the sword, nor shall you
have famine, but I will give you assured peace in this place.' "

14 And the LORD said to me, "The
prophets prophesy lies in My name.
I have not sent them, commanded
them, nor spoken to them; they
prophesy to you a false vision, divination, a worthless thing, and the deceit of their heart. 15 Therefore thus
says the LORD concerning the prophets who prophesy in My name, whom
I did not send, and who say, 'Sword
and famine shall not be in this
land'—'By sword and famine those
prophets shall be consumed!
16 And the people to whom they
prophesy shall be cast out in the
streets of Jerusalem because of the
famine and the sword; they will have
no one to bury them—them nor their
wives, their sons nor their daughters—for I will pour their wickedness
on them.'

17 "Therefore you shall say this
word to them:

'Let my eyes flow with tears
night and day,

And let them not cease;
For the virgin daughter of my
  people
Has been broken with a mighty
  stroke, with a very severe
  blow.
18 If I go out to the field,
Then behold, those slain with
  the sword!
And if I enter the city,
Then behold, those sick from
  famine!
Yes, both prophet and priest go
  about in a land they do not
  know.' "

19 Have You utterly rejected
  Judah?
Has Your soul loathed Zion?
Why have You stricken us so
  that *there is* no healing for
  us?
We looked for peace, but *there*
  was no good;
And for the time of healing, and
  there was trouble.
20 We acknowledge, O LORD, our
  wickedness
And the iniquity of our fathers,
For we have sinned against
  You.
21 Do not abhor *us,* for Your
  name's sake;
Do not disgrace the throne of
  Your glory.
Remember, do not break Your
  covenant with us.
22 Are there any among the idols
  of the nations that can cause
  rain?
Or can the heavens give
  showers?
Are You not He, O LORD our
  God?
Therefore we will wait for You,
Since You have made all these.

15 Then the LORD said to me,
"*Even* if Moses and Samuel
stood before Me, My mind *would* not
be favorable toward this people. Cast
them out of My sight, and let them
go forth. 2 And it shall be, if they say
to you, 'Where should we go?' then
you shall tell them, 'Thus says the
LORD:

"Such as *are* for death, to death;
And such as *are* for the sword,
  to the sword;
And such as *are* for the famine,
  to the famine;

And such as *are* for the
  captivity, to the captivity." '

3 "And I will appoint over them
four forms *of destruction,*" says the
LORD: "the sword to slay, the dogs
to drag, the birds of the heavens and
the beasts of the earth to devour and
destroy. 4 I will hand them over to
trouble, to all kingdoms of the earth,
because of Manasseh the son of
Hezekiah, king of Judah, for what he
did in Jerusalem.

5 "For who will have pity on you,
  O Jerusalem?
Or who will bemoan you?
Or who will turn aside to ask
  how you are doing?
6 You have forsaken Me," says
  the LORD,
"You have gone backward.
Therefore I will stretch out My
  hand against you and destroy
  you;
I am weary of relenting!
7 And I will winnow them with
  a winnowing fan in the gates
  of the land;
I will bereave *them* of children;
I will destroy My people,
Since they do not return from
  their ways.
8 Their widows will be increased
  to Me more than the sand of
  the seas;
I will bring against them,
Against the mother of the
  young men,
A plunderer at noonday;
I will cause anguish and terror
  to fall on them suddenly.

9 "She languishes who has borne
  seven;
She has breathed her last;
Her sun has gone down
While *it was* yet day;
She has been ashamed and
  confounded.
And the remnant of them I will
  deliver to the sword
Before their enemies," says the
  LORD.

10 Woe is me, my mother,
That you have borne me,
A man of strife and a man of
  contention to the whole
  earth!
I have neither lent for interest,

Nor have men lent to me for
   interest.
Every one of them curses me.

11 The LORD said:

"Surely it will be well with your
   remnant;
Surely I will cause the enemy
   to intercede with you
In the time of adversity and in
   the time of affliction.
12 Can anyone break iron,
The northern iron and the
   bronze?
13 Your wealth and your treasures
I will give as plunder without
   price,
Because of all your sins,
Throughout your territories.
14 And I will make *you* cross over
   with*ª* your enemies
Into a land *which* you do not
   know;
For a fire is kindled in My
   anger,
Which shall burn upon you."

15 O LORD, You know;
Remember me and visit me,
And take vengeance for me on
   my persecutors.
In Your enduring patience, do
   not take me away.
Know that for Your sake I have
   suffered rebuke.
16 Your words were found, and I
   ate them,
And Your word was to me the
   joy and rejoicing of my
   heart;
For I am called by Your
   name,
O LORD God of hosts.
17 I did not sit in the assembly of
   the mockers,
Nor did I rejoice;
I sat alone because of Your
   hand,
For You have filled me with
   indignation.
18 Why is my pain perpetual
And my wound incurable,
Which refuses to be healed?
Will You surely be to me like
   an unreliable stream,
As waters *that* fail?

19 Therefore thus says the LORD:

"If you return,
Then I will bring you back;
You shall stand before Me;
If you take out the precious
   from the vile,
You shall be as My mouth.
Let them return to you,
But you must not return to
   them.
20 And I will make you to this
   people a fortified bronze
   wall;
And they will fight against
   you,
But they shall not prevail
   against you;
For I *am* with you to save you
And deliver you," says the
   LORD.
21 "I will deliver you from the hand
   of the wicked,
And I will redeem you from the
   grip of the terrible."

16 The word of the LORD also came to me, saying, 2 "You shall not take a wife, nor shall you have sons or daughters in this place." 3 For thus says the LORD concerning the sons and daughters who are born in this place, and concerning their mothers who bore them and their fathers who begot them in this land: 4 "They shall die gruesome deaths; they shall not be lamented nor shall they be buried, *but* they shall be like refuse on the face of the earth. They shall be consumed by the sword and by famine, and their corpses shall be meat for the birds of heaven and for the beasts of the earth."

5 For thus says the LORD: "Do not enter the house of mourning, nor go to lament or bemoan them; for I have taken away My peace from this people," says the LORD, "lovingkindness and mercies. 6 Both the great and the small shall die in this land. They shall not be buried; neither shall men lament for them, cut themselves, nor make themselves bald for them. 7 Nor shall *men* break *bread* in mourning for them, to comfort them for the dead; nor shall *men* give them the cup of consolation to drink for their father or their mother. 8 Also you shall not go into the house of feasting to sit with them, to eat and drink."

15:14 ªFollowing Masoretic Text and Vulgate; Septuagint, Syriac, and Targum read *cause you to serve* (compare 17:4).

9 For thus says the LORD of hosts, the God of Israel: "Behold, I will cause to cease from this place, before your eyes and in your days, the voice of mirth and the voice of gladness, the voice of the bridegroom and the voice of the bride.

10 "And it shall be, when you show this people all these words, and they say to you, 'Why has the LORD pronounced all this great disaster against us? Or what is our iniquity? Or what is our sin that we have committed against the LORD our God?' 11 then you shall say to them, 'Because your fathers have forsaken Me,' says the LORD; 'they have walked after other gods and have served them and worshiped them, and have forsaken Me and not kept My law. 12 And you have done worse than your fathers, for behold, each one follows the dictates of his own evil heart, so that no one listens to Me. 13 Therefore I will cast you out of this land into a land that you do not know, neither you nor your fathers; and there you shall serve other gods day and night, where I will not show you favor.'

14 "Therefore behold, the days are coming," says the LORD, "that it shall no more be said, 'The LORD lives who brought up the children of Israel from the land of Egypt,' 15 but, 'The LORD lives who brought up the children of Israel from the land of the north and from all the lands where He had driven them.' For I will bring them back into their land which I gave to their fathers.

16 "Behold, I will send for many fishermen," says the LORD, "and they shall fish them; and afterward I will send for many hunters, and they shall hunt them from every mountain and every hill, and out of the holes of the rocks. 17 For My eyes are on all their ways; they are not hidden from My face, nor is their iniquity hidden from My eyes. 18 And first I will repay double for their iniquity and their sin, because they have defiled My land; they have filled My inheritance with the carcasses of their detestable and abominable idols."

19   O LORD, my strength and my
     fortress,

My refuge in the day of
     affliction,
The Gentiles shall come to You
From the ends of the earth and
     say,
   "Surely our fathers have
     inherited lies,
Worthlessness and
     unprofitable things."
20   Will a man make gods for
     himself,
Which are not gods?

21 "Therefore behold, I will this
     once cause them to know,
I will cause them to know
My hand and My might;
And they shall know that My
     name is the LORD.

17 "The sin of Judah is written with
     a pen of iron;
With the point of a diamond it
     is engraved
On the tablet of their heart,
And on the horns of your
     altars,
2   While their children remember
     Their altars and their wooden
     images[a]
By the green trees on the high
     hills.
3   O My mountain in the field,
I will give as plunder your
     wealth, all your treasures,
And your high places of sin
     within all your borders.
4   And you, even yourself,
Shall let go of your heritage
     which I gave you;
And I will cause you to serve
     your enemies
In the land which you do not
     know;
For you have kindled a fire in
     My anger which shall burn
     forever."

5 Thus says the LORD:

   "Cursed is the man who trusts
     in man
And makes flesh his strength,
Whose heart departs from the
     LORD.
6   For he shall be like a shrub in
     the desert,
And shall not see when good
     comes,

17:2 [a]Hebrew Asherim, Canaanite deities

But shall inhabit the parched
places in the wilderness,
In a salt land *which is* not
inhabited.

7 "Blessed *is* the man who trusts
in the LORD,
And whose hope is the LORD.
8 For he shall be like a tree
planted by the waters,
Which spreads out its roots by
the river,
And will not fear*a* when heat
comes;
But its leaf will be green,
And will not be anxious in the
year of drought,
Nor will cease from yielding
fruit.

9 "The heart *is* deceitful above all
things,
And desperately wicked;
Who can know it?
10 I, the LORD, search the heart,
I test the mind,
Even to give every man
according to his ways,
According to the fruit of his
doings.

11 "*As* a partridge that broods but
does not hatch,
So is he who gets riches, but
not by right;
It will leave him in the midst
of his days,
And at his end he will be a
fool."

12 A glorious high throne from the
beginning
Is the place of our sanctuary.
13 O LORD, the hope of Israel,
All who forsake You shall be
ashamed.

"Those who depart from Me
Shall be written in the earth,
Because they have forsaken the
LORD,
The fountain of living waters."

14 Heal me, O LORD, and I shall
be healed;
Save me, and I shall be saved,
For You *are* my praise.
15 Indeed they say to me,
"Where *is* the word of the LORD?
Let it come now!"

16 As for me, I have not hurried
away from *being* a shepherd
who follows You,
Nor have I desired the woeful
day;
You know what came out of my
lips;
It was right there before You.
17 Do not be a terror to me;
You *are* my hope in the day of
doom.
18 Let them be ashamed who
persecute me,
But do not let me be put to
shame;
Let them be dismayed,
But do not let me be dismayed.
Bring on them the day of doom,
And destroy them with double
destruction!

19 Thus the LORD said to me: "Go
and stand in the gate of the children
of the people, by which the kings of
Judah come in and by which they go
out, and in all the gates of Jerusalem;
20 and say to them, 'Hear the word
of the LORD, you kings of Judah, and
all Judah, and all the inhabitants of
Jerusalem, who enter by these gates.
21 Thus says the LORD: "Take heed
to yourselves, and bear no burden on
the Sabbath day, nor bring *it* in by
the gates of Jerusalem; 22 nor carry
a burden out of your houses on the
Sabbath day, nor do any work, but
hallow the Sabbath day, as I commanded your fathers. 23 But they did
not obey nor incline their ear, but
made their neck stiff, that they might
not hear nor receive instruction.
24 "And it shall be, if you heed Me
carefully," says the LORD, "to bring
no burden through the gates of this
city on the Sabbath day, but hallow
the Sabbath day, to do no work in
it, 25 then shall enter the gates of this
city kings and princes sitting on the
throne of David, riding in chariots
and on horses, they and their princes,
accompanied by the men of Judah
and the inhabitants of Jerusalem;
and this city shall remain forever.
26 And they shall come from the cities of Judah and from the places
around Jerusalem, from the land of
Benjamin and from the lowland,
from the mountains and from the
South, bringing burnt offerings and
sacrifices, grain offerings and in-

17:8 *a*Qere and Targum read *see.*

cense, bringing sacrifices of praise to the house of the LORD.

27 "But if you will not heed Me to hallow the Sabbath day, such as not carrying a burden when entering the gates of Jerusalem on the Sabbath day, then I will kindle a fire in its gates, and it shall devour the palaces of Jerusalem, and it shall not be quenched." ' "

18 The word which came to Jeremiah from the LORD, saying: 2 "Arise and go down to the potter's house, and there I will cause you to hear My words." 3 Then I went down to the potter's house, and there he was, making something at the wheel. 4 And the vessel that he made of clay was marred in the hand of the potter; so he made it again into another vessel, as it seemed good to the potter to make.

5 Then the word of the LORD came to me, saying: 6 "O house of Israel, can I not do with you as this potter?" says the LORD. "Look, as the clay *is* in the potter's hand, so *are* you in My hand, O house of Israel! 7 The instant I speak concerning a nation and concerning a kingdom, to pluck up, to pull down, and to destroy *it*, 8 if that nation against whom I have spoken turns from its evil, I will relent of the disaster that I thought to bring upon it. 9 And the instant I speak concerning a nation and concerning a kingdom, to build and to plant *it*, 10 if it does evil in My sight so that it does not obey My voice, then I will relent concerning the good with which I said I would benefit it.

11 "Now therefore, speak to the men of Judah and to the inhabitants of Jerusalem, saying, 'Thus says the LORD: "Behold, I am fashioning a disaster and devising a plan against you. Return now every one from his evil way, and make your ways and your doings good." ' "

12 And they said, "That is hopeless! So we will walk according to our own plans, and we will every one obey the dictates of his evil heart."

13 Therefore thus says the LORD:

"Ask now among the Gentiles,
Who has heard such things?

The virgin of Israel has done a
   very horrible thing.
14 Will *a man* leave the snow-
      water of Lebanon,
   Which comes from the rock of
      the field?
   Will the cold flowing waters be
      forsaken for strange waters?
15 "Because My people have
      forgotten Me,
   They have burned incense to
      worthless idols.
   And they have caused
      themselves to stumble in
      their ways,
   From the ancient paths,
   To walk in pathways and not
      on a highway,
16 To make their land desolate
   and a perpetual hissing;
   Everyone who passes by it will
      be astonished
   And shake his head.
17 I will scatter them as with an
      east wind before the enemy;
   I will show them[a] the back and
      not the face
   In the day of their calamity."

18 Then they said, "Come and let us devise plans against Jeremiah; for the law shall not perish from the priest, nor counsel from the wise, nor the word from the prophet. Come and let us attack him with the tongue, and let us not give heed to any of his words."

19 Give heed to me, O LORD,
   And listen to the voice of those
      who contend with me!
20 Shall evil be repaid for good?
   For they have dug a pit for my
      life.
   Remember that I stood before
      You
   To speak good for them,
   To turn away Your wrath from
      them.
21 Therefore deliver up their
      children to the famine,
   And pour out their *blood*
   By the force of the sword;
   Let their wives *become* widows
   And bereaved of their children.
   Let their men be put to death,
   Their young men *be* slain
   By the sword in battle.

18:17 [a]Following Septuagint, Syriac, Targum, and Vulgate; Masoretic Text reads *look them in.*

22 Let a cry be heard from their
    houses,
  When You bring a troop
    suddenly upon them;
  For they have dug a pit to take
    me,
  And hidden snares for my feet.
23 Yet, LORD, You know all their
    counsel
  Which is against me, to slay
    me.
  Provide no atonement for their
    iniquity,
  Nor blot out their sin from Your
    sight;
  But let them be overthrown
    before You.
  Deal *thus* with them
  In the time of Your anger.

19 Thus says the LORD: "Go and get a potter's earthen flask, and *take* some of the elders of the people and some of the elders of the priests. 2 And go out to the Valley of the Son of Hinnom, which *is* by the entry of the Potsherd Gate; and proclaim there the words that I will tell you, 3 and say, 'Hear the word of the LORD, O kings of Judah and inhabitants of Jerusalem. Thus says the LORD of hosts, the God of Israel: "Behold, I will bring such a catastrophe on this place, that whoever hears of it, his ears will tingle.

4 "Because they have forsaken Me and made this an alien place, because they have burned incense in it to other gods whom neither they, their fathers, nor the kings of Judah have known, and have filled this place with the blood of the innocents 5 (they have also built the high places of Baal, to burn their sons with fire *for* burnt offerings to Baal, which I did not command or speak, nor did it come into My mind), 6 therefore behold, the days are coming," says the LORD, "that this place shall no more be called Tophet or the Valley of the Son of Hinnom, but the Valley of Slaughter. 7 And I will make void the counsel of Judah and Jerusalem in this place, and I will cause them to fall by the sword before their enemies and by the hands of those who seek their lives; their corpses I will give as meat for the birds of the heaven and for the beasts of the earth. 8 I will make this city desolate

and a hissing; everyone who passes by it will be astonished and hiss because of all its plagues. 9 And I will cause them to eat the flesh of their sons and the flesh of their daughters, and everyone shall eat the flesh of his friend in the siege and in the desperation with which their enemies and those who seek their lives shall drive them to despair." '

10 "Then you shall break the flask in the sight of the men who go with you, 11 and say to them, 'Thus says the LORD of hosts: "Even so I will break this people and this city, as *one* breaks a potter's vessel, which cannot be made whole again; and they shall bury *them* in Tophet till *there is* no place to bury. 12 Thus I will do to this place," says the LORD, "and to its inhabitants, and make this city like Tophet. 13 And the houses of Jerusalem and the houses of the kings of Judah shall be defiled like the place of Tophet, because of all the houses on whose roofs they have burned incense to all the host of heaven, and poured out drink offerings to other gods." ' "

14 Then Jeremiah came from Tophet, where the LORD had sent him to prophesy; and he stood in the court of the Lord's house and said to all the people, 15 "Thus says the LORD of hosts, the God of Israel: 'Behold, I will bring on this city and on all her towns all the doom that I have pronounced against it, because they have stiffened their necks that they might not hear My words.' "

20 Now Pashhur the son of Immer, the priest who *was* also chief governor in the house of the LORD, heard that Jeremiah prophesied these things. 2 Then Pashhur struck Jeremiah the prophet, and put him in the stocks that *were* in the high gate of Benjamin, which *was* by the house of the LORD.

3 And it happened on the next day that Pashhur brought Jeremiah out of the stocks. Then Jeremiah said to him, "The LORD has not called your name Pashhur, but Magor-Missabib.*ª* 4 For thus says the LORD: 'Behold, I will make you a terror to yourself and to all your friends; and they shall fall by the sword of their enemies, and your eyes shall see *it.* I will give

20:3 *ª*Literally *Fear on Every Side*

all Judah into the hand of the king of Babylon, and he shall carry them captive to Babylon and slay them with the sword. 5 Moreover I will deliver all the wealth of this city, all its produce, and all its precious things; all the treasures of the kings of Judah I will give into the hand of their enemies, who will plunder them, seize them, and carry them to Babylon. 6 And you, Pashhur, and all who dwell in your house, shall go into captivity. You shall go to Babylon, and there you shall die, and be buried there, you and all your friends, to whom you have prophesied lies.' "

7 O LORD, You induced me, and
      I was persuaded;
   You are stronger than I, and
      have prevailed.
   I am in derision daily;
   Everyone mocks me.
8 For when I spoke, I cried out;
   I shouted, "Violence and
      plunder!"
   Because the word of the LORD
      was made to me
   A reproach and a derision
      daily.
9 Then I said, "I will not make
      mention of Him,
   Nor speak anymore in His
      name."
   But *His word* was in my heart
      like a burning fire
   Shut up in my bones;
   I was weary of holding *it* back,
   And I could not.
10 For I heard many mocking:
      "Fear on every side!"
   "Report," *they say,* "and we will
      report it!"
   All my acquaintances watched
      for my stumbling, *saying,*
   "Perhaps he can be induced;
   Then we will prevail against
      him,
   And we will take our revenge
      on him."

11 But the LORD *is* with me as a
      mighty, awesome One.
   Therefore my persecutors will
      stumble, and will not prevail.
   They will be greatly ashamed,
      for they will not prosper.
   Their everlasting confusion
      will never be forgotten.
12 But, O LORD of hosts,

   You who test the righteous,
   And see the mind and heart,
   Let me see Your vengeance on
      them;
   For I have pleaded my cause
      before You.

13 Sing to the LORD! Praise the
      LORD!
   For He has delivered the life of
      the poor
   From the hand of evildoers.

14 Cursed *be* the day in which I
      was born!
   Let the day not be blessed in
      which my mother bore me!
15 Let the man *be* cursed
   Who brought news to my
      father, saying,
   "A male child has been born to
      you!"
   Making him very glad.
16 And let that man be like the
      cities
   Which the LORD overthrew, and
      did not relent;
   Let him hear the cry in the
      morning
   And the shouting at noon,
17 Because he did not kill me from
      the womb,
   That my mother might have
      been my grave,
   And her womb always
      enlarged *with me.*
18 Why did I come forth from the
      womb to see labor and
      sorrow,
   That my days should be
      consumed with shame?

21 The word which came to Jeremiah from the LORD when King Zedekiah sent to him Pashhur the son of Melchiah, and Zephaniah the son of Maaseiah, the priest, saying, 2 "Please inquire of the LORD for us, for Nebuchadnezzar[a] king of Babylon makes war against us. Perhaps the LORD will deal with us according to all His wonderful works, that *the king* may go away from us."
3 Then Jeremiah said to them, "Thus you shall say to Zedekiah, 4 'Thus says the LORD God of Israel: "Behold, I will turn back the weapons of war that *are* in your hands, with which you fight against the king

21:2 ᵃHebrew *Nebuchadrezzar,* and so elsewhere

of Babylon and the Chaldeans[a] who besiege you outside the walls; and I will assemble them in the midst of this city. 5 I Myself will fight against you with an outstretched hand and with a strong arm, even in anger and fury and great wrath. 6 I will strike the inhabitants of this city, both man and beast; they shall die of a great pestilence. 7 And afterward," says the LORD, "I will deliver Zedekiah king of Judah, his servants and the people, and such as are left in this city from the pestilence and the sword and the famine, into the hand of Nebuchadnezzar king of Babylon, into the hand of their enemies, and into the hand of those who seek their life; and he shall strike them with the edge of the sword. He shall not spare them, or have pity or mercy." '

8 "Now you shall say to this people, 'Thus says the LORD: "Behold, I set before you the way of life and the way of death. 9 He who remains in this city shall die by the sword, by famine, and by pestilence; but he who goes out and defects to the Chaldeans who besiege you, he shall live, and his life shall be as a prize to him. 10 For I have set My face against this city for adversity and not for good," says the LORD. "It shall be given into the hand of the king of Babylon, and he shall burn it with fire." '

11 "And concerning the house of the king of Judah, say, 'Hear the word of the LORD, 12 O house of David! Thus says the LORD:

"Execute judgment in the
    morning;
And deliver him who is
    plundered
Out of the hand of the
    oppressor,
Lest My fury go forth like
    fire
And burn so that no one can
    quench it,
Because of the evil of your
    doings.

13 "Behold, I am against you, O
    inhabitant of the valley,
And rock of the plain," says the
    LORD,
"Who say, 'Who shall come
    down against us?

Or who shall enter our
    dwellings?'
14 But I will punish you according
    to the fruit of your doings,"
    says the LORD;
"I will kindle a fire in its forest,
And it shall devour all things
    around it." ' "

22 Thus says the LORD: "Go down to the house of the king of Judah, and there speak this word, 2 and say, 'Hear the word of the LORD, O king of Judah, you who sit on the throne of David, you and your servants and your people who enter these gates! 3 Thus says the LORD: "Execute judgment and righteousness, and deliver the plundered out of the hand of the oppressor. Do no wrong and do no violence to the stranger, the fatherless, or the widow, nor shed innocent blood in this place. 4 For if you indeed do this thing, then shall enter the gates of this house, riding on horses and in chariots, accompanied by servants and people, kings who sit on the throne of David. 5 But if you will not hear these words, I swear by Myself," says the LORD, "that this house shall become a desolation." ' "

6 For thus says the LORD to the house of the king of Judah:

"You are Gilead to Me,
    The head of Lebanon;
Yet I surely will make you a
    wilderness,
Cities which are not inhabited.
7   I will prepare destroyers
    against you,
Everyone with his weapons;
They shall cut down your
    choice cedars
And cast them into the fire.

8 And many nations will pass by this city; and everyone will say to his neighbor, 'Why has the LORD done so to this great city?' 9 Then they will answer, 'Because they have forsaken the covenant of the LORD their God, and worshiped other gods and served them.' "

10   Weep not for the dead, nor
    bemoan him;
Weep bitterly for him who goes
    away,

For he shall return no more,
Nor see his native country.

11 For thus says the LORD concerning Shallum[a] the son of Josiah, king of Judah, who reigned instead of Josiah his father, who went from this place: "He shall not return here anymore, 12 but he shall die in the place where they have led him captive, and shall see this land no more.

13 "Woe to him who builds his
     house by unrighteousness
And his chambers by injustice,
Who uses his neighbor's
     service without wages
And gives him nothing for his
     work,
14 Who says, 'I will build myself
     a wide house with spacious
     chambers,
And cut out windows for it,
Paneling it with cedar
And painting it with vermilion.'

15 "Shall you reign because you
     enclose yourself in cedar?
Did not your father eat and
     drink,
And do justice and
     righteousness?
Then it was well with him.
16 He judged the cause of the poor
     and needy;
Then it was well.
Was not this knowing Me?"
says the LORD.
17 "Yet your eyes and your heart
     are for nothing but your
     covetousness,
For shedding innocent blood,
And practicing oppression and
     violence."

18 Therefore thus says the LORD concerning Jehoiakim the son of Josiah, king of Judah:

"They shall not lament for him,
     Saying, 'Alas, my brother!' or
     'Alas, my sister!'
They shall not lament for him,
     Saying, 'Alas, master!' or 'Alas,
     his glory!'
19 He shall be buried with the
     burial of a donkey,
Dragged and cast out beyond
     the gates of Jerusalem.

20 "Go up to Lebanon, and cry out,
And lift up your voice in
     Bashan;
Cry from Abarim,
For all your lovers are
     destroyed.
21 I spoke to you in your
     prosperity,
But you said, 'I will not hear.'
This has been your manner
     from your youth,
That you did not obey My
     voice.
22 The wind shall eat up all your
     rulers,
And your lovers shall go into
     captivity;
Surely then you will be
     ashamed and humiliated
For all your wickedness.
23 O inhabitant of Lebanon,
Making your nest in the cedars,
How gracious will you be when
     pangs come upon you,
Like the pain of a woman in
     labor?

24 "As I live," says the LORD, "though Coniah[a] the son of Jehoiakim, king of Judah, were the signet on My right hand, yet I would pluck you off; 25 and I will give you into the hand of those who seek your life, and into the hand of those whose face you fear—the hand of Nebuchadnezzar king of Babylon and the hand of the Chaldeans. 26 So I will cast you out, and your mother who bore you, into another country where you were not born; and there you shall die. 27 But to the land to which they desire to return, there they shall not return.

28 "Is this man Coniah a despised,
     broken idol—
A vessel in which is no
     pleasure?
Why are they cast out, he and
     his descendants,
And cast into a land which they
     do not know?
29 O earth, earth, earth,
Hear the word of the LORD!
30 Thus says the LORD:
'Write this man down as
     childless,
A man who shall not prosper
     in his days;

22:11 [a]Also called Jehoahaz   22:24 [a]Also called Jeconiah and Jehoiachin

For none of his descendants
   shall prosper,
Sitting on the throne of David,
And ruling anymore in
   Judah.' "

23 "Woe to the shepherds who destroy and scatter the sheep of My pasture!" says the LORD. 2 Therefore thus says the LORD God of Israel against the shepherds who feed My people: "You have scattered My flock, driven them away, and not attended to them. Behold, I will attend to you for the evil of your doings," says the LORD. 3 "But I will gather the remnant of My flock out of all countries where I have driven them, and bring them back to their folds; and they shall be fruitful and increase. 4 I will set up shepherds over them who will feed them; and they shall fear no more, nor be dismayed, nor shall they be lacking," says the LORD.

5 "Behold, *the* days are coming,"
   says the LORD,
"That I will raise to David a
   Branch of righteousness;
A King shall reign and prosper,
And execute judgment and
   righteousness in the earth.
6 In His days Judah will be
   saved,
And Israel will dwell safely;
Now this *is* His name by which
He will be called:

THE LORD OUR
RIGHTEOUSNESS.*a*

7 "Therefore, behold, *the* days are coming," says the LORD, "that they shall no longer say, 'As the LORD lives who brought up the children of Israel from the land of Egypt,' 8 but, 'As the LORD lives who brought up and led the descendants of the house of Israel from the north country and from all the countries where I had driven them.' And they shall dwell in their own land."

9 My heart within me is broken
   Because of the prophets;
All my bones shake.
I am like a drunken man,
And like a man whom wine has
   overcome,

Because of the LORD,
And because of His holy words.
10 For the land is full of
   adulterers;
For because of a curse the land
   mourns.
The pleasant places of the
   wilderness are dried up.
Their course of life is evil,
And their might *is* not right.

11 "For both prophet and priest are
   profane;
Yes, in My house I have found
   their wickedness," says the
   LORD.
12 "Therefore their way shall be to
   them
Like slippery *ways;*
In the darkness they shall be
   driven on
And fall in them;
For I will bring disaster on
   them,
The year of their punishment,"
   says the LORD.
13 "And I have seen folly in the
   prophets of Samaria:
They prophesied by Baal
And caused My people Israel to
   err.
14 Also I have seen a horrible
   thing in the prophets of
   Jerusalem:
They commit adultery and
   walk in lies;
They also strengthen the hands
   of evildoers,
So that no one turns back from
   his wickedness.
All of them are like Sodom to
   Me,
And her inhabitants like
   Gomorrah.

15 "Therefore thus says the LORD of hosts concerning the prophets:

'Behold, I will feed them with
   wormwood,
And make them drink the
   water of gall;
For from the prophets of
   Jerusalem
Profaneness has gone out into
   all the land.' "

16 Thus says the LORD of hosts:

23:6 *a*Hebrew *YHWH Tsidkenu*

"Do not listen to the words of
the prophets who prophesy
to you.
They make you worthless;
They speak a vision of their
own heart,
Not from the mouth of the
LORD.

17 They continually say to those
who despise Me,
'The LORD has said, "You shall
have peace" ';
And to everyone who walks
according to the dictates of
his own heart, they say,
'No evil shall come upon you.' "

18 For who has stood in the
counsel of the LORD,
And has perceived and heard
His word?
Who has marked His word and
heard it?

19 Behold, a whirlwind of the
LORD has gone forth in
fury—
A violent whirlwind!
It will fall violently on the head
of the wicked.

20 The anger of the LORD will not
turn back
Until He has executed and
performed the thoughts of
His heart.
In the latter days you will
understand it perfectly.

21 "I have not sent these prophets,
yet they ran.
I have not spoken to them, yet
they prophesied.

22 But if they had stood in My
counsel,
And had caused My people to
hear My words,
Then they would have turned
them from their evil way
And from the evil of their
doings.

23 "Am I a God near at hand," says
the LORD,
"And not a God afar off?

24 Can anyone hide himself in
secret places,
So I shall not see him?" says
the LORD;
"Do I not fill heaven and earth?"
says the LORD.

25 "I have heard what the prophets
have said who prophesy lies in My
name, saying, 'I have dreamed, I
have dreamed!' 26 How long will this
be in the heart of the prophets who
prophesy lies? Indeed they are
prophets of the deceit of their own
heart, 27 who try to make My people
forget My name by their dreams
which everyone tells his neighbor, as
their fathers forgot My name for
Baal.

28 "The prophet who has a dream,
let him tell a dream;
And he who has My word, let
him speak My word
faithfully.
What is the chaff to the
wheat?" says the LORD.

29 "Is not My word like a fire?"
says the LORD,
"And like a hammer that breaks
the rock in pieces?

30 "Therefore behold, I am against
the prophets," says the LORD, "who
steal My words every one from his
neighbor. 31 Behold, I am against the
prophets," says the LORD, "who use
their tongues and say, 'He says.'
32 Behold, I am against those who
prophesy false dreams," says the
LORD, "and tell them, and cause My
people to err by their lies and by their
recklessness. Yet I did not send them
or command them; therefore they
shall not profit this people at all,"
says the LORD.

33 "So when these people or the
prophet or the priest ask you, saying,
'What is the oracle of the LORD?' you
shall then say to them, 'What oracle?'a I will even forsake you," says
the LORD. 34 "And as for the prophet
and the priest and the people who
say, 'The oracle of the LORD!' I will
even punish that man and his house.
35 Thus every one of you shall say
to his neighbor, and every one to his
brother, 'What has the LORD answered?' and, 'What has the LORD
spoken?' 36 And the oracle of the
LORD you shall mention no more. For
every man's word will be his oracle,
for you have perverted the words of
the living God, the LORD of hosts, our
God. 37 Thus you shall say to the
prophet, 'What has the LORD answered you?' and, 'What has the

23:33 aSeptuagint, Targum, and Vulgate read 'You are the burden.'

LORD spoken?' 38 But since you say, 'The oracle of the LORD!' therefore thus says the LORD: 'Because you say this word, "The oracle of the LORD!" and I have sent to you, saying, "Do not say, 'The oracle of the LORD!' " 39 therefore behold, I, even I, will utterly forget you and forsake you, and the city that I gave you and your fathers, and *will cast you* out of My presence. 40 And I will bring an everlasting reproach upon you, and a perpetual shame, which shall not be forgotten.' "

24 The LORD showed me, and there were two baskets of figs set before the temple of the LORD, after Nebuchadnezzar king of Babylon had carried away captive Jeconiah the son of Jehoiakim, king of Judah, and the princes of Judah with the craftsmen and smiths, from Jerusalem, and had brought them to Babylon. 2 One basket *had* very good figs, like the figs *that are* first ripe; and the other basket *had* very bad figs which could not be eaten, they were so bad. 3 Then the LORD said to me, "What do you see, Jeremiah?"

And I said, "Figs, the good figs, very good; and the bad, very bad, which cannot be eaten, they are so bad."

4 Again the word of the LORD came to me, saying, 5 "Thus says the LORD, the God of Israel: 'Like these good figs, so will I acknowledge those who are carried away captive from Judah, whom I have sent out of this place for *their* own good, into the land of the Chaldeans. 6 For I will set My eyes on them for good, and I will bring them back to this land; I will build them and not pull *them* down, and I will plant them and not pluck *them* up. 7 Then I will give them a heart to know Me, that I *am* the LORD; and they shall be My people, and I will be their God, for they shall return to Me with their whole heart.

8 'And as the bad figs which cannot be eaten, they are so bad'—surely thus says the LORD—'so will I give up Zedekiah the king of Judah, his princes, the residue of Jerusalem who remain in this land, and those who dwell in the land of Egypt. 9 I will deliver them to trouble into all the kingdoms of the earth, for *their* harm, *to be* a reproach and a byword, a taunt and a curse, in all places where I shall drive them. 10 And I will send the sword, the famine, and the pestilence among them, till they are consumed from the land that I gave to them and their fathers.' "

25 The word that came to Jeremiah concerning all the people of Judah, in the fourth year of Jehoiakim the son of Josiah, king of Judah (which *was* the first year of Nebuchadnezzar king of Babylon), 2 which Jeremiah the prophet spoke to all the people of Judah and to all the inhabitants of Jerusalem, saying: 3 "From the thirteenth year of Josiah the son of Amon, king of Judah, even to this day, this *is* the twenty-third year in which the word of the LORD has come to me; and I have spoken to you, rising early and speaking, but you have not listened. 4 And the LORD has sent to you all His servants the prophets, rising early and sending *them,* but you have not listened nor inclined your ear to hear. 5 They said, 'Repent now everyone of his evil way and his evil doings, and dwell in the land that the LORD has given to you and your fathers forever and ever. 6 Do not go after other gods to serve them and worship them, and do not provoke Me to anger with the works of your hands; and I will not harm you.' 7 Yet you have not listened to Me," says the LORD, "that you might provoke Me to anger with the works of your hands to your own hurt.

8 "Therefore thus says the LORD of hosts: 'Because you have not heard My words, 9 behold, I will send and take all the families of the north,' says the LORD, 'and Nebuchadnezzar the king of Babylon, My servant, and will bring them against this land, against its inhabitants, and against these nations all around, and will utterly destroy them, and make them an astonishment, a hissing, and perpetual desolations. 10 Moreover I will take from them the voice of mirth and the voice of gladness, the voice of the bridegroom and the voice of the bride, the sound of the millstones and the light of the lamp. 11 And this whole land shall be a desolation *and* an astonishment, and these nations shall serve the king of Babylon seventy years.

12 'Then it will come to pass, when seventy years are completed, *that* I

will punish the king of Babylon and that nation, the land of the Chaldeans, for their iniquity,' says the LORD; 'and I will make it a perpetual desolation. 13 So I will bring on that land all My words which I have pronounced against it, all that is written in this book, which Jeremiah has prophesied concerning all the nations. 14 (For many nations and great kings shall be served by them also; and I will repay them according to their deeds and according to the works of their own hands.)' "

15 For thus says the LORD God of Israel to me: "Take this wine cup of fury from My hand, and cause all the nations, to whom I send you, to drink it. 16 And they will drink and stagger and go mad because of the sword that I will send among them."

17 Then I took the cup from the LORD's hand, and made all the nations drink, to whom the LORD had sent me: 18 Jerusalem and the cities of Judah, its kings and its princes, to make them a desolation, an astonishment, a hissing, and a curse, as it is this day; 19 Pharaoh king of Egypt, his servants, his princes, and all his people; 20 all the mixed multitude, all the kings of the land of Uz, all the kings of the land of the Philistines (namely, Ashkelon, Gaza, Ekron, and the remnant of Ashdod); 21 Edom, Moab, and the people of Ammon; 22 all the kings of Tyre, all the kings of Sidon, and the kings of the coastlands which are across the sea; 23 Dedan, Tema, Buz, and all who are in the farthest corners; 24 all the kings of Arabia and all the kings of the mixed multitude who dwell in the desert; 25 all the kings of Zimri, all the kings of Elam, and all the kings of the Medes; 26 all the kings of the north, far and near, one with another; and all the kingdoms of the world which are on the face of the earth. Also the king of Sheshach[a] shall drink after them.

27 "Therefore you shall say to them, 'Thus says the LORD of hosts, the God of Israel: "Drink, be drunk, and vomit! Fall and rise no more, because of the sword which I will send among you." ' 28 And it shall be, if they refuse to take the cup from your hand to drink, then you shall say to them, 'Thus says the LORD of hosts:

"You shall certainly drink! 29 For behold, I begin to bring calamity on the city which is called by My name, and should you be utterly unpunished? You shall not be unpunished, for I will call for a sword on all the inhabitants of the earth," says the LORD of hosts.'

30 "Therefore prophesy against them all these words, and say to them:

'The LORD will roar from on high,
  And utter His voice from His holy habitation;
He will roar mightily against His fold.
He will give a shout, as those who tread the grapes,
  Against all the inhabitants of the earth.
31 A noise will come to the ends of the earth—
  For the LORD has a controversy with the nations;
He will plead His case with all flesh.
He will give those who are wicked to the sword,' says the LORD."

32 Thus says the LORD of hosts:

"Behold, disaster shall go forth From nation to nation,
And a great whirlwind shall be raised up
  From the farthest parts of the earth.

33 "And at that day the slain of the LORD shall be from one end of the earth even to the other end of the earth. They shall not be lamented, or gathered, or buried; they shall become refuse on the ground.

34 "Wail, shepherds, and cry!
  Roll about in the ashes,
  You leaders of the flock!
For the days of your slaughter and your dispersions are fulfilled;
You shall fall like a precious vessel.
35 And the shepherds will have no way to flee,
  Nor the leaders of the flock to escape.

25:26 [a]A code word for Babylon (compare 51:41)

36 A voice of the cry of the
    shepherds,
And a wailing of the leaders to
    the flock *will be heard.*
For the LORD has plundered
    their pasture,
37 And the peaceful dwellings are
    cut down
Because of the fierce anger of
    the LORD.
38 He has left His lair like the lion;
For their land is desolate
Because of the fierceness of the
    Oppressor,
And because of His fierce
    anger."

26 In the beginning of the reign of Jehoiakim the son of Josiah, king of Judah, this word came from the LORD, saying, 2 "Thus says the LORD: 'Stand in the court of the LORD's house, and speak to all the cities of Judah, which come to worship *in* the LORD's house, all the words that I command you to speak to them. Do not diminish a word. 3 Perhaps everyone will listen and turn from his evil way, that I may relent concerning the calamity which I purpose to bring on them because of the evil of their doings.' 4 And you shall say to them, 'Thus says the LORD: "If you will not listen to Me, to walk in My law which I have set before you, 5 to heed the words of My servants the prophets whom I sent to you, both rising up early and sending *them* (but you have not heeded), 6 then I will make this house like Shiloh, and will make this city a curse to all the nations of the earth." ' "

7 So the priests and the prophets and all the people heard Jeremiah speaking these words in the house of the LORD. 8 Now it happened, when Jeremiah had made an end of speaking all that the LORD had commanded *him* to speak to all the people, that the priests and the prophets and all the people seized him, saying, "You will surely die! 9 Why have you prophesied in the name of the LORD, saying, 'This house shall be like Shiloh, and this city shall be desolate, without an inhabitant'?" And all the people were gathered against Jeremiah in the house of the LORD.

10 When the princes of Judah heard these things, they came up from the king's house to the house of the LORD and sat down in the entry of the New Gate of the LORD's *house.* 11 And the priests and the prophets spoke to the princes and all the people, saying, "This man deserves to die! For he has prophesied against this city, as you have heard with your ears."

12 Then Jeremiah spoke to all the princes and all the people, saying: "The LORD sent me to prophesy against this house and against this city with all the words that you have heard. 13 Now therefore, amend your ways and your doings, and obey the voice of the LORD your God; then the LORD will relent concerning the doom that He has pronounced against you. 14 As for me, here I am, in your hand; do with me as seems good and proper to you. 15 But know for certain that if you put me to death, you will surely bring innocent blood on yourselves, on this city, and on its inhabitants; for truly the LORD has sent me to you to speak all these words in your hearing."

16 So the princes and all the people said to the priests and the prophets, "This man does not deserve to die. For he has spoken to us in the name of the LORD our God."

17 Then certain of the elders of the land rose up and spoke to all the assembly of the people, saying: 18 "Micah of Moresheth prophesied in the days of Hezekiah king of Judah, and spoke to all the people of Judah, saying, 'Thus says the LORD of hosts:

"Zion shall be plowed *like* a
    field,
Jerusalem shall become heaps
    of ruins,
And the mountain of the
    temple[a]
Like the bare hills of the
    forest." ' [b]

19 Did Hezekiah king of Judah and all Judah ever put him to death? Did he not fear the LORD and seek the LORD's favor? And the Lord relented concerning the doom which He had pronounced against them. But we are doing great evil against ourselves."

20 Now there was also a man who prophesied in the name of the LORD,

26:18 [a]Literally *house* [b]Compare Micah 3:12

Urijah the son of Shemaiah of Kirjath Jearim, who prophesied against this city and against this land according to all the words of Jeremiah. 21 And when Jehoiakim the king, with all his mighty men and all the princes, heard his words, the king sought to put him to death; but when Urijah heard *it,* he was afraid and fled, and went to Egypt. 22 Then Jehoiakim the king sent men to Egypt: Elnathan the son of Achbor, and *other* men *who went* with him to Egypt. 23 And they brought Urijah from Egypt and brought him to Jehoiakim the king, who killed him with the sword and cast his dead body into the graves of the common people.

24 Nevertheless the hand of Ahikam the son of Shaphan was with Jeremiah, so that they should not give him into the hand of the people to put him to death.

27 In the beginning of the reign of Jehoiakim*ᵃ* the son of Josiah, king of Judah, this word came to Jeremiah from the LORD, saying,*ᵇ* 2 "Thus says the LORD to me: 'Make for yourselves bonds and yokes, and put them on your neck, 3 and send them to the king of Edom, the king of Moab, the king of the Ammonites, the king of Tyre, and the king of Sidon, by the hand of the messengers who come to Jerusalem to Zedekiah king of Judah. 4 And command them to say to their masters, "Thus says the LORD of hosts, the God of Israel— thus you shall say to your masters: 5 'I have made the earth, the man and the beast that *are* on the ground, by My great power and by My outstretched arm, and have given it to whom it seemed proper to Me. 6 And now I have given all these lands into the hand of Nebuchadnezzar the king of Babylon, My servant; and the beasts of the field I have also given him to serve him. 7 So all nations shall serve him and his son and his son's son, until the time of his land comes; and then many nations and great kings shall make him serve them. 8 And it shall be, *that* the nation and kingdom which will not serve Nebuchadnezzar the king of Babylon, and which will not put its

neck under the yoke of the king of Babylon, that nation I will punish,' says the LORD, 'with the sword, the famine, and the pestilence, until I have consumed them by his hand. 9 Therefore do not listen to your prophets, your diviners, your dreamers, your soothsayers, or your sorcerers, who speak to you, saying, "You shall not serve the king of Babylon." 10 For they prophesy a lie to you, to remove you far from your land; and I will drive you out, and you will perish. 11 But the nations that bring their necks under the yoke of the king of Babylon and serve him, I will let them remain in their own land,' says the LORD, 'and they shall till it and dwell in it.' " .' "

12 I also spoke to Zedekiah king of Judah according to all these words, saying, "Bring your necks under the yoke of the king of Babylon, and serve him and his people, and live! 13 Why will you die, you and your people, by the sword, by the famine, and by the pestilence, as the LORD has spoken against the nation that will not serve the king of Babylon? 14 Therefore do not listen to the words of the prophets who speak to you, saying, 'You shall not serve the king of Babylon,' for they prophesy a lie to you; 15 for I have not sent them," says the LORD, "yet they prophesy a lie in My name, that I may drive you out, and that you may perish, you and the prophets who prophesy to you."

16 Also I spoke to the priests and to all this people, saying, "Thus says the LORD: 'Do not listen to the words of your prophets who prophesy to you, saying, "Behold, the vessels of the LORD's house will now shortly be brought back from Babylon"; for they prophesy a lie to you. 17 Do not listen to them; serve the king of Babylon, and live! Why should this city be laid waste? 18 But if they *are* prophets, and if the word of the LORD is with them, let them now make intercession to the LORD of hosts, that the vessels which are left in the house of the LORD, *in* the house of the king of Judah, and at Jerusalem, do not go to Babylon.'

19 "For thus says the LORD of hosts concerning the pillars, concerning

27:1 *ᵃ*Following Masoretic Text, Targum, and Vulgate; some Hebrew manuscripts, Arabic, and Syriac read *Zedekiah* (compare 27:3, 12; 28:1).   *ᵇ*Septuagint omits verse 1.

the Sea, concerning the carts, and concerning the remainder of the vessels that remain in this city, 20 which Nebuchadnezzar king of Babylon did not take, when he carried away captive Jeconiah the son of Jehoiakim, king of Judah, from Jerusalem to Babylon, and all the nobles of Judah and Jerusalem— 21 yes, thus says the LORD of hosts, the God of Israel, concerning the vessels that remain in the house of the LORD, and in the house of the king of Judah and of Jerusalem: 22 'They shall be carried to Babylon, and there they shall be until the day that I visit them,' says the LORD. 'Then I will bring them up and restore them to this place.' "

28 And it happened in the same year, at the beginning of the reign of Zedekiah king of Judah, in the fourth year *and* in the fifth month, *that* Hananiah the son of Azur the prophet, who *was* from Gibeon, spoke to me in the house of the LORD in the presence of the priests and of all the people, saying, 2 "Thus speaks the LORD of hosts, the God of Israel, saying: 'I have broken the yoke of the king of Babylon. 3 Within two full years I will bring back to this place all the vessels of the LORD's house, that Nebuchadnezzar king of Babylon took away from this place and carried to Babylon. 4 And I will bring back to this place Jeconiah the son of Jehoiakim, king of Judah, with all the captives of Judah who went to Babylon,' says the LORD, 'for I will break the yoke of the king of Babylon.' "

5 Then the prophet Jeremiah spoke to the prophet Hananiah in the presence of the priests and in the presence of all the people who stood in the house of the LORD, 6 and the prophet Jeremiah said, "Amen! The LORD do so; the LORD perform your words which you have prophesied, to bring back the vessels of the LORD's house and all who were carried away captive, from Babylon to this place. 7 Nevertheless hear now this word that I speak in your hearing and in the hearing of all the people: 8 The prophets who have been before me and before you of old prophesied against many countries and great kingdoms—of war and disaster and pestilence. 9 As for the prophet who

prophesies of peace, when the word of the prophet comes to pass, the prophet will be known *as* one whom the LORD has truly sent."

10 Then Hananiah the prophet took the yoke off the prophet Jeremiah's neck and broke it. 11 And Hananiah spoke in the presence of all the people, saying, "Thus says the LORD: 'Even so I will break the yoke of Nebuchadnezzar king of Babylon from the neck of all nations within the space of two full years.' " And the prophet Jeremiah went his way.

12 Now the word of the LORD came to Jeremiah, after Hananiah the prophet had broken the yoke from the neck of the prophet Jeremiah, saying, 13 "Go and tell Hananiah, saying, 'Thus says the LORD: "You have broken the yokes of wood, but you have made in their place yokes of iron." 14 For thus says the LORD of hosts, the God of Israel: "I have put a yoke of iron on the neck of all these nations, that they may serve Nebuchadnezzar king of Babylon; and they shall serve him. I have given him the beasts of the field also." ' "

15 Then the prophet Jeremiah said to Hananiah the prophet, "Hear now, Hananiah, the LORD has not sent you, but you make this people trust in a lie. 16 Therefore thus says the LORD: 'Behold, I will cast you from the face of the earth. This year you shall die, because you have taught rebellion against the LORD.' "

17 So Hananiah the prophet died the same year in the seventh month.

29 Now these *are* the words of the letter that Jeremiah the prophet sent from Jerusalem to the remainder of the elders who were carried away captive—to the priests, the prophets, and all the people whom Nebuchadnezzar had carried away captive from Jerusalem to Babylon. 2 (This happened after Jeconiah the king, the queen mother, the eunuchs, the princes of Judah and Jerusalem, the craftsmen, and the smiths had departed from Jerusalem.) 3 *The letter was sent* by the hand of Elasah the son of Shaphan, and Gemariah the son of Hilkiah, whom Zedekiah king of Judah sent to Babylon, to Nebuchadnezzar king of Babylon, saying,

Open Your Mind to God

Each new year is an appointment to become an authentic optimist.

Each new day is justification for being enthusiastic about life again.

Each dawning is God's invitation to start over and build a new life, beginning with the present moment.

Every new week is an opportunity to make new and noble resolutions! Every Monday morning you have a standing appointment to meet new opportunities!

What does it mean to have faith?

Faith is opening your mind for God's thoughts to flow in—"thoughts of peace and not of evil, to give you a future and a hope" (Jer. 29:11). And when His thoughts flow in, life will change, for you will have a dream. You will see possibilities in the day—the week—the month—the year that is waiting to unfold.

Faith moves mountains. The greatest power in the world is a positive idea.

And the most powerful positive idea is one that comes directly from the God who created the world and broke sunshine through the black of night.

Today open your mind to think God's thoughts. Allow Him to shape you into a new and different person—freed to experience possibility thinking.

Take a moment to pray: *Thank You, God, that I am being born again. Your Holy Spirit is filling my mind with Your thoughts. I am excited about today, and I'm excited about my future. Amen.*

4 Thus says the LORD of hosts, the God of Israel, to all who were carried away captive, whom I have caused to be carried away from Jerusalem to Babylon:

5 Build houses and dwell *in them;* plant gardens and eat their fruit. 6 Take wives and beget sons and daughters; and take wives for your sons and give your daughters to husbands, so that they may bear sons and daughters—that you may be increased there, and not diminished. 7 And seek the peace of the city where I have caused you to be carried away captive, and pray to the LORD for it; for in its peace you will have peace. 8 For thus says the LORD of hosts, the God of Israel: Do not let your prophets and your diviners who are in your midst deceive you, nor listen to your dreams which you cause to be dreamed. 9 For they prophesy falsely to you in My name; I have not sent them, says the LORD.

10 For thus says the LORD: After seventy years are completed at Babylon, I will visit you and perform My good word toward you, and cause you to return to this place. 11 For I know the thoughts that I think toward you, says the LORD, thoughts of peace and not of evil, to give you a future and a hope. 12 Then you will call upon Me and go and pray to Me, and I will listen to you. 13 And you will seek Me and find *Me,* when you search for Me with all your heart. 14 I will be found by you, says the LORD, and I will bring you back from your captivity; I will gather you from all the nations and from all the places where I have driven you, says the LORD, and I will bring you to the place from which I cause you to be carried away captive.

15 Because you have said, "The LORD has raised up prophets for us in Babylon"— 16 therefore thus says the LORD concerning the king who sits on the throne of David, concerning all the people who dwell in this city, and concerning your brethren who have not gone out with you into captivity— 17 thus says the LORD of hosts: Behold, I will send on them the sword, the famine, and the pestilence, and will make them like rotten figs that cannot be eaten, they are so bad. 18 And I will pursue them with the sword, with famine, and with pestilence; and I will deliver them to trouble among all the kingdoms of the earth—to be a curse, an astonishment, a hissing, and a reproach among all the nations where I have driven them, 19 because they have not heeded My words, says the LORD, which I sent to them by My servants the prophets, rising up early and sending *them;* neither would you heed, says the LORD. 20 Therefore hear the word of the LORD, all you of the captivity, whom I have sent from Jerusalem to Babylon.

21 Thus says the LORD of hosts, the God of Israel, concerning Ahab the son of Kolaiah, and Zedekiah the son of Maaseiah, who prophesy a lie to you in My name: Behold, I will deliver them into the hand of Nebuchadnezzar king of Babylon, and he shall slay them before your eyes. 22 And because of them a curse shall be taken up by all the captivity of Judah who *are* in Babylon, saying, "The LORD make you like Zedekiah and Ahab, whom the king of Babylon roasted in the fire"; 23 because they have done disgraceful things in Israel, have committed adultery with their neighbors' wives, and have spoken lying words in My name, which I have not commanded them. Indeed I know, and *am* a witness, says the LORD.

24 You shall also speak to Shemaiah the Nehelamite, saying, 25 Thus speaks the LORD of hosts, the God of Israel,

saying: You have sent letters in your name to all the people who *are* at Jerusalem, to Zephaniah the son of Maaseiah the priest, and to all the priests, saying, 26 "The LORD has made you priest instead of Jehoiada the priest, so that there should be officers *in* the house of the LORD over every man *who* is demented and considers himself a prophet, that you should put him in prison and in the stocks. 27 Now therefore, why have you not rebuked Jeremiah of Anathoth who makes himself a prophet to you? 28 For he has sent to us *in* Babylon, saying, 'This *captivity is* long; build houses and dwell *in them,* and plant gardens and eat their fruit.' "

29 Now Zephaniah the priest read this letter in the hearing of Jeremiah the prophet. 30 Then the word of the LORD came to Jeremiah, saying: 31 Send to all those in captivity, saying, Thus says the LORD concerning Shemaiah the Nehelamite: Because Shemaiah has prophesied to you, and I have not sent him, and he has caused you to trust in a lie— 32 therefore thus says the LORD: Behold, I will punish Shemaiah the Nehelamite and his family: he shall not have anyone to dwell among this people, nor shall he see the good that I will do for My people, says the LORD, because he has taught rebellion against the LORD.

30 The word that came to Jeremiah from the LORD, saying, 2 "Thus speaks the LORD God of Israel, saying: 'Write in a book for yourself all the words that I have spoken to you. 3 For behold, the days are coming,' says the LORD, 'that I will bring back from captivity My people Israel and Judah,' says the LORD. 'And I will cause them to return to the land that I gave to their fathers, and they shall possess it.' "

4 Now these *are* the words that the LORD spoke concerning Israel and Judah.

5 "For thus says the LORD:

'We have heard a voice of
   trembling,
Of fear, and not of peace.
6 Ask now, and see,
Whether a man is ever in labor
   with child?
So why do I see every man *with*
   his hands on his loins
Like a woman in labor,
And all faces turned pale?
7 Alas! For that day *is* great,
So that none *is* like it;
And it *is* the time of Jacob's
   trouble,
But he shall be saved out of it.

8 'For it shall come to pass in that
   day,'
Says the LORD of hosts,
'That I will break his yoke from
   your neck,
And will burst your bonds;
Foreigners shall no more
   enslave them.
9 But they shall serve the LORD
   their God,
And David their king,
Whom I will raise up for them.

10 'Therefore do not fear, O My
   servant Jacob,' says the
   LORD,
'Nor be dismayed, O Israel;
For behold, I will save you from
   afar,
And your seed from the land of
   their captivity.
Jacob shall return, have rest
   and be quiet,
And no one shall make *him*
   afraid.
11 For I *am* with you,' says the
   LORD, 'to save you;
Though I make a full end of all
   nations where I have
   scattered you,
Yet I will not make a complete
   end of you.
But I will correct you in justice,
And will not let you go
   altogether unpunished.'

12 "For thus says the LORD:

'Your affliction *is* incurable,
Your wound *is* severe.
13 *There is* no one to plead your
   cause,
That you may be bound up;

You have no healing
   medicines.
14 All your lovers have forgotten
   you;
   They do not seek you;
   For I have wounded you with
     the wound of an enemy,
   With the chastisement of a
     cruel one,
   For the multitude of your
     iniquities,
   Because your sins have
     increased.
15 Why do you cry about your
   affliction?
   Your sorrow *is* incurable.
   Because of the multitude of
     your iniquities,
   Because your sins have
     increased.
   I have done these things to you.

16 'Therefore all those who devour
   you shall be devoured;
   And all your adversaries, every
     one of them, shall go into
     captivity;
   Those who plunder you shall
     become plunder,
   And all who prey upon you I
     will make a prey.
17 For I will restore health to you
   And heal you of your wounds,'
     says the LORD,
   'Because they called you an
     outcast *saying:*
   "This *is* Zion;
   No one seeks her." '

18 "Thus says the LORD:

   'Behold, I will bring back the
     captivity of Jacob's tents,
   And have mercy on his
     dwelling places;
   The city shall be built upon its
     own mound,
   And the palace shall remain
     according to its own plan.
19 Then out of them shall proceed
   thanksgiving
   And the voice of those who
     make merry;
   I will multiply them, and they
     shall not diminish;
   I will also glorify them, and
     they shall not be small.
20 Their children also shall be as
   before,
   And their congregation shall be
     established before Me;

   And I will punish all who
     oppress them.
21 Their nobles shall be from
     among them,
   And their governor shall come
     from their midst;
   Then I will cause him to draw
     near,
   And he shall approach Me;
   For who *is* this who pledged his
     heart to approach Me?' says
     the LORD.
22 'You shall be My people,
   And I will be your God.' "

23 Behold, the whirlwind of the
   LORD
   Goes forth with fury,
   A continuing whirlwind;
   It will fall violently on the head
     of the wicked.
24 The fierce anger of the LORD
   will not return until He has
   done it,
   And until He has performed the
     intents of His heart.

   In the latter days you will
     consider it.

31 "At the same time," says the
   LORD, "I will be the God of all
the families of Israel, and they shall
be My people."
2 Thus says the LORD:

   "The people who survived the
     sword
   Found grace in the
     wilderness—
   Israel, when I went to give him
     rest."

3 The LORD has appeared of old
   to me, *saying:*
   "Yes, I have loved you with an
     everlasting love;
   Therefore with lovingkindness
     I have drawn you.
4 Again I will build you, and you
     shall be rebuilt,
   O virgin of Israel!
   You shall again be adorned
     with your tambourines,
   And shall go forth in the dances
     of those who rejoice.
5 You shall yet plant vines on the
     mountains of Samaria;
   The planters shall plant and eat
     them as ordinary food.
6 For there shall be a day

When the watchmen will cry on
　Mount Ephraim,
'Arise, and let us go up *to* Zion,
　To the Lord our God.'"

7 For thus says the Lord:

"Sing with gladness for Jacob,
　And shout among the chief of
　　the nations;
Proclaim, give praise, and say,
'O Lord, save Your people,
　The remnant of Israel!'
8　Behold, I will bring them from
　　the north country,
And gather them from the ends
　of the earth,
Among them the blind and the
　lame,
The woman with child
And the one who labors with
　child, together;
A great throng shall return
　there.
9　They shall come with weeping,
And with supplications I will
　lead them.
I will cause them to walk by the
　rivers of waters,
In a straight way in which they
　shall not stumble;
For I am a Father to Israel,
And Ephraim *is* My firstborn.

10 "Hear the word of the Lord, O
　nations,
And declare *it* in the isles afar
　off, and say,
'He who scattered Israel will
　gather him,
And keep him as a shepherd
　does his flock.'
11　For the Lord has redeemed
　Jacob,
And ransomed him from the
　hand of one stronger than he.
12　Therefore they shall come and
　sing in the height of Zion,
Streaming to the goodness of
　the Lord—
For wheat and new wine and
　oil,
For the young of the flock and
　the herd;
Their souls shall be like a well-
　watered garden,
And they shall sorrow no more
　at all.

13 "Then shall the virgin rejoice in
　the dance,

And the young men and the
　old, together;
For I will turn their mourning
　to joy,
Will comfort them,
And make them rejoice rather
　than sorrow.
14　I will satiate the soul of the
　priests with abundance,
And My people shall be
　satisfied with My goodness,
　says the Lord."

15 Thus says the Lord:

"A voice was heard in Ramah,
Lamentation *and* bitter
　weeping,
Rachel weeping for her
　children,
Refusing to be comforted for
　her children,
Because they *are* no more."

16 Thus says the Lord:

"Refrain your voice from
　weeping,
And your eyes from tears;
For your work shall be
　rewarded, says the Lord,
And they shall come back from
　the land of the enemy.
17　There is hope in your future,
　says the Lord,
That *your* children shall come
　back to their own border.

18 "I have surely heard Ephraim
　bemoaning himself:
'You have chastised me, and I
　was chastised,
Like an untrained bull;
Restore me, and I will return,
For You *are* the Lord my God.
19　Surely, after my turning, I
　repented;
And after I was instructed, I
　struck myself on the thigh;
I was ashamed, yes, even
　humiliated,
Because I bore the reproach of
　my youth.'
20　*Is* Ephraim My dear son?
Is he a pleasant child?
For though I spoke against him,
I earnestly remember him
　still;
Therefore My heart yearns for
　him;
I will surely have mercy on
　him, says the Lord.

21 "Set up signposts,
    Make landmarks;
    Set your heart toward the
      highway,
    The way in *which* you went.
    Turn back, O virgin of Israel,
    Turn back to these your cities.
22 How long will you gad about,
    O you backsliding daughter?
    For the LORD has created a new
      thing in the earth—
    A woman shall encompass a
      man."

23 Thus says the LORD of hosts, the God of Israel: "They shall again use this speech in the land of Judah and in its cities, when I bring back their captivity: 'The LORD bless you, O home of justice, *and* mountain of holiness!' 24 And there shall dwell in Judah itself, and in all its cities together, farmers and those going out with flocks. 25 For I have satiated the weary soul, and I have replenished every sorrowful soul."

26 After this I awoke and looked around, and my sleep was sweet to me.

27 "Behold, the days are coming, says the LORD, that I will sow the house of Israel and the house of Judah with the seed of man and the seed of beast. 28 And it shall come to pass, *that* as I have watched over them to pluck up, to break down, to throw down, to destroy, and to afflict, so I will watch over them to build and to plant, says the LORD. 29 In those days they shall say no more:

'The fathers have eaten sour
    grapes,
And the children's teeth are set
    on edge.'

30 But every one shall die for his own iniquity; every man who eats the sour grapes, his teeth shall be set on edge.

31 "Behold, the days are coming, says the LORD, when I will make a new covenant with the house of Israel and with the house of Judah— 32 not according to the covenant that I made with their fathers in the day *that* I took them by the hand to lead them out of the land of Egypt, My covenant which they broke, though I was a husband to them,[a] says the LORD. 33 But this *is* the covenant that I will make with the house of Israel after those days, says the LORD: I will put My law in their minds, and write it on their hearts; and I will be their God, and they shall be My people. 34 No more shall every man teach his neighbor, and every man his brother, saying, 'Know the LORD,' for they all shall know Me, from the least of them to the greatest of them, says the LORD. For I will forgive their iniquity, and their sin I will remember no more."

35 Thus says the LORD,
    Who gives the sun for a light
      by day,
    The ordinances of the moon
      and the stars for a light by
      night,
    Who disturbs the sea,
    And its waves roar
    (The LORD of hosts *is* His
      name):

36 "If those ordinances depart
    From before Me, says the LORD,
    Then the seed of Israel shall
      also cease
    From being a nation before Me
      forever."

37 Thus says the LORD:

"If heaven above can be
    measured,
And the foundations of the
    earth searched out beneath,
I will also cast off all the seed
    of Israel
For all that they have done,
    says the LORD.

38 "Behold, the days are coming, says the LORD, that the city shall be built for the LORD from the Tower of Hananel to the Corner Gate. 39 The surveyor's line shall again extend straight forward over the hill Gareb; then it shall turn toward Goath. 40 And the whole valley of the dead bodies and of the ashes, and all the fields as far as the Brook Kidron, to the corner of the Horse Gate toward the east, *shall be* holy to the LORD. It shall not be plucked up or thrown down anymore forever."

31:32 [a]Following Masoretic Text, Targum, and Vulgate; Septuagint and Syriac read *and I turned away from them.*

32 The word that came to Jeremiah from the LORD in the tenth year of Zedekiah king of Judah, which was the eighteenth year of Nebuchadnezzar. 2 For then the king of Babylon's army besieged Jerusalem, and Jeremiah the prophet was shut up in the court of the prison, which was in the king of Judah's house. 3 For Zedekiah king of Judah had shut him up, saying, "Why do you prophesy and say, 'Thus says the LORD: "Behold, I will give this city into the hand of the king of Babylon, and he shall take it; 4 and Zedekiah king of Judah shall not escape from the hand of the Chaldeans, but shall surely be delivered into the hand of the king of Babylon, and shall speak with him face to face,a and see him eye to eye; 5 then he shall lead Zedekiah to Babylon, and there he shall be until I visit him," says the LORD; "though you fight with the Chaldeans, you shall not succeed" '?"

6 And Jeremiah said, "The word of the LORD came to me, saying, 7 'Behold, Hanamel the son of Shallum your uncle will come to you, saying, "Buy my field which is in Anathoth, for the right of redemption is yours to buy it." ' 8 Then Hanamel my uncle's son came to me in the court of the prison according to the word of the LORD, and said to me, 'Please buy my field that is in Anathoth, which is in the country of Benjamin; for the right of inheritance is yours, and the redemption yours; buy it for yourself.' Then I knew that this was the word of the LORD. 9 So I bought the field from Hanamel, the son of my uncle who was in Anathoth, and weighed out to him the money—seventeen shekels of silver. 10 And I signed the deed and sealed it, took witnesses, and weighed the money on the scales. 11 So I took the purchase deed, both that which was sealed according to the law and custom, and that which was open; 12 and I gave the purchase deed to Baruch the son of Neriah, son of Mahseiah, in the presence of Hanamel my uncle's son, and in the presence of the witnesses who signed the purchase deed, before all the Jews who sat in the court of the prison.

13 "Then I charged Baruch before them, saying, 14 'Thus says the LORD of hosts, the God of Israel: "Take these deeds, both this purchase deed which is sealed and this deed which is open, and put them in an earthen vessel, that they may last many days." 15 For thus says the LORD of hosts, the God of Israel: "Houses and fields and vineyards shall be possessed again in this land." '

16 "Now when I had delivered the purchase deed to Baruch the son of Neriah, I prayed to the LORD, saying: 17 'Ah, Lord GOD! Behold, You have made the heavens and the earth by Your great power and outstretched arm. There is nothing too hard for You. 18 You show lovingkindness to thousands, and repay the iniquity of the fathers into the bosom of their children after them—the Great, the Mighty God, whose name is the LORD of hosts. 19 You are great in counsel and mighty in work, for your eyes are open to all the ways of the sons of men, to give everyone according to his ways and according to the fruit of his doings. 20 You have set signs and wonders in the land of Egypt, to this day, and in Israel and among other men; and You have made Yourself a name, as it is this day. 21 You have brought Your people Israel out of the land of Egypt with signs and wonders, with a strong hand and an outstretched arm, and with great terror; 22 You have given them this land, of which You swore to their fathers to give them—"a land flowing with milk and honey."a 23 And they came in and took possession of it, but they have not obeyed Your voice or walked in Your law. They have done nothing of all that You commanded them to do; therefore You have caused all this calamity to come upon them.

24 'Look, the siege mounds! They have come to the city to take it; and the city has been given into the hand of the Chaldeans who fight against it, because of the sword and famine and pestilence. What You have spoken has happened; there You see it! 25 And You have said to me, O Lord GOD, "Buy the field for money, and take witnesses"!—yet the city has been given into the hand of the Chaldeans." '

26 Then the word of the LORD came to Jeremiah, saying, 27 "Behold, I

32:4 aLiterally mouth to mouth   32:22 aExodus 3:8

am the LORD, the God of all flesh. Is there anything too hard for Me? 28 Therefore thus says the LORD: 'Behold, I will give this city into the hand of the Chaldeans, into the hand of Nebuchadnezzar king of Babylon, and he shall take it. 29 And the Chaldeans who fight against this city shall come and set fire to this city and burn it, with the houses on whose roofs they have offered incense to Baal and poured out drink offerings to other gods, to provoke Me to anger; 30 because the children of Israel and the children of Judah have done only evil before Me from their youth. For the children of Israel have provoked Me only to anger with the work of their hands,' says the LORD. 31 'For this city has been to Me *a provocation of* My anger and My fury from the day that they built it, even to this day; so I will remove it from before My face 32 because of all the evil of the children of Israel and the children of Judah, which they have done to provoke Me to anger—they, their kings, their princes, their priests, their prophets, the men of Judah, and the inhabitants of Jerusalem. 33 And they have turned to Me the back, and not the face; though I taught them, rising up early and teaching *them*, yet they have not listened to receive instruction. 34 But they set their abominations in the house which is called by My name, to defile it. 35 And they built the high places of Baal which *are* in the Valley of the Son of Hinnom, to cause their sons and their daughters to pass through *the fire* to Molech, which I did not command them, nor did it come into My mind that they should do this abomination, to cause Judah to sin.'

36 "Now therefore, thus says the LORD, the God of Israel, concerning this city of which you say, 'It shall be delivered into the hand of the king of Babylon by the sword, by the famine, and by the pestilence: 37 Behold, I will gather them out of all countries where I have driven them in My anger, in My fury, and in great wrath; I will bring them back to this place, and I will cause them to dwell safely. 38 They shall be My people, and I will be their God; 39 then I will give them one heart and one way, that they may

fear Me forever, for the good of them and their children after them. 40 And I will make an everlasting covenant with them, that I will not turn away from doing them good; but I will put My fear in their hearts so that they will not depart from Me. 41 Yes, I will rejoice over them to do them good, and I will assuredly plant them in this land, with all My heart and with all My soul.'

42 "For thus says the LORD: 'Just as I have brought all this great calamity on this people, so I will bring on them all the good that I have promised them. 43 And fields will be bought in this land of which you say, "It *is* desolate, without man or beast; it has been given into the hand of the Chaldeans." 44 Men will buy fields for money, sign deeds and seal *them,* and take witnesses, in the land of Benjamin, in the places around Jerusalem, in the cities of Judah, in the cities of the mountains, in the cities of the lowland, and in the cities of the South; for I will cause their captives to return,' says the LORD."

33 Moreover the word of the LORD came to Jeremiah a second time, while he was still shut up in the court of the prison, saying, 2 "Thus says the LORD who made it, the LORD who formed it to establish it (the LORD *is* His name): 3 'Call to Me, and I will answer you, and show you great and mighty things, which you do not know.'

4 "For thus says the LORD, the God of Israel, concerning the houses of this city and the houses of the kings of Judah, which have been pulled down *to fortify*[a] against the siege mounds and the sword: 5 'They come to fight with the Chaldeans, but *only* to fill their places[a] with the dead bodies of men whom I will slay in My anger and My fury, all for whose wickedness I have hidden My face from this city. 6 Behold, I will bring it health and healing; I will heal them and reveal to them the abundance of peace and truth. 7 And I will cause the captives of Judah and the captives of Israel to return, and will rebuild those places as at the first. 8 I will cleanse them from all their iniquity by which they have sinned against Me, and I will pardon all their

33:4 [a]Compare Isaiah 22:10   33:5 [a]Compare 2 Kings 23:14

iniquities by which they have sinned and by which they have transgressed against Me. 9 Then it shall be to Me a name of joy, a praise, and an honor before all nations of the earth, who shall hear all the good that I do to them; they shall fear and tremble for all the goodness and all the prosperity that I provide for it.'

10 "Thus says the LORD: 'Again there shall be heard in this place— of which you say, "It *is* desolate, without man and without beast"—in the cities of Judah, in the streets of Jerusalem that are desolate, without man and without inhabitant and without beast, 11 the voice of joy and the voice of gladness, the voice of the bridegroom and the voice of the bride, the voice of those who will say:

"Praise the LORD of hosts,
    For the LORD *is* good,
    For His mercy *endures*
       forever"—

and of those *who will* bring the sacrifice of praise into the house of the LORD. For I will cause the captives of the land to return as at the first,' says the LORD.

12 "Thus says the LORD of hosts: 'In this place which is desolate, without man and without beast, and in all its cities, there shall again be a dwelling place of shepherds causing *their* flocks to lie down. 13 In the cities of the mountains, in the cities of the lowland, in the cities of the South, in the land of Benjamin, in the places around Jerusalem, and in the cities of Judah, the flocks shall again pass under the hands of him who counts *them*,' says the LORD.

14 'Behold, the days are coming,' says the LORD, 'that I will perform that good thing which I have promised to the house of Israel and to the house of Judah:

15 'In those days and at that time
    I will cause to grow up to David
    A Branch of righteousness;
    He shall execute judgment and
      righteousness in the earth.
16 In those days Judah will be
    saved,
    And Jerusalem will dwell
      safely.

And this *is the name* by which she will be called:

    THE LORD OUR
    RIGHTEOUSNESS.'*a*

17 "For thus says the LORD: 'David shall never lack a man to sit on the throne of the house of Israel; 18 nor shall the priests, the Levites, lack a man to offer burnt offerings before Me, to kindle grain offerings, and to sacrifice continually.' "

19 And the word of the LORD came to Jeremiah, saying, 20 "Thus says the LORD: 'If you can break My covenant with the day and My covenant with the night, so that there will not be day and night in their season, 21 then My covenant may also be broken with David My servant, so that he shall not have a son to reign on his throne, and with the Levites, the priests, My ministers. 22 As the host of heaven cannot be numbered, nor the sand of the sea measured, so will I multiply the descendants of David My servant and the Levites who minister to Me.' "

23 Moreover the word of the LORD came to Jeremiah, saying, 24 "Have you not considered what these people have spoken, saying, 'The two families which the LORD has chosen, He has also cast them off '? Thus they have despised My people, as if they should no more be a nation before them.

25 "Thus says the LORD: 'If My covenant *is* not with day and night, *and if* I have not appointed the ordinances of heaven and earth, 26 then I will cast away the descendants of Jacob and David My servant, *so* that I will not take *any* of his descendants *to be* rulers over the descendants of Abraham, Isaac, and Jacob. For I will cause their captives to return, and will have mercy on them.' "

34 The word which came to Jeremiah from the LORD, when Nebuchadnezzar king of Babylon and all his army, all the kingdoms of the earth under his dominion, and all the people, fought against Jerusalem and all its cities, saying, 2 "Thus says the LORD, the God of Israel: 'Go and speak to Zedekiah king

33:16 *a*Compare 23:5, 6

of Judah and tell him, "Thus says the LORD: 'Behold, I will give this city into the hand of the king of Babylon, and he shall burn it with fire. 3 And you shall not escape from his hand, but shall surely be taken and delivered into his hand; your eyes shall see the eyes of the king of Babylon, he shall speak with you face to face,[a] and you shall go to Babylon.' " ' 4 Yet hear the word of the LORD, O Zedekiah king of Judah! Thus says the LORD concerning you: 'You shall not die by the sword. 5 You shall die in peace; as in the ceremonies of your fathers, the former kings who were before you, so they shall burn incense for you and lament for you, saying, "Alas, lord!" For I have pronounced the word, says the LORD.' "

6 Then Jeremiah the prophet spoke all these words to Zedekiah king of Judah in Jerusalem, 7 when the king of Babylon's army fought against Jerusalem and all the cities of Judah that were left, against Lachish and Azekah; for only these fortified cities remained of the cities of Judah.

8 This is the word that came to Jeremiah from the LORD, after King Zedekiah had made a covenant with all the people who were at Jerusalem to proclaim liberty to them: 9 that every man should set free his male and female slave—a Hebrew man or woman—that no one should keep a Jewish brother in bondage. 10 Now when all the princes and all the people, who had entered into the covenant, heard that everyone should set free his male and female slaves, that no one should keep them in bondage anymore, they obeyed and let them go. 11 But afterward they changed their minds and made the male and female slaves return, whom they had set free, and brought them into subjection as male and female slaves.

12 Therefore the word of the LORD came to Jeremiah from the LORD, saying, 13 "Thus says the LORD, the God of Israel: 'I made a covenant with your fathers in the day that I brought them out of the land of Egypt, out of the house of bondage, saying, 14 "At the end of seven years let every man set free his Hebrew brother, who has been sold to him; and when he has served you six years, you shall let him go free from you." But your fathers did not obey Me nor incline their ear. 15 Then you recently turned and did what was right in My sight—every man proclaiming liberty to his neighbor; and you made a covenant before Me in the house which is called by My name. 16 Then you turned around and profaned My name, and every one of you brought back his male and female slaves, whom he had set at liberty, at their pleasure, and brought them back into subjection, to be your male and female slaves.'

17 "Therefore thus says the LORD: 'You have not obeyed Me in proclaiming liberty, every one to his brother and every one to his neighbor. Behold, I proclaim liberty to you,' says the LORD—'to the sword, to pestilence, and to famine! And I will deliver you to trouble among all the kingdoms of the earth. 18 And I will give the men who have transgressed My covenant, who have not performed the words of the covenant which they made before Me, when they cut the calf in two and passed between the parts of it— 19 the princes of Judah, the princes of Jerusalem, the eunuchs, the priests, and all the people of the land who passed between the parts of the calf— 20 I will give them into the hand of their enemies and into the hand of those who seek their life. Their dead bodies shall be for meat for the birds of the heaven and the beasts of the earth. 21 And I will give Zedekiah king of Judah and his princes into the hand of their enemies, into the hand of those who seek their life, and into the hand of the king of Babylon's army which has gone back from you. 22 Behold, I will command,' says the LORD, 'and cause them to return to this city. They will fight against it and take it and burn it with fire; and I will make the cities of Judah a desolation without inhabitant.' "

35 The word which came to Jeremiah from the LORD in the days of Jehoiakim the son of Josiah, king of Judah, saying, 2 "Go to the house of the Rechabites, speak to them, and bring them into the house of the

34:3 [a]Literally mouth to mouth

LORD, into one of the chambers, and give them wine to drink."

3 Then I took Jaazaniah the son of Jeremiah, the son of Habazziniah, his brothers and all his sons, and the whole house of the Rechabites, 4 and I brought them into the house of the LORD, into the chamber of the sons of Hanan the son of Igdaliah, a man of God, which *was* by the chamber of the princes, above the chamber of Maaseiah the son of Shallum, the keeper of the door. 5 Then I set before the sons of the house of the Rechabites bowls full of wine, and cups; and I said to them, "Drink wine."

6 But they said, "We will drink no wine, for Jonadab the son of Rechab, our father, commanded us, saying, 'You shall drink no wine, you nor your sons, forever. 7 You shall not build a house, sow seed, plant a vineyard, nor have *any of these;* but all your days you shall dwell in tents, that you may live many days in the land where you are sojourners.' 8 Thus we have obeyed the voice of Jonadab the son of Rechab, our father, in all that he charged us, to drink no wine all our days, we, our wives, our sons, or our daughters, 9 nor to build ourselves houses to dwell in; nor do we have vineyard, field, or seed. 10 But we have dwelt in tents, and have obeyed and done according to all that Jonadab our father commanded us. 11 But it came to pass, when Nebuchadnezzar king of Babylon came up into the land, that we said, 'Come, let us go to Jerusalem for fear of the army of the Chaldeans and for fear of the army of the Syrians.' So we dwell at Jerusalem."

12 Then came the word of the LORD to Jeremiah, saying, 13 "Thus says the LORD of hosts, the God of Israel: 'Go and tell the men of Judah and the inhabitants of Jerusalem, "Will you not receive instruction to obey My words?" says the LORD. 14 "The words of Jonadab the son of Rechab, which he commanded his sons, not to drink wine, are performed; for to this day they drink none, and obey their father's commandment. But although I have spoken to you, rising early and speaking, you did not obey Me. 15 I have also sent to you all My servants the prophets, rising up early and sending *them,* saying, 'Turn now everyone from his evil way, amend your doings, and do not go after other gods to serve them; then you will dwell in the land which I have given you and your fathers.' But you have not inclined your ear, nor obeyed Me. 16 Surely the sons of Jonadab the son of Rechab have performed the commandment of their father, which he commanded them, but this people has not obeyed Me." '

17 "Therefore thus says the LORD God of hosts, the God of Israel: 'Behold, I will bring on Judah and on all the inhabitants of Jerusalem all the doom that I have pronounced against them; because I have spoken to them but they have not heard, and I have called to them but they have not answered.' "

18 And Jeremiah said to the house of the Rechabites, "Thus says the LORD of hosts, the God of Israel: 'Because you have obeyed the commandment of Jonadab your father, and kept all his precepts and done according to all that he commanded you, 19 therefore thus says the LORD of hosts, the God of Israel: "Jonadab the son of Rechab shall not lack a man to stand before Me forever." ' "

36 Now it came to pass in the fourth year of Jehoiakim the son of Josiah, king of Judah, *that* this word came to Jeremiah from the LORD, saying: 2 "Take a scroll of a book and write on it all the words that I have spoken to you against Israel, against Judah, and against all the nations, from the day I spoke to you, from the days of Josiah even to this day. 3 It may be that the house of Judah will hear all the adversities which I purpose to bring upon them, that everyone may turn from his evil way, that I may forgive their iniquity and their sin."

4 Then Jeremiah called Baruch the son of Neriah; and Baruch wrote on a scroll of a book, at the instruction of Jeremiah,[a] all the words of the LORD which He had spoken to him. 5 And Jeremiah commanded Baruch, saying, "I *am* confined, I cannot go into the house of the LORD. 6 You go, therefore, and read from the scroll which you have written at my in-

36:4 [a]Literally *from Jeremiah's mouth*

struction,[a] the words of the LORD, in the hearing of the people in the LORD's house on the day of fasting. And you shall also read them in the hearing of all Judah who come from their cities. 7 It may be that they will present their supplication before the LORD, and everyone will turn from his evil way. For great *is* the anger and the fury that the LORD has pronounced against this people." 8 And Baruch the son of Neriah did according to all that Jeremiah the prophet commanded him, reading from the book the words of the LORD in the LORD's house.

9 Now it came to pass in the fifth year of Jehoiakim the son of Josiah, king of Judah, in the ninth month, *that* they proclaimed a fast before the LORD to all the people in Jerusalem, and to all the people who came from the cities of Judah to Jerusalem. 10 Then Baruch read from the book the words of Jeremiah in the house of the LORD, in the chamber of Gemariah the son of Shaphan the scribe, in the upper court at the entry of the New Gate of the LORD's house, in the hearing of all the people.

11 When Michaiah the son of Gemariah, the son of Shaphan, heard all the words of the LORD from the book, 12 he then went down to the king's house, into the scribe's chamber; and there all the princes were sitting—Elishama the scribe, Delaiah the son of Shemaiah, Elnathan the son of Achbor, Gemariah the son of Shaphan, Zedekiah the son of Hananiah, and all the princes. 13 Then Michaiah declared to them all the words that he had heard when Baruch read the book in the hearing of the people. 14 Therefore all the princes sent Jehudi the son of Nethaniah, the son of Shelemiah, the son of Cushi, to Baruch, saying, "Take in your hand the scroll from which you have read in the hearing of the people, and come." So Baruch the son of Neriah took the scroll in his hand and came to them. 15 And they said to him, "Sit down now, and read it in our hearing." So Baruch read *it* in their hearing.

16 Now it happened, when they had heard all the words, that they looked in fear from one to another, and said to Baruch, "We will surely tell the king of all these words." 17 And they asked Baruch, saying, "Tell us now, how did you write all these words— at his instruction?"[a]

18 So Baruch answered them, "He proclaimed with his mouth all these words to me, and I wrote *them* with ink in the book."

19 Then the princes said to Baruch, "Go and hide, you and Jeremiah; and let no one know where you are."

20 And they went to the king, into the court; but they stored the scroll in the chamber of Elishama the scribe, and told all the words in the hearing of the king. 21 So the king sent Jehudi to bring the scroll, and he took it from Elishama the scribe's chamber. And Jehudi read it in the hearing of the king and in the hearing of all the princes who stood beside the king. 22 Now the king was sitting in the winter house in the ninth month, with *a fire* burning on the hearth before him. 23 And it happened, when Jehudi had read three or four columns, *that the king* cut it with the scribe's knife and cast *it* into the fire that *was* on the hearth, until all the scroll was consumed in the fire that *was* on the hearth. 24 Yet they were not afraid, nor did they tear their garments, the king nor any of his servants who heard all these words. 25 Nevertheless Elnathan, Delaiah, and Gemariah implored the king not to burn the scroll; but he would not listen to them. 26 And the king commanded Jerahmeel the king's[a] son, Seraiah the son of Azriel, and Shelemiah the son of Abdeel, to seize Baruch the scribe and Jeremiah the prophet, but the LORD hid them.

27 Now after the king had burned the scroll with the words which Baruch had written at the instruction of Jeremiah,[a] the word of the LORD came to Jeremiah, saying: 28 "Take yet another scroll, and write on it all the former words that were in the first scroll which Jehoiakim the king of Judah has burned. 29 And you shall say to Jehoiakim king of Judah, 'Thus says the LORD: "You have burned this scroll, saying, 'Why have you written in it that the king of Babylon will certainly come and destroy this land, and cause man

36:6 [a]Literally *from my mouth*   36:17 [a]Literally *with his mouth*   36:26 [a]Hebrew *Hammelech*
36:27 [a]Literally *from Jeremiah's mouth*

and beast to cease from here?' "
30 Therefore thus says the LORD concerning Jehoiakim king of Judah: "He shall have no one to sit on the throne of David, and his dead body shall be cast out to the heat of the day and the frost of the night. 31 I will punish him, his family, and his servants for their iniquity; and I will bring on them, on the inhabitants of Jerusalem, and on the men of Judah all the doom that I have pronounced against them; but they did not heed." ' "

32 Then Jeremiah took another scroll and gave it to Baruch the scribe, the son of Neriah, who wrote on it at the instruction of Jeremiah[a] all the words of the book which Jehoiakim king of Judah had burned in the fire. And besides, there were added to them many similar words.

37 Now King Zedekiah the son of Josiah reigned instead of Coniah the son of Jehoiakim, whom Nebuchadnezzar king of Babylon made king in the land of Judah. 2 But neither he nor his servants nor the people of the land gave heed to the words of the LORD which He spoke by the prophet Jeremiah.

3 And Zedekiah the king sent Jehucal the son of Shelemiah, and Zephaniah the son of Maaseiah, the priest, to the prophet Jeremiah, saying, "Pray now to the LORD our God for us." 4 Now Jeremiah was coming and going among the people, for they had not yet put him in prison. 5 Then Pharaoh's army came up from Egypt; and when the Chaldeans who were besieging Jerusalem heard news of them, they departed from Jerusalem.

6 Then the word of the LORD came to the prophet Jeremiah, saying, 7 "Thus says the LORD, the God of Israel, 'Thus you shall say to the king of Judah, who sent you to Me to inquire of Me: "Behold, Pharaoh's army which has come up to help you will return to Egypt, to their own land. 8 And the Chaldeans shall come back and fight against this city, and take it and burn it with fire." ' 9 Thus says the LORD: 'Do not deceive yourselves, saying, "The Chaldeans will surely depart from us," for they will not depart. 10 For though you

had defeated the whole army of the Chaldeans who fight against you, and there remained *only* wounded men among them, they would rise up, every man in his tent, and burn the city with fire.' "

11 And it happened, when the army of the Chaldeans left *the siege* of Jerusalem for fear of Pharaoh's army, 12 that Jeremiah went out of Jerusalem to go into the land of Benjamin to claim his property there among the people. 13 And when he was in the Gate of Benjamin, a captain of the guard *was* there whose name *was* Irijah the son of Shelemiah, the son of Hananiah; and he seized Jeremiah the prophet, saying, "You are defecting to the Chaldeans!"

14 Then Jeremiah said, "False! I am not defecting to the Chaldeans." But he did not listen to him.

So Irijah seized Jeremiah and brought him to the princes. 15 Therefore the princes were angry with Jeremiah, and they struck him and put him in prison in the house of Jonathan the scribe. For they had made that the prison.

16 When Jeremiah entered the dungeon and the cells, and Jeremiah had remained there many days, 17 then Zedekiah the king sent and took him *out*. The king asked him secretly in his house, and said, "Is there *any* word from the LORD?"

And Jeremiah said, "There is." Then he said, "You shall be delivered into the hand of the king of Babylon!"

18 Moreover Jeremiah said to King Zedekiah, "What offense have I committed against you, against your servants, or against this people, that you have put me in prison? 19 Where now *are* your prophets who prophesied to you, saying, 'The king of Babylon will not come against you or against this land?' 20 Therefore please hear now, O my lord the king. Please, let my petition be accepted before you, and do not make me return to the house of Jonathan the scribe, lest I die there."

21 Then Zedekiah the king commanded that they should commit Jeremiah to the court of the prison, and that they should give him daily a piece of bread from the bakers' street, until all the bread in the city

36:32 [a]Literally *from Jeremiah's mouth*

was gone. Thus Jeremiah remained in the court of the prison.

38 Now Shephatiah the son of Mattan, Gedaliah the son of Pashhur, Jucal*a* the son of Shelemiah, and Pashhur the son of Malchiah heard the words that Jeremiah had spoken to all the people, saying, 2 "Thus says the LORD: 'He who remains in this city shall die by the sword, by famine, and by pestilence; but he who goes over to the Chaldeans shall live; his life shall be as a prize to him, and he shall live.'*a* 3 Thus says the LORD: 'This city shall surely be given into the hand of the king of Babylon's army, which shall take it.'"

4 Therefore the princes said to the king, "Please, let this man be put to death, for thus he weakens the hands of the men of war who remain in this city, and the hands of all the people, by speaking such words to them. For this man does not seek the welfare of this people, but their harm." 5 Then Zedekiah the king said, "Look, he *is* in your hand. For the king can *do* nothing against you." 6 So they took Jeremiah and cast him into the dungeon of Malchiah the king's*a* son, which *was* in the court of the prison, and they let Jeremiah down with ropes. And in the dungeon *there was* no water, but mire. So Jeremiah sank in the mire.

7 Now Ebed-Melech the Ethiopian, one of the eunuchs, who was in the king's house, heard that they had put Jeremiah in the dungeon. When the king was sitting at the Gate of Benjamin, 8 Ebed-Melech went out of the king's house and spoke to the king, saying: 9 "My lord the king, these men have done evil in all that they have done to Jeremiah the prophet, whom they have cast into the dungeon, and he is likely to die from hunger in the place where he is. For *there is* no more bread in the city." 10 Then the king commanded Ebed-Melech the Ethiopian, saying, "Take from here thirty men with you, and lift Jeremiah the prophet out of the dungeon before he dies." 11 So Ebed-Melech took the men with him and went into the house of the king under the treasury, and took from there old clothes and old rags, and let them down by ropes into the dungeon to Jeremiah. 12 Then Ebed-Melech the Ethiopian said to Jeremiah, "Please put these old clothes and rags under your armpits, under the ropes." And Jeremiah did so. 13 So they pulled Jeremiah up with ropes and lifted him out of the dungeon. And Jeremiah remained in the court of the prison.

14 Then Zedekiah the king sent and had Jeremiah the prophet brought to him at the third entrance of the house of the LORD. And the king said to Jeremiah, "I will ask you something. Hide nothing from me."

15 Jeremiah said to Zedekiah, "If I declare *it* to you, will you not surely put me to death? And if I give you advice, you will not listen to me."

16 So Zedekiah the king swore secretly to Jeremiah, saying, "*As* the LORD lives, who made our very souls, I will not put you to death, nor will I give you into the hand of these men who seek your life."

17 Then Jeremiah said to Zedekiah, "Thus says the LORD, the God of hosts, the God of Israel: 'If you surely surrender to the king of Babylon's princes, then your soul shall live; this city shall not be burned with fire, and you and your house shall live. 18 But if you do not surrender to the king of Babylon's princes, then this city shall be given into the hand of the Chaldeans; they shall burn it with fire, and you shall not escape from their hand.'"

19 And Zedekiah the king said to Jeremiah, "I am afraid of the Jews who have defected to the Chaldeans, lest they deliver me into their hand, and they abuse me."

20 But Jeremiah said, "They shall not deliver *you*. Please, obey the voice of the LORD which I speak to you. So it shall be well with you, and your soul shall live. 21 But if you refuse to surrender, this *is* the word that the LORD has shown me: 22 'Now behold, all the women who are left in the king of Judah's house *shall be* surrendered to the king of Babylon's princes, and those *women* shall say:

"Your close friends have set upon you
And prevailed against you;

Your feet have sunk in the
mire,
And they have turned away
again.' "

23 'So they shall surrender all your
wives and children to the Chaldeans.
You shall not escape from their hand,
but shall be taken by the hand of the
king of Babylon. And you shall cause
this city to be burned with fire.' "

24 Then Zedekiah said to Jeremiah,
"Let no one know of these words,
and you shall not die. 25 But if the
princes hear that I have talked with
you, and they come to you and say
to you, 'Declare to us now what you
have said to the king, and also what
the king said to you; do not hide *it*
from us, and we will not put you to
death,' 26 then you shall say to them,
'I presented my request before the
king, that he would not make me return to Jonathan's house to die
there.' "

27 Then all the princes came to
Jeremiah and asked him. And he told
them according to all these words
that the king had commanded. So
they stopped speaking with him, for
the conversation had not been heard.
28 Now Jeremiah remained in the
court of the prison until the day that
Jerusalem was taken. And he was
there when Jerusalem was taken.

39 In the ninth year of Zedekiah
king of Judah, in the tenth
month, Nebuchadnezzar king of
Babylon and all his army came
against Jerusalem, and besieged it.
2 In the eleventh year of Zedekiah,
in the fourth month, on the ninth *day*
of the month, the city was penetrated.
3 Then all the princes of the king
of Babylon came in and sat in the
Middle Gate: Nergal-Sharezer, Sam-
gar-Nebo, Sarsechim, Rabsaris,*ª*
Nergal-Sarezer, Rabmag,*ᵇ* with the
rest of the princes of the king of
Babylon.
4 So it was, when Zedekiah the
king of Judah and all the men of war
saw them, that they fled and went out
of the city by night, by way of the
king's garden, by the gate between
the two walls. And he went out by
way of the plain.*ª* 5 But the Chaldean

army pursued them and overtook
Zedekiah in the plains of Jericho.
And when they had captured him,
they brought him up to Nebuchadnezzar king of Babylon, to Riblah in
the land of Hamath, where he pronounced judgment on him. 6 Then
the king of Babylon killed the sons
of Zedekiah before his eyes in Riblah; the king of Babylon also killed
all the nobles of Judah. 7 Moreover
he put out Zedekiah's eyes, and
bound him with bronze fetters to
carry him off to Babylon. 8 And the
Chaldeans burned the king's house
and the houses of the people with
fire, and broke down the walls of Jerusalem. 9 Then Nebuzaradan the
captain of the guard carried away
captive to Babylon the remnant of
the people who remained in the city
and those who defected to him, with
the rest of the people who remained.
10 But Nebuzaradan the captain of
the guard left in the land of Judah
the poor people, who had nothing,
and gave them vineyards and fields
at the same time.

11 Now Nebuchadnezzar king of
Babylon gave charge concerning
Jeremiah to Nebuzaradan the captain of the guard, saying, 12 "Take
him and look after him, and do him
no harm; but do to him just as he says
to you." 13 So Nebuzaradan the captain of the guard sent Nebushasban,
Rabsaris, Nergal-Sharezer, Rabmag,
and all the king of Babylon's chief
officers; 14 then they sent *someone* to
take Jeremiah from the court of the
prison, and committed him to Gedaliah the son of Ahikam, the son of
Shaphan, that he should take him
home. So he dwelt among the people.

15 Meanwhile the word of the LORD
had come to Jeremiah while he was
shut up in the court of the prison,
saying, 16 "Go and speak to Ebed-
Melech the Ethiopian, saying, 'Thus
says the LORD of hosts, the God of
Israel: "Behold, I will bring My
words upon this city for adversity
and not for good, and they shall be
performed in that day before you.
17 But I will deliver you in that day,"
says the LORD, "and you shall not be
given into the hand of the men of
whom you *are* afraid. 18 For I will
surely deliver you, and you shall not

39:3 *ª*A title, probably *Chief Officer;* also verse 13   *ᵇ*A title, probably *Troop Commander;* also verse 13
39:4 *ª*Or *the arabah,* that is, the Jordan Valley

fall by the sword; but your life shall be as a prize to you, because you have put your trust in Me," says the LORD.' "

40 The word that came to Jeremiah from the LORD after Nebuzaradan the captain of the guard had let him go from Ramah, when he had taken him bound in chains among all who were carried away captive from Jerusalem and Judah, who were carried away captive to Babylon.

2 And the captain of the guard took Jeremiah and said to him: "The LORD your God has pronounced this doom on this place. 3 Now the LORD has brought *it*, and has done just as He said. Because you *people* have sinned against the LORD, and not obeyed His voice, therefore this thing has come upon you. 4 And now look, I free you this day from the chains that *were* on your hand. If it seems good to you to come with me to Babylon, come, and I will look after you. But if it seems wrong for you to come with me to Babylon, remain here. See, all the land *is* before you; wherever it seems good and convenient for you to go, go there."

5 Now while Jeremiah had not yet gone back, *Nebuzaradan said*, "Go back to Gedaliah the son of Ahikam, the son of Shaphan, whom the king of Babylon has made governor over the cities of Judah, and dwell with him among the people. Or go wherever it seems convenient for you to go." So the captain of the guard gave him rations and a gift and let him go. 6 Then Jeremiah went to Gedaliah the son of Ahikam, to Mizpah, and dwelt with him among the people who were left in the land.

7 And when all the captains of the armies who *were* in the fields, they and their men, heard that the king of Babylon had made Gedaliah the son of Ahikam governor in the land, and had committed to him men, women, children, and the poorest of the land who had not been carried away captive to Babylon, 8 then they came to Gedaliah at Mizpah—Ishmael the son of Nethaniah, Johanan and Jonathan the sons of Kareah, Seraiah the son of Tanhumeth, the sons of Ephai the Netophathite, and

Jezaniah[a] the son of a Maachathite, they and their men. 9 And Gedaliah the son of Ahikam, the son of Shaphan, took an oath before them and their men, saying, "Do not be afraid to serve the Chaldeans. Dwell in the land and serve the king of Babylon, and it shall be well with you. 10 As for me, I will indeed dwell at Mizpah and serve the Chaldeans who come to us. But you, gather wine and summer fruit and oil, put *them* in your vessels, and dwell in your cities that you have taken." 11 Likewise, when all the Jews who *were* in Moab, among the Ammonites, in Edom, and who *were* in all the countries, heard that the king of Babylon had left a remnant of Judah, and that he had set over them Gedaliah the son of Ahikam, the son of Shaphan, 12 then all the Jews returned out of all places where they had been driven, and came to the land of Judah, to Gedaliah at Mizpah, and gathered wine and summer fruit in abundance.

13 Moreover Johanan the son of Kareah and all the captains of the forces that *were* in the fields came to Gedaliah at Mizpah, 14 and said to him, "Do you certainly know that Baalis the king of the Ammonites has sent Ishmael the son of Nethaniah to murder you?" But Gedaliah the son of Ahikam did not believe them.

15 Then Johanan the son of Kareah spoke secretly to Gedaliah in Mizpah, saying, "Let me go, please, and I will kill Ishmael the son of Nethaniah, and no one will know *it*. Why should he murder you, so that all the Jews who are gathered to you would be scattered, and the remnant in Judah perish?"

16 But Gedaliah the son of Ahikam said to Johanan the son of Kareah, "You shall not do this thing, for you speak falsely concerning Ishmael."

41 Now it came to pass in the seventh month *that* Ishmael the son of Nethaniah, the son of Elishama, of the royal family and of the officers of the king, came with ten men to Gedaliah the son of Ahikam, at Mizpah. And there they ate bread together in Mizpah. 2 Then Ishmael the son of Nethaniah, and the ten men who were with him, arose and

40:8 [a]Spelled *Jaazaniah* in 2 Kings 25:23

struck Gedaliah the son of Ahikam, the son of Shaphan, with the sword, and killed him whom the king of Babylon had made governor over the land. 3 Ishmael also struck down all the Jews who were with him, *that is,* with Gedaliah at Mizpah, and the Chaldeans who were found there, the men of war.

4 And it happened, on the second day after he had killed Gedaliah, when as yet no one knew *it,* 5 that certain men came from Shechem, from Shiloh, and from Samaria, eighty men with their beards shaved and their clothes torn, having cut themselves, with offerings and incense in their hand, to bring *them* to the house of the LORD. 6 Now Ishmael the son of Nethaniah went out from Mizpah to meet them, weeping as he went along; and it happened as he met them that he said to them, "Come to Gedaliah the son of Ahikam!" 7 So it was, when they came into the midst of the city, that Ishmael the son of Nethaniah killed them *and cast them* into the midst of a pit, he and the men who were with him. 8 But ten men were found among them who said to Ishmael, "Do not kill us, for we have treasures of wheat, barley, oil, and honey in the field." So he desisted and did not kill them among their brethren. 9 Now the pit into which Ishmael had cast all the dead bodies of the men whom he had slain, because of Gedaliah, *was* the same one Asa the king had made for fear of Baasha king of Israel. Ishmael the son of Nethaniah filled it with *the* slain. 10 Then Ishmael carried away captive all the rest of the people who *were* in Mizpah, the king's daughters and all the people who remained in Mizpah, whom Nebuzaradan the captain of the guard had committed to Gedaliah the son of Ahikam. And Ishmael the son of Nethaniah carried them away captive and departed to go over to the Ammonites.

11 But when Johanan the son of Kareah and all the captains of the forces that *were* with him heard of all the evil that Ishmael the son of Nethaniah had done, 12 they took all the men and went to fight with Ishmael the son of Nethaniah; and they found him by the great pool that *is* in Gibeon. 13 So it was, when all the people who *were* with Ishmael saw Johanan the son of Kareah, and all the captains of the forces who *were* with him, that they were glad. 14 Then all the people whom Ishmael had carried away captive from Mizpah turned around and came back, and went to Johanan the son of Kareah. 15 But Ishmael the son of Nethaniah escaped from Johanan with eight men and went to the Ammonites.

16 Then Johanan the son of Kareah, and all the captains of the forces that were with him, took from Mizpah all the rest of the people whom he had recovered from Ishmael the son of Nethaniah after he had murdered Gedaliah the son of Ahikam—the mighty men of war and the women and the children and the eunuchs, whom he had brought back from Gibeon. 17 And they departed and dwelt in the habitation of Chimham, which is near Bethlehem, as they went on their way to Egypt, 18 because of the Chaldeans; for they were afraid of them, because Ishmael the son of Nethaniah had murdered Gedaliah the son of Ahikam, whom the king of Babylon had made governor in the land.

42 Now all the captains of the forces, Johanan the son of Kareah, Jezaniah the son of Hoshaiah, and all the people, from the least to the greatest, came near 2 and said to Jeremiah the prophet, "Please, let our petition be acceptable to you, and pray for us to the LORD your God, for all this remnant (since we are left *but* a few of many, as you can see), 3 that the LORD your God may show us the way in which we should walk and the thing we should do."

4 Then Jeremiah the prophet said to them, "I have heard. Indeed, I will pray to the LORD your God according to your words, and it shall be, *that* whatever the LORD answers you, I will declare *it* to you. I will keep nothing back from you."

5 So they said to Jeremiah, "Let the LORD be a true and faithful witness between us, if we do not do according to everything which the LORD your God sends us by you. 6 Whether *it is* pleasing or displeasing, we will obey the voice of the LORD our God to whom we send you, that it may be well with us when we obey the voice of the LORD our God."

7 And it happened after ten days

that the word of the LORD came to Jeremiah. 8 Then he called Johanan the son of Kareah, all the captains of the forces which *were* with him, and all the people from the least even to the greatest, 9 and said to them, "Thus says the LORD, the God of Israel, to whom you sent me to present your petition before Him: 10 'If you will still remain in this land, then I will build you and not pull *you* down, and I will plant you and not pluck *you* up. For I relent concerning the disaster that I have brought upon you. 11 Do not be afraid of the king of Babylon, of whom you are afraid; do not be afraid of him,' says the LORD, 'for I *am* with you, to save you and deliver you from his hand. 12 And I will show you mercy, that he may have mercy on you and cause you to return to your own land.'

13 "But if you say, 'We will not dwell in this land,' disobeying the voice of the LORD your God, 14 saying, 'No, but we will go to the land of Egypt where we shall see no war, nor hear the sound of the trumpet, nor be hungry for bread, and there we will dwell'— 15 Then hear now the word of the LORD, O remnant of Judah! Thus says the LORD of hosts, the God of Israel: 'If you wholly set your faces to enter Egypt, and go to dwell there, 16 then it shall be *that* the sword which you feared shall overtake you there in the land of Egypt; the famine of which you were afraid shall follow close after you there *in* Egypt; and there you shall die. 17 So shall it be with all the men who set their faces to go to Egypt to dwell there. They shall die by the sword, by famine, and by pestilence. And none of them shall remain or escape from the disaster that I will bring upon them.'

18 "For thus says the LORD of hosts, the God of Israel: 'As My anger and My fury have been poured out on the inhabitants of Jerusalem, so will My fury be poured out on you when you enter Egypt. And you shall be an oath, an astonishment, a curse, and a reproach; and you shall see this place no more.'

19 "The LORD has said concerning you, O remnant of Judah, 'Do not go to Egypt!' Know certainly that I have admonished you this day. 20 For you were hypocrites in your hearts when you sent me to the LORD your God, saying, 'Pray for us to the LORD our God, and according to all that the LORD your God says, so declare to us and we will do *it*.' 21 And I have this day declared *it* to you, but you have not obeyed the voice of the LORD your God, or anything which He has sent you by me. 22 Now therefore, know certainly that you shall die by the sword, by famine, and by pestilence in the place where you desire to go to dwell."

43 Now it happened, when Jeremiah had stopped speaking to all the people all the words of the LORD their God, for which the LORD their God had sent him to them, all these words, 2 that Azariah the son of Hoshaiah, Johanan the son of Kareah, and all the proud men spoke, saying to Jeremiah, "You speak falsely! The LORD our God has not sent you to say, 'Do not go to Egypt to dwell there.' 3 But Baruch the son of Neriah has set you against us, to deliver us into the hand of the Chaldeans, that they may put us to death or carry us away captive to Babylon." 4 So Johanan the son of Kareah, all the captains of the forces, and all the people would not obey the voice of the LORD, to remain in the land of Judah. 5 But Johanan the son of Kareah and all the captains of the forces took all the remnant of Judah who had returned to dwell in the land of Judah, from all nations where they had been driven— 6 men, women, children, the king's daughters, and every person whom Nebuzaradan the captain of the guard had left with Gedaliah the son of Ahikam, the son of Shaphan, and Jeremiah the prophet and Baruch the son of Neriah. 7 So they went to the land of Egypt, for they did not obey the voice of the LORD. And they went as far as Tahpanhes.

8 Then the word of the LORD came to Jeremiah in Tahpanhes, saying, 9 "Take large stones in your hand, and hide them in the sight of the men of Judah, in the clay in the brick courtyard which *is* at the entrance to Pharaoh's house in Tahpanhes; 10 and say to them, 'Thus says the LORD of hosts, the God of Israel: "Behold, I will send and bring Nebuchadnezzar the king of Babylon, My servant, and will set his throne above

these stones that I have hidden. And he will spread his royal pavilion over them. 11 When he comes, he shall strike the land of Egypt *and deliver* to death *those appointed* for death, and to captivity *those appointed* for captivity, and to the sword *those appointed* for the sword. 12 I*a* will kindle a fire in the houses of the gods of Egypt, and he shall burn them and carry them away captive. And he shall array himself with the land of Egypt, as a shepherd puts on his garment, and he shall go out from there in peace. 13 He shall also break the sacred pillars of Beth Shemesh*a* that *are* in the land of Egypt; and the houses of the gods of the Egyptians he shall burn with fire." ' "

44 The word that came to Jeremiah concerning all the Jews who dwell in the land of Egypt, who dwell at Migdol, at Tahpanhes, at Noph,*a* and in the country of Pathros, saying, 2 "Thus says the LORD of hosts, the God of Israel: 'You have seen all the calamity that I have brought on Jerusalem and on all the cities of Judah; and behold, this day they *are* a desolation, and no one dwells in them, 3 because of their wickedness which they have committed to provoke Me to anger, in that they went to burn incense *and* to serve other gods whom they did not know, they nor you nor your fathers. 4 However I have sent to you all My servants the prophets, rising early and sending *them*, saying, "Oh, do not do this abominable thing that I hate!" 5 But they did not listen or incline their ear to turn from their wickedness, to burn no incense to other gods. 6 So My fury and My anger were poured out and kindled in the cities of Judah and in the streets of Jerusalem; and they are wasted *and* desolate, as it is this day.'

7 "Now therefore, thus says the LORD, the God of hosts, the God of Israel: 'Why do you commit *this* great evil against yourselves, to cut off from you man and woman, child and infant, out of Judah, leaving none to remain, 8 in that you provoke Me to wrath with the works of your hands, burning incense to other gods in the land of Egypt where you have gone to dwell, that you may cut yourselves off and be a curse and a reproach among all the nations of the earth? 9 Have you forgotten the wickedness of your fathers, the wickedness of the kings of Judah, the wickedness of their wives, your own wickedness, and the wickedness of your wives, which they committed in the land of Judah and in the streets of Jerusalem? 10 They have not been humbled, to this day, nor have they feared; they have not walked in My law or in My statutes that I set before you and your fathers.'

11 "Therefore thus says the LORD of hosts, the God of Israel: 'Behold, I will set My face against you for catastrophe and for cutting off all Judah. 12 And I will take the remnant of Judah who have set their faces to go into the land of Egypt to dwell there, and they shall all be consumed *and* fall in the land of Egypt. They shall be consumed by the sword *and* by famine. They shall die, from the least to the greatest, by the sword and by famine; and they shall be an oath, an astonishment, a curse and a reproach! 13 For I will punish those who dwell in the land of Egypt, as I have punished Jerusalem, by the sword, by famine, and by pestilence, 14 so that none of the remnant of Judah who have gone into the land of Egypt to dwell there shall escape or survive, lest they return to the land of Judah, to which they desire to return and dwell. For none shall return except those who escape.' "

15 Then all the men who knew that their wives had burned incense to other gods, with all the women who stood by, a great multitude, and all the people who dwelt in the land of Egypt, in Pathros, answered Jeremiah, saying: 16 "As for the word that you have spoken to us in the name of the LORD, we will not listen to you! 17 But we will certainly do whatever has gone out of our own mouth, to burn incense to the queen of heaven and pour out drink offerings to her, as we have done, we and our fathers, our kings and our princes, in the cities of Judah and in the streets of Je-

43:12 *a*Following Masoretic Text and Targum; Septuagint, Syriac, and Vulgate read *He*. 43:13 *a*Literally *House Of The Sun*, ancient On; later called *Heliopolis* 44:1 *a*That is, ancient Memphis rusalem. For *then* we had plenty of food, were well-off, and saw no trouble. 18 But since we stopped burning incense to the queen of heaven and pouring out drink offerings to her, we have lacked everything and have been consumed by the sword and by famine."

19 *The women also said,* "And when we burned incense to the queen of heaven and poured out drink offerings to her, did we make cakes for her, to worship her, and pour out drink offerings to her without our husbands' *permission?*"

20 Then Jeremiah spoke to all the people—the men, the women, and all the people who had given him *that* answer—saying: 21 "The incense that you burned in the cities of Judah and in the streets of Jerusalem, you and your fathers, your kings and your princes, and the people of the land, did not the LORD remember them, and did it *not* come into His mind? 22 So the LORD could no longer bear *it,* because of the evil of your doings *and* because of the abominations which you committed. Therefore your land is a desolation, an astonishment, a curse, and without an inhabitant, as *it is* this day. 23 Because you have burned incense and because you have sinned against the LORD, and have not obeyed the voice of the LORD or walked in His law, in His statutes or in His testimonies, therefore this calamity has happened to you, as *at* this day."

24 Moreover Jeremiah said to all the people and to all the women, "Hear the word of the LORD, all Judah who *are* in the land of Egypt! 25 Thus says the LORD of hosts, the God of Israel, saying: 'You and your wives have spoken with your mouths and fulfilled with your hands, saying, "We will surely keep our vows that we have made, to burn incense to the queen of heaven and pour out drink offerings to her." You will surely keep your vows and perform your vows!' 26 Therefore hear the word of the LORD, all Judah who dwell in the land of Egypt: 'Behold, I have sworn by My great name,' says the LORD, 'that My name shall no more be named in the mouth of any man of Judah in all the land of Egypt, saying, "The Lord GOD lives." 27 Behold, I

will watch over them for adversity and not for good. And all the men of Judah who *are* in the land of Egypt shall be consumed by the sword and by famine, until there is an end to them. 28 Yet a small number who escape the sword shall return from the land of Egypt to the land of Judah; and all the remnant of Judah, who have gone to the land of Egypt to dwell there, shall know whose words will stand, Mine or theirs. 29 And this *shall be* a sign to you,' says the LORD, 'that I will punish you in this place, that you may know that My words will surely stand against you for adversity.'

30 "Thus says the LORD: 'Behold, I will give Pharaoh Hophra king of Egypt into the hand of his enemies and into the hand of those who seek his life, as I gave Zedekiah king of Judah into the hand of Nebuchadnezzar king of Babylon, his enemy who sought his life.' "

45 The word that Jeremiah the prophet spoke to Baruch the son of Neriah, when he had written these words in a book at the instruction of Jeremiah,[a] in the fourth year of Jehoiakim the son of Josiah, king of Judah, saying, 2 "Thus says the LORD, the God of Israel, to you, O Baruch: 3 'You said, "Woe is me now! For the LORD has added grief to my sorrow. I fainted in my sighing, and I find no rest." '

4 "Thus you shall say to him, 'Thus says the LORD: "Behold, what I have built I will break down, and what I have planted I will pluck up, that is, this whole land. 5 And do you seek great things for yourself? Do not seek *them;* for behold, I will bring adversity on all flesh," says the LORD. "But I will give your life to you as a prize in all places, wherever you go." ' "

46 The word of the LORD which came to Jeremiah the prophet against the nations. 2 Against Egypt.

Concerning the army of Pharaoh Necho, king of Egypt, which was by the River Euphrates in Carchemish, and which Nebuchadnezzar king of Babylon defeated in the fourth year of Jehoiakim the son of Josiah, king of Judah:

45:1 *a*Literally *from Jeremiah's mouth*

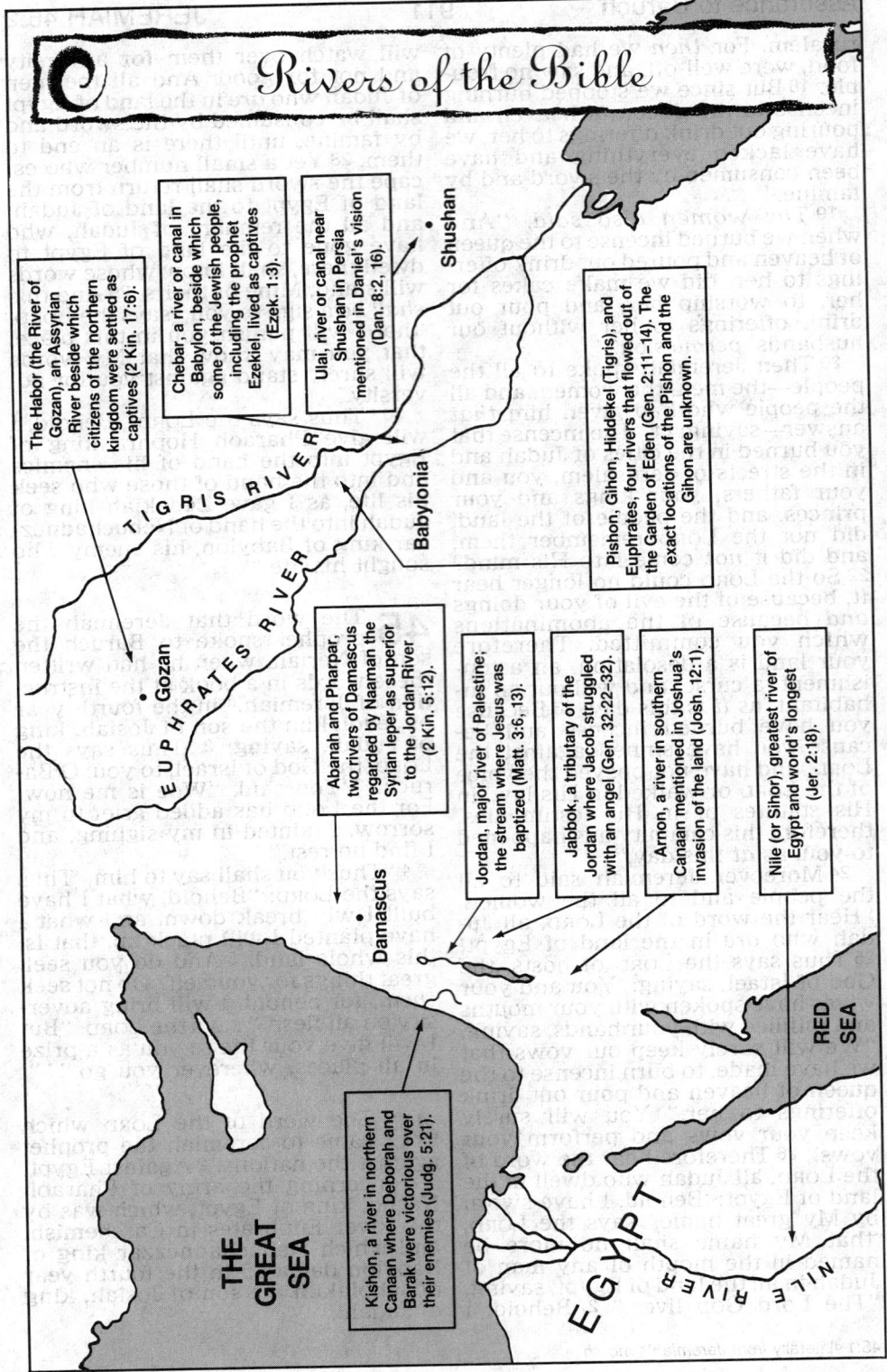

Rivers of the Bible

The Habor (the River of Gozan), an Assyrian River beside which citizens of the northern kingdom were settled as captives (2 Kin. 17:6).

Chebar, a river or canal in Babylon, beside which some of the Jewish people, including the prophet Ezekiel, lived as captives (Ezek. 1:3).

Ulai, river or canal near Shushan in Persia mentioned in Daniel's vision (Dan. 8:2, 16).

Pishon, Gihon, Hiddekel (Tigris), and Euphrates, four rivers that flowed out of the Garden of Eden (Gen. 2:11–14). The exact locations of the Pishon and the Gihon are unknown.

Abanah and Pharpar, two rivers of Damascus regarded by Naaman the Syrian leper as superior to the Jordan River (2 Kin. 5:12).

Jordan, major river of Palestine; the stream where Jesus was baptized (Matt. 3:6, 13).

Jabbok, a tributary of the Jordan where Jacob struggled with an angel (Gen. 32:22–32).

Arnon, a river in southern Canaan mentioned in Joshua's invasion of the land (Josh. 12:1).

Nile (or Sihor), greatest river of Egypt and world's longest (Jer. 2:18).

Kishon, a river in northern Canaan where Deborah and Barak were victorious over their enemies (Judg. 5:21).

Shushan

Babylonia

TIGRIS RIVER

EUPHRATES RIVER

Gozan

Damascus

THE GREAT SEA

EGYPT

NILE RIVER

RED SEA

3 "Order the buckler and shield,
  And draw near to battle!
4 Harness the horses,
  And mount up, you horsemen!
  Stand forth with *your* helmets,
  Polish the spears,
  Put on the armor!
5 Why have I seen them
    dismayed *and* turned back?
  Their mighty ones are beaten
    down;
  They have speedily fled,
  And did not look back,
  For fear *was* all around," says
    the LORD.
6 "Do not let the swift flee away,
  Nor the mighty man escape;
  They will stumble and fall
  Toward the north, by the River
    Euphrates.

7 "Who *is* this coming up like a
    flood,
  Whose waters move like the
    rivers?
8 Egypt rises up like a flood,
  And *its* waters move like the
    rivers;
  And he says, 'I will go up *and*
    cover the earth,
  I will destroy the city and its
    inhabitants.'
9 Come up, O horses, and rage,
    O chariots!
  And let the mighty men come
    forth:
  The Ethiopians and the
    Libyans who handle the
    shield,
  And the Lydians who handle
    and bend the bow.
10 For this *is* the day of the Lord
    GOD of hosts,
  A day of vengeance,
  That He may avenge Himself
    on His adversaries.
  The sword shall devour;
  It shall be satiated and made
    drunk with their blood;
  For the Lord GOD of hosts has
    a sacrifice
  In the north country by the
    River Euphrates.

11 "Go up to Gilead and take balm,
    O virgin, the daughter of
    Egypt;
  In vain you will use many
    medicines;
  You shall not be cured.

12 The nations have heard of your
    shame,
  And your cry has filled the
    land;
  For the mighty man has
    stumbled against the mighty;
  They both have fallen
    together."

13 The word that the LORD spoke
to Jeremiah the prophet, how Nebuchadnezzar king of Babylon would
come *and* strike the land of Egypt.

14 "Declare in Egypt, and proclaim
    in Migdol;
  Proclaim in Noph[a] and in
    Tahpanhes;
  Say, 'Stand fast and prepare
    yourselves,
  For the sword devours all
    around you.'
15 Why are your valiant *men*
    swept away?
  They did not stand
  Because the LORD drove them
    away.
16 He made many fall;
  Yes, one fell upon another.
  And they said, 'Arise!
  Let us go back to our own
    people
  And to the land of our nativity
  From the oppressing sword.'
17 They cried there,
  'Pharaoh, king of Egypt, *is but*
    a noise.
  He has passed by the appointed
    time!'

18 "*As* I live," says the King,
  Whose name *is* the LORD of
    hosts,
  "Surely as Tabor *is* among the
    mountains
  And as Carmel by the sea, *so*
    he shall come.
19 O you daughter dwelling in
    Egypt,
  Prepare yourself to go into
    captivity!
  For Noph[a] shall be waste and
    desolate, without inhabitant.

20 "Egypt *is* a very pretty heifer,
  But destruction comes, it
    comes from the north.
21 Also her mercenaries are in her
    midst like fat bulls,
  For they also are turned back,

46:14 [a]That is, ancient Memphis   46:19 [a]That is, ancient Memphis

They have fled away together.
They did not stand,
For the day of their calamity
   had come upon them,
The time of their punishment.
22 Her noise shall go like a
   serpent,
For they shall march with an
   army
And come against her with
   axes,
Like those who chop wood.

23 "They shall cut down her
   forest," says the LORD,
"Though it cannot be searched,
Because they *are* innumerable,
And more numerous than
   grasshoppers.
24 The daughter of Egypt shall be
   ashamed;
She shall be delivered into the
   hand
Of the people of the north."

25 The LORD of hosts, the God of
Israel, says: "Behold, I will bring
punishment on Amon[a] of No,[b] and
Pharaoh and Egypt, with their gods
and their kings—Pharaoh and those
who trust in him. 26 And I will deliver
them into the hand of those who seek
their lives, into the hand of Nebuchadnezzar king of Babylon and the
hand of his servants. Afterward it
shall be inhabited as in the days of
old," says the LORD.

27 "But do not fear, O My servant
   Jacob,
And do not be dismayed, O
   Israel!
For behold, I will save you from
   afar,
And your offspring from the
   land of their captivity;
Jacob shall return, have rest
   and be at ease;
No one shall make *him* afraid.
28 Do not fear, O Jacob My
   servant," says the LORD,
"For I *am* with you;
For I will make a complete end
   of all the nations
To which I have driven you,
But I will not make a complete
   end of you.
I will rightly correct you,
For I will not leave you wholly
   unpunished."

47 The word of the LORD that
came to Jeremiah the prophet
against the Philistines, before Pharaoh attacked Gaza.
2 Thus says the LORD:

"Behold, waters rise out of the
   north,
And shall be an overflowing
   flood;
They shall overflow the land
   and all that is in it,
The city and those who dwell
   within;
Then the men shall cry,
And all the inhabitants of the
   land shall wail.
3 At the noise of the stamping
   hooves of his strong horses,
At the rushing of his chariots,
At the rumbling of his
   wheels,
The fathers will not look back
   for *their* children,
Lacking courage,
4 Because of the day that
   comes to plunder all the
   Philistines,
To cut off from Tyre and Sidon
   every helper who remains;
For the LORD shall plunder the
   Philistines,
The remnant of the country of
   Caphtor.
5 Baldness has come upon Gaza,
Ashkelon is cut off
With the remnant of their
   valley.
How long will you cut yourself?

6 "O you sword of the LORD,
How long until you are quiet?
Put yourself up into your
   scabbard,
Rest and be still!
7 How can it be quiet,
Seeing the LORD has given it a
   charge
Against Ashkelon and against
   the seashore?
There He has appointed it."

48 Against Moab.
Thus says the LORD of hosts,
the God of Israel:

"Woe to Nebo!
For it is plundered,
Kirjathaim is shamed *and*
   taken;

46:25 [a]A sun god   [b]That is, ancient Thebes

The high stronghold[a] is
  shamed and dismayed—
2 No more praise of Moab.
  In Heshbon they have devised
    evil against her:
  'Come, and let us cut her off as
    a nation.'
  You also shall be cut down, O
    Madmen![a]
  The sword shall pursue you;
3 A voice of crying *shall be* from
    Horonaim:
  'Plundering and great
    destruction!'

4 "Moab is destroyed;
  Her little ones have caused a
    cry to be heard;[a]
5 For in the Ascent of Luhith they
    ascend with continual
    weeping;
  For in the descent of Horonaim
    the enemies have heard a cry
    of destruction.

6 "Flee, save your lives!
  And be like the juniper[a] in the
    wilderness.
7 For because you have trusted
    in your works and your
    treasures,
  You also shall be taken.
  And Chemosh shall go forth
    into captivity,
  His priests and his princes
    together.
8 And the plunderer shall come
    against every city;
  No one shall escape.
  The valley also shall perish,
  And the plain shall be
    destroyed,
  As the LORD has spoken.

9 "Give wings to Moab,
  That she may flee and get
    away;
  For her cities shall be desolate,
  Without any to dwell in them.
10 Cursed *is* he who does the work
    of the LORD deceitfully,
  And cursed *is* he who keeps
    back his sword from blood.

11 "Moab has been at ease from
    his[a] youth;
  He has settled on his dregs,

And has not been emptied from
    vessel to vessel,
  Nor has he gone into captivity.
  Therefore his taste remained in
    him,
  And his scent has not changed.
12 "Therefore behold, the days are
    coming," says the LORD,
  "That I shall send him wine-
    workers
  Who will tip him over
  And empty his vessels
  And break the bottles.
13 Moab shall be ashamed of
    Chemosh,
  As the house of Israel was
    ashamed of Bethel, their
    confidence.

14 "How can you say, 'We *are*
    mighty
  And strong men for the war'?
15 Moab is plundered and gone up
    from her cities;
  Her chosen young men have
    gone down to the slaughter,"
    says the King,
  Whose name *is* the LORD of
    hosts.

16 "The calamity of Moab *is* near
    at hand,
  And his affliction comes
    quickly.
17 Bemoan him, all you who are
    around him;
  And all you who know his
    name,
  Say, 'How the strong staff is
    broken,
  The beautiful rod!'
18 "O daughter inhabiting Dibon,
  Come down from *your* glory,
  And sit in thirst;
  For the plunderer of Moab has
    come against you,
  He has destroyed your
    strongholds.
19 O inhabitant of Aroer,
  Stand by the way and watch;
  Ask him who flees
  And her who escapes;
  Say, 'What has happened?'
20 Moab is shamed, for he is
    broken down.
  Wail and cry!

48:1 [a]Hebrew *Misgab*   48:2 [a]A city of Moab   48:4 [a]Following Masoretic Text, Targum, and Vulgate;
Septuagint reads *Proclaim it in Zoar.*   48:6 [a]Or *Aroer,* a city of Moab   48:11 [a]The Hebrew uses
masculine and feminine pronouns interchangeably in this chapter.

Tell it in Arnon, that Moab is
plundered.

21 "And judgment has come on the
plain country:
On Holon and Jahzah and
Mephaath,
22 On Dibon and Nebo and Beth
Diblathaim,
23 On Kirjathaim and Beth Gamul
and Beth Meon,
24 On Kerioth and Bozrah,
On all the cities of the land of
Moab,
Far or near.
25 The horn of Moab is cut off,
And his arm is broken," says
the LORD.

26 "Make him drunk,
Because he exalted *himself*
against the LORD.
Moab shall wallow in his vomit,
And he shall also be in
derision.
27 For was not Israel a derision to
you?
Was he found among thieves?
For whenever you speak of
him,
You shake *your head in scorn.*

28 You who dwell in Moab,
Leave the cities and dwell in
the rock,
And be like the dove *which*
makes her nest
In the sides of the cave's mouth.

29 "We have heard the pride of
Moab
(He *is* exceedingly proud),
Of his loftiness and arrogance
and pride,
And of the haughtiness of his
heart."

30 "I know his wrath," says the
LORD,
"But it *is* not right;
His lies have made nothing
right.
31 Therefore I will wail for Moab,
And I will cry out for all Moab;
I[a] will mourn for the men of Kir
Heres.
32 O vine of Sibmah! I will weep
for you with the weeping of
Jazer.

Your plants have gone over the
sea,
They reach to the sea of Jazer.
The plunderer has fallen on
your summer fruit and your
vintage.
33 Joy and gladness are taken
From the plentiful field
And from the land of Moab;
I have caused wine to fail from
the winepresses;
No one will tread with joyous
shouting—
Not joyous shouting!

34 "From the cry of Heshbon to
Elealeh and to Jahaz
They have uttered their voice,
From Zoar to Horonaim,
Like a three-year-old heifer;[a]
For the waters of Nimrim also
shall be desolate.

35 "Moreover," says the LORD,
"I will cause to cease in Moab
The one who offers *sacrifices* in
the high places
And burns incense to his gods.
36 Therefore My heart shall wail
like flutes for Moab,
And like flutes My heart shall
wail
For the men of Kir Heres.
Therefore the riches they have
acquired have perished.

37 "For every head *shall be* bald,
and every beard clipped;
On all the hands *shall be* cuts,
and on the loins sackcloth—
38 A general lamentation
On all the housetops of Moab,
And in its streets;
For I have broken Moab like a
vessel in which *is* no
pleasure," says the LORD.
39 "They shall wail:
'How she is broken down!
How Moab has turned her back
with shame!'
So Moab shall be a derision
And a dismay to all those about
her."

40 For thus says the LORD:

"Behold, one shall fly like an
eagle,

48:31 [a]Following Dead Sea Scrolls, Septuagint, and Vulgate; Masoretic Text reads *He.*   48:34 [a]Or *The Third Eglath,* an unknown city (compare Isaiah 15:5)

And spread his wings over
Moab.
41 Kerioth is taken,
And the strongholds are
surprised;
The mighty men's hearts in
Moab on that day shall be
Like the heart of a woman in
birth pangs.
42 And Moab shall be destroyed
as a people,
Because he exalted *himself*
against the LORD.
43 Fear and the pit and the snare
shall be upon you,
O inhabitant of Moab," says the
LORD.
44 He who flees from the fear shall
fall into the pit,
And he who gets out of the pit
shall be caught in the snare.
For upon Moab, upon it I will
bring
The year of their punishment,"
says the LORD.

45 "Those who fled stood under the
shadow of Heshbon
Because of exhaustion.
But a fire shall come out of
Heshbon,
A flame from the midst of
Sihon,
And shall devour the brow of
Moab,
The crown of the head of the
sons of tumult.
46 Woe to you, O Moab!
The people of Chemosh perish;
For your sons have been taken
captive,
And your daughters captive.

47 "Yet I will bring back the
captives of Moab
In the latter days," says the
LORD.

Thus far *is* the judgment of Moab.

49 Against the Ammonites.
Thus says the LORD:

"Has Israel no sons?
Has he no heir?
Why *then* does Milcom[a] inherit
Gad,
And his people dwell in its
cities?

2 Therefore behold, the days are
coming," says the LORD,
"That I will cause to be heard
an alarm of war
In Rabbah of the Ammonites;
It shall be a desolate mound,
And her villages shall be
burned with fire.
Then Israel shall take
possession of his
inheritance," says the LORD.

3 "Wail, O Heshbon, for Ai is
plundered!
Cry, you daughters of Rabbah,
Gird yourselves with sackcloth!
Lament and run to and fro by
the walls;
For Milcom shall go into
captivity
With his priests and his princes
together.
4 Why do you boast in the
valleys,
Your flowing valley, O
backsliding daughter?
Who trusted in her treasures,
saying,
'Who will come against me?'
5 Behold, I will bring fear upon
you,"
Says the Lord GOD of hosts,
"From all those who are around
you;
You shall be driven out,
everyone headlong,
And no one will gather those
who wander off.
6 But afterward I will bring back
The captives of the people of
Ammon," says the LORD.

7 Against Edom.
Thus says the LORD of hosts:

"*Is* wisdom no more in Teman?
Has counsel perished from the
prudent?
Has their wisdom vanished?
8 Flee, turn back, dwell in the
depths, O inhabitants of
Dedan!
For I will bring the calamity of
Esau upon him,
The time *that* I will punish him.
9 If grape-gatherers came to you,
Would they not leave *some*
gleaning grapes?
If thieves by night,

49:1 [a]Hebrew *Malcam*, literally *their king*, a god of the Ammonites; also called *Molech* (compare verse 3)

Would they not destroy until
they have enough?
10 But I have made Esau bare;
I have uncovered his secret
places,[a]
And he shall not be able to hide
himself.
His descendants are plundered,
His brethren and his neighbors,
And he *is* no more.
11 Leave your fatherless children,
I will preserve *them* alive;
And let your widows trust in
Me."

12 For thus says the LORD: "Behold,
those whose judgment *was* not to
drink of the cup have assuredly
drunk. And *are* you the one who will
altogether go unpunished? You shall
not go unpunished, but you shall
surely drink *of it.* 13 For I have sworn
by Myself," says the LORD, "that
Bozrah shall become a desolation, a
reproach, a waste, and a curse. And
all its cities shall be perpetual
wastes."

14 I have heard a message from
the LORD,
And an ambassador has been
sent to the nations:
"Gather together, come against
her,
And rise up to battle!
15 "For indeed, I will make you
small among nations,
Despised among men.
16 Your fierceness has deceived
you,
The pride of your heart,
O you who dwell in the clefts
of the rock,
Who hold the height of the hill!
Though you make your nest as
high as the eagle,
I will bring you down from
there," says the LORD.[a]

17 "Edom also shall be an
astonishment;
Everyone who goes by it will
be astonished
And will hiss at all its plagues.
18 As in the overthrow of Sodom
and Gomorrah
And their neighbors," says the
LORD,
"No one shall remain there,

Nor shall a son of man dwell
in it.

19 "Behold, he shall come up like
a lion from the floodplain[a] of
the Jordan
Against the dwelling place of
the strong;
But I will suddenly make him
run away from her.
And who *is* a chosen *man that*
I may appoint over her?
For who *is* like Me?
Who will arraign Me?
And who *is* that shepherd
Who will withstand Me?"

20 Therefore hear the counsel of
the LORD that He has taken
against Edom,
And His purposes that He has
proposed against the
inhabitants of Teman:
Surely the least of the flock
shall draw them out;
Surely He shall make their
dwelling places desolate with
them.
21 The earth shakes at the noise
of their fall;
At the cry its noise is heard at
the Red Sea.
22 Behold, He shall come up and
fly like the eagle,
And spread His wings over
Bozrah;
The heart of the mighty men of
Edom in that day shall be
Like the heart of a woman in
birth pangs.

23 Against Damascus.

"Hamath and Arpad are
shamed,
For they have heard bad news.
They are fainthearted;
There is trouble on the sea;
It cannot be quiet.
24 Damascus has grown feeble;
She turns to flee,
And fear has seized *her.*
Anguish and sorrows have
taken her like a woman in
labor.
25 Why is the city of praise not
deserted, the city of My joy?
26 Therefore her young men shall
fall in her streets,

49:10 [a]Compare Obadiah 5, 6   49:16 [a]Compare Obadiah 3, 4   49:19 [a]Or *thicket*

And all the men of war shall
be cut off in that day," says
the LORD of hosts.

27 "I will kindle a fire in the wall
of Damascus,
And it shall consume the
palaces of Ben-Hadad."[a]

28 Against Kedar and against the
kingdoms of Hazor, which Nebuchadnezzar king of Babylon shall
strike.

Thus says the LORD:

"Arise, go up to Kedar,
And devastate the men of the
East!

29 Their tents and their flocks
they shall take away.
They shall take for themselves
their curtains,
All their vessels and their
camels;
And they shall cry out to them,
'Fear is on every side!'

30 "Flee, get far away! Dwell in the
depths,
O inhabitants of Hazor!" says
the LORD.
"For Nebuchadnezzar king of
Babylon has taken counsel
against you,
And has conceived a plan
against you.

31 "Arise, go up to the wealthy
nation that dwells securely,"
says the LORD,
"Which has neither gates nor
bars,
Dwelling alone.

32 Their camels shall be for booty,
And the multitude of their
cattle for plunder.
I will scatter to all winds those
in the farthest corners,
And I will bring their calamity
from all its sides," says the
LORD.

33 "Hazor shall be a dwelling for
jackals, a desolation forever;
No one shall reside there,
Nor son of man dwell in it."

34 The word of the LORD that came
to Jeremiah the prophet against
Elam, in the beginning of the reign
of Zedekiah king of Judah, saying,

35 "Thus says the LORD of hosts:

'Behold, I will break the bow of
Elam,
The foremost of their might.

36 Against Elam I will bring the
four winds
From the four quarters of
heaven,
And scatter them toward all
those winds;
There shall be no nations
where the outcasts of Elam
will not go.

37 For I will cause Elam to be
dismayed before their
enemies
And before those who seek
their life.
I will bring disaster upon them,
My fierce anger,' says the
LORD;
'And I will send the sword after
them
Until I have consumed them.

38 I will set My throne in Elam,
And will destroy from there the
king and the princes,' says
the LORD.

39 'But it shall come to pass in the
latter days:
I will bring back the captives
of Elam,' says the LORD."

50 The word that the LORD spoke
against Babylon and against
the land of the Chaldeans by Jeremiah the prophet.

2 "Declare among the nations,
Proclaim, and set up a
standard;
Proclaim—do not conceal it—
Say, 'Babylon is taken, Bel is
shamed.
Merodach[a] is broken in pieces;
Her idols are humiliated,
Her images are broken in
pieces.'

3 For out of the north a nation
comes up against her,
Which shall make her land
desolate,
And no one shall dwell therein.
They shall move, they shall
depart,
Both man and beast.

4 "In those days and in that time,"
says the LORD,

"The children of Israel shall
   come,
They and the children of Judah
   together;
With continual weeping they
   shall come,
And seek the LORD their
   God.
5 They shall ask the way to
   Zion,
With their faces toward it,
   saying,
'Come and let us join ourselves
   to the LORD
In a perpetual covenant
That will not be forgotten.'

6 "My people have been lost
   sheep.
Their shepherds have led them
   astray;
They have turned them away
   on the mountains.
They have gone from mountain
   to hill;
They have forgotten their
   resting place.
7 All who found them have
   devoured them;
And their adversaries said, 'We
   have not offended,
Because they have sinned
   against the LORD, the
   habitation of justice,
The LORD, the hope of their
   fathers.'

8 "Move from the midst of
   Babylon,
Go out of the land of the
   Chaldeans;
And be like the rams before the
   flocks.
9 For behold, I will raise and
   cause to come up against
   Babylon
An assembly of great nations
   from the north country,
And they shall array
   themselves against her;
From there she shall be
   captured.
Their arrows *shall be like those*
   of an expert warrior;[a]
None shall return in vain.
10 And Chaldea shall become
   plunder;
All who plunder her shall be
   satisfied," says the LORD.

11 "Because you were glad,
   because you rejoiced,
You destroyers of My heritage,
Because you have grown fat
   like a heifer threshing grain,
And you bellow like bulls,
12 Your mother shall be deeply
   ashamed.
She who bore you shall be
   ashamed.
Behold, the least of the nations
   shall be a wilderness,
A dry land and a desert.
13 Because of the wrath of the
   LORD
She shall not be inhabited,
But she shall be wholly
   desolate.
Everyone who goes by Babylon
   shall be horrified
And hiss at all her plagues.

14 "Put yourselves in array against
   Babylon all around,
All you who bend the bow;
Shoot at her, spare no arrows,
For she has sinned against the
   LORD.
15 Shout against her all around;
She has given her hand,
Her foundations have fallen,
Her walls are thrown down;
For it *is* the vengeance of the
   LORD.
Take vengeance on her.
As she has done, so do to her.
16 Cut off the sower from
   Babylon,
And him who handles the
   sickle at harvest time.
For fear of the oppressing
   sword
Everyone shall turn to his own
   people,
And everyone shall flee to his
   own land.

17 "Israel *is* like scattered sheep;
The lions have driven *him*
   away.
First the king of Assyria
   devoured him;
Now at last this
   Nebuchadnezzar king of
   Babylon has broken his
   bones."

18 Therefore thus says the LORD of
hosts, the God of Israel:

50:9 [a]Following some Hebrew manuscripts, Septuagint, and Syriac; Masoretic Text, Targum, and Vulgate
read *a warrior who makes childless.*

"Behold, I will punish the king
of Babylon and his land,
As I have punished the king of
Assyria.
19 But I will bring back Israel to
his home,
And he shall feed on Carmel
and Bashan;
His soul shall be satisfied on
Mount Ephraim and Gilead.
20 In those days and in that time,"
says the LORD,
"The iniquity of Israel shall be
sought, but *there shall be*
none;
And the sins of Judah, but they
shall not be found;
For I will pardon those whom
I preserve.

21 "Go up against the land of
Merathaim, against it,
And against the inhabitants of
Pekod.
Waste and utterly destroy
them," says the LORD,
"And do according to all that I
have commanded you.
22 A sound of battle *is* in the
land,
And of great destruction.
23 How the hammer of the whole
earth has been cut apart and
broken!
How Babylon has become a
desolation among the
nations!
I have laid a snare for you;
24 You have indeed been trapped,
O Babylon,
And you were not aware;
You have been found and also
caught,
Because you have contended
against the Lord.
25 The LORD has opened His
armory,
And has brought out the
weapons of His indignation;
For this *is* the work of the Lord
GOD of hosts
In the land of the Chaldeans.
26 Come against her from the
farthest border;
Open her storehouses;
Cast her up as heaps of ruins,
And destroy her utterly;
Let nothing of her be left.
27 Slay all her bulls,

Let them go down to the
slaughter.
Woe to them!
For their day has come, the
time of their punishment.
28 The voice of those who flee and
escape from the land of
Babylon
Declares in Zion the vengeance
of the LORD our God,
The vengeance of His temple.

29 "Call together the archers
against Babylon.
All you who bend the bow,
encamp against it all around;
Let none of them escape.*a*
Repay her according to her
work;
According to all she has done,
do to her;
For she has been proud against
the LORD,
Against the Holy One of Israel.
30 Therefore her young men shall
fall in the streets,
And all her men of war shall
be cut off in that day," says
the LORD.
31 "Behold, I *am* against you,
O most haughty one!" says the
Lord GOD of hosts;
"For your day has come,
The time *that* I will punish
you.*a*
32 The most proud shall stumble
and fall,
And no one will raise him up;
I will kindle a fire in his cities,
And it will devour all around
him."

33 Thus says the LORD of hosts:

"The children of Israel *were*
oppressed,
Along with the children of
Judah;
All who took them captive have
held them fast;
They have refused to let them
go.
34 Their Redeemer *is* strong;
The LORD of hosts *is* His name.
He will thoroughly plead their
case,
That He may give rest to the
land,

And disquiet the inhabitants of
Babylon.

35 "A sword *is* against the
 Chaldeans," says the LORD,
"Against the inhabitants of
 Babylon,
And against her princes and
 her wise men.
36 A sword *is* against the
 soothsayers, and they will be
 fools.
A sword *is* against her mighty
 men, and they will be
 dismayed.
37 A sword *is* against their horses,
Against their chariots,
And against all the mixed
 peoples who *are* in her midst;
And they will become like
 women.
A sword *is* against her
 treasures, and they will be
 robbed.
38 A drought[a] *is* against her
 waters, and they will be dried
 up.
For it *is* the land of carved
 images,
And they are insane with *their*
 idols.

39 "Therefore the wild desert
 beasts shall dwell *there* with
 the jackals,
And the ostriches shall dwell in
 it.
It shall be inhabited no more
 forever,
Nor shall it be dwelt in from
 generation to generation.
40 As God overthrew Sodom and
 Gomorrah
And their neighbors," says the
 LORD,
"*So* no one shall reside there,
Nor son of man dwell in it.

41 "Behold, a people shall come
 from the north,
And a great nation and many
 kings
Shall be raised up from the
 ends of the earth.
42 They shall hold the bow and
 the lance;
They *are* cruel and shall not
 show mercy.

Their voice shall roar like the
 sea;
They shall ride on horses,
Set in array, like a man for the
 battle,
Against you, O daughter of
 Babylon.

43 "The king of Babylon has heard
 the report about them,
And his hands grow feeble;
Anguish has taken hold of him,
Pangs as of a woman in
 childbirth.

44 "Behold, he shall come up like
 a lion from the floodplain[a] of
 the Jordan
Against the dwelling place of
 the strong;
But I will make them suddenly
 run away from her.
And who *is* a chosen *man that*
 I may appoint over her?
For who *is* like Me?
Who will arraign Me?
And who *is* that shepherd
Who will withstand Me?"

45 Therefore hear the counsel of
 the LORD that He has taken
 against Babylon,
And His purposes that He has
 proposed against the land of
 the Chaldeans:
Surely the least of the flock
 shall draw them out;
Surely He will make their
 dwelling place desolate with
 them.
46 At the noise of the taking of
 Babylon
The earth trembles,
And the cry is heard among the
 nations.

51 Thus says the LORD:

"Behold, I will raise up against
 Babylon,
Against those who dwell in Leb
 Kamai,[a]
A destroying wind.
2 And I will send winnowers to
 Babylon,
Who shall winnow her and
 empty her land.

50:38 [a]Following Masoretic Text, Targum, and Vulgate; Syriac reads *sword*; Septuagint omits *A drought
is.* 50:44 [a]Or *thicket* 51:1 [a]A code word for *Chaldea* (Babylonia); may be translated *The Midst of
Those Who Rise Up Against Me*

For in the day of doom
They shall be against her all
around.

3 Against *her* let the archer bend
his bow,
And lift himself up against *her*
in his armor.
Do not spare her young men;
Utterly destroy all her army.

4 Thus the slain shall fall in the
land of the Chaldeans,
And *those* thrust through in her
streets.

5 For Israel is not forsaken, nor
Judah,
By his God, the LORD of hosts,
Though their land was filled
with sin against the Holy One
of Israel."

6 Flee from the midst of Babylon,
And every one save his life!
Do not be cut off in her iniquity,
For this *is* the time of the LORD's
vengeance;
He shall recompense her.

7 Babylon *was* a golden cup in
the LORD's hand,
That made all the earth drunk.
The nations drank her wine;
Therefore the nations are
deranged.

8 Babylon has suddenly fallen
and been destroyed.
Wail for her!
Take balm for her pain;
Perhaps she may be healed.

9 We would have healed
Babylon,
But she is not healed.
Forsake her, and let us go
everyone to his own country;
For her judgment reaches to
heaven and is lifted up to the
skies.

10 The LORD has revealed our
righteousness.
Come and let us declare in Zion
the work of the LORD our
God.

11 Make the arrows bright!
Gather the shields!
The LORD has raised up the
spirit of the kings of the
Medes.
For His plan *is* against Babylon
to destroy it,

Because it *is* the vengeance of
the LORD,
The vengeance for His temple.

12 Set up the standard on the
walls of Babylon;
Make the guard strong,
Set up the watchmen,
Prepare the ambushes.
For the LORD has both devised
and done
What He spoke against the
inhabitants of Babylon.

13 O you who dwell by many
waters,
Abundant in treasures,
Your end has come,
The measure of your
covetousness.

14 The LORD of hosts has sworn
by Himself:
"Surely I will fill you with men,
as with locusts,
And they shall lift up a shout
against you."

15 He has made the earth by His
power;
He has established the world
by His wisdom,
And stretched out the heaven
by His understanding.

16 When He utters *His* voice—
There is a multitude of waters
in the heavens:
"He causes the vapors to ascend
from the ends of the earth;
He makes lightnings for the
rain;
He brings the wind out of His
treasuries."[a]

17 Everyone is dull-hearted,
without knowledge;
Every metalsmith is put to
shame by the carved image;
For his molded image *is*
falsehood,
And *there is* no breath in
them.

18 They *are* futile, a work of
errors;
In the time of their punishment
they shall perish.

19 The Portion of Jacob *is* not like
them,
For He *is* the Maker of all
things;
And *Israel is* the tribe of His
inheritance.
The LORD of hosts *is* His name.

51:16 [a]Psalm 135:7

20 "You *are* My battle-ax *and*
  weapons of war:
For with you I will break the
  nation in pieces;
With you I will destroy
  kingdoms;
21 With you I will break in pieces
  the horse and its rider;
With you I will break in pieces
  the chariot and its rider;
22 With you also I will break in
  pieces man and woman;
With you I will break in pieces
  old and young;
With you I will break in pieces
  the young man and the
  maiden;
23 With you also I will break in
  pieces the shepherd and his
  flock;
With you I will break in pieces
  the farmer and his yoke of
  oxen;
And with you I will break in
  pieces governors and rulers.

24 "And I will repay Babylon
And all the inhabitants of
  Chaldea
For all the evil they have done
In Zion in your sight," says the
  LORD.

25 "Behold, I *am* against you, O
  destroying mountain,
Who destroys all the earth,"
  says the LORD.
"And I will stretch out My hand
  against you,
Roll you down from the rocks,
And make you a burnt
  mountain.
26 They shall not take from you
  a stone for a corner
Nor a stone for a foundation,
But you shall be desolate
  forever," says the LORD.

27 Set up a banner in the land,
Blow the trumpet among the
  nations!
Prepare the nations against
  her,
Call the kingdoms together
  against her:
Ararat, Minni, and Ashkenaz.
Appoint a general against her;
Cause the horses to come up
  like the bristling locusts.
28 Prepare against her the
  nations,
With the kings of the Medes,

Its governors and all its rulers,
All the land of his dominion.
29 And the land will tremble and
  sorrow;
For every purpose of the LORD
  shall be performed against
  Babylon,
To make the land of Babylon
  a desolation without
  inhabitant.
30 The mighty men of Babylon
  have ceased fighting,
They have remained in their
  strongholds;
Their might has failed,
They became *like* women;
They have burned her dwelling
  places,
The bars of her *gate* are
  broken.
31 One runner will run to meet
  another,
And one messenger to meet
  another,
To show the king of Babylon
  that his city is taken on *all*
  sides;
32 The passages are blocked,
The reeds they have burned
  with fire,
And the men of war are
  terrified.

33 For thus says the LORD of hosts,
the God of Israel:

    "The daughter of Babylon *is* like
      a threshing floor
    When it is time to thresh her;
    Yet a little while
    And the time of her harvest will
      come."

34 "Nebuchadnezzar the king of
  Babylon
Has devoured me, he has
  crushed me;
He has made me an empty
  vessel,
He has swallowed me up like
  a monster;
He has filled his stomach with
  my delicacies,
He has spit me out.
35 Let the violence *done* to me and
  my flesh *be* upon Babylon,"
The inhabitant of Zion will say;
"And my blood be upon the
  inhabitants of Chaldea!"
Jerusalem will say.

36 Therefore thus says the LORD:

"Behold, I will plead your case
and take vengeance for
you.
I will dry up her sea and make
her springs dry.
37 Babylon shall become a heap,
A dwelling place for jackals,
An astonishment and a hissing,
Without an inhabitant.
38 They shall roar together like
lions,
They shall growl like lions'
whelps.
39 In their excitement I will
prepare their feasts;
I will make them drunk,
That they may rejoice,
And sleep a perpetual sleep
And not awake," says the
LORD.
40 "I will bring them down
Like lambs to the slaughter,
Like rams with male goats.

41 "Oh, how Sheshach[a] is taken!
Oh, how the praise of the whole
earth is seized!
How Babylon has become
desolate among the nations!
42 The sea has come up over
Babylon;
She is covered with the
multitude of its waves.
43 Her cities are a desolation,
A dry land and a wilderness,
A land where no one dwells,
Through which no son of man
passes.
44 I will punish Bel in Babylon,
And I will bring out of his
mouth what he has
swallowed;
And the nations shall not
stream to him anymore.
Yes, the wall of Babylon shall
fall.

45 "My people, go out of the midst
of her!
And let everyone deliver
himself from the fierce anger
of the LORD.
46 And lest your heart faint,
And you fear for the rumor that
will be heard in the land
(A rumor will come one year,
And after that, in another year
A rumor will come,
And violence in the land,
Ruler against ruler),

47 Therefore behold, the days are
coming
That I will bring judgment on
the carved images of
Babylon;
Her whole land shall be
ashamed,
And all her slain shall fall in
her midst.
48 Then the heavens and the earth
and all that is in them
Shall sing joyously over
Babylon;
For the plunderers shall come
to her from the north," says
the LORD.

49 As Babylon has caused the
slain of Israel to fall,
So at Babylon the slain of all
the earth shall fall.
50 You who have escaped the
sword,
Get away! Do not stand still!
Remember the LORD afar off,
And let Jerusalem come to your
mind.

51 We are ashamed because we
have heard reproach.
Shame has covered our faces,
For strangers have come into
the sanctuaries of the LORD's
house.

52 "Therefore behold, the days are
coming," says the LORD,
"That I will bring judgment on
her carved images,
And throughout all her land the
wounded shall groan.
53 Though Babylon were to mount
up to heaven,
And though she were to fortify
the height of her strength,
Yet from Me plunderers would
come to her," says the LORD.

54 The sound of a cry comes from
Babylon,
And great destruction from the
land of the Chaldeans,
55 Because the LORD is plundering
Babylon
And silencing her loud voice,
Though her waves roar like
great waters,
And the noise of their voice is
uttered,

51:41 [a]A code word for Babylon (compare Jeremiah 25:26)

56 Because the plunderer comes
  against her, against Babylon,
 And her mighty men are taken.
 Every one of their bows is
  broken;
 For the LORD is the God of
  recompense,
 He will surely repay.

57 "And I will make drunk
 Her princes and wise men,
 Her governors, her deputies,
  and her mighty men.
 And they shall sleep a
  perpetual sleep
 And not awake," says the King,
 Whose name is the LORD of
  hosts.

58 Thus says the LORD of hosts:

 "The broad walls of Babylon
  shall be utterly broken,
 And her high gates shall be
  burned with fire;
 The people will labor in vain,
 And the nations, because of the
  fire;
 And they shall be weary."

59 The word which Jeremiah the prophet commanded Seraiah the son of Neriah, the son of Mahseiah, when he went with Zedekiah the king of Judah to Babylon in the fourth year of his reign. And Seraiah was the quartermaster. 60 So Jeremiah wrote in a book all the evil that would come upon Babylon, all these words that are written against Babylon. 61 And Jeremiah said to Seraiah, "When you arrive in Babylon and see it, and read all these words, 62 then you shall say, 'O LORD, You have spoken against this place to cut it off, so that none shall remain in it, neither man nor beast, but it shall be desolate forever.' 63 Now it shall be, when you have finished reading this book, that you shall tie a stone to it and throw it out into the Euphrates. 64 Then you shall say, 'Thus Babylon shall sink and not rise from the catastrophe that I will bring upon her. And they shall be weary.' "
 Thus far are the words of Jeremiah.

52 Zedekiah was twenty-one years old when he became king, and he reigned eleven years in Jerusalem. His mother's name was Hamutal the daughter of Jeremiah of Libnah. 2 He also did evil in the sight of the LORD, according to all that Jehoiakim had done. 3 For because of the anger of the LORD this happened in Jerusalem and Judah, till He finally cast them out from His presence. Then Zedekiah rebelled against the king of Babylon.

4 Now it came to pass in the ninth year of his reign, in the tenth month, on the tenth day of the month, that Nebuchadnezzar king of Babylon and all his army came against Jerusalem and encamped against it; and they built a siege wall against it all around. 5 So the city was besieged until the eleventh year of King Zedekiah. 6 By the fourth month, on the ninth day of the month, the famine had become so severe in the city that there was no food for the people of the land. 7 Then the city wall was broken through, and all the men of war fled and went out of the city at night by way of the gate between the two walls, which was by the king's garden, even though the Chaldeans were near the city all around. And they went by way of the plain.[a]

8 But the army of the Chaldeans pursued the king, and they overtook Zedekiah in the plains of Jericho. All his army was scattered from him. 9 So they took the king and brought him up to the king of Babylon at Riblah in the land of Hamath, and he pronounced judgment on him. 10 Then the king of Babylon killed the sons of Zedekiah before his eyes. And he killed all the princes of Judah in Riblah. 11 He also put out the eyes of Zedekiah; and the king of Babylon bound him in bronze fetters, took him to Babylon, and put him in prison till the day of his death.

12 Now in the fifth month, on the tenth day of the month (which was the nineteenth year of King Nebuchadnezzar king of Babylon), Nebuzaradan, the captain of the guard, who served the king of Babylon, came to Jerusalem. 13 He burned the house of the LORD and the king's house; all the houses of Jerusalem, that is, all the houses of the great, he burned with fire. 14 And all the

52:7 [a]Or the arabah, that is, the Jordan Valley

army of the Chaldeans who *were* with the captain of the guard broke down all the walls of Jerusalem all around. 15 Then Nebuzaradan the captain of the guard carried away captive *some* of the poor people, the rest of the people who remained in the city, the defectors who had deserted to the king of Babylon, and the rest of the craftsmen. 16 But Nebuzaradan the captain of the guard left *some* of the poor of the land as vinedressers and farmers.

17 The bronze pillars that *were* in the house of the LORD, and the carts and the bronze Sea that *were* in the house of the LORD, the Chaldeans broke in pieces, and carried all their bronze to Babylon. 18 They also took away the pots, the shovels, the trimmers, the bowls, the spoons, and all the bronze utensils with which the priests ministered. 19 The basins, the firepans, the bowls, the pots, the lampstands, the spoons, and the cups, whatever *was* solid gold and whatever *was* solid silver, the captain of the guard took away. 20 The two pillars, one Sea, the twelve bronze bulls which *were* under *it, and* the carts, which King Solomon had made for the house of the LORD—the bronze of all these articles was beyond measure. 21 Now *concerning* the pillars: the height of one pillar *was* eighteen cubits, a measuring line of twelve cubits could measure its circumference, and its thickness *was* four fingers; *it was* hollow. 22 A capital of bronze *was* on it; and the height of one capital *was* five cubits, with a network and pomegranates all around the capital, all of bronze. The second pillar, with pomegranates was the same. 23 There were ninety-six pomegranates on the sides; all the pomegranates, all around on the network, *were* one hundred.

24 The captain of the guard took Seraiah the chief priest, Zephaniah the second priest, and the three door-keepers. 25 He also took out of the city an officer who had charge of the men of war, seven men of the king's close associates who were found in the city, the principal scribe of the army who mustered the people of the land, and sixty men of the people of the land who were found in the midst of the city. 26 And Nebuzaradan the captain of the guard took these and brought them to the king of Babylon at Riblah. 27 Then the king of Babylon struck them and put them to death at Riblah in the land of Hamath. Thus Judah was carried away captive from its own land.

28 These *are* the people whom Nebuchadnezzar carried away captive: in the seventh year, three thousand and twenty-three Jews; 29 in the eighteenth year of Nebuchadnezzar he carried away captive from Jerusalem eight hundred and thirty-two persons; 30 in the twenty-third year of Nebuchadnezzar, Nebuzaradan the captain of the guard carried away captive of the Jews seven hundred and forty-five persons. All the persons *were* four thousand six hundred.

31 Now it came to pass in the thirty-seventh year of the captivity of Jehoiachin king of Judah, in the twelfth month, on the twenty-fifth *day* of the month, *that* Evil-Merodach[a] king of Babylon, in the first *year* of his reign, lifted up the head of Jehoiachin king of Judah and brought him out of prison. 32 And he spoke kindly to him and gave him a more prominent seat than those of the kings who *were* with him in Babylon. 33 So Jehoiachin changed from his prison garments, and he ate bread regularly before the king all the days of his life. 34 And as for his provisions, there was a regular ration given him by the king of Babylon, a portion for each day until the day of his death, all the days of his life.

52:31 *a*Or *Awil-Marduk*

Lamentations

Overview of Lamentations

What happens when, after a lifetime of work, a project falls through and failure is the final result? Lamentations deals with that profound question.

The prophet Jeremiah had spent his entire life mourning, praying, and encouraging his people to turn to God. Jeremiah admonished the nation of Judah not to align with and depend upon the mighty nations of Egypt and Babylon. He implored them to put aside the pagan practices they had adopted from these foreign nations and return to pure worship of the true God.

The nation, however, failed to heed Jeremiah's call to repentance. Now, with Jerusalem destroyed by Nebuchadnezzar in 586 B.C., Jeremiah sat among the ashes bemoaning his cherished city. His people had been carried off to captivity, Judah's finest soldiers lay slain on the heights surrounding the city, and the buildings had been burned and reduced to a heap of rubble.

Amidst the outpouring of his poetic lamentations, Jeremiah was able to look to the all-powerful, loving, merciful God.

> Through *the LORD's mercies we are not consumed,*
> *Because His compassions fail not.*
> They are *new every morning;*
> *Great* is *Your faithfulness.*
> *"The LORD* is *my portion," says my soul,*
> *"Therefore I hope in Him!"*
>
> (Lam. 3:22–24)

In the toughest times Jeremiah ever faced, he turned to God with praise, trust, and hope. Trying times are times to triumph! Regardless of the situation, Jeremiah could still praise God. Amidst the affliction, Jeremiah worshiped God.

For the Lord will not cast off forever.
Though He causes grief,
Yet He will show compassion
According to the multitude of His mercies.
(Lam. 3:31, 32)

Jesus in Lamentations

The weeping prophet Jeremiah is a type of Christ, the Prophet who wept over Jerusalem six hundred years after Jeremiah did. Like Jesus, Jeremiah identified himself personally with the suffering and sin in Jerusalem. Jesus later died to redeem Jerusalem and the entire world.

Keys to Lamentations

Key Word: Lamentations. Three themes run through Jeremiah's five laments. First, he mourns over Jerusalem's holocaust when judgment has come. Second, there is a confession of sin and an acknowledgment of God's righteous and holy judgment upon Judah. The third theme is hope in God's future restoration of His people. He will not leave His people in destruction, but will be faithful to His covenant promises.

Key Verse: *"Through* the LORD's mercies we are not consumed, because His compassions fail not. *They are* new every morning; great *is* Your faithfulness" (3:22–23).

Key Chapter: Lamentations 3. Though much of Lamentations deals with destruction and judgment, Jeremiah speaks forth the positive message of God's wonderful promises and character and expresses great faith in His mercy and restoration.

1 How lonely sits the city
That was full of people!
How like a widow is she,
Who *was* great among the
     nations!
The princess among the
     provinces
Has become a slave!

2 She weeps bitterly in the night,
Her tears *are* on her cheeks;
Among all her lovers
She has none to comfort *her*.
All her friends have dealt
     treacherously with her;
They have become her
     enemies.

3 Judah has gone into captivity,
Under affliction and hard
     servitude;
She dwells among the nations,
She finds no rest;
All her persecutors overtake
     her in dire straits.

4 The roads to Zion mourn
Because no one comes to the
     set feasts.
All her gates are desolate;
Her priests sigh,
Her virgins are afflicted,
And she *is* in bitterness.

5 Her adversaries have become
     the master,
Her enemies prosper;
For the LORD has afflicted her
Because of the multitude of her
     transgressions.
Her children have gone into
     captivity before the enemy.

6 And from the daughter of Zion
All her splendor has departed.
Her princes have become like
     deer
That find no pasture,
That flee without strength
Before the pursuer.

7 In the days of her affliction and
     roaming,
Jerusalem remembers all her
     pleasant things
That she had in the days of old.

When her people fell into the
     hand of the enemy,
With no one to help her,
The adversaries saw her
And mocked at her downfall.[a]

8 Jerusalem has sinned gravely,
Therefore she has become
     vile.[a]
All who honored her despise
     her
Because they have seen her
     nakedness;
Yes, she sighs and turns away.

9 Her uncleanness *is* in her
     skirts;
She did not consider her
     destiny;
Therefore her collapse was
     awesome;
She had no comforter.
"O LORD, behold my affliction,
For *the* enemy is exalted!"

10 The adversary has spread his
     hand
Over all her pleasant things;
For she has seen the nations
     enter her sanctuary,
Those whom You commanded
Not to enter Your assembly.

11 All her people sigh,
They seek bread;
They have given their
     valuables for food to restore
     life.
"See, O LORD, and consider,
For I am scorned."

12 "*Is it* nothing to you, all you who
     pass by?
Behold and see
If there is any sorrow like my
     sorrow,
Which has been brought on me,
Which the LORD has inflicted
In the day of His fierce anger.

13 "From above He has sent fire
     into my bones,
And it overpowered them;
He has spread a net for my feet
And turned me back;

1:7 aVulgate reads *her Sabbaths*.   1:8 aSeptuagint and Vulgate read *moved* or *removed*.

He has made me desolate
And faint all the day.

14 "The yoke of my transgressions
was bound;[a]
They were woven together by
His hands,
And thrust upon my neck.
He made my strength fail;
The Lord delivered me into the
hands of *those whom* I am
not able to withstand.

15 "The Lord has trampled
underfoot all my mighty *men*
in my midst;
He has called an assembly
against me
To crush my young men;
The Lord trampled *as* in a
winepress
The virgin daughter of Judah.

16 "For these *things* I weep;
My eye, my eye overflows with
water;
Because the comforter, who
should restore my life,
Is far from me.
My children are desolate
Because the enemy prevailed."

17 Zion spreads out her hands,
But no one comforts her;
The LORD has commanded
concerning Jacob
That those around him *become*
his adversaries;
Jerusalem has become an
unclean thing among them.

18 "The LORD is righteous,
For I rebelled against His
commandment.
Hear now, all peoples,
And behold my sorrow;
My virgins and my young men
Have gone into captivity.

19 "I called for my lovers,
But they deceived me;
My priests and my elders
Breathed their last in the city,
While they sought food
To restore their life.

20 "See, O LORD, that I *am* in
distress;
My soul is troubled;

My heart is overturned within
me,
For I have been very rebellious.
Outside the sword bereaves,
At home *it is* like death.

21 "They have heard that I sigh,
But no one comforts me.
All my enemies have heard of
my trouble;
They are glad that You have
done *it*.
Bring on the day You have
announced,
That they may become like me.

22 "Let all their wickedness come
before You,
And do to them as You have
done to me
For all my transgressions;
For my sighs *are* many,
And my heart *is* faint."

2 How the Lord has covered the
daughter of Zion
With a cloud in His anger!
He cast down from heaven to
the earth
The beauty of Israel,
And did not remember His
footstool
In the day of His anger.

2 The Lord has swallowed up
and has not pitied
All the dwelling places of
Jacob.
He has thrown down in His
wrath
The strongholds of the
daughter of Judah;
He has brought *them* down to
the ground;
He has profaned the kingdom
and its princes.

3 He has cut off in fierce anger
Every horn of Israel;
He has drawn back His right
hand
From before the enemy.
He has blazed against Jacob
like a flaming fire
Devouring all around.

4 Standing like an enemy, He has
bent His bow;
With His right hand, like an
adversary,

1:14 [a]Following Masoretic Text and Targum; Septuagint, Syriac, and Vulgate read *watched over.*

He has slain all *who were*
  pleasing to His eye;
On the tent of the daughter of
  Zion,
He has poured out His fury like
  fire.

5 The Lord was like an enemy.
He has swallowed up Israel,
He has swallowed up all her
  palaces;
He has destroyed her
  strongholds,
And has increased mourning
  and lamentation
In the daughter of Judah.

6 He has done violence to His
  tabernacle,
As if it were a garden;
He has destroyed His place of
  assembly;
The LORD has caused
The appointed feasts and
  Sabbaths to be forgotten in
  Zion.
In His burning indignation He
  has spurned the king and the
  priest.

7 The Lord has spurned His altar,
He has abandoned His
  sanctuary;
He has given up the walls of her
  palaces
Into the hand of the enemy.
They have made a noise in the
  house of the LORD
As on the day of a set feast.

8 The LORD has purposed to
  destroy
The wall of the daughter of
  Zion.
He has stretched out a line;
He has not withdrawn His hand
  from destroying;
Therefore He has caused the
  rampart and wall to lament;
They languished together.

9 Her gates have sunk into the
  ground;
He has destroyed and broken
  her bars.
Her king and her princes *are*
  among the nations;
The Law *is* no more,
And her prophets find no vision
  from the LORD.

10 The elders of the daughter of
  Zion

Sit on the ground *and* keep
  silence;
They throw dust on their heads
And gird themselves with
  sackcloth.
The virgins of Jerusalem
Bow their heads to the ground.

11 My eyes fail with tears,
My heart is troubled;
My bile is poured on the ground
Because of the destruction of
  the daughter of my people,
Because the children and the
  infants
Faint in the streets of the city.

12 They say to their mothers,
  "Where *is* grain and wine?"
As they swoon like the
  wounded
In the streets of the city,
As their life is poured out
In their mothers' bosom.

13 How shall I console you?
To what shall I liken you,
O daughter of Jerusalem?
What shall I compare with you,
  that I may comfort you,
O virgin daughter of Zion?
For your ruin *is* spread wide as
  the sea;
Who can heal you?

14 Your prophets have seen for
  you
False and deceptive visions;
They have not uncovered your
  iniquity,
To bring back your captives,
But have envisioned for you
  false prophecies and
  delusions.

15 All who pass by clap *their*
  hands at you;
They hiss and shake their
  heads
At the daughter of Jerusalem:
"*Is* this the city that is called
  'The perfection of beauty,
The joy of the whole earth'?"

16 All your enemies have opened
  their mouth against you;
They hiss and gnash *their*
  teeth.
They say, "We have swallowed
  her up!
Surely this *is* the day we have
  waited for;

We have found *it*, we have seen
    it!"

17 The Lord has done what He
    purposed;
  He has fulfilled His word
  Which He commanded in days
    of old.
  He has thrown down and has
    not pitied,
  And He has caused an enemy
    to rejoice over you;
  He has exalted the horn of your
    adversaries.

18 Their heart cried out to the
    Lord,
  "O wall of the daughter of Zion,
  Let tears run down like a river
    day and night;
  Give yourself no relief;
  Give your eyes no rest.

19 "Arise, cry out in the night,
  At the beginning of the
    watches;
  Pour out your heart like water
    before the face of the Lord.
  Lift your hands toward Him
  For the life of your young
    children,
  Who faint from hunger at the
    head of every street."

20 "See, O Lord, and consider!
  To whom have You done this?
  Should the women eat their
    offspring,
  The children they have
    cuddled?[a]
  Should the priest and prophet
    be slain
  In the sanctuary of the Lord?

21 "Young and old lie
  On the ground in the streets;
  My virgins and my young men
  Have fallen by the sword;
  You have slain *them* in the day
    of Your anger,
  You have slaughtered *and* not
    pitied.

22 "You have invited as to a feast
    day
  The terrors that surround me.
  In the day of the Lord's anger
  There was no refugee or
    survivor.

Those whom I have borne and
    brought up
  My enemies have destroyed."

3   I *am* the man *who* has seen
    affliction by the rod of His
    wrath.
2 He has led me and made *me*
    walk
  In darkness and not *in* light.
3 Surely He has turned His hand
    against me
  Time and time again
    throughout the day.

4 He has aged my flesh and my
    skin,
  And broken my bones.
5 He has besieged me
  And surrounded *me* with
    bitterness and woe.
6 He has set me in dark places
  Like the dead of long ago.

7 He has hedged me in so that I
    cannot get out;
  He has made my chain heavy.
8 Even when I cry and shout,
  He shuts out my prayer.
9 He has blocked my ways with
    hewn stone;
  He has made my paths
    crooked.

10 He *has been* to me a bear lying
    in wait,
  Like a lion in ambush.
11 He has turned aside my ways
    and torn me in pieces;
  He has made me desolate.
12 He has bent His bow
  And set me up as a target for
    the arrow.

13 He has caused the arrows of
    His quiver
  To pierce my loins.[a]
14 I have become the ridicule of
    all my people—
  Their taunting song all the day.
15 He has filled me with
    bitterness,
  He has made me drink
    wormwood.

16 He has also broken my teeth
    with gravel,
  And covered me with ashes.
17 You have moved my soul far
    from peace;

2:20 [a]Vulgate reads *a span long.*   3:13 [a]Literally *kidneys*

I have forgotten prosperity.
18 And I said, "My strength and
    my hope
Have perished from the LORD."

19 Remember my affliction and
    roaming,
The wormwood and the gall.
20 My soul still remembers
And sinks within me.
21 This I recall to my mind,
Therefore I have hope.

22 *Through* the LORD's mercies we
    are not consumed,
Because His compassions fail
    not.
23 *They are* new every morning;
Great *is* Your faithfulness.
24 "The LORD *is* my portion," says
    my soul,
  "Therefore I hope in Him!"

25 The LORD *is* good to those who
    wait for Him,
To the soul *who* seeks Him.
26 *It is* good that *one* should hope
    and wait quietly
For the salvation of the LORD.
27 *It is* good for a man to bear
The yoke in his youth.

28 Let him sit alone and keep
    silent,
Because *God* has laid *it* on him;
29 Let him put his mouth in the
    dust—
There may yet be hope.
30 Let him give *his* cheek to the
    one who strikes him,
And be full of reproach.

31 For the Lord will not cast off
    forever.
32 Though He causes grief,
Yet He will show compassion
According to the multitude of
    His mercies.
33 For He does not afflict
    willingly,
Nor grieve the children of men.

34 To crush under one's feet
All the prisoners of the earth,
35 To turn aside the justice *due* a
    man
Before the face of the Most
    High,
36 Or subvert a man in his cause—
The Lord does not approve.

37 Who *is* he *who* speaks and it
    comes to pass,
When the Lord has not
    commanded *it*?
38 *Is it* not from the mouth of the
    Most High
That woe and well-being
    proceed?
39 Why should a living man
    complain,
A man for the punishment of
    his sins?

40 Let us search out and examine
    our ways,
And turn back to the LORD;
41 Let us lift our hearts and
    hands
To God in heaven.
42 We have transgressed and
    rebelled;
You have not pardoned.

43 You have covered *Yourself*
    with anger
And pursued us;
You have slain *and* not pitied.
44 You have covered Yourself
    with a cloud,
That prayer should not pass
    through.
45 You have made us an
    offscouring and refuse
In the midst of the peoples.

46 All our enemies
Have opened their mouths
    against us.
47 Fear and a snare have come
    upon us,
Desolation and destruction.
48 My eyes overflow with rivers of
    water
For the destruction of the
    daughter of my people.

49 My eyes flow and do not
    cease,
Without interruption,
50 Till the LORD from heaven
Looks down and sees.
51 My eyes bring suffering to my
    soul
Because of all the daughters of
    my city.

52 My enemies without cause
Hunted me down like a bird.
53 They silenced[a] my life in the pit
And threw stones at me.

3:53 [a]Septuagint reads *put to death.*

54 The waters flowed over my
        head;
    I said, "I am cut off!"

55 I called on Your name, O LORD,
    From the lowest pit.
56 You have heard my voice:
    "Do not hide Your ear
    From my sighing, from my cry
        for help."
57 You drew near on the day I
        called on You,
    And said, "Do not fear!"

58 O Lord, You have pleaded the
        case for my soul;
    You have redeemed my life.
59 O LORD, You have seen *how* I
        am wronged;
    Judge my case.
60 You have seen all their
        vengeance,
    All their schemes against me.

61 You have heard their reproach,
        O LORD,
    All their schemes against me,
62 The lips of my enemies
    And their whispering against
        me all the day.
63 Look at their sitting down and
        their rising up;
    I *am* their taunting song.

64 Repay them, O LORD,
    According to the work of their
        hands.
65 Give them a veiled[a] heart;
    Your curse *be* upon them!
66 In Your anger,
    Pursue and destroy them
    From under the heavens of the
        LORD.

4   How the gold has become dim!
    How changed the fine gold!
    The stones of the sanctuary are
        scattered
    At the head of every street.

2   The precious sons of Zion,
    Valuable as fine gold,
    How they are regarded as clay
        pots,
    The work of the hands of the
        potter!

3   Even the jackals present their
        breasts

To nurse their young;
But the daughter of my people
    is cruel,
Like ostriches in the
    wilderness.

4   The tongue of the infant clings
    To the roof of its mouth for
        thirst;
    The young children ask for
        bread,
    But no one breaks *it* for them.

5   Those who ate delicacies
    Are desolate in the streets;
    Those who were brought up in
        scarlet
    Embrace ash heaps.

6   The punishment of the iniquity
        of the daughter of my people
    Is greater than the punishment
        of the sin of Sodom,
    Which was overthrown in a
        moment,
    With no hand to help her!

7   Her Nazirites[a] were brighter
        than snow
    And whiter than milk;
    They were more ruddy in body
        than rubies,
    Like sapphire in their
        appearance.

8   *Now* their appearance is
        blacker than soot;
    They go unrecognized in the
        streets;
    Their skin clings to their bones,
    It has become as dry as wood.

9   *Those* slain by the sword are
        better off
    Than *those* who die of hunger;
    For these pine away,
    Stricken *for lack* of the fruits
        of the field.

10 The hands of the
        compassionate women
    Have cooked their own
        children;
    They became food for them
    In the destruction of the
        daughter of my people.

11 The LORD has fulfilled His fury,
    He has poured out His fierce
        anger.

3:65 [a]A Jewish tradition reads *sorrow of.*   4:7 [a]Or *nobles*

He kindled a fire in Zion,
And it has devoured its
    foundations.

12 The kings of the earth,
And all inhabitants of the
    world,
Would not have believed
That the adversary and the
    enemy
Could enter the gates of
    Jerusalem—

13 Because of the sins of her
    prophets
And the iniquities of her
    priests,
Who shed in her midst
The blood of the just.

14 They wandered blind in the
    streets;
They have defiled themselves
    with blood,
So that no one would touch
    their garments.

15 They cried out to them,
    "Go away, unclean!
Go away, go away,
    Do not touch us!"
When they fled and wandered,
Those among the nations said,
"They shall no longer dwell
    here."

16 The face[a] of the LORD scattered
    them;
He no longer regards them.
The people do not respect the
    priests
Nor show favor to the elders.

17 Still our eyes failed us,
Watching vainly for our help;
In our watching we watched
For a nation *that* could not
    save *us.*

18 They tracked our steps
So that we could not walk in
    our streets.
Our end was near;
Our days were over,
For our end had come.

19 Our pursuers were swifter
Than the eagles of the heavens.
They pursued us on the
    mountains

And lay in wait for us in the
    wilderness.

20 The breath of our nostrils, the
    anointed of the LORD,
Was caught in their pits,
Of whom we said, "Under his
    shadow
We shall live among the
    nations."

21 Rejoice and be glad, O
    daughter of Edom,
You who dwell in the land of
    Uz!
The cup shall also pass over to
    you
And you shall become drunk
    and make yourself naked.

22 *The punishment of* your
    iniquity is accomplished,
O daughter of Zion;
He will no longer send you into
    captivity.
He will punish your iniquity,
O daughter of Edom;
He will uncover your sins!

5 Remember, O LORD, what has
    come upon us;
Look, and behold our reproach!
2 Our inheritance has been
    turned over to aliens,
And our houses to foreigners.
3 We have become orphans and
    waifs,
Our mothers *are* like widows.

4 We pay for the water we drink,
And our wood comes at a price.
5 *They* pursue at our heels;[a]
We labor *and* have no rest.
6 We have given our hand *to the
    Egyptians
And* the Assyrians, to be
    satisfied with bread.
7 Our fathers sinned *and are* no
    more,
But we bear their iniquities.
8 Servants rule over us;
There is none to deliver *us* from
    their hand.
9 We get our bread *at the risk*
    of our lives,
Because of the sword in the
    wilderness.
10 Our skin is hot as an oven,
Because of the fever of famine.

11　They ravished the women in
　　　Zion,
　　The maidens in the cities of
　　　Judah.
12　Princes were hung up by their
　　　hands,
　　And elders were not respected.
13　Young men ground at the
　　　millstones;
　　Boys staggered under *loads of*
　　　wood.
14　The elders have ceased
　　　gathering at the gate,
　　And the young men from their
　　　music.

15　The joy of our heart has ceased;
　　Our dance has turned into
　　　mourning.
16　The crown has fallen *from* our
　　　head.
　　Woe to us, for we have sinned!

17　Because of this our heart is
　　　faint;
　　Because of these *things* our
　　　eyes grow dim;
18　Because of Mount Zion which
　　　is desolate,
　　With foxes walking about on
　　　it.

19　You, O LORD, remain forever;
　　Your throne from generation to
　　　generation.
20　Why do You forget us
　　　forever,
　　And forsake us for so long a
　　　time?
21　Turn us back to You, O LORD,
　　　and we will be restored;
　　Renew our days as of old,
22　Unless You have utterly
　　　rejected us,
　　And are very angry with us!

Ezekiel

Overview of Ezekiel

A star is best seen at night. This clearly exemplifies Ezekiel's life and presence among his people in an age of war and uncertainty. During stormy times, he stood alone as a beacon to guide and direct those who were failing. Ezekiel was not only a prophet who had many God-given visions, but he had personal vision, fortitude, and the ability to look beyond his present-day circumstances.

Known as "the watchman," Ezekiel probably completed this book by 565 B.C. In a series of prophetic messages, Ezekiel devoted his life to warning of the impending judgment coming upon the nation of Judah. Ezekiel's time was an era of desperation. When surrounding nations were rising in conflict with each other, only those with a strong faith in God would be certain to endure. Ezekiel, whose name means "Strengthened by God," continually and confidently served as a shining light in the nation's darkest hour—the destruction of the temple by Nebuchadnezzar in 586 B.C.

and the subsequent Babylonian captivity. During their captivity, Ezekiel reminded the people that as certain as judgment had come upon them, so would God's comfort and blessings. The prophet believed that failure is never final, but God's love is!

During the captivity, surrounded by negative influences, Ezekiel built up the hopes of the people of returning to their land and rebuilding the temple of God. In the midst of affliction, Ezekiel gave the people God's vision for victory! "I will give you a new heart and put a new spirit within you" (Ezek. 36:26).

Jesus in Ezekiel

The title "Son of Man" occurs some ninety times in Ezekiel. In this book, that title refers to Ezekiel himself, but it was later appropriated by Jesus and He often used it for Himself. In this sense, we may regard Ezekiel as a type of Christ. As such, Ezekiel was empowered as a prophetic voice for the coming Messiah when "the Spirit of the LORD fell" upon him (11:5). We remember Ezekiel when reading Luke's account of the Holy Spirit's falling on Jesus at the Jordan River, empowering Him to begin the messianic age (see Luke 4:18, 19).

Ezekiel 17:22–24 depicts the Messiah as a tender twig that becomes a stately cedar on a lofty mountain, as He is similarly called the Branch in Isaiah (11:1), Jeremiah (23:5; 33:15), and Zechariah (3:8, 6:12). The Messiah is the King who has the right to rule (21:26, 27), and He is the true Shepherd who will deliver and feed His flock (34:11).

Keys to Ezekiel

Key Word: Restoration. Ezekiel's broad purpose is to remind the generation born during the Babylonian exile of the cause of Israel's current destruction, of the coming judgment on the Gentile nations, and of the coming national restoration of Israel. God's glory had earlier departed from Israel, but Ezekiel prophesied that it would return.

Key Verses: "For I will take you from among the nations, gather you out of all countries, and bring you into your own land. Then I will sprinkle clean water on you, and you shall be clean; I will cleanse you from all your filthiness and from all your idols. I will give you a new heart and put a new spirit within you; I will take the heart of stone out of your flesh and give you a heart of flesh" (36:24–26).

Key Chapter: Ezekiel 37. Central to the hope of the restoration of Israel is the vision of the valley of the dry bones. Here we see both God's desire to restore life and His miracle-working power. " 'I will put My Spirit in you, and you shall live, and I will place you in your own land. Then you shall know that I, the LORD, have spoken *it* and performed *it*,' says the LORD" (37:14).

Ezekiel 37 clearly outlines the steps necessary for Israel's future.

1 Now it came to pass in the thirtieth year, in the fourth *month,* on the fifth *day* of the month, as I *was* among the captives by the River Chebar, *that* the heavens were opened and I saw visions[a] of God. 2 On the fifth *day* of the month, which *was* in the fifth year of King Jehoiachin's captivity, 3 the word of the LORD came expressly to Ezekiel the priest, the son of Buzi, in the land of the Chaldeans[a] by the River Chebar; and the hand of the LORD was upon him there.

4 Then I looked, and behold, a whirlwind was coming out of the north, a great cloud with raging fire engulfing itself; and brightness *was* all around it and radiating out of its midst like the color of amber, out of the midst of the fire. 5 Also from within it *came* the likeness of four living creatures. And this *was* their appearance: they had the likeness of a man. 6 Each one had four faces, and each one had four wings. 7 Their legs were straight, and the soles of their feet *were* like the soles of calves' feet. They sparkled like the color of burnished bronze. 8 The hands of a man *were* under their wings on their four sides; and each of the four had faces and wings. 9 Their wings touched one another. *The creatures* did not turn when they went, but each one went straight forward.

10 As for the likeness of their faces, *each* had the face of a man; each of the four had the face of a lion on the right side, each of the four had the face of an ox on the left side, and each of the four had the face of an eagle. 11 Thus *were* their faces. Their wings stretched upward; two *wings* of each one touched one another, and two covered their bodies. 12 And each one went straight forward; they went wherever the spirit wanted to go, and they did not turn when they went.

13 As for the likeness of the living creatures, their appearance *was* like

1:1 [a]Following Masoretic Text, Septuagint, and Vulgate; Syriac and Targum read *a vision.* 1:3 [a]Or *Babylonians,* and so elsewhere in this book burning coals of fire, like the appearance of torches going back and forth among the living creatures. The fire was bright, and out of the fire went lightning. 14 And the living creatures ran back and forth, in appearance like a flash of lightning.

15 Now as I looked at the living creatures, behold, a wheel *was* on the earth beside each living creature with its four faces. 16 The appearance of the wheels and their workings *was* like the color of beryl, and all four had the same likeness. The appearance of their workings *was,* as it were, a wheel in the middle of a wheel. 17 When they moved, they went toward any one of four directions; they did not turn aside when they went. 18 As for their rims, they were so high they were awesome; and their rims *were* full of eyes, all around the four of them. 19 When the living creatures went, the wheels went beside them; and when the living creatures were lifted up from the earth, the wheels were lifted up. 20 Wherever the spirit wanted to go, they went, *because* there the spirit went; and the wheels were lifted together with them, for the spirit of the living creatures*ᵃ was* in the wheels. 21 When those went, *these* went; when those stood, *these* stood; and when those were lifted up from the earth, the wheels were lifted up together with them, for the spirit of the living creatures*ᵃ was* in the wheels.

22 The likeness of the firmament above the heads of the living creatures*ᵃ was* like the color of an awesome crystal, stretched out over their heads. 23 And under the firmament their wings *spread out* straight, one toward another. Each one had two which covered one side, and each one had two which covered the other side of the body. 24 When they went, I heard the noise of their wings, like the noise of many waters, like the voice of the Almighty, a tumult like the noise of an army; and when they stood still, they let down their wings. 25 A voice came from above the firmament that *was* over their heads; whenever they stood, they let down their wings.

26 And above the firmament over their heads *was* the likeness of a throne, in appearance like a sapphire stone; on the likeness of the throne *was* a likeness with the appearance of a man high above it. 27 Also from the appearance of His waist and upward I saw, as it were, the color of amber with the appearance of fire all around within it; and from the appearance of His waist and downward I saw, as it were, the appearance of fire with brightness all around. 28 Like the appearance of a rainbow in a cloud on a rainy day, so *was* the appearance of the brightness all around it. This *was* the appearance of the likeness of the glory of the LORD.

So when I saw *it,* I fell on my face, and I heard a voice of One speaking.

2 And He said to me, "Son of man, stand on your feet, and I will speak to you." 2 Then the Spirit entered me when He spoke to me, and set me on my feet; and I heard Him who spoke to me. 3 And He said to me: "Son of man, I am sending you to the children of Israel, to a rebellious nation that has rebelled against Me; they and their fathers have transgressed against Me to this very day. 4 For *they are* impudent and stubborn children. I am sending you to them, and you shall say to them, 'Thus says the Lord GOD.' 5 As for them, whether they hear or whether they refuse—for they *are* a rebellious house—yet they will know that a prophet has been among them.

6 "And you, son of man, do not be afraid of them nor be afraid of their words, though briers and thorns *are* with you and you dwell among scorpions; do not be afraid of their words or dismayed by their looks, though they *are* a rebellious house. 7 You shall speak My words to them, whether they hear or whether they refuse, for they *are* rebellious. 8 But you, son of man, hear what I say to you. Do not be rebellious like that rebellious house; open your mouth and eat what I give you."

9 Now when I looked, there was a hand stretched out to me; and behold, a scroll of a book *was* in it. 10 Then He spread it before me; and *there was* writing on the inside and on the outside, and written on it

1:20 ᵃLiterally *living creature;* Septuagint and Vulgate read *spirit of life;* Targum reads *creatures.*
1:21 ᵃLiterally *living creature;* Septuagint and Vulgate read *spirit of life;* Targum reads *creatures.*
1:22 ᵃFollowing Septuagint, Targum, and Vulgate; Masoretic Text reads *living creature.*

were lamentations and mourning and woe.

3 Moreover He said to me, "Son of man, eat what you find; eat this scroll, and go, speak to the house of Israel." 2 So I opened my mouth, and He caused me to eat that scroll.

3 And He said to me, "Son of man, feed your belly, and fill your stomach with this scroll that I give you." So I ate, and it was in my mouth like honey in sweetness.

4 Then He said to me: "Son of man, go to the house of Israel and speak with My words to them. 5 For you *are* not sent to a people of unfamiliar speech and of hard language, *but* to the house of Israel, 6 not to many people of unfamiliar speech and of hard language, whose words you cannot understand. Surely, had I sent you to them, they would have listened to you. 7 But the house of Israel will not listen to you, because they will not listen to Me; for all the house of Israel *are* impudent and hardhearted. 8 Behold, I have made your face strong against their faces, and your forehead strong against their foreheads. 9 Like adamant stone, harder than flint, I have made your forehead; do not be afraid of them, nor be dismayed at their looks, though they *are* a rebellious house."

10 Moreover He said to me: "Son of man, receive into your heart all My words that I speak to you, and hear with your ears. 11 And go, get to the captives, to the children of your people, and speak to them and tell them, 'Thus says the Lord GOD,' whether they hear, or whether they refuse."

12 Then the Spirit lifted me up, and I heard behind me a great thunderous voice: "Blessed *is* the glory of the LORD from His place!" 13 I also *heard* the noise of the wings of the living creatures that touched one another, and the noise of the wheels beside them, and a great thunderous noise. 14 So the Spirit lifted me up and took me away, and I went in bitterness, in the heat of my spirit; but the hand of the LORD was strong upon me. 15 Then I came to the captives at Tel Abib, who dwelt by the River Chebar; and I sat where they sat, and remained there astonished among them seven days.

16 Now it came to pass at the end of seven days that the word of the LORD came to me, saying, 17 "Son of man, I have made you a watchman for the house of Israel; therefore hear a word from My mouth, and give them warning from Me: 18 When I say to the wicked, 'You shall surely die,' and you give him no warning, nor speak to warn the wicked from his wicked way, to save his life, that same wicked *man* shall die in his iniquity; but his blood I will require at your hand. 19 Yet, if you warn the wicked, and he does not turn from his wickedness, nor from his wicked way, he shall die in his iniquity; but you have delivered your soul.

20 "Again, when a righteous *man* turns from his righteousness and commits iniquity, and I lay a stumbling block before him, he shall die; because you did not give him warning, he shall die in his sin, and his righteousness which he has done shall not be remembered; but his blood I will require at your hand. 21 Nevertheless if you warn the righteous *man* that the righteous should not sin, and he does not sin, he shall surely live because he took warning; also you will have delivered your soul."

22 Then the hand of the LORD was upon me there, and He said to me, "Arise, go out into the plain, and there I shall talk with you."

23 So I arose and went out into the plain, and behold, the glory of the LORD stood there, like the glory which I saw by the River Chebar; and I fell on my face. 24 Then the Spirit entered me and set me on my feet, and spoke with me and said to me: "Go, shut yourself inside your house. 25 And you, O son of man, surely they will put ropes on you and bind you with them, so that you cannot go out among them. 26 I will make your tongue cling to the roof of your mouth, so that you shall be mute and not be one to rebuke them, for they *are* a rebellious house. 27 But when I speak with you, I will open your mouth, and you shall say to them, 'Thus says the Lord GOD.' He who hears, let him hear; and he who refuses, let him refuse; for they *are* a rebellious house.

4 "You also, son of man, take a clay tablet and lay it before you, and portray on it a city, Jerusalem. 2 Lay siege against it, build a siege

wall against it, and heap up a mound against it; set camps against it also, and place battering rams against it all around. 3 Moreover take for yourself an iron plate, and set it *as* an iron wall between you and the city. Set your face against it, and it shall be besieged, and you shall lay siege against it. This *will be* a sign to the house of Israel.

4 "Lie also on your left side, and lay the iniquity of the house of Israel upon it. *According* to the number of the days that you lie on it, you shall bear their iniquity. 5 For I have laid on you the years of their iniquity, according to the number of the days, three hundred and ninety days; so you shall bear the iniquity of the house of Israel. 6 And when you have completed them, lie again on your right side; then you shall bear the iniquity of the house of Judah forty days. I have laid on you a day for each year.

7 "Therefore you shall set your face toward the siege of Jerusalem; your arm *shall be* uncovered, and you shall prophesy against it. 8 And surely I will restrain you so that you cannot turn from one side to another till you have ended the days of your siege.

9 "Also take for yourself wheat, barley, beans, lentils, millet, and spelt; put them into one vessel, and make bread of them for yourself. *During* the number of days that you lie on your side, three hundred and ninety days, you shall eat it. 10 And your food which you eat *shall be* by weight, twenty shekels a day; from time to time you shall eat it. 11 You shall also drink water by measure, one-sixth of a hin; from time to time you shall drink. 12 And you shall eat it *as* barley cakes; and bake it using fuel of human waste in their sight."

13 Then the LORD said, "So shall the children of Israel eat their defiled bread among the Gentiles, where I will drive them."

14 So I said, "Ah, Lord GOD! In deed I have never defiled myself from my youth till now; I have never eaten what died of itself or was torn by beasts, nor has abominable flesh ever come into my mouth."

15 Then He said to me, "See, I am giving you cow dung instead of human waste, and you shall prepare your bread over it."

16 Moreover He said to me, "Son of man, surely I will cut off the supply of bread in Jerusalem; they shall eat bread by weight and with anxiety, and shall drink water by measure and with dread, 17 that they may lack bread and water, and be dismayed with one another, and waste away because of their iniquity.

5 "And you, son of man, take a sharp sword, take it as a barber's razor, and pass *it* over your head and your beard; then take scales to weigh and divide the hair. 2 You shall burn with fire one-third in the midst of the city, when the days of the siege are finished; then you shall take one-third and strike around *it* with the sword, and one-third you shall scatter in the wind: I will draw out a sword after them. 3 You shall also take a small number of them and bind them in the edge of your *garment*. 4 Then take some of them again and throw them into the midst of the fire, and burn them in the fire. From there a fire will go out into all the house of Israel.

5 "Thus says the Lord GOD: 'This *is* Jerusalem; I have set her in the midst of the nations and the countries all around her. 6 She has rebelled against My judgments by doing wickedness more than the nations, and against My statutes more than the countries that *are* all around her; for they have refused My judgments, and they have not walked in My statutes.' 7 Therefore thus says the Lord GOD: 'Because you have multiplied *disobedience* more than the nations that *are* all around you, have not walked in My statutes nor kept My judgments, nor even done[a] according to the judgments of the nations that *are* all around you'— 8 therefore thus says the Lord GOD: 'Indeed I, even I, *am* against you and will execute judgments in your midst in the sight of the nations. 9 And I will do among you what I have never done, and the like of which I will never do again, because of all your abominations. 10 Therefore fathers

5:7 [a]Following Masoretic Text, Septuagint, Targum, and Vulgate; many Hebrew manuscripts and Syriac read *but have done* (compare 11:12).

shall eat *their* sons in your midst, and sons shall eat their fathers; and I will execute judgments among you, and all of you who remain I will scatter to all the winds.

11 'Therefore, *as* I live,' says the Lord God, 'surely, because you have defiled My sanctuary with all your detestable things and with all your abominations, therefore I will also diminish *you;* My eye will not spare, nor will I have any pity. 12 One-third of you shall die of the pestilence, and be consumed with famine in your midst; and one-third shall fall by the sword all around you; and I will scatter another third to all the winds, and I will draw out a sword after them. 13 'Thus shall My anger be spent, and I will cause My fury to rest upon them, and I will be avenged; and they shall know that I, the Lord, have spoken *it* in My zeal, when I have spent My fury upon them. 14 Moreover I will make you a waste and a reproach among the nations that *are* all around you, in the sight of all who pass by.

15 'So it*a* shall be a reproach, a taunt, a lesson, and an astonishment to the nations that *are* all around you, when I execute judgments among you in anger and in fury and in furious rebukes. I, the Lord, have spoken. 16 When I send against them the terrible arrows of famine which shall be for destruction, which I will send to destroy you, I will increase the famine upon you and cut off your supply of bread. 17 So I will send against you famine and wild beasts, and they will bereave you. Pestilence and blood shall pass through you, and I will bring the sword against you. I, the Lord, have spoken.' "

6 Now the word of the Lord came to me, saying: 2 "Son of man, set your face toward the mountains of Israel, and prophesy against them, 3 and say, 'O mountains of Israel, hear the word of the Lord God! Thus says the Lord God to the mountains, to the hills, to the ravines, and to the valleys: "Indeed I, *even* I, will bring a sword against you, and I will destroy your high places. 4 Then your altars shall be desolate, your incense altars shall be broken, and I will cast down your slain *men* before your idols. 5 And I will lay the corpses of the children of Israel before their idols, and I will scatter your bones all around your altars. 6 In all your dwelling places the cities shall be laid waste, and the high places shall be desolate, so that your altars may be laid waste and made desolate, your idols may be broken and made to cease, your incense altars may be cut down, and your works may be abolished. 7 The slain shall fall in your midst, and you shall know that I *am* the Lord.

8 "Yet I will leave a remnant, so that you may have *some* who escape the sword among the nations, when you are scattered through the countries. 9 Then those of you who escape will remember Me among the nations where they are carried captive, because I was crushed by their adulterous heart which has departed from Me, and by their eyes which play the harlot after their idols; they will loathe themselves for the evils which they committed in all their abominations. 10 And they shall know that I *am* the Lord; I have not said in vain that I would bring this calamity upon them."

11 'Thus says the Lord God: "Pound your fists and stamp your feet, and say, 'Alas, for all the evil abominations of the house of Israel! For they shall fall by the sword, by famine, and by pestilence. 12 He who is far off shall die by the pestilence, he who is near shall fall by the sword, and he who remains and is besieged shall die by the famine. Thus will I spend My fury upon them. 13 Then you shall know that I *am* the Lord, when their slain are among their idols all around their altars, on every high hill, on all the mountaintops, under every green tree, and under every thick oak, wherever they offered sweet incense to all their idols. 14 So I will stretch out My hand against them and make the land desolate, yes, more desolate than the wilderness toward Diblah, in all their dwelling places. Then they shall know that I *am* the Lord.' " '"

7 Moreover the word of the Lord came to me, saying, 2 "And you, son of man, thus says the Lord God to the land of Israel:

5:15 *a*Septuagint, Syriac, Targum, and Vulgate read *you.*

'An end! The end has come
upon the four corners of the
land.
3 Now the end *has come* upon
you,
And I will send My anger
against you;
I will judge you according to
your ways,
And I will repay you for all
your abominations.
4 My eye will not spare you,
Nor will I have pity;
But I will repay your ways,
And your abominations will be
in your midst;
Then you shall know that I *am*
the LORD!'

5 "Thus says the Lord GOD:

'A disaster, a singular disaster;
Behold, it has come!
6 An end has come,
The end has come;
It has dawned for you;
Behold, it has come!
7 Doom has come to you, you
who dwell in the land;
The time has come,
A day of trouble *is* near,
And not of rejoicing in the
mountains.
8 Now upon you I will soon pour
out My fury,
And spend My anger upon you;
I will judge you according to
your ways,
And I will repay you for all
your abominations.
9 'My eye will not spare,
Nor will I have pity;
I will repay you according to
your ways,
And your abominations will be
in your midst.
Then you shall know that I *am*
the LORD who strikes.

10 'Behold, the day!
Behold, it has come!
Doom has gone out;
The rod has blossomed,
Pride has budded.
11 Violence has risen up into a rod
of wickedness;
None of them *shall remain,*
None of their multitude,
None of them;
Nor *shall there be* wailing for
them.

12 The time has come,
The day draws near.

'Let not the buyer rejoice,
Nor the seller mourn,
For wrath *is* on their whole
multitude.
13 For the seller shall not return
to what has been sold,
Though he may still be alive;
For the vision concerns the
whole multitude,
And it shall not turn back;
No one will strengthen himself
Who lives in iniquity.

14 'They have blown the trumpet
and made everyone ready,
But no one goes to battle;
For My wrath *is* on all their
multitude.
15 The sword *is* outside,
And the pestilence and famine
within.
Whoever *is* in the field
Will die by the sword;
And whoever *is* in the city,
Famine and pestilence will
devour him.

16 'Those who survive will escape
and be on the mountains
Like doves of the valleys,
All of them mourning,
Each for his iniquity.
17 Every hand will be feeble,
And every knee will be *as* weak
as water.
18 They will also be girded with
sackcloth;
Horror will cover them;
Shame *will be* on every face,
Baldness on all their heads.

19 'They will throw their silver into
the streets,
And their gold will be like
refuse;
Their silver and their gold will
not be able to deliver them
In the day of the wrath of the
LORD;
They will not satisfy their
souls,
Nor fill their stomachs,
Because it became their
stumbling block of iniquity.

20 'As for the beauty of his
ornaments,
He set it in majesty;
But they made from it

The images of their
  abominations—
Their detestable things;
Therefore I have made it
Like refuse to them.
21 I will give it as plunder
  Into the hands of strangers,
  And to the wicked of the earth
    as spoil;
  And they shall defile it.
22 I will turn My face from them,
  And they will defile My secret
    place;
  For robbers shall enter it and
    defile it.

23 'Make a chain,
  For the land is filled with
    crimes of blood,
  And the city is full of violence.
24 Therefore I will bring the worst
    of the Gentiles,
  And they will possess their
    houses;
  I will cause the pomp of the
    strong to cease,
  And their holy places shall be
    defiled.
25 Destruction comes;
  They will seek peace, but *there
    shall be* none.
26 Disaster will come upon
    disaster,
  And rumor will be upon rumor.
  Then they will seek a vision
    from a prophet;
  But the law will perish from the
    priest,
  And counsel from the elders.

27 'The king will mourn,
  The prince will be clothed with
    desolation,
  And the hands of the common
    people will tremble.
  I will do to them according to
    their way,
  And according to what they
    deserve I will judge them;
  Then they shall know that I *am*
    the LORD!' "

8 And it came to pass in the sixth
  year, in the sixth *month,* on the
fifth *day* of the month, as I sat in my
house with the elders of Judah sitting
before me, that the hand of the Lord
GOD fell upon me there. 2 Then I
looked, and there was a likeness, like
the appearance of fire—from the appearance of His waist and downward, fire; and from His waist and

upward, like the appearance of
brightness, like the color of amber.
3 He stretched out the form of a hand,
and took me by a lock of my hair;
and the Spirit lifted me up between
earth and heaven, and brought me
in visions of God to Jerusalem, to the
door of the north gate of the inner
court, where the seat of the image
of jealousy *was,* which provokes to
jealousy. 4 And behold, the glory of
the God of Israel *was* there, like the
vision that I saw in the plain.

5 Then He said to me, "Son of man,
lift your eyes now toward the north."
So I lifted my eyes toward the north,
and there, north of the altar gate, was
this image of jealousy in the entrance.

6 Furthermore He said to me, "Son
of man, do you see what they are doing, the great abominations that the
house of Israel commits here, to
make Me go far away from My sanctuary? Now turn again, you will see
greater abominations." 7 So He
brought me to the door of the court;
and when I looked, there was a hole
in the wall. 8 Then He said to me,
"Son of man, dig into the wall"; and
when I dug into the wall, there was
a door.

9 And He said to me, "Go in, and
see the wicked abominations which
they are doing there." 10 So I went
in and saw, and there—every sort of
creeping thing, abominable beasts,
and all the idols of the house of Israel, portrayed all around on the
walls. 11 And there stood before them
seventy men of the elders of the
house of Israel, and in their midst
stood Jaazaniah the son of Shaphan.
Each man had a censer in his hand,
and a thick cloud of incense went up.
12 Then He said to me, "Son of man,
have you seen what the elders of the
house of Israel do in the dark, every
man in the room of his idols? For they
say, 'The LORD does not see us, the
LORD has forsaken the land.' "
13 And He said to me, "Turn again,
and you will see greater abominations that they are doing." 14 So He
brought me to the door of the north
gate of the LORD's house; and to my
dismay, women were sitting there
weeping for Tammuz.
15 Then He said to me, "Have you
seen *this,* O son of man? Turn again,
you will see greater abominations
than these." 16 So He brought me into

the inner court of the LORD's house; and there, at the door of the temple of the LORD, between the porch and the altar, *were* about twenty-five men with their backs toward the temple of the LORD and their faces toward the east, and they were worshiping the sun toward the east.

17 And He said to me, "Have you seen *this,* O son of man? Is it a trivial thing to the house of Judah to commit the abominations which they commit here? For they have filled the land with violence; then they have returned to provoke Me to anger. Indeed they put the branch to their nose. 18 Therefore I also will act in fury. My eye will not spare nor will I have pity; and though they cry in My ears with a loud voice, I will not hear them."

9 Then He called out in my hearing with a loud voice, saying, "Let those who have charge over the city draw near, each *with* a deadly weapon in his hand." 2 And suddenly six men came from the direction of the upper gate, which faces north, each with his battle-ax in his hand. One man among them *was* clothed with linen and had a writer's inkhorn at his side. They went in and stood beside the bronze altar.

3 Now the glory of the God of Israel had gone up from the cherub, where it had been, to the threshold of the temple.*a* And He called to the man clothed with linen, who *had* the writer's inkhorn at his side; 4 and the LORD said to him, "Go through the midst of the city, through the midst of Jerusalem, and put a mark on the foreheads of the men who sigh and cry over all the abominations that are done within it."

5 To the others He said in my hearing, "Go after him through the city and kill; do not let your eye spare, nor have any pity. 6 Utterly slay old *and* young men, maidens and little children and women; but do not come near anyone on whom *is* the mark; and begin at My sanctuary." So they began with the elders who *were* before the temple. 7 Then He said to them, "Defile the temple, and fill the courts with the slain. Go out!" And they went out and killed in the city.

8 So it was, that while they were killing them, I was left *alone;* and I fell on my face and cried out, and said, "Ah, Lord GOD! Will You destroy all the remnant of Israel in pouring out Your fury on Jerusalem?"

9 Then He said to me, "The iniquity of the house of Israel and Judah *is* exceedingly great, and the land is full of bloodshed, and the city full of perversity; for they say, 'The LORD has forsaken the land, and the LORD does not see!' 10 And as for Me also, My eye will neither spare, nor will I have pity, *but* I will recompense their deeds on their own head."

11 Just then, the man clothed with linen, who *had* the inkhorn at his side, reported back and said, "I have done as You commanded me."

10 And I looked, and there in the firmament that was above the head of the cherubim, there appeared something like a sapphire stone, having the appearance of the likeness of a throne. 2 Then He spoke to the man clothed with linen, and said, "Go in among the wheels, under the cherub, fill your hands with coals of fire from among the cherubim, and scatter *them* over the city." And he went in as I watched.

3 Now the cherubim were standing on the south side of the temple*a* when the man went in, and the cloud filled the inner court. 4 Then the glory of the LORD went up from the cherub, *and paused* over the threshold of the temple; and the house was filled with the cloud, and the court was full of the brightness of the LORD's glory. 5 And the sound of the wings of the cherubim was heard *even* in the outer court, like the voice of Almighty God when He speaks.

6 Then it happened, when He commanded the man clothed in linen, saying, "Take fire from among the wheels, from among the cherubim," that he went in and stood beside the wheels. 7 And the cherub stretched out his hand from among the cherubim to the fire that *was* among cherubim, and took *some of it* and put *it* into the hands of the *man* clothed with linen, who took *it* and went out. 8 The cherubim appeared

9:3 *a*Literally *house*   10:3 *a*Literally *house,* also in verses 4 and 18 to have the form of a man's hand under their wings.

9 And when I looked, there were four wheels by the cherubim, one wheel by one cherub and another wheel by each other cherub; the wheels appeared *to have* the color of a beryl stone. 10 As for their appearance, all four looked alike—as it were, a wheel in the middle of a wheel. 11 When they went, they went toward *any of* their four directions; they did not turn aside when they went, but followed in the direction the head was facing. They did not turn aside when they went. 12 And their whole body, with their back, their hands, their wings, and the wheels that the four had, *were* full of eyes all around. 13 As for the wheels, they were called in my hearing, "Wheel."

14 Each one had four faces: the first face *was* the face of a cherub, the second face the face of a man, the third the face of a lion, and the fourth the face of an eagle. 15 And the cherubim were lifted up. This *was* the living creature I saw by the River Chebar. 16 When the cherubim went, the wheels went beside them; and when the cherubim lifted their wings to mount up from the earth, the same wheels also did not turn from beside them. 17 When *the cherubim*[a] stood still, *the wheels* stood still, and when one[b] was lifted up, *the other*[c] lifted itself up, for the spirit of the living creature *was* in them.

18 Then the glory of the LORD departed from the threshold of the temple and stood over the cherubim. 19 And the cherubim lifted their wings and mounted up from the earth in my sight. When they went out, the wheels *were* beside them; and they stood at the door of the east gate of the LORD's house, and the glory of the God of Israel *was* above them.

20 This *is* the living creature I saw under the God of Israel by the River Chebar, and I knew they *were* cherubim. 21 Each one had four faces and each one four wings, and the likeness of the hands of a man *was* under their wings. 22 And the likeness of their faces *was* the same *as* the faces which I had seen by the River Chebar, their appearance and their

persons. They each went straight forward.

11 Then the Spirit lifted me up and brought me to the East Gate of the LORD's house, which faces eastward; and there at the door of the gate were twenty-five men, among whom I saw Jaazaniah the son of Azzur, and Pelatiah the son of Benaiah, princes of the people. 2 And He said to me: "Son of man, these *are* the men who devise iniquity and give wicked counsel in this city, 3 who say, '*The time is* not near to build houses; this *city is* the caldron, and we *are* the meat.' 4 Therefore prophesy against them, prophesy, O son of man!"

5 Then the Spirit of the LORD fell upon me, and said to me, "Speak! 'Thus says the LORD: "Thus you have said, O house of Israel; for I know the things that come into your mind. 6 You have multiplied your slain in this city, and you have filled its streets with the slain." 7 Therefore thus says the Lord GOD: "Your slain whom you have laid in its midst, they *are* the meat, and this *city is* the caldron; but I shall bring you out of the midst of it. 8 You have feared the sword; and I will bring a sword upon you," says the Lord GOD. 9 "And I will bring you out of its midst, and deliver you into the hands of strangers, and execute judgments on you. 10 You shall fall by the sword. I will judge you at the border of Israel. Then you shall know that I *am* the LORD. 11 This *city* shall not be your caldron, nor shall you be the meat in its midst. I will judge you at the border of Israel. 12 And you shall know that I *am* the LORD; for you have not walked in My statutes nor executed My judgments, but have done according to the customs of the Gentiles which *are* all around you.'"'

13 Now it happened, while I was prophesying, that Pelatiah the son of Benaiah died. Then I fell on my face and cried with a loud voice, and said, "Ah, Lord GOD! Will You make a complete end of the remnant of Israel?"

14 Again the word of the LORD came to me, saying, 15 "Son of man, your brethren, your relatives, your

10:17 *a*Literally *they*   *b*Literally *they*   *c*Literally *they* countrymen, and all the house of Israel in its entirety, *are* those about whom the inhabitants of Jerusalem have said, 'Get far away from the Lord; this land has been given to us as a possession.' 16 Therefore say, 'Thus says the Lord God: "Although I have cast them far off among the Gentiles, and although I have scattered them among the countries, yet I shall be a little sanctuary for them in the countries where they have gone." ' 17 Therefore say, 'Thus says the Lord God: "I will gather you from the peoples, assemble you from the countries where you have been scattered, and I will give you the land of Israel." ' 18 And they will go there, and they will take away all its detestable things and all its abominations from there. 19 Then I will give them one heart, and I will put a new spirit within them,*a* and take the stony heart out of their flesh, and give them a heart of flesh, 20 that they may walk in My statutes and keep My judgments and do them; and they shall be My people, and I will be their God. 21 But *as for those* whose hearts follow the desire for their detestable things and their abominations, I will recompense their deeds on their own heads," says the Lord God.

22 So the cherubim lifted up their wings, with the wheels beside them, and the glory of the God of Israel *was* high above them. 23 And the glory of the Lord went up from the midst of the city and stood on the mountain, which *is* on the east side of the city.

24 Then the Spirit took me up and brought me in a vision by the Spirit of God into Chaldea,*a* to those in captivity. And the vision that I had seen went up from me. 25 So I spoke to those in captivity of all the things the Lord had shown me.

12 Now the word of the Lord came to me, saying: 2 "Son of man, you dwell in the midst of a rebellious house, which has eyes to see but does not see, and ears to hear but does not hear; for they *are* a rebellious house. 3 "Therefore, son of man, prepare your belongings for captivity, and go into captivity by day in their sight. You shall go from your place into captivity to another place in their sight. It may be that they will consider, though they *are* a rebellious house. 4 By day you shall bring out your belongings in their sight, as though going into captivity; and at evening you shall go in their sight, like those who go into captivity. 5 Dig through the wall in their sight, and carry your belongings out through it. 6 In their sight you shall bear *them* on *your* shoulders *and* carry *them* out at twilight; you shall cover your face, so that you cannot see the ground, for I have made you a sign to the house of Israel."

7 So I did as I was commanded. I brought out my belongings by day, as though going into captivity, and at evening I dug through the wall with my hand. I brought *them* out at twilight, *and* I bore *them* on *my* shoulder in their sight.

8 And in the morning the word of the Lord came to me, saying, 9 "Son of man, has not the house of Israel, the rebellious house, said to you, 'What are you doing?' 10 Say to them, 'Thus says the Lord God: "This burden *concerns* the prince in Jerusalem and all the house of Israel who are among them." ' 11 Say, 'I *am* a sign to you. As I have done, so shall it be done to them; they shall be carried away into captivity.' 12 And the prince who *is* among them shall bear *his belongings* on *his* shoulder at twilight and go out. They shall dig through the wall to carry *them* out through it. He shall cover his face, so that he cannot see the ground with *his* eyes. 13 I will also spread My net over him, and he shall be caught in My snare. I will bring him to Babylon, *to* the land of the Chaldeans; yet he shall not see it, though he shall die there. 14 I will scatter to every wind all who *are* around him to help him, and all his troops; and I will draw out the sword after them.

15 "Then they shall know that I *am* the Lord, when I scatter them among the nations and disperse them throughout the countries. 16 But I will spare a few of their men from the sword, from famine, and from pestilence, that they may declare all their abominations among the Gentiles wherever they go. Then they shall know that I *am* the Lord."

11:19 *a*Literally *you*   11:24 *a*Or *Babylon,* and so elsewhere in this book

17 Moreover the word of the LORD came to me, saying, 18 "Son of man, eat your bread with quaking, and drink your water with trembling and anxiety. 19 And say to the people of the land, 'Thus says the Lord GOD to the inhabitants of Jerusalem *and* to the land of Israel: "They shall eat their bread with anxiety, and drink their water with dread, so that her land may be emptied of all who are in it, because of the violence of all those who dwell in it. 20 Then the cities that are inhabited shall be laid waste, and the land shall become desolate; and you shall know that I *am* the LORD." ' "

21 And the word of the LORD came to me, saying, 22 "Son of man, what *is* this proverb *that* you *people* have about the land of Israel, which says, 'The days are prolonged, and every vision fails'? 23 Tell them therefore, 'Thus says the Lord GOD: "I will lay this proverb to rest, and they shall no more use it as a proverb in Israel." But say to them, "The days are at hand, and the fulfillment of every vision. 24 For no more shall there be any false vision or flattering divination within the house of Israel. 25 For I *am* the LORD. I speak, and the word which I speak will come to pass; it will no more be postponed; for in your days, O rebellious house, I will say the word and perform it," says the Lord GOD.' "

26 Again the word of the LORD came to me, saying, 27 "Son of man, look, the house of Israel is saying, 'The vision that he sees *is* for many days *from now*, and he prophesies of times far off.' 28 Therefore say to them, 'Thus says the Lord GOD: "None of My words will be postponed any more, but the word which I speak will be done," says the Lord GOD.' "

13
And the word of the LORD came to me, saying, 2 "Son of man, prophesy against the prophets of Israel who prophesy, and say to those who prophesy out of their own heart, 'Hear the word of the LORD!' "

3 Thus says the Lord GOD: "Woe to the foolish prophets, who follow their own spirit and have seen nothing! 4 O Israel, your prophets are like foxes in the deserts. 5 You have not gone up into the gaps to build a wall for the house of Israel to stand in bat-

tle on the day of the LORD. 6 They have envisioned futility and false divination, saying, 'Thus says the LORD!' But the LORD has not sent them; yet they hope that the word may be confirmed. 7 Have you not seen a futile vision, and have you not spoken false divination? You say, 'The LORD says,' but I have not spoken."

8 Therefore thus says the Lord GOD: "Because you have spoken nonsense and envisioned lies, therefore I *am* indeed against you," says the Lord GOD. 9 "My hand will be against the prophets who envision futility and who divine lies; they shall not be in the assembly of My people, nor be written in the record of the house of Israel, nor shall they enter into the land of Israel. Then you shall know that I *am* the Lord GOD.

10 "Because, indeed, because they have seduced My people, saying, 'Peace!' when *there is* no peace—and one builds a wall, and they plaster it with untempered *mortar*— 11 say to those who plaster *it* with untempered *mortar,* that it will fall. There will be flooding rain, and you, O great hailstones, shall fall; and a stormy wind shall tear *it* down. 12 Surely, when the wall has fallen, will it not be said to you, 'Where *is* the mortar with which you plastered *it?*' "

13 Therefore thus says the Lord GOD: "I will cause a stormy wind to break forth in My fury; and there shall be a flooding rain in My anger, and great hailstones in fury to consume *it.* 14 So I will break down the wall you have plastered with untempered *mortar,* and bring it down to the ground, so that its foundation will be uncovered; it will fall, and you shall be consumed in the midst of it. Then you shall know that I *am* the LORD.

15 "Thus will I accomplish My wrath on the wall and on those who have plastered it with untempered *mortar;* and I will say to you, 'The wall *is* no *more,* nor those who plastered it, 16 *that is,* the prophets of Israel who prophesy concerning Jerusalem, and who see visions of peace for her when *there is* no peace,' " says the Lord GOD.

17 "Likewise, son of man, set your face against the daughters of your people, who prophesy out of their own heart; prophesy against them,

18 and say, 'Thus says the Lord God: "Woe to the *women* who sew *magic charms* on their sleevesᵃ and make veils for the heads of people of every height to hunt souls! Will you hunt the souls of My people, and keep yourselves alive? 19 And will you profane Me among My people for handfuls of barley and for pieces of bread, killing people who should not die, and keeping people alive who should not live, by your lying to My people who listen to lies?"

20 'Therefore thus says the Lord God: "Behold, I *am* against your *magic* charms by which you hunt souls there like birds. I will tear them from your arms, and let the souls go, the souls you hunt like birds. 21 I will also tear off your veils and deliver My people out of your hand, and they shall no longer be as prey in your hand. Then you shall know that I *am* the Lord. 22 "Because with lies you have made the heart of the righteous sad, whom I have not made sad; and you have strengthened the hands of the wicked, so that he does not turn from his wicked way to save his life. 23 Therefore you shall no longer envision futility nor practice divination; for I will deliver My people out of your hand, and you shall know that I *am* the Lord." ' "

14 Now some of the elders of Israel came to me and sat before me. 2 And the word of the Lord came to me, saying, 3 "Son of man, these men have set up their idols in their hearts, and put before them that which causes them to stumble into iniquity. Should I let Myself be inquired of at all by them?

4 "Therefore speak to them, and say to them, 'Thus says the Lord God: "Everyone of the house of Israel who sets up his idols in his heart, and puts before him what causes him to stumble into iniquity, and then comes to the prophet, I the Lord will answer him who comes, according to the multitude of his idols, 5 that I may seize the house of Israel by their heart, because they are all estranged from Me by their idols." '

6 "Therefore say to the house of Israel, 'Thus says the Lord God: "Re-

pent, turn away from your idols, and turn your faces away from all your abominations. 7 For anyone of the house of Israel, or of the strangers who dwell in Israel, who separates himself from Me and sets up his idols in his heart and puts before him what causes him to stumble into iniquity, then comes to a prophet to inquire of him concerning Me, I the Lord will answer him by Myself. 8 I will set My face against that man and make him a sign and a proverb, and I will cut him off from the midst of My people. Then you shall know that I *am* the Lord.

9 "And if the prophet is induced to speak anything, I the Lord have induced that prophet, and I will stretch out My hand against him and destroy him from among My people Israel. 10 And they shall bear their iniquity; the punishment of the prophet shall be the same as the punishment of the one who inquired, 11 that the house of Israel may no longer stray from Me, nor be profaned anymore with all their transgressions, but that they may be My people and I may be their God," says the Lord God.' "

12 The word of the Lord came again to me, saying: 13 "Son of man, when a land sins against Me by persistent unfaithfulness, I will stretch out My hand against it; I will cut off its supply of bread, send famine on it, and cut off man and beast from it. 14 Even *if* these three men, Noah, Daniel, and Job, were in it, they would deliver *only* themselves by their righteousness," says the Lord God.

15 "If I cause wild beasts to pass through the land, and they empty it, and make it so desolate that no man may pass through because of the beasts, 16 *even though* these three men *were* in it, *as* I live," says the Lord God, "they would deliver neither sons nor daughters; only they would be delivered, and the land would be desolate.

17 "Or *if* I bring a sword on that land, and say, 'Sword, go through the land,' and I cut off man and beast from it, 18 even *though* these three men *were* in it, *as* I live," says the Lord God, "they would deliver neither sons nor daughters, but only

13:18 ᵃLiterally *over all the joints of My hands;* Vulgate reads *under every elbow;* Septuagint and Targum read *on all elbows of the hands.*

Many Logs Burn
Brightly Together

In the Sinai wilderness and southland of Palestine, the Bedouin and his tribe roam the desert land as nomads. The Bedouin depends completely on the resources of the land to meet his needs.

Wood is a scarce and precious commodity in the desert. The Bedouin gathers kindling and branches whenever he has the chance. He will never let the smallest twig pass by, for he never knows when he will find more fuel for his fire. He is most happy when he finds a log from an old acacia tree or trades with another tribe for one.

In the winter months, the desert can be extremely cold. This is when the Bedouin unloads his camels and brings out the largest logs and kindling he has gathered. In careful arrangement, he stacks the kindling together and starts his fire; then when the flames are hot, he adds the logs. He never allows one log to burn alone, for he knows that the fire will not last. Many logs burn brightly together, but take one away and it will not burn long.

Like scarce large pieces of wood in the desert, dreams that come into our minds must be gathered. No dream can be passed by, for you never know when another will come along. When God gives you a dream, grab it, save it and use it! Throw it on the kindling of your time, talents, energies, and education so that they will burn brightly together. We must always hold in our imagination new objectives, greater goals, and loftier dreams. Then when the time is right, throw them on the fire!

they themselves would be delivered. 19 "Or *if* I send a pestilence into that land and pour out My fury on it in blood, and cut off from it man and beast, 20 even *though* Noah, Daniel, and Job *were* in it, *as* I live," says the Lord GOD, "they would deliver neither son nor daughter; they would deliver *only* themselves by their righteousness."

21 For thus says the Lord GOD: "How much more it shall be when I send My four severe judgments on Jerusalem—the sword and famine and wild beasts and pestilence—to cut off man and beast from it? 22 Yet behold, there shall be left in it a remnant who will be brought out, *both* sons and daughters; surely they will come out to you, and you will see their ways and their doings. Then you will be comforted concerning the disaster that I have brought upon Jerusalem, all that I have brought upon it. 23 And they will comfort you, when you see their ways and their doings; and you shall know that I have done nothing without cause that I have done in it," says the Lord GOD.

15 Then the word of the LORD came to me, saying: 2 "Son of man, how is the wood of the vine *better* than any other wood, the vine branch which is among the trees of the forest? 3 Is wood taken from it to make any object? Or can *men* make a peg from it to hang any vessel on? 4 Instead, it is thrown into the fire for fuel; the fire devours both ends of it, and its middle is burned. Is it useful for *any* work? 5 Indeed, when it was whole, no object could be made from it. How much less will it be useful for *any* work when the fire has devoured it, and it is burned?

6 "Therefore thus says the Lord GOD: 'Like the wood of the vine among the trees of the forest, which I have given to the fire for fuel, so I will give up the inhabitants of Jerusalem; 7 and I will set My face against them. They will go out from *one* fire, but *another* fire shall devour them. Then you shall know that I *am* the LORD, when I set My face against them. 8 Thus I will make the land desolate, because they have persisted in unfaithfulness,' says the Lord GOD."

16 Again the word of the LORD came to me, saying, 2 "Son of

man, cause Jerusalem to know her abominations, 3 and say, 'Thus says the Lord GOD to Jerusalem: "Your birth and your nativity *are* from the land of Canaan; your father *was* an Amorite and your mother a Hittite. 4 *As for* your nativity, on the day you were born your navel cord was not cut, nor were you washed in water to cleanse *you;* you were not rubbed with salt nor wrapped in swaddling cloths. 5 No eye pitied you, to do any of these things for you, to have compassion on you; but you were thrown out into the open field, when you yourself were loathed on the day you were born.

6 "And when I passed by you and saw you struggling in your own blood, I said to you in your blood, 'Live!' Yes, I said to you in your blood, 'Live!' 7 I made you thrive like a plant in the field; and you grew, matured, and became very beautiful. *Your* breasts were formed, your hair grew, but you *were* naked and bare.

8 "When I passed by you again and looked upon you, indeed your time *was* the time of love; so I spread My wing over you and covered your nakedness. Yes, I swore an oath to you and entered into a covenant with you, and you became Mine," says the Lord GOD.

9 "Then I washed you in water; yes, I thoroughly washed off your blood, and I anointed you with oil. 10 I clothed you in embroidered cloth and gave you sandals of badger skin; I clothed you with fine linen and covered you with silk. 11 I adorned you with ornaments, put bracelets on your wrists, and a chain on your neck. 12 And I put a jewel in your nose, earrings in your ears, and a beautiful crown on your head. 13 Thus you were adorned with gold and silver, and your clothing *was of* fine linen, silk, and embroidered cloth. You ate *pastry of* fine flour, honey, and oil. You were exceedingly beautiful, and succeeded to royalty. 14 Your fame went out among the nations because of your beauty, for it *was* perfect through My splendor which I had bestowed on you," says the Lord GOD.

15 "But you trusted in your own beauty, played the harlot because of your fame, and poured out your harlotry on everyone passing by who *would have* it. 16 You took some of

your garments and adorned multicolored high places for yourself, and played the harlot on them. *Such things should not happen, nor be.* 17 You have also taken your beautiful jewelry from My gold and My silver, which I had given you, and made for yourself male images and played the harlot with them. 18 You took your embroidered garments and covered them, and you set My oil and My incense before them. 19 Also My food which I gave you—the pastry of fine flour, oil, and honey *which* I fed you—you set it before them as sweet incense; and *so* it was," says the Lord God.

20 "Moreover you took your sons and your daughters, whom you bore to Me, and these you sacrificed to them to be devoured. *Were* your *acts* of harlotry a small matter, 21 that you have slain My children and offered them up to them by causing them to pass through *the fire?* 22 And in all your abominations and acts of harlotry you did not remember the days of your youth, when you were naked and bare, struggling in your blood.

23 "Then it was so, after all your wickedness—'Woe, woe to you!' says the Lord God— 24 *that* you also built for yourself a shrine, and made a high place for yourself in every street. 25 You built your high places at the head of every road, and made your beauty to be abhorred. You offered yourself to everyone who passed by, and multiplied your acts of harlotry. 26 You also committed harlotry with the Egyptians, your very fleshly neighbors, and increased your acts of harlotry to provoke Me to anger.

27 "Behold, therefore, I stretched out My hand against you, diminished your allotment, and gave you up to the will of those who hate you, the daughters of the Philistines, who were ashamed of your lewd behavior. 28 You also played the harlot with the Assyrians, because you were insatiable; indeed you played the harlot with them and still were not satisfied. 29 Moreover you multiplied your acts of harlotry as far as the land of the trader, Chaldea; and even then you were not satisfied.

30 "How degenerate is your heart!" says the Lord God, "seeing you do all these *things,* the deeds of a brazen harlot.

31 "You erected your shrine at the head of every road, and built your high place in every street. Yet you were not like a harlot, because you scorned payment. 32 *You are* an adulterous wife, *who* takes strangers instead of her husband. 33 Men make payment to all harlots, but you made your payments to all your lovers, and hired them to come to you from all around for your harlotry. 34 You are the opposite of *other* women in your harlotry, because no one solicited you to be a harlot. In that you gave payment but no payment was given you, therefore you are the opposite."

35 'Now then, O harlot, hear the word of the Lord! 36 Thus says the Lord God: "Because your filthiness was poured out and your nakedness uncovered in your harlotry with your lovers, and with all your abominable idols, and because of the blood of your children which you gave to them, 37 surely, therefore, I will gather all your lovers with whom you took pleasure, all those you loved, *and* all those you hated; I will gather them from all around against you and will uncover your nakedness to them, that they may see all your nakedness. 38 And I will judge you as women who break wedlock or shed blood are judged; I will bring blood upon you in fury and jealousy. 39 I will also give you into their hand, and they shall throw down your shrines and break down your high places. They shall also strip you of your clothes, take your beautiful jewelry, and leave you naked and bare.

40 "They shall also bring up an assembly against you, and they shall stone you with stones and thrust you through with their swords. 41 They shall burn your houses with fire, and execute judgments on you in the sight of many women; and I will make you cease playing the harlot, and you shall no longer hire lovers. 42 So I will lay to rest My fury toward you, and My jealousy shall depart from you. I will be quiet, and be angry no more. 43 Because you did not remember the days of your youth, but agitated Me*a* with all these *things,* surely I will also recompense your deeds on *your own* head," says

16:43 *a*Following Septuagint, Syriac, Targum, and Vulgate; Masoretic Text reads *were agitated with Me.*

the Lord GOD. "And you shall not commit lewdness in addition to all your abominations.

44 "Indeed everyone who quotes proverbs will use *this* proverb against you: 'Like mother, like daughter!' 45 You *are* your mother's daughter, loathing husband and children; and you *are* the sister of your sisters, who loathed their husbands and children; your mother *was* a Hittite and your father an Amorite. 46 "Your elder sister *is* Samaria, who dwells with her daughters to the north of you; and your younger sister, who dwells to the south of you, *is* Sodom and her daughters. 47 You did not walk in their ways nor act according to their abominations; but, as *if that were* too little, you became more corrupt than they in all your ways.

48 "*As* I live," says the Lord GOD, "neither your sister Sodom nor her daughters have done as you and your daughters have done. 49 Look, this was the iniquity of your sister Sodom: She and her daughter had pride, fullness of food, and abundance of idleness; neither did she strengthen the hand of the poor and needy. 50 And they were haughty and committed abomination before Me; therefore I took them away as I saw fit.*a*

51 "Samaria did not commit half of your sins; but you have multiplied your abominations more than they, and have justified your sisters by all the abominations which you have done. 52 You who judged your sisters, bear your own shame also, because the sins which you committed were more abominable than theirs; they are more righteous than you. Yes, be disgraced also, and bear your own shame, because you justified your sisters.

53 "When I bring back their captives, the captives of Sodom and her daughters, and the captives of Samaria and her daughters, then *I will also bring back* the captives of your captivity among them, 54 that you may bear your own shame and be disgraced by all that you did when you comforted them. 55 When your sisters, Sodom and her daughters, re-

turn to their former state, and Samaria and her daughters return to their former state, then you and your daughters will return to your former state. 56 For your sister Sodom was not a byword in your mouth in the days of your pride, 57 before your wickedness was uncovered. It was like the time of the reproach of the daughters of Syria*a* and all *those* around her, and of the daughters of the Philistines, who despise you everywhere. 58 You have paid for your lewdness and your abominations," says the LORD. 59 For thus says the Lord GOD: "I will deal with you as you have done, who despised the oath by breaking the covenant.

60 "Nevertheless I will remember My covenant with you in the days of your youth, and I will establish an everlasting covenant with you. 61 Then you will remember your ways and be ashamed, when you receive your older and your younger sisters; for I will give them to you for daughters, but not because of My covenant with you. 62 And I will establish My covenant with you. Then you shall know that I *am* the LORD, 63 that you may remember and be ashamed, and never open your mouth anymore because of your shame, when I provide you an atonement for all you have done," says the Lord GOD.' "

17 And the word of the LORD came to me, saying, 2 "Son of man, pose a riddle, and speak a parable to the house of Israel, 3 and say, 'Thus says the Lord GOD:

> "A great eagle with large wings
> 　and long pinions,
> Full of feathers of various
> 　colors,
> Came to Lebanon
> And took from the cedar the
> 　highest branch.
> 4　He cropped off its topmost
> 　young twig
> And carried it to a land of
> 　trade;
> He set it in a city of merchants.
> 5　Then he took some of the seed
> 　of the land
> And planted it in a fertile field;

16:50 *a*Vulgate reads *you saw;* Septuagint reads *he saw;* Targum reads *as was revealed to Me.*
16:57 *a*Following Masoretic Text, Septuagint, Targum, and Vulgate; many Hebrew manuscripts and Syriac read *Edom.*

He placed *it* by abundant
waters
And set it like a willow tree.
6 And it grew and became a
spreading vine of low
stature;
Its branches turned toward
him,
But its roots were under it.
So it became a vine,
Brought forth branches,
And put forth shoots.

7 "But there was another[a] great
eagle with large wings and
many feathers;
And behold, this vine bent its
roots toward him,
And stretched its branches
toward him,
From the garden terrace where
it had been planted,
That he might water it.
8 It was planted in good soil by
many waters,
To bring forth branches, bear
fruit,
And become a majestic vine." '

9 "Say, 'Thus says the Lord GOD:

"Will it thrive?
Will he not pull up its roots,
Cut off its fruit,
And leave it to wither?
All of its spring leaves will
wither,
And no great power or many
people
Will be needed to pluck it up
by its roots.
10 Behold, *it is* planted,
Will it thrive?
Will it not utterly wither when
the east wind touches it?
It will wither in the garden
terrace where it grew." ' "

11 Moreover the word of the LORD
came to me, saying, 12 "Say now to
the rebellious house: 'Do you not
know what these *things* mean?' Tell
them, 'Indeed the king of Babylon
went to Jerusalem and took its king
and princes, and led them with him
to Babylon. 13 And he took the king's
offspring, made a covenant with him,

and put him under oath. He also took
away the mighty of the land,
14 that the kingdom might be brought
low and not lift itself up, *but* that by
keeping his covenant it might stand.
15 But he rebelled against him by
sending his ambassadors to Egypt,
that they might give him horses and
many people. Will he prosper? Will
he who does such *things* escape? Can
he break a covenant and still be delivered?
16 'As I live,' says the Lord GOD,
'surely in the place *where* the king
dwells who made him king, whose
oath he despised and whose covenant he broke—with him in the midst
of Babylon he shall die. 17 Nor will
Pharaoh with *his* mighty army and
great company do anything in the
war, when they heap up a siege
mound and build a wall to cut off
many persons. 18 Since he despised
the oath by breaking the covenant,
and in fact gave his hand and still
did all these *things,* he shall not escape.' "
19 Therefore thus says the Lord
GOD: "As I live, surely My oath which
he despised, and My covenant which
he broke, I will recompense on his
own head. 20 I will spread My net
over him, and he shall be taken in
My snare. I will bring him to Babylon
and try him there for the treason
which he committed against Me.
21 All his fugitives[a] with all his troops
shall fall by the sword, and those
who remain shall be scattered to every wind; and you shall know that I,
the LORD, have spoken."
22 Thus says the Lord GOD: "I will
take also *one* of the highest branches
of the high cedar and set *it* out. I will
crop off from the topmost of its
young twigs a tender one, and will
plant *it* on a high and prominent
mountain. 23 On the mountain height
of Israel I will plant it; and it will
bring forth boughs, and bear fruit,
and be a majestic cedar. Under it will
dwell birds of every sort; in the
shadow of its branches they will
dwell. 24 And all the trees of the field
shall know that I, the LORD, have
brought down the high tree and exalted the low tree, dried up the green
tree and made the dry tree flourish;

17:7 [a]Following Septuagint, Syriac, and Vulgate; Masoretic Text and Targum read *one.*   17:21 [a]Following
Masoretic Text and Vulgate; many Hebrew manuscripts and Syriac read *choice men;* Targum reads *mighty
men;* Septuagint omits *All his fugitives.*

I, the LORD, have spoken and have done *it*."

18 The word of the LORD came to me again, saying, 2 "What do you mean when you use this proverb concerning the land of Israel, saying:

'The fathers have eaten sour grapes,
And the children's teeth are set on edge'?

3 "*As* I live," says the Lord GOD, "you shall no longer use this proverb in Israel.

4 "Behold, all souls are Mine;
The soul of the father
As well as the soul of the son is Mine;
The soul who sins shall die.
5 But if a man is just
And does what is lawful and right;
6 If he has not eaten on the mountains,
Nor lifted up his eyes to the idols of the house of Israel,
Nor defiled his neighbor's wife,
Nor approached a woman during her impurity;
7 If he has not oppressed anyone,
But has restored to the debtor his pledge;
Has robbed no one by violence,
But has given his bread to the hungry
And covered the naked with clothing;
8 If he has not exacted usury
Nor taken any increase,
But has withdrawn his hand from iniquity
And executed true judgment between man and man;
9 *If* he has walked in My statutes
And kept My judgments faithfully—
He *is* just;
He shall surely live!"
Says the Lord GOD.

10 "If he begets a son *who is a* robber
Or a shedder of blood,
Who does any of these *things*
11 And does none of those *duties*,
But has eaten on the mountains
Or defiled his neighbor's wife;

12 If he has oppressed the poor and needy,
Robbed by violence,
Not restored the pledge,
Lifted his eyes to the idols,
Or committed abomination;
13 If he has exacted usury
Or taken increase—
Shall he then live?
He shall not live!
If he has done any of these abominations,
He shall surely die;
His blood shall be upon him.

14 "*If*, however, he begets a son
Who sees all the sins which his father has done,
And considers but does not do likewise;
15 *Who* has not eaten on the mountains,
Nor lifted his eyes to the idols of the house of Israel,
Nor defiled his neighbor's wife;
16 Has not oppressed anyone,
Nor withheld a pledge,
Nor robbed by violence,
But has given his bread to the hungry
And covered the naked with clothing;
17 *Who* has withdrawn his hand from the poor*a*
And not received usury or increase,
But has executed My judgments
And walked in My statutes—
He shall not die for the iniquity of his father;
He shall surely live!

18 "*As for* his father,
Because he cruelly oppressed,
Robbed his brother by violence,
And did what *is* not good among his people,
Behold, he shall die for his iniquity.

19 "Yet you say, 'Why should the son not bear the guilt of the father?' Because the son has done what is lawful and right, and has kept all My statutes and observed them, he shall surely live. 20 The soul who sins shall die. The son shall not bear the guilt of the father, nor the father bear the

18:17 *a*Following Masoretic Text, Targum, and Vulgate; Septuagint reads *iniquity* (compare verse 8).

guilt of the son. The righteousness of the righteous shall be upon himself, and the wickedness of the wicked shall be upon himself.

21 "But if a wicked man turns from all his sins which he has committed, keeps all My statutes, and does what is lawful and right, he shall surely live; he shall not die. 22 None of the transgressions which he has committed shall be remembered against him; because of the righteousness which he has done, he shall live. 23 Do I have any pleasure at all that the wicked should die?" says the Lord GOD, "and not that he should turn from his ways and live?

24 "But when a righteous man turns away from his righteousness and commits iniquity, and does according to all the abominations that the wicked man does, shall he live? All the righteousness which he has done shall not be remembered; because of the unfaithfulness of which he is guilty and the sin which he has committed, because of them he shall die.

25 "Yet you say, 'The way of the Lord is not fair.' Hear now, O house of Israel, is it not My way which is fair, and your ways which are not fair? 26 When a righteous man turns away from his righteousness, commits iniquity, and dies in it, it is because of the iniquity which he has done that he dies. 27 Again, when a wicked man turns away from the wickedness which he committed, and does what is lawful and right, he preserves himself alive. 28 Because he considers and turns away from all the transgressions which he committed, he shall surely live; he shall not die. 29 Yet the house of Israel says, 'The way of the Lord is not fair.' O house of Israel, is it not My ways which are fair, and your ways which are not fair?

30 "Therefore I will judge you, O house of Israel, every one according to his ways," says the Lord GOD. "Repent, and turn from all your transgressions, so that iniquity will not be your ruin. 31 Cast away from you all the transgressions which you have committed, and get yourselves a new heart and a new spirit. For why should you die, O house of Israel? 32 For I have no pleasure in the death of one who dies," says the Lord GOD. "Therefore turn and live!"

19 "Moreover take up a lamentation for the princes of Israel, 2 and say:

'What is your mother? A
　　lioness:
She lay down among the lions;
Among the young lions she
　　nourished her cubs.
3 　She brought up one of her cubs,
And he became a young lion;
He learned to catch prey,
And he devoured men.
4 　The nations also heard of him;
He was trapped in their pit,
And they brought him with
　　chains to the land of Egypt.

5 　'When she saw that she waited,
　　that her hope was lost,
She took another of her cubs
　　and made him a young lion.
6 　He roved among the lions,
And became a young lion;
He learned to catch prey;
He devoured men.
7 　He knew their desolate places,a
And laid waste their cities;
The land with its fullness was
　　desolated
By the noise of his roaring.
8 　Then the nations set against
　　him from the provinces on
　　every side,
And spread their net over him;
He was trapped in their pit.
9 　They put him in a cage with
　　chains,
And brought him to the king of
　　Babylon;
They brought him in nets,
That his voice should no longer
　　be heard on the mountains of
　　Israel.

10 　'Your mother was like a vine in
　　your bloodline,a
Planted by the waters,
Fruitful and full of branches
Because of many waters.
11 　She had strong branches for
　　scepters of rulers.

19:7 aSeptuagint reads He stood in insolence; Targum reads He destroyed its palaces; Vulgate reads He learned to make widows.　19:10 aLiterally blood. Following Masoretic Text, Syriac, and Vulgate; Septuagint reads like a flower on a pomegranate tree; Targum reads in your likeness.

She towered in stature above
   the thick branches,
And was seen in her height
   amid the dense foliage.
12 But she was plucked up in fury,
   She was cast down to the
     ground,
And the east wind dried her
    fruit.
Her strong branches were
   broken and withered;
The fire consumed them.
13 And now she *is* planted in the
   wilderness,
In a dry and thirsty land.
14 Fire has come out from a rod
   of her branches
And devoured her fruit,
So that she has no strong
   branch—a scepter for
   ruling.' "

This *is* a lamentation, and has become a lamentation.

20 It came to pass in the seventh year, in the fifth *month,* on the tenth *day* of the month, *that* certain of the elders of Israel came to inquire of the LORD, and sat before me. 2 Then the word of the LORD came to me, saying, 3 "Son of man, speak to the elders of Israel, and say to them, 'Thus says the Lord GOD: "Have you come to inquire of Me? *As* I live," says the Lord GOD, "I will not be inquired of by you." ' 4 Will you judge them, son of man, will you judge *them?* Then make known to them the abominations of their fathers.

5 "Say to them, 'Thus says the Lord GOD: "On the day when I chose Israel and raised My hand in an oath to the descendants of the house of Jacob, and made Myself known to them in the land of Egypt, I raised My hand in an oath to them, saying, 'I *am* the LORD your God.' 6 On that day I raised My hand in an oath to them, to bring them out of the land of Egypt into a land that I had searched out for them, 'flowing with milk and honey,'*a* the glory of all lands. 7 Then I said to them, 'Each of you, throw away the abominations which are before his eyes, and do not defile yourselves with the idols of Egypt. I *am* the LORD your God.' 8 But they rebelled against Me and would not obey Me. They did not all cast away

the abominations which were before their eyes, nor did they forsake the idols of Egypt. Then I said, 'I will pour out My fury on them and fulfill My anger against them in the midst of the land of Egypt.' 9 But I acted for My name's sake, that it should not be profaned before the Gentiles among whom they *were,* in whose sight I had made Myself known to them, to bring them out of the land of Egypt.

10 "Therefore I made them go out of the land of Egypt and brought them into the wilderness. 11 And I gave them My statutes and showed them My judgments, 'which, *if* a man does, he shall live by them.'*a* 12 Moreover I also gave them My Sabbaths, to be a sign between them and Me, that they might know that I *am* the LORD who sanctifies them. 13 Yet the house of Israel rebelled against Me in the wilderness; they did not walk in My statutes; they despised My judgments, 'which, *if* a man does, he shall live by them';*a* and they greatly defiled My Sabbaths. Then I said I would pour out My fury on them in the wilderness, to consume them. 14 But I acted for My name's sake, that it should not be profaned before the Gentiles, in whose sight I had brought them out. 15 So I also raised My hand in an oath to them in the wilderness, that I would not bring them into the land which I had given *them,* 'flowing with milk and honey,'*a* the glory of all lands, 16 because they despised My judgments and did not walk in My statutes, but profaned My Sabbaths; for their heart went after their idols. 17 Nevertheless My eye spared them from destruction. I did not make an end of them in the wilderness.

18 "But I said to their children in the wilderness, 'Do not walk in the statutes of your fathers, nor observe their judgments, nor defile yourselves with their idols. 19 I *am* the LORD your God: Walk in My statutes, keep My judgments, and do them; 20 hallow My Sabbaths, and they will be a sign between Me and you, that you may know that I *am* the LORD your God.'

21 "Notwithstanding, the children rebelled against Me; they did not

walk in My statutes, and were not careful to observe My judgments, 'which, *if* a man does, he shall live by them';[a] but they profaned My Sabbaths. Then I said I would pour out My fury on them and fulfill My anger against them in the wilderness. 22 Nevertheless I withdrew My hand and acted for My name's sake, that it should not be profaned in the sight of the Gentiles, in whose sight I had brought them out. 23 Also I raised My hand in an oath to those in the wilderness, that I would scatter them among the Gentiles and disperse them throughout the countries, 24 because they had not executed My judgments, but had despised My statutes, profaned My Sabbaths, and their eyes were fixed on their fathers' idols.

25 "Therefore I also gave them up to statutes *that were* not good, and judgments by which they could not live; 26 and I pronounced them unclean because of their ritual gifts, in that they caused all their firstborn to pass through *the fire*, that I might make them desolate and that they might know that I am the Lord." '

27 "Therefore, son of man, speak to the house of Israel, and say to them, 'Thus says the Lord God: "In this too your fathers have blasphemed Me, by being unfaithful to Me. 28 When I brought them into the land *concerning* which I had raised My hand in an oath to give them, and they saw all the high hills and all the thick trees, there they offered their sacrifices and provoked Me with their offerings. There they also sent up their sweet aroma and poured out their drink offerings. 29 Then I said to them, 'What *is* this high place to which you go?' So its name is called Bamah[a] to this day." ' 30 Therefore say to the house of Israel, 'Thus says the Lord God: "Are you defiling yourselves in the manner of your fathers, and committing harlotry according to their abominations? 31 For when you offer your gifts and make your sons pass through the fire, you defile yourselves with all your idols, even to this day. So shall I be inquired of by you, O house of Israel? *As* I live," says the Lord God, "I will not be inquired of by you. 32 What you have in your mind shall never be,

when you say, 'We will be like the Gentiles, like the families in other countries, serving wood and stone.'

33 "*As* I live," says the Lord God, "surely with a mighty hand, with an outstretched arm, and with fury poured out, I will rule over you. 34 I will bring you out from the peoples and gather you out of the countries where you are scattered, with a mighty hand, with an outstretched arm, and with fury poured out. 35 And I will bring you into the wilderness of the peoples, and there I will plead My case with you face to face. 36 Just as I pleaded My case with your fathers in the wilderness of the land of Egypt, so I will plead My case with you," says the Lord God.

37 "I will make you pass under the rod, and I will bring you into the bond of the covenant; 38 I will purge the rebels from among you, and those who transgress against Me; I will bring them out of the country where they dwell, but they shall not enter the land of Israel. Then you will know that I *am* the Lord.

39 "As for you, O house of Israel," thus says the Lord God: "Go, serve every one of you his idols—and hereafter—if you will not obey Me; but profane My holy name no more with your gifts and your idols. 40 For on My holy mountain, on the mountain height of Israel," says the Lord God, "there all the house of Israel, all of them in the land, shall serve Me; there I will accept them, and there I will require your offerings and the firstfruits of your sacrifices, together with all your holy things. 41 I will accept you as a sweet aroma when I bring you out from the peoples and gather you out of the countries where you have been scattered; and I will be hallowed in you before the Gentiles. 42 Then you shall know that I *am* the Lord, when I bring you into the land of Israel, into the country *for* which I raised My hand in an oath to give to your fathers. 43 And there you shall remember your ways and all your doings with which you were defiled; and you shall loathe yourselves in your own sight because of all the evils that you have committed. 44 Then you shall know that I *am* the Lord, when I have

dealt with you for My name's sake, not according to your wicked ways nor according to your corrupt doings, O house of Israel," says the Lord GOD.' "

45 Furthermore the word of the LORD came to me, saying, 46 "Son of man, set your face toward the south; preach against the south and prophesy against the forest land, the South,[a] 47 and say to the forest of the South, 'Hear the word of the LORD! Thus says the Lord GOD: "Behold, I will kindle a fire in you, and it shall devour every green tree and every dry tree in you; the blazing flame shall not be quenched, and all faces from the south to the north shall be scorched by it. 48 All flesh shall see that I, the LORD, have kindled it; it shall not be quenched." ' "

49 Then I said, "Ah, Lord GOD! They say of me, 'Does he not speak parables?' "

21 And the word of the LORD came to me, saying, 2 "Son of man, set your face toward Jerusalem, preach against the holy places, and prophesy against the land of Israel; 3 and say to the land of Israel, 'Thus says the LORD: "Behold, I am against you, and I will draw My sword out of its sheath and cut off both righteous and wicked from you. 4 Because I will cut off both righteous and wicked from you, therefore My sword shall go out of its sheath against all flesh from south to north, 5 that all flesh may know that I, the LORD, have drawn My sword out of its sheath; it shall not return anymore." ' 6 Sigh therefore, son of man, with a breaking heart, and sigh with bitterness before their eyes. 7 And it shall be when they say to you, 'Why are you sighing?' that you shall answer, 'Because of the news; when it comes, every heart will melt, all hands will be feeble, every spirit will faint, and all knees will be weak as water. Behold, it is coming and shall be brought to pass,' says the Lord GOD."

8 Again the word of the LORD came to me, saying, 9 "Son of man, prophesy and say, 'Thus says the LORD!' Say:

'A sword, a sword is sharpened
And also polished!

10 Sharpened to make a dreadful
    slaughter,
Polished to flash like lightning!
Should we then make mirth?
It despises the scepter of My
    son,
As it does all wood.

11 And He has given it to be
    polished,
That it may be handled;
This sword is sharpened, and
    it is polished
To be given into the hand of the
    slayer.'

12 "Cry and wail, son of man;
For it will be against My
    people,
Against all the princes of Israel.
Terrors including the sword
    will be against My people;
Therefore strike your thigh.

13 "Because it is a testing,
And what if the sword despises
    even the scepter?
The scepter shall be no more,"

says the Lord GOD.

14 "You therefore, son of man,
    prophesy,
And strike your hands
    together.
The third time let the sword do
    double damage.
It is the sword that slays,
The sword that slays the great
    men,
That enters their private
    chambers.

15 I have set the point of the sword
    against all their gates,
That the heart may melt and
    many may stumble.
Ah! It is made bright;
It is grasped for slaughter:

16 "Swords at the ready!
Thrust right!
Set your blade!
Thrust left—
Wherever your edge is ordered!

17 "I also will beat My fists
    together,
And I will cause My fury to
    rest;
I, the LORD, have spoken."

18 The word of the LORD came to me again, saying: 19 "And son of

man, appoint for yourself two ways for the sword of the king of Babylon to go; both of them shall go from the same land. Make a sign; put *it* at the head of the road to the city. 20 Appoint a road for the sword to go to Rabbah of the Ammonites, and to Judah, into fortified Jerusalem. 21 For the king of Babylon stands at the parting of the road, at the fork of the two roads, to use divination: he shakes the arrows, he consults the images, he looks at the liver. 22 In his right hand is the divination for Jerusalem: to set up battering rams, to call for a slaughter, to lift the voice with shouting, to set battering rams against the gates, to heap up a *siege* mound, and to build a wall. 23 And it will be to them like a false divination in the eyes of those who have sworn oaths with them; but he will bring their iniquity to remembrance, that they may be taken.

24 "Therefore thus says the Lord GOD: 'Because you have made your iniquity to be remembered, in that your transgressions are uncovered, so that in all your doings your sins appear—because you have come to remembrance, you shall be taken in hand.

25 'Now to you, O profane, wicked prince of Israel, whose day has come, whose iniquity *shall* end, 26 thus says the Lord GOD:

"Remove the turban, and take off the crown;
Nothing *shall remain* the same.
Exalt the humble, and humble the exalted.
27 Overthrown, overthrown,
I will make it overthrown!
It shall be no *longer,*
Until He comes whose right it is,
And I will give it *to Him.*" '

28 "And you, son of man, prophesy and say, 'Thus says the Lord GOD concerning the Ammonites and concerning their reproach,' and say:

'A sword, a sword *is* drawn,
Polished for slaughter,
For consuming, for flashing—
29 While they see false visions for you,
While they divine a lie to you,
To bring you on the necks of the wicked, the slain

Whose day has come,
Whose iniquity *shall* end.
30 'Return *it* to its sheath.
I will judge you
In the place where you were created,
In the land of your nativity.
31 I will pour out My indignation on you;
I will blow against you with the fire of My wrath,
And deliver you into the hands of brutal men *who are* skillful to destroy.
32 You shall be fuel for the fire;
Your blood shall be in the midst of the land.
You shall not be remembered,
For I the LORD have spoken.' "

22 Moreover the word of the LORD came to me, saying, 2 "Now, son of man, will you judge, will you judge the bloody city? Yes, show her all her abominations! 3 Then say, 'Thus says the Lord GOD: "The city sheds blood in her own midst, that her time may come; and she makes idols within herself to defile herself. 4 You have become guilty by the blood which you have shed, and have defiled yourself with the idols which you have made. You have caused your days to draw near, and have come to *the end of* your years; therefore I have made you a reproach to the nations, and a mockery to all countries. 5 *Those* near and *those* far from you will mock you as infamous *and* full of tumult.

6 "Look, the princes of Israel: each one has used his power to shed blood in you. 7 In you they have made light of father and mother; in your midst they have oppressed the stranger; in you they have mistreated the fatherless and the widow. 8 You have despised My holy things and profaned My Sabbaths. 9 In you are men who slander to cause bloodshed; in you are those who eat on the mountains; in your midst they commit lewdness. 10 In you men uncover their fathers' nakedness; in you they violate women who are set apart during their impurity. 11 One commits abomination with his neighbor's wife; another lewdly defiles his daughter-in-law; and another in you violates his sister, his father's daughter. 12 In you they take bribes to shed

blood; you take usury and increase; you have made profit from your neighbors by extortion, and have forgotten Me," says the Lord GOD.

13 "Behold, therefore, I beat My fists at the dishonest profit which you have made, and at the bloodshed which has been in your midst. 14 Can your heart endure, or can your hands remain strong, in the days when I shall deal with you? I, the LORD, have spoken, and will do *it*. 15 I will scatter you among the nations, disperse you throughout the countries, and remove your filthiness completely from you. 16 You shall defile yourself in the sight of the nations; then you shall know that I *am* the LORD." ' "

17 The word of the LORD came to me, saying, 18 "Son of man, the house of Israel has become dross to Me; they *are* all bronze, tin, iron, and lead, in the midst of a furnace; they have become dross from silver. 19 Therefore thus says the Lord GOD: 'Because you have all become dross, therefore behold, I will gather you into the midst of Jerusalem. 20 *As men* gather silver, bronze, iron, lead, and tin into the midst of a furnace, to blow fire on it, to melt *it*; so I will gather *you* in My anger and in My fury, and I will leave *you there* and melt you. 21 Yes, I will gather you and blow on you with the fire of My wrath, and you shall be melted in its midst. 22 As silver is melted in the midst of a furnace, so shall you be melted in its midst; then you shall know that I, the LORD, have poured out My fury on you.' "

23 And the word of the LORD came to me, saying, 24 "Son of man, say to her: 'You *are* a land that is not cleansed[a] or rained on in the day of indignation.' 25 The conspiracy of her prophets[a] in her midst is like a roaring lion tearing the prey; they have devoured people; they have taken treasure and precious things; they have made many widows in her midst. 26 Her priests have violated My law and profaned My holy things; they have not distinguished between the holy and unholy, nor have they made known *the difference* between the unclean and the clean; and they

have hidden their eyes from My Sabbaths, so that I am profaned among them. 27 Her princes in her midst *are* like wolves tearing the prey, to shed blood, to destroy people, and to get dishonest gain. 28 Her prophets plastered them with untempered *mortar,* seeing false visions, and divining lies for them, saying, 'Thus says the Lord GOD,' when the LORD had not spoken. 29 The people of the land have used oppressions, committed robbery, and mistreated the poor and needy; and they wrongfully oppress the stranger. 30 So I sought for a man among them who would make a wall, and stand in the gap before Me on behalf of the land, that I should not destroy it; but I found no one. 31 Therefore I have poured out My indignation on them; I have consumed them with the fire of My wrath; and I have recompensed their deeds on their own heads," says the Lord GOD.

23

The word of the LORD came again to me, saying:

2 "Son of man, there were two women,
The daughters of one mother.
3 They committed harlotry in Egypt,
They committed harlotry in their youth;
Their breasts were there embraced,
Their virgin bosom was there pressed.
4 Their names: Oholah[a] the elder and Oholibah[b] her sister;
They were Mine,
And they bore sons and daughters.
As for their names,
Samaria *is* Oholah, and
Jerusalem *is* Oholibah.

5 "Oholah played the harlot even though she was Mine;
And she lusted for her lovers, the neighboring Assyrians,
6 *Who were* clothed in purple,
Captains and rulers,
All of them desirable young men,
Horsemen riding on horses.

22:24 [a]Following Masoretic Text, Syriac, and Vulgate; Septuagint reads *showered upon.*
22:25 [a]Following Masoretic Text and Vulgate; Septuagint reads *princes;* Targum reads *scribes.*
23:4 [a]Literally *Her Own Tabernacle* [b]Literally *My Tabernacle Is in Her*

7 Thus she committed her
    harlotry with them,
  All of them choice men of
    Assyria;
  And with all for whom she
    lusted,
  With all their idols, she defiled
    herself.
8 She has never given up her
    harlotry *brought* from Egypt,
  For in her youth they had lain
    with her,
  Pressed her virgin bosom,
  And poured out their
    immorality upon her.

9 "Therefore I have delivered her
    Into the hand of her lovers,
  Into the hand of the Assyrians,
    For whom she lusted.
10 They uncovered her
    nakedness,
  Took away her sons and
    daughters,
  And slew her with the sword;
  She became a byword among
    women,
  For they had executed
    judgment on her.

11 "Now although her sister Oholibah saw *this*, she became more corrupt in her lust than she, and in her
harlotry more corrupt than her sister's harlotry.

12 "She lusted for the neighboring
    Assyrians,
  Captains and rulers,
  Clothed most gorgeously,
  Horsemen riding on horses,
  All of them desirable young
    men.
13 Then I saw that she was
    defiled;
  Both *took* the same way.
14 But she increased her harlotry;
  She looked at men portrayed
    on the wall,
  Images of Chaldeans portrayed
    in vermilion,
15 Girded with belts around their
    waists,
  Flowing turbans on their heads,
  All of them looking like
    captains,
  In the manner of the
    Babylonians of Chaldea,
  The land of their nativity.
16 As soon as her eyes saw them,
  She lusted for them

And sent messengers to them
  in Chaldea.

17 "Then the Babylonians came to
    her, into the bed of love,
  And they defiled her with their
    immorality;
  So she was defiled by them,
    and alienated herself from
    them.
18 She revealed her harlotry and
    uncovered her nakedness.
  Then I alienated Myself from
    her,
  As I had alienated Myself from
    her sister.

19 "Yet she multiplied her harlotry
  In calling to remembrance the
    days of her youth,
  When she had played the
    harlot in the land of Egypt.
20 For she lusted for her
    paramours,
  Whose flesh *is like* the flesh of
    donkeys,
  And whose issue *is like* the
    issue of horses.
21 Thus you called to
    remembrance the lewdness
    of your youth,
  When the Egyptians pressed
    your bosom
  Because of your youthful
    breasts.

22 "Therefore, Oholibah, thus says
the Lord GOD:

  'Behold, I will stir up your
    lovers against you,
  From whom you have alienated
    yourself,
  And I will bring them against
    you from every side:
23 The Babylonians,
  All the Chaldeans,
  Pekod, Shoa, Koa,
  All the Assyrians with them,
  All of them desirable young
    men,
  Governors and rulers,
  Captains and men of renown,
  All of them riding on horses.
24 And they shall come against
    you
  With chariots, wagons, and
    war-horses,
  With a horde of people.
  They shall array against you
  Buckler, shield, and helmet all
    around.

'I will delegate judgment to
    them,
And they shall judge you
    according to their judgments.
25 I will set My jealousy against
    you;
And they shall deal furiously
    with you;
They shall remove your nose
    and your ears,
And your remnant shall fall by
    the sword;
They shall take your sons and
    your daughters,
And your remnant shall be
    devoured by fire.
26 They shall also strip you of
    your clothes
And take away your beautiful
    jewelry.
27 'Thus I will make you cease
    your lewdness and your
    harlotry
Brought from the land of
    Egypt,
So that you will not lift your
    eyes to them,
Nor remember Egypt
    anymore.'

28 "For thus says the Lord God:
'Surely I will deliver you into the
hand of those you hate, into the hand
of those from whom you alienated
yourself. 29 They will deal hatefully
with you, take away all you have
worked for, and leave you naked and
bare. The nakedness of your harlotry
shall be uncovered, both your lewdness and your harlotry. 30 I will do
these things to you because you have
gone as a harlot after the Gentiles,
because you have become defiled by
their idols. 31 You have walked in the
way of your sister; therefore I will
put her cup in your hand.'
32 "Thus says the Lord God:

'You shall drink of your sister's
    cup,
The deep and wide one;
You shall be laughed to scorn
And held in derision;
    It contains much.
33 You will be filled with
    drunkenness and sorrow,
The cup of horror and
    desolation,
The cup of your sister Samaria.
34 You shall drink and drain it,
You shall break its shards,

And tear at your own breasts;
For I have spoken,'
Says the Lord God.

35 "Therefore thus says the Lord
God:

'Because you have forgotten Me
    and cast Me behind your
    back,
Therefore you shall bear the
    penalty
Of your lewdness and your
    harlotry.' "

36 The Lord also said to me: "Son
of man, will you judge Oholah and
Oholibah? Then declare to them their
abominations. 37 For they have committed adultery, and blood is on their
hands. They have committed adultery with their idols, and even sacrificed their sons whom they bore to
Me, passing them through the fire,
to devour them. 38 Moreover they
have done this to Me: They have
defiled My sanctuary on the same
day and profaned My Sabbaths.
39 For after they had slain their children for their idols, on the same day
they came into My sanctuary to profane it; and indeed thus they have
done in the midst of My house.
40 "Furthermore you sent for men
to come from afar, to whom a messenger was sent; and there they
came. And you washed yourself for
them, painted your eyes, and
adorned yourself with ornaments.
41 You sat on a stately couch, with a
table prepared before it, on which
you had set My incense and My oil.
42 The sound of a carefree multitude
was with her, and Sabeans were
brought from the wilderness with
men of the common sort, who put
bracelets on their wrists and beautiful crowns on their heads. 43 Then I
said concerning her who had grown
old in adulteries, 'Will they commit
harlotry with her now, and she with
them?' 44 Yet they went in to her, as
men go in to a woman who plays the
harlot; thus they went in to Oholah
and Oholibah, the lewd women.
45 But righteous men will judge them
after the manner of adulteresses, and
after the manner of women who shed
blood, because they are adulteresses,
and blood is on their hands.
46 "For thus says the Lord God:
'Bring up an assembly against them,

give them up to trouble and plunder.
47 The assembly shall stone them
with stones and execute them with
their swords; they shall slay their
sons and their daughters, and burn
their houses with fire. 48 Thus I will
cause lewdness to cease from the
land, that all women may be taught
not to practice your lewdness.
49 They shall repay you for your
lewdness, and you shall pay for your
idolatrous sins. Then you shall know
that I *am* the Lord God.'"

24 Again, in the ninth year, in the
tenth month, on the tenth *day*
of the month, the word of the Lord
came to me, saying, 2 "Son of man,
write down the name of the day, this
very day—the king of Babylon
started his siege against Jerusalem
this very day. 3 And utter a parable
to the rebellious house, and say to
them, 'Thus says the Lord God:

"Put on a pot, set *it* on,
   And also pour water into it.
4 Gather pieces *of meat* in it,
   Every good piece,
   The thigh and the shoulder.
   Fill *it* with choice cuts;
5 Take the choice of the flock.
   Also pile *fuel* bones under it,
   Make it boil well,
   And let the cuts simmer in it."

6 'Therefore thus says the Lord
God:

"Woe to the bloody city,
   To the pot whose scum *is* in it,
   And whose scum is not gone
      from it!
   Bring it out piece by piece,
   On which no lot has fallen.
7 For her blood is in her midst;
   She set it on top of a rock;
   She did not pour it on the
      ground,
   To cover it with dust.
8 That it may raise up fury and
      take vengeance,
   I have set her blood on top of
      a rock,
   That it may not be covered."

9 'Therefore thus says the Lord
God:

"Woe to the bloody city!
   I too will make the pyre great.
10 Heap on the wood,

Kindle the fire;
   Cook the meat well,
   Mix in the spices,
   And let the cuts be burned up.
11 "Then set the pot empty on the
      coals,
   That it may become hot and its
      bronze may burn,
   That its filthiness may be
      melted in it,
   That its scum may be
      consumed.
12 She has grown weary with lies,
   And her great scum has not
      gone from her.
   Let her scum *be* in the fire!
13 In your filthiness *is* lewdness.
   Because I have cleansed you,
      and you were not cleansed,
   You will not be cleansed of
      your filthiness anymore,
   Till I have caused My fury to
      rest upon you.
14 I, the Lord, have spoken *it*;
   It shall come to pass, and I will
      do *it*;
   I will not hold back,
   Nor will I spare,
   Nor will I relent;
   According to your ways
   And according to your deeds
   They*a* will judge you,"
   Says the Lord God.' "

15 Also the word of the Lord came
to me, saying, 16 "Son of man, behold, I take away from you the desire
of your eyes with one stroke; yet you
shall neither mourn nor weep, nor
shall your tears run down. 17 Sigh in
silence, make no mourning for the
dead; bind your turban on your head,
and put your sandals on your feet;
do not cover *your* lips, and do not
eat man's bread *of sorrow*."
18 So I spoke to the people in the
morning, and at evening my wife
died; and the next morning I did as
I was commanded.
19 And the people said to me, "Will
you not tell us what these *things sig-
nify* to us, that you behave so?"
20 Then I answered them, "The
word of the Lord came to me, saying,
21 'Speak to the house of Israel,
"Thus says the Lord God: 'Behold, I
will profane My sanctuary, your arrogant boast, the desire of your eyes,
the delight of your soul; and your
sons and daughters whom you left

24:14 *a*Septuagint, Syriac, Targum, and Vulgate read *I.*

behind shall fall by the sword. 22 And you shall do as I have done; you shall not cover *your* lips nor eat man's bread *of sorrow.* 23 Your turbans shall be on your heads and your sandals on your feet; you shall neither mourn nor weep, but you shall pine away in your iniquities and mourn with one another. 24 Thus Ezekiel is a sign to you; according to all that he has done you shall do; and when this comes, you shall know that I *am* the Lord God.' "

25 'And you, son of man—*will it* not *be* in the day when I take from them their stronghold, their joy and their glory, the desire of their eyes, and that on which they set their minds, their sons and their daughters: 26 on that day one who escapes will come to you to let *you* hear *it* with *your* ears; 27 on that day your mouth will be opened to him who has escaped; you shall speak and no longer be mute. Thus you will be a sign to them, and they shall know that I *am* the Lord.' "

25 The word of the Lord came to me, saying, 2 "Son of man, set your face against the Ammonites, and prophesy against them. 3 Say to the Ammonites, 'Hear the word of the Lord God! Thus says the Lord God: "Because you said, 'Aha!' against My sanctuary when it was profaned, and against the land of Israel when it was desolate, and against the house of Judah when they went into captivity, 4 indeed, therefore, I will deliver you as a possession to the men of the East, and they shall set their encampments among you and make their dwellings among you; they shall eat your fruit, and they shall drink your milk. 5 And I will make Rabbah a stable for camels and Ammon a resting place for flocks. Then you shall know that I *am* the Lord."

6 'For thus says the Lord God: "Because you clapped *your* hands, stamped your feet, and rejoiced in heart with all your disdain for the land of Israel, 7 indeed, therefore, I will stretch out My hand against you, and give you as plunder to the nations; I will cut you off from the peoples, and I will cause you to perish from the countries; I will destroy you, and you shall know that I *am* the Lord."

8 'Thus says the Lord God: "Because Moab and Seir say, 'Look! The house of Judah *is* like all the nations,' 9 therefore, behold, I will clear the territory of Moab of cities, of the cities on its frontier, the glory of the country, Beth Jeshimoth, Baal Meon, and Kirjathaim. 10 To the men of the East I will give it as a possession, together with the Ammonites, that the Ammonites may not be remembered among the nations. 11 And I will execute judgments upon Moab, and they shall know that I *am* the Lord."

12 'Thus says the Lord God: "Because of what Edom did against the house of Judah by taking vengeance, and has greatly offended by avenging itself on them," 13 therefore thus says the Lord God: "I will also stretch out My hand against Edom, cut off man and beast from it, and make it desolate from Teman; Dedan shall fall by the sword. 14 I will lay My vengeance on Edom by the hand of My people Israel, that they may do in Edom according to My anger and according to My fury; and they shall know My vengeance," says the Lord God.

15 'Thus says the Lord God: "Because the Philistines dealt vengefully and took vengeance with a spiteful heart, to destroy because of the old hatred," 16 therefore thus says the Lord God: "I will stretch out My hand against the Philistines, and I will cut off the Cherethites and destroy the remnant of the seacoast. 17 I will execute great vengeance on them with furious rebukes; and they shall know that I *am* the Lord, when I lay My vengeance upon them." ' "

26 And it came to pass in the eleventh year, on the first *day* of the month, *that* the word of the Lord came to me, saying, 2 "Son of man, because Tyre has said against Jerusalem, 'Aha! She is broken who *was* the gateway of the peoples; now she is turned over to me; I shall be filled; she is laid waste.'

3 "Therefore thus says the Lord God: 'Behold, I *am* against you, O Tyre, and will cause many nations to come up against you, as the sea causes its waves to come up. 4 And they shall destroy the walls of Tyre and break down her towers; I will also scrape her dust from her, and make her like the top of a rock.

5 It shall be *a place for* spreading nets in the midst of the sea, for I have spoken,' says the Lord GOD; 'it shall become plunder for the nations. 6 Also her daughter *villages* which *are* in the fields shall be slain by the sword. Then they shall know that I am the LORD.'

7 "For thus says the Lord GOD: 'Behold, I will bring against Tyre from the north Nebuchadnezzar[a] king of Babylon, king of kings, with horses, with chariots, and with horsemen, and an army with many people. 8 He will slay with the sword your daughter *villages* in the fields; he will heap up a siege mound against you, build a wall against you, and raise a defense against you. 9 He will direct his battering rams against your walls, and with his axes he will break down your towers. 10 Because of the abundance of his horses, their dust will cover you; your walls will shake at the noise of the horsemen, the wagons, and the chariots, when he enters your gates, as men enter a city that has been breached. 11 With the hooves of his horses he will trample all your streets; he will slay your people by the sword, and your strong pillars will fall to the ground. 12 They will plunder your riches and pillage your merchandise; they will break down your walls and destroy your pleasant houses; they will lay your stones, your timber, and your soil in the midst of the water. 13 I will put an end to the sound of your songs, and the sound of your harps shall be heard no more. 14 I will make you like the top of a rock; you shall be *a place for* spreading nets, and you shall never be rebuilt, for I the LORD have spoken,' says the Lord GOD.

15 "Thus says the Lord GOD to Tyre: 'Will the coastlands not shake at the sound of your fall, when the wounded cry, when slaughter is made in the midst of you? 16 Then all the princes of the sea will come down from their thrones, lay aside their robes, and take off their embroidered garments; they will clothe themselves with trembling; they will sit on the ground, tremble *every* moment, and be astonished at you. 17 And they will take up a lamentation for you, and say to you:

"How you have perished,
 O one inhabited by seafaring
   men,
 O renowned city,
 Who was strong at sea,
 She and her inhabitants,
 Who caused their terror *to be*
   on all her inhabitants!
18 Now the coastlands tremble on
     the day of your fall;
    Yes, the coastlands by the sea
     are troubled at your
     departure." '

19 "For thus says the Lord GOD: 'When I make you a desolate city, like cities that are not inhabited, when I bring the deep upon you, and great waters cover you, 20 then I will bring you down with those who descend into the Pit, to the people of old, and I will make you dwell in the lowest part of the earth, in places desolate from antiquity, with those who go down to the Pit, so that you may never be inhabited; and I shall establish glory in the land of the living. 21 I will make you a terror, and you *shall be* no *more;* though you are sought for, you will never be found again,' says the Lord GOD."

27 The word of the LORD came again to me, saying, 2 "Now, son of man, take up a lamentation for Tyre, 3 and say to Tyre, 'You who are situated at the entrance of the sea, merchant of the peoples on many coastlands, thus says the Lord GOD:

"O Tyre, you have said,
 'I *am* perfect in beauty.'
4   Your borders *are* in the midst
     of the seas.
    Your builders have perfected
     your beauty.
5   They made all *your* planks of
     fir trees from Senir;
    They took a cedar from
     Lebanon to make you a mast.
6   *Of* oaks from Bashan they
     made your oars;
    The company of Ashurites
     have inlaid your planks
    With ivory from the coasts of
     Cyprus.[a]
7   Fine embroidered linen from

Egypt was what you spread
for your sail;
Blue and purple from the coasts
of Elishah was what covered
you.

8 "Inhabitants of Sidon and Arvad
were your oarsmen;
Your wise men, O Tyre, were
in you;
They became your pilots.
9 Elders of Gebal and its wise
men
Were in you to caulk your
seams;
All the ships of the sea
And their oarsmen were in you
To market your merchandise.

10 "Those from Persia, Lydia,*a* and
Libya*b*
Were in your army as men of
war;
They hung shield and helmet in
you;
They gave splendor to you.
11 Men of Arvad with your army
were on your walls *all*
around,
And the men of Gammad were
in your towers;
They hung their shields on
your walls *all* around;
They made your beauty
perfect.

12 "Tarshish *was* your merchant
because of your many luxury goods.
They gave you silver, iron, tin, and
lead for your goods. 13 Javan, Tubal,
and Meshech *were* your traders.
They bartered human lives and vessels of bronze for your merchandise.
14 Those from the house of Togarmah
traded for your wares with horses,
steeds, and mules. 15 The men of Dedan *were* your traders; many isles
were the market of your hand. They
brought you ivory tusks and ebony
as payment. 16 Syria *was* your merchant because of the abundance of
goods you made. They gave you for
your wares emeralds, purple, embroidery, fine linen, corals, and rubies. 17 Judah and the land of Israel
were your traders. They traded for
your merchandise wheat of Minnith, millet, honey, oil, and balm.
18 Damascus *was* your merchant because of the abundance of goods you

made, because of your many luxury
items, with the wine of Helbon and
with white wool. 19 Dan and Javan
paid for your wares, traversing back
and forth. Wrought iron, cassia, and
cane were among your merchandise.
20 Dedan *was* your merchant in sad-
dlecloths for riding. 21 Arabia and all
the princes of Kedar *were* your regular merchants. They traded with you
in lambs, rams, and goats. 22 The
merchants of Sheba and Raamah
were your merchants. They traded
for your wares the choicest spices,
all kinds of precious stones, and gold.
23 Haran, Canneh, Eden, the merchants of Sheba, Assyria, *and* Chil-
mad *were* your merchants. 24 These
were your merchants in choice
items—in purple clothes, in embroidered garments, in chests of multicolored apparel, in sturdy woven
cords, which were in your marketplace.

25 "The ships of Tarshish were
carriers of your merchandise.
You were filled and very
glorious in the midst of the
seas.
26 Your oarsmen brought you into
many waters,
But the east wind broke you in
the midst of the seas.

27 "Your riches, wares, and
merchandise,
Your mariners and pilots,
Your caulkers and
merchandisers,
All your men of war who *are*
in you,
And the entire company which
is in your midst,
Will fall into the midst of the
seas on the day of your ruin.
28 The common-land will shake at
the sound of the cry of your
pilots.

29 "All who handle the oar,
The mariners,
All the pilots of the sea
Will come down from their
ships *and* stand on the shore.
30 They will make their voice
heard because of you;
They will cry bitterly and cast
dust on their heads;
They will roll about in ashes;

27:10 *a*Hebrew *Lud*   *b*Hebrew *Put*

31 They will shave themselves
completely bald because of
you,
Gird themselves with
sackcloth,
And weep for you
With bitterness of heart *and*
bitter wailing.
32 In their wailing for you
They will take up a
lamentation,
And lament for you:
'What *city is* like Tyre,
Destroyed in the midst of the
sea?
33 'When your wares went out by
sea,
You satisfied many people;
You enriched the kings of the
earth
With your many luxury goods
and your merchandise.
34 But you are broken by the seas
in the depths of the waters;
Your merchandise and the
entire company will fall in
your midst.
35 All the inhabitants of the isles
will be astonished at you;
Their kings will be greatly
afraid,
And *their* countenance will be
troubled.
36 The merchants among the
peoples will hiss at you;
You will become a horror, and
be no more forever.' " ' "

28 The word of the LORD came to
me again, saying, 2 "Son of
man, say to the prince of Tyre, 'Thus
says the Lord GOD:

"Because your heart *is* lifted up,
And you say, 'I *am* a god,
I sit *in* the seat of gods,
In the midst of the seas,'
Yet you *are* a man, and not a
god,
Though you set your heart as
the heart of a god
3 (Behold, you *are* wiser than
Daniel!
There is no secret that can be
hidden from you!
4 With your wisdom and your
understanding
You have gained riches for
yourself,
And gathered gold and silver
into your treasuries;

5 By your great wisdom in trade
you have increased your
riches,
And your heart is lifted up
because of your riches),"
6 'Therefore thus says the Lord
GOD:

"Because you have set your
heart as the heart of a god,
7 Behold, therefore, I will bring
strangers against you,
The most terrible of the
nations;
And they shall draw their
swords against the beauty of
your wisdom,
And defile your splendor.
8 They shall throw you down into
the Pit,
And you shall die the death of
the slain
In the midst of the seas.

9 "Will you still say before him
who slays you,
'I *am* a god'?
But you *shall be* a man, and not
a god,
In the hand of him who slays
you.
10 You shall die the death of the
uncircumcised
By the hand of aliens;
For I have spoken," says the
Lord GOD.' "

11 Moreover the word of the LORD
came to me, saying, 12 "Son of man,
take up a lamentation for the king
of Tyre, and say to him, 'Thus says
the Lord GOD:

"You *were* the seal of perfection,
Full of wisdom and perfect in
beauty.
13 You were in Eden, the garden
of God;
Every precious stone *was* your
covering:
The sardius, topaz, and
diamond,
Beryl, onyx, and jasper,
Sapphire, turquoise, and
emerald with gold.
The workmanship of your
timbrels and pipes
Was prepared for you on the
day you were created.

14 "You *were* the anointed cherub
who covers;

I established you;
You were on the holy mountain
of God;
You walked back and forth in
the midst of fiery stones.
15 You *were* perfect in your ways
from the day you were
created,
Till iniquity was found in you.

16 "By the abundance of your
trading
You became filled with
violence within,
And you sinned;
Therefore I cast you as a
profane thing
Out of the mountain of God;
And I destroyed you, O
covering cherub,
From the midst of the fiery
stones.

17 "Your heart was lifted up
because of your beauty;
You corrupted your wisdom for
the sake of your splendor;
I cast you to the ground,
I laid you before kings,
That they might gaze at you.

18 "You defiled your sanctuaries
By the multitude of your
iniquities,
By the iniquity of your trading;
Therefore I brought fire from
your midst;
It devoured you,
And I turned you to ashes upon
the earth
In the sight of all who saw you.
19 All who knew you among the
peoples are astonished at
you;
You have become a horror,
And *shall be* no more
forever." ' "

20 Then the word of the LORD came
to me, saying, 21 "Son of man, set
your face toward Sidon, and prophesy against her, 22 and say, 'Thus
says the Lord GOD:

"Behold, I *am* against you, O
Sidon;
I will be glorified in your midst;
And they shall know that I *am*
the LORD,

When I execute judgments in
her and am hallowed in her.
23 For I will send pestilence upon
her,
And blood in her streets;
The wounded shall be judged
in her midst
By the sword against her on
every side;
Then they shall know that I *am*
the LORD.

24 "And there shall no longer be a
pricking brier or a painful thorn for
the house of Israel from among all
who *are* around them, who despise
them. Then they shall know that I *am*
the Lord GOD."

25 'Thus says the Lord GOD: "When
I have gathered the house of Israel
from the peoples among whom they
are scattered, and am hallowed in
them in the sight of the Gentiles, then
they will dwell in their own land
which I gave to My servant Jacob.
26 And they will dwell safely there,
build houses, and plant vineyards;
yes, they will dwell securely, when I
execute judgments on all those
around them who despise them. Then
they shall know that I *am* the LORD
their God." ' "

29 In the tenth year, in the tenth
month, on the twelfth *day* of
the month, the word of the LORD
came to me, saying, 2 "Son of man,
set your face against Pharaoh king
of Egypt, and prophesy against him,
and against all Egypt. 3 Speak, and
say, 'Thus says the Lord GOD:

"Behold, I *am* against you,
O Pharaoh king of Egypt,
O great monster who lies in the
midst of his rivers,
Who has said, 'My River[a] *is* my
own;
I have made *it* for myself.'
4 But I will put hooks in your
jaws,
And cause the fish of your
rivers to stick to your scales;
I will bring you up out of the
midst of your rivers,
And all the fish in your rivers
will stick to your scales.
5 I will leave you in the
wilderness,

29:3 [a]That is, the Nile

You and all the fish of your
rivers;
You shall fall on the open field;
You shall not be picked up or
gathered.ᵃ
I have given you as food
To the beasts of the field
And to the birds of the heavens.

6 "Then all the inhabitants of
Egypt
Shall know that I *am* the LORD,
Because they have been a staff
of reed to the house of Israel.
7 When they took hold of you
with the hand,
You broke and tore all their
shoulders;ᵃ
When they leaned on you,
You broke and made all their
backs quiver."

8 'Therefore thus says the Lord
GOD: "Surely I will bring a sword
upon you and cut off from you man
and beast. 9 And the land of Egypt
shall become desolate and waste;
then they will know that I *am* the
LORD, because he said, 'The River *is*
mine, and I have made *it*.' 10 Indeed,
therefore, I *am* against you and
against your rivers, and I will make
the land of Egypt utterly waste and
desolate, from Migdolᵃ *to* Syene, as
far as the border of Ethiopia.
11 Neither foot of man shall pass
through it nor foot of beast pass
through it, and it shall be uninhabited forty years. 12 I will make the
land of Egypt desolate in the midst
of the countries *that are* desolate;
and among the cities *that are* laid
waste, her cities shall be desolate
forty years; and I will scatter the
Egyptians among the nations and
disperse them throughout the countries."

13 'Yet, thus says the Lord GOD: "At
the end of forty years I will gather
the Egyptians from the peoples
among whom they were scattered.
14 I will bring back the captives of
Egypt and cause them to return to
the land of Pathros, to the land of
their origin, and there they shall be
a lowly kingdom. 15 It shall be the
lowliest of kingdoms; it shall never
again exalt itself above the nations,
for I will diminish them so that they
will not rule over the nations anymore. 16 No longer shall it be the confidence of the house of Israel, but will
remind them of *their* iniquity when
they turned to follow them. Then
they shall know that I *am* the Lord
GOD." ' "

17 And it came to pass in the
twenty-seventh year, in the first
month, on the first *day* of the month,
that the word of the LORD came to
me, saying, 18 "Son of man, Nebuchadnezzar king of Babylon caused
his army to labor strenuously against
Tyre; every head *was* made bald, and
every shoulder rubbed raw; yet neither he nor his army received wages
from Tyre, for the labor which they
expended on it. 19 Therefore thus
says the Lord GOD: 'Surely I will give
the land of Egypt to Nebuchadnezzar
king of Babylon; he shall take away
her wealth, carry off her spoil, and
remove her pillage; and that will be
the wages for his army. 20 I have
given him the land of Egypt *for* his
labor, because they worked for Me,'
says the Lord GOD.
21 'In that day I will cause the horn
of the house of Israel to spring forth,
and I will open your mouth to speak
in their midst. Then they shall know
that I *am* the LORD.' "

30 The word of the LORD came to
me again, saying, 2 "Son of
man, prophesy and say, 'Thus says
the Lord GOD:

"Wail, 'Woe to the day!'
3 For the day *is* near,
Even the day of the LORD *is*
near;
It will be a day of clouds, the
time of the Gentiles.
4 The sword shall come upon
Egypt,
And great anguish shall be in
Ethiopia,
When the slain fall in Egypt,
And they take away her wealth,
And her foundations are
broken down.

5 "Ethiopia, Libya,ᵃ Lydia,ᵇ all the
mingled people, Chub, and the men

29:5 ᵃFollowing Masoretic Text, Septuagint, and Vulgate; some Hebrew manuscripts and Targum read
buried. 29:7 ᵃFollowing Masoretic Text and Vulgate; Septuagint and Syriac read *hand.* 29:10 ᵃOr
tower 30:5 ᵃHebrew *Put* ᵇHebrew *Lud*

of the lands who are allied, shall fall with them by the sword."

6 'Thus says the LORD:

"Those who uphold Egypt shall
    fall,
And the pride of her power
    shall come down.
From Migdol *to* Syene
Those within her shall fall by
    the sword,"
Says the Lord GOD.

7 "They shall be desolate in the
    midst of the desolate
    countries,
And her cities shall be in the
    midst of the cities *that are*
    laid waste.
8 Then they will know that I *am*
    the LORD,
When I have set a fire in Egypt
And all her helpers are
    destroyed.
9 On that day messengers shall
    go forth from Me in ships
To make the careless
    Ethiopians afraid,
And great anguish shall come
    upon them,
As on the day of Egypt;
For indeed it is coming!"

10 'Thus says the Lord GOD:

"I will also make a multitude of
    Egypt to cease
By the hand of
    Nebuchadnezzar king of
    Babylon.
11 He and his people with him, the
    most terrible of the nations,
Shall be brought to destroy the
    land;
They shall draw their swords
    against Egypt,
And fill the land with the slain.
12 I will make the rivers dry,
And sell the land into the hand
    of the wicked;
I will make the land waste, and
    all that is in it,
By the hand of aliens.
I, the LORD, have spoken."

13 'Thus says the Lord GOD:

"I will also destroy the idols,
And cause the images to cease
    from Noph;[a]
There shall no longer be
    princes from the land of
    Egypt;
I will put fear in the land of
    Egypt.
14 I will make Pathros desolate,
Set fire to Zoan,
And execute judgments in No.[a]
15 I will pour My fury on Sin,[a] the
    strength of Egypt;
I will cut off the multitude of
    No,
16 And set a fire in Egypt;
Sin shall have great pain,
No shall be split open,
And Noph *shall be in* distress
    daily.
17 The young men of Aven[a] and
    Pi Beseth shall fall by the
    sword,
And these *cities* shall go into
    captivity.
18 At Tehaphnehes[a] the day shall
    also be darkened,[b]
When I break the yokes of
    Egypt there.
And her arrogant strength shall
    cease in her;
As for her, a cloud shall cover
    her,
And her daughters shall go into
    captivity.
19 Thus I will execute judgments
    on Egypt,
Then they shall know that I *am*
    the LORD." ' "

20 And it came to pass in the eleventh year, in the first *month,* on the seventh *day* of the month, *that* the word of the LORD came to me, saying, 21 "Son of man, I have broken the arm of Pharaoh king of Egypt; and see, it has not been bandaged for healing, nor a splint put on to bind it, to make it strong enough to hold a sword. 22 Therefore thus says the Lord GOD: 'Surely I *am* against Pharaoh king of Egypt, and will break his arms, both the strong one and the one that was broken; and I will make the sword fall out of his hand. 23 I will scatter the Egyptians among the nations, and disperse them

throughout the countries. 24 I will strengthen the arms of the king of Babylon and put My sword in his hand; but I will break Pharaoh's arms, and he will groan before him with the groanings of a mortally wounded *man*. 25 Thus I will strengthen the arms of the king of Babylon, but the arms of Pharaoh shall fall down; they shall know that I *am* the LORD, when I put My sword into the hand of the king of Babylon and he stretches it out against the land of Egypt. 26 I will scatter the Egyptians among the nations and disperse them throughout the countries. Then they shall know that I *am* the LORD.' "

31 Now it came to pass in the eleventh year, in the third *month*, on the first *day* of the month, *that* the word of the LORD came to me, saying, 2 "Son of man, say to Pharaoh king of Egypt and to his multitude:

'Whom are you like in your greatness?
3   Indeed Assyria *was* a cedar in Lebanon,
With fine branches that shaded the forest,
And of high stature;
And its top was among the thick boughs.
4   The waters made it grow;
Underground waters gave it height,
With their rivers running around the place where it was planted,
And sent out rivulets to all the trees of the field.
5   'Therefore its height was exalted above all the trees of the field;
Its boughs were multiplied,
And its branches became long because of the abundance of water,
As it sent them out.
6   All the birds of the heavens made their nests in its boughs;
Under its branches all the beasts of the field brought forth their young;

And in its shadow all great nations made their home.
7   'Thus it was beautiful in greatness and in the length of its branches,
Because its roots reached to abundant waters.
8   The cedars in the garden of God could not hide it;
The fir trees were not like its boughs,
And the chestnut[a] trees were not like its branches;
No tree in the garden of God was like it in beauty.
9   I made it beautiful with a multitude of branches,
So that all the trees of Eden envied it,
That *were* in the garden of God.'

10 "Therefore thus says the Lord GOD: 'Because you have increased in height, and it set its top among the thick boughs, and its heart was lifted up in its height, 11 therefore I will deliver it into the hand of the mighty one of the nations, and he shall surely deal with it; I have driven it out for its wickedness. 12 And aliens, the most terrible of the nations, have cut it down and left it; its branches have fallen on the mountains and in all the valleys; its boughs lie broken by all the rivers of the land; and all the peoples of the earth have gone from under its shadow and left it.

13   'On its ruin will remain all the birds of the heavens,
And all the beasts of the field will come to its branches—

14 'So that no trees by the waters may ever again exalt themselves for their height, nor set their tops among the thick boughs, that no tree which drinks water may ever be high enough to reach up to them.

'For they have all been delivered to death,
To the depths of the earth,
Among the children of men who go down to the Pit.'

15 "Thus says the Lord GOD: 'In the day when it went down to hell, I

31:8 [a]Hebrew *armon*

caused mourning. I covered the deep because of it. I restrained its rivers, and the great waters were held back. I caused Lebanon to mourn for it, and all the trees of the field wilted because of it. 16 I made the nations shake at the sound of its fall, when I cast it down to hell together with those who descend into the Pit; and all the trees of Eden, the choice and best of Lebanon, all that drink water, were comforted in the depths of the earth. 17 They also went down to hell with it, with those *slain* by the sword; and *those who were* its *strong* arm dwelt in its shadows among the nations.

18 'To which of the trees in Eden will you then be likened in glory and greatness? Yet you shall be brought down with the trees of Eden to the depths of the earth; you shall lie in the midst of the uncircumcised, with *those* slain by the sword. This *is* Pharaoh and all his multitude,' says the Lord GOD."

32 And it came to pass in the twelfth year, in the twelfth *month,* on the first *day* of the month, *that* the word of the LORD came to me, saying, 2 "Son of man, take up a lamentation for Pharaoh king of Egypt, and say to him:

'You are like a young lion
  among the nations,
And you *are* like a monster in
  the seas,
Bursting forth in your rivers,
Troubling the waters with your
  feet,
And fouling their rivers.'

3 "Thus says the Lord GOD:

'I will therefore spread My net
  over you with a company of
  many people,
And they will draw you up in
  My net.
4 Then I will leave you on the
  land;
I will cast you out on the open
  fields,
And cause to settle on you all
  the birds of the heavens.
And with you I will fill the
  beasts of the whole earth.
5 I will lay your flesh on the
  mountains,

And fill the valleys with your
  carcass.
6 'I will also water the land with
  the flow of your blood,
Even to the mountains;
And the riverbeds will be full
  of you.
7 When *I* put out your light,
I will cover the heavens, and
  make its stars dark;
I will cover the sun with a
  cloud,
And the moon shall not give
  her light.
8 All the bright lights of the
  heavens I will make dark
  over you,
And bring darkness upon your
  land,'
Says the Lord GOD.

9 'I will also trouble the hearts of many peoples, when I bring your destruction among the nations, into the countries which you have not known. 10 Yes, I will make many peoples astonished at you, and their kings shall be horribly afraid of you when I brandish My sword before them; and they shall tremble *every* moment, every man for his own life, in the day of your fall.'

11 "For thus says the Lord GOD: 'The sword of the king of Babylon shall come upon you. 12 By the swords of the mighty warriors, all of them the most terrible of the nations, I will cause your multitude to fall.

'They shall plunder the pomp of
  Egypt,
And all its multitude shall be
  destroyed.
13 Also I will destroy all its
  animals
From beside its great waters;
The foot of man shall muddy
  them no more,
Nor shall the hooves of animals
  muddy them.
14 Then I will make their waters
  clear,
And make their rivers run like
  oil,'
Says the Lord GOD.

15 'When I make the land of Egypt
  desolate,
And the country is destitute of
  all that once filled it,

When I strike all who dwell in
it,
Then they shall know that I *am*
the LORD.

16 'This *is* the lamentation
With which they shall lament
her;
The daughters of the nations
shall lament her;
They shall lament for her, for
Egypt,
And for all her multitude,'
Says the Lord GOD."

17 It came to pass also in the
twelfth year, on the fifteenth *day* of
the month, that the word of the LORD
came to me, saying:

18 "Son of man, wail over the
multitude of Egypt,
And cast them down to the
depths of the earth,
Her and the daughters of the
famous nations,
With those who go down to the
Pit:
19 'Whom do you surpass in
beauty?
Go down, be placed with the
uncircumcised.'

20 "They shall fall in the midst of
those slain by the sword;
She is delivered to the sword,
Drawing her and all her
multitudes.
21 The strong among the mighty
Shall speak to him out of the
midst of hell
With those who help him:
'They have gone down,
They lie with the
uncircumcised, slain by the
sword.'

22 "Assyria *is* there, and all her
company,
With their graves all around
her,
All of them slain, fallen by the
sword.
23 Her graves are set in the
recesses of the Pit,
And her company is all around
her grave,
All of them slain, fallen by the
sword,
Who caused terror in the land
of the living.

24 "There *is* Elam and all her
multitude,
All around her grave,
All of them slain, fallen by the
sword,
Who have gone down
uncircumcised to the lower
parts of the earth,
Who caused their terror in the
land of the living;
Now they bear their shame
with those who go down to
the Pit.
25 They have set her bed in the
midst of the slain,
With all her multitude,
With her graves all around it,
All of them uncircumcised,
slain by the sword;
Though their terror was caused
In the land of the living,
Yet they bear their shame
With those who go down to the
Pit;
It was put in the midst of the
slain.

26 "There *are* Meshech and Tubal
and all their multitudes,
With all their graves around
it,
All of them uncircumcised,
slain by the sword,
Though they caused their
terror in the land of the
living.
27 They do not lie with the mighty
Who are fallen of the
uncircumcised,
Who have gone down to hell
with their weapons of war;
They have laid their swords
under their heads,
But their iniquities will be on
their bones,
Because of the terror of the
mighty in the land of the
living.
28 Yes, you shall be broken in the
midst of the uncircumcised,
And lie with *those* slain by the
sword.

29 "There *is* Edom,
Her kings and all her princes,
Who despite their might
Are laid beside *those* slain by
the sword;
They shall lie with the
uncircumcised,
And with those who go down
to the Pit.

30 There *are* the princes of the
      north,
   All of them, and all the
      Sidonians,
   Who have gone down with the
      slain
   In shame at the terror which
      they caused by their might;
   They lie uncircumcised with
      those slain by the sword,
   And bear their shame with
      those who go down to the Pit.

31 "Pharaoh will see them
   And be comforted over all his
      multitude,
   Pharaoh and all his army,
   Slain by the sword,"
   Says the Lord GOD.

32 "For I have caused My terror in
      the land of the living;
   And he shall be placed in the
      midst of the uncircumcised
   With *those* slain by the sword,
   Pharaoh and all his multitude,"
   Says the Lord GOD.

33 Again the word of the LORD
came to me, saying, 2 "Son of
man, speak to the children of your
people, and say to them: 'When I
bring the sword upon a land, and the
people of the land take a man from
their territory and make him their
watchman, 3 when he sees the sword
coming upon the land, if he blows the
trumpet and warns the people,
4 then whoever hears the sound of
the trumpet and does not take warning, if the sword comes and takes him
away, his blood shall be on his *own*
head. 5 He heard the sound of the
trumpet, but did not take warning;
his blood shall be upon himself. But
he who takes warning will save his
life. 6 But if the watchman sees the
sword coming and does not blow the
trumpet, and the people are not
warned, and the sword comes and
takes *any* person from among them,
he is taken away in his iniquity; but
his blood I will require at the watchman's hand.'
7 "So you, son of man: I have made
you a watchman for the house of Israel; therefore you shall hear a word
from My mouth and warn them for
Me. 8 When I say to the wicked, 'O
wicked *man*, you shall surely die!'
and you do not speak to warn the
wicked from his way, that wicked

man shall die in his iniquity; but his
blood I will require at your hand.
9 Nevertheless if you warn the
wicked to turn from his way, and he
does not turn from his way, he shall
die in his iniquity; but you have delivered your soul.
10 "Therefore you, O son of man,
say to the house of Israel: 'Thus you
say, "If our transgressions and our
sins *lie* upon us, and we pine away
in them, how can we then live?"'
11 Say to them: 'As I live,' says the
Lord GOD, 'I have no pleasure in the
death of the wicked, but that the
wicked turn from his way and live.
Turn, turn from your evil ways! For
why should you die, O house of Israel?'
12 "Therefore you, O son of man,
say to the children of your people:
'The righteousness of the righteous
man shall not deliver him in the day
of his transgression; as for the wickedness of the wicked, he shall not fall
because of it in the day that he turns
from his wickedness; nor shall the
righteous be able to live because of
his righteousness in the day that he
sins.' 13 When I say to the righteous
that he shall surely live, but he trusts
in his own righteousness and commits iniquity, none of his righteous
works shall be remembered; but because of the iniquity that he has committed, he shall die. 14 Again, when
I say to the wicked, 'You shall surely
die,' if he turns from his sin and does
what is lawful and right, 15 *if* the
wicked restores the pledge, gives
back what he has stolen, and walks
in the statutes of life without committing iniquity, he shall surely live; he
shall not die. 16 None of his sins
which he has committed shall be remembered against him; he has done
what is lawful and right; he shall
surely live.
17 "Yet the children of your people
say, 'The way of the LORD is not fair.'
But it is their way which is not fair!
18 When the righteous turns from his
righteousness and commits iniquity,
he shall die because of it. 19 But when
the wicked turns from his wickedness and does what is lawful and
right, he shall live because of it.
20 Yet you say, 'The way of the LORD
is not fair.' O house of Israel, I will
judge every one of you according to
his own ways."
21 And it came to pass in the

twelfth year of our captivity, in the tenth *month,* on the fifth *day* of the month, *that* one who had escaped from Jerusalem came to me and said, "The city has been captured!"

22 Now the hand of the LORD had been upon me the evening before the man came who had escaped. And He had opened my mouth; so when he came to me in the morning, my mouth was opened, and I was no longer mute.

23 Then the word of the LORD came to me, saying: 24 "Son of man, they who inhabit those ruins in the land of Israel are saying, 'Abraham was only one, and he inherited the land. But we *are* many; the land has been given to us as a possession.'

25 "Therefore say to them, 'Thus says the Lord GOD: "You eat *meat* with blood, you lift up your eyes toward your idols, and shed blood. Should you then possess the land? 26 You rely on your sword, you commit abominations, and you defile one another's wives. Should you then possess the land?"'

27 "Say thus to them, 'Thus says the Lord GOD: "*As* I live, surely those who *are* in the ruins shall fall by the sword, and the one who *is* in the open field I will give to the beasts to be devoured, and those who *are* in the strongholds and caves shall die of the pestilence. 28 For I will make the land most desolate, her arrogant strength shall cease, and the mountains of Israel shall be so desolate that no one will pass through. 29 Then they shall know that I *am* the LORD, when I have made the land most desolate because of all their abominations which they have committed."'

30 "As for you, son of man, the children of your people are talking about you beside the walls and in the doors of the houses; and they speak to one another, everyone saying to his brother, 'Please come and hear what the word is that comes from the LORD.' 31 So they come to you as people do, they sit before you *as* My people, and they hear your words, but they do not do them; for with their mouth they show much love, *but* their hearts pursue their *own* gain. 32 Indeed you *are* to them as a very lovely song of one who has a pleasant voice and can play well on an instrument; for they hear your words, but they do not do them. 33 And when

this comes to pass—surely it will come—then they will know that a prophet has been among them."

34 And the word of the LORD came to me, saying, 2 "Son of man, prophesy against the shepherds of Israel, prophesy and say to them, 'Thus says the Lord GOD to the shepherds: "Woe to the shepherds of Israel who feed themselves! Should not the shepherds feed the flocks? 3 You eat the fat and clothe yourselves with the wool; you slaughter the fatlings, *but* you do not feed the flock. 4 The weak you have not strengthened, nor have you healed those who were sick, nor bound up the broken, nor brought back what was driven away, nor sought what was lost; but with force and cruelty you have ruled them. 5 So they were scattered because *there was* no shepherd; and they became food for all the beasts of the field when they were scattered. 6 My sheep wandered through all the mountains, and on every high hill; yes, My flock was scattered over the whole face of the earth, and no one was seeking or searching *for them.*"

7 'Therefore, you shepherds, hear the word of the LORD: 8 "*as* I live," says the Lord GOD, "surely because My flock became a prey, and My flock became food for every beast of the field, because *there was* no shepherd, nor did My shepherds search for My flock, but the shepherds fed themselves and did not feed My flock"— 9 therefore, O shepherds, hear the word of the LORD! 10 Thus says the Lord GOD: "Behold, I *am* against the shepherds, and I will require My flock at their hand; I will cause them to cease feeding the sheep, and the shepherds shall feed themselves no more; for I will deliver My flock from their mouths, that they may no longer be food for them."

11 'For thus says the Lord GOD: "Indeed I Myself will search for My sheep and seek them out. 12 As a shepherd seeks out his flock on the day he is among his scattered sheep, so will I seek out My sheep and deliver them from all the places where they were scattered on a cloudy and dark day. 13 And I will bring them out from the peoples and gather them from the countries, and will bring them to their own land; I will feed them on the mountains of Israel, in

the valleys and in all the inhabited places of the country. 14 I will feed them in good pasture, and their fold shall be on the high mountains of Israel. There they shall lie down in a good fold and feed in rich pasture on the mountains of Israel. 15 I will feed My flock, and I will make them lie down," says the Lord GOD. 16 "I will seek what was lost and bring back what was driven away, bind up the broken and strengthen what was sick; but I will destroy the fat and the strong, and feed them in judgment."

17 'And as for you, O My flock, thus says the Lord GOD: "Behold, I shall judge between sheep and sheep, between rams and goats. 18 Is it too little for you to have eaten up the good pasture, that you must tread down with your feet the residue of your pasture—and to have drunk of the clear waters, that you must foul the residue with your feet? 19 And as for My flock, they eat what you have trampled with your feet, and they drink what you have fouled with your feet."

20 'Therefore thus says the Lord GOD to them: "Behold, I Myself will judge between the fat and the lean sheep. 21 Because you have pushed with side and shoulder, butted all the weak ones with your horns, and scattered them abroad, 22 therefore I will save My flock, and they shall no longer be a prey; and I will judge between sheep and sheep. 23 I will establish one shepherd over them, and he shall feed them—My servant David. He shall feed them and be their shepherd. 24 And I, the LORD, will be their God, and My servant David a prince among them; I, the LORD, have spoken.

25 "I will make a covenant of peace with them, and cause wild beasts to cease from the land; and they will dwell safely in the wilderness and sleep in the woods. 26 I will make them and the places all around My hill a blessing; and I will cause showers to come down in their season; there shall be showers of blessing. 27 Then the trees of the field shall yield their fruit, and the earth shall yield her increase. They shall be safe in their land; and they shall know that I am the LORD, when I have broken the bands of their yoke and delivered them from the hand of those

who enslaved them. 28 And they shall no longer be a prey for the nations, nor shall beasts of the land devour them; but they shall dwell safely, and no one shall make them afraid. 29 I will raise up for them a garden of renown, and they shall no longer be consumed with hunger in the land, nor bear the shame of the Gentiles anymore. 30 Thus they shall know that I, the LORD their God, am with them, and they, the house of Israel, are My people," says the Lord GOD.' "

31 "You are My flock, the flock of My pasture; you are men, and I am your God," says the Lord GOD.

35 Moreover the word of the LORD came to me, saying, 2 "Son of man, set your face against Mount Seir and prophesy against it, 3 and say to it, 'Thus says the Lord GOD:

"Behold, O Mount Seir, I am
    against you;
I will stretch out My hand
    against you,
And make you most desolate;
4 I shall lay your cities waste,
And you shall be desolate.
Then you shall know that I am
    the LORD.

5 "Because you have had an ancient hatred, and have shed the blood of the children of Israel by the power of the sword at the time of their calamity, when their iniquity came to an end, 6 therefore, as I live," says the Lord GOD, "I will prepare you for blood, and blood shall pursue you; since you have not hated blood, therefore blood shall pursue you. 7 Thus I will make Mount Seir most desolate, and cut off from it the one who leaves and the one who returns. 8 And I will fill its mountains with the slain; on your hills and in your valleys and in all your ravines those who are slain by the sword shall fall. 9 I will make you perpetually desolate, and your cities shall be uninhabited; then you shall know that I am the LORD.

10 "Because you have said, 'These two nations and these two countries shall be mine, and we will possess them,' although the LORD was there, 11 therefore, as I live," says the Lord GOD, "I will do according to your anger and according to the envy which

you showed in your hatred against them; and I will make Myself known among them when I judge you. 12 Then you shall know that I *am* the LORD. I have heard all your blasphemies which you have spoken against the mountains of Israel, saying, 'They are desolate; they are given to us to consume.' 13 Thus with your mouth you have boasted against Me and multiplied your words against Me; I have heard *them*."

14 'Thus says the Lord GOD: "The whole earth will rejoice when I make you desolate. 15 As you rejoiced because the inheritance of the house of Israel was desolate, so I will do to you; you shall be desolate, O Mount Seir, as well as all of Edom—all of it! Then they shall know that I *am* the LORD." '

36 "And you, son of man, prophesy to the mountains of Israel, and say, 'O mountains of Israel, hear the word of the LORD! 2 Thus says the Lord GOD: "Because the enemy has said of you, 'Aha! The ancient heights have become our possession,' " ' 3 therefore prophesy, and say, 'Thus says the Lord GOD: "Because they made *you* desolate and swallowed you up on every side, so that you became the possession of the rest of the nations, and you are taken up by the lips of talkers and slandered by the people"— 4 therefore, O mountains of Israel, hear the word of the Lord GOD! Thus says the Lord GOD to the mountains, the hills, the rivers, the valleys, the desolate wastes, and the cities that have been forsaken, which became plunder and mockery to the rest of the nations all around— 5 therefore thus says the Lord GOD: "Surely I have spoken in My burning jealousy against the rest of the nations and against all Edom, who gave My land to themselves as a possession, with wholehearted joy *and* spiteful minds, in order to plunder its open country." '

6 "Therefore prophesy concerning the land of Israel, and say to the mountains, the hills, the rivers, and the valleys, 'Thus says the Lord GOD: "Behold, I have spoken in My jealousy and My fury, because you have borne the shame of the nations." ' 7 Therefore thus says the Lord GOD: "I have raised My hand in an oath that surely the nations that *are* around you shall bear their own shame. 8 But you, O mountains of Israel, you shall shoot forth your branches and yield your fruit to My people Israel, for they are about to come. 9 For indeed I *am* for you, and I will turn to you, and you shall be tilled and sown. 10 I will multiply men upon you, all the house of Israel, all of it; and the cities shall be inhabited and the ruins rebuilt. 11 I will multiply upon you man and beast; and they shall increase and bear young; I will make you inhabited as in former times, and do better *for you* than at your beginnings. Then you shall know that I *am* the LORD. 12 Yes, I will cause men to walk on you, My people Israel; they shall take possession of you, and you shall be their inheritance; no more shall you bereave them *of children*."

13 'Thus says the Lord GOD: "Because they say to you, 'You devour men and bereave your nation *of children*,' 14 therefore you shall devour men no more, nor bereave your nation anymore," says the Lord GOD. 15 Nor will I let you hear the taunts of the nations anymore, nor bear the reproach of the peoples anymore, nor shall you cause your nation to stumble anymore," says the Lord GOD.' "

16 Moreover the word of the LORD came to me, saying: 17 "Son of man, when the house of Israel dwelt in their own land, they defiled it by their own ways and deeds; to Me their way was like the uncleanness of a woman in her customary impurity. 18 Therefore I poured out My fury on them for the blood they had shed on the land, and for their idols *with which* they had defiled it. 19 So I scattered them among the nations, and they were dispersed throughout the countries; I judged them according to their ways and their deeds. 20 When they came to the nations, wherever they went, they profaned My holy name—when they said of them, 'These *are* the people of the LORD, *and* yet they have gone out of His land.' 21 But I had concern for My holy name, which the house of Israel had profaned among the nations wherever they went.

22 "Therefore say to the house of Israel, 'Thus says the Lord GOD: "I do not do *this* for your sake, O house of Israel, but for My holy name's

God Still Makes Miracles

How would you respond if someone challenged your faith with: "Show me a miracle—and I'll believe in it!" You could answer: "Take a look at me—I'm one! Then take a look in the mirror. You'll see another one!"

The fact that you are alive today is nothing short of a miracle! Your life is the continuation of an unbroken genetic string reaching back all the way to the first parents. Look back at your family tree and see how many times the cord came close to being severed. Was it in the Civil War? Was it in a plague epidemic? Was it on a slave ship crossing the waters from Africa to America?

You are a survivor of survivors of survivors! How often you yourself have survived near-death experiences, you will never know!

Your life has a special purpose. There is a reason why you are alive today. You are a walking miracle! Whatever your racial origin, ethnic identification, educational level, or economic bracket, you are special! You are a winner! You are alive!

So give your life totally today to the God who brought you here. Let Jesus Christ—the Ultimate Survivor, who rose from the dead on Easter morning—be your best Friend, and share His wonderful love with the people you come into contact with today. That, at least, is your reason for being here.

God must have believed that you'd be a good person to spread His love around in the world today! God has not let you down. You won't let Him down either. You have every reason to be supergrateful. Think of it: Saved for such a high and holy purpose.

sake, which you have profaned among the nations wherever you went. 23 And I will sanctify My great name, which has been profaned among the nations, which you have profaned in their midst; and the nations shall know that I *am* the LORD," says the Lord GOD, "when I am hallowed in you before their eyes. 24 For I will take you from among the nations, gather you out of all countries, and bring you into your own land. 25 Then I will sprinkle clean water on you, and you shall be clean; I will cleanse you from all your filthiness and from all your idols. 26 I will give you a new heart and put a new spirit within you; I will take the heart of stone out of your flesh and give you a heart of flesh. 27 I will put My Spirit within you and cause you to walk in My statutes, and you will keep My judgments and do *them.* 28 Then you shall dwell in the land that I gave to your fathers; you shall be My people, and I will be your God. 29 I will deliver you from all your uncleannesses. I will call for the grain and multiply it, and bring no famine upon you. 30 And I will multiply the fruit of your trees and the increase of your fields, so that you need never again bear the reproach of famine among the nations. 31 Then you will remember your evil ways and your deeds that *were* not good; and you will loathe yourselves in your own sight, for your iniquities and your abominations. 32 Not for your sake do I do *this,*" says the Lord GOD, "let it be known to you. Be ashamed and confounded for your own ways, O house of Israel!"

33 'Thus says the Lord GOD: "On the day that I cleanse you from all your iniquities, I will also enable *you* to dwell in the cities, and the ruins shall be rebuilt. 34 The desolate land shall be tilled instead of lying desolate in the sight of all who pass by. 35 So they will say, 'This land that was desolate has become like the garden of Eden; and the wasted, desolate, and ruined cities *are now* fortified *and* inhabited.' 36 Then the nations which are left all around you shall know that I, the LORD, have rebuilt the ruined places *and* planted what was desolate. I, the LORD, have spoken *it,* and I will do *it.*"

37 'Thus says the Lord GOD: "I will also let the house of Israel inquire of Me to do this for them: I will increase their men like a flock. 38 Like a flock *offered as* holy *sacrifices,* like the flock at Jerusalem on its feast days, so shall the ruined cities be filled with flocks of men. Then they shall know that I *am* the LORD." ' "

37 The hand of the LORD came upon me and brought me out in the Spirit of the LORD, and set me down in the midst of the valley; and it *was* full of bones. 2 Then He caused me to pass by them all around, and behold, *there were* very many in the open valley; and indeed *they were* very dry. 3 And He said to me, "Son of man, can these bones live?"

So I answered, "O Lord GOD, You know."

4 Again He said to me, "Prophesy to these bones, and say to them, 'O dry bones, hear the word of the LORD! 5 Thus says the Lord GOD to these bones: "Surely I will cause breath to enter into you, and you shall live. 6 I will put sinews on you and bring flesh upon you, cover you with skin and put breath in you; and you shall live. Then you shall know that I *am* the LORD." ' "

7 So I prophesied as I was commanded; and as I prophesied, there was a noise, and suddenly a rattling; and the bones came together, bone to bone. 8 Indeed, as I looked, the sinews and the flesh came upon them, and the skin covered them over; but *there was* no breath in them.

9 Also He said to me, "Prophesy to the breath, prophesy, son of man, and say to the breath, 'Thus says the Lord GOD: "Come from the four winds, O breath, and breathe on these slain, that they may live." ' " 10 So I prophesied as He commanded me, and breath came into them, and they lived, and stood upon their feet, an exceedingly great army.

11 Then He said to me, "Son of man, these bones are the whole house of Israel. They indeed say, 'Our bones are dry, our hope is lost, and we ourselves are cut off!' 12 Therefore prophesy and say to them, 'Thus says the Lord GOD: "Behold, O My people, I will open your graves and cause you to come up from your graves, and bring you into the land of Israel. 13 Then you shall know that I *am* the LORD, when I have

opened your graves, O My people, and brought you up from your graves. 14 I will put My Spirit in you, and you shall live, and I will place you in your own land. Then you shall know that I, the LORD, have spoken it and performed it," says the LORD.' "

15 Again the word of the LORD came to me, saying, 16 "As for you, son of man, take a stick for yourself and write on it: 'For Judah and for the children of Israel, his companions.' Then take another stick and write on it, 'For Joseph, the stick of Ephraim, and for all the house of Israel, his companions.' 17 Then join them one to another for yourself into one stick, and they will become one in your hand.

18 "And when the children of your people speak to you, saying, 'Will you not show us what you mean by these?'— 19 say to them, 'Thus says the Lord GOD: "Surely I will take the stick of Joseph, which is in the hand of Ephraim, and the tribes of Israel, his companions; and I will join them with it, with the stick of Judah, and make them one stick, and they will be one in My hand." ' 20 And the sticks on which you write will be in your hand before their eyes.

21 "Then say to them, 'Thus says the Lord GOD: "Surely I will take the children of Israel from among the nations, wherever they have gone, and will gather them from every side and bring them into their own land; 22 and I will make them one nation in the land, on the mountains of Israel; and one king shall be king over them all; they shall no longer be two nations, nor shall they ever be divided into two kingdoms again. 23 They shall not defile themselves anymore with their idols, nor with their detestable things, nor with any of their transgressions; but I will deliver them from all their dwelling places in which they have sinned, and will cleanse them. Then they shall be My people, and I will be their God.

24 "David My servant shall be king over them, and they shall all have one shepherd; they shall also walk in My judgments and observe My statutes, and do them. 25 Then they shall dwell in the land that I have given to Jacob My servant, where your fathers dwelt; and they shall dwell there, they, their children, and their children's children, forever; and My servant David shall be their prince forever. 26 Moreover I will make a covenant of peace with them, and it shall be an everlasting covenant with them; I will establish them and multiply them, and I will set My sanctuary in their midst forevermore. 27 My tabernacle also shall be with them; indeed I will be their God, and they shall be My people. 28 The nations also will know that I, the LORD, sanctify Israel, when My sanctuary is in their midst forevermore." ' "

38 Now the word of the LORD came to me, saying, 2 "Son of man, set your face against Gog, of the land of Magog, the prince of Rosh,a Meshech, and Tubal, and prophesy against him, 3 and say, 'Thus says the Lord GOD: "Behold, I am against you, O Gog, the prince of Rosh, Meshech, and Tubal. 4 I will turn you around, put hooks into your jaws, and lead you out, with all your army, horses, and horsemen, all splendidly clothed, a great company with bucklers and shields, all of them handling swords. 5 Persia, Ethiopia,a and Libyab are with them, all of them with shield and helmet; 6 Gomer and all its troops; the house of Togarmah from the far north and all its troops— many people are with you.

7 "Prepare yourself and be ready, you and all your companies that are gathered about you; and be a guard for them. 8 After many days you will be visited. In the latter years you will come into the land of those brought back from the sword and gathered from many people on the mountains of Israel, which had long been desolate; they were brought out of the nations, and now all of them dwell safely. 9 You will ascend, coming like a storm, covering the land like a cloud, you and all your troops and many peoples with you."

10 'Thus says the Lord GOD: "On that day it shall come to pass that thoughts will arise in your mind, and you will make an evil plan: 11 You will say, 'I will go up against

---

38:2 aTargum, Vulgate, and Aquila read chief prince of (also verse 3).   38:5 aHebrew Cush   bHebrew Put a land of unwalled villages; I will go to a peaceful people, who dwell safely, all of them dwelling without walls, and having neither bars nor gates'— 12 to take plunder and to take booty, to stretch out your hand against the waste places *that are again* inhabited, and against a people gathered from the nations, who have acquired livestock and goods, who dwell in the midst of the land. 13 Sheba, Dedan, the merchants of Tarshish, and all their young lions will say to you, 'Have you come to take plunder? Have you gathered your army to take booty, to carry away silver and gold, to take away livestock and goods, to take great plunder?' " '

14 "Therefore, son of man, prophesy and say to Gog, 'Thus says the Lord GOD: "On that day when My people Israel dwell safely, will you not know *it*? 15 Then you will come from your place out of the far north, you and many peoples with you, all of them riding on horses, a great company and a mighty army. 16 You will come up against My people Israel like a cloud, to cover the land. It will be in the latter days that I will bring you against My land, so that the nations may know Me, when I am hallowed in you, O Gog, before their eyes." 17 Thus says the Lord GOD: "Are *you* he of whom I have spoken in former days by My servants the prophets of Israel, who prophesied for years in those days that I would bring you against them? 18 " ' "And it will come to pass at the same time, when Gog comes against the land of Israel," says the Lord GOD, "*that* My fury will show in My face. 19 For in My jealousy *and* in the fire of My wrath I have spoken: 'Surely in that day there shall be a great earthquake in the land of Israel, 20 so that the fish of the sea, the birds of the heavens, the beasts of the field, all creeping things that creep on the earth, and all men who *are* on the face of the earth shall shake at My presence. The mountains shall be thrown down, the steep places shall fall, and every wall shall fall to the ground.' 21 I will call for a sword against Gog throughout all My mountains," says the Lord GOD. "Every man's sword will be against his

brother. 22 And I will bring him to judgment with pestilence and bloodshed; I will rain down on him, on his troops, and on the many peoples who *are* with him, flooding rain, great hailstones, fire, and brimstone. 23 Thus I will magnify Myself and sanctify Myself, and I will be known in the eyes of many nations. Then they shall know that I *am* the LORD." '

39 "And you, son of man, prophesy against Gog, and say, 'Thus says the Lord GOD: "Behold, I *am* against you, O Gog, the prince of Rosh,[a] Meshech, and Tubal; 2 and I will turn you around and lead you on, bringing you up from the far north, and bring you against the mountains of Israel. 3 Then I will knock the bow out of your left hand, and cause the arrows to fall out of your right hand. 4 You shall fall upon the mountains of Israel, you and all your troops and the peoples who *are* with you; I will give you to birds of prey of every sort and *to* the beasts of the field to be devoured. 5 You shall fall on the open field; for I have spoken," says the Lord GOD. 6 "And I will send fire on Magog and on those who live in security in the coastlands. Then they shall know that I *am* the LORD. 7 So I will make My holy name known in the midst of My people Israel, and I will not *let them* profane My holy name anymore. Then the nations shall know that I *am* the LORD, the Holy One in Israel. 8 Surely it is coming, and it shall be done," says the Lord GOD. "This *is* the day of which I have spoken.

9 "Then those who dwell in the cities of Israel will go out and set on fire and burn the weapons, both the shields and bucklers, the bows and arrows, the javelins and spears; and they will make fires with them for seven years. 10 They will not take wood from the field nor cut down *any* from the forests, because they will make fires with the weapons; and they will plunder those who plundered them, and pillage those who pillaged them," says the Lord GOD.

11 "It will come to pass in that day *that* I will give Gog a burial place there in Israel, the valley of those who pass by east of the sea; and it

---

39:1 aTargum, Vulgate, and Aquila read *chief prince of.*

will obstruct travelers, because there they will bury Gog and all his multitude. Therefore they will call *it* the Valley of Hamon Gog.*ª* 12 For seven months the house of Israel will be burying them, in order to cleanse the land. 13 Indeed all the people of the land will be burying, and they will gain renown for it on the day that I am glorified," says the Lord GOD. 14 "They will set apart men regularly employed, with the help of a search party,*ª* to pass through the land and bury those bodies remaining on the ground, in order to cleanse it. At the end of seven months they will make a search. 15 The search party will pass through the land; and *when anyone* sees a man's bone, he shall set up a marker by it, till the buriers have buried it in the Valley of Hamon Gog. 16 *The* name of *the* city *will* also *be* Hamonah. Thus they shall cleanse the land." '

17 "And as for you, son of man, thus says the Lord GOD, 'Speak to every sort of bird and to every beast of the field:

"Assemble yourselves and
    come;
Gather together from all sides
    to My sacrificial meal
Which I am sacrificing for you,
A great sacrificial meal on the
    mountains of Israel,
That you may eat flesh and
    drink blood.
18   You shall eat the flesh of the
    mighty,
Drink the blood of the princes
    of the earth,
Of rams and lambs,
Of goats and bulls,
All of them fatlings of Bashan.
19   You shall eat fat till you are
    full,
And drink blood till you are
    drunk,
At My sacrificial meal
Which I am sacrificing for you.
20   You shall be filled at My table
With horses and riders,
With mighty men
And with all the men of war,"
says the Lord GOD.

21 "I will set My glory among the nations; all the nations shall see My judgment which I have executed, and My hand which I have laid on them. 22 So the house of Israel shall know that I *am* the LORD their God from that day forward. 23 The Gentiles shall know that the house of Israel went into captivity for their iniquity; because they were unfaithful to Me, therefore I hid My face from them. I gave them into the hand of their enemies, and they all fell by the sword. 24 According to their uncleanness and according to their transgressions I have dealt with them, and hidden My face from them." '

25 "Therefore thus says the Lord GOD: 'Now I will bring back the captives of Jacob, and have mercy on the whole house of Israel; and I will be jealous for My holy name— 26 after they have borne their shame, and all their unfaithfulness in which they were unfaithful to Me, when they dwelt safely in their *own* land and no one made *them* afraid. 27 When I have brought them back from the peoples and gathered them out of their enemies' lands, and I am hallowed in them in the sight of many nations, 28 then they shall know that I *am* the LORD their God, who sent them into captivity among the nations, but also brought them back to their land, and left none of them captive any longer. 29 And I will not hide My face from them anymore; for I shall have poured out My Spirit on the house of Israel,' says the Lord GOD."

40 In the twenty-fifth year of our captivity, at the beginning of the year, on the tenth *day* of the month, in the fourteenth year after the city was captured, on the very same day the hand of the LORD was upon me; and He took me there. 2 In the visions of God He took me into the land of Israel and set me on a very high mountain; on it toward the south *was* something like the structure of a city. 3 He took me there, and behold, *there was* a man whose appearance *was* like the appearance of bronze. He had a line of flax and a measuring rod in his hand, and he stood in the gateway.

4 And the man said to me, "Son of man, look with your eyes and hear with your ears, and fix your mind on everything I show you; for you *were*

39:11 ªLiterally *The Multitude of Gog*   39:14 ªLiterally *those who pass through* brought here so that I might show *them* to you. Declare to the house of Israel everything you see." 5 Now there was a wall all around the outside of the temple.ᵃ In the man's hand was a measuring rod six cubits *long, each being a* cubit and a handbreadth; and he measured the width of the wall structure, one rod; and the height, one rod.

6 Then he went to the gateway which faced east; and he went up its stairs and measured the threshold of the gateway, *which was* one rod wide, and the other threshold *was* one rod wide. 7 Each gate chamber *was* one rod long and one rod wide; between the gate chambers *was a space of* five cubits; and the threshold of the gateway by the vestibule of the inside gate *was* one rod. 8 He also measured the vestibule of the inside gate, one rod. 9 Then he measured the vestibule of the gateway, eight cubits; and the gateposts, two cubits. The vestibule of the gate *was* on the inside. 10 In the eastern gateway *were* three gate chambers on one side and three on the other; the three *were* all the same size; also the gateposts were of the same size on this side and that side.

11 He measured the width of the entrance to the gateway, ten cubits; *and* the length of the gate, thirteen cubits. 12 *There was* a space in front of the gate chambers, one cubit *on this side* and one cubit on that side; the gate chambers *were* six cubits on this side and six cubits on that side. 13 Then he measured the gateway from the roof of *one* gate chamber to the roof of the other; the width *was* twenty-five cubits, as door faces door. 14 He measured the gateposts, sixty cubits high, and the court all around the gateway *extended* to the gatepost. 15 *From* the front of the entrance gate to the front of the vestibule of the inner gate *was* fifty cubits. 16 *There were* beveled window *frames* in the gate chambers and in their intervening archways on the inside of the gateway all around, and likewise in the vestibules. *There were* windows all around on the inside. And on each gatepost *were* palm trees.

17 Then he brought me into the outer court; and *there were* chambers and a pavement made all around the court; thirty chambers faced the pavement. 18 The pavement was by the side of the gateways, corresponding to the length of the gateways; *this was* the lower pavement. 19 Then he measured the width from the front of the lower gateway to the front of the inner court exterior, one hundred cubits toward the east and the north.

20 On the outer court was also a gateway facing north, and he measured its length and its width. 21 Its gate chambers, three on this side and three on that side, its gateposts and its archways, had the same measurements as the first gate; its length *was* fifty cubits and its width twenty-five cubits. 22 Its windows and those of its archways, and also its palm trees, *had* the same measurements as the gateway facing east; it was ascended by seven steps, and its archway *was* in front of it. 23 A gate of the inner court was opposite the northern gateway, just as the eastern *gateway;* and he measured from gateway to gateway, one hundred cubits.

24 After that he brought me toward the south, and there a gateway was facing south; and he measured its gateposts and archways according to these same measurements. 25 *There were* windows in it and in its archways all around like those windows; its length *was* fifty cubits and its width twenty-five cubits. 26 Seven steps led up to it, and its archway *was* in front of them; and it had palm trees on its gateposts, one on this side and one on that side. 27 *There was* also a gateway on the inner court, facing south; and he measured from gateway to gateway toward the south, one hundred cubits.

28 Then he brought me to the inner court through the southern gateway; he measured the southern gateway according to these same measurements. 29 Also its gate chambers, its gateposts, and its archways *were* according to these same measurements; *there were* windows in it and in its archways all around; *it was* fifty cubits long and twenty-five cubits wide. 30 *There were* archways all around, twenty-five cubits long and five cubits wide. 31 Its archways faced the outer court, palm trees

40:5 ᵃLiterally *house,* and so elsewhere in this book

were on its gateposts, and going up to it *were* eight steps.

32 And he brought me into the inner court facing east; he measured the gateway according to these same measurements. 33 Also its gate chambers, its gateposts, and its archways *were* according to these same measurements; and *there were* windows in it and in its archways all around; it *was* fifty cubits long and twenty-five cubits wide. 34 Its archways faced the outer court, and palm trees *were* on its gateposts on this side and on that side; and going up to it *were* eight steps.

35 Then he brought me to the north gateway and measured *it* according to these same measurements— 36 also its gate chambers, its gateposts, and its archways. It had windows all around; its length *was* fifty cubits and its width twenty-five cubits. 37 Its gateposts faced the outer court, palm trees *were* on its gateposts on this side and on that side, and going up to it *were* eight steps.

38 *There was* a chamber and its entrance by the gateposts of the gateway, where they washed the burnt offering. 39 In the vestibule of the gateway *were* two tables on this side and two tables on that side, on which to slay the burnt offering, the sin offering, and the trespass offering. 40 At the outer side of the vestibule, as one goes up to the entrance of the northern gateway, *were* two tables; and on the other side of the vestibule of the gateway *were* two tables. 41 Four tables *were* on this side and four tables on that side, by the side of the gateway, eight tables on which they slaughtered *the sacrifices.* 42 *There were* also four tables of hewn stone for the burnt offering, one cubit and a half long, one cubit and a half wide, and one cubit high; on these they laid the instruments with which they slaughtered the burnt offering and the sacrifice. 43 Inside *were* hooks, a handbreadth wide, fastened all around; and the flesh of the sacrifices *was* on the tables.

44 Outside the inner gate *were* the chambers for the singers in the inner court, one facing south at the side of the northern gateway, and the other facing north at the side of the southern gateway. 45 Then he said to me, "This chamber which faces south *is* for the priests who have charge of the temple. 46 The chamber which faces north *is* for the priests who have charge of the altar; these *are* the sons of Zadok, from the sons of Levi, who come near the Lord to minister to Him."

47 And he measured the court, one hundred cubits long and one hundred cubits wide, foursquare. The altar *was* in front of the temple. 48 Then he brought me to the vestibule of the temple and measured the doorposts of the vestibule, five cubits on this side and five cubits on that side; and the width of the gateway was three cubits on this side and three cubits on that side. 49 The length of the vestibule *was* twenty cubits, and the width eleven cubits; and by the steps which led up to it *there were* pillars by the doorposts, one on this side and another on that side.

41 Then he brought me into the sanctuary*a* and measured the doorposts, six cubits wide on one side and six cubits wide on the other side—the width of the tabernacle. 2 The width of the entryway *was* ten cubits; and the side walls of the entrance *were* five cubits on this side and five cubits on the other side; and he measured its length, forty cubits, and its width, twenty cubits.

3 Also he went inside and measured the doorposts, two cubits; and the entrance, six cubits *high;* and the width of the entrance, seven cubits. 4 He measured the length, twenty cubits; and the width, twenty cubits, beyond the sanctuary; and he said to me, "This *is* the Most Holy *Place.*"

5 Next, he measured the wall of the temple, six cubits. The width of each side chamber all around the temple *was* four cubits on every side. 6 The side chambers *were* in three stories, one above the other, thirty chambers in each story; they rested on ledges which *were* for the side chambers all around, that they might be supported, but not fastened to the wall of the temple. 7 As one went up from story to story, the side chambers became wider all around, be-

41:1 *a*Hebrew *heykal,* here the main room of the temple, sometimes called the *holy place* (compare Exodus 26:33) cause their supporting ledges in the wall of the temple ascended like steps; therefore the width of the structure increased as one went up *from* the lowest *story* to the highest by way of the middle one. 8 I also saw an elevation all around the temple; it was the foundation of the side chambers, a full rod, *that is,* six cubits *high.* 9 The thickness of the outer wall of the side chambers *was* five cubits, and so also the remaining terrace by the place of the side chambers of the temple. 10 And between *it and* the *wall* chambers was a width of twenty cubits all around the temple on every side. 11 The doors of the side chambers opened on the terrace, one door toward the north and another toward the south; and the width of the terrace *was* five cubits all around.

12 The building that faced the separating courtyard at its western end *was* seventy cubits wide; the wall of the building *was* five cubits thick all around, and its length ninety cubits. 13 So he measured the temple, one hundred cubits long; and the separating courtyard with the building and its walls *was* one hundred cubits long; 14 also the width of the eastern face of the temple, including the separating courtyard, *was* one hundred cubits. 15 He measured the length of the building behind it, facing the separating courtyard, with its galleries on the one side and on the other side, one hundred cubits, as well as the inner temple and the porches of the court, 16 their doorposts and the beveled window frames. And the galleries all around their three stories opposite the threshold were paneled with wood from the ground to the windows—the windows were covered— 17 from the space above the door, even to the inner room,[a] as well as outside, and on every wall all around, inside and outside, by measure.

18 And *it was* made with cherubim and palm trees, a palm tree between cherub and cherub. *Each* cherub had two faces, 19 so that the face of a man *was* toward a palm tree on one side, and the face of a young lion toward a palm tree on the other side; thus *it was* made throughout the temple all around. 20 From the floor to the space above the door, and on the wall of the sanctuary, cherubim and palm trees *were* carved.

21 The doorposts of the temple *were* square, *as was* the front of the sanctuary; their appearance was similar. 22 The altar *was* of wood, three cubits high, and its length two cubits. Its corners, its length, and its sides *were* of wood; and he said to me, "This *is* the table that *is* before the LORD."

23 The temple and the sanctuary had two doors. 24 The doors had two panels *apiece,* two folding panels: two *panels* for one door and two panels for the other *door.* 25 Cherubim and palm trees *were* carved on the doors of the temple just as they *were* carved on the walls. A wooden canopy *was* on the front of the vestibule outside. 26 *There were* beveled window *frames* and palm trees on one side and on the other, on the sides of the vestibule—also on the side chambers of the temple and on the canopies.

42 Then he brought me out into the outer court, by the way toward the north; and he brought me into the chamber which *was* opposite the separating courtyard, and which *was* opposite the building toward the north. 2 Facing the length, *which was* one hundred cubits (the width *was* fifty cubits), was the north door. 3 Opposite the inner court of twenty *cubits,* and opposite the pavement of the outer court, *was* gallery against gallery in three *stories.* 4 In front of the chambers, toward the inside, *was* a walk ten cubits wide, at a distance of one cubit; and their doors faced north. 5 Now the upper chambers *were* shorter, because the galleries took away *space* from them more than from the lower and middle stories of the building. 6 For they *were* in three *stories* and did not have pillars like the pillars of the courts; therefore *the upper level* was shortened more than the lower and middle levels from the ground up. 7 And a wall which *was* outside ran parallel to the chambers, at the front of the chambers, toward the outer court; its length *was* fifty cubits. 8 The length of the chambers toward the outer court *was* fifty cubits, whereas that

41:17 aLiterally *house,* here *the Most Holy Place*

facing the temple *was* one hundred cubits. 9 At the lower chambers *was* the entrance on the east side, as one goes into them from the outer court.

10 Also *there were* chambers in the thickness of the wall of the court toward the east, opposite the separating courtyard and opposite the building. 11 *There was* a walk in front of them also, and their appearance *was* like the chambers which *were* toward the north; they *were* as long and as wide as the others, and all their exits and entrances *were* according to plan. 12 And corresponding to the doors of the chambers that *were* facing south, as one enters them, *there was* a door in front of the walk, the way directly in front of the wall toward the east.

13 Then he said to me, "The north chambers *and* the south chambers, which *are* opposite the separating courtyard, *are* the holy chambers where the priests who approach the Lord shall eat the most holy offerings. There they shall lay the most holy offerings—the grain offering, the sin offering, and the trespass offering—for the place *is* holy. 14 When the priests enter them, they shall not go out of the holy *chamber* into the outer court; but there they shall leave their garments in which they minister, for they *are* holy. They shall put on other garments; then they may approach *that* which *is* for the people."

15 Now when he had finished measuring the inner temple, he brought me out through the gateway that faces toward the east, and measured it all around. 16 He measured the east side with the measuring rod,*a* five hundred rods by the measuring rod all around. 17 He measured the north side, five hundred rods by the measuring rod all around. 18 He measured the south side, five hundred rods by the measuring rod. 19 He came around to the west side *and* measured five hundred rods by the measuring rod. 20 He measured it on the four sides; it had a wall all around, five hundred *cubits* long and five hundred wide, to separate the holy areas from the common.

43 Afterward he brought me to the gate, the gate that faces toward the east. 2 And behold, the glory of the God of Israel came from the way of the east. His voice *was* like the sound of many waters; and the earth shone with His glory. 3 *It was* like the appearance of the vision which I saw—like the vision which I saw when I*a* came to destroy the city. The visions *were* like the vision which I saw by the River Chebar; and I fell on my face. 4 And the glory of the Lord came into the temple by way of the gate which faces toward the east. 5 The Spirit lifted me up and brought me into the inner court; and behold, the glory of the Lord filled the temple.

6 Then I heard *Him* speaking to me from the temple, while a man stood beside me. 7 And He said to me, "Son of man, *this is* the place of My throne and the place of the soles of My feet, where I will dwell in the midst of the children of Israel forever. No more shall the house of Israel defile My holy name, they nor their kings, by their harlotry or with the carcasses of their kings on their high places. 8 When they set their threshold by My threshold, and their doorpost by My doorpost, with a wall between them and Me, they defiled My holy name by the abominations which they committed; therefore I have consumed them in My anger. 9 Now let them put their harlotry and the carcasses of their kings far away from Me, and I will dwell in their midst forever.

10 "Son of man, describe the temple to the house of Israel, that they may be ashamed of their iniquities; and let them measure the pattern. 11 And if they are ashamed of all that they have done, make known to them the design of the temple and its arrangement, its exits and its entrances, its entire design and all its ordinances, all its forms and all its laws. Write *it* down in their sight, so that they may keep its whole design and all its ordinances, and perform them. 12 This *is* the law of the temple: The whole area surrounding the mountaintop *is* most holy. Behold, this *is* the law of the temple.

13 "These are the measurements of the altar in cubits (the *cubit is* one cubit and a handbreadth): the base one cubit high and one cubit wide,

You Are the Salt of the Earth

Jesus often used everyday life experiences when teaching about the kingdom of God. He turned common objects into parables—tools to inspire Christian faith. On one such occasion, Jesus used the compound of ordinary salt, saying, "You are the salt of the earth" (Matt. 5:13).

Salt symbolized many things to the biblical person. Of course, it flavored food as it does today. Yet it was also considered to be pure, part of an acceptable sacrificial offering to God (Ezek. 43:24). And salt was important as a food preservative.

Perhaps Jesus was bringing to His listeners' minds the village of Tarachia, which was in view from where He spoke. This small town's main industry was curing and salting fish. In fact, the town's name means "Salted Fish." Fish, salted and cured there, was a well-known commodity shipped throughout the Roman Empire.

Due to the low elevation of Tarachia in Galilee, 700 feet below sea level, temperatures often exceeded 100 degrees with 80 to 90 percent humidity in the summer. Food spoiled quickly, and the fish they harvested had to be cured and salted immediately.

"You are the salt of the earth." To Jesus' listeners, this was an important image. Like the salt of the biblical world, they, too, were in a preserving position in their community. When we share the love of Jesus Christ, the apostle Paul reminds us in Colossians 4:6 to let our speech be "with grace, seasoned with salt," that it may bless the lives of other people with a positive flavor and spirit. We should share God's covenant of peace and forgiveness with the world. Like salt, may our lives be a pure and acceptable offering of service to our God.

with a rim all around its edge of one span. This *is* the height of the altar: 14 from the base on the ground to the lower ledge, two cubits; the width of the ledge, one cubit; from the smaller ledge to the larger ledge, four cubits; and the width of the ledge, *one* cubit. 15 The altar hearth *is* four cubits high, with four horns extending upward from the hearth. 16 The altar hearth *is* twelve cubits long, twelve wide, square at its four corners; 17 the ledge, fourteen *cubits* long and fourteen wide on its four sides, with a rim of half a cubit around it; its base, one cubit all around; and its steps face toward the east."

18 And He said to me, "Son of man, thus says the Lord GOD: 'These *are* the ordinances for the altar on the day when it is made, for sacrificing burnt offerings on it, and for sprinkling blood on it. 19 You shall give a young bull for a sin offering to the priests, the Levites, who are of the seed of Zadok, who approach Me to minister to Me,' says the Lord GOD. 20 You shall take some of its blood and put *it* on the four horns of the altar, on the four corners of the ledge, and on the rim around it; thus you shall cleanse it and make atonement for it. 21 Then you shall also take the bull of the sin offering, and burn it in the appointed place of the temple, outside the sanctuary. 22 On the second day you shall offer a kid of the goats without blemish for a sin offering; and they shall cleanse the altar, as they cleansed *it* with the bull. 23 When you have finished cleansing *it,* you shall offer a young bull without blemish, and a ram from the flock without blemish. 24 When you offer them before the LORD, the priests shall throw salt on them, and they will offer them up *as* a burnt offering to the LORD. 25 Every day for seven days you shall prepare a goat *for* a sin offering; they shall also prepare a young bull and a ram from the flock, both without blemish. 26 Seven days they shall make atonement for the altar and purify it, and so consecrate *it.* 27 When these days are over it shall be, on the eighth day and thereafter, that the priests shall offer your burnt offerings and your peace offerings on the altar; and I will accept you,' says the Lord GOD."

44 Then He brought me back to the outer gate of the sanctuary which faces toward the east, but it *was* shut. 2 And the LORD said to me, "This gate shall be shut; it shall not be opened, and no man shall enter by it, because the LORD God of Israel has entered by it; therefore it shall be shut. 3 *As for* the prince, *because* he *is* the prince, he may sit in it to eat bread before the LORD; he shall enter by way of the vestibule of the gateway, and go out the same way."

4 Also He brought me by way of the north gate to the front of the temple; so I looked, and behold, the glory of the LORD filled the house of the LORD; and I fell on my face. 5 And the LORD said to me, "Son of man, mark well, see with your eyes and hear with your ears, all that I say to you concerning all the ordinances of the house of the LORD and all its laws. Mark well who may enter the house and all who go out from the sanctuary.

6 "Now say to the rebellious, to the house of Israel, 'Thus says the Lord GOD: "O house of Israel, let Us have no more of all your abominations. 7 When you brought in foreigners, uncircumcised in heart and uncircumcised in flesh, to be in My sanctuary to defile it—My house—and when you offered My food, the fat and the blood, then they broke My covenant because of all your abominations. 8 And you have not kept charge of My holy things, but you have set *others* to keep charge of My sanctuary for you." 9 Thus says the Lord GOD: "No foreigner, uncircumcised in heart or uncircumcised in flesh, shall enter My sanctuary, including any foreigner who *is* among the children of Israel.

10 "And the Levites who went far from Me, when Israel went astray, who strayed away from Me after their idols, they shall bear their iniquity. 11 Yet they shall be ministers in My sanctuary, *as* gatekeepers of the house and ministers of the house; they shall slay the burnt offering and the sacrifice for the people, and they shall stand before them to minister to them. 12 Because they ministered to them before their idols and caused the house of Israel to fall into iniquity, therefore I have raised My hand in an oath against them," says the Lord GOD, "that they shall bear

their iniquity. 13 And they shall not come near Me to minister to Me as priest, nor come near any of My holy things, nor into the Most Holy *Place;* but they shall bear their shame and their abominations which they have committed. 14 Nevertheless I will make them keep charge of the temple, for all its work, and for all that has to be done in it.

15 "But the priests, the Levites, the sons of Zadok, who kept charge of My sanctuary when the children of Israel went astray from Me, they shall come near Me to minister to Me; and they shall stand before Me to offer to Me the fat and the blood," says the Lord GOD. 16 "They shall enter My sanctuary, and they shall come near My table to minister to Me, and they shall keep My charge. 17 And it shall be, whenever they enter the gates of the inner court, that they shall put on linen garments; no wool shall come upon them while they minister within the gates of the inner court or within the house. 18 They shall have linen turbans on their heads and linen trousers on their bodies; they shall not clothe themselves with *anything that causes* sweat. 19 When they go out to the outer court, to the *outer* court to the people, they shall take off their garments in which they have ministered, leave them in the holy chambers, and put on other garments; and in their holy garments they shall not sanctify the people.

20 "They shall neither shave their heads nor let their hair grow long, but they shall keep their hair well trimmed. 21 No priest shall drink wine when he enters the inner court. 22 They shall not take as wife a widow or a divorced woman, but take virgins of the descendants of the house of Israel, or widows of priests.

23 "And they shall teach My people *the difference* between the holy and the unholy, and cause them to discern between the unclean and the clean. 24 In controversy they shall stand as judges, *and* judge it according to My judgments. They shall keep My laws and My statutes in all My appointed meetings, and they shall hallow My Sabbaths.

25 "They shall not defile *themselves* by coming near a dead person.

Only for father or mother, for son or daughter, for brother or unmarried sister may they defile themselves. 26 After he is cleansed, they shall count seven days for him. 27 And on the day that he goes to the sanctuary to minister in the sanctuary, he must offer his sin offering in the inner court," says the Lord GOD.

28 "It shall be, in regard to their inheritance, *that* I *am* their inheritance. You shall give them no possession in Israel, for I *am* their possession. 29 They shall eat the grain offering, the sin offering, and the trespass offering; every dedicated thing in Israel shall be theirs. 30 The best of all firstfruits of any kind, and every sacrifice of any kind from all your sacrifices, shall be the priest's; also you shall give to the priest the first of your ground meal, to cause a blessing to rest on your house. 31 The priests shall not eat anything, bird or beast, that died naturally or was torn *by wild beasts.*

45 "Moreover, when you divide the land by lot into inheritance, you shall set apart a district for the LORD, a holy section of the land; its length *shall be* twenty-five thousand *cubits,* and the width ten thousand. It *shall be* holy throughout its territory all around. 2 Of this there shall be a square plot for the sanctuary, five hundred by five hundred *rods,* with fifty cubits around it for an open space. 3 So this is the district you shall measure: twenty-five thousand *cubits* long and ten thousand wide; in it shall be the sanctuary, the Most Holy *Place.* 4 It shall be a holy *section* of the land, belonging to the priests, the ministers of the sanctuary, who come near to minister to the LORD; it shall be a place for their houses and a holy place for the sanctuary. 5 An *area* twenty-five thousand *cubits* long and ten thousand wide shall belong to the Levites, the ministers of the temple; they shall have twenty chambers as a possession.*a*

6 "You shall appoint as the property of the city *an area* five thousand *cubits* wide and twenty-five thousand long, adjacent to the district of the holy *section;* it shall belong to the whole house of Israel.

45:5 *a*Following Masoretic Text, Targum, and Vulgate; Septuagint reads *a possession, cities of dwelling.*

7 "The prince shall have *a section* on one side and the other of the holy district and the city's property; and bordering on the holy district and the city's property, extending westward on the west side and eastward on the east side, the length *shall be* side by side with one of the *tribal* portions, from the west border to the east border. 8 The land shall be his possession in Israel; and My princes shall no more oppress My people, but they shall give *the rest* of the land to the house of Israel, according to their tribes."

9 'Thus says the Lord GOD: "Enough, O princes of Israel! Remove violence and plundering, execute justice and righteousness, and stop dispossessing My people," says the Lord GOD. 10 "You shall have honest scales, an honest ephah, and an honest bath. 11 The ephah and the bath shall be of the same measure, so that the bath contains one-tenth of a homer, and the ephah one-tenth of a homer; their measure shall be according to the homer. 12 The shekel *shall be* twenty gerahs; twenty shekels, twenty-five shekels, *and* fifteen shekels shall be your mina.

13 "This *is* the offering which you shall offer: you shall give one-sixth of an ephah from a homer of wheat, and one-sixth of an ephah from a homer of barley. 14 The ordinance concerning oil, the bath of oil, *is* one-tenth of a bath from a kor. A kor *is* a homer or ten baths, for ten baths *are* a homer. 15 And one lamb shall be given from a flock of two hundred, from the rich pastures of Israel. These shall be for grain offerings, burnt offerings, and peace offerings, to make atonement for them," says the Lord GOD. 16 "All the people of the land shall give this offering for the prince in Israel. 17 Then it shall be the prince's part *to give* burnt offerings, grain offerings, and drink offerings, at the feasts, the New Moons, the Sabbaths, and at all the appointed seasons of the house of Israel. He shall prepare the sin offering, the grain offering, the burnt offering, and the peace offerings to make atonement for the house of Israel."

18 'Thus says the Lord GOD: "In the first *month,* on the first *day* of the month, you shall take a young bull without blemish and cleanse the sanctuary. 19 The priest shall take some of the blood of the sin offering and put *it* on the doorposts of the temple, on the four corners of the ledge of the altar, and on the gateposts of the gate of the inner court. 20 And so you shall do on the seventh *day* of the month for everyone who has sinned unintentionally or in ignorance. Thus you shall make atonement for the temple.

21 "In the first *month,* on the fourteenth day of the month, you shall observe the Passover, a feast of seven days; unleavened bread shall be eaten. 22 And on that day the prince shall prepare for himself and for all the people of the land a bull *for* a sin offering. 23 On the seven days of the feast he shall prepare a burnt offering to the LORD, seven bulls and seven rams without blemish, daily for seven days, and a kid of the goats daily *for* a sin offering. 24 And he shall prepare a grain offering of one ephah for each bull and one ephah for each ram, together with a hin of oil for each ephah.

25 "In the seventh *month,* on the fifteenth day of the month, at the feast, he shall do likewise for seven days, according to the sin offering, the burnt offering, the grain offering, and the oil."

46 'Thus says the Lord GOD: "The gateway of the inner court that faces toward the east shall be shut the six working days; but on the Sabbath it shall be opened, and on the day of the New Moon it shall be opened. 2 The prince shall enter by way of the vestibule of the gateway from the outside, and stand by the gatepost. The priests shall prepare his burnt offering and his peace offerings. He shall worship at the threshold of the gate. Then he shall go out, but the gate shall not be shut until evening. 3 Likewise the people of the land shall worship at the entrance to this gateway before the LORD on the Sabbaths and the New Moons. 4 The burnt offering that the prince offers to the LORD on the Sabbath day *shall be* six lambs without blemish, and a ram without blemish; 5 and the grain offering *shall be one* ephah for a ram, and the grain offering for the lambs, as much as he wants to give, as well as a hin of oil with every ephah. 6 On the day of the

New Moon *it shall be* a young bull without blemish, six lambs, and a ram; they shall be without blemish. 7 He shall prepare a grain offering of an ephah for a bull, an ephah for a ram, as much as he wants to give for the lambs, and a hin of oil with every ephah. 8 When the prince enters, he shall go in by way of the vestibule of the gateway, and go out the same way.

9 "But when the people of the land come before the LORD on the appointed feast days, whoever enters by way of the north gate to worship shall go out by way of the south gate; and whoever enters by way of the south gate shall go out by way of the north gate. He shall not return by way of the gate through which he came, but shall go out through the opposite gate. 10 The prince shall then be in their midst. When they go in, he shall go in; and when they go out, he shall go out. 11 At the festivals and the appointed feast days the grain offering shall be an ephah for a bull, an ephah for a ram, as much as he wants to give for the lambs, and a hin of oil with every ephah.

12 "Now when the prince makes a voluntary burnt offering or voluntary peace offering to the LORD, the gate that faces toward the east shall then be opened for him; and he shall prepare his burnt offering and his peace offerings as he did on the Sabbath day. Then he shall go out, and after he goes out the gate shall be shut.

13 "You shall daily make a burnt offering to the LORD *of* a lamb of the first year without blemish; you shall prepare it every morning. 14 And you shall prepare a grain offering with it every morning, a sixth of an ephah, and a third of a hin of oil to moisten the fine flour. This grain offering is a perpetual ordinance, to be made regularly to the LORD. 15 Thus they shall prepare the lamb, the grain offering, and the oil, *as* a regular burnt offering every morning."

16 'Thus says the Lord GOD: "If the prince gives a gift *of some* of his inheritance to any of his sons, it shall belong to his sons; it is their possession by inheritance. 17 But if he gives a gift of some of his inheritance to one of his servants, it shall be his until the year of liberty, after which it shall return to the prince. But his inheritance shall belong to his sons; it

shall become theirs. 18 Moreover the prince shall not take any of the people's inheritance by evicting them from their property; he shall provide an inheritance for his sons from his own property, so that none of My people may be scattered from his property." ' "

19 Now he brought me through the entrance, which *was* at the side of the gate, into the holy chambers of the priests which face toward the north; and there a place *was* situated at their extreme western end. 20 And he said to me, "This *is* the place where the priests shall boil the trespass offering and the sin offering, *and* where they shall bake the grain offering, so that they do not bring *them* out into the outer court to sanctify the people."

21 Then he brought me out into the outer court and caused me to pass by the four corners of the court; and in fact, in every corner of the court *there was another* court. 22 In the four corners of the court *were* enclosed courts, forty *cubits* long and thirty wide; all four corners *were* the same size. 23 *There was* a row *of building* stones all around in them, all around the four of them; and cooking hearths were made under the rows of stones all around. 24 And he said to me, "These *are* the kitchens where the ministers of the temple shall boil the sacrifices of the people."

47 Then he brought me back to the door of the temple; and there was water, flowing from under the threshold of the temple toward the east, for the front of the temple faced east; the water was flowing from under the right side of the temple, south of the altar. 2 He brought me out by way of the north gate, and led me around on the outside to the outer gateway that faces east; and there was water, running out on the right side.

3 And when the man went out to the east with the line in his hand, he measured one thousand cubits, and he brought me through the waters; the water *came up to my* ankles. 4 Again he measured one thousand and brought me through the waters; the water *came up to my* knees. Again he measured one thousand and brought me through; the water

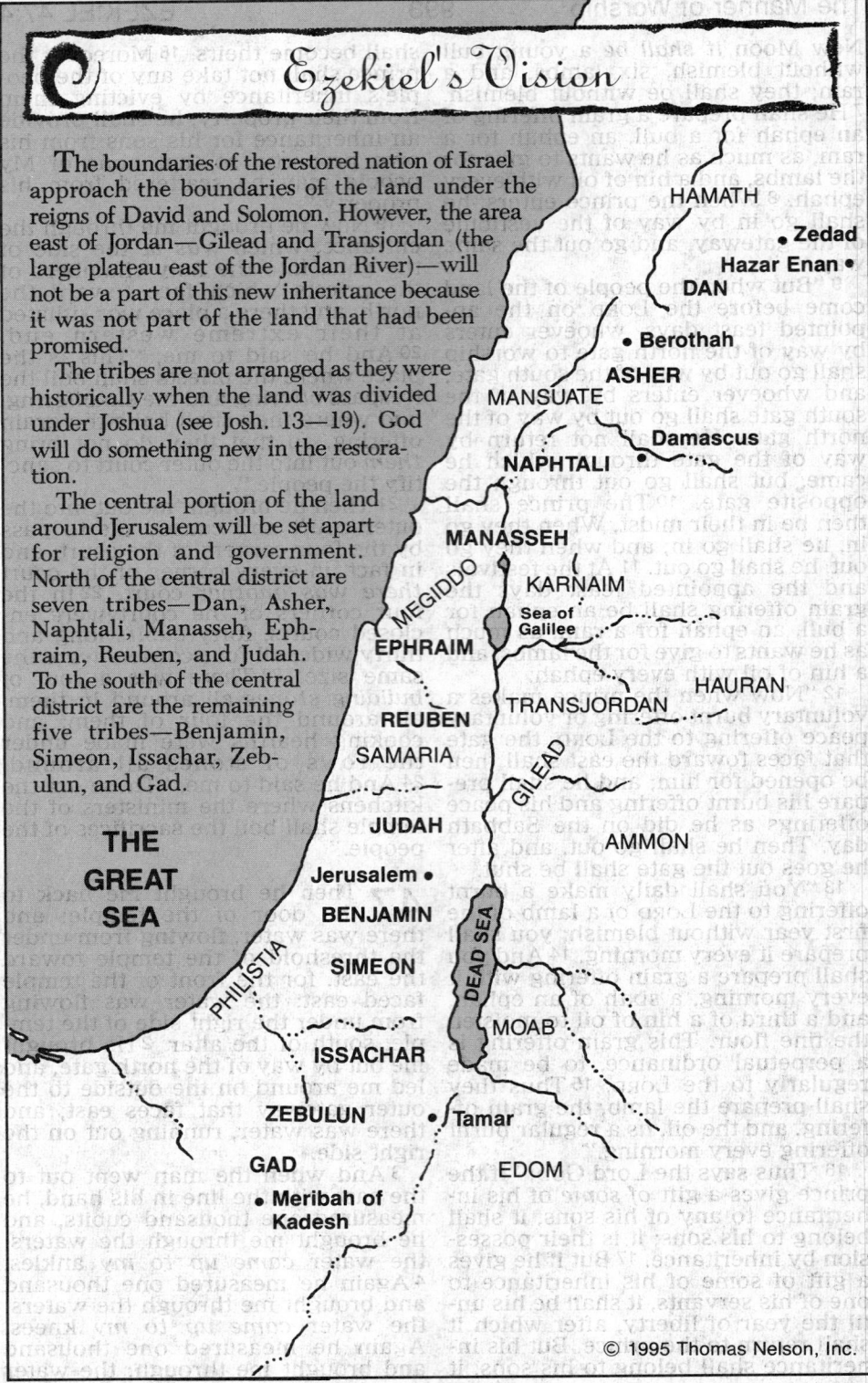

Ezekiel's Vision

The boundaries of the restored nation of Israel approach the boundaries of the land under the reigns of David and Solomon. However, the area east of Jordan—Gilead and Transjordan (the large plateau east of the Jordan River)—will not be a part of this new inheritance because it was not part of the land that had been promised.

The tribes are not arranged as they were historically when the land was divided under Joshua (see Josh. 13—19). God will do something new in the restoration.

The central portion of the land around Jerusalem will be set apart for religion and government. North of the central district are seven tribes—Dan, Asher, Naphtali, Manasseh, Ephraim, Reuben, and Judah. To the south of the central district are the remaining five tribes—Benjamin, Simeon, Issachar, Zebulun, and Gad.

HAMATH

• Zedad

Hazar Enan •

DAN

• Berothah

ASHER

MANSUATE

Damascus

NAPHTALI

MANASSEH

KARNAIM

MEGIDDO

Sea of Galilee

EPHRAIM

HAURAN

REUBEN

TRANSJORDAN

SAMARIA

GILEAD

JUDAH

AMMON

THE GREAT SEA

Jerusalem •

BENJAMIN

SIMEON

DEAD SEA

PHILISTIA

MOAB

ISSACHAR

ZEBULUN   • Tamar

GAD   EDOM

• Meribah of Kadesh

came up to my waist. 5 Again he measured one thousand, *and it was* a river that I could not cross; for the water was too deep, water in which one must swim, a river that could not be crossed. 6 He said to me, "Son of man, have you seen *this?*" Then he brought me and returned me to the bank of the river.

7 When I returned, there, along the bank of the river, *were* very many trees on one side and the other. 8 Then he said to me: "This water flows toward the eastern region, goes down into the valley, and enters the sea. *When it* reaches the sea, *its* waters are healed. 9 And it shall be *that* every living thing that moves, wherever the rivers go, will live. There will be a very great multitude of fish, because these waters go there; for they will be healed, and everything will live wherever the river goes. 10 It shall be *that* fishermen will stand by it from En Gedi to En Eglaim; they will be *places* for spreading their nets. Their fish will be of the same kinds as the fish of the Great Sea, exceedingly many. 11 But its swamps and marshes will not be healed; they will be given over to salt. 12 Along the bank of the river, on this side and that, will grow all *kinds of* trees used for food; their leaves will not wither, and their fruit will not fail. They will bear fruit every month, because their water flows from the sanctuary. Their fruit will be for food, and their leaves for medicine."

13 Thus says the Lord GOD: "These *are* the borders by which you shall divide the land as an inheritance among the twelve tribes of Israel. Joseph *shall have two* portions. 14 You shall inherit it equally with one another; for I raised My hand in an oath to give it to your fathers, and this land shall fall to you as your inheritance.

15 "This *shall be* the border of the land on the north: from the Great Sea, *by* the road to Hethlon, as one goes to Zedad, 16 Hamath, Berothah, Sibraim (which *is* between the border of Damascus and the border of Hamath), to Hazar Hatticon (which *is* on the border of Hauran). 17 Thus the boundary shall be from the Sea to Hazar Enan, the border of Damas-

cus; and as for the north, northward, it is the border of Hamath. *This is* the north side.

18 "On the east side you shall mark out the border from between Hauran and Damascus, and between Gilead and the land of Israel, along the Jordan, and along the eastern side of the sea. *This is* the east side.

19 "The south side, toward the South,[a] *shall be* from Tamar to the waters of Meribah by Kadesh, along the brook to the Great Sea. *This is* the south side, toward the South.

20 "The west side *shall be* the Great Sea, from the *southern* boundary until one comes to a point opposite Hamath. This *is* the west side.

21 "Thus you shall divide this land among yourselves according to the tribes of Israel. 22 It shall be that you will divide it by lot as an inheritance for yourselves, and for the strangers who dwell among you and who bear children among you. They shall be to you as native-born among the children of Israel; they shall have an inheritance with you among the tribes of Israel. 23 And it shall be *that* in whatever tribe the stranger dwells, there you shall give *him* his inheritance," says the Lord GOD.

48 "Now these *are* the names of the tribes: From the northern border along the road to Hethlon at the entrance of Hamath, to Hazar Enan, the border of Damascus northward, in the direction of Hamath, *there shall be* one *section for* Dan from its east to its west side; 2 by the border of Dan, from the east side to the west, one *section for* Asher; 3 by the border of Asher, from the east side to the west, one *section for* Naphtali; 4 by the border of Naphtali, from the east side to the west, one *section for* Manasseh; 5 by the border of Manasseh, from the east side to the west, one *section for* Ephraim; 6 by the border of Ephraim, from the east side to the west, one *section for* Reuben; 7 by the border of Reuben, from the east side to the west, one *section for* Judah; 8 by the border of Judah, from the east side to the west, shall be the district which you shall set apart, twenty-five thousand *cubits* in width, and *in* length the same as one of the

47:19 a Hebrew *Negev*

other portions, from the east side to the west, with the sanctuary in the center.

9 "The district that you shall set apart for the LORD *shall be* twenty-five thousand *cubits* in length and ten thousand in width. 10 To these—to the priests—the holy district shall belong: on the north twenty-five thousand *cubits in length,* on the west ten thousand in width, on the east ten thousand in width, and on the south twenty-five thousand in length. The sanctuary of the LORD shall be in the center. 11 *It shall be* for the priests of the sons of Zadok, who are sanctified, who have kept My charge, who did not go astray when the children of Israel went astray, as the Levites went astray. 12 And *this* district of land that is set apart shall be to them a thing most holy by the border of the Levites.

13 "Opposite the border of the priests, the Levites *shall have an area* twenty-five thousand *cubits* in length and ten thousand in width; its entire length *shall be* twenty-five thousand and its width ten thousand. 14 And they shall not sell or exchange any of it; they may not alienate this best *part* of the land, for *it is* holy to the LORD.

15 "The five thousand *cubits* in width that remain, along the edge of the twenty-five thousand, shall be for general use by the city, for dwellings and common-land; and the city shall be in the center. 16 These *shall be* its measurements: the north side four thousand five hundred *cubits,* the south side four thousand five hundred, the east side four thousand five hundred, and the west side four thousand five hundred. 17 The common-land of the city shall be: to the north two hundred and fifty *cubits,* to the south two hundred and fifty, to the east two hundred and fifty, and to the west two hundred and fifty. 18 The rest of the length, alongside the district of the holy *section, shall be* ten thousand *cubits* to the east and ten thousand to the west. It shall be adjacent to the district of the holy *section,* and its produce shall be food for the workers of the city. 19 The workers of the city, from all the tribes of Israel, shall cultivate it. 20 The entire district *shall be* twenty-five thou-

sand *cubits* by twenty-five thousand *cubits,* foursquare. You shall set apart the holy district with the property of the city.

21 "The rest *shall belong* to the prince, on one side and on the other of the holy district and of the city's property, next to the twenty-five thousand *cubits* of the *holy* district as far as the eastern border, and westward next to the twenty-five thousand as far as the western border, adjacent to the *tribal* portions; *it shall belong* to the prince. It shall be the holy district, and the sanctuary of the temple *shall be* in the center. 22 Moreover, apart from the possession of the Levites and the possession of the city *which are* in the midst of what *belongs* to the prince, *the area* between the border of Judah and the border of Benjamin shall belong to the prince.

23 "As for the rest of the tribes, from the east side to the west, Benjamin *shall have* one *section;* 24 by the border of Benjamin, from the east side to the west, Simeon *shall have* one *section;* 25 by the border of Simeon, from the east side to the west, Issachar *shall have* one *section;* 26 by the border of Issachar, from the east side to the west, Zebulun *shall have* one *section;* 27 by the border of Zebulun, from the east side to the west, Gad *shall have* one *section;* 28 by the border of Gad, on the south side, toward the South,^a the border shall be from Tamar *to* the waters of Meribah *by* Kadesh, along the brook to the Great Sea. 29 This *is* the land which you shall divide by lot as an inheritance among the tribes of Israel, and these *are* their portions," says the Lord GOD.

30 "These *are* the exits of the city. On the north side, measuring four thousand five hundred *cubits* 31 (the gates of the city *shall be* named after the tribes of Israel), the three gates northward: one gate for Reuben, one gate for Judah, and one gate for Levi; 32 on the east side, four thousand five hundred *cubits,* three gates: one gate for Joseph, one gate for Benjamin, and one gate for Dan; 33 on the south side, measuring four thousand five hundred *cubits,* three gates: one gate for Simeon, one gate for Issachar, and one gate for Zebu-

lun; 34 on the west side, four thousand five hundred *cubits* with their three gates: one gate for Gad, one gate for Asher, and one gate for Naphtali. 35 All the way around *shall be* eighteen thousand *cubits;* and the name of the city from *that* day *shall be:* THE LORD *IS* THERE."*a*

48:35 *a*Hebrew *YHWH Shammah*

Daniel

Overview of Daniel

Perhaps one of the greatest possibility thinkers in the Bible is Daniel. Reared in Babylon during the Israelite exile there, Daniel was a godly and wise young man who did not surrender leadership of his life to the forces and people around him.

Written by Daniel about 605–536 B.C., the book records the Jewish plight under King Nebuchadnezzar and Cyrus of Persia. It is truly an uplifting example of the fact that no matter who you are, where you are, and under what circumstances you are, you can overcome any problem.

Three great examples of this thinking stand out in this book. The first is that of Daniel and three young men, Shadrach, Meshach and Abed-Nego. When taken into the household of the king, they were told to forsake their Jewish diets, ordained by God, and to eat only what was served in the king's court. Courageously, the boys challenged the reasoning of this demand. If they could keep to their diets for two weeks, they would prove healthier than their peers. Granted permission, the boys remained on their diets and after the testing period, they excelled in strength and stature over all the rest. God honored their faith!

A second incident and an even more marvelous account of these same young men, minus Daniel, is when they were thrown into a fiery furnace as the death penalty for not bowing down to the false gods. They were willing to die for their faith and God exalted them. They were unscorched and eventually released!

Finally, in the last pages of this book we learn of Daniel in the lions' den. When cast into the den, he was left untouched. God protected him and honored him for his strength and courage.

Daniel and his friends would not surrender leadership of their lives to the forces of society—the images of kings and the false gods of foreign nations. The only one they would surrender leadership to was God. That was possibility thinking in action!

Jesus in Daniel

Jesus is the Great Stone who will crush the kingdoms of this world (2:34, 35, 44), the Son of Man who is given dominion by the Ancient of Days (7:13, 14), and the coming Messiah who will be cut off (9:25, 26). It is likely that Daniel's vision in 10:5–9 was an appearance of the preincarnate Christ (see also Rev. 1:12–16).

Keys to Daniel

Key Word: God's Program for Israel. Daniel was written to encourage the exiled Jews by revealing God's sovereign program for Israel during and after the period of Gentile domination. Daniel repeatedly emphasizes the sovereignty and power of God over human affairs. "The Most High rules in the kingdom of men, and gives it to whomever He chooses" (4:25). The God who directs the forces of history has not deserted His people—even today! We must continue to trust in Him, because His promises are true and sure.

Key Verse: "Daniel answered and said: 'Blessed be the name of God forever and ever, for wisdom and might are His. And He changes the times and the seasons; he removes kings and raises up kings; He gives wisdom to the wise and knowledge to those who have understanding. He reveals deep and secret things; He knows what *is* in the darkness, and light dwells with Him'" (2:20–22).

Key Chapter: Daniel 9. Daniel's prophecy of the seventy weeks (9:24–27) provides the chronological frame for the predictions of Jesus from Daniel's day to the establishment of the kingdom on earth. It is clear that the first sixty-nine weeks were fulfilled at Christ's First Coming.

Some scholars believe that the final week may not be fulfilled until the Second Coming of Jesus Christ (see Matt. 24:15), while others affirm that these words applied to the Roman desecration of the temple in A.D. 70.

1 In the third year of the reign of Jehoiakim king of Judah, Nebuchadnezzar king of Babylon came to Jerusalem and besieged it. 2 And the Lord gave Jehoiakim king of Judah into his hand, with some of the articles of the house of God, which he carried into the land of Shinar to the house of his god; and he brought the articles into the treasure house of his god.

3 Then the king instructed Ashpenaz, the master of his eunuchs, to bring some of the children of Israel and some of the king's descendants and some of the nobles, 4 young men in whom *there was* no blemish, but good-looking, gifted in all wisdom, possessing knowledge and quick to understand, who *had* ability to serve in the king's palace, and whom they might teach the language and literature of the Chaldeans. 5 And the king appointed for them a daily provision of the king's delicacies and of the wine which he drank, and three years of training for them, so that at the end of *that time* they might serve before the king. 6 Now from among those of the sons of Judah were Daniel, Hananiah, Mishael, and Azariah. 7 To them the chief of the eunuchs gave names: he gave Daniel *the name* Belteshazzar; to Hananiah, Shadrach; to Mishael, Meshach; and to Azariah, Abed-Nego.

8 But Daniel purposed in his heart that he would not defile himself with the portion of the king's delicacies, nor with the wine which he drank; therefore he requested of the chief of the eunuchs that he might not defile himself. 9 Now God had brought Daniel into the favor and goodwill of the chief of the eunuchs. 10 And the chief of the eunuchs said to Daniel, "I fear my lord the king, who has appointed your food and drink. For why should he see your faces looking worse than the young men who *are* your age? Then you would endanger my head before the king."

11 So Daniel said to the steward[a] whom the chief of the eunuchs had set over Daniel, Hananiah, Mishael, and Azariah, 12 "Please test your servants for ten days, and let them give us vegetables to eat and water to drink. 13 Then let our appearance be examined before you, and the appearance of the young men who eat the portion of the king's delicacies; and as you see fit, *so* deal with your servants." 14 So he consented with them in this matter, and tested them ten days.

15 And at the end of ten days their features appeared better and fatter in flesh than all the young men who ate the portion of the king's delicacies. 16 Thus the steward took away their portion of delicacies and the wine that they were to drink, and gave them vegetables.

17 As for these four young men, God gave them knowledge and skill in all literature and wisdom; and Daniel had understanding in all visions and dreams.

18 Now at the end of the days, when the king had said that they should be brought in, the chief of the eunuchs brought them in before Nebuchadnezzar. 19 Then the king interviewed[a] them, and among them all none was found like Daniel, Hananiah, Mishael, and Azariah; therefore they served before the king.

1:11 aHebrew *Melzar*, also in verse 16   1:19 aLiterally *talked with them*

20 And in all matters of wisdom *and* understanding about which the king examined them, he found them ten times better than all the magicians *and* astrologers who *were* in all his realm. 21 Thus Daniel continued until the first year of King Cyrus.

2 Now in the second year of Nebuchadnezzar's reign, Nebuchadnezzar had dreams; and his spirit was *so* troubled that his sleep left him. 2 Then the king gave the command to call the magicians, the astrologers, the sorcerers, and the Chaldeans to tell the king his dreams. So they came and stood before the king. 3 And the king said to them, "I have had a dream, and my spirit is anxious to know the dream."

4 Then the Chaldeans spoke to the king in Aramaic,*ª* "O king, live forever! Tell your servants the dream, and we will give the interpretation."

5 The king answered and said to the Chaldeans, "My decision is firm: if you do not make known the dream to me, and its interpretation, you shall be cut in pieces, and your houses shall be made an ash heap. 6 However, if you tell the dream and its interpretation, you shall receive from me gifts, rewards, and great honor. Therefore tell me the dream and its interpretation."

7 They answered again and said, "Let the king tell his servants the dream, and we will give its interpretation."

8 The king answered and said, "I know for certain that you would gain time, because you see that my decision is firm: 9 if you do not make known the dream to me, *there is only* one decree for you! For you have agreed to speak lying and corrupt words before me till the time has changed. Therefore tell me the dream, and I shall know that you can give me its interpretation."

10 The Chaldeans answered the king, and said, "There is not a man on earth who can tell the king's matter; therefore no king, lord, or ruler has *ever* asked such things of any magician, astrologer, or Chaldean. 11 *It is* a difficult thing that the king requests, and there is no other who can tell it to the king except the gods, whose dwelling is not with flesh."

12 For this reason the king was angry and very furious, and gave the command to destroy all the wise *men* of Babylon. 13 So the decree went out, and they began killing the wise *men;* and they sought Daniel and his companions, to kill *them.*

14 Then with counsel and wisdom Daniel answered Arioch, the captain of the king's guard, who had gone out to kill the wise *men* of Babylon; 15 he answered and said to Arioch the king's captain, "Why is the decree from the king so urgent?" Then Arioch made the decision known to Daniel.

16 So Daniel went in and asked the king to give him time, that he might tell the king the interpretation. 17 Then Daniel went to his house, and made the decision known to Hananiah, Mishael, and Azariah, his companions, 18 that they might seek mercies from the God of heaven concerning this secret, so that Daniel and his companions might not perish with the rest of the wise *men* of Babylon. 19 Then the secret was revealed to Daniel in a night vision. So Daniel blessed the God of heaven.

20 Daniel answered and said:

"Blessed be the name of God
    forever and ever,
  For wisdom and might are His.
21 And He changes the times and
    the seasons;
  He removes kings and raises up
    kings;
  He gives wisdom to the wise
  And knowledge to those who
    have understanding.
22 He reveals deep and secret
    things;
  He knows what *is* in the
    darkness,
  And light dwells with Him.

23 "I thank You and praise You,
    O God of my fathers;
  You have given me wisdom
    and might,
  And have now made known to
    me what we asked of You,
  For You have made known to
    us the king's demand."

24 Therefore Daniel went to Arioch, whom the king had appointed

to destroy the wise *men* of Babylon. He went and said thus to him: "Do not destroy the wise *men* of Babylon; take me before the king, and I will tell the king the interpretation."

25 Then Arioch quickly brought Daniel before the king, and said thus to him, "I have found a man of the captives[a] of Judah, who will make known to the king the interpretation."

26 The king answered and said to Daniel, whose name *was* Belteshazzar, "Are you able to make known to me the dream which I have seen, and its interpretation?"

27 Daniel answered in the presence of the king, and said, "The secret which the king has demanded, the wise *men*, the astrologers, the magicians, and the soothsayers cannot declare to the king. 28 But there is a God in heaven who reveals secrets, and He has made known to King Nebuchadnezzar what will be in the latter days. Your dream, and the visions of your head upon your bed, were these: 29 As for you, O king, thoughts came to your *mind while* on your bed, *about* what would come to pass after this; and He who reveals secrets has made known to you what will be. 30 But as for me, this secret has not been revealed to me because I have more wisdom than anyone living, but for *our* sakes who make known the interpretation to the king, and that you may know the thoughts of your heart.

31 "You, O king, were watching; and behold, a great image! This great image, whose splendor *was* excellent, stood before you; and its form *was* awesome. 32 This image's head *was* of fine gold, its chest and arms of silver, its belly and thighs[a] of bronze, 33 its legs of iron, its feet partly of iron and partly of clay.[a] 34 You watched while a stone was cut out without hands, which struck the image on its feet of iron and clay, and broke them in pieces. 35 Then the iron, the clay, the bronze, the silver, and the gold were crushed together, and became like chaff from the summer threshing floors; the wind carried them away so that no trace of them was found. And the stone that struck the image became a

great mountain and filled the whole earth.

36 "This *is* the dream. Now we will tell the interpretation of it before the king. 37 You, O king, *are* a king of kings. For the God of heaven has given you a kingdom, power, strength, and glory; 38 and wherever the children of men dwell, or the beasts of the field and the birds of the heaven, He has given *them* into your hand, and has made you ruler over them all—you *are* this head of gold. 39 But after you shall arise another kingdom inferior to yours; then another, a third kingdom of bronze, which shall rule over all the earth. 40 And the fourth kingdom shall be as strong as iron, inasmuch as iron breaks in pieces and shatters everything; and like iron that crushes, *that kingdom* will break in pieces and crush all the others. 41 Whereas you saw the feet and toes, partly of potter's clay and partly of iron, the kingdom shall be divided; yet the strength of the iron shall be in it, just as you saw the iron mixed with ceramic clay. 42 And *as* the toes of the feet *were* partly of iron and partly of clay, *so* the kingdom shall be partly strong and partly fragile. 43 As you saw iron mixed with ceramic clay, they will mingle with the seed of men; but they will not adhere to one another, just as iron does not mix with clay. 44 And in the days of these kings the God of heaven will set up a kingdom which shall never be destroyed; and the kingdom shall not be left to other people; it shall break in pieces and consume all these kingdoms, and it shall stand forever. 45 Inasmuch as you saw that the stone was cut out of the mountain without hands, and that it broke in pieces the iron, the bronze, the clay, the silver, and the gold—the great God has made known to the king what will come to pass after this. The dream is certain, and its interpretation is sure."

46 Then King Nebuchadnezzar fell on his face, prostrate before Daniel, and commanded that they should present an offering and incense to him. 47 The king answered Daniel, and said, "Truly your God *is* the God of gods, the Lord of kings, and a re-

2:25 [a]Literally *of the sons of the captivity*   2:32 [a]Or *sides*   2:33 [a]Or *baked clay,* and so in verses 34, 35, and 42 vealer of secrets, since you could reveal this secret." 48 Then the king promoted Daniel and gave him many great gifts; and he made him ruler over the whole province of Babylon, and chief administrator over all the wise *men* of Babylon. 49 Also Daniel petitioned the king, and he set Shadrach, Meshach, and Abed-Nego over the affairs of the province of Babylon; but Daniel *sat* in the gate*ᵃ* of the king.

3 Nebuchadnezzar the king made an image of gold, whose height *was* sixty cubits *and* its width six cubits. He set it up in the plain of Dura, in the province of Babylon. 2 And King Nebuchadnezzar sent *word* to gather together the satraps, the administrators, the governors, the counselors, the treasurers, the judges, the magistrates, and all the officials of the provinces, to come to the dedication of the image which King Nebuchadnezzar had set up. 3 So the satraps, the administrators, the governors, the counselors, the treasurers, the judges, the magistrates, and all the officials of the provinces gathered together for the dedication of the image that King Nebuchadnezzar had set up; and they stood before the image that Nebuchadnezzar had set up. 4 Then a herald cried aloud: "To you it is commanded, O peoples, nations, and languages, 5 *that* at the time you hear the sound of the horn, flute, harp, lyre, *and* psaltery, in symphony with all kinds of music, you shall fall down and worship the gold image that King Nebuchadnezzar has set up; 6 and whoever does not fall down and worship shall be cast immediately into the midst of a burning fiery furnace."

7 So at that time, when all the people heard the sound of the horn, flute, harp, *and* lyre, in symphony with all kinds of music, all the people, nations, and languages fell down *and* worshiped the gold image which King Nebuchadnezzar had set up.

8 Therefore at that time certain Chaldeans came forward and accused the Jews. 9 They spoke and said to King Nebuchadnezzar, "O king, live forever! 10 You, O king,

have made a decree that everyone who hears the sound of the horn, flute, harp, lyre, *and* psaltery, in symphony with all kinds of music, shall fall down and worship the gold image; 11 and whoever does not fall down and worship shall be cast into the midst of a burning fiery furnace. 12 There are certain Jews whom you have set over the affairs of the province of Babylon: Shadrach, Meshach, and Abed-Nego; these men, O king, have not paid due regard to you. They do not serve your gods or worship the gold image which you have set up."

13 Then Nebuchadnezzar, in rage and fury, gave the command to bring Shadrach, Meshach, and Abed-Nego. So they brought these men before the king. 14 Nebuchadnezzar spoke, saying to them, "*Is it* true, Shadrach, Meshach, and Abed-Nego, *that* you do not serve my gods or worship the gold image which I have set up? 15 Now if you are ready at the time you hear the sound of the horn, flute, harp, lyre, *and* psaltery, in symphony with all kinds of music, and you fall down and worship the image which I have made, *good!* But if you do not worship, you shall be cast immediately into the midst of a burning fiery furnace. And who *is* the god who will deliver you from my hands?"

16 Shadrach, Meshach, and Abed-Nego answered and said to the king, "O Nebuchadnezzar, we have no need to answer you in this matter. 17 If that *is the case*, our God whom we serve is able to deliver us from the burning fiery furnace, and He will deliver *us* from your hand, O king. 18 But if not, let it be known to you, O king, that we do not serve your gods, nor will we worship the gold image which you have set up."

19 Then Nebuchadnezzar was full of fury, and the expression on his face changed toward Shadrach, Meshach, and Abed-Nego. He spoke and commanded that they heat the furnace seven times more than it was usually heated. 20 And he commanded certain mighty men of valor who *were* in his army to bind Shadrach, Meshach, and Abed-Nego, *and* cast *them* into the burning fiery furnace. 21 Then these men were bound in their coats, their trousers,

2:49 ᵃThat is, the king's court

their turbans, and their *other* garments, and were cast into the midst of the burning fiery furnace. 22 Therefore, because the king's command was urgent, and the furnace exceedingly hot, the flame of the fire killed those men who took up Shadrach, Meshach, and Abed-Nego. 23 And these three men, Shadrach, Meshach, and Abed-Nego, fell down bound into the midst of the burning fiery furnace.

24 Then King Nebuchadnezzar was astonished; and he rose in haste *and* spoke, saying to his counselors, "Did we not cast three men bound into the midst of the fire?"

They answered and said to the king, "True, O king."

25 "Look!" he answered, "I see four men loose, walking in the midst of the fire; and they are not hurt, and the form of the fourth is like the Son of God."*a*

26 Then Nebuchadnezzar went near the mouth of the burning fiery furnace *and* spoke, saying, "Shadrach, Meshach, and Abed-Nego, servants of the Most High God, come out, and come *here*." Then Shadrach, Meshach, and Abed-Nego came from the midst of the fire. 27 And the satraps, administrators, governors, and the king's counselors gathered together, and they saw these men on whose bodies the fire had no power; the hair of their head was not singed nor were their garments affected, and the smell of fire was not on them.

28 Nebuchadnezzar spoke, saying, "Blessed be the God of Shadrach, Meshach, and Abed-Nego, who sent His Angel*a* and delivered His servants who trusted in Him, and they have frustrated the king's word, and yielded their bodies, that they should not serve nor worship any god except their own God! 29 Therefore I make a decree that any people, nation, or language which speaks anything amiss against the God of Shadrach, Meshach, and Abed-Nego shall be cut in pieces, and their houses shall be made an ash heap; because there is no other God who can deliver like this."

30 Then the king promoted Shadrach, Meshach, and Abed-Nego in the province of Babylon.

4 Nebuchadnezzar the king,

To all peoples, nations, and languages that dwell in all the earth:

Peace be multiplied to you.

2 I thought it good to declare the signs and wonders that the Most High God has worked for me.

3 How great *are* His signs,
And how mighty His wonders!
His kingdom *is* an everlasting kingdom,
And His dominion *is* from generation to generation.

4 I, Nebuchadnezzar, was at rest in my house, and flourishing in my palace. 5 I saw a dream which made me afraid, and the thoughts on my bed and the visions of my head troubled me. 6 Therefore I issued a decree to bring in all the wise *men* of Babylon before me, that they might make known to me the interpretation of the dream. 7 Then the magicians, the astrologers, the Chaldeans, and the soothsayers came in, and I told them the dream; but they did not make known to me its interpretation. 8 But at last Daniel came before me (his name *is* Belteshazzar, according to the name of my god; in him *is* the Spirit of the Holy God), and I told the dream before him, *saying:*
9 "Belteshazzar, chief of the magicians, because I know that the Spirit of the Holy God *is* in you, and no secret troubles you, explain to me the visions of my dream that I have seen, and its interpretation.

10 "These *were* the visions of my head *while* on my bed:

"I was looking, and behold,
A tree in the midst of the earth,
And its height was great.
11 The tree grew and became strong;

3:25 *a*Or *a son of the gods*   3:28 *a*Or *angel*

Its height reached to the
   heavens,
And it could be seen to the ends
   of all the earth.
12 Its leaves *were* lovely,
Its fruit abundant,
And in it *was* food for all.
The beasts of the field found
   shade under it,
The birds of the heavens dwelt
   in its branches,
And all flesh was fed from it.

13 "I saw in the visions of my head
while on my bed, and there was
a watcher, a holy one, coming
down from heaven. 14 He cried
aloud and said thus:

'Chop down the tree and cut off
   its branches,
Strip off its leaves and scatter
   its fruit.
Let the beasts get out from
   under it,
And the birds from its
   branches.
15 Nevertheless leave the stump
   and roots in the earth,
Bound with a band of iron and
   bronze,
In the tender grass of the
   field.
Let it be wet with the dew of
   heaven,
And *let* him graze with the
   beasts
On the grass of the earth.'
16 Let his heart be changed from
   that of a man,
Let him be given the heart of
   a beast,
And let seven times*a* pass over
   him.

17 'This decision *is* by the decree
   of the watchers,
And the sentence by the word
   of the holy ones,
In order that the living may
   know
That the Most High rules in the
   kingdom of men,
Gives it to whomever He will,
And sets over it the lowest of
   men.'

18 "This dream I, King
Nebuchadnezzar, have seen.

Now you, Belteshazzar, declare
its interpretation, since all the
wise *men* of my kingdom are
not able to make known to me
the interpretation; but you *are*
able, for the Spirit of the Holy
God *is* in you."

19 Then Daniel, whose name was
Belteshazzar, was astonished
for a time, and his thoughts
troubled him. *So* the king
spoke, and said, "Belteshazzar,
do not let the dream or its
interpretation trouble you."
   Belteshazzar answered and
said, "My lord, *may* the dream
concern those who hate you,
and its interpretation concern
your enemies!

20 "The tree that you saw, which
grew and became strong,
whose height reached to the
heavens and which *could be
seen* by all the earth, 21 whose
leaves *were* lovely and its fruit
abundant, in which *was* food
for all, under which the beasts
of the field dwelt, and in whose
branches the birds of the
heaven had their home—
22 it *is* you, O king, who have
grown and become strong; for
your greatness has grown and
reaches to the heavens, and
your dominion to the end of the
earth.

23 "And inasmuch as the king saw
a watcher, a holy one, coming
down from heaven and saying,
'Chop down the tree and
destroy it, but leave its stump
and roots in the earth, *bound*
with a band of iron and bronze
in the tender grass of the field;
let it be wet with the dew of
heaven, and let him graze with
the beasts of the field, till seven
times pass over him'; 24 this is
the interpretation, O king, and
this is the decree of the Most
High, which has come upon my
lord the king: 25 They shall
drive you from men, your
dwelling shall be with the
beasts of the field, and they
shall make you eat grass like

4:16 *a*Possibly *seven years,* and so in verses 23, 25, and 32 oxen. They shall wet you with the dew of heaven, and seven times shall pass over you, till you know that the Most High rules in the kingdom of men, and gives it to whomever He chooses.

26 "And inasmuch as they gave the command to leave the stump *and* roots of the tree, your kingdom shall be assured to you, after you come to know that Heaven rules. 27 Therefore, O king, let my advice be acceptable to you; break off your sins by *being* righteous, and your iniquities by showing mercy to *the* poor. Perhaps there may be a lengthening of your prosperity."

28 All *this* came upon King Nebuchadnezzar. 29 At the end of the twelve months he was walking about the royal palace of Babylon. 30 The king spoke, saying, "Is not this great Babylon, that I have built for a royal dwelling by my mighty power and for the honor of my majesty?"

31 While the word *was still* in the king's mouth, a voice fell from heaven: "King Nebuchadnezzar, to you it is spoken: the kingdom has departed from you! 32 And they shall drive you from men, and your dwelling *shall be* with the beasts of the field. They shall make you eat grass like oxen; and seven times shall pass over you, until you know that the Most High rules in the kingdom of men, and gives it to whomever He chooses."

33 That very hour the word was fulfilled concerning Nebuchadnezzar; he was driven from men and ate grass like oxen; his body was wet with the dew of heaven till his hair had grown like eagles' *feathers* and his nails like birds' *claws*.

34 And at the end of the time[a] I, Nebuchadnezzar, lifted my eyes to heaven, and my understanding returned to me; and I blessed the Most High and praised and honored Him who lives forever:

For His dominion *is* an
  everlasting dominion,
And His kingdom *is* from
  generation to generation.
35 All the inhabitants of the earth
  are reputed as nothing;
He does according to His will
  in the army of heaven
And *among* the inhabitants of
  the earth.
No one can restrain His hand
Or say to Him, "What have You
  done?"

36 At the same time my reason returned to me, and for the glory of my kingdom, my honor and splendor returned to me. My counselors and nobles resorted to me, I was restored to my kingdom, and excellent majesty was added to me. 37 Now I, Nebuchadnezzar, praise and extol and honor the King of heaven, all of whose works *are* truth, and His ways justice. And those who walk in pride He is able to put down.

5 Belshazzar the king made a great feast for a thousand of his lords, and drank wine in the presence of the thousand. 2 While he tasted the wine, Belshazzar gave the command to bring the gold and silver vessels which his father Nebuchadnezzar had taken from the temple which *had been* in Jerusalem, that the king and his lords, his wives, and his concubines might drink from them. 3 Then they brought the gold vessels that had been taken from the temple of the house of God which *had been* in Jerusalem; and the king and his lords, his wives, and his concubines drank from them. 4 They drank wine, and praised the gods of gold and silver, bronze and iron, wood and stone.

5 In the same hour the fingers of a man's hand appeared and wrote opposite the lampstand on the plaster

4:34 [a]Literally *days*

of the wall of the king's palace; and the king saw the part of the hand that wrote. 6 Then the king's countenance changed, and his thoughts troubled him, so that the joints of his hips were loosened and his knees knocked against each other. 7 The king cried aloud to bring in the astrologers, the Chaldeans, and the soothsayers. The king spoke, saying to the wise *men* of Babylon, "Whoever reads this writing, and tells me its interpretation, shall be clothed with purple and *have* a chain of gold around his neck; and he shall be the third ruler in the kingdom." 8 Now all the king's wise *men* came, but they could not read the writing, or make known to the king its interpretation. 9 Then King Belshazzar was greatly troubled, his countenance was changed, and his lords were astonished.

10 The queen, because of the words of the king and his lords, came to the banquet hall. The queen spoke, saying, "O king, live forever! Do not let your thoughts trouble you, nor let your countenance change. 11 There is a man in your kingdom in whom *is* the Spirit of the Holy God. And in the days of your father, light and understanding and wisdom, like the wisdom of the gods, were found in him; and King Nebuchadnezzar your father—your father the king—made him chief of the magicians, astrologers, Chaldeans, *and* soothsayers. 12 Inasmuch as an excellent spirit, knowledge, understanding, interpreting dreams, solving riddles, and explaining enigmas*ª* were found in this Daniel, whom the king named Belteshazzar, now let Daniel be called, and he will give the interpretation."

13 Then Daniel was brought in before the king. The king spoke, and said to Daniel, "*Are* you that Daniel who is one of the captives*ª* from Judah, whom my father the king brought from Judah? 14 I have heard of you, that the Spirit of God *is* in you, and *that* light and understanding and excellent wisdom are found in you. 15 Now the wise *men*, the astrologers, have been brought in before me, that they should read this writing and make known to me its

interpretation, but they could not give the interpretation of the thing. 16 And I have heard of you, that you can give interpretations and explain enigmas. Now if you can read the writing and make known to me its interpretation, you shall be clothed with purple and *have* a chain of gold around your neck, and shall be the third ruler in the kingdom."

17 Then Daniel answered, and said before the king, "Let your gifts be for yourself, and give your rewards to another; yet I will read the writing to the king, and make known to him the interpretation. 18 O king, the Most High God gave Nebuchadnezzar your father a kingdom and majesty, glory and honor. 19 And because of the majesty that He gave him, all peoples, nations, and languages trembled and feared before him. Whomever he wished, he executed; whomever he wished, he kept alive; whomever he wished, he set up; and whomever he wished, he put down. 20 But when his heart was lifted up, and his spirit was hardened in pride, he was deposed from his kingly throne, and they took his glory from him. 21 Then he was driven from the sons of men, his heart was made like the beasts, and his dwelling *was* with the wild donkeys. They fed him with grass like oxen, and his body was wet with the dew of heaven, till he knew that the Most High God rules in the kingdom of men, and appoints over it whomever He chooses.

22 "But you his son, Belshazzar, have not humbled your heart, although you knew all this. 23 And you have lifted yourself up against the Lord of heaven. They have brought the vessels of His house before you, and you and your lords, your wives and your concubines, have drunk wine from them. And you have praised the gods of silver and gold, bronze and iron, wood and stone, which do not see or hear or know; and the God who *holds* your breath in His hand and owns all your ways, you have not glorified. 24 Then the fingers*ª* of the hand were sent from Him, and this writing was written. 25 "And this is the inscription that was written:

5:12 *ª*Literally *untying knots,* and so in verse 16   5:13 *ª*Literally *of the sons of the captivity*
5:24 *ª*Literally *palm*

MENE,*a* MENE, TEKEL,*b* UPHARSIN.*c*

26 This *is* the interpretation of *each* word. MENE: God has numbered your kingdom, and finished it; 27 TEKEL: You have been weighed in the balances, and found wanting; 28 PERES: Your kingdom has been divided, and given to the Medes and Persians."*a* 29 Then Belshazzar gave the command, and they clothed Daniel with purple and *put* a chain of gold around his neck, and made a proclamation concerning him that he should be the third ruler in the kingdom.

30 That very night Belshazzar, king of the Chaldeans, was slain. 31 And Darius the Mede received the kingdom, *being* about sixty-two years old.

6 It pleased Darius to set over the kingdom one hundred and twenty satraps, to be over the whole kingdom; 2 and over these, three governors, of whom Daniel *was* one, that the satraps might give account to them, so that the king would suffer no loss. 3 Then this Daniel distinguished himself above the governors and satraps, because an excellent spirit *was* in him; and the king gave thought to setting him over the whole realm. 4 So the governors and satraps sought to find *some* charge against Daniel concerning the kingdom; but they could find no charge or fault, because he *was* faithful; nor was there any error or fault found in him. 5 Then these men said, "We shall not find any charge against this Daniel unless we find *it* against him concerning the law of his God."

6 So these governors and satraps thronged before the king, and said thus to him: "King Darius, live forever! 7 All the governors of the kingdom, the administrators and satraps, the counselors and advisors, have consulted together to establish a royal statute and to make a firm decree, that whoever petitions any god or man for thirty days, except you, O king, shall be cast into the den of lions. 8 Now, O king, establish the decree and sign the writing, so that it

cannot be changed, according to the law of the Medes and Persians, which does not alter." 9 Therefore King Darius signed the written decree.

10 Now when Daniel knew that the writing was signed, he went home. And in his upper room, with his windows open toward Jerusalem, he knelt down on his knees three times that day, and prayed and gave thanks before his God, as was his custom since early days.

11 Then these men assembled and found Daniel praying and making supplication before his God. 12 And they went before the king, and spoke concerning the king's decree: "Have you not signed a decree that every man who petitions any god or man within thirty days, except you, O king, shall be cast into the den of lions?"

The king answered and said, "The thing *is* true, according to the law of the Medes and Persians, which does not alter."

13 So they answered and said before the king, "That Daniel, who is one of the captives*a* from Judah, does not show due regard for you, O king, or for the decree that you have signed, but makes his petition three times a day."

14 And the king, when he heard *these* words, was greatly displeased with himself, and set *his* heart on Daniel to deliver him; and he labored till the going down of the sun to deliver him. 15 Then these men approached the king, and said to the king, "Know, O king, that *it is* the law of the Medes and Persians that no decree or statute which the king establishes may be changed."

16 So the king gave the command, and they brought Daniel and cast *him* into the den of lions. *But* the king spoke, saying to Daniel, "Your God, whom you serve continually, He will deliver you." 17 Then a stone was brought and laid on the mouth of the den, and the king sealed it with his own signet ring and with the signets of his lords, that the purpose concerning Daniel might not be changed.

18 Now the king went to his palace and spent the night fasting; and no

5:25 *a*Literally *a mina* (50 shekels) from the verb "to number"   *b*Literally *a shekel* from the verb "to weigh"   *c*Literally *and half-shekels* from the verb "to divide"   5:28 *a*Aramaic *Paras,* consonant with *Peres*
6:13 *a*Literally *of the sons of the captivity*

musicians[a] were brought before him. Also his sleep went from him. 19 Then the king arose very early in the morning and went in haste to the den of lions. 20 And when he came to the den, he cried out with a lamenting voice to Daniel. The king spoke, saying to Daniel, "Daniel, servant of the living God, has your God, whom you serve continually, been able to deliver you from the lions?"

21 Then Daniel said to the king, "O king, live forever! 22 My God sent His angel and shut the lions' mouths, so that they have not hurt me, because I was found innocent before Him; and also, O king, I have done no wrong before you."

23 Now the king was exceedingly glad for him, and commanded that they should take Daniel up out of the den. So Daniel was taken up out of the den, and no injury whatever was found on him, because he believed in his God.

24 And the king gave the command, and they brought those men who had accused Daniel, and they cast *them* into the den of lions—them, their children, and their wives; and the lions overpowered them, and broke all their bones in pieces before they ever came to the bottom of the den.

25 Then King Darius wrote:

To all peoples, nations, and languages that dwell in all the earth:

Peace be multiplied to you.

26   I make a decree that in every dominion of my kingdom *men must* tremble and fear before the God of Daniel.

For He *is* the living God,
And steadfast forever;
His kingdom *is the one* which shall not be destroyed,
And His dominion *shall endure* to the end.
27 He delivers and rescues,
And He works signs and wonders
In heaven and on earth,
Who has delivered Daniel from the power of the lions.

28 So this Daniel prospered in the reign of Darius and in the reign of Cyrus the Persian.

7 In the first year of Belshazzar king of Babylon, Daniel had a dream and visions of his head *while* on his bed. Then he wrote down the dream, telling the main facts.[a]

2 Daniel spoke, saying, "I saw in my vision by night, and behold, the four winds of heaven were stirring up the Great Sea. 3 And four great beasts came up from the sea, each different from the other. 4 The first *was* like a lion, and had eagle's wings. I watched till its wings were plucked off; and it was lifted up from the earth and made to stand on two feet like a man, and a man's heart was given to it.

5 "And suddenly another beast, a second, like a bear. It was raised up on one side, and *had* three ribs in its mouth between its teeth. And they said thus to it: 'Arise, devour much flesh!'

6 "After this I looked, and there was another, like a leopard, which had on its back four wings of a bird. The beast also had four heads, and dominion was given to it.

7 "After this I saw in the night visions, and behold, a fourth beast, dreadful and terrible, exceedingly strong. It had huge iron teeth; it was devouring, breaking in pieces, and trampling the residue with its feet. It *was* different from all the beasts that *were* before it, and it had ten horns. 8 I was considering the horns, and there was another horn, a little one, coming up among them, before whom three of the first horns were plucked out by the roots. And there, in this horn, *were* eyes like the eyes of a man, and a mouth speaking pompous words.

9 "I watched till thrones were put in place,
And the Ancient of Days was seated;
His garment *was* white as snow,
And the hair of His head *was* like pure wool.
His throne *was* a fiery flame,
Its wheels a burning fire;
10 A fiery stream issued

6:18 [a]Exact meaning unknown   7:1 [a]Literally *the head* (or *chief*) *of the words*

And came forth from before
Him.
A thousand thousands
ministered to Him;
Ten thousand times ten
thousand stood before Him.
The court[a] was seated,
And the books were opened.

11 "I watched then because of the sound of the pompous words which the horn was speaking; I watched till the beast was slain, and its body destroyed and given to the burning flame. 12 As for the rest of the beasts, they had their dominion taken away; yet their lives were prolonged for a season and a time.

13 "I was watching in the night
visions,
And behold, *One* like the Son
of Man,
Coming with the clouds of
heaven!
He came to the Ancient of
Days,
And they brought Him near
before Him.
14 Then to Him was given
dominion and glory and a
kingdom,
That all peoples, nations, and
languages should serve Him.
His dominion *is* an everlasting
dominion,
Which shall not pass away,
And His kingdom *the one*
Which shall not be destroyed.

15 "I, Daniel, was grieved in my spirit within *my* body, and the visions of my head troubled me. 16 I came near to one of those who stood by, and asked him the truth of all this. So he told me and made known to me the interpretation of these things: 17 'Those great beasts, which *are* four, *are* four kings[a] which arise out of the earth. 18 But the saints of the Most High shall receive the kingdom, and possess the kingdom forever, even forever and ever.'
19 "Then I wished to know the truth about the fourth beast, which was different from all the others, exceedingly dreadful, *with* its teeth of iron and its nails of bronze, *which* devoured, broke in pieces, and trampled the residue with its feet;

20 and the ten horns that *were* on its head, and the other *horn* which came up, before which three fell, namely, that horn which had eyes and a mouth which spoke pompous words, whose appearance *was* greater than his fellows. 21 "I was watching; and the same horn was making war against the saints, and prevailing against them, 22 until the Ancient of Days came, and a judgment was made *in favor* of the saints of the Most High, and the time came for the saints to possess the kingdom.
23 "Thus he said:

'The fourth beast shall be
A fourth kingdom on earth,
Which shall be different from
all *other* kingdoms,
And shall devour the whole
earth,
Trample it and break it in
pieces.
24 The ten horns *are* ten kings
Who shall arise from this
kingdom.
And another shall rise after
them;
He shall be different from the
first *ones*,
And shall subdue three kings.
25 He shall speak *pompous* words
against the Most High,
Shall persecute[a] the saints of
the Most High,
And shall intend to change
times and law.
Then *the saints* shall be given
into his hand
For a time and times and half
a time.

26 'But the court shall be seated,
And they shall take away his
dominion,
To consume and destroy *it*
forever.
27 Then the kingdom and
dominion,
And the greatness of the
kingdoms under the whole
heaven,
Shall be given to the people, the
saints of the Most High.
His kingdom *is* an everlasting
kingdom,
And all dominions shall serve
and obey Him.'

7:10 aOr *judgment*   7:17 aRepresenting their kingdoms (compare verse 23)   7:25 aLiterally *wear out*

28 "This *is* the end of the account.*a* As for me, Daniel, my thoughts greatly troubled me, and my countenance changed; but I kept the matter in my heart."

8 In the third year of the reign of King Belshazzar a vision appeared *to* me—to me, Daniel—after the one that appeared to me the first time. 2 I saw in the vision, and it so happened while I was looking, that I *was* in Shushan, the citadel, which *is* in the province of Elam; and I saw in the vision that I was by the River Ulai. 3 Then I lifted my eyes and saw, and there, standing beside the river, was a ram which had two horns, and the two horns *were* high; but one *was* higher than the other, and the higher *one* came up last. 4 I saw the ram pushing westward, northward, and southward, so that no animal could withstand him; nor *was there any* that could deliver from his hand, but he did according to his will and became great.

5 And as I was considering, suddenly a male goat came from the west, across the surface of the whole earth, without touching the ground; and the goat *had* a notable horn between his eyes. 6 Then he came to the ram that had two horns, which I had seen standing beside the river, and ran at him with furious power. 7 And I saw him confronting the ram; he was moved with rage against him, attacked the ram, and broke his two horns. There was no power in the ram to withstand him, but he cast him down to the ground and trampled him; and there was no one that could deliver the ram from his hand.

8 Therefore the male goat grew very great; but when he became strong, the large horn was broken, and in place of it four notable ones came up toward the four winds of heaven. 9 And out of one of them came a little horn which grew exceedingly great toward the south, toward the east, and toward the Glorious *Land.* 10 And it grew up to the host of heaven; and it cast down *some* of the host and *some* of the stars to the ground, and trampled them. 11 He even exalted *himself* as

high as the Prince of the host; and by him the daily *sacrifices* were taken away, and the place of His sanctuary was cast down. 12 Because of transgression, an army was given over *to the horn* to oppose the daily *sacrifices;* and he cast truth down to the ground. He did *all this* and prospered.

13 Then I heard a holy one speaking; and *another* holy one said to that certain *one* who was speaking, "How long *will* the vision *be, concerning* the daily *sacrifices* and the transgression of desolation, the giving of both the sanctuary and the host to be trampled underfoot?"

14 And he said to me, "For two thousand three hundred days;*a* then the sanctuary shall be cleansed."

15 Then it happened, when I, Daniel, had seen the vision and was seeking the meaning, that suddenly there stood before me one having the appearance of a man. 16 And I heard a man's voice between *the banks of* the Ulai, who called, and said, "Gabriel, make this *man* understand the vision." 17 So he came near where I stood, and when he came I was afraid and fell on my face; but he said to me, "Understand, son of man, that the vision *refers* to the time of the end."

18 Now, as he was speaking with me, I was in a deep sleep with my face to the ground; but he touched me, and stood me upright. 19 And he said, "Look, I am making known to you what shall happen in the latter time of the indignation; for at the appointed time the end *shall be.* 20 The ram which you saw, having the two horns—*they are* the kings of Media and Persia. 21 And the male goat *is* the kingdom*a* of Greece. The large horn that *is* between its eyes *is* the first king. 22 As for the broken *horn* and the four that stood up in its place, four kingdoms shall arise out of that nation, but not with its power.

23 "And in the latter time of their
    kingdom,
When the transgressors have
    reached their fullness,
A king shall arise,
Having fierce features,

7:28 *a*Literally *the word*   8:14 *a*Literally *evening-mornings*   8:21 *a*Literally *king,* representing his kingdom (compare 7:17, 23)

Who understands sinister
schemes.
24 His power shall be mighty, but
not by his own power;
He shall destroy fearfully,
And shall prosper and thrive;
He shall destroy the mighty,
and *also* the holy people.

25 "Through his cunning
He shall cause deceit to prosper
under his rule;*a*
And he shall exalt *himself* in his
heart.
He shall destroy many in *their*
prosperity.
He shall even rise against the
Prince of princes;
But he shall be broken without
human means.*b*

26 "And the vision of the evenings
and mornings
Which was told is true;
Therefore seal up the vision,
For *it refers* to many days *in
the future*."

27 And I, Daniel, fainted and was
sick for days; afterward I arose and
went about the king's business. I was
astonished by the vision, but no one
understood it.

9 In the first year of Darius the son
of Ahasuerus, of the lineage of the
Medes, who was made king over the
realm of the Chaldeans— 2 in the first
year of his reign I, Daniel, understood by the books the number of the
years *specified* by the word of the
Lord through Jeremiah the prophet,
that He would accomplish seventy
years in the desolations of Jerusalem.
3 Then I set my face toward the
Lord God to make request by prayer
and supplications, with fasting, sackcloth, and ashes. 4 And I prayed to
the Lord my God, and made confession, and said, "O Lord, great and
awesome God, who keeps His covenant and mercy with those who love
Him, and with those who keep His
commandments, 5 we have sinned
and committed iniquity, we have
done wickedly and rebelled, even by
departing from Your precepts and
Your judgments. 6 Neither have we
heeded Your servants the prophets,
who spoke in Your name to our kings

and our princes, to our fathers and
all the people of the land. 7 O Lord,
righteousness *belongs* to You, but to
us shame of face, as *it is* this day—
to the men of Judah, to the inhabitants of Jerusalem and all Israel,
those near and those far off in all the
countries to which You have driven
them, because of the unfaithfulness
which they have committed against
You.
8 "O Lord, to us *belongs* shame of
face, to our kings, our princes, and
our fathers, because we have sinned
against You. 9 To the Lord our God
belong mercy and forgiveness,
though we have rebelled against
Him. 10 We have not obeyed the
voice of the Lord our God, to walk
in His laws, which He set before us
by His servants the prophets.
11 Yes, all Israel has transgressed
Your law, and has departed so as not
to obey Your voice; therefore the
curse and the oath written in the Law
of Moses the servant of God have
been poured out on us, because we
have sinned against Him. 12 And He
has confirmed His words, which He
spoke against us and against our
judges who judged us, by bringing
upon us a great disaster; for under
the whole heaven such has never
been done as what has been done to
Jerusalem.
13 "As *it is* written in the Law of
Moses, all this disaster has come
upon us; yet we have not made our
prayer before the Lord our God, that
we might turn from our iniquities and
understand Your truth. 14 Therefore
the Lord has kept the disaster in
mind, and brought it upon us; for the
Lord our God *is* righteous in all the
works which He does, though we
have not obeyed His voice. 15 And
now, O Lord our God, who brought
Your people out of the land of Egypt
with a mighty hand, and made Yourself a name, as *it is* this day—we have
sinned, we have done wickedly!
16 "O Lord, according to all Your
righteousness, I pray, let Your anger
and Your fury be turned away from
Your city Jerusalem, Your holy
mountain; because for our sins, and
for the iniquities of our fathers, Jerusalem and Your people *are* a reproach to all *those* around us.
17 Now therefore, our God, hear the

8:25 *a*Literally *hand*   *b*Literally *hand*

prayer of Your servant, and his supplications, and for the Lord's sake cause Your face to shine on Your sanctuary, which is desolate. 18 O my God, incline Your ear and hear; open Your eyes and see our desolations, and the city which is called by Your name; for we do not present our supplications before You because of our righteous deeds, but because of Your great mercies. 19 O Lord, hear! O Lord, forgive! O Lord, listen and act! Do not delay for Your own sake, my God, for Your city and Your people are called by Your name."

20 Now while I *was* speaking, praying, and confessing my sin and the sin of my people Israel, and presenting my supplication before the LORD my God for the holy mountain of my God, 21 yes, while I *was* speaking in prayer, the man Gabriel, whom I had seen in the vision at the beginning, being caused to fly swiftly, reached me about the time of the evening offering. 22 And he informed *me*, and talked with me, and said, "O Daniel, I have now come forth to give you skill to understand. 23 At the beginning of your supplications the command went out, and I have come to tell *you*, for you *are* greatly beloved; therefore consider the matter, and understand the vision:

24 "Seventy weeks*a* are determined
For your people and for your
   holy city,
To finish the transgression,
To make an end of*b* sins,
To make reconciliation for
   iniquity,
To bring in everlasting
   righteousness,
To seal up vision and prophecy,
And to anoint the Most Holy.

25 "Know therefore and under-
   stand,
That from the going forth of
   the command
To restore and build Jerusalem
Until Messiah the Prince,
There shall be seven weeks and
   sixty-two weeks;
The street*a* shall be built again,
   and the wall,*b*
Even in troublesome times.

26 "And after the sixty-two weeks
Messiah shall be cut off, but not
   for Himself;
And the people of the prince
   who is to come
Shall destroy the city and the
   sanctuary.
The end of it *shall be* with a
   flood,
And till the end of the war
   desolations are determined.
27 Then he shall confirm a
   covenant with many for one
   week;
But in the middle of the
   week
He shall bring an end to
   sacrifice and offering.
And on the wing of
   abominations shall be one
   who makes desolate,
Even until the consummation,
   which is determined,
Is poured out on the desolate."

10 In the third year of Cyrus king of Persia a message was revealed to Daniel, whose name was called Belteshazzar. The message *was* true, but the appointed time *was* long;*a* and he understood the message, and had understanding of the vision. 2 In those days I, Daniel, was mourning three full weeks. 3 I ate no pleasant food, no meat or wine came into my mouth, nor did I anoint myself at all, till three whole weeks were fulfilled.

4 Now on the twenty-fourth day of the first month, as I was by the side of the great river, that *is,* the Tigris,*a* 5 I lifted my eyes and looked, and behold, a certain man clothed in linen, whose waist *was* girded with gold of Uphaz! 6 His body *was* like beryl, his face like the appearance of lightning, his eyes like torches of fire, his arms and feet like burnished bronze in color, and the sound of his words like the voice of a multitude.

7 And I, Daniel, alone saw the vision, for the men who were with me did not see the vision; but a great terror fell upon them, so that they fled to hide themselves. 8 Therefore I was left alone when I saw this great vision, and no strength remained in me; for my vigor was turned to frailty in me, and I retained no strength.

9:24 *a*Literally *sevens,* and so throughout the chapter *b*Following Qere, Septuagint, Syriac, and Vulgate; Kethib and Theodotion read *To seal up.*   9:25 *a*Or *open square* *b*Or *moat*   10:1 *a*Or *and of great conflict*   10:4 *a*Hebrew *Hiddekel*

9 Yet I heard the sound of his words; and while I heard the sound of his words I was in a deep sleep on my face, with my face to the ground. 10 Suddenly, a hand touched me, which made me tremble on my knees and *on* the palms of my hands. 11 And he said to me, "O Daniel, man greatly beloved, understand the words that I speak to you, and stand upright, for I have now been sent to you." While he was speaking this word to me, I stood trembling. 12 Then he said to me, "Do not fear, Daniel, for from the first day that you set your heart to understand, and to humble yourself before your God, your words were heard; and I have come because of your words. 13 But the prince of the kingdom of Persia withstood me twenty-one days; and behold, Michael, one of the chief princes, came to help me, for I had been left alone there with the kings of Persia. 14 Now I have come to make you understand what will happen to your people in the latter days, for the vision *refers* to *many* days yet *to come*."

15 When he had spoken such words to me, I turned my face toward the ground and became speechless. 16 And suddenly, *one* having the likeness of the sons*a* of men touched my lips; then I opened my mouth and spoke, saying to him who stood before me, "My lord, because of the vision my sorrows have overwhelmed me, and I have retained no strength. 17 For how can this servant of my lord talk with you, my lord? As for me, no strength remains in me now, nor is any breath left in me."

18 Then again, *the one* having the likeness of a man touched me and strengthened me. 19 And he said, "O man greatly beloved, fear not! Peace *be* to you; be strong, yes, be strong!"

So when he spoke to me I was strengthened, and said, "Let my lord speak, for you have strengthened me."

20 Then he said, "Do you know why I have come to you? And now I must return to fight with the prince of Persia; and when I have gone forth, indeed the prince of Greece will come. 21 But I will tell you what is noted in the Scripture of Truth. (No one upholds me against these, except Michael your prince.

11 "Also in the first year of Darius the Mede, I, *even* I, stood up to confirm and strengthen him.) 2 And now I will tell you the truth: Behold, three more kings will arise in Persia, and the fourth shall be far richer than *them* all; by his strength, through his riches, he shall stir up all against the realm of Greece. 3 Then a mighty king shall arise, who shall rule with great dominion, and do according to his will. 4 And when he has arisen, his kingdom shall be broken up and divided toward the four winds of heaven, but not among his posterity nor according to his dominion with which he ruled; for his kingdom shall be uprooted, even for others besides these.

5 "Also the king of the South shall become strong, as well as *one* of his princes; and he shall gain power over him and have dominion. His dominion *shall be* a great dominion. 6 And at the end of *some* years they shall join forces, for the daughter of the king of the South shall go to the king of the North to make an agreement; but she shall not retain the power of her authority, and neither he nor his authority*a* shall stand; but she shall be given up, with those who brought her, and with him who begot her, and with him who strengthened her in *those* times. 7 But from a branch of her roots *one* shall arise in his place, who shall come with an army, enter the fortress of the king of the North, and deal with them and prevail. 8 And he shall also carry their gods captive to Egypt, with their princes*a and* their precious articles of silver and gold; and he shall continue *more* years than the king of the North.

9 "Also *the king of the North* shall come to the kingdom of the king of the South, but shall return to his own land. 10 However his sons shall stir up strife, and assemble a multitude of great forces; and *one* shall certainly come and overwhelm and pass through; then he shall return to his fortress and stir up strife.

11 "And the king of the South shall be moved with rage, and go out and

10:16 *a*Theodotion and Vulgate read *the son;* Septuagint reads *a hand.*   11:6 *a*Literally *arm*   11:8 *a*Or *molded images* fight with him, with the king of the North, who shall muster a great multitude; but the multitude shall be given into the hand of his *enemy.* 12 When he has taken away the multitude, his heart will be lifted up; and he will cast down tens of thousands, but he will not prevail. 13 For the king of the North will return and muster a multitude greater than the former, and shall certainly come at the end of some years with a great army and much equipment.

14 "Now in those times many shall rise up against the king of the South. Also, violent men[a] of your people shall exalt themselves in fulfillment of the vision, but they shall fall. 15 So the king of the North shall come and build a siege mound, and take a fortified city; and the forces[a] of the South shall not withstand *him.* Even his choice troops *shall have* no strength to resist. 16 But he who comes against him shall do according to his own will, and no one shall stand against him. He shall stand in the Glorious Land with destruction in his power.[a]

17 "He shall also set his face to enter with the strength of his whole kingdom, and upright ones[a] with him; thus shall he do. And he shall give him the daughter of women to destroy it; but she shall not stand *with him,* or be for him. 18 After this he shall turn his face to the coastlands, and shall take many. But a ruler shall bring the reproach against them to an end; and with the reproach removed, he shall turn back on him. 19 Then he shall turn his face toward the fortress of his own land; but he shall stumble and fall, and not be found.

20 "There shall arise in his place one who imposes taxes *on* the glorious kingdom; but within a few days he shall be destroyed, but not in anger or in battle. 21 And in his place shall arise a vile person, to whom they will not give the honor of royalty; but he shall come in peaceably, and seize the kingdom by intrigue. 22 With the force[a] of a flood they shall be swept away from before him and be broken, and also the prince of the covenant. 23 And after the

league *is made* with him he shall act deceitfully, for he shall come up and become strong with a small *number of* people. 24 He shall enter peaceably, even into the richest places of the province; and he shall do *what* his fathers have not done, nor his forefathers: he shall disperse among them the plunder, spoil, and riches; and he shall devise his plans against the strongholds, but *only* for a time.

25 "He shall stir up his power and his courage against the king of the South with a great army. And the king of the South shall be stirred up to battle with a very great and mighty army; but he shall not stand, for they shall devise plans against him. 26 Yes, those who eat of the portion of his delicacies shall destroy him; his army shall be swept away, and many shall fall down slain. 27 Both these kings' hearts *shall be* bent on evil, and they shall speak lies at the same table; but it shall not prosper, for the end *will* still *be* at the appointed time. 28 While returning to his land with great riches, his heart shall be *moved* against the holy covenant; so he shall do *damage* and return to his own land.

29 "At the appointed time he shall return and go toward the south; but it shall not be like the former or the latter. 30 For ships from Cyprus[a] shall come against him; therefore he shall be grieved, and return in rage against the holy covenant, and do *damage.*

"So he shall return and show regard for those who forsake the holy covenant. 31 And forces[a] shall be mustered by him, and they shall defile the sanctuary fortress; then they shall take away the daily *sacrifices,* and place *there* the abomination of desolation. 32 Those who do wickedly against the covenant he shall corrupt with flattery; but the people who know their God shall be strong, and carry out *great exploits.* 33 And those of the people who understand shall instruct many; yet *for many* days they shall fall by sword and flame, by captivity and plundering. 34 Now when they fall, they shall be aided with a little help; but many shall join with them by intrigue. 35 And *some* of those of understand-

---

11:14 [a]Or *robbers,* literally *sons of breakage*   11:15 [a]Literally *arms*   11:16 [a]Literally *hand*   11:17 [a]Or *bring equitable terms*   11:22 [a]Literally *arms*   11:30 [a]Hebrew *Kittim,* western lands, especially Cyprus   11:31 [a]Literally *arms* ing shall fall, to refine them, purify *them*, and make *them* white, *until* the time of the end; because *it is* still for the appointed time.

36 "Then the king shall do according to his own will: he shall exalt and magnify himself above every god, shall speak blasphemies against the God of gods, and shall prosper till the wrath has been accomplished; for what has been determined shall be done. 37 He shall regard neither the God[a] of his fathers nor the desire of women, nor regard any god; for he shall exalt himself above *them* all. 38 But in their place he shall honor a god of fortresses; and a god which his fathers did not know he shall honor with gold and silver, with precious stones and pleasant things. 39 Thus he shall act against the strongest fortresses with a foreign god, which he shall acknowledge, *and* advance *its* glory; and he shall cause them to rule over many, and divide the land for gain.

40 "At the time of the end the king of the South shall attack him; and the king of the North shall come against him like a whirlwind, with chariots, horsemen, and with many ships; and he shall enter the countries, overwhelm *them*, and pass through. 41 He shall also enter the Glorious Land, and many *countries* shall be overthrown; but these shall escape from his hand: Edom, Moab, and the prominent people of Ammon. 42 He shall stretch out his hand against the countries, and the land of Egypt shall not escape. 43 He shall have power over the treasures of gold and silver, and over all the precious things of Egypt; also the Libyans and Ethiopians *shall follow* at his heels. 44 But news from the east and the north shall trouble him; therefore he shall go out with great fury to destroy and annihilate many. 45 And he shall plant the tents of his palace between the seas and the glorious holy mountain; yet he shall come to his end, and no one will help him.

12 "At that time Michael shall stand up,
The great prince who stands *watch* over the sons of your people;

And there shall be a time of trouble,
Such as never was since there was a nation,
Even to that time.
And at that time your people shall be delivered,
Every one who is found written in the book.
2   And many of those who sleep in the dust of the earth shall awake,
Some to everlasting life,
Some to shame *and* everlasting contempt.
3   Those who are wise shall shine
Like the brightness of the firmament,
And those who turn many to righteousness
Like the stars forever and ever.

4 "But you, Daniel, shut up the words, and seal the book until the time of the end; many shall run to and fro, and knowledge shall increase."

5 Then I, Daniel, looked; and there stood two others, one on this riverbank and the other on that riverbank. 6 And *one* said to the man clothed in linen, who *was* above the waters of the river, "How long shall the fulfillment of these wonders *be?*"

7 Then I heard the man clothed in linen, who *was* above the waters of the river, when he held up his right hand and his left hand to heaven, and swore by Him who lives forever, that *it shall be* for a time, times, and half *a time;* and when the power of the holy people has been completely shattered, all these *things* shall be finished.

8 Although I heard, I did not understand. Then I said, "My lord, what *shall be* the end of these *things?*"

9 And he said, "Go *your way,* Daniel, for the words *are* closed up and sealed till the time of the end. 10 Many shall be purified, made white, and refined, but the wicked shall do wickedly; and none of the wicked shall understand, but the wise shall understand.

11 "And from the time *that* the daily *sacrifice* is taken away, and the abomination of desolation is set up, *there shall be* one thousand two hun-

11:37 [a]Or *gods*

dred and ninety days. 12 Blessed *is* he who waits, and comes to the one thousand three hundred and thirty-five days.

13 "But you, go *your way* till the end; for you shall rest, and will arise to your inheritance at the end of the days."

Hosea

Overview of Hosea

God used a shocking and dramatic illustration of His love for the people of Israel through the life and marriage of Hosea the prophet to Gomer the prostitute.

Written by the prophet himself sometime between 790 and 710 B.C., the theme of the Book of Hosea is God's unending love despite Israel's unfaithfulness to Him. God used Hosea's marriage and family life to illustrate Israel's relationship with God.

Hosea married Gomer, bringing her into a forgiving, loving relationship with him. But when she returned to her former lovers, Hosea showed his true love for Gomer by seeking her out, forgiving her, and marrying her again.

Hosea's forgiveness of Gomer is especially significant considering that prostitutes in Israel were unclean and not worthy of God's love. Furthermore, such an act of adultery was punishable by death. Yet, Israel, like Gomer, was to be the recipient of God's love and forgiveness. God would seek Israel out and marry her again.

> O Israel, return to the LORD your God,
> For you have stumbled because of your iniquity;
> Take words with you,
> And return to the LORD.
> Say to Him,
> "Take away all iniquity;
> Receive us graciously,
> For we will offer the sacrifices of our lips."

Who is wise?
Let him understand these things.
Who is prudent?
Let him know them.
For the ways of the LORD are right;
The righteous walk in them.
But transgressors stumble in them.

(Hos. 14:1, 2, 9)

Hosea emphasizes God's forgiveness and redeeming love for all people. Even when they failed, God welcomed them back. Failure is never final—but God's love is!

Jesus in Hosea

Matthew 2:15 applies Hosea 11:1 to Christ in Egypt: "When Israel *was* a child, I loved him, and out of Egypt I called My son." Matthew quotes the second half of this verse to show that the Exodus of Israel from Egypt as a new nation was a prophetic type of Israel's Messiah who was also called out of Egypt in his childhood. Both Israel and Christ left Palestine to take refuge in Egypt. Hosea's redemption of his wife Gomer represents Jesus' unconditional love for us. No matter how far we may stray, Jesus is always faithful.

Keys to Hosea

Key Word: Loyal. The key theme of Hosea is God's loyal love for Israel. More than any other Old Testament prophet, Hosea's personal experiences illustrate his prophetic message. In his relationship to Gomer, Hosea portrays God's faithfulness, justice, love, and forgiveness toward His people. The theme of God's holiness is developed in contrast to Israel's corruption and apostasy. God's justice is contrasted with Israel's injustice and His love with her hardness and empty ritual. God's loyal love is ceaseless and unconditional and He constantly woos Israel back to Himself.

Key Verse: " I will heal their backsliding, I will love them freely, for My anger has turned away from him. I will be like the dew to Israel; he shall grow like the lily, and lengthen his roots like Lebanon. His branches shall spread; his beauty shall be like an olive tree, and his fragrance like Lebanon. Those who dwell under his shadow shall return; they shall be revived *like* grain, and grow like a vine" (14:4–7).

Key Chapter: Hosea 4. The nation of Israel has left the knowledge of the truth and followed the idolatrous ways of her pagan neighbors. Hosea 4:6 encouraged them, and encourages us today, to pursue the knowledge of the Lord.

1 The word of the LORD that came to Hosea the son of Beeri, in the days of Uzziah, Jotham, Ahaz, *and* Hezekiah, kings of Judah, and in the days of Jeroboam the son of Joash, king of Israel. 2 When the LORD began to speak by Hosea, the LORD said to Hosea:

"Go, take yourself a wife of
    harlotry
And children of harlotry,
For the land has committed
    great harlotry
By departing from the LORD."

3 So he went and took Gomer the daughter of Diblaim, and she conceived and bore him a son. 4 Then the LORD said to him:

"Call his name Jezreel,
For in a little *while*
I will avenge the bloodshed of
    Jezreel on the house of Jehu,
And bring an end to the
    kingdom of the house of
    Israel.
5   It shall come to pass in that day
That I will break the bow of
    Israel in the Valley of
    Jezreel."

6 And she conceived again and bore a daughter. Then *God* said to him:

"Call her name Lo-Ruhamah,ᵃ
For I will no longer have mercy
    on the house of Israel,
But I will utterly take them
    away.ᵇ
7   Yet I will have mercy on the
    house of Judah,

Will save them by the LORD
    their God,
And will not save them by bow,
Nor by sword or battle,
By horses or horsemen."

8 Now when she had weaned Lo-Ruhamah, she conceived and bore a son. 9 Then *God* said:

"Call his name Lo-Ammi,ᵃ
For you *are* not My people,
And I will not be your *God*.

10 "Yet the number of the children
    of Israel
Shall be as the sand of the sea,
Which cannot be measured or
    numbered.
And it shall come to pass
In the place where it was said
    to them,
'You *are* not My people,'ᵃ
There it shall be said to them,
'You are sons of the living God.'
11 Then the children of Judah and
    the children of Israel
Shall be gathered together,
And appoint for themselves
    one head;
And they shall come up out of
    the land,
For great *will be* the day of
    Jezreel!

2 "Say to your brethren, 'My
    people,'ᵃ
And to your sisters, 'Mercyᵇ *is*
    shown.'
2   Bring charges against your
    mother, bring charges;
For she *is* not My wife, nor *am*
    I her Husband!

Let her put away her harlotries
from her sight,
And her adulteries from
between her breasts;
3 Lest I strip her naked
And expose her, as in the day
she was born,
And make her like a
wilderness,
And set her like a dry land,
And slay her with thirst.

4 "I will not have mercy on her
children,
For they *are* the children of
harlotry.
5 For their mother has played the
harlot;
She who conceived them has
behaved shamefully.
For she said, 'I will go after my
lovers,
Who give *me* my bread and my
water,
My wool and my linen,
My oil and my drink.'

6 "Therefore, behold,
I will hedge up your way with
thorns,
And wall her in,
So that she cannot find her
paths.
7 She will chase her lovers,
But not overtake them;
Yes, she will seek them, but not
find *them.*
Then she will say,
'I will go and return to my first
husband,
For then *it was* better for me
than now.'
8 For she did not know
That I gave her grain, new
wine, and oil,
And multiplied her silver and
gold—
Which they prepared for
Baal.

9 "Therefore I will return and take
away
My grain in its time
And My new wine in its season,
And will take back My wool
and My linen,
Given to cover her nakedness.
10 Now I will uncover her
lewdness in the sight of her
lovers,

And no one shall deliver her
from My hand.
11 I will also cause all her mirth
to cease,
Her feast days,
Her New Moons,
Her Sabbaths—
All her appointed feasts.

12 "And I will destroy her vines
and her fig trees,
Of which she has said,
'These *are* my wages that my
lovers have given me.'
So I will make them a forest,
And the beasts of the field shall
eat them.
13 I will punish her
For the days of the Baals to
which she burned incense.
She decked herself with her
earrings and jewelry,
And went after her lovers;
But Me she forgot," says the
LORD.

14 "Therefore, behold, I will allure
her,
Will bring her into the
wilderness,
And speak comfort to her.
15 I will give her her vineyards
from there,
And the Valley of Achor as a
door of hope;
She shall sing there,
As in the days of her youth,
As in the day when she came
up from the land of Egypt.

16 "And it shall be, in that day,"
Says the LORD,
"*That* you will call Me 'My
Husband,'[a]
And no longer call Me 'My
Master,'[b]
17 For I will take from her mouth
the names of the Baals,
And they shall be remembered
by their name no more.
18 In that day I will make a
covenant for them
With the beasts of the field,
With the birds of the air,
And *with* the creeping things
of the ground.
Bow and sword of battle I will
shatter from the earth,
To make them lie down safely.

2:16 [a]Hebrew *Ishi*   [b]Hebrew *Baali*

19 "I will betroth you to Me
        forever;
    Yes, I will betroth you to Me
    In righteousness and justice,
    In lovingkindness and mercy;
20 I will betroth you to Me in
        faithfulness,
    And you shall know the LORD.

21 "It shall come to pass in that
        day
    That I will answer," says the
        LORD;
    "I will answer the heavens,
    And they shall answer the
        earth.
22 The earth shall answer
    With grain,
    With new wine,
    And with oil;
    They shall answer Jezreel.*a*
23 Then I will sow her for Myself
        in the earth,
    And I will have mercy on *her
        who had* not obtained
        mercy;*a*
    Then I will say to *those who
        were* not My people,*b*
    'You *are* My people!'
    And they shall say, '*You are* my
        God!' "

3 Then the LORD said to me, "Go
again, love a woman *who is* loved
by a lover*a* and is committing adultery, just like the love of the LORD
for the children of Israel, who look
to other gods and love *the* raisin
cakes *of the pagans.*"

2 So I bought her for myself for fifteen *shekels* of silver, and one and
one-half homers of barley. 3 And I
said to her, "You shall stay with me
many days; you shall not play the
harlot, nor shall you have a man—
so, too, *will* I *be* toward you."

4 For the children of Israel shall
abide many days without king or
prince, without sacrifice or sacred
pillar, without ephod or teraphim.
5 Afterward the children of Israel
shall return and seek the LORD their
God and David their king. They shall
fear the LORD and His goodness in
the latter days.

4 Hear the word of the LORD,
    You children of Israel,

For the LORD *brings* a charge
    against the inhabitants of the
    land:

"There is no truth or mercy
    Or knowledge of God in the
    land.
2   By swearing and lying,
    Killing and stealing and
        committing adultery,
    They break all restraint,
    With bloodshed upon
        bloodshed.
3   Therefore the land will mourn;
    And everyone who dwells there
        will waste away
    With the beasts of the field
    And the birds of the air;
    Even the fish of the sea will be
        taken away.

4 "Now let no man contend, or
        rebuke another;
    For your people *are* like those
        who contend with the
        priest.
5   Therefore you shall stumble in
        the day;
    The prophet also shall stumble
        with you in the night;
    And I will destroy your mother.
6   My people are destroyed for
        lack of knowledge.
    Because you have rejected
        knowledge,
    I also will reject you from being
        priest for Me;
    Because you have forgotten the
        law of your God,
    I also will forget your children.

7 "The more they increased,
    The more they sinned against
        Me;
    I will change*a* their glory*b* into
        shame.
8   They eat up the sin of My
        people;
    They set their heart on their
        iniquity.
9   And it shall be: like people, like
        priest.
    So I will punish them for their
        ways,
    And reward them for their
        deeds.
10 For they shall eat, but not have
        enough;

2:22 *a*Literally *God Will Sow*   2:23 *a*Hebrew *lo-ruhamah*   *b*Hebrew *lo-ammi*   3:1 *a*Literally *friend* or
husband   4:7 *a*Following Masoretic Text, Septuagint, and Vulgate; scribal tradition, Syriac, and Targum
read *They will change.*   *b*Following Masoretic Text, Septuagint, Syriac, Targum, and Vulgate; scribal tradition
reads *My glory.*

They shall commit harlotry, but
not increase;
Because they have ceased
obeying the LORD.

11 "Harlotry, wine, and new wine
enslave the heart.
12 My people ask counsel from
their wooden *idols,*
And their staff informs
them.
For the spirit of harlotry has
caused *them* to stray,
And they have played the
harlot against their God.
13 They offer sacrifices on the
mountaintops,
And burn incense on the
hills,
Under oaks, poplars, and
terebinths,
Because their shade *is*
good.
Therefore your daughters
commit harlotry,
And your brides commit
adultery.

14 "I will not punish your
daughters when they commit
harlotry,
Nor your brides when they
commit adultery;
For *the men* themselves go
apart with harlots,
And offer sacrifices with a
ritual harlot.*a*
Therefore people *who* do not
understand will be trampled.

15 "Though you, Israel, play the
harlot,
Let not Judah offend.
Do not come up to Gilgal,
Nor go up to Beth Aven,
Nor swear an oath, *saying,* 'As
the LORD lives'—

16 "For Israel is stubborn
Like a stubborn calf;
Now the LORD will let them
forage
Like a lamb in open country.

17 "Ephraim *is* joined to idols,
Let him alone.
18 Their drink is rebellion,
They commit harlotry
continually.
Her rulers dearly love
dishonor.*a*

19 The wind has wrapped her up
in its wings,
And they shall be ashamed
because of their sacrifices.

5 "Hear this, O priests!
Take heed, O house of Israel!
Give ear, O house of the king!
For yours *is* the judgment,
Because you have been a snare
to Mizpah
And a net spread on Tabor.
2 The revolters are deeply
involved in slaughter,
Though I rebuke them all.
3 I know Ephraim,
And Israel is not hidden from
Me;
For now, O Ephraim, you
commit harlotry;
Israel is defiled.

4 "They do not direct their deeds
Toward turning to their God,
For the spirit of harlotry is in
their midst,
And they do not know the
LORD.
5 The pride of Israel testifies to
his face;
Therefore Israel and Ephraim
stumble in their iniquity;
Judah also stumbles with them.

6 "With their flocks and herds
They shall go to seek the LORD,
But they will not find *Him;*
He has withdrawn Himself
from them.
7 They have dealt treacherously
with the LORD,
For they have begotten pagan
children.
Now a New Moon shall devour
them and their heritage.

8 "Blow the ram's horn in Gibeah,
The trumpet in Ramah!
Cry aloud *at* Beth Aven,
'*Look* behind you, O Benjamin!'
9 Ephraim shall be desolate in
the day of rebuke;
Among the tribes of Israel I
make known what is sure.

10 "The princes of Judah are like
those who remove a
landmark;

I will pour out my wrath on
   them like water.
11 Ephraim is oppressed *and*
   broken in judgment,
Because he willingly walked by
   human precept.
12 Therefore I *will be* to Ephraim
   like a moth,
And to the house of Judah like
   rottenness.

13 "When Ephraim saw his
   sickness,
And Judah *saw* his wound,
Then Ephraim went to Assyria
And sent to King Jareb;
Yet he cannot cure you,
Nor heal you of your wound.
14 For I *will be* like a lion to
   Ephraim,
And like a young lion to the
   house of Judah.
I, *even* I, will tear *them* and go
   away;
I will take *them* away, and no
   one shall rescue.
15 I will return again to My place
Till they acknowledge their
   offense.
Then they will seek My face;
In their affliction they will
   earnestly seek Me."

6 Come, and let us return to the
   LORD;
For He has torn, but He will
   heal us;
He has stricken, but He will
   bind us up.
2 After two days He will revive
   us;
On the third day He will raise
   us up,
That we may live in His sight.
3 Let us know,
Let us pursue the knowledge of
   the LORD.
His going forth is established
   as the morning;
He will come to us like the rain,
Like the latter *and* former rain
   to the earth.

4 "O Ephraim, what shall I do to
   you?
O Judah, what shall I do to you?
For your faithfulness is like a
   morning cloud,
And like the early dew it goes
   away.

5 Therefore I have hewn *them* by
   the prophets,
I have slain them by the words
   of My mouth;
And your judgments *are like*
   light *that* goes forth.
6 For I desire mercy and not
   sacrifice,
And the knowledge of
   God more than burnt
   offerings.

7 "But like men[a] they
   transgressed the covenant;
There they dealt treacherously
   with Me.
8 Gilead *is* a city of evildoers
And defiled with blood.
9 As bands of robbers lie in wait
   for a man,
So the company of priests
   murder on the way to
   Shechem;
Surely they commit lewdness.
10 I have seen a horrible thing in
   the house of Israel:
There *is* the harlotry of
   Ephraim;
Israel is defiled.
11 Also, O Judah, a harvest is
   appointed for you,
When I return the captives of
   My people.

7 "When I would have healed
   Israel,
Then the iniquity of Ephraim
   was uncovered,
And the wickedness of
   Samaria.
For they have committed
   fraud;
A thief comes in;
A band of robbers takes spoil
   outside.
2 They do not consider in their
   hearts
That I remember all their
   wickedness;
Now their own deeds have
   surrounded them;
They are before My face.
3 They make a king glad with
   their wickedness,
And princes with their lies.

4 "They *are* all adulterers.
Like an oven heated by a
   baker—

6:7 [a]Or *like Adam*

He ceases stirring *the fire* after
   kneading the dough,
Until it is leavened.
5 In the day of our king
Princes have made *him* sick,
   inflamed with wine;
He stretched out his hand with
   scoffers.
6 They prepare their heart like
   an oven,
While they lie in wait;
Their baker[a] sleeps all night;
In the morning it burns like a
   flaming fire.
7 They are all hot, like an
   oven,
And have devoured their
   judges;
All their kings have fallen.
None among them calls upon
   Me.

8 "Ephraim has mixed himself
   among the peoples;
Ephraim is a cake unturned.
9 Aliens have devoured his
   strength,
But he does not know *it;*
Yes, gray hairs are here and
   there on him,
Yet he does not know *it.*
10 And the pride of Israel testifies
   to his face,
But they do not return to the
   LORD their God,
Nor seek Him for all this.

11 "Ephraim also is like a silly
   dove, without sense—
They call to Egypt,
They go to Assyria.
12 Wherever they go, I will spread
   My net on them;
I will bring them down like
   birds of the air;
I will chastise them
According to what their
   congregation has heard.

13 "Woe to them, for they have fled
   from Me!
Destruction to them,
Because they have
   transgressed against Me!
Though I redeemed them,
Yet they have spoken lies
   against Me.

14 They did not cry out to Me with
   their heart
When they wailed upon their
   beds.

"They assemble together for[a]
   grain and new wine,
They rebel against Me;[b]
15 Though I disciplined *and*
   strengthened their arms,
Yet they devise evil against Me;
16 They return, *but* not to the
   Most High;[a]
They are like a treacherous
   bow.
Their princes shall fall by the
   sword
For the cursings of their
   tongue.
This *shall be* their derision in
   the land of Egypt.

8 "*Set* the trumpet[a] to your
   mouth!
He shall come like an eagle
   against the house of the
   LORD,
Because they have
   transgressed My covenant
And rebelled against My law.
2 Israel will cry to Me,
'My God, we know You!'
3 Israel has rejected the good;
The enemy will pursue him.

4 "They set up kings, but not by
   Me;
They made princes, but I did
   not acknowledge *them.*
From their silver and gold
They made idols for
   themselves—
That they might be cut off.
5 Your calf is rejected, O
   Samaria!
My anger is aroused against
   them—
How long until they attain to
   innocence?
6 For from Israel *is* even this:
A workman made it, and it *is*
   not God;
But the calf of Samaria shall be
   broken to pieces.

7 "They sow the wind,
And reap the whirlwind.

7:6 [a]Following Masoretic Text and Vulgate; Syriac and Targum read *Their anger;* Septuagint reads
Ephraim.   7:14 [a]Following Masoretic Text and Targum; Vulgate reads *thought upon;* Septuagint reads
slashed themselves for (compare 1 Kings 18:28).   [b]Following Masoretic Text, Syriac, and Targum;
Septuagint omits *They rebel against Me;* Vulgate reads *They departed from Me.*   7:16 [a]Or *upward*
8:1 [a]Hebrew *shophar,* ram's horn

The stalk has no bud;
It shall never produce meal.
If it should produce,
Aliens would swallow it up.
8 Israel is swallowed up;
Now they are among the
Gentiles
Like a vessel in which *is* no
pleasure.
9 For they have gone up to
Assyria,
Like a wild donkey alone by
itself;
Ephraim has hired lovers.
10 Yes, though they have hired
among the nations,
Now I will gather them;
And they shall sorrow a
little,*a*
Because of the burden*b* of the
king of princes.

11 "Because Ephraim has made
many altars for sin,
They have become for him
altars for sinning.
12 I have written for him the great
things of My law,
But they were considered a
strange thing.
13 *For* the sacrifices of My
offerings they sacrifice flesh
and eat *it*,
But the LORD does not accept
them.
Now He will remember their
iniquity and punish their
sins.
They shall return to Egypt.

14 "For Israel has forgotten his
Maker,
And has built temples;*a*
Judah also has multiplied
fortified cities;
But I will send fire upon his
cities,
And it shall devour his
palaces."

9 Do not rejoice, O Israel, with
joy like *other* peoples,
For you have played the harlot
against your God.
You have made love *for* hire on
every threshing floor.
2 The threshing floor and the
winepress
Shall not feed them,

And the new wine shall fail in
her.
3 They shall not dwell in the
LORD's land,
But Ephraim shall return to
Egypt,
And shall eat unclean *things* in
Assyria.
4 They shall not offer wine
offerings to the LORD,
Nor shall their sacrifices be
pleasing to Him.
It shall be like bread of
mourners to them;
All who eat it shall be defiled.
For their bread *shall be* for
their *own* life;
It shall not come into the house
of the LORD.

5 What will you do in the
appointed day,
And in the day of the feast of
the LORD?
6 For indeed they are gone
because of destruction.
Egypt shall gather them up;
Memphis shall bury them.
Nettles shall possess their
valuables of silver;
Thorns *shall be* in their tents.

7 The days of punishment have
come;
The days of recompense have
come.
Israel knows!
The prophet *is* a fool,
The spiritual man *is* insane,
Because of the greatness of
your iniquity and great
enmity.
8 The watchman of Ephraim *is*
with my God;
But the prophet *is* a fowler's*a*
snare in all his ways—
Enmity in the house of his God.
9 They are deeply corrupted,
As in the days of Gibeah.
He will remember their
iniquity;
He will punish their sins.

10 "I found Israel
Like grapes in the wilderness;
I saw your fathers
As the firstfruits on the fig tree
in its first season.

8:10 *a*Or *begin to diminish* *b*Or *oracle* 8:14 *a*Or *palaces* 9:8 *a*That is, one who catches birds in a trap or snare

But they went to Baal Peor,
And separated themselves *to*
    that shame;
They became an abomination
    like the thing they loved.
11 *As for* Ephraim, their glory
    shall fly away like a bird—
No birth, no pregnancy, and no
    conception!
12 Though they bring up their
    children,
Yet I will bereave them to the
    last man.
Yes, woe to them when I depart
    from them!
13 Just as I saw Ephraim like
    Tyre, planted in a pleasant
    place,
So Ephraim will bring out his
    children to the murderer."

14 Give them, O LORD—
What will You give?
Give them a miscarrying womb
And dry breasts!

15 "All their wickedness *is* in
    Gilgal,
For there I hated them.
Because of the evil of their
    deeds
I will drive them from My
    house;
I will love them no more.
All their princes *are* rebellious.
16 Ephraim is stricken,
Their root is dried up;
They shall bear no fruit.
Yes, were they to bear children,
I would kill the darlings of their
    womb."

17 My God will cast them away,
Because they did not obey Him;
And they shall be wanderers
    among the nations.

10 Israel empties *his* vine;
He brings forth fruit for
    himself.
According to the multitude of
    his fruit
He has increased the altars;
According to the bounty of his
    land
They have embellished *his*
    sacred pillars.
2 Their heart is divided;
Now they are held guilty.

He will break down their altars;
He will ruin their sacred pillars.

3 For now they say,
"We have no king,
Because we did not fear the
    LORD.
And as for a king, what would
    he do for us?"
4 They have spoken words,
Swearing falsely in making a
    covenant.
Thus judgment springs up like
    hemlock in the furrows of the
    field.

5 The inhabitants of Samaria
    fear
Because of the calf[a] of Beth
    Aven.
For its people mourn for it,
And its priests shriek for it—
Because its glory has departed
    from it.
6 *The idol* also shall be carried
    to Assyria
As a present for King Jareb.
Ephraim shall receive shame,
And Israel shall be ashamed of
    his own counsel.

7 *As for* Samaria, her king is cut
    off
Like a twig on the water.
8 Also the high places of Aven,
    the sin of Israel,
Shall be destroyed.
The thorn and thistle shall
    grow on their altars;
They shall say to the
    mountains, "Cover us!"
And to the hills, "Fall on us!"

9 "O Israel, you have sinned from
    the days of Gibeah;
There they stood.
The battle in Gibeah against
    the children of iniquity[a]
Did not overtake them.
10 When *it is* My desire, I will
    chasten them.
Peoples shall be gathered
    against them
When I bind them for their two
    transgressions.[a]
11 Ephraim *is* a trained heifer
That loves to thresh *grain;*
But I harnessed her fair neck,

10:5 [a]Literally *calves*   10:9 [a]So read many Hebrew manuscripts, Septuagint, and Vulgate; Masoretic Text
reads *unruliness.*   10:10 [a]Or *in their two habitations*

I will make Ephraim pull *a
    plow.*
Judah shall plow;
Jacob shall break his clods."

12 Sow for yourselves
    righteousness;
Reap in mercy;
Break up your fallow ground,
For *it is* time to seek the LORD,
Till He comes and rains
    righteousness on you.

13 You have plowed wickedness;
You have reaped iniquity.
You have eaten the fruit of lies,
Because you trusted in your
    own way,
In the multitude of your mighty
    men.
14 Therefore tumult shall arise
    among your people,
And all your fortresses shall be
    plundered
As Shalman plundered Beth
    Arbel in the day of battle—
A mother dashed in pieces
    upon *her* children.
15 Thus it shall be done to you, O
    Bethel,
Because of your great
    wickedness.
At dawn the king of Israel
Shall be cut off utterly.

11 "When Israel *was* a child, I loved
    him,
And out of Egypt I called My
    son.
2 *As* they called them,[a]
So they went from them;[b]
They sacrificed to the Baals,
And burned incense to carved
    images.

3 "I taught Ephraim to walk,
Taking them by their arms;[a]
But they did not know that I
    healed them.
4 I drew them with gentle cords,[a]
With bands of love,
And I was to them as those who
    take the yoke from their
    neck.[b]
I stooped *and* fed them.

5 "He shall not return to the land
    of Egypt;

But the Assyrian shall be his
    king,
Because they refused to repent.
6 And the sword shall slash in his
    cities,
Devour his districts,
And consume *them,*
Because of their own counsels.
7 My people are bent on
    backsliding from Me.
Though they call to the Most
    High,[a]
None at all exalt *Him.*

8 "How can I give you up,
    Ephraim?
How can I hand you over,
    Israel?
How can I make you like
    Admah?
How can I set you like
    Zeboiim?
My heart churns within Me;
My sympathy is stirred.
9 I will not execute the fierceness
    of My anger;
I will not again destroy
    Ephraim.
For I *am* God, and not man,
The Holy One in your midst;
And I will not come with
    terror.[a]

10 "They shall walk after the LORD.
He will roar like a lion.
When He roars,
Then *His* sons shall come
    trembling from the west;
11 They shall come trembling like
    a bird from Egypt,
Like a dove from the land of
    Assyria.
And I will let them dwell in
    their houses,"
Says the LORD.

12 "Ephraim has encircled Me with
    lies,
And the house of Israel with
    deceit;
But Judah still walks with God,
Even with the Holy One[a] *who
is* faithful.

12 "Ephraim feeds on the wind,
And pursues the east wind;

11:2 [a]Following Masoretic Text and Vulgate; Septuagint reads *Just as I called them;* Targum interprets as
I sent prophets to a thousand of them.   [b]Following Masoretic Text, Targum, and Vulgate; Septuagint reads
from My face.   11:3 [a]Some Hebrew manuscripts, Septuagint, Syriac, and Vulgate read *My arms.*
11:4 [a]Literally *cords of a man*   [b]Literally *jaws*   11:7 [a]Or *upward*   11:9 [a]Or *I will not enter a city*
11:12 [a]Or *holy ones*

He daily increases lies and
desolation.
Also they make a covenant
with the Assyrians,
And oil is carried to Egypt.

2 "The LORD also *brings* a charge
against Judah,
And will punish Jacob
according to his ways;
According to his deeds He will
recompense him.
3 He took his brother by the heel
in the womb,
And in his strength he
struggled with God.*a*
4 Yes, he struggled with the
Angel and prevailed;
He wept, and sought favor from
Him.
He found Him *in* Bethel,
And there He spoke to us—
5 That is, the LORD God of hosts.
The LORD *is* His memorable
name.
6 So you, by *the help of* your
God, return;
Observe mercy and justice,
And wait on your God
continually.

7 "A cunning Canaanite!
Deceitful scales *are* in his hand;
He loves to oppress.
8 And Ephraim said,
'Surely I have become rich,
I have found wealth for myself;
In all my labors
They shall find in me no
iniquity that *is* sin.'

9 "But I *am* the LORD your God,
Ever since the land of Egypt;
I will again make you dwell in
tents,
As in the days of the appointed
feast.
10 I have also spoken by the
prophets,
And have multiplied visions;
I have given symbols through
the witness of the prophets."

11 Though Gilead *has* idols—
Surely they are vanity—
Though they sacrifice bulls in
Gilgal,
Indeed their altars *shall be*
heaps in the furrows of the
field.

12 Jacob fled to the country of
Syria;
Israel served for a spouse,
And for a wife he tended *sheep.*
13 By a prophet the LORD brought
Israel out of Egypt,
And by a prophet he was
preserved.
14 Ephraim provoked *Him* to
anger most bitterly;
Therefore his Lord will leave
the guilt of his bloodshed
upon him,
And return his reproach upon
him.

13 When Ephraim spoke,
trembling,
He exalted *himself* in Israel;
But when he offended through
Baal *worship*, he died.
2 Now they sin more and more,
And have made for themselves
molded images,
Idols of their silver, according
to their skill;
All of it *is* the work of
craftsmen.
They say of them,
"Let the men who sacrifice*a* kiss
the calves!"
3 Therefore they shall be like the
morning cloud
And like the early dew that
passes away,
Like chaff blown off from a
threshing floor
And like smoke from a
chimney.

4 "Yet I *am* the LORD your God
Ever since the land of Egypt,
And you shall know no God but
Me;
For *there is* no savior besides
Me.
5 I knew you in the wilderness,
In the land of great drought.
6 When they had pasture, they
were filled;
They were filled and their heart
was exalted;
Therefore they forgot Me.

7 "So I will be to them like a lion;
Like a leopard by the road I will
lurk;
8 I will meet them like a bear
deprived *of her cubs*;
I will tear open their rib cage,

The Olive Tree

The ancient olive tree holds an intrinsic beauty to the biblical writer. Its knotted, twisted trunk has dominated the landscape of Israel for thousands of years.

Unlike the country's tall cedars, straight cypresses, and fragrant fruit trees, the beauty of the olive tree is expressed more through function than through outward appearance. To the western mind-set, the tree's form might seem unattractive. Yet, in Hebrew thought, the very nature of the olive tree is lovely.

Throughout the ages, prophets focused on the olive tree to illustrate inner beauty. The tree's value is measured by its service. The delicate olive oil held a prize role in anointing the many kings of the land. For the common person, the oil was needed to fuel their lamps and light their way. Even today, olives and olive oil are staples of the Middle Eastern diet.

The olive branch has long been a symbol of peace and goodwill. Following the great flood, Noah's dove carried an olive twig back to the ark as a sign of God's peace and promise that the waters had receded.

For strength and endurance the olive tree is unsurpassed. Even in the most inhospitable chalky soil of the Judean wilderness, the olive tree is found. Cut back to its roots, the tree will grow back and live thousands of years.

Should we not look at ourselves as the people of Israel look at the olive tree? Like the olive tree, our self-worth is also expressed in service.

Be like an olive tree. Anoint those around you with love. Help light the way. Be a symbol of God's peace. And when people cut you down—grow back. Bloom where you are planted!

And there I will devour them
   like a lion.
The wild beast shall tear them.

9 "O Israel, you are destroyed,[a]
   But your help[b] is from Me.
10 I will be your King;[a]
   Where is any other,
   That he may save you in all
      your cities?
   And your judges to whom you
      said,
   'Give me a king and princes'?
11 I gave you a king in My anger,
   And took him away in My
      wrath.

12 "The iniquity of Ephraim is
      bound up;
   His sin is stored up.
13 The sorrows of a woman in
      childbirth shall come upon
      him.
   He is an unwise son,
   For he should not stay long
      where children are born.

14 "I will ransom them from the
      power of the grave;[a]
   I will redeem them from death.
   O Death, I will be your
      plagues![b]
   O Grave,[c] I will be your
      destruction![d]
   Pity is hidden from My eyes.

15 Though he is fruitful among his
      brethren,
   An east wind shall come;
   The wind of the LORD shall
      come up from the wilderness.
   Then his spring shall become
      dry,
   And his fountain shall be dried
      up.
   He shall plunder the treasury
      of every desirable prize.
16 Samaria is held guilty,[a]
   For she has rebelled against
      her God.
   They shall fall by the sword,
   Their infants shall be dashed in
      pieces,
   And their women with child
      ripped open.

14 O Israel, return to the LORD
      your God,

For you have stumbled because
   of your iniquity;
2 Take words with you,
   And return to the LORD.
   Say to Him,
   "Take away all iniquity;
   Receive us graciously,
   For we will offer the sacrifices[a]
      of our lips.
3 Assyria shall not save us,
   We will not ride on horses,
   Nor will we say anymore to the
      work of our hands,
   'You are our gods.'
   For in You the fatherless finds
      mercy."

4 "I will heal their backsliding,
   I will love them freely,
   For My anger has turned away
      from him.
5 I will be like the dew to
      Israel;
   He shall grow like the lily,
   And lengthen his roots like
      Lebanon.
6 His branches shall spread;
   His beauty shall be like an olive
      tree,
   And his fragrance like
      Lebanon.
7 Those who dwell under his
      shadow shall return;
   They shall be revived like
      grain,
   And grow like a vine.
   Their scent[a] shall be like the
      wine of Lebanon.

8 "Ephraim shall say,
   'What have I to do anymore
      with idols?'
   I have heard and observed
      him.
   I am like a green cypress
      tree;
   Your fruit is found in Me."

9 Who is wise?
   Let him understand these
      things.
   Who is prudent?
   Let him know them.
   For the ways of the LORD are
      right;
   The righteous walk in them,
   But transgressors stumble in
      them.

13:9 [a]Literally it or he destroyed you   [b]Literally in your help   13:10 [a]Septuagint, Syriac, Targum, and
Vulgate read Where is your king?   13:14 [a]Or Sheol   [b]Septuagint reads where is your punishment?
[c]Or Sheol   [d]Septuagint reads Where is your sting?   13:16 [a]Septuagint reads shall be disfigured
14:2 [a]Literally bull calves; Septuagint reads fruit.   14:7 [a]Literally remembrance

Joel

Overview of Joel

The Book of Joel makes a national appeal to the people of Israel about 835 B.C., for repentance based on God's judgment and the promise of deliverance and blessing in the day of the Lord.

Israel was faced with severe plagues and a drought due to their rebellion against God. Joel urges them to see God in the time of calamity and to turn to Him. In the day of distress, God will also bring forth a day of deliverance. He gives them the promise that whoever calls upon the name of the Lord will be saved.

> *So rend your heart, and not your garments;*
> *Return to the LORD your God,*
> *For He is gracious and merciful,*
> *Slow to anger, and of great kindness;*
> *And He relents from doing harm.*
>
> (Joel 2:13)

Joel mentions "the day of the LORD" six times. Perhaps this points to the future and the Second Coming of Christ. Jesus Himself alludes to this reference in Matthew 24 when He speaks of His final return and victory.

Joel encourages the people to change their hearts, which will be visible in their outward actions. God calls them to return to Him, for even in times of great distress, He is gracious and compassionate, slow to anger, and overflowing with lovingkindness. Joel urges them to call on God, to repent, to "turn around." Repentance means to change direction, to set new goals and to establish new standards.

Joel wanted the people to seek God's plan for their lives and to commit themselves to it. For whoever turns to God will not be disappointed!

Lord, forgive me for not having the faith to live the life I should have lived. I am ready to dream your dreams. I am going to live right, think right, pray right, and do right! I am trusting you to give me the power. Together, we shall succeed! Amen.

Jesus in Joel

Jesus promised His disciples that He would send the Holy Spirit after He had ascended to the Father (John 16:7–15). When this was fulfilled on the Day of Pentecost, Peter said, "This is what was spoken by the prophet Joel" (Joel 2:28–32; Acts 2:16–21). As we know, the Holy Spirit is the Spirit of God who has now come to share all of God's goodness and hope with people on earth.

Keys to Joel

Key Word: The Great and Terrible Day of The Lord. Joel looks both forward and backward to the Day of the Lord. He uses the recent locust plague in Israel to illustrate the coming day of judgment when God will directly intervene in human history to vindicate His righteousness. Though this will be a time of unparalleled retribution, it will culminate in great blessing and salvation for all who trust in the Lord (2:18–32; 3:18–21). "And it shall come to pass *that* whoever calls upon the name of the LORD shall be saved" (2:32). Joel is written as a warning to the people to turn their hearts toward God so that He can bless them.

Key Verse: "And it shall come to pass afterward that I will pour out My Spirit on all flesh; your sons and your daughters shall prophesy, your old men shall dream dreams, your young men shall see visions; and also on *My* menservants and on *My* maidservants I will pour out My Spirit in those days" (2:28, 29).

Key Chapter: Joel 2. The prophet calls for Judah's repentance and promises God's repentance (2:13, 14) from His planned judgment upon Judah if they do indeed turn to Him. Though the offer is clearly given, Judah continues to rebel against the Lord, and judgment is to follow. In that judgment, however, is God's promise of His later outpouring, fulfilled initially on the Day of Pentecost and ultimately when Christ returns for the culmination of the Day of the Lord.

1 The word of the LORD that came to Joel the son of Pethuel.

2 Hear this, you elders,
   And give ear, all you
      inhabitants of the land!
   Has *anything like* this
      happened in your days,
   Or even in the days of your
      fathers?

3 Tell your children about it,
   Let your children *tell* their
      children,
   And their children another
      generation.

4 What the chewing locust[a] left,
      the swarming locust has
      eaten;
   What the swarming locust left,
      the crawling locust has
      eaten;
   And what the crawling locust
      left, the consuming locust has
      eaten.

5 Awake, you drunkards, and
      weep;
   And wail, all you drinkers of
      wine,
   Because of the new wine,
   For it has been cut off from
      your mouth.

6 For a nation has come up
      against My land,
   Strong, and without number;
   His teeth *are* the teeth of a lion,
   And he has the fangs of a fierce
      lion.

7 He has laid waste My vine,
   And ruined My fig tree;
   He has stripped it bare and
      thrown *it* away;
   Its branches are made white.

8 Lament like a virgin girded
      with sackcloth
   For the husband of her youth.

9 The grain offering and the
      drink offering
   Have been cut off from the
      house of the LORD;
   The priests mourn, who
      minister to the LORD.

10 The field is wasted,
   The land mourns;
   For the grain is ruined,
   The new wine is dried up,
   The oil fails.

11 Be ashamed, you farmers,
   Wail, you vinedressers,
   For the wheat and the barley;
   Because the harvest of the field
      has perished.

12 The vine has dried up,
   And the fig tree has withered;
   The pomegranate tree,
   The palm tree also,
   And the apple tree—
   All the trees of the field are
      withered;
   Surely joy has withered away
      from the sons of men.

13 Gird yourselves and lament,
      you priests;
   Wail, you who minister before
      the altar;
   Come, lie all night in sackcloth,
   You who minister to my God;
   For the grain offering and the
      drink offering
   Are withheld from the house of
      your God.

14 Consecrate a fast,
   Call a sacred assembly;
   Gather the elders
   And all the inhabitants of the
      land
   Into the house of the LORD your
      God,
   And cry out to the LORD.

15 Alas for the day!
   For the day of the LORD *is* at
      hand;
   It shall come as destruction
      from the Almighty.

16 Is not the food cut off before
      our eyes,
   Joy and gladness from the
      house of our God?

17 The seed shrivels under the
      clods,
   Storehouses are in shambles;
   Barns are broken down,
   For the grain has withered.

18 How the animals groan!
   The herds of cattle are restless,

1:4 ᵃExact identity of these locusts is unknown.

The Prophets of Israel and Judah

The Scriptures teach us where some of the Old Testament prophets were born or where they prophesied.

Samuel, a prophet and a judge, used his hometown of Ramah as a base from which he made his yearly circuit to other places. Two other prophets of the early monarchy, Elijah and Elisha, also had their homes in the Northern Kingdom.

Among the "writing prophets," only Hosea and Jonah were from the North. The exact location of Hosea's home and ministry are unknown. Jonah was from Gath Hepher, but his ministry extended beyond his homeland to the Assyrian city of Nineveh.

Some prophets had homes in the South, but ministered in the North. Amos was from Tekoa, but preached against Baal worship in the Northern city of Bethel. The prophet Micah addressed both Israel and Judah.

The ministry of several prophets centers on Judah and its capital city, Jerusalem. The messages of Isaiah, Jeremiah, Zephaniah, Ezekiel, Haggai, Zechariah, and Malachi span a long time period, but all concern either Jerusalem's imminent destruction and fall or its subsequent restoration.

For some prophets, such as Joel, Obadiah, and Habakkuk, geographical information is lacking. Nahum's home is indicated only by his designation as "the Elkoshite."

? Exact location questionable

THE GREAT SEA

GALILEE

Jonah

Sea of Galilee

Gath Hepher

ISRAEL

Jordan River

Elijah

Abel Meholah?

Tishbe?

Elisha

GILEAD

WILDERNESS

Samuel

Nahum

Ramah

Jeremiah

Anathoth

Jerusalem

Elkosh?

Tekoa

Isaiah   Zephaniah   Zechariah
Ezekiel   Haggai   Malachi

Moresheth Gath

Micah

Amos

DEAD SEA

JUDAH

MOAB

Because they have no pasture;
Even the flocks of sheep suffer
   punishment.ᵃ

19 O LORD, to You I cry out;
For fire has devoured the open
   pastures,
And a flame has burned all the
   trees of the field.
20 The beasts of the field also cry
   out to You,
For the water brooks are dried
   up,
And fire has devoured the open
   pastures.

2 Blow the trumpet in Zion,
And sound an alarm in My holy
   mountain!
Let all the inhabitants of the
   land tremble;
For the day of the LORD is
   coming,
For it is at hand:
2 A day of darkness and
   gloominess,
A day of clouds and thick
   darkness,
Like the morning *clouds* spread
   over the mountains.
A people *come,* great and
   strong,
The like of whom has never
   been;
Nor will there ever be any *such*
   after them,
Even for many successive
   generations.

3 A fire devours before them,
And behind them a flame
   burns;
The land *is* like the Garden of
   Eden before them,
And behind them a desolate
   wilderness;
Surely nothing shall escape
   them.
4 Their appearance is like the
   appearance of horses;
And like swift steeds, so they
   run.
5 With a noise like chariots
Over mountaintops they leap,
Like the noise of a flaming fire
   that devours the stubble,
Like a strong people set in
   battle array.

6 Before them the people writhe
   in pain;
All faces are drained of color.ᵃ
7 They run like mighty men,
They climb the wall like men
   of war;
Every one marches in
   formation,
And they do not break ranks.
8 They do not push one another;
Every one marches in his own
   column.ᵃ
Though they lunge between the
   weapons,
They are not cut down.ᵇ
9 They run to and fro in the city,
They run on the wall;
They climb into the houses,
They enter at the windows like
   a thief.

10 The earth quakes before them,
The heavens tremble;
The sun and moon grow dark,
And the stars diminish their
   brightness.
11 The LORD gives voice before
   His army,
For His camp is very great;
For strong *is the One* who
   executes His word.
For the day of the LORD *is* great
   and very terrible;
Who can endure it?

12 "Now, therefore," says the LORD,
"Turn to Me with all your heart,
With fasting, with weeping,
   and with mourning."
13 So rend your heart, and not
   your garments;
Return to the LORD your God,
For He *is* gracious and
   merciful,
Slow to anger, and of great
   kindness;
And He relents from doing
   harm.
14 Who knows *if* He will turn and
   relent,
And leave a blessing behind
   Him—
A grain offering and a drink
   offering
For the LORD your God?

15 Blow the trumpet in Zion,
Consecrate a fast,
Call a sacred assembly;
16 Gather the people,

1:18 ᵃSeptuagint and Vulgate read *are made desolate.*   2:6 ᵃSeptuagint, Targum, and Vulgate read *gather blackness.*   2:8 ᵃLiterally *his own highway*   ᵇThat is, they are not halted by losses

Sanctify the congregation,
Assemble the elders,
Gather the children and
nursing babes;
Let the bridegroom go out from
his chamber,
And the bride from her
dressing room.

17 Let the priests, who minister to
the LORD,
Weep between the porch and
the altar;
Let them say, "Spare Your
people, O LORD,
And do not give Your heritage
to reproach,
That the nations should rule
over them.
Why should they say among
the peoples,
'Where is their God?' "

18 Then the LORD will be zealous
for His land,
And pity His people.
19 The LORD will answer and say
to His people,
"Behold, I will send you grain
and new wine and oil,
And you will be satisfied by
them;
I will no longer make you a
reproach among the nations.

20 "But I will remove far from you
the northern army,
And will drive him away into
a barren and desolate land,
With his face toward the
eastern sea
And his back toward the
western sea;
His stench will come up,
And his foul odor will rise,
Because he has done
monstrous things."

21 Fear not, O land;
Be glad and rejoice,
For the LORD has done
marvelous things!
22 Do not be afraid, you beasts of
the field;
For the open pastures are
springing up,
And the tree bears its fruit;
The fig tree and the vine yield
their strength.
23 Be glad then, you children of
Zion,

And rejoice in the LORD your
God;
For He has given you the
former rain faithfully,a
And He will cause the rain to
come down for you—
The former rain,
And the latter rain in the first
month.
24 The threshing floors shall be
full of wheat,
And the vats shall overflow
with new wine and oil.

25 "So I will restore to you the
years that the swarming
locust has eaten,
The crawling locust,
The consuming locust,
And the chewing locust,a
My great army which I sent
among you.
26 You shall eat in plenty and be
satisfied,
And praise the name of the
LORD your God,
Who has dealt wondrously
with you;
And My people shall never be
put to shame.
27 Then you shall know that I am
in the midst of Israel:
I am the LORD your God
And there is no other.
My people shall never be put
to shame.

28 "And it shall come to pass
afterward
That I will pour out My Spirit
on all flesh;
Your sons and your daughters
shall prophesy,
Your old men shall dream
dreams,
Your young men shall see
visions.
29 And also on My menservants
and on My maidservants
I will pour out My Spirit in
those days.

30 "And I will show wonders
in the heavens and in the
earth:
Blood and fire and pillars of
smoke.
31 The sun shall be turned into
darkness,
And the moon into blood,

2:23 aOr the teacher of righteousness   2:25 aCompare 1:4

Before the coming of the great
and awesome day of the
LORD.
32 And it shall come to pass
That whoever calls on the
name of the LORD
Shall be saved.
For in Mount Zion and in
Jerusalem there shall be
deliverance,
As the LORD has said,
Among the remnant whom the
LORD calls.

3 "For behold, in those days and
at that time,
When I bring back the captives
of Judah and Jerusalem,
2 I will also gather all nations,
And bring them down to the
Valley of Jehoshaphat;
And I will enter into judgment
with them there
On account of My people, My
heritage Israel,
Whom they have scattered
among the nations;
They have also divided up My
land.
3 They have cast lots for My
people,
Have given a boy *as payment*
for a harlot,
And sold a girl for wine, that
they may drink.

4 "Indeed, what have you to do
with Me,
O Tyre and Sidon, and all the
coasts of Philistia?
Will you retaliate against Me?
But if you retaliate against
Me,
Swiftly and speedily I will
return your retaliation upon
your own head;
5 Because you have taken My
silver and My gold,
And have carried into your
temples My prized
possessions.
6 Also the people of Judah and
the people of Jerusalem
You have sold to the Greeks,
That you may remove them far
from their borders.

7 "Behold, I will raise them
Out of the place to which you
have sold them,

And will return your retaliation
upon your own head.
8 I will sell your sons and your
daughters
Into the hand of the people of
Judah,
And they will sell them to the
Sabeans,*a*
To a people far off;
For the LORD has spoken."

9 Proclaim this among the
nations:
"Prepare for war!
Wake up the mighty men,
Let all the men of war draw
near,
Let them come up.
10 Beat your plowshares into
swords
And your pruning hooks into
spears;
Let the weak say, 'I *am*
strong.' "
11 Assemble and come, all you
nations,
And gather together all around.
Cause Your mighty ones to go
down there, O LORD.

12 "Let the nations be wakened,
and come up to the Valley of
Jehoshaphat;
For there I will sit to judge all
the surrounding nations.
13 Put in the sickle, for the harvest
is ripe.
Come, go down;
For the winepress is full,
The vats overflow—
For their wickedness *is* great."

14 Multitudes, multitudes in the
valley of decision!
For the day of the LORD *is* near
in the valley of decision.
15 The sun and moon will grow
dark,
And the stars will diminish
their brightness.
16 The LORD also will roar from
Zion,
And utter His voice from
Jerusalem;
The heavens and earth will
shake;
But the LORD will be a shelter
for His people,
And the strength of the
children of Israel.

3:8 *a*Literally *Shebaites* (compare Isaiah 60:6 and Ezekiel 27:22)

17 "So you shall know that I *am* the
   LORD your God,
   Dwelling in Zion My holy
   mountain.
   Then Jerusalem shall be holy,
   And no aliens shall ever pass
   through her again."

18 And it will come to pass in that
   day
   That the mountains shall drip
   with new wine,
   The hills shall flow with milk,
   And all the brooks of Judah
   shall be flooded with water;
   A fountain shall flow from the
   house of the LORD

And water the Valley of
   Acacias.

19 "Egypt shall be a desolation,
   And Edom a desolate
   wilderness,
   Because of violence *against* the
   people of Judah,
   For they have shed innocent
   blood in their land.

20 But Judah shall abide forever,
   And Jerusalem from
   generation to generation.

21 For I will acquit them of the
   guilt of bloodshed, whom I
   had not acquitted;
   For the LORD dwells in Zion."

Amos

Overview of Amos

Failure is never final, but God's love and forgiveness is. The Book of Amos is a prime example of God's relationship with the nation of Israel. There was a direct correlation between their obedience to God and His blessings upon them, and their rebellion against God and the resulting circumstances. As a just and perfect God, He sent prophets, including Amos, to help enable His people to return to Him in times of disobedience.

Amos, a shepherd from the village of Tekoa, five miles south of Bethlehem, was living in Israel and prophesied between 760 and 753 B.C. He was called by God to appeal to the people to return to a pure worship of God. The Israelites had taken on the pagan worship and practices of the surrounding nations. Amos pronounced the downfall of these nations and appealed to the Israelites to seek God.

God gave the nation many chances to return to Him, warning them that the worship of these false gods could only produce negative results in their lives. The ancient nation refused to give up their cultic worship and to receive the natural consequences for their rebellion. They were carried off in captivity by the Assyrians.

Amos reveals the forgiving nature of God when he promises restoration and the assurance of God's presence despite their captivity:

> *I will bring back the captives of My people Israel;*
> *They shall build the waste cities and inhabit them;*
> *They shall plant vineyards and drink wine from them;*
> *They shall also make gardens and eat fruit from them.*
> (Amos 9:14)

Jesus in Amos

The clearest anticipation of Christ in Amos is found at the end of the book. He has all authority to judge (9:1—10), but He will also restore His people (9:11–15). He will restore the goodness of life to us!

Keys to Amos

Key Word: The Judgment of Israel. The basic theme of Amos is the coming judgment of Israel because of God's holiness and the people's sin. Because of His righteousness, God will not allow sin to go unpunished indefinitely, but He is infinitely gracious and patient. The people have repeatedly broken every aspect of their covenant relationship with God. Nevertheless, His mercy and love are evident in His offer of deliverance if the people will only turn back to Him.

Key Verses: "Seek good and not evil, that you may live; so the LORD God of hosts will be with you, as you have spoken. Hate evil, love good; establish justice in the gate. It may be that the LORD God of hosts will be gracious to the remnant of Joseph (5:14, 15).

"But let justice run down like water, and righteousness like a mighty stream" (5:24).

"I will bring back the captives of My people Israel; they shall build the waste cities and inhabit *them;* they shall plant vineyards and drink wine from them; they shall also make gardens and eat fruit from them. I will plant them in their land, and no longer shall they be pulled up from the land I have given them," says the LORD your God (9:14, 15).

Key Chapter: Amos 9. Set in the midst of harsh judgments are some of the greatest prophecies of restoration of Israel in all of Scripture. Within just five verses (9:11–15), the future of Israel becomes clear, as the Abrahamic, Davidic, and Palestinian covenants are focused on their climactic fulfillment in the return of the Messiah.

1 The words of Amos, who was among the sheepbreeders[a] of Tekoa, which he saw concerning Israel in the days of Uzziah king of Judah, and in the days of Jeroboam the son of Joash, king of Israel, two years before the earthquake.
2 And he said:

> "The LORD roars from Zion,
> And utters His voice from
>   Jerusalem;
> The pastures of the shepherds
>   mourn,
> And the top of Carmel
>   withers."

3 Thus says the LORD:

> "For three transgressions of
>   Damascus, and for four,
> I will not turn away its
>   *punishment,*
> Because they have threshed
>   Gilead with implements of
>   iron.
4 But I will send a fire into the
>   house of Hazael,
> Which shall devour the palaces
>   of Ben-Hadad.
5 I will also break the *gate* bar
>   of Damascus,

> And cut off the inhabitant from
>   the Valley of Aven,
> And the one who holds the
>   scepter from Beth Eden.
> The people of Syria shall go
>   captive to Kir,"
> Says the LORD.

6 Thus says the LORD:

> "For three transgressions of
>   Gaza, and for four,
> I will not turn away its
>   *punishment,*
> Because they took captive the
>   whole captivity
> To deliver *them* up to Edom.
7 But I will send a fire upon the
>   wall of Gaza,
> Which shall devour its
>   palaces.
8 I will cut off the inhabitant from
>   Ashdod,
> And the one who holds the
>   scepter from Ashkelon;
> I will turn My hand against
>   Ekron,
> And the remnant of the
>   Philistines shall perish,"
> Says the Lord GOD.

9 Thus says the LORD:

1:1 *a*Compare 2 Kings 3:4

"For three transgressions of
    Tyre, and for four,
I will not turn away its
    punishment,
Because they delivered up the
    whole captivity to Edom,
And did not remember the
    covenant of brotherhood.
10 But I will send a fire upon the
    wall of Tyre,
Which shall devour its
    palaces."

11 Thus says the LORD:

"For three transgressions of
    Edom, and for four,
I will not turn away its
    punishment,
Because he pursued his brother
    with the sword,
And cast off all pity;
His anger tore perpetually,
And he kept his wrath forever.
12 But I will send a fire upon
    Teman,
Which shall devour the palaces
    of Bozrah."

13 Thus says the LORD:

"For three transgressions of the
    people of Ammon, and for
    four,
I will not turn away its
    punishment,
Because they ripped open the
    women with child in Gilead,
That they might enlarge their
    territory.
14 But I will kindle a fire in the
    wall of Rabbah,
And it shall devour its palaces,
Amid shouting in the day of
    battle,
And a tempest in the day of the
    whirlwind.
15 Their king shall go into
    captivity,
He and his princes together,"
    Says the LORD.

2 Thus says the LORD:

"For three transgressions of
    Moab, and for four,
I will not turn away its
    punishment,
Because he burned the bones
    of the king of Edom to lime.

2 But I will send a fire upon
    Moab,
And it shall devour the palaces
    of Kerioth;
Moab shall die with tumult,
With shouting *and* trumpet
    sound.
3 And I will cut off the judge from
    its midst,
And slay all its princes with
    him,"
Says the LORD.

4 Thus says the LORD:

"For three transgressions of
    Judah, and for four,
I will not turn away its
    punishment,
Because they have despised the
    law of the LORD,
And have not kept His
    commandments.
Their lies lead them astray,
Lies which their fathers
    followed.
5 But I will send a fire upon
    Judah,
And it shall devour the palaces
    of Jerusalem."

6 Thus says the LORD:

"For three transgressions of
    Israel, and for four,
I will not turn away its
    punishment,
Because they sell the righteous
    for silver,
And the poor for a pair of
    sandals.
7 They pant after[a] the dust of the
    earth *which is* on the head of
    the poor,
And pervert the way of the
    humble.
A man and his father go in to
    the *same* girl,
To defile My holy name.
8 They lie down by every
    altar on clothes taken in
    pledge,
And drink the wine of the
    condemned *in* the house of
    their god.

9 "Yet *it was* I *who* destroyed the
    Amorite before them,
Whose height *was* like the
    height of the cedars,

2:7 *a* Or *trample on*

And he *was as* strong as the
    oaks;
Yet I destroyed his fruit above
And his roots beneath.

10 Also *it was I who* brought you
    up from the land of Egypt,
And led you forty years
    through the wilderness,
To possess the land of the
    Amorite.

11 I raised up some of your sons
    as prophets,
And some of your young men
    as Nazirites.
Is it not so, O you children of
    Israel?"
    Says the LORD.

12 "But you gave the Nazirites wine
    to drink,
And commanded the prophets
    saying,
'Do not prophesy!'

13 "Behold, I am weighed down by
    you,
As a cart full of sheaves is
    weighed down.

14 Therefore flight shall perish
    from the swift,
The strong shall not strengthen
    his power,
Nor shall the mighty deliver
    himself;

15 He shall not stand who handles
    the bow,
The swift of foot shall not
    escape,
Nor shall he who rides a horse
    deliver himself.

16 The most courageous men of
    might
Shall flee naked in that day,"
    Says the LORD.

3 Hear this word that the LORD has
spoken against you, O children of
Israel, against the whole family
which I brought up from the land of
Egypt, saying:

2 "You only have I known of all
    the families of the earth;
Therefore I will punish you for
    all your iniquities."

3 Can two walk together, unless
    they are agreed?

4 Will a lion roar in the forest,
    when he has no prey?
Will a young lion cry out of his
    den, if he has caught
    nothing?

5 Will a bird fall into a snare on
    the earth, where there is no
    trap for it?
Will a snare spring up from the
    earth, if it has caught nothing
    at all?

6 If a trumpet is blown in a city,
    will not the people be
    afraid?
If there is calamity in a city,
    will not the LORD have done
    it?

7 Surely the Lord GOD does
    nothing,
Unless He reveals His secret to
    His servants the prophets.

8 A lion has roared!
Who will not fear?
The Lord GOD has spoken!
Who can but prophesy?

9 "Proclaim in the palaces at
    Ashdod,
And in the palaces in the land
    of Egypt, and say:
'Assemble on the mountains of
    Samaria;
See great tumults in her midst,
And the oppressed within her.

10 For they do not know to do
    right,'
    Says the LORD,
'Who store up violence and
    robbery in their palaces.' "

11 Therefore thus says the Lord
GOD:

"An adversary *shall be* all
    around the land;
He shall sap your strength from
    you,
And your palaces shall be
    plundered."

12 Thus says the LORD:

"As a shepherd takes from the
    mouth of a lion
Two legs or a piece of an ear,
So shall the children of Israel
    be taken out
Who dwell in Samaria—
In the corner of a bed and on
    the edge*a* of a couch!

13 Hear and testify against the
    house of Jacob,"

3:12 *a* The Hebrew is uncertain.

Says the Lord GOD, the God of
hosts,
14 "That in the day I punish Israel
for their transgressions,
I will also visit *destruction* on
the altars of Bethel;
And the horns of the altar shall
be cut off
And fall to the ground.
15 I will destroy the winter house
along with the summer
house;
The houses of ivory shall
perish,
And the great houses shall
have an end,"
Says the LORD.

4 Hear this word, you cows of
Bashan, who *are* on the
mountain of Samaria,
Who oppress the poor,
Who crush the needy,
Who say to your husbands,[a]
"Bring *wine*, let us drink!"
2 The Lord GOD has sworn by His
holiness:
"Behold, the days shall come
upon you
When He will take you away
with fishhooks,
And your posterity with
fishhooks.
3 You will go out *through* broken
walls,
Each one straight ahead of her,
And you will be cast into
Harmon,"
Says the LORD.

4 "Come to Bethel and transgress,
At Gilgal multiply
transgression;
Bring your sacrifices every
morning,
Your tithes every three days.[a]
5 Offer a sacrifice of
thanksgiving with leaven,
Proclaim *and* announce the
freewill offerings;
For this you love,
You children of Israel!"
Says the Lord GOD.
6 "Also I gave you cleanness of
teeth in all your cities.
And lack of bread in all your
places;
Yet you have not returned to
Me,"
Says the LORD.

7 "I also withheld rain from you,
When *there were* still three
months to the harvest.
I made it rain on one city,
I withheld rain from another
city.
One part was rained upon,
And where it did not rain the
part withered.
8 So two *or* three cities wandered
to another city to drink
water,
But they were not satisfied;
Yet you have not returned to
Me,"
Says the LORD.

9 "I blasted you with blight and
mildew.
When your gardens increased,
Your vineyards,
Your fig trees,
And your olive trees,
The locust devoured *them*;
Yet you have not returned to
Me,"
Says the LORD.

10 "I sent among you a plague after
the manner of Egypt;
Your young men I killed with
a sword,
Along with your captive
horses;
I made the stench of your
camps come up into your
nostrils;
Yet you have not returned to
Me,"
Says the LORD.

11 "I overthrew *some* of you,
As God overthrew Sodom and
Gomorrah,
And you were like a firebrand
plucked from the burning;
Yet you have not returned to
Me,"
Says the LORD.

12 "Therefore thus will I do to you,
O Israel;
Because I will do this to you,
Prepare to meet your God, O
Israel!"

13 For behold,
He who forms mountains,
And creates the wind,
Who declares to man what his[a]
thought *is*,

4:1 [a]Literally *their lords* or *their masters*   4:4 [a]Or *years* (compare Deuteronomy 14:28)   4:13 [a]Or *His*

And makes the morning
    darkness,
Who treads the high places of
    the earth—
The LORD God of hosts *is* His
    name.

5 Hear this word which I take up
  against you, a lamentation, O
house of Israel:

2   The virgin of Israel has fallen;
    She will rise no more.
    She lies forsaken on her land;
    There is no one to raise her up.

3 For thus says the Lord GOD:

    "The city that goes out by a
        thousand
    Shall have a hundred left,
    And that which goes out by a
        hundred
    Shall have ten left to the house
        of Israel."

4 For thus says the LORD to the
house of Israel:

    "Seek Me and live;
5   But do not seek Bethel,
    Nor enter Gilgal,
    Nor pass over to Beersheba;
    For Gilgal shall surely go into
        captivity,
    And Bethel shall come to
        nothing.
6   Seek the LORD and live,
    Lest He break out like fire *in*
        the house of Joseph,
    And devour *it,*
    With no one to quench *it* in
        Bethel—
7   You who turn justice to
        wormwood,
    And lay righteousness to rest
        in the earth!"

8   He made the Pleiades and
        Orion;
    He turns the shadow of death
        into morning
    And makes the day dark as
        night;
    He calls for the waters of the
        sea
    And pours them out on the face
        of the earth;
    The LORD *is* His name.
9   He rains ruin upon the strong,
    So that fury comes upon the
        fortress.

10   They hate the one who rebukes
        in the gate,
    And they abhor the one who
        speaks uprightly.
11   Therefore, because you tread
        down the poor
    And take grain taxes from
        him,
    Though you have built houses
        of hewn stone,
    Yet you shall not dwell in them;
    You have planted pleasant
        vineyards,
    But you shall not drink wine
        from them.
12   For I know your manifold
        transgressions
    And your mighty sins:
    Afflicting the just *and* taking
        bribes;
    Diverting the poor *from justice*
        at the gate.
13   Therefore the prudent keep
        silent at that time,
    For it *is* an evil time.

14   Seek good and not evil,
    That you may live;
    So the LORD God of hosts will
        be with you,
    As you have spoken.
15   Hate evil, love good;
    Establish justice in the gate.
    It may be that the LORD God of
        hosts
    Will be gracious to the remnant
        of Joseph.

16 Therefore the LORD God of hosts,
the Lord, says this:

    "There shall be wailing in all
        streets,
    And they shall say in all the
        highways,
    'Alas! Alas!'
    They shall call the farmer to
        mourning,
    And skillful lamenters to
        wailing.
17   In all vineyards *there shall be*
        wailing,
    For I will pass through you,"
    Says the LORD.

18   Woe to you who desire the day
        of the LORD!
    For what good *is* the day of the
        LORD to you?
    It *will be* darkness, and not
        light.

19 It *will be* as though a man fled
  from a lion,
And a bear met him!
Or *as though* he went into the
  house,
Leaned his hand on the wall,
And a serpent bit him!

20 *Is* not the day of the LORD
  darkness, and not light?
Is it not very dark, with no
  brightness in it?

21 "I hate, I despise your feast
  days,
And I do not savor your sacred
  assemblies.

22 Though you offer Me burnt
  offerings and your grain
  offerings,
I will not accept *them,*
Nor will I regard your fattened
  peace offerings.

23 Take away from Me the noise
  of your songs,
For I will not hear the melody
  of your stringed instruments.

24 But let justice run down like
  water,
And righteousness like a
  mighty stream.

25 "Did you offer Me sacrifices and
  offerings
In the wilderness forty years,
O house of Israel?

26 You also carried Sikkuth*ᵃ* your
  king*ᵇ*
And Chiun,*ᶜ* your idols,
The star of your gods,
Which you made for
  yourselves.

27 Therefore I will send you into
  captivity beyond Damascus,"
Says the LORD, whose name *is*
  the God of hosts.

6 Woe to you *who are* at ease in
  Zion,
And trust in Mount Samaria,
Notable persons in the chief
  nation,
To whom the house of Israel
  comes!

2 Go over to Calneh and see;
And from there go to Hamath
  the great;
Then go down to Gath of the
  Philistines.

Are you better than these
  kingdoms?
Or is their territory greater
  than your territory?

3 *Woe to* you who put far off the
  day of doom,
Who cause the seat of violence
  to come near;

4 Who lie on beds of ivory,
Stretch out on your couches,
Eat lambs from the flock
And calves from the midst of
  the stall;

5 Who sing idly to the sound of
  stringed instruments,
And invent for yourselves
  musical instruments like
  David;

6 Who drink wine from bowls,
And anoint yourselves with the
  best ointments,
But are not grieved for the
  affliction of Joseph.

7 Therefore they shall now go
  captive as the first of the
  captives,
And those who recline at
  banquets shall be removed.

8 The Lord GOD has sworn by
  Himself,
The LORD God of hosts says:
"I abhor the pride of Jacob,
And hate his palaces;
Therefore I will deliver up *the*
  city
And all that is in it."

9 Then it shall come to pass, that
if ten men remain in one house, they
shall die. 10 And when a relative *of
the dead,* with one who will burn *the
bodies,* picks up the bodies*ᵃ* to take
them out of the house, he will say to
one inside the house, "*Are there* any
more with you?"
Then someone will say, "None."
And he will say, "Hold your
tongue! For we dare not mention the
name of the LORD."

11 For behold, the LORD gives a
  command:
He will break the great house
  into bits,
And the little house into
  pieces.

5:26 *ᵃ*A pagan deity   *ᵇ*Septuagint and Vulgate read *tabernacle of Moloch.*   *ᶜ*A pagan deity   6:10 *ᵃ*Literally
bones

12 Do horses run on rocks?
Does *one* plow *there* with
     oxen?
Yet you have turned justice into
     gall,
And the fruit of righteousness
     into wormwood,
13 You who rejoice over Lo
     Debar,*a*
Who say, "Have we not taken
     Karnaim*b* for ourselves
By our own strength?"

14 "But, behold, I will raise up a
     nation against you,
O house of Israel,"
Says the LORD God of hosts;
"And they will afflict you from
     the entrance of Hamath
To the Valley of the Arabah."

7 Thus the Lord GOD showed me:
Behold, He formed locust swarms
at the beginning of the late crop; indeed *it was* the late crop after the
king's mowings. 2 And so it was,
when they had finished eating the
grass of the land, that I said:

"O Lord GOD, forgive, I pray!
Oh, that Jacob may stand,
For he *is* small!"
3   *So* the LORD relented
          concerning this.
"It shall not be," said the LORD.

4 Thus the Lord GOD showed me:
Behold, the Lord GOD called for conflict by fire, and it consumed the
great deep and devoured the territory. 5 Then I said:

"O Lord GOD, cease, I pray!
Oh, that Jacob may stand,
For he *is* small!"
6   *So* the LORD relented
          concerning this.
"This also shall not be," said the
     Lord GOD.

7 Thus He showed me: Behold, the
Lord stood on a wall *made* with a
plumb line, with a plumb line in His
hand. 8 And the LORD said to me,
"Amos, what do you see?"
And I said, "A plumb line."
Then the Lord said:

"Behold, I am setting a plumb
     line

In the midst of My people
     Israel;
I will not pass by them
     anymore.
9 The high places of Isaac shall
     be desolate,
And the sanctuaries of Israel
     shall be laid waste.
I will rise with the sword
     against the house of
     Jeroboam."

10 Then Amaziah the priest of
Bethel sent to Jeroboam king of Israel, saying, "Amos has conspired
against you in the midst of the house
of Israel. The land is not able to bear
all his words. 11 For thus Amos has
said:

'Jeroboam shall die by the
     sword,
And Israel shall surely be led
     away captive
From their own land.' "

12 Then Amaziah said to Amos:

"Go, you seer!
Flee to the land of Judah.
There eat bread,
And there prophesy.
13 But never again prophesy at
     Bethel,
For it *is* the king's sanctuary,
And it *is* the royal residence."

14 Then Amos answered, and said
to Amaziah:

"I *was* no prophet,
Nor *was* I a son of a prophet,
But I *was* a sheepbreeder*a*
And a tender of sycamore fruit.
15 Then the LORD took me as I
     followed the flock,
And the LORD said to me,
'Go, prophesy to My people
     Israel.'
16 Now therefore, hear the word
     of the LORD:
You say, 'Do not prophesy
     against Israel,
And do not spout against the
     house of Isaac.'

17 "Therefore thus says the LORD:

'Your wife shall be a harlot in
     the city;

6:13 *a*Literally *Nothing*   *b*Literally *Horns,* symbol of strength   7:14 *a*Compare 2 Kings 3:4

Your sons and daughters shall
fall by the sword;
Your land shall be divided by
survey line;
You shall die in a defiled land;
And Israel shall surely be led
away captive
From his own land.' "

8 Thus the Lord GOD showed me:
Behold, a basket of summer fruit.
2 And He said, "Amos, what do you
see?"
So I said, "A basket of summer
fruit."
Then the LORD said to me:

"The end has come upon My
people Israel;
I will not pass by them
anymore.
3 And the songs of the temple
Shall be wailing in that day,"
Says the Lord GOD—
"Many dead bodies everywhere,
They shall be thrown out in
silence."

4 Hear this, you who swallow up[a]
the needy,
And make the poor of the land
fail,

5 Saying:

"When will the New Moon be
past,
That we may sell grain?
And the Sabbath,
That we may trade wheat?
Making the ephah small and
the shekel large,
Falsifying the scales by
deceit,
6 That we may buy the poor for
silver,
And the needy for a pair of
sandals—
Even sell the bad wheat?"

7 The LORD has sworn by the
pride of Jacob:
"Surely I will never forget any
of their works.
8 Shall the land not tremble for
this,
And everyone mourn who
dwells in it?

All of it shall swell like the
River,[a]
Heave and subside
Like the River of Egypt.

9 "And it shall come to pass in that
day," says the Lord GOD,
"That I will make the sun go
down at noon,
And I will darken the earth in
broad daylight;
10 I will turn your feasts into
mourning,
And all your songs into
lamentation;
I will bring sackcloth on every
waist,
And baldness on every head;
I will make it like mourning for
an only *son,*
And its end like a bitter day.

11 "Behold, the days are coming,"
says the Lord GOD,
"That I will send a famine on the
land,
Not a famine of bread,
Nor a thirst for water,
But of hearing the words of the
LORD.
12 They shall wander from sea to
sea,
And from north to east;
They shall run to and fro,
seeking the word of the LORD,
But shall not find *it.*

13 "In that day the fair virgins
And strong young men
Shall faint from thirst.
14 Those who swear by the sin[a]
of Samaria,
Who say,
'As your god lives, O Dan!'
And, 'As the way of Beersheba
lives!'
They shall fall and never rise
again."

9 I saw the Lord standing by the altar, and He said:

"Strike the doorposts, that the
thresholds may shake,
And break them on the heads
of them all.
I will slay the last of them with
the sword.

8:4 [a]Or *trample on* (compare 2:7)   8:8 [a]That is, the Nile; some Hebrew manuscripts, Septuagint, Syriac, Targum, and Vulgate read *River* (compare 9:5); Masoretic Text reads *the light.*   8:14 [a]Or *Ashima,* a Syrian goddess

He who flees from them shall
  not get away,
And he who escapes from them
  shall not be delivered.

2 "Though they dig into hell,ᵃ
  From there My hand shall take
    them;
  Though they climb up to
    heaven,
  From there I will bring them
    down;
3 And though they hide
    themselves on top of Carmel,
  From there I will search and
    take them;
  Though they hide from My
    sight at the bottom of the sea,
  From there I will command the
    serpent, and it shall bite
    them;
4 Though they go into captivity
    before their enemies,
  From there I will command the
    sword,
  And it shall slay them.
  I will set My eyes on them for
    harm and not for good."

5 The Lord GOD of hosts,
  He who touches the earth and
    it melts,
  And all who dwell there mourn;
  All of it shall swell like the
    River,ᵃ
  And subside like the River of
    Egypt.
6 He who builds His layers in the
    sky,
  And has founded His strata in
    the earth;
  Who calls for the waters of the
    sea,
  And pours them out on the face
    of the earth—
  The LORD is His name.

7 "Are you not like the people of
    Ethiopia to Me,
  O children of Israel?" says the
    LORD.
  "Did I not bring up Israel from
    the land of Egypt,
  The Philistines from Caphtor,
  And the Syrians from Kir?

8 "Behold, the eyes of the Lord
    GOD are on the sinful
    kingdom,

And I will destroy it from the
  face of the earth;
Yet I will not utterly destroy the
  house of Jacob,"
Says the LORD.

9 "For surely I will command,
  And will sift the house of Israel
    among all nations,
  As grain is sifted in a sieve;
  Yet not the smallest grain shall
    fall to the ground.
10 All the sinners of My people
    shall die by the sword,
  Who say, 'The calamity shall
    not overtake nor confront
    us.'

11 "On that day I will raise
    up
  The tabernacleᵃ of David,
    which has fallen down,
  And repair its damages;
  I will raise up its ruins,
  And rebuild it as in the days of
    old;
12 That they may possess the
    remnant of Edom,ᵃ
  And all the Gentiles who are
    called by My name,"
  Says the LORD who does this
    thing.

13 "Behold, the days are coming,"
    says the LORD,
  "When the plowman shall
    overtake the reaper,
  And the treader of grapes him
    who sows seed;
  The mountains shall drip with
    sweet wine,
  And all the hills shall flow with
    it.
14 I will bring back the captives
    of My people Israel;
  They shall build the waste
    cities and inhabit them;
  They shall plant vineyards and
    drink wine from them;
  They shall also make
    gardens and eat fruit from
    them.
15 I will plant them in their
    land,
  And no longer shall they be
    pulled up
  From the land I have given
    them,"
  Says the LORD your God.

9:2 ᵃOr Sheol   9:5 ᵃThat is, the Nile   9:11 ᵃLiterally booth, figure of a deposed dynasty
9:12 ᵃSeptuagint reads mankind.

Obadiah

Overview of Obadiah

Obadiah is a prophetic announcement of the destruction of the ancient kingdom of Edom. According to this book, we learn that the Edomites were heartless scavengers who looked with joy upon the destruction of God's people. They cowardly assisted the warring armies, possibly the ancient Babylonians, in defeating the Israelites.

> Indeed, you should not have gazed on their
> affliction
> In the day of their calamity,
> Nor laid hands on their substance
> In the day of their calamity.
> You should not have stood at the crossroads
> To cut off those among them who escaped;
> Nor should you have delivered up those among them
> who remained
> In the day of distress.
>
> (Obad. 13, 14)

Scholars differ as to the date of this book. Some place it during the ninth century B.C., corresponding to the destruction of Jerusalem by Jehoram, while others believe it was written in 586 B.C. during the onslaught by Nebuchadnezzar. The book contains only twenty-one verses, making it difficult to determine the time, situation, and the attacking enemy from the text itself.

Obadiah was an obscure prophet who probably lived in the southern kingdom of Judah. Nothing is known of his hometown or family, but it is not likely that he came out of the kingly or priestly line, because his father is not mentioned (1:1). There are thirteen Obadiahs in the Old Testament, and some scholars have attempted to identify the author of this book with one of the other twelve. Four of the better prospects are: (1) the officer in Ahab's palace who hid God's prophets in a cave (1 Kin. 18:3); (2) one of the officials sent out by Jehoshaphat to teach the law in the cities of Judah (2 Chr. 17:7); (3) one of the overseers who took part in repairing the temple under Josiah (2 Chr. 34:12); or (4) a priest in the time of Nehemiah (Neh. 10:5).

Obadiah, whose name means "Servant of Yahweh," assures the people of Israel that God will overcome their enemy. He foretells them that God will deal justly with those who have wronged them.

Although Obadiah is the shortest book in the Old Testament, its message is one of the strongest. God will defeat all evil and negative forces in our lives and provide the ultimate victory over our enemies and problems. He will raise up positive leaders to establish His kingdom. God is greater than our greatest problems and stronger than our strongest foe!

Jesus in Obadiah

The Book of Obadiah pictures Jesus in three ways. First, He is seen as the Judge of the nations (15–16). Second, He is pictured as the Savior of Israel (17–20). Third, Obadiah reveals Jesus as the Possessor of the kingdom (21).

Keys to Obadiah

Key Word: The Judgment of Edom. The major theme of Obadiah is a declaration of impending judgment on Edom because the Edomites have been cruel and arrogant toward the people of Judah. Through the prophet, God says to Edom: "I will make you small among the nations" (2); "the pride of your heart has deceived you" (3); "how you will be cut off!" (5); "how Esau shall be searched out!" (6); "your mighty men, O Teman, shall be dismayed" (9); "shame shall cover you" (10); "as you have done, it shall be done to you" (15). Even the last few verses, which primarily deal with Israel, speak of Edom's downfall (17–21).

The secondary theme of Obadiah is the future restoration of Israel and faithfulness of Yahweh to His covenant promises.

Key Verses: "For *your* violence against your brother Jacob, shame shall cover you, and you shall be cut off forever" (10).

"Then saviors shall come to Mount Zion to judge the mountains of Esau, and the kingdom shall be the LORD's" (21).

1 The vision of Obadiah.

    Thus says the Lord GOD
      concerning Edom
    (We have heard a report from
      the LORD,
    And a messenger has been
      sent among the nations,
      saying,
    "Arise, and let us rise up against
      her for battle"):

2 "Behold, I will make you small
    among the nations;
    You shall be greatly despised.
3 The pride of your heart has
    deceived you,
    You who dwell in the clefts of
      the rock,
    Whose habitation is high;
    You who say in your heart,
    'Who will bring me down to the
      ground?'
4 Though you ascend *as* high as
    the eagle,
    And though you set your nest
      among the stars,
    From there I will bring you
      down," says the LORD.

5 "If thieves had come to you,
    If robbers by night—
    Oh, how you will be cut off!—
    Would they not have stolen till
      they had enough?
    If grape-gatherers had come to
      you,
    Would they not have left *some*
      gleanings?
6 "Oh, how Esau shall be searched
    out!
    How his hidden treasures shall
      be sought after!
7 All the men in your
    confederacy
    Shall force you to the border;
    The men at peace with you
    Shall deceive you *and* prevail
      against you.
    Those who eat your bread shall
      lay a trap[a] for you.
    No one is aware of it.

8 "Will I not in that day," says the
    LORD,

    "Even destroy the wise *men*
      from Edom,
    And understanding from the
      mountains of Esau?
9 Then your mighty men, O
    Teman, shall be dismayed,
    To the end that everyone from
      the mountains of Esau
    May be cut off by slaughter.

10 "For violence against your
      brother Jacob,
    Shame shall cover you,
    And you shall be cut off
      forever.
11 In the day that you stood on the
      other side—
    In the day that strangers
      carried captive his forces,
    When foreigners entered his
      gates
    And cast lots for Jerusalem—
    Even you *were* as one of
      them.

12 "But you should not have
      gazed on the day of your
      brother
    In the day of his captivity;[a]
    Nor should you have rejoiced
      over the children of Judah
    In the day of their destruction;
    Nor should you have spoken
      proudly
    In the day of distress.
13 You should not have entered
      the gate of My people
    In the day of their calamity.
    Indeed, you should not have
      gazed on their affliction
    In the day of their calamity,
    Nor laid *hands* on their
      substance
    In the day of their calamity.
14 You should not have stood at
      the crossroads
    To cut off those among them
      who escaped;
    Nor should you have delivered
      up those among them who
      remained
    In the day of distress.

15 "For the day of the LORD upon
      all the nations *is* near;

7 [a]Or *wound,* or *plot*   12 [a]Literally *on the day he became a foreigner*

As you have done, it shall be
 done to you;
Your reprisal shall return upon
 your own head.
16 For as you drank on my holy
 mountain,
 So shall all the nations drink
 continually;
 Yes, they shall drink, and
 swallow,
 And they shall be as though
 they had never been.

17 "But on Mount Zion there shall
 be deliverance,
 And there shall be holiness;
 The house of Jacob shall
 possess their
 possessions.
18 The house of Jacob shall be a
 fire,
 And the house of Joseph a
 flame;
 But the house of Esau *shall be*
 stubble;
 They shall kindle them and
 devour them,

And no survivor shall *remain*
 of the house of Esau,"
For the LORD has spoken.

19 The South*a* shall possess the
 mountains of Esau,
 And the Lowland shall possess
 Philistia.
 They shall possess the fields of
 Ephraim
 And the fields of Samaria.
 Benjamin *shall possess* Gilead.
20 And the captives of this host of
 the children of Israel
 Shall possess the land of the
 Canaanites
 As far as Zarephath.
 The captives of Jerusalem who
 are in Sepharad
 Shall possess the cities of the
 South.*a*
21 Then saviors*a* shall come to
 Mount Zion
 To judge the mountains of
 Esau,
 And the kingdom shall be the
 LORD'S.

19 *a*Hebrew *Negev*   20 *a*Hebrew *Negev*   21 *a*Or *deliverers*

Jonah

Overview of Jonah

The Book of Jonah is best known for the story of the prophet's three days in the belly of a fish. But the main message of this book is a powerful affirmation of God's love and forgiveness for all people.

Written sometime between 782 and 753 B.C., probably by Jonah himself, the book records Jonah's experience in learning of God's mercy. The only Old Testament prophet from the region of Galilee, a Gentile area known as "the circle" (of the nations), Jonah lived in the town of Gath Hepher, located three miles from Nazareth. Jonah, a Jew, was given a mission by God to go to the Gentile nation and its capital Nineveh.

During Jonah's time, there was much hatred from the Israelites toward the Gentiles. God called Jonah to travel to Nineveh so that he could encourage the people, his natural enemies, to turn to God. Jonah failed to recognize God's love for all persons and fled in the opposite direction toward Tarshish.

Jonah writes a lively, spirited autobiography of his travel by sea, where he was thrown overboard, swallowed by a great fish, and finally spit up on the shore. God's message finally got through to him. Jonah went to the city of Nineveh, where the people listened to his words and turned to God.

Jonah argued with God that he was not needed by God to begin with. He fled because he was embarrassed, afraid, and did not want to feel awkward. God could have made the city repent without Jonah's presence. Yet God made it clear that He does His greatest works through His smallest people. He used Jonah as a vessel of His truth, to proclaim that His loving kindness is for all people.

The greatest power in the world is a positive idea. And the most powerful positive idea is one that comes from God. Faith is opening your mind to God's thought. God will do great things through people dedicated to Him.

Jesus in Jonah

Jonah is the only prophet to whom Jesus likened Himself. "But He answered and said to them, 'An evil and adulterous generation seeks after a sign, and no sign will be given to it except the sign of the prophet Jonah. For as Jonah was three days and three nights in the belly of the great fish, so will the Son of Man be three days and three nights in the heart of the earth. The men on Nineveh will rise in the judgment with this generation and condemn it, because they repented at the preaching of Jonah; and indeed a greater than Jonah is here'" (Matt. 12:39–41). Jonah's experience is a type of the death, burial, and resurrection of Christ. (The Hebrew idiom, "three days and three nights," requires only a portion of the first and third days).

Keys to Jonah

Key Word: Revival. God's lovng concern for the Gentiles is not exclusive to the New Testament. More than seven hundred years before the birth of Christ, God commissioned the Hebrew prophet Jonah to proclaim a message of repentance to the Assyrians. Jewish nationalism, however, blinded both God's prophets and covenant people to His worldwide purposes of salvation. The story of Jonah is one of the clearest demonstrations of God's love and mercy for all mankind in the entire Scriptures.

Key Verses: "Those who regard worthless idols forsake their own Mercy. But I will sacrifice to You with the voice of thanksgiving; I will pay what I have vowed. Salvation *is* of the LORD" (2:8, 9).

"So he prayed to the LORD, and said, 'Ah, LORD, was this not what I said when I was still in my country? Therefore I fled previously to Tarshish; for I know that You *are* a gracious and merciful God, slow to anger and abundant in lovingkindness, One who relents from doing harm'" (4:2).

Key Chapter: Jonah 3. The third chapter of Jonah records perhaps the greatest revival of all time as the entire city of Ninevah "[believes] God, and [proclaims] a fast," and cries out to God. No matter how bad a city or a nation or an individual may appear, positive change is always possible!

1 Now the word of the LORD came to Jonah the son of Amittai, saying, 2 "Arise, go to Nineveh, that great city, and cry out against it; for their wickedness has come up before Me." 3 But Jonah arose to flee to Tarshish from the presence of the LORD. He went down to Joppa, and found a ship going to Tarshish; so he paid the fare, and went down into it, to go with them to Tarshish from the presence of the LORD.

4 But the LORD sent out a great wind on the sea, and there was a mighty tempest on the sea, so that the ship was about to be broken up.

5 Then the mariners were afraid; and every man cried out to his god, and threw the cargo that *was* in the ship into the sea, to lighten the load.[a] But Jonah had gone down into the lowest parts of the ship, had lain down, and was fast asleep.

6 So the captain came to him, and said to him, "What do you mean, sleeper? Arise, call on your God; perhaps your God will consider us, so that we may not perish."

7 And they said to one another, "Come, let us cast lots, that we may know for whose cause this trouble *has come* upon us." So they cast lots, and the lot fell on Jonah. 8 Then they said to him, "Please tell us! For whose cause *is* this trouble upon us? What is your occupation? And where do you come from? What is your country? And of what people are you?"

1:5 *a*Literally *from upon them*

9 So he said to them, "I *am* a Hebrew; and I fear the LORD, the God of heaven, who made the sea and the dry *land*."

10 Then the men were exceedingly afraid, and said to him, "Why have you done this?" For the men knew that he fled from the presence of the LORD, because he had told them.

11 Then they said to him, "What shall we do to you that the sea may be calm for us?"—for the sea was growing more tempestuous.

12 And he said to them, "Pick me up and throw me into the sea; then the sea will become calm for you. For I know that this great tempest *is* because of me."

13 Nevertheless the men rowed hard to return to land, but they could not, for the sea continued to grow more tempestuous against them. 14 Therefore they cried out to the LORD and said, "We pray, O LORD, please do not let us perish for this man's life, and do not charge us with innocent blood; for You, O LORD, have done as it pleased You." 15 So they picked up Jonah and threw him into the sea, and the sea ceased from its raging. 16 Then the men feared the LORD exceedingly, and offered a sacrifice to the LORD and took vows.

17 Now the LORD had prepared a great fish to swallow Jonah. And Jonah was in the belly of the fish three days and three nights.

2 Then Jonah prayed to the LORD his God from the fish's belly. 2 And he said:

"I cried out to the LORD because
    of my affliction,
And He answered me.

"Out of the belly of Sheol I
    cried,
And You heard my voice.
3   For You cast me into the deep,
Into the heart of the seas,
And the floods surrounded me;
All Your billows and Your
    waves passed over me.
4   Then I said, 'I have been cast
out of Your sight;
Yet I will look again toward
Your holy temple.'

5   The waters surrounded me,
even to my soul;
The deep closed around me;
Weeds were wrapped around
my head.
6   I went down to the moorings
of the mountains;
The earth with its bars *closed*
behind me forever;
Yet You have brought up my
life from the pit,
O LORD, my God.

7   "When my soul fainted within
me,
I remembered the LORD;
And my prayer went *up* to You,
Into Your holy temple.

8   "Those who regard worthless
idols
Forsake their own Mercy.
9   But I will sacrifice to You
With the voice of thanksgiving;
I will pay what I have vowed.
Salvation *is* of the LORD."

10 So the LORD spoke to the fish, and it vomited Jonah onto dry *land*.

3 Now the word of the LORD came to Jonah the second time, saying, 2 "Arise, go to Nineveh, that great city, and preach to it the message that I tell you." 3 So Jonah arose and went to Nineveh, according to the word of the LORD. Now Nineveh was an exceedingly great city, a three-day journey[a] *in extent.* 4 And Jonah began to enter the city on the first day's walk. Then he cried out and said, "Yet forty days, and Nineveh shall be overthrown!"

5 So the people of Nineveh believed God, proclaimed a fast, and put on sackcloth, from the greatest to the least of them. 6 Then word came to the king of Nineveh; and he arose from his throne and laid aside his robe, covered *himself* with sackcloth and sat in ashes. 7 And he caused *it* to be proclaimed and published throughout Nineveh by the decree of the king and his nobles, saying,

Let neither man nor beast, herd nor flock, taste anything; do not let them eat, or drink water. 8 But let man and beast be covered with sackcloth, and cry mightily to God;

3:3 *a*Exact meaning unknown

yes, let every one turn from his evil way and from the violence that is in his hands. 9 Who can tell *if* God will turn and relent, and turn away from His fierce anger, so that we may not perish?

10 Then God saw their works, that they turned from their evil way; and God relented from the disaster that He had said He would bring upon them, and He did not do it.

4 But it displeased Jonah exceedingly, and he became angry. 2 So he prayed to the LORD, and said, "Ah, LORD, was not this what I said when I was still in my country? Therefore I fled previously to Tarshish; for I know that You *are* a gracious and merciful God, slow to anger and abundant in lovingkindness, One who relents from doing harm. 3 Therefore now, O LORD, please take my life from me, for *it is* better for me to die than to live!"

4 Then the LORD said, "*Is it* right for you to be angry?"

5 So Jonah went out of the city and sat on the east side of the city. There he made himself a shelter and sat under it in the shade, till he might see what would become of the city. 6 And the LORD God prepared a plant[a] and made it come up over Jonah, that it might be shade for his head to deliver him from his misery. So Jonah was very grateful for the plant. 7 But as morning dawned the next day God prepared a worm, and *it so* damaged the plant that it withered. 8 And it happened, when the sun arose, that God prepared a vehement east wind; and the sun beat on Jonah's head, so that he grew faint. Then he wished death for himself, and said, "*It is* better for me to die than to live."

9 Then God said to Jonah, "*Is it* right for you to be angry about the plant?"

And he said, "*It is* right for me to be angry, even to death!"

10 But the LORD said, "You have had pity on the plant for which you have not labored, nor made it grow, which came up in a night and perished in a night. 11 And should I not pity Nineveh, that great city, in which are more than one hundred and twenty thousand persons who cannot discern between their right hand and their left—and much livestock?"

4:6 *a*Hebrew *kikayon*, exact identity unknown

Micah

Overview of Micah

Micah was one of the many prophets God raised up to keep His light shining during a difficult and sorrowful time in the history of Judah and Israel. He was from the promised city of Moresheth in Judah, overlooking the fertile coastal plain of the Mediterranean Sea. The book was written between 735 and 710 B.C.

A beautiful account of hope in the face of hardship, mercy in time of distress, and promise in the moment of confusion, Micah recounts how God will restore His people after captivity. In the midst of pending destruction, Micah foretells the coming birth of the Messiah. The birthplace, Bethlehem, was a tiny insignificant village, but from there God would raise up the Deliverer.

> But you, Bethlehem Ephrathah,
> Though *you are little among the thousands of Judah,*
> Yet *out of you shall come forth to Me*
> The One to be Ruler in Israel,
> Whose goings forth are from of old,
> From everlasting.
>
> (Mic. 5:2)

Almost every chapter of Micah includes a positive inspirational promise for the people of Israel to hold on to in their times of despair. He assures them of the restoration of Israel and of their future mercy before God:

> Therefore I will look to the LORD;
> I will wait for the God of my salvation;
> My God will hear me.
>
> (Mic. 7:7)

Micah's name means "Who is Like Yahweh." In reminding his readers of God's gracious love and mercy, Micah assures them that God is able to forgive their sins completely:

> Who is a God like You,
> Pardoning iniquity
> And passing over the transgression of the remnant of
>   His heritage?
> He does not retain His anger forever,
> Because He delights in mercy.
>
> (Mic. 7:18)

Jesus in Micah

Micah 5:2 is one of the clearest and most important of all Old Testament prophecies: "But you, Bethlehem Ephrathah, *though* you are little among the thousands of Judah, *yet* out of you shall come forth to Me the One to be Ruler in Israel, whose goings forth *are* from of old, from everlasting." This prophecy about the birthplace and eternity of the Messiah was made seven hundred years before His birth. The chief priests and scribes paraphrased this verse in Matthew 2:5, 6 when questioned about the birthplace of the Messiah. Micah 2:12, 13; 4:1–8; and 5:4, 5 offer some of the best Old Testament descriptions of the righteous reign of Christ over the whole earth.

Keys to Micah

Key Word: Judgment and Restoration. Micah exposes the injustice of Judah and the righteousness and justice of God. The first two-thirds of the book deal with sin and judgment, while the last third is a message of hope and consolation. God's justice will triumph and the divine Deliverer will come. True peace and justice will prevail only when the Messiah reigns. Micah 6:8 summarizes what God wants to see in His people: justice and equity tempered with mercy and compassion, as the results of a humble and obedient relationship with Him.

Key Verses: "He has shown you, O man, what *is* good; and what does the LORD require of you but to do justly, to love mercy, and to walk humbly with your God? (6:8).

"Who *is* a God like You, pardoning iniquity and passing over the transgression of the remnant of His heritage? He does not retain His anger forever, because He delights *in* mercy" (7:18).

Key Chapters: Micah 6; 7. The closing section of Micah describes a courtroom scene. God has a case against His people and has called the mountains and hills to serve as the jury. God's case is that the people have replaced heartfelt worship with empty ritual, thinking that this is all God requires. They have divorced God's standards of justice from their daily dealings in order to cover up their unscrupulous practices. They have failed to see what God really wants of man. There can only be one verdict: guilty.

Nevertheless, the book closes with a note of hope. This God of judgment also delights to extend mercy. No wonder the prophet exclaims, "Therefore I will look to the LORD; I will wait for the God of my salvation; my God will hear me" (7:7).

1 The word of the LORD that came to Micah of Moresheth in the days of Jotham, Ahaz, *and* Hezekiah, kings of Judah, which he saw concerning Samaria and Jerusalem.

2　Hear, all you peoples!
　Listen, O earth, and all that is in it!
　Let the Lord GOD be a witness against you,
　The Lord from His holy temple.

3　For behold, the LORD is coming out of His place;
　He will come down
　And tread on the high places of the earth.

4　The mountains will melt under Him,
　And the valleys will split
　Like wax before the fire,
　Like waters poured down a steep place.

5　All this is for the transgression of Jacob
　And for the sins of the house of Israel.
　What *is* the transgression of Jacob?
　Is it not Samaria?

And what *are* the high places
　of Judah?
Are they not Jerusalem?

6 "Therefore I will make Samaria
　　a heap of ruins in the field,
　Places for planting a vineyard;
　I will pour down her stones into
　　the valley,
　And I will uncover her
　　foundations.
7 All her carved images shall be
　　beaten to pieces,
　And all her pay as a harlot shall
　　be burned with the fire;
　All her idols I will lay desolate,
　For she gathered *it* from the
　　pay of a harlot,
　And they shall return to the pay
　　of a harlot."

8 Therefore I will wail and howl,
　I will go stripped and naked;
　I will make a wailing like the
　　jackals
　And a mourning like the
　　ostriches,
9 For her wounds *are* incurable.
　For it has come to Judah;
　It has come to the gate of My
　　people—
　To Jerusalem.

10 Tell *it* not in Gath,
　Weep not at all;
　In Beth Aphrah[a]
　Roll yourself in the dust.
11 Pass by in naked shame, you
　　inhabitant of Shaphir;
　The inhabitant of Zaanan[a] does
　　not go out.
　Beth Ezel mourns;
　Its place to stand is taken away
　　from you.

12 For the inhabitant of Maroth
　　pined[a] for good,
　But disaster came down from
　　the LORD
　To the gate of Jerusalem.
13 O inhabitant of Lachish,
　Harness the chariot to the swift
　　steeds
　(She *was* the beginning of sin
　　to the daughter of Zion),
　For the transgressions of Israel
　　were found in you.

14 Therefore you shall give
　　presents to Moresheth
　　Gath;[a]
　The houses of Achzib[b] *shall be*
　　a lie to the kings of Israel.
15 I will yet bring an heir to you,
　　O inhabitant of Mareshah;[a]
　The glory of Israel shall come
　　to Adullam.
16 Make yourself bald and cut off
　　your hair,
　Because of your precious
　　children;
　Enlarge your baldness like an
　　eagle,
　For they shall go from you into
　　captivity.

2 Woe to those who devise
　　iniquity,
　And work out evil on their
　　beds!
　At morning light they practice
　　it,
　Because it is in the power of
　　their hand.
2 They covet fields and take
　　them by violence,
　Also houses, and seize *them*.
　So they oppress a man and his
　　house,
　A man and his inheritance.

3 Therefore thus says the LORD:

　"Behold, against this family I am
　　devising disaster,
　From which you cannot remove
　　your necks;
　Nor shall you walk haughtily,
　For this *is* an evil time.
4 In that day one shall take up a
　　proverb against you,
　And lament with a bitter
　　lamentation, saying:
　'We are utterly destroyed!
　He has changed the heritage of
　　my people;
　How He has removed *it* from
　　me!
　To a turncoat He has divided
　　our fields.' "
5 Therefore you will have no one
　　to determine boundaries[a] by
　　lot
　In the assembly of the LORD.

6 "Do not prattle," *you say to
    those* who prophesy.
   So they shall not prophesy to
    you;[a]
   They shall not return insult for
    insult.[b]
7 *You who are* named the house
    of Jacob:
   "Is the Spirit of the LORD
    restricted?
   Are these His doings?
   Do not My words do good
   To him who walks uprightly?

8 "Lately My people have risen up
    as an enemy—
   You pull off the robe with the
    garment
   From those who trust *you,* as
    they pass by,
   Like men returned from war.
9 The women of My people you
    cast out
   From their pleasant houses;
   From their children
   You have taken away My glory
    forever.

10 "Arise and depart,
   For this *is* not *your* rest;
   Because it is defiled, it shall
    destroy,
   Yes, with utter destruction.
11 If a man should walk in a false
    spirit
   And speak a lie, *saying,*
   'I will prophesy to you of wine
    and drink,'
   Even he would be the prattler
    of this people.

12 "I will surely assemble all of
    you, O Jacob,
   I will surely gather the remnant
    of Israel;
   I will put them together like
    sheep of the fold,[a]
   Like a flock in the midst of their
    pasture;
   They shall make a loud noise
    because of *so many* people.
13 The one who breaks open will
    come up before them;
   They will break out,
   Pass through the gate,
   And go out by it;
   Their king will pass before
    them,
   With the LORD at their head."

3 And I said:

   "Hear now, O heads of Jacob,
   And you rulers of the house of
    Israel:
   Is it not for you to know
    justice?
2 You who hate good and love
    evil;
   Who strip the skin from My
    people,[a]
   And the flesh from their bones;
3 Who also eat the flesh of My
    people,
   Flay their skin from them,
   Break their bones,
   And chop *them* in pieces
   Like *meat* for the pot,
   Like flesh in the caldron."

4 Then they will cry to the LORD,
   But He will not hear them;
   He will even hide His face from
    them at that time,
   Because they have been evil in
    their deeds.

5 Thus says the LORD concerning
    the prophets
   Who make my people stray;
   Who chant "Peace"
   While they chew with their
    teeth,
   But who prepare war against
    him
   Who puts nothing into their
    mouths:
6 "Therefore you shall have night
    without vision,
   And you shall have darkness
    without divination;
   The sun shall go down on the
    prophets,
   And the day shall be dark for
    them.
7 So the seers shall be ashamed,
   And the diviners abashed;
   Indeed they shall all cover their
    lips;
   For *there is* no answer from
    God."

8 But truly I am full of power by
    the Spirit of the LORD,
   And of justice and might,
   To declare to Jacob his
    transgression
   And to Israel his sin.
9 Now hear this,

2:6 [a]Literally *to these*   [b]Vulgate reads *He shall not take shame.*   2:12 [a]Hebrew *Bozrah*   3:2 [a]Literally
them

You heads of the house of
Jacob
And rulers of the house of
Israel,
Who abhor justice
And pervert all equity,
10 Who build up Zion with
bloodshed
And Jerusalem with iniquity:
11 Her heads judge for a bribe,
Her priests teach for pay,
And her prophets divine for
money.
Yet they lean on the LORD, and
say,
"Is not the LORD among us?
No harm can come upon us."
12 Therefore because of you
Zion shall be plowed *like* a
field,
Jerusalem shall become heaps
of ruins,
And the mountain of the
temple*a*
Like the bare hills of the forest.

4 Now it shall come to pass in the
latter days
That the mountain of the
LORD's house
Shall be established on the top
of the mountains,
And shall be exalted above the
hills;
And peoples shall flow to it.
2 Many nations shall come and
say,
"Come, and let us go up to the
mountain of the LORD,
To the house of the God of
Jacob;
He will teach us His ways,
And we shall walk in His
paths."
For out of Zion the law shall
go forth,
And the word of the LORD from
Jerusalem.
3 He shall judge between many
peoples,
And rebuke strong nations afar
off;
They shall beat their swords
into plowshares,
And their spears into pruning
hooks;
Nation shall not lift up sword
against nation,
Neither shall they learn war
anymore.*a*

4 But everyone shall sit under
his vine and under his fig
tree,
And no one shall make *them*
afraid;
For the mouth of the LORD of
hosts has spoken.
5 For all people walk each in the
name of his god,
But we will walk in the name
of the LORD our God
Forever and ever.

6 "In that day," says the LORD,
"I will assemble the lame,
I will gather the outcast
And those whom I have
afflicted;
7 I will make the lame a remnant,
And the outcast a strong
nation;
So the LORD will reign over
them in Mount Zion
From now on, even forever.
8 And you, O tower of the
flock,
The stronghold of the daughter
of Zion,
To you shall it come,
Even the former dominion shall
come,
The kingdom of the daughter
of Jerusalem."

9 Now why do you cry aloud?
Is there no king in your midst?
Has your counselor perished?
For pangs have seized you like
a woman in labor.
10 Be in pain, and labor to bring
forth,
O daughter of Zion,
Like a woman in birth pangs.
For now you shall go forth from
the city,
You shall dwell in the field,
And to Babylon you shall go.
There you shall be delivered;
There the LORD will redeem you
From the hand of your enemies.
11 Now also many nations have
gathered against you,
Who say, "Let her be defiled,
And let our eye look upon
Zion."
12 But they do not know the
thoughts of the LORD,
Nor do they understand His
counsel;

3:12 *a*Literally *house*   4:3 *a*Compare Isaiah 2:2–4

For He will gather them like
sheaves to the threshing
floor.

13 "Arise and thresh, O daughter of
Zion;
For I will make your horn
iron,
And I will make your hooves
bronze;
You shall beat in pieces many
peoples;
I will consecrate their gain to
the LORD,
And their substance to the Lord
of the whole earth."

5 Now gather yourself in troops,
O daughter of troops;
He has laid siege against us;
They will strike the judge of
Israel with a rod on the
cheek.

2 "But you, Bethlehem Ephrathah,
Though you are little among
the thousands of Judah,
Yet out of you shall come forth
to Me
The One to be Ruler in Israel,
Whose goings forth *are* from of
old,
From everlasting."

3 Therefore He shall give them
up,
Until the time *that* she who is
in labor has given birth;
Then the remnant of His
brethren
Shall return to the children of
Israel.

4 And He shall stand and feed
His flock
In the strength of the LORD,
In the majesty of the name of
the LORD His God;
And they shall abide,
For now He shall be great
To the ends of the earth;

5 And this *One* shall be peace.

When the Assyrian comes into
our land,
And when he treads in our
palaces,
Then we will raise against him
Seven shepherds and eight
princely men.

6 They shall waste with the
sword the land of Assyria,
And the land of Nimrod at its
entrances;
Thus He shall deliver *us* from
the Assyrian,
When he comes into our
land
And when he treads within our
borders.

7 Then the remnant of Jacob
Shall be in the midst of many
peoples,
Like dew from the LORD,
Like showers on the grass,
That tarry for no man
Nor wait for the sons of
men.

8 And the remnant of Jacob
Shall be among the Gentiles,
In the midst of many peoples,
Like a lion among the beasts
of the forest,
Like a young lion among flocks
of sheep,
Who, if he passes through,
Both treads down and tears in
pieces,
And none can deliver.

9 Your hand shall be lifted
against your adversaries,
And all your enemies shall be
cut off.

10 "And it shall be in that day,"
says the LORD,
"That I will cut off your horses
from your midst
And destroy your chariots.

11 I will cut off the cities of your
land
And throw down all your
strongholds.

12 I will cut off sorceries from
your hand,
And you shall have no
soothsayers.

13 Your carved images I will also
cut off,
And your sacred pillars from
your midst;
You shall no more worship the
work of your hands;

14 I will pluck your wooden
images[a] from your midst;
Thus I will destroy your
cities.

15 And I will execute vengeance
in anger and fury
On the nations that have not
heard."[a]

5:14 [a]Hebrew *Asherim,* Canaanite deities   5:15 [a]Or *obeyed*

6 Hear now what the LORD says:

"Arise, plead your case before
    the mountains,
And let the hills hear your
    voice.
2 Hear, O you mountains, the
    LORD's complaint,
And you strong foundations of
    the earth;
For the LORD has a complaint
    against His people,
And He will contend with
    Israel.

3 "O My people, what have I done
    to you?
And how have I wearied you?
    Testify against Me.
4 For I brought you up from the
    land of Egypt,
I redeemed you from the house
    of bondage;
And I sent before you Moses,
    Aaron, and Miriam.
5 O My people, remember now
What Balak king of Moab
    counseled,
And what Balaam the son of
    Beor answered him,
From Acacia Grove[a] to Gilgal,
That you may know the
    righteousness of the
    LORD."

6 With what shall I come before
    the LORD,
And bow myself before the
    High God?
Shall I come before Him with
    burnt offerings,
With calves a year old?
7 Will the LORD be pleased with
    thousands of rams,
Ten thousand rivers of oil?
Shall I give my firstborn for my
    transgression,
The fruit of my body for the sin
    of my soul?

8 He has shown you, O man,
    what is good;
And what does the LORD
    require of you
But to do justly,
To love mercy,
And to walk humbly with your
    God?

9 The LORD's voice cries to the
    city—
Wisdom shall see Your name:

"Hear the rod!
Who has appointed it?
10 Are there yet the treasures of
    wickedness
In the house of the wicked,
And the short measure that is
    an abomination?
11 Shall I count pure those with
    the wicked scales,
And with the bag of deceitful
    weights?
12 For her rich men are full of
    violence,
Her inhabitants have spoken
    lies,
And their tongue is deceitful in
    their mouth.

13 "Therefore I will also make you
    sick by striking you,
By making you desolate
    because of your sins.
14 You shall eat, but not be
    satisfied;
Hunger[a] shall be in your
    midst.
You may carry some away,[b]
    but shall not save them;
And what you do rescue I will
    give over to the sword.

15 "You shall sow, but not reap;
You shall tread the olives, but
    not anoint yourselves with
    oil;
And make sweet wine, but not
    drink wine.
16 For the statutes of Omri are
    kept;
All the works of Ahab's house
    are done;
And you walk in their counsels,
That I may make you a
    desolation,
And your inhabitants a hissing.
Therefore you shall bear the
    reproach of My people."[a]

7 Woe is me!
For I am like those who gather
    summer fruits,
Like those who glean vintage
    grapes;
There is no cluster to eat

6:5 [a]Hebrew *Shittim* (compare Numbers 25:1; Joshua 2:1, 3:1)   6:14 [a]Or *Emptiness* or *Humiliation*
[b]Targum and Vulgate read *You shall take hold*.   6:16 [a]Following Masoretic Text, Targum, and Vulgate;
Septuagint reads *of nations*.

Of the first-ripe fruit *which* my
soul desires.
2 The faithful *man* has perished
from the earth,
And *there is* no one upright
among men.
They all lie in wait for blood;
Every man hunts his brother
with a net.

3 That they may successfully do
evil with both hands—
The prince asks *for gifts,*
The judge *seeks* a bribe,
And the great *man* utters his
evil desire;
So they scheme together.
4 The best of them *is* like a brier;
The most upright *is sharper*
than a thorn hedge;
The day of your watchman and
your punishment comes;
Now shall be their perplexity.

5 Do not trust in a friend;
Do not put your confidence in
a companion;
Guard the doors of your
mouth
From her who lies in your
bosom.
6 For son dishonors father,
Daughter rises against her
mother,
Daughter-in-law against her
mother-in-law;
A man's enemies *are* the men
of his own household.
7 Therefore I will look to the
LORD;
I will wait for the God of my
salvation;
My God will hear me.

8 Do not rejoice over me, my
enemy;
When I fall, I will arise;
When I sit in darkness,
The LORD *will be* a light to me.
9 I will bear the indignation of
the LORD,
Because I have sinned against
Him,
Until He pleads my case
And executes justice for me.
He will bring me forth to the
light;
I will see His righteousness.

10 Then *she who is* my enemy will
see,
And shame will cover her who
said to me,
"Where is the LORD your God?"
My eyes will see her;
Now she will be trampled down
Like mud in the streets.

11 *In* the day when your walls are
to be built,
In that day the decree shall go
far and wide.*a*
12 *In* that day they*a* shall come to
you
From Assyria and the fortified
cities,*b*
From the fortress*c* to the River,*d*
From sea to sea,
And mountain *to* mountain.
13 Yet the land shall be desolate
Because of those who dwell in
it,
And for the fruit of their deeds.

14 Shepherd Your people with
Your staff,
The flock of Your heritage,
Who dwell solitarily *in* a
woodland,
In the midst of Carmel;
Let them feed *in* Bashan and
Gilead,
As in days of old.

15 "As in the days when you came
out of the land of Egypt,
I will show them*a* wonders."

16 The nations shall see and be
ashamed of all their might;
They shall put *their* hand over
their mouth;
Their ears shall be deaf.
17 They shall lick the dust like a
serpent;
They shall crawl from their
holes like snakes of the earth.
They shall be afraid of the LORD
our God,
And shall fear because of
You.
18 Who *is* a God like You,
Pardoning iniquity
And passing over the
transgression of the remnant
of His heritage?

7:11 *a*Or *the boundary shall be extended*   7:12 *a*Literally *he,* collective of the captives   *b*Hebrew *arey mazor,* possibly *cities of Egypt*   *c*Hebrew *mazor,* possibly *Egypt*   *d*That is, the Euphrates   7:15 *a*Literally *him,* collective for the captives

He does not retain His anger
    forever,
    Because He delights *in* mercy.
19 He will again have compassion
    on us,
    And will subdue our
    iniquities.

You will cast all our[a] sins
    Into the depths of the sea.
20 You will give truth to Jacob
    And mercy to Abraham,
    Which You have sworn to our
    fathers
    From days of old.

7:19 aLiterally *their*

Nahum

Overview of Nahum

The Book of Nahum was written by the prophet of the same name sometime between 663 and 612 B.C. During these years, the Assyrian empire was at its height. God called the prophet Nahum to the city of Nineveh, which was the capital of the Assyrian kingdom. Because the Assyrian armies were terribly cruel and violent, their destruction was imminent. Nahum's responsibility was to warn the city of this impending doom. In this short book, we see that Nahum was indeed faithful to the call God had given him.

The prophet Nahum was a courageous individual who was willing to stand up for the oppressed people in the face of wickedly arrogant Assyrians. He was not afraid to face the Assyrian army. Though he was only one man, he insisted on doing right.

Though he was called to preach destruction to the Assyrians, Nahum, whose name means "Comfort," also expresses the comfort of God to his people in the face of cruel opposition. Nahum proves that God is stronger than the wickedness of the Assyrian.

The LORD has His way
In the whirlwind and in the storm,
And the clouds are the dust of His
    feet.
He rebukes the sea and makes it dry,
And dries up all the rivers.

Bashan and Carmel wither,
And the flower of Lebanon wilts.
The mountains quake before Him,
The hills melt,
And the earth heaves at His presence,
Yes, the world and all who dwell in it.
(Nah. 1:3–5)

Nahum and the people of Judah depended on God's ability, not their own ability. They knew that God was stronger and bigger than any problem—even the mighty Assyrian empire! With God, they could not fail!

Jesus in Nahum

While there are no direct messianic prophecies in Nahum, the divine attributes in 1:2–8 are consistent with Christ's work as the judge of the nations in His second advent.

Keys to Nahum

Key Word: Nineveh Judged. The great city of Nineveh seemed an invincible stronghold for Assyria. By Nahum's word as a prophet, Nineveh would fall before the Babylonian onslaught, never to be rebuilt. None of the resources of the mighty city would withstand the divine judgment brought at Nahum's word.

Key Verses: "The LORD *is* good, a stronghold in the day of trouble; and He knows those who trust in Him. But with an overflowing flood He will make an utter end of its place, and darkness will pursue His enemies" (1:7, 8).

"Behold, I *am* against you," says the LORD of hosts; "I will lift your skirts over your face, I will show the nations your nakedness, and the kingdoms your shame. I will cast abominable filth upon you, make you vile, and make you a spectacle. It shall come to pass *that* all who look upon you will flee from you, and say, 'Nineveh is laid waste! Who will bemoan her?' Where shall I seek comforters for you?" (3:5, 6).

Key Chapter: Nahum 1. In this chapter, the principles of divine judgment resulting in the decree of Nineveh's fall are recorded. Assyria's arrogance and cruelty have been judged by God, and the great city will fall under God's mighty hand of destruction.

Nahum 1:2–8 portrays the patience, power, holiness and justice of the living God. The God who is slow to wrath settles His accounts in full. This book concerns Nineveh's downfall, but is written for the comfort of the surviving kingdom—Judah (1:15; 2:2).

1 The burden[a] against Nineveh. The book of the vision of Nahum the Elkoshite.

2 God *is* jealous, and the LORD avenges;
The LORD avenges and *is* furious.
The LORD will take vengeance on His adversaries,
And He reserves *wrath* for His enemies;
3 The LORD *is* slow to anger and great in power,
And will not at all acquit *the wicked.*

The LORD has His way
In the whirlwind and in the storm,
And the clouds *are* the dust of His feet.
4 He rebukes the sea and makes it dry,
And dries up all the rivers.
Bashan and Carmel wither,
And the flower of Lebanon wilts.
5 The mountains quake before Him,
The hills melt,
And the earth heaves[a] at His presence,
Yes, the world and all who dwell in it.
6 Who can stand before His indignation?
And who can endure the fierceness of His anger?

His fury is poured out like fire,
And the rocks are thrown down by Him.

7 The LORD *is* good,
A stronghold in the day of trouble;
And He knows those who trust in Him.
8 But with an overflowing flood
He will make an utter end of its place,
And darkness will pursue His enemies.
9 What do you conspire against the LORD?
He will make an utter end *of it.*
Affliction will not rise up a second time.
10 For while tangled *like* thorns,
And while drunken *like* drunkards,
They shall be devoured like stubble fully dried.
11 From you comes forth *one*
Who plots evil against the LORD,
A wicked counselor.

12 Thus says the LORD:

"Though *they are* safe, and likewise many,
Yet in this manner they will be cut down
When he passes through.
Though I have afflicted you,
I will afflict you no more;

1:1 [a]Or *oracle*   1:5 [a]Targum reads *burns.*

13 For now I will break off his
    yoke from you,
    And burst your bonds apart."

14 The LORD has given a command
    concerning you:
    "Your name shall be
    perpetuated no longer.
    Out of the house of your gods
    I will cut off the carved image
    and the molded image.
    I will dig your grave,
    For you are vile."

15 Behold, on the mountains
    The feet of him who brings
    good tidings,
    Who proclaims peace!
    O Judah, keep your appointed
    feasts,
    Perform your vows.
    For the wicked one shall no
    more pass through you;
    He is utterly cut off.

2 He who scatters[a] has come up
    before your face.
    Man the fort!
    Watch the road!
    Strengthen *your* flanks!
    Fortify *your* power mightily.

2 For the LORD will restore the
    excellence of Jacob
    Like the excellence of Israel,
    For the emptiers have emptied
    them out
    And ruined their vine
    branches.

3 The shields of his mighty men
    are made red,
    The valiant men *are* in scarlet.
    The chariots *come* with flaming
    torches
    In the day of his preparation,
    And the spears are
    brandished.[a]

4 The chariots rage in the streets,
    They jostle one another in the
    broad roads;
    They seem like torches,
    They run like lightning.

5 He remembers his nobles;
    They stumble in their walk;
    They make haste to her walls,
    And the defense is prepared.

6 The gates of the rivers are
    opened,
    And the palace is dissolved.

7 It is decreed:[a]
    She shall be led away captive,
    She shall be brought up;
    And her maidservants shall
    lead *her* as with the voice of
    doves,
    Beating their breasts.

8 Though Nineveh of old *was* like
    a pool of water,
    Now they flee away.
    "Halt! Halt!" *they cry;*
    But no one turns back.

9 Take spoil of silver!
    Take spoil of gold!
    There is no end of treasure,
    Or wealth of every desirable
    prize.

10 She is empty, desolate, and
    waste!
    The heart melts, and the knees
    shake;
    Much pain *is* in every side,
    And all their faces are drained
    of color.[a]

11 Where *is* the dwelling of the
    lions,
    And the feeding place of the
    young lions,
    Where the lion walked, the
    lioness *and* lion's cub,
    And no one made *them*
    afraid?

12 The lion tore in pieces enough
    for his cubs,
    Killed for his lionesses,
    Filled his caves with prey,
    And his dens with flesh.

13 "Behold, I *am* against you," says
the LORD of hosts, "I will burn your[a]
chariots in smoke, and the sword
shall devour your young lions; I will
cut off your prey from the earth, and
the voice of your messengers shall
be heard no more."

3 Woe to the bloody city!
    It *is* all full of lies *and* robbery.
    Its victim never departs.

2 The noise of a whip
    And the noise of rattling
    wheels,
    Of galloping horses,
    Of clattering chariots!

2:1 ᵃVulgate reads *he who destroys.*   2:3 ᵃLiterally *the cypresses are shaken;* Septuagint and Syriac
read *the horses rush about;* Vulgate reads *the drivers are stupefied.*   2:7 ᵃHebrew *Huzzab*
2:10 ᵃCompare Joel 2:6   2:13 ᵃLiterally *her*

3 Horsemen charge with
   bright sword and glittering
   spear.
   There is a multitude of slain,
   A great number of bodies,
   Countless corpses—
   They stumble over the
   corpses—
4 Because of the multitude of
   harlotries of the seductive
   harlot,
   The mistress of sorceries,
   Who sells nations through her
   harlotries,
   And families through her
   sorceries.

5 "Behold, I *am* against you," says
   the LORD of hosts;
   "I will lift your skirts over your
   face,
   I will show the nations your
   nakedness,
   And the kingdoms your shame.
6 I will cast abominable filth
   upon you,
   Make you vile,
   And make you a spectacle.
7 It shall come to pass *that* all
   who look upon you
   Will flee from you, and say,
   'Nineveh is laid waste!
   Who will bemoan her?'
   Where shall I seek comforters
   for you?"

8 Are you better than No Amon[a]
   That was situated by the
   River,[b]
   That had the waters around
   her,
   Whose rampart *was* the sea,
   Whose wall *was* the sea?
9 Ethiopia and Egypt *were* her
   strength,
   And *it was* boundless;
   Put and Lubim were your[a]
   helpers.
10 Yet she *was* carried away,
   She went into captivity;
   Her young children also were
   dashed to pieces
   At the head of every street;
   They cast lots for her
   honorable men,
   And all her great men were
   bound in chains.
11 You also will be drunk;
   You will be hidden;

   You also will seek refuge from
   the enemy.
12 All your strongholds *are* fig
   trees with ripened figs:
   If they are shaken,
   They fall into the mouth of the
   eater.
13 Surely, your people in your
   midst *are* women!
   The gates of your land are wide
   open for your enemies;
   Fire shall devour the bars of
   your *gates.*

14 Draw your water for the siege!
   Fortify your strongholds!
   Go into the clay and tread the
   mortar!
   Make strong the brick kiln!
15 There the fire will devour you,
   The sword will cut you off;
   It will eat you up like a locust.

   Make yourself many—like the
   locust!
   Make yourself many—like the
   swarming locusts!
16 You have multiplied your
   merchants more than the
   stars of heaven.
   The locust plunders and flies
   away.
17 Your commanders *are* like
   swarming locusts,
   And your generals like great
   grasshoppers,
   Which camp in the hedges on
   a cold day;
   When the sun rises they flee
   away,
   And the place where they *are*
   is not known.

18 Your shepherds slumber, O
   king of Assyria;
   Your nobles rest *in the dust.*
   Your people are scattered on
   the mountains,
   And no one gathers them.
19 Your injury *has* no healing,
   Your wound is severe.
   All who hear news of you
   Will clap *their* hands over
   you,
   For upon whom has not your
   wickedness passed
   continually?

3:8 [a]That is, ancient Thebes; Targum and Vulgate read *populous Alexandria.*   [b]Literally *rivers,* that is, the Nile and the surrounding canals   3:9 [a]Septuagint reads *her.*

Habakkuk

Overview of Habakkuk

Tough times never last but tough people do! Habakkuk continually trusted God in the face of all adversity.

The Book of Habakkuk concerns a message of invasion as told by Habakkuk, or "one who embraces," to the people of Judah between 609 to 597 B.C. A contemporary of Zephaniah and Jeremiah, Habakkuk was called by God to forewarn the people of coming destruction by the Chaldeans.

Although he was the bearer of bad news, Habakkuk said that in any generation, "the just shall live by his faith" (Hab. 2:4). This particular verse is quoted three times in the New Testament as one of the great promises of God. The positively oriented personality derives its strength from faith and can stand in confidence and can trust in God while facing tough times.

Habakkuk placed his trust in God, despite not totally understanding the reasons for and outcome of the situation of Judah's destruction. This prophet is not afraid to talk about the tough issues with his God, yet with the heart of a psalmist, he praises God in all circumstances. Without food, and with isolation, Habakkuk is sustained by faith and God's faithfulness.

> Yet I will rejoice in the LORD,
> I will joy in the God of my salvation.
> The LORD God is my strength;
> He will make my feet like deer's feet,
> And He will make me walk on my high hills.
> (Hab. 3:18, 19)

Set in a dialogue with God, Habakkuk learns to take his problems to God, and to learn more of God's person, power and plan. Then he knows he can trust the Lord, no matter what God brings to pass. He ends the book praising God and acknowledging His wisdom.

Jesus in Habakkuk

The word salvation appears three times in 3:13, 18 and is the root word from which the name Jesus is derived (cf. Matt. 1:21). When He comes again, "the earth will be filled with the knowledge of the glory of the LORD, as the waters cover the sea" (2:14).

Keys to Habakkuk

Key Word: "The Just Shall Live by His Faith." This book is about Habakkuk's struggles within himself as he sees men flagrantly violating God's law. He wants to know why they remain unpunished. God answers that the coming storm of fierce Babylonian troops will be God's chosen instrument to punish sinful Judah. Habakkuk has questions when God reveals His choice of a more wicked country as a rod for Judah's punishment. God answers Habakkuk's reasoning with His wisdom, and calls Habakkuk to trust Him.

Key Verses: "Behold the proud, his soul is not upright in him; but the just shall live by his faith" (2:4).

"Though the fig tree may not blossom, nor fruit be on the vines; though the labor of the olive may fail, and the fields yield no food; though the flock may be cut off from the fold, and there be no herd in the stalls—yet I will rejoice in the LORD, I will joy in the God of my salvation (3:17–18).

Key Chapter: Habakkuk 3. This chapter is a triumphant climax to this book. The first and second chapters contrast each other. They reveal mystery rather than certainty, and complaining questions over the affirmation of confidence. Poetic and gracious, chapter three sings the praises of a constant Creator, showing His glory in history and in the future.

1 The burden[a] which the prophet Habakkuk saw.

2 O LORD, how long shall I cry,
And You will not hear?
Even cry out to You,
    "Violence!"
And You will not save.
3 Why do You show me iniquity,
And cause *me* to see trouble?
For plundering and violence
    are before me;
There is strife, and contention
    arises.
4 Therefore the law is powerless,
And justice never goes forth.
For the wicked surround the
    righteous;
Therefore perverse judgment
    proceeds.

5 "Look among the nations and
    watch—
Be utterly astounded!
For *I will* work a work in your
    days
Which you would not believe,
    though it were told *you.*
6 For indeed I am raising up the
    Chaldeans,
A bitter and hasty nation
Which marches through the
    breadth of the earth,
To possess dwelling places
    that are not theirs.
7 They are terrible and dreadful;
Their judgment and their
    dignity proceed from
    themselves.
8 Their horses also are swifter
    than leopards,
And more fierce than evening
    wolves.
Their chargers charge ahead;
Their cavalry comes from afar;
They fly as the eagle *that*
    hastens to eat.

9 "They all come for violence;
Their faces are set *like* the east
    wind.
They gather captives like sand.
10 They scoff at kings,
And princes are scorned by
    them.
They deride every stronghold,

For they heap up earthen
    mounds and seize it.
11 Then *his* mind[a] changes, and he
    transgresses;
He commits offense,
Ascribing this power to his
    god."

12 Are You not from everlasting,
O LORD my God, my Holy
    One?
We shall not die.
O LORD, You have appointed
    them for judgment;
O Rock, You have marked
    them for correction.
13 *You are* of purer eyes than to
    behold evil,
And cannot look on
    wickedness.
Why do You look on those who
    deal treacherously,
And hold Your tongue when
    the wicked devours
A *person* more righteous than
    he?
14 *Why* do You make men like
    fish of the sea,
Like creeping things *that have*
    no ruler over them?

15 They take up all of them with
    a hook,
They catch them in their net,
And gather them in their
    dragnet.
Therefore they rejoice and are
    glad.
16 Therefore they sacrifice to their
    net,
And burn incense to their
    dragnet;
Because by them their share *is*
    sumptuous
And their food plentiful.
17 Shall they therefore empty
    their net,
And continue to slay nations
    without pity?

2 I will stand my watch
And set myself on the rampart,
And watch to see what He will
    say to me,
And what I will answer when
    I am corrected.

1:1 *a*Or *oracle*   1:11 *a*Literally *spirit* or *wind*

Pursue Your Vision

If I asked you to draw a picture, how would you go about it? You'd probably reach for a blank piece of paper and some pencils or crayons. Or you'd reach for a canvas, with oil paints and brushes.

I am no artist, but I can teach you how to draw pictures in the mind. Your mind is the canvas. Your willpower is the brush. Your thoughts are the oils and colors. Within your mind is an incredible assortment of colors; every idea is a potential color! Begin to "see" ideas in "color." Ideas that are happy can be colored red, yellow. Depressing thoughts? Color them gray. Angry thoughts? Color them black. Loving thoughts? Color them blue. Forward moving, growth ideas? Color them green!

Today choose to become an artist with ideas. No training is necessary. God gives gifts of imagination—your thoughts. Now use your creativity to draw the mental image of the dream accomplished. See the finished project in the mind.

> The me I see is the me I'll be.
> If I cannot see it, I will never be it.
> Until I believe it, I will never achieve it!

It may be helpful to you to actually take out a blank piece of paper and draw a picture of what you want to accomplish. Sketches on paper plant images on the brain. The subconscious, like a roll of undeveloped film, picks up the image and the picture is drawn. And at this very moment faith moves into a motivational phase. Energy and enthusiasm begin to be released.

Have fun! Become an artist with ideas.

O God, give me a vision, a mental picture of the person you want me to be, the project you want me to pursue, the objectives you want me to manage toward actualization. I open my mind like a screen to the Holy Spirit. I will paint the pictures within my imagination now. Thank You, God. Amen.

2 Then the LORD answered me and said:

"Write the vision
And make *it* plain on tablets,
That he may run who reads it.
3   For the vision *is* yet for an
      appointed time;
But at the end it will speak, and
      it will not lie.
Though it tarries, wait for it;
Because it will surely come,
It will not tarry.

4   "Behold the proud,
His soul is not upright in him;
But the just shall live by his
      faith.

5   "Indeed, because he
      transgresses by wine,
He is a proud man,
And he does not stay at home.
Because he enlarges his desire
      as hell,*a*
And he *is* like death, and
      cannot be satisfied,
He gathers to himself all
      nations
And heaps up for himself all
      peoples.

6   "Will not all these take up a
      proverb against him,
And a taunting riddle against
      him, and say,
'Woe to him who increases
What is not his—how long?
And to him who loads himself
      with many pledges'?*a*
7   Will not your creditors*a* rise up
      suddenly?
Will they not awaken who
      oppress you?
And you will become their
      booty.
8   Because you have plundered
      many nations,
All the remnant of the people
      shall plunder you,
Because of men's blood
And the violence of the land
      and the city,
And of all who dwell in it.

9   "Woe to him who covets evil
      gain for his house,

That he may set his nest on
      high,
That he may be delivered from
      the power of disaster!
10   You give shameful counsel to
      your house,
Cutting off many peoples,
And sin *against* your soul.
11   For the stone will cry out from
      the wall,
And the beam from the timbers
      will answer it.

12   "Woe to him who builds a town
      with bloodshed,
Who establishes a city by
      iniquity!
13   Behold, *is it* not of the LORD of
      hosts
That the peoples labor to feed
      the fire,*a*
And nations weary themselves
      in vain?
14   For the earth will be filled
With the knowledge of the
      glory of the LORD,
As the waters cover the sea.

15   "Woe to him who gives drink to
      his neighbor,
Pressing*a* *him* to your bottle,
Even to make *him* drunk,
That you may look on his
      nakedness!
16   You are filled with shame
      instead of glory.
You also—drink!
And be exposed as
      uncircumcised!*a*
The cup of the LORD's right
      hand *will be* turned against
      you,
And utter shame will be on
      your glory.
17   For the violence *done to*
      Lebanon will cover you,
And the plunder of beasts
      which made them afraid,
Because of men's blood
And the violence of the land
      and the city,
And of all who dwell in it.

18   "What profit is the image, that
      its maker should carve it,
The molded image, a teacher of
      lies,

2:5 *a*Or *Sheol*   2:6 *a*Syriac and Vulgate read *thick clay.*   2:7 *a*Literally *those who bite you*
2:13 *a*Literally *for what satisfies fire,* that is, for what is of no lasting value   2:15 *a*Literally *Attaching* or
Joining   2:16 *a*Dead Sea Scrolls and Septuagint read *And reel!;* Syriac and Vulgate read *And fall fast
asleep!*

That the maker of its mold
    should trust in it,
To make mute idols?
19 Woe to him who says to wood,
    'Awake!'
To silent stone, 'Arise! It shall
    teach!'
Behold, it is overlaid with gold
    and silver,
Yet in it there is no breath at
    all.

20 "But the LORD is in His holy
    temple.
Let all the earth keep silence
    before Him."

3 A prayer of Habakkuk the
prophet, on Shigionoth.ᵃ

2 O LORD, I have heard your
    speech *and* was afraid;
O LORD, revive Your work in
    the midst of the years!
In the midst of the years make
    it known;
In wrath remember mercy.

3 God came from Teman,
The Holy One from Mount
    Paran.   Selah

His glory covered the heavens,
And the earth was full of His
    praise.
4 *His* brightness was like the
    light;
He had rays *flashing* from His
    hand,
And there His power *was*
    hidden.
5 Before Him went pestilence,
And fever followed at His
    feet.

6 He stood and measured the
    earth;
He looked and startled the
    nations.
And the everlasting mountains
    were scattered,
The perpetual hills bowed.
His ways *are* everlasting.
7 I saw the tents of Cushan in
    affliction;
The curtains of the land of
    Midian trembled.

8 O LORD, were *You* displeased
    with the rivers,

Was Your anger against the
    rivers,
Was Your wrath against the
    sea,
That You rode on Your horses,
Your chariots of salvation?
9 Your bow was made quite
    ready;
Oaths were sworn over *Your*
    arrows.ᵃ   Selah

You divided the earth with
    rivers.
10 The mountains saw You *and*
    trembled;
The overflowing of the water
    passed by.
The deep uttered its voice,
And lifted its hands on high.
11 The sun and moon stood still
    in their habitation;
At the light of Your arrows
    they went,
At the shining of Your
    glittering spear.
12 You marched through the land
    in indignation;
You trampled the nations in
    anger.
13 You went forth for the
    salvation of Your people,
For salvation with Your
    Anointed.
You struck the head from the
    house of the wicked,
By laying bare from foundation
    to neck.   Selah

14 You thrust through with his
    own arrows
The head of his villages.
They came out like a whirlwind
    to scatter me;
Their rejoicing was like
    feasting on the poor in secret.
15 You walked through the sea
    with Your horses,
Through the heap of great
    waters.

16 When I heard, my body
    trembled;
My lips quivered at *the* voice;
Rottenness entered my bones;
And I trembled in myself,
That I might rest in the day of
    trouble.
When he comes up to the
    people,

3:1 ᵃExact meaning unknown   3:9 ᵃLiterally *rods* or *tribes* (compare verse 14)

He will invade them with his troops.

17 Though the fig tree may not blossom,
Nor fruit be on the vines;
Though the labor of the olive may fail,
And the fields yield no food;
Though the flock may be cut off from the fold,
And there be no herd in the stalls—

18 Yet I will rejoice in the LORD,
I will joy in the God of my salvation.

19 The LORD God[a] is my strength;
He will make my feet like deer's *feet*,
And He will make me walk on my high hills.

To the Chief Musician. With my stringed instruments.

3:19 *a*Hebrew *YHWH Adonai*

Zephaniah

Overview of Zephaniah

Although the Book of Zephaniah describes the destruction of Judah, Philistia, Moab, Ammon, Ethiopia, and Assyria by the mighty nation of Babylon, the underlying theme is God's gracious ability and power to heal these nations' wounds.

Zephaniah was written by the prophet whose name means "Hidden by Yahweh" between 640 and 612 B.C. Only three chapters long, Zephaniah points to a positive future for all nations who turn to God. Zephaniah was confident that through the coming disaster, those who would remain true to God would stand firm and receive God's goodness. In asking them to seek God, Zephaniah assured the nations that no one was too far from God's love, no nation was too small for His power!

Powerful promises dominate the close of the book, telling the people to respond positively to God's unending love:

"The LORD your God in your midst,
The Mighty One, will save;
He will rejoice over you with gladness,

> *He will quiet you with His love,*
> *He will rejoice over you with singing."*
> *"At that time I will bring you back,*
> *Even at the time I gather you;*
> *For I will give you fame and praise*
> *Among all the peoples of the earth,*
> *When I return your captives before your eyes,"*
> *Says the LORD.*
>
> (Zeph. 3:17, 20)

God has the power to save and restore the nations to Himself. Zephaniah encourages them to focus on their prospects, not their problems! Their opportunities, not their obstacles! Their future, not their failures!

Jesus in Zephaniah

Jesus alluded to the prophet Zephaniah two times (Matt. 13:41; Matt. 24:29). Both of these passages refer to the second coming of Christ. Although the Messiah is not specifically mentioned in this book, it is clear He fulfills the great promises of 3:9–20. He will gather His people and reign in victory: "The LORD has taken away your judgments, He has cast out your enemy. The King of Israel, the LORD, *is* in your midst; you shall see disaster no more" (3:15).

Keys to Zephaniah

Key Word: The Day of the Lord. No one escapes from God's authority and dominion. The Day of the Lord will have universal impact when God calls the nations to account in His presence. To some degree, the day has already come for Judah and all the nations mentioned (2:4–15), but there is a future day when all the earth will be judged. Zephaniah 3:9–20 says that day will also be a day of blessing after judgment is through. A righteous remnant will survive and all who call upon God, Jew or Gentile, will be blessed.

God will regather and restore His people, and the world will rejoice.

Key Verses: "The great day of the LORD *is* near; *it is* near and hastens quickly. The noise of the day of the LORD is bitter; there the mighty men shall cry out. That day *is* a day of wrath, a day of trouble and distress, a day of devastation and desolation, a day of darkness and gloominess, a day of clouds and thick darkness" (1:14–15).

"Seek the LORD, all you meek of the earth, who have upheld His justice. Seek righteousness, seek humility. It may be that you will be hidden in the day of the LORD's anger" (2:3).

Key Chapter: Zephaniah 3. The last chapter of the book records the two distinct parts of the day of the Lord: judgment and restoration. Following the conversion of the nation, Israel is finally fully restored. Under the righteous rule of God, Israel fully inherits the blessings contained in the biblical covenants.

1 The word of the LORD which came to Zephaniah the son of Cushi, the son of Gedaliah, the son of Amariah, the son of Hezekiah, in the days of Josiah the son of Amon, king of Judah.

2 "I will utterly consume everything
From the face of the land,"
Says the LORD;
3 "I will consume man and beast;
I will consume the birds of the heavens,
The fish of the sea,
And the stumbling blocks*a*
along with the wicked.
I will cut off man from the face of the land,"
Says the LORD.

4 "I will stretch out My hand against Judah,
And against all the inhabitants of Jerusalem.
I will cut off every trace of Baal from this place,
The names of the idolatrous priests*a* with the *pagan* priests—
5 Those who worship the host of heaven on the housetops;
Those who worship and swear *oaths* by the LORD,

But who *also* swear by Milcom;*a*
6 Those who have turned back from *following* the LORD,
And have not sought the LORD, nor inquired of Him."

7 Be silent in the presence of the Lord GOD;
For the day of the LORD *is* at hand,
For the LORD has prepared a sacrifice;
He has invited*a* His guests.

8 "And it shall be,
In the day of the LORD's sacrifice,
That I will punish the princes and the king's children,
And all such as are clothed with foreign apparel.
9 In the same day I will punish
All those who leap over the threshold,*a*
Who fill their masters' houses with violence and deceit.

10 "And there shall be on that day," says the LORD,
"The sound of a mournful cry from the Fish Gate,
A wailing from the Second Quarter,

1:3 *a*Figurative of idols   1:4 *a*Hebrew *chemarim* (compare Leviticus 18:21)   1:5 *a*Or *Malcam,* an Ammonite god, also called *Molech*   1:7 *a*Literally *set apart, consecrated*   1:9 *a*Compare 1 Samuel 5:5

And a loud crashing from the hills.

11 Wail, you inhabitants of
Maktesh![a]
For all the merchant people are
cut down;
All those who handle money
are cut off.

12 "And it shall come to pass at that
time
That I will search Jerusalem
with lamps,
And punish the men
Who are settled in
complacency,[a]
Who say in their heart,
'The LORD will not do good,
Nor will He do evil.'

13 Therefore their goods shall
become booty,
And their houses a desolation;
They shall build houses, but not
inhabit *them;*
They shall plant vineyards, but
not drink their wine."

14 The great day of the LORD *is*
near;
It is near and hastens quickly.
The noise of the day of the
LORD is bitter;
There the mighty men shall cry
out.

15 That day *is* a day of wrath,
A day of trouble and distress,
A day of devastation and
desolation,
A day of darkness and
gloominess,
A day of clouds and thick
darkness,

16 A day of trumpet and alarm
Against the fortified cities
And against the high towers.

17 "I will bring distress upon men,
And they shall walk like blind
men,
Because they have sinned
against the LORD;
Their blood shall be poured out
like dust,
And their flesh like refuse."

18 Neither their silver nor their
gold
Shall be able to deliver them
In the day of the LORD's wrath;

But the whole land shall be
devoured
By the fire of His jealousy,
For He will make speedy
riddance
Of all those who dwell in the
land.

2 Gather yourselves together,
yes, gather together,
O undesirable[a] nation,

2 Before the decree is issued,
Or the day passes like chaff,
Before the LORD's fierce anger
comes upon you,
Before the day of the LORD's
anger comes upon you!

3 Seek the LORD, all you meek of
the earth,
Who have upheld His justice.
Seek righteousness, seek
humility.
It may be that you will be
hidden
In the day of the LORD's anger.

4 For Gaza shall be forsaken,
And Ashkelon desolate;
They shall drive out Ashdod at
noonday,
And Ekron shall be uprooted.

5 Woe to the inhabitants of the
seacoast,
The nation of the Cherethites!
The word of the LORD *is* against
you,
O Canaan, land of the
Philistines:
"I will destroy you;
So there shall be no
inhabitant."

6 The seacoast shall be pastures,
With shelters[a] for shepherds
and folds for flocks.

7 The coast shall be for the
remnant of the house of
Judah;
They shall feed *their* flocks
there;
In the houses of Ashkelon they
shall lie down at evening.
For the LORD their God will
intervene for them,
And return their captives.

8 "I have heard the reproach of
Moab,
And the insults of the people of
Ammon,

1:11 [a]Literally *Mortar,* a market district of Jerusalem   1:12 [a]Literally *on their lees,* that is, settled like the
dregs of wine   2:1 [a]Or *shameless*   2:6 [a]Literally *excavations,* either underground huts or cisterns

With which they have
  reproached My people,
And made arrogant threats
  against their borders.
9 Therefore, as I live,"
Says the LORD of hosts, the God
  of Israel,
  "Surely Moab shall be like
    Sodom,
And the people of Ammon like
  Gomorrah—
Overrun with weeds and
  saltpits,
And a perpetual desolation.
The residue of My people shall
  plunder them,
And the remnant of My people
  shall possess them."

10 This they shall have for their
  pride,
Because they have reproached
  and made arrogant threats
Against the people of the LORD
  of hosts.
11 The LORD *will be* awesome to
  them,
For He will reduce to nothing
  all the gods of the earth;
People shall worship Him,
Each one from his place,
Indeed all the shores of the
  nations.

12 "You Ethiopians also,
You shall be slain by My
  sword."

13 And He will stretch out His
  hand against the north,
Destroy Assyria,
And make Nineveh a
  desolation,
As dry as the wilderness.
14 The herds shall lie down in her
  midst,
Every beast of the nation.
Both the pelican and the
  bittern
Shall lodge on the capitals *of*
  her *pillars;*
Their voice shall sing in the
  windows;
Desolation *shall be* at the
  threshold;
For He will lay bare the cedar
  work.
15 This is the rejoicing city
That dwelt securely,

That said in her heart,
  "I *am it,* and *there is* none
    besides me."
How has she become a
  desolation,
A place for beasts to lie down!
Everyone who passes by her
Shall hiss and shake his fist.

3 Woe to her who is rebellious
  and polluted,
To the oppressing city!
2 She has not obeyed *His* voice,
She has not received
  correction;
She has not trusted in the LORD,
She has not drawn near to her
  God.

3 Her princes in her midst *are*
  roaring lions;
Her judges *are* evening wolves
That leave not a bone till
  morning.
4 Her prophets are insolent,
  treacherous people;
Her priests have polluted the
  sanctuary,
They have done violence to the
  law.
5 The LORD *is* righteous in her
  midst,
He will do no unrighteousness.
Every morning He brings His
  justice to light;
He never fails,
But the unjust knows no
  shame.

6 "I have cut off nations,
Their fortresses are devastated;
I have made their streets
  desolate,
With none passing by.
Their cities are destroyed;
There is no one, no inhabitant.
7 I said, 'Surely you will fear Me,
You will receive instruction'—
So that her dwelling would not
  be cut off,
Despite everything for which I
  punished her.
But they rose early and
  corrupted all their deeds.

8 "Therefore wait for Me," says
  the LORD,
"Until the day I rise up for
  plunder;*a*

3:8 *a*Septuagint and Syriac read *for witness;* Targum reads *for the day of My revelation for judgment;*
Vulgate reads *for the day of My resurrection that is to come.*

Affirm Your Faith

Just as the people of Israel were to trust God fearlessly and joyfully (Zeph. 3:13, 14), so should we.

Deliberately exercise your faith in these ways:

Trust that God has inspired you to begin and that He will surely guide you.
Thank God—today—that He has a plan for your life.
Seek and serve God's will.
Walk the walk of faith.
Think God's thoughts.
Set goals.
Chart a course.
Believe that you will succeed.
Discipline your mind to weed out negative thoughts.
Reject all thoughts of discouragement.
See yourself making steady progress.
Base your ultimate success on the character of God.
God never starts a project and abandons it!
God is no quitter. He is a finisher!

God gave you a dream; motivated you to set a goal; and He will keep stimulating you to succeed. Keep on believing in success, knowing that success is inevitable as long as you focus your belief on eventual success.

Determine to make your life an exclamation mark! Surely God wants you to be successful. He certainly does not dream up plans for people to fail at! Because you are responsible for your life, decide to succeed. Believe you will make it.

Remember the promise found in Philippians 1:6: God, who has begun a good work in you, will complete it!

My determination *is* to gather
  the nations
To My assembly of kingdoms,
To pour on them My
  indignation,
All my fierce anger;
All the earth shall be devoured
With the fire of My jealousy.

9 "For then I will restore to the
    peoples a pure language,
  That they all may call on the
    name of the Lord,
  To serve Him with one
    accord.
10 From beyond the rivers of
    Ethiopia
  My worshipers,
  The daughter of My dispersed
    ones,
  Shall bring My offering.
11 In that day you shall not be
    shamed for any of your deeds
  In which you transgress
    against Me;
  For then I will take away from
    your midst
  Those who rejoice in your
    pride,
  And you shall no longer be
    haughty
  In My holy mountain.
12 I will leave in your midst
  A meek and humble people,
  And they shall trust in the
    name of the Lord.
13 The remnant of Israel shall do
    no unrighteousness
  And speak no lies,
  Nor shall a deceitful tongue be
    found in their mouth;
  For they shall feed *their* flocks
    and lie down,
  And no one shall make *them*
    afraid."

14 Sing, O daughter of Zion!
  Shout, O Israel!
  Be glad and rejoice with all
    your heart,

O daughter of Jerusalem!
15 The Lord has taken away your
    judgments,
  He has cast out your enemy.
  The King of Israel, the Lord, *is*
    in your midst;
  You shall see[a] disaster no
    more.

16 In that day it shall be said to
    Jerusalem:
  "Do not fear;
  Zion, let not your hands be
    weak.
17 The Lord your God in your
    midst,
  The Mighty One, will save;
  He will rejoice over you with
    gladness,
  He will quiet *you* with His
    love,
  He will rejoice over you with
    singing."

18 "I will gather those who sorrow
    over the appointed assembly,
  Who are among you,
  To whom its reproach *is* a
    burden.
19 Behold, at that time
  I will deal with all who afflict
    you;
  I will save the lame,
  And gather those who were
    driven out;
  I will appoint them for praise
    and fame
  In every land where they were
    put to shame.
20 At that time I will bring you
    back,
  Even at the time I gather
    you;
  For I will give you fame and
    praise
  Among all the peoples of the
    earth,
  When I return your captives
    before your eyes,"
  Says the Lord.

3:15 [a]Some Hebrew manuscripts, Septuagint, and Bomberg read *see;* Masoretic Text and Vulgate read *fear.*

Haggai

Overview of Haggai

Haggai is a poignant, hard-hitting book to encourage people to get started and never quit! Written after Israel's return from exile in Babylon in 520 B.C., Haggai motivated the people to believe in themselves and to undertake the task of rebuilding the temple in Jerusalem. Although Haggai was very old, about eighty, he was strong enough to rally the people behind him.

Haggai was faced with innumerable naysayers who imagined every excuse possible not to build the temple. They said they must wait for "the right time" to begin, for the necessary funds, and for the large number of people and material needed for the task. Haggai, being elderly, may have seen Solomon's temple in all its glory before its destruction. For he had a vision of what they could do with their time, talents, and ability—if they only applied themselves.

Haggai told the people that they did not have a material problem, they had a motivational problem. They did not have a money problem, they had an idea problem. They only needed to do two things to be successful. Get started. And never quit!

Postponing tough decisions is the direct result of a lack of faith. All types of obstacles had led the Israelites to a place of pessimism and spiritual lethargy. Haggai's prophecy shook them from their preoccupation with building their own houses to refocus on building God's house.

Jesus in Haggai

The role of the second temple in God's redemptive plan is foretold in Haggai 2:9. Herod the Great spent a fortune on the temple's refurnishing and improvement. Every time Christ came into the temple, God's incarnate glory filled the place.

Christ is also portrayed in the person of Zerubbabel: "I will take you, Zerubbabel . . . and will make you like a signet ring; for I have chosen you" (2:23). Zerubbabel becomes the center of the messianic line and is like a signet ring, sealing both branches together.

Keys to Haggai

Key Word: Reconstruction. Haggai's basic theme is clear: the remnant of God must reorder its priorities and complete the temple before God can bless their efforts. The people must discover that their hardships are divinely given symptoms of their spiritual disease. When they place God first, Haggai says, He will bring joy and prosperity to His people.

Key Verses: "Thus says the LORD of hosts: 'Consider your ways! Go up to the mountains and bring wood and build the temple, that I may take pleasure in it and be glorified,' says the LORD" (1:7, 8).

"' And I will shake all nations, and they shall come to the Desire of All Nations, and I will fill this temple with glory,' says the LORD of hosts. 'The silver *is* Mine, and the gold *is* Mine,' says the LORD of hosts. 'The glory of this latter temple shall be greater than the former,' says the LORD of hosts. 'And in this place I will give peace,' says the LORD of hosts" (2:7–9).

Key Chapter: Haggai 2. Verses 6–9 record some of the most startling prophecies in Scripture: "I will shake heaven and earth, the sea and dry land" and "they shall come to the Desire of All Nations" and "in this place I will give peace."

1 In the second year of King Darius, in the sixth month, on the first day of the month, the word of the LORD came by Haggai the prophet to Zerubbabel the son of Shealtiel, governor of Judah, and to Joshua the son of Jehozadak, the high priest, saying, 2 "Thus speaks the LORD of hosts, saying: 'This people says, "The time has not come, the time that the LORD's house should be built." ' "

3 Then the word of the LORD came by Haggai the prophet, saying, 4 "Is it time for you yourselves to dwell in your paneled houses, and this temple[a] to lie in ruins?" 5 Now therefore, thus says the LORD of hosts: "Consider your ways!

6   "You have sown much, and
       bring in little;
     You eat, but do not have
       enough;
     You drink, but you are not
       filled with drink;
     You clothe yourselves, but no
       one is warm;
     And he who earns wages,
     Earns wages to put into a bag
       with holes."

7 Thus says the LORD of hosts: "Consider your ways! 8 Go up to the mountains and bring wood and build the temple, that I may take pleasure in it and be glorified," says the LORD. 9 "You looked for much, but indeed it came to little; and when you brought it home, I blew it away. Why?" says the LORD of hosts. "Because of My house that is in ruins, while every one of you runs to his own house. 10 Therefore the heavens above you withhold the dew, and the earth withholds its fruit. 11 For I called for a drought on the land and the mountains, on the grain and the new wine and the oil, on whatever the ground brings forth, on men and livestock, and on all the labor of your hands."

12 Then Zerubbabel the son of Shealtiel, and Joshua the son of Jehozadak, the high priest, with all the remnant of the people, obeyed the voice of the LORD their God, and the words of Haggai the prophet, as the LORD their God had sent him; and the people feared the presence of the LORD. 13 Then Haggai, the LORD's messenger, spoke the LORD's message to the people, saying, "I am with you, says the LORD." 14 So the LORD stirred up the spirit of Zerubbabel the son of Shealtiel, governor of Judah, and the spirit of Joshua the son of Jehozadak, the high priest, and the spirit of all the remnant of the people; and they came and worked on the house of the LORD of hosts, their God, 15 on the twenty-fourth day of the sixth month, in the second year of King Darius.

2 In the seventh month, on the twenty-first of the month, the word of the LORD came by Haggai the prophet, saying: 2 "Speak now to Zerubbabel the son of Shealtiel, governor of Judah, and to Joshua the son of Jehozadak, the high priest, and to the remnant of the people, saying: 3 'Who is left among you who saw this temple[a] in its former glory? And how do you see it now? In comparison with it, is this not in your eyes as nothing? 4 Yet now be strong, Zerubbabel,' says the LORD; 'and be strong, Joshua, son of Jehozadak, the high priest; and be strong, all you people of the land,' says the LORD, 'and work; for I am with you,' says the LORD of hosts. 5 'According to the word that I covenanted with you when you came out of Egypt, so My Spirit remains among you; do not fear!'

6 "For thus says the LORD of hosts: 'Once more (it is a little while) I will shake heaven and earth, the sea and dry land; 7 and I will shake all nations, and they shall come to the Desire of All Nations,[a] and I will fill this temple with glory,' says the LORD of hosts. 8 'The silver is Mine, and the gold is Mine,' says the LORD of hosts. 9 'The glory of this latter temple shall be greater than the former,' says the LORD of hosts. 'And in this place I

1:4 [a]Literally house, and so in verse 8   2:3 [a]Literally house, and so in verses 7 and 9   2:7 [a]Or the desire of all nations will give peace,' says the Lord of hosts."

10 On the twenty-fourth *day* of the ninth *month,* in the second year of Darius, the word of the Lord came by Haggai the prophet, saying, 11 "Thus says the Lord of hosts: 'Now, ask the priests *concerning the law,* saying, 12 "If one carries holy meat in the fold of his garment, and with the edge he touches bread or stew, wine or oil, or any food, will it become holy?" ' "

Then the priests answered and said, "No."

13 And Haggai said, "If *one who is* unclean *because* of a dead body touches any of these, will it be unclean?"

So the priests answered and said, "It shall be unclean."

14 Then Haggai answered and said, " 'So is this people, and so is this nation before Me,' says the Lord, 'and so is every work of their hands; and what they offer there is unclean.

15 'And now, carefully consider from this day forward: from before stone was laid upon stone in the temple of the Lord— 16 since those *days,* when *one* came to a heap of twenty ephahs, there were *but* ten; when *one* came to the wine vat to draw out fifty baths from the press, there were *but* twenty. 17 I struck you with blight and mildew and hail in all the labors of your hands; yet you did not *turn* to Me,' says the Lord. 18 'Consider now from this day forward, from the twenty-fourth day of the ninth month, from the day that the foundation of the Lord's temple was laid— consider it: 19 Is the seed still in the barn? As yet the vine, the fig tree, the pomegranate, and the olive tree have not yielded *fruit. But* from this day I will bless *you.* ' "

20 And again the word of the Lord came to Haggai on the twenty-fourth day of the month, saying, 21 "Speak to Zerubbabel, governor of Judah, saying:

'I will shake heaven and
  earth.
22 I will overthrow the throne of
  kingdoms;
I will destroy the strength of
  the Gentile kingdoms.
I will overthrow the chariots
And those who ride in them;
The horses and their riders
  shall come down,
Every one by the sword of his
  brother.

23 'In that day,' says the Lord of hosts, 'I will take you, Zerubbabel My servant, the son of Shealtiel,' says the Lord, 'and will make you like a signet *ring;* for I have chosen you,' says the Lord of hosts.' "

Zechariah

Overview of Zechariah

Zechariah has been relevant to people during every age. The prophet wrote the book, at least the first eight chapters, as a very young man in the years 520 to 518 B.C. Zechariah continued the message of the earlier prophet Haggai. He encouraged the people of Israel to complete the temple of God. His message supplemented Haggai's by urging the people to build up the spiritual quality of their lives. Zechariah also inspired a proper attitude in worship.

Through a series of God-given visions, Zechariah extends the people's perspective to look beyond their present circumstances to the future. Zechariah reminded them that God had a plan for their future in the coming of the Messiah. God promised to work miraculous events for His people.

Having just returned from years of Babylonian captivity, it was difficult for the Israelites to feel secure in establishing long-term goals. Zechariah gave the people hope and vision to trust and see a bright future as they planned ahead. This enabled them to complete the temple and to develop a positive, worshipful attitude toward God.

> For the seed shall be *prosperous*,
> The vine shall give its fruit,
> The ground shall give her increase,
> And the heavens shall give their dew—
> I will cause the remnant of this people
> To possess all these.
> And it shall come to pass
> That *just as you were a curse among the nations*,
> O house of Judah and house of Israel,
> So I will save you, and you shall be a blessing.
> Do not fear,
> Let your hands be strong.
> (Zech. 8:12, 13)

Zechariah taught the people that though they did not know what the future held, they knew the God who held the future.

Jesus in Zechariah

Very clear messianic passages abound in this book: Christ is shown in His two advents as both Servant and King, Man and God. Jesus is anticipated as: the angel of the Lord (3:1, 2), the righteous Branch (3:8; 6:12, 13); the stone with seven eyes (3:9); the King-Priest (6:13); the humble King (9:9, 10); the cornerstone, tent peg, and battle bow (10:4); the good Shepherd rejected and sold for thirty shekels of silver, the price of a slave (11:4–13); the pierced one (12:10); the cleansing fountain (13:1); the smitten Shepherd who is abandoned (13:7); and the coming Judge and righteous King (14).

Keys to Zechariah

Key Word: Prepare. The first eight chapters frequently allude to the temple and its completion. As they build the temple, they are building their future, because the Messiah will use this structure when He brings salvation. Zechariah affirms God's faithfulness to Israel and the covenants He has made with her. This book outlines God's program for His people during the times of the Gentiles until Jesus returns to deliver Israel and reign over all. This book also promotes spiritual revival.

Key Verses: "Thus says the LORD: 'I will return to Zion, and dwell in the midst of Jerusalem. Jerusalem shall be called the City of Truth, the Mountain of the LORD of hosts, the Holy Mountain'" (8:3).

"Rejoice greatly, O daughter of Zion! Shout, O daughter of Jerusalem! Behold, your King is coming to you; He *is* just and having salvation, lowly and riding on a donkey, a colt, the foal of a donkey" (9:9).

Key Chapter: Zechariah 14. The book builds to a climactic finish in this chapter when Zechariah discloses the last siege of Jerusalem, the initial victory over the enemies of Israel, the cleaving of the Mount of Olives, the Lord's defense of Jerusalem when He appears on Olivet, judgment on the confederated nations, topographical changes in the land of Israel, the Feast of Tabernacles, and the ultimate holiness of Jerusalem and her people.

1 In the eighth month of the second year of Darius, the word of the LORD came to Zechariah the son of Berechiah, the son of Iddo the prophet, saying, 2 "The LORD has been very angry with your fathers. 3 Therefore say to them, 'Thus says the LORD of hosts: "Return to Me," says the LORD of hosts, "and I will return to you," says the LORD of hosts. 4 "Do not be like your fathers, to whom the former prophets preached, saying, 'Thus says the LORD of hosts: "Turn now from your evil ways and your evil deeds."' But

they did not hear nor heed Me," says the LORD.

5 "Your fathers, where *are* they?
And the prophets, do they live forever?
6 Yet surely My words and My statutes,
Which I commanded My servants the prophets,
Did they not overtake your fathers?

"So they returned and said:

'Just as the LORD of hosts
    determined to do to us,
According to our ways and
    according to our deeds,
So He has dealt with us.' "

7 On the twenty-fourth day of the eleventh month, which is the month Shebat, in the second year of Darius, the word of the LORD came to Zechariah the son of Berechiah, the son of Iddo the prophet: 8 I saw by night, and behold, a man riding on a red horse, and it stood among the myrtle trees in the hollow; and behind him *were* horses: red, sorrel, and white. 9 Then I said, "My lord, what *are* these?" So the angel who talked with me said to me, "I will show you what they *are*."

10 And the man who stood among the myrtle trees answered and said, "These *are the ones* whom the LORD has sent to walk to and fro throughout the earth."

11 So they answered the Angel of the LORD, who stood among the myrtle trees, and said, "We have walked to and fro throughout the earth, and behold, all the earth is resting quietly."

12 Then the Angel of the LORD answered and said, "O LORD of hosts, how long will You not have mercy on Jerusalem and on the cities of Judah, against which You were angry these seventy years?"

13 And the LORD answered the angel who talked to me, *with* good *and* comforting words. 14 So the angel who spoke with me said to me, "Proclaim, saying, 'Thus says the LORD of hosts:

"I am zealous for Jerusalem
    And for Zion with great
      zeal.
15 I am exceedingly angry with
    the nations at ease;
For I was a little angry,
And they helped—*but* with evil
    intent."

16 'Therefore thus says the LORD:

"I am returning to Jerusalem
    with mercy;
My house shall be built in it,"
    says the LORD of hosts,

"And a *surveyor's* line shall be
    stretched out over
    Jerusalem." '

17 "Again proclaim, saying, 'Thus says the LORD of hosts:

"My cities shall again spread out
    through prosperity;
The LORD will again comfort
    Zion,
And will again choose
    Jerusalem." ' "

18 Then I raised my eyes and looked, and there *were* four horns. 19 And I said to the angel who talked with me, "What *are* these?"

So he answered me, "These *are* the horns that have scattered Judah, Israel, and Jerusalem."

20 Then the LORD showed me four craftsmen. 21 And I said, "What are these coming to do?"

So he said, "These *are* the horns that scattered Judah, so that no one could lift up his head; but the craftsmen[a] are coming to terrify them, to cast out the horns of the nations that lifted up *their* horn against the land of Judah to scatter it."

2 Then I raised my eyes and looked, and behold, a man with a measuring line in his hand. 2 So I said, "Where are you going?"

And he said to me, "To measure Jerusalem, to see what *is* its width and what *is* its length."

3 And there *was* the angel who talked with me, going out; and another angel was coming out to meet him, 4 who said to him, "Run, speak to this young man, saying: 'Jerusalem shall be inhabited *as* towns without walls, because of the multitude of men and livestock in it. 5 For I,' says the LORD, 'will be a wall of fire all around her, and I will be the glory in her midst.' "

6 "Up, up! Flee from the land of the north," says the LORD; "for I have spread you abroad like the four winds of heaven," says the LORD. 7 Up, Zion! Escape, you who dwell with the daughter of Babylon."

8 For thus says the LORD of hosts: "He sent Me after glory, to the nations which plunder you; for he who

1:21 ªLiterally *these*

Announce Your Intentions

An angel spoke these words to Zechariah: "Who *are* you, O great mountain? Before Zerubbabel *you shall become* a plain! And he shall bring forth the capstone with shouts of 'Grace, grace to it!'" (Zech. 4:7). The walk of faith is a progressive walk that leads us up the steps of faith in action.

Faith takes the first step by dreaming. It climbs higher through drawing mental pictures, and it takes a giant step upward through the public announcement of your goals!

This is one of the most frightening steps that you can take in the walk of faith. As long as you keep your mental picture to yourself and secretly harbor your unspoken desires, then the dreaming is relatively safe. But once you open your mouth and tell the world what you intend to do, then you place your reputation as a believable person on the line. Now you must either produce or be proven unreliable at best and a phony at worst.

Many biblical heroes and prophets faced ridicule—even condemnation—when announcing God's plan. Noah, Joshua, Jesus—their public announcements of faith were the first step in obeying and realizing God's unique plan for their lives. The public declaration of commitment intensifies the risk. You can immediately expect opposition and criticism to come out of the woodwork. Negative thinkers will leap forward—"It can't be done," "It won't work," "Somebody else tried it and failed." Or they'll attack your motives.

But rest assured of this: Just as criticism and opposition will come, so support will come from unknown and unexpected sources. The power of a positive idea is greater than the power of a negative idea. Ask God for His strength.

touches you touches the apple of His eye. 9 For surely I will shake My hand against them, and they shall become spoil for their servants. Then you will know that the LORD of hosts has sent Me.

10 "Sing and rejoice, O daughter of Zion! For behold, I am coming and I will dwell in your midst," says the LORD. 11 Many nations shall be joined to the LORD in that day, and they shall become My people. And I will dwell in your midst. Then you will know that the LORD of hosts has sent Me to you. 12 And the LORD will take possession of Judah as His inheritance in the Holy Land, and will again choose Jerusalem. 13 Be silent, all flesh, before the LORD, for He is aroused from His holy habitation!"

3 Then he showed me Joshua the high priest standing before the Angel of the LORD, and Satan standing at his right hand to oppose him. 2 And the LORD said to Satan, "The LORD rebuke you, Satan! The LORD who has chosen Jerusalem rebuke you! Is this not a brand plucked from the fire?"

3 Now Joshua was clothed with filthy garments, and was standing before the Angel. 4 Then He answered and spoke to those who stood before Him, saying, "Take away the filthy garments from him." And to him He said, "See, I have removed your iniquity from you, and I will clothe you with rich robes."

5 And I said, "Let them put a clean turban on his head."

So they put a clean turban on his head, and they put the clothes on him. And the Angel of the LORD stood by.

6 Then the Angel of the LORD admonished Joshua, saying, 7 "Thus says the LORD of hosts:

'If you will walk in My ways,
And if you will keep My command,
Then you shall also judge My house,
And likewise have charge of My courts;
I will give you places to walk
Among these who stand here.

8 'Hear, O Joshua, the high priest,
You and your companions who sit before you,
For they are a wondrous sign;
For behold, I am bringing forth My Servant the BRANCH.
9 For behold, the stone
That I have laid before Joshua:
Upon the stone are seven eyes.
Behold, I will engrave its inscription,'
Says the LORD of hosts,
'And I will remove the iniquity of that land in one day.
10 In that day,' says the LORD of hosts,
'Everyone will invite his neighbor
Under his vine and under his fig tree.' "

4 Now the angel who talked with me came back and wakened me, as a man who is wakened out of his sleep. 2 And he said to me, "What do you see?"

So I said, "I am looking, and there is a lampstand of solid gold with a bowl on top of it, and on the stand seven lamps with seven pipes to the seven lamps. 3 Two olive trees are by it, one at the right of the bowl and the other at its left." 4 So I answered and spoke to the angel who talked with me, saying, "What are these, my lord?"

5 Then the angel who talked with me answered and said to me, "Do you not know what these are?"

And I said, "No, my lord."

6 So he answered and said to me:

"This is the word of the LORD to Zerubbabel:
'Not by might nor by power, but by My Spirit,'
Says the LORD of hosts.
7 'Who are you, O great mountain?
Before Zerubbabel you shall become a plain!
And he shall bring forth the capstone
With shouts of "Grace, grace to it!" ' "

8 Moreover the word of the LORD came to me, saying:

9 "The hands of Zerubbabel
Have laid the foundation of this
temple;[a]
His hands shall also finish *it*.
Then you will know
That the LORD of hosts has sent
Me to you.

10 For who has despised the day
of small things?
For these seven rejoice to see
The plumb line in the hand of
Zerubbabel.
They are the eyes of the LORD,
Which scan to and fro
throughout the whole
earth."

11 Then I answered and said to
him, "What *are* these two olive
trees—at the right of the lampstand
and at its left?" 12 And I further answered and said to him, "What *are*
these two olive branches that *drip*
into the receptacles[a] of the two gold
pipes from which the golden *oil*
drains?"

13 Then he answered me and said,
"Do you not know what these *are*?"
And I said, "No, my lord."

14 So he said, "These *are* the two
anointed ones, who stand beside the
Lord of the whole earth."

5 Then I turned and raised my
eyes, and saw there a flying
scroll.

2 And he said to me, "What do you
see?"

So I answered, "I see a flying
scroll. Its length *is* twenty cubits and
its width ten cubits."

3 Then he said to me, "This *is* the
curse that goes out over the face of
the whole earth: 'Every thief shall be
expelled,' according *to* this side of
the scroll; and, 'Every perjurer shall
be expelled,' according *to* that side
of it."

4 "I will send out *the curse*," says
the LORD of hosts;
"It shall enter the house of the
thief
And the house of the one who
swears falsely by My name.
It shall remain in the midst of
his house
And consume it, with its timber
and stones."

5 Then the angel who talked with
me came out and said to me, "Lift
your eyes now, and see what this *is*
that goes forth."

6 So I asked, "What *is* it?" And he
said, "It *is* a basket[a] that is going
forth."

He also said, "This *is* their resem-
blance throughout the earth: 7 Here
is a lead disc lifted up, and this *is* a
woman sitting inside the basket";
8 then he said, "This *is* Wickedness!"
And he thrust her down into the basket, and threw the lead cover[a] over
its mouth. 9 Then I raised my eyes
and looked, and there *were* two
women, coming with the wind in
their wings; for they had wings like
the wings of a stork, and they lifted
up the basket between earth and
heaven.

10 So I said to the angel who talked
with me, "Where are they carrying
the basket?"

11 And he said to me, "To build a
house for it in the land of Shinar;[a]
when it is ready, *the basket* will be
set there on its base."

6 Then I turned and raised my eyes
and looked, and behold, four
chariots *were* coming from between
two mountains, and the mountains
were mountains of bronze. 2 With the
first chariot *were* red horses, with
the second chariot black horses,
3 with the third chariot white horses,
and with the fourth chariot dappled
horses—strong *steeds*. 4 Then I answered and said to the angel who
talked with me, "What *are* these, my
lord?"

5 And the angel answered and said
to me, "These *are* four spirits of
heaven, who go out from *their* station
before the Lord of all the earth.
6 The one with the black horses is going to the north country, the white
are going after them, and the dappled
are going toward the south country."
7 Then the strong *steeds* went out, eager to go, that they might walk to and
fro throughout the earth. And He
said, "Go, walk to and fro throughout
the earth." So they walked to and
fro throughout the earth. 8 And He
called to me, and spoke to me, saying, "See, those who go toward the
north country have given rest

---

to My Spirit in the north country."
9 Then the word of the LORD came to me, saying: 10 "Receive *the gift* from the captives—from Heldai, Tobijah, and Jedaiah, who have come from Babylon—and go the same day and enter the house of Josiah the son of Zephaniah. 11 Take the silver and gold, make an elaborate crown, and set *it* on the head of Joshua the son of Jehozadak, the high priest. 12 Then speak to him, saying, 'Thus says the LORD of hosts, saying:

"Behold, the Man whose name
  is the BRANCH!
From His place He shall branch
  out,
And He shall build the temple
  of the LORD;
13 Yes, He shall build the temple
  of the LORD.
He shall bear the glory,
And shall sit and rule on His
  throne;
So He shall be a priest on His
  throne,
And the counsel of peace shall
  be between them both."' '

14 "Now the elaborate crown shall be for a memorial in the temple of the LORD for Helem,*a* Tobijah, Jedaiah, and Hen the son of Zephaniah. 15 Even those from afar shall come and build the temple of the LORD. Then you shall know that the LORD of hosts has sent Me to you. And *this* shall come to pass if you diligently obey the voice of the LORD your God."

7 Now in the fourth year of King Darius it came to pass *that* the word of the LORD came to Zechariah, on the fourth day of the ninth month, Chislev, 2 when *the people*a sent Sherezer,*b* with Regem-Melech and his men, *to* the house of God,*c* to pray before the LORD, 3 *and* to ask the priests who *were* in the house of the LORD of hosts, and the prophets, saying, "Should I weep in the fifth month and fast as I have done for so many years?"
4 Then the word of the LORD of hosts came to me, saying, 5 "Say to all the people of the land, and to the priests: 'When you fasted and mourned in the fifth and seventh *months* during those seventy years, did you really fast for Me—for Me? 6 When you eat and when you drink, do you not eat and drink *for yourselves*? 7 *Should you* not *have obeyed* the words which the LORD proclaimed through the former prophets when Jerusalem and the cities around it were inhabited and prosperous, and the South*a* and the Lowland were inhabited?' "
8 Then the word of the LORD came to Zechariah, saying, 9 "Thus says the LORD of hosts:

'Execute true justice,
Show mercy and compassion
Everyone to his brother.
10   Do not oppress the widow or
  the fatherless,
The alien or the poor.
Let none of you plan evil in his
  heart
Against his brother.'

11 But they refused to heed, shrugged their shoulders, and stopped their ears so that they could not hear. 12 Yes, they made their hearts like flint, refusing to hear the law and the words which the LORD of hosts had sent by His Spirit through the former prophets. Thus great wrath came from the LORD of hosts. 13 Therefore it happened, *that* just as He proclaimed and they would not hear, so they called out and I would not listen," says the LORD of hosts. 14 "But I scattered them with a whirlwind among all the nations which they had not known. Thus the land became desolate after them, so that no one passed through or returned; for they made the pleasant land desolate."

8 Again the word of the LORD of hosts came, saying, 2 "Thus says the LORD of hosts:

'I am zealous for Zion with
  great zeal;
With great fervor I am zealous
  for her.'

3 "Thus says the LORD:

6:14 aFollowing Masoretic Text, Targum, and Vulgate; Syriac reads *for Heldai* (compare verse 10); Septuagint reads *for the patient ones.*   7:2 aLiterally *they* (compare verse 5)   bOr *Sar-Ezer*   cHebrew *Bethel*   7:7 aHebrew *Negev*

'I will return to Zion,
And dwell in the midst of
Jerusalem.
Jerusalem shall be called the
City of Truth,
The Mountain of the LORD of
hosts,
The Holy Mountain.'

4 "Thus says the LORD of hosts:

'Old men and old women shall
again sit
In the streets of Jerusalem,
Each one with his staff in his
hand
Because of great age.
5 The streets of the city
Shall be full of boys and girls
Playing in its streets.'

6 "Thus says the LORD of hosts:

'If it is marvelous in the eyes of
the remnant of this people in
these days,
Will it also be marvelous in My
eyes?'
Says the LORD of hosts.

7 "Thus says the LORD of hosts:

'Behold, I will save My people
from the land of the east
And from the land of the west;
8 I will bring them back,
And they shall dwell in the
midst of Jerusalem.
They shall be My people
And I will be their God,
In truth and righteousness.'

9 "Thus says the LORD of hosts:

'Let your hands be strong,
You who have been hearing in
these days
These words by the mouth of
the prophets,
Who spoke in the day the
foundation was laid
For the house of the LORD of
hosts,
That the temple might be built.
10 For before these days
There were no wages for man
nor any hire for beast;
There was no peace from the
enemy for whoever went out
or came in;

For I set all men, everyone,
against his neighbor.

11 'But now I will not treat the remnant of this people as in the former
days,' says the LORD of hosts.

12 'For the seed shall be
prosperous,
The vine shall give its fruit,
The ground shall give her
increase,
And the heavens shall give
their dew—
I will cause the remnant of this
people
To possess all these.
13 And it shall come to pass
That just as you were a curse
among the nations,
O house of Judah and house of
Israel,
So I will save you, and you
shall be a blessing.
Do not fear,
Let your hands be strong.'

14 "For thus says the LORD of hosts:

'Just as I determined to punish
you
When your fathers provoked
Me to wrath,'
Says the LORD of hosts,
'And I would not relent,
15 So again in these days
I am determined to do good
To Jerusalem and to the house
of Judah.
Do not fear.
16 These are the things you shall
do:
Speak each man the truth to his
neighbor;
Give judgment in your gates for
truth, justice, and peace;
17 Let none of you think evil in
your[a] heart against your
neighbor;
And do not love a false oath.
For all these are things that I
hate,'
Says the LORD."

18 Then the word of the LORD of
hosts came to me, saying, 19 "Thus
says the LORD of hosts:

'The fast of the fourth month,
The fast of the fifth,

8:17 aLiterally his

Allow God to Do the Unexpected

When Jesus rode into Jerusalem on a donkey during Passover week, His reception was overwhelming. Multitudes rushed out to greet Him, shouting, "Hosanna! Blessed is He who comes in the name of the Lord!" (Mark 11:9). They threw palm branches and garments down into Jesus' path as they welcomed Him into the city.

The people had been yearning for a messiah. They longed for a political leader to lead them in a revolt against Rome. Their actions confirm that they expected Jesus to assume this role. "Hosanna," meaning "Save now," in the Jewish religion was often a salute to kings. Their shouts of "Blessed is He who comes in the name of the Lord," referred to a kingly political leader who would deliver the Jews from the oppression of the Romans. As they threw palm branches in front of Jesus they performed an act that represented freedom.

Many coins used in the temple during the New Testament period bear inscriptions of palm branches. This was a symbol of Jewish nationalism. The Romans had reason to be concerned by Jewish solidarity.

But God did not send Jesus to simply establish a political kingdom. Christ's kingdom was much, much more. Not until after His death and resurrection did the disciples and the other followers realize what Jesus' kingdom was all about. It did not consist of swords, arms, and a political dictatorship. Rather, His was a kingdom of love, hope, and forgiveness.

The people all expected a king, a political messiah. But God did the unexpected. He did the impossible. When God raised Jesus Christ from the dead, He freed the people from the oppression of sin, death, and despair. Unlock your thinking and lock in your faith. Allow God to do the unexpected. Let Him accomplish the impossible in your life!

The fast of the seventh,
And the fast of the tenth,
Shall be joy and gladness and
cheerful feasts
For the house of Judah.
Therefore love truth and
peace.'

20 "Thus says the LORD of hosts:

'Peoples shall yet come,
Inhabitants of many cities;
21 The inhabitants of one *city*
shall go to another, saying,
"Let us continue to go and pray
before the LORD,
And seek the LORD of hosts.
I myself will go also."
22 Yes, many peoples and strong
nations
Shall come to seek the LORD of
hosts in Jerusalem,
And to pray before the LORD.'

23 "Thus says the LORD of hosts: 'In
those days ten men from every language of the nations shall grasp the
sleeve of a Jewish man, saying, "Let
us go with you, for we have heard
that God *is* with you." ' "

9 The burden[a] of the word of the
LORD
Against the land of Hadrach,
And Damascus its resting
place
(For the eyes of men
And all the tribes of Israel
Are on the LORD);
2 Also *against* Hamath, *which*
borders on it,
And *against* Tyre and Sidon,
though they are very wise.

3 For Tyre built herself a tower,
Heaped up silver like the dust,
And gold like the mire of the
streets.
4 Behold, the LORD will cast her
out;
He will destroy her power in
the sea,
And she will be devoured by
fire.

5 Ashkelon shall see *it* and fear;
Gaza also shall be very
sorrowful;
And Ekron, for He dried up her
expectation.

The king shall perish from
Gaza,
And Ashkelon shall not be
inhabited.

6 "A mixed race shall settle in
Ashdod,
And I will cut off the pride of
the Philistines.
7 I will take away the blood from
his mouth,
And the abominations from
between his teeth.
But he who remains, even he
shall be for our God,
And shall be like a leader in
Judah,
And Ekron like a Jebusite.
8 I will camp around My house
Because of the army,
Because of him who passes by
and him who returns.
No more shall an oppressor
pass through them,
For now I have seen with My
eyes.

9 "Rejoice greatly, O daughter of
Zion!
Shout, O daughter of
Jerusalem!
Behold, your King is coming to
you;
He *is* just and having salvation,
Lowly and riding on a donkey,
A colt, the foal of a donkey.
10 I will cut off the chariot from
Ephraim
And the horse from Jerusalem;
The battle bow shall be cut off.
He shall speak peace to the
nations;
His dominion *shall be* 'from sea
to sea,
And from the River to the ends
of the earth.'[a]

11 "As for you also,
Because of the blood of your
covenant,
I will set your prisoners free
from the waterless pit.
12 Return to the stronghold,
You prisoners of hope.
Even today I declare
That I will restore double to
you.
13 For I have bent Judah, My *bow,*
Fitted the bow with Ephraim,

9:1 [a]Or *oracle*   9:10 [a]Psalm 72:8

And raised up your sons, O
   Zion,
Against your sons, O Greece,
And made you like the sword
   of a mighty man.''

14 Then the LORD will be seen over
   them,
And His arrow will go forth like
   lightning.
The Lord GOD will blow the
   trumpet,
And go with whirlwinds from
   the south.
15 The LORD of hosts will defend
   them;
They shall devour and subdue
   with slingstones.
They shall drink *and* roar as if
   with wine;
They shall be filled *with blood*
   like basins,
Like the corners of the altar.
16 The LORD their God will save
   them in that day,
As the flock of His people.
For they *shall be like* the jewels
   of a crown,
Lifted like a banner over His
   land—
17 For how great is its[a] goodness
And how great its[b] beauty!
Grain shall make the young
   men thrive,
And new wine the young
   women.

10 Ask the LORD for rain
In the time of the latter rain.[a]
The LORD will make flashing
   clouds;
He will give them showers of
   rain,
Grass in the field for everyone.

2 For the idols[a] speak delusion;
The diviners envision lies,
And tell false dreams;
They comfort in vain.
Therefore *the people* wend
   their way like sheep;
They are in trouble because
   there is no shepherd.

3 "My anger is kindled against the
   shepherds,
And I will punish the
   goatherds.
For the LORD of hosts will visit
   His flock,

The house of Judah,
And will make them as His
   royal horse in the battle.
4 From him comes the
   cornerstone,
From him the tent peg,
From him the battle bow,
From him every ruler[a] together.
5 They shall be like mighty men,
Who tread down *their enemies*
In the mire of the streets in the
   battle.
They shall fight because the
   LORD is with them,
And the riders on horses shall
   be put to shame.

6 "I will strengthen the house of
   Judah,
And I will save the house of
   Joseph.
I will bring them back,
Because I have mercy on them.
They shall be as though I had
   not cast them aside;
For I *am* the LORD their God,
And I will hear them.
7 *Those of* Ephraim shall be like
   a mighty man,
And their heart shall rejoice as
   if with wine.
Yes, their children shall see *it*
   and be glad;
Their heart shall rejoice in the
   LORD.
8 I will whistle for them and
   gather them,
For I will redeem them;
And they shall increase as they
   once increased.

9 "I will sow them among the
   peoples,
And they shall remember Me
   in far countries;
They shall live, together with
   their children,
And they shall return.
10 I will also bring them back
   from the land of Egypt,
And gather them from Assyria.
I will bring them into the land
   of Gilead and Lebanon,
Until no *more room* is found for
   them.
11 He shall pass through the sea
   with affliction,
And strike the waves of the sea:
All the depths of the River[a]
   shall dry up.

9:17 [a]Or *His*   [b]Or *His*   10:1 [a]That is, spring rain   10:2 [a]Hebrew *teraphim*   10:4 [a]Or *despot*
10:11 [a]That is, the Nile

Then the pride of Assyria shall
   be brought down,
And the scepter of Egypt shall
   depart.

12 "So I will strengthen them in the
   LORD,
And they shall walk up and
   down in His name,"
Says the LORD.

11 Open your doors, O Lebanon,
   That fire may devour your
     cedars.
2   Wail, O cypress, for the cedar
   has fallen,
Because the mighty *trees* are
   ruined.
Wail, O oaks of Bashan,
For the thick forest has come
   down.
3   *There is* the sound of wailing
   shepherds!
For their glory is in ruins.
There is the sound of roaring
   lions!
For the pride*ᵃ* of the Jordan is
   in ruins.

4 Thus says the LORD my God,
"Feed the flock for slaughter,
5 whose owners slaughter them and
feel no guilt; those who sell them say,
'Blessed be the LORD, for I am rich';
and their shepherds do not pity them.
6 For I will no longer pity the inhabitants of the land," says the LORD. "But
indeed I will give everyone into his
neighbor's hand and into the hand
of his king. They shall attack the
land, and I will not deliver *them* from
their hand."

7 So I fed the flock for slaughter,
in particular the poor of the flock.*ᵃ* I
took for myself two staffs: the one I
called Beauty,*ᵇ* and the other I called
Bonds;*ᶜ* and I fed the flock. 8 I dismissed the three shepherds in one
month. My soul loathed them, and
their soul also abhorred me.
9 Then I said, "I will not feed you.
Let what is dying die, and what is
perishing perish. Let those that are
left eat each other's flesh." 10 And I
took my staff, Beauty, and cut it in
two, that I might break the covenant
which I had made with all the peoples. 11 So it was broken on that day.
Thus the poor*ᵃ* of the flock, who were

watching me, knew that it *was* the
word of the LORD. 12 Then I said to
them, "If it is agreeable to you, give
me my wages; and if not, refrain."
So they weighed out for my wages
thirty *pieces* of silver.
13 And the LORD said to me,
"Throw it to the potter"—that
princely price they set on me. So I
took the thirty *pieces* of silver and
threw them into the house of the
LORD for the potter. 14 Then I cut in
two my other staff, Bonds, that I
might break the brotherhood between Judah and Israel.
15 And the LORD said to me, "Next,
take for yourself the implements of
a foolish shepherd. 16 For indeed I
will raise up a shepherd in the land
who will not care for those who are
cut off, nor seek the young, nor heal
those that are broken, nor feed those
that still stand. But he will eat the
flesh of the fat and tear their hooves
in pieces.

17 "Woe to the worthless shepherd,
   Who leaves the flock!
A sword *shall be* against his
   arm
And against his right eye;
His arm shall completely
   wither,
And his right eye shall be
   totally blinded."

12 The burden*ᵃ* of the word of the
   LORD against Israel. Thus says
the LORD, who stretches out the heavens, lays the foundation of the earth,
and forms the spirit of man within
him: 2 "Behold, I will make Jerusalem a cup of drunkenness to all the
surrounding peoples, when they lay
siege against Judah and Jerusalem.
3 And it shall happen in that day that
I will make Jerusalem a very heavy
stone for all peoples; all who would
heave it away will surely be cut in
pieces, though all nations of the earth
are gathered against it. 4 In that day,"
says the LORD, "I will strike every
horse with confusion, and its rider
with madness; I will open My eyes
on the house of Judah, and will strike
every horse of the peoples with blindness. 5 And the governors of Judah
shall say in their heart, 'The inhabitants of Jerusalem *are* my strength

11:3 *ᵃ*Or *floodplain, thicket*   11:7 *ᵃ*Following Masoretic Text, Targum, and Vulgate; Septuagint reads *for
the Canaanites.*   *ᵇ*Or *Grace,* and so in verse 10   *ᶜ*Or *Unity,* and so in verse 14   11:11 *ᵃ*Following
Masoretic Text, Targum, and Vulgate; Septuagint reads *the Canaanites.*   12:1 *ᵃ*Or *oracle*

in the LORD of hosts, their God.'
6 In that day I will make the governors of Judah like a firepan in the woodpile, and like a fiery torch in the sheaves; they shall devour all the surrounding peoples on the right hand and on the left, but Jerusalem shall be inhabited again in her own place—Jerusalem.

7 "The LORD will save the tents of Judah first, so that the glory of the house of David and the glory of the inhabitants of Jerusalem shall not become greater than that of Judah. 8 In that day the LORD will defend the inhabitants of Jerusalem; the one who is feeble among them in that day shall be like David, and the house of David *shall be* like God, like the Angel of the LORD before them. 9 It shall be in that day *that* I will seek to destroy all the nations that come against Jerusalem.

10 "And I will pour on the house of David and on the inhabitants of Jerusalem the Spirit of grace and supplication; then they will look on Me whom they pierced. Yes, they will mourn for Him as one mourns for *his* only *son,* and grieve for Him as one grieves for a firstborn. 11 In that day there shall be a great mourning in Jerusalem, like the mourning at Hadad Rimmon in the plain of Megiddo.[a] 12 And the land shall mourn, every family by itself: the family of the house of David by itself, and their wives by themselves; the family of the house of Nathan by itself, and their wives by themselves; 13 the family of the house of Levi by itself, and their wives by themselves; the family of Shimei by itself, and their wives by themselves; 14 all the families that remain, every family by itself, and their wives by themselves.

13 "In that day a fountain shall be opened for the house of David and for the inhabitants of Jerusalem, for sin and for uncleanness.

2 "It shall be in that day," says the LORD of hosts, "*that* I will cut off the names of the idols from the land, and they shall no longer be remembered. I will also cause the prophets and the unclean spirit to depart from the land. 3 It shall come to pass *that* if anyone still prophesies, then his father and mother who begot him will say to him, 'You shall not live, because you have spoken lies in the name of the LORD.' And his father and mother who begot him shall thrust him through when he prophesies.

4 "And it shall be in that day *that* every prophet will be ashamed of his vision when he prophesies; they will not wear a robe of coarse hair to deceive. 5 But he will say, 'I *am* no prophet, I *am* a farmer; for a man taught me to keep cattle from my youth.' 6 And *one* will say to him, 'What are these wounds between your arms?'[a] Then he will answer, '*Those* with which I was wounded in the house of my friends.'

7   "Awake, O sword, against My
        Shepherd,
     Against the Man who is My
        Companion,"
   Says the LORD of hosts.
   "Strike the Shepherd,
     And the sheep will be
        scattered;
     Then I will turn My hand
        against the little ones.
8   And it shall come to pass in all
        the land,"
   Says the LORD,
   "*That* two-thirds in it shall be
        cut off *and* die,
     But *one*-third shall be left in
        it:
9   I will bring the *one*-third
        through the fire,
     Will refine them as silver is
        refined,
     And test them as gold is tested.
     They will call on My name,
     And I will answer them.
   I will say, 'This *is* My people';
     And each one will say, 'The
        LORD *is* my God.' "

14 Behold, the day of the LORD is
        coming,
     And your spoil will be divided
        in your midst.
2   For I will gather all the nations
        to battle against Jerusalem;
     The city shall be taken,
     The houses rifled,
     And the women ravished.
     Half of the city shall go into
        captivity,

12:11 [a]Hebrew *Megiddon*   13:6 [a]Or *hands*

But the remnant of the people
    shall not be cut off from the
    city.

3   Then the LORD will go forth
And fight against those
    nations,
As He fights in the day of
    battle.
4   And in that day His feet will
    stand on the Mount of Olives,
Which faces Jerusalem on the
    east.
And the Mount of Olives shall
    be split in two,
From east to west,
Making a very large valley;
Half of the mountain shall
    move toward the north
And half of it toward the south.

5   Then you shall flee *through* My
    mountain valley,
For the mountain valley shall
    reach to Azal.
Yes, you shall flee
As you fled from the
    earthquake
In the days of Uzziah king of
    Judah.

Thus the LORD my God will
    come,
And all the saints with You.*a*

6   It shall come to pass in that day
That there will be no light;
The lights will diminish.
7   It shall be one day
Which is known to the LORD—
Neither day nor night.
But at evening time it shall
    happen
That it will be light.

8   And in that day it shall be
That living waters shall flow
    from Jerusalem,
Half of them toward the eastern
    sea
And half of them toward the
    western sea;
In both summer and winter it
    shall occur.
9   And the LORD shall be King
    over all the earth.
In that day it shall be—
"The LORD *is* one,"*a*
And His name one.

10 All the land shall be turned into
a plain from Geba to Rimmon south
of Jerusalem. *Jerusalem*a shall be
raised up and inhabited in her place
from Benjamin's Gate to the place of
the First Gate and the Corner Gate,
and *from* the Tower of Hananel to
the king's winepresses.

11   *The people* shall dwell in it;
And no longer shall there be
    utter destruction,
But Jerusalem shall be safely
    inhabited.

12 And this shall be the plague with
which the LORD will strike all the people who fought against Jerusalem:

Their flesh shall dissolve while
    they stand on their feet,
Their eyes shall dissolve in
    their sockets,
And their tongues shall
    dissolve in their mouths.

13   It shall come to pass in that day
That a great panic from the
    LORD will be among them.
Everyone will seize the hand of
    his neighbor,
And raise his hand against his
    neighbor's hand;
14   Judah also will fight at
    Jerusalem.
And the wealth of all the
    surrounding nations
Shall be gathered together:
Gold, silver, and apparel in
    great abundance.

15   Such also shall be the plague
On the horse *and* the mule,
On the camel and the donkey,
And on all the cattle that will
    be in those camps.
So *shall* this plague *be.*

16 And it shall come to pass *that*
everyone who is left of all the nations
which came against Jerusalem shall
go up from year to year to worship
the King, the LORD of hosts, and to
keep the Feast of Tabernacles.
17 And it shall be *that* whichever of
the families of the earth do not come
up to Jerusalem to worship the King,
the LORD of hosts, on them there will
be no rain. 18 If the family of Egypt

14:5 *a*Or *you;* Septuagint, Targum, and Vulgate read *Him.*   14:9 *a*Compare Deuteronomy 6:4
14:10 *a*Literally *She*

will not come up and enter in, they *shall have* no *rain;* they shall receive the plague with which the LORD strikes the nations who do not come up to keep the Feast of Tabernacles. 19 This shall be the punishment of Egypt and the punishment of all the nations that do not come up to keep the Feast of Tabernacles.

20 In that day "HOLINESS TO THE LORD" shall be *engraved* on the bells of the horses. The pots in the LORD's house shall be like the bowls before the altar. 21 Yes, every pot in Jerusalem and Judah shall be holiness to the LORD of hosts.[a] Everyone who sacrifices shall come and take them and cook in them. In that day there shall no longer be a Canaanite in the house of the LORD of hosts.

14:21 aOr on every pot . . . shall be (engraved) "HOLINESS TO THE LORD OF HOSTS"

Malachi

Overview of Malachi

The Book of Malachi was written sometime between 450 and 400 B.C. following Israel's return from captivity in Babylon. Malachi sought to bring the people back to God, encouraging them to shed the pagan life-style they had adopted while in exile.

The temple in Jerusalem had been rebuilt, but the people were ignorant as to how they were to worship God. General lack of belief in God's providential care led the people to steal from the temple by not tithing. Their life-styles revealed a lack of trust in God's ability to provide for their needs.

Malachi presented twenty-three probing questions between God and the people in a self-examining essay. He allowed the nation to see for itself that they had turned from God. Malachi then assured them that God loved them and had promised to make them "My jewels" (Mal. 3:17). By affirming God's love toward them, Malachi was able to prepare their hearts for a relationship with God.

Malachi was one in a long series of prophets that God raised up to keep His light of love, hope, and forgiveness shining. Malachi was the last prophet in the Old Testament. His words to the people prepared them for the "four hundred silent years," during which they would have no other prophets to lead them. Generations were to cling to the hope of the coming Messiah for over four centuries, during which they would suffer greatly under Alexander the Great, the Seleucids, The Ptolemies, and the Romans.

Malachi not only taught them to await the Savior of the world, but to live a positive life of faith. He urged them to give freely, promising that by doing so God would return their gifts sevenfold. The words of Malachi enabled the people to trust God and to take Him at His word. Then they were able to live positively and hold on to hope!

Jesus in Malachi

The Book of Malachi is the prelude to four hundred years of prophetic silence, broken by the words of John the Baptist: "Behold! The Lamb of God, who takes away the sin of the world" (John 1:29). Malachi predicted the coming of this messenger who cleared the way for Christ in His first coming (3:1, cf. Is. 40:3). Malachi 3:2–5 jumps ahead in time to predict Christ's second advent.

Keys to Malachi

Key Word: Messenger. The divine dialogue in this book appeals to Israel to break down the disbelief, disappointment and discouragement of the years and to look for God's concern. Malachi preaches repentance for the flow of God's divine blessings to begin. Malachi reminds the people of a day of reckoning when God judges the righteous and the wicked. But he also reminds the people that a messenger will come and redemption will follow.

Key Verses: "You have wearied the LORD with your words; yet you say, 'In what way have we wearied *Him?*' In that you say, 'Everyone who does evil *is* good in the sight of the LORD, and He delights in them' or 'Where *is* the God of justice?'

"'Behold I send My messenger, and he will prepare the way before Me. And the Lord, whom you seek, will suddenly come to His temple, even the Messenger of the covenant, in whom you delight. Behold, He is coming,' says the LORD of hosts" (2:17—3:1).

Key Chapter: Malachi 3. The last book of the Old Testament concludes with a dramatic prophecy of the coming of the Lord and John the Baptist. "I will send My messenger, and he will prepare the way before Me" (3:1). Four hundred years later, Israel flocked to the Jordan River to hear "the

voice of one crying in the wilderness: 'Prepare the way of
the LORD'" (Matt. 3:3). The prophetic silence was broken,
and Malachi 3 and 4 go on to record the coming of the Messiah and His forerunner.

1 The burden[a] of the word of the
LORD to Israel by Malachi.

2 "I have loved you," says the
   LORD.
   "Yet you say, 'In what way have
      You loved us?'
   Was not Esau Jacob's
      brother?"
   Says the LORD.
   "Yet Jacob I have loved;
3 But Esau I have hated,
   And laid waste his mountains
      and his heritage
   For the jackals of the
      wilderness."

4 Even though Edom has said,
   "We have been impoverished,
   But we will return and build the
      desolate places,"

Thus says the LORD of hosts:

   "They may build, but I will
      throw down;
   They shall be called the
      Territory of Wickedness,
   And the people against whom
      the LORD will have
      indignation forever.
5 Your eyes shall see,
   And you shall say,
   'The LORD is magnified beyond
      the border of Israel.'

6 "A son honors *his* father,
   And a servant *his* master.

If then I am the Father,
Where *is* My honor?
And if I *am* a Master,
Where *is* My reverence?
Says the LORD of hosts
To you priests who despise My
   name.
Yet you say, 'In what way have
   we despised Your name?'

7 "You offer defiled food on My
   altar,
But say,
'In what way have we defiled
   You?'
By saying,
'The table of the LORD is
   contemptible.'
8 And when you offer the blind
   as a sacrifice,
Is it not evil?
And when you offer the lame
   and sick,
Is it not evil?
Offer it then to your governor!
Would he be pleased with you?
Would he accept you
   favorably?"
Says the LORD of hosts.

9 "But now entreat God's favor,
   That He may be gracious to us.
   While this is being *done* by
      your hands,
   Will He accept you favorably?"
   Says the LORD of hosts.
10 "Who *is there* even among you
      who would shut the doors,

1:1 *a*Or *oracle*

So that you would not kindle
fire *on* My altar in vain?
I have no pleasure in you,"
Says the LORD of hosts,
"Nor will I accept an offering
from your hands.
11 For from the rising of the sun,
even to its going down,
My name *shall be* great among
the Gentiles;
In every place incense *shall be*
offered to My name,
And a pure offering;
For My name shall be great
among the nations,"
Says the LORD of hosts.

12 "But you profane it,
In that you say,
'The table of the LORD*a* is
defiled;
And its fruit, its food, *is*
contemptible.'
13 You also say,
'Oh, what a weariness!'
And you sneer at it,"
Says the LORD of hosts.
"And you bring the stolen, the
lame, and the sick;
Thus you bring an offering!
Should I accept this from your
hand?"
Says the LORD.
14 "But cursed *be* the deceiver
Who has in his flock a male,
And takes a vow,
But sacrifices to the Lord what
is blemished—
For I *am* a great King,"
Says the LORD of hosts,
"And My name *is to be* feared
among the nations.

2 "And now, O priests, this
commandment is for you.
2 If you will not hear,
And if you will not take *it* to
heart,
To give glory to My name,"
Says the LORD of hosts,
"I will send a curse upon you,
And I will curse your blessings.
Yes, I have cursed them
already,
Because you do not take *it* to
heart.

3 "Behold, I will rebuke your
descendants
And spread refuse on your
faces,

The refuse of your solemn
feasts;
And *one* will take you away
with it.
4 Then you shall know that I
have sent this commandment
to you,
That My covenant with Levi
may continue,"
Says the LORD of hosts.
5 "My covenant was with him, *one*
of life and peace,
And I gave them to him *that
he might* fear *Me;*
So he feared Me
And was reverent before My
name.
6 The law of truth*a* was in his
mouth,
And injustice was not found on
his lips.
He walked with Me in peace
and equity,
And turned many away from
iniquity.

7 "For the lips of a priest should
keep knowledge,
And *people* should seek the law
from his mouth;
For he is the messenger of the
LORD of hosts.
8 But you have departed from the
way;
You have caused many to
stumble at the law.
You have corrupted the
covenant of Levi,"
Says the LORD of hosts.
9 "Therefore I also have made you
contemptible and base
Before all the people,
Because you have not kept My
ways
But have shown partiality in
the law."

10 Have we not all one Father?
Has not one God created us?
Why do we deal treacherously
with one another
By profaning the covenant of
the fathers?
11 Judah has dealt treacherously,
And an abomination has been
committed in Israel and in
Jerusalem,
For Judah has profaned
The LORD's holy *institution*
which He loves:

1:12 *a*Following Bomberg; Masoretic Text reads *Lord.*   2:6 *a*Or *true instruction*

He has married the daughter of a foreign god.

12 May the LORD cut off from the tents of Jacob
The man who does this, being awake and aware,[a]
Yet who brings an offering to the LORD of hosts!

13 And this is the second thing you do:
You cover the altar of the LORD with tears,
With weeping and crying;
So He does not regard the offering anymore,
Nor receive it with goodwill from your hands.

14 Yet you say, "For what reason?"
Because the LORD has been witness
Between you and the wife of your youth,
With whom you have dealt treacherously;
Yet she is your companion
And your wife by covenant.

15 But did He not make them one,
Having a remnant of the Spirit?
And why one?
He seeks godly offspring.
Therefore take heed to your spirit,
And let none deal treacherously with the wife of his youth.

16 "For the LORD God of Israel says
That He hates divorce,
For it covers one's garment with violence,"
Says the LORD of hosts.
"Therefore take heed to your spirit,
That you do not deal treacherously."

17 You have wearied the LORD with your words;
Yet you say,
"In what way have we wearied Him?"
In that you say,
"Everyone who does evil
Is good in the sight of the LORD,
And He delights in them,"
Or, "Where is the God of justice?"

3 "Behold, I send My messenger,
And he will prepare the way before Me.
And the Lord, whom you seek,
Will suddenly come to His temple,
Even the Messenger of the covenant,
In whom you delight.
Behold, He is coming,"
Says the LORD of hosts.

2 "But who can endure the day of His coming?
And who can stand when He appears?
For He is like a refiner's fire
And like launderers' soap.

3 He will sit as a refiner and a purifier of silver;
He will purify the sons of Levi,
And purge them as gold and silver,
That they may offer to the LORD
An offering in righteousness.

4 "Then the offering of Judah and Jerusalem
Will be pleasant to the LORD,
As in the days of old,
As in former years.

5 And I will come near you for judgment;
I will be a swift witness
Against sorcerers,
Against adulterers,
Against perjurers,
Against those who exploit wage earners and widows and orphans,
And against those who turn away an alien—
Because they do not fear Me,"
Says the LORD of hosts.

6 "For I am the LORD, I do not change;
Therefore you are not consumed, O sons of Jacob.

7 Yet from the days of your fathers
You have gone away from My ordinances
And have not kept them.
Return to Me, and I will return to you,"
Says the LORD of hosts.
"But you said,
'In what way shall we return?'

2:12 [a]Talmud and Vulgate read teacher and student.

Called to Prepare the Way

John the Baptist was unique to modern man. He was called by God to prepare the way for the earthly ministry of Jesus Christ.

The son of Elizabeth and Zacharias, a priest who carried out important temple functions, John the Baptist grew up in Jerusalem surrounded with a comfortable, cosmopolitan lifestyle. In society's terms, he had everything he wanted—prestige and religious stature. Yet when it came time for him to carry out his calling, he left his family and went to live in the wilderness of Judea. Here he lived a nomadic lifestyle. The Bible records that he ate locusts and honey, perhaps a way of describing yogurt—the sweet milk of goats and the locust plant which grows wild in the wilderness.

John the Baptist carried on the majority of his ministry within earshot of the New Testament village of Jericho. Soon throngs of people from the mountains of Judea, Samaria, and beyond the Jordan came to hear John the Baptist. John encouraged them to believe in God. Romans, Jews, Samaritans, women—he accepted them all into a symbolic act of baptism and preparation for the coming of the Messiah, Jesus Christ.

A common practice among kings in ancient times was to send forth a scout to insure the road was safe, clear, and prepared before their journey. This was John the Baptist's task, only the road he made ready was the hearts and minds of men and women. He was "the voice of one crying in the wilderness: Prepare the way of the LORD; make His paths straight" (Matt. 3:3).

Those familiar with Jewish prophecies expected Elijah to come before the Messiah. When John the Baptist's disciples asked Jesus whether or not he was the Messiah, Jesus told them to inform John that "*the* blind see, *the* lame walk, *the* lepers are cleansed, *the* deaf hear, *the* dead are raised, *the* poor have the gospel preached to them" (Luke 7:22). Jesus then explained to His listeners, "What did you go out into the wilderness to see? . . . A prophet? [Elijah] . . . there is not a greater prophet than John the Baptist" (Luke 7:24–28).

In the Old Testament, Elijah was taken up into heaven just outside of Jericho. The fact that John the Baptist practiced most of his ministry in the very same district must have stirred his listeners to remember the prophetic call, "Behold, I will send you Elijah the prophet" (Mal. 4:5).

John the Baptist prepared the way for Jesus Christ. Now that Christ has come, our responsibility continues to be the same: to prepare the hearts of men and women for the Good News of Jesus Christ. We are messengers called to prepare the way where we are, with whom we meet, and with what we have. Like John the Baptist, we can encourage others to believe in God. Our lives can be a living message of God's positive love and joy. Let us be bold enough to get out of our comfortable existence and share the exciting news—Jesus Christ has come!

8 "Will a man rob God?
   Yet you have robbed Me!
   But you say,
   'In what way have we robbed
      You?'
   In tithes and offerings.
9 You are cursed with a
      curse,
   For you have robbed Me,
   Even this whole nation.
10 Bring all the tithes into the
      storehouse,
   That there may be food in My
      house,
   And try Me now in this,"
   Says the LORD of hosts,
   "If I will not open for you the
      windows of heaven
   And pour out for you *such*
      blessing
   That *there will* not *be room*
      enough *to receive it.*

11 "And I will rebuke the devourer
      for your sakes,
   So that he will not destroy the
      fruit of your ground,
   Nor shall the vine fail to bear
      fruit for you in the field,"
   Says the LORD of hosts;
12 And all nations will call you
      blessed,
   For you will be a delightful
      land,"
   Says the LORD of hosts.

13 "Your words have been harsh
      against Me,"
   Says the LORD,
   "Yet you say,
   'What have we spoken against
      You?'
14 You have said,
   'It is useless to serve God;
   What profit *is it* that we have
      kept His ordinance,
   And that we have walked as
      mourners
   Before the LORD of hosts?
15 So now we call the proud
      blessed,
   For those who do wickedness
      are raised up;
   They even tempt God and go
      free.' "

16 Then those who feared the
      LORD spoke to one another,
   And the LORD listened and
      heard *them*;

So a book of remembrance was
   written before Him
For those who fear the LORD
And who meditate on His
   name.
17 "They shall be Mine," says the
      LORD of hosts,
   "On the day that I make them
      My jewels.*a*
   And I will spare them
   As a man spares his own son
      who serves him."
18 Then you shall again discern
   Between the righteous and the
      wicked,
   Between one who serves God
   And one who does not serve
      Him.

4 "For behold, the day is coming,
      Burning like an oven,
   And all the proud, yes, all who
      do wickedly will be stubble.
   And the day which is coming
      shall burn them up,"
   Says the LORD of hosts,
   "That will leave them neither
      root nor branch.
2 But to you who fear My name
   The Sun of Righteousness shall
      arise
   With healing in His wings;
   And you shall go out
   And grow fat like stall-fed
      calves.
3 You shall trample the wicked,
   For they shall be ashes under
      the soles of your feet
   On the day that I do *this*,"
   Says the LORD of hosts.

4 "Remember the Law of Moses,
      My servant,
   Which I commanded him in
      Horeb for all Israel,
   With the statutes and
      judgments.
5 Behold, I will send you Elijah
      the prophet
   Before the coming of the great
      and dreadful day of the LORD.
6 And he will turn
   The hearts of the fathers to the
      children,
   And the hearts of the children
      to their fathers,
   Lest I come and strike the earth
      with a curse."

3:17 *a*Literally *special treasure*

The
New Testament

Matthew

Overview of Matthew

M atthew writes to let his readers know that Jesus Christ is indeed the King of the Jews. Himself a Jew, Matthew writes this Gospel to his countrymen, telling them that the long-awaited Messiah has come, bringing salvation and hope to those who believe.

Matthew is the most orderly account of the good news of Jesus Christ, tracing the genealogy of Jesus with a carefully selected series of Old Testament quotations as proof of His birth, His ministry and the miraculous fulfillment of God's covenant promises. Almost exclusively, Matthew incorporates the phrase "that it might be fulfilled which was spoken by the prophets."

Matthew was among many Jewish youth who memorized the Law and the Prophets by rote. Four New Testament synagogues have been discovered in Palestine. Three of these have a room known as the "midrash" room. "Midrash" refers to the compiling of the Old Testament verses from various portions of Scripture in order to present evidence from the Law. Matthew uses a similar compilation technique to present Jesus Christ as the Messiah who fulfilled all the Old Testament prophecies concerning the Promised One.

Although Matthew is Jewish in his orientation, he writes with a Gentile slant. This is most likely due to his association with the Romans and Greeks when he served as a tax collector. He flavors his presentation with a universal outlook, especially when he records Jesus' last words:

Go therefore and make disciples of all the nations, baptizing them in the name of the Father and of the Son and of the Holy Spirit, teaching them to observe all things that I have commanded you; and lo, I am with you always, even to the end of the age."

(Matt. 28:19, 20)

Jesus in Matthew

Matthew presents Jesus as Israel's promised messianic King (1:23; 2:2, 6; 3:17; 4:15–17; 21:5, 9; 22:44, 45; 26:64; 27:11, 27–37). The phrase "the kingdom of heaven" appears thirty-two times in Matthew, but nowhere else in the New Testament. "That what was spoken through the prophet might be fulfilled" appears nine times in this Gospel, showing Matthew's scriptural assertion of Christ as Messiah. Jesus is revealed in Matthew as the Son of Man (24:30ff.), the "Servant" of the Lord (12:17–21), and the "Son of David."

Keys to Matthew

Key Words: Jesus the King. Through Old Testament prophecies, Matthew validates Jesus' lineage, His birthplace, His flight into Egypt, His announcement by John the Baptist, and His confrontation with Satan in the desert. After four hundred years of prophetic silence, Jesus the King arrives.

Key Verses: "Simon Peter answered and said, 'You are the Christ, the Son of the living God.' Jesus answered and said to him, 'Blessed are you, Simon Bar-Jonah, for flesh and blood has not revealed *this* to you, but My Father who is in heaven. And I also say to you that you are Peter, and on this rock I will build My church, and the gates of Hades shall not prevail against it. And I will give you the keys of the kingdom of heaven, and whatever you bind on earth will be bound in heaven, and whatever you loose on earth will be loosed in heaven'" (16:16–19).

"And Jesus came and spoke to them, saying, 'All authority has been given to Me in heaven and on earth. Go therefore and make disciples of all the nations, baptizing them in the name of the Father and of the Son and of the Holy Spirit, teaching them to observe all things that I have commanded you; and lo, I am with you always, *even* to the end of the age.' Amen" (28:18–20).

Key Chapter: Matthew 12. The turning point of Matthew comes in the twelfth chapter when the Pharisees, acting as the leadership of Israel, formally reject Jesus Christ as the Messiah, attributing His power to Satan. Christ's ministry changes immediately with new teachings in parables, increased attention to His disciples, and His repeated statement that His death is now near.

1 The book of the genealogy of Jesus Christ, the Son of David, the Son of Abraham:

2 Abraham begot Isaac, Isaac begot Jacob, and Jacob begot Judah and his brothers. 3 Judah begot Perez and Zerah by Tamar, Perez begot Hezron, and Hezron begot Ram. 4 Ram begot Amminadab, Amminadab begot Nahshon, and Nahshon begot Salmon. 5 Salmon begot Boaz by Rahab, Boaz begot Obed by Ruth, Obed begot Jesse, 6 and Jesse begot David the king.

David the king begot Solomon by her *who had been the wife*[a] of Uriah. 7 Solomon begot Rehoboam, Rehoboam begot Abijah, and Abijah begot Asa.[a] 8 Asa begot Jehoshaphat, Jehoshaphat begot Joram, and Joram begot Uzziah. 9 Uzziah begot Jotham, Jotham begot Ahaz, and Ahaz begot Hezekiah. 10 Hezekiah begot Manasseh, Manasseh begot Amon,[a] and Amon begot Josiah. 11 Josiah begot Jeconiah and his brothers about the time they were carried away to Babylon.

12 And after they were brought to Babylon, Jeconiah begot Shealtiel, and Shealtiel begot Zerubbabel. 13 Zerubbabel begot Abiud, Abiud begot Eliakim, and Eliakim begot Azor. 14 Azor begot Zadok, Zadok begot Achim, and Achim begot Eliud. 15 Eliud begot Eleazar, Eleazar begot Matthan, and Matthan begot Jacob. 16 And Jacob begot Joseph the husband of Mary, of whom was born Jesus who is called Christ.

17 So all the generations from Abraham to David *are* fourteen generations, from David until the captivity in Babylon *are* fourteen generations, and from the captivity in Babylon until the Christ *are* fourteen generations.

18 Now the birth of Jesus Christ was as follows: After His mother Mary was betrothed to Joseph, before they came together, she was found with child of the Holy Spirit. 19 Then Joseph her husband, being a just *man,* and not wanting to make her a public example, was minded to put her away secretly. 20 But while he thought about these things, behold, an angel of the Lord appeared to him in a dream, saying, "Joseph, son of David, do not be afraid to take to you Mary your wife, for that which is conceived in her is of the Holy Spirit. 21 And she will bring forth a Son, and you shall call His name JESUS, for He will save His people from their sins."

22 So all this was done that it might be fulfilled which was spoken by the Lord through the prophet, saying: 23 *"Behold, the virgin shall be with child, and bear a Son, and they shall call His name Immanuel,"*[a] which is translated, "God with us."

24 Then Joseph, being aroused from sleep, did as the angel of the Lord commanded him and took to him his wife, 25 and did not know her till she had brought forth her firstborn Son.[a] And he called His name JESUS.

2 Now after Jesus was born in Bethlehem of Judea in the days of Herod the king, behold, wise men from the East came to Jerusalem, 2 saying, "Where is He who has been born King of the Jews? For we have seen His star in the East and have come to worship Him."

3 When Herod the king heard *this,* he was troubled, and all Jerusalem with him. 4 And when he had gathered all the chief priests and scribes of the people together, he inquired of them where the Christ was to be born.

5 So they said to him, "In Bethlehem of Judea, for thus it is written by the prophet:

6   'But you, Bethlehem, in the land of Judah,
    Are not the least among the rulers of Judah;
    For out of you shall come a Ruler

The King by Might— The King by Right

The obscure village of Bethlehem is located in the southland of Judah, a remote corner of the world where Abraham, Isaac, Jacob, and David the shepherd king, roamed the arid hillsides. The town's name literally means "house of bread." It was into this house of bread that Jesus, the Bread of Life, was born.

At the Child's birth, His newlywed parents, Joseph and Mary, named Him Joshua, meaning "God Saves." But the world would know Him by His Greek name, Jesus. Following the thirty-three-day waiting period for new mothers, the young family journeyed to Jerusalem to offer their sacrifice at the temple. Theirs was a poor person's sacrifice: two small birds. It was at the temple that two Jerusalemites, Simeon and Anna, told Jesus' parents that they foresaw great things in the Child's future.

Jesus was immediately accepted as a king by wise men and humble working-class shepherds alike. But there was one man in the vicinity who was not happy about a baby born ruler of his people—that was the ruthless King Herod. Things began to turn sour in Herod's mind when he was visited in his plush Jerusalem palace by three trained specialists in the fields of natural sciences, astrology, and medicine. They reported their knowledge of an ancient prophecy by Micah that a ruler of Israel would come from Bethlehem.

For one who had acquired possession of his kingdom by political ingenuity, daring military campaign, and murderous persecution, this birth of a king was not easy to accept. Before, when his throne was threatened, Herod put to death anyone he remotely suspected, including many of his in-laws, one of his wives, and four of his sons. Now, he attempted trickery to enlist the help of the palace visitors, saying he also wanted to worship the Child, while hiding in his heart his intention of killing the infant.

Herod's plan was exposed to Joseph and Mary and the wise men by messengers sent from God. The wise men returned home by a different route, while Mary and Joseph found safety in Egypt. Herod attempted to solve the "infant king" problem by slaying every male in the region two years old and younger.

Herod probably sent his soldiers from the magnificent fortress palace, Herodian, to carry out his orders. The close proximity of Bethlehem to the Herodian vividly accents the contrast between Herod's cruel, material kingdom and the spiritual, life-giving kingdom of Jesus. Herod was a king by might. Jesus was a king by right. Born the Son of God, His divine birthright gave Him the authority and the power to establish God's kingdom forever!

*Who will shepherd My people
Israel.'"a*

7 Then Herod, when he had secretly called the wise men, determined from them what time the star appeared. 8 And he sent them to Bethlehem and said, "Go and search carefully for the young Child, and when you have found *Him,* bring back word to me, that I may come and worship Him also."
9 When they heard the king, they departed; and behold, the star which they had seen in the East went before them, till it came and stood over where the young Child was. 10 When they saw the star, they rejoiced with exceedingly great joy. 11 And when they had come into the house, they saw the young Child with Mary His mother, and fell down and worshiped Him. And when they had opened their treasures, they presented gifts to Him: gold, frankincense, and myrrh.
12 Then, being divinely warned in a dream that they should not return to Herod, they departed for their own country another way.
13 Now when they had departed, behold, an angel of the Lord appeared to Joseph in a dream, saying, "Arise, take the young Child and His mother, flee to Egypt, and stay there until I bring you word; for Herod will seek the young Child to destroy Him."
14 When he arose, he took the young Child and His mother by night and departed for Egypt, 15 and was there until the death of Herod, that it might be fulfilled which was spoken by the Lord through the prophet, saying, *"Out of Egypt I called My Son."a*
16 Then Herod, when he saw that he was deceived by the wise men, was exceedingly angry; and he sent forth and put to death all the male children who were in Bethlehem and in all its districts, from two years old and under, according to the time which he had determined from the wise men. 17 Then was fulfilled what was spoken by Jeremiah the prophet, saying:

18 *"A voice was heard in
Ramah,*

*Lamentation, weeping, and
great mourning,
Rachel weeping for her
children,
Refusing to be comforted,
Because they are no more."a*

19 Now when Herod was dead, behold, an angel of the Lord appeared in a dream to Joseph in Egypt, 20 saying, "Arise, take the young Child and His mother, and go to the land of Israel, for those who sought the young Child's life are dead." 21 Then he arose, took the young Child and His mother, and came into the land of Israel.
22 But when he heard that Archelaus was reigning over Judea instead of his father Herod, he was afraid to go there. And being warned by God in a dream, he turned aside into the region of Galilee. 23 And he came and dwelt in a city called Nazareth, that it might be fulfilled which was spoken by the prophets, "He shall be called a Nazarene."

3 In those days John the Baptist came preaching in the wilderness of Judea, 2 and saying, "Repent, for the kingdom of heaven is at hand!" 3 For this is he who was spoken of by the prophet Isaiah, saying:

*"The voice of one crying in the
wilderness:
'Prepare the way of the* LORD;
Make His paths straight.'"a

4 Now John himself was clothed in camel's hair, with a leather belt around his waist; and his food was locusts and wild honey. 5 Then Jerusalem, all Judea, and all the region around the Jordan went out to him 6 and were baptized by him in the Jordan, confessing their sins.
7 But when he saw many of the Pharisees and Sadducees coming to his baptism, he said to them, "Brood of vipers! Who warned you to flee from the wrath to come? 8 Therefore bear fruits worthy of repentance, 9 and do not think to say to yourselves, 'We have Abraham as *our* father.' For I say to you that God is able to raise up children to Abraham from these stones. 10 And even now the ax is laid to the root of the trees. There-

2:6 aMicah 5:2   2:15 aHosea 11:1   2:18 aJeremiah 31:15   3:3 aIsaiah 40:3

fore every tree which does not bear good fruit is cut down and thrown into the fire. 11 I indeed baptize you with water unto repentance, but He who is coming after me is mightier than I, whose sandals I am not worthy to carry. He will baptize you with the Holy Spirit and fire.*a* 12 His winnowing fan *is* in His hand, and He will thoroughly clean out His threshing floor, and gather His wheat into the barn; but He will burn up the chaff with unquenchable fire."

13 Then Jesus came from Galilee to John at the Jordan to be baptized by him. 14 And John *tried to* prevent Him, saying, "I need to be baptized by You, and are You coming to me?"

15 But Jesus answered and said to him, "Permit *it to be so* now, for thus it is fitting for us to fulfill all righteousness." Then he allowed Him.

16 When He had been baptized, Jesus came up immediately from the water; and behold, the heavens were opened to Him, and He*a* saw the Spirit of God descending like a dove and alighting upon Him. 17 And suddenly a voice *came* from heaven, saying, "This is My beloved Son, in whom I am well pleased."

4 Then Jesus was led up by the Spirit into the wilderness to be tempted by the devil. 2 And when He had fasted forty days and forty nights, afterward He was hungry. 3 Now when the tempter came to Him, he said, "If You are the Son of God, command that these stones become bread."

4 But He answered and said, "It is written, *'Man shall not live by bread alone, but by every word that proceeds from the mouth of God.'"a*

5 Then the devil took Him up into the holy city, set Him on the pinnacle of the temple, 6 and said to Him, "If You are the Son of God, throw Yourself down. For it is written:

'He shall give His angels charge over you,'

and,

'In their hands they shall bear you up,

Lest you dash your foot against a stone.'"a

7 Jesus said to him, "It is written again, *'You shall not tempt the LORD your God.'"a*

8 Again, the devil took Him up on an exceedingly high mountain, and showed Him all the kingdoms of the world and their glory. 9 And he said to Him, "All these things I will give You if You will fall down and worship me."

10 Then Jesus said to him, "Away with you,*a* Satan! For it is written, *'You shall worship the LORD your God, and Him only you shall serve.'"b*

11 Then the devil left Him, and behold, angels came and ministered to Him.

12 Now when Jesus heard that John had been put in prison, He departed to Galilee. 13 And leaving Nazareth, He came and dwelt in Capernaum, which is by the sea, in the regions of Zebulun and Naphtali, 14 that it might be fulfilled which was spoken by Isaiah the prophet, saying:

15 *"The land of Zebulun and the land of Naphtali,*
By the way of the sea, beyond the Jordan,
Galilee of the Gentiles:
16 *The people who sat in darkness have seen a great light,*
And upon those who sat in the region and shadow of death Light has dawned."a

17 From that time Jesus began to preach and to say, "Repent, for the kingdom of heaven is at hand."

18 And Jesus, walking by the Sea of Galilee, saw two brothers, Simon called Peter, and Andrew his brother, casting a net into the sea; for they were fishermen. 19 Then He said to them, "Follow Me, and I will make you fishers of men." 20 They immediately left *their* nets and followed Him.

21 Going on from there, He saw two other brothers, James *the son* of Zebedee, and John his brother, in the boat with Zebedee their father, mending their nets. He called them, 22 and immediately they left the boat

and their father, and followed Him. 23 And Jesus went about all Galilee, teaching in their synagogues, preaching the gospel of the kingdom, and healing all kinds of sickness and all kinds of disease among the people. 24 Then His fame went throughout all Syria; and they brought to Him all sick people who were afflicted with various diseases and torments, and those who were demon-possessed, epileptics, and paralytics; and He healed them. 25 Great multitudes followed Him—from Galilee, and *from* Decapolis, Jerusalem, Judea, and beyond the Jordan.

5 And seeing the multitudes, He went up on a mountain, and when He was seated His disciples came to Him. 2 Then He opened His mouth and taught them, saying:

3   "Blessed *are* the poor in spirit,
     For theirs is the kingdom of
        heaven.
4   Blessed *are* those who mourn,
     For they shall be comforted.
5   Blessed *are* the meek,
     For they shall inherit the
        earth.
6   Blessed *are* those who hunger
        and thirst for
        righteousness,
     For they shall be filled.
7   Blessed *are* the merciful,
     For they shall obtain mercy.
8   Blessed *are* the pure in heart,
     For they shall see God.
9   Blessed *are* the peacemakers,
     For they shall be called sons
        of God.
10   Blessed are those who are
        persecuted for
        righteousness' sake,
     For theirs is the kingdom of
        heaven.

11 "Blessed are you when they revile and persecute you, and say all kinds of evil against you falsely for My sake. 12 Rejoice and be exceedingly glad, for great *is* your reward in heaven, for so they persecuted the prophets who were before you.

13 "You are the salt of the earth; but if the salt loses its flavor, how shall it be seasoned? It is then good for nothing but to be thrown out and trampled underfoot by men.

14 "You are the light of the world. A city that is set on a hill cannot be hidden. 15 Nor do they light a lamp and put it under a basket, but on a lampstand, and it gives light to all *who are* in the house. 16 Let your light so shine before men, that they may see your good works and glorify your Father in heaven.

17 "Do not think that I came to destroy the Law or the Prophets. I did not come to destroy but to fulfill. 18 For assuredly, I say to you, till heaven and earth pass away, one jot or one tittle will by no means pass from the law till all is fulfilled. 19 Whoever therefore breaks one of the least of these commandments, and teaches men so, shall be called least in the kingdom of heaven; but whoever does and teaches *them,* he shall be called great in the kingdom of heaven. 20 For I say to you, that unless your righteousness exceeds *the righteousness* of the scribes and Pharisees, you will by no means enter the kingdom of heaven.

21 "You have heard that it was said to those of old, '*You shall not murder,*ᵃ and whoever murders will be in danger of the judgment.' 22 But I say to you that whoever is angry with his brother without a causeᵃ shall be in danger of the judgment. And whoever says to his brother, 'Raca!' shall be in danger of the council. But whoever says, 'You fool!' shall be in danger of hell fire. 23 Therefore if you bring your gift to the altar, and there remember that your brother has something against you, 24 leave your gift there before the altar, and go your way. First be reconciled to your brother, and then come and offer your gift. 25 Agree with your adversary quickly, while you are on the way with him, lest your adversary deliver you to the judge, the judge hand you over to the officer, and you be thrown into prison. 26 Assuredly, I say to you, you will by no means get out of there till you have paid the last penny.

27 "You have heard that it was said to those of old,ᵃ '*You shall not commit adultery.*'ᵇ 28 But I say to you that whoever looks at a woman to lust for her has already committed adultery with her in his heart. 29 If your right

5:21 ᵃExodus 20:13; Deuteronomy 5:17   5:22 ᵃNU-Text omits *without a cause.*   5:27 ᵃNU-Text and M-Text omit *to those of old.*   ᵇExodus 20:14; Deuteronomy 5:18

You Are the Light of the World

"You are the light of the world. A city that is set on a hill cannot be hidden" (Matt. 5:14).

Jesus spoke this promise to His followers while overlooking the beautiful Sea of Galilee. Surrounded on all sides by high mountains, the lake is twelve miles long and seven miles wide. Nestled between these hills and the lake were many Jewish towns from which villagers came to hear Jesus.

Every evening the Jewish people had a constant reminder of the oppression of their Roman overlords. At sundown, the mighty Roman legions lit bonfires at their hilltop command post as they guarded and maintained the famous thoroughfares, the *Via Maris*, and the King's Highway. In the first century as many as twelve to fourteen legions, each consisting of six thousand men, were stationed in Galilee. Their fires were a spectacular sight from anywhere on the lake.

Jesus' illustration dramatically punctuated His teaching on the kingdom of God. His call to be a "light—a city that is set on a hill" was a challenge to His listeners. Archaeologists have discovered that as many as ninety Greco-Roman towns were set on the eastern hills. The lights from the town lamps burned brightly above the sea below. The faith of Jesus' listeners was to be as visible and bright to the people around them as were the lights from the towns and camps that lit up the evening sky.

Jesus' call is as alive today as it was when the bonfires encircled the Sea of Galilee. Your life will burn with enthusiasm and joy when you announce and advance the kingdom of God. It may begin with lighting one candle by touching one person in your world today. But soon the fire will spread. Your life will be a mighty roaring bonfire encircling your world with the warmth of God's love!

eye causes you to sin, pluck it out and cast *it* from you; for it is more profitable for you that one of your members perish, than for your whole body to be cast into hell. 30 And if your right hand causes you to sin, cut it off and cast *it* from you; for it is more profitable for you that one of your members perish, than for your whole body to be cast into hell.

31 "Furthermore it has been said, 'Whoever divorces his wife, let him give her a certificate of divorce.' 32 But I say to you that whoever divorces his wife for any reason except sexual immorality*a* causes her to commit adultery; and whoever marries a woman who is divorced commits adultery.

33 "Again you have heard that it was said to those of old, 'You shall not swear falsely, but shall perform your oaths to the Lord.' 34 But I say to you, do not swear at all: neither by heaven, for it is God's throne; 35 nor by the earth, for it is His footstool; nor by Jerusalem, for it is the city of the great King. 36 Nor shall you swear by your head, because you cannot make one hair white or black. 37 But let your 'Yes' be 'Yes,' and your 'No,' 'No.' For whatever is more than these is from the evil one.

38 "You have heard that it was said, *'An eye for an eye and a tooth for a tooth.'a* 39 But I tell you not to resist an evil person. But whoever slaps you on your right cheek, turn the other to him also. 40 If anyone wants to sue you and take away your tunic, let him have *your* cloak also. 41 And whoever compels you to go one mile, go with him two. 42 Give to him who asks you, and from him who wants to borrow from you do not turn away.

43 "You have heard that it was said, *'You shall love your neighbora* and hate your enemy.' 44 But I say to you, love your enemies, bless those who curse you, do good to those who hate you, and pray for those who spitefully use you and persecute you,*a* 45 that you may be sons of your Father in heaven; for He makes His sun rise on the evil and on the good, and sends rain on the just and on the

unjust. 46 For if you love those who love you, what reward have you? Do not even the tax collectors do the same? 47 And if you greet your brethren*a* only, what do you do more *than others?* Do not even the tax collectors*b* do so? 48 Therefore you shall be perfect, just as your Father in heaven is perfect.

6 "Take heed that you do not do your charitable deeds before men, to be seen by them. Otherwise you have no reward from your Father in heaven. 2 Therefore, when you do a charitable deed, do not sound a trumpet before you as the hypocrites do in the synagogues and in the streets, that they may have glory from men. Assuredly, I say to you, they have their reward. 3 But when you do a charitable deed, do not let your left hand know what your right hand is doing, 4 that your charitable deed may be in secret; and your Father who sees in secret will Himself reward you openly.*a*

5 "And when you pray, you shall not be like the hypocrites. For they love to pray standing in the synagogues and on the corners of the streets, that they may be seen by men. Assuredly, I say to you, they have their reward. 6 But you, when you pray, go into your room, and when you have shut your door, pray to your Father who *is* in the secret *place;* and your Father who sees in secret will reward you openly.*a* 7 And when you pray, do not use vain repetitions as the heathen *do.* For they think that they will be heard for their many words.

8 "Therefore do not be like them. For your Father knows the things you have need of before you ask Him. 9 In this manner, therefore, pray:

> Our Father in heaven,
> Hallowed be Your name.
> 10   Your kingdom come.
> Your will be done
> On earth as *it is* in heaven.
> 11   Give us this day our daily
>   bread.
> 12   And forgive us our debts,
> As we forgive our debtors.

13 And do not lead us into
      temptation,
      But deliver us from the evil one.
      For Yours is the kingdom and
        the power and the glory
        forever. Amen.*a*

14 "For if you forgive men their
trespasses, your heavenly Father will
also forgive you. 15 But if you do not
forgive men their trespasses, neither
will your Father forgive your trespasses.

16 "Moreover, when you fast, do
not be like the hypocrites, with a sad
countenance. For they disfigure their
faces that they may appear to men
to be fasting. Assuredly, I say to you,
they have their reward. 17 But you,
when you fast, anoint your head and
wash your face, 18 so that you do not
appear to men to be fasting, but to
your Father who *is* in the secret
place; and your Father who sees in
secret will reward you openly.*a*

19 "Do not lay up for yourselves
treasures on earth, where moth and
rust destroy and where thieves break
in and steal; 20 but lay up for yourselves treasures in heaven, where
neither moth nor rust destroys and
where thieves do not break in and
steal. 21 For where your treasure is,
there your heart will be also.

22 "The lamp of the body is the
eye. If therefore your eye is good,
your whole body will be full of
light. 23 But if your eye is bad, your
whole body will be full of darkness.
If therefore the light that is in you
is darkness, how great *is* that darkness!

24 "No one can serve two masters;
for either he will hate the one and
love the other, or else he will be loyal
to the one and despise the other. You
cannot serve God and mammon.

25 "Therefore I say to you, do not
worry about your life, what you will
eat or what you will drink; nor about
your body, what you will put on. Is
not life more than food and the body
more than clothing? 26 Look at the
birds of the air, for they neither sow
nor reap nor gather into barns; yet
your heavenly Father feeds them.
Are you not of more value than they?
27 Which of you by worrying can add
one cubit to his stature?

28 "So why do you worry about

clothing? Consider the lilies of the
field, how they grow: they neither toil
nor spin; 29 and yet I say to you that
even Solomon in all his glory was not
arrayed like one of these. 30 Now if
God so clothes the grass of the field,
which today is, and tomorrow is
thrown into the oven, *will He* not
much more *clothe* you, O you of little
faith?

31 "Therefore do not worry, saying,
'What shall we eat?' or 'What shall
we drink?' or 'What shall we wear?'
32 For after all these things the Gentiles seek. For your heavenly Father
knows that you need all these things.
33 But seek first the kingdom of God
and His righteousness, and all these
things shall be added to you.
34 Therefore do not worry about tomorrow, for tomorrow will worry
about its own things. Sufficient for
the day *is* its own trouble.

7 "Judge not, that you be not
   judged. 2 For with what judgment
you judge, you will be judged; and
with the measure you use, it will be
measured back to you. 3 And why do
you look at the speck in your brother's eye, but do not consider the
plank in your own eye? 4 Or how can
you say to your brother, 'Let me remove the speck from your eye'; and
look, a plank *is* in your own eye?
5 Hypocrite! First remove the plank
from your own eye, and then you will
see clearly to remove the speck from
your brother's eye.

6 "Do not give what is holy to the
dogs; nor cast your pearls before
swine, lest they trample them under
their feet, and turn and tear you in
pieces.

7 "Ask, and it will be given to you;
seek, and you will find; knock, and
it will be opened to you. 8 For everyone who asks receives, and he who
seeks finds, and to him who knocks
it will be opened. 9 Or what man is
there among you who, if his son asks
for bread, will give him a stone?
10 Or if he asks for a fish, will he give
him a serpent? 11 If you then, being
evil, know how to give good gifts to
your children, how much more will
your Father who is in heaven give
good things to those who ask Him!
12 Therefore, whatever you want
men to do to you, do also to them,

6:13 *a*NU-Text omits *For Yours* through *Amen.*   6:18 *a*NU-Text and M-Text omit *openly.*

A House Built on Rock

On the slopes above the northwest shores of the Sea of Galilee sat the ancient Jewish village of Chorazin. Matthew records that in this town many of Jesus' miracles took place (see Matt. 11:21). This village was also the origin of one of Jesus' most familiar teachings—the parable of two houses. Archaeologists have discovered first-and-second-century remnants of the town which indicate that the village was built on the rocky slopes of the hill and in the adjacent waterbed below.

In this region a major mountain range running east to west caught most of the country's rainfall during the winter months of January and February. As much as thirty-seven inches of rain falls in a two-month span. The high amount of rainfall causes flash floods in several watershed systems, including the Wadi Ammud, where Chorazin is located. These wadis naturally drained mountain water to the lake below.

Even today, it is common to see a ten-foot wall of water burst suddenly upon the plains surrounding the lake. Jesus vividly described the sudden floods that often roared without warning from the mountains. "Whoever hears these sayings of Mine, and does them, I will liken him to a wise man who built his house on the rock: and the rain descended, the floods came, and the winds blew and beat on that house; and it did not fall, for it was founded on the rock. But everyone who hears these sayings of Mine, and does not do them, will be like a foolish man who built his house on the sand: and the rain descended, the floods came, and the winds blew and beat on that house; and it fell. And great was its fall" (Matt. 7:24–27).

Many structures of ancient houses from Jesus' day still stand on rocks high above. But in the sandy wadi below, only rubble remains, bearing witness to the homes crushed by sudden, calamitous downpours.

What is the foundation of your life? Set it high and firm on the rock of Jesus by hearing and doing what He says. Build your life on Him. When the winds and rains of life's problems suddenly descend on you, you will not fall—for you are founded on the rock (see 1 Cor. 10:4).

for this is the Law and the Prophets.

13 "Enter by the narrow gate; for wide *is* the gate and broad *is* the way that leads to destruction, and there are many who go in by it. 14 Because*a* narrow *is* the gate and difficult *is* the way which leads to life, and there are few who find it.

15 "Beware of false prophets, who come to you in sheep's clothing, but inwardly they are ravenous wolves. 16 You will know them by their fruits. Do men gather grapes from thornbushes or figs from thistles? 17 Even so, every good tree bears good fruit, but a bad tree bears bad fruit. 18 A good tree cannot bear bad fruit, nor *can* a bad tree bear good fruit. 19 Every tree that does not bear good fruit is cut down and thrown into the fire. 20 Therefore by their fruits you will know them.

21 "Not everyone who says to Me, 'Lord, Lord,' shall enter the kingdom of heaven, but he who does the will of My Father in heaven. 22 Many will say to Me in that day, 'Lord, Lord, have we not prophesied in Your name, cast out demons in Your name, and done many wonders in Your name?' 23 And then I will declare to them, 'I never knew you; depart from Me, you who practice lawlessness!'

24 "Therefore whoever hears these sayings of Mine, and does them, I will liken him to a wise man who built his house on the rock: 25 and the rain descended, the floods came, and the winds blew and beat on that house; and it did not fall, for it was founded on the rock.

26 "But everyone who hears these sayings of Mine, and does not do them, will be like a foolish man who built his house on the sand: 27 and the rain descended, the floods came, and the winds blew and beat on that house; and it fell. And great was its fall."

28 And so it was, when Jesus had ended these sayings, that the people were astonished at His teaching, 29 for He taught them as one having authority, and not as the scribes.

8 When He had come down from the mountain, great multitudes followed Him. 2 And behold, a leper came and worshiped Him, saying, "Lord, if You are willing, You can make me clean."

3 Then Jesus put out *His* hand and touched him, saying, "I am willing; be cleansed." Immediately his leprosy was cleansed.

4 And Jesus said to him, "See that you tell no one; but go your way, show yourself to the priest, and offer the gift that Moses commanded, as a testimony to them."

5 Now when Jesus had entered Capernaum, a centurion came to Him, pleading with Him, 6 saying, "Lord, my servant is lying at home paralyzed, dreadfully tormented."

7 And Jesus said to him, "I will come and heal him."

8 The centurion answered and said, "Lord, I am not worthy that You should come under my roof. But only speak a word, and my servant will be healed. 9 For I also am a man under authority, having soldiers under me. And I say to this *one,* 'Go,' and he goes; and to another, 'Come,' and he comes; and to my servant, 'Do this,' and he does *it.*"

10 When Jesus heard *it,* He marveled, and said to those who followed, "Assuredly, I say to you, I have not found such great faith, not even in Israel! 11 And I say to you that many will come from east and west, and sit down with Abraham, Isaac, and Jacob in the kingdom of heaven. 12 But the sons of the kingdom will be cast out into outer darkness. There will be weeping and gnashing of teeth." 13 Then Jesus said to the centurion, "Go your way; and as you have believed, so let it be done for you." And his servant was healed that same hour.

14 Now when Jesus had come into Peter's house, He saw his wife's mother lying sick with a fever. 15 So He touched her hand, and the fever left her. And she arose and served them.*a*

16 When evening had come, they brought to Him many who were demon-possessed. And He cast out the spirits with a word, and healed all who were sick, 17 that it might be fulfilled which was spoken by Isaiah the prophet, saying:

7:14 *a*NU-Text and M-Text read *How . . . !*   8:15 *a*NU-Text and M-Text read *Him.*

Stilling the Storm

The Sea of Galilee is only twelve miles long, seven miles wide and seven hundred feet deep. Yet over these waters come some of the most ferocious, vicious storms in the Middle East.

The Sea of Galilee is located scarcely fifty miles from the coast of the Mediterranean Sea. To the northeast of its shores, the Syro-Phoenician mountains of Lebanon rise. When a low pressure system comes off the Mediterranean and clashes with a high pressure system from these mountains, the calm surface of the Sea of Galilee can be suddenly transformed into a raging storm with waves fifteen to twenty feet high.

There is constant danger for fishermen caught out on the lake in the springtime and early fall, when the storms most frequently occur. During these seasons, the weather may be perfect when the fishermen leave shore—not a cloud in the sky—but within minutes the sky becomes overcast and large swells mount to toss their boats about.

Mark 4:36–41 records just such a day when Jesus and His disciples had gone out on the sea. "A great windstorm arose, and the waves beat into the boat, so that it was already filling" (v. 37). Jesus, who had been asleep, now rose, and standing in the middle of the boat, rebuked the storm saying, "Peace, be still!" (v. 39). Immediately the storm subsided. The disciples wondered among themselves, "Who can this be, that even the wind and the sea obey Him" (v. 41).

There are times in our lives when everything seems to be calm. But like one of the sudden storms on the Sea of Galilee, problems can suddenly arise, transforming our lives into a raging storm of stress and difficulty. Without someone to turn to, these problems seem overwhelming. Yet with faith in God, we rest assured that the voice of Jesus and the presence of God will still any storm of problems with a word: "Peace, be still!"

*"He Himself took our
infirmities
And bore our sicknesses."[a]*

18 And when Jesus saw great multitudes about Him, He gave a command to depart to the other side. 19 Then a certain scribe came and said to Him, "Teacher, I will follow You wherever You go."

20 And Jesus said to him, "Foxes have holes and birds of the air *have* nests, but the Son of Man has nowhere to lay *His* head."

21 Then another of His disciples said to Him, "Lord, let me first go and bury my father."

22 But Jesus said to him, "Follow Me, and let the dead bury their own dead."

23 Now when He got into a boat, His disciples followed Him. 24 And suddenly a great tempest arose on the sea, so that the boat was covered with the waves. But He was asleep. 25 Then His disciples came to *Him* and awoke Him, saying, "Lord, save us! We are perishing!"

26 But He said to them, "Why are you fearful, O you of little faith?" Then He arose and rebuked the winds and the sea, and there was a great calm. 27 So the men marveled, saying, "Who can this be, that even the winds and the sea obey Him?"

28 When He had come to the other side, to the country of the Gergesenes,[a] there met Him two demon-possessed *men,* coming out of the tombs, exceedingly fierce, so that no one could pass that way. 29 And suddenly they cried out, saying, "What have we to do with You, Jesus, You Son of God? Have You come here to torment us before the time?"

30 Now a good way off from them there was a herd of many swine feeding. 31 So the demons begged Him, saying, "If You cast us out, permit us to go away[a] into the herd of swine."

32 And He said to them, "Go." So when they had come out, they went into the herd of swine. And suddenly the whole herd of swine ran violently down the steep place into the sea, and perished in the water.

33 Then those who kept *them* fled; and they went away into the city and told everything, including what *had happened* to the demon-possessed *men.* 34 And behold, the whole city came out to meet Jesus. And when they saw Him, they begged *Him* to depart from their region.

9 So He got into a boat, crossed over, and came to His own city. 2 Then behold, they brought to Him a paralytic lying on a bed. When Jesus saw their faith, He said to the paralytic, "Son, be of good cheer; your sins are forgiven you."

3 And at once some of the scribes said within themselves, "This Man blasphemes!"

4 But Jesus, knowing their thoughts, said, "Why do you think evil in your hearts? 5 For which is easier, to say, '*Your* sins are forgiven you,' or to say, 'Arise and walk'? 6 But that you may know that the Son of Man has power on earth to forgive sins"—then He said to the paralytic, "Arise, take up your bed, and go to your house." 7 And he arose and departed to his house.

8 Now when the multitudes saw *it,* they marveled[a] and glorified God, who had given such power to men.

9 As Jesus passed on from there, He saw a man named Matthew sitting at the tax office. And He said to him, "Follow Me." So he arose and followed Him.

10 Now it happened, as Jesus sat at the table in the house, *that* behold, many tax collectors and sinners came and sat down with Him and His disciples. 11 And when the Pharisees saw *it,* they said to His disciples, "Why does your Teacher eat with tax collectors and sinners?"

12 When Jesus heard *that,* He said to them, "Those who are well have no need of a physician, but those who are sick. 13 But go and learn what *this* means: '*I desire mercy and not sacrifice.*'[a] For I did not come to call the righteous, but sinners, to repentance."[b]

14 Then the disciples of John came to Him, saying, "Why do we and the Pharisees fast often,[a] but Your disciples do not fast?"

15 And Jesus said to them, "Can the

8:17 [a]Isaiah 53:4   8:28 [a]NU-Text reads *Gadarenes.*   8:31 [a]NU-Text reads *send us.*   9:8 [a]NU-Text reads *were afraid.*   9:13 [a]Hosea 6:6   [b]NU-Text omits *to repentance.*   9:14 [a]NU-Text brackets *often* as disputed.

Reach Out in Faith

In the ancient Middle East, certain prophets, places, and objects were said to have had specific healing powers. People from all corners of the Roman Empire came to sit in the healing waters of Galilee's hot springs. The pool of Bethesda in Jerusalem was also reported by the apostle in John 5:1–4 to have miraculous healing properties.

The concept of a divine touch and healing power was prevalent in the Jewish culture of Jesus' day, according to many accounts in the Gospels. People looked to "holy men," as well as to physicians for healing.

The physician, gospel-writer Luke, told how Jesus was passing through a crowd one day en route to the house of an important Capernaum ruler whose daughter was dying (see Luke 8:41–48). A woman who had been plagued with an ailment for twelve years and who had received no cure from many doctors' visits reached out to touch Jesus' hem and was healed. Suddenly, He turned and asked who had touched Him. He told the disciples He knew that power had gone out from Him. The woman stepped forward reluctantly and admitted she had believed if she could simply touch the hem of Jesus' garment, she would be healed. Jesus told her to rejoice because her faith had made her well.

When we reach out in faith to touch God, He always acknowledges us. Our Lord is never too busy, and He is always ready to be an unending source of strength and healing power. When we approach God with positive faith, He says to us, "Be of good cheer . . . your faith has made you well" (Matt. 9:22).

friends of the bridegroom mourn as long as the bridegroom is with them? But the days will come when the bridegroom will be taken away from them, and then they will fast. 16 No one puts a piece of unshrunk cloth on an old garment; for the patch pulls away from the garment, and the tear is made worse. 17 Nor do they put new wine into old wineskins, or else the wineskins break, the wine is spilled, and the wineskins are ruined. But they put new wine into new wineskins, and both are preserved."

18 While He spoke these things to them, behold, a ruler came and worshiped Him, saying, "My daughter has just died, but come and lay Your hand on her and she will live." 19 So Jesus arose and followed him, and so *did* His disciples.

20 And suddenly, a woman who had a flow of blood for twelve years came from behind and touched the hem of His garment. 21 For she said to herself, "If only I may touch His garment, I shall be made well." 22 But Jesus turned around, and when He saw her He said, "Be of good cheer, daughter; your faith has made you well." And the woman was made well from that hour.

23 When Jesus came into the ruler's house, and saw the flute players and the noisy crowd wailing, 24 He said to them, "Make room, for the girl is not dead, but sleeping." And they ridiculed Him. 25 But when the crowd was put outside, He went in and took her by the hand, and the girl arose. 26 And the report of this went out into all that land.

27 When Jesus departed from there, two blind men followed Him, crying out and saying, "Son of David, have mercy on us!"

28 And when He had come into the house, the blind men came to Him. And Jesus said to them, "Do you believe that I am able to do this?"

They said to Him, "Yes, Lord."

29 Then He touched their eyes, saying, "According to your faith let it be to you." 30 And their eyes were opened. And Jesus sternly warned them, saying, "See *that* no one

knows *it*." 31 But when they had departed, they spread the news about Him in all that country.

32 As they went out, behold, they brought to Him a man, mute and demon-possessed. 33 And when the demon was cast out, the mute spoke. And the multitudes marveled, saying, "It was never seen like this in Israel!"

34 But the Pharisees said, "He casts out demons by the ruler of the demons."

35 Then Jesus went about all the cities and villages, teaching in their synagogues, preaching the gospel of the kingdom, and healing every sickness and every disease among the people.*a* 36 But when He saw the multitudes, He was moved with compassion for them, because they were weary*a* and scattered, like sheep having no shepherd. 37 Then He said to His disciples, "The harvest truly *is* plentiful, but the laborers *are* few. 38 Therefore pray the Lord of the harvest to send out laborers into His harvest."

10 And when He had called His twelve disciples to *Him,* He gave them power *over* unclean spirits, to cast them out, and to heal all kinds of sickness and all kinds of disease. 2 Now the names of the twelve apostles are these: first, Simon, who is called Peter, and Andrew his brother; James the *son* of Zebedee, and John his brother; 3 Philip and Bartholomew; Thomas and Matthew the tax collector; James the *son* of Alphaeus, and Lebbaeus, whose surname was*a* Thaddaeus; 4 Simon the Cananite,*a* and Judas Iscariot, who also betrayed Him.

5 These twelve Jesus sent out and commanded them, saying: "Do not go into the way of the Gentiles, and do not enter a city of the Samaritans. 6 But go rather to the lost sheep of the house of Israel. 7 And as you go, preach, saying, 'The kingdom of heaven is at hand.' 8 Heal the sick, cleanse the lepers, raise the dead,*a* cast out demons. Freely you have received, freely give. 9 Provide neither gold nor silver nor copper in your money belts, 10 nor bag for *your* journey, nor two tunics, nor sandals, nor

---

9:35 *a*NU-Text omits *among the people.* 　　9:36 *a*NU-Text and M-Text read *harassed.* 　　10:3 *a*NU-Text omits *Lebbaeus, whose surname was.* 　10:4 *a*NU-Text reads *Cananaean.* 　10:8 *a*NU-Text reads *raise the dead, cleanse the lepers;* M-Text omits *raise the dead.*

staffs; for a worker is worthy of his food.

11 "Now whatever city or town you enter, inquire who in it is worthy, and stay there till you go out. 12 And when you go into a household, greet it. 13 If the household is worthy, let your peace come upon it. But if it is not worthy, let your peace return to you. 14 And whoever will not receive you nor hear your words, when you depart from that house or city, shake off the dust from your feet. 15 Assuredly, I say to you, it will be more tolerable for the land of Sodom and Gomorrah in the day of judgment than for that city!

16 "Behold, I send you out as sheep in the midst of wolves. Therefore be wise as serpents and harmless as doves. 17 But beware of men, for they will deliver you up to councils and scourge you in their synagogues. 18 You will be brought before governors and kings for My sake, as a testimony to them and to the Gentiles. 19 But when they deliver you up, do not worry about how or what you should speak. For it will be given to you in that hour what you should speak; 20 for it is not you who speak, but the Spirit of your Father who speaks in you.

21 "Now brother will deliver up brother to death, and a father *his* child; and children will rise up against parents and cause them to be put to death. 22 And you will be hated by all for My name's sake. But he who endures to the end will be saved. 23 When they persecute you in this city, flee to another. For assuredly, I say to you, you will not have gone through the cities of Israel before the Son of Man comes.

24 "A disciple is not above *his* teacher, nor a servant above his master. 25 It is enough for a disciple that he be like his teacher, and a servant like his master. If they have called the master of the house Beelzebub,*a* how much more *will they call* those of his household! 26 Therefore do not fear them. For there is nothing covered that will not be revealed, and hidden that will not be known.

27 "Whatever I tell you in the dark, speak in the light; and what you hear in the ear, preach on the housetops. 28 And do not fear those who kill the body but cannot kill the soul. But rather fear Him who is able to destroy both soul and body in hell. 29 Are not two sparrows sold for a copper coin? And not one of them falls to the ground apart from your Father's will. 30 But the very hairs of your head are all numbered. 31 Do not fear therefore; you are of more value than many sparrows.

32 "Therefore whoever confesses Me before men, him I will also confess before My Father who is in heaven. 33 But whoever denies Me before men, him I will also deny before My Father who is in heaven.

34 "Do not think that I came to bring peace on earth. I did not come to bring peace but a sword. 35 For I have come to *'set a man against his father, a daughter against her mother, and a daughter-in-law against her mother-in-law';* 36 and *'a man's enemies will be those of his own household.'a* 37 He who loves father or mother more than Me is not worthy of Me. And he who loves son or daughter more than Me is not worthy of Me. 38 And he who does not take his cross and follow after Me is not worthy of Me. 39 He who finds his life will lose it, and he who loses his life for My sake will find it.

40 "He who receives you receives Me, and he who receives Me receives Him who sent Me. 41 He who receives a prophet in the name of a prophet shall receive a prophet's reward. And he who receives a righteous man in the name of a righteous man shall receive a righteous man's reward. 42 And whoever gives one of these little ones only a cup of cold *water* in the name of a disciple, assuredly, I say to you, he shall by no means lose his reward."

11 Now it came to pass, when Jesus finished commanding His twelve disciples, that He departed from there to teach and to preach in their cities.

2 And when John had heard in prison about the works of Christ, he sent two of*a* his disciples 3 and said to Him, "Are You the Coming One, or do we look for another?"

4 Jesus answered and said to them, "Go and tell John the things which you hear and see: 5 *The* blind see

10:25 *a*NU-Text and M-Text read *Beelzebul.*   10:36 *a*Micah 7:6   11:2 *a*NU-Text reads *by* for *two of.*

and *the* lame walk; *the* lepers are cleansed and *the* deaf hear; *the* dead are raised up and *the* poor have the gospel preached to them. 6 And blessed is he who is not offended because of Me."

7 As they departed, Jesus began to say to the multitudes concerning John: "What did you go out into the wilderness to see? A reed shaken by the wind? 8 But what did you go out to see? A man clothed in soft garments? Indeed, those who wear soft *clothing* are in kings' houses. 9 But what did you go out to see? A prophet? Yes, I say to you, and more than a prophet. 10 For this is *he* of whom it is written:

> 'Behold, I send My messenger
>   before Your face,
> Who will prepare Your way
>   before You.'ᵃ

11 "Assuredly, I say to you, among those born of women there has not risen one greater than John the Baptist; but he who is least in the kingdom of heaven is greater than he. 12 And from the days of John the Baptist until now the kingdom of heaven suffers violence, and the violent take it by force. 13 For all the prophets and the law prophesied until John. 14 And if you are willing to receive *it,* he is Elijah who is to come. 15 He who has ears to hear, let him hear!

16 "But to what shall I liken this generation? It is like children sitting in the marketplaces and calling to their companions, 17 and saying:

> 'We played the flute for you,
>   And you did not dance;
> We mourned to you,
>   And you did not lament.'

18 For John came neither eating nor drinking, and they say, 'He has a demon.' 19 The Son of Man came eating and drinking, and they say, 'Look, a glutton and a winebibber, a friend of tax collectors and sinners!' But wisdom is justified by her children."ᵃ

20 Then He began to rebuke the cities in which most of His mighty works had been done, because they did not repent: 21 "Woe to you, Chorazin! Woe to you, Bethsaida! For if the mighty works which were done in you had been done in Tyre and Sidon, they would have repented long ago in sackcloth and ashes. 22 But I say to you, it will be more tolerable for Tyre and Sidon in the day of judgment than for you. 23 And you, Capernaum, who are exalted to heaven, will beᵃ brought down to Hades; for if the mighty works which were done in you had been done in Sodom, it would have remained until this day. 24 But I say to you that it shall be more tolerable for the land of Sodom in the day of judgment than for you."

25 At that time Jesus answered and said, "I thank You, Father, Lord of heaven and earth, that You have hidden these things from *the* wise and prudent and have revealed them to babes. 26 Even so, Father, for so it seemed good in Your sight. 27 All things have been delivered to Me by My Father, and no one knows the Son except the Father. Nor does anyone know the Father except the Son, and *the one* to whom the Son wills to reveal *Him.* 28 Come to Me, all *you* who labor and are heavy laden, and I will give you rest. 29 Take My yoke upon you and learn from Me, for I am gentle and lowly in heart, and you will find rest for your souls. 30 For My yoke *is* easy and My burden is light."

12 At that time Jesus went through the grainfields on the Sabbath. And His disciples were hungry, and began to pluck heads of grain and to eat. 2 And when the Pharisees saw *it,* they said to Him, "Look, Your disciples are doing what is not lawful to do on the Sabbath!"

3 But He said to them, "Have you not read what David did when he was hungry, he and those who were with him: 4 how he entered the house of God and ate the showbread which was not lawful for him to eat, nor for those who were with him, but only for the priests? 5 Or have you not read in the law that on the Sabbath the priests in the temple profane the Sabbath, and are blameless? 6 Yet I say to you that in this place there is *One* greater than the temple.

11:10 ᵃMalachi 3:1   11:19 ᵃNU-Text reads *works.*   11:23 ᵃNU-Text reads *will you be exalted to heaven? No, you will be.*

7 But if you had known what *this* means, '*I desire mercy and not sacrifice,*'*a* you would not have condemned the guiltless. 8 For the Son of Man is Lord even*a* of the Sabbath.''

9 Now when He had departed from there, He went into their synagogue. 10 And behold, there was a man who had a withered hand. And they asked Him, saying, ''Is it lawful to heal on the Sabbath?''—that they might accuse Him.

11 Then He said to them, ''What man is there among you who has one sheep, and if it falls into a pit on the Sabbath, will not lay hold of it and lift *it* out? 12 Of how much more value then is a man than a sheep? Therefore it is lawful to do good on the Sabbath.'' 13 Then He said to the man, ''Stretch out your hand.'' And he stretched *it* out, and it was restored as whole as the other. 14 Then the Pharisees went out and plotted against Him, how they might destroy Him.

15 But when Jesus knew *it,* He withdrew from there. And great multitudes*a* followed Him, and He healed them all. 16 Yet He warned them not to make Him known, 17 that it might be fulfilled which was spoken by Isaiah the prophet, saying:

18 *''Behold! My Servant whom I*
* have chosen,*
* My Beloved in whom My soul*
*   is well pleased!*
* I will put My Spirit upon Him,*
* And He will declare justice to*
*   the Gentiles.*
19 *He will not quarrel nor cry*
*   out,*
* Nor will anyone hear His voice*
*   in the streets.*
20 *A bruised reed He will not*
*   break,*
* And smoking flax He will not*
*   quench,*
* Till He sends forth justice to*
*   victory;*
21 *And in His name Gentiles will*
*   trust.''a*

22 Then one was brought to Him who was demon-possessed, blind and mute; and He healed him, so that the blind and*a* mute man both spoke and saw. 23 And all the multitudes were amazed and said, ''Could this be the Son of David?''

24 Now when the Pharisees heard *it* they said, ''This *fellow* does not cast out demons except by Beelzebub,*a* the ruler of the demons.''

25 But Jesus knew their thoughts, and said to them: ''Every kingdom divided against itself is brought to desolation, and every city or house divided against itself will not stand. 26 If Satan casts out Satan, he is divided against himself. How then will his kingdom stand? 27 And if I cast out demons by Beelzebub, by whom do your sons cast *them* out? Therefore they shall be your judges. 28 But if I cast out demons by the Spirit of God, surely the kingdom of God has come upon you. 29 Or how can one enter a strong man's house and plunder his goods, unless he first binds the strong man? And then he will plunder his house. 30 He who is not with Me is against Me, and he who does not gather with Me scatters abroad.

31 ''Therefore I say to you, every sin and blasphemy will be forgiven men, but the blasphemy *against* the Spirit will not be forgiven men. 32 Anyone who speaks a word against the Son of Man, it will be forgiven him; but whoever speaks against the Holy Spirit, it will not be forgiven him, either in this age or in the *age* to come.

33 ''Either make the tree good and its fruit good, or else make the tree bad and its fruit bad; for a tree is known by *its* fruit. 34 Brood of vipers! How can you, being evil, speak good things? For out of the abundance of the heart the mouth speaks. 35 A good man out of the good treasure of his heart*a* brings forth good things, and an evil man out of the evil treasure brings forth evil things. 36 But I say to you that for every idle word men may speak, they will give account of it in the day of judgment. 37 For by your words you will be justified, and by your words you will be condemned.''

38 Then some of the scribes and Pharisees answered, saying,

12:7 *a*Hosea 6:6   12:8 *a*NU-Text and M-Text omit *even.*   12:15 *a*NU-Text brackets *multitudes* as disputed.   12:21 *a*Isaiah 42:1–4   12:22 *a*NU-Text omits *blind and.*   12:24 *a*NU-Text and M-Text read *Beelzebul.*   12:35 *a*NU-Text and M-Text omit *of his heart.*

"Teacher, we want to see a sign from You."

39 But He answered and said to them, "An evil and adulterous generation seeks after a sign, and no sign will be given to it except the sign of the prophet Jonah. 40 For as Jonah was three days and three nights in the belly of the great fish, so will the Son of Man be three days and three nights in the heart of the earth. 41 The men of Nineveh will rise up in the judgment with this generation and condemn it, because they repented at the preaching of Jonah; and indeed a greater than Jonah is here. 42 The queen of the South will rise up in the judgment with this generation and condemn it, for she came from the ends of the earth to hear the wisdom of Solomon; and indeed a greater than Solomon is here.

43 "When an unclean spirit goes out of a man, he goes through dry places, seeking rest, and finds none. 44 Then he says, 'I will return to my house from which I came.' And when he comes, he finds it empty, swept, and put in order. 45 Then he goes and takes with him seven other spirits more wicked than himself, and they enter and dwell there; and the last state of that man is worse than the first. So shall it also be with this wicked generation."

46 While He was still talking to the multitudes, behold, His mother and brothers stood outside, seeking to speak with Him. 47 Then one said to Him, "Look, Your mother and Your brothers are standing outside, seeking to speak with You."

48 But He answered and said to the one who told Him, "Who is My mother and who are My brothers?" 49 And He stretched out His hand toward His disciples and said, "Here are My mother and My brothers! 50 For whoever does the will of My Father in heaven is My brother and sister and mother."

13 On the same day Jesus went out of the house and sat by the sea. 2 And great multitudes were gathered together to Him, so that He got into a boat and sat; and the whole multitude stood on the shore. 3 Then He spoke many things to them in parables, saying: "Behold, a sower went out to sow. 4 And as he sowed, some seed fell by the wayside; and the birds came and devoured them. 5 Some fell on stony places, where they did not have much earth; and they immediately sprang up because they had no depth of earth. 6 But when the sun was up they were scorched, and because they had no root they withered away. 7 And some fell among thorns, and the thorns sprang up and choked them. 8 But others fell on good ground and yielded a crop: some a hundredfold, some sixty, some thirty. 9 He who has ears to hear, let him hear!"

10 And the disciples came and said to Him, "Why do You speak to them in parables?"

11 He answered and said to them, "Because it has been given to you to know the mysteries of the kingdom of heaven, but to them it has not been given. 12 For whoever has, to him more will be given, and he will have abundance; but whoever does not have, even what he has will be taken away from him. 13 Therefore I speak to them in parables, because seeing they do not see, and hearing they do not hear, nor do they understand. 14 And in them the prophecy of Isaiah is fulfilled, which says:

'Hearing you will hear and shall not understand,
And seeing you will see and not perceive;
15 For the hearts of this people have grown dull.
Their ears are hard of hearing,
And their eyes they have closed,
Lest they should see with their eyes and hear with their ears,
Lest they should understand with their hearts and turn,
So that I should[a] heal them.'[b]

16 But blessed are your eyes for they see, and your ears for they hear; 17 for assuredly, I say to you that many prophets and righteous men desired to see what you see, and did not see it, and to hear what you hear, and did not hear it.

18 "Therefore hear the parable of the sower: 19 When anyone hears the word of the kingdom, and does not

13:15 aNU-Text and M-Text read would.   bIsaiah 6:9, 10

The Mustard Seed

Mustard trees grow in abundance beside the Sea of Galilee and in the southern hill country of Judea on the Mount of Olives. These trees are not individually planted by local farmers, but by birds and the wind carrying their seeds and scattering them about. Once rooted, the trees grow to a height of eight to twelve feet. In the springtime, these colorful yellow plants are found with birds nesting among their branches.

Jesus taught that the kingdom of God is like both the tiny mustard seed and the full-grown mustard tree. Small or large, God's providential care is there for its growth. To Jesus' listeners, the mustard seed symbolized something small and apparently lifeless. Yet they knew when it was sown, it would spring to life as a full, growing tree. In another parable, Jesus said, "Unless a grain of wheat falls into the ground and dies, it remains alone; but if it dies, it produces much grain" (John 12:24). Paul also drew from this teaching when he said about our bodies, "This mortal has put on immortality" (1 Cor. 15:54). So, then, a seed and the death of the seed bring forth life and renewed faith.

We can be confident that out of the tiniest of possibilities, God will raise and establish His kingdom. Out of our little beginnings He will reap a full harvest. Whether you have a great task or a small responsibility, do it joyfully, for out of your endeavors God will raise bountiful blessings. Remember, anyone can count the seeds in an apple, but only God can count the apples in a seed!

understand *it*, then the wicked *one* comes and snatches away what was sown in his heart. This is he who received seed by the wayside. 20 But he who received the seed on stony places, this is he who hears the word and immediately receives it with joy; 21 yet he has no root in himself, but endures only for a while. For when tribulation or persecution arises because of the word, immediately he stumbles. 22 Now he who received seed among the thorns is he who hears the word, and the cares of this world and the deceitfulness of riches choke the word, and he becomes unfruitful. 23 But he who received seed on the good ground is he who hears the word and understands *it*, who indeed bears fruit and produces: some a hundredfold, some sixty, some thirty."

24 Another parable He put forth to them, saying: "The kingdom of heaven is like a man who sowed good seed in his field; 25 but while men slept, his enemy came and sowed tares among the wheat and went his way. 26 But when the grain had sprouted and produced a crop, then the tares also appeared. 27 So the servants of the owner came and said to him, 'Sir, did you not sow good seed in your field? How then does it have tares?' 28 He said to them, 'An enemy has done this.' The servants said to him, 'Do you want us then to go and gather them up?' 29 But he said, 'No, lest while you gather up the tares you also uproot the wheat with them. 30 Let both grow together until the harvest, and at the time of harvest I will say to the reapers, "First gather together the tares and bind them in bundles to burn them, but gather the wheat into my barn." ' "

31 Another parable He put forth to them, saying: "The kingdom of heaven is like a mustard seed, which a man took and sowed in his field, 32 which indeed is the least of all the seeds; but when it is grown it is greater than the herbs and becomes a tree, so that the birds of the air come and nest in its branches."

33 Another parable He spoke to them: "The kingdom of heaven is like leaven, which a woman took and hid in three measures*a* of meal till it was all leavened."

34 All these things Jesus spoke to the multitude in parables; and without a parable He did not speak to them, 35 that it might be fulfilled which was spoken by the prophet, saying:

> "I will open My mouth in parables;
> I will utter things kept secret from the foundation of the world."*a*

36 Then Jesus sent the multitude away and went into the house. And His disciples came to Him, saying, "Explain to us the parable of the tares of the field."

37 He answered and said to them: "He who sows the good seed is the Son of Man. 38 The field is the world, the good seeds are the sons of the kingdom, but the tares are the sons of the wicked *one*. 39 The enemy who sowed them is the devil, the harvest is the end of the age, and the reapers are the angels. 40 Therefore as the tares are gathered and burned in the fire, so it will be at the end of this age. 41 The Son of Man will send out His angels, and they will gather out of His kingdom all things that offend, and those who practice lawlessness, 42 and will cast them into the furnace of fire. There will be wailing and gnashing of teeth. 43 Then the righteous will shine forth as the sun in the kingdom of their Father. He who has ears to hear, let him hear!

44 "Again, the kingdom of heaven is like treasure hidden in a field, which a man found and hid; and for joy over it he goes and sells all that he has and buys that field.

45 "Again, the kingdom of heaven is like a merchant seeking beautiful pearls, 46 who, when he had found one pearl of great price, went and sold all that he had and bought it.

47 "Again, the kingdom of heaven is like a dragnet that was cast into the sea and gathered some of every kind, 48 which, when it was full, they drew to shore; and they sat down and gathered the good into vessels, but threw the bad away. 49 So it will be at the end of the age. The angels will come forth, separate the wicked from among the just, 50 and cast them into

---

13:33 *a*Greek *sata*, approximately two pecks in all   13:35 *a*Psalm 78:2

the furnace of fire. There will be wailing and gnashing of teeth."

51 Jesus said to them,[a] "Have you understood all these things?"

They said to Him, "Yes, Lord."[b]

52 Then He said to them, "Therefore every scribe instructed concerning[a] the kingdom of heaven is like a householder who brings out of his treasure *things* new and old."

53 Now it came to pass, when Jesus had finished these parables, that He departed from there. 54 When He had come to His own country, He taught them in their synagogue, so that they were astonished and said, "Where did this *Man* get this wisdom and *these* mighty works? 55 Is this not the carpenter's son? Is not His mother called Mary? And His brothers James, Joses,[a] Simon, and Judas? 56 And His sisters, are they not all with us? Where then did this *Man* get all these things?" 57 So they were offended at Him.

But Jesus said to them, "A prophet is not without honor except in his own country and in his own house." 58 Now He did not do many mighty works there because of their unbelief.

14 At that time Herod the tetrarch heard the report about Jesus 2 and said to his servants, "This is John the Baptist; he is risen from the dead, and therefore these powers are at work in him." 3 For Herod had laid hold of John and bound him, and put *him* in prison for the sake of Herodias, his brother Philip's wife. 4 Because John had said to him, "It is not lawful for you to have her." 5 And although he wanted to put him to death, he feared the multitude, because they counted him as a prophet.

6 But when Herod's birthday was celebrated, the daughter of Herodias danced before them and pleased Herod. 7 Therefore he promised with an oath to give her whatever she might ask.

8 So she, having been prompted by her mother, said, "Give me John the Baptist's head here on a platter." 9 And the king was sorry; nevertheless, because of the oaths and because of those who sat with him, he commanded *it* to be given *to her.*

10 So he sent and had John beheaded in prison. 11 And his head was brought on a platter and given to the girl, and she brought *it* to her mother. 12 Then his disciples came and took away the body and buried it, and went and told Jesus.

13 When Jesus heard *it*, He departed from there by boat to a deserted place by Himself. But when the multitudes heard it, they followed Him on foot from the cities. 14 And when Jesus went out He saw a great multitude; and He was moved with compassion for them, and healed their sick. 15 When it was evening, His disciples came to Him, saying, "This is a deserted place, and the hour is already late. Send the multitudes away, that they may go into the villages and buy themselves food."

16 But Jesus said to them, "They do not need to go away. You give them something to eat."

17 And they said to Him, "We have here only five loaves and two fish."

18 He said, "Bring them here to Me." 19 Then He commanded the multitudes to sit down on the grass. And He took the five loaves and the two fish, and looking up to heaven, He blessed and broke and gave the loaves to the disciples; and the disciples gave to the multitudes. 20 So they all ate and were filled, and they took up twelve baskets full of the fragments that remained. 21 Now those who had eaten were about five thousand men, besides women and children.

22 Immediately Jesus made His disciples get into the boat and go before Him to the other side, while He sent the multitudes away. 23 And when He had sent the multitudes away, He went up on the mountain by Himself to pray. Now when evening came, He was alone there. 24 But the boat was now in the middle of the sea,[a] tossed by the waves, for the wind was contrary.

25 Now in the fourth watch of the night Jesus went to them, walking on the sea. 26 And when the disciples saw Him walking on the sea, they were troubled, saying, "It is a ghost!" And they cried out for fear.

27 But immediately Jesus spoke to

13:51 [a]NU-Text omits *Jesus said to them.*   [b]NU-Text omits *Lord.*   13:52 [a]Or *for.*   13:55 [a]NU-Text reads *Joseph.*   14:24 [a]NU-Text reads *many furlongs away from the land.*

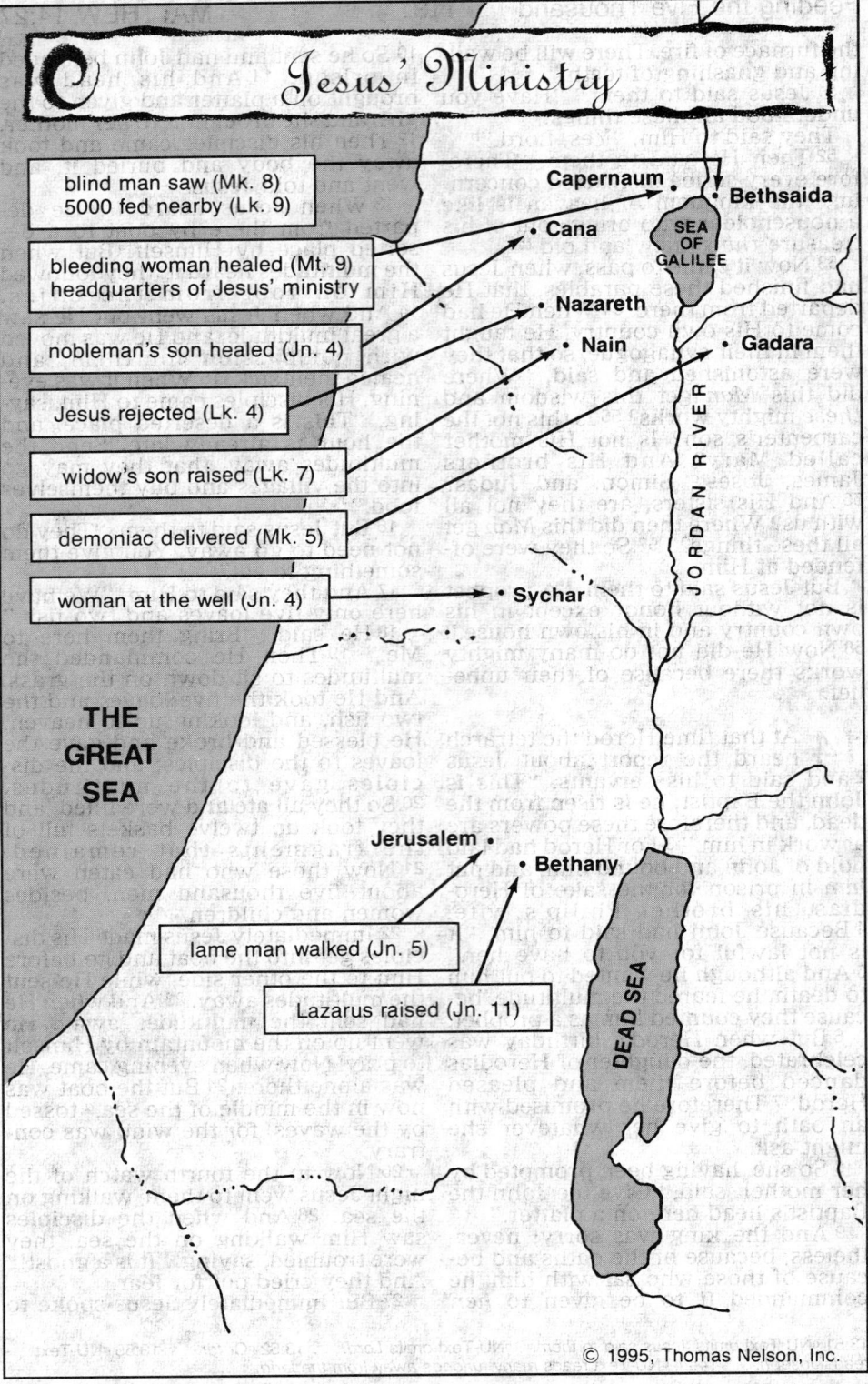

Jesus' Ministry

blind man saw (Mk. 8)
5000 fed nearby (Lk. 9)

bleeding woman healed (Mt. 9)
headquarters of Jesus' ministry

nobleman's son healed (Jn. 4)

Jesus rejected (Lk. 4)

widow's son raised (Lk. 7)

demoniac delivered (Mk. 5)

woman at the well (Jn. 4)

THE GREAT SEA

Capernaum

Bethsaida

SEA OF GALILEE

Cana

Nazareth

Nain

Gadara

JORDAN RIVER

Sychar

Jerusalem

Bethany

lame man walked (Jn. 5)

Lazarus raised (Jn. 11)

DEAD SEA

them, saying, "Be of good cheer! It is I; do not be afraid."

28 And Peter answered Him and said, "Lord, if it is You, command me to come to You on the water."

29 So He said, "Come." And when Peter had come down out of the boat, he walked on the water to go to Jesus. 30 But when he saw that the wind *was* boisterous,*a* he was afraid; and beginning to sink he cried out, saying, "Lord, save me!"

31 And immediately Jesus stretched out *His* hand and caught him, and said to him, "O you of little faith, why did you doubt?" 32 And when they got into the boat, the wind ceased.

33 Then those who were in the boat came and*a* worshiped Him, saying, "Truly You are the Son of God."

34 When they had crossed over, they came to the land of*a* Gennesaret. 35 And when the men of that place recognized Him, they sent out into all that surrounding region, brought to Him all who were sick, 36 and begged Him that they might only touch the hem of His garment. And as many as touched *it* were made perfectly well.

15

Then the scribes and Pharisees who were from Jerusalem came to Jesus, saying, 2 "Why do Your disciples transgress the tradition of the elders? For they do not wash their hands when they eat bread."

3 He answered and said to them, "Why do you also transgress the commandment of God because of your tradition? 4 For God commanded, saying, 'Honor your father and your mother';*a* and, 'He who curses father or mother, let him be put to death.'*b* 5 But you say, 'Whoever says to his father or mother, "Whatever profit you might have received from me *is* a gift *to* God"— 6 then he need not honor his father or mother.'*a* Thus you have made the commandment*b* of God of no effect by your tradition. 7 Hypocrites! Well did Isaiah prophesy about you, saying:

8 'These people draw near to Me with their mouth,
And honor Me with their lips,
But their heart is far from Me.
9 And in vain they worship Me,
Teaching as doctrines the commandments of men.'"*a*

10 When He had called the multitude to *Himself,* He said to them, "Hear and understand: 11 Not what goes into the mouth defiles a man; but what comes out of the mouth, this defiles a man."

12 Then His disciples came and said to Him, "Do You know that the Pharisees were offended when they heard this saying?"

13 But He answered and said, "Every plant which My heavenly Father has not planted will be uprooted. 14 Let them alone. They are blind leaders of the blind. And if the blind leads the blind, both will fall into a ditch."

15 Then Peter answered and said to Him, "Explain this parable to us."

16 So Jesus said, "Are you also still without understanding? 17 Do you not yet understand that whatever enters the mouth goes into the stomach and is eliminated? 18 But those things which proceed out of the mouth come from the heart, and they defile a man. 19 For out of the heart proceed evil thoughts, murders, adulteries, fornications, thefts, false witness, blasphemies. 20 These are the things which defile a man, but to eat with unwashed hands does not defile a man."

21 Then Jesus went out from there and departed to the region of Tyre and Sidon. 22 And behold, a woman of Canaan came from that region and cried out to Him, saying, "Have mercy on me, O Lord, Son of David! My daughter is severely demon-possessed."

23 But He answered her not a word. And His disciples came and urged Him, saying, "Send her away, for she cries out after us."

24 But He answered and said, "I was not sent except to the lost sheep of the house of Israel."

14:30 *a*NU-Text brackets *that* and *boisterous* as disputed.   14:33 *a*NU-Text omits *came and.*
14:34 *a*NU-Text reads *came to land at.*   15:4 *a*Exodus 20:12; Deuteronomy 5:16   *b*Exodus 21:17
15:6 *a*NU-Text omits *or mother.*   *b*NU-Text reads *word.*   15:8 *a*NU-Text omits *draw near to Me with their mouth, And.*   15:9 *a*Isaiah 29:13

25 Then she came and worshiped Him, saying, "Lord, help me!"

26 But He answered and said, "It is not good to take the children's bread and throw it to the little dogs."

27 And she said, "Yes, Lord, yet even the little dogs eat the crumbs which fall from their masters' table."

28 Then Jesus answered and said to her, "O woman, great is your faith! Let it be to you as you desire." And her daughter was healed from that very hour.

29 Jesus departed from there, skirted the Sea of Galilee, and went up on the mountain and sat down there. 30 Then great multitudes came to Him, having with them the lame, blind, mute, maimed, and many others; and they laid them down at Jesus' feet, and He healed them. 31 So the multitude marveled when they saw the mute speaking, the maimed made whole, the lame walking, and the blind seeing; and they glorified the God of Israel.

32 Now Jesus called His disciples to Himself and said, "I have compassion on the multitude, because they have now continued with Me three days and have nothing to eat. And I do not want to send them away hungry, lest they faint on the way."

33 Then His disciples said to Him, "Where could we get enough bread in the wilderness to fill such a great multitude?"

34 Jesus said to them, "How many loaves do you have?"

And they said, "Seven, and a few little fish."

35 So He commanded the multitude to sit down on the ground. 36 And He took the seven loaves and the fish and gave thanks, broke them and gave them to His disciples; and the disciples gave to the multitude. 37 So they all ate and were filled, and they took up seven large baskets full of the fragments that were left. 38 Now those who ate were four thousand men, besides women and children. 39 And He sent away the multitude, got into the boat, and came to the region of Magdala.ᵃ

16 Then the Pharisees and Sadducees came, and testing Him asked that He would show them a sign from heaven. 2 He answered and said to them, "When it is evening you say, 'It will be fair weather, for the sky is red'; 3 and in the morning, 'It will be foul weather today, for the sky is red and threatening.' Hypocrites!ᵃ You know how to discern the face of the sky, but you cannot discern the signs of the times. 4 A wicked and adulterous generation seeks after a sign, and no sign shall be given to it except the sign of the prophetᵃ Jonah." And He left them and departed.

5 Now when His disciples had come to the other side, they had forgotten to take bread. 6 Then Jesus said to them, "Take heed and beware of the leaven of the Pharisees and the Sadducees."

7 And they reasoned among themselves, saying, "It is because we have taken no bread."

8 But Jesus, being aware of it, said to them, "O you of little faith, why do you reason among yourselves because you have brought no bread?ᵃ 9 Do you not yet understand, or remember the five loaves of the five thousand and how many baskets you took up? 10 Nor the seven loaves of the four thousand and how many large baskets you took up? 11 How is it you do not understand that I did not speak to you concerning bread?—but to beware of the leaven of the Pharisees and Sadducees." 12 Then they understood that He did not tell them to beware of the leaven of bread, but of the doctrine of the Pharisees and Sadducees.

13 When Jesus came into the region of Caesarea Philippi, He asked His disciples, saying, "Who do men say that I, the Son of Man, am?"

14 So they said, "Some say John the Baptist, some Elijah, and others Jeremiah or one of the prophets."

15 He said to them, "But who do you say that I am?"

16 Simon Peter answered and said, "You are the Christ, the Son of the living God."

17 Jesus answered and said to him, "Blessed are you, Simon Bar-Jonah, for flesh and blood has not revealed this to you, but My Father who is in heaven. 18 And I also say to you that you are Peter, and on this rock I will

15:39 ᵃNU-Text reads Magadan.   16:3 ᵃNU-Text omits Hypocrites.   16:4 ᵃNU-Text omits the prophet.   16:8 ᵃNU-Text reads you have no bread.

build My church, and the gates of Hades shall not prevail against it. 19 And I will give you the keys of the kingdom of heaven, and whatever you bind on earth will be bound in heaven, and whatever you loose on earth will be loosed*a* in heaven."

20 Then He commanded His disciples that they should tell no one that He was Jesus the Christ.

21 From that time Jesus began to show to His disciples that He must go to Jerusalem, and suffer many things from the elders and chief priests and scribes, and be killed, and be raised the third day.

22 Then Peter took Him aside and began to rebuke Him, saying, "Far be it from You, Lord; this shall not happen to You!"

23 But He turned and said to Peter, "Get behind Me, Satan! You are an offense to Me, for you are not mindful of the things of God, but the things of men."

24 Then Jesus said to His disciples, "If anyone desires to come after Me, let him deny himself, and take up his cross, and follow Me. 25 For whoever desires to save his life will lose it, but whoever loses his life for My sake will find it. 26 For what profit is it to a man if he gains the whole world, and loses his own soul? Or what will a man give in exchange for his soul? 27 For the Son of Man will come in the glory of His Father with His angels, and then He will reward each according to his works. 28 Assuredly, I say to you, there are some standing here who shall not taste death till they see the Son of Man coming in His kingdom."

17 Now after six days Jesus took Peter, James, and John his brother, led them up on a high mountain by themselves; 2 and He was transfigured before them. His face shone like the sun, and His clothes became as white as the light. 3 And behold, Moses and Elijah appeared to them, talking with Him. 4 Then Peter answered and said to Jesus, "Lord, it is good for us to be here; if You wish, let us*a* make here three tabernacles: one for You, one for Moses, and one for Elijah."

5 While he was still speaking, behold, a bright cloud overshadowed them; and suddenly a voice came out of the cloud, saying, "This is My beloved Son, in whom I am well pleased. Hear Him!" 6 And when the disciples heard *it*, they fell on their faces and were greatly afraid. 7 But Jesus came and touched them and said, "Arise, and do not be afraid." 8 When they had lifted up their eyes, they saw no one but Jesus only.

9 Now as they came down from the mountain, Jesus commanded them, saying, "Tell the vision to no one until the Son of Man is risen from the dead."

10 And His disciples asked Him, saying, "Why then do the scribes say that Elijah must come first?"

11 Jesus answered and said to them, "Indeed, Elijah is coming first*a* and will restore all things. 12 But I say to you that Elijah has come already, and they did not know him but did to him whatever they wished. Likewise the Son of Man is also about to suffer at their hands." 13 Then the disciples understood that He spoke to them of John the Baptist.

14 And when they had come to the multitude, a man came to Him, kneeling down to Him and saying, 15 "Lord, have mercy on my son, for he is an epileptic*a* and suffers severely; for he often falls into the fire and often into the water. 16 So I brought him to Your disciples, but they could not cure him."

17 Then Jesus answered and said, "O faithless and perverse generation, how long shall I be with you? How long shall I bear with you? Bring him here to Me." 18 And Jesus rebuked the demon, and it came out of him; and the child was cured from that very hour.

19 Then the disciples came to Jesus privately and said, "Why could we not cast it out?"

20 So Jesus said to them, "Because of your unbelief;*a* for assuredly, I say to you, if you have faith as a mustard seed, you will say to this mountain, 'Move from here to there,' and it will move; and nothing will be impossible for you. 21 However, this kind does

---

16:19 *a*Or *will have been bound . . . will have been loosed*   17:4 *a*NU-Text reads *I will.*
17:11 *a*NU-Text omits *first.*   17:15 *a*Literally *moonstruck*   17:20 *a*NU-Text reads *little faith.*

The Lost Sheep

The Gospel of Luke records that the Pharisees were adamantly opposed to Jesus eating with tax gatherers and other "immoral" people, and they murmured when He associated with unrighteous men and women (Luke 15:2). Jesus responded to their grumblings: "A man had one hundred sheep, but upon counting them discovered there were only ninety-nine. One was missing. Immediately the man went in search of the lost sheep." It was an almost daily occurrence in a shepherd's life to look for a sheep that had strayed from the flock. Jesus used this story to illustrate God's love for each one of his children.

Today, in the Judean wilderness, a shepherd will appoint other shepherds to watch his flock while he goes to find a lost sheep. In the twisted folds and narrow canyon gullies of the wilderness, it is easy for a sheep to stray into the open mouth of a cave or wander aimlessly down an adjacent riverbed. The shepherd will search and call out for the lost sheep, sometimes throwing stones at the mouths of caves to scare a sheep out of hiding.

On one such occasion, in 1948, while searching for his lost sheep, a young shepherd boy threw a stone into a cave. He heard the sound of pottery breaking. It turned out to be containers of the famous Dead Sea Scrolls, which held the earliest manuscripts of the Old Testament.

Once a shepherd has found his sheep, he will place the lamb on his shoulder, grabbing its feet with one hand, while keeping his other hand free to hold his staff and defend himself against attacking animals. The shepherd can often be heard singing, rejoicing that the sheep that was lost is now found.

Jesus' answer to the Pharisees reveals that God is constantly guarding and caring for His sheep. He, especially, goes to great effort to find those who have gone astray from His flock. God sent Jesus Christ into the world specifically to seek and save that which was lost (Luke 19:10).

In our lives, let us look to Jesus, the Good Shepherd, keeping our eyes on Him and heeding His call. When we go astray, we can be confident that He will come and search for us. He will find us, lift us up on His shoulders and bring us safely home. Then there will be much rejoicing—for the sheep that was lost is now found!

not go out except by prayer and fasting."[a]

22 Now while they were staying[a] in Galilee, Jesus said to them, "The Son of Man is about to be betrayed into the hands of men, 23 and they will kill Him, and the third day He will be raised up." And they were exceedingly sorrowful.

24 When they had come to Capernaum,[a] those who received the *temple* tax came to Peter and said, "Does your Teacher not pay the *temple* tax?"

25 He said, "Yes."

And when he had come into the house, Jesus anticipated him, saying, "What do you think, Simon? From whom do the kings of the earth take customs or taxes, from their sons or from strangers?"

26 Peter said to Him, "From strangers."

Jesus said to him, "Then the sons are free. 27 Nevertheless, lest we offend them, go to the sea, cast in a hook, and take the fish that comes up first. And when you have opened its mouth, you will find a piece of money;[a] take that and give it to them for Me and you."

18 At that time the disciples came to Jesus, saying, "Who then is greatest in the kingdom of heaven?"

2 Then Jesus called a little child to Him, set him in the midst of them, 3 and said, "Assuredly, I say to you, unless you are converted and become as little children, you will by no means enter the kingdom of heaven. 4 Therefore whoever humbles himself as this little child is the greatest in the kingdom of heaven. 5 Whoever receives one little child like this in My name receives Me.

6 "But whoever causes one of these little ones who believe in Me to sin, it would be better for him if a millstone were hung around his neck, and he were drowned in the depth of the sea. 7 Woe to the world because of offenses! For offenses must come, but woe to that man by whom the offense comes!

8 "If your hand or foot causes you to sin, cut it off and cast *it* from you. It is better for you to enter into life lame or maimed, rather than having two hands or two feet, to be cast into the everlasting fire. 9 And if your eye causes you to sin, pluck it out and cast *it* from you. It is better for you to enter into life with one eye, rather than having two eyes, to be cast into hell fire.

10 "Take heed that you do not despise one of these little ones, for I say to you that in heaven their angels always see the face of My Father who is in heaven. 11 For the Son of Man has come to save that which was lost.[a]

12 "What do you think? If a man has a hundred sheep, and one of them goes astray, does he not leave the ninety-nine and go to the mountains to seek the one that is straying? 13 And if he should find it, assuredly, I say to you, he rejoices more over that *sheep* than over the ninety-nine that did not go astray. 14 Even so it is not the will of your Father who is in heaven that one of these little ones should perish.

15 "Moreover if your brother sins against you, go and tell him his fault between you and him alone. If he hears you, you have gained your brother. 16 But if he will not hear, take with you one or two more, that 'by the mouth of two or three witnesses every word may be established.'[a] 17 And if he refuses to hear them, tell *it* to the church. But if he refuses even to hear the church, let him be to you like a heathen and a tax collector.

18 "Assuredly, I say to you, whatever you bind on earth will be bound in heaven, and whatever you loose on earth will be loosed in heaven.

19 "Again I say[a] to you that if two of you agree on earth concerning anything that they ask, it will be done for them by My Father in heaven. 20 For where two or three are gathered together in My name, I am there in the midst of them."

21 Then Peter came to Him and said, "Lord, how often shall my brother sin against me, and I forgive him? Up to seven times?"

22 Jesus said to him, "I do not say to you, up to seven times, but up to seventy times seven. 23 Therefore the

17:21 [a]NU-Text omits this verse.   17:22 [a]NU-Text reads *gathering together.*   17:24 [a]NU-Text reads *Capharnaum* (here and elsewhere).   17:27 [a]Greek *stater*, the exact amount to pay the temple tax (didrachma) for two.   18:11 [a]NU-Text omits this verse.   18:16 [a]Deuteronomy 19:15   18:19 [a]NU-Text and M-Text read *Again, assuredly, I say.*

kingdom of heaven is like a certain king who wanted to settle accounts with his servants. 24 And when he had begun to settle accounts, one was brought to him who owed him ten thousand talents. 25 But as he was not able to pay, his master commanded that he be sold, with his wife and children and all that he had, and that payment be made. 26 The servant therefore fell down before him, saying, 'Master, have patience with me, and I will pay you all.' 27 Then the master of that servant was moved with compassion, released him, and forgave him the debt.

28 "But that servant went out and found one of his fellow servants who owed him a hundred denarii; and he laid hands on him and took *him* by the throat, saying, 'Pay me what you owe!' 29 So his fellow servant fell down at his feet*a* and begged him, saying, 'Have patience with me, and I will pay you all.'*b* 30 And he would not, but went and threw him into prison till he should pay the debt. 31 So when his fellow servants saw what had been done, they were very grieved, and came and told their master all that had been done. 32 Then his master, after he had called him, said to him, 'You wicked servant! I forgave you all that debt because you begged me. 33 Should you not also have had compassion on your fellow servant, just as I had pity on you?' 34 And his master was angry, and delivered him to the torturers until he should pay all that was due to him.

35 "So My heavenly Father also will do to you if each of you, from his heart, does not forgive his brother his trespasses."*a*

19 Now it came to pass, when Jesus had finished these sayings, *that* He departed from Galilee and came to the region of Judea beyond the Jordan. 2 And great multitudes followed Him, and He healed them there.

3 The Pharisees also came to Him, testing Him, and saying to Him, "Is it lawful for a man to divorce his wife for *just* any reason?"

4 And He answered and said to them, "Have you not read that He who made*a them* at the beginning *'made them male and female,'b* 5 and said, *'For this reason a man shall leave his father and mother and be joined to his wife, and the two shall become one flesh'?a* 6 So then, they are no longer two but one flesh. Therefore what God has joined together, let not man separate."

7 They said to Him, "Why then did Moses command to give a certificate of divorce, and to put her away?"

8 He said to them, "Moses, because of the hardness of your hearts, permitted you to divorce your wives, but from the beginning it was not so. 9 And I say to you, whoever divorces his wife, except for sexual immorality,*a* and marries another, commits adultery; and whoever marries her who is divorced commits adultery."

10 His disciples said to Him, "If such is the case of the man with *his* wife, it is better not to marry."

11 But He said to them, "All cannot accept this saying, but only *those* to whom it has been given: 12 For there are eunuchs who were born thus from *their* mother's womb, and there are eunuchs who were made eunuchs by men, and there are eunuchs who have made themselves eunuchs for the kingdom of heaven's sake. He who is able to accept *it,* let him accept *it.*"

13 Then little children were brought to Him that He might put *His* hands on them and pray, but the disciples rebuked them. 14 But Jesus said, "Let the little children come to Me, and do not forbid them; for of such is the kingdom of heaven." 15 And He laid *His* hands on them and departed from there.

16 Now behold, one came and said to Him, "Good*a* Teacher, what good thing shall I do that I may have eternal life?"

17 So He said to him, "Why do you call Me good?*a* No one *is* good but One, *that is,* God.*b* But if you want to enter into life, keep the commandments."

18 He said to Him, "Which ones?" Jesus said, "'*You shall not murder,*' '*You shall not commit adultery,*' '*You shall not steal,*' '*You shall not bear*

18:29 *a*NU-Text omits *at his feet.*   *b*NU-Text and M-Text omit *all.*   18:35 *a*NU-Text omits *his trespasses.*   19:4 *a*NU-Text reads *created.*   *b*Genesis 1:27; 5:2   19:5 *a*Genesis 2:24   19:9 *a*Or *fornication*   19:16 *a*NU-Text omits *Good.*   19:17 *a*NU-Text reads *Why do you ask Me about what is good?*   *b*NU-Text reads *There is One who is good.*

false witness,' 19 'Honor your father and your mother,'ᵃ and, 'You shall love your neighbor as yourself.'"ᵇ

20 The young man said to Him, "All these things I have kept from my youth.ᵃ What do I still lack?"

21 Jesus said to him, "If you want to be perfect, go, sell what you have and give to the poor, and you will have treasure in heaven; and come, follow Me."

22 But when the young man heard that saying, he went away sorrowful, for he had great possessions.

23 Then Jesus said to His disciples, "Assuredly, I say to you that it is hard for a rich man to enter the kingdom of heaven. 24 And again I say to you, it is easier for a camel to go through the eye of a needle than for a rich man to enter the kingdom of God."

25 When His disciples heard it, they were greatly astonished, saying, "Who then can be saved?"

26 But Jesus looked at them and said to them, "With men this is impossible, but with God all things are possible."

27 Then Peter answered and said to Him, "See, we have left all and followed You. Therefore what shall we have?"

28 So Jesus said to them, "Assuredly I say to you, that in the regeneration, when the Son of Man sits on the throne of His glory, you who have followed Me will also sit on twelve thrones, judging the twelve tribes of Israel. 29 And everyone who has left houses or brothers or sisters or father or mother or wifeᵃ or children or lands, for My name's sake, shall receive a hundredfold, and inherit eternal life. 30 But many who are first will be last, and the last first.

20 "For the kingdom of heaven is like a landowner who went out early in the morning to hire laborers for his vineyard. 2 Now when he had agreed with the laborers for a denarius a day, he sent them into his vineyard. 3 And he went out about the third hour and saw others standing idle in the marketplace, 4 and said to them, 'You also go into the vineyard, and whatever is right I will give you.'

So they went. 5 Again he went out about the sixth and the ninth hour, and did likewise. 6 And about the eleventh hour he went out and found others standing idle,ᵃ and said to them, 'Why have you been standing here idle all day?' 7 They said to him, 'Because no one hired us.' He said to them, 'You also go into the vineyard, and whatever is right you will receive.'ᵃ

8 "So when evening had come, the owner of the vineyard said to his steward, 'Call the laborers and give them their wages, beginning with the last to the first.' 9 And when those came who were hired about the eleventh hour, they each received a denarius. 10 But when the first came, they supposed that they would receive more; and they likewise received each a denarius. 11 And when they had received it, they complained against the landowner, 12 saying, 'These last men have worked only one hour, and you made them equal to us who have borne the burden and the heat of the day.' 13 But he answered one of them and said, 'Friend, I am doing you no wrong. Did you not agree with me for a denarius? 14 Take what is yours and go your way. I wish to give to this last man the same as to you. 15 Is it not lawful for me to do what I wish with my own things? Or is your eye evil because I am good?' 16 So the last will be first, and the first last. For many are called, but few chosen."ᵃ

17 Now Jesus, going up to Jerusalem, took the twelve disciples aside on the road and said to them, 18 "Behold, we are going up to Jerusalem, and the Son of Man will be betrayed to the chief priests and to the scribes; and they will condemn Him to death, 19 and deliver Him to the Gentiles to mock and to scourge and to crucify. And the third day He will rise again."

20 Then the mother of Zebedee's sons came to Him with her sons, kneeling down and asking something from Him.

21 And He said to her, "What do you wish?"

She said to Him, "Grant that these

19:19 ᵃExodus 20:12–16; Deuteronomy 5:16–20 ᵇLeviticus 19:18 19:20 ᵃNU-Text omits from my youth. 19:29 ᵃNU-Text omits or wife. 20:6 ᵃNU-Text omits idle. 20:7 ᵃNU-Text omits the last clause of this verse. 20:16 ᵃNU-Text omits the last sentence of this verse.

two sons of mine may sit, one on Your right hand and the other on the left, in Your kingdom."

22 But Jesus answered and said, "You do not know what you ask. Are you able to drink the cup that I am about to drink, and be baptized with the baptism that I am baptized with?"[a]

They said to Him, "We are able."

23 So He said to them, "You will indeed drink My cup, and be baptized with the baptism that I am baptized with;[a] but to sit on My right hand and on My left is not Mine to give, but it is for those for whom it is prepared by My Father."

24 And when the ten heard it, they were greatly displeased with the two brothers. 25 But Jesus called them to Himself and said, "You know that the rulers of the Gentiles lord it over them, and those who are great exercise authority over them. 26 Yet it shall not be so among you; but whoever desires to become great among you, let him be your servant. 27 And whoever desires to be first among you, let him be your slave— 28 just as the Son of Man did not come to be served, but to serve, and to give His life a ransom for many."

29 Now as they went out of Jericho, a great multitude followed Him. 30 And behold, two blind men sitting by the road, when they heard that Jesus was passing by, cried out, saying, "Have mercy on us, O Lord, Son of David!"

31 Then the multitude warned them that they should be quiet; but they cried out all the more, saying, "Have mercy on us, O Lord, Son of David!"

32 So Jesus stood still and called them, and said, "What do you want Me to do for you?"

33 They said to Him, "Lord, that our eyes may be opened." 34 So Jesus had compassion and touched their eyes. And immediately their eyes received sight, and they followed Him.

21 Now when they drew near Jerusalem, and came to Bethphage,[a] at the Mount of Olives, then Jesus sent two disciples, 2 saying to them, "Go into the village opposite you, and immediately you will find a donkey tied, and a colt with her. Loose them and bring them to Me. 3 And if anyone says anything to you, you shall say, 'The Lord has need of them,' and immediately he will send them."

4 All[a] this was done that it might be fulfilled which was spoken by the prophet, saying:

5   "Tell the daughter of Zion,
    'Behold, your King is coming to you,
    Lowly, and sitting on a donkey,
    A colt, the foal of a donkey.' "[a]

6 So the disciples went and did as Jesus commanded them. 7 They brought the donkey and the colt, laid their clothes on them, and set Him[a] on them. 8 And a very great multitude spread their clothes on the road; others cut down branches from the trees and spread them on the road. 9 Then the multitudes who went before and those who followed cried out, saying:

    "Hosanna to the Son of David!
    'Blessed is He who comes in the name of the Lord!'[a]
    Hosanna in the highest!"

10 And when He had come into Jerusalem, all the city was moved, saying, "Who is this?"

11 So the multitudes said, "This is Jesus, the prophet from Nazareth of Galilee."

12 Then Jesus went into the temple of God[a] and drove out all those who bought and sold in the temple, and overturned the tables of the money changers and the seats of those who sold doves. 13 And He said to them, "It is written, 'My house shall be called a house of prayer,'[a] but you have made it a 'den of thieves.' "[b]

14 Then the blind and the lame came to Him in the temple, and He healed them. 15 But when the chief priests and scribes saw the wonderful things that He did, and the children crying out in the temple and saying, "Hosanna to the Son of David!" they were indignant 16 and said

---

20:22 [a]NU-Text omits and be baptized with the baptism that I am baptized with.   20:23 [a]NU-Text omits and be baptized with the baptism that I am baptized with.   21:1 [a]M-Text reads Bethsphage.
21:4 [a]NU-Text omits All.   21:5 [a]Zechariah 9:9   21:7 [a]NU-Text reads and He sat.   21:9 [a]Psalm 118:26   21:12 [a]NU-Text omits of God.   21:13 [a]Isaiah 56:7   [b]Jeremiah 7:11

Faith to Move Mountains

Two thousand years ago, Jesus Christ and His disciples stood on the Mount of Olives. They had just completed a twenty-six-mile journey from Jericho to Jerusalem. Before them was the Golden City with its magnificent temple set like a jewel among the beautiful Judean hills. Beyond lay an unforgettable view of the glistening blue Mediterranean Sea, nearly always visible on the clear spring days of Passover. Behind them to the east was the vast desert stretching down to the salt-filled sea.

Here on the Mount of Olives, Christ's words about faith were vividly illustrated. Perhaps He stooped down, grabbed a handful of the chalky mountain soil and let it sift through His fingers as He pointed to the seas within view, and declared, "If you have faith and do not doubt, you will not only do what was done to the fig tree, but also if you say to this mountain, 'Be removed and be cast into the sea,' it will be done" (Matt. 21:21).

During this season, the Mount of Olives is colorfully alive with a patchwork of red anemones, poppies, and bright yellow mustard tree flowers. The disciples had only to look at the golden mustard plant to remember the tiny seed from which it was sown.

A faith that small can move mountains. It can move the mountains in your life today! How do you get this mountain-moving faith? Christ Himself told us, "And whatever things you ask in prayer, believing, you will receive" (Matt. 21:22).

to Him, "Do You hear what these are saying?"

And Jesus said to them, "Yes. Have you never read,

> 'Out of the mouth of babes and
>   nursing infants
> You have perfected praise'? "[a]

17 Then He left them and went out of the city to Bethany, and He lodged there.

18 Now in the morning, as He returned to the city, He was hungry. 19 And seeing a fig tree by the road, He came to it and found nothing on it but leaves, and said to it, "Let no fruit grow on you ever again." Immediately the fig tree withered away.

20 And when the disciples saw it, they marveled, saying, "How did the fig tree wither away so soon?"

21 So Jesus answered and said to them, "Assuredly, I say to you, if you have faith and do not doubt, you will not only do what was done to the fig tree, but also if you say to this mountain, 'Be removed and be cast into the sea,' it will be done. 22 And whatever things you ask in prayer, believing, you will receive."

23 Now when He came into the temple, the chief priests and the elders of the people confronted Him as He was teaching, and said, "By what authority are You doing these things? And who gave You this authority?"

24 But Jesus answered and said to them, "I also will ask you one thing, which if you tell Me, I likewise will tell you by what authority I do these things: 25 The baptism of John— where was it from? From heaven or from men?"

And they reasoned among themselves, saying, "If we say, 'From heaven,' He will say to us, 'Why then did you not believe him?' 26 But if we say, 'From men,' we fear the multitude, for all count John as a prophet."

27 So they answered Jesus and said, "We do not know."

And He said to them, "Neither will I tell you by what authority I do these things.

28 "But what do you think? A man had two sons, and he came to the first and said, 'Son, go, work today in my vineyard.' 29 He answered and said,

'I will not,' but afterward he regretted it and went. 30 Then he came to the second and said likewise. And he answered and said, 'I go, sir,' but he did not go. 31 Which of the two did the will of his father?"

They said to Him, "The first."

Jesus said to them, "Assuredly, I say to you that tax collectors and harlots enter the kingdom of God before you. 32 For John came to you in the way of righteousness, and you did not believe him; but tax collectors and harlots believed him; and when you saw it, you did not afterward relent and believe him.

33 "Hear another parable: There was a certain landowner who planted a vineyard and set a hedge around it, dug a winepress in it and built a tower. And he leased it to vinedressers and went into a far country. 34 Now when vintage-time drew near, he sent his servants to the vinedressers, that they might receive its fruit. 35 And the vinedressers took his servants, beat one, killed one, and stoned another. 36 Again he sent other servants, more than the first, and they did likewise to them. 37 Then last of all he sent his son to them, saying, 'They will respect my son.' 38 But when the vinedressers saw the son, they said among themselves, 'This is the heir. Come, let us kill him and seize his inheritance.' 39 So they took him and cast him out of the vineyard and killed him.

40 "Therefore, when the owner of the vineyard comes, what will he do to those vinedressers?"

41 They said to Him, "He will destroy those wicked men miserably, and lease his vineyard to other vinedressers who will render to him the fruits in their seasons."

42 Jesus said to them, "Have you never read in the Scriptures:

> 'The stone which the builders
>   rejected
> Has become the chief
>   cornerstone.
> This was the LORD's doing,
> And it is marvelous in our
>   eyes'?[a]

43 "Therefore I say to you, the kingdom of God will be taken from you and given to a nation bearing the

21:16 [a]Psalm 8:2   21:42 [a]Psalm 118:22, 23

fruits of it. 44 And whoever falls on this stone will be broken; but on whomever it falls, it will grind him to powder."

45 Now when the chief priests and Pharisees heard His parables, they perceived that He was speaking of them. 46 But when they sought to lay hands on Him, they feared the multitudes, because they took Him for a prophet.

22 And Jesus answered and spoke to them again by parables and said: 2 "The kingdom of heaven is like a certain king who arranged a marriage for his son, 3 and sent out his servants to call those who were invited to the wedding; and they were not willing to come. 4 Again, he sent out other servants, saying, 'Tell those who are invited, "See, I have prepared my dinner; my oxen and fatted cattle *are* killed, and all things *are* ready. Come to the wedding." ' 5 But they made light of it and went their ways, one to his own farm, another to his business. 6 And the rest seized his servants, treated *them* spitefully, and killed *them.* 7 But when the king heard *about it,* he was furious. And he sent out his armies, destroyed those murderers, and burned up their city. 8 Then he said to his servants, 'The wedding is ready, but those who were invited were not worthy. 9 Therefore go into the highways, and as many as you find, invite to the wedding.' 10 So those servants went out into the highways and gathered together all whom they found, both bad and good. And the wedding *hall* was filled with guests.

11 "But when the king came in to see the guests, he saw a man there who did not have on a wedding garment. 12 So he said to him, 'Friend, how did you come in here without a wedding garment?' And he was speechless. 13 Then the king said to the servants, 'Bind him hand and foot, take him away, and*a* cast *him* into outer darkness; there will be weeping and gnashing of teeth.'

14 "For many are called, but few *are* chosen."

15 Then the Pharisees went and plotted how they might entangle Him in *His* talk. 16 And they sent to Him their disciples with the Herodians, saying, "Teacher, we know that You are true, and teach the way of God in truth; nor do You care about anyone, for You do not regard the person of men. 17 Tell us, therefore, what do You think? Is it lawful to pay taxes to Caesar, or not?"

18 But Jesus perceived their wickedness, and said, "Why do you test Me, *you* hypocrites? 19 Show Me the tax money."

So they brought Him a denarius. 20 And He said to them, "Whose image and inscription *is* this?"

21 They said to Him, "Caesar's."

And He said to them, "Render therefore to Caesar the things that are Caesar's, and to God the things that are God's." 22 When they had heard *these words,* they marveled, and left Him and went their way.

23 The same day the Sadducees, who say there is no resurrection, came to Him and asked Him, 24 saying: "Teacher, Moses said that if a man dies, having no children, his brother shall marry his wife and raise up offspring for his brother. 25 Now there were with us seven brothers. The first died after he had married, and having no offspring, left his wife to his brother. 26 Likewise the second also, and the third, even to the seventh. 27 Last of all the woman died also. 28 Therefore, in the resurrection, whose wife of the seven will she be? For they all had her."

29 Jesus answered and said to them, "You are mistaken, not knowing the Scriptures nor the power of God. 30 For in the resurrection they neither marry nor are given in marriage, but are like angels of God*a* in heaven. 31 But concerning the resurrection of the dead, have you not read what was spoken to you by God, saying, 32 *'I am the God of Abraham, the God of Isaac, and the God of Jacob'?a* God is not the God of the dead, but of the living." 33 And when the multitudes heard *this,* they were astonished at His teaching.

34 But when the Pharisees heard that He had silenced the Sadducees, they gathered together. 35 Then one of them, a lawyer, asked *Him a question,* testing Him, and saying, 36 "Teacher, which *is* the great commandment in the law?"

22:13 *a*NU-Text omits *take him away, and.*   22:30 *a*NU-Text omits *of God.*   22:32 *a*Exodus 3:6, 15

37 Jesus said to him, " *'You shall love the LORD your God with all your heart, with all your soul, and with all your mind.'* [a] 38 This is *the* first and great commandment. 39 And *the* second *is* like it: *'You shall love your neighbor as yourself.'* [a] 40 On these two commandments hang all the Law and the Prophets."

41 While the Pharisees were gathered together, Jesus asked them, 42 saying, "What do you think about the Christ? Whose Son is He?" They said to Him, *"The Son* of David."

43 He said to them, "How then does David in the Spirit call Him *'Lord,'* saying:

44 *'The LORD said to my Lord,*
   "Sit at My right hand,
     Till I make Your enemies Your
        footstool"' ? [a]

45 If David then calls Him *'Lord,'* how is He his Son?" 46 And no one was able to answer Him a word, nor from that day on did anyone dare question Him anymore.

23 Then Jesus spoke to the multitudes and to His disciples, 2 saying: "The scribes and the Pharisees sit in Moses' seat. 3 Therefore whatever they tell you to observe, [a] *that* observe and do, but do not do according to their works; for they say, and do not do. 4 For they bind heavy burdens, hard to bear, and lay *them* on men's shoulders; but they *themselves* will not move them with one of their fingers. 5 But all their works they do to be seen by men. They make their phylacteries broad and enlarge the borders of their garments. 6 They love the best places at feasts, the best seats in the synagogues, 7 greetings in the marketplaces, and to be called by men, 'Rabbi, Rabbi.' 8 But you, do not be called 'Rabbi'; for One is your Teacher, the Christ, [a] and you are all brethren. 9 Do not call anyone on earth your father; for One is your Father, He who is in heaven. 10 And do not be called teachers; for One is your Teacher, the Christ. 11 But he who is greatest among you shall be your servant. 12 And whoever exalts himself will be humbled, and he who humbles himself will be exalted.

13 "But woe to you, scribes and Pharisees, hypocrites! For you shut up the kingdom of heaven against men; for you neither go in *yourselves,* nor do you allow those who are entering to go in. 14 Woe to you, scribes and Pharisees, hypocrites! For you devour widows' houses, and for a pretense make long prayers. Therefore you will receive greater condemnation. [a]

15 "Woe to you, scribes and Pharisees, hypocrites! For you travel land and sea to win one proselyte, and when he is won, you make him twice as much a son of hell as yourselves.

16 "Woe to you, blind guides, who say, 'Whoever swears by the temple, it is nothing; but whoever swears by the gold of the temple, he is obliged *to perform it.'* 17 Fools and blind! For which is greater, the gold or the temple that sanctifies [a] the gold? 18 And, 'Whoever swears by the altar, it is nothing; but whoever swears by the gift that is on it, he is obliged *to perform it.'* 19 Fools and blind! For which is greater, the gift or the altar that sanctifies the gift? 20 Therefore he who swears by the altar, swears by it and by all things on it. 21 He who swears by the temple, swears by it and by Him who dwells [a] in it. 22 And he who swears by heaven, swears by the throne of God and by Him who sits on it.

23 "Woe to you, scribes and Pharisees, hypocrites! For you pay tithe of mint and anise and cummin, and have neglected the weightier *matters* of the law: justice and mercy and faith. These you ought to have done, without leaving the others undone. 24 Blind guides, who strain out a gnat and swallow a camel!

25 "Woe to you, scribes and Pharisees, hypocrites! For you cleanse the outside of the cup and dish, but inside they are full of extortion and self-indulgence. [a] 26 Blind Pharisee, first cleanse the inside of the cup and dish, that the outside of them may be clean also.

27 "Woe to you, scribes and Pharisees, hypocrites! For you are like

---

22:37 *a* Deuteronomy 6:5   22:39 *a* Leviticus 19:18   22:44 *a* Psalm 110:1   23:3 *a* NU-Text omits *to observe.*   23:8 *a* NU-Text omits *the Christ.*   23:14 *a* NU-Text omits this verse.   23:17 *a* NU-Text reads *sanctified.*   23:21 *a* M-Text reads *dwelt.*   23:25 *a* M-Text reads *unrighteousness.*

whitewashed tombs which indeed appear beautiful outwardly, but inside are full of dead *men's* bones and all uncleanness. 28 Even so you also outwardly appear righteous to men, but inside you are full of hypocrisy and lawlessness.

29 "Woe to you, scribes and Pharisees, hypocrites! Because you build the tombs of the prophets and adorn the monuments of the righteous, 30 and say, 'If we had lived in the days of our fathers, we would not have been partakers with them in the blood of the prophets.'

31 "Therefore you are witnesses against yourselves that you are sons of those who murdered the prophets. 32 Fill up, then, the measure of your fathers' *guilt*. 33 Serpents, brood of vipers! How can you escape the condemnation of hell? 34 Therefore, indeed, I send you prophets, wise men, and scribes: *some* of them you will kill and crucify, and *some* of them you will scourge in your synagogues and persecute from city to city, 35 that on you may come all the righteous blood shed on the earth, from the blood of righteous Abel to the blood of Zechariah, son of Berechiah, whom you murdered between the temple and the altar. 36 Assuredly, I say to you, all these things will come upon this generation.

37 "O Jerusalem, Jerusalem, the one who kills the prophets and stones those who are sent to her! How often I wanted to gather your children together, as a hen gathers her chicks under *her* wings, but you were not willing! 38 See! Your house is left to you desolate; 39 for I say to you, you shall see Me no more till you say, '*Blessed is He who comes in the name of the Lord!*'"[a]

24 Then Jesus went out and departed from the temple, and His disciples came up to show Him the buildings of the temple. 2 And Jesus said to them, "Do you not see all these things? Assuredly, I say to you, not *one* stone shall be left here upon another, that shall not be thrown down."

3 Now as He sat on the Mount of Olives, the disciples came to Him privately, saying, "Tell us, when will these things be? And what *will be* the sign of Your coming, and of the end of the age?"

4 And Jesus answered and said to them: "Take heed that no one deceives you. 5 For many will come in My name, saying, 'I am the Christ,' and will deceive many. 6 And you will hear of wars and rumors of wars. See that you are not troubled; for all[a] *these things* must come to pass, but the end is not yet. 7 For nation will rise against nation, and kingdom against kingdom. And there will be famines, pestilences,[a] and earthquakes in various places. 8 All these *are* the beginning of sorrows.

9 "Then they will deliver you up to tribulation and kill you, and you will be hated by all nations for My name's sake. 10 And then many will be offended, will betray one another, and will hate one another. 11 Then many false prophets will rise up and deceive many. 12 And because lawlessness will abound, the love of many will grow cold. 13 But he who endures to the end shall be saved. 14 And this gospel of the kingdom will be preached in all the world as a witness to all the nations, and then the end will come.

15 "Therefore when you see the '*abomination of desolation,*'[a] spoken of by Daniel the prophet, standing in the holy place" (whoever reads, let him understand), 16 "then let those who are in Judea flee to the mountains. 17 Let him who is on the housetop not go down to take anything out of his house. 18 And let him who is in the field not go back to get his clothes. 19 But woe to those who are pregnant and to those who are nursing babies in those days! 20 And pray that your flight may not be in winter or on the Sabbath. 21 For then there will be great tribulation, such as has not been since the beginning of the world until this time, no, nor ever shall be. 22 And unless those days were shortened, no flesh would be saved; but for the elect's sake those days will be shortened.

23 "Then if anyone says to you, 'Look, here *is* the Christ!' or 'There!' do not believe *it*. 24 For false christs and false prophets will rise and show great signs and wonders to deceive,

23:39 [a]Psalm 118:26   24:6 [a]NU-Text omits *all.*   24:7 [a]NU-Text omits *pestilences.*   24:15 [a]Daniel 11:31; 12:11

if possible, even the elect. 25 See, I have told you beforehand.

26 "Therefore if they say to you, 'Look, He is in the desert!' do not go out; *or* 'Look, *He is* in the inner rooms!' do not believe *it*. 27 For as the lightning comes from the east and flashes to the west, so also will the coming of the Son of Man be. 28 For wherever the carcass is, there the eagles will be gathered together.

29 "Immediately after the tribulation of those days the sun will be darkened, and the moon will not give its light; the stars will fall from heaven, and the powers of the heavens will be shaken. 30 Then the sign of the Son of Man will appear in heaven, and then all the tribes of the earth will mourn, and they will see the Son of Man coming on the clouds of heaven with power and great glory. 31 And He will send His angels with a great sound of a trumpet, and they will gather together His elect from the four winds, from one end of heaven to the other.

32 "Now learn this parable from the fig tree: When its branch has already become tender and puts forth leaves, you know that summer *is* near. 33 So you also, when you see all these things, know that it*a* is near—at the doors! 34 Assuredly, I say to you, this generation will by no means pass away till all these things take place. 35 Heaven and earth will pass away, but My words will by no means pass away.

36 "But of that day and hour no one knows, not even the angels of heaven,*a* but My Father only. 37 But as the days of Noah *were,* so also will the coming of the Son of Man be. 38 For as in the days before the flood, they were eating and drinking, marrying and giving in marriage, until the day that Noah entered the ark, 39 and did not know until the flood came and took them all away, so also will the coming of the Son of Man be. 40 Then two *men* will be in the field: one will be taken and the other left. 41 Two *women will be* grinding at the mill: one will be taken and the other left. 42 Watch therefore, for you do not know what hour*a* your Lord is coming. 43 But know this, that if the master of the house

had known what hour the thief would come, he would have watched and not allowed his house to be broken into. 44 Therefore you also be ready, for the Son of Man is coming at an hour you do not expect.

45 "Who then is a faithful and wise servant, whom his master made ruler over his household, to give them food in due season? 46 Blessed *is* that servant whom his master, when he comes, will find so doing. 47 Assuredly, I say to you that he will make him ruler over all his goods. 48 But if that evil servant says in his heart, 'My master is delaying his coming,'*a* 49 and begins to beat *his* fellow servants, and to eat and drink with the drunkards, 50 the master of that servant will come on a day when he is not looking for *him* and at an hour that he is not aware of, 51 and will cut him in two and appoint *him* his portion with the hypocrites. There shall be weeping and gnashing of teeth.

25 "Then the kingdom of heaven shall be likened to ten virgins who took their lamps and went out to meet the bridegroom. 2 Now five of them were wise, and five *were* foolish. 3 Those who *were* foolish took their lamps and took no oil with them, 4 but the wise took oil in their vessels with their lamps. 5 But while the bridegroom was delayed, they all slumbered and slept.

6 "And at midnight a cry was *heard:* 'Behold, the bridegroom is coming;*a* go out to meet him!' 7 Then all those virgins arose and trimmed their lamps. 8 And the foolish said to the wise, 'Give us *some* of your oil, for our lamps are going out.' 9 But the wise answered, saying, '*No,* lest there should not be enough for us and you; but go rather to those who sell, and buy for yourselves.' 10 And while they went to buy, the bridegroom came, and those who were ready went in with him to the wedding; and the door was shut.

11 "Afterward the other virgins came also, saying, 'Lord, Lord, open to us!' 12 But he answered and said, 'Assuredly, I say to you, I do not know you.'

13 "Watch therefore, for you know

24:33 *a*Or He   24:36 *a*NU-Text adds *nor the Son.*   24:42 *a*NU-Text reads *day.*   24:48 *a*NU-Text omits
his coming.   25:6 *a*NU-Text omits *is coming.*

neither the day nor the hour[a] in which the Son of Man is coming.

14 "For *the kingdom of heaven is* like a man traveling to a far country, *who* called his own servants and delivered his goods to them. 15 And to one he gave five talents, to another two, and to another one, to each according to his own ability; and immediately he went on a journey. 16 Then he who had received the five talents went and traded with them, and made another five talents. 17 And likewise he who *had received* two gained two more also. 18 But he who had received one went and dug in the ground, and hid his lord's money. 19 After a long time the lord of those servants came and settled accounts with them.

20 "So he who had received five talents came and brought five other talents, saying, 'Lord, you delivered to me five talents; look, I have gained five more talents besides them.' 21 His lord said to him, 'Well *done,* good and faithful servant; you were faithful over a few things, I will make you ruler over many things. Enter into the joy of your lord.' 22 He also who had received two talents came and said, 'Lord, you delivered to me two talents; look, I have gained two more talents besides them.' 23 His lord said to him, 'Well *done,* good and faithful servant; you have been faithful over a few things, I will make you ruler over many things. Enter into the joy of your lord.'

24 "Then he who had received the one talent came and said, 'Lord, I knew you to be a hard man, reaping where you have not sown, and gathering where you have not scattered seed. 25 And I was afraid, and went and hid your talent in the ground. Look, *there* you have *what is* yours.' 26 "But his lord answered and said to him, 'You wicked and lazy servant, you knew that I reap where I have not sown, and gather where I have not scattered seed. 27 So you ought to have deposited my money with the bankers, and at my coming I would have received back my own with interest. 28 Therefore take the talent from him, and give *it* to him who has ten talents.

29 'For to everyone who has, more will be given, and he will have abundance; but from him who does not have, even what he has will be taken away. 30 And cast the unprofitable servant into the outer darkness. There will be weeping and gnashing of teeth.'

31 "When the Son of Man comes in His glory, and all the holy[a] angels with Him, then He will sit on the throne of His glory. 32 All the nations will be gathered before Him, and He will separate them one from another, as a shepherd divides *his* sheep from the goats. 33 And He will set the sheep on His right hand, but the goats on the left. 34 Then the King will say to those on His right hand, 'Come, you blessed of My Father, inherit the kingdom prepared for you from the foundation of the world: 35 for I was hungry and you gave Me food; I was thirsty and you gave Me drink; I was a stranger and you took Me in; 36 I *was* naked and you clothed Me; I was sick and you visited Me; I was in prison and you came to Me.'

37 "Then the righteous will answer Him, saying, 'Lord, when did we see You hungry and feed *You,* or thirsty and give *You* drink? 38 When did we see You a stranger and take *You* in, or naked and clothe *You?* 39 Or when did we see You sick, or in prison, and come to You?' 40 And the King will answer and say to them, 'Assuredly, I say to you, inasmuch as you did *it* to one of the least of these My brethren, you did *it* to Me.'

41 "Then He will also say to those on the left hand, 'Depart from Me, you cursed, into the everlasting fire prepared for the devil and his angels: 42 for I was hungry and you gave Me no food; I was thirsty and you gave Me no drink; 43 I was a stranger and you did not take Me in, naked and you did not clothe Me, sick and in prison and you did not visit Me.'

44 "Then they also will answer Him,[a] saying, 'Lord, when did we see You hungry or thirsty or a stranger or naked or sick or in prison, and did not minister to You?' 45 Then He will answer them, saying, 'Assuredly, I say to you, inasmuch as you did not do *it* to one of the least of these, you did not do *it* to Me.' 46 And these will

25:13 [a]NU-Text omits the rest of this verse. 25:31 [a]NU-Text omits *holy.* 25:44 [a]NU-Text and M-Text omit *Him.*

go away into everlasting punishment, but the righteous into eternal life."

26 Now it came to pass, when Jesus had finished all these sayings, *that* He said to His disciples, 2 "You know that after two days is the Passover, and the Son of Man will be delivered up to be crucified."

3 Then the chief priests, the scribes,[a] and the elders of the people assembled at the palace of the high priest, who was called Caiaphas, 4 and plotted to take Jesus by trickery and kill *Him*. 5 But they said, "Not during the feast, lest there be an uproar among the people."

6 And when Jesus was in Bethany at the house of Simon the leper, 7 a woman came to Him having an alabaster flask of very costly fragrant oil, and she poured *it* on His head as He sat *at the table*. 8 But when His disciples saw *it*, they were indignant, saying, "Why this waste? 9 For this fragrant oil might have been sold for much and given to *the* poor."

10 But when Jesus was aware of *it*, He said to them, "Why do you trouble the woman? For she has done a good work for Me. 11 For you have the poor with you always, but Me you do not have always. 12 For in pouring this fragrant oil on My body, she did *it* for My burial. 13 Assuredly, I say to you, wherever this gospel is preached in the whole world, what this woman has done will also be told as a memorial to her."

14 Then one of the twelve, called Judas Iscariot, went to the chief priests 15 and said, "What are you willing to give me if I deliver Him to you?" And they counted out to him thirty pieces of silver. 16 So from that time he sought opportunity to betray Him.

17 Now on the first *day of the Feast* of Unleavened Bread the disciples came to Jesus, saying to Him, "Where do You want us to prepare for You to eat the Passover?"

18 And He said, "Go into the city to a certain man, and say to him, 'The Teacher says, "My time is at hand; I will keep the Passover at your house with My disciples." '"

19 So the disciples did as Jesus had directed them; and they prepared the Passover.

20 When evening had come, He sat down with the twelve. 21 Now as they were eating, He said, "Assuredly, I say to you, one of you will betray Me."

22 And they were exceedingly sorrowful, and each of them began to say to Him, "Lord, is it I?"

23 He answered and said, "He who dipped *his* hand with Me in the dish will betray Me. 24 The Son of Man indeed goes just as it is written of Him, but woe to that man by whom the Son of Man is betrayed! It would have been good for that man if he had not been born."

25 Then Judas, who was betraying Him, answered and said, "Rabbi, is it I?"

He said to him, "You have said it."

26 And as they were eating, Jesus took bread, blessed[a] and broke *it*, and gave *it* to the disciples and said, "Take, eat; this is My body."

27 Then He took the cup, and gave thanks, and gave *it* to them, saying, "Drink from it, all of you. 28 For this is My blood of the new[a] covenant, which is shed for many for the remission of sins. 29 But I say to you, I will not drink of this fruit of the vine from now on until that day when I drink it new with you in My Father's kingdom."

30 And when they had sung a hymn, they went out to the Mount of Olives.

31 Then Jesus said to them, "All of you will be made to stumble because of Me this night, for it is written:

'I will strike the Shepherd,
    And the sheep of the flock will
        be scattered.'[a]

32 But after I have been raised, I will go before you to Galilee."

33 Peter answered and said to Him, "Even if all are made to stumble because of You, I will never be made to stumble."

34 Jesus said to him, "Assuredly, I say to you that this night, before the rooster crows, you will deny Me three times."

35 Peter said to Him, "Even if I

26:3 [a]NU-Text omits *the scribes*.   26:26 [a]M-Text reads *gave thanks for*.   26:28 [a]NU-Text omits *new*.   26:31 [a]Zechariah 13:7

have to die with You, I will not deny You!"

And so said all the disciples.

36 Then Jesus came with them to a place called Gethsemane, and said to the disciples, "Sit here while I go and pray over there." 37 And He took with Him Peter and the two sons of Zebedee, and He began to be sorrowful and deeply distressed. 38 Then He said to them, "My soul is exceedingly sorrowful, even to death. Stay here and watch with Me."

39 He went a little farther and fell on His face, and prayed, saying, "O My Father, if it is possible, let this cup pass from Me; nevertheless, not as I will, but as You *will*."

40 Then He came to the disciples and found them sleeping, and said to Peter, "What! Could you not watch with Me one hour? 41 Watch and pray, lest you enter into temptation. The spirit indeed *is* willing, but the flesh *is* weak."

42 Again, a second time, He went away and prayed, saying, "O My Father, if this cup cannot pass away from Me unless[a] I drink it, Your will be done." 43 And He came and found them asleep again, for their eyes were heavy.

44 So He left them, went away again, and prayed the third time, saying the same words. 45 Then He came to His disciples and said to them, "Are *you* still sleeping and resting? Behold, the hour is at hand, and the Son of Man is being betrayed into the hands of sinners. 46 Rise, let us be going. See, My betrayer is at hand."

47 And while He was still speaking, behold, Judas, one of the twelve, with a great multitude with swords and clubs, came from the chief priests and elders of the people.

48 Now His betrayer had given them a sign, saying, "Whomever I kiss, He is the One; seize Him." 49 Immediately he went up to Jesus and said, "Greetings, Rabbi!" and kissed Him.

50 But Jesus said to him, "Friend, why have you come?"

Then they came and laid hands on Jesus and took Him. 51 And suddenly, one of those *who were* with Jesus stretched out *his* hand and drew his sword, struck the servant of the high priest, and cut off his ear.

52 But Jesus said to him, "Put your sword in its place, for all who take the sword will perish[a] by the sword. 53 Or do you think that I cannot now pray to My Father, and He will provide Me with more than twelve legions of angels? 54 How then could the Scriptures be fulfilled, that it must happen thus?"

55 In that hour Jesus said to the multitudes, "Have you come out, as against a robber, with swords and clubs to take Me? I sat daily with you, teaching in the temple, and you did not seize Me. 56 But all this was done that the Scriptures of the prophets might be fulfilled."

Then all the disciples forsook Him and fled.

57 And those who had laid hold of Jesus led *Him* away to Caiaphas the high priest, where the scribes and the elders were assembled. 58 But Peter followed Him at a distance to the high priest's courtyard. And he went in and sat with the servants to see the end.

59 Now the chief priests, the elders,[a] and all the council sought false testimony against Jesus to put Him to death, 60 but found none. Even though many false witnesses came forward, they found none.[a] But at last two false witnesses[b] came forward 61 and said, "This *fellow* said, 'I am able to destroy the temple of God and to build it in three days.'"

62 And the high priest arose and said to Him, "Do You answer nothing? What *is it* these men testify against You?" 63 But Jesus kept silent. And the high priest answered and said to Him, "I put You under oath by the living God: Tell us if You are the Christ, the Son of God!"

64 Jesus said to him, "*It is as* you said. Nevertheless, I say to you, hereafter you will see the Son of Man sitting at the right hand of the Power, and coming on the clouds of heaven."

65 Then the high priest tore his clothes, saying, "He has spoken blasphemy! What further need do we have of witnesses? Look, now you have heard His blasphemy! 66 What do you think?"

26:42 [a]NU-Text reads *if this may not pass away unless.*   26:52 [a]M-Text reads *die.*   26:59 [a]NU-Text omits *the elders.*   26:60 [a]NU-Text puts a comma after *but found none,* does not capitalize *Even,* and omits *they found none.*   [b]NU-Text omits *false witnesses.*

The King Forever

Jesus Christ was tried before Pontius Pilate in the Roman praetorium inside the Antonia fortress. Here, Rome's legions were garrisoned overlooking the temple of Jerusalem. This large pavement area, consisting of huge limestone blocks weighing several tons each, has been unearthed.

Archaeologists have discovered etched into the stone pavement of the praetorium a playing board for a game known among the Roman soldiers as "king for a day." Shapes of squares, pie-like slices, and rectangles were cut into the surface of the unearthed stone. Dice made from sheep's knucklebones were cast onto these marks. The soldier who threw his dice on just the right shape won the game. His reward was to be "king for a day."

As king, the soldier was dressed in a beautiful purple robe imported from the city of Colossae, where the special purple dye was extracted from seashells. This particular style of robe was reserved for royalty, and the colored dye was often reserved by emperors exclusively for their use. In addition to the robe, the "king" received a crown, scepter, and anything else he wished, including wine, women, and song. But there was one catch. At the end of the day, the "king" was put to death.

This game sheds new light on the Romans' mocking and scourging of Jesus. They beat Him, dressed Him in a purple robe, gave Him a crown of thorns and told Him to save Himself. By mocking Jesus, the Roman and Herodian soldiers saw an opportunity to play the "king for a day" game in a perverse and twisted manner.

Unknown to them, the "king" they mocked was not just another man. In fact, He was and is the true King. His love was evident for those who crucified Him when He cried out from the cross, "Father, forgive them, for they do not know what they do" (Luke 23:34).

Jesus, the Son of God, was not simply to be king for the day, for the cords of death could not hold Him. By His resurrection He revealed that He was and is King forever!

They answered and said, "He is deserving of death."

67 Then they spat in His face and beat Him; and others struck *Him* with the palms of their hands, 68 saying, "Prophesy to us, Christ! Who is the one who struck You?"

69 Now Peter sat outside in the courtyard. And a servant girl came to him, saying, "You also were with Jesus of Galilee."

70 But he denied it before *them* all, saying, "I do not know what you are saying."

71 And when he had gone out to the gateway, another *girl* saw him and said to those *who were* there, "This *fellow* also was with Jesus of Nazareth."

72 But again he denied with an oath, "I do not know the Man!"

73 And a little later those who stood by came up and said to Peter, "Surely you also are *one* of them, for your speech betrays you."

74 Then he began to curse and swear, *saying,* "I do not know the Man!"

Immediately a rooster crowed. 75 And Peter remembered the word of Jesus who had said to him, "Before the rooster crows, you will deny Me three times." So he went out and wept bitterly.

27 When morning came, all the chief priests and elders of the people plotted against Jesus to put Him to death. 2 And when they had bound Him, they led Him away and delivered Him to Pontius*ᵃ* Pilate the governor.

3 Then Judas, His betrayer, seeing that He had been condemned, was remorseful and brought back the thirty pieces of silver to the chief priests and elders, 4 saying, "I have sinned by betraying innocent blood."

And they said, "What *is that* to us? You see *to it!*"

5 Then he threw down the pieces of silver in the temple and departed, and went and hanged himself.

6 But the chief priests took the silver pieces and said, "It is not lawful to put them into the treasury, because they are the price of blood." 7 And they consulted together and bought with them the potter's field,

to bury strangers in. 8 Therefore that field has been called the Field of Blood to this day.

9 Then was fulfilled what was spoken by Jeremiah the prophet, saying, *"And they took the thirty pieces of silver, the value of Him who was priced,* whom they of the children of Israel priced, 10 *and gave them for the potter's field, as the* LORD *directed me."ᵃ*

11 Now Jesus stood before the governor. And the governor asked Him, saying, "Are You the King of the Jews?"

Jesus said to him, "*It is as* you say." 12 And while He was being accused by the chief priests and elders, He answered nothing.

13 Then Pilate said to Him, "Do You not hear how many things they testify against You?" 14 But He answered him not one word, so that the governor marveled greatly.

15 Now at the feast the governor was accustomed to releasing to the multitude one prisoner whom they wished. 16 And at that time they had a notorious prisoner called Barabbas.*ᵃ* 17 Therefore, when they had gathered together, Pilate said to them, "Whom do you want me to release to you? Barabbas, or Jesus who is called Christ?" 18 For he knew that they had handed Him over because of envy.

19 While he was sitting on the judgment seat, his wife sent to him, saying, "Have nothing to do with that just Man, for I have suffered many things today in a dream because of Him."

20 But the chief priests and elders persuaded the multitudes that they should ask for Barabbas and destroy Jesus. 21 The governor answered and said to them, "Which of the two do you want me to release to you?"

They said, "Barabbas!"

22 Pilate said to them, "What then shall I do with Jesus who is called Christ?"

They all said to him, "Let Him be crucified!"

23 Then the governor said, "Why, what evil has He done?"

But they cried out all the more, saying, "Let Him be crucified!"

24 When Pilate saw that he could

27:2 ᵃNU-Text omits *Pontius.* 27:10 ᵃJeremiah 32:6–9 27:16 ᵃNU-Text reads *Jesus Barabbas.*

The Centurion

Among the Roman ranks stationed in Judea during the time of Christ were the crack tenth and twelfth legions. From these superior troops came the soldiers and their centurion commander who crucified Christ. This Roman centurion was a highly trained officer who commanded over one hundred men. Under his authority the soldiers beat, mocked, and eventually nailed Jesus to the cross. They were well experienced in crucifying criminals. The centurion, himself a veteran who had witnessed and carried out numerous crucifixions, realized that there was something mysteriously different about *this* crucifixion! In his understanding, Jesus had done nothing worthy of death. Having observed the entire scene of Jesus' death, the centurion declared, "Truly this was the Son of God!" (Matt. 27:54).

Roman emperors often requested that divine homage be paid only to themselves. Worship or admiration of other gods was punishable by death. Well aware of these consequences, the centurion boldly declared his faith. Even though he played a part in Jesus' crucifixion, the centurion could accept God's love and forgiveness.

We must also be bold and worship God when others mock Him. We, too, must accept God's love and forgiveness and make a positive declaration of our faith.

not prevail at all, but rather *that* a tumult was rising, he took water and washed *his* hands before the multitude, saying, "I am innocent of the blood of this just Person.*a* You see to it."

25 And all the people answered and said, "His blood *be* on us and on our children."

26 Then he released Barabbas to them; and when he had scourged Jesus, he delivered *Him* to be crucified.

27 Then the soldiers of the governor took Jesus into the Praetorium and gathered the whole garrison around Him. 28 And they stripped Him and put a scarlet robe on Him. 29 When they had twisted a crown of thorns, they put *it* on His head, and a reed in His right hand. And they bowed the knee before Him and mocked Him, saying, "Hail, King of the Jews!" 30 Then they spat on Him, and took the reed and struck Him on the head. 31 And when they had mocked Him, they took the robe off Him, put His *own* clothes on Him, and led Him away to be crucified.

32 Now as they came out, they found a man of Cyrene, Simon by name. Him they compelled to bear His cross. 33 And when they had come to a place called Golgotha, that is to say, Place of a Skull, 34 they gave Him sour*a* wine mingled with gall to drink. But when He had tasted *it*, He would not drink.

35 Then they crucified Him, and divided His garments, casting lots,*a* that it might be fulfilled which was spoken by the prophet:

> "They divided My garments
>   among them,
> And for My clothing they cast
>   lots."*b*

36 Sitting down, they kept watch over Him there. 37 And they put up over His head the accusation written against Him:

THIS IS JESUS
THE KING OF THE JEWS.

38 Then two robbers were crucified with Him, one on the right and another on the left.

39 And those who passed by blasphemed Him, wagging their heads 40 and saying, "You who destroy the temple and build *it* in three days, save Yourself! If You are the Son of God, come down from the cross."

41 Likewise the chief priests also, mocking with the scribes and elders,*a* said, 42 "He saved others; Himself He cannot save. If He is the King of Israel,*a* let Him now come down from the cross, and we will believe Him.*b* 43 He trusted in God; let Him deliver Him now if He will have Him; for He said, 'I am the Son of God.'"

44 Even the robbers who were crucified with Him reviled Him with the same thing.

45 Now from the sixth hour until the ninth hour there was darkness over all the land. 46 And about the ninth hour Jesus cried out with a loud voice, saying, "Eli, Eli, lama sabachthani?" that is, *"My God, My God, why have You forsaken Me?"a*

47 Some of those who stood there, when they heard *that*, said, "This Man is calling for Elijah!" 48 Immediately one of them ran and took a sponge, filled *it* with sour wine and put *it* on a reed, and offered it to Him to drink.

49 The rest said, "Let Him alone; let us see if Elijah will come to save Him."

50 And Jesus cried out again with a loud voice, and yielded up His spirit.

51 Then, behold, the veil of the temple was torn in two from top to bottom; and the earth quaked, and the rocks were split, 52 and the graves were opened; and many bodies of the saints who had fallen asleep were raised; 53 and coming out of the graves after His resurrection, they went into the holy city and appeared to many.

54 So when the centurion and those with him, who were guarding Jesus, saw the earthquake and the things that had happened, they feared greatly, saying, "Truly this was the Son of God!"

55 And many women who followed Jesus from Galilee, ministering to Him, were there looking on from

---

27:24 *a*NU-Text omits *just*.   27:34 *a*NU-Text omits *sour*.   27:35 *a*NU-Text and M-Text omit the rest of this verse.   *b*Psalm 22:18   27:41 *a*M-Text reads *with the scribes, the Pharisees, and the elders*.
27:42 *a*NU-Text reads *He is the King of Israel!*   *b*NU-Text and M-Text read *we will believe in Him*.
27:46 *a*Psalm 22:1

afar, 56 among whom were Mary Magdalene, Mary the mother of James and Joses,[a] and the mother of Zebedee's sons.

57 Now when evening had come, there came a rich man from Arimathea, named Joseph, who himself had also become a disciple of Jesus. 58 This man went to Pilate and asked for the body of Jesus. Then Pilate commanded the body to be given to him. 59 When Joseph had taken the body, he wrapped it in a clean linen cloth, 60 and laid it in his new tomb which he had hewn out of the rock; and he rolled a large stone against the door of the tomb, and departed. 61 And Mary Magdalene was there, and the other Mary, sitting opposite the tomb.

62 On the next day, which followed the Day of Preparation, the chief priests and Pharisees gathered together to Pilate, 63 saying, "Sir, we remember, while He was still alive, how that deceiver said, 'After three days I will rise.' 64 Therefore command that the tomb be made secure until the third day, lest His disciples come by night[a] and steal Him away, and say to the people, 'He has risen from the dead.' So the last deception will be worse than the first."

65 Pilate said to them, "You have a guard; go your way, make it as secure as you know how." 66 So they went and made the tomb secure, sealing the stone and setting the guard.

28 Now after the Sabbath, as the first day of the week began to dawn, Mary Magdalene and the other Mary came to see the tomb. 2 And behold, there was a great earthquake; for an angel of the Lord descended from heaven, and came and rolled back the stone from the door,[a] and sat on it. 3 His countenance was like lightning, and his clothing as white as snow. 4 And the guards shook for fear of him, and became like dead men.

5 But the angel answered and said to the women, "Do not be afraid, for I know that you seek Jesus who was crucified. 6 He is not here; for He is risen, as He said. Come, see the place where the Lord lay. 7 And go quickly and tell His disciples that He is risen from the dead, and indeed He is going before you into Galilee; there you will see Him. Behold, I have told you."

8 So they went out quickly from the tomb with fear and great joy, and ran to bring His disciples word.

9 And as they went to tell His disciples,[a] behold, Jesus met them, saying, "Rejoice!" So they came and held Him by the feet and worshiped Him. 10 Then Jesus said to them, "Do not be afraid. Go and tell My brethren to go to Galilee, and there they will see Me."

11 Now while they were going, behold, some of the guard came into the city and reported to the chief priests all the things that had happened. 12 When they had assembled with the elders and consulted together, they gave a large sum of money to the soldiers, 13 saying, "Tell them, 'His disciples came at night and stole Him away while we slept.' 14 And if this comes to the governor's ears, we will appease him and make you secure." 15 So they took the money and did as they were instructed; and this saying is commonly reported among the Jews until this day.

16 Then the eleven disciples went away into Galilee, to the mountain which Jesus had appointed for them. 17 When they saw Him, they worshiped Him; but some doubted.

18 And Jesus came and spoke to them, saying, "All authority has been given to Me in heaven and on earth. 19 Go therefore[a] and make disciples of all the nations, baptizing them in the name of the Father and of the Son and of the Holy Spirit, 20 teaching them to observe all things that I have commanded you; and lo, I am with you always, even to the end of the age." Amen.[a]

27:56 [a]NU-Text reads Joseph.   27:64 [a]NU-Text omits by night.   28:2 [a]NU-Text omits from the door.
28:9 [a]NU-Text omits the first clause of this verse.   28:19 [a]M-Text omits therefore.   28:20 [a]NU-Text omits Amen.

Mark

Overview of Mark

Mark is the shortest and is thought to be the earliest Gospel, written about A.D. 45–65. John Mark was the apostle Peter's *amanuensis*—a Greek word meaning scribe or secretary. It is most probable that Mark recorded the eyewitness accounts of Peter. This Gospel may have been written while Peter and Mark were in prison in Rome. Mark pays careful attention to translate Aramaic expressions to Latin and Greek for his Gentile readers.

Mark is the second in the arrangement of the three synoptic Gospels (meaning "to see together"). A major theme throughout the Gospel of Mark is the urgency of belief in Jesus Christ and the kingdom of God. The word "immediately" occurs repeatedly: at Jesus' baptism "immediately . . . He saw the heavens parting and the Spirit descending upon Him like a dove" (Mark 1:10); Jesus called the disciples and "immediately [they] left their nets" (Mark 1:18); "immediately His fame spread throughout all the region around Galilee" (Mark 1:28); "immediately the leprosy left him, and he was cleansed" (Mark 1:42). Mark wants to convince his readers of the urgency to evangelize the Jewish people and the Gentile nations. After spending time with Jesus, the disciples must now do what Jesus had prepared them for—to carry on His ministry.

Mark was a "do it now" person! He knew that the biggest obstacle was getting started. After spending three years with Jesus, he witnessed how his Lord acted—immediately, to heal human hurts and sufferings. In this Gospel the service and sacrifice of Jesus are revealed chapter by chapter.

The Gospel of Mark not only gives us a greater understanding of our Lord, but an attitude and life-style which we can follow.

Jesus in Mark

Mark emphasizes the public ministry of Jesus, moving straight into the activities of the obedient, compassionate

Christ. Mark clearly identifies the source of Jesus' power, identifying Him as the Son of God.

Keys to Mark

Key Word: Jesus the Servant. Even in the first verse, it is obvious that this Gospel centers on the person and mission of the Son of God. Mark's theme is captured well in 10:45 where Jesus is both Servant and Redeemer of men (cf. Phil. 2:5–11). Mark's narrative relates Christ's teachings and His works, showing how they authenticate each other. The Gospel is obviously evangelistic, written to Gentiles having no knowledge of Old Testament theology.

Key Verses: "Yet it shall not be so among you; but whoever desires to become great among you shall be your servant. And whoever of you desires to be first shall be slave of all. For even the Son of Man did not come to be served, but to serve, and to give His life a ransom for many" (10:43–45).

"When He had called the people to *Himself,* with His disciples also, He said to them, 'Whoever desires to come after Me, let him deny himself, and take up his cross, and follow Me. For whoever desires to save his life will lose it, but whoever loses his life for My sake and the gospel's will save it. For what will it profit a man if he gains the whole world, and loses his own soul? Or what will a man give in exchange for his soul?'" (8:34–37).

Key Chapter: Mark 8. As in Matthew, Mark's Gospel has a pivotal chapter, showing a change of emphasis in Jesus' ministry. Peter's confession of Jesus as the Christ marks a validation of the Messiah through man's voice. Jesus now begins to fortify His men for the suffering and death that will soon follow. Jesus' steps take him closer daily to Jerusalem, where He demonstrates His servanthood by means of the cross, perfecting righteousness and purchasing redemption by blood for God's children.

1 The beginning of the gospel of Jesus Christ, the Son of God. 2 As it is written in the Prophets:[a]

> "Behold, I send My messenger
> before Your face,
> Who will prepare Your way
> before You."[b]
>
> 3 "The voice of one crying in the wilderness:
> 'Prepare the way of the LORD;
> Make His paths straight.'"[a]

4 John came baptizing in the wilderness and preaching a baptism of repentance for the remission of sins. 5 Then all the land of Judea, and those from Jerusalem, went out to him and were all baptized by him in the Jordan River, confessing their sins.

6 Now John was clothed with camel's hair and with a leather belt around his waist, and he ate locusts and wild honey. 7 And he preached, saying, "There comes One after me who is mightier than I, whose sandal strap I am not worthy to stoop down and loose. 8 I indeed baptized you with water, but He will baptize you with the Holy Spirit."

9 It came to pass in those days that Jesus came from Nazareth of Galilee, and was baptized by John in the Jordan. 10 And immediately, coming up from[a] the water, He saw the heavens parting and the Spirit descending upon Him like a dove. 11 Then a voice came from heaven, "You are My beloved Son, in whom I am well pleased."

12 Immediately the Spirit drove Him into the wilderness. 13 And He was there in the wilderness forty days, tempted by Satan, and was with the wild beasts; and the angels ministered to Him.

14 Now after John was put in prison, Jesus came to Galilee, preaching the gospel of the kingdom[a] of God, 15 and saying, "The time is fulfilled, and the kingdom of God is at hand. Repent, and believe in the gospel."

16 And as He walked by the Sea of Galilee, He saw Simon and Andrew his brother casting a net into the sea; for they were fishermen. 17 Then Jesus said to them, "Follow Me, and I will make you become fishers of men." 18 They immediately left their nets and followed Him.

19 When He had gone a little farther from there, He saw James the son of Zebedee, and John his brother, who also were in the boat mending their nets. 20 And immediately He called them, and they left their father Zebedee in the boat with the hired servants, and went after Him.

21 Then they went into Capernaum, and immediately on the Sabbath He entered the synagogue and taught. 22 And they were astonished at His teaching, for He taught them as one having authority, and not as the scribes.

23 Now there was a man in their synagogue with an unclean spirit. And he cried out, 24 saying, "Let us alone! What have we to do with You, Jesus of Nazareth? Did You come to destroy us? I know who You are—the Holy One of God!"

25 But Jesus rebuked him, saying, "Be quiet, and come out of him!" 26 And when the unclean spirit had convulsed him and cried out with a loud voice, he came out of him. 27 Then they were all amazed, so that they questioned among themselves, saying, "What is this? What new doctrine is this? For with authority[a] He commands even the unclean spirits, and they obey Him." 28 And immediately His fame spread throughout all the region around Galilee.

29 Now as soon as they had come out of the synagogue, they entered the house of Simon and Andrew, with James and John. 30 But Simon's wife's mother lay sick with a fever, and they told Him about her at once. 31 So He came and took her by the hand and lifted her up, and immediately the fever left her. And she served them.

32 At evening, when the sun had

1:2 [a]NU-Text reads Isaiah the prophet.   [b]Malachi 3:1   1:3 [a]Isaiah 40:3   1:10 [a]NU-Text reads out of.   1:14 [a]NU-Text omits of the kingdom.   1:27 [a]NU-Text reads What is this? A new doctrine with authority.

Peter's House in Capernaum

Archaeologists believe they have unearthed the house of the disciple Peter in Capernaum. Numerous fishhooks and coins from the time of Christ have been found in the house, indicating that it was a fisherman's dwelling. First-century inscriptions showing early Christian respect of the site as Peter's house provide written and pictorial evidence to support this claim.

In the course of Jesus' ministry, He spent many days in Capernaum. On one such occasion, Jesus taught in Peter's home. While He was teaching, a group of men attempted to bring a paralyzed man to Jesus to be healed. With the crowds pressing in on all sides of the house, an impossible situation faced this small band of believers.

Determined to conquer all obstacles, the men climbed to the roof of the house and raised the paralytic on a stretcher to the rooftop. The tile roof was quickly disassembled, and the sick man was then lowered on the stretcher to Jesus in the room below. Jesus recognized their display of faith and determination. Even though a situation barred them from getting to Jesus, the men moved forward, for they knew that Jesus was the answer. In response to their faith, Jesus healed the paralytic.

Throughout the Gospels we read of other incidents where people did everything they could to get to Jesus. They traveled hundreds of miles in adverse conditions, paid toll taxes, and suffered persecution and rejection. Why? They knew that Jesus had the healing power and the touch they needed.

What obstacle prevents you from getting close to Jesus? You know He is the answer. Make Him your goal. Look at obstacles as opportunities. Be determined and persistent. When faced with a mountain of a problem—find a way through! Jeremiah 29:13 promises, "And you will seek Me and find *Me*, when you search for me with all your heart."

set, they brought to Him all who were sick and those who were demon-possessed. 33 And the whole city was gathered together at the door. 34 Then He healed many who were sick with various diseases, and cast out many demons; and He did not allow the demons to speak, because they knew Him.

35 Now in the morning, having risen a long while before daylight, He went out and departed to a solitary place; and there He prayed. 36 And Simon and those *who were* with Him searched for Him. 37 When they found Him, they said to Him, "Everyone is looking for You."

38 But He said to them, "Let us go into the next towns, that I may preach there also, because for this purpose I have come forth."

39 And He was preaching in their synagogues throughout all Galilee, and casting out demons.

40 Now a leper came to Him, imploring Him, kneeling down to Him and saying to Him, "If You are willing, You can make me clean."

41 Then Jesus, moved with compassion, stretched out *His* hand and touched him, and said to him, "I am willing; be cleansed." 42 As soon as He had spoken, immediately the leprosy left him, and he was cleansed. 43 And He strictly warned him and sent him away at once, 44 and said to him, "See that you say nothing to anyone; but go your way, show yourself to the priest, and offer for your cleansing those things which Moses commanded, as a testimony to them."

45 However, he went out and began to proclaim *it* freely, and to spread the matter, so that Jesus could no longer openly enter the city, but was outside in deserted places; and they came to Him from every direction.

2 And again He entered Capernaum after *some* days, and it was heard that He was in the house. 2 Immediately*a* many gathered together, so that there was no longer room to receive *them*, not even near the door. And He preached the word to them. 3 Then they came to Him, bringing a paralytic who was carried by four *men.* 4 And when they could

not come near Him because of the crowd, they uncovered the roof where He was. So when they had broken through, they let down the bed on which the paralytic was lying. 5 When Jesus saw their faith, He said to the paralytic, "Son, your sins are forgiven you."

6 And some of the scribes were sitting there and reasoning in their hearts, 7 "Why does this *Man* speak blasphemies like this? Who can forgive sins but God alone?"

8 But immediately, when Jesus perceived in His spirit that they reasoned thus within themselves, He said to them, "Why do you reason about these things in your hearts? 9 Which is easier, to say to the paralytic, 'Your sins are forgiven you,' or to say, 'Arise, take up your bed and walk'? 10 But that you may know that the Son of Man has power on earth to forgive sins"—He said to the paralytic, 11 "I say to you, arise, take up your bed, and go to your house." 12 Immediately he arose, took up the bed, and went out in the presence of them all, so that all were amazed and glorified God, saying, "We never saw *anything* like this!"

13 Then He went out again by the sea; and all the multitude came to Him, and He taught them. 14 As He passed by, He saw Levi the *son* of Alphaeus sitting at the tax office. And He said to him, "Follow Me." So he arose and followed Him.

15 Now it happened, as He was dining in *Levi's* house, that many tax collectors and sinners also sat together with Jesus and His disciples; for there were many, and they followed Him. 16 And when the scribes and*a* Pharisees saw Him eating with the tax collectors and sinners, they said to His disciples, "How *is it* that He eats and drinks with tax collectors and sinners?"

17 When Jesus heard *it*, He said to them, "Those who are well have no need of a physician, but those who are sick. I did not come to call *the* righteous, but sinners, to repentance."*a* 18 The disciples of John and of the Pharisees were fasting. Then they came and said to Him, "Why do the disciples of John and of the Pharisees fast, but Your disciples do not fast?"

2:2 *a*NU-Text omits *Immediately.*   2:16 *a*NU-Text reads *of the.*   2:17 *a*NU-Text omits *to repentance.*

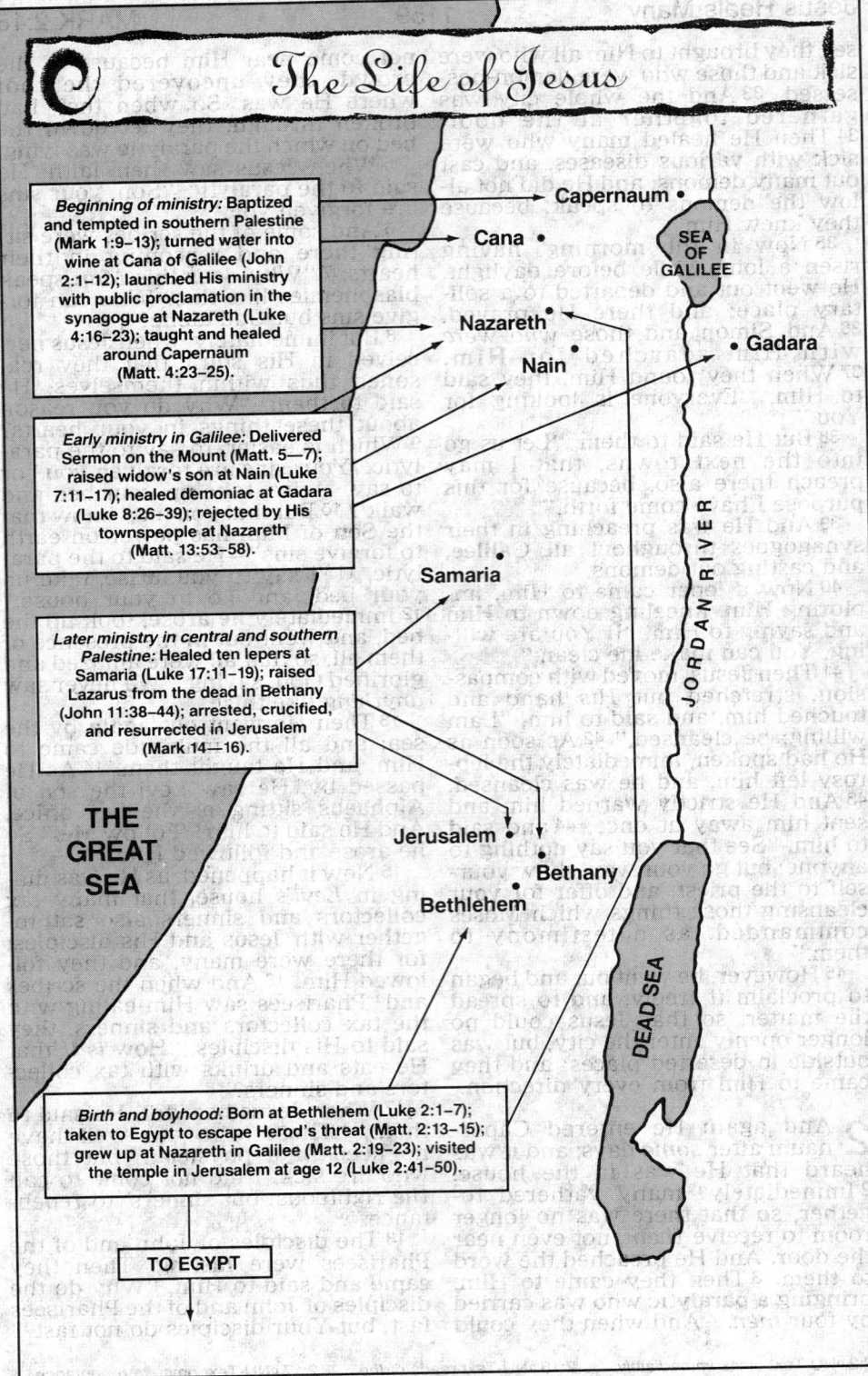

The Life of Jesus

Beginning of ministry: Baptized and tempted in southern Palestine (Mark 1:9–13); turned water into wine at Cana of Galilee (John 2:1–12); launched His ministry with public proclamation in the synagogue at Nazareth (Luke 4:16–23); taught and healed around Capernaum (Matt. 4:23–25).

Early ministry in Galilee: Delivered Sermon on the Mount (Matt. 5—7); raised widow's son at Nain (Luke 7:11–17); healed demoniac at Gadara (Luke 8:26–39); rejected by His townspeople at Nazareth (Matt. 13:53–58).

Later ministry in central and southern Palestine: Healed ten lepers at Samaria (Luke 17:11–19); raised Lazarus from the dead in Bethany (John 11:38–44); arrested, crucified, and resurrected in Jerusalem (Mark 14—16).

Birth and boyhood: Born at Bethlehem (Luke 2:1–7); taken to Egypt to escape Herod's threat (Matt. 2:13–15); grew up at Nazareth in Galilee (Matt. 2:19–23); visited the temple in Jerusalem at age 12 (Luke 2:41–50).

Capernaum

Cana

SEA OF GALILEE

Nazareth

Nain

Gadara

Samaria

JORDAN RIVER

THE GREAT SEA

Jerusalem

Bethany

Bethlehem

DEAD SEA

TO EGYPT

19 And Jesus said to them, "Can the friends of the bridegroom fast while the bridegroom is with them? As long as they have the bridegroom with them they cannot fast. 20 But the days will come when the bridegroom will be taken away from them, and then they will fast in those days. 21 No one sews a piece of unshrunk cloth on an old garment; or else the new piece pulls away from the old, and the tear is made worse. 22 And no one puts new wine into old wineskins; or else the new wine bursts the wineskins, the wine is spilled, and the wineskins are ruined. But new wine must be put into new wineskins."

23 Now it happened that He went through the grainfields on the Sabbath; and as they went His disciples began to pluck the heads of grain. 24 And the Pharisees said to Him, "Look, why do they do what is not lawful on the Sabbath?"

25 But He said to them, "Have you never read what David did when he was in need and hungry, he and those with him: 26 how he went into the house of God *in the days* of Abiathar the high priest, and ate the showbread, which is not lawful to eat except for the priests, and also gave some to those who were with him?"

27 And He said to them, "The Sabbath was made for man, and not man for the Sabbath. 28 Therefore the Son of Man is also Lord of the Sabbath."

3 And He entered the synagogue again, and a man was there who had a withered hand. 2 So they watched Him closely, whether He would heal him on the Sabbath, so that they might accuse Him. 3 And He said to the man who had the withered hand, "Step forward." 4 Then He said to them, "Is it lawful on the Sabbath to do good or to do evil, to save life or to kill?" But they kept silent. 5 And when He had looked around at them with anger, being grieved by the hardness of their hearts, He said to the man, "Stretch out your hand." And he stretched *it* out, and his hand was restored as whole as the other.[a] 6 Then the Pharisees went out and immediately plotted with the Herodians against Him, how they might destroy Him.

7 But Jesus withdrew with His disciples to the sea. And a great multitude from Galilee followed Him, and from Judea 8 and Jerusalem and Idumea and beyond the Jordan; and those from Tyre and Sidon, a great multitude, when they heard how many things He was doing, came to Him. 9 So He told His disciples that a small boat should be kept ready for Him because of the multitude, lest they should crush Him. 10 For He healed many, so that as many as had afflictions pressed about Him to touch Him. 11 And the unclean spirits, whenever they saw Him, fell down before Him and cried out, saying, "You are the Son of God." 12 But He sternly warned them that they should not make Him known.

13 And He went up on the mountain and called to *Him* those He Himself wanted. And they came to Him. 14 Then He appointed twelve,[a] that they might be with Him and that He might send them out to preach, 15 and to have power to heal sicknesses and[a] to cast out demons: 16 Simon,[a] to whom He gave the name Peter; 17 James the *son* of Zebedee and John the brother of James, to whom He gave the name Boanerges, that is, "Sons of Thunder"; 18 Andrew, Philip, Bartholomew, Matthew, Thomas, James the *son* of Alphaeus, Thaddaeus, Simon the Cananite; 19 and Judas Iscariot, who also betrayed Him. And they went into a house.

20 Then the multitude came together again, so that they could not so much as eat bread. 21 But when His own people heard *about this*, they went out to lay hold of Him, for they said, "He is out of His mind."

22 And the scribes who came down from Jerusalem said, "He has Beelzebub," and, "By the ruler of the demons He casts out demons."

23 So He called them to *Himself* and said to them in parables: "How can Satan cast out Satan? 24 If a kingdom is divided against itself, that kingdom cannot stand. 25 And if a house is divided against itself, that

3:5 aNU-Text omits *as whole as the other.*
3:15 aNU-Text omits *to heal sicknesses and.*
3:14 aNU-Text adds *whom He also named apostles.*
3:16 aNU-Text reads *and He appointed the twelve:
Simon . . . .*

house cannot stand. 26 And if Satan has risen up against himself, and is divided, he cannot stand, but has an end. 27 No one can enter a strong man's house and plunder his goods, unless he first binds the strong man. And then he will plunder his house.

28 "Assuredly, I say to you, all sins will be forgiven the sons of men, and whatever blasphemies they may utter; 29 but he who blasphemes against the Holy Spirit never has forgiveness, but is subject to eternal condemnation"— 30 because they said, "He has an unclean spirit."

31 Then His brothers and His mother came, and standing outside they sent to Him, calling Him. 32 And a multitude was sitting around Him; and they said to Him, "Look, Your mother and Your brothersª are outside seeking You."

33 But He answered them, saying, "Who is My mother, or My brothers?" 34 And He looked around in a circle at those who sat about Him, and said, "Here are My mother and My brothers! 35 For whoever does the will of God is My brother and My sister and mother."

4 And again He began to teach by the sea. And a great multitude was gathered to Him, so that He got into a boat and sat in it on the sea; and the whole multitude was on the land facing the sea. 2 Then He taught them many things by parables, and said to them in His teaching:

3 "Listen! Behold, a sower went out to sow. 4 And it happened, as he sowed, that some seed fell by the wayside; and the birds of the airª came and devoured it. 5 Some fell on stony ground, where it did not have much earth; and immediately it sprang up because it had no depth of earth. 6 But when the sun was up it was scorched, and because it had no root it withered away. 7 And some seed fell among thorns; and the thorns grew up and choked it, and it yielded no crop. 8 But other seed fell on good ground and yielded a crop that sprang up, increased and produced: some thirtyfold, some sixty, and some a hundred."

9 And He said to them,ª "He who has ears to hear, let him hear!"

10 But when He was alone, those around Him with the twelve asked Him about the parable. 11 And He said to them, "To you it has been given to know the mystery of the kingdom of God; but to those who are outside, all things come in parables, 12 so that

'Seeing they may see and not perceive,
And hearing they may hear and not understand;
Lest they should turn,
And their sins be forgiven them.'"ª

13 And He said to them, "Do you not understand this parable? How then will you understand all the parables? 14 The sower sows the word. 15 And these are the ones by the wayside where the word is sown. When they hear, Satan comes immediately and takes away the word that was sown in their hearts. 16 These likewise are the ones sown on stony ground who, when they hear the word, immediately receive it with gladness; 17 and they have no root in themselves, and so endure only for a time. Afterward, when tribulation or persecution arises for the word's sake, immediately they stumble. 18 Now these are the ones sown among thorns; they are the ones who hear the word, 19 and the cares of this world, the deceitfulness of riches, and the desires for other things entering in choke the word, and it becomes unfruitful. 20 But these are the ones sown on good ground, those who hear the word, accept it, and bear fruit: some thirtyfold, some sixty, and some a hundred."

21 Also He said to them, "Is a lamp brought to be put under a basket or under a bed? Is it not to be set on a lampstand? 22 For there is nothing hidden which will not be revealed, nor has anything been kept secret but that it should come to light. 23 If anyone has ears to hear, let him hear."

24 Then He said to them, "Take heed what you hear. With the same measure you use, it will be measured to you; and to you who hear, more will be given. 25 For whoever has, to

3:32 ªNU-Text and M-Text add and Your sisters.   4:4 ªNU-Text and M-Text omit of the air.
4:9 ªNU-Text and M-Text omit to them.   4:12 ªIsaiah 6:9, 10

The Gadarene Demoniac

On the southern shores of the Sea of Galilee, towering cliffs stretch down to the lake. In the face of these sea-salted cliffs are many honeycombed caves. In one such cave lived a demon-possessed man who for many years prevented travelers from passing along the road that ran from the cliffs to the sea. The Bible tells us he harassed them and frightened them. Each time the demoniac was put in chains, he broke free. He was one of the most feared men of the region.

During one of Jesus' trips to the cliffs near the eastern shore of the lake, He entered the area of Gadara, a Gentile region known for its pig farms. Upon seeing Jesus, the Gadarene demoniac ran to him, bowed down, and worshipped Him. The demons within this man asked Jesus to leave him alone. Seeing the man's great need, Jesus commanded the demons to leave him, and Jesus asked, "What is your name?" The demons answered, "My name *is* Legion; for we are many" (Mark 5:9). Immediately, Jesus commanded the demons to leave the man and to go into the 2,000 pigs feeding nearby. The demons entered the swine who ran down the steep cliff and into the sea. Normally pigs will swim well, but in this case they drowned.

The people from the region of Gadara had two choices for response to Jesus' miracle: to be excited that Jesus healed the man; or to be deeply disturbed that Jesus destroyed their main source of income. Witnesses ran into the city and told the townspeople what had happened. When the entire city of Gadara went out and saw the healed man and that the pigs were no longer grazing on the hillside, they were afraid and asked Jesus to leave because He had destroyed their major industry.

The people chose to look at what they had lost, not what Jesus had given them. They did not see the value of a restored human being, but the loss of their livelihood. They did not understand that the God who healed the demon-possessed man could have provided all of their needs if they only asked.

The healed man wanted to travel with Jesus, but Jesus had other plans for him. Jesus said, "Go home to your friends, and tell them what great thing the Lord has done for you, and how He has had compassion on you" (Mark 5:19). So the healed man departed, proclaimed throughout Decapolis what Jesus had done, and all the people marveled.

In every situation in our lives we have the opportunity to choose the positive perspective. Look at what Jesus has given you. In all aspects of life, look at what you have been given that is valuable rather than at what of lesser value you've temporarily lost! As Christians we are "looking unto Jesus, the author and finisher of *our* faith, who for the joy that was set before Him endured the cross, despising the shame, and has sat down at the right hand of the throne of God" (Heb. 12:2).

him more will be given; but whoever does not have, even what he has will be taken away from him."

26 And He said, "The kingdom of God is as if a man should scatter seed on the ground, 27 and should sleep by night and rise by day, and the seed should sprout and grow, he himself does not know how. 28 For the earth yields crops by itself: first the blade, then the head, after that the full grain in the head. 29 But when the grain ripens, immediately he puts in the sickle, because the harvest has come."

30 Then He said, "To what shall we liken the kingdom of God? Or with what parable shall we picture it? 31 It is like a mustard seed which, when it is sown on the ground, is smaller than all the seeds on earth; 32 but when it is sown, it grows up and becomes greater than all herbs, and shoots out large branches, so that the birds of the air may nest under its shade."

33 And with many such parables He spoke the word to them as they were able to hear it. 34 But without a parable He did not speak to them. And when they were alone, He explained all things to His disciples.

35 On the same day, when evening had come, He said to them, "Let us cross over to the other side." 36 Now when they had left the multitude, they took Him along in the boat as He was. And other little boats were also with Him. 37 And a great windstorm arose, and the waves beat into the boat, so that it was already filling. 38 But He was in the stern, asleep on a pillow. And they awoke Him and said to Him, "Teacher, do You not care that we are perishing?" 39 Then He arose and rebuked the wind, and said to the sea, "Peace, be still!" And the wind ceased and there was a great calm. 40 But He said to them, "Why are you so fearful? How is it that you have no faith?"[a] 41 And they feared exceedingly, and said to one another, "Who can this be, that even the wind and the sea obey Him!"

5 Then they came to the other side of the sea, to the country of the Gadarenes.[a] 2 And when He had come out of the boat, immediately there met Him out of the tombs a man with an unclean spirit, 3 who had his dwelling among the tombs; and no one could bind him,[a] not even with chains, 4 because he had often been bound with shackles and chains. And the chains had been pulled apart by him, and the shackles broken in pieces; neither could anyone tame him. 5 And always, night and day, he was in the mountains and in the tombs, crying out and cutting himself with stones.

6 When he saw Jesus from afar, he ran and worshiped Him. 7 And he cried out with a loud voice and said, "What have I to do with You, Jesus, Son of the Most High God? I implore You by God that You do not torment me."

8 For He said to him, "Come out of the man, unclean spirit!" 9 Then He asked him, "What is your name?"

And he answered, saying, "My name is Legion; for we are many." 10 Also he begged Him earnestly that He would not send them out of the country.

11 Now a large herd of swine was feeding there near the mountains. 12 So all the demons begged Him, saying, "Send us to the swine, that we may enter them." 13 And at once Jesus[a] gave them permission. Then the unclean spirits went out and entered the swine (there were about two thousand); and the herd ran violently down the steep place into the sea, and drowned in the sea.

14 So those who fed the swine fled, and they told it in the city and in the country. And they went out to see what it was that had happened. 15 Then they came to Jesus, and saw the one who had been demon-possessed and had the legion, sitting and clothed and in his right mind. And they were afraid. 16 And those who saw it told them how it happened to him who had been demon-possessed, and about the swine. 17 Then they began to plead with Him to depart from their region.

18 And when He got into the boat, he who had been demon-possessed begged Him that he might be with Him. 19 However, Jesus did not per-

4:40 [a]NU-Text reads Have you still no faith?   5:1 [a]NU-Text reads Gerasenes.   5:3 [a]NU-Text adds anymore.   5:13 [a]NU-Text reads And He gave.

mit him, but said to him, "Go home to your friends, and tell them what great things the Lord has done for you, and how He has had compassion on you." 20 And he departed and began to proclaim in Decapolis all that Jesus had done for him; and all marveled.

21 Now when Jesus had crossed over again by boat to the other side, a great multitude gathered to Him; and He was by the sea. 22 And behold, one of the rulers of the synagogue came, Jairus by name. And when he saw Him, he fell at His feet 23 and begged Him earnestly, saying, "My little daughter lies at the point of death. Come and lay Your hands on her, that she may be healed, and she will live." 24 So *Jesus* went with him, and a great multitude followed Him and thronged Him.

25 Now a certain woman had a flow of blood for twelve years, 26 and had suffered many things from many physicians. She had spent all that she had and was no better, but rather grew worse. 27 When she heard about Jesus, she came behind *Him* in the crowd and touched His garment. 28 For she said, "If only I may touch His clothes, I shall be made well."

29 Immediately the fountain of her blood was dried up, and she felt in *her* body that she was healed of the affliction. 30 And Jesus, immediately knowing in Himself that power had gone out of Him, turned around in the crowd and said, "Who touched My clothes?"

31 But His disciples said to Him, "You see the multitude thronging You, and You say, 'Who touched Me?'"

32 And He looked around to see her who had done this thing. 33 But the woman, fearing and trembling, knowing what had happened to her, came and fell down before Him and told Him the whole truth. 34 And He said to her, "Daughter, your faith has made you well. Go in peace, and be healed of your affliction."

35 While He was still speaking, *some* came from the ruler of the synagogue's *house* who said, "Your daughter is dead. Why trouble the Teacher any further?"

36 As soon as Jesus heard the word that was spoken, He said to the ruler of the synagogue, "Do not be afraid; only believe." 37 And He permitted no one to follow Him except Peter, James, and John the brother of James. 38 Then He came to the house of the ruler of the synagogue, and saw a tumult and those who wept and wailed loudly. 39 When He came in, He said to them, "Why make this commotion and weep? The child is not dead, but sleeping."

40 And they ridiculed Him. But when He had put them all outside, He took the father and the mother of the child, and those *who were* with Him, and entered where the child was lying. 41 Then He took the child by the hand, and said to her, "Talitha, cumi," which is translated, "Little girl, I say to you, arise." 42 Immediately the girl arose and walked, for she was twelve years *of age*. And they were overcome with great amazement. 43 But He commanded them strictly that no one should know it, and said that *something* should be given her to eat.

6 Then He went out from there and came to His own country, and His disciples followed Him. 2 And when the Sabbath had come, He began to teach in the synagogue. And many hearing *Him* were astonished, saying, "Where *did* this Man *get* these things? And what wisdom *is* this which is given to Him, that such mighty works are performed by His hands! 3 Is this not the carpenter, the Son of Mary, and brother of James, Joses, Judas, and Simon? And are not His sisters here with us?" So they were offended at Him.

4 But Jesus said to them, "A prophet is not without honor except in his own country, among his own relatives, and in his own house." 5 Now He could do no mighty work there, except that He laid His hands on a few sick people and healed *them*. 6 And He marveled because of their unbelief. Then He went about the villages in a circuit, teaching.

7 And He called the twelve to *Himself*, and began to send them out two by two, and gave them power over unclean spirits. 8 He commanded them to take nothing for the journey except a staff—no bag, no bread, no copper in *their* money belts— 9 but to wear sandals, and not to put on two tunics.

10 Also He said to them, "In what-

ever place you enter a house, stay there till you depart from that place. 11 And whoever[a] will not receive you nor hear you, when you depart from there, shake off the dust under your feet as a testimony against them.[b] Assuredly, I say to you, it will be more tolerable for Sodom and Gomorrah in the day of judgment than for that city!"

12 So they went out and preached that *people* should repent. 13 And they cast out many demons, and anointed with oil many who were sick, and healed *them*.

14 Now King Herod heard *of Him*, for His name had become well known. And he said, "John the Baptist is risen from the dead, and therefore these powers are at work in him."

15 Others said, "It is Elijah."

And others said, "It is the Prophet, or[a] like one of the prophets."

16 But when Herod heard, he said, "This is John, whom I beheaded; he has been raised from the dead!" 17 For Herod himself had sent and laid hold of John, and bound him in prison for the sake of Herodias, his brother Philip's wife; for he had married her. 18 Because John had said to Herod, "It is not lawful for you to have your brother's wife."

19 Therefore Herodias held it against him and wanted to kill him, but she could not; 20 for Herod feared John, knowing that he *was* a just and holy man, and he protected him. And when he heard him, he did many things, and heard him gladly.

21 Then an opportune day came when Herod on his birthday gave a feast for his nobles, the high officers, and the chief *men* of Galilee. 22 And when Herodias' daughter herself came in and danced, and pleased Herod and those who sat with him, the king said to the girl, "Ask me whatever you want, and I will give *it* to you." 23 He also swore to her, "Whatever you ask me, I will give you, up to half my kingdom."

24 So she went out and said to her mother, "What shall I ask?"

And she said, "The head of John the Baptist!"

25 Immediately she came in with haste to the king and asked, saying, "I want you to give me at once the head of John the Baptist on a platter."

26 And the king was exceedingly sorry; *yet*, because of the oaths and because of those who sat with him, he did not want to refuse her. 27 Immediately the king sent an executioner and commanded his head to be brought. And he went and beheaded him in prison, 28 brought his head on a platter, and gave it to the girl; and the girl gave it to her mother. 29 When his disciples heard *of it*, they came and took away his corpse and laid it in a tomb.

30 Then the apostles gathered to Jesus and told Him all things, both what they had done and what they had taught. 31 And He said to them, "Come aside by yourselves to a deserted place and rest a while." For there were many coming and going, and they did not even have time to eat. 32 So they departed to a deserted place in the boat by themselves.

33 But the multitudes[a] saw them departing, and many knew Him and ran there on foot from all the cities. They arrived before them and came together to Him. 34 And Jesus, when He came out, saw a great multitude and was moved with compassion for them, because they were like sheep not having a shepherd. So He began to teach them many things. 35 When the day was now far spent, His disciples came to Him and said, "This is a deserted place, and already the hour *is* late. 36 Send them away, that they may go into the surrounding country and villages and buy themselves bread;[a] for they have nothing to eat."

37 But He answered and said to them, "You give them something to eat."

And they said to Him, "Shall we go and buy two hundred denarii worth of bread and give them *something* to eat?"

38 But He said to them, "How many loaves do you have? Go and see."

And when they found out they said, "Five, and two fish."

39 Then He commanded them to

6:11 aNU-Text reads *whatever place*. bNU-Text omits the rest of this verse. 6:15 aNU-Text and M-Text omit *or*.   6:33 aNU-Text and M-Text read *they*.   6:36 aNU-Text reads *something to eat* and omits the rest of verse.

The Other Side

A major portion of Jesus' ministry took place around the shores of the Sea of Galilee, an area widely influenced by Roman and Greek civilizations. This influence was primarily felt on the eastern shores of the sea where the cities were separated culturally, religiously, and geographically from the Jewish cities of Capernaum, Chorazin, and Bethsaida, located on the lake's western shores. According to Matthew, Jesus concentrated His teachings and miracles in these Jewish towns. This area was known by the Jewish population as "our side."

On occasion Jesus traveled to "the other side" to teach the people. This phrase refers not only to the eastern side of the Sea of Galilee, but more culturally and religiously to the Gentile region. "The other side" was a specific reference given by the Jewish villagers to the Greek and Roman centers located on the other side of the lake, including the cities of Hippus, Gergesa, and Gadara.

According to the Gospels, thousands of people followed Jesus to the other side. This was no easy task for the Jews. Whether they journeyed by boat or land, Rome levied heavy sea and land taxes to finance their wars in Europe. Travel to the predominantly Gentile region was greatly discouraged by the religious community. Once there, the food of the Gentiles was uneatable under the Jewish dietary laws. Those who traveled with young families found the ten-to-twenty-mile journey even more difficult.

Despite the physical, cultural, and religious obstacles of travel to "the other side," the Bible records that on two occasions there were crowds of four thousand and five thousand people to hear Jesus. We know that these were mostly Jewish villagers who had traveled a long distance to hear Jesus. Since there were many Gentile towns nearby, their complaints about having nothing to eat can be interpreted that there was no food available for the Jewish diet. The Gospels say that Jesus, out of compassion, provided fish and bread for the hungry multitudes.

Sometimes people may ridicule us, often it will take time out of our busy schedules, and it will certainly run contrary to the status quo for us to follow Jesus. Yet the reward for doing so remains the same: "He received them and spoke to them about the kingdom of God, and healed those who had need of healing . . . So they all ate and were filled" (Luke 9:11, 17). Jesus filled their spiritual *and* material needs.

make them all sit down in groups on the green grass. 40 So they sat down in ranks, in hundreds and in fifties. 41 And when He had taken the five loaves and the two fish, He looked up to heaven, blessed and broke the loaves, and gave *them* to His disciples to set before them; and the two fish He divided among *them* all. 42 So they all ate and were filled. 43 And they took up twelve baskets full of fragments and of the fish. 44 Now those who had eaten the loaves were about*a* five thousand men.

45 Immediately He made His disciples get into the boat and go before Him to the other side, to Bethsaida, while He sent the multitude away. 46 And when He had sent them away, He departed to the mountain to pray. 47 Now when evening came, the boat was in the middle of the sea; and He *was* alone on the land. 48 Then He saw them straining at rowing, for the wind was against them. Now about the fourth watch of the night He came to them, walking on the sea, and would have passed them by. 49 And when they saw Him walking on the sea, they supposed it was a ghost, and cried out; 50 for they all saw Him and were troubled. But immediately He talked with them and said to them, "Be of good cheer! It is I; do not be afraid." 51 Then He went up into the boat to them, and the wind ceased. And they were greatly amazed in themselves beyond measure, and marveled. 52 For they had not understood about the loaves, because their heart was hardened.

53 When they had crossed over, they came to the land of Gennesaret and anchored there. 54 And when they came out of the boat, immediately the people recognized Him, 55 ran through that whole surrounding region, and began to carry about on beds those who were sick to wherever they heard He was. 56 Wherever He entered, into villages, cities, or the country, they laid the sick in the marketplaces, and begged Him that they might just touch the hem of His garment. And as many as touched Him were made well.

7 Then the Pharisees and some of the scribes came together to Him, having come from Jerusalem. 2 Now when*a* they saw some of His disciples eat bread with defiled, that is, with unwashed hands, they found fault. 3 For the Pharisees and all the Jews do not eat unless they wash *their* hands in a special way, holding the tradition of the elders. 4 *When they come* from the marketplace, they do not eat unless they wash. And there are many other things which they have received and hold, *like* the washing of cups, pitchers, copper vessels, and couches.

5 Then the Pharisees and scribes asked Him, "Why do Your disciples not walk according to the tradition of the elders, but eat bread with unwashed hands?"

6 He answered and said to them, "Well did Isaiah prophesy of you hypocrites, as it is written:

> 'This people honors Me with
> 　　their lips,
> But their heart is far from Me.
> 7　And in vain they worship Me,
> 　　Teaching as doctrines the
> 　　commandments of men.'*a*

8 For laying aside the commandment of God, you hold the tradition of men*a*—the washing of pitchers and cups, and many other such things you do."

9 He said to them, "*All* too well you reject the commandment of God, that you may keep your tradition. 10 For Moses said, 'Honor your father and your mother';*a* and, 'He who curses father or mother, let him be put to death.'*b* 11 But you say, 'If a man says to his father or mother, "Whatever profit you might have received from me *is* Corban"—' (that is, a gift *to* God), 12 then you no longer let him do anything for his father or his mother, 13 making the word of God of no effect through your tradition which you have handed down. And many such things you do."

14 When He had called all the multitude to *Himself,* He said to them, "Hear Me, everyone, and understand: 15 There is nothing that enters

6:44 *a*NU-Text and M-Text omit *about.*　7:2 *a*NU-Text omits *when* and *they found fault.*　7:7 *a*Isaiah 29:13　7:8 *a*NU-Text omits the rest of this verse.　7:10 *a*Exodus 20:12; Deuteronomy 5:16　*b*Exodus 21:17

a man from outside which can defile him; but the things which come out of him, those are the things that defile a man. 16 If anyone has ears to hear, let him hear!"[a]

17 When He had entered a house away from the crowd, His disciples asked Him concerning the parable. 18 So He said to them, "Are you thus without understanding also? Do you not perceive that whatever enters a man from outside cannot defile him, 19 because it does not enter his heart but his stomach, and is eliminated, *thus* purifying all foods?"[a] 20 And He said, "What comes out of a man, that defiles a man. 21 For from within, out of the heart of men, proceed evil thoughts, adulteries, fornications, murders, 22 thefts, covetousness, wickedness, deceit, lewdness, an evil eye, blasphemy, pride, foolishness. 23 All these evil things come from within and defile a man."

24 From there He arose and went to the region of Tyre and Sidon.[a] And He entered a house and wanted no one to know *it*, but He could not be hidden. 25 For a woman whose young daughter had an unclean spirit heard about Him, and she came and fell at His feet. 26 The woman was a Greek, a Syro-Phoenician by birth, and she kept asking Him to cast the demon out of her daughter. 27 But Jesus said to her, "Let the children be filled first, for it is not good to take the children's bread and throw *it* to the little dogs."

28 And she answered and said to Him, "Yes, Lord, yet even the little dogs under the table eat from the children's crumbs."

29 Then He said to her, "For this saying go your way; the demon has gone out of your daughter."

30 And when she had come to her house, she found the demon gone out, and her daughter lying on the bed.

31 Again, departing from the region of Tyre and Sidon, He came through the midst of the region of Decapolis to the Sea of Galilee. 32 Then they brought to Him one who was deaf and had an impediment in his speech, and they begged Him to put His hand on him. 33 And He took him aside from the multitude, and put His

fingers in his ears, and He spat and touched his tongue. 34 Then, looking up to heaven, He sighed, and said to him, "Ephphatha," that is, "Be opened."

35 Immediately his ears were opened, and the impediment of his tongue was loosed, and he spoke plainly. 36 Then He commanded them that they should tell no one; but the more He commanded them, the more widely they proclaimed *it*. 37 And they were astonished beyond measure, saying, "He has done all things well. He makes both the deaf to hear and the mute to speak."

8 In those days, the multitude being very great and having nothing to eat, Jesus called His disciples *to Him* and said to them, 2 "I have compassion on the multitude, because they have now continued with Me three days and have nothing to eat. 3 And if I send them away hungry to their own houses, they will faint on the way; for some of them have come from afar."

4 Then His disciples answered Him, "How can one satisfy these people with bread here in the wilderness?"

5 He asked them, "How many loaves do you have?"

And they said, "Seven."

6 So He commanded the multitude to sit down on the ground. And He took the seven loaves and gave thanks, broke *them* and gave *them* to His disciples to set before *them*; and they set *them* before the multitude. 7 They also had a few small fish; and having blessed them, He said to set them also before *them*. 8 So they ate and were filled, and they took up seven large baskets of leftover fragments. 9 Now those who had eaten were about four thousand. And He sent them away, 10 immediately got into the boat with His disciples, and came to the region of Dalmanutha.

11 Then the Pharisees came out and began to dispute with Him, seeking from Him a sign from heaven, testing Him. 12 But He sighed deeply in His spirit, and said, "Why does this gen-

7:16 [a]NU-Text omits this verse.   7:19 [a]NU-Text ends quotation with *eliminated*, setting off the final clause as Mark's comment that Jesus has declared all foods clean.   7:24 [a]NU-Text omits *and Sidon*.

eration seek a sign? Assuredly, I say to you, no sign shall be given to this generation."

13 And He left them, and getting into the boat again, departed to the other side. 14 Now the disciples*a* had forgotten to take bread, and they did not have more than one loaf with them in the boat. 15 Then He charged them, saying, "Take heed, beware of the leaven of the Pharisees and the leaven of Herod."

16 And they reasoned among themselves, saying, "*It is* because we have no bread."

17 But Jesus, being aware of *it,* said to them, "Why do you reason because you have no bread? Do you not yet perceive nor understand? Is your heart still*a* hardened? 18 Having eyes, do you not see? And having ears, do you not hear? And do you not remember? 19 When I broke the five loaves for the five thousand, how many baskets full of fragments did you take up?"

They said to Him, "Twelve."

20 "Also, when I broke the seven for the four thousand, how many large baskets full of fragments did you take up?"

And they said, "Seven."

21 So He said to them, "How *is it* you do not understand?"

22 Then He came to Bethsaida; and they brought a blind man to Him, and begged Him to touch him. 23 So He took the blind man by the hand and led him out of the town. And when He had spit on his eyes and put His hands on him, He asked him if he saw anything.

24 And he looked up and said, "I see men like trees, walking."

25 Then He put *His* hands on his eyes again and made him look up. And he was restored and saw everyone clearly. 26 Then He sent him away to his house, saying, "Neither go into the town, nor tell anyone in the town."*a*

27 Now Jesus and His disciples went out to the towns of Caesarea Philippi; and on the road He asked His disciples, saying to them, "Who do men say that I am?"

28 So they answered, "John the Baptist; but some *say,* Elijah; and others, one of the prophets."

29 He said to them, "But who do you say that I am?"

Peter answered and said to Him, "You are the Christ."

30 Then He strictly warned them that they should tell no one about Him.

31 And He began to teach them that the Son of Man must suffer many things, and be rejected by the elders and chief priests and scribes, and be killed, and after three days rise again. 32 He spoke this word openly. Then Peter took Him aside and began to rebuke Him. 33 But when He had turned around and looked at His disciples, He rebuked Peter, saying, "Get behind Me, Satan! For you are not mindful of the things of God, but the things of men."

34 When He had called the people to *Himself,* with His disciples also, He said to them, "Whoever desires to come after Me, let him deny himself, and take up his cross, and follow Me. 35 For whoever desires to save his life will lose it, but whoever loses his life for My sake and the gospel's will save it. 36 For what will it profit a man if he gains the whole world, and loses his own soul? 37 Or what will a man give in exchange for his soul? 38 For whoever is ashamed of Me and My words in this adulterous and sinful generation, of him the Son of Man also will be ashamed when He comes in the glory of His Father with the holy angels."

9 And He said to them, "Assuredly, I say to you that there are some standing here who will not taste death till they see the kingdom of God present with power."

2 Now after six days Jesus took Peter, James, and John, and led them up on a high mountain apart by themselves; and He was transfigured before them. 3 His clothes became shining, exceedingly white, like snow, such as no launderer on earth can whiten them. 4 And Elijah appeared to them with Moses, and they were talking with Jesus. 5 Then Peter answered and said to Jesus, "Rabbi, it is good for us to be here; and let us make three tabernacles: one for You, one for Moses, and one for Elijah"— 6 because he did not know

---

8:14 *a*NU-Text and M-Text read *they.*   8:17 *a*NU-Text omits *still.*   8:26 *a*NU-Text reads *"Do not even go into the town."*

Faith Makes the Impossible Possible

Peter, James, and John were given a glimpse of glory when they saw Jesus transfigured on the mountain (Mark 9:2). Faith is the process of *acting upon glorious assumptions.*

If you attempt to achieve an objective that is easily reached, then you are not moving within the circle of faith.

Faith is not necessary unless your projects are humanly impossible.

Unless there is strong reason to doubt, you are not living in the higher altitude of real faith.

You must commit yourself to projects where there is a possibility of failure before you can claim to be walking the walk of faith.

How does faith move us forward when success is uncertain? Faith moves us onward by giving us the courage to act upon positive assumptions. We assume that:

• With the help of God, the impossible can be possible.

• There will never be progress until someone acts upon a grand assumption. Surely, you have the right to assume that God, who made your dream, will also make it possible for you to succeed.

Keep moving forward, steadily, assuming that when you reach the door it will swing open! Noah assumed the rains would come. Moses moved toward the Red Sea, assuming that a way would clear for him to cross it. Joshua assumed the walls would fall.

Begin your faith walk with prayer:

O God, with Your help today, I believe the impossible can be possible. I assume that my problems are solvable; that help will be forthcoming; that new breakthroughs will come my way; and that positive and exciting new healings will flow into me. I believe that today's assumptions will become tomorrow's grand accomplishments! Thank You, God. Amen.

what to say, for they were greatly afraid.

7 And a cloud came and overshadowed them; and a voice came out of the cloud, saying, "This is My beloved Son. Hear Him!" 8 Suddenly, when they had looked around, they saw no one anymore, but only Jesus with themselves.

9 Now as they came down from the mountain, He commanded them that they should tell no one the things they had seen, till the Son of Man had risen from the dead. 10 So they kept this word to themselves, questioning what the rising from the dead meant.

11 And they asked Him, saying, "Why do the scribes say that Elijah must come first?"

12 Then He answered and told them, "Indeed, Elijah is coming first and restores all things. And how is it written concerning the Son of Man, that He must suffer many things and be treated with contempt? 13 But I say to you that Elijah has also come, and they did to him whatever they wished, as it is written of him."

14 And when He came to the disciples, He saw a great multitude around them, and scribes disputing with them. 15 Immediately, when they saw Him, all the people were greatly amazed, and running to *Him,* greeted Him. 16 And He asked the scribes, "What are you discussing with them?"

17 Then one of the crowd answered and said, "Teacher, I brought You my son, who has a mute spirit. 18 And wherever it seizes him, it throws him down; he foams at the mouth, gnashes his teeth, and becomes rigid. So I spoke to Your disciples, that they should cast it out, but they could not."

19 He answered him and said, "O faithless generation, how long shall I be with you? How long shall I bear with you? Bring him to Me." 20 Then they brought him to Him. And when he saw Him, immediately the spirit convulsed him, and he fell on the ground and wallowed, foaming at the mouth.

21 So He asked his father, "How long has this been happening to him?"

And he said, "From childhood.

22 And often he has thrown him both into the fire and into the water to destroy him. But if You can do anything, have compassion on us and help us."

23 Jesus said to him, "If you can believe,[a] all things *are* possible to him who believes."

24 Immediately the father of the child cried out and said with tears, "Lord, I believe; help my unbelief!"

25 When Jesus saw that the people came running together, He rebuked the unclean spirit, saying to it, "Deaf and dumb spirit, I command you, come out of him and enter him no more!" 26 Then *the spirit* cried out, convulsed him greatly, and came out of him. And he became as one dead, so that many said, "He is dead." 27 But Jesus took him by the hand and lifted him up, and he arose.

28 And when He had come into the house, His disciples asked Him privately, "Why could we not cast it out?"

29 So He said to them, "This kind can come out by nothing but prayer and fasting."[a]

30 Then they departed from there and passed through Galilee, and He did not want anyone to know *it.* 31 For He taught His disciples and said to them, "The Son of Man is being betrayed into the hands of men, and they will kill Him. And after He is killed, He will rise the third day." 32 But they did not understand this saying, and were afraid to ask Him.

33 Then He came to Capernaum. And when He was in the house He asked them, "What was it you disputed among yourselves on the road?" 34 But they kept silent, for on the road they had disputed among themselves who *would be the* greatest. 35 And He sat down, called the twelve, and said to them, "If anyone desires to be first, he shall be last of all and servant of all." 36 Then He took a little child and set him in the midst of them. And when He had taken him in His arms, He said to them, 37 "Whoever receives one of these little children in My name receives Me; and whoever receives Me, receives not Me but Him who sent Me."

38 Now John answered Him, saying, "Teacher, we saw someone who

---

9:23 [a]NU-Text reads *"If You can! All things. . . ."*   9:29 [a]NU-Text omits *and fasting.*

does not follow us casting out demons in Your name, and we forbade him because he does not follow us."

39 But Jesus said, "Do not forbid him, for no one who works a miracle in My name can soon afterward speak evil of Me. 40 For he who is not against us is on our[a] side. 41 For whoever gives you a cup of water to drink in My name, because you belong to Christ, assuredly, I say to you, he will by no means lose his reward.

42 "But whoever causes one of these little ones who believe in Me to stumble, it would be better for him if a millstone were hung around his neck, and he were thrown into the sea. 43 If your hand causes you to sin, cut it off. It is better for you to enter into life maimed, rather than having two hands, to go to hell, into the fire that shall never be quenched— 44 where

'Their worm does not die,
And the fire is not quenched.'[a]

45 And if your foot causes you to sin, cut it off. It is better for you to enter life lame, rather than having two feet, to be cast into hell, into the fire that shall never be quenched— 46 where

'Their worm does not die,
And the fire is not quenched.'[a]

47 And if your eye causes you to sin, pluck it out. It is better for you to enter the kingdom of God with one eye, rather than having two eyes, to be cast into hell fire— 48 where

'Their worm does not die,
And the fire is not quenched.'[a]

49 "For everyone will be seasoned with fire,[a] and every sacrifice will be seasoned with salt. 50 Salt *is* good, but if the salt loses its flavor, how will you season it? Have salt in yourselves, and have peace with one another."

10 Then He arose from there and came to the region of Judea by the other side of the Jordan. And multitudes gathered to Him again, and as He was accustomed, He taught them again.

2 The Pharisees came and asked Him, "Is it lawful for a man to divorce *his* wife?" testing Him.

3 And He answered and said to them, "What did Moses command you?"

4 They said, "Moses permitted *a man* to write a certificate of divorce, and to dismiss *her.*"

5 And Jesus answered and said to them, "Because of the hardness of your heart he wrote you this precept. 6 But from the beginning of the creation, God *'made them male and female.'[a]* 7 *'For this reason a man shall leave his father and mother and be joined to his wife,* 8 *and the two shall become one flesh';[a]* so then they are no longer two, but one flesh. 9 Therefore what God has joined together, let not man separate."

10 In the house His disciples also asked Him again about the same matter. 11 So He said to them, "Whoever divorces his wife and marries another commits adultery against her. 12 And if a woman divorces her husband and marries another, she commits adultery."

13 Then they brought little children to Him, that He might touch them; but the disciples rebuked those who brought *them.* 14 But when Jesus saw *it,* He was greatly displeased and said to them, "Let the little children come to Me, and do not forbid them; for of such is the kingdom of God. 15 Assuredly, I say to you, whoever does not receive the kingdom of God as a little child will by no means enter it." 16 And He took them up in His arms, laid *His* hands on them, and blessed them.

17 Now as He was going out on the road, one came running, knelt before Him, and asked Him, "Good Teacher, what shall I do that I may inherit eternal life?"

18 So Jesus said to him, "Why do you call Me good? No one *is* good but One, *that is,* God. 19 You know the commandments: *'Do not commit adultery,' 'Do not murder,' 'Do not steal,' 'Do not bear false witness,' 'Do*

9:40 [a]M-Text reads *against you is on your side.*   9:44 [a]NU-Text omits this verse.   9:46 [a]NU-Text omits the last clause of verse 45 and all of verse 46.   9:48 [a]Isaiah 66:24   9:49 [a]NU-Text omits the rest of this verse.   10:6 [a]Genesis 1:27; 5:2   10:8 [a]Genesis 2:24

not defraud,' *'Honor your father and your mother.'"*[a]

20 And he answered and said to Him, "Teacher, all these things I have kept from my youth."

21 Then Jesus, looking at him, loved him, and said to him, "One thing you lack: Go your way, sell whatever you have and give to the poor, and you will have treasure in heaven; and come, take up the cross, and follow Me."

22 But he was sad at this word, and went away sorrowful, for he had great possessions.

23 Then Jesus looked around and said to His disciples, "How hard it is for those who have riches to enter the kingdom of God!" 24 And the disciples were astonished at His words. But Jesus answered again and said to them, "Children, how hard it is for those who trust in riches[a] to enter the kingdom of God! 25 It is easier for a camel to go through the eye of a needle than for a rich man to enter the kingdom of God."

26 And they were greatly astonished, saying among themselves, "Who then can be saved?"

27 But Jesus looked at them and said, "With men *it is* impossible, but not with God; for with God all things are possible."

28 Then Peter began to say to Him, "See, we have left all and followed You."

29 So Jesus answered and said, "Assuredly, I say to you, there is no one who has left house or brothers or sisters or father or mother or wife[a] or children or lands, for My sake and the gospel's, 30 who shall not receive a hundredfold now in this time—houses and brothers and sisters and mothers and children and lands, with persecutions—and in the age to come, eternal life. 31 But many *who are* first will be last, and the last first."

32 Now they were on the road, going up to Jerusalem, and Jesus was going before them; and they were amazed. And as they followed they were afraid. Then He took the twelve aside again and began to tell them the things that would happen to Him: 33 "Behold, we are going up to Jerusalem, and the Son of Man will be betrayed to the chief priests and to the scribes; and they will condemn Him to death and deliver Him to the Gentiles; 34 and they will mock Him, and scourge Him, and spit on Him, and kill Him. And the third day He will rise again."

35 Then James and John, the sons of Zebedee, came to Him, saying, "Teacher, we want You to do for us whatever we ask."

36 And He said to them, "What do you want Me to do for you?"

37 They said to Him, "Grant us that we may sit, one on Your right hand and the other on Your left, in Your glory."

38 But Jesus said to them, "You do not know what you ask. Are you able to drink the cup that I drink, and be baptized with the baptism that I am baptized with?"

39 They said to Him, "We are able."

So Jesus said to them, "You will indeed drink the cup that I drink, and with the baptism I am baptized with you will be baptized; 40 but to sit on My right hand and on My left is not Mine to give, but *it is for those* for whom it is prepared."

41 And when the ten heard *it,* they began to be greatly displeased with James and John. 42 But Jesus called them to *Himself* and said to them, "You know that those who are considered rulers over the Gentiles lord it over them, and their great ones exercise authority over them. 43 Yet it shall not be so among you; but whoever desires to become great among you shall be your servant. 44 And whoever of you desires to be first shall be slave of all. 45 For even the Son of Man did not come to be served, but to serve, and to give His life a ransom for many."

46 Now they came to Jericho. As He went out of Jericho with His disciples and a great multitude, blind Bartimaeus, the son of Timaeus, sat by the road begging. 47 And when he heard that it was Jesus of Nazareth, he began to cry out and say, "Jesus, Son of David, have mercy on me!"

48 Then many warned him to be quiet; but he cried out all the more, "Son of David, have mercy on me!"

49 So Jesus stood still and commanded him to be called.

10:19 [a]Exodus 20:12–16; Deuteronomy 5:16–20   10:24 [a]NU-Text omits *for those who trust in riches.*
10:29 [a]NU-Text omits *or wife.*

Then they called the blind man, saying to him, "Be of good cheer. Rise, He is calling you."

50 And throwing aside his garment, he rose and came to Jesus.

51 So Jesus answered and said to him, "What do you want Me to do for you?"

The blind man said to Him, "Rabboni, that I may receive my sight."

52 Then Jesus said to him, "Go your way; your faith has made you well." And immediately he received his sight and followed Jesus on the road.

11 Now when they drew near Jerusalem, to Bethphage[a] and Bethany, at the Mount of Olives, He sent two of His disciples; 2 and He said to them, "Go into the village opposite you; and as soon as you have entered it you will find a colt tied, on which no one has sat. Loose it and bring it. 3 And if anyone says to you, 'Why are you doing this?' say, 'The Lord has need of it,' and immediately he will send it here."

4 So they went their way, and found the[a] colt tied by the door outside on the street, and they loosed it. 5 But some of those who stood there said to them, "What are you doing, loosing the colt?"

6 And they spoke to them just as Jesus had commanded. So they let them go. 7 Then they brought the colt to Jesus and threw their clothes on it, and He sat on it. 8 And many spread their clothes on the road, and others cut down leafy branches from the trees and spread them on the road. 9 Then those who went before and those who followed cried out, saying:

"Hosanna!
'Blessed is He who comes in the
name of the LORD!'[a]
10 Blessed is the kingdom of our
father David
That comes in the name of the
Lord![a]
Hosanna in the highest!"

11 And Jesus went into Jerusalem and into the temple. So when He had looked around at all things, as the hour was already late, He went out to Bethany with the twelve.

12 Now the next day, when they had come out from Bethany, He was hungry. 13 And seeing from afar a fig tree having leaves, He went to see if perhaps He would find something on it. When He came to it, He found nothing but leaves, for it was not the season for figs. 14 In response Jesus said to it, "Let no one eat fruit from you ever again."

And His disciples heard it.

15 So they came to Jerusalem. Then Jesus went into the temple and began to drive out those who bought and sold in the temple, and overturned the tables of the money changers and the seats of those who sold doves. 16 And He would not allow anyone to carry wares through the temple. 17 Then He taught, saying to them, "Is it not written, 'My house shall be called a house of prayer for all nations'?[a] But you have made it a 'den of thieves.'"[b]

18 And the scribes and chief priests heard it and sought how they might destroy Him; for they feared Him, because all the people were astonished at His teaching. 19 When evening had come, He went out of the city.

20 Now in the morning, as they passed by, they saw the fig tree dried up from the roots. 21 And Peter, remembering, said to Him, "Rabbi, look! The fig tree which You cursed has withered away."

22 So Jesus answered and said to them, "Have faith in God. 23 For assuredly, I say to you, whoever says to this mountain, 'Be removed and be cast into the sea,' and does not doubt in his heart, but believes that those things he says will be done, he will have whatever he says. 24 Therefore I say to you, whatever things you ask when you pray, believe that you receive them, and you will have them.

25 "And whenever you stand praying, if you have anything against anyone, forgive him, that your Father in heaven may also forgive you your trespasses. 26 But if you do not forgive, neither will your Father in heaven forgive your trespasses."[a]

27 Then they came again to Jerusa-

11:1 [a]M-Text reads Bethsphage.   11:4 [a]NU-Text and M-Text read a.   11:9 [a]Psalm 118:26
11:10 [a]NU-Text omits in the name of the Lord.   11:17 [a]Isaiah 56:7   [b]Jeremiah 7:11   11:26 [a]NU-Text omits this verse.

lem. And as He was walking in the temple, the chief priests, the scribes, and the elders came to Him. 28 And they said to Him, "By what authority are You doing these things? And who gave You this authority to do these things?"

29 But Jesus answered and said to them, "I also will ask you one question; then answer Me, and I will tell you by what authority I do these things: 30 The baptism of John—was it from heaven or from men? Answer Me."

31 And they reasoned among themselves, saying, "If we say, 'From heaven,' He will say, 'Why then did you not believe him?' 32 But if we say, 'From men' "—they feared the people, for all counted John to have been a prophet indeed. 33 So they answered and said to Jesus, "We do not know."

And Jesus answered and said to them, "Neither will I tell you by what authority I do these things."

12 Then He began to speak to them in parables: "A man planted a vineyard and set a hedge around it, dug a place for the wine vat and built a tower. And he leased it to vinedressers and went into a far country. 2 Now at vintage-time he sent a servant to the vinedressers, that he might receive some of the fruit of the vineyard from the vinedressers. 3 And they took him and beat him and sent him away empty-handed. 4 Again he sent them another servant, and at him they threw stones,a wounded him in the head, and sent him away shamefully treated. 5 And again he sent another, and him they killed; and many others, beating some and killing some. 6 Therefore still having one son, his beloved, he also sent him to them last, saying, 'They will respect my son.' 7 But those vinedressers said among themselves, 'This is the heir. Come, let us kill him, and the inheritance will be ours.' 8 So they took him and killed him and cast him out of the vineyard.

9 "Therefore what will the owner of the vineyard do? He will come and destroy the vinedressers, and give the vineyard to others. 10 Have you not even read this Scripture:

'The stone which the builders
    rejected
Has become the chief
    cornerstone.
11 This was the LORD's
    doing,
And it is marvelous in our
    eyes'? "a

12 And they sought to lay hands on Him, but feared the multitude, for they knew He had spoken the parable against them. So they left Him and went away.

13 Then they sent to Him some of the Pharisees and the Herodians, to catch Him in His words. 14 When they had come, they said to Him, "Teacher, we know that You are true, and care about no one; for You do not regard the person of men, but teach the way of God in truth. Is it lawful to pay taxes to Caesar, or not? 15 Shall we pay, or shall we not pay?"

But He, knowing their hypocrisy, said to them, "Why do you test Me? Bring Me a denarius that I may see it." 16 So they brought it.

And He said to them, "Whose image and inscription is this?" They said to Him, "Caesar's."

17 And Jesus answered and said to them, "Render to Caesar the things that are Caesar's, and to God the things that are God's."

And they marveled at Him.

18 Then some Sadducees, who say there is no resurrection, came to Him; and they asked Him, saying: 19 "Teacher, Moses wrote to us that if a man's brother dies, and leaves his wife behind, and leaves no children, his brother should take his wife and raise up offspring for his brother. 20 Now there were seven brothers. The first took a wife; and dying, he left no offspring. 21 And the second took her, and he died; nor did he leave any offspring. And the third likewise. 22 So the seven had her and left no offspring. Last of all the woman died also. 23 Therefore, in the resurrection, when they rise, whose wife will she be? For all seven had her as wife."

24 Jesus answered and said to them, "Are you not therefore mistaken, because you do not know the Scriptures nor the power of God?

12:4 aNU-Text omits and at him they threw stones.   12:11 aPsalm 118:22, 23

The Widow's Mite

The temple area was crowded and noisy as usual. Richly robed merchants deposited large amounts of money in the temple treasury box on the grand staircase. One woman, clothed in black, dropped two mites for her offering, pausing for a quiet prayer.

Jesus observed the scene, and said to the crowd, "This poor widow has put in more than all those who have given to the treasury; for they all put in out of their abundance, but she out of her poverty put in all she had, her whole livelihood" (Mark 12:43, 44).

The Bible labels the woman a widow. In ancient times, widows had little or no means of income. They were dependent on the gifts of relatives or friends. In this case, Jesus reveals that she gave all she had to live on.

The widow gave two "mites"—the smallest denomination in circulation. A Greek copper coin, the mite is worth a mere fraction of a penny. Two mites would not even equal one cent. Yet Jesus commended this woman for the large amount she gave.

The story of the widow's mites is a beautiful illustration of right-spirited giving. While other merchants gave large amounts of their wealth, their offering was for recognition and the praise of onlookers. The widow, however, displayed a heart of gratitude to God, despite the loss of her husband and lack of financial security. She could still trust God for her basic needs, thereby enabling her to give out of her need.

We can learn much from the poor widow who gave all she had to live on. Let us, with equal gratitude, give to God the talents, time, energy, and financial resources we have to live on. And then with trust and confidence watch as God uses and works through our offerings. For we have the promise of Jesus: "Give, and it will be given to you: good measure, pressed down, shaken together, and running over" (Luke 6:38).

25 For when they rise from the dead, they neither marry nor are given in marriage, but are like angels in heaven. 26 But concerning the dead, that they rise, have you not read in the book of Moses, in the *burning bush passage*, how God spoke to him, saying, *'I am the God of Abraham, the God of Isaac, and the God of Jacob'*?*a* 27 He is not the God of the dead, but the God of the living. You are therefore greatly mistaken."

28 Then one of the scribes came, and having heard them reasoning together, perceiving*a* that He had answered them well, asked Him, "Which is the first commandment of all?"

29 Jesus answered him, "The first of all the commandments *is: 'Hear, O Israel, the* LORD *our God, the* LORD *is one.* 30 *And you shall love the* LORD *your God with all your heart, with all your soul, with all your mind, and with all your strength.'a* This *is* the first commandment.*b* 31 And the second, like *it, is* this: *'You shall love your neighbor as yourself.'a* There is no other commandment greater than these."

32 So the scribe said to Him, "Well *said,* Teacher. You have spoken the truth, for there is one God, and there is no other but He. 33 And to love Him with all the heart, with all the understanding, with all the soul,*a* and with all the strength, and to love one's neighbor as oneself, is more than all the whole burnt offerings and sacrifices."

34 Now when Jesus saw that he answered wisely, He said to him, "You are not far from the kingdom of God."

But after that no one dared question Him.

35 Then Jesus answered and said, while He taught in the temple, "How *is it* that the scribes say that the Christ is the Son of David? 36 For David himself said by the Holy Spirit:

> *'The* LORD *said to my Lord,*
> *"Sit at My right hand,*
>   *Till I make Your enemies Your*
>   *footstool."'a*

37 Therefore David himself calls Him *'Lord'*; how is He *then* his Son?"

And the common people heard Him gladly.

38 Then He said to them in His teaching, "Beware of the scribes, who desire to go around in long robes, *love* greetings in the marketplaces, 39 the best seats in the synagogues, and the best places at feasts, 40 who devour widows' houses, and for a pretense make long prayers. These will receive greater condemnation."

41 Now Jesus sat opposite the treasury and saw how the people put money into the treasury. And many *who were* rich put in much. 42 Then one poor widow came and threw in two mites,*a* which make a quadrans. 43 So He called His disciples to *Himself* and said to them, "Assuredly, I say to you that this poor widow has put in more than all those who have given to the treasury; 44 for they all put in out of their abundance, but she out of her poverty put in all that she had, her whole livelihood."

13 Then as He went out of the temple, one of His disciples said to Him, "Teacher, see what manner of stones and what buildings *are here!*"

2 And Jesus answered and said to him, "Do you see these great buildings? Not *one* stone shall be left upon another, that shall not be thrown down."

3 Now as He sat on the Mount of Olives opposite the temple, Peter, James, John, and Andrew asked Him privately, 4 "Tell us, when will these things be? And what *will be* the sign when all these things will be fulfilled?"

5 And Jesus, answering them, began to say: "Take heed that no one deceives you. 6 For many will come in My name, saying, 'I am *He*,' and will deceive many. 7 But when you hear of wars and rumors of wars, do not be troubled; for *such things* must happen, but the end *is* not yet. 8 For nation will rise against nation, and kingdom against kingdom. And there will be earthquakes in various places, and there will be famines and

---

12:26 *a*Exodus 3:6, 15   12:28 *a*NU-Text reads *seeing.*   12:30 *a*Deuteronomy 6:4, 5   *b*NU-Text omits this sentence.   12:31 *a*Leviticus 19:18   12:33 *a*NU-Text omits *with all the soul.*   12:36 *a*Psalm 110:1   12:42 *a*Greek *lepta*, very small copper coins worth a fraction of a penny troubles.*a* These *are* the beginnings of sorrows.

9 "But watch out for yourselves, for they will deliver you up to councils, and you will be beaten in the synagogues. You will be brought*a* before rulers and kings for My sake, for a testimony to them. 10 And the gospel must first be preached to all the nations. 11 But when they arrest *you* and deliver you up, do not worry beforehand, or premeditate*a* what you will speak. But whatever is given you in that hour, speak that; for it is not you who speak, but the Holy Spirit. 12 Now brother will betray brother to death, and a father *his* child; and children will rise up against parents and cause them to be put to death. 13 And you will be hated by all for My name's sake. But he who endures to the end shall be saved.

14 "So when you see the *'abomination of desolation,'a* spoken of by Daniel the prophet,*b* standing where it ought not" (let the reader understand), "then let those who are in Judea flee to the mountains. 15 Let him who is on the housetop not go down into the house, nor enter to take anything out of his house. 16 And let him who is in the field not go back to get his clothes. 17 But woe to those who are pregnant and to those who are nursing babies in those days! 18 And pray that your flight may not be in winter. 19 For *in* those days there will be tribulation, such as has not been since the beginning of the creation which God created until this time, nor ever shall be. 20 And unless the Lord had shortened those days, no flesh would be saved; but for the elect's sake, whom He chose, He shortened the days.

21 "Then if anyone says to you, 'Look, here *is* the Christ!' or, 'Look, *He is* there!' do not believe it. 22 For false christs and false prophets will rise and show signs and wonders to deceive, if possible, even the elect. 23 But take heed; see, I have told you all things beforehand.

24 "But in those days, after that tribulation, the sun will be darkened, and the moon will not give its light; 25 the stars of heaven will fall, and the powers in the heavens will be shaken. 26 Then they will see the Son of Man coming in the clouds with great power and glory. 27 And then He will send His angels, and gather together His elect from the four winds, from the farthest part of earth to the farthest part of heaven.

28 "Now learn this parable from the fig tree: When its branch has already become tender, and puts forth leaves, you know that summer is near. 29 So you also, when you see these things happening, know that it*a* is near—at the doors! 30 Assuredly, I say to you, this generation will by no means pass away till all these things take place. 31 Heaven and earth will pass away, but My words will by no means pass away.

32 "But of that day and hour no one knows, not even the angels in heaven, nor the Son, but only the Father. 33 Take heed, watch and pray; for you do not know when the time is. 34 *It is* like a man going to a far country, who left his house and gave authority to his servants, and to each his work, and commanded the doorkeeper to watch. 35 Watch therefore, for you do not know when the master of the house is coming—in the evening, at midnight, at the crowing of the rooster, or in the morning— 36 lest, coming suddenly, he find you sleeping. 37 And what I say to you, I say to all: Watch!"

14 After two days it was the Passover and *the Feast* of Unleavened Bread. And the chief priests and the scribes sought how they might take Him by trickery and put *Him* to death. 2 But they said, "Not during the feast, lest there be an uproar of the people."

3 And being in Bethany at the house of Simon the leper, as He sat at the table, a woman came having an alabaster flask of very costly oil of spikenard. Then she broke the flask and poured *it* on His head. 4 But there were some who were indignant among themselves, and said, "Why was this fragrant oil wasted? 5 For it might have been sold for

---

13:8 *a*NU-Text omits *and troubles.*   13:9 *a*NU-Text and M-Text read *will stand.*   13:11 *a*NU-Text omits *or premeditate.*   13:14 *a*Daniel 11:31; 12:11   *b*NU-Text omits *spoken of by Daniel the prophet.*   13:29 *a*Or *He*

A Man with a Pitcher

Be prepared to do the uncommon when God calls you. One such individual in the New Testament was simply referred to as "a man . . . carrying a pitcher."

During the final week before our Lord's crucifixion, Jesus called Peter and John and asked them to go into the city of Jerusalem to prepare the Passover meal. There they would see a man carrying a pitcher. They were to follow him as he led the disciples to the room where Jesus would eat the Last Supper with His disciples (Mark 14:13).

We know nothing more about the man whom God instructed to carry the pitcher of water. But from the culture and time we do know that he was called to do something out of the ordinary. In the society of the New Testament, it was most common to see a woman, not a man, carrying a jar or a pitcher of water. Yet his call from God was clear, and he carried out his task. By doing so, he earned a place in history by leading the disciples to the room where they would share their last meal together during Jesus' earthly ministry.

At this meal, Jesus instituted the Lord's Supper of the New Covenant, which to this day serves as a holy communion of new life and forgiveness to people everywhere.

By faithfully following God's call, the man with the pitcher served God and Jesus Christ in a unique way. He was the "man behind the scenes" in one of the greatest events of the world.

When God calls you with certainty to perform a task that is uncommon or unusual, do it with total commitment. For you never know when you will be serving God's children in a special way.

more than three hundred denarii and given to the poor." And they criticized her sharply.

6 But Jesus said, "Let her alone. Why do you trouble her? She has done a good work for Me. 7 For you have the poor with you always, and whenever you wish you may do them good; but Me you do not have always. 8 She has done what she could. She has come beforehand to anoint My body for burial. 9 Assuredly, I say to you, wherever this gospel is preached in the whole world, what this woman has done will also be told as a memorial to her."

10 Then Judas Iscariot, one of the twelve, went to the chief priests to betray Him to them. 11 And when they heard it, they were glad, and promised to give him money. So he sought how he might conveniently betray Him.

12 Now on the first day of Unleavened Bread, when they killed the Passover lamb, His disciples said to Him, "Where do You want us to go and prepare, that You may eat the Passover?"

13 And He sent out two of His disciples and said to them, "Go into the city, and a man will meet you carrying a pitcher of water; follow him. 14 Wherever he goes in, say to the master of the house, 'The Teacher says, "Where is the guest room in which I may eat the Passover with My disciples?" ' 15 Then he will show you a large upper room, furnished and prepared; there make ready for us."

16 So His disciples went out, and came into the city, and found it just as He had said to them; and they prepared the Passover.

17 In the evening He came with the twelve. 18 Now as they sat and ate, Jesus said, "Assuredly, I say to you, one of you who eats with Me will betray Me."

19 And they began to be sorrowful, and to say to Him one by one, "Is it I?" And another said, "Is it I?"*a*

20 He answered and said to them, "It is one of the twelve, who dips with Me in the dish. 21 The Son of Man indeed goes just as it is written of Him, but woe to that man by whom the Son of Man is betrayed! It would

have been good for that man if he had never been born."

22 And as they were eating, Jesus took bread, blessed and broke it, and gave it to them and said, "Take, eat;*a* this is My body."

23 Then He took the cup, and when He had given thanks He gave it to them, and they all drank from it. 24 And He said to them, "This is My blood of the new*a* covenant, which is shed for many. 25 Assuredly, I say to you, I will no longer drink of the fruit of the vine until that day when I drink it new in the kingdom of God."

26 And when they had sung a hymn, they went out to the Mount of Olives.

27 Then Jesus said to them, "All of you will be made to stumble because of Me this night,*a* for it is written:

> 'I will strike the Shepherd,
> And the sheep will be
> scattered.'*b*

28 "But after I have been raised, I will go before you to Galilee."

29 Peter said to Him, "Even if all are made to stumble, yet I will not be."

30 Jesus said to him, "Assuredly, I say to you that today, even this night, before the rooster crows twice, you will deny Me three times."

31 But he spoke more vehemently, "If I have to die with You, I will not deny You!"

And they all said likewise.

32 Then they came to a place which was named Gethsemane; and He said to His disciples, "Sit here while I pray." 33 And He took Peter, James, and John with Him, and He began to be troubled and deeply distressed. 34 Then He said to them, "My soul is exceedingly sorrowful, even to death. Stay here and watch."

35 He went a little farther, and fell on the ground, and prayed that if it were possible, the hour might pass from Him. 36 And He said, "Abba, Father, all things are possible for You. Take this cup away from Me; nevertheless, not what I will, but what You will."

37 Then He came and found them

14:19 *a*NU-Text omits this sentence.   14:22 *a*NU-Text omits eat.   14:24 *a*NU-Text omits new.
14:27 *a*NU-Text omits because of Me this night.   *b*Zechariah 13:7

sleeping, and said to Peter, "Simon, are you sleeping? Could you not watch one hour? 38 Watch and pray, lest you enter into temptation. The spirit indeed *is* willing, but the flesh *is* weak."

39 Again He went away and prayed, and spoke the same words. 40 And when He returned, He found them asleep again, for their eyes were heavy; and they did not know what to answer Him.

41 Then He came the third time and said to them, "Are you still sleeping and resting? It is enough! The hour has come; behold, the Son of Man is being betrayed into the hands of sinners. 42 Rise, let us be going. See, My betrayer is at hand."

43 And immediately, while He was still speaking, Judas, one of the twelve, with a great multitude with swords and clubs, came from the chief priests and the scribes and the elders. 44 Now His betrayer had given them a signal, saying, "Whomever I kiss, He is the One; seize Him and lead *Him* away safely."

45 As soon as He had come, immediately he went up to Him and said to Him, "Rabbi, Rabbi!" and kissed Him.

46 Then they laid their hands on Him and took Him. 47 And one of those who stood by drew his sword and struck the servant of the high priest, and cut off his ear.

48 Then Jesus answered and said to them, "Have you come out, as against a robber, with swords and clubs to take Me? 49 I was daily with you in the temple teaching, and you did not seize Me. But the Scriptures must be fulfilled."

50 Then they all forsook Him and fled.

51 Now a certain young man followed Him, having a linen cloth thrown around *his* naked *body.* And the young men laid hold of him, 52 and he left the linen cloth and fled from them naked.

53 And they led Jesus away to the high priest; and with him were assembled all the chief priests, the elders, and the scribes. 54 But Peter followed Him at a distance, right into the courtyard of the high priest. And he sat with the servants and warmed himself at the fire.

55 Now the chief priests and all the council sought testimony against Jesus to put Him to death, but found none. 56 For many bore false witness against Him, but their testimonies did not agree.

57 Then some rose up and bore false witness against Him, saying, 58 "We heard Him say, 'I will destroy this temple made with hands, and within three days I will build another made without hands.'" 59 But not even then did their testimony agree.

60 And the high priest stood up in the midst and asked Jesus, saying, "Do You answer nothing? What *is it* these men testify against You?" 61 But He kept silent and answered nothing.

Again the high priest asked Him, saying to Him, "Are You the Christ, the Son of the Blessed?"

62 Jesus said, "I am. And you will see the Son of Man sitting at the right hand of the Power, and coming with the clouds of heaven."

63 Then the high priest tore his clothes and said, "What further need do we have of witnesses? 64 You have heard the blasphemy! What do you think?"

And they all condemned Him to be deserving of death.

65 Then some began to spit on Him, and to blindfold Him, and to beat Him, and to say to Him, "Prophesy!" And the officers struck Him with the palms of their hands.*a*

66 Now as Peter was below in the courtyard, one of the servant girls of the high priest came. 67 And when she saw Peter warming himself, she looked at him and said, "You also were with Jesus of Nazareth."

68 But he denied it, saying, "I neither know nor understand what you are saying." And he went out on the porch, and a rooster crowed.

69 And the servant girl saw him again, and began to say to those who stood by, "This is one of them." 70 But he denied it again.

And a little later those who stood by said to Peter again, "Surely you are *one* of them; for you are a Galilean, and your speech shows *it.*"*a*

71 Then he began to curse and swear, "I do not know this Man of whom you speak!"

14:65 *a*NU-Text reads *received Him with slaps.*   14:70 *a*NU-Text omits *and your speech shows it.*

72 A second time *the* rooster crowed. Then Peter called to mind the word that Jesus had said to him, "Before the rooster crows twice, you will deny Me three times." And when he thought about it, he wept.

15 Immediately, in the morning, the chief priests held a consultation with the elders and scribes and the whole council; and they bound Jesus, led *Him* away, and delivered *Him* to Pilate. 2 Then Pilate asked Him, "Are You the King of the Jews?"

He answered and said to him, "*It is as* you say."

3 And the chief priests accused Him of many things, but He answered nothing. 4 Then Pilate asked Him again, saying, "Do You answer nothing? See how many things they testify against You!"*a* 5 But Jesus still answered nothing, so that Pilate marveled.

6 Now at the feast he was accustomed to releasing one prisoner to them, whomever they requested. 7 And there was one named Barabbas, *who was* chained with his fellow rebels; they had committed murder in the rebellion. 8 Then the multitude, crying aloud,*a* began to ask *him to do* just as he had always done for them. 9 But Pilate answered them, saying, "Do you want me to release to you the King of the Jews?" 10 For he knew that the chief priests had handed Him over because of envy.

11 But the chief priests stirred up the crowd, so that he should rather release Barabbas to them. 12 Pilate answered and said to them again, "What then do you want me to do with *Him* whom you call the King of the Jews?"

13 So they cried out again, "Crucify Him!"

14 Then Pilate said to them, "Why, what evil has He done?"

But they cried out all the more, "Crucify Him!"

15 So Pilate, wanting to gratify the crowd, released Barabbas to them; and he delivered Jesus, after he had scourged *Him,* to be crucified.

16 Then the soldiers led Him away into the hall called Praetorium, and they called together the whole garrison. 17 And they clothed Him with purple; and they twisted a crown of thorns, put it on His *head,* 18 and began to salute Him, "Hail, King of the Jews!" 19 Then they struck Him on the head with a reed and spat on Him; and bowing the knee, they worshiped Him. 20 And when they had mocked Him, they took the purple off Him, put His own clothes on Him, and led Him out to crucify Him.

21 Then they compelled a certain man, Simon a Cyrenian, the father of Alexander and Rufus, as he was coming out of the country and passing by, to bear His cross. 22 And they brought Him to the place Golgotha, which is translated, Place of a Skull. 23 Then they gave Him wine mingled with myrrh to drink, but He did not take *it.* 24 And when they crucified Him, they divided His garments, casting lots for them to determine what every man should take.

25 Now it was the third hour, and they crucified Him. 26 And the inscription of His accusation was written above:

THE KING OF THE JEWS.

27 With Him they also crucified two robbers, one on His right and the other on His left. 28 So the Scripture was fulfilled*a* which says, *"And He was numbered with the transgressors."b*

29 And those who passed by blasphemed Him, wagging their heads and saying, "Aha! *You* who destroy the temple and build *it* in three days, 30 save Yourself, and come down from the cross!"

31 Likewise the chief priests also, mocking among themselves with the scribes, said, "He saved others; Himself He cannot save. 32 Let the Christ, the King of Israel, descend now from the cross, that we may see and believe."*a*

Even those who were crucified with Him reviled Him.

33 Now when the sixth hour had come, there was darkness over the whole land until the ninth hour. 34 And at the ninth hour Jesus cried out with a loud voice, saying, "Eloi,

Eloi, lama sabachthani?" which is translated, *"My God, My God, why have You forsaken Me?"ᵃ*

35 Some of those who stood by, when they heard *that*, said, "Look, He is calling for Elijah!" 36 Then someone ran and filled a sponge full of sour wine, put *it* on a reed, and offered *it* to Him to drink, saying, "Let Him alone; let us see if Elijah will come to take Him down."

37 And Jesus cried out with a loud voice, and breathed His last.

38 Then the veil of the temple was torn in two from top to bottom. 39 So when the centurion, who stood opposite Him, saw that He cried out like this and breathed His last,ᵃ he said, "Truly this Man was the Son of God!"

40 There were also women looking on from afar, among whom were Mary Magdalene, Mary the mother of James the Less and of Joses, and Salome, 41 who also followed Him and ministered to Him when He was in Galilee, and many other women who came up with Him to Jerusalem.

42 Now when evening had come, because it was the Preparation Day, that is, the day before the Sabbath, 43 Joseph of Arimathea, a prominent council member, who was himself waiting for the kingdom of God, coming and taking courage, went in to Pilate and asked for the body of Jesus. 44 Pilate marveled that He was already dead; and summoning the centurion, he asked him if He had been dead for some time. 45 So when he found out from the centurion, he granted the body to Joseph. 46 Then he bought fine linen, took Him down, and wrapped Him in the linen. And he laid Him in a tomb which had been hewn out of the rock, and rolled a stone against the door of the tomb. 47 And Mary Magdalene and Mary *the mother* of Joses observed where He was laid.

16 Now when the Sabbath was past, Mary Magdalene, Mary *the mother* of James, and Salome bought spices, that they might come and anoint Him. 2 Very early in the morning, on the first *day* of the week, they came to the tomb when the sun had risen. 3 And they said among themselves, "Who will roll away the stone from the door of the tomb for us?" 4 But when they looked up, they saw that the stone had been rolled away—for it was very large. 5 And entering the tomb, they saw a young man clothed in a long white robe sitting on the right side; and they were alarmed.

6 But he said to them, "Do not be alarmed. You seek Jesus of Nazareth, who was crucified. He is risen! He is not here. See the place where they laid Him. 7 But go, tell His disciples—and Peter—that He is going before you into Galilee; there you will see Him, as He said to you."

8 So they went out quicklyᵃ and fled from the tomb, for they trembled and were amazed. And they said nothing to anyone, for they were afraid.

9 Now when *He* rose early on the first *day* of the week, He appeared first to Mary Magdalene, out of whom He had cast seven demons. 10 She went and told those who had been with Him, as they mourned and wept. 11 And when they heard that He was alive and had been seen by her, they did not believe.

12 After that, He appeared in another form to two of them as they walked and went into the country. 13 And they went and told *it* to the rest, *but* they did not believe them either.

14 Later He appeared to the eleven as they sat at the table; and He rebuked their unbelief and hardness of heart, because they did not believe those who had seen Him after He had risen. 15 And He said to them, "Go into all the world and preach the gospel to every creature. 16 He who believes and is baptized will be saved; but he who does not believe will be condemned. 17 And these signs will follow those who believe: In My name they will cast out demons; they will speak with new tongues; 18 theyᵃ will take up serpents; and if they drink anything deadly, it will by no means hurt them; they will lay hands on the sick, and they will recover."

15:34 ᵃPsalm 22:1　　15:39 ᵃNU-Text reads *that He thus breathed His last.*　　16:8 ᵃNU-Text and M-Text omit *quickly.*　　16:18 ᵃNU-Text reads *and in their hands they will.*

19 So then, after the Lord had spoken to them, He was received up into heaven, and sat down at the right hand of God. 20 And they went out and preached everywhere, the Lord working with *them* and confirming the word through the accompanying signs. Amen.*a*

16:20 *a*Verses 9–20 are bracketed in NU-Text as not original. They are lacking in Codex Sinaiticus and Codex Vaticanus, although nearly all other manuscripts of Mark contain them.

Luke

Overview of Luke

The Gospel of Luke presents a detailed, historical account of the life of Jesus Christ. With great accuracy and clarity, Luke portrays the Son of God as a compassionate, unprejudiced, accepting, and forgiving person. Written about A.D. 60, Luke is the third of the synoptic Gospels, and from his writing, we gain a better understanding of the chronological events in the life of Christ.

Luke presents the Jesus who broke down religious, cultural, social, and economic barriers—a Jesus who constantly laid down His life as the Son of God to reach out to sinful man. Jesus challenged the status quo by befriending outcasts and associating with people of poor reputations.

Jesus confounded traditional messianic expectations of a king. Luke's account of the Savior's birth in a manger presents a vivid picture of the seemingly unsuitable birthplace of our Lord. His ministry and life did not meet all the expectations the people had for a Messiah who would be a political deliverer. Yet, Luke points out the kingship and humanity of the Awaited One who would deliver salvation to all who believed.

But if you love those who love you, what credit is that to you? For even sinners love those who love them. . . . But love your enemies, do good, and lend, hoping for nothing in return; and your reward will be great, and you will be sons of the Most High. For He is kind to the unthankful and evil."

(Luke 6:32, 35)

Through His death and resurrection, Jesus faced and conquered His greatest enemy. His victory over death far exceeded the beliefs of even His most faithful followers. As Luke discloses, Jesus constantly preached, taught, and lived the unexpected. Jesus Christ truly was and is today the greatest possibility thinker that ever lived!

Jesus in Luke

The humanity and compassion of Jesus are repeatedly stressed in Luke's Gospel. The most complete account of Christ's ancestry, birth, and development are given by the detail-oriented physician Luke. Jesus is the Son of Man, ideal in His identification with sorrow and the plight of sinful man. Jesus alone fulfills the Greek ideal of human perfection, as He carries men's sorrows and offers the gift of salvation with His blood.

Keys to Luke

Key Word: Jesus the Son of Man. Luke's prologue clearly states the theme of this Gospel: "to write to you an orderly account . . . that you may know the certainty of those things in which you were instructed" (1:3, 4). Luke's account creates an accurate chronology of Jesus as He ministered to Gentiles and nonbelievers. The divinity and humanity of Jesus are clearly shown by Luke's recording of Christ's feelings and humanity more than any other Gospel record.

Key Verses: "It seemed good to me also, having had perfect understanding of all things from the very first, to write to you an orderly account, most excellent Theophilus, that you may know the certainty of those things in which you were instructed" (1:3, 4).

"For the Son of Man has come to seek and to save that which was lost" (19:10).

Key Chapter: Luke 15. Captured in three parables of the Lost Sheep, Lost Coin, and Lost Son is the crux of this Gospel: that God through Christ has come to seek and to save that which was lost.

1 Inasmuch as many have taken in hand to set in order a narrative of those things which have been fulfilled[a] among us, 2 just as those who from the beginning were eyewitnesses and ministers of the word delivered them to us, 3 it seemed good to me also, having had perfect understanding of all things from the very first, to write to you an orderly account, most excellent Theophilus, 4 that you may know the certainty of those things in which you were instructed.

5 There was in the days of Herod, the king of Judea, a certain priest named Zacharias, of the division of Abijah. His wife *was* of the daughters of Aaron, and her name *was* Elizabeth. 6 And they were both righteous before God, walking in all the commandments and ordinances of the Lord blameless. 7 But they had no child, because Elizabeth was barren, and they were both well advanced in years.

8 So it was, that while he was serving as priest before God in the order of his division, 9 according to the custom of the priesthood, his lot fell to burn incense when he went into the temple of the Lord. 10 And the whole multitude of the people was praying outside at the hour of incense. 11 Then an angel of the Lord appeared to him, standing on the right side of the altar of incense. 12 And when Zacharias saw *him,* he was troubled, and fear fell upon him.

13 But the angel said to him, "Do not be afraid, Zacharias, for your prayer is heard; and your wife Elizabeth will bear you a son, and you shall call his name John. 14 And you will have joy and gladness, and many will rejoice at his birth. 15 For he will be great in the sight of the Lord, and shall drink neither wine nor strong drink. He will also be filled with the Holy Spirit, even from his mother's womb. 16 And he will turn many of the children of Israel to the Lord their God. 17 He will also go before Him in the spirit and power of Elijah, '*to turn the hearts of the fathers to the children,*'[a] and the disobedient to the wisdom of the just, to make ready a people prepared for the Lord."

18 And Zacharias said to the angel, "How shall I know this? For I am an old man, and my wife is well advanced in years."

19 And the angel answered and said to him, "I am Gabriel, who stands in the presence of God, and was sent to speak to you and bring you these glad tidings. 20 But behold, you will be mute and not able to speak until the day these things take place, because you did not believe my words which will be fulfilled in their own time."

21 And the people waited for Zacharias, and marveled that he lingered so long in the temple. 22 But when he came out, he could not speak to them; and they perceived that he had seen a vision in the temple, for he beckoned to them and remained speechless.

23 So it was, as soon as the days of his service were completed, that

1:1 *aOr are most surely believed* 1:17 aMalachi 4:5, 6

he departed to his own house.
24 Now after those days his wife Elizabeth conceived; and she hid herself five months, saying, 25 "Thus the Lord has dealt with me, in the days when He looked on *me*, to take away my reproach among people."

26 Now in the sixth month the angel Gabriel was sent by God to a city of Galilee named Nazareth, 27 to a virgin betrothed to a man whose name was Joseph, of the house of David. The virgin's name *was* Mary. 28 And having come in, the angel said to her, "Rejoice, highly favored *one*, the Lord *is* with you; blessed *are* you among women!"*a*

29 But when she saw *him*,*a* she was troubled at his saying, and considered what manner of greeting this was. 30 Then the angel said to her, "Do not be afraid, Mary, for you have found favor with God. 31 And behold, you will conceive in your womb and bring forth a Son, and shall call His name Jesus. 32 He will be great, and will be called the Son of the Highest; and the Lord God will give Him the throne of His father David. 33 And He will reign over the house of Jacob forever, and of His kingdom there will be no end."

34 Then Mary said to the angel, "How can this be, since I do not know a man?"

35 And the angel answered and said to her, "*The* Holy Spirit will come upon you, and the power of the Highest will overshadow you; therefore, also, that Holy One who is to be born will be called the Son of God. 36 Now indeed, Elizabeth your relative has also conceived a son in her old age; and this is now the sixth month for her who was called barren. 37 For with God nothing will be impossible."

38 Then Mary said, "Behold the maidservant of the Lord! Let it be to me according to your word." And the angel departed from her.

39 Now Mary arose in those days and went into the hill country with haste, to a city of Judah, 40 and entered the house of Zacharias and greeted Elizabeth. 41 And it happened, when Elizabeth heard the greeting of Mary, that the babe leaped in her womb; and Elizabeth was filled with the Holy Spirit.

42 Then she spoke out with a loud voice and said, "Blessed *are* you among women, and blessed *is* the fruit of your womb! 43 But why *is* this *granted* to me, that the mother of my Lord should come to me? 44 For indeed, as soon as the voice of your greeting sounded in my ears, the babe leaped in my womb for joy. 45 Blessed *is* she who believed, for there will be a fulfillment of those things which were told her from the Lord."

46 And Mary said:

"My soul magnifies the Lord,
47   And my spirit has rejoiced in God my Savior.
48   For He has regarded the lowly state of His maidservant;
      For behold, henceforth all generations will call me blessed.
49   For He who is mighty has done great things for me,
      And holy *is* His name.
50   And His mercy *is* on those who fear Him
      From generation to generation.
51   He has shown strength with His arm;
      He has scattered *the* proud in the imagination of their hearts.
52   He has put down the mighty from *their* thrones,
      And exalted *the* lowly.
53   He has filled *the* hungry with good things,
      And *the* rich He has sent away empty.
54   He has helped His servant Israel,
      In remembrance of *His* mercy,
55   As He spoke to our fathers,
      To Abraham and to his seed forever."

56 And Mary remained with her about three months, and returned to her house.

57 Now Elizabeth's full time came for her to be delivered, and she brought forth a son. 58 When her neighbors and relatives heard how the Lord had shown great mercy to her, they rejoiced with her.

59 So it was, on the eighth day, that they came to circumcise the child; and they would have called him by

---

the name of his father, Zacharias.
60 His mother answered and said,
"No; he shall be called John."

61 But they said to her, "There is
no one among your relatives who is
called by this name." 62 So they made
signs to his father—what he would
have him called.

63 And he asked for a writing tablet, and wrote, saying, "His name
is John." So they all marveled.
64 Immediately his mouth was
opened and his tongue *loosed*, and
he spoke, praising God. 65 Then fear
came on all who dwelt around them;
and all these sayings were discussed
throughout all the hill country of Judea. 66 And all those who heard *them*
kept *them* in their hearts, saying,
"What kind of child will this be?"
And the hand of the Lord was with
him.

67 Now his father Zacharias was
filled with the Holy Spirit, and prophesied, saying:

68 "Blessed *is* the Lord God of
     Israel,
     For He has visited and
       redeemed His people,
69   And has raised up a horn of
       salvation for us
     In the house of His servant
       David,
70   As He spoke by the mouth of
       His holy prophets,
     Who *have been* since the world
       began,
71   That we should be saved from
       our enemies
     And from the hand of all who
       hate us,
72   To perform the mercy *promised*
       to our fathers
     And to remember His holy
       covenant,
73   The oath which He swore to
       our father Abraham:
74   To grant us that we,
     Being delivered from the hand
       of our enemies,
     Might serve Him without fear,
75   In holiness and righteousness
       before Him all the days of our
       life.
76   And you, child, will be called
       the prophet of the Highest;
     For you will go before the face
       of the Lord to prepare His
       ways,

77   To give knowledge of salvation
       to His people
     By the remission of their sins,
78   Through the tender mercy of
       our God,
     With which the Dayspring
       from on high has visited[a] us;
79   To give light to those who sit
       in darkness and the shadow
       of death,
     To guide our feet into the way
       of peace."

80 So the child grew and became
strong in spirit, and was in the deserts till the day of his manifestation
to Israel.

2 And it came to pass in those days
that a decree went out from Caesar Augustus that all the world
should be registered. 2 This census
first took place while Quirinius was
governing Syria. 3 So all went to be
registered, everyone to his own city.

4 Joseph also went up from Galilee,
out of the city of Nazareth, into Judea, to the city of David, which is
called Bethlehem, because he was of
the house and lineage of David,
5 to be registered with Mary, his betrothed wife,[a] who was with child.
6 So it was, that while they were
there, the days were completed for
her to be delivered. 7 And she
brought forth her firstborn Son, and
wrapped Him in swaddling cloths,
and laid Him in a manger, because
there was no room for them in the
inn.

8 Now there were in the same country shepherds living out in the fields,
keeping watch over their flock by
night. 9 And behold,[a] an angel of the
Lord stood before them, and the
glory of the Lord shone around them,
and they were greatly afraid.
10 Then the angel said to them, "Do
not be afraid, for behold, I bring you
good tidings of great joy which will
be to all people. 11 For there is born
to you this day in the city of David
a Savior, who is Christ the Lord.
12 And this *will be* the sign to you:
You will find a Babe wrapped in
swaddling cloths, lying in a manger."
13 And suddenly there was with the
angel a multitude of the heavenly
host praising God and saying:

1:78 [a]NU-Text reads *shall visit*.   2:5 [a]NU-Text omits *wife*.   2:9 [a]NU-Text omits *behold*.

14 "Glory to God in the highest,
  And on earth peace, goodwill
    toward men!"*a*

15 So it was, when the angels had gone away from them into heaven, that the shepherds said to one another, "Let us now go to Bethlehem and see this thing that has come to pass, which the Lord has made known to us." 16 And they came with haste and found Mary and Joseph, and the Babe lying in a manger. 17 Now when they had seen *Him,* they made widely*a* known the saying which was told them concerning this Child. 18 And all those who heard *it* marveled at those things which were told them by the shepherds. 19 But Mary kept all these things and pondered *them* in her heart. 20 Then the shepherds returned, glorifying and praising God for all the things that they had heard and seen, as it was told them.

21 And when eight days were completed for the circumcision of the Child,*a* His name was called JESUS, the name given by the angel before He was conceived in the womb.

22 Now when the days of her purification according to the law of Moses were completed, they brought Him to Jerusalem to present *Him* to the Lord 23 (as it is written in the law of the Lord, *"Every male who opens the womb shall be called holy to the LORD"*),*a* 24 and to offer a sacrifice according to what is said in the law of the Lord, *"A pair of turtledoves or two young pigeons."a*

25 And behold, there was a man in Jerusalem whose name was Simeon, and this man was just and devout, waiting for the Consolation of Israel, and the Holy Spirit was upon him. 26 And it had been revealed to him by the Holy Spirit that he would not see death before he had seen the Lord's Christ. 27 So he came by the Spirit into the temple. And when the parents brought in the Child Jesus, to do for Him according to the custom of the law, 28 he took Him up in his arms and blessed God and said:

29 "Lord, now You are letting Your
    servant depart in peace,
    According to Your word;
30 For my eyes have seen Your
    salvation
31 Which You have prepared
    before the face of all peoples,
32 A light to *bring* revelation to
    the Gentiles,
    And the glory of Your people
    Israel."

33 And Joseph and His mother*a* marveled at those things which were spoken of Him. 34 Then Simeon blessed them, and said to Mary His mother, "Behold, this *Child* is destined for the fall and rising of many in Israel, and for a sign which will be spoken against 35 (yes, a sword will pierce through your own soul also), that the thoughts of many hearts may be revealed."

36 Now there was one, Anna, a prophetess, the daughter of Phanuel, of the tribe of Asher. She was of a great age, and had lived with a husband seven years from her virginity; 37 and this woman *was* a widow of about eighty-four years,*a* who did not depart from the temple, but served God with fastings and prayers night and day. 38 And coming in that instant she gave thanks to the Lord,*a* and spoke of Him to all those who looked for redemption in Jerusalem.

39 So when they had performed all things according to the law of the Lord, they returned to Galilee, to their *own* city, Nazareth. 40 And the Child grew and became strong in spirit,*a* filled with wisdom; and the grace of God was upon Him.

41 His parents went to Jerusalem every year at the Feast of the Passover. 42 And when He was twelve years old, they went up to Jerusalem according to the custom of the feast. 43 When they had finished the days, as they returned, the Boy Jesus lingered behind in Jerusalem. And Joseph and His mother*a* did not know *it;* 44 but supposing Him to have been in the company, they went a day's journey, and sought Him among *their* relatives and acquaintances. 45 So when they did not find Him,

2:14 *a*NU-Text reads *toward men of goodwill.*   2:17 *a*NU-Text omits *widely.*   2:21 *a*NU-Text reads *for His circumcision.*   2:23 *a*Exodus 13:2, 12, 15   2:24 *a*Leviticus 12:8   2:33 *a*NU-Text reads *And His father and mother.*   2:37 *a*NU-Text reads *a widow until she was eighty-four.*   2:38 *a*NU-Text reads *to God.*   2:40 *a*NU-Text omits *in spirit.*   2:43 *a*NU-Text reads *And His parents.*

they returned to Jerusalem, seeking Him. 46 Now so it was *that* after three days they found Him in the temple, sitting in the midst of the teachers, both listening to them and asking them questions. 47 And all who heard Him were astonished at His understanding and answers. 48 So when they saw Him, they were amazed; and His mother said to Him, "Son, why have You done this to us? Look, Your father and I have sought You anxiously."

49 And He said to them, "Why did you seek Me? Did you not know that I must be about My Father's business?" 50 But they did not understand the statement which He spoke to them.

51 Then He went down with them and came to Nazareth, and was subject to them, but His mother kept all these things in her heart. 52 And Jesus increased in wisdom and stature, and in favor with God and men.

3 Now in the fifteenth year of the reign of Tiberius Caesar, Pontius Pilate being governor of Judea, Herod being tetrarch of Galilee, his brother Philip tetrarch of Iturea and the region of Trachonitis, and Lysanias tetrarch of Abilene, 2 while Annas and Caiaphas were high priests,[a] the word of God came to John the son of Zacharias in the wilderness. 3 And he went into all the region around the Jordan, preaching a baptism of repentance for the remission of sins, 4 as it is written in the book of the words of Isaiah the prophet, saying:

> "The voice of one crying in the wilderness:
> 'Prepare the way of the LORD;
> Make His paths straight.
> 5 Every valley shall be filled
> And every mountain and hill brought low;
> The crooked places shall be made straight
> And the rough ways smooth;
> 6 And all flesh shall see the salvation of God.' "[a]

7 Then he said to the multitudes that came out to be baptized by him, "Brood of vipers! Who warned you to flee from the wrath to come? 8 Therefore bear fruits worthy of repentance, and do not begin to say to yourselves, 'We have Abraham as our father.' For I say to you that God is able to raise up children to Abraham from these stones. 9 And even now the ax is laid to the root of the trees. Therefore every tree which does not bear good fruit is cut down and thrown into the fire."

10 So the people asked him, saying, "What shall we do then?"

11 He answered and said to them, "He who has two tunics, let him give to him who has none; and he who has food, let him do likewise."

12 Then tax collectors also came to be baptized, and said to him, "Teacher, what shall we do?"

13 And he said to them, "Collect no more than what is appointed for you."

14 Likewise the soldiers asked him, saying, "And what shall we do?"

So he said to them, "Do not intimidate anyone or accuse falsely, and be content with your wages."

15 Now as the people were in expectation, and all reasoned in their hearts about John, whether he was the Christ or not, 16 John answered, saying to all, "I indeed baptize you with water; but One mightier than I is coming, whose sandal strap I am not worthy to loose. He will baptize you with the Holy Spirit and fire. 17 His winnowing fan is in His hand, and He will thoroughly clean out His threshing floor, and gather the wheat into His barn; but the chaff He will burn with unquenchable fire."

18 And with many other exhortations he preached to the people. 19 But Herod the tetrarch, being rebuked by him concerning Herodias, his brother Philip's wife,[a] and for all the evils which Herod had done, 20 also added this, above all, that he shut John up in prison.

21 When all the people were baptized, it came to pass that Jesus also was baptized; and while He prayed, the heaven was opened. 22 And the Holy Spirit descended in bodily form like a dove upon Him, and a voice came from heaven which said, "You are My beloved Son; in You I am well pleased."

23 Now Jesus Himself began *His ministry at* about thirty years of age, being (as was supposed) *the* son of Joseph, *the son* of Heli, 24 *the son* of Matthat,[a] *the son* of Levi, *the son* of Melchi, *the son* of Janna, *the son* of Joseph, 25 *the son* of Mattathiah, *the son* of Amos, *the son* of Nahum, *the son* of Esli, *the son* of Naggai, 26 *the son* of Maath, *the son* of Mattathiah, *the son* of Semei, *the son* of Joseph, *the son* of Judah, 27 *the son* of Joannas, *the son* of Rhesa, *the son* of Zerubbabel, *the son* of Shealtiel, *the son* of Neri, 28 *the son* of Melchi, *the son* of Addi, *the son* of Cosam, *the son* of Elmodam, *the son* of Er, 29 *the son* of Jose, *the son* of Eliezer, *the son* of Jorim, *the son* of Matthat, *the son* of Levi, 30 *the son* of Simeon, *the son* of Judah, *the son* of Joseph, *the son* of Jonan, *the son* of Eliakim, 31 *the son* of Melea, *the son* of Menan, *the son* of Mattathah, *the son* of Nathan, *the son* of David, 32 *the son* of Jesse, *the son* of Obed, *the son* of Boaz, *the son* of Salmon, *the son* of Nahshon, 33 *the son* of Amminadab, *the son* of Ram, *the son* of Hezron, *the son* of Perez, *the son* of Judah, 34 *the son* of Jacob, *the son* of Isaac, *the son* of Abraham, *the son* of Terah, *the son* of Nahor, 35 *the son* of Serug, *the son* of Reu, *the son* of Peleg, *the son* of Eber, *the son* of Shelah, 36 *the son* of Cainan, *the son* of Arphaxad, *the son* of Shem, *the son* of Noah, *the son* of Lamech, 37 *the son* of Methuselah, *the son* of Enoch, *the son* of Jared, *the son* of Mahalalel, *the son* of Cainan, 38 *the son* of Enosh, *the son* of Seth, *the son* of Adam, *the son* of God.

4 Then Jesus, being filled with the Holy Spirit, returned from the Jordan and was led by the Spirit into[a] the wilderness, 2 being tempted for forty days by the devil. And in those days He ate nothing, and afterward, when they had ended, He was hungry.

3 And the devil said to Him, "If You are the Son of God, command this stone to become bread."

4 But Jesus answered him, saying,[a] "It is written, 'Man shall not live by bread alone, but by every word of God.' "[b]

5 Then the devil, taking Him up on a high mountain, showed Him[a] all the kingdoms of the world in a moment of time. 6 And the devil said to Him, "All this authority I will give You, and their glory; for this has been delivered to me, and I give it to whomever I wish. 7 Therefore, if You will worship before me, all will be Yours."

8 And Jesus answered and said to him, "Get behind Me, Satan![a] For[b] it is written, 'You shall worship the LORD your God, and Him only you shall serve.' "[c]

9 Then he brought Him to Jerusalem, set Him on the pinnacle of the temple, and said to Him, "If You are the Son of God, throw Yourself down from here. 10 For it is written:

'He shall give His angels charge
    over you,
  To keep you,'

11 and,

'In their hands they shall bear
    you up,
  Lest you dash your foot against
    a stone.' "[a]

12 And Jesus answered and said to him, "It has been said, 'You shall not tempt the LORD your God.' "[a]

13 Now when the devil had ended every temptation, he departed from Him until an opportune time.

14 Then Jesus returned in the power of the Spirit to Galilee, and news of Him went out through all the surrounding region. 15 And He taught in their synagogues, being glorified by all.

16 So He came to Nazareth, where He had been brought up. And as His custom was, He went into the synagogue on the Sabbath day, and stood up to read. 17 And He was handed the book of the prophet Isaiah. And when He had opened the book, He found the place where it was written:

3:24 [a]This and several other names in the genealogy are spelled somewhat differently in the NU-Text. Since the New King James Version uses the Old Testament spelling for persons mentioned in the New Testament, these variations, which come from the Greek, have not been footnoted.   4:1 [a]NU-Text reads in.   4:4 [a]Deuteronomy 8:3   [b]NU-Text omits *but by every word of God.*   4:5 [a]NU-Text reads *And taking Him up, he showed Him.*   4:8 [a]NU-Text omits *Get behind Me, Satan.*   [b]NU-Text and M-Text omit *For.*   [c]Deuteronomy 6:13   4:11 [a]Psalm 91:11, 12   4:12 [a]Deuteronomy 6:16

18 "The Spirit of the LORD is upon
    Me,
    Because He has anointed Me
    To preach the gospel to the
        poor;
    He has sent Me to heal the
        brokenhearted,a
    To proclaim liberty to the
        captives
    And recovery of sight to the
        blind,
    To set at liberty those who are
        oppressed;
19 To proclaim the acceptable
        year of the LORD."a

20 Then He closed the book, and gave
it back to the attendant and sat
down. And the eyes of all who were
in the synagogue were fixed on Him.
21 And He began to say to them, "Today this Scripture is fulfilled in your
hearing." 22 So all bore witness to
Him, and marveled at the gracious
words which proceeded out of His
mouth. And they said, "Is this not Joseph's son?"

23 He said to them, "You will surely
say this proverb to Me, 'Physician,
heal yourself! Whatever we have
heard done in Capernaum,a do also
here in Your country.' " 24 Then He
said, "Assuredly, I say to you, no
prophet is accepted in his own country. 25 But I tell you truly, many widows were in Israel in the days of Elijah, when the heaven was shut up
three years and six months, and
there was a great famine throughout
all the land; 26 but to none of them
was Elijah sent except to Zarephath,a
in the region of Sidon, to a woman
who was a widow. 27 And many lepers were in Israel in the time of Elisha
the prophet, and none of them was
cleansed except Naaman the Syrian."

28 So all those in the synagogue,
when they heard these things, were
filled with wrath, 29 and rose up and
thrust Him out of the city; and they
led Him to the brow of the hill on
which their city was built, that they
might throw Him down over the cliff.
30 Then passing through the midst of
them, He went His way.

31 Then He went down to Capernaum, a city of Galilee, and was

teaching them on the Sabbaths.
32 And they were astonished at His
teaching, for His word was with authority. 33 Now in the synagogue
there was a man who had a spirit of
an unclean demon. And he cried out
with a loud voice, 34 saying, "Let us
alone! What have we to do with You,
Jesus of Nazareth? Did You come to
destroy us? I know who You are—
the Holy One of God!"

35 But Jesus rebuked him, saying,
"Be quiet, and come out of him!" And
when the demon had thrown him in
their midst, it came out of him and
did not hurt him. 36 Then they were
all amazed and spoke among themselves, saying, "What a word this is!
For with authority and power He
commands the unclean spirits, and
they come out." 37 And the report
about Him went out into every place
in the surrounding region.

38 Now He arose from the synagogue and entered Simon's house.
But Simon's wife's mother was sick
with a high fever, and they made
request of Him concerning her.
39 So He stood over her and rebuked
the fever, and it left her. And immediately she arose and served them.

40 When the sun was setting, all
those who had any that were sick
with various diseases brought them
to Him; and He laid His hands on every one of them and healed them.
41 And demons also came out of
many, crying out and saying, "You
are the Christ,a the Son of God!"

And He, rebuking them, did not allow them to speak, for they knew
that He was the Christ.

42 Now when it was day, He departed and went into a deserted
place. And the crowd sought Him
and came to Him, and tried to keep
Him from leaving them; 43 but He
said to them, "I must preach the kingdom of God to the other cities also,
because for this purpose I have been
sent." 44 And He was preaching in
the synagogues of Galilee.a

5 So it was, as the multitude
pressed about Him to hear the
word of God, that He stood by the
Lake of Gennesaret, 2 and saw two
boats standing by the lake; but the

4:18 aNU-Text omits to heal the brokenhearted.   4:19 aIsaiah 61:1, 2   4:23 aHere and elsewhere the
NU-Text spelling is Capharnaum.   4:26 aGreek Sarepta   4:41 aNU-Text omits the Christ.
4:44 aNU-Text reads Judea.

Let Down Your Nets

Working as a fisherman in Jesus' day was a hard, toilsome occupation. Most of the fishing was done at night near the shores, usually by dragging a net between two boats in hopes of catching fish. Fishing was done close to shore where the fish hid under the many rocks and boulders. It was not uncommon to fish throughout the night, only to return home with nothing.

One morning, Peter and his brother, Andrew, and their partners, James and John, were mending their nets by the shores of the Sea of Galilee. Jesus asked Peter to launch out into the deep water and let down his nets for a catch. Peter responded, "Master, we have toiled all night and caught nothing; nevertheless at Your word I will let down the net" (Luke 5:5).

Jesus was asking Peter to fish in broad daylight, at a carpenter's direction. Peter and Andrew went out into the deep water in one boat, dragging a net over the side in the middle of the day. It was a step of obedience and faith that Jesus rewarded. "When they had done this, they caught a great number of fish, and their net was breaking. So they signaled to *their* partners in the other boat to come and help them. And they came and filled both the boats, so that they began to sink" (Luke 5:6, 7).

Jesus wanted to unlock Peter's limited thinking to understand what faith in God could do. Jesus wants us, like Peter, to realize that when we think we have exhausted all possibilities, we haven't!

We may have toiled in the usual manner for days, months, or even years. But God calls us to cast our nets one more time, to try again when we have run out of hope, to believe in His ability, not our ability. Then when we have done the uncommon, in obedience, through faith God will reward us. Our nets will overflow!

fishermen had gone from them and were washing *their* nets. 3 Then He got into one of the boats, which was Simon's, and asked him to put out a little from the land. And He sat down and taught the multitudes from the boat.

4 When He had stopped speaking, He said to Simon, "Launch out into the deep and let down your nets for a catch."

5 But Simon answered and said to Him, "Master, we have toiled all night and caught nothing; nevertheless at Your word I will let down the net." 6 And when they had done this, they caught a great number of fish, and their net was breaking. 7 So they signaled to *their* partners in the other boat to come and help them. And they came and filled both the boats, so that they began to sink. 8 When Simon Peter saw *it*, he fell down at Jesus' knees, saying, "Depart from me, for I am a sinful man, O Lord!"

9 For he and all who were with him were astonished at the catch of fish which they had taken; 10 and so also *were* James and John, the sons of Zebedee, who were partners with Simon. And Jesus said to Simon, "Do not be afraid. From now on you will catch men." 11 So when they had brought their boats to land, they forsook all and followed Him.

12 And it happened when He was in a certain city, that behold, a man who was full of leprosy saw Jesus; and he fell on *his* face and implored Him, saying, "Lord, if You are willing, You can make me clean."

13 Then He put out *His* hand and touched him, saying, "I am willing; be cleansed." Immediately the leprosy left him. 14 And He charged him to tell no one, "But go and show yourself to the priest, and make an offering for your cleansing, as a testimony to them, just as Moses commanded."

15 However, the report went around concerning Him all the more; and great multitudes came together to hear, and to be healed by Him of their infirmities. 16 So He Himself *often* withdrew into the wilderness and prayed.

17 Now it happened on a certain day, as He was teaching, that there were Pharisees and teachers of the law sitting by, who had come out of every town of Galilee, Judea, and Jerusalem. And the power of the Lord was *present* to heal them.*a* 18 Then behold, men brought on a bed a man who was paralyzed, whom they sought to bring in and lay before Him. 19 And when they could not find how they might bring him in, because of the crowd, they went up on the housetop and let him down with *his* bed through the tiling into the midst before Jesus.

20 When He saw their faith, He said to him, "Man, your sins are forgiven you."

21 And the scribes and the Pharisees began to reason, saying, "Who is this who speaks blasphemies? Who can forgive sins but God alone?"

22 But when Jesus perceived their thoughts, He answered and said to them, "Why are you reasoning in your hearts? 23 Which is easier, to say, 'Your sins are forgiven you,' or to say, 'Rise up and walk'? 24 But that you may know that the Son of Man has power on earth to forgive sins" —He said to the man who was paralyzed, "I say to you, arise, take up your bed, and go to your house."

25 Immediately he rose up before them, took up what he had been lying on, and departed to his own house, glorifying God. 26 And they were all amazed, and they glorified God and were filled with fear, saying, "We have seen strange things today!"

27 After these things He went out and saw a tax collector named Levi, sitting at the tax office. And He said to him, "Follow Me." 28 So he left all, rose up, and followed Him.

29 Then Levi gave Him a great feast in his own house. And there were a great number of tax collectors and others who sat down with them. 30 And their scribes and the Pharisees*a* complained against His disciples, saying, "Why do You eat and drink with tax collectors and sinners?"

31 Jesus answered and said to them, "Those who are well have no need of a physician, but those who are sick. 32 I have not come to call

the righteous, but sinners, to repentance."

33 Then they said to Him, "Why do*a* the disciples of John fast often and make prayers, and likewise those of the Pharisees, but Yours eat and drink?"

34 And He said to them, "Can you make the friends of the bridegroom fast while the bridegroom is with them? 35 But the days will come when the bridegroom will be taken away from them; then they will fast in those days."

36 Then He spoke a parable to them: "No one puts a piece from a new garment on an old one;*a* otherwise the new makes a tear, and also the piece that was *taken* out of the new does not match the old. 37 And no one puts new wine into old wineskins; or else the new wine will burst the wineskins and be spilled, and the wineskins will be ruined. 38 But new wine must be put into new wineskins, and both are preserved.*a* 39 And no one, having drunk old *wine,* immediately*a* desires new; for he says, 'The old is better.' "*b*

6 Now it happened on the second Sabbath after the first*a* that He went through the grainfields. And His disciples plucked the heads of grain and ate *them,* rubbing *them* in *their* hands. 2 And some of the Pharisees said to them, "Why are you doing what is not lawful to do on the Sabbath?"

3 But Jesus answering them said, "Have you not even read this, what David did when he was hungry, he and those who were with him: 4 how he went into the house of God, took and ate the showbread, and also gave some to those with him, which is not lawful for any but the priests to eat?" 5 And He said to them, "The Son of Man is also Lord of the Sabbath."

6 Now it happened on another Sabbath, also, that He entered the synagogue and taught. And a man was there whose right hand was withered. 7 So the scribes and Pharisees watched Him closely, whether He would heal on the Sabbath, that they

might find an accusation against Him. 8 But He knew their thoughts, and said to the man who had the withered hand, "Arise and stand here." And he arose and stood. 9 Then Jesus said to them, "I will ask you one thing: Is it lawful on the Sabbath to do good or to do evil, to save life or to destroy?"*a* 10 And when He had looked around at them all, He said to the man,*a* "Stretch out your hand." And he did so, and his hand was restored as whole as the other.*b* 11 But they were filled with rage, and discussed with one another what they might do to Jesus.

12 Now it came to pass in those days that He went out to the mountain to pray, and continued all night in prayer to God. 13 And when it was day, He called His disciples to *Himself;* and from them He chose twelve whom He also named apostles: 14 Simon, whom He also named Peter, and Andrew his brother; James and John; Philip and Bartholomew; 15 Matthew and Thomas; James the *son* of Alphaeus, and Simon called the Zealot; 16 Judas *the son* of James, and Judas Iscariot who also became a traitor.

17 And He came down with them and stood on a level place with a crowd of His disciples and a great multitude of people from all Judea and Jerusalem, and from the seacoast of Tyre and Sidon, who came to hear Him and be healed of their diseases, 18 as well as those who were tormented with unclean spirits. And they were healed. 19 And the whole multitude sought to touch Him, for power went out from Him and healed *them* all.

20 Then He lifted up His eyes toward His disciples, and said:

"Blessed *are you* poor,
    For yours is the kingdom of
      God.
21 Blessed *are you* who hunger
     now,
    For you shall be filled,
    Blessed *are you* who weep now,
    For you shall laugh.
22 Blessed are you when men hate
     you,

5:33 *a*NU-Text omits *Why do,* making the verse a statement.   5:36 *a*NU-Text reads *No one tears a piece from a new garment and puts it on an old one.*   5:38 *a*NU-Text omits *and both are preserved.*
5:39 *a*NU-Text omits *immediately.*   *b*NU-Text reads *good.*   6:1 *a*NU-Text reads *on a Sabbath.*
6:9 *a*M-Text reads *to kill.*   6:10 *a*NU-Text and M-Text read *to him.*   *b*NU-Text omits *as whole as the other.*

And when they exclude you,
And revile *you*, and cast out
   your name as evil,
For the Son of Man's sake.
23 Rejoice in that day and leap for
   joy!
For indeed your reward *is*
   great in heaven,
For in like manner their
   fathers did to the prophets.
24 "But woe to you who are rich,
For you have received your
   consolation.
25   Woe to you who are full,
For you shall hunger.
Woe to you who laugh now,
For you shall mourn and
   weep.
26   Woe to you*a* when all*b* men
   speak well of you,
For so did their fathers to the
   false prophets.

27 "But I say to you who hear: Love your enemies, do good to those who hate you, 28 bless those who curse you, and pray for those who spitefully use you. 29 To him who strikes you on the *one* cheek, offer the other also. And from him who takes away your cloak, do not withhold *your* tunic either. 30 Give to everyone who asks of you. And from him who takes away your goods do not ask *them* back. 31 And just as you want men to do to you, you also do to them likewise.

32 "But if you love those who love you, what credit is that to you? For even sinners love those who love them. 33 And if you do good to those who do good to you, what credit is that to you? For even sinners do the same. 34 And if you lend *to those* from whom you hope to receive back, what credit is that to you? For even sinners lend to sinners to receive as much back. 35 But love your enemies, do good, and lend, hoping for nothing in return; and your reward will be great, and you will be sons of the Most High. For He is kind to the unthankful and evil. 36 Therefore be merciful, just as your Father also is merciful.

37 "Judge not, and you shall not be judged. Condemn not, and you shall not be condemned. Forgive, and you will be forgiven. 38 Give, and it will be given to you: good measure, pressed down, shaken together, and running over will be put into your bosom. For with the same measure that you use, it will be measured back to you."

39 And He spoke a parable to them: "Can the blind lead the blind? Will they not both fall into the ditch? 40 A disciple is not above his teacher, but everyone who is perfectly trained will be like his teacher. 41 And why do you look at the speck in your brother's eye, but do not perceive the plank in your own eye? 42 Or how can you say to your brother, 'Brother, let me remove the speck that *is* in your eye,' when you yourself do not see the plank that *is* in your own eye? Hypocrite! First remove the plank from your own eye, and then you will see clearly to remove the speck that is in your brother's eye.

43 "For a good tree does not bear bad fruit, nor does a bad tree bear good fruit. 44 For every tree is known by its own fruit. For *men* do not gather figs from thorns, nor do they gather grapes from a bramble bush. 45 A good man out of the good treasure of his heart brings forth good; and an evil man out of the evil treasure of his heart*a* brings forth evil. For out of the abundance of the heart his mouth speaks.

46 "But why do you call Me 'Lord, Lord,' and not do the things which I say? 47 Whoever comes to Me, and hears My sayings and does them, I will show you whom he is like: 48 He is like a man building a house, who dug deep and laid the foundation on the rock. And when the flood arose, the stream beat vehemently against that house, and could not shake it, for it was founded on the rock.*a* 49 But he who heard and did nothing is like a man who built a house on the earth without a foundation, against which the stream beat vehemently; and immediately it fell.*a* And the ruin of that house was great."

7 Now when He concluded all His sayings in the hearing of the people, He entered Capernaum. 2 And a certain centurion's servant, who was dear to him, was sick and

---

6:26 *a*NU-Text and M-Text omit *to you.* *b*M-Text omits *all.*   6:45 *a*NU-Text omits *treasure of his heart.*
6:48 *a*NU-Text reads *for it was well built.*   6:49 *a*NU-Text reads *collapsed.*

ready to die. 3 So when he heard about Jesus, he sent elders of the Jews to Him, pleading with Him to come and heal his servant. 4 And when they came to Jesus, they begged Him earnestly, saying that the one for whom He should do this was deserving, 5 "for he loves our nation, and has built us a synagogue."

6 Then Jesus went with them. And when He was already not far from the house, the centurion sent friends to Him, saying to Him, "Lord, do not trouble Yourself, for I am not worthy that You should enter under my roof. 7 Therefore I did not even think myself worthy to come to You. But say the word, and my servant will be healed. 8 For I also am a man placed under authority, having soldiers under me. And I say to one, 'Go,' and he goes; and to another, 'Come,' and he comes; and to my servant, 'Do this,' and he does *it*."

9 When Jesus heard these things, He marveled at him, and turned around and said to the crowd that followed Him, "I say to you, I have not found such great faith, not even in Israel!" 10 And those who were sent, returning to the house, found the servant well who had been sick.*a*

11 Now it happened, the day after, *that* He went into a city called Nain; and many of His disciples went with Him, and a large crowd. 12 And when He came near the gate of the city, behold, a dead man was being carried out, the only son of his mother; and she was a widow. And a large crowd from the city was with her. 13 When the Lord saw her, He had compassion on her and said to her, "Do not weep." 14 Then He came and touched the open coffin, and those who carried *him* stood still. And He said, "Young man, I say to you, arise." 15 So he who was dead sat up and began to speak. And He presented him to his mother.

16 Then fear came upon all, and they glorified God, saying, "A great prophet has risen up among us"; and, "God has visited His people." 17 And this report about Him went throughout all Judea and all the surrounding region.

18 Then the disciples of John reported to him concerning all these things. 19 And John, calling two of his disciples to *him*, sent *them* to Jesus,*a* saying, "Are You the Coming One, or do we look for another?"

20 When the men had come to Him, they said, "John the Baptist has sent us to You, saying, 'Are You the Coming One, or do we look for another?' " 21 And that very hour He cured many of infirmities, afflictions, and evil spirits; and to many blind He gave sight.

22 Jesus answered and said to them, "Go and tell John the things you have seen and heard: that *the* blind see, *the* lame walk, *the* lepers are cleansed, *the* deaf hear, *the* dead are raised, *the* poor have the gospel preached to them. 23 And blessed is *he* who is not offended because of Me."

24 When the messengers of John had departed, He began to speak to the multitudes concerning John: "What did you go out into the wilderness to see? A reed shaken by the wind? 25 But what did you go out to see? A man clothed in soft garments? Indeed those who are gorgeously appareled and live in luxury are in kings' courts. 26 But what did you go out to see? A prophet? Yes, I say to you, and more than a prophet. 27 This is *he* of whom it is written:

> 'Behold, I send My messenger
>   before Your face,
> Who will prepare Your way
>   before You.'*a*

28 For I say to you, among those born of women there is not a greater prophet than John the Baptist;*a* but he who is least in the kingdom of God is greater than he."

29 And when all the people heard *Him*, even the tax collectors justified God, having been baptized with the baptism of John. 30 But the Pharisees and lawyers rejected the will of God for themselves, not having been baptized by him.

31 And the Lord said,*a* "To what then shall I liken the men of this generation, and what are they like? 32 They are like children sitting in the

7:10 *a*NU-Text omits *who had been sick.*   7:19 *a*NU-Text reads *the Lord.*   7:27 *a*Malachi 3:1
7:28 *a*NU-Text reads *there is none greater than John.*   7:31 *a*NU-Text and M-Text omit *And the Lord said.*

Forgiven More

He was called a friend of sinners. And so He was, for Jesus disgraced no one, but openly offered forgiveness and love to the lowest of society. Unimpressed with status, He ignored prestige, but honored praise.

While dining at the home of Simon the Pharisee, Jesus had an unusual experience. Upon entering the house, He was not extended the customary greeting of a kiss, nor did a servant offer to wash His feet. Jesus ignored this obvious offense and reclined to join in the feast.

The banquet, which was open to the public, was suddenly interrupted by a woman's outcry. This woman was known as the city prostitute. Falling at Jesus' feet, she assumed the role of the host. She revealed an alabaster flask filled with expensive fragrant oil. The woman poured the oil over Jesus' feet, anointing Him as an honored guest. Her tears of joy fell to wash His feet, as she kissed them in a supreme act of devotion. Realizing that she had no towel to dry His feet, the woman let down her hair to wipe them clean. No woman in the Middle East would let down her hair in front of a man who was not her husband. Doing so was considered immoral and was possibly punishable by death. Desperate to express her love and gratitude for her new life in Jesus, she put aside the standards of her culture to worship Him.

Simon, the snubbed Pharisee, chose not to express His outrage at the woman's behavior. Oblivious to the depth and sincerity of her gratitude, he saw only her "unrighteousness." Simon felt that if Jesus were righteous, He would have banished the woman from His presence.

Jesus then told Simon a story about two men in debt to the same creditor. One owed fifty denarii and the other owed five hundred. When they could not pay their debts, the creditor forgave them both. Jesus asked Simon, "Tell Me, therefore, which of them will love Him more?" Simon answered correctly by saying, "I suppose the *one* whom He forgave more" (Luke 7:42, 43).

Love is a response to grace. The woman loved Jesus more because she had been forgiven more. Unconcerned with the rules of her culture, she poured forth her praise and joy in gratitude to Jesus.

We who have also been forgiven can love more. Like the woman do not hold back from praising and thanking God because of what people might think. Give Him your gratitude freely!

marketplace and calling to one another, saying:

> 'We played the flute for you,
> And you did not dance;
> We mourned to you,
> And you did not weep.'

33 For John the Baptist came neither eating bread nor drinking wine, and you say, 'He has a demon.' 34 The Son of Man has come eating and drinking, and you say, 'Look, a glutton and a winebibber, a friend of tax collectors and sinners!' 35 But wisdom is justified by all her children."

36 Then one of the Pharisees asked Him to eat with him. And He went to the Pharisee's house, and sat down to eat. 37 And behold, a woman in the city who was a sinner, when she knew that *Jesus* sat at the table in the Pharisee's house, brought an alabaster flask of fragrant oil, 38 and stood at His feet behind *Him* weeping; and she began to wash His feet with her tears, and wiped *them* with the hair of her head; and she kissed His feet and anointed *them* with the fragrant oil. 39 Now when the Pharisee who had invited Him saw *this*, he spoke to himself, saying, "This man, if He were a prophet, would know who and what manner of woman *this is* who is touching Him, for she is a sinner."

40 And Jesus answered and said to him, "Simon, I have something to say to you."

So he said, "Teacher, say it."

41 "There was a certain creditor who had two debtors. One owed five hundred denarii, and the other fifty. 42 And when they had nothing with which to repay, he freely forgave them both. Tell Me, therefore, which of them will love him more?"

43 Simon answered and said, "I suppose the *one* whom he forgave more."

And He said to him, "You have rightly judged." 44 Then He turned to the woman and said to Simon, "Do you see this woman? I entered your house; you gave Me no water for My feet, but she has washed My feet with her tears and wiped *them* with the hair of her head. 45 You gave Me no kiss, but this woman has not ceased to kiss My feet since the time I came

in. 46 You did not anoint My head with oil, but this woman has anointed My feet with fragrant oil. 47 Therefore I say to you, her sins, *which are* many, are forgiven, for she loved much. But to whom little is forgiven, *the same* loves little."

48 Then He said to her, "Your sins are forgiven."

49 And those who sat at the table with Him began to say to themselves, "Who is this who even forgives sins?"

50 Then He said to the woman, "Your faith has saved you. Go in peace."

8 Now it came to pass, afterward, that He went through every city and village, preaching and bringing the glad tidings of the kingdom of God. And the twelve *were* with Him, 2 and certain women who had been healed of evil spirits and infirmities—Mary called Magdalene, out of whom had come seven demons, 3 and Joanna the wife of Chuza, Herod's steward, and Susanna, and many others who provided for Him[a] from their substance.

4 And when a great multitude had gathered, and they had come to Him from every city, He spoke by a parable: 5 "A sower went out to sow his seed. And as he sowed, some fell by the wayside; and it was trampled down, and the birds of the air devoured it. 6 Some fell on rock; and as soon as it sprang up, it withered away because it lacked moisture. 7 And some fell among thorns, and the thorns sprang up with it and choked it. 8 But others fell on good ground, sprang up, and yielded a crop a hundredfold." When He had said these things He cried, "He who has ears to hear, let him hear!"

9 Then His disciples asked Him, saying, "What does this parable mean?"

10 And He said, "To you it has been given to know the mysteries of the kingdom of God, but to the rest *it is given* in parables, that

> 'Seeing they may not see,
> And hearing they may not
>   understand.'[a]

11 "Now the parable is this: The seed is the word of God. 12 Those by

8:3 [a]NU-Text and M-Text read *them*.   8:10 [a]Isaiah 6:9

the wayside are the ones who hear;
then the devil comes and takes away
the word out of their hearts, lest they
should believe and be saved.
13 But the ones on the rock *are those*
who, when they hear, receive the
word with joy; and these have no
root, who believe for a while and
in time of temptation fall away.
14 Now the ones *that* fell among
thorns are those who, when they
have heard, go out and are choked
with cares, riches, and pleasures of
life, and bring no fruit to maturity.
15 But the ones *that* fell on the good
ground are those who, having heard
the word with a noble and good
heart, keep *it* and bear fruit with patience.
16 "No one, when he has lit a lamp,
covers it with a vessel or puts *it* under a bed, but sets *it* on a lampstand,
that those who enter may see the
light. 17 For nothing is secret that will
not be revealed, nor *anything* hidden
that will not be known and come to
light. 18 Therefore take heed how you
hear. For whoever has, to him *more*
will be given; and whoever does not
have, even what he seems to have
will be taken from him."
19 Then His mother and brothers
came to Him, and could not approach
Him because of the crowd. 20 And it
was told Him *by some,* who said,
"Your mother and Your brothers are
standing outside, desiring to see
You."
21 But He answered and said to
them, "My mother and My brothers
are these who hear the word of God
and do it."
22 Now it happened, on a certain
day, that He got into a boat with His
disciples. And He said to them, "Let
us cross over to the other side of the
lake." And they launched out.
23 But as they sailed He fell asleep.
And a windstorm came down on the
lake, and they were filling *with water,* and were in jeopardy. 24 And
they came to Him and awoke Him,
saying, "Master, Master, we are perishing!"
Then He arose and rebuked the
wind and the raging of the water.
And they ceased, and there was a
calm. 25 But He said to them, "Where
is your faith?"

And they were afraid, and marveled, saying to one another, "Who
can this be? For He commands even
the winds and water, and they obey
Him!"
26 Then they sailed to the country
of the Gadarenes,*a* which is opposite
Galilee. 27 And when He stepped out
on the land, there met Him a certain
man from the city who had demons
for a long time. And he wore no
clothes,*a* nor did he live in a house
but in the tombs. 28 When he saw Jesus, he cried out, fell down before
Him, and with a loud voice said,
"What have I to do with You, Jesus,
Son of the Most High God? I beg You,
do not torment me!" 29 For He had
commanded the unclean spirit to
come out of the man. For it had often
seized him, and he was kept under
guard, bound with chains and shackles; and he broke the bonds and was
driven by the demon into the wilderness.
30 Jesus asked him, saying, "What
is your name?"
And he said, "Legion," because
many demons had entered him.
31 And they begged Him that He
would not command them to go out
into the abyss.
32 Now a herd of many swine was
feeding there on the mountain. So
they begged Him that He would permit them to enter them. And He permitted them. 33 Then the demons
went out of the man and entered the
swine, and the herd ran violently
down the steep place into the lake
and drowned.
34 When those who fed *them* saw
what had happened, they fled and
told *it* in the city and in the country.
35 Then they went out to see what
had happened, and came to Jesus,
and found the man from whom the
demons had departed, sitting at the
feet of Jesus, clothed and in his
right mind. And they were afraid.
36 They also who had seen *it* told
them by what means he who had
been demon-possessed was healed.
37 Then the whole multitude of the
surrounding region of the Gadarenes*a* asked Him to depart from
them, for they were seized with great
fear. And He got into the boat and
returned.

8:26 *a*NU-Text reads *Gerasenes.* 8:27 *a*NU-Text reads *who had demons and for a long time wore no
clothes.* 8:37 *a*NU-Text reads *Gerasenes.*

Never Look Back

In teaching total commitment, Jesus used an illustration familiar to all His listeners. "No one, having put his hand to the plow, and looking back, is fit for the kingdom of God" (Luke 9:62). During the planting season in the Middle East, farmers can be seen plowing their fields throughout the land. Plowing in biblical Palestine took a tremendous amount of effort. The light, wooden plow pulled by oxen or donkeys, required the worker to direct all his strength and attention to the task of plowing straight furrows. Among the laborers, it was totally unacceptable to look back after "putting his hand to the plow." In fact, in many parts of the Middle East while traveling or working, to look back is thought to bring the ultimate misfortune upon oneself.

If the farmer plows unevenly and looks back, it only results in an even more crooked furrow. If he looks back at all, his weight is taken off the plow, prohibiting him from making an even furrow in the earth.

Jesus calls us to focus all of our attention and strength on serving God and His kingdom. Jesus encourages us to look forward, not back toward our past mistakes. The apostle Paul also exemplifies this attitude when he says, "Forgetting those things which are behind . . . I press toward the goal for the prize of the upward call of God in Christ Jesus" (Phil. 3:13, 14).

Put your hand to the plow today and never look back. Then you will truly be fit for the kingdom of God. You can say with certainty, I have locked the door on yesterday and have thrown the key away; tomorrow has no fears for me since I have found today!

38 Now the man from whom the demons had departed begged Him that he might be with Him. But Jesus sent him away, saying, 39 "Return to your own house, and tell what great things God has done for you." And he went his way and proclaimed throughout the whole city what great things Jesus had done for him.

40 So it was, when Jesus returned, that the multitude welcomed Him, for they were all waiting for Him. 41 And behold, there came a man named Jairus, and he was a ruler of the synagogue. And he fell down at Jesus' feet and begged Him to come to his house, 42 for he had an only daughter about twelve years of age, and she was dying.

But as He went, the multitudes thronged Him. 43 Now a woman, having a flow of blood for twelve years, who had spent all her livelihood on physicians and could not be healed by any, 44 came from behind and touched the border of His garment. And immediately her flow of blood stopped.

45 And Jesus said, "Who touched Me?"

When all denied it, Peter and those with him*a* said, "Master, the multitudes throng and press You, and You say, 'Who touched Me?' "*b*

46 But Jesus said, "Somebody touched Me, for I perceived power going out from Me." 47 Now when the woman saw that she was not hidden, she came trembling; and falling down before Him, she declared to Him in the presence of all the people the reason she had touched Him and how she was healed immediately.

48 And He said to her, "Daughter, be of good cheer;*a* your faith has made you well. Go in peace."

49 While He was still speaking, someone came from the ruler of the synagogue's *house,* saying to him, "Your daughter is dead. Do not trouble the Teacher."*a*

50 But when Jesus heard *it,* He answered him, saying, "Do not be afraid; only believe, and she will be made well." 51 When He came into the house, He permitted no one to go in*a* except Peter, James, and John,*b* and the father and mother of the girl.

52 Now all wept and mourned for her; but He said, "Do not weep; she is not dead, but sleeping." 53 And they ridiculed Him, knowing that she was dead.

54 But He put them all outside,*a* took her by the hand and called, saying, "Little girl, arise." 55 Then her spirit returned, and she arose immediately. And He commanded that she be given *something* to eat. 56 And her parents were astonished, but He charged them to tell no one what had happened.

9 Then He called His twelve disciples together and gave them power and authority over all demons, and to cure diseases. 2 He sent them to preach the kingdom of God and to heal the sick. 3 And He said to them, "Take nothing for the journey, neither staffs nor bag nor bread nor money; and do not have two tunics apiece.

4 "Whatever house you enter, stay there, and from there depart. 5 And whoever will not receive you, when you go out of that city, shake off the very dust from your feet as a testimony against them."

6 So they departed and went through the towns, preaching the gospel and healing everywhere.

7 Now Herod the tetrarch heard of all that was done by Him; and he was perplexed, because it was said by some that John had risen from the dead, 8 and by some that Elijah had appeared, and by others that one of the old prophets had risen again. 9 Herod said, "John I have beheaded, but who is this of whom I hear such things?" So he sought to see Him.

10 And the apostles, when they had returned, told Him all that they had done. Then He took them and went aside privately into a deserted place belonging to the city called Bethsaida. 11 But when the multitudes knew *it,* they followed Him; and He received them and spoke to them about the kingdom of God, and healed those who had need of healing. 12 When the day began to wear away, the twelve came and said to Him, "Send the multitude away, that they may go into the surrounding

8:45 *a*NU-Text omits *and those with him.*   *b*NU-Text omits *and You say, 'Who touched Me?'*
8:48 *a*NU-Text omits *be of good cheer.*   8:49 *a*NU-Text adds *anymore.*   8:51 *a*NU-Text adds *with Him.*   *b*NU-Text and M-Text read *Peter, John, and James.*   8:54 *a*NU-Text omits *put them all outside.*

Galilee to Jerusalem

The Jewish people often journeyed from Galilee to Jerusalem. Some traveled throughout the year for business reasons, but most went to Jerusalem to observe the Passover. The popular route passed directly through Samaria. However, some Jews chose not to travel through Samaria because of the traditional animosity between the Jews and the Samaritans. Devout Jews shunned Samaritans because of the idolatry and intermarriage they practiced. Samaritans often "bullied" or robbed Jews as they passed through Samaria. The Jews who wanted to avoid Samaria traveled from Galilee through Jericho to Jerusalem.

THE GREAT SEA

Capernaum

Sea of Galilee

GALILEE

Scythopolis

SAMARIA

DECAPOLIS

Samaria
Sychar

JORDAN RIVER

Bethel

Jericho

Jerusalem

PEREA

JUDEA

DEAD SEA

© 1995, Thomas Nelson, Inc.

towns and country, and lodge and get provisions; for we are in a deserted place here."

13 But He said to them, "You give them something to eat."

And they said, "We have no more than five loaves and two fish, unless we go and buy food for all these people." 14 For there were about five thousand men.

Then He said to His disciples, "Make them sit down in groups of fifty." 15 And they did so, and made them all sit down.

16 Then He took the five loaves and the two fish, and looking up to heaven, He blessed and broke *them*, and gave *them* to the disciples to set before the multitude. 17 So they all ate and were filled, and twelve baskets of the leftover fragments were taken up by them.

18 And it happened, as He was alone praying, *that* His disciples joined Him, and He asked them, saying, "Who do the crowds say that I am?"

19 So they answered and said, "John the Baptist, but some *say* Elijah; and others *say* that one of the old prophets has risen again."

20 He said to them, "But who do you say that I am?"

Peter answered and said, "The Christ of God."

21 And He strictly warned and commanded them to tell this to no one, 22 saying, "The Son of Man must suffer many things, and be rejected by the elders and chief priests and scribes, and be killed, and be raised the third day."

23 Then He said to *them* all, "If anyone desires to come after Me, let him deny himself, and take up his cross daily,*a* and follow Me. 24 For whoever desires to save his life will lose it, but whoever loses his life for My sake will save it. 25 For what profit is it to a man if he gains the whole world, and is himself destroyed or lost? 26 For whoever is ashamed of Me and My words, of him the Son of Man will be ashamed when He comes in His *own* glory, and *in His* Father's, and of the holy angels. 27 But I tell you truly, there are some standing here who shall not taste death till they see the kingdom of God."

28 Now it came to pass, about eight days after these sayings, that He took Peter, John, and James and went up on the mountain to pray. 29 As He prayed, the appearance of His face was altered, and His robe *became* white *and* glistening. 30 And behold, two men talked with Him, who were Moses and Elijah, 31 who appeared in glory and spoke of His decease which He was about to accomplish at Jerusalem. 32 But Peter and those with him were heavy with sleep; and when they were fully awake, they saw His glory and the two men who stood with Him. 33 Then it happened, as they were parting from Him, *that* Peter said to Jesus, "Master, it is good for us to be here; and let us make three tabernacles: one for You, one for Moses, and one for Elijah"— not knowing what he said.

34 While he was saying this, a cloud came and overshadowed them; and they were fearful as they entered the cloud. 35 And a voice came out of the cloud, saying, "This is My beloved Son.*a* Hear Him!" 36 When the voice had ceased, Jesus was found alone. But they kept quiet, and told no one in those days any of the things they had seen.

37 Now it happened on the next day, when they had come down from the mountain, that a great multitude met Him. 38 Suddenly a man from the multitude cried out, saying, "Teacher, I implore You, look on my son, for he is my only child. 39 And behold, a spirit seizes him, and he suddenly cries out; it convulses him so that he foams *at the mouth;* and it departs from him with great difficulty, bruising him. 40 So I implored Your disciples to cast it out, but they could not."

41 Then Jesus answered and said, "O faithless and perverse generation, how long shall I be with you and bear with you? Bring your son here." 42 And as he was still coming, the demon threw him down and convulsed *him.* Then Jesus rebuked the unclean spirit, healed the child, and gave him back to his father.

43 And they were all amazed at the majesty of God.

But while everyone marveled at all the things which Jesus did, He said to His disciples, 44 "Let these words

9:23 *a*M-Text omits *daily.*   9:35 *a*NU-Text reads *This is My Son, the Chosen One.*

sink down into your ears, for the Son of Man is about to be betrayed into the hands of men." 45 But they did not understand this saying, and it was hidden from them so that they did not perceive it; and they were afraid to ask Him about this saying.

46 Then a dispute arose among them as to which of them would be greatest. 47 And Jesus, perceiving the thought of their heart, took a little child and set him by Him, 48 and said to them, "Whoever receives this little child in My name receives Me; and whoever receives Me receives Him who sent Me. For he who is least among you all will be great."

49 Now John answered and said, "Master, we saw someone casting out demons in Your name, and we forbade him because he does not follow with us."

50 But Jesus said to him, "Do not forbid *him,* for he who is not against us*a* is on our*b* side."

51 Now it came to pass, when the time had come for Him to be received up, that He steadfastly set His face to go to Jerusalem, 52 and sent messengers before His face. And as they went, they entered a village of the Samaritans, to prepare for Him. 53 But they did not receive Him, because His face was *set* for the journey to Jerusalem. 54 And when His disciples James and John saw *this,* they said, "Lord, do You want us to command fire to come down from heaven and consume them, just as Elijah did?"*a*

55 But He turned and rebuked them,*a* and said, "You do not know what manner of spirit you are of. 56 For the Son of Man did not come to destroy men's lives but to save *them.*"*a* And they went to another village.

57 Now it happened as they journeyed on the road, *that* someone said to Him, "Lord, I will follow You wherever You go."

58 And Jesus said to him, "Foxes have holes and birds of the air *have* nests, but the Son of Man has nowhere to lay *His* head."

59 Then He said to another, "Follow Me."

But he said, "Lord, let me first go and bury my father."

60 Jesus said to him, "Let the dead bury their own dead, but you go and preach the kingdom of God."

61 And another also said, "Lord, I will follow You, but let me first go *and* bid them farewell who are at my house."

62 But Jesus said to him, "No one, having put his hand to the plow, and looking back, is fit for the kingdom of God."

10 After these things the Lord appointed seventy others also,*a* and sent them two by two before His face into every city and place where He Himself was about to go. 2 Then He said to them, "The harvest truly *is* great, but the laborers *are* few; therefore pray the Lord of the harvest to send out laborers into His harvest. 3 Go your way; behold, I send you out as lambs among wolves. 4 Carry neither money bag, knapsack, nor sandals; and greet no one along the road. 5 But whatever house you enter, first say, 'Peace to this house.' 6 And if a son of peace is there, your peace will rest on it; if not, it will return to you. 7 And remain in the same house, eating and drinking such things as they give, for the laborer is worthy of his wages. Do not go from house to house. 8 Whatever city you enter, and they receive you, eat such things as are set before you. 9 And heal the sick there, and say to them, 'The kingdom of God has come near to you.' 10 But whatever city you enter, and they do not receive you, go out into its streets and say, 11 'The very dust of your city which clings to us*a* we wipe off against you. Nevertheless know this, that the kingdom of God has come near you.' 12 But*a* I say to you that it will be more tolerable in that Day for Sodom than for that city. 13 "Woe to you, Chorazin! Woe to you, Bethsaida! For if the mighty works which were done in you had been done in Tyre and Sidon, they would have repented long ago, sitting in sackcloth and ashes. 14 But it will be more tolerable for Tyre and Si-

---

9:50 *a*NU-Text reads *you.*   *b*NU-Text reads *your.*   9:54 *a*NU-Text omits *just as Elijah did.*
9:55 *a*NU-Text omits the rest of this verse.   9:56 *a*NU-Text omits the first sentence of this verse.
10:1 *a*NU-Text reads *seventy-two others.*   10:11 *a*NU-Text reads *our feet.*   10:12 *a*NU-Text and M-Text omit *But.*

The Good Samaritan

The story of the Good Samaritan is a powerful illustration of how we should meet the needs of other people. Against the historical background, this parable is even more challenging.

During New Testament times, there was a great division between the Jewish populace and their neighbors, the Samaritans. Their disagreements centered around a religious point. The Samaritans believed the true place of worship was in Samaria on Mount Gerizim; the Jews held that the temple at Jerusalem was the rightful place.

The Jews disliked the Samaritans so much that they chose not to go near their towns. Even when they traveled to Galilee, they avoided the direct route through Samaria and took the longer, more arduous trip through the wilderness, through Jericho, and up the desert Rift Valley.

This road, from Jerusalem to Jericho, was known as Maale Addumin, meaning, "the ascent of blood." For here thieves and robbers often attacked the travelers.

It was along this road that Jesus told the story of the Good Samaritan. A Jewish man was traveling this route when thieves jumped him, beat him, and left him for dead. Shortly thereafter, a Levitical priest traveled by, but upon seeing the man, crossed the road and left him. Soon after, another Jewish man passed by and also offered no assistance. Finally, a Samaritan, who normally did not journey on this road, came upon the beaten man. Not only did he stop, but he carried the Jew to an inn where he paid two days' wages to insure the man's rest and recovery.

Jesus commended the Samaritan for truly having love for his neighbor. Despite his religious, cultural, and ethnic differences, the Samaritan reached out to meet the needs of the Jew.

In the same manner, we must look out for the needs of those around us. We can put away our prejudices and sacrifice our time, money, and energy to help heal the spiritual, emotional, and physical needs of both our neighbors and strangers. Matthew 25:34–40 says Jesus will honor those who feed and clothe a stranger because they are in need. As you serve others, you're serving Jesus Himself.

don at the judgment than for you. 15 And you, Capernaum, who are exalted to heaven, will be brought down to Hades.[a] 16 He who hears you hears Me, he who rejects you rejects Me, and he who rejects Me rejects Him who sent Me.''

17 Then the seventy[a] returned with joy, saying, ''Lord, even the demons are subject to us in Your name.''

18 And He said to them, ''I saw Satan fall like lightning from heaven. 19 Behold, I give you the authority to trample on serpents and scorpions, and over all the power of the enemy, and nothing shall by any means hurt you. 20 Nevertheless do not rejoice in this, that the spirits are subject to you, but rather[a] rejoice because your names are written in heaven.''

21 In that hour Jesus rejoiced in the Spirit and said, ''I thank You, Father, Lord of heaven and earth, that You have hidden these things from *the* wise and prudent and revealed them to babes. Even so, Father, for so it seemed good in Your sight. 22 All[a] things have been delivered to Me by My Father, and no one knows who the Son is except the Father, and who the Father is except the Son, and *the one* to whom the Son wills to reveal *Him.''*

23 Then He turned to *His* disciples and said privately, ''Blessed *are* the eyes which see the things you see; 24 for I tell you that many prophets and kings have desired to see what you see, and have not seen *it,* and to hear what you hear, and have not heard *it.''*

25 And behold, a certain lawyer stood up and tested Him, saying, ''Teacher, what shall I do to inherit eternal life?''

26 He said to him, ''What is written in the law? What is your reading *of it?''*

27 So he answered and said, '''*You shall love the* LORD *your God with all your heart, with all your soul, with all your strength, and with all your mind,'*[a] and '*your neighbor as yourself.'''*[b]

28 And He said to him, ''You have answered rightly; do this and you will live.''

29 But he, wanting to justify himself, said to Jesus, ''And who is my neighbor?''

30 Then Jesus answered and said: ''A certain *man* went down from Jerusalem to Jericho, and fell among thieves, who stripped him of his clothing, wounded *him,* and departed, leaving *him* half dead. 31 Now by chance a certain priest came down that road. And when he saw him, he passed by on the other side. 32 Likewise a Levite, when he arrived at the place, came and looked, and passed by on the other side. 33 But a certain Samaritan, as he journeyed, came where he was. And when he saw him, he had compassion. 34 So he went to *him* and bandaged his wounds, pouring on oil and wine; and he set him on his own animal, brought him to an inn, and took care of him. 35 On the next day, when he departed,[a] he took out two denarii, gave *them* to the innkeeper, and said to him, 'Take care of him; and whatever more you spend, when I come again, I will repay you.' 36 So which of these three do you think was neighbor to him who fell among the thieves?''

37 And he said, ''He who showed mercy on him.''

Then Jesus said to him, ''Go and do likewise.''

38 Now it happened as they went that He entered a certain village; and a certain woman named Martha welcomed Him into her house. 39 And she had a sister called Mary, who also sat at Jesus'[a] feet and heard His word. 40 But Martha was distracted with much serving, and she approached Him and said, ''Lord, do You not care that my sister has left me to serve alone? Therefore tell her to help me.''

41 And Jesus[a] answered and said to her, ''Martha, Martha, you are worried and troubled about many things. 42 But one thing is needed, and Mary has chosen that good part, which will not be taken away from her.''

11 Now it came to pass, as He was praying in a certain place,

---

10:15 [a]NU-Text reads *will you be exalted to heaven? You will be thrust down to Hades!*
10:17 [a]NU-Text reads *seventy-two.*　　10:20 [a]NU-Text and M-Text omit *rather.*　　10:22 [a]M-Text reads *And turning to the disciples He said, ''All . . . .*　　10:27 [a]Deuteronomy 6:5　　[b]Leviticus 19:18
10:35 [a]NU-Text omits *when he departed.*　　10:39 [a]NU-Text reads *the Lord's.*　　10:41 [a]NU-Text reads *the Lord.*

Teach Us to Pray

The disciples often observed Jesus retreating alone to the mountains to pray. It seemed as if He gained some intangible strength from His time alone. Wanting to learn more about this divine communication, the disciples asked Jesus, "Lord, teach us to pray" (Luke 11:1).

In first-century Judaism, prayer was most often done by priests and high holy men openly in the temple. They stood on the temple stairs, bowing and praying dramatically. The older the priest and the longer his shawl, the holier he was.

Every day at noon, the Sanhedrin, consisting of the Pharisees and Sadducees, met for afternoon prayer. Their prayer rituals were intense. Each member held a phylactery, a three-inch square black wooden box. Inscribed on the surface of the box was the name of God. Inside were four sacred passages from the Torah. Attached to the phylactery were long leather straps. During the prayers, the priests wrapped these straps around their arms. Their chants in Hebrew could be heard throughout the temple area.

Jesus, however, demonstrated a different attitude toward prayer when He said:

> And when you pray, you shall not be like the hypocrites. For they love to pray standing in the synagogues and on the corners of the streets, that they may be seen by men. Assuredly, I say to you, they have their reward. But you, when you pray, go into your room, and when you have shut your door, pray to your Father who *is* in the secret *place;* and your Father who sees in secret will reward you openly. And when you pray, do not use vain repetitions as the heathen *do.* For they think that they will be heard for their many words. Therefore do not be like them. For your Father knows the things you have need of before you ask Him. (Matt. 6:5–8)

Jesus' pattern of true prayer is the Lord's Prayer. It is interesting that Jesus chose the reverent term "Our Father," or *Avinu* in Hebrew to begin the Lord's Prayer. Later, Jesus makes it clear to us we also have the privilege to call God "Abba," meaning "Daddy," an intimate term of affection.

It is evident that in our prayers we should come to God with an attitude of reverence and worship, yet also with a feeling of a close, intimate relationship with our Father. He knows our needs, even before we ask. And He will meet them.

when He ceased, *that* one of His disciples said to Him, "Lord, teach us to pray, as John also taught his disciples."

2 So He said to them, "When you pray, say:

> Our Father in heaven,^a
> Hallowed be Your name.
> Your kingdom come.^b
> Your will be done
> On earth as *it is* in heaven.
> 3   Give us day by day our daily
>   bread.
> 4   And forgive us our sins,
>   For we also forgive everyone
>   who is indebted to us.
>   And do not lead us into
>   temptation,
>   But deliver us from the evil
>   one."^a

5 And He said to them, "Which of you shall have a friend, and go to him at midnight and say to him, 'Friend, lend me three loaves; 6 for a friend of mine has come to me on his journey, and I have nothing to set before him'; 7 and he will answer from within and say, 'Do not trouble me; the door is now shut, and my children are with me in bed; I cannot rise and give to you'? 8 I say to you, though he will not rise and give to him because he is his friend, yet because of his persistence he will rise and give him as many as he needs.

9 "So I say to you, ask, and it will be given to you; seek, and you will find; knock, and it will be opened to you. 10 For everyone who asks receives, and he who seeks finds, and to him who knocks it will be opened. 11 If a son asks for bread^a from any father among you, will he give him a stone? Or if *he asks* for a fish, will he give him a serpent instead of a fish? 12 Or if he asks for an egg, will he offer him a scorpion? 13 If you then, being evil, know how to give good gifts to your children, how much more will *your* heavenly Father give the Holy Spirit to those who ask Him!"

14 And He was casting out a demon, and it was mute. So it was, when the demon had gone out, that the mute spoke; and the multitudes marveled. 15 But some of them said, "He casts out demons by Beelzebub,^a the ruler of the demons."

16 Others, testing *Him,* sought from Him a sign from heaven. 17 But He, knowing their thoughts, said to them: "Every kingdom divided against itself is brought to desolation, and a house *divided* against a house falls. 18 If Satan also is divided against himself, how will his kingdom stand? Because you say I cast out demons by Beelzebub. 19 And if I cast out demons by Beelzebub, by whom do your sons cast *them* out? Therefore they will be your judges. 20 But if I cast out demons with the finger of God, surely the kingdom of God has come upon you. 21 When a strong man, fully armed, guards his own palace, his goods are in peace. 22 But when a stronger than he comes upon him and overcomes him, he takes from him all his armor in which he trusted, and divides his spoils. 23 He who is not with Me is against Me, and he who does not gather with Me scatters.

24 "When an unclean spirit goes out of a man, he goes through dry places, seeking rest; and finding none, he says, 'I will return to my house from which I came.' 25 And when he comes, he finds *it* swept and put in order. 26 Then he goes and takes with *him* seven other spirits more wicked than himself, and they enter and dwell there; and the last *state* of that man is worse than the first."

27 And it happened, as He spoke these things, that a certain woman from the crowd raised her voice and said to Him, "Blessed *is* the womb that bore You, and *the* breasts which nursed You!"

28 But He said, "More than that, blessed *are* those who hear the word of God and keep it!"

29 And while the crowds were thickly gathered together, He began to say, "This is an evil generation. It seeks a sign, and no sign will be given to it except the sign of Jonah the prophet.^a 30 For as Jonah became a sign to the Ninevites, so also the Son of Man will be to this generation. 31 The queen of the South will rise

---

11:2 ^aNU-Text omits *Our* and *in heaven.*   ^bNU-Text omits the rest of this verse.   11:4 ^aNU-Text omits *But deliver us from the evil one.*   11:11 ^aNU-Text omits the words from *bread* through *for* in the next sentence.   11:15 ^aNU-Text and M-Text read *Beelzebul.*   11:29 ^aNU-Text omits *the prophet.*

up in the judgment with the men of this generation and condemn them, for she came from the ends of the earth to hear the wisdom of Solomon; and indeed a greater than Solomon *is* here. 32 The men of Nineveh will rise up in the judgment with this generation and condemn it, for they repented at the preaching of Jonah; and indeed a greater than Jonah *is* here.

33 "No one, when he has lit a lamp, puts *it* in a secret place or under a basket, but on a lampstand, that those who come in may see the light. 34 The lamp of the body is the eye. Therefore, when your eye is good, your whole body also is full of light. But when *your eye* is bad, your body also *is* full of darkness. 35 Therefore take heed that the light which is in you is not darkness. 36 If then your whole body *is* full of light, having no part dark, *the* whole *body* will be full of light, as when the bright shining of a lamp gives you light."

37 And as He spoke, a certain Pharisee asked Him to dine with him. So He went in and sat down to eat. 38 When the Pharisee saw *it,* he marveled that He had not first washed before dinner.

39 Then the Lord said to him, "Now you Pharisees make the outside of the cup and dish clean, but your inward part is full of greed and wickedness. 40 Foolish ones! Did not He who made the outside make the inside also? 41 But rather give alms of such things as you have; then indeed all things are clean to you.

42 "But woe to you Pharisees! For you tithe mint and rue and all manner of herbs, and pass by justice and the love of God. These you ought to have done, without leaving the others undone. 43 Woe to you Pharisees! For you love the best seats in the synagogues and greetings in the marketplaces. 44 Woe to you, scribes and Pharisees, hypocrites!*a* For you are like graves which are not seen, and the men who walk over *them* are not aware *of them.*"

45 Then one of the lawyers answered and said to Him, "Teacher, by saying these things You reproach us also."

46 And He said, "Woe to you also,

lawyers! For you load men with burdens hard to bear, and you yourselves do not touch the burdens with one of your fingers. 47 Woe to you! For you build the tombs of the prophets, and your fathers killed them. 48 In fact, you bear witness that you approve the deeds of your fathers; for they indeed killed them, and you build their tombs. 49 Therefore the wisdom of God also said, 'I will send them prophets and apostles, and *some* of them they will kill and persecute,' 50 that the blood of all the prophets which was shed from the foundation of the world may be required of this generation, 51 from the blood of Abel to the blood of Zechariah who perished between the altar and the temple. Yes, I say to you, it shall be required of this generation.

52 "Woe to you lawyers! For you have taken away the key of knowledge. You did not enter in yourselves, and those who were entering in you hindered."

53 And as He said these things to them,*a* the scribes and the Pharisees began to assail *Him* vehemently, and to cross-examine Him about many things, 54 lying in wait for Him, and seeking to catch Him in something He might say, that they might accuse Him.*a*

12 In the meantime, when an innumerable multitude of people had gathered together, so that they trampled one another, He began to say to His disciples first *of all,* "Beware of the leaven of the Pharisees, which is hypocrisy. 2 For there is nothing covered that will not be revealed, nor hidden that will not be known. 3 Therefore whatever you have spoken in the dark will be heard in the light, and what you have spoken in the ear in inner rooms will be proclaimed on the housetops.

4 "And I say to you, My friends, do not be afraid of those who kill the body, and after that have no more that they can do. 5 But I will show you whom you should fear: Fear Him who, after He has killed, has power to cast into hell; yes, I say to you, fear Him!

6 "Are not five sparrows sold for

11:44 *a*NU-Text omits *scribes and Pharisees, hypocrites.* 11:53 *a*NU-Text reads *And when He left there.* 11:54 *a*NU-Text omits *and seeking* and *that they might accuse Him.*

two copper coins?a And not one of them is forgotten before God. 7 But the very hairs of your head are all numbered. Do not fear therefore; you are of more value than many sparrows.

8 "Also I say to you, whoever confesses Me before men, him the Son of Man also will confess before the angels of God. 9 But he who denies Me before men will be denied before the angels of God.

10 "And anyone who speaks a word against the Son of Man, it will be forgiven him; but to him who blasphemes against the Holy Spirit, it will not be forgiven.

11 "Now when they bring you to the synagogues and magistrates and authorities, do not worry about how or what you should answer, or what you should say. 12 For the Holy Spirit will teach you in that very hour what you ought to say."

13 Then one from the crowd said to Him, "Teacher, tell my brother to divide the inheritance with me."

14 But He said to him, "Man, who made Me a judge or an arbitrator over you?" 15 And He said to them, "Take heed and beware of covetousness,a for one's life does not consist in the abundance of the things he possesses."

16 Then He spoke a parable to them, saying: "The ground of a certain rich man yielded plentifully. 17 And he thought within himself, saying, 'What shall I do, since I have no room to store my crops?' 18 So he said, 'I will do this: I will pull down my barns and build greater, and there I will store all my crops and my goods. 19 And I will say to my soul, "Soul, you have many goods laid up for many years; take your ease; eat, drink, and be merry." ' 20 But God said to him, 'Fool! This night your soul will be required of you; then whose will those things be which you have provided?'

21 "So is he who lays up treasure for himself, and is not rich toward God."

22 Then He said to His disciples, "Therefore I say to you, do not worry about your life, what you will eat; nor about the body, what you will put on. 23 Life is more than food, and the body is more than clothing. 24 Consider the ravens, for they neither sow nor reap, which have neither storehouse nor barn; and God feeds them. Of how much more value are you than the birds? 25 And which of you by worrying can add one cubit to his stature? 26 If you then are not able to do the least, why are you anxious for the rest? 27 Consider the lilies, how they grow: they neither toil nor spin; and yet I say to you, even Solomon in all his glory was not arrayed like one of these. 28 If then God so clothes the grass, which today is in the field and tomorrow is thrown into the oven, how much more will He clothe you, O you of little faith?

29 "And do not seek what you should eat or what you should drink, nor have an anxious mind. 30 For all these things the nations of the world seek after, and your Father knows that you need these things. 31 But seek the kingdom of God, and all these thingsa shall be added to you.

32 "Do not fear, little flock, for it is your Father's good pleasure to give you the kingdom. 33 Sell what you have and give alms; provide yourselves money bags which do not grow old, a treasure in the heavens that does not fail, where no thief approaches nor moth destroys. 34 For where your treasure is, there your heart will be also.

35 "Let your waist be girded and your lamps burning; 36 and you yourselves be like men who wait for their master, when he will return from the wedding, that when he comes and knocks they may open to him immediately. 37 Blessed are those servants whom the master, when he comes, will find watching. Assuredly, I say to you that he will gird himself and have them sit down to eat, and will come and serve them. 38 And if he should come in the second watch, or come in the third watch, and find them so, blessed are those servants. 39 But know this, that if the master of the house had known what hour the thief would come, he would have watched anda not allowed his house to be broken into. 40 Therefore you also be ready, for the Son of Man is coming at an hour you do not expect."

12:6 aGreek assarion, a coin of very small value   12:15 aNU-Text reads all covetousness.
12:31 aNU-Text reads His kingdom, and these things.   12:39 aNU-Text reads he would not have allowed.

41 Then Peter said to Him, "Lord, do You speak this parable *only* to us, or to all *people?*"

42 And the Lord said, "Who then is that faithful and wise steward, whom *his* master will make ruler over his household, to give *them their* portion of food in due season? 43 Blessed *is* that servant whom his master will find so doing when he comes. 44 Truly, I say to you that he will make him ruler over all that he has. 45 But if that servant says in his heart, 'My master is delaying his coming,' and begins to beat the male and female servants, and to eat and drink and be drunk, 46 the master of that servant will come on a day when he is not looking for *him,* and at an hour when he is not aware, and will cut him in two and appoint *him* his portion with the unbelievers. 47 And that servant who knew his master's will, and did not prepare *himself* or do according to his will, shall be beaten with many *stripes.* 48 But he who did not know, yet committed things deserving of stripes, shall be beaten with few. For everyone to whom much is given, from him much will be required; and to whom much has been committed, of him they will ask the more.

49 "I came to send fire on the earth, and how I wish it were already kindled! 50 But I have a baptism to be baptized with, and how distressed I am till it is accomplished! 51 Do *you* suppose that I came to give peace on earth? I tell you, not at all, but rather division. 52 For from now on five in one house will be divided: three against two, and two against three. 53 Father will be divided against son and son against father, mother against daughter and daughter against mother, mother-in-law against her daughter-in-law and daughter-in-law against her mother-in-law."

54 Then He also said to the multitudes, "Whenever *you see* a cloud rising out of the west, immediately you say, 'A shower is coming'; and so it is. 55 And when you see the south wind blow, you say, 'There will be hot weather'; and there is. 56 Hypocrites! You can discern the face of the sky and of the earth, but how *is it* you do not discern this time?

57 "Yes, and why, even of yourselves, do you not judge what is right? 58 When you go with your adversary to the magistrate, make every effort along the way to settle with him, lest he drag you to the judge, the judge deliver you to the officer, and the officer throw you into prison. 59 I tell you, you shall not depart from there till you have paid the very last mite."

13 There were present at that season some who told Him about the Galileans whose blood Pilate had mingled with their sacrifices. 2 And Jesus answered and said to them, "Do you suppose that these Galileans were worse sinners than all *other* Galileans, because they suffered such things? 3 I tell you, no; but unless you repent you will all likewise perish. 4 Or those eighteen on whom the tower in Siloam fell and killed them, do you think that they were worse sinners than all *other* men who dwelt in Jerusalem? 5 I tell you, no; but unless you repent you will all likewise perish."

6 He also spoke this parable: "A certain *man* had a fig tree planted in his vineyard, and he came seeking fruit on it and found none. 7 Then he said to the keeper of his vineyard, 'Look, for three years I have come seeking fruit on this fig tree and find none. Cut it down; why does it use up the ground?' 8 But he answered and said to him, 'Sir, let it alone this year also, until I dig around it and fertilize *it.* 9 And if it bears fruit, *well.* But if not, after that*a* you can cut it down.'"

10 Now He was teaching in one of the synagogues on the Sabbath. 11 And behold, there was a woman who had a spirit of infirmity eighteen years, and was bent over and could in no way raise *herself* up. 12 But when Jesus saw her, He called *her* to *Him* and said to her, "Woman, you are loosed from your infirmity." 13 And He laid *His* hands on her, and immediately she was made straight, and glorified God.

14 But the ruler of the synagogue answered with indignation, because Jesus had healed on the Sabbath; and he said to the crowd, "There are six days on which men ought to work;

13:9 *a*NU-Text reads *And if it bears fruit after that, well. But if not, you can cut it down.*

Compel Them to Come In

In the course of Jesus' ministry, He taught His disciples through a parable to extend an invitation for everyone to come and sit at a banquet feast in the kingdom of God. "Go out into the highways and hedges, and compel *them* to come in, that my house may be filled" (Luke 14:23).

The highways referred to in Jesus' parable were the famous Via Maris and King's Highway which ran through Gentile regions. The hedges, byways, indicated the smaller connecting travel routes. These passed through the remote Jewish villages. In teaching His disciples to go into the highways and byways, Jesus extended His invitation to enter God's kingdom to both the Gentile and the Jew. God's forgiveness and love are offered to all mankind.

Jesus implored an attitude still evident today when inviting someone to dine. Jesus said, "Compel them to come in." A common practice in the Middle East is to invite someone for dinner, knowing full well that the person will turn down the invitation the first time. As a matter of fact, it is not courteous to accept at first. It is expected that the host will invite you again and insist that you come.

A common dinner invitation dialogue might sound like this:
"Oh, please come and dine at our house."
"Oh, no, we couldn't. Thank you very much anyway."
"No, we insist that you come."
"Oh, we really couldn't."
"Oh, but you must come. We have so much to give you. We have prepared everything for you. We have you in our minds, thoughts, and prayers. Please come and honor us with your presence."

Then the invited guest will say, "Well, if you've done all that, we can do nothing but come. Of course we'll be there."

This is the persistent attitude that Jesus wishes His disciples to convey to people about God's love and forgiveness by inviting them to share in the kingdom of God. Though many will turn it down upon the first, second, and third request, the call is to continually insist and invite them to share in Jesus' love and forgiveness.

Who can you share a positive experience of joy and forgiveness with in your world? What highways and byways can you travel to meet and share with others the love of Jesus Christ? Compel them to come in!

therefore come and be healed on them, and not on the Sabbath day."

15 The Lord then answered him and said, "Hypocrite!ᵃ Does not each one of you on the Sabbath loose his ox or donkey from the stall, and lead *it* away to water it? 16 So ought not this woman, being a daughter of Abraham, whom Satan has bound— think of it—for eighteen years, be loosed from this bond on the Sabbath?" 17 And when He said these things, all His adversaries were put to shame; and all the multitude rejoiced for all the glorious things that were done by Him.

18 Then He said, "What is the kingdom of God like? And to what shall I compare it? 19 It is like a mustard seed, which a man took and put in his garden; and it grew and became a largeᵃ tree, and the birds of the air nested in its branches."

20 And again He said, "To what shall I liken the kingdom of God? 21 It is like leaven, which a woman took and hid in three measuresᵃ of meal till it was all leavened."

22 And He went through the cities and villages, teaching, and journeying toward Jerusalem. 23 Then one said to Him, "Lord, are there few who are saved?"

And He said to them, 24 "Strive to enter through the narrow gate, for many, I say to you, will seek to enter and will not be able. 25 When once the Master of the house has risen up and shut the door, and you begin to stand outside and knock at the door, saying, 'Lord, Lord, open for us,' and He will answer and say to you, 'I do not know you, where you are from,' 26 then you will begin to say, 'We ate and drank in Your presence, and You taught in our streets.' 27 But He will say, 'I tell you I do not know you, where you are from. Depart from Me, all you workers of iniquity.' 28 There will be weeping and gnashing of teeth, when you see Abraham and Isaac and Jacob and all the prophets in the kingdom of God, and yourselves thrust out. 29 They will come from the east and the west, from the north and the south, and sit down in the kingdom of God. 30 And indeed there are last who will

be first, and there are first who will be last."

31 On that very dayᵃ some Pharisees came, saying to Him, "Get out and depart from here, for Herod wants to kill You."

32 And He said to them, "Go, tell that fox, 'Behold, I cast out demons and perform cures today and tomorrow, and the third *day* I shall be perfected.' 33 Nevertheless I must journey today, tomorrow, and the *day* following; for it cannot be that a prophet should perish outside of Jerusalem.

34 "O Jerusalem, Jerusalem, the one who kills the prophets and stones those who are sent to her! How often I wanted to gather your children together, as a hen *gathers* her brood under *her* wings, but you were not willing! 35 See! Your house is left to you desolate; and assuredly,ᵃ I say to you, you shall not see Me until *the time* comes when you say, '*Blessed is He who comes in the name of the Lord!*'"ᵇ

14 Now it happened, as He went into the house of one of the rulers of the Pharisees to eat bread on the Sabbath, that they watched Him closely. 2 And behold, there was a certain man before Him who had dropsy. 3 And Jesus, answering, spoke to the lawyers and Pharisees, saying, "Is it lawful to heal on the Sabbath?"ᵃ

4 But they kept silent. And He took *him* and healed him, and let him go. 5 Then He answered them, saying, "Which of you, having a donkeyᵃ or an ox that has fallen into a pit, will not immediately pull him out on the Sabbath day?" 6 And they could not answer Him regarding these things.

7 So He told a parable to those who were invited, when He noted how they chose the best places, saying to them: 8 "When you are invited by anyone to a wedding feast, do not sit down in the best place, lest one more honorable than you be invited by him; 9 and he who invited you and him come and say to you, 'Give place to this man,' and then you begin with shame to take the lowest place. 10 But when you are invited, go and

---

13:15 ᵃNU-Text and M-Text read *Hypocrites*.   13:19 ᵃNU-Text omits *large*.   13:21 ᵃGreek *sata*, approximately two pecks in all   13:31 ᵃNU-Text reads *In that very hour*.   13:35 ᵃNU-Text and M-Text omit *assuredly*.   ᵇPsalm 118:26   14:3 ᵃNU-Text adds *or not*.   14:5 ᵃNU-Text and M-Text read *son*.

The Lost Coin

"What woman, having ten silver coins, if she loses one coin, does not light a lamp, sweep the house, and search carefully until she finds *it*? And when she has found *it*, she calls *her* friends and neighbors together, saying, 'Rejoice with me, for I have found the piece which I lost!' Likewise, I say to you, there is joy in the presence of the angels of God over one sinner who repents" (Luke 15:8–10).

The ancient dress of Palestinian women helps illuminate this parable of Jesus. The coin for which the woman searched so diligently held immense value for her—not simply because of monetary worth, but because it was probably the type of coin attached to the headdress of the woman's dowry. Even today Bedouin women in Palestine wear ten, fifty, even one hundred coins attached to the scarfs that cover their heads. The coin this woman lost had special sentimental value to her.

By lighting a lamp and sweeping her floor, the woman did everything she could to help locate the lost coin. Perhaps a shimmer of light bouncing off the coin would help her detect it. Maybe the tinkling sound made by the coin as the broom would loosened it from its lodging place between the basaltic stone cracks would reveal its location.

Like the woman who searched for her coin, we can be assured that we are special to God. Like the one sentimental coin, we hold unique value and worth to our Father. For we are His valued possession, giving glory to Him. We can have the confidence that He will light our way, look for us, and when He finds us, pick us up and rejoice.

sit down in the lowest place, so that when he who invited you comes he may say to you, 'Friend, go up higher.' Then you will have glory in the presence of those who sit at the table with you. 11 For whoever exalts himself will be humbled, and he who humbles himself will be exalted."

12 Then He also said to him who invited Him, "When you give a dinner or a supper, do not ask your friends, your brothers, your relatives, nor rich neighbors, lest they also invite you back, and you be repaid. 13 But when you give a feast, invite *the* poor, *the* maimed, *the* lame, *the* blind. 14 And you will be blessed, because they cannot repay you; for you shall be repaid at the resurrection of the just."

15 Now when one of those who sat at the table with Him heard these things, he said to Him, "Blessed *is* he who shall eat bread*a* in the kingdom of God!"

16 Then He said to him, "A certain man gave a great supper and invited many, 17 and sent his servant at supper time to say to those who were invited, 'Come, for all things are now ready.' 18 But they all with one *accord* began to make excuses. The first said to him, 'I have bought a piece of ground, and I must go and see it. I ask you to have me excused.' 19 And another said, 'I have bought five yoke of oxen, and I am going to test them. I ask you to have me excused.' 20 Still another said, 'I have married a wife, and therefore I cannot come.' 21 So that servant came and reported these things to his master. Then the master of the house, being angry, said to his servant, 'Go out quickly into the streets and lanes of the city, and bring in here *the* poor and *the* maimed and *the* lame and *the* blind.' 22 And the servant said, 'Master, it is done as you commanded, and still there is room.' 23 Then the master said to the servant, 'Go out into the highways and hedges, and compel *them* to come in, that my house may be filled. 24 For I say to you that none of those men who were invited shall taste my supper.' "

25 Now great multitudes went with Him. And He turned and said to them, 26 "If anyone comes to Me and does not hate his father and mother, wife and children, brothers and sisters, yes, and his own life also, he cannot be My disciple. 27 And whoever does not bear his cross and come after Me cannot be My disciple. 28 For which of you, intending to build a tower, does not sit down first and count the cost, whether he has *enough* to finish *it*— 29 lest, after he has laid the foundation, and is not able to finish, all who see *it* begin to mock him, 30 saying, 'This man began to build and was not able to finish.' 31 Or what king, going to make war against another king, does not sit down first and consider whether he is able with ten thousand to meet him who comes against him with twenty thousand? 32 Or else, while the other is still a great way off, he sends a delegation and asks conditions of peace. 33 So likewise, whoever of you does not forsake all that he has cannot be My disciple.

34 "Salt *is* good; but if the salt has lost its flavor, how shall it be seasoned? 35 It is neither fit for the land nor for the dunghill, *but* men throw it out. He who has ears to hear, let him hear!"

15 Then all the tax collectors and the sinners drew near to Him to hear Him. 2 And the Pharisees and scribes complained, saying, "This Man receives sinners and eats with them." 3 So He spoke this parable to them, saying:

4 "What man of you, having a hundred sheep, if he loses one of them, does not leave the ninety-nine in the wilderness, and go after the one which is lost until he finds it? 5 And when he has found *it*, he lays *it* on his shoulders, rejoicing. 6 And when he comes home, he calls together *his* friends and neighbors, saying to them, 'Rejoice with me, for I have found my sheep which was lost!' 7 I say to you that likewise there will be more joy in heaven over one sinner who repents than over ninety-nine just persons who need no repentance.

8 "Or what woman, having ten silver coins,*a* if she loses one coin, does not light a lamp, sweep the house,

The Prodigal Son

Throughout Jesus' ministry, He occasionally drew from Jewish culture to illustrate His truths. Perhaps one of His most familiar stories is that of the Prodigal Son. Similar parables were also used by the rabbis of His day, but Jesus gave them fresh new meanings.

The story of the Prodigal Son focuses on an average young man from a small village in the Jordan River valley. This town is in Perea, a sparsely populated Jewish area south of Galilee on the road to Jerusalem. His father is a wealthy landowner whose many servants care for his fields and flocks of his land.

Like any other boy his age, the son dreams of his future and autonomy. He may have looked dreamily into the mountains surrounding his village in the Gentile Decapolis, known for its Greek temples, art, games, and literature. It is considered the "far-off land," reflecting not its geographical distance, but its cultural distance from the religious beliefs of the Jewish population.

One day, consumed by wanderlust, the young boy leaves behind his family and makes haste for this pagan country. Here the story tells that he "wasted his possessions with prodigal living" (Luke 15:13). At this time, a great famine sweeps over the land, bringing severe hardship to the mountainous Decapolis region. The Perean area is not affected, however, for it is located seven hundred feet below sea level. Its several underground springs keep the land fertile and alive. The young boy, now moneyless and hungry, persuades a local farmer to let him care for his hogs. Upon realizing that the hogs he feeds have a better life than he does, the boy decides to return home with hopes of being hired as a servant on his father's farm (see Luke 15:15–19).

Here the rabbinical teaching explains that once someone leaves his faith and indulges in the culture and religion of the Greek cities, he is considered dead. The father cannot forgive his son for his wanderings and sins in the Gentile land. The boy is cut off from his family, friends, and religion forever.

Jesus, however, gives this story a new ending. Now, the boy receives forgiveness from his father, who celebrates his homecoming by killing a fatted calf and throwing a feast. No longer is man cut off from God. Instead, there is much rejoicing. Man is forgiven because of the Father's great love. 1 John 3:1 tells us, "Behold what manner of love the Father has bestowed on us, that we should be called the children of God!"

and search carefully until she finds *it?* 9 And when she has found *it,* she calls *her* friends and neighbors together, saying, 'Rejoice with me, for I have found the piece which I lost!' 10 Likewise, I say to you, there is joy in the presence of the angels of God over one sinner who repents."

11 Then He said: "A certain man had two sons. 12 And the younger of them said to *his* father, 'Father, give me the portion of goods that falls *to me.*' So he divided to them *his* livelihood. 13 And not many days after, the younger son gathered all together, journeyed to a far country, and there wasted his possessions with prodigal living. 14 But when he had spent all, there arose a severe famine in that land, and he began to be in want. 15 Then he went and joined himself to a citizen of that country, and he sent him into his fields to feed swine. 16 And he would gladly have filled his stomach with the pods that the swine ate, and no one gave him *anything.*

17 "But when he came to himself, he said, 'How many of my father's hired servants have bread enough and to spare, and I perish with hunger! 18 I will arise and go to my father, and will say to him, "Father, I have sinned against heaven and before you, 19 and I am no longer worthy to be called your son. Make me like one of your hired servants."'

20 "And he arose and came to his father. But when he was still a great way off, his father saw him and had compassion, and ran and fell on his neck and kissed him. 21 And the son said to him, 'Father, I have sinned against heaven and in your sight, and am no longer worthy to be called your son.'

22 "But the father said to his servants, 'Bring*a* out the best robe and put *it* on him, and put a ring on his hand and sandals on *his* feet. 23 And bring the fatted calf here and kill *it,* and let us eat and be merry; 24 for this my son was dead and is alive again; he was lost and is found.' And they began to be merry.

25 "Now his older son was in the field. And as he came and drew near to the house, he heard music and dancing. 26 So he called one of the servants and asked what these things meant. 27 And he said to him, 'Your brother has come, and because he has received him safe and sound, your father has killed the fatted calf.' 28 "But he was angry and would not go in. Therefore his father came out and pleaded with him. 29 So he answered and said to *his* father, 'Lo, these many years I have been serving you; I never transgressed your commandment at any time; and yet you never gave me a young goat, that I might make merry with my friends. 30 But as soon as this son of yours came, who has devoured your livelihood with harlots, you killed the fatted calf for him.'

31 "And he said to him, 'Son, you are always with me, and all that I have is yours. 32 It was right that we should make merry and be glad, for your brother was dead and is alive again, and was lost and is found.' "

16 He also said to His disciples: "There was a certain rich man who had a steward, and an accusation was brought to him that this man was wasting his goods. 2 So he called him and said to him, 'What is this I hear about you? Give an account of your stewardship, for you can no longer be steward.'

3 "Then the steward said within himself, 'What shall I do? For my master is taking the stewardship away from me. I cannot dig; I am ashamed to beg. 4 I have resolved what to do, that when I am put out of the stewardship, they may receive me into their houses.'

5 "So he called every one of his master's debtors to *him,* and said to the first, 'How much do you owe my master?' 6 And he said, 'A hundred measures*a* of oil.' So he said to him, 'Take your bill, and sit down quickly and write fifty.' 7 Then he said to another, 'And how much do you owe?' So he said, 'A hundred measures*a* of wheat.' And he said to him, 'Take your bill, and write eighty.' 8 So the master commended the unjust steward because he had dealt shrewdly. For the sons of this world are more shrewd in their generation than the sons of light.

9 "And I say to you, make friends for yourselves by unrighteous mam-

---

15:22 *a*NU-Text reads *Quickly bring.*   16:6 *a*Greek *batos,* eight or nine gallons each (Old Testament *bath*)   16:7 *a*Greek *koros,* ten or twelve bushels each (Old Testament *kor*) mon, that when you fail,[a] they may receive you into an everlasting home. 10 He who *is* faithful in *what is* least is faithful also in much; and he who is unjust in *what is* least is unjust also in much. 11 Therefore if you have not been faithful in the unrighteous mammon, who will commit to your trust the true *riches?* 12 And if you have not been faithful in what is another man's, who will give you what is your own?

13 "No servant can serve two masters; for either he will hate the one and love the other, or else he will be loyal to the one and despise the other. You cannot serve God and mammon."

14 Now the Pharisees, who were lovers of money, also heard all these things, and they derided Him. 15 And He said to them, "You are those who justify yourselves before men, but God knows your hearts. For what is highly esteemed among men is an abomination in the sight of God.

16 "The law and the prophets *were* until John. Since that time the kingdom of God has been preached, and everyone is pressing into it. 17 And it is easier for heaven and earth to pass away than for one tittle of the law to fail.

18 "Whoever divorces his wife and marries another commits adultery; and whoever marries her who is divorced from *her* husband commits adultery.

19 "There was a certain rich man who was clothed in purple and fine linen and fared sumptuously every day. 20 But there was a certain beggar named Lazarus, full of sores, who was laid at his gate, 21 desiring to be fed with the crumbs which fell[a] from the rich man's table. Moreover the dogs came and licked his sores. 22 So it was that the beggar died, and was carried by the angels to Abraham's bosom. The rich man also died and was buried. 23 And being in torments in Hades, he lifted up his eyes and saw Abraham afar off, and Lazarus in his bosom.

24 "Then he cried and said, 'Father Abraham, have mercy on me, and send Lazarus that he may dip the tip of his finger in water and cool my tongue; for I am tormented in this flame.' 25 But Abraham said, 'Son, remember that in your lifetime you received your good things, and likewise Lazarus evil things; but now he is comforted and you are tormented. 26 And besides all this, between us and you there is a great gulf fixed, so that those who want to pass from here to you cannot, nor can those from there pass to us.'

27 "Then he said, 'I beg you therefore, father, that you would send him to my father's house, 28 for I have five brothers, that he may testify to them, lest they also come to this place of torment.' 29 Abraham said to him, 'They have Moses and the prophets; let them hear them.' 30 And he said, 'No, father Abraham; but if one goes to them from the dead, they will repent.' 31 But he said to him, 'If they do not hear Moses and the prophets, neither will they be persuaded though one rise from the dead.'"

17 Then He said to the disciples, "It is impossible that no offenses should come, but woe *to him* through whom they do come! 2 It would be better for him if a millstone were hung around his neck, and he were thrown into the sea, than that he should offend one of these little ones. 3 Take heed to yourselves. If your brother sins against you,[a] rebuke him; and if he repents, forgive him. 4 And if he sins against you seven times in a day, and seven times in a day returns to you,[a] saying, 'I repent,' you shall forgive him."

5 And the apostles said to the Lord, "Increase our faith."

6 So the Lord said, "If you have faith as a mustard seed, you can say to this mulberry tree, 'Be pulled up by the roots and be planted in the sea,' and it would obey you. 7 And which of you, having a servant plowing or tending sheep, will say to him when he has come in from the field, 'Come at once and sit down to eat'? 8 But will he not rather say to him, 'Prepare something for my supper, and gird yourself and serve me till I have eaten and drunk, and afterward you will eat and drink'? 9 Does he thank that servant because he did the things that were commanded him? I think not.[a] 10 So like-

16:9 [a]NU-Text reads *it fails.*   16:21 [a]NU-Text reads *with what fell.*   17:3 [a]NU-Text omits *against you.*   17:4 [a]M-Text omits *to you.*   17:9 [a]NU-Text ends verse with *commanded;* M-Text omits *him.*

Return to Give Thanks

Leprosy was a dreaded and deadly disease in the Middle East during the time of Christ. According to Jewish Levitical law, lepers were to live in isolation outside the city, and they were not to come in contact with any "clean" person. Theirs a life of uncleanness, having contact only with each other.

It was one such group that Jesus came upon when traveling through the area of Perea on His way to Jerusalem. Their cries for help did not go unheard. Having compassion on them, Jesus healed the lepers of their disease. He told them to go before the Levitical priests to show themselves as clean. This practice of the Levitical law was the leper's one hope to return and live a normal life in society.

In faith, the lepers journeyed to the priests. As they began their travel, the disease left them. They went before the priests who confirmed they were well. Of the ten lepers that Jesus healed, only one took the time and energy to return to find and thank Jesus for what He had done.

In the same manner, Jesus heals us of our emotional, spiritual, and physical diseases. Yet how often do we return to thank Him? We must, like the one leper, return to give thanks. It is easy to cry out to God when we are in pain. But when we are surrounded with prosperity, may we also acknowledge Him for His gifts. The one leper who returned was a Samaritan—the least likely to come back to Jesus. But despite the cultural barriers between the Jews and Samaritans, the leper did return.

Let us not be held back by anything, but let us always make the effort to have a grateful heart before our Lord.

wise you, when you have done all those things which you are commanded, say, 'We are unprofitable servants. We have done what was our duty to do.' "

11 Now it happened as He went to Jerusalem that He passed through the midst of Samaria and Galilee. 12 Then as He entered a certain village, there met Him ten men who were lepers, who stood afar off. 13 And they lifted up *their* voices and said, "Jesus, Master, have mercy on us!"

14 So when He saw *them*, He said to them, "Go, show yourselves to the priests." And so it was that as they went, they were cleansed.

15 And one of them, when he saw that he was healed, returned, and with a loud voice glorified God, 16 and fell down on *his* face at His feet, giving Him thanks. And he was a Samaritan.

17 So Jesus answered and said, "Were there not ten cleansed? But where *are* the nine? 18 Were there not any found who returned to give glory to God except this foreigner?" 19 And He said to him, "Arise, go your way. Your faith has made you well."

20 Now when He was asked by the Pharisees when the kingdom of God would come, He answered them and said, "The kingdom of God does not come with observation; 21 nor will they say, 'See here!' or 'See there!'ᵃ For indeed, the kingdom of God is within you."

22 Then He said to the disciples, "The days will come when you will desire to see one of the days of the Son of Man, and you will not see *it*. 23 And they will say to you, 'Look here!' or 'Look there!'ᵃ Do not go after *them* or follow *them*. 24 For as the lightning that flashes out of one *part* under heaven shines to the other *part* under heaven, so also the Son of Man will be in His day. 25 But first He must suffer many things and be rejected by this generation. 26 And as it was in the days of Noah, so it will be also in the days of the Son of Man: 27 They ate, they drank, they married wives, they were given in marriage, until the day that Noah entered the ark, and the flood came and destroyed them all. 28 Likewise as it was also in the days of Lot: They ate, they drank, they bought, they sold, they planted, they built; 29 but on the day that Lot went out of Sodom it rained fire and brimstone from heaven and destroyed *them* all. 30 Even so will it be in the day when the Son of Man is revealed.

31 "In that day, he who is on the housetop, and his goods *are* in the house, let him not come down to take them away. And likewise the one who is in the field, let him not turn back. 32 Remember Lot's wife. 33 Whoever seeks to save his life will lose it, and whoever loses his life will preserve it. 34 I tell you, in that night there will be two *men* in one bed: the one will be taken and the other will be left. 35 Two *women* will be grinding together: the one will be taken and the other left. 36 Two *men* will be in the field: the one will be taken and the other left."ᵃ

37 And they answered and said to Him, "Where, Lord?"

So He said to them, "Wherever the body is, there the eagles will be gathered together."

18 Then He spoke a parable to them, that men always ought to pray and not lose heart, 2 saying: "There was in a certain city a judge who did not fear God nor regard man. 3 Now there was a widow in that city; and she came to him, saying, 'Get justice for me from my adversary.' 4 And he would not for a while; but afterward he said within himself, 'Though I do not fear God nor regard man, 5 yet because this widow troubles me I will avenge her, lest by her continual coming she weary me.' "

6 Then the Lord said, "Hear what the unjust judge said. 7 And shall God not avenge His own elect who cry out day and night to Him, though He bears long with them? 8 I tell you that He will avenge them speedily. Nevertheless, when the Son of Man comes, will He really find faith on the earth?"

9 Also He spoke this parable to some who trusted in themselves that they were righteous, and despised others: 10 "Two men went up to the

---

17:21 ᵃNU-Text reverses *here* and *there*.   17:23 ᵃNU-Text reverses *here* and *there*.   17:36 ᵃNU-Text and M-Text omit verse 36.

temple to pray, one a Pharisee and the other a tax collector. 11 The Pharisee stood and prayed thus with himself, 'God, I thank You that I am not like other men—extortioners, unjust, adulterers, or even as this tax collector. 12 I fast twice a week; I give tithes of all that I possess.' 13 And the tax collector, standing afar off, would not so much as raise *his* eyes to heaven, but beat his breast, saying, 'God, be merciful to me a sinner!' 14 I tell you, this man went down to his house justified *rather* than the other; for everyone who exalts himself will be humbled, and he who humbles himself will be exalted."

15 Then they also brought infants to Him that He might touch them; but when the disciples saw *it*, they rebuked them. 16 But Jesus called them to *Him* and said, "Let the little children come to Me, and do not forbid them; for of such is the kingdom of God. 17 Assuredly, I say to you, whoever does not receive the kingdom of God as a little child will by no means enter it."

18 Now a certain ruler asked Him, saying, "Good Teacher, what shall I do to inherit eternal life?"

19 So Jesus said to him, "Why do you call Me good? No one *is* good but One, *that is*, God. 20 You know the commandments: '*Do not commit adultery,*' '*Do not murder,*' '*Do not steal,*' '*Do not bear false witness,*' '*Honor your father and your mother.*'"*a*

21 And he said, "All these things I have kept from my youth."

22 So when Jesus heard these things, He said to him, "You still lack one thing. Sell all that you have and distribute to the poor, and you will have treasure in heaven; and come, follow Me."

23 But when he heard this, he became very sorrowful, for he was very rich.

24 And when Jesus saw that he became very sorrowful, He said, "How hard it is for those who have riches to enter the kingdom of God! 25 For it is easier for a camel to go through the eye of a needle than for a rich man to enter the kingdom of God."

26 And those who heard it said, "Who then can be saved?"

27 But He said, "The things which are impossible with men are possible with God."

28 Then Peter said, "See, we have left all*a* and followed You."

29 So He said to them, "Assuredly, I say to you, there is no one who has left house or parents or brothers or wife or children, for the sake of the kingdom of God, 30 who shall not receive many times more in this present time, and in the age to come eternal life."

31 Then He took the twelve aside and said to them, "Behold, we are going up to Jerusalem, and all things that are written by the prophets concerning the Son of Man will be accomplished. 32 For He will be delivered to the Gentiles and will be mocked and insulted and spit upon. 33 They will scourge *Him* and kill Him. And the third day He will rise again."

34 But they understood none of these things; this saying was hidden from them, and they did not know the things which were spoken.

35 Then it happened, as He was coming near Jericho, that a certain blind man sat by the road begging. 36 And hearing a multitude passing by, he asked what it meant. 37 So they told him that Jesus of Nazareth was passing by. 38 And he cried out, saying, "Jesus, Son of David, have mercy on me!"

39 Then those who went before warned him that he should be quiet; but he cried out all the more, "Son of David, have mercy on me!"

40 So Jesus stood still and commanded him to be brought to Him. And when he had come near, He asked him, 41 saying, "What do you want Me to do for you?"

He said, "Lord, that I may receive my sight."

42 Then Jesus said to him, "Receive your sight; your faith has made you well." 43 And immediately he received his sight, and followed Him, glorifying God. And all the people, when they saw *it*, gave praise to God.

19 Then *Jesus* entered and passed through Jericho. 2 Now behold, *there was* a man named Zacchaeus who was a chief tax collector, and he was rich. 3 And he sought to see

18:20 *a*Exodus 20:12–16; Deuteronomy 5:16–20   18:28 *a*NU-Text reads *our own*.

Change Your Direction

Of the incredible assortment of religions in the world, why have I chosen Christianity? Because it is true. Because it deals with the problems of sin, negativity, antisocial behavior, and psychological aberrations in the most redemptive, positive way possible! It forthrightly recognizes the reality of sin. It does not try to explain it away, permitting us to keep indulging in lusts that deprive us or another person of our dignity.

Positive Christianity has at its heart a God who demonstrates perfect love. He loves us after He has seen us at our worst. That's forgiveness. Just read and consider the story of Jesus' response to the tax collector Zacchaeus, for example (Luke 19:1–10).

And forgiveness requires repentance. Repentance obviously includes regret, remorse, and a genuine sorrow for negative behavior. But it is not self-condemnation. The word *repentance* is used to translate a Greek word, *metanoia*, meaning to "turn around." Repentance means to change directions—set new goals and establish new standards. Pick up on God's dream for your life! 1. Positive repentance recognizes doubt as the real sin. So repentance is a decision to share faith. 2. Positive repentance also makes daring decisions; to seek to fulfill God's plan for my life regardless of the price!

You may choose to make this your prayer: *Lord, forgive me for not having the faith to live the life I should have lived. I am now ready to dream Your dreams, to carry the cross, and to pay the price. I pledge to live right, think right, pray right, and do right! I am trusting You to give me the power. Together, we shall succeed. Thank You, Lord. Amen.*

who Jesus was, but could not because of the crowd, for he was of short stature. 4 So he ran ahead and climbed up into a sycamore tree to see Him, for He was going to pass that *way*. 5 And when Jesus came to the place, He looked up and saw him,*a* and said to him, "Zacchaeus, make haste and come down, for today I must stay at your house." 6 So he made haste and came down, and received Him joyfully. 7 But when they saw *it*, they all complained, saying, "He has gone to be a guest with a man who is a sinner."

8 Then Zacchaeus stood and said to the Lord, "Look, Lord, I give half of my goods to the poor; and if I have taken anything from anyone by false accusation, I restore fourfold."

9 And Jesus said to him, "Today salvation has come to this house, because he also is a son of Abraham; 10 for the Son of Man has come to seek and to save that which was lost."

11 Now as they heard these things, He spoke another parable, because He was near Jerusalem and because they thought the kingdom of God would appear immediately. 12 Therefore He said: "A certain nobleman went into a far country to receive for himself a kingdom and to return. 13 So he called ten of his servants, delivered to them ten minas,*a* and said to them, 'Do business till I come.' 14 But his citizens hated him, and sent a delegation after him, saying, 'We will not have this *man* to reign over us.'

15 "And so it was that when he returned, having received the kingdom, he then commanded these servants, to whom he had given the money, to be called to him, that he might know how much every man had gained by trading. 16 Then came the first, saying, 'Master, your mina has earned ten minas.' 17 And he said to him, 'Well *done,* good servant; because you were faithful in a very little, have authority over ten cities.' 18 And the second came, saying, 'Master, your mina has earned five minas.' 19 Likewise he said to him, 'You also be over five cities.'

20 "Then another came, saying, 'Master, here is your mina, which I have kept put away in a handkerchief. 21 For I feared you, because you are an austere man. You collect what you did not deposit, and reap what you did not sow.' 22 And he said to him, 'Out of your own mouth I will judge you, *you* wicked servant. You knew that I was an austere man, collecting what I did not deposit and reaping what I did not sow. 23 Why then did you not put my money in the bank, that at my coming I might have collected it with interest?'

24 "And he said to those who stood by, 'Take the mina from him, and give *it* to him who has ten minas.' 25 ("But they said to him, 'Master, he has ten minas.') 26 For I say to you, that to everyone who has will be given; and from him who does not have, even what he has will be taken away from him. 27 But bring here those enemies of mine, who did not want me to reign over them, and slay *them* before me.' "

28 When He had said this, He went on ahead, going up to Jerusalem. 29 And it came to pass, when He drew near to Bethphage*a* and Bethany, at the mountain called Olivet, *that* He sent two of His disciples, 30 saying, "Go into the village opposite *you,* where as you enter you will find a colt tied, on which no one has ever sat. Loose it and bring *it here.* 31 And if anyone asks you, 'Why are you loosing *it?*' thus you shall say to him, 'Because the Lord has need of it.' "

32 So those who were sent went their way and found *it* just as He had said to them. 33 But as they were loosing the colt, the owners of it said to them, "Why are you loosing the colt?"

34 And they said, "The Lord has need of him." 35 Then they brought him to Jesus. And they threw their own clothes on the colt, and they set Jesus on him. 36 And as He went, *many* spread their clothes on the road.

37 Then, as He was now drawing near the descent of the Mount of Olives, the whole multitude of the disciples began to rejoice and praise God with a loud voice for all the mighty works they had seen, 38 saying:

" 'Blessed is the King who
      comes in the name of the
      LORD!'ª
  Peace in heaven and glory in
      the highest!"

39 And some of the Pharisees called to Him from the crowd, "Teacher, rebuke Your disciples."

40 But He answered and said to them, "I tell you that if these should keep silent, the stones would immediately cry out."

41 Now as He drew near, He saw the city and wept over it, 42 saying, "If you had known, even you, especially in this your day, the things *that make* for your peace! But now they are hidden from your eyes. 43 For days will come upon you when your enemies will build an embankment around you, surround you and close you in on every side, 44 and level you, and your children within you, to the ground; and they will not leave in you one stone upon another, because you did not know the time of your visitation."

45 Then He went into the temple and began to drive out those who bought and sold in it,ª 46 saying to them, "It is written, *'My house is*ª *a house of prayer,'*ᵇ but you have made it a *'den of thieves.'* "ᶜ

47 And He was teaching daily in the temple. But the chief priests, the scribes, and the leaders of the people sought to destroy Him, 48 and were unable to do anything; for all the people were very attentive to hear Him.

20 Now it happened on one of those days, as He taught the people in the temple and preached the gospel, *that* the chief priests and the scribes, together with the elders, confronted *Him* 2 and spoke to Him, saying, "Tell us, by what authority are You doing these things? Or who is he who gave You this authority?"

3 But He answered and said to them, "I also will ask you one thing, and answer Me: 4 The baptism of John—was it from heaven or from men?"

5 And they reasoned among themselves, saying, "If we say, 'From heaven,' He will say, 'Why thenª did

you not believe him?' 6 But if we say, 'From men,' all the people will stone us, for they are persuaded that John was a prophet." 7 So they answered that they did not know where *it was* from.

8 And Jesus said to them, "Neither will I tell you by what authority I do these things."

9 Then He began to tell the people this parable: "A certain man planted a vineyard, leased it to vinedressers, and went into a far country for a long time. 10 Now at vintage-time he sent a servant to the vinedressers, that they might give him some of the fruit of the vineyard. But the vinedressers beat him and sent *him* away empty-handed. 11 Again he sent another servant; and they beat him also, treated *him* shamefully, and sent *him* away empty-handed. 12 And again he sent a third; and they wounded him also and cast *him* out.

13 "Then the owner of the vineyard said, 'What shall I do? I will send my beloved son. Probably they will respect *him* when they see him.' 14 But when the vinedressers saw him, they reasoned among themselves, saying, 'This is the heir. Come, let us kill him, that the inheritance may be ours.' 15 So they cast him out of the vineyard and killed *him*. Therefore what will the owner of the vineyard do to them? 16 He will come and destroy those vinedressers and give the vineyard to others."

And when they heard *it* they said, "Certainly not!"

17 Then He looked at them and said, "What then is this that is written:

'The stone which the builders
      rejected
  Has become the chief
      cornerstone'?ª

18 Whoever falls on that stone will be broken; but on whomever it falls, it will grind him to powder."

19 And the chief priests and the scribes that very hour sought to lay hands on Him, but they feared the peopleª—for they knew He had spoken this parable against them.

20 So they watched *Him*, and sent

Render to God What Is God's

In New Testament Palestine, the Jews suffered under heavy taxation by their Roman oppressors. The Emperor demanded a tribute tax be paid as divine homage to himself. He ordered the agriculture to be taxed. The travel roads, buildings, fishing licenses, and even animals were taxed.

More than two-thirds of a person's earned income was taxed and payable to the Roman authorities. The Jewish people carried the burden of taxes to pay for the Roman wars at the other end of the empire. In addition, the Jewish people were obligated to pay temple and religious taxes. The question of taxation was a hotly contested issue during Jesus' time. Much blood was shed in tax revolts prior to and following Jesus' ministry.

One day while Jesus taught at the temple, some Pharisees and Herodians, trying to trick Jesus, asked him whether it was lawful to pay taxes to Caesar or not. While doing so, they held up a denarius. This event took place outside the main temple enclosure, for coins with images of man or beast were forbidden in the temple area.

Jesus raised His voice above the crowd and declared, "Render therefore to Caesar the things that are Caesar's, and to God the things that are God's" (Matt. 22:21). His answer satisfied the Herodian authorities and the Pharisees. It also pointed out to His followers that although they were taxed unjustly in many cases, they should not become so preoccupied with hatred and rebellion that they would be unable to spread the message of God's love and forgiveness. The Jewish people were burdened with taxes beyond reason, but Jesus taught them not to focus on the money due Caesar. Jesus knew man could not have a heart divided between mammon and God, or money would become the object of their worship (Matt. 6:24).

Caesar's image was indelibly minted on the coin, whereas Jews were forbidden to make any image of God. This was to recognize that God is above His creation as well as in His creation.

Jesus taught not against Caesar but against the worries induced by paying tribute to Caesar. In times of injustice, do not become overly concerned or robbed of the joy of serving God fully with your time, talents, and abilities. Render to God what is God's. Present yourself to God, "a living sacrifice, holy, acceptable to God," as Romans 12:1 directs.

spies who pretended to be righteous, that they might seize on His words, in order to deliver Him to the power and the authority of the governor.

21 Then they asked Him, saying, "Teacher, we know that You say and teach rightly, and You do not show personal favoritism, but teach the way of God in truth: 22 Is it lawful for us to pay taxes to Caesar or not?"

23 But He perceived their craftiness, and said to them, "Why do you test Me?ᵃ 24 Show Me a denarius. Whose image and inscription does it have?"

They answered and said, "Caesar's."

25 And He said to them, "Render therefore to Caesar the things that are Caesar's, and to God the things that are God's."

26 But they could not catch Him in His words in the presence of the people. And they marveled at His answer and kept silent.

27 Then some of the Sadducees, who deny that there is a resurrection, came to *Him* and asked Him, 28 saying: "Teacher, Moses wrote to us *that* if a man's brother dies, having a wife, and he dies without children, his brother should take his wife and raise up offspring for his brother. 29 Now there were seven brothers. And the first took a wife, and died without children. 30 And the secondᵃ took her as wife, and he died childless. 31 Then the third took her, and in like manner the seven also; and they left no children,ᵃ and died. 32 Last of all the woman died also. 33 Therefore, in the resurrection, whose wife does she become? For all seven had her as wife."

34 Jesus answered and said to them, "The sons of this age marry and are given in marriage. 35 But those who are counted worthy to attain that age, and the resurrection from the dead, neither marry nor are given in marriage; 36 nor can they die anymore, for they are equal to the angels and are sons of God, being sons of the resurrection. 37 But even Moses showed in the *burning bush passage* that the dead are raised, when he called the Lord *'the God of Abraham, the God of Isaac, and the God of Jacob.'ᵃ* 38 For He is not the God of the dead but of the living, for all live to Him."

39 Then some of the scribes answered and said, "Teacher, You have spoken well." 40 But after that they dared not question Him anymore.

41 And He said to them, "How can they say that the Christ is the Son of David? 42 Now David himself said in the Book of Psalms:

'The LORD said to my Lord,
"Sit at My right hand,
43 Till I make Your enemies Your
footstool." 'ᵃ

44 Therefore David calls Him 'Lord'; how is He then his Son?"

45 Then, in the hearing of all the people, He said to His disciples, 46 "Beware of the scribes, who desire to go around in long robes, love greetings in the marketplaces, the best seats in the synagogues, and the best places at feasts, 47 who devour widows' houses, and for a pretense make long prayers. These will receive greater condemnation."

21 And He looked up and saw the rich putting their gifts into the treasury, 2 and He saw also a certain poor widow putting in two mites. 3 So He said, "Truly I say to you that this poor widow has put in more than all; 4 for all these out of their abundance have put in offerings for God,ᵃ but she out of her poverty put in all the livelihood that she had."

5 Then, as some spoke of the temple, how it was adorned with beautiful stones and donations, He said, 6 "These things which you see—the days will come in which not *one* stone shall be left upon another that shall not be thrown down."

7 So they asked Him, saying, "Teacher, but when will these things be? And what sign *will there be* when these things are about to take place?"

8 And He said: "Take heed that you not be deceived. For many will come in My name, saying, 'I am *He*,' and, 'The time has drawn near.' Thereforeᵃ do not go after them. 9 But when you hear of wars and commotions, do not be terrified; for these things

---

20:23 ᵃNU-Text omits *Why do you test Me?*   20:30 ᵃNU-Text ends verse 30 here.   20:31 ᵃNU-Text and M-Text read *the seven also left no children.*   20:37 ᵃExodus 3:6, 15   20:43 ᵃPsalm 110:1
21:4 ᵃNU-Text omits *for God.*   21:8 ᵃNU-Text omits *Therefore.*

must come to pass first, but the end *will not come* immediately."

10 Then He said to them, "Nation will rise against nation, and kingdom against kingdom. 11 And there will be great earthquakes in various places, and famines and pestilences; and there will be fearful sights and great signs from heaven. 12 But before all these things, they will lay their hands on you and persecute *you*, delivering *you* up to the synagogues and prisons. You will be brought before kings and rulers for My name's sake. 13 But it will turn out for you as an occasion for testimony. 14 Therefore settle *it* in your hearts not to meditate beforehand on what you will answer; 15 for I will give you a mouth and wisdom which all your adversaries will not be able to contradict or resist. 16 You will be betrayed even by parents and brothers, relatives and friends; and they will put *some* of you to death. 17 And you will be hated by all for My name's sake. 18 But not a hair of your head shall be lost. 19 By your patience possess your souls.

20 "But when you see Jerusalem surrounded by armies, then know that its desolation is near. 21 Then let those who are in Judea flee to the mountains, let those who are in the midst of her depart, and let not those who are in the country enter her. 22 For these are the days of vengeance, that all things which are written may be fulfilled. 23 But woe to those who are pregnant and to those who are nursing babies in those days! For there will be great distress in the land and wrath upon this people. 24 And they will fall by the edge of the sword, and be led away captive into all nations. And Jerusalem will be trampled by Gentiles until the times of the Gentiles are fulfilled.

25 "And there will be signs in the sun, in the moon, and in the stars; and on the earth distress of nations, with perplexity, the sea and the waves roaring; 26 men's hearts failing them from fear and the expectation of those things which are coming on the earth, for the powers of the heavens will be shaken. 27 Then they will see the Son of Man coming in a cloud with power and great glory.

28 Now when these things begin to happen, look up and lift up your heads, because your redemption draws near."

29 Then He spoke to them a parable: "Look at the fig tree, and all the trees. 30 When they are already budding, you see and know for yourselves that summer is now near. 31 So you also, when you see these things happening, know that the kingdom of God is near. 32 Assuredly, I say to you, this generation will by no means pass away till all things take place. 33 Heaven and earth will pass away, but My words will by no means pass away.

34 "But take heed to yourselves, lest your hearts be weighed down with carousing, drunkenness, and cares of this life, and that Day come on you unexpectedly. 35 For it will come as a snare on all those who dwell on the face of the whole earth. 36 Watch therefore, and pray always that you may be counted worthy*a* to escape all these things that will come to pass, and to stand before the Son of Man."

37 And in the daytime He was teaching in the temple, but at night He went out and stayed on the mountain called Olivet. 38 Then early in the morning all the people came to Him in the temple to hear Him.

22 Now the Feast of Unleavened Bread drew near, which is called Passover. 2 And the chief priests and the scribes sought how they might kill Him, for they feared the people.

3 Then Satan entered Judas, surnamed Iscariot, who was numbered among the twelve. 4 So he went his way and conferred with the chief priests and captains, how he might betray Him to them. 5 And they were glad, and agreed to give him money. 6 So he promised and sought opportunity to betray Him to them in the absence of the multitude.

7 Then came the Day of Unleavened Bread, when the Passover must be killed. 8 And He sent Peter and John, saying, "Go and prepare the Passover for us, that we may eat."

9 So they said to Him, "Where do You want us to prepare?"

10 And He said to them, "Behold,

21:36 *a*NU-Text reads *may have strength.*

Gethsemane

The Garden of Gethsemane is located outside of Jerusalem across the Kidron Valley on the slopes of the Mount of Olives. Filled with beautiful, old, twisted olive trees, Gethsemane means "Garden of the Olive Press."

As Jesus and His disciples went to the garden, they passed through Jerusalem late at night, sometime between eleven and twelve o'clock. The last flickering lights of families sharing the Passover meal, celebrating God's deliverance from Egypt, glowed from inside the houses along the city streets. When the small band arrived in Gethsemane, the disciples, tired and full from the feast, retired under the many trees.

Jesus, however, knowing what was before Him, prayed in anguish to God for help and strength. He knew that all things were possible with God, and even asked God to take away the "cup" He was called upon to drink. Yet our Lord added the phase, "Nevertheless not My will, but Yours, be done" (Luke 22:42). How dejected and saddened Jesus must have been as He knelt in the olive grove. Even His closest friends slept during His greatest time of need. Yet Jesus knew God would stand by and strengthen Him to carry out His purpose to redeem the lost and hurting world.

In the darkness of the night, the sound of horses on the limestone block streets was soon heard. Light from the torches carried by the Roman cohort also revealed the faces of the temple officers, chief priests, elders, scribes, and Judas Iscariot. When Judas gave Jesus the betrayal kiss, he probably used the common Passover greeting to kiss a friend or relative on both cheeks.

Jesus asked the Roman soldiers, "Whom are you seeking?" They answered Him, "Jesus of Nazareth." Jesus replied, "I am *He*" (John 18:4, 5). Immediately, the Romans drew back and fell to the ground. The Romans probably expected Jesus to be a revolutionary with a band of followers like so many others who had revolted against Rome in Jerusalem. The fact that a cohort, consisting of six hundred men, came to arrest Jesus indicates they anticipated a fight.

After speaking a word of release to His followers, Jesus was alone to be taken to trial for crimes He never committed. His disciples and friends had deserted Him, but Jesus had confidence and the knowledge that God would never desert Him. Jesus' demonstration of faith in God allows us the confidence that even when trials come and our friends and companions desert us, God will offer us the same protection and love He gave to His Son. Isaiah 53:7 foretold Jesus' arrest and punishment by death as a picture of a lamb led to slaughter. And Isaiah 53:11 added that Jesus' travail would result in the justification of many!

when you have entered the city, a man will meet you carrying a pitcher of water; follow him into the house which he enters. 11 Then you shall say to the master of the house, 'The Teacher says to you, "Where is the guest room where I may eat the Passover with My disciples?" ' 12 Then he will show you a large, furnished upper room; there make ready."

13 So they went and found it just as He had said to them, and they prepared the Passover.

14 When the hour had come, He sat down, and the twelve[a] apostles with Him. 15 Then He said to them, "With *fervent* desire I have desired to eat this Passover with you before I suffer; 16 for I say to you, I will no longer eat of it until it is fulfilled in the kingdom of God."

17 Then He took the cup, and gave thanks, and said, "Take this and divide *it* among yourselves; 18 for I say to you,[a] I will not drink of the fruit of the vine until the kingdom of God comes."

19 And He took bread, gave thanks and broke *it,* and gave *it* to them, saying, "This is My body which is given for you; do this in remembrance of Me."

20 Likewise He also *took* the cup after supper, saying, "This cup *is* the new covenant in My blood, which is shed for you. 21 But behold, the hand of My betrayer *is* with Me on the table. 22 And truly the Son of Man goes as it has been determined, but woe to that man by whom He is betrayed!"

23 Then they began to question among themselves, which of them it was who would do this thing.

24 Now there was also a dispute among them, as to which of them should be considered the greatest. 25 And He said to them, "The kings of the Gentiles exercise lordship over them, and those who exercise authority over them are called 'benefactors.' 26 But not so *among* you; on the contrary, he who is greatest among you, let him be as the younger, and he who governs as he who serves. 27 For who *is* greater, he who sits at the table, or he who serves? *Is* it not he who sits at the table? Yet I am

among you as the One who serves. 28 "But you are those who have continued with Me in My trials. 29 And I bestow upon you a kingdom, just as My Father bestowed *one* upon Me, 30 that you may eat and drink at My table in My kingdom, and sit on thrones judging the twelve tribes of Israel."

31 And the Lord said,[a] "Simon, Simon! Indeed, Satan has asked for you, that he may sift *you* as wheat. 32 But I have prayed for you, that your faith should not fail; and when you have returned to *Me,* strengthen your brethren."

33 But he said to Him, "Lord, I am ready to go with You, both to prison and to death."

34 Then He said, "I tell you, Peter, the rooster shall not crow this day before you will deny three times that you know Me."

35 And He said to them, "When I sent you without money bag, knapsack, and sandals, did you lack anything?"

So they said, "Nothing."

36 Then He said to them, "But now, he who has a money bag, let him take *it,* and likewise a knapsack; and he who has no sword, let him sell his garment and buy one. 37 For I say to you that this which is written must still be accomplished in Me: 'And He *was numbered with the transgressors.'*[a] For the things concerning Me have an end."

38 So they said, "Lord, look, here *are* two swords."

And He said to them, "It is enough."

39 Coming out, He went to the Mount of Olives, as He was accustomed, and His disciples also followed Him. 40 When He came to the place, He said to them, "Pray that you may not enter into temptation."

41 And He was withdrawn from them about a stone's throw, and He knelt down and prayed, 42 saying, "Father, if it is Your will, take this cup away from Me; nevertheless not My will, but Yours, be done." 43 Then an angel appeared to Him from heaven, strengthening Him. 44 And being in agony, He prayed more earnestly. Then His sweat be-

22:14 [a]NU-Text omits *twelve.* 22:18 [a]NU-Text adds *from now on.* 22:31 [a]NU-Text omits *And the Lord said.* 22:37 [a]Isaiah 53:12

came like great drops of blood falling down to the ground.[a]

45 When He rose up from prayer, and had come to His disciples, He found them sleeping from sorrow. 46 Then He said to them, "Why do you sleep? Rise and pray, lest you enter into temptation."

47 And while He was still speaking, behold, a multitude; and he who was called Judas, one of the twelve, went before them and drew near to Jesus to kiss Him. 48 But Jesus said to him, "Judas, are you betraying the Son of Man with a kiss?"

49 When those around Him saw what was going to happen, they said to Him, "Lord, shall we strike with the sword?" 50 And one of them struck the servant of the high priest and cut off his right ear.

51 But Jesus answered and said, "Permit even this." And He touched his ear and healed him.

52 Then Jesus said to the chief priests, captains of the temple, and the elders who had come to Him, "Have you come out, as against a robber, with swords and clubs? 53 When I was with you daily in the temple, you did not try to seize Me. But this is your hour, and the power of darkness."

54 Having arrested Him, they led Him and brought Him into the high priest's house. But Peter followed at a distance. 55 Now when they had kindled a fire in the midst of the courtyard and sat down together, Peter sat among them. 56 And a certain servant girl, seeing him as he sat by the fire, looked intently at him and said, "This man was also with Him."

57 But he denied Him,[a] saying, "Woman, I do not know Him."

58 And after a little while another saw him and said, "You also are of them."

But Peter said, "Man, I am not!"

59 Then after about an hour had passed, another confidently affirmed, saying, "Surely this *fellow* also was with Him, for he is a Galilean."

60 But Peter said, "Man, I do not know what you are saying!"

Immediately, while he was still speaking, the rooster[a] crowed.

61 And the Lord turned and looked at Peter. Then Peter remembered the word of the Lord, how He had said to him, "Before the rooster crows,[a] you will deny Me three times." 62 So Peter went out and wept bitterly.

63 Now the men who held Jesus mocked Him and beat Him. 64 And having blindfolded Him, they struck Him on the face and asked Him,[a] saying, "Prophesy! Who is the one who struck You?" 65 And many other things they blasphemously spoke against Him.

66 As soon as it was day, the elders of the people, both chief priests and scribes, came together and led Him into their council, saying, 67 "If You are the Christ, tell us."

But He said to them, "If I tell you, you will by no means believe. 68 And if I also ask *you*, you will by no means answer Me or let *Me* go.[a] 69 Hereafter the Son of Man will sit on the right hand of the power of God."

70 Then they all said, "Are You then the Son of God?"

So He said to them, "You *rightly* say that I am."

71 And they said, "What further testimony do we need? For we have heard it ourselves from His own mouth."

23 Then the whole multitude of them arose and led Him to Pilate. 2 And they began to accuse Him, saying, "We found this *fellow* perverting the[a] nation, and forbidding to pay taxes to Caesar, saying that He Himself is Christ, a King."

3 Then Pilate asked Him, saying, "Are You the King of the Jews?"

He answered him and said, "*It is as* you say."

4 So Pilate said to the chief priests and the crowd, "I find no fault in this Man."

5 But they were the more fierce, saying, "He stirs up the people, teaching throughout all Judea, beginning from Galilee to this place."

6 When Pilate heard of Galilee,[a] he asked if the Man were a Galilean. 7 And as soon as he knew that He

22:44 [a]NU-Text brackets verses 43 and 44 as not in the original text.   22:57 [a]NU-Text reads *denied it*. 22:60 [a]NU-Text and M-Text read *a rooster*.   22:61 [a]NU-Text adds *today*.   22:64 [a]NU-Text reads *And having blindfolded Him, they asked Him*.   22:68 [a]NU-Text omits *also* and *Me or let Me go*. 23:2 [a]NU-Text reads *our*.   23:6 [a]NU-Text omits *of Galilee*.

belonged to Herod's jurisdiction, he sent Him to Herod, who was also in Jerusalem at that time. 8 Now when Herod saw Jesus, he was exceedingly glad; for he had desired for a long *time* to see Him, because he had heard many things about Him, and he hoped to see some miracle done by Him. 9 Then he questioned Him with many words, but He answered him nothing. 10 And the chief priests and scribes stood and vehemently accused Him. 11 Then Herod, with his men of war, treated Him with contempt and mocked *Him,* arrayed Him in a gorgeous robe, and sent Him back to Pilate. 12 That very day Pilate and Herod became friends with each other, for previously they had been at enmity with each other.

13 Then Pilate, when he had called together the chief priests, the rulers, and the people, 14 said to them, "You have brought this Man to me, as one who misleads the people. And indeed, having examined *Him* in your presence, I have found no fault in this Man concerning those things of which you accuse Him; 15 no, neither did Herod, for I sent you back to him;*a* and indeed nothing deserving of death has been done by Him. 16 I will therefore chastise Him and release *Him*" 17 (for it was necessary for him to release one to them at the feast).*a*

18 And they all cried out at once, saying, "Away with this *Man,* and release to us Barabbas"— 19 who had been thrown into prison for a certain rebellion made in the city, and for murder.

20 Pilate, therefore, wishing to release Jesus, again called out to them. 21 But they shouted, saying, "Crucify *Him,* crucify Him!"

22 Then he said to them the third time, "Why, what evil has He done? I have found no reason for death in Him. I will therefore chastise Him and let *Him* go."

23 But they were insistent, demanding with loud voices that He be crucified. And the voices of these men and of the chief priests prevailed.*a* 24 So Pilate gave sentence that it should be as they requested. 25 And

he released to them*a* the one they requested, who for rebellion and murder had been thrown into prison; but he delivered Jesus to their will.

26 Now as they led Him away, they laid hold of a certain man, Simon a Cyrenian, who was coming from the country, and on him they laid the cross that he might bear *it* after Jesus.

27 And a great multitude of the people followed Him, and women who also mourned and lamented Him. 28 But Jesus, turning to them, said, "Daughters of Jerusalem, do not weep for Me, but weep for yourselves and for your children. 29 For indeed the days are coming in which they will say, 'Blessed *are* the barren, wombs that never bore, and breasts which never nursed!' 30 Then they will begin *'to say to the mountains, "Fall on us!" and to the hills, "Cover us!" '*a 31 For if they do these things in the green wood, what will be done in the dry?"

32 There were also two others, criminals, led with Him to be put to death. 33 And when they had come to the place called Calvary, there they crucified Him, and the criminals, one on the right hand and the other on the left. 34 Then Jesus said, "Father, forgive them, for they do not know what they do."*a*

And they divided His garments and cast lots. 35 And the people stood looking on. But even the rulers with them sneered, saying, "He saved others; let Him save Himself if He is the Christ, the chosen of God."

36 The soldiers also mocked Him, coming and offering Him sour wine, 37 and saying, "If You are the King of the Jews, save Yourself."

38 And an inscription also was written over Him in letters of Greek, Latin, and Hebrew:*a*

THIS IS THE KING
OF THE JEWS.

39 Then one of the criminals who were hanged blasphemed Him, saying, "If You are the Christ,*a* save Yourself and us."

40 But the other, answering, rebuked him, saying, "Do you not even

---

23:15 *a*NU-Text reads *for he sent Him back to us.*   23:17 *a*NU-Text omits verse 17.   23:23 *a*NU-Text omits *and of the chief priests.*   23:25 *a*NU-Text and M-Text omit *to them.*   23:30 *a*Hosea 10:8
23:34 *a*NU-Text brackets the first sentence as a later addition.   23:38 *a*NU-Text omits *written* and *in letters of Greek, Latin, and Hebrew.*   23:39 *a*NU-Text reads *Are You not the Christ?*

The Empty Tomb— A Silent Witness

Through the centuries various theories have been advanced to explain away the resurrection of Jesus Christ. Yet, in light of the facts concerning Jesus' death and burial, these theories remain unconvincing.

After Jesus Christ was crucified under Roman authority, His body was taken down from the cross to be buried. As was the custom of the day, His body was wrapped in approximately one hundred pounds of preserving burial ointment. He was then placed in the tomb of a Jerusalem Sanhedrin member, Joseph of Arimathea.

A Roman guard, consisting of twelve men from the empire's crack legion, was stationed in front of Jesus' tomb. The soldiers were under orders that no one was to come near the tomb. Should they leave their post for any reason, the punishment was death. The Roman and Jewish leaders secured the burial place of Jesus by ordering a heavy stone to be placed in front of the tomb's opening. Finally, the emperor's seal of authority was fixed to the stone covering the tomb. Anyone who broke the seal was punished by death.

Yet, somehow, three days later the tomb of Christ was empty. The followers of Jesus claimed that He had risen from the dead. Did He? If not, what were the alternatives? Could the Jewish leaders have stolen the body? No, for they had no motive and certainly could not have overpowered the Roman soldiers. Also, they would have produced the body to disprove the resurrection claims of the Christians.

Could the disciples have stolen the body? These men, who abandoned Jesus at

His arrest and crucifixion, did not possess the military power or any other means to over-throw twelve of the emperor's top guards, who were within shouting distance of the entire Roman garrison. On the contrary, the disciples were frightened and secretly hid in the city. Could the women have stolen the body? Three women moving an enormous stone after overpowering twelve Roman soldiers is hardly plausible.

It has been suggested that Jesus Christ was not completely dead; somehow He regained consciousness in the cold tomb; rid himself of one hundred pounds of ointment; pushed a two-ton stone away; overpowered twelve Roman soldiers; then walked into the city on feet that had been pierced by nails, and appeared to His disciples and followers as the Lord of Life.

All of these theories are preposterous. The only possible explanation is that Jesus Christ was resurrected from the dead by the power of God the Father on the morning we now call Easter. The empty tomb still stands as a silent witness inviting even the most crit-ical skeptic to examine the evidence concerning Jesus Christ's resurrection.

You may ask, "Then where does faith come in?" Christian faith is based on his-torical reality, not blind subjectivity. There is much evidence supporting the resurrection of Jesus which can be examined by anyone who wishes to approach Scripture from a his-torical perspective.

Yet there remains another very important aspect of our faith. That is commit-ment to the resurrected Jesus Christ. This level of commitment always goes beyond the knowledge of the facts.

There is sufficient physical and historical evidence to warrant belief in the risen Christ. But faith is required by God of believers. With belief comes assurance and rest, Hebrews 4:3 says.

In 1 Peter 3:15, the apostle Peter also urges us to become familiar with the facts concerning Christ's resurrection so we can give intelligent, reasonable answers of the hope within us to anyone who should ask.

fear God, seeing you are under the same condemnation? 41 And we indeed justly, for we receive the due reward of our deeds; but this Man has done nothing wrong." 42 Then he said to Jesus, "Lord,ᵃ remember me when You come into Your kingdom."

43 And Jesus said to him, "Assuredly, I say to you, today you will be with Me in Paradise."

44 Now it wasᵃ about the sixth hour, and there was darkness over all the earth until the ninth hour. 45 Then the sun was darkened,ᵃ and the veil of the temple was torn in two. 46 And when Jesus had cried out with a loud voice, He said, "Father, 'into Your hands I commit My spirit.'"ᵃ Having said this, He breathed His last.

47 So when the centurion saw what had happened, he glorified God, saying, "Certainly this was a righteous Man!"

48 And the whole crowd who came together to that sight, seeing what had been done, beat their breasts and returned. 49 But all His acquaintances, and the women who followed Him from Galilee, stood at a distance, watching these things.

50 Now behold, there was a man named Joseph, a council member, a good and just man. 51 He had not consented to their decision and deed. He was from Arimathea, a city of the Jews, who himself was also waitingᵃ for the kingdom of God. 52 This man went to Pilate and asked for the body of Jesus. 53 Then he took it down, wrapped it in linen, and laid it in a tomb that was hewn out of the rock, where no one had ever lain before. 54 That day was the Preparation, and the Sabbath drew near.

55 And the women who had come with Him from Galilee followed after, and they observed the tomb and how His body was laid. 56 Then they returned and prepared spices and fragrant oils. And they rested on the Sabbath according to the commandment.

24 Now on the first day of the week, very early in the morning, they, and certain other women with them,ᵃ came to the tomb bringing the spices which they had prepared. 2 But they found the stone rolled away from the tomb. 3 Then they went in and did not find the body of the Lord Jesus. 4 And it happened, as they were greatlyᵃ perplexed about this, that behold, two men stood by them in shining garments. 5 Then, as they were afraid and bowed their faces to the earth, they said to them, "Why do you seek the living among the dead? 6 He is not here, but is risen! Remember how He spoke to you when He was still in Galilee, 7 saying, 'The Son of Man must be delivered into the hands of sinful men, and be crucified, and the third day rise again.'"

8 And they remembered His words. 9 Then they returned from the tomb and told all these things to the eleven and to all the rest. 10 It was Mary Magdalene, Joanna, Mary the mother of James, and the other women with them, who told these things to the apostles. 11 And their words seemed to them like idle tales, and they did not believe them. 12 But Peter arose and ran to the tomb; and stooping down, he saw the linen cloths lyingᵃ by themselves; and he departed, marveling to himself at what had happened.

13 Now behold, two of them were traveling that same day to a village called Emmaus, which was seven milesᵃ from Jerusalem. 14 And they talked together of all these things which had happened. 15 So it was, while they conversed and reasoned, that Jesus Himself drew near and went with them. 16 But their eyes were restrained, so that they did not know Him.

17 And He said to them, "What kind of conversation is this that you have with one another as you walk and are sad?"ᵃ

18 Then the one whose name was Cleopas answered and said to Him, "Are You the only stranger in Jerusalem, and have You not known the things which happened there in these days?"

23:42 ᵃNU-Text reads And he said, "Jesus, remember me.
23:45 ᵃNU-Text reads obscured.   23:46 ᵃPsalm 31:5   23:44 ᵃNU-Text adds already.
24:1 ᵃNU-Text omits and certain other women with them.   23:51 ᵃNU-Text reads who was waiting.
24:12 ᵃNU-Text omits lying.   24:13 ᵃLiterally sixty stadia   24:4 ᵃNU-Text omits greatly.
And they stood still, looking sad.   24:17 ᵃNU-Text reads as you walk?

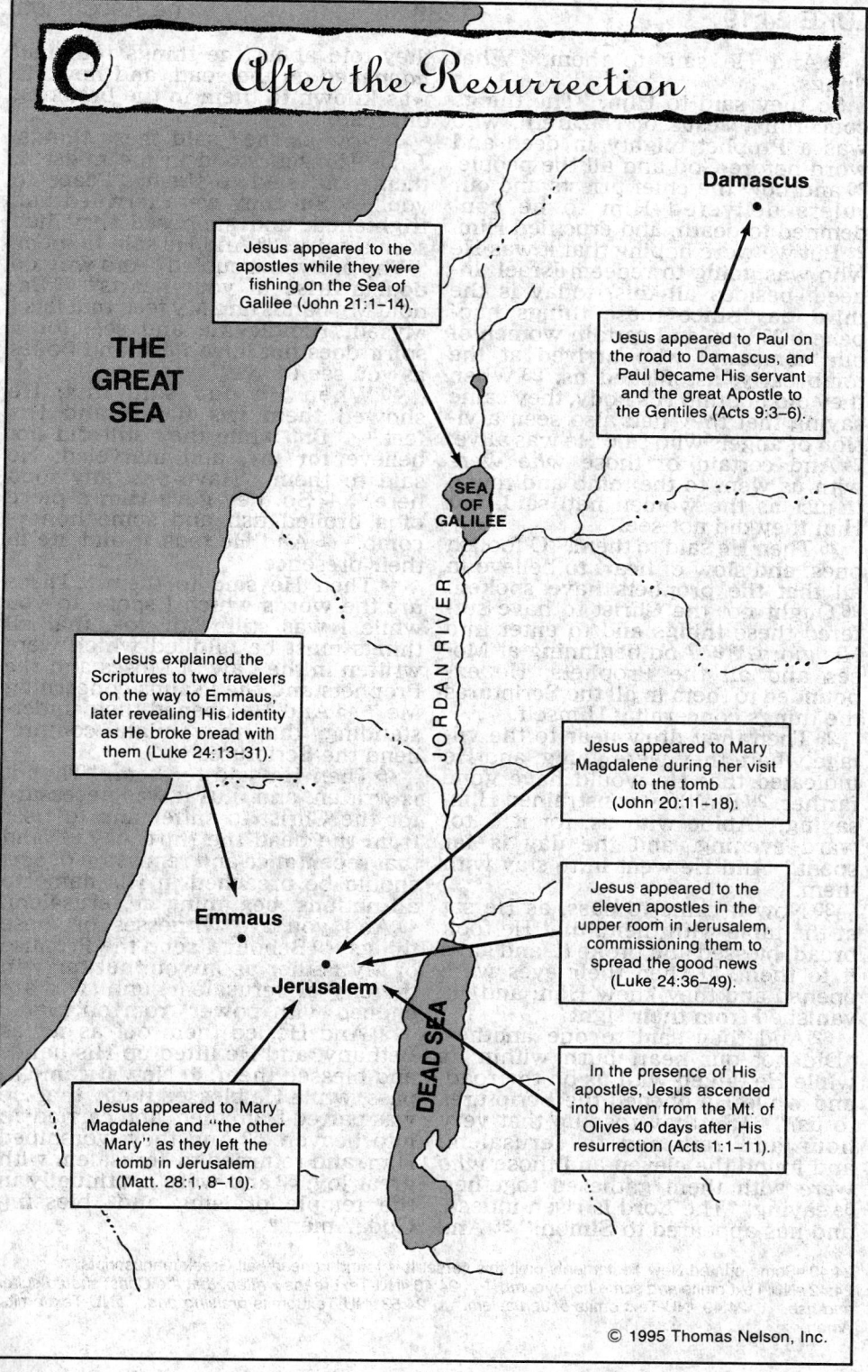

After the Resurrection

Damascus

Jesus appeared to the apostles while they were fishing on the Sea of Galilee (John 21:1–14).

Jesus appeared to Paul on the road to Damascus, and Paul became His servant and the great Apostle to the Gentiles (Acts 9:3–6).

THE GREAT SEA

SEA OF GALILEE

JORDAN RIVER

Jesus explained the Scriptures to two travelers on the way to Emmaus, later revealing His identity as He broke bread with them (Luke 24:13–31).

Jesus appeared to Mary Magdalene during her visit to the tomb (John 20:11–18).

Jesus appeared to the eleven apostles in the upper room in Jerusalem, commissioning them to spread the good news (Luke 24:36–49).

Emmaus

Jerusalem

DEAD SEA

Jesus appeared to Mary Magdalene and ''the other Mary'' as they left the tomb in Jerusalem (Matt. 28:1, 8–10).

In the presence of His apostles, Jesus ascended into heaven from the Mt. of Olives 40 days after His resurrection (Acts 1:1–11).

© 1995 Thomas Nelson, Inc.

19 And He said to them, "What things?"

So they said to Him, "The things concerning Jesus of Nazareth, who was a Prophet mighty in deed and word before God and all the people, 20 and how the chief priests and our rulers delivered Him to be condemned to death, and crucified Him. 21 But we were hoping that it was He who was going to redeem Israel. Indeed, besides all this, today is the third day since these things happened. 22 Yes, and certain women of our company, who arrived at the tomb early, astonished us. 23 When they did not find His body, they came saying that they had also seen a vision of angels who said He was alive. 24 And certain of those *who were* with us went to the tomb and found *it* just as the women had said; but Him they did not see."

25 Then He said to them, "O foolish ones, and slow of heart to believe in all that the prophets have spoken! 26 Ought not the Christ to have suffered these things and to enter into His glory?" 27 And beginning at Moses and all the Prophets, He expounded to them in all the Scriptures the things concerning Himself.

28 Then they drew near to the village where they were going, and He indicated that He would have gone farther. 29 But they constrained Him, saying, "Abide with us, for it is toward evening, and the day is far spent." And He went in to stay with them.

30 Now it came to pass, as He sat at the table with them, that He took bread, blessed and broke *it*, and gave it to them. 31 Then their eyes were opened and they knew Him; and He vanished from their sight.

32 And they said to one another, "Did not our heart burn within us while He talked with us on the road, and while He opened the Scriptures to us?" 33 So they rose up that very hour and returned to Jerusalem, and found the eleven and those *who were* with them gathered together, 34 saying, "The Lord is risen indeed, and has appeared to Simon!" 35 And they told about the things *that had happened* on the road, and how He was known to them in the breaking of bread.

36 Now as they said these things, Jesus Himself stood in the midst of them, and said to them, "Peace to you." 37 But they were terrified and frightened, and supposed they had seen a spirit. 38 And He said to them, "Why are you troubled? And why do doubts arise in your hearts? 39 Behold My hands and My feet, that it is I Myself. Handle Me and see, for a spirit does not have flesh and bones as you see I have."

40 When He had said this, He showed them His hands and His feet.*a* 41 But while they still did not believe for joy, and marveled, He said to them, "Have you any food here?" 42 So they gave Him a piece of a broiled fish and some honeycomb.*a* 43 And He took *it* and ate in their presence.

44 Then He said to them, "These *are* the words which I spoke to you while I was still with you, that all things must be fulfilled which were written in the Law of Moses and *the* Prophets and *the* Psalms concerning Me." 45 And He opened their understanding, that they might comprehend the Scriptures.

46 Then He said to them, "Thus it is written, and thus it was necessary for the Christ to suffer and to rise*a* from the dead the third day, 47 and that repentance and remission of sins should be preached in His name to all nations, beginning at Jerusalem. 48 And you are witnesses of these things. 49 Behold, I send the Promise of My Father upon you; but tarry in the city of Jerusalem*a* until you are endued with power from on high."

50 And He led them out as far as Bethany, and He lifted up His hands and blessed them. 51 Now it came to pass, while He blessed them, that He was parted from them and carried up into heaven. 52 And they worshiped Him, and returned to Jerusalem with great joy, 53 and were continually in the temple praising and*a* blessing God. Amen.*b*

24:40 *a*Some printed New Testaments omit this verse. It is found in nearly all Greek manuscripts.
24:42 *a*NU-Text omits *and some honeycomb.*　　24:46 *a*NU-Text reads *written, that the Christ should suffer and rise.*　　24:49 *a*NU-Text omits *of Jerusalem.*　　24:53 *a*NU-Text omits *praising and.*　　*b*NU-Text omits *Amen.*

John

Overview of John

The apostle John, in an artistic theological masterpiece, presents the love of God as demonstrated in the person and work of Jesus Christ. Written probably between A.D. 80 and 90, John's aim is to reveal Jesus as the incarnate Word of God, who came to establish the proper relationship between God and man.

John's Gospel is theological in its treatment of the events in the life of Jesus Christ. More than the three synoptic Gospels, John gives his readers a personal look into the love God has for the world. "For God so loved the world that He gave His only begotten Son, that whoever believes in Him should not perish but have everlasting life" (John 3:16).

Identified as the disciple "whom Jesus loved," John was a Palestinian Jew whose meticulous attention to numbers and names indicates he was an eyewitness to the events of the Gospel.

John records some of the prayers and teachings of Jesus that are not mentioned in the other Gospels. He includes the "I am" passages in which Jesus reveals the relationship between God and man.

I am the bread of life (John 6:48).
I am the light of the world (John 8:12).
I am the door of the sheep (John 10:7).
I am the good shepherd (John 10:11).
I am the resurrection and the life (John 11:25).
I am the way, the truth, and the life (John 14:6).
I am the true vine (John 15:1).

In chapters 15—17, John interweaves the experience of loving relationships with others to a dependence upon a right relationship with God. Jesus Himself is the great vehicle of God's love for us, presenting us as His friends before God. "Greater love has no one than this, than to lay down one's life for his friends" (John 15:13).

John truly is the "Gospel of Love" as Jesus brings us into a loving relationship with God and others. Then we can go out and proclaim, "God loves you and so do I."

Jesus in John

John powerfully states the deity of the incarnate Son of God. "A Man called Jesus" (9:11) is also "Christ, the Son of the living God" (6:69). The deity of Christ can be seen in the seven statements: "I am." The seven signs (chapters 1—12) and the five witnesses (5:30–40) also point to His divine character. Some of the most crucial affirmations of Christ's deity are found in John 1:1, 8:58, 10:30, 14:9, and 20:28.

The humanity of Jesus can also be seen in John 4:6, 4:7, 5:19, 11:35, 12:27 and chapter 19. Jesus, the Word, is fully God (1:1), yet fully human (1:14). John portrays the living Word of God as He walked on earth.

Keys to John

Key Word: Believe Jesus is the Son of God. This Gospel of John clearly states its purpose: "But these are written that you may believe that Jesus is the Christ, the Son of God, and that believing you may have life in His name" (20:31). John gives mighty intellectual and spiritual proof for conviction about Jesus as God's Son. The Gospel calls the hearer to faith and eternal life.

Key Verses: "He came to His own, and His own did not receive Him. But as many as received Him, to them He gave the right to become children of God, to those who believe in His name: who were born, not of blood, nor of the will of the flesh, nor of the will of man, but of God" (1:11–13).

"And truly Jesus did many other signs in the presence of His disciples, which are not written in this book; but these are written that you may believe that Jesus is the Christ, the Son of God, and that believing you may have life in His name" (20:30, 31).

Key Chapter: John 3. John 3:16 is the most often preached verse in all of Scripture. Captured in it is the essence of the Gospel: Salvation is a gift of God obtainable only through faith in Jesus. The conversation with Nicodemus and the testimony of John the Baptist provide the setting that clearly points out that the only way to the Kingdom of God is to be "born again."

1 In the beginning was the Word, and the Word was with God, and the Word was God. 2 He was in the beginning with God. 3 All things were made through Him, and without Him nothing was made that was made. 4 In Him was life, and the life was the light of men. 5 And the light shines in the darkness, and the darkness did not comprehend*a* it.

6 There was a man sent from God, whose name *was* John. 7 This man came for a witness, to bear witness of the Light, that all through him might believe. 8 He was not that Light, but *was sent* to bear witness of that Light. 9 That was the true Light which gives light to every man coming into the world.*a*

10 He was in the world, and the world was made through Him, and the world did not know Him. 11 He came to His own,*a* and His own*b* did not receive Him. 12 But as many as received Him, to them He gave the right to become children of God, to those who believe in His name: 13 who were born, not of blood, nor of the will of the flesh, nor of the will of man, but of God.

14 And the Word became flesh and dwelt among us, and we beheld His glory, the glory as of the only begotten of the Father, full of grace and truth.

15 John bore witness of Him and cried out, saying, "This was He of whom I said, 'He who comes after me is preferred before me, for He was before me.' "

16 And*a* of His fullness we have all received, and grace for grace. 17 For the law was given through Moses, *but* grace and truth came through Jesus Christ. 18 No one has seen God at any time. The only begotten Son,*a* who is in the bosom of the Father, He has declared *Him.*

19 Now this is the testimony of John, when the Jews sent priests and Levites from Jerusalem to ask him, "Who are you?"

20 He confessed, and did not deny, but confessed, "I am not the Christ."

21 And they asked him, "What then? Are you Elijah?"

He said, "I am not."

"Are you the Prophet?"

And he answered, "No."

22 Then they said to him, "Who are you, that we may give an answer to those who sent us? What do you say about yourself?"

23 He said: "I *am*

    'The voice of one crying in the wilderness:

    "Make straight the way of the LORD," 'a*

as the prophet Isaiah said."

24 Now those who were sent were from the Pharisees. 25 And they asked him, saying, "Why then do you baptize if you are not the Christ, nor Elijah, nor the Prophet?"

26 John answered them, saying, "I baptize with water, but there stands One among you whom you do not know. 27 It is He who, coming after me, is preferred before me, whose sandal strap I am not worthy to loose."

28 These things were done in Bethabara*a* beyond the Jordan, where John was baptizing.

29 The next day John saw Jesus coming toward him, and said, "Behold! The Lamb of God who takes away the sin of the world! 30 This is He of whom I said, 'After me comes a Man who is preferred before me, for He was before me.' 31 I did not know Him; but that He should be revealed to Israel, therefore I came baptizing with water."

32 And John bore witness, saying, "I saw the Spirit descending from heaven like a dove, and He remained upon Him. 33 I did not know Him, but He who sent me to baptize with water said to me, 'Upon whom you see the Spirit descending, and remaining on Him, this is He who baptizes with the Holy Spirit.' 34 And I have seen and testified that this is the Son of God."

Family of God

Jesus placed us in the most intimate relationship with God—calling us sons and daughters. In the ancient world, the firstborn son of a household possessed great authority and power. He was the first in the line of succession to his father's household. Everything under his father's jurisdiction and authority was granted by birthright to the oldest son.

Of particular interest was the son's power to grant freedom to slaves and to adopt other people as members of his family. These adopted sons and daughters were then granted the same privileges as the son. This cultural background forms the basis for Jesus' statement, "Therefore if the Son makes you free, you shall be free indeed" (John 8:36).

As the Son of God, Jesus has the sole right to free us of our sin, guilt, low self-esteem, and negative self-image. He grants us to share in an intimate relationship similar to the one He possesses with God His Father. We are given the right to speak to God as *Abba,* meaning "Daddy," instead of the more traditional address of *Avinu,* meaning "Our Father." In Jesus' day it was unthinkable to address God the Creator of the universe in such intimate terms. Throughout the New Testament this privilege was extolled by all of the early Christians and teachers. Paul assures us, in Galatians 4:4–7, that we have received the spirit of adoption as sons and daughters of God and that we can cry out 'Abba, Father.' "

We have been granted a birthright by the firstborn Son of God, Jesus Christ, who has adopted us into the family of God. Ephesians 1:5 relates how it pleased Abba, Father to adopt sons and daughters for Himself.

35 Again, the next day, John stood with two of his disciples. 36 And looking at Jesus as He walked, he said, "Behold the Lamb of God!"

37 The two disciples heard him speak, and they followed Jesus. 38 Then Jesus turned, and seeing them following, said to them, "What do you seek?"

They said to Him, "Rabbi" (which is to say, when translated, Teacher), "where are You staying?"

39 He said to them, "Come and see." They came and saw where He was staying, and remained with Him that day (now it was about the tenth hour).

40 One of the two who heard John *speak,* and followed Him, was Andrew, Simon Peter's brother. 41 He first found his own brother Simon, and said to him, "We have found the Messiah" (which is translated, the Christ). 42 And he brought him to Jesus.

Now when Jesus looked at him, He said, "You are Simon the son of Jonah.a You shall be called Cephas" (which is translated, A Stone).

43 The following day Jesus wanted to go to Galilee, and He found Philip and said to him, "Follow Me." 44 Now Philip was from Bethsaida, the city of Andrew and Peter. 45 Philip found Nathanael and said to him, "We have found Him of whom Moses in the law, and also the prophets, wrote—Jesus of Nazareth, the son of Joseph."

46 And Nathanael said to him, "Can anything good come out of Nazareth?"

Philip said to him, "Come and see."

47 Jesus saw Nathanael coming toward Him, and said of him, "Behold, an Israelite indeed, in whom is no deceit!"

48 Nathanael said to Him, "How do You know me?"

Jesus answered and said to him, "Before Philip called you, when you were under the fig tree, I saw you."

49 Nathanael answered and said to Him, "Rabbi, You are the Son of God! You are the King of Israel!"

50 Jesus answered and said to him, "Because I said to you, 'I saw you under the fig tree,' do you believe? You will see greater things than these." 51 And He said to him, "Most assuredly, I say to you, hereaftera you shall see heaven open, and the angels of God ascending and descending upon the Son of Man."

2 On the third day there was a wedding in Cana of Galilee, and the mother of Jesus was there. 2 Now both Jesus and His disciples were invited to the wedding. 3 And when they ran out of wine, the mother of Jesus said to Him, "They have no wine."

4 Jesus said to her, "Woman, what does your concern have to do with Me? My hour has not yet come."

5 His mother said to the servants, "Whatever He says to you, do *it.*"

6 Now there were set there six waterpots of stone, according to the manner of purification of the Jews, containing twenty or thirty gallons apiece. 7 Jesus said to them, "Fill the waterpots with water." And they filled them up to the brim. 8 And He said to them, "Draw *some* out now, and take *it* to the master of the feast." And they took *it.* 9 When the master of the feast had tasted the water that was made wine, and did not know where it came from (but the servants who had drawn the water knew), the master of the feast called the bridegroom. 10 And he said to him, "Every man at the beginning sets out the good wine, and when the *guests* have well drunk, then the inferior. You have kept the good wine until now!"

11 This beginning of signs Jesus did in Cana of Galilee, and manifested His glory; and His disciples believed in Him.

12 After this He went down to Capernaum, He, His mother, His brothers, and His disciples; and they did not stay there many days.

13 Now the Passover of the Jews was at hand, and Jesus went up to Jerusalem. 14 And He found in the temple those who sold oxen and sheep and doves, and the money changers doing business. 15 When He had made a whip of cords, He drove them all out of the temple, with the sheep and the oxen, and poured out the changers' money and overturned the tables. 16 And He said to those who sold doves, "Take these things away! Do not make My Father's house a house of merchandise!"

1:42 aNU-Text reads *John.*   1:51 aNU-Text omits *hereafter.*

The Spirit of God

Jesus drew from God's creation to describe the nature of God. To illustrate the Spirit of God, Jesus likened it to the wind. In the well-known dialogue with Nicodemus, Jesus said, "The wind blows where it wishes, and you hear the sound of it, but cannot tell where it comes from and where it goes. So is everyone who is born of the Spirit" (John 3:8).

The winds of Jerusalem shift constantly. Exposed on the top of a ridge, the city has winds coming from every direction of the compass. The nature of the winds also varies from a hot east desert wind to a cool Mediterranean breeze. In the course of a day, the winds can shift four or five times.

We cannot physically see the Spirit of God. But just as we see evidence of the wind blowing through the trees, so we can see the effects of the Spirit of God at work in our lives. We hear the rush and rustle of the wind in nature. Likewise, we hear the Spirit of God in the words and deeds of His people.

As a Jew, Jesus sometimes spoke in the Hebrew language. The same word for wind, *ruah*, also means spirit. In the play on words, Jesus gave a beautiful description of the Spirit of God.

When the first Christians received the Spirit, as recorded in the second chapter of Acts, He came with the rushing sound of a wind. We do not always know when and how the Spirit of God comes into our lives anymore than we can see the wind. God's Spirit may come to us suddenly like the rushing of a wind, or quietly like a cool, soft breeze.

Throughout our lives, we must be aware of God's Spirit and always welcome Him. For then we will let other people "see" and "hear" God's Spirit as they watch His effects in our lives. Like the winds of Jerusalem, the Spirit of God can come to people in many ways, yet the effect is the same—a new birth!

17 Then His disciples remembered that it was written, *"Zeal for Your house has eaten*[a] *Me up."*[b]

18 So the Jews answered and said to Him, "What sign do You show to us, since You do these things?"

19 Jesus answered and said to them, "Destroy this temple, and in three days I will raise it up."

20 Then the Jews said, "It has taken forty-six years to build this temple, and will You raise it up in three days?"

21 But He was speaking of the temple of His body. 22 Therefore, when He had risen from the dead, His disciples remembered that He had said this to them;[a] and they believed the Scripture and the word which Jesus had said.

23 Now when He was in Jerusalem at the Passover, during the feast, many believed in His name when they saw the signs which He did. 24 But Jesus did not commit Himself to them, because He knew all *men*, 25 and had no need that anyone should testify of man, for He knew what was in man.

3 There was a man of the Pharisees named Nicodemus, a ruler of the Jews. 2 This man came to Jesus by night and said to Him, "Rabbi, we know that You are a teacher come from God; for no one can do these signs that You do unless God is with him."

3 Jesus answered and said to him, "Most assuredly, I say to you, unless one is born again, he cannot see the kingdom of God."

4 Nicodemus said to Him, "How can a man be born when he is old? Can he enter a second time into his mother's womb and be born?"

5 Jesus answered, "Most assuredly, I say to you, unless one is born of water and the Spirit, he cannot enter the kingdom of God. 6 That which is born of the flesh is flesh, and that which is born of the Spirit is spirit. 7 Do not marvel that I said to you, 'You must be born again.' 8 The wind blows where it wishes, and you hear the sound of it, but cannot tell where it comes from and where it goes. So is everyone who is born of the Spirit."

9 Nicodemus answered and said to Him, "How can these things be?"

10 Jesus answered and said to him, "Are you the teacher of Israel, and do not know these things? 11 Most assuredly, I say to you, We speak what We know and testify what We have seen, and you do not receive Our witness. 12 If I have told you earthly things and you do not believe, how will you believe if I tell you heavenly things? 13 No one has ascended to heaven but He who came down from heaven, *that is*, the Son of Man who is in heaven.[a] 14 And as Moses lifted up the serpent in the wilderness, even so must the Son of Man be lifted up, 15 that whoever believes in Him should not perish but[a] have eternal life. 16 For God so loved the world that He gave His only begotten Son, that whoever believes in Him should not perish but have everlasting life. 17 For God did not send His Son into the world to condemn the world, but that the world through Him might be saved.

18 "He who believes in Him is not condemned; but he who does not believe is condemned already, because he has not believed in the name of the only begotten Son of God. 19 And this is the condemnation, that the light has come into the world, and men loved darkness rather than light, because their deeds were evil. 20 For everyone practicing evil hates the light and does not come to the light, lest his deeds should be exposed. 21 But he who does the truth comes to the light, that his deeds may be clearly seen, that they have been done in God."

22 After these things Jesus and His disciples came into the land of Judea, and there He remained with them and baptized. 23 Now John also was baptizing in Aenon near Salim, because there was much water there. And they came and were baptized. 24 For John had not yet been thrown into prison.

25 Then there arose a dispute between *some* of John's disciples and the Jews about purification. 26 And they came to John and said to him, "Rabbi, He who was with you beyond the Jordan, to whom you have testified—behold, He is bap-

(handwritten margin notes: "course in miracles me love/ light / Where there is love cannot be true / evil")

---

tizing, and all are coming to Him!"

27 John answered and said, "A man can receive nothing unless it has been given to him from heaven. 28 You yourselves bear me witness, that I said, 'I am not the Christ,' but, 'I have been sent before Him.' 29 He who has the bride is the bridegroom; but the friend of the bridegroom, who stands and hears him, rejoices greatly because of the bridegroom's voice. Therefore this joy of mine is fulfilled. 30 He must increase, but I *must* decrease. 31 He who comes from above is above all; he who is of the earth is earthly and speaks of the earth. He who comes from heaven is above all. 32 And what He has seen and heard, that He testifies; and no one receives His testimony. 33 He who has received His testimony has certified that God is true. 34 For He whom God has sent speaks the words of God, for God does not give the Spirit by measure. 35 The Father loves the Son, and has given all things into His hand. 36 He who believes in the Son has everlasting life; and he who does not believe the Son shall not see life, but the wrath of God abides on him."

4 Therefore, when the Lord knew that the Pharisees had heard that Jesus made and baptized more disciples than John 2 (though Jesus Himself did not baptize, but His disciples), 3 He left Judea and departed again to Galilee. 4 But He needed to go through Samaria.

5 So He came to a city of Samaria which is called Sychar, near the plot of ground that Jacob gave to his son Joseph. 6 Now Jacob's well was there. Jesus therefore, being wearied from *His* journey, sat thus by the well. It was about the sixth hour.

7 A woman of Samaria came to draw water. Jesus said to her, "Give Me a drink." 8 For His disciples had gone away into the city to buy food.

9 Then the woman of Samaria said to Him, "How is it that You, being a Jew, ask a drink from me, a Samaritan woman?" For Jews have no dealings with Samaritans.

10 Jesus answered and said to her, "If you knew the gift of God, and who it is who says to you, 'Give Me a drink,' you would have asked Him, and He would have given you living water."

11 The woman said to Him, "Sir, You have nothing to draw with, and the well is deep. Where then do You get that living water? 12 Are You greater than our father Jacob, who gave us the well, and drank from it himself, as well as his sons and his livestock?"

13 Jesus answered and said to her, "Whoever drinks of this water will thirst again, 14 but whoever drinks of the water that I shall give him will never thirst. But the water that I shall give him will become in him a fountain of water springing up into everlasting life."

15 The woman said to Him, "Sir, give me this water, that I may not thirst, nor come here to draw."

16 Jesus said to her, "Go, call your husband, and come here."

17 The woman answered and said, "I have no husband."

Jesus said to her, "You have well said, 'I have no husband,' 18 for you have had five husbands, and the one whom you now have is not your husband; in that you spoke truly."

19 The woman said to Him, "Sir, I perceive that You are a prophet. 20 Our fathers worshiped on this mountain, and you *Jews* say that in Jerusalem is the place where one ought to worship."

21 Jesus said to her, "Woman, believe Me, the hour is coming when you will neither on this mountain, nor in Jerusalem, worship the Father. 22 You worship what you do not know; we know what we worship, for salvation is of the Jews. 23 But the hour is coming, and now is, when the true worshipers will worship the Father in spirit and truth; for the Father is seeking such to worship Him. 24 God *is* Spirit, and those who worship Him must worship in spirit and truth."

25 The woman said to Him, "I know that Messiah is coming" (who is called Christ). "When He comes, He will tell us all things."

26 Jesus said to her, "I who speak to you am *He.*"

27 And at this *point* His disciples came, and they marveled that He talked with a woman; yet no one said, "What do You seek?" or, "Why are You talking with her?"

28 The woman then left her waterpot, went her way into the city, and said to the men, 29 "Come, see a Man

If you don't believe you can't see the light

A Nobleman's Journey to Cana

A beautiful illustration of one man's faith took place in the small village of Cana in Galilee. An important official of Herod's court in Tiberias heard that Jesus was in the area. A few days earlier this nobleman's son had contracted a severe illness and was at the point of death.

Jesus' reputation had preceded Him, for the nobleman believed Jesus was sent by God and could heal his son. So the next morning, at sunrise, the nobleman set out on the twenty-mile journey from Capernaum to Cana. When he arrived in Cana, the nobleman implored Jesus to return to Capernaum and heal his son. Jesus, realizing the time and distance involved in the official's journey, knew the man had great faith in God. Jesus told the official to return home—his son was alive and well. The nobleman believed Jesus and immediately began the descent back to Capernaum.

While the official completed his journey to Capernaum, his servants ran to meet him, explaining the good news. His son was alive and well. The official asked what time the fever had left the boy. The servants replied, "Yesterday at the seventh hour the fever left him" (John 4:52). The official noted the time (one o'clock—the seventh hour) and knew it was Jesus' words that healed the boy. Scripture says miraculous salvation came to him and his whole household because of the miraculous healing.

Our faith, like the nobleman's, must first believe God can help us. Second, we must make the effort to go to God and ask Him to meet our needs. Then we must take God at His word, letting the peace and confidence of His faithfulness fill our hearts and minds. And when we find our problem solved, our hurts healed, and our lives renewed—note the time. Give the credit to God to whom it is due.

who told me all things that I ever did. Could this be the Christ?" 30 Then they went out of the city and came to Him.

31 In the meantime His disciples urged Him, saying, "Rabbi, eat."

32 But He said to them, "I have food to eat of which you do not know."

33 Therefore the disciples said to one another, "Has anyone brought Him *anything* to eat?"

34 Jesus said to them, "My food is to do the will of Him who sent Me, and to finish His work. 35 Do you not say, 'There are still four months and *then* comes the harvest'? Behold, I say to you, lift up your eyes and look at the fields, for they are already white for harvest! 36 And he who reaps receives wages, and gathers fruit for eternal life, that both he who sows and he who reaps may rejoice together. 37 For in this the saying is true: 'One sows and another reaps.' 38 I sent you to reap that for which you have not labored; others have labored, and you have entered into their labors."

39 And many of the Samaritans of that city believed in Him because of the word of the woman who testified, "He told me all that I *ever* did." 40 So when the Samaritans had come to Him, they urged Him to stay with them; and He stayed there two days. 41 And many more believed because of His own word.

42 Then they said to the woman, "Now we believe, not because of what you said, for we ourselves have heard *Him* and we know that this is indeed the Christ,ᵃ the Savior of the world."

43 Now after the two days He departed from there and went to Galilee. 44 For Jesus Himself testified that a prophet has no honor in his own country. 45 So when He came to Galilee, the Galileans received Him, having seen all the things He did in Jerusalem at the feast; for they also had gone to the feast.

46 So Jesus came again to Cana of Galilee where He had made the water wine. And there was a certain nobleman whose son was sick at Capernaum. 47 When he heard that Jesus had come out of Judea into Galilee, he went to Him and implored Him to come down and heal his son, for he was at the point of death. 48 Then Jesus said to him, "Unless you *people* see signs and wonders, you will by no means believe."

49 The nobleman said to Him, "Sir, come down before my child dies!"

50 Jesus said to him, "Go your way; your son lives." So the man believed the word that Jesus spoke to him, and he went his way. 51 And as he was now going down, his servants met him and told *him,* saying, "Your son lives!"

52 Then he inquired of them the hour when he got better. And they said to him, "Yesterday at the seventh hour the fever left him." 53 So the father knew that *it was* at the same hour in which Jesus said to him, "Your son lives." And he himself believed, and his whole household.

54 This again *is* the second sign Jesus did when He had come out of Judea into Galilee.

5 After this there was a feast of the Jews, and Jesus went up to Jerusalem. 2 Now there is in Jerusalem by the Sheep *Gate* a pool, which is called in Hebrew, Bethesda,ᵃ having five porches. 3 In these lay a great multitude of sick people, blind, lame, paralyzed, waiting for the moving of the water. 4 For an angel went down at a certain time into the pool and stirred up the water; then whoever stepped in first, after the stirring of the water, was made well of whatever disease he had.ᵃ 5 Now a certain man was there who had an infirmity thirty-eight years. 6 When Jesus saw him lying there, and knew that he already had been *in that condition* a long time, He said to him, "Do you want to be made well?"

7 The sick man answered Him, "Sir, I have no man to put me into the pool when the water is stirred up; but while I am coming, another steps down before me."

8 Jesus said to him, "Rise, take up your bed and walk." 9 And immediately the man was made well, took up his bed, and walked.

And that day was the Sabbath. 10 The Jews therefore said to him who was cured, "It is the Sabbath;

4:42 ᵃNU-Text omits *the Christ.*   5:2 ᵃNU-Text reads *Bethzatha.*   5:4 ᵃNU-Text omits *waiting for the moving of the water* at the end of verse 3, and all of verse 4.

it is not lawful for you to carry your bed."

11 He answered them, "He who made me well said to me, 'Take up your bed and walk.'"

12 Then they asked him, "Who is the Man who said to you, 'Take up your bed and walk'?" 13 But the one who was healed did not know who it was, for Jesus had withdrawn, a multitude being in *that* place. 14 Afterward Jesus found him in the temple, and said to him, "See, you have been made well. Sin no more, lest a worse thing come upon you."

15 The man departed and told the Jews that it was Jesus who had made him well.

16 For this reason the Jews persecuted Jesus, and sought to kill Him,*a* because He had done these things on the Sabbath. 17 But Jesus answered them, "My Father has been working until now, and I have been working."

18 Therefore the Jews sought all the more to kill Him, because He not only broke the Sabbath, but also said that God was His Father, making Himself equal with God. 19 Then Jesus answered and said to them, "Most assuredly, I say to you, the Son can do nothing of Himself, but what He sees the Father do; for whatever He does, the Son also does in like manner. 20 For the Father loves the Son, and shows Him all things that He Himself does; and He will show Him greater works than these, that you may marvel. 21 For as the Father raises the dead and gives life to *them,* even so the Son gives life to whom He will. 22 For the Father judges no one, but has committed all judgment to the Son, 23 that all should honor the Son just as they honor the Father. He who does not honor the Son does not honor the Father who sent Him.

24 "Most assuredly, I say to you, he who hears My word and believes in Him who sent Me has everlasting life, and shall not come into judgment, but has passed from death into life. 25 Most assuredly, I say to you, the hour is coming, and now is, when the dead will hear the voice of the Son of God; and those who hear will live. 26 For as the Father has life in Himself, so He has granted the Son to have life in Himself, 27 and has given

Him authority to execute judgment also, because He is the Son of Man. 28 Do not marvel at this; for the hour is coming in which all who are in the graves will hear His voice 29 and come forth—those who have done good, to the resurrection of life, and those who have done evil, to the resurrection of condemnation. 30 I can of Myself do nothing. As I hear, I judge; and My judgment is righteous, because I do not seek My own will but the will of the Father who sent Me.

31 "If I bear witness of Myself, My witness is not true. 32 There is another who bears witness of Me, and I know that the witness which He witnesses of Me is true. 33 You have sent to John, and he has borne witness to the truth. 34 Yet I do not receive testimony from man, but I say these things that you may be saved. 35 He was the burning and shining lamp, and you were willing for a time to rejoice in his light. 36 But I have a greater witness than John's; for the works which the Father has given Me to finish—the very works that I do—bear witness of Me, that the Father has sent Me. 37 And the Father Himself, who sent Me, has testified of Me. You have neither heard His voice at any time, nor seen His form. 38 But you do not have His word abiding in you, because whom He sent, Him you do not believe. 39 You search the Scriptures, for in them you think you have eternal life; and these are they which testify of Me. 40 But you are not willing to come to Me that you may have life.

41 "I do not receive honor from men. 42 But I know you, that you do not have the love of God in you. 43 I have come in My Father's name, and you do not receive Me; if another comes in his own name, him you will receive. 44 How can you believe, who receive honor from one another, and do not seek the honor that *comes* from the only God? 45 Do not think that I shall accuse you to the Father; there is *one* who accuses you—Moses, in whom you trust. 46 For if you believed Moses, you would believe Me; for he wrote about Me. 47 But if you do not believe his writings, how will you believe My words?"

5:16 *a*NU-Text omits *and sought to kill Him.*

6 After these things Jesus went over the Sea of Galilee, which is *the Sea* of Tiberias. 2 Then a great multitude followed Him, because they saw His signs which He performed on those who were diseased. 3 And Jesus went up on the mountain, and there He sat with His disciples. 4 Now the Passover, a feast of the Jews, was near. 5 Then Jesus lifted up *His* eyes, and seeing a great multitude coming toward Him, He said to Philip, "Where shall we buy bread, that these may eat?" 6 But this He said to test him, for He Himself knew what He would do.

7 Philip answered Him, "Two hundred denarii worth of bread is not sufficient for them, that every one of them may have a little."

8 One of His disciples, Andrew, Simon Peter's brother, said to Him, 9 "There is a lad here who has five barley loaves and two small fish, but what are they among so many?"

10 Then Jesus said, "Make the people sit down." Now there was much grass in the place. So the men sat down, in number about five thousand. 11 And Jesus took the loaves, and when He had given thanks He distributed *them* to the disciples, and the disciples[a] to those sitting down; and likewise of the fish, as much as they wanted. 12 So when they were filled, He said to His disciples, "Gather up the fragments that remain, so that nothing is lost." 13 Therefore they gathered *them* up, and filled twelve baskets with the fragments of the five barley loaves which were left over by those who had eaten. 14 Then those men, when they had seen the sign that Jesus did, said, "This is truly the Prophet who is to come into the world."

15 Therefore when Jesus perceived that they were about to come and take Him by force to make Him king, He departed again to the mountain by Himself alone.

16 Now when evening came, His disciples went down to the sea, 17 got into the boat, and went over the sea toward Capernaum. And it was already dark, and Jesus had not come to them. 18 Then the sea arose because a great wind was blowing.

19 So when they had rowed about three or four miles,[a] they saw Jesus walking on the sea and drawing near the boat; and they were afraid. 20 But He said to them, "It is I; do not be afraid." 21 Then they willingly received Him into the boat, and immediately the boat was at the land where they were going.

22 On the following day, when the people who were standing on the other side of the sea saw that there was no other boat there, except that one which His disciples had entered,[a] and that Jesus had not entered the boat with His disciples, but His disciples had gone away alone— 23 however, other boats came from Tiberias, near the place where they ate bread after the Lord had given thanks— 24 when the people therefore saw that Jesus was not there, nor His disciples, they also got into boats and came to Capernaum, seeking Jesus. 25 And when they found Him on the other side of the sea, they said to Him, "Rabbi, when did You come here?"

26 Jesus answered them and said, "Most assuredly, I say to you, you seek Me, not because you saw the signs, but because you ate of the loaves and were filled. 27 Do not labor for the food which perishes, but for the food which endures to everlasting life, which the Son of Man will give you, because God the Father has set His seal on Him."

28 Then they said to Him, "What shall we do, that we may work the works of God?"

29 Jesus answered and said to them, "This is the work of God, that you believe in Him whom He sent."

30 Therefore they said to Him, "What sign will You perform then, that we may see it and believe You? What work will You do? 31 Our fathers ate the manna in the desert; as it is written, 'He gave them bread from heaven to eat.'"[a]

32 Then Jesus said to them, "Most assuredly, I say to you, Moses did not give you the bread from heaven, but My Father gives you the true bread from heaven. 33 For the bread of God is He who comes down from heaven and gives life to the world."

6:11 [a]NU-Text omits *to the disciples, and the disciples.* 6:19 [a]Literally *twenty-five or thirty stadia*
6:22 [a]NU-Text omits *that* and *which His disciples had entered.* 6:31 [a]Exodus 16:4; Nehemiah 9:15;
Psalm 78:24

34 Then they said to Him, "Lord, give us this bread always."

35 And Jesus said to them, "I am the bread of life. He who comes to Me shall never hunger, and he who believes in Me shall never thirst. 36 But I said to you that you have seen Me and yet do not believe. 37 All that the Father gives Me will come to Me, and the one who comes to Me I will by no means cast out. 38 For I have come down from heaven, not to do My own will, but the will of Him who sent Me. 39 This is the will of the Father who sent Me, that of all He has given Me I should lose nothing, but should raise it up at the last day. 40 And this is the will of Him who sent Me, that everyone who sees the Son and believes in Him may have everlasting life; and I will raise him up at the last day."

41 The Jews then complained about Him, because He said, "I am the bread which came down from heaven." 42 And they said, "Is not this Jesus, the son of Joseph, whose father and mother we know? How is it then that He says, 'I have come down from heaven'?"

43 Jesus therefore answered and said to them, "Do not murmur among yourselves. 44 No one can come to Me unless the Father who sent Me draws him; and I will raise him up at the last day. 45 It is written in the prophets, 'And they shall all be taught by God.'ᵃ Therefore everyone who has heard and learnedᵇ from the Father comes to Me. 46 Not that anyone has seen the Father, except He who is from God; He has seen the Father. 47 Most assuredly, I say to you, he who believes in Meᵃ has everlasting life. 48 I am the bread of life. 49 Your fathers ate the manna in the wilderness, and are dead. 50 This is the bread which comes down from heaven, that one may eat of it and not die. 51 I am the living bread which came down from heaven. If anyone eats of this bread, he will live forever; and the bread that I shall give is My flesh, which I shall give for the life of the world."

52 The Jews therefore quarreled among themselves, saying, "How can this Man give us His flesh to eat?"

53 Then Jesus said to them, "Most assuredly, I say to you, unless you eat the flesh of the Son of Man and drink His blood, you have no life in you. 54 Whoever eats My flesh and drinks My blood has eternal life, and I will raise him up at the last day. 55 For My flesh is food indeed,ᵃ and My blood is drink indeed. 56 He who eats My flesh and drinks My blood abides in Me, and I in him. 57 As the living Father sent Me, and I live because of the Father, so he who feeds on Me will live because of Me. 58 This is the bread which came down from heaven—not as your fathers ate the manna, and are dead. He who eats this bread will live forever."

59 These things He said in the synagogue as He taught in Capernaum.

60 Therefore many of His disciples, when they heard this, said, "This is a hard saying; who can understand it?"

61 When Jesus knew in Himself that His disciples complained about this, He said to them, "Does this offend you? 62 What then if you should see the Son of Man ascend where He was before? 63 It is the Spirit who gives life; the flesh profits nothing. The words that I speak to you are spirit, and they are life. 64 But there are some of you who do not believe." For Jesus knew from the beginning who they were who did not believe, and who would betray Him. 65 And He said, "Therefore I have said to you that no one can come to Me unless it has been granted to him by My Father."

66 From that time many of His disciples went back and walked with Him no more. 67 Then Jesus said to the twelve, "Do you also want to go away?"

68 But Simon Peter answered Him, "Lord, to whom shall we go? You have the words of eternal life. 69 Also we have come to believe and know that You are the Christ, the Son of the living God."ᵃ

70 Jesus answered them, "Did I not choose you, the twelve, and one of you is a devil?" 71 He spoke of Judas Iscariot, the son of Simon, for it was he who would betray Him, being one of the twelve.

6:45 ᵃIsaiah 54:13   ᵇM-Text reads hears and has learned.   6:47 ᵃNU-Text omits in Me.
6:55 ᵃNU-Text reads true food and true drink.   6:69 ᵃNU-Text reads You are the Holy One of God.

Expect the Unexpected

During the New Testament period, the Jewish people had rigid expectations. They yearned for a Messiah and they specifically expected Him to come from Bethlehem in Judea. They were right. Jesus was born in Bethlehem. However, when He was a baby His parents fled with Him to Egypt to escape death at the hand of cruel Herod. When they returned to the land, they settled in the town of Nazareth.

Nazareth probably comes from the Hebrew word for "branch"—exactly as the prophet Isaiah (53:2) foretold that the Messiah would grow up like a "tender plant" or a "young branch" for the Lord. An insignificant village in New Testament times, Nathanael suggests that nothing good could come out of Nazareth (see John 1:46). It was a simple fact that all the great leaders of Israel came from Jerusalem or another major city in Judea.

The only other prophet from this region was Jonah, whose village, Gath Hepher, was located one-and-a-half miles from Nazareth. The village where Jesus was reared is never mentioned in the Old Testament and had little status in the New Testament.

Because they expected the Messiah to come from Bethlehem, the Jewish leaders completely fought Jesus' claim as the Son of God. Set in their ways, they failed to recognize the One they waited for. One day, while Jesus taught in the temple, the leaders asked Him, "Has not the Scripture said that the Christ comes from the seed of David and from the town of Bethlehem?" (John 7:42). The crowd sought to apprehend Jesus, but had no accusation to bring against Him. Their expectations limited God. When Jesus, the true Messiah finally came to them, they could not accept Him because He did not fit into the plans they had created in their minds regarding *how* the Promised One would come.

Do not limit God with your locked-in thinking. Allow God to touch you, reach you, and come to you in unexpected ways through people, places, and events in life you never dreamed of before. Proverbs 2:6 says, "The LORD gives wisdom; from His mouth *come* knowledge and understanding."

7 After these things Jesus walked in Galilee; for He did not want to walk in Judea, because the Jews[a] sought to kill Him. 2 Now the Jews' Feast of Tabernacles was at hand. 3 His brothers therefore said to Him, "Depart from here and go into Judea, that Your disciples also may see the works that You are doing. 4 For no one does anything in secret while he himself seeks to be known openly. If You do these things, show Yourself to the world." 5 For even His brothers did not believe in Him.

6 Then Jesus said to them, "My time has not yet come, but your time is always ready. 7 The world cannot hate you, but it hates Me because I testify of it that its works are evil. 8 You go up to this feast. I am not yet[a] going up to this feast, for My time has not yet fully come." 9 When He had said these things to them, He remained in Galilee.

10 But when His brothers had gone up, then He also went up to the feast, not openly, but as it were in secret. 11 Then the Jews sought Him at the feast, and said, "Where is He?" 12 And there was much complaining among the people concerning Him. Some said, "He is good"; others said, "No, on the contrary, He deceives the people." 13 However, no one spoke openly of Him for fear of the Jews.

14 Now about the middle of the feast Jesus went up into the temple and taught. 15 And the Jews marveled, saying, "How does this Man know letters, having never studied?" 16 Jesus[a] answered them and said, "My doctrine is not Mine, but His who sent Me. 17 If anyone wills to do His will, he shall know concerning the doctrine, whether it is from God or whether I speak on My own authority. 18 He who speaks from himself seeks his own glory; but He who seeks the glory of the One who sent Him is true, and no unrighteousness is in Him. 19 Did not Moses give you the law, yet none of you keeps the law? Why do you seek to kill Me?"

20 The people answered and said, "You have a demon. Who is seeking to kill You?"

21 Jesus answered and said to them, "I did one work, and you all marvel. 22 Moses therefore gave you circumcision (not that it is from Moses, but from the fathers), and you circumcise a man on the Sabbath. 23 If a man receives circumcision on the Sabbath, so that the law of Moses should not be broken, are you angry with Me because I made a man completely well on the Sabbath? 24 Do not judge according to appearance, but judge with righteous judgment."

25 Now some of them from Jerusalem said, "Is this not He whom they seek to kill? 26 But look! He speaks boldly, and they say nothing to Him. Do the rulers know indeed that this is truly[a] the Christ? 27 However, we know where this Man is from; but when the Christ comes, no one knows where He is from."

28 Then Jesus cried out, as He taught in the temple, saying, "You both know Me, and you know where I am from; and I have not come of Myself, but He who sent Me is true, whom you do not know. 29 But[a] I know Him, for I am from Him, and He sent Me."

30 Therefore they sought to take Him; but no one laid a hand on Him, because His hour had not yet come. 31 And many of the people believed in Him, and said, "When the Christ comes, will He do more signs than these which this *Man* has done?"

32 The Pharisees heard the crowd murmuring these things concerning Him, and the Pharisees and the chief priests sent officers to take Him. 33 Then Jesus said to them,[a] "I shall be with you a little while longer, and *then* I go to Him who sent Me. 34 You will seek Me and not find *Me,* and where I am you cannot come."

35 Then the Jews said among themselves, "Where does He intend to go that we shall not find Him? Does He intend to go to the Dispersion among the Greeks and teach the Greeks? 36 What is this thing that He said, 'You will seek Me and not find Me, and where I am you cannot come'?"

37 On the last day, that great *day* of the feast, Jesus stood and cried out, saying, "If anyone thirsts, let him come to Me and drink. 38 He who believes in Me, as the Scripture has

---

7:1 [a]That is, the ruling authorities *Jesus.* 7:26 [a]NU-Text omits *truly.* omit *to them.* 7:8 [a]NU-Text omits *yet.* 7:29 [a]NU-Text and M-Text omit *But.* 7:16 [a]NU-Text and M-Text read *So* 7:33 [a]NU-Text and M-Text

Find a Hurt and Heal It!

When the time came for Jesus to begin His public ministry, He left Nazareth and settled in Capernaum by the Sea of Galilee. Of all the places in Palestine—why did Jesus go there?

The Gospels and other sources from the New Testament period tell us that multitudes of sick, crippled, paralytics, lepers, lame, blind, and deaf people already lived by the Sea of Galilee before Jesus settled in the region. Why did they go there?

The Sea of Galilee is located in a volcanic region seven hundred feet below sea level. Molten lava deep within the earth streams from natural rock fissures and heats the many springs around the lake. People of the Greco-Roman world of the New Testament period believed these hot springs had healing powers. They built cities near these pools and erected beautiful marble bathhouses with inlaid mosaic floors. Businessmen and physicians charged high fees, exploiting the sick who sat in these baths.

Here in the region where people were suffering, Jesus came to heal them and demonstrate the kingdom of God. He found out where they were and went to them. Jesus knew that those who were sick needed a Physician (Matt. 9:12). Today, Jesus finds us and comes to us where we are. Whether we hurt from a lack of joy, low self-worth, guilt from an unhealthy life-style, or a physical affliction—Jesus, the Great Physician, heals us.

Because many people are afraid to come to Jesus for help, we must first go to them with an attitude of concern. When they know that we will not turn away, they can freely accept our help. Let us be like our Lord Jesus Christ as we exude joy, build others up, and aid in their physical needs. We, like our Lord, will seek for the lost (Luke 19:10) and introduce them to the lover of their soul, the healer of their body.

said, out of his heart will flow rivers of living water." 39 But this He spoke concerning the Spirit, whom those believing[a] in Him would receive; for the Holy[b] Spirit was not yet given, because Jesus was not yet glorified.

40 Therefore many[a] from the crowd, when they heard this saying, said, "Truly this is the Prophet." 41 Others said, "This is the Christ."

But some said, "Will the Christ come out of Galilee? 42 Has not the Scripture said that the Christ comes from the seed of David and from the town of Bethlehem, where David was?" 43 So there was a division among the people because of Him. 44 Now some of them wanted to take Him, but no one laid hands on Him.

45 Then the officers came to the chief priests and Pharisees, who said to them, "Why have you not brought Him?"

46 The officers answered, "No man ever spoke like this Man!"

47 Then the Pharisees answered them, "Are you also deceived? 48 Have any of the rulers or the Pharisees believed in Him? 49 But this crowd that does not know the law is accursed."

50 Nicodemus (he who came to Jesus by night,[a] being one of them) said to them, 51 "Does our law judge a man before it hears him and knows what he is doing?"

52 They answered and said to him, "Are you also from Galilee? Search and look, for no prophet has arisen[a] out of Galilee."

53 And everyone went to his own house.[a]

8

But Jesus went to the Mount of Olives.

2 Now early[a] in the morning He came again into the temple, and all the people came to Him; and He sat down and taught them. 3 Then the scribes and Pharisees brought to Him a woman caught in adultery. And when they had set her in the midst, 4 they said to Him, "Teacher, this woman was caught[a] in adultery, in the very act. 5 Now Moses, in the law, commanded[a] us that such should be stoned.[b] But what do You say?"[c] 6 This they said, testing Him, that they might have something of which to accuse Him. But Jesus stooped down and wrote on the ground with His finger, as though He did not hear.[a]

7 So when they continued asking Him, He raised Himself up[a] and said to them, "He who is without sin among you, let him throw a stone at her first." 8 And again He stooped down and wrote on the ground. 9 Then those who heard it, being convicted by their conscience,[a] went out one by one, beginning with the oldest even to the last. And Jesus was left alone, and the woman standing in the midst. 10 When Jesus had raised Himself up and saw no one but the woman, He said to her,[a] "Woman, where are those accusers of yours?[b] Has no one condemned you?"

11 She said, "No one, Lord."

And Jesus said to her, "Neither do I condemn you; go and[a] sin no more."

12 Then Jesus spoke to them again, saying, "I am the light of the world. He who follows Me shall not walk in darkness, but have the light of life."

13 The Pharisees therefore said to Him, "You bear witness of Yourself; Your witness is not true."

14 Jesus answered and said to them, "Even if I bear witness of Myself, My witness is true, for I know where I came from and where I am going; but you do not know where I come from and where I am going. 15 You judge according to the flesh; I judge no one. 16 And yet if I do judge, My judgment is true; for I am not alone, but I am with the Father who sent Me. 17 It is also written in your law that the testimony of two men is true. 18 I am One who bears witness of Myself, and the Father who sent Me bears witness of Me."

7:39 [a]NU-Text reads who believed.   [b]NU-Text omits Holy.   7:40 [a]NU-Text reads some.
7:50 [a]NU-Text reads before.   7:52 [a]NU-Text reads is to rise.   7:53 [a]The words And everyone through sin no more (8:11) are bracketed by NU-Text as not original. They are present in over 900 manuscripts.   8:2 [a]M-Text reads very early.   8:4 [a]M-Text reads we found this woman.
8:5 [a]M-Text reads in our law Moses commanded.   [b]NU-Text and M-Text read to stone such.   [c]M-Text adds about her.   8:6 [a]NU-Text and M-Text omit as though He did not hear.   8:7 [a]M-Text reads He looked up.   8:9 [a]NU-Text and M-Text omit being convicted by their conscience.   8:10 [a]NU-Text omits and saw no one but the woman; M-Text reads He saw her and said.   [b]NU-Text and M-Text omit of yours.   8:11 [a]NU-Text and M-Text add from now on.

19 Then they said to Him, "Where is Your Father?"

Jesus answered, "You know neither Me nor My Father. If you had known Me, you would have known My Father also."

20 These words Jesus spoke in the treasury, as He taught in the temple; and no one laid hands on Him, for His hour had not yet come.

21 Then Jesus said to them again, "I am going away, and you will seek Me, and will die in your sin. Where I go you cannot come."

22 So the Jews said, "Will He kill Himself, because He says, 'Where I go you cannot come'?"

23 And He said to them, "You are from beneath; I am from above. You are of this world; I am not of this world. 24 Therefore I said to you that you will die in your sins; for if you do not believe that I am *He,* you will die in your sins."

25 Then they said to Him, "Who are You?"

And Jesus said to them, "Just what I have been saying to you from the beginning. 26 I have many things to say and to judge concerning you, but He who sent Me is true; and I speak to the world those things which I heard from Him."

27 They did not understand that He spoke to them of the Father.

28 Then Jesus said to them, "When you lift up the Son of Man, then you will know that I am *He,* and *that* I do nothing of Myself; but as My Father taught Me, I speak these things. 29 And He who sent Me is with Me. The Father has not left Me alone, for I always do those things that please Him." 30 As He spoke these words, many believed in Him.

31 Then Jesus said to those Jews who believed Him, "If you abide in My word, you are My disciples indeed. 32 And you shall know the truth, and the truth shall make you free."

33 They answered Him, "We are Abraham's descendants, and have never been in bondage to anyone. How *can* you say, 'You will be made free'?"

34 Jesus answered them, "Most assuredly, I say to you, whoever commits sin is a slave of sin. 35 And a slave does not abide in the house for-

ever, *but* a son abides forever. 36 Therefore if the Son makes you free, you shall be free indeed.

37 "I know that you are Abraham's descendants, but you seek to kill Me, because My word has no place in you. 38 I speak what I have seen with My Father, and you do what you have seen with*ᵃ* your father."

39 They answered and said to Him, "Abraham is our father."

Jesus said to them, "If you were Abraham's children, you would do the works of Abraham. 40 But now you seek to kill Me, a Man who has told you the truth which I heard from God. Abraham did not do this. 41 You do the deeds of your father."

Then they said to Him, "We were not born of fornication; we have one Father—God."

42 Jesus said to them, "If God were your Father, you would love Me, for I proceeded forth and came from God; nor have I come of Myself, but He sent Me. 43 Why do you not understand My speech? Because you are not able to listen to My word. 44 You are of *your* father the devil, and the desires of your father you want to do. He was a murderer from the beginning, and *does not* stand in the truth, because there is no truth in him. When he speaks a lie, he speaks from his own *resources,* for he is a liar and the father of it. 45 But because I tell the truth, you do not believe Me. 46 Which of you convicts Me of sin? And if I tell the truth, why do you not believe Me? 47 He who is of God hears God's words; therefore you do not hear, because you are not of God."

48 Then the Jews answered and said to Him, "Do we not say rightly that You are a Samaritan and have a demon?"

49 Jesus answered, "I do not have a demon; but I honor My Father, and you dishonor Me. 50 And I do not seek My *own* glory; there is One who seeks and judges. 51 Most assuredly, I say to you, if anyone keeps My word he shall never see death."

52 Then the Jews said to Him, "Now we know that You have a demon! Abraham is dead, and the prophets; and You say, 'If anyone keeps My word he shall never taste death.' 53 Are You greater than our

8:38 ᵃNU-Text reads *heard from.*

Sent by God

Throughout Jesus' ministry, He communicated that He was uniquely sent from God. A common phrase spoken by Jesus was "the very works that I do—bear witness of Me, that the Father has sent Me" (John 5:36).

Such emphasis was placed on this truth that the Gospel of John records the word *sent* twenty-five times in the first nine chapters. John 8 and 9 tell of a heated discussion on this subject between some of the religious leaders and Jesus. Jesus claimed that He was sent from God and was equal with God. Some of the Pharisees and Sadducees adamantly denied His claim.

This dispute came to a climax as Jesus and His disciples left the temple area. Again, Jesus asserted this fact. "I must work the works of Him who sent Me while it is day; the night is coming when no one can work. As long as I am in the world, I am the light of the world" (John 9:4, 5). Having said all this, Jesus approached a blind man outside the temple. He made mud and placed it on the man's eyes and said, "Go, wash in the pool of Siloam (which is translated, Sent)" (John 9:7). The fact that Siloam means *sent* is a clear challenge by Jesus for everyone to examine His works and ultimately His claims.

After the blind man washed in the pool, he came back with his sight fully restored, just as Jesus had said. He and his parents were immediately questioned on the issue of where Jesus was sent from. His parents refused to answer for fear of being put out of the synagogue. But the blind man confidently answered, "Why, this is a marvelous thing, that you do not know where He is from . . . Since the world began it has been unheard of that anyone opened the eyes of one who was born blind. If this Man were not from God, He could do nothing" (John 9:30, 32, 33).

Later in His ministry, after His resurrection, Jesus disclosed to His followers this incredible truth; "As the Father has sent Me, I also send you" (John 20:21).

The healed blind man believed Jesus' words and experienced His works. By believing Christ's claim, we can confidently answer the question, "Where was this Man sent from?"

father Abraham, who is dead? And the prophets are dead. Who do You make Yourself out to be?"

54 Jesus answered, "If I honor Myself, My honor is nothing. It is My Father who honors Me, of whom you say that He is your[a] God. 55 Yet you have not known Him, but I know Him. And if I say, 'I do not know Him,' I shall be a liar like you; but I do know Him and keep His word. 56 Your father Abraham rejoiced to see My day, and he saw it and was glad."

57 Then the Jews said to Him, "You are not yet fifty years old, and have You seen Abraham?"

58 Jesus said to them, "Most assuredly, I say to you, before Abraham was, I AM."

59 Then they took up stones to throw at Him; but Jesus hid Himself and went out of the temple,[a] going through the midst of them, and so passed by.

9 Now as Jesus passed by, He saw a man who was blind from birth. 2 And His disciples asked Him, saying, "Rabbi, who sinned, this man or his parents, that he was born blind?"

3 Jesus answered, "Neither this man nor his parents sinned, but that the works of God should be revealed in him. 4 I[a] must work the works of Him who sent Me while it is day; the night is coming when no one can work. 5 As long as I am in the world, I am the light of the world."

6 When He had said these things, He spat on the ground and made clay with the saliva; and He anointed the eyes of the blind man with the clay. 7 And He said to him, "Go, wash in the pool of Siloam" (which is translated, Sent). So he went and washed, and came back seeing.

8 Therefore the neighbors and those who previously had seen that he was blind[a] said, "Is not this he who sat and begged?"

9 Some said, "This is he." Others said, "He is like him."[a]

He said, "I am he."

10 Therefore they said to him, "How were your eyes opened?"

11 He answered and said, "A Man called Jesus made clay and anointed my eyes and said to me, 'Go to the pool of[a] Siloam and wash.' So I went and washed, and I received sight."

12 Then they said to him, "Where is He?"

He said, "I do not know."

13 They brought him who formerly was blind to the Pharisees. 14 Now it was a Sabbath when Jesus made the clay and opened his eyes. 15 Then the Pharisees also asked him again how he had received his sight. He said to them, "He put clay on my eyes, and I washed, and I see."

16 Therefore some of the Pharisees said, "This Man is not from God, because He does not keep the Sabbath."

Others said, "How can a man who is a sinner do such signs?" And there was a division among them.

17 They said to the blind man again, "What do you say about Him because He opened your eyes?"

He said, "He is a prophet."

18 But the Jews did not believe concerning him, that he had been blind and received his sight, until they called the parents of him who had received his sight. 19 And they asked them, saying, "Is this your son, who you say was born blind? How then does he now see?"

20 His parents answered them and said, "We know that this is our son, and that he was born blind; 21 but by what means he now sees we do not know, or who opened his eyes we do not know. He is of age; ask him. He will speak for himself."

22 His parents said these things because they feared the Jews, for the Jews had agreed already that if anyone confessed that He was Christ, he would be put out of the synagogue. 23 Therefore his parents said, "He is of age; ask him."

24 So they again called the man who was blind, and said to him, "Give God the glory! We know that this Man is a sinner."

25 He answered and said, "Whether He is a sinner or not I do not know. One thing I know: that though I was blind, now I see."

26 Then they said to him again, "What did He do to you? How did He open your eyes?"

Jesus the Good Shepherd

Jesus' parable of the Good Shepherd is deeply rooted in the everyday responsibilities of a shepherd. His listeners could easily visualize each aspect of His teaching as He detailed how He cares for His flock.

Even today, the duties of a shepherd are much the same as they were when Jesus first taught this parable. The shepherd's daily routine begins by leading his flock out to the wilderness to pasture. There in the hot, dry countryside he must find food and water for his sheep and guard against wild animals and thieves.

Jesus presents the unique relationship held between a sheepherder and his flock. "I am the good shepherd; and I know My *sheep,* and am known by My own. . . . My sheep hear My voice, and I know them, and they follow Me" (John 10:14, 27).

Each shepherd has a specific call which readily identifies him when he summons the flock, usually a clicking sound or a high-pitched shrill. Often several shepherds and their flocks intermingle while refreshing at small wilderness streams. Once the sheep have been watered, a shepherd will call his flock from the larger group of hundreds of sheep and his small flock will emerge to follow him.

As dusk approaches, shepherds voice their own calls to lead their flocks through the narrow canyon gullies, where they make use of the natural sheepfolds formed by the twisted geological structure of the land. Here the sheep are fed, watered, and kept for the night, secured on three sides by the steep canyon walls. The wider outlet is narrowed by building a wall of stones and thorn branches. The shepherd leaves a small entranceway at the intersection of the walls where he takes his watch post and actually serves as the door to guard his flock. No animal or thief is able to enter the fold without passing by the shepherd. When the safety of the morning dawn arrives, the shepherd calls his sheep and leads them out to find pasture.

Jesus drew directly from this practice. "I am the door. If anyone enters by Me, he will be saved, and will go in and out and find pasture. The thief does not come except to steal, and to kill, and to destroy. I have come that they may have life, and that they may have *it* more abundantly" (John 10:9, 10).

27 He answered them, "I told you already, and you did not listen. Why do you want to hear *it* again? Do you also want to become His disciples?"

28 Then they reviled him and said, "You are His disciple, but we are Moses' disciples. 29 We know that God spoke to Moses; *as for* this *fellow*, we do not know where He is from."

30 The man answered and said to them, "Why, this is a marvelous thing, that you do not know where He is from; yet He has opened my eyes! 31 Now we know that God does not hear sinners; but if anyone is a worshiper of God and does His will, He hears him. 32 Since the world began it has been unheard of that anyone opened the eyes of one who was born blind. 33 If this Man were not from God, He could do nothing."

34 They answered and said to him, "You were completely born in sins, and are you teaching us?" And they cast him out.

35 Jesus heard that they had cast him out; and when He had found him, He said to him, "Do you believe in the Son of God?"[a]

36 He answered and said, "Who is He, Lord, that I may believe in Him?"

37 And Jesus said to him, "You have both seen Him and it is He who is talking with you."

38 Then he said, "Lord, I believe!" And he worshiped Him.

39 And Jesus said, "For judgment I have come into this world, that those who do not see may see, and that those who see may be made blind."

40 Then *some* of the Pharisees who were with Him heard these words, and said to Him, "Are we blind also?"

41 Jesus said to them, "If you were blind, you would have no sin; but now you say, 'We see.' Therefore your sin remains.

10 "Most assuredly, I say to you, he who does not enter the sheepfold by the door, but climbs up some other way, the same is a thief and a robber. 2 But he who enters by the door is the shepherd of the sheep. 3 To him the doorkeeper opens, and the sheep hear his voice; and he calls his own sheep by name and leads them out. 4 And when he brings out his own sheep, he goes before them;

and the sheep follow him, for they know his voice. 5 Yet they will by no means follow a stranger, but will flee from him, for they do not know the voice of strangers." 6 Jesus used this illustration, but they did not understand the things which He spoke to them.

7 Then Jesus said to them again, "Most assuredly, I say to you, I am the door of the sheep. 8 All who *ever* came before Me[a] are thieves and robbers, but the sheep did not hear them. 9 I am the door. If anyone enters by Me, he will be saved, and will go in and out and find pasture. 10 The thief does not come except to steal, and to kill, and to destroy. I have come that they may have life, and that they may have *it* more abundantly.

11 "I am the good shepherd. The good shepherd gives His life for the sheep. 12 But a hireling, *he who is* not the shepherd, one who does not own the sheep, sees the wolf coming and leaves the sheep and flees; and the wolf catches the sheep and scatters them. 13 The hireling flees because he is a hireling and does not care about the sheep. 14 I am the good shepherd; and I know My *sheep*, and am known by My own. 15 As the Father knows Me, even so I know the Father; and I lay down My life for the sheep. 16 And other sheep I have which are not of this fold; them also I must bring, and they will hear My voice; and there will be one flock *and* one shepherd.

17 "Therefore My Father loves Me, because I lay down My life that I may take it again. 18 No one takes it from Me, but I lay it down of Myself. I have power to lay it down, and I have power to take it again. This command I have received from My Father."

19 Therefore there was a division again among the Jews because of these sayings. 20 And many of them said, "He has a demon and is mad. Why do you listen to Him?"

21 Others said, "These are not the words of one who has a demon. Can a demon open the eyes of the blind?"

22 Now it was the Feast of Dedication in Jerusalem, and it was winter. 23 And Jesus walked in the temple, in Solomon's porch. 24 Then the Jews surrounded Him and said to Him,

9:35 [a]NU-Text reads *Son of Man*.　　10:8 [a]M-Text omits *before Me*.

"How long do You keep us in doubt? If You are the Christ, tell us plainly." 25 Jesus answered them, "I told you, and you do not believe. The works that I do in My Father's name, they bear witness of Me. 26 But you do not believe, because you are not of My sheep, as I said to you.[a] 27 My sheep hear My voice, and I know them, and they follow Me. 28 And I give them eternal life, and they shall never perish; neither shall anyone snatch them out of My hand. 29 My Father, who has given them to Me, is greater than all; and no one is able to snatch them out of My Father's hand. 30 I and My Father are one."

31 Then the Jews took up stones again to stone Him. 32 Jesus answered them, "Many good works I have shown you from My Father. For which of those works do you stone Me?"

33 The Jews answered Him, saying, "For a good work we do not stone You, but for blasphemy, and because You, being a Man, make Yourself God."

34 Jesus answered them, "Is it not written in your law, 'I said, "You are gods" '?[a] 35 If He called them gods, to whom the word of God came (and the Scripture cannot be broken), 36 do you say of Him whom the Father sanctified and sent into the world, 'You are blaspheming,' because I said, 'I am the Son of God'? 37 If I do not do the works of My Father, do not believe Me; 38 but if I do, though you do not believe Me, believe the works, that you may know and believe[a] that the Father is in Me, and I in Him." 39 Therefore they sought again to seize Him, but He escaped out of their hand.

40 And He went away again beyond the Jordan to the place where John was baptizing at first, and there He stayed. 41 Then many came to Him and said, "John performed no sign, but all the things that John spoke about this Man were true." 42 And many believed in Him there.

11 Now a certain man was sick, Lazarus of Bethany, the town of Mary and her sister Martha. 2 It was that Mary who anointed the Lord with fragrant oil and wiped His feet with her hair, whose brother Lazarus was sick. 3 Therefore the sisters sent to Him, saying, "Lord, behold, he whom You love is sick."

4 When Jesus heard that, He said, "This sickness is not unto death, but for the glory of God, that the Son of God may be glorified through it."

5 Now Jesus loved Martha and her sister and Lazarus. 6 So, when He heard that he was sick, He stayed two more days in the place where He was. 7 Then after this He said to the disciples, "Let us go to Judea again."

8 The disciples said to Him, "Rabbi, lately the Jews sought to stone You, and are You going there again?"

9 Jesus answered, "Are there not twelve hours in the day? If anyone walks in the day, he does not stumble, because he sees the light of this world. 10 But if one walks in the night, he stumbles, because the light is not in him." 11 These things He said, and after that He said to them, "Our friend Lazarus sleeps, but I go that I may wake him up."

12 Then His disciples said, "Lord, if he sleeps he will get well." 13 However, Jesus spoke of his death, but they thought that He was speaking about taking rest in sleep.

14 Then Jesus said to them plainly, "Lazarus is dead. 15 And I am glad for your sakes that I was not there, that you may believe. Nevertheless let us go to him."

16 Then Thomas, who is called the Twin, said to his fellow disciples, "Let us also go, that we may die with Him."

17 So when Jesus came, He found that he had already been in the tomb four days. 18 Now Bethany was near Jerusalem, about two miles[a] away. 19 And many of the Jews had joined the women around Martha and Mary, to comfort them concerning their brother.

20 Then Martha, as soon as she heard that Jesus was coming, went and met Him, but Mary was sitting in the house. 21 Now Martha said to Jesus, "Lord, if You had been here, my brother would not have died. 22 But even now I know that what-

10:26 [a]NU-Text omits as I said to you.   10:34 [a]Psalm 82:6   10:38 [a]NU-Text reads understand.
11:18 [a]Literally fifteen stadia

ever You ask of God, God will give You."

23 Jesus said to her, "Your brother will rise again."

24 Martha said to Him, "I know that he will rise again in the resurrection at the last day."

25 Jesus said to her, "I am the resurrection and the life. He who believes in Me, though he may die, he shall live. 26 And whoever lives and believes in Me shall never die. Do you believe this?"

27 She said to Him, "Yes, Lord, I believe that You are the Christ, the Son of God, who is to come into the world."

28 And when she had said these things, she went her way and secretly called Mary her sister, saying, "The Teacher has come and is calling for you." 29 As soon as she heard *that*, she arose quickly and came to Him. 30 Now Jesus had not yet come into the town, but was*ª* in the place where Martha met Him. 31 Then the Jews who were with her in the house, and comforting her, when they saw that Mary rose up quickly and went out, followed her, saying, "She is going to the tomb to weep there."*ª*

32 Then, when Mary came where Jesus was, and saw Him, she fell down at His feet, saying to Him, "Lord, if You had been here, my brother would not have died."

33 Therefore, when Jesus saw her weeping, and the Jews who came with her weeping, He groaned in the spirit and was troubled. 34 And He said, "Where have you laid him?"

They said to Him, "Lord, come and see."

35 Jesus wept. 36 Then the Jews said, "See how He loved him!"

37 And some of them said, "Could not this Man, who opened the eyes of the blind, also have kept this man from dying?"

38 Then Jesus, again groaning in Himself, came to the tomb. It was a cave, and a stone lay against it. 39 Jesus said, "Take away the stone."

Martha, the sister of him who was dead, said to Him, "Lord, by this time there is a stench, for he has been *dead* four days."

40 Jesus said to her, "Did I not say to you that if you would believe you would see the glory of God?" 41 Then they took away the stone *from the place* where the dead man was lying.*ª* And Jesus lifted up *His* eyes and said, "Father, I thank You that You have heard Me. 42 And I know that You always hear Me, but because of the people who are standing by I said *this*, that they may believe that You sent Me." 43 Now when He had said these things, He cried with a loud voice, "Lazarus, come forth!" 44 And he who had died came out bound hand and foot with graveclothes, and his face was wrapped with a cloth. Jesus said to them, "Loose him, and let him go."

45 Then many of the Jews who had come to Mary, and had seen the things Jesus did, believed in Him. 46 But some of them went away to the Pharisees and told them the things Jesus did. 47 Then the chief priests and the Pharisees gathered a council and said, "What shall we do? For this Man works many signs. 48 If we let Him alone like this, everyone will believe in Him, and the Romans will come and take away both our place and nation."

49 And one of them, Caiaphas, being high priest that year, said to them, "You know nothing at all, 50 nor do you consider that it is expedient for us*ª* that one man should die for the people, and not that the whole nation should perish." 51 Now this he did not say on his own *authority;* but being high priest that year he prophesied that Jesus would die for the nation, 52 and not for that nation only, but also that He would gather together in one the children of God who were scattered abroad.

53 Then, from that day on, they plotted to put Him to death. 54 Therefore Jesus no longer walked openly among the Jews, but went from there into the country near the wilderness, to a city called Ephraim, and there remained with His disciples.

55 And the Passover of the Jews was near, and many went from the country up to Jerusalem before the

---

11:30 *ª*NU-Text adds *still.*   11:31 *ª*NU-Text reads *supposing that she was going to the tomb to weep there.*   11:41 *ª*NU-Text omits *from the place where the dead man was lying.*   11:50 *ª*NU-Text reads *you.*

Passover, to purify themselves.
56 Then they sought Jesus, and spoke among themselves as they stood in the temple, "What do you think—that He will not come to the feast?" 57 Now both the chief priests and the Pharisees had given a command, that if anyone knew where He was, he should report *it*, that they might seize Him.

12 Then, six days before the Passover, Jesus came to Bethany, where Lazarus was who had been dead,*a* whom He had raised from the dead. 2 There they made Him a supper; and Martha served, but Lazarus was one of those who sat at the table with Him. 3 Then Mary took a pound of very costly oil of spikenard, anointed the feet of Jesus, and wiped His feet with her hair. And the house was filled with the fragrance of the oil.

4 But one of His disciples, Judas Iscariot, Simon's *son*, who would betray Him, said, 5 "Why was this fragrant oil not sold for three hundred denarii*a* and given to the poor?" 6 This he said, not that he cared for the poor, but because he was a thief, and had the money box; and he used to take what was put in it.

7 But Jesus said, "Let her alone; she has kept*a* this for the day of My burial. 8 For the poor you have with you always, but Me you do not have always."

9 Now a great many of the Jews knew that He was there; and they came, not for Jesus' sake only, but that they might also see Lazarus, whom He had raised from the dead. 10 But the chief priests plotted to put Lazarus to death also, 11 because on account of him many of the Jews went away and believed in Jesus.

12 The next day a great multitude that had come to the feast, when they heard that Jesus was coming to Jerusalem, 13 took branches of palm trees and went out to meet Him, and cried out:

> "Hosanna!
> 'Blessed is He who comes in the
>   name of the LORD!'*a*
> The King of Israel!"

14 Then Jesus, when He had found a young donkey, sat on it; as it is written:

> 15 "Fear not, daughter of Zion;
>   Behold, your King is coming,
>   Sitting on a donkey's colt."*a*

16 His disciples did not understand these things at first; but when Jesus was glorified, then they remembered that these things were written about Him and *that* they had done these things to Him.

17 Therefore the people, who were with Him when He called Lazarus out of his tomb and raised him from the dead, bore witness. 18 For this reason the people also met Him, because they heard that He had done this sign. 19 The Pharisees therefore said among themselves, "You see that you are accomplishing nothing. Look, the world has gone after Him!"

20 Now there were certain Greeks among those who came up to worship at the feast. 21 Then they came to Philip, who was from Bethsaida of Galilee, and asked him, saying, "Sir, we wish to see Jesus."

22 Philip came and told Andrew, and in turn Andrew and Philip told Jesus.

23 But Jesus answered them, saying, "The hour has come that the Son of Man should be glorified. 24 Most assuredly, I say to you, unless a grain of wheat falls into the ground and dies, it remains alone; but if it dies, it produces much grain. 25 He who loves his life will lose it, and he who hates his life in this world will keep it for eternal life. 26 If anyone serves Me, let him follow Me; and where I am, there My servant will be also. If anyone serves Me, him *My* Father will honor.

27 "Now My soul is troubled, and what shall I say? 'Father, save Me from this hour'? But for this purpose I came to this hour. 28 "Father, glorify Your name."

Then a voice came from heaven, *saying,* "I have both glorified *it* and will glorify *it* again."

29 Therefore the people who stood by and heard *it* said that it had thundered. Others said, "An angel has spoken to Him."

12:1 *a*NU-Text omits *who had been dead.*   12:5 *a*About one year's wages for a worker.
12:7 *a*NU-Text reads *that she may keep.*   12:13 *a*Psalm 118:26   12:15 *a*Zechariah 9:9

Servant of All

Jesus Christ is the greatest servant the world has ever known. At the Last Supper, Jesus exemplified the real meaning of love and service when, as Lord and Teacher, He willingly washed the feet of His disciples. In doing so, Jesus demonstrated the humble role of service to others, which all leaders must be willing to pattern.

In both the ancient and modern Middle East the feet are considered the dirtiest part of the body. Usually covered only by open sandals, feet are constantly dusty and dirty during the summer months. In the winter, the rain turns the rendzina soils and the black basaltic earth into thick, wet mud, making it impassable in many parts of the area. One step in the mire leaves large clods of mud stuck to the feet.

In biblical times it was customary to remove sandals before entering a household. The host or hostess would supply water and towels for the guest of their house to wash with. The Gospels record that at the Last Supper Jesus began to wash each of the disciples' feet, taking upon Himself the lowliest of all tasks. When Jesus began to wash Peter's feet, the fisherman objected vehemently. His Lord was too far above this degrading act. Yet Jesus replied clearly, "Do you know what I have done to you? You call Me Teacher and Lord, and you say well, for *so* I am. If I then, *your* Lord and Teacher, have washed your feet, you also ought to wash one another's feet. For I have given you an example, that you should do as I have done to you" (John 13:12–15).

Who can you serve today in an unusual and unexpected way? When God brings a seemingly humbling, degrading responsibility into your life, follow Jesus' pattern of service: "If anyone desires to be first, he shall be last of all and servant of all" (Mark 9:35).

30 Jesus answered and said, "This voice did not come because of Me, but for your sake. 31 Now is the judgment of this world; now the ruler of this world will be cast out. 32 And I, if I am lifted up from the earth, will draw all *peoples* to Myself." 33 This He said, signifying by what death He would die.

34 The people answered Him, "We have heard from the law that the Christ remains forever; and how *can* You say, 'The Son of Man must be lifted up'? Who is this Son of Man?"

35 Then Jesus said to them, "A little while longer the light is with you. Walk while you have the light, lest darkness overtake you; he who walks in darkness does not know where he is going. 36 While you have the light, believe in the light, that you may become sons of light." These things Jesus spoke, and departed, and was hidden from them.

37 But although He had done so many signs before them, they did not believe in Him, 38 that the word of Isaiah the prophet might be fulfilled, which he spoke:

"Lord, who has believed our
    report?
And to whom has the arm of
    the Lord been revealed?"ᵃ

39 Therefore they could not believe, because Isaiah said again:

40 "He has blinded their eyes and
    hardened their hearts,
Lest they should see with their
    eyes,
Lest they should understand
    with their hearts and turn,
So that I should heal them."ᵃ

41 These things Isaiah said whenᵃ he saw His glory and spoke of Him. 42 Nevertheless even among the rulers many believed in Him, but because of the Pharisees they did not confess *Him*, lest they should be put out of the synagogue; 43 for they loved the praise of men more than the praise of God.

44 Then Jesus cried out and said, "He who believes in Me, believes not in Me but in Him who sent Me. 45 And he who sees Me sees Him who

sent Me. 46 I have come *as* a light into the world, that whoever believes in Me should not abide in darkness. 47 And if anyone hears My words and does not believe,ᵃ I do not judge him; for I did not come to judge the world but to save the world. 48 He who rejects Me, and does not receive My words, has that which judges him— the word that I have spoken will judge him in the last day. 49 For I have not spoken on My own *authority*; but the Father who sent Me gave Me a command, what I should say and what I should speak. 50 And I know that His command is everlasting life. Therefore, whatever I speak, just as the Father has told Me, so I speak."

13 Now before the feast of the Passover, when Jesus knew that His hour had come that He should depart from this world to the Father, having loved His own who were in the world, He loved them to the end.

2 And supper being ended,ᵃ the devil having already put it into the heart of Judas Iscariot, Simon's *son*, to betray Him, 3 Jesus, knowing that the Father had given all things into His hands, and that He had come from God and was going to God, 4 rose from supper and laid aside His garments, took a towel and girded Himself. 5 After that, He poured water into a basin and began to wash the disciples' feet, and to wipe *them* with the towel with which He was girded. 6 Then He came to Simon Peter. And *Peter* said to Him, "Lord, are You washing my feet?"

7 Jesus answered and said to him, "What I am doing you do not understand now, but you will know after this."

8 Peter said to Him, "You shall never wash my feet!"

Jesus answered him, "If I do not wash you, you have no part with Me."

9 Simon Peter said to Him, "Lord, not my feet only, but also *my* hands and *my* head!"

10 Jesus said to him, "He who is bathed needs only to wash *his* feet, but is completely clean; and you are clean, but not all of you." 11 For He

12:38 ᵃIsaiah 53:1   12:40 ᵃIsaiah 6:10   12:41 ᵃNU-Text reads *because.*   12:47 ᵃNU-Text reads *keep them.*   13:2 ᵃNU-Text reads *And during supper.*

In My Father's House

There were several different kinds of dwellings in Jesus' day. Some people lived in tents and others in caves, but most lived in houses built of stone. In Hebrew, these stone houses were called *beit (beth)*. The word *beth* means not only a place of shelter, but also of love, protection, sharing, peace, fellowship, hospitality, and friendship.

Often, when a family builds a new house or moves, there is great excitement and rejoicing. In some cultures, the owner or head of the household goes into the house before the other family members in order to prepare everything for them. When every room is perfectly arranged for each family member, the head of the family brings everyone together into the new house.

Jesus knew of this custom when He spoke of our future in heaven with Him. "In My Father's house are many mansions; if *it were* not *so,* I would have told you. I go to prepare a place for you . . . I will come again and recieve you to Myself, that where I am, *there* you may be also" (John 14:2, 3).

The disciples traveling with Jesus undoubtedly were exposed to the itinerant ways of their teacher. How refreshing it must have been for them to hear that Jesus was providing a true place of rest and care for them!

This promise is for us as well. Jesus has declared that our future with Him is secure. Our "homecoming" in heaven will be filled with joy as we meet our Lord. Jesus Himself will welcome us. Until then, let us live in joy and expectation for that day when we enter our eternal home.

knew who would betray Him; therefore He said, "You are not all clean."

12 So when He had washed their feet, taken His garments, and sat down again, He said to them, "Do you know what I have done to you? 13 You call Me Teacher and Lord, and you say well, for so I am. 14 If I then, your Lord and Teacher, have washed your feet, you also ought to wash one another's feet. 15 For I have given you an example, that you should do as I have done to you. 16 Most assuredly, I say to you, a servant is not greater than his master; nor is he who is sent greater than he who sent him. 17 If you know these things, blessed are you if you do them.

18 "I do not speak concerning all of you. I know whom I have chosen; but that the Scripture may be fulfilled, 'He who eats bread with Me^a has lifted up his heel against Me.'^b 19 Now I tell you before it comes, that when it does come to pass, you may believe that I am He. 20 Most assuredly, I say to you, he who receives whomever I send receives Me; and he who receives Me receives Him who sent Me."

21 When Jesus had said these things, He was troubled in spirit, and testified and said, "Most assuredly, I say to you, one of you will betray Me." 22 Then the disciples looked at one another, perplexed about whom He spoke.

23 Now there was leaning on Jesus' bosom one of His disciples, whom Jesus loved. 24 Simon Peter therefore motioned to him to ask who it was of whom He spoke.

25 Then, leaning back^a on Jesus' breast, he said to Him, "Lord, who is it?"

26 Jesus answered, "It is he to whom I shall give a piece of bread when I have dipped it." And having dipped the bread, He gave it to Judas Iscariot, the son of Simon. 27 Now after the piece of bread, Satan entered him. Then Jesus said to him, "What you do, do quickly." 28 But no one at the table knew for what reason He said this to him. 29 For some thought, because Judas had the money box,

that Jesus had said to him, "Buy those things we need for the feast," or that he should give something to the poor.

30 Having received the piece of bread, he then went out immediately. And it was night.

31 So, when he had gone out, Jesus said, "Now the Son of Man is glorified, and God is glorified in Him. 32 If God is glorified in Him, God will also glorify Him in Himself, and glorify Him immediately. 33 Little children, I shall be with you a little while longer. You will seek Me; and as I said to the Jews, 'Where I am going, you cannot come,' so now I say to you. 34 A new commandment I give to you, that you love one another; as I have loved you, that you also love one another. 35 By this all will know that you are My disciples, if you have love for one another."

36 Simon Peter said to Him, "Lord, where are You going?"

Jesus answered him, "Where I am going you cannot follow Me now, but you shall follow Me afterward."

37 Peter said to Him, "Lord, why can I not follow You now? I will lay down my life for Your sake."

38 Jesus answered him, "Will you lay down your life for My sake? Most assuredly, I say to you, the rooster shall not crow till you have denied Me three times.

14 "Let not your heart be troubled; you believe in God, believe also in Me. 2 In My Father's house are many mansions;^a if it were not so, I would have told you. I go to prepare a place for you.^b 3 And if I go and prepare a place for you, I will come again and receive you to Myself; that where I am, there you may be also. 4 And where I go you know, and the way you know."

5 Thomas said to Him, "Lord, we do not know where You are going, and how can we know the way?"

6 Jesus said to him, "I am the way, the truth, and the life. No one comes to the Father except through Me.

7 "If you had known Me, you would have known My Father also; and

13:18 ^aNU-Text reads My bread. ^bPsalm 41:9 13:25 ^aNU-Text and M-Text add thus. 14:2 ^aLiterally dwellings ^bNU-Text adds a word which would cause the text to read either if it were not so, would I have told you that I go to prepare a place for you? or if it were not so I would have told you; for I go to prepare a place for you.

The Vineyard and the Vinedresser

When the biblical vinedresser prepared to plant his field, he found a use for everything. First he cleared the rocky Judean soil of stones and thistles. The stones he cleared were built into a watchtower and protective wall enclosing the field. The thorns were then placed on top of the wall, serving as a natural barbed wire to keep wild animals out.

Today the vineyards in Palestine are unlike those seen growing on trellises above the ground. Instead, the vines grow along the surface of the earth. In the warm spring and early summer months, the vine cannot depend on rainfall for its water. In the early morning hours there is enough moisture available from the night's dew to water the plants. However, once the sun rises high overhead, the ground quickly cracks and dries before the water has soaked in.

To ensure that the vine has sufficient water, the vinedresser will lift up the vine and support it with a rock. In doing so, the vinedresser allows the morning moisture to seep into the ground under the vine. The plant then shades the earth from the sun to enable the water to completely soak in. Some of the branches are naturally arched and allow this process without the support of rocks. Others are heavy and must be cut back to prevent the branches from crushing the fruit. Jesus illustrates this process in John 15. "I am the true vine, and My Father is the vinedresser. Every branch in Me that does not bear fruit He takes away; and every branch that bears fruit He prunes, that it may bear more fruit" (John 15:1, 2).

The Greek word translated "takes away" refers to the death of an unfruitful believer or the eventual judgment of his labors (v. 6). This Greek word can also be translated "lifts up," which would then indicate the vinedresser's activities. This correlates perfectly with the ministry that Jesus has as He builds us up until we are able to bear fruit as vital Christians.

Jesus is the vine, and we are the branches. When we, for whatever reason, do not have the strength, knowledge, or maturity to bear fruit, He lifts us up. He supports us so we can bear fruit. And when we are heavy with this fruit, He prunes us of the things that would weigh us down in life so we can bear more fruit. What is this fruit? Jesus explains at the end of His parable. "Go and bear fruit, and *that* your fruit should remain . . . These things I command you, that you love one another" (John 15:16, 17).

from now on you know Him and have seen Him."

8 Philip said to Him, "Lord, show us the Father, and it is sufficient for us."

9 Jesus said to him, "Have I been with you so long, and yet you have not known Me, Philip? He who has seen Me has seen the Father; so how can you say, 'Show us the Father'? 10 Do you not believe that I am in the Father, and the Father in Me? The words that I speak to you I do not speak on My own *authority;* but the Father who dwells in Me does the works. 11 Believe Me that I *am* in the Father and the Father in Me, or else believe Me for the sake of the works themselves.

12 "Most assuredly, I say to you, he who believes in Me, the works that I do he will do also; and greater *works* than these he will do, because I go to My Father. 13 And whatever you ask in My name, that I will do, that the Father may be glorified in the Son. 14 If you ask*a* anything in My name, I will do *it.*

15 "If you love Me, keep*a* My commandments. 16 And I will pray the Father, and He will give you another Helper, that He may abide with you forever— 17 the Spirit of truth, whom the world cannot receive, because it neither sees Him nor knows Him; but you know Him, for He dwells with you and will be in you. 18 I will not leave you orphans; I will come to you.

19 "A little while longer and the world will see Me no more, but you will see Me. Because I live, you will live also. 20 At that day you will know that I *am* in My Father, and you in Me, and I in you. 21 He who has My commandments and keeps them, it is he who loves Me. And he who loves Me will be loved by My Father, and I will love him and manifest Myself to him."

22 Judas (not Iscariot) said to Him, "Lord, how is it that You will manifest Yourself to us, and not to the world?"

23 Jesus answered and said to him, "If anyone loves Me, he will keep My word; and My Father will love him, and We will come to him and make Our home with him. 24 He who does not love Me does not keep My words; and the word which you hear is not Mine but the Father's who sent Me.

25 "These things I have spoken to you while being present with you. 26 But the Helper, the Holy Spirit, whom the Father will send in My name, He will teach you all things, and bring to your remembrance all things that I said to you. 27 Peace I leave with you, My peace I give to you; not as the world gives do I give to you. Let not your heart be troubled, neither let it be afraid. 28 You have heard Me say to you, 'I am going away and coming *back* to you.' If you loved Me, you would rejoice because I said,*a* 'I am going to the Father,' for My Father is greater than I.

29 "And now I have told you before it comes, that when it does come to pass, you may believe. 30 I will no longer talk much with you, for the ruler of this world is coming, and he has nothing in Me. 31 But that the world may know that I love the Father, and as the Father gave Me commandment, so I do. Arise, let us go from here.

15 "I am the true vine, and My Father is the vinedresser. 2 Every branch in Me that does not bear fruit He takes away;*a* and every *branch* that bears fruit He prunes, that it may bear more fruit. 3 You are already clean because of the word which I have spoken to you. 4 Abide in Me, and I in you. As the branch cannot bear fruit of itself, unless it abides in the vine, neither can you, unless you abide in Me.

5 "I am the vine, you *are* the branches. He who abides in Me, and I in him, bears much fruit; for without Me you can do nothing. 6 If anyone does not abide in Me, he is cast out as a branch and is withered; and they gather them and throw *them* into the fire, and they are burned. 7 If you abide in Me, and My words abide in you, you will*a* ask what you desire, and it shall be done for you. 8 By this My Father is glorified, that you bear much fruit; so you will be My disciples.

9 "As the Father loved Me, I also have loved you; abide in My love.

14:14 *a*NU-Text adds *Me.*   14:15 *a*NU-Text reads *you will keep.*   14:28 *a*NU-Text omits *I said.*
15:2 *a*Or *lifts up*   15:7 *a*NU-Text omits *you will.*

10 If you keep My commandments, you will abide in My love, just as I have kept My Father's commandments and abide in His love.

11 "These things I have spoken to you, that My joy may remain in you, and *that* your joy may be full. 12 This is My commandment, that you love one another as I have loved you. 13 Greater love has no one than this, than to lay down one's life for his friends. 14 You are My friends if you do whatever I command you. 15 No longer do I call you servants, for a servant does not know what his master is doing; but I have called you friends, for all things that I heard from My Father I have made known to you. 16 You did not choose Me, but I chose you and appointed you that you should go and bear fruit, and *that* your fruit should remain, that whatever you ask the Father in My name He may give you. 17 These things I command you, that you love one another.

18 "If the world hates you, you know that it hated Me before *it hated* you. 19 If you were of the world, the world would love its own. Yet because you are not of the world, but I chose you out of the world, therefore the world hates you. 20 Remember the word that I said to you, 'A servant is not greater than his master.' If they persecuted Me, they will also persecute you. If they kept My word, they will keep yours also. 21 But all these things they will do to you for My name's sake, because they do not know Him who sent Me. 22 If I had not come and spoken to them, they would have no sin, but now they have no excuse for their sin. 23 He who hates Me hates My Father also. 24 If I had not done among them the works which no one else did, they would have no sin; but now they have seen and also hated both Me and My Father. 25 But *this happened* that the word might be fulfilled which is written in their law, 'They hated Me without a cause.'[a]

26 "But when the Helper comes, whom I shall send to you from the Father, the Spirit of truth who proceeds from the Father, He will testify of Me. 27 And you also will bear witness, because you have been with Me from the beginning.

16 "These things I have spoken to you, that you should not be made to stumble. 2 They will put you out of the synagogues; yes, the time is coming that whoever kills you will think that he offers God service. 3 And these things they will do to you[a] because they have not known the Father nor Me. 4 But these things I have told you, that when the[a] time comes, you may remember that I told you of them.

"And these things I did not say to you at the beginning, because I was with you. 5 "But now I go away to Him who sent Me, and none of you asks Me, 'Where are You going?' 6 But because I have said these things to you, sorrow has filled your heart. 7 Nevertheless I tell you the truth. It is to your advantage that I go away; for if I do not go away, the Helper will not come to you; but if I depart, I will send Him to you. 8 And when He has come, He will convict the world of sin, and of righteousness, and of judgment: 9 of sin, because they do not believe in Me; 10 of righteousness, because I go to My Father and you see Me no more; 11 of judgment, because the ruler of this world is judged.

12 "I still have many things to say to you, but you cannot bear *them* now. 13 However, when He, the Spirit of truth, has come, He will guide you into all truth; for He will not speak on His own *authority*, but whatever He hears He will speak; and He will tell you things to come. 14 He will glorify Me, for He will take of what is Mine and declare *it* to you. 15 All things that the Father has are Mine. Therefore I said that He will take of Mine and declare *it* to you.[a]

16 "A little while, and you will not see Me; and again a little while, and you will see Me, because I go to the Father."

17 Then *some* of His disciples said among themselves, "What is this that He says to us, 'A little while, and you will not see Me; and again a little while, and you will see Me'; and, 'because I go to the Father'?" 18 They

said therefore, "What is this that He says, 'A little while'? We do not know what He is saying."

19 Now Jesus knew that they desired to ask Him, and He said to them, "Are you inquiring among yourselves about what I said, 'A little while, and you will not see Me; and again a little while, and you will see Me'? 20 Most assuredly, I say to you that you will weep and lament, but the world will rejoice; and you will be sorrowful, but your sorrow will be turned into joy. 21 A woman, when she is in labor, has sorrow because her hour has come; but as soon as she has given birth to the child, she no longer remembers the anguish, for joy that a human being has been born into the world. 22 Therefore you now have sorrow; but I will see you again and your heart will rejoice, and your joy no one will take from you.

23 "And in that day you will ask Me nothing. Most assuredly, I say to you, whatever you ask the Father in My name He will give you. 24 Until now you have asked nothing in My name. Ask, and you will receive, that your joy may be full.

25 "These things I have spoken to you in figurative language; but the time is coming when I will no longer speak to you in figurative language, but I will tell you plainly about the Father. 26 In that day you will ask in My name, and I do not say to you that I shall pray the Father for you; 27 for the Father Himself loves you, because you have loved Me, and have believed that I came forth from God. 28 I came forth from the Father and have come into the world. Again, I leave the world and go to the Father."

29 His disciples said to Him, "See, now You are speaking plainly, and using no figure of speech! 30 Now we are sure that You know all things, and have no need that anyone should question You. By this we believe that You came forth from God."

31 Jesus answered them, "Do you now believe? 32 Indeed the hour is coming, yes, has now come, that you will be scattered, each to his own, and will leave Me alone. And yet I am not alone, because the Father is with Me. 33 These things I have spo-

ken to you, that in Me you may have peace. In the world you will*a* have tribulation; but be of good cheer, I have overcome the world."

17 Jesus spoke these words, lifted up His eyes to heaven, and said: "Father, the hour has come. Glorify Your Son, that Your Son also may glorify You, 2 as You have given Him authority over all flesh, that He should*a* give eternal life to as many as You have given Him. 3 And this is eternal life, that they may know You, the only true God, and Jesus Christ whom You have sent. 4 I have glorified You on the earth. I have finished the work which You have given Me to do. 5 And now, O Father, glorify Me together with Yourself, with the glory which I had with You before the world was.

6 "I have manifested Your name to the men whom You have given Me out of the world. They were Yours, You gave them to Me, and they have kept Your word. 7 Now they have known that all things which You have given Me are from You. 8 For I have given to them the words which You have given Me; and they have received *them*, and have known surely that I came forth from You; and they have believed that You sent Me.

9 "I pray for them. I do not pray for the world but for those whom You have given Me, for they are Yours. 10 And all Mine are Yours, and Yours are Mine, and I am glorified in them. 11 Now I am no longer in the world, but these are in the world, and I come to You. Holy Father, keep through Your name those whom You have given Me,*a* that they may be one as We *are*. 12 While I was with them in the world,*a* I kept them in Your name. Those whom You gave Me I have kept;*b* and none of them is lost except the son of perdition, that the Scripture might be fulfilled. 13 But now I come to You, and these things I speak in the world, that they may have My joy fulfilled in themselves. 14 I have given them Your word; and the world has hated them because they are not of the world, just as I am not of the world. 15 I do not pray

---

16:33 *a*NU-Text and M-Text omit *will*.   17:2 *a*M-Text reads *shall*.   17:11 *a*NU-Text and M-Text read *keep them through Your name which You have given Me*.   17:12 *a*NU-Text omits *in the world*.
*b*NU-Text reads *in Your name which You gave Me. And I guarded them* (or *it*).

Peter—Denial to Declaration

On the evening of Jesus Christ's trial and crucifixion, the apostle Peter was in a severe state of depression. Hours earlier, Peter had boldly asserted that he would never deny his Master. Yet later, during Christ's trial, Peter sat crouching in fear, warming himself by a fire. A servant of the high priest's court approached Peter and for the third time asked if he knew Jesus. Peter flatly denied his Lord. Upon his denial, a rooster crowed—fulfilling Jesus' word to Peter that he would deny the Lord three times before dawn. Peter ran out weeping bitterly.

The house of Caiaphas, the high priest, the scene of Jesus' trial before the Sanhedrin, has been unearthed in Jerusalem. The find included many coins, including both Roman and those used exclusively in the temple. A major thoroughfare ran through the courtyard where Jesus was tried. Hebrew inscriptions including the word *corban* meaning "sacrificial gift" were found etched above the lintel of the door. It was in this courtyard that Peter denied Jesus.

For many years Peter had stood by Jesus. He left his fishing nets to follow his Lord wholeheartedly. He stood up for Christ many times in many places before many people. Even hours earlier in the Garden of Gethsemane, Peter boldly was ready to fight for Him. Yet when Jesus was in His most desperate hour of need, Peter abandoned Him.

The emotional scars left on Peter's life must have been devastating. Yet within forty days Peter stood in the Jerusalem temple proclaiming Jesus before three thousand people. This speech took place only one hundred yards from where he had flatly denied Christ as his Lord and Savior. What happened? Why the change in Peter? Three days after Peter's denial, the young fisherman witnessed the risen Christ. Jesus' love and forgiveness freed Peter from the emotional scars seared upon his heart.

Many times we may deny Jesus, unintentionally or willfully, choosing not to include Him in our lives. But we are assured with confidence that Jesus Christ has given us His kingdom. There is no sin too great, too severe, or too scary to separate us from the love of God.

Let Jesus Christ's love turn your broken heart into wholeness, your denials into declarations of His love and forgiveness for all mankind. Then like Peter, go and proclaim boldly what your Lord has done!

that You should take them out of the world, but that You should keep them from the evil one. 16 They are not of the world, just as I am not of the world. 17 Sanctify them by Your truth. Your word is truth. 18 As You sent Me into the world, I also have sent them into the world. 19 And for their sakes I sanctify Myself, that they also may be sanctified by the truth.

20 "I do not pray for these alone, but also for those who will*a* believe in Me through their word; 21 that they all may be one, as You, Father, *are* in Me, and I in You; that they also may be one in Us, that the world may believe that You sent Me. 22 And the glory which You gave Me I have given them, that they may be one just as We are one: 23 I in them, and You in Me; that they may be made perfect in one, and that the world may know that You have sent Me, and have loved them as You have loved Me.

24 "Father, I desire that they also whom You gave Me may be with Me where I am, that they may behold My glory which You have given Me; for You loved Me before the foundation of the world. 25 O righteous Father! The world has not known You, but I have known You; and these have known that You sent Me. 26 And I have declared to them Your name, and will declare *it*, that the love with which You loved Me may be in them, and I in them."

18 When Jesus had spoken these words, He went out with His disciples over the Brook Kidron, where there was a garden, which He and His disciples entered. 2 And Judas, who betrayed Him, also knew the place; for Jesus often met there with His disciples. 3 Then Judas, having received a detachment *of troops*, and officers from the chief priests and Pharisees, came there with lanterns, torches, and weapons. 4 Jesus therefore, knowing all things that would come upon Him, went forward and said to them, "Whom are you seeking?"

5 They answered Him, "Jesus of Nazareth."

Jesus said to them, "I am *He*." And Judas, who betrayed Him, also stood with them. 6 Now when He said to them, "I am *He*," they drew back and fell to the ground.

7 Then He asked them again, "Whom are you seeking?"

And they said, "Jesus of Nazareth."

8 Jesus answered, "I have told you that I am *He*. Therefore, if you seek Me, let these go their way," 9 that the saying might be fulfilled which He spoke, "Of those whom You gave Me I have lost none."

10 Then Simon Peter, having a sword, drew it and struck the high priest's servant, and cut off his right ear. The servant's name was Malchus.

11 So Jesus said to Peter, "Put your sword into the sheath. Shall I not drink the cup which My Father has given Me?"

12 Then the detachment *of troops* and the captain and the officers of the Jews arrested Jesus and bound Him. 13 And they led Him away to Annas first, for he was the father-in-law of Caiaphas who was high priest that year. 14 Now it was Caiaphas who advised the Jews that it was expedient that one man should die for the people.

15 And Simon Peter followed Jesus, and so *did* another*a* disciple. Now that disciple was known to the high priest, and went with Jesus into the courtyard of the high priest. 16 But Peter stood at the door outside. Then the other disciple, who was known to the high priest, went out and spoke to her who kept the door, and brought Peter in. 17 Then the servant girl who kept the door said to Peter, "You are not also *one* of this Man's disciples, are you?"

He said, "I am not."

18 Now the servants and officers who had made a fire of coals stood there, for it was cold, and they warmed themselves. And Peter stood with them and warmed himself.

19 The high priest then asked Jesus about His disciples and His doctrine.

20 Jesus answered him, "I spoke openly to the world. I always taught in synagogues and in the temple, where the Jews always meet,*a* and in secret I have said nothing. 21 Why do

---

17:20 *a*NU-Text and M-Text omit *will*.   18:15 *a*M-Text reads *the other*.   18:20 *a*NU-Text reads *where*
all the Jews meet.

you ask Me? Ask those who have heard Me what I said to them. Indeed they know what I said."

22 And when He had said these things, one of the officers who stood by struck Jesus with the palm of his hand, saying, "Do You answer the high priest like that?"

23 Jesus answered him, "If I have spoken evil, bear witness of the evil; but if well, why do you strike Me?"

24 Then Annas sent Him bound to Caiaphas the high priest.

25 Now Simon Peter stood and warmed himself. Therefore they said to him, "You are not also *one* of His disciples, are you?"

He denied *it* and said, "I am not!"

26 One of the servants of the high priest, a relative *of him* whose ear Peter cut off, said, "Did I not see you in the garden with Him?" 27 Peter then denied again; and immediately a rooster crowed.

28 Then they led Jesus from Caiaphas to the Praetorium, and it was early morning. But they themselves did not go into the Praetorium, lest they should be defiled, but that they might eat the Passover. 29 Pilate then went out to them and said, "What accusation do you bring against this Man?"

30 They answered and said to him, "If He were not an evildoer, we would not have delivered Him up to you."

31 Then Pilate said to them, "You take Him and judge Him according to your law."

Therefore the Jews said to him, "It is not lawful for us to put anyone to death," 32 that the saying of Jesus might be fulfilled which He spoke, signifying by what death He would die.

33 Then Pilate entered the Praetorium again, called Jesus, and said to Him, "Are You the King of the Jews?"

34 Jesus answered him, "Are you speaking for yourself about this, or did others tell you this concerning Me?"

35 Pilate answered, "Am I a Jew? Your own nation and the chief priests have delivered You to me. What have You done?"

36 Jesus answered, "My kingdom is not of this world. If My kingdom were of this world, My servants would fight, so that I should not be delivered to the Jews; but now My kingdom is not from here."

37 Pilate therefore said to Him, "Are You a king then?"

Jesus answered, "You say *rightly* that I am a king. For this cause I was born, and for this cause I have come into the world, that I should bear witness to the truth. Everyone who is of the truth hears My voice."

38 Pilate said to Him, "What is truth?" And when he had said this, he went out again to the Jews, and said to them, "I find no fault in Him at all.

39 "But you have a custom that I should release someone to you at the Passover. Do you therefore want me to release to you the King of the Jews?"

40 Then they all cried again, saying, "Not this Man, but Barabbas!" Now Barabbas was a robber.

19 So then Pilate took Jesus and scourged *Him*. 2 And the soldiers twisted a crown of thorns and put *it* on His head, and they put on Him a purple robe. 3 Then they said,[a] "Hail, King of the Jews!" And they struck Him with their hands.

4 Pilate then went out again, and said to them, "Behold, I am bringing Him out to you, that you may know that I find no fault in Him."

5 Then Jesus came out, wearing the crown of thorns and the purple robe. And *Pilate* said to them, "Behold the Man!"

6 Therefore, when the chief priests and officers saw Him, they cried out, saying, "Crucify *Him*, crucify *Him!*"

Pilate said to them, "You take Him and crucify *Him*, for I find no fault in Him."

7 The Jews answered him, "We have a law, and according to our[a] law He ought to die, because He made Himself the Son of God."

8 Therefore, when Pilate heard that saying, he was the more afraid, 9 and went again into the Praetorium, and said to Jesus, "Where are You from?" But Jesus gave him no answer.

10 Then Pilate said to Him, "Are You not speaking to me? Do You not know that I have power to cru-

---

19:3 [a]NU-Text reads *And they came up to Him and said.*   19:7 [a]NU-Text reads *the law.*

cify You, and power to release You?"

11 Jesus answered, "You could have no power at all against Me unless it had been given you from above. Therefore the one who delivered Me to you has the greater sin."

12 From then on Pilate sought to release Him, but the Jews cried out, saying, "If you let this Man go, you are not Caesar's friend. Whoever makes himself a king speaks against Caesar."

13 When Pilate therefore heard that saying, he brought Jesus out and sat down in the judgment seat in a place that is called The Pavement, but in Hebrew, Gabbatha. 14 Now it was the Preparation Day of the Passover, and about the sixth hour. And he said to the Jews, "Behold your King!"

15 But they cried out, "Away with Him, away with Him! Crucify Him!"

Pilate said to them, "Shall I crucify your King?"

The chief priests answered, "We have no king but Caesar!"

16 Then he delivered Him to them to be crucified. Then they took Jesus and led Him away.ᵃ

17 And He, bearing His cross, went out to a place called the Place of a Skull, which is called in Hebrew, Golgotha, 18 where they crucified Him, and two others with Him, one on either side, and Jesus in the center. 19 Now Pilate wrote a title and put it on the cross. And the writing was:

JESUS OF NAZARETH,
THE KING OF THE JEWS.

20 Then many of the Jews read this title, for the place where Jesus was crucified was near the city; and it was written in Hebrew, Greek, and Latin. 21 Therefore the chief priests of the Jews said to Pilate, "Do not write, 'The King of the Jews,' but, 'He said, "I am the King of the Jews."'"

22 Pilate answered, "What I have written, I have written."

23 Then the soldiers, when they had crucified Jesus, took His garments and made four parts, to each soldier a part, and also the tunic. Now the tunic was without seam, woven from the top in one piece. 24 They said therefore among themselves, "Let us not tear it, but cast lots for it, whose it shall be," that the Scripture might be fulfilled which says:

"They divided My garments among them,
And for My clothing they cast lots."ᵃ

Therefore the soldiers did these things.

25 Now there stood by the cross of Jesus His mother, and His mother's sister, Mary the wife of Clopas, and Mary Magdalene. 26 When Jesus therefore saw His mother, and the disciple whom He loved standing by, He said to His mother, "Woman, behold your son!" 27 Then He said to the disciple, "Behold your mother!" And from that hour that disciple took her to his own home.

28 After this, Jesus, knowingᵃ that all things were now accomplished, that the Scripture might be fulfilled, said, "I thirst!" 29 Now a vessel full of sour wine was sitting there; and they filled a sponge with sour wine, put it on hyssop, and put it to His mouth. 30 So when Jesus had received the sour wine, He said, "It is finished!" And bowing His head, He gave up His spirit.

31 Therefore, because it was the Preparation Day, that the bodies should not remain on the cross on the Sabbath (for that Sabbath was a high day), the Jews asked Pilate that their legs might be broken, and that they might be taken away. 32 Then the soldiers came and broke the legs of the first and of the other who was crucified with Him. 33 But when they came to Jesus and saw that He was already dead, they did not break His legs. 34 But one of the soldiers pierced His side with a spear, and immediately blood and water came out. 35 And he who has seen has testified, and his testimony is true; and he knows that he is telling the truth, so that you may believe. 36 For these things were done that the Scripture should be fulfilled, "Not one of His bones shall be broken."ᵃ 37 And again another Scripture says, "They shall look on Him whom they pierced."ᵃ

38 After this, Joseph of Arimathea,

19:16 ᵃNU-Text omits and led Him away.   19:24 ᵃPsalm 22:18   19:28 ᵃM-Text reads seeing.
19:36 ᵃExodus 12:46; Numbers 9:12; Psalm 34:20   19:37 ᵃZechariah 12:10

Where Jesus Lay

North of the city of Jerusalem are the famous Sanhedrin tombs, hewn out of the chalky mountainside. Over seventy of these tombs, thought to be the burial place of the Jewish Sanhedrin, have been unearthed. Each dates to the era of Christ. The unique architectural style of these tombs represents the burial customs of the Jewish people in the first century. This style lasted only a short time, and the design fits the exact description of Jesus' tomb as recorded in the Scriptures.

The Gospels report that on the first Easter morning, after Mary Magdalene's report of the missing stone, John and Peter ran to the tomb (see John 20:1–8). John stooped to look into the tomb, while Peter went on inside.

Entrance into the Sanhedrin tombs also required one to stoop down to enter the two-to-three-foot opening. Sealed with a two-ton stone, the entryway led to a ten-foot-square chamber, with waist-high slabs on each side of the walls. Here bodies were placed to be anointed. John 20:12 reports how Mary saw two angels at the head and foot of where Jesus' body had lain to be anointed. Jesus' grave clothes were neatly rolled and folded, separate from the head cloth on these slabs.

Jesus was, in fact, buried in the tomb of Joseph of Arimathea, a member of the Sanhedrin. Another Sanhedrin member, Nicodemus, also helped in the burial process. Not all Jews, including the religious leaders, wanted to see Jesus crucified. We understand from this account that some actually served the Lord in this most unusual way. By burying Jesus, Nicodemus and Joseph of Arimathea risked ridicule, slander, and excommunication. Their courage and belief were great.

The literally accurate description of Jesus' empty tomb is strong, contemporary, eyewitness evidence of His resurrection.

The cords of death could not hold the power of God. On the third day, Jesus rose again. The empty tomb is the greatest witness of the deity and victory of Jesus Christ. With faith we can go and proclaim what the angel told the women that first Easter morning, "He is not here; for He is risen, as He said" (Matt.28:6). Like Nicodemus and Joseph of Arimathea, let us have courage to serve our Lord in unique and unusual ways.

being a disciple of Jesus, but secretly, for fear of the Jews, asked Pilate that he might take away the body of Jesus; and Pilate gave *him* permission. So he came and took the body of Jesus. 39 And Nicodemus, who at first came to Jesus by night, also came, bringing a mixture of myrrh and aloes, about a hundred pounds. 40 Then they took the body of Jesus, and bound it in strips of linen with the spices, as the custom of the Jews is to bury. 41 Now in the place where He was crucified there was a garden, and in the garden a new tomb in which no one had yet been laid. 42 So there they laid Jesus, because of the Jews' Preparation *Day,* for the tomb was nearby.

20 Now the first *day* of the week Mary Magdalene went to the tomb early, while it was still dark, and saw *that* the stone had been taken away from the tomb. 2 Then she ran and came to Simon Peter, and to the other disciple, whom Jesus loved, and said to them, "They have taken away the Lord out of the tomb, and we do not know where they have laid Him."

3 Peter therefore went out, and the other disciple, and were going to the tomb. 4 So they both ran together, and the other disciple outran Peter and came to the tomb first. 5 And he, stooping down and looking in, saw the linen cloths lying *there;* yet he did not go in. 6 Then Simon Peter came, following him, and went into the tomb; and he saw the linen cloths lying *there,* 7 and the handkerchief that had been around His head, not lying with the linen cloths, but folded together in a place by itself. 8 Then the other disciple, who came to the tomb first, went in also; and he saw and believed. 9 For as yet they did not know the Scripture, that He must rise again from the dead. 10 Then the disciples went away again to their own homes.

11 But Mary stood outside by the tomb weeping, and as she wept she stooped down *and looked* into the tomb. 12 And she saw two angels in white sitting, one at the head and the other at the feet, where the body of Jesus had lain. 13 Then they said to

her, "Woman, why are you weeping?"

She said to them, "Because they have taken away my Lord, and I do not know where they have laid Him."

14 Now when she had said this, she turned around and saw Jesus standing *there,* and did not know that it was Jesus. 15 Jesus said to her, "Woman, why are you weeping? Whom are you seeking?"

She, supposing Him to be the gardener, said to Him, "Sir, if You have carried Him away, tell me where You have laid Him, and I will take Him away."

16 Jesus said to her, "Mary!"

She turned and said to Him,[a] "Rabboni!" (which is to say, Teacher).

17 Jesus said to her, "Do not cling to Me, for I have not yet ascended to My Father; but go to My brethren and say to them, 'I am ascending to My Father and your Father, and *to* My God and your God.'"

18 Mary Magdalene came and told the disciples that she had seen the Lord,[a] and *that* He had spoken these things to her.

19 Then, the same day at evening, being the first *day* of the week, when the doors were shut where the disciples were assembled,[a] for fear of the Jews, Jesus came and stood in the midst, and said to them, "Peace *be* with you." 20 When He had said this, He showed them *His* hands and His side. Then the disciples were glad when they saw the Lord.

21 So Jesus said to them again, "Peace to you! As the Father has sent Me, I also send you." 22 And when He had said this, He breathed on *them,* and said to them, "Receive the Holy Spirit. 23 If you forgive the sins of any, they are forgiven them; if you retain the *sins* of any, they are retained."

24 Now Thomas, called the Twin, one of the twelve, was not with them when Jesus came. 25 The other disciples therefore said to him, "We have seen the Lord."

So he said to them, "Unless I see in His hands the print of the nails, and put my finger into the print of the nails, and put my hand into His side, I will not believe."

26 And after eight days His disci-

Believe It Before You See It

The apostle Thomas has often been criticized for his lack of faith concerning the resurrection of Jesus Christ. During one of Jesus' resurrection appearances, He came to the disciples when they were hiding together in a room in Jerusalem when Thomas was not present. Later the disciples told Thomas that they had seen Jesus (John 20:24). Thomas boldly declared, "Unless I see in His hands the print of the nails, and put my finger into the print of the nails, and put my hand into His side, I will not believe" (John 20:25).

Eight days later, Jesus again appeared to the disciples still in hiding. This time Thomas was present. Jesus said to Thomas, " 'Reach your finger here, and look at My hands; and reach your hand *here,* and put *it* into My side. Do not be unbelieving, but believing.' And Thomas answered and said to Him, 'My Lord and my God!' Jesus said to him, 'Thomas, because you have seen Me, you have believed. Blessed *are* those who have not seen and *yet* have believed' " (John 20:27–29).

Earlier in Jesus' ministry, when He faced mounting resistance from Jewish leaders in Jerusalem, all of the disciples tried to persuade Him not to return to Judea. Thomas was the only disciple who boldly proclaimed, "Let us also go, that we may die with Him" (John 11:16).

Thomas was willing to make a commitment and stick with it. The difficulty for Thomas was not his lack of faith in Jesus, but his concrete thinking. When Jesus was alive and there was hope for a political messianic kingdom led by Jesus, Thomas was willing to die for His cause. But once Jesus was dead, Thomas's dream of freedom from the Roman overlords was finished. His locked-in thinking kept him from envisioning and believing an even greater Kingdom.

Thomas teaches us not to pour our own plans in concrete, so that we block God's greater plans and purposes. Allow God to do the impossible in your life. Commit yourself completely as Thomas did. But do not allow locked-in thinking to keep you from anticipating a different result. You have to believe it before you see it!

ples were again inside, and Thomas with them. Jesus came, the doors being shut, and stood in the midst, and said, "Peace to you!" 27 Then He said to Thomas, "Reach your finger here, and look at My hands; and reach your hand *here*, and put *it* into My side. Do not be unbelieving, but believing."

28 And Thomas answered and said to Him, "My Lord and my God!"

29 Jesus said to him, "Thomas,*a* because you have seen Me, you have believed. Blessed *are* those who have not seen and *yet* have believed."

30 And truly Jesus did many other signs in the presence of His disciples, which are not written in this book; 31 but these are written that you may believe that Jesus is the Christ, the Son of God, and that believing you may have life in His name.

21 After these things Jesus showed Himself again to the disciples at the Sea of Tiberias, and in this way He showed *Himself*: 2 Simon Peter, Thomas called the Twin, Nathanael of Cana in Galilee, the *sons* of Zebedee, and two others of His disciples were together. 3 Simon Peter said to them, "I am going fishing."

They said to him, "We are going with you also." They went out and immediately*a* got into the boat, and that night they caught nothing. 4 But when the morning had now come, Jesus stood on the shore; yet the disciples did not know that it was Jesus. 5 Then Jesus said to them, "Children, have you any food?"

They answered Him, "No."

6 And He said to them, "Cast the net on the right side of the boat, and you will find *some*." So they cast, and now they were not able to draw it in because of the multitude of fish.

7 Therefore that disciple whom Jesus loved said to Peter, "It is the Lord!" Now when Simon Peter heard that it was the Lord, he put on *his* outer garment (for he had removed it), and plunged into the sea. 8 But the other disciples came in the little boat (for they were not far from land, but about two hundred cubits), dragging the net with fish. 9 Then, as soon as they had come to land, they

saw a fire of coals there, and fish laid on it, and bread. 10 Jesus said to them, "Bring some of the fish which you have just caught."

11 Simon Peter went up and dragged the net to land, full of large fish, one hundred and fifty-three; and although there were so many, the net was not broken. 12 Jesus said to them, "Come *and* eat breakfast." Yet none of the disciples dared ask Him, "Who are You?"—knowing that it was the Lord. 13 Jesus then came and took the bread and gave it to them, and likewise the fish.

14 This *is* now the third time Jesus showed Himself to His disciples after He was raised from the dead.

15 So when they had eaten breakfast, Jesus said to Simon Peter, "Simon, *son* of Jonah,*a* do you love Me more than these?"

He said to Him, "Yes, Lord; You know that I love You."

He said to him, "Feed My lambs."

16 He said to him again a second time, "Simon, *son* of Jonah,*a* do you love Me?"

He said to Him, "Yes, Lord; You know that I love You."

He said to him, "Tend My sheep."

17 He said to him the third time, "Simon, *son* of Jonah,*a* do you love Me?" Peter was grieved because He said to him the third time, "Do you love Me?"

And he said to Him, "Lord, You know all things; You know that I love You."

Jesus said to him, "Feed My sheep. 18 Most assuredly, I say to you, when you were younger, you girded yourself and walked where you wished; but when you are old, you will stretch out your hands, and another will gird you and carry *you* where you do not wish." 19 This He spoke, signifying by what death he would glorify God. And when He had spoken this, He said to him, "Follow Me."

20 Then Peter, turning around, saw the disciple whom Jesus loved following, who also had leaned on His breast at the supper, and said, "Lord, who is the one who betrays You?" 21 Peter, seeing him, said to Jesus, "But Lord, what *about* this man?"

22 Jesus said to him, "If I will that

20:29 *a*NU-Text and M-Text omit *Thomas*.   21:3 *a*NU-Text omits *immediately*.   21:15 *a*NU-Text reads *John*.   21:16 *a*NU-Text reads *John*.   21:17 *a*NU-Text reads *John*.

Respect Those Around You

Wow! Talk about a challenge. Is it possible to know and respect *all* people? That would take a mountain of faith!

Is it possible to honor crude and cruel persons who destroy life and love? Yes. We do not condone their behavior, but we recognize that they are still souls for whom Christ died on the cross. And we can still pause to pray, "God have mercy on their souls."

On a far more practical level, the challenge you and I have is to respect the people with whom we live, work, and closely relate. Can we respect them after we've seen them at their worst? Can we honor them as beautiful human beings even after their weaknesses have been grossly exposed? The answer must be a resounding YES. Consider how Jesus restored Peter to service even after this disciple had denied his Lord and Master three times (see John 21:15–19).

How can our faith perform this miracle? Quite simply. Our faith reminds us that we, too, are imperfect human beings. Our faith reminds us that God loves us even though He knows us better than anybody else! And if God loves in spite of what we are, He will give us the grace to pass that charitable spirit along!

In gratitude for God's grace and forgiveness, pray: *I thank You today, O God my Father, for honoring me even after I have disappointed You, for treating me like a noble person even after I have been guilty of disgraceful behavior in Your sight. Help me now to treat my fellow human beings with no less respect than You have shown me.*

Thank You, Father, for this faith. It's working miracles. Amen.

he remain till I come, what *is that* to you? You follow Me."

23 Then this saying went out among the brethren that this disciple would not die. Yet Jesus did not say to him that he would not die, but, "If I will that he remain till I come, what *is that* to you?"

24 This is the disciple who testifies of these things, and wrote these things; and we know that his testimony is true.

25 And there are also many other things that Jesus did, which if they were written one by one, I suppose that even the world itself could not contain the books that would be written. Amen.

Acts

Overview of Acts

The Book of Acts is one of the most fascinating accounts of the power of possibility thinking. When Jesus Christ instilled His Spirit into the lives of twelve men, they went out to literally change the world!

Written in the early 60s A.D., Acts is the account of the initial spread of Christianity. It was written by Luke, the same author whose Gospel bears his name. Luke gives a firsthand account of the events surrounding the early church. He personally accompanied Paul during several evangelistic trips through Syria, Asia Minor, Greece, and Rome where they planted and nourished many new churches. (This is indicated by the pronouns "we" and "us" found in Acts 16:10–17; 20:5—21:18; and 27:1—28:16).

Luke writes this book to Christian Gentiles who were interested in this newly found faith. The book is addressed to Theophilus (Acts 1:1). This name (meaning "lover of God") could refer to an individual who wanted to know more about Christianity or to a people who truly loved God.

Acts presents the origin of our faith with extreme accuracy. Archaeologists confirm that Luke was among the most reliable historians of antiquity. A master of the Greek language, Luke gives the most detailed account of the early church of all the Gospels and Epistles.

Acts portrays the success of the gospel as it spread like wildfire from Jerusalem to Rome in only thirty years. In the face of persecution, the early church's growth and development are inspiring. Numerous lists of cities, dates, events, persons, and their beliefs throughout the Roman empire are recorded here as nowhere else in the entire New Testament.

The Christian Church all began with twelve men and a few women who lived and walked with our Lord. Once afraid of their Roman overlords, these possibility thinkers caught the vision and Spirit of God. Like a small spring that bursts forth into a mighty river, the message and love of Jesus Christ trickled down from the heights of Jerusalem and roared out to change the world forever!

Jesus in Acts

The resurrected Christ is central in the sermons and apologetics of the Book of Acts. The apostolic testimony of Christ's resurrection and the infilling power of the Holy Spirit on the day of Pentecost all point to Jesus as both Lord and Christ (2:22–36 and 10:34–43). Salvation and the substantiating works of God the Spirit are themes of this book that records the earliest acts of the Christian church as they preached eternal life through belief in the risen Jesus.

Keys to Acts

Key Word: Growth. This book is unique in its account of the period of and following Jesus' ascension. It serves as the historical link between the Gospels and the Epistles. The Book of Acts is written in a personal view by Luke to show the progressive spread of the gospel through the newly empowered believers. Theologically, Acts is written to present Christianity apologetically, as distinct from Judaism, but also as its fulfillment. The book covers the one-generation transition of the primarily Jewish body of Christ to the predominantly Gentile membership.

Key Verses: "But you shall receive power when the Holy Spirit has come upon you; and you shall be witnesses to Me in Jerusalem, and in all Judea and Samaria, and to the ends of the earth" (1:8).

"And they continued steadfastly in the apostles' doctrine and fellowship, in the breaking of bread, and in prayers. Then fear came upon every soul, and many wonders and signs were done through the apostles. Now all who believed were together, and had all things in common, and sold their possessions and goods, and divided them among all, as anyone had need. So continuing daily with one accord in the temple, and breaking bread from house to house, they ate their food with gladness and simplicity of heart, praising God and having favor with all the people. And the Lord added to the church daily those who were being saved" (2:42–47).

Key Chapter: Acts 2. Chapter 2 records the earth-changing events of the Day of Pentecost when the Holy Spirit comes, fulfilling Christ's promise that He would send the Comforter. The Holy Spirit transforms the lives of a small band of praying believers into a worldwide church that is ever fulfilling Jesus' great call to preach the gospel to all the world.

1 The former account I made, O Theophilus, of all that Jesus began both to do and teach, 2 until the day in which He was taken up, after He through the Holy Spirit had given commandments to the apostles whom He had chosen, 3 to whom He also presented Himself alive after His suffering by many infallible proofs, being seen by them during forty days and speaking of the things pertaining to the kingdom of God.

4 And being assembled together with *them,* He commanded them not to depart from Jerusalem, but to wait for the Promise of the Father, "which," *He said,* "you have heard from Me; 5 for John truly baptized with water, but you shall be baptized with the Holy Spirit not many days from now." 6 Therefore, when they had come together, they asked Him, saying, "Lord, will You at this time restore the kingdom to Israel?" 7 And He said to them, "It is not for you to know times or seasons which the Father has put in His own authority. 8 But you shall receive power when the Holy Spirit has come upon you; and you shall be witnesses to Me*a* in Jerusalem, and in all Judea and Samaria, and to the end of the earth."

9 Now when He had spoken these things, while they watched, He was taken up, and a cloud received Him out of their sight. 10 And while they looked steadfastly toward heaven as He went up, behold, two men stood by them in white apparel, 11 who also said, "Men of Galilee, why do you stand gazing up into heaven? This *same* Jesus, who was taken up from you into heaven, will so come in like manner as you saw Him go into heaven."

12 Then they returned to Jerusalem from the mount called Olivet, which is near Jerusalem, a Sabbath day's journey. 13 And when they had entered, they went up into the upper room where they were staying: Peter, James, John, and Andrew; Philip and Thomas; Bartholomew and Matthew; James *the son* of Alphaeus and Simon the Zealot; and Judas *the son* of James. 14 These all continued with one accord in prayer and supplication,*a* with the women and Mary the mother of Jesus, and with His brothers.

15 And in those days Peter stood up in the midst of the disciples*a* (altogether the number of names was about a hundred and twenty), and said, 16 "Men *and* brethren, this Scripture had to be fulfilled, which the Holy Spirit spoke before by the mouth of David concerning Judas, who became a guide to those who arrested Jesus; 17 for he was numbered with us and obtained a part in this ministry."

18 (Now this man purchased a field with the wages of iniquity; and falling headlong, he burst open in the middle and all his entrails gushed out. 19 And it became known to all those dwelling in Jerusalem; so that field is called in their own language, Akel Dama, that is, Field of Blood.)

20 "For it is written in the book of Psalms:

1:8 *a*NU-Text reads My witnesses.   1:14 *a*NU-Text omits and supplication.   1:15 *a*NU-Text reads brethren.

The Nations of Pentecost

Pentecost, a Jewish feast also known as the Feast of Weeks, marked the completion of the barley harvest. On this annual holiday about 50 days after the resurrection of Jesus, Jewish people from throughout the Roman Empire were gathered in the city of Jerusalem to observe this great religious holiday. When the Holy Spirit was poured out on the apostles, they began to speak with "other tongues," and these people from other nations understood them perfectly (Acts 2:5–13). This map shows the different regions of the Roman Empire represented in Jerusalem on the Day of Pentecost.

Go into All the World

During Jesus' ministry, He specifically told His disciples that, following His death and resurrection, they would see Him in Galilee. Jesus spent a great deal of His early ministry there.

Galilee means "Circle" (of the nations). Here, the ancient world's highways crisscrossed to find outlets at the coastal cities of Phoenicia and the desert capitals of Ammon and Damascus. Galilee was the place where Jesus began His ministry—healing the lame to walk, giving sight to the blind, and healing all who were brought to Him.

Following Jesus' resurrection, the angel at the tomb told the women to go quickly and tell the disciples that Jesus was going before them into Galilee. There they would see Him. As these followers made their journey to Galilee, Jesus appeared to them on a high mountain. Through this appearance, Jesus completed the final victory over death; and in the "Circle" (of the nations) He commissioned His disciples to carry the good news of His resurrection and God's love and forgiveness to all lands, cultures, and peoples. That commission continues to us today. Like the first disciples, we should share our faith with all people. We have the same comforting promise that Jesus gave to His disciples before His ascension: "And lo, I am with you always" (Matt. 28:20).

'Let his dwelling place be
　desolate,
And let no one live in it';[a]

and,

'Let[b] another take his office.'[c]

21 "Therefore, of these men who have accompanied us all the time that the Lord Jesus went in and out among us, 22 beginning from the baptism of John to that day when He was taken up from us, one of these must become a witness with us of His resurrection."

23 And they proposed two: Joseph called Barsabas, who was surnamed Justus, and Matthias. 24 And they prayed and said, "You, O Lord, who know the hearts of all, show which of these two You have chosen 25 to take part in this ministry and apostleship from which Judas by transgression fell, that he might go to his own place." 26 And they cast their lots, and the lot fell on Matthias. And he was numbered with the eleven apostles.

2 When the Day of Pentecost had fully come, they were all with one accord[a] in one place. 2 And suddenly there came a sound from heaven, as of a rushing mighty wind, and it filled the whole house where they were sitting. 3 Then there appeared to them divided tongues, as of fire, and one sat upon each of them. 4 And they were all filled with the Holy Spirit and began to speak with other tongues, as the Spirit gave them utterance.

5 And there were dwelling in Jerusalem Jews, devout men, from every nation under heaven. 6 And when this sound occurred, the multitude came together, and were confused, because everyone heard them speak in his own language. 7 Then they were all amazed and marveled, saying to one another, "Look, are not all these who speak Galileans? 8 And how is it that we hear, each in our own language in which we were born? 9 Parthians and Medes and Elamites, those dwelling in Mesopotamia, Judea and Cappadocia, Pontus and Asia, 10 Phrygia and Pamphylia, Egypt and the parts of Libya adjoining Cyrene, visitors from Rome, both Jews and proselytes, 11 Cretans and Arabs—we hear them speaking in our own tongues the wonderful works of God." 12 So they were all amazed and perplexed, saying to one another, "Whatever could this mean?"

13 Others mocking said, "They are full of new wine."

14 But Peter, standing up with the eleven, raised his voice and said to them, "Men of Judea and all who dwell in Jerusalem, let this be known to you, and heed my words. 15 For these are not drunk, as you suppose, since it is only the third hour of the day. 16 But this is what was spoken by the prophet Joel:

17 'And it shall come to pass in the
　　last days, says God,
　That I will pour out of My Spirit
　　on all flesh;
　Your sons and your daughters
　　shall prophesy,
　Your young men shall see
　　visions,
　Your old men shall dream
　　dreams.
18 And on My menservants and
　　on My maidservants
　I will pour out My Spirit in
　　those days;
　And they shall prophesy.
19 I will show wonders in heaven
　　above
　And signs in the earth beneath:
　Blood and fire and vapor of
　　smoke.
20 The sun shall be turned into
　　darkness,
　And the moon into blood,
　Before the coming of the great
　　and awesome day of the
　　LORD.
21 And it shall come to pass
　That whoever calls on the
　　name of the LORD
　Shall be saved.'[a]

22 "Men of Israel, hear these words: Jesus of Nazareth, a Man attested by God to you by miracles, wonders, and signs which God did through Him in your midst, as you yourselves also know— 23 Him, being delivered by the determined purpose and foreknowledge of God, you have taken[a] by lawless hands, have

---

1:20 [a]Psalm 69:25　　[b]Psalm 109:8　　[c]Greek episkopen
2:21 [a]Joel 2:28–32　　2:23 [a]NU-Text omits have taken.　　2:1 [a]NU-Text reads together.

crucified, and put to death; 24 whom God raised up, having loosed the pains of death, because it was not possible that He should be held by it. 25 For David says concerning Him:

'I foresaw the LORD always
     before my face,
For He is at my right hand, that
     I may not be shaken.
26 Therefore my heart rejoiced,
     and my tongue was glad;
Moreover my flesh also will
     rest in hope.
27 For You will not leave my soul
     in Hades,
Nor will You allow Your Holy
     One to see corruption.
28 You have made known to me
     the ways of life;
You will make me full of joy
     in Your presence.'a

29 "Men and brethren, let me speak freely to you of the patriarch David, that he is both dead and buried, and his tomb is with us to this day. 30 Therefore, being a prophet, and knowing that God had sworn with an oath to him that of the fruit of his body, according to the flesh, He would raise up the Christ to sit on his throne,a 31 he, foreseeing this, spoke concerning the resurrection of the Christ, that His soul was not left in Hades, nor did His flesh see corruption. 32 This Jesus God has raised up, of which we are all witnesses. 33 Therefore being exalted to the right hand of God, and having received from the Father the promise of the Holy Spirit, He poured out this which you now see and hear. 34 "For David did not ascend into the heavens, but he says himself:

'The LORD said to my Lord,
   "Sit at My right hand,
35 Till I make Your enemies Your
     footstool." 'a

36 "Therefore let all the house of Israel know assuredly that God has made this Jesus, whom you crucified, both Lord and Christ."

37 Now when they heard this, they were cut to the heart, and said to Peter and the rest of the apostles, "Men

and brethren, what shall we do?"

38 Then Peter said to them, "Repent, and let every one of you be baptized in the name of Jesus Christ for the remission of sins; and you shall receive the gift of the Holy Spirit. 39 For the promise is to you and to your children, and to all who are afar off, as many as the Lord our God will call."

40 And with many other words he testified and exhorted them, saying, "Be saved from this perverse generation." 41 Then those who gladlya received his word were baptized; and that day about three thousand souls were added to them. 42 And they continued steadfastly in the apostles' doctrine and fellowship, in the breaking of bread, and in prayers. 43 Then fear came upon every soul, and many wonders and signs were done through the apostles. 44 Now all who believed were together, and had all things in common, 45 and sold their possessions and goods, and divided them among all, as anyone had need.

46 So continuing daily with one accord in the temple, and breaking bread from house to house, they ate their food with gladness and simplicity of heart, 47 praising God and having favor with all the people. And the Lord added to the churcha daily those who were being saved.

3 Now Peter and John went up together to the temple at the hour of prayer, the ninth hour. 2 And a certain man lame from his mother's womb was carried, whom they laid daily at the gate of the temple which is called Beautiful, to ask alms from those who entered the temple; 3 who, seeing Peter and John about to go into the temple, asked for alms. 4 And fixing his eyes on him, with John, Peter said, "Look at us." 5 So he gave them his attention, expecting to receive something from them. 6 Then Peter said, "Silver and gold I do not have, but what I do have I give you: In the name of Jesus Christ of Nazareth, rise up and walk." 7 And he took him by the right hand and lifted him up, and immediately his feet and ankle bones re-

---

2:28 aPsalm 16:8–11   2:30 aNU-Text omits according to the flesh, He would raise up the Christ and completes the verse with He would seat one on his throne.   2:35 aPsalm 110:1   2:41 aNU-Text omits gladly.   2:47 aNU-Text omits to the church.

Take a Leap of Faith

Faith is often called a "leap." How appropriate! How else could you possibly move from one point to another when there is no direct link?

How do you cross over a crevice when there is no bridge?

Faith is leaping across gaps that exist between

- the goals achieved and the goals still pursued
- the known and the unknown
- the actual and the possible
- the "I have it" and the "I want it"
- youth and maturity
- sickness and health
- sin and forgiveness
- life and death.

Yes, there is always a chasm between today and tomorrow. You may not be sure you can cope with tomorrow. But by a running leap you can jump into tomorrow with expectancy! There is always a chasm between your present achievements and your unfulfilled hopes and dreams. By faith you make the leap--and grow! Consider the leap of the man (lame from birth) who was healed in Jesus' name! (see Acts 3:8).

There is always a chasm between where you are and where you're going--by faith make the leap forward!

What lies ahead? Tomorrow? Next week? Next month? Next year? Beyond this life? Believe in faith! Believe in believers! Believe in God! Believe in Jesus Christ! Believe in tomorrow, and take the leap of faith!

ceived strength. 8 So he, leaping up, stood and walked and entered the temple with them—walking, leaping, and praising God. 9 And all the people saw him walking and praising God. 10 Then they knew that it was he who sat begging alms at the Beautiful Gate of the temple; and they were filled with wonder and amazement at what had happened to him.

11 Now as the lame man who was healed held on to Peter and John, all the people ran together to them in the porch which is called Solomon's, greatly amazed. 12 So when Peter saw *it*, he responded to the people: "Men of Israel, why do you marvel at this? Or why look so intently at us, as though by our own power or godliness we had made this man walk? 13 The God of Abraham, Isaac, and Jacob, the God of our fathers, glorified His Servant Jesus, whom you delivered up and denied in the presence of Pilate, when he was determined to let *Him* go. 14 But you denied the Holy One and the Just, and asked for a murderer to be granted to you, 15 and killed the Prince of life, whom God raised from the dead, of which we are witnesses. 16 And His name, through faith in His name, has made this man strong, whom you see and know. Yes, the faith which *comes* through Him has given him this perfect soundness in the presence of you all.

17 "Yet now, brethren, I know that you did *it* in ignorance, as *did* also your rulers. 18 But those things which God foretold by the mouth of all His prophets, that the Christ would suffer, He has thus fulfilled. 19 Repent therefore and be converted, that your sins may be blotted out, so that times of refreshing may come from the presence of the Lord, 20 and that He may send Jesus Christ, who was preached to you before,[a] 21 whom heaven must receive until the times of restoration of all things, which God has spoken by the mouth of all His holy prophets since the world began. 22 For Moses truly said to the fathers, 'The LORD your God will raise up for you a Prophet like me from your brethren. Him you shall hear in all things, whatever He says to you. 23 And it shall be that every soul who will not hear that Prophet shall be utterly destroyed from among the people.'[a] 24 Yes, and all the prophets, from Samuel and those who follow, as many as have spoken, have also foretold[a] these days. 25 You are sons of the prophets, and of the covenant which God made with our fathers, saying to Abraham, 'And in your seed all the families of the earth shall be blessed.'[a] 26 To you first, God, having raised up His Servant Jesus, sent Him to bless you, in turning away every one *of you* from your iniquities."

4 Now as they spoke to the people, the priests, the captain of the temple, and the Sadducees came upon them, 2 being greatly disturbed that they taught the people and preached in Jesus the resurrection from the dead. 3 And they laid hands on them, and put *them* in custody until the next day, for it was already evening. 4 However, many of those who heard the word believed; and the number of the men came to be about five thousand.

5 And it came to pass, on the next day, that their rulers, elders, and scribes, 6 as well as Annas the high priest, Caiaphas, John, and Alexander, and as many as were of the family of the high priest, were gathered together at Jerusalem. 7 And when they had set them in the midst, they asked, "By what power or by what name have you done this?"

8 Then Peter, filled with the Holy Spirit, said to them, "Rulers of the people and elders of Israel: 9 If we this day are judged for a good deed *done* to a helpless man, by what means he has been made well, 10 let it be known to you all, and to all the people of Israel, that by the name of Jesus Christ of Nazareth, whom you crucified, whom God raised from the dead, by Him this man stands here before you whole. 11 This is the 'stone which was rejected by you builders, which has become the chief cornerstone.'[a] 12 Nor is there salvation in any other, for there is no other name under heaven

---

3:20 [a]NU-Text and M-Text read *Christ Jesus, who was ordained for you before.*   3:23 [a]Deuteronomy 18:15, 18, 19   3:24 [a]NU-Text and M-Text read *proclaimed.*   3:25 [a]Genesis 22:18; 26:4; 28:14   4:11 [a]Psalm 118:22

The Spread of the Gospel

Philip and Peter, two of the original apostles of Jesus, were the first to preach the gospel throughout Palestine in the cities around Jerusalem in response to the command of Jesus, "You shall be witnesses to Me in Jerusalem, and in all Judea and Samaria, and to the end of the earth" (Acts 1:8). In later years, the apostle Paul became the great missionary of the Gentiles, proclaiming Christ in other nations throughout the Roman Empire.

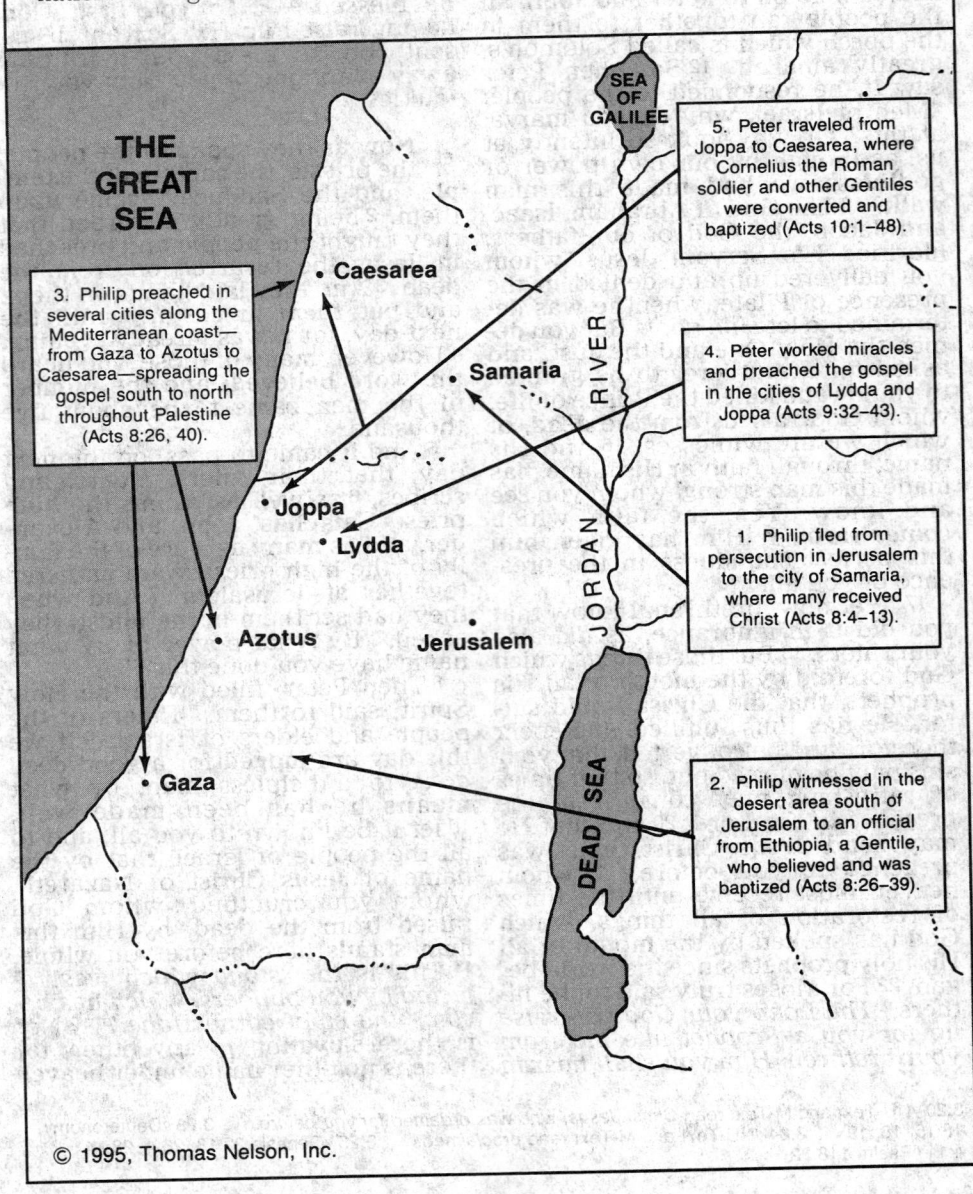

THE GREAT SEA

SEA OF GALILEE

5. Peter traveled from Joppa to Caesarea, where Cornelius the Roman soldier and other Gentiles were converted and baptized (Acts 10:1–48).

• Caesarea

3. Philip preached in several cities along the Mediterranean coast—from Gaza to Azotus to Caesarea—spreading the gospel south to north throughout Palestine (Acts 8:26, 40).

• Samaria

JORDAN RIVER

4. Peter worked miracles and preached the gospel in the cities of Lydda and Joppa (Acts 9:32–43).

• Joppa
• Lydda

1. Philip fled from persecution in Jerusalem to the city of Samaria, where many received Christ (Acts 8:4–13).

• Azotus   Jerusalem

DEAD SEA

• Gaza

2. Philip witnessed in the desert area south of Jerusalem to an official from Ethiopia, a Gentile, who believed and was baptized (Acts 8:26–39).

given among men by which we must be saved."

13 Now when they saw the boldness of Peter and John, and perceived that they were uneducated and untrained men, they marveled. And they realized that they had been with Jesus. 14 And seeing the man who had been healed standing with them, they could say nothing against it. 15 But when they had commanded them to go aside out of the council, they conferred among themselves, 16 saying, "What shall we do to these men? For, indeed, that a notable miracle has been done through them *is* evident to all who dwell in Jerusalem, and we cannot deny *it.* 17 But so that it spreads no further among the people, let us severely threaten them, that from now on they speak to no man in this name."

18 So they called them and commanded them not to speak at all nor teach in the name of Jesus. 19 But Peter and John answered and said to them, "Whether it is right in the sight of God to listen to you more than to God, you judge. 20 For we cannot but speak the things which we have seen and heard." 21 So when they had further threatened them, they let them go, finding no way of punishing them, because of the people, since they all glorified God for what had been done. 22 For the man was over forty years old on whom this miracle of healing had been performed.

23 And being let go, they went to their own *companions* and reported all that the chief priests and elders had said to them. 24 So when they heard that, they raised their voice to God with one accord and said: "Lord, You *are* God, who made heaven and earth and the sea, and all that is in them, 25 who by the mouth of Your servant David*ᵃ* have said:

'Why did the nations rage,
And the people plot vain things?
26   The kings of the earth took their stand,
And the rulers were gathered together
Against the Lᴏʀᴅ and against His Christ.'*ᵃ*

27 "For truly against Your holy Servant Jesus, whom You anointed, both Herod and Pontius Pilate, with the Gentiles and the people of Israel, were gathered together 28 to do whatever Your hand and Your purpose determined before to be done. 29 Now, Lord, look on their threats, and grant to Your servants that with all boldness they may speak Your word, 30 by stretching out Your hand to heal, and that signs and wonders may be done through the name of Your holy Servant Jesus."

31 And when they had prayed, the place where they were assembled together was shaken; and they were all filled with the Holy Spirit, and they spoke the word of God with boldness.

32 Now the multitude of those who believed were of one heart and one soul; neither did anyone say that any of the things he possessed was his own, but they had all things in common. 33 And with great power the apostles gave witness to the resurrection of the Lord Jesus. And great grace was upon them all. 34 Nor was there anyone among them who lacked; for all who were possessors of lands or houses sold them, and brought the proceeds of the things that were sold, 35 and laid *them* at the apostles' feet; and they distributed to each as anyone had need.

36 And Joses,*ᵃ* who was also named Barnabas by the apostles (which is translated Son of Encouragement), a Levite of the country of Cyprus, 37 having land, sold *it,* and brought the money and laid *it* at the apostles' feet.

5 But a certain man named Ananias, with Sapphira his wife, sold a possession. 2 And he kept back *part* of the proceeds, his wife also being aware *of it,* and brought a certain part and laid *it* at the apostles' feet. 3 But Peter said, "Ananias, why has Satan filled your heart to lie to the Holy Spirit and keep back *part* of the price of the land for yourself? 4 While it remained, was it not your own? And after it was sold, was it not in your own control? Why have you conceived this thing in your heart? You have not lied to men but to God."

4:25 ᵃNU-Text reads *who through the Holy Spirit, by the mouth of our father, Your servant David.*
4:26 ᵃPsalm 2:1, 2   4:36 ᵃNU-Text reads *Joseph.*

5 Then Ananias, hearing these words, fell down and breathed his last. So great fear came upon all those who heard these things. 6 And the young men arose and wrapped him up, carried *him* out, and buried *him*.

7 Now it was about three hours later when his wife came in, not knowing what had happened. 8 And Peter answered her, "Tell me whether you sold the land for so much?"

She said, "Yes, for so much."

9 Then Peter said to her, "How is it that you have agreed together to test the Spirit of the Lord? Look, the feet of those who have buried your husband *are* at the door, and they will carry you out." 10 Then immediately she fell down at his feet and breathed her last. And the young men came in and found her dead, and carrying *her* out, buried *her* by her husband. 11 So great fear came upon all the church and upon all who heard these things.

12 And through the hands of the apostles many signs and wonders were done among the people. And they were all with one accord in Solomon's Porch. 13 Yet none of the rest dared join them, but the people esteemed them highly. 14 And believers were increasingly added to the Lord, multitudes of both men and women, 15 so that they brought the sick out into the streets and laid *them* on beds and couches, that at least the shadow of Peter passing by might fall on some of them. 16 Also a multitude gathered from the surrounding cities to Jerusalem, bringing sick people and those who were tormented by unclean spirits, and they were all healed.

17 Then the high priest rose up, and all those who *were* with him (which is the sect of the Sadducees), and they were filled with indignation, 18 and laid their hands on the apostles and put them in the common prison. 19 But at night an angel of the Lord opened the prison doors and brought them out, and said, 20 "Go, stand in the temple and speak to the people all the words of this life."

21 And when they heard *that*, they entered the temple early in the morn-ing and taught. But the high priest and those with him came and called the council together, with all the elders of the children of Israel, and sent to the prison to have them brought.

22 But when the officers came and did not find them in the prison, they returned and reported, 23 saying, "Indeed we found the prison shut securely, and the guards standing outside[a] before the doors; but when we opened them, we found no one inside!" 24 Now when the high priest,[a] the captain of the temple, and the chief priests heard these things, they wondered what the outcome would be. 25 So one came and told them, saying,[a] "Look, the men whom you put in prison are standing in the temple and teaching the people!"

26 Then the captain went with the officers and brought them without violence, for they feared the people, lest they should be stoned. 27 And when they had brought them, they set *them* before the council. And the high priest asked them, 28 saying, "Did we not strictly command you not to teach in this name? And look, you have filled Jerusalem with your doctrine, and intend to bring this Man's blood on us!"

29 But Peter and the *other* apostles answered and said: "We ought to obey God rather than men. 30 The God of our fathers raised up Jesus whom you murdered by hanging on a tree. 31 Him God has exalted to His right hand *to be* Prince and Savior, to give repentance to Israel and forgiveness of sins. 32 And we are His witnesses to these things, and *so* also *is* the Holy Spirit whom God has given to those who obey Him."

33 When they heard *this,* they were furious and plotted to kill them. 34 Then one in the council stood up, a Pharisee named Gamaliel, a teacher of the law held in respect by all the people, and commanded them to put the apostles outside for a little while. 35 And he said to them: "Men of Israel, take heed to yourselves what you intend to do regarding these men. 36 For some time ago Theudas rose up, claiming to be somebody. A number of men, about four hundred, joined him. He was slain, and all who obeyed him were

5:23 aNU-Text and M-Text omit *outside*. 5:24 aNU-Text omits *the high priest*. 5:25 aNU-Text and M-Text omit *saying*.

scattered and came to nothing. 37 After this man, Judas of Galilee rose up in the days of the census, and drew away many people after him. He also perished, and all who obeyed him were dispersed. 38 And now I say to you, keep away from these men and let them alone; for if this plan or this work is of men, it will come to nothing; 39 but if it is of God, you cannot overthrow it—lest you even be found to fight against God."

40 And they agreed with him, and when they had called for the apostles and beaten *them*, they commanded that they should not speak in the name of Jesus, and let them go. 41 So they departed from the presence of the council, rejoicing that they were counted worthy to suffer shame for His*a* name. 42 And daily in the temple, and in every house, they did not cease teaching and preaching Jesus *as* the Christ.

6 Now in those days, when *the number of* the disciples was multiplying, there arose a complaint against the Hebrews by the Hellenists,*a* because their widows were neglected in the daily distribution. 2 Then the twelve summoned the multitude of the disciples and said, "It is not desirable that we should leave the word of God and serve tables. 3 Therefore, brethren, seek out from among you seven men of *good* reputation, full of the Holy Spirit and wisdom, whom we may appoint over this business; 4 but we will give ourselves continually to prayer and to the ministry of the word."

5 And the saying pleased the whole multitude. And they chose Stephen, a man full of faith and the Holy Spirit, and Philip, Prochorus, Nicanor, Timon, Parmenas, and Nicolas, a proselyte from Antioch, 6 whom they set before the apostles; and when they had prayed, they laid hands on them.

7 Then the word of God spread, and the number of the disciples multiplied greatly in Jerusalem, and a great many of the priests were obedient to the faith.

8 And Stephen, full of faith*a* and power, did great wonders and signs

among the people. 9 Then there arose some from what is called the Synagogue of the Freedmen (Cyrenians, Alexandrians, and those from Cilicia and Asia), disputing with Stephen. 10 And they were not able to resist the wisdom and the Spirit by which he spoke. 11 Then they secretly induced men to say, "We have heard him speak blasphemous words against Moses and God." 12 And they stirred up the people, the elders, and the scribes; and they came upon *him*, seized him, and brought *him* to the council. 13 They also set up false witnesses who said, "This man does not cease to speak blasphemous*a* words against this holy place and the law; 14 for we have heard him say that this Jesus of Nazareth will destroy this place and change the customs which Moses delivered to us." 15 And all who sat in the council, looking steadfastly at him, saw his face as the face of an angel.

7 Then the high priest said, "Are these things so?"

2 And he said, "Brethren and fathers, listen: The God of glory appeared to our father Abraham when he was in Mesopotamia, before he dwelt in Haran, 3 and said to him, 'Get out of your country and from your relatives, and come to a land that I will show you.'*a* 4 Then he came out of the land of the Chaldeans and dwelt in Haran. And from there, when his father was dead, He moved him to this land in which you now dwell. 5 And God gave him no inheritance in it, not even *enough* to set his foot on. But even when *Abraham* had no child, He promised to give it to him for a possession, and to his descendants after him. 6 But God spoke in this way: that his descendants would dwell in a foreign land, and that they would bring them into bondage and oppress *them* four hundred years. 7 'And the nation to whom they will be in bondage I will judge,'*a* said God, 'and after that they shall come out and serve Me in this place.'*b* 8 Then He gave him the covenant of circumcision; and so *Abraham* begot Isaac and circumcised him on the eighth day; and Isaac

5:41 *a*NU-Text reads *the name;* M-Text reads *the name of Jesus.*   6:1 *a*That is, Greek-speaking Jews.
6:8 *a*NU-Text reads *grace.*   6:13 *a*NU-Text omits *blasphemous.*   7:3 *a*Genesis 12:1
7:7 *a*Genesis 15:14   *b*Exodus 3:12

begot Jacob, and Jacob *begot* the twelve patriarchs.

9 "And the patriarchs, becoming envious, sold Joseph into Egypt. But God was with him 10 and delivered him out of all his troubles, and gave him favor and wisdom in the presence of Pharaoh, king of Egypt; and he made him governor over Egypt and all his house. 11 Now a famine and great trouble came over all the land of Egypt and Canaan, and our fathers found no sustenance. 12 But when Jacob heard that there was grain in Egypt, he sent out our fathers first. 13 And the second *time* Joseph was made known to his brothers, and Joseph's family became known to the Pharaoh. 14 Then Joseph sent and called his father Jacob and all his relatives to *him*, seventy-five*ᵃ* people. 15 So Jacob went down to Egypt; and he died, he and our fathers. 16 And they were carried back to Shechem and laid in the tomb that Abraham bought for a sum of money from the sons of Hamor, *the father* of Shechem.

17 "But when the time of the promise drew near which God had sworn to Abraham, the people grew and multiplied in Egypt 18 till another king arose who did not know Joseph. 19 This man dealt treacherously with our people, and oppressed our forefathers, making them expose their babies, so that they might not live. 20 At this time Moses was born, and was well pleasing to God; and he was brought up in his father's house for three months. 21 But when he was set out, Pharaoh's daughter took him away and brought him up as her own son. 22 And Moses was learned in all the wisdom of the Egyptians, and was mighty in words and deeds.

23 "Now when he was forty years old, it came into his heart to visit his brethren, the children of Israel. 24 And seeing one of *them* suffer wrong, he defended and avenged him who was oppressed, and struck down the Egyptian. 25 For he supposed that his brethren would have understood that God would deliver them by his hand, but they did not understand. 26 And the next day he appeared to two of them as they were fighting, and *tried to* reconcile them, saying,

'Men, you are brethren; why do you wrong one another?' 27 But he who did his neighbor wrong pushed him away, saying, '*Who made you a ruler and a judge over us?* 28 *Do you want to kill me as you did the Egyptian yesterday?*'ᵃ 29 Then, at this saying, Moses fled and became a dweller in the land of Midian, where he had two sons.

30 "And when forty years had passed, an Angel of the Lord*ᵃ* appeared to him in a flame of fire in a bush, in the wilderness of Mount Sinai. 31 When Moses saw *it*, he marveled at the sight; and as he drew near to observe, the voice of the Lord came to him, 32 saying, '*I am the God of your fathers—the God of Abraham, the God of Isaac, and the God of Jacob.*'ᵃ And Moses trembled and dared not look. 33 '*Then the* LORD *said to him, "Take your sandals off your feet, for the place where you stand is holy ground. 34 I have surely seen the oppression of My people who are in Egypt; I have heard their groaning and have come down to deliver them. And now come, I will send you to Egypt."* 'ᵃ

35 "This Moses whom they rejected, saying, '*Who made you a ruler and a judge?*'ᵃ is the one God sent *to be* a ruler and a deliverer by the hand of the Angel who appeared to him in the bush. 36 He brought them out, after he had shown wonders and signs in the land of Egypt, and in the Red Sea, and in the wilderness forty years.

37 "This is that Moses who said to the children of Israel,*ᵃ* '*The* LORD *your God will raise up for you a Prophet like me from your brethren. Him you shall hear.*'ᵇ

38 "This is he who was in the congregation in the wilderness with the Angel who spoke to him on Mount Sinai, and *with* our fathers, the one who received the living oracles to give to us, 39 whom our fathers would not obey, but rejected. And in their hearts they turned back to Egypt, 40 saying to Aaron, '*Make us gods to go before us; as for this Moses who brought us out of the land of Egypt, we do not know what has become of him.*'ᵃ 41 And they made a calf in those days, offered sacrifices to the

7:14 ᵃOr *seventy* (compare Exodus 1:5) 7:28 ᵃExodus 2:14 7:30 ᵃNU-Text omits *of the Lord.*
7:32 ᵃExodus 3:6, 15 7:34 ᵃExodus 3:5, 7, 8, 10 7:35 ᵃExodus 2:14 7:37 ᵃDeuteronomy 18:15
ᵇNU-Text and M-Text omit *Him you shall hear.* 7:40 ᵃExodus 32:1, 23

The Unnamed Men and Women

The early Christians in Jerusalem enjoyed a tremendous amount of freedom sharing their newfound faith. They taught openly in the temple and in the "Freed Man's Synagogue," which was recently discovered in Jerusalem.

Between A.D. 40 and 60, however, resistance mounted from the Jewish leaders in the Jerusalem temple (see Acts 4). One church leader, Stephen, was stoned to death outside the city walls because he was falsely accused of blasphemy (see Acts 6:13). The Jerusalem congregation was eventually forced to scatter throughout Judea and Samaria. The Acts 8:4 account says that because of persecution "those who were scattered went everywhere preaching the word."

Freedom was not enough. These dear saints faced their changing circumstances, realizing the objective God gave them was not simply to meet in seclusion, but to share His message of love and forgiveness with all people. They believed in management by objectives. So they split up into missionary teams and took the gospel to as many cities as possible along the coast of Africa, Palestine, Greece, and Rome.

The Book of Acts does not mention specifically all the early Christians other than to say they shared the Good News with those who lived along the coast of Palestine. The unnamed people in the Book of Acts did not care who got the credit. They simply wanted to make sure God's work was done.

What can you do in your world today to share God's love, regardless of who gets the credit? Remember God does His greatest works and His greatest projects through His smallest people!

idol, and rejoiced in the works of their own hands. 42 Then God turned and gave them up to worship the host of heaven, as it is written in the book of the Prophets:

> 'Did you offer Me slaughtered
>   animals and sacrifices during
>   forty years in the wilderness,
>   O house of Israel?
> 43 You also took up the tabernacle
>   of Moloch,
>   And the star of your god
>   Remphan,
>   Images which you made to
>   worship;
>   And I will carry you away
>   beyond Babylon.'a

44 "Our fathers had the tabernacle of witness in the wilderness, as He appointed, instructing Moses to make it according to the pattern that he had seen, 45 which our fathers, having received it in turn, also brought with Joshua into the land possessed by the Gentiles, whom God drove out before the face of our fathers until the days of David, 46 who found favor before God and asked to find a dwelling for the God of Jacob. 47 But Solomon built Him a house.

48 "However, the Most High does not dwell in temples made with hands, as the prophet says:

> 49 'Heaven is My throne,
>   And earth is My footstool.
>   What house will you build for
>   Me? says the LORD,
>   Or what is the place of My rest?
> 50 Has My hand not made all
>   these things?'a

51 "You stiff-necked and uncircumcised in heart and ears! You always resist the Holy Spirit; as your fathers did, so do you. 52 Which of the prophets did your fathers not persecute? And they killed those who foretold the coming of the Just One, of whom you now have become the betrayers and murderers, 53 who have received the law by the direction of angels and have not kept it."

54 When they heard these things they were cut to the heart, and they gnashed at him with their teeth. 55 But he, being full of the Holy Spirit, gazed into heaven and saw the glory of God, and Jesus standing at the right hand of God, 56 and said, "Look! I see the heavens opened and the Son of Man standing at the right hand of God!"

57 Then they cried out with a loud voice, stopped their ears, and ran at him with one accord; 58 and they cast him out of the city and stoned him. And the witnesses laid down their clothes at the feet of a young man named Saul. 59 And they stoned Stephen as he was calling on God and saying, "Lord Jesus, receive my spirit." 60 Then he knelt down and cried out with a loud voice, "Lord, do not charge them with this sin." And when he had said this, he fell asleep.

8 Now Saul was consenting to his death.

At that time a great persecution arose against the church which was at Jerusalem; and they were all scattered throughout the regions of Judea and Samaria, except the apostles. 2 And devout men carried Stephen to his burial, and made great lamentation over him.

3 As for Saul, he made havoc of the church, entering every house, and dragging off men and women, committing them to prison.

4 Therefore those who were scattered went everywhere preaching the word. 5 Then Philip went down to the a city of Samaria and preached Christ to them. 6 And the multitudes with one accord heeded the things spoken by Philip, hearing and seeing the miracles which he did. 7 For unclean spirits, crying with a loud voice, came out of many who were possessed; and many who were paralyzed and lame were healed. 8 And there was great joy in that city.

9 But there was a certain man called Simon, who previously practiced sorcery in the city and astonished the people of Samaria, claiming that he was someone great, 10 to whom they all gave heed, from the least to the greatest, saying, "This man is the great power of God." 11 And they heeded him because he had astonished them with his sorceries for a long time. 12 But when they believed Philip as he preached the

Great People—Ordinary People

Great people are just ordinary people with an extraordinary amount of determination. One such man among the first disciples was the evangelist, Philip. When Philip went down to the city of Samaria, Acts 8:5, 6 says, multitudes who heard him speak and saw the miracles he did came to Christ. With great joy, they were baptized, receiving the Holy Spirit. Even a magician named Simon was converted.

It is significant that Philip began his ministry in Samaria, a region where no upstanding Jew from the Jerusalem area was ever seen. God used Philip to cut through cultural and ethnic barriers.

A beautiful example of Philip's ministry is seen where he met an Ethiopian eunuch on the road from Jerusalem to Gaza. The eunuch was reading Isaiah 53:7, a passage concerning the Messiah. Philip seized the opportunity, approached the eunuch, and, answering his questions, shared with him the fulfillment of the messianic prophecy in the person and work of Jesus Christ. The Ethiopian eunuch believed and was baptized. The new convert continued his journey to North Africa, where, tradition tells us, he founded the first Christian church in Ethiopia.

Philip continued his work in the coastal cities of Palestine, finally settling in Caesarea. Here he shared the gospel with many people of diverse cultural, religious, and ethnic backgrounds.

In the New Testament period, Caesarea was the largest Greco-Roman city on the coast of Palestine. People from all corners of the empire walked through its gates to trade their wares and share news of events elsewhere in the empire.

Philip saw Caesarea as an opportunity to multiply his resources by sharing with as many sources as possible. Who knows how many people he was responsible for converting? Only God can count the apples in one seed.

Where can you plant a seed in your world today? What dream has God instilled in you? Multiply your resources—share your faith. Remember: great people are just ordinary people with an extraordinary amount of determination!

things concerning the kingdom of God and the name of Jesus Christ, both men and women were baptized. 13 Then Simon himself also believed; and when he was baptized he continued with Philip, and was amazed, seeing the miracles and signs which were done.

14 Now when the apostles who were at Jerusalem heard that Samaria had received the word of God, they sent Peter and John to them, 15 who, when they had come down, prayed for them that they might receive the Holy Spirit. 16 For as yet He had fallen upon none of them. They had only been baptized in the name of the Lord Jesus. 17 Then they laid hands on them, and they received the Holy Spirit.

18 And when Simon saw that through the laying on of the apostles' hands the Holy Spirit was given, he offered them money, 19 saying, "Give me this power also, that anyone on whom I lay hands may receive the Holy Spirit."

20 But Peter said to him, "Your money perish with you, because you thought that the gift of God could be purchased with money! 21 You have neither part nor portion in this matter, for your heart is not right in the sight of God. 22 Repent therefore of this your wickedness, and pray God if perhaps the thought of your heart may be forgiven you. 23 For I see that you are poisoned by bitterness and bound by iniquity."

24 Then Simon answered and said, "Pray to the Lord for me, that none of the things which you have spoken may come upon me."

25 So when they had testified and preached the word of the Lord, they returned to Jerusalem, preaching the gospel in many villages of the Samaritans.

26 Now an angel of the Lord spoke to Philip, saying, "Arise and go toward the south along the road which goes down from Jerusalem to Gaza." This is desert. 27 So he arose and went. And behold, a man of Ethiopia, a eunuch of great authority under Candace the queen of the Ethiopians, who had charge of all her treasury, and had come to Jerusalem to worship, 28 was returning. And sitting in his chariot, he was reading Isaiah the prophet. 29 Then the Spirit said to Philip, "Go near and overtake this chariot."

30 So Philip ran to him, and heard him reading the prophet Isaiah, and said, "Do you understand what you are reading?"

31 And he said, "How can I, unless someone guides me?" And he asked Philip to come up and sit with him. 32 The place in the Scripture which he read was this:

"He was led as a sheep to the slaughter;
And as a lamb before its shearer is silent,
So He opened not His mouth.
33 In His humiliation His justice was taken away,
And who will declare His generation?
For His life is taken from the earth."ᵃ

34 So the eunuch answered Philip and said, "I ask you, of whom does the prophet say this, of himself or of some other man?" 35 Then Philip opened his mouth, and beginning at this Scripture, preached Jesus to him. 36 Now as they went down the road, they came to some water. And the eunuch said, "See, here is water. What hinders me from being baptized?"

37 Then Philip said, "If you believe with all your heart, you may."

And he answered and said, "I believe that Jesus Christ is the Son of God."ᵃ

38 So he commanded the chariot to stand still. And both Philip and the eunuch went down into the water, and he baptized him. 39 Now when they came up out of the water, the Spirit of the Lord caught Philip away, so that the eunuch saw him no more; and he went on his way rejoicing. 40 But Philip was found at Azotus. And passing through, he preached in all the cities till he came to Caesarea.

9 Then Saul, still breathing threats and murder against the disciples of the Lord, went to the high priest 2 and asked letters from him to the synagogues of Damascus, so that if

---

8:33 ᵃIsaiah 53:7, 8   8:37 ᵃNU-Text and M-Text omit this verse. It is found in Western texts, including the Latin tradition.

The City of Damascus

Damascus is the oldest continually inhabited city in the world. As the current capital of Syria, the city is located on the border of some of the most important highways in the ancient Near Eastern world. Because of its ideal location, the city has always been an important trade center. Its name may be derived from a patterned cloth known as damask, its most important export item in Old Testament times (Ezek. 27:18).

According to Josephus, the founder of Damascus was Uz, grandson of Shem (Gen. 5:32; 10:21, 23). Its strategic location as a trading center brought Damascus into conflict with Israel on numerous occasions as it sought to regulate the flow of trade into all parts of the ancient Near East.

After periods of dominance by the Assyrians and the Persians, Damascus was conquered by Alexander the Great in 333 B.C. Later it became the capital of the Roman province of Syria. In the early years of Roman influence in Syria, many Jews from Judaea moved to Damascus. The city had a large Jewish community during New Testament times.

All references to Damascus in the New Testament are associated with the apostle Paul's conversion and early ministry. He was blinded in a vision while traveling to Damascus to persecute early Christians (Acts 9:1–8). After his conversion, Paul went to the house of Judas on "Straight Street" in Damascus. There he met Ananias, a Christian citizen of the city who healed Paul's blindness (Acts 9:10–22). After regaining his sight, Paul preached in the Jewish synagogue in Damascus, astonishing those who remembered him as a persecutor of the Christian faith. Eventually Paul was forced to flee Damascus because of threats on his life.

Damascus is still a trading center filled with open-air markets and crowded streets, some of which are very similar to those which Paul might have visited.

he found any who were of the Way, whether men or women, he might bring them bound to Jerusalem.

3 As he journeyed he came near Damascus, and suddenly a light shone around him from heaven. 4 Then he fell to the ground, and heard a voice saying to him, "Saul, Saul, why are you persecuting Me?"

5 And he said, "Who are You, Lord?"

Then the Lord said, "I am Jesus, whom you are persecuting.*a* It *is* hard for you to kick against the goads."

6 So he, trembling and astonished, said, "Lord, what do You want me to do?"

Then the Lord *said* to him, "Arise and go into the city, and you will be told what you must do."

7 And the men who journeyed with him stood speechless, hearing a voice but seeing no one. 8 Then Saul arose from the ground, and when his eyes were opened he saw no one. But they led him by the hand and brought *him* into Damascus. 9 And he was three days without sight, and neither ate nor drank.

10 Now there was a certain disciple at Damascus named Ananias; and to him the Lord said in a vision, "Ananias."

And he said, "Here I am, Lord."

11 So the Lord *said* to him, "Arise and go to the street called Straight, and inquire at the house of Judas for *one* called Saul of Tarsus, for behold, he is praying. 12 And in a vision he has seen a man named Ananias coming in and putting *his* hand on him, so that he might receive his sight."

13 Then Ananias answered, "Lord, I have heard from many about this man, how much harm he has done to Your saints in Jerusalem. 14 And here he has authority from the chief priests to bind all who call on Your name."

15 But the Lord said to him, "Go, for he is a chosen vessel of Mine to bear My name before Gentiles, kings, and the children of Israel. 16 For I will show him how many things he must suffer for My name's sake."

17 And Ananias went his way and entered the house; and laying his hands on him he said, "Brother Saul, the Lord Jesus,*a* who appeared to you

on the road as you came, has sent me that you may receive your sight and be filled with the Holy Spirit."

18 Immediately there fell from his eyes *something* like scales, and he received his sight at once; and he arose and was baptized.

19 So when he had received food, he was strengthened. Then Saul spent some days with the disciples at Damascus.

20 Immediately he preached the Christ*a* in the synagogues, that He is the Son of God.

21 Then all who heard were amazed, and said, "Is this not he who destroyed those who called on this name in Jerusalem, and has come here for that purpose, so that he might bring them bound to the chief priests?"

22 But Saul increased all the more in strength, and confounded the Jews who dwelt in Damascus, proving that this *Jesus* is the Christ.

23 Now after many days were past, the Jews plotted to kill him. 24 But their plot became known to Saul. And they watched the gates day and night, to kill him. 25 Then the disciples took him by night and let *him* down through the wall in a large basket.

26 And when Saul had come to Jerusalem, he tried to join the disciples; but they were all afraid of him, and did not believe that he was a disciple. 27 But Barnabas took him and brought *him* to the apostles. And he declared to them how he had seen the Lord on the road, and that He had spoken to him, and how he had preached boldly at Damascus in the name of Jesus. 28 So he was with them at Jerusalem, coming in and going out. 29 And he spoke boldly in the name of the Lord Jesus and disputed against the Hellenists, but they attempted to kill him. 30 When the brethren found out, they brought him down to Caesarea and sent him out to Tarsus.

31 Then the churches*a* throughout all Judea, Galilee, and Samaria had peace and were edified. And walking in the fear of the Lord and in the comfort of the Holy Spirit, they were multiplied.

32 Now it came to pass, as Peter

9:5 *a*NU-Text and M-Text omit the last sentence of verse 5 and begin verse 6 with *But arise and go.*
9:17 *a*M-Text omits *Jesus.*   9:20 *a*NU-Text reads *Jesus.*   9:31 *a*NU-Text reads *church . . . was edified.*

went through all *parts of the country*, that he also came down to the saints who dwelt in Lydda. 33 There he found a certain man named Aeneas, who had been bedridden eight years and was paralyzed. 34 And Peter said to him, "Aeneas, Jesus the Christ heals you. Arise and make your bed." Then he arose immediately. 35 So all who dwelt at Lydda and Sharon saw him and turned to the Lord.

36 At Joppa there was a certain disciple named Tabitha, which is translated Dorcas. This woman was full of good works and charitable deeds which she did. 37 But it happened in those days that she became sick and died. When they had washed her, they laid *her* in an upper room. 38 And since Lydda was near Joppa, and the disciples had heard that Peter was there, they sent two men to him, imploring *him* not to delay in coming to them. 39 Then Peter arose and went with them. When he had come, they brought *him* to the upper room. And all the widows stood by him weeping, showing the tunics and garments which Dorcas had made while she was with them. 40 But Peter put them all out, and knelt down and prayed. And turning to the body he said, "Tabitha, arise." And she opened her eyes, and when she saw Peter she sat up. 41 Then he gave her *his* hand and lifted her up; and when he had called the saints and widows, he presented her alive. 42 And it became known throughout all Joppa, and many believed on the Lord. 43 So it was that he stayed many days in Joppa with Simon, a tanner.

10 There was a certain man in Caesarea called Cornelius, a centurion of what was called the Italian Regiment, 2 a devout *man* and one who feared God with all his household, who gave alms generously to the people, and prayed to God always. 3 About the ninth hour of the day he saw clearly in a vision an angel of God coming in and saying to him, "Cornelius!"

4 And when he observed him, he was afraid, and said, "What is it, lord?"

So he said to him, "Your prayers and your alms have come up for a memorial before God. 5 Now send men to Joppa, and send for Simon whose surname is Peter. 6 He is lodging with Simon, a tanner, whose house is by the sea.*ª* He will tell you what you must do." 7 And when the angel who spoke to him had departed, Cornelius called two of his household servants and a devout soldier from among those who waited on him continually. 8 So when he had explained all *these* things to them, he sent them to Joppa.

9 The next day, as they went on their journey and drew near the city, Peter went up on the housetop to pray, about the sixth hour. 10 Then he became very hungry and wanted to eat; but while they made ready, he fell into a trance 11 and saw heaven opened and an object like a great sheet bound at the four corners, descending to him and let down to the earth. 12 In it were all kinds of four-footed animals of the earth, wild beasts, creeping things, and birds of the air. 13 And a voice came to him, "Rise, Peter; kill and eat."

14 But Peter said, "Not so, Lord! For I have never eaten anything common or unclean."

15 And a voice *spoke* to him again the second time, "What God has cleansed you must not call common." 16 This was done three times. And the object was taken up into heaven again.

17 Now while Peter wondered within himself what this vision which he had seen meant, behold, the men who had been sent from Cornelius had made inquiry for Simon's house, and stood before the gate. 18 And they called and asked whether Simon, whose surname was Peter, was lodging there.

19 While Peter thought about the vision, the Spirit said to him, "Behold, three men are seeking you. 20 Arise therefore, go down and go with them, doubting nothing; for I have sent them."

21 Then Peter went down to the men who had been sent to him from Cornelius,*ª* and said, "Yes, I am he whom you seek. For what reason have you come?"

22 And they said, "Cornelius *the*

10:6 *ª*NU-Text and M-Text omit the last sentence of this verse.   10:21 *ª*NU-Text and M-Text omit *who had been sent to him from Cornelius.*

centurion, a just man, one who fears God and has a good reputation among all the nation of the Jews, was divinely instructed by a holy angel to summon you to his house, and to hear words from you." 23 Then he invited them in and lodged *them*.

On the next day Peter went away with them, and some brethren from Joppa accompanied him.

24 And the following day they entered Caesarea. Now Cornelius was waiting for them, and had called together his relatives and close friends. 25 As Peter was coming in, Cornelius met him and fell down at his feet and worshiped *him*. 26 But Peter lifted him up, saying, "Stand up; I myself am also a man." 27 And as he talked with him, he went in and found many who had come together. 28 Then he said to them, "You know how unlawful it is for a Jewish man to keep company with or go to one of another nation. But God has shown me that I should not call any man common or unclean. 29 Therefore I came without objection as soon as I was sent for. I ask, then, for what reason have you sent for me?"

30 So Cornelius said, "Four days ago I was fasting until this hour; and at the ninth hour*a* I prayed in my house, and behold, a man stood before me in bright clothing, 31 and said, 'Cornelius, your prayer has been heard, and your alms are remembered in the sight of God. 32 Send therefore to Joppa and call Simon here, whose surname is Peter. He is lodging in the house of Simon, a tanner, by the sea.*a* When he comes, he will speak to you.' 33 So I sent to you immediately, and you have done well to come. Now therefore, we are all present before God, to hear all the things commanded you by God."

34 Then Peter opened *his* mouth and said: "In truth I perceive that God shows no partiality. 35 But in every nation whoever fears Him and works righteousness is accepted by Him. 36 The word which *God* sent to the children of Israel, preaching peace through Jesus Christ—He is Lord of all— 37 that word you know, which was proclaimed throughout all Judea, and began from Galilee after

the baptism which John preached: 38 how God anointed Jesus of Nazareth with the Holy Spirit and with power, who went about doing good and healing all who were oppressed by the devil, for God was with Him. 39 And we are witnesses of all things which He did both in the land of the Jews and in Jerusalem, whom they*a* killed by hanging on a tree. 40 Him God raised up on the third day, and showed Him openly, 41 not to all the people, but to witnesses chosen before by God, *even* to us who ate and drank with Him after He arose from the dead. 42 And He commanded us to preach to the people, and to testify that it is He who was ordained by God *to be* Judge of the living and the dead. 43 To Him all the prophets witness that, through His name, whoever believes in Him will receive remission of sins."

44 While Peter was still speaking these words, the Holy Spirit fell upon all those who heard the word. 45 And those of the circumcision who believed were astonished, as many as came with Peter, because the gift of the Holy Spirit had been poured out on the Gentiles also. 46 For they heard them speak with tongues and magnify God.

Then Peter answered, 47 "Can anyone forbid water, that these should not be baptized who have received the Holy Spirit just as we *have?*" 48 And he commanded them to be baptized in the name of the Lord. Then they asked him to stay a few days.

11 Now the apostles and brethren who were in Judea heard that the Gentiles had also received the word of God. 2 And when Peter came up to Jerusalem, those of the circumcision contended with him, 3 saying, "You went in to uncircumcised men and ate with them!"

4 But Peter explained *it* to them in order from the beginning, saying: 5 "I was in the city of Joppa praying; and in a trance I saw a vision, an object descending like a great sheet, let down from heaven by four corners; and it came to me. 6 When I observed it intently and considered, I saw four-footed animals of the earth, wild

10:30 *a*NU-Text reads *Four days ago to this hour, at the ninth hour.* 10:32 *a*NU-Text omits the last sentence of this verse. 10:39 *a*NU-Text and M-Text add *also.*

beasts, creeping things, and birds of the air. 7 And I heard a voice saying to me, 'Rise, Peter; kill and eat.' 8 But I said, 'Not so, Lord! For nothing common or unclean has at any time entered my mouth.' 9 But the voice answered me again from heaven, 'What God has cleansed you must not call common.' 10 Now this was done three times, and all were drawn up again into heaven. 11 At that very moment, three men stood before the house where I was, having been sent to me from Caesarea. 12 Then the Spirit told me to go with them, doubting nothing. Moreover these six brethren accompanied me, and we entered the man's house. 13 And he told us how he had seen an angel standing in his house, who said to him, 'Send men to Joppa, and call for Simon whose surname is Peter, 14 who will tell you words by which you and all your household will be saved.' 15 And as I began to speak, the Holy Spirit fell upon them, as upon us at the beginning. 16 Then I remembered the word of the Lord, how He said, 'John indeed baptized with water, but you shall be baptized with the Holy Spirit.' 17 If therefore God gave them the same gift as *He gave* us when we believed on the Lord Jesus Christ, who was I that I could withstand God?''

18 When they heard these things they became silent; and they glorified God, saying, "Then God has also granted to the Gentiles repentance to life.''

19 Now those who were scattered after the persecution that arose over Stephen traveled as far as Phoenicia, Cyprus, and Antioch, preaching the word to no one but the Jews only. 20 But some of them were men from Cyprus and Cyrene, who, when they had come to Antioch, spoke to the Hellenists, preaching the Lord Jesus. 21 And the hand of the Lord was with them, and a great number believed and turned to the Lord.

22 Then news of these things came to the ears of the church in Jerusalem, and they sent out Barnabas to go as far as Antioch. 23 When he came and had seen the grace of God, he was glad, and encouraged them all that with purpose of heart they should continue with the Lord.

24 For he was a good man, full of the Holy Spirit and of faith. And a great many people were added to the Lord.

25 Then Barnabas departed for Tarsus to seek Saul. 26 And when he had found him, he brought him to Antioch. So it was that for a whole year they assembled with the church and taught a great many people. And the disciples were first called Christians in Antioch.

27 And in these days prophets came from Jerusalem to Antioch. 28 Then one of them, named Agabus, stood up and showed by the Spirit that there was going to be a great famine throughout all the world, which also happened in the days of Claudius Caesar. 29 Then the disciples, each according to his ability, determined to send relief to the brethren dwelling in Judea. 30 This they also did, and sent it to the elders by the hands of Barnabas and Saul.

12 Now about that time Herod the king stretched out *his* hand to harass some from the church. 2 Then he killed James the brother of John with the sword. 3 And because he saw that it pleased the Jews, he proceeded further to seize Peter also. Now it was *during* the Days of Unleavened Bread. 4 So when he had arrested him, he put *him* in prison, and delivered *him* to four squads of soldiers to keep him, intending to bring him before the people after Passover.

5 Peter was therefore kept in prison, but constant*ᵃ* prayer was offered to God for him by the church. 6 And when Herod was about to bring him out, that night Peter was sleeping, bound with two chains between two soldiers; and the guards before the door were keeping the prison. 7 Now behold, an angel of the Lord stood by *him,* and a light shone in the prison; and he struck Peter on the side and raised him up, saying, "Arise quickly!" And his chains fell off *his* hands. 8 Then the angel said to him, "Gird yourself and tie on your sandals"; and so he did. And he said to him, "Put on your garment and follow me." 9 So he went out and followed him, and did not know that what was done by the angel was real, but thought he was seeing a vision.

12:5 ᵃNU-Text reads *constantly* (or *earnestly*).

Son of Encouragement

Often we read the Bible and come across names like Priscilla, Aquila, and Onesimus. We see their names once and never hear from them again. One of these names is Barnabas.

Barnabas means, "son of encouragement." He is introduced to us in the Book of Acts, first as a supporter of the church (4:36, 37) and later (9:27) as a defender of the newly converted Paul after Paul's reputation hindered his acceptance by the apostles.

When Barnabas was finished with this task, the Jerusalem church desperately needed someone to take control of the young church in Antioch, Syria. They were looking for someone strong, steady, and firm, who could be an encouragement to build up the people in their newfound faith.

The church in Antioch, Syria was surrounded with all sorts of mystery religions. It was easy for the new Christians to be persuaded to let false doctrines infiltrate the church. So the Jerusalem church turned to someone they could count on. Barnabas was active in the leadership of the church in Antioch.

Barnabas may have spent many years there, during which time he may have discipled John Mark, the apostle who wrote the Gospel of Mark, although the Bible does not directly record any of this information. We have to rely on indirect references in the Bible, as well as extrabiblical literature to surmise what Barnabas's life was like.

But from all that is recorded of him in Scripture, it is evident that Barnabas was one of those people who did not care who got all the credit, as long as he was serving God with his talents, gifts, and abilities.

Remember, God can do wonderful things through someone who does not really care who gets the credit. Perhaps God has given you the gift of encouragement. Be that special person of encouragement to someone in your life. First Corinthians 14:12 says to "*let it be* for the edification of the church *that* you seek to excel" with whatever spiritual gift you have. You may not be recognized by everyone, but remember, God sees your good works and He rewards you!

Paul's First Journey

On his first of four missionary journeys, Paul and Barnabus were sent out from the church at Antioch. They traveled to the nearby cities of Galatia in Asia Minor. Although Paul encountered some opposition by some synagogues, most of the Jewish synagogues in these cities provided him a platform for preaching the gospel. The first missionary journey included the cities of Antioch, Iconium, Lystra, Derbe, Seleucia, Salamis, Paphos, Attalia, and Perga.

10 When they were past the first and the second guard posts, they came to the iron gate that leads to the city, which opened to them of its own accord; and they went out and went down one street, and immediately the angel departed from him.

11 And when Peter had come to himself, he said, "Now I know for certain that the Lord has sent His angel, and has delivered me from the hand of Herod and from all the expectation of the Jewish people."

12 So, when he had considered this, he came to the house of Mary, the mother of John whose surname was Mark, where many were gathered together praying. 13 And as Peter knocked at the door of the gate, a girl named Rhoda came to answer. 14 When she recognized Peter's voice, because of her gladness she did not open the gate, but ran in and announced that Peter stood before the gate. 15 But they said to her, "You are beside yourself!" Yet she kept insisting that it was so. So they said, "It is his angel."

16 Now Peter continued knocking; and when they opened the door and saw him, they were astonished. 17 But motioning to them with his hand to keep silent, he declared to them how the Lord had brought him out of the prison. And he said, "Go, tell these things to James and to the brethren." And he departed and went to another place.

18 Then, as soon as it was day, there was no small stir among the soldiers about what had become of Peter. 19 But when Herod had searched for him and not found him, he examined the guards and commanded that they should be put to death.

And he went down from Judea to Caesarea, and stayed there.

20 Now Herod had been very angry with the people of Tyre and Sidon; but they came to him with one accord, and having made Blastus the king's personal aide their friend, they asked for peace, because their country was supplied with food by the king's country.

21 So on a set day Herod, arrayed in royal apparel, sat on his throne and gave an oration to them. 22 And the people kept shouting, "The voice of a god and not of a man!" 23 Then immediately an angel of the Lord struck him, because he did not give glory to God. And he was eaten by worms and died.

24 But the word of God grew and multiplied.

25 And Barnabas and Saul returned from[a] Jerusalem when they had fulfilled their ministry, and they also took with them John whose surname was Mark.

13 Now in the church that was at Antioch there were certain prophets and teachers: Barnabas, Simeon who was called Niger, Lucius of Cyrene, Manaen who had been brought up with Herod the tetrarch, and Saul. 2 As they ministered to the Lord and fasted, the Holy Spirit said, "Now separate to Me Barnabas and Saul for the work to which I have called them." 3 Then, having fasted and prayed, and laid hands on them, they sent them away.

4 So, being sent out by the Holy Spirit, they went down to Seleucia, and from there they sailed to Cyprus. 5 And when they arrived in Salamis, they preached the word of God in the synagogues of the Jews. They also had John as their assistant.

6 Now when they had gone through the island[a] to Paphos, they found a certain sorcerer, a false prophet, a Jew whose name was Bar-Jesus, 7 who was with the proconsul, Sergius Paulus, an intelligent man. This man called for Barnabas and Saul and sought to hear the word of God. 8 But Elymas the sorcerer (for so his name is translated) withstood them, seeking to turn the proconsul away from the faith. 9 Then Saul, who also is called Paul, filled with the Holy Spirit, looked intently at him 10 and said, "O full of all deceit and all fraud, you son of the devil, you enemy of all righteousness, will you not cease perverting the straight ways of the Lord? 11 And now, indeed, the hand of the Lord is upon you, and you shall be blind, not seeing the sun for a time."

And immediately a dark mist fell on him, and he went around seeking someone to lead him by the hand. 12 Then the proconsul believed, when he saw what had been done, being

---

12:25 aNU-Text and M-Text read to.   13:6 aNU-Text reads the whole island.

astonished at the teaching of the Lord.

13 Now when Paul and his party set sail from Paphos, they came to Perga in Pamphylia; and John, departing from them, returned to Jerusalem. 14 But when they departed from Perga, they came to Antioch in Pisidia, and went into the synagogue on the Sabbath day and sat down. 15 And after the reading of the Law and the Prophets, the rulers of the synagogue sent to them, saying, "Men *and* brethren, if you have any word of exhortation for the people, say on."

16 Then Paul stood up, and motioning with *his* hand said, "Men of Israel, and you who fear God, listen: 17 The God of this people Israel*a* chose our fathers, and exalted the people when they dwelt as strangers in the land of Egypt, and with an uplifted arm He brought them out of it. 18 Now for a time of about forty years He put up with their ways in the wilderness. 19 And when He had destroyed seven nations in the land of Canaan, He distributed their land to them by allotment.

20 "After that He gave *them* judges for about four hundred and fifty years, until Samuel the prophet. 21 And afterward they asked for a king; so God gave them Saul the son of Kish, a man of the tribe of Benjamin, for forty years. 22 And when He had removed him, He raised up for them David as king, to whom also He gave testimony and said, '*I have found David*a the *son* of Jesse, *a man after My own heart,* who will do all My will.'*b* 23 From this man's seed, according to *the* promise, God raised up for Israel a Savior—Jesus—*a* 24 after John had first preached, before His coming, the baptism of repentance to all the people of Israel. 25 And as John was finishing his course, he said, 'Who do you think I am? I am not *He.* But behold, there comes One after me, the sandals of whose feet I am not worthy to loose.'

26 "Men *and* brethren, sons of the family of Abraham, and those among you who fear God, to you the word of this salvation has been sent. 27 For those who dwell in Jerusalem,

and their rulers, because they did not know Him, nor even the voices of the Prophets which are read every Sabbath, have fulfilled *them* in condemning *Him.* 28 And though they found no cause for death *in Him,* they asked Pilate that He should be put to death. 29 Now when they had fulfilled all that was written concerning Him, they took *Him* down from the tree and laid *Him* in a tomb. 30 But God raised Him from the dead. 31 He was seen for many days by those who came up with Him from Galilee to Jerusalem, who are His witnesses to the people. 32 And we declare to you glad tidings—that promise which was made to the fathers. 33 God has fulfilled this for us their children, in that He has raised up Jesus. As it is also written in the second Psalm:

'*You are My Son,*
    Today I have begotten
        You.'*a*

34 "And that He raised Him from the dead, no more to return to corruption, He has spoken thus:

'*I will give you the sure mercies*
    of David.'*a*

35 "Therefore He also says in another Psalm:

'*You will not allow Your Holy*
    One to see corruption.'*a*

36 "For David, after he had served his own generation by the will of God, fell asleep, was buried with his fathers, and saw corruption; 37 but He whom God raised up saw no corruption. 38 Therefore let it be known to you, brethren, that through this Man is preached to you the forgiveness of sins; 39 and by Him everyone who believes is justified from all things from which you could not be justified by the law of Moses. 40 Beware therefore, lest what has been spoken in the prophets come upon you:

41 '*Behold, you despisers,*
    Marvel and perish!
    For I work a work in your
        days,

13:17 aM-Text omits *Israel.*   13:22 aPsalm 89:20   b1 Samuel 13:14   13:23 aM-Text reads *for Israel salvation.*   13:33 aPsalm 2:7   13:34 aIsaiah 55:3   13:35 aPsalm 16:10

> *A work which you will by no
> means believe,
> Though one were to declare it
> to you.' "*[a]

42 So when the Jews went out of the synagogue,[a] the Gentiles begged that these words might be preached to them the next Sabbath. 43 Now when the congregation had broken up, many of the Jews and devout proselytes followed Paul and Barnabas, who, speaking to them, persuaded them to continue in the grace of God.

44 On the next Sabbath almost the whole city came together to hear the word of God. 45 But when the Jews saw the multitudes, they were filled with envy; and contradicting and blaspheming, they opposed the things spoken by Paul. 46 Then Paul and Barnabas grew bold and said, "It was necessary that the word of God should be spoken to you first; but since you reject it, and judge yourselves unworthy of everlasting life, behold, we turn to the Gentiles. 47 For so the Lord has commanded us:

> *'I have set you as a light to the
> Gentiles,
> That you should be for
> salvation to the ends of the
> earth.' "*[a]

48 Now when the Gentiles heard this, they were glad and glorified the word of the Lord. And as many as had been appointed to eternal life believed.

49 And the word of the Lord was being spread throughout all the region. 50 But the Jews stirred up the devout and prominent women and the chief men of the city, raised up persecution against Paul and Barnabas, and expelled them from their region. 51 But they shook off the dust from their feet against them, and came to Iconium. 52 And the disciples were filled with joy and with the Holy Spirit.

14 Now it happened in Iconium that they went together to the synagogue of the Jews, and so spoke that a great multitude both of the Jews and of the Greeks believed.

2 But the unbelieving Jews stirred up the Gentiles and poisoned their minds against the brethren. 3 Therefore they stayed there a long time, speaking boldly in the Lord, who was bearing witness to the word of His grace, granting signs and wonders to be done by their hands.

4 But the multitude of the city was divided: part sided with the Jews, and part with the apostles. 5 And when a violent attempt was made by both the Gentiles and Jews, with their rulers, to abuse and stone them, 6 they became aware of it and fled to Lystra and Derbe, cities of Lycaonia, and to the surrounding region. 7 And they were preaching the gospel there.

8 And in Lystra a certain man without strength in his feet was sitting, a cripple from his mother's womb, who had never walked. 9 *This* man heard Paul speaking. Paul, observing him intently and seeing that he had faith to be healed, 10 said with a loud voice, "Stand up straight on your feet!" And he leaped and walked. 11 Now when the people saw what Paul had done, they raised their voices, saying in the Lycaonian *language,* "The gods have come down to us in the likeness of men!" 12 And Barnabas they called Zeus, and Paul, Hermes, because he was the chief speaker. 13 Then the priest of Zeus, whose temple was in front of their city, brought oxen and garlands to the gates, intending to sacrifice with the multitudes.

14 But when the apostles Barnabas and Paul heard this, they tore their clothes and ran in among the multitude, crying out 15 and saying, "Men, why are you doing these things? We also are men with the same nature as you, and preach to you that you should turn from these useless things to the living God, who made the heaven, the earth, the sea, and all things that are in them, 16 who in bygone generations allowed all nations to walk in their own ways. 17 Nevertheless He did not leave Himself without witness, in that He did good, gave us rain from heaven and fruitful seasons, filling our hearts with food and gladness." 18 And with these sayings they could scarcely re-

---

13:41 [a]Habakkuk 1:5   13:42 [a]Or *And when they went out of the synagogue of the Jews;* NU-Text reads *And when they went out of the synagogue, they begged.*   13:47 [a]Isaiah 49:6

Followers of the Way

In biblical times, people's names had specific meanings. They often revealed the city or village from which a person came, such as Jesus of Nazareth or Joseph of Arimathea. Another rationale for choosing a name was to show a certain characteristic about the person. For instance, Nathanael means "God has given." Joshua translates "Jehovah saves."

Ancient Middle Eastern names were carefully chosen, for they were an honor, considered to be a gift of God. Strong evidence in the New Testament and first-century inscriptions support the practice that when people became Christians, they often changed their names. We know, for instance, that Saul changed his name to Paul.

The early Christians, primarily of Jewish heritage, converted to Christianity either through personal contact with Jesus or by the message of the disciples. At that time, they were known as "followers of the Way." This name was derived from Jesus' statement, "I am the way, the truth, and the life. No one comes to the Father except through Me" (John 14:6).

Paul directly referred to this name when he made his defense before the Roman authorities and the Jewish council as recorded in the Book of Acts. Speaking of his fight against Christianity before his conversion, Paul said, "I persecuted this Way to the death" (Acts 22:4).

In the latter part of the first century A.D., the followers of the Way became known as "Nazarenes." Eventually they took on the name "Christian" meaning "Christ one." This is in keeping with the promise in Isaiah 62:2 that God would give true believers a new name, the name God would Himself name.

New life in Christ is a new beginning when we take a new name—the name of Christ. As a Christian, it may not always be easy to live up to the meaning of our name, yet the reward for living by faith is immeasurable. During the early centuries, many Christians came under persecution. They were asked, "Are you a Christian?" If they answered in the affirmative, they were often thrown to the lions or other means of being put to death.

We may or may not suffer persecution for our faith, yet we can learn a vital lesson from these early believers. They understood that their spiritual lives through Christ far surpassed physical and personal success without Christ. For as Paul wrote, "To live *is* Christ, and to die *is* gain" (Phil. 1:21).

As Christians we walk in the power and life of Jesus Christ. Loving Him ends our old selfish, negative life. We take on His name and a positive, fulfilling life for God. In faith, like the early Christians, we believe that every end is a new beginning. And we proudly wear our new name "Christian."

The City of Antioch

Situated on the most important trade routes of the day, Antioch was an ideal city for a flourishing missions-minded church that was destined to play a key role in the expansion of early Christianity. Seleuchus I founded the city about 300 B.C. and named it for his father, Antiochus. Antioch served as the capital of the Roman province of Syria during the New Testament times.

Located on the east bank of the Orontes River, Antioch was about 16 miles from the Mediterranean Sea and about 300 miles north of Jerusalem. With a population of more than half a million, it was the third largest city of the Roman Empire, ranking behind only Rome and Alexandria.

Under the Roman rulers, Antioch became one of the most beautiful cities of the Roman Empire. Its main street, about two miles long, was paved with marble and flanked on both sides by hundreds of columns, which supported ornamented porches and balconies (see Street of Colonnades on map). Its cultural splendor and beautiful buildings, including the temple of Artemis, the amphitheater, and royal palaces, contributed to its reputation as the "Paris of the Ancient World" among scholars and researchers.

Antioch was also a city of many philosophies and cults. It prided itself on its toleration. But many citizens sought a more significant religious experience than the old Greek and Roman gods offered. Many accepted the gospel and committed themselves to Christ. Because this church was made up of both Gentiles and Jews, city officials sought a name that would distinguish them from other religious groups. They nicknamed them Christians, meaning "Christ Followers" or "People of Christ," and the name stuck. According to the Book of Acts, "the disciples were called Christians first in Antioch" (Acts 11:26).

Except for Jerusalem, Antioch played a larger part in the early life of the Christian church than any other city of the Roman Empire. It became the birthplace of foreign missions as Paul used the Antioch church as a base of operations for his missionary tours into Asia Minor.

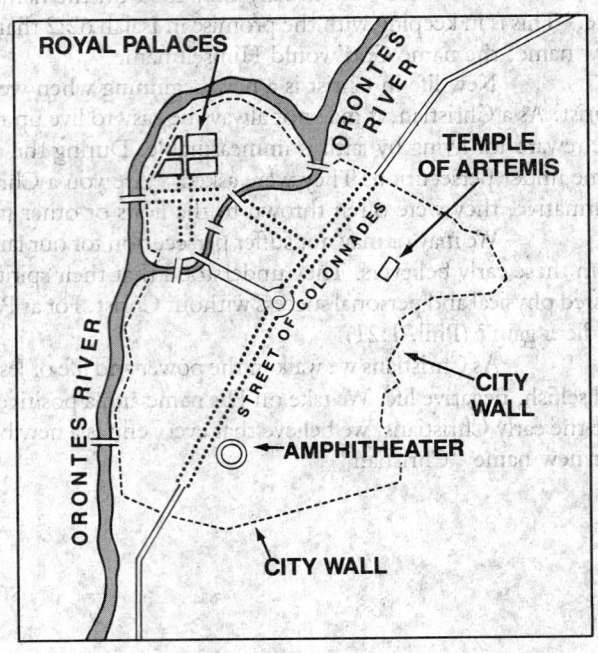

strain the multitudes from sacrificing to them.

19 Then Jews from Antioch and Iconium came there; and having persuaded the multitudes, they stoned Paul *and* dragged *him* out of the city, supposing him to be dead. 20 However, when the disciples gathered around him, he rose up and went into the city. And the next day he departed with Barnabas to Derbe.

21 And when they had preached the gospel to that city and made many disciples, they returned to Lystra, Iconium, and Antioch, 22 strengthening the souls of the disciples, exhorting *them* to continue in the faith, and *saying,* "We must through many tribulations enter the kingdom of God." 23 So when they had appointed elders in every church, and prayed with fasting, they commended them to the Lord in whom they had believed. 24 And after they had passed through Pisidia, they came to Pamphylia. 25 Now when they had preached the word in Perga, they went down to Attalia. 26 From there they sailed to Antioch, where they had been commended to the grace of God for the work which they had completed.

27 Now when they had come and gathered the church together, they reported all that God had done with them, and that He had opened the door of faith to the Gentiles. 28 So they stayed there a long time with the disciples.

15 And certain *men* came down from Judea and taught the brethren, "Unless you are circumcised according to the custom of Moses, you cannot be saved." 2 Therefore, when Paul and Barnabas had no small dissension and dispute with them, they determined that Paul and Barnabas and certain others of them should go up to Jerusalem, to the apostles and elders, about this question.

3 So, being sent on their way by the church, they passed through Phoenicia and Samaria, describing the conversion of the Gentiles; and they caused great joy to all the brethren. 4 And when they had come to Jerusalem, they were received by the church and the apostles and the elders; and they reported all things that God had done with them. 5 But some of the sect of the Pharisees who believed rose up, saying, "It is necessary to circumcise them, and to command *them* to keep the law of Moses."

6 Now the apostles and elders came together to consider this matter. 7 And when there had been much dispute, Peter rose up and said to them: "Men and brethren, you know that a good while ago God chose among us, that by my mouth the Gentiles should hear the word of the gospel and believe. 8 So God, who knows the heart, acknowledged them by giving them the Holy Spirit, just as *He did* to us, 9 and made no distinction between us and them, purifying their hearts by faith. 10 Now therefore, why do you test God by putting a yoke on the neck of the disciples which neither our fathers nor we were able to bear? 11 But we believe that through the grace of the Lord Jesus Christ*a* we shall be saved in the same manner as they."

12 Then all the multitude kept silent and listened to Barnabas and Paul declaring how many miracles and wonders God had worked through them among the Gentiles. 13 And after they had become silent, James answered, saying, "Men *and* brethren, listen to me: 14 Simon has declared how God at the first visited the Gentiles to take out of them a people for His name. 15 And with this the words of the prophets agree, just as it is written:

16 'After this I will return
   And will rebuild the tabernacle
      of David, which has fallen
      down;
   I will rebuild its ruins,
   And I will set it up;
17 So that the rest of mankind
      may seek the LORD,
   Even all the Gentiles who are
      called by My name,
   Says the LORD who does all
      these things.'*a*

18 "Known to God from eternity are all His works.*a* 19 Therefore I judge that we should not trouble

---

15:11 *a*NU-Text and M-Text omit *Christ*.   15:17 *a*Amos 9:11, 12   15:18 *a*NU-Text reads *Says the Lord, who makes these things known from eternity (of old)*.

Paul's Second Journey

Paul began his second missionary journey in Jerusalem with his friend, Silas. They visited the churches of Galatia (see map of Paul's first journey) but went further. Young Timothy joined Paul and Silas in Lystra and the three men traveled to Macedonia and Achaia (present-day Greece). On this journey, the Philippian jailer was saved, the Bereans "searched the Scriptures daily" (Acts 17:11), and Paul preached at the Areopagus in Athens (17:22–32). Paul then ministered further in Corinth.

those from among the Gentiles who are turning to God, 20 but that we write to them to abstain from things polluted by idols, *from* sexual immorality,*a* *from* things strangled, and *from* blood. 21 For Moses has had throughout many generations those who preach him in every city, being read in the synagogues every Sabbath."

22 Then it pleased the apostles and elders, with the whole church, to send chosen men of their own company to Antioch with Paul and Barnabas, *namely,* Judas who was also named Barsabas,*a* and Silas, leading men among the brethren. 23 They wrote this *letter* by them:

The apostles, the elders, and the brethren,

To the brethren who are of the Gentiles in Antioch, Syria, and Cilicia:

Greetings.

24   Since we have heard that some who went out from us have troubled you with words, unsettling your souls, saying, "*You must* be circumcised and keep the law"*a*—to whom we gave no *such* commandment— 25 it seemed good to us, being assembled with one accord, to send chosen men to you with our beloved Barnabas and Paul, 26 men who have risked their lives for the name of our Lord Jesus Christ. 27 We have therefore sent Judas and Silas, who will also report the same things by word of mouth. 28 For it seemed good to the Holy Spirit, and to us, to lay upon you no greater burden than these necessary things: 29 that you abstain from things offered to idols, from blood, from things strangled, and from sexual immorality.*a* If you keep yourselves from these, you will do well.

Farewell.

30 So when they were sent off, they came to Antioch; and when they had gathered the multitude together, they delivered the letter. 31 When they had read it, they rejoiced over its encouragement. 32 Now Judas and Silas, themselves being prophets also, exhorted and strengthened the brethren with many words. 33 And after they had stayed *there* for a time, they were sent back with greetings from the brethren to the apostles.*a*

34 However, it seemed good to Silas to remain there.*a* 35 Paul and Barnabas also remained in Antioch, teaching and preaching the word of the Lord, with many others also.

36 Then after some days Paul said to Barnabas, "Let us now go back and visit our brethren in every city where we have preached the word of the Lord, *and see* how they are doing." 37 Now Barnabas was determined to take with them John called Mark. 38 But Paul insisted that they should not take with them the one who had departed from them in Pamphylia, and had not gone with them to the work. 39 Then the contention became so sharp that they parted from one another. And so Barnabas took Mark and sailed to Cyprus; 40 but Paul chose Silas and departed, being commended by the brethren to the grace of God. 41 And he went through Syria and Cilicia, strengthening the churches.

16 Then he came to Derbe and Lystra. And behold, a certain disciple was there, named Timothy, *the* son of a certain Jewish woman who believed, but his father *was* Greek. 2 He was well spoken of by the brethren who were at Lystra and Iconium. 3 Paul wanted to have him go on with him. And he took *him* and circumcised him because of the Jews who were in that region, for they all knew that his father was Greek. 4 And as they went through the cities, they delivered to them the decrees to keep, which were determined by the apostles and elders at Jerusalem. 5 So the churches were strengthened in the faith, and increased in number daily.

6 Now when they had gone through Phrygia and the region of Galatia, they were forbidden by the Holy

---

15:20 *a*Or *fornication*   15:22 *a*NU-Text and M-Text read *Barsabbas.* "*You must be circumcised and keep the law*".   15:29 *a*Or *fornication*   15:33 *a*NU-Text reads *to those who had sent them.*   15:34 *a*NU-Text and M-Text omit this verse.

Spirit to preach the word in Asia. 7 After they had come to Mysia, they tried to go into Bithynia, but the Spirit[a] did not permit them. 8 So passing by Mysia, they came down to Troas. 9 And a vision appeared to Paul in the night. A man of Macedonia stood and pleaded with him, saying, "Come over to Macedonia and help us." 10 Now after he had seen the vision, immediately we sought to go to Macedonia, concluding that the Lord had called us to preach the gospel to them.

11 Therefore, sailing from Troas, we ran a straight course to Samothrace, and the next day came to Neapolis, 12 and from there to Philippi, which is the foremost city of that part of Macedonia, a colony. And we were staying in that city for some days. 13 And on the Sabbath day we went out of the city to the riverside, where prayer was customarily made; and we sat down and spoke to the women who met there. 14 Now a certain woman named Lydia heard us. She was a seller of purple from the city of Thyatira, who worshiped God. The Lord opened her heart to heed the things spoken by Paul. 15 And when she and her household were baptized, she begged us, saying, "If you have judged me to be faithful to the Lord, come to my house and stay." So she persuaded us.

16 Now it happened, as we went to prayer, that a certain slave girl possessed with a spirit of divination met us, who brought her masters much profit by fortune-telling. 17 This girl followed Paul and us, and cried out, saying, "These men are the servants of the Most High God, who proclaim to us the way of salvation." 18 And this she did for many days.

But Paul, greatly annoyed, turned and said to the spirit, "I command you in the name of Jesus Christ to come out of her." And he came out that very hour. 19 But when her masters saw that their hope of profit was gone, they seized Paul and Silas and dragged them into the marketplace to the authorities.

20 And they brought them to the magistrates, and said, "These men, being Jews, exceedingly trouble our city; 21 and they teach customs which are not lawful for us, being Romans, to receive or observe." 22 Then the multitude rose up together against them; and the magistrates tore off their clothes and commanded them to be beaten with rods. 23 And when they had laid many stripes on them, they threw them into prison, commanding the jailer to keep them securely. 24 Having received such a charge, he put them into the inner prison and fastened their feet in the stocks.

25 But at midnight Paul and Silas were praying and singing hymns to God, and the prisoners were listening to them. 26 Suddenly there was a great earthquake, so that the foundations of the prison were shaken; and immediately all the doors were opened and everyone's chains were loosed. 27 And the keeper of the prison, awaking from sleep and seeing the prison doors open, supposing the prisoners had fled, drew his sword and was about to kill himself. 28 But Paul called with a loud voice, saying, "Do yourself no harm, for we are all here."

29 Then he called for a light, ran in, and fell down trembling before Paul and Silas. 30 And he brought them out and said, "Sirs, what must I do to be saved?"

31 So they said, "Believe on the Lord Jesus Christ, and you will be saved, you and your household." 32 Then they spoke the word of the Lord to him and to all who were in his house. 33 And he took them the same hour of the night and washed their stripes. And immediately he and all his family were baptized. 34 Now when he had brought them into his house, he set food before them; and he rejoiced, having believed in God with all his household.

35 And when it was day, the magistrates sent the officers, saying, "Let those men go."

36 So the keeper of the prison reported these words to Paul, saying, "The magistrates have sent to let you go. Now therefore depart, and go in peace."

37 But Paul said to them, "They have beaten us openly, uncondemned Romans, and have thrown us into prison. And now do they put us out secretly? No indeed! Let them come themselves and get us out."

16:7 [a]NU-Text adds of Jesus.

38 And the officers told these words to the magistrates, and they were afraid when they heard that they were Romans. 39 Then they came and pleaded with them and brought *them* out, and asked *them* to depart from the city. 40 So they went out of the prison and entered *the house of* Lydia; and when they had seen the brethren, they encouraged them and departed.

17 Now when they had passed through Amphipolis and Apollonia, they came to Thessalonica, where there was a synagogue of the Jews. 2 Then Paul, as his custom was, went in to them, and for three Sabbaths reasoned with them from the Scriptures, 3 explaining and demonstrating that the Christ had to suffer and rise again from the dead, and *saying,* "This Jesus whom I preach to you is the Christ." 4 And some of them were persuaded; and a great multitude of the devout Greeks, and not a few of the leading women, joined Paul and Silas.

5 But the Jews who were not persuaded, becoming envious,*a* took some of the evil men from the marketplace, and gathering a mob, set all the city in an uproar and attacked the house of Jason, and sought to bring them out to the people. 6 But when they did not find them, they dragged Jason and some brethren to the rulers of the city, crying out, "These who have turned the world upside down have come here too. 7 Jason has harbored them, and these are all acting contrary to the decrees of Caesar, saying there is another king—Jesus." 8 And they troubled the crowd and the rulers of the city when they heard these things. 9 So when they had taken security from Jason and the rest, they let them go.

10 Then the brethren immediately sent Paul and Silas away by night to Berea. When they arrived, they went into the synagogue of the Jews. 11 These were more fair-minded than those in Thessalonica, in that they received the word with all readiness, and searched the Scriptures daily *to find out* whether these things were so. 12 Therefore many of them believed, and also not a few of the

Greeks, prominent women as well as men. 13 But when the Jews from Thessalonica learned that the word of God was preached by Paul at Berea, they came there also and stirred up the crowds. 14 Then immediately the brethren sent Paul away, to go to the sea; but both Silas and Timothy remained there. 15 So those who conducted Paul brought him to Athens; and receiving a command for Silas and Timothy to come to him with all speed, they departed.

16 Now while Paul waited for them at Athens, his spirit was provoked within him when he saw that the city was given over to idols. 17 Therefore he reasoned in the synagogue with the Jews and with the *Gentile* worshipers, and in the marketplace daily with those who happened to be there. 18 Then*a* certain Epicurean and Stoic philosophers encountered him. And some said, "What does this babbler want to say?"

Others said, "He seems to be a proclaimer of foreign gods," because he preached to them Jesus and the resurrection.

19 And they took him and brought him to the Areopagus, saying, "May we know what this new doctrine *is* of which you speak? 20 For you are bringing some strange things to our ears. Therefore we want to know what these things mean." 21 For all the Athenians and the foreigners who were there spent their time in nothing else but either to tell or to hear some new thing.

22 Then Paul stood in the midst of the Areopagus and said, "Men of Athens, I perceive that in all things you are very religious; 23 for as I was passing through and considering the objects of your worship, I even found an altar with this inscription:

TO THE UNKNOWN GOD.

Therefore, the One whom you worship without knowing, Him I proclaim to you: 24 God, who made the world and everything in it, since He is Lord of heaven and earth, does not dwell in temples made with hands. 25 Nor is He worshiped with men's hands, as though He needed anything, since He gives to all life,

---

17:5 *a*NU-Text omits *who were not persuaded;* M-Text omits *becoming envious.*   17:18 *a*NU-Text and M-Text add *also.*

Paul's Third Journey

On his third missionary journey, Paul visited the churches of Galatia for a third time, and then settled in Ephesus for more than two years. Upon leaving Ephesus, Paul traveled again to Macedonia and Achaia (Greece) for a three-month stay. He returned to Asia by way of Macedonia. On this journey, Paul wrote 1 Corinthians (from Ephesus), 2 Corinthians (from Macedonia), and Romans (from Corinth).

BLACK SEA

SYRIA

Antioch

Tarsus

CYPRUS

Tyre
Ptolemais
Caesarea
Jerusalem

BITHYNIA

GALATIA

Iconium
Lystra
Derbe

PHRYGIA

MYSIA

ASIA Antioch
Ephesus
Miletus

Troas
Assos

Patara

Rhodes

Philippi
Neapolis

MACEDONIA

Amphipolis
Thessalonica
Berea

Apollonia

Athens

ACHAIA

Corinth

THE
GREAT
SEA

breath, and all things. 26 And He has made from one blood*a* every nation of men to dwell on all the face of the earth, and has determined their preappointed times and the boundaries of their dwellings, 27 so that they should seek the Lord, in the hope that they might grope for Him and find Him, though He is not far from each one of us; 28 for in Him we live and move and have our being, as also some of your own poets have said, 'For we are also His offspring.' 29 Therefore, since we are the offspring of God, we ought not to think that the Divine Nature is like gold or silver or stone, something shaped by art and man's devising. 30 Truly, these times of ignorance God overlooked, but now commands all men everywhere to repent, 31 because He has appointed a day on which He will judge the world in righteousness by the Man whom He has ordained. He has given assurance of this to all by raising Him from the dead."

32 And when they heard of the resurrection of the dead, some mocked, while others said, "We will hear you again on this *matter*." 33 So Paul departed from among them. 34 However, some men joined him and believed, among them Dionysius the Areopagite, a woman named Damaris, and others with them.

18 After these things Paul departed from Athens and went to Corinth. 2 And he found a certain Jew named Aquila, born in Pontus, who had recently come from Italy with his wife Priscilla (because Claudius had commanded all the Jews to depart from Rome); and he came to them. 3 So, because he was of the same trade, he stayed with them and worked; for by occupation they were tentmakers. 4 And he reasoned in the synagogue every Sabbath, and persuaded both Jews and Greeks.

5 When Silas and Timothy had come from Macedonia, Paul was compelled by the Spirit, and testified to the Jews *that* Jesus *is* the Christ. 6 But when they opposed him and blasphemed, he shook *his* garments and said to them, "Your blood *be* upon your *own* heads; I *am* clean. From now on I will go to the Gen-

tiles." 7 And he departed from there and entered the house of a certain *man* named Justus,*a* *one* who worshiped God, whose house was next door to the synagogue. 8 Then Crispus, the ruler of the synagogue, believed on the Lord with all his household. And many of the Corinthians, hearing, believed and were baptized.

9 Now the Lord spoke to Paul in the night by a vision, "Do not be afraid, but speak, and do not keep silent; 10 for I am with you, and no one will attack you to hurt you; for I have many people in this city." 11 And he continued *there* a year and six months, teaching the word of God among them.

12 When Gallio was proconsul of Achaia, the Jews with one accord rose up against Paul and brought him to the judgment seat, 13 saying, "This *fellow* persuades men to worship God contrary to the law."

14 And when Paul was about to open *his* mouth, Gallio said to the Jews, "If it were a matter of wrongdoing or wicked crimes, O Jews, there would be reason why I should bear with you. 15 But if it is a question of words and names and your own law, look *to it* yourselves; for I do not want to be a judge of such *matters*." 16 And he drove them from the judgment seat. 17 Then all the Greeks*a* took Sosthenes, the ruler of the synagogue, and beat *him* before the judgment seat. But Gallio took no notice of these things.

18 So Paul still remained a good while. Then he took leave of the brethren and sailed for Syria, and Priscilla and Aquila *were* with him. He had *his* hair cut off at Cenchrea, for he had taken a vow. 19 And he came to Ephesus, and left them there; but he himself entered the synagogue and reasoned with the Jews. 20 When they asked *him* to stay a longer time with them, he did not consent, 21 but took leave of them, saying, "I must by all means keep this coming feast in Jerusalem;*a* but I will return again to you, God willing." And he sailed from Ephesus.

22 And when he had landed at Caesarea, and gone up and greeted the church, he went down to Antioch. 23 After he had spent some time

---

17:26 *a*NU-Text omits *blood.*   18:7 *a*NU-Text reads *Titius Justus.*   18:17 *a*NU-Text reads *they all.*
18:21 *a*NU-Text omits *I must* through *Jerusalem.*

there, he departed and went over the region of Galatia and Phrygia in order, strengthening all the disciples.

24 Now a certain Jew named Apollos, born at Alexandria, an eloquent man *and* mighty in the Scriptures, came to Ephesus. 25 This man had been instructed in the way of the Lord; and being fervent in spirit, he spoke and taught accurately the things of the Lord, though he knew only the baptism of John. 26 So he began to speak boldly in the synagogue. When Aquila and Priscilla heard him, they took him aside and explained to him the way of God more accurately. 27 And when he desired to cross to Achaia, the brethren wrote, exhorting the disciples to receive him; and when he arrived, he greatly helped those who had believed through grace; 28 for he vigorously refuted the Jews publicly, showing from the Scriptures that Jesus is the Christ.

19 And it happened, while Apollos was at Corinth, that Paul, having passed through the upper regions, came to Ephesus. And finding some disciples 2 he said to them, "Did you receive the Holy Spirit when you believed?"

So they said to him, "We have not so much as heard whether there is a Holy Spirit."

3 And he said to them, "Into what then were you baptized?"

So they said, "Into John's baptism."

4 Then Paul said, "John indeed baptized with a baptism of repentance, saying to the people that they should believe on Him who would come after him, that is, on Christ Jesus."

5 When they heard *this*, they were baptized in the name of the Lord Jesus. 6 And when Paul had laid hands on them, the Holy Spirit came upon them, and they spoke with tongues and prophesied. 7 Now the men were about twelve in all.

8 And he went into the synagogue and spoke boldly for three months, reasoning and persuading concerning the things of the kingdom of God. 9 But when some were hardened and did not believe, but spoke evil of the

Way before the multitude, he departed from them and withdrew the disciples, reasoning daily in the school of Tyrannus. 10 And this continued for two years, so that all who dwelt in Asia heard the word of the Lord Jesus, both Jews and Greeks.

11 Now God worked unusual miracles by the hands of Paul, 12 so that even handkerchiefs or aprons were brought from his body to the sick, and the diseases left them and the evil spirits went out of them. 13 Then some of the itinerant Jewish exorcists took it upon themselves to call the name of the Lord Jesus over those who had evil spirits, saying, "We*a* exorcise you by the Jesus whom Paul preaches." 14 Also there were seven sons of Sceva, a Jewish chief priest, who did so.

15 And the evil spirit answered and said, "Jesus I know, and Paul I know; but who are you?"

16 Then the man in whom the evil spirit was leaped on them, overpowered*a* them, and prevailed against them,*b* so that they fled out of that house naked and wounded. 17 This became known both to all Jews and Greeks dwelling in Ephesus; and fear fell on them all, and the name of the Lord Jesus was magnified. 18 And many who had believed came confessing and telling their deeds. 19 Also, many of those who had practiced magic brought their books together and burned *them* in the sight of all. And they counted up the value of them, and *it* totaled fifty thousand *pieces* of silver. 20 So the word of the Lord grew mightily and prevailed.

21 When these things were accomplished, Paul purposed in the Spirit, when he had passed through Macedonia and Achaia, to go to Jerusalem, saying, "After I have been there, I must also see Rome." 22 So he sent into Macedonia two of those who ministered to him, Timothy and Erastus, but he himself stayed in Asia for a time.

23 And about that time there arose a great commotion about the Way. 24 For a certain man named Demetrius, a silversmith, who made silver shrines of Diana,*a* brought no small profit to the craftsmen. 25 He called

19:13 *a*NU-Text reads *I*.   19:16 *a*M-Text reads *and they overpowered*.   *b*NU-Text reads *both of them*.
19:24 *a*Greek *Artemis*

them together with the workers of similar occupation, and said: "Men, you know that we have our prosperity by this trade. 26 Moreover you see and hear that not only at Ephesus, but throughout almost all Asia, this Paul has persuaded and turned away many people, saying that they are not gods which are made with hands. 27 So not only is this trade of ours in danger of falling into disrepute, but also the temple of the great goddess Diana may be despised and her magnificence destroyed,*a* whom all Asia and the world worship."

28 Now when they heard *this,* they were full of wrath and cried out, saying, "Great *is* Diana of the Ephesians!" 29 So the whole city was filled with confusion, and rushed into the theater with one accord, having seized Gaius and Aristarchus, Macedonians, Paul's travel companions. 30 And when Paul wanted to go in to the people, the disciples would not allow him. 31 Then some of the officials of Asia, who were his friends, sent to him pleading that he would not venture into the theater. 32 Some therefore cried one thing and some another, for the assembly was confused, and most of them did not know why they had come together. 33 And they drew Alexander out of the multitude, the Jews putting him forward. And Alexander motioned with his hand, and wanted to make his defense to the people. 34 But when they found out that he was a Jew, all with one voice cried out for about two hours, "Great *is* Diana of the Ephesians!"

35 And when the city clerk had quieted the crowd, he said: "Men of Ephesus, what man is there who does not know that the city of the Ephesians is temple guardian of the great goddess Diana, and of the *image* which fell down from Zeus? 36 Therefore, since these things cannot be denied, you ought to be quiet and do nothing rashly. 37 For you have brought these men here who are neither robbers of temples nor blasphemers of your*a* goddess. 38 Therefore, if Demetrius and his fellow craftsmen have a case against anyone, the courts are open and there are proconsuls. Let them bring charges against one another. 39 But if you have any other inquiry to make, it shall be determined in the lawful assembly. 40 For we are in danger of being called in question for today's uproar, there being no reason which we may give to account for this disorderly gathering." 41 And when he had said these things, he dismissed the assembly.

20 After the uproar had ceased, Paul called the disciples to *himself,* embraced *them,* and departed to go to Macedonia. 2 Now when he had gone over that region and encouraged them with many words, he came to Greece 3 and stayed three months. And when the Jews plotted against him as he was about to sail to Syria, he decided to return through Macedonia. 4 And Sopater of Berea accompanied him to Asia—also Aristarchus and Secundus of the Thessalonians, and Gaius of Derbe, and Timothy, and Tychicus and Trophimus of Asia. 5 These men, going ahead, waited for us at Troas. 6 But we sailed away from Philippi after the Days of Unleavened Bread, and in five days joined them at Troas, where we stayed seven days.

7 Now on the first *day* of the week, when the disciples came together to break bread, Paul, ready to depart the next day, spoke to them and continued his message until midnight. 8 There were many lamps in the upper room where they*a* were gathered together. 9 And in a window sat a certain young man named Eutychus, who was sinking into a deep sleep. He was overcome by sleep; and as Paul continued speaking, he fell down from the third story and was taken up dead. 10 But Paul went down, fell on him, and embracing *him* said, "Do not trouble yourselves, for his life is in him." 11 Now when he had come up, had broken bread and eaten, and talked a long while, even till daybreak, he departed. 12 And they brought the young man in alive, and they were not a little comforted.

13 Then we went ahead to the ship and sailed to Assos, there intending to take Paul on board; for so he had given orders, intending himself to go

19:27 *a*NU-Text reads *she be deposed from her magnificence.*   19:37 *a*NU-Text reads *our.*
20:8 *a*NU-Text and M-Text read *we.*

on foot. 14 And when he met us at Assos, we took him on board and came to Mitylene. 15 We sailed from there, and the next *day* came opposite Chios. The following *day* we arrived at Samos and stayed at Trogyllium. The next *day* we came to Miletus. 16 For Paul had decided to sail past Ephesus, so that he would not have to spend time in Asia; for he was hurrying to be at Jerusalem, if possible, on the Day of Pentecost.

17 From Miletus he sent to Ephesus and called for the elders of the church. 18 And when they had come to him, he said to them: "You know, from the first day that I came to Asia, in what manner I always lived among you, 19 serving the Lord with all humility, with many tears and trials which happened to me by the plotting of the Jews; 20 how I kept back nothing that was helpful, but proclaimed it to you, and taught you publicly and from house to house, 21 testifying to Jews, and also to Greeks, repentance toward God and faith toward our Lord Jesus Christ. 22 And see, now I go bound in the spirit to Jerusalem, not knowing the things that will happen to me there, 23 except that the Holy Spirit testifies in every city, saying that chains and tribulations await me. 24 But none of these things move me; nor do I count my life dear to myself,*a* so that I may finish my race with joy, and the ministry which I received from the Lord Jesus, to testify to the gospel of the grace of God.

25 "And indeed, now I know that you all, among whom I have gone preaching the kingdom of God, will see my face no more. 26 Therefore I testify to you this day that I *am* innocent of the blood of all *men*. 27 For I have not shunned to declare to you the whole counsel of God. 28 Therefore take heed to yourselves and to all the flock, among which the Holy Spirit has made you overseers, to shepherd the church of God*a* which He purchased with His own blood. 29 For I know this, that after my departure savage wolves will come in among you, not sparing the flock. 30 Also from among yourselves men will rise up, speaking perverse

things, to draw away the disciples after themselves. 31 Therefore watch, and remember that for three years I did not cease to warn everyone night and day with tears.

32 "So now, brethren, I commend you to God and to the word of His grace, which is able to build you up and give you an inheritance among all those who are sanctified. 33 I have coveted no one's silver or gold or apparel. 34 Yes,*a* you yourselves know that these hands have provided for my necessities, and for those who were with me. 35 I have shown you in every way, by laboring like this, that you must support the weak. And remember the words of the Lord Jesus, that He said, 'It is more blessed to give than to receive.'"

36 And when he had said these things, he knelt down and prayed with them all. 37 Then they all wept freely, and fell on Paul's neck and kissed him, 38 sorrowing most of all for the words which he spoke, that they would see his face no more. And they accompanied him to the ship.

21 Now it came to pass, that when we had departed from them and set sail, running a straight course we came to Cos, the following *day* to Rhodes, and from there to Patara. 2 And finding a ship sailing over to Phoenicia, we went aboard and set sail. 3 When we had sighted Cyprus, we passed it on the left, sailed to Syria, and landed at Tyre; for there the ship was to unload her cargo. 4 And finding disciples,*a* we stayed there seven days. They told Paul through the Spirit not to go up to Jerusalem. 5 When we had come to the end of those days, we departed and went on our way; and they all accompanied us, with wives and children, till *we were* out of the city. And we knelt down on the shore and prayed. 6 When we had taken our leave of one another, we boarded the ship, and they returned home.

7 And when we had finished *our* voyage from Tyre, we came to Ptolemais, greeted the brethren, and stayed with them one day. 8 On the next *day* we who were Paul's companions*a* departed and came to Cae-

20:24 *a*NU-Text reads *But I do not count my life of any value or dear to myself.*   20:28 *a*M-Text reads *of the Lord and God.*   20:34 *a*NU-Text and M-Text omit *Yes.*   21:4 *a*NU-Text reads *the disciples.*
21:8 *a*NU-Text omits *who were Paul's companions.*

sarea, and entered the house of Philip the evangelist, who was *one* of the seven, and stayed with him. 9 Now this man had four virgin daughters who prophesied. 10 And as we stayed many days, a certain prophet named Agabus came down from Judea. 11 When he had come to us, he took Paul's belt, bound his *own* hands and feet, and said, "Thus says the Holy Spirit, 'So shall the Jews at Jerusalem bind the man who owns this belt, and deliver *him* into the hands of the Gentiles.' "

12 Now when we heard these things, both we and those from that place pleaded with him not to go up to Jerusalem. 13 Then Paul answered, "What do you mean by weeping and breaking my heart? For I am ready not only to be bound, but also to die at Jerusalem for the name of the Lord Jesus."

14 So when he would not be persuaded, we ceased, saying, "The will of the Lord be done."

15 And after those days we packed and went up to Jerusalem. 16 Also some of the disciples from Caesarea went with us and brought with them a certain Mnason of Cyprus, an early disciple, with whom we were to lodge.

17 And when we had come to Jerusalem, the brethren received us gladly. 18 On the following *day* Paul went in with us to James, and all the elders were present. 19 When he had greeted them, he told in detail those things which God had done among the Gentiles through his ministry. 20 And when they heard *it*, they glorified the Lord. And they said to him, "You see, brother, how many myriads of Jews there are who have believed, and they are all zealous for the law; 21 but they have been informed about you that you teach all the Jews who are among the Gentiles to forsake Moses, saying that they ought not to circumcise *their* children nor to walk according to the customs. 22 What then? The assembly must certainly meet, for they will[a] hear that you have come. 23 Therefore do what we tell you: We have four men who have taken a vow. 24 Take them and be purified with them, and pay their expenses so that

they may shave *their* heads, and that all may know that those things of which they were informed concerning you are nothing, but *that* you yourself also walk orderly and keep the law. 25 But concerning the Gentiles who believe, we have written *and* decided that they should observe no such thing,[a] except that they should keep themselves from *things* offered to idols, from blood, from things strangled, and from sexual immorality."

26 Then Paul took the men, and the next day, having been purified with them, entered the temple to announce the expiration of the days of purification, at which time an offering should be made for each one of them.

27 Now when the seven days were almost ended, the Jews from Asia, seeing him in the temple, stirred up the whole crowd and laid hands on him, 28 crying out, "Men of Israel, help! This is the man who teaches all *men* everywhere against the people, the law, and this place; and furthermore he also brought Greeks into the temple and has defiled this holy place." 29 (For they had previously[a] seen Trophimus the Ephesian with him in the city, whom they supposed that Paul had brought into the temple.)

30 And all the city was disturbed; and the people ran together, seized Paul, and dragged him out of the temple; and immediately the doors were shut. 31 Now as they were seeking to kill him, news came to the commander of the garrison that all Jerusalem was in an uproar. 32 He immediately took soldiers and centurions, and ran down to them. And when they saw the commander and the soldiers, they stopped beating Paul. 33 Then the commander came near and took him, and commanded *him* to be bound with two chains; and he asked who he was and what he had done. 34 And some among the multitude cried one thing and some another.

So when he could not ascertain the truth because of the tumult, he commanded him to be taken into the barracks. 35 When he reached the stairs, he had to be carried by the soldiers

---

21:22 [a]NU-Text reads *What then is to be done? They will certainly.*   21:25 [a]NU-Text omits *that they should observe no such thing, except.*   21:29 [a]M-Text omits *previously.*

because of the violence of the mob. 36 For the multitude of the people followed after, crying out, "Away with him!"

37 Then as Paul was about to be led into the barracks, he said to the commander, "May I speak to you?"

He replied, "Can you speak Greek? 38 Are you not the Egyptian who some time ago stirred up a rebellion and led the four thousand assassins out into the wilderness?"

39 But Paul said, "I am a Jew from Tarsus, in Cilicia, a citizen of no mean city; and I implore you, permit me to speak to the people."

40 So when he had given him permission, Paul stood on the stairs and motioned with his hand to the people. And when there was a great silence, he spoke to *them* in the Hebrew language, saying,

22 "Brethren and fathers, hear my defense before you now." 2 And when they heard that he spoke to them in the Hebrew language, they kept all the more silent.

Then he said: 3 "I am indeed a Jew, born in Tarsus of Cilicia, but brought up in this city at the feet of Gamaliel, taught according to the strictness of our fathers' law, and was zealous toward God as you all are today. 4 I persecuted this Way to the death, binding and delivering into prisons both men and women, 5 as also the high priest bears me witness, and all the council of the elders, from whom I also received letters to the brethren, and went to Damascus to bring in chains even those who were there to Jerusalem to be punished.

6 "Now it happened, as I journeyed and came near Damascus at about noon, suddenly a great light from heaven shone around me. 7 And I fell to the ground and heard a voice saying to me, 'Saul, Saul, why are you persecuting Me?' 8 So I answered, 'Who are You, Lord?' And He said to me, 'I am Jesus of Nazareth, whom you are persecuting.'

9 "And those who were with me indeed saw the light and were afraid,[a] but they did not hear the voice of Him who spoke to me. 10 So I said, 'What shall I do, Lord?' And the Lord said to me, 'Arise and go into Damascus, and there you will be told all things

which are appointed for you to do.' 11 And since I could not see for the glory of that light, being led by the hand of those who were with me, I came into Damascus.

12 "Then a certain Ananias, a devout man according to the law, having a good testimony with all the Jews who dwelt *there,* 13 came to me; and he stood and said to me, 'Brother Saul, receive your sight.' And at that same hour I looked up at him. 14 Then he said, 'The God of our fathers has chosen you that you should know His will, and see the Just One, and hear the voice of His mouth. 15 For you will be His witness to all men of what you have seen and heard. 16 And now why are you waiting? Arise and be baptized, and wash away your sins, calling on the name of the Lord.'

17 "Now it happened, when I returned to Jerusalem and was praying in the temple, that I was in a trance 18 and saw Him saying to me, 'Make haste and get out of Jerusalem quickly, for they will not receive your testimony concerning Me.' 19 So I said, 'Lord, they know that in every synagogue I imprisoned and beat those who believe on You. 20 And when the blood of Your martyr Stephen was shed, I also was standing by consenting to his death,[a] and guarding the clothes of those who were killing him.' 21 Then He said to me, 'Depart, for I will send you far from here to the Gentiles.' "

22 And they listened to him until this word, and *then* they raised their voices and said, "Away with such a *fellow* from the earth, for he is not fit to live!" 23 Then, as they cried out and tore off *their* clothes and threw dust into the air, 24 the commander ordered him to be brought into the barracks, and said that he should be examined under scourging, so that he might know why they shouted so against him. 25 And as they bound him with thongs, Paul said to the centurion who stood by, "Is it lawful for you to scourge a man who is a Roman, and uncondemned?"

26 When the centurion heard *that,* he went and told the commander, saying, "Take care what you do, for this man is a Roman."

27 Then the commander came and

22:9 aNU-Text omits *and were afraid.*   22:20 aNU-Text omits *to his death.*

said to him, "Tell me, are you a Roman?"

He said, "Yes."

28 The commander answered, "With a large sum I obtained this citizenship."

And Paul said, "But I was born a citizen."

29 Then immediately those who were about to examine him withdrew from him; and the commander was also afraid after he found out that he was a Roman, and because he had bound him.

30 The next day, because he wanted to know for certain why he was accused by the Jews, he released him from his bonds, and commanded the chief priests and all their council to appear, and brought Paul down and set him before them.

23 Then Paul, looking earnestly at the council, said, "Men and brethren, I have lived in all good conscience before God until this day." 2 And the high priest Ananias commanded those who stood by him to strike him on the mouth. 3 Then Paul said to him, "God will strike you, you whitewashed wall! For you sit to judge me according to the law, and do you command me to be struck contrary to the law?"

4 And those who stood by said, "Do you revile God's high priest?"

5 Then Paul said, "I did not know, brethren, that he was the high priest; for it is written, 'You shall not speak evil of a ruler of your people.' "a

6 But when Paul perceived that one part were Sadducees and the other Pharisees, he cried out in the council, "Men and brethren, I am a Pharisee, the son of a Pharisee; concerning the hope and resurrection of the dead I am being judged!"

7 And when he had said this, a dissension arose between the Pharisees and the Sadducees; and the assembly was divided. 8 For Sadducees say that there is no resurrection—and no angel or spirit; but the Pharisees confess both. 9 Then there arose a loud outcry. And the scribes of the Pharisees' party arose and protested, saying, "We find no evil in this man; but if a spirit or an angel has spoken to him, let us not fight against God."a

10 Now when there arose a great dissension, the commander, fearing lest Paul might be pulled to pieces by them, commanded the soldiers to go down and take him by force from among them, and bring him into the barracks.

11 But the following night the Lord stood by him and said, "Be of good cheer, Paul; for as you have testified for Me in Jerusalem, so you must also bear witness at Rome."

12 And when it was day, some of the Jews banded together and bound themselves under an oath, saying that they would neither eat nor drink till they had killed Paul. 13 Now there were more than forty who had formed this conspiracy. 14 They came to the chief priests and elders, and said, "We have bound ourselves under a great oath that we will eat nothing until we have killed Paul. 15 Now you, therefore, together with the council, suggest to the commander that he be brought down to you tomorrow,a as though you were going to make further inquiries concerning him; but we are ready to kill him before he comes near."

16 So when Paul's sister's son heard of their ambush, he went and entered the barracks and told Paul. 17 Then Paul called one of the centurions to him and said, "Take this young man to the commander, for he has something to tell him." 18 So he took him and brought him to the commander and said, "Paul the prisoner called me to him and asked me to bring this young man to you. He has something to say to you."

19 Then the commander took him by the hand, went aside, and asked privately, "What is it that you have to tell me?"

20 And he said, "The Jews have agreed to ask that you bring Paul down to the council tomorrow, as though they were going to inquire more fully about him. 21 But do not yield to them, for more than forty of them lie in wait for him, men who have bound themselves by an oath that they will neither eat nor drink till they have killed him; and now they are ready, waiting for the promise from you."

22 So the commander let the young

23:5 aExodus 22:28   23:9 aNU-Text omits last clause and reads what if a spirit or an angel has spoken to him?   23:15 aNU-Text omits tomorrow.

man depart, and commanded *him*, "Tell no one that you have revealed these things to me."

23 And he called for two centurions, saying, "Prepare two hundred soldiers, seventy horsemen, and two hundred spearmen to go to Caesarea at the third hour of the night; 24 and provide mounts to set Paul on, and bring *him* safely to Felix the governor." 25 He wrote a letter in the following manner:

26   Claudius Lysias,

To the most excellent governor Felix:

Greetings.

27   This man was seized by the Jews and was about to be killed by them. Coming with the troops I rescued him, having learned that he was a Roman. 28 And when I wanted to know the reason they accused him, I brought him before their council. 29 I found out that he was accused concerning questions of their law, but had nothing charged against him deserving of death or chains. 30 And when it was told me that the Jews lay in wait for the man,*a* I sent him immediately to you, and also commanded his accusers to state before you the charges against him.

Farewell.

31 Then the soldiers, as they were commanded, took Paul and brought *him* by night to Antipatris. 32 The next day they left the horsemen to go on with him, and returned to the barracks. 33 When they came to Caesarea and had delivered the letter to the governor, they also presented Paul to him. 34 And when the governor had read *it,* he asked what province he was from. And when he understood that *he was* from Cilicia, 35 he said, "I will hear you when your accusers also have come." And he commanded him to be kept in Herod's Praetorium.

24 Now after five days Ananias the high priest came down with the elders and a certain orator *named* Tertullus. These gave evidence to the governor against Paul.

2 And when he was called upon, Tertullus began his accusation, saying: "Seeing that through you we enjoy great peace, and prosperity is being brought to this nation by your foresight, 3 we accept *it* always and in all places, most noble Felix, with all thankfulness. 4 Nevertheless, not to be tedious to you any further, I beg you to hear, by your courtesy, a few words from us. 5 For we have found this man a plague, a creator of dissension among all the Jews throughout the world, and a ringleader of the sect of the Nazarenes. 6 He even tried to profane the temple, and we seized him,*a* and wanted to judge him according to our law. 7 But the commander Lysias came by and with great violence took *him* out of our hands, 8 commanding his accusers to come to you. By examining him yourself you may ascertain all these things of which we accuse him." 9 And the Jews also assented,*a* maintaining that these things were so.

10 Then Paul, after the governor had nodded to him to speak, answered: "Inasmuch as I know that you have been for many years a judge of this nation, I do the more cheerfully answer for myself, 11 because you may ascertain that it is no more than twelve days since I went up to Jerusalem to worship. 12 And they neither found me in the temple disputing with anyone nor inciting the crowd, either in the synagogues or in the city. 13 Nor can they prove the things of which they now accuse me. 14 But this I confess to you, that according to the Way which they call a sect, so I worship the God of my fathers, believing all things which are written in the Law and in the Prophets. 15 I have hope in God, which they themselves also accept, that there will be a resurrection of *the* dead,*a* both of *the* just and *the*

23:30 *a*NU-Text reads *there would be a plot against the man.*   24:6 *a*NU-Text ends the sentence here and omits the rest of verse 6, all of verse 7, and the first clause of verse 8.   24:9 *a*NU-Text and M-Text read *joined the attack.*   24:15 *a*NU-Text omits *of the dead.*

Appeal to Caesar

Perhaps one of Paul's greatest assets was that he was an uncommon person committed to uncommon goals. He was willing to attempt great things for God because he knew the power of the gospel (see Rom. 1:16).

Because of his witness, Paul suffered many imprisonments. One was at Caesarea by the Sea, the great coastal city of Palestine. Here Paul spent two years in prison and appeared before two governors who tried his case: Festus and Felix.

Festus decided Paul was to be granted freedom; but Paul declined his own release in favor of a greater goal. He wished to stay in prison in order to have the chance to speak to Caesar. As a Roman citizen, Paul had the right to appeal his case to the emperor. Festus told Paul he would have been set free had it not been for this request. Paul had appealed to Caesar, so to Caesar he would go (see Acts 24—26).

Paul was willing to attempt to do great things for God, even if it meant further imprisonment. But the cost was worth the opportunity to speak to one of the world's great leaders about the greatest event in history. The Book of Philippians reveals the outcome of Paul's plan. "All the saints greet you, but especially those who are of Caesar's household" (Phil. 4:22). Paul's message of Jesus Christ infiltrated the mighty kingdom of Caesar. All it took was one man's commitment to an uncommon goal.

What goal would you set for yourself if you knew you would not fail? Who is the Caesar—the greater authority, the powerful overlord—in your life? Appeal to Caesar; speak of Christ confidently no matter what the personal cost. Remember Paul's words and be encouraged: "Being confident of this very thing, that He who has begun a good work in you will complete *it* until the day of Jesus Christ" (Phil. 1:6).

unjust. 16 This *being* so, I myself always strive to have a conscience without offense toward God and men.

17 "Now after many years I came to bring alms and offerings to my nation, 18 in the midst of which some Jews from Asia found me purified in the temple, neither with a mob nor with tumult. 19 They ought to have been here before you to object if they had anything against me. 20 Or else let those who are *here* themselves say if they found any wrongdoing^a in me while I stood before the council, 21 unless *it is* for this one statement which I cried out, standing among them, 'Concerning the resurrection of the dead I am being judged by you this day.' "

22 But when Felix heard these things, having more accurate knowledge of *the* Way, he adjourned the proceedings and said, "When Lysias the commander comes down, I will make a decision on your case." 23 So he commanded the centurion to keep Paul and to let *him* have liberty, and told him not to forbid any of his friends to provide for or visit him.

24 And after some days, when Felix came with his wife Drusilla, who was Jewish, he sent for Paul and heard him concerning the faith in Christ. 25 Now as he reasoned about righteousness, self-control, and the judgment to come, Felix was afraid and answered, "Go away for now; when I have a convenient time I will call for you." 26 Meanwhile he also hoped that money would be given him by Paul, that he might release him.^a Therefore he sent for him more often and conversed with him.

27 But after two years Porcius Festus succeeded Felix; and Felix, wanting to do the Jews a favor, left Paul bound.

25 Now when Festus had come to the province, after three days he went up from Caesarea to Jerusalem. 2 Then the high priest^a and the chief men of the Jews informed him against Paul; and they petitioned him, 3 asking a favor against him, that he would summon him to Jerusalem—while *they* lay in ambush

along the road to kill him. 4 But Festus answered that Paul should be kept at Caesarea, and that he himself was going *there* shortly. 5 "Therefore," he said, "let those who have authority among you go down with *me* and accuse this man, to see if there is any fault in him."

6 And when he had remained among them more than ten days, he went down to Caesarea. And the next day, sitting on the judgment seat, he commanded Paul to be brought. 7 When he had come, the Jews who had come down from Jerusalem stood about and laid many serious complaints against Paul, which they could not prove, 8 while he answered for himself, "Neither against the law of the Jews, nor against the temple, nor against Caesar have I offended in anything at all."

9 But Festus, wanting to do the Jews a favor, answered Paul and said, "Are you willing to go up to Jerusalem and there be judged before me concerning these things?"

10 So Paul said, "I stand at Caesar's judgment seat, where I ought to be judged. To the Jews I have done no wrong, as you very well know. 11 For if I am an offender, or have committed anything deserving of death, I do not object to dying; but if there is nothing in these things of which these men accuse me, no one can deliver me to them. I appeal to Caesar."

12 Then Festus, when he had conferred with the council, answered, "You have appealed to Caesar? To Caesar you shall go!"

13 And after some days King Agrippa and Bernice came to Caesarea to greet Festus. 14 When they had been there many days, Festus laid Paul's case before the king, saying: "There is a certain man left a prisoner by Felix, 15 about whom the chief priests and the elders of the Jews informed *me*, when I was in Jerusalem, asking for a judgment against him. 16 To them I answered, 'It is not the custom of the Romans to deliver any man to destruction^a before the accused meets the accusers face to face, and has opportunity to answer for himself concerning the

charge against him.' 17 Therefore when they had come together, without any delay, the next day I sat on the judgment seat and commanded the man to be brought in. 18 When the accusers stood up, they brought no accusation against him of such things as I supposed, 19 but had some questions against him about their own religion and about a certain Jesus, who had died, whom Paul affirmed to be alive. 20 And because I was uncertain of such questions, I asked whether he was willing to go to Jerusalem and there be judged concerning these matters. 21 But when Paul appealed to be reserved for the decision of Augustus, I commanded him to be kept till I could send him to Caesar."

22 Then Agrippa said to Festus, "I also would like to hear the man myself."

"Tomorrow," he said, "you shall hear him."

23 So the next day, when Agrippa and Bernice had come with great pomp, and had entered the auditorium with the commanders and the prominent men of the city, at Festus' command Paul was brought in. 24 And Festus said: "King Agrippa and all the men who are here present with us, you see this man about whom the whole assembly of the Jews petitioned me, both at Jerusalem and here, crying out that he was not fit to live any longer. 25 But when I found that he had committed nothing deserving of death, and that he himself had appealed to Augustus, I decided to send him. 26 I have nothing certain to write to my lord concerning him. Therefore I have brought him out before you, and especially before you, King Agrippa, so that after the examination has taken place I may have something to write. 27 For it seems to me unreasonable to send a prisoner and not to specify the charges against him."

26 Then Agrippa said to Paul, "You are permitted to speak for yourself."

So Paul stretched out his hand and answered for himself: 2 "I think myself happy, King Agrippa, because today I shall answer for myself before you concerning all the things of which I am accused by the Jews, 3 especially because you are expert in all customs and questions which have to do with the Jews. Therefore I beg you to hear me patiently.

4 "My manner of life from my youth, which was spent from the beginning among my own nation at Jerusalem, all the Jews know. 5 They knew me from the first, if they were willing to testify, that according to the strictest sect of our religion I lived a Pharisee. 6 And now I stand and am judged for the hope of the promise made by God to our fathers. 7 To this *promise* our twelve tribes, earnestly serving *God* night and day, hope to attain. For this hope's sake, King Agrippa, I am accused by the Jews. 8 Why should it be thought incredible by you that God raises the dead?

9 "Indeed, I myself thought I must do many things contrary to the name of Jesus of Nazareth. 10 This I also did in Jerusalem, and many of the saints I shut up in prison, having received authority from the chief priests; and when they were put to death, I cast my vote against *them*. 11 And I punished them often in every synagogue and compelled *them* to blaspheme; and being exceedingly enraged against them, I persecuted *them* even to foreign cities.

12 "While thus occupied, as I journeyed to Damascus with authority and commission from the chief priests, 13 at midday, O king, along the road I saw a light from heaven, brighter than the sun, shining around me and those who journeyed with me. 14 And when we all had fallen to the ground, I heard a voice speaking to me and saying in the Hebrew language, 'Saul, Saul, why are you persecuting Me? *It is* hard for you to kick against the goads.' 15 So I said, 'Who are You, Lord?' And He said, 'I am Jesus, whom you are persecuting. 16 But rise and stand on your feet; for I have appeared to you for this purpose, to make you a minister and a witness both of the things which you have seen and of the things which I will yet reveal to you. 17 I will deliver you from the *Jewish* people, as well as *from* the Gentiles, to whom I now*a* send you, 18 to open

26:17 *a*NU-Text and M-Text omit *now*.

their eyes, *in order* to turn *them* from darkness to light, and *from* the power of Satan to God, that they may receive forgiveness of sins and an inheritance among those who are sanctified by faith in Me.'

19 "Therefore, King Agrippa, I was not disobedient to the heavenly vision, 20 but declared first to those in Damascus and in Jerusalem, and throughout all the region of Judea, and *then* to the Gentiles, that they should repent, turn to God, and do works befitting repentance. 21 For these reasons the Jews seized me in the temple and tried to kill *me.* 22 Therefore, having obtained help from God, to this day I stand, witnessing both to small and great, saying no other things than those which the prophets and Moses said would come— 23 that the Christ would suffer, that He would be the first to rise from the dead, and would proclaim light to the *Jewish* people and to the Gentiles."

24 Now as he thus made his defense, Festus said with a loud voice, "Paul, you are beside yourself! Much learning is driving you mad!"

25 But he said, "I am not mad, most noble Festus, but speak the words of truth and reason. 26 For the king, before whom I also speak freely, knows these things; for I am convinced that none of these things escapes his attention, since this thing was not done in a corner. 27 King Agrippa, do you believe the prophets? I know that you do believe."

28 Then Agrippa said to Paul, "You almost persuade me to become a Christian."

29 And Paul said, "I would to God that not only you, but also all who hear me today, might become both almost and altogether such as I am, except for these chains."

30 When he had said these things, the king stood up, as well as the governor and Bernice and those who sat with them; 31 and when they had gone aside, they talked among themselves, saying, "This man is doing nothing deserving of death or chains."

32 Then Agrippa said to Festus, "This man might have been set free if he had not appealed to Caesar."

27 And when it was decided that we should sail to Italy, they delivered Paul and some other prisoners to *one* named Julius, a centurion of the Augustan Regiment. 2 So, entering a ship of Adramyttium, we put to sea, meaning to sail along the coasts of Asia. Aristarchus, a Macedonian of Thessalonica, was with us. 3 And the next *day* we landed at Sidon. And Julius treated Paul kindly and gave *him* liberty to go to his friends and receive care. 4 When we had put to sea from there, we sailed under *the shelter of* Cyprus, because the winds were contrary. 5 And when we had sailed over the sea which is off Cilicia and Pamphylia, we came to Myra, *a city* of Lycia. 6 There the centurion found an Alexandrian ship sailing to Italy, and he put us on board.

7 When we had sailed slowly many days, and arrived with difficulty off Cnidus, the wind not permitting us to proceed, we sailed under *the shelter of* Crete off Salmone. 8 Passing it with difficulty, we came to a place called Fair Havens, near the city *of* Lasea.

9 Now when much time had been spent, and sailing was now dangerous because the Fast was already over, Paul advised them, 10 saying, "Men, I perceive that this voyage will end with disaster and much loss, not only of the cargo and ship, but also our lives." 11 Nevertheless the centurion was more persuaded by the helmsman and the owner of the ship than by the things spoken by Paul. 12 And because the harbor was not suitable to winter in, the majority advised to set sail from there also, if by any means they could reach Phoenix, a harbor of Crete opening toward the southwest and northwest, *and* winter *there.*

13 When the south wind blew softly, supposing that they had obtained *their* desire, putting out to sea, they sailed close by Crete. 14 But not long after, a tempestuous head wind arose, called Euroclydon.ᵃ 15 So when the ship was caught, and could not head into the wind, we let *her* drive. 16 And running under *the shelter of* an island called Clauda,ᵃ we secured the skiff with difficulty. 17 When they had taken it on board,

27:14 ᵃNU-Text reads *Euraquilon.*   27:16 ᵃNU-Text reads *Cauda.*

they used cables to undergird the ship; and fearing lest they should run aground on the Syrtis[a] Sands, they struck sail and so were driven. 18 And because we were exceedingly tempest-tossed, the next *day* they lightened the ship. 19 On the third *day* we threw the ship's tackle overboard with our own hands. 20 Now when neither sun nor stars appeared for many days, and no small tempest beat on *us*, all hope that we would be saved was finally given up.

21 But after long abstinence from food, then Paul stood in the midst of them and said, "Men, you should have listened to me, and not have sailed from Crete and incurred this disaster and loss. 22 And now I urge you to take heart, for there will be no loss of life among you, but only of the ship. 23 For there stood by me this night an angel of the God to whom I belong and whom I serve, 24 saying, 'Do not be afraid, Paul; you must be brought before Caesar; and indeed God has granted you all those who sail with you.' 25 Therefore take heart, men, for I believe God that it will be just as it was told me. 26 However, we must run aground on a certain island."

27 Now when the fourteenth night had come, as we were driven up and down in the Adriatic *Sea*, about midnight the sailors sensed that they were drawing near some land. 28 And they took soundings and found *it* to be twenty fathoms; and when they had gone a little farther, they took soundings again and found *it* to be fifteen fathoms. 29 Then, fearing lest we should run aground on the rocks, they dropped four anchors from the stern, and prayed for day to come. 30 And as the sailors were seeking to escape from the ship, when they had let down the skiff into the sea, under pretense of putting out anchors from the prow, 31 Paul said to the centurion and the soldiers, "Unless these men stay in the ship, you cannot be saved." 32 Then the soldiers cut away the ropes of the skiff and let it fall off.

33 And as day was about to dawn, Paul implored *them* all to take food, saying, "Today is the fourteenth day you have waited and continued without food, and eaten nothing. 34 Therefore I urge you to take nourishment, for this is for your survival, since not a hair will fall from the head of any of you." 35 And when he had said these things, he took bread and gave thanks to God in the presence of them all; and when he had broken *it* he began to eat. 36 Then they were all encouraged, and also took food themselves. 37 And in all we were two hundred and seventy-six persons on the ship. 38 So when they had eaten enough, they lightened the ship and threw out the wheat into the sea.

39 When it was day, they did not recognize the land; but they observed a bay with a beach, onto which they planned to run the ship if possible. 40 And they let go the anchors and left *them* in the sea, meanwhile loosing the rudder ropes; and they hoisted the mainsail to the wind and made for shore. 41 But striking a place where two seas met, they ran the ship aground; and the prow stuck fast and remained immovable, but the stern was being broken up by the violence of the waves.

42 And the soldiers' plan was to kill the prisoners, lest any of them should swim away and escape. 43 But the centurion, wanting to save Paul, kept them from *their* purpose, and commanded that those who could swim should jump *overboard* first and get to land, 44 and the rest, some on boards and some on *parts* of the ship. And so it was that they all escaped safely to land.

28 Now when they had escaped, they then found out that the island was called Malta. 2 And the natives showed us unusual kindness; for they kindled a fire and made us all welcome, because of the rain that was falling and because of the cold. 3 But when Paul had gathered a bundle of sticks and laid *them* on the fire, a viper came out because of the heat, and fastened on his hand. 4 So when the natives saw the creature hanging from his hand, they said to one another, "No doubt this man is a murderer, whom, though he has escaped the sea, yet justice does not allow to live." 5 But he shook off the creature into the fire and suffered no harm. 6 However, they were expecting that

27:17 [a]M-Text reads *Syrtes*.

he would swell up or suddenly fall down dead. But after they had looked for a long time and saw no harm come to him, they changed their minds and said that he was a god.

7 In that region there was an estate of the leading citizen of the island, whose name was Publius, who received us and entertained us courteously for three days. 8 And it happened that the father of Publius lay sick of a fever and dysentery. Paul went in to him and prayed, and he laid his hands on him and healed him. 9 So when this was done, the rest of those on the island who had diseases also came and were healed. 10 They also honored us in many ways; and when we departed, they provided such things as were necessary.

11 After three months we sailed in an Alexandrian ship whose figurehead was the Twin Brothers, which had wintered at the island. 12 And landing at Syracuse, we stayed three days. 13 From there we circled round and reached Rhegium. And after one day the south wind blew; and the next day we came to Puteoli, 14 where we found brethren, and were invited to stay with them seven days. And so we went toward Rome. 15 And from there, when the brethren heard about us, they came to meet us as far as Appii Forum and Three Inns. When Paul saw them, he thanked God and took courage.

16 Now when we came to Rome, the centurion delivered the prisoners to the captain of the guard; but Paul was permitted to dwell by himself with the soldier who guarded him.

17 And it came to pass after three days that Paul called the leaders of the Jews together. So when they had come together, he said to them: "Men *and* brethren, though I have done nothing against our people or the customs of our fathers, yet I was delivered as a prisoner from Jerusalem into the hands of the Romans, 18 who, when they had examined me, wanted to let *me* go, because there was no cause for putting me to death. 19 But when the Jews*a* spoke against *it,* I was compelled to appeal to Caesar, not that I had anything of which to accuse my nation. 20 For this rea-

son therefore I have called for you, to see *you* and speak with *you,* because for the hope of Israel I am bound with this chain."

21 Then they said to him, "We neither received letters from Judea concerning you, nor have any of the brethren who came reported or spoken any evil of you. 22 But we desire to hear from you what you think; for concerning this sect, we know that it is spoken against everywhere."

23 So when they had appointed him a day, many came to him at *his* lodging, to whom he explained and solemnly testified of the kingdom of God, persuading them concerning Jesus from both the Law of Moses and the Prophets, from morning till evening. 24 And some were persuaded by the things which were spoken, and some disbelieved. 25 So when they did not agree among themselves, they departed after Paul had said one word: "The Holy Spirit spoke rightly through Isaiah the prophet to our*a* fathers, 26 saying,

'Go to this people and say:
"Hearing you will hear, and
    shall not understand;
And seeing you will see, and
    not perceive;
27 For the hearts of this people
    have grown dull.
Their ears are hard of hearing,
And their eyes they have
    closed,
Lest they should see with their
    eyes and hear with their
    ears,
Lest they should understand
    with their hearts and turn,
So that I should heal them." '*a*

28 "Therefore let it be known to you that the salvation of God has been sent to the Gentiles, and they will hear it!" 29 And when he had said these words, the Jews departed and had a great dispute among themselves.*a*

30 Then Paul dwelt two whole years in his own rented house, and received all who came to him, 31 preaching the kingdom of God and teaching the things which concern the Lord Jesus Christ with all confidence, no one forbidding him.

28:19 *a*That is, the ruling authorities   28:25 *a*NU-Text reads *your.*   28:27 *a*Isaiah 6:9, 10
28:29 *a*NU-Text omits this verse.

Romans

Overview of Romans

R ome in A.D. 56 was the seat of one of the greatest empires the world has ever known. Its mighty Emperors Caligula, Claudius, and then Nero, ruled in lavish dominion over Rome's one million inhabitants. Roman law and forms of worship dominated the culture, demanding the attention and respect in the hearts of men and women. Here, a tiny sect known as "Christians" flourished.

To these believers Paul wrote the longest of his thirteen New Testament letters, introducing himself in advance of his upcoming visit. Sometimes called "Paul's testament," Romans presents a beautifully detailed doctrinal statement of Christianity.

Paul presents the need for all people to realize their position before God—one which falls short of God's glorious design and plan for their lives. But by an act of God's grace and by faith, people are restored to their rightful relationship with God. Because of the confidence of forgiveness, all believers can present their talents, gifts, and abilities—whatever they are—as an act of worship to God. The exhortations of Paul in Romans are practical directions for living a life justified by the grace of Jesus Christ.

Paul also encourages his readers to realize that God is in control when he says "all things work together for good to those who love God" (Rom. 8:28). He also comforts them with the knowledge that nothing can separate them from the love of God. This scripture was especially appropriate for the Roman church, as they faced much persecution from both their Roman overlords and the Jews who lived in the capital. Yet, the church in Rome grew to be a great center of faith that today echoes around the world.

Paul, who later died a martyr's death in Rome, spoke well of the vitality of faith for believers. The knowledge of God's grace and forgiveness frees us not only from sin, but from anxiety, guilt, depression, and a negative self-image. The stress flows out and salvation flows in!

Jesus in Romans

Paul presents Christ as the second Adam whose righteousness and substitutionary death have provided justification for all who will place their faith in Him. Christ is shown as the gracious gift of God to sinful man, having borne God's condemnation and wrath for their sinfulness. The resurrected Christ becomes the basis for the believer's redemption, justification, reconciliation, salvation, and glorification.

Keys to Romans

Key Words: Righteousness. The theme of Romans is seen in 1:16, where God offers the gift of righteousness to everyone who comes to Christ by faith. Paul eloquently writes of God's sovereign plan of salvation; of the Jews' and Gentiles' places within that plan; and of God's desire for harmony and righteousness between the two groups. Romans moves the reader from positional truth to practical truth, and mentions the key words, "righteousness," "faith," "law," "all," and "sin" over sixty times.

Key Verses: "For I am not ashamed of the gospel of Christ, for it is the power of God to salvation for everyone who believes, for the Jew first and also for the Greek. For in it the righteousness of God is revealed from faith to faith; as it is written, *The just shall live by faith*'" (1:16, 17).

"But now the righteousness of God apart from the law is revealed, being witnessed by the Law and the Prophets, even the righteousness of God, through faith in Jesus Christ, to all and on all who believe. For there is no difference; for all have sinned and fall short of the glory of God, being justified freely by His grace through the redemption that is in Christ Jesus, whom God set forth *as* a propitiation by His blood, through faith, to demonstrate His righteousness, because in His forbearance God had passed over the sins that were previously committed" (3:21–25).

Key Chapters: Romans 6—8. Foundational to all teaching on the spiritual life is the central passage of Romans 6—8. This passage shows how to be delivered from sin, how to live a balanced life under grace, and how to live the victorious Christian life through the power of the Holy Spirit. Many consider this the principal passage on being conformed to the image of Jesus Christ.

1 Paul, a bondservant of Jesus Christ, called *to be* an apostle, separated to the gospel of God 2 which He promised before through His prophets in the Holy Scriptures, 3 concerning His Son Jesus Christ our Lord, who was born of the seed of David according to the flesh, 4 *and* declared *to be* the Son of God with power according to the Spirit of holiness, by the resurrection from the dead. 5 Through Him we have received grace and apostleship for obedience to the faith among all nations for His name, 6 among whom you also are the called of Jesus Christ;

7 To all who are in Rome, beloved of God, called *to be* saints:

Grace to you and peace from God our Father and the Lord Jesus Christ.

8 First, I thank my God through Jesus Christ for you all, that your faith is spoken of throughout the whole world. 9 For God is my witness, whom I serve with my spirit in the gospel of His Son, that without ceasing I make mention of you always in my prayers, 10 making request if, by some means, now at last I may find a way in the will of God to come to you. 11 For I long to see you, that I may impart to you some spiritual gift, so that you may be established— 12 that is, that I may be encouraged together with you by the mutual faith both of you and me.

13 Now I do not want you to be unaware, brethren, that I often planned to come to you (but was hindered until now), that I might have some fruit among you also, just as among the other Gentiles. 14 I am a debtor both to Greeks and to barbarians, both to wise and to unwise. 15 So, as much as is in me, *I am* ready to preach the gospel to you who are in Rome also.

16 For I am not ashamed of the gospel of Christ,[a] for it is the power of God to salvation for everyone who believes, for the Jew first and also for the Greek. 17 For in it the righteousness of God is revealed from faith to faith; as it is written, *"The just shall live by faith."*[a]

18 For the wrath of God is revealed from heaven against all ungodliness and unrighteousness of men, who suppress the truth in unrighteousness, 19 because what may be known of God is manifest in them, for God has shown *it* to them. 20 For since the creation of the world His invisible *attributes* are clearly seen, being understood by the things that are made, *even* His eternal power and Godhead, so that they are without excuse, 21 because, although they knew God, they did not glorify *Him* as God, nor were thankful, but became futile in their thoughts, and their foolish hearts were darkened. 22 Professing to be wise, they became fools, 23 and changed the glory of the incorruptible God into an image made like corruptible man—and birds and four-footed animals and creeping things.

24 Therefore God also gave them up to uncleanness, in the lusts of their hearts, to dishonor their bodies among themselves, 25 who exchanged the truth of God for the lie, and worshiped and served the creature rather than the Creator, who is blessed forever. Amen.

26 For this reason God gave them up to vile passions. For even their women exchanged the natural use for what is against nature. 27 Likewise also the men, leaving the natural use of the woman, burned in their lust for one another, men with men committing what is shameful, and receiving in themselves the penalty of their error which was due.

28 And even as they did not like to retain God in *their* knowledge, God gave them over to a debased mind, to do those things which are not fitting; 29 being filled with all unrighteousness, sexual immorality,[a] wickedness, covetousness, maliciousness; full of envy, murder, strife, deceit, evil-mindedness; *they are* whisperers, 30 backbiters, haters of God, violent, proud, boasters, inventors of evil things, disobedient to parents,

Gathered in One Accord

Faith is fantastic! The positive fruits and by-products that will spring up in our lives as we walk this walk of faith are too numerous to count. Yet, let's examine just one of the assets of this risky business called faith. When you make the decision to become a believer, you put yourself in the company of brave people, the possibility thinkers. That carries an immediate reward. Every time you make a new commitment, you meet new friends. You experience the joy of the company of people who laugh, sing, pray, and are generally enthusiastic. Romans 1:12 speaks of the encouragement we share with others of the same faith.

Faith is aligning yourself with the up-and-comers. The believer is drawn into the circle of eagles while the doubter sides with the lame-duck crowd. The insecure person who hesitates to make the plunge finds himself in the company of shrinking violets and withering flowers. The price he pays for his security is a creeping awareness that life is passing him by.

Today reaffirm your commitment to be a believer! Don't miss the chance at excitement in life: *There is a train pulling out of the station. On it I see people who are laughing, excited, and enthusiastic. I will jump on board with them—now! I will join the crowd of positive people who are going places and doing great things.*

I choose to be a believer. I am parting company with the losers. Thank You for leading the way, Jesus Christ. I am aligning myself with the up-and-comers. I feel an aliveness within me now. Is this Your presence, Lord? This keen and energizing vibrancy within me? Thank You, Lord!

31 undiscerning, untrustworthy, unloving, unforgiving,ᵃ unmerciful; 32 who, knowing the righteous judgment of God, that those who practice such things are deserving of death, not only do the same but also approve of those who practice them.

2 Therefore you are inexcusable, O man, whoever you are who judge, for in whatever you judge another you condemn yourself; for you who judge practice the same things. 2 But we know that the judgment of God is according to truth against those who practice such things. 3 And do you think this, O man, you who judge those practicing such things, and doing the same, that you will escape the judgment of God? 4 Or do you despise the riches of His goodness, forbearance, and longsuffering, not knowing that the goodness of God leads you to repentance? 5 But in accordance with your hardness and your impenitent heart you are treasuring up for yourself wrath in the day of wrath and revelation of the righteous judgment of God, 6 who "will render to each one according to his deeds":ᵃ 7 eternal life to those who by patient continuance in doing good seek for glory, honor, and immortality; 8 but to those who are self-seeking and do not obey the truth, but obey unrighteousness—indignation and wrath, 9 tribulation and anguish, on every soul of man who does evil, of the Jew first and also of the Greek; 10 but glory, honor, and peace to everyone who works what is good, to the Jew first and also to the Greek. 11 For there is no partiality with God.

12 For as many as have sinned without law will also perish without law, and as many as have sinned in the law will be judged by the law 13 (for not the hearers of the law are just in the sight of God, but the doers of the law will be justified; 14 for when Gentiles, who do not have the law, by nature do the things in the law, these, although not having the law, are a law to themselves, 15 who show the work of the law written in their hearts, their conscience also bearing witness, and between

themselves *their* thoughts accusing or else excusing *them*) 16 in the day when God will judge the secrets of men by Jesus Christ, according to my gospel.

17 Indeedᵃ you are called a Jew, and rest on the law, and make your boast in God, 18 and know *His* will, and approve the things that are excellent, being instructed out of the law, 19 and are confident that you yourself are a guide to the blind, a light to those who are in darkness, 20 an instructor of the foolish, a teacher of babes, having the form of knowledge and truth in the law. 21 You, therefore, who teach another, do you not teach yourself? You who preach that a man should not steal, do you steal? 22 You who say, "Do not commit adultery," do you commit adultery? You who abhor idols, do you rob temples? 23 You who make your boast in the law, do you dishonor God through breaking the law? 24 For *"the name of God is blasphemed among the Gentiles because of you,"*ᵃ as it is written.

25 For circumcision is indeed profitable if you keep the law; but if you are a breaker of the law, your circumcision has become uncircumcision. 26 Therefore, if an uncircumcised man keeps the righteous requirements of the law, will not his uncircumcision be counted as circumcision? 27 And will not the physically uncircumcised, if he fulfills the law, judge you who, *even* with *your* written *code* and circumcision, *are* a transgressor of the law? 28 For he is not a Jew who *is one* outwardly, nor *is* circumcision that which *is* outward in the flesh; 29 but *he is* a Jew who *is one* inwardly; and circumcision *is that* of the heart, in the Spirit, not in the letter; whose praise *is* not from men but from God.

3 What advantage then has the Jew, or what *is* the profit of circumcision? 2 Much in every way! Chiefly because to them were committed the oracles of God. 3 For what if some did not believe? Will their unbelief make the faithfulness of God without effect? 4 Certainly not! Indeed, let God be true but every man a liar. As it is written:

1:31 ᵃNU-Text omits *unforgiving*.   2:6 ᵃPsalm 62:12; Proverbs 24:12   2:17 ᵃNU-Text reads *But if.*
2:24 ᵃIsaiah 52:5; Ezekiel 36:22

Forgiveness for Everyone

During the Passover meal, Jesus demonstrated an attitude of forgiveness unparalleled in the history of man.

It was the Passover custom for the meal's host to dip the sop (bread) in lamb stew and give it to the most honored guest at the banquet table. Jesus told His disciples that whoever dipped *"his* hand with Me in the dish" (Matt. 26:23) was the one who would betray Him. Knowing what Judas was going to do, Jesus still honored him and extended to him an offering of forgiveness. The partaking of a meal was a traditional Jewish covenant of peace and forgiveness. By giving Judas the sop, Jesus offered him peace and forgiveness if he would accept it. Judas must have recognized this symbolism, yet he chose to rebel and turn away.

If Jesus could forgive a chosen disciple who betrayed Him, can He not also forgive us? Jesus' love is sufficient to forgive even the greatest sins. We can be confident of His love and forgiveness no matter who we are, what we have done, or what we will ever do in the future. Colossians 1:14 and Ephesians 1:7 both say, "In Him we have redemption through His blood, the forgiveness of sins."

What wonderful confidence we can have in the assurance that Jesus Christ forgives all our sins—past, present, and future—if we only accept His forgiveness!

*"That You may be justified in
   Your words,
And may overcome when You
   are judged."ᵃ*

5 But if our unrighteousness demonstrates the righteousness of God, what shall we say? *Is* God unjust who inflicts wrath? (I speak as a man.) 6 Certainly not! For then how will God judge the world?
7 For if the truth of God has increased through my lie to His glory, why am I also still judged as a sinner? 8 And *why* not *say,* "Let us do evil that good may come"?—as we are slanderously reported and as some affirm that we say. Their condemnation is just.
9 What then? Are we better *than they?* Not at all. For we have previously charged both Jews and Greeks that they are all under sin.
10 As it is written:

   *"There is none righteous, no, not
      one;*
11   *There is none who
      understands;
   There is none who seeks after
      God.*
12   *They have all turned aside;
   They have together become
      unprofitable;
   There is none who does good,
      no, not one."ᵃ*
13 *"Their throat is an open tomb;
   With their tongues they have
      practiced deceit";ᵃ
   "The poison of asps is under
      their lips";ᵇ*
14 *"Whose mouth is full of cursing
      and bitterness."ᵃ*
15 *"Their feet are swift to shed
      blood;*
16   *Destruction and misery are in
      their ways;*
17   *And the way of peace they have
      not known."ᵃ*
18 *"There is no fear of God before
      their eyes."ᵃ*

19 Now we know that whatever the law says, it says to those who are under the law, that every mouth may be stopped, and all the world may become guilty before God. 20 Therefore by the deeds of the law no flesh will

be justified in His sight, for by the law *is* the knowledge of sin.
21 But now the righteousness of God apart from the law is revealed, being witnessed by the Law and the Prophets, 22 even the righteousness of God, through faith in Jesus Christ, to all and on allᵃ who believe. For there is no difference; 23 for all have sinned and fall short of the glory of God, 24 being justified freely by His grace through the redemption that is in Christ Jesus, 25 whom God set forth *as* a propitiation by His blood, through faith, to demonstrate His righteousness, because in His forbearance God had passed over the sins that were previously committed, 26 to demonstrate at the present time His righteousness, that He might be just and the justifier of the one who has faith in Jesus.
27 Where *is* boasting then? It is excluded. By what law? Of works? No, but by the law of faith. 28 Therefore we conclude that a man is justified by faith apart from the deeds of the law. 29 Or *is* He the God of the Jews only? *Is* He not also the God of the Gentiles? Yes, of the Gentiles also, 30 since *there is* one God who will justify the circumcised by faith and the uncircumcised through faith. 31 Do we then make void the law through faith? Certainly not! On the contrary, we establish the law.

4 What then shall we say that Abraham our father has found according to the flesh?ᵃ 2 For if Abraham was justified by works, he has *something* to boast about, but not before God. 3 For what does the Scripture say? *"Abraham believed God, and it was accounted to him for righteousness."ᵃ* 4 Now to him who works, the wages are not counted as grace but as debt.
5 But to him who does not work but believes on Him who justifies the ungodly, his faith is accounted for righteousness, 6 just as David also describes the blessedness of the man to whom God imputes righteousness apart from works:

7 *"Blessed are those whose
      lawless deeds are forgiven,*

3:4 ᵃPsalm 51:4   3:12 ᵃPsalms 14:1–3; 53:1–3; Ecclesiastes 7:20   3:13 ᵃPsalm 5:9   ᵇPsalm 140:3
3:14 ᵃPsalm 10:7   3:17 ᵃIsaiah 59:7, 8   3:18 ᵃPsalm 36:1   3:22 ᵃNU-Text omits *and on all.*
4:1 ᵃOr *Abraham our (fore)father according to the flesh has found?*   4:3 ᵃGenesis 15:6

Asia Minor

Asia Minor, also called Anatolia, was a peninsula situated in the extreme western part of the Asian continent. This peninsula was bounded on the north by the Black Sea, the Sea of Marmara, and the Dardanelles; by the Aegean Sea on the west; and by Syria and by the Great Sea on the south. Biblical Asia Minor corresponds roughly to the modern-day nation of Turkey.

In the New Testament, the term "Asia" is often unclear. It sometimes refers to the entire peninsula of Asia Minor, but more often refers to the part of Asia which sits in the western part of the peninsula.

© 1995, Thomas Nelson, Inc.

And whose sins are covered;
8 Blessed is the man to whom the
LORD shall not impute sin."[a]

9 Does this blessedness then come
upon the circumcised only, or upon
the uncircumcised also? For we say
that faith was accounted to Abraham
for righteousness. 10 How then was
it accounted? While he was circumcised, or uncircumcised? Not while
circumcised, but while uncircumcised. 11 And he received the sign of
circumcision, a seal of the righteousness of the faith which he had while
still uncircumcised, that he might be
the father of all those who believe,
though they are uncircumcised, that
righteousness might be imputed to
them also, 12 and the father of circumcision to those who not only are
of the circumcision, but who also
walk in the steps of the faith which
our father Abraham had while still
uncircumcised.

13 For the promise that he would
be the heir of the world was not to
Abraham or to his seed through the
law, but through the righteousness of
faith. 14 For if those who are of the
law are heirs, faith is made void and
the promise made of no effect,
15 because the law brings about
wrath; for where there is no law
there is no transgression.

16 Therefore it is of faith that it
might be according to grace, so that
the promise might be sure to all the
seed, not only to those who are of
the law, but also to those who are of
the faith of Abraham, who is the father of us all 17 (as it is written, "I
have made you a father of many nations"[a]) in the presence of Him
whom he believed—God, who gives
life to the dead and calls those things
which do not exist as though they
did; 18 who, contrary to hope, in hope
believed, so that he became the father of many nations, according to
what was spoken, "So shall your descendants be."[a] 19 And not being
weak in faith, he did not consider his
own body, already dead (since he
was about a hundred years old), and
the deadness of Sarah's womb.
20 He did not waver at the promise
of God through unbelief, but was
strengthened in faith, giving glory to

God, 21 and being fully convinced
that what He had promised He was
also able to perform. 22 And therefore "it was accounted to him for
righteousness."[a]

23 Now it was not written for his
sake alone that it was imputed to
him, 24 but also for us. It shall be imputed to us who believe in Him who
raised up Jesus our Lord from the
dead, 25 who was delivered up because of our offenses, and was raised
because of our justification.

5 Therefore, having been justified
by faith, we have[a] peace with God
through our Lord Jesus Christ,
2 through whom also we have access
by faith into this grace in which we
stand, and rejoice in hope of the
glory of God. 3 And not only that, but
we also glory in tribulations, knowing that tribulation produces perseverance; 4 and perseverance, character; and character, hope. 5 Now hope
does not disappoint, because the love
of God has been poured out in our
hearts by the Holy Spirit who was
given to us.

6 For when we were still without
strength, in due time Christ died for
the ungodly. 7 For scarcely for a righteous man will one die; yet perhaps
for a good man someone would even
dare to die. 8 But God demonstrates
His own love toward us, in that while
we were still sinners, Christ died for
us. 9 Much more then, having now
been justified by His blood, we shall
be saved from wrath through Him.
10 For if when we were enemies we
were reconciled to God through the
death of His Son, much more, having
been reconciled, we shall be saved
by His life. 11 And not only that, but
we also rejoice in God through our
Lord Jesus Christ, through whom we
have now received the reconciliation.

12 Therefore, just as through one
man sin entered the world, and death
through sin, and thus death spread
to all men, because all sinned—
13 (For until the law sin was in the
world, but sin is not imputed when
there is no law. 14 Nevertheless death
reigned from Adam to Moses, even
over those who had not sinned according to the likeness of the transgression of Adam, who is a type of

4:8 [a]Psalm 32:1, 2   4:17 [a]Genesis 17:5   4:18 [a]Genesis 15:5   4:22 [a]Genesis 15:6   5:1 [a]Another
ancient reading is, let us have peace.

Faith Can Fill Your Life

The apostle Paul wrote: "Having been justified by faith, we have peace with God through our Lord Jesus Christ, through whom also we have access by faith into this grace in which we stand, and rejoice in hope of the glory of God" (Rom. 5:1, 2).

Faith is a choice, not an argument.

It is a decision, not a debate.

It is a commitment, not a controversy.

Faith fulfills some need in your heart.

Even the super-affluent are attracted to faith; they soon realize that all of their wealth, social standing, and personal power leave a void in their lives. When you have more money than you can enjoy, what is left?

We suspect that out there, somewhere, there is always something more. From where does this intuition for "something more" come? It is built into our nature.

Be careful what you want—you'll get it! Wanting is believing, and believing produces results. Strong faith is often the expression of deep desire. On the other hand, doubt is the lack of desire. A host of conscious or subconscious forces can keep you from wanting to believe. Fears of what God might do *to* your life or *in* your life can keep you from wanting to believe. Internalized guilt can make the possibility of God a threatening concept. Deep-seated, negative emotions can kill the desire to believe, leaving you with a negative inclination to doubt. Having trouble believing? Why don't you want to believe?

In Psalm 37:3, 4 we read God's promise of blessings upon faith: "Trust in the LORD, and do good; dwell in the land, and feed on His faithfulness. Delight yourself also in the LORD, and He shall give you the desires of your heart."

Him who was to come. 15 But the free gift *is* not like the offense. For if by the one man's offense many died, much more the grace of God and the gift by the grace of the one Man, Jesus Christ, abounded to many. 16 And the gift *is* not like *that which came* through the one who sinned. For the judgment *which came* from one *offense resulted* in condemnation, but the free gift *which came* from many offenses *resulted* in justification. 17 For if by the one man's offense death reigned through the one, much more those who receive abundance of grace and of the gift of righteousness will reign in life through the One, Jesus Christ.)

18 Therefore, as through one man's offense *judgment* came to all men, resulting in condemnation, even so through one Man's righteous act *the free gift came* to all men, resulting in justification of life. 19 For as by one man's disobedience many were made sinners, so also by one Man's obedience many will be made righteous.

20 Moreover the law entered that the offense might abound. But where sin abounded, grace abounded much more, 21 so that as sin reigned in death, even so grace might reign through righteousness to eternal life through Jesus Christ our Lord.

6 What shall we say then? Shall we continue in sin that grace may abound? 2 Certainly not! How shall we who died to sin live any longer in it? 3 Or do you not know that as many of us as were baptized into Christ Jesus were baptized into His death? 4 Therefore we were buried with Him through baptism into death, that just as Christ was raised from the dead by the glory of the Father, even so we also should walk in newness of life.

5 For if we have been united together in the likeness of His death, certainly we also shall be *in the likeness* of *His* resurrection, 6 knowing this, that our old man was crucified with *Him,* that the body of sin might be done away with, that we should no longer be slaves of sin. 7 For he who has died has been freed from sin. 8 Now if we died with Christ, we believe that we shall also live with Him, 9 knowing that Christ, having been raised from the dead, dies no more. Death no longer has dominion

over Him. 10 For *the death* that He died, He died to sin once for all; but *the life* that He lives, He lives to God. 11 Likewise you also, reckon yourselves to be dead indeed to sin, but alive to God in Christ Jesus our Lord.

12 Therefore do not let sin reign in your mortal body, that you should obey it in its lusts. 13 And do not present your members *as* instruments of unrighteousness to sin, but present yourselves to God as being alive from the dead, and your members *as* instruments of righteousness to God. 14 For sin shall not have dominion over you, for you are not under law but under grace.

15 What then? Shall we sin because we are not under law but under grace? Certainly not! 16 Do you not know that to whom you present yourselves slaves to obey, you are that one's slaves whom you obey, whether of sin *leading* to death, or of obedience *leading* to righteousness? 17 But God be thanked that *though* you were slaves of sin, yet you obeyed from the heart that form of doctrine to which you were delivered. 18 And having been set free from sin, you became slaves of righteousness. 19 I speak in human *terms* because of the weakness of your flesh. For just as you presented your members *as* slaves of uncleanness, and of lawlessness *leading* to *more* lawlessness, so now present your members *as* slaves *of* righteousness for holiness.

20 For when you were slaves of sin, you were free in regard to righteousness. 21 What fruit did you have then in the things of which you are now ashamed? For the end of those things *is* death. 22 But now having been set free from sin, and having become slaves of God, you have your fruit to holiness, and the end, everlasting life. 23 For the wages of sin *is* death, but the gift of God *is* eternal life in Christ Jesus our Lord.

7 Or do you not know, brethren (for I speak to those who know the law), that the law has dominion over a man as long as he lives? 2 For the woman who has a husband is bound by the law to *her* husband as long as he lives. But if the husband dies, she is released from the law of *her* husband. 3 So then if, while *her* husband lives, she marries another man, she will be called an adulteress; but if her husband dies, she is free from that law, so that she is no adulteress, though she has married another man. 4 Therefore, my brethren, you also have become dead to the law through the body of Christ, that you may be married to another—to Him who was raised from the dead, that we should bear fruit to God. 5 For when we were in the flesh, the sinful passions which were aroused by the law were at work in our members to bear fruit to death. 6 But now we have been delivered from the law, having died to what we were held by, so that we should serve in the newness of the Spirit and not *in* the oldness of the letter.

7 What shall we say then? *Is* the law sin? Certainly not! On the contrary, I would not have known sin except through the law. For I would not have known covetousness unless the law had said, *"You shall not covet."*[a] 8 But sin, taking opportunity by the commandment, produced in me all *manner of evil* desire. For apart from the law sin *was* dead. 9 I was alive once without the law, but when the commandment came, sin revived and I died. 10 And the commandment, which *was* to *bring* life, I found to *bring* death. 11 For sin, taking occasion by the commandment, deceived me, and by it killed *me.* 12 Therefore the law *is* holy, and the commandment holy and just and good.

13 Has then what is good become death to me? Certainly not! But sin, that it might appear sin, was producing death in me through what is good, so that sin through the commandment might become exceedingly sinful. 14 For we know that the law is spiritual, but I am carnal, sold under sin. 15 For what I am doing, I do not understand. For what I will to do, that I do not practice; but what I hate, that I do. 16 If, then, I do what I will not to do, I agree with the law that *it is* good. 17 But now, *it is* no longer I who do it, but sin that dwells in me. 18 For I know that in me (that is, in my flesh) nothing good dwells; for to will is present with me, but *how* to perform what is good I do not find. 19 For the good that I will *to do,* I do not do; but the evil I will not *to do,* that I practice. 20 Now if I do what I

will not *to do,* it is no longer I who do it, but sin that dwells in me.

21 I find then a law, that evil is present with me, the one who wills to do good. 22 For I delight in the law of God according to the inward man. 23 But I see another law in my members, warring against the law of my mind, and bringing me into captivity to the law of sin which is in my members. 24 O wretched man that I am! Who will deliver me from this body of death? 25 I thank God—through Jesus Christ our Lord!

So then, with the mind I myself serve the law of God, but with the flesh the law of sin.

8 *There is* therefore now no condemnation to those who are in Christ Jesus,[a] who do not walk according to the flesh, but according to the Spirit. 2 For the law of the Spirit of life in Christ Jesus has made me free from the law of sin and death. 3 For what the law could not do in that it was weak through the flesh, God *did* by sending His own Son in the likeness of sinful flesh, on account of sin: He condemned sin in the flesh, 4 that the righteous requirement of the law might be fulfilled in us who do not walk according to the flesh but according to the Spirit. 5 For those who live according to the flesh set their minds on the things of the flesh, but those *who live* according to the Spirit, the things of the Spirit. 6 For to be carnally minded *is* death, but to be spiritually minded *is* life and peace. 7 Because the carnal mind *is* enmity against God; for it is not subject to the law of God, nor indeed can be. 8 So then, those who are in the flesh cannot please God.

9 But you are not in the flesh but in the Spirit, if indeed the Spirit of God dwells in you. Now if anyone does not have the Spirit of Christ, he is not His. 10 And if Christ *is* in you, the body *is* dead because of sin, but the Spirit *is* life because of righteousness. 11 But if the Spirit of Him who raised Jesus from the dead dwells in you, He who raised Christ from the dead will also give life to your mortal bodies through His Spirit who dwells in you.

12 Therefore, brethren, we are debtors—not to the flesh, to live accord-

7:7 aExodus 20:17; Deuteronomy 5:21   8:1 aNU-Text omits the rest of this verse.

You Can Do It!

Faith is an inner conviction.

It is an unshakable assurance that "we are more than conquerors through Him [Jesus] who loved us" (see Rom. 8:37–39).

It is the profound "knowing" that comes before reality confirms it.

Faith is a sense of destiny: "It's possible." "It's going to happen."

Faith is knowing that you can do it. The person who walks the walk of faith knows he can solve his problem!

He *knows* that he can detach himself from that awful habit.

He *knows* he can extricate himself from his negative enslavements.

The person who walks the walk of faith faces his projects, affirming:

I *know* I can do it—*if* God will help me. And I'm sure God wants to help me!

I know I can do it *when* I'm totally dedicated to Him, which I really am!

I know I can do it *after* everything is in readiness. And I am trusting God to help me get my act together!

I know I can do it *only* with the help of my Lord. He is my Best Friend. He wants me to succeed.

"I can do all things through Christ who strengthens me" (Phil. 4:13). I know it's possible after all.

Deep down in your heart, you know it will work out. An unquenchable confidence keeps fueling your feelings that you're going to make it.

Again and again the person who succeeds does so because he or she doesn't know it is impossible!

ing to the flesh. 13 For if you live according to the flesh you will die; but if by the Spirit you put to death the deeds of the body, you will live. 14 For as many as are led by the Spirit of God, these are sons of God. 15 For you did not receive the spirit of bondage again to fear, but you received the Spirit of adoption by whom we cry out, "Abba, Father." 16 The Spirit Himself bears witness with our spirit that we are children of God, 17 and if children, then heirs—heirs of God and joint heirs with Christ, if indeed we suffer with *Him*, that we may also be glorified together.

18 For I consider that the sufferings of this present time are not worthy *to be compared* with the glory which shall be revealed in us. 19 For the earnest expectation of the creation eagerly waits for the revealing of the sons of God. 20 For the creation was subjected to futility, not willingly, but because of Him who subjected *it* in hope; 21 because the creation itself also will be delivered from the bondage of corruption into the glorious liberty of the children of God. 22 For we know that the whole creation groans and labors with birth pangs together until now. 23 Not only *that*, but we also who have the firstfruits of the Spirit, even we ourselves groan within ourselves, eagerly waiting for the adoption, the redemption of our body. 24 For we were saved in this hope, but hope that is seen is not hope; for why does one still hope for what he sees? 25 But if we hope for what we do not see, we eagerly wait for *it* with perseverance.

26 Likewise the Spirit also helps in our weaknesses. For we do not know what we should pray for as we ought, but the Spirit Himself makes intercession for us[a] with groanings which cannot be uttered. 27 Now He who searches the hearts knows what the mind of the Spirit *is,* because He makes intercession for the saints according to *the will of* God.

28 And we know that all things work together for good to those who love God, to those who are the called according to *His* purpose. 29 For whom He foreknew, He also predestined *to be* conformed to the image of His Son, that He might be the

firstborn among many brethren. 30 Moreover whom He predestined, these He also called; whom He called, these He also justified; and whom He justified, these He also glorified.

31 What then shall we say to these things? If God *is* for us, who *can be* against us? 32 He who did not spare His own Son, but delivered Him up for us all, how shall He not with Him also freely give us all things? 33 Who shall bring a charge against God's elect? *It is* God who justifies. 34 Who *is* he who condemns? *It is* Christ who died, and furthermore is also risen, who is even at the right hand of God, who also makes intercession for us. 35 Who shall separate us from the love of Christ? *Shall* tribulation, or distress, or persecution, or famine, or nakedness, or peril, or sword? 36 As it is written:

> "For Your sake we are killed all
>   day long;
> We are accounted as sheep for
>   the slaughter."[a]

37 Yet in all these things we are more than conquerors through Him who loved us. 38 For I am persuaded that neither death nor life, nor angels nor principalities nor powers, nor things present nor things to come, 39 nor height nor depth, nor any other created thing, shall be able to separate us from the love of God which is in Christ Jesus our Lord.

9 I tell the truth in Christ, I am not lying, my conscience also bearing me witness in the Holy Spirit, 2 that I have great sorrow and continual grief in my heart. 3 For I could wish that I myself were accursed from Christ for my brethren, my countrymen[a] according to the flesh, 4 who are Israelites, to whom *pertain* the adoption, the glory, the covenants, the giving of the law, the service *of God,* and the promises; 5 of whom *are* the fathers and from whom, according to the flesh, Christ *came,* who is over all, *the* eternally blessed God. Amen.

6 But it is not that the word of God has taken no effect. For they *are* not all Israel who *are* of Israel, 7 nor *are* they all children because they are the

---

8:26 [a]NU-Text omits *for us.*   8:36 [a]Psalm 44:22   9:3 [a]Or *relatives* seed of Abraham; but, *"In Isaac your seed shall be called."ᵃ* 8 That is, those who *are* the children of the flesh, these *are* not the children of God; but the children of the promise are counted as the seed. 9 For this *is* the word of promise: *"At this time I will come and Sarah shall have a son."ᵃ*

10 And not only *this,* but when Rebecca also had conceived by one man, *even* by our father Isaac 11 (for *the children* not yet being born, nor having done any good or evil, that the purpose of God according to election might stand, not of works but of Him who calls), 12 it was said to her, *"The older shall serve the younger."ᵃ* 13 As it is written, *"Jacob I have loved, but Esau I have hated."ᵃ*

14 What shall we say then? *Is there* unrighteousness with God? Certainly not! 15 For He says to Moses, *"I will have mercy on whomever I will have mercy, and I will have compassion on whomever I will have compassion."ᵃ* 16 So then *it is* not of him who wills, nor of him who runs, but of God who shows mercy. 17 For the Scripture says to the Pharaoh, *"For this very purpose I have raised you up, that I may show My power in you, and that My name may be declared in all the earth."ᵃ* 18 Therefore He has mercy on whom He wills, and whom He wills He hardens.

19 You will say to me then, "Why does He still find fault? For who has resisted His will?" 20 But indeed, O man, who are you to reply against God? Will the thing formed say to him who formed *it,* "Why have you made me like this?" 21 Does not the potter have power over the clay, from the same lump to make one vessel for honor and another for dishonor?

22 *What* if God, wanting to show *His* wrath and to make His power known, endured with much longsuffering the vessels of wrath prepared for destruction, 23 and that He might make known the riches of His glory on the vessels of mercy, which He had prepared beforehand for glory, 24 *even* us whom He called, not of the Jews only, but also of the Gentiles?

25 As He says also in Hosea:

*"I will call them My people, who were not My people,
And her beloved, who was not beloved."ᵃ*
26 *"And it shall come to pass in the place where it was said to them,
'You are not My people,'
There they shall be called sons of the living God."ᵃ*

27 Isaiah also cries out concerning Israel:ᵃ

*"Though the number of the children of Israel be as the sand of the sea,
The remnant will be saved.*
28 *For He will finish the work and cut it short in righteousness,
Because the* LORD *will make a short work upon the earth."ᵃ*

29 And as Isaiah said before:

"Unless the LORD *of Sabaothᵃ had left us a seed,
We would have become like Sodom,
And we would have been made like Gomorrah."ᵇ*

30 What shall we say then? That Gentiles, who did not pursue righteousness, have attained to righteousness, even the righteousness of faith; 31 but Israel, pursuing the law of righteousness, has not attained to the law of righteousness.ᵃ 32 Why? Because *they did* not *seek it* by faith, but as it were, by the works of the law.ᵃ For they stumbled at that stumbling stone. 33 As it is written:

*"Behold, I lay in Zion a stumbling stone and rock of offense,
And whoever believes on Him will not be put to shame."ᵃ*

10 Brethren, my heart's desire and prayer to God for Israelᵃ is that they may be saved. 2 For I bear them

---

9:7 ᵃGenesis 21:12   9:9 ᵃGenesis 18:10, 14   9:12 ᵃGenesis 25:23   9:13 ᵃMalachi 1:2, 3
9:15 ᵃExodus 33:19   9:17 ᵃExodus 9:16   9:25 ᵃHosea 2:23   9:26 ᵃHosea 1:10   9:27 ᵃIsaiah
10:22, 23   9:28 ᵃNU-Text reads *For the Lord will finish the work and cut it short upon the earth.*
9:29 ᵃLiterally, in Hebrew, *Hosts*   ᵇIsaiah 1:9   9:31 ᵃNU-Text omits *of righteousness.*   9:32 ᵃNU-Text
reads *by works.*   9:33 ᵃIsaiah 8:14; 28:16   10:1 ᵃNU-Text reads *them.*

witness that they have a zeal for God, but not according to knowledge. 3 For they being ignorant of God's righteousness, and seeking to establish their own righteousness, have not submitted to the righteousness of God. 4 For Christ *is* the end of the law for righteousness to everyone who believes.

5 For Moses writes about the righteousness which is of the law, *"The man who does those things shall live by them."ᵃ* 6 But the righteousness of faith speaks in this way, *"Do not say in your heart, 'Who will ascend into heaven?' "ᵃ* (that is, to bring Christ down *from above*) 7 or, *" 'Who will descend into the abyss?' "ᵃ* (that is, to bring Christ up from the dead). 8 But what does it say? *"The word is near you, in your mouth and in your heart"ᵃ* (that is, the word of faith which we preach): 9 that if you confess with your mouth the Lord Jesus and believe in your heart that God has raised Him from the dead, you will be saved. 10 For with the heart one believes unto righteousness, and with the mouth confession is made unto salvation. 11 For the Scripture says, *"Whoever believes on Him will not be put to shame."ᵃ* 12 For there is no distinction between Jew and Greek, for the same Lord over all is rich to all who call upon Him. 13 For *"whoever calls on the name of the LORD shall be saved."ᵃ*

14 How then shall they call on Him in whom they have not believed? And how shall they believe in Him of whom they have not heard? And how shall they hear without a preacher? 15 And how shall they preach unless they are sent? As it is written:

> *"How beautiful are the feet of*
> *   those who preach the gospel*
> *   of peace,ᵃ*
> *Who bring glad tidings of good*
> *   things!"ᵇ*

16 But they have not all obeyed the gospel. For Isaiah says, *"Lord, who has believed our report?"ᵃ* 17 So then faith *comes* by hearing, and hearing by the word of God.

18 But I say, have they not heard? Yes indeed:

> *"Their sound has gone out to all*
> *   the earth,*
> *And their words to the ends of*
> *   the world."ᵃ*

19 But I say, did Israel not know? First Moses says:

> *"I will provoke you to jealousy*
> *   by those who are not a*
> *   nation,*
> *I will move you to anger by a*
> *   foolish nation."ᵃ*

20 But Isaiah is very bold and says:

> *"I was found by those who did*
> *   not seek Me;*
> *I was made manifest to those*
> *   who did not ask for Me."ᵃ*

21 But to Israel he says:

> *"All day long I have stretched*
> *   out My hands*
> *To a disobedient and contrary*
> *   people."ᵃ*

11 I say then, has God cast away His people? Certainly not! For I also am an Israelite, of the seed of Abraham, *of* the tribe of Benjamin. 2 God has not cast away His people whom He foreknew. Or do you not know what the Scripture says of Elijah, how he pleads with God against Israel, saying, 3 *"LORD, they have killed Your prophets and torn down Your altars, and I alone am left, and they seek my life"? ᵃ* 4 But what does the divine response say to him? *"I have reserved for Myself seven thousand men who have not bowed the knee to Baal."ᵃ* 5 Even so then, at this present time there is a remnant according to the election of grace. 6 And if by grace, then *it is* no longer of works; otherwise grace is no longer grace.ᵃ But if *it is* of works, it is no longer grace; otherwise work is no longer work.

7 What then? Israel has not obtained what it seeks; but the elect

---

10:5 ᵃLeviticus 18:5   10:6 ᵃDeuteronomy 30:12
30:14   10:11 ᵃIsaiah 28:16   10:13 ᵃJoel 2:32
Who.   ᵇIsaiah 52:7; Nahum 1:15   10:16 ᵃIsaiah 53:1
32:21   10:20 ᵃIsaiah 65:1   10:21 ᵃIsaiah 65:2
11:6 ᵃNU-Text omits the rest of this verse.   10:7 ᵃDeuteronomy 30:13   10:8 ᵃDeuteronomy
10:15 ᵃNU-Text omits *preach the gospel of peace,*
10:18 ᵃPsalm 19:4   10:19 ᵃDeuteronomy
11:3 ᵃ1 Kings 19:10, 14   11:4 ᵃ1 Kings 19:18

have obtained it, and the rest were blinded. 8 Just as it is written:

"God has given them a spirit of stupor,
Eyes that they should not see
And ears that they should not hear,
To this very day."a

9 And David says:

"Let their table become a snare and a trap,
A stumbling block and a recompense to them.
10 Let their eyes be darkened, so that they do not see,
And bow down their back always."a

11 I say then, have they stumbled that they should fall? Certainly not! But through their fall, to provoke them to jealousy, salvation has come to the Gentiles. 12 Now if their fall is riches for the world, and their failure riches for the Gentiles, how much more their fullness!

13 For I speak to you Gentiles; inasmuch as I am an apostle to the Gentiles, I magnify my ministry, 14 if by any means I may provoke to jealousy those who are my flesh and save some of them. 15 For if their being cast away is the reconciling of the world, what will their acceptance be but life from the dead?

16 For if the firstfruit is holy, the lump is also holy; and if the root is holy, so are the branches. 17 And if some of the branches were broken off, and you, being a wild olive tree, were grafted in among them, and with them became a partaker of the root and fatness of the olive tree, 18 do not boast against the branches. But if you do boast, remember that you do not support the root, but the root supports you. 19 You will say then, "Branches were broken off that I might be grafted in." 20 Well said. Because of unbelief they were broken off, and you stand by faith. Do not be haughty, but fear. 21 For if God did not spare the natural branches, He may not spare you either.

22 Therefore consider the goodness and severity of God: on those who fell, severity; but toward you, goodness,a if you continue in His goodness. Otherwise you also will be cut off. 23 And they also, if they do not continue in unbelief, will be grafted in, for God is able to graft them in again. 24 For if you were cut out of the olive tree which is wild by nature, and were grafted contrary to nature into a cultivated olive tree, how much more will these, who are natural branches, be grafted into their own olive tree?

25 For I do not desire, brethren, that you should be ignorant of this mystery, lest you should be wise in your own opinion, that blindness in part has happened to Israel until the fullness of the Gentiles has come in. 26 And so all Israel will be saved,a as it is written:

"The Deliverer will come out of Zion,
And He will turn away ungodliness from Jacob;
27 For this is My covenant with them,
When I take away their sins."a

28 Concerning the gospel they are enemies for your sake, but concerning the election they are beloved for the sake of the fathers. 29 For the gifts and the calling of God are irrevocable. 30 For as you were once disobedient to God, yet have now obtained mercy through their disobedience, 31 even so these also have now been disobedient, that through the mercy shown you they also may obtain mercy. 32 For God has committed them all to disobedience, that He might have mercy on all.

33 Oh, the depth of the riches both of the wisdom and knowledge of God! How unsearchable are His judgments and His ways past finding out!

34 "For who has known the mind of the LORD?
Or who has become His counselor?"a
35 "Or who has first given to Him
And it shall be repaid to him?"a

11:8 aDeuteronomy 29:4; Isaiah 29:10   11:10 aPsalm 69:22, 23   11:22 aNU-Text adds of God.
11:26 aOr delivered   11:27 aIsaiah 59:20, 21   11:34 aIsaiah 40:13; Jeremiah 23:18   11:35 aJob 41:11

The Art of Asking Loving Questions

Romans 12:16 gives a clue to the secret of dynamic success in business, religion, and interpersonal relationships: learning to question *respectfully*. Switch from the accusatory approach to the inquisitive approach.

You demonstrate great respect toward your colleague, friend, co-laborer, or family when you ask questions rather than level charges.

Because of training, conditioning, and human nature, most people impulsively react negatively when they spot an activity that appears to be offensive. They immediately pass judgment, express disagreement, and thereby promptly provoke an argument.

Faith does not react in such an irresponsible and unstudied way. Rather, faith motivates us to use the interrogative approach!

We need to ask questions—questions that do not intimidate, but sincerely try to understand: "Am I understanding you correctly?" "Can you help me understand the reason you have done this?"

Learn to develop the skill of asking questions that are success-oriented—questions that will buy time, questions that will disarm an adversary, questions that will protect you from polarization.

If you want to learn the art of positive communication, then pray: *Father, forgive me for passing judgment irresponsibly when I should have been questioning wisely, for accusing unjustly when I should have been inquiring sincerely. Forgive me for preaching sermons when I should have been listening. Amen.*

36 For of Him and through Him and to Him *are* all things, to whom *be* glory forever. Amen.

12 I beseech you therefore, brethren, by the mercies of God, that you present your bodies a living sacrifice, holy, acceptable to God, *which is* your reasonable service. 2 And do not be conformed to this world, but be transformed by the renewing of your mind, that you may prove what *is* that good and acceptable and perfect will of God.

3 For I say, through the grace given to me, to everyone who is among you, not to think *of himself* more highly than he ought to think, but to think soberly, as God has dealt to each one a measure of faith. 4 For as we have many members in one body, but all the members do not have the same function, 5 so we, *being* many, are one body in Christ, and individually members of one another. 6 Having then gifts differing according to the grace that is given to us, *let us use them:* if prophecy, *let us prophesy* in proportion to our faith; 7 or ministry, *let us use it* in *our* ministering; he who teaches, in teaching; 8 he who exhorts, in exhortation; he who gives, with liberality; he who leads, with diligence; he who shows mercy, with cheerfulness.

9 *Let* love *be* without hypocrisy. Abhor what is evil. Cling to what is good. 10 *Be* kindly affectionate to one another with brotherly love, in honor giving preference to one another; 11 not lagging in diligence, fervent in spirit, serving the Lord; 12 rejoicing in hope, patient in tribulation, continuing steadfastly in prayer; 13 distributing to the needs of the saints, given to hospitality.

14 Bless those who persecute you; bless and do not curse. 15 Rejoice with those who rejoice, and weep with those who weep. 16 Be of the same mind toward one another. Do not set your mind on high things, but associate with the humble. Do not be wise in your own opinion.

17 Repay no one evil for evil. Have regard for good things in the sight of all men. 18 If it is possible, as much as depends on you, live peaceably with all men. 19 Beloved, do not avenge yourselves, but *rather* give place to wrath; for it is written, *"Vengeance is Mine, I will repay,"ª* says the Lord. 20 Therefore

> *"If your enemy is hungry, feed him;*
> *If he is thirsty, give him a drink;*
> *For in so doing you will heap*
> *coals of fire on his head."ª*

21 Do not be overcome by evil, but overcome evil with good.

13 Let every soul be subject to the governing authorities. For there is no authority except from God, and the authorities that exist are appointed by God. 2 Therefore whoever resists the authority resists the ordinance of God, and those who resist will bring judgment on themselves. 3 For rulers are not a terror to good works, but to evil. Do you want to be unafraid of the authority? Do what is good, and you will have praise from the same. 4 For he is God's minister to you for good. But if you do evil, be afraid; for he does not bear the sword in vain; for he is God's minister, an avenger to *execute* wrath on him who practices evil. 5 Therefore *you* must be subject, not only because of wrath but also for conscience' sake. 6 For because of this you also pay taxes, for they are God's ministers attending continually to this very thing. 7 Render therefore to all their due: taxes to whom taxes *are due,* customs to whom customs, fear to whom fear, honor to whom honor.

8 Owe no one anything except to love one another, for he who loves another has fulfilled the law. 9 For the commandments, *"You shall not commit adultery," "You shall not murder," "You shall not steal," "You shall not bear false witness,"ª "You shall not covet,"ᵇ* and if *there is* any other commandment, are *all* summed up in this saying, namely, *"You shall love your neighbor as yourself."ᶜ* 10 Love does no harm to a neighbor; therefore love *is* the fulfillment of the law.

11 And *do* this, knowing the time,

12:19 ªDeuteronomy 32:35   12:20 ªProverbs 25:21, 22   13:9 ªNU-Text omits *"You shall not bear false witness."*   ᵇExodus 20:13–15, 17; Deuteronomy 5:17–19, 21   ᶜLeviticus 19:18

that now *it is* high time to awake out of sleep; for now our salvation *is* nearer than when we *first* believed. 12 The night is far spent, the day is at hand. Therefore let us cast off the works of darkness, and let us put on the armor of light. 13 Let us walk properly, as in the day, not in revelry and drunkenness, not in lewdness and lust, not in strife and envy. 14 But put on the Lord Jesus Christ, and make no provision for the flesh, to *fulfill its* lusts.

14 Receive one who is weak in the faith, *but* not to disputes over doubtful things. 2 For one believes he may eat all things, but he who is weak eats *only* vegetables. 3 Let not him who eats despise him who does not eat, and let not him who does not eat judge him who eats; for God has received him. 4 Who are you to judge another's servant? To his own master he stands or falls. Indeed, he will be made to stand, for God is able to make him stand.

5 One person esteems *one* day above another; another esteems every day *alike*. Let each be fully convinced in his own mind. 6 He who observes the day, observes *it* to the Lord;*a* and he who does not observe the day, to the Lord he does not observe *it*. He who eats, eats to the Lord, for he gives God thanks; and he who does not eat, to the Lord he does not eat, and gives God thanks. 7 For none of us lives to himself, and no one dies to himself. 8 For if we live, we live to the Lord; and if we die, we die to the Lord. Therefore, whether we live or die, we are the Lord's. 9 For to this end Christ died and rose*a* and lived again, that He might be Lord of both the dead and the living. 10 But why do you judge your brother? Or why do you show contempt for your brother? For we shall all stand before the judgment seat of Christ.*a* 11 For it is written:

> "As I live, says the LORD,
> Every knee shall bow to Me,
> And every tongue shall confess
> to God."*a*

12 So then each of us shall give account of himself to God. 13 Therefore let us not judge one another anymore, but rather resolve this, not to put a stumbling block or a cause to fall in *our* brother's way.

14 I know and am convinced by the Lord Jesus that *there is* nothing unclean of itself; but to him who considers anything to be unclean, to him *it is* unclean. 15 Yet if your brother is grieved because of *your* food, you are no longer walking in love. Do not destroy with your food the one for whom Christ died. 16 Therefore do not let your good be spoken of as evil; 17 for the kingdom of God is not eating and drinking, but righteousness and peace and joy in the Holy Spirit. 18 For he who serves Christ in these things*a is* acceptable to God and approved by men.

19 Therefore let us pursue the things *which make* for peace and the things by which one may edify another. 20 Do not destroy the work of God for the sake of food. All things indeed *are* pure, but *it is* evil for the man who eats with offense. 21 *It is* good neither to eat meat nor drink wine nor *do anything* by which your brother stumbles or is offended or is made weak.*a* 22 Do you have faith?*a* Have *it* to yourself before God. Happy *is* he who does not condemn himself in what he approves. 23 But he who doubts is condemned if he eats, because *he does* not *eat* from faith; for whatever *is* not from faith is sin.*a*

15 We then who are strong ought to bear with the scruples of the weak, and not to please ourselves. 2 Let each of us please *his* neighbor for *his* good, leading to edification. 3 For even Christ did not please Himself; but as it is written, *"The reproaches of those who reproached You fell on Me."a* 4 For whatever things were written before were written for our learning, that we through the patience and comfort of the Scriptures might have hope. 5 Now may the God of patience and comfort grant you to be like-minded toward one another, according to

---

14:6 *a*NU-Text omits the rest of this sentence.   14:9 *a*NU-Text omits *and rose*.   14:10 *a*NU-Text reads *of God*.   14:11 *a*Isaiah 45:23   14:18 *a*NU-Text reads *this*.   14:21 *a*NU-Text omits *or is offended or is made weak*.   14:22 *a*NU-Text reads *The faith which you have—have*.   14:23 *a*M-Text puts Romans 16:25–27 here.   15:3 *a*Psalm 69:9

Christ Jesus, 6 that you may with one mind *and* one mouth glorify the God and Father of our Lord Jesus Christ.

7 Therefore receive one another, just as Christ also received us,*a* to the glory of God. 8 Now I say that Jesus Christ has become a servant to the circumcision for the truth of God, to confirm the promises *made* to the fathers, 9 and that the Gentiles might glorify God for *His* mercy, as it is written:

> "For this reason I will confess
>   to You among the Gentiles,
> And sing to Your name."*a*

10 And again he says:

> "Rejoice, O Gentiles, with His
>   people!"*a*

11 And again:

> "Praise the LORD, all you
>   Gentiles!
> Laud Him, all you peoples!"*a*

12 And again, Isaiah says:

> "There shall be a root of Jesse;
> And He who shall rise to reign
>   over the Gentiles,
> In Him the Gentiles shall
>   hope."*a*

13 Now may the God of hope fill you with all joy and peace in believing, that you may abound in hope by the power of the Holy Spirit.

14 Now I myself am confident concerning you, my brethren, that you also are full of goodness, filled with all knowledge, able also to admonish one another.*a* 15 Nevertheless, brethren, I have written more boldly to you on *some* points, as reminding you, because of the grace given to me by God, 16 that I might be a minister of Jesus Christ to the Gentiles, ministering the gospel of God, that the offering of the Gentiles might be acceptable, sanctified by the Holy Spirit. 17 Therefore I have reason to glory in Christ Jesus in the things *which pertain* to God. 18 For I will not dare to speak of any of those things which Christ has not accomplished through me, in word and deed, to make the Gentiles obedient— 19 in mighty signs and wonders, by the power of the Spirit of God, so that from Jerusalem and round about to Illyricum I have fully preached the gospel of Christ. 20 And so I have made it my aim to preach the gospel, not where Christ was named, lest I should build on another man's foundation, 21 but as it is written:

> "To whom He was not
>   announced, they shall see;
> And those who have not heard
>   shall understand."*a*

22 For this reason I also have been much hindered from coming to you. 23 But now no longer having a place in these parts, and having a great desire these many years to come to you, 24 whenever I journey to Spain, I shall come to you.*a* For I hope to see you on my journey, and to be helped on my way there by you, if first I may enjoy your *company* for a while. 25 But now I am going to Jerusalem to minister to the saints. 26 For it pleased those from Macedonia and Achaia to make a certain contribution for the poor among the saints who are in Jerusalem. 27 It pleased them indeed, and they are their debtors. For if the Gentiles have been partakers of their spiritual things, their duty is also to minister to them in material things. 28 Therefore, when I have performed this and have sealed to them this fruit, I shall go by way of you to Spain. 29 But I know that when I come to you, I shall come in the fullness of the blessing of the gospel*a* of Christ.

30 Now I beg you, brethren, through the Lord Jesus Christ, and through the love of the Spirit, that you strive together with me in prayers to God for me, 31 that I may be delivered from those in Judea who do not believe, and that my service for Jerusalem may be acceptable to the saints, 32 that I may come to you with joy by the will of God, and may be refreshed together with you. 33 Now the God of peace *be* with you all. Amen.

15:7 *a*NU-Text and M-Text read *you.*   15:9 *a*2 Samuel 22:50; Psalm 18:49   15:10 *a*Deuteronomy 32:43   15:11 *a*Psalm 117:1   15:12 *a*Isaiah 11:10   15:14 *a*M-Text reads *others.*   15:21 *a*Isaiah 52:15   15:24 *a*NU-Text omits *I shall come to you* (and joins *Spain* with the next sentence).   15:29 *a*NU-Text omits *of the gospel.*

16 I commend to you Phoebe our sister, who is a servant of the church in Cenchrea, 2 that you may receive her in the Lord in a manner worthy of the saints, and assist her in whatever business she has need of you; for indeed she has been a helper of many and of myself also.

3 Greet Priscilla and Aquila, my fellow workers in Christ Jesus, 4 who risked their own necks for my life, to whom not only I give thanks, but also all the churches of the Gentiles. 5 Likewise *greet* the church that is in their house.

Greet my beloved Epaenetus, who is the firstfruits of Achaia*ᵃ* to Christ. 6 Greet Mary, who labored much for us. 7 Greet Andronicus and Junia, my countrymen and my fellow prisoners, who are of note among the apostles, who also were in Christ before me.

8 Greet Amplias, my beloved in the Lord. 9 Greet Urbanus, our fellow worker in Christ, and Stachys, my beloved. 10 Greet Apelles, approved in Christ. Greet those who are of the *household* of Aristobulus. 11 Greet Herodion, my countryman.*ᵃ* Greet those who are of the *household* of Narcissus who are in the Lord.

12 Greet Tryphena and Tryphosa, who have labored in the Lord. Greet the beloved Persis, who labored much in the Lord. 13 Greet Rufus, chosen in the Lord, and his mother and mine. 14 Greet Asyncritus, Phlegon, Hermas, Patrobas, Hermes, and the brethren who are with them. 15 Greet Philologus and Julia, Nereus and his sister, and Olympas, and all the saints who are with them.

16 Greet one another with a holy kiss. The*ᵃ* churches of Christ greet you.

17 Now I urge you, brethren, note those who cause divisions and offenses, contrary to the doctrine which you learned, and avoid them. 18 For those who are such do not serve our Lord Jesus*ᵃ* Christ, but their own belly, and by smooth words and flattering speech deceive the hearts of the simple. 19 For your obedience has become known to all. Therefore I am glad on your behalf; but I want you to be wise in what is good, and simple concerning evil. 20 And the God of peace will crush Satan under your feet shortly.

The grace of our Lord Jesus Christ *be* with you. Amen.

21 Timothy, my fellow worker, and Lucius, Jason, and Sosipater, my countrymen, greet you.

22 I, Tertius, who wrote *this* epistle, greet you in the Lord.

23 Gaius, my host and *the host* of the whole church, greets you. Erastus, the treasurer of the city, greets you, and Quartus, a brother. 24 The grace of our Lord Jesus Christ *be* with you all. Amen.*ᵃ*

25 Now to Him who is able to establish you according to my gospel and the preaching of Jesus Christ, according to the revelation of the mystery kept secret since the world began 26 but now has been made manifest, and by the prophetic Scriptures has been made known to all nations, according to the commandment of the everlasting God, for obedience to the faith— 27 to God, alone wise, *be* glory through Jesus Christ forever. Amen.*ᵃ*

16:5 *ᵃ*NU-Text reads *Asia.*   16:11 *ᵃ*Or *relative*   16:16 *ᵃ*NU-Text reads *All the churches.*
16:18 *ᵃ*NU-Text and M-Text omit *Jesus.*   16:24 *ᵃ*NU-Text omits this verse.   16:27 *ᵃ*M-Text puts Romans 16:25–27 after Romans 14:23.

First Corinthians

Overview of First Corinthians

It is a constant challenge for Christians to bloom where they are planted! This is what the apostle Paul encouraged the Corinthians to do.

The First Epistle to the Corinthians was written by the apostle Paul while in Ephesus to the young and struggling church in the city of Corinth, Greece. Throughout this letter, Paul encourages the church to live up to its calling from God.

The city of Corinth was a wealthy trade center because of its established seaport and a strong military fortress built on solid rock hundreds of feet above the Corinthian plain. Corinth was known for its immoral behavior. One ancient writer explained that to be called a "Corinthian" was to be called a fornicator. It was in this environment that Paul wrote to the young, floundering church he had helped establish.

Paul spent more than one and a half years in Corinth during A.D. 50 and 51. He later returned on another journey to the church sometime between A.D. 53 and 54. Paul corresponded more with this body of believers than any other church in the New Testament period, most likely to deal with the serious problems facing the Christians there.

Throughout First Corinthians we learn that the young believers were led off track by their surroundings. Immoral acts were infiltrating the church, Paul's apostleship was questioned, and even the resurrection of Jesus Christ was denied. Paul treats these problems from both a theological and a practical viewpoint. He encourages the church to become unified and demonstrate their oneness through love. Paul reminds them that even though they may be talented, devoted, generous, and faithful, if love is absent, there can be no profit. He implores them to make love their aim.

Paul's patience in confirming and encouraging the Corinthian church indicates his love in action; Paul's vision was to build up the Corinthian church. By doing so, he also was built up. Paul demonstrates in this letter that love truly equals obedience to God in words and actions.

Jesus in First Corinthians

This book proclaims the relevance of Christ to every area of the believer's life. Jesus "became for us wisdom from God—and righteousness and sanctification and redemption—" (1:30), and Paul addresses this theme in his letter to the church at Corinth, which desperately needed Christ's wisdom.

Keys to First Corinthians

Key Word: Correction. This Epistle applies Christian principles to correct carnality in the individual and in church life. The cross of Christ is the central message to transform the individual's life in the face of immorality and to unify the body of believers' disunity. This letter is a corrective response by Paul to promote unity in relationships and worship within the Church, and is tempered by Paul's tender heart of concern for them.

Key Verses: "Or do you not know that your body is the temple of the Holy Spirit *who is* in you, whom you have from God, and you are not your own? For you were bought at a price; therefore glorify God in your body and in your spirit, which are God's" (6:19, 20).

"Therefore let him who thinks he stands take heed lest he fall. No temptation has overtaken you except such as is common to man; but God *is* faithful, who will not allow you to be tempted beyond what you are able, but with the temptation will also make the way of escape, that you may be able to bear *it*" (10:12, 13).

Key Chapter: First Corinthians 13. This chapter is often read at weddings and found in sermon texts as the best scriptural definition of love. This book primarily reveals love as an action in stark contrast to popular belief that love is an emotion. This is why God's love is best revealed in John 3:16: "For God so loved the world that He gave . . ."

1 Paul, called *to be* an apostle of Jesus Christ through the will of God, and Sosthenes *our* brother,

2 To the church of God which is at Corinth, to those who are sanctified in Christ Jesus, called *to be* saints, with all who in every place call on

Important Capital Cities

Capital of province of Syria during Roman period; missionary base for Paul and Barnabas (Acts 13:1–3).

Important biblical seaport built by Herod the Great and named for Caesar Augustus; became Roman provincial capital of Jewish nation for 600 years.

Religious capital of the Jewish people during the Roman occupation.

Capital of the Roman province of Asia; location of the "compromising" church addressed by John (Rev. 2:12–17).

Capital of the Roman province of Macedonia; Paul founded a church here (Acts 17:1–4).

Capital city of the Roman Empire and present capital of Italy; the apostle Paul was imprisoned and probably executed at Rome (Acts 28:16).

Capital of the Roman province of Achaia in ancient Greece; thriving trade and shipping center when Paul arrived here to establish a church (Acts 18:1).

Capital of ancient Greece; center of culture and politics during Greece's golden age; visited by Paul on his second missionary journey (Acts 17:16–34).

Capital of Egypt during the Greek and Roman periods; established by Alexander the Great; home of Apollos (Acts 18:24).

• Antioch

• Caesarea

• Jerusalem

• Pergamos

ASIA

THE GREAT SEA

• Alexandria

E G Y P T

RED SEA

MACEDONIA

ACHAIA

• Thessalonica

Athens

Corinth

ADRIATIC SEA

• Rome

the name of Jesus Christ our Lord, both theirs and ours:

3 Grace to you and peace from God our Father and the Lord Jesus Christ. 4 I thank my God always concerning you for the grace of God which was given to you by Christ Jesus, 5 that you were enriched in everything by Him in all utterance and all knowledge, 6 even as the testimony of Christ was confirmed in you, 7 so that you come short in no gift, eagerly waiting for the revelation of our Lord Jesus Christ, 8 who will also confirm you to the end, *that you may be* blameless in the day of our Lord Jesus Christ. 9 God *is* faithful, by whom you were called into the fellowship of His Son, Jesus Christ our Lord.

10 Now I plead with you, brethren, by the name of our Lord Jesus Christ, that you all speak the same thing, and *that* there be no divisions among you, but *that* you be perfectly joined together in the same mind and in the same judgment. 11 For it has been declared to me concerning you, my brethren, by those of Chloe's *household*, that there are contentions among you. 12 Now I say this, that each of you says, "I am of Paul," or "I am of Apollos," or "I am of Cephas," or "I am of Christ." 13 Is Christ divided? Was Paul crucified for you? Or were you baptized in the name of Paul?

14 I thank God that I baptized none of you except Crispus and Gaius, 15 lest anyone should say that I had baptized in my own name. 16 Yes, I also baptized the household of Stephanas. Besides, I do not know whether I baptized any other. 17 For Christ did not send me to baptize, but to preach the gospel, not with wisdom of words, lest the cross of Christ should be made of no effect.

18 For the message of the cross is foolishness to those who are perishing, but to us who are being saved it is the power of God. 19 For it is written:

"I will destroy the wisdom of the wise,
And bring to nothing the

understanding of the prudent."[a]

20 Where *is* the wise? Where *is* the scribe? Where *is* the disputer of this age? Has not God made foolish the wisdom of this world? 21 For since, in the wisdom of God, the world through wisdom did not know God, it pleased God through the foolishness of the message preached to save those who believe. 22 For Jews request a sign, and Greeks seek after wisdom; 23 but we preach Christ crucified, to the Jews a stumbling block and to the Greeks[a] foolishness, 24 but to those who are called, both Jews and Greeks, Christ the power of God and the wisdom of God. 25 Because the foolishness of God is wiser than men, and the weakness of God is stronger than men.

26 For you see your calling, brethren, that not many wise according to the flesh, not many mighty, not many noble, *are called.* 27 But God has chosen the foolish things of the world to put to shame the wise, and God has chosen the weak things of the world to put to shame the things which are mighty; 28 and the base things of the world and the things which are despised God has chosen, and the things which are not, to bring to nothing the things that are, 29 that no flesh should glory in His presence. 30 But of Him you are in Christ Jesus, who became for us wisdom from God—and righteousness and sanctification and redemption— 31 that, as it is written, *"He who glories, let him glory in the LORD."*[a]

2 And I, brethren, when I came to you, did not come with excellence of speech or of wisdom declaring to you the testimony[a] of God. 2 For I determined not to know anything among you except Jesus Christ and Him crucified. 3 I was with you in weakness, in fear, and in much trembling. 4 And my speech and my preaching *were* not with persuasive words of human[a] wisdom, but in demonstration of the Spirit and of power, 5 that your faith should not be in the wisdom of men but in the power of God.

1:19 [a]Isaiah 29:14   1:23 [a]NU-Text reads *Gentiles.*   1:31 [a]Jeremiah 9:24   2:1 [a]NU-Text reads
mystery.   2:4 [a]NU-Text omits *human.*

You Are Living Stones

The architecture of the temple in the New Testament period is a fascinating work of art. Started by Herod the Great, approximately 20 B.C., the temple was completed somewhere around A.D. 27, forty-six years later.

Made from solid limestone quarried from the hills around Jerusalem, the temple stood as one of the great buildings of the ancient world. The ancient historian Josephus, lauded the structure. "He who has not seen the Jerusalem temple has not seen a beautiful building."

Recent archaeological excavations have focused on exposing remains of the temple mount, the enclosure upon which the New Testament temple was built. Already archaeological teams have unearthed temple stones ranging in size from forty tons to seven hundred tons. The builders of the temple quarried large blocks of limestone, with which they employed an ancient architectural design known as "headers and stretchers." Stones of equal length were placed in an alternate pattern. The first block was lined up with the end of the stone facing outside—the length of it going into the building. The second stone was situated so the side or length faced outside. The subsequent stone was like the first. This pattern continued around the base of the structure.

In addition, the builders left two inches of space between each stone. This was done so that when the heat of the summer came and the temple stones expanded, they would have room to push outward. In the coolness of winter, the limestone contracted giving the temple remarkable flexibility to hold up through severe winters or intense summer heat. The temple had room to breathe. Each stone was placed one upon the other with a half-inch tilt inward, until it reached hundreds of feet in height.

The apostle Peter reminds us in 1 Peter 2:5 of the beauty of another temple—a spiritual house—when he asks us to be built together, dependent upon one another in loving relationships as "living stones." We are choice stones built upon the foundation of Jesus Christ. Like the stones from the temple two thousand years ago, we must be in place with our relationship to Jesus, the Chief Cornerstone, well established. We expand and contract when the heat of problems and cold of negative influences come our way. First Peter 2:9 says then we "may proclaim the praises of Him . . ."

6 However, we speak wisdom among those who are mature, yet not the wisdom of this age, nor of the rulers of this age, who are coming to nothing. 7 But we speak the wisdom of God in a mystery, the hidden *wisdom* which God ordained before the ages for our glory, 8 which none of the rulers of this age knew; for had they known, they would not have crucified the Lord of glory.

9 But as it is written:

> "Eye has not seen, nor ear heard,
> Nor have entered into the heart of man
> The things which God has prepared for those who love Him."[a]

10 But God has revealed *them* to us through His Spirit. For the Spirit searches all things, yes, the deep things of God. 11 For what man knows the things of a man except the spirit of the man which is in him? Even so no one knows the things of God except the Spirit of God. 12 Now we have received, not the spirit of the world, but the Spirit who is from God, that we might know the things that have been freely given to us by God.

13 These things we also speak, not in words which man's wisdom teaches but which the Holy[a] Spirit teaches, comparing spiritual things with spiritual. 14 But the natural man does not receive the things of the Spirit of God, for they are foolishness to him; nor can he know *them*, because they are spiritually discerned. 15 But he who is spiritual judges all things, yet he himself is *rightly* judged by no one. 16 For *"who has known the mind of the Lord that he may instruct Him?"*[a] But we have the mind of Christ.

3 And I, brethren, could not speak to you as to spiritual *people* but as to carnal, as to babes in Christ. 2 I fed you with milk and not with solid food; for until now you were not able *to receive it,* and even now you are still not able; 3 for you are still carnal. For where *there are* envy, strife, and divisions among you, are you not carnal and behaving like *mere* men? 4 For when one says, "I am of Paul," and another, "I *am* of Apollos," are you not carnal?

5 Who then is Paul, and who *is* Apollos, but ministers through whom you believed, as the Lord gave to each one? 6 I planted, Apollos watered, but God gave the increase. 7 So then neither he who plants is anything, nor he who waters, but God who gives the increase. 8 Now he who plants and he who waters are one, and each one will receive his own reward according to his own labor.

9 For we are God's fellow workers; you are God's field, *you are* God's building. 10 According to the grace of God which was given to me, as a wise master builder I have laid the foundation, and another builds on it. But let each one take heed how he builds on it. 11 For no other foundation can anyone lay than that which is laid, which is Jesus Christ. 12 Now if anyone builds on this foundation *with* gold, silver, precious stones, wood, hay, straw, 13 each one's work will become clear; for the Day will declare it, because it will be revealed by fire; and the fire will test each one's work, of what sort it is. 14 If anyone's work which he has built on *it* endures, he will receive a reward. 15 If anyone's work is burned, he will suffer loss; but he himself will be saved, yet so as through fire.

16 Do you not know that you are the temple of God and *that* the Spirit of God dwells in you? 17 If anyone defiles the temple of God, God will destroy him. For the temple of God is holy, which *temple* you are.

18 Let no one deceive himself. If anyone among you seems to be wise in this age, let him become a fool that he may become wise. 19 For the wisdom of this world is foolishness with God. For it is written, *"He catches the wise in their own craftiness"*;[a] 20 and again, *"The Lord knows the thoughts of the wise, that they are futile."*[a] 21 Therefore let no one boast in men. For all things are yours: 22 whether Paul or Apollos or Cephas, or the world or life or death, or things present or things to come—

2:9 [a]Isaiah 64:4　　2:13 [a]NU-Text omits *Holy.*　　2:16 [a]Isaiah 40:13　　3:19 [a]Job 5:13　　3:20 [a]Psalm 94:11

all are yours. 23 And you *are* Christ's, and Christ *is* God's.

4 Let a man so consider us, as servants of Christ and stewards of the mysteries of God. 2 Moreover it is required in stewards that one be found faithful. 3 But with me it is a very small thing that I should be judged by you or by a human court.*a* In fact, I do not even judge myself. 4 For I know of nothing against myself, yet I am not justified by this; but He who judges me is the Lord. 5 Therefore judge nothing before the time, until the Lord comes, who will both bring to light the hidden things of darkness and reveal the counsels of the hearts. Then each one's praise will come from God.

6 Now these things, brethren, I have figuratively transferred to myself and Apollos for your sakes, that you may learn in us not to think beyond what is written, that none of you may be puffed up on behalf of one against the other. 7 For who makes you differ *from another?* And what do you have that you did not receive? Now if you did indeed receive *it,* why do you boast as if you had not received *it?*

8 You are already full! You are already rich! You have reigned as kings without us—and indeed I could wish you did reign, that we also might reign with you! 9 For I think that God has displayed us, the apostles, last, as men condemned to death; for we have been made a spectacle to the world, both to angels and to men. 10 We *are* fools for Christ's sake, but you *are* wise in Christ! We *are* weak, but you *are* strong! You *are* distinguished, but we *are* dishonored! 11 To the present hour we both hunger and thirst, and we are poorly clothed, and beaten, and homeless. 12 And we labor, working with our own hands. Being reviled, we bless; being persecuted, we endure; 13 being defamed, we entreat. We have been made as the filth of the world, the offscouring of all things until now.

14 I do not write these things to shame you, but as my beloved children I warn you. 15 For though you might have ten thousand instructors in Christ, yet *you do* not *have* many fathers; for in Christ Jesus I have begotten you through the gospel. 16 Therefore I urge you, imitate me. 17 For this reason I have sent Timothy to you, who is my beloved and faithful son in the Lord, who will remind you of my ways in Christ, as I teach everywhere in every church.

18 Now some are puffed up, as though I were not coming to you. 19 But I will come to you shortly, if the Lord wills, and I will know, not the word of those who are puffed up, but the power. 20 For the kingdom of God *is* not in word but in power. 21 What do you want? Shall I come to you with a rod, or in love and a spirit of gentleness?

5 It is actually reported *that there is* sexual immorality among you, and such sexual immorality as is not even named*a* among the Gentiles— that a man has his father's wife! 2 And you are puffed up, and have not rather mourned, that he who has done this deed might be taken away from among you. 3 For I indeed, as absent in body but present in spirit, have already judged (as though I were present) him who has so done this deed. 4 In the name of our Lord Jesus Christ, when you are gathered together, along with my spirit, with the power of our Lord Jesus Christ, 5 deliver such a one to Satan for the destruction of the flesh, that his spirit may be saved in the day of the Lord Jesus.*a*

6 Your glorying *is* not good. Do you not know that a little leaven leavens the whole lump? 7 Therefore purge out the old leaven, that you may be a new lump, since you truly are unleavened. For indeed Christ, our Passover, was sacrificed for us.*a* 8 Therefore let us keep the feast, not with old leaven, nor with the leaven of malice and wickedness, but with the unleavened *bread* of sincerity and truth.

9 I wrote to you in my epistle not to keep company with sexually immoral people. 10 Yet I certainly *did* not *mean* with the sexually immoral people of this world, or with the covetous, or extortioners, or idolaters, since then you would need to go out

4:3 *a* Literally *day*   5:1 *a* NU-Text omits *named.*   5:5 *a* NU-Text omits *Jesus.*   5:7 *a* NU-Text omits *for us.*

of the world. 11 But now I have written to you not to keep company with anyone named a brother, who is sexually immoral, or covetous, or an idolater, or a reviler, or a drunkard, or an extortioner—not even to eat with such a person.

12 For what *have* I *to do* with judging those also who are outside? Do you not judge those who are inside? 13 But those who are outside God judges. Therefore *"put away from yourselves the evil person."*[a]

6 Dare any of you, having a matter against another, go to law before the unrighteous, and not before the saints? 2 Do you not know that the saints will judge the world? And if the world will be judged by you, are you unworthy to judge the smallest matters? 3 Do you not know that we shall judge angels? How much more, things that pertain to this life? 4 If then you have judgments concerning things pertaining to this life, do you appoint those who are least esteemed by the church to judge? 5 I say this to your shame. Is it so, that there is not a wise man among you, not even one, who will be able to judge between his brethren? 6 But brother goes to law against brother, and that before unbelievers!

7 Now therefore, it is already an utter failure for you that you go to law against one another. Why do you not rather accept wrong? Why do you not rather *let yourselves* be cheated? 8 No, you yourselves do wrong and cheat, and *you do* these things *to your* brethren! 9 Do you not know that the unrighteous will not inherit the kingdom of God? Do not be deceived. Neither fornicators, nor idolaters, nor adulterers, nor homosexuals,[a] nor sodomites, 10 nor thieves, nor covetous, nor drunkards, nor revilers, nor extortioners will inherit the kingdom of God. 11 And such were some of you. But you were washed, but you were sanctified, but you were justified in the name of the Lord Jesus and by the Spirit of our God.

12 All things are lawful for me, but all things are not helpful. All things are lawful for me, but I will not be brought under the power of any.

13 Foods for the stomach and the stomach for foods, but God will destroy both it and them. Now the body *is* not for sexual immorality but for the Lord, and the Lord for the body. 14 And God both raised up the Lord and will also raise us up by His power.

15 Do you not know that your bodies are members of Christ? Shall I then take the members of Christ and make *them* members of a harlot? Certainly not! 16 Or do you not know that he who is joined to a harlot is one body *with her*? For *"the two,"* He says, *"shall become one flesh."*[a] 17 But he who is joined to the Lord is one spirit *with Him*.

18 Flee sexual immorality. Every sin that a man does is outside the body, but he who commits sexual immorality sins against his own body. 19 Or do you not know that your body is the temple of the Holy Spirit *who is* in you, whom you have from God, and you are not your own? 20 For you were bought at a price; therefore glorify God in your body[a] and in your spirit, which are God's.

7 Now concerning the things of which you wrote to me:

It is good for a man not to touch a woman. 2 Nevertheless, because of sexual immorality, let each man have his own wife, and let each woman have her own husband. 3 Let the husband render to his wife the affection due her, and likewise also the wife to her husband. 4 The wife does not have authority over her own body, but the husband *does*. And likewise the husband does not have authority over his own body, but the wife *does*. 5 Do not deprive one another except with consent for a time, that you may give yourselves to fasting and prayer; and come together again so that Satan does not tempt you because of your lack of self-control. 6 But I say this as a concession, not as a commandment. 7 For I wish that all men were even as I myself. But each one has his own gift from God, one in this manner and another in that.

8 But I say to the unmarried and to the widows: It is good for them if they remain even as I am; 9 but if

5:13 [a]Deuteronomy 17:7; 19:19; 22:21, 24; 24:7   6:9 [a]That is, catamites   6:16 [a]Genesis 2:24
6:20 [a]NU-Text ends the verse at *body*.

they cannot exercise self-control, let them marry. For it is better to marry than to burn *with passion.*

10 Now to the married I command, *yet* not I but the Lord: A wife is not to depart from *her* husband. 11 But even if she does depart, let her remain unmarried or be reconciled to *her* husband. And a husband is not to divorce *his* wife.

12 But to the rest I, not the Lord, say: If any brother has a wife who does not believe, and she is willing to live with him, let him not divorce her. 13 And a woman who has a husband who does not believe, if he is willing to live with her, let her not divorce him. 14 For the unbelieving husband is sanctified by the wife, and the unbelieving wife is sanctified by the husband; otherwise your children would be unclean, but now they are holy. 15 But if the unbeliever departs, let him depart; a brother or a sister is not under bondage in such *cases.* But God has called us to peace. 16 For how do you know, O wife, whether you will save *your* husband? Or how do you know, O husband, whether you will save *your* wife?

17 But as God has distributed to each one, as the Lord has called each one, so let him walk. And so I ordain in all the churches. 18 Was anyone called while circumcised? Let him not become uncircumcised. Was anyone called while uncircumcised? Let him not be circumcised. 19 Circumcision is nothing and uncircumcision is nothing, but keeping the commandments of God *is what matters.* 20 Let each one remain in the same calling in which he was called. 21 Were you called *while* a slave? Do not be concerned about it; but if you can be made free, rather use *it.* 22 For he who is called in the Lord *while* a slave is the Lord's freedman. Likewise he who is called *while* free is Christ's slave. 23 You were bought at a price; do not become slaves of men. 24 Brethren, let each one remain with God in that *state* in which he was called.

25 Now concerning virgins: I have no commandment from the Lord; yet I give judgment as one whom the Lord in His mercy *has made* trustworthy. 26 I suppose therefore that this is good because of the present distress—that *it is* good for a man to remain as he is: 27 Are you bound to a wife? Do not seek to be loosed. Are you loosed from a wife? Do not seek a wife. 28 But even if you do marry, you have not sinned; and if a virgin marries, she has not sinned. Nevertheless such will have trouble in the flesh, but I would spare you.

29 But this I say, brethren, the time *is* short, so that from now on even those who have wives should be as though they had none, 30 those who weep as though they did not weep, those who rejoice as though they did not rejoice, those who buy as though they did not possess, 31 and those who use this world as not misusing *it.* For the form of this world is passing away.

32 But I want you to be without care. He who is unmarried cares for the things of the Lord—how he may please the Lord. 33 But he who is married cares about the things of the world—how he may please *his* wife. 34 There is[a] a difference between a wife and a virgin. The unmarried woman cares about the things of the Lord, that she may be holy both in body and in spirit. But she who is married cares about the things of the world—how she may please *her* husband. 35 And this I say for your own profit, not that I may put a leash on you, but for what is proper, and that you may serve the Lord without distraction.

36 But if any man thinks he is behaving improperly toward his virgin, if she is past the flower of youth, and thus it must be, let him do what he wishes. He does not sin; let them marry. 37 Nevertheless he who stands steadfast in his heart, having no necessity, but has power over his own will, and has so determined in his heart that he will keep his virgin,[a] does well. 38 So then he who gives her[a] in marriage does well, but he who does not give *her* in marriage does better.

39 A wife is bound by law as long as her husband lives; but if her husband dies, she is at liberty to be married to whom she wishes, only in the Lord. 40 But she is happier if she remains as she is, according to my judgment—and I think I also have the Spirit of God.

7:34 [a]M-Text adds *also.*   7:37 [a]Or *virgin daughter*   7:38 [a]NU-Text reads *his own virgin.*

8 Now concerning things offered to idols: We know that we all have knowledge. Knowledge puffs up, but love edifies. 2 And if anyone thinks that he knows anything, he knows nothing yet as he ought to know. 3 But if anyone loves God, this one is known by Him.

4 Therefore concerning the eating of things offered to idols, we know that an idol *is* nothing in the world, and that *there is* no other God but one. 5 For even if there are so-called gods, whether in heaven or on earth (as there are many gods and many lords), 6 yet for us *there is* one God, the Father, of whom *are* all things, and we for Him; and one Lord Jesus Christ, through whom *are* all things, and through whom we *live.*

7 However, *there is* not in everyone that knowledge; for some, with consciousness of the idol, until now eat *it* as a thing offered to an idol; and their conscience, being weak, is defiled. 8 But food does not commend us to God; for neither if we eat are we the better, nor if we do not eat are we the worse.

9 But beware lest somehow this liberty of yours become a stumbling block to those who are weak. 10 For if anyone sees you who have knowledge eating in an idol's temple, will not the conscience of him who is weak be emboldened to eat those things offered to idols? 11 And because of your knowledge shall the weak brother perish, for whom Christ died? 12 But when you thus sin against the brethren, and wound their weak conscience, you sin against Christ. 13 Therefore, if food makes my brother stumble, I will never again eat meat, lest I make my brother stumble.

9 Am I not an apostle? Am I not free? Have I not seen Jesus Christ our Lord? Are you not my work in the Lord? 2 If I am not an apostle to others, yet doubtless I am to you. For you are the seal of my apostleship in the Lord.

3 My defense to those who examine me is this: 4 Do we have no right to eat and drink? 5 Do we have no right to take along a believing wife, as *do* also the other apostles, the brothers of the Lord, and Cephas? 6 Or *is it* only Barnabas and I *who* have no right to refrain from working? 7 Who ever goes to war at his own expense? Who plants a vineyard and does not eat of its fruit? Or who tends a flock and does not drink of the milk of the flock?

8 Do I say these things as a *mere* man? Or does not the law say the same also? 9 For it is written in the law of Moses, *"You shall not muzzle an ox while it treads out the grain."*ᵃ Is it oxen God is concerned about? 10 Or does He say *it* altogether for our sakes? For our sakes, no doubt, *this* is written, that he who plows should plow in hope, and he who threshes in hope should be partaker of his hope. 11 If we have sown spiritual things for you, *is it* a great thing if we reap your material things? 12 If others are partakers of *this* right over you, *are* we not even more?

Nevertheless we have not used this right, but endure all things lest we hinder the gospel of Christ. 13 Do you not know that those who minister the holy things eat *of the things* of the temple, and those who serve at the altar partake of *the offerings of* the altar? 14 Even so the Lord has commanded that those who preach the gospel should live from the gospel.

15 But I have used none of these things, nor have I written these things that it should be done so to me; for it *would be* better for me to die than that anyone should make my boasting void. 16 For if I preach the gospel, I have nothing to boast of, for necessity is laid upon me; yes, woe is me if I do not preach the gospel! 17 For if I do this willingly, I have a reward; but if against my will, I have been entrusted with a stewardship. 18 What is my reward then? That when I preach the gospel, I may present the gospel of Christᵃ without charge, that I may not abuse my authority in the gospel.

19 For though I am free from all *men,* I have made myself a servant to all, that I might win the more; 20 and to the Jews I became as a Jew, that I might win Jews; to those *who are* under the law, as under the law,ᵃ

9:9 ᵃDeuteronomy 25:4   9:18 ᵃNU-Text omits *of Christ.*   9:20 ᵃNU-Text adds *though not being myself under the law.*

The Games

"Run in such a way that you may obtain *it*" (1 Cor. 9:24).

Everywhere in the New Testament world, Greek society left its mark on the culture and religion of the people. Perhaps one of the greatest contributions was that of the Olympic Games.

Held every four years in Greece since its inception, the Olympic Games quickly became world renowned. There was scarcely a city in the Roman Empire where mention of the games did not excite a discussion. Many cities were anxious to host the games. Two cities in Palestine were granted this honor: Dor and Samaria.

During the reign of King Herod in Palestine, he built magnificent accommodations for the games. In Assyria, he constructed a hippodrome larger than the one in Rome, as well as gladiator stadiums and other facilities. In Samaria, Herod built horse racing stadiums and theaters to host plays for visitors attending the games. The ancient historian, Josephus, records that over one-hundred-foot-high marble pillars visible from the seashore were also built in Samaria.

The writers of the New Testament were also influenced by the Greeks and the Olympic Games. The apostle Paul encourages his readers to "press toward the goal for the prize of the upward call of God in Christ Jesus" (Phil. 3:14). He urges believers to run in such a way that they may win. Paul compares the Christian life-style to the continuous training and preparation for the games.

As Christians, we must bring our thoughts and abilities to their fullest potential by training, exercising, and demonstrating them before God and others. God has given you a unique gift—who you are. And He wants to honor you at the end of your race. But you must train, grow, and run with endurance your life's race.

that I might win those *who are* under the law; 21 to those *who are* without law, as without law (not being without law toward God,*a* but under law toward Christ*b*), that I might win those *who are* without law; 22 to the weak I became as*a* weak, that I might win the weak. I have become all things to all *men,* that I might by all means save some. 23 Now this I do for the gospel's sake, that I may be partaker of it with *you.*

24 Do you not know that those who run in a race all run, but one receives the prize? Run in such a way that you may obtain *it.* 25 And everyone who competes *for the prize* is temperate in all things. Now they *do it* to obtain a perishable crown, but we *for* an imperishable *crown.* 26 Therefore I run thus: not with uncertainty. Thus I fight: not as *one who* beats the air. 27 But I discipline my body and bring *it* into subjection, lest, when I have preached to others, I myself should become disqualified.

10 Moreover, brethren, I do not want you to be unaware that all our fathers were under the cloud, all passed through the sea, 2 all were baptized into Moses in the cloud and in the sea, 3 all ate the same spiritual food, 4 and all drank the same spiritual drink. For they drank of that spiritual Rock that followed them, and that Rock was Christ. 5 But with most of them God was not well pleased, for *their bodies* were scattered in the wilderness.

6 Now these things became our examples, to the intent that we should not lust after evil things as they also lusted. 7 And do not become idolaters as *were* some of them. As it is written, *"The people sat down to eat and drink, and rose up to play."*a 8 Nor let us commit sexual immorality, as some of them did, and in one day twenty-three thousand fell; 9 nor let us tempt Christ, as some of them also tempted, and were destroyed by serpents; 10 nor complain, as some of them also complained, and were destroyed by the destroyer. 11 Now all*a* these things happened to them as examples, and they were written for our admonition, upon

whom the ends of the ages have come.

12 Therefore let him who thinks he stands take heed lest he fall. 13 No temptation has overtaken you except such as is common to man; but God *is* faithful, who will not allow you to be tempted beyond what you are able, but with the temptation will also make the way of escape, that you may be able to bear *it.*

14 Therefore, my beloved, flee from idolatry. 15 I speak as to wise men; judge for yourselves what I say. 16 The cup of blessing which we bless, is it not the communion of the blood of Christ? The bread which we break, is it not the communion of the body of Christ? 17 For we, *though* many, are one bread *and* one body; for we all partake of that one bread.

18 Observe Israel after the flesh: Are not those who eat of the sacrifices partakers of the altar? 19 What am I saying then? That an idol is anything, or what is offered to idols is anything? 20 Rather, that the things which the Gentiles sacrifice they sacrifice to demons and not to God, and I do not want you to have fellowship with demons. 21 You cannot drink the cup of the Lord and the cup of demons; you cannot partake of the Lord's table and of the table of demons. 22 Or do we provoke the Lord to jealousy? Are we stronger than He?

23 All things are lawful for me,*a* but not all things are helpful; all things are lawful for me,*b* but not all things edify. 24 Let no one seek his own, but each one the other's *well-being.*

25 Eat whatever is sold in the meat market, asking no questions for conscience' sake; 26 for *"the earth is the* LORD'S, *and all its fullness."*a

27 If any of those who do not believe invites you *to dinner,* and you desire to go, eat whatever is set before you, asking no question for conscience' sake. 28 But if anyone says to you, "This was offered to idols," do not eat it for the sake of the one who told you, and for conscience' sake;*a* for *"the earth is the* LORD'S, *and all its fullness."*b 29 "Conscience," I say, not your own, but that of the other. For why is my lib-

---

9:21 *a*NU-Text reads *God's law.*   *b*NU-Text reads *Christ's law.*   9:22 *a*NU-Text omits *as.*
10:7 *a*Exodus 32:6   10:11 *a*NU-Text omits *all.*   10:23 *a*NU-Text omits *for me.*   *b*NU-Text omits *for me.*   10:26 *a*Psalm 24:1   10:28 *a*NU-Text omits the rest of this verse.   *b*Psalm 24:1

erty judged by another *man's* conscience? 30 But if I partake with thanks, why am I evil spoken of for *the food* over which I give thanks?

31 Therefore, whether you eat or drink, or whatever you do, do all to the glory of God. 32 Give no offense, either to the Jews or to the Greeks or to the church of God, 33 just as I also please all *men* in all *things,* not seeking my own profit, but the *profit* of many, that they may be saved.

11 Imitate me, just as I also *imitate* Christ.

2 Now I praise you, brethren, that you remember me in all things and keep the traditions just as I delivered *them* to you. 3 But I want you to know that the head of every man is Christ, the head of woman *is* man, and the head of Christ *is* God. 4 Every man praying or prophesying, having *his* head covered, dishonors his head. 5 But every woman who prays or prophesies with *her* head uncovered dishonors her head, for that is one and the same as if her head were shaved. 6 For if a woman is not covered, let her also be shorn. But if it is shameful for a woman to be shorn or shaved, let her be covered. 7 For a man indeed ought not to cover *his* head, since he is the image and glory of God; but woman is the glory of man. 8 For man is not from woman, but woman from man. 9 Nor was man created for the woman, but woman for the man. 10 For this reason the woman ought to have *a symbol of* authority on *her* head, because of the angels. 11 Nevertheless, neither *is* man independent of woman, nor woman independent of man, in the Lord. 12 For as woman *came* from man, even so man also *comes* through woman; but all things are from God. 13 Judge among yourselves. Is it proper for a woman to pray to God with her head uncovered? 14 Does not even nature itself teach you that if a man has long hair, it is a dishonor to him? 15 But if a woman has long hair, it is a glory to her; for *her* hair is given to her[a] for a covering. 16 But if anyone seems to be conten-

tious, we have no such custom, nor *do* the churches of God.

17 Now in giving these instructions I do not praise *you,* since you come together not for the better but for the worse. 18 For first of all, when you come together as a church, I hear that there are divisions among you, and in part I believe it. 19 For there must also be factions among you, that those who are approved may be recognized among you. 20 Therefore when you come together in one place, it is not to eat the Lord's Supper. 21 For in eating, each one takes his own supper ahead of *others;* and one is hungry and another is drunk. 22 What! Do you not have houses to eat and drink in? Or do you despise the church of God and shame those who have nothing? What shall I say to you? Shall I praise you in this? I do not praise *you.*

23 For I received from the Lord that which I also delivered to you: that the Lord Jesus on the *same* night in which He was betrayed took bread; 24 and when He had given thanks, He broke *it* and said, "Take, eat;[a] this is My body which is broken[b] for you; do this in remembrance of Me." 25 In the same manner *He* also *took* the cup after supper, saying, "This cup is the new covenant in My blood. This do, as often as you drink *it,* in remembrance of Me."

26 For as often as you eat this bread and drink this cup, you proclaim the Lord's death till He comes.

27 Therefore whoever eats this bread or drinks *this* cup of the Lord in an unworthy manner will be guilty of the body and blood[a] of the Lord. 28 But let a man examine himself, and so let him eat of the bread and drink of the cup. 29 For he who eats and drinks in an unworthy manner[a] eats and drinks judgment to himself, not discerning the Lord's[b] body. 30 For this reason many *are* weak and sick among you, and many sleep. 31 For if we would judge ourselves, we would not be judged. 32 But when we are judged, we are chastened by the Lord, that we may not be condemned with the world.

33 Therefore, my brethren, when you come together to eat, wait for

---

11:15 [a]M-Text omits *to her.*   11:24 [a]NU-Text omits *Take, eat.*   [b]NU-Text omits *broken.*
11:27 [a]NU-Text and M-Text read *the blood.*   11:29 [a]NU-Text omits *in an unworthy manner.*
[b]NU-Text omits *Lord's.*

one another. 34 But if anyone is hungry, let him eat at home, lest you come together for judgment. And the rest I will set in order when I come.

12 Now concerning spiritual *gifts,* brethren, I do not want you to be ignorant: 2 You know that[a] you were Gentiles, carried away to these dumb idols, however you were led. 3 Therefore I make known to you that no one speaking by the Spirit of God calls Jesus accursed, and no one can say that Jesus is Lord except by the Holy Spirit.

4 There are diversities of gifts, but the same Spirit. 5 There are differences of ministries, but the same Lord. 6 And there are diversities of activities, but it is the same God who works all in all. 7 But the manifestation of the Spirit is given to each one for the profit *of all:* 8 for to one is given the word of wisdom through the Spirit, to another the word of knowledge through the same Spirit, 9 to another faith by the same Spirit, to another gifts of healings by the same[a] Spirit, 10 to another the working of miracles, to another prophecy, to another discerning of spirits, to another *different* kinds of tongues, to another the interpretation of tongues. 11 But one and the same Spirit works all these things, distributing to each one individually as He wills.

12 For as the body is one and has many members, but all the members of that one body, being many, are one body, so also *is* Christ. 13 For by one Spirit we were all baptized into one body—whether Jews or Greeks, whether slaves or free—and have all been made to drink into[a] one Spirit. 14 For in fact the body is not one member but many.

15 If the foot should say, "Because I am not a hand, I am not of the body," is it therefore not of the body? 16 And if the ear should say, "Because I am not an eye, I am not of the body," is it therefore not of the body? 17 If the whole body *were* an eye, where *would* be the hearing? If the whole *were* hearing, where *would* be the smelling? 18 But now God has set the members, each one of them, in the body just as He pleased.

19 And if they *were* all one member, where *would* the body *be?* 20 But now indeed *there are* many members, yet one body. 21 And the eye cannot say to the hand, "I have no need of you"; nor again the head to the feet, "I have no need of you." 22 No, much rather, those members of the body which seem to be weaker are necessary. 23 And those *members* of the body which we think to be less honorable, on these we bestow greater honor; and our unpresentable *parts* have greater modesty, 24 but our presentable *parts* have no need. But God composed the body, having given greater honor to that *part* which lacks it, 25 that there should be no schism in the body, but *that* the members should have the same care for one another. 26 And if one member suffers, all the members suffer with *it;* or if one member is honored, all the members rejoice with *it.*

27 Now you are the body of Christ, and members individually. 28 And God has appointed these in the church: first apostles, second prophets, third teachers, after that miracles, then gifts of healings, helps, administrations, varieties of tongues. 29 *Are* all apostles? *Are* all prophets? *Are* all teachers? *Are* all workers of miracles? 30 Do all have gifts of healings? Do all speak with tongues? Do all interpret? 31 But earnestly desire the best[a] gifts. And yet I show you a more excellent way.

13 Though I speak with the tongues of men and of angels, but have not love, I have become sounding brass or a clanging cymbal. 2 And though I have *the gift of* prophecy, and understand all mysteries and all knowledge, and though I have all faith, so that I could remove mountains, but have not love, I am nothing. 3 And though I bestow all my goods to feed *the poor,* and though I give my body to be burned,[a] but have not love, it profits me nothing.

4 Love suffers long *and* is kind; love does not envy; love does not parade itself, is not puffed up; 5 does not behave rudely, does not seek its own, is not provoked, thinks

---

12:2 [a]NU-Text and M-Text add *when.*   12:9 [a]NU-Text reads *one.*   12:13 [a]NU-Text omits *into.*
12:31 [a]NU-Text reads *greater.*   13:3 [a]NU-Text reads *so I may boast.*

Washing the Windows of the Soul

If you tune in positive thoughts and censor out negative ones, will these dynamic exercises of a daily, disciplined faith keep the windows of your soul sparkling continually? No, not completely. As we all know, accidents can dent a new car; spills can stain clean clothes, upsets can frustrate a patient person; thoughtless interruptions can disturb quiet meditation.

In Holland, Dutch people wash their windows every morning, even if there is no dirt on them, no rainfall to stain the glass, no heavy dew to dry and leave a misty film.

Faith is washing the windows of your soul, every morning beginning the new day bright with God's love, and each night washing away the film of negativity.

Have you ever noticed how quickly windows that were once clean can lose their sparkle? A film comes over them and clouds the reflection of the sun.

Is the sparkle of faith gone from the window panes of your soul? Is the reflection of God's love clouded in your life? Ask the Holy Spirit to come in each morning and evening to wash the windows of your soul. Remember, the Spirit of God lives in you to brighten your life with love and faith!

Lord, make my life a window for Your light to shine through, a mirror to reflect Your love to everyone I meet. Amen.

no evil; 6 does not rejoice in iniquity, but rejoices in the truth; 7 bears all things, believes all things, hopes all things, endures all things.

8 Love never fails. But whether *there are* prophecies, they will fail; whether *there are* tongues, they will cease; whether *there is* knowledge, it will vanish away. 9 For we know in part and we prophesy in part. 10 But when that which is perfect has come, then that which is in part will be done away.

11 When I was a child, I spoke as a child, I understood as a child, I thought as a child; but when I became a man, I put away childish things. 12 For now we see in a mirror, dimly, but then face to face. Now I know in part, but then I shall know just as I also am known.

13 And now abide faith, hope, love, these three; but the greatest of these *is* love.

14 Pursue love, and desire spiritual *gifts*, but especially that you may prophesy. 2 For he who speaks in a tongue does not speak to men but to God, for no one understands *him;* however, in the spirit he speaks mysteries. 3 But he who prophesies speaks edification and exhortation and comfort to men. 4 He who speaks in a tongue edifies himself, but he who prophesies edifies the church. 5 I wish you all spoke with tongues, but even more that you prophesied; for*a* he who prophesies *is* greater than he who speaks with tongues, unless indeed he interprets, that the church may receive edification.

6 But now, brethren, if I come to you speaking with tongues, what shall I profit you unless I speak to you either by revelation, by knowledge, by prophesying, or by teaching? 7 Even things without life, whether flute or harp, when they make a sound, unless they make a distinction in the sounds, how will it be known what is piped or played? 8 For if the trumpet makes an uncertain sound, who will prepare for battle? 9 So likewise you, unless you utter by the tongue words easy to understand, how will it be known what is spoken? For you will be speaking into the air. 10 There are, it

may be, so many kinds of languages in the world, and none of them *is* without significance. 11 Therefore, if I do not know the meaning of the language, I shall be a foreigner to him who speaks, and he who speaks *will be* a foreigner to me. 12 Even so you, since you are zealous for spiritual *gifts, let it be* for the edification of the church *that* you seek to excel.

13 Therefore let him who speaks in a tongue pray that he may interpret. 14 For if I pray in a tongue, my spirit prays, but my understanding is unfruitful. 15 What is *the conclusion* then? I will pray with the spirit, and I will also pray with the understanding. I will sing with the spirit, and I will also sing with the understanding. 16 Otherwise, if you bless with the spirit, how will he who occupies the place of the uninformed say "Amen" at your giving of thanks, since he does not understand what you say? 17 For you indeed give thanks well, but the other is not edified.

18 I thank my God I speak with tongues more than you all; 19 yet in the church I would rather speak five words with my understanding, that I may teach others also, than ten thousand words in a tongue.

20 Brethren, do not be children in understanding; however, in malice be babes, but in understanding be mature. 21 In the law it is written:

"With men of other tongues and
   other lips
I will speak to this people;
And yet, for all that, they will
   not hear Me,"*a*

says the Lord. 22 Therefore tongues are for a sign, not to those who believe but to unbelievers; but prophesying is not for unbelievers but for those who believe. 23 Therefore if the whole church comes together in one place, and all speak with tongues, and there come in *those who are* uninformed or unbelievers, will they not say that you are out of your mind? 24 But if all prophesy, and an unbeliever or an uninformed person comes in, he is convinced by all, he is convicted by all. 25 And thus*a* the secrets of his heart are revealed; and so, falling

14:5 *a*NU-Text reads *and.*   14:21 *a*Isaiah 28:11, 12   14:25 *a*NU-Text omits *And thus.*

down on *his* face, he will worship God and report that God is truly among you.

26 How is it then, brethren? Whenever you come together, each of you has a psalm, has a teaching, has a tongue, has a revelation, has an interpretation. Let all things be done for edification. 27 If anyone speaks in a tongue, *let there be* two or at the most three, *each* in turn, and let one interpret. 28 But if there is no interpreter, let him keep silent in church, and let him speak to himself and to God. 29 Let two or three prophets speak, and let the others judge. 30 But if *anything* is revealed to another who sits by, let the first keep silent. 31 For you can all prophesy one by one, that all may learn and all may be encouraged. 32 And the spirits of the prophets are subject to the prophets. 33 For God is not *the author* of confusion but of peace, as in all the churches of the saints.

34 Let your*ᵃ* women keep silent in the churches, for they are not permitted to speak; but *they are* to be submissive, as the law also says. 35 And if they want to learn something, let them ask their own husbands at home; for it is shameful for women to speak in church.

36 Or did the word of God come *originally* from you? Or *was it* you only that it reached? 37 If anyone thinks himself to be a prophet or spiritual, let him acknowledge that the things which I write to you are the commandments of the Lord. 38 But if anyone is ignorant, let him be ignorant.*ᵃ*

39 Therefore, brethren, desire earnestly to prophesy, and do not forbid to speak with tongues. 40 Let all things be done decently and in order.

15 Moreover, brethren, I declare to you the gospel which I preached to you, which also you received and in which you stand, 2 by which also you are saved, if you hold fast that word which I preached to you—unless you believed in vain.

3 For I delivered to you first of all that which I also received: that Christ died for our sins according to the Scriptures, 4 and that He was buried, and that He rose again the third day

according to the Scriptures, 5 and that He was seen by Cephas, then by the twelve. 6 After that He was seen by over five hundred brethren at once, of whom the greater part remain to the present, but some have fallen asleep. 7 After that He was seen by James, then by all the apostles. 8 Then last of all He was seen by me also, as by one born out of due time.

9 For I am the least of the apostles, who am not worthy to be called an apostle, because I persecuted the church of God. 10 But by the grace of God I am what I am, and His grace toward me was not in vain; but I labored more abundantly than they all, yet not I, but the grace of God *which was* with me. 11 Therefore, whether *it was* I or they, so we preach and so you believed.

12 Now if Christ is preached that He has been raised from the dead, how do some among you say that there is no resurrection of the dead? 13 But if there is no resurrection of the dead, then Christ is not risen. 14 And if Christ is not risen, then our preaching *is* empty and your faith *is* also empty. 15 Yes, and we are found false witnesses of God, because we have testified of God that He raised up Christ, whom He did not raise up—if in fact the dead do not rise. 16 For if *the* dead do not rise, then Christ is not risen. 17 And if Christ is not risen, your faith *is* futile; you are still in your sins! 18 Then also those who have fallen asleep in Christ have perished. 19 If in this life only we have hope in Christ, we are of all men the most pitiable.

20 But now Christ is risen from the dead, *and* has become the firstfruits of those who have fallen asleep. 21 For since by man *came* death, by Man also *came* the resurrection of the dead. 22 For as in Adam all die, even so in Christ all shall be made alive. 23 But each one in his own order: Christ the firstfruits, afterward those *who are* Christ's at His coming. 24 Then *comes* the end, when He delivers the kingdom to God the Father, when He puts an end to all rule and all authority and power. 25 For He must reign till He has put all enemies under His feet. 26 The last enemy

14:34 ᵃNU-Text omits *your.*   14:38 ᵃNU-Text reads *If anyone does not recognize this, he is not recognized.*

that will be destroyed *is* death. 27 For *"He has put all things under His feet."*[a] But when He says "all things are put under *Him*," *it is* evident that He who put all things under Him is excepted. 28 Now when all things are made subject to Him, then the Son Himself will also be subject to Him who put all things under Him, that God may be all in all.

29 Otherwise, what will they do who are baptized for the dead, if the dead do not rise at all? Why then are they baptized for the dead? 30 And why do we stand in jeopardy every hour? 31 I affirm, by the boasting in you which I have in Christ Jesus our Lord, I die daily. 32 If, in the manner of men, I have fought with beasts at Ephesus, what advantage *is it* to me? If *the* dead do not rise, *"Let us eat and drink, for tomorrow we die!"*[a]

33 Do not be deceived: "Evil company corrupts good habits." 34 Awake to righteousness, and do not sin; for some do not have the knowledge of God. I speak *this* to your shame.

35 But someone will say, "How are the dead raised up? And with what body do they come?" 36 Foolish one, what you sow is not made alive unless it dies. 37 And what you sow, you do not sow that body that shall be, but mere grain—perhaps wheat or some other *grain.* 38 But God gives it a body as He pleases, and to each seed its own body.

39 All flesh *is* not the same flesh, but *there is* one *kind of* flesh[a] of men, another flesh of animals, another of fish, *and* another of birds.

40 *There are* also celestial bodies and terrestrial bodies; but the glory of the celestial *is* one, and the *glory* of the terrestrial *is* another. 41 *There is* one glory of the sun, another glory of the moon, and another glory of the stars; for *one* star differs from *another* star in glory.

42 So also *is* the resurrection of the dead. *The body* is sown in corruption, it is raised in incorruption. 43 It is sown in dishonor, it is raised in glory. It is sown in weakness, it is raised in power. 44 It is sown a natural body,

it is raised a spiritual body. There is a natural body, and there is a spiritual body. 45 And so it is written, *"The first man Adam became a living being."*[a] The last Adam *became* a life-giving spirit.

46 However, the spiritual is not first, but the natural, and afterward the spiritual. 47 The first man *was* of the earth, *made* of dust; the second Man *is* the Lord[a] from heaven. 48 As *was* the *man* of dust, so also *are* those *who are made* of dust; and as *is* the heavenly *Man,* so also *are* those *who are* heavenly. 49 And as we have borne the image of the *man* of dust, we shall also bear[a] the image of the heavenly *Man.*

50 Now this I say, brethren, that flesh and blood cannot inherit the kingdom of God; nor does corruption inherit incorruption. 51 Behold, I tell you a mystery: We shall not all sleep, but we shall all be changed— 52 in a moment, in the twinkling of an eye, at the last trumpet. For the trumpet will sound, and the dead will be raised incorruptible, and we shall be changed. 53 For this corruptible must put on incorruption, and this mortal *must* put on immortality. 54 So when this corruptible has put on incorruption, and this mortal has put on immortality, then shall be brought to pass the saying that is written: *"Death is swallowed up in victory."*[a]

55 *"O Death, where is your sting?*[a]
   O Hades, where is your
      victory?"*[b]

56 The sting of death *is* sin, and the strength of sin *is* the law. 57 But thanks *be* to God, who gives us the victory through our Lord Jesus Christ.

58 Therefore, my beloved brethren, be steadfast, immovable, always abounding in the work of the Lord, knowing that your labor is not in vain in the Lord.

16 Now concerning the collection for the saints, as I have given orders to the churches of Galatia, so you must do also: 2 On the first *day*

15:27 [a]Psalm 8:6   15:32 [a]Isaiah 22:13   15:39 [a]NU-Text and M-Text omit *of flesh.*   15:45 [a]Genesis 2:7   15:47 [a]NU-Text omits *the Lord.*   15:49 [a]M-Text reads *let us also bear.*   15:54 [a]Isaiah 25:8   15:55 [a]Hosea 13:14   [b]NU-Text reads *O Death, where is your victory? O Death, where is your sting?*

Success in Failure

Often faith meets success at the point of failure. For example, the pole vaulter who runs and then vaults over the bar a little higher each time never really knows how high he can jump until he fails to scale the bar.

He succeeds when he fails!

For failure isn't a matter of not reaching your goal! Failure is failing to give your project all that you have!

Success is achieving the maximum of your potential in the situation you are in. The apostle Paul encouraged his readers to "be steadfast, immovable, always abounding in the work of the Lord, knowing that your labor is not in vain in the Lord" (1 Cor. 15:58). When you honestly have attempted your ultimate best, then you have been successful, in spite of failure. The people who are really failures are the people who set their standards so low, keep the bar at such a safe level, that they never run the risk of failure.

Faith is daring to face an embarrassing failure. It's only after the pole vaulter knocks down the bar raised to its highest level that he knows he's jumped as high as he can--today!

Success comes at the point where we can't do any better than we are doing at this moment. The applause doesn't come until you've given all you have to give. Spectators love the winners and they love the losers, as long as both give it their best!

Make this prayer your own: *Dear God, thank You for this boost You have given me today. I understand now that I really am not a failure. I am succeeding because I am doing my very best. Thank You for Your confidence in me. I will keep on keeping on! To God be the glory. Amen.*

of the week let each one of you lay something aside, storing up as he may prosper, that there be no collections when I come. 3 And when I come, whomever you approve by *your* letters I will send to bear your gift to Jerusalem. 4 But if it is fitting that I go also, they will go with me.

5 Now I will come to you when I pass through Macedonia (for I am passing through Macedonia). 6 And it may be that I will remain, or even spend the winter with you, that you may send me on my journey, wherever I go. 7 For I do not wish to see you now on the way; but I hope to stay a while with you, if the Lord permits.

8 But I will tarry in Ephesus until Pentecost. 9 For a great and effective door has opened to me, and *there are* many adversaries.

10 And if Timothy comes, see that he may be with you without fear; for he does the work of the Lord, as I also *do*. 11 Therefore let no one despise him. But send him on his journey in peace, that he may come to me; for I am waiting for him with the brethren.

12 Now concerning *our* brother Apollos, I strongly urged him to come to you with the brethren, but he was quite unwilling to come at this time; however, he will come when he has a convenient time.

13 Watch, stand fast in the faith, be brave, be strong. 14 Let all *that* you *do* be done with love.

15 I urge you, brethren—you know the household of Stephanas, that it is the firstfruits of Achaia, and *that* they have devoted themselves to the ministry of the saints— 16 that you also submit to such, and to everyone who works and labors with *us*.

17 I am glad about the coming of Stephanas, Fortunatus, and Achaicus, for what was lacking on your part they supplied. 18 For they refreshed my spirit and yours. Therefore acknowledge such men.

19 The churches of Asia greet you. Aquila and Priscilla greet you heartily in the Lord, with the church that is in their house. 20 All the brethren greet you.

Greet one another with a holy kiss.

21 The salutation with my own hand—Paul's.

22 If anyone does not love the Lord Jesus Christ, let him be accursed.*a* O Lord, come!*b*

23 The grace of our Lord Jesus Christ *be* with you. 24 My love *be* with you all in Christ Jesus. Amen.

16:22 *a*Greek *anathema*   *b*Aramaic *Maranatha*

Second Corinthians

Overview of Second Corinthians

The second letter from Paul to the Corinthians is a great example of expecting the best in others. It is also the most emotional of all Paul's letters. Writing in A.D. 55, Paul corresponds with a church that had a history of serious problems. This church is shaken by false teachers who have undermined Paul's work in Corinth. In this Epistle, Paul humbly defends his apostleship, and appeals for separation

from defilement and for fulfillment of the Corinthian believers' promises to God in the ministry of giving.

Paul is joyful to learn, upon Titus' return from Corinth,
that the church has repented and returned to a positive,
productive Christian lifestyle. The book overflows with
promises and affirmations as he continues to build up the
believers. "If anyone *is* in Christ, *he is* a new creation; old
things have passed away; behold, all things have become
new" (2 Cor. 5:17).

The Corinthian church, exposed to persecution and cultural isolation, hears Paul continue to exhort them to press
on with God's support: "*We are* hard pressed on every side,
yet not crushed; *we are* perplexed, but not in despair; persecuted, but not forsaken; struck down, but not destroyed" (2
Cor. 4:8, 9).

Paul told the Corinthians to expect the best in their lives
and in other people. To do so, they needed to connect with
God's power. "Not that we are sufficient of ourselves to
think of anything as *being* from ourselves, but our sufficiency *is* from God" (2 Cor. 3:5).

Faith calls us to believe in the best. If you believe the
best will happen and it does not, you lose nothing! For you
have the joy of anticipating something wonderful. The happiness that comes through positive anticipation pays divi-
dends instantaneously. Each smile, every happy heartbeat,
every elegant thought is an immediate reward. Paul had
the skill and sensitivity to motivate, inspire, and remain
devoted to the Corinthians in their time of need.

Jesus in Second Corinthians

Christ is presented as the believer's comfort (1:5), triumph (2:14), Lord (4:5), light (4:6), judge (5:10), reconciliation (5:19), substitute (5:21), gift (9:15), owner (10:7), and
power (12:9) in this Pauline Epistle.

Keys to Second Corinthians

Key Word: Defense. Paul speaks in defense of his apostolic credentials and authority in this book. There is still a
rebellious minority in the church at Corinth. False teachers have influenced this group to dismiss Paul's teachings
as unworthy. Paul, while forced to take steps to quell the
dissension, expresses his joy that the true gospel of Jesus

Christ has triumphed in Corinth, and he acknowledges the godly sorrow of the true believers.

Key Verses: "For we do not preach ourselves, but Christ Jesus the Lord, and ourselves your bondservants for Jesus' sake. For it is the God who commmanded light to shine out of darkness, who has shone in our hearts to *give* the light of the knowledge of the glory of God in the face of Jesus Christ" (4:5, 6).

"Therefore, if anyone *is* in Christ, *he is* a new creation; old things have passed away; behold, all things have become new. Now all things *are* of God, who has reconciled us to Himself through Jesus Christ, and has given us the ministry of reconciliation, that is, that God was in Christ reconciling the world to Himself, not imputing their trespasses to them, and has committed to us the word of reconciliation" (5:17–19).

Key Chapters: Second Corinthians 8–9. Chapters 8 and 9 of this book are one unit, revealing God's plan for giving. This section reveals the principle for giving (8:1–6), the purpose for giving (8:7–15), the policy to be followed in giving (8:16—9:5), and the promises to be realized in giving (9:6–15).

1 Paul, an apostle of Jesus Christ by the will of God, and Timothy *our* brother,

To the church of God which is at Corinth, with all the saints who are in all Achaia:

2 Grace to you and peace from God our Father and the Lord Jesus Christ.

3 Blessed *be* the God and Father of our Lord Jesus Christ, the Father of mercies and God of all comfort, 4 who comforts us in all our tribulation, that we may be able to comfort those who are in any trouble, with the comfort with which we ourselves are comforted by God. 5 For as the sufferings of Christ abound in us, so our consolation also abounds through Christ. 6 Now if we are afflicted, *it is* for your consolation and salvation, which is effective for enduring the same sufferings which we also suffer. Or if we are comforted, *it is* for your consolation and salvation. 7 And our hope for you *is* steadfast, because we know that as you are partakers of the sufferings, so

Speak of God's Presence

A greeting in biblical times served as a constant reminder of God's presence among men and women. Not one day passed when the name of God was not invoked as a blessing to give hope, or encouragement, or exhortation.

This practice has continued for thousands of years. Many common phrases in the everyday language of the Middle East today contain the name of God and share His presence:

> Good morning, may God's light be upon you.
> Hurry up, let's go. O God, help.
> Hello, may the peace of God come upon you.
> May the peace of God be with you also.
> How is it going? How is God with you?
> Take care, go under the protection and hand of God.
> Get well soon. May God give you health and strength.

This style of language is also reflected throughout the New Testament. Many of the Epistles include greetings and benedictions similar to those heard in the Middle East today.

> But may the God of all grace . . . perfect, establish, strengthen, and settle *you*. (1 Pet. 5:10)

> Grace to you and peace from God our Father and the Lord Jesus Christ. (2 Cor. 1:2)

> And *whatever* you do in word or deed, *do* all in the name of the Lord Jesus, giving thanks to God the Father through Him. (Col. 3:17)

By keeping the name of God in everyday language, the biblical reader as well as modern men and women in the Middle East is constantly reminded of God's presence and power at work in their lives. It is recognition of God's involvement in even the most common events.

In today's society, it may seem awkward to speak of God's existence and presence so openly to strangers. However, we can also demonstrate God's love in action to those with whom we come in contact. The writer of Hebrews tells us to "consider one another in order to stir up love and good works . . . exhorting *one another*" as we see the days pass until Jesus returns (Heb. 10:24–25).

It is not enough to simply love in word, but we must love in deed. By uplifting, encouraging, planting God's positive thoughts, meeting needs, healing hurts, and speaking of our faith, we truly make the presence of God known and loved in others' lives.

also *you will partake* of the consolation.

8 For we do not want you to be ignorant, brethren, of our trouble which came to us in Asia: that we were burdened beyond measure, above strength, so that we despaired even of life. 9 Yes, we had the sentence of death in ourselves, that we should not trust in ourselves but in God who raises the dead, 10 who delivered us from so great a death, and does*a* deliver us; in whom we trust that He will still deliver *us,* 11 you also helping together in prayer for us, that thanks may be given by many persons on our*a* behalf for the gift *granted* to us through many.

12 For our boasting is this: the testimony of our conscience that we conducted ourselves in the world in simplicity and godly sincerity, not with fleshly wisdom but by the grace of God, and more abundantly toward you. 13 For we are not writing any other things to you than what you read or understand. Now I trust you will understand, even to the end 14 (as also you have understood us in part), that we are your boast as you also *are* ours, in the day of the Lord Jesus.

15 And in this confidence I intended to come to you before, that you might have a second benefit— 16 to pass by way of you to Macedonia, to come again from Macedonia to you, and be helped by you on my way to Judea. 17 Therefore, when I was planning this, did I do it lightly? Or the things I plan, do I plan according to the flesh, that with me there should be Yes, Yes, and No, No? 18 But *as* God *is* faithful, our word to you was not Yes and No. 19 For the Son of God, Jesus Christ, who was preached among you by us—by me, Silvanus, and Timothy—was not Yes and No, but in Him was Yes. 20 For all the promises of God in Him *are* Yes, and in Him Amen, to the glory of God through us. 21 Now He who establishes us with you in Christ and has anointed us *is* God, 22 who also has sealed us and given us the Spirit in our hearts as a guarantee.

23 Moreover I call God as witness against my soul, that to spare you I came no more to Corinth. 24 Not that we have dominion over your faith, but are fellow workers for your joy; for by faith you stand.

2 But I determined this within myself, that I would not come again to you in sorrow. 2 For if I make you sorrowful, then who is he who makes me glad but the one who is made sorrowful by me?

3 And I wrote this very thing to you, lest, when I came, I should have sorrow over those from whom I ought to have joy, having confidence in you all that my joy is *the joy* of you all. 4 For out of much affliction and anguish of heart I wrote to you, with many tears, not that you should be grieved, but that you might know the love which I have so abundantly for you.

5 But if anyone has caused grief, he has not grieved me, but all of you to some extent—not to be too severe. 6 This punishment which *was inflicted* by the majority *is* sufficient for such a man, 7 so that, on the contrary, you *ought* rather to forgive and comfort *him,* lest perhaps such a one be swallowed up with too much sorrow. 8 Therefore I urge you to reaffirm *your* love to him. 9 For to this end I also wrote, that I might put you to the test, whether you are obedient in all things. 10 Now whom you forgive anything, I also *forgive.* For if indeed I have forgiven anything, I have forgiven*a* that one for your sakes in the presence of Christ, 11 lest Satan should take advantage of us; for we are not ignorant of his devices.

12 Furthermore, when I came to Troas to *preach* Christ's gospel, and a door was opened to me by the Lord, 13 I had no rest in my spirit, because I did not find Titus my brother; but taking my leave of them, I departed for Macedonia.

14 Now thanks *be* to God who always leads us in triumph in Christ, and through us diffuses the fragrance of His knowledge in every place. 15 For we are to God the fragrance of Christ among those who are being saved and among those who are perishing. 16 To the one *we are* the aroma of death *leading* to death, and to the other the aroma of life *leading*

1:10 *a*NU-Text reads *shall.*   1:11 *a*M-Text reads *your behalf.*   2:10 *a*NU-Text reads *indeed, what I have forgiven, if I have forgiven anything, I did it for your sakes.*

to life. And who *is* sufficient for these things? 17 For we are not, as so many,*a* peddling the word of God; but as of sincerity, but as from God, we speak in the sight of God in Christ.

3 Do we begin again to commend ourselves? Or do we need, as some *others,* epistles of commendation to you or *letters* of commendation from you? 2 You are our epistle written in our hearts, known and read by all men; 3 clearly *you are* an epistle of Christ, ministered by us, written not with ink but by the Spirit of the living God, not on tablets of stone but on tablets of flesh, *that is,* of the heart.

4 And we have such trust through Christ toward God. 5 Not that we are sufficient of ourselves to think of anything as *being* from ourselves, but our sufficiency *is* from God, 6 who also made us sufficient as ministers of the new covenant, not of the letter but of the Spirit;*a* for the letter kills, but the Spirit gives life.

7 But if the ministry of death, written *and* engraved on stones, was glorious, so that the children of Israel could not look steadily at the face of Moses because of the glory of his countenance, which *glory* was passing away, 8 how will the ministry of the Spirit not be more glorious? 9 For if the ministry of condemnation *had* glory, the ministry of righteousness exceeds much more in glory. 10 For even what was made glorious had no glory in this respect, because of the glory that excels. 11 For if what is passing away *was* glorious, what remains *is* much more glorious.

12 Therefore, since we have such hope, we use great boldness of speech— 13 unlike Moses, *who* put a veil over his face so that the children of Israel could not look steadily at the end of what was passing away. 14 But their minds were blinded. For until this day the same veil remains unlifted in the reading of the Old Testament, because the *veil* is taken away in Christ. 15 But even to this day, when Moses is read, a veil lies on their heart. 16 Nevertheless when one turns to the Lord, the veil is taken away. 17 Now the Lord is the Spirit; and where the Spirit of the Lord *is,* there *is* liberty. 18 But we all,

with unveiled face, beholding as in a mirror the glory of the Lord, are being transformed into the same image from glory to glory, just as by the Spirit of the Lord.

4 Therefore, since we have this ministry, as we have received mercy, we do not lose heart. 2 But we have renounced the hidden things of shame, not walking in craftiness nor handling the word of God deceitfully, but by manifestation of the truth commending ourselves to every man's conscience in the sight of God. 3 But even if our gospel is veiled, it is veiled to those who are perishing, 4 whose minds the god of this age has blinded, who do not believe, lest the light of the gospel of the glory of Christ, who is the image of God, should shine on them. 5 For we do not preach ourselves, but Christ Jesus the Lord, and ourselves your bondservants for Jesus' sake. 6 For it is the God who commanded light to shine out of darkness, who has shone in our hearts to *give* the light of the knowledge of the glory of God in the face of Jesus Christ.

7 But we have this treasure in earthen vessels, that the excellence of the power may be of God and not of us. 8 *We are* hard pressed on every side, yet not crushed; *we are* perplexed, but not in despair; 9 persecuted, but not forsaken; struck down, but not destroyed— 10 always carrying about in the body the dying of the Lord Jesus, that the life of Jesus also may be manifested in our body. 11 For we who live are always delivered to death for Jesus' sake, that the life of Jesus also may be manifested in our mortal flesh. 12 So then death is working in us, but life in you.

13 And since we have the same spirit of faith, according to what is written, *"I believed and therefore I spoke,"a* we also believe and therefore speak, 14 knowing that He who raised up the Lord Jesus will also raise us up with Jesus, and will present *us* with you. 15 For all things *are* for your sakes, that grace, having spread through the many, may cause thanksgiving to abound to the glory of God.

16 Therefore we do not lose heart.

2:17 *a*M-Text reads *the rest.*   3:6 *a*Or *spirit*   4:13 *a*Psalm 116:10

Breathing Faith

It's important to understand that a believer is a normal person—that walking by faith (2 Cor. 5:7) is the mark of normality. A persistently negative and cynical attitude is a mark of emotional illness.

Birds were designed to fly. The air under the wings of a bird is a natural habitat of the flying fowl.

Water is the natural habitat of the fish.

Faith is the native air to be breathed in and out by human beings.

It is normal to have faith. It is abnormal to be cynical. Therefore you welcome all stimuli that would encourage you to have faith. Reject all negative forces that would destroy faith and replace it with unbelief.

When you practice positive belief, you are more controlled by positive emotions—love, joy, courage, faith, enthusiasm.

These are the qualities of an emotionally healthy person. Persons who are not breathing the natural air of faith, but are breathing the polluted air of doubt and unbelief, are quickly susceptible to a lower morality. They are quickly consumed by negative emotions—all of which are measured and marked as symptoms of something less than true wholeness and health as a human being.

You were created to be a believer!

Faith is finding your native air.

Give gratitude to God: *Thank You, Father, for causing me to be a normal, healthy human being by motivating me to walk the walk of faith. Amen.*

Even though our outward man is perishing, yet the inward *man* is being renewed day by day. 17 For our light affliction, which is but for a moment, is working for us a far more exceeding *and* eternal weight of glory, 18 while we do not look at the things which are seen, but at the things which are not seen. For the things which are seen *are* temporary, but the things which are not seen *are* eternal.

5 For we know that if our earthly house, *this* tent, is destroyed, we have a building from God, a house not made with hands, eternal in the heavens. 2 For in this we groan, earnestly desiring to be clothed with our habitation which is from heaven, 3 if indeed, having been clothed, we shall not be found naked. 4 For we who are in *this* tent groan, being burdened, not because we want to be unclothed, but further clothed, that mortality may be swallowed up by life. 5 Now He who has prepared us for this very thing *is* God, who also has given us the Spirit as a guarantee.

6 So *we are* always confident, knowing that while we are at home in the body we are absent from the Lord. 7 For we walk by faith, not by sight. 8 We are confident, yes, well pleased rather to be absent from the body and to be present with the Lord. 9 Therefore we make it our aim, whether present or absent, to be well pleasing to Him. 10 For we must all appear before the judgment seat of Christ, that each one may receive the things *done* in the body, according to what he has done, whether good or bad. 11 Knowing, therefore, the terror of the Lord, we persuade men; but we are well known to God, and I also trust are well known in your consciences.

12 For we do not commend ourselves again to you, but give you opportunity to boast on our behalf, that you may have *an answer* for those who boast in appearance and not in heart. 13 For if we are beside ourselves, *it is* for God; or if we are of sound mind, *it is* for you. 14 For the love of Christ compels us, because we judge thus: that if One died for all, then all died; 15 and He died for all, that those who live should live no longer for themselves, but for Him who died for them and rose again.

16 Therefore, from now on, we regard no one according to the flesh. Even though we have known Christ according to the flesh, yet now we know *Him thus* no longer. 17 Therefore, if anyone *is* in Christ, *he is* a new creation; old things have passed away; behold, all things have become new. 18 Now all things *are* of God, who has reconciled us to Himself through Jesus Christ, and has given us the ministry of reconciliation, 19 that is, that God was in Christ reconciling the world to Himself, not imputing their trespasses to them, and has committed to us the word of reconciliation.

20 Now then, we are ambassadors for Christ, as though God were pleading through us: we implore *you* on Christ's behalf, be reconciled to God. 21 For He made Him who knew no sin *to be* sin for us, that we might become the righteousness of God in Him.

6 We then, *as* workers together *with Him* also plead with *you* not to receive the grace of God in vain. 2 For He says:

> "In an acceptable time I have
>   heard you,
> And in the day of salvation I
>   have helped you."[a]

Behold, now *is* the accepted time; behold, now *is* the day of salvation. 3 We give no offense in anything, that our ministry may not be blamed. 4 But in all *things* we commend ourselves as ministers of God: in much patience, in tribulations, in needs, in distresses, 5 in stripes, in imprisonments, in tumults, in labors, in sleeplessness, in fastings; 6 by purity, by knowledge, by longsuffering, by kindness, by the Holy Spirit, by sincere love, 7 by the word of truth, by the power of God, by the armor of righteousness on the right hand and on the left, 8 by honor and dishonor, by evil report and good report; as deceivers, and *yet* true; 9 as unknown, and *yet* well known; as dying, and behold we live; as chastened, and *yet* not killed; 10 as sorrowful, yet always rejoicing; as poor, yet making many rich; as having nothing, and *yet* possessing all things.

11 O Corinthians! We have spoken openly to you, our heart is wide open. 12 You are not restricted by us, but you are restricted by your *own* affections. 13 Now in return for the same (I speak as to children), you also be open.

14 Do not be unequally yoked together with unbelievers. For what fellowship has righteousness with lawlessness? And what communion has light with darkness? 15 And what accord has Christ with Belial? Or what part has a believer with an unbeliever? 16 And what agreement has the temple of God with idols? For you*ᵃ* are the temple of the living God. As God has said:

"I will dwell in them
And walk among them.
I will be their God,
And they shall be My people."*ᵇ*

17 Therefore

"Come out from among them
And be separate, says the Lord.
Do not touch what is unclean,
And I will receive you."*ᵃ*
18 "I will be a Father to you,
And you shall be My sons and daughters,
Says the LORD Almighty."*ᵃ*

7 Therefore, having these promises, beloved, let us cleanse ourselves from all filthiness of the flesh and spirit, perfecting holiness in the fear of God.

2 Open *your hearts* to us. We have wronged no one, we have corrupted no one, we have cheated no one. 3 I do not say *this* to condemn; for I have said before that you are in our hearts, to die together and to live together. 4 Great *is* my boldness of speech toward you, great *is* my boasting on your behalf. I am filled with comfort. I am exceedingly joyful in all our tribulation.

5 For indeed, when we came to Macedonia, our bodies had no rest, but we were troubled on every side. Outside *were* conflicts, inside *were* fears. 6 Nevertheless God, who comforts the downcast, comforted us by the coming of Titus, 7 and not only by his coming, but also by the consolation with which he was comforted in you, when he told us of your earnest desire, your mourning, your zeal for me, so that I rejoiced even more.

8 For even if I made you sorry with my letter, I do not regret it; though I did regret it. For I perceive that the same epistle made you sorry, though only for a while. 9 Now I rejoice, not that you were made sorry, but that your sorrow led to repentance. For you were made sorry in a godly manner, that you might suffer loss from us in nothing. 10 For godly sorrow produces repentance *leading* to salvation, not to be regretted; but the sorrow of the world produces death. 11 For observe this very thing, that you sorrowed in a godly manner: What diligence it produced in you, *what* clearing *of yourselves*, *what* indignation, *what* fear, *what* vehement desire, *what* zeal, *what* vindication! In all *things* you proved yourselves to be clear in this matter. 12 Therefore, although I wrote to you, *I did* not *do it* for the sake of him who had done the wrong, nor for the sake of him who suffered wrong, but that our care for you in the sight of God might appear to you.

13 Therefore we have been comforted in your comfort. And we rejoiced exceedingly more for the joy of Titus, because his spirit has been refreshed by you all. 14 For if in anything I have boasted to him about you, I am not ashamed. But as we spoke all things to you in truth, even so our boasting to Titus was found true. 15 And his affections are greater for you as he remembers the obedience of you all, how with fear and trembling you received him. 16 Therefore I rejoice that I have confidence in you in everything.

8 Moreover, brethren, we make known to you the grace of God bestowed on the churches of Macedonia: 2 that in a great trial of affliction the abundance of their joy and their deep poverty abounded in the riches of their liberality. 3 For I bear witness that according to *their* ability, yes, and beyond *their* ability,

6:16 *ᵃ*NU-Text reads *we.*   *ᵇ*Leviticus 26:12; Jeremiah 32:38; Ezekiel 37:27   6:17 *ᵃ*Isaiah 52:11; Ezekiel 20:34, 41   6:18 *ᵃ*2 Samuel 7:14

they were freely willing, 4 imploring us with much urgency that we would receive[a] the gift and the fellowship of the ministering to the saints. 5 And not *only* as we had hoped, but they first gave themselves to the Lord, and *then* to us by the will of God. 6 So we urged Titus, that as he had begun, so he would also complete this grace in you as well. 7 But as you abound in everything— in faith, in speech, in knowledge, in all diligence, and in your love for us—*see* that you abound in this grace also.

8 I speak not by commandment, but I am testing the sincerity of your love by the diligence of others. 9 For you know the grace of our Lord Jesus Christ, that though He was rich, yet for your sakes He became poor, that you through His poverty might become rich.

10 And in this I give advice: It is to your advantage not only to be doing what you began and were desiring to do a year ago; 11 but now you also must complete the doing *of it;* that as *there was* a readiness to desire *it,* so *there* also *may be* a completion out of what *you* have. 12 For if there is first a willing mind, *it is* accepted according to what one has, *and* not according to what he does not have.

13 For *I do* not *mean* that others should be eased and you burdened; 14 but by an equality, *that* now at this time your abundance *may supply* their lack, that their abundance also may supply your lack—that there may be equality. 15 As it is written, *"He who gathered much had nothing left over, and he who gathered little had no lack."*[a]

16 But thanks *be* to God who puts[a] the same earnest care for you into the heart of Titus. 17 For he not only accepted the exhortation, but being more diligent, he went to you of his own accord. 18 And we have sent with him the brother whose praise *is* in the gospel throughout all the churches, 19 and not only *that,* but who was also chosen by the churches to travel with us with this gift, which is administered by us to the glory of the Lord Himself and *to show* your

ready mind, 20 avoiding this: that anyone should blame us in this lavish gift which is administered by us— 21 providing honorable things, not only in the sight of the Lord, but also in the sight of men.

22 And we have sent with them our brother whom we have often proved diligent in many things, but now much more diligent, because of the great confidence which *we have* in you. 23 If *anyone inquires* about Titus, *he is* my partner and fellow worker concerning you. Or if our brethren *are inquired about, they are* messengers of the churches, the glory of Christ. 24 Therefore show to them, and[a] before the churches the proof of your love and of our boasting on your behalf.

9 Now concerning the ministering to the saints, it is superfluous for me to write to you; 2 for I know your willingness, about which I boast of you to the Macedonians, that Achaia was ready a year ago; and your zeal has stirred up the majority. 3 Yet I have sent the brethren, lest our boasting of you should be in vain in this respect, that, as I said, you may be ready; 4 lest if *some* Macedonians come with me and find you unprepared, we (not to mention you!) should be ashamed of this confident boasting.[a] 5 Therefore I thought it necessary to exhort the brethren to go to you ahead of time, and prepare your generous gift beforehand, which *you had* previously promised, that it may be ready as *a matter of* generosity and not as a grudging obligation.

6 But this *I say:* He who sows sparingly will also reap sparingly, and he who sows bountifully will also reap bountifully. 7 *So let* each one *give* as he purposes in his heart, not grudgingly or of necessity; for God loves a cheerful giver. 8 And God *is* able to make all grace abound toward you, that you, always having all sufficiency in all *things,* may have an abundance for every good work. 9 As it is written:

"He has dispersed abroad,
He has given to the poor;

His righteousness endures forever.''[a]

10 Now may[a] He who supplies seed to the sower, and bread for food, supply and multiply the seed you have *sown* and increase the fruits of your righteousness, 11 while *you are* enriched in everything for all liberality, which causes thanksgiving through us to God. 12 For the administration of this service not only supplies the needs of the saints, but also is abounding through many thanksgivings to God, 13 while, through the proof of this ministry, they glorify God for the obedience of your confession to the gospel of Christ, and for *your* liberal sharing with them and all *men,* 14 and by their prayer for you, who long for you because of the exceeding grace of God in you. 15 Thanks *be* to God for His indescribable gift!

10 Now I, Paul, myself am pleading with you by the meekness and gentleness of Christ—who in presence *am* lowly among you, but being absent am bold toward you. 2 But I beg *you* that when I am present I may not be bold with that confidence by which I intend to be bold against some, who think of us as if we walked according to the flesh. 3 For though we walk in the flesh, we do not war according to the flesh. 4 For the weapons of our warfare *are* not carnal but mighty in God for pulling down strongholds, 5 casting down arguments and every high thing that exalts itself against the knowledge of God, bringing every thought into captivity to the obedience of Christ, 6 and being ready to punish all disobedience when your obedience is fulfilled.

7 Do you look at things according to the outward appearance? If anyone is convinced in himself that he is Christ's, let him again consider this in himself, that just as he *is* Christ's, even so we *are* Christ's.[a] 8 For even if I should boast somewhat more about our authority, which the Lord gave us[a] for edification and not for your destruction, I shall not be ashamed— 9 lest I seem to terrify you

by letters. 10 "For *his* letters," they say, "*are* weighty and powerful, but *his* bodily presence *is* weak, and *his* speech contemptible." 11 Let such a person consider this, that what we are in word by letters when we are absent, such *we will* also *be* in deed when we are present.

12 For we dare not class ourselves or compare ourselves with those who commend themselves. But they, measuring themselves by themselves, and comparing themselves among themselves, are not wise. 13 We, however, will not boast beyond measure, but within the limits of the sphere which God appointed us—a sphere which especially includes you. 14 For we are not overextending ourselves (as though *our authority* did not extend to you), for it was to you that we came with the gospel of Christ; 15 not boasting of things beyond measure, *that is,* in other men's labors, but having hope, *that* as your faith is increased, we shall be greatly enlarged by you in our sphere, 16 to preach the gospel in the *regions* beyond you, *and* not to boast in another man's sphere of accomplishment.

17 But *"he who glories, let him glory in the* LORD.*"*[a] 18 For not he who commends himself is approved, but whom the Lord commends.

11 Oh, that you would bear with me in a little folly—and indeed you do bear with me. 2 For I am jealous for you with godly jealousy. For I have betrothed you to one husband, that I may present *you as* a chaste virgin to Christ. 3 But I fear, lest somehow, as the serpent deceived Eve by his craftiness, so your minds may be corrupted from the simplicity[a] that is in Christ. 4 For if he who comes preaches another Jesus whom we have not preached, or *if* you receive a different spirit which you have not received, or a different gospel which you have not accepted—you may well put up with it!

5 For I consider that I am not at all inferior to the most eminent apostles. 6 Even though *I am* untrained in speech, yet *I am* not in knowledge.

9:9 [a]Psalm 112:9   9:10 [a]NU-Text reads *Now He who supplies . . . will supply . . . .*   10:7 [a]NU-Text reads *even as we are.*   10:8 [a]NU-Text omits *us.*   10:17 [a]Jeremiah 9:24   11:3 [a]NU-Text adds *and purity.*

But we have been thoroughly manifested[a] among you in all things.

7 Did I commit sin in humbling myself that you might be exalted, because I preached the gospel of God to you free of charge? 8 I robbed other churches, taking wages *from them* to minister to you. 9 And when I was present with you, and in need, I was a burden to no one, for what I lacked the brethren who came from Macedonia supplied. And in everything I kept myself from being burdensome to you, and so I will keep *myself*. 10 As the truth of Christ is in me, no one shall stop me from this boasting in the regions of Achaia. 11 Why? Because I do not love you? God knows!

12 But what I do, I will also continue to do, that I may cut off the opportunity from those who desire an opportunity to be regarded just as we are in the things of which they boast. 13 For such *are* false apostles, deceitful workers, transforming themselves into apostles of Christ. 14 And no wonder! For Satan himself transforms himself into an angel of light. 15 Therefore *it is* no great thing if his ministers also transform themselves into ministers of righteousness, whose end will be according to their works.

16 I say again, let no one think me a fool. If otherwise, at least receive me as a fool, that I also may boast a little. 17 What I speak, I speak not according to the Lord, but as it were, foolishly, in this confidence of boasting. 18 Seeing that many boast according to the flesh, I also will boast. 19 For you put up with fools gladly, since you *yourselves* are wise! 20 For you put up with it if one brings you into bondage, if one devours *you,* if one takes *from you,* if one exalts himself, if one strikes you on the face. 21 To *our* shame I say that we were too weak for that! But in whatever anyone is bold—I speak foolishly—I am bold also.

22 Are they Hebrews? So *am* I. Are they Israelites? So *am* I. Are they the seed of Abraham? So *am* I. 23 Are they ministers of Christ?—I speak as a fool—I *am* more: in labors more abundant, in stripes above measure, in prisons more frequently, in deaths often. 24 From the Jews five times I received forty *stripes* minus one. 25 Three times I was beaten with rods; once I was stoned; three times I was shipwrecked; a night and a day I have been in the deep; 26 *in* journeys often, *in* perils of waters, *in* perils of robbers, *in* perils of *my own* countrymen, *in* perils of the Gentiles, *in* perils in the city, *in* perils in the wilderness, *in* perils in the sea, *in* perils among false brethren; 27 in weariness and toil, in sleeplessness often, in hunger and thirst, in fastings often, in cold and nakedness— 28 besides the other things, what comes upon me daily: my deep concern for all the churches. 29 Who is weak, and I am not weak? Who is made to stumble, and I do not burn *with indignation*?

30 If I must boast, I will boast in the things which concern my infirmity. 31 The God and Father of our Lord Jesus Christ, who is blessed forever, knows that I am not lying. 32 In Damascus the governor, under Aretas the king, was guarding the city of the Damascenes with a garrison, desiring to arrest me; 33 but I was let down in a basket through a window in the wall, and escaped from his hands.

12 It is doubtless[a] not profitable for me to boast. I will come to visions and revelations of the Lord: 2 I know a man in Christ who fourteen years ago—whether in the body I do not know, or whether out of the body I do not know, God knows—such a one was caught up to the third heaven. 3 And I know such a man— whether in the body or out of the body I do not know, God knows— 4 how he was caught up into Paradise and heard inexpressible words, which it is not lawful for a man to utter. 5 Of such a one I will boast; yet of myself I will not boast, except in my infirmities. 6 For though I might desire to boast, I will not be a fool; for I will speak the truth. But I refrain, lest anyone should think of me above what he sees me *to be* or hears from me.

7 And lest I should be exalted above measure by the abundance of the revelations, a thorn in the flesh was given to me, a messenger of Satan to buffet me, lest I be exalted

---

11:6 [a]NU-Text omits *been.*   12:1 [a]NU-Text reads *necessary, though not profitable, to boast.*

above measure. 8 Concerning this thing I pleaded with the Lord three times that it might depart from me. 9 And He said to me, "My grace is sufficient for you, for My strength is made perfect in weakness." Therefore most gladly I will rather boast in my infirmities, that the power of Christ may rest upon me. 10 Therefore I take pleasure in infirmities, in reproaches, in needs, in persecutions, in distresses, for Christ's sake. For when I am weak, then I am strong.

11 I have become a fool in boasting;*a* you have compelled me. For I ought to have been commended by you; for in nothing was I behind the most eminent apostles, though I am nothing. 12 Truly the signs of an apostle were accomplished among you with all perseverance, in signs and wonders and mighty deeds. 13 For what is it in which you were inferior to other churches, except that I myself was not burdensome to you? Forgive me this wrong!

14 Now *for* the third time I am ready to come to you. And I will not be burdensome to you; for I do not seek yours, but you. For the children ought not to lay up for the parents, but the parents for the children. 15 And I will very gladly spend and be spent for your souls; though the more abundantly I love you, the less I am loved.

16 But be that *as it may,* I did not burden you. Nevertheless, being crafty, I caught you by cunning! 17 Did I take advantage of you by any of those whom I sent to you? 18 I urged Titus, and sent our brother with *him.* Did Titus take advantage of you? Did we not walk in the same spirit? Did *we* not *walk* in the same steps?

19 Again, do you think*a* that we excuse ourselves to you? We speak before God in Christ. But *we do* all things, beloved, for your edification. 20 For I fear lest, when I come, I shall not find you such as I wish, and *that* I shall be found by you such as you do not wish; lest *there be* contentions, jealousies, outbursts of wrath, selfish ambitions, backbitings, whisperings, conceits, tumults; 21 lest,

when I come again, my God will humble me among you, and I shall mourn for many who have sinned before and have not repented of the uncleanness, fornication, and lewdness which they have practiced.

13 This *will be* the third *time* I am coming to you. *"By the mouth of two or three witnesses every word shall be established."*a 2 I have told you before, and foretell as if I were present the second time, and now being absent I write*a* to those who have sinned before, and to all the rest, that if I come again I will not spare— 3 since you seek a proof of Christ speaking in me, who is not weak toward you, but mighty in you. 4 For though He was crucified in weakness, yet He lives by the power of God. For we also are weak in Him, but we shall live with Him by the power of God toward you.

5 Examine yourselves *as to* whether you are in the faith. Test yourselves. Do you not know yourselves, that Jesus Christ is in you?— unless indeed you are disqualified. 6 But I trust that you will know that we are not disqualified. 7 Now I*a* pray to God that you do no evil, not that we should appear approved, but that you should do what is honorable, though we may seem disqualified. 8 For we can do nothing against the truth, but for the truth. 9 For we are glad when we are weak and you are strong. And this also we pray, that you may be made complete. 10 Therefore I write these things being absent, lest being present I should use sharpness, according to the authority which the Lord has given me for edification and not for destruction.

11 Finally, brethren, farewell. Become complete. Be of good comfort, be of one mind, live in peace; and the God of love and peace will be with you.

12 Greet one another with a holy kiss.

13 All the saints greet you.

14 The grace of the Lord Jesus Christ, and the love of God, and the communion of the Holy Spirit *be* with you all. Amen.

12:11 *a*NU-Text omits *in boasting.*   12:19 *a*NU-Text reads *You have been thinking for a long time. . . .*
13:1 *a*Deuteronomy 19:15   13:2 *a*NU-Text omits *I write.*   13:7 *a*NU-Text reads *we.*

Galatians

Overview of Galatians

*T*he apostle Paul wrote this letter to the Christians in the region of Galatia sometime between A.D. 49 and 55, from either Antioch or Ephesus.

In essence, he writes to tell them that what we are is God's gift to us and what we become is our gift to God!

Paul writes to remind all Christians that our relationship with God is a gift of grace, not earned by the works of the law. As Christians, we are freed from rules and regulations such as those dictated by Jewish legalism. Our perfection before God is not earned, but is freely given when we place our faith in Jesus Christ. In Him, we can find our self-worth because of His death on the cross. Since God has made us alive in the Spirit, our lives should reflect the love and positive attitudes that come from knowing Jesus Christ in a very real and personal way.

Paul encourages Christians to continue doing good to one another, reminding us that we are heirs to an inheritance given freely to us by God through Jesus Christ. That is an inheritance to become sons and daughters of God. As God's children, we have the right to address God in the most intimate terms, as Abba or "Daddy."

Freed from the law, we can now fulfill the law in one action—love God and love others.

For you, brethren, have been called to liberty; only do not use liberty as an opportunity for the flesh, but through love serve one another. . . . And let us not grow weary while doing good, for in due season we shall reap if we do not lose heart.

(Gal. 5:13; 6:9)

The cross of Christ was the premier demonstration of God's sacrificial love. We can reenact this demonstration when we live out the greeting, "God loves you and so do I!"

Jesus in Galatians

Jesus has freed believers from bondage to the law (legalism) and to sin (license) and has placed them in a position of liberty. The transforming cross provides for the believers' deliverance from the curse of sin, law, and self.

Keys to Galatians

Key Word: Freedom from the Law. This Epistle shows that the believer is no longer under the law but is saved only by grace. It has been said that Judaism was the cradle of Christianity, but also that it was very nearly its grave as well. God raised up Paul as the Moses of the Christian church to deliver them from this bondage. Galatians is the Christian's Declaration of Independence. The power of the Holy Spirit enables the Christian to enjoy freedom within the law of love.

Key Verses: "I have been crucified with Christ; it is no longer I who live, but Christ lives in me; and the *life* which I now live in the flesh I live by faith in the Son of God, who loved me and gave Himself for me. I do not set aside the grace of God; for if righteousness *comes* through the law, then Christ died in vain" (2:20, 21).

"Stand fast therefore in the liberty by which Christ has made us free, and do not be entangled again with a yoke of bondage" (5:1).

Key Chapter: Galatians 5. The impact of the truth about freedom is staggering: freedom must not be used "as an opportunity for the flesh, but through love serve one another" (5:13). This chapter records the power and the results of that freedom—the fruit of the Spirit.

1 Paul, an apostle (not from men nor through man, but through Jesus Christ and God the Father who raised Him from the dead), 2 and all the brethren who are with me,

To the churches of Galatia:

3 Grace to you and peace from God the Father and our Lord Jesus Christ, 4 who gave Himself for our sins, that He might deliver us from this present evil age, according to the will of our God and Father, 5 to whom *be* glory forever and ever. Amen.

6 I marvel that you are turning away so soon from Him who called you in the grace of Christ, to a different gospel, 7 which is not another; but there are some who trouble you and want to pervert the gospel of Christ. 8 But even if we, or an angel from heaven, preach any other gospel to you than what we have preached to you, let him be accursed. 9 As we have said before, so now I say again, if anyone preaches any other gospel to you than what you have received, let him be accursed.

10 For do I now persuade men, or God? Or do I seek to please men? For if I still pleased men, I would not be a bondservant of Christ.

11 But I make known to you, brethren, that the gospel which was preached by me is not according to man. 12 For I neither received it from man, nor was I taught *it,* but *it came* through the revelation of Jesus Christ.

13 For you have heard of my former conduct in Judaism, how I persecuted the church of God beyond measure and *tried to* destroy it. 14 And I advanced in Judaism beyond many of my contemporaries in my own nation, being more exceedingly zealous for the traditions of my fathers.

15 But when it pleased God, who separated me from my mother's womb and called *me* through His grace, 16 to reveal His Son in me, that I might preach Him among the Gentiles, I did not immediately confer with flesh and blood, 17 nor did I go up to Jerusalem to those *who were* apostles before me; but I went to Arabia, and returned again to Damascus.

18 Then after three years I went up to Jerusalem to see Peter,*a* and remained with him fifteen days. 19 But I saw none of the other apostles except James, the Lord's brother. 20 (Now *concerning* the things which I write to you, indeed, before God, I do not lie.)

21 Afterward I went into the regions of Syria and Cilicia. 22 And I was unknown by face to the churches of Judea which *were* in Christ. 23 But they were hearing only, "He who formerly persecuted us now preaches the faith which he once *tried to* destroy." 24 And they glorified God in me.

2 Then after fourteen years I went up again to Jerusalem with Barnabas, and also took Titus with *me.* 2 And I went up by revelation, and communicated to them that gospel which I preach among the Gentiles, but privately to those who were of reputation, lest by any means I might run, or had run, in vain. 3 Yet not even Titus who *was* with me, being a Greek, was compelled to be circumcised. 4 And *this occurred* because of false brethren secretly brought in (who came in by stealth to spy out our liberty which we have in Christ Jesus, that they might bring us into bondage), 5 to whom we did not yield submission even for an hour, that the truth of the gospel might continue with you.

6 But from those who seemed to be something—whatever they were, it makes no difference to me; God shows personal favoritism to no man—for those who seemed *to be something* added nothing to me. 7 But on the contrary, when they saw that the gospel for the uncircumcised had been committed to me, as *the gospel* for the circumcised *was* to Peter 8 (for He who worked effectively in Peter for the apostleship to the circumcised also worked effectively in me toward the Gentiles), 9 and when James, Cephas, and John, who

1:18 *a*NU-Text reads *Cephas.*

The Churches of Galatia

In the Book of Galatians, the apostle Paul was most likely writing to a group of churches in the Roman Province of Galatia, located in South Central Asia Minor. On their first missionary journey, Paul and Barnabus established churches in the following cities: Antioch, Iconium, Lystra, and Derbe. Also noted on this map are the important cities of Jerusalem and Antioch, as well as Paul's hometown of Tarsus.

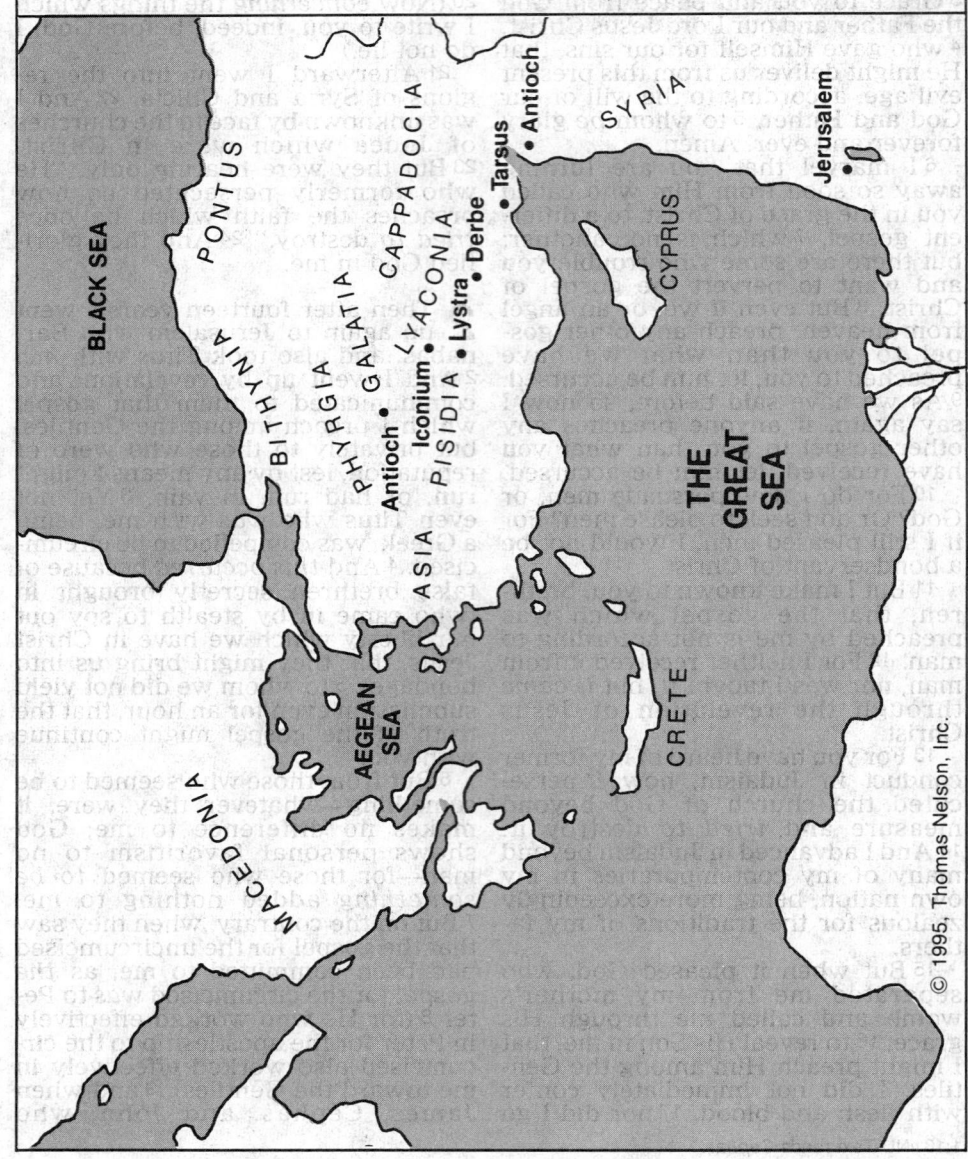

BLACK SEA

PONTUS

BITHYNIA

PHYRGIA

GALATIA

CAPPADOCIA

ASIA

PISIDIA

LYCAONIA

Iconium

Antioch

Lystra

Derbe

Tarsus

Antioch

SYRIA

CYPRUS

Jerusalem

THE GREAT SEA

CRETE

AEGEAN SEA

MACEDONIA

seemed to be pillars, perceived the grace that had been given to me, they gave me and Barnabas the right hand of fellowship, that we *should go* to the Gentiles and they to the circumcised. 10 *They desired* only that we should remember the poor, the very thing which I also was eager to do.

11 Now when Peter[a] had come to Antioch, I withstood him to his face, because he was to be blamed; 12 for before certain men came from James, he would eat with the Gentiles; but when they came, he withdrew and separated himself, fearing those who were of the circumcision. 13 And the rest of the Jews also played the hypocrite with him, so that even Barnabas was carried away with their hypocrisy.

14 But when I saw that they were not straightforward about the truth of the gospel, I said to Peter before *them* all, "If you, being a Jew, live in the manner of Gentiles and not as the Jews, why do you[a] compel Gentiles to live as Jews?[b] 15 We *who are* Jews by nature, and not sinners of the Gentiles, 16 knowing that a man is not justified by the works of the law but by faith in Jesus Christ, even we have believed in Christ Jesus, that we might be justified by faith in Christ and not by the works of the law; for by the works of the law no flesh shall be justified.

17 "But if, while we seek to be justified by Christ, we ourselves also are found sinners, *is* Christ therefore a minister of sin? Certainly not! 18 For if I build again those things which I destroyed, I make myself a transgressor. 19 For I through the law died to the law that I might live to God. 20 I have been crucified with Christ; it is no longer I who live, but Christ lives in me; and the *life* which I now live in the flesh I live by faith in the Son of God, who loved me and gave Himself for me. 21 I do not set aside the grace of God; for if righteousness *comes* through the law, then Christ died in vain."

3 O foolish Galatians! Who has bewitched you that you should not obey the truth,[a] before whose eyes Jesus Christ was clearly portrayed among you[b] as crucified? 2 This only I want to learn from you: Did you receive the Spirit by the works of the law, or by the hearing of faith? 3 Are you so foolish? Having begun in the Spirit, are you now being made perfect by the flesh? 4 Have you suffered so many things in vain—if indeed *it was* in vain?

5 Therefore He who supplies the Spirit to you and works miracles among you, *does He do it* by the works of the law, or by the hearing of faith?— 6 just as Abraham "*believed God, and it was accounted to him for righteousness.*"[a] 7 Therefore know that *only* those who are of faith are sons of Abraham. 8 And the Scripture, foreseeing that God would justify the Gentiles by faith, preached the gospel to Abraham beforehand, *saying, "In you all the nations shall be blessed.*"[a] 9 So then those who *are* of faith are blessed with believing Abraham.

10 For as many as are of the works of the law are under the curse; for it is written, "*Cursed is everyone who does not continue in all things which are written in the book of the law, to do them.*"[a] 11 But that no one is justified by the law in the sight of God *is* evident, for "*the just shall live by faith.*"[a] 12 Yet the law is not of faith, but "*the man who does them shall live by them.*"[a]

13 Christ has redeemed us from the curse of the law, having become a curse for us (for it is written, "*Cursed is everyone who hangs on a tree*"[a]), 14 that the blessing of Abraham might come upon the Gentiles in Christ Jesus, that we might receive the promise of the Spirit through faith.

15 Brethren, I speak in the manner of men: Though *it is* only a man's covenant, yet *if it is* confirmed, no one annuls or adds to it. 16 Now to Abraham and his Seed were the promises made. He does not say, "And to seeds," as of many, but as of one, "*And to your Seed,*"[a] who is Christ. 17 And this I say, *that* the law, which was four hundred and thirty years later, cannot annul the cove-

2:11 [a]NU-Text reads *Cephas.*   2:14 [a]NU-Text reads *how can you.*   [b]Some interpreters stop the quotation here.   3:1 [a]NU-Text omits *that you should not obey the truth.*   [b]NU-Text omits *among you.*
3:6 [a]Genesis 15:6   3:8 [a]Genesis 12:3; 18:18; 22:18; 26:4; 28:14   3:10 [a]Deuteronomy 27:26
3:11 [a]Habakkuk 2:4   3:12 [a]Leviticus 18:5   3:13 [a]Deuteronomy 21:23   3:16 [a]Genesis 12:7; 13:15; 24:7

nant that was confirmed before by God in Christ,*a* that it should make the promise of no effect. 18 For if the inheritance *is* of the law, *it is* no longer of promise; but God gave *it* to Abraham by promise.

19 What purpose then *does* the law serve? It was added because of transgressions, till the Seed should come to whom the promise was made; *and it was* appointed through angels by the hand of a mediator. 20 Now a mediator does not *mediate* for one *only*, but God is one.

21 *Is* the law then against the promises of God? Certainly not! For if there had been a law given which could have given life, truly righteousness would have been by the law. 22 But the Scripture has confined all under sin, that the promise by faith in Jesus Christ might be given to those who believe. 23 But before faith came, we were kept under guard by the law, kept for the faith which would afterward be revealed. 24 Therefore the law was our tutor *to bring us* to Christ, that we might be justified by faith. 25 But after faith has come, we are no longer under a tutor.

26 For you are all sons of God through faith in Christ Jesus. 27 For as many of you as were baptized into Christ have put on Christ. 28 There is neither Jew nor Greek, there is neither slave nor free, there is neither male nor female; for you are all one in Christ Jesus. 29 And if you *are* Christ's, then you are Abraham's seed, and heirs according to the promise.

4 Now I say *that* the heir, as long as he is a child, does not differ at all from a slave, though he is master of all, 2 but is under guardians and stewards until the time appointed by the father. 3 Even so we, when we were children, were in bondage under the elements of the world. 4 But when the fullness of the time had come, God sent forth His Son, born*a* of a woman, born under the law, 5 to redeem those who were under the law, that we might receive the adoption as sons.

6 And because you are sons, God has sent forth the Spirit of His Son

into your hearts, crying out, "Abba, Father!" 7 Therefore you are no longer a slave but a son, and if a son, then an heir of*a* God through Christ.

8 But then, indeed, when you did not know God, you served those which by nature are not gods. 9 But now after you have known God, or rather are known by God, how *is it that* you turn again to the weak and beggarly elements, to which you desire again to be in bondage? 10 You observe days and months and seasons and years. 11 I am afraid for you, lest I have labored for you in vain.

12 Brethren, I urge you to become like me, for I *became* like you. You have not injured me at all. 13 You know that because of physical infirmity I preached the gospel to you at the first. 14 And my trial which was in my flesh you did not despise or reject, but you received me as an angel of God, *even* as Christ Jesus. 15 What*a* then was the blessing you enjoyed? For I bear you witness that, if possible, you would have plucked out your own eyes and given them to me. 16 Have I therefore become your enemy because I tell you the truth?

17 They zealously court you, *but* for no good; yes, they want to exclude you, that you may be zealous for them. 18 But it is good to be zealous in a good thing always, and not only when I am present with you. 19 My little children, for whom I labor in birth again until Christ is formed in you, 20 I would like to be present with you now and to change my tone; for I have doubts about you.

21 Tell me, you who desire to be under the law, do you not hear the law? 22 For it is written that Abraham had two sons: the one by a bondwoman, the other by a freewoman. 23 But he *who was* of the bondwoman was born according to the flesh, and he of the freewoman through promise, 24 which things are symbolic. For these are the*a* two covenants: the one from Mount Sinai which gives birth to bondage, which is Hagar— 25 for this Hagar is Mount Sinai in Arabia, and corresponds to Jerusalem which now is, and is in bondage with her children— 26 but the Jerusa-

Change Your Thoughts
and Change Your World

The apostle Paul was a Jewish Roman citizen from the bustling city of Tarsus in the province of Cilicia. As a young boy, he spent much time in the small Jewish village of Gishalav in northern Galilee. His relatives probably fought in the major revolts against Rome in A.D. 66. About the age of twelve, Paul, then known as Saul, began his studies in Jerusalem under the famous Rabbi Gamaliel. Saul excelled in his knowledge of the Jewish law and customs. He was at the top of his class. Eventually he rose to a prominent position in the synagogue at Jerusalem.

Here he met Stephen and other early Christians. Protecting his Jewish forefathers' laws and traditions, Saul joined in the fight against the "heretics" known as "followers of the Way."

Saul zealously persecuted many early church members, rounding up men, women and children to bring them in to kill them. During one such pursuit, as Saul journeyed from Jerusalem to Damascus, the resurrected Christ appeared to him. Through this stunning encounter, Saul was converted and eventually his name was changed to Paul.

Then Paul became one of the most enthusiastic, outspoken leaders of the early Christian movement. But it did not happen overnight. Following Paul's conversion, he spent fourteen years in training. Paul realized that Christ was the goal of the law he had been taught. He had to unlearn all of the legalism of his upbringing. With the Holy Spirit's guidance, he filtered out the negative use of doctrines which taught judgment and arguments, and replaced them with the fruit of the Spirit: "love, joy, peace, longsuffering, kindness, goodness, faithfulness, gentleness, and self-control. Against such there is no law" (Gal. 5:22–23). Paul renewed his energy by renewing his mind. Jesus was the fulfillment of the law, the freedom to which the law pointed.

If you change your thoughts, you can change your world. Paul taught us: "Finally, brethren, whatever things are true, whatever things *are* noble, whatever things *are* just, whatever things *are* pure, whatever things *are* lovely, whatever things *are* of good report, if *there is* any virtue and if *there is* anything praiseworthy—meditate on these things . . . and the God of peace will be with you" (Phil. 4:8–9).

lem above is free, which is the mother of us all. 27 For it is written:

"Rejoice, O barren,
You who do not bear!
Break forth and shout,
You who are not in labor!
For the desolate has many
   more children
Than she who has a husband."ᵃ

28 Now we, brethren, as Isaac *was*, are children of promise. 29 But, as he who was born according to the flesh then persecuted him *who was born* according to the Spirit, even so *it is* now. 30 Nevertheless what does the Scripture say? *"Cast out the bondwoman and her son, for the son of the bondwoman shall not be heir with the son of the freewoman."*ᵃ 31 So then, brethren, we are not children of the bondwoman but of the free.

5 Stand fast therefore in the liberty by which Christ has made us free,ᵃ and do not be entangled again with a yoke of bondage. 2 Indeed I, Paul, say to you that if you become circumcised, Christ will profit you nothing. 3 And I testify again to every man who becomes circumcised that he is a debtor to keep the whole law. 4 You have become estranged from Christ, you who *attempt to* be justified by law; you have fallen from grace. 5 For we through the Spirit eagerly wait for the hope of righteousness by faith. 6 For in Christ Jesus neither circumcision nor uncircumcision avails anything, but faith working through love.

7 You ran well. Who hindered you from obeying the truth? 8 This persuasion does not *come* from Him who calls you. 9 A little leaven leavens the whole lump. 10 I have confidence in you, in the Lord, that you will have no other mind; but he who troubles you shall bear his judgment, whoever he is.

11 And I, brethren, if I still preach circumcision, why do I still suffer persecution? Then the offense of the cross has ceased. 12 I could wish that those who trouble you would even cut themselves off!

13 For you, brethren, have been called to liberty; only do not *use* liberty as an opportunity for the flesh, but through love serve one another. 14 For all the law is fulfilled in one word, *even* in this: *"You shall love your neighbor as yourself."*ᵃ 15 But if you bite and devour one another, beware lest you be consumed by one another!

16 I say then: Walk in the Spirit, and you shall not fulfill the lust of the flesh. 17 For the flesh lusts against the Spirit, and the Spirit against the flesh; and these are contrary to one another, so that you do not do the things that you wish. 18 But if you are led by the Spirit, you are not under the law.

19 Now the works of the flesh are evident, which are: adultery,ᵃ fornication, uncleanness, lewdness, 20 idolatry, sorcery, hatred, contentions, jealousies, outbursts of wrath, selfish ambitions, dissensions, heresies, 21 envy, murders,ᵃ drunkenness, revelries, and the like; of which I tell you beforehand, just as I also told *you* in time past, that those who practice such things will not inherit the kingdom of God.

22 But the fruit of the Spirit is love, joy, peace, longsuffering, kindness, goodness, faithfulness, 23 gentleness, self-control. Against such there is no law. 24 And those *who are* Christ's have crucified the flesh with its passions and desires. 25 If we live in the Spirit, let us also walk in the Spirit. 26 Let us not become conceited, provoking one another, envying one another.

6 Brethren, if a man is overtaken in any trespass, you who *are* spiritual restore such a one in a spirit of gentleness, considering yourself lest you also be tempted. 2 Bear one another's burdens, and so fulfill the law of Christ. 3 For if anyone thinks himself to be something, when he is nothing, he deceives himself. 4 But let each one examine his own work, and then he will have rejoicing in himself alone, and not in another. 5 For each one shall bear his own load.

6 Let him who is taught the word

4:27 ᵃIsaiah 54:1   4:30 ᵃGenesis 21:10   5:1 ᵃNU-Text reads *For freedom Christ has made us free; stand fast therefore.*   5:14 ᵃLeviticus 19:18   5:19 ᵃNU-Text omits *adultery.*   5:21 ᵃNU-Text omits *murders.*

share in all good things with him who teaches.

7 Do not be deceived, God is not mocked; for whatever a man sows, that he will also reap. 8 For he who sows to his flesh will of the flesh reap corruption, but he who sows to the Spirit will of the Spirit reap everlasting life. 9 And let us not grow weary while doing good, for in due season we shall reap if we do not lose heart. 10 Therefore, as we have opportunity, let us do good to all, especially to those who are of the household of faith.

11 See with what large letters I have written to you with my own hand! 12 As many as desire to make a good showing in the flesh, these *would* compel you to be circumcised, only that they may not suffer perse-

cution for the cross of Christ. 13 For not even those who are circumcised keep the law, but they desire to have you circumcised that they may boast in your flesh. 14 But God forbid that I should boast except in the cross of our Lord Jesus Christ, by whom*a* the world has been crucified to me, and I to the world. 15 For in Christ Jesus neither circumcision nor uncircumcision avails anything, but a new creation.

16 And as many as walk according to this rule, peace and mercy *be* upon them, and upon the Israel of God.

17 From now on let no one trouble me, for I bear in my body the marks of the Lord Jesus.

18 Brethren, the grace of our Lord Jesus Christ *be* with your spirit. Amen.

6:14 *a*Or *by which* (the cross)

Ephesians

Overview of Ephesians

The apostle Paul wrote this letter to the Christians in Ephesus around A.D. 60, while imprisoned in Rome. This Epistle presents an all-powerful God and His wise and loving design for the world.

Ephesians teaches us how to share in the life of the risen Christ. Most relevant to church doctrine, this letter discusses the nature of the church and how it should be demonstrated to the world.

Rich in promises, Ephesians presents confident passages which Christians can draw upon today. God "is able to do exceedingly abundantly above all that we ask or think, according to the power that works in us" (Eph. 3:20). We are assured of "the love of Christ which passes knowledge" (Eph. 3:19). Our talents and gifts can be used to build up the church and to help us more fully understand Jesus Christ and share Him with others (Eph. 4:7–16).

The pagan culture of the city of Ephesus surrounded the Christians there with immoral and negative influences. Worship of the goddess Diana with its ceremonial prostitution was a trademark of the city. The city was known as a place of refuge where murderers, thieves, and robbers could live freely.

Against this negative environment, the church was encouraged to live a positive Christian lifestyle. Negative influences can be battled successfully by relying on the positive power of God. As Christians we can put on the armor of God to defeat the negative forces which would destroy us.

Stand therefore, having girded your waist with truth, having put on the breastplate of righteousness, and having shod your feet with the preparation of the gospel of peace; above all, taking the shield of faith with which you will be able to quench all the fiery darts of the wicked one. And take the helmet of salvation, and the sword of the Spirit, which is the word of God.

(Eph. 6:14–17)

Jesus in Ephesians

Paul's important phrase "in Christ," or its equivalent, appears in Ephesians more than in any other New Testament book. The believer is in Christ, in the heavenly places in Christ, chosen in Him, adopted through Christ, in the Beloved, redeemed in Him, given an inheritance in Him, sealed in Him, made alive together with Christ, raised and seated with Him, created in Christ, brought near by His blood, growing in Christ, a partaker of the promise in Christ, and given access through faith in Him.

Keys to Ephesians

Key Word: Building the Body of Christ. Ephesians was not written to correct specific errors in a local church, but to prevent problems in the church as a whole by encouraging the body of Christ to maturity in Him. It was also written to make believers more aware of their position in Christ because this is the basis for their practice on every level of life.

Key Verses: "For by grace you have been saved through faith, and that not of yourselves; *it is* the gift of God, not of works, lest anyone should boast. For we are His workmanship, created in Christ Jesus for good works, which God prepared beforehand that we should walk in them" (2:8–10).

"I, therefore, the prisoner of the Lord, beseech you to walk worthy of the calling with which you were called, with all lowliness and gentleness, with longsuffering, bearing with one another in love, endeavoring to keep the unity of the Spirit in the bond of peace" (4:1–3).

Key Chapter: Ephesians 6. Even though the Christian is blessed "with every spiritual blessing in the heavenly *places* in Christ" (1:3), spiritual warfare is still the daily experience of the Christian while in the world. Chapter 6 is the clearest advice for how to "be strong in the Lord and in the power of His might" (6:10).

1 Paul, an apostle of Jesus Christ by the will of God,

To the saints who are in Ephesus, and faithful in Christ Jesus:

2 Grace to you and peace from God our Father and the Lord Jesus Christ.
3 Blessed *be* the God and Father of our Lord Jesus Christ, who has blessed us with every spiritual blessing in the heavenly *places* in Christ, 4 just as He chose us in Him before the foundation of the world, that we should be holy and without blame before Him in love, 5 having predestined us to adoption as sons by Jesus Christ to Himself, according to the good pleasure of His will, 6 to the praise of the glory of His grace, by which He made us accepted in the Beloved.
7 In Him we have redemption through His blood, the forgiveness of sins, according to the riches of His grace 8 which He made to abound to-

ward us in all wisdom and prudence, 9 having made known to us the mystery of His will, according to His good pleasure which He purposed in Himself, 10 that in the dispensation of the fullness of the times He might gather together in one all things in Christ, both*a* which are in heaven and which are on earth—in Him. 11 In Him also we have obtained an inheritance, being predestined according to the purpose of Him who works all things according to the counsel of His will, 12 that we who first trusted in Christ should be to the praise of His glory.
13 In Him you also *trusted,* after you heard the word of truth, the gospel of your salvation; in whom also, having believed, you were sealed with the Holy Spirit of promise, 14 who*a* is the guarantee of our inheritance until the redemption of the purchased possession, to the praise of His glory.
15 Therefore I also, after I heard of

1:10 *a*NU-Text and M-Text omit *both.*   1:14 *a*NU-Text reads *which.*

Grace Is a Gift from God

What's the best gift that faith can deliver to your life? Ephesians 2:8 says: "For by grace you have been saved through faith, and that not of yourselves; *it is* the gift of God."

The best gift faith delivers is the gift of salvation from sin. It is the peace of mind that comes from knowing that Christ died for your sins on the cross.

It is the serenity of spirit that comes over you when you know God has pardoned you.

It is the mental health you experience when old guilt is gone.

How can you earn this salvation?

You can't. A gift is something you can only accept. If you earn it, then it becomes a salary—not a gift!

You are pardoned, forgiven, and saved by the grace of God. And what is grace? It is God's love in action for those who don't deserve it.

Grace is the most beautiful word in the English language. Nothing is more valuable than

- a gift that is given when you don't deserve it.
- love before you've earned it.
- credit when it is not justified.

One of the hardest things for an honorable person to do is to accept something he has not earned. This explains why people so often resist accepting the gospel of Jesus Christ, salvation by the grace of God.

Today make a great leap of faith, and embrace God's grace. Accept His understanding and forgiveness. Trust Him not only to cleanse you of sin and negativity, but also to inspire you to treat other persons the same way. You will soon begin to realize that you are *forgiven not through the good works you do, but to do good works!*

your faith in the Lord Jesus and your love for all the saints, 16 do not cease to give thanks for you, making mention of you in my prayers: 17 that the God of our Lord Jesus Christ, the Father of glory, may give to you the spirit of wisdom and revelation in the knowledge of Him, 18 the eyes of your understanding[a] being enlightened; that you may know what is the hope of His calling, what are the riches of the glory of His inheritance in the saints, 19 and what is the exceeding greatness of His power toward us who believe, according to the working of His mighty power 20 which He worked in Christ when He raised Him from the dead and seated Him at His right hand in the heavenly places, 21 far above all principality and power and might and dominion, and every name that is named, not only in this age but also in that which is to come.

22 And He put all things under His feet, and gave Him to be head over all things to the church, 23 which is His body, the fullness of Him who fills all in all.

2 And you He made alive, who were dead in trespasses and sins, 2 in which you once walked according to the course of this world, according to the prince of the power of the air, the spirit who now works in the sons of disobedience, 3 among whom also we all once conducted ourselves in the lusts of our flesh, fulfilling the desires of the flesh and of the mind, and were by nature children of wrath, just as the others. 4 But God, who is rich in mercy, because of His great love with which He loved us, 5 even when we were dead in trespasses, made us alive together with Christ (by grace you have been saved), 6 and raised us up together, and made us sit together in the heavenly places in Christ Jesus, 7 that in the ages to come He might show the exceeding riches of His grace in His kindness toward us in Christ Jesus. 8 For by grace you have been saved through faith, and that not of yourselves; it is the gift of God, 9 not of works, lest anyone should boast. 10 For we are His workmanship, created in Christ Jesus for good works, which God prepared before-

hand that we should walk in them.

11 Therefore remember that you, once Gentiles in the flesh—who are called Uncircumcision by what is called the Circumcision made in the flesh by hands— 12 that at that time you were without Christ, being aliens from the commonwealth of Israel and strangers from the covenants of promise, having no hope and without God in the world. 13 But now in Christ Jesus you who once were far off have been brought near by the blood of Christ.

14 For He Himself is our peace, who has made both one, and has broken down the middle wall of separation, 15 having abolished in His flesh the enmity, that is, the law of commandments contained in ordinances, so as to create in Himself one new man from the two, thus making peace, 16 and that He might reconcile them both to God in one body through the cross, thereby putting to death the enmity. 17 And He came and preached peace to you who were afar off and to those who were near. 18 For through Him we both have access by one Spirit to the Father.

19 Now, therefore, you are no longer strangers and foreigners, but fellow citizens with the saints and members of the household of God, 20 having been built on the foundation of the apostles and prophets, Jesus Christ Himself being the chief cornerstone, 21 in whom the whole building, being fitted together, grows into a holy temple in the Lord, 22 in whom you also are being built together for a dwelling place of God in the Spirit.

3 For this reason I, Paul, the prisoner of Christ Jesus for you Gentiles— 2 if indeed you have heard of the dispensation of the grace of God which was given to me for you, 3 how that by revelation He made known to me the mystery (as I have briefly written already, 4 by which, when you read, you may understand my knowledge in the mystery of Christ), 5 which in other ages was not made known to the sons of men, as it has now been revealed by the Spirit to His holy apostles and prophets: 6 that the Gentiles should be fellow heirs, of the same body, and partak-

1:18 [a]NU-Text and M-Text read hearts.

The City of Ephesus

Ephesus was an important city on the western coast of Asia Minor where the apostle Paul founded a church. As the most favorable seaport in the Roman province of Asia, this city was the most important trade center west of Tarsus. Today the city lies in swampy ruins about six miles from the sea because of centuries of silting from the Cayster River.

During Paul's years in Ephesus, the city was a cultural center with a population of about 300,000 people. Ephesus boasted of a great amphitheater, which seated 25,000 people. The city also had a number of gymnasiums, baths, and impressive public buildings.

Religion was a prominent feature of life in Ephesus. The temple of Artemis (or Diana, her Roman name) ranked as one of the Seven Wonders of the Ancient World. As the daughter of Zeus, Artemis was variously known as the moon goddess, the goddess of hunting, and the patroness of young girls. The Ephesians took pride in the beautiful temple, which was supported by scores of stone columns (see map).

The church at Ephesus may have been established by Priscilla and Aquila (Acts 18:18, 19). It was about two years old when Paul settled in the city. Timothy was also involved in ministry at Ephesus (1 Tim. 1:3). Paul taught daily in the lecture hall of Tyrannus (Acts 19:9). Influence from Paul's three-year ministry likely resulted in the planting of churches in the Lycus River Valley at Laodicea, Hierapolis, and Colosse. The apostle wrote 1 Corinthians during his Ephesian ministry.

Some time after Paul's ministry, the apostle John settled and ministered at Ephesus. Exiled on the Isle of Patmos off the coast of Ephesus, he addressed the Book of Revelation to the seven churches of Asia Minor, which included the congregation at Ephesus (Rev. 1:11; 2:1–7). The traditional tomb of John is located at the Church of St. John in Ephesus.

City of Ephesus.

ers of His promise in Christ through the gospel, 7 of which I became a minister according to the gift of the grace of God given to me by the effective working of His power.

8 To me, who am less than the least of all the saints, this grace was given, that I should preach among the Gentiles the unsearchable riches of Christ, 9 and to make all see what *is* the fellowship*a* of the mystery, which from the beginning of the ages has been hidden in God who created all things through Jesus Christ;*b* 10 to the intent that now the manifold wisdom of God might be made known by the church to the principalities and powers in the heavenly *places,* 11 according to the eternal purpose which He accomplished in Christ Jesus our Lord, 12 in whom we have boldness and access with confidence through faith in Him. 13 Therefore I ask that you do not lose heart at my tribulations for you, which is your glory.

14 For this reason I bow my knees to the Father of our Lord Jesus Christ,*a* 15 from whom the whole family in heaven and earth is named, 16 that He would grant you, according to the riches of His glory, to be strengthened with might through His Spirit in the inner man, 17 that Christ may dwell in your hearts through faith; that you, being rooted and grounded in love, 18 may be able to comprehend with all the saints what *is* the width and length and depth and height— 19 to know the love of Christ which passes knowledge; that you may be filled with all the fullness of God.

20 Now to Him who is able to do exceedingly abundantly above all that we ask or think, according to the power that works in us, 21 to Him *be* glory in the church by Christ Jesus to all generations, forever and ever. Amen.

4 I, therefore, the prisoner of the Lord, beseech you to walk worthy of the calling with which you were called, 2 with all lowliness and gentleness, with longsuffering, bearing with one another in love, 3 endeavoring to keep the unity of the Spirit in the bond of peace. 4 *There is* one body and one Spirit, just as you were called in one hope of your calling; 5 one Lord, one faith, one baptism; 6 one God and Father of all, who *is* above all, and through all, and in you*a* all.

7 But to each one of us grace was given according to the measure of Christ's gift. 8 Therefore He says:

> "When He ascended on high,
> He led captivity captive,
> And gave gifts to men."*a*

9 (Now this, *"He ascended"*—what does it mean but that He also first*a* descended into the lower parts of the earth? 10 He who descended is also the One who ascended far above all the heavens, that He might fill all things.)

11 And He Himself gave some *to be* apostles, some prophets, some evangelists, and some pastors and teachers, 12 for the equipping of the saints for the work of ministry, for the edifying of the body of Christ, 13 till we all come to the unity of the faith and of the knowledge of the Son of God, to a perfect man, to the measure of the stature of the fullness of Christ; 14 that we should no longer be children, tossed to and fro and carried about with every wind of doctrine, by the trickery of men, in the cunning craftiness of deceitful plotting, 15 but, speaking the truth in love, may grow up in all things into Him who is the head—Christ— 16 from whom the whole body, joined and knit together by what every joint supplies, according to the effective working by which every part does its share, causes growth of the body for the edifying of itself in love.

17 This I say, therefore, and testify in the Lord, that you should no longer walk as the rest of the*a* Gentiles walk, in the futility of their mind, 18 having their understanding darkened, being alienated from the life of God, because of the ignorance that is in them, because of the blindness of their heart; 19 who, being past feeling, have given themselves over to lewdness, to work all uncleanness with greediness.

3:9 *a*NU-Text and M-Text read *stewardship (dispensation).*   *b*NU-Text omits *through Jesus Christ.*
3:14 *a*NU-Text omits *of our Lord Jesus Christ.*   4:6 *a*NU-Text omits *you;* M-Text reads *us.*   4:8 *a*Psalm 68:18   4:9 *a*NU-Text omits *first.*   4:17 *a*NU-Text omits *rest of the.*

God's Dream is Yours

What's the purpose of life anyway?
Only to eat, drink, work, play?
Or do you have a brain designed to dream dreams? The apostle Paul wrote: "Be renewed in the spirit of your mind" (Eph. 4:23).
Is your mind created to be an architect, drawing plans?
Can you imagine beautiful accomplishments?
Think of this:

The human being
is the only creature in the universe
that has the capacity for exercising creative imagination!

This divine quality of *dreaming*
what you want to be,
where you want to go,
what you'd love to do,
projects you hope to achieve,
goals you'd like to reach—
all of this makes you human
and the most unique creature in all of creation!

You really are "made in the image" of the Creator—God!
So you are fulfilling your destiny
as a child of God in human flesh
when you start dreaming the beautiful
dreams God Himself is inspiring in your mind.

A radio is designed to pick up the sounds that are here in this room now!
A television is engineered to pick up the moving pictures that are in the airwaves around you now.
Your mind was invented and created by God to pick up the messages and mental pictures He is sending your way.
That's exciting!
Faith is dreaming God's dreams!

20 But you have not so learned Christ, 21 if indeed you have heard Him and have been taught by Him, as the truth is in Jesus: 22 that you put off, concerning your former conduct, the old man which grows corrupt according to the deceitful lusts, 23 and be renewed in the spirit of your mind, 24 and that you put on the new man which was created according to God, in true righteousness and holiness.

25 Therefore, putting away lying, *"Let each one of you speak truth with his neighbor,"*ᵃ for we are members of one another. 26 *"Be angry, and do not sin"*:ᵃ do not let the sun go down on your wrath, 27 nor give place to the devil. 28 Let him who stole steal no longer, but rather let him labor, working with *his* hands what is good, that he may have something to give him who has need. 29 Let no corrupt word proceed out of your mouth, but what is good for necessary edification, that it may impart grace to the hearers. 30 And do not grieve the Holy Spirit of God, by whom you were sealed for the day of redemption. 31 Let all bitterness, wrath, anger, clamor, and evil speaking be put away from you, with all malice. 32 And be kind to one another, tenderhearted, forgiving one another, even as God in Christ forgave you.

5 Therefore be imitators of God as dear children. 2 And walk in love, as Christ also has loved us and given Himself for us, an offering and a sacrifice to God for a sweet-smelling aroma.

3 But fornication and all uncleanness or covetousness, let it not even be named among you, as is fitting for saints; 4 neither filthiness, nor foolish talking, nor coarse jesting, which are not fitting, but rather giving of thanks. 5 For this you know,ᵃ that no fornicator, unclean person, nor covetous man, who is an idolater, has any inheritance in the kingdom of Christ and God. 6 Let no one deceive you with empty words, for because of these things the wrath of God comes upon the sons of disobedience. 7 Therefore do not be partakers with them.

8 For you were once darkness, but now *you are* light in the Lord. Walk as children of light 9 (for the fruit of the Spiritᵃ *is* in all goodness, righteousness, and truth), 10 finding out what is acceptable to the Lord. 11 And have no fellowship with the unfruitful works of darkness, but rather expose *them*. 12 For it is shameful even to speak of those things which are done by them in secret. 13 But all things that are exposed are made manifest by the light, for whatever makes manifest is light. 14 Therefore He says:

"Awake, you who sleep,
Arise from the dead,
And Christ will give you light."

15 See then that you walk circumspectly, not as fools but as wise, 16 redeeming the time, because the days are evil.

17 Therefore do not be unwise, but understand what the will of the Lord *is*. 18 And do not be drunk with wine, in which is dissipation; but be filled with the Spirit, 19 speaking to one another in psalms and hymns and spiritual songs, singing and making melody in your heart to the Lord, 20 giving thanks always for all things to God the Father in the name of our Lord Jesus Christ, 21 submitting to one another in the fear of God.ᵃ

22 Wives, submit to your own husbands, as to the Lord. 23 For the husband is head of the wife, as also Christ is head of the church; and He is the Savior of the body. 24 Therefore, just as the church is subject to Christ, so *let* the wives *be* to their own husbands in everything.

25 Husbands, love your wives, just as Christ also loved the church and gave Himself for her, 26 that He might sanctify and cleanse her with the washing of water by the word, 27 that He might present her to Himself a glorious church, not having spot or wrinkle or any such thing, but that she should be holy and without blemish. 28 So husbands ought to love their own wives as their own bodies; he who loves his wife loves himself. 29 For no one ever hated his own flesh, but nourishes and cherishes it, just as the Lord *does* the church. 30 For we are members of His

4:25 ᵃZechariah 8:16   4:26 ᵃPsalm 4:4   5:5 ᵃNU-Text reads *For know this.*   5:9 ᵃNU-Text reads *light.*   5:21 ᵃNU-Text reads *Christ.*

body,[a] of His flesh and of His bones. 31 *"For this reason a man shall leave his father and mother and be joined to his wife, and the two shall become one flesh."*[a] 32 This is a great mystery, but I speak concerning Christ and the church. 33 Nevertheless let each one of you in particular so love his own wife as himself, and let the wife *see* that she respects *her* husband.

6 Children, obey your parents in the Lord, for this is right. 2 *"Honor your father and mother,"*[a] which is the first commandment with promise: 3 *"that it may be well with you and you may live long on the earth."*

4 And you, fathers, do not provoke your children to wrath, but bring them up in the training and admonition of the Lord.

5 Bondservants, be obedient to those who are your masters according to the flesh, with fear and trembling, in sincerity of heart, as to Christ; 6 not with eyeservice, as menpleasers, but as bondservants of Christ, doing the will of God from the heart, 7 with good will doing service, as to the Lord, and not to men, 8 knowing that whatever good anyone does, he will receive the same from the Lord, whether *he is* a slave or free.

9 And you, masters, do the same things to them, giving up threatening, knowing that your own Master also[a] is in heaven, and there is no partiality with Him.

10 Finally, my brethren, be strong in the Lord and in the power of His might. 11 Put on the whole armor of God, that you may be able to stand against the wiles of the devil. 12 For we do not wrestle against flesh and blood, but against principalities, against powers, against the rulers of the darkness of this age,[a] against spiritual *hosts* of wickedness in the heavenly *places.* 13 Therefore take up the whole armor of God, that you may be able to withstand in the evil day, and having done all, to stand.

14 Stand therefore, having girded your waist with truth, having put on the breastplate of righteousness, 15 and having shod your feet with the preparation of the gospel of peace; 16 above all, taking the shield of faith with which you will be able to quench all the fiery darts of the wicked one. 17 And take the helmet of salvation, and the sword of the Spirit, which is the word of God; 18 praying always with all prayer and supplication in the Spirit, being watchful to this end with all perseverance and supplication for all the saints— 19 and for me, that utterance may be given to me, that I may open my mouth boldly to make known the mystery of the gospel, 20 for which I am an ambassador in chains; that in it I may speak boldly, as I ought to speak.

21 But that you also may know my affairs *and* how I am doing, Tychicus, a beloved brother and faithful minister in the Lord, will make all things known to you; 22 whom I have sent to you for this very purpose, that you may know our affairs, and *that* he may comfort your hearts.

23 Peace to the brethren, and love with faith, from God the Father and the Lord Jesus Christ. 24 Grace *be* with all those who love our Lord Jesus Christ in sincerity. Amen.

5:30 [a]NU-Text omits the rest of this verse.   5:31 [a]Genesis 2:24   6:2 [a]Deuteronomy 5:16
6:9 [a]NU-Text reads *He who is both their Master and yours.*   6:12 [a]NU-Text reads *rulers of this darkness.*

Philippians

Overview of Philippians

$\mathcal{T}$he Book of Philippians is a motivational, goal-oriented letter, inspiring the Christians in Philippi and those throughout the world today to believe that they can do great things for God!

Paul wrote this Epistle while imprisoned in Rome about A.D. 61. His words of faith, though he was captive, are filled with determination and confidence to serve God no matter what the cost. Paul confirms that there is no gain without pain: "For to me, to live *is* Christ, and to die *is* gain" (Phil. 1:21).

The people of Philippi are presented with specific goals to strive toward in this letter: to become like-minded; to love one another; and to focus their thoughts on what is true, honest, just, pure, lovely, of good report, virtuous, and praiseworthy. Paul encourages them to filter out negative thoughts and to be controlled by positive thoughts. Then they can let worry drain out and let God's peace flow in.

Paul reminds them that what they do and what they become will be determined by the thoughts and goals they pursue. Their greatest asset is that God is working in and through them. "Being confident of this very thing, that He who has begun a good work in you will complete *it* until the day of Jesus Christ" (Phil. 1:6). And, "It is God who works in you both to will and to do for *His* good pleasure" (Phil. 2:13).

In Philippians we discover that a true Christian has a mind through which Christ thinks, a heart through which Christ loves, a tongue through which Christ speaks, a face through which Christ glows, and a hand through which Christ lifts!

Jesus in Philippians

Paul gives several portraits of Jesus in this Epistle. In chapter 1, Paul sees Jesus as his life. In chapter 2, Jesus is the model of true humility. Chapter 3 presents Him as the One "who will transform our lowly body that it may be conformed to His glorious body" (3:21). In chapter 4, He is the source of Paul's power over circumstances.

Keys to Philippians

Key Word: To Live Is Christ. Every chapter in Philippians resounds with the theme of the centrality of Jesus in the Christian's life: "Let this mind be in you which was also in Christ Jesus" (2:5); "I also count all things loss for the excellence of the knowledge of Christ Jesus" (3:8); "I can do all things through Christ who strengthens me" (4:13).

Key Verses: "For to me, to live *is* Christ, and to die *is* gain" (1:21).

"I know how to be abased, and I know how to abound. Everywhere and in all things I have learned both to be full and to be hungry, both to abound and to suffer need" (4:12).

Key Chapter: Philippians 2. The grandeur of the truth of the New Testament seldom exceeds the revelation of the humility of Jesus Christ when He left heaven to become a servant of man. Jesus is clearly the Christian's example.

1 Paul and Timothy, bondservants of Jesus Christ,

To all the saints in Christ Jesus who are in Philippi, with the bishops[a] and deacons:

2 Grace to you and peace from God our Father and the Lord Jesus Christ.

3 I thank my God upon every remembrance of you, 4 always in every prayer of mine making request for you all with joy, 5 for your fellowship in the gospel from the first day until now, 6 being confident of this very thing, that He who has begun a good work in you will complete it until the day of Jesus Christ; 7 just as it is right for me to think this of you all, because I have you in my heart, inasmuch as both in my chains and in the defense and confirmation of the gospel, you all are partakers with me of grace. 8 For God is my witness, how greatly I long for you all with the affection of Jesus Christ.

9 And this I pray, that your love may abound still more and more in knowledge and all discernment, 10 that you may approve the things that are excellent, that you may be sincere and without offense till the day of Christ, 11 being filled with the fruits of righteousness which are by Jesus Christ, to the glory and praise of God.

12 But I want you to know, brethren, that the things which happened to me have actually turned out for the furtherance of the gospel, 13 so that it has become evident to the whole palace guard, and to all the rest, that my chains are in Christ; 14 and most of the brethren in the Lord, having become confident by my chains, are much more bold to speak the word without fear.

15 Some indeed preach Christ even from envy and strife, and some also from goodwill: 16 The former[a] preach Christ from selfish ambition, not sincerely, supposing to add affliction to my chains; 17 but the latter out of love, knowing that I am appointed for the defense of the gospel. 18 What then? Only that in every way, whether in pretense or in truth, Christ is preached; and in this I rejoice, yes, and will rejoice.

19 For I know that this will turn out for my deliverance through your prayer and the supply of the Spirit of Jesus Christ, 20 according to my earnest expectation and hope that in nothing I shall be ashamed, but with all boldness, as always, so now also Christ will be magnified in my body, whether by life or by death. 21 For to me, to live is Christ, and to die is gain. 22 But if I live on in the flesh, this will mean fruit from my labor; yet what I shall choose I cannot tell. 23 For[a] I am hard pressed between the two, having a desire to depart and be with Christ, which is far better. 24 Nevertheless to remain in the flesh is more needful for you. 25 And being confident of this, I know that I shall remain and continue with you all for your progress and joy of faith, 26 that your rejoicing for me may be more abundant in Jesus Christ by my coming to you again.

27 Only let your conduct be worthy of the gospel of Christ, so that whether I come and see you or am absent, I may hear of your affairs, that you stand fast in one spirit, with one mind striving together for the faith of the gospel, 28 and not in any way terrified by your adversaries, which is to them a proof of perdition, but to you of salvation,[a] and that from God. 29 For to you it has been granted on behalf of Christ, not only to believe in Him, but also to suffer for His sake, 30 having the same conflict which you saw in me and now hear is in me.

2 Therefore if there is any consolation in Christ, if any comfort of love, if any fellowship of the Spirit, if any affection and mercy, 2 fulfill my joy by being like-minded, having the same love, being of one accord, of one mind. 3 Let nothing be done through selfish ambition or conceit,

1:1 [a]Literally overseers and M-Text read But. 1:16 [a]NU-Text reverses the contents of verses 16 and 17. 1:23 [a]NU-Text 1:28 [a]NU-Text reads of your salvation.

Press Toward the Goal

Our positive faith in Jesus Christ can be divided into three major steps:

1. Intellectual—When you walk the walk of faith you use your head. Be smart about it.
2. Emotional—Be inwardly secure enough that you do not fear the mysterious and marvelous geysering of positive emotions. Enthusiasm is a mark of health. However, it's not enough to merely "experience a religious feeling." In fact, many people with a strong faith never do have an emotional conversion experience. It's possible to be "born again" and not know the exact hour or time.
3. Volitional—Faith must be applied to daily life. The word *volition* means an act of choosing.

Faith moves from emotional and intellectual stages to a volitional stage when you are determined and disciplined. All great athletes who have won medals or earned crowns have done so because of tremendous faith. They believed they could win! And *then* they exploded with an inner willpower. Paul the apostle wrote: "I press toward the goal for the prize of the upward call of God in Christ Jesus" (Phil. 3:14).

Have you discovered this capacity in yourself? It's there. If you have experienced it, you know what I mean. But if you haven't, you need to believe that there is a lot more within you than you have ever experienced. It begins to surface when faith becomes an act of the will, when belief is translated into dynamic willpower. Only then will you realize the prize—the higher calling of God in Jesus Christ.

Ask God to help you discover the power that comes from within you when you make up your mind wholeheartedly to pursue your objective relentlessly.

but in lowliness of mind let each esteem others better than himself. 4 Let each of you look out not only for his own interests, but also for the interests of others.

5 Let this mind be in you which was also in Christ Jesus, 6 who, being in the form of God, did not consider it robbery to be equal with God, 7 but made Himself of no reputation, taking the form of a bondservant, *and* coming in the likeness of men. 8 And being found in appearance as a man, He humbled Himself and became obedient to *the point of* death, even the death of the cross. 9 Therefore God also has highly exalted Him and given Him the name which is above every name, 10 that at the name of Jesus every knee should bow, of those in heaven, and of those on earth, and of those under the earth, 11 and *that* every tongue should confess that Jesus Christ *is* Lord, to the glory of God the Father.

12 Therefore, my beloved, as you have always obeyed, not as in my presence only, but now much more in my absence, work out your own salvation with fear and trembling; 13 for it is God who works in you both to will and to do for *His* good pleasure.

14 Do all things without complaining and disputing, 15 that you may become blameless and harmless, children of God without fault in the midst of a crooked and perverse generation, among whom you shine as lights in the world, 16 holding fast the word of life, so that I may rejoice in the day of Christ that I have not run in vain or labored in vain.

17 Yes, and if I am being poured out *as a drink offering* on the sacrifice and service of your faith, I am glad and rejoice with you all. 18 For the same reason you also be glad and rejoice with me.

19 But I trust in the Lord Jesus to send Timothy to you shortly, that I also may be encouraged when I know your state. 20 For I have no one like-minded, who will sincerely care for your state. 21 For all seek their own, not the things which are of Christ Jesus. 22 But you know his proven character, that as a son with

his father he served with me in the gospel. 23 Therefore I hope to send him at once, as soon as I see how it goes with me. 24 But I trust in the Lord that I myself shall also come shortly.

25 Yet I considered it necessary to send to you Epaphroditus, my brother, fellow worker, and fellow soldier, but your messenger and the one who ministered to my need; 26 since he was longing for you all, and was distressed because you had heard that he was sick. 27 For indeed he was sick almost unto death; but God had mercy on him, and not only on him but on me also, lest I should have sorrow upon sorrow. 28 Therefore I sent him the more eagerly, that when you see him again you may rejoice, and I may be less sorrowful. 29 Receive him therefore in the Lord with all gladness, and hold such men in esteem; 30 because for the work of Christ he came close to death, not regarding his life, to supply what was lacking in your service toward me.

3 Finally, my brethren, rejoice in the Lord. For me to write the same things to you *is* not tedious, but for you *it is* safe.

2 Beware of dogs, beware of evil workers, beware of the mutilation! 3 For we are the circumcision, who worship God in the Spirit,*a* rejoice in Christ Jesus, and have no confidence in the flesh, 4 though I also might have confidence in the flesh. If anyone else thinks he may have confidence in the flesh, I more so: 5 circumcised the eighth day, of the stock of Israel, *of* the tribe of Benjamin, a Hebrew of the Hebrews; concerning the law, a Pharisee; 6 concerning zeal, persecuting the church; concerning the righteousness which is in the law, blameless.

7 But what things were gain to me, these I have counted loss for Christ. 8 Yet indeed I also count all things loss for the excellence of the knowledge of Christ Jesus my Lord, for whom I have suffered the loss of all things, and count them as rubbish, that I may gain Christ 9 and be found in Him, not having my own righteousness, which *is* from the law, but

3:3 *a*NU-Text and M-Text read *who worship in the Spirit of God.*

What is Your Goal?

Faith is not merely thinking holy and happy thoughts. God's thoughts must take the form of good and godly goals (Phil. 3:12–14).

No act of faith is more dynamic, more constructive, than setting high goals! Have you noticed how negative thinkers avoid setting goals of any kind?

"Goals—who needs them? I'll just wing it, thank you. I prefer to roll with the punches." "I don't want to get trapped by a commitment. Isn't that what happens when you set a goal?" "I've had enough disappointments. I don't want to be set up only to be let down. Goals? No more failures, thank you." Failure is not a matter of failing to meet your goal. Failure is not making the most of the possibilities seen and unseen, known and unknown, in your present and in your future! Jesus' parable of the talents (Matt. 25:14–30) clearly exemplifies this negative approach. The one who buried his talent in the field took no responsibility—goal setting—and reaped what he sowed—nothing. The man who set goals and wisely invested his talent was praised by Jesus for taking positive action.

Use faith to set positive goals, and you'll be sure to rise to the higher plateau. Try it, and you'll find that . . .

- you'll be farther ahead tomorrow than you are today. Even a little can turn out to be a lot!
- you'll be a happier person. When you're focused on goals, you are distracted from worries.
- you'll feel that your life has value!

Goals—what are they anyway? They are impossible problems waiting to be solved by someone with this incredible power called faith! So get set to set goals, and move upward!

that which *is* through faith in Christ, the righteousness which is from God by faith; 10 that I may know Him and the power of His resurrection, and the fellowship of His sufferings, be ing conformed to His death, 11 if, by any means, I may attain to the resurrection from the dead.

12 Not that I have already attained, or am already perfected; but I press on, that I may lay hold of that for which Christ Jesus has also laid hold of me. 13 Brethren, I do not count myself to have apprehended; but one thing *I do*, forgetting those things which are behind and reaching forward to those things which are ahead, 14 I press toward the goal for the prize of the upward call of God in Christ Jesus.

15 Therefore let us, as many as are mature, have this mind; and if in anything you think otherwise, God will reveal even this to you. 16 Nevertheless, to *the degree* that we have already attained, let us walk by the same rule,*a* let us be of the same mind.

17 Brethren, join in following my example, and note those who so walk, as you have us for a pattern. 18 For many walk, of whom I have told you often, and now tell you even weeping, *that they are* the enemies of the cross of Christ: 19 whose end *is* destruction, whose god *is their* belly, and *whose* glory *is* in their shame—who set their mind on earthly things. 20 For our citizenship is in heaven, from which we also eagerly wait for the Savior, the Lord Jesus Christ, 21 who will transform our lowly body that it may be conformed to His glorious body, according to the working by which He is able even to subdue all things to Himself.

4 Therefore, my beloved and longed-for brethren, my joy and crown, so stand fast in the Lord, beloved.

2 I implore Euodia and I implore Syntyche to be of the same mind in the Lord. 3 And*a* I urge you also, true companion, help these women who labored with me in the gospel, with Clement also, and the rest of my fellow workers, whose names *are* in the Book of Life.

4 Rejoice in the Lord always. Again I will say, rejoice!

5 Let your gentleness be known to all men. The Lord *is* at hand.

6 Be anxious for nothing, but in everything by prayer and supplication, with thanksgiving, let your requests be made known to God; 7 and the peace of God, which surpasses all understanding, will guard your hearts and minds through Christ Jesus.

8 Finally, brethren, whatever things are true, whatever things *are* noble, whatever things *are* just, whatever things *are* pure, whatever things *are* lovely, whatever things *are* of good report, if *there is* any virtue and if *there is* anything praiseworthy—meditate on these things. 9 The things which you learned and received and heard and saw in me, these do, and the God of peace will be with you.

10 But I rejoiced in the Lord greatly that now at last your care for me has flourished again; though you surely did care, but you lacked opportunity. 11 Not that I speak in regard to need, for I have learned in whatever state I am, to be content: 12 I know how to be abased, and I know how to abound. Everywhere and in all things I have learned both to be full and to be hungry, both to abound and to suffer need. 13 I can do all things through Christ*a* who strengthens me.

14 Nevertheless you have done well that you shared in my distress. 15 Now you Philippians know also that in the beginning of the gospel, when I departed from Macedonia, no church shared with me concerning giving and receiving but you only. 16 For even in Thessalonica you sent *aid* once and again for my necessities. 17 Not that I seek the gift, but I seek the fruit that abounds to your account. 18 Indeed I have all and abound. I am full, having received from Epaphroditus the things *sent* from you, a sweet-smelling aroma, an acceptable sacrifice, well pleasing to God. 19 And my God shall supply all your need according to His riches in glory by

Set Your Mind on Things Above

Philippians 4:8 makes it clear that a faith committed to success in the pursuit of an excellent and noble idea will require fine-tuning. Fine-tuning happens as you develop the practice of filtering the thoughts that come through your mind. Gradually your conscious level will rise as it relates in sensitivity to

what is positive and what is negative,
what is good and what is evil,
what is constructive and what is destructive,
what is healthy and what is unhealthy.

Your faith will be strengthened or weakened on a daily basis by the thoughts that enter your mind. You can choose many of your thoughts by selecting the reading material, the television programs, and the deliberate exposures that you choose to encounter.

Still, there are the thousands of unsolicited stimuli that hit the average brain from a variety of unpredictable sources in the course of a single day. Consequently, a filtering system must be built into your mind that screens out the negative while allowing the positive to pass through. Philippians 4:8 gives you the blueprint for establishing a six-layer mental filtering system.

1. Is it true?
2. Is it noble?
3. Is it just?
4. Is it pure?
5. Is it lovely?
6. Is it positive?

Now meditate on these things!

Christ Jesus. 20 Now to our God and Father *be* glory forever and ever. Amen.

21 Greet every saint in Christ Jesus. The brethren who are with me greet

you. 22 All the saints greet you, but especially those who are of Caesar's household.

23 The grace of our Lord Jesus Christ be with you all.*a* Amen.

4:23 *a*NU-Text reads *your spirit.*

Overview of Colossians

Paul wrote this letter to the Christians at Colossae from Rome about A.D. 60. The Colossians were mostly converted Gentiles who lived in the cosmopolitan city known for its fine wools and dyes, located on the major trade route between east and west in Asia Minor (modern Turkey).

To Christians in a city greatly influenced by its neighbors, Paul writes to encourage them in their newfound faith, warning them not to adopt any foreign doctrines or untruths into their belief and worship. It would have been easy for the Colossians to incorporate Jewish legalism, Greek philosophical speculative religion, and other pagan ideas because they had constant contact with the east and its mysticism.

Paul encourages his readers with the truth that Jesus Christ is the image of the invisible God and that through Him all things were created and are held together. He speaks of the mystery of God "which is Christ in you, the hope of glory" (Col.1:27). Paul holds up high ideals for the Colossians, and by sharing these goals with them he is confident his readers will live up to them.

The Colossians were able to believe in themselves because they knew that Paul believed in them. He made their destiny quite clear: "When Christ *who is* our life appears, then you also will appear with Him in glory" (Col. 3:4).

If Paul believed the best about the Christians in Colossae, who were faced with numerous negative obstacles to their faith, should we not also believe the best about ourselves and others? For with God as our strength we will succeed!

Jesus in Colossians

In Colossians, Paul eloquently describes Jesus' supreme position in all the universe: "the head of all principality and power" (2:10), the Lord of creation, and the Author of reconciliation. He is the basis for the believer's hope, the source of the believer's power for a new life, the believer's Redeemer and Reconciler, the embodiment of full deity, the Creator and Sustainer of all things, the Head of the church, the resurrected God-Man, and the all-sufficient Savior.

Keys to Colossians

Key Word: The Preeminence of Jesus. The resounding theme in Colossians is the preeminence and sufficiency of Jesus in all things. Paul's purpose is to refute a threatening heresy that is devaluing Jesus. This false teaching is countered by a positive presentation of His true attributes and accomplishments. A proper view of Jesus is the antidote for heresy. A firm adherence to the true gospel will give them stability and resistance to opposing influences.

Key Verses: "For in Him dwells all the fullness of the Godhead bodily; and you are complete in Him, who is the head of all principality and power" (2:9, 10).

"If then you were raised with Christ, seek those things which are above, where Christ is, sitting at the right hand of God. Set your mind on things above, not on things on the earth" (3:1, 3).

Key Chapter: Colossians 3. Chapter 3 links the three themes of Colossians together, showing their cause and effect relationships. Because the believer is risen with Christ, he is to put off the old man and put on the new, which will result in holiness in all relationships.

1 Paul, an apostle of Jesus Christ by the will of God, and Timothy our brother,

2 To the saints and faithful brethren in Christ *who are* in Colosse:

Grace to you and peace from God our Father and the Lord Jesus Christ.*a*

3 We give thanks to the God and Father of our Lord Jesus Christ, praying always for you, 4 since we heard of your faith in Christ Jesus and of your love for all the saints; 5 because of the hope which is laid up for you in heaven, of which you heard before in the word of the truth of the gospel, 6 which has come to you, as *it has* also in all the world, and is bringing forth fruit,*a* as *it is* also among you since the day you heard and knew the grace of God in truth; 7 as you also learned from Epaphras, our dear fellow servant, who is a faithful minister of Christ on your behalf, 8 who also declared to us your love in the Spirit.

9 For this reason we also, since the day we heard it, do not cease to pray for you, and to ask that you may be filled with the knowledge of His will in all wisdom and spiritual understanding; 10 that you may walk worthy of the Lord, fully pleasing *Him,* being fruitful in every good work and increasing in the knowledge of God; 11 strengthened with all might, according to His glorious power, for all patience and longsuffering with joy; 12 giving thanks to the Father who has qualified us to be partakers of the inheritance of the saints in the light. 13 He has delivered us from the power of darkness and conveyed *us* into the kingdom of the Son of His love, 14 in whom we have redemption through His blood,*a* the forgiveness of sins.

15 He is the image of the invisible God, the firstborn over all creation. 16 For by Him all things were created that are in heaven and that are on earth, visible and invisible, whether thrones or dominions or principalities or powers. All things were created through Him and for Him. 17 And He is before all things, and in Him all things consist. 18 And He is the head of the body, the church, who is the beginning, the firstborn from the dead, that in all things He may have the preeminence.

19 For it pleased *the Father that* in Him all the fullness should dwell, 20 and by Him to reconcile all things to Himself, by Him, whether things on earth or things in heaven, having made peace through the blood of His cross.

21 And you, who once were alienated and enemies in your mind by wicked works, yet now He has reconciled 22 in the body of His flesh through death, to present you holy, and blameless, and above reproach in His sight— 23 if indeed you continue in the faith, grounded and steadfast, and are not moved away from the hope of the gospel which you heard, which was preached to every creature under heaven, of which I, Paul, became a minister.

24 I now rejoice in my sufferings for

1:2 *a*NU-Text omits *and the Lord Jesus Christ.*   1:6 *a*NU-Text and M-Text add *and growing.*
1:14 *a*NU-Text and M-Text omit *through His blood.*

Hidden Treasure

The Bible and history have much to say about hidden treasure. People of the biblical world often stored great amounts of wealth in the ground for safekeeping. The earth itself was the central bank of the ancient world. If a warring army or band of thieves plundered or robbed a village, they would not find the town's treasure, for it was hidden secretly in the field. In Jesus' parable of the talents, one servant buried his money (Matt. 25:25). Solomon said, "Search for [wisdom] as *for* hidden treasures" (Prov. 2:4).

The famous Dead Sea Scrolls contain a document known as "The Copper Scroll" that describes sixty-four hiding places of buried treasure. Many scholars of biblical studies and archaeology believe that the Qumran community, who lived near the Dead Sea, hid these scrolls from the invading Roman army in A.D. 68. On several occasions in modern times, archaeologists or farmers plowing fields have unearthed thousands of coins, jewelry, gold, silver, or pearls hidden in the countryside.

There are three ways of locating these ancient hidden treasures. The first is to find an antique map describing the treasure's location. The second is to stumble across the treasure when you are traveling or if you are, for some reason, plowing a field. And the third is simply to have someone tell you where it is.

Regardless of how treasure was found in biblical times, it belonged to the owner of the field in which it was buried. Jesus said, "Again, the kingdom of heaven is like treasure hidden in a field, which a man found and hid; and for joy over it he goes and sells all that he has and buys that field" (Matt. 13:44).

The hidden treasure Jesus spoke of is the kingdom of God. When you enter into a relationship with God and discover the riches of knowing Him, you will put all your efforts into getting to know Him better, through reading His Word, prayer, and service. Then you will discover with the apostle Paul, "In [Christ] are hidden all the treasures of wisdom and knowledge" (Col. 2:3).

you, and fill up in my flesh what is lacking in the afflictions of Christ, for the sake of His body, which is the church, 25 of which I became a minister according to the stewardship from God which was given to me for you, to fulfill the word of God, 26 the mystery which has been hidden from ages and from generations, but now has been revealed to His saints. 27 To them God willed to make known what are the riches of the glory of this mystery among the Gentiles: which*a* is Christ in you, the hope of glory. 28 Him we preach, warning every man and teaching every man in all wisdom, that we may present every man perfect in Christ Jesus. 29 To this *end* I also labor, striving according to His working which works in me mightily.

2 For I want you to know what a great conflict I have for you and those in Laodicea, and *for* as many as have not seen my face in the flesh, 2 that their hearts may be encouraged, being knit together in love, and *attaining* to all riches of the full assurance of understanding, to the knowledge of the mystery of God, both of the Father and*a* of Christ, 3 in whom are hidden all the treasures of wisdom and knowledge.

4 Now this I say lest anyone should deceive you with persuasive words. 5 For though I am absent in the flesh, yet I am with you in spirit, rejoicing to see your *good* order and the steadfastness of your faith in Christ.

6 As you therefore have received Christ Jesus the Lord, so walk in Him, 7 rooted and built up in Him and established in the faith, as you have been taught, abounding in it*a* with thanksgiving.

8 Beware lest anyone cheat you through philosophy and empty deceit, according to the tradition of men, according to the basic principles of the world, and not according to Christ. 9 For in Him dwells all the fullness of the Godhead bodily; 10 and you are complete in Him, who is the head of all principality and power.

11 In Him you were also circumcised with the circumcision made without hands, by putting off the body of the sins*a* of the flesh, by the circumcision of Christ, 12 buried with Him in baptism, in which you also were raised with *Him* through faith in the working of God, who raised Him from the dead. 13 And you, being dead in your trespasses and the uncircumcision of your flesh, He has made alive together with Him, having forgiven you all trespasses, 14 having wiped out the handwriting of requirements that was against us, which was contrary to us. And He has taken it out of the way, having nailed it to the cross. 15 Having disarmed principalities and powers, He made a public spectacle of them, triumphing over them in it.

16 So let no one judge you in food or in drink, or regarding a festival or a new moon or sabbaths, 17 which are a shadow of things to come, but the substance is of Christ. 18 Let no one cheat you of your reward, taking delight in *false* humility and worship of angels, intruding into those things which he has not*a* seen, vainly puffed up by his fleshly mind, 19 and not holding fast to the Head, from whom all the body, nourished and knit together by joints and ligaments, grows with the increase *that is* from God.

20 Therefore,*a* if you died with Christ from the basic principles of the world, why, as *though* living in the world, do you subject yourselves to regulations— 21 "Do not touch, do not taste, do not handle," 22 which all concern things which perish with the using—according to the commandments and doctrines of men? 23 These things indeed have an appearance of wisdom in self-imposed religion, *false* humility, and neglect of the body, *but are* of no value against the indulgence of the flesh.

3 If then you were raised with Christ, seek those things which are above, where Christ is, sitting at the right hand of God. 2 Set your mind on things above, not on things on the earth. 3 For you died, and your life is hidden with Christ in God. 4 When Christ *who is* our life ap-

---

1:27 *a*M-Text reads *who.*   2:2 *a*NU-Text omits *both of the Father and.*   2:7 *a*NU-Text omits *in it.*
2:11 *a*NU-Text omits *of the sins.*   2:18 *a*NU-Text omits *not.*   2:20 *a*NU-Text and M-Text omit *Therefore.*

Co-Workers with God

Work held a religious significance to the people of the biblical world. To them the term "work" meant people and God working together. God was considered at the center of both work and play. Without His help, man's endeavors could not be successful. When asked the question, "How is the harvest?" the sowers in the fields replied, "God is working bountifully." Even today, Christians implore God's help in their daily tasks. Asking God's assistance in daily functions is an essential aspect of everyday life (see Phil. 4:19).

Jesus expressed an intimate relationship between His work and God's work. "My Father has been working until now, and I have been working" (John 5:17). The miracles Jesus performed in the presence of many people bear witness that God worked in and through Him. Jesus declared, "This is the work of God, that you believe in Him whom He sent" (John 6:29).

The early apostles also realized the need of God's power in their work of evangelizing the nations. Paul said, "*Whatever* you do in word or deed, *do* all in the name of the Lord Jesus . . ." (Col. 3:17). Having God work through us and help us insures that whatever work we undertake will be His work and have His blessings. Jesus Himself promised us that the works He did we also will do (see John 14:12). After a long life of sharing in God's work, Paul assures his readers in Philippians that God is at work in Christians to accomplish His good pleasure.

Whatever we do, we can be confident that God will work through us as we abide in Him. John 15:5 says, "I am the vine, you *are* the branches. He who abides in Me, and I in him, bears much fruit; for without Me you can do nothing."

pears, then you also will appear with Him in glory.

5 Therefore put to death your members which are on the earth: fornication, uncleanness, passion, evil desire, and covetousness, which is idolatry. 6 Because of these things the wrath of God is coming upon the sons of disobedience, 7 in which you yourselves once walked when you lived in them.

8 But now you yourselves are to put off all these: anger, wrath, malice, blasphemy, filthy language out of your mouth. 9 Do not lie to one another, since you have put off the old man with his deeds, 10 and have put on the new *man* who is renewed in knowledge according to the image of Him who created him, 11 where there is neither Greek nor Jew, circumcised nor uncircumcised, barbarian, Scythian, slave *nor* free, but Christ *is* all and in all.

12 Therefore, as *the* elect of God, holy and beloved, put on tender mercies, kindness, humility, meekness, longsuffering; 13 bearing with one another, and forgiving one another, if anyone has a complaint against another; even as Christ forgave you, so you also *must do.* 14 But above all these things put on love, which is the bond of perfection. 15 And let the peace of God rule in your hearts, to which also you were called in one body; and be thankful. 16 Let the word of Christ dwell in you richly in all wisdom, teaching and admonishing one another in psalms and hymns and spiritual songs, singing with grace in your hearts to the Lord. 17 And *whatever* you do in word or deed, *do* all in the name of the Lord Jesus, giving thanks to God the Father through Him.

18 Wives, submit to your own husbands, as is fitting in the Lord.

19 Husbands, love your wives and do not be bitter toward them.

20 Children, obey your parents in all things, for this is well pleasing to the Lord.

21 Fathers, do not provoke your children, lest they become discouraged.

22 Bondservants, obey in all things your masters according to the flesh, not with eyeservice, as men-pleasers, but in sincerity of heart, fearing God. 23 And whatever you do, do it heartily, as to the Lord and not to men, 24 knowing that from the Lord you will receive the reward of the inheritance; for[a] you serve the Lord Christ. 25 But he who does wrong will be repaid for what he has done, and there is no partiality.

4 Masters, give your bondservants what is just and fair, knowing that you also have a Master in heaven.

2 Continue earnestly in prayer, being vigilant in it with thanksgiving; 3 meanwhile praying also for us, that God would open to us a door for the word, to speak the mystery of Christ, for which I am also in chains, 4 that I may make it manifest, as I ought to speak.

5 Walk in wisdom toward those *who are* outside, redeeming the time. 6 *Let* your speech always *be* with grace, seasoned with salt, that you may know how you ought to answer each one.

7 Tychicus, a beloved brother, faithful minister, and fellow servant in the Lord, will tell you all the news about me. 8 I am sending him to you for this very purpose, that he[a] may know your circumstances and comfort your hearts, 9 with Onesimus, a faithful and beloved brother, who is *one* of you. They will make known to you all things which *are happening* here.

10 Aristarchus my fellow prisoner greets you, with Mark the cousin of Barnabas (about whom you received instructions: if he comes to you, welcome him), 11 and Jesus who is called Justus. These *are my* only fellow workers for the kingdom of God who are of the circumcision; they have proved to be a comfort to me.

12 Epaphras, who is *one* of you, a bondservant of Christ, greets you, always laboring fervently for you in prayers, that you may stand perfect and complete[a] in all the will of God. 13 For I bear him witness that he has a great zeal[a] for you, and those who are in Laodicea, and those in Hierapolis. 14 Luke the beloved physician and Demas greet you. 15 Greet the

---

3:24 [a]NU-Text omits *for.*   4:8 [a]NU-Text reads *you may know our circumstances and he may.*
4:12 [a]NU-Text reads *fully assured.*   4:13 [a]NU-Text reads *concern.*

Season Your World

What precisely does it mean to let your speech be seasoned with salt (Col. 4:6)? Can you imagine how bland food would be without salt? That's precisely what happens in an institution—whether it's a club, church, or legislative body—without new ideas and creative opportunities.

A community, state, country, or life becomes very matter-of-fact until a possibility thinker steps in. When he dreams great dreams, he seasons life. When he speaks a wholesome word, he creates

- beauty where there was drabness.
- excellence where there was mediocrity.
- excitement where there were only ho-hum attitudes.

Watch out, world, wherever there is a possibility thinker, life is never going to be the same again!

When possibilities begin to bounce around and big ideas produce big projects, a sleepy little town starts awakening! This is the exciting challenge!

Put some energy and enthusiasm in the lives of people around you! Dynamic leaders who season the world with fulfilling plans can liven things up in a hurry!

Determine to be wholesome seasoning in the feast of life, thanking God for this opportunity. Amen.

brethren who are in Laodicea, and Nymphas and the church that *is* in his*a* house.

16 Now when this epistle is read among you, see that it is read also in the church of the Laodiceans, and that you likewise read the epistle from Laodicea. 17 And say to Archippus, "Take heed to the ministry which you have received in the Lord, that you may fulfill it."

18 This salutation by my own hand—Paul. Remember my chains. Grace *be* with you. Amen.

4:15 *a*NU-Text reads *Nympha . . . . her house.*

First Thessalonians

Overview of First Thessalonians

God is stronger and bigger than any problem! With Him you can overcome any obstacle!

First Thessalonians was written between A.D. 50 and 51 by Paul from Corinth to the Christians in Thessalonica, Greece. These new believers were facing tough persecution from both the Jews and the Gentiles.

Paul had personally evangelized the Thessalonians, and several people came to know Jesus Christ because of his message. But the outraged Jewish population forced Paul to escape by night to the city of Berea, sixty miles away. When a group of Jews followed Paul, he had to flee a second time to the city of Athens.

After Paul left, the new church was the focus of persecution. Paul writes to encourage them and to rejoice with his friends as they grow in their faith. They have remained steadfast despite the troubles, he notes, and have even grown stronger during their trials. Paul commends them for turning their thoughts to God, not to their problems.

We give thanks to God always for you all, making mention of you in our prayers, remembering without ceasing your work of faith, labor of love, and patience of hope in our Lord Jesus Christ in the sight of our God and Father.

(1 Thess. 1:2, 3)

Paul was not unfamiliar with persecution because of a faithful testimony. He had experienced trouble throughout the Roman Empire. Even so, he had learned to focus his efforts on the present in light of the Second Coming of Jesus Christ. This is what he urges the Thessalonians to do. The present life, despite its problems, is a precious gift from God and should be enjoyed. Paul assures them that God's faithful ability can accomplish anything in their lives: "He who calls you *is* faithful, who also will do *it*" (1 Thess. 5:24). God is stronger and bigger than any problem!

Jesus in First Thessalonians

Jesus is the believer's hope of salvation both now and at His coming. When He returns, He will deliver, reward, perfect, resurrect, and sanctify all who trust Him.

Keys to First Thessalonians

Key Word: Holiness in Light of Jesus' Return. Throughout this letter is an unmistakable emphasis upon steadfastness in the Lord and a continuing growth in faith and love in view of the return of Jesus. The theme is not only His return, but also the life of the believer in every practical relationship, each aspect of which can be transformed and illuminated by the glorious prospect of His eventual return.

Key Verses: "And may the Lord make you increase and abound in love to one another and to all, just as we *do* to you, so that He may establish your hearts blameless in holiness before our God and Father at the coming of our Lord Jesus Christ with all His saints" (3:12, 13).

"For the Lord Himself will descend from heaven with a shout, with the voice of an archangel, and with the trumpet of God. And the dead in Christ will rise first. Then we who are alive *and* remain shall be caught up together with them in the clouds to meet the Lord in the air. And thus we shall always be with the Lord. Therefore comfort one another with these words" (4:16–18).

Key Chapter: First Thessalonians 4. Chapter 4 includes the central passage of the Epistles on the coming of the Lord, when the dead in Christ shall rise, and those who remain are caught up together with them in the clouds.

1
Paul, Silvanus, and Timothy,

To the church of the Thessalonians in God the Father and the Lord Jesus Christ:

Grace to you and peace from God our Father and the Lord Jesus Christ.[a]

2 We give thanks to God always for you all, making mention of you in our prayers, 3 remembering without ceasing your work of faith, labor of love, and patience of hope in our Lord Jesus Christ in the sight of our God and Father, 4 knowing, beloved brethren, your election by God. 5 For our gospel did not come to you in word only, but also in power, and in the Holy Spirit and in much assurance, as you know what kind of men we were among you for your sake.

6 And you became followers of us and of the Lord, having received the word in much affliction, with joy of the Holy Spirit, 7 so that you became examples to all in Macedonia and Achaia who believe. 8 For from you the word of the Lord has sounded forth, not only in Macedonia and Achaia, but also in every place. Your faith toward God has gone out, so that we do not need to say anything. 9 For they themselves declare concerning us what manner of entry we had to you, and how you turned to God from idols to serve the living and true God, 10 and to wait for His Son from heaven, whom He raised from the dead, *even* Jesus who delivers us from the wrath to come.

2
For you yourselves know, brethren, that our coming to you was not in vain. 2 But even[a] after we had suffered before and were spitefully treated at Philippi, as you know, we were bold in our God to speak to you the gospel of God in much conflict. 3 For our exhortation *did* not *come* from error or uncleanness, nor *was it* in deceit.

4 But as we have been approved by God to be entrusted with the gospel, even so we speak, not as pleasing men, but God who tests our hearts. 5 For neither at any time did we use flattering words, as you know, nor a cloak for covetousness—God *is* witness. 6 Nor did we seek glory from men, either from you or from others, when we might have made demands as apostles of Christ. 7 But we were gentle among you, just as a nursing *mother* cherishes her own children. 8 So, affectionately longing for you, we were well pleased to impart to you not only the gospel of God, but also our own lives, because you had become dear to us. 9 For you remember, brethren, our labor and toil; for laboring night and day, that we might not be a burden to any of you, we preached to you the gospel of God.

10 You *are* witnesses, and God *also*, how devoutly and justly and blamelessly we behaved ourselves among you who believe; 11 as you know how

1:1 [a]NU-Text omits *from God our Father and the Lord Jesus Christ.*   2:2 [a]NU-Text and M-Text omit *even.*

In the Name of God

Some *trust* in chariots, and some in horses;
But we will remember the name of the LORD our God (Ps. 20:7).

In ancient times, it was customary to invoke the name of a ruler or king to validate authority. Letters were sent between pharaohs, princes, and emperors bearing the scarab seal or signet ring imprint of the name of the monarch who sent the epistle. Messengers presenting themselves before kings were introduced as coming in the name of the ruler who sent them.

Much evidence has been unearthed indicating that names played a dominant role in the ancient Middle East society. Various forms of communication have been found containing the names of Thutmose III, Sennacherib, Alexander the Great, Cleopatra, and the Roman caesars. Greetings were exchanged, victories declared, cities built, peace made, and worship invoked in the name of rulers and gods.

This belief that the name had special power was so important that people put their trust in the name they considered to have supreme authority. To ridicule or curse the name of a ruler or god was to make an assault on the individual.

The concept of going in the name of a ruler carried over into the New Testament period and is often reflected in the words of Jesus. In teaching His disciples how to pray, Jesus asked them to respect or "hallow" the name of God (see Matt. 6:9). Jesus told His followers that belief in His name would grant them eternal life.

The New Testament apostles declared that at the name of Jesus every knee should bow (see Phil. 2:10). Many of the Epistles open with an invocation mentioning the name of Jesus. Spiritual victories and great power and authority were associated with His name.

In our lives, this power of the name of Jesus is as real as it was in the early church. If we place our trust in Him and in our God, then we have access to *the* greatest authority and power. In our daily existence, we may hear people talk about how they work for a large, important company, how they take pride in their family name, or how they act under the auspices of a specific title. This is all fine. But as Christians, we come in the name of the supreme authority. We come in the name of the Lord. And we have the promises that He gave to us: "Whatever things you ask in prayer, believing, you will receive" (Matt. 21:22). "And nothing will be impossible for you" (Matt. 17:20).

we exhorted, and comforted, and charged[a] every one of you, as a father *does* his own children, 12 that you would walk worthy of God who calls you into His own kingdom and glory.

13 For this reason we also thank God without ceasing, because when you received the word of God which you heard from us, you welcomed *it* not *as* the word of men, but as it is in truth, the word of God, which also effectively works in you who believe. 14 For you, brethren, became imitators of the churches of God which are in Judea in Christ Jesus. For you also suffered the same things from your own countrymen, just as they *did* from the Judeans, 15 who killed both the Lord Jesus and their own prophets, and have persecuted us; and they do not please God and are contrary to all men, 16 forbidding us to speak to the Gentiles that they may be saved, so as always to fill up *the measure of* their sins; but wrath has come upon them to the uttermost.

17 But we, brethren, having been taken away from you for a short time in presence, not in heart, endeavored more eagerly to see your face with great desire. 18 Therefore we wanted to come to you—even I, Paul, time and again—but Satan hindered us. 19 For what *is* our hope, or joy, or crown of rejoicing? *Is it* not even you in the presence of our Lord Jesus Christ at His coming? 20 For you are our glory and joy.

3 Therefore, when we could no longer endure it, we thought it good to be left in Athens alone, 2 and sent Timothy, our brother and minister of God, and our fellow laborer in the gospel of Christ, to establish you and encourage you concerning your faith, 3 that no one should be shaken by these afflictions; for you yourselves know that we are appointed to this. 4 For, in fact, we told you before when we were with you that we would suffer tribulation, just as it happened, and you know. 5 For this reason, when I could no longer endure it, I sent to know your faith, lest by some means the tempter had tempted you, and our labor might be in vain.

6 But now that Timothy has come to us from you, and brought us good news of your faith and love, and that you always have good remembrance of us, greatly desiring to see us, as we also *to see* you— 7 therefore, brethren, in all our affliction and distress we were comforted concerning you by your faith. 8 For now we live, if you stand fast in the Lord.

9 For what thanks can we render to God for you, for all the joy with which we rejoice for your sake before our God, 10 night and day praying exceedingly that we may see your face and perfect what is lacking in your faith?

11 Now may our God and Father Himself, and our Lord Jesus Christ, direct our way to you. 12 And may the Lord make you increase and abound in love to one another and to all, just as we *do* to you, 13 so that He may establish your hearts blameless in holiness before our God and Father at the coming of our Lord Jesus Christ with all His saints.

4 Finally then, brethren, we urge and exhort in the Lord Jesus that you should abound more and more, just as you received from us how you ought to walk and to please God; 2 for you know what commandments we gave you through the Lord Jesus.

3 For this is the will of God, your sanctification: that you should abstain from sexual immorality; 4 that each of you should know how to possess his own vessel in sanctification and honor, 5 not in passion of lust, like the Gentiles who do not know God; 6 that no one should take advantage of and defraud his brother in this matter, because the Lord *is* the avenger of all such, as we also forewarned you and testified. 7 For God did not call us to uncleanness, but in holiness. 8 Therefore he who rejects *this* does not reject man, but God, who has also given[a] us His Holy Spirit.

9 But concerning brotherly love you have no need that I should write to you, for you yourselves are taught by God to love one another; 10 and indeed you do so toward all the brethren who are in all Macedonia. But we urge you, brethren, that you increase more and more; 11 that you also aspire to lead a quiet life, to mind your own business, and

2:11 [a]NU-Text and M-Text read *implored*.   4:8 [a]NU-Text reads *who also gives*.

The City of Thessalonica

Thessalonica was founded in 315 B.C. by the Macedonian king Cassander. He named the city after his wife Thessalonica, sister of the Greek military conqueror, Alexander the Great. The apostle Paul worked for several months in Thessalonica and later addressed two letters (1 and 2 Thessalonians) to the church in this city.

Paul visited Thessalonica in the early fifties during his second missionary journey through the Roman province of Macedonia (Acts 17:1–9). The church that he worked with here consisted of former members of the Jewish synagogue, as well as non-Jews from pagan backgrounds. The tender words with which Paul addressed the Thessalonians make it clear that he developed strong affection for the Thessalonian church (1 Thess. 2:1–12).

Thessalonica's natural harbor made it a vital trading center, which brought in people from many places. This may have been why it was selected as the site for a church. At the time of his visit, Thessalonica was the most populous city in the entire Roman province of Macedonia.

Roman influence on Thessalonica is evident in the city's physical structure. Vital to the city's prosperity was the Egnatian Way, a Roman military highway which provided a route to the empire's eastern provinces. This route still serves as one of the main streets for modern Thessalonica (known as Salonika). Roman arches stood at Thessalonica's two entrances to the Egnatian Way. The one built in A.D. 297 to honor the Roman emperor Galerius remains intact.

Thessalonica's importance is also demonstrated by the great wall that surrounded the city, portions of which are still standing. The modern wall was built after Paul's time, but it was constructed on the foundations of the old city wall from the New Testament era.

Thessalonica's natural harbor made it a vital trading center, which brought in people from many places.

to work with your own hands, as we commanded you, 12 that you may walk properly toward those who are outside, and *that* you may lack nothing.

13 But I do not want you to be ignorant, brethren, concerning those who have fallen asleep, lest you sorrow as others who have no hope. 14 For if we believe that Jesus died and rose again, even so God will bring with Him those who sleep in Jesus.*a*

15 For this we say to you by the word of the Lord, that we who are alive *and* remain until the coming of the Lord will by no means precede those who are asleep. 16 For the Lord Himself will descend from heaven with a shout, with the voice of an archangel, and with the trumpet of God. And the dead in Christ will rise first. 17 Then we who are alive *and* remain shall be caught up together with them in the clouds to meet the Lord in the air. And thus we shall always be with the Lord. 18 Therefore comfort one another with these words.

5 But concerning the times and the seasons, brethren, you have no need that I should write to you. 2 For you yourselves know perfectly that the day of the Lord so comes as a thief in the night. 3 For when they say, "Peace and safety!" then sudden destruction comes upon them, as labor pains upon a pregnant woman. And they shall not escape. 4 But you, brethren, are not in darkness, so that this Day should overtake you as a thief. 5 You are all sons of light and sons of the day. We are not of the night nor of darkness. 6 Therefore let us not sleep, as others *do*, but let us watch and be sober. 7 For those who sleep, sleep at night, and those who get drunk are drunk at night.

8 But let us who are of the day be sober, putting on the breastplate of faith and love, and *as* a helmet the hope of salvation. 9 For God did not appoint us to wrath, but to obtain salvation through our Lord Jesus Christ, 10 who died for us, that whether we wake or sleep, we should live together with Him.

11 Therefore comfort each other and edify one another, just as you also are doing.

12 And we urge you, brethren, to recognize those who labor among you, and are over you in the Lord and admonish you, 13 and to esteem them very highly in love for their work's sake. Be at peace among yourselves.

14 Now we exhort you, brethren, warn those who are unruly, comfort the fainthearted, uphold the weak, be patient with all. 15 See that no one renders evil for evil to anyone, but always pursue what is good both for yourselves and for all.

16 Rejoice always, 17 pray without ceasing, 18 in everything give thanks; for this is the will of God in Christ Jesus for you.

19 Do not quench the Spirit. 20 Do not despise prophecies. 21 Test all things; hold fast what is good. 22 Abstain from every form of evil.

23 Now may the God of peace Himself sanctify you completely; and may your whole spirit, soul, and body be preserved blameless at the coming of our Lord Jesus Christ. 24 He who calls you *is* faithful, who also will do *it*.

25 Brethren, pray for us.

26 Greet all the brethren with a holy kiss.

27 I charge you by the Lord that this epistle be read to all the holy*a* brethren.

28 The grace of our Lord Jesus Christ *be* with you. Amen.

4:14 *a*Or those who through Jesus sleep   5:27 *a*NU-Text omits *holy*.

Second Thessalonians

Overview of Second Thessalonians

The Thessalonians are outstanding examples of Christian believers who stood firm in their faith and showed love and charity toward each other. Second Thessalonians is the second of Paul's letters from Corinth to these believers, written only a few months following his first correspondence in A.D. 51.

Possibly due to their location on the Via Egnatia, the famous highway from Rome to the east, the Thessalonians were exposed to itinerant false teachers who claimed that the Second Coming of Christ was about to take place. In response, the people had left their jobs and businesses to await the Lord's return.

Paul exhorts them to return to work and to be patient, trusting God's timing for Jesus' return. He urges them not to be so heavenly minded that they are no earthly good.

Paul encourages the Thessalonians to continue living the positive Christian life-style to which they have committed themselves. Paul prays that God may give them peace in every circumstance, knowing that God is with them. God's presence is not to be just in the future; it's in the present also!

Therefore, brethren, stand fast and hold the traditions which you were taught, whether by word or our epistle. Now may our Lord Jesus Christ Himself, and our God and Father, who has loved us and given us everlasting consolation and good hope by grace, comfort your hearts and establish you in every good word and work.

(2 Thess. 2:15–17)

Jesus in Second Thessalonians

The return of Jesus is mentioned more times in the New Testament than any other doctrine, and this is certainly the major concept in chapters 1 and 2 of this Epistle. The return of the Lord Jesus is a reassuring and joyful hope for believers, but His revelation from heaven holds awesome and terrifying implications for those who have not trusted in Him.

Keys to Second Thessalonians

Key Word: Understanding the Day of the Lord. The theme of this Epistle is an understanding of the Day of the Lord and how it affects believers' everyday lives. Some of the believers have abandoned their work and have begun to live off of other people, apparently assuming that the end is at hand. Paul commands them to follow his example by supporting themselves and instructs the rest of the church to discipline them if they fail to do so.

Key Verses: "Not to be soon shaken in mind or troubled, either by spirit or by word or by letter, as if from us, as though the day of Christ had come. Let no one deceive you by any means; for *that Day will not come* unless the falling away comes first, and the man of sin is revealed, the son of perdition" (2:2, 3).

"Now may the Lord direct your hearts into the love of God and into the patience of Christ. But we command you, brethren, in the name of our Lord Jesus Christ, that you withdraw from every brother who walks disorderly and not according to the tradition which he received from us" (3:5, 6).

Key Chapter: Second Thessalonians 2. The second chapter is written to correct the false teaching that the Day of the Lord has already come upon the Thessalonian church. This teaching, coupled with afflictions they have been suffering, is causing a great disturbance among the believers who wonder when their "gathering together to Him" (2:1) will take place. Paul makes it clear that certain identifiable events will precede that day and that those events have not yet occurred.

1 Paul, Silvanus, and Timothy,

To the church of the Thessalonians in God our Father and the Lord Jesus Christ:

2 Grace to you and peace from God our Father and the Lord Jesus Christ.

3 We are bound to thank God always for you, brethren, as it is fitting, because your faith grows exceedingly, and the love of every one of you all abounds toward each other, 4 so that we ourselves boast of you among the churches of God for your patience and faith in all your persecutions and tribulations that you endure, 5 *which is* manifest evidence of the righteous judgment of God, that you may be counted worthy of the kingdom of God, for which you also suffer; 6 since *it is* a righteous thing with God to repay with tribulation those who trouble you, 7 and to *give* you who are troubled rest with us when the Lord Jesus is revealed from heaven with His mighty angels, 8 in flaming fire taking vengeance on those who do not know God, and on those who do not obey the gospel of our Lord Jesus Christ. 9 These shall be punished with everlasting destruction from the presence of the Lord and from the glory of His power, 10 when He comes, in that Day, to be glorified in His saints and to be admired among all those who believe,*a* because our testimony among you was believed.

11 Therefore we also pray always for you that our God would count you worthy of *this* calling, and fulfill all the good pleasure of *His* goodness and the work of faith with power, 12 that the name of our Lord Jesus Christ may be glorified in you, and you in Him, according to the grace of our God and the Lord Jesus Christ.

2 Now, brethren, concerning the coming of our Lord Jesus Christ and our gathering together to Him, we ask you, 2 not to be soon shaken in mind or troubled, either by spirit or by word or by letter, as if from us, as though the day of Christ*a* had come. 3 Let no one deceive you by any means; for *that Day will not come* unless the falling away comes first, and the man of sin*a* is revealed, the son of perdition, 4 who opposes and exalts himself above all that is called God or that is worshiped, so that he sits as God*a* in the temple of God, showing himself that he is God.

5 Do you not remember that when I was still with you I told you these things? 6 And now you know what is restraining, that he may be revealed in his own time. 7 For the mystery of lawlessness is already at work; only He*a* who now restrains *will do so* until He*b* is taken out of the way. 8 And then the lawless one will be revealed, whom the Lord will consume with the breath of His mouth and destroy with the brightness of His coming. 9 The coming of the *lawless one* is according to the working of Satan, with all power, signs, and lying wonders, 10 and with all unrighteous deception among those who perish, because they did not receive the love of the truth, that they might be saved. 11 And for this reason God will send them strong delusion, that they should believe the lie, 12 that they all may be condemned who did not believe the truth but had pleasure in unrighteousness.

13 But we are bound to give thanks to God always for you, brethren beloved by the Lord, because God from the beginning chose you for salvation through sanctification by the Spirit and belief in the truth, 14 to which He called you by our gospel, for the obtaining of the glory of our Lord Jesus Christ. 15 Therefore, brethren, stand fast and hold the traditions which you were taught, whether by word or our epistle.

16 Now may our Lord Jesus Christ Himself, and our God and Father, who has loved us and given *us* everlasting consolation and good hope by grace, 17 comfort your hearts and es-

1:10 *a*NU-Text and M-Text read *have believed.*   2:2 *a*NU-Text reads *the Lord.*   2:3 *a*NU-Text reads
lawlessness.   2:4 *a*NU-Text omits *as God.*   2:7 *a*Or *he*   *b*Or *he*

tablish you in every good word and work.

3 Finally, brethren, pray for us, that the word of the Lord may run *swiftly* and be glorified, just as *it is* with you, 2 and that we may be delivered from unreasonable and wicked men; for not all have faith.

3 But the Lord is faithful, who will establish you and guard *you* from the evil one. 4 And we have confidence in the Lord concerning you, both that you do and will do the things we command you.

5 Now may the Lord direct your hearts into the love of God and into the patience of Christ.

6 But we command you, brethren, in the name of our Lord Jesus Christ, that you withdraw from every brother who walks disorderly and not according to the tradition which he*a* received from us. 7 For you yourselves know how you ought to follow us, for we were not disorderly among you; 8 nor did we eat anyone's bread free of charge, but worked with labor and toil night and day, that we might not be a burden to any of you,

9 not because we do not have authority, but to make ourselves an example of how you should follow us.

10 For even when we were with you, we commanded you this: If anyone will not work, neither shall he eat. 11 For we hear that there are some who walk among you in a disorderly manner, not working at all, but are busybodies. 12 Now those who are such we command and exhort through our Lord Jesus Christ that they work in quietness and eat their own bread.

13 But *as for* you, brethren, do not grow weary *in* doing good. 14 And if anyone does not obey our word in this epistle, note that person and do not keep company with him, that he may be ashamed. 15 Yet do not count *him* as an enemy, but admonish *him* as a brother.

16 Now may the Lord of peace Himself give you peace always in every way. The Lord *be* with you all.

17 The salutation of Paul with my own hand, which is a sign in every epistle; so I write.

18 The grace of our Lord Jesus Christ *be* with you all. Amen.

3:6 *a*NU-Text and M-Text read *they.*

First Timothy

Overview of First Timothy

E ncouragement is one of the greatest gifts you will ever give or receive. Never be afraid to accept or offer encouragement when it is in your power to do so.

First Timothy, Second Timothy, and Titus are known as the Pastoral Epistles. Written around A.D. 62, from Macedonia, the letters to Timothy contain advice to a young pastor regarding the church in Ephesus.

Paul encourages Timothy in his work, urging him not to be ashamed of his youth. Even though he is young, God will use him. The goal of Timothy's instruction should be love from a pure heart, a good conscience, and sincere faith. "Let no one despise your youth, but be an example to the believers in word, in conduct, in love, in spirit, in faith, in purity" (1 Tim. 4:12).

Although this book deals primarily with church matters, it also offers possibility thinking attitudes. Paul encourages Timothy to help his congregation establish wisdom and right values. He points out that contentment does not come from possessions, but comes from a positive attitude toward life.

Finally, Paul urges Timothy not to neglect the gift that God has given him. He should train his faith with self-discipline, as does an athlete. "Meditate on these things; give yourself entirely to them, that your progress may be evident to all" (1 Tim. 4:15).

This great letter of inspiration points out a dynamic lesson to Timothy and to all people hoping to do the work of God: What you are is God's gift to you. What you become is your gift to God!

Lord, make my life a window for Your light to shine through and a mirror to reflect Your love to all I meet! Amen.

Jesus in First Timothy

Jesus is the "one Mediator between God and men" (2:5), and "God was manifested in the flesh, justified in the Spirit, seen by angels, preached among the Gentiles, believed on in the world, received up in glory" (3:16). He is the source of spiritual strength, faith, and love. He "came into the world to save sinners" (1:15) and "gave Himself a ransom for all" (2:6).

Keys to First Timothy

Key Word: Leadership Manual for Church Organization. Paul writes this letter as a reference manual for leadership so that Timothy will have effective guidance for his work during Paul's absence in Macedonia. Paul wants to encourage and exhort his younger assistant to become an example to others, exercise his spiritual gifts, and "fight the good fight of faith" (6:12). Timothy's personal and public life must be above reproach; and he must be ready to deal with matters of false teaching, organization, discipline, proclamation of the Scriptures, poverty and wealth, and the roles of various groups in the church.

Key Verses: "But if I am delayed, *I write* so that you may know how you ought to conduct yourself in the house of God, which is the church of the living God, the pillar and ground of the truth. And without controversy great is the mystery of godliness: God was manifested in the flesh, justified in the Spirit, seen by angels, preached among the Gentiles, believed on in the world, received up in glory" (3:15, 16).

"But you, O man of God, . . . pursue righteousness, godliness, faith, love, patience, gentleness. Fight the good fight of faith, lay hold on eternal life, to which you were also called and have confessed the good confession in the presence of many witnesses" (6:11, 12).

Key Chapter: First Timothy 3. Listed in chapter 3 are the qualifications for the leaders of God's church, the elders and deacons. Notably absent are qualities of worldly success or position. Instead, Paul enumerates character qualities demonstrating that true leadership emanates from our walk with God rather than from achievements or vocational success.

1 Paul, an apostle of Jesus Christ, by the commandment of God our Savior and the Lord Jesus Christ, our hope,

2 To Timothy, a true son in the faith:

Grace, mercy, *and* peace from God our Father and Jesus Christ our Lord.
3 As I urged you when I went into Macedonia—remain in Ephesus that you may charge some that they teach no other doctrine, 4 nor give heed to fables and endless genealogies, which cause disputes rather than godly edification which is in faith. 5 Now the purpose of the commandment is love from a pure heart, *from*

a good conscience, and *from* sincere faith, 6 from which some, having strayed, have turned aside to idle talk, 7 desiring to be teachers of the law, understanding neither what they say nor the things which they affirm.

8 But we know that the law *is* good if one uses it lawfully, 9 knowing this: that the law is not made for a righteous person, but for *the* lawless and insubordinate, for *the* ungodly and for sinners, for *the* unholy and profane, for murderers of fathers and murderers of mothers, for manslayers, 10 for fornicators, for sodomites, for kidnappers, for liars, for perjurers, and if there is any other thing that is contrary to sound doctrine,

11 according to the glorious gospel of the blessed God which was committed to my trust.

12 And I thank Christ Jesus our Lord who has enabled me, because He counted me faithful, putting *me* into the ministry, 13 although I was formerly a blasphemer, a persecutor, and an insolent man; but I obtained mercy because I did *it* ignorantly in unbelief. 14 And the grace of our Lord was exceedingly abundant, with faith and love which are in Christ Jesus. 15 This *is* a faithful saying and worthy of all acceptance, that Christ Jesus came into the world to save sinners, of whom I am chief. 16 However, for this reason I obtained mercy, that in me first Jesus Christ might show all longsuffering, as a pattern to those who are going to believe on Him for everlasting life. 17 Now to the King eternal, immortal, invisible, to God who alone is wise,*a* *be* honor and glory forever and ever. Amen.

18 This charge I commit to you, son Timothy, according to the prophecies previously made concerning you, that by them you may wage the good warfare, 19 having faith and a good conscience, which some having rejected, concerning the faith have suffered shipwreck, 20 of whom are Hymenaeus and Alexander, whom I delivered to Satan that they may learn not to blaspheme.

2 Therefore I exhort first of all that supplications, prayers, intercessions, *and* giving of thanks be made for all men, 2 for kings and all who are in authority, that we may lead a quiet and peaceable life in all godliness and reverence. 3 For this *is* good and acceptable in the sight of God our Savior, 4 who desires all men to be saved and to come to the knowledge of the truth. 5 For *there is* one God and one Mediator between God and men, *the* Man Christ Jesus, 6 who gave Himself a ransom for all, to be testified in due time, 7 for which I was appointed a preacher and an apostle—I am speaking the truth in Christ*a* *and* not lying—a teacher of the Gentiles in faith and truth.

8 I desire therefore that the men pray everywhere, lifting up holy hands, without wrath and doubting; 9 in like manner also, that the women adorn themselves in modest apparel, with propriety and moderation, not with braided hair or gold or pearls or costly clothing, 10 but, which is proper for women professing godliness, with good works. 11 Let a woman learn in silence with all submission. 12 And I do not permit a woman to teach or to have authority over a man, but to be in silence. 13 For Adam was formed first, then Eve. 14 And Adam was not deceived, but the woman being deceived, fell into transgression. 15 Nevertheless she will be saved in childbearing if they continue in faith, love, and holiness, with self-control.

3 This *is* a faithful saying: If a man desires the position of a bishop,*a* he desires a good work. 2 A bishop then must be blameless, the husband of one wife, temperate, soberminded, of good behavior, hospitable, able to teach; 3 not given to wine, not violent, not greedy for money,*a* but gentle, not quarrelsome, not covetous; 4 one who rules his own house well, having *his* children in submission with all reverence 5 (for if a man does not know how to rule his own house, how will he take care of the church of God?); 6 not a novice, lest being puffed up with pride he fall into the *same* condemnation as the devil. 7 Moreover he must have a good testimony among those who are outside, lest he fall into reproach and the snare of the devil.

8 Likewise deacons *must be* reverent, not double-tongued, not given to much wine, not greedy for money, 9 holding the mystery of the faith with a pure conscience. 10 But let these also first be tested; then let them serve as deacons, being *found* blameless. 11 Likewise, *their* wives *must be* reverent, not slanderers, temperate, faithful in all things. 12 Let deacons be the husbands of one wife, ruling *their* children and their own houses well. 13 For those who have served well as deacons obtain for themselves a good standing and great boldness in the faith which is in Christ Jesus.

14 These things I write to you,

1:17 *a*NU-Text reads *to the only God.*   2:7 *a*NU-Text omits *in Christ.*   3:1 *a*Literally *overseer* 3:3 *a*NU-Text omits *not greedy for money.*

though I hope to come to you shortly; 15 but if I am delayed, *I write* so that you may know how you ought to conduct yourself in the house of God, which is the church of the living God, the pillar and ground of the truth. 16 And without controversy great is the mystery of godliness:

> God[a] was manifested in the
>   flesh,
> Justified in the Spirit,
> Seen by angels,
> Preached among the Gentiles,
> Believed on in the world,
> Received up in glory.

4 Now the Spirit expressly says that in latter times some will depart from the faith, giving heed to deceiving spirits and doctrines of demons, 2 speaking lies in hypocrisy, having their own conscience seared with a hot iron, 3 forbidding to marry, *and commanding* to abstain from foods which God created to be received with thanksgiving by those who believe and know the truth. 4 For every creature of God *is* good, and nothing is to be refused if it is received with thanksgiving; 5 for it is sanctified by the word of God and prayer.

6 If you instruct the brethren in these things, you will be a good minister of Jesus Christ, nourished in the words of faith and of the good doctrine which you have carefully followed. 7 But reject profane and old wives' fables, and exercise yourself toward godliness. 8 For bodily exercise profits a little, but godliness is profitable for all things, having promise of the life that now is and of that which is to come. 9 This *is* a faithful saying and worthy of all acceptance. 10 For to this *end* we both labor and suffer reproach,[a] because we trust in the living God, who is *the* Savior of all men, especially of those who believe. 11 These things command and teach.

12 Let no one despise your youth, but be an example to the believers in word, in conduct, in love, in spirit,[a] in faith, in purity. 13 Till I come, give attention to reading, to exhortation, to doctrine. 14 Do not neglect the gift that is in you, which was given you by prophecy with the laying on of the hands of the eldership. 15 Meditate on these things; give yourself entirely to them, that your progress may be evident to all. 16 Take heed to yourself and to the doctrine. Continue in them, for in doing this you will save both yourself and those who hear you.

5 Do not rebuke an older man, but exhort *him* as a father, younger men as brothers, 2 older women as mothers, younger women as sisters, with all purity.

3 Honor widows who are really widows. 4 But if any widow has children or grandchildren, let them first learn to show piety at home and to repay their parents; for this is good and[a] acceptable before God. 5 Now she who is really a widow, and left alone, trusts in God and continues in supplications and prayers night and day. 6 But she who lives in pleasure is dead while she lives. 7 And these things command, that they may be blameless. 8 But if anyone does not provide for his own, and especially for those of his household, he has denied the faith and is worse than an unbeliever.

9 Do not let a widow under sixty years old be taken into the number, *and not unless* she has been the wife of one man, 10 well reported for good works: if she has brought up children, if she has lodged strangers, if she has washed the saints' feet, if she has relieved the afflicted, if she has diligently followed every good work.

11 But refuse *the* younger widows; for when they have begun to grow wanton against Christ, they desire to marry, 12 having condemnation because they have cast off their first faith. 13 And besides they learn *to be* idle, wandering about from house to house, and not only idle but also gossips and busybodies, saying things which they ought not. 14 Therefore I desire that *the* younger *widows* marry, bear children, manage the house, give no opportunity to the adversary to speak reproachfully. 15 For some have already turned aside after Satan. 16 If any believing man or[a] woman has widows, let them relieve them, and do not let the

---

3:16 aNU-Text reads *Who.*   4:10 aNU-Text reads *we labor and strive.*   4:12 aNU-Text omits *in spirit.*   5:4 aNU-Text and M-Text omit *good and.*   5:16 aNU-Text omits *man or.*

church be burdened, that it may relieve those who are really widows.

17 Let the elders who rule well be counted worthy of double honor, especially those who labor in the word and doctrine. 18 For the Scripture says, *"You shall not muzzle an ox while it treads out the grain,"*[a] and, "The laborer *is* worthy of his wages."[b] 19 Do not receive an accusation against an elder except from two or three witnesses. 20 Those who are sinning rebuke in the presence of all, that the rest also may fear.

21 I charge *you* before God and the Lord Jesus Christ and the elect angels that you observe these things without prejudice, doing nothing with partiality. 22 Do not lay hands on anyone hastily, nor share in other people's sins; keep yourself pure.

23 No longer drink only water, but use a little wine for your stomach's sake and your frequent infirmities.

24 Some men's sins are clearly evident, preceding *them* to judgment, but those of some *men* follow later. 25 Likewise, the good works *of some* are clearly evident, and those that are otherwise cannot be hidden.

6 Let as many bondservants as are under the yoke count their own masters worthy of all honor, so that the name of God and *His* doctrine may not be blasphemed. 2 And those who have believing masters, let them not despise *them* because they are brethren, but rather serve *them* because those who are benefited are believers and beloved. Teach and exhort these things.

3 If anyone teaches otherwise and does not consent to wholesome words, *even* the words of our Lord Jesus Christ, and to the doctrine which accords with godliness, 4 he is proud, knowing nothing, but is obsessed with disputes and arguments over words, from which come envy, strife, reviling, evil suspicions, 5 useless wranglings[a] of men of corrupt minds and destitute of the truth, who suppose that godliness is a *means of* gain. From such withdraw yourself.[b]

6 Now godliness with contentment is great gain. 7 For we brought nothing into *this* world, *and it is* certain[a] we can carry nothing out. 8 And having food and clothing, with these we shall be content. 9 But those who desire to be rich fall into temptation and a snare, and *into* many foolish and harmful lusts which drown men in destruction and perdition. 10 For the love of money is a root of all *kinds of* evil, for which some have strayed from the faith in their greediness, and pierced themselves through with many sorrows.

11 But you, O man of God, flee these things and pursue righteousness, godliness, faith, love, patience, gentleness. 12 Fight the good fight of faith, lay hold on eternal life, to which you were also called and have confessed the good confession in the presence of many witnesses. 13 I urge you in the sight of God who gives life to all things, and *before* Christ Jesus who witnessed the good confession before Pontius Pilate, 14 that you keep *this* commandment without spot, blameless until our Lord Jesus Christ's appearing, 15 which He will manifest in His own time, *He who is* the blessed and only Potentate, the King of kings and Lord of lords, 16 who alone has immortality, dwelling in unapproachable light, whom no man has seen or can see, to whom *be* honor and everlasting power. Amen.

17 Command those who are rich in this present age not to be haughty, nor to trust in uncertain riches but in the living God, who gives us richly all things to enjoy. 18 *Let them* do good, that they be rich in good works, ready to give, willing to share, 19 storing up for themselves a good foundation for the time to come, that they may lay hold on eternal life.

20 O Timothy! Guard what was committed to your trust, avoiding the profane *and* idle babblings and contradictions of what is falsely called knowledge— 21 by professing it some have strayed concerning the faith.

Grace *be* with you. Amen.

5:18 [a]Deuteronomy 25:4   [b]Luke 10:7   6:5 [a]NU-Text and M-Text read *constant friction.*   [b]NU-Text omits this sentence.   6:7 [a]NU-Text omits *and it is certain.*

Second Timothy

Overview of Second Timothy

Second Timothy is a work of great inspiration by the apostle Paul. Probably written in A.D. 67 while he was imprisoned in Rome, this letter demonstrates Paul's positive attitude despite the negative circumstances of his life.

Paul writes the young pastor Timothy to encourage him and to continue his training. Now sixty years old, Paul hopes to share his insights of over thirty years of preaching the Gospel. As he writes to Timothy, we learn that the apostle is facing a death sentence and that the Christians who once supported him have now deserted him.

> For this reason I also suffer these things; nevertheless I am not ashamed, for I know whom I have believed and am persuaded that He is able to keep what I have committed to Him until that Day.
>
> (2 Tim. 1:12)

Nonetheless, Paul's letter contains positive, faith-building news. He never expresses bitterness toward those who have forsaken him. In spite of being abandoned, he neither condemns nor criticizes anyone. He seeks only to build up others and to continue the ministry that God has given him.

> I have fought the good fight, I have finished the race, I have kept the faith. Finally, there is laid up for me the crown of righteousness, which the Lord, the righteous Judge, will give to me on that Day, and not to me only but also to all who have loved His appearing.
>
> (2 Tim. 4:7, 8)

While awaiting final trial, Paul helps to convert members of Caesar's household. During the greatest test of his faith, Paul overcomes with possibility thinking! He knows that a star is best seen at night. He knows that even though his friends have left him, God will never leave him. Paul is confident that God will help him to keep on keeping on. He knows that tough times never last, but tough people do!

Jesus in Second Timothy

Jesus appeared on earth, "abolished death and brought life and immortality to light through the gospel" (1:10). He rose from the dead and provides salvation and eternal glory; for if believers "died with Him" they will "also live with Him" (2:11). All who love His appearing will receive "the crown of righteousness" (4:8) and "reign with Him" (2:12).

Keys to Second Timothy

Key Word: Endurance in the Pastoral Ministry. In this letter, Paul commissions Timothy to faithfully endure and carry on the work that the condemned apostle must now relinquish. Timothy is in great need of encouragement because of the hardships he is facing, and Paul uses this letter to instruct him about handling persecution from the secular authorities, and dissension and deception from within the church. As a spiritual father, Paul urges his young helper to overcome his natural timidity and to boldly proclaim the gospel, even if it means that he will suffer for doing so.

Key Verses: "You therefore must endure hardship as a good soldier of Jesus Christ. No one engaged in warfare entangles himself with the affairs of *this* life, that he may please him who enlisted him as a soldier" (2:3, 4).

"But you must continue in the things which you have learned and been assured of, knowing from whom you have learned *them,* and that from childhood you have known the Holy Scriptures, which are able to make you wise for salvation through faith which is in Christ Jesus. All Scripture *is* . . . profitable for doctrine, for reproof, for correction, for instruction in righteousness, that the man of God may be complete, thoroughly equipped for every good work" (3:14–17).

Key Chapter: Second Timothy 2. The second chapter of Second Timothy ought to be required daily reading for every pastor and full-time Christian worker. Paul lists the keys to an enduring successful ministry: a reproducing ministry, an enduring ministry, a studying ministry, and a holy ministry.

1 Paul, an apostle of Jesus Christ*a* by the will of God, according to the promise of life which is in Christ Jesus,

2 To Timothy, a beloved son:

Grace, mercy, *and* peace from God the Father and Christ Jesus our Lord. 3 I thank God, whom I serve with a pure conscience, as *my* forefathers *did,* as without ceasing I remember you in my prayers night and day, 4 greatly desiring to see you, being mindful of your tears, that I may be filled with joy, 5 when I call to remembrance the genuine faith that is in you, which dwelt first in your grandmother Lois and your mother Eunice, and I am persuaded is in you also. 6 Therefore I remind you to stir up the gift of God which is in you through the laying on of my hands. 7 For God has not given us a spirit of fear, but of power and of love and of a sound mind.

8 Therefore do not be ashamed of the testimony of our Lord, nor of me His prisoner, but share with me in the sufferings for the gospel according to the power of God, 9 who has saved us and called *us* with a holy calling, not according to our works, but according to His own purpose and grace which was given to us in Christ Jesus before time began, 10 but has now been revealed by the appearing of our Savior Jesus Christ, *who* has abolished death and brought life and immortality to light through the gospel, 11 to which I was appointed a preacher, an apostle, and a teacher of the Gentiles.*a* 12 For this reason I also suffer these things; nevertheless I am not ashamed, for I know whom I have believed and am persuaded that He is able to keep what I have committed to Him until that Day.

13 Hold fast the pattern of sound words which you have heard from me, in faith and love which are in Christ Jesus. 14 That good thing which was committed to you, keep by the Holy Spirit who dwells in us.

15 This you know, that all those in Asia have turned away from me, among whom are Phygellus and Hermogenes. 16 The Lord grant mercy to the household of Onesiphorus, for he often refreshed me, and was not ashamed of my chain; 17 but when he arrived in Rome, he sought me out very zealously and found *me.* 18 The Lord grant to him that he may find mercy from the Lord in that Day—and you know very well how many ways he ministered *to me*a at Ephesus.

2 You therefore, my son, be strong in the grace that is in Christ Jesus. 2 And the things that you have heard from me among many witnesses, commit these to faithful men who will be able to teach others also. 3 You therefore must endure*a* hardship as a good soldier of Jesus Christ. 4 No one engaged in warfare entangles himself with the affairs of *this* life, that he may please him who enlisted him as a soldier. 5 And also if anyone competes in athletics, he is not crowned unless he competes according to the rules. 6 The hardworking farmer must be first to partake of the crops. 7 Consider what I say, and may*a* the Lord give you understanding in all things.

8 Remember that Jesus Christ, of the seed of David, was raised from the dead according to my gospel, 9 for which I suffer trouble as an evildoer, *even* to the point of chains; but the word of God is not chained. 10 Therefore I endure all things for the sake of the elect, that they also may obtain the salvation which is in Christ Jesus with eternal glory. 11 *This is* a faithful saying:

> For if we died with *Him,*
>   We shall also live with *Him.*
> 12 If we endure,
>   We shall also reign with *Him.*
> If we deny *Him,*
>   He also will deny us.

1:1 *a*NU-Text and M-Text read *Christ Jesus.*   1:11 *a*NU-Text omits *of the Gentiles.*   1:18 *aTo me is* from the Vulgate and a few Greek manuscripts.   2:3 *a*NU-Text reads *You must share.*   2:7 *a*NU-Text reads *the Lord will give you.*

13 If we are faithless,
   He remains faithful;
   He cannot deny Himself.

14 Remind *them* of these things, charging *them* before the Lord not to strive about words to no profit, to the ruin of the hearers. 15 Be diligent to present yourself approved to God, a worker who does not need to be ashamed, rightly dividing the word of truth. 16 But shun profane *and* idle babblings, for they will increase to more ungodliness. 17 And their message will spread like cancer. Hymenaeus and Philetus are of this sort, 18 who have strayed concerning the truth, saying that the resurrection is already past; and they overthrow the faith of some. 19 Nevertheless the solid foundation of God stands, having this seal: "The Lord knows those who are His," and, "Let everyone who names the name of Christ[a] depart from iniquity."

20 But in a great house there are not only vessels of gold and silver, but also of wood and clay, some for honor and some for dishonor. 21 Therefore if anyone cleanses himself from the latter, he will be a vessel for honor, sanctified and useful for the Master, prepared for every good work. 22 Flee also youthful lusts; but pursue righteousness, faith, love, peace with those who call on the Lord out of a pure heart. 23 But avoid foolish and ignorant disputes, knowing that they generate strife. 24 And a servant of the Lord must not quarrel but be gentle to all, able to teach, patient, 25 in humility correcting those who are in opposition, if God perhaps will grant them repentance, so that they may know the truth, 26 and *that* they may come to their senses *and escape* the snare of the devil, having been taken captive by him to *do* his will.

3 But know this, that in the last days perilous times will come: 2 For men will be lovers of themselves, lovers of money, boasters, proud, blasphemers, disobedient to parents, unthankful, unholy, 3 unloving, unforgiving, slanderers, without self-control, brutal, despisers of good, 4 traitors, headstrong, haughty, lovers of pleasure rather than lovers of God, 5 having a form of godliness but denying its power. And from such people turn away! 6 For of this sort are those who creep into households and make captives of gullible women loaded down with sins, led away by various lusts, 7 always learning and never able to come to the knowledge of the truth. 8 Now as Jannes and Jambres resisted Moses, so do these also resist the truth: men of corrupt minds, disapproved concerning the faith; 9 but they will progress no further, for their folly will be manifest to all, as theirs also was.

10 But you have carefully followed my doctrine, manner of life, purpose, faith, longsuffering, love, perseverance, 11 persecutions, afflictions, which happened to me at Antioch, at Iconium, at Lystra—what persecutions I endured. And out of *them* all the Lord delivered me. 12 Yes, and all who desire to live godly in Christ Jesus will suffer persecution. 13 But evil men and impostors will grow worse and worse, deceiving and being deceived. 14 But you must continue in the things which you have learned and been assured of, knowing from whom you have learned *them,* 15 and that from childhood you have known the Holy Scriptures, which are able to make you wise for salvation through faith which is in Christ Jesus.

16 All Scripture *is* given by inspiration of God, and *is* profitable for doctrine, for reproof, for correction, for instruction in righteousness, 17 that the man of God may be complete, thoroughly equipped for every good work.

4 I charge *you* therefore before God and the Lord Jesus Christ, who will judge the living and the dead at[a] His appearing and His kingdom: 2 Preach the word! Be ready in season *and* out of season. Convince, rebuke, exhort, with all longsuffering and teaching. 3 For the time will come when they will not endure sound doctrine, but according to their own desires, *because* they have itching ears, they will heap up for themselves teachers; 4 and they will turn *their* ears away from the truth, and be turned aside to fables.

2:19 aNU-Text and M-Text read *the Lord.*   4:1 aNU-Text omits *therefore* and reads *and by* for *at.*

5 But you be watchful in all things, endure afflictions, do the work of an evangelist, fulfill your ministry.

6 For I am already being poured out as a drink offering, and the time of my departure is at hand. 7 I have fought the good fight, I have finished the race, I have kept the faith. 8 Finally, there is laid up for me the crown of righteousness, which the Lord, the righteous Judge, will give to me on that Day, and not to me only but also to all who have loved His appearing.

9 Be diligent to come to me quickly; 10 for Demas has forsaken me, having loved this present world, and has departed for Thessalonica—Crescens for Galatia, Titus for Dalmatia. 11 Only Luke is with me. Get Mark and bring him with you, for he is useful to me for ministry. 12 And Tychicus I have sent to Ephesus. 13 Bring the cloak that I left with Carpus at Troas when you come—and the books, especially the parchments.

14 Alexander the coppersmith did me much harm. May the Lord re-pay him according to his works. 15 You also must beware of him, for he has greatly resisted our words.

16 At my first defense no one stood with me, but all forsook me. May it not be charged against them.

17 But the Lord stood with me and strengthened me, so that the message might be preached fully through me, and that all the Gentiles might hear. Also I was delivered out of the mouth of the lion. 18 And the Lord will deliver me from every evil work and preserve me for His heavenly kingdom. To Him be glory forever and ever. Amen!

19 Greet Prisca and Aquila, and the household of Onesiphorus. 20 Erastus stayed in Corinth, but Trophimus I have left in Miletus sick.

21 Do your utmost to come before winter.

Eubulus greets you, as well as Pudens, Linus, Claudia, and all the brethren.

22 The Lord Jesus Christ[a] be with your spirit. Grace be with you. Amen.

4:22 aNU-Text omits *Jesus Christ*.

Titus

Overview of Titus

P aul taught Titus to believe that his church had real possibilities. In any environment the church can grow and prosper.

The apostle Paul wrote this letter from Greece between A.D. 62 and 65 to Titus, a Christian pastor residing on the island of Crete. The major thrust of the book concerns the administration of the churches at Crete.

Paul commends Titus, encouraging him to be a great pastor. Titus's earnestness as a successful church leader is mentioned as a challenging example to the Corinthians. Titus must meet some challenges of his own in guiding the churches. He must continue to rebuke the legalistic or mythical influences that creep into the church. Paul exhorts Titus to speak things which adorn the doctrine of God, those words which are positive, inspirational, and uplifting. Titus is to be a positive leader and is not to surrender leadership to his problems; Titus is to take control of the situation to reshape, reorganize, and rejuvenate the church so that it will share the positive, life-giving message of Jesus Christ with a dying world.

Titus is encouraged to focus his thoughts on God and the blessed hope of Jesus Christ's return. Paul urges him to focus on God and not on his problems. For we are saved through faith in Jesus Christ, the demonstration of God's love for us.

For the grace of God that brings salvation has appeared to all men, teaching us that, denying ungodliness and worldly lusts, we should live soberly, righteously, and godly in the present age, looking for the blessed hope and glorious appearing of our great God and Savior Jesus Christ.

(Titus 2:11–13)

Jesus in Titus

The deity and redemptive work of Jesus are beautifully stated in 2:13, 14: "Looking for the blessed hope and glorious appearing of our great God and Savior Jesus Christ, who gave Himself for us, that He might redeem us from every lawless deed and purify for Himself *His* own special people, zealous for good works."

Keys to Titus

Key Word: Conduct Manual for Church Living. This brief letter focuses on Titus's role and responsibility in the organization and supervision of the churches in Crete. It is written to strengthen and exhort Titus to firmly exercise his authority as an apostolic representative to churches that need to be put in order, refuting false teachers and dissenters and replacing immoral behavior with good deeds.

Key Verses: "For this reason I left you in Crete, that you should set in order the things that are lacking, and appoint elders in every city as I commanded you" (1:5).

"This is a faithful saying, and these things I want you to

affirm constantly, that those who have believed in God should be careful to maintain good works. These things are good and profitable to men" (3:8).

Key Chapter: Titus 2. Summarized in Titus 2 are the key commands to be obeyed which insure godly relationships within the church. Paul includes all categories of people, instructing them to show "all good fidelity, that they may adorn the doctrine of God our Savior in all things" (2:10).

1 Paul, a bondservant of God and an apostle of Jesus Christ, according to the faith of God's elect and the acknowledgment of the truth which accords with godliness, 2 in hope of eternal life which God, who cannot lie, promised before time began, 3 but has in due time manifested His word through preaching, which was committed to me according to the commandment of God our Savior;

4 To Titus, a true son in *our* common faith:

Grace, mercy, *and* peace from God the Father and the Lord Jesus Christ[a] our Savior.

5 For this reason I left you in Crete, that you should set in order the things that are lacking, and appoint elders in every city as I commanded you— 6 if a man is blameless, the husband of one wife, having faithful children not accused of dissipation or insubordination. 7 For a bishop[a] must be blameless, as a steward of God, not self-willed, not quick-tempered, not given to wine, not violent, not greedy for money, 8 but hospitable, a lover of what is good, soberminded, just, holy, self-controlled, 9 holding fast the faithful word as he has been taught, that he may be able, by sound doctrine, both to exhort and convict those who contradict.

10 For there are many insubordi-

1:4 aNU-Text reads *and* Christ Jesus.   1:7 aLiterally *overseer*

Creative Mediation

Walking the walk of faith will ultimately lead you to a clearing where the sun can shine gloriously upon your well-lived life! How can you be sure that the walk of faith will lead to such a happy ending? Read Paul's advice to Titus in Titus 3:8, 9. By its very nature, faith cultivates a positive mental attitude toward conflicts.

If you anticipate problems and tensions after making a commitment, you are not necessarily guilty of negative thinking.

For the truth is, any time you press forward toward your goal, you will create conflict.

You can be sure that not everyone will agree with you!

However, in the face of conflict, the positive person has a creative attitude toward problems, whereas a negative person has a destructive and complicating attitude toward conflict.

Negative thinkers become defensive when they face conflicts.

Positive thinkers become peacemakers when they face conflicts.

When you walk the walk of faith, you discipline yourself to resolve conflicts. Resolving conflicts always starts with a resolution:

I will manage the conflict and will not allow the conflict to manage me!

I will not allow the conflict to collide, clash, or collapse the commitments I have made.

I will be more patient and determined to turn the conflict around and in the process become healthier and happier than I was before!

Resolve to win out over the conflict!

nate, both idle talkers and deceivers, especially those of the circumcision, 11 whose mouths must be stopped, who subvert whole households, teaching things which they ought not, for the sake of dishonest gain. 12 One of them, a prophet of their own, said, "Cretans *are* always liars, evil beasts, lazy gluttons." 13 This testimony is true. Therefore rebuke them sharply, that they may be sound in the faith, 14 not giving heed to Jewish fables and commandments of men who turn from the truth. 15 To the pure all things are pure, but to those who are defiled and unbelieving nothing is pure; but even their mind and conscience are defiled. 16 They profess to know God, but in works they deny Him, being abominable, disobedient, and disqualified for every good work.

2 But as for you, speak the things which are proper for sound doctrine: 2 that the older men be sober, reverent, temperate, sound in faith, in love, in patience; 3 the older women likewise, that they be reverent in behavior, not slanderers, not given to much wine, teachers of good things— 4 that they admonish the young women to love their husbands, to love their children, 5 to be discreet, chaste, homemakers, good, obedient to their own husbands, that the word of God may not be blasphemed.

6 Likewise, exhort the young men to be sober-minded, 7 in all things showing yourself *to be* a pattern of good works; in doctrine *showing* integrity, reverence, incorruptibility,*a* 8 sound speech that cannot be condemned, that one who is an opponent may be ashamed, having nothing evil to say of you.*a*

9 *Exhort* bondservants to be obedient to their own masters, to be well pleasing in all *things,* not answering back, 10 not pilfering, but showing all good fidelity, that they may adorn the doctrine of God our Savior in all things.

11 For the grace of God that brings salvation has appeared to all men, 12 teaching us that, denying ungodliness and worldly lusts, we should live soberly, righteously, and godly in the present age, 13 looking for the blessed hope and glorious appearing of our great God and Savior Jesus Christ, 14 who gave Himself for us, that He might redeem us from every lawless deed and purify for Himself *His* own special people, zealous for good works.

15 Speak these things, exhort, and rebuke with all authority. Let no one despise you.

3 Remind them to be subject to rulers and authorities, to obey, to be ready for every good work, 2 to speak evil of no one, to be peaceable, gentle, showing all humility to all men. 3 For we ourselves were also once foolish, disobedient, deceived, serving various lusts and pleasures, living in malice and envy, hateful and hating one another. 4 But when the kindness and the love of God our Savior toward man appeared, 5 not by works of righteousness which we have done, but according to His mercy He saved us, through the washing of regeneration and renewing of the Holy Spirit, 6 whom He poured out on us abundantly through Jesus Christ our Savior, 7 that having been justified by His grace we should become heirs according to the hope of eternal life.

8 This is a faithful saying, and these things I want you to affirm constantly, that those who have believed in God should be careful to maintain good works. These things are good and profitable to men.

9 But avoid foolish disputes, genealogies, contentions, and strivings about the law; for they are unprofitable and useless. 10 Reject a divisive man after the first and second admonition, 11 knowing that such a person is warped and sinning, being self-condemned.

12 When I send Artemas to you, or Tychicus, be diligent to come to me at Nicopolis, for I have decided to spend the winter there. 13 Send Zenas the lawyer and Apollos on their journey with haste, that they may lack nothing. 14 And let our *people* also learn to maintain good works, to *meet* urgent needs, that they may not be unfruitful.

15 All who *are* with me greet you. Greet those who love us in the faith.

Grace *be* with you all. Amen.

2:7 *a*NU-Text omits *incorruptibility*.   2:8 *a*NU-Text and M-Text read *us*.

Philemon

Overview of Philemon

Forgiveness is the language of love! This is the theme of the Epistle to Philemon. This book was written between A.D. 58 and 63, during Paul's first Roman imprisonment. It is the shortest of all of Paul's letters.

During Paul's imprisonment, he met an ex-slave named Onesimus, who had been caught stealing from his master, Philemon. Now Paul writes to Philemon pleading for him to accept Onesimus as a brother and to forgive him for his former actions. Paul reminds Philemon that because of Onesimus' newfound faith in Christ, he would be a benefit to his brothers and sisters in the church at Colosse.

The apostle Paul encourages Philemon to forgive Onesimus so that he can live up to the true meaning of his name, "useful." In a play on words, Paul reminds Philemon that if the useful one, Onesimus, is accepted back, he can truly become useful for Philemon and the church.

Onesimus was accepted back into the church and a later tradition tells us that Onesimus became a bishop in the church at Ephesus.

Because of Philemon's forgiveness and the forgiveness of others, Onesimus truly was able to become "the useful one." The Book of Philemon is a beautiful illustration of what can be accomplished in a person's life when complete forgiveness is given and accepted. Forgiveness brings change.

Whether you need to change and forgive someone else, or change and forgive yourself, this book positively illustrates the rewards for doing so. A humble prayer is the right start: *I am willing, wanting, and waiting to change into the person You want me to be, Lord. Amen.*

Jesus in Philemon

The forgiveness that the believer finds in Christ is beautifully portrayed by analogy in Philemon. Onesimus is guilty of a great offense, but Paul intercedes for him. He becomes Onesimus' substitute by assuming his debt. By Philemon's gracious forgiveness, Onesimus is restored and placed in a new relationship with his master. Paul's advocacy before Philemon is parallel to Jesus' work of mediation before the Father on our behalf.

Keys to Philemon

Key Word: Forgiveness. The Book of Philemon develops the transition from bondage to brotherhood that is brought about by Christian love and forgiveness. Just as Philemon was shown mercy through the grace of Christ, so he must graciously forgive his repentant runaway, who has returned as a brother in Christ. Paul wrote this letter as his personal appeal that Philemon receive Onesimus even as he would receive Paul.

Key Verses: "No longer as a slave but more than a slave—a beloved brother, especially to me but how much more to you, both in the flesh and in the Lord. If then you count me as a partner, receive him as *you would* me" (vv. 16, 17).

"I thank my God, making mention of you always in my prayers, hearing of your love and faith which you have toward the Lord Jesus and toward all the saints, that the sharing of your faith may become effective by the acknowledgment of every good thing which is in you in Christ Jesus" (vv. 4–6).

Servants are First

It takes two to make a miracle. When a believing human being merges his will with God's power, miracles happen. Miracles require faith—and faith is often spelled *w-o-r-k*.

There is a great misconception today that faith is simply a matter of asking God to perform a miracle, sitting back, and waiting for it to happen. Don't be misled! Positive Christians don't do great things for God by manipulating others simply to achieve their own selfish goals. They reach their goals by working toward them after they've prayed through their plans!

Jesus Himself encouraged the pursuit of greatness. But our Lord made it clear that the pathway to success is the path of service. If you want to be great—be prepared to be a servant. Serving does not come naturally. Even the disciples had to be reminded of this truth again and again, and they had Jesus as their Personal Trainer!

Service works in all areas of life, even in the business world. In a free country, people buy only the products and services that meet their needs. The professional person who becomes ego-involved instead of human-service-oriented soon finds himself in trouble.

Today, ask yourself: Have I been sitting back just waiting for God to pour out blessings in my life without making an effort myself? Am I willing to join with God to make a miracle? I believe it will happen as I become a servant.

1 Paul, a prisoner of Christ Jesus, and Timothy *our* brother,

To Philemon our beloved *friend* and fellow laborer, 2 to the beloved*a* Apphia, Archippus our fellow soldier, and to the church in your house:

3 Grace to you and peace from God our Father and the Lord Jesus Christ.

4 I thank my God, making mention of you always in my prayers, 5 hearing of your love and faith which you have toward the Lord Jesus and toward all the saints, 6 that the sharing of your faith may become effective by the acknowledgment of every good thing which is in you*a* in Christ Jesus. 7 For we have*a* great joy*b* and consolation in your love, because the hearts of the saints have been refreshed by you, brother.

8 Therefore, though I might be very bold in Christ to command you what is fitting, 9 *yet* for love's sake I rather appeal *to you*—being such a one as Paul, the aged, and now also a prisoner of Jesus Christ— 10 I appeal to you for my son Onesimus, whom I have begotten *while* in my chains, 11 who once was unprofitable to you, but now is profitable to you and to me.

12 I am sending him back.*a* You therefore receive him, that is, my own heart, 13 whom I wished to keep with me, that on your behalf he might minister to me in my chains for the gospel. 14 But without your consent I wanted to do nothing, that your good deed might not be by compulsion, as it were, but voluntary.

15 For perhaps he departed for a while for this *purpose,* that you might receive him forever, 16 no longer as a slave but more than a slave—a beloved brother, especially to me but how much more to you, both in the flesh and in the Lord.

17 If then you count me as a partner, receive him as *you would* me. 18 But if he has wronged you or owes anything, put that on my account. 19 I, Paul, am writing with my own hand. I will repay—not to mention to you that you owe me even your own self besides. 20 Yes, brother, let me have joy from you in the Lord; refresh my heart in the Lord.

21 Having confidence in your obedience, I write to you, knowing that you will do even more than I say. 22 But, meanwhile, also prepare a guest room for me, for I trust that through your prayers I shall be granted to you.

23 Epaphras, my fellow prisoner in Christ Jesus, greets you, 24 *as do* Mark, Aristarchus, Demas, Luke, my fellow laborers.

25 The grace of our Lord Jesus Christ *be* with your spirit. Amen.

2 *a*NU-Text reads *to our sister Apphia.*   6 *a*NU-Text and M-Text read *us.*   7 *a*NU-Text reads *had.* *b*M-Text reads *thanksgiving.*   12 *a*NU-Text reads *back to you in person, that is, my own heart.*

Hebrews

Overview of Hebrews

Although the author of the Book of Hebrews is unknown, scholars have placed the date of writing in the 60s A.D., prior to the destruction of the Jerusalem temple in A.D. 70. Some feel this Epistle may have been written by either Paul, Barnabas, Luke, or Apollos.

A work of highly polished Greek literature, this book is rivaled in the New Testament in its mastery of the language only by Luke and Acts. Its recipients were Jewish Christians, possibly those living in Rome.

The theme of Hebrews is the superiority of Jesus Christ over Judaism. In a step-by-step outline, the author reveals how Jesus is the Great High Priest according to the order of Melchizedek. The author knew that his readers had a great understanding of and familiarity with the Old Testament, having been trained as upright Jews. Therefore, he draws from over twenty-nine passages and fifty-three symbolic illustrations of the Old Testament to show how Christianity embodies the New Covenant between God and His people.

Faith is also a dominant thread which runs throughout the book. The famous "faith chapter," Hebrews 11, recounts the lives of great possibility thinkers of the Bible as an inspiration for us to have a similar enduring faith, looking to the same eternal God to supply our needs.

With great encouragement and exhortation, this book builds up the faith of all believers, bringing them into a more vital relationship with Jesus Christ.

Jesus in Hebrews

Hebrews presents Jesus as the divine-human Prophet, Priest, and King. His deity and humanity are asserted with equal force, and over twenty titles are used to describe His attributes and accomplishments—titles such as: Heir of all things, Apostle and High Priest, Mediator, Author and Perfecter of faith. He is superior to all who went before and offers the supreme sacrifice, priesthood, and covenant.

Keys to Hebrews

Key Word: The Superiority of Christ. The basic theme of Hebrews is found in the word *better,* describing the superiority of Jesus in His person and work. The words *perfect* and *heavenly* are also prominent. He offers a better revelation, position, priesthood, covenant, sacrifice, and power. The writer develops this theme to prevent the readers from giving up the substance for the shadow by abandoning Jesus and retreating into the old Judaic system. This Epistle was also written to exhort them to become mature in Christ and to put away their spiritual dullness and degeneration.

Key Verses: "Seeing then that we have a great High Priest who has passed through the heavens, Jesus the Son of God, let us hold fast *our* confession. For we do not have a High Priest who cannot sympathize with our weaknesses, but was in all *points* tempted as *we are, yet* without sin. Let us therefore come boldly to the throne of grace, that we may obtain mercy and find grace to help in time of need" (4:14–16).

"Therefore we also, since we are surrounded by so great a cloud of witnesses, let us lay aside every weight, and the sin which so easily ensnares *us,* and let us run with endurance the race that is set before us, looking unto Jesus, the author and finisher of *our* faith, who for the joy that was set before Him endured the cross, despising the shame, and has sat down at the right hand of the throne of God" (12:1, 2).

Key Chapter: Hebrews 11. The hall of fame of the Scriptures is located in Hebrews 11 and records those who willingly took God at His word even when there was nothing to cling to but His promise. Inherent to all those listed is the recognition that "without faith *it is* impossible to please *Him,* for he who comes to God must believe that He is, and *that* He is a rewarder of those who diligently seek Him" (11:6).

1 God, who at various times and in various ways spoke in time past to the fathers by the prophets, ² has in these last days spoken to us by *His* Son, whom He has appointed heir of all things, through whom also He made the worlds; 3 who being the brightness of *His* glory and the express image of His person, and upholding all things by the word of His power, when He had by Himself[a] purged our[b] sins, sat down at the right hand of the Majesty on high, 4 having become so much better than the angels, as He has by inheritance obtained a more excellent name than they.

5 For to which of the angels did He ever say:

"You are My Son,
Today I have begotten You"?[a]

And again:

"I will be to Him a Father,
And He shall be to Me a Son"?[b]

6 But when He again brings the firstborn into the world, He says:

"Let all the angels of God
worship Him."[a]

7 And of the angels He says:

"Who makes His angels spirits
And His ministers a flame of
fire."[a]

8 But to the Son He says:

"Your throne, O God, is forever
and ever;
A scepter of righteousness is
the scepter of Your kingdom.
9   You have loved righteousness
and hated lawlessness;
Therefore God, Your God, has
anointed You
With the oil of gladness more
than Your companions."[a]

10 And:

"You, LORD, in the beginning
laid the foundation of the
earth,
And the heavens are the work
of Your hands.
11 They will perish, but You
remain;
And they will all grow old like
a garment;
12 Like a cloak You will fold them
up,
And they will be changed.

But You are the same,
And Your years will not fail."[a]

13 But to which of the angels has He ever said:

"Sit at My right hand,
Till I make Your enemies Your
footstool"?[a]

14 Are they not all ministering spirits sent forth to minister for those who will inherit salvation?

2 Therefore we must give the more earnest heed to the things we have heard, lest we drift away. 2 For if the word spoken through angels proved steadfast, and every transgression and disobedience received a just reward, 3 how shall we escape if we neglect so great a salvation, which at the first began to be spoken by the Lord, and was confirmed to us by those who heard Him, 4 God also bearing witness both with signs and wonders, with various miracles, and gifts of the Holy Spirit, according to His own will?

5 For He has not put the world to come, of which we speak, in subjection to angels. 6 But one testified in a certain place, saying:

"What is man that You are
mindful of him,
Or the son of man that You
take care of him?
7   You have made him a little
lower than the angels;
You have crowned him with
glory and honor,[a]
And set him over the works of
Your hands.
8   You have put all things in
subjection under his feet."[a]

For in that He put all in subjection under him, He left nothing that is not put under him. But now we do not yet see all things put under him. 9 But we see Jesus, who was made a little lower than the angels, for the suffering of death crowned with glory and honor, that He, by the grace of God, might taste death for everyone.

The Life of Paul

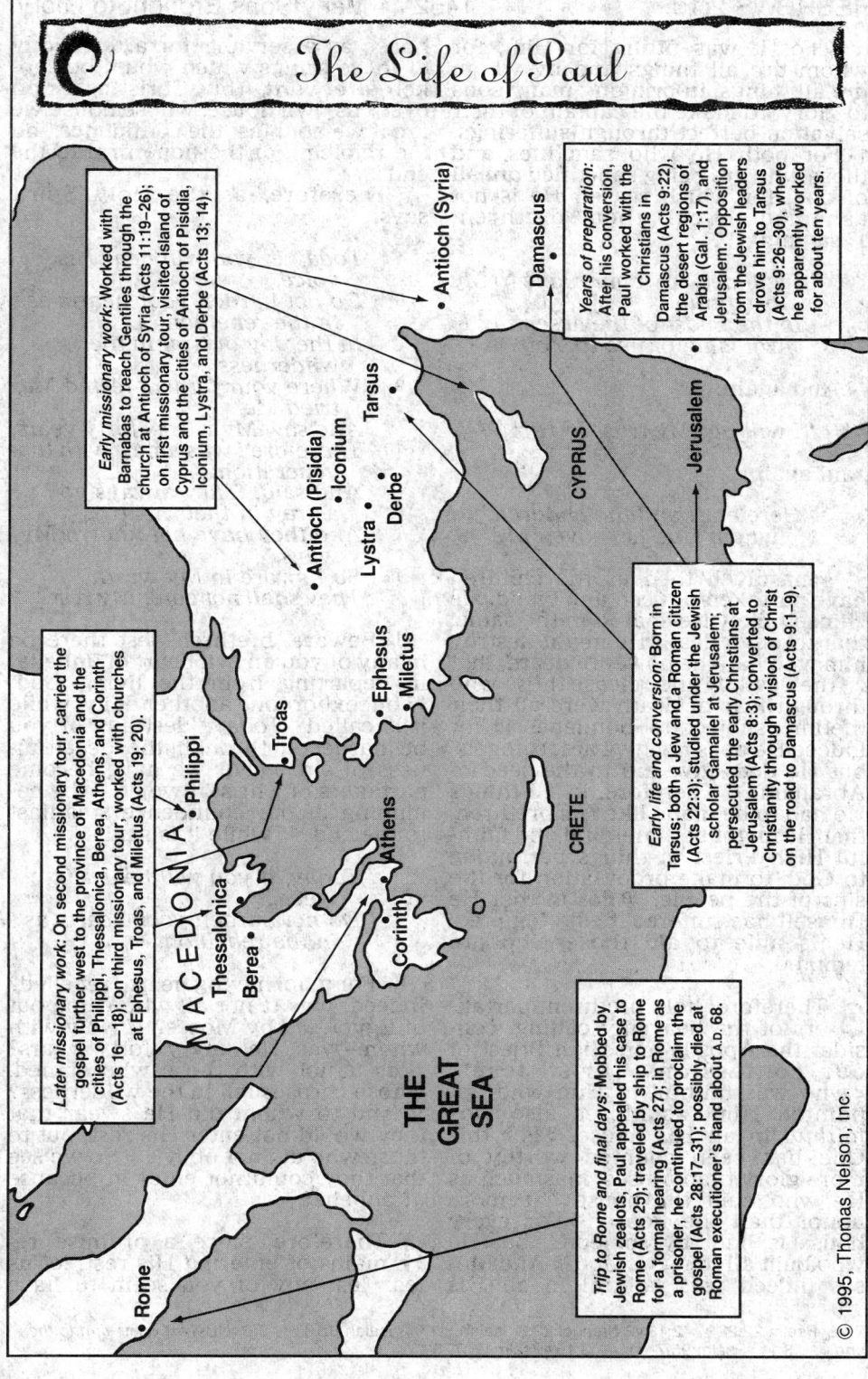

Early missionary work: Worked with Barnabas to reach Gentiles through the church at Antioch of Syria (Acts 11:19–26); on first missionary tour, visited island of Cyprus and the cities of Antioch of Pisidia, Iconium, Lystra, and Derbe (Acts 13; 14).

Years of preparation: After his conversion, Paul worked with the Christians in Damascus (Acts 9:22), the desert regions of Arabia (Gal. 1:17), and Jerusalem. Opposition from the Jewish leaders drove him to Tarsus (Acts 9:26–30), where he apparently worked for about ten years.

Early life and conversion: Born in Tarsus; both a Jew and a Roman citizen (Acts 22:3); studied under the Jewish scholar Gamaliel at Jerusalem; persecuted the early Christians at Jerusalem (Acts 8:3); converted to Christianity through a vision of Christ on the road to Damascus (Acts 9:1–9).

Later missionary work: On second missionary tour, carried the gospel further west to the province of Macedonia and the cities of Philippi, Thessalonica, Berea, Athens, and Corinth (Acts 16—18); on third missionary tour, worked with churches at Ephesus, Troas, and Miletus (Acts 19; 20).

Trip to Rome and final days: Mobbed by Jewish zealots, Paul appealed his case to Rome (Acts 25); traveled by ship to Rome for a formal hearing (Acts 27); in Rome as a prisoner, he continued to proclaim the gospel (Acts 28:17–31); possibly died at Roman executioner's hand about A.D. 68.

Antioch (Syria)
Damascus
CYPRUS
Jerusalem
Tarsus
Antioch (Pisidia)
Iconium
Lystra
Derbe
Troas
Ephesus
Miletus
MACEDONIA
Philippi
Thessalonica
Berea
Corinth
Athens
CRETE
THE GREAT SEA
Rome

10 For it was fitting for Him, for whom *are* all things and by whom *are* all things, in bringing many sons to glory, to make the captain of their salvation perfect through sufferings. 11 For both He who sanctifies and those who are being sanctified *are* all of one, for which reason He is not ashamed to call them brethren, 12 saying:

> "I will declare Your name to My brethren;
> In the midst of the assembly I will sing praise to You."ᵃ

13 And again:

> "I will put My trust in Him."ᵃ

And again:

> "Here am I and the children whom God has given Me."ᵇ

14 Inasmuch then as the children have partaken of flesh and blood, He Himself likewise shared in the same, that through death He might destroy him who had the power of death, that is, the devil, 15 and release those who through fear of death were all their lifetime subject to bondage. 16 For indeed He does not give aid to angels, but He does give aid to the seed of Abraham. 17 Therefore, in all things He had to be made like *His* brethren, that He might be a merciful and faithful High Priest in things *pertaining* to God, to make propitiation for the sins of the people. 18 For in that He Himself has suffered, being tempted, He is able to aid those who are tempted.

3 Therefore, holy brethren, partakers of the heavenly calling, consider the Apostle and High Priest of our confession, Christ Jesus, 2 who was faithful to Him who appointed Him, as Moses also *was faithful* in all His house. 3 For this One has been counted worthy of more glory than Moses, inasmuch as He who built the house has more honor than the house. 4 For every house is built by someone, but He who built all things *is* God. 5 And Moses indeed *was* faithful in all His house as a servant, for a testimony of those things which would be spoken *afterward,* 6 but Christ as a Son over His own house, whose house we are if we hold fast the confidence and the rejoicing of the hope firm to the end.ᵃ

7 Therefore, as the Holy Spirit says:

> "Today, if you will hear His voice,
> 8   Do not harden your hearts as in the rebellion,
>   In the day of trial in the wilderness,
> 9   Where your fathers tested Me, tried Me,
>   And saw My works forty years.
> 10 Therefore I was angry with that generation,
>   And said, 'They always go astray in their heart,
>   And they have not known My ways.'
> 11 So I swore in My wrath,
>   'They shall not enter My rest.' "ᵃ

12 Beware, brethren, lest there be in any of you an evil heart of unbelief in departing from the living God; 13 but exhort one another daily, while it is called "Today," lest any of you be hardened through the deceitfulness of sin. 14 For we have become partakers of Christ if we hold the beginning of our confidence steadfast to the end, 15 while it is said:

> "Today, if you will hear His voice,
> Do not harden your hearts as in the rebellion."ᵃ

16 For who, having heard, rebelled? Indeed, *was it* not all who came out of Egypt, *led* by Moses? 17 Now with whom was He angry forty years? *Was it* not with those who sinned, whose corpses fell in the wilderness? 18 And to whom did He swear that they would not enter His rest, but to those who did not obey? 19 So we see that they could not enter in because of unbelief.

4 Therefore, since a promise remains of entering His rest, let us fear lest any of you seem to have

2:12 ᵃPsalm 22:22   2:13 ᵃ2 Samuel 22:3; Isaiah 8:17   ᵇIsaiah 8:18   3:6 ᵃNU-Text omits *firm to the end.*   3:11 ᵃPsalm 95:7–11   3:15 ᵃPsalm 95:7, 8 come short of it. 2 For indeed the gospel was preached to us as well as to them; but the word which they heard did not profit them,[a] not being mixed with faith in those who heard it. 3 For we who have believed do enter that rest, as He has said:

"So I swore in My wrath,
'They shall not enter My rest,' "[a]

although the works were finished from the foundation of the world. 4 For He has spoken in a certain place of the seventh day in this way: "And God rested on the seventh day from all His works";[a] 5 and again in this place: "They shall not enter My rest."[a]

6 Since therefore it remains that some must enter it, and those to whom it was first preached did not enter because of disobedience, 7 again He designates a certain day, saying in David, "Today," after such a long time, as it has been said:

"Today, if you will hear His voice,
Do not harden your hearts."[a]

8 For if Joshua had given them rest, then He would not afterward have spoken of another day. 9 There remains therefore a rest for the people of God. 10 For he who has entered His rest has himself also ceased from his works as God did from His.

11 Let us therefore be diligent to enter that rest, lest anyone fall according to the same example of disobedience. 12 For the word of God is living and powerful, and sharper than any two-edged sword, piercing even to the division of soul and spirit, and of joints and marrow, and is a discerner of the thoughts and intents of the heart. 13 And there is no creature hidden from His sight, but all things are naked and open to the eyes of Him to whom we must give account.

14 Seeing then that we have a great High Priest who has passed through the heavens, Jesus the Son of God, let us hold fast our confession. 15 For we do not have a High Priest who cannot sympathize with our weaknesses, but was in all points tempted as we are, yet without sin. 16 Let us therefore come boldly to the throne of grace, that we may obtain mercy and find grace to help in time of need.

5 For every high priest taken from among men is appointed for men in things pertaining to God, that he may offer both gifts and sacrifices for sins. 2 He can have compassion on those who are ignorant and going astray, since he himself is also subject to weakness. 3 Because of this he is required as for the people, so also for himself, to offer sacrifices for sins. 4 And no man takes this honor to himself, but he who is called by God, just as Aaron was.

5 So also Christ did not glorify Himself to become High Priest, but it was He who said to Him:

"You are My Son,
Today I have begotten You."[a]

6 As He also says in another place:

"You are a priest forever
According to the order of Melchizedek";[a]

7 who, in the days of His flesh, when He had offered up prayers and supplications, with vehement cries and tears to Him who was able to save Him from death, and was heard because of His godly fear, 8 though He was a Son, yet He learned obedience by the things which He suffered. 9 And having been perfected, He became the author of eternal salvation to all who obey Him, 10 called by God as High Priest "according to the order of Melchizedek," 11 of whom we have much to say, and hard to explain, since you have become dull of hearing.

12 For though by this time you ought to be teachers, you need someone to teach you again the first principles of the oracles of God; and you have come to need milk and not solid food. 13 For everyone who partakes only of milk is unskilled in the word of righteousness, for he is a babe. 14 But solid food belongs to those who are of full age, that is, those who

4:2 [a]NU-Text and M-Text read profit them, since they were not united by faith with those who heeded it.
4:3 [a]Psalm 95:11   4:4 [a]Genesis 2:2   4:5 [a]Psalm 95:11   4:7 [a]Psalm 95:7, 8   5:5 [a]Psalm 2:7
5:6 [a]Psalm 110:4

by reason of use have their senses exercised to discern both good and evil.

6 Therefore, leaving the discussion of the elementary *principles* of Christ, let us go on to perfection, not laying again the foundation of repentance from dead works and of faith toward God, 2 of the doctrine of baptisms, of laying on of hands, of resurrection of the dead, and of eternal judgment. 3 And this we will*a* do if God permits.

4 For *it is* impossible for those who were once enlightened, and have tasted the heavenly gift, and have become partakers of the Holy Spirit, 5 and have tasted the good word of God and the powers of the age to come, 6 if they fall away,*a* to renew them again to repentance, since they crucify again for themselves the Son of God, and put *Him* to an open shame.

7 For the earth which drinks in the rain that often comes upon it, and bears herbs useful for those by whom it is cultivated, receives blessing from God; 8 but if it bears thorns and briers, *it is* rejected and near to being cursed, whose end *is* to be burned.

9 But, beloved, we are confident of better things concerning you, yes, things that accompany salvation, though we speak in this manner. 10 For God *is* not unjust to forget your work and labor of*a* love which you have shown toward His name, *in that* you have ministered to the saints, and do minister. 11 And we desire that each one of you show the same diligence to the full assurance of hope until the end, 12 that you do not become sluggish, but imitate those who through faith and patience inherit the promises.

13 For when God made a promise to Abraham, because He could swear by no one greater, He swore by Himself, 14 saying, *"Surely blessing I will bless you, and multiplying I will multiply you."*a 15 And so, after he had patiently endured, he obtained the promise. 16 For men indeed swear by the greater, and an oath for confirmation *is* for them an end of all dispute. 17 Thus God, determining to show more abundantly to the heirs of promise the immutability of His counsel, confirmed *it* by an oath, 18 that by two immutable things, in which it *is* impossible for God to lie, we might*a* have strong consolation, who have fled for refuge to lay hold of the hope set before *us*.

19 This *hope* we have as an anchor of the soul, both sure and steadfast, and which enters the Presence *behind* the veil, 20 where the forerunner has entered for us, *even* Jesus, having become High Priest forever according to the order of Melchizedek.

7 For this Melchizedek, king of Salem, priest of the Most High God, who met Abraham returning from the slaughter of the kings and blessed him, 2 to whom also Abraham gave a tenth part of all, first being translated "king of righteousness," and then also king of Salem, meaning "king of peace," 3 without father, without mother, without genealogy, having neither beginning of days nor end of life, but made like the Son of God, remains a priest continually.

4 Now consider how great this man *was*, to whom even the patriarch Abraham gave a tenth of the spoils. 5 And indeed those who are of the sons of Levi, who receive the priesthood, have a commandment to receive tithes from the people according to the law, that is, from their brethren, though they have come from the loins of Abraham; 6 but he whose genealogy is not derived from them received tithes from Abraham and blessed him who had the promises. 7 Now beyond all contradiction the lesser is blessed by the better. 8 Here mortal men receive tithes, but there he *receives them*, of whom it is witnessed that he lives. 9 Even Levi, who receives tithes, paid tithes through Abraham, so to speak, 10 for he was still in the loins of his father when Melchizedek met him.

11 Therefore, if perfection were through the Levitical priesthood (for under it the people received the law), what further need *was there* that another priest should rise according to the order of Melchizedek, and not be called according to the order of

---

6:3 *a*M-Text reads *let us do.*   6:6 *a*Or *and have fallen away.*   6:10 *a*NU-Text omits *labor of.*
6:14 *a*Genesis 22:17   6:18 *a*M-Text omits *might.*

Aaron? 12 For the priesthood being changed, of necessity there is also a change of the law. 13 For He of whom these things are spoken belongs to another tribe, from which no man has officiated at the altar.

14 For *it is* evident that our Lord arose from Judah, of which tribe Moses spoke nothing concerning priesthood.*a* 15 And it is yet far more evident if, in the likeness of Melchizedek, there arises another priest 16 who has come, not according to the law of a fleshly commandment, but according to the power of an endless life. 17 For He testifies:*a*

> "*You are a priest forever*
> *According to the order of*
> *Melchizedek."*b*

18 For on the one hand there is an annulling of the former commandment because of its weakness and unprofitableness, 19 for the law made nothing perfect; on the other hand, *there is the* bringing in of a better hope, through which we draw near to God.

20 And inasmuch as *He was* not *made priest* without an oath 21 (for they have become priests without an oath, but He with an oath by Him who said to Him:

> "*The LORD has sworn*
> *And will not relent,*
> '*You are a priest forever*a*
> *According to the order of*
> *Melchizedek'* "),*b*

22 by so much more Jesus has become a surety of a better covenant.

23 Also there were many priests, because they were prevented by death from continuing. 24 But He, because He continues forever, has an unchangeable priesthood. 25 Therefore He is also able to save to the uttermost those who come to God through Him, since He always lives to make intercession for them.

26 For such a High Priest was fitting for us, *who is* holy, harmless, undefiled, separate from sinners, and has become higher than the heavens; 27 who does not need daily, as those high priests, to offer up sacrifices, first for His own sins and then for the people's, for this He did once for all when He offered up Himself. 28 For the law appoints as high priests men who have weakness, but the word of the oath, which came after the law, *appoints* the Son who has been perfected forever.

8 Now *this is* the main point of the things we are saying: We have such a High Priest, who is seated at the right hand of the throne of the Majesty in the heavens, 2 a Minister of the sanctuary and of the true tabernacle which the Lord erected, and not man.

3 For every high priest is appointed to offer both gifts and sacrifices. Therefore *it is* necessary that this One also have something to offer. 4 For if He were on earth, He would not be a priest, since there are priests who offer the gifts according to the law; 5 who serve the copy and shadow of the heavenly things, as Moses was divinely instructed when he was about to make the tabernacle. For He said, "*See that you make all things according to the pattern shown you on the mountain."*a* 6 But now He has obtained a more excellent ministry, inasmuch as He is also Mediator of a better covenant, which was established on better promises.

7 For if that first *covenant* had been faultless, then no place would have been sought for a second. 8 Because finding fault with them, He says: "*Behold, the days are coming, says the LORD, when I will make a new covenant with the house of Israel and with the house of Judah— 9 not according to the covenant that I made with their fathers in the day when I took them by the hand to lead them out of the land of Egypt; because they did not continue in My covenant, and I disregarded them, says the LORD. 10 For this is the covenant that I will make with the house of Israel after those days, says the LORD: I will put My laws in their mind and write them on their hearts; and I will be their God, and they shall be My people. 11 None of them shall teach his neighbor, and none his brother, saying, 'Know the LORD,' for all shall know Me, from the least of them to*

7:14 *a*NU-Text reads *priests.*   7:17 *a*NU-Text reads *it is testified.*   *b*Psalm 110:4   7:21 *a*NU-Text ends the quotation here.   *b*Psalm 110:4   8:5 *a*Exodus 25:40

the greatest of them. 12 For I will be merciful to their unrighteousness, and their sins and their lawless deeds[a] I will remember no more."[b]

13 In that He says, "A new covenant," He has made the first obsolete. Now what is becoming obsolete and growing old is ready to vanish away.

9 Then indeed, even the first *covenant* had ordinances of divine service and the earthly sanctuary. 2 For a tabernacle was prepared: the first *part,* in which *was* the lampstand, the table, and the showbread, which is called the sanctuary; 3 and behind the second veil, the part of the tabernacle which is called the Holiest of All, 4 which had the golden censer and the ark of the covenant overlaid on all sides with gold, in which *were* the golden pot that had the manna, Aaron's rod that budded, and the tablets of the covenant; 5 and above it were the cherubim of glory overshadowing the mercy seat. Of these things we cannot now speak in detail.

6 Now when these things had been thus prepared, the priests always went into the first part of the tabernacle, performing *the services.* 7 But into the second part the high priest *went* alone once a year, not without blood, which he offered for himself and *for* the people's sins *committed* in ignorance; 8 the Holy Spirit indicating this, that the way into the Holiest of All was not yet made manifest while the first tabernacle was still standing. 9 It *was* symbolic for the present time in which both gifts and sacrifices are offered which cannot make him who performed the service perfect in regard to the conscience— 10 *concerned* only with foods and drinks, various washings, and fleshly ordinances imposed until the time of reformation.

11 But Christ came *as* High Priest of the good things to come,[a] with the greater and more perfect tabernacle not made with hands, that is, not of this creation. 12 Not with the blood of goats and calves, but with His own blood He entered the Most Holy Place once for all, having obtained eternal redemption. 13 For if the blood of bulls and goats and the ashes of a heifer, sprinkling the unclean, sanctifies for the purifying of the flesh, 14 how much more shall the blood of Christ, who through the eternal Spirit offered Himself without spot to God, cleanse your conscience from dead works to serve the living God? 15 And for this reason He is the Mediator of the new covenant, by means of death, for the redemption of the transgressions under the first covenant, that those who are called may receive the promise of the eternal inheritance.

16 For where there *is* a testament, there must also of necessity be the death of the testator. 17 For a testament *is* in force after men are dead, since it has no power at all while the testator lives. 18 Therefore not even the first *covenant* was dedicated without blood. 19 For when Moses had spoken every precept to all the people according to the law, he took the blood of calves and goats, with water, scarlet wool, and hyssop, and sprinkled both the book itself and all the people, 20 saying, *"This is the blood of the covenant which God has commanded you."*[a] 21 Then likewise he sprinkled with blood both the tabernacle and all the vessels of the ministry. 22 And according to the law almost all things are purified with blood, and without shedding of blood there is no remission.

23 Therefore *it was* necessary that the copies of the things in the heavens should be purified with these, but the heavenly things themselves with better sacrifices than these. 24 For Christ has not entered the holy places made with hands, *which are* copies of the true, but into heaven itself, now to appear in the presence of God for us; 25 not that He should offer Himself often, as the high priest enters the Most Holy Place every year with blood of another— 26 He then would have had to suffer often since the foundation of the world; but now, once at the end of the ages, He has appeared to put away sin by the sacrifice of Himself. 27 And as it is appointed for men to die once, but after this the judgment, 28 so Christ was offered once to bear the sins of many. To those who ea-

---

8:12 [a]NU-Text omits *and their lawless deeds.*   [b]Jeremiah 31:31–34   9:11 [a]NU-Text reads *that have come.*   9:20 [a]Exodus 24:8

gerly wait for Him He will appear a second time, apart from sin, for salvation.

10 For the law, having a shadow of the good things to come, *and* not the very image of the things, can never with these same sacrifices, which they offer continually year by year, make those who approach perfect. 2 For then would they not have ceased to be offered? For the worshipers, once purified, would have had no more consciousness of sins. 3 But in those *sacrifices there is* a reminder of sins every year. 4 For *it is* not possible that the blood of bulls and goats could take away sins.

5 Therefore, when He came into the world, He said:

"*Sacrifice and offering You did not desire,
But a body You have prepared for Me.*
6   *In burnt offerings and sacrifices for sin
You had no pleasure.*
7   *Then I said, 'Behold, I have come—
In the volume of the book it is written of Me—
To do Your will, O God.' "a*

8 Previously saying, *"Sacrifice and offering, burnt offerings, and offerings for sin You did not desire, nor had pleasure in them"* (which are offered according to the law), 9 then He said, *"Behold, I have come to do Your will, O God."a* He takes away the first that He may establish the second. 10 By that will we have been sanctified through the offering of the body of Jesus Christ once *for all.*

11 And every priest stands ministering daily and offering repeatedly the same sacrifices, which can never take away sins. 12 But this Man, after He had offered one sacrifice for sins forever, sat down at the right hand of God, 13 from that time waiting till His enemies are made His footstool. 14 For by one offering He has perfected forever those who are being sanctified.

15 But the Holy Spirit also wit-

nesses to us; for after He had said before,

16 *"This is the covenant that I will make with them after those days, says the Lord: I will put My laws into their hearts, and in their minds I will write them,"a* 17 then He adds, *"Their sins and their lawless deeds I will remember no more."a* 18 Now where there is remission of these, *there is* no longer an offering for sin.

19 Therefore, brethren, having boldness to enter the Holiest by the blood of Jesus, 20 by a new and living way which He consecrated for us, through the veil, that is, His flesh, 21 and *having* a High Priest over the house of God, 22 let us draw near with a true heart in full assurance of faith, having our hearts sprinkled from an evil conscience and our bodies washed with pure water. 23 Let us hold fast the confession of *our* hope without wavering, for He who promised *is* faithful. 24 And let us consider one another in order to stir up love and good works, 25 not forsaking the assembling of ourselves together, as *is* the manner of some, but exhorting *one another,* and so much the more as you see the Day approaching.

26 For if we sin willfully after we have received the knowledge of the truth, there no longer remains a sacrifice for sins, 27 but a certain fearful expectation of judgment, and fiery indignation which will devour the adversaries. 28 Anyone who has rejected Moses' law dies without mercy on the testimony of two or three witnesses. 29 Of how much worse punishment, do you suppose, will he be thought worthy who has trampled the Son of God underfoot, counted the blood of the covenant by which he was sanctified a common thing, and insulted the Spirit of grace? 30 For we know Him who said, *"Vengeance is Mine, I will repay,"a* says the Lord.*b* And again, *"The Lord will judge His people."c* 31 It is a fearful thing to fall into the hands of the living God.

32 But recall the former days in which, after you were illuminated, you endured a great struggle with sufferings: 33 partly while you were made a spectacle both by reproaches

10:7 aPsalm 40:6–8   10:9 aNU-Text and M-Text omit O God.   10:16 aJeremiah 31:33
10:17 aJeremiah 31:34   10:30 aDeuteronomy 32:35   bNU-Text omits says the Lord.   cDeuteronomy 32:36

Speak Confidence

Practice all the faith you can by complimenting yourself honestly, genuinely, and fluently! Be effervescent in complimenting yourself today.

As Christians we sometimes become so programmed to humility, coupled with the awareness that we can accomplish nothing without the grace of God and the goodness of our Lord, that we fail to give ourselves adequate credit.

God knows you and I need a pat on the back. There are nobler dreams that God wants us to pursue; there are bigger battles to be fought. The need to endure to the end compels us to give ourselves all the motivation possible.

Self-congratulatory remarks—in the privacy of your prayer time with God—are in order!

In the presence of God, in the privacy of prayer, take time to applaud the great human being that you really are!

You are a redeemed child of God! Let your light shine!

Try complimenting yourself every morning when you begin the day by praying.

Thank You, Father, for giving me enough faith in myself, and in Your goodness to me, to give myself these compliments! I thank You that I have been created with a mind capable of dreaming dreams! I thank You that I have a heart through which the love of Jesus Christ can flow to human beings around me. I thank You that I do have talents, abilities, and gifts that You can use. I thank You, God, that my life is definitely on the right road. Stay with me, Father, all the way. Amen.

and tribulations, and partly while you became companions of those who were so treated; 34 for you had compassion on me[a] in my chains, and joyfully accepted the plundering of your goods, knowing that you have a better and an enduring possession for yourselves in heaven.[b] 35 Therefore do not cast away your confidence, which has great reward. 36 For you have need of endurance, so that after you have done the will of God, you may receive the promise:

37 "For yet a little while,
    And He[a] who is coming will
        come and will not tarry.
38 Now the[a] just shall live by
        faith;
    But if anyone draws back,
    My soul has no pleasure in
        him."[b]

39 But we are not of those who draw back to perdition, but of those who believe to the saving of the soul.

11 Now faith is the substance of things hoped for, the evidence of things not seen. 2 For by it the elders obtained a good testimony.

3 By faith we understand that the worlds were framed by the word of God, so that the things which are seen were not made of things which are visible.

4 By faith Abel offered to God a more excellent sacrifice than Cain, through which he obtained witness that he was righteous, God testifying of his gifts; and through it he being dead still speaks.

5 By faith Enoch was taken away so that he did not see death, "and was not found, because God had taken him";[a] for before he was taken he had this testimony, that he pleased God. 6 But without faith it is impossible to please Him, for he who comes to God must believe that He is, and that He is a rewarder of those who diligently seek Him.

7 By faith Noah, being divinely warned of things not yet seen, moved with godly fear, prepared an ark for the saving of his household, by which he condemned the world and became

heir of the righteousness which is according to faith.

8 By faith Abraham obeyed when he was called to go out to the place which he would receive as an inheritance. And he went out, not knowing where he was going. 9 By faith he dwelt in the land of promise as in a foreign country, dwelling in tents with Isaac and Jacob, the heirs with him of the same promise; 10 for he waited for the city which has foundations, whose builder and maker is God.

11 By faith Sarah herself also received strength to conceive seed, and she bore a child[a] when she was past the age, because she judged Him faithful who had promised. 12 Therefore from one man, and him as good as dead, were born as many as the stars of the sky in multitude—innumerable as the sand which is by the seashore.

13 These all died in faith, not having received the promises, but having seen them afar off were assured of them,[a] embraced them and confessed that they were strangers and pilgrims on the earth. 14 For those who say such things declare plainly that they seek a homeland. 15 And truly if they had called to mind that country from which they had come out, they would have had opportunity to return. 16 But now they desire a better, that is, a heavenly country. Therefore God is not ashamed to be called their God, for He has prepared a city for them.

17 By faith Abraham, when he was tested, offered up Isaac, and he who had received the promises offered up his only begotten son, 18 of whom it was said, "In Isaac your seed shall be called,"[a] 19 concluding that God was able to raise him up, even from the dead, from which he also received him in a figurative sense.

20 By faith Isaac blessed Jacob and Esau concerning things to come.

21 By faith Jacob, when he was dying, blessed each of the sons of Joseph, and worshiped, leaning on the top of his staff.

22 By faith Joseph, when he was dying, made mention of the depar-

10:34 aNU-Text reads the prisoners instead of me in my chains.   bNU-Text omits in heaven.
10:37 aOr that which   10:38 aNU-Text reads my just one.   bHabakkuk 2:3, 4   11:5 aGenesis 5:24
11:11 aNU-Text omits she bore a child.   11:13 aNU-Text and M-Text omit were assured of them.
11:18 aGenesis 21:12

Take a Positive Plunge

Hebrews 12:1 encourages us to "run with endurance the race that is set before us." The running of a race provides an exciting illustration of faith. The runner jumps at the starting gun, even though he cannot be sure he will win. But one thing is certain. The person who does not start can never win!

This means that another truth becomes markedly evident: *Every starter is a winner.* The losers are those who never tried. If you need to be sure that you will win, if you need to be confident of success *before* you make a commitment, *then you are not walking the walk of faith!*

It is the element of uncertainty that adds excitement to life. The predictable always produces boredom. The element of the unpredictable always generates the interest and involvement of spectator and participant alike.

So the person who walks the walk of faith is alive and is keeping others alive, speculating on his success. He is news, because he has entered the race before he is positive that he can win.

God's promises are not offered to the "play-it-safe" spectator in the stands, but to the "let's-take-a-chance" player in the middle of the game!

Take this positive plunge: Today double-check your life. Have you plunged ahead with the new opportunities that came to your mind only a day or two ago? If not, then today step on the starting line, put both hands to the ground. Step up on tiptoe, and look ahead at the course. Then, run the race. This time, don't be a spectator in the stands, but be a *contestant!*

ture of the children of Israel, and gave instructions concerning his bones.

23 By faith Moses, when he was born, was hidden three months by his parents, because they saw *he was* a beautiful child; and they were not afraid of the king's command.

24 By faith Moses, when he became of age, refused to be called the son of Pharaoh's daughter, 25 choosing rather to suffer affliction with the people of God than to enjoy the passing pleasures of sin, 26 esteeming the reproach of Christ greater riches than the treasures in*a* Egypt; for he looked to the reward.

27 By faith he forsook Egypt, not fearing the wrath of the king; for he endured as seeing Him who is invisible. 28 By faith he kept the Passover and the sprinkling of blood, lest he who destroyed the firstborn should touch them.

29 By faith they passed through the Red Sea as by dry *land, whereas* the Egyptians, attempting *to do* so, were drowned.

30 By faith the walls of Jericho fell down after they were encircled for seven days. 31 By faith the harlot Rahab did not perish with those who did not believe, when she had received the spies with peace.

32 And what more shall I say? For the time would fail me to tell of Gideon and Barak and Samson and Jephthah, also *of* David and Samuel and the prophets: 33 who through faith subdued kingdoms, worked righteousness, obtained promises, stopped the mouths of lions, 34 quenched the violence of fire, escaped the edge of the sword, out of weakness were made strong, became valiant in battle, turned to flight the armies of the aliens. 35 Women received their dead raised to life again.

Others were tortured, not accepting deliverance, that they might obtain a better resurrection. 36 Still others had trial of mockings and scourgings, yes, and of chains and imprisonment. 37 They were stoned, they were sawn in two, were tempted,*a* were slain with the sword. They wandered about in sheepskins and goatskins, being destitute, af-

flicted, tormented— 38 of whom the world was not worthy. They wandered in deserts and mountains, *in* dens and caves of the earth.

39 And all these, having obtained a good testimony through faith, did not receive the promise, 40 God having provided something better for us, that they should not be made perfect apart from us.

12 Therefore we also, since we are surrounded by so great a cloud of witnesses, let us lay aside every weight, and the sin which so easily ensnares *us*, and let us run with endurance the race that is set before us, 2 looking unto Jesus, the author and finisher of *our* faith, who for the joy that was set before Him endured the cross, despising the shame, and has sat down at the right hand of the throne of God.

3 For consider Him who endured such hostility from sinners against Himself, lest you become weary and discouraged in your souls. 4 You have not yet resisted to bloodshed, striving against sin. 5 And you have forgotten the exhortation which speaks to you as to sons:

"My son, do not despise the
      chastening of the LORD,
Nor be discouraged when you
      are rebuked by Him;
6   For whom the LORD loves He
      chastens,
      And scourges every son whom
      He receives."*a*

7 If*a* you endure chastening, God deals with you as with sons; for what son is there whom a father does not chasten? 8 But if you are without chastening, of which all have become partakers, then you are illegitimate and not sons. 9 Furthermore, we have had human fathers who corrected *us*, and we paid *them* respect. Shall we not much more readily be in subjection to the Father of spirits and live? 10 For they indeed for a few days chastened *us* as seemed *best* to them, but He for *our* profit, that *we* may be partakers of His holiness. 11 Now no chastening seems to be joyful for the present, but painful; nevertheless, afterward it yields the peace

11:26 *a*NU-Text and M-Text read *of*.   11:37 *a*NU-Text omits *were tempted*.   12:6 *a*Proverbs 3:11, 12
12:7 *a*NU-Text and M-Text read *It is for discipline that you endure; God.*

able fruit of righteousness to those who have been trained by it.

12 Therefore strengthen the hands which hang down, and the feeble knees, 13 and make straight paths for your feet, so that what is lame may not be *dislocated*, but rather be healed.

14 Pursue peace with all *people*, and holiness, without which no one will see the Lord: 15 looking carefully lest anyone fall short of the grace of God; lest any root of bitterness springing up cause trouble, and by this many become defiled; 16 lest there *be* any fornicator or profane person like Esau, who for one morsel of food sold his birthright. 17 For you know that afterward, when he wanted to inherit the blessing, he was rejected, for he found no place for repentance, though he sought it diligently with tears.

18 For you have not come to the mountain that*a* may be touched and that burned with fire, and to blackness and darkness*b* and tempest, 19 and the sound of a trumpet and the voice of words, so that those who heard *it* begged that the word should not be spoken to them anymore. 20 (For they could not endure what was commanded: *"And if so much as a beast touches the mountain, it shall be stoned*a* or shot with an arrow."*b* 21 And so terrifying was the sight that Moses said, *"I am exceedingly afraid and trembling."*a*)

22 But you have come to Mount Zion and to the city of the living God, the heavenly Jerusalem, to an innumerable company of angels, 23 to the general assembly and church of the firstborn *who are* registered in heaven, to God the Judge of all, to the spirits of just men made perfect, 24 to Jesus the Mediator of the new covenant, and to the blood of sprinkling that speaks better things than *that of* Abel.

25 See that you do not refuse Him who speaks. For if they did not escape who refused Him who spoke on earth, much more *shall we not escape* if we turn away from Him who *speaks* from heaven, 26 whose voice then shook the earth; but now He has

promised, saying, *"Yet once more I shake*a* not only the earth, but also heaven."*b* 27 Now this, *"Yet once more,"* indicates the removal of those things that are being shaken, as of things that are made, that the things which cannot be shaken may remain.

28 Therefore, since we are receiving a kingdom which cannot be shaken, let us have grace, by which we may*a* serve God acceptably with reverence and godly fear. 29 For our God *is* a consuming fire.

13 Let brotherly love continue. 2 Do not forget to entertain strangers, for by so *doing* some have unwittingly entertained angels. 3 Remember the prisoners as if chained with them—those who are mistreated—since you yourselves are in the body also.

4 Marriage *is* honorable among all, and the bed undefiled; but fornicators and adulterers God will judge.

5 *Let your* conduct *be* without covetousness; *be* content with such things as you have. For He Himself has said, *"I will never leave you nor forsake you."*a* 6 So we may boldly say:

> *"The LORD is my helper;*
> *I will not fear.*
> *What can man do to me?"*a*

7 Remember those who rule over you, who have spoken the word of God to you, whose faith follow, considering the outcome of *their* conduct. 8 Jesus Christ *is* the same yesterday, today, and forever. 9 Do not be carried about*a* with various and strange doctrines. For *it is* good that the heart be established by grace, not with foods which have not profited those who have been occupied with them.

10 We have an altar from which those who serve the tabernacle have no right to eat. 11 For the bodies of those animals, whose blood is brought into the sanctuary by the high priest for sin, are burned outside the camp. 12 Therefore Jesus also,

---

12:18 *a*NU-Text reads *to that which.*   *b*NU-Text reads *gloom.*   12:20 *a*NU-Text and M-Text omit the rest of this verse.   *b*Exodus 19:12, 13   12:21 *a*Deuteronomy 9:19   12:26 *a*NU-Text reads *will shake.*   *b*Haggai 2:6   12:28 *a*M-Text omits *may.*   13:5 *a*Deuteronomy 31:6, 8; Joshua 1:5   13:6 *a*Psalm 118:6   13:9 *a*NU-Text and M-Text read *away.*

that He might sanctify the people with His own blood, suffered outside the gate. 13 Therefore let us go forth to Him, outside the camp, bearing His reproach. 14 For here we have no continuing city, but we seek the one to come. 15 Therefore by Him let us continually offer the sacrifice of praise to God, that is, the fruit of *our* lips, giving thanks to His name. 16 But do not forget to do good and to share, for with such sacrifices God is well pleased.

17 Obey those who rule over you, and be submissive, for they watch out for your souls, as those who must give account. Let them do so with joy and not with grief, for that would be unprofitable for you.

18 Pray for us; for we are confident that we have a good conscience, in all things desiring to live honorably. 19 But I especially urge *you* to do this,

that I may be restored to you the sooner.

20 Now may the God of peace who brought up our Lord Jesus from the dead, that great Shepherd of the sheep, through the blood of the everlasting covenant, 21 make you complete in every good work to do His will, working in you[a] what is well pleasing in His sight, through Jesus Christ, to whom *be* glory forever and ever. Amen.

22 And I appeal to you, brethren, bear with the word of exhortation, for I have written to you in few words. 23 Know that *our* brother Timothy has been set free, with whom I shall see you if he comes shortly.

24 Greet all those who rule over you, and all the saints. Those from Italy greet you.

25 Grace *be* with you all. Amen.

13:21 *a*NU-Text and M-Text read *us*.

James

Overview of James

Written by James, the half-brother of Jesus, between A.D. 45 and 50, James is a letter to all Jewish Christians or "the twelve tribes which are scattered abroad" (James 1:1).

James is the most practical of all the Epistles, emphasizing that love and Christian faith must be demonstrated in deeds. The letter encourages faith to be lived out by sharing and helping one another. James also encouraged his readers to stand fast in the face of trials:

My brethren, count it all joy when you fall into various trials, knowing that the testing of your faith produces patience. But let patience have its perfect work, that you may be perfect and complete, lacking nothing. If any of you lacks wisdom, let him ask of God, who gives to all liberally and without reproach, and it will be given to him.

(James 1:2–5)

James must have witnessed his brother Jesus' attitude of concern for those who were in need. Perhaps this is why he appeals to us not to be simply hearers of the Word, but doers of the Word by caring for the poor, visiting the sick and depressed, and helping widows. We should be a light of hope when others are going through tough times.

James encourages us not to judge but to welcome back with lovingkindness those who have not lived up to their faith. James tells us to be like Jesus, who touched the lives of all people—to find a need and fill it, find a hurt and heal it!

Jesus in James

Compared to other New Testament writers, James says little about Jesus, and yet his Epistle is virtually saturated with allusions to the teaching of Jesus. The Sermon on the Mount is especially prominent in James' thinking. This letter, like Jesus' most well-known speech, concerns the practical aspects of faith in Him.

Keys to James

Key Word: Faith That Works. Throughout his Epistle, James centers on the characteristics of true faith. He effectively uses these characteristics as a series of tests to help his readers evaluate the quality of their relationship to Jesus. The purpose of this work is not doctrinal or apologetic but practical. James seeks to challenge these believers to examine the quality of their daily lives in terms of attitudes and actions. A genuine faith will produce real changes in a person's conduct and character, and the absence of change is a symptom of a dead faith.

Key Verses: "So then, my beloved brethren, let every man be swift to hear, slow to speak, slow to wrath; for the wrath of man does not produce the righteousness of God. Therefore lay aside all filthiness and overflow of wickedness, and receive with meekness the implanted word, which is able to save your souls. But be doers of the word, and not hearers only, deceiving yourselves" (1:19–22).

"What *does it* profit, my brethren, if someone says he has faith but does not have works? Can faith save him? If a brother or sister is naked and destitute of daily food, and one of you says to them, 'Depart in peace, be warmed and filled,' but you do not give them the things which are needed for the body, what *does it* profit? Thus also faith by itself, if it does not have works, is dead" (2:14–17).

Key Chapter: James 1. One of the most difficult areas of life for the Christian is that of testing and temptations. James reveals our correct response to each: to testings, count them all joy; to temptations, realize that God is not their source.

1 James, a bondservant of God and of the Lord Jesus Christ,

To the twelve tribes which are scattered abroad:

Greetings.

2 My brethren, count it all joy when you fall into various trials, 3 knowing that the testing of your faith produces patience. 4 But let patience have *its* perfect work, that you may be perfect and complete, lacking nothing. 5 If any of you lacks wisdom, let him ask of God, who gives to all liberally and without reproach, and it will be given to him. 6 But let him ask in faith, with no doubting, for he who doubts is like a wave of the sea driven and tossed by the wind. 7 For let not that man suppose that he will receive anything from the Lord; 8 *he is* a double-minded man, unstable in all his ways.

9 Let the lowly brother glory in his exaltation, 10 but the rich in his hu-miliation, because as a flower of the field he will pass away. 11 For no sooner has the sun risen with a burning heat than it withers the grass; its flower falls, and its beautiful appearance perishes. So the rich man also will fade away in his pursuits.

12 Blessed *is* the man who endures temptation; for when he has been approved, he will receive the crown of life which the Lord has promised to those who love Him. 13 Let no one say when he is tempted, "I am tempted by God"; for God cannot be tempted by evil, nor does He Himself tempt anyone. 14 But each one is tempted when he is drawn away by his own desires and enticed. 15 Then, when desire has conceived, it gives birth to sin; and sin, when it is full-grown, brings forth death.

16 Do not be deceived, my beloved brethren. 17 Every good gift and every perfect gift is from above, and comes down from the Father of lights, with whom there is no varia-

Have Faith in Your Faith

Jesus' half-brother James wrote: "Let [those who seek wisdom] ask in faith, with no doubting, for he who doubts is like a wave of the sea driven and tossed by the wind" (James 1:6). It is quite apparent that the believer in God and the Bible has as strong a foundation for a rational system of belief as any doubter has for the philosophy of irreligion he has fabricated.

Faith in God will
   increase your moral strength,
      increase your days of joy,
         reduce your days of despair.

Jesus is our cornerstone—our guide on our walk of faith. When doubts surface, remember what Jesus said, what He did, and where His faith stood:

Jesus believed in God. He believed in prayer.

He believed in heaven and hell and eternal life.

He believed in salvation.

He believed in every single human being.

He believed in possibility thinking and He believed in faith.

If your doubts collide and clash with the viewpoint of Jesus Christ, it is the better part of wisdom to believe the Believer and doubt the doubter. Then you are on your way to a great life.

tion or shadow of turning. 18 Of His own will He brought us forth by the word of truth, that we might be a kind of firstfruits of His creatures.

19 So then,*a* my beloved brethren, let every man be swift to hear, slow to speak, slow to wrath; 20 for the wrath of man does not produce the righteousness of God.

21 Therefore lay aside all filthiness and overflow of wickedness, and receive with meekness the implanted word, which is able to save your souls.

22 But be doers of the word, and not hearers only, deceiving yourselves. 23 For if anyone is a hearer of the word and not a doer, he is like a man observing his natural face in a mirror; 24 for he observes himself, goes away, and immediately forgets what kind of man he was. 25 But he who looks into the perfect law of liberty and continues *in it*, and is not a forgetful hearer but a doer of the work, this one will be blessed in what he does.

26 If anyone among you*a* thinks he is religious, and does not bridle his tongue but deceives his own heart, this one's religion *is* useless. 27 Pure and undefiled religion before God and the Father is this: to visit orphans and widows in their trouble, *and* to keep oneself unspotted from the world.

2 My brethren, do not hold the faith of our Lord Jesus Christ, *the Lord* of glory, with partiality. 2 For if there should come into your assembly a man with gold rings, in fine apparel, and there should also come in a poor man in filthy clothes, 3 and you pay attention to the one wearing the fine clothes and say to him, "You sit here in a good place," and say to the poor man, "You stand there," or, "Sit here at my footstool," 4 have you not shown partiality among yourselves, and become judges with evil thoughts?

5 Listen, my beloved brethren: Has God not chosen the poor of this world *to be* rich in faith and heirs of the kingdom which He promised to those who love Him? 6 But you have dishonored the poor man. Do not the rich oppress you and drag you into the courts? 7 Do they not blaspheme that noble name by which you are called?

8 If you really fulfill *the* royal law according to the Scripture, *"You shall love your neighbor as yourself,"a* you do well; 9 but if you show partiality, you commit sin, and are convicted by the law as transgressors. 10 For whoever shall keep the whole law, and yet stumble in one *point,* he is guilty of all. 11 For He who said, *"Do not commit adultery,"a* also said, *"Do not murder."b* Now if you do not commit adultery, but you do murder, you have become a transgressor of the law. 12 So speak and so do as those who will be judged by the law of liberty. 13 For judgment is without mercy to the one who has shown no mercy. Mercy triumphs over judgment.

14 What *does it* profit, my brethren, if someone says he has faith but does not have works? Can faith save him? 15 If a brother or sister is naked and destitute of daily food, 16 and one of you says to them, "Depart in peace, be warmed and filled," but you do not give them the things which are needed for the body, what *does it* profit? 17 Thus also faith by itself, if it does not have works, is dead.

18 But someone will say, "You have faith, and I have works." Show me your faith without your*a* works, and I will show you my faith by my*b* works. 19 You believe that there is one God. You do well. Even the demons believe—and tremble! 20 But do you want to know, O foolish man, that faith without works is dead?*a* 21 Was not Abraham our father justified by works when he offered Isaac his son on the altar? 22 Do you see that faith was working together with his works, and by works faith was made perfect? 23 And the Scripture was fulfilled which says, *"Abraham believed God, and it was accounted to him for righteousness."a* And he was called the friend of God. 24 You see then that a man is justified by works, and not by faith only.

25 Likewise, was not Rahab the harlot also justified by works when

1:19 *a*NU-Text reads *Know (this)* or *(This) you know.*   1:26 *a*NU-Text omits *among you.*   2:8 *a*Leviticus 19:18   2:11 *a*Exodus 20:14; Deuteronomy 5:18   *b*Exodus 20:13; Deuteronomy 5:17   2:18 *a*NU-Text omits *your.*   *b*NU-Text omits *my.*   2:20 *a*NU-Text reads *useless.*   2:23 *a*Genesis 15:6

she received the messengers and sent *them* out another way?

26 For as the body without the spirit is dead, so faith without works is dead also.

3 My brethren, let not many of you become teachers, knowing that we shall receive a stricter judgment. 2 For we all stumble in many things. If anyone does not stumble in word, he *is* a perfect man, able also to bridle the whole body. 3 Indeed,*a* we put bits in horses' mouths that they may obey us, and we turn their whole body. 4 Look also at ships: although they are so large and are driven by fierce winds, they are turned by a very small rudder wherever the pilot desires. 5 Even so the tongue is a little member and boasts great things.

See how great a forest a little fire kindles! 6 And the tongue *is* a fire, a world of iniquity. The tongue is so set among our members that it defiles the whole body, and sets on fire the course of nature; and it is set on fire by hell. 7 For every kind of beast and bird, of reptile and creature of the sea, is tamed and has been tamed by mankind. 8 But no man can tame the tongue. *It is* an unruly evil, full of deadly poison. 9 With it we bless our God and Father, and with it we curse men, who have been made in the similitude of God. 10 Out of the same mouth proceed blessing and cursing. My brethren, these things ought not to be so. 11 Does a spring send forth fresh *water* and bitter from the same opening? 12 Can a fig tree, my brethren, bear olives, or a grapevine bear figs? Thus no spring yields both salt water and fresh.*a*

13 Who *is* wise and understanding among you? Let him show by good conduct *that* his works *are done* in the meekness of wisdom. 14 But if you have bitter envy and self-seeking in your hearts, do not boast and lie against the truth. 15 This wisdom does not descend from above, but *is* earthly, sensual, demonic. 16 For where envy and self-seeking *exist,* confusion and every evil thing *are* there. 17 But the wisdom that is from above is first pure, then peaceable, gentle, willing to yield, full of mercy and good fruits, without partiality and without hypocrisy. 18 Now the fruit of righteousness is sown in peace by those who make peace.

4 Where do wars and fights *come* from among you? Do *they* not *come* from your *desires for* pleasure that war in your members? 2 You lust and do not have. You murder and covet and cannot obtain. You fight and war. Yet*a* you do not have because you do not ask. 3 You ask and do not receive, because you ask amiss, that you may spend *it* on your pleasures. 4 Adulterers and*a* adulteresses! Do you not know that friendship with the world is enmity with God? Whoever therefore wants to be a friend of the world makes himself an enemy of God. 5 Or do you think that the Scripture says in vain, "The Spirit who dwells in us yearns jealously"?

6 But He gives more grace. Therefore He says:

> "God resists the proud,
> But gives grace to the
>   humble."*a*

7 Therefore submit to God. Resist the devil and he will flee from you. 8 Draw near to God and He will draw near to you. Cleanse *your* hands, *you* sinners; and purify *your* hearts, *you* double-minded. 9 Lament and mourn and weep! Let your laughter be turned to mourning and *your* joy to gloom. 10 Humble yourselves in the sight of the Lord, and He will lift you up.

11 Do not speak evil of one another, brethren. He who speaks evil of a brother and judges his brother, speaks evil of the law and judges the law. But if you judge the law, you are not a doer of the law but a judge. 12 There is one Lawgiver,*a* who is able to save and to destroy. Who*b* are you to judge another?*c*

13 Come now, you who say, "Today or tomorrow we will*a* go to such and such a city, spend a year there, buy and sell, and make a profit"; 14 whereas you do not know what

---

3:3 *a*NU-Text reads *Now if.*   3:12 *a*NU-Text reads *Neither can a salty spring produce fresh water.*
4:2 *a*NU-Text and M-Text omit *Yet.*   4:4 *a*NU-Text omits *Adulterers and.*   4:6 *a*Proverbs 3:34
4:12 *a*NU-Text adds *and Judge.*   *b*NU-Text and M-Text read *But who.*   *c*NU-Text reads *a neighbor.*
4:13 *a*M-Text reads *let us.*

will happen tomorrow. For what *is* your life? It is even a vapor that appears for a little time and then vanishes away. 15 Instead you *ought* to say, "If the Lord wills, we shall live and do this or that." 16 But now you boast in your arrogance. All such boasting is evil.

17 Therefore, to him who knows to do good and does not do *it,* to him it is sin.

5 Come now, *you* rich, weep and howl for your miseries that are coming upon *you!* 2 Your riches are corrupted, and your garments are moth-eaten. 3 Your gold and silver are corroded, and their corrosion will be a witness against you and will eat your flesh like fire. You have heaped up treasure in the last days. 4 Indeed the wages of the laborers who mowed your fields, which you kept back by fraud, cry out; and the cries of the reapers have reached the ears of the Lord of Sabaoth.*ª* 5 You have lived on the earth in pleasure and luxury; you have fattened your hearts as*ª* in a day of slaughter. 6 You have condemned, you have murdered the just; he does not resist you.

7 Therefore be patient, brethren, until the coming of the Lord. See *how* the farmer waits for the precious fruit of the earth, waiting patiently for it until it receives the early and latter rain. 8 You also be patient. Establish your hearts, for the coming of the Lord is at hand.

9 Do not grumble against one another, brethren, lest you be condemned.*ª* Behold, the Judge is standing at the door! 10 My brethren, take the prophets, who spoke in the name of the Lord, as an example of suffering and patience. 11 Indeed we count them blessed who endure. You have heard of the perseverance of Job and seen the end *intended by* the Lord—that the Lord is very compassionate and merciful.

12 But above all, my brethren, do not swear, either by heaven or by earth or with any other oath. But let your "Yes" be "Yes," and *your* "No," "No," lest you fall into judgment.*ª*

13 Is anyone among you suffering? Let him pray. Is anyone cheerful? Let him sing psalms. 14 Is anyone among you sick? Let him call for the elders of the church, and let them pray over him, anointing him with oil in the name of the Lord. 15 And the prayer of faith will save the sick, and the Lord will raise him up. And if he has committed sins, he will be forgiven. 16 Confess *your* trespasses*ª* to one another, and pray for one another, that you may be healed. The effective, fervent prayer of a righteous man avails much. 17 Elijah was a man with a nature like ours, and he prayed earnestly that it would not rain; and it did not rain on the land for three years and six months. 18 And he prayed again, and the heaven gave rain, and the earth produced its fruit.

19 Brethren, if anyone among you wanders from the truth, and someone turns him back, 20 let him know that he who turns a sinner from the error of his way will save a soul*ª* from death and cover a multitude of sins.

5:4 *ª*Literally, in Hebrew, *Hosts*   5:5 *ª*NU-Text omits *as.*   5:9 *ª*NU-Text and M-Text read *judged.*
5:12 *ª*M-Text reads *hypocrisy.*   5:16 *ª*NU-Text reads *Therefore confess your sins.*   5:20 *ª*NU-Text reads *his soul.*

First Peter

Overview of First Peter

The apostle Peter was a bold individual who accompanied Jesus throughout His ministry. Peter's life had been transformed by the risen Lord Jesus Christ—from the depths of despair to the heights of hope! Peter wanted his readers to know that the resurrection of Jesus Christ was not accomplished behind a curtain of obscurity but was open to the scrutiny and examination of the entire world!

The apostle wrote this letter to Christians in Asia Minor who were suffering great persecution. Written between A.D. 63 and 64, most likely from Rome, First Peter has often been called the "Epistle of Hope."

The Christian life, as Peter reveals, must be a life of hope. This may seem inconceivable to those suffering for their faith. Yet Peter encourages them to stay true to their calling by God. Their faith is being tested through fire the way gold is refined. Peter promises that with hope, they will stand true.

Peter also discussed the effect that these believers' positive Christian lifestyles can have on the unbelieving society around them. He urges them to fervently love one another and strangers as well.

Peter realized that encouragement was the key to keeping alive the faith and the dream of these early Christians. He offered them the vital ingredient to their success—hope!

Blessed be the God and Father of our Lord Jesus Christ, who according to His abundant mercy has begotten us again to a living hope through the resurrection of Jesus Christ from the dead, to an inheritance incorruptible and undefiled and that does not fade away, reserved in heaven for you.

(1 Pet. 1:3, 4)

Jesus in First Peter

The Epistle presents Jesus as the believer's example and hope in times of suffering in a spiritually hostile world. He is the basis for the Christian's living hope and inheritance, and the love relationship with Him is a source of inexpressible joy. His suffering and death provide redemption for all who trust in Him. Jesus is the Chief Shepherd and Overseer of believers, and when He appears, those who know Him will be glorified.

Keys to First Peter

Key Word: Suffering for the Cause of Christ. Knowing that his readers will be facing more persecution than ever before, Peter writes this letter to give them a divine perspective on these trials so that they will be able to endure them without wavering in their faith. They should not be surprised at their ordeal because the One they follow also suffered and died. Rather, they should count it a privilege to share the sufferings of Jesus. Peter therefore exhorts them to be sure that their hardships are not being caused by their own wrongdoings, but for their Christian testimony.

Key Verses: "Of this salvation the prophets have inquired and searched carefully, who prophesied of the grace *that would come* to you, searching what, or what manner of time, the Spirit of Christ who was in them was indicating when He testified beforehand the sufferings of Christ and the glories that would follow. To them it was revealed that, not to themselves, but to us they were ministering the things which now have been reported to you through those who have preached the gospel to you by the Holy Spirit sent from heaven—things which angels desire to look into" (1:10–12).

"Beloved, do not think it strange concerning the fiery trial which is to try you, as though some strange thing happened to you; but rejoice to the extent that you partake of Christ's sufferings, that when His glory is revealed, you may also be glad with exceeding joy" (4:12, 13).

Key Chapter: First Peter 4. Central in the New Testament revelation concerning how to handle persecution and suffering caused by one's Christian testimony is First Peter 4. Not only is Jesus' suffering to be our model, but also we are to rejoice that we can share in His suffering.

1 Peter, an apostle of Jesus Christ, To the pilgrims of the Dispersion in Pontus, Galatia, Cappadocia, Asia, and Bithynia, 2 elect according to the foreknowledge of God the Father, in sanctification of the Spirit, for obedience and sprinkling of the blood of Jesus Christ:

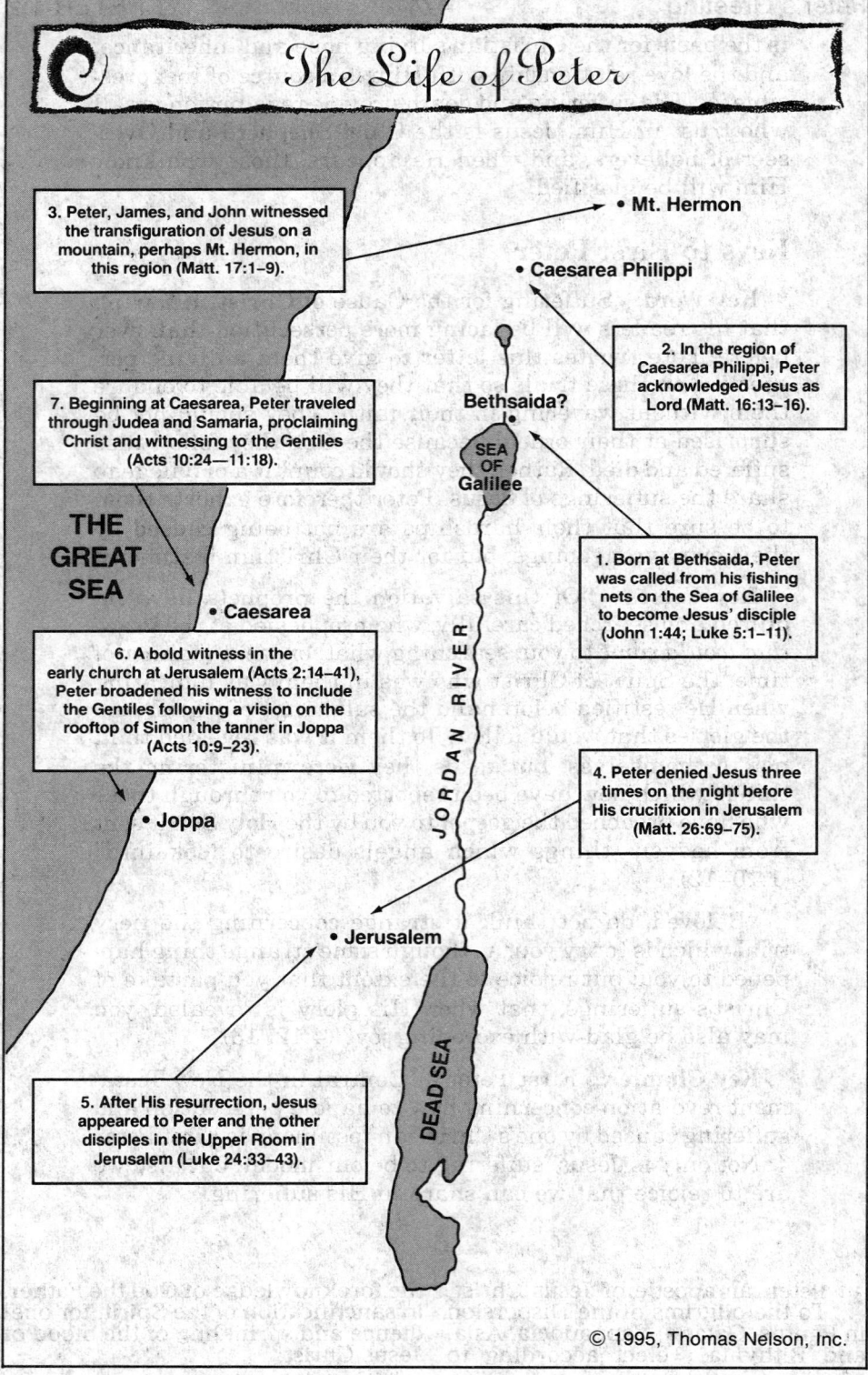

The Life of Peter

3. Peter, James, and John witnessed the transfiguration of Jesus on a mountain, perhaps Mt. Hermon, in this region (Matt. 17:1–9).

• Mt. Hermon

• Caesarea Philippi

2. In the region of Caesarea Philippi, Peter acknowledged Jesus as Lord (Matt. 16:13–16).

Bethsaida?

SEA OF Galilee

7. Beginning at Caesarea, Peter traveled through Judea and Samaria, proclaiming Christ and witnessing to the Gentiles (Acts 10:24—11:18).

1. Born at Bethsaida, Peter was called from his fishing nets on the Sea of Galilee to become Jesus' disciple (John 1:44; Luke 5:1–11).

THE GREAT SEA

• Caesarea

JORDAN RIVER

6. A bold witness in the early church at Jerusalem (Acts 2:14–41), Peter broadened his witness to include the Gentiles following a vision on the rooftop of Simon the tanner in Joppa (Acts 10:9–23).

4. Peter denied Jesus three times on the night before His crucifixion in Jerusalem (Matt. 26:69–75).

• Joppa

• Jerusalem

DEAD SEA

5. After His resurrection, Jesus appeared to Peter and the other disciples in the Upper Room in Jerusalem (Luke 24:33–43).

Grace to you and peace be multiplied.

3 Blessed *be* the God and Father of our Lord Jesus Christ, who according to His abundant mercy has begotten us again to a living hope through the resurrection of Jesus Christ from the dead, 4 to an inheritance incorruptible and undefiled and that does not fade away, reserved in heaven for you, 5 who are kept by the power of God through faith for salvation ready to be revealed in the last time.

6 In this you greatly rejoice, though now for a little while, if need be, you have been grieved by various trials, 7 that the genuineness of your faith, *being* much more precious than gold that perishes, though it is tested by fire, may be found to praise, honor, and glory at the revelation of Jesus Christ, 8 whom having not seen[a] you love. Though now you do not see *Him*, yet believing, you rejoice with joy inexpressible and full of glory, 9 receiving the end of your faith—the salvation of *your* souls.

10 Of this salvation the prophets have inquired and searched carefully, who prophesied of the grace *that would come* to you, 11 searching what, or what manner of time, the Spirit of Christ who was in them was indicating when He testified beforehand the sufferings of Christ and the glories that would follow. 12 To them it was revealed that, not to themselves, but to us[a] they were ministering the things which now have been reported to you through those who have preached the gospel to you by the Holy Spirit sent from heaven—things which angels desire to look into.

13 Therefore gird up the loins of your mind, be sober, and rest your hope fully upon the grace that is to be brought to you at the revelation of Jesus Christ; 14 as obedient children, not conforming yourselves to the former lusts, *as* in your ignorance; 15 but as He who called you *is* holy, you also be holy in all *your* conduct, 16 because it is written, *"Be holy, for I am holy."*[a]

17 And if you call on the Father, who without partiality judges according to each one's work, conduct yourselves throughout the time of your stay *here* in fear; 18 knowing that you were not redeemed with corruptible things, *like* silver or gold, from your aimless conduct *received* by tradition from your fathers, 19 but with the precious blood of Christ, as of a lamb without blemish and without spot. 20 He indeed was foreordained before the foundation of the world, but was manifest in these last times for you 21 who through Him believe in God, who raised Him from the dead and gave Him glory, so that your faith and hope are in God.

22 Since you have purified your souls in obeying the truth through the Spirit[a] in sincere love of the brethren, love one another fervently with a pure heart, 23 having been born again, not of corruptible seed but incorruptible, through the word of God which lives and abides forever,[a] 24 because

"All flesh is as grass,
    And all the glory of man[a] as the
        flower of the grass.
The grass withers,
    And its flower falls away,
25 But the word of the LORD
        endures forever."[a]

Now this is the word which by the gospel was preached to you.

2 Therefore, laying aside all malice, all deceit, hypocrisy, envy, and all evil speaking, 2 as newborn babes, desire the pure milk of the word, that you may grow thereby,[a] 3 if indeed you have tasted that the Lord *is* gracious.

4 Coming to Him *as to* a living stone, rejected indeed by men, but chosen by God *and* precious, 5 you also, as living stones, are being built up a spiritual house, a holy priesthood, to offer up spiritual sacrifices acceptable to God through Jesus Christ. 6 Therefore it is also contained in the Scripture,

"Behold, I lay in Zion
    A chief cornerstone, elect,
        precious,

1:8 [a]M-Text reads *known.*   1:12 [a]NU-Text and M-Text read *you.*   1:16 [a]Leviticus 11:44, 45; 19:2; 20:7   1:22 [a]NU-Text omits *through the Spirit.*   1:23 [a]NU-Text omits *forever.*   1:24 [a]NU-Text reads *all its glory.*   1:25 [a]Isaiah 40:6–8   2:2 [a]NU-Text adds *up to salvation.*

> And he who believes on Him
> will by no means be put to
> shame."[a]

7 Therefore, to you who believe, He *is* precious; but to those who are disobedient,[a]

> "The stone which the builders
> rejected
> Has become the chief
> cornerstone,"[b]

8 and

> "A stone of stumbling
> And a rock of offense."[a]

They stumble, being disobedient to the word, to which they also were appointed.

9 But you *are* a chosen generation, a royal priesthood, a holy nation, His own special people, that you may proclaim the praises of Him who called you out of darkness into His marvelous light; 10 who once *were* not a people but *are* now the people of God, who had not obtained mercy but now have obtained mercy.

11 Beloved, I beg *you* as sojourners and pilgrims, abstain from fleshly lusts which war against the soul, 12 having your conduct honorable among the Gentiles, that when they speak against you as evildoers, they may, by *your* good works which they observe, glorify God in the day of visitation.

13 Therefore submit yourselves to every ordinance of man for the Lord's sake, whether to the king as supreme, 14 or to governors, as to those who are sent by him for the punishment of evildoers and *for the* praise of those who do good. 15 For this is the will of God, that by doing good you may put to silence the ignorance of foolish men— 16 as free, yet not using liberty as a cloak for vice, but as bondservants of God. 17 Honor all *people*. Love the brotherhood. Fear God. Honor the king.

18 Servants, *be* submissive to *your* masters with all fear, not only to the good and gentle, but also to the harsh. 19 For this *is* commendable, if because of conscience toward God one endures grief, suffering wrongfully. 20 For what credit *is it* if, when you are beaten for your faults, you take it patiently? But when you do good and suffer, if you take it patiently, this *is* commendable before God. 21 For to this you were called, because Christ also suffered for us,[a] leaving us[b] an example, that you should follow His steps:

> 22 "Who committed no sin,
> Nor was deceit found in His
> mouth";[a]

23 who, when He was reviled, did not revile in return; when He suffered, He did not threaten, but committed *Himself* to Him who judges righteously; 24 who Himself bore our sins in His own body on the tree, that we, having died to sins, might live for righteousness—by whose stripes you were healed. 25 For you were like sheep going astray, but have now returned to the Shepherd and Overseer[a] of your souls.

3 Wives, likewise, *be* submissive to your own husbands, that even if some do not obey the word, they, without a word, may be won by the conduct of their wives, 2 when they observe your chaste conduct *accompanied* by fear. 3 Do not let your adornment be *merely* outward—arranging the hair, wearing gold, or putting on *fine* apparel— 4 rather *let it be* the hidden person of the heart, with the incorruptible *beauty* of a gentle and quiet spirit, which is very precious in the sight of God. 5 For in this manner, in former times, the holy women who trusted in God also adorned themselves, being submissive to their own husbands, 6 as Sarah obeyed Abraham, calling him lord, whose daughters you are if you do good and are not afraid with any terror.

7 Husbands, likewise, dwell with *them* with understanding, giving honor to the wife, as to the weaker vessel, and as *being* heirs together of the grace of life, that your prayers may not be hindered.

8 Finally, all *of you be* of one mind,

2:6 [a]Isaiah 28:16   2:7 [a]NU-Text reads to those who disbelieve.   [b]Psalm 118:22   2:8 [a]Isaiah 8:14
2:21 [a]NU-Text reads you.   [b]NU-Text and M-Text read you.   2:22 [a]Isaiah 53:9   2:25 [a]Greek Episkopos

having compassion for one another; love as brothers, *be* tenderhearted, *be* courteous;[a] 9 not returning evil for evil or reviling for reviling, but on the contrary blessing, knowing that you were called to this, that you may inherit a blessing. 10 For

> "He who would love life
> And see good days,
> Let him refrain his tongue from evil,
> And his lips from speaking deceit.
> 11 Let him turn away from evil and do good;
> Let him seek peace and pursue it.
> 12 For the eyes of the LORD are on the righteous,
> And His ears are open to their prayers;
> But the face of the LORD is against those who do evil."[a]

13 And who *is* he who will harm you if you become followers of what is good? 14 But even if you should suffer for righteousness' sake, *you are* blessed. *"And do not be afraid of their threats, nor be troubled."*[a] 15 But sanctify the Lord God[a] in your hearts, and always *be* ready to *give* a defense to everyone who asks you a reason for the hope that is in you, with meekness and fear; 16 having a good conscience, that when they defame you as evildoers, those who revile your good conduct in Christ may be ashamed. 17 For *it is* better, if it is the will of God, to suffer for doing good than for doing evil.

18 For Christ also suffered once for sins, the just for the unjust, that He might bring us[a] to God, being put to death in the flesh but made alive by the Spirit, 19 by whom also He went and preached to the spirits in prison, 20 who formerly were disobedient, when once the Divine longsuffering waited[a] in the days of Noah, while *the* ark was being prepared, in which a few, that is, eight souls, were saved through water. 21 There is also an antitype which now saves us—baptism (not the removal of the filth of the

flesh, but the answer of a good conscience toward God), through the resurrection of Jesus Christ, 22 who has gone into heaven and is at the right hand of God, angels and authorities and powers having been made subject to Him.

4 Therefore, since Christ suffered for us[a] in the flesh, arm yourselves also with the same mind, for he who has suffered in the flesh has ceased from sin, 2 that he no longer should live the rest of *his* time in the flesh for the lusts of men, but for the will of God. 3 For we *have spent* enough of our past lifetime[a] in doing the will of the Gentiles—when we walked in lewdness, lusts, drunkenness, revelries, drinking parties, and abominable idolatries. 4 In regard to these, they think it strange that you do not run with *them* in the same flood of dissipation, speaking evil of *you.* 5 They will give an account to Him who is ready to judge the living and the dead. 6 For this reason the gospel was preached also to those who are dead, that they might be judged according to men in the flesh, but live according to God in the spirit.

7 But the end of all things is at hand; therefore be serious and watchful in your prayers. 8 And above all things have fervent love for one another, for *"love will cover a multitude of sins."*[a] 9 *Be* hospitable to one another without grumbling. 10 As each one has received a gift, minister it to one another, as good stewards of the manifold grace of God. 11 If anyone speaks, *let him speak* as the oracles of God. If anyone ministers, *let him do it* as with the ability which God supplies, that in all things God may be glorified through Jesus Christ, to whom belong the glory and the dominion forever and ever. Amen.

12 Beloved, do not think it strange concerning the fiery trial which is to try you, as though some strange thing happened to you; 13 but rejoice to the extent that you partake of Christ's sufferings, that when His glory is revealed, you may also be glad with exceeding joy. 14 If you are

---

3:8 [a]NU-Text reads *humble.*   3:12 [a]Psalm 34:12–16   3:14 [a]Isaiah 8:12   3:15 [a]NU-Text reads *Christ as Lord.*   3:18 [a]NU-Text and M-Text read *you.*   3:20 [a]NU-Text and M-Text read *when the longsuffering of God waited patiently.*   4:1 [a]NU-Text omits *for us.*   4:3 [a]NU-Text reads *time.*   4:8 [a]Proverbs 10:12

Replace Stress with Success

As you walk the walk of faith and discipline yourself to seek positive possibilities in every situation, you will still face such realities as sickness, separation from loved ones, and even death.

You can't escape the raw realities of life,
but you can shape them!

You either shape life's realities, or they ravage your mind until you're devastated with worry.

How can faith help you dissolve life's anxieties?

Faith faces the worries and anxieties one at a time. If you imagined all of the possible painful experiences you might encounter from birth until the end of your life all at once, you could not handle it. A bridge cannot handle all the traffic that passes over it at one time. Bridges are designed to handle moving traffic. So faith is designed to handle anxieties one at a time. Deal with only your immediate pressures. Let tomorrow's worries wait until then.

Faith erases anxieties and worries. By the time you've spaced your anxieties, you will have erased many of them! Many anxieties that remain can be erased by transferring them to a Higher Department. Turn them over to God. He specializes in problems you are incapable of handling.

Faith replaces anxieties. If anxieties and worries still remain after prayer, then faith replaces them. It says: I'll replace worry with work. I'll replace anxiety with ambition. I'll replace depression with new drive. I'll replace stress with success!

Faith and I will win. Thank You, Lord.

reproached for the name of Christ, blessed *are you,* for the Spirit of glory and of God rests upon you.*a* On their part He is blasphemed, but on your part He is glorified. 15 But let none of you suffer as a murderer, a thief, an evildoer, or as a busybody in other people's matters. 16 Yet if *anyone suffers* as a Christian, let him not be ashamed, but let him glorify God in this matter.*a*

17 For the time *has come* for judgment to begin at the house of God; and if *it begins* with us first, what will *be* the end of those who do not obey the gospel of God? 18 Now

> "If the righteous one is scarcely saved,
> Where will the ungodly and the sinner appear?"*a*

19 Therefore let those who suffer according to the will of God commit their souls *to Him* in doing good, as to a faithful Creator.

5 The elders who are among you I exhort, I who am a fellow elder and a witness of the sufferings of Christ, and also a partaker of the glory that will be revealed: 2 Shepherd the flock of God which is among you, serving as overseers, not by compulsion but willingly,*a* not for dishonest gain but eagerly; 3 nor as being lords over those entrusted to you, but being examples to the flock; 4 and when the Chief Shepherd appears, you will receive

the crown of glory that does not fade away.

5 Likewise you younger people, submit yourselves to *your* elders. Yes, all of *you* be submissive to one another, and be clothed with humility, for

> "God resists the proud,
> But gives grace to the humble."*a*

6 Therefore humble yourselves under the mighty hand of God, that He may exalt you in due time, 7 casting all your care upon Him, for He cares for you.

8 Be sober, be vigilant; because*a* your adversary the devil walks about like a roaring lion, seeking whom he may devour. 9 Resist him, steadfast in the faith, knowing that the same sufferings are experienced by your brotherhood in the world. 10 But may*a* the God of all grace, who called us*b* to His eternal glory by Christ Jesus, after you have suffered a while, perfect, establish, strengthen, and settle *you.* 11 To Him *be* the glory and the dominion forever and ever. Amen.

12 By Silvanus, our faithful brother as I consider him, I have written to you briefly, exhorting and testifying that this is the true grace of God in which you stand.

13 She who is in Babylon, elect together with *you,* greets you; and *so does* Mark my son. 14 Greet one another with a kiss of love.

Peace to you all who are in Christ Jesus. Amen.

4:14 *a*NU-Text omits the rest of this verse.   4:16 *a*NU-Text reads *name.*   4:18 *a*Proverbs 11:31
5:2 *a*NU-Text adds *according to God.*   5:5 *a*Proverbs 3:34   5:8 *a*NU-Text and M-Text omit *because.*   5:10 *a*NU-Text reads *But the God of all grace . . . will perfect, establish, strengthen, and settle you.*   *b*NU-Text and M-Text read *you.*

Second Peter

Overview of Second Peter

The second letter of Peter to Christians in Asia Minor was written shortly before Peter's martyrdom, probably in A.D. 64. Peter knew his death was imminent, yet he displays strong positive characteristics by encouraging other Christians also suffering persecution to focus their thoughts on God's "exceedingly great and precious promises."

Peter reminds his readers that their faith is based on the historical certainty of Jesus Christ's resurrection: "For we did not follow cunningly devised fables when we made known to you the power and coming of our Lord Jesus Christ, but were eyewitnesses of His majesty" (2 Pet. 1:16). This personal conviction carried Peter from the small fishing village of Bethsaida on the shores of the Sea of Galilee to the mighty pagan center of Rome. And this same faith would carry them through any difficult and trying time.

Because they lived on the famous travel route connecting the east with Rome, Christians in Asia Minor were exposed to many strange ideas and false religions. Peter warns them not to mix the negative doctrines of these false religions with their positive Christian faith.

It would have been easy for these Christians to give in to persecution and false doctrines, yet Peter encouraged them to fix their hope on the power of God and Christ's second coming. They had the strength to do this because God had given them everything that pertained to life and godliness. They were not intimidated by the impossibilities of their surroundings, but they were motivated by the greater possibility—life in Jesus Christ!

Jesus in Second Peter

Apart from the first verse of his Epistle, Peter employs the title *Lord* every time he names the Savior. The Lord Jesus Christ is the source of full knowledge and power for the attainment of spiritual maturity. Peter recalls the glory of Christ's transfiguration on the holy mountain and anticipates His coming, when the whole world, not just three men on a mountain, will behold His glory.

Keys to Second Peter

Key Word: Guard Against False Teachers. This letter is written to expose the dangerous and seductive work of false teachers, and to warn believers to be on their guard so that they will not be "led away with the error of the wicked" (3:17). It is also written to exhort readers to "grow in the grace and knowledge of our Lord and Savior Jesus Christ" (3:18), because this growth into Christian maturity is the best defense against spiritual counterfeits.

Key Verses: "Knowing this first, that no prophecy of Scripture is of any private interpretation, for prophecy never came by the will of man, but holy men of God spoke *as they were* moved by the Holy Spirit" (1:20, 21).

"The Lord is not slack concerning *His* promise, as some count slackness, but is longsuffering toward us, not willing that any should perish but that all should come to repentance. But the day of the Lord will come as a thief in the night, in which the heavens will pass away with a great noise, and the elements will melt with fervent heat; both the earth and the works that are in it will be burned up. Therefore, since all these things will be dissolved, what manner *of persons* ought you to be in holy conduct and godliness" (3:9–11).

Key Chapter: Second Peter 1. The Scripture clearest in defining the relationship between God and man on the issue of inspiration is contained in 1:19–21. Three distinct principles surface: that the interpretation of Scriptures is not limited to a favored elect but is open for all who rightly divide the truth; that the divinely inspired prophet did not initiate the Scripture himself; and that the Holy Spirit (not the emotion or circumstances of the moment) moved holy men.

1 Simon Peter, a bondservant and apostle of Jesus Christ,

To those who have obtained like precious faith with us by the righteousness of our God and Savior Jesus Christ:

2 Grace and peace be multiplied to you in the knowledge of God and of

Keep Working On Yourself

Does 2 Peter 1:5-7 show where the path of faith leads? Will we never reach a point where we have it made? Does this mean we will constantly have to improve ourselves?

Absolutely! That's what spares us from death. For plateaus are boring. Nothing is as dull as yesterday's race when it is over! Who cares to look at the bumper stickers of last year's political campaign? We must always be living in today—and tomorrow!

It is exciting to know that the real stimulation of life never needs to diminish with age. It comes as you make constant commitments to new projects that hold creative challenge.

You can continue to feel young as long as you live, because a youthful attitude is basically a commitment to progress. You can have that no matter how old you are! The walk of faith calls you to improve yourself constantly, consistently, and continually!

Choose one of the qualities described in 2 Peter 1:5–7, and concentrate on improving yourself. Your goal may be increased

faith,
virtue,
knowledge,
self-control,
perseverance,
godliness,
kindness, or
love.

With any of these as your focus, your life will remain fruitful no matter how old you are! Thank God for this glorious promise.

Jesus our Lord, 3 as His divine power has given to us all things that *pertain* to life and godliness, through the knowledge of Him who called us by glory and virtue, 4 by which have been given to us exceedingly great and precious promises, that through these you may be partakers of the divine nature, having escaped the corruption *that is* in the world through lust.

5 But also for this very reason, giving all diligence, add to your faith virtue, to virtue knowledge, 6 to knowledge self-control, to self-control perseverance, to perseverance godliness, 7 to godliness brotherly kindness, and to brotherly kindness love. 8 For if these things are yours and abound, *you will be* neither barren nor unfruitful in the knowledge of our Lord Jesus Christ. 9 For he who lacks these things is shortsighted, even to blindness, and has forgotten that he was cleansed from his old sins.

10 Therefore, brethren, be even more diligent to make your call and election sure, for if you do these things you will never stumble; 11 for so an entrance will be supplied to you abundantly into the everlasting kingdom of our Lord and Savior Jesus Christ.

12 For this reason I will not be negligent to remind you always of these things, though you know and are established in the present truth. 13 Yes, I think it is right, as long as I am in this tent, to stir you up by reminding *you,* 14 knowing that shortly I *must* put off my tent, just as our Lord Jesus Christ showed me. 15 Moreover I will be careful to ensure that you always have a reminder of these things after my decease.

16 For we did not follow cunningly devised fables when we made known to you the power and coming of our Lord Jesus Christ, but were eyewitnesses of His majesty. 17 For He received from God the Father honor and glory when such a voice came to Him from the Excellent Glory: "This is My beloved Son, in whom I am well pleased." 18 And we heard this voice which came from heaven when we were with Him on the holy mountain.

19 And so we have the prophetic word confirmed,[a] which you do well to heed as a light that shines in a dark place, until the day dawns and the morning star rises in your hearts; 20 knowing this first, that no prophecy of Scripture is of any private interpretation,[a] 21 for prophecy never came by the will of man, but holy men of God[a] spoke *as they were* moved by the Holy Spirit.

2 But there were also false prophets among the people, even as there will be false teachers among you, who will secretly bring in destructive heresies, even denying the Lord who bought them, *and* bring on themselves swift destruction. 2 And many will follow their destructive ways, because of whom the way of truth will be blasphemed. 3 By covetousness they will exploit you with deceptive words; for a long time their judgment has not been idle, and their destruction does[a] not slumber.

4 For if God did not spare the angels who sinned, but cast *them* down to hell and delivered *them* into chains of darkness, to be reserved for judgment; 5 and did not spare the ancient world, but saved Noah, *one of* eight *people,* a preacher of righteousness, bringing in the flood on the world of the ungodly; 6 and turning the cities of Sodom and Gomorrah into ashes, condemned *them* to destruction, making *them* an example to those who afterward would live ungodly; 7 and delivered righteous Lot, *who was* oppressed by the filthy conduct of the wicked 8 (for that righteous man, dwelling among them, tormented *his* righteous soul from day to day by seeing and hearing *their* lawless deeds)— 9 *then* the Lord knows how to deliver the godly out of temptations and to reserve the unjust under punishment for the day of judgment, 10 and especially those who walk according to the flesh in the lust of uncleanness and despise authority. *They are* presumptuous, self-willed. They are not afraid to speak evil of dignitaries, 11 whereas angels, who are greater in power and might, do not bring a reviling accusation against them before the Lord.

12 But these, like natural brute

I Will Build My Church

One of the most remarkable elements of our faith is that Jesus Christ has called us to fulfill His ministry—to help build His church. If He trusts us—how can we do less?

Near the end of His earthly ministry, Jesus took his closest disciples to a high mountain in northern Galilee. Here in the region of Caesarea Philippi was a major seat of political and religious power.

The area was known for its pagan worship and divine homage to political rulers. The Canaanite god Baal and the Greek gods Pan and Aphrodite inspired devotion from their followers. Caesar Augustus, Mark Antony, Nero, and Claudius elevated themselves to the rank of deity and demanded political homage from their subjects.

Among the Jews, the Gentile cities of Caesarea Philippi, Jaffa, Ptolemais, Caesarea, Rome, Tyre, and Sidon were all feared and branded the "gates of hell." No upright Jew would go near these pagan centers.

Against this background, Jesus summoned His disciples to make a decision. " 'But who do you say that I am?' Simon Peter answered and said, 'You are the Christ, the Son of the living God.' Jesus answered and said to him, 'Blessed are you, Simon Bar-Jonah, for flesh and blood has not revealed *this* to you, but My Father who is in heaven . . . you are Peter, and on this rock I will build My church, and the gates of Hades shall not prevail against it' " (Matt. 16:15–18). This was a spiritual reference to "the rulers of the darkness of this age" (Eph. 6:12) with cultural and historical relevance.

Not until after Jesus' death and resurrection did Peter understand the full meaning of his Lord's commission. Inspired by Christ's promise, Peter fulfilled his call. He was the first disciple to bring the Good News of Jesus Christ to the cities of Jaffa, Caesarea, and Rome. He put aside his prejudice, hatred, and contempt for the cities known as the "gates of hell." God gave him the message of love, hope, and forgiveness for all mankind.

One simple fisherman from the shores of Galilee walked straight into the gates of hell to build the foundation of the church of God, and nothing prevailed against him.

beasts made to be caught and destroyed, speak evil of the things they do not understand, and will utterly perish in their own corruption, 13 *and* will receive the wages of unrighteousness, *as* those who count it pleasure to carouse in the daytime. *They are* spots and blemishes, carousing in their own deceptions while they feast with you, 14 having eyes full of adultery and that cannot cease from sin, enticing unstable souls. *They have* a heart trained in covetous practices, *and are* accursed children. 15 They have forsaken the right way and gone astray, following the way of Balaam the *son* of Beor, who loved the wages of unrighteousness; 16 but he was rebuked for his iniquity: a dumb donkey speaking with a man's voice restrained the madness of the prophet.

17 These are wells without water, clouds*a* carried by a tempest, for whom is reserved the blackness of darkness forever.*b*

18 For when they speak great swelling *words* of emptiness, they allure through the lusts of the flesh, through lewdness, the ones who have actually escaped*a* from those who live in error. 19 While they promise them liberty, they themselves are slaves of corruption; for by whom a person is overcome, by him also he is brought into bondage. 20 For if, after they have escaped the pollutions of the world through the knowledge of the Lord and Savior Jesus Christ, they are again entangled in them and overcome, the latter end is worse for them than the beginning. 21 For it would have been better for them not to have known the way of righteousness, than having known *it,* to turn from the holy commandment delivered to them. 22 But it has happened to them according to the true proverb: *"A dog returns to his own vomit,"a* and, "a sow, having washed, to her wallowing in the mire."

3 Beloved, I now write to you this second epistle (in *both of* which I stir up your pure minds by way of reminder), 2 that you may be mindful of the words which were spoken be-

fore by the holy prophets, and of the commandment of us,*a* the apostles of the Lord and Savior, 3 knowing this first: that scoffers will come in the last days, walking according to their own lusts, 4 and saying, "Where is the promise of His coming? For since the fathers fell asleep, all things continue as *they were* from the beginning of creation." 5 For this they willfully forget: that by the word of God the heavens were of old, and the earth standing out of water and in the water, 6 by which the world *that* then existed perished, being flooded with water. 7 But the heavens and the earth *which* are now preserved by the same word, are reserved for fire until the day of judgment and perdition of ungodly men.

8 But, beloved, do not forget this one thing, that with the Lord one day *is* as a thousand years, and a thousand years as one day. 9 The Lord is not slack concerning *His* promise, as some count slackness, but is longsuffering toward us,*a* not willing that any should perish but that all should come to repentance.

10 But the day of the Lord will come as a thief in the night, in which the heavens will pass away with a great noise, and the elements will melt with fervent heat; both the earth and the works that are in it will be burned up.*a* 11 Therefore, since all these things will be dissolved, what manner *of persons* ought you to be in holy conduct and godliness, 12 looking for and hastening the coming of the day of God, because of which the heavens will be dissolved, being on fire, and the elements will melt with fervent heat? 13 Nevertheless we, according to His promise, look for new heavens and a new earth in which righteousness dwells.

14 Therefore, beloved, looking forward to these things, be diligent to be found by Him in peace, without spot and blameless; 15 and consider *that* the longsuffering of our Lord *is* salvation—as also our beloved brother Paul, according to the wisdom given to him, has written to you, 16 as also in all his epistles, speaking in them of these things, in which are

---

2:17 *a*NU-Text reads *and mists.* *b*NU-Text omits *forever.*   2:18 *a*NU-Text reads *are barely escaping.*
2:22 *a*Proverbs 26:11   3:2 *a*NU-Text and M-Text read *commandment of the apostles of your Lord and Savior* or *commandment of your apostles of the Lord and Savior.*   3:9 *a*NU-Text reads *you.*
3:10 *a*NU-Text reads *laid bare* (literally *found*).

some things hard to understand, which untaught and unstable *people* twist to their own destruction, as *they do* also the rest of the Scriptures.

17 You therefore, beloved, since you know *this* beforehand, beware lest you also fall from your own steadfastness, being led away with the error of the wicked; 18 but grow in the grace and knowledge of our Lord and Savior Jesus Christ.

To Him *be* the glory both now and forever. Amen.

First John

Overview of First John

The First Epistle of John was written by the apostle John sometime in the 80s or 90s of the first century. John, the son of Zebedee, most likely wrote this letter prior to being banished to the island of Patmos by the Roman Emperor Domitian.

John's aim was to strengthen his readers, Christians in Asia Minor, to give them knowledge, joy, and assurance in their faith. He also hoped to build their confidence and self-esteem as they realized that God was faithful to forgive their sins and wipe any guilt from their lives. Then they could truly be free to carry out God's command to love one another.

John reminds us that love is not just by word, but by deed and truth. The life of a believer is more than just saying "I love you." The life of a believer is living love out! John writes about a common false doctrine that denied the humanity of Jesus Christ. In today's society, we often face another argument—that Jesus was not really God. John assures his readers from a firsthand experience that Jesus is fully God and fully man and that His unique purpose is to restore fellowship between men and women and their Creator Father.

John encourages his readers to be practical and action-oriented in living out their faith. In urging Christians to demonstrate love, he makes it clear that love is not love until you give it away!

Beloved, let us love one another, for love is of God; and everyone who loves is born of God and knows God. He who does not love does not know God, for God is love. In this the love of God was manifested toward us, that God has sent His only begotten Son into the world, that we might live through Him. . . . Beloved, if God so loved us, we also ought to love one another.

(1 John 4:7–9, 11)

Jesus in First John

Jesus' blood continually cleanses the believer from all sin, and He is our righteous Advocate before the Father. This Epistle places particular emphasis on the incarnation of God the Son and the identity of Jesus as the Christ by refuting gnostic doctrine. Jesus Christ "came by water and blood" (5:6). He was the same indivisible person from the beginning (His baptism) to the end (His crucifixion) of His public ministry.

Keys to First John

Key Word: Fellowship with God. John wants his readers to have assurance of the indwelling God through their abiding relationship with Him. Belief in Jesus should be manifested in the practice of righteousness and love for the brethren, which in turn produces joy and confidence before God. John writes this Epistle to encourage this kind of fellowship and to emphasize the importance of holding fast to apostolic doctrine.

Key Verses: "That which we have seen and heard we declare to you, that you also may have fellowship with us; and truly our fellowship *is* with the Father and with His Son Jesus Christ. And these things we write to you that your joy may be full" (1:3, 4).

"And this is the testimony: that God has given us eternal life, and this life is in His Son. He who has the Son has life; he who does not have the Son of God does not have life. These things I have written to you who believe in the name of the Son of God, that you may know that you have eternal life, and that you may *continue to* believe in the name of the Son of God" (5:11–13).

Key Chapter: First John 1. The two central passages for continued fellowship with God are John 15 and First John

1. John 15 relates the positive side of fellowship, that is, abiding in Christ. First John 1 unfolds the other side, pointing out that when Christians do not abide in Christ, they must seek forgiveness before fellowship can be restored.

1 That which was from the beginning, which we have heard, which we have seen with our eyes, which we have looked upon, and our hands have handled, concerning the Word of life— 2 the life was manifested, and we have seen, and bear witness, and declare to you that eternal life which was with the Father and was manifested to us— 3 that which we have seen and heard we declare to you, that you also may have fellowship with us; and truly our fellowship *is* with the Father and with His Son Jesus Christ. 4 And these things we write to you that your*a* joy may be full.

5 This is the message which we have heard from Him and declare to you, that God is light and in Him is no darkness at all. 6 If we say that we have fellowship with Him, and walk in darkness, we lie and do not practice the truth. 7 But if we walk in the light as He is in the light, we have fellowship with one another, and the blood of Jesus Christ His Son cleanses us from all sin.

8 If we say that we have no sin, we deceive ourselves, and the truth is not in us. 9 If we confess our sins, He is faithful and just to forgive us *our* sins and to cleanse us from all unrighteousness. 10 If we say that we have not sinned, we make Him a liar, and His word is not in us.

2 My little children, these things I write to you, so that you may not sin. And if anyone sins, we have an Advocate with the Father, Jesus Christ the righteous. 2 And He Himself is the propitiation for our sins, and not for ours only but also for the whole world.

3 Now by this we know that we know Him, if we keep His commandments. 4 He who says, "I know Him," and does not keep His commandments, is a liar, and the truth is not in him. 5 But whoever keeps His word, truly the love of God is perfected in him. By this we know that we are in Him. 6 He who says he abides in Him ought himself also to walk just as He walked.

7 Brethren,*a* I write no new commandment to you, but an old commandment which you have had from the beginning. The old commandment is the word which you heard from the beginning.*b* 8 Again, a new commandment I write to you, which thing is true in Him and in you, because the darkness is passing away, and the true light is already shining.

9 He who says he is in the light, and hates his brother, is in darkness until now. 10 He who loves his brother abides in the light, and there is no cause for stumbling in him. 11 But he who hates his brother is in darkness and walks in darkness, and does not know where he is going, because the darkness has blinded his eyes.

12   I write to you, little children,
    Because your sins are
      forgiven you for His
      name's sake.

1:4 *a*NU-Text and M-Text read *our.*   2:7 *a*NU-Text reads *Beloved.*   *b*NU-Text omits *from the beginning.*

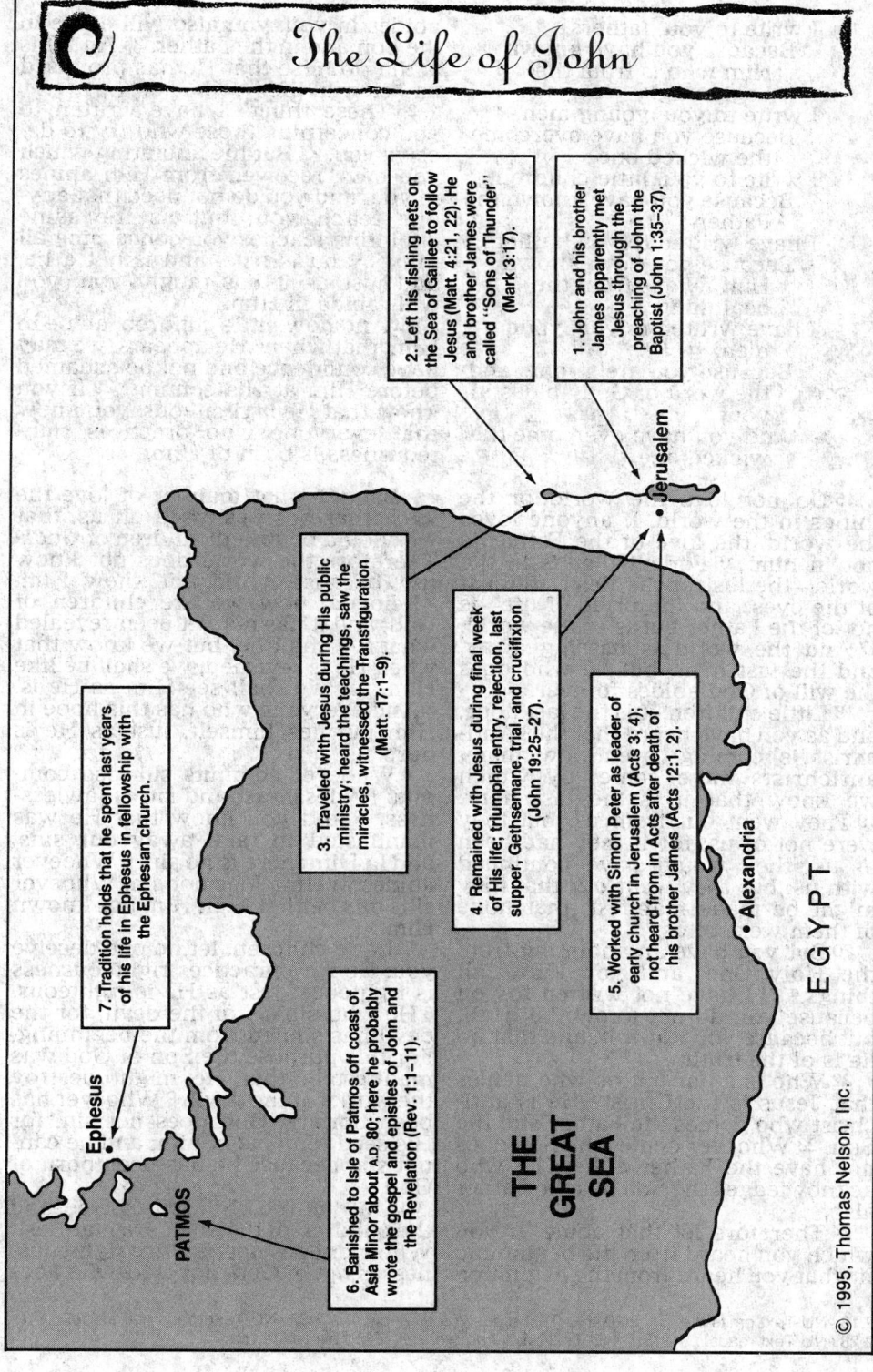

The Life of John

2. Left his fishing nets on the Sea of Galilee to follow Jesus (Matt. 4:21, 22). He and brother James were called "Sons of Thunder" (Mark 3:17).

1. John and his brother James apparently met Jesus through the preaching of John the Baptist (John 1:35–37).

3. Traveled with Jesus during His public ministry; heard the teachings, saw the miracles, witnessed the Transfiguration (Matt. 17:1–9).

4. Remained with Jesus during final week of His life; triumphal entry, rejection, last supper, Gethsemane, trial, and crucifixion (John 19:25–27).

5. Worked with Simon Peter as leader of early church in Jerusalem (Acts 3; 4); not heard from in Acts after death of his brother James (Acts 12:1, 2).

7. Tradition holds that he spent last years of his life in Ephesus in fellowship with the Ephesian church.

6. Banished to Isle of Patmos off coast of Asia Minor about A.D. 80; here he probably wrote the gospel and epistles of John and the Revelation (Rev. 1:1–11).

Jerusalem

Ephesus

PATMOS

THE GREAT SEA

Alexandria

E G Y P T

13　I write to you, fathers,
　　　Because you have known
　　　　Him *who is* from the
　　　　beginning.
　　I write to you, young men,
　　　Because you have overcome
　　　　the wicked one.
　　I write to you, little children,
　　　Because you have known the
　　　　Father.
14　I have written to you, fathers,
　　　Because you have known
　　　　Him *who is* from the
　　　　beginning.
　　I have written to you, young
　　　men,
　　　Because you are strong, and
　　　　the word of God abides in
　　　　you,
　　And you have overcome the
　　　wicked one.

15 Do not love the world or the things in the world. If anyone loves the world, the love of the Father is not in him. 16 For all that *is* in the world—the lust of the flesh, the lust of the eyes, and the pride of life—is not of the Father but is of the world. 17 And the world is passing away, and the lust of it; but he who does the will of God abides forever.

18 Little children, it is the last hour; and as you have heard that the*a* Antichrist is coming, even now many antichrists have come, by which we know that it is the last hour. 19 They went out from us, but they were not of us; for if they had been of us, they would have continued with us; but *they went out* that they might be made manifest, that none of them were of us.

20 But you have an anointing from the Holy One, and you know all things.*a* 21 I have not written to you because you do not know the truth, but because you know it, and that no lie is of the truth.

22 Who is a liar but he who denies that Jesus is the Christ? He is antichrist who denies the Father and the Son. 23 Whoever denies the Son does not have the Father either; he who acknowledges the Son has the Father also.

24 Therefore let that abide in you which you heard from the beginning. If what you heard from the beginning

abides in you, you also will abide in the Son and in the Father. 25 And this is the promise that He has promised us—eternal life.

26 These things I have written to you concerning those who *try to* deceive you. 27 But the anointing which you have received from Him abides in you, and you do not need that anyone teach you; but as the same anointing teaches you concerning all things, and is true, and is not a lie, and just as it has taught you, you will*a* abide in Him.

28 And now, little children, abide in Him, that when*a* He appears, we may have confidence and not be ashamed before Him at His coming. 29 If you know that He is righteous, you know that everyone who practices righteousness is born of Him.

3 Behold what manner of love the Father has bestowed on us, that we should be called children of God!*a* Therefore the world does not know us,*b* because it did not know Him. 2 Beloved, now we are children of God; and it has not yet been revealed what we shall be, but we know that when He is revealed, we shall be like Him, for we shall see Him as He is. 3 And everyone who has this hope in Him purifies himself, just as He is pure.

4 Whoever commits sin also commits lawlessness, and sin is lawlessness. 5 And you know that He was manifested to take away our sins, and in Him there is no sin. 6 Whoever abides in Him does not sin. Whoever sins has neither seen Him nor known Him.

7 Little children, let no one deceive you. He who practices righteousness is righteous, just as He is righteous. 8 He who sins is of the devil, for the devil has sinned from the beginning. For this purpose the Son of God was manifested, that He might destroy the works of the devil. 9 Whoever has been born of God does not sin, for His seed remains in him; and he cannot sin, because he has been born of God.

10 In this the children of God and the children of the devil are manifest: Whoever does not practice righteousness is not of God, nor *is* he who does

2:18 *a*NU-Text omits *the.*　　2:20 *a*NU-Text reads *you all know.*　　2:27 *a*NU-Text reads *you abide.*
2:28 *a*NU-Text reads *if.*　　3:1 *a*NU-Text adds *And we are.*　*b*M-Text reads *you.*

God Loves You and So Do I!

One day, while teaching in the temple, Jesus was asked by a Pharisee, "Teacher, which *is* the great commandment in the law?" Jesus replied, "You shall love the LORD your God with all your heart, with all your soul, and with all your mind" (Matt. 22:36, 37).

Then he added, "And *the* second is like it: You shall love your neighbor as yourself" (Matt. 22:39). This term *like* can be understood as "equal." The two commandments are contingent, each dependent upon the other.

Jesus lived a life that was worthy of this teaching, for throughout His ministry His goal was to reveal the love of God through His love for all people. He taught His disciples, "As the Father loved Me, I also have loved you" (John 15:9). "A new commandment I give to you, that you love one another" (John 13:34).

The supreme act of love came when Jesus willingly died on the cross to bring us into an intimate relationship with God. Through the cross, Jesus declared His love for all people. Because of His love in our lives, we now can love each other.

The cross itself symbolizes this relationship of love. Like the vertical post of the cross, our lives must receive the love of God from above. Then like outstretched arms in a horizontal position, we can extend this love to others. As God loves us so we should love each other.

Our lives can reflect this relationship, because from the love of God we receive the feeling of self-worth that enables us to love other people without fear of rejection. Then we can live a life which truly says, "God loves you and so do I!"

not love his brother. 11 For this is the message that you heard from the beginning, that we should love one another, 12 not as Cain *who* was of the wicked one and murdered his brother. And why did he murder him? Because his works were evil and his brother's righteous.

13 Do not marvel, my brethren, if the world hates you. 14 We know that we have passed from death to life, because we love the brethren. He who does not love *his* brother*ᵃ* abides in death. 15 Whoever hates his brother is a murderer, and you know that no murderer has eternal life abiding in him.

16 By this we know love, because He laid down His life for us. And we also ought to lay down *our* lives for the brethren. 17 But whoever has this world's goods, and sees his brother in need, and shuts up his heart from him, how does the love of God abide in him?

18 My little children, let us not love in word or in tongue, but in deed and in truth. 19 And by this we know*ᵃ* that we are of the truth, and shall assure our hearts before Him. 20 For if our heart condemns us, God is greater than our heart, and knows all things. 21 Beloved, if our heart does not condemn us, we have confidence toward God. 22 And whatever we ask we receive from Him, because we keep His commandments and do those things that are pleasing in His sight. 23 And this is His commandment: that we should believe on the name of His Son Jesus Christ and love one another, as He gave us*ᵃ* commandment.

24 Now he who keeps His commandments abides in Him, and He in him. And by this we know that He abides in us, by the Spirit whom He has given us.

4 Beloved, do not believe every spirit, but test the spirits, whether they are of God; because many false prophets have gone out into the world. 2 By this you know the Spirit of God: Every spirit that confesses that Jesus Christ has come in the flesh is of God, 3 and every spirit that does not confess that Jesus Christ

has come in the flesh*ᵃ* is not of God. And this is the *spirit* of the Antichrist, which you have heard was coming, and is now already in the world.

4 You are of God, little children, and have overcome them, because He who is in you is greater than he who is in the world. 5 They are of the world. Therefore they speak *as* of the world, and the world hears them. 6 We are of God. He who knows God hears us; he who is not of God does not hear us. By this we know the spirit of truth and the spirit of error.

7 Beloved, let us love one another, for love is of God; and everyone who loves is born of God and knows God. 8 He who does not love does not know God, for God is love. 9 In this the love of God was manifested toward us, that God has sent His only begotten Son into the world, that we might live through Him. 10 In this is love, not that we loved God, but that He loved us and sent His Son *to be* the propitiation for our sins. 11 Beloved, if God so loved us, we also ought to love one another.

12 No one has seen God at any time. If we love one another, God abides in us, and His love has been perfected in us. 13 By this we know that we abide in Him, and He in us, because He has given us of His Spirit. 14 And we have seen and testify that the Father has sent the Son *as* Savior of the world. 15 Whoever confesses that Jesus is the Son of God, God abides in him, and he in God. 16 And we have known and believed the love that God has for us. God is love, and he who abides in love abides in God, and God in him.

17 Love has been perfected among us in this: that we may have boldness in the day of judgment; because as He is, so are we in this world. 18 There is no fear in love; but perfect love casts out fear, because fear involves torment. But he who fears has not been made perfect in love. 19 We love Him*ᵃ* because He first loved us.

20 If someone says, "I love God," and hates his brother, he is a liar; for he who does not love his brother whom he has seen, how can*ᵃ* he love God whom he has not seen? 21 And

---

3:14 *ᵃNU-Text omits *his brother*.   3:19 *ᵃNU-Text reads *we shall know*.   3:23 *ᵃM-Text omits *us*.
4:3 *ᵃNU-Text omits *that* and *Christ has come in the flesh*.   4:19 *ᵃNU-Text omits *Him*.   4:20 *ᵃNU-Text reads *he cannot*.

this commandment we have from Him: that he who loves God *must* love his brother also.

5 Whoever believes that Jesus is the Christ is born of God, and everyone who loves Him who begot also loves him who is begotten of Him. 2 By this we know that we love the children of God, when we love God and keep His commandments. 3 For this is the love of God, that we keep His commandments. And His commandments are not burdensome. 4 For whatever is born of God overcomes the world. And this is the victory that has overcome the world—our*a* faith. 5 Who is he who overcomes the world, but he who believes that Jesus is the Son of God?

6 This is He who came by water and blood—Jesus Christ; not only by water, but by water and blood. And it is the Spirit who bears witness, because the Spirit is truth. 7 For there are three that bear witness in heaven: the Father, the Word, and the Holy Spirit; and these three are one. 8 And there are three that bear witness on earth:*a* the Spirit, the water, and the blood; and these three agree as one.

9 If we receive the witness of men, the witness of God is greater; for this is the witness of God which*a* He has testified of His Son. 10 He who believes in the Son of God has the witness in himself; he who does not believe God has made Him a liar, because he has not believed the testimony that God has given of His Son. 11 And this is the testimony: that God

has given us eternal life, and this life is in His Son. 12 He who has the Son has life; he who does not have the Son of God does not have life. 13 These things I have written to you who believe in the name of the Son of God, that you may know that you have eternal life,*a* and that you may *continue to* believe in the name of the Son of God.

14 Now this is the confidence that we have in Him, that if we ask anything according to His will, He hears us. 15 And if we know that He hears us, whatever we ask, we know that we have the petitions that we have asked of Him.

16 If anyone sees his brother sinning a sin *which does* not *lead* to death, he will ask, and He will give him life for those who commit sin not *leading* to death. There is sin *leading* to death. I do not say that he should pray about that. 17 All unrighteousness is sin, and there is sin not *leading* to death.

18 We know that whoever is born of God does not sin; but he who has been born of God keeps himself,*a* and the wicked one does not touch him.

19 We know that we are of God, and the whole world lies *under the sway of* the wicked one.

20 And we know that the Son of God has come and has given us an understanding, that we may know Him who is true; and we are in Him who is true, in His Son Jesus Christ. This is the true God and eternal life.

21 Little children, keep yourselves from idols. Amen.

5:4 *a*M-Text reads *your*. 5:8 *a*NU-Text and M-Text omit the words from *in heaven* (verse 7) through *on earth* (verse 8). Only four or five very late manuscripts contain these words in Greek. 5:9 *a*NU-Text reads *God, that*. 5:13 *a*NU-Text omits the rest of this verse. 5:18 *a*NU-Text reads *him*.

Second John

Overview of Second John

The Second Epistle of John is a powerful illustration that love means staying involved. Written in the late 80s or early 90s A.D., probably from Ephesus and possibly to a nearby church, this letter shows John's continual concern for and involvement with this congregation.

The phrase "to the elect lady and her children" (v. 1) is probably a literary device which refers to the church as a whole rather than a specific person. John encourages the Christians to beware of the many false teachers in the region of Ephesus who did not teach the truth of Jesus Christ. John also commends them for their walk of faith. He urges them to continue living with the greatest positive influence they can demonstrate—love.

What is perfect love? There are three levels of love: "I love you because I need you"; "I love you because I want you"; and "I love you because you need me." John demonstrates that truly the latter is the definition of perfect love. This is what Christian love is all about. John points his readers to the source of perfect love—Jesus Christ!

John's commitment to his fellow Christians affirms his message. Love means staying involved!

Jesus in Second John

John refutes the same error regarding the person of Jesus in this Epistle as he did in his first Epistle. Again he stresses that those "who do not confess Jesus Christ *as* coming in the flesh" (v. 7) are deceivers who must be avoided. One must abide "in the doctrine of Christ" (v. 9) to have a relationship with God. The doctrine of the person and work of Jesus Christ affects every other area of theology.

Keys to Second John

Key Word: Avoid Fellowship with False Teachers. The basic theme of this brief letter is steadfastness in the practice and purity of the apostolic doctrine that the readers "have heard from the beginning" (v. 6). John writes it as a reminder to continue walking in obedience to God's commandment to love one another. His primary purpose is to deliver a warning not to associate with or assist teachers who do not acknowledge the truth about Jesus Christ.

Key Verses: "And now I plead with you, lady, not as though I wrote a new commandment to you, but that which we have had from the beginning: that we love one another. This is love, that we walk according to His commandments. This is the commandment, that as you have heard from the beginning, you should walk in it" (vv. 5, 6).

"Whoever transgresses and does not abide in the doctrine of Christ does not have God. He who abides in the doctrine of Christ has both the Father and the Son. If anyone comes to you and does not bring this doctrine, do not receive him into your house nor greet him" (vv. 9, 10).

1 The Elder,

To the elect lady and her children, whom I love in truth, and not only I, but also all those who have known the truth, 2 because of the truth which abides in us and will be with us forever:

3 Grace, mercy, *and* peace will be with you*ᵃ* from God the Father and from the Lord Jesus Christ, the Son of the Father, in truth and love.

4 I rejoiced greatly that I have found *some* of your children walking in truth, as we received commandment from the Father. 5 And now I plead with you, lady, not as though I wrote a new commandment to you, but that which we have had from the beginning: that we love one another. 6 This is love, that we walk according to His commandments. This is the commandment, that as you have heard from the beginning, you should walk in it.

7 For many deceivers have gone out into the world who do not confess Jesus Christ *as* coming in the flesh. This is a deceiver and an antichrist. 8 Look to yourselves, that we*ᵃ* do not lose those things we worked for, but *that* we*ᵇ* may receive a full reward.

9 Whoever transgresses*ᵃ* and does not abide in the doctrine of Christ does not have God. He who abides in the doctrine of Christ has both the Father and the Son. 10 If anyone comes to you and does not bring this doctrine, do not receive him into your house nor greet him; 11 for he who greets him shares in his evil deeds.

12 Having many things to write to you, I did not wish *to do so* with paper and ink; but I hope to come to you and speak face to face, that our joy may be full.

13 The children of your elect sister greet you. Amen.

3 *ᵃ*NU-Text and M-Text read *us*.   8 *ᵃ*NU-Text reads *you*.   *ᵇ*NU-Text reads *you*.   9 *ᵃ*NU-Text reads *goes ahead*.

Third John

Overview of Third John

T his letter is the third of John's short messages of encouragement, written most likely from Ephesus in the late 80s or early 90s A.D.

This brief Epistle was written to Gaius, a close friend who had demonstrated his love and faith by generous hospitality, and to other Christians living probably in the province of Asia. John's greatest joy was to hear that these believers with whom he had been in continual contact were still walking in the truth. They kept on keeping on in the faith.

Third John portrays the church as a family bound together by the bonds of love, with its members extending gracious hospitality toward one another. The church must guard against selfish ambition and factious jealousy, which threaten pure Christian fellowship. At the same time, church members must be vigilant to maintain positive, loving relationships with each other.

At this point in John's life, he was elderly and was the sole survivor of those who had personally walked with Jesus when He was on earth. Perhaps because John had lived an itinerant life-style with Jesus, he understood the need for hospitality to Christians and traveling ministers. He urges believers to go out of their way to take in and provide for the men and women traveling and spreading the gospel of Christ throughout Asia Minor. John asks them to continue living in love. As believers in Jesus Christ, they had the opportunity to help spread the message of faith by their support and encouragement of the evangelists. From their small seeds of love, enormous harvests of goodness would abound. We, too, can sow seeds of love in our world today. Love is going out of our way!

Jesus in Third John

Unlike First and Second John, Third John makes no mention of the name of Jesus Christ. But verse 7 says "they went forth for His name's sake," an indirect reference to our Lord.

John presents Jesus as the Truth and encourages all believers to walk in the light of His truth. Devotion to Christ is the only motivation for genuine teachers in their itinerant ministries.

The lives of Gaius and Demetrius were in harmony with Jesus' teachings and gave strong testimony to the power of His love. On the other hand, Diotrephes reveals a life in contrast to the commands of Christ.

Let us be like Gaius and Demetrius—positive examples of faithful followers of Christ.

Keys to Third John

Key Word: Enjoy Fellowship with the Brethren. The basic theme of this letter is to enjoy and continue to have fellowship (hospitality) with fellow believers, especially those who are journeying to spread the gospel. This is contrasted between the truth and servanthood of Gaius and the error and selfishness of Diotrephes.

Key Verses: "Beloved, I pray that you may prosper in all things and be in health, just as your soul prospers" (v. 2).

"I have no greater joy than to hear that my children walk in truth" (v. 4).

"Beloved, you do faithfully whatever you do for the brethren and for strangers, who have borne witness of your love before the church. *If* you send them forward on their journey in a manner worthy of God, you will do well" (vv. 5, 6).

"Beloved, do not imitate what is evil, but what is good. He who does good is of God, but he who does evil has not seen God" (v. 11).

1 The Elder,

To the beloved Gaius, whom I love in truth:

2 Beloved, I pray that you may prosper in all things and be in health, just as your soul prospers. 3 For I rejoiced greatly when brethren came and testified of the truth *that is* in you, just as you walk in the truth. 4 I have no greater joy than to hear that my children walk in truth.ᵃ

5 Beloved, you do faithfully whatever you do for the brethren andᵃ for strangers, 6 who have borne witness of your love before the church. *If* you send them forward on their journey in a manner worthy of God, you will do well, 7 because they went forth for His name's sake, taking nothing from the Gentiles. 8 We therefore ought to receiveᵃ such, that we may become fellow workers for the truth.

9 I wrote to the church, but Dio-trephes, who loves to have the pre-eminence among them, does not receive us. 10 Therefore, if I come, I will call to mind his deeds which he does, prating against us with malicious words. And not content with that, he himself does not receive the brethren, and forbids those who wish to, putting *them* out of the church.

11 Beloved, do not imitate what is evil, but what is good. He who does good is of God, butᵃ he who does evil has not seen God.

12 Demetrius has a *good* testimony from all, and from the truth itself. And we also bear witness, and you know that our testimony is true.

13 I had many things to write, but I do not wish to write to you with pen and ink; 14 but I hope to see you shortly, and we shall speak face to face.

Peace to you. Our friends greet you. Greet the friends by name.

4 ᵃNU-Text reads *the truth.*   5 ᵃNU-Text adds *especially.*   8 ᵃNU-Text reads *support.*   11 ᵃNU-Text and M-Text omit *but.*

Jude

Overview of Jude

Unveil yourself to the love of God and involve yourself in the lives of others. This is the message of Jude's Epistle.

Jude was written by the half-brother of Jesus Christ, Jude, to Christians everywhere, encouraging them to be built up in their faith. Jude warns against the negative influences that could weaken their faith and devotion to Jesus. He calls their attention to false teachers and heretics who are immoral, covetous, proud, and divisive. By building up their faith, they can remain positive and strong.

Jude knew the importance of trusting his life to the most powerful person in the universe—Jesus Christ.

But you, beloved, building yourselves up on your most holy faith, praying in the Holy Spirit, keep yourselves in the love of God, looking for the mercy of our Lord Jesus Christ unto eternal life.

(Jude 20, 21)

Jude has one of the most beautiful benedictions in the entire New Testament. Expressing confidence in God's ability to lift up, to strengthen, and to help us live positively, these words of faith are as meaningful today, with the many negative forces of people and circumstances, as they were to the first-century Christians.

Now to Him who is able to keep you from stumbling,
And to present you faultless
Before the presence of His glory with exceeding joy,
To God our Savior,
Who alone is wise,
Be glory and majesty,
Dominion and power,
Both now and forever.
Amen.

(Jude 24, 25)

Jesus in Jude

In contrast to those who stand condemned by their licentiousness and denial of Jesus, the believer is "preserved in Jesus Christ" (v. 1). Jude tells his readers to keep abiding in the love of God, trusting Jesus' mercy to bring them to eternal life and trusting His indwelling Spirit to keep them from stumbling.

Keys to Jude

Key Word: Contend for the Faith. This Epistle is intensely concerned with the threat of heretical teachers in the church and the believer's proper response to that threat. The contents reveal two major purposes: first, to condemn the practices of the ungodly libertines who were infesting the churches and corrupting believers; and second, to counsel the readers to stand firm, grow in their faith, and contend for the truth. The readers are encouraged to reach out to those who have been misled by false teachers.

Key Verses: "Beloved, while I was very diligent to write to you concerning our common salvation, I found it necessary to write to you exhorting you to contend earnestly for the faith which was once for all delivered to the saints" (v. 3).

"But you, beloved, building yourselves up on your most holy faith, praying in the Holy Spirit, keep yourselves in the love of God, looking for the mercy of our Lord Jesus Christ unto eternal life" (vv. 20, 21).

1 Jude, a bondservant of Jesus Christ, and brother of James,

To those who are called, sanctified[a] by God the Father, and preserved in Jesus Christ:

2 Mercy, peace, and love be multiplied to you.

3 Beloved, while I was very diligent to write to you concerning our common salvation, I found it necessary to write to you exhorting you to contend earnestly for the faith which was once for all delivered to the saints. 4 For certain men have crept in unnoticed, who long ago were marked out for this condemnation, ungodly men, who turn the grace of our God into lewdness and deny the only Lord God[a] and our Lord Jesus Christ.

5 But I want to remind you, though you once knew this, that the Lord, having saved the people out of the land of Egypt, afterward destroyed those who did not believe. 6 And the angels who did not keep their proper domain, but left their own abode, He has reserved in everlasting chains under darkness for the judgment of the great day; 7 as Sodom and Gomorrah, and the cities around them in a similar manner to these, having given themselves over to sexual immorality and gone after strange flesh, are set forth as an example, suffering the vengeance of eternal fire.

8 Likewise also these dreamers defile the flesh, reject authority, and speak evil of dignitaries. 9 Yet Michael the archangel, in contending with the devil, when he disputed about the body of Moses, dared not bring against him a reviling accusation, but said, "The Lord rebuke you!" 10 But these speak evil of whatever they do not know; and whatever they know naturally, like brute beasts, in these things they corrupt themselves. 11 Woe to them! For they have gone in the way of Cain, have run greedily in the error of Balaam for profit, and perished in the rebellion of Korah.

12 These are spots in your love feasts, while they feast with you without fear, serving only themselves. They are clouds without water, carried about[a] by the winds; late autumn trees without fruit, twice dead, pulled up by the roots; 13 raging waves of the sea, foaming up their own shame; wandering stars for whom is reserved the blackness of darkness forever.

14 Now Enoch, the seventh from Adam, prophesied about these men also, saying, "Behold, the Lord comes with ten thousands of His saints, 15 to execute judgment on all, to convict all who are ungodly among them of all their ungodly deeds which they have committed in an ungodly way, and of all the harsh things which ungodly sinners have spoken against Him."

16 These are grumblers, complainers, walking according to their own lusts; and they mouth great swelling words, flattering people to gain advantage. 17 But you, beloved, remember the words which were spoken before by the apostles of our Lord Jesus Christ: 18 how they told you that there would be mockers in the last time who would walk according to their own ungodly lusts. 19 These are sensual persons, who cause divisions, not having the Spirit.

20 But you, beloved, building yourselves up on your most holy faith, praying in the Holy Spirit, 21 keep yourselves in the love of God, looking for the mercy of our Lord Jesus Christ unto eternal life.

22 And on some have compassion, making a distinction;[a] 23 but others save with fear, pulling them out of the fire,[a] hating even the garment defiled by the flesh.

24   Now to Him who is able to keep
          you[a] from stumbling,

1 [a]NU-Text reads beloved.   4 [a]NU-Text omits God.   12 [a]NU-Text and M-Text read along.
22 [a]NU-Text reads who are doubting (or making distinctions).   23 [a]NU-Text adds and on some have
mercy with fear and omits with fear in first clause.   24 [a]M-Text reads them.

And to present *you* faultless
Before the presence of His
   glory with exceeding
   joy,
25 To God our Savior,[a]

Who alone is wise,[b]
Be glory and majesty,
Dominion and power,[c]
Both now and forever.
Amen.

25 [a]NU-Text reads *To the only God, our Savior* and omits *wise.*   [b]NU-Text adds *through Jesus Christ our Lord.*   [c]NU-Text adds *Before all time.*

Revelation

Overview of Revelation

Every end is a new beginning.

The Book of Revelation was written in the 90s A.D. by the apostle John during his exile on the island of Patmos. It was addressed to seven churches in Asia Minor.

Revelation has been called the "treatise for hard times" because its audience was suffering severe persecution. Christianity was growing in numbers but was constantly in direct conflict with the morals and religions of the time. In addition, the political powers opposed any lordship other than Caesar's. The church was in a life-and-death struggle.

John assures the believers that the outcome of history is in God's hands. In a series of visions, God reveals to John in prophetic symbolism the Second Coming of Jesus Christ and the creation of a new world. John also forewarns the church that tough times are coming, but they must hold on to hope. God will gain victory over the negative forces and evil powers in the world.

Tough times never last, but tough people do! Who are tough people? Tough people are those who believe in God and His ability to overcome negative, evil powers and establish a positive, life-giving world!

Through the Revelation to John we are assured that the end of the world will be a new beginning. God will restore believers to their rightful position with God in the new creation.

And he showed me a pure river of water of life, clear as crystal, proceeding from the throne of God and of the Lamb. In the middle of its street, and on either side of the river, was the tree of life, which bore twelve fruits, each tree yielding its fruit every month. The leaves of the tree were for the healing of the nations.

(Rev. 22:1, 2)

The curse of death will be removed and all believers will have access to the Tree of Life from which man was banished in the Garden of Eden. Jesus offers everyone the chance to eat of the Tree of Life and drink freely of the Water of Life.

Let us look to Jesus, the Alpha and Omega, the Beginning and the End, the First and the Last. Every end truly is a new beginning!

Jesus in Revelation

Revelation has much to say about all three persons of the Godhead, but it is especially clear in its presentation of the awesome resurrected Christ who has received all authority to judge the earth. The book is indeed "The Revelation of Jesus Christ" since it comes from Him and centers on Him. It begins with a vision of His glory, wisdom, and power, and portrays His authority over the entire world. He is the Lamb who was slain and declared worthy to open the book of judgment. His righteous wrath is poured out upon the whole earth, and He returns in power to judge His enemies and to reign as the Lord over all. He will rule forever over the heavenly city in the presence of all who know Him.

Keys to Revelation

Key Word: The Revelation of the Coming of Christ. Revelation is the most difficult biblical book to interpret, inviting several approaches. Advocates of each approach agree that the book was written to assure the recipients of the ultimate triumph of Jesus over all who rise up against Him and His saints. The readers were facing dark times of persecution, and even worse times would follow. Therefore they needed to be encouraged to persevere by standing firm in Christ in view of God's plan for the righteous and the wicked. The book was also written to challenge complacent Christians to stop compromising with the world.

Key Verses: "And God will wipe away every tear from their eyes; there shall be no more death, nor sorrow, nor crying. There shall be no more pain, for the former things have passed away . . . Behold, I make all things new" (21:4, 5).

Key Chapters: Revelation 19—22. When the end of history is fully understood, its impact radically affects the present. In Revelation 19—22 the plans of God for the last days and for all of eternity are recorded in explicit terms. Careful study of and obedience to them will bring the blessings that are promised. Uppermost in the mind and deep in the heart should be guarded the words of Jesus, "Surely I am coming quickly" (22:20).

1 The Revelation of Jesus Christ, which God gave Him to show His servants—things which must shortly take place. And He sent and signified *it* by His angel to His servant John, 2 who bore witness to the word of God, and to the testimony of Jesus Christ, to all things that he saw. 3 Blessed *is* he who reads and those who hear the words of this prophecy, and keep those things which are written in it; for the time *is* near.

4 John, to the seven churches which are in Asia:

Grace to you and peace from Him who is and who was and who is to come, and from the seven Spirits who are before His throne, 5 and from Jesus Christ, the faithful witness, the firstborn from the dead, and the ruler over the kings of the earth.

To Him who loved us and washed[a] us from our sins in His own blood, 6 and has made us kings[a] and priests to His God and Father, to Him *be* glory and dominion forever and ever. Amen.

7 Behold, He is coming with clouds, and every eye will see Him, even they who pierced Him. And all the tribes of the earth will mourn because of Him. Even so, Amen.

8 "I am the Alpha and the Omega, *the* Beginning and *the* End,"[a] says the Lord,[b] "who is and who was and who is to come, the Almighty."

9 I, John, both[a] your brother and companion in the tribulation and kingdom and patience of Jesus Christ, was on the island that is called Patmos for the word of God and for the testimony of Jesus Christ. 10 I was in the Spirit on the Lord's Day, and I heard behind me a loud voice, as of a trumpet, 11 saying, "I am the Alpha and the Omega, the First and the Last," and,[a] "What you see, write in a book and send *it* to the seven churches which are in Asia:[b] to Ephesus, to Smyrna, to Pergamos, to Thyatira, to Sardis, to Philadelphia, and to Laodicea."

12 Then I turned to see the voice that spoke with me. And having turned I saw seven golden lampstands, 13 and in the midst of the seven lampstands *One* like the Son of Man, clothed with a garment down to the feet and girded about the chest with a golden band. 14 His head and hair *were* white like wool, as white as snow, and His eyes like a flame of fire; 15 His feet *were* like fine brass, as if refined in a furnace, and His voice as the sound of many waters; 16 He had in His right hand seven stars, out of His mouth went a sharp two-edged sword, and His countenance *was* like the sun shining in its strength. 17 And when I saw Him, I fell at His feet as dead. But He laid His right hand on me, saying to me,[a] "Do not be afraid; I am the First and the Last. 18 I *am* He who lives, and was dead, and behold, I am alive forevermore. Amen. And I have

---

1:5 [a]NU-Text reads *loves us and freed;* M-Text reads *loves us and washed.*   1:6 [a]NU-Text and M-Text read *a kingdom.*   1:8 [a]NU-Text and M-Text omit *the Beginning and the End.*   [b]NU-Text and M-Text add *God.*   1:9 [a]NU-Text and M-Text omit *both.*   1:11 [a]NU-Text and M-Text omit *I am* through third *and.*   [b]NU-Text and M-Text omit *which are in Asia.*   1:17 [a]NU-Text and M-Text omit *to me.*

The Aegean Sea Region

BLACK SEA

THE GREAT SEA

THRACE

MYSIA

• Troas

• Pergamos

• Thyatira

• Smyrna

• Sardis

• Philadelphia

• Laodicea

ASIA

• Ephesus

RHODES

MACEDONIA

Philippi •

Thessalonica •

Berea •

SAMOTHRACE

LESBOS

CHIOS

SAMOS

PATMOS

AEGEAN SEA

Athens •

Corinth •

ACHAIA

THE GREAT SEA

the keys of Hades and of Death. 19 Write*a* the things which you have seen, and the things which are, and the things which will take place after this. 20 The mystery of the seven stars which you saw in My right hand, and the seven golden lampstands: The seven stars are the angels of the seven churches, and the seven lampstands which you saw*a* are the seven churches.

2 "To the angel of the church of Ephesus write,

'These things says He who holds the seven stars in His right hand, who walks in the midst of the seven golden lampstands: 2 "I know your works, your labor, your patience, and that you cannot bear those who are evil. And you have tested those who say they are apostles and are not, and have found them liars; 3 and you have persevered and have patience, and have labored for My name's sake and have not become weary. 4 Nevertheless I have *this* against you, that you have left your first love. 5 Remember therefore from where you have fallen; repent and do the first works, or else I will come to you quickly and remove your lampstand from its place—unless you repent. 6 But this you have, that you hate the deeds of the Nicolaitans, which I also hate.

7 "He who has an ear, let him hear what the Spirit says to the churches. To him who overcomes I will give to eat from the tree of life, which is in the midst of the Paradise of God." '

8 "And to the angel of the church in Smyrna write,

'These things says the First and the Last, who was dead, and came to life: 9 "I know your works, tribulation, and poverty (but you are rich); and *I know* the blasphemy of those who say they are Jews and are not, but *are* a synagogue of Satan. 10 Do not fear any of those things which you are about to suffer. Indeed, the devil is about to throw *some* of you into prison, that you may be tested, and you will have tribulation ten days. Be faithful until death, and I will give you the crown of life.

11 "He who has an ear, let him hear what the Spirit says to the churches. He who overcomes shall not be hurt by the second death." '

12 "And to the angel of the church in Pergamos write,

'These things says He who has the sharp two-edged sword: 13 "I know your works, and where you dwell, where Satan's throne *is*. And you hold fast to My name, and did not deny My faith even in the days in which Antipas *was* My faithful martyr, who was killed among you, where Satan dwells. 14 But I have a few things against you, because you have there those who hold the doctrine of Balaam, who taught Balak to put a stumbling block before the children of Israel, to eat things sacrificed to idols, and to commit sexual immorality. 15 Thus you also have those who hold the doctrine of the Nicolaitans, which thing I hate.*a* 16 Repent, or else I will come to you quickly and will fight against them with the sword of My mouth.

17 "He who has an ear, let him hear what the Spirit says to the churches. To him who overcomes I will give some of the hidden manna to eat. And I will give him a white stone, and on the stone a new name written which no one knows except him who receives *it*." '

18 "And to the angel of the church in Thyatira write,

'These things says the Son of God, who has eyes like a flame of fire, and His feet like fine brass: 19 I know your works, love, service, faith,*a* and your patience; and *as* for your works, the last *are* more than the first. 20 Nevertheless I have a few things against you, because you allow*a* that woman*b* Jezebel, who calls herself a prophetess, to teach and seduce*c* My servants to commit sexual immorality and eat things sacrificed to idols. 21 And I gave her time to repent of her sexual immorality, and she did not repent.*a* 22 Indeed I will cast her into a sickbed, and those who commit adultery with her into great tribu-

---

1:19 *a*NU-Text and M-Text read *Therefore, write.*   1:20 *a*NU-Text and M-Text omit *which you saw.* 2:15 *a*NU-Text and M-Text read *likewise* for *which thing I hate.*   2:19 *a*NU-Text and M-Text read *faith, service.*   2:20 *a*NU-Text and M-Text read *I have against you that you tolerate.*   *b*M-Text reads *your wife Jezebel.*   *c*NU-Text and M-Text read *and teaches and seduces.*   2:21 *a*NU-Text and M-Text read *time to repent, and she does not want to repent of her sexual immorality.*

The Seven Churches

Part of John's vision in the Revelation consists of Jesus' messages to seven churches in Asia Minor. The letters addressed the following concerns in each church. Jesus encouraged the church at Ephesus to return to her first love. The church at Smyrna was exhorted to remain faithful in the face of persecution. Jesus spoke to the church at Pergamos about their willingness to compromise their faith. The church at Thytira had become corrupt, so Jesus warned them to hold fast to His teachings. The church at Sardis had a few faithful people, but was a dead church. Jesus inspired them to be watchful and strong. The church at Philadelphia was known for their good works. Jesus encouraged them to continue as overcomers. Jesus spoke to the church at Laodicea about "being lukewarm" and spiritually pretentious. He told them to repent and be strong.

2. Message to Smyrna: "Be faithful until death, and I will give you the crown of life" (Rev. 2:10).

3. Message to Pergamos: "But I have a few things against you" (Rev. 2:14).

4. Message to Thyatira: "But hold fast what you have till I come" (Rev. 2:25).

5. Message to Sardis: "That you have a name that you are alive, but you are dead" (Rev. 3:1).

6. Message to Philadelphia: "I have set before you an open door" (Rev. 3:8).

7. Message to Laodicea: "That you are neither cold nor hot" (Rev. 3:15).

1. Message to Ephesus: "That you have left your first love" (Rev. 2:4).

John received his vision and wrote the Revelation while in exile on this island in the Aegean Sea (Rev. 1:1, 9).

MYSIA

ASIA

AEGEAN SEA

ISLE OF PATMOS

Pergamos
Thyatira
Sardis
Smyrna
Philadelphia
Ephesus
Laodicea

lation, unless they repent of their[a] deeds. 23 I will kill her children with death, and all the churches shall know that I am He who searches the minds and hearts. And I will give to each one of you according to your works.

24 "Now to you I say, and[a] to the rest in Thyatira, as many as do not have this doctrine, who have not known the depths of Satan, as they say, I will[b] put on you no other burden. 25 But hold fast what you have till I come. 26 And he who overcomes, and keeps My works until the end, to him I will give power over the nations—

27 'He shall rule them with a rod
        of iron;
    They shall be dashed to pieces
        like the potter's vessels'[a]—

as I also have received from My Father; 28 and I will give him the morning star.

29 "He who has an ear, let him hear what the Spirit says to the churches." '

3 "And to the angel of the church in Sardis write,

'These things says He who has the seven Spirits of God and the seven stars: "I know your works, that you have a name that you are alive, but you are dead. 2 Be watchful, and strengthen the things which remain, that are ready to die, for I have not found your works perfect before God.[a] 3 Remember therefore how you have received and heard; hold fast and repent. Therefore if you will not watch, I will come upon you as a thief, and you will not know what hour I will come upon you. 4 You[a] have a few names even in Sardis who have not defiled their garments; and they shall walk with Me in white, for they are worthy. 5 He who overcomes shall be clothed in white garments, and I will not blot out his name from the Book of Life; but I will confess his name before My Father and before His angels.

6 "He who has an ear, let him hear what the Spirit says to the churches." '

7 "And to the angel of the church in Philadelphia write,

'These things says He who is holy, He who is true, *"He who has the key of David, He who opens and no one shuts, and shuts and no one opens":*[a] 8 I know your works. See, I have set before you an open door, and no one can shut it;[a] for you have a little strength, have kept My word, and have not denied My name. 9 Indeed I will make *those* of the synagogue of Satan, who say they are Jews and are not, but lie—indeed I will make them come and worship before your feet, and to know that I have loved you. 10 Because you have kept My command to persevere, I also will keep you from the hour of trial which shall come upon the whole world, to test those who dwell on the earth. 11 Behold,[a] I am coming quickly! Hold fast what you have, that no one may take your crown. 12 He who overcomes, I will make him a pillar in the temple of My God, and he shall go out no more. I will write on him the name of My God and the name of the city of My God, the New Jerusalem, which comes down out of heaven from My God. And *I will write on him* My new name.

13 "He who has an ear, let him hear what the Spirit says to the churches." '

14 "And to the angel of the church of the Laodiceans[a] write,

'These things says the Amen, the Faithful and True Witness, the Beginning of the creation of God: 15 "I know your works, that you are neither cold nor hot. I could wish you were cold or hot. 16 So then, because you are lukewarm, and neither cold nor hot,[a] I will vomit you out of My mouth. 17 Because you say, 'I am rich, have become wealthy, and have need of nothing'—and do not know that you are wretched, miserable, poor, blind, and naked— 18 I counsel you to buy from Me gold refined in the fire, that you may be rich; and white garments, that you may be clothed, *that* the shame of your

---

2:22 [a]NU-Text and M-Text read *her.*   2:24 [a]NU-Text and M-Text omit *and.*   [b]NU-Text and M-Text omit *will.*   2:27 [a]Psalm 2:9   3:2 [a]NU-Text and M-Text read *My God.*   3:4 [a]NU-Text and M-Text read *Nevertheless you have a few names in Sardis.*   3:7 [a]Isaiah 22:22   3:8 [a]NU-Text and M-Text read *which no one can shut.*   3:11 [a]NU-Text and M-Text omit *Behold.*   3:14 [a]NU-Text and M-Text read *in Laodicea.*   3:16 [a]NU-Text and M-Text read *hot nor cold.*

Reason to Believe

The total dedication and commitment of the early disciples to their newfound faith is strong evidence for the truth of the New Testament and the resurrection of Jesus Christ.

A look at the disciples' lives gives added insight into the power of God's Son. Twelve men from various walks of life left everything to follow Jesus. They traveled with Him for approximately three years, but upon Jesus' arrest and crucifixion each one fled and hid in fear. Yet something incredible happened shortly thereafter, for within a few days after Jesus' death and burial, the disciples proclaimed God's love and forgiveness through the death and resurrection of Jesus Christ openly and bravely.

Their commitment to this belief cannot be explained in any psychological terms, other than they believed what they claimed actually happened.

Several of the disciples had a strong dislike, and in some cases even hatred, for the Gentile nations. Yet, remarkably, their attitudes changed to embrace their Gentile brothers. They insisted on traveling to obscure places to share God's love and forgiveness to people of all races. They claimed that Jesus Christ, the Son of God, was crucified and rose from the dead, thereby giving all people hope over their greatest foe—death.

According to tradition, eleven of the twelve disciples suffered a martyr's death for what they believed, preached, and taught. Herod had James killed by the sword in Palestine (Acts 12:2). What we know of the deaths of the other disciples is shrouded in tradition. Philip was said to have been hanged in Hierapolis in Asia Minor. Matthew was killed by the sword in Parthia. Andrew was crucified on an X-shaped cross in Patrae in Achaia. Mark was dragged to pieces by the people in Alexandria in front of the great idol, Serapis. Peter was crucified upside down in Rome. Paul had his head cut off in Rome. Jude was crucified in Edessa. Thomas was killed by a spear thrust through his side in India. Bartholomew was beaten and crucified in Asia Minor. Luke was nailed to an olive tree by a pagan priest in Greece. John was the only disciple who did not die for his faith. But even he was said to have been boiled in a cauldron of scalding oil, but survived and was banished to the island of Patmos by the Emperor Domitian.

If the disciples knew the resurrection of Jesus Christ was a hoax, or could be explained in any other way, they would not have been willing to die for their faith. Throughout history, many martyrs have died for something that was true. But few have died for what they knew to be a lie. It is virtually impossible to gather twelve men or women together and have them propagate a lie, spread it everywhere so that people believe it, and die for it, knowing it to be a lie. It is a psychological impossibility. The disciples and hundreds of other first-century martyrs knew the resurrection of Jesus Christ was the truth, and they sealed their testimony in their own blood.

Because of their faith, commitment, and dedication, we have the confidence that what they recorded, taught, and preached was true. We can believe wholeheartedly with them the statement of Jesus, "I am the resurrection and the life. He who believes in Me, though he may die, he shall live" (John 11:25).

nakedness may not be revealed; and anoint your eyes with eye salve, that you may see. 19 As many as I love, I rebuke and chasten. Therefore be zealous and repent. 20 Behold, I stand at the door and knock. If anyone hears My voice and opens the door, I will come in to him and dine with him, and he with Me. 21 To him who overcomes I will grant to sit with Me on My throne, as I also overcame and sat down with My Father on His throne.

22 "He who has an ear, let him hear what the Spirit says to the churches." ' "

4 After these things I looked, and behold, a door *standing* open in heaven. And the first voice which I heard *was* like a trumpet speaking with me, saying, "Come up here, and I will show you things which must take place after this."

2 Immediately I was in the Spirit; and behold, a throne set in heaven, and *One* sat on the throne. 3 And He who sat there was[a] like a jasper and a sardius stone in appearance; and *there was* a rainbow around the throne, in appearance like an emerald. 4 Around the throne *were* twenty-four thrones, and on the thrones I saw twenty-four elders sitting, clothed in white robes; and they had crowns[a] of gold on their heads. 5 And from the throne proceeded lightnings, thunderings and voices.[a] Seven lamps of fire *were* burning before the throne, which are the[b] seven Spirits of God.

6 Before the throne *there was*[a] a sea of glass, like crystal. And in the midst of the throne, and around the throne, *were* four living creatures full of eyes in front and in back. 7 The first living creature *was* like a lion, the second living creature like a calf, the third living creature had a face like a man, and the fourth living creature *was* like a flying eagle. 8 *The* four living creatures, each having six wings, were full of eyes around and within. And they do not rest day or night, saying:

"Holy, holy, holy,[a]
Lord God Almighty,
Who was and is and is to
come!"

9 Whenever the living creatures give glory and honor and thanks to Him who sits on the throne, who lives forever and ever, 10 the twenty-four elders fall down before Him who sits on the throne and worship Him who lives forever and ever, and cast their crowns before the throne, saying:

11 "You are worthy, O Lord,[a]
To receive glory and honor and
power;
For You created all things,
And by Your will they exist[b]
and were created."

5 And I saw in the right *hand* of Him who sat on the throne a scroll written inside and on the back, sealed with seven seals. 2 Then I saw a strong angel proclaiming with a loud voice, "Who is worthy to open the scroll and to loose its seals?" 3 And no one in heaven or on the earth or under the earth was able to open the scroll, or to look at it. 4 So I wept much, because no one was found worthy to open and read[a] the scroll, or to look at it. 5 But one of the elders said to me, "Do not weep. Behold, the Lion of the tribe of Judah, the Root of David, has prevailed to open the scroll and to loose[a] its seven seals."

6 And I looked, and behold,[a] in the midst of the throne and of the four living creatures, and in the midst of the elders, stood a Lamb as though it had been slain, having seven horns and seven eyes, which are the seven Spirits of God sent out into all the earth. 7 Then He came and took the scroll out of the right hand of Him who sat on the throne.

8 Now when He had taken the scroll, the four living creatures and the twenty-four elders fell down before the Lamb, each having a harp, and golden bowls full of incense, which are the prayers of the saints. 9 And they sang a new song, saying:

4:3 [a]M-Text omits *And He who sat there was* (which makes the description in verse 3 modify the throne rather than God).   4:4 [a]NU-Text and M-Text read *robes, with crowns.*   4:5 [a]NU-Text and M-Text read *voices, and thunderings.*   [b]M-Text omits *the.*   4:6 [a]NU-Text and M-Text add *something like.*   4:8 [a]M-Text has *holy* nine times.   4:11 [a]NU-Text and M-Text read *our Lord and God.*   [b]NU-Text and M-Text read *existed.*   5:4 [a]NU-Text and M-Text omit *and read.*   5:5 [a]NU-Text and M-Text omit *to loose.*   5:6 [a]NU-Text and M-Text read *I saw in the midst . . . a Lamb standing.*

"You are worthy to take the
  scroll,
And to open its seals;
For You were slain,
And have redeemed us to God
  by Your blood
Out of every tribe and tongue
  and people and nation,
10 And have made us*a* kings*b* and
  priests to our God;
And we*c* shall reign on the
  earth."

11 Then I looked, and I heard the
voice of many angels around the
throne, the living creatures, and the
elders; and the number of them was
ten thousand times ten thousand, and
thousands of thousands, 12 saying
with a loud voice:

"Worthy is the Lamb who was
  slain
To receive power and riches
  and wisdom,
And strength and honor and
  glory and blessing!"

13 And every creature which is in
heaven and on the earth and under
the earth and such as are in the sea,
and all that are in them, I heard saying:

"Blessing and honor and glory
  and power
Be to Him who sits on the
  throne,
And to the Lamb, forever and
  ever!"*a*

14 Then the four living creatures
said, "Amen!" And the twenty-four*a*
elders fell down and worshiped Him
who lives forever and ever.*b*

6 Now I saw when the Lamb
  opened one of the seals;*a* and I
heard one of the four living creatures
saying with a voice like thunder,
"Come and see." 2 And I looked, and
behold, a white horse. He who sat on
it had a bow; and a crown was given
to him, and he went out conquering
and to conquer.
3 When He opened the second seal,

I heard the second living creature
saying, "Come and see."*a* 4 Another
horse, fiery red, went out. And it was
granted to the one who sat on it to
take peace from the earth, and that
people should kill one another; and
there was given to him a great sword.
5 When He opened the third seal,
I heard the third living creature say,
"Come and see." So I looked, and behold, a black horse, and he who sat
on it had a pair of scales in his hand.
6 And I heard a voice in the midst of
the four living creatures saying, "A
quart*a* of wheat for a denarius,*b* and
three quarts of barley for a denarius;
and do not harm the oil and the
wine."
7 When He opened the fourth seal,
I heard the voice of the fourth living
creature saying, "Come and see."
8 So I looked, and behold, a pale
horse. And the name of him who sat
on it was Death, and Hades followed
with him. And power was given to
them over a fourth of the earth, to
kill with sword, with hunger, with
death, and by the beasts of the earth.
9 When He opened the fifth seal, I
saw under the altar the souls of those
who had been slain for the word of
God and for the testimony which
they held. 10 And they cried with a
loud voice, saying, "How long, O
Lord, holy and true, until You judge
and avenge our blood on those who
dwell on the earth?" 11 Then a white
robe was given to each of them; and
it was said to them that they should
rest a little while longer, until both
the number of their fellow servants
and their brethren, who would be
killed as they *were,* was completed.
12 I looked when He opened the
sixth seal, and behold,*a* there was a
great earthquake; and the sun became black as sackcloth of hair, and
the moon*b* became like blood.
13 And the stars of heaven fell to the
earth, as a fig tree drops its late figs
when it is shaken by a mighty wind.
14 Then the sky receded as a scroll
when it is rolled up, and every mountain and island was moved out of its
place. 15 And the kings of the earth,
the great men, the rich men, the com-

5:10 *a*NU-Text and M-Text read *them.* *b*NU-Text reads *a kingdom.* *c*NU-Text and M-Text read *they.*
5:13 *a*M-Text adds *Amen.* 5:14 *a*NU-Text and M-Text omit *twenty-four.* *b*NU-Text and M-Text omit *Him
who lives forever and ever.* 6:1 *a*NU-Text and M-Text read *seven seals.* 6:3 *a*NU-Text and M-Text
omit *and see.* 6:6 *a*Greek *choinix;* that is, approximately one quart *b*This was approximately one day's
wage for a worker. 6:12 *a*NU-Text and M-Text omit *behold.* *b*NU-Text and M-Text read *the whole moon.*

manders,[a] the mighty men, every slave and every free man, hid themselves in the caves and in the rocks of the mountains, 16 and said to the mountains and rocks, "Fall on us and hide us from the face of Him who sits on the throne and from the wrath of the Lamb! 17 For the great day of His wrath has come, and who is able to stand?"

7 After these things I saw four angels standing at the four corners of the earth, holding the four winds of the earth, that the wind should not blow on the earth, on the sea, or on any tree. 2 Then I saw another angel ascending from the east, having the seal of the living God. And he cried with a loud voice to the four angels to whom it was granted to harm the earth and the sea, 3 saying, "Do not harm the earth, the sea, or the trees till we have sealed the servants of our God on their foreheads." 4 And I heard the number of those who were sealed. One hundred *and* forty-four thousand of all the tribes of the children of Israel *were* sealed:

5 of the tribe of Judah twelve
   thousand *were* sealed;[a]
   of the tribe of Reuben twelve
   thousand *were* sealed;
   of the tribe of Gad twelve
   thousand *were* sealed;
6 of the tribe of Asher twelve
   thousand *were* sealed;
   of the tribe of Naphtali twelve
   thousand *were* sealed;
   of the tribe of Manasseh twelve
   thousand *were* sealed;
7 of the tribe of Simeon twelve
   thousand *were* sealed;
   of the tribe of Levi twelve
   thousand *were* sealed;
   of the tribe of Issachar twelve
   thousand *were* sealed;
8 of the tribe of Zebulun twelve
   thousand *were* sealed;
   of the tribe of Joseph twelve
   thousand *were* sealed;
   of the tribe of Benjamin twelve
   thousand *were* sealed.

9 After these things I looked, and behold, a great multitude which no one could number, of all nations, tribes, peoples, and tongues, standing before the throne and before the Lamb, clothed with white robes, with palm branches in their hands, 10 and crying out with a loud voice, saying, "Salvation *belongs* to our God who sits on the throne, and to the Lamb!" 11 All the angels stood around the throne and the elders and the four living creatures, and fell on their faces before the throne and worshiped God, 12 saying:

"Amen! Blessing and glory and
   wisdom,
Thanksgiving and honor and
   power and might,
Be to our God forever and ever.
   Amen."

13 Then one of the elders answered, saying to me, "Who are these arrayed in white robes, and where did they come from?"
14 And I said to him, "Sir,[a] you know."
So he said to me, "These are the ones who come out of the great tribulation, and washed their robes and made them white in the blood of the Lamb. 15 Therefore they are before the throne of God, and serve Him day and night in His temple. And He who sits on the throne will dwell among them. 16 They shall neither hunger anymore nor thirst anymore; the sun shall not strike them, nor any heat; 17 for the Lamb who is in the midst of the throne will shepherd them and lead them to living fountains of waters.[a] And God will wipe away every tear from their eyes."

8 When He opened the seventh seal, there was silence in heaven for about half an hour. 2 And I saw the seven angels who stand before God, and to them were given seven trumpets. 3 Then another angel, having a golden censer, came and stood at the altar. He was given much incense, that he should offer *it* with the prayers of all the saints upon the golden altar which was before the throne. 4 And the smoke of the incense, with the prayers of the saints, ascended before God from the angel's hand. 5 Then the angel took the

---

6:15 [a]NU-Text and M-Text read *the commanders, the rich men.*   7:5 [a]In NU-Text and M-Text *were sealed* is stated only in verses 5a and 8c; the words are understood in the remainder of the passage.
7:14 [a]NU-Text and M-Text read *My lord.*   7:17 [a]NU-Text and M-Text read *to fountains of the waters of life.*

censer, filled it with fire from the altar, and threw *it* to the earth. And there were noises, thunderings, lightnings, and an earthquake.

6 So the seven angels who had the seven trumpets prepared themselves to sound.

7 The first angel sounded: And hail and fire followed, mingled with blood, and they were thrown to the earth.*a* And a third of the trees were burned up, and all green grass was burned up.

8 Then the second angel sounded: And *something* like a great mountain burning with fire was thrown into the sea, and a third of the sea became blood. 9 And a third of the living creatures in the sea died, and a third of the ships were destroyed.

10 Then the third angel sounded: And a great star fell from heaven, burning like a torch, and it fell on a third of the rivers and on the springs of water. 11 The name of the star is Wormwood. A third of the waters became wormwood, and many men died from the water, because it was made bitter.

12 Then the fourth angel sounded: And a third of the sun was struck, a third of the moon, and a third of the stars, so that a third of them were darkened. A third of the day did not shine, and likewise the night.

13 And I looked, and I heard an angel*a* flying through the midst of heaven, saying with a loud voice, "Woe, woe, woe to the inhabitants of the earth, because of the remaining blasts of the trumpet of the three angels who are about to sound!"

9 Then the fifth angel sounded: And I saw a star fallen from heaven to the earth. To him was given the key to the bottomless pit. 2 And he opened the bottomless pit, and smoke arose out of the pit like the smoke of a great furnace. So the sun and the air were darkened because of the smoke of the pit. 3 Then out of the smoke locusts came upon the earth. And to them was given power, as the scorpions of the earth have power. 4 They were commanded not to harm the grass of the earth, or any green thing, or any tree, but only those men who do not have the seal

of God on their foreheads. 5 And they were not given *authority* to kill them, but to torment them *for* five months. Their torment *was* like the torment of a scorpion when it strikes a man. 6 In those days men will seek death and will not find it; they will desire to die, and death will flee from them.

7 The shape of the locusts was like horses prepared for battle. On their heads were crowns of something like gold, and their faces *were* like the faces of men. 8 They had hair like women's hair, and their teeth were like lions' *teeth.* 9 And they had breastplates like breastplates of iron, and the sound of their wings *was* like the sound of chariots with many horses running into battle. 10 They had tails like scorpions, and there were stings in their tails. Their power *was* to hurt men five months. 11 And they had as king over them the angel of the bottomless pit, whose name in Hebrew *is* Abaddon, but in Greek he has the name Apollyon.

12 One woe is past. Behold, still two more woes are coming after these things.

13 Then the sixth angel sounded: And I heard a voice from the four horns of the golden altar which is before God, 14 saying to the sixth angel who had the trumpet, "Release the four angels who are bound at the great river Euphrates." 15 So the four angels, who had been prepared for the hour and day and month and year, were released to kill a third of mankind. 16 Now the number of the army of the horsemen *was* two hundred million; I heard the number of them. 17 And thus I saw the horses in the vision: those who sat on them had breastplates of fiery red, hyacinth blue, and sulfur yellow; and the heads of the horses *were* like the heads of lions; and out of their mouths came fire, smoke, and brimstone. 18 By these three *plagues* a third of mankind was killed—by the fire and the smoke and the brimstone which came out of their mouths. 19 For their power*a* is in their mouth and in their tails; for their tails *are* like serpents, having heads; and with them they do harm.

20 But the rest of mankind, who were not killed by these plagues, did

8:7 *a*NU-Text and M-Text add *And a third of the earth was burned up.*   8:13 *a*NU-Text and M-Text read *eagle.*   9:19 *a*NU-Text and M-Text read *the power of the horses.*

not repent of the works of their hands, that they should not worship demons, and idols of gold, silver, brass, stone, and wood, which can neither see nor hear nor walk. 21 And they did not repent of their murders or their sorceries[a] or their sexual immorality or their thefts.

10 I saw still another mighty angel coming down from heaven, clothed with a cloud. And a rainbow *was* on his head, his face *was* like the sun, and his feet like pillars of fire. 2 He had a little book open in his hand. And he set his right foot on the sea and *his* left *foot* on the land, 3 and cried with a loud voice, as *when* a lion roars. When he cried out, seven thunders uttered their voices. 4 Now when the seven thunders uttered their voices,[a] I was about to write; but I heard a voice from heaven saying to me,[b] "Seal up the things which the seven thunders uttered, and do not write them."

5 The angel whom I saw standing on the sea and on the land raised up his hand[a] to heaven 6 and swore by Him who lives forever and ever, who created heaven and the things that are in it, the earth and the things that are in it, and the sea and the things that are in it, that there should be delay no longer, 7 but in the days of the sounding of the seventh angel, when he is about to sound, the mystery of God would be finished, as He declared to His servants the prophets.

8 Then the voice which I heard from heaven spoke to me again and said, "Go, take the little book which is open in the hand of the angel who stands on the sea and on the earth."

9 So I went to the angel and said to him, "Give me the little book."

And he said to me, "Take and eat it; and it will make your stomach bitter, but it will be as sweet as honey in your mouth."

10 Then I took the little book out of the angel's hand and ate it, and it was as sweet as honey in my mouth. But when I had eaten it, my stomach became bitter. 11 And he[a] said to me, "You must prophesy again about many peoples, nations, tongues, and kings."

11 Then I was given a reed like a measuring rod. And the angel stood,[a] saying, "Rise and measure the temple of God, the altar, and those who worship there. 2 But leave out the court which is outside the temple, and do not measure it, for it has been given to the Gentiles. And they will tread the holy city underfoot *for* forty-two months. 3 And I will give *power* to my two witnesses, and they will prophesy one thousand two hundred and sixty days, clothed in sackcloth."

4 These are the two olive trees and the two lampstands standing before the God[a] of the earth. 5 And if anyone wants to harm them, fire proceeds from their mouth and devours their enemies. And if anyone wants to harm them, he must be killed in this manner. 6 These have power to shut heaven, so that no rain falls in the days of their prophecy; and they have power over waters to turn them to blood, and to strike the earth with all plagues, as often as they desire.

7 When they finish their testimony, the beast that ascends out of the bottomless pit will make war against them, overcome them, and kill them. 8 And their dead bodies *will lie* in the street of the great city which spiritually is called Sodom and Egypt, where also our[a] Lord was crucified. 9 Then *those* from the peoples, tribes, tongues, and nations will see their dead bodies three-and-a-half days, and not allow[a] their dead bodies to be put into graves. 10 And those who dwell on the earth will rejoice over them, make merry, and send gifts to one another, because these two prophets tormented those who dwell on the earth.

11 Now after the three-and-a-half days the breath of life from God entered them, and they stood on their feet, and great fear fell on those who saw them. 12 And they[a] heard a loud voice from heaven saying to them, "Come up here." And they ascended to heaven in a cloud, and their enemies saw them. 13 In the same hour

9:21 [a]NU-Text and M-Text read *drugs*.   10:4 [a]NU-Text and M-Text read *sounded*.   [b]NU-Text and M-Text omit *to me*.   10:5 [a]NU-Text and M-Text read *right hand*.   10:11 [a]NU-Text and M-Text read *they*.   11:1 [a]NU-Text and M-Text omit *And the angel stood*.   11:4 [a]NU-Text and M-Text read *Lord*.   11:8 [a]NU-Text and M-Text read *their*.   11:9 [a]NU-Text and M-Text read *nations see . . . and will not allow*.   11:12 [a]M-Text reads *I*.

there was a great earthquake, and a tenth of the city fell. In the earthquake seven thousand people were killed, and the rest were afraid and gave glory to the God of heaven.

14 The second woe is past. Behold, the third woe is coming quickly.

15 Then the seventh angel sounded: And there were loud voices in heaven, saying, "The kingdoms*a* of this world have become *the kingdoms* of our Lord and of His Christ, and He shall reign forever and ever!" 16 And the twenty-four elders who sat before God on their thrones fell on their faces and worshiped God, 17 saying:

"We give You thanks, O Lord
    God Almighty,
    The One who is and who was
        and who is to come,*a*
    Because You have taken Your
        great power and reigned.
18 The nations were angry, and
        Your wrath has come,
    And the time of the dead, that
        they should be judged,
    And that You should reward
        Your servants the prophets
        and the saints,
    And those who fear Your
        name, small and great,
    And should destroy those who
        destroy the earth."

19 Then the temple of God was opened in heaven, and the ark of His covenant*a* was seen in His temple. And there were lightnings, noises, thunderings, an earthquake, and great hail.

12 Now a great sign appeared in heaven: a woman clothed with the sun, with the moon under her feet, and on her head a garland of twelve stars. 2 Then being with child, she cried out in labor and in pain to give birth.

3 And another sign appeared in heaven: behold, a great, fiery red dragon having seven heads and ten horns, and seven diadems on his heads. 4 His tail drew a third of the stars of heaven and threw them to the earth. And the dragon stood before the woman who was ready to give birth, to devour her Child as soon as it was born. 5 She bore a male Child who was to rule all nations with a rod of iron. And her Child was caught up to God and His throne. 6 Then the woman fled into the wilderness, where she has a place prepared by God, that they should feed her there one thousand two hundred and sixty days.

7 And war broke out in heaven: Michael and his angels fought with the dragon; and the dragon and his angels fought, 8 but they did not prevail, nor was a place found for them*a* in heaven any longer. 9 So the great dragon was cast out, that serpent of old, called the Devil and Satan, who deceives the whole world; he was cast to the earth, and his angels were cast out with him.

10 Then I heard a loud voice saying in heaven, "Now salvation, and strength, and the kingdom of our God, and the power of His Christ have come, for the accuser of our brethren, who accused them before our God day and night, has been cast down. 11 And they overcame him by the blood of the Lamb and by the word of their testimony, and they did not love their lives to the death. 12 Therefore rejoice, O heavens, and you who dwell in them! Woe to the inhabitants of the earth and the sea! For the devil has come down to you, having great wrath, because he knows that he has a short time."

13 Now when the dragon saw that he had been cast to the earth, he persecuted the woman who gave birth to the male *Child*. 14 But the woman was given two wings of a great eagle, that she might fly into the wilderness to her place, where she is nourished for a time and times and half a time, from the presence of the serpent. 15 So the serpent spewed water out of his mouth like a flood after the woman, that he might cause her to be carried away by the flood. 16 But the earth helped the woman, and the earth opened its mouth and swallowed up the flood which the dragon had spewed out of his mouth. 17 And the dragon was enraged with the woman, and he went to make war with the rest of her offspring, who keep the commandments of God and have the testimony of Jesus Christ.*a*

11:15 *a*NU-Text and M-Text read *kingdom . . . has become.* *is to come.*   11:19 *a*M-Text reads *the covenant of the Lord.*   12:17 *a*NU-Text and M-Text omit *Christ.*   11:17 *a*NU-Text and M-Text omit *and who is to come.*   12:8 *a*M-Text reads *him.*

13 Then I*a* stood on the sand of the sea. And I saw a beast rising up out of the sea, having seven heads and ten horns,*b* and on his horns ten crowns, and on his heads a blasphemous name. 2 Now the beast which I saw was like a leopard, his feet were like *the feet of* a bear, and his mouth like the mouth of a lion. The dragon gave him his power, his throne, and great authority. 3 And *I saw* one of his heads as if it had been mortally wounded, and his deadly wound was healed. And all the world marveled and followed the beast. 4 So they worshiped the dragon who gave authority to the beast; and they worshiped the beast, saying, "Who *is* like the beast? Who is able to make war with him?"

5 And he was given a mouth speaking great things and blasphemies, and he was given authority to continue*a* for forty-two months. 6 Then he opened his mouth in blasphemy against God, to blaspheme His name, His tabernacle, and those who dwell in heaven. 7 It was granted to him to make war with the saints and to overcome them. And authority was given him over every tribe,*a* tongue, and nation. 8 All who dwell on the earth will worship him, whose names have not been written in the Book of Life of the Lamb slain from the foundation of the world.

9 If anyone has an ear, let him hear. 10 He who leads into captivity shall go into captivity; he who kills with the sword must be killed with the sword. Here is the patience and the faith of the saints.

11 Then I saw another beast coming up out of the earth, and he had two horns like a lamb and spoke like a dragon. 12 And he exercises all the authority of the first beast in his presence, and causes the earth and those who dwell in it to worship the first beast, whose deadly wound was healed. 13 He performs great signs, so that he even makes fire come down from heaven on the earth in the sight of men. 14 And he deceives those*a* who dwell on the earth by those signs which he was granted to do in the sight of the beast, telling those who dwell on the earth to make an image to the beast who was wounded by the sword and lived. 15 He was granted *power* to give breath to the image of the beast, that the image of the beast should both speak and cause as many as would not worship the image of the beast to be killed. 16 He causes all, both small and great, rich and poor, free and slave, to receive a mark on their right hand or on their foreheads, 17 and that no one may buy or sell except one who has the mark or*a* the name of the beast, or the number of his name.

18 Here is wisdom. Let him who has understanding calculate the number of the beast, for it is the number of a man: His number *is* 666.

14 Then I looked, and behold, a*a* Lamb standing on Mount Zion, and with Him one hundred *and* forty-four thousand, having*b* His Father's name written on their foreheads. 2 And I heard a voice from heaven, like the voice of many waters, and like the voice of loud thunder. And I heard the sound of harpists playing their harps. 3 They sang as it were a new song before the throne, before the four living creatures, and the elders; and no one could learn that song except the hundred *and* forty-four thousand who were redeemed from the earth. 4 These are the ones who were not defiled with women, for they are virgins. These are the ones who follow the Lamb wherever He goes. These were redeemed*a* from *among* men, *being* firstfruits to God and to the Lamb. 5 And in their mouth was found no deceit,*a* for they are without fault before the throne of God.*b*

6 Then I saw another angel flying in the midst of heaven, having the everlasting gospel to preach to those who dwell on the earth—to every nation, tribe, tongue, and people— 7 saying with a loud voice, "Fear God and give glory to Him, for the hour of His judgment has come; and worship Him who made heaven and earth, the sea and springs of water."

13:1 *a*NU-Text reads *he.*   *b*NU-Text and M-Text read *ten horns and seven heads.*   13:5 *a*M-Text reads *make war.*   13:7 *a*NU-Text and M-Text add *and people.*   13:14 *a*M-Text reads *my own people.*   13:17 *a*NU-Text and M-Text omit *or.*   14:1 *a*NU-Text and M-Text read *the.*   *b*NU-Text and M-Text add *His name and.*   14:4 *a*M-Text adds *by Jesus.*   14:5 *a*NU-Text and M-Text read *falsehood.*   *b*NU-Text and M-Text omit *before the throne of God.*

8 And another angel followed, saying, "Babylon[a] is fallen, is fallen, that great city, because she has made all nations drink of the wine of the wrath of her fornication."

9 Then a third angel followed them, saying with a loud voice, "If anyone worships the beast and his image, and receives *his* mark on his forehead or on his hand, 10 he himself shall also drink of the wine of the wrath of God, which is poured out full strength into the cup of His indignation. He shall be tormented with fire and brimstone in the presence of the holy angels and in the presence of the Lamb. 11 And the smoke of their torment ascends forever and ever; and they have no rest day or night, who worship the beast and his image, and whoever receives the mark of his name."

12 Here is the patience of the saints; here *are* those[a] who keep the commandments of God and the faith of Jesus.

13 Then I heard a voice from heaven saying to me,[a] "Write: 'Blessed *are* the dead who die in the Lord from now on.'"

"Yes," says the Spirit, "that they may rest from their labors, and their works follow them."

14 Then I looked, and behold, a white cloud, and on the cloud sat *One* like the Son of Man, having on His head a golden crown, and in His hand a sharp sickle. 15 And another angel came out of the temple, crying with a loud voice to Him who sat on the cloud, "Thrust in Your sickle and reap, for the time has come for You[a] to reap, for the harvest of the earth is ripe." 16 So He who sat on the cloud thrust in His sickle on the earth, and the earth was reaped.

17 Then another angel came out of the temple which is in heaven, he also having a sharp sickle.

18 And another angel came out from the altar, who had power over fire, and he cried with a loud cry to him who had the sharp sickle, saying, "Thrust in your sharp sickle and gather the clusters of the vine of the earth, for her grapes are fully ripe."

19 So the angel thrust his sickle into the earth and gathered the vine of the earth, and threw *it* into the great winepress of the wrath of God. 20 And the winepress was trampled outside the city, and blood came out of the winepress, up to the horses' bridles, for one thousand six hundred furlongs.

15 Then I saw another sign in heaven, great and marvelous: seven angels having the seven last plagues, for in them the wrath of God is complete.

2 And I saw *something* like a sea of glass mingled with fire, and those who have the victory over the beast, over his image and over his mark[a] *and* over the number of his name, standing on the sea of glass, having harps of God. 3 They sing the song of Moses, the servant of God, and the song of the Lamb, saying:

"Great and marvelous *are* Your
  works,
Lord God Almighty!
Just and true *are* Your
  ways,
O King of the saints![a]
4   Who shall not fear You, O
  Lord, and glorify Your
  name?
For *You* alone *are* holy.
For all nations shall come and
  worship before You,
For Your judgments have been
  manifested."

5 After these things I looked, and behold,[a] the temple of the tabernacle of the testimony in heaven was opened. 6 And out of the temple came the seven angels having the seven plagues, clothed in pure bright linen, and having their chests girded with golden bands. 7 Then one of the four living creatures gave to the seven angels seven golden bowls full of the wrath of God who lives forever and ever. 8 The temple was filled with smoke from the glory of God and from His power, and no one was able to enter the temple till the seven plagues of the seven angels were completed.

14:8 [a]NU-Text reads *Babylon the great is fallen, is fallen, which has made;* M-Text reads *Babylon the great is fallen. She has made.*   14:12 [a]NU-Text and M-Text omit *here are those.*   14:13 [a]NU-Text and M-Text omit *to me.*   14:15 [a]NU-Text and M-Text omit *for You.*   15:2 [a]NU-Text and M-Text omit *over his mark.*   15:3 [a]NU-Text and M-Text read *nations.*   15:5 [a]NU-Text and M-Text omit *behold.*

16 Then I heard a loud voice from the temple saying to the seven angels, "Go and pour out the bowls[a] of the wrath of God on the earth."

2 So the first went and poured out his bowl upon the earth, and a foul and loathsome sore came upon the men who had the mark of the beast and those who worshiped his image.

3 Then the second angel poured out his bowl on the sea, and it became blood as of a dead *man;* and every living creature in the sea died.

4 Then the third angel poured out his bowl on the rivers and springs of water, and they became blood. 5 And I heard the angel of the waters saying:

"You are righteous, O Lord,[a]
  The One who is and who was
    and who is to be,[b]
  Because You have judged these
    things.
6   For they have shed the blood
    of saints and prophets,
  And You have given them
    blood to drink.
  For[a] it is their just due."

7 And I heard another from[a] the altar saying, "Even so, Lord God Almighty, true and righteous *are* Your judgments."

8 Then the fourth angel poured out his bowl on the sun, and power was given to him to scorch men with fire. 9 And men were scorched with great heat, and they blasphemed the name of God who has power over these plagues; and they did not repent and give Him glory.

10 Then the fifth angel poured out his bowl on the throne of the beast, and his kingdom became full of darkness; and they gnawed their tongues because of the pain. 11 They blasphemed the God of heaven because of their pains and their sores, and did not repent of their deeds.

12 Then the sixth angel poured out his bowl on the great river Euphrates, and its water was dried up, so that the way of the kings from the east might be prepared. 13 And I saw three unclean spirits like frogs *coming* out of the mouth of the dragon, out of the mouth of the beast, and out of the mouth of the false prophet. 14 For they are spirits of demons, performing signs, *which* go out to the kings of the earth and[a] of the whole world, to gather them to the battle of that great day of God Almighty.

15 "Behold, I am coming as a thief. Blessed *is* he who watches, and keeps his garments, lest he walk naked and they see his shame."

16 And they gathered them together to the place called in Hebrew, Armageddon.[a]

17 Then the seventh angel poured out his bowl into the air, and a loud voice came out of the temple of heaven, from the throne, saying, "It is done!" 18 And there were noises and thunderings and lightnings; and there was a great earthquake, such a mighty and great earthquake as had not occurred since men were on the earth. 19 Now the great city was divided into three parts, and the cities of the nations fell. And great Babylon was remembered before God, to give her the cup of the wine of the fierceness of His wrath. 20 Then every island fled away, and the mountains were not found. 21 And great hail from heaven fell upon men, *each hailstone* about the weight of a talent. Men blasphemed God because of the plague of the hail, since that plague was exceedingly great.

17 Then one of the seven angels who had the seven bowls came and talked with me, saying to me,[a] "Come, I will show you the judgment of the great harlot who sits on many waters, 2 with whom the kings of the earth committed fornication, and the inhabitants of the earth were made drunk with the wine of her fornication."

3 So he carried me away in the Spirit into the wilderness. And I saw a woman sitting on a scarlet beast *which was* full of names of blasphemy, having seven heads and ten horns. 4 The woman was arrayed in purple and scarlet, and adorned with gold and precious stones and pearls, having in her hand a golden cup full

of abominations and the filthiness of her fornication.[a] 5 And on her forehead a name *was* written:

MYSTERY,
BABYLON THE GREAT,
THE MOTHER OF HARLOTS
AND OF THE ABOMINATIONS
OF THE EARTH.

6 I saw the woman, drunk with the blood of the saints and with the blood of the martyrs of Jesus. And when I saw her, I marveled with great amazement.

7 But the angel said to me, "Why did you marvel? I will tell you the mystery of the woman and of the beast that carries her, which has the seven heads and the ten horns. 8 The beast that you saw was, and is not, and will ascend out of the bottomless pit and go to perdition. And those who dwell on the earth will marvel, whose names are not written in the Book of Life from the foundation of the world, when they see the beast that was, and is not, and yet is.[a]

9 "Here *is* the mind which has wisdom: The seven heads are seven mountains on which the woman sits. 10 There are also seven kings. Five have fallen, one is, *and* the other has not yet come. And when he comes, he must continue a short time. 11 The beast that was, and is not, is himself also the eighth, and is of the seven, and is going to perdition.

12 "The ten horns which you saw are ten kings who have received no kingdom as yet, but they receive authority for one hour as kings with the beast. 13 These are of one mind, and they will give their power and authority to the beast. 14 These will make war with the Lamb, and the Lamb will overcome them, for He is Lord of lords and King of kings; and those *who are* with Him *are* called, chosen, and faithful."

15 Then he said to me, "The waters which you saw, where the harlot sits, are peoples, multitudes, nations, and tongues. 16 And the ten horns which you saw on[a] the beast, these will hate the harlot, make her desolate and

naked, eat her flesh and burn her with fire. 17 For God has put it into their hearts to fulfill His purpose, to be of one mind, and to give their kingdom to the beast, until the words of God are fulfilled. 18 And the woman whom you saw is that great city which reigns over the kings of the earth."

18 After these things I saw another angel coming down from heaven, having great authority, and the earth was illuminated with his glory. 2 And he cried mightily[a] with a loud voice, saying, "Babylon the great is fallen, is fallen, and has become a dwelling place of demons, a prison for every foul spirit, and a cage for every unclean and hated bird! 3 For all the nations have drunk of the wine of the wrath of her fornication, the kings of the earth have committed fornication with her, and the merchants of the earth have become rich through the abundance of her luxury."

4 And I heard another voice from heaven saying, "Come out of her, my people, lest you share in her sins, and lest you receive of her plagues. 5 For her sins have reached[a] to heaven, and God has remembered her iniquities. 6 Render to her just as she rendered to you,[a] and repay her double according to her works; in the cup which she has mixed, mix double for her. 7 In the measure that she glorified herself and lived luxuriously, in the same measure give her torment and sorrow; for she says in her heart, 'I sit *as* queen, and am no widow, and will not see sorrow.' 8 Therefore her plagues will come in one day—death and mourning and famine. And she will be utterly burned with fire, for strong *is* the Lord God who judges[a] her.

9 "The kings of the earth who committed fornication and lived luxuriously with her will weep and lament for her, when they see the smoke of her burning, 10 standing at a distance for fear of her torment, saying, 'Alas, alas, that great city Babylon, that mighty city! For in one hour your judgment has come.'

17:4 [a]M-Text reads *the filthiness of the fornication of the earth.*   17:8 [a]NU-Text and M-Text read *and shall be present.*   17:16 [a]NU-Text and M-Text read *saw, and the beast.*   18:2 [a]NU-Text and M-Text omit *mightily.*   18:5 [a]NU-Text and M-Text read *have been heaped up.*   18:6 [a]NU-Text and M-Text omit *to you.*   18:8 [a]NU-Text and M-Text read *has judged.*

11 "And the merchants of the earth will weep and mourn over her, for no one buys their merchandise anymore: 12 merchandise of gold and silver, precious stones and pearls, fine linen and purple, silk and scarlet, every kind of citron wood, every kind of object of ivory, every kind of object of most precious wood, bronze, iron, and marble; 13 and cinnamon and incense, fragrant oil and frankincense, wine and oil, fine flour and wheat, cattle and sheep, horses and chariots, and bodies and souls of men. 14 The fruit that your soul longed for has gone from you, and all the things which are rich and splendid have gone from you,a and you shall find them no more at all. 15 The merchants of these things, who became rich by her, will stand at a distance for fear of her torment, weeping and wailing, 16 and saying, 'Alas, alas, that great city that was clothed in fine linen, purple, and scarlet, and adorned with gold and precious stones and pearls! 17 For in one hour such great riches came to nothing.' Every shipmaster, all who travel by ship, sailors, and as many as trade on the sea, stood at a distance 18 and cried out when they saw the smoke of her burning, saying, 'What is like this great city?'

19 "They threw dust on their heads and cried out, weeping and wailing, and saying, 'Alas, alas, that great city, in which all who had ships on the sea became rich by her wealth! For in one hour she is made desolate.'

20 "Rejoice over her, O heaven, and you holy apostlesa and prophets, for God has avenged you on her!"

21 Then a mighty angel took up a stone like a great millstone and threw it into the sea, saying, "Thus with violence the great city Babylon shall be thrown down, and shall not be found anymore. 22 The sound of harpists, musicians, flutists, and trumpeters shall not be heard in you anymore. No craftsman of any craft shall be found in you anymore, and the sound of a millstone shall not be heard in you anymore. 23 The light of a lamp shall not shine in you anymore, and the voice of bridegroom and bride shall not be heard in you

anymore. For your merchants were the great men of the earth, for by your sorcery all the nations were deceived. 24 And in her was found the blood of prophets and saints, and of all who were slain on the earth."

19 After these things I hearda a loud voice of a great multitude in heaven, saying, "Alleluia! Salvation and glory and honor and power belong to the Lordb our God! 2 For true and righteous are His judgments, because He has judged the great harlot who corrupted the earth with her fornication; and He has avenged on her the blood of His servants shed by her." 3 Again they said, "Alleluia! Her smoke rises up forever and ever!" 4 And the twenty-four elders and the four living creatures fell down and worshiped God who sat on the throne, saying, "Amen! Alleluia!" 5 Then a voice came from the throne, saying, "Praise our God, all you His servants and those who fear Him, botha small and great!"

6 And I heard, as it were, the voice of a great multitude, as the sound of many waters and as the sound of mighty thunderings, saying, "Alleluia! For thea Lord God Omnipotent reigns! 7 Let us be glad and rejoice and give Him glory, for the marriage of the Lamb has come, and His wife has made herself ready." 8 And to her it was granted to be arrayed in fine linen, clean and bright, for the fine linen is the righteous acts of the saints.

9 Then he said to me, "Write: 'Blessed are those who are called to the marriage supper of the Lamb!'" And he said to me, "These are the true sayings of God." 10 And I fell at his feet to worship him. But he said to me, "See that you do not do that! I am your fellow servant, and of your brethren who have the testimony of Jesus. Worship God! For the testimony of Jesus is the spirit of prophecy."

11 Now I saw heaven opened, and behold, a white horse. And He who sat on him was called Faithful and True, and in righteousness He judges and makes war. 12 His eyes were like a flame of fire, and on His head were

18:14 aNU-Text and M-Text read been lost to you.   18:20 aNU-Text and M-Text read saints and
apostles.   19:1 aNU-Text and M-Text add something like.   bNU-Text and M-Text omit the Lord.
19:5 aNU-Text and M-Text omit both.   19:6 aNU-Text and M-Text read our.

many crowns. He had*a* a name written that no one knew except Himself. 13 He *was* clothed with a robe dipped in blood, and His name is called The Word of God. 14 And the armies in heaven, clothed in fine linen, white and clean,*a* followed Him on white horses. 15 Now out of His mouth goes a sharp*a* sword, that with it He should strike the nations. And He Himself will rule them with a rod of iron. He Himself treads the winepress of the fierceness and wrath of Almighty God. 16 And He has on *His* robe and on His thigh a name written:

KING OF KINGS
AND LORD OF LORDS.

17 Then I saw an angel standing in the sun; and he cried with a loud voice, saying to all the birds that fly in the midst of heaven, "Come and gather together for the supper of the great God,*a* 18 that you may eat the flesh of kings, the flesh of captains, the flesh of mighty men, the flesh of horses and of those who sit on them, and the flesh of all *people,* free*a* and slave, both small and great."

19 And I saw the beast, the kings of the earth, and their armies, gathered together to make war against Him who sat on the horse and against His army. 20 Then the beast was captured, and with him the false prophet who worked signs in his presence, by which he deceived those who received the mark of the beast and those who worshiped his image. These two were cast alive into the lake of fire burning with brimstone. 21 And the rest were killed with the sword which proceeded from the mouth of Him who sat on the horse. And all the birds were filled with their flesh.

20 Then I saw an angel coming down from heaven, having the key to the bottomless pit and a great chain in his hand. 2 He laid hold of the dragon, that serpent of old, who is *the* Devil and Satan, and bound him for a thousand years; 3 and he cast him into the bottomless pit, and shut him up, and set a seal on him, so that he should deceive the nations no more till the thousand years were finished. But after these things he must be released for a little while.

4 And I saw thrones, and they sat on them, and judgment was committed to them. Then *I saw* the souls of those who had been beheaded for their witness to Jesus and for the word of God, who had not worshiped the beast or his image, and had not received *his* mark on their foreheads or on their hands. And they lived and reigned with Christ for a*a* thousand years. 5 But the rest of the dead did not live again until the thousand years were finished. This *is* the first resurrection. 6 Blessed and holy *is* he who has part in the first resurrection. Over such the second death has no power, but they shall be priests of God and of Christ, and shall reign with Him a thousand years.

7 Now when the thousand years have expired, Satan will be released from his prison 8 and will go out to deceive the nations which are in the four corners of the earth, Gog and Magog, to gather them together to battle, whose number *is* as the sand of the sea. 9 They went up on the breadth of the earth and surrounded the camp of the saints and the beloved city. And fire came down from God out of heaven and devoured them. 10 The devil, who deceived them, was cast into the lake of fire and brimstone where*a* the beast and the false prophet *are.* And they will be tormented day and night forever and ever.

11 Then I saw a great white throne and Him who sat on it, from whose face the earth and the heaven fled away. And there was found no place for them. 12 And I saw the dead, small and great, standing before God,*a* and books were opened. And another book was opened, which is *the Book* of Life. And the dead were judged according to their works, by the things which were written in the books. 13 The sea gave up the dead who were in it, and Death and Hades delivered up the dead who were in them. And they were judged, each

---

19:12 *a*M-Text adds *names written, and.*   19:14 *a*NU-Text and M-Text read *pure white linen.*
19:15 *a*M-Text adds *two-edged.*   19:17 *a*NU-Text and M-Text read *the great supper of God.*
19:18 *a*NU-Text and M-Text read *both free.*   20:4 *a*M-Text reads *the.*   20:10 *a*NU-Text and M-Text add *also.*   20:12 *a*NU-Text and M-Text read *the throne.*

one according to his works. 14 Then Death and Hades were cast into the lake of fire. This is the second death.*a* 15 And anyone not found written in the Book of Life was cast into the lake of fire.

21 Now I saw a new heaven and a new earth, for the first heaven and the first earth had passed away. Also there was no more sea. 2 Then I, John,*a* saw the holy city, New Jerusalem, coming down out of heaven from God, prepared as a bride adorned for her husband. 3 And I heard a loud voice from heaven saying, "Behold, the tabernacle of God *is* with men, and He will dwell with them, and they shall be His people. God Himself will be with them *and be* their God. 4 And God will wipe away every tear from their eyes; there shall be no more death, nor sorrow, nor crying. There shall be no more pain, for the former things have passed away."

5 Then He who sat on the throne said, "Behold, I make all things new." And He said to me,*a* "Write, for these words are true and faithful."

6 And He said to me, "It is done!*a* I am the Alpha and the Omega, the Beginning and the End. I will give of the fountain of the water of life freely to him who thirsts. 7 He who overcomes shall inherit all things,*a* and I will be his God and he shall be My son. 8 But the cowardly, unbelieving,*a* abominable, murderers, sexually immoral, sorcerers, idolaters, and all liars shall have their part in the lake which burns with fire and brimstone, which is the second death."

9 Then one of the seven angels who had the seven bowls filled with the seven last plagues came to me*a* and talked with me, saying, "Come, I will show you the bride, the Lamb's wife."*b* 10 And he carried me away in the Spirit to a great and high mountain, and showed me the great city, the holy*a* Jerusalem, descending out of heaven from God, 11 having the

glory of God. Her light *was* like a most precious stone, like a jasper stone, clear as crystal. 12 Also she had a great and high wall with twelve gates, and twelve angels at the gates, and names written on them, which are *the names* of the twelve tribes of the children of Israel: 13 three gates on the east, three gates on the north, three gates on the south, and three gates on the west.

14 Now the wall of the city had twelve foundations, and on them were the names*a* of the twelve apostles of the Lamb. 15 And he who talked with me had a gold reed to measure the city, its gates, and its wall. 16 The city is laid out as a square; its length is as great as its breadth. And he measured the city with the reed: twelve thousand furlongs. Its length, breadth, and height are equal. 17 Then he measured its wall: one hundred *and* forty-four cubits, *according* to the measure of a man, that is, of an angel. 18 The construction of its wall was *of* jasper; and the city *was* pure gold, like clear glass. 19 The foundations of the wall of the city *were* adorned with all kinds of precious stones: the first foundation *was* jasper, the second sapphire, the third chalcedony, the fourth emerald, 20 the fifth sardonyx, the sixth sardius, the seventh chrysolite, the eighth beryl, the ninth topaz, the tenth chrysoprase, the eleventh jacinth, and the twelfth amethyst. 21 The twelve gates *were* twelve pearls: each individual gate was of one pearl. And the street of the city *was* pure gold, like transparent glass.

22 But I saw no temple in it, for the Lord God Almighty and the Lamb are its temple. 23 The city had no need of the sun or of the moon to shine in it,*a* for the glory*b* of God illuminated it. The Lamb *is* its light. 24 And the nations of those who are saved*a* shall walk in its light, and the kings of the earth bring their glory and honor into it.*b* 25 Its gates shall not be shut at all by day (there shall be no night there). 26 And they shall

---

20:14 *a*NU-Text and M-Text add *the lake of fire.*   21:2 *a*NU-Text and M-Text omit *John.*
21:5 *a*NU-Text and M-Text omit *to me.*   21:6 *a*M-Text omits *It is done.*   21:7 *a*M-Text reads *overcomes, I shall give him these things.*   21:8 *a*M-Text adds *and sinners.*   21:9 *a*NU-Text and M-Text omit *to me.* *b*M-Text reads *I will show you the woman, the Lamb's bride.*   21:10 *a*NU-Text and M-Text omit *the great* and read *the holy city, Jerusalem.*   21:14 *a*NU-Text and M-Text read *twelve names.*
21:23 *a*NU-Text and M-Text omit *in it.* *b*M-Text reads *the very glory.*   21:24 *a*NU-Text and M-Text omit *of those who are saved.* *b*M-Text reads *the glory and honor of the nations to Him.*

bring the glory and the honor of the nations into it.[a] 27 But there shall by no means enter it anything that defiles, or causes[a] an abomination or a lie, but only those who are written in the Lamb's Book of Life.

22 And he showed me a pure[a] river of water of life, clear as crystal, proceeding from the throne of God and of the Lamb. 2 In the middle of its street, and on either side of the river, *was* the tree of life, which bore twelve fruits, each *tree* yielding its fruit every month. The leaves of the tree *were* for the healing of the nations. 3 And there shall be no more curse, but the throne of God and of the Lamb shall be in it, and His servants shall serve Him. 4 They shall see His face, and His name *shall be* on their foreheads. 5 There shall be no night there: They need no lamp nor light of the sun, for the Lord God gives them light. And they shall reign forever and ever.

6 Then he said to me, "These words *are* faithful and true." And the Lord God of the holy[a] prophets sent His angel to show His servants the things which must shortly take place.

7 "Behold, I am coming quickly! Blessed *is* he who keeps the words of the prophecy of this book."

8 Now I, John, saw and heard[a] these things. And when I heard and saw, I fell down to worship before the feet of the angel who showed me these things.

9 Then he said to me, "See *that you do* not *do that.* For[a] I am your fellow servant, and of your brethren the prophets, and of those who keep the words of this book. Worship God."

10 And he said to me, "Do not seal the words of the prophecy of this book, for the time is at hand. 11 He who is unjust, let him be unjust still; he who is filthy, let him be filthy still; he who is righteous, let him be righteous[a] still; he who is holy, let him be holy still."

12 "And behold, I am coming quickly, and My reward *is* with Me, to give to every one according to his work. 13 I am the Alpha and the Omega, *the* Beginning and *the* End, the First and the Last."[a]

14 Blessed *are* those who do His commandments,[a] that they may have the right to the tree of life, and may enter through the gates into the city. 15 But[a] outside *are* dogs and sorcerers and sexually immoral and murderers and idolaters, and whoever loves and practices a lie.

16 "I, Jesus, have sent My angel to testify to you these things in the churches. I am the Root and the Offspring of David, the Bright and Morning Star."

17 And the Spirit and the bride say, "Come!" And let him who hears say, "Come!" And let him who thirsts come. Whoever desires, let him take the water of life freely.

18 For[a] I testify to everyone who hears the words of the prophecy of this book: If anyone adds to these things, God will add[b] to him the plagues that are written in this book; 19 and if anyone takes away from the words of the book of this prophecy, God shall take away[a] his part from the Book[b] of Life, from the holy city, and *from* the things which are written in this book.

20 He who testifies to these things says, "Surely I am coming quickly." Amen. Even so, come, Lord Jesus!

21 The grace of our Lord Jesus Christ *be* with you all.[a] Amen.

21:26 [a]M-Text adds *that they may enter in.* 21:27 [a]NU-Text and M-Text read *anything profane, nor one who causes.* 22:1 [a]NU-Text and M-Text omit *pure.* 22:6 [a]NU-Text and M-Text read *spirits of the prophets.* 22:8 [a]NU-Text and M-Text read *am the one who heard and saw.* 22:9 [a]NU-Text and M-Text omit *For.* 22:11 [a]NU-Text and M-Text read *do right.* 22:13 [a]NU-Text and M-Text read *the First and the Last, the Beginning and the End.* 22:14 [a]NU-Text reads *wash their robes.* 22:15 [a]NU-Text and M-Text omit *But.* 22:18 [a]NU-Text and M-Text omit *For.* [b]M-Text reads *may God add.* 22:19 [a]M-Text reads *may God take away.* [b]NU-Text and M-Text read *tree of life.* 22:21 [a]NU-Text reads *with all;* M-Text reads *with all the saints.*

Special Helps

The Greatest Possibility Thinker
Who Ever Lived

The Greatest Possibility Thinker
Who Ever Lived

Impossibility Thinking

You know what that is?
It's the kind of thinking that says:
"It's impossible!"
"It won't work."
"It'll never happen."
"I haven't got what it takes."
"Why bother to try?"
So
JESUS should have been
the world's greatest impossibility
thinker
For He had *nothing* going for Him.

JESUS was

a member of a despised minority,
a citizen of an occupied country,
a nobody as far as the Romans were
concerned,
a joke to the occupying power,
a nuisance to His fellow Jews.

JESUS lived among an oppressed,
cynical, and
embittered people!

Taxes were oppressive.
Freedom was unknown.
Survival was uncertain.
Religion was restrictive, negative,
and joyless.

Yet Jesus never made an inflammatory
speech, never organized a guerilla
force, and never led a march on
Jerusalem or Rome.

JESUS inherited no illustrious name.

His father was a common laborer.
His mother was a simple, homespun
type.
His uncles and aunts; who were they?
His grandparents? Nobodies!

He could never point with pride to a
prestigious address. Rather
He came from a city reputed to be
culturally deprived and morally
corrupt.
"Can anything good come out of
Nazareth?"
was a common expression.

JESUS was uneducated.
Whatever His schooling was, it was
simple. The only account of His writing
was a note He scribbled in the sand.
He had
No academic degrees,
No certificates of special merit,
award or achievement:
No trophies or medals;
And He never received an honorary
doctorate of divinity degree!

JESUS lived and died untraveled. He
never visited the exciting, glamorous
world outside His own country. He saw
none of the sights so important to the
secular world of His day. Like

The glistening temples of Athens:
with the Parthenon on the acropolis
holding the golden statue of Athena;

The Greatest Possibility Thinker

or
Rome—with its impressive forum,
colosseum, and theatres: or
The marble, pillar-lined streets of
Alexandria.
Or the spectacular city of Ephesus!

All He saw was people: lonely, hurting,
sick, depressed, fearful, troubled hearts!
It made Him cry!

JESUS never became an intimate friend
of men of power and influence.

He had no "big connections"—V.I.P.'s
did not seek Him out. Had He ever
been asked for letters of character
reference—who could He list? No
peer professors; famous authors;
powerful politicians; ranking
generals; or lordly churchmen.

He couldn't have been a
name-dropper if He wanted to!
(Except to say—as He did—that He
and God were very close.)

JESUS had no organization.

His followers were men with

broken speech,
rough hands, and
cracked fingernails.

They were
unpolished, uncultured,
unlettered, and ignorant failures,

In many ways, and in critical times,
they proved to be
unstable,
uncertain,
undependable, and
disappointing.

Yes,
JESUS knew

ingratitude,
rejection,
misunderstanding, and
betrayal!

JESUS—by all the psychological laws of
human development, should have lived
and died a

judgmental,
frustrated,
critical,
angry,
unbelieving,
cynical,
rebellious,
violence-prone,
emotionally-deprived,
radically militant revolutionary!

JESUS lived and died in poverty. He had:

No home of His own,
No insurance policy,
No Social Security card,
No retirement plan:
He performed a miracle to raise the
money to pay His taxes!

His estate? He left behind only one
simple robe, a cheap prize to entice
the gambling soldiers at the cross.

So He died empty-handed—except
for fresh wounds—leaving no fortune
and no heirs.

JESUS remained unmarried,
a single adult
all His life.

So He spent His years without the
encouragement,

1528

comfort, or
companionship
of a wife or children.

In a society where children were a
man's greatest treasure, He died
never having fathered a single son or
daughter.

So He died.
Childless.

JESUS
Think of it: At His death

He was only thirty-three years
old!
He was so young.
He died before His mother!
He was not given a half-century,
or more, to make His mark,
write His books, build His
empire, and conquer the world.

This—at least and at last—should
have made Him a
cynical impossibility thinker, crying
out through tight
lips, and bitter tears:

"It isn't fair!"
"I'm too young to die!"
"Others live long and
longer—why can't I?"
"O God—give me more time!"

JESUS—
Where was His Heavenly Father
when Jesus needed Him most?

JESUS—
All His life He was good, kind, and
loving, and very religious.
Every Sabbath—He was in the
synagogue.
The Holy Scriptures—how He loved
to read them.

Prayer? His life was a prayer for all
seasons!

JESUS—
How He loved His Heavenly Father.
How He trusted His Heavenly Father.
How He served His Heavenly Father.

JESUS—
Now on His cross—when He needs
His God most—
God seems to have abandoned Him.

This man, Jesus, turned out to be

THE WORLD'S GREATEST
POSSIBILITY THINKER!

No founder of any religion ever used the
word *possible* more than Jesus did!

"For with God all things are possible"
(Mark 10:27).

"The things which are impossible with
men are possible with God" (Luke
18:27).

"All things *are* possible to him who
believes" (Mark 9:23).

"Father, all things *are* possible" (Mark
14:36).

"If you have faith as a mustard seed, you
will say to this mountain, 'Move . . .' and
nothing will be impossible" (Matt.
17:20).

"With God nothing will be impossible"
(Luke 1:37).

"With men *it is* impossible, but not with
God" (Mark 10:27).

"With God all things are possible" (Matt.
19:26).

1529

The Greatest Possibility Thinker

To **JESUS**

Every problem was a possibility in disguise.

Sickness—was an opportunity for healing.
Sin—was an opportunity for forgiveness.
Sorrow—was an opportunity for compassion.

Personal abuse was an opportunity to leave a good impression and show the world how possibility thinkers react!

To **JESUS**

Every person was a gold mine of undiscovered hidden possibilities!

Peter? A tough-talking fisherman:
    But—he could make a great
    leader of a great new church.
Mary Magdalene? A common prostitute:
    But—she could become a
    sensitive, sweet soul. She could
    one day anoint His body for
    burial.
Matthew? A vulgar materialist:
    But—he had possibilities to
    become a great writer! Even the
    gospel!

No wonder Jesus rushed to meet the outcast, riff-raff of humanity!

To **JESUS**

The important fact about you and me
    is not that
    WE ARE SINNERS
    But that
    WE CAN BE SAINTS.

So Jesus never called any person a sinner! He became angry only with religious people who made people feel they were miserable, guilty sinners.

Instead Jesus rushed to build—in the worst of sinners—a belief that they, too, could be saved for inspiring service!

So
JESUS proclaimed the greatest possibility:

The immeasurable

MERCY
OF
GOD

To **JESUS**

the whole world was
    jammed,
    pregnant,
    loaded,
    bulging, with
        untapped,
        undiscovered,
        undetected

POSSIBILITIES!

JESUS really believed in the
    supreme possibilities!

Jesus preached these grand possibilities:

Man *can* be born again!
Character *can* be changed!
You *can* become a new person!
Life *can* be beautiful!
There *is* a solution to every problem!
There *is* a light behind every shadow!

Yes,
JESUS had an unshakeable faith in these ultimate possibilities:

God exists!
Life goes on beyond death!
Heaven is for real!

He was prepared to prove it:
by dying—and rising again!

He saw the possibility of
ultimate justice!
So
He had as much to say about hell as
He did about heaven.

JESUS
Saw the possibility of heaven and hell
in eternity.
He also saw the possibility of a transformed world—
here on planet earth.
He was impressed by what the world
could become—
never depressed by what the world
was.
He truly believed in the possibility of
transformed lives.
He truly believed that common people can become
uncommonly powerful.
He knew without a shadow of doubt
that ordinary persons
could become extraordinary persons
if they could
become possibility thinkers.

So He would give self-confidence to
inferiority-complexed people.
He would make it possible for guilt-
infected, failure-plagued, problem-
swamped persons to start loving
themselves and stop hating themselves!

What enormous self-confidence this great
Possibility Thinker had! Listen to what
Christ said:

"I am the good shepherd" (John
10:11).

"I am the door. If anyone enters by
Me, he will be saved" (John 10:9).

"I am the bread of life" (John 6:35).

"I am the vine, you *are* the branches.
He who abides in Me, and I in him,
bears much fruit" (John 15:5).

"I am the way, the truth, and the life.
No one comes to the Father, except
through Me" (John 14:6).

"I am the resurrection and the life.
He who believes in Me, though he
may die, he shall live" (John 11:25).

Then came the end. He was accused of
stirring up the people. He was placed on
trial. He was charged with blasphemy.
Did He not claim to be the promised
Messiah? At least, did He not allow
people to get the impression that He was
the Son of God? In His public trial He was
challenged to deny His deity, to withdraw
His blasphemous statements, and clear up
the confused minds of the simple people
who believed Him to be God visiting
earth in human form.

But He could not tell a lie, so He
remained silent. The verdict was
predictable: death by crucifixion! A
crowd gathered to see how a possibility
thinker dies. How did He die? He died
seeing and seizing the possibilities of the
moment! He practiced what He had
preached all His life! He turned the hell
into a heaven.

For here was His chance to save the soul
of a lost thief who was being crucified
beside Him.

This was a spectacular opportunity to
dramatically teach all men of all ages to
come that death can be a grand reunion
with God!

The Greatest Possibility Thinker

So His last spoken words were loaded with great expectations. "Father, into Your hands I commend My spirit" (Luke 23:46).

There was a final gasp—and He was gone. The Roman commander in charge of the execution turned away—converted on the spot, he was overheard saying, "Certainly this was a righteous Man!" (Luke 23:47).

The body was taken down and sealed in a tomb. Then it happened! Easter! He was resurrected. He came back to life again.

Why do we believe this fantastic tale? Because of the incredible change in His followers. They saw Him alive again. Where they were cowards, they became fearless proclaimers in the city streets—in daylight! Where they were impossibility thinkers—they became possibility thinkers!

Think Now About Your Personal Possibilities

Today, twenty centuries later, Christ literally lives in millions of human beings all around the world! By His death He solved His greatest problem. What was that? He could only be in one place at a time. Now, through the power of His Holy Spirit, He is able to live in millions of lives all around this world! Think of the possibilities:

> **Christ can infiltrate**
> **any race,**
> **any religion,**
> **any community,**
> **any country!**

THE GOOD NEWS IS— CHRIST CAN LIVE IN— EVEN YOU

That is what it is all about!

BEING A CHRISTIAN IS offering yourself to Him

Your mind—for Christ to think through,
Your heart—for Christ to love through,
Your lips—for Christ to speak through,
Your hands—for Christ to touch through!

Just imagine what possibilities for exciting living this opens up to you!

If Christ can live within you then it is possible for you, too,

> To—Turn your problems into opportunities!
> To—Tackle your opportunities and succeed!
> To—Dream great dreams and make them come true!
> To—Switch from jealousy and self-pity to really caring about others who are much worse off than you are.
> To—Pick up the broken hopes and start over again!
> To—See great possibilities in those unattractive people!
> To—Become a truly beautiful person—like Jesus!

Your Prayer for a New and Exciting Life

Jesus Christ—I've come to see that many things are possible that I never before believed were possible.

I believe it's possible—that You were sent by God into the world to be my Savior. I accept You now.

I believe it's possible—eternal life!

I believe it's possible—that Christ is alive this moment and trying to penetrate my life through my brain as I read these words!

I believe it's possible—for His Holy Spirit to live within me! I confess my sin. I ask Christ to save me. I invite Him to come into my life. I believe it's possible!

Amen.

Now pray this Possibility-Thinking Prayer every day:

**Lord, show me the person
You want to speak to
through my life today.**

Amen.

The Life of the Greatest Possibility Thinker

*J*esus of Nazareth was undoubtedly the greatest possibility thinker who ever lived. Ever since His world-changing life, death and resurrection, people have told and retold the wonderful drama of the things He did and the possibilities to which His life pointed us. The Bible records four of those stories. The accounts of Jesus' life found in the Bible were written by people who had intimate knowledge of what He did and what He said. The miracle of these accounts is that each gives us a slightly different perspective of Jesus in only one or two dimensions, or paint Him only in shades of one color. But with all four gospel accounts, we see a full-dimensioned possibility thinker. With all four accounts we see the personality of a man resplendently painted in all colors of the palette.

In the following pages you will find an outline of the four-fold drama of Jesus' life as recorded in the Gospels of Matthew, Mark, Luke and John. Look closely at those parts of the story told only by one of the biblical writers. Then compare those parts of the drama told by two or more of the writers.

Then, on page 1545 you will find a list of the greatest stories Jesus told to people who came to Him. Also, you will find on page 1546 a list of the greatest miracles Jesus performed. Become acquainted with the wonderful story of Jesus, the Greatest Possibility Thinker Who Ever Lived. Discover the great possibilities God has planned for you, too!

Jesus' Life in Four Dramas

Date	Event	Location	Matthew	Mark	Luke	John
INTRODUCTIONS TO JESUS CHRIST						
	(1) Luke's Introduction				1:1–4	
	(2) Pre-Fleshly State of Christ					1:1–18
	(3) Genealogy of Jesus Christ		1:1–17		3:23–38	
BIRTH, INFANCY, AND ADOLESCENCE OF JESUS AND JOHN THE BAPTIST						
7 B.C.	(1) Announcement of Birth of John	Jerusalem (Temple)			1:5–25	
7 or 6 B.C.	(2) Announcement of Birth of Jesus to the Virgin	Nazareth			1:26–38	
c. 5 B.C.	(3) Song of Elizabeth to Mary	Hill Country of Judea			1:39–45	
	(4) Mary's Song of Praise				1:46–56	
5 B.C.	(5) Birth, Infancy, and Purpose for Future of John the Baptist	Judea			1:57–80	
	(6) Announcement of Jesus' Birth to Joseph	Nazareth	1:18–25			
5–4 B.C.	(7) Birth of Jesus Christ	Bethlehem	1:24, 25		2:1–7	
	(8) Proclamation by the Angels	Near Bethlehem			2:8–14	
	(9) The Visit of Homage by Shepherds	Bethlehem			2:15–20	
	(10) Jesus' Circumcision	Bethlehem			2:21	
4 B.C.	(11) First Temple Visit with Acknowledgments by Simeon and Anna	Jerusalem			2:22–38	
	(12) Visit of the Wise Men	Jerusalem & Bethlehem	2:1–12			
	(13) Flight into Egypt and Massacre of Innocents	Bethlehem, Jerusalem & Egypt	2:13–18			
	(14) From Egypt to Nazareth with Jesus		2:19–23		2:39	
Afterward	(15) Childhood of Jesus	Nazareth			2:40, 51	
A.D. 7–8	(16) Jesus, 12 Years Old, Visits the Temple	Jerusalem			2:41–50	
Afterward	(17) 18-Year Account of Jesus' Adolescence and Adulthood	Nazareth			2:51, 52	
TRUTHS ABOUT JOHN THE BAPTIST						
C. A.D. 25–27	(1) John's Ministry Begins	Judean Wilderness	3:1	1:1–4	3:1, 2	1:19–28

Jesus' Life in Four Dramas

Date	Event	Location	Matthew	Mark	Luke	John
C. A.D. 25–27	(2) Man and Message (3) His Picture of Jesus (4) His Courage		3:2–12 3:11, 12 14:4–12	1:2–8 1:7, 8	3:3–14 3:15–18 3:19, 20	 1:26, 27
BEGINNING OF JESUS' MINISTRY						
C. A.D. 27	(1) Jesus Baptized (2) Jesus Tempted (3) Calls First Disciples (4) The First Miracle (5) First Stay in Capernaum	Jordan River Wilderness Beyond Jordan Cana in Galilee (Capernaum is "His" city)	3:13–17 4:1–11	1:9–11 1:12, 13	3:21–23 4:1–13	1:29–34 1:35–51 2:1–11 2:12
A.D. 27	(6) First Cleansing of the Temple (7) Received at Jerusalem (8) Teaches Nicode- mus About Sec- ond Birth (9) Co-Ministry with John (10) Leaves for Galilee (11) Samaritan Woman at Jacob's Well (12) Returns to Galilee	Jerusalem Judea Judea Judea Judea Samaria	 4:12	 1:14 1:15	 4:14 4:15	2:13–22 2:23–25 3:1–21 3:22–30 4:1–4 4:5–42 4:43–45
THE GALILEAN MINISTRY OF JESUS						
A.D. 27–29						
A.D. 27	(1) Healing of the Nobleman's Son (2) Rejected at Nazareth (3) Moved to Capernaum (4) Four Become Fishers of Men (5) Demoniac Healed on the Sabbath Day (6) Peter's Mother-in- Law Cured, Plus Others	Cana Nazareth Capernaum Sea of Galilee Capernaum Capernaum	 4:13–17 4:18–22 8:14–17	 1:16–20 1:21–28 1:29–34	 4:16–30 5:1–11 4:31–37 4:38–41	4:46–54
C. A.D. 27	(7) First Preaching Tour of Galilee (8) Leper Healed and Response Re- corded (9) Paralytic Healed (10) Matthew's Call and Reception Held (11) Disciples Defended via a Parable	Galilee Galilee Capernaum Capernaum Capernaum	4:23–25 8:1–4 9:1–8 9:9–13 9:14–17	1:35–39 1:40–45 2:1–12 2:13–17 2:18–22	4:42–44 5:12–16 5:17–26 5:27–32 5:33–39	
A.D. 28	(12) Goes to Jerusa- lem for Second Passover; Heals Lame Man	Jerusalem				5:1–47

Date	Event	Location	Matthew	Mark	Luke	John
A.D. 28	(13) Plucked Grain Precipitates Sabbath Controversy	En Route to Galilee	12:1–8	2:23–28	6:1–5	
	(14) Withered Hand Healed Causes Another Sabbath Controversy	Galilee	12:9–14	3:1–6	6:6–11	
	(15) Multitudes Healed	Sea of Galilee	12:15–21	3:7–12	6:17–19	
	(16) Twelve Apostles Selected After a Night of Prayer	Near Capernaum		3:13–19	6:12–16	
	(17) Sermon on the Mt.	Near Capernaum	5:1—7:29		6:20–49	
	(18) Centurion's Servant Healed	Capernaum	8:5–13		7:1–10	
	(19) Raises Widow's Son from Dead	Nain			7:11–17	
	(20) Jesus Allays John's Doubts	Galilee	11:2–19		7:18–35	
	(21) Woes Upon the Privileged		11:20–30			
	(22) A Sinful Woman Anoints Jesus	Simon's House, Capernaum			7:36–50	
	(23) Another Tour of Galilee	Galilee			8:1–3	
	(24) Jesus Accused of Blasphemy	Capernaum	12:22–37	3:20–30	11:14–23	
	(25) Jesus' Answer to a Demand for a Sign	Capernaum	12:38–45		11:24–26, 29–36	
	(26) Mother, Brothers Seek Audience	Capernaum	12:46–50	3:31–35	8:19–21	
	(27) Famous Parables of Sower, Seed, Tares, Mustard Seed, Leaven, Treasure, Pearl, Dragnet, Lamp Told	By Sea of Galilee	13:1–52	4:1–34	8:4–18	
	(28) Sea Made Serene	Sea of Galilee	8:23–27	4:35–41	8:22–25	
	(29) Gadarene Demoniac Healed	E. Shore of Galilee	8:28–34	5:1–20	8:26–39	
	(30) Jairus's Daughter Raised and Woman with Hemorrhage Healed		9:18–26	5:21–43	8:40–56	
	(31) Two Blind Men's Sight Restored		9:27–31			
	(32) Mute Demoniac Healed		9:32–34			
	(33) Nazareth's Second Rejection of Christ	Nazareth	13:53–58	6:1–6		
	(34) Twelve Sent Out		9:35—11:1	6:7–13	9:1–6	
	(35) Fearful Herod Beheads John	Galilee	14:1–12	6:14–29	9:7–9	
Spring A.D. 29	(36) Return of 12, Jesus Withdraws, 5000 Fed	Near Bethsaida	14:13–21	6:30–44	9:10–17	6:1–14
	(37) Walks on the Water	Sea of Galilee	14:22–33	6:45–52		6:15–21

Jesus' Life in Four Dramas

Date	Event	Location	Matthew	Mark	Luke	John
Spring A.D. 29	(38) Sick of Gennesaret Healed	Gennesaret	14:34–36	6:53–56		
	(39) Peak of Popularity Passes in Galilee	Capernaum				6:22–71; 7:1
A.D. 29	(40) Traditions Attacked		15:1–20	7:1–23		
	(41) Aborted Retirement in Phoenicia: Syro-Phoenician Healed	Phoenicia	15:21–28	7:24–30		
	(42) Afflicted Healed	Decapolis	15:29–31	7:31–37		
	(43) 4000 Fed	Decapolis	15:32–39	8:1–9		
	(44) Pharisees Increase Attack	Magdala	16:1–4	8:10–13		
	(45) Disciples' Carelessness Condemned; Blind Man Healed		16:5–12	8:14–26		
	(46) Peter Confesses Jesus Is the Christ	Near Caesarea Philippi	16:13–20	8:27–30	9:18–21	
	(47) Jesus Foretells His Death	Caesarea Philippi	16:21–26	8:31–38	9:22–25	
	(48) Kingdom Promised		16:27, 28	9:1	9:26, 27	
	(49) The Transfiguration	Mountain Unnamed	17:1–13	9:2–13	9:28–36	
	(50) Epileptic Healed	Mt. of Transfiguration	17:14–21	9:14–29	9:37–42	
	(51) Again Tells of Death, Resurrection	Galilee	17:22, 23	9:30–32	9:43–45	
	(52) Taxes Paid	Capernaum	17:24–27			
	(53) Disciples Contend About Greatness; Jesus Defines; also Patience, Loyalty, Forgiveness	Capernaum	18:1–35	9:33–50	9:46–62	
	(54) Jesus Rejects Brothers' Advice	Galilee				7:2–9
c. Sept. A.D. 29	(55) Galilee Departure and Samaritan Rejection		19:1		9:51–56	7:10
	(56) Cost of Discipleship		8:18–22		9:57–62	

LAST JUDEAN AND PEREAN MINISTRY OF JESUS

Date	Event	Location	Matthew	Mark	Luke	John
A.D. 29–30						
Oct. A.D. 29	(1) Feast of Tabernacles	Jerusalem				7:2, 10–52
	(2) Forgiveness of Adulteress	Jerusalem				7:53— 8:11
A.D. 29	(3) Christ—the Light of the World	Jerusalem				8:12–20
	(4) Pharisees Can't Meet the Prophecy; Thus Try to Destroy the Prophet	Jerusalem—Temple				8:21–59

Date	Event	Location	Matthew	Mark	Luke	John
A.D. 29	(5) Man Born Blind Healed; Following Consequences	Jerusalem				9:1–41
	(6) Parable of the Good Shepherd	Jerusalem				10:1–21
	(7) The Service of the Seventy	{ Probably Judea			10:1–24	
	(8) Lawyer Hears the Story of the Good Samaritan	Judea (?)			10:25–37	
	(9) The Hospitality of Martha and Mary	Bethany			10:38–42	
	(10) Another Lesson on Prayer	Judea (?)			11:1–13	
	(11) Accused of Connection with Beelzebub				11:14–36	
	(12) Judgment Against Lawyers and Pharisees				11:37–54	
	(13) Jesus Deals with Hypocrisy, Covetousness, Worry, and Alertness				12:1–59	
	(14) Repent or Perish				13:1–5	
	(15) Barren Fig Tree				13:6–9	
	(16) Crippled Woman Healed on Sabbath				13:10–17	
	(17) Parables of Mustard Seed and Leaven	{ Probably Perea			13:18–21	
Winter A.D. 29	(18) Feast of Dedication	Jerusalem				10:22–39
	(19) Withdrawal Beyond Jordan					10:40–42
	(20) Begins Teaching Return to Jerusalem with Special Words About Herod	Perea			13:22–35	
	(21) Meal with a Pharisee Ruler Occasions Healing Man with Dropsy; Parables of Ox, Best Places, and Great Supper				14:1–24	
	(22) Demands of Discipleship	Perea			14:25–35	
	(23) Parables of Lost Sheep, Coin, Son				15:1–32	
	(24) Parables of Unjust Steward, Rich Man and Lazarus				16:1–31	
	(25) Lessons on Service, Faith, Influence				17:1–10	
	(26) Resurrection of Lazarus	{ Perea to Bethany				11:1–44
	(27) Reaction to It: Withdrawal of Jesus					11:45–54

Jesus' Life in Four Dramas

Date	Event	Location	Matthew	Mark	Luke	John
A.D. 30	(28) Begins Last Journey to Jerusalem via Samaria & Galilee	{ Samaria, Galilee			17:11	
	(29) Heals Ten Lepers				17:12–19	
	(30) Lessons on the Coming Kingdom				17:20–37	
	(31) Parables: Persistent Widow, Pharisee and Tax Collector				18:1–14	
	(32) Doctrine on Divorce		19:1–12	10:1–12		
	(33) Jesus Blesses Children: Objections	Perea	19:13–15	10:13–16	18:15–17	
	(34) Rich Young Ruler	Perea	19:16–30	10:17–31	18:18–30	
	(35) Laborers of the 11th Hour		20:1–16			
	(36) Foretells Death and Resurrection	{ Near Jordan	20:17–19	10:32–34	18:31–34	
	(37) Ambition of James and John		20:20–28	10:35–45		
	(38) Blind Bartimaeus Healed	Jericho		10:46–52	18:35–43	
	(39) Interview with Zacchaeus	Jericho			19:1–10	
	(40) Parable: the Minas	Jericho			19:11–27	
	(41) Returns to Home of Mary and Martha	Bethany				{ 11:55—12:1
	(42) Plot to Kill Lazarus	Bethany				12:9–11

JESUS' FINAL WEEK OF WORK AT JERUSALEM

Date	Event	Location	Matthew	Mark	Luke	John
Spring A.D. 30						
Sunday	(1) Triumphal Entry	Bethany, Jerusalem, Bethany	21:1–9	11:1–11	19:28–44	12:12–19
Monday	(2) Fig Tree Cursed and Temple Cleansed	{ Bethany to Jerusalem	21:10–19	11:12–18	19:45–48	
	(3) The Attraction of Sacrifice	Jerusalem				12:20–50
Tuesday	(4) Withered Fig Tree Testifies	{ Bethany to Jerusalem	21:20–22	11:19–26		
	(5) Sanhedrin Challenges Jesus. Answered by Parables: Two Sons, Wicked Vinedressers and Marriage Feast	Jerusalem	{ 21:23—22:14	{ 11:27—12:12	20:1–19	
	(6) Tribute to Caesar	Jerusalem	22:15–22	12:13–17	20:20–26	
	(7) Sadducees Question the Resurrection	Jerusalem	22:23–33	12:18–27	20:27–40	

1542

Date	Event	Location	Matthew	Mark	Luke	John
Tuesday	(8) Pharisees Question Commandments	Jerusalem	22:34–40	12:28–34		
	(9) Jesus and David	Jerusalem	22:41–46	12:35–37	20:41–44	
	(10) Jesus' Last Sermon	Jerusalem	23:1–39	12:38–40	20:45–47	
	(11) Widow's Mite	Jerusalem		12:41–44	21:1–4	
	(12) Jesus Tells of the Future	Mt. of Olives	24:1–51	13:1–37	21:5–36	
	(13) Parables: Ten Virgins, Talents, The Day of Judgment	Mt. of Olives	25:1–46			
	(14) Jesus Tells Date of Crucifixion		26:1–5	14:1, 2	22:1, 2	
	(15) Anointing by Mary at Simon's Feast	Bethany	26:6–13	14:3–9		12:2–8
	(16) Judas Contracts the Betrayal		26:14–16	14:10, 11	22:3–6	
Thursday	(17) Preparation for the Passover	Jerusalem	26:17–19	14:12–16	22:7–13	
Thursday P.M.	(18) Passover Eaten, Jealousy Rebuked	Jerusalem	26:20	14:17	{ 22:14–16, 24–30	
	(19) Feet Washed	Upper Room				13:1–20
	(20) Judas Revealed, Defects	Upper Room	26:21–25	14:18–21	22:21–23	13:21–30
	(21) Jesus Warns About Further Desertion; Cries of Loyalty	Upper Room	26:31–35	14:27–31	22:31–38	13:31–38
	(22) Institution of the Lord's Supper	Upper Room	26:26–29	14:22–25	22:17–20	
	(23) Last Speech to the Apostles and Intercessory Prayer	Jerusalem				{ 14:1— 17:26
Thursday-Friday	(24) The Grief of Gethsemane	Mt. of Olives	{ 26:30, 36–46	{ 14:26, 32–42	22:39–46	18:1
Friday	(25) Betrayal, Arrest, Desertion	Gethsemane	26:47–56	14:43–52	22:47–53	18:2–12
	(26) First Examined by Annas	Jerusalem				{ 18:12–14, 19–23
	(27) Trial by Caiaphas and Council; Following Indignities	Jerusalem	{ 26:57, 59–68	{ 14:53, 55–65	{ 22:54, 63–65	18:24
	(28) Peter's Triple Denial	Jerusalem	{ 26:58, 69–75	{ 14:54, 66–72	22:54–62	{ 18:15–18, 25–27
	(29) Condemnation by the Council	Jerusalem	27:1	15:1	22:66–71	
	(30) Suicide of Judas	Jerusalem	27:3–10			
	(31) First Appearance Before Pilate	Jerusalem	{ 27:2, 11–14	15:1–5	23:1–7	18:28–38
	(32) Jesus Before Herod	Jerusalem			23:6–12	
	(33) Second Appearance Before Pilate	Jerusalem	27:15–26	15:6–15	23:13–25	{ 18:39— 19:16
	(34) Mockery by Roman Soldiers	Jerusalem	27:27–30	15:16–19		
	(35) Led to Golgotha	Jerusalem	27:31–34	15:20–23	23:26–33	19:16, 17
	(36) 6 Events of First 3 Hours on Cross	Calvary	27:35–44	15:24–32	23:33–43	19:18–27

Jesus' Life in Four Dramas

Date	Event	Location	Matthew	Mark	Luke	John
Friday	(37) Last 3 Hours on Cross	Calvary	27:45–50	15:33–37	23:44–46	19:28–30
	(38) Events Attending Jesus' Death		27:51–56	15:38–41	{ 23:45, 47–49	
	(39) Burial of Jesus	Jerusalem	27:57–60	15:42–46	23:50–54	19:31–42
Friday-	(40) Tomb Sealed	Jerusalem	27:61–66		23:55, 56	
Saturday	(41) Women Watch	Jerusalem		15:47		

THE RESURRECTION THROUGH THE ASCENSION

Date	Event	Location	Matthew	Mark	Luke	John
A.D. 30						
Dawn of First Day (Sunday, "Lord's Day")	(1) Women Visit the Tomb	Near Jerusalem	28:1–10	16:1–8	24:1–11	
	(2) Peter and John See the Empty Tomb				24:12	20:1–10
	(3) Jesus' Appearance to Mary Magdalene	Jerusalem		16:9–11		20:11–18
	(4) Jesus' Appearance to the Other Women	Jerusalem	28:9, 10			
	(5) Guards' Report of the Resurrection		28:11–15			
Sunday Afternoon	(6) Jesus' Appearance to Two Disciples on Way to Emmaus			16:12, 13	24:13–35	
Late Sunday	(7) Jesus' Appearance to Ten Disciples Without Thomas	Jerusalem			24:36–43	20:19–25
One Week Later	(8) Appearance to Disciples with Thomas	Jerusalem				20:26–31
During 40 Days until Ascension	(9) Jesus' Appearance to Seven Disciples by Sea of Galilee	Galilee				21:1–25
	(10) Great Commission		28:16–20	16:14–18	24:44–49	
	(11) The Ascension	Mt. Olivet		16:19, 20	24:50–53	

The Stories Jesus Told

PARABLE	MATTHEW	MARK	LUKE
1. Lamp Under a Basket	5:14–16	4:21, 22	8:16, 17 11:33–36
2. A Wise Man Builds on Rock and a Foolish Man Builds on Sand	7:24–27		6:47–49
3. Unshrunk (New) Cloth on an Old Garment	9:16	2:21	5:36
4. New Wine in Old Wineskins	9:17	2:22	5:37, 38
5. The Sower	13:3–23	4:2–20	8:4–15
6. The Tares (Weeds)	13:24–30		
7. The Mustard Seed	13:31, 32	4:30–32	13:18, 19
8. The Leaven	13:33		13:20, 21
9. The Hidden Treasure	13:44		
10. The Pearl of Great Price	13:45, 46		
11. The Dragnet	13:47–50		
12. The Lost Sheep	18:12–14		15:3–7
13. The Unforgiving Servant	18:23–35		
14. The Workers in the Vineyard	20:1–16		
15. The Two Sons	21:28–32		
16. The Wicked Vinedressers	21:33–45	12:1–12	20:9–19
17. The Wedding Feast	22:2–14		
18. The Fig Tree	24:32–44	13:28–32	21:29–33
19. The Wise and Foolish Virgins	25:1–13		
20. The Talents	25:14–30		
21. The Growing Seed		4:26–29	
22. The Absent Householder		13:33–37	
23. The Creditor and Two Debtors			7:41–43
24. The Good Samaritan			10:30–37
25. A Friend in Need			11:5–13
26. The Rich Fool			12:16–21
27. The Faithful Servant and the Evil Servant			12:35–40
28. Faithful and Wise Steward			12:42–48
29. The Barren Fig Tree			13:6–9
30. The Great Supper			14:16–24
31. Building a Tower and a King Making War			14:25–35
32. The Lost Coin			15:8–10
33. The Lost Son			15:11–32
34. The Unjust Steward			16:1–13
35. The Rich Man and Lazarus			16:19–31
36. Unprofitable Servants			17:7–10
37. The Persistent Widow			18:1–8
38. The Pharisee and the Tax Collector			18:9–14
39. The Minas (Pounds)			19:11–27

The Miracles Jesus Performed

MIRACLE	MATTHEW	MARK	LUKE	JOHN
1. Cleansing a Leper	8:2	1:40	5:12	
2. Healing a Centurion's Servant (of paralysis)	8:5		7:1	
3. Healing Peter's Mother-in-law	8:14	1:30	4:38	
4. Healing the Sick at Evening	8:16	1:32	4:40	
5. Stilling the Storm	8:23	4:35	8:22	
6. Demons Entering a Herd of Swine	8:28	5:1	8:26	
7. Healing a Paralytic	9:2	2:3	5:18	
8. Raising the Ruler's Daughter	9:18, 23	5:22, 35	8:40, 49	
9. Healing the Hemorrhaging Woman	9:20	5:25	8:43	
10. Healing Two Blind Men	9:27			
11. Curing a Demon-possessed, Mute Man	9:32			
12. Healing a Man's Withered Hand	12:9	3:1	6:6	
13. Curing a Demon-possessed, Blind and Mute Man	12:22		11:14	
14. Feeding the Five Thousand	14:13	6:30	9:10	6:1
15. Walking on the Sea	14:25	6:48		6:19
16. Healing the Gentile Woman's Daughter	15:21	7:24		
17. Feeding the Four Thousand	15:32	8:1		
18. Healing the Epileptic Boy	17:14	9:17	9:38	
19. Temple Tax in the Fish's Mouth	17:24			
20. Healing Two Blind Men	20:30	10:46	18:35	
21. Withering the Fig Tree	21:18	11:12		
22. Casting Out an Unclean Spirit		1:23	4:33	
23. Healing a Deaf Mute		7:31		
24. Healing a Blind Paralytic at Bethsaida		8:22		
25. Escape from the Hostile Multitude			4:30	
26. Draught of Fish			5:1	
27. Raising of a Widow's Son at Nain			7:11	
28. Healing the Infirm, Bent Woman			13:11	
29. Healing the Man with Dropsy			14:1	
30. Cleansing the Ten Lepers			17:11	
31. Restoring a Servant's Ear			22:51	
32. Turning Water into Wine				2:1
33. Healing the Nobleman's Son (of fever)				4:46
34. Healing an Infirm Man at Bethesda				5:1
35. Healing the Man Born Blind				9:1
36. Raising of Lazarus				11:43
37. Second Draught of Fish				21:1

Prayers for Positive Faith

Morning Affirmation

The sky is bright, my Father, with the morning light. Always after night there is a new day. Always after winter there is a springtime. Always after the seed is dropped in the soil to die, new life springs forth. Always after the tough times, there comes the recovery. Always, my Father, when a penitent, contrite heart bows in repentance before you, there comes the joy of fresh pardon. And so now, my Father, I come, expecting good things to happen, for I have stepped into the circle of Your love, and I find mercy and Your peace here. Strength is coming like a warm rain driven by warm winds. Healing is coming through the living Christ. Thank You, Father. Amen.

Thank You, Lord, that You have come to give us affirmation as persons, salvation as sinners, to turn us into the potential people of being a part of this world's solution, messengers of real love. Thank You, Jesus Christ, I accept You as my Savior. I accept You for all the forgiveness that I need. I embrace Your holy cross, and by the sacrifice of Your precious life, I have been made clean. What can wash away my sin? Nothing but the blood of Jesus. Amen.

Morning Meditation

Thank You, Father, that the dawning has come. The sun is shining. The birds are singing and the flowers are blooming. Clouds are sliding silently through the soundless sea of space, and there is a Spirit that is moving in my mind and heart now. You are here and I am waiting. Bless me, O Father, in the name of Christ. Amen.

A Prayer for Inner Peace

You will keep him in perfect peace whose mind is stayed on You, O Lord. My face changes when I focus on Christ. My heart changes when I focus on Christ. My mind changes when I focus on His cross. Jesus Christ, I really remember You, I really love You, and now I want to show it by saying, Jesus Christ come into my life, save me from my sin, cleanse me from my negative thinking, fill me with Your positive thoughts, fill me with Your Holy Spirit, and may we walk together through the best years of my life. Amen.

A Prayer for Support

O Lord my God, my rock upon whom I build my dreams.
I come to You today to feel again Your mighty strength.

As the foundation of a great building silently supports its beautiful burden.

So may I feel You carry me and my dreams along
in Your supportive arms of love.

And as the fortress gallantly protects a vulnerable city from deadly assaults, so
wrap me in Your protective arms of love, so that I may feel Your
protection.

As the granite landmarks remain immovable in the midst of the shifting sands,
so I fix my eyes on You, my unchanging point of reference—when I
become confused and lost in the maze of today's values.

And so, Lord, I build my dreams on Your love—my solid Rock.

And I ask for Your protection on my dream from the negative assaults
that come my way.

I look to You for guidance, lest my dreams lose their true direction which is
toward You and Your glory.

Thank You for hearing my prayer, for sending me Jesus, my Friend,
my Lord, and my Rock.

A Perfect Friend

Thank You, Jesus, when I am lonely, You give me love.
When I am guilty, You grant me forgiveness.
When I doubt, You give faith.
When I have a searching mind and heart, You give direction.
When I feel empty, You fill me with joy.
God, You never fail me. You are here now. Your are born within me now.
You are saving me by Your grace. It will be a joyous day. Amen.

A New Dawn

O Lord, it is good to sing praises to You in the morning.
To consider Your guidance during the day, and to remember
      Your faithfulness at sunset.

As each day dawns with new opportunities and unexpected surprises,
      I am grateful for the gift of fresh beginnings.
And as I pursue the dreams You send my way, I am conscious
      of Your ever-present guiding hand.

When I become confused, I can feel You gently lead.
When I tire, You carry me along.
When I stumble and fall, You pick me up.

And so as I journey to the end of my day, I rejoice and am eternally grateful
      to You for the difference You have made.
Without You my life would be empty, dark, and broken.
But instead You have come bringing life, light, and healing.
And so I thank You and praise You! Amen.

The Lord's Prayer

I sense an inner strength surging within me now.
I sense an inner joy breaking forth all around me.
I feel Your loving presence as I focus my prayers
      for _____ before You,
      the loving and eternal God of us all.
Teach us to pray, as Your Son taught, saying . . .

"Our Father in heaven,
Hallowed be Your name.
Your kingdom come.
Your will be done
On earth as *it is* in heaven.
Give us this day our daily bread.
And forgive us our debts,
As we forgive our debtors.
And do not lead us into temptation,
But deliver us from the evil one.
For Yours is the kingdom and the power
      and the glory forever. Amen."

Mountains to Climb

Our Father, I come to You today to bless Your Holy Name.
You are great and You are loving.
Send me Your peace, Your presence, and Your courage.

For I find myself with tall mountains to climb, rough roads to trod, deep valleys
    to forge, and vast oceans to bridge.

As people in days of old knelt to be knighted before their king, so I bend my
    knee before You, O King of Kings and Lord of Lords.

May I feel Your tap on my shoulder, Your healing touch in my life. And when I
    arise may I stand taller and stronger than ever before.

For I know that there is no mountain too tall to climb, no ocean too vast to
    bridge, no race too long to run, and no world too large to overcome
    with the help of Your powerful and mighty hand.

I thank You, O Lord, for making all these things possible through Jesus Christ,
    Your Son. Amen.

A Prayer of Dependence

Dear Lord, I come to You in much the same way that sheep return to their
    shepherd.
I have been stubborn in the past and have wandered from Your care.
I have become confused and lost my way.
And I have run into thorns that have cut deep.
But now, I run with my arms open wide to You.
For as a shepherd protects his sheep, so You lift me, O Lord, in Your protective
    arms above the overwhelming times of life.
And as a shepherd guides his sheep, so You sustain me with the words of life
    in Your book, the Bible.
And as a shepherd loves his sheep, so I feel Your forgiving hand of love heal the
    hurts within my heart today.

Thank You, gentle Shepherd.
I will love and praise You forevermore.

New Possibilities

O Lord, I praise You this morning and sing songs of joy because of the peace,
the love, and the hope that You have given me.

I look expectantly to the new dreams You want me to dream, the new goals
You want me to reach, and the new mountains You want me to climb.

As I scale the mountain trail, I pray that You will refresh me with unexpected
meadows along the way, that You will shelter me when I am beset
by storms. And that You will give me the grace to look for the gold mines
in the detours.

I have within me the capacity to be a gem, a jewel, and a light
to those who are struggling around me.
So help me, Lord, to discover the possibilities that You have put
in each new day.
Help me to see the face that needs Your smile, open my ears to the cries
of our hurting world, and give me the courage to touch the lives
that so desperately need You.

I praise You, I love You, and I trust You, O Lord,
my strength and my Redeemer. Amen.

Choose Life

O Lord, my God, whose power and might is stronger than anything
I might ever face.
I know that You are watching me in every step I take, leading me toward
the abundant life You have planned for me.

Today, as every day, I am faced with decisions.

I must choose. Will I respond negatively or positively to the ideas
You will bring my way?

Will I align myself with loneliness or brighten someone's day?

Will I look anxiously toward tomorrow with fear, or will I place my life
in Your care and face my future with hope?

Prayers for Positive Faith

O Lord, I am so grateful for the gift of choice. I have the ability to choose.

And with Your help and guidance,
I can choose happiness,
I can choose joy,
I can choose love,
I can choose life.

And so I praise You and thank You through whose mercy
and grace my life is full.

Because of You I can live and love abundantly.

Thank You, Lord.

A Prayer for a New Day

Dear Heavenly Father:
Thank You for the new day that awaits me today,
And for the new possibilities that
You have put into my tomorrows.

I rejoice this morning in the knowledge that with the nights come new days,
With the winter comes the spring, and
With the Cross comes the Resurrection.

Just as the buds of green leaves appear on dry, barren trees,
As the tender sprouts push their way through the stubborn soil, so, O Lord,
may I feel the creativity You have planted within me push its way
through my barren times,
To bloom into a beautiful, new idea, a fresh concept, and an unexpected
opportunity.

Just as the shafts of sunshine send their bright, warm rays across the empty
black night, so, O Lord, this morning send positive thoughts into my
mind to erase the negative influences that have blinded me.
Thank You, Lord, for new days and for new life.

The Presence of God

Thank You, Father, for the light that surrounds me, for
     the hope that surges into me, for
     the love that controls my mood.
I am experiencing Your presence. Praise be to You, O God.
I worship You, the Eternal Source of all Life.

I thank You for the joy I have in knowing You as my personal Lord and Savior.
I thank You that I know what it is like to have You in the center of my being.
I pray that You will fill my heart right now with a warmth that will spread
     throughout my body and that I will feel Your Holy Spirit penetrating
     and moving throughout me, giving me a direction and an aim and a goal
     in life.
O Lord, I pray that in this hour You will inspire me and motivate me and give
     me the drive to be Your voice in my world.

This I pray in Your Son's name. Amen.

A Prayer for New Hope

O Father, I look around me to see the beautiful world
     which You have given me.

The majestic mountains, the restful blue skies, and the towering trees
     are all the handiwork of Your greatness.

As the wistful breezes stir the air, so, O Lord, stir my heart and fill my life
     with Your loving Spirit.

Reach down and touch my life with Yours.
For with Your special touch, O Lord, I am changed.

I gain new hope, when all around I see despair.
I receive new faith, when struggles and hurts are great.
I am bathed in Your peace, when tensions and worries abound.
And bright ideas come, when all possibilities seem lost.

So it is no wonder that I am glad that I come with praise and thankfulness.
For I know that Your goodness will never end.

I rejoice in the assurance that even now You are leading me into new
and challenging possibilities.

Hear me now as I pray. Amen.

A Prayer for the Church

Thank You, Father, that You have created a church,
a collection of human beings,
ecclesia, the called-out people,
those people who have accepted Christ
as Savior and Lord
and now offer themselves—bodies,
minds, and souls.

Through the Holy Spirit,
these, Your family,
carry out Christ's love and caring
in an alienated lonely world.
Thank You, Father.

May Your blessings rest upon each minister
and each lay person in their duties.

Strengthen the work of the church
that the world may discover
that there is another life they never tasted.
The life and the love of Jesus
who can save us from our shame,
our sins,
our unbelief,
our scepticism,
our cynicism,
and can fill us with emotional power
of health and wholeness.

Thank You, God, for the church,
a place where we offer ourselves as volunteers
in this the work of God,
an opportunity and a challenge
to find our place
to be minds through
which Christ can think,
hands through which Christ can lift,
faces through which He can smile,
voices through which He can talk and sing,
examples through which others can be led in the Way.

Grace, mercy, and God's peace
be with you, my fellow ministers
of Christ's church.

May the doors of Your church always be open wide
to all who wish to come—from the mountains,
from the seashore, from the roadside,
from homes and hotels.

May they be open to all—
the lovely and unlovely,
the deserted, the lonely,
the doubting, and the believing.

May the doors of Your church, O God,
be always a gateway to joyful
and abundant living.

The door by which all—young and old,
rich and poor, may enter into
a relationship with Jesus Christ
as Lord and Savior.

An Intimate Prayer

Dear God, as I reach out to grasp the hand of a friend, or a stranger,
Even so now, O God, I reach out to You.

You are there, reaching out to me, You reach out—out of the sky, out of the
    heavens, out of the Scriptures, You reach out from the cross—
Because You want to give me new life.

O God, thank You for what You can do, for what You are doing, and for what
    You are waiting anxiously to do in me.
Move in and show me the treasures that are waiting to be discovered in me—
Treasures of health and physical fitness,
Prosperity instead of poverty, joy instead of despair, love instead of loneliness.

I thank You, Lord, that my impossibilities are Your opportunities.

O God, hear me as I reach out with my struggling, faltering, stumbling,
    clumsy faith.
Help me to trust these moments of faith and to doubt my doubts in Your name,
    my Lord.

God's Goodness

O Lord, my God, my Guide and Friend, it is good to sing praises to You
    and to remember Your faithfulness and steadfast love.

I am reminded that as the sun rises every morning and as the waves roll in
    unceasingly, so Your love is just as unending.

Friendships come and go,
opportunities ebb and flow,
but Your love and care for me is as constant as the seasons
    and as endless as the heavens.
For that, O Lord, I am forever grateful.

No matter how confused I may become,
no matter how lost I may seem to be,
I can run to Your loving arms, there to regain my bearings and set out again,
for I want to feel Your love, so I can in turn love.
I want to be upheld by Your strength, and in turn strengthen.
I want to be renewed by Your grace and then go and glow for You.

Hear my prayer this morning, O Lord, and grant unto me Your peace. Amen.

Tune into God's Thoughts

Thank You, Father, that my mind is designed to pick up Your thoughts and that my heart has been created to welcome the feeling of love, Your Spirit within.

Thank You, Father, that I can in this time of prayer, have the freedom to reach out and let the thoughts that are in me come out. Touch them, bless them, and ordain them to become the seeds of better living. Grace, mercy, and God's peace is with You now. Amen.

Thank You, Lord, that You have called me to develop the potential and the possibility that is built into every one of Your children and that includes me. Release, O God, within me the attitude, "I can do it, with the help of God." Let it begin with me now.

Jesus Christ, I want to thank You, that You have come to be my Savior, my Lord, my Best Friend. Thank You for walking with me and talking with me.

Thank You for the joy we share as we walk in prayer. Father, whisper in my ear to give me a dream for today, a dream that makes life wonderful and eternity exciting. Amen.

Renewal

Thank You, Father, for bringing me to a path that leads to light, for causing me to see the spark and to follow it, for tuning my ear to hear the still, small voice of the Spirit and to listen.

Thank You, God, for the good things that are happening deep within my spirit at this moment. Thank You, Jesus Christ, that You have not forgotten me, even when I have forgotten You. And now we are together.

Father, thank You for Jesus Christ, my beautiful Lord and Savior, who came to forgive me of my sins. By His incarnation He has honored me, by His crucifixion, He has placed a value on my soul, by His resurrection, He has taken early retirement and given me His good job, spreading love around.

Jesus Christ, You are the Great Repairer of the breach; You are the restorer of paths to dwell in, and You have called me to carry on in Your good name. Give me this day the strength to do it well. Amen.

A Prayer for Healing

Jesus Christ, You are alive. You have given me the Good News. Life is abundant, and now life is eternal to those who know You and that includes me. "God so loved the world that He gave His only begotten Son, that whoever believes in Him should not perish but have everlasting life."

You have promised it, Lord. "I am the resurrection and the life. He who believes in Me, though he may die, he shall live." You have promised that if I have faith as the grain of a mustard seed, I can say to my mountain, "move" and nothing will be impossible. Jesus Christ, look at me. You know who I am. You know where I come from. You know what problems I carry in my heart, and my mind, and in my physical, organic body.

O Lord, you know a lot more about me than I do. A lot more about me than any doctor, any psychiatrist, or any counselor knows.

O God, give me the gift of faith. I receive this gift, and I feel a warm glow. Your faith is flowing from my mind, across my face, across my lips, down my neck, and through my body. I am feeling the healing presence of the God of all eternity. In the name of my Lord, I praise You, and I thank You, Jesus Christ. Amen.

For Others in Need

I thank You, Father, for the blessings that are being poured into my life with
  every passing moment in this time of prayer.

I sense that my mind is being cleansed of negative thoughts, my soul is being
  purged and washed clean, and my heart is being filled with love, peace,
  joy, hope, and faith.

O God, many around me today and this past week have traveled over rough
  roads; others have traveled through low valleys of pain and trouble; still
  others are climbing steep mountains. Through laughter and tears we work
  and live together in Your world. For each of these, my brothers and
  sisters—Your children, I pray today.

Some have had exciting awards and others crushing blows, and so I pray the
  prayer with the psalmist,

Every morning I shall praise Him for His kindness, every evening I shall
  rejoice in all His faithfulness.

I remember especially . . .

_____

_____

_____

(Use for names of others to pray for today).

To Give Something Back

Lord, thank You for what You have given to me, and Lord, help me to give
something back. Let me go out today and try to lift up those who are really
hurting. Dear Jesus, I thank You that You have taught me that God loves me.
Do something wonderful in my life, Lord, not for my sake, but for the sake of
people who are hungry and lost. Amen.

A Prayer for Tough Times

Thank You, Father, that I am surrounded by light. There are no gloomy corners
in Your presence. The sun filters through the clouds and no shadow can ever
turn the starlight off.

Thank You, Father, that after winter comes spring, after death comes a new
resurrection, and so I wait for the rock to crack and for the flower to
open into blossom today through my faith in You.

I experience Your grace, mercy, and peace now. I do not understand it, so I
rejoice in experiencing it. Amen.

A Prayer of Thanksgiving

I come to You now with so much to thank You for.
As your child I want to shout for joy and sing Your praises for all You have done
 for me.

Thank You for these moments when I withdraw from the world's pressures and
 anxieties into a quiet place where the sun is shining and the green trees
 are bending against blue skies, the flowers are blooming, the grass is
 green, and the water is clean.

There is a fresh fragrance in the air and I sense it is the presence of my God
 whose love and peace is filling my life now.

Father, give me now the courage to step into life with new drive and motivation.
Help me to channel the creative ideas You give me into beautiful life-changing
 goals.
Give me the strength to hold on to hope as I meet the many challenges
 throughout the day.

And Lord, give me love as I share with others all the things You have
 done in my life.
So I may say with integrity to those I meet,
"God loves you and so do I." Amen.

The Blessings of Christmas

O loving Father, as the joy of morning bursts through the sky,
So I come before You bringing songs of joy and praise.
I rejoice in the Good News of the birth of Your Son, knowing that my heart
    will take wings as it is filled with the love of Christmas.

With the birth of Christ in my life, I receive the gift of love in my heart.
And as the star of hope brought light to a dark world that night,
So illuminate all negative thoughts within me with the bright light of faith.

For as Christmas captured God's dream of bringing me back to Him, so now
    crystalize my courage so I can dream new dreams and sight new stars.
And with the Christ child as my north star, I look expectantly to a New Year,
Knowing that Your Spirit will shine in splendor in my life.

Christmas Prayer

O Father, as the burst of an infant's cry penetrated a dark, silent night,

So may Your love fill my life this morning with the joy of Christmastime.

For that Child, Your Son, has brought a star of hope and a prism of peace
    into a world needing a guiding light.

Now I come to thank You and join the angels in singing,
"Glory to God in the highest."

For with the birth of Your Son, my own life is reborn, giving me

Peace, even in the midst of turbulence,
Hope, despite despair,
Joy, in place of sorrow, and
Love, to overcome all strife and tensions.

So now, I gratefully receive Your gift of Your Son, the Christmas Child,
    and I celebrate with carols of song and praise. Amen.

A Prayer of Commitment

What a beautiful thing You can do, O God, in a human being. You are able to take a manger and turn it into a cradle of a king. And You can come and live inside a man, a woman, or a child sometimes cracked, chipped, splintered, battered, and as rough as a manger and transform them into beautiful creations.

Thank You for what You will do in my life now, for I kneel before You and welcome You in, Lord Jesus. When I rise from my kneeling prayer, may I stand taller than I ever have before and face the sun knowing that God is my Friend, into all eternity. I ask this prayer in the name of my Savior who taught us to pray together saying, Our Father . . . .

O God, I feel that this is a moment of great decision for many people. I am so thankful, Father, that we have the opportunities to change our minds. O God, the innkeeper did not have a second chance, we do. I want to thank You now, O Lord, that You want to live within us, You want to build us up, You want to save our immortal souls for heaven. O God, thank You. Amen.

A Prayer of Blessing

And now may the Lord bless you and keep you.
May the Lord make His face to shine upon you
and be gracious unto you,
and may God give to you His peace
in your going out
and in your coming in,
in your lying down
and in your rising up,
in your labor and in your leisure,
in your laughter and in your tears,
until you come to stand before Jesus
in that day in which there is no
sunset and no dawning. Amen.

Positive Verses for Possibility Thinking

Positive Verses for Possibility Thinking

*T*he Bible is filled with positive motivational verses to enable you to live a happy and fulfilled life. This unique key to these verses will help you to unlock the power of God's truth. It includes modern words that describe your world. Whether you are feeling anxious or ambitious, concerned or confident, stressful or successful, this possibility thinker's index will lead you to the verse that meets your needs.

Acceptance—John 5:24; 6:51; 2 Cor. 6:2

Accomplishment—Matt. 7:17; Gal. 6:9; Col. 3:17

Action—Deut. 1:21; Matt. 25:36, 40; John 14:12

Affection—John 13:34; Rom. 12:10; 1 Thess. 2:8

Analyzation—Josh. 24:15; John 7:17

Anxiety—Matt. 6:25, 34; Rom. 8:28; Phil. 4:6; 1 Pet. 5:6, 7

Application—Prov. 2:2; John 15:14

Aspiration—Matt. 5:6; 6:21; Phil. 3:12; 1 Thess. 4:11

Assurance—Heb. 12:5–11

Attainment—John 14:14; 3 John 2

Attitude—Matt. 5:16, 44; John 14:15; Rom. 12:16; Phil. 2:5

Beauty—Ps. 149:4; Zech. 9:16, 17; Rom. 10:15

Beginning—John 1:1–3; Col. 3:10

Belief—Matt. 8:2, 13; 16:13, 16; 21:22; Rom. 10:10, 11; 2 Cor. 4:13

Beneficial—Ps. 1:1–3; John 15:7; 1 Thess. 5:15

Benevolence—Acts 20:35

Blessed—Rev. 1:3

Celebration—Neh. 8:10–12; Esth. 9:19

Challenge—Deut. 1:21

Change—Matt. 18:3; 1 Cor. 15:51; 2 Cor. 5:17

Cheerfulness—Jas. 5:13

Cleansing—2 Cor. 7:1; Eph. 5:25–27; 1 John 1:7, 9

Contentment—1 Tim. 6:8

Comfort—Matt. 5:4; 2 Cor. 1:4; 2 Thess. 2:16, 17

Commission—Matt. 10:16; John 20:21; Acts 1:8

Commitment—Matt. 10:22; 1 Cor. 9:24; Luke 9:23

Completion—Job 5:26; 2 Tim. 4:6–8

Concentration—Matt. 7:7, 8; John 9:4; Rom. 15:20; 1 Cor. 9:24; Phil. 3:14

Confidence—Matt. 10:32; 16:18; Eph. 6:14–18; Phil. 1:6; 4:13

Courage—Deut. 31:6; 1 Cor. 16:13

Creation—Gen. 5:1; Matt. 12:35; 2 Cor. 5:17

Death—Matt. 4:16; 16:28; John 11:25; 1 Cor. 15:22, 26; 2 Tim. 1:10

Decision—Deut. 30:19; Prov. 16:33

Delight—Job 33:26; 1 Cor. 1:31

Deliverance—Prov. 21:31

Dependence—Ex. 13:21; Deut. 7:9; 2 Cor. 3:5; 1 Thess. 5:24

Depression—Prov. 12:25

Design—Ps. 8:1; Eph. 4:16

Desire—Matt. 6:20, 33; 13:44–46; Luke 9:23; Rom. 14:19; Phil. 4:6

Development—Ps. 1:1–3; Mark 4:8; 1 Cor.13:11, 12

Dignity—Phil. 1:27; Col. 1:10

Discipline—1 Thess. 5:14; 2 Tim. 2:3–5

Doubt—Matt. 14:31; 2 Cor. 5:7

Edification—1 Cor. 8:1

Education—Deut. 6:6, 7; Matt. 5:19; 28:20; Col. 1:28

Encouragement—1 Sam. 23:16, 17; 1 Cor. 1:4–7; Col. 3:16

Endurance—Matt. 24:13; 1 Cor. 4:12; 2 Cor. 4:8, 9; 2 Tim. 2:12

Enjoyment—Ps. 4:7; 16:9

Enthusiasm—Ex. 15:2; 1 Thess. 2:13; 3:9

Esteem—Rom. 13:9; Phil. 2:3; 1 Tim. 4:4

Examination—Ps. 26:2; 2 Cor. 13:5

Example—Matt. 20:26–28; Rom. 10:17; 2 Cor. 3:18; 1 Tim. 4:12

Excellence—Ps.8:1; 2 Cor. 4:7

Experience—Rom. 15:13; Eph. 1:18, 19

Positive Verses

Failure—Job 10:12; 42:10

Faith—Matt. 9:29; 17:20; Rom. 10:17; 12:3, 2 Cor. 5:7; Gal. 3:11

Faithfulness—Rev. 2:10

Fear—Matt. 10:28; 17:7; Mark 5:36; 6:50

Fellowship—Acts 2:42

Focus—Phil. 4:8

Follower—Matt. 4:19; 16:24; Mark 1:17; 8:34

Forgiveness—Matt. 6:12, 14; Mark 2:5; Rom. 12:14; Eph. 1:7; Col. 3:13

Foundation—Ps. 1:3; 2 Cor. 1:21, 22; Col. 2:7; 1 Thess. 3:13; 1 Pet. 5:10

Fulfillment—Matt. 5:17, 18

Future—Matt. 6:30, 34; Rom. 8:28

Gain—Deut. 28:11; Mark 8:36; Phil. 3:7; 1 Tim. 6:6

Gift—Luke 11:11–13; 1 Tim. 4:14; James 1:17

Glory—2 Cor. 4:17; 1 Thess. 2:12

Good Deeds—Prov. 3:27; Gal. 6:9; Phil. 2:4

Goodness—Rom. 2:4

Grace—Deut. 7:6–9; John 1:14, 17; Rom. 3:24

Gratitude—Ps. 7:17; 1 Thess. 2:13

Greatness—Matt. 5:19; 20:26; 23:11; Eph. 1:19

Grief—Job 9:27; Ps. 3:4; 4:1; 6:2; John 16:20, 22

Growth—Deut. 32:11; Mark 4:32

Guidance—Ps. 77:20

Healing—Rev. 22:2

Heart—1 Sam. 16:7; Matt. 5:8; 6:21; Luke 6:45

Honesty—Lev. 19:35; Prov. 12:22

Honor—Ex. 20:12; Deut. 5:16; John 12:26; Eph. 6:2, 3; Col. 3:24

Hope—Rom. 5:5; 8:25; 12:12; 1 Cor. 9:10

Humility—2 Chr. 7:14; Matt. 18:4; 23:12; James 4:10

Hunger—Matt. 5:6; 6:11, 25, 26; John 6:35

Ideal—Gen. 1:27; Matt. 26:39; 1 Tim. 1:17; 3:16

Identity—Phil. 3:21; Col. 2:10; 1 John 3:1

Inheritance—Eph. 1:11

Imagination—Ps. 2:8; John 14:12–14

Implementation—Matt. 7:24, 25; Luke 11:28

Impossibility—Matt. 19:26; Mark 10:27; Luke 18:27

Improvement—1 Chr. 28:9; Eph. 3:19

Increase—1 Cor. 3:6, 7; 1 Thess. 3:12, 13; 4:10

Influence—1 Tim. 4:12; 2 Tim. 2:2

Intercession—Rom. 8:26, 27, 34; 1 Tim. 2:5; Heb. 9:15; James 5:16

Investment—Matt. 13:12, 23; 25:29; 2 Cor. 9:6

Involvement—Gen. 14:14–16; Luke 10:33–35

Joy—Ps. 9:1, 2; Luke 2:10, 11; John 15:11; Col. 1:11

Judgment—Ps. 7:8; 9:4, 8; Rom. 14:13

Justification—Rom. 3:30; Gal. 3:8

Keep (on)—2 Cor. 4:8, 9; Phil. 1:6

Keep (up)—Gal. 6:9

Kindness—Ps. 117:2; Gal. 6:9, 10; Col. 3:12

Kingdom—Rev. 11:15

Knowledge—Rom. 11:33; 1 Cor. 12:8; Col. 1:9

Labor—John 4:36; 5:17; 1 Cor. 15:58; 1 Thess. 1:3; 2:9

Laughter—Gen. 21:6; Eccl. 3:1, 4

Leadership—John 4:42; 8:12; Rom. 14:9; Col. 1:16, 17

Learning—Prov. 1:7–9; Matt. 11:29

Liberty—John 5:24; 8:32, 36; 2 Cor. 3:17; Gal. 5:13

Limitless—Matt. 21:21; Mark 9:23; 11:23; Eph. 3:20

Longsuffering—Eph. 4:1, 2

Loss—Mark 8:36; Luke 15:8, 9

Love—1 Cor. 13:4–8, 13; Col. 3:14; 1 Thess. 3:12; 1 Tim. 1:5; 1 John 3:18, 23; 4:7, 8

Maintenance—Gal. 6:9; 1 Thess. 1:3; Titus 3:8

Majesty—Job 37:22

Maturity—Matt. 20:26; 1 Cor. 13:11, 12; Phil. 1:27; Col. 2:6, 7

Measurement—Deut. 25:15; Rom. 12:3

Meditation—Ps. 19:14; 119:97; Jer. 32:17

Mercy—Eph. 1:7; 2:8; Jude 2

Might—2 Cor. 4:7; Eph. 1:19

Motivation—Col. 1:10; 2 Pet. 3:14; 1 John 4:19

Need—Nah. 1:7; Heb. 4:16; 1 Pet. 5:7

Negative—Job 2:10; Hab. 3:17, 18; 1 Pet. 3:10, 11

Newness—Rom. 7:6

Nurturing—1 Thess. 2:7, 8; Col. 2:6, 7

Obedience—Col. 3:20; 1 John 5:3

Oneness—Matt. 19:6; Rom. 14:8; 1 Cor. 6:15, 19, 20; 12:12; John 17:21–23

Opinion—2 Tim. 2:25

Opportunity—2 Cor. 6:2; Gal. 6:10

Pardon—Rom. 12:14; Eph. 1:7; 1 John 1:9

Patience—Rom. 12:12; James 1:3, 4; 5:8

Peace—Rom. 12:18; 14:19; Eph. 2:14; Phil. 4:7

Perception—Rom. 10:17

Perfection—Phil. 3:12; Col. 1:28

Perseverance—2 Cor. 4:8; Gal. 6:9; Phil. 4:13

Persistence—Luke 18:1; 1 Tim. 6:12

Plan—Prov. 16:9; 21:5

Positive—1 Thess. 2:12; 5:15

Power—Mic. 3:8

Praise—Rev. 19:5

Preparation—Eph. 6:14–18; 2 Tim. 2:21

Promise—Eph. 3:20; 1 Pet. 1:3, 4; 2 Pet. 1:4

Prudence—Prov. 1:2–4

Purity—1 Thess. 4:7; 2 Tim. 2:22

Purpose—Rom. 14:7, 8; 15:20; 2 Cor. 5:9; Col. 3:23

Pursuit—1 Cor. 14:1; Phil. 3:12–14; 1 Thess. 5:15; 1 Tim. 6:11

Put Aside—1 Cor. 13:11; Phil. 3:13

Qualification—Col. 1:12

Quality—2 Tim. 2:15; 1 Pet. 5:10

Quest—Col. 3:2; 1 Pet. 3:11

Question—Jer. 33:3; Phil. 4:6; 1 John 5:14, 15

Quiet—Is. 30:15; 1 Thess. 4:11; 1 Tim. 2:1, 2

Quitting—Phil. 4:13

Race—1 Cor. 9:24, 26; Phil. 2:16

Radiance—Matt. 5:16; 2 Cor. 4:6; Phil. 2:15

Reaching Out—Phil. 3:12–14

Readiness—Acts 17:11

Reality—Eccl. 1:10; John 14:2

Receive—1 Cor. 15:3; 1 Thess. 2:13

Reconciliation—Col. 1:19, 20

Redemption—Heb. 9:12

Rejoice—Ps. 118:24; Rom. 12:15; 1 Thess. 5:16–18; 1 Pet. 1:8

Reliance—2 Chr. 13:18; Is. 50:10; 1 Thess. 5:24

Renewal—Rom. 12:2; 2 Cor. 4:16; Eph. 4:23, 24

Representative—2 Cor. 2:14; 3:18

Request—Phil. 4:6; Col. 4:2

Rest—Jer. 6:16

Restoration—Jer. 30:17

Results—Rom. 5:3, 4; Gal. 6:8–10

Revival—Ps. 85:6; 119:25; Is. 57:15

Reward—1 Cor. 9:25; Phil. 3:14; Col. 3:10; James 1:12

Salvation—John 3:16; 1 Tim. 2:4; 1 John 1:9; 5:13

Sanctuary—Ez. 11:16

Satisfaction—Ps. 17:15; 91:16; 105:40; John 4:14

See—John 1:50; 9:25

Security—Ps. 94:22

Self-esteem—1 Cor. 6:20; Eph. 2:10; Phil. 3:21; Col. 2:10; 1 Tim. 4:4

Service—Eph. 6:5–7

Skepticism—Luke 1:18, 19; John 20:27–29

Speech—2 Cor. 4:13; Col. 4:6

Starting Point—2 Cor. 5:7

Steadfastness—1 Cor. 15:58; Phil. 2:16; 1 Tim. 6:12; Rev. 3:11

Strength—Jer. 1:18; 2 Cor. 12:9, 10; Col. 1:10, 11; 2 Tim. 2:1

Stress—2 Cor. 4:8, 9, 17

Success—2 Cor. 3:5; Phil. 1:6; 3:14

Support—Rom. 12:10, 13–15; 1 John 3:16

Sureness—2 Tim. 1:12; Heb. 3:6; 1 John 2:28

Talent—Rom. 14:12; 1 Tim. 4:14

Test—Ps. 17:3; James 1:2–4; 1 Pet. 1:6, 7

Thanksgiving—Ps. 100:4; 2 Cor. 9:15; Heb. 13:15

Tough Times—Phil. 4:6; 2 Thess. 3:3; 2 Tim. 1:7; 2:3

Transformation—2 Cor. 3:18; Col. 3:4

Transition—Ps. 103:26; Is. 40:31

Treasures—Matt. 13:52

Trial—James 1:2–4; 1 Pet. 1:6, 7

Triumph—1 Cor. 10:13; 15:57

Trust—Ps. 40:4; Eph. 1:13

Positive Verses

Truth—1 Cor. 13:6; Eph. 4:21; 1 John 3:18

Try—Phil. 2:16; 3:12-14

Uncertainty—Job 19:25, 26; John 14:1-3; 1 John 2:26, 27

Understanding—Prov. 8:9; Phil. 4:7; Col. 2:2; 1 John 5:20

Unemployed—Ps. 37:5; Prov. 16:9; Jer. 29:11, 12; Rom. 8:28

Unfolding—Col. 2:3

Unity—Gen. 2:24; Mark 10:9; 1 Cor. 12:4-7, 12

Unknown—Jer. 29:11; 33:3

Uplift—Is. 40:31; Jer. 29:12

Useful—Rom. 12:1; 2 Tim. 2:21

Validity—1 Cor. 15:3-8; 1 John 5:6, 7

Value—Luke 12:7, 24; Phil. 3:21

Venture—Num. 13:30; Matt. 25:16, 17, 20-23

Victory—Eph. 3:20; 1 John 2:14; 4:4; 5:4, 5

Vision—Jer. 33:3; Eph. 1:18

Watchfulness—1 Cor. 16:13; Eph. 6:18; 2 Tim. 4:5

Weakness—Rom. 8:26; 2 Cor. 12:9, 10; 13:4; Heb. 4:15

Weary—Is. 40:31; Gal. 6:9; 2 Thess. 3:13

Weeping—Is. 65:19

Winning—1 Cor. 9:24; 2 Tim. 4:7

Wisdom—Prov. 2:6, 7; Eph. 3:19; Col. 1:9; James 3:17

Witness—Matt. 24:14; Acts 1:8; 22:15

Work—1 Cor. 9:10; Phil. 2:13; Col. 1:10; 1 Tim. 5:18

Yearning—Song 5:4; Is. 63:15

Yielding—1 John 2:6

Youth—Eccl. 11:9; Jer. 1:7, 8; 1 Tim. 4:12

Zeal—1 Cor. 9:16-21; 2 Cor. 9:2

Concordance

CONCORDANCE

This Concordance is designed to help you locate important occurrences of significant words, phrases, and proper names found in the Bible. Words and phrases are referenced with Scripture quotations, in which the first letter of the word or phrase, italicized, stands for the entire word or phrase. Phrases are cross-referenced under every major word of the phrase except the first. When looking up a word, be sure to check for related forms of the word and for phrases beginning with that word.

Proper names are defined by descriptive phrases and Scripture references. If a name applies to more than one person, place, or group (see ABIJAH, below), the different identities are distinguished by the dash ("———").

AARON
Ancestry and family of, Ex 6:16–20, 23
Helper and prophet to Moses, Ex 4:13–31; 7:1, 2
Appears before Pharaoh, Ex 5:1–4
Performs miracles, Ex 7:9, 10, 19, 20
Supports Moses' hands, Ex 17:10–12
Ascends Mt. Sinai; sees God's glory, Ex 19:24; 24:1, 9, 10
Judges Israel in Moses' absence, Ex 24:14
Chosen by God as priest, Ex 28:1
Consecrated, Ex 29; Lev 8
Duties prescribed, Ex 30:7–10
Tolerates Israel's idolatry, Ex 32
Priestly ministry begins, Lev 9
Sons offer profane fire; Aaron's humble response, Lev 10
Conspires against Moses, Num 12:1–16
Rebelled against by Korah, Num 16
Intercedes to stop plague, Num 16:45–48
Rod buds to confirm his authority, Num 17:1–10
With Moses, fails at Meribah, Num 20:1–13
Dies; son succeeds him as priest, Num 20:23–29
His priesthood compared:
with Melchizedek's, Heb 7:11–19
with Christ's, Heb 9:6–15, 23–28

ABADDON
Angel of the bottomless pit, Rev 9:11

ABASED
I know how to be *a* . . . . Phil 4:12

ABBA
And He said, "*A* . . . . . . Mark 14:36
by whom we cry out, "*A* . . . Rom 8:15
crying out, "*A* . . . . Gal 4:6

ABED-NEGO
Babylonian name given to Azariah, a Hebrew captive, Dan 1:7
Appointed by Nebuchadnezzar, Dan 2:49
Refuses to serve idols; cast into furnace but delivered, Dan 3:12–30

ABEL
Adam's second son, Gen 4:2
His offering accepted, Gen 4:4
Murdered by Cain, Gen 4:8
His sacrifice offered by faith, Heb 11:4

ABEL BETH MAACHAH
Captured by Tiglath-Pileser, 2 Kin 15:29
Refuge of Sheba; saved from destruction, 2 Sam 20:14–22
Seized by Ben-Hadad, 1 Kin 15:20

ABEL MEHOLAH
A city a few miles east of Jabesh Gilead, Judg 7:22; 1 Kin 4:12
Elisha's native city, 1 Kin 19:16

ABHOR
My soul shall not *a* . . . . Lev 26:11

Therefore I *a* myself . . . . Job 42:6
nations will *a* him . . . . Prov 24:24
a the pride of Jacob . . . . Amos 6:8
A what is evil . . . . Rom 12:9

ABHORRED
a His own inheritance . . . . . . Ps 106:40
he who is *a* by the . . . . Prov 22:14
and their soul also *a* . . . . Zech 11:8

ABHORRENCE
They shall be an *a* . . . . Is 66:24

ABHORRENT
you have made us *a* . . . . Ex 5:21

ABHORS
So that his life *a* . . . . Job 33:20

ABIATHAR
A priest who escapes Saul at Nob, 1 Sam 22:20–23
Becomes high priest under David, 1 Sam 23:6, 9–12
Remains faithful to David, 2 Sam 15:24–29
Informs David about Ahithophel, 2 Sam 15:34–36
Supports Adonijah's usurpation, 1 Kin 1:7, 9, 25
Deposed by Solomon, 1 Kin 2:26, 27, 35

ABIDE
nor *a* in its paths . . . . Job 24:13
LORD, who may *a* . . . . Ps 15:1
He shall *a* before God . . . . Ps 61:7
the Most High shall *a* . . . . Ps 91:1
"If you *a* in My word . . . . . . John 8:31
And a slave does not *a* . . . . . John 8:35
Helper, that He may *a* . . . . John 14:16
A in Me and I in you . . . . . . John 15:4
If you *a* in Me . . . . John 15:7
a in My love . . . . John 15:9
And now *a* faith . . . . 1 Cor 13:13
does the love of God *a* . . . 1 John 3:17
this we know that we *a* . . . 1 John 4:13

ABIDES
even He who *a* from of old . . Ps 55:19
He who *a* in Me . . . . John 15:5
lives and *a* forever . . . . 1 Pet 1:23
will of God *a* forever . . . . . 1 John 2:17

ABIDING
not have His word *a* . . . . John 5:38
has eternal life *a* . . . . 1 John 3:15

ABIEZRITES
Relatives of Gideon; rally to his call, Judg 6:11, 24, 34

ABIGAIL
Wise wife of foolish Nabal, 1 Sam 25:3
Appeases David and becomes his wife, 1 Sam 25:14–42
Mother of Chileab, 2 Sam 3:3

ABIHU
Second son of Aaron, Ex 6:23
Offers profane fire and dies, Lev 10:1–7

ABIJAH
Samuel's second son; follows corrupt ways, 1 Sam 8:2, 3
——— Descendant of Aaron; head of an office of priests, 1 Chr 24:3, 10
Zechariah belongs to division of, Luke 1:5
——— Son of Jeroboam I, 1 Kin 14:1–18
——— Another name for King Abijam, 2 Chr 11:20

ABIJAM (or Abijah)
King of Judah, 1 Kin 14:31
Follows the sins of his father, 1 Kin 15:1–7
Defeats Jeroboam and takes cities, 2 Chr 13:13–20

ABILENE
A province or tetrarchy of Syria, Luke 3:1

ABILITY
who had *a* to serve . . . . Dan 1:4
according to his own *a* . . . . Matt 25:15
and beyond their *a* . . . . 2 Cor 8:3
a which God supplies . . . . . . 1 Pet 4:11

ABIMELECH
King of Gerar; takes Sarah in ignorance, Gen 20:1–18
Makes treaty with Abraham, Gen 21:22–34
——— A second king of Gerar; sends Isaac away, Gen 26:1–16
Makes treaty with Isaac, Gen 26:17–33
——— Gideon's son by a concubine, Judg 8:31
Conspires to become king, Judg 9

ABINADAB
A man of Kirjath Jearim in whose house the ark was kept, 1 Sam 7:1, 2
——— The second of Jesse's eight sons, 1 Sam 16:8
Serves in Saul's army, 1 Sam 17:13
——— A son of Saul slain at Mt. Gilboa, 1 Sam 31:1–8
Bones of, buried by men of Jabesh, 1 Chr 10:1–12

ABIRAM
Reubenite who conspired against Moses, Num 16:1–50

ABISHAG
A Shunammite employed as David's nurse, 1 Kin 1:1–4, 15
Witnessed David's choice of Solomon as successor, 1 Kin 1:15–31
Adonijah slain for desiring to marry her, 1 Kin 2:13–25

ABISHAI
David's nephew; joins Joab in blood revenge against Abner, 2 Sam 2:18–24
Loyal to David during Absalom's and Sheba's rebellion, 2 Sam 16:9–12; 20:1–6, 10

Rebuked by David, 2 Sam 16:9–12;
19:21–23
His exploits, 2 Sam 21:16, 17; 23:18;
1 Chr 18:12, 13

ABLE

you are *a* to number . . . . Gen 15:5
the LORD was not *a* . . . . . . Num 14:16
shall give as he is *a* . . . . . Deut 16:17
For who is *a* to judge . . . . . . 1 Kin 3:9
should be *a* to offer . . . . . . 1 Chr 29:14
who is *a* to build Him . . . . . 2 Chr 2:6
"The LORD is *a* . . . . 2 Chr 25:9
Who then is *a* to stand . . . . . Job 41:10
gold will not be *a* to . . . . . . Ezek 7:19
God whom we serve is *a* . . . . Dan 3:17
in pride He is *a* to abase . . . . Dan 4:37
God is *a* to raise up . . . . Matt 3:9
believe that I am *a* . . . . Matt 9:28
fear Him who is *a* . . . . Matt 10:28
Are you *a* to drink the . . . . Matt 20:22
enter and will not be *a* . . . Luke 13:24
was not *a* to finish . . . . . . Luke 14:30
be *a* to contradict or . . . . . Luke 21:15
shall be *a* to separate . . . . . Rom 8:39
God is *a* to make him . . . . . Rom 14:4
Now to Him who is *a* . . . . . Rom 16:25
beyond what you are *a* . . 1 Cor 10:13
And God is *a* to make . . . . . 2 Cor 9:8
may be *a* to comprehend . . . Eph 3:18
that you may be *a* to . . . . . . Eph 6:13
hospitable, *a* to teach . . . . . 1 Tim 3:2
persuaded that He is *a* . . . . 2 Tim 1:12
learning and never *a* . . . . . 2 Tim 3:7
being tempted, He is *a* . . . . Heb 2:18
Therefore He is also *a* to . . . Heb 7:25
that God was *a* to . . . . Heb 11:19
a also to bridle the . . . . . . James 3:2
to Him who is *a* . . . . Jude 24
was *a* to open the scroll, ... Rev 5:3
has come, and who is *a* . . . . Rev 6:17

ABNER

Saul's cousin; commander of his army,
1 Sam 14:50, 51
Rebuked by David, 1 Sam 26:5, 14–16
Supports Ishbosheth; defeated by
David's men; kills Asahel, 2 Sam
2:8–32
Makes covenant with David, 2 Sam
3:6–21
Killed by Joab; mourned by David,
2 Sam 3:22–39

ABODE

but left their own *a* . . . . Jude 6

ABOLISHED

your works may be *a* . . . . . . Ezek 6:6
having *a* in His flesh . . . . . . Eph 2:15
Christ, who has *a* . . . . 2 Tim 1:10

ABOMINABLE

not make yourselves *a* . . . . Lev 11:43
They have done *a* . . . . Ps 14:1
your grave like an *a* . . . . Is 14:19
Oh, do not do this *a* . . . . . . Jer 44:4
they deny Him, being *a* . . . . Titus 1:16
and *a* idolatries . . . . 1 Pet 4:3
unbelieving, *a*, murderers . . . Rev 21:8

ABOMINATION

every shepherd is an *a* . . . . Gen 46:34
If we sacrifice the *a* . . . . Ex 8:26
You have made me an *a* . . . . Ps 88:8
yes, seven are an *a* . . . . Prov 6:16
wickedness is an *a* . . . . Prov 8:7
Dishonest scales are an *a* . . . Prov 11:1
the scoffer is an *a* . . . . Prov 24:9
even his prayer is an *a* . . . . Prov 28:9
An unjust man is an *a* . . . . Prov 29:27
incense is an *a* to Me . . . . Is 1:13
and place there the *a* . . . . . . Dan 11:31
the *a* of desolation . . . . Dan 12:11
the '*a* of desolation,' . . . . . Matt 24:15

ABOMINATIONS

to follow the *a* . . . . Deut 18:9
delights in their *a* . . . . Is 66:3
will put away your *a* . . . . Jer 4:1
your harlotry, your *a* . . . . . Jer 13:27
will see greater *a* . . . . Ezek 8:6
a which they commit . . . . . Ezek 8:17
you, throw away the *a* . . . . Ezek 20:7
show her all her *a* . . . . Ezek 22:2
a golden cup full of *a* . . . . . Rev 17:4
of the *a* of the earth . . . . . . Rev 17:5

ABOUND

lawlessness will *a* . . . . Matt 24:12
the offense might *a* . . . . Rom 5:20
sin that grace may *a* . . . . Rom 6:1
thanksgiving to *a* . . . . 2 Cor 4:15
to make all grace *a* . . . . 2 Cor 9:8
and I know how to *a* . . . . . . Phil 4:12
that you should *a* . . . . 1 Thess 4:1
things are yours and *a* . . . . . 2 Pet 1:8

ABOUNDED

But where sin *a* . . . . Rom 5:20

ABOUNDING

and *a* in goodness and . . . . . Ex 34:6
and *a* in mercy . . . . Ps 103:8
immovable, always *a* . . . . 1 Cor 15:58
a in it with thanksgiving . . . . Col 2:7

ABOVE

that is in heaven *a* . . . . Ex 20:4
"He sent from *a* . . . . 2 Sam 22:17
A it stood seraphim . . . . Is 6:2
nor a servant *a* his . . . . . . Matt 10:24
He who comes from *a* . . . . . John 3:31
beneath; I am from *a* . . . . . . John 8:23
been given you from *a* . . . . John 19:11
of all, who is *a* all . . . . Eph 4:6
the name which is *a* . . . . Phil 2:9
things which are *a* . . . . Col 3:1
perfect gift is from *a* . . . . . James 1:17

ABRAHAM

Ancestry and family, Gen 11:26–31
Receives God's call; enters Canaan,
Gen 12:1–6
Promised Canaan by God; pitches tent
near Bethel, Gen 12:7, 8
Deceives Egyptians concerning Sarai,
Gen 12:11–20
Separates from Lot; inherits Canaan,
Gen 13
Rescues Lot from captivity, Gen
14:11–16
Gives a tithe to Melchizedek; refuses
spoil, Gen 14:18–24
Covenant renewed; promised a son,
Gen 15
Takes Hagar as concubine; Ishmael
born, Gen 16
Name changed from Abram; circumci-
sion commanded, Gen 17
Entertains Lord and angels, Gen
18:1–15
Intercedes for Sodom, Gen 18:16–33
Deceives Abimelech concerning Sarah,
Gen 20
Birth of Isaac, Gen 21:1–7
Sends Hagar and Ishmael away, Gen
21:9–14
Offers Isaac in obedience to God, Gen
22:1–19
Finds wife for Isaac, Gen 24
Marries Keturah; fathers other chil-
dren; dies, Gen 25:1–10
Friend of God, 2 Chr 20:7
Justified by faith, Rom 4:1–12
Father of true believers, Rom 4:11–25
In the line of faith, Heb 11:8–10
Eternal home of, in heaven, Luke
16:19–25

A was circumcised . . . . Gen 17:26
bore *A* a son in his . . . . Gen 21:2
A circumcised his son . . . . . . Gen 21:4
A was one hundred . . . . Gen 21:5
God tested *A*, and . . . . Gen 22:1
A said, "My son, God . . . . . Gen 22:8
A begot Isaac . . . . Gen 25:19
His covenant with *A* . . . . Ex 2:24
I swore to give to *A* . . . . Ex 6:8
which I swore to *A* . . . . . . Num 32:11
which He made with *A* . . . 1 Chr 16:16
O seed of *A* His servant . . . . Ps 105:6
LORD, who redeemed *A* . . . . Is 29:22
descendants of *A* My . . . . Is 41:8
David, the Son of *A* . . . . Matt 1:1
to you, before *A* was . . . . . John 8:58
For if *A* was justified . . . . . . Rom 4:2
A believed God, and . . . . Rom 4:3
are of the faith of *A* . . . . . . Rom 4:16
of *A* might come upon . . . . . Gal 3:14
Now to *A* and his Seed . . . . Gal 3:16
that *A* had two sons . . . . Gal 4:22
also *A* gave a tenth . . . . Heb 7:2
By faith *A* obeyed when . . . Heb 11:8
By faith *A*, when he . . . . . . Heb 11:17
A believed God, and . . . . . James 2:23
as Sarah obeyed *A*, ... 1 Pet 3:6

ABRAM

See ABRAHAM

ABRONAH

Israelite encampment, Num 33:34

ABSALOM

Son of David, 2 Sam 3:3
Kills Amnon for raping Tamar; flees
from David, 2 Sam 13:20–39
Returns through Joab's intrigue; recon-
ciled to David, 2 Sam 14
Attempts to usurp throne, 2 Sam
15:1—18:8
Caught and killed by Joab, 2 Sam
18:9–18
Mourned by David, 2 Sam 18:19—19:8

ABSENT

For I indeed, as *a* . . . . 1 Cor 5:3
in the body we are *a* . . . . . . 2 Cor 5:6

ABSTAIN

we write to them to *a* . . . . . Acts 15:20
A from every form . . . . . . 1 Thess 5:22
and commanding to *a* . . . . . 1 Tim 4:3
a from fleshly lusts . . . . 1 Pet 2:11

ABUNDANCE

is the sound of *a* . . . . 1 Kin 18:41
workmen with you in *a* . . 1 Chr 22:15
flourish, and *a* of peace . . . . . Ps 72:7
eyes bulge with *a* . . . . Ps 73:7
nor he who loves *a* . . . . Eccl 5:10
delight itself in *a* . . . . Is 55:2
out of the *a* of the heart . . . Matt 12:34
put in out of their *a* . . . . . . Mark 12:44
not consist in the *a* . . . . . . Luke 12:15
of affliction the *a* . . . . 2 Cor 8:2
above measure by the *a* . . 2 Cor 12:7
rich through the *a* . . . . Rev 18:3

ABUNDANT

in judgment and *a* . . . . Job 37:23
a in mercy to all those . . . . . . Ps 86:5
Longsuffering and *a* . . . . . . Ps 86:15
Him is *a* redemption . . . . . . Ps 130:7
placed it by *a* waters . . . . . Ezek 17:5
lovely and its fruit *a* . . . . . . Dan 4:21
slow to anger and *a* . . . . Jon 4:2
in labors more *a* . . . . 2 Cor 11:23
may be more *a* in Jesus . . . . Phil 1:26
Lord was exceedingly *a* . . . 1 Tim 1:14
a mercy has begotten . . . . . . 1 Pet 1:3

ABUNDANTLY

a satisfied with the . . . . Ps 36:8
may have it more *a* . . . . John 10:10
to do exceedingly *a* . . . . . . Eph 3:20
to show more *a* to the . . . . . Heb 6:17

ACACIA

make an ark of a wood .....Ex 25:10
make a table of a wood .....Ex 25:23

ACACIA GROVE

Spies sent from, Josh 2:1
Israel's last camp before crossing the
Jordan, Josh 3:1

ACCEPT

For I will a him ....Job 42:8
a your burnt sacrifice ....Ps 20:3
offering, I will not a ....Jer 14:12
Should I a this from ....Mal 1:13

ACCEPTABLE

sought to find a ....Eccl 12:10
a time I have heard ....Is 49:8
proclaim the a year ....Is 61:2
proclaim the a year ....Luke 4:19
is that good and a ....Rom 12:2
finding out what is a ....Eph 5:10
For this is good and a .....1 Tim 2:3
spiritual sacrifices a ....1 Pet 2:5

ACCEPTABLY

we may serve God a .....Heb 12:28

ACCEPTED

Behold, now is the a ......2 Cor 6:2
by which He made us a .....Eph 1:6

ACCESS

we have a by faith ....Rom 5:2
we have boldness and a ....Eph 3:12

ACCOMPLISHED

today the LORD has a ....1 Sam 11:13
A desire a is sweet to .....Prov 13:19
must still be a in Me ....Luke 22:37
all things were now a ....John 19:28

ACCORD

See WITH ONE ACCORD
and Israel with one a ....Josh 9:2
serve Him with one a ....Zeph 3:9
continued with one a ....Acts 1:14
daily with one a ....Acts 2:46
what a has Christ with ....2 Cor 6:15
love, being of one a ....Phil 2:2

ACCORDING TO THE FLESH

You judge a; I judge .....John 8:15
of the seed of David a.......Rom 1:3
who do not walk a ....Rom 8:1
not many wise a ....1 Cor 1:26
do I plan a, that with ......2 Cor 1:17
we regard no one a ....2 Cor 5:16
we do not war a ....2 Cor 10:3
that many boast a ....2 Cor 11:18
as he who was born a ....Gal 4:29
those who walk a ....2 Pet 2:10

ACCORDING TO THE LAW

a of his separation ....Num 6:21
let it be done a ....Ezra 10:3
a of the Medes ....Dan 6:8
of her purification a .....Luke 2:22
performed all things a ....Luke 2:39
Ananias, a devout man a ..Acts 22:12
you sit to judge me a .....Acts 23:3
who has come, not a ......Heb 7:16
a almost all things are ......Heb 9:22
(which are offered a ......Heb 10:8

ACCORDING TO THE WORD OF THE LORD

Moses numbered them a ...Num 3:16
in the land of Moab, a ....Deut 34:5
booty for themselves, a ....Josh 8:27
they had obtained a ....Josh 22:9
him and killed him, a .....1 Kin 13:26
he had destroyed him, a ..1 Kin 15:29
he set up its gates, a .....1 Kin 16:34
jar of oil run dry, a ......1 Kin 17:16
a which he had spoken ...1 Kin 22:38
barley for a shekel, a ......2 Kin 7:16
David king over Israel, a ..1 Chr 11:3
So I got a sash a ....Jer 13:2

ACCOUNT

they will give a of it ....Matt 12:36
The former a I made ....Acts 1:1
each of us shall give a ....Rom 14:12
put that on my a ....Philem 18
those who must give a .....Heb 13:17

ACCOUNTED

and He a it to him ....Gen 15:6
And that was a to him .....Ps 106:31
his faith is a for ....Rom 4:5
a as sheep for the ....Rom 8:36
and it was a to him ....Gal 3:6
and it was a to him ......James 2:23

ACCURSED

he who is hanged is a .....Deut 21:23
regarding the a things ....Josh 7:1
years old shall be a ....Is 65:20
not know the law is a ......John 7:49
that I myself were a ....Rom 9:3
calls Jesus a, and no .....1 Cor 12:3
let him be a ....Gal 1:8

ACCUSATION

they wrote an a against ....Ezra 4:6
over His head the a ......Matt 27:37
they might find an a ....Luke 6:7
Do not receive an a ....1 Tim 5:19
not bring a reviling a ......2 Pet 2:11

ACCUSE

anyone or a falsely ....Luke 3:14
they began to a Him .....Luke 23:2
think that I shall a........John 5:45

ACCUSED

forward and a the Jews .....Dan 3:8
while He was being a .....Matt 27:12

ACCUSER

a of our brethren ....Rev 12:10

ACCUSERS

Let my a be clothed ....Ps 109:29
meets the a face to ....Acts 25:16

ACCUSING

their thoughts a or else ....Rom 2:15

ACHAIA

Visited by Paul, Acts 18:1, 12
Apollos preaches in, Acts 18:24–28
Gospel proclaimed throughout, 1 Thess
1:7, 8

ACHAN (or Achar)

Sin of, caused Israel's defeat, Josh
7:1–15
Stoned to death, Josh 7:16–25
Sin of, recalled, Josh 22:20
Also called Achar, 1 Chr 2:7

ACHISH

A king of Gath, 1 Sam 21:10–15
David seeks refuge with, 1 Sam
27:1–12
Forced by Philistine lords to expel
David, 1 Sam 29:1–11
Receives Shimei's servants, 1 Kin 2:39,
40

ACHOR, VALLEY OF

Site of Achan's stoning, Josh 7:24–26
On Judah's boundary, Josh 15:7
Promises concerning, Is 65:10

ACHSAH

A daughter of Caleb, 1 Chr 2:49
Given to Othniel, Josh 15:16–19
Given springs of water, Judg 1:12–15

ACKNOWLEDGE

did he a his brothers ....Deut 33:9
a my transgressions ....Ps 51:3
in all your ways a ....Prov 3:6
and Israel does not a ....Is 63:16
Only a your iniquity ....Jer 3:13
let him a that the ....1 Cor 14:37

arose and went to Nineveh, a . Jon 3:3

ACKNOWLEDGED

of Israel, and God a them ....Ex 2:25
a my sin to You ....Ps 32:5

ACKNOWLEDGES

there is no one who a ....Ps 142:4
he who a the Son has ....1 John 2:23

ACQUAINT

a yourself with Him ....Job 22:21

ACQUAINTANCES

You have put away my a ....Ps 88:8
All my a watched for ....Jer 20:10
all His a, and the women .Luke 23:49

ACQUAINTED

a with all my ways ....Ps 139:3
a Man of sorrows and a ....Is 53:3

ACQUIRE

a possessions for ....Gen 34:10

ACQUIRED

he has a all this wealth .....Gen 31:1
I have a as my wife ....Ruth 4:10
I a male and female ....Eccl 2:7

ACQUIT

at all a the wicked ....Nah 1:3

ACQUITTED

struck him shall be a ....Ex 21:19
of the ox shall be a ....Ex 21:28
that you may be a ....Is 43:26
whom I had not a ....Joel 3:21

ACT

a corruptly and make ......Deut 4:25
seen every great a ....Deut 11:7
hear in heaven, and a .....1 Kin 8:32
hear from heaven, and a ..2 Chr 6:23
Thus you shall a in ......2 Chr 19:9
is time for You to a ......Ps 119:126
His a, His unusual a ....Is 28:21
O Lord, listen and a ....Dan 9:19
adultery, in the very a .....John 8:4

ACTED

if you have a in truth .....Judg 9:16
But Jehu a deceptively, .. 2 Kin 10:19
a more wickedly than ....2 Kin 21:11

ACTIONS

by Him a are weighed .....1 Sam 2:3

ACTS

LORD, the righteous a ....Judg 5:11
His a to the children ....Ps 103:7
declare Your mighty a ......Ps 145:4
of Your awesome a ....Ps 145:6

ADAM

Creation of, Gen 1:26, 27; 2:7
Given dominion over the earth, Gen
1:28–30
Given a wife, Gen 2:18–25
Temptation, fall, and exile from Eden,
Gen 3
Children of, Gen 4:1, 2; 5:3, 4
Transgression results in sin and death,
Rom 5:12–14
———— Last or second Adam, an appella-
tion of Christ, Rom 5:14, 15; 1 Cor
15:20–24, 45–48

ADD

The LORD shall a to me ....Gen 30:24
You shall not a ....Deut 4:2
you shall not a to it ....Deut 12:32
A iniquity to their ....Ps 69:27
Do not a to His words ....Prov 30:6
by worrying can a one .....Matt 6:27
by worrying can a one ....Luke 12:25
a to your faith virtue, to ....2 Pet 1:5
Gold will a to him the .....Rev 22:18

ADDED

things shall be a ....Matt 6:33
And the Lord a to the ....Acts 2:47
many people were a ......Acts 11:24

It was *a* because of ....Gal 3:19

ADDS
and He *a* no sorrow ......Prov 10:22
no one annuls or *a* to it .....Gal 3:15
If anyone *a* to these ....Rev 22:18

ADMINISTERS
a justice for the ....Deut 10:18

ADMONISH
also to *a* one another .....Rom 15:14
a him as a brother ......2 Thess 3:15

ADMONISHED
further, my son, be *a* .....Eccl 12:12
Angel of the LORD *a* ....Zech 3:6

ADMONISHING
a one another in ....Col 3:16

ADMONITION
were written for our *a* ....1 Cor 10:11
in the training and *a* ....Eph 6:4

ADONI-ZEDEK
An Amorite king of Jerusalem, Josh
   10:1–5
Defeated and slain by Joshua, Josh
   10:6–27

ADONIJAH
David's fourth son, 2 Sam 3:2, 4
Attempts to usurp throne, 1 Kin 1:5–53
Desires Abishag as wife, 1 Kin 2:13–18
Executed by Solomon, 1 Kin 2:19–25

ADONIRAM (or Adoram)
Official under David, Solomon, and
   Rehoboam, 2 Sam 20:24; 1 Kin 5:14;
   12:18
Stoned by angry Israelites, 1 Kin 12:18
Called Hadoram, 2 Chr 10:18

ADOPTION
received the Spirit of *a* .....Rom 8:15
waiting for the *a* ....Rom 8:23
to whom pertain the *a* ......Rom 9:4
we might receive the *a* .....Gal 4:5
a as sons by Jesus ....Eph 1:5

ADORN
a the monuments ....Matt 23:29
also, that the women *a* .....1 Tim 2:9

ADORNED
By His Spirit He *a* ....Job 26:13
You shall again be *a* ....Jer 31:4
temple, how it was *a* ......Luke 21:5
also *a* themselves ....1 Pet 3:5
prepared as a bride *a* ......Rev 21:2

ADRIFT
A among the dead ....Ps 88:5

ADULLAM
A town of Canaan, Gen 38:1, 12, 20;
   Josh 12:7, 15; 15:20, 35
David seeks refuge in caves of,
   1 Sam 23:13–17

ADULTERER
the *a* and the adulteress ....Lev 20:10
The eye of the *a* ....Job 24:15

ADULTERERS
the land is full of *a* ....Jer 23:10
nor idolaters, nor *a* ....1 Cor 6:9
a God will judge ....Heb 13:4
A and adulteresses ....James 4:4

ADULTERIES
I have seen your *a* ....Jer 13:27
her sight, and her *a* ....Hos 2:2
evil thoughts, *a* ....Mark 7:21

ADULTEROUS
evil and a generation .....Matt 12:39

ADULTERY
You shall not commit *a* ....Ex 20:14
You shall not commit *a* ...Deut 5:18
Whoever commits *a* ....Prov 6:32
Israel had committed *a* .....Jer 3:8

have committed *a* with .....Jer 29:23
a with their idols ....Ezek 23:37
and is committing *a* ....Hos 3:1
already committed *a* ....Matt 5:28
is divorced commits *a* .....Matt 5:32
You shall not commit *a* ...Matt 19:18
another commits *a* ....Mark 10:11
husband commits *a* ......Luke 16:18
a woman caught in *a* ....John 8:3
which are: *a*, fornication, ...Gal 5:19
having eyes full of *a* ......2 Pet 2:14
those who commit *a* ....Rev 2:22

ADVANCED
Joshua was old, *a* in ......Josh 13:1
I am old, *a* in age ....Josh 23:2
David was old, *a* in years ..1 Kin 1:1
were both well *a* in years ..Luke 1:7
wife is well *a* in years .....Luke 1:18
I *a* in Judaism beyond ......Gal 1:14

ADVANTAGE
a will it be to You ....Job 35:3
man has no *a* over ....Eccl 3:19
a that I go away ....John 16:7
What *a* then has the ....Rom 3:1
Satan should take *a* ......2 Cor 2:11
no one should take *a* .....1 Thess 4:6
people to gain *a* ....Jude 16

ADVERSARIES
The *a* of the LORD ....1 Sam 2:10
rid Myself of My *a* ....Is 1:24
a will not be able ....Luke 21:15
and there are many *a* .....1 Cor 16:9
terrified by your *a* ....Phil 1:28
will devour the *a* ....Heb 10:27

ADVERSARY
in the way as an *a* ......Num 22:22
battle he become our *a* ...1 Sam 29:4
how long will the *a* ....Ps 74:10
a has spread his hand .....Lam 1:10
Agree with your *a* ....Matt 5:25
for me from my *a* ....Luke 18:3
opportunity to the *a* ......1 Tim 5:14
your *a* the devil walks ......1 Pet 5:8

ADVERSITIES
you from all your *a* .....1 Sam 10:19
known my soul in *a* ....Ps 31:7

ADVERSITY
them with every *a* ....2 Chr 15:6
I shall never be in *a* ....Ps 10:6
from the days of *a* ....Ps 94:13
brother is born for *a* ......Prov 17:17
faint in the day of *a* ......Prov 24:10
the day of *a* consider ......Eccl 7:14
you the bread of *a* ....Is 30:20

ADVICE
And blessed is your *a* ....1 Sam 25:33
in this I give my *a* ....2 Cor 8:10

ADVOCATE
we have an A with the ....1 John 2:1

AENON
A place near Salim where John the
   Baptist baptized, John 3:22, 23

AFAR
and worship from *a* ....Ex 24:1
sons shall come from *a* .....Is 60:4
and not a God *a* ....Jer 23:23
and saw Abraham *a* ......Luke 16:23
to all who are *a* ....Acts 2:39
to you who were *a* ....Eph 2:17
but having seen them *a* ....Heb 11:13

AFFAIRS
he will guide his *a* ....Ps 112:5
I may hear of your *a* ....Phil 1:27
himself with the *a* ....2 Tim 2:4

AFFECTION
to his wife the *a* ....1 Cor 7:3
for you all with the *a* ....Phil 1:8

if any *a* and mercy ....Phil 2:1

AFFECTIONATE
Be kindly *a* to one ....Rom 12:10

AFFIRM
you to *a* constantly ....Titus 3:8

AFFLICT
a them with their ....Ex 1:11
oath to *a* her soul ....Num 30:13
may be bound to *a* you ....Judg 16:6
a the descendants ....1 Kin 11:39
will hear, and *a* them ....Ps 55:19
a Your heritage ....Ps 94:5
a man to *a* his soul ....Is 58:5
to destroy, and to *a* ......Jer 31:28
For He does not *a* ....Lam 3:33
deal with all who *a* ....Zeph 3:19

AFFLICT YOUR SOULS
shall *a*, and do no work ....Lev 16:29
you shall *a*, and offer .....Lev 23:27
You shall *a*; you shall not ..Num 29:7

AFFLICTED
"Why have You *a* ....Num 11:11
and the Almighty has *a* ...Ruth 1:21
To him who is *a* ....Job 6:14
hears the cry of the *a* .....Job 34:28
You *a* the peoples ....Ps 44:2
Before I was *a* ....Ps 119:67
I am a very much ....Ps 119:107
Many a time they have *a* ..Ps 129:1
the cause of the *a* ....Ps 140:12
days of the *a* are evil .....Prov 15:15
Smitten by God, and *a* .....Is 53:4
oppressed and He was *a* ....Is 53:7
"O you *a* one, tossed ....Is 54:11
Why have we *a* our............Is 58:3
and satisfy the *a* ....Is 58:10
her virgins are *a* ....Lam 1:4
she has relieved the *a* .....1 Tim 5:10
being destitute, *a* ....Heb 11:37

AFFLICTING
A the just and taking ....Amos 5:12

AFFLICTION
in the land of my *a* ....Gen 41:52
the bread of *a* ....Deut 16:3
indeed look on the *a* .....1 Sam 1:11
LORD saw that the *a* .....2 Kin 14:26
a take hold of me ....Job 30:16
days of *a* confront me .....Job 30:27
held in the cords of *a* .....Job 36:8
of death, bound in *a* ......Ps 107:10
is my comfort in my *a* .....Ps 119:50
and it is an evil *a* ....Eccl 6:2
a He was afflicted ....Is 63:9
refuge in the day of *a* .....Jer 16:19
"O LORD, behold my *a* .....Lam 1:9
not grieved for the *a* ......Amos 6:6
For our light *a* ....2 Cor 4:17
supposing to add *a* ....Phil 1:16
the word in much *a* ......1 Thess 1:6

AFFLICTIONS
Many are the *a* of the .....Ps 34:19
in the *a* of Christ ....Col 1:24
shaken by these *a* ....1 Thess 3:3
persecutions, *a*, which ....2 Tim 3:11
in all things, endure *a*, ...2 Tim 4:5

AFFORD
poor and cannot *a* it .....Lev 14:21
such as he can *a* ....Lev 14:30

AFRAID
See DO NOT BE AFRAID
garden, and I was *a* ....Gen 3:10
saying,, "Do not be *a* ....Gen 15:1
his face, for he was *a* ......Ex 3:6
none will make you *a* ......Lev 26:6
you shall not be *a* in ....Deut 1:17
of whom you are *a* ....Deut 7:19
do not be *a* of them ....Deut 20:1
Do not be *a* of the ......2 Kin 25:24

David was *a* of God . . . . . . 1 Chr 13:12
I will not be *a* of ten . . . . Ps 3:6
ungodliness made me *a* . . . . . . Ps 18:4
Of whom shall I be *a* . . . . Ps 27:1
Do not be *a* when one . . . . Ps 49:16
Whenever I am *a* . . . . Ps 56:3
farthest parts are *a* . . . . Ps 65:8
you will not be *a* . . . . Prov 3:24
nor be *a* of their threats . . . . . . Is 8:12
be *a* of the Assyrian . . . . Is 10:24
I will trust and not be *a* . . . . . . Is 12:2
no one will make them *a* . . . . . . Is 17:2
Do not fear, nor be *a* . . . . Is 44:8
that you should be *a* . . . . Is 51:12
Do not be *a* of their faces, ... Jer 1:8
dream which made me *a* . . . . Dan 4:5
Then the mariners were *a* . . . . Jon 1:5
It is I; do not be *a* . . . . Matt 14:27
Do not be *a*; only believe . . Mark 5:36
Do not be *a*, Zacharias, ... Luke 1:13
Do not be *a*, Mary, for . . . . Luke 1:30
not be *a* of those who . . . . . Luke 12:4
neither let it be *a* . . . . John 14:27
"Do not be *a*, Paul . . . . . . Acts 27:24
if you do evil, be *a* . . . . Rom 13:4
do good and are not *a* . . . . . . 1 Pet 3:6

AFTERWARD
A he will let you go . . . . Ex 11:1
a we will speak . . . . Job 18:2
a receive me to glory . . . . Ps 73:24
you shall follow Me *a* . . . . . John 13:36
the firstfruits, *a* . . . . 1 Cor 15:23

AGAG
A king of Amalek in Balaam's prophecy, Num 24:7
——— Amalekite king spared by Saul,
  but slain by Samuel, 1 Sam 15:8,
  9, 20–24, 32, 33

AGAIN
See BORN AGAIN
day He will rise *a* . . . . Matt 20:19
'You must be born *a* . . . . John 3:7
to renew them *a* . . . . Heb 6:6
having been born *a* . . . . 1 Pet 1:23

AGAINST
See SINNED AGAINST THE LORD; SINNED
  AGAINST YOU
his hand shall be *a* . . . . Gen 16:12
I will set My face *a* . . . . Lev 20:3
come to 'set a man *a* . . . . . Matt 10:35
or house divided *a* . . . . Matt 12:25
not with Me is *a* Me . . . . . . Matt 12:30
blasphemy *a* the Spirit . . . . Matt 12:31
For nation will rise *a* . . . . . . Matt 24:7
out, as *a* a robber . . . . Matt 26:55
I have sinned *a* . . . . Luke 15:18
lifted up his heel *a* . . . . John 13:18
LORD and *a* His Christ . . . . . Acts 4:26
to kick *a* the goads . . . . Acts 9:5
all men everywhere *a* . . . . . Acts 21:28
let us not fight *a* . . . . Acts 23:9
a the promises of God . . . . . . Gal 3:21
we do not wrestle *a* . . . . Eph 6:12
I have a few things *a* . . . . . . Rev 2:20

AGE
well advanced in *a* . . . . Gen 18:11
Israel were dim with *a* . . . . Gen 48:10
the flower of their *a* . . . . . 1 Sam 2:33
the grave at a full *a* . . . . Job 5:26
a is as nothing . . . . Ps 39:5
and in the *a* to come . . . . . Mark 10:30
"The sons of this *a* . . . . . . Luke 20:34
He is of *a*; ask him . . . . John 9:21
who are of full *a* . . . . Heb 5:14
the powers of the *a* . . . . Heb 6:5

AGE TO COME
in this age or in the *a* . . . . . Matt 12:32
in the *a*, eternal life . . . . . Mark 10:30
in the *a* eternal life . . . . . . Luke 18:30
the powers of the *a* . . . . Heb 6:5

AGED
Wisdom is with *a* . . . . Job 12:12
a one as Paul, the *a* . . . . Philem 9

AGES
ordained before the *a* . . . . . 1 Cor 2:7
in other *a* was not . . . . Eph 3:5
at the end of the *a* . . . . Heb 9:26

AGONY
And being in *a* . . . . Luke 22:44

AGREE
A with your adversary . . . . Matt 5:25
that if two of you *a* . . . . Matt 18:19
testimonies did not *a* . . . . Mark 14:56
and these three *a* . . . . 1 John 5:8

AGREED
unless they are *a* . . . . Amos 3:3
they were glad, and *a* . . . . Luke 22:5

AGREEMENT
with Sheol we are in *a* . . . . . Is 28:15
the North to make an *a* . . . . Dan 11:6
what *a* has the temple . . . . 2 Cor 6:16

AHAB
A wicked king of Israel, 1 Kin 16:29
Marries Jezebel; promotes Baal wor-
  ship, 1 Kin 16:31–33; 18:17–46
Denounced by Elijah, 1 Kin 17:1
Wars against Ben-Hadad, 1 Kin
  20:1–43
Covets Naboth's vineyard, 1 Kin
  21:1–16
Death predicted; repentance delays
  judgment, 1 Kin 21:17–29
Goes to war in spite of Micaiah's warn-
  ing; killed in battle, 1 Kin. 22:1–37
Prophecy concerning, fulfilled, 1 Kin
  22:38
——— Lying prophet, Jer 29:21–23

AHASUERUS
The father of Darius the Mede, Dan
  9:1
——— Persian king, probably Xerxes I,
  486–465 B.C., Ezra 4:6; Esth 1:1
Makes Esther queen, Esth 2:16, 17
Orders Jews annihilated, by Haman's
  advice, Esth 3:8–15
Reverses decree at Esther's request,
  Esth 7; 8
Exalts Mordecai, Esth 10:1–3

AHAZ
King of Judah; pursues idolatry; submits to Assyrian rule; desecrates
  the temple, 2 Kin 16
Defeated by Syria and Israel, 2 Chr
  28:5–15
Comforted by Isaiah; refuses to ask a
  sign, Is 7:1–17

AHAZIAH
King of Israel; son of Ahab and Jezebel;
  worships Baal, 1 Kin 22:51–53
Falls through lattice; calls on Baal-
  Zebub; dies according to Elijah's
  word, 2 Kin 1:2–18
——— King of Judah; Ahab's son-in-law;
  reigns wickedly, 2 Kin 8:25–29; 2 Chr
  22:1–6
Killed by Jehu, 2 Kin 9:27–29; 2 Chr
  22:7–9

AHIJAH
A prophet of Shiloh who foretells division of Solomon's kingdom,
  1 Kin 11:29–39
Foretells elimination of Jeroboam's
  line, 1 Kin 14:1–18
A writer of prophecy, 2 Chr 9:29

AHIKAM
Sent in Josiah's mission to Huldah,
  2 Kin 22:12–14
Protects Jeremiah, Jer 26:24

The father of Gedaliah, governor under
  Nebuchadnezzar, 2 Kin 25:22; Jer
  39:14

AHIMAAZ
A son of Zadok the high priest, 1 Chr
  6:8, 9
Warns David of Absalom's plans,
  2 Sam 15:27, 36
First to tell David of Absalom's defeat,
  2 Sam 18:19–30

AHIMELECH
High priest in Saul's reign; helps David,
  1 Sam 21:1–9
Betrayed and killed by Doeg; son Abi-
  athar escapes, 1 Sam 22:9–20
David writes concerning, Ps 52:title

AHINOAM
Wife of David, 1 Sam 25:43; 27:3; 30:5,
  18
Mother of Amnon, 2 Sam 3:2

AHITHOPHEL
David's counselor, 2 Sam 15:12
Joins Absalom's insurrection; counsels
  him, 2 Sam 15:31; 16:20–23
His counsel rejected; commits suicide,
  2 Sam 17:1–23

AI
Israel defeated at, Josh 7:2–5
Israel destroys completely, Josh 8:1–28

AIDE
the king's personal *a* . . . . . . Acts 12:20

AIJALON
Amorites not driven from, Judg 1:35
Miracle there, Josh 10:12, 13
City of refuge, 1 Chr 6:66–69
Fortified by Rehoboam, 2 Chr 11:5, 10
Captured by Philistines, 2 Chr 28:18

AIR
the birds of the *a* . . . . Gen 1:26
of the *a* have nests . . . . Luke 9:58
as one who beats the *a* . . . . 1 Cor 9:26
be speaking into the *a* . . . . . 1 Cor 14:9
of the power of the *a* . . . . Eph 2:2
the Lord in the *a* . . . . 1 Thess 4:17
his bowl into the *a* . . . . Rev 16:17

AKEL DAMA
Field called "Field of Blood," Acts 1:19

AKRABBIM
An "ascent" on the south of the Dead
  Sea, Num 34:4
One border of Judah, Josh 15:3

ALABASTER
mosaic pavement of *a* . . . . . . Esth 1:6
an *a* flask of very costly . . . Matt 26:7
woman came having an *a* . Mark 14:3
brought an *a* flask of . . . . . . Luke 7:37

ALARM
to sound the *a* against . . . . 2 Chr 13:12
A day of trumpet and *a* . . . . Zeph 1:16

ALEXANDER
A member of the high-priestly family,
  Acts 4:6
——— A Jew in Ephesus, Acts 19:33, 34
——— An apostate condemned by Paul,
  1 Tim 1:19, 20

ALEXANDRIA
Men of, persecute Stephen, Acts 6:9
Paul sails in ship of, Acts 27:6

ALGUM
a logs from Lebanon, ... 2 Chr 2:8
Ophir, brought *a* wood . . . . 2 Chr 9:10
a wood for the house . . . . . 2 Chr 9:11

ALIEN
because you were an *a* . . . . Deut 23:7
I am an *a* in their . . . . Job 19:15
who turn away an *a* . . . . Mal 3:5

ALIENATED
a herself from them ......Ezek 23:17
darkened, being *a* ....Eph 4:18
you, who once were *a* ......Col 1:21

ALIENS
For we are *a* and ....1 Chr 29:15
For I have loved *a* ....Jer 2:25
A have devoured his ....Hos 7:9
without Christ, being *a* ....Eph 2:12
the armies of the *a* ....Heb 11:34

ALIGHTING
dove and *a* upon Him .....Matt 3:16

ALIKE
All things come *a* ....Eccl 9:2
esteems every day *a* ....Rom 14:5

ALIVE
in the ark remained *a* ......Gen 7:23
with them went down *a* ...Num 16:33
Lord your God are *a* ....Deut 4:4
I kill and I make *a* ....Deut 32:39
Let them go down *a* ......Ps 55:15
he preserves himself *a* ...Ezek 18:27
heard that He was *a* .....Mark 16:11
son was dead and is *a* ...Luke 15:24
presented Himself *a* ....Acts 1:3
dead indeed to sin, but *a* ...Rom 6:11
I was *a* once without ......Rom 7:9
all shall be made *a* ......1 Cor 15:22
trespasses, made us *a* ......Eph 2:5
flesh, He has made *a* .....Col 2:13
that we who are *a* ....1 Thess 4:15
the flesh but made *a* ......1 Pet 3:18
and behold, I am *a* ....Rev 1:18
a name that you are *a* ......Rev 3:1
These two were cast *a* ....Rev 19:20

ALL
See WITH ALL YOUR HEART
for this is man's *a* ....Eccl 12:13

ALL THE DAYS OF HIS LIFE
he shall read it *a* ....Deut 17:19
give him to the LORD *a*...1 Sam 1:11
I have made him ruler *a* ...1 Kin 11:34
He commanded him *a* ....1 Kin 15:5
toils under the sun *a* ......Eccl 5:18
before the king *a* ....Jer 52:33

ALL THE EARTH
over the cattle, over *a* ......Gen 1:26
alive on the face of *a* ......Gen 7:3
confused the language of *a* .Gen 11:9
Shall not the Judge of *a* ...Gen 18:25
there is none like Me in *a* ...Ex 9:14
going the way of *a* ....Josh 23:14
I go the way of *a*; ....1 Kin 2:2
a sought the presence ....1 Kin 10:24
Sing to the LORD, *a*; .....1 Chr 16:23
Let *a* fear the LORD; ....Ps 33:8
A shall worship You ....Ps 66:4
I have gathered *a* ....Is 10:14
that made *a* drunk ....Jer 51:7
which shall rule over *a* .....Dan 2:39
Let *a* keep silence ....Hab 2:20
was darkness over *a* .....Luke 23:44
sound has gone out to *a* ...Rom 10:18
of God sent out into *a* ......Rev 5:6

ALL THE SAINTS
God will come, and *a* ......Zech 14:5
your love for *a* ....Eph 1:15
less than the least of *a* .....Eph 3:8
able to comprehend with *a* .Eph 3:18
and supplication for *a* .....Eph 6:18
your love for *a* ....Col 1:4
with the prayers of *a* ....Rev 8:3

ALLELUIA
Again they said, "*A* ......Rev 19:3

ALLOW
a Your Holy One ....Ps 16:10
a My faithfulness ....Ps 89:33
nor do you *a* those ....Matt 23:13

a Your Holy One...........Acts 2:27
who will not *a* you to be . . 1 Cor 10:13

ALLOWED
bygone generations *a* .....Acts 14:16

ALLURE
behold, I will *a* ....Hos 2:14
they *a* through the lusts ....2 Pet 2:18

ALMIGHTY
I am *A* God; walk before ....Gen 17:1
May God *A* bless you, and . .Gen 28:3
and to Jacob, as God *A* ......Ex 6:3
for the *A* has dealt very .....Ruth 1:20
does the *A* pervert justice ...Job 8:3
find out the limits of the *A* ..Job 11:7
of the wrath of the *A* ......Job 21:20
your delight in the *A* ......Job 22:26
breath of the *A* gives me ...Job 33:4
under the shadow of the *A* ...Ps 91:1
as destruction from the *A* ....Is 13:6
as destruction from the *A* ..Joel 1:15
and who is to come, the *A* ..Rev 1:8
holy, holy, Lord God *A* ......Rev 4:8
Even so, Lord God *A* ....Rev 16:7
fierceness and wrath of *A* ..Rev 19:15

ALMOND
a blossoms on one ....Ex 25:33
a tree blossoms ....Eccl 12:5
branch of an *a* tree ....Jer 1:11

ALMOST
for me, my feet had *a* ....Ps 73:2
a persuade me to ....Acts 26:28
a all things are ....Heb 9:22

ALMS
But rather give *a* ....Luke 11:41
you have and give *a* ......Luke 12:33
I came to bring *a* ....Acts 24:17

ALOES
with myrrh and *a* ....Ps 45:8
my bed with myrrh, *a* .....Prov 7:17
mixture of myrrh and *a* ...John 19:39

ALOUD
And he wept *a*, and the .....Gen 45:2
many shouted *a* for joy ....Ezra 3:12
them sing *a* on their beds ...Ps 149:5
Wisdom calls *a* outside ....Prov 1:20
Cry *a* at Beth Aven ....Hos 5:8

ALPHA
I am the *A* and the ....Rev 1:8
I am the *A* and the ....Rev 22:13

ALTAR
Then Noah built an *a* ....Gen 8:20
he built an *a* to the LORD. . . Gen 12:7
built an *a* there ....Gen 13:18
Abraham built an *a* ....Gen 22:9
son and laid him on the *a* . .Gen 22:9
So he built an *a* there .....Gen 26:25
make an *a* there to God ....Gen 35:1
And Moses built an *a* ......Ex 17:15
An *a* of earth you ....Ex 20:24
two sides of the *a* ....Ex 27:7
incense *a* of acacia wood ...Ex 37:25
a shall be kept ....Lev 6:9
it to you upon the *a* ....Lev 17:11
offering for the *a* ....Num 7:84
a to the LORD your God ....Deut 27:5
Joshua built an *a* ....Josh 8:30
a great, impressive *a* .....Josh 22:10
called the *a* a Witness .....Josh 22:34
and tear down the *a* ......Judg 6:25
early and built an *a* ....Judg 21:4
built an *a* to the LORD ....1 Sam 7:17
Saul built an *a* ....1 Sam 14:35
"Go up, erect an *a* ....2 Sam 24:18
built there an *a* ....2 Sam 24:25
a which he had made ....1 Kin 12:33
cried out against the *a* ....1 Kin 13:2
set up an *a* for Baal ......1 Kin 16:32
he repaired the *a* ....1 Kin 18:30
a according to all that ....2 Kin 16:11

built there an *a* ....1 Chr 21:26
made a bronze *a* ....2 Chr 4:1
a of gold and the tables ...2 Chr 4:19
he restored the *a* ....2 Chr 15:8
worship before one *a* ....2 Chr 32:12
repaired the *a* of the .....2 Chr 33:16
the *a* of the God of ....Ezra 3:2
I will go to the *a* ....Ps 43:4
tongs from the *a* ....Is 6:6
there will be an *a* ....Is 19:19
Lord has spurned His *a* .....Lam 2:7
The *a* was in front ....Ezek 40:47
you cover the *a* ....Mal 2:13
your gift to the *a* ....Matt 5:23
swears by the *a* ....Matt 23:18
I even found an *a* ....Acts 17:23
the offerings of the *a* ......1 Cor 9:13
partakers of the *a* ....1 Cor 10:18
We have an *a* from ......Heb 13:10
Isaac his son on the *a* ....James 2:21
under the *a* the souls ......Rev 6:9
and stood at the *a* ....Rev 8:3
horns of the golden *a* ......Rev 9:13
angel came out from the *a* .Rev 14:18

ALTARS
a Hezekiah has taken ....2 Kin 18:22
Even Your *a*, O LORD ......Ps 84:3
on the horns of your *a* .....Jer 17:1
a shall be broken ....Ezek 6:4
has made many *a* ....Hos 8:11
a shall be heaps ....Hos 12:11
destruction on the *a* ......Amos 3:14
and torn down Your *a* ....Rom 11:3

ALTER
put their hand to *a* it .....Ezra 6:12
Nor *a* the word ....Ps 89:34
Persians, which does not *a*. .Dan 6:8
Persians, which does not *a* . .Dan 6:12

ALTERED
of His face was *a* ....Luke 9:29

ALWAYS
delight, rejoicing *a* ....Prov 8:30
the poor with you *a* ......Matt 26:11
Me you do not have *a* ....Matt 26:11
lo, I am with you *a* ....Matt 28:20
'Son, you are *a* ....Luke 15:31
men *a* ought to pray ......Luke 18:1
immovable, *a* abounding .1 Cor 15:58
Rejoice in the Lord *a* ....Phil 4:4
thus we shall *a* ....1 Thess 4:17
a be ready to give *a* ....1 Pet 3:15

AM
See HERE I AM; I AM WITH YOU
to Moses, "I A WHO I A .....Ex 3:14
First and I *a* the Last ....Is 44:6
in My name, I *a* there .....Matt 18:20
I *a* the bread of life ....John 6:35
I *a* the light of the ....John 8:12
I *a* from above ....John 8:23
Abraham was, I A ....John 8:58
I *a* the door ....John 10:9
I *a* the good shepherd ....John 10:11
I *a* the resurrection ......John 11:25
to him, "I *a* the way ......John 14:6
of God I *a* what I *a* .....1 Cor 15:10

AMALEK
Grandson of Esau, Gen 36:11, 12
A chief of Edom, Gen 36:16
First among nations, Num 24:20

AMALEKITES
Destruction predicted, Ex 17:14; Deut
25:17–19
Defeated by Israel, Ex 17:8–13; Judg
7:12–25; 1 Sam 14:47, 48; 27:8, 9;
1 Chr 4:42, 43
Overcome Israel, Num 14:39–45; Judg
3:13

AMASA
Commands Absalom's rebels, 2 Sam
17:25

Made David's commander, 2 Sam 19:13
Treacherously killed by Joab, 2 Sam
20:9–12
Death avenged, 1 Kin 2:28–34

AMAZED
the multitudes were *a* ..... Matt 12:23
trembled and were *a* ...... Mark 16:8
saw Him, they were *a* ..... Luke 2:48
Then they were all *a* and .... Acts 2:7
with Philip, and was *a* ..... Acts 8:13

AMAZIAH
King of Judah; kills his father's assassi-
nators, 2 Kin 14:1–6; 2 Chr 25:1–4
Hires troops from Israel; is rebuked by
a man of God; sends troops home,
2 Chr 25:5–10
Defeats Edomites; worships their gods,
2 Chr 25:11–16
Wars with Israel, 2 Kin 14:8–14; 2 Chr
25:17–24
Killed by conspirators, 2 Chr 25:25–28

AMBASSADOR
but a faithful *a* .... Prov 13:17
for which I am an *a* .... Eph 6:20

AMBASSADORS
which sends *a* by sea .... Is 18:2
cry outside, the *a* .... Is 33:7
we are *a* for Christ .... 2 Cor 5:20

AMBITION
Christ from selfish *a* .... Phil 1:16
through selfish *a* .... Phil 2:3

AMBUSH
Lay an *a* for the city .... Josh 8:2
a all around Gibeah ...... Judg 20:29
son heard of their *a* .... Acts 23:16
they lay in *a* along .... Acts 25:3

AMEN
shall say, "A, so be it ...... Num 5:22
answer and say, 'A ...... Deut 27:15
the people said, "A!" ..... 1 Chr 16:36
all the people say, "A!" ..... Ps 106:48
and the glory forever. A. ... Matt 6:13
to the end of the age." A. .. Matt 28:20
accompanying signs. A. .. Mark 16:20
and blessing God. A. ..... Luke 24:53
that would be written. A. . John 21:25
uninformed say "A .... 1 Cor 14:16
are Yes, and in Him A ... 2 Cor 1:20
These things says the A ..... Rev 3:14
creatures said, "A .... Rev 5:14
I am coming quickly". A. .. Rev 22:20

AMEND
A your ways and your .... Jer 7:3
from his evil way, *a* .... Jer 35:15

AMETHYST
an agate, and an *a* .... Ex 28:19
the twelfth *a* .... Rev 21:20

AMMON
A nation fathered by Lot, Gen 19:36,
38

AMMONITES
Excluded from assembly for hostility
to Israel, Deut 23:3–6
Propose cruel treaty; conquered by
Saul, 1 Sam 11:1–3, 11
Abuse David's ambassadors; con-
quered by his army, 2 Sam 10:1–14
Harass postexilic Jews, Neh 4:3, 7, 8
Defeated by Israel and Judah, Judg
11:4–33; 2 Chr 20:1–25; 27:5, 6
Prophecies concerning, Ps 83:1–18; Jer
25:9–21; Ezek 25:1–7; Amos 1:13–15;
Zeph 2:9–11

AMNON
A son of David, 2 Sam 3:2
Rapes his half sister, 2 Sam 13:1–18
Killed by Absalom, 2 Sam 13:19–29

AMON
King of Judah, 2 Kin 21:18, 19
Follows evil, 2 Chr 33:22, 23
Killed by conspiracy, 2 Kin 21:23, 24
—— A governor of Samaria, 1 Kin
22:10, 26

AMORITES
Defeated by Joshua, Josh 10:1–43
Not driven out of Canaan, Judg
1:34–36
Put to forced labor under Solomon,
1 Kin 9:20, 21

AMOS
A prophet of Israel, Amos 1:1
Pronounces judgment against nations,
Amos 1:1–3, 15
Denounces Israel's sins, Amos 4:1—7:9
Condemns Amaziah, the priest of
Bethel, Amos 7:10–17
Predicts Israel's downfall, Amos
9:1–10
Foretells great blessings, Amos
9:11–15

AMPHIPOLIS
A city in Macedonia visited by Paul,
Acts 17:1

AMRAM
Son of Kohath, Num 3:17–19
The father of Aaron, Moses and
Miriam, Ex 6:18–20; 1 Chr 6:3

ANAKIM
A race of giants; very strong, Num
13:28–33; Deut 2:10, 11, 21
Defeated:
by Joshua, Josh 10:36–39; 11:21
by Caleb, Josh 14:6–15

ANANIAS
Disciple at Jerusalem; slain for lying
to God, Acts 5:1–11
—— A Christian disciple at Damascus,
Acts 9:10–19; 22:12–16
—— A Jewish high priest, Acts 23:1–5

ANATHOTH
A Levitical city in Benjamin, Josh 21:18
Jeremiah's birthplace; he buys prop-
erty there, Jer 1:1; 32:6–15
To be invaded by Assyria, Is 10:30

ANCHOR
hope we have as an *a* ...... Heb 6:19

ANCIENT
Do not remove the *a* ..... Prov 23:10
a times that I .... Is 37:26
until the *A* of Days .... Dan 7:22

ANDREW
A disciple of John the Baptist, then of
Christ, Matt 4:18, 19; John 1:40–42
Enrolled among the Twelve, Matt
10:2
Mentioned, Mark 13:3, 4; John 6:8, 9;
12:20–22; Acts 1:13

ANGEL
Now the *A* of the Lord ..... Gen 16:7
A who has redeemed me .. Gen 48:16
"Behold, I send an *A* ...... Ex 23:20
the donkey saw the *A* .... Num 22:23
For I have seen the *A* ..... Judg 6:22
Manoah said to the *A* ..... Judg 13:17
in my sight as an *a* ...... 1 Sam 29:9
a who was destroying ... 2 Sam 24:16
night that the *a* .... 2 Kin 19:35
the *A* of His Presence .... Is 63:9
struggled with the *A* .... Hos 12:4
standing before the *A* .... Zech 3:3
like God, like the *A* .... Zech 12:8
things, behold, an *a* .... Matt 1:20
for an *a* of the Lord .... Matt 28:2
Then an *a* of the Lord ..... Luke 1:11
And behold, an *a* .... Luke 2:9

a appeared to Him from .. Luke 22:43
For an *a* went down at ...... John 5:4
a has spoken to Him ..... John 12:29
But at night an *a* .... Acts 5:19
A who appeared to him .... Acts 7:35
Then immediately an *a* .... Acts 12:23
and no *a* or spirit .... Acts 23:8
a has spoken to him .... Acts 23:9
by me this night an *a* .... Acts 27:23
himself into an *a* .... 2 Cor 11:14
even if we, or an *a* .... Gal 1:8
Then I saw a strong *a* ...... Rev 5:2
over them the *a* .... Rev 9:11
Then I saw an *a* .... Rev 19:17
Jesus, have sent My *a* ..... Rev 22:16

ANGEL OF GOD
the *a* called to Hagar ...... Gen 21:17
Then the *A* spoke to me ... Gen 31:11
A, who went before the .... Ex 14:19
the *A* came to the woman .. Judg 13:9
the king is like the *a* ..... 2 Sam 19:27
in a vision an *a* coming .... Acts 10:3
you received me as an *a*. ... Gal 4:14

ANGEL OF THE LORD
A found her by a spring .... Gen 16:7
the *A* called to Abraham ... Gen 22:15
A appeared to him in a flame . Ex 3:2
the donkey saw the *A* .... Num 22:23
the *A* came up from Gilgal .. Judg 2:1
the *A* appeared to him ..... Judg 6:12
A appeared to the woman .. Judg 13:3
A was by the threshing .. 2 Sam 24:16
a said to Elijah .... 2 Kin 1:3
a went out, and killed .... 2 Kin 19:35
in the land, with the *a* .... 1 Chr 21:12
The *a* encamps all around .... Ps 34:7
let the *a* pursue them .... Ps 35:6
A, who stood among the ... Zech 1:11
priest standing before the *A* . Zech 3:1
like the *A* before them ... Zech 12:8
a appeared to him in a ..... Matt 1:20
an *a* appeared to Joseph .. Matt 2:13
a descended from heaven, .. Matt 28:2
an *a* appeared to him, ... Luke 1:11
an *a* opened the prison .... Acts 5:19
a spoke to Philip, saying ... Acts 8:26
an *a* stood by him, ... Acts 12:7
an *a* struck him, ... Acts 12:23

ANGELS
If He charges His *a* .... Job 4:18
lower than the *a* .... Ps 8:5
He shall give His *a* .... Ps 91:11
Praise Him, all His *a* .... Ps 148:2
He shall give His *a* .... Matt 4:6
a will come forth .... Matt 13:49
a always see the face ..... Matt 18:10
but are like *a* of God .... Matt 22:30
not even the *a* of heaven .. Matt 24:36
and all the holy *a* .... Matt 25:31
twelve legions of *a* ...... Matt 26:53
the presence of the *a* ..... Luke 15:10
was carried by the *a* ..... Luke 16:22
are equal to the *a* .... Luke 20:36
And she saw two *a* .... John 20:12
that we shall judge *a* ...... 1 Cor 6:3
head, because of the *a* .... 1 Cor 11:10
and worship of *a* .... Col 2:18
with His mighty *a* .... 2 Thess 1:7
the Spirit, seen by *a* ...... 1 Tim 3:16
much better than the *a* ...... Heb 1:4
does not give aid to *a* ...... Heb 2:16
company of *a*, to the ...... Heb 12:22
unwittingly entertained *a* ... Heb 13:2
things which *a* desire ..... 1 Pet 1:12
did not spare the *a* .... 2 Pet 2:4
a who did not keep .... Jude 6
Michael and his *a* .... Rev 12:7

ANGER
See SLOW TO ANGER
Cursed be their *a* .... Gen 49:7

sun, that the fierce *a* ...... Num 25:4
fierceness of His *a* .... Deut 13:17
heat of this great *a* .... Deut 29:24
So the *a* of the LORD ..... Judg 10:7
to provoke Me to *a* .... 1 Kin 16:2
For His *a* is but for a .... Ps 30:5
let Your wrathful *a* .... Ps 69:24
a time He turned His *a* .... Ps 78:38
made a path for His *a* ..... Ps 78:50
You prolong Your *a* .... Ps 85:5
the power of Your *a* .... Ps 90:11
gracious, slow to *a* .... Ps 103:8
Nor will He keep His *a* .... Ps 103:9
harsh word stirs up *a* ..... Prov 15:1
a sins against his own ..... Prov 20:2
a rests in the bosom ...... Eccl 7:9
a the Holy One of .... Is 1:4
a is not turned away .... Is 5:25
a is turned away .... Is 12:1
'I will not cause My *a* ..... Jer 3:12
For great is the *a* .... Jer 36:7
and I will send My *a* ...... Ezek 7:3
does not retain His *a* ...... Mic 7:18
fierceness of His *a* .... Nah 1:6
a is kindled against .... Zech 10:3
around at them with *a* ..... Mark 3:5
bitterness, wrath, *a* .... Eph 4:31

ANGER OF THE LORD
a was kindled against Moses. Ex 4:14
a was aroused against ..... Num 25:3
a burned against the ...... Josh 7:1
a was hot against Israel ... Judg 2:14
a was aroused against ..... 2 Sam 6:7
a was aroused against ..... 2 Kin 13:3
a is aroused against His ...... Is 5:25
a will not turn back ...... Jer 23:20
because of the *a* this ...... Jer 52:3

ANGRY
Cain, "Why are you *a* ...... Gen 4:6
"Let not the Lord be *a* ..... Gen 18:30
the Son, lest He be *a* .... Ps 2:12
judge, and God is *a* .... Ps 7:11
When once You are *a* ...... Ps 76:7
Will you be *a* forever ...... Ps 79:5
friendship with an *a* ..... Prov 22:24
backbiting tongue an *a* ... Prov 25:23
a man stirs up strife ..... Prov 29:22
in your spirit to be *a* ...... Eccl 7:9
I was *a* with My people ..... Is 47:6
nor will I always be *a* ...... Is 57:16
covetousness I was *a* ...... Is 57:17
right for you to be *a* .... Jon 4:4
LORD has been very *a* ...... Zech 1:2
I am exceedingly *a* .... Zech 1:15
you that whoever is *a* ..... Matt 5:22
"Be *a*, and do not sin" ..... Eph 4:26
Therefore I was *a* .... Heb 3:10
with whom was He *a* .... Heb 3:17
The nations were *a* .... Rev 11:18

ANGUISH
a has come upon me ...... 2 Sam 1:9
a make him afraid .... Job 15:24
I will be in *a* over my ...... Ps 38:18
and *a* have overtaken ..... Ps 119:143
longer remembers the *a* .. John 16:21
tribulation and *a* .... Rom 2:9
much affliction and *a* ..... 2 Cor 2:4

ANIMAL
of every clean *a* .... Gen 7:2
Whoever kills an *a* .... Lev 24:18
the life of his *a* .... Prov 12:10
set him on his own *a* ..... Luke 10:34

ANIMALS
of *a* after their kind ...... Gen 6:20
sacrifices of fat *a* .... Ps 66:15
of four-footed *a* .... Acts 10:12
and four-footed *a* .... Rom 1:23

ANISE
tithe of mint and *a* .... Matt 23:23

ANNA
Aged prophetess, Luke 2:36–38

ANNAS
A Jewish high priest, Luke 3:2
Christ appeared before, John 18:12–24
Peter and John appeared before, Acts 4:6

ANNUL
and who will *a* .... Is 14:27
years later, cannot *a* ...... Gal 3:17

ANNULLING
one hand there is an *a* ..... Heb 7:18

ANNULS
is confirmed, no one *a* ..... Gal 3:15

ANOINT
You shall *a* them .... Ex 28:41
but you shall not *a* .... Deut 28:40
you shall *a* for Me the .... 1 Sam 16:3
a yourself with oil .... 2 Sam 14:2
a my head with oil .... Ps 23:5
Arise, you princes, *a* .... Is 21:5
a the Most Holy .... Dan 9:24
when you fast, *a* .... Matt 6:17
a My body for burial ...... Mark 14:8
they might come and *a* .... Mark 16:1
a your eyes with eye ...... Rev 3:18

ANOINTED
See LORD'S ANOINTED
the priest, who is *a* .... Lev 16:32
"Surely the LORD's *a* ...... 1 Sam 16:6
destroy the LORD's *a* ...... 2 Sam 1:14
he cursed the LORD's *a* .. 2 Sam 19:21
shows mercy to His *a* .... 2 Sam 22:51
"Do not touch My *a* ...... 1 Chr 16:22
the LORD saves His *a* ...... Ps 20:6
because the LORD has *a* ..... Is 61:1
"These are the two *a* ...... Zech 4:14
Because He has *a* .... Luke 4:18
but this woman has *a* ..... Luke 7:46
the eyes of the .... John 9:6
It was that Mary who *a* ... John 11:2
Jesus, whom You *a* .... Acts 4:27
and has *a* us is God ...... 2 Cor 1:21

ANOINTING
also made the holy *a* ...... Ex 37:29
pray over him, *a* him ..... James 5:14
But you have an *a* .... 1 John 2:20
but as the same *a* .... 1 John 2:27

ANOTHER
See LOVE ONE ANOTHER
that you love one *a* ...... John 13:34
and He will give you *a* .... John 14:16
'Let *a* take his office ...... Acts 1:20

ANSWER
will give Pharaoh an *a* .... Gen 41:16
a I should take back ...... 2 Sam 24:13
Him, he could not *a* .... Job 9:3
Call, and I will *a* .... Job 13:22
how shall I *a* Him .... Job 31:14
and you shall *a* .... Job 40:7
the day that I call, *a* ...... Ps 102:2
In Your faithfulness *a* ..... Ps 143:1
a turns away wrath .... Prov 15:1
A man has joy by the *a* ... Prov 15:23
He who gives a right *a* ... Prov 24:26
a a fool according .... Prov 26:4
was there none to *a* .... Is 50:2
for there is no *a* .... Mic 3:7
or what you should *a* ..... Luke 12:11
you may have an *a* .... 2 Cor 5:12
ought to *a* each one .... Col 4:6

ANSWERS
a a matter before he ...... Prov 18:13
but the rich *a* roughly ..... Prov 18:23
money *a* everything ...... Eccl 10:19

ANT
Go to the *a*, you sluggard ... Prov 6:6

ANTICHRIST
heard that the *A* .... 1 John 2:18
a who denies the .... 1 John 2:22
is the spirit of the *A* ...... 1 John 4:3
is a deceiver and an *a* ...... 2 John 7

ANTIOCH
———— In Syria:
First Gentile church established, Acts 11:19–21
Disciples first called "Christians" in, Acts 11:26
Church commissions Paul, Acts 13:1–4; 15:35–41
Church troubled by Judaizers, Acts 15:1–4; Gal 2:11–21
———— In Pisidia:
Paul visits; Jews reject the gospel, Acts 13:14, 42–51

ANTIPATRIS
A city between Jerusalem and Caesarea, Acts 23:31

ANTITYPE
a which now saves us ..... 1 Pet 3:21

ANXIETIES
the multitude of my *a* ...... Ps 94:19
Try me, and know my *a* ... Ps 139:23

ANXIETY
A in the heart of man ..... Prov 12:25
eat their bread with *a* ..... Ezek 12:19

ANXIOUS
drink, nor have an *a* ...... Luke 12:29
Be *a* for nothing .... Phil 4:6

APART
See SET APART
that you shall set *a* .... Ex 13:12
she shall be set *a* .... Lev 15:19
the LORD has set *a* .... Ps 4:3
justified by faith *a* .... Rom 3:28

APHEK
A town in the Plain of Sharon, Josh 12:18
Site of Philistine camp, 1 Sam 4:1; 29:1
———— A city in Jezreel, 1 Kin 20:26–30
Syria's defeat prophesied here, 2 Kin 13:14–19

APOLLOS
An Alexandrian Jew; instructed by Aquila and Priscilla and sent to Achaia, Acts 18:24–28
Referred to as having ministered in Corinth, 1 Cor 1:12; 3:4, 22; 4:6; 16:12

APOLLONIA
A town between Amphipolis and Thessalonica, Acts 17:1

APOLLYON
Angel of the bottomless pit, Rev 9:11

APOSTLE
called to be an *a* .... Rom 1:1
inasmuch as I am an *a* .... Rom 11:13
Am I not an *a* .... 1 Cor 9:1
the signs of an *a* were .... 2 Cor 12:12
a preacher and an *a* .... 1 Tim 2:7
consider the *A* and High .... Heb 3:1

APOSTLES
See TWELVE APOSTLES
names of the twelve *a* ..... Matt 10:2
whom He also named *a* ... Luke 6:13
displayed us, the *a* .... 1 Cor 4:9
am the least of the *a* ..... 1 Cor 15:9
to the most eminent *a* .... 2 Cor 11:5
themselves into *a* .... 2 Cor 11:13
none of the other *a* .... Gal 1:19
gave some to be *a* .... Eph 4:11
who say they are *a* .... Rev 2:2
heaven, and you holy *a* ... Rev 18:20

APOSTLESHIP
in this ministry and *a* ..... Acts 1:25

received grace and a . . . . Rom 1:5
are the seal of my a . . . . 1 Cor 9:2
in Peter for the a . . . . Gal 2:8

APPAREL
is glorious in His a . . . . Is 63:1
clothed with foreign a . . . . . Zeph 1:8
by them in white a . . . . Acts 1:10
themselves in modest a . . . . 1 Tim 2:9
gold rings, in fine a . . . . James 2:2
or putting on fine a . . . . 1 Pet 3:3

APPEAL
I a to Caesar . . . . Acts 25:11
love's sake I rather a . . . . Philem 9

APPEAR
and let the dry land a . . . . Gen 1:9
all your males shall a . . . . . . Ex 23:17
all Israel comes to a . . . . . Deut 31:11
shall I come and a . . . . Ps 42:2
Let Your work a . . . . Ps 90:16
He shall a in His . . . . Ps 102:16
doings your sins a . . . . Ezek 21:24
faces that they may a . . . . . Matt 6:16
also outwardly a . . . . Matt 23:28
kingdom of God would a . Luke 19:11
For we must all a . . . . 2 Cor 5:10
for Him He will a . . . . Heb 9:28
and the sinner a . . . . 1 Pet 4:18

APPEARANCE
Do not look at his a . . . . . . 1 Sam 16:7
a is blacker than soot . . . . . Lam 4:8
As He prayed, the a . . . . . . Luke 9:29
judge according to a . . . . . . John 7:24
those who boast in a . . . . . 2 Cor 5:12
to the outward a . . . . 2 Cor 10:7
found in a as a man . . . . Phil 2:8
indeed have an a . . . . Col 2:23

APPEARED
See LORD APPEARED TO
an angel of the Lord a . . . . . Luke 1:11
who a in glory and . . . . Luke 9:31
brings salvation has a . . . . . Titus 2:11
of the ages, He has a . . . . . . Heb 9:26

APPEARING
Lord Jesus Christ's a . . . . . 1 Tim 6:14
been revealed by the a . . . . 2 Tim 1:10
and the dead at His a . . . . . . 2 Tim 4:1
who have loved His a . . . . . 2 Tim 4:8
hope and glorious a . . . . Titus 2:13

APPEARS
can stand when He a . . . . Mal 3:2
who is our life a . . . . Col 3:4
the Chief Shepherd a . . . . . 1 Pet 5:4
in Him, that when He a . . 1 John 2:28

APPETITE
or satisfy the a . . . . Job 38:39
are a man given to a . . . . . . Prov 23:2

APPII FORUM
A town about 40 miles south of Rome
  where Christians came to meet Paul,
  Acts 28:15

APPLE
He kept him as the a . . . . . Deut 32:10
And my law as the a . . . . Prov 7:2
Like an a tree among . . . . . . Song 2:3
touches the a of His eye . . . . Zech 2:8

APPLES
fitly spoken is like a . . . . . . Prov 25:11
refresh me with a . . . . Song 2:5

APPLIED
a my heart to know . . . . Eccl 7:25

APPOINT
I will even a terror . . . . Lev 26:16
a each of them to his . . . . . . Num 4:19
a me ruler over the . . . . . . 2 Sam 6:21
a salvation for walls . . . . Is 26:1
For God did not a . . . . 1 Thess 5:9
a elders in every city . . . . . . Titus 1:5

APPOINTED
You have a his limits . . . . . . Job 14:5
To release those a . . . . Ps 102:20
And as it is a for men . . . . . . Heb 9:27

APPOINTED FEASTS
to the LORD at your a . . . . Num 29:39
your a my soul hates . . . . Is 1:14
her Sabbaths, all her a . . . . . Hos 2:11
O Judah, keep your a . . . . . . Nah 1:15

APPOINTED TIME
At the a I will return to . . . Gen 18:14
keep the Passover at its a . . . Num 9:2
the morning till the a . . . 2 Sam 24:15
at the a the end shall be . . . . Dan 8:19
end will still be at the a . . . Dan 11:27
vision is yet for an a . . . . Hab 2:3

APPROACH
a anyone who is near . . . . . . Lev 18:6
And cause to a You . . . . Ps 65:4
year, make those who a . . . . Heb 10:1

APPROACHING
take delight in a God . . . . Is 58:2
as you see the Day a . . . . . . Heb 10:25

APPROVE
their posterity who a . . . . . . Ps 49:13
do the same but also a . . . . . Rom 1:32
a the things that . . . . Rom 2:18
a the things that are . . . . Phil 1:10

APPROVED
to God and a by men . . . . Rom 14:18
to present yourself a . . . . . . 2 Tim 2:15
when he has been a . . . . . . James 1:12

APRONS
a were brought from his . . Acts 19:12

AQUEDUCT
stood by the a . . . . 2 Kin 18:17
at the end of the a . . . . Is 7:3
he stood by the a . . . . Is 36:2

AQUILA
Paul's host in Corinth, Acts 18:2, 3
Travels to Syria and Ephesus with Paul,
  Acts 18:18, 19
Instructs Apollos, Acts 18:24–26
Esteemed by Paul, Rom 16:3, 4

AR
A chief Moabite city, Num 21:15
On Israel's route, Deut 2:18
Destroyed by Sihon, Num 21:28
Destroyed by God, Is 15:1

ARABIA
Pays tribute to Solomon, 1 Kin 10:14, 15
Plunders Jerusalem, 2 Chr 21:16, 17
Defeated by Uzziah, 2 Chr 26:1, 7
Denounced by prophets, Is 21:13–17

ARARAT
Site of ark's landing, Gen 8:4
Assassins flee to, 2 Kin 19:37; Is 37:38

ARAUNAH (or Ornan)
A Jebusite, 2 Sam 24:15–25
His threshing floor bought by David,
  2 Sam 24:18–25
becomes site of temple, 2 Chr 3:1
Also called Ornan, 1 Chr 21:18–28

ARBITRATOR
a judge or an a over . . . . . Luke 12:14

ARCHANGEL
with the voice of an a . . . 1 Thess 4:16
Yet Michael the a . . . . Jude 9

ARCHELAUS
Son of Herod the Great, Matt 2:22

AREOPAGUS
Paul preaches at, Acts 17:18–34

ARGUMENTS
fill my mouth with a . . . . Job 23:4
casting down a and . . . . . . 2 Cor 10:5

ARIEL
Ezra's friend, Ezra 8:15–17
——— Name applied to Jerusalem,
  Is 29:1, 2, 7

ARISE
needy, now I will a . . . . Ps 12:5
A for our help . . . . Ps 44:26
Let God a . . . . Ps 68:1
A, shine; for your light . . . . . . Is 60:1
But the LORD will a . . . . Is 60:2
Righteousness shall a . . . . . . Mal 4:2
I will a and go to . . . . Luke 15:18
you who sleep, a . . . . Eph 5:14

ARISTARCHUS
A Macedonian Christian, Acts 19:29
Accompanies Paul, Acts 20:1, 4
Imprisoned with Paul, Col 4:10

ARK
Make yourself an a . . . . Gen 6:14
two of every sort into the a . Gen 6:19
Then the a rested . . . . Gen 8:4
she took an a of bulrushes . . . Ex 2:3
in the a you shall put . . . . . . Ex 25:21
Bezalel made the a . . . . Ex 37:1
seat which is on the a . . . . . Lev 16:2
the a which I had made . . . . Deut 10:5
"Cross over before the a . . . Josh 4:5
"Take up the a . . . . Josh 6:6
Let us bring the a . . . . 1 Sam 4:3
Also the a of God . . . . 1 Sam 4:11
a of God was captured . . . . 1 Sam 4:19
Philistines took the a . . . . . 1 Sam 5:1
the a remained in Kirjath . 1 Sam 7:2
out his hand to the a . . . . . 2 Sam 6:6
brought the a of the . . . . . . 2 Sam 6:17
Nothing was in the a . . . . . . 1 Kin 8:9
his hand to hold the a . . . . 1 Chr 13:9
the holy a in the house . . . 2 Chr 35:3
golden censer and the a . . . . Heb 9:4
prepared an a for the . . . . . Heb 11:7
of Noah, while the a . . . . . . 1 Pet 3:20
in heaven, and the a . . . . . Rev 11:19

ARM
with an outstretched a . . . . . . Ex 6:6
"Has the LORD's a . . . . . . Num 11:23
With him is an a . . . . 2 Chr 32:8
a that has no strength . . . . . Job 26:2
Have you an a like God . . . . Job 40:9
Break the a of the . . . . Ps 10:15
You have a mighty a . . . . . . Ps 89:13
a have gained Him the . . . . . . Ps 98:1
a shall rule for Him . . . . Is 40:10
therefore His own a . . . . Is 59:16
strength with His a . . . . Luke 1:51
with an uplifted a . . . . Acts 13:17
a yourselves also with . . . . . 1 Pet 4:1

ARMAGEDDON
See MEGIDDO
Possible site of final battle, Rev 16:16

ARMED
You have a me with . . . . . 2 Sam 22:40
a strong man, fully a . . . . . Luke 11:21

ARMIES
make captains of the a . . . . Deut 20:9
"I defy the a of Israel . . . . 1 Sam 17:10
any number to His a . . . . . . Job 25:3
not go out with our a . . . . . . Ps 60:10
And he sent out his a . . . . . . Matt 22:7
surrounded by a . . . . Luke 21:20
And the a in heaven . . . . . Rev 19:14
the earth, and their a . . . . . Rev 19:19

ARMOR
but he put his a . . . . 1 Sam 17:54
spears, put on the a . . . . Jer 46:4
let us put on the a . . . . Rom 13:12
Put on the whole a . . . . Eph 6:11

ARMORBEARER
to the young man, his a . . . . Judg 9:54

ARMS (cont.)

Jonathan said to his *a* ... 1 Sam 14:12
he became his *a* .... 1 Sam 16:21
Saul said to his *a* .... 1 Sam 31:4
his *a* would not, for he ... 1 Chr 10:4
when his *a* saw that Saul . 1 Chr 10:5

ARMS

are the everlasting *a* ...... Deut 33:27
into the clash of *a* .... Job 39:21
It is God who *a* .... Ps 18:32
My *a* will judge the .... Is 51:5
wounds between your *a* ... Zech 13:6
took them up in His *a* .. Mark 10:16
took Him up in his *a* ..... Luke 2:28

ARMY

the multitude of an *a* ...... Ps 33:16
an exceedingly great *a* .... Ezek 37:10
the number of the *a* .... Rev 9:16

ARNON

Boundary between Moab and Ammon,
Num 21:13, 26
Border of Reuben, Deut 3:12, 16
Ammonites reminded of, Judg
11:18–26

AROER

A town in east Jordan; rebuilt by Gadites, Num 32:34; Deut 2:36
Assigned to Reuben, Deut 3:12
Ruled by Amorites, Josh 12:2; 13:9, 10,
16

AROMA

smelled a soothing *a* .... Gen 8:21
To the one we are the *a* .. 2 Cor 2:16
for a sweet-smelling *a* ...... Eph 5:2
a sweet-smelling *a* .... Phil 4:18

AROSE

younger *a* and lay with .... Gen 19:35
a and crossed the river .... Gen 31:21
behold, my sheaf *a* .... Gen 37:7
there *a* a new king .... Ex 1:8
Deborah *a* and went ...... Judg 4:9
until I, Deborah, *a* .... Judg 5:7
a a mother in Israel .... Judg 5:7
Samuel *a* and went to Eli, . 1 Sam 3:6
David *a* and fled .... 1 Sam 21:10
LORD *a* against His .... 2 Chr 36:16
Then I *a* in the night .... Neh 2:12
Esther *a* and stood before ... Esth 8:4
I *a* to open for my beloved .. Song 5:5
the king *a* very early .... Dan 6:19
afterward I *a* and went .... Dan 8:27
Jonah *a* to flee to .... Jon 1:3
And she *a* and served ..... Matt 8:15
tempest *a* on the sea ...... Matt 8:24
He *a* and rebuked .... Matt 8:26
all those virgins *a* and .... Matt 25:7
a great windstorm ...... Mark 4:37
a and rebuked the wind ... Mark 4:39
a against the church .... Acts 8:1
he *a* and was baptized ...... Acts 9:18
with Him after He *a* ...... Acts 10:41
a dissension *a* between .... Acts 23:7
smoke *a* out of the pit ...... Rev 9:2

AROUSED

the LORD was greatly *a* ... Num 11:10
his wrath was *a* because .... Num 32:2
Then Joseph, being *a* ..... Matt 1:24

ARPHAXAD

A son of Shem, Gen 10:22, 24
Born two years after the flood, Gen
11:10–13
An ancestor of Christ, Luke 3:36

ARRAY

a against Gibeah .... Judg 20:30
battle *a* against Israel ...... 1 Sam 4:2
drew up in battle *a* .... 1 Sam 17:2
a yourself with glory ...... Job 40:10

ARRAYED

his glory was not *a* .... Matt 6:29

"Who are these *a* .... Rev 7:13
The woman was *a* .... Rev 17:4

ARREST

come up to *a* Samson ..... Judg 15:10
the altar, saying, "A him .. 1 Kin 13:4
when they *a* you .... Mark 13:11

ARROGANCE

Pride and *a* and the .... Prov 8:13
I will halt the *a* .... Is 13:11

ARROGANT

the fruit of the *a* .... Is 10:12
sanctuary, your *a* boast ... Ezek 24:21

ARROW

deliverance and the *a* .... 2 Kin 13:17
a cannot make him flee .... Job 41:28
make ready their *a* .... Ps 11:2
a that flies by day .... Ps 91:5
a sword, and a sharp *a* .... Prov 25:18
Their tongue is an *a* .... Jer 9:8
as a target for the *a* .... Lam 3:12

ARROWS

He sent out *a* and .... 2 Sam 22:15
a pierce me deeply .... Ps 38:2
There He broke the *a* ...... Ps 76:3
Like *a* in the hand of .... Ps 127:4
He has caused the *a* ...... Lam 3:13
were sworn over Your *a* ..... Hab 3:9

ARTAXERXES

Artaxerxes I, king of Persia (465–425
B.C.), authorizes Ezra's mission to
Jerusalem, Ezra 7:1–28
Temporarily halts rebuilding program
at Jerusalem, Ezra 4:7–23
Authorizes Nehemiah's mission, Neh
2:1–10
Permits Nehemiah to return, Neh 13:6

ARTISAN

gifted *a* in whom .... Ex 36:1
the skillful *a*, and the expert ... Is 3:3

ARTISTIC

a designs of cherubim ...... Ex 26:1
to design *a* works .... Ex 31:4
a designs of cherubim ...... Ex 36:8
linen, into *a* designs .... Ex 39:3

AS IT IS WRITTEN

A in the Law of Moses, ... Dan 9:13
of Man indeed goes just *a* . Matt 26:24
A in the Prophets: "Behold, . Mark 1:2
of you hypocrites, *a* ...... Mark 7:6
whatever they wished, *a* .. Mark 9:13
a, 'He gave them bread .... Mark 6:31
donkey, sat on it; *a* .... John 12:14
a, "The just shall live ...... Rom 1:17
Israel will be saved, *a* ..... Rom 11:26
but *a*, "The reproaches of . Rom 15:3

ASA

Third king of Judah; restores true worship, 1 Kin 15:8–15; 2 Chr 14; 15
Hires Ben-Hadad against Baasha; rebuked by a prophet, 1 Kin 15:16–22;
2 Chr 16:1–10
Diseased, seeks physicians rather than
the Lord, 2 Chr 16:12
Death and burial, 2 Chr 16:13, 14

ASAHEL

David's nephew; captain in his army;
noted for valor, 2 Sam 2:18; 23:24;
1 Chr 2:16; 27:7
Killed by Abner, 2 Sam 2:19–23
Avenged by Joab, 2 Sam 3:27, 30

ASAPH

A Levite choir leader under David and
Solomon, 1 Chr 15:16–19; 16:1–7;
2 Chr 5:6, 12
Twelve psalms assigned to, 2 Chr
29:30; Ps 50; 73–83

ASCEND

Who may *a* into the .... Ps 24:3

If I *a* into heaven .... Ps 139:8
'I will *a* into heaven .... Is 14:13
a as high as the eagle .... Obad 4
see the Son of Man *a* ..... John 6:62

ASCENDED

You have *a* on high .... Ps 68:18
Who has *a* into heaven .... Prov 30:4
No one has *a* to heaven .... John 3:13
"When He *a* on high .... Eph 4:8
also the One who *a* .... Eph 4:10
And they *a* to heaven ...... Rev 11:12

ASCENDING

angels of God were *a* ...... Gen 28:12
the angels of God *a* .... John 1:51

ASCRIBE

a greatness to our God .... Deut 32:3
I will *a* righteousness to .... Job 36:3
A strength to God .... Ps 68:34

ASENATH

Daughter of Poti-Pherah and wife of
Joseph, Gen 41:45
Mother of Manasseh and Ephraim, Gen
41:50–52; 46:20

ASHAMED

O my God, I am too *a* and ... Ezra 9:6
all my enemies be *a* .... Ps 6:10
Let me not be *a* .... Ps 25:2
who waits on You be *a* ...... Ps 25:3
The wise men are *a* .... Jer 8:9
forsake You shall be *a* ..... Jer 17:13
And Israel shall be *a* ...... Hos 10:6
For whoever is *a* .... Mark 8:38
am not *a* of the gospel .... Rom 1:16
nothing I shall be *a* .... Phil 1:20
Therefore God is not *a* .... Heb 11:16
in Christ may be *a* .... 1 Pet 3:16
let him not be *a* .... 1 Pet 4:16
and not be *a* before ...... 1 John 2:28

ASHDOD

One of five Philistine cities, Josh 13:3
Seat of Dagon worship, 1 Sam 5:1–8
Opposes Nehemiah, Neh 4:7
Women of, marry Jews, Neh 13:23, 24
Called Azotus, Acts 8:40

ASHER

Jacob's second son by Zilpah, Gen
30:12, 13
Goes to Egypt with Jacob, Gen 46:8,
17
Blessed by Jacob, Gen 49:20
——— Tribe of:
Census of, Num 1:41; 26:47
Slow to fight against Canaanites, Judg
1:31, 32; 5:17
Among Gideon's army, Judg 6:35; 7:23
A godly remnant among, 2 Chr 30:11

ASHERAH

The female counterpart of Baal, Judg
3:7; 1 Kin 18:19
Image of, erected by Manasseh in the
temple, 2 Kin 21:7
Vessels of, destroyed by Josiah, 2 Kin
23:4
——— Translated "wooden images,"
idols used in the worship of Asherah,
Ex 34:13; Deut 12:3; 16:21; 1 Kin
16:32, 33; 2 Kin 23:6, 7

ASHES

are proverbs of *a* .... Job 13:12
become like dust and *a* .... Job 30:19
For I have eaten *a* .... Ps 102:9
He feeds on *a*; a deceived .... Is 44:20
sackcloth and sat in *a* ...... Jon 3:6
in sackcloth and *a* .... Luke 10:13
and the *a* of a heifer .... Heb 9:13

ASHKELON

One of five Philistine cities, Josh 13:3;
Jer 47:5, 7

Captured by Judah, Judg 1:18
Men of, killed by Samson, Judg 14:19, 20
Repossessed by Philistines, 1 Sam 6:17; 2 Sam 1:20
Doom of, pronounced by the prophets, Jer 47:5, 7; Amos 1:8; Zeph 2:4, 7; Zech 9:5

ASHTAROTH
A city in Bashan; residence of King Og, Deut 1:4; Josh 12:4
Captured by Israel, Josh 9:10
—— A general designation of the Canaanite female deities, 1 Sam 7:3, 4; 31:10

ASHTORETH
A mother-goddess worshiped by the Philistines, 1 Sam 31:10
Israel ensnared by, Judg 2:13; 10:6
Worshiped by Solomon, 1 Kin 11:5, 33
Destroyed by Josiah, 2 Kin 23:13

ASIA
Paul forbidden to preach in, Acts 16:6
Paul's later ministry in, Acts 19:1–26
Seven churches of, Rev 1:4, 11

ASIDE
See TURN ASIDE
lay something a, storing ...1 Cor 16:2
lay a all filthiness ....James 1:21
Therefore, laying a ....1 Pet 2:1

ASK
"Why is it that you a ......Gen 32:29
when your children a ....Josh 4:6
"A a sign for yourself ....Is 7:11
They shall a the way ....Jer 50:5
the young children a ....Lam 4:4
A the LORD for rain in .....Zech 10:1
whatever things you a ..Matt 21:22
a, and it will be ....Luke 11:9
that whatever You a ....John 11:22
a anything in My ....John 14:14
in that day you will a .....John 16:23
something, let them a ...1 Cor 14:35
above all that we a ....Eph 3:20
wisdom, let him a ....James 1:5
But let him a in faith .....James 1:6
because you do not a .....James 4:2
hears us, whatever we a . 1 John 5:15

ASKS
For everyone who a ......Matt 7:8
if his son a for bread ......Matt 7:9
Or if he a for a fish ......Luke 11:11

ASLEEP
down, and was fast a ....Jon 1:5
But He was a ....Matt 8:24
but some have fallen a ...1 Cor 15:6
those who are a ....1 Thess 4:15
the fathers fell a ....2 Pet 3:4

ASSEMBLE
A the men of Judah ......2 Sam 20:4
a the outcasts of Israel .....Is 11:12
A yourselves, and let ......Jer 4:5
I will a them in the midst ...Jer 21:4
A yourselves and come ...Ezek 39:17
a a multitude of great .....Dan 11:10
A and come, all you ......Joel 3:11
I will surely a all of you ...Mic 2:12

ASSEMBLED
a all the congregation .....Num 1:18
Israel a together at Shiloh . Josh 18:1
Solomon a the elders ....1 Kin 8:1
David a the children of ....1 Chr 15:4
of the God of Israel a .....Ezra 9:4
Israel were a with fasting ...Neh 9:1
who were at Shushan a ....Esth 9:18
behold, the kings a........Ps 48:4
elders of the people a at ....Matt 26:3
with him were a all the .. Mark 14:53

the disciples were a ......John 20:19
a together was shaken .....Acts 4:31
being a with one accord, .. Acts 15:25

ASSEMBLING
not forsaking the a ....Heb 10:25

ASSEMBLY
to kill this whole a ....Ex 16:3
It is a sacred a ....Lev 23:36
a I will praise You ....Ps 22:22
I have hated the a ....Ps 26:5
also in the a of the ....Ps 89:5
to be feared in the a ....Ps 89:7
will rest in the a of the .... Prov 21:16
fast, call a sacred a ....Joel 1:14
people, sanctify the a ......Joel 2:15
a I will sing praise ....Heb 2:12
to the general a ....Heb 12:23
come into your a ....James 2:2

ASSHUR
One of the sons of Shem; progenitor of the Assyrians, Gen 10:22; 1 Chr 1:17
—— The chief god of the Assyrians; seen in names like Ashurbanipal (Osnapper), Ezra 4:10
—— A city in Assyria or the nation of Assyria, Num 24:22, 24

ASSOS
A seaport of Mysia in Asia to which Paul walked, Acts 20:13

ASSURANCE
night, and have no a .....Deut 28:66
riches of the full a ....Col 2:2
Spirit and in much a .....1 Thess 1:5
to the full of hope ....Heb 6:11
a true heart in full a ....Heb 10:22

ASSURE
a our hearts before ....1 John 3:19

ASSURED
I will give you a peace .....Jer 14:13
learned and been a ....2 Tim 3:14

ASSUREDLY, I SAY TO YOU
"For a, till heaven and ....Matt 5:18
"A, you will by no means .. Matt 5:26
A, they have their reward... Matt 6:2
"A, I have not found such . Matt 8:10
"A, it will be more ....Matt 10:15
For a, you will not have ... Matt 10:23
a, he shall by no means ... Matt 10:42
"A, among those born of . Matt 11:11
"a that many prophets ... Matt 13:17
"A, there are some ......Matt 16:28
for a, if you have faith ....Matt 17:20
"A, unless you are ....Matt 18:3
a, he rejoices more over ..Matt 18:13
"A, whatever you bind ...Matt 18:18
"A that it is hard for a ... Matt 19:23
"A, that in the ....Matt 19:28
"A, if you have faith and .. Matt 21:21
"A that tax collectors ....Matt 21:31
"A, all these things will .. Matt 23:36
A, not one stone shall be .. Matt 24:2
"A, this generation will ...Matt 24:34
"A that he will make .....Matt 24:47
'A, I do not know you.' .. .Matt 25:12
'A, inasmuch as you did .. Matt 25:40
'A, inasmuch as you did .. Matt 25:45
A, wherever this gospel .. Matt 26:13
"A, one of you will betray . Matt 26:21
"A that this night, before . Matt 26:34
"A, all sins will be ....Mark 3:28
A, no sign shall be given . Mark 8:12
A, whoever does not .....Mark 10:15
"A, there is no one who .. Mark 10:29
a, whoever says to this ...Mark 11:23
"A that this poor widow .. Mark 12:43
"A, I will no longer .....Mark 14:25
"A, no prophet is accepted . Luke 4:24
A that he will gird ....Luke 12:37

a, you shall not see Me ...Luke 13:35
"A, today you will be .....Luke 23:43
"Most a, hereafter you .....John 1:51
"Most a, unless one is born . John 3:3
"Most a, We speak what ...John 3:11
"Most a, the Son can do ...John 5:19
"Most a, he who hears .....John 5:24
"Most a, the hour is ......John 5:25
"Most a, you seek Me, not . John 6:26
"Most a, Moses did not ....John 6:32
"Most a, he who believes . . John 6:47
"Most a, unless you eat ...John 6:53
"Most a, whoever commits . John 8:34
"Most a, if anyone keeps . John 8:51
"Most a, before Abraham . John 8:58
"Most a, he who does not . John 10:1
"Most a, I am the door of . . John 10:7
"Most a, unless a grain ... John 12:24
Most a, he who receives . John 13:20
"Most a, he who believes . John 14:12
"Most a that you will .....John 16:20
Most a, whatever you ask . John 16:23
"Most a, when you were .. John 21:18

ASSYRIA (or Asshur)
Founded by Nimrod, Gen 10:8–12; Mic 5:6
Agent of God's purposes, Is 7:17–20; 10:5, 6
Attacks and finally conquers Israel, 2 Kin 15:19, 20, 29; 17:3–41
Invades and threatens Judah, 2 Kin 18:13–37
Hezekiah prays for help against; army miraculously slain, 2 Kin 19:1–35
Prophecies concerning, Num 24:22–24; Is 10:12–19; 14:24, 25; 19:23–25; Hos 10:6; 11:5; Nah 3:1–19

ASTONISHED
dwell in it shall be a .....Lev 26:32
who passes by it will be a . 1 Kin 9:8
I sat a until the evening .....Ezra 9:4
are a at His rebuke ....Job 26:11
Just as many were a ....Is 52:14
Be a, O heavens, at ....Jer 2:12
remained there a ....Ezek 3:15
was a for a time, and his .. Dan 4:19
that the people were a ....Matt 7:28
so that they were a ....Matt 13:54
disciples were a at His .. Mark 10:24
who heard Him were a ....Luke 2:47
a at the catch of fish ......Luke 5:9
her parents were a, ...Luke 8:56
at the tomb early, a us ...Luke 24:22
So he, trembling and a, ...Acts 9:6
who believed were a, ...Acts 10:45
saw him, they were a ....Acts 12:16
being a at the teaching ...Acts 13:12

ASTONISHMENT
you shall become an a ....Deut 28:37
a has taken hold ....Jer 8:21

ASTRAY
is a people who go a ....Ps 95:10
a fool, shall not go a ....Is 35:8
Their lies lead them a .....Amos 2:4
and one of them goes a .. Matt 18:12
They always go a ....Heb 3:10
like sheep going a ....1 Pet 2:25

ASTROLOGERS
the a, the stargazers ....Is 47:13
the magicians, the a ....Dan 2:2
bring in the a ....Dan 5:7

AT THE RIGHT HAND
Son of Man sitting a ......Matt 26:64
heaven, and sat down a ...Mark 16:19
Jesus standing a of God ....Acts 7:55
who is even a of God, ...Rom 8:34
sat down a of the Majesty ....Heb 1:3
Priest, who is seated a .....Heb 8:1
heaven and is a of God, ...1 Pet 3:22

ATE

she took of its fruit and *a* . . . Gen 3:6
near to him, and he *a* . . . . . Gen 27:25
I *a* all of it before . . . . Gen 27:33
gaunt cows *a* up the seven . . Gen 41:4
a manna forty years . . . . Ex 16:35
died, you arose and *a* . . . . 2 Sam 12:21
Men *a* angels' food . . . . Ps 78:25
I *a* them, and Your word . . . Jer 15:16
I *a* it, and it was in my . . . . . Ezek 3:3
all *a* and were filled . . . . . . Matt 14:20
all *a* and were filled . . . . . . Matt 15:37
he *a* locusts and wild . . . . . . Mark 1:6
a the showbread . . . . Mark 2:26
all *a* and were filled . . . . . . Mark 6:42
they *a* and were filled . . . . . Mark 8:8
all *a* and were filled . . . . . . Luke 9:17
Our fathers *a* the manna . . . John 6:31
men and *a* with them . . . . Acts 11:3
a the same spiritual . . . . . . 1 Cor 10:3
a it, and it was as sweet . . . Rev 10:10

ATHALIAH

Daughter of Ahab and Jezebel, 2 Kin
8:18, 26; 2 Chr 22:2, 3
Kills royal children; usurps throne,
2 Kin 11:1–3; 2 Chr 22:10, 11
Killed in priestly uprising, 2 Kin
11:4–16; 2 Chr 23:1–21

ATHENS

Paul preaches in, Acts 17:15–34
Paul resides in, 1 Thess 3:1

ATONEMENT

a year he shall make *a* . . . . . Ex 30:10
priest shall make *a* . . . . Lev 16:30
the blood that makes *a* . . . . Lev 17:11
for it is the Day of *A* . . . . . . Lev 23:28
what shall I make *a* . . . . . 2 Sam 21:3
offerings to make *a* . . . . . . Neh 10:33
a is provided for . . . . Prov 16:6
there will be no *a* . . . . Is 22:14
I provide you an *a* . . . . Ezek 16:63

ATTACK

the Midianites, and *a* . . . . . Num 25:17
men go up and *a* Ai . . . . Josh 7:3
a Amalek, and utterly . . . . 1 Sam 15:3
got ready to *a* the city . . . . 1 Kin 20:12
a Jerusalem and create . . . . . Neh 4:8
king of the South shall *a* . . Dan 11:40
no one will *a* you to hurt . . Acts 18:10

ATTACKED

a the Rephaim in . . . . Gen 14:5
who *a* Midian in the . . . . . . Gen 36:35
they *a* them until they left . . Josh 11:8
he *a* the army while the . . . . Judg 8:11
Jonathan *a* the garrison . . 1 Sam 13:3
a Ziklag and burned it . . . . 1 Sam 30:1
David *a* the Philistines . . . . 2 Sam 8:1
a Judah, and carried . . . . . 2 Chr 28:17
a the ram, and broke . . . . . . Dan 8:7
a the house of Jason . . . . . . Acts 17:5

ATTAIN

It is high, I cannot *a* . . . . . . Ps 139:6
understanding will *a* . . . . . . Prov 1:5
How long until they *a* . . . . . Hos 5:5
worthy to *a* that age . . . . . Luke 20:35
by any means, I may *a* . . . . Phil 3:11

ATTALIA

A seaport of Pamphylia from which
Paul sailed to Antioch, Acts 14:25

ATTEND

just cause, O LORD, *a* . . . . Ps 17:1
And *a* to the voice of . . . . Ps 86:6
behold, I will *a* . . . . Jer 23:2

ATTENTION

My son, give *a* to my . . . . . Prov 4:20
Till I come, give *a* . . . . 1 Tim 4:13
and you pay *a* to the . . . . . James 2:3

ATTENTIVE

Let Your ears be *a* . . . . Ps 130:2

the people were very *a* . . . Luke 19:48

ATTESTED

a Man *a* by God to you . . . . Acts 2:22

AUSTERE

because you are an *a* . . . . Luke 19:21

AUTHOR

For God is not the *a* . . . . . 1 Cor 14:33
He became the *a* . . . . Heb 5:9
unto Jesus, the *a* . . . . Heb 12:2

AUTHORITIES

magistrates and *a* . . . . . . Luke 12:11
a that exist are . . . . Rom 13:1
subject to rulers and *a* . . . . Titus 3:1
of God, angels and *a* . . . . . 1 Pet 3:22

AUTHORITY

Jew, wrote with full *a* . . . . Esth 9:29
the righteous are in *a* . . . . Prov 29:2
them as one having *a* . . . . Matt 7:29
a man under *a* . . . . Matt 8:9
who are great exercise *a* . . Matt 20:25
"All *a* has been given . . . . . Matt 28:18
ones exercise *a* over . . . . . Mark 10:42
By what *a* are You . . . . . . Mark 11:28
a I will give You . . . . Luke 4:6
His word was with *a* . . . . . Luke 4:32
a over all demons . . . . Luke 9:1
and has given Him *a* . . . . . John 5:27
You have given Him *a* . . . . . John 17:2
has put in His own *a* . . . . . . Acts 1:7
For there is no *a* . . . . Rom 13:1
a over her own body . . . . . 1 Cor 7:4
to have a symbol of *a* . . . 1 Cor 11:10
end to all rule and all *a* . . 1 Cor 15:24
and all who are in *a* . . . . . . 1 Tim 2:2
have *a* over a man . . . . 1 Tim 2:12
and rebuke with all *a* . . . . . Titus 2:15
defile the flesh, reject *a* . . . . Jude 8
his throne, and great *a* . . . . Rev 13:2
they receive *a* for one . . . . Rev 17:12

AUTUMN

a trees without fruit . . . . Jude 12

AVAILS

nor uncircumcision *a* . . . . . . Gal 5:6
of a righteous man *a* . . . . James 5:16

AVEN

The city of On in Egypt near Cairo;
known as Heliopolis, Gen 41:45;
Ezek 30:17
—— A name contemptuously applied
to Bethel, Hos 10:5, 8
—— Valley in Syria, Amos 1:5

AVENGE

for He will *a* the . . . . Deut 32:43
you that He will *a* . . . . Luke 18:8
Beloved, do not *a* . . . . Rom 12:19
a our blood on those . . . . . . Rev 6:10

AVENGER

The *a* of blood . . . . Num 35:19
the enemy and the *a* . . . . Ps 8:2
God's minister, an *a* . . . . . . Rom 13:4
the Lord is the *a* . . . . 1 Thess 4:6

AVENGES

It is God who *a* . . . . 2 Sam 22:48
When He *a* blood . . . . Ps 9:12

AVOID

a foolish and ignorant . . . . 2 Tim 2:23
a foolish disputes . . . . Titus 3:9

AWAKE

be satisfied when I *a* . . . . . . Ps 17:15
I lie *a* and am like . . . . Ps 102:7
A, lute and harp . . . . Ps 108:2
My eyes are *a* through . . . . Ps 119:148
A, O north wind . . . . Song 4:16
but my heart is *a* . . . . Song 5:2
of the earth shall *a* . . . . Dan 12:2
it is high time to *a* . . . . Rom 13:11
A to righteousness . . . . . . 1 Cor 15:34

"*A*, you who sleep . . . . Eph 5:14

AWARE

Before I was even *a* . . . . . . Song 6:12
hour that he is not *a* of . . . Matt 24:50
But Jesus, being *a* of it . . . Mark 8:17
hour when he is not *a* . . . . Luke 12:46
his wife also being *a* . . . . . . Acts 5:2

AWAY

the wind drives *a* . . . . Ps 1:4
Do not cast me *a* . . . . Ps 51:11
A time to cast *a* . . . . Eccl 3:5
fair one, and come *a* . . . . . Song 2:10
and the shadows flee *a* . . . Song 2:17
minded to put her *a* . . . . . . Matt 1:19
and earth will pass *a* . . . . Matt 24:35
and steal Him *a* . . . . Matt 27:64
the rich He has sent *a* . . . . Luke 1:53
of God who takes *a* . . . . . . John 1:29
"I am going *a*, and you . . . John 8:21
they cried out, "*A* . . . . John 19:15
"They have taken *a* . . . . . . John 20:2
crying out, "*A* with him . . . Acts 21:36
the veil is taken *a* . . . . 2 Cor 3:14
Barnabas was carried *a* . . . . Gal 2:13
unless the falling *a* . . . . . 2 Thess 2:3
in Asia have turned *a* . . . . 2 Tim 1:15
heard, lest we drift *a* . . . . . . Heb 2:1
if they fall *a*, to renew . . . . . Heb 6:6
which can never take *a* . . . Heb 10:11
that does not fade *a* . . . . . . 1 Pet 5:4
the world is passing *a* . . . . 1 John 2:17
and the heaven fled *a* . . . . Rev 20:11
if anyone takes *a* . . . . Rev 22:19

AWE

the world stand in *a* . . . . Ps 33:8
my heart stands in *a* . . . . . Ps 119:161

AWESOME

How *a* is this place . . . . . . Gen 28:17
a thing that I will do . . . . . . Ex 34:10
God, the great and *a* . . . . . Deut 7:21
God, mighty and *a* . . . . . . Deut 10:17
a things which your eyes . Deut 10:21
a name, THE LORD . . . . . . Deut 28:58
Angel of God, very *a* . . . . . Judg 13:6
a deeds for Your land . . . . 2 Sam 7:23
a deeds, by driving out . . 1 Chr 17:21
heaven, O great and *a* . . . . . Neh 1:5
the Lord, great and *a* . . . . . Neh 4:14
a God, Who keeps . . . . Neh 9:32
show Yourself *a* . . . . Job 10:16
with God is *a* majesty . . . . . Job 37:22
hand shall teach You *a* . . . . . Ps 45:4
LORD Most High is *a* . . . . Ps 47:2
By *a* deeds in . . . . Ps 65:5
a are Your works . . . . Ps 66:3
He is *a* in His doing . . . . Ps 66:5
O God, You are more *a* . . . Ps 68:35
He is *a* to the kings . . . . . . Ps 76:12
Your great and *a* name . . . . . Ps 99:3
a things by the Red Sea . . Ps 106:22
Holy and *a* is His name . . . Ps 111:9
of the might of Your *a* . . . Ps 145:6
When You did *a* things . . . . Is 64:3
with me as a mighty, *a* . . Jer 20:11
her collapse was *a* . . . . Lam 1:9
so high they were *a* . . . . . Ezek 1:18
color of an *a* crystal . . . . . Ezek 1:22
its form was *a* . . . . Dan 2:31
"O Lord, great and *a* . . . . . . Dan 9:4
The LORD will be *a* . . . . . . Zeph 2:11

AWL

his ear with an *a* . . . . Ex 21:6
you shall take an *a* . . . . . . Deut 15:17

AWOKE

Noah *a* from his wine . . . . Gen 9:24
Jacob *a* from his sleep . . . . Gen 28:16
I *a*, for the LORD sustained . . . . Ps 3:5
Then the Lord *a* as . . . . . . Ps 78:65
came to Him and *a* Him, . . . Matt 8:25
they *a* Him and said to . . . . Mark 4:38

came to Him and *a* Him, . . . Luke 8:24

AX
a stroke with the *a* . . . . Deut 19:5
Abimelech took an *a* . . . . Judg 9:48
a tree, the iron *a* . . . . 2 Kin 6:5
If the *a* is dull, and one . . . . Eccl 10:10
a boast itself against . . . . Is 10:15
And even now the *a* . . . . Matt 3:10

AZARIAH
A prophet who encourages King Asa, 2 Chr 15:1–8
——— Son of King Jehoshaphat, 2 Chr 21:2
——— King of Judah, 2 Kin 15:1
——— A high priest who rebukes King Uzziah, 2 Chr 26:16–20
——— Chief priest in the time of Hezekiah, 2 Chr 31:9, 10
——— The Hebrew name of Abed-Nego, Dan 1:7

AZEKAH
Camp of Goliath, 1 Sam 17:1, 4, 17
Besieged by Nebuchadnezzar, Jer 34:7

AZMAVETH
A village near Jerusalem, Neh 12:29
Also called Beth Azmaveth, Neh 7:28

AZOTUS
A city which Philip the evangelist visited, Acts 8:40

BAAL (or Baals)
Deities of Canaanite polytheism, Judg 10:10–14
The male god of the Phoenicians and Canaanites; the counterpart of the female Ashtaroth, 2 Kin 23:5
Nature of the worship of, 1 Kin 18:26, 28; 19:18; Ps 106:28; Jer 7:9; 19:5; Hos 9:10; 13:1, 2
Worshiped by Israelites, Num 25:1–5; Judg 2:11–14; 3:7; 6:28–32; 1 Kin 16:31, 32; 2 Kin 21:3; Jer 11:13; Hos 2:8
Ahaz makes images to, 2 Chr 28:1–4
Overthrown by Elijah, 1 Kin 18:17–40
by Josiah, 2 Kin 23:4, 5
Denounced by prophets, Jer 19:4–6; Ezek 16:1, 2, 20, 21
Historic retrospect, Rom 11:4

BAAL PEOR (or Baal of Peor)
A Moabite god; worshiped by Israelites, Num 25:1–9

BAAL PERAZIM
Site of David's victory over the Philistines, 2 Sam 5:18–20
Same as Perazim, Is 28:21

BAAL-ZEBUB
A Philistine god at Ekron, 2 Kin 1:2
Ahaziah inquires of, 2 Kin 1:2, 6, 16
Also called Beelzebub, Matt 10:25; 12:24

BAALAH
A town also known as Kirjath Jearim, Josh 15:9, 10

BAALS
Deities of Canaanite polytheism, Judg 10:10–14
Ensnare Israelites, Judg 2:11–14; 3:7
Ahaz makes images to, 2 Chr 28:1–4

BAANAH
A murderer of Ishbosheth, 2 Sam 4:1–12

BAASHA
Usurps throne of Israel; his evil reign; wars with Judah, 1 Kin 15:16—16:7

BABBLER
b is no different . . . . Eccl 10:11
"What does this *b* . . . . Acts 17:18

BABBLINGS
the profane and idle *b* . . . 1 Tim 6:20

BABE
the *b* leaped in my . . . . Luke 1:44
You will find a B . . . . Luke 2:12
righteousness, for he is a *b* . Heb 5:13

BABEL, TOWER OF
A huge brick structure intended to magnify man and preserve the unity of the race, Gen 11:1–4
Objectives of, thwarted by God, Gen 11:5–9

BABES
Out of the mouth of *b* . . . . Ps 8:2
b shall rule over them . . . . Is 3:4
revealed them to *b* . . . . . . Matt 11:25
'Out of the mouth of *b* . . . . Matt 21:16
foolish, a teacher of *b* . . . . . . Rom 2:20
as to carnal, as to *b* . . . . 1 Cor 3:1
as newborn *b*, desire . . . . 1 Pet 2:2

BABYLON
Built by Nimrod; Tower of Babel, Gen 10:8–10; 11:1–9
Descriptions of, Is 13:19; 14:4; Jer 51:44; Dan 4:30
Jews carried captive to, 2 Kin 25:1–21; 2 Chr 36:5–21
Inhabitants of, described, Is 47:1, 9–13; Jer 50:35–38; Dan 5:1–3
Prophecies concerning, Is 13:1–22; Jer 21:1–7; 25:9–12; 27:5–8; 29:10; Jer 50:1–46; Dan 2:31–38; 7:2–4
The prophetic city, Rev 14:8; 16:19; 17:1—18:24

BACK
Jordan turned *b* . . . . Ps 114:3
but a rod is for the *b* . . . . . . Prov 10:13
a rod for the fool's *b* . . . . Prov 26:3
I gave My *b* to those . . . . Is 50:6
cast Me behind your *b* . . . . Ezek 23:35
found Him, bring *b* word . . . . Matt 2:8
plow, and looking *b* . . . . . . Luke 9:62
they drew *b* and fell . . . . John 18:6
I am sending him *b* . . . . Philem 12
of those who draw *b* . . . . . . Heb 10:39
someone turns him *b* . . . . . James 5:19
inside and on the *b* . . . . Rev 5:1

BACKBITERS
b, haters of God . . . . Rom 1:30

BACKBITING
b tongue an angry . . . . Prov 25:23

BACKSLIDER
The *b* in heart will be . . . . . Prov 14:14

BACKSLIDINGS
b will rebuke you . . . . Jer 2:19
And I will heal your *b* . . . . . . Jer 3:22
b have increased . . . . Jer 5:6
for our *b* are many . . . . Jer 14:7

BACKWARD
fell off the seat *b* . . . . 1 Sam 4:18
shadow ten degrees *b* . . . . 2 Kin 20:11

BAD
speak to you either *b* . . . . . . Gen 24:50
good for *b* or *b* for good . . . . Lev 27:10
trouble is like a *b* tooth . . . Prov 25:19
as the *b* figs which cannot . . . Jer 24:8
if your eye is *b*, your . . . . Matt 6:23
b tree bears *b* fruit . . . . Matt 7:17
a *b* tree bear good . . . . Luke 6:43
whether good or *b* . . . . 2 Cor 5:10

BADGER
covering of *b* skins . . . . Ex 26:14
sandals of *b* skin . . . . Ezek 16:10

BAG
is sealed up in a *b* . . . . Job 14:17

wages to put into a *b* . . . . Hag 1:6
nor *b* for your journey . . . . Matt 10:10

BAKE
b twelve cakes with it . . . . . . Lev 24:5

BAKED
b unleavened cakes . . . . Ex 12:39
b unleavened bread . . . . . 1 Sam 28:24

BAKER
the butler and the *b* . . . . Gen 40:1
an oven heated by a *b* . . . . . . Hos 7:4

BAKERS
of bread from the *b* . . . . Jer 37:21

BAKES
kindles it and *b* bread . . . . . . Is 44:15

BALAAM
Sent by Balak to curse Israel, Num 22:5–7; Josh 24:9
Hindered by talking donkey, Num 22:22–35; 2 Pet 2:16
Curse becomes a blessing, Deut 23:4, 5; Josh 24:10
Prophecies of, Num 23:7–10, 18–24; 24:3–9, 15–24
N.T. references to, 2 Pet 2:15, 16; Jude 11; Rev 2:14

BALAK
A Moabite king, Num 22:4
Hires Balaam to curse Israel, Num 22—24

BALANCE
and the hills in a *b* . . . . Is 40:12

BALANCES
weighed in the *b* . . . . Dan 5:27

BALD
shall not make any *b* . . . . . . Lev 21:5
every head shall be *b* . . . . . . Jer 48:37
completely *b* because . . . . Ezek 27:31

BALDHEAD
Go up, you *b* . . . . 2 Kin 2:23

BALM
a little *b* and a little . . . . . . Gen 43:11
Is there no *b* in Gilead . . . . . . Jer 8:22

BAN
No person under the *b* . . . . . Lev 27:29

BAND
A *b* of robbers takes . . . . Hos 7:1
with a golden *b* . . . . Rev 1:13

BANDS
their *b* shall be silver . . . . . . Ex 27:10
broken the *b* of your yoke . Lev 26:13
broken the *b* of their . . . . . Ezek 34:27
with *b* of love, and I was . . . . Hos 11:4
girded with golden *b* . . . . . . Rev 15:6

BANDAGED
him, and *b* his wounds . . . Luke 10:34

BANISHED
bring his *b* one home . . . . 2 Sam 14:13
he *b* the perverted . . . . 1 Kin 15:12

BANK
cows on the *b* of the river . . . Gen 41:3
the reeds by the river's *b* . . . . . Ex 2:3
along the *b* of the river, ... Ezek 47:7
put my money in the *b* . . . . Luke 19:23

BANKERS
my money with the *b* . . . . . Matt 25:27

BANKS
the *b* of the Jordan . . . . Num 13:29
overflows all its *b* . . . . Josh 3:15
overflowed all its *b* . . . . . . 1 Chr 12:15
b of scented herbs . . . . Song 5:13
the *b* of the Ulai . . . . Dan 8:16

BANNER
his *b* over me was love . . . . . Song 2:4
a *b* to the people . . . . Is 11:10

BANNERS (cont.)
a *b* for the nations .... Is 11:12
lift up a *b* for the peoples .... Is 62:10
Set up a *b* in the land ..... Jer 51:27
a *b* over His land .... Zech 9:16

BANNERS
we will set up our *b* .... Ps 20:5
They set up their *b* .... Ps 74:4
as an army with *b* .... Song 6:4

BANQUET
b that I have prepared .... Esth 5:4
companions make a *b* .... Job 41:6
lords, came to the *b* .... Dan 5:10

BANQUETING
He brought me to the *b* ..... Song 2:4

BANQUETS
b shall be removed .... Amos 6:7

BAPTISM
coming to his *b* .... Matt 3:7
b that I am baptized ...... Matt 20:22
The *b* of John—where .... Matt 21:25
a *b* of repentance .... Mark 1:4
baptized with the *b* that .. Mark 10:38
The *b* of John—was it .... Mark 11:30
a *b* of repentance .... Luke 3:3
But I have a *b* to be ..... Luke 12:50
The *b* of John—was it .... Luke 20:4
from the *b* of John .... Acts 1:22
b which John preached .... Acts 10:37
b of repentance to all ..... Acts 13:24
only the *b* of John .... Acts 18:25
said, "Into John's *b* .... Acts 19:3
a *b* of repentance .... Acts 19:4
with Him through *b* ...... Rom 6:4
Lord, one faith, one *b* ...... Eph 4:5
buried with Him in *b* ...... Col 2:12
now saves us—*b* .... 1 Pet 3:21

BAPTISMS
of the doctrine of *b* .... Heb 6:2

BAPTIZE
I indeed *b* you with .... Matt 3:11
He will *b* you with .... Mark 1:8
b you with the Holy .... Luke 3:16
"Why then do you *b* .... John 1:25
me to *b* with water .... John 1:33
Himself did not *b* .... John 4:2
did not send me to *b* ..... 1 Cor 1:17

BAPTIZED
b by him in the Jordan, ... Matt 3:6
at the Jordan to be *b* by .... Matt 3:13
"I need to be *b* by You .... Matt 3:14
When He had been *b* ...... Matt 3:16
were all *b* by him .... Mark 1:5
was *b* by John .... Mark 1:9
b with the baptism that .. Mark 10:38
b with you will be *b* ..... Mark 10:39
and is *b* will be saved .... Mark 16:16
came out to be *b* .... Luke 3:7
also came to be *b* .... Luke 3:12
Jesus also was *b* .... Luke 3:21
not having been *b* .... Luke 7:30
with them and *b* .... John 3:22
b more disciples .... John 4:1
for John truly *b* with water .. Acts 1:5
every one of you be *b* ..... Acts 2:38
received his word were *b* .. Acts 2:41
men and women were *b* ... Acts 8:12
he was *b* he continued .... Acts 8:13
only been *b* in the name .... Acts 8:16
hinders me from being *b* .... Acts 8:36
water, and he *b* him .... Acts 8:38
he arose and was *b* .... Acts 9:18
these should not be *b* .... Acts 10:47
be *b* in the name .... Acts 10:48
you shall be *b* with ...... Acts 11:16
her household were *b* ..... Acts 16:15
all his family were *b* ..... Acts 16:33
believed and were *b* ...... Acts 18:8
Into what then were you *b* .. Acts 19:3
Arise and be *b*, and wash .. Acts 22:16

were *b* into Christ .... Rom 6:3
I thank God that I *b* .... 1 Cor 1:14
b the household .... 1 Cor 1:16
all were *b* into Moses ..... 1 Cor 10:2
Spirit we were all *b* ...... 1 Cor 12:13
who are *b* for the dead ... 1 Cor 15:29
as many of you as were *b* ... Gal 3:27

BAPTIZING
b them in the name of .... Matt 28:19
b in the wilderness .... Mark 1:4
where John was *b* .... John 1:28
therefore I came *b* .... John 1:31
John also was *b* in Aenon .. John 3:23
behold, He is *b* .... John 3:26
where John was *b* .... John 10:40

BAR-JESUS (or Elymas)
A Jewish false prophet, Acts 13:6–12

BAR-JONAH
Surname of Simon (Peter), Matt 16:17

BARABBAS
A murderer released in place of Jesus,
Matt 27:16–26; Acts 3:14, 15

BARAK
Defeats Jabin, Judg 4:1–24
A man of faith, Heb 11:32

BARBARIAN
nor uncircumcised, *b* .... Col 3:11

BARBARIANS
to Greeks and to *b* ...:..... Rom 1:14

BARE
make yourselves *b* .... Is 32:11
The LORD has made *b* .... Is 52:10

BAREFOOT
covered and went *b* ..... 2 Sam 15:30
walking naked and *b* .... Is 20:2

BARLEY
a land of wheat and *b* ...... Deut 8:8
loaf of *b* bread tumbled .... Judg 7:13
beginning of *b* harvest .... Ruth 1:22
who has five *b* loaves ...... John 6:9
and three quarts of *b* .... Rev 6:6

BARN
seed still in the *b* .... Hag 2:19
the wheat into my *b* ...... Matt 13:30
storehouse nor *b* .... Luke 12:24

BARNABAS
A disciple from Cyprus; gives property,
Acts 4:36, 37
Supports Paul, Acts 9:27
Ministers in Antioch, Acts 11:22–30
Travels with Paul, Acts 12:25; 13–15
Breaks with Paul over John Mark, Acts
15:36–39

BARNS
so your *b* will be filled ..... Prov 3:10
b are broken down .... Joel 1:17
reap nor gather into *b* ...... Matt 6:26
I will pull down my *b* .... Luke 12:18

BARREN
But Sarai was *b* .... Gen 11:30
b has borne seven .... 1 Sam 2:5
He grants the *b* .... Ps 113:9
"Sing, O *b*, you who have .... Is 54:1
'Blessed are the *b* .... Luke 23:29
"Rejoice, O *b*, you who do ... Gal 4:27
you will be neither *b* ...... 2 Pet 1:8

BARRENNESS
A fruitful land into *b* ...... Ps 107:34

BARS
has strengthened the *b* ..... Ps 147:13
bronze and cut the *b* .... Is 45:2
the earth with its *b* .... Jon 2:6

BARSABAS
Nominated to replace Judas, Acts 1:23
Sent to Antioch, Acts 15:22

BARTHOLOMEW
Called Nathanael, John 1:45, 46
One of the twelve apostles, Matt 10:3;
Acts 1:13

BARTIMAEUS
Blind beggar healed by Jesus, Mark
10:46–52

BARUCH
Son of Neriah, Jer 32:12, 13
Jeremiah's faithful friend and scribe,
Jer 36:4–32

BARZILLAI
Supplies David with food, 2 Sam
17:27–29
Age restrains him from following
David, 2 Sam 19:31–39

BASE
the elder, and the *b* .... Is 3:5
and the *b* things of .... 1 Cor 1:28

BASHAN
Conquered by Israel, Num 21:33–35
Assigned to Manasseh, Deut 3:13
Conquered by Hazael, king of Syria,
2 Kin 10:32, 33

BASIC
to the *b* principles .... Col 2:8
b principles of the world .... Col 2:20

BASIN
poured water into a *b* ...... John 13:5

BASINS
its shovels and its *b* .... Ex 27:3
b of silver, trimmers ...... 2 Kin 12:13
gold for the forks, the *b* .. 1 Chr 28:17
filled with blood like *b* ..... Zech 9:15

BASKET
the *b* on my head .... Gen 40:17
the *b* out of your hand .... Deut 26:4
Blessed shall be your *b* .... Deut 28:5
Cursed shall be your *b* .... Deut 28:17
b had very good figs .... Jer 24:2
"A *b* of summer fruit ...... Amos 8:2
lifted up the *b* between ..... Zech 5:9
and put it under a *b* .... Matt 5:15
under a *b*, but on a ...... Luke 11:33
I was let down in a *b* ..... 2 Cor 11:33

BASKETS
there were three white *b* ... Gen 40:16
and there were two *b* .... Jer 24:1
they took up twelve *b* ..... Matt 14:20
took up seven large *b* ..... Matt 15:37

BATHED
My sword shall be *b* .... Is 34:5
to him, "He who is *b* ..... John 13:10

BATHSHEBA
Wife of Uriah, taken by David, 2 Sam
11
Her first child dies, 2 Sam 12:14–19
Bears Solomon, 2 Sam 12:24
Secures throne for Solomon, 1 Kin
1:15–31
Deceived by Adonijah, 1 Kin 2:13–25

BATS
To the moles and *b* .... Is 2:20

BATTLE
b is the LORD's ......,..... 1 Sam 17:47
out to God in the *b* .... 1 Chr 5:20
strength for the *b* .... Ps 18:39
shield and sword of *b* .... Ps 76:3
for the day of *b* .... Prov 21:31
the *b* to the strong .... Eccl 9:11
who turn back the *b* .... Is 28:6
A sound of *b* is in the ..... Jer 50:22
who will prepare for *b*? ... 1 Cor 14:8
became valiant in *b* .... Heb 11:34
gather them to the *b* ...... Rev 16:14

BATTLE-AX
You are My *b* .... Jer 51:20

each with his *b* in his hand . . Ezek 9:2

BATTLEMENT
upon her a *b* of silver . . . . . . Song 8:9

BATTLES
before us and fight our *b* . . 1 Sam 8:20
to fight our *b* . . . . 2 Chr 32:8

BDELLIUM
B and the onyx stone . . . . Gen 2:12
like the color of *b* . . . . Num 11:7

BE FRUITFUL AND MULTIPLY
blessed them, saying, "*B* . . . . Gen 1:22
on the earth, and *b* . . . . Gen 8:17
"*B*, and fill the earth . . . . Gen 9:1
B; a nation and a . . . . Gen 35:11

BE GLAD AND REJOICE
I will *b* in You; I will . . . . Ps 9:2
I will *b* in Your mercy, ... Ps 31:7
We will *b* in you . . . . Song 1:4
we will *b* in His salvation . . . . . Is 25:9
you also *b* with me . . . . Phil 2:18
us *b* and give Him glory, . . . Rev 19:7

BE OF GOOD CHEER
to the paralytic, "Son, *b* . . . . . Matt 9:2
her He said, "*B*, daughter . . Matt 9:22
to them, saying, "*B* . . . . . . Matt 14:27
man, saying to him, "*B* . . Mark 10:49
b, I have overcome . . . . John 16:33
by him and said, "*B* . . . . Acts 23:11

BEAM
on a carrying *b* . . . . Num 4:10
like a weaver's *b* . . . . 1 Sam 17:7
the *b* from the timbers . . . . . Hab 2:11

BEAMS
paneled the temple with *b* . . 1 Kin 6:9
cedar *b* on the pillars . . . . . . 1 Kin 7:2
the *b* and doorposts . . . . 2 Chr 3:7
make *b* for the gates . . . . Neh 2:8
bones are like *b* . . . . Job 40:18
He lays the *b* of His . . . . Ps 104:3
b of our houses are cedar . . Song 1:17

BEAR
greater than I can *b* . . . . Gen 4:13
whom Sarah shall *b* . . . . . . Gen 17:21
not *b* false witness . . . . Ex 20:16
from the paw of the *b* . . . 1 Sam 17:37
they shall *b* you up in . . . . . . Ps 91:12
b a broken spirit . . . . Prov 18:14
be clean, you who *b* . . . . Is 52:11
b their iniquities . . . . Is 53:11
LORD could no longer *b* . . . . Jer 44:22
b deprived of her cubs . . . . Hos 13:8
lion, and a *b* met him . . . . . Amos 5:19
He shall *b* the glory . . . . . . Zech 6:13
child, and a Son . . . . Matt 1:23
A good tree cannot *b* . . . . . . Matt 7:18
how long shall I *b* . . . . Matt 17:17
by, to *b* His cross . . . . Mark 15:21
wife Elizabeth will *b* . . . . . . Luke 1:13
And whoever does not *b* . . Luke 14:27
in Me that does not *b* . . . . . John 15:2
for he does not *b* . . . . Rom 13:4
are strong ought to *b* . . . . . . Rom 15:1
you may be able to *b* . . . . 1 Cor 10:13
B one another's . . . . Gal 6:2
I *b* in my body the . . . . Gal 6:17
b the sins of many . . . . Heb 9:28
like the feet of a *b* . . . . Rev 13:2

BEAR FRUIT
take root downward, and *b* . . Is 37:31
bring forth branches, *b*, . . . Ezek 17:8
shall the vine fail to *b* . . . . . Mal 3:11
the word, accept it, and *b* . Mark 4:20
it and *b* with patience . . . . Luke 8:15
does not *b* He takes away . . John 15:2
branch cannot *b* of itself, . . John 15:4
that we should *b* to God . . . Rom 7:4

our members to *b* to death . . Rom 7:5

BEAR WITNESS
you *b* that you approve . . . Luke 11:48
to *b* of the Light, ... John 1:7
If I *b* of Myself, ... John 5:31
"You *b* of Yourself . . . . John 8:13
Father's name, they *b* . . . . John 10:25
And you also will *b* . . . . . . John 15:27
I should *b* to the truth . . . . John 18:37
must also *b* at Rome . . . . . Acts 23:11
we have seen, and *b*, and . . 1 John 1:2
three who *b* in heaven . . . . 1 John 5:7
three that *b* on earth: . . . . . 1 John 5:8

BEARD
the edges of your *b* . . . . Lev 19:27
I caught it by its *b* . . . . . 1 Sam 17:35
took Amasa by the *b* . . . . 2 Sam 20:9
Running down on the *b* . . . . Ps 133:2

BEARING
goes forth weeping, *b* . . . . . Ps 126:6
And He, *b* His cross . . . . . John 19:17
b with one another . . . . Col 3:13
the camp, *b* His reproach . . Heb 13:13

BEARS
Every branch that *b* . . . . . . John 15:2
b all things, believes . . . . . 1 Cor 13:7
it is the Spirit who *b* . . . . . 1 John 5:6

BEAST
b has devoured him . . . . Gen 37:20
You preserve man and *b* . . . . Ps 36:6
I was like a *b* before . . . . . . Ps 73:22
to the *b* its food . . . . Ps 147:9
b touches the mountain . . . Heb 12:20
And I saw a *b* rising . . . . Rev 13:1
Then I saw another *b* . . . . . . Rev 13:11
the mark of the *b* . . . . Rev 19:20

BEASTS
are we counted as *b* . . . . Job 18:3
The *b* go into dens . . . . Job 37:8
like the *b* that perish . . . . . . Ps 49:12
I have fought with *b* . . . . 1 Cor 15:32
naturally, like brute *b* . . . . . . Jude 10

BEAT
I will *b* down his foes . . . . . . Ps 89:23
You shall *b* him with a . . . . Prov 23:14
b their swords into . . . . Is 2:4
you shall *b* in pieces . . . . . . Mic 4:13
spat in His face and *b* . . . . Matt 26:67
but *b* his breast . . . . Luke 18:13

BEATEN
and you will be *b* . . . . Mark 13:9
his will, shall be *b* . . . . Luke 12:47
Three times I was *b* . . . . . 2 Cor 11:25
when you are *b* for your . . . 1 Pet 2:20

BEATS
one who *b* the air . . . . 1 Cor 9:26

BEAUTIFUL
of men, that they were *b* . . . . Gen 6:2
woman of *b* countenance . . Gen 12:11
that she was very *b* . . . . . . Gen 12:14
woman was very *b* . . . . Gen 24:16
she is *b* to behold . . . . Gen 26:7
but Rachel was *b* . . . . Gen 29:17
he was a *b* child . . . . Ex 2:2
the captives a *b* woman . . . Deut 21:11
a *b* Babylonian garment . . . . Josh 7:21
and *b* appearance . . . . 1 Sam 25:3
woman was very *b* . . . . 2 Sam 11:2
a woman of *b* . . . . 2 Sam 14:27
she was *b* to behold . . . . Esth 1:11
woman was lovely and *b* . . . Esth 2:7
b as the daughters of Job . . Job 42:15
B in elevation, the joy . . . . . . Ps 48:2
has made everything *b* . . . . Eccl 3:11
my love, you are as *b* . . . . . Song 6:4
How *b* are your feet . . . . . . Song 7:1
of the LORD shall be *b* . . . . Is 4:2
How *b* upon the . . . . Is 52:7

a *b* heritage of the hosts . . . . Jer 3:19
became very *b* . . . . Ezek 16:7
a *b* crown on your head . . . Ezek 16:12
You were exceedingly *b* . . Ezek 16:13
b crowns on their heads . . Ezek 23:42
b with a multitude . . . . Ezek 31:9
indeed appear *b* . . . . Matt 23:27
adorned with *b* stones . . . . Luke 21:5
temple which is called *B* . . . . Acts 3:2
begging alms at the *B* . . . . . Acts 3:10
How *b* are the feet . . . . Rom 10:15
they saw he was a *b* . . . . . Heb 11:23
b appearance perishes . . . . James 1:11

BEAUTIFY
b the humble with . . . . Ps 149:4
b the place of My . . . . Is 60:13

BEAUTY
for glory and for *b* . . . . Ex 28:2
"The *b* of Israel is . . . . 2 Sam 1:19
in the *b* of holiness . . . . . . 1 Chr 16:29
show her *b* to the people . . . Esth 1:11
let *b* preparations be given . . Esth 2:3
yourself with glory and *b* . . Job 40:10
To behold the *b* . . . . Ps 27:4
greatly desire your *b* . . . . . . Ps 45:11
Zion, the perfection of *b* . . . . Ps 50:2
b of the LORD our God . . . . . Ps 90:17
do not lust after her *b* . . . . Prov 6:25
and *b* is passing . . . . Prov 31:30
branding instead of *b* . . . . Is 3:24
glorious *b* is a fading . . . . Is 28:1
see the King in His *b* . . . . . . Is 33:17
no *b* that we should . . . . Is 53:2
to give them *b* for ashes . . . . Is 61:3
'the perfection of *b* . . . . . . Lam 2:15
b to be abhorred . . . . Ezek 16:25
said, 'I am perfect in *b* . . . Ezek 27:3
wisdom and perfect in *b* . . Ezek 28:12
of God was like it in *b* . . . Ezek 31:8
the one I called *B* . . . . Zech 11:7
the incorruptible *b* . . . . 1 Pet 3:4

BECAME
man *b* a living being . . . . Gen 2:7
to the Jews I *b* as a Jew . . 1 Cor 9:20
like me, for I *b* like you . . . . Gal 4:12

BED
house, if I make my *b* . . . . . Job 17:13
I remember You on my *b* . . . . Ps 63:6
if I make my *b* in hell . . . . . Ps 139:8
Also our *b* is green . . . . Song 1:16
b is too short to stretch . . . . Is 28:20
you have set your *b* . . . . Is 57:7
"Arise, take up your *b* . . . . . Matt 9:6
be two men in one *b* . . . . . Luke 17:34
and the *b* undefiled . . . . Heb 13:4

BEDRIDDEN
had been *b* eight years . . . . Acts 9:33

BEDROOM
lying on his bed in his *b* . . 2 Sam 4:7
her brother in the *b* . . . . . 2 Sam 13:10
and his nurse in the *b* . . . . 2 Kin 11:2

BEDS
sing aloud on their *b* . . . . . . Ps 149:5
shall rest in their *b* . . . . Is 57:2
who lie on *b* of ivory . . . . . Amos 6:4

BEDSTEAD
his *b* was an iron *b* . . . . . . Deut 3:11

BEE
Egypt, and for the *b* . . . . Is 7:18

BEELZEBUB
Jesus accused of serving, Matt 10:25; 12:24–27

BEER LAHAI ROI
Angel meets Hagar there, Gen 16:7–14
Isaac dwells in, Gen 24:62

BEERSHEBA
God appears there to Hagar, Gen 21:14–19

to Isaac, Gen 26:23–25
to Jacob, Gen 46:1–5
to Elijah, 1 Kin 19:3–7
Oaths sworn there by Abraham, Gen 21:31–33
by Isaac, Gen 26:26–33

BEFALL
calamity *b* him . . . . Gen 42:4
b you in the last days . . . . Gen 49:1
No evil shall *b* you . . . . Ps 91:10

BEFOREHAND
do not worry *b* . . . . Mark 13:11
told you all things *b* . . . . . Mark 13:23
not to meditate *b* . . . . . . Luke 21:14
when He testified *b* . . . . 1 Pet 1:11

BEG
I would *b* mercy of my . . . . . . Job 9:15
I am ashamed to *b* . . . . Luke 16:3
b you as sojourners . . . . 1 Pet 2:11

BEGAN
Then men *b* to call on . . . . . Gen 4:26
since the world *b* . . . . Luke 1:70

BEGETS
b a scoffer does . . . . Prov 17:21
b a wise child will . . . . Prov 23:24
b a hundred children . . . . Eccl 6:3

BEGGAR
lifts the *b* from the ash . . . . . 1 Sam 2:8
there was a certain *b* . . . . . Luke 16:20

BEGGARLY
weak and *b* elements . . . . Gal 4:9

BEGGED
So the demons *b* Him, ... Matt 8:31
they *b* Him to depart . . . . Matt 8:34
b him, saying, 'Have . . . . . . Matt 18:29
b Him to put His hand . . . . Mark 7:32
b Him earnestly, saying . . . . Luke 7:4
b Him to come to his . . . . . Luke 8:41
not this he who sat and *b* . . . John 9:8
the Gentiles *b* that these . . Acts 13:42
those who heard it *b* . . . . . . Heb 12:19

BEGINNING
b God created the . . . . Gen 1:1
Though your *b* was . . . . Job 8:7
of the LORD is the *b* . . . . Ps 111:10
that God does from *b* . . . . . . Eccl 3:11
who made them at the *b* . . . . Matt 19:4
In the *b* was the Word . . . . . . John 1:1
This *b* of signs Jesus . . . . . John 2:11
a murderer from the *b* . . . . John 8:44
with Me from the *b* . . . . . . John 15:27
the *b*, the firstborn . . . . Col 1:18
having neither *b* . . . . Heb 7:3
True Witness, the *B* . . . . Rev 3:14
and the Omega, the *B* . . . . . . Rev 21:6

BEGOTTEN
See ONLY BEGOTTEN SON
today I have *b* You . . . . Ps 2:7
heart, 'Who has *b* . . . . Is 49:21
glory as of the only *b* . . . . . John 1:14
Christ Jesus I have *b* . . . . . . 1 Cor 4:15
abundant mercy has *b* . . . . . . 1 Pet 1:3
loves him who is *b* . . . . 1 John 5:1

BEGUN
Having *b* in the Spirit . . . . Gal 3:3
that He who has *b* . . . . Phil 1:6

BEHALF
to speak on God's *b* . . . . Job 36:2
you on Christ's *b* . . . . 2 Cor 5:20
has been granted on *b* . . . . . Phil 1:29

BEHAVE
I will *b* wisely in a . . . . Ps 101:2
does not *b* rudely . . . . 1 Cor 13:5

BEHAVED
sent him, and *b* wisely . . . . 1 Sam 18:5
and blamelessly we *b* . . . . 1 Thess 2:10

BEHAVIOR
of good *b*, hospitable . . . . 1 Tim 3:2
they be reverent in *b* . . . . Titus 2:3

BEHEADED
he sent and had John *b* . . . Matt 14:10
those who had been *b* . . . . . Rev 20:4

BEHEMOTH
Described, Job 40:15–24

BEHOLD
the eyes to *b* the sun . . . . . . Eccl 11:7
B, you are fair . . . . Song 1:15
B, the virgin shall . . . . Is 7:14
Judah, "*B* your God . . . . Is 40:9
B the Lamb of God . . . . . . John 1:36
I am, that they may *b* . . . . . John 17:24
to them, "*B* the Man . . . . . . John 19:5
B what manner of love . . . . 1 John 3:1

BEHOLDING
with unveiled face, *b* . . . . . . 2 Cor 3:18

BEING
man became a living *b* . . . . . . Gen 2:7
God while I have my *b* . . . . Ps 104:33
move and have our *b* . . . . . Acts 17:28
who, *b* in the form of . . . . . . Phil 2:6

BEL
Patron god of Babylon, Is 46:1; Jer 50:2; 51:44

BELIEF
by the Spirit and *b* . . . . . . 2 Thess 2:13

BELIEVE
b me or listen to my voice . . . . . Ex 4:1
will they not *b* Me . . . . Num 14:11
did not *b* the LORD . . . . Deut 1:32
I did not *b* the words . . . . . . 1 Kin 10:7
B in the LORD your God . . 2 Chr 20:20
did not *b* in His wondrous . . . Ps 78:32
which you would not *b* . . . . . . Hab 1:5
ones who *b* in Me to sin . . . . Matt 18:6
'Why then did you not *b* . . Matt 21:25
cross, and we will *b* Him . . Matt 27:42
Repent, and *b* . . . . Mark 1:15
Do not be afraid; only *b* . . . Mark 5:36
tears, "Lord, I *b* . . . . Mark 9:24
b in Me to stumble . . . . Mark 9:42
b that you receive . . . . Mark 11:24
that we may see and *b* . . . Mark 15:32
because they did not *b* . . . . Mark 16:14
have no root, who *b* . . . . . . Luke 8:13
only *b*, and she will . . . . . . Luke 8:50
will by no means *b* . . . . . . Luke 22:67
and slow of heart to *b* . . . . Luke 24:25
all through him might *b* . . . . . John 1:7
to those who *b* . . . . John 1:12
how will you *b* . . . . John 3:12
Now we *b*, not because . . . . John 4:42
sent, Him you do not *b* . . . . John 5:38
we may see it and *b* . . . . . . John 6:30
we have come to *b* . . . . John 6:69
brothers did not *b* in Him . . . John 7:5
not *b* that I am He . . . . John 8:24
to him, "Do you *b* . . . . John 9:35
not *b*, because you . . . . John 10:26
b that the Father is in Me . John 10:38
b that You are the Christ . John 11:27
this, that they may *b* . . . . . John 11:42
they did not *b* in Him . . . . . John 12:37
may *b* that I am He . . . . . . John 13:19
you *b* in God, *b* also in . . . . John 14:1
B Me that I am in . . . . John 14:11
we *b* that You came . . . . . . John 16:30
b that You sent Me . . . . John 17:21
truth, so that you may *b* . . John 19:35
into His side, I will not *b* . . John 20:25
written that you may *b* . . . John 20:31
word of the gospel and *b* . . Acts 15:7
"*B* on the Lord Jesus . . . . . Acts 16:31
b on Him who would . . . . . . Acts 19:4
King Agrippa, do you *b* . . . Acts 26:27
to all and on all who *b* . . . . . Rom 3:22

father of all those who *b* . . . Rom 4:11
the Lord Jesus and *b* . . . . . . Rom 10:9
And how shall they *b* . . . . . Rom 10:14
to save those who *b* . . . . . . 1 Cor 1:21
a wife who does not *b* . . . . 1 Cor 7:12
I spoke," we also *b* . . . . 2 Cor 4:13
given to those who *b* . . . . Gal 3:22
Christ, not only to *b* . . . . Phil 1:29
if we *b* that Jesus died . . . 1 Thess 4:14
should *b* the lie . . . . 2 Thess 2:11
of those who *b* . . . . 1 Tim 4:10
comes to God must *b* . . . . . . Heb 11:6
Even the demons *b* . . . . . . James 2:19
to you who *b*, He . . . . 1 Pet 2:7
should *b* on the name . . . . 1 John 3:23
Beloved, do not *b* . . . . 1 John 4:1
written to you who *b* . . . . . 1 John 5:13

BELIEVED
And he *b* in the LORD . . . . . . Gen 15:6
So the people *b* . . . . Ex 4:31
b that I would see the . . . . . Ps 27:13
Who has *b* our report . . . . Is 53:1
people of Nineveh *b* . . . . Jon 3:5
Blessed is she who *b* . . . . . Luke 1:45
they *b* the Scripture . . . . . . John 2:22
because he has not *b* . . . . . John 3:18
of that city *b* in Him . . . . . John 4:39
you *b* Moses, you would . . . John 5:46
Jesus did, *b* in Him . . . . . . John 11:45
who has *b* our report . . . . John 12:38
and he saw and *b* . . . . John 20:8
seen Me, you have *b* . . . . John 20:29
who heard the word *b* . . . . . Acts 4:4
of those who *b* were of . . . . Acts 4:32
appointed to eternal life *b* . Acts 13:48
Holy Spirit when you *b* . . . . Acts 19:2
"Abraham *b* God . . . . Rom 4:3
in whom they have not *b* . . Rom 10:14
than when we first *b* . . . . . Rom 13:11
unless you *b* in vain . . . . . . 1 Cor 15:2
'I *b* and therefore I spoke . 2 Cor 4:13
b God, and it was accounted . Gal 3:6
b on in the world . . . . 1 Tim 3:16
I know whom I have *b* . . . . 2 Tim 1:12
b the love that God has . . 1 John 4:16

BELIEVERS
be an example to the *b* . . . 1 Tim 4:12
are benefited are *b* . . . . 1 Tim 6:2

BELIEVES
See HE WHO BELIEVES
The simple *b* every . . . . Prov 14:15
possible to him who *b* . . . . Mark 9:23
b that those things he . . . . Mark 11:23
He who *b* and is . . . . Mark 16:16
that whoever *b* in Him . . . . . John 3:16
He who *b* in the Son . . . . . . John 3:36
b in Him who sent Me . . . . . John 5:24
who *b* in Me shall never . . . John 6:35
b in Him may have . . . . John 6:40
he who *b* in Me has . . . . . . John 6:47
He who *b* in Me, as the . . . John 7:38
He who *b* in Me, though . . John 11:25
He who *b* in Me . . . . John 12:44
whoever *b* in Him . . . . Acts 10:43
Him everyone who *b* is . . . Acts 13:39
for everyone who *b* . . . . . . Rom 1:16
to everyone who *b* . . . . Rom 10:4
with the heart one *b* . . . . . Rom 10:10
b all things, hopes all . . . . 1 Cor 13:7
Whoever *b* that Jesus is . . 1 John 5:1
he who *b* that Jesus is . . . . 1 John 5:5
b in the Son of God . . . . . 1 John 5:10

BELIEVING
you ask in prayer, *b* . . . . . Matt 21:22
b you may have life . . . . . . John 20:31
take along a *b* wife . . . . 1 Cor 9:5
blessed with *b* Abraham . . . . Gal 3:9
those who have *b* masters . 1 Tim 6:2

BELLY
On your *b* you shall go . . . . Gen 3:14

And Jonah was in the *b* .....Jon 1:17
three nights in the *b* .....Matt 12:40
whose glory is their *b* ....Phil 3:19

BELONG
interpretations *b* to God ....Gen 40:8
highest heavens *b* to .....Deut 10:14
secret things *b* to ....Deut 29:29
"Dominion and fear *b* ....Job 25:2
shields of the earth *b* ....Ps 47:9
things also *b* to the wise .. Prov 24:23
To the Lord our God *b* ......Dan 9:9
My name, because you *b* .. Mark 9:41
to whom *b* the glory ....1 Pet 4:11

BELONGS
offering that *b* to the LORD .. Lev 7:20
Salvation to the LORD ....Ps 3:8
that power *b* to God ....Ps 62:11
to You, O Lord, *b* mercy ....Ps 62:12
shield *b* to the LORD.........Ps 89:18
to whom vengeance *b* ....Ps 94:1
righteousness *b* to You .....Dan 9:7
solid food *b* to those ....Heb 5:14
b to another tribe ....Heb 7:13
"Salvation *b* to our God .....Rev 7:10

BELOVED
"The *b* of the Lord ....Deut 33:12
so He gives His *b* ....Ps 127:2
of myrrh is my *b* ....Song 1:13
My *b* is mine, and I am ... Song 2:16
b more than another ....Song 5:9
Where has your *b* ....Song 6:1
leaning upon her *b* ....Song 8:5
a song of my *B* ....Is 5:1
for you are greatly *b* ....Dan 9:23
"This is My *b* Son ....Matt 3:17
election they are *b* ....Rom 11:28
us accepted in the *B* ....Eph 1:6
Luke the *b* physician ....Col 4:14
than a slave as a *b* ....Philem 16
"This is My *b* Son ....2 Pet 1:17
our *b* brother Paul ....2 Pet 3:15
the saints and the *b* ....Rev 20:9

BELOVED SON
saying, "This is My *b*. .....Matt 3:17
"This is My *b*, in whom ...Matt 17:5
I will send my *b*. ....Luke 20:13
To Timothy, a *b*: ....2 Tim 1:2

BELSHAZZAR
King of Babylon; Daniel interprets his
dream, Dan 5

BELT
with a leather *b* ....Matt 3:4
us, he took Paul's *b* ....Acts 21:11

BELTESHAZZAR
Daniel's Babylonian name, Dan 1:7

BEMOAN
Or who will *b* you ....Jer 15:5
for the dead, nor *b* ....Jer 22:10

BEN-AMMI
Son of Lot; father of the Ammonites,
Gen 19:38

BEN-HADAD
Ben-Hadad I, king of Damascus; hired
by Asa, king of Judah, to attack Baasha, king of Israel, 1 Kin 15:18–21
——— Ben-Hadad II, king of Damascus;
makes war on Ahab, king of Israel,
1 Kin 20
Falls in siege against Samaria, 2 Kin
6:24–33; 7:6–20
Killed by Hazael, 2 Kin 8:7–15
——— Ben-Hadad III, king of Damascus;
loses all Israelite conquests made by
Hazael, his father, 2 Kin 13:3–25

BEN-ONI
Rachel's name for Benjamin, Gen
35:16–18

BENAIAH
The son of Jehoiada; a mighty man,
2 Sam 23:20–23
Faithful to David, 2 Sam 15:18; 20:23
Escorts Solomon to the throne, 1 Kin
1:38–40
Executes Adonijah, Joab and Shimei,
1 Kin 2:25, 29–34, 46
——— A Pirathonite; another of David's
mighty men, 2 Sam 23:30
Divisional commander, 1 Chr 27:14

BEND
The wicked *b* their bow ......Ps 11:2

BENEATH
and on the earth *b* ....Deut 4:39
"You are from *b* ....John 8:23

BENEFACTORS
them are called '*b* ....Luke 22:25

BENEFIT
That I may see the *b* ....Ps 106:5
people who could not *b* ....Is 30:5
might have a second *b* ....2 Cor 1:15

BENEFITS
daily loads us with *b* ....Ps 68:19
forget not all His *b* ....Ps 103:2
for all His *b* toward me ....Ps 116:12

BENJAMIN
Jacob's youngest son, Gen 35:16–20
Taken to Egypt against Jacob's wishes,
Gen 42—45
Jacob's prophecy concerning, Gen
49:27
——— Tribe of:
Families of, Num 26:38–41
Territory allotted to, Josh 18:11–28
Attacked by remaining tribes for con-
doning sin of Gibeah, Judg 20:12–48
Wives provided for remnant of, Judg
21:1–23
Tribe of Saul, 1 Sam 9:1, 2
of Paul, Phil 3:5

BENT
have *b* their bow, ...Ps 37:14
and all their bows *b* ....Is 5:28
behold, this vine *b* ....Ezek 17:7
hearts shall be *b* on evil ...Dan 11:27
I have *b* Judah, My bow, ...Zech 9:13
was *b* over and could ....Luke 13:11

BEREA
A city of Macedonia; visited by Paul,
Acts 17:10–15

BEREAVE
I will *b* them of ....Jer 15:7
no more shall you *b* ......Ezek 36:12
children, yet I will *b* ....Hos 9:12

BERNICE
Sister of Herod Agrippa II, Acts 25:13,
23
Hears Paul's defense, Acts 26:1–30

BERODACH-BALADAN
See MERODACH-BALADAN
A king of Babylon, 2 Kin 20:12–19

BERYL
fourth row, a *b* ....Ex 28:20
a *b*, an onyx ....Ex 39:13
rods of gold set with *b* .....Song 5:14
was like the color of *b* .....Ezek 1:16
the color of a *b* ....Ezek 10:9
topaz, and diamond, *b* ....Ezek 28:13
His body was like *b* ....Dan 10:6
chrysolite, the eighth *b* ....Rev 21:20

BESEECH
Return, we *b* You ....Ps 80:14
b you therefore ....Rom 12:1
of the LORD, *b* you to ....Eph 4:1

BESIDE
He leads me *b* the ....Ps 23:2

"Paul, you are *b* ....Acts 26:24
For if we are *b* ....2 Cor 5:13

BESIEGED
Joab *b* the city ....2 Sam 11:16
went up and *b* Samaria ....2 Kin 6:24
and the city was *b* ....2 Kin 24:10
of cucumbers, as a *b* city ......Is 1:8
army *b* Jerusalem ....Jer 32:2
to Jerusalem and *b* it ....Dan 1:1

BEST
with the *b* ointments ....Amos 6:6
b seats in the synagogues .. Matt 23:6
b places at feasts ....Mark 12:39
sit down in the *b* place ....Luke 14:8
'Bring out the *b* ....Luke 15:22
earnestly desire the *b* ....1 Cor 12:31

BESTOW
LORD, that He may *b*........Ex 32:29
b greater honor ....1 Cor 12:23

BESTOWED
love the Father has *b* ......1 John 3:1

BETH HORON
Twin towns of Ephraim, Josh 16:3, 5
Fortified by Solomon, 2 Chr 8:3–5
Prominent in battles, Josh 10:10–14;
1 Sam 13:18

BETH PEOR
Town near Pisgah, Deut 3:29
Moses buried near, Deut 34:6
Assigned to Reubenites, Josh 13:15, 20

BETH SHAN (or Beth Shean)
A town in Issachar, Josh 17:11–16
Saul's corpse hung up at, 1 Sam
31:10–13; 2 Sam 21:12–14

BETH SHEMESH
Ark brought to, 1 Sam 6:12–19
Joash defeats Amaziah at, 2 Kin 14:11
Taken by Philistines, 2 Chr 28:18

BETHABARA
A place beyond the Jordan where John
baptized, John 1:28

BETHANY
A town on the Mt. of Olives, Luke 19:29
Home of Lazarus, John 11:1
Home of Simon, the leper, Matt 26:6
Jesus visits there, Mark 11:1, 11, 12
Scene of the ascension, Luke 24:50, 51

BETHEL
Abram settles near, Gen 12:7, 8
Site of Abram's altar, Gen 13:3, 4
Site of Jacob's vision of the ladder, Gen
28:10–19
Jacob returns to, Gen 35:1–15
Samuel judges there, 1 Sam 7:15, 16
Site of worship and sacrifice, 1 Sam
10:3
Center of idolatry, 1 Kin 12:28–33
Josiah destroys altars of, 2 Kin 23:4,
15–20
Denounced by prophets, 1 Kin 13:1–10;
Amos 7:10–13; Jer 48:13; Hos 10:15

BETHESDA
Jerusalem pool, John 5:2–4

BETHLEHEM
Originally called Ephrath, Gen 35:16
Rachel buried there, Gen 35:19
Home of Naomi and Boaz, Ruth 1:1,
19; 4:9–11
Home of David, 1 Sam 16:1–18
Predicted place of Messiah's birth, Mic
5:2
Christ born there, Matt 2:1; Luke
2:4–7; John 7:42
Infants of, killed by Herod, Matt
2:16–18

BETHPHAGE
Village near Bethany, Mark 11:1

Near Mt. of Olives, Matt 21:1

BETHSAIDA
A city of Galilee, Mark 6:45
Home of Andrew, Peter and Philip,
John 1:44; 12:21
Blind man healed there, Mark 8:22, 23
5,000 fed nearby, Luke 9:10–17
Unbelief of, denounced, Matt 11:21;
Luke 10:13

BETRAY
the outcasts, do not *b* .... Is 16:3
you, one of you will *b* ..... Matt 26:21
Now brother will *b* ...... Mark 13:12

BETRAYED
Man is about to be *b* ..... Matt 17:22
in which He was *b* ...... 1 Cor 11:23

BETRAYER
See, My *b* is at hand ..... Matt 26:46

BETRAYING
"Judas, are you *b* .... Luke 22:48

BETRAYS
who is the one who *b* ..... John 21:20

BETROTH
"You shall *b* a wife ...... Deut 28:30
"I will *b* you to Me ....,.... Hos 2:19

BETROTHED
a virgin who is not *b* .... Ex 22:16
finds a *b* young woman .. Deut 22:25
I *b* myself for a .... 2 Sam 3:14
mother Mary was *b* to ..... Matt 1:18
to a virgin *b* to a man ..... Luke 1:27
For I have *b* you to .... 2 Cor 11:2

BETTER
obey is *b* than sacrifice .. 1 Sam 15:22
It is *b* to trust in .... Ps 118:8
B is a little with the ...... Prov 15:16
B is a dry morsel .... Prov 17:1
B is the poor who .... Prov 19:1
B to dwell in .... Prov 21:19
b is a neighbor .... Prov 27:10
B a handful with .... Eccl 4:6
Two are *b* than one .... Eccl 4:9
B a poor and wise .... Eccl 4:13
were the former days *b* ..... Eccl 7:10
features appeared *b* .... Dan 1:15
For it is *b* to marry .... 1 Cor 7:9
Christ, which is far *b* .... Phil 1:23
b than the angels .... Heb 1:4
b things concerning .... Heb 6:9
b things than that .... Heb 12:24

BEULAH
A symbol of true Israel, Is 62:4, 5

BEVERAGE
lacks no blended *b* .... Song 7:2

BEWAIL
Israel, *b* the burning .... Lev 10:6
b my virginity .... Judg 11:37
I will *b* the vine .... Is 16:9

BEWARE
"*B* of false prophets .... Matt 7:15
b of evil workers .... Phil 3:2
B lest anyone cheat .... Col 2:8

BEWILDERED
"They are *b* by the land ..... Ex 14:3

BEWITCHED
b you that you should .... Gal 3:1

BEYOND
b what is written .... 1 Cor 4:6
yes, and *b* their ability ..... 2 Cor 8:3
advanced in Judaism *b* ..... Gal 1:14

BEZALEL
Hur's grandson, 1 Chr 2:20
Tabernacle builder, Ex 31:1–11;
35:30–35

BEZER
A city of refuge in the territory of
Reuben, Deut 4:43; John 20:8

BILDAD
One of Job's friends, Job 2:11
Makes three speeches, Job 8:1–22;
18:1–21; 25:1–6

BILHAH
Rachel's maid, Gen 29:29
The mother of Dan and Naphtali, Gen
30:1–8
Commits incest with Reuben, Gen
35:22

BILLOWS
b have gone over me .... Ps 42:7
all Your *b* and Your .... Jon 2:3

BIND
b them as a sign .... Deut 6:8
b this line of scarlet .... Josh 2:18
b the cluster of the .... Job 38:31
b the wild ox in the .... Job 39:10
b the sacrifice with cords .. Ps 118:27
b them around your .... Prov 3:3
B them continually upon ... Prov 6:21
B them on your fingers ..... Prov 7:3
B up the testimony .... Is 8:16
but He will *b* us up .... Hos 6:1
and whatever you *b* .... Matt 16:19
'*B* him hand and foot ..... Matt 22:13
b heavy burdens .... Matt 23:4
b the man who owns this .. Acts 21:11

BINDS
first *b* the strong man ..... Matt 12:29

BIRD
the blood of the *b* .... Lev 14:52
with him as with a *b* .... Job 41:5
soul, "Flee as a *b* .... Ps 11:1
has escaped as a *b* .... Ps 124:7
b hastens to the snare ...... Prov 7:23
for a *b* of the air may ..... Eccl 10:20
fly away like a *b* .... Hos 9:11
unclean and hated *b* .... Rev 18:2

BIRDS
b will eat your flesh .... Gen 40:19
b make their nests .... Ps 104:17
b caught in a snare .... Eccl 9:12
Look at the *b* of the .... Matt 6:26
"Foxes have holes and *b* ... Matt 8:20

BIRTH
cursed the day of his *b* ...... Job 3:1
heaven, who gives it *b* ..... Job 38:29
makes the deer give *b* ...... Ps 29:9
the day of one's *b* .... Eccl 7:1
bring to the time of *b* ...... Is 66:9
the deer also gave *b* ...... Jer 14:5
no *b*, no pregnancy .... Hos 9:11
Now the *b* of Jesus .... Matt 1:18
will rejoice at his *b* .... Luke 1:14
who was blind from *b* ...... John 9:1
labors with *b* pangs .... Rom 8:22
conceived, it gives *b* ..... James 1:15

BIRTHDAY
which was Pharaoh's *b* .... Gen 40:20
b gave a feast for his ..... Mark 6:21

BIRTHRIGHT
"Sell me your *b* .... Gen 25:31
Esau despised his *b* ...... Gen 25:34
according to his *b* .... Gen 43:33
of food sold his *b* .... Heb 12:16

BIRTHSTOOLS
see them on the *b* .... Ex 1:16

BISHOP
the position of a *b* .... 1 Tim 3:1
b must be blameless ...... Titus 1:7

BIT
and they *b* the people ..... Num 21:6
be harnessed with *b* .... Ps 32:9

BITE
A serpent may *b* .... Eccl 10:11
But if you *b* and .... Gal 5:15

BITHYNIA
The Spirit keeps Paul from, Acts 16:7
Peter writes to Christians of, 1 Pet 1:1

BITS
the great house into *b* ..... Amos 6:11
Indeed, we put *b* .... James 3:3

BITTER
made their lives *b* .... Ex 1:14
b herbs they shall eat it ..... Ex 12:8
to those who are *b* .... Prov 31:6
who put *b* for sweet .... Is 5:20
and do not be *b* .... Col 3:19
But if you have *b* .... James 3:14
make your stomach *b* ..... Rev 10:9

BITTERLY
has dealt very *b* .... Ruth 1:20
And Hezekiah wept *b* ..... 2 Kin 20:3
he went out and wept *b* ... Matt 26:75

BITTERNESS
man dies in the *b* ......:.... Job 21:25
heart knows its own *b* .... Prov 14:10
all my years in the *b* .... Is 38:15
you are poisoned by *b* ..... Acts 8:23
b springing up cause ..... Heb 12:15

BLACK
My skin grows *b* ......:.... Job 30:30
wavy, and *b* as a raven ..... Song 5:11
one hair white or *b* .... Matt 5:36
a *b* horse and he who sat ... Rev 6:5
and the sun became *b* ..... Rev 6:12

BLACKNESS
the heavens with *b* .... Is 50:3
whom is reserved the *b* .... Jude 13

BLACKSMITH
no *b* to be found .... 1 Sam 13:19
The *b* with the tongs .... Is 44:12
I have created the *b* .... Is 54:16

BLADE
went in after the *b* .... Judg 3:22
first the *b*, then the head .. Mark 4:28

BLAME
that anyone should *b* ..... 2 Cor 8:20
be holy and without *b* ...... Eph 1:4

BLAMELESS
walk before Me and be *b* ... Gen 17:1
You shall be *b* .... Deut 18:13
b before Him, and I ..... 2 Sam 22:24
and that man was *b* .... Job 1:1
a *b* and upright man .... Job 1:8
a *b* and upright man .... Job 2:3
will not cast away the *b* ..... Job 8:20
though I were *b* .... Job 9:20
b who is ridiculed .... Job 12:4
make your ways *b* .... Job 22:3
I was also *b* before Him .... Ps 18:23
Then I shall be *b* .... Ps 19:13
Mark the *b* man .... Ps 37:37
when You speak, and *b* ..... Ps 51:4
Let my heart be *b* .... Ps 119:80
the *b* will remain .... Prov 2:21
righteousness of the *b* ..... Prov 11:5
the *b* in their ways .... Prov 11:20
the *b* will inherit good .... Prov 28:10
Sabbath, and are *b* .... Matt 12:5
end, that you may be *b* .... 1 Cor 1:8
that you may become *b* ... Phil 2:15
which is in the law, *b* ...... Phil 3:6
you holy, and *b* .... Col 1:22
your hearts *b* in .... 1 Thess 3:13
body be preserved *b* .... 1 Thess 5:23
bishop then must be *b* ..... 1 Tim 3:2
deacons, being found *b* ... 1 Tim 3:10
man is *b*, the husband ..... Titus 1:6
a bishop must be *b* .... Titus 1:7
without spot and *b* .... 2 Pet 3:14

BLAMELESSLY
b we behaved .... 1 Thess 2:10

BLANKET
covered him with a *b* ......Judg 4:18

BLASPHEME
b Your name forever ....Ps 74:10
compelled them to *b* ......Acts 26:11
may learn not to *b* ....1 Tim 1:20
b that noble name ....James 2:7
God, to *b* His name ....Rev 13:6

BLASPHEMED
a foolish people has *b* ....Ps 74:18
b continually every ....Is 52:5
who passed by *b* Him .....Matt 27:39
who were hanged *b* .....Luke 23:39
The name of God is *b* .....Rom 2:24
doctrine may not be *b* ......1 Tim 6:1
On their part He is *b* ......1 Pet 4:14
great heat, and they *b* ......Rev 16:9

BLASPHEMER
I was formerly a *b* ....1 Tim 1:13

BLASPHEMERS
boasters, proud, *b* ....2 Tim 3:2

BLASPHEMES
b the name of the LORD ....Lev 24:16
"This Man *b*!" ....Matt 9:3
who *b* against the Holy ...Mark 3:29
to him who *b* against .....Luke 12:10

BLASPHEMIES
false witness, *b* ....Matt 15:19
is this who speaks *b* ....Luke 5:21
great things and *b* ....Rev 13:5

BLASPHEMY
trouble and rebuke and *b* .....Is 37:3
but the *b* against ....Matt 12:31
"He has spoken *b* ....Matt 26:65
You have heard the *b* ....Mark 14:64
not stone You, but for *b* ...John 10:33
mouth in *b* against God ....Rev 13:6
was full of names of *b* ......Rev 17:3

BLAST
By the *b* of God they ....Job 4:9
for the *b* of the terrible ....Is 25:4

BLASTED
"I *b* you with blight ....Amos 4:9

BLEATING
"What then is this *b* .....1 Sam 15:14

BLEMISH
shall be without *b* ....Ex 12:5
LORD, a ram without *b* .....Lev 6:6
be holy and without *b* ......Eph 5:27
as of a lamb without *b* ....1 Pet 1:19

BLEMISHED
to the Lord what is *b* ....Mal 1:14

BLESS
I will *b* you and make ......Gen 12:2
b those who *b* you ....Gen 12:3
blessing I will *b* you ......Gen 22:17
I will *b* you and multiply ..Gen 26:24
b you before I die ....Gen 27:4
"B me—me also ....Gen 27:34
You go unless You *b* ......Gen 32:26
He will *b* your bread ......Ex 23:25
"The LORD *b* you and ......Num 6:24
whom you *b* is blessed ....Num 22:6
Gerizim to *b* the people ...Deut 27:12
returned to *b* his house ..1 Chr 16:43
b the LORD at all ....Ps 34:1
b with their mouth ....Ps 62:4
b You while I live ....Ps 63:4
b His holy name ....Ps 103:1
b the house of Israel ......Ps 115:12
b those who fear the ....Ps 115:13
b you in the name of ....Ps 129:8
I will abundantly *b* ....Ps 132:15
this day forward I will *b* ...Hag 2:19
b those who curse ....Luke 6:28
B those who persecute ....Rom 12:14
Being reviled, we *b* ....1 Cor 4:12

of blessing which we *b* ...1 Cor 10:16
"blessing I will *b* you ....Heb 6:14
With it we *b* our God .....James 3:9

BLESS THE LORD
then you shall *b* your God ..Deut 8:10
the assembly, "Now *b* ...1 Chr 29:20
Stand up and *b* ....Neh 9:5
I will *b* who has given ......Ps 16:7
the congregations I will *b* ...Ps 26:12
I will *b* at all times; ....Ps 34:1
B, O my soul; and all ......Ps 103:1
B, O my soul! O LORD ....Ps 104:1
we will *b* from this time ...Ps 115:18
b, all you servants ....Ps 134:1
B, O house of Israel! ....Ps 135:19

BLESSED
And God *b* them ....Gen 1:22
God *b* the seventh day ....Gen 2:3
God *b* Noah and his sons ....Gen 9:1
the earth shall be *b* ....Gen 12:3
b be those who ....Gen 27:29
indeed he shall be *b* .....Gen 27:33
b the Sabbath day ....Ex 20:11
he whom you bless is *b* ....Num 22:6
b, and I cannot reverse ...Num 23:20
B is he who blesses ....Num 24:9
B shall you be in the city ...Deut 28:3
b among women is Jael ...Judg 5:24
grew, and the LORD *b* .....Judg 13:24
the LORD *b* Obed-Edom ...2 Sam 6:11
You have *b* the work of ....Job 1:10
B is the man who walks ....Ps 1:1
B is the man to whom ....Ps 32:2
B is the nation whose ......Ps 33:12
B is he who considers ....Ps 41:1
B are those who keep ....Ps 106:3
B is he who comes ....Ps 118:26
b who fears the LORD ....Ps 128:4
rise up and call her *b* ...Prov 31:28
nations will call you *b* ......Mal 3:12
B are the poor in ....Matt 5:3
B are those who mourn ....Matt 5:4
B are the meek ....Matt 5:5
B are those who hunger ....Matt 5:6
B are the merciful ....Matt 5:7
B are the pure in ....Matt 5:8
B are the peacemakers .....Matt 5:9
B are those who are ......Matt 5:10
B are you when they ......Matt 5:11
b is he who is not ....Matt 11:6
b are your eyes ....Matt 13:16
B is He who comes ....Matt 21:9
hand, 'Come, you *b* ....Matt 25:34
Jesus took bread, *b* ....Matt 26:26
b are you among women ..Luke 1:28
'B is He who comes ....Luke 13:35
know these things, *b* .....John 13:17
B are those who have .....John 20:29
'It is more *b* to give ......Acts 20:35
the Creator, who is *b* ......Rom 1:25
all, the eternally *b* ....Rom 9:5
B be the God and Father ...2 Cor 1:3
b with believing Abraham ....Gal 3:9
B be the God and ....Eph 1:3
b God which was ....1 Tim 1:11
the lesser is *b* by the better ..Heb 7:7
this one will be *b* ....James 1:25
B is he who reads ....Rev 1:3
'B are the dead who ....Rev 14:13
B is he who watches ....Rev 16:15
B are those who are ....Rev 19:9
B and holy is he who ....Rev 20:6
B is he who keeps the ....Rev 22:7
B are those who do His ....Rev 22:14

BLESSED BE THE LORD
B God of my master ......Gen 24:27
"B, who has delivered you ..Ex 18:10
"B, who has not left you ...Ruth 4:14
"B, who has pleaded ...1 Sam 25:39
'B God of Israel, who .....1 Kin 1:48
B God of Israel from .....1 Chr 16:36

B God of our fathers, ...Ezra 7:27
B, because He has heard ....Ps 28:6
B, for he has shown me .....Ps 31:21
B, who daily loads us ....Ps 68:19
B, who has not given us .....Ps 124:6
B my Rock, who trains ......Ps 144:1

BLESSING
and you shall be a *b* .....Gen 12:2
the *b* of Abraham ....Gen 28:4
I will command My *b* .....Lev 25:21
before you today a *b* ......Deut 11:26
LORD will command the *b* ..Deut 28:8
life and death, *b* ....Deut 30:19
exalted above all *b* ....Neh 9:5
The *b* of a perishing ....Job 29:13
Your *b* is upon Your ....Ps 3:8
did not delight in *b* ....Ps 109:17
The *b* of the LORD ....Prov 10:22
My *b* on your offspring .....Is 44:3
shall be showers of *b* ....Ezek 34:26
relent, and leave a *b* ......Joel 2:14
and you shall be a *b* ......Zech 8:13
pour out for you such *b* .....Mal 3:10
the fullness of the *b* ......Rom 15:29
b which we bless ....1 Cor 10:16
that the *b* of Abraham ......Gal 3:14
with every spiritual *b* ......Eph 1:3
cultivated, receives *b* ......Heb 6:7
"Surely *b* I will bless you ...Heb 6:14
to inherit the *b* ....Heb 12:17
same mouth proceed *b* ...James 3:10
honor and glory and *b* .....Rev 5:12

BLESSINGS
of the law, the *b* ....Josh 8:34
B are on the head of ....Prov 10:6

BLEW
b them into the Red Sea ....Ex 10:19
b the trumpets, and the .....Josh 6:8
Then Saul *b* the trumpet ..1 Sam 13:3
the priests regularly *b* ....1 Chr 16:6
came, and the winds *b* ....Matt 7:25

BLIGHT
"I blasted you with *b* ....Amos 4:9
I struck you with *b* ....Hag 2:17

BLIND
I was eyes to the *b* ....Job 29:15
B yourselves and be ....Is 29:9
To open *b* eyes ....Is 42:7
I will bring the *b* ....Is 42:16
b people who have eyes ......Is 43:8
His watchmen are *b* ....Is 56:10
They wandered *b* ....Lam 4:14
when you offer the *b* ....Mal 1:8
The *b* see and the lame ....Matt 11:5
if the *b* leads the *b* ....Matt 15:14
of sight to the *b* ....Luke 4:18
to Him, "Are we *b* ....John 9:40
miserable, poor, *b* ....Rev 3:17

BLINDED
b their eyes and ....John 12:40
and the rest were *b* ....Rom 11:7
of this age has *b* ....2 Cor 4:4
the darkness has *b* ....1 John 2:11

BLINDFOLD
to *b* Him, and to beat ....Mark 14:65

BLINDS
a bribe, for a bribe *b* ......Deut 16:19

BLOCK
See STUMBLING BLOCK
not to put a stumbling *b* ...Rom 14:13
the Jews a stumbling *b* ....1 Cor 1:23

BLOOD
See FLESH AND BLOOD; INNOCENT
BLOOD
of your brother's *b* ....Gen 4:10
life, that is, its *b* ....Gen 9:4
b shall be shed ....Gen 9:6
the tunic in the *b* ....Gen 37:31

you are a husband of *b* ...... Ex 4:25
river were turned to *b* ..... Ex 7:20
when I see the *b*, I will ...... Ex 12:13
the *b* of the covenant .... Ex 24:8
b that makes atonement ... Lev 17:11
b sustains its life .... Lev 17:14
do not cover my *b* .... Job 16:18
is there in my *b* .... Ps 30:9
And condemn innocent *b* .... Ps 94:21
hands are full of *b* .... Is 1:15
also disclose her *b* .... Is 26:21
to you in your *b* .... Ezek 16:6
And the moon into *b* ...... Joel 2:31
to the *b* of Zechariah ..... Matt 23:35
For this is My *b* .... Matt 26:28
betraying innocent *b* ...... Matt 27:4
called the Field of *B* ...... Matt 27:8
b of this just Person ...... Matt 27:24
"His *b* be on us and ...... Matt 27:25
new covenant in My *b* .... Luke 22:20
b falling down .... Luke 22:44
were born, not of *b* ...... John 1:13
b has eternal life .... John 6:54
that is, Field of *B* .... Acts 1:19
the moon into *b* .... Acts 2:20
b every nation of men ... Acts 17:26
with His own *b* .... Acts 20:28
propitiation by His *b* ...... Rom 3:25
justified by His *b* .... Rom 5:9
communion of the *b* .... 1 Cor 10:16
b cannot inherit .... 1 Cor 15:50
confer with flesh and *b* ... Gal 1:16
redemption through His *b* .... Eph 1:7
brought near by the *b* ..... Eph 2:13
against flesh and *b* ...... Eph 6:12
peace through the *b* .... Col 1:20
His own *b* He entered ..... Heb 9:12
"This is the *b* of the ...... Heb 9:20
are purified with *b* .... Heb 9:22
the Holiest by the *b* .... Heb 10:19
sprinkling of the *b* ...... 1 Pet 1:2
with the precious *b* ...... 1 Pet 1:19
b of Jesus Christ His ... 1 John 1:7
the water, and the *b* ...... 1 John 5:8
our sins in His own *b* ...... Rev 1:5
us to God by Your *b* ...... Rev 5:9
moon became like *b* ...... Rev 6:12
them white in the *b* ...... Rev 7:14
the sea became *b* ...... Rev 8:8
overcame him by the *b* ... Rev 12:11
with the *b* of the martyrs ... Rev 17:6
a robe dipped in *b* .... Rev 19:13

BLOODSHED
me from the guilt of *b* ...... Ps 51:14
the land is full of *b* .... Ezek 9:9
build up Zion with *b* ...... Mic 3:10

BLOODTHIRSTY
The LORD abhors the *b* .... Ps 5:6
B and deceitful men .... Ps 55:23

BLOSSOM
Israel shall *b* and bud ...... Is 27:6
and *b* as the rose .... Is 35:1
the fig tree may not *b* ..... Hab 3:17

BLOT
b me out of Your book ...... Ex 32:32
say that He would *b* ..... 2 Kin 14:27
from my sins, and *b* .... Ps 51:9
and I will not *b* .... Rev 3:5

BLOTTED
Let them be *b* out of ...... Ps 69:28
I have *b* out, like a thick ... Is 44:22
your sins may be *b* .... Acts 3:19

BLOW
b the trumpets over ...... Num 10:10
priests shall *b* the .... Josh 6:4
When I *b* the trumpet ..... Judg 7:18
an east wind to *b* .... Ps 78:26
B upon my garden .... Song 4:16
with a very severe *b* ...... Jer 14:17
B the trumpet in Zion ...... Joel 2:1

Lord GOD will *b* the........ Zech 9:14

BLOWS
B that hurt cleanse .... Prov 20:30
breath of the LORD *b*........ Is 40:7
The wind *b* where it .... John 3:8

BLUE
b, purple, and scarlet .... Ex 25:4
pomegranates of *b* .... Ex 28:33
tabernacle door, of *b* ...... Ex 36:37
spread a *b* cloth .... Num 4:7
put a *b* thread in the ...... Num 15:38
made the veil of *b* .... 2 Chr 3:14
royal apparel of *b* .... Esth 8:15
of fiery red, hyacinth *b* ..... Rev 9:17

BLUSH
did they know how to *b* .... Jer 6:15

BOANERGES
Surname of James and John. Mark
3:17

BOAST
puts on his armor *b* ...... 1 Kin 20:11
soul shall make its *b* .... Ps 34:2
God we *b* all day long ...... Ps 44:8
and make your *b* .... Rom 2:17
that we are your *b* .... 2 Cor 1:14
you, and not to *b* .... 2 Cor 10:16
that I also may *b* .... 2 Cor 11:16
lest anyone should *b* .... Eph 2:9
your hearts, do not *b* .... James 3:14

BOASTERS
God, violent, proud, *b* ...... Rom 1:30
lovers of money, *b* .... 2 Tim 3:2

BOASTFUL
b shall not stand .... Ps 5:5
I was envious of the *b* .... Ps 73:3

BOASTING
Where is *b* then .... Rom 3:27
should make my *b* .... 1 Cor 9:15
you, great is my *b* .... 2 Cor 7:4
All such *b* is evil .... James 4:16

BOASTS
Whoever falsely *b* .... Prov 25:14

BOAT
in the *b* with Zebedee ..... Matt 4:21
So He got into a *b* .... Matt 9:1
disciples get into the *b* .... Matt 14:22
by *b* to the other side .... Mark 5:21
in the *b* by themselves ... Mark 6:32
b was in the middle ..... Mark 6:47
b with His disciples .... Luke 8:22
immediately the *b* was ..... John 6:21

BOAZ
A wealthy Bethlehemite. Ruth 2:1,
4–18
Husband of Ruth. Ruth 4:10–13
Ancestor of Christ. Matt 1:5
——— Pillar of the temple. 1 Kin 7:21

BODIES
valley of the dead *b* .... Jer 31:40
b a living sacrifice .... Rom 12:1
not know that your *b* ..... 1 Cor 6:15
also celestial *b* .... 1 Cor 15:40
wives as their own *b* ...... Eph 5:28
and chariots, and *b* ...... Rev 18:13

BODILY
b form like a dove .... Luke 3:22
b presence is weak ...... 2 Cor 10:10
of the Godhead *b* .... Col 2:9
b exercise profits .... 1 Tim 4:8

BODY
b clings to the ground ...... Ps 44:25
b is carved ivory .... Song 5:14
b was wet with the dew .... Dan 4:33
of the *b* is the eye .... Matt 6:22
those who kill the *b* ...... Matt 10:28
Take, eat; this is My *b* .... Matt 26:26
and asked for the *b* ...... Matt 27:58

around his naked *b* ...... Mark 14:51
of the temple of His *b* ...... John 2:21
deliver me from this *b* ..... Rom 7:24
redemption of our *b* ...... Rom 8:23
members in one *b* .... Rom 12:4
and the Lord for the *b* ..... 1 Cor 6:13
against his own *b* .... 1 Cor 6:18
not know that your *b* ...... 1 Cor 6:19
glorify God in your *b* ..... 1 Cor 6:20
But I discipline my *b* ...... 1 Cor 9:27
one bread and one *b* ..... 1 Cor 10:17
b which is broken .... 1 Cor 11:24
be guilty of the *b* .... 1 Cor 11:27
For as the *b* is one .... 1 Cor 12:12
baptized into one *b* ...... 1 Cor 12:13
b is not one member ..... 1 Cor 12:14
are the *b* of Christ .... 1 Cor 12:27
though I give my *b* .... 1 Cor 13:3
It is sown a natural *b* .... 1 Cor 15:44
both to God in one *b* ...... Eph 2:16
be magnified in my *b* ...... Phil 1:20
in the *b* of His flesh .... Col 1:22
by putting off the *b* .... Col 2:11
and neglect of the *b* ...... Col 2:23
were called in one *b* ...... Col 3:15
b You have prepared ...... Heb 10:5
the offering of the *b* ...... Heb 10:10
For as the *b* without ..... James 2:26
our sins in His own *b* ..... 1 Pet 2:24

BOILS
Job with painful *b* .... Job 2:7

BOISTEROUS
that the wind was *b* ...... Matt 14:30

BOLD
the righteous are *b* .... Prov 28:1
whatever anyone is *b* ... 2 Cor 11:21
are much more *b* .... Phil 1:14

BOLDLY
I may open my mouth *b* ... Eph 6:19
therefore come *b* .... Heb 4:16
So we may *b* say .... Heb 13:6

BOLDNESS
Great is my *b* of .... 2 Cor 7:4
in whom we have *b* .... Eph 3:12
but with all *b* .... Phil 1:20
standing and great *b* ..... 1 Tim 3:13
brethren, having *b* ...... Heb 10:19
that we may have *b* ..... 1 John 4:17

BOND
bring you into the *b* ...... Ezek 20:37
of the Spirit in the *b* .... Eph 4:3
love, which is the *b* .... Col 3:14

BONDAGE
because of the *b* .... Ex 2:23
out of the house of *b* ...... Ex 13:14
receive the spirit of *b* ..... Rom 8:15
might bring us into *b* ...... Gal 2:4
which gives birth to *b* ..... Gal 4:24
again with a yoke of *b* ..... Gal 5:1
lifetime subject to *b* ...... Heb 2:15
he is brought into *b* ...... 2 Pet 2:19

BONDS
"Let us break Their *b* .... Ps 2:3
the other I called *B* ...... Zech 11:7

BONDSERVANT
Paul, a *b* of Jesus Christ, ... Rom 1:1
would not be a *b* of Christ ... Gal 1:10
who is one of you, a *b* ...... Col 4:12
Paul, a *b* of God and an .... Titus 1:1
James, a *b* of God and of .. James 1:1
Simon Peter, a *b* and ...... 2 Pet 1:1
Jude, a *b* of Jesus Christ, ... Jude 1

BONDSERVANTS
your *b* for Jesus' sake ..... 2 Cor 4:5
B, be obedient to .... Eph 6:5
as men-pleasers, but as *b* ... Eph 6:6
Paul and Timothy, *b* of .... Phil 1:1
B, obey in all things .... Col 3:22

Masters, give your *b* ....Col 4:1
Exhort *b* to be obedient ..... Titus 2:9
for vice, but as *b* ....1 Pet 2:16

BONDWOMAN
"Cast out this *b* ....Gen 21:10
the one by a *b* ....Gal 4:22

BONE
"This is now *b* of my ....Gen 2:23
b clings to my skin ....Job 19:20
bonds came together, *b* ....Ezek 37:7

BONES
shall carry up my *b* ....Gen 50:25
which made all my *b* ....Job 4:14
His *b* are like beams ....Job 40:18
I can count all My *b* ....Ps 22:17
and my *b* waste away ....Ps 31:10
I kept silent, my *b* ....Ps 32:3
the wind, or how the *b* ....Eccl 11:5
say to them, 'O dry *b* ......Ezek 37:4
b are the whole house ....Ezek 37:11
of dead men's *b* ....Matt 23:27
b shall be broken ....John 19:36
concerning his *b* ....Heb 11:22

BOOK
you will find in the *b* ......Ezra 4:15
distinctly from the *b* ....Neh 8:8
were inscribed in a *b* ......Job 19:23
"Search from the *b* ....Is 34:16
'Write in a *b* for ....Jer 30:2
found written in the *b* ......Dan 12:1
so a *b* of remembrance .....Mal 3:16
are written in the *b* ....Gal 3:10
sprinkled both the *b* ....Heb 9:19
in the Lamb's *B* ....Rev 21:27
the prophecy of this *b* .....Rev 22:18
the words of the *b* ....Rev 22:19

BOOK OF LIFE
whose names are in the *B* ....Phil 4:3
out his name from the *B* ....Rev 3:5
written in the *B* of the .....Rev 13:8
not written in the *B* ....Rev 17:8
opened, which is the *B* .....Rev 20:12
found written in the *B* .....Rev 20:15
written in the Lamb's *B* ....Rev 21:27
away his part from the *B* ..Rev 22:19

BOOK OF THE LAW
are written in this *B*. ....Deut 30:10
Take this *B*, and put it .....Deut 31:26
This *B* shall not depart ......Josh 1:8
that is written in the *B* .....Josh 8:34
that is written in the *B* .....Josh 23:6
"I have found the *B* ....2 Kin 22:8
the words of the *B* ....2 Kin 22:11
in Judah, and had the *B* ...2 Chr 17:9
the scribe to bring the *B* ...Neh 8:1
written in the *b* ....Gal 3:10

BOOKS
b there is no end ....Eccl 12:12
not contain the *b* ....John 21:25
magic brought their *b* ....Acts 19:19
God, and *b* were opened ...Rev 20:12

BOOTH
b which a watchman ......Job 27:18
of Zion is left as a *b* ....Is 1:8

BOOTHS
dwell in *b* for seven ....Lev 23:42
in *b* during the feast ....Neh 8:14

BORDER
pillar to the LORD at its *b* ....Is 19:19

BORDERS
and enlarge your *b* ....Ex 34:24
makes peace in your *b* .....Ps 147:14
and enlarge the *b* ....Matt 23:5

BORE
conceived and *b* Cain ......Gen 4:1
And to Sarah who *b* ....Is 51:2
b the sin of many ....Is 53:12

and He *b* them and ....Is 63:9
b our sicknesses ....Matt 8:17
who Himself *b* our sins ....1 Pet 2:24
b a male Child who was ....Rev 12:5

BORN
"Every son who is *b* ....Ex 1:22
yet man is *b* to trouble ......Job 5:7
"Man who is *b* ....Job 14:1
'This one was *b* ....Ps 87:4
A time to be *b* ....Eccl 3:2
unto us a Child is *b* ....Is 9:6
Or shall a nation be *b* ......Is 66:8
b Jesus who is called ....Matt 1:16
For there is *b* to you ....Luke 2:11
unless one is *b* again ......John 3:3
That which is *b* ....John 3:6
For this cause I was *b* .....John 18:37
me also, as by one *b* ......1 Cor 15:8
of the bondwoman was *b* ....Gal 4:23
having been *b* again ....1 Pet 1:23
who loves is *b* of God .....1 John 4:7
is the Christ is *b* ....1 John 5:1
know that whoever is *b* ..1 John 5:18

BORN AGAIN
unless one is *b*. ....John 3:3
'You must be *b* ....John 3:7
having been *b*, not of ......1 Pet 1:23

BORNE
had *b* him no children ......Gen 16:1
the barren has *b* seven ....1 Sam 2:5
not my son whom I had *b* ..1 Kin 3:21
'I have *b* chastening ....Job 34:31
Surely He has *b* our griefs ....Is 53:4
you who have not *b* ....Is 54:1
you have *b* the shame .....Ezek 36:6
who have *b* the burden ...Matt 20:12
And as we have *b* ....1 Cor 15:49

BORROWER
b is servant to the ....Prov 22:7
lender, so with the *b* ....Is 24:2

BORROWS
The wicked *b* and does ......Ps 37:21

BOSOM
man take fire to his *b* ......Prov 6:27
consolation of her *b* ....Is 66:11
angels to Abraham's *b* ....Luke 16:22
Son, who is in the *b* ....John 1:18
leaning on Jesus' *b* ....John 13:23

BOTTLE
tears into Your *b* ....Ps 56:8
b shall be filled ....Jer 13:12

BOTTOM
they sank to the *b* ....Ex 15:5
in two from top to *b* ......Matt 27:51
in two from top to *b* .....Mark 15:38

BOTTOMLESS
given the key to the *b* ....Rev 9:1
ascend out of the *b* ....Rev 17:8
the key to the *b* ....Rev 20:1

BOTTOMLESS PIT
given the key to the *b* ....Rev 9:1
the angel of the *b*, ...Rev 9:11
ascends out of the *b* ......Rev 11:7
ascend out of the *b* ....Rev 17:8
having the key to the *b* ....Rev 20:1
cast him into the *b* ....Rev 20:3

BOUGH
Joseph is a fruitful *b* ......Gen 49:22
cut down a *b* from the .....Judg 9:48
lop off the *b* with terror .....Is 10:33
will be as a forsaken *b* ......Is 17:9

BOUGHS
cedars with its *b* ....Ps 80:10
She sent out her *b* ....Ps 80:11

BOUGHT
the hand of him who *b* ....Lev 25:28
not your Father, who *b* ....Deut 32:6

b the threshing floor .....2 Sam 24:24
b the field from ....Jer 32:9
all that he had and *b* ......Matt 13:46
For you were *b* at a ....1 Cor 6:20
denying the Lord who *b* .....2 Pet 2:1

BOUND
he *b* Isaac his son ....Gen 22:9
she *b* the scarlet cord ......Josh 2:21
b him with two new ......Judg 15:13
b him with bronze ....Judg 16:21
of the wicked have *b* ......Ps 119:61
cast three men *b* ....Dan 3:24
b the waters in a ....Prov 30:4
not been closed or *b* ....Is 1:6
on earth will be *b* ....Matt 16:19
b hand and foot with .....John 11:44
b at the four corners ......Acts 10:11
And see, now I go *b* ......Acts 20:22
of Israel I am *b* ....Acts 28:20
who has a husband is *b* .....Rom 7:2
Are you *b* to a wife ....1 Cor 7:27
Devil and Satan, and *b* ....Rev 20:2

BOUNDARY
b that they may not ....Ps 104:9

BOUNDS
You shall set *b* ....Ex 19:12
I will set your *b* ....Ex 23:31

BOUNTIFUL
the miser said to be *b* ....Is 32:5
you into a *b* country ....Jer 2:7

BOUNTIFULLY
Because He has dealt *b* ....Ps 13:6
and he who sows *b* ....2 Cor 9:6

BOW
sons *b* down to you ....Gen 27:29
brothers indeed come to *b* ...Gen 37:10
b remained in strength ....Gen 49:24
You shall not *b* ....Ex 23:24
to serve them and *b* ....Judg 2:19
b is renewed in my ....Job 29:20
Judah the Song of the *B* ..2 Sam 1:18
will not trust in my *b* ....Ps 44:6
He breaks the *b* ....Ps 46:9
like a deceitful *b* ....Ps 78:57
let us worship and *b* ....Ps 95:6
B down Your heavens ......Ps 144:5
Me every knee shall *b* ....Is 45:23
not save them by *b* ....Hos 1:7
knee shall *b* to Me ....Rom 14:11
For this reason I *b* ....Eph 3:14
Jesus every knee should *b* ..Phil 2:10
who sat on it had a *b* ....Rev 6:2

BOWED
stood all around and *b* ......Gen 37:7
b the heavens also ......2 Sam 22:10
whose knees have not *b* ..1 Kin 19:18
They have *b* down and .....Ps 20:8
And they *b* the knee ......Matt 27:29
men who have not *b* ....Rom 11:4

BOWED THEIR HEADS
then they *b* and worshiped ...Ex 4:31
So the people *b* ....Ex 12:27
b and prostrated ....1 Chr 29:20
b and worshiped the Lord ...Neh 8:6

BOWL
his hand in the *b* ....Prov 19:24
or the golden *b* ....Eccl 12:6
and poured out his *b* ....Rev 16:2

BOWLS
who drink wine from *b* ......Amos 6:6
a harp, and golden *b* ....Rev 5:8
Go and pour out the *b* ......Rev 16:1
who had the seven *b* ....Rev 21:9

BOWS
"The *b* of the mighty ......1 Sam 2:4

BOWSTRING
He has loosed my *b* ....Job 30:11

BOX 22 CONCORDANCE

BOX
Judas had the money *b* ... John 13:29

BOY
b to Hagar, and sent her ... Gen 21:14
Do not sin against the *b*' .. Gen 42:22
the *b* Samuel ministered ...1 Sam 3:1
B Jesus lingered behind ...Luke 2:43

BOYS
Shall be full of *b* ....Zech 8:5

BOZRAH
City of Edom, Gen 36:33
Destruction, foretold, Amos 1:12
Figurative of Messiah's victory, Is 63:1

BRACELET
b that was on his arm, ...2 Sam 1:10

BRACELETS
two *b* for her wrists ....Gen 24:22
of gold: armlets and *b* ....Num 31:50
b on their wrists ....Ezek 23:42

BRAIDED
not with *b* hair or ....1 Tim 2:9

BRAMBLE
gather grapes from a *b* ....Luke 6:44

BRANCH
blossoms on one *b* ....Ex 25:33
b will not be green ....Job 15:32
from Israel, both a *b* ....Is 9:14
B shall grow out of ....Is 11:1
raise to David a *B* ....Jer 23:5
grow up to David a *B* ......Jer 33:15
forth My Servant the *B* ....Zech 3:8
whose name is the *B* ......Zech 6:12
b has already become .....Matt 24:32
b that bears fruit He ....John 15:2
b cannot bear fruit ....John 15:4
he is cast out as a *b* ....John 15:6

BRANCHES
in the sun, and his *b* ....Job 8:16
and bring forth *b* ....Job 14:9
and cut down the *b* ....Is 18:5
and its *b* are broken ....Jer 11:16
His *b* shall spread ....Hos 14:6
of the air nested in its *b* ..Luke 13:19
vine, you are the *b* ....John 15:5
root is holy, so are the *b* ..Rom 11:16
b were broken off ....Rom 11:17

BRAND
Is this not a *b* plucked ......Zech 3:2

BRASS
become sounding *b* ....1 Cor 13:1
feet were like fine *b* ....Rev 1:15

BRAVE
in the faith, be *b* ....1 Cor 16:13

BREACH
before Him in the *b* ....Ps 106:23
the Repairer of the *B* ....Is 58:12

BREACHES
Heal its *b*, for it is ....Ps 60:2

BREAD
See FEAST OF UNLEAVENED BREAD;
   UNLEAVENED BREAD
face you shall eat *b* ....Gen 3:19
of Salem brought out *b* ....Gen 14:18
"Behold, I will rain *b* ....Ex 16:4
shall eat unleavened *b* ......Ex 23:15
not live by *b* alone ....Deut 8:3
lives, I do not have *b* .....1 Kin 17:12
new wine, a land of the *b* ..2 Kin 18:32
that his life abhors *b* ......Job 33:20
people as they eat *b* ....Ps 14:4
Can He give *b* also ....Ps 78:20
up late, to eat the *b* ....Ps 127:2
her poor with *b* ....Ps 132:15
For they eat the *b* ....Prov 4:17
b eaten in secret is ....Prov 9:17
B gained by deceit is .....Prov 20:17

Go, eat your *b* with ....Eccl 9:7
Cast your *b* upon the ......Eccl 11:1
b will be given him ....Is 33:16
for what is not *b* ....Is 55:2
to share your *b* ....Is 58:7
We get our *b* at the ....Lam 5:9
who give me my *b* ....Hos 2:5
For their *b* shall be ....Hos 9:4
And lack of *b* in all ....Amos 4:6
these stones become *b* .....Matt 4:3
not live by *b* alone ....Matt 4:4
this day our daily *b* ....Matt 6:11
eating, Jesus took *b* ....Matt 26:26
no bag, no *b*, no copper ....Mark 6:8
is he who shall eat *b* .....Luke 14:15
gives you the true *b* ....John 6:32
I am the *b* of life ....John 6:48
having dipped the *b* ....John 13:26
b which we break ....1 Cor 10:16
He was betrayed took *b* ..1 Cor 11:23
as you eat this *b* ....1 Cor 11:26
did we eat anyone's *b* ....2 Thess 3:8
and eat their own *b* .....2 Thess 3:12

BREADTH
is as great as its *b* ....Rev 21:16

BREAK
that you shall *b* his yoke ..Gen 27:40
nor shall you *b* one of its ....Ex 12:46
lest the LORD *b* out against ..Ex 19:22
B off the golden earrings ....Ex 32:2
b their bones and ....Num 24:8
never *b* My covenant ......Judg 2:1
torment my soul, and *b* .....Job 19:2
They *b* up my path ....Job 30:13
B their teeth in their ....Ps 58:6
And now they *b* down ......Ps 74:6
b My statutes and do ....Ps 89:31
covenant I will not *b* ......Ps 89:34
reed He will not *b* ....Is 42:3
and that you *b* every yoke ....Is 58:6
your light shall *b* forth ......Is 58:8
Remember, do not *b* ....Jer 14:21
b your fallow ground, ...Hos 10:12
and where thieves *b* in ....Matt 6:19
reed He will not *b* ....Matt 12:20
they did not *b* His legs ....John 19:33
together to *b* bread ....Acts 20:7
bread which we *b* ....1 Cor 10:16
B forth and shout, ...Gal 4:27

BREAKING
in the *b* of bread ....Acts 2:42
b bread from house to .....Acts 2:46
weeping and *b* my heart ...Acts 21:13
dishonor God through *b* ....Rom 2:23

BREAKS
He *b* in pieces mighty .....Job 34:24
My soul *b* with longing .....Ps 119:20
Until the day *b* ....Song 2:17
Whoever therefore *b* ......Matt 5:19

BREAST
back on Jesus' *b* ....John 13:25

BREASTPLATE
a *b*, an ephod ....Ex 28:4
righteousness as a *b* ....Is 59:17
having put on the *b* ....Eph 6:14

BREASTS
blessings of the *b* ....Gen 49:25
on My mother's *b* ....Ps 22:9
doe, let her *b* satisfy ....Prov 5:19
Your two *b* are like ....Song 4:5
b which nursed You ......Luke 11:27
done, beat their *b* ....Luke 23:48

BREATH
nostrils the *b* of life ....Gen 2:7
at the blast of the *b* ......2 Sam 22:16
that there was no *b* ......1 Kin 17:17
perish, and by the *b* ....Job 4:9
as long as my *b* ....Job 27:3
has made me, and the *b* ...Job 33:4

You take away their *b* .....Ps 104:29
Man is like a *b* ....Ps 144:4
everything that has *b* ....Ps 150:6
they all have one *b* ....Eccl 3:19
from it, who gives *b* ....Is 42:5
"Surely I will cause *b* .....Ezek 37:5
God who holds your *b* .....Dan 5:23
gives to all life, *b* ....Acts 17:25
consume with the *b* .....2 Thess 2:8
power to give *b* ....Rev 13:15

BREATH OF LIFE
into his nostrils the *b* ....Gen 2:7
flesh in which is the *b* ......Gen 6:17
flesh in which is the *b* .....Gen 7:15
b from God entered them ..Rev 11:11

BREATHE
me, and such as *b* ....Ps 27:12
winds, O breath, and *b* ....Ezek 37:9

BREATHED
and *b* into his nostrils the ....Gen 2:7
a loud voice, and *b* His ...Mark 15:37
He *b* on them, and said ...John 20:22
fell down and *b* his last .....Acts 5:5
at his feet and *b* her last ....Acts 5:10

BREATHES
indeed he *b* his last ....Job 14:10

BRETHREN
presence of all his *b* ....Gen 16:12
be lifted above his *b* ....Deut 17:20
how good it is for *b* to .....Ps 133:1
and you are all *b* ....Matt 23:8
least of these My *b* ....Matt 25:40
Go and tell My *b* ....Matt 28:10
Men and *b*, this Scripture ..Acts 1:16
six *b* accompanied me ....Acts 11:12
firstborn among many *b* ...Rom 8:29
to judge between his *b* .....1 Cor 6:5
thus sin against the *b* .....1 Cor 8:12
over five hundred *b* ....1 Cor 15:6
perils among false *b* .....2 Cor 11:26
b secretly brought ....Gal 2:4
Finally, my *b*, be strong ....Eph 6:10
Greet all the *b* with .....1 Thess 5:26
to be made like His *b* ....Heb 2:17
sincere love of the *b* ......1 Pet 1:22
because we love the *b* ....1 John 3:14
our lives for the *b* ....1 John 3:16
does not receive the *b* .....3 John 10
for the accuser of our *b* ...Rev 12:10
of your *b* the prophets ......Rev 22:9

BRIBE
you shall take no *b* ....Ex 23:8
b blinds the eyes ....Deut 16:19
b debases the heart ....Eccl 7:7

BRIBERY
consume the tents of *b* .....Job 15:34

BRIBES
hand is full of *b* ....Ps 26:10
but he who hates *b* ....Prov 15:27
but he who receives *b* ......Prov 29:4
everyone loves *b* ....Is 1:23
the just and taking *b* ......Amos 5:12

BRICK
people straw to make *b* ....Ex 5:7
incense on altars of *b* ....Is 65:3
Make strong the *b* ....Nah 3:14

BRICKS
"Come, let us make *b* ......Gen 11:3
b which they made ....Ex 5:8
deliver the quota of *b* ......Ex 5:18
b have fallen down ....Is 9:10

BRIDE
them on you as a *b* ....Is 49:18
He who has the *b* ....John 3:29
I will show you the *b* ......Rev 21:9
the Spirit and the *b* ....Rev 22:17

BRIDEGROOM
righteousness, as a *b* ....Is 61:10

and as the *b* rejoices .... Is 62:5
mourn as long as the *b* ..... Matt 9:15
b will be taken away .... Matt 9:15
went out to meet the *b* ..... Matt 25:1
b fast while the .... Mark 2:19
the friend of the *b* .... John 3:29

BRIDLE
harnessed with bit and *b* ..... Ps 32:9
b the whole body ....James 3:2

BRIER
b shall come up the .... Is 55:13
longer be a pricking *b* ... Ezek 28:24
of them is like a *b* .... Mic 7:4

BRIERS
there shall come up *b* .... Is 5:6
their words, though *b* .... Ezek 2:6

BRIGHTER
Her Nazirites were *b* .... Lam 4:7
a light from heaven, *b* .... Acts 26:13

BRIGHTNESS
From the *b* before Him .. 2 Sam 22:13
and kings to the *b* .... Is 60:3
goes forth as *b* .... Is 62:1
very dark, with no *b* ...... Amos 5:20
who being the *b* .... Heb 1:3

BRIMSTONE
Then the LORD rained *b*.... Gen 19:24
b is scattered on his .... Job 18:15
fire, smoke, and *b* .... Rev 9:17
the lake of fire and *b* .... Rev 20:10

BRING
LORD your God will *b* ...... Deut 30:3
b back his soul .... Job 33:30
for they *b* down .... Ps 55:3
Lord said, "I will *b* .... Ps 68:22
B forth your strong .... Is 41:21
He will *b* forth justice .... Is 42:3
b My righteousness .... Is 46:13
Though they *b* up their .... Hos 9:12
she will *b* forth a Son ..... Matt 1:21
b no fruit to maturity .... Luke 8:14
this Man's blood .... Acts 5:28
Who shall *b* a charge ..... Rom 8:33
b Christ down from .... Rom 10:6
b Christ up from the ...... Rom 10:7
even so God will *b* ..... 1 Thess 4:14

BROAD
set me in a *b* place .... Ps 118:5
b is the way that .... Matt 7:13
their phylacteries *b* .... Matt 23:5

BROKE
b them at the foot of ...... Ex 32:19
b open the fountain .... Ps 74:15
covenant which they *b* ..... Jer 31:32
He blessed and *b* .... Matt 14:19
b the flask and poured .... Mark 14:3
b the legs of the .... John 19:32

BROKEN
he has *b* My covenant ..... Gen 17:14
I am like a *b* vessel .... Ps 31:12
their bows shall be *b* ...... Ps 37:15
He has *b* his covenant ...... Ps 55:20
heart the spirit is *b* .... Prov 15:13
b spirit dries the .... Prov 17:22
but who can bear a *b* ..... Prov 18:14
in the staff of this *b* .... Is 36:6
heart within me is *b* .... Jer 23:9
is oppressed and *b* .... Hos 5:11
this stone will be *b* .... Matt 21:44
Scripture cannot be *b* ..... John 10:35
is My body which is *b* .... 1 Cor 11:24

BROKENHEARTED
He heals the *b* and .... Ps 147:3
sent Me to heal the *b* .... Is 61:1
sent Me to heal the *b* ..... Luke 4:18

BRONZE
So Moses made a *b* .... Num 21:9

your head shall be *b* ..... Deut 28:23
b serpent that Moses ..... 2 Kin 18:4
Or is my flesh *b* .... Job 6:12
b as rotten wood .... Job 41:27
broken the gates of *b* ..... Ps 107:16
b I will bring .... Is 60:17
b walls against the .... Jer 1:18
people a fortified *b* .... Jer 15:20
a third kingdom of *b* ..... Dan 2:39
make your hooves *b* .... Mic 4:13
were mountains of *b* ...... Zech 6:1

BROOD
The *b* of evildoers .... Is 14:20
B of vipers .... Matt 12:34
hen gathers her *b* .... Luke 13:34

BROOD OF VIPERS
he said to them, "*B*........ Matt 3:7
*B! How can you, being .... Matt 12:34
Serpents, *b! How can .... Matt 23:33
baptized by him, "*B* ...... Luke 3:7

BROOK
stones from the *b* .... 1 Sam 17:40
shall drink of the *b* .... Ps 110:7
disciples over the *B* ...... John 18:1

BROOK CHERITH
God hides Elijah here and the ravens
feed him, 1 Kin 17:3–6

BROOKS
good land, a land of *b* .... Deut 8:7
b that pass away .... Job 6:15
for the water *b* .... Ps 42:1

BROTHER
"Where is Abel your *b* ...... Gen 4:9
he were my friend or *b* ..... Ps 35:14
speak against your *b* .... Ps 50:20
and a *b* is born for .... Prov 17:17
b offended is harder ...... Prov 18:19
has neither son nor *b* ..... Eccl 4:8
and do not trust any *b* ..... Jer 9:4
he pursued his *b* .... Amos 1:11
Was not Esau Jacob's *b* ..... Mal 1:2
b will deliver up .... Matt 10:21
how often shall my *b* ..... Matt 18:21
"Teacher, tell my *b* .... Luke 12:13
b will rise again .... John 11:23
do you judge your *b* ..... Rom 14:10
b goes to law against ..... 1 Cor 6:6
shall the weak *b* .... 1 Cor 8:11
slave—a beloved *b* .... Philem 16
He who loves his *b* ...... 1 John 2:10
and murdered his *b* ...... 1 John 3:12
Whoever hates his *b* ..... 1 John 3:15
b sinning a sin which .... 1 John 5:16
I, John, both your *b* .... Rev 1:9

BROTHERHOOD
the covenant of *b* .... Amos 1:9
I might break the *b* ...... Zech 11:14
Love the *b* .... 1 Pet 2:17
experienced by your *b* ..... 1 Pet 5:9

BROTHERLY
to one another with *b* ..... Rom 12:10
b love continue .... Heb 13:1

BROTHER'S
Am I my *b* keeper .... Gen 4:9
at the speck in your *b* ..... Matt 7:3

BROTHERS
My *b* have dealt .... Job 6:15
a stranger to my *b* .... Ps 69:8
is My mother, or My *b* ..... Mark 3:33
b are these who hear ..... Luke 8:21
b did not believe .... John 7:5
love as *b*, be tenderhearted .. 1 Pet 3:8

BROUGHT
He *b* out His people ...... Ps 105:43
The king has *b* me into ..... Song 1:4
to heaven, will be *b* ..... Luke 10:15

BRUISE
He shall *b* your head ...... Gen 3:15

LORD binds up the *b* ...... Is 30:26
the LORD to *b* Him .... Is 53:10

BRUISED
b reed He will not .... Is 42:3
He was *b* for our .... Is 53:5
b reed He will not .... Matt 12:20

BRUTAL
b men who are .... Ezek 21:31

BUCKET
are as a drop in a *b* .... Is 40:15

BUCKLER
be your shield and *b* .... Ps 91:4

BUD
it bring forth and *b* .... Is 55:10

BUFFET
of Satan to *b* me .... 2 Cor 12:7

BUILD
b ourselves a city........... Gen 11:4
cities which you did not *b* .. Deut 6:10
shall *b* with whole stones .. Deut 27:6
b an altar to the LORD...... Judg 6:26
will *b* him a sure house ... 1 Sam 2:35
"Would you *b* a house ..... 2 Sam 7:5
b a temple for the name ... 1 Kin 8:17
that the LORD will *b* ...... 1 Chr 17:10
Solomon who shall *b* ..... 1 Chr 28:6
able to *b* Him a temple .... 2 Chr 2:6
b the house of the LORD .... Ezra 1:5
and let us *b* the wall of .... Neh 2:17
B the walls of Jerusalem ... Ps 51:18
labor in vain who *b* .... Ps 127:1
afterward *b* your house ... Prov 24:27
down, and a time to *b* ..... Eccl 3:3
house that you will *b* .... Is 66:1
I will *b* them and not ...... Jer 24:6
Who *b* up Zion with .... Mic 3:10
b the desolate places .... Mal 1:4
'This man began to *b* ..... Luke 14:30
What house will you *b* ..... Acts 7:49
b you up and give you .... Acts 20:32
named, lest I should *b* ..... Rom 15:20
For if I *b* again .... Gal 2:18

BUILDER
me, as a wise master *b* ... 1 Cor 3:10
foundations, whose *b* ..... Heb 11:10

BUILDERS
The stone which the *b* ..... Ps 118:22
The stone which the *b* .... Matt 21:42
The stone which the *b* .... Mark 12:10
The stone which the *b* .... Luke 20:17
was rejected by you *b* ..... Acts 4:11
The stone which the *b* .... 1 Pet 2:7

BUILDING
field, you are God's *b* ..... 1 Cor 3:9
destroyed, we have a *b* .... 2 Cor 5:1
in whom the whole *b* ..... Eph 2:21
But you, beloved, *b* .... Jude 20

BUILDS
The LORD *b* up.............. Ps 147:2
The wise woman *b* .... Prov 14:1
one take heed how he *b* .. 1 Cor 3:10

BUILT
Wisdom has *b* her house ... Prov 9:1
my works great, I *b* .... Eccl 2:4
Babylon, that I have *b* ..... Dan 4:30
to a wise man who *b* ..... Matt 7:24
a foolish man who *b* ...... Matt 7:26
work which he has *b* ..... 1 Cor 3:14
having been *b* on the ...... Eph 2:20
rooted and *b* up in Him .... Col 2:7
For every house is *b* .... Heb 3:4
stones, are being *b* .... 1 Pet 2:5

BULL
I will not take a *b* .... Ps 50:9
like an untrained *b* .... Jer 31:18

BULLS
in the blood of *b* .... Is 1:11

For if the blood of *b* .... Heb 9:13

BULRUSHES
she took an ark of *b* .... Ex 2:3

BULWARKS
Mark well her *b* .... Ps 48:13
for walls and *b* .... Is 26:1

BUNDLE
each man's *b* of money .... Gen 42:35
A *b* of myrrh is my .... Song 1:13

BURDEN
You have laid the *b* .... Num 11:11
one knows his own *b* ..... 2 Chr 6:29
so that I am a *b* .... Job 7:20
Cast your *b* on the .... Ps 55:22
the grasshopper is a *b* .... Eccl 12:5
in that day that his *b* .... Is 10:27
its reproach is a *b* .... Zeph 3:18
easy and My *b* is light .... Matt 11:30
upon you no greater *b* ... Acts 15:28
as it may, I did not *b* ..... 2 Cor 12:16
we might not be a *b* ..... 1 Thess 2:9
on you no other *b* .... Rev 2:24

BURDENED
but you have *b* Me with ...... Is 43:24
were *b* beyond measure .... 2 Cor 1:8
this tent groan, being *b* ..... 2 Cor 5:4
be eased and you *b* .... 2 Cor 8:13
not let the church be *b* .... 1 Tim 5:16

BURDENS
and looked at their *b* .... Ex 2:11
For they bind heavy *b* ..... Matt 23:4
Bear one another's *b* .... Gal 6:2

BURDENSOME
b task God has given .... Eccl 1:13
his life will be *b* .... Is 15:4
I myself was not *b* .... 2 Cor 12:13
commandments are not *b* .. 1 John 5:3

BURIAL
as property for a *b* place .. Gen 23:20
indeed he has no *b* .... Eccl 6:3
she did it for My *b* .... Matt 26:12
to anoint My body for *b* ... Mark 14:8
for the day of My *b* .... John 12:7
Stephen to his *b* .... Acts 8:2

BURIED
and there will I be *b* .... Ruth 1:17
I saw the wicked *b* .... Eccl 8:10
away the body and *b* ..... Matt 14:12
also died and was *b* .... Luke 16:22
Therefore we were *b* .... Rom 6:4
and that He was *b* .... 1 Cor 15:4
b with Him in baptism ...... Col 2:12

BURN
the bush does not *b* .... Ex 3:3
that My wrath may *b* ...... Ex 32:10
b their chariots .... Josh 11:6
both will *b* together........... Is 1:31
"Did not our heart *b* .... Luke 24:32
eat her flesh and *b* .... Rev 17:16

BURNED
If anyone's work is *b* ...... 1 Cor 3:15
my body to be *b* .... 1 Cor 13:3
whose end is to be *b* .... Heb 6:8
be touched and that *b* .... Heb 12:18
are *b* outside the camp .... Heb 13:11
in it will be *b* .... 2 Pet 3:10
all green grass was *b* .... Rev 8:7

BURNING
b torch that passed .... Gen 15:17
with severe *b* fever .... Deut 28:22
on his lips like a *b* .... Prov 16:27
b fire shut up in my .... Jer 20:9
b jealousy against the ..... Ezek 36:5
plucked from the *b* .... Amos 4:11
a great mountain *b* .... Rev 8:8
fell from heaven, *b* .... Rev 8:10

BURNT
offered *b* offerings .... Gen 8:20

---

lamb for a *b* offering .... Gen 22:7
and *b* offerings, that .... Ex 10:25
took a *b* offering and .... Ex 18:12
shall set the altar of the *b* .... Ex 40:6
is a *b* sacrifice of the herd .... Lev 1:3
And they offered on it *b* .... Josh 8:31
offer a *b* sacrifice with .... Judg 6:26
if you offer a *b* offering ... Judg 13:16
accepted a *b* offering ..... Judg 13:23
b offerings on that altar .... 1 Kin 3:4
offered *b* offerings .... 1 Kin 9:25
offer *b* offerings on it, ... Ezra 3:2
delight in *b* offering .... Ps 51:16
b offerings are not .... Jer 6:20
sacrificing *b* offerings ..... Ezek 43:18
Though you offer Me *b* ... Amos 5:22

BURST
it is ready to *b* .... Job 32:19
with doors, when it *b* ..... Job 38:8
the new wine will *b* .... Luke 5:37
falling headlong, he *b* ...... Acts 1:18

BURY
b your dead in the .... Gen 23:6
was no one to *b* them .... Ps 79:3
go and *b* my father .... Matt 8:21
and let the dead *b* .... Matt 8:22

BUSH
from the midst of a *b* .... Ex 3:2
Him who dwelt in the *b* ... Deut 33:16
to him in the *b* .... Acts 7:35

BUSINESS
in ships, who do *b* .... Ps 107:23
farm, another to his *b* .... Matt 22:5
about My Father's *b* .... Luke 2:49

BUSYBODIES
at all, but are *b* .... 2 Thess 3:11
but also gossips and *b* .... 1 Tim 5:13

BUT I SAY TO YOU
B that whoever is angry .... Matt 5:22
B that whoever looks ...... Matt 5:28
B that whoever divorces .... Matt 5:32
B, do not swear at all ...... Matt 5:34
B, love your enemies, ... Matt 5:44
B, it will be more .... Matt 11:22
B that for every idle ...... Matt 12:36
B that Elijah has come .... Matt 17:12
B, I will not drink of ...... Matt 26:29
B that Elijah has also ..... Mark 9:13
B who hear: Love .... Luke 6:27
B that it will be more .... Luke 10:12

BUTLER
b did not remember .... Gen 40:23

BUTTER
So he took *b* and milk ...... Gen 18:8
were smoother than *b* ..... Ps 55:21
of milk produces *b* .... Prov 30:33

BUY
in Egypt to *b* grain .... Gen 41:57
B it back in the presence .... Ruth 4:4
b the threshing floor .... 2 Sam 24:21
B the truth, and do not ... Prov 23:23
Yes, come, *b* wine and .... Is 55:1
B the field for money, and .. Jer 32:25
will *b* fields for money ..... Jer 32:44
that we may *b* the poor .... Amos 8:6
b food for all these .... Luke 9:13
"*B* those things we .... John 13:29
rejoice, those who *b* ...... 1 Cor 7:30
spend a year there, *b* ..... James 4:13
I counsel you to *b* .... Rev 3:18
and that no one may *b* .... Rev 13:17

BUYER
nothing," cries the *b* ...... Prov 20:14
as with the *b*, so with .... Is 24:2
'Let not the *b* rejoice ...... Ezek 7:12

BUYS
a field and *b* it .... Prov 31:16
has and *b* that field ..... Matt 13:44

---

b their merchandise .... Rev 18:11

BYGONE
b generations .... Acts 14:16

BYWORD
But He has made me a *b* ... Job 17:6
You made us a *b* .... Ps 44:14

CAESAR
——— Augustus Caesar (31 B.C.–A.D. 14):
Decree of brings Joseph and Mary to
Bethlehem, Luke 2:1
——— Tiberius Caesar (A.D. 14–37):
Christ's ministry dated by, Luke
3:1–23
Tribute paid to, Matt 22:17–21
Jews side with, John 19:12
——— Claudius Caesar (A.D. 41–54):
Famine in time of, Acts 11:28
Banished Jews from Rome, Acts 18:2
——— Nero Caesar (A.D. 54–68):
Paul appealed to, Acts 25:8–12
Christian converts in household of,
Phil 4:22
Paul tried before, 2 Tim 4:16–18
Called Augustus, Acts 25:21

CAESAREA
Roman capital of Palestine, Acts 12:19;
23:33
Paul escorted to, Acts 23:23–33
Paul imprisoned at; appeals to Caesar,
Acts 25:4, 8–13
Peter preaches at, Acts 10:34–43
Paul preaches at, Acts 9:26–30; 18:22;
21:8

CAESAREA PHILIPPI
A city in northern Palestine; scene of
Peter's great confession, Matt
16:13–20
Probable site of the transfiguration,
Matt 17:1–3

CAGE
c is full of birds .... Jer 5:27
foul spirit, and a *c* .... Rev 18:2

CAIAPHAS
Son-in-law of Annas; high priest, John
18:13
Makes prophecy, John 11:49–52
Jesus appears before, John 18:23, 24
Apostles appear before, Acts 4:1–22

CAIN
Adam's first son, Gen 4:1
His offering rejected, Gen 4:2–7; Heb
11:4
Murders Abel; is exiled; settles in Nod,
Gen 4:8–17
A type of evil, Jude 11

CAKE
Ephraim is a *c* .... Hos 7:8

CAKES
Sustain me with *c* .... Song 2:5
and love the raisin *c* .... Hos 3:1

CALAMITIES
refuge, until these *c* .... Ps 57:1

CALAMITY
for the day of their *c* ..... Deut 32:35
will laugh at your *c* .... Prov 1:26
c shall come suddenly ..... Prov 6:15
If there is *c* in a .... Amos 3:6

CALCULATED
c the dust of the .... Is 40:12

CALDRON
this city is the *c* .... Ezek 11:3

CALEB
Sent as spy; gives good report; rewarded, Num 13:2, 6, 27, 30; 14:5–9,
24–38

Inherits Hebron, Josh 14:6–15
Conquers his territory with Othniel's
help, Josh 15:13–19

CALF
and made a molded c . . . . Ex 32:4
They made a c in Horeb . . . . Ps 106:19
is, than a fatted c . . . . Prov 15:17
like a stubborn c . . . . Hos 4:16
Your c is rejected . . . . Hos 8:5
And bring the fatted c . . . . Luke 15:23
creature like a c . . . . Rev 4:7

CALL
Then men began to c . . . . . . Gen 4:26
I c heaven and earth . . . . Deut 4:26
I did not c, my son . . . . 1 Sam 3:6
I will c to the LORD . . . . . . 1 Sam 12:17
c their lands after . . . . Ps 49:11
To you, O men, I c . . . . Prov 8:4
c upon Him while He . . . . Is 55:6
c the Sabbath a delight, ... Is 58:13
'C to Me, and I will . . . . Jer 33:3
Arise, c on your God . . . . Jon 1:6
They will c on My name . . . Zech 13:9
c His name JESUS . . . . Matt 1:21
c the righteous . . . . Matt 9:13
Why do you c Me good . . Mark 10:18
shall c his name John . . . . Luke 1:13
shall c His name JESUS . . . . Luke 1:31
Lord our God will c . . . . Acts 2:39
you must not c common . . . Acts 10:15
c them My people . . . . Rom 9:25
then shall they c . . . . Rom 10:14
For God did not c . . . . 1 Thess 4:7
Let him c for the elders . . . James 5:14
c and election sure . . . . 2 Pet 1:10

CALLED
c the light Day . . . . Gen 1:5
c his wife's name Eve . . . . . . Gen 3:20
"I, the LORD, have c . . . . Is 42:6
I have c you by your . . . . Is 43:1
The LORD has c Me from . . . . . Is 49:1
and out of Egypt I c . . . . . . Hos 11:1
"Out of Egypt I c . . . . Matt 2:15
a city c Nazareth . . . . Matt 2:23
For many are c . . . . Matt 20:16
to those who are the c . . . . . Rom 8:28
these He also c . . . . Rom 8:30
But God has c us to . . . . . . 1 Cor 7:15
praises of Him who c . . . . . . 1 Pet 2:9
knowledge of Him who c . . . 2 Pet 1:3
c children of God . . . . 1 John 3:1

CALLED BY MY NAME
if My people who are c . . . . 2 Chr 7:14
everyone who is c . . . . Is 43:7
a nation that was not c . . . . . . Is 65:1
this house which is c . . . . Jer 7:10
the city which is c . . . . Jer 25:29
house which is c . . . . Jer 32:34
the Gentiles who are c . . . . Amos 9:12
the Gentiles who are c . . . . Acts 15:17

CALLING
the gifts and the c . . . . Rom 11:29
For you see your c . . . . 1 Cor 1:26
remain in the same c . . . . . . 1 Cor 7:20
to walk worthy of the c . . . . . . Eph 4:1
in one hope of your c . . . . Eph 4:4
us with a holy c . . . . 2 Tim 1:9
of the heavenly c . . . . Heb 3:1

CALLS
c them all by name . . . . Ps 147:4
there is no one who c . . . . Is 64:7
David himself c . . . . Mark 12:37
c his own sheep . . . . John 10:3
For "whoever c . . . . Rom 10:13

CALM
the sea will become c . . . . . . Jon 1:12
there was a great c . . . . . . Matt 8:26

CALMED
Surely I have c . . . . Ps 131:2

CALVARY
Christ crucified there, Luke 23:33
Same as "Golgotha" in Hebrew, John
19:17

CALVES
made two c of gold . . . . . . 1 Kin 12:28
their cow c without . . . . Job 21:10
like stall-fed c . . . . Mal 4:2
blood of goats and c . . . . Heb 9:12
he took the blood of c . . . . . Heb 9:19

CAMEL
it is easier for a c . . . . Matt 19:24
and swallow a c . . . . Matt 23:24

CAMEL'S
John was clothed with c . . . . Mark 1:6

CAMP
"This is God's c . . . . Gen 32:2
who went before the c . . . . . Ex 14:19
to Him, outside the c . . . . . Heb 13:13

CAN
I c do all things . . . . Phil 4:13

CANA
A village of upper Galilee; home of Na-
thanael, John 21:2
Site of Christ's first miracle, John
2:1–11
Healing at, John 4:46–54

CANAAN
A son of Ham, Gen 10:6
Cursed by Noah, Gen 9:20–25
———— Promised Land, Gen 12:5
Boundaries of, Gen 10:19
God's promises concerning, giv
Abraham, Gen 12:1–3
to Isaac, Gen 26:2, 3
to Jacob, Gen 28:10–13
to Israel, Ex 3:8   7–21
Conquest of, announced, G Num
preceded by spying expec
13:1–33   1–35
delayed by unbelief, Nu sh
accomplished by the L
23:1–16   1:21,
achieved only in part,
27–36

CANAANITES
Israelites commande   e their gods.
drive them out; no
Ex 23:23–33   ns, Lev 18:24–
shun their abomi
30
not make coven or intermarry
with them, De 1–3

CANCER
will spread lik . . . . 2 Tim 2:17

CANE
bought Me n veet c . . . . Is 43:24
Sheba, and et c . . . . Jer 6:20

CANOPIE
He made d ness c . . . . . 2 Sam 22:12

CANOPY
His c ar our Him was . . . . . Ps 18:11

CAPERNAUM
Simon Pe r's home, Mark 1:21, 29
Christ p forms healings there, Matt
8:5–1 9:1–8; Mark 1:21–28; John
4:46–4
prea es there, Mark 9:33–50; John
6:2–71
use as headquarters, Matt 4:13–17
p nounces judgment upon, Matt
1:23, 24

CAPPADOCIA
Jews from, at Pentecost, Acts 2:1, 9
Christians of, addressed by Peter, 1 Pet
1:1

CAPSTO . . . . Zech 4:7
bring for

CAPTA . . . . Gen 39:1
c of the he . . . 2 Sam 17:25
made c . . . . . . 2 Kin 25:11
Nebu c . . . . Prov 6:7
whic e c . . . . . . John 18:12
of t guard . . . . . Acts 28:16
to t

CA tivity c . . . . Ps 68:18
h , O c . . . . Is 52:2
now go c . . . . Amos 6:7
away c . . . . Luke 21:24
ptivity c . . . . Eph 4:8

/ES
ng back the c . . . . . Amos 9:14
turn their c . . . . Zeph 2:7
c of gullible women . . 2 Tim 3:6

TIVITY
ng you back from c . . . . Deut 30:3
gh, You have led c . . . . . Ps 68:18
udah has gone into c . . . . . . Lam 1:3
from David until the c . . . . Matt 1:17
and bringing me into c . . . . Rom 7:23
every thought into c . . . . . 2 Cor 10:5
on high, He led c . . . . Eph 4:8
shall go into c . . . . Rev 13:10

CARCASS
honey were in the c . . . . . . Judg 14:8
For wherever the c . . . . . Matt 24:28

CARE
and let her c for him . . . . 1 Kin 1:2
into the c of Hegai the . . . . . Esth 2:8
Your c has preserved my . . . Job 10:12
the LORD will take c of me . . Ps 27:10
do You c about anyone, . . . Matt 22:16
to an inn, and took c of . . . Luke 10:34
"Lord, do You not c . . . . . . Luke 10:40
not c about the sheep . . . . . John 10:13
you to be without c . . . . . . 1 Cor 7:32
same c for one another . . . 1 Cor 12:25
but that our c for you . . . . . 2 Cor 7:12
who will sincerely c . . . . Phil 2:20
that now at last your c for . . Phil 4:10
how will he take c . . . . 1 Tim 3:5
that You take c of him . . . . . . Heb 2:6
casting all your c . . . . 1 Pet 5:7

CARED
he said, not that he c . . . . . . John 12:6

CAREFUL
c to observe all the . . . . . . Deut 17:19
shall be c to observe . . . . 2 Kin 17:37
c to maintain good works . . Titus 3:8

CAREFULLY
c keep all these . . . . Deut 11:22
choose his friends c . . . . . . Prov 12:26
than love c concealed . . . . . Prov 27:5
I shall walk c all my . . . . Is 38:15
you have c followed . . . . . . 1 Tim 4:6

CARELESS
but he who is c . . . . Prov 19:16

CARES
no one c for my soul . . . . . . Ps 142:4
and are choked with c . . . . Luke 8:14
He who is unmarried c . . . . 1 Cor 7:32
for He c for you . . . . 1 Pet 5:7

CARMEL
City of Judah, Josh 15:55
Site of Saul's victory, 1 Sam 15:12
———— A mountain of Palestine, Josh
19:26
Scene of Elijah's triumph, 1 Kin
18:19–45
Elisha visits, 2 Kin 2:25

CARNAL
spiritual, but I am c . . . . Rom 7:14

c mind is enmity ... [Rom] 8:7
for you are still c ..... [1 Cor] 3:3
our warfare are not c .. 3:3

CARNALLY
..0:4
we may know them c ..
that we may know him c :5
c minded is death 2

CAROUSE
count it pleasure to c ....

CAROUSING
be weighed down with c .. Lu

CARPENTER
Is this not the c .... Ma

CARRIED
the LORD your God c .. Deut
and c our sorrows .... Is
parted from them and c .. Luke 24
c me away in the .... Rev 17

CARRY
shall c me out of Egypt .... Gen 47:30
you shall c up my bones .... Ex 13:19
longer c the tabernacle .. 1 Chr 23:26
their hands cannot c ...... Job 5:12
c them away like a ..... Ps 90:5
to gray hairs I will c you .. Is 46:4
and c out great exploits ... Dan 11:32
I am not worthy to c ..... Matt 3:11
C neither money bag ... Luke 10:4
for you to c your bed ..... John 5:10
c you where you do not .. John 21:18
it is certain we can c ..... 1 Tim 6:7

CARRYING
a man will meet you c .... Mark 14:13
always c about in the ..... 2 Cor 4:10

CART
ark of the LORD on the c .. 1 Sam 6:11
ark of God on a new c .. 2 Sam 6:3
Every c had four bronze .. 1 Kin 7:30
and sin as if with a c rope .. Is 5:18
as a c is weighed down .. Amos 2:13

CARTS
and Joseph gave them c ... Gen 45:21
made ten c of bronze ... 1 Kin 7:27
the ten c, and ten lavers .. 1 Kin 7:43
one Sea, and the c ... 2 Kin 25:16

CARVE
that its maker should c it ... Hab 2:18

CARVED
for yourself a c image ...... Ex 20:4
shall burn the c images .... Deut 7:25
the c images of their gods .. Deut 12:3
son, to make a c image .... Judg 17:3
Micah's c image which ... Judg 18:31
Then he c cherubim .... 1 Kin 6:35
He even set a c image, ... 2 Chr 33:7
to shame who serve c .... Ps 97:7
workman to prepare a c .... Is 40:20
the c images of Babylon .. Jer 51:47
I will cut off the c image .. Nah 1:14

CASE
God has judged my c ..... Gen 30:6
c that is too hard .... Deut 1:17
I have prepared my c ..... Job 13:18
I would present my c ..... Job 23:4
"Present your c .... Is 41:21
plead His c with all flesh .. Jer 25:31
My c with you face to ... Ezek 20:35
plead your c before the ..... Mic 6:1
Him, until He pleads my c ... Mic 7:9
Festus laid Paul's c ...... Acts 25:14

CASSIA
myrrh and aloes and c ...... Ps 45:8

CAST
C out this bondwoman .... Gen 21:10
c him into this pit which ... Gen 37:22
c longing eyes on Joseph ... Gen 39:7
c it before Pharaoh............ Ex 7:9

army He has c into the sea ... Ex 15:4
that I may c lots for you .... Josh 18:6
c two pillars of bronze ..... 1 Kin 7:15
they c lots for their duty, .. 1 Chr 25:8
they c Pur (that is, the lot) ... Esth 3:7
had c Pur (that is, the lot). .. Esth 9:24
When they c you down .... Job 22:29
c away Their cords from ...... Ps 2:3
c upon You from birth ...... Ps 22:10
for My clothing they c lots .. Ps 22:18
Why are you c down .... Ps 42:5
But You have c us off ...... Ps 44:9
c me away from Your .... Ps 51:11
C your burden on the .... Ps 55:22
He c on them the .... Ps 78:49
the LORD will not c......... Ps 94:14
me up and c me away ...... Ps 102:10
The lot is c into the lap. ... Prov 16:33
the people c off restraint .. Prov 29:18
and the earth shall .... Is 26:19
My sight, as I have c .... Jer 7:15
C away from you all ...... Ezek 18:31
Did we not c three men ... Dan 3:24
brought Daniel and c ...... Dan 6:16
all our sins into .... Mic 7:19
whole body to be c ...... Matt 5:29
out demons in Your ..... Matt 7:22
kingdom will be c ...... Matt 8:12
ts, to c them out ...... Matt 10:1
if I c out demons by .. Matt 12:27
othing they c lots ... Matt 27:35
atan c out Satan ..... Mark 3:23
name they will c .. Mark 16:17
h sons c them out .. Luke 11:19
Her to c into hell .... Luke 12:5
by tents and c lots .. Luke 23:34
C ans c out .... John 6:37
c upon the right ...... John 21:6
C our people .... Rom 11:1
c away bondwoman .. Gal 4:30
c their confidence ... Heb 10:35
the great s before ..... Rev 4:10
c him into ron was c .. Rev 12:9
was c into bottomless ... Rev 20:3
lake of fire .. Rev 20:15

CAST OUT DEMONS
c in Your name
raise the dead ...... Matt 7:22
"This fellow c ...... Matt 10:8
heal sickness, not c ... Matt 12:24
In My name they will c .. Mark 3:15
And if I c by Be... ... Mark 16:17
that fox, 'Behold ...pub. .. Luke 11:19
...... Luke 13:32

CASTING
nation which I am ...... Lev 20:23
Andrew his brother ..... Matt 4:18
c down arguments ...... 2 Cor 10:5
c all your care ...... 1 Pet 5:7

CASTING OUT DEMONS
all Galilee, and c ... Mark 1:39
who does not follow us .. Mark 9:38
someone c in Your nme .. Luke 9:49

CASTLE
are like the bars of a c .. Prov 18:19

CASTS
If Satan c out Satan ... Matt 12:26
perfect love c out ..... 1 John 4:18

CATASTROPHE
bring such a c on this place .. Jer 19:3
not rise from the c that I .. Jer 51:64

CATCH
in wait to c the poor ...... Ps 10:9
c Him in His words ..... Mark 12:13
down your nets for a c .. Luke 5:4
From now on you will c .. Luke 5:10
seeking to c Him in ..... Luke 11:54
they could not c Him in .. Luke 20:26

CATCHES
and the wolf c the .... John 10:12

c the wise in their .... 1 Cor 3:19

CATERPILLAR
their crops to the c .... Ps 78:46

CATTLE
c you shall take as .... Josh 8:2
does not let their c .... Ps 107:38

CAUGHT
behind him was a ram c ... Gen 22:13
and that night they c ...... John 21:3
Spirit of the Lord c .... Acts 8:39
her Child was c up .... Rev 12:5

CAUSE
I would commit my c .... Job 5:8
my enemy without c .... Ps 7:4
hate me without a c .... Ps 35:19
c His face to shine .... Ps 67:1
C me to know the way ..... Ps 143:8
one to plead his c ...... Prov 18:17
God, Who pleads the c ...... Is 51:22
He judged the c .... Jer 22:16
brother without a c .... Matt 5:22
hated Me without a c ..... John 15:25
For this c I was born .... John 18:37

CAUSED
not c it to rain on the earth .. Gen 2:5
LORD God c a deep sleep.... Gen 2:21
LORD c the sea to go back ... Ex 14:21
Jonathan again c .... 1 Sam 20:37
pagan women c even him .. Neh 13:26
c the dawn to know its ..... Job 38:12
which You have c me ...... Ps 119:49
I have c to be carried ..... Jer 29:4
the LORD has c the .... Lam 2:6
He c me to eat that scroll ... Ezek 3:2

CAVALRY
and cities for his c .... 1 Kin 9:19
on a horse with the c ..... 1 Kin 20:20
their c comes from afar ...... Hab 1:8

CAVE
daughters dwelt in a c ..... Gen 19:30
field and the c that is in ... Gen 23:11
him in the c of Machpelah .. Gen 25:9
in a c at Makkedah .... Josh 10:16
escaped to the c of ...... 1 Sam 22:1
hidden them, fifty to a c ... 1 Kin 18:4
It was a c, and a stone .... John 11:38

CAVES
the people hid in c .... 1 Sam 13:6
rocks, and into the c .... Is 2:19
in dens and c of the .... Heb 11:38

CEASE
and night shall not c .... Gen 8:22
Why should the work c ...... Neh 6:3
There the wicked c .... Job 3:17
He makes wars c .... Ps 46:9
C listening to .... Prov 19:27
when the grinders c .... Eccl 12:3
C to do evil .... Is 1:16
eyes flow and do not c, ... Lam 3:49
cause all her mirth to c .... Hos 2:11
they did not c teaching ..... Acts 5:42
tongues, they will c ...... 1 Cor 13:8
do not c to give .... Eph 1:16
do not c to pray for .... Col 1:9

CEASED
c building the city .... Gen 11:8
the sea, and the sea c ...... Jon 1:15
this woman has not c to ... Luke 7:45
offense of the cross has c ... Gal 5:11

CEASES
for the godly man c .... Ps 12:1

CEASING
c your work of faith ...... 1 Thess 1:3
thank God without c ... 1 Thess 2:13
pray without c .... 1 Thess 5:17

CEDAR
dwell in a house of c....... 2 Sam 7:2

He shall grow like a c . . . . Ps 92:12
of our houses are c . . . . Song 1:17
it, paneling it with c . . . . Jer 22:14
Indeed Assyria was a c . . . . Ezek 31:3

CEDARS
the LORD breaks the c . . . . Ps 29:5
c of Lebanon which He . . . . Ps 104:16

CELEBRATE
you shall c your sabbath . . . Lev 23:32
You shall c it in the . . . . Lev 23:41
to c the dedication with . . . . Neh 12:27
c yearly the fourteenth . . . . Esth 9:21

CELEBRATED
Herod's birthday was c . . . . . Matt 14:6

CELESTIAL
but the glory of the c . . . . . 1 Cor 15:40

CENCHREA
A harbor of Corinth, Acts 18:18
Home of Phoebe, Rom 16:1

CENSER
Aaron, each took his c . . . . . Lev 10:1
Each man had a c . . . . . . Ezek 8:11
which had the golden c . . . . . Heb 9:4
the angel took the c . . . . Rev 8:5

CENSUS
When you take the c of . . . . . Ex 30:12
"Take a c of all the . . . . Num 1:2
Take a c of the people . . . . . Num 26:4
Israel because of this c . . 1 Chr 27:24
the c in which David . . . . . 2 Chr 2:17
c first took place while . . . . . Luke 2:2
in the days of the c . . . . Acts 5:37

CENTER
the sanctuary in the c . . . . . Ezek 48:8
side, and Jesus in the c . . . John 19:18

CENTURION
c came to Him, pleading . . . . Matt 8:5
when the c, who stood . . . . Mark 15:39
when the c saw what . . . . . Luke 23:47
Cornelius the c, a just . . . . . Acts 10:22
said to the c who stood . . . . Acts 22:25
a c of the Augustan . . . . Acts 27:1

CENTURION'S
a certain c servant, who . . . . Luke 7:2

CEPHAS
Aramaic for Peter, John 1:42

CERAMIC
the iron mixed with c clay . . Dan 2:41

CEREMONIALLY
Israel and cleanse them c . . . Num 8:6

CEREMONIES
rites and you shall keep . . . Num 9:3
as in the c of your fathers, . . . Jer 34:5

CERTAIN
a c man of Bethlehem, ... Ruth 1:1
Know for c that on the . . . . 1 Kin 2:42
a c man clothed in linen, . . . Dan 10:5
was a c landowner . . . . Matt 21:33
into the city to a c man . . . Matt 26:18
But a c Samaritan, as he . . Luke 10:33
A c man had a fig tree . . . . . Luke 13:6
A c man gave a great . . . Luke 14:16
A c man had two sons . . . . Luke 15:11
There was a c rich man . . . . Luke 16:1
there was a c beggar . . . . Luke 16:20
there was a c nobleman . . . John 4:46
c we can carry nothing . . . . 1 Tim 6:7
He designates a c day . . . . . . Heb 4:7
a c fearful expectation . . . . Heb 10:27

CERTAINLY NOT
C! Indeed, let God be true . . . Rom 3:4
C! For then how will God . . . Rom 3:6
the law through faith? C! . . . Rom 3:31
C! How shall we who died . . Rom 6:2
law but under grace? C . . . . Rom 6:15
Is the law sin? C . . . . Rom 7:7

C! But sin, that it might . . . . Rom 7:13
with God? C . . . . Rom 9:14
cast away His people? C . . . Rom 11:1
C! But through their fall, . . Rom 11:11
members of a harlot? C . . . 1 Cor 6:15
a minister of sin? C . . . . Gal 2:17
C! For if there had been . . . . . Gal 3:21

CERTAINTY
make you know the c . . . . . Prov 22:21
you may know the c . . . . Luke 1:4

CERTIFICATE
writes her a c of divorce . . . Deut 24:1
Where is the c of your . . . . Is 50:1
given her a c of divorce . . . . . . Jer 3:8
a man to write a c . . . . Mark 10:4

CERTIFIED
His testimony has c . . . . John 3:33

CHAFF
c that a storm . . . . Job 21:18
c which the wind . . . . Ps 1:4
Let them be like c . . . . Ps 35:5
be chased like the c . . . . Is 17:13
You shall conceive c . . . . Is 33:11
the day passes like c . . . . . Zeph 2:2
He will burn up the c . . . . . Matt 3:12

CHAIN
He has made my c . . . . Lam 3:7
pit and a great c . . . . Rev 20:1

CHAINED
of God is not c . . . . 2 Tim 2:9
the prisoners as if c . . . . Heb 13:3

CHAINS
their kings with c . . . . Ps 149:8
your neck with c . . . . Song 1:10
And his c fell off . . . . Acts 12:7
am, except for these c . . . . Acts 26:29
Remember my c . . . . Col 4:18
minister to me in my c . . . . Philem 13
delivered them into c . . . . 2 Pet 2:4

CHAINWORK
with wreaths of c . . . . 1 Kin 7:17
carved palm trees and c . . . . 2 Chr 3:5

CHAIR
and a table and a c . . . . 2 Kin 4:10

CHALCEDONY
sapphire, the third c . . . . . . Rev 21:19

CHALDEA
Originally, the southern portion of Babylonia, Gen 11:31
Applied later to all Babylonia, Dan 3:8
Abram came from, Gen 11:28–31

CHALDEANS
Attack Job, Job 1:17
Nebuchadnezzar, king of, 2 Kin 24:1
Jerusalem defeated by, 2 Kin 25:1–21
Babylon, "the glory of," Is 13:19
Predicted captivity of Jews among, Jer 25:1–26
God's agent, Hab 1:6

CHALK
he marks one out with c . . . . . Is 44:13

CHALKSTONES
c that are beaten to dust . . . . . Is 27:9

CHAMBER
went into his c and wept . . Gen 43:30
in his cool private c) . . . . . . Judg 3:20
into an inner c to hide . . . 2 Chr 18:24
go out from his c . . . . Joel 2:16

CHAMBERS
and the c of the south . . . . Job 9:9
brought me into his c . . . . . . Song 1:4
and his c by injustice . . . . . . Jer 22:13

CHAMPION
And a c went out from . . . . 1 Sam 17:4

CHANCE
time and c happen to . . . . . . Eccl 9:11

CHANGE
c his countenance . . . . Job 14:20
c the night into day . . . . Job 17:12
and who can make Him c . . Job 23:13
Because they do not c . . . . . Ps 55:19
a cloak You will c . . . . Ps 102:26
with those given to c . . . . . Prov 24:21
Can the Ethiopian c . . . . . . Jer 13:23
c times and law . . . . Dan 7:25
c their glory into . . . . Hos 4:7
the LORD, I do not c . . . . Mal 3:6
now and to c my tone . . . . . Gal 4:20
there is also a c . . . . Heb 7:12

CHANGED
c my wages ten times, ... Gen 31:7
c his clothing, and came . . . Gen 41:14
them, and they will be c . . . Ps 102:26
But My people have c . . . . . . Jer 2:11
his countenance was c, ... Dan 5:9
c the glory of the . . . . Rom 1:23
but we shall all be c . . . . 1 Cor 15:51
up, and they will be c . . . . . Heb 1:12
the priesthood being c . . . . . Heb 7:12

CHANGERS'
and poured out the c . . . . . John 2:15

CHANGES
c the times and the . . . . Dan 2:21

CHANNELS
c of the sea were seen . . . . . Ps 18:15

CHANT
who c "Peace" while . . . . Mic 3:5

CHARACTER
and c, hope . . . . Rom 5:4
you know his proven c . . . . . Phil 2:22

CHARCOAL
As c is to burning coals, . . Prov 26:21

CHARGE
My voice and kept My c . . . Gen 26:5
shall not c him interest . . . . Ex 22:25
You shall not c interest . . . Deut 23:19
in c of the music . . . . 1 Chr 15:22
kept the c of their God . . . . Neh 12:45
not sin nor c God with . . . . . . Job 1:22
His angels c over you . . . . . . Ps 91:11
His angels c over you . . . . . Matt 4:6
His angels c over You . . . . . Luke 4:10
not c them with this sin . . . . Acts 7:60
shall bring a c against . . . . . Rom 8:33
of Christ without c . . . . 1 Cor 9:18
of God to you free of c . . . . 2 Cor 11:7
anyone's bread free of c . . 2 Thess 3:8
This c I commit to you, . . . 1 Tim 1:18

CHARGED
May it not be c . . . . 2 Tim 4:16

CHARIOT
He took off their c . . . . Ex 14:25
that suddenly a c . . . . 2 Kin 2:11
makes the clouds His c . . . Ps 104:3
and overtake this c . . . . Acts 8:29

CHARIOTEERS
killed seven hundred c . . 2 Sam 10:18

CHARIOTS
the clatter of his c . . . . Judg 5:28
Some trust in c . . . . Ps 20:7
The c of God are . . . . Ps 68:17

CHARITABLE
you do not do your c . . . . . . Matt 6:1
that your c deed . . . . Matt 6:4
c deeds which she . . . . Acts 9:36

CHARM
C is deceitful and . . . . Prov 31:30

CHARMED
may bite when it is not c . . Eccl 10:11
vipers which cannot be c . . . . Jer 8:17

CHARMERS
heed the voice of c . . . . Ps 58:5

CHARMS
the perfume boxes, the, c, ... Is 3:20
have scattered your c to ..... Jer 3:13
who sew magic c .... Ezek 13:18

CHASE
Five of you shall c .... Lev 26:8
How could one c .... Deut 32:30
angel of the LORD c .... Ps 35:5

CHASTE
may present you as a c .. 2 Cor 11:2
to be discreet, c .... Titus 2:5
c conduct accompanied .. 1 Pet 3:2

CHASTEN
C your son while there .... Prov 19:18
is My desire, I will c .... Hos 10:10
a father does not c .... Heb 12:7
I love, I rebuke and c ...... Rev 3:19

CHASTENED
c my soul with fasting ...... Ps 69:10
c every morning .... Ps 73:14
The LORD has c me .... Ps 118:18
In vain I have c .... Jer 2:30
c us as seemed best ...... Heb 12:10

CHASTENING
have not seen the c .... Deut 11:2
do not despise the c .... Job 5:17
'I have borne c .... Job 34:31
a prayer when Your c ..... Is 26:16
if you are without c .... Heb 12:8
Now no c seems to be ..... Heb 12:11

CHASTENS
the LORD your God c you .... Deut 8:5
the LORD loves He c .... Heb 12:6

CHASTISE
and I, even I, will c .... Lev 26:28
c them according .... Hos 7:12
I will therefore c .... Luke 23:22

CHASTISED
father c you with whips... 1 Kin 12:11
have c me, and I was c .... Jer 31:18

CHASTISEMENT
the c for our peace .... Is 53:5

CHATTER
c leads only to poverty .... Prov 14:23

CHEAT
'You shall not c .... Lev 19:13
Beware lest anyone c .... Col 2:8

CHEATED
let yourselves be c .... 1 Cor 6:7
we have c no one .... 2 Cor 7:2

CHEBAR
River in Babylonia, Ezek 1:3
Site of Ezekiel's visions, Ezek 10:15, 20

CHEDORLAOMER
A king of Elam; invaded Canaan, Gen 14:1–16

CHEEK
Let him give his c .... Lam 3:30
with a rod on the c .... Mic 5:1
on your right c .... Matt 5:39

CHEEKBONE
my enemies on the c .... Ps 3:7

CHEEKS
c are lovely with .... Song 1:10
His c are like a bed .... Song 5:13
struck Me, and My c .... Is 50:6

CHEER
See BE OF GOOD CHEER
and let your heart c .... Eccl 11:9
"Son, be of good c .... Matt 9:2

CHEERFUL
makes a c countenance ... Prov 15:13
for God loves a c .... 2 Cor 9:7
Is anyone c? Let him ..... James 5:13

CHEERFULNESS
shows mercy, with c ...... Rom 12:8

CHEESE
and curdle me like c ...... Job 10:10

CHEMOSH
The god of the Moabites, Num 21:29
Children sacrificed to, 2 Kin 3:26, 27
Solomon builds altars to, 1 Kin 11:7
Josiah destroys altars of, 2 Kin 23:13

CHERISHES
but nourishes and c .... Eph 5:29
as a nursing mother c .... 1 Thess 2:7

CHERUB
Make one c at one end. ..... Ex 25:19
c at one end on this side .... Ex 37:8
He rode upon a c ...... 2 Sam 22:11
other c was ten cubits ..... 1 Kin 6:25
And He rode upon a c. ...... Ps 18:10
the wheels, under the c .... Ezek 10:2
anointed c who covers .... Ezek 28:14
tree between c and c .... Ezek 41:18

CHERUBIM
and He placed c .... Gen 3:24
shall make two c of gold ... Ex 25:18
an artistic design of c .... Ex 26:31
dwells between the c ...... 2 Sam 6:2
two c of olive wood ..... 1 Kin 6:23
out the wings of the c so .. 1 Kin 6:27
were lions, oxen, and c .... 1 Kin 7:29
its panels he engraved c ... 1 Kin 7:36
under the wings of the c ... 1 Kin 8:6
c overshadowed the ark .... 2 Chr 5:8
dwell between the c .... Ps 80:1
who dwells between the c ... Is 37:16
fire from among the c .... Ezek 10:2
above it were the c .... Heb 9:5

CHEST
offering in a c by its side . 1 Sam 6:8
the c with the gold rats ... 1 Sam 6:11
the priest took a c .... 2 Kin 12:9
came and emptied the c .. 2 Chr 24:11

CHESTNUT
c trees, peeled white ...... Gen 30:37

CHEW
or does not c the cud, is .... Lev 11:26

CHEWING
What the c locust left, the .... Joel 1:4
the c locust, my great .... Joel 2:25

CHICKS
gathers her c under her ... Matt 23:37

CHIEF
is white and ruddy, c ..... Song 5:10
of whom I am c .... 1 Tim 1:15
Zion a c cornerstone .... 1 Pet 2:6
has become the c .... 1 Pet 2:7
C Shepherd appears .... 1 Pet 5:4

CHILD
See WITH CHILD
she is with c by harlotry ... Gen 38:24
that he was a beautiful c ...... Ex 2:2
c grew, and she brought ..... Ex 2:10
the c shall be a Nazirite .... Judg 13:5
the c ministered to the .... 1 Sam 2:11
c Samuel grew in stature . 1 Sam 2:26
named the c Ichabod ..... 1 Sam 4:21
her dead c in my bosom .. 1 Kin 3:20
Divide the living c in two .. 1 Kin 3:25
soul of the c came back .. 1 Kin 17:22
flesh of the c became ..... 2 Kin 4:34
Like a weaned c .... Ps 131:2
c is known by his .... Prov 20:11
Train up a c in the .... Prov 22:6
before the C shall know...... Is 7:16
For unto us a C .... Is 9:6
c shall lead them .... Is 11:6
When Israel was a c .... Hos 11:1
with c of the Holy Spirit ... Matt 1:18

virgin shall be with c...... Matt 1:23
He took a little c .... Mark 9:36
of God as a little c ...... Mark 10:15
kind of c will this be ...... Luke 1:66
So the c grew and .... Luke 1:80
the circumcision of the C .. Luke 2:21
When I was a c .... 1 Cor 13:11
She bore a male C .... Rev 12:5

CHILDBEARING
she will be saved in c .... 1 Tim 2:15

CHILDBIRTH
pain as a woman in c .... Is 13:8

CHILDHOOD
from your flesh, for c ..... Eccl 11:10
And he said, "From c ..... Mark 9:21
c you have known .... 2 Tim 3:15

CHILDISH
I put away c things ...... 1 Cor 13:11

CHILDLESS
give me, seeing I go c ..... Gen 15:2
this man down as c .... Jer 22:30

CHILDREN
See LITTLE CHILDREN
she bore Jacob no c .... Gen 30:1
and all of you are c .... Ps 82:6
c are a heritage .... Ps 127:3
He has blessed your c .... Ps 147:13
let the c of Zion be .... Ps 149:2
c are blessed after ...... Prov 20:7
c rise up and call her .... Prov 31:28
c are their oppressors .... Is 3:12
c whom the LORD has....... Is 8:18
be the peace of your c ..... Is 54:13
they are My people, c .... Is 63:8
the hearts of the c .... Mal 4:6
c will rise up against ..... Matt 10:21
and become as little c .... Matt 18:3
c were brought to Him .... Matt 19:13
"Let the little c .... Matt 19:14
the right to become c ..... John 1:12
you were Abraham's c .... John 8:39
spirit that we are c ...... Rom 8:16
but as my beloved c ..... 1 Cor 4:14
Brethren, do not be c .... 1 Cor 14:20
c ought not to lay up ..... 2 Cor 12:14
and were by nature c ...... Eph 2:3
should no longer be c ...... Eph 4:14
Walk as c of light .... Eph 5:8
and harmless, c of God .... Phil 2:15
now we are c of God ..... 1 John 3:2
that we love the c .... 1 John 5:2
to hear that my c .... 3 John 4

CHILDREN'S
are really ours and our c .. Gen 31:16
the c children to the third ... Ex 34:7
His righteousness to c .... Ps 103:17
you see your c children ... Ps 128:6
inheritance to his c ...... Prov 13:22
C children are the crown .. Prov 17:6
the c teeth are set on edge . Jer 31:29
good to take the c bread .. Matt 15:26
eat from the c crumbs ..... Mark 7:28

CHILION
Elimelech's son, Ruth 1:2
Orpah's deceased husband, Ruth 1:4, 5
Boaz redeems his estate, Ruth 4:9

CHINNERETH (or Chinneroth)
Fortified city in Naphtali, Deut 3:17
A region bordering the Sea of Galilee, 1 Kin 15:20
Same as the plain of Gennesaret, Matt 14:34
——— The O.T. name for the Sea of Galilee, Num 34:11
Also called Lake of Gennesaret, Luke 5:1

CHOICE
rather than c gold .... Prov 8:10

CHOIR
c went the opposite way, .. Neh 12:38

CHOKE
things entering in c the .... Mark 4:19

CHOKED
thorns sprang up and c .... Matt 13:7
are c with cares, riches, ... Luke 8:14

CHOOSE
therefore c life .... Deut 30:19
c none of his ways .... Prov 3:31
evil and c the good .... Is 7:15
will still c Israel .... Is 14:1
will again c Jerusalem ..... Zech 1:17
You did not c Me, but I .. John 15:16
yet what I shall c .... Phil 1:22

CHOOSES
in the way He c .... Ps 25:12

CHOSE
a good while ago God c .... Acts 15:7
just as He c us in Him .... Eph 1:4
from the beginning c .... 2 Thess 2:13

CHOSEN
the LORD has c you to be ... Deut 14:2
has c them to minister to .. Deut 21:5
c the son of Jesse to ..... 1 Sam 20:30
of Jacob, His c .... 1 Chr 16:13
I have c Jerusalem .... 2 Chr 6:6
I have c David to be over .. 2 Chr 6:6
people He has c .... Ps 33:12
a covenant with My c .... Ps 89:3
c the way of truth .... Ps 119:30
A good name is to be c .... Prov 22:1
servant whom I have c .... Is 43:10
Is it a fast that I have c .... Is 58:5
c that good part .... Luke 10:42
I know whom I have c .... John 13:18
c you that you should ..... Acts 22:14
c the foolish things .... 1 Cor 1:27
Has God not c the poor ... James 2:5
But you are a c .... 1 Pet 2:9

CHRIST
See JESUS; LORD JESUS CHRIST; LOVE
OF CHRIST; YOU ARE THE CHRIST
Preexistence of, Ps 2:7; John 8:58; Col
1:15–18
Birth of, from a virgin, Is 7:14; Matt
1:18–25
Deity of, Is 9:6; John 1:1, 14, 18; 20:28,
29; Rom 9:5; Heb 1:8
Humanity of, Gen 3:15; Matt 22:45;
Luke 3:38; John 1:14; 1 Cor 15:45–
47; Gal 4:4; Phil 2:5–11; 1 Tim 2:5
Character of:
omnipotent, Matt 28:18
omniscient, Col 2:3
omnipresent, Matt 18:20
eternal, John 1:1, 2, 15
holy, Luke 1:35
righteous, Is 53:11
just, Zech 9:9
guileless, 1 Pet 2:22
sinless, 2 Cor 5:21
spotless, 1 Pet 1:19
innocent, Matt 27:4
gentle, Matt 11:29
merciful, Heb 2:17
humble, Phil 2:8
forgiving, Luke 23:34
Mission of:
do God's will, John 6:38
save sinners, Luke 19:10
destroy Satan's works, Heb 2:14;
1 John 3:8
fulfill the O.T., Matt 5:17
give life, John 10:10, 28
complete revelation, Heb 1:1
Worshiped by:
O.T. saints, Josh 5:13–15

demons, Mark 5:2, 6
men, John 9:38
angels, Heb 1:6
disciples, Luke 24:52
saints in glory, Rev 7:9, 10
all, Phil 2:10, 11
O.T. types of:
Adam, Rom 5:14
Abel, Heb 12:24
Moses, Deut 18:15
Passover, 1 Cor 5:7
manna, John 6:32
bronze serpent, John 3:14
genealogy of Jesus C .... Matt 1:1
Jesus who is called C .... Matt 1:16
"You are the C .... Matt 16:16
do you think about the C .. Matt 22:42
if You are the C .... Matt 26:63
of the gospel of Jesus C, ... Mark 1:1
You are the C .... Mark 8:29
Are You the C, the Son .. Mark 14:61
a Savior, who is C .... Luke 2:11
and said, "The C of God ... Luke 9:20
that He Himself is C ...... Luke 23:2
is translated, the C) .... John 1:41
the law that the C .... John 12:34
believe that Jesus is the C. John 20:31
crucified, both Lord and C .. Acts 2:36
preaching Jesus as the C ... Acts 5:42
he preached the C .... Acts 9:20
that this Jesus is the C ..... Acts 9:22
Jesus the C heals .... Acts 9:34
the C had to suffer and ..... Acts 17:3
that Jesus is the C .... Acts 18:28
that the C would suffer, ... Acts 26:23
His Son Jesus C our Lord .. Rom 1:3
faith in Jesus C to all and .. Rom 3:22
through our Lord Jesus C ... Rom 5:1
in due time C died for the ... Rom 5:6
through our Lord Jesus C .. Rom 5:11
through the One, Jesus C .. Rom 5:17
that just as C was raised .... Rom 6:4
life in C Jesus our Lord .... Rom 6:23
law through the body of C . Rom 7:4
those who are in C Jesus .... Rom 8:1
have the Spirit of C .... Rom 8:9
and joint heirs with C ..... Rom 8:17
It is C who died .... Rom 8:34
C came, who is over all ..... Rom 9:5
C is the end of the law ..... Rom 10:4
many, are one body in C ... Rom 12:5
put on the Lord Jesus C .. Rom 13:14
For to this end C died ...... Rom 14:9
C did not please .... Rom 15:3
just as C also received us, .. Rom 15:7
serve our Lord Jesus C ... Rom 16:18
are sanctified in C Jesus .... 1 Cor 1:2
Is C divided .... 1 Cor 1:13
For C did not send me to .. 1 Cor 1:17
we preach C crucified ..... 1 Cor 1:23
Him you are in C Jesus .... 1 Cor 1:30
among you except Jesus C . 1 Cor 2:2
is laid, which is Jesus C .. 1 Cor 3:11
indeed C, our Passover, ... 1 Cor 5:7
bodies are members of C . 1 Cor 6:15
Lord Jesus C, through ...... 1 Cor 8:6
you sin against C .... 1 Cor 8:12
and that Rock was C ...... 1 Cor 10:4
just as I also imitate C ..... 1 Cor 11:1
head of every man is C .... 1 Cor 11:3
you are the body of C .... 1 Cor 12:27
that C died for our sins ... 1 Cor 15:3
if C is not risen, then ..... 1 Cor 15:14
even so in C all shall be ... 1 Cor 15:22
our Lord Jesus C .... 1 Cor 15:57
sufferings of C abound .... 2 Cor 1:5
leads us in triumph in C, .. 2 Cor 2:14
you are an epistle of C ..... 2 Cor 3:3
veil is taken away in C .. 2 Cor 3:14
gospel of the glory of C .... 2 Cor 4:4
the judgment seat of C ... 2 Cor 5:10
if anyone is in C .... 2 Cor 5:17

accord has C with Belial .. 2 Cor 6:15
and gentleness of C .... 2 Cor 10:1
as a chaste virgin to C ... 2 Cor 11:2
to pervert the gospel of C .... Gal 1:7
which we have in C Jesus, ... Gal 2:4
to be justified by C .... Gal 2:17
been crucified with C ...... Gal 2:20
your Seed," who is C ...... Gal 3:16
before by God in C .... Gal 3:17
through faith in C Jesus .... Gal 3:26
until C is formed in you, ... Gal 4:19
which C has made us free .... Gal 5:1
become estranged from C .... Gal 5:4
cross of our Lord Jesus C .. Gal 6:14
the heavenly places in C .... Eph 1:3
in one all things in C, ... Eph 1:10
which He worked in C ...... Eph 1:20
C (by grace you have been ... Eph 2:5
time you were without C .. Eph 2:12
Jesus C Himself being ..... Eph 2:20
unsearchable riches of C .... Eph 3:8
C may dwell in your .... Eph 3:17
stature of the fullness of C .. Eph 4:13
Him who is the head—C ... Eph 4:15
even as God in C forgave .. Eph 4:32
C will give you light .... Eph 5:14
C is head of the church ... Eph 5:23
just as C also loved the ..... Eph 5:25
or in truth, C is preached .. Phil 1:18
to me, to live is C .... Phil 1:21
to depart and be with C .... Phil 1:23
worthy of the gospel of C .. Phil 1:27
which was also in C Jesus .. Phil 2:5
confess that Jesus C .... Phil 2:11
I have counted loss for C .. Phil 3:7
enemies of the cross of C .. Phil 3:18
C who strengthens .... Phil 4:13
riches in glory by C Jesus .. Phil 4:19
of your faith in C Jesus ...... Col 1:4
which is C in you .... Col 1:27
every man perfect in C ..... Col 1:28
of the Father and of C .... Col 2:2
received C Jesus the Lord .... Col 2:6
but the substance is of C .... Col 2:17
you were raised with C ...... Col 3:1
hidden with C in God .... Col 3:3
C who is our life .... Col 3:4
C is all and in all .... Col 3:11
Let the word of C dwell ..... Col 3:16
dead in C will rise first .. 1 Thess 4:16
our Lord Jesus C, ... 1 Thess 5:9
and the Lord Jesus C ..... 2 Thess 1:2
of our Lord Jesus C ...... 2 Thess 2:1
of our Lord Jesus C ..... 2 Thess 2:14
I thank C Jesus our Lord .. 1 Tim 1:12
that C Jesus came into .... 1 Tim 1:15
first Jesus C might show .. 1 Tim 1:16
and men, the Man C ...... 1 Tim 2:5
in C Jesus before time ..... 2 Tim 1:9
good soldier of C .... 2 Tim 2:3
in C Jesus with eternal ... 2 Tim 2:10
in C Jesus will suffer ,.... 2 Tim 3:12
faith which is in C Jesus .. 2 Tim 3:15
and the Lord Jesus C, ... 2 Tim 4:1
God and Savior Jesus C ... Titus 2:13
of our confession, C Jesus, .. Heb 3:1
C as a Son over His own ..... Heb 3:6
C if we hold the beginning .. Heb 3:14
So also C did not glorify ... Heb 5:5
elementary principles of C .. Heb 6:1
But C came as High Priest .. Heb 9:11
more shall the blood of C .. Heb 9:14
For C has not entered the ... Heb 9:24
C was offered once to bear .. Heb 9:28
body of Jesus C once for .. Heb 10:10
Jesus C is the same .... Heb 13:8
of the blood of Jesus C ..... 1 Pet 1:2
Spirit of C who was in ..... 1 Pet 1:11
the precious blood of C .... 1 Pet 1:19
because C also suffered .... 1 Pet 2:21
For C also suffered once ... 1 Pet 3:18
resurrection of Jesus C ... 1 Pet 3:21

for the name of C .... 1 Pet 4:14
God and Savior Jesus C .... 2 Pet 1:1
of our Lord Jesus C ...... 2 Pet 1:16
C His Son cleanses us ..... 1 John 1:7
Jesus C the righteous ..... 1 John 2:1
denies that Jesus is the C . 1 John 2:22
name of His Son Jesus C . 1 John 3:23
confesses that Jesus C .... 1 John 4:2
that Jesus is the C .... 1 John 5:1
true, in His Son Jesus C . 1 John 5:20
of C does not have God .... 2 John 9
and our Lord Jesus C .... Jude 4
The Revelation of Jesus C .... Rev 1:1
from Jesus C, the faithful .... Rev 1:5
the testimony of Jesus C .... Rev 1:9
of our Lord and of His C, .. Rev 11:15
of His C have come ...... Rev 12:10
and reigned with C .... Rev 20:4
be priests of God and of C .. Rev 20:6

CHRISTIAN
me to become a C .... Acts 26:28
anyone suffers as a C ..... 1 Pet 4:16

CHRISTIANS
were first called C ...... Acts 11:26

CHRIST'S
you are C, and Christ is ... 1 Cor 3:23
We are fools for C' sake, .. 1 Cor 4:10
are C at His coming ...... 1 Cor 15:23
in himself that he is C, ... 2 Cor 10:7
if you are C, then you are ... Gal 3:29
partake of C sufferings .... 1 Pet 4:13

CHRISTS
For false c and .... Matt 24:24

CHRYSOLITE
sardius, the seventh c ..... Rev 21:20

CHRYSOPRASE
ninth topaz, the tenth c .... Rev 21:20

CHURCH
rock I will build My c ..... Matt 16:18
them, tell it to the c .... Matt 18:17
c daily those who were .... Acts 2:47
elders in every c .... Acts 14:23
do you despise the c ..... 1 Cor 11:22
persecuted the c of God .. 1 Cor 15:9
over all things to the c .... Eph 1:22
be made known by the c ... Eph 3:10
also loved the c .... Eph 5:25
Himself a glorious c ...... Eph 5:27
as the Lord does the c .... Eph 5:29
no c shared with me ...... Phil 4:15
body, which is the c ...... Col 1:24
is the c of the living ...... 1 Tim 3:15
and do not let the c ...... 1 Tim 5:16
general assembly and c .... Heb 12:23
To the angel of the c ...... Rev 2:1

CHURCHES
strengthening the c ...... Acts 15:41
The c of Christ greet ..... Rom 16:16
imitators of the c .... 1 Thess 2:14
John, to the seven c .... Rev 1:4
angels of the seven c ..... Rev 1:20
these things in the c ..... Rev 22:16

CHURNING
For as the c of milk ...... Prov 30:33

CHURNS
My heart c within Me ..... Hos 11:8

CILICIA
Paul's homeland, Acts 21:39
Students from, argued with Stephen,
Acts 6:9
Paul labors in, Gal 1:21

CINNAMON
sweet-smelling c .... Ex 30:23
saffron, calamus and c, ... Song 4:14
c and incense, fragrant .... Rev 18:13

CIRCLE
He walks above the c ..... Job 22:14

when He drew a c .... Prov 8:27
who sits above the c ...... Is 40:22

CIRCUIT
of heaven, and its c .... Ps 19:6
comes again on its c ...... Eccl 1:6

CIRCUMCISE
c the foreskin of your .... Deut 10:16
LORD your God will c ..... Deut 30:6
C yourselves to the .... Jer 4:4
is necessary to c them .... Acts 15:5

CIRCUMCISED
among you shall be c ..... Gen 17:10
day Abraham was c ...... Gen 17:26
Abraham c his son Isaac ... Gen 21:4
every male was c, all .... Gen 34:24
let all his males be c ..... Ex 12:48
of Egypt, had not been c ... Josh 5:5
c him on the eighth day .... Acts 7:8
who will justify the c ..... Rom 3:30
While he was c .... Rom 4:10
the gospel for the c .... Gal 2:7
if you become c .... Gal 5:2
c the eighth day .... Phil 3:5
In Him you were also c ... Col 2:11

CIRCUMCISION
him the covenant of c ..... Acts 7:8
c that which is outward .... Rom 2:28
c is that of the heart ..... Rom 2:29
a servant to the c .... Rom 15:8
C is nothing and .... 1 Cor 7:19
Christ Jesus neither c ..... Gal 5:6
For we are the c .... Phil 3:3
circumcised with the c .... Col 2:11
those of the c .... Titus 1:10

CIRCUMSPECTLY
then that you walk c ..... Eph 5:15

CISTERN
waters of his own c ..... 2 Kin 18:31
from your own c .... Prov 5:15

CISTERNS
and hewn themselves c .... Jer 2:13
went to the c and found ... Jer 14:3

CITIES
He overthrew those c .... Gen 19:25
repair the ruined c .... Is 61:4
c are a wilderness .... Is 64:10
c will be laid waste .... Jer 4:7
three parts, and the c .... Rev 16:19

CITIZEN
But I was born a c ...... Acts 22:28

CITIZENS
But his c hated him ..... Luke 19:14
but fellow c with the ..... Eph 2:19

CITIZENSHIP
sum I obtained this c ..... Acts 22:28
For our c is in heaven .... Phil 3:20

CITY
See HOLY CITY
And he built a c .... Gen 4:17
shall make glad the c ..... Ps 46:4
c shall flourish .... Ps 72:16
They found no c .... Ps 107:4
c that is compact .... Ps 122:3
the LORD guards the c ..... Ps 127:1
at the entry of the c ..... Prov 8:3
c has become a harlot ...... Is 1:21
upon Zion, the c .... Is 33:20
after the holy c .... Is 48:2
How lonely sits the c ..... Lam 1:1
Nineveh, that great c ..... Jon 4:11
c that dwelt securely .... Zeph 2:15
to the oppressing c .... Zeph 3:1
c called Nazareth .... Matt 2:23
c that is set on a .... Matt 5:14
He has prepared a c ..... Heb 11:16
Zion and to the c .... Heb 12:22
have no continuing c ..... Heb 13:14

will tread the holy c ...... Rev 11:2
fallen, that great c ...... Rev 14:8
and the beloved c .... Rev 20:9
John, saw the holy c ..... Rev 21:2
c was pure gold .... Rev 21:18
c had no need of the ..... Rev 21:23
the gates into the c ..... Rev 22:14

CITY OF DAVID
of Zion (that is, the C .... 2 Sam 5:7
with him into the C ...... 2 Sam 6:10
was buried in the C ...... 1 Kin 2:10
of the Lord from the C .... 1 Kin 8:1
was buried in the C ..... 1 Kin 11:43
for himself in the C ...... 1 Chr 15:1
the Millo in the C .... 2 Chr 32:5
the west side of the C .... 2 Chr 32:30
that go down from the C ... Neh 3:15
up the stairs of the C, ... Neh 12:37
the damage to the c, ... Is 22:9
into Judea, to the c, ... Luke 2:4
this day in the c a Savior, .. Luke 2:11

CLAD
was c with zeal as a cloak ... Is 59:17

CLAMOROUS
A foolish woman is c ..... Prov 9:13

CLANGING
brass or a c cymbal ...... 1 Cor 13:1

CLAP
c their hands at him ..... Job 27:23
Oh, c your hands .... Ps 47:1
let the rivers c .... Ps 98:8
of the field shall c .... Is 55:12

CLAUDIUS LYSIAS
Roman commander who protected
Paul, Acts 24:22–24, 26

CLAY
dwell in houses of c .... Job 4:19
have made me like c ...... Job 10:9
are defenses of c .... Job 13:12
been formed out of c ..... Job 33:6
takes on form like c ..... Job 38:14
pit, out of the miry c ...... Ps 40:2
be esteemed as the c ...... Is 29:16
Shall the c say to him ...... Is 45:9
We are the c, and You ...... Is 64:8
"Look, as the c .... Jer 18:6
iron and partly of c ...... Dan 2:33
blind man with the c ..... John 9:6
have power over the c .... Rom 9:21
but also of wood and c ... 2 Tim 2:20

CLEAN
seven each of every c ..... Gen 7:2
outside the camp to a c .... Lev 4:12
all who are c may eat of it .. Lev 7:19
between unclean and c .... Lev 10:10
shall be c from the flow ... Lev 12:7
shall pronounce him c .... Lev 13:23
wash his clothes and be c .. Lev 13:34
wash in them and be c .... 2 Kin 5:12
all of them were ritually c .. Ezra 6:20
pure, and I am c in your ... Job 11:4
Who can bring a c .... Job 14:4
He who has c hands and ... Ps 24:4
hyssop, and I shall be c ..... Ps 51:7
Create in me a c heart, ... Ps 51:10
I have made my heart c, ... Prov 20:9
make yourselves c .... Is 1:16
the midst of her, be c ..... Is 52:11
Then I will sprinkle c .... Ezek 36:25
c out His threshing ...... Matt 3:12
You can make me c .... Matt 8:2
outside of them may be c . Matt 23:26
wrapped it in a c linen ... Matt 27:59
all things are c .... Luke 11:41
but is completely c ...... John 13:10
"You are not all c ...... John 13:11
You are already c .... John 15:3
your own heads; I am c ... Acts 18:6

CLEANNESS
according to the c of .... 2 Sam 22:21
According to the c of my .... Ps 18:20
Also I gave you c of teeth .. Amos 4:6

CLEANSE
You shall c the altar .... Ex 29:36
and c them ceremonially .... Num 8:6
and c my hands with soap, .. Job 9:30
C me from secret .... Ps 19:12
and c me from my sin ...... Ps 51:2
How can a young man c .... Ps 119:9
I will c you from all ...... Ezek 36:25
they shall c the altar ...... Ezek 43:22
c the lepers, raise .... Matt 10:8
For you c the outside ..... Matt 23:25
let us c ourselves from all .. 2 Cor 7:1
might sanctify and c .... Eph 5:26
c your conscience .... Heb 9:14
C your hands .... James 4:8
us our sins and to c .... 1 John 1:9

CLEANSED
He who is to be c shall ...... Lev 14:8
Surely I have c .... Ps 73:13
and you were not c ...... Ezek 24:13
the sanctuary shall be c .... Dan 8:14
I am willing; be c." .... Matt 8:3
the lepers are c .... Matt 11:5
they went, they were c .. Luke 17:14
"Were there not ten c .... Luke 17:17
God has c you must .... Acts 10:15

CLEANSES
Therefore if anyone c ..... 2 Tim 2:21
Jesus Christ His Son c ... 1 John 1:7

CLEAR
c shining after rain .... 2 Sam 23:4
fair as the moon, c .... Song 6:10
yourselves to be c .... 2 Cor 7:11
like a jasper stone, c ...... Rev 21:11
of life, c as crystal .... Rev 22:1

CLEARLY
I not c reveal Myself ..... 1 Sam 2:27
you will see c to remove .... Matt 7:5
hour of the day he saw c ... Acts 10:3
c portrayed among you .... Gal 3:1
men's sins are c evident .. 1 Tim 5:24

CLEARS
by no means c the guilty .. Num 14:18

CLEFTS
to go into the c .... Is 2:21
valleys and in the c .... Is 7:19
you who dwell in the c .... Jer 49:16

CLERK
c had quieted the .... Acts 19:35

CLIFF
secret places of the c ...... Song 2:14

CLIMB
go into thickets and c ...... Jer 4:29
mighty men, they c .... Joel 2:7
though they c up to .... Amos 9:2

CLIMBED
c up into a sycamore tree .. Luke 19:4

CLIMBS
c up some other way ...... John 10:1

CLING
and that you may c ...... Deut 30:20
to her, "Do not c .... John 20:17
C to what is good .... Rom 12:9

CLINGS
and My tongue c .... Ps 22:15
My soul c to the dust ..... Ps 119:25

CLOAK
c You will change them .... Ps 102:26
let him have your c .... Matt 5:40
c You will fold them .... Heb 1:12
using liberty as a c .... 1 Pet 2:16

CLODS
The c of the valley .... Job 21:33

CLOSE
c friends abhor me .... Job 19:19
of Christ he came c .... Phil 2:30

CLOSED
c up the flesh in its place ... Gen 2:21
LORD had c her womb .... 1 Sam 1:5
and has c your eyes ...... Is 29:10
for the words are c .... Dan 12:9
the deep c around me ..... Jon 2:5
Then He c the book, and .. Luke 4:20
their eyes they have c ..... Acts 28:27

CLOSER
sticks c than a brother .... Prov 18:24

CLOTH
a piece of unshrunk c ..... Matt 9:16
in a clean linen c .... Matt 27:59

CLOTHE
c them with tunics .... Ex 40:14
c me with skin and .... Job 10:11
c her priests with .... Ps 132:16
His enemies I will c .... Ps 132:18
Though you c yourself ..... Jer 4:30
He not much more c ...... Matt 6:30

CLOTHED
of skin, and c them .... Gen 3:21
Have you c his neck ...... Job 39:19
off my sackcloth and c ..... Ps 30:11
The pastures are c .... Ps 65:13
the LORD is c .... Ps 93:1
You are c with honor ..... Ps 104:1
c himself with cursing ..... Ps 109:18
Let Your priests be c ...... Ps 132:9
all her household is c ..... Prov 31:21
c you with fine linen ...... Ezek 16:10
A man c in soft .... Matt 11:8
I was naked and you c .... Matt 25:36
legion, sitting and c ...... Mark 5:15
And they c Him with .... Mark 15:17
rich man who was c ...... Luke 16:19
desiring to be c .... 2 Cor 5:2
that you may be c .... Rev 3:18
a woman c with the sun ... Rev 12:1
He was c with a robe ..... Rev 19:13

CLOTHES
See TORE HIS CLOTHES
c will abhor me .... Job 9:31
c became shining .... Mark 9:3
many spread their c ..... Luke 19:36
laid down their c .... Acts 7:58
and tore off their c .... Acts 22:23
a poor man in filthy c ..... James 2:2

CLOTHING
c they cast lots .... Ps 22:18
c is woven with gold ...... Ps 45:13
will provide your c .... Prov 27:26
and honor are her c ...... Prov 31:25
of vengeance for c .... Is 59:17
the body more than .... Matt 6:25
do you worry about c ..... Matt 6:28
to you in sheep's c .... Matt 7:15
those who wear soft c .... Matt 11:8
c as white as snow .... Matt 28:3
c they cast lots .... John 19:24
before me in bright c ..... Acts 10:30

CLOTHS
wrapped in swaddling c ... Luke 2:12
in, saw the linen c .... John 20:5

CLOUD
My rainbow in the c ...... Gen 9:13
rainbow shall be in the c .. Gen 9:16
day in a pillar of c .... Ex 13:21
c covered the mountain ... Ex 24:15
c descended and stood .... Ex 33:9
the c above the mercy seat . Lev 16:2
that the c of incense may .. Lev 16:13
that the c filled the house .. 1 Kin 8:10

CLOUD (continued)
LORD, was filled with a c .. 2 Chr 5:13
would dwell in the dark c .. 2 Chr 6:1
c did not depart .... Neh 9:19
He led them with the c ..... Ps 78:14
his favor is like a c .... Prov 16:15
like a c of dew in the heat .. Is 18:4
these who fly like a c .... Is 60:8
rainbow in a c on a ...... Ezek 1:28
like a morning c .... Hos 6:4
behold, a bright c .... Matt 17:5
c came and overshadowed . Luke 9:34
of Man coming in a c ..... Luke 21:27
c received Him out of ...... Acts 1:9
were under the c .... 1 Cor 10:1
by so great a c .... Heb 12:1
ascended to heaven in a c .. Rev 11:12

CLOUDS
a morning without c ...... 2 Sam 23:4
c poured out water .... Ps 77:17
and hail, snow and c ...... Ps 148:8
c drop down the dew ...... Prov 3:20
he who regards the c ...... Eccl 11:4
of Man coming on the c ... Matt 24:30
with them in the c .... 1 Thess 4:17
are c without water .... Jude 12
He is coming with c .... Rev 1:7

CLOUDY
them by day with a c ...... Neh 9:12
spoke to them in the c ..... Ps 99:7

CLOVEN
the hoof, having c .... Lev 11:3
chew the cud or have c .... Deut 14:7

CLUNG
but Ruth c to her .... Ruth 1:14
Solomon c to these in ..... 1 Kin 11:2

CLUSTER
beloved is to me a c .... Song 1:14
wine is found in the c .... Is 65:8

CNIDUS
City of Asia Minor on Paul's voyage,
Acts 27:7

COAL
in his hand a live c .... Is 6:6
it shall not be a c .... Is 47:14

COALS
wicked He will rain c ...... Ps 11:6
c were kindled by it .... Ps 18:8
let burning c fall .... Ps 140:10
Can one walk on hot c ..... Prov 6:28
so you will heap c .... Prov 25:22
doing you will heap c ..... Rom 12:20

COARSE
robe of c hair to deceive ... Zech 13:4
nor c jesting, which are .... Eph 5:4

COBRA
it becomes c venom ...... Job 20:14
c that stops its ear .... Ps 58:4
the lion and the c .... Ps 91:13

COBRA'S
shall play by the c .... Is 11:8

CODE
even with your written c ... Rom 2:27

COFFIN
and he was put in a c ..... Gen 50:26
David followed the c ...... 2 Sam 3:31
touched the open c .... Luke 7:14

COIN
sold for a copper c .... Matt 10:29
if she loses one c .... Luke 15:8

COLD
and harvest, c and .... Gen 8:22
can stand before His c ..... Ps 147:17
Like the c of snow in ..... Prov 25:13
c water to a weary .... Prov 25:25
c water in the name of .... Matt 10:42
of many will grow c ...... Matt 24:12

that you are neither c ...... Rev 3:15

COLLECTED
coming I might have c .... Luke 19:23

COLLECTION
from Jerusalem the c ...... 2 Chr 24:6
concerning the c .... 1 Cor 16:1

COLLECTOR
See TAX COLLECTOR; TAX COLLECTORS
AND SINNERS

COLOR
c like the c of bdellium .... Num 11:7
the c of burnished bronze ... Ezek 1:7
c of an awesome crystal ... Ezek 1:22
the c of a beryl stone ...... Ezek 10:9
all faces are drained of c .... Joel 2:6

COLORS
him a tunic of many c ..... Gen 37:3
on a robe of many c ..... 2 Sam 13:18
stones of various c, all .... 1 Chr 29:2

COLOSSE
A city in Asia Minor, Col 1:2
Evangelized by Epaphras, Col 1:7
Not visited by Paul, Col 2:1
Paul writes against errors of, Col
2:16–23

COLT
and his donkey's c .... Gen 49:11
on a donkey, a c .... Zech 9:9
on a donkey, a c .... Matt 21:5
own clothes on the c ..... Luke 19:35

COME
then does wisdom c .... Job 28:20
of glory shall c .... Ps 24:7
Our God shall c .... Ps 50:3
You all flesh will c .... Ps 65:2
C with me from Lebanon ... Song 4:8
He will c and save you .... Is 35:4
who have no money, C ...... Is 55:1
Your kingdom c .... Matt 6:10
C to Me .... Matt 11:28
For many will c .... Matt 24:5
Israel, let Him now c ..... Matt 27:42
If anyone desires to c ...... Luke 9:23
kingdom of God has c ..... Luke 10:9
I have c in My .... John 5:43
and I have not c .... John 7:28
thirsts, let him c .... John 7:37
c that they may have ..... John 10:10
c as a light into the ...... John 12:46
I will c to you .... John 14:18
If I had not c .... John 15:22
savage wolves will c ..... Acts 20:29
O Lord, c .... 1 Cor 16:22
the door, I will c .... Rev 3:20
the bride say, "C .... Rev 22:17

COMELINESS
He has no form or c .... Is 53:2

COMES
Who is this who c .... Is 63:1
'Come,' and he c .... Matt 8:9
Lord's death till He c ..... 1 Cor 11:26
Then c the end .... 1 Cor 15:24

COMFORT
one will c us concerning ... Gen 5:29
daughters arose to c him .. Gen 37:35
speak c to your servants .. 2 Sam 19:7
with him, and to c him ...... Job 2:11
and Your staff, they c .... Ps 23:4
And c me on every side ..... Ps 71:21
is my c in my affliction ..... Ps 119:50
kindness be for my c ...... Ps 119:76
When will you c .... Ps 119:82
go up to the c of my bed .... Ps 132:3
yes, c My people .... Is 40:1
For the LORD will c .... Is 51:3
c all who mourn .... Is 61:2
comforts, so I will c you ..... Is 66:13
she has none to c her ...... Lam 1:2

wilderness, and speak c to .. Hos 2:14
the LORD will again c ..... Zech 1:17
c them concerning their .. John 11:19
in the c of the Holy Spirit, .. Acts 9:31
c of the Scriptures might ... Rom 15:4
and exhortation and c to ... 1 Cor 14:3
and God of all c .... 2 Cor 1:3
trouble, with the c .... 2 Cor 1:4
that he may c your hearts .. Eph 6:22
in Christ, if any c .... Phil 2:1
and c your hearts, ... Col 4:8
c one another .... 1 Thess 4:18
c each other and edify ... 1 Thess 5:11
c your hearts and ...... 2 Thess 2:17

COMFORTED
So Isaac was c after .... Gen 24:67
c them and spoke kindly .. Gen 50:21
David c Bathsheba ...... 2 Sam 12:24
soul refused to be c .... Ps 77:2
For the LORD has c .... Is 49:13
refusing to be c .... Jer 31:15
children, refusing to be c .. Matt 2:18
mourn, for they shall be c ... Matt 5:4
but now he is c .... Luke 16:25
they were not a little c .... Acts 20:12
ourselves are c by God ..... 2 Cor 1:4

COMFORTER
but they have no c .... Eccl 4:1
She had no c .... Lam 1:9

COMFORTERS
because he has sent c to .. 2 Sam 10:3
miserable c are you all ..... Job 16:2
for c, but I found none ...... Ps 69:20

COMFORTS
the army, as one who c .... Job 29:25
I, even I, am He who c .... Is 51:12
him, and restore c .... Is 57:18
one whom his mother c ..... Is 66:13
who c us in all our .... 2 Cor 1:4
who c the downcast .... 2 Cor 7:6

COMING
your salvation is c .... Is 62:11
behold, the day is c .... Mal 4:1
but He who is c .... Matt 3:11
"Are You the C .... Matt 11:3
be the sign of Your c ..... Matt 24:3
is delaying his c .... Matt 24:48
see the Son of Man c .... Mark 13:26
mightier than I is c ...... Luke 3:16
are Christ's at His c ...... 1 Cor 15:23
to you the power and c ... 2 Pet 1:16
the promise of His c ...... 2 Pet 3:4
Behold, I am c .... Rev 3:11
"Behold, I am c .... Rev 22:7
"Surely I am c .... Rev 22:20

COMMAND
in order that he may c ..... Gen 18:19
shall speak all that I c you .... Ex 7:2
transgress the c of the .... Num 14:41
add to the word which I c ... Deut 4:2
I c you today you must be .... Deut 8:1
Whatever I c you, be ..... Deut 12:32
therefore I c you, saying .. Deut 15:11
"The LORD will c .... Deut 28:8
in that I c you .... Deut 30:16
today, which you shall c ... Deut 32:46
c His lovingkindness .... Ps 42:8
c victories for Jacob .... Ps 44:4
you, and whatever I c you .... Jer 1:7
to them all that I c you ...... Jer 1:17
to all that I c .... Jer 11:4
that I c you to speak to ..... Jer 26:2
c that these stones .... Matt 4:3
if it is You, c .... Matt 14:28
c fire to come down ...... Luke 9:54
c I have received .... John 10:18
And I know that His c .... John 12:50
if you do whatever I c .... John 15:14
These things I c you, ... John 15:17
do the things we c .... 2 Thess 3:4

C those who are rich in .. 1 Tim 6:17
kept My c to persevere ..... Rev 3:10

COMMANDED
See LORD COMMANDED
the LORD God c the man .... Gen 2:16
to all that the LORD c him .... Gen 7:5
Joseph c his servants the ... Gen 50:2
just as the LORD c them, ... Ex 7:6
which the LORD c him........ Ex 19:7
just as the LORD my God c .. Deut 4:5
LORD c us to observe all .... Deut 6:24
Have I not c you .... Josh 1:9
did so, as the LORD c ..... 2 Sam 5:25
which I c your fathers .... 2 Kin 17:13
to all that I have c them ... 2 Kin 21:8
do all that I have c them .. 2 Chr 33:8
"Have you c the .... Job 38:12
He c, and it stood fast .... Ps 33:9
Which He c our fathers, ... Ps 78:5
c His covenant forever ..... Ps 111:9
For there the LORD c .... Ps 133:3
of the LORD, for He c ...... Ps 148:5
things that I have c you .. Matt 28:20
Even so the LORD has c ... 1 Cor 9:14
it is the God who c .... 2 Cor 4:6
not endure what was c .... Heb 12:20

COMMANDER
the c of his army, spoke ... Gen 21:22
but as C of the army of .... Josh 5:14
c of his army was Sisera,.... Judg 4:2
c over His inheritance .... 1 Sam 10:1
Abner, the c of the ...... 1 Sam 17:55
Joab the c of the army ..... 1 Kin 1:19
have a message for you, C .. 2 Kin 9:5
Rehum the c and Shimshai .. Ezra 4:8
news came to the c of ..... Acts 21:31
But the c Lysias came by ... Acts 24:7

COMMANDMENT
to the c of the LORD, ... Ex 17:1
numbered at the c of the ... Num 3:39
shall keep every c which ... Deut 11:8
heed to do the c .... Josh 22:5
observe the law and the c . 2 Chr 14:4
according to the c of ..... 2 Chr 29:25
c of the LORD is pure........ Ps 19:8
c is exceedingly broad ... Ps 119:96
For the c is a lamp .... Prov 6:23
Me is taught by the c .... Is 29:13
which is the great c ...... Matt 22:36
is the first and great c .... Matt 22:38
no other c greater than ... Mark 12:31
according to the c .... Luke 23:56
A new c I give to .... John 13:34
the Father gave Me c .... John 14:31
is My c, that you love ..... John 15:12
whom we gave no such c .. Acts 15:24
law, but when the c .... Rom 7:9
the c might become .... Rom 7:13
and if there is any other c .. Rom 13:9
as a concession, not as a c .. 1 Cor 7:6
I speak not by c, but .... 2 Cor 8:8
which is the first c .... Eph 6:2
have a c to receive tithes ..... Heb 7:5
the holy c delivered to ..... 2 Pet 2:21
of the c of us, the apostles .. 2 Pet 3:2
c is the word which ...... 1 John 2:7
And this is His c .... 1 John 3:23
as we received c .... 2 John 4
I wrote a new c to you ..... 2 John 5
This is the c that as you ..... 2 John 6

COMMANDMENTS
love Me and keep My c ..... Ex 20:6
c which I have written, ... Ex 24:12
covenant, the Ten C ...... Ex 34:28
he gave them as c all that ... Ex 34:32
you shall keep My c ...... Lev 22:31
all the c of the LORD and .. Num 15:39
perform the Ten C .... Deut 4:13
love Me and keep My c .... Deut 5:10
to observe all these c ...... Deut 6:25

love Him and Keep His c ... Deut 7:9
first writing, the Ten C .... Deut 10:4
judgments, and His c ..... Deut 11:1
obey the c of the LORD ... Deut 11:27
c which I command you .... Deut 28:1
your God, to keep His c ... Deut 30:10
His ways, to keep His c ... Josh 22:5
keep His statutes, His c .... 1 Kin 2:3
ways, and to keep His c ... 1 Kin 8:58
statutes and keep His c ... 1 Kin 8:61
steadfast to observe My c . 1 Chr 28:7
heart to keep Your c .... 1 Chr 29:19
You and observe Your c ..... Neh 1:5
of God, but keep His c ...... Ps 78:7
who remember His c ...... Ps 103:18
delights greatly in His c .... Ps 112:1
do not hide Your c .... Ps 119:19
myself in Your c .... Ps 119:47
for I believe Your c .... Ps 119:66
Your c are faithful .... Ps 119:86
c more than gold ...... Ps 119:127
Fear God and keep His c, .. Eccl 12:13
that you had heeded My c ... Is 48:18
those who keep His c ...... Dan 9:4
one of the least of these c .. Matt 5:19
as doctrines the c .... Matt 15:9
enter into life, keep the c .. Matt 19:17
c hang all the Law .... Matt 22:40
You know the c .... Mark 10:19
The first of all the c is .... Mark 12:29
God, walking in all the c .... Luke 1:6
You know the c .... Luke 18:20
He who has My c .... John 14:21
If you keep My c, you .... John 15:10
For the c, "You shall not .. Rom 13:9
keeping the c of God is .... 1 Cor 7:19
the law of c contained in ... Eph 2:15
according to the c .... Col 2:22
Him, if we keep His c ... 1 John 2:3
because we keep His c ... 1 John 3:22
he who keeps His c ..... 1 John 3:24
love God and keep His c .. 1 John 5:2
walk according to His c .... 2 John 6
keep the c of God and ..... Rev 12:17
who keep the c of God .... Rev 14:12

COMMANDS
treasure my c within you .... Prov 2:1
let your heart keep my c .... Prov 3:1
wise in heart will receive c . Prov 10:8
with authority He c .... Mark 1:27
c all men everywhere .... Acts 17:30

COMMEND
I c you to God and to the .. Acts 20:32
But food does not c .... 1 Cor 8:8
begin again to c ourselves .. 2 Cor 3:1
those who c themselves .. 2 Cor 10:12

COMMENDABLE
For this is c, if because .... 1 Pet 2:19
patiently, this is c .... 1 Pet 2:20

COMMENDED
A man will be c .... Prov 12:8
c the unjust steward .... Luke 16:8
where they had been c .... Acts 14:26

COMMENDING
of the truth c .... 2 Cor 4:2

COMMENDS
but whom the Lord c ..... 2 Cor 10:18

COMMIT
"You shall not c .... Ex 20:14
You shall not c adultery .... Deut 5:18
c a trespass in the .... Josh 22:20
C your works to the ...... Prov 16:3
mammon, who will c ...... Luke 16:11
into Your hands I c ...... Luke 23:46
But Jesus did not c .... John 2:24
c sexual immorality ...... 1 Cor 10:8
c these to faithful .... 2 Tim 2:2
if you do not c adultery ... James 2:11
c their souls to Him ...... 1 Pet 4:19

c sin not leading .... 1 John 5:16
to c sexual immorality ..... Rev 2:14

COMMITS
to you, whoever c .... John 8:34
sin also c lawlessness ..... 1 John 3:4

COMMITTED
For My people have c ..... Jer 2:13
c things deserving .... Luke 12:48
For God has c them all .... Rom 11:32
Guard what was c .... 1 Tim 6:20
"Who c no sin .... 1 Pet 2:22
c Himself to Him who ..... 1 Pet 2:23

COMMON
of the c people sins ...... Lev 4:27
poor have this in c ...... Prov 22:2
c people heard Him ..... Mark 12:37
had all things in c .... Acts 2:44
never eaten anything c ... Acts 10:14
not call any man c ...... Acts 10:28
a true son in our c .... Titus 1:4
concerning our c .... Jude 3

COMMOTION
there arose a great c ..... Acts 19:23

COMMUNED
I c with my heart .... Eccl 1:16

COMMUNION
bless, is it not the c ..... 1 Cor 10:16
c has light with .... 2 Cor 6:14
c of the Holy Spirit ...... 2 Cor 13:14

COMPANION
a man my equal, My c .... Ps 55:13
I am a c of all who ...... Ps 119:63
the Man who is My C .... Zech 13:7
urge you also, true c ...... Phil 4:3
your brother and c .... Rev 1:9

COMPANIONS
are rebellious, and c .... Is 1:23
and calling to their c ..... Matt 11:16
more than Your c .... Heb 1:9
while you became c ...... Heb 10:33

COMPANY
great was the c .... Ps 68:11
epistle not to keep c ...... 1 Cor 5:9
c corrupts good habits .... 1 Cor 15:33
and do not keep c ...... 2 Thess 3:14
to an innumerable c ...... Heb 12:22

COMPARABLE
make him a helper c to ..... Gen 2:18

COMPARE
may desire cannot c ...... Prov 3:15
likeness will you c to Him ... Is 40:18
c ourselves with those .... 2 Cor 10:12

COMPARED
the heavens can be c ...... Ps 89:6
may desire cannot be c ... Prov 8:11
are not worthy to be c .... Rom 8:18

COMPASSION
will have c on whom I will .. Ex 33:19
show you mercy, have c . Deut 13:17
have c on you, and gather . Deut 30:3
His people and have c . Deut 32:36
yearned with c for her .... 1 Kin 3:26
had c on them, and ...... 2 Kin 13:23
will be treated with c by .. 2 Chr 30:9
He, being full of c .... Ps 78:38
are a God full of c .... Ps 86:15
have c on Your servants .... Ps 90:13
He will have c on His ..... Ps 135:14
is gracious and full of c ... Ps 145:8
not have c on the son of ... Is 49:15
will return and have c .... Jer 12:15
yet He will show c .... Lam 3:32
for you, to have c on you .. Ezek 16:5
He will again have c on us .. Mic 7:19
c everyone to his .... Zech 7:9
He was moved with c .... Matt 9:36
moved with c for them .... Matt 14:14

have c on the multitude, .. Matt 15:32
was moved with c .... Matt 18:27
also have had c .... Matt 18:33
So Jesus had c and ...... Matt 20:34
Jesus, moved with c, put .. Mark 1:41
moved with c for them ... Mark 6:34
"I have c on the .... Mark 8:2
saw him and had c ...... Luke 15:20
whomever I will have c ... Rom 9:15
He can have c on those ..... Heb 5:2
of one mind, having c ..... 1 Pet 3:8
And on some have c .... Jude 22

COMPASSIONATE
c women have cooked .... Lam 4:10
the Lord is very c .... James 5:11

COMPASSIONS
because His c fail not ..... Lam 3:22

COMPEL
c them to come in .... Luke 14:23
why do you c Gentiles to .... Gal 2:14

COMPELLED
they c to bear His cross ... Matt 27:32
Macedonia, Paul was c .... Acts 18:5
and c them to blaspheme .. Acts 26:11
was c to be circumcised ..... Gal 2:3

COMPELS
the spirit within me c ..... Job 32:18
And whoever c .... Matt 5:41
the love of Christ c ...... 2 Cor 5:14

COMPETES
everyone who c for the .. 1 Cor 9:25
if anyone c in athletics .... 2 Tim 2:5

COMPLACENCY
slay them, and the c ...... Prov 1:32
who are settled in c ..... Zeph 1:12

COMPLAIN
should a living man c ..... Lam 3:39

COMPLAINED
and you c in your .... Deut 1:27
but c in their tents .... Ps 106:25
some of them also c ..... 1 Cor 10:10

COMPLAINERS
These are grumblers, c ..... Jude 16

COMPLAINING
all things without c ...... Phil 2:14

COMPLAINT
"Even today my c .... Job 23:2
I pour out my c .... Ps 142:2
for the LORD has a c ...... Mic 6:2
if anyone has a c .... Col 3:13

COMPLAINTS
Who has c .... Prov 23:29
laid many serious c ...... Acts 25:7

COMPLETE
would also c this grace .... 2 Cor 8:6
must c the doing of it .... 2 Cor 8:11
that you may be made c ... 2 Cor 13:9
work in you will c .... Phil 1:6
and you are c in Him ...... Col 2:10
and c in all the will of God .. Col 4:12
of God may be c .... 2 Tim 3:17
make you c in every ...... Heb 13:21
you may be perfect and c . James 1:4
the wrath of God is c ..... Rev 15:1

COMPLETED
Moses had c writing ..... Deut 31:24
house of the LORD was c . 2 Chr 8:16
is built and the walls c .... Ezra 4:13
when these days were c .... Esth 1:5
when seventy years are c .. Jer 25:12
days were c for her to be ... Luke 2:6
work which they had c .... Acts 14:26
killed as they were, was c ... Rev 6:11

COMPLETELY
person shall be c cut off .. Num 15:31
did not c drive them out .... Judg 1:28

filthiness c from you . . . . . Ezek 22:15
I made a man c well . . . . . . John 7:23
You were c born in sins, . . . John 9:34
his feet, but is c clean . . . . John 13:10
Himself sanctify you c . . . 1 Thess 5:23

COMPOSED
But God c the body . . . . . . 1 Cor 12:24

COMPREHEND
which we cannot c . . . . Job 37:5
c my path and my lying . . . . . Ps 139:3
the darkness did not c . . . . John 1:5
may be able to c . . . . Eph 3:18

CONCEAL
Almighty I will not c . . . . Job 27:11
c pride from man . . . . Job 33:17
of God to c a matter . . . . . . Prov 25:2

CONCEALED
c Your lovingkindness . . . . . . Ps 40:10
than love carefully c . . . . . . Prov 27:5

CONCEIT
selfish ambition or c . . . . Phil 2:3

CONCEITED
Let us not become c . . . . Gal 5:26

CONCEIVE
the virgin shall c . . . . Is 7:14
And behold, you will c . . . Luke 1:31

CONCEIVED
in sin my mother c . . . . Ps 51:5
when desire has c . . . . James 1:15

CONCERN
Neither do I c myself . . . . Ps 131:1
c for My holy name, ... Ezek 36:21
may the dream c those . . . Dan 4:19
the things which c . . . . Acts 28:31
my deep c for all the . . . . . 2 Cor 11:28

CONCERNED
Is it oxen God is c . . . . 1 Cor 9:9
c only with foods and . . . . . . Heb 9:10

CONCESSION
But I say this as a c . . . . 1 Cor 7:6

CONCILIATION
c pacifies great . . . . Eccl 10:4

CONCLUSION
Let us hear the c . . . . Eccl 12:13

CONCUBINE
with Bilhah his father's c . . Gen 35:22
c who was in Shechem . . . . . Judg 8:31
He took for himself a c . . . . Judg 19:1
Saul had a c, whose . . . . . . 2 Sam 3:7
to Keturah, Abraham's c . . 1 Chr 1:32

CONCUBINES
And David took more c . . 2 Sam 5:13
Go in to your father's c . . 2 Sam 16:21
and three hundred c . . . . . . 1 Kin 11:3
eunuch who kept the c . . . . . Esth 2:14
sixty queens and eighty c . . . Song 6:8

CONDEMN
say to God, 'Do not c . . . . . . Job 10:2
Would you c Me that you . . . Job 40:8
who is he who will c Me . . . . . Is 50:9
they will c Him to death, . . Matt 20:18
C not, and you shall not . . . Luke 6:37
world to c the world . . . . . . John 3:17
her, "Neither do I c . . . . John 8:11
judge another you c . . . . Rom 2:1
is he who does not c . . . . . Rom 14:22
I do not say this to c . . . . . . 2 Cor 7:3
our heart does not c . . . . . 1 John 3:21

CONDEMNATION
will receive greater c . . . . . Matt 23:14
can you escape the c . . . . . Matt 23:33
subject to eternal c . . . . . . Mark 3:29
And this is the c . . . . John 3:19
the resurrection of c . . . . . . John 5:29
Their c is just . . . . Rom 3:8
therefore now no c . . . . Rom 8:1

of c had glory . . . . 2 Cor 3:9
having c because they . . . . 1 Tim 5:12
marked out for this c . . . . Jude 4

CONDEMNED
David's heart c him . . . . . 2 Sam 24:10
words you will be c . . . . . . Matt 12:37
and you shall not be c . . . . Luke 6:37
does not believe is c . . . . . . John 3:18
Has no one c you . . . . John 8:10
c sin in the flesh . . . . Rom 8:3
he who doubts is c if he . . Rom 14:23
last, as men c to death . . . . 1 Cor 4:9
by which he c the world . . . . Heb 11:7
brethren, lest you be c . . . . James 5:9
c them to destruction, ... 2 Pet 2:6

CONDEMNS
Who is he who c . . . . Rom 8:34
For if our heart c . . . . 1 John 3:20

CONDUCT
c yourselves like men . . . . . 1 Sam 4:9
who are of upright c . . . . . . Ps 37:14
c yourself in the . . . . 1 Tim 3:15
c that his works are . . . . . James 3:13
to each one's work, c . . . . . 1 Pet 1:17
from your aimless c . . . . . . 1 Pet 1:18
may be won by the c . . . . . . 1 Pet 3:1

CONFERRED
c with the chief priests . . . . Luke 22:4
they c among themselves, . . Acts 4:15
when he had c with the . . . Acts 25:12

CONFESS
c my transgressions . . . . Ps 32:5
that if you c with . . . . Rom 10:9
every tongue shall c . . . . . . Rom 14:11
C your trespasses . . . . James 5:16
If we c our sins . . . . 1 John 1:9
but I will c his name . . . . Rev 3:5

CONFESSED
stood and c their sins . . . . . . Neh 9:2
did not deny, but c, "I . . . . John 1:20
c that He was Christ . . . . . . John 9:22
c the good confession . . . . 1 Tim 6:12

CONFESSES
prosper, but whoever c . . . Prov 28:13
Every spirit that c that . . . 1 John 4:2
c that Jesus is the . . . . . . 1 John 4:15

CONFESSION
of Israel, and make c . . . . . Josh 7:19
with the mouth c . . . . Rom 10:10
c to the gospel of Christ . . 2 Cor 9:13
confessed the good c . . . . . 1 Tim 6:12
witnessed the good c . . . . . 1 Tim 6:13
High Priest of our c . . . . Heb 3:1
let us hold fast our c . . . . . . Heb 4:14

CONFIDENCE
fine gold, 'You are my c' . . . Job 31:24
You who are the c . . . . Ps 65:5
the Lord than to put c . . . . . Ps 118:8
the Lord will be your c . . . . Prov 3:26
c shall be your . . . . Is 30:15
Jesus Christ with all c . . . . Acts 28:31
having c in you all that . . . . 2 Cor 2:3
Jesus, and have no c . . . . Phil 3:3
we have c in the Lord . . . . 2 Thess 3:4
if we hold fast the c . . . . Heb 3:6
do not cast away your c, . . Heb 10:35
appears, we may have c . . 1 John 2:28
Now this is the c that . . . . 1 John 5:14

CONFIDENT
me, in this I will be c . . . . . . Ps 27:3
I myself am c . . . . Rom 15:14
so we are always c . . . . 2 Cor 5:6
become c by my chains . . . . Phil 1:14
we are c that we have a . . . Heb 13:18

CONFINED
saying, "I am c . . . . Jer 36:5
the Scripture has c . . . . Gal 3:22

CONFIRM
c the promises . . . . Rom 15:8

who will also c . . . . 1 Cor 1:8

CONFIRMATION
c of the gospel, you all . . . . . Phil 1:7
an oath for c is for them . . . Heb 6:16

CONFIRMED
covenant that was c . . . . Gal 3:17
by the Lord, and was c . . . . Heb 2:3
c it by an oath . . . . Heb 6:17
prophetic word is . . . . 2 Pet 1:19

CONFIRMING
c the word through the . . . Mark 16:20

CONFLICT
having the same c . . . . Phil 1:30
to know what a great c . . . . . Col 2:1

CONFLICTS
Outside were c . . . . 2 Cor 7:5

CONFORMED
predestined to be c . . . . . . Rom 8:29
And do not be c . . . . Rom 12:2
sufferings, being c . . . . Phil 3:10
body that it may be c . . . . . Phil 3:21

CONFOUNDED
who seek You be c . . . . Ps 69:6
ashamed and c who seek . . . Ps 70:2
c the Jews who dwelt in . . . Acts 9:22

CONFRONTED
They c me in the day . . . . 2 Sam 22:19
The snares of death c me . . . Ps 18:5
c Him as He was . . . . Matt 21:23
with the elders, c Him . . . . Luke 20:1

CONFUSE
c their language . . . . Gen 11:7

CONFUSED
there the Lord c . . . . Gen 11:9
the assembly was c . . . . . . Acts 19:32

CONFUSION
I will cause c among all . . . . Ex 23:27
blindness and c of heart . . Deut 28:28
c who plot my hurt . . . . Ps 35:4
us drink the wine of c . . . . . . Ps 60:3
strike every horse with c . . . Zech 12:4
city was filled with c . . . . . Acts 19:29
author of c but of peace . . 1 Cor 14:33
and self-seeking exist, c . . James 3:16

CONGREGATION
Nor sinners in the c . . . . Ps 1:5
the c of the wicked . . . . Ps 22:16
God stands in the c . . . . Ps 82:1
is he who was in the c . . . . Acts 7:38
the c had broken up, ... Acts 13:43

CONIAH
King of Judah, Jer 22:24, 28
Same as Jehoiachin, 2 Kin 24:8

CONJURES
or one who c spells, or a . . Deut 18:11

CONQUER
conquering and to c . . . . Rev 6:2

CONQUERORS
we are more than c . . . . . . Rom 8:37

CONSCIENCE
convicted by their c . . . . John 8:9
strive to have a c . . . . Acts 24:16
c also bearing witness, ... Rom 2:15
I am not lying, my c . . . . Rom 9:1
wrath but also for c . . . . . . Rom 13:5
and their c, being weak, is . . 1 Cor 8:7
no questions for c . . . . 1 Cor 10:25
by another man's c . . . . . . 1 Cor 10:29
c in the sight of God . . . . . 2 Cor 4:2
faith with a pure c . . . . 1 Tim 3:9
having their own c . . . . 1 Tim 4:2
mind and c are defiled . . . . Titus 1:15
to God, cleanse your c . . . . Heb 9:14
from an evil c and our . . . . Heb 10:22
having a good c . . . . 1 Pet 3:16

CONSCIENCE'
wrath but also for c sake ...Rom 13:5
no questions for c sake ...1 Cor 10:25

CONSECRATE
"C to Me all the ....Ex 13:2
c himself this day ....1 Chr 29:5
the trumpet in Zion, c .....Joel 2:15
c their gain to the ....Mic 4:13

CONSECRATED
c this house which you .....1 Kin 9:3

CONSENT
entice you, do not c ....Prov 1:10
and does not c to ....1 Tim 6:3

CONSENTED
you saw a thief, you c ....Ps 50:18
He had not c to their .....Luke 23:51

CONSENTING
Now Saul was c to his ....Acts 8:1

CONSIDER
When I c Your heavens ....Ps 8:3
c her palaces ....Ps 48:13
c carefully what is ....Prov 23:1
who weighs the hearts c ..Prov 24:12
not c that poverty will ....Prov 28:22
turned myself to c wisdom ..Eccl 2:12
C the work of God ....Eccl 7:13
My people do not c ....Is 1:3
c the operation ....Is 5:12
your God will c ....Jon 1:6
"C your ways ....Hag 1:5
C the lilies of the ....Matt 6:28
but do not c the plank in ...Matt 7:3
C the ravens ....Luke 12:24
Let a man so c us ....1 Cor 4:1
c the Apostle and High ......Heb 3:1
c how great this man ....Heb 7:4
c one another in order ....Heb 10:24
c Him who endured ....Heb 12:3

CONSIDERS
c all their works ....Ps 33:15
Blessed is he who c the......Ps 41:1
She c a field and buys it ..Prov 31:16

CONSIST
not c in the abundance ...Luke 12:15
in Him all things c ....Col 1:17

CONSOLATION
waiting for the C ....Luke 2:25
have received your c ......Luke 6:24
abound in us, so our c .....2 Cor 1:5
if there is any c ....Phil 2:1
given us everlasting c ...2 Thess 2:16
we might have strong c .....Heb 6:18

CONSOLATIONS
Are the c of God too ....Job 15:11

CONSOLE
c those who mourn ....Is 61:3

CONSPIRE
What do you c against ....Nah 1:9

CONSTANT
c prayer was offered ....Acts 12:5

CONSULT
They only c to cast ....Ps 62:4

CONSULTED
c together against ....Ps 83:3

CONSUME
your midst, lest I c ....Ex 33:3
this great fire will c .....Deut 5:25
C them in wrath ....Ps 59:13
whom the Lord will c .....2 Thess 2:8

CONSUMED
but the bush was not c ....Ex 3:2
c the burnt sacrifice ......1 Kin 18:38
For we have been c ....Ps 90:7
mercies we are not c ....Lam 3:22
beware lest you be c ....Gal 5:15

CONSUMING
the Lord was like a c ....Ex 24:17
before you as a c ....Deut 9:3
our God is a c fire ....Heb 12:29

CONSUMMATION
I have seen the c ....Ps 119:96

CONSUMPTION
will strike you with c .....Deut 28:22

CONTAIN
of heavens cannot c ....2 Chr 2:6
c the books that ....John 21:25

CONTEMPT
He pours c on princes ....Job 12:21
wicked comes, c comes ....Prov 18:3
and everlasting c ....Dan 12:2
and be treated with c .....Mark 9:12

CONTEMPTIBLE
of the Lord is c..............Mal 1:7
also have made you c ....Mal 2:9
and his speech c ....2 Cor 10:10

CONTEND
show me why You c ....Job 10:2
Will you c for God ....Job 13:8
let us c together ....Is 43:26
for I will c with him ....Is 49:25
then how can you c ....Jer 12:5
c earnestly for the ....Jude 3

CONTENDED
Therefore the people ......Ex 17:2

CONTENDING
in c with the devil, when .....Jude 9

CONTENT
heard that, he was c .....Lev 10:20
Oh, that we had been c, ...Josh 7:7
and be c with your wages ..Luke 3:14
state I am, to be c ....Phil 4:11
these we shall be c ....1 Tim 6:8
covetousness; be c ....Heb 13:5

CONTENTION
lips enter into c ....Prov 18:6
and c will leave ....Prov 22:10
strife and a man of c ....Jer 15:10

CONTENTIONS
Casting lots causes c .....Prov 18:18
sorcery, hatred, c ....Gal 5:20
genealogies, c ....Titus 3:9

CONTENTIOUS
than with a c and ....Prov 21:19
shared with a c woman ...Prov 25:24
anyone seems to be c ....1 Cor 11:16

CONTENTMENT
c is great gain ....1 Tim 6:6

CONTINUAL
a merry heart has a c ....Prov 15:15
in wrath with a c ....Is 14:6
c coming she weary me ....Luke 18:5
c grief in my heart ....Rom 9:2

CONTINUALLY
heart was only evil c ....Gen 6:5
His praise shall c ....Ps 34:1
and Your truth c ....Ps 40:11
of God endures c ....Ps 52:1
I keep Your law c ....Ps 119:44
Before Me c are grief ....Jer 6:7
and wait on your God c ....Hos 12:6
will give ourselves c ....Acts 6:4
remains a priest c ....Heb 7:3
c offer the sacrifice ....Heb 13:15

CONTINUE
kingdom shall not c .....1 Sam 13:14
c Your lovingkindness .....Ps 36:10
tells lies shall not c ....Ps 101:7
persuaded them to c ......Acts 13:43
Shall we c in sin that ......Rom 6:1
if you c in His goodness ..Rom 11:22
who does not c in all ....Gal 3:10

CONTINUED
c prospering until he ......Gen 26:13
as she c praying before ...1 Sam 1:12
for the sea c to grow more ..Jon 1:13
c with Me three days .....Matt 15:32
c all night in prayer to ....Luke 6:12
c steadfastly in the ....Acts 2:42
Now Peter c knocking .....Acts 12:16
c his message until ....Acts 20:7
and c without food, and ..Acts 27:33
us, they would have c ....1 John 2:19

CONTINUES
But He, because He c ....Heb 7:24
law of liberty and c ......James 1:25

CONTINUING
c daily with one accord .....Acts 2:46
c steadfastly in prayer ....Rom 12:12
here we have no c city ....Heb 13:14

CONTRADICTIONS
idle babblings and c ......1 Tim 6:20

CONTRARY
for the wind was c ....Matt 14:24
to worship God c ....Acts 18:13
me to be struck c to the .....Acts 23:3
c to hope, in hope ....Rom 4:18
were grafted c to nature ..Rom 11:24
and these are c ....Gal 5:17
against us, which was c to ...Col 2:14
please God and are c ....1 Thess 2:15
other thing that is c ......1 Tim 1:10

CONTRIBUTION
to make a certain c ....Rom 15:26

CONTRITE
saves such as have a c ...Ps 34:18
a broken and a c ....Ps 51:17
with him who has a c ....Is 57:15
poor and of a c spirit ....Is 66:2

CONTROVERSY
another, matters of c.......Deut 17:8
For the Lord has a c ....Jer 25:31
without c great is ....1 Tim 3:16

CONVERSION
describing the c...........Acts 15:3

CONVERTED
unless you are c ....Matt 18:3
Repent therefore and be c, ..Acts 3:19

CONVERTING
Lord is perfect, c the soul ...Ps 19:7

CONVEYED
of darkness and c ....Col 1:13

CONVICT
He has come, He will c ....John 16:8
c those who contradict ......Titus 1:9
c all who are ungodly ....Jude 15

CONVICTED
c by their conscience, ...John 8:9
sin, and are c by the law ...James 2:9

CONVICTS
Which of you c.............John 8:46

CONVINCED
I am c that none of these ..Acts 26:26
Let each be fully c ....Rom 14:5
he is c by all, he is ....1 Cor 14:24
If anyone is c in himself ...2 Cor 10:7

CONVOCATION
day there shall be a holy c ..Ex 12:16
of solemn rest, a holy c .....Lev 23:3
of trumpets, a holy c ......Lev 23:24

CONVULSED
unclean spirit had c him ... Mark 1:26
immediately the spirit c ... Mark 9:20

COOKED
c their own children .... Lam 4:10

COOL
in the garden in the c .... Gen 3:8
and c my tongue .... Luke 16:24

COPIES
necessary that the c .... Heb 9:23
hands, which are c .... Heb 9:24

COPPER
hills you can dig c .... Deut 8:9
c in your money belts ..... Matt 10:9
of cups, pitchers, c .... Mark 7:4
sold for two c coins .... Luke 12:6

COPPERSMITH
c did me much harm ...... 2 Tim 4:14

COPY
who serve the c .... Heb 8:5

CORBAN
from me is C (that is, ... Mark 7:11

CORD
this line of scarlet c .... Josh 2:18
And a threefold c .... Eccl 4:12
before the silver c .... Eccl 12:6

CORDS
cut in pieces the c .... Ps 129:4
he is caught in the c .... Prov 5:22
draw iniquity with c .... Is 5:18
them with gentle c .... Hos 11:4
had made a whip of c ...... John 2:15

CORIANDER
it was like white c seed ..... Ex 16:31
manna was like c seed ..... Num 11:7

CORINTH
Paul labors at, Acts 18:1–18
Site of church, 1 Cor 1:2
Visited by Apollos, Acts 19:1

CORNELIUS
A religious Gentile, Acts 10:1–48

CORNER
cut off a c of Saul's robe .. 1 Sam 24:4
Jerusalem at the C Gate ... 2 Chr 26:9
dwell in a c of a housetop .. Prov 21:9
in the c of a bed and on ... Amos 3:12
was not done in a c .... Acts 26:26

CORNERS
its horns on its four c .... Ex 27:2
in the tassels of the c ..... Num 15:38
sheet bound at the four c .. Acts 10:11
at the four c of the earth ..... Rev 7:1

CORNERSTONE
Or who laid its c .... Job 38:6
has become the chief c ..... Ps 118:22
stone, a precious c .... Is 28:16
become the chief c .... Matt 21:42
has become the chief c ..... Acts 4:11
Himself being the chief c ... Eph 2:20
in Zion a chief c .... 1 Pet 2:6

CORPSE
c was thrown on the ...... 1 Kin 13:24
c trodden underfoot .... Is 14:19

CORRECT
with rebukes You c .... Ps 39:11
C your son, and he will ... Prov 29:17
But I will c you in .... Jer 30:11

CORRECTED
human fathers who c .... Heb 12:9

CORRECTION
nor detest His c .... Prov 3:11
but he who refuses c ...... Prov 10:17
but he who hates c .... Prov 12:1
rod of c will drive it ...... Prov 22:15
Do not withhold c .... Prov 23:13

they received no c .... Jer 2:30
for reproof, for c .... 2 Tim 3:16

CORRECTS
is the man whom God c ..... Job 5:17
the LORD loves He c .... Prov 3:12

CORRODED
and silver are c .... James 5:3

CORRUPT
earth also was c before ..... Gen 6:11
the sons of Eli were c ..... 1 Sam 2:12
have together become c ..... Ps 14:3
have together become c ..... Ps 53:3
old man which grows c ..... Eph 4:22
Let no c word .... Eph 4:29
men of c minds .... 2 Tim 3:8
in these things they c .... Jude 10

CORRUPTED
for all flesh had c .... Gen 6:12
we have c no one .... 2 Cor 7:2
so your minds may be c ... 2 Cor 11:3
Your riches are c .... James 5:2
the great harlot who c ..... Rev 19:2

CORRUPTIBLE
For this c must put on .... 1 Cor 15:53
redeemed with c things .... 1 Pet 1:18

CORRUPTION
Your Holy One to see c ..... Ps 16:10
God raised up saw no c ... Acts 13:37
from the bondage of c ..... Rom 8:21
The body is sown in c .... 1 Cor 15:42
c inherit incorruption .... 1 Cor 15:50
of the flesh reap c .... Gal 6:8
having escaped the c .... 2 Pet 1:4
perish in their own c ..... 2 Pet 2:12

COST
and count the c .... Luke 14:28

COSTLY
foundation was of c .... 1 Kin 7:10
of very c oil of spikenard . Mark 14:3
or pearls or c clothing ...... 1 Tim 2:9

COSTS
which c me nothing ..... 2 Sam 24:24

COUCH
He went up to my c .... Gen 49:4
I drench my c with my .... Ps 6:6
Behold, it is Solomon's c ... Song 3:7

COULD
has done what she c ..... Mark 14:8
c remove mountains ...... 1 Cor 13:2
which no one c number ...... Rev 7:9

COUNCIL
shall be in danger of the c .. Matt 5:22
all the c sought false ..... Matt 26:59
a prominent c member .... Mark 15:43
Pharisees gathered a c .... John 11:47
and called the c together ... Acts 5:21
all the c of the elders, ... Acts 22:5

COUNCILS
deliver you up to c .... Mark 13:9

COUNSEL
and strength, He has c .... Job 12:13
the c of the wicked is ...... Job 21:16
when the friendly c .... Job 29:4
is this who darkens c ...... Job 38:2
who walks not in the c .... Ps 1:1
We took sweet c .... Ps 55:14
guide me with Your c ...... Ps 73:24
you disdained all my c .... Prov 1:25
have none of my c .... Prov 1:30
Where there is no c ...... Prov 11:14
C in the heart of man .... Prov 20:5
by wise c wage war ...... Prov 20:18
whom did He take c .... Is 40:14
You are great in c .... Jer 32:19
according to the c .... Eph 1:11
immutability of His c ...... Heb 6:17
I c you to buy from .... Rev 3:18

COUNSELOR
be called Wonderful, C .... Is 9:6
but there was no c .... Is 41:28
Has your c perished .... Mic 4:9
who has become His c .... Rom 11:34

COUNSELORS
c there is safety .... Prov 11:14

COUNT
c the people of Israel ..... 2 Sam 24:4
I can c all My bones .... Ps 22:17
all c John as a prophet .... Matt 21:26
c my life dear to .... Acts 20:24
c me as a partner .... Philem 17
c it all joy when you fall ... James 1:2
His promise, as some c .... 2 Pet 3:9

COUNTED
Even a fool is c .... Prov 17:28
c as the small dust .... Is 40:15
the wages are not c .... Rom 4:4
me, these I have c loss for ... Phil 3:7
He c me faithful .... 1 Tim 1:12
who rule well be c .... 1 Tim 5:17
c the blood of the .... Heb 10:29

COUNTENANCE
The LORD lift up His c ..... Num 6:26
c they did not cast .... Job 29:24
up the light of Your c .... Ps 4:6
His c is like Lebanon ...... Song 5:15
hypocrites, with a sad c ... Matt 6:16
His c was like .... Matt 28:3
of the glory of his c .... 2 Cor 3:7
sword, and His c .... Rev 1:16

COUNTRY
See FAR COUNTRY
"Get out of your c .... Gen 12:1
but you shall go to my c .... Gen 24:4
us pass through your c .... Num 20:17
Israel to search out the c ... Josh 2:2
an end of dividing the c ... Josh 19:51
the c was quiet for forty ... Judg 8:28
dwell in the c of Moab ..... Ruth 1:1
the c of the Philistines ... 1 Sam 27:11
good news from a far c .... Prov 25:25
you into a bountiful c. ...... Jer 2:7
their own c another way ... Matt 2:12
honor except in his own c . Matt 13:57
and went into a far c .... Matt 21:33
the c of the Gadarenes ..... Mark 5:1
go into the surrounding c .. Mark 6:36
and went into a far c ..... Mark 12:1
there were in the same c .... Luke 2:8
journeyed to a far c, ... Luke 15:13
as in a foreign c .... Heb 11:9
that is, a heavenly c .... Heb 11:16

COUNTRYMEN
for my brethren, my c ...... Rom 9:3

COUNTS
c the number of the stars .... Ps 147:4

COURAGE
strong and of good c ...... Deut 31:6
c in anyone because of ..... Josh 2:11
the prophet, he took c .... 2 Chr 15:8
Be of good c, and do it ..... Ezra 10:4
his c against the king of ... Dan 11:25
thanked God and took c ... Acts 28:15

COURAGEOUS
Only be strong and very c. .. Josh 1:7
Be strong and c .... 2 Chr 32:7

COURSE
and sets on fire the c ..... James 3:6

COURT
the c of the tabernacle ...... Ex 27:9
men, and they come to c, .. Deut 25:1
made the c of the priests ... 2 Chr 4:9
the inner c to the king ..... Esth 4:11
appoint my day in c .... Job 9:19
many would c your favor ... Job 11:19
Do not go hastily to c ..... Prov 25:8

up in the c of the prison . . . . . Jer 32:2
cloud filled the inner c . . . . . Ezek 10:3
me into the outer c . . . . Ezek 40:17
by you or by a human c . . . . 1 Cor 4:3
They zealously c you . . . . Gal 4:17

COURTEOUS
be tenderhearted, be c . . . . . . 1 Pet 3:8

COURTS
he may dwell in Your c . . . . . . Ps 65:4
even faints for the c . . . . Ps 84:2
flourish in the c . . . . Ps 92:13
and into His c . . . . Ps 100:4
drink it in My holy c . . . . Is 62:9

COVENANT
See NEW COVENANT
I will establish My c . . . . Gen 6:18
I establish My c with you . . . . Gen 9:9
the LORD made a c . . . . Gen 15:18
I will make My c between . . Gen 17:2
for Me, behold, My c . . . . . . Gen 17:4
My voice and keep My c . . . . . Ex 19:5
he took the Book of the C . . . Ex 24:7
as a perpetual c . . . . Ex 31:16
it is a c of salt . . . . Num 18:19
c which He commanded . . . . Deut 4:13
the c which He made . . . . . . Deut 29:1
never break My c with . . . . . . Judg 2:1
a c before the LORD . . . . . . 1 Sam 23:18
is the c of the LORD . . . . 1 Kin 8:21
You, who keep Your c . . . . . 1 Kin 8:23
of the Book of the C . . . . . 2 Kin 23:2
Remember His c forever . 1 Chr 16:15
You, who keep Your c . . . 2 Chr 6:14
of the Book of the C . . . . 2 Chr 34:30
You who keep Your c . . . . Neh 1:5
"I have made a c . . . . Job 31:1
will show them His c . . . . Ps 25:14
c shall stand firm . . . . Ps 89:28
has remembered His c . . . . . Ps 105:8
sons will keep My c . . . . Ps 132:12
forgets the c of her God . . . . Prov 2:17
and give You as a c . . . . Is 42:6
with them an everlasting c . . . Is 61:8
the words of this c . . . . Jer 11:2
I will make a new c . . . . . . Jer 31:31
'I made a c with your . . . . . . Jer 34:13
a c of peace with them . . Ezek 37:26
c with many for one week . . Dan 9:27
they transgressed the c . . . . . Hos 6:7
I might break the c . . . . . . Zech 11:10
and your wife by c . . . . Mal 2:14
the Messenger of the c . . . . . Mal 3:1
is My blood of the new c . . Matt 26:28
My blood of the new c . . . Mark 14:24
cup is the new c . . . . Luke 22:20
the new c in My blood . . . . 1 Cor 11:25
as ministers of the new c . . . 2 Cor 3:6
c that was confirmed . . . . Gal 3:17
Mediator of a better c . . . . . . Heb 8:6
c had been faultless . . . . Heb 8:7
He says, "A new c . . . . Heb 8:13
the Mediator of the new c . . . Heb 9:15
Mediator of the new c . . . . Heb 12:24
of the everlasting c . . . . Heb 13:20

COVENANTED
your kingdom, as I c . . . . . . 2 Chr 7:18
to the word that I c . . . . Hag 2:5

COVENANTS
the glory, the c . . . . Rom 9:4
these are the two c . . . . Gal 4:24

COVER
the rock, and will c . . . . Ex 33:22
He shall c you with . . . . Ps 91:4
c Yourself with light . . . . Ps 104:2
LORD as the waters c . . . . Is 11:9
and will no more c . . . . Is 26:21
from the wind and a c . . . . . . Is 32:2
and to the hills, 'C us . . . . Luke 23:30
not to c his head . . . . 1 Cor 11:7
c a multitude of sins . . . . . James 5:20

love will c a multitude of . . . . 1 Pet 4:8

COVERED
The depths have c . . . . Ex 15:5
c my transgressions as . . . . . Job 31:33
Whose sin is c . . . . Ps 32:1
the wings of a dove c . . . . . . Ps 68:13
You have c all their sin . . . . . . Ps 85:2
You c me in my . . . . Ps 139:13
with two he c his face . . . . Is 6:2
of Jacob will be c . . . . Is 27:9
You have c Yourself . . . . . . Lam 3:44
For there is nothing c . . . . Matt 10:26

COVERING
spread a cloud for a c . . . . . Ps 105:39
make sackcloth their c . . . . . . Is 50:3
given to her for a c . . . . . . 1 Cor 11:15

COVERINGS
and made themselves c . . . . . Gen 3:7

COVET
"You shall not c . . . . Ex 20:17
c fields and take them . . . . . . Mic 2:2
You murder and c . . . . James 4:2

COVETED
c no one's silver . . . . Acts 20:33

COVETOUS
nor thieves, nor c . . . . 1 Cor 6:10
trained in c practices . . . . . . 2 Pet 2:14

COVETOUSNESS
but he who hates c . . . . . . Prov 28:16
for nothing but your c . . . . . Jer 22:17
heed and beware of c . . . . Luke 12:15
would not have known c . . . . Rom 7:7
all uncleanness or c . . . . Eph 5:3
conduct be without c . . . . . . Heb 13:5

COWARDLY
the c, unbelieving . . . . Rev 21:8

COWS
out of the river seven c . . . . Gen 41:2
c ate up the first seven . . . Gen 41:20
take two milk c which . . . . . 1 Sam 6:7
you c of Bashan, who are . . Amos 4:1

CRAFTILY
His people, to deal c . . . . . Ps 105:25

CRAFTINESS
wise in their own c . . . . Job 5:13
not walking in c . . . . 2 Cor 4:2
deceived Eve by his c . . . . 2 Cor 11:3
in the cunning c . . . . Eph 4:14

CRAFTSMAN
instructor of every c . . . . . . Gen 4:22
c encouraged the . . . . Is 41:7
c stretches out his . . . . Is 44:13

CRAFTSMEN
all the c who were doing . . . . Ex 36:4
and the Valley of C . . . . . . Neh 11:35
no small profit to the c . . . . Acts 19:24

CRAFTY
Jonadab was a very c . . . . 2 Sam 13:3
the devices of the c . . . . Job 5:12
They have taken c . . . . Ps 83:3
of a harlot, and a c . . . . Prov 7:10
Nevertheless, being c . . . . 2 Cor 12:16

CRANE
Like a c or a swallow . . . . . . Is 38:14

CRAVES
and his soul still c . . . . Is 29:8

CRAVING
yielded to intense c . . . . . . Num 11:4
who had yielded to c . . . . . Num 11:34

CREAM
she brought out c . . . . Judg 5:25
were bathed with c . . . . Job 29:6

CREATE
C in me a clean heart, ... Ps 51:10

then the LORD will c above . . . . . Is 4:5
peace and c calamity . . . . Is 45:7
Who did not c it in vain . . . . Is 45:18
For behold, I c . . . . Is 65:17
to c in Himself one new . . . . Eph 2:15

CREATED
God c the heavens . . . . Gen 1:1
God c great sea creatures . . Gen 1:21
So God c man in His . . . . . . Gen 1:27
earth when they were c . . . . . Gen 2:4
the day that God c man . . . . . . Gen 5:1
man whom I have c . . . . Gen 6:7
God c man on the earth . . . . Deut 4:32
south, You have c them . . . . Ps 89:12
You c all the children of . . . . . Ps 89:47
c may praise the LORD . . . . . Ps 102:18
Spirit, they are c . . . . Ps 104:30
and they were c . . . . Ps 148:5
and see who has c . . . . Is 40:26
of Israel has c . . . . Is 41:20
LORD, Who c the heavens . . . . Is 42:5
says the LORD, who c you . . . . Is 43:1
I, the LORD, have c it . . . . Is 45:8
They are c now and not . . . . . . Is 48:7
I have c the blacksmith . . . . . Is 54:16
For the LORD has c . . . . Jer 31:22
place where you were c . . . Ezek 21:30
on the day you were c . . . Ezek 28:13
Has not one God c . . . . Mal 2:10
which God c until this . . . . Mark 13:19
nor any other c thing . . . . . . Rom 8:39
Nor was man c for the . . . . 1 Cor 11:9
c in Christ Jesus . . . . Eph 2:10
hidden in God who c . . . . Eph 3:9
new man which was c . . . . . . Eph 4:24
Him all things were c . . . . . . Col 1:16
from foods which God c . . . 1 Tim 4:3
for You c all things . . . . Rev 4:11
who c heaven and the . . . . . Rev 10:6

CREATION
the beginning of the c . . . . . Mark 10:6
beginning of the c which . Mark 13:19
since the c of the world . . . . Rom 1:20
c was subjected . . . . Rom 8:20
know that the whole c . . . . . Rom 8:22
Christ, he is a new c . . . . . 2 Cor 5:17
anything, but a new c . . . . . . Gal 6:15
firstborn over all c . . . . Col 1:15
that is, not of this c . . . . Heb 9:11
from the beginning of c . . . 2 Pet 3:4
Beginning of the c of God . . . Rev 3:14

CREATOR
Remember now your C . . . . . Eccl 12:1
God, the LORD, the C . . . . . . Is 40:28
rather than the C . . . . Rom 1:25
good, as to a faithful C . . . 1 Pet 4:19

CREATURE
See LIVING CREATURE
every living c that is with . . . Gen 9:12
living c with its four . . . . . . Ezek 1:15
the gospel to every c . . . . Mark 16:15
For every c of God is . . . . . 1 Tim 4:4
And there is no c . . . . Heb 4:13
And every c which is . . . . . . Rev 5:13
and every living c . . . . Rev 16:3

CREATURES
See LIVING CREATURES
created great sea c . . . . Gen 1:21
firstfruits of His c . . . . James 1:18
were four living c . . . . Rev 4:6

CREDIT
who love you, what c . . . . . Luke 6:32
For what c is it if . . . . 1 Pet 2:20

CREDITOR
Every c who has lent . . . . . Deut 15:2
c is coming to take my . . . 2 Kin 4:1
c seize all that he . . . . Ps 109:11
There was a certain c . . . . Luke 7:41

CREEP
beasts of the forest c . . . . . Ps 104:20

sort are those who c .... 2 Tim 3:6

CREEPING
c thing and beast of .... Gen 1:24
every sort of c thing ...... Ezek 8:10
animals and c things ...... Rom 1:23

CREPT
For certain men have c ...... Jude 4

CRETE
Paul visits, Acts 27:7–21
Titus dispatched to, Titus 1:5
Inhabitants of, evil and lazy, Titus 1:12

CRIB
donkey its master's c .... Is 1:3

CRIED
he c with an exceedingly .. Gen 27:34
the poor who c out .... Job 29:12
They c to You .... Ps 22:5
of the depths I have c ...... Ps 130:1
of the belly of Sheol I c ...... Jon 2:2
beginning to sink he c .... Matt 14:30
Jesus c out and said ..... John 12:44
they c out, "Away with ... John 19:15

CRIES
your brother's blood c ..... Gen 4:10
with vehement c .... Heb 5:7

CRIMES
land is filled with c .... Ezek 7:23

CRIMINALS
also two others, c .... Luke 23:32

CRIMSON
blue, and purple, and c .. 2 Chr 3:14
though they are red like c ..... Is 1:18

CRIPPLE
c from his mother's womb .. Acts 14:8

CRISPUS
Chief ruler of synagogue of Corinth,
Acts 18:8
Baptized by Paul, 1 Cor 1:14

CROOKED
perverse and c generation .. Deut 32:5
turn aside to their c .... Ps 125:5
whose ways are c .... Prov 2:15
What is c cannot be made .. Eccl 1:15
what He has made c .... Eccl 7:13
c places shall be made .... Is 40:4
c places straight .... Is 45:2
c places shall be made ..... Luke 3:5
in the midst of a c .... Phil 2:15

CROSS
I would not c over the .... Deut 4:21
But when you c over the .. Deut 12:10
does not take his c .... Matt 10:38
and take up his c .... Matt 16:24
compelled to bear His c .. Matt 27:32
down from the c .... Matt 27:40
and take up his c .... Mark 8:34
and take up his c daily, ... Luke 9:23
does not bear his c ...... Luke 14:27
And He, bearing His c, .. John 19:17
lest the c of Christ .... 1 Cor 1:17
offense of the c has ceased .. Gal 5:11
persecution for the c .... Gal 6:12
boast except in the c ...... Gal 6:14
one body through the c ..... Eph 2:16
even the death of the c ..... Phil 2:8
the enemies of the c ...... Phil 3:18
through the blood of His c ... Col 1:20
having nailed it to the c ..... Col 2:14
Him endured the c .... Heb 12:2

CROW
rooster will not c this ..... Luke 22:34

CROWD
shall not follow a c .... Ex 23:2

CROWN
the holy c on the turban ..... Ex 29:6
You set a c of pure .... Ps 21:3

c the year with Your .... Ps 65:11
have profaned his c .... Ps 89:39
upon Himself His c .... Ps 132:18
The c of the wise is .... Prov 14:24
head is a c of glory .... Prov 16:31
Woe to the c of pride .... Is 28:1
hosts will be for a c .... Is 28:5
c has fallen from our ...... Lam 5:16
they had twisted a c ..... Matt 27:29
wearing the c of thorns .... John 19:5
obtain a perishable c ..... 1 Cor 9:25
brethren, my joy and c ...... Phil 4:1
or joy, or c of rejoicing .. 1 Thess 2:19
laid up for me the c .... 2 Tim 4:8
he will receive the c ...... James 1:12
you will receive the c of .. 1 Pet 5:4
I will give you the c of life .. Rev 2:10
no one may take your c .... Rev 3:11
on His head a golden c .... Rev 14:14

CROWNED
angels, and You have c .... Ps 8:5
but the prudent are c ... Prov 14:18
athletics, he is not c .... 2 Tim 2:5
You have c him with glory ... Heb 2:7

CROWNS
and they had c of gold ...... Rev 4:4
on his horns ten c .... Rev 13:1
His head were many c ..... Rev 19:12

CRUCIFIED
be delivered up to be c ... Matt 26:2
"Let Him be c .... Matt 27:22
robbers were c with Him .. Matt 27:38
you seek Jesus who was c .. Matt 28:5
scourged Him, to be c .... Mark 15:15
third hour, and they c .... Mark 15:25
of Nazareth, who was c ... Mark 16:6
Calvary, there they c ..... Luke 23:33
of sinful men, and be c .... Luke 24:7
to death, and c Him ...... Luke 24:20
Him to them to be c ...... John 19:16
c there was a garden ..... John 19:41
lawless hands, have c ..... Acts 2:23
of Nazareth, whom you c, .. Acts 4:10
that our old man was c ..... Rom 6:6
Was Paul c for you .... 1 Cor 1:13
but we preach Christ c.... 1 Cor 1:23
Jesus Christ and Him c ..... 1 Cor 2:2
they would not have c ..... 1 Cor 2:8
though He was c .... 2 Cor 13:4
I have been c with Christ .... Gal 2:20
portrayed among you as c .... Gal 3:1
c the flesh with its passions .. Gal 5:24
the world has been c to me .. Gal 6:14
where also our Lord was c .. Rev 11:8

CRUCIFY
and to scourge and to c ... Matt 20:19
them you will kill and c ... Mark 15:34
out again, "C Him .... Mark 15:13
saying, "C Him, c Him ... Luke 23:21
I have power to c You ..... John 19:10
"Shall I c your King ...... John 19:15
since they c again .... Heb 6:6

CRUEL
wrath, for it is c .... Gen 49:7
spirit and c bondage .... Ex 6:9
hate me with c hatred ..... Ps 25:19
of the wicked are c .... Prov 12:10

CRUELTY
of c are in their .... Gen 49:5
the haunts of c .... Ps 74:20
c you have ruled .... Ezek 34:4

CRUMBS
eat from the children's c .. Mark 7:28
c which fell from the ..... Luke 16:21

CRUSH
that a foot may c .... Job 39:15
that your foot may c .... Ps 68:23
the poor, who c .... Amos 4:1
of peace will c .... Rom 16:20

CRUSHED
in the dust, who are c ...... Job 4:19
c my life to the .... Ps 143:3
every side, yet not c .... 2 Cor 4:8

CRUST
man is reduced to a c ..... Prov 6:26

CRY
and their c came up to ...... Ex 2:23
of oppressions they c ...... Job 35:9
heart and my flesh c .... Ps 84:2
I c out with my whole ..... Ps 119:145
Does not wisdom c .... Prov 8:1
"What shall I c .... Is 40:6
nor lift up a c .... Jer 7:16
c mightily to God .... Jon 3:8
at midnight a c .... Matt 25:6
His own elect who c ...... Luke 18:7

CRYING
"The voice of one c .... Matt 3:3
nor sorrow, nor c .... Rev 21:4

CRYSTAL
nor c can equal it .... Job 28:17
your gates of c .... Is 54:12
of an awesome c .... Ezek 1:22
a sea of glass, like c .... Rev 4:6

CUBIT
shall finish it to a c .... Gen 6:16
can add one c .... Matt 6:27

CUCUMBERS
in Egypt, the c .... Num 11:5
a hut in a garden of c .... Is 1:8

CUD
c or those that have cloven .. Lev 11:4
the c or have cloven .... Deut 14:7

CUMI
Talitha, c," which is .... Mark 5:41

CUNNING
the serpent was more c ..... Gen 3:1
c comes quickly .... Job 5:13
c craftiness of deceitful ..... Eph 4:14

CUP
My c runs over .... Ps 23:5
waters of a full c are .... Ps 73:10
the Lord there is a c .... Ps 75:8
I will take up the c .... Ps 116:13
the dregs of the c .... Is 51:17
men give them the c .... Jer 16:7
"Take this wine c .... Jer 25:15
The c of the Lord's........ Hab 2:16
make Jerusalem a c .... Zech 12:2
little ones only a c .... Matt 10:42
will indeed drink My c ... Matt 20:23
cleanse the inside of the c .. Matt 23:26
Then He took the c ...... Matt 26:27
possible, let this c .... Matt 26:39
c of water to drink in My .. Mark 9:41
the outside of the c ...... Luke 11:39
c is the new covenant ..... Luke 22:20
this c away from Me ..... Luke 22:42
cannot drink the c ...... 1 Cor 10:21
c is the new covenant .... 1 Cor 11:25
the c of His indignation .... Rev 14:10
to give her the c .... Rev 16:19
c full of abominations...... Rev 17:4

CURE
but they could not c ...... Matt 17:16
and to c diseases .... Luke 9:1

CURES
and perform c .... Luke 13:32

CURSE
c the ground for man's ..... Gen 8:21
will c him who curses you .. Gen 12:3
your c be on me, my son .. Gen 27:13
c a ruler of your .... Ex 22:28
You shall not c the deaf .... Lev 19:14
c this people for me .... Num 22:6
Balaam, "Neither c ...... Num 23:25

your God turned the c . . . . . Deut 23:5
on Mount Ebal to c . . . . . . Deut 27:13
c which I have set before . . Deut 30:1
said to him, 'C David . . . . 2 Sam 16:10
the c into a blessing . . . . Neh 13:2
C God and die . . . . Job 2:9
mouth, but they c . . . . Ps 62:4
Let them c, but You bless . . Ps 109:28
The c of the LORD is . . . . Prov 3:33
So a c without cause shall . . Prov 26:2
Do not c the king . . . . Eccl 10:20
the c has devoured . . . . Is 24:6
a byword, a taunt and a c . . . Jer 24:9
This is the c that goes out . . . Zech 5:3
a c among the nations . . . . . Zech 8:13
"I will send a c . . . . Mal 2:2
are cursed with a c . . . . Mal 3:9
bless those who cry you, ... Luke 6:28
bless and do not c . . . . Rom 12:14
law are under the c . . . . Gal 3:10
us from the c of the law, ... Gal 3:13
Father, and with it we c . . . James 3:9
there shall be no more c . . . . Rev 22:3

CURSED
c more than all cattle . . . . Gen 3:14
C is the man who . . . . Jer 17:5
c is he who keeps . . . . Jer 48:10
'Depart from Me, you c . . . Matt 25:41
C is everyone who hangs . . . . Gal 3:13
and near to being c . . . . Heb 6:8

CURSES
I will curse him who c . . . . . . Gen 12:3
'For everyone who c . . . . . . Lev 20:9
write these c in a book . . . . Num 5:23
c his father or his . . . . Prov 20:20
'He who c father or . . . . Mark 7:10

CURSINGS
by the sword for the c . . . . . Hos 7:16

CURTAIN
of each c shall be . . . . Ex 26:2
the heavens like a c . . . . Ps 104:2

CUSH
Ham's oldest son, 1 Chr 1:8–10
——— Another name for Ethiopia, Is 18:1

CUSHAN-RISHATHAIM
Mesopotamian king; oppresses Israel,
Judg 3:8
Othniel delivers Israel from, Judg 3:9,
10

CUSTOM
to me, as Your c . . . . Ps 119:132
according to the c . . . . Acts 15:1
we have no such c . . . . . . 1 Cor 11:16

CUT
confidence shall be c . . . . Job 8:14
evildoers shall be c . . . . Ps 37:9
the wicked will be c . . . . Prov 2:22
c off your supply of bread . . Ezek 5:16
your navel cord was not c . . Ezek 16:4
stone was c out without . . . . Dan 2:34
that I will c off the names . . . Zech 13:2
not bear good fruit is c . . . . . Matt 3:10
causes you to sin, c . . . . Matt 5:30
and will c him in . . . . Matt 24:51
him whose ear Peter c . . . . John 18:26
He had his hair c . . . . Acts 18:18

CYMBAL
or a clanging c . . . . 1 Cor 13:1

CYPRUS
Mentioned in prophecies, Num 24:24;
Is 23:1–12; Jer 2:10
Christians preach to Jews of, Acts
11:19, 20
Paul and Barnabas visit, Acts 13:4–13;
15:39

CYRENE
A Greek colonial city in North Africa;
home of Simon the cross-bearer,
Matt 27:32

Synagogue of, Acts 6:9
Christians from, become missionaries,
Acts 11:20

CYRUS
King of Persia, referred to as God's
anointed, Is 44:28—45:1

DAGON
The national god of the Philistines,
Judg 16:23
Falls before ark, 1 Sam 5:1–5

DAILY
much as they gather d . . . . . . Ex 16:5
d He shall be praised . . . . Ps 72:15
to me, watching d . . . . Prov 8:34
Yet they seek Me d . . . . Is 58:2
Give us this day our d . . . . . Matt 6:11
I sat d with you . . . . Matt 26:55
take up his cross d . . . . Luke 9:23
the Scriptures d . . . . Acts 17:11
our Lord, I die d . . . . 1 Cor 15:31
stands ministering d . . . . . . Heb 10:11

DALMATIA
A region east of the Adriatic Sea; Titus
departs for, 2 Tim 4:10

DAMASCUS
Capital of Syria; captured by David;
ruled by enemy kings, 2 Sam 8:5, 6;
1 Kin 11:23, 24; 15:18
Elisha's prophecy in, 2 Kin 8:7–15
Taken by Assyrians, 2 Kin 16:9
Prophecy concerning, Is 8:3, 4
Paul converted on road to; first
preaches there, Acts 9:1–22
escapes from, 2 Cor 11:32, 33
revisits, Gal 1:17

DAN
Jacob's son by Bilhah, Gen 30:5, 6
Prophecy concerning, Gen 49:16, 17
——— Tribe of:
Numbered, Num 1:38, 39
Blessed, Deut 33:22
Receive their inheritance, Josh
19:40–47
Fall into idolatry, Judg 18:1–31
——— Town, northern boundary of Is-
rael, Judg 20:1
Called Leshem; captured by Danites,
Josh 19:47
Center of idolatry, 1 Kin 12:28–30
Destroyed by Ben-Hadad, 1 Kin 15:20

DANCE
and their children d . . . . Job 21:11
His name with the d . . . . Ps 149:3
mourn, and a time to d . . . . . Eccl 3:4
d has turned into . . . . Lam 5:15
and you did not d . . . . Matt 11:17

DANCED
Then David d before . . . . . 2 Sam 6:14
daughter of Herodias d . . . . Matt 14:6

DANCING
saw the calf and the d . . . . . Ex 32:19
me my mourning into d . . . . . Ps 30:11
he heard music and d . . . Luke 15:25

DANIEL
Taken to Babylon; refuses Nebuchad-
nezzar's foods, Dan 1
Interprets dreams; honored by king,
Dan 2
Interprets handwriting on wall; hon-
ored by Belshazzar, Dan 5:10–29
Appointed to high office; conspired
against and thrown to lions, Dan
6:1–23
Visions of four beasts, ram and goat,
Dan 7; 8

Intercedes for Israel, Dan 9:1–19
Further visions, Dan 9:20—12:13

DARE
someone would even d . . . . . . Rom 5:7
D any of you . . . . 1 Cor 6:1

DARIUS
Darius the Mede, son of Ahasuerus;
made king of the Chaldeans, Dan 9:1
Succeeds Belshazzar, Dan 5:30, 31
Co-ruler with Cyrus, Dan 6:28
——— Darius Hystaspis (522–486 B.C.),
king of all Persia; temple work dated
by his reign, Ezra 4:5, 24
Confirms Cyrus's royal edict, Ezra
6:1–14
——— Darius the Persian (423–404 B.C.);
priestly records kept during his
reign, Neh 12:22

DARK
dwell in the d cloud . . . . . . 1 Kin 8:12
I am d, but lovely . . . . Song 1:5
d place of the earth . . . . Is 45:19
d places like the dead . . . . . . Lam 3:6
and makes the day d . . . . . . Amos 5:8
and the day shall be d . . . . . . Mic 3:6
I tell you in the d . . . . Matt 10:27
while it was still d . . . . John 20:1
shines in a d place . . . . 2 Pet 1:19

DARKENED
so that the land was d . . . . . . Ex 10:15
Let their eyes be d . . . . Ps 69:23
their understanding d . . . . . . Eph 4:18

DARKNESS
d He called Night . . . . Gen 1:5
shall enlighten my d . . . . 2 Sam 22:29
through the deep d . . . . Job 22:13
Those who sat in d . . . . Ps 107:10
d shall not hide . . . . Ps 139:12
d have seen a great light . . . . . . Is 9:2
I will make d light . . . . Is 42:16
and deep d the people . . . . Is 60:2
Israel, or a land of d . . . . Jer 2:31
body will be full of d . . . . . . Matt 6:23
cast out into outer d . . . . . . Matt 8:12
and the power of d . . . . . Luke 22:53
d rather than light . . . . John 3:19
d does not know . . . . John 12:35
For you were once d . . . . Eph 5:8
the rulers of the d . . . . Eph 6:12
us from the power of d . . . . . . Col 1:13
of the night nor of d . . . . . 1 Thess 5:5
and to blackness and d . . . . Heb 12:18
called you out of d . . . . 1 Pet 2:9
blackness of d forever . . . . . 2 Pet 2:17
and in Him is no d . . . . 1 John 1:5
Him, and walk in d . . . . 1 John 1:6
d is passing away . . . . 1 John 2:8
blackness of d forever . . . . . . Jude 13

DARTS
quench all the fiery d . . . . . . Eph 6:16

DASH
You shall d them to . . . . Ps 2:9
lest you d your foot . . . . Matt 4:6

DASHED
hand, O LORD, has d . . . . . . Ex 15:6
also will be d to . . . . Is 13:16
infants shall be d . . . . Hos 13:16

DATHAN
Joins Korah's rebellion, Num 16:1–35
Swallowed up by the earth, Ps 106:17

DAUGHTER
I am the d of Bethuel, ... Gen 24:24
Dinah the d of Leah . . . . . . Gen 34:1
Jochebed the d of Levi . . . Num 26:59
had neither son nor d . . . . Judg 11:34
cry of the d of my people . . . . Jer 8:19
the virgin d of my people . . . Jer 14:17

O virgin, the *d* of Egypt ....Jer 46:11
"Rejoice greatly, O *d* ....Zech 9:9
My *d* has just died, ...Matt 9:18
Be of good cheer, *d* ....Matt 9:22
being a *d* of Abraham, ...Luke 13:16
"Fear not, *d* of Zion ......John 12:15
the son of Pharaoh's *d* ....Heb 11:24

DAUGHTER-IN-LAW

Judah said to Tamar his *d* . Gen 38:11
the Moabitess her *d* with ...Ruth 1:22
lewdly defiles his *d* ......Ezek 22:11
d against her ....Mic 7:6
a *d* against her ....Matt 10:35

DAUGHTERS

he had sons and *d* ....Gen 5:4
of God saw the *d* ....Gen 6:2
Thus both the *d* of Lot .....Gen 19:36
years for your two *d* ......Gen 31:41
the *d* of Zelophehad ....Num 27:1
not give them our *d* as .....Judg 21:7
Turn back, my *d* ....Ruth 1:11
O *d* of Israel, weep over ..2 Sam 1:24
d wore such apparel .....2 Sam 13:18
beautiful as the *d* of Job ..Job 42:15
Kings' *d* are among Your .....Ps 45:9
Let the *d* of Judah be glad, ..Ps 48:11
The leech has two *d* ......Prov 30:15
"Many *d* have done well ...Prov 31:29
a bird, and all the *d* ....Eccl 12:4
O *d* of Jerusalem, like the ...Song 1:5
"Because the *d* of Zion are ..Is 3:16
d shall go into captivity ...Ezek 30:18
your *d* shall prophesy ......Joel 2:28
D of Jerusalem, do not ...Luke 23:28
d shall prophesy ....Acts 2:17
man had four virgin *d* .....Acts 21:9
shall be My sons and *d* ....2 Cor 6:18
whose *d* you are if you ......1 Pet 3:6

DAVID

See CITY OF DAVID; HOUSE OF DAVID;
   SEED OF DAVID; SON OF DAVID;
   THRONE OF DAVID
Anointed by Samuel, 1 Sam 16:1–13
Becomes royal harpist, 1 Sam 16:14–23
Defeats Goliath, 1 Sam 17
Makes covenant with Jonathan, 1 Sam
   18:1–4
Honored by Saul; loved by the people;
   Saul becomes jealous, 1 Sam 18:5–16
Wins Michal as wife, 1 Sam 18:17–30
Flees from Saul, 1 Sam 19; 20;
   21:10—22:5; 23:14–29
Eats the holy bread, 1 Sam 21:1–6; Matt
   12:3, 4
Saves Keilah from Philistines, 1 Sam
   23:1–13
Twice spares Saul's life, 1 Sam
   24:1–22; 26:1–25
Anger at Nabal appeased by Abigail;
   marries her, 1 Sam 25:2–42
Allies with the Philistines, 1 Sam
   27:1—28:2
Rejected by them, 1 Sam 29
Avenges destruction of Ziklag, 1 Sam
   30
Mourns death of Saul and Jonathan,
   2 Sam 1
Anointed king of Judah, 2 Sam 2:1–7
War with Saul's house; Abner defects
   to David, 2 Sam 3:1, 6–21
Mourns Abner's death, 2 Sam 3:28–39
Punishes Ishbosheth's murderers,
   2 Sam 4
Anointed king of all Israel, 2 Sam
   5:1–5
Conquers Jerusalem; makes it his capi-
   tal, 2 Sam 5:6–16
Defeats Philistines, 2 Sam 5:17–25
Brings ark to Jerusalem, 2 Sam 6
Receives eternal covenant, 2 Sam 7
Further conquests, 2 Sam 8; 10

Shows mercy to Mephibosheth,
   2 Sam 9
Commits adultery and murder, 2 Sam
   11
Rebuked by Nathan; repents, 2 Sam
   12:1–23; Ps 32; 51
Absalom's rebellion, 2 Sam 15—18
Mourns Absalom's death, 2 Sam
   18:33—19:8
Shows himself merciful, 2 Sam
   19:18–39
Sheba's rebellion, 2 Sam 19:40—20:22
Avenges the Gibeonites, 2 Sam
   21:1–14
Song of deliverance, 2 Sam 22
Sins by numbering the people, 2 Sam
   24:1–17
Buys threshing floor to build altar,
   2 Sam 24:18–25
Secures Solomon's succession, 1 Kin
   1:5–53
Instructions to Solomon, 1 Kin 2:1–11
Last words, 2 Sam 23:1–7
Inspired by Spirit, Matt 22:43
As prophet, Acts 2:29–34
Faith of, Heb 11:32–34

DAY

See LAST DAY; THIRD DAY
God called the light *D* ......Gen 1:5
blessed the seventh *d* ....Gen 2:3
garden in the cool of the *d* ...Gen 3:8
on that *d* all the fountains ..Gen 7:11
and *d* and night ....Gen 8:22
"Swear to me as of this *d* ..Gen 25:33
shall observe this *d* ....Ex 12:17
a certain quota every *d* .....Ex 16:4
sixth *d* bread for two days ...Ex 16:29
rested on the seventh *d* .....Ex 16:30
Remember the Sabbath *d* ....Ex 20:8
eaten the same *d* ....Lev 19:6
seventh *d* shall be a holy ...Lev 23:8
be the *D* of Atonement ....Lev 23:27
clothes on the seventh *d* ..Num 31:24
and in the cloud by *d* ......Deut 1:33
This *d* you are to cross ....Deut 2:18
witness against you this *d* ..Deut 4:26
the *d* of their calamity ....Deut 32:35
you shall meditate in it *d* ....Josh 1:8
"This *d* I have rolled away ..Josh 5:9
grain, on the very same *d* ..Josh 5:11
has been no *d* like that ....Josh 10:14
rebel this *d* against the ....Josh 22:16
You are witnesses this *d* ....Ruth 4:10
on the *d* of battle, that ...1 Sam 13:22
the victory that *d* was ....2 Sam 19:2
This *d* is a *d* of good news, ..2 Kin 7:9
This *d* is a *d* of trouble, ...2 Kin 19:3
of a pit on a snowy *d* .....1 Chr 11:22
d of the foundation of ....2 Chr 8:16
Be still, for the *d* is holy ....Neh 8:11
made it a *d* of feasting .....Esth 9:18
and cursed the *d* ....Job 3:1
for the *d* of battle and .....Job 38:23
d utters speech ....Ps 19:2
For a *d* in Your courts .....Ps 84:10
In the *d* of my trouble ....Ps 86:7
d the LORD has made ......Ps 118:24
not strike you by *d* ....Ps 121:6
night shines as the *d* ......Ps 139:12
unto the perfect *d* ....Prov 4:18
do not know what a *d* .....Prov 27:1
the *d* when the keepers .....Eccl 12:3
Until the *d* breaks and .....Song 4:6
In that *d* the Branch of the ...Is 4:2
in the *d* of your fast you ......Is 58:3
tears, that I might weep *d* .....Jer 9:1
My covenant with the *d* ....Jer 33:20
a cloud on a rainy *d*, so ...Ezek 1:28
Behold, the *d* ....Ezek 7:10
on the *d* of the LORD ......Ezek 13:5
the *d* you were created ...Ezek 28:15

life, in the *d* of your fall ..Ezek 32:10
knees three times that *d* ....Dan 6:10
you shall stumble in the *d* ...Hos 4:5
a *d* of clouds and thick ......Joel 2:2
For the *d* of the LORD ......Joel 2:11
who put far off the *d* ......Amos 6:3
next *d* God prepared a ....Jon 4:7
the *d* of your watchman ......Mic 7:4
for the *d* of the LORD ......Zeph 1:7
who has despised the *d* ....Zech 4:10
neither *d* nor night ....Zech 14:7
who can endure the *d* ......Mal 3:2
d our daily bread ....Matt 6:11
and Gomorrah in the *d* ....Matt 10:15
d when I drink it new ....Matt 26:29
this *d* in the city of David ..Luke 2:11
you seven times in a *d* ....Luke 17:4
and the third *d* rise again ..Luke 24:7
sent Me while it is *d* ....John 9:4
great and awesome *d* ......Acts 2:20
person esteems one *d* .....Rom 14:5
D will declare it ....1 Cor 3:13
again the third *d* ....1 Cor 15:4
d I have been in the ......2 Cor 11:25
perfectly that the *d* ....1 Thess 5:2
and sons of the *d* ....1 Thess 5:5
He designates a certain *d* ....Heb 4:7
God in the *d* of visitation . 1 Pet 2:12
with the Lord one *d* ....2 Pet 3:8
great *d* of God Almighty ...Rev 16:14

DAY OF THE LORD

For the *d* of hosts shall ......Is 2:12
Wail, for the *d* is at hand .....Is 13:6
the holy *d* honorable, ...Is 58:13
is the *d* God of hosts, ...Jer 46:10
stand in battle on the *d* ...Ezek 13:5
is near, even the *d* ....Ezek 30:3
For the *d* is at hand; ....Joel 1:15
the great and awesome *d* ..Joel 2:31
For what good is the *d* ....Amos 5:18
d upon all the nations .....Obad 15
for the *d* is at hand, ...Zeph 1:7
the great and dreadful *d* ...Mal 4:5
the great and awesome *d* ..Acts 2:20
may be saved in the *d* .....1 Cor 5:5
also are ours, in the *d* ....2 Cor 1:14
d will come as a thief ......2 Pet 3:10

DAYS

See ALL THE DAYS OF HIS LIFE; LAST
   DAYS
seasons, and for *d* ....Gen 1:14
rain on the earth forty *d* .....Gen 7:4
He who is eight *d* old .....Gen 17:12
Seven *d* you shall eat ......Ex 12:15
Six *d* you shall gather it, ...Ex 16:26
Six *d* you shall labor ....Ex 20:9
that your *d* may be long ....Deut 5:16
d are swifter than a ....Job 7:6
Let me alone, for my *d* .....Job 7:16
of woman is of few *d* ......Job 14:1
blessed the latter *d* ....Job 42:12
me all the *d* of my life ......Ps 23:6
The *d* of our lives are ......Ps 90:10
teach us to number our *d* ...Ps 90:12
For my *d* are consumed ....Ps 102:3
I remember the *d* of old ....Ps 143:5
for length of *d* and long ....Prov 3:2
of the LORD prolongs *d*....Prov 10:27
evil all the *d* of her life ....Prov 31:12
"Why were the former *d* ....Eccl 7:10
Before the difficult *d* ....Eccl 12:1
and tested them ten *d* .....Dan 1:14
He had fasted forty *d* ......Matt 4:2
But the *d* will come when ..Matt 9:15
those *d* were shortened ...Matt 24:22
had shortened those *d* ...Mark 13:20
the *d* were completed ......Luke 2:6
But the *d* will come when ..Luke 5:35
raise it up in three *d* ......John 2:20
he has been dead four *d* ..John 11:39
by them during forty *d* .....Acts 1:3

You observe d and . . . . Gal 4:10
life and see good d . . . . 1 Pet 3:10
will come in the last d. . . . . . 2 Pet 3:3
two hundred and sixty d. . . . . Rev 11:3

DAYSPRING
with which the D . . . . Luke 1:78

DEACONS
with the bishops and d . . . . . . Phil 1:1
d must be reverent . . . . 1 Tim 3:8
d be the husbands . . . . 1 Tim 3:12

DEAD
See RAISED FROM THE DEAD; RAISED
   HIM FROM THE DEAD
"We shall all be d . . . . Ex 12:33
he stood between the d . . . Num 16:48
work wonders for the d . . . . Ps 88:10
who have long been d . . . . . Ps 143:3
But the d know nothing . . . . . Eccl 9:5
shall cast out the d . . . . Is 26:19
d bury their own d . . . . Matt 8:22
d are raised up and . . . . Matt 11:5
not the God of the d . . . . . Matt 22:32
for this my son was d . . . . Luke 15:24
d will hear the voice . . . . . . John 5:25
was raised from the d . . . . . . Rom 6:4
yourselves to be d . . . . Rom 6:11
from the law sin was d . . . . . Rom 7:8
be Lord of both the d . . . . . Rom 14:9
resurrection of the d . . . . . 1 Cor 15:12
baptized for the d . . . . 1 Cor 15:29
made alive, who were d . . . . . Eph 2:1
And the d in Christ . . . . . . 1 Thess 4:16
d while she sleeps . . . . 1 Tim 5:6
without works is d . . . . . . James 2:26
d did not live again . . . . Rev 20:5
And the d were judged . . . . . Rev 20:12

DEAD SEA
Called the:
Salt Sea, Gen 14:3
Sea of the Arabah, Deut 3:17

DEADLY
they drink anything d . . . . Mark 16:18
evil, full of d poison . . . . James 3:8
d wound was healed . . . . Rev 13:3

DEADNESS
the d of Sarah's womb . . . . . Rom 4:19

DEAF
makes the mute, the d . . . . . . Ex 4:11
d shall hear the words . . . . . Is 29:18
d shall be unstopped . . . . Is 35:5
d as My messenger . . . . Is 42:19
d who have ears . . . . Is 43:8
their ears shall be d . . . . Mic 7:16
are cleansed and the d . . . . . Matt 11:5

DEAL
Do you thus d with the . . . . . Deut 32:6
My Servant shall d . . . . Is 52:13

DEAR
servant, who was d to him . . Luke 7:2
count my life d to myself . . Acts 20:24
of God as d children . . . . Eph 5:1
you had become to us . . 1 Thess 2:8

DEARLY
I have given the d beloved . . . Jer 12:7
rulers d love dishonor . . . . . . Hos 4:18

DEATH
See SECOND DEATH; SHADOW OF
   DEATH
Let me die the d . . . . Num 23:10
d parts you and me . . . . . . Ruth 1:17
and the shadow of d . . . . . . Job 10:21
You will bring me to d . . . . . Job 30:23
For in d there is no . . . . Ps 6:5
I sleep the sleep of d . . . . . . Ps 13:3
of the shadow of d . . . . Ps 23:4
my soul from d . . . . Ps 56:13
can live and not see d . . . . . . Ps 89:48
house leads down to d . . . . Prov 2:18
who hate me love d . . . . Prov 8:36

D and life are in the . . . . . Prov 18:21
swallow up d forever . . . . Is 25:8
no pleasure in the d . . . . . . Ezek 18:32
redeem them from d . . . . . Hos 13:14
turns the shadow of d . . . . . Amos 5:8
who shall not taste d . . . . . Matt 16:28
but has passed from d . . . . . John 5:24
he shall never see d . . . . John 8:51
Nevertheless d reigned . . . . . Rom 5:14
as sin reigned in d . . . . Rom 5:21
D no longer has . . . . Rom 6:9
the wages of sin is d . . . . . . Rom 6:23
to bear fruit to d . . . . Rom 7:5
proclaim the Lord's d . . . . 1 Cor 11:26
since by man came d . . . . . 1 Cor 15:21
D is swallowed up in . . . . . 1 Cor 15:54
The sting of d is sin . . . . . . 1 Cor 15:56
we are the aroma of d . . . . . 2 Cor 2:16
d is working in us . . . . 2 Cor 4:12
the world produces d . . . . . . 2 Cor 7:10
to the point of d . . . . Phil 2:8
d crowned with glory . . . . Heb 2:9
who had the power of d . . . Heb 2:14
that he did not see d . . . . Heb 11:5
brings forth d . . . . James 1:15
to God, being put to d . . . . 1 Pet 3:18
is sin leading to d . . . . 1 John 5:16
Be faithful until d . . . . Rev 2:10
Over such the second d . . . . Rev 20:6
shall be no more d . . . . Rev 21:4
which is the second d . . . . . . Rev 21:8

DEBATE
D your case with your . . . . . Prov 25:9
you fast for strife and d . . . . . . Is 58:4

DEBIR
City of Judah; captured by Joshua, Josh
   10:38, 39
Recaptured by Othniel; formerly called
   Kirjath Sepher, Josh 15:15–17; Judg
   1:11–13

DEBORAH
A prophetess and judge, Judg 4:4–14
Composed song of triumph, Judg
   5:1–31

DEBT
everyone who was in d . . . 1 Sam 22:2
sell the oil and pay your d . . 2 Kin 4:7
the exacting of every d . . . . Neh 10:31
and forgave him the d . . . . Matt 18:27
counted as grace but as d . . . Rom 4:4

DEBTOR
I am a d both to . . . . Rom 1:14
that he is a d to keep . . . . Gal 5:3

DEBTORS
as we forgive our d . . . . Matt 6:12
of his master's d . . . . Luke 16:5
brethren, we are d . . . . Rom 8:12
and they are their d . . . . Rom 15:27

DEBTS
forgive us our d, as we . . . . . Matt 6:12

DECAPOLIS
Multitudes from follow Jesus, Matt
   4:25
Jesus heals demon-possessed,
   preaches in, Mark 5:20

DECEIT
spirit there is no d . . . . Ps 32:2
from speaking d . . . . Ps 34:13
d shall not dwell . . . . Ps 101:7
D is in the heart of . . . . . . Prov 12:20
Nor was any d in His . . . . Is 53:9
They hold fast to d . . . . Jer 8:5
in whom is no d . . . . John 1:47
"O full of all d . . . . Acts 13:10
philosophy and empty d . . . . . Col 2:8
no sin, nor was d . . . . 1 Pet 2:22
mouth was found no d . . . . . Rev 14:5

DECEITFUL
deliver me from the d . . . . Ps 43:1

d men shall not . . . . Ps 55:23
of the wicked are d . . . . Prov 12:5
of an enemy are d . . . . Prov 27:6
"The heart is d . . . . Jer 17:9
are false apostles, d . . . . . 2 Cor 11:13

DECEITFULLY
an idol, nor sworn d . . . . Ps 24:4
the word of God d . . . . 2 Cor 4:2

DECEITFULNESS
this world and the d . . . . . Matt 13:22
hardened through the d . . . . Heb 3:13

DECEIVE
'Do not d yourselves . . . . . . Jer 37:9
rise up and d many . . . . . . Matt 24:11
signs and wonders to d . . . Matt 24:24
Let no one d himself . . . . . 1 Cor 3:18
Let no one d you with . . . . . . Eph 5:6
we have no sin, we d . . . . . 1 John 1:8
children, let no one d you . . 1 John 3:7
go out to d the nations . . . . . Rev 20:8

DECEIVED
"The serpent d . . . . Gen 3:13
Why then have you d me . . Gen 29:25
Why have you d us . . . . Josh 9:22
d heart has turned him . . . . . Is 44:20
heed that you not be d . . . Luke 21:8
Are you also d . . . . John 7:47
by the commandment, d . . . Rom 7:11
Do not be d . . . . 1 Cor 6:9
as the serpent d . . . . 2 Cor 11:3
Do not be d, God is not . . . . Gal 6:7
but the woman being d . . . 1 Tim 2:14
deceiving and being d . . . . 2 Tim 3:13
Do not be d, my beloved . James 1:16
all the nations were d . . . . . Rev 18:23
who d them . . . . Rev 20:10

DECEIVER
"But cursed be the d . . . . . . Mal 1:14
how that d said . . . . Matt 27:63
This is a d and an . . . . 2 John 7

DECEIVES
heed that no one d . . . . . . Matt 24:4
d his own heart . . . . James 1:26
Satan, who d the whole . . . . Rev 12:9

DECEIVING
giving heed to d spirits . . . . 1 Tim 4:1
and worse, d and being . . 2 Tim 3:13
hearers only, d . . . . James 1:22

DECENTLY
all things be done d . . . . . 1 Cor 14:40

DECEPTION
d all the day long . . . . Ps 38:12

DECEPTIVE
you with d words . . . . 2 Pet 2:3

DECISION
but its every d . . . . Prov 16:33
in the valley of d . . . . Joel 3:14

DECLARE
D His glory among the . . . 1 Chr 16:24
I will d the decree . . . . Ps 2:7
The heavens d the . . . . Ps 19:1
d Your name to My . . . . Ps 22:22
d what He had done . . . . . . Ps 66:16
d that the LORD is . . . . Ps 92:15
d His generation . . . . Is 53:8
what is Mine and d it to . . John 16:14
who will d His generation . . Acts 8:33
we d to you glad tidings . . . Acts 13:32
"I will d Your name . . . . Heb 2:12
seen and heard we d . . . . . 1 John 1:3

DECLARED
the Father, He has d . . . . . . John 1:18
and d to be the Son of . . . . . Rom 1:4

DECREE
King Cyrus issued a d to . . . Ezra 5:13
Moreover I issue a d as to . . Ezra 6:8
let a royal d go out from . . . . Esth 1:19

let a *d* be written that they .. Esth 3:9
"I will declare the *d* .... Ps 2:7
d which shall not pass ...... Ps 148:6
Woe to those who *d* .... Is 10:1
by a perpetual *d* .... Jer 5:22
is by the *d* of the watchers . . Dan 4:17
Nineveh by the *d* of the .... Jon 3:7
in those days that a *d* ...... Luke 2:1

DEDICATED
house and has not *d* ...... Deut 20:5
every *d* thing in .... Ezek 44:29
first covenant was *d* .... Heb 9:18

DEDICATION
sacrifices at the *d* .... Ezra 6:17
it was the Feast of *D* ..... John 10:22

DEED
What *d* is this you have .. . Gen 44:15
d has been done .... Judg 19:30
So I took the purchase *d*, .. . Jer 32:11
you do a charitable *d* ...... Matt 6:2
a Prophet mighty in *d* .... Luke 24:19
you do in word or *d* .... Col 3:17
us from every lawless *d*.... Titus 2:14
your good *d* might not ..... Philem 14
or in tongue, but in *d* ..... 1 John 3:18

DEEDS
works and Your mighty *d* . . Deut 3:24
make known His *d* .... 1 Chr 16:8
Declare His *d* among .... Ps 9:11
them according to their *d* ..... Ps 28:4
d You did in their days, ... Ps 44:1
awesome in *d* in righteousness . . Ps 65:5
vengeance on their *d* .... Ps 99:8
Make known His *d* .... Ps 105:1
harlot by their own *d* ..... Ps 106:39
against the *d* of the wicked .. Ps 141:5
man according to his *d* .... Prov 24:12
declare His *d* among .... Is 12:4
they surpass the *d* .... Jer 5:28
their *d* on their own head .. Ezek 9:10
charitable *d* before men .... Matt 6:1
the *d* of your fathers ..... Luke 11:48
because their *d* .... John 3:19
You do the *d* of your ...... John 8:41
mighty in words and *d* .... Acts 7:22
one according to his *d* .... Rom 2:6
apart from the *d* of the law . Rom 3:28
you put to death the *d* ..... Rom 8:13
off the old man with his *d* .. . Col 3:9
shares in his evil *d* .... 2 John 11
that you hate the *d* of the .... Rev 2:6
did not repent of their *d*.... Rev 16:11

DEEP
LORD God caused a *d* ...... Gen 2:21
He lays up the *d* .... Ps 33:7
D calls unto *d* .... Ps 42:7
In His hand are the *d* .... Ps 95:4
His wonders in the *d* ..... Ps 107:24
put out in *d* darkness ..... Prov 20:20
led them through the *d* ..... Is 63:13
d closed around me .... Jon 2:5
d uttered its voice .... Hab 3:10
"Launch out into the *d* .... Luke 5:4
I have been in the *d* ..... 2 Cor 11:25

DEEPER
D than Sheol .... Job 11:8

DEEPLY
Drink, yes, drink *d* .... Song 5:1
But He sighed *d* .... Mark 8:12

DEER
"Naphtali is a *d* .... Gen 49:21
my feet like the feet of *d* .. Ps 18:33
As the *d* pants for the .... Ps 42:1
shall leap like a *d* .... Is 35:6

DEER'S
will make my feet like *d* ... Hab 3:19

DEFEATED
and Israel was *d* .... 1 Sam 4:10

DEFECT
who has any *d* .... Lev 21:17

DEFEND
'For I will *d* this .... 2 Kin 19:34
d my own ways before ..... Job 13:15
for joy, because You *d* ...... Ps 5:11
of the God of Jacob *d* you ... Ps 20:1
D the poor and .... Ps 82:3
d the fatherless .... Is 1:17
of hosts *d* Jerusalem .... Is 31:5
The LORD of hosts will *d* ... Zech 9:15

DEFENDER
a *d* of widows .... Ps 68:5

DEFENSE
For wisdom is a *d* .... Eccl 7:12
d will be the fortress .... Is 33:16
am appointed for the *d* .... Phil 1:17
d no one stood with me ... 2 Tim 4:16
be ready to give a *d* ...... 1 Pet 3:15

DEFERRED
Hope *d* makes the heart ... Prov 13:12

DEFILE
the heart, and they *d* ..... Matt 15:18
also these dreamers *d* .... Jude 8

DEFILED
had *d* Dinah his daughter ... Gen 34:5
d the dwelling place .... Ps 74:7
For your hands are *d* .... Is 59:3
lest they should be *d* ..... John 18:28
and has *d* this holy place ... Acts 21:28
being weak, is *d* .... 1 Cor 8:7
and conscience are *d* ..... Titus 1:15
even the garment *d* .... Jude 23
have not *d* their garments .... Rev 3:4

DEFILES
mouth, this *d* a man ...... Matt 15:11
d the temple of God .... 1 Cor 3:17
it anything that *d* .... Rev 21:27

DEFRAUD
d his brother in this ...... 1 Thess 4:6

DEGENERATE
before Me into the *d* .... Jer 2:21
d is your heart .... Ezek 16:30

DEGREES
go forward ten *d* .... 2 Kin 20:9

DELAIAH
Son of Shemaiah; urges Jehoiakim not
to burn Jeremiah's scroll, Jer 36:12,
25

DELICACIES
let me eat of their *d* .... Ps 141:4
Do not desire his *d* .... Prov 23:3
of the king's *d* .... Dan 1:5

DELICATE
Leah's eyes were *d*, but .... Gen 29:17
be called tender and *d* .... Is 47:1
a lovely and *d* woman .... Jer 6:2

DELIGHT
the LORD as great *d* ..... 1 Sam 15:22
And his heart took *d* .... 2 Chr 17:6
your *d* in the Almighty ..... Job 22:26
Will he *d* himself in .... Job 27:10
But his *d* is in the .... Ps 1:2
ones, in whom is all my *d* .... Ps 16:3
D yourself also in the .... Ps 37:4
I *d* to do Your will .... Ps 40:8
You do not *d* in burnt ...... Ps 51:16
They *d* in lies .... Ps 62:4
the peoples who *d* in war ..... Ps 68:30
I will *d* myself in Your ..... Ps 119:16
commandments, For I *d* ... Ps 119:35
For Your law is my *d* ..... Ps 119:77
Your law had been my *d* .... Ps 119:92
And Your law is my *d* .... Ps 119:174
does not *d* in the strength .. Ps 147:10
For scorners *d* in their ..... Prov 1:22
d in the perversity of the ... Prov 2:14

d ourselves with love ...... Prov 7:18
And I was daily His *d* ...... Prov 8:30
but a just weight is His *d* ... Prov 11:1
truthfully are His *d* ...... Prov 12:22
will give *d* to your soul .... Prov 29:17
in his shade with great *d* ... Song 2:3
His *d* is in the fear of the ..... Is 11:3
gold, they will not *d* in it ..... Is 13:17
And let your soul *d* .... Is 55:2
call the Sabbath a *d* .... Is 58:13
that in which I do not *d* .... Is 65:12
For in these I *d*," says the ... Jer 9:24
eyes, the *d* of your soul ... Ezek 24:21
For I *d* in the law of .... Rom 7:22
taking *d* in false humility .... Col 2:18

DELIGHTED
The LORD *d* only in ...... Deut 10:15
d greatly in David .... 1 Sam 19:1
because He *d* in me .... 2 Sam 22:20
who *d* in you, setting you ...2 Chr 9:8
me because He *d* in me ..... Ps 18:19

DELIGHTS
whom the king *d* to honor ... Esth 6:6
Him, since He *d* in ...... Ps 22:8
the LORD, and He *d* in his... Ps 37:23
the son in whom he *d* ...... Prov 3:12
O love, with your *d* .... Song 7:6
For the LORD *d* in you...... Is 62:4
forever, because He *d* ...... Mic 7:18

DELILAH
Deceives Samson, Judg 16:4–22

DELIVER
d them out of the hand .... Ex 3:8
will *d* him into your hand' ... Judg 4:7
The LORD will *d* us ...... 2 Kin 18:32
He shall *d* you in six .... Job 5:19
is no one who can *d* .... Job 10:7
'D him from going down ... Job 33:24
Let Him *d* Him .... Ps 22:8
d their soul from .... Ps 33:19
I will *d* him and honor ..... Ps 91:15
d you from the immoral ... Prov 2:16
wickedness will not *d* ...... Eccl 8:8
have I no power to *d* .... Is 50:2
we serve is able to *d* .... Dan 3:17
into temptation, but *d* ..... Matt 6:13
let Him *d* Him now if .... Matt 27:43
d such a one to Satan ...... 1 Cor 5:5
And the Lord will *d* ...... 2 Tim 4:18
d the godly out of .... 2 Pet 2:9

DELIVERANCE
d He gives to His king ...... Ps 18:50
but *d* is of the LORD...... Prov 21:31
not accepting *d* .... Heb 11:35

DELIVERED
d the poor who cried ...... Job 29:12
for You have *d* my soul .... Ps 56:13
For He has *d* the life ...... Jer 20:13
All things have been *d* .... Matt 11:27
who was *d* up because ..... Rom 4:25
But now we have been *d* ... Rom 7:6
who *d* us from so great ....2 Cor 1:10
was once for all *d* .... Jude 3

DELIVERER
the LORD raised up a *d* ..... Judg 3:9
LORD raised up a *d* for ..... Judg 3:15
my fortress and my *d* .... 2 Sam 22:2
LORD gave Israel a *d*...... 2 Kin 13:5
You are my help and my *d* .. Ps 40:17
My high tower and my *d* ... Ps 144:2
d by the hand of the Angel . Acts 7:35
D will come out of .... Rom 11:26

DELIVERERS
d who saved them .... Neh 9:27

DELIVERS
d the kingdom to God .... 1 Cor 15:24
even Jesus who *d* ....1 Thess 1:10

DELUSION
send them strong *d* ......2 Thess 2:11

DEMAS
Follows Paul, Col 4:14
Forsakes Paul, 2 Tim 4:10

DEMETRIUS
A silversmith at Ephesus, Acts
19:24–31
—— A good Christian, 3 John 12

DEMON
when the *d* was cast out ....Matt 9:33
they say, 'He has a *d* ...Matt 11:18
Jesus rebuked the *d*.......Matt 17:18
the *d* out of her daughter ..Mark 7:26
a spirit of an unclean *d* ....Luke 4:33
you say, 'He has a *d*.......Luke 7:33
was driven by the *d* into ...Luke 8:29
d threw him down and ....Luke 9:42
He was casting out a *d* ...Luke 11:14
You have a *d*.............John 7:20
and have a *d*.............John 8:48
He has a *d* and is mad ...John 10:20

DEMON-POSSESSED
and those who were *d*......Matt 4:24
to Him many who were *d* ..Matt 8:16
there met Him two *d* men..Matt 8:28
Him a man, mute and *d* ...Matt 9:32
to Him who was *d*.......Matt 12:22
daughter is severely ....Matt 15:22
and those who were *d*......Mark 1:32
one who had been *d*......Mark 5:15
had been *d* was healed ....Luke 8:36

DEMONIC
is earthly, sensual, *d* .....James 3:15

DEMONS
See CAST OUT DEMONS; CASTING OUT
DEMONS
They sacrificed to *d*.......Deut 32:17
their daughters to *d*........Ps 106:37
cast out *d* in Your name ....Matt 7:22
d begged Him, saying....Matt 8:31
He casts out *d* ....Matt 9:34
raise the dead, cast out *d* ...Matt 10:8
except by Beelzebub ......Matt 12:24
and cast out many *d* ......Mark 1:34
and to cast out *d* ....Mark 3:15
d begged Him, saying......Mark 5:12
they cast out many *d* ......Mark 6:13
out *d* in Your name ....Mark 9:38
He had cast seven *d*......Mark 16:9
name they will cast out *d* .Mark 16:17
And *d* also came out of ...Luke 4:41
whom had come seven *d* ....Luke 8:2
many *d* had entered ....Luke 8:30
authority over all *d* ....Luke 9:1
casting out *d* in Your ......Luke 9:49
the *d* are subject.........Luke 10:17
casts out *d* by Beelzebub .Luke 11:15
fox, 'Behold, I cast out *d* ..Luke 13:32
Lord and the cup of *d* ....1 Cor 10:21
spirits and doctrines of *d* ...1 Tim 4:1
Even the *d* believe.......James 2:19
they should not worship *d* ..Rev 9:20
For they are spirits of *d* ....Rev 16:14
a dwelling place of *d* ......Rev 18:2

DEMONSTRATE
faith, to *d* His ....Rom 3:25

DEMONSTRATES
d His own love toward ......Rom 5:8

DEMONSTRATION
but in *d* of the Spirit and ...1 Cor 2:4

DEN
in the viper's *d* ....Is 11:8
by My name, become a *d* ....Jer 7:11
cast him into the *d* ....Dan 6:16
it a '*d* of thieves ....Matt 21:13

DENARIUS
the laborers for a *d* ....Matt 20:2
they brought Him a *d* ....Matt 22:19
quart of wheat for a *d* .....Rev 6:6

DENIED
before men will be *d* ....Luke 12:9
Peter then *d* again ....John 18:27
d the Holy One and the ....Acts 3:14
things cannot be *d* ....Acts 19:36
household, he has *d* ....1 Tim 5:8
word, and have not *d* ....Rev 3:8

DENIES
But whoever *d* Me ....Matt 10:33
d that Jesus is the ....1 John 2:22

DENS
lie down in their *d* ....Ps 104:22
and mountains, in *d* ......Heb 11:38

DENY
lest you *d* your God ......Josh 24:27
place, then it will *d* him .....Job 8:18
lest I be full and *d* ....Prov 30:9
him I will also *d* before ...Matt 10:33
let him *d* himself ....Matt 16:24
will *d* Me three times .....Matt 26:34
who *d* that there is a .....Luke 20:27
confessed, and did not *d* ...John 1:20
He cannot *d* Himself ......2 Tim 2:13
in works they *d* ....Titus 1:16
d the only Lord ....Jude 4
d My faith even ....Rev 2:13

DENYING
but *d* its power ....2 Tim 3:5
d ungodliness and.........Titus 2:12
d the Lord who bought ......2 Pet 2:1

DEPART
scepter shall not *d* ....Gen 49:10
they say to God, '*D* ....Job 21:14
D from evil and do good ....Ps 34:14
fear the Lord and *d*.........Prov 3:7
the mountains, shall *d* ......Is 54:10
on the left hand, '*D* ......Matt 25:41
will *d* from the faith ....1 Tim 4:1

DEPARTED
the day that you *d* ....Deut 9:7

DEPARTING
heart of unbelief in *d* ......Heb 3:12

DEPARTS
His spirit *d*, he returns to ....Ps 146:4
But if the unbeliever *d* .....1 Cor 7:15

DEPARTURE
d savage wolves will ......Acts 20:29
and the time of my *d* ....2 Tim 4:6

DEPRESSION
of man causes *d* ....Prov 12:25

DEPRIVE
d myself of good ....Eccl 4:8
d one another except ....1 Cor 7:5

DEPRIVED
like a bear *d* of her cubs ....Hos 13:8

DEPTH
because they had no *d* .....Matt 13:5
nor height nor *d* ....Rom 8:39
Oh, the *d* of the ....Rom 11:33
width and length and *d* ....Eph 3:18

DEPTHS
d have covered them.........Ex 15:5
The *d* also trembled ....Ps 77:16
my soul from the *d* ....Ps 86:13
led them through the *d* .....Ps 106:9
go down again to the *d* ....Ps 107:26
d I was brought forth ....Prov 8:24
our sins into the *d* ....Mic 7:19
have not known the *d* ....Rev 2:24

DERANGED
the nations are *d* ....Jer 51:7

DERBE
Paul visits, Acts 14:6, 20
Paul meets Timothy at, Acts 16:1

DERISION
shall hold them in *d* ....Ps 2:4

I am in *d* daily ....Jer 20:7

DESCEND
His glory shall not *d* ....Ps 49:17
d now from the cross ....Mark 15:32
Lord Himself will *d* ......1 Thess 4:16
This wisdom does not *d* ..James 3:15

DESCENDANTS
All you *d* of Jacob ....Ps 22:23
d shall inherit the ....Ps 25:13
pour My Spirit on your *d* .....Is 44:3
In the Lord all the *d*........Is 45:25
none of his *d* shall prosper ..Jer 22:30
"We are Abraham's *d* ....John 8:33
So shall your *d* be ....Rom 4:18

DESCENDED
because the Lord *d*.........Ex 19:18
that He also first *d* ....Eph 4:9
He who *d* is also the ....Eph 4:10

DESCENDING
were ascending and *d* ....Gen 28:12
"I saw the Spirit *d*........John 1:32
God ascending and *d* .....John 1:51
the holy Jerusalem, *d* .....Rev 21:10

DESERT
And tested God in the *d* ....Ps 106:14
d shall rejoice and blossom ...Is 35:1
and rivers in the *d* ....Is 43:19
her *d* like the garden of ....Is 51:3
'Look, He is in the *d* .....Matt 24:26
ate the manna in the *d* ....John 6:31

DESERTED
d place by Himself ....Matt 14:13

DESERTS
led them through the *d* .....Is 48:21
They wandered in *d* ......Heb 11:38

DESERVE
to them what they *d* ....Ps 28:4
d I will judge them ....Ezek 7:27

DESIGN
with an artistic *d* ....Ex 26:31
may keep its whole *d* .....Ezek 43:11

DESIRABLE
the eyes, and a tree *d* ....Gen 3:6
d that we should leave ......Acts 6:2

DESIRE
d shall be for your ....Gen 3:16
and you shall not *d* your ....Deut 5:21
is all the *d* of Israel .....1 Sam 9:20
salvation and all my *d* ....2 Sam 23:5
I *d* to reason with God ......Job 13:3
for we do not *d* ....Job 21:14
boasts of his heart's *d* ......Ps 10:3
heard the *d* of the humble ...Ps 10:17
him his heart's *d* ....Ps 21:2
and offering You did not *d* ...Ps 40:6
Behold, You *d* truth in ......Ps 51:6
confused Who *d* my hurt .....Ps 70:2
upon earth that I *d* ....Ps 73:25
the *d* of the wicked ....Ps 112:10
and satisfy the *d* ....Ps 145:16
all the things you may *d* ....Prov 3:15
all the things one may *d* ....Prov 8:11
d of the righteous will ....Prov 10:24
The *d* of the righteous is ..Prov 11:23
The *d* of the lazy ....Prov 21:25
nor *d* to be with them .....Prov 24:1
a burden, and *d* fails ......Eccl 12:5
and his *d* is toward me ....Song 7:10
the *d* of our soul is ....Is 26:8
beauty that we should *d* .....Is 53:2
the *d* of their eyes, and ...Ezek 24:25
For I *d* mercy and not ....Hos 6:6
great man utters his evil *d* ...Mic 7:3
d mercy and not sacrifice ..Matt 9:13
d I have desired ....Luke 22:15
"Father, I *d* that ....John 17:24
all manner of evil *d* ....Rom 7:8
Brethren, my heart's *d* ...Rom 10:1

d the best gifts . . . . 1 Cor 12:31
d spiritual gifts . . . . 1 Cor 14:1
was a readiness to *d* . . . . . . 2 Cor 8:11
the two, having a *d* . . . . Phil 1:23
passion, evil *d* . . . . Col 3:5
offering You did not *d* . . . . . Heb 10:5
But now they *d* a better . . . . Heb 11:16
d has conceived . . . . James 1:15
angels to look into . . . . 1 Pet 1:12
d the pure milk of the . . . . 1 Pet 2:2

DESIRED
d are they than gold . . . . Ps 19:10
One thing I have *d* . . . . Ps 27:4
guides them to their *d* . . . . . Ps 107:30
What is *d* in a man is . . . . . Prov 19:22
Whatever my eyes *d* . . . . Eccl 2:10
desire I have *d* . . . . Luke 22:15

DESIRES
all that your heart *d* . . . . . . 2 Sam 3:21
Who is the man who *d* . . . . . . Ps 34:12
shall give you the *d* . . . . Ps 37:4
the *d* of the wicked . . . . Ps 140:8
soul of a lazy man *d* . . . . . . Prov 13:4
for himself of all he *d* . . . . . . Eccl 6:2
d to come after Me . . . . . . Matt 16:24
d to become great . . . . Matt 20:26
the *d* for other things . . Mark 4:19
wine, immediately *d* new . . Luke 5:39
the devil, and the *d* . . . . John 8:44
with its passions and *d* . . . . . Gal 5:24
fulfilling the *d* of the flesh . . . Eph 2:3
If a man *d* the position . . . . . 1 Tim 3:1
according to their own *d* . . 2 Tim 4:3
away by his own *d* . . . . . . James 1:14
not come from your *d* . . . . James 4:1
Whoever *d*, let him take . . . Rev 22:17

DESIRING
earnestly *d* to be clothed . . . 2 Cor 5:2
d to be teachers of the . . . . 1 Tim 1:7
in all things *d* to live . . . . . . Heb 13:18

DESOLATE
on me, for I am *d* . . . . Ps 25:16
the wilderness in a *d* . . . . Ps 107:4
my children and am *d* . . . . . . Is 49:21
any more be termed *D* . . . . . . Is 62:4
to make your land *d* . . . . Jer 4:7
house is left to you *d* . . . . Matt 23:38
one hour she is made *d* . . . Rev 18:19

DESOLATION
the 'abomination of *d* . . . . Matt 24:15
then know that its *d* . . . . . Luke 21:20

DESOLATIONS
Lord, who has made *d* . . . . . . Ps 46:8

DESPAIRED
turned my heart and *d* . . . . Eccl 2:20
strength, so that we *d* . . . . 2 Cor 1:8

DESPERATELY
he flees *d* from its . . . . Job 27:22

DESPISE
if you *d* My statutes . . . . . . Lev 26:15
d Me shall be lightly . . . . . 1 Sam 2:30
I *d* my life . . . . Job 9:21
but fools *d* wisdom . . . . Prov 1:7
People do not *d* a thief if . . Prov 6:30
d your mother when she . . Prov 23:22
Because you *d* this word . . . . . Is 30:12
d your feast days . . . . Amos 5:21
to you priests who *d* . . . . Mal 1:6
one and *d* the other . . . . Matt 6:24
d one of these little ones . . Matt 18:10
d the riches of His . . . . Rom 2:4
d the church of God . . . . . 1 Cor 11:22
Therefore let no one *d* . . . 1 Cor 16:11
Do not *d* prophecies . . . . . 1 Thess 5:20
Let no one *d* your youth . . 1 Tim 4:12
do not *d* the chastening of . . Heb 12:5
and *d* authority . . . . 2 Pet 2:10

DESPISED
mistress became *d* in her . . . Gen 16:4

Esau *d* his birthright . . . . . . Gen 25:34
you have *d* the Lord . . . . . . Num 11:20
she *d* him in her heart . . . . 2 Sam 6:16
men, and *d* by the people . . . . . Ps 22:6
d the counsel of the Most . . Ps 107:11
perverse heart will be *d* . . . . Prov 12:8
poor man's wisdom is *d* . . . . Eccl 9:16
it would be utterly *d* . . . . Song 8:7
d the word of the Holy . . . . Is 5:24
He is *d* and rejected . . . . Is 53:3
have *d* My holy things . . . . . Ezek 22:8
For who has *d* the day of . . Zech 4:10
righteous, and *d* others . . Luke 18:9
the things which are *d* . . . . 1 Cor 1:28

DESPISES
wisdom *d* his neighbor . . . . Prov 11:12
d the word will be . . . . Prov 13:13
d his neighbor sins . . . . Prov 14:21
but a foolish man *d* . . . . . . Prov 15:20
d the scepter of My . . . . . . Ezek 21:10

DESPISING
the cross, *d* the shame . . . . . . Heb 12:2

DESTINED
this Child is *d* for the fall . . Luke 2:34

DESTINY
did not consider her *d* . . . . . . Lam 1:9

DESTITUTE
the prayer of the *d* . . . . Ps 102:17
of corrupt minds and *d* . . . . 1 Tim 6:5
sister is naked and *d* . . . . . James 2:15

DESTROY
d the righteous . . . . Gen 18:23
d all the wicked . . . . Ps 101:8
of the Lord I will *d* . . . . Ps 118:10
the wicked He will *d* . . . . . . Ps 145:20
Why should you *d* . . . . Eccl 7:16
shall not hurt nor *d* . . . . Is 11:9
have mercy, but will *d* . . . . . Jer 13:14
d them with double . . . . Jer 17:18
I did not come to *d* . . . . Matt 5:17
where moth and rust *d* . . . . Matt 6:19
Him who is able to *d* . . . . . Matt 10:28
I am able to *d* the temple . . Matt 26:61
Barabbas and *d* Jesus . . . . Matt 27:20
You who *d* the temple . . . . Matt 27:40
'I will *d* this temple . . . . . . Mark 14:58
to save life or to *d* . . . . Luke 6:9
d men's lives but to . . . . . . Luke 9:56
D this temple, and in . . . . . . John 2:19
and to kill, and to *d* . . . . . . John 10:10
d the work of God for . . . . . Rom 14:20
d the wisdom of the . . . . . . 1 Cor 1:19
God will *d* him . . . . 1 Cor 3:17
foods, but God will *d* . . . . . 1 Cor 6:13
d with the brightness of . . 2 Thess 2:8
able to save and to *d* . . . . . James 4:12
He might *d* the works . . . . . 1 John 3:8

DESTROYED
d all living things . . . . Gen 7:23
d those who hated me . . . 2 Sam 22:41
My people are *d* . . . . Hos 4:6
"O Israel, you are *d* . . . . Hos 13:9
house, this tent, is *d* . . . . . . 2 Cor 5:1

DESTROYER
the paths of the *d* . . . . Ps 17:4
him who is a great *d* . . . . . Prov 18:9
destroyed by the *d* . . . . . . 1 Cor 10:10

DESTRUCTION
not be afraid of *d* . . . . Job 5:21
D has no covering . . . . Job 26:6
d come upon him . . . . Ps 35:8
cast them down to *d* . . . . . . Ps 73:18
You turn man to *d* . . . . Ps 90:3
d that lays waste . . . . Ps 91:6
your life from *d* . . . . Ps 103:4
d will come to the . . . . Prov 10:29
Pride goes before *d* . . . . . . Prov 16:18
d the heart of a man . . . . . Prov 18:12

---

called the City of *D* . . . . Is 19:18
neither wasting nor *d* . . . . Is 60:18
heifer, but *d* comes . . . . Jer 46:20
wrath prepared for *d* . . . . . . Rom 9:22
one to Satan for the *d* . . . . . 1 Cor 5:5
whose end is *d* . . . . Phil 3:19
then sudden *d* . . . . 1 Thess 5:3
with everlasting *d* . . . . 2 Thess 1:9
which drown men in *d* . . . . 1 Tim 6:9
twist to their own . . . . 2 Pet 3:16

DESTRUCTIVE
bring in *d* heresies . . . . 2 Pet 2:1

DETERMINED
Since his days are *d* . . . . Job 14:5
of hosts will make a *d* . . . . . Is 10:23
"Seventy weeks are *d* . . . . Dan 9:24
d their preappointed . . . . Acts 17:26
For I *d* not to know . . . . 1 Cor 2:2

DETESTABLE
shall not eat any *d* . . . . Deut 14:3

DEVICE
there is no work or *d* . . . . . Eccl 9:10

DEVICES
not ignorant of his *d* . . . . . 2 Cor 2:11

DEVIL
See SATAN
Titles of:
 Abaddon, Apollyon, angel of the
  bottomless pit, Rev 9:11
 accuser, Rev 12:10
 adversary, 1 Pet 5:8
 Beelzebub, prince of demons, Matt
  12:24
 Belial, 2 Cor 6:15
 evil one, Matt 6:13; Luke 11:4
 god of this age, 2 Cor 4:4
 murderer, father of lies, John 8:44
 prince of the power of the air, Eph
  2:2
 ruler of darkness, Eph 6:12
 ruler of this world, John 14:30
 Satan, Luke 10:18
 serpent, Gen 3:4
 serpent of Rev 20:2
 wicked one, Matt 13:19
Origin of, in heaven, Is 14:12–20; Rev
 12:7–9
Power and activities of:
 tempted Eve, Gen 3:1
 tempted David, 1 Chr 21:1
 accused and tormented Job, Job 1:6—
  2:10
 opposed Joshua the high priest, Zech
  3:1
 tempted Jesus, Matt 4:1–11; Mark
  3:22–28; Luke 22:31
 entered Judas at betrayal, Luke 22:3;
  John 13:27
 deceives and ensnares, 2 Cor 11:3–15;
  1 Tim 3:6, 7; Rev 20:7, 8
 works in evildoers, Acts 13:8–10; Eph
  2:2
 accuses believers before God, Rev
  12:10
 Believers must resist, 2 Cor 2:10, 11;
  Eph 6:11–16; James 4:7; 1 Pet 5:8, 9;
  1 John 2:13
 His defeat by Christ, Gen 3:15; Rev
  12:10–12; 20:7–10

to be tempted by the *d* . . . . . . Matt 4:1
who sowed them is the *d* . . Matt 13:39
prepared for the *d* . . . . Matt 25:41
forty days by the *d* . . . . Luke 4:2
then the *d* comes and . . . . . . Luke 8:12
and one of you is a *d* . . . . . . John 6:70
of your father the *d* . . . . John 8:44
d having already put . . . . John 13:2
oppressed by the *d* . . . . Acts 10:38
fraud, you son of the *d* . . . . Acts 13:10

give place to the *d* . . . . Eph 4:27
the wiles of the *d* . . . . Eph 6:11
condemnation as the *d* . . . . . 1 Tim 3:6
the snare of the *d* . . . . 2 Tim 2:26
of death, that is, the *d* . . . . . . Heb 2:14
Resist the *d* and he . . . . James 4:7
d walks about like a . . . . 1 Pet 5:8
the works of the *d* . . . . 1 John 3:8
contending with the *d* . . . . Jude 9
Indeed, the *d* is about . . . . . . Rev 2:10
serpent of old, called the *D* . . Rev 12:9
the *d* has come down to . . . . Rev 12:12
serpent of old, who is the *D* . Rev 20:2
d, who deceived them . . . . . . Rev 20:10

DEVIOUS
crooked, and who are *d* . . . . Prov 2:15

DEVISE
Do not *d* evil against . . . . Prov 3:29
Woe to those who *d* . . . . Mic 2:1

DEVISES
d wickedness on his . . . . Ps 36:4
he *d* evil continually . . . . Prov 6:14
d wicked plans to . . . . Is 32:7
But a generous man *d* . . . . Is 32:8

DEVOID
He who is *d* of wisdom . . . . Prov 11:12

DEVOTE
d rashly something as . . . . Prov 20:25

DEVOTED
d offering is most . . . . Lev 27:28
"Every *d* thing in . . . . Num 18:14
Your servant, who is *d* . . . . Ps 119:38

DEVOUR
A fire shall *d* before . . . . Ps 50:3
For you *d* widows' . . . . Matt 23:14
bite and *d* one another . . . . . . Gal 5:15
seeking whom he may *d* . . . . 1 Pet 5:8
d her Child as . . . . Rev 12:4

DEVOURED
Some wild beast has *d* . . . . Gen 37:20
rebel, you shall be *d* . . . . Is 1:20
the curse has *d* . . . . Is 24:6
Your sword has *d* . . . . Jer 2:30
For shame has *d* . . . . Jer 3:24
have *d* their judges . . . . Hos 7:7
trees, the locust *d* . . . . Amos 4:9
birds came and *d* them . . . . Matt 13:4
of heaven and *d* them . . . . . . Rev 20:9

DEVOURER
I will rebuke the *d* . . . . Mal 3:11

DEVOURING
You love all *d* words . . . . Ps 52:4
the flame of *d* fire . . . . Is 29:6

DEVOUT
man was just and *d* . . . . Luke 2:25
d men carried Stephen . . . . . . Acts 8:2
d soldier from among . . . . . . Acts 10:7
d proselytes followed Paul . Acts 13:43

DEW
God give you of the *d* . . . . . Gen 27:28
shall also drop *d* . . . . Deut 33:28
have the *d* of Your youth . . . . Ps 110:3
his favor is like a *d* . . . . Prov 19:12
a cloud of *d* in the heat . . . . . . Is 18:4
your *d* is like the *d* . . . . Is 26:19
like the early *d* . . . . Hos 6:4
many peoples, like *d* . . . . Mic 5:7

DIADEM
LORD, and a royal *d* . . . . Is 62:3

DIADEMS
ten horns, and seven *d* . . . . . Rev 12:3

DIAL
d by which it had gone . . . . Is 38:8

DIAMOND
a sapphire, and a *d* . . . . Ex 28:18
d it is engraved . . . . Jer 17:1

the sardius, topaz, and *d* . . Ezek 28:13

DIANA
Worship of at Ephesus creates uproar,
Acts 19:23–41

DIBON
Amorite town, Num 21:30
Taken by Israel, Num 32:2–5
Destruction of, foretold, Jer 48:18, 22

DICTATES
according to the *d* . . . . Jer 23:17

DIE
it you shall surely *d* . . . . Gen 2:17
you touch it, lest you *d* . . . . . . Gen 3:3
the land of Egypt shall *d* . . . . . Ex 11:5
Where you *d*, I will *d* . . . . . . Ruth 1:17
but a person shall *d* . . . . 2 Chr 25:4
Curse God and *d* . . . . Job 2:9
sees wise men *d* . . . . Ps 49:10
I shall not *d*, but live . . . . . . Ps 118:17
He shall *d* for lack of . . . . . . Prov 5:23
but fools *d* for lack of . . . . . Prov 10:21
hates correction will *d* . . . . Prov 15:10
with a rod, he will not *d* . . . Prov 23:13
who are appointed to *d* . . . . . Prov 31:8
how does a wise man *d* . . . . Eccl 2:16
born, and a time to *d* . . . . Eccl 3:2
why should you *d* . . . . Eccl 7:17
drink, for tomorrow we *d* . . . . Is 22:13
their worm does not *d* . . . . . . Is 66:24
every one shall *d* for his . . . . Jer 31:30
wicked way, he shall *d* . . . . Ezek 3:19
the soul who sins shall *d* . . Ezek 18:4
man, you shall surely *d* . . . Ezek 33:8
"Even if I have to *d* . . . . . . Matt 26:35
their worm does not *d* . . . . Mark 9:44
nor can they *d* . . . . Luke 20:36
eat of it and not *d* . . . . John 6:50
to you that you will *d* . . . . . . John 8:24
though he may *d* . . . . John 11:25
that one man should *d* . . . . John 11:50
that Jesus would *d* . . . . John 11:51
our law He ought to *d* . . . . . John 19:7
righteous man will one *d* . . . . Rom 5:7
the flesh you will *d* . . . . Rom 8:13
if we *d*, we *d* to the Lord . . . Rom 14:8
For as in Adam all *d* . . . . . . 1 Cor 15:22
Jesus our Lord, I *d* daily . 1 Cor 15:31
and to *d* is gain . . . . Phil 1:21
for men to *d* once . . . . Heb 9:27
are the dead who *d* . . . . Rev 14:13

DIED
And all flesh *d* . . . . Gen 7:21
"Oh, that we had *d* . . . . Ex 16:3
himself with fire, and *d* . . 1 Kin 16:18
Hadad *d* also . . . . 1 Chr 1:51
So Saul *d* for his . . . . 1 Chr 10:13
was that the beggar *d* . . . . . Luke 16:22
in due time Christ *d* . . . . Rom 5:6
Christ *d* for us . . . . Rom 5:8
For he who has *d* . . . . Rom 6:7
Now if we *d* with . . . . Rom 6:8
sin revived and I *d* . . . . Rom 7:9
For to this end Christ *d* . . . . . Rom 14:9
perish, for whom Christ *d* . 1 Cor 8:11
that Christ *d* for our sins . . 1 Cor 15:3
that if One *d* for all . . . . 2 Cor 5:14
and He *d* for all . . . . 2 Cor 5:15
through the law *d* . . . . Gal 2:19
if you *d* with Christ from . . . Col 2:20
For you *d*, and your life is . . . . Col 3:3
believe that Jesus *d* . . . . . 1 Thess 4:14
who *d* for us . . . . 1 Thess 5:10
for if we *d* with Him . . . . . . 2 Tim 2:11
These all *d* in faith . . . . Heb 11:13
having *d* to sins . . . . 1 Pet 2:24

DIES
If a man *d*, shall he live . . . . Job 14:14
When a wicked man *d* . . . . . Prov 11:7
into the ground and *d* . . . . . John 12:24
if the husband *d*, she is . . . . . Rom 7:2

and no one *d* to himself . . . . Rom 14:7
made alive unless it *d* . . . . 1 Cor 15:36

DIFFERENCE
the LORD will make a *d* . . . . Ex 9:4
d between the unclean . . . . Ezek 22:26
the *d* between the holy . . . . Ezek 44:23
For there is no *d* . . . . Rom 3:22
were, it makes no *d* to me . . . . Gal 2:6

DIFFERENCES
There are *d* of ministries . . . 1 Cor 12:5

DIFFERENT
he has a *d* spirit in him . . . Num 14:24
with *d* kinds of seed . . . . . . Deut 22:9
each *d* from the other . . . . . . Dan 7:3
d kinds of tongues . . . . 1 Cor 12:10
if you receive a *d* spirit . . . . 2 Cor 11:4
of Christ, to a *d* gospel, ... Gal 1:6

DIFFERING
Having then gifts *d* . . . . Rom 12:6

DIFFERS
for one star *d* from . . . . 1 Cor 15:41

DIFFICULT
d is the way which leads . . . Matt 7:14

DIFFUSED
By what way is light *d* . . . . . Job 38:24

DIFFUSES
us *d* the fragrance . . . . 2 Cor 2:14

DIG
wells which you did not *d* . . . Deut 6:11
Son of man, *d* into the . . . . . . Ezek 8:8
Though they *d* into hell . . . . Amos 9:2
I cannot *d*; I am ashamed . . Luke 16:3

DIGNITARIES
afraid to speak evil of *d* . . . . 2 Pet 2:10
and speak evil of *d* . . . . Jude 8

DILIGENCE
your heart with all *d* . . . . . . Prov 4:23
d is man's precious . . . . Prov 12:27
he who leads, with *d* . . . . . . Rom 12:8
not lagging in *d*, fervent . . Rom 12:11
d it produced in you . . . . . . 2 Cor 7:11
of your love by the *d* . . . . . . 2 Cor 8:8
giving all *d*, add to your . . . . 2 Pet 1:5

DILIGENT
d in sanctifying . . . . 2 Chr 29:34
and my spirit makes *d* . . . . . . Ps 77:6
hand of the *d* makes rich . . . Prov 10:4
of the *d* will rule . . . . Prov 12:24
d shall be made rich . . . . . . Prov 13:4
proved *d* in many things . . . 2 Cor 8:22
d to come to me quickly . . . . 2 Tim 4:9
Let us therefore be *d* . . . . Heb 4:11
be *d* to be found by Him . . . 2 Pet 3:14

DILIGENTLY
if you *d* obey the voice of . . Deut 28:1
seek that will find me . . . . . . Prov 8:17
d followed every good . . . . . 1 Tim 5:10
he sought it *d* with tears . . . Heb 12:17

DIM
His eyes were not *d* . . . . . . Deut 34:7
the windows grow *d* . . . . Eccl 12:3
the gold has become *d* . . . . . . Lam 4:1

DIMINISH
stars *d* their brightness . . . . . Joel 2:10
the lights will *d* . . . . Zech 14:6

DIMLY
we see in a mirror, *d* . . . . . 1 Cor 13:12

DINAH
Daughter of Leah, Gen 30:20, 21
Defiled by Shechem, Gen 34:1–24
Avenged by brothers, Gen 34:25–31

DINE
asked Him to *d* with . . . . . . Luke 11:37
come in to him and *d* . . . . . . Rev 3:20

DINNER
Better is a *d* of herbs . . . . . Prov 15:17

I have prepared my *d* . . . . . Matt 22:4
invites you to *d* . . . . 1 Cor 10:27

DIOTREPHES
Unruly church member, 3 John 9, 10

DIP
d them in the blood . . . . Lev 14:51
d it in the water, ... Num 19:18
let him *d* his foot in oil . . . . Deut 33:24
d your piece of bread . . . . . Ruth 2:14
d the tip of his finger in . . Luke 16:24

DIPPED
d the tunic in the blood . . . . Gen 37:31
d his finger in the . . . . Lev 9:9
d seven times in the . . . . . . 2 Kin 5:14
of bread when I have *d* . . John 13:26
clothed with a robe *d* . . . . . Rev 19:13

DIRECT
the morning I will *d* . . . . Ps 5:3
and He shall *d* your paths . . . Prov 3:6
d their work in truth . . . . Is 61:8
Now may the Lord *d* . . . . . 2 Thess 3:5

DIRT
I cast them out like *d* . . . . Ps 18:42
cast up mire and *d* . . . . Is 57:20

DISAPPEARS
As water *d* from the . . . . . . Job 14:11

DISARMED
d principalities . . . . Col 2:15

DISARMS
and *d* the mighty . . . . Job 12:21

DISASTER
bring *d* on the house . . . . . 1 Kin 14:10
I am fashioning a *d* . . . . Jer 18:11
war and *d* and pestilence . . . . Jer 28:8
D will come upon . . . . Ezek 7:26
you shall see *d* . . . . Zeph 3:15
voyage will end with *d* . . . . Acts 27:10

DISCERN
Can I *d* between the . . . . 2 Sam 19:35
Then you shall again *d* . . . . . Mal 3:18
d the face of the sky . . . . . . Matt 16:3
senses exercised to *d* . . . . . . Heb 5:14

DISCERNED
they are spiritually *d* . . . . . . 1 Cor 2:14

DISCERNER
d of the thoughts . . . . Heb 4:12

DISCERNING
not *d* the Lord's body . . . . 1 Cor 11:29
another *d* of spirits, to . . . . 1 Cor 12:10

DISCERNMENT
and takes away the *d* . . . . . Job 12:20

DISCERNS
a wise man's heart *d* . . . . Eccl 8:5

DISCIPLE
d is not above his . . . . Matt 10:24
in the name of a *d* . . . . Matt 10:42
he cannot be My *d* . . . . . . Luke 14:26
the *d* whom He loved . . . . . John 19:26
d whom Jesus loved . . . . . . John 21:7
the *d* whom Jesus loved . . John 21:20

DISCIPLES
See TWELVE DISCIPLES
but Your *d* do not fast . . . . . Matt 9:14
called His twelve *d* to . . . . . Matt 10:1
d transgress the . . . . Matt 15:2
took the twelve *d* . . . . Matt 20:17
all the *d* forsook Him . . . . . Matt 26:56
make *d* of all the nations, . Matt 28:19
with His *d* to the sea . . . . . . Mark 3:7
called His *d* to Himself . . . . Luke 6:13
His *d* believed in Him . . . . . John 2:11
many of His *d* went back . . John 6:66
My word, you are My *d* . . . John 8:31
to become His *d* . . . . John 9:27
but we are Moses' *d* . . . . . . John 9:28
His *d* did not understand . . John 12:16

know that you are My *d* . . John 13:35
so you will be My *d* . . . . . . John 15:8
Then the *d* were glad . . . . . John 20:20
of the *d* was multiplying, ... Acts 6:1
the *d* were first called . . . . . Acts 11:26
souls of the *d*, exhorting . . . Acts 14:22
strengthening all the *d* . . . . Acts 18:23

DISCIPLES'
began to wash the *d* feet . . . John 13:5

DISCIPLINE
Harsh *d* is for him who . . . Prov 15:10
I *d* my body and bring . . . . . 1 Cor 9:27

DISCIPLINES
but he who loves him *d* . . . Prov 13:24

DISCLOSE
d my dark saying . . . . Ps 49:4

DISCORD
and one who sows *d* . . . . . . Prov 6:19

DISCOURAGE
why will you *d* the heart . . . Num 32:7

DISCOURAGED
do not fear or be *d* . . . . Deut 1:21
will not fail nor be *d* . . . . Is 42:4
lest they become *d* . . . . Col 3:21
you become weary and *d* . . . Heb 12:3
d when you are rebuked . . . . Heb 12:5

DISCREET
d, chaste, homemakers, ... Titus 2:5

DISCRETION
D will preserve you . . . . Prov 2:11
out knowledge and *d* . . . . . . Prov 8:12
woman who lacks *d* . . . . . . Prov 11:22
The *d* of a man makes . . . . Prov 19:11
the heavens at His *d* . . . . . . Jer 10:12

DISEASE
Shall I recover from this *d* . . 2 Kin 8:8
in his *d* he did not seek . . 2 Chr 16:12
all kinds of *d* among the . . Matt 4:23
every *d* among the people . . Matt 9:35
well of whatever *d* he had . . John 5:4

DISEASES
Who heals all your *d*, ... Ps 103:3
afflicted with various *d* . . . . Matt 4:24
various *d* brought them . . . Luke 4:40
all demons, and to cure *d* . . Luke 9:1
d left them and the evil . . . . Acts 19:12

DISFIGURE
nor shall you *d* the edges . . Lev 19:27
d their faces that . . . . Matt 6:16

DISGRACE
plead my *d* against me, ... Job 19:5
do not *d* the throne of . . . . . Jer 14:21

DISGRACEFUL
he had done a *d* thing . . . . . Gen 34:7
done a *d* thing in Israel . . . . Josh 7:15
Do not do this *d* thing . . 2 Sam 13:12

DISGUISES
and he *d* his face . . . . Job 24:15
He who hates, *d* . . . . Prov 26:24

DISHONEST GAIN
turned aside after *d* . . . . 1 Sam 8:3
for the sake of *d* . . . . Titus 1:11
not for *d* but eagerly . . . . . . 1 Pet 5:2

DISHONESTY
Wealth gained by *d* will . . . Prov 13:11

DISHONOR
d who wish me evil . . . . Ps 40:14
with *d* comes reproach . . . . . Prov 18:3
d the pride of all . . . . Is 23:9
Her rulers dearly love *d* . . . . Hos 4:18
My Father, and you *d* Me . . John 8:49
d their bodies among . . . . . . Rom 1:24
and another for *d* . . . . Rom 9:21
long hair, it is a *d* to . . . . . 1 Cor 11:14

It is sown in *d* . . . . 1 Cor 15:43
by honor and *d* . . . . 2 Cor 6:8
honor and some for *d* . . . . . 2 Tim 2:20

DISHONORED
but we are *d* . . . . 1 Cor 4:10
But you have *d* the . . . . James 2:6

DISHONORS
For son of father . . . . Mic 7:6
covered, *d* his head . . . . . . 1 Cor 11:4

DISOBEDIENCE
d many were made . . . . Rom 5:19
works in the sons of *d* . . . . . . Eph 2:2
d received a just . . . . Heb 2:2

DISOBEDIENT
Nevertheless they were *d* . . . Neh 9:26
the *d* to the wisdom of . . . . Luke 1:17
out My hands to a *d* . . . . . Rom 10:21
you were once *d* to God . . . Rom 11:30
d to parents, unthankful, . . . 2 Tim 3:2
d, deceived, serving . . . . Titus 3:3
They stumble, being *d* . . . . . 1 Pet 2:8
who formerly were *d* . . . . . . 1 Pet 3:20

DISORDERLY
for this *d* gathering . . . . Acts 19:40
brother who walks *d* . . . . . 2 Thess 3:6

DISPENSATION
d of the fullness of . . . . Eph 1:10
d of the grace of God . . . . . . Eph 3:2

DISPERSE
d them throughout the . . . . Ezek 20:23

DISPERSION
intend to go to the *D* . . . . . John 7:35
the pilgrims of the *D* . . . . . . 1 Pet 1:1

DISPLEASE
LORD see it, and it *d*. . . . . . Prov 24:18

DISPLEASED
that David had done *d* . . . 2 Sam 11:27
You have been *d* . . . . Ps 60:1
they were greatly *d* . . . . . . Matt 20:24
it, He was greatly *d* . . . . . Mark 10:14

DISPUTE
Now there was also a *d* . . . Luke 22:24

DISPUTED
when he *d* about the body . . . . Jude 9

DISPUTER
Where is the *d* of this . . . . 1 Cor 1:20

DISPUTES
d rather than godly . . . . 1 Tim 1:4
but is obsessed with *d* . . . . . 1 Tim 6:4
foolish and ignorant *d* . . . . 2 Tim 2:23
But avoid foolish *d* . . . . Titus 3:9

DISQUALIFIED
myself should become *d* . . . 1 Cor 9:27
indeed you are *d* . . . . 2 Cor 13:5
though we may seem *d* . . . . 2 Cor 13:7

DISQUIETED
And why are you *d* . . . . Ps 42:5

DISSENSION
had no small *d* and . . . . Acts 15:2
this, a *d* arose between . . . . . Acts 23:7
a creator of *d* among all . . . Acts 24:5

DISSENSIONS
selfish ambitions, *d* . . . . Gal 5:20

DISSIPATION
not accused of *d* . . . . Titus 1:6
in the same flood of *d* . . . . . 1 Pet 4:4

DISSOLVED
of heaven shall be *d* . . . . Is 34:4
the heavens will be *d* . . . . . 2 Pet 3:12

DISTINCTION
and made no *d* . . . . Acts 15:9
For there is no *d* . . . . Rom 10:12
compassion, making a *d* . . . . Jude 22

DISTRACTED
But Martha was *d* with . . . Luke 10:40

DISTRESS
me in the day of my d . . . . . Gen 35:3
When you are in d . . . . Deut 4:30
my life from every d . . . . . . 1 Kin 1:29
you out of dire d . . . . Job 36:16
keep you from d . . . . Job 36:19
d them in His deep . . . . Ps 2:5
on the LORD in d . . . . Ps 118:5
a whirlwind, when d . . . . . . Prov 1:27
and on the earth d . . . . . . Luke 21:25
tribulation, or d . . . . Rom 8:35
of the present d . . . . 1 Cor 7:26

DISTRESSED
was greatly afraid and d . . . . Gen 32:7
Israel was severely d . . . . . . Judg 10:9
David was greatly d . . . . . 1 Sam 30:6
the queen was deeply d . . . . Esth 4:4
heart within me is d . . . . Ps 143:4
not be upon her who is d . . . . . Is 9:1
troubled and deeply d . . . Mark 14:33
and how d I am till it is . . . Luke 12:50

DISTRESSES
bring me out of my d . . . . . . Ps 25:17

DISTRESSING
d spirit from the LORD . . 1 Sam 16:14
Now the d spirit from . . . . 1 Sam 19:9

DISTRIBUTE
that you have and d . . . . . Luke 18:22

DISTRIBUTED
and they d to each as . . . . . . Acts 4:35
But as God has d . . . . 1 Cor 7:17

DISTRIBUTING
d to the needs of the . . . . . Rom 12:13

DITCH
will fall into a d . . . . Matt 15:14

DIVERSE
D weights are an . . . . Prov 20:23

DIVERSITIES
There are d of gifts . . . . 1 Cor 12:4
there are d of activities, . . . 1 Cor 12:6

DIVIDE
D the living child . . . . . . 1 Kin 3:25
d My garments among . . . . . . Ps 22:18
d their tongues . . . . Ps 55:9
d the spoil with the . . . . . . Prov 16:19
d the inheritance . . . . Luke 12:13
"Take this and d . . . . Luke 22:17

DIVIDED
and the waters were d . . . . . Ex 14:21
death they were not d . . . . 2 Sam 1:23
And You d the sea . . . . Neh 9:11
"Who has d a channel . . . . . Job 38:25
shall they ever be d . . . . . Ezek 37:22
kingdom has been d . . . . . . Dan 5:28
your land shall be d . . . . . . Amos 7:17
"Every kingdom d . . . . . . Matt 12:25
and a house d against . . . Luke 11:17
in one house will be d . . . Luke 12:52
So he d to them his . . . . . . Luke 15:12
they d His garments and . Luke 23:34
d My garments among . . . . John 19:24
appeared to them d . . . . Acts 2:3
d them among all . . . . Acts 2:45
Is Christ d? Was Paul . . . . . 1 Cor 1:13
the great city was d . . . . . . Rev 16:19

DIVIDES
at home d the spoil . . . . Ps 68:12

DIVIDING
rightly d the word of . . . . . 2 Tim 2:15

DIVINATION
shall you practice d . . . . . . Lev 19:26
D is on the lips of . . . . . . Prov 16:10
darkness without d . . . . Mic 3:6
a spirit of d met us . . . . . Acts 16:16

DIVINE
futility and who d . . . . . . Ezek 13:9

and her prophets d . . . . Mic 3:11
d service and the . . . . Heb 9:1
d power has given . . . . 2 Pet 1:3

DIVINERS
your prophets, your d . . . . . Jer 27:9

DIVISION
So there was a d . . . . John 7:43
piercing even to the d . . . . Heb 4:12

DIVISIONS
note those who cause d . . . Rom 16:17
and that there be no d . . . . 1 Cor 1:10
envy, strife, and d . . . . 1 Cor 3:3
hear that there are d . . . . . 1 Cor 11:18
persons, who cause d . . . . . . Jude 19

DIVISIVE
Reject a d man after . . . . . . Titus 3:10

DIVORCE
cannot d her all his days . . Deut 22:19
her a certificate of d . . . . . . Deut 24:1
of your mother's d . . . . Is 50:1
given her a certificate of d . . . Jer 3:8
Israel says that He hates d . . Mal 2:16
give her a certificate of d . . Matt 5:31
to d his wife for just any . . . Matt 19:3
a certificate of d . . . . Mark 10:4
husband is not to d his . . . . 1 Cor 7:11

DIVORCED
d from her husband . . . . Lev 21:7
A widow or a d woman . . . . Lev 21:14
daughter is a widow or d . . Lev 22:13
vow of a widow or a d . . . . Num 30:9
d her must not take her . . . Deut 24:4
a widow or a d woman . . . Ezek 44:22
is d commits adultery . . . . . Matt 5:32
is d from her husband . . . . Luke 16:18

DIVORCES
say, 'If a man d his wife . . . . Jer 3:1
said, 'Whoever d his wife . . Matt 5:31
whoever d his wife . . . . . . Matt 19:9
Whoever d his wife . . . . . . Mark 10:11
Whoever d his wife . . . . . . Luke 16:18

DO
set in them to d evil . . . . . . Eccl 8:11
I will also d it . . . . Is 46:11
men to d to you, d . . . . Matt 7:12
d this and you will . . . . . Luke 10:28
He sees the Father d . . . . . John 5:19
without Me you can d . . . . . John 15:5
"Sirs, what must I d . . . . . . Acts 16:30
d evil that good may . . . . . . Rom 3:8
For what I will to d . . . . . . Rom 7:15
good that I will to d . . . . . . Rom 7:19
or whatever you d, d . . . . 1 Cor 10:31
d all things through . . . . . . Phil 4:13
d in word or deed, d . . . . . . Col 3:17
d good and to share . . . . . Heb 13:16
and d this or that . . . . James 4:15

DO NOT BE AFRAID
vision, saying, "D, Abram . . Gen 15:1
said to the people, "D . . . . . Ex 14:13
d, and do not tremble . . . . Deut 20:3
Lord said to Joshua, "D . . . Josh 11:6
d of him." So he arose . . . . 2 Kin 1:15
D of the words . . . . 2 Kin 19:6
D of sudden terror, ... Prov 3:25
D of their faces, for . . . . Jer 1:8
"D to serve the Chaldeans . . . Jer 40:9
And you, son of man, ... Ezek 2:6
D, you beasts of the . . . . . . Joel 2:22
"Joseph, son of David, d . . . Matt 1:20
It is I; d . . . . Matt 14:27
"Arise, and d . . . . Matt 17:7
said to the women, "D . . . . Matt 28:5
of the synagogue, "D . . . . Mark 5:36
angel said to him, "D . . . . . Luke 1:13
"D, Mary, for you have . . . . Luke 1:30
angel said to them, "D . . . . Luke 2:10
Jesus said to Simon, "D . . . . Luke 5:10

d of those who kill the . . . . Luke 12:4
"D, but speak . . . . Acts 18:9
"D, Paul; you must . . . . . . Acts 27:24
saying to me, "D . . . . Rev 1:17

DO NOT FEAR
d, for I am with you. . . . . . Gen 26:24
d to go down to Egypt, ... Gen 46:3
D; for God has come . . . . . . Ex 20:20
d or be discouraged . . . . . . Deut 1:21
d the gods of the . . . . Judg 6:10
d, you shall not die . . . . . . Judg 6:23
D. You have done all . . . . 1 Sam 12:20
D, for I will surely . . . . 1 Sam 9:7
Elijah said to her, "D: . . . 1 Kin 17:13
D, for those who are with . 2 Kin 6:16
d or be fainthearted . . . . Is 7:4
fearful-hearted, "Be strong, d . Is 35:4
d the reproach of men, ... Is 51:7
d, O My servant Jacob,' . . . . Jer 30:10
said to me, "D, Daniel . . . . Dan 10:12
remains among you; d . . . . . Hag 2:5
D, let your hands be . . . . . Zech 8:13
d them. For there is . . . . . Matt 10:26
D therefore; you are of . . . Luke 12:7
D any of those things . . . . . Rev 2:10

DOCTRINE
said, 'My d is pure . . . . Job 11:4
for I give you good d . . . . . . Prov 4:2
idol is a worthless d . . . . . . Jer 10:8
of bread, but of the d . . . . Matt 16:12
What new d is this . . . . . . Mark 1:27
"My d is not Mine . . . . . . John 7:16
Jerusalem with your d . . . . Acts 5:28
heart that form of d . . . . . . Rom 6:17
with every wind of d . . . . . Eph 4:14
is contrary to sound d . . . . 1 Tim 1:10
followed my d . . . . 2 Tim 3:10
is profitable for d . . . . 2 Tim 3:16
not endure sound d . . . . . . 2 Tim 4:3
in d showing integrity . . . . . Titus 2:7
they may adorn the d . . . . Titus 2:10
not abide in the d . . . . 2 John 9

DOCTRINES
the commandments and d . . . Col 2:22
spirits and d of demons . . . 1 Tim 4:1
various and strange d . . . . . Heb 13:9

DOEG
An Edomite; chief of Saul's herdsmen,
1 Sam 21:7
Betrays David, 1 Sam 22:9, 10
Kills 85 priests, 1 Sam 22:18, 19

DOERS
of God, but the d . . . . Rom 2:13
But be d of the word . . . . James 1:22

DOG
to David, "Am I a d . . . . 1 Sam 17:43
they growl like a d . . . . Ps 59:6
d returns to his own . . . . . Prov 26:11
d is better than a . . . . Eccl 9:4
d returns to his own . . . . . 2 Pet 2:22

DOGS
you shall throw it to the d . . . Ex 22:31
The d shall eat whoever . . . 1 Kin 14:11
The d shall eat Jezebel . . . 2 Kin 9:10
Yes, they are greedy d . . . . . . Is 56:11
what is holy to the d . . . . . Matt 7:6
d eat the crumbs which . . . Matt 15:27
Moreover the d came . . . . Luke 16:21
But outside are d . . . . Rev 22:15

DOMINION
let them have d . . . . Gen 1:26
"D and fear belong . . . . Job 25:2
made him to have d . . . . Ps 8:6
let them not have d . . . . Ps 19:13
besides You have had d . . . . Is 26:13
d is an everlasting . . . . Dan 4:34
sin shall not have d . . . . . . Rom 6:14
Not that we have d . . . . . . 2 Cor 1:24
glory and majesty, d . . . . . . Jude 25

DONKEY
d saw the Angel .... Num 22:23
Does the wild *d* .... Job 6:5
d its master's crib .... Is 1:3
and riding on a *d* .... Zech 9:9
colt, the foal of a *d* .... Matt 21:5
He had found a young *d* .. John 12:14
d speaking with a .... 2 Pet 2:16

DONKEY'S
d colt is born a man .... Job 11:12

DONKEYS
d quench their thirst .... Ps 104:11
a chariot of *d* .... Is 21:7
And the wild *d* stood .... Jer 14:6

DOOM
for the day of *d* .... Prov 16:4

DOOR
sin lies at the *d* .... Gen 4:7
keep watch over the *d* ...... Ps 141:3
d turns on its hinges ...... Prov 26:14
stone against the *d* .... Matt 27:60
to you, I am the *d* .... John 10:7
and effective *d* .... 1 Cor 16:9
d was opened to me by ... 2 Cor 2:12
would open to us a *d* .... Col 4:3
is standing at the *d* .... James 5:9
before you an open *d* .... Rev 3:8
I stand at the *d* .... Rev 3:20
and behold, a *d* .... Rev 4:1

DOORKEEPER
I would rather be a *d* .... Ps 84:10
To him the *d* .... John 10:3

DOORPOSTS
write them on the *d* .... Deut 6:9
"Strike them on the *d* .... Amos 9:1

DOORS
up, you everlasting *d* .... Ps 24:7
the entrance of the *d* .... Prov 8:3
when the *d* are shut in ..... Eccl 12:4
who would shut the *d* .... Mal 1:10

DOR
City captured by Joshua and assigned
to Manasseh, Josh 12:23; 17:11; Judg
1:27

DORCAS
Disciple at Joppa, also called Tabitha;
raised to life, Acts 9:36–42

DOTHAN
Ancient town where Joseph was sold,
Gen 37:14–25
Elisha strikes Syrians at, 2 Kin 6:8–23

DOUBLE
Please let a *d* portion of .... 2 Kin 2:9
from the LORD's hand *d* ...... Is 40:2
first I will repay *d* .... Jer 16:18
worthy of *d* honor .... 1 Tim 5:17
and repay her *d* .... Rev 18:6

DOUBLE-MINDED
I hate the *d* .... Ps 119:113
he is a *d* man .... James 1:8
your hearts, you *d* .... James 4:8

DOUBT
life shall hang in *d* .... Deut 28:66
faith, why did you *d* ...... Matt 14:31
does not *d* in his heart ... Mark 11:23
No *d* this man is a .... Acts 28:4

DOUBTING
without wrath and *d* .... 1 Tim 2:8
in faith, with no *d* .... James 1:6

DOUBTS
And why do *d* arise in .... Luke 24:38
for I have *d* about you ...... Gal 4:20
doubting, for he who *d* .... James 1:6

DOUGH
d before it was leavened, ... Ex 12:34

DOVE
d found no resting .... Gen 8:9
I had wings like a *d* .... Ps 55:6

I mourned like a *d* .... Is 38:14
also is like a silly *d* .... Hos 7:11
descending like a *d* .... Matt 3:16

DOVES
and moan sadly like *d* ...... Is 59:11
and harmless as *d* .... Matt 10:16
of those who sold *d* ...... Matt 21:12

DOWNCAST
who comforts the *d* .... 2 Cor 7:6

DRAGNET
gather them in their *d* ..... Hab 1:15
d that was cast .... Matt 13:47

DRAGON
a great, fiery red *d* .... Rev 12:3
fought with the *d* .... Rev 12:7
they worshiped the *d* ...... Rev 13:4
He laid hold of the *d* ...... Rev 20:2

DRAIN
wicked of the earth *d* .... Ps 75:8

DRAINED
all faces are *d* .... Joel 2:6

DRANK
them, and they all *d* ..... Mark 14:23
d with Him after He .... Acts 10:41
d the same spiritual .... 1 Cor 10:4

DRAW
d honey from the rock .... Deut 32:13
me to *d* near to God .... Ps 73:28
and the years *d* .... Eccl 12:1
D me away .... Song 1:4
Woe to those who *d* .... Is 5:18
with joy you will *d* .... Is 12:3
"*D* some out now .... John 2:8
You have nothing to *d* ...... John 4:11
will *d* all peoples .... John 12:32
let us *d* near with a .... Heb 10:22
who *d* back to perdition ... Heb 10:39
D near to God and He ..... James 4:8

DRAWN
The wicked have *d* .... Ps 37:14
tempted when he is *d* ..... James 1:14

DRAWS
and my life *d* near to .... Ps 88:3
your redemption *d* .... Luke 21:28
the Father who sent Me *d* .. John 6:44
but if anyone *d* back ...... Heb 10:38

DREAD
fear of you and the *d* .... Gen 9:2
begin to put the *d* .... Deut 2:25

DREADFUL
of the great and *d* .... Mal 4:5

DREAM
Now Joseph had a *d* .... Gen 37:5
We each have had a *d* ..... Gen 40:8
I speak to him in a *d* ...... Num 12:6
will fly away like a *d* .... Job 20:8
As a *d* when one awakes ... Ps 73:20
like those who *d* .... Ps 126:1
For a *d* comes through ...... Eccl 5:3
her, shall be as a *d* .... Is 29:7
prophet who has a *d* ...... Jer 23:28
do not let the *d* .... Dan 4:19
your old men shall *d* ...... Joel 2:28
to Joseph in a *d* .... Matt 2:13
things today in a *d* .... Matt 27:19
your old men shall *d* ...... Acts 2:17

DREAMERS
d defile the flesh .... Jude 8

DREAMS
in the multitude of *d* .... Eccl 5:7
when a hungry man *d* .... Is 29:8
Nebuchadnezzar had *d* ...... Dan 2:1

DREGS
d shall all the wicked .... Ps 75:8
has settled on his *d* .... Jer 48:11

DREW
and *d* for all his camels .... Gen 24:20

Because I *d* him out of .... Ex 2:10
d me out of many waters .... Ps 18:16
and *d* his sword, struck ... Matt 26:51

DRIED
My strength is *d* .... Ps 22:15
of her blood was *d* .... Mark 5:29
saw the fig tree *d* .... Mark 11:20
and its water was *d* .... Rev 16:12

DRIFT
have heard, lest we *d* .... Heb 2:1

DRINK
"What shall we *d* .... Ex 15:24
"Do not *d* wine or .... Lev 10:9
and let him *d* of the .... Job 21:20
gave me vinegar to *d* .... Ps 69:21
D water from your own ... Prov 5:15
mocker, strong *d* .... Prov 20:1
lest they *d* and forget ..... Prov 31:5
Give strong *d* to him ...... Prov 31:6
Let him *d* and forget ...... Prov 31:7
d your wine with a .... Eccl 9:7
follow intoxicating *d* .... Is 5:11
mixing intoxicating *d* .... Is 5:22
d the milk of the .... Is 60:16
My servants shall *d* .... Is 65:13
bosom, that you may *d* ...... Is 66:11
d water by measure .... Ezek 4:11
"Bring wine, let us *d* .... Amos 4:1
to you of wine and *d* .... Mic 2:11
and you gave Me no *d* ..... Matt 25:42
that day when I *d* .... Matt 26:29
mingled with gall to *d* ..... Matt 27:34
with myrrh to *d* .... Mark 15:23
to her, "Give Me a *d* .... John 4:7
him come to Me and *d* ...... John 7:37
d wine nor do anything ... Rom 14:21
do, as often as you *d* ..... 1 Cor 11:25
all been made to *d* ...... 1 Cor 12:13
No longer *d* only water ... 1 Tim 5:23
has made all nations *d* ...... Rev 14:8

DRINKS
to her, "Whoever *d* .... John 4:13
d My blood has eternal ..... John 6:54
For he who eats and *d* .... 1 Cor 11:29
For the earth which *d* .... Heb 6:7

DRIP
immoral woman *d* honey .... Prov 5:3
d as the honeycomb .... Song 4:11
shall *d* with new wine, the .. Joel 3:18

DRIPPED
my hands *d* with myrrh, ... Song 5:5

DRIPPING
wife are a continual *d* ..... Prov 19:13
His lips are lilies, *d* .... Song 5:13

DRIVE
Little by little I will *d* .... Ex 23:30
then you shall *d* out all .... Num 33:52
not utterly *d* them out ..... Josh 17:13
but they could not *d* out .... Judg 1:19
of the wicked *d* .... Ps 36:11
so *d* them away .... Ps 68:2
will *d* it far from him ...... Prov 22:15
They shall *d* you from ...... Dan 4:25
I will *d* them from My ...... Hos 9:15
temple and began to *d* ... Mark 11:15

DRIVEN
They were *d* out from .... Job 30:5
Let them be *d* backward .... Ps 40:14
sail and so were *d* .... Acts 27:17
a wave of the sea *d* ...... James 1:6

DROP
They *d* on the pastures ..... Ps 65:12
the nations are as a *d* ...... Is 40:15

DROSS
of the earth like *d* .... Ps 119:119
Take away the *d* .... Prov 25:4
purge away your *d* .... Is 1:25
of Israel has become *d* .... Ezek 22:18

DROUGHT
through a land of d ....Jer 2:6
in the year of d ....Jer 17:8
For I called for a d ....Hag 1:11

DROVE
So He d out the man ......Gen 3:24
temple of God d .....Matt 21:12
a whip of cords, He d ...John 2:15

DROWN
nor can the floods d ....Song 8:7
harmful lusts which d ....1 Tim 6:9

DROWSINESS
d will clothe a ....Prov 23:21

DRUNK
of the wine and was d .....Gen 9:21
d my wine with my milk ....Song 5:1
you afflicted, and d ....Is 51:21
My anger, made them d .....Is 63:6
be satiated and made d ....Jer 46:10
the guests have well d ....John 2:10
For these are not d ....Acts 2:15
and another is d ....1 Cor 11:21
And do not be d ....Eph 5:18
and those who get d ....1 Thess 5:7
the earth were made d .....Rev 17:2
I saw the woman, d ......Rev 17:6

DRUNKARD
d could be included ......Deut 29:19
d is a proverb in the ....Prov 26:9
to and fro like a d ....Is 24:20
or a reviler, or a d ....1 Cor 5:11

DRUNKEN
I am like a d man ....Jer 23:9

DRUNKENNESS
will be filled with d ......Ezek 23:33
Jerusalem a cup of d.......Zech 12:2
with carousing, d.......Luke 21:34
not in revelry and d......Rom 13:13
envy, murders, d.........Gal 5:21
lusts, d, revelries ....1 Pet 4:3

DRUSILLA
Wife of Felix; hears Paul, Acts 24:24,
25

DRY
place, and let the d ....Gen 1:9
made the sea into d ....Ex 14:21
It was d on the fleece ......Judg 6:40
I will d up her sea ....Jer 51:36
d tree flourish ....Ezek 17:24
will make the rivers d ....Ezek 30:12
will be done in the d .....Luke 23:31

DUE
because it is your d ....Lev 10:13
their food in d season .....Ps 104:27
pay all that was d ......Matt 18:34
d time Christ died ....Rom 5:6
to whom taxes are d ....Rom 13:7
d season we shall ....Gal 6:9
exalt you in d time ....1 Pet 5:6

DUG
that I have d this well .....Gen 21:30
father's servants had d ....Gen 26:15
in my grave which I d for ...Gen 50:5
They have d a pit before ....Ps 57:6
the pit is d for the wicked ...Ps 94:13
proud have d pits for me ....Ps 119:85
He d it up and cleared out .....Is 5:2
to the Euphrates and d .....Jer 13:7
d a winepress in it and ...Matt 21:33
d in the ground, and hid ...Matt 25:18
who d deep and laid ......Luke 6:48

DULL
heart of this people d ....Is 6:10
people have grown d ....Matt 13:15
you have become d ....Heb 5:11

DUMB
the tongue of the d ....Is 35:6
"Deaf and d spirit ....Mark 9:25

DUNGHILL
the land nor for the d .....Luke 14:35

DUST
formed man of the d ....Gen 2:7
d you shall return ....Gen 3:19
descendants as the d ......Gen 13:16
now, I who am but d .....Gen 18:27
"Who can count the d ....Num 23:10
lay your gold in the d .....Job 22:24
and repent in d ....Job 42:6
Will the d praise You ......Ps 30:9
like the whirling d ....Ps 83:13
show favor to her d ....Ps 102:14
remembers that we are d ...Ps 103:14
or the primal d ....Prov 8:26
all are from the d ....Eccl 3:20
counted as the small d .....Is 40:15
They shall lick the d ....Mic 7:17
city, shake off the d ......Matt 10:14
image of the man of d ....1 Cor 15:49

DUTY
the d of a husband's ......Deut 25:5
d of a close relative ......Ruth 3:13
done what was our d .....Luke 17:10

DWELL
O LORD, make me d ....Ps 4:8
Who may d in Your holy ....Ps 15:1
He himself shall d ....Ps 25:13
d in the land, and feed on ...Ps 37:3
the LORD God might d .....Ps 68:18
of my God than d ....Ps 84:10
Him, that glory may d ......Ps 85:9
Woe is me, that I d ....Ps 120:5
better to d in a corner ....Prov 25:24
he will d on high ....Is 33:16
into Egypt to d there ....Is 52:4
"I d in the high and ....Is 57:15
Restorer of Streets to D In ...Is 58:12
"They shall no longer d ....Lam 4:15
they enter and d there ....Matt 12:45
of Judea and all who d .....Acts 2:14
"I will d in them ....2 Cor 6:16
that Christ may d ....Eph 3:17
the fullness should ....Col 1:19
the word of Christ d ....Col 3:16
men, and He will d ....Rev 21:3

DWELLER
fled and became a d ....Acts 7:29

DWELLING
A people d alone ....Num 23:9
is the way to the d ....Job 38:19
built together for a d .....Eph 2:22
a foreign country, d ....Heb 11:9

DWELLS
He who d in the secret ......Ps 91:1
but the Father who d .....John 14:10
do it, but sin that d ....Rom 7:17
the Spirit of God d ....Rom 8:9
from the dead d ....Rom 8:11
the Spirit of God d ....1 Cor 3:16
d all the fullness ....Col 2:9
which righteousness d .....2 Pet 3:13
you, where Satan d ....Rev 2:13

DWELT
Egypt, and Jacob d ....Ps 105:23
became flesh and d ....John 1:14
By faith he d in the ....Heb 11:9

DYING
I do not object to d ....Acts 25:11
in the body the d ....2 Cor 4:10
Jacob, when he was d .....Heb 11:21

EAGLE
As an e stirs up its ....Deut 32:11
e swooping on its prey ......Job 9:26
fly away like an e ....Prov 23:5

The way of an e ....Prov 30:19
nest as high as the e .....Jer 49:16
had the face of an e ......Ezek 1:10
like a flying e ....Rev 4:7
two wings of a great e ....Rev 12:14

EAGLES
up with wings like e ....Is 40:31
are swifter than e ....Jer 4:13
e will be gathered ....Matt 24:28

EAGLES'
how I bore you on e ....Ex 19:4

EAR
shall pierce his e ....Ex 21:6
Does not the e test ....Job 12:11
Bow down Your e ....Ps 31:2
And the e of the wise .....Prov 18:15
He awakens My e ....Is 50:4
e is uncircumcised ....Jer 6:10
what you hear in the e ....Matt 10:27
cut off his right e ....John 18:10
not seen, nor e heard ......1 Cor 2:9
if the e should say ....1 Cor 12:16
He who has an e ....Rev 2:7

EARLY
Very e in the morning .....Mark 16:2
arrived at the tomb e .....Luke 24:22

EARNEST
must give the more e ....Heb 2:1

EARNESTLY
if you e obey My ....Deut 11:13
He prayed more e ....Luke 22:44
in this we groan, e ....2 Cor 5:2
e that it would not ......James 5:17
you to contend e ....Jude 3

EARS
both his e will tingle .....2 Kin 21:12
Whoever shuts his e .....Prov 21:13
And hear with their e ....Is 6:10
He who has e ....Matt 11:15
e are hard of hearing ....Matt 13:15
they have itching e ....2 Tim 4:3
e are open to their ....1 Pet 3:12

EARS TO HEAR
eyes to see and e, ...Deut 29:4
e but does not hear ....Ezek 12:2
He who has e, ...Matt 11:15
He who has e, ...Matt 13:9
He who has e, ...Matt 13:43
"He who has e, ...Mark 4:9
If anyone has e, ...Mark 4:23
If anyone has e, ...Mark 7:16
"He who has e, ...Luke 8:8
He who has e, ...Luke 14:35

EARTH
See ALL THE EARTH; HEAVEN AND
EARTH
The e was without form .....Gen 1:2
God called the dry land E ...Gen 1:10
caused it to rain on the e ...Gen 2:5
The e also was corrupt .....Gen 6:11
a wind to pass over the e ...Gen 8:1
and multiply, and fill the e ...Gen 9:1
the whole e was populated ..Gen 9:19
and struck the dust of the e ..Ex 8:17
the e is the LORD's ....Ex 9:29
the e swallowed them.......Ex 15:12
"Lest the e swallow us ....Num 16:34
or that is in the e beneath ...Deut 5:8
e which is under you .....Deut 28:23
e to witness against ....Deut 31:28
fell to the e on his face ......Josh 7:6
the e trembled ....Judg 5:4
e are the LORD's ....1 Sam 2:8
the e quaked ....1 Sam 14:15
"I go the way of all the e ...1 Kin 2:2
the e was divided ....1 Chr 1:19
to the LORD, all the e .....1 Chr 16:23
coming to judge the e ....1 Chr 16:33

service for man on e . . . . Job 7:1
He hangs the e on . . . . Job 26:7
foundations of the e . . . . Job 38:4
tried in a furnace of e . . . . Ps 12:6
e is the LORD's . . . . Ps 24:1
the shields of the e . . . . Ps 47:9
You visit the e . . . . Ps 65:9
You had formed the e . . . . Ps 90:2
let the e be moved . . . . Ps 99:1
glory is above the e . . . . . . Ps 148:13
wisdom founded the e . . . . . Prov 3:19
there was ever an e . . . . . . Prov 8:23
For three things the e . . . . . Prov 30:21
e abides forever . . . . Eccl 1:4
heaven, and you on e . . . . Eccl 5:2
the fruit of the e . . . . Is 4:2
for the meek of the e . . . . Is 11:4
the e shall be full of . . . . Is 11:9
curse has devoured the e . . . . . Is 24:6
a dark place of the e . . . . Is 45:19
the foundations of the e . . . . . Is 51:16
are higher than the e . . . . Is 55:9
e is My footstool . . . . Is 66:1
new e which I will make . . . . . Is 66:22
O e, e, e, hear the word . . . . Jer 22:29
lifted me up between e . . . . . . Ezek 8:3
and the e shone with . . . . . Ezek 43:2
a tree in the midst of the e . . Dan 4:10
in heaven and on e . . . . Dan 6:27
The e shall answer . . . . Hos 2:22
I will darken the e . . . . Amos 8:9
e will be filled . . . . Hab 2:14
Let all the e keep silence . . . Hab 2:20
shall inherit the e . . . . Matt 5:5
heaven and e pass away . . . Matt 5:18
e as it is in heaven . . . . Matt 6:10
treasures on e, where . . . . . Matt 6:19
whatever you bind on e . . . Matt 18:18
of the e will mourn . . . . . . Matt 24:30
Me in heaven and on e . . . . Matt 28:18
all the seeds on e . . . . Mark 4:31
and e will pass away . . . . Mark 13:31
on e peace, goodwill . . . . . Luke 2:14
power on e to forgive . . . . . Luke 5:24
find faith on the e . . . . Luke 18:8
e is My footstool . . . . Acts 7:49
then shook the e . . . . Heb 12:26
e which are now . . . . 2 Pet 3:7
heavens and a new e . . . . 2 Pet 3:13
all the tribes of the e . . . . Rev 1:7
"Do not harm the e . . . . Rev 7:3
he was cast to the e . . . . . . Rev 12:9
the e helped the woman . . . Rev 12:16
on the e will worship him . . Rev 13:8
and the e was reaped . . . . Rev 14:16
the e was illuminated . . . . . Rev 18:1
from whose face the e . . . . Rev 20:11
new heaven and a new e . . . Rev 21:1

EARTHEN
holy water in an e vessel . . . Num 5:17
a potter's e flask . . . . Jer 19:1
treasure in e vessels . . . . 2 Cor 4:7

EARTHLY
If I have told you e . . . . John 3:12
that if our e house . . . . 2 Cor 5:1
their mind on e things . . . . . Phil 3:19
from above, but is e . . . . . . James 3:15

EARTHQUAKE
LORD was not in the e . . . . 1 Kin 19:11
as you fled from the e . . . . . Zech 14:5
there was a great e . . . . Matt 28:2
there was a great e . . . . . Acts 16:26
there was a great e . . . . Rev 6:12
e as had not occurred . . . . . Rev 16:18

EARTHQUAKES
And there will be e . . . . Mark 13:8

EASE
I was at e, but He has . . . . . Job 16:12
you women who are at e . . . . Is 32:9
to you who are at e . . . . Amos 6:1

take your e; eat, drink . . . Luke 12:19

EASIER
Which is e, to say . . . . Mark 2:9
It is e for a camel . . . . . . Mark 10:25
e for heaven and earth . . . Luke 16:17

EAST
goes toward the e . . . . Gen 2:14
e of the garden of Eden . . . . Gen 3:24
the LORD brought an e . . . . . Ex 10:13
e wind scattered . . . . Job 38:24
As far as the e . . . . Ps 103:12
descendants from the e . . . . . Is 43:5
wise men from the E . . . . . . Matt 2:1
many will come from e . . . . . Matt 8:11
will come from the e . . . . . Luke 13:29
e might be prepared . . . . . . Rev 16:12

EASTWARD
planted a garden e in Eden . . Gen 2:8

EASY
My yoke is e and My . . . . . Matt 11:30

EAT
you may freely e . . . . Gen 2:16
e dust all the days . . . . Gen 3:14
'You shall not e . . . . Gen 3:17
you shall e the herb . . . . Gen 3:18
e of my game . . . . Gen 27:19
brethren to e bread . . . . Gen 31:54
you shall e it in haste . . . . . . Ex 12:11
No foreigner shall e it . . . . . . Ex 12:43
may not e the life . . . . Deut 12:23
dogs shall e Jezebel . . . . . . 2 Kin 9:10
my people as they e . . . . Ps 53:4
love it will e its fruit . . . . . . Prov 18:21
E only as much as you . . . . Prov 25:16
good to e much honey . . . . Prov 25:27
e your bread with joy . . . . . . Eccl 9:7
Curds and honey He shall e . . . Is 7:15
You shall e this year such . . . Is 37:30
lion shall e straw . . . . Is 65:25
e this scroll . . . . Ezek 3:1
on your couches, e . . . . Amos 6:4
e the flesh of My . . . . Mic 3:3
life, what you will e . . . . . . Matt 6:25
even the little dogs e . . . . . Matt 15:27
You to e the Passover . . . . Matt 26:17
I may e the Passover . . . . Mark 14:14
e; this is My body . . . . . . Mark 14:22
what you will e . . . . Luke 12:22
food to e of which you . . . . John 4:32
give us His flesh to e . . . . . John 6:52
"Rise, Peter; kill and e." . . . Acts 10:13
e nor drink till they have . . Acts 23:21
one believes he may e . . . . . Rom 14:2
e meat nor drink wine . . . . Rom 14:21
I will never again e . . . . . . 1 Cor 8:13
e whatever is set . . . . 1 Cor 10:27
e; this is My body . . . . . . 1 Cor 11:24
neither shall he e . . . . 2 Thess 3:10
have no right to e . . . . Heb 13:10
e your flesh like fire . . . . . . James 5:3
"Take and e it . . . . Rev 10:9

EATEN
Have you e from the . . . . . . Gen 3:11
It shall be e the same day . . . Lev 19:6
Your house has e me up . . . . Ps 69:9
e my honeycomb with my . . Song 5:1
bad figs which cannot be e . . Jer 24:8
e the fruit of lies . . . . Hos 10:13
And he was e by worms . . Acts 12:23

EATING
by e with the blood . . . . . 1 Sam 14:33
sons and daughters were e . . Job 1:13
e swine's flesh . . . . Is 66:17
neither e nor drinking . . . . Matt 11:18
the flood, they were e . . . . Matt 24:38
as they were e, He said . . . Matt 26:21
Pharisees saw Him e . . . . . Mark 2:16
in the same house, e . . . . . Luke 10:7
e in an idol's temple . . . . . 1 Cor 8:10

in e, each one takes . . . . . 1 Cor 11:21

EATS
The righteous e . . . . Prov 13:25
receives sinners and e . . . . . Luke 15:2
Whoever e My flesh . . . . . . John 6:54
e this bread will live . . . . . . John 6:58
e despise him who does . . . . Rom 14:3
He who e, e to the . . . . Rom 14:6
an unworthy manner e . . . 1 Cor 11:29

EBAL
Mountain in Samaria, Deut 27:12, 13
Stones of the Law erected upon, Deut
   27:1–8; Josh 8:30–35

EBED-MELECH
Ethiopian eunuch; rescues Jeremiah,
   Jer 38:7–13
Promised divine protection, Jer
   39:15–18

EBENEZER
Site of Israel's defeat, 1 Sam 4:1–10
Ark transferred from, 1 Sam 5:1
Site of memorial stone, 1 Sam 7:10, 12

EBER
Great-grandson of Shem, Gen
   10:21–24; 1 Chr 1:25
Progenitor of the:
   Hebrews, Gen 11:16–26
   Arabians and Arameans, Gen
   10:25–30
Ancestor of Christ, Luke 3:35

EDEN
First home of mankind, Gen 2:8–15
Zion becomes like, Is 51:3
Called the "garden of God," Ezek 28:13

EDIFICATION
his good, leading to e . . . . . Rom 15:2
prophesies speaks e . . . . . . 1 Cor 14:3
things are done for e . . . . 1 Cor 14:26
the Lord gave us for e . . . . 2 Cor 10:8
has given me for e . . . . . . 2 Cor 13:10
rather than godly e . . . . 1 Tim 1:4

EDIFIES
puffs up, but love e . . . . . . 1 Cor 8:1
he who prophesies e . . . . . 1 Cor 14:4

EDIFY
but not all things e . . . . . . 1 Cor 10:23
and e one another . . . . . . 1 Thess 5:11

EDIFYING
of the body for the e . . . . . . Eph 4:16

EDOM
Name given to Esau, Gen 25:30
——— Land of Esau; called Seir, Gen 32:3
Called Edom and Idumea, Mark 3:8
People of, cursed, Is 34:5, 6

EDOMITES
Descendants of Esau, Gen 36:9
Refuse passage to Israel, Num
   20:18–20
Hostile to Israel, Gen 27:40; 1 Sam
   14:47; 2 Chr 20:10; Ps 137:7
Prophecies concerning, Gen 27:37; Is
   34:5–17; Ezek 25:12–14; 35:5–7;
   Amos 9:11, 12

EDREI
Capital of Bashan, Deut 3:10
Site of Og's defeat, Num 21:33–35

EFFECT
of the peoples of no e . . . . . Ps 33:10
of no e by your tradition . . . Matt 15:6
promise made of no e . . . . . Rom 4:14
make the promise of no e . . Gal 3:17

EFFECTIVELY
for He who worked e . . . . . . Gal 2:8
e works in you who . . . . . 1 Thess 2:13

EGG
in the white of an e . . . . Job 6:6

Or if he asks for an *e* . . . . . Luke 11:12

EGLON
City of Judah, Josh 15:39

EGYPT
Abram visits, Gen 12:10
Joseph sold into, Gen 37:28, 36
Joseph becomes leader in, Gen 39:1–4
Hebrews move to, Gen 46:5–7
Hebrews persecuted in, Ex 1:15–22
Plagues on, Ex 7—11
Israel leaves, Ex 12:31–33
Army of, perishes, Ex 14:26–28
Prophecies concerning, Gen 15:13; Is
   19:18–25; Ezek 29:14, 15; 30:24, 25;
   Matt 2:15

EHUD
Son of Gera, Judg 3:15
Slays Eglon, Judg 3:16–26

EIGHT
Isaac when he was *e* days . . Gen 21:4
Jesse, and who had *e* . . . . 1 Sam 17:12
Josiah was *e* years old . . . 2 Kin 22:1
e days were completed . . . . Luke 2:21
about *e* days after these . . . Luke 9:28
bedridden *e* years . . . . Acts 9:33
a few, that is, *e* . . . . 1 Pet 3:20
saved Noah, one of *e* . . . . 2 Pet 2:5

EIGHTH
shall sow in the *e* year . . . . Lev 25:22
So it was, on the *e* day . . . . Luke 1:59
circumcised the *e* day, of . . . . Phil 3:5

EIGHTY
Moses was *e* years old . . . . Ex 7:7
land had rest for *e* years . . . Judg 3:30
I am today *e* years old . . . 2 Sam 19:35
with him were *e* priests . . 2 Chr 26:17
strength they are *e* years . . . . Ps 90:10
your bill, and write *e* . . . . . . Luke 16:7

EKRON
Philistine city, Josh 13:3
Captured by Judah, Judg 1:18
Assigned to Dan, Josh 19:40, 43
Ark sent to, 1 Sam 5:10
Denounced by the prophets, Jer 25:9,
   20

EL BETHEL
Site of Jacob's altar, Gen 35:6, 7

ELAH
King of Israel, 1 Kin 16:6, 8–10

ELAMITES
Descendants of Shem, Gen 10:22
Destruction of, Jer 49:34–39
In Persian Empire, Ezra 4:9
Jews from, at Pentecost, Acts 2:9

ELATH
Seaport on Red Sea, 1 Kin 9:26
Built by Azariah, 2 Kin 14:21, 22
Captured by Syrians, 2 Kin 16:6
Same as Ezion Geber, 2 Chr 8:17

ELDER
clothes of her *e* son Esau . . Gen 27:15
The *e* and honorable . . . . Is 9:15
against an *e* except . . . . 1 Tim 5:19
I who am a fellow *e* . . . . 1 Pet 5:1
The *E*. To the elect lady . . . . . 2 John 1
The *E*. To the beloved . . . . 3 John 1

ELDERS
See TWENTY-FOUR ELDERS
and seventy of the *e* . . . . Ex 24:1
called for the *e* of Israel . . . . Josh 24:1
the advice of the *e* . . . . 2 Chr 10:13
And teach his *e* . . . . Ps 105:22
in the company of the *e* . . . . Ps 107:32
and counsel from the *e* . . . Ezek 7:26
the tradition of the *e* . . . Matt 15:2
many things from the *e* . . . Matt 16:21
e of the people plotted . . . . . Matt 27:1

be rejected by the *e* . . . . . . Luke 9:22
e who had come to Him . . Luke 22:52
the people, the *e* . . . . Acts 6:12
they had appointed *e* . . . . . . Acts 14:23
e came together to . . . . Acts 15:6
and called for the *e* . . . . Acts 20:17
e who rule well be . . . . 1 Tim 5:17
lacking, and appoint *e* . . . . . . Titus 1:5
e obtained a good . . . . Heb 11:2
Let him call for the *e* . . . . James 5:14
e who are among you I . . . . . 1 Pet 5:1
I saw twenty-four *e* . . . . Rev 4:4
twenty-four *e* fall down . . . . . Rev 4:10
the twenty-four *e* fell down . . Rev 5:8

ELDERSHIP
of the hands of the *e* . . . . . . 1 Tim 4:14

ELEAZAR
Son of Aaron; succeeds him as high
   priest, Ex 6:23, 25; 28:1; Lev 10:6, 7;
   Num 3:32; 20:25–28; Josh 14:1; 24:33

ELECT
whom I uphold, My *E* . . . . Is 42:1
and Israel My *e* . . . . Is 45:4
e shall long enjoy the . . . . Is 65:22
gather together His *e* . . . . Matt 24:31
e have obtained it . . . . Rom 11:7
e according to the . . . . 1 Pet 1:2
a chief cornerstone, *e* . . . . . 1 Pet 2:6
e sister greet you . . . . 2 John 13

ELECTION
e they are beloved . . . . Rom 11:28
call and *e* sure . . . . 2 Pet 1:10

ELEMENTS
weak and beggarly *e* . . . . Gal 4:9
e will melt with . . . . 2 Pet 3:10

ELEVEN
and his *e* sons . . . . Gen 32:22
the *e* stars bowed down . . . . . Gen 37:9
e disciples went away . . . . Matt 28:16
and found the *e* . . . . Luke 24:33
numbered with the *e* . . . . Acts 1:26

ELI
Officiates in Shiloh, 1 Sam 1:3
Blesses Hannah, 1 Sam 1:12–19
Becomes Samuel's guardian, 1 Sam
   1:20–28
Samuel ministers before, 1 Sam 2:11
Sons of, 1 Sam 2:12–17
Rebukes sons, 1 Sam 2:22–25
Rebuked by a man of God, 1 Sam
   2:27–36
Instructs Samuel, 1 Sam 3:1–18
Death of, 1 Sam 4:15–18

ELIAB
Brother of David, 1 Sam 16:5–13
Fights in Saul's army, 1 Sam 17:13
Discounts David's worth, 1 Sam 17:28,
   29

ELIAKIM
Son of Hilkiah, 2 Kin 18:18
Confers with Rabshakeh, Is 36:4,
   11–22
Sent to Isaiah, Is 37:2–5
Becomes type of the Messiah,
   Is 22:20–25
——— Son of King Josiah, 2 Kin 23:34
Name changed to Jehoiakim, 2 Chr
   36:4

ELIASHIB
High priest, Neh 12:10
Rebuilds Sheep Gate, Neh 3:1, 20, 21
Allies with foreigners, Neh 13:4, 5, 28

ELIHU
David's brother, 1 Chr 27:18
Called Eliab, 1 Sam 16:6
——— One who reproved Job and his
   friends, Job 32:2, 4–6

ELIJAH
Denounces Ahab; goes into hiding; fed
   by ravens, 1 Kin 17:1–7
Dwells with widow; performs miracles
   for her, 1 Kin 17:8–24
Sends message to Ahab; overthrows
   prophets of Baal, 1 Kin 18:1–40
Brings rain, 1 Kin 18:41–45
Flees from Jezebel; fed by angels, 1 Kin
   19:1–8
Receives revelation from God, 1 Kin
   19:9–18
Condemns Ahab, 1 Kin 21:15–29
Condemns Ahaziah; fire consumes
   troops sent against him, 2 Kin
   1:1–16
Taken up to heaven, 2 Kin 2:1–15
Appears with Christ in transfiguration,
   Matt 17:1–4
Type of John the Baptist, Mal 4:5, 6;
   Luke 1:17

ELIMELECH
Naomi's husband, Ruth 1:1–3; 2:1, 3;
   4:3–9

ELIPHAZ
One of Job's friends, Job 2:11
Rebukes Job, Job 4:1, 5
Is forgiven, Job 42:7–9

ELISHA
Chosen as Elijah's successor; follows
   him, 1 Kin 19:16–21
Witnesses Elijah's translation; receives
   his spirit and mantle, 2 Kin 2:1–18
Performs miracles, 2 Kin 2:19–25;
   4:1—6:23
Prophesies victory over Moab; fulfilled,
   2 Kin 3:11–27
Prophesies end of siege; fulfilled,
   2 Kin 7
Prophesies death of Ben-Hadad, 2 Kin
   8:7–15
Sends servant to anoint Jehu, 2 Kin
   9:1–3
Last words and death; miracle performed by his bones, 2 Kin 13:14–21

ELIZABETH
Barren wife of Zacharias, Luke 1:5–7
Conceives a son, Luke 1:13, 24, 25
Salutation to Mary, Luke 1:36–45
Mother of John the Baptist, Luke
   1:57–60

ELIZAPHAN
Chief of Kohathites, Num 3:30
Heads family, 1 Chr 15:5, 8
Family consecrated, 2 Chr 29:12–16

ELKANAH
Father of Samuel, 1 Sam 1:1–23
——— Son of Korah, Ex 6:24
Escapes judgment, Num 26:11

ELNATHAN
Father of Nehushta, 2 Kin 24:8
Goes to Egypt, Jer 26:22
Entreats with king, Jer 36:25

ELOQUENT
"O my Lord, I am not *e* . . . . . . Ex 4:10
an *e* man and mighty . . . . . Acts 18:24

ELYMAS
Arabic name of Bar-Jesus, a false
   prophet, Acts 13:6–12

EMBALM
to *e* his father . . . . Gen 50:2

EMBANKMENT
will build an *e* . . . . Luke 19:43

EMBRACE
you shall *e* a son . . . . 2 Kin 4:16
a time to *e*, and a time . . . . Eccl 3:5

EMBRACED
and have *e* other gods . . . . . . 1 Kin 9:9

be *e* in the arms of .... Prov 5:20
e them, and departed to .... Acts 20:1
e them, and confessed ..... Heb 11:13

EMBRACES
his right hand *e* me .... Song 2:6

EMERALD
sardius, a topaz, and an *e* ... Ex 28:17
turquoise, and *e* with .... Ezek 28:13
chalcedony, the fourth *e* ... Rev 21:19

EMERALDS
for your wares *e* .... Ezek 27:16

EMMAUS
Town near Jerusalem, Luke 24:13–18

EMPTY
And the pit was *e* .... Gen 37:24
appear before Me *e* .... Ex 23:15
e pitchers, and torches ..... Judg 7:16
after *e* things which .... 1 Sam 12:21
comfort me with *e* words .. Job 21:34
not listen to *e* talk .... Job 35:13
Lord makes the earth *e* ...... Is 24:1
trust in *e* words .... Is 59:4
comes, he finds it *e* ...... Matt 12:44
He has sent away *e* .... Luke 1:53
you with *e* words .... Eph 5:6

EMPTY-HANDED
sent me away *e* .... Gen 31:42
appear before Me *e* .... Ex 34:20
'Do not go *e* to your ...... Ruth 3:17
and sent him away *e* ..... Mark 12:3

EMPTY-HEADED
e man will be wise .... Job 11:12

EN DOR
Town of Manasseh which was the
home of the witch whom Saul consulted, Josh 17:11; 1 Sam 28:1–10;
Ps 83:9, 10

EN GEDI
Occupied by the Amorites, Gen 14:7
Assigned to Judah, Josh 15:62, 63
David's hiding place, 1 Sam 23:29
Noted for vineyards, Song 1:14

EN HAKKORE
Miraculous spring, Judg 15:14–19

EN ROGEL
Fountain outside Jerusalem, 2 Sam
17:17
Seat of Adonijah's plot, 1 Kin 1:5–9

ENABLED
our Lord who has *e* .... 1 Tim 1:12

ENCHANTER
and the expert *e* .... Is 3:3

ENCOURAGE
e him and strengthen him .. Deut 3:28
e you concerning your .... 1 Thess 3:2

ENCOURAGED
is, that I may be *e* .... Rom 1:12
and all may be *e* .... 1 Cor 14:31
their hearts may be *e* ...... Col 2:2

ENCOURAGEMENT
Hezekiah gave *e* to .... 2 Chr 30:22
translated Son of *E)* ...... Acts 4:36
they rejoiced over its *e* .... Acts 15:31

END
at the *e* of forty days .... Gen 8:6
one cherub at one *e* ...... Ex 25:19
at the *e* of forty days .... Deut 9:11
the *e* of every seven years .. Deut 15:1
made an *e* of dividing ..... Josh 19:51
yet your latter *e* .... Job 8:7
Man puts an *e* to darkness .. Job 28:3
from one *e* of heaven .... Ps 19:6
make me to know my *e* ..... Ps 39:4
Your years will have no *e* .. Ps 102:27
shall keep it to the *e* ...... Ps 119:33
e is the way of death ..... Prov 14:12

not be blessed at the *e* .... Prov 20:21
There was no *e* of all ...... Eccl 4:16
The *e* of a thing is better ..... Eccl 7:8
and peace there will be no *e* .... Is 9:7
Declaring the *e* .... Is 46:10
Our *e* was near .... Lam 4:18
whose iniquity shall *e* .... Ezek 21:25
shall endure to the *e* ...... Dan 6:26
the time of the *e* .... Dan 8:17
until the time of the *e* ..... Dan 11:35
what shall be the *e* .... Dan 12:8
e has come upon my ...... Amos 8:2
to the *e* will be saved .... Matt 10:22
the harvest is the *e* ...... Matt 13:39
to pass, but the *e* .... Matt 24:6
always, even to the *e* .... Matt 28:20
there will be no *e* .... Luke 1:33
He loved them to the *e* .... John 13:1
to the *e* of the earth .... Acts 1:8
the *e* of those things is .... Rom 6:21
For Christ is the *e* .... Rom 10:4
the hope firm to the *e* ...... Heb 3:6
steadfast to the *e* .... Heb 3:14
but now, once at the *e* ..... Heb 9:26
of Job and seen the *e* .... James 5:11
the *e* of your faith .... 1 Pet 1:9
But the *e* of all .... 1 Pet 4:7
what will be the *e* .... 1 Pet 4:17
the latter *e* is worse .... 2 Pet 2:20
My works until the *e* ...... Rev 2:26
Beginning and the *E* ...... Rev 22:13

ENDEAVORING
e to keep the unity .... Eph 4:3

ENDED
the seventh day God *e* His ... Gen 2:2
that her warfare is *e* .... Is 40:2
is past, the summer is *e* ..... Jer 8:20
Jesus had *e* these sayings .. Matt 7:28
had *e* every temptation .... Luke 4:13
supper being *e*, the devil ... John 13:2

ENDLESS
and *e* genealogies .... 1 Tim 1:4
to the power of an *e* .... Heb 7:16

ENDS
cherubim at the two *e* of .... Ex 25:19
judge the *e* of the earth ... 1 Sam 2:10
looks to the *e* of the earth .. Job 28:24
All the *e* of the world .... Ps 22:27
all the *e* of the earth have .... Ps 98:3
established all the *e* .... Prov 30:4
Creator of the *e* of the ..... Is 40:28
from the *e* of the earth ..... Is 42:10
she came from the *e* ...... Matt 12:42
salvation to the *e* .... Acts 13:47
their words to the *e* ...... Rom 10:18

ENDURANCE
For you have need of *e* .... Heb 10:36
run with *e* the race that ..... Heb 12:1

ENDURE
But the Lord shall *e* .... Ps 9:7
weeping may *e* for a night .... Ps 30:5
as the sun and moon *e* ...... Ps 72:5
His name shall *e* .... Ps 72:17
heart, Him I will not *e* ..... Ps 101:5
glory of the Lord *e* .... Ps 104:31
nor does a crown *e* .... Prov 27:24
Can your heart *e* .... Ezek 22:14
e only for a time .... Mark 4:17
persecuted, we *e* .... 1 Cor 4:12
must *e* hardship .... 2 Tim 2:3
Therefore I *e* all .... 2 Tim 2:10
If you *e* chastening .... Heb 12:7
them blessed who *e* ..... James 5:11

ENDURED
what persecutions I *e* .... 2 Tim 3:11
he had patiently *e* .... Heb 6:15
e as seeing Him who ...... Heb 11:27
For consider Him who *e* .... Heb 12:3

ENDURES
See HIS MERCY ENDURES FOREVER

goodness of God *e* .... Ps 52:1
And His truth *e* .... Ps 100:5
his righteousness *e* forever .. Ps 112:3
truth of the Lord *e* forever .. Ps 117:2
For His mercy *e* .... Ps 136:1
But he who *e* to the ...... Matt 10:22
e only for a while .... Matt 13:21
for the food which *e* ..... John 6:27
he has built on it *e* .... 1 Cor 3:14
hopes all things, *e* .... 1 Cor 13:7
is the man who *e* .... James 1:12
word of the Lord *e* ...... 1 Pet 1:25

ENDURING
the Lord is clean, *e* .... Ps 19:9
e possession for .... Heb 10:34

ENEMIES
See LOVE YOUR ENEMIES
an enemy to your *e* .... Ex 23:22
Your *e* be scattered ...... Num 10:35
I took you to curse my *e* .. Num 23:11
Lord will cause your *e* .... Deut 28:7
from the hand of our *e* .. 1 Sam 12:10
your *e* from before you .... 2 Sam 7:9
be saved from my *e* ..... 2 Sam 22:4
Let all my *e* be ashamed ..... Ps 6:10
be saved from my *e* .... Ps 18:3
delivers me from my *e* .... Ps 18:48
the presence of my *e* ...... Ps 23:5
Let not my *e* triumph ...... Ps 25:2
But my *e* are vigorous ...... Ps 38:19
arise, let His *e* be scattered .. Ps 68:1
e will lick the dust .... Ps 72:9
Your *e* with Your mighty .... Ps 89:10
Your *e* Your footstool ..... Ps 110:1
me wiser than my *e* ...... Ps 119:98
rescued us from our *e*, ... Ps 136:24
I count them my *e* .... Ps 139:22
makes even his *e* to be ..... Prov 16:7
e are the men of his .... Mic 7:6
darkness will pursue His *e* ... Nah 1:8
to you, love your *e* .... Matt 5:44
a man's *e* will be those .... Matt 10:36
be saved from our *e* .... Luke 1:71
Your *e* Your footstool .... Luke 20:43
e we were reconciled ...... Rom 5:10
the gospel they are *e* ..... Rom 11:28
till He has put all *e* ...... 1 Cor 15:25
were alienated and *e* .... Col 1:21
His *e* are made His .... Heb 10:13
and devours their *e* .... Rev 11:5

ENEMY
then I will be an *e* .... Ex 23:22
out the *e* from before ..... Deut 33:27
David's *e* continually .... 1 Sam 18:29
delivered your *e* into .... 1 Sam 26:8
Haman, the *e* of the Jews .... Esth 8:1
regard me as Your *e* ...... Job 13:24
He counts me as His *e* ..... Job 33:10
or have plundered my *e* ...... Ps 7:4
You may silence the *e* .... Ps 8:2
e does not triumph .... Ps 41:11
e who reproaches me ...... Ps 55:12
a strong tower from the *e* ... Ps 61:3
e has persecuted my .... Ps 143:3
If your *e* is hungry .... Prov 25:21
kisses of an *e* are .... Prov 27:6
the *e* comes in like .... Is 59:19
with the wound of an *e* .... Jer 30:14
rejoice over me, my *e* ...... Mic 7:8
and hate your *e* .... Matt 5:43
The *e* who sowed them ... Matt 13:39
all the power of the *e* .... Luke 10:19
"If your *e* hungers .... Rom 12:20
last *e* that will be ...... 1 Cor 15:26
become your *e* because ..... Gal 4:16
not count him as an *e* ... 2 Thess 3:15
makes himself an *e* ...... James 4:4

ENGRAVE
two onyx stones and *e* ..... Ex 28:9
e its inscription .... Zech 3:9

ENJOY
e its sabbaths as long ...... Lev 26:34
therefore *e* pleasure .... Eccl 2:1
e the good of all his labor .. Eccl 3:13
richly all things to *e* ...... 1 Tim 6:17
than to *e* the passing ..... Heb 11:25

ENJOYMENT
So I commended *e* .... Eccl 8:15

ENLARGES
He *e* nations .... Job 12:23
e his desire as hell .... Hab 2:5

ENLIGHTEN
E my eyes, lest I sleep .... Ps 13:3
the LORD my God will *e* ..... Ps 18:28

ENLIGHTENED
those who were once *e* ...... Heb 6:4

ENMITY
And I will put *e* .... Gen 3:15
the carnal mind is *e* .... Rom 8:7
in His flesh the *e* .... Eph 2:15
putting to death the *e* ...... Eph 2:16
with the world is *e* .... James 4:4

ENOCH
Father of Methuselah, Gen 5:21
Walks with God, Gen 5:22
Taken up to heaven, Gen 5:24
Prophecy of, cited, Jude 14, 15

ENOUGH
four never say, "*E* .... Prov 30:15
It is *e*! The hour has ....Mark 14:41
servants have bread *e* .... Luke 15:17

ENRAGED
being exceedingly *e* .... Acts 26:11
And the dragon was *e* ..... Rev 12:17

ENRAPTURED
And always be *e* .... Prov 5:19

ENRICHED
that you were *e* .... 1 Cor 1:5
while you are *e* .... 2 Cor 9:11

ENSNARED
The wicked is *e* .... Prov 12:13

ENSNARES
sin which so easily *e* ...... Heb 12:1

ENTANGLE
how they might *e* .... Matt 22:15

ENTANGLES
engaged in warfare *e* .... 2 Tim 2:4

ENTER
'They shall not *e* My rest .... Ps 95:11
E into His gates .... Ps 100:4
Do not *e* into judgment ...... Ps 143:2
E into the rock .... Is 2:10
He shall *e* into peace .... Is 57:2
Jonah began to *e* the city on .. Jon 3:4
you will by no means *e* .... Matt 5:20
"*E* by the narrow .... Matt 7:13
Lord,' shall *e* the kingdom .. Matt 7:21
city or town you *e* .... Matt 10:11
e into life with one eye .... Matt 18:9
e the kingdom of God ... Matt 19:24
E into the joy of your ..... Matt 25:21
and pray, lest you *e* .... Matt 26:41
e a strong man's .... Mark 3:27
child will by no means *e* . Mark 10:15
e the kingdom of God .... Mark 10:24
Whatever house you *e* ...... Luke 9:4
"Strive to *e* through ...... Luke 13:24
Can he *e* a second time ..... John 3:4
cannot *e* the kingdom ...... John 3:5
you, he who does not *e* ... John 10:1
who have believed do *e* ...... Heb 4:3
e the Holiest by the ...... Heb 10:19
e the temple till the .... Rev 15:8
e through the gates .... Rev 22:14

ENTERED
day that Noah *e* the ark ... Matt 24:38

went out and *e* the swine .. Mark 5:13
as they *e* the cloud .... Luke 9:34
day that Noah *e* the ark .. Luke 17:27
Then Satan *e* Judas .... Luke 22:3
through one man sin *e* .... Rom 5:12
ear heard, nor have *e* ...... 1 Cor 2:9
he who has *e* His rest ...... Heb 4:10
the forerunner has *e* ...... Heb 6:20
e the Most Holy Place ..... Heb 9:12

ENTERS
If anyone *e* by Me .... John 10:9
e the Presence behind ..... Heb 6:19

ENTHRONED
You are holy, *e* in .... Ps 22:3
LORD sat *e* at the Flood ..... Ps 29:10

ENTICED
his own desires and *e* .... James 1:14

ENTICING
e speech she caused .... Prov 7:21
e unstable souls .... 2 Pet 2:14

ENTIRELY
give yourself *e* to them .... 1 Tim 4:15

ENTRANCE
The *e* of Your words ...... Ps 119:130
e will be supplied .... 2 Pet 1:11

ENTREAT
"*E* me not to leave you .... Ruth 1:16
"But now *e* God's favor ...... Mal 1:9
being defamed, we *e* ...... 1 Cor 4:13

ENTREATED
man of God the LORD .... 1 Kin 13:6
e our God for this .... Ezra 8:23

ENTRUSTED
e with a stewardship ...... 1 Cor 9:17
e with the gospel .... 1 Thess 2:4

ENVIOUS
For I was *e* of the .... Ps 73:3
Do not be *e* of evil .... Prov 24:1
patriarchs, becoming *e* ...... Acts 7:9

ENVY
e slays a simple .... Job 5:2
e the oppressor .... Prov 3:31
e is rottenness .... Prov 14:30
not let your heart *e* .... Prov 23:17
e have now perished .... Eccl 9:6
Him over because of *e* .... Matt 27:18
full of *e*, murder .... Rom 1:29
not in strife and *e* .... Rom 13:13
where there are *e*, strife ... 1 Cor 3:3
love does not *e* .... 1 Cor 13:4
e, murders, drunkenness .... Gal 5:21
preach Christ even from *e* .. Phil 1:15
living in malice and *e* ...... Titus 3:3
For where *e* and .... James 3:16
deceit, hypocrisy, *e* .... 1 Pet 2:1

EPAPHRAS
Leader of the Colossian church, Col 1:7, 8
Suffers as a prisoner in Rome, Philem 23

EPAPHRODITUS
Messenger from Philippi, Phil 2:25–27
Brings a gift to Paul, Phil 4:18

EPHES DAMMIM
Philistine encampment, 1 Sam 17:1
Called Pasdammim, 1 Chr 11:13

EPHESUS
Paul visits, Acts 18:18–21
Miracles done here, Acts 19:11–21
Demetrius stirs up riot in, Acts 19:24–29
Elders of, addressed by Paul at Miletus, Acts 20:17–38
Letter sent to, Eph 1:1
Site of one of seven churches, Rev 1:11

EPHOD
stones to be set in the *e* ..... Ex 25:7

a breastplate, an *e* .... Ex 28:4
made the *e* of gold, blue ..... Ex 39:2
and put the *e* on him .... Lev 8:7
Gideon made it into an *e* ... Judg 8:27
a shrine, and made an *e* .... Judg 17:5
a child, wearing a linen *e* . 1 Sam 2:18
was wearing an *e* .... 1 Sam 14:3
"Bring the *e* here .... 1 Sam 23:9
brought the *e* to David .... 1 Sam 30:7
was wearing a linen *e* .... 2 Sam 6:14

EPHRAIM
Joseph's younger son, Gen 41:52
Obtains Jacob's blessing, Gen 48:8–20
—— Tribe of:
Predictions concerning, Gen 48:20
Territory assigned to, Josh 16:1–10
Assist Deborah, Judg 5:14, 15
Assist Gideon, Judg 7:24, 25
Quarrel with Gideon, Judg 8:1–3
Quarrel with Jephthah, Judg 12:1–4
Leading tribe of kingdom of Israel, Is 7:2–17
Provoke God by sin, Hos 12:7–14
Many of, join Judah, 2 Chr 15:8, 9
Captivity of, predicted, Hos 9:3–17
Messiah promised to, Zech 9:9–13

EPHRATHAH
Ancient name of Bethlehem, Ruth 4:11
Prophecy concerning, Mic 5:2

EPHRON
Hittite who sold Machpelah to Abraham, Gen 23:8–20

EPICUREANS
Sect of pleasure-loving philosophers, Acts 17:18

EPISTLE
You are our *e* written ...... 2 Cor 3:2
you are an *e* .... 2 Cor 3:3
by word or our *e* .... 2 Thess 2:15
our word in this *e* .... 2 Thess 3:14
is a sign in every *e* ...... 2 Thess 3:17

EPISTLES
e of commendation to ...... 2 Cor 3:1
as also in all his *e* .... 2 Pet 3:16

EQUAL
it was you, a man my *e* ..... Ps 55:13
and you made them *e* .... Matt 20:12
they are *e* to the angels ... Luke 20:36
making Himself *e* .... John 5:18
it robbery to be *e* .... Phil 2:6

EQUALITY
that there may be *e* .... 2 Cor 8:14

EQUITY
You have established *e* .... Ps 99:4
judgment, and *e* .... Prov 1:3
and *e* cannot enter .... Is 59:14
and pervert all *e* .... Mic 3:9
with Me in peace and *e* ...... Mal 2:6

ER
Son of Judah, Gen 38:1–7; 46:12

ERASTUS
Paul's friend at Ephesus, Acts 19:21, 22; 2 Tim 4:20
Treasurer of Corinth, Rom 16:23

ERR
you cause you to *e* .... Is 3:12
My people Israel to *e* ...... Jer 23:13

ERROR
God that it was an *e* .... Eccl 5:6
utter *e* against the LORD....... Is 32:6
nor was there any *e* .... Dan 6:4
e which was due .... Rom 1:27
a sinner from the *e* .... James 5:20
led away with the *e* .... 2 Pet 3:17
and the spirit of *e* .... 1 John 4:6
run greedily in the *e* .... Jude 11

ERRORS
can understand his *e* .... Ps 19:12

ESARHADDON
Son of Sennacherib; king of Assyria
(681–669 B.C.), 2 Kin 19:36, 37

ESAU
Isaac's favorite son, Gen 25:25–28
Sells his birthright, Gen 25:29–34
Deprived of blessing; seeks to kill
 Jacob, Gen 27
Reconciled to Jacob, Gen 33:1–17
Descendants of, Gen 36

ESCAPE
E to the mountains . . . . Gen 19:17
Do not let one of them e . . 1 Kin 18:40
and they shall not e . . . . Job 11:20
Shall they e by . . . . Ps 56:7
speaks lies will not e . . . . Prov 19:5
who fears God will e . . . . Eccl 7:18
and how shall we e . . . . Is 20:6
who does such things e . . . Ezek 17:15
nothing shall e them . . . . Joel 2:3
How can you e the . . . . Matt 23:33
e all these things . . . . Luke 21:36
same, that you will e . . . . Rom 2:3
also make the way of e . . 1 Cor 10:13
And they shall not e . . . . . 1 Thess 5:3
e the snare of the devil . . . . 2 Tim 2:26
how shall we e if we . . . . Heb 2:3
e who refused Him who . . . . Heb 12:25

ESCAPED
I alone have e to tell . . . . Job 1:15
my flesh, and I have e . . . . . Job 19:20
Our soul has e as a . . . . Ps 124:7
all e safely to land . . . . . . Acts 27:44
having e the corruption . . . . . 2 Pet 1:4
after they have e . . . . 2 Pet 2:20

ESH-BAAL
Son of Saul, 1 Chr 8:33

ESHCOL
Valley near Hebron, Num 13:22–27;
 Deut 1:24

ESTABLISH
But I will e My covenant . . . . Gen 6:18
I will e the throne of his . . 2 Sam 7:13
to e them forever . . . . 2 Chr 9:8
'Your seed I will e . . . . Ps 89:4
e the work of our . . . . Ps 90:17
E Your word to Your . . . . . . Ps 119:38
e an everlasting . . . . Ezek 16:60
e justice in the gate . . . . . . Amos 5:15
seeking to e their own . . . . . Rom 10:3
to Him who is able to e . . . Rom 16:25
He may e your hearts . . . 1 Thess 3:13
e you in every good . . . . . 2 Thess 2:17
faithful, who will e . . . . 2 Thess 3:3
that He may e the second . . . Heb 10:9
E your hearts . . . . James 5:8
a while, perfect, e . . . . 1 Pet 5:10

ESTABLISHED
He not made you and e . . . . Deut 32:6
also is firmly e . . . . 1 Chr 16:30
David my father be e . . . . . . 2 Chr 1:9
e it upon the waters . . . . Ps 24:2
a rock, and e my steps . . . . . . Ps 40:2
e a testimony in Jacob . . . . . . Ps 78:5
It shall be e forever . . . . Ps 89:37
Your throne is e . . . . Ps 93:2
LORD has e His throne . . . . Ps 103:19
let all your ways be e . . . . . Prov 4:26
e the clouds above . . . . Prov 8:28
lip shall be e forever . . . . . Prov 12:19
your thoughts will be e . . . . Prov 16:3
by understanding it is e . . . Prov 24:3
house shall be e . . . . Is 2:2
In mercy the throne will be e . . Is 16:5
by His power, He has e . . . Jer 10:12
every word may be e . . . . . Matt 18:16
built up in Him and e . . . . Col 2:7
covenant, which was e . . . . . . Heb 8:6
that the heart be e . . . . Heb 13:9

ESTABLISHES
The king e the land by . . . . . Prov 29:4
Now He who e us with . . . . 2 Cor 1:21

ESTEEM
high wall in his own e . . . . Prov 18:11
and we did not e . . . . Is 53:3
e others better than . . . . Phil 2:3
and hold such men in e . . . . Phil 2:29
e them very highly . . . . . . 1 Thess 5:13

ESTEEMED
For what is highly e . . . . . Luke 16:15
those who are least e . . . . . 1 Cor 6:4

ESTEEMS
One person e one day . . . . . Rom 14:5

ESTHER
Selected for harem, Esth 2:7–16
Chosen to be queen, Esth 2:17, 18
Agrees to intercede for her people,
 Esth 4
Invites king to banquet, Esth 5:1–8
Denounces Haman; obtains reversal of
 decree, Esth 7:1—8:8
Establishes Purim, Esth 9:29–32

ESTRANGED
The wicked are e . . . . Ps 58:3
because they are all e . . . . . Ezek 14:5
You have become e . . . . Gal 5:4

ETAM
Rock where Samson took refuge, Judg
 15:8–19

ETERNAL
e God is your refuge . . . . . Deut 33:27
For man goes to his e . . . . . Eccl 12:5
I do that I may have e . . . . Matt 19:16
and inherit e life . . . . Matt 19:29
the righteous into e life . . . Matt 25:46
that I may inherit e life . . . Mark 10:17
in the age to come, e . . . . Mark 10:30
not perish but have e . . . . . . John 3:16
gathers fruit for e life . . . . . . John 4:36
you think you have e . . . . . . John 5:39
drinks My blood has e life . John 6:54
the words of e life . . . . John 6:68
And I give them e life . . . . John 10:28
that He should give e . . . . . John 17:2
And this is e life . . . . John 17:3
e life to those who by . . . . . . Rom 2:7
righteousness to e . . . . Rom 5:21
the gift of God is e . . . . Rom 6:23
e weight of glory . . . . 2 Cor 4:17
are not seen are e . . . . 2 Cor 4:18
not made with hands, e . . . . 2 Cor 5:1
to the King e, immortal . . . 1 Tim 1:17
lay hold on e life . . . . 1 Tim 6:12
e life which God . . . . Titus 1:2
to the hope of e life . . . . Titus 3:7
and of e judgment . . . . Heb 6:2
obtained e redemption . . . . . Heb 9:12
e life which was . . . . 1 John 1:2
has promised us— e life . . . 1 John 2:25
that no murderer has e . . . 1 John 3:15
God has given us e . . . . 1 John 5:11
that you have e life . . . . . . 1 John 5:13
the true God and e life . . . 1 John 5:20
Jesus Christ unto e . . . . Jude 21

ETERNAL LIFE
that I may have e . . . . Matt 19:16
the righteous into e . . . . . . Matt 25:46
in the age to come, e . . . . Mark 10:30
I do to inherit e . . . . Luke 10:25
not perish but have e . . . . . . John 3:15
and gathers fruit for e . . . . . John 4:36
you think you have e . . . . . . John 5:39
You have the words of e . . . John 6:68
will keep it for e . . . . John 12:25
is e, that they may know . . . John 17:3
had been appointed to e . . Acts 13:48
e to those who by patient . . . Rom 2:7
righteousness to e . . . . Rom 5:21

the gift of God is e . . . . Rom 6:23
lay hold on e . . . . 1 Tim 6:12
in hope of e which God, ... Titus 1:2
declare to you that e . . . . . 1 John 1:2
He has promised us e . . . . 1 John 2:25
no murderer has e . . . . 1 John 3:15
that God has given us e . . 1 John 5:11
Lord Jesus Christ unto e . . . . Jude 21

ETERNITY
Also He has put e . . . . Eccl 3:11
One who inhabits e . . . . Is 57:15

ETHAM
Israel's encampment, Ex 13:20

ETHIOPIA
See CUSH
Hostile to Israel and Judah, 2 Chr 12:2,
 3; 14:9–15; Is 43:3; Dan 11:43
Prophecies against, Is 20:1–6; Ezek
 30:4–9

ETHIOPIANS
Skin of, unchangeable, Jer 13:23

EUNICE
Mother of Timothy, 2 Tim 1:5

EUNUCH
eczema or scab, or is a e . . . Lev 21:20
Hegai the king's e . . . . Esth 2:3
of Ethiopia, a e . . . . Acts 8:27

EUNUCHS
seven e who served . . . . Esth 1:10
be e in the palace . . . . Is 39:7
Ethiopian, one of the e . . . . . Jer 38:7
the master of his e . . . . Dan 1:3
have made themselves e . . . Matt 19:12

EUPHRATES
River of Eden, Gen 2:14
Boundary of Promised Land, Gen
 15:18; 1 Kin 4:21, 24
Scene of battle, Jer 46:2, 6, 10
Angels bound there, Rev 9:14

EUTYCHUS
Sleeps during Paul's sermon, Acts 20:9
Restored to life, Acts 20:12

EVANGELIST
house of Philip the e . . . . . . Acts 21:8
do the work of an e . . . . 2 Tim 4:5

EVANGELISTS
some prophets, some e . . . . . Eph 4:11

EVEN
E in laughter the heart . . . Prov 14:13
E a child is known . . . . Prov 20:11
e nature itself teach . . . . . 1 Cor 11:14
e denying the Lord who . . . . 2 Pet 2:1

EVENING
the e and the morning were . . Gen 1:5
quails came up at e . . . . Ex 16:13
At e they return . . . . Ps 59:6
e it is cut down and . . . . Ps 90:6
of my hands as the e . . . . . . Ps 141:2
e do not withhold your . . . . Eccl 11:6
and more fierce than e . . . . . Hab 1:8
When it is e you say, 'It . . . Matt 16:2
when e came, the boat . . . . Mark 6:47
in the e, at midnight . . . . Mark 13:35
it is toward e . . . . Luke 24:29

EVER
shall reign forever and e . . . Ex 15:18
No razor has e come . . . . . . Judg 16:17
were the upright e cut off . . . . Job 4:7
Let them e shout for joy, ... Ps 5:11
eyes are e toward the LORD . . Ps 25:15
He is e merciful . . . . Ps 37:26
Or e You had formed . . . . Ps 90:2
Your name forever and e . . . . Ps 145:1
shines e brighter unto . . . . . Prov 4:18
there was e an earth . . . . Prov 8:23
even forever and e . . . . Dan 7:18
time, no, nor e shall be . . . Matt 24:21
eat fruit from you e . . . . . . Mark 11:14

all things that I e did ......John 4:29
"No man e spoke like ......John 7:46
be glory forever and e ....Gal 1:5
no one e hated his own ......Eph 5:29
the angels has He e said ....Heb 1:13
to the Lamb, forever and e ..Rev 5:13
shall reign forever and e ..Rev 11:15

EVERLASTING
for an e covenant ....Gen 17:7
are the e arms ....Deut 33:27
God of Israel from e ....1 Chr 16:36
His mercy is e ....Ps 100:5
of the LORD is from e .....Ps 103:17
to Israel as an e covenant ..Ps 105:10
righteousness is an e .....Ps 119:142
lead me in the way e .....Ps 139:24
Your kingdom is an e .....Ps 145:13
E Father, Prince of Peace ....Is 9:6
in YAH, the LORD, is e........Is 26:4
e joy on their heads ....Is 35:10
I will make an e covenant .....Is 55:3
will be to you an e ....Is 60:19
from E is Your name ....Is 63:16
loved you with an e love ....Jer 31:3
awake, some to e life ......Dan 12:2
cast into the e fire ....Matt 18:8
away into e punishment ....Matt 25:46
not perish but have e .....John 3:16
springing up into e life ...John 4:14
Him who sent Me has e ...John 5:24
endures to e life ....John 6:27
in Him may have e ....John 6:40
believes in Me has e .....John 6:47
unworthy of e life ....Acts 13:46
and the end, e life ....Rom 6:22
of the Spirit reap e ....Gal 6:8
e destruction from the ....2 Thess 1:9
reserved in e chains ....Jude 6

EVERLASTING LIFE
Some to e, some to shame ..Dan 12:2
not perish but have e .....John 3:16
springing up into e .....John 4:14
e and shall not come......John 5:24
food which endures to e ...John 6:27
His command is e ....John 12:50
yourselves unworthy of e .Acts 13:46
holiness, and the end, e ...Rom 6:22
will of the Spirit reap e .....Gal 6:8
to believe on Him for e ....1 Tim 1:16

EVERYONE
said, 'Repent now e ....Jer 25:5
e who is born of the ....John 3:8
E who is of the truth ....John 18:37

EVIDENCE
my e is on high ....Job 16:19
e of things not seen ....Heb 11:1

EVIDENT
the sight of God is e ....Gal 3:11
of some are clearly e ......1 Tim 5:25
e that our Lord arose ......Heb 7:14

EVIL
knowledge of good and e ....Gen 2:9
knowing good and e ....Gen 3:5
his heart was only e ....Gen 6:5
repaid e for good ....Gen 44:4
e have been the ....Gen 47:9
you meant e against me ...Gen 50:20
follow a crowd to do e .....Ex 23:2
e in the sight of the ....Num 32:13
the e from your midst ....Deut 13:5
and good, death and e ....Deut 30:15
Saul plotted e against ....1 Sam 23:9
rebellious and e city ....Ezra 4:12
feared God and shunned e ....Job 1:1
e shall touch you ....Job 5:19
I looked for good, e ....Job 30:26
nor shall e dwell ....Ps 5:4
Nor does e to his neighbor ..Ps 15:3
I will fear no e ....Ps 23:4
Keep your tongue from e ...Ps 34:13

E shall slay the ....Ps 34:21
he does not abhor e ....Ps 36:4
Depart from e, and do ......Ps 37:27
done this e in Your sight ....Ps 51:4
e more than good ....Ps 52:3
e shall befall you ....Ps 91:10
love the LORD, hate e.......Ps 97:10
not be afraid of e tidings ....Ps 112:7
feet from every e way .....Ps 119:101
preserve you from all e .....Ps 121:7
secure, without fear of e ...Prov 1:33
LORD and depart from e ....Prov 3:7
of the LORD is to hate e......Prov 8:13
To do e is like sport ......Prov 10:23
shall be filled with e .....Prov 12:21
e will bow before the .....Prov 14:19
Keeping watch on the e ....Prov 15:3
is to depart from e ....Prov 16:17
Whoever rewards e ....Prov 17:13
A prudent man forsees e ..Prov 22:3
e all the days of her ......Prov 31:12
vanity and a great e ....Eccl 2:21
There is a severe e ....Eccl 5:13
of men are full of e ....Eccl 9:3
put away e from your .....Eccl 11:10
to those who call e ....Is 5:20
his eyes from seeing e ......Is 33:15
is taken away from e ....Is 57:1
of peace and not of e ......Jer 29:11
commit this great e ....Jer 44:7
Seek good and not e ......Amos 5:14
turn from his e way ....Jon 3:8
"Turn now from your e ....Zech 1:4
not to resist an e person ....Matt 5:39
His sun rise on the e ....Matt 5:45
deliver us from the e ....Matt 6:13
If you then, being e ....Matt 7:11
"Why do you think e ....Matt 9:4
e treasure brings ....Matt 12:35
"An e and adulterous ....Matt 12:39
to do good or to do e ......Mark 3:4
proceed e thoughts ....Mark 7:21
what e has He done ......Mark 15:14
to the unthankful and e ....Luke 6:35
e treasure of his heart ....Luke 6:45
If you then, being e .....Luke 11:13
everyone practicing e ......John 3:20
them from the e one ......John 17:15
bear witness of the e .....John 18:23
the e spirits went out .....Acts 19:12
'You shall not speak e of ...Acts 23:5
e I will not to do ....Rom 7:19
then a law, that e ....Rom 7:21
done any good or e ....Rom 9:11
Abhor what is e ....Rom 12:9
Repay no one e for ....Rom 12:17
not be overcome by e .....Rom 12:21
to good works, but to e ....Rom 13:3
good be spoken of as e ....Rom 14:16
simple concerning e ....Rom 16:19
provoked, thinks no e ....1 Cor 13:5
"E company corrupts ....1 Cor 15:33
from this present age ....Gal 1:4
e speaking be put away ....Eph 4:31
withstand in the e day ......Eph 6:13
from every form of e ....1 Thess 5:22
a root of all kinds of e .....1 Tim 6:10
an e heart of unbelief ......Heb 3:12
cannot be tempted by e ...James 1:13
speaks e of a brother ....James 4:11
envy, and all e speaking ...1 Pet 2:1
refrain his tongue from e ...1 Pet 3:10
against those who do e ....1 Pet 3:12
he who does e has not ....3 John 11

EVIL-MERODACH
Babylonian king (562–560 B.C.), 2 Kin
25:27–30

EVIL-MINDEDNESS
strife, deceit, e ....Rom 1:29

EVIL ONE
than these is from the e ....Matt 5:37

But deliver us from the e ...Matt 6:13
But deliver us from the e ...Luke 11:4
keep them from the e .....John 17:15
guard you from the e .....2 Thess 3:3

EVILDOER
LORD shall repay the e ....2 Sam 3:39
An e gives heed to false ....Prov 17:4
"If He were not an e ......John 18:30
suffer trouble as an e ......2 Tim 2:9
a thief, an e ....1 Pet 4:15

EVILDOERS
Do not fret because of e ......Ps 37:1
e shall be cut off ....Ps 37:9
Depart from me, you e ...Ps 119:115
iniquity, a brood of e ....Is 1:4
e shall never be ....Is 14:20
against you as e ....1 Pet 2:12

EVILS
e have surrounded me......Ps 40:12
have committed two e ......Jer 2:13

EXALT
God, and I will e ....Ex 15:2
do you e yourselves ......Num 16:3
e the horn of His ....1 Sam 2:10
e His name together ....Ps 34:3
E the LORD our God.........Ps 99:5
Let them e Him ....Ps 107:32
are my God, I will e ....Ps 118:28
if I do not e Jerusalem .....Ps 137:6
E her, and she will ....Prov 4:8
into heaven, I will e ....Is 14:13
I will e You, I will praise .....Is 25:1
E the humble ....Ezek 21:26
and he shall e himself .....Dan 8:25
He may e you in due time ...1 Pet 5:6

EXALTATION
e comes neither from ......Ps 75:6
who rejoice in My e ....Is 13:3
brother glory in his e .....James 1:9

EXALTED
Let God be e ....2 Sam 22:47
So the LORD e Solomon ..1 Chr 29:25
built You an e house ....2 Chr 6:2
name, which is e ....Neh 9:5
e for a little while ....Job 24:4
God is e by His power .....Job 36:22
when vileness is e ....Ps 12:8
God of my salvation be e .....Ps 18:46
Be e, O LORD, in Your ......Ps 21:13
I will be e among the ....Ps 46:10
Be e, O God, above ....Ps 57:5
righteous shall be e ....Ps 75:10
favor our horn is e ....Ps 89:17
You are e far above ....Ps 97:9
hand of the LORD is e .....Ps 118:16
His name alone is e ....Ps 148:13
upright the city is e ....Prov 11:11
LORD alone shall be e ....Is 2:11
His name is e ....Is 12:4
The LORD is e, for He dwells ..Is 33:5
valley shall be e ....Is 40:4
and humble the e ....Ezek 21:26
e above the hills ....Mic 4:1
humbles himself will be e ..Matt 23:12
Him God has e ....Acts 5:31
And lest I should be e .....2 Cor 12:7
also has highly e ....Phil 2:9

EXALTS
down one, and another ....Ps 75:7
Righteousness e ....Prov 14:34
whoever e himself will ....Luke 14:11
high thing that e ....2 Cor 10:5
e himself above all ....2 Thess 2:4

EXAMINE
E me, O LORD............Ps 26:2
e our ways, and turn ....Lam 3:40
But let a man e ....1 Cor 11:28
But let each one e ....Gal 6:4

EXAMPLE 56 CONCORDANCE

EXAMPLE
to make her a public *e* ..... Matt 1:19
I have given you an *e* .... John 13:15
in following my *e* .... Phil 3:17
to make ourselves an *e* ..2 Thess 3:9
youth, but be an *e* .... 1 Tim 4:12
us, leaving us an *e* .... 1 Pet 2:21
making them an *e* .... 2 Pet 2:6
are set forth as an *e* .... Jude 7

EXAMPLES
happened to them as *e* ...1 Cor 10:11
so that you became *e* .....1 Thess 1:7
to you, but being *e* .... 1 Pet 5:3

EXCEEDING
for us a far more *e* .... 2 Cor 4:17
the *e* greatness of .... Eph 1:19
He might show the *e* .... Eph 2:7
also be glad with *e* joy ..... 1 Pet 4:13

EXCEEDINGLY
prevailed *e* on the earth ....Gen 7:19
your *e* great reward ....Gen 15:1
your descendants *e* .... Gen 16:10
and grew *e* mighty .... Ex 1:7
for the LORD must be *e* .... 1 Chr 22:5
You have made him *e* .... Ps 21:6
let them rejoice *e* .... Ps 68:3
and I love them *e* .... Ps 119:167
is far off and *e* deep .... Eccl 7:24
it displeased Jonah *e* .... Jon 4:1
rejoiced with *e* great joy ....Matt 2:10
e high mountain .... Matt 4:8
Rejoice and be *e* .... Matt 5:12
they were *e* sorrowful ..... Matt 26:22
e white, like snow .... Mark 9:3
"My soul is *e* sorrowful ... Mark 14:34
Him who is able to do *e* .... Eph 3:20
our Lord was *e* abundant .. 1 Tim 1:14
given to us *e* great .... 2 Pet 1:4

EXCEEDS
your righteousness *e* ...... Matt 5:20

EXCEL
you His angels, who *e* ....Ps 103:20
but you *e* them all .... Prov 31:29
that you seek to *e* .... 1 Cor 14:12

EXCELLENCE
e You have overthrown ...... Ex 15:7
did not come with *e* .... 1 Cor 2:1
the *e* of the power .... 2 Cor 4:7
things loss for the *e* .... Phil 3:8

EXCELLENT
He is *e* in power .... Job 37:23
How *e* is Your name in all .... Ps 8:1
It shall be as *e* oil .... Ps 141:5
to His *e* greatness .... Ps 150:2
will speak of *e* things .... Prov 8:6
An *e* wife is the crown of ...Prov 12:4
like Lebanon, *e* .... Song 5:15
for He has done *e* .... Is 12:5
in counsel and *e* .... Is 28:29
Inasmuch as an *e* .... Dan 5:12
the things that are *e* .... Rom 2:18
show you a more *e* way ..1 Cor 12:31
the things that are *e* .... Phil 1:10
a more *e* name .... Heb 1:4
e sacrifice than Cain .... Heb 11:4
came to Him from the *E* ...2 Pet 1:17

EXCELS
Do you see a man who *e* ...Prov 22:29
I saw that wisdom *e* .... Eccl 2:13
of the glory that *e* .... 2 Cor 3:10

EXCHANGE
give in *e* for his soul ...... Matt 16:26

EXCHANGED
Nor can it be *e* .... Job 28:17
e the truth of God for ...... Rom 1:25
For even their women *e* .... Rom 1:26

EXCLUDE
you, and when they *e* ...... Luke 6:22

they want to *e* you .... Gal 4:17

EXCUSE
God be angry at your *e* ...... Eccl 5:6
but now they have no *e* .... John 15:22
they are without *e* .... Rom 1:20
do you think that we *e* ....2 Cor 12:19

EXCUSES
began to make *e* .... Luke 14:18

EXECUTE
nor *e* His fierce wrath ...1 Sam 28:18
e vengeance on the .... Ps 149:7
if you thoroughly *e* .... Jer 7:5
E judgment and .... Jer 22:3
e the fierceness .... Hos 11:9
'*E* true justice .... Zech 7:9
e judgment also .... John 5:27
e wrath on him who .... Rom 13:4

EXECUTES
by the judgment He *e* ...... Ps 9:16
e righteousness .... Ps 103:6
e justice for the .... Ps 146:7
One whose *e* His word ...... Joel 2:11
e justice for me .... Mic 7:9

EXERCISE
those who are great *e* ....Matt 20:25
e yourself toward .... 1 Tim 4:7
e profits a little .... 1 Tim 4:8

EXERCISED
have their senses *e* .... Heb 5:14

EXHORT
we command and *e* .....2 Thess 3:12
I *e* first of all .... 1 Tim 2:1
e him as a father .... 1 Tim 5:1
and *e* these things .... 1 Tim 6:2
Convince, rebuke, *e* .... 2 Tim 4:2
doctrine, both to *e* .... Titus 1:9
e the young men .... Titus 2:6
Speak these things, *e* ...... Titus 2:15
e one another .... Heb 3:13

EXHORTATION
you have any word of *e* ...Acts 13:15
he who exhorts, in *e* ...... Rom 12:8
to reading, to *e* .... 1 Tim 4:13
with the word of *e* .... Heb 13:22

EXHORTED
For I earnestly *e* .... Jer 11:7
e and strengthened .... Acts 15:32
as you know how we *e* ..1 Thess 2:11

EXILE
and also an *e* from ......2 Sam 15:19
The captive *e* hastens .... Is 51:14

EXIST
things which do not *e* ...... Rom 4:17
by Your will they *e* .... Rev 4:11

EXPECT
an hour you do not *e* ..... Luke 12:40

EXPECTATION
The *e* of the poor .... Ps 9:18
God alone, for my *e* .... Ps 62:5
the people were in *e* ...... Luke 3:15
For the earnest *e* .... Rom 8:19
a certain fearful *e* .... Heb 10:27

EXPECTING
e to receive something ...... Acts 3:5

EXPEDIENT
e for us that one man ..... John 11:50

EXPERT
and the *e* enchanter .... Is 3:3
those of an *e* warrior .... Jer 50:9
because you are *e* .... Acts 26:3

EXPLAIN
was no one who could *e* ... Gen 41:24
days they could not *e* ..... Judg 14:14
"*E* this parable to us ...... Matt 15:15
to say, and hard to *e* .... Heb 5:11

EXPLAINED
He *e* all things to His ...... Mark 4:34
e to him the way of God ... Acts 18:26

EXPLOIT
e all your laborers .... Is 58:3
against those who *e* .... Mal 3:5
they will *e* you with .... 2 Pet 2:3

EXPOSED
his deeds should be *e* ..... John 3:20
all things that are *e* .... Eph 5:13

EXPOUNDED
He *e* to them in all ...... Luke 24:27

EXPRESS
man cannot *e* it .... Eccl 1:8
of His glory and the *e* ...... Heb 1:3

EXPRESSLY
of the LORD came *e* .... Ezek 1:3
Now the Spirit *e* .... 1 Tim 4:1

EXTEND
none to *e* mercy to him ....Ps 109:12
"Behold, I will *e* .... Is 66:12
did not *e* to you .... 2 Cor 10:14

EXTINGUISHED
broken, my days are *e* ..... Job 17:1
They are *e*, they are .... Is 43:17

EXTOL
I will *e* You .... Ps 30:1
e Him who rides .... Ps 68:4

EXTOLLED
e with my tongue .... Ps 66:17
shall be exalted and *e* ...... Is 52:13

EXTORTION
e gathers it for him .... Prov 28:8
your neighbors by *e* ..... Ezek 22:12
they are full of *e* .... Matt 23:25

EXTORTIONERS
nor *e* will inherit .... 1 Cor 6:10

EXULT
in anguish I would *e* .... Job 6:10

EYE
e for *e*, tooth for tooth ..... Ex 21:24
your *e* be evil against .... Deut 15:9
the ear, but now my *e* ..... Job 42:5
me as the apple of Your *e* ...Ps 17:8
guide you with My *e* .... Ps 32:8
Behold, the *e* of the .... Ps 33:18
He who formed the *e* ...... Ps 94:9
with the *e* causes trouble .. Prov 10:10
and the seeing *e* .... Prov 20:12
who has a generous *e* ..... Prov 22:9
A man with an evil *e* ..... Prov 28:22
e that mocks his .... Prov 30:17
e is not satisfied .... Eccl 1:8
labors, nor is his *e* .... Eccl 4:8
for they shall see *e* .... Is 52:8
e seen any God besides .... Is 64:4
the apple of His *e* .... Zech 2:8
If your right *e* causes ...... Matt 5:29
it was said, 'An *e* .... Matt 5:38
lamp of the body is the *e* ... Matt 6:22
plank in your own *e* .... Matt 7:3
e causes you to sin .... Matt 18:9
Or is your *e* evil .... Matt 20:15
e causes you to sin .... Mark 9:47
when your *e* is good ...... Luke 11:34
the *e* of a needle .... Luke 18:25
"*E* has not seen .... 1 Cor 2:9
"Because I am not an *e* ...1 Cor 12:16
whole body were an *e* ...1 Cor 12:17
the twinkling of an *e* .... 1 Cor 15:52
every *e* will see Him .... Rev 1:7
your eyes with *e* salve ..... Rev 3:18

EYELIDS
His eyes behold, His *e* ...... Ps 11:4
e look right before .... Prov 4:25
slumber to your *e* .... Prov 6:4

EYES

e will be opened .... Gen 3:5
"Lift your e now and ...... Gen 13:14
Abraham lifted his e ...... Gen 22:13
the e of Israel were dim ... Gen 48:10
and you can be our e ..... Num 10:31
hallow Me in the e of .... Num 20:12
Your e have seen what the .. Deut 4:3
frontlets between your e .... Deut 6:8
right in his own e .... Deut 12:8
in the e of the LORD....... Deut 13:18
e to see and ears to hear .. Deut 29:4
thorns in your e .... Josh 23:13
found favor in your e ...... Ruth 2:10
open his e that he may .... 2 Kin 6:17
she put paint on her e .... 2 Kin 9:30
My e will be open .... 2 Chr 7:15
For the e of the LORD...... 2 Chr 16:9
God may enlighten our e ... Ezra 9:8
Do You have e of flesh ..... Job 10:4
And my e shall behold .... Job 19:27
His e are on their ways ... Job 24:23
I was e to the blind ...... Job 29:15
e observe from afar .... Job 39:29
e are secretly fixed .... Ps 10:8
His e behold, His eyelids .... Ps 11:4
enlightening the e.......... Ps 19:8
e are ever toward the ..... Ps 25:15
is before my e .... Ps 26:3
The e of the LORD are ..... Ps 34:15
His e observe the nations .... Ps 66:7
e fail while I wait .... Ps 69:3
e shall you look .... Ps 91:8
E they have, but they .... Ps 115:5
marvelous in our e .... Ps 118:23
Open my e, that I may see .. Ps 119:18
I will lift up my e .... Ps 121:1
our e look to the LORD ... Ps 123:2
not give sleep to my e ...... Ps 132:4
e saw my substance ...... Ps 139:16
wise in your own e .... Prov 3:7
not depart from your e ..... Prov 3:21
e look straight ahead ...... Prov 4:25
is right in his own e ...... Prov 12:15
The e of the LORD are ..... Prov 15:3
but the e of a fool .... Prov 17:24
Will you set your e .... Prov 23:5
Who has redness of e ..... Prov 23:29
be wise in his own e ...... Prov 26:5
so the e of man are ...... Prov 27:20
pure in its own e .... Prov 30:12
The wise man's e .... Eccl 2:14
e than the wandering .... Eccl 6:9
You have dove's e .... Song 1:15
the e of the lofty .... Is 5:15
e have seen the King .... Is 6:5
lest they see with their e ..... Is 6:10
of the book, and the e ..... Is 29:18
open Your e, O LORD .... Is 37:17
e fail from looking .... Is 38:14
O LORD, are not Your e..... Jer 5:3
Who have e and see .... Jer 5:21
e will weep bitterly .... Jer 13:17
For I will set My e .... Jer 24:6
your e from tears .... Jer 31:16
rims were full of e .... Ezek 1:18
full of e all around ...... Ezek 10:12
e to see but does .... Ezek 12:2
that horn which had e ..... Dan 7:20
horn between his e .... Dan 8:5
e like torches of fire, ... Dan 10:6
the e of the Lord GOD ..... Amos 9:8
You are of purer e .... Hab 1:13
their e were opened ...... Matt 9:30
But blessed are your e.... Matt 13:16
their e were heavy .... Matt 26:43
it is marvelous in our e .. Mark 12:11
Hades, he lifted up his e .. Luke 16:23
raise his e to heaven ..... Luke 18:13
lift up your e and look ..... John 4:35
"He put clay on my e ...... John 9:15
e of one who was born .... John 9:32

fixing his e on him .... Acts 3:4
e they have closed .... Acts 28:27
e that they should not ..... Rom 11:8
plucked out your own e .... Gal 4:15
e of your understanding ... Eph 1:18
have seen with our e ..... 1 John 1:1
the lust of the e .... 1 John 2:16
as snow, and His e .... Rev 1:14
and anoint your e .... Rev 3:18
creatures full of e .... Rev 4:6
horns and seven e .... Rev 5:6
tear from their e .... Rev 21:4

EYESERVICE

not with e, as .... Eph 6:6
the flesh, not with e .... Col 3:22

EYEWITNESSES

the beginning were e ...... Luke 1:2
e of His majesty .... 2 Pet 1:16

EZEKIEL

Sent to rebellious Israel, Ezek 2; 3
Prophesies by symbolic action:
siege of Jerusalem, Ezek 4
destruction of Jerusalem, Ezek 5
captivity of Judah, Ezek 12:1–20
destruction of the temple, Ezek
24:15–27
Visions of:
God's glory, Ezek 1:4–28
abominations, Ezek 8:5–18
valley of dry bones, Ezek 37:1–14
messianic times, Ezek 40—48
river of life, Ezek 47:1–5
Parables, allegories, dirges of, Ezek 15;
16; 17; 19; 23; 24

EZION GEBER

See ELATH
Town on the Red Sea, 1 Kin 9:26
Israelite encampment, Num 33:35
Seaport of Israel's navy, 1 Kin 22:48

EZRA

Scribe, priest and reformer of post-
exilic times; commissioned by
Artaxerxes, Ezra 7
Returns with exiles to Jerusalem,
Ezra 8
Institutes reforms, Ezra 9
Reads the Law, Neh 8
Assists in dedication of wall, Neh
12:27–43

FABLES

nor give heed to f .... 1 Tim 1:4
be turned aside to f .... 2 Tim 4:4
cunningly devised f .... 2 Pet 1:16

FACE

was on the f of the deep ..... Gen 1:2
In the sweat of your f you .. Gen 3:19
"For I have seen God f .... Gen 32:30
shall see my f no more .... Gen 44:23
Joseph fell on his father's f . Gen 50:1
LORD spoke to Moses f to f .. Ex 33:11
f shone while he .... Ex 34:29
he put a veil on his f .... Ex 34:33
the LORD make His f ...... Num 6:25
I will hide My f from ...... Deut 31:17
his f in his mantle .... 1 Kin 19:13
Then he turned his f ..... 2 Kin 20:2
seek His f evermore ..... 1 Chr 16:11
and pray and seek My f .. 2 Chr 7:14
not turn His f from you ... 2 Chr 30:9
Why is your f sad, since ... Neh 2:2
curse You to Your f .... Job 1:11
I will put off my sad f and ... Job 9:27
and lift up your f to God ... Job 22:26
He shall see His f with joy .. Job 33:26
me, I will see Your f .... Ps 17:15
"Your f, LORD, I will seek.... Ps 27:8

Do not hide Your f from ... Ps 27:9
Why do You hide Your f ... Ps 44:24
and cause His f to shine ... Ps 67:1
Do not hide Your f from ... Ps 102:2
Make Your f shine upon .. Ps 119:135
As in water f reflects ..... Prov 27:19
of his f is changed .... Eccl 8:1
I have set My f like a flint ... Is 50:7
sins have hidden His f .... Is 59:2
I have made your f .... Ezek 3:8
set your f against Gog, of .. Ezek 38:2
but to us shame of f .... Dan 9:7
before Your f .... Matt 11:10
to discern the f of the sky .. Matt 16:3
f shone like the sun ...... Matt 17:2
of His f was altered ...... Luke 9:29
His f to go to Jerusalem ... Luke 9:51
they struck Him on the f .. Luke 22:64
always before my f .... Acts 2:25
his f as the f of an angel ... Acts 6:15
dimly, but then f .... 1 Cor 13:12
look steadily at the f ...... 2 Cor 3:7
with unveiled f .... 2 Cor 3:18
one strikes you on the f .. 2 Cor 11:20
withstood him to his f ...... Gal 2:11
that we may see your f .. 1 Thess 3:10
his natural f in a .... James 1:23
but the f of the LORD...... 1 Pet 3:12
creature had a f like a man ... Rev 4:7
They shall see His f .... Rev 22:4

FACE TO FACE

For I have seen God f, ... Gen 32:30
the Lord spoke to Moses f .. Ex 33:11
I speak with him f .... Num 12:8
the LORD talked with you f .. Deut 5:4
whom the LORD knew f .. Deut 34:10
Angel of the LORD f......... Judg 6:22
My case with you f .... Ezek 20:35
mirror, dimly, but then f .. 1 Cor 13:12

FACES

f were not ashamed ...... Ps 34:5
wipe away tears from all f .... Is 25:8
hid, as it were, our f .... Is 53:3
be afraid of their f .... Jer 1:8
and all f turned pale ...... Jer 30:6
Each one had four f ...... Ezek 1:6
the gate that f toward the .. Ezek 43:1
your f looking worse than .. Dan 1:10
all f are drained of color .... Joel 2:6
they disfigure their f ...... Matt 6:16
fell on their f before the ..... Rev 7:11

FACTIONS

there must also be f ...... 1 Cor 11:19

FADE

we all f as a leaf............. Is 64:6
and the leaf shall f .... Jer 8:13
rich man also will f ...... James 1:11
and that does not f .... 1 Pet 1:4
of glory that does not f .... 1 Pet 5:4

FADES

withers, the flower f .... Is 40:7

FAIL

eyes shall look and f ...... Deut 28:32
man's heart f because .... 1 Sam 17:32
You shall not f to have a .. 1 Kin 8:25
eyes of the wicked will f ... Job 11:20
flesh and my heart f .... Ps 73:26
of the thirsty to f .... Is 32:6
not one of these shall f .... Is 34:16
their tongues f .... Is 41:17
whose waters do not f .... Is 58:11
have caused wine to f ..... Jer 48:33
His compassions f not .... Lam 3:22
of the olive may f .... Hab 3:17
nor shall the vine f .... Mal 3:11
heavens that does not f .. Luke 12:33
that when you f .... Luke 16:9
tittle of the law to f ...... Luke 16:17
faith should not f .... Luke 22:32
prophecies, they will f ..... 1 Cor 13:8

Your years will not *f* .... Heb 1:12
For the time would *f* .... Heb 11:32

FAILED
Not a word *f* of any .... Josh 21:45
My relatives have *f* .... Job 19:14
Has His promise *f* .... Ps 77:8
refuge has *f* me .... Ps 142:4

FAILING
men's hearts *f* .... Luke 21:26

FAILS
my strength *f* because .... Ps 31:10
Therefore my heart *f* me ... Ps 40:12
my spirit *f* .... Ps 143:7
and every vision *f* .... Ezek 12:22
wine is dried up, the oil *f* ... Joel 1:10
He never *f*, but the unjust ... Zeph 3:5
Love never *f* .... 1 Cor 13:8

FAINT
If you *f* in the day of .... Prov 24:10
the youths shall *f* .... Is 40:30
shall walk and not *f* .... Is 40:31
my heart is *f* in me .... Jer 8:18
and the infants *f* .... Lam 2:11

FAINTED
thirsty, their soul *f* .... Ps 107:5

FAINTHEARTED
unruly, comfort the *f* .... 1 Thess 5:14

FAINTS
longs, yes, even *f* .... Ps 84:2
My soul *f* for Your .... Ps 119:81
And the whole heart *f* .... Is 1:5
the earth, neither *f* .... Is 40:28

FAIR
Behold, you are *f* .... Song 1:15
How *f* and how pleasant ... Song 7:6
of the Lord is not *f* .... Ezek 18:25
My ways which are *f* .... Ezek 18:29
say, 'It will be *f* weather ... Matt 16:2
to a place called *F* .... Acts 27:8
what is just and *f* .... Col 4:1

FAIR HAVENS
Harbor of Crete at which Paul landed,
Acts 27:8

FAIR-MINDED
These were more *f* .... Acts 17:11

FAIRER
f than the sons .... Ps 45:2

FAIREST
another beloved, O *f* .... Song 5:9
your beloved gone, O *f* ..... Song 6:1

FAITH
in whom is no *f* .... Deut 32:20
shall live by his *f* .... Hab 2:4
you, O you of little *f* .... Matt 6:30
not found such great *f* ..... Matt 8:10
your *f* has made you well .. Matt 9:22
"O you of little *f* .... Matt 14:31
woman, great is your *f* .... Matt 15:28
f as a mustard seed .... Matt 17:20
that you have no *f* .... Mark 4:40
to them, "Have *f* .... Mark 11:22
not found such great *f* ..... Luke 7:9
you, O you of little *f* .... Luke 12:28
"Increase our *f* .... Luke 17:5
will He really find *f* .... Luke 18:8
through *f* in His name .... Acts 3:16
a man full of *f* .... Acts 6:5
the Holy Spirit and of *f* .... Acts 11:24
that he had *f* to be healed .. Acts 14:9
were strengthened in the *f* .. Acts 16:5
are sanctified by *f* .... Acts 26:18
for obedience to the *f* .... Rom 1:5
that your *f* is spoken of ..... Rom 1:8
God is revealed from *f* .... Rom 1:17
God, through *f* .... Rom 3:22
f apart from the deeds ..... Rom 3:28

his *f* is accounted for .... Rom 4:5
f which he had while still .. Rom 4:11
f is made void and the ..... Rom 4:14
those who are of the *f* ..... Rom 4:16
And not being weak in *f* ... Rom 4:19
having been justified by *f* .. Rom 5:1
of *f* speaks in this way ..... Rom 10:6
f which we preach .... Rom 10:8
f comes by hearing .... Rom 10:17
and you stand by *f* .... Rom 11:20
each one a measure of *f* .... Rom 12:3
in proportion to our *f* .... Rom 12:6
Do you have *f* .... Rom 14:22
whatever is not from *f* .... Rom 14:23
that your *f* should not be ... 1 Cor 2:5
though I have all *f* .... 1 Cor 13:2
And now abide *f* .... 1 Cor 13:13
your *f* is also empty .... 1 Cor 15:14
stand fast in the *f* .... 1 Cor 16:13
For we walk by *f* .... 2 Cor 5:7
as your *f* is increased .... 2 Cor 10:15
now preaches the *f* which ... Gal 1:23
law but by *f* in Jesus Christ .. Gal 2:16
the flesh I live by *f* .... Gal 2:20
or by the hearing of *f* .... Gal 3:2
f are sons of Abraham .... Gal 3:7
the just shall live by *f* .... Gal 3:11
the law is not of *f* .... Gal 3:12
of the Spirit through *f* .... Gal 3:14
But before *f* came .... Gal 3:23
But after *f* has come .... Gal 3:25
f working through love .... Gal 5:6
of the household of *f* .... Gal 6:10
been saved through *f* .... Eph 2:8
one Lord, one *f* .... Eph 4:5
to the unity of the *f* .... Eph 4:13
taking the shield of *f* .... Eph 6:16
for the *f* of the gospel .... Phil 1:27
established in the *f* .... Col 2:7
your work of *f* .... 1 Thess 1:3
on the breastplate of *f* .... 1 Thess 5:8
work of *f* with power .... 2 Thess 1:11
for not all have *f* .... 2 Thess 3:2
a true son in the *f* .... 1 Tim 1:2
edification which is in *f* .... 1 Tim 1:4
having *f* and a good .... 1 Tim 1:19
if they continue in *f*, love . 1 Tim 2:15
the mystery of the *f* .... 1 Tim 3:9
great boldness in the *f* .... 1 Tim 3:13
in love, in spirit, in *f* .... 1 Tim 4:12
he has denied the *f* .... 1 Tim 5:8
righteousness, godliness, *f* . 1 Tim 6:11
Fight the good fight of *f* ... 1 Tim 6:12
I have kept the *f* .... 2 Tim 4:7
in our common *f* .... Titus 1:4
temperate, sound in *f* .... Titus 2:2
not being mixed with *f* .... Heb 4:2
of *f* toward God, ... Heb 6:1
those who through *f* .... Heb 6:12
in full assurance of *f* .... Heb 10:22
the just shall live by *f* ..... Heb 10:38
f is the substance .... Heb 11:1
without *f* it is .... Heb 11:6
These all died in *f* .... Heb 11:13
good testimony through *f* .. Heb 11:39
author and finisher of our *f* . Heb 12:2
whose *f* follow .... Heb 13:7
your *f* produces patience ... James 1:3
But let him ask in *f* .... James 1:6
someone says he has *f* .... James 2:14
Show me your *f* .... James 2:18
f without works is dead .... James 2:20
and not by *f* only .... James 2:24
f will save the sick .... James 5:15
the genuineness of your *f* .. 1 Pet 1:7
receiving the end of your *f* . 1 Pet 1:9
him, steadfast in the *f* ..... 1 Pet 5:9
add to your *f* virtue .... 2 Pet 1:5
on your most holy *f* .... Jude 20
works, love, service, *f* .... Rev 2:19
the patience and the *f* ..... Rev 13:10
of God and the *f* .... Rev 14:12

FAITHFUL
he is *f* in all My house ..... Num 12:7
God, He is God, the *f* .... Deut 7:9
found his heart *f* .... Neh 9:8
f disappear from among ..... Ps 12:1
LORD preserves the *f* .... Ps 31:23
whose spirit was not *f* .... Ps 78:8
eyes shall be on the *f* .... Ps 101:6
commandments are *f* .... Ps 119:86
are righteous and very *f* .. Ps 119:138
f spirit conceals a .... Prov 11:13
A *f* witness does not lie ... Prov 14:5
But who can find a *f* .... Prov 20:6
A *f* man will abound .... Prov 28:20
the LORD who is *f* .... Is 49:7
f witness between us .... Jer 42:5
or fault, because he was *f* .... Dan 6:4
the Holy One who is *f* ..... Hos 11:12
"Who then is a *f* .... Matt 24:45
good and *f* servant .... Matt 25:23
"Who then is that *f* .... Luke 12:42
He who is *f* in what .... Luke 16:10
if you have not been *f* ..... Luke 16:12
have judged me to be *f* .... Acts 16:15
God is *f*, by whom .... 1 Cor 1:9
that one be found *f* .... 1 Cor 4:2
is my beloved and *f* .... 1 Cor 4:17
God is *f*, who will not .... 1 Cor 10:13
But as God is *f* .... 2 Cor 1:18
f minister in the LORD ...... Eph 6:21
f brethren in Christ .... Col 1:2
He who calls you is *f* ..... 1 Thess 5:24
because He counted me *f* . 1 Tim 1:12
This is a *f* saying and .... 1 Tim 1:15
temperate, *f* in all things .. 1 Tim 3:11
commit these to *f* men .... 2 Tim 2:2
f High Priest in .... Heb 2:17
as Moses also was *f* .... Heb 3:2
Moses indeed was *f* .... Heb 3:5
He who promised is *f* ..... Heb 10:23
judged Him *f* who had .... Heb 11:11
He is *f* and just to .... 1 John 1:9
Be *f* until death .... Rev 2:10
words are true and *f* .... Rev 21:5

FAITHFULNESS
righteousness and his *f* .. 1 Sam 26:23
for in their *f* they .... 2 Chr 31:18
f reaches to the clouds .... Ps 36:5
I have declared Your *f* .... Ps 40:10
Your *f* to all generations .... Ps 89:1
f You shall establish .... Ps 89:2
Your *f* also surrounds .... Ps 89:8
allow My *f* to fail .... Ps 89:33
and Your *f* every night .... Ps 89:33
f endures to all .... Ps 119:90
In Your *f* answer me .... Ps 143:1
counsels of old are *f* .... Is 25:1
great is Your *f* .... Lam 3:23
your *f* is like a morning ...... Hos 6:4
unbelief make the *f* .... Rom 3:3
kindness, goodness, *f* .... Gal 5:22

FAITHLESS
the words of the *f* .... Prov 22:12
"O *f* and perverse .... Matt 17:17
"O *f* generation .... Mark 9:19
If we are *f*, He remains .... 2 Tim 2:13

FALL
a deep sleep to *f* .... Gen 2:21
but do not let me *f* .... 2 Sam 24:14
Let them *f* by their .... Ps 5:10
Though he *f*, he shall not .... Ps 37:24
For I am ready to *f* .... Ps 38:17
Yes, all kings shall *f* .... Ps 72:11
A thousand may *f* at your ... Ps 91:7
Let the wicked *f* into their .. Ps 141:10
LORD upholds all who *f* ... Ps 145:14
but a prating fool will *f* .... Prov 10:8
the wicked will *f* by his ... Prov 11:5
no counsel, the people *f* ... Prov 11:14
trusts in his riches will *f* .. Prov 11:28
haughty spirit before a *f* .. Prov 16:18

but the wicked shall *f* ..... Prov 24:16
digs a pit will *f* .... Prov 26:27
For if they *f*, one will lift .... Eccl 4:10
both he who helps will *f* ...... Is 31:3
all their host shall *f* .... Is 34:4
men shall utterly *f* .... Is 40:30
"Will they *f* and not rise ..... Jer 8:4
F and rise no more .... Jer 25:27
proud shall stumble and *f* ... Jer 50:32
of music, you shall *f* .... Dan 3:5
if You will *f* down .... Matt 4:9
And great was its *f* .... Matt 7:27
the blind, both will *f* ...... Matt 15:14
f from their masters' ...... Matt 15:27
the stars will *f* .... Matt 24:29
Child is destined for the *f* ... Luke 2:34
"I saw Satan *f* .... Luke 10:18
they will *f* by the edge .... Luke 21:24
might *f* on some .... Acts 5:15
f short of the glory of ...... Rom 3:23
that they should *f* .... Rom 11:11
block or a cause to *f* in ... Rom 14:13
take heed lest he *f* ...... 1 Cor 10:12
with pride he *f* .... 1 Tim 3:6
be rich *f* into temptation ... 1 Tim 6:9
if they *f* away .... Heb 6:6
to *f* into the hands of the .. Heb 10:31
lest anyone *f* short of ...... Heb 12:15
it all joy when you *f* ...... James 1:2
and rocks, "*F* on us .... Rev 6:16

FALLEN

has your countenance *f* ...... Gen 4:6
terror of you has *f* on us .... Josh 2:9
f on its face to the earth ... 1 Sam 5:3
who reproach You have *f* ..... Ps 69:9
you are *f* from heaven .... Is 14:12
"Babylon is *f* .... Is 21:9
Babylon has suddenly *f* .... Jer 51:8
you have *f* from grace .... Gal 5:4
who have *f* asleep .... 1 Thess 4:13
And I saw a star *f* .... Rev 9:1
"Babylon is *f* .... Rev 14:8

FALLING

and my feet from *f* .... Ps 116:8
and *f* down before Him .... Luke 8:47
great drops of blood *f* .... Luke 22:44
f away comes first .... 2 Thess 2:3

FALLS

when your enemy *f* ...... Prov 24:17
who is alone when he *f* .... Eccl 4:10
not one of them *f* to the ... Matt 10:29
And whoever *f* .... Matt 21:44
divided against a house *f* .. Luke 11:17
wheat *f* into the ground ... John 12:24
master he stands or *f* ...... Rom 14:4
grass; its flower *f* .... James 1:11
withers, and its flower *f* .... 1 Pet 1:24
so that no rain *f* .... Rev 11:6

FALSE

"You shall not bear *f* ...... Ex 20:16
shall not bear *f* witness .... Deut 5:20
I hate every *f* way .... Ps 119:104
f witness who speaks lies .. Prov 6:19
gives heed to *f* lips .... Prov 17:4
f witness shall perish ..... Prov 21:28
the *f* pen of the scribe ...... Jer 8:8
walk in a *f* spirit .... Mic 2:11
and do not love a *f* .... Zech 8:17
"Beware of *f* prophets ..... Matt 7:15
shall not bear *f* witness .... Matt 19:18
f christs and *f* .... Matt 24:24
at last two *f* witnesses .... Matt 26:60
f prophets will rise ...... Mark 13:22
and we are found *f* ...... 1 Cor 15:15
among *f* brethren .... 2 Cor 11:26
of *f* brethren secretly .... Gal 2:4
taking delight in *f* humility .. Col 2:18
f prophets have gone ...... 1 John 4:1
f teachers among you ...... 2 Pet 2:1
mouth of the *f* prophet ..... Rev 16:13

FALSE PROPHETS

Beware of *f*, who come to .. Matt 7:15
many *f* will rise up .... Matt 24:11
false christs and *f* .... Matt 24:24
f will rise and show ..... Mark 13:22
their fathers to the *f* ...... Luke 6:26
But there were also *f* ...... 2 Pet 2:1
many *f* have gone out ..... 1 John 4:1

FALSE WITNESS

You shall not bear *f* .... Ex 20:16
a *f* who speaks lies. .... Prov 6:19
But a *f*, deceit .... Prov 12:17
f will not go unpunished .. Prov 19:5
A man who bears *f* ...... Prov 25:18
thefts, *f*, blasphemies ..... Matt 15:19
bore *f* against Him ...... Mark 14:56

FALSEHOOD

since *f* remains in your ..... Job 21:34
If I have walked with *f* ..... Job 31:5
those who speak *f* .... Ps 5:6
and brings forth *f* .... Ps 7:14
For their deceit is *f* ...... Ps 119:118
remove *f* and lies far ...... Prov 30:8
under *f* we have hidden .... Is 28:15
offspring of *f* .... Is 57:4
and trusted in *f* .... Jer 13:25

FALSELY

it, and swears *f* .... Lev 6:3
shall not steal, nor deal *f* ... Lev 19:11
nor have we dealt *f* .... Ps 44:17
Whoever *f* boasts of ...... Prov 25:14
surely they swear *f* .... Jer 5:2
prophesy *f* to you .... Jer 29:9
words, swearing *f* .... Hos 10:4
of evil against you *f* ...... Matt 5:11
anyone or accuse *f* ...... Luke 3:14
f called knowledge .... 1 Tim 6:20

FAME

his *f* spread throughout ... Josh 6:27
Sheba heard of the *f* ...... 1 Kin 10:1
exceed the *f* of which .... 1 Kin 10:7
his *f* spread throughout all ... Esth 9:4
endures forever, Your *f* ... Ps 135:13
heard My *f* nor seen .... Is 66:19
Your *f* went out .... Ezek 16:14
them for praise and *f* ..... Zeph 3:19
Then His *f* went .... Matt 4:24

FAMILIAR

to mediums and *f* spirits ... Lev 19:31
and *f* spirits, to prostitute .... Lev 20:6
Even my own *f* friend .... Ps 41:9

FAMILIES

in you all the *f* .... Gen 12:3
in your seed all the *f* of ... Gen 28:14
and all the *f* of the nations .. Ps 22:27
God sets the solitary in *f* ... Ps 68:6
and makes their *f* .... Ps 107:41
the God of all the *f* .... Jer 31:1
f which the LORD has ...... Jer 33:24
of all the *f* of the earth .... Amos 3:2
in your seed all the *f* ...... Acts 3:25

FAMILY

that man and against his *f* ... Lev 20:5
against the whole *f* .... Amos 3:1
shall mourn, every *f* ..... Zech 12:12
Joseph's *f* became known .. Acts 7:13
sons of the *f* of Abraham .. Acts 13:26
f were baptized .... Acts 16:33
from whom the whole *f* .... Eph 3:15

FAMINE

Now there was a *f* .... Gen 12:10
besides the first *f* that was .. Gen 26:1
seven years of *f* will arise .. Gen 41:30
the *f* was severe in the ..... Gen 43:1
the LORD has called for a *f* .. 2 Kin 8:1
In *f* He shall redeem you .... Job 5:20
keep them alive in *f* .... Ps 33:19
He called for a *f* .... Ps 105:16
and destruction, *f* .... Is 51:19

shall die by the sword, by *f* .. Jer 21:9
send the sword, the *f* ..... Jer 24:10
of the fever of *f* .... Lam 5:10
I will increase the *f* ...... Ezek 5:16
there arose a severe *f* ..... Luke 15:14
a *f* and great trouble came .. Acts 7:11
or persecution, or *f*, or ..... Rom 8:35

FAMINES

And there will be *f* .... Matt 24:7

FAMISH

righteous soul to *f* .... Prov 10:3

FAMISHED

honorable men are *f* .... Is 5:13

FAMOUS

and may his name be *f* .... Ruth 4:14

FAN

not to *f* or to cleanse ...... Jer 4:11
His winnowing *f* .... Matt 3:12

FANCIES

with their own *f* .... Prov 1:31

FAR

removed my brothers *f* ..... Job 19:13
Your judgments are *f* ...... Ps 10:5
Be not *f* from Me .... Ps 22:11
those who are *f* .... Ps 73:27
The LORD is *f* from the .... Prov 15:29
but it was *f* from me ...... Eccl 7:23
removed their hearts *f* ...... Is 29:13
Those near and those *f* ... Ezek 22:5
their heart is *f* from ...... Matt 15:8
going to a *f* country ...... Mark 13:34
though He is not *f* .... Acts 17:27
you who once were *f* ...... Eph 2:13

FAR BE IT FROM ME

"*F* that I should do so ..... Gen 44:17
'*F*; for those who honor ... 1 Sam 2:30
f that I should sin .... 1 Sam 12:23
F! Let not the king ...... 1 Sam 22:15
f, that I should swallow .. 2 Sam 20:20
"*F*, O LORD, that .... 2 Sam 23:17
"*F*, O my God, that ...... 1 Chr 11:19
F that I should say .... Job 27:5

FAR COUNTRY

"We have come from a *f* .... Josh 9:6
good news from a *f* ...... Prov 25:25
f, from the end of heaven ..... Is 13:5
from a *f*, from Babylon .... Is 39:3
and went into a *f* ...... Matt 21:33
man traveling to a *f* ...... Matt 25:14
a *f*, and there wasted ..... Luke 15:13
nobleman went into a *f* ... Luke 19:12
and went into a *f* .... Luke 20:9

FARMER

The hard-working *f* ...... 2 Tim 2:6
See how the *f* waits ...... James 5:7

FASHIONED

have made me and *f* .... Job 10:8

FASHIONS

He *f* their hearts .... Ps 33:15

FAST

"But you who held *f* to the .. Deut 4:4
serve Him and hold *f* to .... Deut 13:4
For he held *f* to the LORD .. 2 Kin 18:6
My maids and I will *f* ..... Esth 4:16
commanded, and it stood *f* .... Ps 33:9
of your *f* you find pleasure .... Is 58:3
f that I have chosen .... Is 58:5
they *f*, I will not hear ...... Jer 14:12
Consecrate a *f*, call a .... Joel 1:14
believed God, proclaimed a *f* .. Jon 3:5
"Moreover, when you *f* .... Matt 6:16
disciples do not *f* .... Matt 9:14
f while the bridegroom is .. Mark 2:19
I *f* twice a week .... Luke 18:12
if you hold *f* that word .... 1 Cor 15:2
stand *f* in the faith, be .... 1 Cor 16:13
holding *f* the word of life ... Phil 2:16
you stand *f* in the Lord ... 1 Thess 3:8

holding *f* the faithful word .. Titus 1:9
hold *f* our confession .... Heb 4:14
hold *f* the confession ...... Heb 10:23
Hold *f* what you have .... Rev 3:11

FASTED

and *f* seven days .... 1 Sam 31:13
the child, and David *f* .. 2 Sam 12:16
f and entreated our God .... Ezra 8:23
'Why have we *f* .... Is 58:3
'When you *f* and .... Zech 7:5
And when He had *f* .... Matt 4:2
Then, having *f* and prayed .. Acts 13:3

FASTENED

were its foundations *f* .... Job 38:6
'the peg that is *f* .... Is 22:25

FASTING

I was *f* and praying before ... Neh 1:4
humbled myself with *f* ...... Ps 35:13
are weak through *f* .... Ps 109:24
house on the day of *f* ...... Jer 36:6
and spent the night *f* ...... Dan 6:18
with all your heart, with *f* ... Joel 2:12
not appear to men to be *f* .. Matt 6:18
except by prayer and *f* .... Matt 17:21
I was *f* until this hour ...... Acts 10:30
give yourselves to *f* .... 1 Cor 7:5

FASTINGS

but served God with *f* ...... Luke 2:37
in sleeplessness, in *f* .... 2 Cor 6:5

FAT

the first seven, the *f* cows .. Gen 41:20
and you will eat the *f* ...... Gen 45:18
f is the LORD'S .... Lev 3:16
Now Eglon was a very *f* .... Judg 3:17
have closed up their *f* ...... Ps 17:10

FATHER

See GOD THE FATHER; HEAVENLY
      FATHER

man shall leave his *f* .... Gen 2:24
saw the nakedness of his *f* .. Gen 9:22
and you shall be a *f* .... Gen 17:4
the lineage of our *f* .... Gen 19:32
his *f* blessed him .... Gen 27:41
God of my *f* has been with .. Gen 31:5
Esau was the *f* of the ...... Gen 36:43
f loved him more than all ... Gen 37:4
Thus his *f* wept for him .... Gen 37:35
'Is your *f* still alive .... Gen 43:7
bring my *f* down here ...... Gen 45:13
God, the God of your *f* ..... Gen 46:3
to meet his *f* Israel .... Gen 46:29
went up to bury his *f* ...... Gen 50:7
Honor your *f* and your ...... Ex 20:12
Honor your *f* and your ..... Deut 5:16
obey the voice of his *f* ..... Deut 21:18
of Jesse, the *f* of David .... Ruth 4:17
son, and I will be his *F* ... 1 Chr 22:10
son, and I will be his *F* ... 1 Chr 28:6
'You are my *f* .... Job 17:14
I was a *f* to the poor ...... Job 29:16
When my *f* and my mother .. Ps 27:10
A *f* of the fatherless .... Ps 68:5
f pities his children .... Ps 103:13
the instruction of a *f* .... Prov 4:1
wise son makes a glad *f* .... Prov 10:1
wise son makes a glad *f* ... Prov 15:20
glory of children is their *f* .. Prov 17:6
the *f* of a fool has no joy .. Prov 17:21
son is a grief to his *f* ...... Prov 17:25
curses his *f* or his .... Prov 20:20
f of the righteous will ..... Prov 23:24
makes his *f* rejoice .... Prov 29:3
that curses its *f* .... Prov 30:11
God, Everlasting *F* .... Is 9:6
Your first *f* sinned .... Is 43:27
You, O LORD, are our *F* ..... Is 63:16
time cry to Me, My *F* ...... Jer 3:4
for I am a *F* to Israel ...... Jer 31:9
for the iniquity of his *f* .... Ezek 18:17
not bear the guilt of the *f* . Ezek 18:20

"A son honors his *f* .... Mal 1:6
Have we not all one *F* ... Mal 2:10
your *F* who sees in secret ... Matt 6:4
your heavenly *F* will also .. Matt 6:14
neither will your *F* forgive .. Matt 6:15
your heavenly *F* knows .... Matt 6:32
much more will your *F* .... Matt 7:11
He who loves *f* .... Matt 10:37
does anyone know the *F* .. Matt 11:27
'He who curses *f* .... Matt 15:4
My *F* who is in heaven .... Matt 18:10
a man shall leave his *f* .... Matt 19:5
for One is your *F* .... Matt 23:9
you blessed of My *F* ...... Matt 25:34
"O My *F*, if this cup ...... Matt 26:42
in the name of the *F* ..... Matt 28:19
F with the holy angels .... Mark 8:38
a man shall leave his *f* ... Mark 10:7
the Son, but only the *F* .. Mark 13:32
"Abba, *F*, all things are . Mark 14:36
Your *f* and I have sought . Luke 2:48
just as your *F* also is .. Luke 6:36
first go and bury my *f* ... Luke 9:59
who the Son is but the *F* . Luke 10:22
bread from any *f* among .. Luke 11:11
F give the Holy Spirit to .. Luke 11:13
F will be divided .... Luke 12:53
does not hate his *f* .... Luke 14:26
arise and go to my *f* ..... Luke 15:18
'I beg you therefore, *f* .... Luke 16:27
"*F*, if it is Your will ...... Luke 22:42
"*F*, forgive them, for ..... Luke 23:34
only begotten of the *F* .... John 1:14
F loves the Son .... John 3:35
worship the *F* in spirit .... John 4:23
F has been working ...... John 5:17
what He sees the *F* do .... John 5:19
F raises the dead .... John 5:21
F judges no one .... John 5:22
not honor the *F* who sent . John 5:23
All that the *F* gives Me ... John 6:37
He has seen the *F* .... John 6:46
F who sent Me bears ..... John 8:18
but as My *F* taught Me, I .. John 8:28
we have one *F* .... John 8:41
he is a liar and the *f* of it .. John 8:44
I and My *F* are one ...... John 10:30
and believe that the *F* .... John 10:38
"*F*, I thank You that ..... John 11:41
F, glorify Your name ..... John 12:28
"Lord, show us the *F* ..... John 14:8
seen Me has seen the *F* .... John 14:9
believe that I am in the *F* . John 14:10
because I go to My *F* ..... John 14:12
And I will pray the *F* ..... John 14:16
will be loved by My *F* ... John 14:21
'I am going to the *F* ..... John 14:28
F is the vinedresser .... John 15:1
whatever you ask the *F* ... John 15:16
you ask the *F* in My ..... John 16:23
came forth from the *F* .... John 16:28
And now, O *F*, glorify Me .. John 17:5
yet ascended to My *F* .... John 20:17
F the promise of the Holy .. Acts 2:33
that he might be the *F* ..... Rom 4:11
"I have made you a *f* ..... Rom 4:17
we cry out, "Abba, *F*." .... Rom 8:15
F of our Lord Jesus ...... Rom 15:6
F of mercies and God of .... 2 Cor 1:3
"I will be a *F* to you ...... 2 Cor 6:18
by one Spirit to the *F* ..... Eph 2:18
I bow my knees to the *F* of .. Eph 3:14
one God and *F* of all .... Eph 4:6
a man shall leave his *f* and .. Eph 5:31
F be glory forever and ...... Phil 4:20
For it pleased the *F* that in .. Col 1:19
f does his own children .. 1 Thess 2:11
but exhort him as a *f* ...... 1 Tim 5:1
"I will be to Him a *F* ...... Heb 1:5
without *f*, without mother .... Heb 7:3
whom a *f* does not chasten .. Heb 12:7
comes down from the *F* ... James 1:17

we bless our God and *F* .... James 3:9
if you call on the *F* .... 1 Pet 1:17
an Advocate with the *F* .... 1 John 2:1
love of the *F* is not in .... 1 John 2:15
love the *F* has bestowed ... 1 John 3:1
and testify that the *F* ..... 1 John 4:14
F, the Word, and the ...... 1 John 5:7
his name before My *F* ...... Rev 3:5

FATHER IN HEAVEN

and glorify your *F* .... Matt 5:16
may be sons of your *F* .... Matt 5:45
just as your *F* is perfect .... Matt 5:48
no reward from your *F* ..... Matt 6:1
Our *F*, hallowed be Your .... Matt 6:9
who does the will of My *F* . Matt 7:21
does the will of My *F* ... Matt 12:50
done for them by My *F* ... Matt 18:19
F may also forgive you ... Mark 11:25
Our *F*, hallowed be .... Luke 11:2

FATHER'S

Joseph fell on his *f* face ..... Gen 50:1
he and his *f* household .... Gen 50:22
my *f* God, and I will exalt .... Ex 15:2
When I was my *f* son .... Prov 4:3
keep your *f* command .... Prov 6:20
heeds his *f* instruction ..... Prov 13:1
you in My *F* kingdom .... Matt 26:29
I must be about My *F* ..... Luke 2:49
many of my *f* hired ...... Luke 15:17
Do not make My *F* house .. John 2:16
works that I do in My *F* . John 10:25
F house are many .... John 14:2
the *F* who sent Me ...... John 14:24
that a man has his *f* .... 1 Cor 5:1

FATHERLESS

afflict any widow or *f* child .. Ex 22:22
and your children *f* .... Ex 22:24
justice for the *f* .... Deut 10:18
my hand against the *f* ..... Job 31:21
the helper of the *f* .... Ps 10:14
to do justice to the *f* .... Ps 10:18
father of the *f*, a defender .... Ps 68:5
Let his children be *f* ...... Ps 109:9
He relieves the *f* .... Ps 146:9
the fields of the *f* .... Prov 23:10
do not defend the *f* .... Is 1:23
they may rob the *f* .... Is 10:2
You the *f* finds mercy .... Hos 14:3
the widow or the *f* .... Zech 7:10

FATHERS

bury me with my *f* .... Gen 49:29
swore to your *f* to give you ... Ex 13:5
the iniquity of the *f* .... Ex 20:5
the LORD swore to your *f* ... Deut 1:8
f make you a thousand ..... Deut 1:11
the iniquity of the *f* upon .... Deut 5:9
the LORD God of our *f* ..... Ezra 7:27
f trusted in You .... Ps 22:4
sojourner, as all my *f* were .. Ps 39:12
our ears, O God, our *f* ...... Ps 44:1
He commanded our *f* .... Ps 78:5
did in the sight of their *f* .... Ps 78:12
have sinned with our *f* ..... Ps 106:6
that I gave to your *f* forever ... Jer 7:7
f have eaten sour grapes ... Jer 31:29
f have eaten sour grapes ... Ezek 18:2
for the iniquities of our *f* .... Dan 9:16
f provoked Me to wrath .... Zech 8:14
For so did their *f* to the .... Luke 6:26
Our *f* worshiped on this .... John 4:20
f ate the manna .... John 6:31
f nor we were able to ..... Acts 15:10
of whom are the *f* .... Rom 9:5
you do not have many *f* ... 1 Cor 4:15
unaware that all our *f* ..... 1 Cor 10:1
f, do not provoke .... Eph 6:4
F, do not provoke your .... Col 3:21
where your *f* tested Me ..... Heb 3:9

FATLING

and the *f* together .... Is 11:6

FATNESS
as with marrow and *f* . . . . Ps 63:5
of the root and *f* . . . . Rom 11:17

FATTED
f cattle are killed . . . . Matt 22:4
has killed the *f* . . . . Luke 15:27

FATTENED
f your hearts as . . . . James 5:5

FATTER
f in flesh than all the . . . . . . Dan 1:15

FAULT
find no charge or *f* . . . . Dan 6:4
tell him his *f* between . . . . . Matt 18:15
I have found no *f* . . . . Luke 23:14
does He still find *f* . . . . Rom 9:19
of God without *f* . . . . Phil 2:15
for they are without *f* . . . . . . Rev 14:5

FAULTLESS
covenant had been *f* . . . . Heb 8:7
to present you *f* . . . . Jude 24

FAULTS
"I remember my *f* . . . . Gen 41:9
me from secret *f* . . . . Ps 19:12
are beaten for your *f* . . . . . . 1 Pet 2:20

FAVOR
Joseph found *f* in his sight . . Gen 39:4
nor show *f* to the young . . . Deut 28:50
"Let me find *f* in your . . . . Ruth 2:13
f in his sight more than all . . Esth 2:17
granted me life and *f* . . . . . . Job 10:12
with *f* You will surround . . . . . Ps 5:12
His *f* is for life . . . . Ps 30:5
who *f* my righteous cause . . Ps 35:27
the *f* You have toward . . . . . . Ps 106:4
find *f* and high esteem . . . . . Prov 3:4
obtains *f* from the LORD . . . Prov 8:35
A good man obtains *f* . . . . . Prov 12:2
understanding gains *f* . . . . Prov 13:15
his *f* is like a cloud . . . . . . Prov 16:15
but his *f* is like dew . . . . . . Prov 19:12
loving *f* rather than silver . . Prov 22:1
in My *f* I have had mercy . . . . Is 60:10
and seek the LORD's *f* . . . . . Jer 26:19
brought Daniel into the *f* . . . . Dan 1:9
have found *f* with God . . . . Luke 1:30
and stature, and in *f* . . . . . . Luke 2:52
God and having *f* . . . . Acts 2:47
troubles, and gave him *f* . . . Acts 7:10
to do the Jews a *f* . . . . Acts 24:27

FAVORABLE
And will He be *f* . . . . Ps 77:7
LORD, You have been *f* . . . . . . Ps 85:1

FAVORED
because You *f* them . . . . Ps 44:3
"Rejoice, highly *f* . . . . Luke 1:28

FAVORITISM
do not show personal *f* . . Luke 20:21
God shows personal *f* . . . . Gal 2:6

FEAR
See DO NOT FEAR
do not *f*, for I am with . . . . . Gen 26:24
this and live, for I *f* God . . . Gen 42:18
not *f* to go down to Egypt . . . Gen 46:3
f the people of the . . . . Num 14:9
not *f* or be discouraged . . . . Deut 1:21
to put the dread and *f* . . . . . Deut 2:25
f Me all the days . . . . Deut 4:10
You shall *f* the LORD . . . . Deut 6:13
f Him, and keep His . . . . . . Deut 13:4
book, that you may *f* . . . . . Deut 28:58
do not *f* nor be dismayed . . . Deut 31:8
said, "Does Job *f* . . . . Job 1:9
Yes, you cast off *f* . . . . Job 15:4
houses are safe from *f* . . . . . Job 21:9
"Dominion and *f* belong . . . Job 25:2
Surely no *f* of me will . . . . . . Job 33:7
He mocks at *f* . . . . Job 39:22

they are in great *f* . . . . Ps 14:5
You who *f* the LORD . . . . Ps 22:23
of death, I will *f* . . . . Ps 23:4
with those who *f* Him . . . . . . Ps 25:14
whom shall I *f* . . . . Ps 27:1
me, my heart shall not *f* . . . . . Ps 27:3
Let all the earth *f* . . . . Ps 33:8
on those who *f* Him . . . . Ps 33:18
around those who *f* Him . . . . . Ps 34:7
Oh, *f* the LORD . . . . Ps 34:9
there is no *f* of God . . . . Ps 36:1
they are in great *f* . . . . Ps 53:5
hear, all you who *f* . . . . Ps 66:16
ends of the earth shall *f* . . . . . Ps 67:7
f You as long as the . . . . Ps 72:5
heart to *f* Your name . . . . Ps 86:11
LORD pities those who *f* . . . Ps 103:13
those who *f* the LORD . . . . . Ps 115:13
Let those who *f* the LORD . . . Ps 118:4
f You will be glad . . . . Ps 119:74
pleasure in those who *f* . . . Ps 147:11
by the *f* of the LORD one . . Prov 16:6
The *f* of man brings a . . . . . Prov 29:25
it, that men should *f* . . . . Eccl 3:14
F God and keep His . . . . Eccl 12:13
let Him be your *f* . . . . Is 8:13
their *f* toward Me is taught . . . Is 29:13
"Be strong, do not *f* . . . . Is 35:4
F not, for I am with you . . . . . Is 41:10
F not, for I have redeemed . . . . Is 43:1
not *f* the reproach of men . . . . Is 51:7
Do not *f*, for you will not . . . . Is 54:4
the *f* of Me is not in you . . . . Jer 2:19
Do you not *f* Me . . . . Jer 5:22
who would not *f* . . . . Jer 10:7
but I will put My *f* . . . . Jer 32:40
greatly beloved, *f* not . . . . . Dan 10:19
who *f* My name the Sun . . . . Mal 4:2
f Him who is able . . . . Matt 10:28
serve Him without *f* . . . . . . Luke 1:74
Then *f* came upon all . . . . . Luke 7:16
"Do not *f*, little flock . . . . . Luke 12:32
a judge who did not *f* . . . . . Luke 18:2
failing them from *f* . . . . . . Luke 21:26
"Do you not even *f* . . . . . . Luke 23:40
of bondage again to *f* . . . . . . Rom 8:15
f to whom *f*, honor to . . . . . . Rom 13:7
holiness in the *f* of God . . . . 2 Cor 7:1
another in the *f* of God . . . . . Eph 5:21
your own salvation with *f* . . . Phil 2:12
the rest also may *f* . . . . 1 Tim 5:20
given us a spirit of *f* . . . . 2 Tim 1:7
those who through *f* . . . . Heb 2:15
His rest, let us *f* . . . . Heb 4:1
because of His godly *f* . . . . . . Heb 5:7
F God. Honor the king . . . . . 1 Pet 2:17
love casts out *f* . . . . 1 John 4:18
Do not *f* any of . . . . Rev 2:10
"F God and give glory . . . . . . Rev 14:7
servants and those who *f* . . . Rev 19:5

FEAR OF THE LORD
f fell on the people . . . . 1 Sam 11:7
f fell on all the . . . . 2 Chr 17:10
f, that is wisdom, ... Job 28:28
The *f* is clean, enduring . . . . . Ps 19:9
I will teach you the *f* . . . . Ps 34:11
The *f* is the beginning of . . . Ps 111:10
The *f* is the beginning of . . . . Prov 1:7
The *f* is to hate evil; . . . . Prov 8:13
The *f* is the beginning of . . . . Prov 9:10
The *f* prolongs days . . . . . . Prov 10:27
The *f* is a fountain of . . . . . Prov 14:27
a little with the *f* . . . . Prov 15:16
The *f* is the instruction . . . . Prov 15:33
The *f* leads to life, ... Prov 19:23
By humility and the *f* . . . . . . Prov 22:4
of knowledge and of the *f* . . . . Is 11:2
His delight is in the *f*. . . . . Is 11:3
And walking in the *f* . . . . . . Acts 9:31

FEAR THE LORD
That you may *f* your God, . . . Deut 6:2

require of you, but to *f* . . . . Deut 10:12
that they may learn to *f* . . . Deut 31:12
f, serve Him in sincerity . . . Josh 24:14
them how they should *f* . . 2 Kin 17:28
he honors those who *f* . . . . . . Ps 15:4
who *f*, trust in the LORD; . . . Ps 115:11
F and depart from evil . . . . . . Prov 3:7
"Let us now *f* . . . . Jer 5:24
I *f*, the God of heaven. . . . . . . Jon 1:9

FEARED
But the midwives *f* . . . . Ex 1:17
so the people *f* the LORD . . . Ex 14:31
He is also to be *f* . . . . . . 1 Chr 16:25
f God more than . . . . Neh 7:2
thing I greatly *f* has come . . . Job 3:25
Yourself, are to be *f* . . . . Ps 76:7
God is greatly to be *f* . . . . Ps 89:7
He is to be *f* above all gods . . . Ps 96:4
Then those who *f* . . . . Mal 3:16
they *f* greatly, saying . . . . . Matt 27:54
Him, for they *f* the people . . . Luke 22:2
one who *f* God with all his . . Acts 10:2

FEARFUL
f in praises, doing . . . . Ex 15:11
them, "Why are you *f* . . . . . Matt 8:26
there will be *f* sights . . . . . Luke 21:11
It is a *f* thing to . . . . Heb 10:31

FEARFUL-HEARTED
to those who are *f* . . . . Is 35:4

FEARFULLY
f and wonderfully made . . . Ps 139:14

FEARFULNESS
F and trembling have . . . . Ps 55:5
f has seized the . . . . Is 33:14

FEARING
is devoted to *f* You . . . . Ps 119:38
woman, *f* and trembling . . Mark 5:33
sincerity of heart, *f* . . . . Col 3:22
forsook Egypt, not *f* . . . . . . Heb 11:27

FEARS
upright man, one who *f* . . . . . Job 1:8
Who is the man that *f* . . . . . Ps 25:12
me from all my *f* . . . . Ps 34:4
every one who *f* the LORD . . . Ps 128:1
in his uprightness *f* . . . . . . Prov 14:2
a woman who *f* the LORD . . Prov 31:30
an oath as he who *f* . . . . Eccl 9:2
every nation whoever *f* . . . Acts 10:35
f has not been made . . . . . 1 John 4:18

FEAST
Then he made them a *f* . . . Gen 19:3
F of Unleavened Bread . . . . . Ex 12:17
keep a *f* to Me in the year . . . Ex 23:14
and the F of Harvest . . . . Ex 23:16
F of Ingathering . . . . Ex 23:16
observe the F of Weeks . . . . . Ex 34:22
F of the Passover be left . . . . Ex 34:25
F of Tabernacles for . . . . . . Lev 23:34
and you shall keep a *f* . . . . Num 29:12
the F of Esther, for all his . . . Esth 2:18
moon, on our solemn *f* day . . Ps 81:3
f is made for laughter . . . . Eccl 10:19
f day the terrors that . . . . . Lam 2:22
hate, I despise your *f* . . . . . Amos 5:21
"Not during the *f*, lest . . . . Mark 14:2
every year at the F . . . . Luke 2:41
by anyone to a wedding *f* . . Luke 14:8
when you give a *f* . . . . Luke 14:13
Now the Passover, a *f* . . . . . John 6:4
the *f* Jesus went up into . . . . John 7:14
great day of the *f* . . . . John 7:37
Now before the *f* of the . . . . John 13:1
let us keep the *f* . . . . 1 Cor 5:8

FEAST OF DEDICATION
Now it was the F . . . . John 10:22

FEAST OF HARVEST
and the F, the firstfruits . . . . . Ex 23:16

FEAST OF INGATHERING
F at the end of the year. . . . . Ex 23:16
and the *F* at the year's end . Ex 34:22

FEAST OF TABERNACLES
the *F* for seven days . . . . . . Lev 23:34
observe the *F* seven . . . . . . Deut 16:13
year of release, at the *F* . . . Deut 31:10
They also kept the *F*. . . . . . . Ezra 3:4
and to keep the *F* . . . . Zech 14:16
Now the Jews' *F* . . . . John 7:2

FEAST OF UNLEAVENED BREAD
you shall observe the *F* . . . . Ex 12:17
You shall keep the *F* . . . . . . Ex 23:15
F you shall keep. Seven . . . . Ex 34:18
Jerusalem to keep the *F* . 2 Chr 30:13
And they kept the *F*. . . . . . . Ezra 6:22
on the first day of the *F* . . Matt 26:17
the Passover and the *F* . . . Mark 14:1
Now the *F* drew near. . . . . Luke 22:1

FEAST OF WEEKS
you shall observe the *F* . . . . Ex 34:22
at your *f*, you shall have . . Num 28:26
you shall keep the *F* . . . . . Deut 16:10

FEASTING
house full of *f* with strife . . . Prov 17:1
go to the house of *f* . . . . Eccl 7:2

FEASTS
See APPOINTED FEASTS
These are the *f* of the LORD. . Lev 23:4
in your appointed *f* . . . . . . Num 10:10
Moons and on the set *f* . . . 1 Chr 23:31
I will turn your *f* . . . . Amos 8:10
the best places at *f* . . . . . . Luke 20:46
spots in your love *f* . . . . Jude 12

FEATHERS
shall cover you with His *f* . . . Ps 91:4

FED
f me all my life long . . . . Gen 48:15
and *f* you with manna . . . . . . Deut 8:3
but the shepherds *f* . . . . . . Ezek 34:8
They *f* him with grass like . . Dan 5:21
So those who *f* the swine . . Mark 5:14
desiring to be *f* with the . . Luke 16:21
f you with milk and . . . . 1 Cor 3:2

FEEBLE
strengthened the *f* . . . . Job 4:4
And there was none *f* . . . . Ps 105:37
And my flesh is *f* . . . . Ps 109:24
and make firm the *f* knees . . . . Is 35:3
Every hand will be *f* . . . . . Ezek 7:17
hang down. and the *f* . . . . Heb 12:12

FEED
ravens to *f* you there . . . . . 1 Kin 17:4
and *f* on His faithfulness . . . . . Ps 37:3
death shall *f* on them . . . . . Ps 49:14
of the righteous *f* . . . . Prov 10:21
He will *f* His flock like a . . . . Is 40:11
and *f* your flocks . . . . Is 61:5
f you with knowledge . . . . . . Jer 3:15
over them who will *f* them . . . Jer 23:4
I will *f* My flock, and I . . . Ezek 34:15
to him. "*F* My lambs . . . . John 21:15
to him. "*F* My sheep . . . . . John 21:17
your enemy hungers. . . . Rom 12:20
my goods to *f* the poor . . . 1 Cor 13:3

FEEDS
"Ephraim *f* on the wind . . . . Hos 12:1
your heavenly Father *f* . . . . Matt 6:26
he who *f* on Me will live . . . John 6:57

FEET
See UNDER HIS FEET
your sandals off your *f* . . . . . Ex 3:5
not worn out on your *f* . . . Deut 29:5
f touched the dry land . . . . Josh 4:18
So she lay at his *f* . . . . Ruth 3:14
was lame in both his *f* . . . 2 Sam 9:13
so my *f* did not slip . . . . . 2 Sam 22:37

in places forgotten by *f* . . . . Job 28:4
I was *f* to the lame . . . . Job 29:15
all things under his *f* . . . . Ps 8:6
He makes my *f* like the . . . . Ps 18:33
pierced My hands and My *f* . . Ps 22:16
You have set my *f* . . . . Ps 31:8
and set my *f* upon a rock . . . . Ps 40:2
does not allow our *f* . . . . Ps 66:9
f had almost stumbled . . . . . . Ps 73:2
and my *f* from falling . . . . . Ps 116:8
f from every evil way . . . . Ps 119:101
word is a lamp to my *f* . . . Ps 119:105
f have been standing . . . . . . Ps 122:2
For their *f* run to . . . . Prov 1:16
Her *f* go down to death . . . . Prov 5:5
f that are swift in running . . Prov 6:18
spreads a net for his *f* . . . . Prov 29:5
with two he covered his *f* . . . . Is 6:2
sandals off your *f* . . . . Is 20:2
called him to His *f* . . . . Is 41:2
up the dust of your *f* . . . . . Is 49:23
mountains are the *f* . . . . Is 52:7
place of My *f* glorious . . . . . Is 60:13
have not restrained their *f* . . Jer 14:10
its *f* partly of iron and . . . . Dan 2:33
f like burnished bronze in . . Dan 10:6
are the dust of His *f* . . . . . . Nah 1:3
on the mountains the *f* of . . Nah 1:15
make my *f* like deer's *f* . . . Hab 3:19
in that day His *f* . . . . Zech 14:4
off the dust from your *f* . . . Matt 10:14
two hands or two *f* . . . . . . Matt 18:8
saw Him, he fell at His *f* . . Mark 5:22
she came and fell at His *f* . . Mark 7:25
rather than having two *f* . . Mark 9:45
began to wash His *f* . . . . . Luke 7:38
sitting at the *f* of Jesus . . . Luke 8:35
also sat at Jesus' *f* . . . . . . Luke 10:39
and sandals on his *f* . . . . . Luke 15:22
My hands and My *f* . . . . . . Luke 24:39
wash the disciples' *f* . . . . . John 13:5
wash one another's *f* . . . . John 13:14
and the other at the *f* . . . . John 20:12
up, and immediately his *f* . . . Acts 3:7
at the apostles' *f* . . . . Acts 4:35
your sandals off your *f* . . . . Acts 7:33
his own hands and *f* . . . . . Acts 21:11
f are swift to shed . . . . Rom 3:15
beautiful are the *f* . . . . . . Rom 10:15
all things under His *f* . . . . 1 Cor 15:27
put all things under His *f* . . . Eph 1:22
and having shod your *f* . . . Eph 6:15
straight paths for your *f* . . . Heb 12:13
fell at His *f* as dead . . . . . . Rev 1:17
And I fell at his *f* . . . . Rev 19:10

FELIX
Governor of Judea; letter addressed to.
Acts 23:24–30
Paul's defense before. Acts 24:1–27

FELL
f on his neck and kissed . . . Gen 33:4
Joseph *f* on his father's . . . Gen 50:1
Saul took a sword and *f* . . 1 Sam 31:4
ax head *f* into the water . . . 2 Kin 6:5
Saul took a sword and *f* . . . 1 Chr 10:4
fear of the Jews *f* upon . . . Esth 8:17
fire of God *f* from heaven . . . Job 1:16
foes, they stumbled and *f* . . . Ps 27:2
f on my face, and I heard . . Ezek 1:28
Spirit of the LORD *f* upon . . Ezek 11:5
f down bound into the . . . . . Dan 3:23
lots, and the lot *f* on Jonah . . Jon 1:7
on that house; and it *f* . . . . Matt 7:27
seed *f* by the wayside . . . . Matt 13:4
others *f* on good ground . . . Matt 13:8
saw Him, he *f* at His feet . . Mark 5:22
as they sailed He *f* asleep . . Luke 8:23
f among thieves . . . . Luke 10:30
the tower in Siloam *f* . . . . . Luke 13:4
f from the rich man's . . . . Luke 16:21
she *f* down at His feet . . . John 11:32

and the lot *f* on Matthias . . . Acts 1:26
f down and breathed his . . . . Acts 5:5
had said this, he *f* asleep . . Acts 7:60
ready, he *f* into a trance . . Acts 10:10
the Holy Spirit *f* upon all . . Acts 10:44
his chains *f* off his hands . . Acts 12:7
he *f* down from the third . . . Acts 20:9
who reproached You *f* on . . Rom 15:3
f down after they were . . . Heb 11:30
elders *f* down before . . . . Rev 5:8
of heaven *f* to the earth . . . Rev 6:13
a great star *f* from heaven . . Rev 8:10
four living creatures *f* . . . . . Rev 19:4

FELLOW
f servants who owed . . . . Matt 18:28
begins to beat his *f* . . . . . Matt 24:49
f worker concerning . . . . . . 2 Cor 8:23
f citizens with the . . . . Eph 2:19
Gentiles should be *f* . . . . Eph 3:6
rest of my *f* workers . . . . Phil 4:3
These are my only *f* . . . . Col 4:11
that we may become *f* . . . . . . 3 John 8
I am your *f* servant . . . . . . Rev 19:10

FELLOWSHIP
doctrine and *f* . . . . Acts 2:42
were called into the *f* . . . . 1 Cor 1:9
not want you to have *f* . . . 1 Cor 10:20
f has righteousness . . . . 2 Cor 6:14
the right hand of *f* . . . . Gal 2:9
And have no *f* with the . . . . Eph 5:11
for your *f* in the . . . . Phil 1:5
of love, if any *f* . . . . Phil 2:1
and the *f* of His . . . . Phil 3:10
also may have *f* . . . . 1 John 1:3
we say that we have *f* . . . . 1 John 1:6
the light, we have *f* . . . . . . 1 John 1:7

FEMALE
male and *f* He created . . . . . Gen 1:27
they shall be male and *f* . . . Gen 6:19
ark to Noah, male and *f* . . . . Gen 7:9
has borne a male or a *f* . . . . Lev 12:7
made them male and *f* . . . . Matt 19:4
there is neither male nor *f* . . Gal 3:28

FENCE
and a tottering *f* . . . . Ps 62:3

FENCED
He has *f* up my way . . . . . . Job 19:8

FERTILIZE
I dig around it and *f* . . . . . . Luke 13:8

FERVENT
f desire I have desired . . . . Luke 22:15
and being *f* in spirit . . . . . . Acts 18:25
f in spirit, serving the . . . . Rom 12:11
f prayer of a . . . . James 5:16
all things have *f* . . . . 1 Pet 4:8
will melt with *f* . . . . 2 Pet 3:10

FERVENTLY
you, always laboring *f* . . . . . Col 4:12
love one another *f* . . . . 1 Pet 1:22

FESTIVAL
night when a holy *f* . . . . Is 30:29
or regarding a *f* . . . . Col 2:16

FESTUS
Governor of Judea, Acts 24:27
Paul's defense made to, Acts 25:1–22

FETCH
f my knowledge from . . . . . Job 36:3

FETTERS
hurt his feet with *f* . . . . . . Ps 105:18
their nobles with *f* . . . . Ps 149:8

FEVER
f which shall consume . . . . Lev 26:16
my bones burn with *f* . . . . Job 30:30
mother lying sick with a *f* . . Matt 8:14
immediately the *f* left her . . Mark 1:31
and rebuked the *f* . . . . Luke 4:39
of Publius lay sick of a *f* . . . Acts 28:8

FEW

f and evil have been .... Gen 47:9
f days and full of .... Job 14:1
Let his days be *f* .... Ps 109:8
let your words be *f* .... Eccl 5:2
there are *f* who find it ..... Matt 7:14
but the laborers are *f* ..... Matt 9:37
called, but *f* chosen ..... Matt 20:16
"Lord, are there *f* .... Luke 13:23
prepared, in which a *f* .. 1 Pet 3:20
I have a *f* things .... Rev 2:20

FIDELITY

but showing all good *f* .... Titus 2:10

FIELD

and to every beast of the *f* . Gen 2:20
f which the LORD has...... Gen 27:27
gleaned in the *f* after the .... Ruth 2:3
even the beasts of the *f* ...... Ps 8:7
Let the *f* be joyful .... Ps 96:12
as a flower of the *f*, so he .. Ps 103:15
went by the *f* of the lazy .. Prov 24:30
She considers a *f* and ..... Prov 31:16
to house; they add *f* .... Is 5:8
becomes a fruitful *f* .... Is 32:15
is like the flower of the *f* ..... Is 40:6
beast of the *f* will honor ... Is 43:20
all the trees of the *f* shall .... Is 55:12
"Buy the *f* for money .... Jer 32:25
thrive like a plant in the *f* .. Ezek 16:5
shall be plowed like a *f* ..... Mic 3:12
Consider the lilies of the *f* .. Matt 6:28
clothes the grass of the *f* .. Matt 6:30
The *f* is the world .... Matt 13:38
and buys that *f* .... Matt 13:44
let him who is in the *f* .... Matt 24:18
f has been called the ...... Matt 27:8
which today is in the *f* .... Luke 12:28
Two men will be in the *f* .. Luke 17:36
you are God's *f* .... 1 Cor 3:9
the *f* he will pass away .. James 1:10

FIELD OF BLOOD

A field bought as a cemetery for Judas's
burial. Matt 27:1–10
Predicted in the O.T., Zech 11:12, 13

FIELDS

and sends waters on the *f* .... Job 5:10
nor enter the *f* of the ...... Prov 23:10
f yield no food .... Hab 3:17
living out in the *f* .... Luke 2:8
eyes and look at the *f* ..... John 4:35

FIERCE

the *f* wrath of our God .... Ezra 10:14
f wrath has gone over me ... Ps 88:16
A *f* lion is in the streets ... Prov 26:13
the *f* anger of the LORD .... Jer 4:8
in the day of His *f* anger ... Lam 1:12
turn away from His *f* anger .. Jon 3:9
the tombs, exceedingly *f* ... Matt 8:28
are driven by *f* winds ..... James 3:4

FIERCENESS

f has deceived you .... Jer 49:16
the winepress of the *f* ..... Rev 19:15

FIERY

the LORD sent *f* serpents.... Num 21:6
right hand came a *f* .... Deut 33:2
shall make them as a *f* ...... Ps 21:9
their flocks to *f* lightning .... Ps 78:48
offspring will be a *f* .... Is 14:29
burning *f* furnace .... Dan 3:6
from the burning *f* furnace .. Dan 3:17
f darts of the wicked one .... Eph 6:16
concerning the *f* trial ...... 1 Pet 4:12
horse, *f* red, went out ...... Rev 6:4
f red dragon having .... Rev 12:3

FIFTEEN

about *f* thousand all who .... Judg 8:10
add to your days *f* years .. 2 Kin 20:6
remained with him *f* days ... Gal 1:18

FIFTH

morning were the *f* day ..... Gen 1:23

He opened the *f* seal .... Rev 6:9
the *f* angel poured out ...... Rev 16:10

FIFTY

nine hundred and *f* years ... Gen 9:29
Suppose there were *f* ..... Gen 18:24
f prophets of Baal, and ... 1 Kin 18:19
denarii, and the other *f* .... Luke 7:41
sit down in groups of *f* ..... Luke 9:14
down quickly and write *f* .. Luke 16:6
"You are not yet *f* years ... John 8:57

FIG

f leaves together .... Gen 3:7
f trees and pomegranates.... Deut 8:8
his vine and his *f* .... 1 Kin 4:25
from his own *f* tree ...... 2 Kin 18:31
fruit falling from a *f* .... Is 34:4
and the *f* tree has withered .. Joel 1:12
f tree and the vine yield .... Joel 2:22
f tree may not blossom ..... Hab 3:17
immediately the *f* tree .... Matt 21:19
parable from the *f* tree .... Matt 24:32
saw the *f* tree dried up ... Mark 11:20
fruit on this *f* .... Luke 13:7
"Look at the *f* .... Luke 21:29
'I saw you under the *f* ..... John 1:50
Can a *f* tree .... James 3:12
f tree drops its late .... Rev 6:13

FIGHT

The LORD will *f* for you .... Ex 14:14
like men, and *f* .... 1 Sam 4:9
you go with me to *f* ...... 1 Kin 22:4
Our God will *f* for us .... Neh 4:20
My servants would *f* ..... John 18:36
to him, let us not *f* .... Acts 23:9
Thus I *f*: not as one who ... 1 Cor 9:26
F the good *f* .... 1 Tim 6:12
have fought the good *f* .... 2 Tim 4:7
You *f* and war .... James 4:2

FIGHTS

your God is He who *f* .... Josh 23:10
because my lord *f* .... 1 Sam 25:28
f come from among .... James 4:1

FIGS

puts forth her green *f* ..... Song 2:13
f set before the .... Jer 24:1
from thornbushes or *f* ..... Matt 7:16
men do not gather *f* ...... Luke 6:44
or a grapevine bear *f* ..... James 3:12

FIGURATIVELY

brethren, I have *f* .... 1 Cor 4:6

FIGURE

using no *f* of speech ...... John 16:29

FILL

f the earth and subdue ...... Gen 1:28
multiply, and *f* the earth ..... Gen 9:1
their sacks with grain ..... Gen 42:25
"*F* four waterpots .... 1 Kin 18:33
He will yet *f* your mouth ... Job 8:21
f my mouth with .... Job 23:4
wealth, that I may *f* .... Prov 8:21
out of his wings will *f* the ..... Is 8:8
"Do I not *f* heaven .... Jer 23:24
f this temple with .... Hag 2:7
f such a great multitude .. Matt 15:33
"*F* the waterpots .... John 2:7
hope *f* you with all joy .... Rom 15:13
that He might *f* .... Eph 4:10
so as always to *f* .... 1 Thess 2:16

FILLED

f her pitcher, and came ... Gen 24:16
you shall be *f* with bread .... Ex 16:12
the LORD *f* the tabernacle.... Ex 40:34
all the earth shall be *f* ..... Num 14:21
f the house of the LORD... 1 Kin 8:11
So they ate and were *f* ..... Neh 9:25
the whole earth be *f* .... Ps 72:19
they are *f* with good ...... Ps 104:28
Then our mouth was *f* ..... Ps 126:2

barns will be *f* with .... Prov 3:10
of his lips he shall be *f* .... Prov 18:20
for they shall be *f* .... Matt 5:6
they all ate and were *f* .... Matt 14:20
"Let the children be *f* ..... Mark 7:27
in spirit, *f* with wisdom ... Luke 2:40
f with the Holy Spirit ...... Luke 4:1
were *f* with fear, saying .... Luke 5:26
he would gladly have *f* ... Luke 15:16
they *f* them up to the brim ... John 2:7
f twelve baskets with the .... John 6:13
sorrow has *f* your heart .... John 16:6
were all *f* with the Holy ..... Acts 2:4
why has Satan *f* your heart ... Acts 5:3
being *f* with all .... Rom 1:29
full of goodness, *f* .... Rom 15:14
that you may be *f* .... Eph 3:19
but be *f* with the Spirit ..... Eph 5:18
being *f* with the fruits ...... Phil 1:11
peace, be warmed and *f* .. James 2:16

FILLED WITH THE HOLY SPIRIT

He will also be *f* .... Luke 1:15
and Elizabeth was *f* ...... Luke 1:41
father Zacharias was *f* .... Luke 1:67
Then Jesus, being *f* ...... Luke 4:1
And they were all *f* .... Acts 2:4
Peter, *f*, said to them ...... Acts 4:8
and they were all *f*, ... Acts 4:31
your sight and be *f* .... Acts 9:17
who also is called Paul, *f*, ... Acts 13:9

FILTH

has washed away the *f* .... Is 4:4
been made as the *f* ...... 1 Cor 4:13
the removal of the *f* ...... 1 Pet 3:21

FILTHINESS

from all your *f* .... Ezek 36:25
ourselves from all *f* .... 2 Cor 7:1
lay aside all *f* .... James 1:21
abominations and the *f* .... Rev 17:4

FILTHY

is abominable and *f* .... Job 15:16
with *f* garments .... Zech 3:3
malice, blasphemy, *f* ...... Col 3:8
poor man in *f* clothes ..... James 2:2
oppressed by the *f* .... 2 Pet 2:7
let him be *f* .... Rev 22:11

FIND

"If I *f* in Sodom fifty ...... Gen 18:26
not *f* the household idols ... Gen 31:35
Can we *f* such a one as .... Gen 41:38
straw where you can *f* it ..... Ex 5:11
that I may *f* grace in Your ... Ex 33:13
sure your sin will *f* .... Num 32:23
you will *f* Him if you seek .. Deut 4:29
"Let me *f* favor in your ..... Ruth 2:13
f the arrows which I ..... 1 Sam 20:36
f in the book of the .... Ezra 4:15
Can you *f* out the limits of .. Job 11:7
knew where I might *f* Him .. Job 23:3
Almighty, we cannot *f* ..... Job 37:23
but they will not *f* me ..... Prov 1:28
life to those who *f* .... Prov 4:22
seek me diligently will *f* ... Prov 8:17
word wisely will *f* good .... Prov 16:20
can *f* a virtuous wife ...... Prov 31:10
that no one can *f* .... Eccl 3:11
waters, for you will *f* ...... Eccl 11:1
if you *f* my beloved .... Song 5:8
f Me, when you search for .. Jer 29:13
seek, and you will *f* .... Matt 7:7
and there are few who *f* it .. Matt 7:14
for My sake will *f* .... Matt 10:39
will *f* a piece of money .... Matt 17:27
when he comes, will *f* .... Matt 24:46
you will *f* a colt tied ...... Mark 11:2
he *f* you sleeping .... Mark 13:36
f a Babe wrapped .... Luke 2:12
seek, and you will *f* .... Luke 11:9
you will *f* a colt tied ..... Luke 19:30

f no fault in this Man . . . . . . Luke 23:4
seek Me and not *f* Me . . . . . . John 7:34
not *f* them in the prison . . . Acts 5:22
I *f* then a law . . . . Rom 7:21
f grace to help in . . . . Heb 4:16
seek death and will not *f* it . . . Rev 9:6

FINDING
great things past *f* . . . . Job 9:10
rest; and *f* none . . . . . . Luke 11:24
and His ways past *f* . . . . . . Rom 11:33

FINDS
one who *f* great treasure . . Ps 119:162
the man who *f* wisdom . . . . . Prov 3:13
whoever *f* me *f* life . . . . Prov 8:35
f a wife *f* a good . . . . Prov 18:22
Whatever your hand *f* . . . . . . Eccl 9:10
You the fatherless *f* mercy . . Hos 14:3
and he who seeks *f* . . . . Matt 7:8
f his life will lose . . . . Matt 10:39
he *f* it empty, swept, and . . Matt 12:44
and he who seeks *f* . . . . . . Luke 11:10
carefully until she *f* it . . . . . Luke 15:8

FINE
ate up the seven *f* looking . . Gen 41:4
Then I beat them as *f* . . . 2 Sam 22:43
gold, yea, than much *f* . . . . . Ps 19:10
than gold, yes, than *f* gold . . Prov 8:19
f gold is a wise . . . . Prov 25:12
her clothing is *f* linen . . . . . Prov 31:22
set on bases of *f* gold . . . . . Song 5:15
more rare than *f* . . . . Is 13:12
and for *f* clothing . . . . Is 23:18
how changed the *f* . . . . Lam 4:1
Then he bought *f* linen . . . Mark 15:46
rings, in *f* apparel . . . . James 2:2
His feet were like *f* brass . . . Rev 1:15
for the *f* linen is the . . . . Rev 19:8

FINGER
written with the *f* . . . . Ex 31:18
written with the *f* of God . . . Deut 9:10
f shall be thicker . . . . 1 Kin 12:10
the pointing of the *f* . . . . Is 58:9
demons with the *f* of . . . . Luke 11:20
dip the tip of his *f* . . . . . . Luke 16:24
the ground with His *f* . . . . . John 8:6
"Reach your *f* . . . . John 20:27

FINGERS
the work of Your *f* . . . . Ps 8:3
he points with his *f* . . . . . . Prov 6:13
Bind them on your *f* . . . . Prov 7:3
that which their own *f* . . . . Is 2:8
In the same hour the *f* of a . . . Dan 5:5
with one of their *f* . . . . Matt 23:4
put His *f* in his ears . . . . . Mark 7:33

FINISH
We *f* our years like a sigh . . . . Ps 90:9
to *f* the transgression . . . . . Dan 9:24
he has enough to *f* . . . . . . Luke 14:28
has given Me to *f* . . . . John 5:36
so that I may *f* . . . . Acts 20:24

FINISHED
house of the LORD was *f* . . 1 Kin 7:51
f the work which You . . . . . John 17:4
He said, "It is *f* . . . . John 19:30
I have *f* the race . . . . 2 Tim 4:7
thousand years were *f* . . . . . Rev 20:3

FIRE
rained brimstone and *f* . . . . Gen 19:24
to him in a flame of *f* . . . . Ex 3:2
the pillar of *f* by night . . . . . Ex 13:22
descended upon it in *f* . . . . . Ex 19:18
made, burned it in the *f* . . . . Ex 32:20
by day, and *f* was over . . . . . Ex 40:38
profane *f* before the LORD . . Lev 10:1
through the *f* to Molech . . . Lev 18:21
like the appearance of *f* . . . . Num 9:15
the *f* was quenched . . . . . . Num 11:2
from the midst of the *f* . . . . Deut 5:24
God, who answers by *f* . . . 1 Kin 18:24

the *f* of the LORD fell . . . . . 1 Kin 18:38
LORD was not in the *f* . . . . 1 Kin 19:12
of *f* appeared with horses . . 2 Kin 2:11
I was musing, the *f* . . . . Ps 39:3
we went through *f* . . . . Ps 66:12
they have set *f* . . . . Ps 74:7
f goes before Him . . . . Ps 97:3
His ministers a flame of *f* . . . Ps 104:4
f and hail, snow and . . . . . . Ps 148:8
burns as the *f* . . . . Is 9:18
says the LORD, whose *f* . . . . . Is 31:9
you walk through the *f* . . . . . Is 43:2
f that burns all the . . . . Is 65:5
My fury come forth like *f* . . . . Jer 4:4
their daughters in the *f* . . . . Jer 7:31
His waist and downward, *f* . . Ezek 8:2
in the midst of the *f* . . . . . . Dan 3:25
the smell of *f* was not on . . . Dan 3:27
He break out like *f* . . . . Amos 5:6
for conflict by *f* . . . . Amos 7:4
a brand plucked from the *f* . . Zech 3:2
like a refiner's *f* . . . . Mal 3:2
the Holy Spirit and *f* . . . . . Matt 3:11
chaff with unquenchable *f* . Matt 3:12
shall be in danger of hell *f* . . Matt 5:22
he often falls into the *f* . . . Matt 17:15
into the everlasting *f* . . . . . Matt 25:41
f is not quenched . . . . Mark 9:44
"I came to send *f* . . . . Luke 12:49
tongues, as of *f* . . . . Acts 2:3
off the creature into the *f* . . Acts 28:5
coals of *f* on his head . . . . Rom 12:20
f taking vengeance . . . . . . 2 Thess 1:8
His ministers a flame of *f* . . . Heb 1:7
and that burned with *f* . . . . Heb 12:18
our God is a consuming *f* . . Heb 12:29
And the tongue is a *f* . . . . James 3:6
vengeance of eternal *f* . . . . . . Jude 7
His eyes like a flame of *f* . . . Rev 1:14
f came down from God . . . . Rev 20:9
into the lake of *f* . . . . Rev 20:14

FIREBRAND
f plucked from the . . . . . . Amos 4:11

FIREBRANDS
a madman who throws *f* . . Prov 26:18
two stubs of smoking *f* . . . . . . Is 7:4

FIRM
their strength is *f* . . . . Ps 73:4
shall stand *f* with him . . . . . Ps 89:28
Take *f* hold of instruction . . Prov 4:13
f the feeble knees . . . . Is 35:3
of the hope *f* to the . . . . Heb 3:6

FIRMAMENT
Thus God made the *f* . . . . . . Gen 1:7
f shows His handiwork . . . . . . Ps 19:1
in His mighty *f* . . . . Ps 150:1
brightness of the *f* . . . . Dan 12:3

FIRST
the morning were the *f* day . . Gen 1:5
cows ate up the *f* seven . . . . Gen 41:20
The *f* of the firstfruits of . . . Ex 23:19
"Give the *f* woman the . . . 1 Kin 3:27
The *f* one to plead his . . . . Prov 18:17
f father sinned . . . . Is 43:27
the F and I am the Last . . . . . Is 44:6
f was like a lion, and had . . . Dan 7:4
F be reconciled to your . . . . Matt 5:24
seek *f* the kingdom of . . . . Matt 6:33
F remove the plank from . . . . Matt 7:5
unless he *f* binds the . . . . Matt 12:29
man is worse than the *f* . . . Matt 12:45
who are *f* will be last . . . . Matt 19:30
desires to be *f* . . . . Matt 20:27
This is the *f* and great . . . . Matt 22:38
f the blade, then the . . . . . Mark 4:28
that Elijah must come *f* . . . Mark 9:11
f shall be slave . . . . Mark 10:44
the *f* commandment . . . . . Mark 12:30
And the gospel must *f* . . . . Mark 13:10
He appeared *f* to Mary . . . Mark 16:9

let me *f* go and bury my . . . Luke 9:59
f He must suffer many . . . . Luke 17:25
f took a wife, and died . . . Luke 20:29
f found his own brother . . . . John 1:41
him throw a stone at her *f* . . John 8:7
disciples were *f* called . . . . Acts 11:26
evil, of the Jew *f* . . . . Rom 2:9
"Or who has *f* given . . . . . Rom 11:35
f apostles, second . . . . . . 1 Cor 12:28
f man Adam became a . . . 1 Cor 15:45
f a willing mind . . . . 2 Cor 8:12
that we who *f* trusted . . . . . . Eph 1:12
the *f* commandment with . . . Eph 6:2
in Christ will rise *f* . . . 1 Thess 4:16
the falling away comes *f* . . 2 Thess 2:3
Therefore I exhort *f* of all . . . 1 Tim 2:1
For Adam was formed *f* . . . 1 Tim 2:13
let them *f* learn to show . . . 1 Tim 5:4
to teach you again the *f* . . . Heb 5:12
f covenant had been . . . . Heb 8:7
from above is *f* pure . . . . . James 3:17
knowing this *f*, that no . . . 2 Pet 1:20
this *f*: that scoffers will . . . . 2 Pet 3:3
love Him because He *f* . . . 1 John 4:19
I am the F and the . . . . Rev 1:17
you have left your *f* . . . . Rev 2:4
The *f* angel sounded . . . . Rev 8:7
is the *f* resurrection . . . . Rev 20:5
f earth had passed away . . . . Rev 21:1

FIRST AND THE LAST
and the Omega, the F . . . . . Rev 1:11
not be afraid; I am the F . . . Rev 1:17
These things says the F . . . . . Rev 2:8
and the End, the F . . . . Rev 22:13

FIRST-RIPE
f fruit which my soul . . . . Mic 7:1

FIRSTBORN
"I am Esau your *f* . . . . Gen 27:19
"Israel is My son, My *f* . . . . . Ex 4:22
LORD struck all the *f* . . . . . Ex 12:29
"Consecrate to Me all the *f* . . Ex 13:2
was the *f* of Israel . . . . Num 26:5
destroyed all the *f* in Egypt . . Ps 78:51
I will make him My *f* . . . . . . Ps 89:27
Shall I give my *f* . . . . Mic 6:7
as one grieves for a *f* . . . . Zech 12:10
brought forth her *f* . . . . Matt 1:25
brought forth her *f* Son . . . Luke 2:7
that He might be the *f* . . . . Rom 8:29
invisible God, the *f* . . . . . . Col 1:15
the beginning, the *f* . . . . . . Col 1:18
witness, the *f* from . . . . Rev 1:5

FIRSTFRUIT
For if the *f* is holy . . . . . . Rom 11:16

FIRSTFRUITS
the *f* of your harvest to . . . Lev 23:10
bring the *f* of our ground . . Neh 10:35
with the *f* of all your . . . . . . Prov 3:9
also who have the *f* . . . . . Rom 8:23
and has become the *f* . . . 1 Cor 15:20
order: Christ the *f* . . . . . 1 Cor 15:23
might be a kind of *f* . . . . . James 1:18
among men, being *f* . . . . . Rev 14:4

FISH
over the *f* of the sea . . . . . Gen 1:28
f taken in a cruel net . . . . . Eccl 9:12
had prepared a great *f* . . . . Jon 1:17
do You make men like *f* . . . Hab 1:14
Or if he asks for a *f* . . . . . Matt 7:10
belly of the great *f* . . . . . . Matt 12:40
five loaves and two *f* . . . . Matt 14:17
and likewise the *f* . . . . . . John 21:13

FISHERMEN
The *f* also will mourn . . . . . . Is 19:8
I will send for many *f* . . . . Jer 16:16

FISHERS
and I will make you *f* . . . . Matt 4:19

FIT
and looking back, is *f* . . . . Luke 9:62

FITTING
Therefore it is not *f* for the . . Esth 3:8
Is it *f* to say to a . . . . Job 34:18
Luxury is not *f* . . . . Prov 19:10
so honor is not *f* . . . . Prov 26:1
things which are not *f* . . . . . Rom 1:28
husbands, as is *f* in the . . . . . . Col 3:18
a High Priest was *f* . . . . Heb 7:26

FIVE
bring out those *f* kings . . . . Josh 10:22
f smooth stones . . . . 1 Sam 17:40
about *f* thousand men . . . Matt 14:21
and *f* were foolish . . . . Matt 25:2
to one he gave *f* talents . . . Matt 25:15
Are not *f* sparrows sold . . Luke 12:6
bought *f* yoke of oxen . . . . Luke 14:19
you have had *f* husbands . . John 4:18
speak *f* words with my . . . 1 Cor 14:19

FIXED
f My limit for it . . . . Job 38:10
is a great gulf *f* . . . . Luke 16:26

FLAME
appeared to him in a *f* . . . . . . Ex 3:2
f will dry out his . . . . Job 15:30
His ministers a *f* of fire . . . . . Ps 104:4
f consumes the chaff . . . . Is 5:24
and his Holy One for a *f* . . . . Is 10:17
and tempest and the *f* . . . . . . Is 29:6
nor shall the *f* scorch you . . . . Is 43:2
hot, the *f* of the fire killed . . Dan 3:22
behind them a *f* . . . . Joel 2:3
am tormented in this *f* . . . . Luke 16:24
and His ministers a *f* . . . . Heb 1:7
and His eyes like a *f* . . . . Rev 1:14

FLAMES
the LORD divides the *f* . . . . . . Ps 29:7

FLAMING
f sword which turned . . . . . . Gen 3:24
f fire in their land . . . . Ps 105:32
in *f* fire taking . . . . 2 Thess 1:8

FLANKS
Strengthen your *f* . . . . Nah 2:1

FLASK
alabaster *f* of fragrant oil . . Luke 7:37

FLATTER
I do not know how to *f* . . . . . Job 32:22
They *f* with their . . . . Ps 5:9

FLATTERED
Nevertheless they *f* . . . . Ps 78:36

FLATTERING
f mouth works ruin . . . . . . Prov 26:28
f speech deceive . . . . Rom 16:18
any time did we use *f* . . . . 1 Thess 2:5
swelling words, *f* . . . . Jude 16

FLATTERS
with one who *f* with . . . . . . Prov 20:19
f his neighbor spreads . . . . . Prov 29:5

FLATTERY
shall corrupt with *f* . . . . . . Dan 11:32

FLAVOR
the salt loses its *f* . . . . Matt 5:13

FLAVORLESS
f food be eaten . . . . Job 6:6

FLAX
f He will not quench . . . . Is 42:3
f He will not quench . . . . . Matt 12:20

FLED
Moses *f* from the face of . . . . Ex 2:15
f before the men of Ai . . . . . Josh 7:4
The sea saw it and *f* . . . . . . Ps 114:3
who have *f* for refuge . . . . . . Heb 6:18

FLEE
f away secretly . . . . Gen 31:27
those who hate You *f* . . . . Num 10:35
such a man as I *f* . . . . Neh 6:11
who see me outside *f* . . . . . . Ps 31:11

Or where can I *f* . . . . Ps 139:7
wicked *f* when no one . . . . . Prov 28:1
And the shadows *f* . . . . Song 2:17
f to Egypt, and stay there . . Matt 2:13
who are in Judea *f* . . . . . . Matt 24:16
F sexual immorality . . . . . . 1 Cor 6:18
f these things and . . . . 1 Tim 6:11
F also youthful lusts . . . . . . 2 Tim 2:22
devil and he will *f* . . . . . . James 4:7

FLEECE
there is dew on the *f* only . . Judg 6:37

FLESH
See ACCORDING TO THE FLESH
bone of my bones and *f* . . . . Gen 2:23
shall become one *f* . . . . Gen 2:24
f had corrupted their . . . . . Gen 6:12
f I shall see God . . . . Job 19:26
My *f* also will rest in . . . . Ps 16:9
What can *f* do to me . . . . Ps 56:4
f longs for You in a dry . . . . . Ps 63:1
that they were but *f* . . . . Ps 78:39
my heart and my *f* . . . . Ps 84:2
Who gives food to all *f* . . . Ps 136:25
f shall bless His holy . . . . . Ps 145:21
It will be health to your *f* . . . Prov 3:8
and health to all their *f* . . . . Prov 4:22
mouth cause your *f* to sin . . Eccl 5:6
is wearisome to the *f* . . . . Eccl 12:12
And all *f* shall see it . . . . Is 40:5
"All *f* is grass . . . . Is 40:6
give them a heart of *f* . . . Ezek 11:19
of stone out of your *f* . . . Ezek 36:26
out My Spirit on all *f* . . . . . Joel 2:28
Be silent, all *f*, before the . . Zech 2:13
two shall become one *f* . . Matt 19:5
were shortened, no *f* . . . . Matt 24:22
is willing, but the *f* is . . . . Matt 26:41
shall become one *f* . . . . . . Mark 10:8
but the *f* is weak . . . . Mark 14:38
f shall see the salvation . . . Luke 3:6
And the Word became *f* . . . John 1:14
is born of the *f* is *f* . . . . John 3:6
I shall give is My *f* . . . . John 6:51
unless you eat the *f* . . . . . . John 6:53
Whoever eats My *f* and . . . John 6:54
For My *f* is food indeed . . . John 6:55
f profits nothing . . . . John 6:63
according to the *f* . . . . John 8:15
Him authority over all *f* . . . John 17:2
out of My Spirit on all *f* . . . Acts 2:17
did His *f* see corruption . . . Acts 2:31
no *f* will be justified in . . . Rom 3:20
when we were in the *f* . . . . . Rom 7:5
in my *f*) nothing good . . . . . Rom 7:18
of God, but with the *f* . . . . Rom 7:25
not walk according to the *f* . . Rom 8:1
on the things of the *f* . . . . . Rom 8:5
in the *f* cannot please God . . Rom 8:8
you are not in the *f* . . . . Rom 8:9
to the *f* you will die . . . . . . Rom 8:13
no provision for the *f* . . . . Rom 13:14
f should glory in His . . . . . . 1 Cor 1:29
for the destruction of the *f* . . 1 Cor 5:5
"shall become one *f* . . . . . . 1 Cor 6:16
there is one kind of *f* . . . . . 1 Cor 15:39
no one according to the *f* . . 2 Cor 5:16
from all filthiness of the *f* . . 2 Cor 7:1
war according to the *f* . . . . 2 Cor 10:3
immediately confer with *f* . . Gal 1:16
law no *f* shall be justified . . . Gal 2:16
which I now live in the *f* . . . Gal 2:20
not fulfill the lust of the *f* . . Gal 5:16
For the *f* lusts . . . . Gal 5:17
have crucified the *f* . . . . Gal 5:24
his *f* will of the *f* reap . . . . . Gal 6:8
good showing in the *f* . . . . Gal 6:12
may boast in your *f* . . . . . . Gal 6:13
one ever hated his own *f* . . . Eph 5:29
two shall become one *f* . . . Eph 5:31
have no confidence in the *f* . . Phil 3:3
of His *f* through death . . . . . Col 1:22

was manifested in the *f* . . 1 Tim 3:16
the veil, that is, His *f* . . . . Heb 10:20
f has ceased from sin . . . . . 1 Pet 4:1
of his time in the *f* . . . . 1 Pet 4:2
the lust of the *f* . . . . 1 John 2:16
has come in the *f* . . . . 1 John 4:2
dreamers defile the *f* . . . . Jude 8

FLESH AND BLOOD
f has not revealed this . . . Matt 16:17
f cannot inherit the . . . . . 1 Cor 15:50
do not wrestle against *f* . . . . Eph 6:12
have partaken of *f* . . . . Heb 2:14

FLESHLY
f wisdom but by the . . . . . . 2 Cor 1:12
law of a *f* commandment . . . . Heb 7:16
f lusts which war against . . 1 Pet 2:11

FLIES
will send swarms of *f* . . . . Ex 8:21
He sent swarms of *f* . . . . Ps 78:45
of the arrow that *f* by day . . . Ps 91:5
Dead *f* putrefy the . . . . Eccl 10:1

FLIGHT
put ten thousand to *f* . . . Deut 32:30
f shall perish from . . . . Amos 2:14
And pray that your *f* . . . . Matt 24:20
turned to *f* the armies of . . . Heb 11:34

FLINT
will seem like *f* . . . . Is 5:28
set My face like a *f* . . . . Is 50:7

FLINTY
out of the *f* rock . . . . Deut 8:15
oil from the *f* rock . . . . . . Deut 32:13

FLOAT
and he made the iron *f* . . . 2 Kin 6:6

FLOCK
of the firstborn of his *f* . . . . . Gen 4:4
Go now to the *f* and bring . . Gen 27:9
pass through all your *f* . . . Gen 30:32
put them with Laban's *f* . . . Gen 30:40
Moses was tending the *f* . . . . . Ex 3:1
Your people like a *f* . . . . Ps 77:20
wilderness like a *f* . . . . Ps 78:52
lead Joseph like a *f* . . . . Ps 80:1
their families like a *f* . . . . . Ps 107:41
the footsteps of the *f* . . . . . . Song 1:8
He will feed His *f* . . . . Is 40:11
with the shepherd of His *f* . . . Is 63:11
"You have scattered My *f* . . . Jer 23:2
gather the remnant of My *f* . . Jer 23:3
oil, for the young of the *f* . . . Jer 31:12
you do not feed the *f* . . . . . Ezek 34:3
are My *f*, the *f* . . . . Ezek 34:31
though the *f* be cut . . . . Hab 3:17
my God, "Feed the *f* . . . . . . Zech 11:4
sheep of the *f* will be . . . . . Matt 26:31
watch over their *f* by night . . Luke 2:8
"Do not fear, little *f* . . . . . Luke 12:32
there will be one *f* . . . . John 10:16
and to all the *f* . . . . Acts 20:28
not sparing the *f* . . . . Acts 20:29
of the milk of the *f* . . . . 1 Cor 9:7
Shepherd the *f* of God . . . . . 1 Pet 5:2
examples to the *f* . . . . 1 Pet 5:3

FLOCKS
fed the rest of Laban's *f* . . . Gen 30:36
their little ones, their *f* . . . . . Gen 50:8
Also take your *f* and your . . . Ex 12:32
are clothed with *f* . . . . Ps 65:13
the *f* of your companions . . . Song 1:7
lion among *f* of sheep . . . . . . Mic 5:8
for they shall feed their *f* . . Zeph 3:13

FLOOD
the waters of the *f* . . . . Gen 7:10
a *f* to destroy all flesh . . . . . Gen 9:15
on the earth after the *f* . . . Gen 10:32
sat enthroned at the *F* . . . . . Ps 29:10
them away like a *f* . . . . Ps 90:5
enemy comes in like a *f* . . . . Is 59:19

FLOODS (continued)

the days before the *f* ...... Matt 24:38
when the *f* arose, the ...... Luke 6:48
bringing in the *f* .... 2 Pet 2:5
of his mouth like a *f* ...... Rev 12:15

FLOODS
me, and the *f* of .... Ps 18:4
f on the dry ground .... Is 44:3
and the *f* surrounded me .... Jon 2:3
rain descended, the *f* ...... Matt 7:25

FLOOR
down to the threshing *f* ..... Ruth 3:6
came to the threshing *f* .... Ruth 3:14
bought the threshing *f* ... 2 Sam 24:24
clean out His threshing *f* .. Matt 3:12
clean out His threshing *f* .. Luke 3:17

FLOUR
a handful of *f* in a bin .... 1 Kin 17:12
bin of *f* was not used up .. 1 Kin 17:16
"Then bring some *f* .... 2 Kin 4:41

FLOURISH
the righteous shall *f* .... Ps 72:7
f in the courts of our God ... Ps 92:13
tent of the upright will *f* ... Prov 14:11

FLOURISHED
your care for me has *f* ...... Phil 4:10

FLOURISHES
In the morning it *f* .... Ps 90:6

FLOW
f away as waters which ...... Ps 58:7
and the waters *f* .... Ps 147:18
that its spices may *f* ...... Song 4:16
all nations shall *f* .... Is 2:2
and peoples shall *f* to it ...... Mic 4:1
who had a *f* of blood ...... Matt 9:20
f of blood for twelve ...... Mark 5:25
immediately her *f* of ...... Luke 8:44
of his heart will *f* .... John 7:38

FLOWER
comes forth like a *f* .... Job 14:2
as a *f* of the field .... Ps 103:15
beauty is a fading *f* .... Is 28:4
is like the *f* of the .... Is 40:6
grass withers, the *f* .... Is 40:7
if she is past the *f* .... 1 Cor 7:36
of man as the *f* .... 1 Pet 1:24

FLOWERS
f appear on the earth ...... Song 2:12

FLOWING
'a land *f* with milk .... Deut 6:3
of wisdom is a *f* .... Prov 18:4
the Gentiles like a *f* .... Is 66:12

FLUTE
play the harp and *f* .... Gen 4:21
sound of the horn, *f* .... Dan 3:5
saw the *f* players .... Matt 9:23
"We played the *f* for you .. Luke 7:32

FLUTES
instruments and *f* .... Ps 150:4

FLUTISTS
harpists, musicians, *f* ...... Rev 18:22

FLY
let birds *f* above the earth ...Gen 1:20
I would *f* away and be .... Ps 55:6
soon cut off, and we *f* ...... Ps 90:10
they *f* away, like an .... Prov 23:5
being caused to *f* swiftly .... Dan 9:21

FLYING
a *f* swallow, so a curse ..... Prov 26:2

FOAL
a colt, the *f* of a donkey ..... Zech 9:9
a colt, the *f* of a donkey .... Matt 21:5

FOAMS
so that he *f* at the mouth ... Luke 9:39

FOE
and scattered the *f* .... Ps 18:14

FOES
my enemies and *f* .... Ps 27:2
I will beat down his *f* ...... Ps 89:23

FOLD
are not of this *f* .... John 10:16
a cloak You will *f* .... Heb 1:12

FOLDING
slumber, a little *f* .... Prov 6:10
f of the hands to sleep .... Prov 24:33

FOLLOW
willing to *f* me to this land .. Gen 24:5
f what is altogether ...... Deut 16:20
If the LORD is God, *f* ..... I Kin 18:21
shall *f* me all the days .... Ps 23:6
to Me, you who *f* .... Is 51:1
"*F* Me, and I will make ..... Matt 4:19
f You wherever You go ... Matt 8:19
"*F* Me, and let the dead ... Matt 8:22
He said to him, "*F* .... Matt 9:9
f after Me is not worthy ... Matt 10:38
his cross, and *f* Me ...... Matt 16:24
up his cross, and *f* .... Mark 8:34
someone who does not *f* .. Mark 9:38
the cross, and *f* Me ...... Mark 10:21
signs will *f* those who .... Mark 16:17
he does not *f* with us ...... Luke 9:49
I will *f* You wherever ...... Luke 9:57
said to another, "*F* Me ..... Luke 9:59
not go after them or *f* ..... Luke 17:23
and come, *f* Me .... Luke 18:22
f him into the house ...... Luke 22:10
the sheep *f* him, for they ... John 10:4
will by no means *f* .... John 10:5
serves Me, let him *f* ...... John 12:26
on your garment and *f* ...... Acts 12:8
those of some men *f* ...... 1 Tim 5:24
God to you, whose faith *f* .. Heb 13:7
that you should *f* .... 1 Pet 2:21
f the Lamb wherever He .... Rev 14:4
and their works *f* .... Rev 14:13

FOLLOWED
f the LORD my God .... Josh 14:8
LORD took me as I *f* ...... Amos 7:15
left their nets and *f* Him ... Matt 4:20
great multitudes *f* Him ...... Matt 8:1
Peter *f* Him at a distance .. Matt 26:58
women who *f* Jesus ...... Matt 27:55
we have left all and *f* ..... Mark 10:28
sight and *f* Jesus .... Mark 10:52
This girl *f* Paul and us .... Acts 16:17
spiritual Rock that *f* ...... 1 Cor 10:4
diligently *f* every good .... 1 Tim 5:10
carefully *f* my doctrine .... 2 Tim 3:10

FOLLOWING
if you turn away from *f* ... Num 32:15
away this day from *f* the .. Josh 22:16
back from *f* after you ...... Ruth 1:16
continue *f* the LORD ..... 1 Sam 12:14
f the sheep, to be ruler ... 2 Sam 7:8
away from *f* the LORD .... 2 Chr 25:27
turned, and seeing them *f* .. John 1:38
whom Jesus loved *f* ..... John 21:20
join in *f* my example .... Phil 3:17
f the way of Balaam .... 2 Pet 2:15

FOLLOWS
My soul *f* close behind ...... Ps 63:8
but he who *f* frivolity is .. Prov 12:11
loves him who *f* .... Prov 15:9
f Me shall not walk .... John 8:12

FOLLY
taken much notice of *f* ..... Job 35:15
not turn back to *f* .... Ps 85:8
F is joy to him who is ..... Prov 15:21
correction of fools is *f* .... Prov 16:22
F is set in great .... Eccl 10:6

FOOD
you it shall be for *f* .... Gen 1:29
that lives shall be *f* .... Gen 9:3
stranger, giving him *f* .... Deut 10:18

He gives *f* in abundance ... Job 36:31
he may bring forth *f* ...... Ps 104:14
Who gives *f* to all .... Ps 136:25
Much *f* is in the .... Prov 13:23
feed me with the *f* .... Prov 30:8
their *f* in the summer ..... Prov 30:25
night, and provides *f* ..... Prov 31:15
f which you eat shall ..... Ezek 4:10
I ate no pleasant *f* .... Dan 10:3
the fields yield no *f* .... Hab 3:17
that there may be *f* .... Mal 3:10
is worthy of his *f* .... Matt 10:10
to give them *f* in due ..... Matt 24:45
and you gave Me *f* .... Matt 25:35
and he who has *f* .... Luke 3:11
Life is more than *f* .... Luke 12:23
I have *f* to eat of which ... John 4:32
f is to do the will of Him ... John 4:34
for the *f* which perishes ... John 6:27
have you any *f* .... John 21:5
they ate their *f* .... Acts 2:46
our hearts with *f* .... Acts 14:17
destroy with your *f* ...... Rom 14:15
f makes my brother ...... 1 Cor 8:13
the same spiritual *f* .... 1 Cor 10:3
sower, and bread for *f* .... 2 Cor 9:10
And having *f* and .... 1 Tim 6:8
and not solid *f* .... Heb 5:12
But solid *f* belongs to ...... Heb 5:14
of *f* sold his birthright ..... Heb 12:16
destitute of daily *f* .... James 2:15

FOODS
F for the stomach .... 1 Cor 6:13
f which God created ...... 1 Tim 4:3

FOOL
I have played the *f* ...... 1 Sam 26:21
Should Abner die as a *f* .. 2 Sam 3:33
f has said in his .... Ps 14:1
or as a *f* to the correction .. Prov 7:22
is like sport to a *f* .... Prov 10:23
f will be servant .... Prov 11:29
f is right in his own ...... Prov 12:15
f lays open his folly ...... Prov 13:16
A *f* despises his father's .... Prov 15:5
a hundred blows on a *f* ... Prov 17:10
is too lofty for a *f* .... Prov 24:7
Do not answer a *f* .... Prov 26:4
"As it happens to the *f*, it .. Eccl 2:15
A *f* also multiplies words .. Eccl 10:14
whoever says, 'You *f* ..... Matt 5:22
But God said to him, '*F* .. Luke 12:20
let him become a *f* that ... 1 Cor 3:18
I speak as a *f* .... 2 Cor 11:23
I have become a *f* .... 2 Cor 12:11

FOOLISH
of the *f* women speaks ..... Job 2:10
I was so *f* and .... Ps 73:22
f pulls it down with ...... Prov 14:1
f man squanders it ...... Prov 21:20
"For My people are *f* ...... Jer 4:22
f hearts were darkened .... Rom 1:21
Has not God made *f* ...... 1 Cor 1:20
But God has chosen the *f* .. 1 Cor 1:27
O *f* Galatians .... Gal 3:1
nor *f* talking, nor coarse ... Eph 5:4
But avoid *f* and ignorant .. 2 Tim 2:23
were also once *f* .... Titus 3:3
But avoid *f* disputes ...... Titus 3:9

FOOLISHLY
man acts *f*, and a man .... Prov 14:17
I speak *f*—I am bold ...... 2 Cor 11:21

FOOLISHNESS
O God, You know my *f* ...... Ps 69:5
Forsake *f* and live .... Prov 9:6
of fools proclaims *f* ...... Prov 12:23
The *f* of a man twists ..... Prov 19:3
F is bound up in the ...... Prov 22:15
devising of *f* is sin .... Prov 24:9
person will speak *f* .... Is 32:6
of the cross is *f* .... 1 Cor 1:18

FOOLS

f despise wisdom . . . . Prov 1:7
folly of *f* is deceit . . . . Prov 14:8
F mock at sin . . . . Prov 14:9
has no pleasure in *f* . . . . Eccl 5:4
F and blind! . . . . Matt 23:17
to be wise, they became *f* . . Rom 1:22
We are *f* for Christ's . . . . . 1 Cor 4:10
not as *f* but as wise . . . . Eph 5:15

FOOT

your *f* will tread upon . . . . Josh 1:3
your sandal off your *f* . . . . . Josh 5:15
f has trodden shall be . . . . . Josh 14:9
dash your *f* against a stone . . Ps 91:12
will not allow your *f* . . . . . . Ps 121:3
f will not stumble . . . . Prov 3:23
From the sole of the *f* . . . . Is 1:6
you turn away your *f* . . . . . . Is 58:13
dash your *f* against a stone . . Matt 4:6
f causes you to sin . . . . Matt 18:8
you dash your *f* . . . . Luke 4:11
If the *f* should say . . . . . . 1 Cor 12:15

FOOTMEN

have run with the *f* . . . . Jer 12:5

FOOTSTEPS

f were not known . . . . Ps 77:19
and shall make His *f* . . . . . . Ps 85:13

FOOTSTOOL

God, and worship at His *f* . . . . Ps 99:5
Your enemies Your *f* . . . . . . Ps 110:1
throne, and earth is My *f* . . . . Is 66:1
by the earth, for it is His *f* . . Matt 5:35
Your enemies Your *f* . . . . . Matt 22:44
throne, and earth is My *f* . . . Acts 7:49
"Sit here at my *f* . . . . James 2:3

FORBID

come to Me, and do not *f* . . Matt 19:14
said, "Do not *f* him . . . . . . Mark 9:39
"Can anyone *f* water . . . . . Acts 10:47
prophesy, and do not *f* . . . 1 Cor 14:39
f that I should boast . . . . Gal 6:14

FORBIDDEN

LORD your God has *f* you . . . Deut 4:23
they were *f* by the Holy . . . . Acts 16:6

FORBIDDING

confidence, no one *f* . . . . . Acts 28:31
f us to speak to the . . . . . . 1 Thess 2:16
f to marry . . . . 1 Tim 4:3

FORCE

violent take it by *f* . . . . Matt 11:12
come and take Him by *f* . . . John 6:15
a testament is in *f* . . . . Heb 9:17

FORCEFUL

f are right words . . . . Job 6:25

FORCES

Though they join *f* . . . . Prov 11:21

FOREFATHERS

f who refused to hear . . . . . . Jer 11:10
and oppressed our *f* . . . . Acts 7:19
conscience, as my *f* . . . . 2 Tim 1:3

FOREHEADS

strong against their *f* . . . . . . Ezek 3:8
put a mark on the *f* . . . . Ezek 9:4
seal of God on their *f* . . . . . . Rev 9:4
his mark on their *f* . . . . Rev 20:4

FOREIGN

been a stranger in a *f* land . . Ex 2:22
put away the *f* gods . . . . . . Josh 24:23
loved many *f* women . . . . . 1 Kin 11:1
the LORD's song in a *f* land . . Ps 137:4
set out *f* seedlings . . . . Is 17:10
promise as in a *f* country . . . Heb 11:9

FOREIGN GODS

"put away the *f* . . . . Gen 35:2

---

to jealousy with *f;* . . . . Deut 32:16
the LORD and serve *f* . . . . . . Josh 24:20
So they put away the *f* . . . . . Judg 10:16
then put away the *f* . . . . . . 1 Sam 7:3
the altars of the *f* . . . . 2 Chr 14:3
He took away the *f* . . . . . . 2 Chr 33:15
forsaken Me and served *f* . . . . Jer 5:19
to be a proclaimer of *f* . . . . Acts 17:18

FOREIGNER

"I am a *f* and a . . . . Gen 23:4
of me, since I am a *f* . . . . . . Ruth 2:10
to God except this *f* . . . . . Luke 17:18
who speaks will be a *f* . . . 1 Cor 14:11

FOREIGNERS

from the hand of *f* . . . . Ps 144:11
with the children of *f* . . . . Is 2:6
f shall build up your . . . . Is 60:10
f who were there . . . . Acts 17:21
longer strangers and *f* . . . . . Eph 2:19

FOREKNEW

For whom He *f* . . . . Rom 8:29
His people whom He *f* . . . . . Rom 11:2

FOREKNOWLEDGE

purpose and *f* of God . . . . . . Acts 2:23
according to the *f* . . . . 1 Pet 1:2

FOREORDAINED

He indeed was *f* . . . . 1 Pet 1:20

FORERUNNER

f has entered for us . . . . Heb 6:20

FORESAW

"I *f* the LORD . . . . Acts 2:25

FORESEEING

f that God would . . . . Gal 3:8

FORESEES

A prudent man *f* . . . . Prov 22:3

FORESKINS

in the flesh of your *f* . . . . . . Gen 17:11
f of the Philistines . . . . 1 Sam 18:25

FOREST

beast of the *f* is Mine . . . . . . Ps 50:10
See how great a *f* . . . . James 3:5

FORESTS

and strips the *f* . . . . Ps 29:9

FORETOLD

have also *f* these days . . . . . . Acts 3:24
killed those who *f* . . . . Acts 7:52

FOREVER

See HIS MERCY ENDURES FOREVER
and eat, and live *f* . . . . Gen 3:22
shall not strive with man *f* . . . Gen 6:3
This is My name *f* . . . . Ex 3:15
and they shall inherit it *f* . . . Ex 32:13
to our children *f* . . . . Deut 29:29
has loved Israel *f* . . . . 1 Kin 10:9
for His mercy endures *f* . . . 2 Chr 5:13
for His mercy endures *f* . . . 2 Chr 7:3
I would not live *f* . . . . Job 7:16
from this generation *f* . . . . . . Ps 12:7
LORD sits as King *f* . . . . Ps 29:10
Do not cast us off *f* . . . . Ps 44:23
throne, O God, is *f* . . . . Ps 45:6
"You are a priest *f* . . . . Ps 110:4
His mercy endures *f* . . . . Ps 118:1
F, O LORD, Your word is . . . . Ps 119:89
be moved, but abides *f* . . . . . Ps 125:1
From this time forth and *f* . . Ps 125:2
This is My resting place *f* . . Ps 132:14
name, O LORD, endures *f* . . . Ps 135:13
His mercy endures *f* . . . . . . Ps 136:1
will bless Your name *f* . . . . . Ps 145:1
bless His holy name *f* . . . . . Ps 145:21
who keeps truth *f* . . . . Ps 146:6
The LORD shall reign *f* . . . . . Ps 146:10
also established them *f* . . . . . Ps 148:6
lip shall be established *f* . . . Prov 12:19
for riches are not *f* . . . . Prov 27:24
Trust in the LORD *f* . . . . Is 26:4

---

of our God stands *f* . . . . Is 40:8
My salvation will be *f* . . . . Is 51:6
will not cast off *f* . . . . Lam 3:31
be the name of God *f* . . . . . Dan 2:20
Like the stars *f* . . . . Dan 12:3
of the LORD our God *f* . . . . . . Mic 4:5
and the glory *f* . . . . Matt 6:13
eats this bread will live *f* . . . John 6:58
the Christ remains *f* . . . . . . John 12:34
He may abide with you *f* . . . John 14:16
righteousness endures *f* . . . 2 Cor 9:9
who is blessed *f* . . . . 2 Cor 11:31
to whom be glory *f* . . . . Gal 1:5
generation, *f* and ever . . . . . . Eph 3:21
and Father be glory *f* . . . . . . Phil 4:20
throne, O God, is *f* . . . . Heb 1:8
"You are a priest *f* . . . . Heb 5:6
f according to the order of . . Heb 6:20
has been perfected *f* . . . . . . Heb 7:28
one sacrifice for sins *f* . . . . Heb 10:12
yesterday, today, and *f* . . . . Heb 13:8
lives and abides *f* . . . . 1 Pet 1:23
of the LORD endures *f* . . . . . 1 Pet 1:25
blackness of darkness *f* . . . . . Jude 13
power, both now and *f* . . . . . . Jude 25
throne, and to the Lamb, *f* . . Rev 5:13
And they shall reign *f* . . . . . Rev 22:5

FOREVERMORE

Blessed be the LORD *f* . . . . . Ps 89:52
this time forth and *f* . . . . . . Ps 113:2
behold, I am alive *f* . . . . Rev 1:18

FOREWARNED

all such, as we also *f* . . . . . 1 Thess 4:6

FORGAVE

f the iniquity of my . . . . Ps 32:5
and *f* him the debt . . . . Matt 18:27
I *f* you all that debt . . . . . . Matt 18:32
to repay, he freely *f* . . . . . . Luke 7:42
the one whom he *f* more . . . Luke 7:43
God in Christ *f* . . . . Eph 4:32
even as Christ *f* . . . . Col 3:13

FORGED

The proud have *f* . . . . Ps 119:69

FORGERS

But you *f* of lies . . . . Job 13:4

FORGET

"For God has made me *f* . . Gen 41:51
yourselves, lest you *f* . . . . . . Deut 4:23
f the covenant of your . . . . . Deut 4:31
f the LORD who brought . . . Deut 6:12
the paths of all who *f* . . . . . . Job 8:13
all the nations that *f* . . . . Ps 9:17
this, you who *f* God . . . . Ps 50:22
f the works of God . . . . Ps 78:7
I will not *f* Your word . . . . . Ps 119:16
If I *f* you, O Jerusalem . . . . Ps 137:5
My son, do not *f* . . . . Prov 3:1
f her nursing child . . . . Is 49:15
f the LORD your Maker . . . . . . Is 51:13
virgin *f* her ornaments . . . . . Jer 2:32
f your work and labor . . . . . . Heb 6:10
Do not *f* to entertain . . . . . . Heb 13:2
But do not *f* to do good . . . . Heb 13:16
do not *f* this one thing . . . . . 2 Pet 3:8

FORGETFUL

not a *f* hearer but a doer . . James 1:25

FORGETFULNESS

in the land of *f* . . . . Ps 88:12

FORGETS

f the covenant of her . . . . . . Prov 2:17
and immediately *f* . . . . James 1:24

FORGETTING

f those things which . . . . Phil 3:13

FORGIVE

please *f* my sin only this . . . . Ex 10:17
if You will *f* their sin . . . . . . Ex 32:32
dwelling place, and *f* . . . . . . 1 Kin 8:39
f their sin and heal . . . . 2 Chr 7:14

good, and ready to f . . . . Ps 86:5
For I will f their iniquity . . . . . Jer 31:34
O Lord, hear! O Lord, f . . . . . Dan 9:19
And f us our debts . . . . Matt 6:12
Father will also f . . . . Matt 6:14
f men their trespasses . . . . . Matt 6:15
sin against me, and I f . . . . Matt 18:21
his heart, does not f . . . . Matt 18:35
Who can f sins but God . . . Mark 2:7
f him, that your Father . . . . Mark 11:25
if you do not f, neither . . . . Mark 11:26
power on earth to f sins . . . Luke 5:24
F, and you will be . . . . Luke 6:37
f us our sins, for we also . . . Luke 11:4
and if he repents, f him . . . . Luke 17:3
'I repent,' you shall f him . . . Luke 17:4
f them, for they do not . . . . Luke 23:34
f the sins of any . . . . John 20:23
you ought rather to f . . . . . . 2 Cor 2:7
anything, I also f . . . . 2 Cor 2:10
F me this wrong . . . . 2 Cor 12:13
f us our sins and to . . . . 1 John 1:9

FORGIVEN
transgression is f . . . . Ps 32:1
sins be f them . . . . Mark 4:12
to whom little is f . . . . Luke 7:47
of your heart may be f . . . . Acts 8:22
indeed I have f . . . . 2 Cor 2:10
f you all trespasses . . . . Col 2:13
sins, he will be f . . . . James 5:15
your sins are f . . . . 1 John 2:12

FORGIVENESS
But there is f with . . . . Ps 130:4
God belong mercy and f . . . . Dan 9:9
never has f, but is subject . . Mark 3:29
preached to you the f . . . . Acts 13:38
they may receive f . . . . Acts 26:18
His blood, the f . . . . Eph 1:7
His blood, the f of sins . . . . . . Col 1:14

FORGIVES
f all your iniquities . . . . Ps 103:3
"Who is this who even f . . . Luke 7:49

FORGIVING
tenderhearted, f . . . . Eph 4:32
and f one another . . . . Col 3:13

FORGOT
remember Joseph, but f . . . . Gen 40:23
f the LORD their God . . . . Judg 3:7
f His works and His . . . . Ps 78:11
They soon f His works . . . . . Ps 106:13

FORGOTTEN
f the God who fathered . . . Deut 32:18
needy shall not always be f . . . Ps 9:18
"Why have You f . . . . Ps 42:9
If we had f the name . . . . Ps 44:20
memory of them is f . . . . Eccl 9:5
you will not be f . . . . Is 44:21
And my Lord has f . . . . Is 49:14
I have f prosperity . . . . Lam 3:17
not one of them is f . . . . Luke 12:6
f the exhortation . . . . Heb 12:5
f that he was cleansed . . . . . 2 Pet 1:9

FORM
earth was without f . . . . Gen 1:2
he sees the f of the LORD . . . Num 12:8
of the words, but saw no f . . Deut 4:12
Who would f a god or . . . . Is 44:10
f the light and create . . . . Is 45:7
He has no f or comeliness . . . . Is 53:2
descended in bodily f . . . . . Luke 3:22
time, nor seen His f . . . . John 5:37
having the f of knowledge . . Rom 2:20
For the f of this . . . . 1 Cor 7:31
who, being in the f . . . . Phil 2:6
the f of a bondservant . . . . . . Phil 2:7
Abstain from every f . . . . 1 Thess 5:22
having a f of godliness . . . . . 2 Tim 3:5

FORMED
And the LORD God f . . . . Gen 2:7

And His hands f . . . . Ps 95:5
f my inward parts . . . . Ps 139:13
f everything gives the . . . . . Prov 26:10
say of him who f . . . . Is 29:16
Me there was no God f . . . . . . Is 43:10
This people I have f . . . . Is 43:21
No weapon f against you . . . Is 54:17
"Before I f you in . . . . Jer 1:5
Will the thing f say to . . . . . Rom 9:20
until Christ is f . . . . Gal 4:19
For Adam was f first . . . . . . 1 Tim 2:13

FORMER
according to the f . . . . Gen 40:13
not remember f inquiries . . . . Ps 79:8
f lovingkindness . . . . Ps 89:49
f days better than . . . . Eccl 7:10
Who gives rain, both the f . . . Jer 5:24
f rain to the earth . . . . Hos 6:3
the f rain, and the latter . . . Joel 2:23
f prophets preached . . . . Zech 1:4
through the f prophets . . . . Zech 7:12
The f account I made, O . . . . Acts 1:1
f conduct in Judaism . . . . Gal 1:13
your f conduct, the old . . . . . Eph 4:22
yourselves to the f lusts . . . 1 Pet 1:14
in f times, the holy women . . 1 Pet 3:5
f things have passed . . . . . . Rev 21:4

FORMS
clay say to him who f . . . . Is 45:9
f the spirit of man . . . . Zech 12:1

FORNICATION
"We were not born of f . . . John 8:41
adultery, f, uncleanness . . . . Gal 5:19
of the wrath of her f . . . . . . Rev 14:8

FORNICATOR
you know, that no f . . . . Eph 5:5
lest there be any f . . . . Heb 12:16

FORNICATORS
but f and adulterers . . . . Heb 13:4

FORSAKE
but if you f Him . . . . 2 Chr 15:2
and did not f them . . . . Neh 9:17
mercies You did not f . . . . . . Neh 9:19
Do not leave me nor f me . . . Ps 27:9
father and my mother f me . . Ps 27:10
Cease from anger, and f . . . . . Ps 37:8
And does not f His saints . . . Ps 37:28
"If his sons f My law . . . . . . Ps 89:30
f His inheritance . . . . Ps 94:14
But I did not f Your . . . . Ps 119:87
father, and do not f . . . . Prov 1:8
Let not mercy and truth f . . . Prov 3:3
worthless idols f . . . . Jon 2:8
of you does not f . . . . Luke 14:33
never leave you nor f . . . . . . Heb 13:5

FORSAKEN
My God, why have You f . . . Ps 22:1
seen the righteous f . . . . Ps 37:25
you dread will be f . . . . Is 7:16
cities will be as a f . . . . Is 17:9
a mere moment I have f . . . . Is 54:7
no longer be termed F . . . . . Is 62:4
they have f Me . . . . Jer 2:13
My God, why have You f . . Matt 27:46
persecuted, but not f . . . . . . 2 Cor 4:9
for Demas has f . . . . 2 Tim 4:10
f the right way . . . . 2 Pet 2:15

FORSAKES
f the companion of her . . . . Prov 2:17
and f them will have . . . . . . Prov 28:13

FORSAKING
f the assembling . . . . Heb 10:25

FORSOOK
f God who made him . . . . . Deut 32:15
all the disciples f . . . . Matt 26:56
with me, but all f . . . . 2 Tim 4:16
By faith he f Egypt . . . . Heb 11:27

FORT
Man the f! . . . . Nah 2:1

FORTRESS
LORD is my rock, my f . . . 2 Sam 22:2
my rock of refuge, a f . . . . . . Ps 31:2
He is my refuge and my f . . . Ps 91:2

FORTUNE-TELLING
masters much profit by f . . Acts 16:16

FORTY
to rain on the earth f days . . . Gen 7:4
to pass, at the end of f days . . Gen 8:6
not do it for the sake of f . . Gen 18:29
Isaac was f years old . . . . . . Gen 25:20
Esau was f years old . . . . . . Gen 26:34
F days were required . . . . Gen 50:3
Israel ate manna f years . . . Ex 16:35
mountain f days and f . . . . . . Ex 24:18
LORD f days and f nights . . . Ex 34:28
out the land after f days . . Num 13:25
in the wilderness f years . . Num 14:33
f days, for each day you . . . Num 14:34
in the wilderness f years . . Num 32:13
These f years the LORD . . . . . Deut 2:7
f years in the wilderness . . . Deut 8:2
foot swell these f years . . . . Deut 8:4
first, f days and f nights . . . Deut 9:18
f nights I kept prostrating . . Deut 9:25
mountain f days and f . . . . Deut 10:10
F blows he may give him . . Deut 25:3
f years old when Moses . . . Josh 14:7
land had rest for f years . . . Judg 3:11
the Philistines for f years . . Judg 13:1
judged Israel f years . . . . . 1 Sam 4:18
presented himself f . . . . . . 1 Sam 17:16
f nights as far as Horeb . . . 1 Kin 19:8
For f years I was grieved . . . Ps 95:10
f days, and Nineveh shall . . . Jon 3:4
when He had fasted f days . . Matt 4:2
for f days by the devil . . . . Luke 4:2
seen by them during f days . . Acts 1:3
when he was f years old . . . . Acts 7:23
when f years had passed . . . Acts 7:30
f who had formed this . . . . Acts 23:13
more than f of them lie . . . . Acts 23:21
f stripes minus one . . . . . . 2 Cor 11:24
and saw My works f years . . . Heb 3:9
was He angry f years . . . . . . Heb 3:17

FORWARD
David from that day f . . . 1 Sam 16:13
David from that day f . . . . 1 Sam 18:9

FOUGHT
f against me without . . . . Ps 109:3
I have f the good fight, I . . . 2 Tim 4:7

FOUL
My wounds are f . . . . Ps 38:5
f weather today . . . . Matt 16:3
a prison for every f . . . . Rev 18:2

FOUND
f a helper comparable . . . . . Gen 2:20
Why have I f favor in . . . . . Ruth 2:10
where can wisdom be f . . . Job 28:12
when You may be f . . . . Ps 32:6
f My servant David . . . . Ps 89:20
a thousand I have f . . . . Eccl 7:28
this only I have f . . . . Eccl 7:29
f the one I love . . . . Song 3:4
LORD while He may be f . . . . . Is 55:6
none was f like Daniel . . . . . Dan 1:19
he f them ten times better . . Dan 1:20
balances, and f wanting . . . . Dan 5:27
any error or fault f in him . . Dan 6:4
f Daniel praying and . . . . Dan 6:11
your fruit is f . . . . Hos 14:8
and when you have f Him . . Matt 2:8
not f such great faith . . . . . Matt 8:10
when he had f one pearl . . Matt 13:46
f nothing on it but leaves . . Matt 21:19
f them sleeping, and said . . Matt 26:40
have f favor with God . . . . Luke 1:30
they f Him in the temple . . Luke 2:46
fruit on it and f none . . . . . Luke 13:6

he was lost and is *f* . . . . Luke 15:24
they *f* the stone rolled . . . . . Luke 24:2
f the Messiah" (which . . . . . John 1:41
we *f* the prison shut . . . . Acts 5:23
I even *f* an altar with . . . . . . Acts 17:23
I *f* to death . . . . Rom 7:10
that one be *f* faithful . . . . . . 1 Cor 4:2
and be *f* in Him . . . . Phil 3:9
being *f* blameless . . . . 1 Tim 3:10
be diligent to be *f* . . . . 2 Pet 3:14
anyone not *f* written in . . . . Rev 20:15

FOUNDATION
he shall lay its *f* . . . . Josh 6:26
His *f* is in the holy . . . . Ps 87:1
and justice are the *f* . . . . Ps 89:14
Of old You laid the *f* . . . . . . Ps 102:25
has an everlasting *f* . . . . Prov 10:25
deep and laid the *f* . . . . Luke 6:48
the earth without a *f* . . . . . . Luke 6:49
loved Me before the *f* . . . . . John 17:24
I have laid the *f* . . . . 1 Cor 3:10
f can anyone lay than . . . . . 1 Cor 3:11
us in Him before the *f* . . . . . . Eph 1:4
the solid *f* of God . . . . 2 Tim 2:19
not laying again the *f* . . . . Heb 6:1
Lamb slain from the *f* . . . . . . Rev 13:8
the first *f* was jasper . . . . . . Rev 21:19

FOUNDATIONS
when I laid the *f* . . . . Job 38:4
f are destroyed . . . . Ps 11:3
You who laid the *f* . . . . Ps 104:5
shall raise up the *f* . . . . Is 58:12
that the *f* of the prison . . . . Acts 16:26
The *f* of the wall . . . . Rev 21:19

FOUNDED
For He has *f* it upon . . . . Ps 24:2
by wisdom *f* the earth . . . . . Prov 3:19
shake it, for it was *f* . . . . . . Luke 6:48

FOUNTAIN
Let your *f* be blessed . . . . . . Prov 5:18
Immediately the *f* of her . . . Mark 5:29
will become in him a *f* . . . . John 4:14
I will give of the *f* of the . . . . Rev 21:6

FOUNTAINS
on that day all the *f* . . . . Gen 7:11
f be dispersed abroad . . . . . . Prov 5:16
when there were no *f* . . . . . . Prov 8:24
lead them to living *f* . . . . Rev 7:17

FOUR
became *f* riverheads . . . . Gen 2:10
prophets are *f* hundred . . . 1 Kin 18:22
Each one had *f* faces . . . . . Ezek 10:14
and each one *f* wings . . . . . Ezek 10:21
I see *f* men loose, walking . . Dan 3:25
f great beasts came up . . . . . . Dan 7:3
f kingdoms shall arise . . . . . . Dan 8:22
are *f* spirits of heaven . . . . . . Zech 6:5
ate were *f* thousand . . . . . Matt 15:38
been in the tomb *f* days . . . John 11:17
sheet bound at the *f* . . . . . . Acts 10:11
Now this man had *f* virgin . . Acts 21:9
were *f* living creatures full . . . Rev 4:6
the *f* angels to whom it was . . Rev 7:2

FOWLER
you from the snare of the *f* . . Ps 91:3
bird from the hand of the *f* . Prov 6:5

FOX
build, if even a *f* . . . . Neh 4:3
"Go, tell that *f* . . . . Luke 13:32

FOXES
caught three hundred *f* . . . . Judg 15:4
f that spoil the vines . . . . . Song 2:15
F have holes and birds . . . . Luke 9:58

FRAGMENTS
f that remained . . . . Matt 14:20
of the leftover *f* . . . . Luke 9:17
baskets with the *f* . . . . John 6:13

FRAGRANCE
garments is like the *f* . . . . . Song 4:11
was filled with the *f* . . . . . . John 12:3
we are to God the *f* . . . . . . 2 Cor 2:15

FRAGRANT
the merchant's *f* powders . . . Song 3:6
flask of very costly *f* oil . . . . Matt 26:7
an alabaster flask of *f* oil . . . Luke 7:37
prepared spices and *f* . . . . Luke 23:56
was this *f* oil not sold . . . . . John 12:5
f oil and frankincense . . . . . Rev 18:13

FRAIL
that I may know how *f* . . . . . . Ps 39:4

FRAME
For He knows our *f* . . . . . . Ps 103:14
f was not hidden . . . . Ps 139:15

FRAMED
that the worlds were *f* . . . . . Heb 11:3

FRANKINCENSE
oil on it, and put *f* on it . . . . . . Lev 2:1
with myrrh and *f* . . . . Song 3:6
gold, *f*, and myrrh . . . . Matt 2:11
incense, fragrant oil and *f* . . Rev 18:13

FREE
and the servant is *f* . . . . Job 3:19
let the oppressed go *f* . . . . Is 58:6
'You will be made *f* . . . . John 8:33
if the Son makes you *f* . . . . . John 8:36
And having been set *f* . . . . . Rom 6:18
now having been set *f* . . . . . Rom 6:22
Jesus has made me *f* . . . . . . Rom 8:2
Am I not *f* . . . . 1 Cor 9:1
is neither slave nor *f* . . . . Gal 3:28
Jerusalem above is *f* . . . . . . Gal 4:26
Christ has made us *f* . . . . Gal 5:1
he is a slave or *f* . . . . Eph 6:8
poor, *f* and slave . . . . Rev 13:16

FREED
has died has been *f* . . . . Rom 6:7

FREEDMAN
slave is the Lord's *f* . . . . . . 1 Cor 7:22

FREEDOM
The LORD gives *f* to the . . . . . . Ps 146:7

FREELY
the garden you may *f* . . . . . . Gen 2:16
I will love them *f* . . . . Hos 14:4
F you have received . . . . . . Matt 10:8
f give us all things . . . . Rom 8:32
that have been *f* . . . . 1 Cor 2:12
the water of life *f* . . . . Rev 22:17

FREEWOMAN
the other by a *f* . . . . Gal 4:22
with the son of the *f* . . . . Gal 4:30

FRESH
My glory is *f* within . . . . Job 29:20
they shall be *f* . . . . Ps 92:14
both salt water and *f* . . . . James 3:12

FRETS
and his heart *f* . . . . Prov 19:3

FRIEND
a man speaks to his *f* . . . . . . Ex 33:11
of Abraham Your *f* . . . . . . 2 Chr 20:7
though he were my *f* . . . . . . Ps 35:14
f You have put far from me . . Ps 88:18
f loves at all times . . . . Prov 17:17
f who sticks closer . . . . Prov 18:24
not forsake your own *f* . . . . Prov 27:10
a *f* of tax collectors . . . . . . Matt 11:19
of you shall have a *f* . . . . . . Luke 11:5
f Lazarus sleeps . . . . John 11:11
you are not Caesar's *f* . . . . John 19:12
Philemon our beloved *f* . . . Philem 1
he was called the *f* . . . . . . James 2:23
wants to be a *f* . . . . James 4:4

FRIENDLY
friends must himself be *f* . . Prov 18:24

FRIENDS
and hate your *f* . . . . 2 Sam 19:6
My *f* scorn me . . . . Job 16:20
f have forgotten me . . . . Job 19:14
the rich has many *f* . . . . . . Prov 14:20
one's life for his *f* . . . . John 15:13
You are My *f* . . . . John 15:14
I have called you *f* . . . . John 15:15
to forbid any of his *f* . . . . . Acts 24:23

FRIENDSHIP
no *f* with an angry man . . . . Prov 22:24
that *f* with the world . . . . . . James 4:4

FROGS
your territory with *f* . . . . Ex 8:2
f coming out of the . . . . Rev 16:13

FRONTLETS
on your hand and as *f* . . . . . Ex 13:16
and they shall be as *f* . . . . . . Deut 6:8

FROZEN
the broad waters are *f* . . . . . Job 37:10

FRUIT
See BEAR FRUIT
and showed them the *f* . . . . Num 13:26
Blessed shall be the *f* . . . . . Deut 28:4
brings forth its *f* . . . . Ps 1:3
f is better than gold . . . . Prov 8:19
The *f* of the righteous . . . . Prov 11:30
with good by the *f* . . . . Prov 12:14
f was sweet to my . . . . Song 2:3
they shall eat the *f* . . . . Is 3:10
like the first *f* . . . . Is 28:4
"I create the *f* . . . . Is 57:19
f is found in Me . . . . Hos 14:8
does not bear good *f* . . . . . . Matt 3:10
good tree bears good *f* . . . . Matt 7:17
not drink of this *f* . . . . Matt 26:29
and blessed is the *f* . . . . . . Luke 1:42
life, and bring no *f* . . . . Luke 8:14
and he came seeking *f* . . . . Luke 13:6
And if it bears *f* . . . . Luke 13:9
branch that bears *f* . . . . John 15:2
that you bear much *f* . . . . . . John 15:8
should go and bear *f* . . . . . John 15:16
f did you have then in . . . . . Rom 6:21
God, you have your *f* . . . . . Rom 6:22
that we should bear *f* . . . . . . Rom 7:4
But the *f* of the Spirit is . . . . Gal 5:22
(for the *f* of the Spirit is . . . . Eph 5:9
but I seek the *f* . . . . Phil 4:17
yields the peaceable *f* . . . . . Heb 12:11
the *f* of our lips, giving . . . . Heb 13:15
Now the *f* of . . . . James 3:18
precious *f* of the earth . . . . James 5:7
autumn trees without *f* . . . . . Jude 12
tree yielding its *f* . . . . Rev 22:2

FRUITFUL
See BE FRUITFUL AND MULTIPLY
them, saying, "Be *f* . . . . Gen 1:22
a *f* bough, a *f* . . . . Gen 49:22
wife shall be like a *f* . . . . . . Ps 128:3
heaven and *f* seasons . . . . Acts 14:17
pleasing Him, being *f* . . . . . . Col 1:10

FRUITS
Therefore bear *f* . . . . Matt 3:8
know them by their *f* . . . . . Matt 7:16
and increase the *f* . . . . 2 Cor 9:10
being filled with the *f* of . . . Phil 1:11
of mercy and good *f* . . . . . James 3:17
which bore twelve *f* . . . . . . Rev 22:2

FUEL
people shall be as *f* . . . . Is 9:19
into the fire for *f* . . . . Ezek 15:4

FUGITIVE
A *f* and a vagabond . . . . . . Gen 4:12

FULFILL
the LORD, to *f* his vow . . . . . Lev 22:21
And you shall *f* . . . . 1 Kin 5:9
f all your petitions . . . . Ps 20:5

f the desire of those .... Ps 145:19
for us to *f* all .... Matt 3:15
come to destroy but to *f* .... Matt 5:17
for the flesh, to *f* its lusts .. Rom 13:14
f the law of Christ .... Gal 6:2
f my joy by being .... Phil 2:2
and *f* all the good .... 2 Thess 1:11
evangelist, *f* your ministry .. 2 Tim 4:5
If you really *f* .... James 2:8

FULFILLED
be *f* which was spoken by .. Matt 1:22
the law till all is *f* .... Matt 5:18
could the Scriptures be *f* .. Matt 26:54
is *f*, and the kingdom ...... Mark 1:15
is *f* in your hearing .... Luke 4:21
of the Gentiles are *f* .... Luke 21:24
all things must be *f* ...... Luke 24:44
this joy of mine is *f* .... John 3:29
the Scripture may be *f* .... John 13:18
My joy *f* in themselves .... John 17:13
this Scripture had to be *f* ... Acts 1:16
they had *f* their ministry ... Acts 12:25
of the law might be *f* ...... Rom 8:4
loves another has *f* .... Rom 13:8
For all the law is *f* .... Gal 5:14
the words of God are *f* ..... Rev 17:17

FULFILLMENT
for there will be a *f* .... Luke 1:45
love is the *f* of the .... Rom 13:10

FULL
I went out *f* .... Ruth 1:21
For I am *f* of words .... Job 32:18
of the LORD is *f* .... Ps 29:4
who has his quiver *f* .... Ps 127:5
Lest I be *f* and deny ...... Prov 30:9
yet the sea is not *f* .... Eccl 1:7
the whole earth is *f* .... Is 6:3
and it was *f* of bones ..... Ezek 37:1
But truly I am *f* .... Mic 3:8
whole body will be *f* ...... Matt 6:22
of the Father, *f* of grace ... John 1:14
your joy may be *f* .... John 15:11
chose Stephen, a man *f* .... Acts 6:5
You are already *f* .... 1 Cor 4:8
learned both to be *f* .... Phil 4:12
I am *f*, having received ...... Phil 4:18
in *f* assurance of faith ..... Heb 10:22
that your joy may be *f* ...... 1 John 1:4
we may receive a *f* reward .. 2 John 8

FULL-GROWN
and sin, when it is *f* ..... James 1:15

FULLNESS
satisfied with the *f* .... Ps 36:8
f we have all received ..... John 1:16
to Israel until the *f* .... Rom 11:25
But when the *f* of the ...... Gal 4:4
dispensation of the *f* .... Eph 1:10
filled with all the *f* .... Eph 3:19
Him dwells all the *f* .... Col 2:9

FULLY
did not *f* follow the LORD .. 1 Kin 11:6
time has not yet *f* come ..... John 7:8
Pentecost had *f* come .... Acts 2:1
being *f* convinced that ...... Rom 4:21
f preached the gospel .... Rom 15:19
f pleasing Him, being .... Col 1:10
preached *f* through me .... 2 Tim 4:17
rest your hope *f* upon the .. 1 Pet 1:13

FUME
Why do you *f* with envy ..... Ps 68:16

FUNCTION
do not have the same *f* .... Rom 12:4

FURIOUS
You have been *f* .... Ps 89:38
f man do not go .... Prov 22:24
fury and in *f* rebukes ...... Ezek 5:15
LORD avenges and is *f* ...... Nah 1:2
this, they were *f* .... Acts 5:33

FURIOUSLY
for he drives *f* .... 2 Kin 9:20

FURNACE
you out of the iron *f* ...... Deut 4:20
tested you in the *f* .... Is 48:10
of a burning fiery *f* .... Dan 3:6
cast them into the *f* ...... Matt 13:42
the smoke of a great *f* ...... Rev 9:2

FURNISHED
also *f* her table .... Prov 9:2
a large upper room, *f* .... Mark 14:15

FURNISHINGS
and the pattern of all its *f* .... Ex 25:9
tabernacle and all its *f* .... Num 1:50
Solomon and all the *f* ..... 1 Kin 7:48
all the holy *f* that were in ... 2 Chr 5:5

FURY
F is not in Me .... Is 27:4
they are full of the *f* .... Is 51:20
f to His adversaries .... Is 59:18
My own *f*, it sustained ...... Is 63:5
even in anger and *f* .... Jer 21:5
and I will cause My *f* ..... Ezek 5:13
Thus will I spend My *f* ..... Ezek 6:12
in anger and *f* on the ...... Mic 5:15

FUTILE
For it is not a *f* thing ...... Deut 32:47
of the peoples are *f* .... Jer 10:3
wise, that they are *f* ...... 1 Cor 3:20
risen, your faith is *f* ...... 1 Cor 15:17

FUTILITY
allotted months of *f* .... Job 7:3
f have You created all ...... Ps 89:47
was subjected to *f* .... Rom 8:20

FUTURE
for the *f* of that man .... Ps 37:37
the *f* of the wicked .... Ps 37:38
to give you a *f* and a hope .. Jer 29:11
to many days in the *f* ...... Dan 8:26

GAAL
Son of Ebed; vilifies Abimelech, Judg 9:26–41

GAASH
Hill of Ephraim, Judg 2:9
Joshua buried near, Josh 24:30

GABBATHA
Place of Pilate's court, John 19:13

GABRIEL
Messenger archangel; interprets Daniel's vision, Dan 8:16–27
Reveals the prophecy of 70 weeks, Dan 9:21–27
Announces John's birth, Luke 1:11–22
Announces Christ's birth, Luke 1:26–38
Stands in God's presence, Luke 1:19

GAD
Son of Jacob by Zilpah, Gen 30:10, 11
Blessed by Jacob, Gen 49:19
―――― Tribe of:
Census of, Num 1:24, 25
Territory of, Num 32:20–36
Captivity of, 1 Chr 5:26
Later references to, Rev 7:5
―――― Prophet in David's reign, 1 Sam 22:5
Message of, to David, 2 Sam 24:10–16

GADARENES (or Gergesenes)
People east of the Sea of Galilee, Mark 5:1
Healing of demon-possessed in territory of, Matt 8:28–34

GAIN
See DISHONEST GAIN

aside after dishonest *g* .... 1 Sam 8:3
they did not *g* possession ..... Ps 44:3
That we may *g* a heart of .... Ps 90:12
g than fine gold .... Prov 3:14
He who is greedy for *g* .... Prov 15:27
will have no lack of *g* ..... Prov 31:11
a time to *g* .... Eccl 3:6
to get dishonest *g* .... Ezek 22:27
him who covets evil *g* ...... Hab 2:9
and to die is *g* .... Phil 1:21
what things were *g* to me .... Phil 3:7
rubbish, that I may *g* .... Phil 3:8
is a means of *g* .... 1 Tim 6:5
contentment is great *g* ..... 1 Tim 6:6
the sake of dishonest *g* .... Titus 1:11
for dishonest *g* .... 1 Pet 5:2
people to *g* advantage .... Jude 16

GAINED
which he had *g* .... Gen 31:18
g in the land of Canaan .... Gen 36:6
have *g* Him the victory .... Ps 98:1
Wealth *g* by dishonesty ... Prov 13:11
Bread *g* by deceit is ...... Prov 20:17
An inheritance *g* hastily .. Prov 20:21
g more wisdom than all .... Eccl 1:16
you have *g* your brother .. Matt 18:15
received two *g* two more .. Matt 25:17
g five more talents .... Matt 25:20

GAINS
understanding *g* favor .... Prov 13:15
g the whole world .... Matt 16:26

GAIUS
Companion of Paul, Acts 19:29
―――― Convert at Derbe, Acts 20:4
―――― Paul's host at Corinth, Rom 16:23; 1 Cor 1:14

GALATIA
Paul visits, Acts 16:6; 18:23
Paul writes to Christians in, Gal 1:1
Peter writes to Christians in, 1 Pet 1:1

GALILEANS
Speech of, Mark 14:70
Faith of, John 4:45
Pilate's cruelty toward, Luke 13:1, 2

GALILEE
Prophecies concerning, Deut 33:18–23; Is 9:1, 2
Dialect of, distinctive, Matt 26:73
Herod's jurisdiction over, Luke 3:1
Christ's contacts with, Matt 2:22; 4:12–25; 26:32; 27:55; John 4:1, 3

GALILEE, SEA OF
Scene of many events in Christ's life, Mark 7:31
Called Chinnereth, Num 34:11
Later called Gennesaret, Luke 5:1

GALL
grapes are grapes of *g* .... Deut 32:32
They also gave me *g* .... Ps 69:21
the wormwood and the *g* ... Lam 3:19
turned justice into *g* ...... Amos 6:12
wine mingled with *g* ...... Matt 27:34

GALLIO
Roman proconsul of Achaia, dismisses charges against Paul, Acts 18:12–17

GALLONS
twenty or thirty *g* apiece .... John 2:6

GALLOWS
both were hanged on a *g* .... Esth 2:23
should be hanged on the *g* .. Esth 9:25

GAMALIEL
Famous Jewish teacher, Acts 22:3
Respected by people, Acts 5:34–39

GAME
because he ate of his *g* .... Gen 25:28
Bring me *g* and make .... Gen 27:7

GAP
and stand in the *g* .... Ezek 22:30

GARDEN

Lord God planted a *g* . . . . Gen 2:8
g enclosed is my . . . . Song 4:12
like a watered *g* . . . . Is 58:11
Eden, the *g* of God . . . . . . Ezek 28:13
raise up for them a *g* . . . . Ezek 34:29
where there was a *g* . . . . . . John 18:1
in the *g* a new tomb . . . . . . John 19:41

GARDENER

Him to be the *g* . . . . John 20:15

GARDENS

I made myself *g* . . . . Eccl 2:5
plant and eat their . . . . Jer 29:5

GARLANDS

brought oxen and *g* . . . . Acts 14:13

GARLIC

the onions, and the *g* . . . . . . Num 11:5

GARMENT

and Japheth took a *g* . . . . Gen 9:23
like a hairy *g* all over . . . . . Gen 25:25
she caught him by his *g* . . . Gen 39:12
she kept his *g* with her . . . . Gen 39:16
beautiful Babylonian *g* . . . . . Josh 7:21
put on your best *g* . . . . Ruth 3:3
g that is moth-eaten . . . . Job 13:28
made sackcloth my *g* . . . . . . Ps 69:11
with light as with a *g* . . . . . . Ps 104:2
one who takes away a *g* . . Prov 25:20
the *g* of praise for the . . . . Is 61:3
the hem of His *g* . . . . Matt 9:20
have on a wedding *g* . . . . Matt 22:11
cloth on an old *g* . . . . Mark 2:21
throwing aside his *g* . . . . . Mark 10:50
all grow old like a *g* . . . . Heb 1:11
hating even the *g* . . . . Jude 23

GARMENTS

took off her widow's *g* . . . . . Gen 38:14
the *g* of her widowhood . . . Gen 38:19
g did not wear out on . . . . Deut 8:4
and old *g* on themselves . . . . Josh 9:5
our *g* and our sandals . . . . . . Josh 9:13
cut off their *g* in the . . . . . . 2 Sam 10:4
Why are your *g* hot . . . . Job 37:17
They divide My *g* . . . . Ps 22:18
She makes linen *g* and . . . . Prov 31:24
g always be white . . . . Eccl 9:8
g rolled in blood . . . . Is 9:5
from Edom, with dyed *g* . . . . . Is 63:1
nor were their *g* affected . . . . Dan 3:27
your heart, and not your *g* . . Joel 2:13
Take away the filthy *g* . . . . . Zech 3:4
man clothed in soft *g* . . . . . Matt 11:8
and divided His *g* . . . . Matt 27:35
by them in shining *g* . . . . . . Luke 24:4
and laid aside His *g* . . . . . . John 13:4
divided My *g* among . . . . . . John 19:24
g which Dorcas had made . . Acts 9:39
g are moth-eaten . . . . James 5:2
be clothed in white *g* . . . . Rev 3:5

GARRISON

gathered the whole *g* . . . . Matt 27:27
Damascenes with a *g* . . . . 2 Cor 11:32

GATE

sitting in the *g* of Sodom . . . . Gen 19:1
Boaz went up to the *g* . . . . . . Ruth 4:1
people who were at the *g* . . Ruth 4:11
This is the *g* of the . . . . Ps 118:20
by the narrow *g* . . . . Matt 7:13
Because narrow is the *g* . . . . Matt 7:14
by the Sheep *G* a pool . . . . . John 5:2
laid daily at the *g* . . . . Acts 3:2
she did not open the *g* . . . . Acts 12:14
suffered outside the *g* . . . . Heb 13:12
each individual *g* . . . . Rev 21:21

GATES

possess the *g* of those . . . . . Gen 24:60
g are burned with fire . . . . Neh 1:3

I commanded the *g* to be . . Neh 13:19
they go down to the *g* . . . . . Job 17:16
up your heads, O you *g* . . . . . Ps 24:7
The Lord loves the *g* . . . . Ps 87:2
Enter into His *g* with . . . . Ps 100:4
Open to me the *g* . . . . Ps 118:19
watching daily at my *g* . . . . Prov 8:34
is known in the *g* . . . . Prov 31:23
praise her in the *g* . . . . Prov 31:31
go through the *g* . . . . Is 62:10
and the *g* of Hades . . . . Matt 16:18
wall with twelve *g* . . . . Rev 21:12
g were twelve pearls . . . . Rev 21:21
g shall not be shut . . . . Rev 21:25

GATH

Philistine city, 1 Sam 6:17
Ark carried to, 1 Sam 5:8
David takes refuge in, 1 Sam 21:10–15
David's second flight to, 1 Sam
27:3–12
Captured by David, 1 Chr 18:1
Destruction of, prophetic, Amos 6:1–3
Name becomes proverbial, Mic 1:10

GATH HEPHER

Birthplace of Jonah, 2 Kin 14:25

GATHER

g my soul with sinners . . . . . . Ps 26:9
G My saints together . . . . Ps 50:5
and a time to *g* stones . . . . . . Eccl 3:5
g the lambs with His . . . . Is 40:11
g His wheat into the . . . . Matt 3:12
sow nor reap nor *g* . . . . Matt 6:26
Do men *g* grapes from . . . . . Matt 7:16
g where I have not . . . . Matt 25:26
g together His elect . . . . Mark 13:27
who does not *g* with Me . . Luke 11:23
often I wanted to *g* your . . Luke 13:34
G up the fragments that . . . . John 6:12
of the times He might *g* . . . . Eph 1:10

GATHERED

g little had no lack . . . . Ex 16:18
And *g* out of the lands . . . . . Ps 107:3
g some of every kind . . . . . Matt 13:47
g together in My name . . . . Matt 18:20
the nations will be *g* . . . . . Matt 25:32
many were *g* together . . . . . Acts 12:12
g the church together . . . . . Acts 14:27
when Paul had *g* a bundle . . Acts 28:3
when you are *g* together . . . . 1 Cor 5:4
who *g* much had nothing . . . 2 Cor 8:15
they *g* them together . . . . . . Rev 16:16

GATHERING

g together of the waters . . . . Gen 1:10
widow was there *g* . . . . . . 1 Kin 17:10
I am *g* a couple of sticks . . 1 Kin 17:12
they were three days *g* . . 2 Chr 20:25
He gives the work of *g* . . . . Eccl 2:26
g where you have not . . . . . Matt 25:24
g a mob, set all the city in . . Acts 17:5
for this disorderly *g* . . . . . . Acts 19:40
g together to Him . . . . 2 Thess 2:1

GATHERS

g the waters of the . . . . Ps 33:7
His heart *g* iniquity . . . . Ps 41:6
He *g* together the outcasts . . Ps 147:2
g her food in the . . . . Prov 6:8
He who *g* in summer is a . . Prov 10:5
he who *g* by labor will . . . . Prov 13:11
extortion *g* it for him who . . Prov 28:8
The Lord God, who *g* . . . . . . Is 56:8
together, as a hen *g* . . . . . Matt 23:37

GAUNT

out of the river, ugly and *g* . . Gen 41:3
g and ugly cows ate up . . . . Gen 41:20

GAVE

So Adam *g* names to all . . . . Gen 2:20
She also *g* to her husband . . Gen 3:6
to be with me, she *g* . . . . Gen 3:12
he *g* him a tithe of all . . . . . Gen 14:20

g her to her husband . . . . Gen 16:3
and *g* the lad a drink . . . . . Gen 21:19
hand, and *g* him a drink . . . . Gen 24:18
Abraham *g* all that he had . . Gen 25:5
Jacob *g* Esau bread and . . . Gen 25:34
which God *g* to Abraham . . . Gen 28:4
g him favor in the sight . . . . Gen 39:21
Joseph *g* a command . . . . . . Gen 42:25
it *g* light by night to the . . . . Ex 14:20
He *g* Moses two tablets of . . Ex 31:18
So they *g* it to me, and I . . . . Ex 32:24
g the children of Israel . . . . Num 13:32
stone and *g* them to me . . . . Deut 5:22
the Lord *g* me the two . . . . . . Deut 9:11
g you on this side of the . . . . Josh 1:14
g it as an inheritance . . . . . . Josh 11:23
So he *g* her the upper . . . . . . Josh 15:19
The Lord *g* them rest all . . Josh 21:44
Samson *g* a feast there . . . . Judg 14:10
g the changes of clothing . . Judg 14:19
therefore I *g* her to your . . . Judg 15:2
Lord *g* her conception . . . . . Ruth 4:13
g birth, for her labor . . . . . 1 Sam 4:19
God *g* him another heart . . 1 Sam 10:9
g it to David, with his . . . . 1 Sam 18:4
Saul *g* him Michal . . . . 1 Sam 18:27
So the priest *g* him holy . . 1 Sam 21:6
g him the sword of . . . . . . 1 Sam 22:10
this woman also *g* birth . . . 1 Kin 3:18
God *g* Solomon wisdom . . . 1 Kin 4:29
Hiram *g* Solomon cedar . . . 1 Kin 5:10
g to King Solomon . . . . . . 1 Kin 10:10
g a commandment . . . . . . 1 Chr 14:12
David *g* his son . . . . 1 Chr 28:11
g it to the workmen . . . . . . 2 Chr 34:10
Hilkiah *g* the book to . . . . 2 Chr 34:15
Josiah *g* the lay people . . . 2 Chr 35:7
so he readily *g* beauty . . . . . Esth 2:9
g gifts according to the . . . . Esth 2:18
He also *g* him a copy of . . . . Esth 4:8
and *g* it to Mordecai . . . . Esth 8:2
return to God who *g* it . . . . Eccl 12:7
of the eunuchs *g* names . . . . Dan 1:7
and *g* them vegetables . . . . Dan 1:16
God *g* them knowledge . . . . Dan 1:17
g him many great gifts . . . . Dan 2:48
Belshazzar *g* the command . . Dan 5:2
g thanks before his God . . . Dan 6:10
He *g* them power over . . . . Matt 10:1
g You this authority . . . . . Matt 21:23
hungry and you *g* Me . . . . Matt 25:35
g thanks, and *g* it to . . . . Matt 26:27
g Him sour wine . . . . Matt 27:34
platter, and *g* it to . . . . . . Mark 6:28
To many blind He *g* sight . . Luke 7:21
g Me no water for My . . . . Luke 7:44
g them to the innkeeper . . Luke 10:35
no one *g* him anything . . . Luke 15:16
saw it, *g* praise to God . . . Luke 18:43
to them He *g* the right to . . John 1:12
that He *g* His only . . . . John 3:16
Those whom You *g* . . . . . . John 17:12
glory which You *g* Me . . . . John 17:22
head, He *g* up His spirit . . . John 19:30
tongues, as the Spirit *g* . . . . Acts 2:4
great power the apostles *g* . . Acts 4:33
who *g* alms generously to . . Acts 10:2
g us rain from heaven . . . . Acts 14:17
God also *g* them up . . . . . . Rom 1:24
but God *g* the increase . . . 1 Cor 3:6
but first *g* themselves to . . 2 Cor 8:5
but God *g* it to Abraham . . . Gal 3:18
g Him to be head over all . . Eph 1:22
captive, and *g* gifts to men . . Eph 4:8
He Himself *g* some to be . . Eph 4:11
Abraham *g* a tenth part of . . Heb 7:2
and the heaven *g* rain . . . James 5:18
g Him glory, so that your . . 1 Pet 1:21
He *g* us commandment . . . 1 John 3:23
which God *g* Him to show . . Rev 1:1
g to the seven angels . . . . . . Rev 15:7
The sea *g* up the dead . . . . Rev 20:13

GAVE HIMSELF
who g for our sins, ... Gal 1:4
who loved me and g . . . . . . Gal 2:20
loved the church and g . . . . . Eph 5:25
who g a ransom for all, ... 1 Tim 2:6
who g for us, ... Titus 2:14

GAZA
Philistine city, Josh 13:3
Samson removes the gates of, Judg 16:1–3
Samson taken there as prisoner; his revenge, Judg 16:21–31
Sin of, condemned, Amos 1:6, 7
Philip journeys to, Acts 8:26

GAZED
g into heaven and saw . . . . . Acts 7:55

GAZING
why do you stand g . . . . Acts 1:11

GEBA
Levite city in Benjamin, Josh 18:24; 21:17
Rebuilt by Asa, 1 Kin 15:22

GEDALIAH
Made governor of Judah, 2 Kin 25:22–26
Befriends Jeremiah, Jer 40:5, 6
Murdered by Ishmael, Jer 41:2, 18

GEHAZI
Elisha's servant; seeks reward from Naaman, 2 Kin 5:20–24
Afflicted with leprosy, 2 Kin 5:25–27
Relates Elisha's deeds to Jehoram, 2 Kin 8:4–6

GEMS
your stones with colorful g . . . Is 54:11

GENEALOGIES
fables and endless g . . . . 1 Tim 1:4

GENEALOGY
The book of the g . . . . Matt 1:1
mother, without g . . . . Heb 7:3

GENERAL
g assembly and church . . . . Heb 12:23

GENERATE
that they g strife . . . . 2 Tim 2:23

GENERATION
See THIS GENERATION
before Me in this g . . . . Gen 7:1
the third and the fourth g . . . . Ex 34:7
to the third and fourth g . . Num 14:18
until all the g that had . . . . . Num 32:13
perverse and crooked g . . . . Deut 32:5
another g arose after . . . . Judg 2:10
Telling to the g to come . . . . . . Ps 78:4
That the g to come might . . . . . Ps 78:6
stubborn and rebellious g . . . . Ps 78:8
The g of the upright . . . . Ps 112:2
g shall praise Your . . . . Ps 145:4
g that curses its . . . . Prov 30:11
g that is pure in its . . . . . . Prov 30:12
One g passes away . . . . Eccl 1:4
to g it shall lie waste . . . . Is 34:10
who will declare His g . . . . Is 53:8
O g, see the word of the . . . . . Jer 2:31
His dominion is from g to g . . . Dan 4:3
kingdom is from g to g . . . . Dan 4:34
their children another g . . . . . Joel 1:3
what shall I liken this g . . . Matt 11:16
and adulterous g . . . . Matt 12:39
this g will by no . . . . Matt 24:34
O faithless g, how long . . . . Mark 9:19
fear Him from g to g . . . . . Luke 1:50
be required of this g . . . . . . Luke 11:50
g than the sons of light . . . Luke 16:8
g will by no means pass . . Luke 21:32
from this perverse g . . . . Acts 2:40
who will declare His g . . . . Acts 8:33
I was angry with that g . . . . Heb 3:10

GENTLENESS
g has made me great . . . . Ps 18:35

But you are a chosen g . . . . . 1 Pet 2:9

GENERATIONS
a just man, perfect in his g . . . Gen 6:9
with you, for perpetual g . . . . Gen 9:12
according to their g . . . . Gen 10:32
male child in your g . . . . Gen 17:12
is My memorial to all g . . . . . Ex 3:15
g of those who hate Me . . . . . Ex 20:5
fourth g of those who hate . . Deut 5:9
mercy for a thousand g . . . . . Deut 7:9
grandchildren for four g . . . Job 42:16
plans of His heart to all g . . . Ps 33:11
be remembered in all g . . . . . Ps 45:17
Your praise to all g . . . . Ps 79:13
Your faithfulness to all g . . . . . Ps 89:1
our dwelling place in all g . . . . Ps 90:1
His truth endures to all g . . . . Ps 100:5
for a thousand g . . . . Ps 105:8
endures to all g . . . . Ps 119:90
a crown endure for four g . . . Prov 27:24
g will call me blessed . . . . . . Luke 1:48
from ages and from g . . . . . . Col 1:26

GENEROSITY
be ready as a matter of g . . . 2 Cor 9:5

GENEROUS
uphold me by Your g Spirit . . Ps 51:12
g soul will be made . . . . Prov 11:25
g eye will be blessed . . . . . . Prov 22:9
no longer be called g . . . . Is 32:5
g man devises g . . . . Is 32:8

GENEROUSLY
gave alms g to the people . . Acts 10:2

GENNESARET
See GALILEE

GENTILE
with the G worshipers . . . . Acts 17:17

GENTILES
G were separated . . . . Gen 10:5
Rejoice, O G, with His . . . . Deut 32:43
O LORD, among the G . . . . 2 Sam 22:50
Why should the G say, ... Ps 115:2
Praise the LORD, all you G . . . Ps 117:1
for the G shall seek Him . . . . , Is 11:10
as a light to the G . . . . Is 42:6
G shall come to your . . . . Is 60:3
the riches of the G . . . . Is 61:6
The G shall see your . . . . Is 62:2
the glory of the G like a . . . . . Is 66:12
all the G who are called . . . Amos 9:12
shall be among the G . . . . Mic 5:8
be great among the G . . . . . . Mal 1:11
all these things the G . . . . . . Matt 6:32
into the way of the G . . . . . . Matt 10:5
revelation to the G . . . . Luke 2:32
times of the G are . . . . Luke 21:24
bear My name before G . . . . Acts 9:15
poured out on the G . . . . . Acts 10:45
a light to the G . . . . Acts 13:47
blasphemed among the G . . Rom 2:24
also the God of the G . . . . . . Rom 3:29
even named among the G . . . 1 Cor 5:1
in perils of the G, in . . . . . . 2 Cor 11:26
he would eat with the G . . . . . Gal 2:12
mystery among the G . . . . Col 1:27
a teacher of the G . . . . 1 Tim 2:7
and a teacher of the G . . . . 2 Tim 1:11
nothing from the G . . . . 3 John 7

GENTLE
g tongue breaks a bone . . . Prov 25:15
I drew them with g cords, . . . Hos 11:4
from Me, for I am g . . . . Matt 11:29
But we were g among . . . . 1 Thess 2:7
to be peaceable, g . . . . Titus 3:2
pure, then peaceable, g . . . James 3:17
only to the good and g . . . . . 1 Pet 2:18
ornament of a g and quiet . . 1 Pet 3:4

love and a spirit of g . . . . . . 1 Cor 4:21
g, self-control . . . . Gal 5:23
all lowliness and g . . . . Eph 4:2
Let your g be known to . . . . . Phil 4:5
love, patience, g . . . . 1 Tim 6:11

GERAR
Town of Philistia, Gen 10:19
Visited by Abraham, Gen 20:1–18
Visited by Isaac, Gen 26:1–17
Abimelech, king of, Gen 26:1, 26

GERIZIM
See MOUNT GERIZIM

GERSHOM (or Gershon)
Son of Moses, Ex 2:21, 22
Circumcised, Ex 4:25
Founder of Levite family, 1 Chr 23:14–16

GESHUR
Inhabitants of, not expelled by Israel, Josh 13:13
Talmai, king of, grandfather of Absalom, 2 Sam 3:3
Absalom flees to, 2 Sam 13:37, 38

GETHSEMANE
Garden near Jerusalem, Matt 26:30, 36
Often visited by Christ, Luke 22:39
Scene of Christ's agony and betrayal, Matt 26:36–56; John 18:1–12

GEZER
Canaanite city, Josh 10:33
Inhabitants not expelled, Josh 16:10
Given as dowry of Pharaoh's daughter, 1 Kin 9:15–17

GHOST
supposed it was a g . . . . Mark 6:49

GIBEAH
Town of Benjamin; known for wickedness, Judg 19:12–30
Destruction of, Judg 20:1–48
Saul's birthplace, 1 Sam 10:26
Saul's political capital, 1 Sam 15:34
Wickedness of, long remembered, Hos 9:9

GIBEON
Sun stands still at, Josh 10:12
Location of tabernacle, 1 Chr 16:39
Joab struck Amasa at, 2 Sam 20:8–10
Joab killed at, 1 Kin 2:28–34
Site of Solomon's sacrifice and dream, 1 Kin 3:5–15

GIBEONITES
Trick Joshua into making treaty; subjected to forced labor, Josh 9:3–27
Rescued by Joshua, Josh 10
Massacred by Saul; avenged by David, 2 Sam 21:1–9

GIDEON
Called by an angel, Judg 6:11–24
Destroys Baal's altar, Judg 6:25–32
Fleece confirms call from God, Judg 6:36–40
Miraculous victory over the Midianites, Judg 7
Takes revenge on Succoth and Penuel, Judg 8:4–21
Refuses kingship; makes an ephod, Judg 8:22–28
Fathers 71 sons; dies, Judg 8:29–35

GIFT
g makes room for him . . . . Prov 18:16
A g in secret pacifies . . . . . Prov 21:14
it is the g of God . . . . Eccl 3:13
Receive the g from the . . . . . Zech 6:10
bring your g to the altar . . . . Matt 5:23
swears by the g that is . . . . Matt 23:18
altar that sanctifies the g . . . Matt 23:19
is Corban''—'(that is, a g . . Mark 7:11

"If you knew the *g* . . . . John 4:10
the *g* of the Holy Spirit . . . . . Acts 2:38
thought that the *g* of God . . . Acts 8:20
the *g* of the Holy . . . . Acts 10:45
same *g* as He gave us . . . . . Acts 11:17
to you some spiritual *g* . . . . . Rom 1:11
But the free *g* is not . . . . Rom 5:15
of the *g* of righteousness . . . Rom 5:17
but the *g* of God is . . . . Rom 6:23
each one has his own *g* . . . . . 1 Cor 7:7
though I have the *g* . . . . 1 Cor 13:2
it is the *g* of God . . . . Eph 2:8
Not that I seek the *g* . . . . Phil 4:17
Do not neglect the *g* . . . . . . 1 Tim 4:14
you to stir up the *g* . . . . 2 Tim 1:6
tasted the heavenly *g* . . . . Heb 6:4
Every good and every . . James 1:17
one has received a *g* . . . . . . 1 Pet 4:10

GIFTED
the women who were *g* . . . . . Ex 35:25
but good-looking, *g* . . . . Dan 1:4

GIFTS
g you shall offer . . . . Num 18:29
You have received *g* . . . . Ps 68:18
and Seba will offer *g* . . . . Ps 72:10
though you give many *g* . . . Prov 6:35
to one who gives *g* . . . . Prov 19:6
how to give good *g* . . . . . . Matt 7:11
rich putting their *g* . . . . Luke 21:1
Having then *g* differing . . . . Rom 12:6
are diversities of *g* . . . . 1 Cor 12:4
and desire spiritual *g* . . . . . 1 Cor 14:1
captive, and gave *g* . . . . Eph 4:8

GIHON
River of Eden, Gen 2:13
—— Spring outside Jerusalem, 1 Kin
1:33–45
Source of water supply, 2 Chr 32:30

GILBOA
Range of limestone hills in Issachar,
1 Sam 28:4
Scene of Saul's death, 1 Sam 31:1–9
Under David's curse, 2 Sam 1:17, 21

GILEAD
Plain east of the Jordan; taken from
the Amorites and assigned to Gad,
Reuben, and Manasseh, Num
21:21–31; 32:33–40; Deut 3:12, 13;
Josh 13:24–31
Ishbosheth rules over, 2 Sam 2:8, 9
David takes refuge in, 2 Sam 17:21–26
Conquered by Hazael, 2 Kin 10:32, 33
Balm of, figurative of national healing,
Jer 8:22

GILGAL
Site of memorial stones, circumcision,
first Passover in the Promised Land,
Josh 4:19—5:12
Site of Gibeonite covenant, Josh
9:3–15
One location on Samuel's circuit, 1 Sam
7:15, 16
Saul made king and later rejected,
1 Sam 11:15; 13:4–15
Denounced for idolatry, Hos 9:15

GIRD
G Your sword upon Your . . . . Ps 45:3
of wrath You shall *g* . . . . . . Ps 76:10
I will *g* you, though you . . . . . . Is 45:5
and another will *g* . . . . John 21:18
Therefore *g* up the . . . . 1 Pet 1:13

GIRDED
a towel and *g* Himself . . . . . John 13:4
down to the feet and *g* . . . . . . Rev 1:13

GIRGASHITES
Descendants of Canaan, Gen 10:15, 16
Land of, given to Abraham's descen-
dants, Gen 15:18, 21
Delivered to Israel, Josh 24:11

GITTITES
600 follow David, 2 Sam 15:18–23

GIVE
g thanks to the LORD . . . . . 1 Chr 16:8
g me wisdom and . . . . 2 Chr 1:10
G ear to my prayer . . . . Ps 17:1
G to them according . . . . Ps 28:4
g you the desires . . . . Ps 37:4
Yes, the LORD will *g* . . . . Ps 85:12
G me understanding . . . . . . Ps 119:34
g me your heart . . . . Prov 23:26
You will *g* truth to . . . . Mic 7:20
G to him who asks . . . . Matt 5:42
G us this day our . . . . Matt 6:11
what you have and *g* . . . . . Matt 19:21
authority I will *g* . . . . Luke 4:6
g them eternal life . . . . John 10:28
new commandment I *g* . . . : John 13:34
but what I do have I *g* . . . . . . Acts 3:6
g us all things . . . . Rom 8:32
G no offense . . . . 1 Cor 10:32
So let each one *g* . . . . 2 Cor 9:7
nor *g* place to the devil . . . . . Eph 4:27
g him who has need . . . . Eph 4:28
g thanks to God . . . . 2 Thess 2:13
g yourself entirely . . . . 1 Tim 4:15
good works, ready to *g* . . . . 1 Tim 6:18
and always be ready to *g* . . 1 Pet 3:15
They will *g* an account to . . . 1 Pet 4:5
I will *g* you the crown of . . . . Rev 2:10
I will *g* him a white stone, . . . Rev 2:17
I will *g* him the morning . . . . Rev 2:28
"*G* me the little book . . . . . . Rev 10:9
I will *g* of the fountain of . . . . Rev 21:6
g to every one according . . . Rev 22:12

GIVEN
I have *g* every green herb . . . Gen 1:30
land which He has *g* you . . . Deut 8:10
will tread upon I have *g* . . . . Josh 1:3
I had *g* rest to Israel from . . Josh 23:1
see, I have *g* you a wise . . . . 1 Kin 3:12
He has *g* us rest on . . . . 2 Chr 14:7
she was *g* whatever she . . . . . Esth 2:13
You have *g* me wisdom . . . . . Dan 2:23
Ask and it will be *g* to you . . Matt 7:7
to him more will be *g* . . . . . Matt 13:12
nor are *g* in marriage . . . . . Matt 22:30
has, more will be *g* . . . . Matt 25:29
to whom much is *g* . . . . Luke 12:48
and are *g* in marriage . . . . Luke 20:34
My body which is *g* for . . . Luke 22:19
law was *g* through Moses . . John 1:17
has *g* Him authority to . . . . John 5:27
g Me I should lose . . . . John 6:39
Spirit was not yet *g* . . . . John 7:39
have been freely *g* . . . . 1 Cor 2:12
g us the Spirit in our . . . . . . 2 Cor 1:22
g according to the . . . . Eph 4:7
utterance may be *g* to me . . . Eph 6:19
not *g* to wine . . . . 1 Tim 3:3
God has not *g* us a spirit . . . 2 Tim 1:7
All Scripture is *g* by . . . . . . 2 Tim 3:16
robe was *g* to each of . . . . . . Rev 6:11

GIVES
He who *g* to the poor . . . . . Prov 28:27
For God *g* wisdom and . . . . Eccl 2:26
g life to the world . . . . John 6:33
All that the Father *g* . . . . . . John 6:37
The good shepherd *g* . . . . . John 10:11
not as the world *g* . . . . John 14:27
g us richly all things . . . . . . 1 Tim 6:17
who *g* to all liberally . . . . . James 1:5
g grace to the humble . . . . . James 4:6

GLAD
See BE GLAD AND REJOICE
g of heart for the good . . . . 2 Chr 7:10
I will be *g* and . . . . Ps 9:2
my heart is *g* . . . . Ps 16:9
Be *g* in the LORD and . . . . Ps 32:11
streams shall make *g* . . . . Ps 46:4

And wine that makes *g* . . . . Ps 104:15
I will be *g* in the LORD . . . . . Ps 104:34
I was *g* when they said . . . . . Ps 122:1
son makes a *g* father . . . . . . Prov 10:1
We will be *g* and rejoice . . . Song 1:4
Be *g* and rejoice with all . . . Zeph 3:14
shall see it and be *g* . . . . . . Zech 10:7
and be exceedingly *g* . . . . . . Matt 5:12
bring you these *g* tidings . . . Luke 1:19
bringing the *g* tidings of . . . . Luke 8:1
make merry and be *g* . . . . . Luke 15:32
he saw it and was *g* . . . . John 8:56
Let us be *g* and rejoice . . . . . Rev 19:7

GLADNESS
in the day of your *g* . . . . . . Num 10:10
day of feasting and *g* . . . . . . Esth 9:17
You have put *g* in my . . . . Ps 4:7
me hear joy and *g* . . . . Ps 51:8
Serve the LORD with *g* . . . . . Ps 100:2
shall obtain joy and *g* . . . . . . Is 35:10
They shall obtain joy and *g* . . Is 51:11
over you with *g* . . . . Zeph 3:17
receive it with *g* . . . . Mark 4:16
they ate their food with *g* . . Acts 2:46
You with the oil of *g* more . . . Heb 1:9

GLASS
there was a sea of *g* . . . . Rev 4:6
like transparent *g* . . . . Rev 21:21

GLORIFIED
the people I must be *g* . . . . . Lev 10:3
and they *g* the God of . . . . . Matt 15:31
Jesus was not yet *g* . . . . John 7:39
when Jesus was *g* . . . . John 12:16
By this My Father is *g* . . . . . John 15:8
I have *g* You on the . . . . John 17:4
g His Servant Jesus . . . . Acts 3:13
these He also *g* . . . . Rom 8:30
things God may be *g* . . . . . . 1 Pet 4:11

GLORIFY
My altar, and I will *g* . . . . Is 60:7
g your Father in . . . . Matt 5:16
"Father, *g* Your name . . . . John 12:28
He will *g* Me . . . . John 16:14
And now, O Father, *g* . . . . . . John 17:5
what death he would *g* . . . John 21:19
God, they did not *g* . . . . Rom 1:21
therefore *g* God in . . . . 1 Cor 6:20
also Christ did not *g* . . . . Heb 5:5
ashamed, but let him *g* . . . . 1 Pet 4:16

GLORIOUS
g in holiness, fearful in . . . . Ex 15:11
daughter is all *g* . . . . Ps 45:13
And blessed be His *g* . . . . . . Ps 72:19
G things are spoken . . . . Ps 87:3
is honorable and *g* . . . . Ps 111:3
g splendor of Your . . . . Ps 145:5
habitation, holy and *g* . . . . . . Is 63:15
also enter the *G* Land . . . . . Dan 11:41
engraved on stones, was *g* . . 2 Cor 3:7
it to Himself a *g* . . . . Eph 5:27
be conformed to His *g* . . . . . Phil 3:21
g appearing of our . . . . Titus 2:13

GLORY
"Please, show me Your *g* . . . Ex 33:18
filled with the *g* of the . . . . Num 14:21
g has departed from . . . . . . 1 Sam 4:21
G in His holy name . . . . . . 1 Chr 16:10
a shield for me, my *g* . . . . Ps 3:3
who have set Your *g* . . . . Ps 8:1
Who is this King of *g* . . . . Ps 24:8
the place where Your *g* . . . . . Ps 26:8
Your power and Your *g* . . . . . Ps 63:2
shall speak of the *g* . . . . . . Ps 145:11
wise shall inherit *g* . . . . Prov 3:35
head is a crown of *g*, if . . . Prov 16:31
The *g* of young men is . . . . Prov 20:29
It is the *g* of God to . . . . Prov 25:2
"*G* to the righteous . . . . Is 24:16
g I will not give . . . . Is 42:8
g will be seen upon . . . . Is 60:2

brightness of the LORD's *g* . . Ezek 10:4
then be likened in *g* . . . . . . Ezek 31:18
I will set My *g* among . . . . Ezek 39:21
I will change their *g* . . . . Hos 4:7
and I will be the *g* . . . . Zech 2:5
He shall bear the *g* . . . . Zech 6:13
that they may have *g* . . . . Matt 6:2
the power and the *g* . . . . Matt 6:13
g was not arrayed . . . . Matt 6:29
Man will come in the *g* . . . Matt 16:27
with power and great *g* . . . Matt 24:30
"*G* to God in the . . . . Luke 2:14
and we beheld His *g* . . . . . . John 1:14
and manifested His *g* . . . . . John 2:11
I do not seek My own *g* . . . . John 8:50
"Give God the *g* . . . . John 9:24
g which I had with You . . . John 17:5
g which You gave Me I . . . John 17:22
he did not give *g* . . . . Acts 12:23
doing good seek for *g* . . . . . . Rom 2:7
in faith, giving *g* . . . . Rom 4:20
the adoption, the *g* . . . . Rom 9:4
the riches of His *g* . . . . Rom 9:23
God, alone wise, be *g* . . . . Rom 16:27
who glories, let him *g* . . . . 1 Cor 1:31
but woman is the *g* . . . . 1 Cor 11:7
of the *g* that excels . . . . 2 Cor 3:10
of the gospel of the *g* . . . . . 2 Cor 4:4
eternal weight of *g* . . . . 2 Cor 4:17
who glories, let him *g* . . . . 2 Cor 10:17
to His riches in *g* . . . . Phil 4:19
appear with Him in *g* . . . . . . Col 3:4
For you are our *g* . . . . 1 Thess 2:20
You crowned him with *g* . . . . Heb 2:7
many sons to *g* . . . . Heb 2:10
grass, and all the *g* . . . . . . 1 Pet 1:24
to whom belong the *g* . . . . 1 Pet 4:11
for the Spirit of *g* . . . . 1 Pet 4:14
To Him be the *g* and the . . 1 Pet 5:11
the presence of His *g* . . . . . Jude 24
O Lord, to receive *g* . . . . . . Rev 4:11

GLORY OF GOD

The heavens declare the *g* . . . . Ps 19:1
unto death, but for the *g* . . . John 11:4
into heaven and saw the *g* . . Acts 7:55
fall short of the *g* . . . . Rom 3:23
do all to the *g* . . . . 1 Cor 10:31
he is the image and *g* . . . . 1 Cor 11:7
g in the face of Jesus . . . . . . 2 Cor 4:6
with smoke from the *g* . . . . . Rev 15:8
having the *g* . . . . Rev 21:11
for the *g* illuminated it . . . . Rev 21:23

GLORY OF THE LORD

g appeared in the cloud . . . . . Ex 16:10
g rested on Mount Sinai, . . . Ex 24:16
g filled the tabernacle . . . . . . Ex 40:34
the *g* will appear to you . . . . . Lev 9:6
g appeared in the . . . . Num 14:10
the *g* appeared to all . . . . Num 16:19
and the *g* appeared . . . . . . Num 16:42
the *g* appeared to them . . . . Num 20:6
the *g* filled the house . . . . . . 1 Kin 8:11
the *g* filled the temple . . . . . 2 Chr 7:1
May the *g* endure forever . . Ps 104:31
They shall see the *g* . . . . Is 35:2
the *g* shall be revealed, ... Is 40:5
the *g* is risen upon you . . . . . . Is 60:1
of the likeness of the *g* . . . . Ezek 1:28
behold, the *g* stood there . . . Ezek 3:23
the *g* went up . . . . Ezek 10:4
the *g* came into the . . . . . . Ezek 43:4
g filled the house of the . . . . Ezek 44:4
the knowledge of the *g* . . . . Hab 2:14
the *g* shone around them, . . . Luke 2:9
as in a mirror the *g*, ... 2 Cor 3:18
by us to the *g* . . . . 2 Cor 8:19

GLORYING

Your *g* is not good . . . . 1 Cor 5:6

GLUTTON

g will come to poverty . . . Prov 23:21
you say, 'Look, a *g* . . . . Luke 7:34

GLUTTONS

companion of *g* shames . . . . Prov 28:7
evil beasts, lazy *g* . . . . Titus 1:12

GNASHING

will be weeping and *g* . . . . . Matt 8:12

GO

He said, "Let Me *g* . . . . Gen 32:26
'Let My people *g* . . . . Ex 5:1
Presence does not *g* . . . . . . Ex 33:15
for wherever you *g* . . . . Ruth 1:16
"Look, I *g* forward . . . . Job 23:8
For I used to *g* with the . . . . . Ps 42:4
g astray as soon as . . . . Ps 58:3
I will *g* in the strength of . . . . Ps 71:16
Those who *g* down to . . . . . Ps 107:23
Where can I *g* from . . . . Ps 139:7
G to the ant . . . . Prov 6:6
All *g* to one place . . . . Eccl 3:20
of mourning than to *g* . . . . . Eccl 7:2
out of Zion shall *g* forth . . . . . Is 2:3
You wherever You *g* . . . . . . Matt 8:19
do not *g* out . . . . Matt 24:26
He said to them, "*G* . . . . Mark 16:15
And I say to one, '*G* . . . . . . Luke 7:8
also want to *g* away . . . . . . John 6:67
to whom shall we *g* . . . . . . John 6:68
g you cannot come . . . . John 8:21
I *g* to prepare a place . . . . . John 14:2
will do, because I *g* . . . . . . John 14:12
seek Me, let these *g* . . . . . . John 18:8
and he shall *g* out no more . . Rev 3:12

GOADS

of the wise are like *g* . . . . . Eccl 12:11
to kick against the *g* . . . . Acts 9:5

GOAL

I press toward the *g* . . . . Phil 3:14

GOATS

drink the blood of *g* . . . . Ps 50:13
his sheep from the *g* . . . . . Matt 25:32
with the blood of *g* . . . . Heb 9:12
g could take away . . . . Heb 10:4

GOD

See ANGEL OF GOD; GLORY OF GOD;
HAND OF GOD; HOUSE OF GOD;
KINGDOM OF GOD; LORD GOD OF
HOSTS; LORD GOD OF ISRAEL; LOVE
OF GOD; LOVE THE LORD YOUR GOD;
MAN OF GOD; PEOPLE OF GOD; POWER
OF GOD; RIGHTEOUSNESS OF GOD;
SON OF GOD; SONS OF GOD; SPIRIT OF
GOD; THINGS OF GOD; THRONE OF
GOD; WILL OF GOD; WORD OF GOD;
WRATH OF GOD

Names of:
God, Gen 1:1
LORD God, Gen 2:4
God Most High, Gen 14:18–22
Lord GOD, Gen 15:2, 8
Almighty God, Gen 17:1, 2
I AM, Ex 3:14
Jealous, Ex 34:14
Eternal God, Deut 33:27
Living God, Josh 3:10
God of hosts, Ps 80:7
LORD of hosts, Is 1:24
Holy One of Israel, Is 43:3, 14, 15
Mighty God, Jer 32:18
God of heaven, Jon 1:9
Heavenly Father, Matt 6:26
King eternal, 1 Tim 1:17
only Potentate, 1 Tim 6:15
Father of lights, James 1:17
Manifestations of:
face of, Gen 32:30
voice of, Deut 5:22–26
glory of, Ex 40:34, 35
Angel of, Gen 16:7–13
name of, Ex 34:5–7
form of, Num 12:6–8

Nature of:
spirit, John 4:24
one, Deut 6:4
personal, John 17:1–3
trinitarian, 2 Cor 13:14

Attributes of:
incomparable, 2 Sam 7:22
invisible, John 1:18
inscrutable, Is 40:28
unchangeable, Num 23:19
unequaled, Is 40:13–25
unsearchable, Rom 11:33, 34
infinite, 1 King 8:27
eternal, Is 57:15
omnipotent, Jer 32:17, 27
omnipresent, Ps 139:7–12
omniscient, 1 John 3:20
foreknowing, Is 48:3, 5
wise, Acts 15:18
holy, Rev 4:8
impartial, 1 Pet 1:17
just, Ps 89:14
longsuffering, Ex 34:6, 7
love, 1 John 4:8, 16
mercy, Lam 3:22, 23
truth, Ps 117:2
vengeance, Deut 32:34–41
wrath, Deut 32:22

G created the heavens . . . . . . Gen 1:1
Abram of *G* Most High . . . . Gen 14:19
and I will be their *G* . . . . . . Gen 17:8
hands of the Mighty *G* . . . . Gen 49:24
the *G* of Abraham . . . . Ex 3:6
He is my *G* . . . . Ex 15:2
Stand before *G* for the . . . . . . Ex 18:19
"I am the LORD your *G* . . . . . . Ex 20:2
"This is your *g* . . . . Ex 32:4
G is not a man . . . . Num 23:19
G is a consuming fire . . . . . . Deut 4:24
great and awesome *G* . . . . . Deut 7:21
my people, and your *G* . . . . . Ruth 1:16
know that there is a *G* . . 1 Sam 17:46
a rock, except our *G* . . . . . 2 Sam 22:32
If the LORD is *G* . . . . 1 Kin 18:21
G is greater than all . . . . 2 Chr 2:5
G is greater than . . . . Job 33:12
"Behold, *G* is mighty . . . . . . Job 36:5
"Behold, *G* is great . . . . . . Job 36:26
You have been My *G* . . . . . . Ps 22:10
"Where is your *G* . . . . Ps 42:3
G is our refuge . . . . Ps 46:1
G is in the midst of . . . . Ps 46:5
G is the King of all . . . . Ps 47:7
The Mighty One, *G* . . . . Ps 50:1
I am *G*, your *G* . . . . Ps 50:7
me a clean heart, O *G* . . . . . . Ps 51:10
Our *G* is the *G* . . . . Ps 68:20
Who is so great a *G* . . . . Ps 77:13
Restore us, O *G* . . . . Ps 80:7
You alone are *G* . . . . Ps 86:10
Exalt the LORD our *G* . . . . Ps 99:9
Yes, our *G* is merciful . . . . . . Ps 116:5
give thanks to the *G* . . . . . . Ps 136:26
For *G* is in heaven . . . . Eccl 5:2
Counselor, Mighty *G* . . . . Is 9:6
G is my salvation . . . . Is 12:2
Behold, this is our *G* . . . . Is 25:9
"Behold your *G* . . . . Is 40:9
Is there a *G* besides . . . . Is 44:8
to Zion, "Your *G* . . . . Is 52:7
stricken, smitten by *G* . . . . . . Is 53:4
and I will be their *G* . . . . . . Jer 31:33
and I saw visions of *G* . . . . . Ezek 1:1
Who is a *G* like You . . . . Mic 7:18
translated, "*G* with us." . . . . Matt 1:23
in *G* my Savior . . . . Luke 1:47
the Word was with *G* . . . . . . John 1:1
enter the kingdom of *G* . . . . John 3:5
For *G* so loved the . . . . John 3:16
has certified that *G* . . . . . . John 3:33
G is Spirit, and those . . . . . John 4:24

"My Lord and my *G* . . . . . John 20:28
Christ is the Son of *G* . . . . . Acts 8:37
To the Unknown *G* . . . . . . Acts 17:23
Indeed, let *G* be true . . . . Rom 3:4
If *G* is for us . . . . Rom 8:31
G is faithful . . . . 1 Cor 1:9
us there is one *G* . . . . 1 Cor 8:6
G shall supply all . . . . Phil 4:19
and I will be their *G* . . . . . . Heb 8:10
G is a consuming fire . . . . Heb 12:29
G is greater than our . . . . 1 John 3:20
for *G* is love . . . . 1 John 4:8
No one has seen *G* . . . . . . 1 John 4:12
in the temple of My *G* . . . . . Rev 3:12
gave glory to the *G* . . . . . . Rev 11:13
G Himself will be . . . . Rev 21:3
and I will be his *G* . . . . Rev 21:7

GOD THE FATHER
G has set His seal on Him . . John 6:27
the kingdom to *G* . . . . 1 Cor 15:24
through Jesus Christ and *G* . . . Gal 1:1
G and our Lord Jesus Christ . . Gal 1:3
for all things to *G* . . . . Eph 5:20
love with faith, from *G* . . . . Eph 6:23
to the glory of *G* . . . . Phil 2:11
giving thanks to *G* . . . . Col 3:17
in *G* and the Lord Jesus . . 1 Thess 1:1
mercy, and peace from *G* . . 2 Tim 1:2
mercy, and peace from *G* . . . Titus 1:4
the foreknowledge of *G* . . . . 1 Pet 1:2
For He received from *G* . . . 2 Pet 1:17
G and from the Lord Jesus . . 2 John 3
sanctified by *G*, and . . . . Jude 1

GODDESS
after Ashtoreth the *g* . . . . . . 1 Kin 11:5
of the great *g* Diana . . . . . . Acts 19:35

GODHEAD
eternal power and *G* . . . . . . Rom 1:20
the fullness of the *G* . . . . Col 2:9

GODLINESS
is the mystery of *g* . . . . 1 Tim 3:16
g is profitable . . . . 1 Tim 4:8
Now *g* with contentment . . . 1 Tim 6:6
having a form of *g* . . . . 2 Tim 3:5
pertain to life and *g* . . . . 2 Pet 1:3
to perseverance *g* . . . . 2 Pet 1:6

GODLY
Himself him who is *g* . . . . Ps 4:3
everyone who is *g* . . . . Ps 32:6
who desire to live *g* . . . . . . 2 Tim 3:12
righteously, and *g* . . . . Titus 2:12
reverence and *g* fear . . . . . . Heb 12:28
to deliver the *g* . . . . 2 Pet 2:9

GODS
See FOREIGN GODS
your God is God of *g* . . . . . Deut 10:17
the household *g* . . . . 2 Kin 23:24
He judges among the *g* . . . . . Ps 82:1
I said, "You are *g* . . . . Ps 82:6
yourselves with *g* . . . . Is 57:5
If He called them . . . . John 10:35
g have come down to . . . . . Acts 14:11

GOG
Prince of Rosh, Meshech, and Tubal, Ezek 38:2, 3
—— Leader of the final battle, Rev 20:8–15

GOLAN
City of refuge, Josh 20:8, 21:27

GOLD
And the *g* of that land . . . . . Gen 2:12
a mercy seat of pure *g* . . . . . Ex 25:17
multiply silver and *g* . . . . . Deut 17:17
"If I have made *g* . . . . Job 31:24
yea, than much fine *g* . . . . . . Ps 19:10
is like apples of *g* . . . . Prov 25:11
is Mine, and the *g* . . . . Hag 2:8
g I do not have . . . . Acts 3:6

with braided hair or *g* . . . . . 1 Tim 2:9
a man with *g* rings . . . . James 2:2
Your *g* and silver are . . . . . James 5:3
more precious than *g* . . . . . . 1 Pet 1:7
like silver or *g* . . . . 1 Pet 1:18
of the city was pure *g* . . . . . Rev 21:21

GOLDEN
g bell and a pomegranate . . . Ex 28:34
g tumors and five *g* rats . . . . 1 Sam 6:4
from the *g* calves that . . . . 2 Kin 10:29
or the *g* bowl is broken, or . . Eccl 12:6
the seven *g* lampstands . . . . Rev 1:20
and *g* bowls full of incense, . . Rev 5:8
g altar which is before . . . . . Rev 9:13
having in her hand a *g* cup . . Rev 17:4

GOLGOTHA
Where Jesus died, Matt 27:33–35

GOLIATH
Giant of Gath, 1 Sam 17:4
Killed by David, 1 Sam 17:50
—— Brother of above; killed by El-hanan, 2 Sam 21:19

GOMER
Son of Japheth, Gen 10:2, 3; 1 Chr 1:5, 6
Northern nation, Ezek 38:6
—— Wife of Hosea, Hos 1:2, 3

GOMORRAH
See SODOM AND GOMORRAH
With Sodom, defeated by Chedor-laomer; Lot captured, Gen 14:8–12
Destroyed by God, Gen 19:23–29
Later references to, Is 1:10; Amos 4:11; Matt 10:15

GONE
I am *g* like a shadow . . . . Ps 109:23
I have *g* astray like a . . . . . Ps 119:176
the word has *g* out of . . . . Is 45:23
like sheep have *g* . . . . Is 53:6

GOOD
See BE OF GOOD CHEER; LORD IS GOOD
God saw that it was *g* . . . . Gen 1:10
but God meant it for *g* . . . . . Gen 50:20
LORD has promised *g* . . . . . Num 10:29
you have spoken is *g* . . . . . 2 Kin 20:19
seeking the *g* of his . . . . Esth 10:3
Shall we indeed accept *g* . . . . . Job 2:10
"Who will show us any *g* . . . . . . Ps 4:6
is none who does *g* . . . . Ps 14:1
G and upright is the . . . . Ps 25:8
that he may see *g* . . . . Ps 34:12
Truly God is *g* to . . . . Ps 73:1
g man deals graciously . . . . . Ps 112:5
Your Spirit is *g* . . . . Ps 143:10
g man obtains favor . . . . Prov 12:2
g word makes it glad . . . . . Prov 12:25
on the evil and the *g* . . . . . . Prov 15:3
A merry heart does *g* . . . . . Prov 17:22
who knows what is *g* . . . . Eccl 6:12
learn to do *g* . . . . Is 1:17
Zion, you who bring *g* . . . . . . Is 40:9
tidings of *g* things . . . . Is 52:7
talked to me, with *g* . . . . . . Zech 1:13
said, "Be of *g* cheer . . . . . . Matt 9:22
A *g* man out of the . . . . Matt 12:35
"*G* Teacher, what *g* . . . . . Matt 19:16
No one is *g* but One . . . . . Matt 19:17
For she has done a *g* . . . . . Matt 26:10
behold, I bring you *g* . . . . . . Luke 2:10
love your enemies, do *g* . . . . Luke 6:35
"Can anything *g* come . . . . John 1:46
Some said, "He is *g* . . . . John 7:12
who went about doing *g* . . . Acts 10:38
For he was a *g* man . . . . . . Acts 11:24
in that He did *g* . . . . Acts 14:17
g man someone would . . . . . . Rom 5:7
in my flesh) nothing *g* . . . . . Rom 7:18
overcome evil with *g* . . . . . Rom 12:21
according to the *g* pleasure . . Eph 1:5

fruitful in every *g* . . . . Col 1:10
know that the law is *g* . . . . . 1 Tim 1:8
may wage the *g* warfare . . 1 Tim 1:18
For this is *g* and . . . . 1 Tim 2:3
bishop, he desires a *g* . . . . 1 Tim 3:1
for this is *g* and . . . . 1 Tim 5:4
a *g* soldier of Jesus Christ . . 2 Tim 2:3
prepared for every *g* . . . . . 2 Tim 2:21
I have fought the *g* fight . . 2 Tim 4:7
and have tasted the *g* . . . . . . Heb 6:5
obtained a *g* testimony . . . . . Heb 11:2
Every *g* gift and every . . . James 1:17
g days, let him refrain . . . . . 1 Pet 3:10
to suffer for doing *g* . . . . . . 1 Pet 3:17
g stewards of the . . . . 1 Pet 4:10

GOOD WORKS
that they may see your *g* . . . Matt 5:16
"Many *g* I have shown . . . John 10:32
woman was full of *g* . . . . . . Acts 9:36
in Christ Jesus for *g*, ... Eph 2:10
godliness, with *g* . . . . 1 Tim 2:10
well reported for *g*; . . . . . . 1 Tim 5:10
g of some are clearly, ... 1 Tim 5:25
that they be rich in *g* . . . . . 1 Tim 6:18
to be a pattern of *g* . . . . Titus 2:7
stir up love and *g* . . . . Heb 10:24
by your *g* which they . . . . . 1 Pet 2:12

GOODNESS
"I will make all My *g* . . . . . . Ex 33:19
and abounding in *g* . . . . Ex 34:6
"You are my Lord, my *g* . . . . Ps 16:2
Surely *g* and mercy . . . . Ps 23:6
that I would see the *g* . . . . . Ps 27:13
how great is Your *g* . . . . Ps 31:19
The *g* of God endures . . . . . . Ps 52:1
how great is its *g* . . . . Zech 9:17
the riches of His *g* . . . . Rom 2:4
consider the *g* and . . . . Rom 11:22
kindness, *g* . . . . Gal 5:22

GOODS
When *g* increase . . . . Eccl 5:11
and plunder his *g* . . . . Matt 12:29
ruler over all his *g* . . . . Matt 24:47
"Soul, you have many *g* . . . Luke 12:19
man was wasting his *g* . . . . Luke 16:1
I give half of my *g* . . . . Luke 19:8
has this world's *g* . . . . 1 John 3:17

GOSHEN
District of Egypt where Israel lived; the best of the land, Gen 45:10; 46:28, 29; 47:1–11

GOSPEL
See PREACH THE GOSPEL
The beginning of the *g* . . . . . Mark 1:1
and believe in the *g* . . . . . . Mark 1:15
g must first be preached . . Mark 13:10
to testify to the *g* . . . . . . Acts 20:24
separated to the *g* . . . . Rom 1:1
not ashamed of the *g* . . . . . Rom 1:16
should live from the *g* . . . . 1 Cor 9:14
if our *g* is veiled . . . . 2 Cor 4:3
to a different *g* . . . . Gal 1:6
of truth, the *g* . . . . Eph 1:13
the mystery of the *g* . . . . . . Eph 6:19
g which you heard . . . . Col 1:23
the everlasting *g* . . . . Rev 14:6

GOSSIPS
only idle but also *g* . . . . 1 Tim 5:13

GOVERNMENT
and the *g* will be upon . . . . Is 9:6

GRACE
But Noah found *g* . . . . Gen 6:8
G is poured upon Your . . . . . Ps 45:2
The LORD will give *g* . . . . . . Ps 84:11
the Spirit of *g* . . . . Zech 12:10
and the *g* of God was . . . . . Luke 2:40
g and truth came . . . . John 1:17
And great *g* was upon . . . . . Acts 4:33
G to you and peace . . . . Rom 1:7

receive abundance of *g* .... Rom 5:17
g is no longer *g* .... Rom 11:6
The *g* of our Lord .... Rom 16:20
For you know the *g* .... 2 Cor 8:9
"My *g* is sufficient .... 2 Cor 12:9
The *g* of the Lord .... 2 Cor 13:14
you have fallen from *g* .... Gal 5:4
to the riches of His *g* .... Eph 1:7
g you have been saved ...... Eph 2:8
dispensation of the *g* .... Eph 3:2
g was given according .... Eph 4:7
G be with all those .... Eph 6:24
G to you and peace .... 1 Thess 1:1
according to the *g* of .... 2 Thess 1:12
and good hope by *g* ..... 2 Thess 2:16
be strong in the *g* that is ... 2 Tim 2:1
the *g* of God that brings ... Titus 2:11
been justified by His *g* we ... Titus 3:7
G be with you all .... Titus 3:15
insulted the Spirit of *g* .... Heb 10:29
shaken, let us have *g* ..... Heb 12:28
But He gives more *g* ...... James 4:6
who prophesied of the *g* .. 1 Pet 1:10
together of the *g* of life ... 1 Pet 3:7
this is the true *g* .... 1 Pet 5:12
but grow in the *g* .... 2 Pet 3:18

GRACIOUS
he said, "God be *g* ..... Gen 43:29
I will be *g* to whom I ...... Ex 33:19
then He is *g* to him .... Job 33:24
wise man's mouth are *g* .. Eccl 10:12
of hosts will be *g* .... Amos 5:15
know that You are a *g* ...... Jon 4:2
that He may be *g* .... Mal 1:9
at the *g* words which ..... Luke 4:22
that the Lord is *g* .... 1 Pet 2:3

GRACIOUSLY
God has dealt *g* with me ... Gen 33:11
A good man deals *g* and ... Ps 112:5
receive us *g*, for we will .... Hos 14:2

GRAFT
able to *g* them in again ... Rom 11:23

GRAFTED
in unbelief, will be *g* ..... Rom 11:23

GRAIN
Israel went to buy *g* .... Gen 42:5
it treads out the *g* .... Deut 25:4
You provide their *g* .... Ps 65:9
be an abundance of *g* ...... Ps 72:16
him who withholds *g* ..... Prov 11:26
be revived like *g* .... Hos 14:7
G shall make the young .... Zech 9:17
to pluck heads of *g* .... Matt 12:1
unless a *g* of wheat ...... John 12:24
it treads out the *g* .... 1 Cor 9:9

GRAINFIELDS
the *g* on the Sabbath ...... Matt 12:1
He went through the *g* ..... Luke 6:1

GRANT
and *g* us Your salvation ...... Ps 85:7
G that these two .... Matt 20:21
who overcomes I will *g* ..... Rev 3:21

GRANTED
has *g* me my petition .... 1 Sam 1:27
It shall be *g* you .... Esth 5:6
he *g* the body to Joseph .. Mark 15:45
g to him by My Father .... John 6:65
it was *g* to harm the earth .... Rev 7:2
He was *g* power to give .... Rev 13:15

GRAPEVINE
olives, or a *g* bear figs .... James 3:12

GRAPES
in the blood of *g* .... Gen 49:11
their *g* are *g* of gall ... Deut 32:32
g give a good smell .... Song 2:13
vines have tender *g* .... Song 2:15
brought forth wild *g* .... Is 5:2
Yet gleaning *g* will be .... Is 17:6

No *g* shall be on the vine .... Jer 8:13
have eaten sour *g* .... Ezek 18:2
Do men gather *g* .... Matt 7:16
g are fully ripe .... Rev 14:18

GRASPING
all is vanity and *g* .... Eccl 1:14

GRASS
they were as the *g* ..... 2 Kin 19:26
offspring like the *g* .... Job 5:25
g which grows up .... Ps 90:5
his days are like *g* .... Ps 103:15
The *g* withers .... Is 40:7
so clothes the *g* .... Matt 6:30
to sit down on the *g* ..... Matt 14:19
"All flesh is as *g* .... 1 Pet 1:24

GRASSHOPPERS
inhabitants are like *g* .... Is 40:22
generals like great *g* ...... Nah 3:17

GRAVE
g does not come .... Job 7:9
for the *g* as my house ..... Job 17:13
my soul up from the *g* ...... Ps 30:3
the power of the *g* .... Ps 49:15
or wisdom in the *g* .... Eccl 9:10
And they made His *g* .... Is 53:9
the power of the *g* .... Hos 13:14

GRAVES
there were no *g* .... Ex 14:11
and the *g* were opened .... Matt 27:52
g which are not .... Luke 11:44
g will hear His voice ...... John 5:28

GRAY
would bring down my *g* ... Gen 42:38
the man of *g* hairs ...... Deut 32:25
of old men is their *g* ..... Prov 20:29

GRAZE
cow and bear shall *g* .... Is 11:7
let him *g* with the beasts ... Dan 4:15

GREAT
God made two *g* lights ...... Gen 1:16
and make your name *g* ...... Gen 12:2
With *g* wrestlings I have .... Gen 30:8
there was a *g* cry in Egypt .. Ex 12:30
have committed a *g* sin ..... Ex 32:30
shall shout with a *g* shout ... Josh 6:5
were *g* resolves of heart .... Judg 5:15
He has done us this *g* .... 1 Sam 6:9
For the LORD is *g* .... 1 Chr 16:25
I build will be *g* .... 2 Chr 2:5
"The work is *g* .... Neh 4:19
Who does *g* things .... Job 5:9
G men are not always .... Job 32:9
in the *g* assembly .... Ps 22:25
g are Your works .... Ps 92:5
my God, You are very *g* .... Ps 104:1
"The LORD has done *g* ..... Ps 126:2
g is the sum of them ...... Ps 139:17
in the place of the *g* ...... Prov 25:6
g is the Holy One .... Is 12:6
And do you seek *g* .... Jer 45:5
g is Your faithfulness ..... Lam 3:23
The *g* day of the LORD .... Zeph 1:14
he shall be called *g* ...... Matt 5:19
one pearl of *g* price ..... Matt 13:46
desires to become *g* ..... Matt 20:26
and *g* commandment ...... Matt 22:38
a *g* windstorm arose, and ... Mark 4:37
g multitude followed ...... Mark 5:24
he had *g* possessions .... Mark 10:22
She was of a *g* age, and ... Luke 2:36
g drops of blood .... Luke 22:44
before the coming of the *g* ... Acts 2:20
did *g* wonders and signs ..... Acts 6:8
that he was someone *g* ...... Acts 8:9
"G is Diana of the .... Acts 19:28
that I have *g* sorrow .... Rom 9:2
a *g* and effective door ... 1 Cor 16:9
because of His *g* love with ... Eph 2:4
This is a *g* mystery, but I .... Eph 5:32

without controversy *g* ..... 1 Tim 3:16
with contentment is *g* ...... 1 Tim 6:6
But in a *g* house .... 2 Tim 2:20
appearing of our *g* .... Titus 2:13
See how *g* a forest .... James 3:5
g men, the rich men ...... Rev 6:15
Babylon the G .... Rev 17:5
Then I saw a *g* white ...... Rev 20:11
the dead, small and *g* ..... Rev 20:12

GREATER
the throne will I be *g* ..... Gen 41:40
g than all the gods .... Ex 18:11
whose appearance was *g* ... Dan 7:20
kingdom of heaven is *g* ... Matt 11:11
place there is One *g* ...... Matt 12:6
g than Jonah is here ..... Matt 12:41
g than Solomon is here ... Matt 12:42
g things than these ..... John 1:50
g than our father .... John 4:12
a servant is not *g* ...... John 13:16
G love has no one .... John 15:13
'A servant is not *g* ...... John 15:20
parts have *g* modesty ... 1 Cor 12:23
he who prophesies is *g* ... 1 Cor 14:5
swear by no one *g* .... Heb 6:13
condemns us, God is *g* ... 1 John 3:20
witness of God is *g* ...... 1 John 5:9

GREATEST
little child is the *g* .... Matt 18:4
be considered the *g* ..... Luke 22:24
but the *g* of these is ..... 1 Cor 13:13

GREATNESS
And in the *g* of Your ...... Ex 15:7
According to the *g* .... Ps 79:11
g is unsearchable .... Ps 145:3
I will declare Your *g* ..... Ps 145:6
I have attained *g* .... Eccl 1:16
traveling in the *g* .... Is 63:1
is the exceeding *g* .... Eph 1:19

GREECE
Paul preaches in, Acts 17:16–31
Daniel's vision of, Dan 8:21

GREED
part is full of *g* .... Luke 11:39

GREEDINESS
all uncleanness with *g* ..... Eph 4:19
the faith in their *g* ...... 1 Tim 6:10

GREEDY
of everyone who is *g* ...... Prov 1:19
not violent, not *g* .... 1 Tim 3:3
not violent, not *g* .... Titus 1:7

GREEK
written in Hebrew, G ..... John 19:20
and also for the G .... Rom 1:16
with me, being a G .... Gal 2:3
is neither Jew nor G .... Gal 3:28

GREEKS
Natives of Greece, Joel 3:6; Acts 16:1
Spiritual state of, Rom 10:12
Some believe, Acts 14:1

GREEN
and under every *g* tree ... 2 Kin 17:10
lie down in *g* pastures .... Ps 23:2

GREET
g your brethren only ...... Matt 5:47
G one another with a ..... 1 Cor 16:20
into your house nor *g* ..... 2 John 10
G the friends by name ..... 3 John 14

GREETED
and *g* Elizabeth .... Luke 1:40

GREW
Pharaoh's heart *g* hard ...... Ex 7:13
Samuel *g* before the ..... 1 Sam 2:21
and you *g*, matured, and ... Ezek 16:7
g exceedingly great toward .. Dan 8:9
and the thorns *g* up and ... Mark 4:7
And the Child *g* .... Luke 2:40

But the word of God *g* .... Acts 12:24
the word of the Lord *g* .... Acts 19:20

GRIEF
burden and his own *g* ..... 2 Chr 6:29
g were fully weighed .... Job 6:2
Though I speak, my *g* ...... Job 16:6
observe trouble and *g* ...... Ps 10:14
of mirth may be *g* .... Prov 14:13
much wisdom is much *g* .... Eccl 1:18
and acquainted with *g* .... Is 53:3
joy and not with *g* .... Heb 13:17

GRIEVE
g the children of men ...... Lam 3:33
g the Holy Spirit .... Eph 4:30

GRIEVED
earth, and He was *g* .... Gen 6:6
Has not my soul *g* .... Job 30:25
forty years I was *g* .... Ps 95:10
a woman forsaken and *g* ...... Is 54:6
g His Holy Spirit .... Is 63:10
with anger, being *g* .... Mark 3:5
Peter was *g* because ...... John 21:17

GRINDERS
when the *g* cease .... Eccl 12:3

GRINDING
the sound of *g* is low ...... Eccl 12:4
g the faces of the poor .... Is 3:15
Two women will be *g* .... Matt 24:41

GROAN
The dying *g* in the .... Job 24:12
even we ourselves *g* .... Rom 8:23
who are in this tent *g* ...... 2 Cor 5:4

GROANED
He *g* in the spirit and .... John 11:33

GROANING
So God heard their *g* .... Ex 2:24
I am weary with my *g* .... Ps 6:6
Then Jesus, again *g* ...... John 11:38

GROANINGS
g which cannot .... Rom 8:26

GROPE
And you shall *g* .... Deut 28:29
They *g* in the dark .... Job 12:25
We *g* for the wall like .... Is 59:10
hope that they might *g* .... Acts 17:27

GROUND
"Cursed is the *g* .... Gen 3:17
you stand is holy *g* .... Ex 3:5
up your fallow *g* .... Jer 4:3
give its fruit, the *g* .... Zech 8:12
others fell on good *g* ...... Matt 13:8
bought a piece of *g* .... Luke 14:18
God, the pillar and *g* ...... 1 Tim 3:15

GROUNDED
being rooted and *g* .... Eph 3:17

GROUPS
sit down in *g* of fifty .... Luke 9:14

GROW
they will all *g* old like ...... Ps 102:26
the horn of David *g* .... Ps 132:17
the earth will *g* old like ...... Is 51:6
you shall go out and *g* .... Mal 4:2
truth in love, may *g* .... Eph 4:15
and they will all *g* .... Heb 1:11
but *g* in the grace and ..... 2 Pet 3:18

GROWN
plants *g* up in their youth .. Ps 144:12
They have *g* fat, they are .... Jer 5:28
this people have *g* dull .... Matt 13:15
this people have *g* dull .... Acts 28:27

GROWS
shall eat every tree which *g* .. Ex 10:5
what *g* of its own accord ... Lev 25:11
It *g* old because of all my ...... Ps 6:7
when it is sown, it *g* up .... Mark 4:32
g into a holy temple in the .. Eph 2:21

---

your faith *g* exceedingly .. 2 Thess 1:3

GROWTH
causes *g* of the body for .... Eph 4:16

GRUDGINGLY
in his heart, not *g* .... 2 Cor 9:7

GRUMBLERS
These are *g* .... Jude 16

GUARANTEE
in our hearts as a *g* .... 2 Cor 1:22
us the Spirit as a *g* .... 2 Cor 5:5
who is the *g* of our .... Eph 1:14

GUARD
g the way to the tree .... Gen 3:24
I will *g* my ways, lest I sin .... Ps 39:1
will be your rear *g* .... Is 52:12
g the doors of your .... Mic 7:5
we were kept under *g* .... Gal 3:23
to the whole palace *g* ...... Phil 1:13
g your hearts and minds ..... Phil 4:7
g you from the evil one .. 2 Thess 3:3
G what was committed .... 1 Tim 6:20

GUARDIANS
but is under *g* and .... Gal 4:2

GUARDS
Unless the LORD *g* .... Ps 127:1
And the *g* shook for .... Matt 28:4

GUIDANCE
and excellent in *g* .... Is 28:29

GUIDE
I will *g* you with My eye ..... Ps 32:8
He will be our *g* .... Ps 48:14
Father, You are the *g* .... Jer 3:4
g our feet into the .... Luke 1:79
has come, He will *g* ...... John 16:13
Judas, who became a *g* ..... Acts 1:16
you yourself are a *g* .... Rom 2:19

GUIDES
Woe to you, blind *g* ...... Matt 23:16
unless someone *g* .... Acts 8:31

GUILT
they accept their *g* .... Lev 26:41
g has grown up to the .... Ezra 9:6
of your fathers' *g* .... Matt 23:32

GUILTLESS
g who takes His name ...... Ex 20:7
have condemned the *g* .... Matt 12:7

GUILTY
"We are truly *g* .... Gen 42:21
we have been very *g* .... Ezra 9:7
the world may become *g* ... Rom 3:19
in one point, he is *g* ...... James 2:10

GULF
you there is a great *g* ..... Luke 16:26

HABAKKUK
Prophet in Judah just prior to Babylonian invasion, Hab 1:1
Prayer of, in praise of God, Hab 3:1–19

HABITATION
to Your holy *h* .... Ex 15:13
Is God in His holy *h* .... Ps 68:5
in a peaceful *h* .... Is 32:18
from His holy *h* .... Zech 2:13
be clothed with our *h* ...... 2 Cor 5:2

HACHILAH
Hill in the Wilderness of Ziph where David hid, 1 Sam 23:19–26

HADADEZER
King of Zobah, 2 Sam 8:3–13
Defeated by David, 2 Sam 10:6–19

HADASSAH
Esther's Jewish name, Esth 2:7

HADES
be brought down to *H* .... Matt 11:23
H shall not prevail .... Matt 16:18
being in torments in *H* .... Luke 16:23
not leave my soul in *H* ..... Acts 2:27
I have the keys of *H* .... Rev 1:18
H were cast into the .... Rev 20:14

HAGAR
Sarah's servant; bears Ishmael to Abraham, Gen 16
Abraham sends her away; God comforts her, Gen 21:9–21
Paul explains symbolic meaning of, Gal 4:22–31

HAGGAI
Postexilic prophet; contemporary of Zechariah, Ezra 5:1, 2; 6:14; Hag 1:1

HAGGITH
One of David's wives, 2 Sam 3:4
Mother of Adonijah, 1 Kin 1:5

HAIL
cause very heavy *h* .... Ex 9:18
seen the treasury of *h* ...... Job 38:22
He casts out His *h* .... Ps 147:17
h will sweep away the .... Is 28:17
of the plague of the *h* ..... Rev 16:21

HAILSTONES
clouds passed with *h* .... Ps 18:12

HAIR
bring down my gray *h* ..... Gen 42:38
shaved his consecrated *h* .. Num 6:19
h of his head began to ...... Judg 16:22
he cut the *h* of his .... 2 Sam 14:26
the *h* on my body stood ..... Job 4:15
Your *h* is like a flock .... Song 4:1
h had grown like eagles' .... Dan 4:33
you cannot make one *h* .... Matt 5:36
clothed with camel's *h* ..... Mark 1:6
But not a *h* of your .... Luke 21:18
wiped His feet with her *h* .. John 11:2
He had his *h* cut off at .... Acts 18:18
since not a *h* will fall .... Acts 27:34
if a woman has long *h* .... 1 Cor 11:15
not with braided *h* .... 1 Tim 2:9
arranging the *h* .... 1 Pet 3:3
h were white like wool, ... Rev 1:14
black as sackcloth of *h*, ... Rev 6:12
h like women's *h* .... Rev 9:8

HAIRS
are more than the *h* .... Ps 40:12
h I will carry you .... Is 46:4
yes, gray *h* are here .... Hos 7:9
But the very *h* .... Matt 10:30

HAIRY
h garment all over .... Gen 25:25
A *h* man wearing a leather .. 2 Kin 1:8

HAKKOZ
Descendant of Aaron, 1 Chr 24:1, 10
Called Koz, Ezra 2:61, 62
Descendants of, kept from priesthood, Neh 7:63, 64

HALF
h of it in the morning and ... Lev 6:20
h the tribe of Manasseh .... Josh 22:9
h of the people followed .. 1 Kin 16:21
up to *h* the kingdom .... Esth 5:6
you, up to *h* my kingdom .. Mark 6:23
I give *h* of my goods to .... Luke 19:8
h a time, from the .... Rev 12:14

HALLOW
hosts, Him you shall *h* .... Is 8:13
h the Holy One of .... Is 29:23
h the Sabbath day .... Jer 17:24

HALLOWED
the Sabbath day and *h* ...... Ex 20:11
but I will be *h* .... Lev 22:32
who is holy shall be *h* .... Is 5:16

heaven, *h* be Your name ....Matt 6:9

HAM
Noah's youngest son, Gen 5:32
Enters ark, Gen 7:7
His immoral behavior merits Noah's curse, Gen 9:22–25
Father of descendants of repopulated earth, Gen 10:6–20

HAMAN
Plots to destroy Jews, Esth 3:3–15
Invited to Esther's banquet, Esth 5:1–14
Forced to honor Mordecai, Esth 6:5–14
Hanged on his own gallows, Esth 7:1–10

HAMATH
Israel's northern boundary, Num 34:8; 1 Kin 8:65; Ezek 47:16–20
Conquered, 2 Kin 18:34; Jer 49:23
Israelites exiled there, Is 11:11

HAMMER
h that breaks the rock ......Jer 23:29
How the *h* of the whole .....Jer 50:23

HAMOR
Sells land to Jacob, Gen 33:18–20; Acts 7:16
Killed by Jacob's sons, Gen 34:1–31

HAMSTRUNG
their self-will they *h* an ox ..Gen 49:6
David *h* all the chariot .....2 Sam 8:4

HANANI
Father of Jehu the prophet, 1 Kin 16:1, 7
Rebukes Asa; confined to prison, 2 Chr 16:7–10
———— Nehemiah's brother; brings news concerning the Jews, Neh 1:2
Becomes a governor of Jerusalem, Neh 7:2

HANANIAH
False prophet who contradicts Jeremiah, Jer 28:1–17
———— Hebrew name of Shadrach, Dan 1:6, 7, 11

HAND
See AT THE RIGHT HAND; HIS RIGHT HAND; MY RIGHT HAND; STRETCH OUT MY HAND; STRETCHED OUT HIS HAND
lest he put out his *h* ....Gen 3:22
h shall be against ....Gen 16:12
your *h* under my thigh .....Gen 24:2
h toward Israel's right *h* ...Gen 48:13
What is that in your *h* ....Ex 4:2
took the rod of God in his *h* ..Ex 4:20
tooth for tooth, *h* ....Ex 21:24
lay his *h* on the bull's head ...Lev 4:4
Egypt with a mighty *h* .....Deut 9:26
and strengthened his *h* ..1 Sam 23:16
Uzzah put out his *h* ....2 Sam 6:6
let us fall into the *h* .....2 Sam 24:14
Then, by the good *h* ....Ezra 8:18
He would loose His *h* ....Job 6:9
he stretches out his *h* ......Job 15:25
that your own right *h* ......Job 40:14
h has held me up ....Ps 18:35
My times are in Your *h* .....Ps 31:15
and night Your *h* ....Ps 32:4
Your right *h* is full ....Ps 48:10
Let Your *h* be upon the .....Ps 80:17
h shall be established ....Ps 89:21
"Sit at My right *h* ....Ps 110:1
days is in her right *h* ......Prov 3:16
heart is in the *h* ....Prov 21:1
Whatever your *h* finds .....Eccl 9:10
is at his right *h* ....Eccl 10:2
do not withhold your *h* .....Eccl 11:6
His left *h* is under my ......Song 8:3

My *h* has laid the ....Is 48:13
Behold, the LORD's *h* ....Is 59:1
are the work of Your *h* ....Is 64:8
the clay is in the potter's *h* ...Jer 18:6
Am I a God near at *h* ....Jer 23:23
and incense in their *h*, to .....Jer 41:5
h under their wings ....Ezek 10:8
a measuring rod in his *h* ...Ezek 40:3
of a man's *h* appeared ....Dan 5:5
a *h* touched me, which ....Dan 10:10
of heaven is at *h* ....Matt 3:2
if your right *h* causes ......Matt 5:30
do not let your left *h* ....Matt 6:3
h causes you to sin ....Mark 9:43
sitting at the right *h* .....Mark 14:62
delivered from the *h* ......Luke 1:74
Sit at My right *h*, ...Acts 2:34
at the right *h* of God ....Acts 7:55
is even at the right *h* ......Rom 8:34
Because I am not a *h* ....1 Cor 12:15
with my own *h* ....1 Cor 16:21
the right *h* of fellowship ......Gal 2:9
by the *h* of a mediator .....Gal 3:19
to you with my own *h* ......Gal 6:11
The Lord is at *h* ....Phil 4:5
sitting at the right *h* of God ...Col 3:1
"Sit at My right *h* ....Heb 1:13
right *h* of the throne of the ...Heb 8:1
down at the right *h* ....Heb 10:12
of the Lord is at *h* ....James 5:8
in His right *h* seven stars ...Rev 1:16
stars in His right *h* ....Rev 2:1

HAND OF GOD
the *h* was very heavy ....1 Sam 5:11
the *h* was on Judah .....2 Chr 30:12
the *h* has struck me ....Job 19:21
was from the *h* ....Eccl 2:24
their works are in the *h* ....Eccl 9:1
under the mighty *h*, ...1 Pet 5:6

HAND OF THE LORD
the *h* was against them, ...Deut 2:15
earth may know the *h*, ...Josh 4:24
of Israel out of the *h* .....Josh 22:31
h has gone out against .....Ruth 1:13
h was heavy on the ....1 Sam 5:6
h was against the ....1 Sam 7:13
let us fall into the *h* .....2 Sam 24:14
h came upon Elijah; ......1 Kin 18:46
the *h* came upon him ......2 Kin 3:15
according to the *h* ....Ezra 7:6
h my God was upon me ....Ezra 7:28
the *h* has done this ....Job 12:9
the right *h* does valiantly ...Ps 118:15
king's heart is in the *h* ....Prov 21:1
crown of glory in the *h* .....Is 62:3
the *h* shall be known ....Is 66:14
the *h* was strong upon me ...Ezek 3:14
the *h* came upon me ....Ezek 37:1
And the *h* was with him ...Luke 1:66
And the *h* was with them ...Acts 11:21
the *h* is upon you, ...Acts 13:11

HANDIWORK
firmament shows His *h* ....Ps 19:1

HANDKERCHIEFS
so that even *h* or aprons ..Acts 19:12

HANDLE
h the law did not know ......Jer 2:8
H Me and see ....Luke 24:39
do not taste, do not *h* ....Col 2:21

HANDLED
and our hands have *h* .....1 John 1:1

HANDS
the *h* are the *h* ....Gen 27:22
and Hur supported his *h* ....Ex 17:12
Moses had laid his *h* on ....Deut 34:9
here we are, in your *h* .....Josh 9:25
took his life in his *h* .....1 Sam 19:5
put my life in my *h* ....1 Sam 28:21
but His *h* make whole ....Job 5:18

and cleanse my *h* ....Job 9:30
h have made me and ....Job 10:8
They pierced My *h* ....Ps 22:16
washed my *h* in innocence ..Ps 73:13
establish the work of our *h* ...Ps 90:17
In their *h* they shall bear ....Ps 91:12
h formed the dry land ....Ps 95:5
stretches out her *h* ....Prov 31:19
say, 'He has no *h* ....Is 45:9
strike your *h* together ....Ezek 21:14
was cut out without *h* .....Dan 2:34
on the palms of my *h* ......Dan 10:10
The *h* of Zerubbabel have ...Zech 4:9
than having two *h* ....Matt 18:8
will lay *h* on the sick .....Mark 16:18
into Your *h* I commit .....Luke 23:46
Behold My *h* and My .....Luke 24:39
only, but also my *h* ....John 13:9
h the print of the ....John 20:25
his chains fell off his *h* .....Acts 12:7
know that these *h* ....Acts 20:34
and he laid his *h* on him ...Acts 28:8
a house not made with *h* ....2 Cor 5:1
his *h* what is good ....Eph 4:28
made without *h* ....Col 2:11
lifting up holy *h* ....1 Tim 2:8
the laying on of the *h* .....1 Tim 4:14
Do not lay *h* on anyone ...1 Tim 5:22
the laying on of my *h* .....2 Tim 1:6
baptisms, of laying on of *h* ...Heb 6:2
not made with *h* ....Heb 9:11
to fall into the *h* ....Heb 10:31
Cleanse your *h*, you ....James 4:8
and our *h* have handled, ...1 John 1:1
foreheads or on their *h* ....Rev 20:4

HANDWRITING
having wiped out the *h* ......Col 2:14

HANG
They will *h* on him all the ....Is 22:24
commandments *h* all the ...Matt 22:40
the hands which *h* down ..Heb 12:12

HANGED
for he who is *h* ....Deut 21:23
went and *h* himself ....Matt 27:5

HANGS
h the earth on nothing ......Job 26:7
is everyone who *h* ....Gal 3:13

HANNAH
Barren wife of Elkanah; prays for a son, 1 Sam 1:1–18
Bears Samuel and dedicates him to the Lord, 1 Sam 1:19–28
Magnifies God, 1 Sam 2:1–10

HANUN
King of Ammon; disgraces David's ambassadors and is defeated by him, 2 Sam 10:1–14

HAPPEN
show us what will *h* ....Is 41:22
understand what will *h* ....Dan 10:14
not know what will *h* .....James 4:14

HAPPINESS
one year, and bring *h* .....Deut 24:5

HAPPY
h are these your servants ...2 Chr 9:7
H is the man who has ......Ps 127:5
H are the people who ......Ps 144:15
H is the man who finds .....Prov 3:13
mercy on the poor, *h* .....Prov 14:21
trusts in the LORD, *h* .....Prov 16:20
h is he who keeps ....Prov 29:18
H is he who does not .....Rom 14:22

HARAN
Abraham's younger brother, Gen 11:26–31
———— City of Mesopotamia, Gen 11:31
Abraham leaves, Gen 12:4, 5
Jacob dwells at, Gen 29:4–35

HARASS
and Judah shall not *h* . . . . Is 11:13
h some from the church . . . . Acts 12:1

HARD
Is anything too *h* . . . . Gen 18:14
Pharaoh's heart is *h* . . . . Ex 7:14
test him with *h* questions . . 1 Kin 10:1
His heart is as *h* . . . . Job 41:24
shown Your people *h* . . . . Ps 60:3
of the unfaithful is *h* . . . . . . Prov 13:15
h to bear, and lay them . . . . Matt 23:4
I knew you to be a *h* . . . . . Matt 25:24
"This is a *h* saying . . . . John 6:60
It is *h* for you to kick . . . . Acts 9:5
are some things *h* . . . . 2 Pet 3:16

HARDEN
But I will *h* his heart . . . . Ex 4:21
Do not *h* your hearts . . . . Ps 95:8
h your hearts as . . . . Heb 3:8

HARDENED
But Pharaoh *h* his . . . . Ex 8:32
Who has *h* himself . . . . Job 9:4
their heart was *h* . . . . Mark 6:52
eyes and *h* their hearts . . . John 12:40
lest any of you be *h* . . . . Heb 3:13

HARDENS
A wicked man *h* his . . . . . . Prov 21:29
h his heart will fall . . . . . . Prov 28:14
whom He wills He *h* . . . . . . Rom 9:18

HARDER
brother offended is *h* to . . . Prov 18:19
their faces *h* than rock . . . . . . Jer 5:3
h than flint, I have made . . . . Ezek 3:9

HARDSHIP
h that has befallen us . . . . . Num 20:14
h as a good soldier . . . . 2 Tim 2:3

HARLOT
play the *h* with their gods . . . Ex 34:16
shall be no ritual *h* . . . . . . Deut 23:17
of a *h* named Rahab . . . . Josh 2:1
h is a deep pit . . . . Prov 23:27
the deeds of a brazen *h* . . . Ezek 16:30
Oholah played the *h* . . . . . . Ezek 23:5
you, Israel, play the *h*, let . . . Hos 4:15
h is one body with . . . . 1 Cor 6:16
h Rahab did not perish . . . . Heb 11:31
of the great *h* who . . . . Rev 17:1

HARLOTRIES
the land with your *h* . . . . Jer 3:2
Let her put away her *h* . . . . . . Hos 2:2

HARLOTRY
through her casual *h* . . . . Jer 3:9
the lewdness of your *h* . . . . . Jer 13:27
let them put their *h* . . . . . . Ezek 43:9
are the children of *h* . . . . Hos 2:4
Ephraim, you commit *h* . . . . . Hos 5:3
for the spirit of *h* . . . . Hos 5:4

HARLOTS
his blood while the *h* . . . . . 1 Kin 22:38
h enter the kingdom . . . . . Matt 21:31
Great, The Mother of *H* . . . . Rev 17:5

HARM
do My prophets no *h* . . . . . 1 Chr 16:22
they thought to do me *h* . . . . . Neh 6:2
those who sought their *h* . . . . Esth 9:2
it only causes *h* . . . . Ps 37:8
and do My prophets no *h* . . . Ps 105:15
and I will not *h* you . . . . Jer 25:6
Do yourself no *h*, for we . . . Acts 16:28
Love does no *h* to a . . . . . . Rom 13:10
and do not *h* the oil . . . . Rev 6:6
Do not *h* the earth, the . . . . . . Rev 7:3

HARMLESS
become blameless and *h* . . . . Phil 2:15
for us, who is holy, *h* . . . . . . Heb 7:26

HARMONIOUS
the harp, with *h* sound . . . . . . Ps 92:3

HAROD
Well near Gideon's camp, Judg 7:1

HARP
those who play the *h* . . . . . . Gen 4:21
skillful player on the *h* . . 1 Sam 16:16
Praise the LORD with the *h* . . . Ps 33:2
Sing to the LORD with the *h* . . . Ps 98:5
On a *h* of ten strings I will . . Ps 144:9
with the lute and *h* . . . . Ps 150:3
Lamb, each having a *h* . . . . . . Rev 5:8

HARPS
to direct with *h* on the . . . . 1 Chr 15:21
We hung our *h* upon the . . . . Ps 137:2
playing their *h* . . . . Rev 14:2
of glass, having *h* of God . . . . Rev 15:2

HARSH
a *h* word stirs up anger . . . . Prov 15:1
"Your words have been *h* . . . Mal 3:13
but also to the *h* . . . . 1 Pet 2:18

HARVEST
See FEAST OF HARVEST
seedtime and *h* . . . . Gen 8:22
to death in the days of *h* . . 2 Sam 21:9
He who sleeps in *h* is a . . . . Prov 10:5
to the joy of *h* . . . . Is 9:3
cloud of dew in the heat of *h* . . Is 18:4
shall eat up your *h* . . . . Jer 5:17
"The *h* is past . . . . Jer 8:20
of her *h* will come . . . . Jer 51:33
the sickle, for the *h* is ripe . . Joel 3:13
h truly is plentiful . . . . Matt 9:37
pray the Lord of the *h* . . . . Matt 9:38
sickle, because the *h* . . . . . . Mark 4:29
pray the Lord of the *h* to . . Luke 10:2
already white for *h* . . . . John 4:35
the *h* of the earth is . . . . . . Rev 14:15

HASTE
you shall eat it in *h* . . . . Ex 12:11
For I said in my *h* . . . . Ps 31:22
And they came with *h* . . . . . Luke 2:16
"Zacchaeus, make *h* . . . . . . Luke 19:5

HASTEN
be multiplied who *h* . . . . Ps 16:4
Do not *h* in your . . . . Eccl 7:9
I, the LORD, will *h* . . . . Is 60:22

HASTENING
h the coming of the . . . . 2 Pet 3:12

HASTENS
and he sins who *h* . . . . Prov 19:2
with an evil eye *h* . . . . Prov 28:22
is near and *h* quickly . . . . . . Zeph 1:14

HASTILY
utter anything *h* . . . . Eccl 5:2
lay hands on anyone *h* . . . . 1 Tim 5:22

HASTY
Do you see a man *h* . . . . . . Prov 29:20

HATE
'You shall not *h* . . . . Lev 19:17
h all workers of . . . . Ps 5:5
h the righteous shall . . . . . . Ps 34:21
love the LORD, *h* evil . . . . . . Ps 97:10
h every false way . . . . Ps 119:104
h the double-minded . . . . . Ps 119:113
I *h* and abhor lying . . . . . . Ps 119:163
love, and a time to *h* . . . . . . Eccl 3:8
h robbery for burnt . . . . Is 61:8
H evil, love good . . . . Amos 5:15
I *h*, I despise your feast . . . Amos 5:21
You who *h* good and . . . . Mic 3:2
either he will *h* the one . . . . Matt 6:24
but what I *h*, that I do . . . . . Rom 7:15
Nicolaitans, which I also *h* . . . Rev 2:6
these will *h* the harlot, ... Rev 17:16

HATED
So Esau *h* Jacob because . . Gen 27:41
they *h* knowledge . . . . Prov 1:29
Therefore I *h* life . . . . Eccl 2:17

h all my labor in . . . . Eccl 2:18
but Esau I have *h* . . . . Mal 1:3
And you will be *h* . . . . Matt 10:22
have seen and also *h* . . . . . John 15:24
h Me without a cause . . . . John 15:25
world has *h* them . . . . John 17:14
but Esau I have *h* . . . . Rom 9:13
For no one ever *h* . . . . Eph 5:29
and *h* lawlessness . . . . Heb 1:9

HATEFUL
h woman when she is . . . . . Prov 30:23
in malice and envy, *h* . . . . . Titus 3:3

HATERS
The *h* of the LORD . . . . Ps 81:15
backbiters, *h* of God . . . . . . Rom 1:30

HATES
six things the LORD *h* . . . . . . Prov 6:16
lose it, and he who *h* . . . . . John 12:25
"If the world *h* . . . . John 15:18
h his brother is . . . . 1 John 2:11

HATING
h even the garment defiled . . . Jude 23

HATRED
I hate them with perfect *h* . . Ps 139:22

HAUGHTY
Your eyes are on the *h* . . 2 Sam 22:28
bring down *h* looks . . . . Ps 18:27
my heart is not *h* . . . . Ps 131:1
h spirit before a fall . . . . . . Prov 16:18
A proud and *h* man . . . . Prov 21:24
Do not be *h*, but fear . . . . . Rom 11:20
age not to be *h* . . . . 1 Tim 6:17

HAUNTS
are full of the *h* . . . . Ps 74:20

HAURAN
District southeast of Mt. Hermon, Ezek 47:16

HAVE MERCY
h on me, and hear my prayer . . Ps 4:1
h on me, for I am . . . . Ps 25:16
H upon me, O God, ... Ps 51:1
arise and *h* on Zion; . . . . . . Ps 102:13
and forsakes them will *h* . . Prov 28:13
nor *h* on their fatherless . . . . . Is 9:17
the Lord will *h* . . . . Is 14:1
will *h* on His afflicted . . . . . . Is 49:13
not pity nor spare nor *h* . . . . Jer 13:14
I will surely *h* on him," . . . . Jer 31:20
captives of Jacob, and *h* . . Ezek 39:25
I will no longer *h* . . . . Hos 1:6
how long will You not *h* . . . . Zech 1:12
"Son of David, *h* on us . . . . Matt 9:27
"*H* on me, O Lord . . . . Matt 15:22
Lord, *h* on my son, ... Matt 17:15
"*H* on us, O Lord, ... Matt 20:30
"Jesus, Son of David, *h* . . Mark 10:47
'Father Abraham, *h* . . . . . . Luke 16:24
"Jesus, Master, *h* on us . . . Luke 17:13
"Jesus, Son of David, *h* . . . Luke 18:38
"I will *h* on whomever . . . . . Rom 9:15
that He might *h* on all . . . . . Rom 11:32

HAVEN
shall dwell by the *h* . . . . . . Gen 49:13
to their desired *h* . . . . Ps 107:30

HAVOC
for Saul, he made *h* . . . . Acts 8:3

HAY
precious stones, wood, *h* . . 1 Cor 3:12

HAZAEL
Anointed king of Syria by Elijah, 1 Kin 19:15–17
Elisha predicts his taking the throne, 2 Kin 8:7–15
Oppresses Israel, 2 Kin 8:28, 29; 10:32, 33; 12:17, 18; 13:3–7, 22

HAZAR ENAN
Village of north Palestine, Num 34:9, 10

HAZEROTH

Scene of sedition of Miriam and Aaron, Num 11:35—12:16

HAZOR

Royal Canaanite city destroyed by Joshua, Josh 11:1–13
Rebuilt and assigned to Naphtali, Josh 19:32, 36
Army of, defeated by Deborah and Barak, Judg 4:1–24

HE WHO BELIEVES

H and is baptized .... Mark 16:16
H in Him is not .... John 3:18
H in the Son has .... John 3:36
h in Me shall never thirst .. John 6:35
h in Me has everlasting .... John 6:47
H in Me, as the Scripture .. John 7:38
H, though he may die, ... John 11:25
and said, "*H* in Me, ... John 12:44
h in Me, the works that .. John 14:12
precious, and *h* on Him .... 1 Pet 2:6
the world, but *h* .... 1 John 5:5
H in the Son of God ...... 1 John 5:10

HEAD

He shall bruise your *h* ...... Gen 3:15
white baskets on my *h* ..... Gen 40:16
on the *h* of the bed .... Gen 47:31
your right hand on his *h* ... Gen 48:18
shall come upon his *h* .... 1 Sam 1:11
a bronze helmet on his *h* .. 1 Sam 17:5
and cut off his *h* with .... 1 Sam 17:51
crown from his *h* .... 2 Sam 12:30
put ashes on her *h* .... 2 Sam 13:19
and dust on his *h* .... 2 Sam 15:32
My *h*, my *h*!" .... 2 Kin 4:19
is with us as our *h* ...... 2 Chr 13:12
my skin, and laid my *h* .... Job 16:15
return upon his own *h* ..... Ps 7:16
of pure gold upon his *h* ..... Ps 21:3
the lip, they shake the *h* ... Ps 22:7
You anoint my *h* with oil ... Ps 23:5
than the hairs of my *h* ..... Ps 40:12
the precious oil upon the *h* .. Ps 133:2
The silver-haired *h* is a ... Prov 16:31
old men is their gray *h* ... Prov 20:29
coals of fire on his *h* ..... Prov 25:22
h is covered with dew ..... Song 5:2
The whole *h* is sick .... Is 1:5
it to bow down his *h* .... Is 58:5
For every *h* shall be bald ... Jer 48:37
visions of my *h* troubled ... Dan 4:5
could lift up his *h* .... Zech 1:21
you swear by your *h* ...... Matt 5:36
you fast, anoint your *h* .... Matt 6:17
Baptist's *h* here on a .... Matt 14:8
first the blade, then the *h* .. Mark 4:28
and poured it on His *h* .... Mark 14:3
thorns, put it on His *h* .... Mark 15:17
did not anoint My *h* with .. Luke 7:46
has nowhere to lay His *h* .. Luke 9:58
bowing His *h*, He gave .... John 19:30
coals of fire on his *h* ...... Rom 12:20
having his *h* covered ...... 1 Cor 11:4
or prophesies with her *h* ... 1 Cor 11:5
and gave Him to be *h* ..... Eph 1:22
For the husband is *h* ..... Eph 5:23
His *h* and his hair .... Rev 1:14
having on His *h* a golden .. Rev 14:14
His *h* were many crowns .. Rev 19:12

HEADS

See BOWED THEIR HEADS
men to ride over our *h* ..... Ps 66:12
Him, wagging their *h* ..... Matt 27:39
dragon having seven *h* ..... Rev 12:3

HEAL

I wound and I *h* .... Deut 32:39
surely I will *h* you .... 2 Kin 20:5
O LORD, *h* me............... Ps 6:2
H my soul, for I have ...... Ps 41:4
time to kill, and a time to *h* .. Eccl 3:3

sent Me to *h* the .... Is 61:1
h your backslidings .... Jer 3:22
who can *h* you .... Lam 2:13
torn, but He will *h* .... Hos 6:1
h all kinds of sickness ...... Matt 10:1
H the sick, cleanse .... Matt 10:8
to *h* on the Sabbath ...... Matt 12:10
so that I should *h* .... Matt 13:15
power to *h* sicknesses ..... Mark 3:15
sent Me to *h* the .... Luke 4:18
Physician, *h* yourself ..... Luke 4:23

HEALED

I have *h* this water .... 2 Kin 2:21
His word and *h* them ...... Ps 107:20
And return and be *h* .... Is 6:10
His stripes we are *h* .... Is 53:5
h the hurt of My .... Jer 6:14
When I would have *h* .... Hos 7:1
and He *h* them .... Matt 4:24
and my servant will be *h* .. Matt 8:8
and *h* all who were sick, ... Matt 8:16
Jesus' feet, and He *h* ..... Matt 15:30
be *h* of their diseases, ... Luke 6:17
demon-possessed was *h* ... Luke 8:36
h the child, and gave him .. Luke 9:42
touched his ear and *h* .... Luke 22:51
and they were all *h* .... Acts 5:16
he had faith to be *h* .... Acts 14:9
but rather be *h* .... Heb 12:13
that you may be *h* .... James 5:16
whose stripes you were *h* .. 1 Pet 2:24
his deadly wound was *h* .... Rev 13:3

HEALING

h shall spring forth .... Is 58:8
so that there is no *h* .... Jer 14:19
Your injury has no *h* .... Nah 3:19
shall arise with *h* .... Mal 4:2
and *h* all kinds of .... Matt 4:23
h all who were oppressed . Acts 10:38
tree were for the *h* .... Rev 22:2

HEALINGS

to another gifts of *h* .... 1 Cor 12:9
Do all have gifts of *h* ..... 1 Cor 12:30

HEALS

h all your diseases .... Ps 103:3
He *h* the broken-hearted .... Ps 147:3
h the stroke of their .... Is 30:26
Jesus the Christ *h* .... Acts 9:34

HEALTH

It will be *h* to your flesh, ... Prov 3:8
and *h* to all their flesh ..... Prov 4:22
of the wise promotes *h* .... Prov 12:18
to the soul and *h* .... Prov 16:24
and for a time of *h* .... Jer 8:15
no recovery for the *h* ...... Jer 8:22
For I will restore *h* to you .. Jer 30:17
all things and be in *h* ...... 3 John 2

HEAP

This *h* is a witness .... Gen 31:48
I could *h* up words .... Job 16:4
sea together as a *h* .... Ps 33:7
so you will *h* coals of .... Prov 25:22
ears, they will *h* .... 2 Tim 4:3

HEAPS

Though he *h* up silver ..... Job 27:16

HEAR

See EARS TO HEAR
with us, and we will *h* .... Ex 20:19
Me, I will surely *h* their .... Ex 22:23
"*H*, O Israel: The LORD ..... Deut 6:4
Him you shall *h* .... Deut 18:15
of the oxen which I *h* .... 1 Sam 15:14
You *h* the supplication of . 1 Kin 8:30
h in heaven Your .... 1 Kin 8:43
H me when I call .... Ps 4:1
O You who *h* prayer .... Ps 65:2
h what God the LORD....... Ps 85:8
ear, shall He not *h* .... Ps 94:9
h the words of the .... Prov 22:17

h rather than to give .... Eccl 5:1
H, O heavens, and give ear ..... Is 1:2
H, you who are afar .... Is 33:13
Let the earth *h* .... Is 34:1
I have made you *h* new ...... Is 48:6
I spoke, you did not *h* ...... Is 65:12
cleansed and the deaf *h* .... Matt 11:5
'Hearing you will *h* .... Matt 13:14
if he will not *h* .... Matt 18:16
"Take heed what you *h* .... Mark 4:24
ears, do you not *h* .... Mark 8:18
h the sound of it .... John 3:8
that God does not *h* .... John 9:31
My sheep *h* My voice ...... John 10:27
And how shall they *h* .... Rom 10:14
man be swift to *h* .... James 1:19
those who *h* the words of ... Rev 1:3
h what the Spirit says........ Rev 2:7
has an ear, let him *h* ...... Rev 13:9

HEARD

h the sound of the .... Gen 3:8
h their cry because of .... Ex 3:7
you only *h* a voice .... Deut 4:12
certainly God has *h* .... Ps 66:19
quietly, should be *h* .... Eccl 9:17
Have you not *h* .... Is 40:21
world men have not *h* ...... Is 64:4
Who has *h* such a thing ..... Is 66:8
h Ephraim bemoaning ...... Jer 31:18
that they will be *h* .... Matt 6:7
h the word believed .... Acts 4:4
I say, have they not *h* ..... Rom 10:18
not seen, nor ear *h* .... 1 Cor 2:9
h inexpressible words ..... 2 Cor 12:4
things that you have *h* .... 2 Tim 2:2
the things we have *h* .... Heb 2:1
the word which they *h* ...... Heb 4:2
from death, and was *h* ...... Heb 5:7
which we have *h* .... 1 John 1:1
Lord's Day, and I *h* .... Rev 1:10

HEARER

if anyone is a *h* .... James 1:23
is not a forgetful *h* .... James 1:25

HEARERS

for not the *h* of the .... Rom 2:13
impart grace to the *h* ...... Eph 4:29
of the word, and not *h* .... James 1:22

HEARING

and read in the *h* .... Ex 24:7
Book of Moses in the *h* .... Neh 13:1
Do not speak in the *h* ...... Prov 23:9
'Keep on *h*, but do not .... Is 6:9
h they do not .... Matt 13:13
h they may hear .... Mark 4:12
If the whole were *h* ...... 1 Cor 12:17
or by the *h* of faith .... Gal 3:2
have become dull of *h* ..... Heb 5:11

HEARS

for Your servant *h* .... 1 Sam 3:9
out, and the LORD *h* .... Ps 34:17
He who *h* you *h* Me ..... Luke 10:16
of God *h* God's words ..... John 8:47
And if anyone *h* .... John 12:47
who is of the truth *h* ..... John 18:37
He who knows God *h* ..... 1 John 4:6
And let him who *h* .... Rev 22:17

HEART

See UPRIGHT IN HEART; WITH ALL YOUR HEART
h was only evil .... Gen 6:5
for you know the *h* .... Ex 23:9
as many as had a willing *h* .. Ex 35:22
h the LORD had put .... Ex 36:2
seek Him with all your *h* .. Deut 4:29
the foreskin of your *h* .... Deut 10:16
whatever your *h* desires .. Deut 14:26
and confusion of *h* .... Deut 28:28
will circumcise your *h* .... Deut 30:6
incline your *h* to the ..... Josh 24:23
great searchings of *h* ..... Judg 5:16

Hannah spoke in her *h* ... 1 Sam 1:13
h rejoices in the LORD...... 1 Sam 2:1
God gave him another *h* .. 1 Sam 10:9
a man after His own *h* ... 1 Sam 13:14
LORD looks at the *h*....... 1 Sam 16:7
his *h* died within him, ... 1 Sam 25:37
despised him for her *h* .... 2 Sam 6:16
David's *h* condemned .... 2 Sam 24:10
and understanding *h* ..... 1 Kin 3:12
largeness of *h* like the ..... 1 Kin 4:29
h to build a temple for ..... 1 Kin 8:18
My eyes and My *h* will be .. 1 Kin 9:3
his wives turned his *h* .... 1 Kin 11:4
Ezra had prepared his *h* .... Ezra 7:10
He pierces my *h* .... Job 16:13
How my *h* yearns within ... Job 19:27
For God made my *h* ...... Job 23:16
My *h* is in turmoil and ..... Job 30:27
within your *h* on your bed .. Ps 4:4
My *h* also instructs me ...... Ps 16:7
your *h* live forever .... Ps 22:26
h is overflowing .... Ps 45:1
My *h* is steadfast .... Ps 57:7
Thus my *h* was grieved ..... Ps 73:21
my *h* and my flesh cry....... Ps 84:2
h is set on pilgrimage .... Ps 84:5
may gain a *h* of wisdom ..... Ps 90:12
h shall depart from me ...... Ps 101:4
look and a proud *h* .... Ps 101:5
with my whole *h* .... Ps 111:1
With my whole *h* I have .... Ps 119:10
I have hidden in my *h* ...... Ps 119:11
h is not haughty .... Ps 131:1
O God, and know my *h* .... Ps 139:23
h makes a cheerful .... Prov 15:13
The king's *h* is in the ...... Prov 21:1
as he thinks in his *h* .... Prov 23:7
with a wicked *h* .... Prov 26:23
h reveals the man .... Prov 27:19
trusts in his own *h* .... Prov 28:26
The *h* of the wise is .... Eccl 7:4
and a wise man's *h* .... Eccl 8:5
h yearned for him .... Song 5:4
and the whole *h* .... Is 1:5
h shall resound .... Is 16:11
the yearning of Your *h* ...... Is 63:15
the mind and the *h* .... Jer 11:20
h is deceitful above .... Jer 17:9
I will give them a *h* .... Jer 24:7
therefore My *h* yearns ...... Jer 31:20
and take the stony *h* ..... Ezek 11:19
get yourselves a new *h* .... Ezek 18:31
uncircumcised in *h* .... Ezek 44:7
are the pure in *h* .... Matt 5:8
is, there your *h* .... Matt 6:21
of the *h* proceed evil ..... Matt 15:19
does not doubt in his *h* .. Mark 11:23
Did not our *h* burn ..... Luke 24:32
h will flow rivers .... John 7:38
"Let not your *h* .... John 14:1
believed were of one *h* .... Acts 4:32
Satan filled your *h* .... Acts 5:3
h is not right in the .... Acts 8:21
is that of the *h* .... Rom 2:29
h that God has raised ...... Rom 10:9
with the *h* one believes ... Rom 10:10
in sincerity of *h* .... Eph 6:5
refresh my *h* in the .... Philem 20
always go astray in their *h* .. Heb 3:10
and shuts up his *h* ...... 1 John 3:17
if our *h* condemns us ..... 1 John 3:20

HEARTILY
you do, do it *h* .... Col 3:23

HEARTS
God tests the *h* .... Ps 7:9
who seek God, your *h* .... Ps 69:32
let the *h* of those .... Ps 105:3
And he will turn the *h* ...... Mal 4:6
h failing them from ...... Luke 21:26
purifying their *h* .... Acts 15:9
will guard your *h* .... Phil 4:7

of God rule in your *h* .... Col 3:15

HEAT
and harvest, cold and *h*, ... Gen 8:22
storm, a shade from the *h* ..... Is 25:4
in the *h* of my spirit .... Ezek 3:14
will melt with fervent *h* .... 2 Pet 3:12

HEATHEN
repetitions as the *h* .... Matt 6:7
him be to you like a *h* ... Matt 18:17

HEAVEN
See FATHER IN HEAVEN; HOST OF
   HEAVEN; KINGDOM OF HEAVEN
called the firmament *H* ...... Gen 1:8
High, Possessor of *h* .... Gen 14:19
called to him from *h* ...... Gen 22:11
multiply as the stars of *h* ... Gen 26:4
give you of the dew of *h* ... Gen 27:28
and this is the gate of *h* ... Gen 28:17
with blessings of *h* above .. Gen 49:25
out his rod toward *h* .... Ex 9:23
rain bread from *h* for you ... Ex 16:4
Out of *h* He let you hear ... Deut 4:36
precious things of *h* ...... Deut 33:13
foundations of *h* quaked .. 2 Sam 22:8
the host of *h* standing .... 1 Kin 22:19
came down from *h* .... 2 Kin 1:12
Elijah into *h* by a .... 2 Kin 2:1
would make windows in *h* .. 2 Kin 7:2
Behold, the *h* and the .... 2 Chr 6:18
The LORD's throne is in *h* .... Ps 11:4
LORD looks down from *h* ..... Ps 14:2
Whom have I in *h* but You .. Ps 73:25
word is settled in *h* ...... Ps 119:89
For God is in *h* .... Eccl 5:2
"*H* is My throne .... Is 66:1
"If *h* above can be .... Jer 31:37
and the birds of the *h* ..... Dan 2:38
come to know that *H* .... Dan 4:26
though they climb up to *h* .. Amos 9:2
These are four spirits of *h* ... Zech 6:5
for the kingdom of *h* .... Matt 3:2
your Father in *h* .... Matt 5:16
Our Father in *h*, hallowed ... Matt 6:9
on earth as it is in *h* ...... Matt 6:10
H and earth will .... Matt 24:35
from Him a sign from *h* .... Mark 8:11
but are like angels in *h* ... Mark 12:25
with the clouds of *h* ..... Mark 14:62
prayed, the *h* was opened .. Luke 3:21
fall like lightning from *h* .. Luke 10:18
names are written in *h* ... Luke 10:20
done on earth as it is in *h* .. Luke 11:2
will be more joy in *h* ..... Luke 15:7
have sinned against *h* .... Luke 15:18
descending from *h* like a ... John 1:32
you shall see *h* open .... John 1:51
one has ascended to *h* ..... John 3:13
the true bread from *h* ...... John 6:32
a voice came from *h* ...... John 12:28
sheet, let down from *h* .... Acts 11:5
the whole family in *h* .... Eph 3:15
laid up for you in *h* .... Col 1:5
and the *h* gave rain ...... James 5:18
there was silence in *h* ...... Rev 8:1
sign appeared in *h* .... Rev 12:1
Now I saw a new *h* .... Rev 21:1

HEAVEN AND EARTH
High, Possessor of *h* ...... Gen 14:19
"I call *h* to witness .... Deut 4:26
You have made *h* ...... 2 Kin 19:15
of Israel, who made *h* ..... 2 Chr 2:12
servants of the God of *h* ... Ezra 5:11
Let *h* praise Him, the seas .. Ps 69:34
the LORD, who made *h* ..... Ps 121:2
LORD who made *h* bless ..... Ps 134:3
who made *h*, the sea, and .. Ps 146:6
You have made *h* .... Is 37:16
"do I not fill *h*?" says ..... Jer 23:24
the ordinances of *h* .... Jer 33:25
I will shake *h*, the sea and ... Hag 2:6

till *h* pass away, one jot .... Matt 5:18
Father, Lord of *h* .... Matt 11:25
"*H* will pass away, but .... Matt 24:35
You are God, who made *h*.. Acts 4:24
the whole family in *h* ...... Eph 3:15
worship Him who made *h* ... Rev 14:7

HEAVENLY
h host praising God .... Luke 2:13
if I tell you *h* things .... John 3:12
are those who are *h* ...... 1 Cor 15:48
the image of the *h* Man .. 1 Cor 15:49
blessing in the *h* .... Eph 1:3
the *h* places in Christ Jesus .. Eph 2:6
and powers in the *h* places .. Eph 3:10
wickedness in the *h* places .. Eph 6:12
and have tasted the *h* ...... Heb 6:4
h things themselves .... Heb 9:23
a better, that is, a *h* ...... Heb 11:16
the living God, the *h* ...... Heb 12:22

HEAVENLY FATHER
your *h* will also forgive .... Matt 6:14
yet your *h* feeds them ..... Matt 6:26
h knows that you need ..... Matt 6:32
My *h* has not planted ..... Matt 15:13
"So My *h* also will do .... Matt 18:35
your *h* give the Holy ...... Luke 11:13

HEAVENS
I will make your *h* .... Lev 26:19
and the highest *h* .... Deut 10:14
h cannot contain .... 1 Kin 8:27
the LORD made the *h* ..... 1 Chr 16:26
Till the *h* are no more ..... Job 14:12
in the *h* shall laugh .... Ps 2:4
h declare the glory .... Ps 19:1
Let the *h* declare His .... Ps 50:6
h can be compared .... Ps 89:6
The *h* are Yours .... Ps 89:11
For as the *h* are high ..... Ps 103:11
When He prepared the *h* ... Prov 8:27
h are higher than the .... Is 55:9
behold, I create new *h* ..... Is 65:17
and behold, the *h* .... Matt 3:16
h will be shaken .... Matt 24:29
h are the work of Your .... Heb 1:10
h will pass away .... 2 Pet 3:10

HEAVINESS
and I am full of *h* .... Ps 69:20
My soul melts from *h* ..... Ps 119:28

HEAVY
the bondage was *h* .... Neh 5:18

HEBREW
Term applied to:
   Abram, Gen 14:13
   Israelites, 1 Sam 4:6, 9
   Jews, Acts 6:1
   Paul, Phil 3:5

HEBRON
Abram, Isaac, and Jacob dwell there,
   Gen 13:18; 23:2–20; 35:27
Visited by spies, Num 13:21, 22
Defeated by Joshua, Josh 10:1–37
Caleb's inheritance, Josh 14:12–15
David's original capital; sons born
   there, 2 Sam 2:1–3, 11; 3:2–5
Site of Absalom's rebellion, 2 Sam
   15:7–10

HEDGE
behold, I will *h* up your ...... Hos 2:6
sharper than a thorn *h* ...... Mic 7:4
a vineyard and set a *h* .... Mark 12:1

HEDGED
and whom God has *h* .... Job 3:23
You have *h* me behind ..... Ps 139:5
He has *h* me in so that ..... Lam 3:7

HEED
See TAKE HEED
By taking *h* according ...... Ps 119:9
if you *h* Me carefully ...... Jer 17:24

and let us not give *h* . . . . Jer 18:18
Take *h*, watch and pray . . Mark 13:33
stands take *h* lest he . . . . . 1 Cor 10:12
nor give *h* to fables . . . . 1 Tim 1:4
giving *h* to deceiving . . . . 1 Tim 4:1
the more earnest *h* . . . . Heb 2:1

HEEDS
h counsel is wise . . . . Prov 12:15

HEEL
you shall bruise His *h* . . . . . Gen 3:15
took hold of Esau's *h* . . . . . Gen 25:26
has lifted up his *h* . . . . Ps 41:9
Me has lifted up his *h* . . . . John 13:18

HEIFER
a red *h* without blemish . . . . Num 19:2
not plowed with my *h* . . . . . Judg 14:18
goats and the ashes of a *h* . . Heb 9:13

HEIGHT
"Is not God in the *h* . . . . Job 22:12
looked down from the *h* . . . . Ps 102:19
nor *h* nor depth . . . . Rom 8:39
length and depth and *h* . . . . . Eph 3:18

HEIR
own body shall be your *h* . . . Gen 15:4
Has he no *h* . . . . Jer 49:1
Now I say that the *h* . . . . Gal 4:1
if a son, then an *h* . . . . Gal 4:7
He has appointed *h* . . . . Heb 1:2
the world and became *h* . . . . Heb 11:7

HEIRS
of God and joint *h* . . . . Rom 8:17
should be fellow *h* . . . . Eph 3:6
be rich in faith and *h* . . . . . James 2:5
vessel, and as being *h* . . . . . . 1 Pet 3:7

HELAM
Place between Damascus and Hamath
   where David defeated Syrians,
   2 Sam 10:16–19

HELL
shall be turned into *h* . . . . Ps 9:17
go down alive into *h* . . . . Ps 55:15
house is the way to *h* . . . . . . Prov 7:27
his soul from *h* . . . . Prov 23:14
H and Destruction are . . . . . Prov 27:20
"*H* from beneath is . . . . Is 14:9
be in danger of *h* fire . . . . . . Matt 5:22
to be cast into *h* . . . . Matt 18:9
the condemnation of *h* . . . . Matt 23:33
power to cast into *h* . . . . Luke 12:5
it is set on fire by *h* . . . . James 3:6

HELLENISTS
Greek-speaking Jews, Acts 6:1
Hostile to Paul, Acts 9:29
Gospel preached to, Acts 11:20

HELMET
a breastplate, and a *h* . . . . Is 59:17
And take the *h* of . . . . Eph 6:17
and love, and as a *h* . . . . . . 1 Thess 5:8

HELP
the shield of your *h* . . . . . . Deut 33:29
Is my *h* not within me . . . . . . Job 6:13
"There is no *h* for him . . . . . . Ps 3:2
May He send you *h* . . . . Ps 20:2
He is our *h* and our . . . . Ps 33:20
yet praise Him, the *h* . . . . . . Ps 42:11
A very present *h* . . . . Ps 46:1
Give us *h* from trouble . . . . . Ps 60:11
God, make haste to *h* . . . . . . Ps 71:12
"I have given *h* . . . . Ps 89:19
the Lord had been my *h* . . . . Ps 94:17
there was none to *h* . . . . Ps 107:12
He is their *h* and . . . . Ps 115:9
Our *h* is in the name . . . . Ps 124:8
let no one *h* him . . . . Prov 28:17
h my unbelief . . . . Mark 9:24
tell her to *h* me . . . . Luke 10:40
and find grace to *h* . . . . Heb 4:16

HELPED
far the Lord has *h* . . . . 1 Sam 7:12

h the people to . . . . Neh 8:7
fall, but the Lord *h* . . . . Ps 118:13
of salvation I have *h* . . . . Is 49:8
h His servant Israel . . . . . . Luke 1:54

HELPER
I will make him a *h* . . . . Gen 2:18
Behold, God is my *h* . . . . Ps 54:4
give you another *H* . . . . John 14:16
"But when the *H* . . . . John 15:26
she has been a *h* . . . . Rom 16:2
"The Lord is my *h* . . . . Heb 13:6

HELPFUL
all things are not *h* . . . . 1 Cor 6:12

HELPS
the Spirit also *h* . . . . Rom 8:26
gifts of healings, *h* . . . . 1 Cor 12:28

HEM
and touched the *h* . . . . Matt 9:20
might only touch the *h* . . . . Matt 14:36

HEMAN
Composer of a psalm, Ps 88:title

HEMLOCK
judgment springs up like *h* . . Hos 10:4

HEN
as a *h* gathers her chicks . . Matt 23:37
as a *h* gathers her brood . . Luke 13:34

HENNA
is to me a cluster of *h* . . . . . Song 1:14
fragrant *h* with spikenard . . Song 4:13

HERB
the *h* that yields seed, and . . Gen 1:11
every green *h* for food . . . . . Gen 1:30
struck every *h* of the field . . . Ex 9:25
ate every *h* of the land . . . . . Ex 10:15
raindrops on the tender *h* . . Deut 32:2
field and the green *h* . . . . . 2 Kin 19:26
And wither as the green *h* . . . Ps 37:2
the field and the green *h* . . . . Is 37:27

HERBS
with bitter *h* they shall eat . . . Ex 12:8
bread and bitter *h* . . . . Num 9:11
a dinner of *h* where love . . Prov 15:17

HERD
And Abraham ran to the *h* . . Gen 18:7
a burnt sacrifice of the *h* . . . . Lev 1:3
tithe of the *h* or the flock . . Lev 27:32
there be no *h* in the stalls . . . Hab 3:17
into the *h* of swine . . . . Matt 8:31

HERE
Then I said, "*H* am I . . . . Is 6:8

HERE I AM
And he said, "*H* . . . . Gen 22:1
And he answered him, "*H* . . Gen 27:1
'Jacob.' And I said, '*H* . . . . Gen 31:11
So he said to him, "*H* . . . . . Gen 37:13
Jacob!" And he said, "*H* . . . Gen 46:2
Moses!" And he said, "*H* . . . . . Ex 3:4
And he answered, "*H* . . . . . 1 Sam 3:4
"*H*. Witness against me . . 1 Sam 12:3
h, let Him do to me as . . . 2 Sam 15:26
h, the first to come . . . . . 2 Sam 19:20
nor let the eunuch say, "*H* . . . Is 56:3
cry, and He will say, '*H* . . . . . Is 58:9
I said, '*H*, *h*.' to a nation . . . . Is 65:1
h, in your hand; do with . . . Jer 26:14
And he said, "*H* . . . . Acts 9:10

HERESIES
dissensions, *h* . . . . Gal 5:20
in destructive *h* . . . . 2 Pet 2:1

HERITAGE
give it to you as a *h* . . . . Ex 6:8
have given me the *h* . . . . Ps 61:5
for that is his *h* . . . . Eccl 3:22
for it is his *h* . . . . Eccl 5:18
This is the *h* of the . . . . Is 54:17
of My people, My *h* . . . . Joel 3:2

The flock of Your *h* . . . . Mic 7:14

HERMES
Paul acclaimed as, Acts 14:12

HERMON
Highest mountain (9,166 ft.) in Syria;
   also called Sirion, Shenir, Deut
   3:8, 9

HEROD
——— Herod the Great, procurator of
   Judea (37–4 B.C.), Luke 1:5
Inquires about Jesus' birth, Matt
   2:3–8
Slays infants of Bethlehem, Matt
   2:12–18
——— Herod Antipas, the tetrarch, ruler
   of Galilee and Perea (4 B.C.–A.D. 39),
   Luke 3:1
Imprisons John the Baptist, Luke
   3:18–21
Has John the Baptist beheaded, Matt
   14:1–12
Disturbed about Jesus, Luke 9:7–9
Jesus sent to him, Luke 23:7–11
——— Herod Agrippa I (A.D. 37–44), Acts
   12:1, 19
Kills James, Acts 12:1, 2
Imprisons Peter, Acts 12:3–11, 19
Slain by an angel, Acts 12:20–23
——— Herod Agrippa II (A.D. 53–70);
   called Agrippa and King Agrippa,
   Acts 25:22–24, 26
Festus tells him about Paul, Acts
   25:13–27
Paul makes a defense before, Acts
   26:1–32

HERODIANS
Join Pharisees against Jesus, Mark 3:6
Seek to trap Jesus, Matt 22:15–22
Jesus warns against, Mark 8:15

HERODIAS
Granddaughter of Herod the Great;
   plots John's death, Matt 14:3–12
Married her uncle, Mark 6:17, 18

HESHBON
Ancient Moabite city; taken by Moses,
   Num 21:23–34
Assigned to Reubenites, Num 32:1–37
Prophecies concerning, Is 15:1–4;
   16:8–14; Jer 48:2, 34, 35

HETH
Son of Canaan, Gen 10:15
Abraham buys field from sons of, Gen
   23:3–20
Esau marries daughters of, Gen 27:46

HEW
H for yourself two tablets . . Deut 10:1

HEWN
she has *h* out her seven . . . . . Prov 9:1
in a tomb that was *h* . . . . . Luke 23:53

HEZEKIAH
Righteous king of Judah; reforms tem-
   ple and worship, 2 Chr 29—31
Wars with Assyria; prayer for deliver-
   ance is answered, 2 Kin 18:7—19:37
His sickness and recovery; thanks-
   giving, 2 Kin 20:1–11; Is 38:9–22
Boasts to Babylonian ambassadors,
   2 Kin 20:12–19
Death, 2 Kin 20:20, 21

HID
naked; and I *h* myself . . . . . Gen 3:10
child, she *h* him three . . . . . . Ex 2:2
Egyptian and *h* him in the . . . . Ex 2:12
she *h* the messengers . . . . . Josh 6:25
David *h* in the field . . . . . 1 Sam 20:24
they *h* him and his nurse . . 2 Kin 11:2
And we *h*, as it were, our . . . . Is 53:3
and *h* his lord's money . . . . Matt 25:18

she *h* herself five months, .. Luke 1:24
h in three measures of .... Luke 13:21
but Jesus *h* Himself and ... John 8:59
h themselves in the caves ... Rev 6:15

HIDDEKEL
Hebrew name of the river Tigris, Gen
2:14; Dan 10:4

HIDDEN
and the LORD has *h*........ 2 Kin 4:27
It is *h* from the eyes .... Job 28:21
h Your righteousness .... Ps 40:10
and my sins are not *h* ...... Ps 69:5
Your word I have *h*........ Ps 119:11
h riches of secret places ...... Is 45:3
there His power was *h*....... Hab 3:4
h that will not .... Matt 10:26
the *h* wisdom which God ... 1 Cor 2:7
bring to light the *h*......... 1 Cor 4:5
have renounced the *h* ...... 2 Cor 4:2
rather let it be the *h* .... 1 Pet 3:4
give some of the *h* .... Rev 2:17

HIDE
h by the Brook Cherith, ... 1 Kin 17:3
If me under the shadow .... Ps 17:8
tabernacle He shall *h* me ..... Ps 27:5
You shall *h* them in .... Ps 31:20
O God, and do not *h* .... Ps 55:1
You *h* Your face .... Ps 104:29
darkness shall not *h* .... Ps 139:12
You are God, who *h*........ Is 45:15
h yourself from your .... Is 58:7
"Fall on us and *h* .... Rev 6:16

HIDES
He *h* His face .... Ps 10:11

HIDING
You are my *h* place .... Ps 32:7
A man will be as a *h* .... Is 32:2

HIEL
Native of Bethel; rebuilds Jericho,
1 Kin 16:34
Fulfills Joshua's curse, Josh 6:26

HIGH
See MOST HIGH
priest of God Most *H* ...... Gen 14:18
For the LORD Most *H*........ Ps 47:2
h is Your right hand .... Ps 89:13
are on *h* forevermore .... Ps 92:8
the LORD is on *h*........... Ps 138:6
"I dwell in the *h*........... Is 57:15
know that the Most *H* ...... Dan 4:17
whose habitation is *h*........ Obad 3
up on a *h* mountain by ..... Matt 17:1
your mind on *h* things .... Rom 12:16
h thing that exalts .... 2 Cor 10:5
and faithful *H* Priest .... Heb 2:17

HIGH PLACE
people today on the *h*...... 1 Sam 9:12
coming down from the *h* .. 1 Sam 10:5
great *h*: Solomon offered .... 1 Kin 3:4
Solomon built a *h* for ..... 1 Kin 11:7
h which Jeroboam the .... 2 Kin 23:15
h that was at Gibeon .... 1 Chr 16:39
Moab is weary on the *h* ...... Is 16:12
made a *h* for yourself in ... Ezek 16:24
this *h* to which you go?' .. Ezek 20:29

HIGH PLACES
I will destroy your *h* .... Lev 26:30
him up to the *h* of Baal .... Num 22:41
demolish all their *h* .... Num 33:52
shall tread down their *h* .. Deut 33:29
Israel is slain on your *h* ... 2 Sam 1:19
and sets me on my *h* .... 2 Sam 22:34
people sacrificed at the *h* ... 1 Kin 3:2
made shrines on the *h* .... 1 Kin 12:31
the *h* were not removed .. 1 Kin 15:14
He removed the *h* and .... 2 Kin 18:4
to burn incense on the *h* .. 2 Kin 23:5
He also removed the *h* .... 2 Chr 14:5

threw down the *h* and ..... 2 Chr 31:1
taken away His *h* .... 2 Chr 32:12
h, the wooden images ..... 2 Chr 34:3
He makes peace in His *h* .... Job 25:2
deer, and sets me on my *h* ... Ps 18:33
Him to anger with their *h* ... Ps 78:58
to the *h* to weep. Moab will ... Is 15:2
have built the *h* of Tophet ... Jer 7:31
your *h* of sin within all ...... Jer 17:3
I will destroy your *h* ...... Ezek 6:3
adorned multicolored *h* ... Ezek 16:16
of their kings on their *h*.... Ezek 43:7
Also the *h* of Aven, the sin ... Hos 10:8
who treads the *h* of the ... Amos 4:13

HIGH PRIEST
'And he who is the *h*...... Lev 21:10
until the death of the *h* ... Num 35:25
"Go up to Hilkiah the *h*... 2 Kin 22:4
h, was a son-in-law of ..... Neh 13:28
son of Jehozadak, the *h* .... Hag 1:1
showed me Joshua the *h* ... Zech 3:1
at the palace of the *h* ..... Matt 26:3
days of Abiathar the *h* .... Mark 2:26
servant of the *h*, and .... Mark 14:47
Caiaphas, being *h* that .... John 11:49
the courtyard of the *h* .... John 18:15
Annas the *h*, Caiaphas, ... Acts 4:6
of the Lord, went to the *h*.... Acts 9:1
h Ananias commanded ..... Acts 23:2
a merciful and faithful *H*.... Heb 2:17
we have a great *H* who .... Heb 4:14
we do not have a *H* who .... Heb 4:15
called by God as *H* .... Heb 5:10
H forever according to the .. Heb 6:20
We have such a *H*, who is .. Heb 8:1
h went alone once a year .... Heb 9:7
H over the house of God .. Heb 10:21

HIGHER
They are *h* than heaven ..... Job 11:8
you, 'Friend, go up *h*..... Luke 14:10
h than the heavens .... Heb 7:26

HIGHEST
the *h* heavens belong to ... Deut 10:14
Hosanna in the *h*!........ Matt 21:9
the power of the *H* will ... Luke 1:35
Glory to God in the *h* ..... Luke 2:14
and glory in the *h* .... Luke 19:38

HIGHLY
Rejoice, *h* favored one ... Luke 1:28
also has *h* exalted Him ...... Phil 2:9

HIGHWAY
of the upright is a *h*...... Prov 15:19
in the desert a *h* .... Is 40:3
up, build up the *h* .... Is 62:10

HIGHWAYS
h shall be elevated .... Is 49:11
go into the *h* .... Matt 22:9

HILKIAH
Shallum's son, 1 Chr 6:13
High priest in Josiah's reign, 2 Chr
34:9–22
Oversees temple work, 2 Kin 22:4–7
Finds the Book of the Law, 2 Kin
22:8–14
Aids in reformation, 2 Kin 23:4

HILL
My King on My holy *h* .... Ps 2:6
h cannot be hidden .... Matt 5:14
and *h* brought low .... Luke 3:5
to the brow of the *h* ...... Luke 4:29

HILLS
of the everlasting *h*........ Gen 49:26
possess is a land of *h* .... Deut 11:11
of the *h* are His also .... Ps 95:4
up my eyes to the *h* .... Ps 121:1
settled, before the *h*....... Prov 8:25

HINDER
takes away, who can *h* ...... Job 9:12

all things lest we *h* .... 1 Cor 9:12

HINDERED
come to you (but was *h* .... Rom 1:13
Who *h* you from obeying ..... Gal 5:7
prayers may not be *h* .... 1 Pet 3:7

HINDERS
h me from being baptized .. Acts 8:36

HINNOM, VALLEY OF THE SON OF
See TOPHET
Place near Jerusalem used for human
sacrifice, 2 Kin 23:10; 2 Chr 28:3; Jer
7:31, 32; 19:1–15

HIP
socket of Jacob's *h* .... Gen 32:25

HIRAM
King of Tyre; provided materials for
David's palace and Solomon's temple, 2 Sam 5:11; 1 Kin 5:1–12;
9:10–14, 26–28; 10:11; 1 Chr 14:1

HIRE
h laborers for his .... Matt 20:1

HIRED
h man who eagerly .... Job 7:2
as the years of a *h* man ..... Is 16:14
h about the eleventh hour .. Matt 20:9
h servants have bread .... Luke 15:17

HIRELING
The *h* flees because .... John 10:13

HIS MERCY ENDURES FOREVER
for He is good! For *H* .... 1 Chr 16:34
"For He is good, for *H* .... 2 Chr 5:13
"Praise the LORD, for *H* .. 2 Chr 20:21
For *H* toward Israel." .... Ezra 3:11
for He is good! For *H* ...... Ps 106:1
for He is good! For *H* ...... Ps 107:1
for He is good! For *H* ...... Ps 118:1
for He is good! For *H* ...... Ps 136:1
the LORD is good, for *H*.... Jer 33:11

HIS RIGHT HAND
Ephraim with *h* toward .... Gen 48:13
on the thumb of *h*, and on ... Lev 8:23
on *H* and on His left ..... 1 Kin 22:19
the saving strength of *H* ...... Ps 20:6
H and His holy arm have ..... Ps 98:1
A wise man's heart is at *h* .. Eccl 10:2
is under my head, and *h* .... Song 2:6
The LORD has sworn by *H*.... Is 62:8
He has drawn back *H* from .. Lam 2:3
when he held up *h* and his .. Dan 12:7
Satan standing at *h* to ...... Zech 3:1
will set the sheep on *H* .... Matt 25:33
a reed in *H*. And they ..... Matt 27:29
God has exalted to *H* ...... Acts 5:31
seated Him at *H* in .... Eph 1:20
He had in *H* seven stars ..... Rev 1:16
holds the seven stars in *H* .... Rev 2:1

HITTITES
One of seven Canaanite nations, Deut
7:1
Israelites intermarry with, Judg 3:5, 6;
1 Kin 11:1; Ezra 9:1, 2

HIVITES
One of seven Canaanite nations, Deut
7:1
Esau intermarries with, Gen 36:2
Gibeonites belong to, Josh 9:3, 7

HOLD
he took *h* of his father's ... Gen 48:17
for we must *h* a feast to the .. Ex 10:9
sorrow will take *h* of the .... Ex 15:14
trembling will take *h* of ..... Ex 15:15
took *h* of the doors of the .. Judg 16:3
took *h* of the horns of the .. 1 Kin 1:50
enough to *h* two seahs.... 1 Kin 18:32

out his hand to *h* the ark .. 1 Chr 13:9
Take *h* of shield and .... Ps 35:2
h my eyelids open .... Ps 77:4
right hand shall *h* .... Ps 139:10
LORD your God, will *h* .... Is 41:13
cisterns that can *h* no ...... Jer 2:13
I cannot *h* my peace .... Jer 4:19
Herod had laid *h* of John .. Matt 14:3
who had laid *h* of Jesus ... Matt 26:57
you *h* the tradition of men .. Mark 7:8
h fast that word .... 1 Cor 15:2
h fast our confession .... Heb 4:14
h fast and repent .... Rev 3:3
H fast what you have, that .. Rev 3:11

HOLES
"Foxes have *h* .... Matt 8:20

HOLIER
near me, for I am *h* .... Is 65:5

HOLIEST
the way into the *H* .... Heb 9:8
to enter the *H* by the ...... Heb 10:19

HOLINESS
You, glorious in *h* .... Ex 15:11
H to the LORD .... Ex 28:36
LORD in the beauty of *h* .. 1 Chr 16:29
has spoken in His *h* .... Ps 60:6
I have sworn by My *h* ...... Ps 89:35
h adorns Your house .... Ps 93:5
the Highway of *H* .... Is 35:8
to the Spirit of *h* .... Rom 1:4
spirit, perfecting *h* .... 2 Cor 7:1
uncleanness, but in *h* ...... 1 Thess 4:7
be partakers of His *h* ...... Heb 12:10

HOLY
See MOST HOLY PLACE

where you stand is *h* .... Ex 3:5
rest, a *h* Sabbath to the .... Ex 16:23
priests and a *h* nation ...... Ex 19:6
day, to keep it *h* .... Ex 20:8
put the *h* crown on the ..... Ex 29:6
the altar shall be most *h* ... Ex 29:37
It shall be a *h* anointing oil .. Ex 30:25
distinguish between *h* ..... Lev 10:10
the LORD your God am *h* .... Lev 19:2
the priest is *h* to his God .. Lev 21:7
all the congregation is *h* ... Num 16:3
"No one is *h* like the ...... 1 Sam 2:2
priest gave him *h* bread .. 1 Sam 21:6
the *h* ark in the house ..... 2 Chr 35:3
h seed is mixed .... Ezra 9:2
This day is *h* to the LORD .... Neh 8:9
h ones will you turn .... Job 5:1
LORD is in His *h* temple....... Ps 11:4
may dwell in Your *h* hill ..... Ps 15:1
H One to see corruption ..... Ps 16:10
God sits on His *h* .... Ps 47:8
God, in His *h* mountain....... Ps 48:1
my life, for I am *h* .... Ps 86:2
"*H, h, h* is the LORD........... Is 6:3
H One of Israel, in truth ..... Is 10:20
destroy in all My *h* .... Is 11:9
hallow the *H* One of Jacob .. Is 29:23
Redeemer, the *H* One of ..... Is 41:14
call them The *H* People ..... Is 62:12
It shall be the *h* district ... Ezek 48:21
Spirit of the *H* God is in .... Dan 4:9
I heard a *h* one speaking ... Dan 8:13
the *h* angels with Him .... Matt 25:31
name of Your *h* Servant .... Acts 4:30
if the firstfruit is *h* .... Rom 11:16
bodies a living sacrifice, *h* .. Rom 12:1
one another with a *h* ...... Rom 16:16
that we should be *h* .... Eph 1:4
lifting up *h* hands, without .. 1 Tim 2:8
called us with a *h* calling .. 2 Tim 1:9
has not entered the *h* ...... Heb 9:24
He who called you is *h* .... 1 Pet 1:15
it is written, "Be *h* .... 1 Pet 1:16
a *h* priesthood, to offer up ... 1 Pet 2:5
a *h* nation, His own special .. 1 Pet 2:9

you to be in *h* conduct ..... 2 Pet 3:11
says He who is *h* .... Rev 3:7
H, h, h, Lord God .... Rev 4:8
For You alone are *h* .... Rev 15:4
is *h*, let him be *h* .... Rev 22:11

HOLY CITY
dwell in Jerusalem, the *h* ... Neh 11:1
call themselves after the *h* .... Is 48:2
O Jerusalem, the *h* .... Is 52:1
people and for your *h* ..... Dan 9:24
took Him up into the *h* ..... Matt 4:5
they went into the *h* and .. Matt 27:53
they will tread the *h* under .. Rev 11:2
Then I, John, saw the *h* .... Rev 21:2
Book of Life, from the *h* ... Rev 22:19

HOLY NAME
and profane My *h* .... Lev 20:3
Glory in His *h*; let .... 1 Chr 16:10
You a house for Your *h* .. 1 Chr 29:16
remembrance of His *h* ...... Ps 30:4
we have trusted in His *h* .... Ps 33:21
remembrance of His *h* ...... Ps 97:12
is within me, bless His *h* ... Ps 103:1
Glory in His *h*; let the ...... Ps 105:3
to give thanks to Your *h* ... Ps 106:47
all flesh shall bless His *h* .. Ps 145:21
profane My *h* no more .... Ezek 20:39
I had concern for My *h* .... Ezek 36:21
be jealous for My *h* ...... Ezek 39:25
same girl, to defile My *h* ... Amos 2:7

HOLY ONE OF ISRAEL
on high? Against the *H* ... 2 Kin 19:22
sing with the harp, O *H* ..... Ps 71:22
And our king to the *H* ...... Ps 89:18
have provoked to anger the *H* .. Is 1:4
depend on the LORD, the *H* ... Is 10:20
great is the *H* in your midst ... Is 12:6
and your Redeemer, the *H* ... Is 41:14
LORD who is faithful, the *H*... Is 49:7
of the LORD, Zion of the *H* .. Is 60:14
the LORD, against the *H*..... Jer 50:29

HOLY PLACE
between the *h* and the ...... Ex 26:33
when he goes into the *h* .... Ex 28:29
sweet incense for the *h* ..... Ex 31:11
it shall be eaten in a *h* ..... Lev 6:16
any time into the *H* inside ... Lev 16:2
most *h* you shall eat ...... Num 18:10
sanctuary, as the Most *H* .. 1 Kin 6:16
the needs of the *h*, and ... 1 Chr 23:32
And he made the Most *H* .. 2 Chr 3:8
H, under the wings of the .. 2 Chr 5:7
the rubbish from the *h* .... 2 Chr 29:5
stand in the *h* according .. 2 Chr 35:5
to give us a peg in His *h* .... Ezra 9:8
who may stand in His *h*? .... Ps 24:3
the *h* of the tabernacle of ..... Ps 46:4
as in Sinai, in the *H* .... Ps 68:17
"I dwell in the high and *h* .... Is 57:15
"This is the Most *H* .... Ezek 41:4
standing in the *h* .... Matt 24:15
words against this *h* and ... Acts 6:13
and has defiled this *h* .... Acts 21:28
He entered the Most *H* ..... Heb 9:12
priest enters the Most *H* .... Heb 9:25

HOLY SPIRIT
See FILLED WITH THE HOLY SPIRIT
Affirmed as divine:
 called God, Acts 5:3, 4
 joined with the Father and the Son,
  Matt 28:19; 2 Cor 13:14
 eternal, Heb 9:14
 omnipotent, Luke 1:35
 omniscient, 1 Cor 2:10, 11
 omnipresent, Ps 139:7–13
 Creator, Gen 1:2
 sovereign, 1 Cor 12:6, 11
 new creation, John 3:3, 8
 sin against, unforgiveable, Matt 12:31,
  32

Work of:
 speaks in Scripture, Acts 1:16, 17;
  28:25; 2 Tim 3:16
 role in Christ's ministry, Matt 3:16;
  12:28; Luke 1:35; 4:1, 17, 18; Rom 1:4;
  1 Tim 3:16; Heb 9:14
 regenerates, John 3:3, 5
 indwells, Rom 8:11
 anoints, 1 John 2:20, 27
 baptizes, Acts 2:17–41
 guides, John 16:13
 empowers, Mic 3:8
 sanctifies, Rom 15:16; 2 Thess 2:13
 bears witness, Rom 8:16; Heb 10:15
 helps, John 14:16–26
 gives joy, Rom 14:17
 gives discernment, 1 Cor 2:10–16;
  1 John 4:1–6
 bears fruit, Gal 5:22, 23
 gives gifts, 1 Cor 12:3–11
 comforts, Acts 9:31
 illuminates the mind, 1 Cor 2:12, 13;
  Eph 1:16, 17
 reveals things of God, Is 40:13, 14;
  1 Cor 2:10, 13
Promised, Joel 2:28–32
Received by disciples, Acts 2:1–21
Received by Gentiles, Acts 10:45
Persons filled by:
 Bezalel, Ex 31:2
 Jesus, Luke 4:1
 John the Baptist, Luke 1:15, 60
 Elizabeth, Luke 1:41
 Zacharias, Luke 1:67
 Pentecost Christians, Acts 2:1–4
 Peter, Acts 4:8
 seven deacons, Acts 6:3–5
 Stephen, Acts 7:55
 Barnabas, Acts 11:22, 24
 Paul, Acts 13:9
 certain disciples, Acts 13:52

not take Your *H* from me .... Ps 51:11
rebelled and grieved His *H* ... Is 63:10
found with child of the *H* ... Matt 1:18
baptize you with the *H* ..... Matt 3:11
speaks against the *H*, it ... Matt 12:32
of the Son and of the *H* ... Matt 28:19
himself said by the *H* ..... Mark 12:36
who speak, but the *H* .... Mark 13:11
filled with the *H*, even .... Luke 1:15
was filled with the *H* ...... Luke 1:41
the *H*, and prophesied ..... Luke 1:67
and the *H* was upon him .... Luke 2:25
And the *H* descended in .... Luke 3:22
being filled with the *H* ...... Luke 4:1
Father give the *H* .... Luke 11:13
the *H* was not yet given .... John 7:39
"But the Helper, the *H* .... John 14:26
to them, "Receive the *H* .. John 20:22
be baptized with the *H* ...... Acts 1:5
receive power when the *H* ... Acts 1:8
were all filled with the *H* .... Acts 2:4
the promise of the *H* ...... Acts 2:33
receive the gift of the *H* .... Acts 2:38
Peter, filled with the *H* ..... Acts 4:8
were all filled with the *H* .... Acts 4:31
to lie to the *H* and keep ..... Acts 5:3
full of the *H* and wisdom ... Acts 6:3
You always resist the *H* .... Acts 7:51
they might receive the *H* .... Acts 8:15
and be filled with the *H* .... Acts 9:17
in the comfort of the *H* ..... Acts 9:31
the *H* fell upon all those ... Acts 10:44
the *H* fell upon them, as ... Acts 11:15
the *H* said, "Now separate .. Acts 13:2
with joy and with the *H* .... Acts 13:52
by giving them the *H* just ... Acts 15:8
it seemed good to the *H* ... Acts 15:28
were forbidden by the *H*.... Acts 16:6
the *H* testifies in every .... Acts 20:23
H has made you .... Acts 20:28

HOME (cont.)

says the *H*, "So shall the .. Acts 21:11
out in our hearts by the *H* ... Rom 5:5
me witness in the *H* .... Rom 9:1
peace and joy in the *H* .... Rom 14:17
sanctified by the *H* .... Rom 15:16
but which the *H* teaches .. 1 Cor 2:13
is the temple of the *H* ..... 1 Cor 6:19
is Lord except by the *H* ... 1 Cor 12:3
by kindness, by the *H* ...... 2 Cor 6:6
were sealed with the *H* of ... Eph 1:13
And do not grieve the *H* .... Eph 4:30
by the *H* who dwells ...... 2 Tim 1:14
and renewing of the *H* .... Titus 3:5
miracles, and gifts of the *H* .. Heb 2:4
become partakers of the *H* .. Heb 6:4
were moved by the *H* ...... 2 Pet 1:21
the Word, and the *H* ...... 1 John 5:7

HOME

LORD has brought me *h* .... Ruth 1:21
sparrow has found a *h* .... Ps 84:3
the stork has her *h* .... Ps 104:17
to his eternal *h* .... Eccl 12:5
said to him, "Go *h* .... Mark 5:19
into an everlasting *h* ...... Luke 16:9
to him and make Our *h* ... John 14:23
took her to his own *h* .... John 19:27
let him eat at *h* .... 1 Cor 11:34
own husbands at *h* .... 1 Cor 14:35
that while we are at *h* ...... 2 Cor 5:6
to show piety at *h* .... 1 Tim 5:4

HOMELESS

and beaten, and *h* .... 1 Cor 4:11

HOMEMAKERS

be discreet, chaste, *h* .... Titus 2:5

HOMOSEXUALS

nor adulterers, nor *h*, nor ... 1 Cor 6:9

HONEST

we are *h* men .... Gen 42:11

HONEY

See MILK AND HONEY
flowing with milk and *h* ..Num 16:13
"What is sweeter than *h* ..Judg 14:18
I tasted a little of this *h* .. 1 Sam 14:29
Sweeter also than *h* and ..... Ps 19:10
and with *h* from the .... Ps 81:16
sweeter than *h* to my ..... Ps 119:103
My son, eat *h* because .... Prov 24:13
not good to eat much *h* ... Prov 25:27
h and milk are under ..... Song 4:11
was locusts and wild *h* .... Matt 3:4
sweet as *h* in my mouth .... Rev 10:10

HONEYCOMB

than honey and the *h* ...... Ps 19:10
words are like a *h* .... Prov 16:24
fish and some *h* .... Luke 24:42

HONOR

H your father and your .... .Ex 20:12
both riches and *h* .... 1 Kin 3:13
the king delights to *h* ...... Esth 6:6
earth, and lay my *h* .... Ps 7:5
A man who is in *h* .... Ps 49:20
Sing out the *h* of His ...... Ps 66:2
will deliver him and *h* ...... Ps 91:15
H and majesty are .... Ps 96:6
h have all His saints ...... Ps 149:9
H the LORD with your ...... Prov 3:9
before *h* is humility ...... Prov 15:33
h is not fitting .... Prov 26:1
spirit will retain *h* .... Prov 29:23
Father, where is My *h* ...... Mal 1:6
is not without *h* .... Matt 13:57
'*H* your father and your .... Matt 15:4
h the Son just as they .... John 5:23
"I do not receive *h* ...... John 5:41
but I *h* My Father .... John 8:49
"If I *h* Myself .... John 8:54
him My Father will *h* .... John 12:26
make one vessel for *h* ..... Rom 9:21
to whom fear, *h* .... Rom 13:7
we bestow greater *h* ..... 1 Cor 12:23

sanctification and *h* ...... 1 Thess 4:4
alone is wise, be *h* .... 1 Tim 1:17
worthy of double *h* .... 1 Tim 5:17
and clay, some for *h* ...... 2 Tim 2:20
no man takes this *h* .... Heb 5:4
H the king .... 1 Pet 2:17
from God the Father *h* ..... 2 Pet 1:17
give glory and *h* .... Rev 4:9

HONORABLE

of God, and he is an *h* ... 1 Sam 9:6
His work is an *h* .... Ps 111:3
It is *h* for a man to .... Prov 20:3
traders are the *h* .... Is 23:8
holy day of the LORD *h* ... Is 58:13
providing *h* things .... 2 Cor 8:21
Marriage is *h* among ...... Heb 13:4
having your conduct *h* ..... 1 Pet 2:12

HONORABLY

desiring to live *h* .... Heb 13:18

HONORS

h those who fear the .... Ps 15:4
'This people *h* Me .... Mark 7:6
It is My Father who *h* ..... John 8:54

HOOKS

will lament who cast *h* .... Is 19:8
spears into pruning *h* .... Mic 4:3

HOOVES

those that have cloven *h* .... Lev 11:4
I will make your *h* bronze ... Mic 4:13

HOPE

I should say I have *h* ...... Ruth 1:12
are spent without *h* .... Job 7:6
so You destroy the *h* ...... Job 14:19
where then is my *h* .... Job 17:15
h He has uprooted .... Job 19:10
also will rest in *h* .... Ps 16:9
heart, all you who *h* .... Ps 31:24
My *h* is in You .... Ps 39:7
For You are my *h* .... Ps 71:5
I *h* in Your word .... Ps 119:147
O Israel, *h* in the .... Ps 130:7
h will not be cut .... Prov 23:18
There is more *h* .... Prov 26:12
the living there is *h* .... Eccl 9:4
O the *H* of Israel .... Jer 14:8
good that one should *h* .... Lam 3:26
Achor as a door of *h* ...... Hos 2:15
you prisoners of *h* .... Zech 9:12
I have *h* in God .... Acts 24:15
to *h*, in *h* believed .... Rom 4:18
and rejoice in *h* .... Rom 5:2
h does not disappoint ...... Rom 5:5
h that is seen is .... Rom 8:24
But if we *h* for what ...... Rom 8:25
And now abide faith, *h* ... 1 Cor 13:13
life only we have *h* ...... 1 Cor 15:19
may know what is the *h* .... Eph 1:18
were called in one *h* .... Eph 4:4
h which is laid .... Col 1:5
Christ in you, the *h* .... Col 1:27
For what is our *h* .... 1 Thess 2:19
others who have no *h* ... 1 Thess 4:13
and as a helmet the *h* .... 1 Thess 5:8
Jesus Christ, our *h* .... 1 Tim 1:1
in *h* of eternal life .... Titus 1:2
for the blessed *h* .... Titus 2:13
to lay hold of the *h* .... Heb 6:18
of a better *h* .... Heb 7:19
us again to a living *h* ...... 1 Pet 1:3
you a reason for the *h* .... 1 Pet 3:15
who has this *h* in Him ..... 1 John 3:3

HOPED

substance of things *h* ...... Heb 11:1

HOPHNI

Wicked son of Eli, 1 Sam 1:3; 2:12–17,
22–25
Prophecy against, 1 Sam 2:27–36;
3:11–14
Carries ark into battle; killed, 1 Sam
4:1–11

HOR

Mountain of Edom; scene of Aaron's
death, Num 20:22–29; 33:37–39

HOREB

See SINAI
God appears to Moses at, Ex 3:1–22
Water flows from, Ex 17:6
Elijah lodged here 40 days, 1 Kin
19:8, 9

HORITES

Inhabitants of Mt. Seir, Gen 36:20
Defeated by Chedorlaomer, Gen
14:5, 6
Driven out by Esau's descendants, Gen
36:20–29; Deut 2:12, 22

HORMAH

Destroyed by Israel, Num 21:1–3

HORN

my shield and the *h* .... Ps 18:2
h will be exalted .... Ps 112:9
goat had a notable *h* .... Dan 8:5
and has raised up a *h* .... Luke 1:69

HORRIBLE

h thing has been .... Jer 5:30
I have seen a *h* .... Hos 6:10

HORROR

and behold, *h* and .... Gen 15:12
sorrow, the cup of *h* ..... Ezek 23:33
you will become a *h* ..... Ezek 27:36

HORSE

The *h* and its rider He ...... Ex 15:1
Have you given the *h* ...... Job 39:19
h is a vain hope .... Ps 33:17
the strength of the *h* ..... Ps 147:10
h is prepared for the ...... Prov 21:31
and behold, a white *h* .... Rev 6:2
and behold, a black *h* .... Rev 6:5
and behold, a pale *h* .... Rev 6:8
and behold, a white *h* ..... Rev 19:11

HORSES

seen servants on *h* .... Eccl 10:7
h are swifter than .... Jer 4:13
Do *h* run on rocks .... Amos 6:12
we put bits in *h* .... James 3:3

HOSANNA

H in the highest .... Matt 21:9

HOSEA

Son of Beeri, prophet of the northern
kingdom, Hos 1:1

HOSHEA

Original name of Joshua, the son of
Nun, Deut 32:44; Num 13:8, 16
——— Israel's last king; usurps throne,
2 Kin 15:30
Reigns wickedly; Israel taken to
Assyria during his reign, 2 Kin
17:1–23

HOSPITABLE

of good behavior, *h* .... 1 Tim 3:2
Be *h* to one another .... 1 Pet 4:9

HOST

who brings out their *h* ..... Is 40:26
of the heavenly *h* .... Luke 2:13

HOST OF HEAVEN

all the *h*, you feel driven ... Deut 4:19
throne, and all the *h* ..... 1 Kin 22:19
worshiped all the *h* ...... 2 Kin 17:16
and for all the *h* .... 2 Kin 23:4
The *h* worships You .... Neh 9:6
All the *h* shall be dissolved .... Is 34:4
the moon and all the *h* ...... Jer 8:2
burned incense to all the *h* .. Jer 19:13
the *h* cannot be numbered .. Jer 33:22
And it grew up to the *h* .. Dan 8:10
them up to worship the *h* ... Acts 7:42

HOSTILITY

Him who endured such *h* ... Heb 12:3

HOSTS

See LORD GOD OF HOSTS; LORD OF
HOSTS

name of the LORD of *h* . . . 1 Sam 17:45
As the LORD of *h* lives . . . . 1 Kin 18:15
The LORD of *h* is with . . . . Ps 46:7
LORD, all you His *h* . . . . Ps 103:21
praise Him, all His *h* . . . . Ps 148:2
word of the LORD of *h* . . . . Is 39:5
LORD of *h* is His name . . . . Is 47:4
against spiritual *h* . . . . Eph 6:12

HOT

of the LORD was *h* . . . . Judg 2:14
My heart was *h* within . . . . Ps 39:3
are neither cold nor *h* . . . . . . Rev 3:15

HOUND

My enemies would *h* . . . . Ps 56:2

HOUR

h what you should . . . . Matt 10:19
day and *h* no one knows . . Matt 24:36
Man is coming at an *h* . . . . Matt 24:44
Behold, the *h* is at . . . . Matt 26:45
But this is your *h* . . . . Luke 22:53
h has not yet come . . . . John 2:4
But the *h* is coming . . . . John 4:23
h has come that the . . . . . . John 12:23
save Me from this *h* . . . . . . John 12:27
"Father, the *h* has come . . . . John 17:1
will not know what *h* . . . . . . Rev 3:3
keep you from the *h* . . . . . . Rev 3:10

HOURS

Are there not twelve *h* . . . . John 11:9

HOUSE

from your father's *h* . . . . . . Gen 12:1
But as for me and my *h* . . Josh 24:15
h appointed for all . . . . Job 30:23
with them to the *h* . . . . Ps 42:4
the goodness of Your *h* . . . . . Ps 65:4
For her *h* leads down . . . . . . Prov 2:18
Through wisdom a *h* . . . . . . Prov 24:3
better to go to the *h* . . . . Eccl 7:2
of the *h* tremble . . . . Eccl 12:3
to the *h* of the God of . . . . Is 2:3
to those who join in . . . . Is 5:8
h was filled with . . . . Is 6:4
'Set your *h* in order . . . . Is 38:1
h shall be called a . . . . Is 56:7
built his *h* on the rock . . . . Matt 7:24
and beat on that *h* . . . . Matt 7:25
blew and beat on that *h* . . . Matt 7:27
had come into Peter's *h* . . . Matt 8:14
came into the ruler's *h* . . . . Matt 9:23
sheep of the *h* of Israel . . . Matt 10:6
h divided against . . . . Matt 12:25
enter a strong man's *h* . . . Matt 12:29
h shall be called a . . . . Matt 21:13
Your *h* is left to you . . . . . . Matt 23:38
the *h* of Simon the leper . . Matt 26:6
no one who has left *h* . . . . Mark 10:29
My *h* shall be called a *h* . . Mark 11:17
the *h* of Zacharias . . . . Luke 1:40
bed, and go to your *h* . . . . . Luke 5:24
ruin of that *h* was great . . . Luke 6:49
Whatever *h* you enter . . . . . . Luke 9:4
h may be filled . . . . Luke 14:23
light a lamp, sweep the *h* . . Luke 15:8
has come to this *h* . . . . Luke 19:9
make My Father's *h* . . . . John 2:16
for Your *h* has eaten Me . . . John 2:17
the *h* was filled with the . . . John 12:3
h are many mansions . . . . . John 14:2
bread from *h* to *h*, they . . . . Acts 2:46
hour I prayed in my *h* . . . . Acts 10:30
in the *h* of Simon . . . . Acts 10:32
publicly and from *h* . . . . . . Acts 20:20
in his own rented *h* . . . . . . Acts 28:30
church that is in their *h* . . . Rom 16:5
a *h* not made with hands, . . 2 Cor 5:1
who rules his own *h* . . . . . . 1 Tim 3:4
children, manage the *h* . . . . 1 Tim 5:14

in a great *h* there are . . . . . 2 Tim 2:20
the church in your *h* . . . . Philem 2
has more honor than the *h* . . . Heb 3:3
For every *h* is built . . . . Heb 3:4
His own *h*, whose *h* . . . . Heb 3:6
Priest over the *h* of God . . . Heb 10:21
being built up a spiritual *h* . . 1 Pet 2:5
to begin at the *h* of God . . . . 1 Pet 4:17
him into your *h* . . . . 2 John 1:10

HOUSE OF DAVID

a covenant with the *h* . . . . 1 Sam 20:16
house of Saul and the *h* . . . . 2 Sam 3:1
rebellion against the *h* . . . . 1 Kin 12:19
may return to the *h* . . . . . . 1 Kin 12:26
shall be born to the *h* . . . . . 1 Kin 13:2
away from the *h* . . . . 1 Kin 14:8
shall not dwell in the *h* . . . 2 Chr 8:11
would not destroy the *h* . . . 2 Chr 21:7
the wall, beyond the *h* . . . . . Neh 12:37
the thrones of the *h* . . . . . . Ps 122:5
And it was told to the *h* . . . . . . Is 7:2
The key of the *h* I will lay . . . Is 22:22
'O *h*!' Thus says the LORD: . . . Jer 21:12
h shall be like God . . . . Zech 12:8
was Joseph, of the *h* . . . . . Luke 1:27

HOUSE OF GOD

none other than the *h* . . . . Gen 28:17
the *h* was in Shiloh . . . . . Judg 18:31
of the tabernacle of the *h* . . 1 Chr 6:48
stones to build the *h* . . . . . 1 Chr 22:2
all the service of the *h* . . . 1 Chr 28:21
King Solomon for the *h* . . . 2 Chr 4:11
of the LORD filled the *h* . . . 2 Chr 5:14
people dedicated the *h* . . . . . 2 Chr 7:5
also brought into the *h* . . . 2 Chr 15:18
with them in the *h* . . . . . . 2 Chr 22:12
articles from the *h* . . . . . . 2 Chr 36:18
freewill offerings for the *h* . . Ezra 1:4
oversee the work of the *h* . . . Ezra 3:8
or the courts of the *h* . . . . . Neh 8:16
"Why is the *h* forsaken?" . . Neh 13:11
I went with them to the *h* . . . Ps 42:4
a green olive tree in the *h* . . Ps 52:8
walked to the *h* in the . . . . . Ps 55:14
when you go to the *h* . . . . . . Eccl 5:1
the articles of the *h* . . . . Dan 1:2
from the temple of the *h* . . . Dan 5:3
how he entered the *h* and . . Matt 12:4
conduct yourself in the *h* . . 1 Tim 3:15
High Priest over the *h* . . . . Heb 10:21
to begin at the *h* . . . . 1 Pet 4:17

HOUSE OF THE LORD

you shall bring into the *h* . . . Ex 23:19
price of a dog to the *h* . . . . Deut 23:18
into the treasury of the *h* . . . Josh 6:24
she went up to the *h* . . . . . 1 Sam 1:7
brought him to the *h* . . . . . 1 Sam 1:24
he went into the *h* and . . . 2 Sam 12:20
his own house, and the *h* . . . 1 Kin 3:1
he began to build the *h* . . . . 1 Kin 6:1
the cloud filled the *h* . . . . . 1 Kin 8:10
hidden with her in the *h* . . . 2 Kin 11:3
the damage of the *h* . . . . . 2 Kin 12:12
service of song in the *h* . . . 1 Chr 6:31
David said, "This is the *h* . . 1 Chr 22:1
began to build the *h* . . . . . . 2 Chr 3:1
for the *h* was finished . . . . . 2 Chr 5:1
So the *h* was completed. . . 2 Chr 8:16
heart on repairing the *h* . . 2 Chr 24:4
cut off from the *h* . . . . . . 2 Chr 26:21
of the *h* to cleanse it . . . . 2 Chr 29:16
built altars in the *h* . . . . . 2 Chr 33:4
of the Law in the *h* . . . . . 2 Chr 34:15
from the *h* to Babylon . . . . 2 Chr 36:7
build the *h* God of Israel . . . Ezra 1:3
heart, to beautify the *h* . . . . Ezra 7:27
I will dwell in the *h* forever . . . Ps 23:6
that I may dwell in the *h* . . . . Ps 27:4
who are planted in the *h* . . . Ps 92:13
"Let us go into the *h* . . . . . Ps 122:1
Hezekiah went up to the *h* . . Is 37:14

these words in the *h* . . . . . . Jer 26:7
of praise into the *h*. For I . . Jer 33:11
He burned the *h* and the . . . Jer 52:13
noise in the *h* as on the . . . Lam 2:7
LORD filled the *h*; and I . . Ezek 44:4
it shall not come into the *h* . . Hos 9:4
shall flow from the *h* . . . . . . Joel 3:18
came and worked on the *h* . . Hag 1:14
priests who were in the *h* . . Zech 7:3

HOUSEHOLD

over the ways of her *h* . . . Prov 31:27
If the *h* is worthy . . . . Matt 10:13
be those of his own *h* . . . . Matt 10:36
make ruler over his *h* . . . . Luke 12:42
h were baptized . . . . Acts 16:15
saved, you and your *h* . . . . Acts 16:31
also baptized the *h* . . . . . . 1 Cor 1:16
the *h* of Stephanas . . . . . . 1 Cor 16:15
those who are of the *h* . . . . Gal 6:10
who are of Caesar's *h* . . . . Phil 4:22
mercy to the *h* of . . . . 2 Tim 1:16
ark for the saving of his *h* . . Heb 11:7

HOUSEHOLDER

h who brings out of . . . . . . Matt 13:52

HOUSEHOLDS

that He provided *h* for . . . . . . Ex 1:21
heads of the fathers' *h* . . . Ezra 10:16
those who creep into *h* . . . . 2 Tim 3:6
who subvert whole *h* . . . . . . Titus 1:11

HOUSES

h are safe from fear . . . . Job 21:9
Yet He filled their *h* . . . . Job 22:18
is that their *h* will last . . . . . Ps 49:11
H and riches are an . . . . . . Prov 19:14
who has left *h* or . . . . Matt 19:29
you devour widows' *h* . . . . Matt 23:14
Do you not have *h* . . . . . . 1 Cor 11:22

HOUSETOP

dwell in a corner of a *h* . . . Prov 25:24
they went up on the *h* . . . . Luke 5:19
went up on the *h* to pray, . . . Acts 10:9

HOUSETOPS

herb, as the grass on the *h* . . Is 37:27
ear, preach on the *h* . . . . . Matt 10:27
be proclaimed on the *h* . . . . Luke 12:3

HOVERING

Spirit of God was *h* . . . . Gen 1:2

HOW

"*H* can this be . . . . Luke 1:34
H long do You keep . . . . . . John 10:24
h you turned to God . . . . . 1 Thess 1:9

HULDAH

Wife of Shallum, 2 Kin 22:14
Foretells Jerusalem's ruin, 2 Kin
22:15–17; 2 Chr 34:22–25
Exempts Josiah from trouble, 2 Kin
22:18–20

HUMAN

broken without *h* means . . . Dan 8:25
for joy that a *h* being . . . . . John 16:21
I speak in *h* terms . . . . Rom 6:19
words of *h* wisdom . . . . . . 1 Cor 2:4
we have had *h* fathers . . . . Heb 12:9

HUMBLE

man Moses was very *h* . . . Num 12:3
h you and test you . . . . Deut 8:2
who is proud, and *h* . . . . . Job 40:11
the cry of the *h* . . . . Ps 9:12
Do not forget the *h* . . . . . . Ps 10:12
the desire of the *h* . . . . . . Ps 10:17
H He guides in justice . . . . . Ps 25:9
h shall hear of it and . . . . . Ps 34:2
LORD lifts up the *h* . . . . . Ps 147:6
h spirit with the . . . . Prov 16:19
contrite and *h* spirit . . . . . Is 57:15
a meek and *h* people . . . . Zeph 3:12
associate with the *h* . . . . . Rom 12:16
gives grace to the *h* . . . . . James 4:6

H yourselves in the . . . . James 4:10
gives grace to the *h* . . . . 1 Pet 5:5
h yourselves under the . . . . . . 1 Pet 5:6

HUMBLED
h himself greatly . . . . 2 Chr 33:12
as a man, He *h* Himself . . . . . . Phil 2:8

HUMBLES
h Himself to behold . . . . Ps 113:6

HUMILIATION
to plunder, and to *h* . . . . Ezra 9:7
h His justice was . . . . Acts 8:33
but the rich in his *h* . . . . . James 1:10

HUMILITY
By *h* and the fear of . . . . . . Prov 22:4
righteousness, seek *h* . . . . Zeph 2:3
the Lord with all *h* . . . . . . Acts 20:19
delight in false *h* . . . . Col 2:18
mercies, kindness, *h* . . . . Col 3:12
h correcting those . . . . 2 Tim 2:25
gentle, showing all *h* . . . . Titus 3:2
and be clothed with *h* . . . . . . 1 Pet 5:5

HUNDRED
Adam lived were nine *h* . . . . . Gen 5:5
of Lamech were seven *h* . . . . Gen 5:31
of Jacob's life was one *h* . . Gen 47:28
Joseph lived one *h* and . . . . Gen 50:22
one *h* cubits long for one . . . . . Ex 27:9
of which was one *h* . . . . Num 7:13
for a *h* foreskins of the . . . 2 Sam 3:14
one *h* summer fruits . . . . . 2 Sam 16:1
had taken one *h* prophets . . 1 Kin 18:4

HUNDREDFOLD
in the same year a *h* . . . . Gen 26:12
some a *h*, some sixty . . . . . Matt 13:8
receive a *h* now in this . . . Mark 10:30
up, and yielded a crop a *h* . . Luke 8:8

HUNGER
you, allowed you to *h* . . . . . . Deut 8:3
lack and suffer *h* . . . . Ps 34:10
They shall neither *h* . . . . Is 49:10
likely to die from *h* . . . . Jer 38:9
are those who *h* . . . . Matt 5:6
for you shall *h* . . . . Luke 6:25
to Me shall never *h* . . . . John 6:35
present hour we both *h* . . . . 1 Cor 4:11
They shall neither *h* . . . . Rev 7:16

HUNGRY
bread from the *h* . . . . Job 22:7
and fills the *h* . . . . Ps 107:9
gives food to the *h* . . . . Ps 146:7
h soul every bitter . . . . Prov 27:7
your soul to the *h* . . . . Is 58:10
for I was *h* and you . . . . . . Matt 25:35
when did we see You *h* . . . Matt 25:37
and one is *h* and . . . . . . 1 Cor 11:21
But if anyone is *h* . . . . 1 Cor 11:34
to be full and to be *h* . . . . . . Phil 4:12

HUNT
Yet you *h* my life to . . . . . 1 Sam 24:11
h the violent man . . . . Ps 140:11
h the souls of My . . . . Ezek 13:18

HUNTER
Nimrod the mighty *h* . . . . . . Gen 10:9
Esau was a skillful *h* . . . . . Gen 25:27

HUR
Man of Judah; of Caleb's house, 1 Chr
2:18–20
Supports Moses' hands, Ex 17:10–12
Aids Aaron, Ex 24:14

HURAM
Master craftsman of Solomon's temple,
1 Kin 7:13–40, 45; 2 Chr 2:13, 14

HURT
h a woman with child . . . . Ex 21:22
who plot my *h* . . . . Ps 35:4
but I was not *h* . . . . Prov 23:35
another to his own *h* . . . . Eccl 8:9

They shall not *h* . . . . Is 11:9
of my people I am *h* . . . . Jer 8:21
Woe is me for my *h* . . . . Jer 10:19
it will by no means *h* . . . . Mark 16:18
shall not be *h* by the . . . . Rev 2:11

HUSBAND
She also gave to her *h* . . . . . . Gen 3:6
desire shall be for your *h* . . . Gen 3:16
"Surely you are a *h* . . . . Ex 4:25
Uriah her *h* was dead . . . . 2 Sam 11:26
h safely trusts her . . . . . Prov 31:11
Her *h* is known in the . . . . . Prov 31:23
your Maker is your *h* . . . . Is 54:5
though I was a *h* . . . . Jer 31:32
you will call Me "My *H* . . . . . Hos 2:16
I have no *h* . . . . John 4:17
now have is not your *h* . . . . . John 4:18
But if the *h* dies, she is . . . . . . Rom 7:2
woman have her own *h* . . . . . 1 Cor 7:2
For the unbelieving *h* . . . . . 1 Cor 7:14
you will save your *h* . . . . . . 1 Cor 7:16
betrothed you to one *h* . . . . 2 Cor 11:2
For the *h* is head of . . . . Eph 5:23
the *h* of one wife . . . . 1 Tim 3:2
a bride adorned for her *h* . . . Rev 21:2

HUSBANDS
them ask their own *h* . . . . . 1 Cor 14:35
H, love your wives . . . . Eph 5:25
H, love your wives and do . . . Col 3:19
Let deacons be the *h* . . . . . 1 Tim 3:12
women to love their *h* . . . . . . Titus 2:4
submissive to your own *h* . . . 1 Pet 3:1

HUSHAI
Archite; David's friend, 2 Sam
15:32–37
Feigns sympathy with Absalom, 2 Sam
16:16–19
Defeats Ahithophel's advice, 2 Sam
17:5–23

HYACINTH
h blue, and sulfur yellow . . . . Rev 9:17

HYMENAEUS
False teacher excommunicated by
Paul, 1 Tim 1:19, 20

HYMN
they had sung a *h* . . . . Matt 26:30

HYMNS
praying and singing *h* . . . . . Acts 16:25
in psalms and *h* . . . . Eph 5:19

HYPOCRISY
you are full of *h* . . . . Matt 23:28
Pharisees, which is *h* . . . . . Luke 12:1
Let love be without *h* . . . . . Rom 12:9
away with their *h* . . . . Gal 2:13
and without *h* . . . . James 3:17
malice, all deceit, *h* . . . . 1 Pet 2:1

HYPOCRITE
of the *h* shall perish . . . . . . Job 8:13
and the joy of the *h* . . . . . . Job 20:5
is the hope of the *h* . . . . Job 27:8
for everyone is a *h* . . . . Is 9:17
also played the *h* . . . . Gal 2:13

HYPOCRITES
"But the *h* in heart . . . . Job 36:13
will I go in with *h* . . . . Ps 26:4
For you were *h* . . . . Jer 42:20
not be like the *h* . . . . Matt 6:5
do you test Me, you *h* . . . . Matt 22:18
and Pharisees, *h* . . . . Matt 23:13

HYSSOP
Purge me with *h* . . . . Ps 51:7
sour wine, put it on *h* . . . . John 19:29

I AM WITH YOU
do not fear, for *I*, I will . . . Gen 26:24
"Behold, *I* and will keep . . . Gen 28:15

Fear not, for *I*; be not . . . . . . Is 41:10
I to deliver you," says the . . . . Jer 1:8
prevail against you; for *I* . . . Jer 15:20
For *I*,' says the LORD, 'to . . . Jer 30:11
I, to save you and deliver . . . Jer 42:11
saying, "*I*, says the LORD." . . Hag 1:13
and lo, *I* always, even to . . Matt 28:20
I, and no one will attack . . Acts 18:10
absent in the flesh, yet *I* in . . . Col 2:5

I WILL BE WITH YOU
"Dwell in this land, and *I* . . . Gen 26:3
to your family, and *I* . . . . . . Gen 31:3
I swore to them, and *I* . . . Deut 31:23
as I was with Moses, so *I* . . . Josh 1:5
"Surely *I*, and you shall . . . . Judg 6:16
David did, then *I* . . . . 1 Kin 11:38
pass through the waters, *I* . . . Is 43:2

IBZAN
Judge of Israel; father of 60 children,
Judg 12:8, 9

ICE
dark because of the *i* . . . . Job 6:16

ICHABOD
Son of Phinehas, 1 Sam 4:19–22

ICONIUM
City of Asia Minor; visited by Paul, Acts
13:51
Many converts in, Acts 14:1–6

IDDO
Leader of Jews at Casiphia, Ezra
8:17–20
——— Seer whose writings are cited,
2 Chr 9:29

IDLE
For they are *i* . . . . Ex 5:8
i person will suffer . . . . Prov 19:15
i word men may speak . . . Matt 12:36
saw others standing *i* . . . . . Matt 20:3
they learn to be *i* . . . . 1 Tim 5:13
both *i* talkers and . . . . Titus 1:10

IDLENESS
not eat the bread of *i* . . . . . Prov 31:27
through *i* of the hands the . . . Eccl 10:18
food, and abundance of *i* . . Ezek 16:49

IDLY
They speak *i* everyone with . . Ps 12:2

IDOL
lifted up his soul to an *i* . . . . . Ps 24:4
if he blesses an *i* . . . . Is 66:3
a wooden *i* is a worthless . . . Jer 10:8
that an *i* is nothing . . . . 1 Cor 8:4
thing offered to an *i* . . . . 1 Cor 8:7
That an *i* is anything . . . . . 1 Cor 10:19

IDOLATER
or covetous, or an *i* . . . . 1 Cor 5:11
man, who is an *i* . . . . Eph 5:5

IDOLATERS
fornicators, nor *i* . . . . 1 Cor 6:9
immoral, sorcerers, *i* . . . . . . Rev 21:8
and murderers and *i* . . . . . . Rev 22:15

IDOLATRIES
and abominable *i* . . . . 1 Pet 4:3

IDOLATROUS
he removed the *i* priests . . . 2 Kin 23:5
I have not sat with *i* mortals . Ps 26:4
pay for your *i* sins . . . . Ezek 23:49
the names of the *i* priests . . . Zeph 1:4

IDOLATRY
beloved, flee from *i* . . . . . . 1 Cor 10:14
i, sorcery, hatred . . . . Gal 5:20
covetousness, which is *i* . . . . Col 3:5

IDOLS
stolen the household *i* . . . . . Gen 31:19
of the peoples are *i* . . . . Ps 96:5
i are silver and gold . . . . . . Ps 115:4
land is also full of *i* . . . . Is 2:8

IDUMEA

insane with their *i* . . . . Jer 50:38
in the room of his *i* . . . . Ezek 8:12
from their wooden *i* . . . . Hos 4:12
who regard worthless *i* . . . . . . Jon 2:8
i speak delusion . . . . Zech 10:2
things polluted by *i* . . . . . . Acts 15:20
You who abhor *i* . . . . Rom 2:22
This was offered to *i* . . . . . 1 Cor 10:28
keep yourselves from *i* . . . 1 John 5:21
worship demons, and *i* . . . . . . Rev 9:20

IDUMEA
Name used by Greeks and Romans to
designate Edom, Mark 3:8

IGNORANCE
unintentionally or in *i* . . . . Ezek 45:20
that you did it in *i* . . . . Acts 3:17
i God overlooked . . . . Acts 17:30
sins committed in *i* . . . . Heb 9:7
to silence the *i* . . . . 1 Pet 2:15

IGNORANT
I was so foolish and *i* . . . . Ps 73:22
though Abraham was *i* . . . . . . Is 63:16
For they being *i* of God's . . . Rom 10:3
be *i* of this mystery . . . . Rom 11:25
not want you to be *i* . . . . 1 Cor 12:1
But if anyone is *i* . . . . 1 Cor 14:38
i disputes, knowing that . . 2 Tim 2:23
on those who are *i* . . . . Heb 5:2

IGNORANTLY
because I did it *i* . . . . 1 Tim 1:13

IJON
Town of Naphtali; captured by Ben-
Hadad, 1 Kin 15:20
Captured by Tiglath-Pileser, 2 Kin
15:29

ILL
God sent a spirit of *i* will . . . Judg 9:23
David, and it became *i* . . . 2 Sam 12:15
bed and pretend to be *i* . . . 2 Sam 13:5
go *i* with him who is . . . . . . Job 20:26

ILLEGITIMATE
then you are *i* . . . . Heb 12:8

ILLUMINATED
after you were *i* . . . . Heb 10:32
and the earth was *i* . . . . Rev 18:1
for the glory of God *i* . . . . . Rev 21:23

ILLYRICUM
Paul preaches in, Rom 15:19

IMAGE
See WOODEN IMAGE; WOODEN IMAGES
Us make man in Our *i* . . . . . . Gen 1:26
yourselves a carved *i* . . . . . Deut 4:16
shall despise their *i* . . . . Ps 73:20
the king made an *i* . . . . Dan 3:1
to them, "Whose *i* . . . . . . Matt 22:20
since he is the *i* . . . . 1 Cor 11:7
He is the *i* of the . . . . Col 1:15
and not the very *i* . . . . Heb 10:1
the beast and his *i* . . . . Rev 14:9
who worshiped his *i* . . . . . . Rev 19:20

IMAGINATION
although the *i* of man's . . . . . Gen 8:21
the proud in the *i* . . . . Luke 1:51

IMITATE
I urge you, *i* me . . . . 1 Cor 4:16
as I also *i* Christ . . . . 1 Cor 11:1
i those who through . . . . Heb 6:12

IMMANUEL
shall call His name *I* . . . . Is 7:14
shall call His name *I* . . . . . . Matt 1:23

IMMEDIATELY
I the fig tree withered . . . . Matt 21:19
i the Spirit drove Him . . . . . Mark 1:12
i they left their nets and . . . Mark 1:18
hear, Satan comes *i* . . . . Mark 4:15
i he puts in the sickle, ... Mark 4:29
I his mouth was opened . . . Luke 1:64

i her flow of blood . . . . Luke 8:44
stones would *i* cry out . . . . Luke 19:40
I sent to you *i*, and you . . . . Acts 10:33
i an angel of the Lord . . . . Acts 12:23
I did not *i* confer with flesh . . Gal 1:16
i forgets what kind of . . . . James 1:24
I I was in the Spirit . . . . Rev 4:2

IMMORAL
lips of an *i* woman drip . . . . . Prov 5:3
i woman is a deep pit . . . . Prov 22:14
with sexually *i* people . . . . . 1 Cor 5:9
murderers, sexually *i* . . . . . . Rev 21:8

IMMORALITY
except sexual *i* . . . . Matt 5:32
wife, except for sexual *i* . . . Matt 19:9
and from sexual *i* . . . . Acts 15:29
unrighteousness, sexual *i* . . Rom 1:29
i as is not even named . . . . . 1 Cor 5:1
Flee sexual *i* . . . . 1 Cor 6:18
abstain from sexual *i* . . . 1 Thess 4:3
themselves over to sexual *i* . . Jude 7
to repent of her sexual *i* . . . Rev 2:21

IMMORTAL
to the King eternal, *i* . . . . . 1 Tim 1:17

IMMORTALITY
glory, honor, and *i* . . . . Rom 2:7
mortal must put on *i* . . . . 1 Cor 15:53
who alone has *i* . . . . 1 Tim 6:16
and brought life and *i* . . . . . 2 Tim 1:10

IMMOVABLE
be steadfast, *i* . . . . 1 Cor 15:58

IMMUTABLE
that by two *i* things . . . . Heb 6:18

IMPART
see you, that I may *i* . . . . . . Rom 1:11
that it may *i* grace . . . . Eph 4:29

IMPENITENT
i heart you are . . . . Rom 2:5

IMPERISHABLE
but we for an *i* crown . . . . . 1 Cor 9:25

IMPLANTED
with meekness the *i* . . . . . James 1:21

IMPORTED
had horses *i* from Egypt . . 1 Kin 10:28
i from Egypt a chariot . . . . . 2 Chr 1:17

IMPOSSIBLE
and nothing will be *i* . . . . . . Matt 17:20
"With men this is *i* . . . . Matt 19:26
God nothing will be *i* . . . . . . Luke 1:37
It is *i* that no offenses . . . . . Luke 17:1
For it is *i* for those who . . . . . Heb 6:4
which it is *i* for God to lie . . . Heb 6:18
without faith it is *i* . . . . Heb 11:6

IMPOSTORS
i will grow worse . . . . 2 Tim 3:13

IMPRISONMENT
and of chains and *i* . . . . Heb 11:36

IMPRISONMENTS
in stripes, in *i* . . . . 2 Cor 6:5

IMPULSIVE
but he who is *i* . . . . Prov 14:29

IMPURITY
during her *i* shall be . . . . . . Lev 15:20
cleansed from her *i* . . . . . 2 Sam 11:4
end to another with their *i* . . Ezra 9:11
a woman during her *i* . . . . . Ezek 18:6

IMPUTE
"Do not let my lord *i* . . . . 2 Sam 19:19
the LORD does not *i* . . . . Ps 32:2
the LORD shall not *i* . . . . Rom 4:8

IMPUTED
bloodshed shall be *i* . . . . . . Lev 17:4
might be *i* to them . . . . Rom 4:11
alone that it was *i* . . . . Rom 4:23
but sin is not *i* . . . . Rom 5:13

IMPUTES
i righteousness apart . . . . . . Rom 4:6

IN MY NAME
which He speaks *i* . . . . Deut 18:19
to speak a word *i* . . . . Deut 18:20
i his horn shall be exalted. . . Ps 89:24
prophets prophesy lies *i* . . Jer 14:14
prophesy falsely to you *i* . . . Jer 29:9
little child like this *i* . . . . . . Matt 18:5
are gathered together *i* . . . Matt 18:20
many will come *i*, saying . . Matt 24:5
who works a miracle *i* . . . . Mark 9:39
cup of water to drink *i* . . . . Mark 9:41
I they will cast out . . . . . . Mark 16:17
whatever you ask *i* . . . . . . John 14:13
the Father will send *i* . . . . John 14:26
you ask the Father *i* . . . . . John 15:16
day you will ask *i* . . . . John 16:26

IN THE WORLD
He was *i*, and the world . . . . John 1:10
"As long as I am *i*, I am . . . . . John 9:5
His own who were *i* . . . . . . John 13:1
I you will have . . . . John 16:33
"Now I am no longer *i* . . . . John 17:11
I was with them *i* . . . . John 17:12
until the law sin was *i* . . . . . Rom 5:13
an idol is nothing *i* . . . . 1 Cor 8:4
we conducted ourselves *i* . 2 Cor 1:12
no hope and without God *i* . . Eph 2:12
you shine as lights *i* . . . . . . Phil 2:15
why, as though living *i* . . . . . Col 2:20
believed on *i*, received . . . . 1 Tim 3:16
the corruption that is *i* . . . . 2 Pet 1:4
the world or the things *i* . . 1 John 2:15
greater than he who is *i* . . 1 John 4:4

INCENSE
oil and for the sweet *i* . . . . . . Ex 25:6
lamps, he shall burn *i* on it . . Ex 30:7
perpetual *i* before the LORD . . Ex 30:8
the pure *i* of sweet spices, . . Ex 37:29
the cloud of *i* may cover . . . Lev 16:13
put *i* in it, and each of . . . . Num 16:17
burned *i* at the high places . 1 Kin 3:3
be set before You as *i* . . . . . . Ps 141:2
i is an abomination to Me . . . . Is 1:13
i to the queen of heaven . . . Jer 44:18
oil and My *i* before them . . Ezek 16:18
In every place *i* shall be . . . . Mal 1:11
his lot fell to burn *i* when . . Luke 1:9
right side of the altar of *i* . . Luke 1:11
golden bowls full of *i* . . . . . . Rev 5:8
the smoke of the *i*, with . . . . Rev 8:4
cinnamon and *i*, fragrant . . Rev 18:13

INCLINE
i your heart to the . . . . Josh 24:23
I Your ear to me, and hear . . Ps 17:6
I Your ear to my cry . . . . Ps 88:2
I my heart to Your . . . . Ps 119:36
i my heart to any evil . . . . . Ps 141:4
i your ear to my sayings . . . Prov 4:20
not obey Me or *i* their ear . . . Jer 7:26
O my God, *i* Your ear and . . Dan 9:18

INCORRUPTIBLE
the glory of the *i* . . . . Rom 1:23
dead will be raised *i* . . . . 1 Cor 15:52
to an inheritance *i* . . . . 1 Pet 1:4
corruptible seed but *i* . . . . . 1 Pet 1:23
i beauty of a gentle . . . . 1 Pet 3:4

INCORRUPTION
it is raised in *i* . . . . 1 Cor 15:42
corruption inherit *i* . . . . . . 1 Cor 15:50
must put on *i* . . . . 1 Cor 15:53

INCREASE
if riches *i*, do not set . . . . . . Ps 62:10
the LORD give you *i* . . . . . . Ps 115:14
hear and *i* learning . . . . Prov 1:5
When goods *i*, they . . . . Eccl 5:11
Of the *i* of His . . . . Is 9:7
and knowledge shall *i* . . . . . Dan 12:4

Lord, "*I* our faith .... Luke 17:5
He must *i*, but I must ...... John 3:30
but God gave the *i* .... 1 Cor 3:6
grows with the *i* .... Col 2:19
for they will *i* .... 2 Tim 2:16

INCREASED
The waters *i* and .... Gen 7:17
i your mercy which you ... Gen 19:19
nation and *i* its joy .... Is 9:3
And Jesus *i* in wisdom ..... Luke 2:52

INCREASES
i knowledge *i* sorrow .... Eccl 1:18
who have no might He *i* ..... Is 40:29

INCREDIBLE
should it be thought *i* .... Acts 26:8

INCURABLE
My wound is *i* .... Job 34:6
'Your affliction is *i* ...... Jer 30:12
Your sorrow is *i* .... Jer 30:15

INDEBTED
everyone who is *i* .... Luke 11:4

INDEED
i it was very good .... Gen 1:31
"But will God *i* .... 1 Kin 8:27
"Behold, an Israelite *i* ... John 1:47

INDIA
Eastern limit of Persian Empire, Esth
1:1

INDICATING
the Holy Spirit *i* .... Heb 9:8
who was in them was *i* .... 1 Pet 1:11

INDIGNANT
saw it, they were *i* .... Matt 26:8

INDIGNATION
of His anger, wrath, *i* ...... Ps 78:49
I has taken hold .... Ps 119:53
in whose hand is My *i* ..... Is 10:5
For the *i* of the LORD .... Is 34:2
have filled me with *i* ..... Jer 15:17
can stand before His *i* ..... Nah 1:6
i which will devour .... Heb 10:27
into the cup of His *i* ...... Rev 14:10

INDIVIDUALLY
He fashions their hearts *i* .... Ps 33:15
i members of one another .. Rom 12:5
Christ, and members *i* .... 1 Cor 12:27

INDUCED
O LORD, You *i* me .... Jer 20:7
if the prophet is *i* .... Ezek 14:9

INDULGENCE
no value against the *i* ...... Col 2:23

INEXCUSABLE
Therefore you are *i* .... Rom 2:1

INEXPRESSIBLE
Paradise and heard *i* ..... 2 Cor 12:4
you rejoice with joy *i* .... 1 Pet 1:8

INFALLIBLE
suffering by many *i* .... Acts 1:3

INFANTS
i who never saw .... Job 3:16
i You have ordained .... Ps 8:2
i You have perfected ...... Matt 21:16
they also brought *i* .... Luke 18:15

INFERIOR
another kingdom *i* .... Dan 2:39
that I am not at all *i* ...... 2 Cor 11:5

INFIRMITIES
"He Himself took our *i* .... Matt 8:17
boast, except in my *i* ..... 2 Cor 12:5
and your frequent *i* .... 1 Tim 5:23

INFIRMITY
a spirit of *i* eighteen ...... Luke 13:11
had an *i* thirty-eight years .. John 5:5
i I preached the gospel to .... Gal 4:13

INFLAMING
i yourselves with gods .... Is 57:5

INGATHERING
the Feast of *I* at the year's .. Ex 34:22

INHABIT
the wicked will not *i* ...... Prov 10:30
cities and *i* them .... Amos 9:14

INHABITANT
Cry out and shout, O *i* .... Is 12:6
And the *i* will not say .... Is 33:24

INHABITANTS
He looks on all the *i* .... Ps 33:14
give ear, all *i* .... Ps 49:1
Let the *i* of Sela sing .... Is 42:11
Woe to the *i* of the .... Rev 12:12

INHABITED
rejoicing in His *i* .... Prov 8:31
'You shall be *i* .... Is 44:26
who formed it to be *i* ...... Is 45:18

INHERIT
i the iniquities .... Job 13:26
descendants shall *i* .... Ps 25:13
The righteous shall *i* .... Ps 37:29
The wise shall *i* .... Prov 3:35
love me to *i* wealth .... Prov 8:21
The simple *i* folly .... Prov 14:18
the blameless will *i* .... Prov 28:10
i the kingdom prepared ... Matt 25:34
I do that I may *i* .... Mark 10:17
unrighteous will not *i* ...... 1 Cor 6:9
you may *i* a blessing .... 1 Pet 3:9
who overcomes shall *i* ...... Rev 21:7

INHERITANCE
"You shall have no *i* ...... Num 18:20
is the place of His *i* .... Deut 32:9
the portion of my *i* .... Ps 16:5
yes, I have a good *i* .... Ps 16:6
i shall be forever .... Ps 37:18
He will choose our *i* .... Ps 47:4
You confirmed Your *i* ...... Ps 68:9
the tribe of Your *i* .... Ps 74:2
i gained hastily .... Prov 20:21
right of *i* is yours .... Jer 32:8
i has been turned .... Lam 5:2
will arise to your *i* .... Dan 12:13
And God gave him no *i* ...... Acts 7:5
and give you an *i* .... Acts 20:32
For if the *i* is of the .... Gal 3:18
we have obtained an *i* ...... Eph 1:11
be partakers of the *i* .... Col 1:12
receive as an *i* .... Heb 11:8
to an *i* incorruptible .... 1 Pet 1:4

INIQUITIES
How many are my *i* .... Job 13:23
i have overtaken me .... Ps 40:12
I prevail against me .... Ps 65:3
forgives all your *i* .... Ps 103:3
LORD, should mark *i* .... Ps 130:3
was bruised for our *i* .... Is 53:5
He shall bear their *i* ...... Is 53:11
i have separated you .... Is 59:2

INIQUITY
See WORKERS OF INIQUITY
God, visiting the *i* of the ..... Ex 20:5
He has not observed *i* .... Num 23:21
wicked brings forth *i* .... Ps 7:14
O LORD, pardon my *i* .... Ps 25:11
i I have not hidden .... Ps 32:5
was brought forth in *i* ...... Ps 51:5
If I regard *i* in my .... Ps 66:18
Add *i* to their *i* .... Ps 69:27
workers of *i* flourish .... Ps 92:7
i boast in themselves .... Ps 94:4
Shall the throne of *i* .... Ps 94:20
let no *i* have dominion .... Ps 119:133
i will reap sorrow .... Prov 22:8
a people laden with *i* .... Is 1:4
i is taken away .... Is 6:7

INFLAMING
has laid on Him the *i* .... Is 53:6
will remember their *i* .... Hos 9:9
to those who devise *i* .... Mic 2:1
like You, pardoning *i* .... Mic 7:18
all you workers of *i* .... Luke 13:27
a fire, a world of *i* .... James 3:6

INJUSTICE
of truth and without *i* ...... Deut 32:4
i shuts her mouth .... Job 5:16
i have your fathers .... Jer 2:5

INK
us, written not with *i* .... 2 Cor 3:3
do so with paper and *i* .... 2 John 12

INN
room for them in the *i* ...... Luke 2:7
brought him to an *i* .... Luke 10:34

INNOCENCE
of my heart and *i* .... Gen 20:5
washed my hands in *i* ...... Ps 73:13

INNOCENT
do not kill the *i* .... Ex 23:7
a bribe to slay an *i* .... Deut 27:25
i will divide the .... Job 27:17
a bribe against the *i* .... Ps 15:5
because I was found *i* ...... Dan 6:22
by betraying *i* blood ...... Matt 27:4
saying, "I am *i* .... Matt 27:24
this day that I am *i* .... Acts 20:26

INNOCENT BLOOD
"lest *i* be shed in the ...... Deut 19:10
against *i*, to kill David .... 1 Sam 19:5
the *i* which Joab shed ..... 1 Kin 2:31
shed very much *i* .... 2 Kin 21:16
righteous, and condemn *i* .... Ps 94:21
And shed *i*, the blood ...... Ps 106:38
tongue, hands that shed *i* .... Prov 6:17
they make haste to shed *i* ... Is 59:7
do not shed *i* in this place ..... Jer 7:6
you will surely bring *i* ...... Jer 26:15
for they have shed *i* .... Joel 3:19
do not charge us with *i* ..... Jon 1:14
sinned by betraying *i* ...... Matt 27:4

INNUMERABLE
i as the sand which is ..... Heb 11:12
i company of angels ...... Heb 12:22

INQUIRE
went to *i* of the LORD ...... Gen 25:22
a man went to *i* of God .... 1 Sam 9:9
I may go to her and *i* ..... 1 Sam 28:7
sent you to Me to *i* of Me ... Jer 37:7
i who in it is worthy ...... Matt 10:11
to *i* more fully about him .. Acts 23:20

INQUIRED
children of Israel *i* .... Judg 20:27
Therefore David *i* .... 1 Sam 23:2
the LORD, nor *i* of Him ..... Zeph 1:6
the prophets have *i* .... 1 Pet 1:10

INQUIRY
shall make careful *i* ...... Deut 19:18

INSANE
images, and they are *i* ..... Jer 50:38
the spiritual man is *i* .... Hos 9:7

INSCRIBED
Oh, that they were *i* ...... Job 19:23
See, I have *i* you on .... Is 49:16

INSCRIPTION
wrote on it an *i* like the ..... Ex 39:30
image and *i* is this .... Matt 22:20
the *i* of His accusation .... Mark 15:26
found an altar with this *i* .. Acts 17:23

INSPIRATION
is given by *i* of God .... 2 Tim 3:16

INSTRUCT
good Spirit to *i* them ...... Neh 9:20
I will *i* you and teach .... Ps 32:8
is the man whom You *i* .... Ps 94:12

the LORD that he may *i* .... 1 Cor 2:16
If you *i* the brethren in ...... 1 Tim 4:6

INSTRUCTED
Surely you have *i* .... Job 4:3
counsel, and who *i* .... Is 40:14
This man had been *i* ...... Acts 18:25
are excellent, being *i* .... Rom 2:18
Moses was divinely *i* .... Heb 8:5

INSTRUCTION
also opens their ear to *i* .... Job 36:10
seeing you hate *i* .... Ps 50:17
despise wisdom and *i* ...... Prov 1:7
Take firm hold of *i* .... Prov 4:13
He shall die for lack of *i* ... Prov 5:23
Hear *i* and be wise .... Prov 8:33
Give *i* to a wise man .... Prov 9:9
i loves knowledge .... Prov 12:1
fool despises his father's *i* .. Prov 15:5
Cease listening to *i* .... Prov 19:27
Apply your heart to *i* ...... Prov 23:12
you have written at my *i*, ... Jer 36:6
for correction, for *i* .... 2 Tim 3:16

INSTRUCTORS
have ten thousand *i* .... 1 Cor 4:15

INSTRUCTS
My heart also *i* .... Ps 16:7
He who *i* the nations .... Ps 94:10

INSTRUMENT
to Him with an *i* .... Ps 33:2
on an *i* of ten strings .... Ps 92:3

INSTRUMENTS
i of cruelty are in .... Gen 49:5
on harps, on stringed *i* ..... 2 Sam 6:5
by *i* of music .... 1 Chr 15:16
with stringed *i* .... 2 Chr 20:28
cymbals and stringed *i* .... Neh 12:27
for Himself *i* of death .... Ps 7:13
with stringed *i* .... Ps 150:4
and musical *i* of all kinds .... Eccl 2:8
i of unrighteousness .... Rom 6:13

INSUBORDINATE
for the lawless and *i* .... 1 Tim 1:9
For there are many *i* .... Titus 1:10

INSUBORDINATION
of dissipation or *i* .... Titus 1:6

INSULT
shall not return *i* for *i* .... Mic 2:6

INSULTED
will be mocked and *i* .... Luke 18:32
i the Spirit of grace .... Heb 10:29

INSULTS
nor be afraid of their *i* .... Is 51:7

INTEGRITY
In the *i* of my heart .... Gen 20:5
walked, in *i* of heart and .... 1 Kin 9:4
he holds fast to his *i* .... Job 2:3
that God may know my *i* .... Job 31:6
Let *i* and uprightness .... Ps 25:21
I have walked in my *i* .... Ps 26:1
You uphold me in my *i* ...... Ps 41:12
with *i* walks securely ...... Prov 10:9
The *i* of the upright .... Prov 11:3
poor who walks in his *i* .... Prov 19:1
man walks in his *i* .... Prov 20:7
i than one perverse in his . Prov 28:6
in doctrine showing *i* ...... Titus 2:7

INTELLIGENT
Sergius Paulus, an *i* .... Acts 13:7

INTENT
that every *i* of the thoughts .. Gen 6:5
all the *i* of the thoughts .... 1 Chr 28:9
brings it with wicked *i* .... Prov 21:27
to the *i* that we should ..... 1 Cor 10:6

INTERCEDE
the LORD, who will *i* ...... 1 Sam 2:25

INTERCESSION
of many, and made *i* .... Is 53:12

Spirit Himself makes *i* ..... Rom 8:26
always lives to make *i* ...... Heb 7:25

INTERCESSOR
that there was no *i* .... Is 59:16

INTEREST
shall not charge him *i* ...... Ex 22:25
men lent to me for *i* .... Jer 15:10
collected it with *i* .... Luke 19:23

INTERPRET
could *i* them for Pharaoh ... Gen 41:8
Do all *i* .... 1 Cor 12:30
pray that he may *i* .... 1 Cor 14:13
in turn, and let one *i* ..... 1 Cor 14:27

INTERPRETATION
"This is the *i* .... Gen 40:12
who knows the *i* of a thing '.. Eccl 8:1
you tell the dream and its *i* .. Dan 2:6
to another the *i* .... 1 Cor 12:10
a revelation, has an *i* ..... 1 Cor 14:26
of any private *i* .... 2 Pet 1:20

INTERPRETATIONS
Do not *i* belong to God ..... Gen 40:8
that you can give *i* .... Dan 5:16

INTOXICATING
not drink wine or *i* drink .... Lev 10:9

INTRIGUE
seize the kingdom by *i* .... Dan 11:21
join with them by *i* .... Dan 11:34

INTRUDING
i into those things which .... Col 2:18

INVENT
but you *i* them in your own .. Neh 6:8
i for yourselves musical .... Amos 6:5

INVISIBLE
of the world His *i* .... Rom 1:20
is the image of the *i* .... Col 1:15
eternal, immortal, *i* .... 1 Tim 1:17
as seeing Him who is *i* .... Heb 11:27

INVITE
i Jesse to the sacrifice .... 1 Sam 16:3
he did not *i* Nathan the .... 1 Kin 1:10
you find, *i* to the wedding .. Matt 22:9
lest they also *i* you back .. Luke 14:12

INVITED
so Absalom *i* all the ..... 2 Sam 13:23
has *i* all the sons of the .... 1 Kin 1:19
Queen Esther *i* no one but .. Esth 5:12
were *i* to the wedding ...... Matt 22:3
who had *i* Him saw this .... Luke 7:39
to those who were *i* .... Luke 14:7
were *i* to the wedding .... John 2:2
he *i* them in and lodged ... Acts 10:23
were *i* to stay with them .. Acts 28:14

INWARD
i part is destruction .... Ps 5:9
Both the *i* thought .... Ps 64:6
You have formed my *i* ..... Ps 139:13
God according to the *i* ..... Rom 7:22
i man is being renewed .... 2 Cor 4:16

INWARDLY
i they are ravenous .... Matt 7:15
is a Jew who is one *i* ...... Rom 2:29

IRON
make your heavens like *i* .. Lev 26:19
was an *i* bedstead .... Deut 3:11
He will put a yoke of *i* .... Deut 28:48
i picks and *i* axes, and .... 2 Sam 12:31
He regards *i* as straw ...... Job 41:27
i sharpens *i* .... Prov 27:17
and your neck was an *i* ...... Is 48:4
its feet partly of *i* .... Dan 2:33
seared with a hot *i* .... 1 Tim 4:2
all nations with a rod of *i* ... Rev 12:5

IRREVOCABLE
calling of God are *i* .... Rom 11:29

ISAAC
Promised heir of the covenant, Gen 17:16–21

Born and circumcised, Gen 21:1–7
Offered up as a sacrifice, Gen 22:1–19
Marries Rebekah, Gen 24:62–67
Prays for children; prefers Esau, Gen 25:21–28
Dealings with Abimelech, king of Gerar, Gen 26:1–31
Mistakenly blesses Jacob, Gen 27:1—28:5
Dies in his old age, Gen 35:28, 29
N.T. references to, Luke 3:34; Gal 4:21–31; Heb 11:9, 20

ISAIAH
Prophet during reigns of Uzziah, Jotham, Ahaz, and Hezekiah, Is 1:1
Responds to prophetic call, Is 6:1–13
Prophesies to Hezekiah, 2 Kin 19; 20
Writes Uzziah's biography, 2 Chr 26:22
Writes Hezekiah's biography, 2 Chr 32:32
Quoted in N.T., Matt 1:22, 23; 3:3; 8:17; 12:17–21; Luke 4:17–19; Acts 13:34; Rom 9:27, 29; 10:16, 20, 21; 11:26, 27; 15:12; 1 Pet 2:22

ISCARIOT, JUDAS
Listed among the Twelve, Mark 3:14, 19; Luke 6:16
Criticizes Mary, John 12:3–6
Identified as betrayer, John 13:21–30
Takes money to betray Christ, Matt 26:14–16
Betrays Christ with a kiss, Mark 14:43–45
Repents and commits suicide, Matt 27:3–10
His place filled, Acts 1:15–26

ISHBOSHETH
One of Saul's sons; made king, 2 Sam 2:8–10
Offends Abner, 2 Sam 3:7–11
Slain; his assassins executed, 2 Sam 4:1–12

ISHMAEL
Abram's son by Hagar, Gen 16:3, 4, 11–16
Circumcised, Gen 17:25
Scoffs at Isaac's feast; exiled with his mother, Gen 21:8–21
His sons; his death, Gen 25:12–18
—— Son of Nethaniah; kills Gedaliah, 2 Kin 25:22–26

ISHMAELITES
Settle at Havilah, Gen 25:17, 18
Joseph sold to, Gen 37:25–28
Sell Joseph to Potiphar, Gen 39:1

ISLAND
aground on a certain *i* .... Acts 27:26
the leading citizen of the *i* .. Acts 28:7
i was moved out of its ...... Rev 6:14
Then every *i* fled away .... Rev 16:20

ISLES
the multitude of *i* be glad ..... Ps 97:1
declare it in the *i* afar off ... Jer 31:10
many *i* were the market .. Ezek 27:15
i will be astonished at .... Ezek 27:35

ISRAEL
See HOLY ONE OF ISRAEL; LORD GOD OF ISRAEL
Used to refer to:
Jacob, Gen 32:28
descendants of Jacob, Gen 49:16, 28
ten northern tribes (in contrast to Judah), 1 Sam 11:8
restored nation after exile, Ezra 9:1
true church, Gal 6:16

be called Jacob, but *I* ...... Gen 32:28
"Hear, O *I*: The LORD .... Deut 6:4
shepherd My people *I* ...... 2 Sam 7:7

Jacob rejoice and *I* be glad ...Ps 14:7
Redeem *I*, O God, out of .....Ps 25:22
Truly God is good to *I* ....Ps 73:1
O *I*, if you will listen to Me ...Ps 81:8
When *I* went out of Egypt, ..Ps 114:1
Let *I* now say, "His mercy ...Ps 118:2
O *I*, hope in the LORD ....Ps 130:7
Let *I* rejoice in their Maker ..Ps 149:2
will shepherd My people *I* ...Matt 2:6
great faith, not even in *I* ...Matt 8:10
sheep of the house of *I* .....Matt 10:6
the twelve tribes of *I* .....Matt 19:28
If He is the King of *I*, let ..Matt 27:42
helped His servant *I* ....Luke 1:54
of his manifestation to *I* ...Luke 1:80
Are you the teacher of *I*, ...John 3:10
restore the kingdom to *I* .....Acts 1:6
God raised up for *I* a ......Acts 13:23
because for the hope of *I* ..Acts 28:20
For they are not all *I* ....Rom 9:6
so all *I* will be saved ....Rom 11:26
Observe *I* after the flesh ..1 Cor 10:18
and upon the *I* of God ....Gal 6:16
eighth day, of the stock of *I* ..Phil 3:5
with the house of *I* ....Heb 8:8
children of *I* were sealed .....Rev 7:4
tribes of the children of *I* ..Rev 21:12

ISRAELITES
Afflicted in Egypt, Ex 1:12–22
Escape from Egypt, Ex 12:29–42, 50;
  13:17–22
Receive law at Sinai, Ex 19
Idolatry and rebellion of, Ex 32; Num
  13; 14
Wander in the wilderness, Num
  14:26–39
Cross Jordan; conquer Canaan, Josh
  4; 12
Ruled by judges, Judg 2
Saul chosen as king, 1 Sam 10
Kingdom divided, 1 Kin 12
Northern kingdom carried captive,
  2 Kin 17
Southern kingdom carried captive,
  2 Kin 24
70 years in exile, 2 Chr 36:20, 21
Return after exile, Ezra 1:1–5
Nation rejects Christ, Matt 27:20–27
Nation destroyed, Luke 21:20–24

ISSACHAR
Jacob's fifth son, Gen 30:17, 18
—— Tribe of:
Genealogy of, 1 Chr 7:1–5
Prophecy concerning, Gen 49:14, 15
Census at Sinai, Num 1:28, 29
Inheritance of, Josh 19:17–23

ISSUED
King Darius *i* a decree ......Ezra 6:1
be *i* as law in every ....Esth 3:14
i as a decree in every .....Esth 8:13
A fiery stream *i* and came ..Dan 7:10
before the decree is *i*.......Zeph 2:2

IT IS WRITTEN
as *i* in the Law of Moses ....1 Kin 2:3
as *i* in this Book of ....2 Kin 23:21
Feast of Tabernacles, as *i*...Ezra 3:4
trees, to make booths, as *i* ..Neh 8:15
in the scroll of the Book *i*.....Ps 40:7
"Behold, *i* before Me: I will ...Is 65:6
"As *i* in the Law of Moses ..Dan 9:13
for thus *i* by the prophet: ....Matt 2:5
"*I*, 'Man shall not live by ...Matt 4:4
throw Yourself down. For *i* ..Matt 4:6
"*I* again, 'You shall not .....Matt 4:7
i, 'You shall worship ......Matt 4:10
"For this is he of whom *i* ..Matt 11:10
"*I*, 'My house shall be .....Matt 21:13
i: 'I will strike the ....Matt 26:31
"Thus *i*, and thus it was ..Luke 24:46
"*I* in the prophets, 'And ....John 6:45

i in the book of Psalms ....Acts 1:20
i, 'You shall not speak .....Acts 23:5
volume of the book *i* ......Heb 10:7
because *i*, "Be holy, for ...1 Pet 1:16

ITALIAN
was called the *I* Regiment ..Acts 10:1

ITALY
Jews expelled from, Acts 18:2
Paul sails for, Acts 27:1, 6
Christians in, Acts 28:14

ITCHING
they have *i* ears ....2 Tim 4:3

ITHAMAR
Youngest son of Aaron, Ex 6:23
Consecrated as priest, Ex 28:1
Duty entrusted to, Ex 38:21
Jurisdiction over Gershonites and
  Merarites, Num 4:21–33

ITINERANT
i Jewish exorcists ....Acts 19:13

ITUREA
Region ruled by Herod Philip, Luke 3:1

IVORY
made a great throne of *i* ..1 Kin 10:18
Out of the *i* palaces ....Ps 45:8
neck is like an *i* tower .....Song 7:4
lie on beds of *i*, stretch ....Amos 6:4

JABBOK
River entering the Jordan about 20
  miles north of the Dead Sea, Num
  21:24
Scene of Jacob's conflict, Gen
  32:22–32
Boundary marker, Deut 3:16

JABESH GILEAD
Consigned to destruction, Judg
  21:8–15
Saul defeats the Ammonites at, 1 Sam
  11:1–11
Citizens of, rescue Saul's body, 1 Sam
  31:11–13
David thanks citizens of, 2 Sam 2:4–7

JABIN
Canaanite king of Hazor; leads confed-
  eracy against Joshua, Josh 11:1–14
—— Another king of Hazor; oppresses
  Israelites, Judg 4:2
Defeated by Deborah and Barak, Judg
  4:3–24
Immortalized in poetry, Judg 5:1–31

JACHIN
One of two pillars in front of Solomon's
  temple, 1 Kin 7:21, 22

JACINTH
third row, a *j*, an agate, ...Ex 28:19
the eleventh *j* ....Rev 21:20

JACKALS
it shall be a habitation of *j* ...Is 34:13
make a wailing like the *j* .....Mic 1:8

JACOB
Son of Isaac and Rebekah; Rebekah's
  favorite, Gen 25:21–28
Obtains birthright, Gen 25:29–34
Obtains blessing meant for Esau; flees,
  Gen 27:1—28:5
Sees vision of ladder, Gen 28:10–22
Serves Laban for Rachel and Leah, Gen
  29:1–30
Fathers children, Gen 29:31—30:24
Flees from, makes covenant with
  Laban, Gen 30:25—31:55
Makes peace with Esau, Gen 32:1–21;
  33:1–17

Wrestles with God, Gen 32:22–32
Returns to Bethel; renamed Israel, Gen
  35:1–15
Shows preference for Joseph, Gen 37:3
Mourns Joseph's disappearance, Gen
  37:32–35
Sends sons to Egypt for food, Gen
  42:1–5
Reluctantly allows Benjamin to go, Gen
  43:1–15
Moves his household to Egypt, Gen
  45:25—47:12
Blesses his sons and grandsons; dies,
  Gen 48; 49
Buried in Canaan, Gen 50:1–14

JACOB'S WELL
Christ teaches a Samaritan woman at,
  John 4:5–26

JAEL
Wife of Heber the Kenite; kills Sisera,
  Judg 4:17–22
Praised by Deborah, Judg 5:24–27

JAIR
Manassite warrior; conquers towns in
  Gilead, Num 32:41; Deut 3:14
—— Eighth judge of Israel, Judg
  10:3–5

JAIRUS
Ruler of the synagogue; Jesus raises
  his daughter, Mark 5:22–24, 35–43

JAMES
Son of Zebedee, called as disciple, Matt
  4:21, 22; Luke 5:10, 11
One of the Twelve, Matt 10:2; Mark 3:17
Zealous for the Lord, Luke 9:52–54
Ambitious for honor, Mark 10:35–45
Witnesses transfiguration, Matt
  17:1–9
Martyred by Herod Agrippa, Acts 12:2
—— Son of Alphaeus; one of the
  Twelve, Matt 10:3, 4
Called "the Less," Mark 15:40
—— Jesus' half brother, Matt 13:55, 56;
  Gal 1:19
Becomes leader of Jerusalem Council
  and Jerusalem church, Acts
  15:13–22; Gal 2:9
Author of an epistle, James 1:1

JANNES AND JAMBRES
Two Egyptian magicians; oppose
  Moses, Ex 7:11–22; 2 Tim 3:8

JANOAH
Town of Naphtali, 2 Kin 15:29

JAPHETH
One of Noah's three sons, Gen 5:32
Receives blessing, Gen 9:20–27
His descendants occupy Asia Minor
  and Europe, Gen 10:2–5

JARED
Father of Enoch, Gen 5:15–20
Ancestor of Noah, 1 Chr 1:2
Ancestor of Christ, Luke 3:37

JASHER
Book of, quoted, Josh 10:13

JASON
Welcomes Paul at Thessalonica, Acts
  17:5–9
Described as Paul's kinsman, Rom
  16:21

JASPER
a beryl, an onyx, and a *j* ....Ex 28:20
beryl, onyx, and *j* ....Ezek 28:13
stone, like a *j* stone, clear ..Rev 21:11

JAVAN
Son of Japheth, Gen 10:2, 4
Descendants of, to receive good news,
  Is 66:19, 20

JAVELINS
bows and arrows, the *j* . . . . . Ezek 39:9

JAW
or pierce his *j* with a hook . . Job 41:2

JAWBONE
a fresh *j* of a donkey . . . . . . Judg 15:15

JAWS
My tongue clings to My *j* . . . . Ps 22:15
bridle in the *j* of the people . . Is 30:28
I will put hooks in your *j* . . Ezek 29:4
put hooks into your *j* . . . . . . Ezek 38:4

JEALOUS
your God, am a *j* God . . . . Ex 20:5
LORD, whose name is J . . . . . . Ex 34:14
he becomes *j* of his wife, . . . Num 5:14
a consuming fire, a *j* . . . . . . Deut 4:24
I will be *j* for My holy . . . . Ezek 39:25
For I am *j* for you . . . . 2 Cor 11:2

JEALOUSY
They provoked Him to *j* . . . Deut 32:16
Will Your *j* burn like . . . . Ps 79:5
j is a husband's . . . . Prov 6:34
as strong as death, *j* . . . . Song 8:6
will provoke you to *j* . . . . . . Rom 10:19
fall, to provoke them to *j* . . Rom 11:11
provoke the Lord to *j* . . . . 1 Cor 10:22
for you with godly *j* . . . . 2 Cor 11:2

JEBUS
Canaanite name of Jerusalem before
captured by David, 1 Chr 11:4–8

JEBUSITES
Descendants of Canaan, Gen 15:18–21;
Num 13:29
Defeated by Joshua, Josh 11:1–12
Not driven from Jerusalem; later con-
quered by David, Judg 1:21; 2 Sam
5:6–8
Put to forced labor under Solomon,
1 Kin 9:20, 21

JECONIAH
See JEHOIACHIN
Variant form of Jehoiachin, 1 Chr 3:16,
17
Abbreviated to Coniah, Jer 22:24, 28

JEDIDIAH
Name given to Solomon by Nathan,
2 Sam 12:24, 25

JEDUTHUN
Levite musician appointed by David,
1 Chr 16:41, 42
Heads a family of musicians, 2 Chr
5:12
Name appears in psalm titles, Ps 39;
62; 77

JEGAR SAHADUTHA
Name given by Laban to memorial
stones, Gen 31:46, 47

JEHOAHAZ
Son and successor of Jehu, king of
Israel, 2 Kin 10:35
Seeks the Lord in defeat, 2 Kin 13:2–9
———— Son and successor of Josiah, king
of Judah, 2 Kin 23:30–34
Called Shallum, 1 Chr 3:15
———— Another form of Ahaziah, young-
est son of King Joram, 2 Chr 21:17

JEHOASH
See JOASH

JEHOIACHIN
Son of Jehoiakim; next to the last king
of Judah, 2 Kin 24:8
Deported to Babylon, 2 Kin 24:8–16
Liberated by Evil-Merodach, Jer
52:31–34

JEHOIADA
High priest during reign of Joash, 2 Kin
11:4—12:16
Instructs Joash, 2 Kin 12:2

JEHOIAKIM
Wicked king of Judah; son of Josiah;
serves Pharaoh and Nebuchadnez-
zar, 2 Kin 23:34—24:7
Taken captive to Babylon, 2 Chr
36:6–8
Kills prophet Urijah, Jer 26:20–23
Destroys Jeremiah's scroll; cursed by
God, Jer 36

JEHORAM (or Joram)
Wicked king of Judah; son of
Jehoshaphat, 2 Kin 8:16–24
Marries Athaliah, 2 Kin 8:18, 19
Kills his brothers, 2 Chr 21:2, 4
Elijah prophesies against him; proph-
ecy fulfilled, 2 Chr 21:12–20
———— Wicked king of Israel; son of Ahab,
2 Kin 3:1–3
Counseled by Elisha, 2 Kin 3; 5:8;
6:8–12
Wounded in battle, 2 Kin 8:28, 29
Killed by Jehu, 2 Kin 9:14–26

JEHOSHAPHAT
Righteous king of Judah; son of Asa,
1 Kin 22:41–50
Goes to war with Ahab against Syria,
1 Kin 22:1–36
Institutes reforms; sends out teachers
of the Law, 2 Chr 17:6–9; 19
His enemies defeated through his faith,
2 Chr 20:1–30

JEHOZABAD
Son of a Moabitess; assassinates Joash,
2 Kin 12:20, 21
Put to death, 2 Chr 25:3

JEHU
Prophet; denounces Baasha, 1 Kin
16:1–7
Rebukes Jehoshaphat, 2 Chr 19:2, 3
———— Commander under Ahab;
anointed king, 1 Kin 19:16; 2 Kin
9:1–13
Destroys the house of Ahab, 2 Kin
9:14—10:30
Turns away from the Lord; dies, 2 Kin
10:31–36

JEHUDI
Reads Jeremiah's scroll, Jer 36:14, 21,
23

JEOPARDY
stand in *j* every hour . . . . . 1 Cor 15:30

JEPHTHAH
Gilead's son by a harlot, Judg 11:1
Driven out, then brought back to com-
mand army against Ammonites,
Judg 11:2–28
Sacrifices his daughter to fulfill a vow,
Judg 11:29–40
Chastises Ephraim, Judg 12:1–7

JEREMIAH
Prophet under Josiah, Jehoiakim, and
Zedekiah, Jer 1:1–3
Called by God, Jer 1:4–9
Forbidden to marry, Jer 16:2
Imprisoned by Pashhur, Jer 20:1–6
Prophecy written, destroyed, rewritten,
Jer 36
Accused of defection and imprisoned;
released by Zedekiah, Jer 37
Cast into dungeon; rescued; prophesies
to Zedekiah, Jer 38
Set free by Nebuchadnezzar, Jer
39:11—40:6

Forcibly taken to Egypt, Jer 43:5–7

JERICHO
City near the Jordan, Num 22:1
Called the city of palm trees, Deut 34:3;
2 Chr 28:15
Miraculously defeated by Joshua,
Josh 6
Rebuilt by Hiel, 1 Kin 16:34
Visited by Jesus, Matt 20:29–34; Luke
19:1–10

JEROBOAM
Son of Nebat; receives prophecy that
he will be king, 1 Kin 11:26–40
Made king; leads revolt against
Rehoboam, 1 Kin 12:1–24
Sets up idols, 1 Kin 12:25–33
Rebuked by a man of God, 1 Kin
13:1–10
Judgment on house of, 1 Kin
13:33—14:20
———— Wicked king of Israel; son of
Joash; successful in war, 2 Kin
14:23–29
Prophecy concerning, Amos 7:7–13

JERUBBAAL
Name given to Gideon for destroying
Baal's altar, Judg 6:32

JERUSALEM
Originally called Salem, Gen 14:18
Jebusite city, Josh 15:8; Judg 1:8, 21
King of, defeated by Joshua, Josh
10:5–23
Conquered by David; made capital,
2 Sam 5:6–9
Ark brought to, 2 Sam 6:12–17; 1 Kin
8:1–13
Saved from plague, 2 Sam 24:16
Temple built and dedicated here, 1 Kin
6; 8:14–66
Suffers in war, 1 Kin 14:25–27; 2 Kin
14:13, 14; Is 7:1
Miraculously saved, 2 Kin 19:31–36
Captured by Babylon, 2 Kin
24:10—25:21; Jer 39:1–8
Exiles return and rebuild temple, Ezra
1:1–4; 2:1
Walls of, dedicated, Neh 12:27–47
Christ enters as King, Matt 21:4–11
Christ laments for, Matt 23:37; Luke
19:41–44
Church born in, Acts 2
Christians of, persecuted, Acts 4

Jebusite city (which is J) . . . Josh 15:8
in J he reigned . . . . 2 Sam 5:5
were born to him in J . . . . . 2 Sam 5:14
ark of God back to J . . . . 2 Sam 15:29
yourself a house in J . . . . . . 1 Kin 2:36
a lamp before Me in J . . . . 1 Kin 11:36
Solomon reigned in J . . . . 1 Kin 11:42
Rehoboam came to J . . . . 1 Kin 12:21
gave him a lamp in J . . . . . . 1 Kin 15:4
down the wall of J from . . 2 Kin 14:13
up to J to make war . . . . . . 2 Kin 16:5
before this altar in J' . . . . . 2 Kin 18:22
should deliver J from . . . . 2 Kin 18:35
J shall not be given into . . 2 Kin 19:10
daughter of J has . . . . 2 Kin 19:21
I will stretch over J the . . 2 Kin 21:13
(She dwelt in J in the . . . 2 Kin 22:14
elders of Judah and J to . . 2 Kin 23:1
burned them outside J . . . . 2 Kin 23:4
from J to Babylon . . . . 2 Kin 24:15
his army came against J . . 2 Kin 25:1
the walls of J all around . . 2 Kin 25:10
J into captivity by the . . . . 1 Chr 6:15
house of the LORD in J . . . . 1 Chr 6:32
Now in J the children of . . . 1 Chr 9:3
and all Israel went to J . . . 1 Chr 11:4
took more wives in J . . . . . . 1 Chr 14:3

all Israel together at *J*, to . . 1 Chr 15:3
angel to *J* to destroy it . . . 1 Chr 21:15
they may dwell in *J* . . . . . . 1 Chr 23:25
David assembled at *J* all . . 1 Chr 28:1
gold as common in *J* as . . 2 Chr 1:15
the LORD at *J* on Mount . . . . 2 Chr 3:1
Solomon reigned in *J* . . . . 2 Chr 9:30
So Rehoboam dwelt in *J* . . 2 Chr 11:5
of Judah and came to *J* . . . 2 Chr 12:4
him in the city, in *J* . . . . . 2 Chr 28:27
the altars that were in *J* . . 2 Chr 30:14
against the God of *J* . . . . 2 Chr 32:19
the inhabitants of *J* . . . . . 2 Chr 32:26
to *J* into his kingdom . . . 2 Chr 33:13
and the inhabitants of *J* . 2 Chr 35:18
of the LORD which is in *J* . . Ezra 2:68
together as one man to *J* . . . Ezra 3:1
out of the captivity to *J* . . . . Ezra 3:8
the temple which is in *J* . . . . Ezra 6:5
to bring them to *J* to the . . . Ezra 8:30
a wall in Judah and *J* . . . . . . Ezra 9:9
that they must gather at *J* . . Ezra 10:7
I came to *J* and was there . . . Neh 2:11
let us build the wall of *J* . . . . Neh 2:17
to come and attack *J* . . . . Neh 4:8
it was, at the gates of *J* . . . . Neh 13:19
build the walls of *J* . . . . Ps 51:18
In the midst of you, O *J* . . . Ps 116:19
J is built as a city that is . . . Ps 122:3
If I forget you, O *J*, let my . . . Ps 137:5
The LORD builds up *J* . . . . . . Ps 147:2
was king over Israel in *J* . . . Eccl 1:12
you, O daughters of *J* . . . . . Song 5:8
as Tirzah, lovely as *J*, ... Song 6:4
snare to the inhabitants of *J* . . Is 8:14
of Zion, the hill of *J* . . . . Is 10:32
numbered the houses of *J* . . Is 22:10
watchmen on your walls, O *J* . . Is 62:6
a wilderness, *J* a desolation . . Is 64:10
yes, proclaim against *J*, ... Jer 4:16
Be instructed, O *J*, lest My . . . Jer 6:8
will make *J* a heap of ruins . . Jer 9:11
the cry of *J* has gone up . . . . Jer 14:2
reigned eleven years in *J* . . . . Jer 52:1
J has become an unclean . . . Lam 1:7
and portray on it a city, *J* . . . Ezek 4:1
me in visions of God to *J* . . . . Ezek 8:3
Oholah, and *J* is Oholibah . . . Ezek 23:4
build *J* until Messiah the . . . . Dan 9:25
then *J* shall be holy, and . . . . Joel 3:17
utters His voice from *J* . . . . . Amos 1:2
The captives of *J* who are . . . Obad 20
You not have mercy on *J* . . . Zech 1:12
To measure *J*, to see what . . . Zech 2:2
again in her own place—*J* . . Zech 12:6
to *J* to worship the King . . . Zech 14:17
from the East came to *J* . . . . Matt 2:1
that He must go to *J* . . . . . Matt 16:21
O *J*, *J*, the one who . . . . . Matt 23:37
we are going up to *J* . . . . . . Mark 10:33
Jesus lingered behind in *J* . Luke 2:43
you see *J* surrounded . . . . Luke 21:20
Daughters of *J*, do not . . . . Luke 23:28
but tarry in the city of *J* . Luke 24:49
J before the Passover . . . . John 11:55
be witnesses to Me in *J* . . . . . Acts 1:8
were gathered together at *J* . . Acts 4:6
you have filled *J* with . . . . . . Acts 5:28
Lord, they returned to *J* . . . . Acts 8:25
bring them bound to *J* . . . . . . Acts 9:2
when Saul had come to *J* . . . Acts 9:26
when Peter came up to *J* . . . Acts 11:2
came from *J* to Antioch . . . Acts 11:27
bound in the spirit to *J* . . . . Acts 20:22
shall the Jews at *J* bind . . . Acts 21:11
I went up to *J* to worship . . Acts 24:11
he was willing to go to *J* . . . Acts 25:20
the saints who are in *J* . . . . Rom 15:26
to bear your gift to *J* . . . . . . 1 Cor 16:3
corresponds to *J* which . . . . . Gal 4:25
city of My God, the New *J* . . Rev 3:12
saw the holy city, New *J* . . . Rev 21:2

JESHIMON
Wilderness west of the Dead Sea,
1 Sam 23:19, 24

JESHUA (or Joshua)
Postexilic high priest; returns with
Zerubbabel, Ezra 2:2
Aids in rebuilding temple, Ezra 3:2–8
Also called Joshua; seen in vision,
Zech 3:1–10

JESHURUN
Poetic name of endearment for Israel,
Deut 32:15

JESSE
Grandson of Ruth and Boaz, Ruth
4:17–22
Father of David, 1 Sam 16:1–13
Mentioned in prophecy, Is 11:1, 10

JESTING
talking, nor coarse *j* . . . . Eph 5:4

JESUS
See CHRIST; LORD JESUS CHRIST
birth of *J* Christ was as . . . . Matt 1:18
shall call His name *J* . . . . . . Matt 1:21
J was led up by the . . . . Matt 4:1
These twelve *J* sent . . . . . . Matt 10:5
and laid hands on *J* . . . . . . Matt 26:50
Barabbas and destroy *J* . . . Matt 27:20
we to do with You, *J* . . . . . . Mark 1:24
J withdrew with His . . . . Mark 3:7
J said, "Do not forbid . . . . Mark 9:39
J went into Jerusalem . . . . Mark 11:11
as they were eating, *J* . . . . Mark 14:22
and he delivered *J* . . . . Mark 15:15
J increased in wisdom . . . . . Luke 2:52
J said, "Who touched . . . . . Luke 8:45
J rebuked the unclean . . . . Luke 9:42
J said to him, "Foxes . . . . . Luke 9:58
sought to see who *J* was . . Luke 19:3
near to *J* to kiss Him . . . . Luke 22:47
J Himself stood in the . . . Luke 24:36
truth came through *J* . . . . . . John 1:17
J said to him, "Rise, take . . . . John 5:8
J lifted up His eyes . . . . John 6:5
they saw *J* walking on . . . . John 6:19
But *J* stooped down and . . . John 8:6
J wept . . . . John 11:35
anointed the feet of *J* . . . . John 12:3
J was crucified . . . . John 19:20
other things that *J* did . . . . John 21:25
This *J* God has raised . . . . . Acts 2:32
of Your holy Servant *J* . . . . Acts 4:30
believed on the Lord *J* . . . Acts 11:17
baptized into Christ *J* . . . . . Rom 6:3
Spirit of life in Christ *J* . . . . Rom 8:2
your mouth the Lord *J* . . . Rom 10:9
among you except *J* . . . . . . 1 Cor 2:2
the day of the Lord *J* . . . . . . 1 Cor 5:5
heavenly places in Christ *J* . . Eph 2:6
that at the name of *J* every . . Phil 2:10
perfect in Christ *J* . . . . Col 1:28
exhort in the Lord *J* . . . . . 1 Thess 4:1
But we see *J*, who was . . . . . . Heb 2:9
J the Son of God, let us . . . . Heb 4:14
looking unto *J*, the author . . Heb 12:2
J Christ the righteous . . . . 1 John 2:1
that *J* is the Son of God . . . 1 John 5:5
Revelation of *J* Christ . . . . Rev 1:1
Even so, come, Lord *J* . . . . Rev 22:20

JETHER
Gideon's oldest son, Judg 8:20, 21

JETHRO
Priest of Midian; becomes Moses'
father-in-law, Ex 2:16–22
Blesses Moses' departure, Ex 4:18
Visits and counsels Moses, Ex 18
Also called Reuel, Num 10:29

JEW
J whose name was . . . . Esth 2:5

is it that You, being a *J* . . . . . John 4:9
Am I a *J*? . . . . John 18:35
found out that he was a *J* . Acts 19:34
I am indeed a *J*, born in . . . Acts 22:3
believes, for the *J* first . . . . . Rom 1:16
who does evil, of the *J* first . . Rom 2:9
he is not a *J* who is one . . . Rom 2:28
advantage then has the *J* . . . Rom 3:1
no distinction between *J* . . Rom 10:12
Jews I became as a *J* . . . . . 1 Cor 9:20
If you, being a *J*, live in . . . . Gal 2:14
is neither *J* nor Greek . . . . . Gal 3:28
is neither Greek nor *J* . . . . . . Col 3:11

JEWELS
your thighs are like *j* . . . . . . Songs 7:1
that I make them My *j* . . . . . . Mal 3:17

JEWISH
against their *J* brethren . . . . . Neh 5:1
J descent, you will not . . . . . Esth 6:13
a *J* brother in bondage . . . . . Jer 34:9
expectation of the *J* . . . . . . Acts 12:11
J exorcists took it upon . . . Acts 19:13
light to the *J* people and . . Acts 26:23
giving heed to *J* fables . . . . Titus 1:14

JEWS
See KING OF THE JEWS
Jesus born King of the, Matt 2:2
Salvation comes through the, John
4:22; Acts 11:19; Rom 1:16; 2:9, 10
Reject Christ, Matt 27:21–25
Reject the gospel, Acts 13:42–46

the elders of the *J* build . . . . Ezra 6:7
are these feeble *J* doing . . . . . Neh 4:2
J who were at Shushan . . . Esth 9:18
sent letters to all the *J* . . . . Esth 9:30
I am afraid of the *J* who . . . Jer 38:19
of the *J* seven hundred . . . . Jer 52:30
There are certain *J* whom . . Dan 3:12
You the King of the *J* . . . . Matt 27:11
of purification of the *J* . . . . . John 2:6
for salvation is of the *J* . . . . John 4:22
those *J* who believed Him . John 8:31
the *J* took up stones . . . . . John 10:31
The King of the *J* . . . . John 19:19
dwelling in Jerusalem *J* . . . Acts 2:5
confounded the *J* who . . . . Acts 9:22
in the land of the *J* . . . . . . Acts 10:39
in the synagogues of the *J* . Acts 13:5
But the *J* stirred up the . . . Acts 13:50
refuted the *J* publicly, ... Acts 18:28
the God of the *J* only . . . . . Rom 3:29
J a stumbling block . . . . . . 1 Cor 1:23
whether *J* or Greeks, ... 1 Cor 12:13
From the *J* five times I . . . . 2 Cor 11:24
compel Gentiles to live as *J* . . Gal 2:14
of those who say they are *J* . Rev 2:9
Satan, who say they are *J* . . . Rev 3:9

JEZEBEL
Ahab's idolatrous wife, 1 Kin 16:31
Her abominable acts, 1 Kin 18:4, 13;
19:1, 2; 21:1–16
Death prophesied; prophecy fulfilled,
1 Kin 21:23; 2 Kin 9:7, 30–37
——— Type of paganism in the church,
Rev 2:20

JEZREEL
Ahab's capital, 1 Kin 18:45; 21:1
Ahab's family destroyed at, 1 Kin
21:23; 2 Kin 9:30–37; 10:1–11

JOAB
David's nephew; commands his army,
2 Sam 2:10–32; 8:16; 10:1–14; 11:1,
14–25; 20:1–23
Kills Abner, 2 Sam 3:26, 27
Intercedes for Absalom, 2 Sam 14:1–33
Remains loyal to David; kills Absalom,
2 Sam 18:1–5, 9–17
Demoted; kills Amasa, 2 Sam 19:13;
20:8–10

JOANNA *(continued)*

Opposes census, 2 Sam 24:1–9; 1 Chr 21:1–6
Supports Adonijah, 1 Kin 1:7
Solomon orders his death in obedience to David's command, 1 Kin 2:1–6, 28–34

JOANNA

Wife of Chuza, Herod's steward, Luke 8:1–3
With others, heralds Christ's resurrection, Luke 23:55, 56

JOASH (or Jehoash)

Son of Ahaziah; saved from Athaliah's massacre and crowned by Jehoiada, 2 Kin 11:1–12
Repairs the temple, 2 Kin 12:1–16
Turns away from the Lord and is killed, 2 Chr 24:17–25
—— Wicked king of Israel; son of Jehoahaz, 2 Kin 13:10–25
Defeats Amaziah in battle, 2 Kin 14:8–15; 2 Chr 25:17–24

JOB

Model of righteousness, Job 1:1–5
His faith tested, Job 1:6—2:10
Debates with his three friends; complains to God, Job 3—33
Elihu intervenes, Job 34—37
God's answer, Job 38—41
Humbles himself and repents, Job 42:1–6
Restored to prosperity, Job 42:10–17

JOCHEBED

Daughter of Levi; mother of Miriam, Aaron, and Moses, Ex 6:20

JOEL

Preexilic prophet, Joel 1:1
Quoted in N.T., Acts 2:16

JOGBEHAH

Town in Gilead, Judg 8:11

JOHANAN

Military leader of Judah; warns Gedaliah of Ishmael's plot, Jer 40:13–16
Avenges Gedaliah; takes the people to Egypt, Jer 41:11–18

JOHN

The apostle, son of Zebedee; called as disciple, Matt 4:21, 22; Luke 5:1–11
Chosen as one of the Twelve, Matt 10:2
Especially close to Christ, Matt 17:1–9; Mark 13:3; John 13:23–25; 19:26, 27; 20:2–8; 21:7, 20
Ambitious and overzealous, Mark 10:35–41; Luke 9:54–56
Sent to prepare the Passover, Luke 22:8–13
With Peter, heals a man and is arrested, Acts 3:1—4:22
Goes on missionary trip with Peter, Acts 8:14–25
Exiled on Patmos, Rev 1:9
Author of Gospel, three epistles, and the Revelation, John 21:23–25; 1 John; 2 John; 3 John; Rev 1:1
—— The Baptist; O.T. prophecy concerning, Is 40:3–5; Mal 4:5
His birth announced and accomplished, Luke 1:11–20, 57–80
Preaches repentance, Luke 3:1–20
Bears witness to Christ, John 1:19–36; 3:25–36
Baptizes Jesus, Matt 3:13–17
Jesus speaks about, Matt 11:7–19
Identified with Elijah, Matt 11:13, 14
Herod imprisons and kills, Matt 14:3–12
—— Surnamed Mark: *see* MARK

JOIN

Woe to those who *j* .... Is 5:8
'Come and let us *j* .... Jer 50:5
of the rest dared *j* .... Acts 5:13

JOINED

and mother and be *j* ...... Gen 2:24
for him who is *j* .... Eccl 9:4
"Ephraim is *j* .... Hos 4:17
what God has *j* .... Matt 19:6
you be perfectly *j* .... 1 Cor 1:10
But he who is *j* .... 1 Cor 6:17
the whole body, *j* .... Eph 4:16

JOINT

j as He wrestled .... Gen 32:25
My bones are out of *j* ...... Ps 22:14
j heirs with Christ .... Rom 8:17
by what every *j* .... Eph 4:16

JOINTS

and knit together by *j* ...... Col 2:19
and spirit, and of *j* .... Heb 4:12

JOKTAN

See ARABIA
Descendants of Shem, Gen. 10:21, 25

JONADAB (or Jehonadab)

David's nephew; encourages Amnon in sin, 2 Sam 13:3–5, 32–36
—— Son of Rechab; father of the Rechabites, Jer 35:5–19
Helps Jehu overthrow Baal, 2 Kin 10:15–28

JONAH

Prophet sent to Nineveh; rebels and is punished, Jon 1
Repents and is saved, Jon 2
Preaches in Nineveh, Jon 3
Becomes angry at God's mercy, Jon 4
Type of Christ's resurrection, Matt 12:39, 40

JONATHAN

King Saul's eldest son; his exploits in battle, 1 Sam 13:2, 3; 14:1–14, 49
Saved from his father's wrath, 1 Sam 14:24–45
Makes covenant with David; protects him from Saul, 1 Sam 18:1–4; 19:1–7; 20:1–42; 23:15–18
Killed by Philistines, 1 Sam 31:2, 8
Mourned by David; his son provided for, 2 Sam 1:17–27; 9:1–8
—— Son of high priest Abiathar; faithful to David, 2 Sam 15:26–36; 17:15–22
Informs Adonijah of Solomon's coronation, 1 Kin 1:41–49

JOPPA

Scene of Peter's vision, Acts 10:5–23, 32

JORAM

See JEHORAM

JORDAN RIVER

Lot dwells near, Gen 13:8–13
Canaan's eastern boundary, Num 34:12
Moses forbidden to cross, Deut 3:27
Miraculous dividing of, for Israel, Josh 3:1–17
by Elijah, 2 Kin 2:5–8
by Elisha, 2 Kin 2:13,14
Naaman healed in, 2 Kin 5:10–14
John baptizes in, Matt 3:6, 13–17

JOSEPH

Son of Jacob by Rachel, Gen 30:22–24
Loved by Jacob; hated by his brothers, Gen 37:3–11
Sold into slavery, Gen 37:12–36
Unjustly imprisoned in Egypt, Gen 39:1–23
Interprets dreams in prison, Gen 40:1–23

Wins Pharaoh's favor, Gen 41:1–44
Prepares Egypt for famine, Gen 41:45–57
Sells grain to his brothers, Gen 42—44
Reveals identity and reconciles with brothers; sends for Jacob, Gen 45:1–28
Settles family in Egypt, Gen 47:1–12
His sons blessed by Jacob, Gen 48:1–22
Blessed by Jacob, Gen 49:22–26
Buries his father; reassures his brothers, Gen 50:1–21
His death, Gen 50:22–26
—— Husband of Mary, Jesus' mother, Matt 1:16
Visited by angel, Matt 1:19–25
Takes Mary to Bethlehem, Luke 2:3–7
Protects Jesus from Herod, Matt 2:13–23
Jesus subject to, Luke 2:51
—— Secret disciple from Arimathea; donates tomb and assists in Christ's burial, Mark 15:42–46; Luke 23:50–53; John 19:38–42

JOSES

One of Jesus' half brothers, Matt 13:55
—— The name of Barnabas, Acts 4:36

JOSHUA

See JESHUA
—— Leader of Israel succeeding Moses, Num 27:18–23
Leads battle against Amalek, Ex 17:8–16
Sent as spy into Canaan; reports favorably, Num 13:16–25; 14:6–9
Assumes command, Josh 1:1–18
Sends spies to Jericho, Josh 2:1
Leads Israel across Jordan, Josh 3:1–17
Sets up commemorative stones, Josh 4:1–24
Circumcises the people, Josh 5:2–9
Conquers Jericho, Josh 5:13—6:27
Punishes Achan, Josh 7:10–26
Conquers Canaan, Josh 8—12
Divides the land, Josh 13—19
Addresses rulers, Josh 23:1–16
Addresses the people, Josh 24:1–28
His death, Josh 24:29, 30

JOSIAH

Righteous king of Judah; son of Amon, 2 Kin 22:1, 2
Repairs the temple, 2 Kin 22:3–9
Hears the Law; spared for his humility, 2 Kin 22:10–20
Institutes reforms, 2 Kin 23:1–25
Killed in battle, 2 Chr 35:20–25

JOT

one *j* or one tittle .... Matt 5:18

JOTHAM

Gideon's youngest son; escapes Abimelech's massacre, Judg 9:5
Utters prophetic parable, Judg 9:7–21
—— Righteous king of Judah; son of Azariah, 2 Kin 15:32–38; 2 Chr 27:1–9

JOURNEY

us go three days' *j* .... Ex 3:18
busy, or he is on a *j* ...... 1 Kin 18:27
he has gone on a long *j* .... Prov 7:19
city, a three-day *j* in extent ... Jon 3:3
nor bag for your *j*, nor .... Matt 10:10
he went on a *j* .... Matt 25:15
Nevertheless I must *j* ...... Luke 13:33
wearied from His *j* .... John 4:6
may send me on my *j* ...... 1 Cor 16:6
j in a manner worthy of ..... 3 John 6

JOY

Lord your God with *j* ..... Deut 28:47
of Obed-Edom with *j* ..... 1 Chr 15:25
the *j* of the Lord is your .... Neh 8:10
heart to sing for *j* .... Job 29:13
presence is fullness of *j* ..... Ps 16:11
j comes in the morning .... Ps 30:5
To God my exceeding *j* ..... Ps 43:4
me the *j* of Your salvation ... Ps 51:12
sow in tears shall reap in *j* .. Ps 126:5
You according to the *j* .... Is 9:3
j you will draw water .... Is 12:3
everlasting *j* on their heads .. Is 51:11
ashes, the oil of *j* .... Is 61:3
j shall be theirs .... Is 61:7
shall sing for *j* .... Is 65:14
word was to me the *j* ...... Jer 15:16
I will *j* in the God of my .... Hab 3:18
receives it with *j* .... Matt 13:20
Enter into the *j* .... Matt 25:21
in my womb for *j* .... Luke 1:44
good tidings of great *j* ..... Luke 2:10
there will be more *j* .... Luke 15:7
did not believe for *j* ...... Luke 24:41
My *j* may remain in ...... John 15:11
will be turned into *j* ...... John 16:20
that your *j* may be full .... John 16:24
they may have My *j* ...... John 17:13
finish my race with *j* ..... Acts 20:24
peace and *j* in the Holy ... Rom 14:17
fill you with all *j* .... Rom 15:13
that my *j* is the *j* .... 2 Cor 2:3
the Spirit is love, *j* .... Gal 5:22
brethren, my *j* and .... Phil 4:1
longsuffering with *j* .... Col 1:11
with *j* of the Holy Spirit... 1 Thess 1:6
are our glory and *j* ...... 1 Thess 2:20
that I may be filled with *j* ..2 Tim 1:4
j that was set before ...... Heb 12:2
count it all *j* .... James 1:2
j inexpressible and full ... 1 Pet 1:8
with exceeding *j* .... 1 Pet 4:13
that your *j* may be full .... 1 John 1:4
that our *j* may be full .... 2 John 12
I have no greater *j* .... 3 John 4
His glory with exceeding *j* .. Jude 24

JOYFUL

And my soul shall be *j* ...... Ps 35:9
Make a *j* shout to the ...... Ps 100:1
of prosperity be *j* .... Eccl 7:14
and make them *j* .... Is 56:7
soul shall be *j* in my God .... Is 61:10
I am exceedingly *j* .... 2 Cor 7:4
to be *j* for the present ..... Heb 12:11

JOYFULLY

Let us shout *j* to the Rock .... Ps 95:1
shout *j* before the Lord ...... Ps 98:6
j accepted the plundering .. Heb 10:34

JOZACHAR

Assassin of Joash, 2 Kin 12:19–21
Called Zabad, 2 Chr 24:26

JUBAL

Son of Lamech, Gen 4:21

JUBILEE

cause the trumpet of the *J* ...Lev 25:9
For it is the *J* .... Lev 25:12
his field after the *J*, then .. Lev 27:18
In the Year of *J* the field .. Lev 27:24
the *J* of the children .... Num 36:4

JUDAH

Son of Jacob and Leah, Gen 29:30–35
Intercedes for Joseph, Gen 37:26, 27
Fails in duty to Tamar, Gen 38:1–30
Offers himself as Benjamin's ransom,
Gen 44:18–34
Jacob bestows birthright on, Gen
49:3–10
Accepted the blessing of Christ, Matt 1:3, 16
—— Tribe of:
Prophecy concerning, Gen 49:8–12

Numbered at Sinai, Num 1:26, 27
Territory assigned to, Josh 15:1–63
Leads in conquest of Canaan, Judg
1:1–19
Makes David king, 2 Sam 2:1–11
Loyal to David and his house, 2 Sam
20:1, 2; 1 Kin 12:20
Becomes leader of southern kingdom,
1 Kin 14:21, 22
Taken to Babylon, 2 Kin 24:1–16
Returns after exile, 2 Chr 36:20–23

JUDAISM

And I advanced in *J* .... Gal 1:14

JUDAS

Judas Lebbaeus, surnamed Thad-
daeus, Matt 10:3
One of the Twelve, Luke 6:13, 16
Offers a question, John 14:22
—— Judas Barsabas, a chief deputy,
Acts 15:22–32
—— Betrayer of Christ: *see* ISCARIOT

JUDE (or Judas)

Half brother of Christ, Matt 13:55
Does not believe in Christ, John 7:5
Becomes Christ's disciple, Acts 1:14
Writes an epistle, Jude 1

JUDEA

Christ born in, Matt 2:1, 5, 6
Hostile toward Christ, John 7:1
Gospel preached in, Acts 8:1, 4
Churches established in, Acts 9:31

JUDGE

The Lord *j* between .... Gen 16:5
Dan shall *j* his people as ... Gen 49:16
you a price and a *j* over us ... Ex 2:14
Moses sat to *j* the people .... Ex 18:13
For the Lord will *j* .... Deut 32:36
the Lord was with the *j* .... Judg 2:18
coming to *j* the earth ..... 1 Chr 16:33
and judges who may *j* all .. Ezra 7:25
He shall *j* the world in .... Ps 9:8
How long will you *j* unjustly ..Ps 82:2
Arise, O God, *j* the earth ..... Ps 82:8
Rise up, O *J* of the .... Ps 94:2
He is coming to *j* the earth .. Ps 96:13
He shall *j* the world, and .... Ps 98:9
the Lord will *j* His people .. Ps 135:14
j righteously, and plead .... Prov 31:9
sword the Lord will *j* .... Is 66:16
deliver you to the *j* .... Matt 5:25
"*J* not, that you be not ...... Matt 7:1
"Man, who made Me a *j* .. Luke 12:14
j who did not fear God .... Luke 18:2
As I hear, I *j* .... John 5:30
Do not *j* according .... John 7:24
I *j* no one .... John 8:15
j the world but to .... John 12:47
this, O man, you who *j* ..... Rom 2:3
then how will God *j* .... Rom 3:6
Therefore let us not *j* ...... Rom 14:13
the saints will *j* the world ... 1 Cor 6:2
that we shall *j* angels ...... 1 Cor 6:3
J among yourselves .... 1 Cor 11:13
let no one *j* you in .... Col 2:16
Christ, who will *j* .... 2 Tim 4:1
Lord, the righteous *J* ...... 2 Tim 4:8
heaven, to God the *J* ...... Heb 12:23
and adulterers God will *j* .... Heb 13:4
are you to *j* another .... James 4:12
the *J* is standing at the ..... James 5:9
who is ready to *j* the living .. 1 Pet 4:5
holy and true, until You *j* ...Rev 6:10

JUDGED

God has *j* my case .... Gen 30:6
So they *j* the people at all ... Ex 18:26
upon him, and he *j* Israel ... Judg 3:10
Samuel *j* Israel all the .... 1 Sam 7:15
condemn him when he is *j* ... Ps 37:33
He *j* the cause of the poor .. Jer 22:16
You who *j* your sisters, ... Ezek 16:52

Judge not, that you be not *j* . Matt 7:1
You have rightly *j* .... Luke 7:43
ruler of this world is *j* .... John 16:11
being *j* by you this day .... Acts 24:21
law will be *j* by the law ... Rom 2:12
overcome when You are *j* ... Rom 3:4
world will be *j* by you ...... 1 Cor 6:2
But when we are *j* .... 1 Cor 11:32
be *j* by the law of liberty .. James 2:12
the dead were *j* according .. Rev 20:12

JUDGES

j who delivered .... Judg 2:16
in the days when the *j* ...... Ruth 1:1
said to the *j*, "Take heed .. 2 Chr 19:6
Surely He is God who *j* .... Ps 58:11
He *j* among the gods .... Ps 82:1
He makes the *j* of the ...... Is 40:23
j are evening wolves .... Zeph 3:3
For the Father *j* .... John 5:22
he who is spiritual *j* ...... 1 Cor 2:15
j me is the Lord .... 1 Cor 4:4
who without partiality *j* ... 1 Pet 1:17
Him who *j* righteously ..... 1 Pet 2:23

JUDGMENT

Aaron shall bear the *j* of ... Ex 28:30
show partiality in *j* .... Deut 1:17
David administered *j* ..... 2 Sam 8:15
Does God subvert *j* .... Job 8:3
Teach me good *j* .... Ps 119:66
instructs him in right *j* ..... Is 28:26
from prison and from *j* ..... Is 53:8
I will also speak *j* .... Jer 4:12
j was made in favor of ..... Dan 7:22
be in danger of the *j* ...... Matt 5:21
For with what *j* you judge ... Matt 7:2
in the day of *j* than for .... Matt 11:22
will rise up in the *j* .... Matt 12:42
shall not come into *j* ...... John 5:24
and My *j* is righteous ..... John 5:30
but judge with righteous *j* .. John 7:24
if I do judge, My *j* .... John 8:16
For *j* I have come into ..... John 9:39
Now is the *j* of this .... John 12:31
the righteous *j* of God ..... Rom 1:32
j which came from one .... Rom 5:16
all stand before the *j* ...... Rom 14:10
yet I give *j* as one whom ... 1 Cor 7:25
eats and drinks *j* .... 1 Cor 11:29
appear before the *j* .... 2 Cor 5:10
preceding them to *j* .... 1 Tim 5:24
after this the *j* .... Heb 9:27
For *j* is without mercy ... James 2:13
receive a stricter *j* .... James 3:1
time has come for *j* .... 1 Pet 4:17
a long time their *j* .... 2 Pet 2:3
boldness in the day of *j* .. 1 John 4:17
darkness for the *j* .... Jude 6
the hour of His *j* has come .. Rev 14:7
hour your *j* has come ..... Rev 18:10
j was committed to them .... Rev 20:4

JUDGMENTS

The *j* of the Lord are .... Ps 19:9
j are a great deep .... Ps 36:6
I dread, for Your *j* .... Ps 119:39
statutes nor kept My *j* ..... Ezek 5:7
had not executed My *j* .... Ezek 20:24
unsearchable are His *j* .... Rom 11:33
righteous are His *j* .... Rev 19:2

JUG

So she opened a *j* of milk .. Judg 4:19
j of water by Saul's ...... 1 Sam 26:12

JULIUS

Roman centurion assigned to guard
Paul, Acts 27:1–44

JUST

Noah was a *j* man .... Gen 6:9
I have done *j* as you told ... Gen 27:19
j as the Lord commanded .. Num 26:4
J as the gazelle and the ... Deut 12:22
a perfect and *j* weight ..... Deut 25:15

JUSTICE (continued)

j as my strength was ...... Josh 14:11
Hear a *j* cause .... Ps 17:1
the path of the *j* is like ..... Prov 4:18
j weight is His delight ...... Prov 11:1
It is a joy for the *j* .... Prov 21:15
j man who perishes .... Eccl 7:15
For there is not a *j* .... Eccl 7:20
way of the *j* is uprightness .... Is 26:7
the blood of the *j* .... Lam 4:13
j shall live by his .... Hab 2:4
He is *j* and having .... Zech 9:9
her husband, being a *j* ..... Matt 1:19
resurrection of the *j* ...... Luke 14:14
j persons who need no ..... Luke 15:7
the Holy One and the J ..... Acts 3:14
dead, both of the *j* .... Acts 24:15
j shall live by faith .... Rom 1:17
that He might be *j* .... Rom 3:26
the *j* shall live by faith ...... Gal 3:11
j as you were called in one ... Eph 4:4
j as Christ also loved the .... Eph 5:25
whatever things are *j* .... Phil 4:8
received a *j* reward, ... Heb 2:2
j men made perfect .... Heb 12:23
have murdered the *j* ...... James 5:6
He is faithful and *j* .... 1 John 1:9
J and true are Your .... Rev 15:3

JUSTICE

to do righteousness and *j* .. Gen 18:19
after many to pervert *j* ...... Ex 23:2
for all His ways are *j* ...... Deut 32:4
bribes, and perverted *j* ..... 1 Sam 8:3
to discern *j* .... 1 Kin 3:11
the Almighty pervert *j* .... Job 8:3
gives *j* to the oppressed ..... Job 36:6
j as the noonday .... Ps 37:6
and Your poor with *j* .... Ps 72:2
Do *j* to the afflicted .... Ps 82:3
and *j* are the .... Ps 89:14
j for all who are oppressed .. Ps 103:6
He guards the paths of *j*, ... Prov 2:8
revenues without *j* .... Prov 16:8
do not understand *j* .... Prov 28:5
j the measuring line .... Is 28:17
the LORD is a God of *j*........ Is 30:18
He will bring forth *j* .... Is 42:1
No one calls for *j* .... Is 59:4
J is turned back .... Is 59:14
I, the LORD, love *j* .... Is 61:8
you, O home of *j* .... Jer 31:23
plundering, execute *j* ...... Ezek 45:9
truth, and His ways *j* .... Dan 4:37
observe mercy and *j* .... Hos 12:6
who turn *j* to wormwood ... Amos 5:7
'Execute true *j* .... Zech 7:9
"Where is the God of *j* ...... Mal 2:17
And He will declare *j* ...... Matt 12:18
of herbs, and pass by *j* .... Luke 11:42
His humiliation His *j* .... Acts 8:33

JUSTIFICATION

because of our *j* .... Rom 4:25
offenses resulted in *j* ...... Rom 5:16
men, resulting in *j* .... Rom 5:18

JUSTIFIED

Me that you may be *j* .... Job 40:8
of Israel shall be *j* .... Is 45:25
words you will be *j* ...... Matt 12:37
But wisdom is *j* .... Luke 7:35
j rather than the .... Luke 18:14
who believes is *j* .... Acts 13:39
"That You may be *j* .... Rom 3:4
law no flesh will be *j* ...... Rom 3:20
j freely by His grace .... Rom 3:24
having been *j* by .... Rom 5:1
these He also *j* .... Rom 8:30
but you were *j* .... 1 Cor 6:11
that we might be *j* .... Gal 2:16
who attempt to be *j* .... Gal 5:4
j in the Spirit .... 1 Tim 3:16
then that a man is *j* ...... James 2:24
the harlot also *j* .... James 2:25

JUSTIFIER

be just and the *j* .... Rom 3:26

JUSTIFIES

He who *j* the wicked ...... Prov 17:15
It is God who *j* .... Rom 8:33

JUSTIFY

j the wicked for a .... Is 5:23
wanting to *j* himself ...... Luke 10:29
"You are those who *j* ..... Luke 16:15
is one God who will *j* ...... Rom 3:30
that God would *j* .... Gal 3:8

JUSTLY

of you but to do *j* .... Mic 6:8
And we indeed *j* .... Luke 23:41
how devoutly and *j* ..... 1 Thess 2:10

JUSTUS

Surname of Joseph, a disciple, Acts
   1:23
——— Man of Corinth; befriends Paul,
   Acts 18:7
——— Fellow worker of Paul, also called
   Jesus, Col 4:11

KADESH

Spies sent from, Num 13:3, 26
Moses strikes rock at, Num 20:1–13
Boundary in the new Israel, Ezek 47:19

KADESH BARNEA

Boundary of Promised Land, Num
   34:1–4
Limit of Joshua's military campaign,
   Josh 10:41

KARNAIM

Conquered region, Amos 6:13

KEDESH

Town in south Judah, Josh 15:23
——— Levite city in Issachar, 1 Chr 6:72

KEDESH NAPHTALI

City of refuge, Josh 21:27, 32
Home of Barak, Judg 4:6

KEEP

k you wherever you .... Gen 28:15
day, to *k* it holy .... Ex 20:8
and *k* My judgments ...... Lev 25:18
k all My commandments .. 1 Kin 6:12
and that You would *k* ...... 1 Chr 4:10
Even he who cannot *k* ...... Ps 22:29
K my soul, and deliver me ... Ps 25:20
do not *k* silence .... Ps 35:22
k Your righteous .... Ps 119:106
k them in the midst of ..... Prov 4:21
K your heart with all ...... Prov 4:23
a time to *k* silence .... Eccl 3:7
k your appointed feasts, ... Nah 1:15
Let all the earth *k* .... Hab 2:20
k the commandments ..... Matt 19:17
charge over you, to *k* ...... Luke 4:10
If you love Me, *k* .... John 14:15
k through Your name ..... John 17:11
orderly and *k* the law ..... Acts 21:24
and *k* the traditions .... 1 Cor 11:2
Let your women *k* .... 1 Cor 14:34
a debtor to *k* the whole law .. Gal 5:3
k the unity of the .... Eph 4:3
k yourself pure .... 1 Tim 5:22
He is able to *k* what I ...... 2 Tim 1:12
to *k* oneself unspotted ..... James 1:27
k His commandments ..... 1 John 2:3
k His commandments ..... 1 John 3:22
k yourselves from idols .. 1 John 5:21
k yourselves in the .... Jude 21
k you from stumbling .... Jude 24
k those things .... Rev 1:3
I also will *k* you from the ... Rev 3:10
of those who *k* the words ... Rev 22:9

KEEPER

Am I my brother's *k* .... Gen 4:9

of the *k* of the prison ...... Gen 39:21
The LORD is your *k* .... Ps 121:5
me the *k* of the vineyards ... Song 1:6
to the *k* of his vineyard .... Luke 13:7
of the prison, awaking .... Acts 16:27

KEEPERS

in the day when the *k* ...... Eccl 12:3

KEEPS

the faithful God who *k* .... Deut 7:9
God, Who *k* covenant and .. Neh 9:32
who *k* you will not slumber .. Ps 121:3
k truth forever .... Ps 146:6
k his way preserves .... Prov 16:17
k the commandment .... Prov 19:16
Whoever *k* the law is a ..... Prov 28:7
none of you *k* the law ...... John 7:19
born of God *k* himself .... 1 John 5:18
and *k* his garments .... Rev 16:15

KEILAH

Town of Judah; rescued from Philistines by David, 1 Sam 23:1–5
Prepares to betray David; he escapes,
   1 Sam 23:6–13

KENITES

Canaanite tribe whose land is promised
   to Abraham's seed, Gen 15:19
Subjects of Balaam's prophecy, Num
   24:20–22
Settle with Judahites, Judg 1:16
Spared by Saul in war with Amalekites,
   1 Sam 15:6

KEPT

shall be *k* burning on it ...... Lev 6:9
be *k* as a sign against ..... Num 17:10
He *k* him as the apple of .. Deut 32:10
For I have *k* the ways .... 2 Sam 22:22
k what You promised ...... 2 Chr 6:15
Now Josiah *k* a Passover .. 2 Chr 35:1
desolate she *k* Sabbath .. 2 Chr 36:21
brethren who *k* the gates, .. Neh 11:19
gatekeepers *k* the charge .. Neh 12:45
that *k* a pilgrim feast .... Ps 42:4
vineyard I have *k* .... Song 1:6
when a holy festival is *k* ... Is 30:29
k charge of My .... Ezek 44:15
we have *k* His ordinance .... Mal 3:14
these things I have *k* ...... Matt 19:20
But Jesus *k* silent .... Matt 26:63
she *k* asking Him to cast ... Mark 7:26
all these things I have *k* .. Mark 10:20
k all these things .... Luke 2:19
love, just as I have *k* ...... John 15:10
If they *k* My word, they ... John 15:20
You gave Me I have *k* ..... John 17:12
k back part of the .... Acts 5:2
k secret since the world ... Rom 16:25
I have *k* the faith .... 2 Tim 4:7
who are *k* by the power .... 1 Pet 1:5
Because you have *k* My ..... Rev 3:10

KETURAH

Abraham's second wife, Gen 25:1
Sons of:
   listed, Gen 25:1, 2
   given gifts and sent away, Gen 25:6

KEY

The *k* of the house of .... Is 22:22
have taken away the *k* ... Luke 11:52
"He who has the *k* .... Rev 3:7
heaven, having the *k* ...... Rev 20:1

KEYS

I will give you the *k* ...... Matt 16:19
And I have the *k* .... Rev 1:18

KIBROTH HATTAAVAH

Burial site of Israelites slain by God,
   Num 11:33–35

KICK

is hard for you to *k* .... Acts 9:5

KIDNAPPERS

for sodomites, for *k* .... 1 Tim 1:10

KIDNAPS

"He who *k* a man and . . . . Ex 21:16

KIDRON

Valley near Jerusalem; crossed by David and Christ, 2 Sam 15:23; John 18:1

Idols dumped there, 2 Chr 29:16

KILL

who finds me will *k* . . . . Gen 4:14
k the Passover lamb . . . . Ex 12:21
I *k* and I make alive . . . . . . Deut 32:39
"Am I God, to *k* . . . . 2 Kin 5:7
a time to *k* . . . . Eccl 3:3
to save life or to *k* . . . . Mark 3:4
of them they will *k* . . . . Luke 11:49
afraid of those who *k* . . . . . Luke 12:4
Why do you seek to *k* . . . . . . John 7:19
except to steal, and to *k* . . . John 10:10
"Rise, Peter; *k* and eat . . . . Acts 10:13
was about to *k* himself . . . . . Acts 16:27
to *k* with sword, with . . . . Rev 6:8

KILLED

Abel his brother and *k* . . . . . . Gen 4:8
For I have *k* a man for . . . . . . Gen 4:23
LORD *k* all the firstborn . . . . . Ex 13:15
Your servant has *k* . . . . . . 1 Sam 17:36
for Your sake we are *k* . . . . . Ps 44:22
and scribes, and be *k* . . . . . Matt 16:21
Siloam fell and *k* them . . . . Luke 13:4
k the Prince of life . . . . Acts 3:15
me, and by it *k* me . . . . Rom 7:11
"For Your sake we are *k* . . . Rom 8:36
who *k* both the Lord . . . . 1 Thess 2:15
martyr, who was *k* . . . . Rev 2:13

KILLS

"The LORD *k* and . . . . 1 Sam 2:6
the one who *k* the . . . . Matt 23:37
for the letter *k* . . . . 2 Cor 3:6

KIND

animals after their *k* . . . . . . Gen 6:20
breed with another *k* . . . . . Lev 19:19
k can come out by . . . . Mark 9:29
For He is *k* to the . . . . Luke 6:35
suffers long and is *k* . . . . . 1 Cor 13:4
is one *k* of flesh of men, . . 1 Cor 15:39
And be *k* to one . . . . Eph 4:32
forgets what *k* of man . . . . James 1:24

KINDLED

When His wrath is *k* . . . . Ps 2:12
I, the LORD, have *k* . . . . . Ezek 20:48
wish it were already *k* . . . . Luke 12:49
they *k* a fire and made us . . Acts 28:2

KINDLY

The LORD deal *k* . . . . Ruth 1:8
Julius treated Paul *k* . . . . . Acts 27:3
k affectionate to one . . . . . Rom 12:10

KINDNESS

may the LORD show *k* . . . . 2 Sam 2:6
anger, abundant in *k* . . . . . Neh 9:17
me His marvelous *k* . . . . . . Ps 31:21
For His merciful *k* . . . . Ps 117:2
tongue is the law of *k* . . . . Prov 31:26
k shall not depart . . . . Is 54:10
I remember you, the *k* . . . . . Jer 2:2
by longsuffering, by *k* . . . . 2 Cor 6:6
longsuffering, *k* . . . . Gal 5:22
But when the *k* and the . . . . Titus 3:4
and to brotherly *k* . . . . 2 Pet 1:7

KING

Then Melchizedek *k* . . . . . Gen 14:18
days there was no *k* . . . . . Judg 17:6
said, "Give us a *k* . . . . 1 Sam 8:6
"Long live the *k* . . . . 1 Sam 10:24
they anointed David *k* . . . . 2 Sam 2:4
Yet I have set My *K* . . . . Ps 2:6
The LORD is *K* forever . . . . . Ps 10:16
K answer us when . . . . Ps 20:9
And the *K* of glory . . . . Ps 24:7
k is saved by the . . . . Ps 33:16

k Your judgments . . . . Ps 72:1
For God is my *K* . . . . Ps 74:12
do who succeeds the *k* . . . . Eccl 2:12
out of prison to be *k* . . . . . . Eccl 4:14
when your *k* is a child . . . . Eccl 10:16
In the year that *K* . . . . Is 6:1
k will reign in . . . . Is 32:1
the LORD is our *K* . . . . Is 33:22
Is not her *K* in her . . . . Jer 8:19
and the everlasting *K* . . . . . Jer 10:10
k of Babylon, *k* . . . . Ezek 26:7
I gave you a *k* in My . . . . . Hos 13:11
the LORD shall be *K* . . . . . Zech 14:9
He who has been born *K* . . . Matt 2:2
This Is Jesus the *K* . . . . . Matt 27:37
by force to make Him *k* . . . . John 6:15
"Behold your *K* . . . . John 19:14
there is another *k* . . . . Acts 17:7
Now to the *K* eternal . . . . . . 1 Tim 1:17
only Potentate, the *K* . . . . . 1 Tim 6:15
this Melchizedek, *k* . . . . Heb 7:1
Honor the *k* . . . . 1 Pet 2:17
K of kings and Lord of . . . . Rev 19:16

KING OF THE JEWS

He who has been born *K* . . . Matt 2:2
saying, "Are You the *K* . . . Matt 27:11
This Is Jesus the *K* . . . . . Matt 27:37
to release to you the *K* . . . . Mark 15:9
salute Him, "Hail, *K* . . . . . Mark 15:18
"If You are the *K* . . . . Luke 23:37
'He said, "I am the *K* . . . . . John 19:21

KINGDOM

you shall be to Me a *k* . . . . . Ex 19:6
LORD has torn the *k* . . . . . 1 Sam 15:28
Yours is the *k* . . . . 1 Chr 29:11
k is the LORD's . . . . Ps 22:28
the scepter of Your *k* . . . . . Ps 45:6
in heaven, and His *k* . . . . . Ps 103:19
is an everlasting *k* . . . . Ps 145:13
k which shall never be . . . . . Dan 2:44
High rules in the *k* . . . . Dan 4:17
Your *k* has been divided, . . Dan 5:28
and glory and a *k* . . . . Dan 7:14
k shall be the LORD's . . . . . . Obad 21
for Yours is the *k* . . . . Matt 6:13
Baptist until now the *k* . . . . Matt 11:12
are the sons of the *k* . . . . . Matt 13:38
k all things that offend . . . Matt 13:41
up to half of my *k* . . . . Mark 6:23
Blessed is the *k* of our . . . Mark 11:10
nation, and *k* against . . . . Mark 13:8
of His *k* there will be no . . . Luke 1:33
k of God has come near . . . Luke 10:9
k come, Your will be done . . Luke 11:2
k divided against . . . . Luke 11:17
to give you the *k* . . . . Luke 12:32
of such is the *k* of God . . . Luke 18:16
against nation, and *k* . . . . Luke 21:10
at My table in My *k* . . . . . Luke 22:30
You come into Your *k* . . . . Luke 23:42
he cannot enter the *k* . . . . . John 3:5
If My *k* were of this . . . . . John 18:36
preaching the *k* of God . . . Acts 20:25
when He delivers the *k* . . . 1 Cor 15:24
in the *k* of Christ and God . . Eph 5:5
you into His own *k* . . . . . 1 Thess 2:12
the scepter of Your *k* . . . . . Heb 1:8
we are receiving a *k* . . . . . Heb 12:28
into the everlasting *k* . . . . . 2 Pet 1:11

KINGDOM OF GOD

But seek first the *k* . . . . . . Matt 6:33
k has come upon you . . . . Matt 12:28
rich man to enter the *k* . . . Matt 19:24
harlots enter the *k* . . . . . . Matt 21:31
the *k* will be taken . . . . . . Matt 21:43
the gospel of the *k* . . . . . . Mark 1:14
the *k* is at hand . . . . Mark 1:15
the mystery of the *k* . . . . . Mark 4:11
what shall we liken the *k* . . Mark 4:30
death till they see the *k* . . . Mark 9:1
enter the *k* with one eye . . Mark 9:47

for of such is the *k* . . . . . Mark 10:14
riches to enter the *k* . . . . Mark 10:23
are not far from the *k* . . . Mark 12:34
I drink it new in the *k* . . . Mark 14:25
waiting for the *k* . . . . Mark 15:43
"I must preach the *k* . . . . . Luke 4:43
poor, for yours is the *k* . . . Luke 6:20
he who is least in the *k* . . . Luke 7:28
preach the *k* and to heal . . . Luke 9:2
you go and preach the *k* . . . Luke 9:60
back, is fit for the *k* . . . . . Luke 9:62
all the prophets in the *k* . . Luke 13:28
shall eat bread in the *k* . . . Luke 14:15
k has been preached . . . . . Luke 16:16
k does not come with . . . . Luke 17:20
the *k* is within you . . . . . . Luke 17:21
for the sake of the *k* . . . . . Luke 18:29
thought the *k* would . . . . . Luke 19:11
know that the *k* is near . . . Luke 21:31
he cannot see the *k* . . . . . . John 3:3
things pertaining to the *k* . . . Acts 1:3
tribulations enter the *k* . . . Acts 14:22
testified of the *k* . . . . Acts 28:23
the *k* is not eating and . . . Rom 14:17
the *k* is not in word . . . . . 1 Cor 4:20
will not inherit the *k* . . . . . 1 Cor 6:9
cannot inherit the *k* . . . . . 1 Cor 15:50
will not inherit the *k* . . . . . Gal 5:21
fellow workers for the *k* . . . Col 4:11
counted worthy of the *k* . . 2 Thess 1:5

KINGDOM OF HEAVEN

"Repent, for the *k* . . . . Matt 3:2
for theirs is the *k* . . . . Matt 5:10
by no means enter the *k* . . . Matt 5:20
Lord, shall enter the *k* . . . . . Matt 7:21
Isaac, and Jacob in the *k* . . Matt 8:11
'The *k* is at hand . . . . Matt 10:7
who is least in the *k* . . . . . Matt 11:11
the mysteries of the *k* . . . . Matt 13:11
The *k* is like a man . . . . . . Matt 13:24
k is like a mustard seed, . . Matt 13:31
The *k* is like leaven. . . . . . Matt 13:33
the *k* is like treasure . . . . Matt 13:44
k is like a dragnet . . . . . . Matt 13:47
you the keys of the *k* . . . . Matt 16:19
then is greatest in the *k* . . . Matt 18:1
by no means enter the *k* . . . Matt 18:3
is the greatest in the *k* . . . Matt 18:4
k is like a certain king . . . Matt 18:23
for of such is the *k* . . . . . Matt 19:14
a rich man to enter the *k* . . Matt 19:23
k is like a landowner . . . . . Matt 20:1
k is like a certain king . . . Matt 22:2
you shut up the *k* . . . . . . Matt 23:13
k shall be likened . . . . Matt 25:1
the *k* is like a man . . . . . . Matt 25:14

KINGDOMS

the *k* were moved . . . . Ps 46:6
tremble, who shook it . . . . . . Is 14:16
showed Him all the *k* . . . . . Matt 4:8
have become the *k* . . . . . . Rev 11:15

KINGS

The *k* of the earth set . . . . . . Ps 2:2
k shall fall down . . . . Ps 72:11
He is awesome to the *k* . . . Ps 76:12
By me *k* reign . . . . Prov 8:15
He will stand before *k* . . . Prov 22:29
k is unsearchable . . . . Prov 25:3
that which destroys *k* . . . . Prov 31:3
it is not for *k* to drink . . . . Prov 31:4
K shall be your foster . . . . . Is 49:23
"They set up *k* . . . . Hos 8:4
before governors and *k* . . . Matt 10:18
k have desired to see . . . . Luke 10:24
You have reigned as *k* . . . 1 Cor 4:8
and has made us *k* . . . . Rev 1:6
that the way of the *k* . . . . . Rev 16:12
may eat the flesh of *k* . . . . Rev 19:18

KIR HARESETH

Fortified city of Moab, 2 Kin 3:25; Is 15:1; 16:7

KIRJATH ARBA
Ancient name of Hebron, Gen 23:2
Possessed by Judah, Judg 1:10

KIRJATH JEARIM
Gibeonite town, Josh 9:17
Ark taken from, 1 Chr 13:5

KISH
Benjamite of Gibeah; father of King
Saul, 1 Sam 9:1–3

KISHON
River of north Palestine; Sisera's army
swept away by, Judg 4:7, 13
Elijah executes prophets of Baal at,
1 Kin 18:40

KISS
K the Son, lest He be . . . . Ps 2:12
Let him *k* me with the . . . . . . Song 1:2
who sacrifice *k* the calves . . . Hos 13:2
Whomever I *k*, He is . . . . . Mark 14:44
You gave Me no *k* . . . . Luke 7:45
drew near to Jesus to *k* . . . Luke 22:47
another with a holy *k* . . . . . Rom 16:16
another with a holy *k* . . . . 2 Cor 13:12
with a holy *k* . . . . 1 Thess 5:26
one another with a *k* . . . . . . 1 Pet 5:14

KISSED
they *k* one another . . . . 1 Sam 20:41
and peace have *k* each. . . . . . Ps 85:10
Rabbi!" and *k* Him . . . . . . Matt 26:49
and she *k* His feet and . . . . Luke 7:38

KITTIM
See CYPRUS
Descendants of Javan, Gen 10:4

KNEE
that to Me every *k* . . . . Is 45:23
And they bowed the *k* . . . . Matt 27:29
have not bowed the *k* . . . . . Rom 11:4
every *k* shall bow to . . . . . . Rom 14:11
of Jesus every *k* . . . . Phil 2:10

KNEES
make firm the feeble *k* . . . . Is 35:3
be dandled on her *k* . . . . Is 66:12
this reason I bow my *k* . . . . Eph 3:14
and the feeble *k* . . . . Heb 12:12

KNEW
k that they were naked . . . . . Gen 3:7
Adam *k* Eve his wife . . . . Gen 4:1
in the womb I *k* . . . . Jer 1:5
to them, 'I never *k* . . . . Matt 7:23
k what was in man . . . . John 2:25
For He made Him who *k* . . 2 Cor 5:21

KNIFE
fire in his hand, and a *k* . . . . Gen 22:6
his house he took a *k* . . . . . Judg 19:29
put a *k* to your throat if . . . . Prov 23:2
cut it with the scribe's *k* . . . . Jer 36:23

KNIT
of Jonathan was *k* . . . . 1 Sam 18:1
k me together with . . . . Job 10:11
be encouraged, being *k* . . . . . . Col 2:2

KNOCK
k, and it will be . . . . Matt 7:7
at the door and *k* . . . . Rev 3:20

KNOW
k good and evil . . . . Gen 3:22
and I did not *k* . . . . Gen 28:16
Egypt, who did not *k* Joseph . . Ex 1:8
k that I am the LORD . . . . Ex 6:7
'I *k* you by name, and you . . Ex 33:12
way, that I may *k* You . . . . . Ex 33:13
to *k* how to do all manner . . . Ex 36:1
Therefore *k* that the LORD . . Deut 7:9
k what was in your heart . . . Deut 8:2
You should *k* in your heart . . Deut 8:5
that you may *k* the way by . . . Josh 3:4
might be taught to *k* war, . . . Judg 3:2
Samuel did not yet *k* the . . . 1 Sam 3:7

k that there is a God . . . . 1 Sam 17:46
I *k* that this is a holy man . . 2 Kin 4:9
k that there is no God . . . . . 2 Kin 5:15
you, my son Solomon, *k* . . . 1 Chr 28:9
Hear it, and *k* for . . . . Job 5:27
and *k* nothing, because . . . . . . Job 8:9
k that my Redeemer . . . . . . Job 19:25
'What does God *k* . . . . Job 22:13
k Your name will put . . . . Ps 9:10
Now I *k* that the LORD saves . . Ps 20:6
k that I am God . . . . Ps 46:10
make me to *k* wisdom . . . . Ps 51:6
O God, and *k* my heart . . . Ps 139:23
k wisdom and instruction, . . . Prov 1:2
to *k* understanding . . . . Prov 4:1
set my heart to *k* wisdom . . . Eccl 1:17
that He may *k* to refuse the . . . Is 7:15
Egyptians will *k* the LORD . . . . Is 19:21
But I *k* your dwelling place . . Is 37:28
do not *k* nor understand . . . . Is 44:18
All flesh shall *k* that I, the . . . Is 49:26
My people shall *k* My name . . Is 52:6
call a nation you do not *k* . . . Is 55:5
language you do not *k* . . . . . . Jer 5:15
nor did they *k* how to blush . . Jer 6:15
Who can *k* it . . . . Jer 17:9
saying, 'K the LORD . . . . Jer 31:34
you shall *k* that I am . . . . . . Ezek 6:13
of the field shall *k* that I . . . Ezek 17:24
Gentiles shall *k* that . . . . . . Ezek 39:23
is anxious to *k* the dream . . . . Dan 2:3
you may *k* the thoughts . . . . . Dan 2:30
I wished to *k* the truth . . . . . Dan 7:19
you shall *k* no God but Me . . Hos 13:4
For I *k* your manifold . . . . . . Amos 5:12
for you to *k* justice . . . . Mic 3:1
did not *k* her till she had . . . . Matt 1:25
You *k* how to discern the . . . Matt 16:3
k that summer is near . . . . Matt 24:32
k what hour your Lord . . . . Matt 24:42
an oath, "I do not *k* . . . . . . Matt 26:72
I do not *k* the Man . . . . Matt 26:74
k the mystery of the . . . . Mark 4:11
k the commandments . . . . . Mark 10:19
do not *k* what you ask . . . Mark 10:38
do not *k* what manner of . . Luke 9:55
k how to give good gifts . . Luke 11:13
k that its desolation is . . . . Luke 21:20
the world did not *k* . . . . John 1:10
We speak what We *k* . . . . . . John 3:11
k what we worship . . . . John 4:22
k that You are the Christ . . . John 6:69
k that you are Abraham's . . John 8:37
we *k* that God does not . . . . . John 9:31
hear My voice, and I *k* . . . . John 10:27
If you *k* these things . . . . . . John 13:17
k whom I have chosen . . . . John 13:18
we are sure that You *k* . . . John 16:30
k that I love You . . . . John 21:15
k times or seasons . . . . Acts 1:7
and said, "Jesus I *k* . . . . . . Acts 19:15
we *k* that all things work . . . Rom 8:28
wisdom did not *k* . . . . 1 Cor 1:21
nor can he *k* them . . . . 1 Cor 2:14
For we *k* in part and . . . . . 1 Cor 13:9
k a man in Christ who . . . . 2 Cor 12:2
when you did not *k* God, ... Gal 4:8
k the love of Christ . . . . Eph 3:19
k Him and the power . . . . . . Phil 3:10
abased, and I *k* how to . . . . . Phil 4:12
k how to possess his . . . . . 1 Thess 4:4
k what is restraining . . . . . 2 Thess 2:6
k whom I have believed . . . 2 Tim 1:12
so that they may *k* . . . . 2 Tim 2:25
this we *k* that we *k* Him . . 1 John 2:3
He who says, "I *k* . . . . 1 John 2:4
and you *k* all things . . . . . . 1 John 2:20
By this we *k* love . . . . 1 John 3:16
k that we are of the . . . . . . 1 John 3:19
k that He abides . . . . 1 John 3:24
k that we are of God . . . . . 1 John 5:19
"I *k* your works . . . . Rev 2:2

KNOWING
like God, *k* good and evil . . . . Gen 3:5
k their thoughts, said, ... Matt 9:4
not *k* the Scriptures nor . . . Matt 22:29
k all things that would . . . . . John 18:4
k that tribulation produces . . Rom 5:3
k that your labor is not . . . 1 Cor 15:58
k that He who raised up . . 2 Cor 4:14
k that while we are at . . . . . 2 Cor 5:6
k that I am appointed for . . . Phil 1:17
k that you also have a . . . . . . Col 4:1
k that you have a better . . . Heb 10:34
not *k* where he was going . . Heb 11:8
k that the testing of your . . James 1:3
k that the same sufferings . . 1 Pet 5:9

KNOWLEDGE
and the tree of the *k* . . . . Gen 2:9
and understanding, in *k* . . . Ex 35:31
LORD is the God of *k*. . . . . . 1 Sam 2:3
give me wisdom and *k*. . . . . 2 Chr 1:10
Can anyone teach God *k* . . . Job 21:22
who is perfect in *k* . . . . Job 36:4
unto night reveals *k* . . . . Ps 19:2
me good judgment and *k* . . . Ps 119:66
k is too wonderful . . . . Ps 139:6
LORD is the beginning of *k* . . Prov 1:7
k the depths were . . . . Prov 3:20
k rather than choice . . . . . . Prov 8:10
Wise people store up *k* . . . Prov 10:14
prudent man conceals *k* . . . Prov 12:23
k is easy to him who . . . . . . Prov 14:6
k spares his words . . . . Prov 17:27
a soul to be without *k* . . . . . Prov 19:2
by *k* the rooms are filled . . . Prov 24:4
of *k* increases strength . . . . Prov 24:5
and he who increases *k* . . . . Eccl 1:18
k is that wisdom . . . . Eccl 7:12
no work or device or *k* . . . . . Eccl 9:10
Whom will he teach *k* . . . . . . Is 28:9
His *k* My righteous Servant . . Is 53:11
k shall increase . . . . Dan 12:4
you have rejected *k* . . . . Hos 4:6
taken away the key of *k* . . . Luke 11:52
having more accurate *k* . . . Acts 24:22
to retain God in their *k* . . . . Rom 1:28
having the form of *k* . . . . . . Rom 2:20
by the law is the *k* of sin . . . Rom 3:20
K puffs up, but love . . . . 1 Cor 8:1
to another the word of *k* . . 1 Cor 12:8
all mysteries and all *k* . . . . 1 Cor 13:2
whether there is *k* . . . . 1 Cor 13:8
of His *k* in every place . . . . 2 Cor 2:14
to give the light of the *k* . . . 2 Cor 4:6
by purity, by *k*, by . . . . 2 Cor 6:6
against the *k* of God . . . . . . 2 Cor 10:5
Christ which passes *k* . . . . . Eph 3:19
k of His will in all wisdom . . . Col 1:9
treasures of wisdom and *k* . . . Col 2:3
is falsely called *k* . . . . 1 Tim 6:20
faith virtue, to virtue *k* . . . . 2 Pet 1:5
in the grace and *k* . . . . 2 Pet 3:18

KNOWN
In Judah God is *k* . . . . Ps 76:1
my mouth will make *k* . . . . . Ps 89:1
If you had *k* Me . . . . John 8:19
My sheep, and am *k* . . . . . . John 10:14
The world has not *k* . . . . . . John 17:25
peace they have not *k* . . . . . Rom 3:17
I would not have *k* . . . . Rom 7:7
"For who has *k* . . . . Rom 11:34
after you have *k* . . . . Gal 4:9
requests be made *k* . . . . Phil 4:6
k the Holy Scriptures . . . . . 2 Tim 3:15
have not *k* the depths of . . . . Rev 2:24

KNOWS
For God *k* that in . . . . Gen 3:5
k the secrets of the . . . . Ps 44:21
he understands and *k* . . . . . . Jer 9:24
k what is in the . . . . Dan 2:22
k those who trust . . . . Nah 1:7
k the things you have . . . . . . Matt 6:8

and hour no one *k* . . . . Matt 24:36
k who the Son is . . . . Luke 10:22
but God *k* your hearts . . . . Luke 16:15
searches the hearts *k* . . . . . . Rom 8:27
k the things of God . . . . 1 Cor 2:11
The LORD *k* the thoughts . . 1 Cor 3:20
k those who are His . . . . . . 2 Tim 2:19
to him who *k* to do . . . . . . James 4:17
and *k* all things . . . . 1 John 3:20
written which no one *k* . . . . Rev 2:17

KOHATH
Second son of Levi, Gen 46:8, 11
Brother of Jochebed, mother of Aaron
and Moses, Ex 6:16–20

KOHATHITES
Numbered, Num 3:27, 28
Duties assigned to, Num 4:15–20
Leaders of temple music, 1 Chr
6:31–38; 2 Chr 20:19

KORAH
Leads rebellion against Moses and
Aaron; supernaturally destroyed,
Num 16:1–35
Sons of, not destroyed, Num 26:9–11

LABAN
Son of Bethuel; brother of Rebekah;
father of Leah and Rachel, Gen 24:15,
24, 29; 29:16
Agrees to Rebekah's marriage to Isaac,
Gen 24:50, 51
Entertains Jacob, Gen 29:1–14
Substitutes Leah for Rachel, Gen
29:15–30
Agrees to division of cattle; grows re-
sentful of Jacob, Gen 30:25—31:2
Pursues Jacob and makes covenant
with him, Gen 31:21–55

LABOR
Six days you shall *l* . . . . Ex 20:9
why then do I *l* . . . . Job 9:29
their boast is only *l* . . . . Ps 90:10
The *l* of the righteous . . . . . Prov 10:16
l will increase . . . . Prov 13:11
l there is profit . . . . Prov 14:23
things are full of *l* . . . . Eccl 1:8
has man for all his *l* . . . . Eccl 2:22
He shall see the *l* . . . . Is 53:11
"Before she was in *l* . . . . Is 66:7
from the womb to see *l* . . . . Jer 20:18
to Me, all you who *l* . . . . . Matt 11:28
Do not *l* for the . . . . John 6:27
knowing that your *L* . . . . . 1 Cor 15:58
but rather let him *l* . . . . Eph 4:28
mean fruit from my *l* . . . . . . Phil 1:22
your work of faith, *l* . . . . . 1 Thess 1:3
forget your work and *l* . . . . . Heb 6:10
your works, your *l* . . . . Rev 2:2

LABORED
l more abundantly than . . 1 Cor 15:10
for you, lest I have *l* . . . . Gal 4:11

LABORERS
but the *l* are few . . . . Matt 9:37

LABORING
of a *l* man is sweet . . . . Eccl 5:12
l night and day . . . . 1 Thess 2:9

LABORS
The person who *l* . . . . Prov 16:26
is no end to all his *l* . . . . Eccl 4:8
entered into their *l* . . . . . . John 4:38
creation groans and *l* . . . . . . Rom 8:22
l more abundant . . . . 2 Cor 11:23
may rest from their *l* . . . . . Rev 14:13

LACHISH
Defeated by Joshua, Josh 10:3–33
Taken by Sennacherib, 2 Kin 18:13–17;
Is 36:1, 2; 37:8

LACK
the city for *l* of five . . . . Gen 18:28
gathered little had no *l* . . . . . . Ex 16:18
'you shall not *l* a man on . . . 1 Kin 2:4
anyone perish for *l* . . . . Job 31:19
the LORD shall not *l* . . . . Ps 34:10
fools die for *l* of wisdom . . Prov 10:21
for *l* of justice there is . . . . Prov 13:23
to the poor will not *l* . . . . . Prov 28:27
l a man to stand before . . . . . Jer 35:19
for *l* of knowledge . . . . Hos 4:6
What do I still *l* . . . . Matt 19:20
"One thing you *l* . . . . Mark 10:21
did you *l* anything . . . . Luke 22:35
of your *l* of self-control . . . . 1 Cor 7:5
may supply their *l* . . . . 2 Cor 8:14
gathered little had no *l* . . . . 2 Cor 8:15

LACKED
among them who *l* . . . . Acts 4:34

LACKING
is *l* cannot be numbered . . . . Eccl 1:15
to supply what was *l* in . . . . Phil 2:30
the things that are *l* . . . . Titus 1:5
and complete, *l* nothing . . . . James 1:4

LACKS
woman who *l* discretion . . Prov 11:22
who *l* understanding . . . . . . Prov 28:16
to that part which *l* . . . . . 1 Cor 12:24
If any of you *l* wisdom . . . . James 1:5
he who *l* these things is . . . . 2 Pet 1:9

LAD
and gave the *l* a drink . . . . . Gen 21:19
lay your hand on the *l* . . . . . Gen 22:12
said, "The *l* is no more . . . . Gen 37:30
'The *l* cannot leave his . . . Gen 44:30
As the *l* ran, he shot an . . 1 Sam 20:36
"There is a *l* here who has . . John 6:9

LADDER
and behold, a *l* . . . . Gen 28:12

LADEN
nation, a people *l* . . . . Is 1:4
and are heavy *l* . . . . Matt 11:28

LADIES
wisest *l* answered her . . . . . . Judg 5:29
very day the noble *l* . . . . Esth 1:18

LADY
'I shall be a *l* . . . . Is 47:7
To the elect *l* . . . . 2 John 1

LAGGING
not *l* in diligence . . . . Rom 12:11

LAHAI ROI
Name of a well, Gen 16:7, 14
Same as Beer Lahai Roi, Gen 24:62

LAID
l him on the altar . . . . Gen 22:9
l up the food in the cities . . Gen 41:48
and *l* it in the reeds by the . . . . Ex 2:3
l the staff on the face of . . 2 Kin 4:31
l the foundation of the . . . . Ezra 5:16
But man dies and is *l* . . . . . . Job 14:10
You *l* the foundation . . . . Ps 102:25
He has *l* waste My vine . . . . . Joel 1:7
have *l* the foundation of . . . . Zech 4:9
even now the ax is *l* to . . . . Matt 3:10
the place where they *l* . . . . . Mark 16:6
l Him in a manger . . . . Luke 2:7
l the foundation on the . . . . Luke 6:48
"Where have you *l* . . . . John 11:34
l aside His garments . . . . . . John 13:4
where You have *l* Him . . . . John 20:15
l it at the apostles' feet . . . . . Acts 4:37
and he *l* his hands on him . . Acts 28:8
I have *l* the foundation . . . . 1 Cor 3:10
He *l* down His life . . . . 1 John 3:16
He *l* His right hand on me . . Rev 1:17

LAISH
Called Leshem, Josh 19:47; Judg 18:29
Taken by Danites, Judg 18:7, 14, 27

LAKE
by the *L* of Gennesaret . . . . . Luke 5:1
to the other side of the *l* . . . Luke 8:22
cast alive into the *l* . . . . Rev 19:20

LAMB
but where is the *l* . . . . Gen 22:7
a *l* for a household . . . . Ex 12:3
and kill the Passover *l* . . . . . . Ex 12:21
took the poor man's *l* . . . . 2 Sam 12:4
shall dwell with the *l* . . . . Is 11:6
He was led as a *l* . . . . Is 53:7
l shall feed together . . . . Is 65:25
The *L* of God who takes . . . John 1:29
as a *l* before its shearer . . . . Acts 8:32
of Christ, as of a *l* . . . . 1 Pet 1:19
the elders, stood a *L* . . . . Rev 5:6
"Worthy is the *L* . . . . Rev 5:12
by the blood of the *L* . . . . . Rev 12:11
Book of Life of the *L* . . . . . . Rev 13:8
supper of the *L* . . . . Rev 19:9

LAMB'S
the bride, the *L* wife . . . . . . Rev 21:9
in the *L* Book of Life . . . . . . Rev 21:27

LAMBS
slaughtered the Passover *l* . . Ezra 6:20
O little hills, like *l* . . . . Ps 114:6
with the blood of *l* and . . . . . Is 34:6
gather the *l* with His arm . . . . Is 40:11
out as *l* among wolves . . . . Luke 10:3
"Feed My *l* . . . . John 21:15

LAME
l take the prey . . . . Is 33:23
l shall leap like a . . . . Is 35:6
when you offer the *l* . . . . Mal 1:8
blind see and the *l* . . . . Matt 11:5
And a certain man *l* . . . . Acts 3:2
so that what is *l* . . . . Heb 12:13

LAMECH
Son of Methushael, of Cain's race, Gen
4:17, 18
—— Son of Methuselah; father of Noah,
Gen 5:25–31

LAMENT
l the daughter of . . . . Judg 11:40
king sang a *l* over Abner . . 2 Sam 3:33
Her gates shall *l* and mourn . . Is 3:26
"They shall not *l* for him, . . . Jer 22:18
they shall *l* for her . . . . Ezek 32:16
to you, and you did not *l* . . . Matt 11:17
that you will weep and *l* . . . John 16:20
L and mourn and weep . . . . James 4:9
l for her, when they see . . . . . Rev 18:9

LAMENTATION
a great and very solemn *l* . . Gen 50:10
with this *l* over Saul and . . 2 Sam 1:17
was heard in Ramah, *l* . . . . . Jer 31:15
l in the daughter of Judah . . . Lam 2:5
was heard in Ramah, *l* . . . . . Matt 2:18
and made great *l* . . . . Acts 8:2

LAMP
For You are my *l* . . . . 2 Sam 22:29
"How often is the *l* . . . . Job 21:17
You will light my *l* . . . . Ps 18:28
Your word is a *l* . . . . Ps 119:105
the *l* of the wicked . . . . Prov 13:9
his *l* will be put out . . . . . . Prov 20:20
Nor do they light a *l* . . . . . . Matt 5:15
"The *l* of the body . . . . Matt 6:22
when he has lit a *l* . . . . Luke 8:16
l gives you light . . . . Luke 11:36
does not light a *l* . . . . Luke 15:8
burning and shining *l* . . . . . John 5:35
l shall not shine . . . . Rev 18:23
They need no *l* nor . . . . Rev 22:5

LAMPS
he made its seven *l* . . . . Ex 37:23
Jerusalem with *l* . . . . Zeph 1:12

and trimmed their *l* .... Matt 25:7
Seven *l* of fire .... Rev 4:5

LAMPSTAND
branches of the *l* .... Ex 25:32
and there is a *l* .... Zech 4:2
a basket, but on a *l* .... Matt 5:15
in which was the *l* .... Heb 9:2
and remove your *l* .... Rev 2:5

LAND
and let the dry *l* appear ...... Gen 1:9
God called the dry *l* Earth .. Gen 1:10
dwelt in the *l* of Nod .... Gen 4:16
l that I will show you .... Gen 12:1
I will give this *l* .... Gen 12:7
was a famine in the *l* ...... Gen 12:10
Is not the whole *l* before ... Gen 13:9
walk in the *l* through its ... Gen 13:17
I have given this *l* .... Gen 15:18
arise, get out of this *l* ..... Gen 31:13
the best of the *l* of Egypt . Gen 45:18
dwell in the *l* of Goshen ... Gen 46:34
a stranger in a foreign *l* ..... Ex 2:22
l flowing with milk .... Ex 3:8
to a *l* flowing with milk and .. Ex 3:17
the *l* of their pilgrimage ...... Ex 6:4
firstborn in the *l* of Egypt .. Ex 12:12
and the *l* vomits out its .... Lev 18:25
for the *l* is Mine .... Lev 25:23
I will give peace in the *l* .... Lev 26:6
And all the tithe of the *l* .. Lev 27:30
spy out the *l* of Canaan .. Num 13:17
evil report about the *l* ..... Num 14:37
l is subdued before the .... Num 32:22
possess the good *l* .... Deut 6:18
a *l* of wheat and barley .... Deut 8:8
He will bless you in the *l* .. Deut 28:8
the produce of your *l* .... Deut 28:51
l which I am giving .... Josh 1:2
to go in to possess the *l* .... Josh 1:11
Joshua took the whole *l* ... Josh 11:23
Joshua divided the *l*...... Josh 18:10
to return to the *l* of Judah .. Ruth 1:7
sold the piece of *l* which .... Ruth 4:3
spiritists from the *l* .... 1 Sam 28:9
In the *l* of the living .... Ps 27:13
dwell in the *l*, and feed on .... Ps 37:3
turned the sea into dry *l* .... Ps 66:6
in the *l* of forgetfulness ..... Ps 88:12
l was polluted with blood ... Ps 106:38
dry *l* into watersprings ..... Ps 107:35
for You like a thirsty *l* ..... Ps 143:6
is heard in our *l* .... Song 2:12
they will see the *l* .... Is 33:17
a *l* of grain and new wine .... Is 36:17
and your *l* shall be married ... Is 62:4
Bethlehem, in the *l*........ Matt 2:6
put out a little from the *l* .... Luke 5:3
price of the *l* for yourself .... Acts 5:3
and his left foot on the *l* .... Rev 10:2

LAND OF THE LIVING
nor is it found in the *l* ..... Job 28:13
of the LORD in the *l* ...... Ps 27:13
uproot you from the *l* .... Ps 52:5
before the LORD in the *l* .... Ps 116:9
my portion in the *l* .... Ps 142:5
the LORD in the *l* .... Is 38:11
cut off from the *l* .... Is 53:8
establish glory in the *l* .... Ezek 26:20

LANDMARK
your neighbor's *l* .... Deut 19:14
remove the ancient *l* ...... Prov 22:28
those who remove a *l* .... Hos 5:10

LANDS
We have mortgaged our *l* .... Neh 5:3
to scatter them in the *l* .... Ps 106:27
or wife or children or *l*.... Matt 19:29
of *l* or houses sold them .... Acts 4:34

LANGUAGE
whole earth had one *l* ..... Gen 11:1
there confuse their *l* ...... Gen 11:7

is no speech nor *l* .... Ps 19:3
a people of strange *l* .... Ps 114:1
the peoples a pure *l* .... Zeph 3:9
speak in his own *l* .... Acts 2:6
blasphemy, filthy *l* .... Col 3:8

LANGUAGES
according to their *l* .... Gen 10:20
be, so many kinds of *l* .... 1 Cor 14:10

LAODICEA
Paul's concern for, Col 2:1; 4:12–16
Letter to church of, Rev 3:14–22

LAST
See FIRST AND THE LAST
He shall stand at *l* .... Job 19:25
First and I am the L .... Is 44:6
l man the same as .... Matt 20:14
l will be first .... Matt 20:16
are first who will be *l* .... Luke 13:30
raise him up at the *l* day ... John 6:40
On the *l* day, that great .... John 7:37
come to pass in the *l* days .. Acts 2:17
The *l* enemy that will be .. 1 Cor 15:26
eye, at the *l* trumpet ..... 1 Cor 15:52
has in these *l* days spoken ... Heb 1:2
children, it is the *l* ...... 1 John 2:18
the First and the L .... Rev 1:11
l are more than the first .... Rev 2:19

LAST DAY
raise it up at the *l* .... John 6:39
the resurrection at the *l* ... John 11:24
will judge him in the *l* .... John 12:48

LAST DAYS
shall befall you in the *l* ..... Gen 49:1
come to pass in the *l* ...... Acts 2:17
in the *l* perilous times .... 2 Tim 3:1
these *l* spoken to us .... Heb 1:2
up treasure in the *l* .... James 5:3
will come in the *l* .... 2 Pet 3:3

LATE
to rise up early, to sit up *l* ... Ps 127:2
and already the hour is *l* .. Mark 6:35
l autumn trees without ...... Jude 12
as a fig tree drops its *l* ..... Rev 6:13

LATIN
in Hebrew, Greek, and L .. John 19:20

LATTER
people in the *l* days ..... Dan 10:14
former rain, and the *l* ..... Joel 2:23
The glory of this *l* temple .... Hag 2:9
l times some will .... 1 Tim 4:1
the early and *l* rain ...... James 5:7
l end is worse for them .... 2 Pet 2:20

LATTICE
I looked through my *l* ...... Prov 7:6
gazing through the *l* .... Song 2:9

LAUGH
Why did Sarah *l* .... Gen 18:13
"God has made me *l* ...... Gen 21:6
sits in the heavens shall *l* ..... Ps 2:4
You, O LORD, shall *l* .... Ps 59:8
to weep, and a time to *l* ..... Eccl 3:4
Woe to you who *l* .... Luke 6:25

LAUGHS
he *l* at the threat of .... Job 41:29
The Lord *l* at him .... Ps 37:13

LAUGHTER
was filled with *l* .... Ps 126:2
your *l* be turned to .... James 4:9

LAUNDERER
such as no *l* on earth can ... Mark 9:3

LAVER
also make a *l* of bronze .... Ex 30:18
l contained forty baths .... 1 Kin 7:38

LAW
See ACCORDING TO THE LAW; BOOK
  OF THE LAW; UNDER THE LAW;
  WORKS OF THE LAW

stones a copy of the *l* ..... Josh 8:32
When He made a *l* .... Job 28:26
The *l* of the LORD is .... Ps 19:7
The *l* of his God is in ...... Ps 37:31
I delight in Your *l* .... Ps 119:70
The *l* of Your mouth is ..... Ps 119:72
l is my delight .... Ps 119:77
Oh, how I love Your *l* ...... Ps 119:97
And Your *l* is truth ...... Ps 119:142
and the *l* a light .... Prov 6:23
is he who keeps the *l* .... Prov 29:18
shall go forth the *l* .... Is 2:3
l will proceed from Me ...... Is 51:4
in whose heart is My *l* ...... Is 51:7
the L is no more .... Lam 2:9
The *l* of truth was in ...... Mal 2:6
to destroy the L .... Matt 5:17
for this is the L .... Matt 7:12
l prophesied until John .. Matt 11:13
hang all the L and the .... Matt 22:40
one tittle of the *l* to fail ... Luke 16:17
l was given through .... John 1:17
"Does our *l* judge a .... John 7:51
a teacher of the *l* held in ... Acts 5:34
and keep the *l* .... Acts 15:24
are all zealous for the *l* .... Acts 21:20
man according to the *l* .... Acts 22:12
l is the knowledge .... Rom 3:20
By what *l*? Of works? ...... Rom 3:27
because the *l* brings .... Rom 4:15
when there is no *l* .... Rom 5:13
you are not under *l* .... Rom 6:14
have become dead to the *l* .... Rom 7:4
Is the *l* sin .... Rom 7:7
For we know that the *l* ..... Rom 7:14
warring against the *l* ...... Rom 7:23
For the *l* of the Spirit of .... Rom 8:2
For what the *l* could ...... Rom 8:3
A wife is bound by *l* as .... 1 Cor 7:39
who are without *l* .... 1 Cor 9:21
strength of sin is the *l* ... 1 Cor 15:56
l that I might live .... Gal 2:19
Spirit by the works of the *l* ... Gal 3:2
under guard by the *l* ...... Gal 3:23
the *l* was our tutor .... Gal 3:24
born under the *l* .... Gal 4:4
l is fulfilled in one .... Gal 5:14
and so fulfill the *l* of Christ ... Gal 6:2
concerning the *l*, a Pharisee .. Phil 3:5
to be teachers of the *l* ..... 1 Tim 1:7
l is not made for a .... 1 Tim 1:9
and strivings about the *l* ... Titus 3:9
into the perfect *l* .... James 1:25
fulfill the royal *l*, ... James 2:8

LAW AND THE PROPHETS
them, for this is the L ..... Matt 7:12
hang all the L .... Matt 22:40
The *l* were until John. ... Luke 16:16
being witnessed by the L ... Rom 3:21

LAW OF MOSES
the stones a copy of the *l* ... Josh 8:32
a skilled scribe in the L .... Ezra 7:6
bring the Book of the L ...... Neh 8:1
oath written in the L ...... Dan 9:11
the L, My servant .... Mal 4:4
according to the *l* .... Luke 2:22
were written in the L ...... Luke 24:44
Sabbath, so that the *l* ..... John 7:23
not be justified by the *l* .... Acts 13:39
them to keep the *l* .... Acts 15:5

LAW OF THE LORD
that you may keep the *l* .. 1 Chr 22:12
that he forsook the L ...... 2 Chr 12:1
themselves to the L .... 2 Chr 31:4
his heart to seek the L .... Ezra 7:10
his delight is in the *l* .... Ps 1:2
l is perfect, converting ...... Ps 19:7
way, who walk in the *l* ..... Ps 119:1
they have rejected the *l* ..... Is 5:24
who will not hear the *l* ..... Is 30:9
'We are wise, and the *l* ..... Jer 8:8

they have despised the *l*. . . . .Amos 2:4
things according to the *l* . . .Luke 2:39

LAWFUL
doing what is not *l* . . . . .Matt 12:2
Is it *l* to pay taxes . . . . . . .Matt 22:17
All things are *l*. . . . . .1 Cor 6:12

LAWGIVER
Judah is My *l* . . . . .Ps 60:7
the LORD is our *L*. . . . . .Is 33:22
There is one *L* . . . . .James 4:12

LAWLESS
l one will be revealed . . . . .2 Thess 2:8
and hearing their *l*. . . . . .2 Pet 2:8

LAWLESSNESS
Me, you who practice *l* . . . . .Matt 7:23
l is already at work. . . . . . .2 Thess 2:7
and hated *l* . . . . .Heb 1:9
and sin is *l* . . . . .1 John 3:4

LAWYERS
l rejected the will of . . . . . . .Luke 7:30
Woe to you also, *l* . . . . . . .Luke 11:46

LAY
l it on the wood, but put . .1 Kin 18:23
I *l* down and slept . . . . .Ps 3:5
I will *l* your stones with . . . . . .Is 54:11
Do not *l* up for yourselves . .Matt 6:19
nowhere to *l* His head . . . . .Matt 8:20
I have power to *l* it down . .John 10:18
Will you *l* down your life . .John 13:38
l hands may receive . . . . .Acts 8:19
Do not *l* hands on . . . . .1 Tim 5:22
let us *l* aside every weight. . .Heb 12:1
l aside all filthiness . . . . . . .James 1:21
"Behold, I *l* in Zion a chief . .1 Pet 2:6

LAYING
l on of the apostles' hands . .Acts 8:18
the *l* on of my hands . . . . . . .2 Tim 1:6
not *l* again the foundation . . . .Heb 6:1
of *l* on of hands, of . . . . .Heb 6:2
l aside all malice, all deceit . .1 Pet 2:1

LAYS
'God *l* up one's iniquity . . . . .Job 21:19
He *l* up the deep in . . . . .Ps 33:7
He *l* the beams of His . . . . . . .Ps 104:3
which the LORD *l* on him . . . . .Is 30:32
l the foundation of the . . . . .Zech 12:1
he who *l* up treasure . . . . .Luke 12:21
he *l* it on his shoulders. . . . .Luke 15:5

LAZARUS
Beggar described in a parable, Luke
16:20–25
—— Brother of Mary and Martha;
raised from the dead, John 11:1–44
Attends a supper, John 12:1, 2
Jews seek to kill, John 12:9–11

LAZINESS
L casts one into a . . . . .Prov 19:15
l the building decays . . . . . .Eccl 10:18

LAZY
l man will be put to . . . . . . .Prov 12:24
l man does not roast . . . . . .Prov 12:27
soul of a *l* man desires . . . . .Prov 13:4
l man buries his hand . . . . .Prov 19:24
by the field of the *l* . . . . . . .Prov 24:30
l man is wiser in his . . . . . .Prov 26:16
wicked and *l* servant . . . . .Matt 25:26
liars, evil beasts, *l* . . . . .Titus 1:12

LEAD
pillar of cloud to *l* the way . .Ex 13:21
they sank like *l* . . . . .Ex 15:10
L me in Your truth and . . . . . .Ps 25:5
And *l* me in a smooth path . .Ps 27:11
L me and guide me . . . . .Ps 31:3
L me to the rock that is . . . . .Ps 61:2
Your hand shall *l* . . . . .Ps 139:10
a little child shall *l* them . . . . .Is 11:6
I will *l* them in paths they . . . .Is 42:16

l is consumed by the fire . . . . .Jer 6:29
bronze, tin, iron, and *l* . . . .Ezek 22:18
tin, and *l* for your goods . . .Ezek 27:12
threw the *l* cover over its . . . .Zech 5:8
And do not *l* us into . . . . . . .Matt 6:13
"Can the blind *l* . . . . .Luke 6:39
not *l* us into temptation . . . .Luke 11:4
someone to *l* him by the . . .Acts 13:11
aspire to *l* a quiet life . . . .1 Thess 4:11
that we may *l* a quiet and . .1 Tim 2:2
to *l* them out of the land of . . .Heb 8:9
sin which does not *l* to . . . .1 John 5:16
l them to living fountains . . .Rev 7:17

LEADING
l men among the . . . . .Acts 15:22
not a few of the *l* women . . . .Acts 17:4
of lawlessness *l* to more . . . .Rom 6:19
his good, *l* to edification . . . .Rom 15:2
sin not *l* to death . . . . .1 John 5:16

LEADS
He *l* me beside the . . . . .Ps 23:2
He *l* me in the paths . . . . .Ps 23:3
And if the blind *l* . . . . .Matt 15:14
by name and *l* them out . . . .John 10:3
the goodness of God *l* . . . . . .Rom 2:4

LEAF
plucked olive *l* . . . . .Gen 8:11
Will You frighten a *l* . . . . . . .Job 13:25
l will be green . . . . .Jer 17:8

LEAH
Laban's eldest daughter; given to Jacob
deceitfully, Gen 29:16–27
Unloved by Jacob, but bears children,
Gen 29:30–35; 30:16–21

LEAN
all your heart, and *l* . . . . .Prov 3:5
Yet they *l* on the LORD . . . . . .Mic 3:11

LEANING
Then, *l* back on Jesus' . . . .John 13:25
l on the top of his . . . . .Heb 11:21

LEANNESS
request, but sent *l* . . . . .Ps 106:15
of hosts, will send *l* . . . . .Is 10:16

LEAP
by my God I can *l* . . . . .Ps 18:29
Then the lame shall *l* . . . . .Is 35:6

LEAPED
the rams which *l* upon . . . . .Gen 31:10
they *l* about the altar . . . . .1 Kin 18:26
the babe *l* in her womb . . . .Luke 1:41
and he *l* and walked . . . . . .Acts 14:10

LEAPING
saw King David *l* . . . . .2 Sam 6:16
walking, *l*, and praising . . . . .Acts 3:8

LEARN
it, may hear and *l* . . . . .Deut 31:13
l Your statutes. . . . . .Ps 119:71
lest you *l* his ways . . . . . . .Prov 22:25
l to do good . . . . .Is 1:17
neither shall they *l* . . . . .Is 2:4
My yoke upon you and *l* . . .Matt 11:29
Let a woman *l* in . . . . .1 Tim 2:11
let our people also *l* . . . . . .Titus 3:14
no one could *l* that song . . . .Rev 14:3

LEARNED
Me the tongue of the *l* . . . . . . .Is 50:4
who has heard and *l* . . . . . .John 6:45
have not so *l* Christ . . . . . . .Eph 4:20
in all things I have *l* . . . . . . .Phil 4:12
l obedience by the . . . . .Heb 5:8

LEARNING
hear and increase *l* . . . . .Prov 1:5
l is driving you mad . . . . . .Acts 26:24
were written for our *l* . . . . . .Rom 15:4

LEAST
Judah, are not the *l* . . . . .Matt 2:6

so, shall be called *l* . . . . . . .Matt 5:19
For I am the *l* of the . . . . . .1 Cor 15:9

LEATHER
everything made of *l* . . . . .Num 31:20
wearing a *l* belt around . . . . .2 Kin 1:8
with a *l* belt around his . . . .Mark 1:6

LEAVE
a man shall *l* his . . . . .Gen 2:24
He will not *l* you nor . . . . . .Deut 31:6
For You will not *l* . . . . .Ps 16:10
do not *l* me nor . . . . .Ps 27:9
"I will never *l* . . . . .Heb 13:5

LEAVEN
day you shall remove *l* . . . . .Ex 12:15
of heaven is like *l* . . . . . . .Matt 13:33
and beware of the *l* . . . . . . .Matt 16:6
know that a little *l* . . . . .1 Cor 5:6
l leavens the whole . . . . .Gal 5:9

LEAVENED
For whoever eats *l* bread . . . .Ex 12:15
shall eat no *l* bread with . . . .Deut 16:3
of meal till it was all *l* . . . .Matt 13:33

LEAVES
and they sewed fig *l* . . . . .Gen 3:7
nothing on it but *l* . . . . . . .Matt 21:19
l the sheep and flees . . . . .John 10:12
The *l* of the tree . . . . .Rev 22:2

LEBANON
Part of Israel's inheritance, Josh
13:5–7
Not completely conquered, Judg
3:1–3
Source of materials for temple, 1 Kin
5:2–18; Ezra 3:7
Mentioned in prophecy, Is 10:34; 29:17;
35:2; Ezek 17:3; Hos 14:5–7

LEBBAEUS
See JUDAS
Surname of Judas (Jude), Matt 10:3

LEBONAH
Town north of Shiloh, Judg 21:19

LED
l the people around by . . . . . .Ex 13:18
I have *l* you forty years in . .Deut 29:5
so the LORD alone *l* . . . . . .Deut 32:12
have *l* captivity captive . . . . . .Ps 68:18
l them forth by the . . . . .Ps 107:7
He was *l* as a lamb to the . . . . .Is 53:7
and be *l* out with peace . . . . . .Is 55:12
l them by the right . . . . .Is 63:12
have *l* them astray . . . . .Jer 50:6
Then Jesus was *l* up by the . .Matt 4:1
l Him out to crucify . . . . . .Mark 15:20
"He was *l* as a sheep to . . . . .Acts 8:32
For as many as are *l* . . . . . . .Rom 8:14
sorrow *l* to repentance . . . . .2 Cor 7:9
if you are *l* by the Spirit . . . . .Gal 5:18
l captivity captive . . . . .Eph 4:8
l away by various . . . . .2 Tim 3:6

LEFT
Lie also on your *l* side . . . .Ezek 4:4
l hand know what your . . . . .Matt 6:3
"See, we have *l* . . . . .Matt 19:27
And everyone who has *l* . . .Matt 19:29
on My *l* is not Mine to . . . .Mark 10:40
right hand and on the *l* . . . .2 Cor 6:7

LEGACY
shame shall be the *l* . . . . . . .Prov 3:35

LEGION
"My name is *L* . . . . .Mark 5:9
"*L*," because many . . . . .Luke 8:30

LEGIONS
twelve *l* of angels . . . . .Matt 26:53

LEGS
Like the *l* of the lame . . . .Prov 26:7
l are pillars of . . . . .Song 5:15
did not break His *l* . . . . . . .John 19:33

LEHI
Samson kills Philistines at, Judg 15:9–19

LEMUEL
King taught by his mother, Prov 31:1–31

LEND
"If you *l* money to .... Ex 22:25
l him sufficient .... Deut 15:8
And if you *l* to those ...... Luke 6:34
l me three loaves .... Luke 11:5

LENDER
is servant to the *l* .... Prov 22:7
as with the *l* .... Is 24:2

LENDING
and my servants, am *l* ...... Neh 5:10

LENDS
ever merciful, and *l* .... Ps 37:26
deals graciously and *l* ...... Ps 112:5
has pity on the poor *l* ..... Prov 19:17

LENGTH
The *l* of the ark shall .... Gen 6:15
is your life and the *l* ...... Deut 30:20
L of days is in her .... Prov 3:16
l is as great as its .... Rev 21:16

LENGTHENS
a shadow when it *l* .... Ps 109:23

LEOPARD
the *l* shall lie down .... Is 11:6
or the *l* its spots .... Jer 13:23

LEPER
put out of the camp every *l* .. Num 5:2
and there she was, a *l* .... Num 12:10
King Uzziah was a *l* ..... 2 Chr 26:21
l came and worshiped .... Matt 8:2
house of Simon the *l* ...... Mark 14:3

LEPERS
And when these *l* .... 2 Kin 7:8
the sick, cleanse the *l* ..... Matt 10:8
And many *l* were in .... Luke 4:27
ten men who were *l* ..... Luke 17:12

LEPROSY
This is the law of *l* .... Lev 14:57
he would heal him of his *l* ..2 Kin 5:3
l broke out on his .... 2 Chr 26:19
immediately the *l* left him .. Luke 5:13

LEPROUS
out, behold, his hand was *l* ... Ex 4:6
Miriam became *l* .... Num 12:10
out from his presence *l* .... 2 Kin 5:27
his forehead, he was *l* .... 2 Chr 26:20

LET
"L there be light" .... Gen 1:3
L the little children .... Matt 19:14

LETTER
they delivered the *l* .... Acts 15:30
the Spirit, and not in the *l* .. Rom 2:29
the oldness of the *l* .... Rom 7:6
for the *l* kills .... 2 Cor 3:6
you sorry with my *l* .... 2 Cor 7:8
or by word or by *l* .... 2 Thess 2:2

LETTERS
does this Man know *l* ...... John 7:15
or *l* of commendation ...... 2 Cor 3:1
"For his *l*," they say ...... 2 Cor 10:10
with what large *l* .... Gal 6:11

LEVI
Third son of Jacob and Leah, Gen 29:34
Avenges rape of Dinah, Gen 34:25–31
Jacob's prophecy concerning, Gen 49:5–7
Ancestor of Moses and Aaron, Ex 6:16–27

LEVIATHAN
"Can you draw out L .... Job 41:1
L which You have made ... Ps 104:26

LEVITE
"Is not Aaron the L .... Ex 4:14
Likewise a L, when he .... Luke 10:32
a L of the country of ...... Acts 4:36

LEVITES
Rewarded for dedication, Ex 32:26–29
Appointed over tabernacle, Num 1:47–54
Substituted for Israel's firstborn, Num 3:12–45
Consecrated to the Lord's service, Num 8:5–26
Cities assigned to, Num 35:2–8; Josh 14:3, 4; 1 Chr 6:54–81
Organized for temple service, 1 Chr 9:14–34; 23:1—26:28

LEVITICAL
were through the L .... Heb 7:11

LEWDNESS
wickedness, deceit, *l* ...... Mark 7:22
drunkenness, not in *l* .... Rom 13:13
themselves over to *l* .... Eph 4:19
when we walked in *l* .... 1 Pet 4:3

LIAR
a *l* listens eagerly to a ..... Prov 17:4
for he is a *l* and the .... John 8:44
but every man a *l* .... Rom 3:4
we make Him a *l* .... 1 John 1:10
Who is a *l* but he who .... 1 John 2:22
his brother, he is a *l* .... 1 John 4:20
God has made Him a *l* .... 1 John 5:10

LIARS
"All men are *l* .... Ps 116:11
Cretans are always *l* .... Titus 1:12
and have found them *l* ...... Rev 2:2
l shall have their .... Rev 21:8

LIBERALITY
he who gives, with *l* ...... Rom 12:8
the riches of their *l* .... 2 Cor 8:2

LIBERALLY
who gives to all *l* .... James 1:5

LIBERTY
year, and proclaim *l* ...... Lev 25:10
And I will walk at *l* .... Ps 119:45
to proclaim *l* to the .... Is 61:1
to proclaim *l* to the .... Luke 4:18
into the glorious *l* .... Rom 8:21
For why is my *l* .... 1 Cor 10:29
Lord is, there is *l* .... 2 Cor 3:17
therefore in the *l* .... Gal 5:1
l as an opportunity .... Gal 5:13
the perfect law of *l* ...... James 1:25
yet not using *l* .... 1 Pet 2:16

LIBNAH
Canaanite city, captured by Joshua, Josh 10:29, 30
Given to Aaron's descendants, Josh 21:13

LIBYA
Mentioned in prophecy, Ezek 30:5; Dan 11:43
Jews from, present at Pentecost, Acts 2:1–10

LICE
so that it may become *l* ...... Ex 8:16
and *l* in all their territory ... Ps 105:31

LIE
man, that He should *l* .... Num 23:19
to Samuel, "Go, *l* down .... 1 Sam 3:5
For now I will *l* .... Job 7:21
I will not *l* to David .... Ps 89:35
forged a *l* against me ...... Ps 119:69
leopard shall *l* down with ..... Is 11:6
prophesy a *l* to you in My .. Jer 29:21
heart to *l* to the Holy Spirit .. Acts 5:3
Do not *l* to one .... Col 3:9
God, who cannot *l* .... Titus 1:2

do not boast and *l* .... James 3:14
know it, and that no *l* .... 1 John 2:21
an abomination or a *l* ...... Rev 21:27

LIED
They have *l* about the .... Jer 5:12
You have not *l* to men ...... Acts 5:4

LIES
sin *l* at the door .... Gen 4:7
not say, "Here *l* Jezebel .. 2 Kin 9:37
He *l* in wait secretly .... Ps 10:9
speak *l* shall be stopped ... Ps 63:11
and he who speaks *l* ...... Prov 19:5
She also *l* in wait as for ... Prov 23:28
prophesy *l* in My name .... Jer 14:14
they shall speak *l* at the ... Dan 11:27
l in the name of the LORD .. Zech 13:3
speaking *l* in hypocrisy ... 1 Tim 4:2
and the whole world *l* .... 1 John 5:19

LIFE
See ALL THE DAYS OF HIS LIFE; BOOK
OF LIFE; BREATH OF LIFE; ETERNAL
LIFE; EVERLASTING LIFE; TREE OF
LIFE; WATER OF LIFE
the breath of *l* .... Gen 2:7
l was also in the .... Gen 2:9
I will require the *l* of man .... Gen 9:5
then you shall give *l* .... Ex 21:23
For the *l* of the .... Lev 17:11
before you today I .... Deut 30:15
You have granted me *l* ..... Job 10:12
in whose hand is the *l* .... Job 12:10
God takes away his *l* ...... Job 27:8
with the light of *l* .... Job 33:30
He will redeem their *l* ..... Ps 72:14
word has given me *l* ...... Ps 119:50
blessing—L forevermore .... Ps 133:3
regain the paths of *l* .... Prov 2:19
She is a tree of *l* .... Prov 3:18
so they will be *l* .... Prov 3:22
finds me finds *l* .... Prov 8:35
the *l* of his animal .... Prov 12:10
LORD is a fountain of *l* .... Prov 14:27
l winds upward for the .... Prov 15:24
thief hates his own *l* ..... Prov 29:24
is that wisdom gives *l* ..... Eccl 7:12
I have cut off my *l* .... Is 38:12
you the way of *l* .... Jer 21:8
l shall be as a prize .... Jer 39:18
not worry about your *l* .... Matt 6:25
l does not consist .... Luke 12:15
L is more than food ...... Luke 12:23
l was the light .... John 1:4
so the Son gives *l* .... John 5:21
as the Father has *l* .... John 5:26
spirit, and they are *l* .... John 6:63
have the light of *l* .... John 8:12
and I lay down My *l* ...... John 10:15
resurrection and the *l* ..... John 11:25
you lay down your *l* ...... John 13:38
God, who gives *l* .... Rom 4:17
that pertain to this *l* .... 1 Cor 6:3
Lord Jesus, that the *l* ..... 2 Cor 4:10
l which I now live .... Gal 2:20
l is hidden with .... Col 3:3
of God who gives *l* .... 1 Tim 6:13
For what is your *l* .... James 4:14
that pertain to *l* .... 2 Pet 1:3
l was manifested .... 1 John 1:2
and the pride of *l* .... 1 John 2:16
has given us eternal *l* ..... 1 John 5:11
who has the Son has *l* ... 1 John 5:12
the Lamb's Book of L ...... Rev 21:27
right to the tree of *l* .... Rev 22:14
the water of *l* freely .... Rev 22:17
from the Book of L .... Rev 22:19

LIFT
"L your eyes now and .... Gen 13:14
l up His countenance ...... Num 6:26
L up your heads .... Ps 24:7
I will *l* up my hands .... Ps 63:4

I will *l* up my eyes to . . . . Ps 121:1
l up your voice like a . . . . Is 58:1
l up a banner for the . . . . Is 62:10
l our hearts and hands . . . . . Lam 3:41
Nation shall not *l* up sword . . . Mic 4:3
Lord, and He will *l* . . . . . . James 4:10

LIFTED
l up the ark, and it rose . . . . . Gen 7:17
Then Abraham *l* his eyes . . Gen 22:13
Esau *l* up his voice and . . . . Gen 27:38
he *l* up the rod and struck . . . . Ex 7:20
when your heart is *l* up . . . . Deut 8:14
O LORD, for You have *l* . . . . Ps 30:1
l up his heel against me . . . . . . Ps 41:9
your heart is *l* up . . . . Ezek 28:2
l like a banner over His . . . Zech 9:16
He *l* up His eyes toward . . . Luke 6:20
in Hades, he *l* up his . . . . . Luke 16:23
l up His hands and . . . . . . Luke 24:50
the Son of Man be *l* . . . . . . John 3:14
And I, if I am *l* . . . . John 12:32
of Man must be *l* . . . . John 12:34
l up his heel against Me . . John 13:18
l up His eyes to heaven . . . . John 17:1

LIFTING
while *l* up their hands . . . . Neh 8:6
The *l* up of my hands as . . . . . Ps 141:2
l up holy hands, without . . . . 1 Tim 2:8

LIFTS
He brings low and *l* up . . . . 1 Sam 2:7
the One who *l* up my head . . . . Ps 3:3
The LORD *l* up the humble . . . Ps 147:6

LIGAMENTS
together by joints and *l* . . . . . Col 2:19

LIGHT
"Let there be *l* . . . . Gen 1:3
God called the *l* Day . . . . Gen 1:5
had *l* in their dwellings . . . . . Ex 10:23
pillar of fire to give them *l* . . Ex 13:21
of pressed olives for the *l* . . . Ex 27:20
he shall be like the *l* of . . . 2 Sam 23:4
by night, to show them *l* . . . . Neh 9:19
"The *l* of the wicked . . . . Job 18:5
l will shine on your . . . . Job 22:28
the wicked their *l* . . . . Job 38:15
to the dwelling of *l* . . . . Job 38:19
LORD, lift up the *l* . . . . Ps 4:6
For You will *l* my lamp . . . . . . Ps 18:28
The LORD is my *l* . . . . Ps 27:1
Oh, send out Your *l* . . . . Ps 43:3
L is sown for the . . . . Ps 97:11
and He has given us *l* . . . . . Ps 118:27
and a *l* to my path . . . . Ps 119:105
Him, all you stars of *l* . . . . . . Ps 148:3
The *l* of the righteous . . . . . . Prov 13:9
The *l* of the eyes . . . . Prov 15:30
The LORD gives *l* . . . . Prov 29:13
Truly the *l* is sweet . . . . Eccl 11:7
let us walk in the *l* . . . . Is 2:5
l is darkened by the . . . . Is 5:30
because there is no *l* . . . . Is 8:20
moon will be as the *l* . . . . . . Is 30:26
darkness *l* before them . . . . . Is 42:16
l shall break forth . . . . Is 58:8
for your *l* has come . . . . Is 60:1
shall come to your *l* . . . . Is 60:3
be your everlasting *l* . . . . Is 60:20
gives the sun for a *l* . . . . . . Jer 31:35
moon shall not give her *l* . . Ezek 32:7
like *l* that goes forth . . . . Hos 6:5
have seen a great *l* . . . . Matt 4:16
"You are the *l* . . . . Matt 5:14
Let your *l* so shine . . . . Matt 5:16
body will be full of *l* . . . . . . Matt 6:22
moon will not give its *l* . . . . Matt 24:29
take heed that the *l* . . . . . . Luke 11:35
than the sons of *l* . . . . Luke 16:8
and the life was the *l* . . . . . . John 1:4
That was the true *L* . . . . John 1:9
darkness rather than *l* . . . . . John 3:19

evil hates the *l* . . . . John 3:20
truth comes to the *l* . . . . . . John 3:21
saying, "I am the *l* . . . . John 8:12
believe in the *l* . . . . John 12:36
I have come as a *l* . . . . . . John 12:46
to *l* the hidden things . . . . . . 1 Cor 4:5
God who commanded *l* . . . . 2 Cor 4:6
Walk as children of *l* . . . . Eph 5:8
You are all sons of *l* . . . . . 1 Thess 5:5
and immortality to *l* . . . . . . 2 Tim 1:10
into His marvelous *l* . . . . 1 Pet 2:9
do well to heed as a *l* . . . . . . 2 Pet 1:19
to you, that God is *l* . . . . 1 John 1:5
l as He is in the . . . . 1 John 1:7
says he is in the *l* . . . . 1 John 2:9
l of a lamp shall not . . . . . . Rev 18:23
The Lamb is its *l* . . . . Rev 21:23
Lord God gives them *l* . . . . . Rev 22:5

LIGHTEN
L the yoke which . . . . 1 Kin 12:9
the sea, to *l* the load . . . . Jon 1:5

LIGHTLY
this, did I do it *l* . . . . 2 Cor 1:17

LIGHTNING
For as the *l* comes . . . . Matt 24:27
countenance was like *l* . . . . Matt 28:3
saw Satan fall like *l* . . . . . . Luke 10:18

LIGHTNINGS
were thunderings and *l* . . . . Ex 19:16
the *l* lit up the world . . . . Ps 77:18
l light the world . . . . Ps 97:4
the throne proceeded *l* . . . . . . Rev 4:5

LIGHTS
"Let there be *l* . . . . Gen 1:14
when Aaron *l* the lamps at . . . Ex 30:8
Him who made great *l* . . . . . Ps 136:7
whom you shine as *l* . . . . . . Phil 2:15
from the Father of *l* . . . . . . James 1:17

LIKE
"Who is *l* You . . . . Ex 15:11
L a lily among thorns . . . . . . Song 2:2
be made *l* His brethren . . . . Heb 2:17

LIKE-MINDED
grant you to be *l* . . . . Rom 15:5
For I have no one *l* . . . . Phil 2:20

LIKEN
To whom will you *l* Me . . . . . . Is 46:5
shall I *l* this generation . . . Matt 11:16
shall I *l* the kingdom . . . . Luke 13:20

LIKENESS
according to Our *l* . . . . Gen 1:26
carved image—any *l* . . . . . . Ex 20:4
when I awake in Your *l* . . . . . Ps 17:15
in the *l* of His death . . . . Rom 6:5
His own Son in the *l* . . . . Rom 8:3
and coming in the *l* . . . . Phil 2:7

LILIES
were in the shape of *l* . . . . . 1 Kin 7:22
his lips are *l*, dripping . . . . . Song 5:13
feeds his flock among the *l* . . Song 6:3
the *l*, how they grow . . . . . Luke 12:27

LILY
the *l* of the valleys . . . . Song 2:1
Like a *l* among thorns . . . . . Song 2:2
shall grow like the *l* . . . . Hos 14:5

LIMIT
Do you *l* wisdom to . . . . Job 15:8
to the sea its *l* . . . . Prov 8:29

LIMITED
l the Holy One of . . . . Ps 78:41

LINE
l has gone out through . . . . . . Ps 19:4
upon precept, *l* upon *l* . . . . Is 28:10
I am setting a plumb *l* . . . . . Amos 7:8

LINEAGE
was of the house and *l* . . . . . Luke 2:4

LINEN
him in garments of fine *l* . . Gen 41:42
artistically woven of fine *l* . . Ex 39:27
shall put on his *l* garment . . . Lev 6:10
with the *l* turban he shall . . . . Lev 16:4
take off the *l* garments . . . . . Lev 16:23
child, wearing a *l* ephod . . 1 Sam 2:18
David also wore a *l* . . . . . . 1 Chr 15:27
her clothing is fine *l* . . . . . . Prov 31:22
get yourself a *l* sash . . . . Jer 13:1
to the man clothed with *l* . . . . Ezek 9:3
heard the man clothed in *l* . . Dan 12:7
wrapped it in a clean *l* . . Matt 27:59
wrapped Him in the *l* . . . . Mark 15:46
in purple and fine *l* . . . . . . Luke 16:19
strips of *l* with the spices . . John 19:40
saw the *l* cloths lying . . . . . . John 20:5
that was clothed in fine *l* . . Rev 18:12
l is the righteous . . . . Rev 19:8

LINGER
Those who *l* long at . . . . . Prov 23:30
salvation shall not *l* . . . . Is 46:13

LINGERED
the Boy Jesus *l* behind . . . . . Luke 2:43

LINTEL
on the *l* of the houses . . . . Ex 12:7
the *l* and doorposts were . . 1 Kin 6:31

LION
he lies down as a *l* . . . . Gen 49:9
he tore the *l* apart as one . . Judg 14:6
when a *l* or a bear . . . . . . 1 Sam 17:34
is like the heart of a *l* . . . 2 Sam 17:10
l standing by the corpse . . 1 Kin 13:28
Killed a *l* in the midst . . . . 1 Chr 11:22
like a fierce *l* . . . . Job 10:16
l shall eat straw . . . . Is 11:7
face of a *l* on the right . . . . Ezek 1:10
the third the face of a *l* . . . Ezek 10:14
the face of a young *l* . . . . . Ezek 41:19
For I will be like a *l* . . . . Hos 5:14
about like a roaring *l* . . . . . . 1 Pet 5:8
living creature was like a *l* . . Rev 4:7
the *L* of the tribe of Judah . . . Rev 5:5

LION'S
Judah is a *l* whelp . . . . Gen 49:9

LIONS
Twelve *l* stood there . . . . 1 Kin 10:20
My soul is among *l* . . . . Ps 57:4
be cast into the den of *l* . . . . Dan 6:7
the mouths of *l* . . . . Heb 11:33
were like the heads of *l* . . . . Rev 9:17

LIPS
of uncircumcised *l* . . . . Ex 6:12
off all flattering *l* . . . . Ps 12:3
Let the lying *l* . . . . Ps 31:18
The *l* of the righteous . . . . Prov 10:21
but the *l* of knowledge . . . . Prov 20:15
am a man of unclean *l* . . . . Is 6:5
with stammering *l* and . . . . . . Is 28:11
I create the fruit of the *l* . . . . Is 57:19
offer the sacrifices of our *l* . . Hos 14:2
honors Me with their *l* . . . . . Mark 7:6
asps is under their *l* . . . . . . Rom 3:13
other *l* I will speak . . . . . . 1 Cor 14:21
that is, the fruit of our *l* . . . Heb 13:15
from evil, and his *l* . . . . . . 1 Pet 3:10

LISTEN
L now to my voice . . . . Ex 18:19
would not *l* to Balaam . . . . Deut 23:5
not *l* to their judges . . . . Judg 2:17
But do not *l* to Hezekiah . . 2 Kin 18:32
L carefully to Me . . . . Is 55:2
O Lord, *l* and act . . . . Dan 9:19
"*L*! Behold, a sower went . . . Mark 4:3
you are not able to *l* . . . . . . John 8:43
Why do you *l* to Him . . . . . John 10:20
you who fear God, *l* . . . . . Acts 13:16

LISTENED
God *l* to Leah, and she . . . . Gen 30:17

the LORD *l* to the voice of .. Num 21:3
But the LORD *l* to me ...... Deut 9:19
l to the voice of Manoah ... Judg 13:9
and the LORD *l* to him ..... 2 Kin 13:4
the LORD *l* to Hezekiah ... 2 Chr 30:20
Yet you have not *l* to Me .... Jer 25:7
"Men, you should have *l* .. Acts 27:21

LISTENS
but whoever *l* to me ...... Prov 1:33

LITTLE
l foxes that spoil the ...... Song 2:15
We have a *l* sister .... Song 8:8
upon line, here a *l* .... Is 28:10
though you are *l* .... Mic 5:2
indeed it came to *l* .... Hag 1:9
for I was a *l* angry .... Zech 1:15
l ones only a cup .... Matt 10:42
"O you of *l* faith .... Matt 14:31
Whoever receives one *l* .... Matt 18:5
to whom *l* is forgiven ..... Luke 7:47
"Let the *l* children come .. Luke 18:16
faithful in a very *l* .... Luke 19:17
gathered *l* had no lack .... 2 Cor 8:15
l leaven leavens the whole .... Gal 5:9
exercise profits a *l* .... 1 Tim 4:8
made him a *l* lower than .... Heb 2:7
"For yet a *l* while .... Heb 10:37
the tongue is a *l* member .. James 3:5
L children, keep .... 1 John 5:21
"Give me the *l* book .... Rev 10:9

LITTLE CHILDREN
converted and become as *l* .. Matt 18:3
l were brought to Him .... Matt 19:13
receives one of these *l* .... Mark 9:37
"Let the *l* come to Me, .. Mark 10:14
L, I shall be with you ..... John 13:33
My *l*, for whom I labor .... Gal 4:19
l, these things I write ...... 1 John 2:1
I write to you, *l*, ... 1 John 2:12
now, *l*, abide in Him, ... 1 John 2:28
L, let no one deceive ...... 1 John 3:7
You are of God, *l*, ... 1 John 4:4
L, keep yourselves from .... 1 John 5:21

LIVE
eat, and *l* forever .... Gen 3:22
a man does, he shall *l* ..... Lev 18:5
I would not *l* forever ...... Job 7:16
L joyfully with the .... Eccl 9:9
by these things men *l* ...... Is 38:16
sin, he shall surely *l* ...... Ezek 3:21
"Seek Me and *l* .... Amos 5:4
but the just shall *l* .... Hab 2:4
l by bread alone .... Matt 4:4
who feeds on Me will *l* .... John 6:57
Because I *l*, you will *l* ... John 14:19
for in Him we *l* .... Acts 17:28
those who *l* according to .... Rom 8:5
l peaceably with all ...... Rom 12:18
should *l* from the gospel .. 1 Cor 9:14
as dying, and behold we *l* .. 2 Cor 6:9
l in the manner of Gentiles .. Gal 2:14
the life which I now *l* ..... Gal 2:20
"the just shall *l* by faith ..... Gal 3:11
If we *l* in the Spirit .... Gal 5:25
to me, to *l* is Christ .... Phil 1:21
l godly in Christ .... 2 Tim 3:12
the just shall *l* by faith .... Heb 10:38
Father of spirits and *l* ..... Heb 12:9
to *l* honorably .... Heb 13:18
l according to God in .... 1 Pet 4:6
l again until the thousand ... Rev 20:5

LIVED
our religion I *l* a Pharisee .. Acts 26:5
died and rose and *l* ...... Rom 14:9
walked when you *l* in them .. Col 3:7
And they *l* and reigned .... Rev 20:4

LIVES
but man *l* by every .... Deut 8:3
know that my Redeemer *l* .. Job 19:25
days of our *l* are seventy .... Ps 90:10

have risked their *l* .... Acts 15:26
He *l* to God .... Rom 6:10
For none of us *l* .... Rom 14:7
He *l* by the power of God .. 2 Cor 13:4
but Christ *l* in me .... Gal 2:20
at all while the testator *l* .... Heb 9:17
to lay down our *l* ...... 1 John 3:16
I am He who *l* .... Rev 1:18

LIVING
See LAND OF THE LIVING
and man became a *l* .... Gen 2:7
in the light of the *l* .... Ps 56:13
l will take it to heart ...... Eccl 7:2
l know that they will ...... Eccl 9:5
Why should a *l* man ...... Lam 3:39
the dead, but of the *l* ..... Matt 22:32
Why do you seek the *l* .... Luke 24:5
I am the *l* bread .... John 6:51
will flow rivers of *l* water .. John 7:38
to be Judge of the *l* ...... Acts 10:42
your bodies a *l* sacrifice .... Rom 12:1
the church of the *l* God .... 1 Tim 3:15
who will judge the *l* ...... 2 Tim 4:1
the word of God is *l* ...... Heb 4:12
the hands of the *l* God .... Heb 10:31
to Him as to a *l* stone ..... 1 Pet 2:4
ready to judge the *l* .... 1 Pet 4:5
l creature was like a .... Rev 4:7
the four *l* creatures .... Rev 7:11

LIVING CREATURE
earth bring forth the *l* ..... Gen 1:24
Adam called each *l*, ... Gen 2:19
every *l* that is with you ..... Gen 9:10
and every *l* of all flesh ..... Gen 9:15
every *l* that moves .... Lev 11:46
each *l* with its four .... Ezek 1:15
This was the *l* I saw ...... Ezek 10:15
the spirit of the *l* .... Ezek 10:17
first *l* was like a lion, ... Rev 4:7
I heard the second *l* ...... Rev 6:3
l in the sea died .... Rev 16:3

LIVING CREATURES
with an abundance of *l*, ... Gen 1:20
likeness of four *l* .... Ezek 1:5
the wings of the *l* .... Ezek 3:13
four *l* full of eyes .... Rev 4:6
four *l* said, "Amen!" ..... Rev 5:14
the *l* in the sea died, ... Rev 8:9
before the four *l* .... Rev 14:3
one of the four *l* .... Rev 15:7
l fell down and worshiped .. Rev 19:4

LO-AMMI
Symbolic name of Hosea's son, Hos
1:8, 9

LO-RUHAMAH
Symbolic name of Hosea's daughter,
Hos 1:6

LOAD
into the sea, to lighten the *l* .. Jon 1:5
you *l* men with burdens .. Luke 11:46
shall bear his own *l* .... Gal 6:5

LOADED
they *l* their donkeys with .. Gen 42:26
l them on donkeys ...... 1 Sam 25:18
women *l* down with sins .. 2 Tim 3:6

LOAF
l of barley bread tumbled .. Judg 7:13
l with them in the boat .... Mark 8:14

LOATHE
I *l* my life .... Job 7:16
l themselves for the .... Ezek 6:9

LOATHSOME
but a wicked man is *l* ..... Prov 13:5

LOAVES
have here only five *l* ..... Matt 14:17
He took the seven *l* ...... Matt 15:36
lend me three *l* .... Luke 11:5
you ate of the *l* .... John 6:26

LOCKS
If you weave the seven *l* .. Judg 16:13
his *l* are wavy, and black .. Song 5:11

LOCUST
What the chewing *l* .... Joel 1:4
left, the swarming *l* .... Joel 1:4

LOCUSTS
as numerous as *l* .... Judg 7:12
He spoke, and *l* came ...... Ps 105:34
the *l* have no king .... Prov 30:27
and his food was *l* .... Matt 3:4
waist, and he ate *l* .... Mark 1:6
out of the smoke *l* .... Rev 9:3

LODGED
them in and *l* them ...... Acts 10:23
children, if she has *l* ..... 1 Tim 5:10

LOFTILY
they speak *l* .... Ps 73:8

LOFTY
haughty, nor my eyes *l* .... Ps 131:1
Wisdom is too *l* .... Prov 24:7
l are their eyes .... Prov 30:13
and *L* One who.......... Is 57:15

LOINS
gird up the *l* of your ...... 1 Pet 1:13

LONELY
How *l* sits the city that was .. Lam 1:1

LONG
your days may be *l* .... Deut 5:16
said, "*L* live the king .... 1 Sam 10:24
who *l* for death .... Job 3:21
me the thing that I *l* ...... Job 6:8
I *l* for Your salvation ..... Ps 119:174
the appointed time was *l* ... Dan 10:1
l as the bridegroom is ..... Matt 9:15
How I shall I bear with .... Mark 9:19
go around in *l* robes ..... Mark 12:38
make *l* prayers .... Luke 20:47
we are killed all day *l* ..... Rom 8:36
Love suffers *l* and is kind .. 1 Cor 13:4
how greatly I *l* .... Phil 1:8
"How *l*, O LORD, holy and ... Rev 6:10

LONGING
wife cast *l* eyes on Joseph .. Gen 39:7
David said with *l*, "Oh .. 2 Sam 23:15
For He satisfies the *l* soul .. Ps 107:9
since he was *l* for you all ... Phil 2:26

LONGSUFFERING
and gracious, *l* .... Ps 86:15
is love, joy, peace, *l* .... Gal 5:22
and gentleness, with *l* ..... Eph 4:2
for all patience and *l* ..... Col 1:11
might show all *l* .... 1 Tim 1:16
when once the Divine *l* ... 1 Pet 3:20
and consider that the *l* .... 2 Pet 3:15

LOOK
Do not *l* behind you ...... Gen 19:17
l down from heaven .... Ps 80:14
who has a haughty *l* ...... Ps 101:5
A proud *l*, a lying .... Prov 6:17
that day a man will *l* ...... Is 17:7
L upon Zion .... Is 33:20
"*L* to Me, and be saved .... Is 45:22
l to the rock from which .... Is 51:1
we *l* for light .... Is 59:9
we *l* for justice .... Is 59:11
"*L* among the nations .... Hab 1:5
l on Me whom they ...... Zech 12:10
L at the birds of the air ... Matt 6:26
why do you *l* at the speck .. Matt 7:3
say to you, '*L* here ...... Luke 17:23
L at the fig tree .... Luke 21:29
and *l* at My hands .... John 20:27
l on their threats .... Acts 4:29
L! I see the heavens ...... Acts 7:56
of Israel could not *l* ...... 2 Cor 3:7
while we do not *l* .... 2 Cor 4:18
Let each of you *l* .... Phil 2:4

angels desire to *l* into ...... 1 Pet 1:12
l for new heavens and a ...2 Pet 3:13
L to yourselves .... 2 John 8
open the scroll, or to *l* at it ...Rev 5:3

LOOKED
But when I *l* for good ...... Job 30:26
They *l* to Him and were ...... Ps 34:5
For He *l* down from the ....Ps 102:19
He *l* for justice .... Is 5:7
"We *l* for peace .... Jer 8:15
"You *l* for much .... Hag 1:9
the Lord turned and *l*.....Luke 22:61
for he *l* to the reward ....Heb 11:26

LOOKING
the plow, and *l* back ...... Luke 9:62
l for the blessed hope ...... Titus 2:13
l unto Jesus, the author ..... Heb 12:2
l carefully lest .... Heb 12:15
l for the mercy of.......... Jude 21

LOOKS
Absalom for his good *l* ..2 Sam 14:25
Then he *l* at men and ...... Job 33:27
God *l* down from heaven .....Ps 53:2
The lofty *l* of man .... Is 2:11
to you that whoever *l* ..... Matt 5:28

LOOM
and the web from the *l* .....Judg 16:14
cuts me off from the *l* .... Is 38:12

LOOSE
l the armor of kings .... Is 45:1
and whatever you *l* ...... Matt 16:19
said to them, "L him ...... John 11:44

LOOSED
You have *l* my bonds ......Ps 116:16
the silver cord is *l* .... Eccl 12:6
on earth will be *l* in .... Matt 16:19
his tongue was *l*, and he ... Mark 7:35
l from your infirmity .....Luke 13:12
be *l* from this bond ......Luke 13:16
l the pains of death .... Acts 2:24
everyone's chains were *l* .. Acts 16:26
Do not seek to be *l* .... 1 Cor 7:27

LORD
See ANGEL OF THE LORD; ANGER
   OF THE LORD; BLESS THE LORD;
   BLESSED BE THE LORD; DAY OF THE
   LORD; FEAR OF THE LORD; FEAR
   THE LORD; GLORY OF THE LORD;
   HAND OF THE LORD; HOUSE OF THE
   LORD; LAW OF THE LORD; LOVE THE
   LORD YOUR GOD; PRAISE THE LORD;
   REJOICE IN THE LORD; SEEK THE
   LORD; SERVE THE LORD; SINNED
   AGAINST THE LORD; SPIRIT OF THE
   LORD; VOICE OF THE LORD; VOW TO
   THE LORD; WAIT ON THE LORD; WAY
   OF THE LORD; WRATH OF THE LORD
L is my strength .... Ex 15:2
L is a man of war .... Ex 15:3
L our God, the *L*........... Deut 6:4
sacrifice to the *L* your ..... Deut 17:1
may know that the *L* ...... 1 Kin 8:60
If the *L* is God .... 1 Kin 18:21
You alone are the *L* .... Neh 9:6
The *L* of hosts .... Ps 24:10
belongs to the *L* .... Ps 89:18
let us sing to the *L* .... Ps 95:1
L is the great God .... Ps 95:3
Gracious is the *L* .... Ps 116:5
L surrounds His people .....Ps 125:2
The *L* is righteous .... Ps 129:4
L is near to all who .... Ps 145:18
L is a God of justice .... Is 30:18
L Our Righteousness ..... Jer 23:6
L has done marvelous ..... Joel 2:21
L God is my strength ...... Hab 3:19
"The *L* is one .... Zech 14:9
shall not tempt the *L*....... Matt 4:7
shall worship the *L* .... Matt 4:10

Son of Man is also *L* ...... Mark 2:28
who is Christ the *L* ....Luke 2:11
why do you call Me '*L* ..... Luke 6:46
L is risen indeed .... Luke 24:34
call Me Teacher and *L* .... John 13:13
He is *L* of all .... Acts 10:36
'Who are You, *L* .... Acts 26:15
with your mouth the *L* ..... Rom 10:9
Greek, for the same *L* ..... Rom 10:12
say that Jesus is *L* ...... 1 Cor 12:3
second Man is the *L* .... 1 Cor 15:47
the Spirit of the *L* .... 2 Cor 3:17
that Jesus Christ is *L* ...... Phil 2:11
and deny the only *L* .... Jude 4
L God Omnipotent .... Rev 19:6

LORD APPEARED TO
Then the *L* Abram and ..... Gen 12:7
the *L* Abram and said to ... Gen 17:1
L him by the terebinth ...... Gen 18:1
Then the *L* him and said ... Gen 26:2
Then the glory of the *L* .... Lev 9:23
glory of the *L* them .... Num 20:6
L Solomon in a dream ...... 1 Kin 3:5
L Solomon the second ..... 1 Kin 9:2

LORD COMMANDED
all that the *L* him .... Gen 7:5
L Moses and Aaron, ... Ex 12:50
words which the *L* him ...... Ex 19:7
the thing which the *L*........ Ex 35:4
The *L* this to be given ...... Lev 7:36
which the *L* Moses .... Lev 27:34
As the *L* Moses, so he ..... Num 1:19
as the *L* Moses, all .... Num 15:36
Moses did as the *L* ...... Num 27:22
statutes which the *L* ...... Num 30:16
the *L* us to observe .... Deut 6:24
not kept what the *L*...... 1 Sam 13:14
David did so, as the *L* ...2 Sam 5:25
So the *L* the angel, ... 1 Chr 21:27
there the *L* the blessing .....Ps 133:3
the Euphrates, as the *L* ..... Jer 13:5
did as the angel of the *L* ...Matt 1:24

LORD GOD OF HOSTS
the *L* was with him .... 2 Sam 5:10
very zealous for the *L* .... 1 Kin 19:10
who wait for You, O *L*........ Ps 69:6
Restore us, O *L*; .... Ps 80:19
O *L*, hear my prayer; .... Ps 84:8
Therefore thus says the *L*: ... Is 10:24
L in the Valley of Vision ..... Is 22:5
I have heard from the *L*, ... Is 28:22
called by Your name, O *L* .... Jer 15:16
this is the day of the *L* .... Jer 46:10
the work of the *L* .... Jer 50:25
the *L* is his name .... Amos 4:13
The *L*, he who touches ..... Amos 9:5

LORD GOD OF ISRAEL
Pharaoh, "Thus says the *L* ... Ex 5:1
before the Lord, the *L* ..... Ex 34:23
give glory to the *L*, ... Josh 7:19
built an altar to the *L* ...... Josh 8:30
sworn to them by the *L* .... Josh 9:19
the *L* fought for Israel .... Josh 10:42
L was their inheritance ... Josh 13:33
your heart to the *L*........ Josh 24:23
will sing praise to the *L* ..... Judg 5:3
"O *L*, why has this come ... Judg 21:3
be given you by the *L*, ... Ruth 2:12
Saul said to the *L* ...... 1 Sam 14:41
"O *L*, Your servant ...... 1 Sam 23:10
Blessed is the *L* .... 1 Sam 25:32
L: 'I anointed you .... 2 Sam 12:7
'Blessed be the *L* .... 1 Kin 1:48
for the name of the *L* ..... 1 Kin 8:17
turned away from the *L* .... 1 Kin 11:9
provoked the *L* to anger .. 1 Kin 15:30
O *L*, the One who .... 2 Kin 19:15
the ark of the *L* .... 1 Chr 15:12
build a house for the *L* .... 1 Chr 22:6
"The *L* has given rest .... 1 Chr 23:25

their heart to seek the *L* .. 2 Chr 11:16
they turned to the *L*...... 2 Chr 15:4
the Passover to the *L* ..... 2 Chr 30:1
build the house of the *L* .... Ezra 1:3
in order to seek the *L* ..... Ezra 6:21
Blessed be the *L*, from ..... Ps 41:13
Blessed is the *L*, for he ..... Luke 1:68

LORD HAS SPOKEN
son's wife, as the *L* ...... Gen 24:51
that the *L* we will do .... Ex 19:8
the statutes which the *L* ... Lev 10:11
which the *L* to Moses ..... Num 15:22
For the *L* of David .... 2 Sam 3:18
the sign which the *L* ...... 1 Kin 13:3
the mouth of the *L* .... Is 1:20
for the mouth of the *L* ...... Is 40:5
not be proud, for the *L* ..... Jer 13:15
Hear this word that the *L* .. Amos 3:1

LORD IS GOOD
taste and see that the *L*..... Ps 34:8
For the *L*; His mercy .... Ps 100:5
Praise the Lord, for the *L*... Ps 135:3
L to all, and His .... Ps 145:9
Lord of hosts, for the *L* .... Jer 33:11
The *L* to those who wait .... Lam 3:25
The *L*, a stronghold .... Nah 1:7

LORD JESUS CHRIST
we believed on the *L* ..... Acts 11:17
the grace of the *L*....... Acts 15:11
for the name of our *L* .... Acts 15:26
"Believe on the *L* .... Acts 16:31
with God through our *L* ..... Rom 5:1
in God through our *L* ...... Rom 5:11
But put on the *L* .... Rom 13:14
do not serve our *L* .... Rom 16:18
the revelation of our *L* ..... 1 Cor 1:7
in the day of our *L* .... 1 Cor 1:8
victory through our *L* .... 1 Cor 15:57
does not love the *L* ...... 1 Cor 16:22
know the grace of our *L* .... 2 Cor 8:9
in the cross of our *L* .... Gal 6:14
in the name of our *L*....... Eph 5:20
for the Savior, the *L* .... Phil 3:20
presence of our *L* ...... 1 Thess 2:19
salvation through our *L* ... 1 Thess 5:9
at the coming of our *L* ... 1 Thess 5:23
obey the gospel of our *L* .. 2 Thess 1:8
the coming of our *L* ...... 2 Thess 2:1
hold the faith of our *L* ..... James 2:1
in the knowledge of *L*....... 2 Pet 1:8
just as our *L* showed me ... 2 Pet 1:14
Lord God and our *L* .... Jude 4
by the apostles of our *L* ..... Jude 17
The grace of our *L* .... Rev 22:21

LORD OF HOSTS
to the *L* in Shiloh .... 1 Sam 1:3
"O *L*, if You will indeed .. 1 Sam 1:11
L, who dwells between .... 1 Sam 4:4
in the name of the *L* ..... 1 Sam 17:45
'*L* is the God over Israel ..2 Sam 7:26
The zeal of the *L*........ 2 Kin 19:31
the *L* was with him .... 1 Chr 11:9
The *L*, He is the King ..... Ps 24:10
The *L* is with us; .... Ps 46:7
Your tabernacle, O *L*........ Ps 84:1
Unless the *L* had left to ...... Is 1:9
For the day of the *L* .... Is 2:12
vineyard of the *L* .... Is 5:7
Holy, holy, holy is the *L* ..... Is 6:3
The *L*, Him you shall .... Is 8:13
The zeal of the *L* .... Is 9:7
Through the wrath of the *L* ... Is 9:19
in the wrath of the *L* ...... Is 13:13
L will reign on Mount Zion .. Is 24:23
In that day the *L* .... Is 28:5
O *L*, God of Israel .... Is 37:16
his Redeemer, the *L* .... Is 44:6
is your husband, the *L* ...... Is 54:5
But, O *L*, You who test ..... Jer 20:12
of the living God, the *L* ..... Jer 23:36

intercession to the *L* . . . . Jer 27:18
the *L* is His name . . . . Jer 31:35
Praise the *L*, for the Lord . . . Jer 33:11
by his God, the *L* . . . . Jer 51:5
The *L* has sworn . . . . Jer 51:14
the people of the *L* . . . . Zeph 2:10
on the house of the *L* . . . . . . Hag 1:14
with glory," says the *L* . . . . . . Hag 2:7
"Return to me," says the *L* . . . Zech 1:3
"O *L*, how long will You . . . Zech 1:12
L has sent me . . . . Zech 2:9
My Spirit,' says the *L* . . . . . . Zech 4:6
wrath came from the *L* . . . Zech 7:12
the Mountain of the *L* . . . . . . Zech 8:3
shall come to seek the *L* . . . Zech 8:22
The *L* will defend them . . . . Zech 9:15
worship the King, the *L* . . . Zech 14:16
a great King," says the *L* . . . Mal 1:14
is the messenger of the *L* . . . . Mal 2:7
return to you, says the *L* . . . Mal 3:7

LORD OF LORDS
God of gods and *L* . . . . . Deut 10:17
give thanks to the *L* . . . . . Ps 136:3
King of kings and *L* . . . . . 1 Tim 6:15
He is *L* and King of kings . . Rev 17:14
King of kings and *L* . . . . . Rev 19:16

LORD WAS WITH HIM
master saw that the *L* . . . . . Gen 39:3
Samuel grew, and the *L* . . 1 Sam 3:19
David, because the *L* . . 1 Sam 18:12
ways, and the *L* . . . . 1 Sam 18:14
The *L*; he prospered . . . . . . 2 Kin 18:7
And the hand of the *L* . . . . Luke 1:66

LORD'S ANOINTED
"Surely the *L* is before . . . . 1 Sam 16:6
to my master, the *L* . . . . . . 1 Sam 24:6
his hand against the *L* . . . 1 Sam 26:9
hand to destroy the *L* . . . . 2 Sam 1:14
he cursed the *L* . . . . 2 Sam 19:21

LORDS
many gods and many *l* . . . . . 1 Cor 8:5
nor as being *l* over . . . . 1 Pet 5:3
for He is Lord of *l* . . . . Rev 17:14

LORDSHIP
Gentiles exercise *l* . . . . Luke 22:25

LOSE
gain, and a time to *l* . . . . Eccl 3:6
save his life will *l* . . . . Matt 16:25
reap if we do not *l* . . . . Gal 6:9
that we do not *l* . . . . 2 John 8

LOSES
but if the salt *l* . . . . Matt 5:13
and *l* his own soul . . . . Matt 16:26
if she *l* one coin . . . . Luke 15:8
l his life will preserve . . . Luke 17:33

LOSS
he will suffer *l* . . . . 1 Cor 3:15
count all things *l* . . . . Phil 3:8

LOST
are dry, our hope is *l* . . . . Ezek 37:11
save that which was *l* . . . . . Matt 18:11
the one which is *l* . . . . Luke 15:4
my sheep which was *l* . . . . . Luke 15:6
the piece which I *l* . . . . Luke 15:9
and none of them is *l* . . . . . John 17:12
You gave Me I have *l* . . . . . . John 18:9

LOT
Abram's nephew; accompanies him,
Gen 11:27—12:5; 13:1
Separates from Abram, Gen 13:5–12
Rescued by Abram, Gen 14:12–16
Saved from Sodom for his hospitality,
Gen 19:1–29
Tricked into committing incest, Gen
19:30–38

LOT
shall be divided by *l* . . . . . . Num 26:55
You maintain my *l* . . . . Ps 16:5

cast in your *l* among . . . . . . Prov 1:14
l is cast into the lap . . . . . . Prov 16:33

LOT'S WIFE
Disobedient, becomes pillar of salt,
Gen 19:26
Event to be remembered, Luke 17:32

LOTS
l causes contentions . . . . . Prov 18:18
garments, casting *l* . . . . . . Mark 15:24
And they cast their *l* . . . . . . Acts 1:26

LOUD
I cried out with a *l* . . . . Gen 39:14
Him with *l* cymbals . . . . Ps 150:5
cried out with a *l* . . . . Matt 27:46
I heard behind me a *l* . . . . . . Rev 1:10

LOVE
l your neighbor as . . . . Lev 19:18
l the Lord your God . . . . Deut 6:5
your *l* to me was . . . . 2 Sam 1:26
How long will you *l* . . . . Ps 4:2
Oh, *l* the Lord . . . . Ps 31:23
l righteousness . . . . Ps 45:7
he has set his *l* . . . . Ps 91:14
Oh, how I *l* Your law . . . . . . Ps 119:97
peace have those who *l* . . Ps 119:165
preserves all who *l* . . . . . . Ps 145:20
us take our fill of *l* . . . . Prov 7:18
l covers all sins . . . . Prov 10:12
a time to *l* . . . . Eccl 3:8
People know neither *l* . . . . . . Eccl 9:1
l is better than wine . . . . . . Song 1:2
banner over me was *l* . . . . . Song 2:4
stir up nor awaken *l* . . . . . . Song 3:5
I will give you my *l* . . . . Song 7:12
l is as strong as death . . . . . Song 8:6
waters cannot quench *l* . . . . Song 8:7
time was the time of *l* . . . . Ezek 16:8
backsliding, I will *l* . . . . Hos 14:4
do justly, to *l* mercy . . . . . . Mic 6:8
to you, *l* your enemies . . . . Matt 5:44
l those who *l* you . . . . Matt 5:46
which of them will *l* . . . . . . Luke 7:42
you do not have the *l* . . . . . . John 5:42
if you have *l* for one . . . . . . John 13:35
"If you *l* Me, keep My . . . . John 14:15
and My Father will *l* . . . . . John 14:23
l one another as I . . . . John 15:12
l has no one than this . . . . John 15:13
l Me more than these . . . . John 21:15
of Jonah, do you *l* . . . . John 21:16
because the *l* of God . . . . . . Rom 5:5
Let *l* be without . . . . Rom 12:9
to *l* one another . . . . Rom 13:8
L does no harm to a . . . . . Rom 13:10
up, but *l* edifies . . . . 1 Cor 8:1
L suffers long and is . . . . . . 1 Cor 13:4
L never fails . . . . 1 Cor 13:8
greatest of these is *l* . . . . . . 1 Cor 13:13
For the *l* of Christ . . . . 2 Cor 5:14
and the God of *l* . . . . 2 Cor 13:11
of the Spirit is *l* . . . . Gal 5:22
rooted and grounded in *l* . . . Eph 3:17
the edifying of itself in *l* . . . Eph 4:16
Husbands, *l* your wives . . . . Eph 5:25
if any comfort of *l* . . . . Phil 2:1
of the Son of His *l* . . . . Col 1:13
being knit together in *l* . . . . . Col 2:2
l your wives and do . . . . . . Col 3:19
breastplate of faith and *l* . . 1 Thess 5:8
the commandment is *l* . . . . . 1 Tim 1:5
continue in faith, *l* . . . . 1 Tim 2:15
word, in conduct, in *l* . . . . . 1 Tim 4:12
For the *l* of money is . . . . . . 1 Tim 6:10
l their husbands . . . . Titus 2:4
Let brotherly *l* . . . . Heb 13:1
having not seen you *l* . . . . . . 1 Pet 1:8
L the brotherhood . . . . 1 Pet 2:17
for "*l* will cover a . . . . 1 Pet 4:8
with a kiss of *l* . . . . 1 Pet 5:14
brotherly kindness *l* . . . . . . 2 Pet 1:7
loves the world, the *l* . . . . 1 John 2:15

we *l* the brethren . . . . 1 John 3:14
By this we know *l* . . . . 1 John 3:16
him, how does the *l* . . . . . 1 John 3:17
Beloved, let us *l* . . . . 1 John 4:7
know God, for God is *l* . . . 1 John 4:8
In this is *l* . . . . 1 John 4:10
If we *l* one another . . . . . . 1 John 4:12
L has been perfected . . . . 1 John 4:17
There is no fear in *l* . . . . . 1 John 4:18
l Him because He first . . . 1 John 4:19
who loves God must *l* . . . 1 John 4:21
For this is the *l* . . . . 1 John 5:3
and *l* be multiplied to you . . . . Jude 2
are spots in your *l* feasts . . . . Jude 12
have left your first *l* . . . . Rev 2:4
your works, *l*, service . . . . . Rev 2:19
and they did not *l* . . . . Rev 12:11

LOVE OF CHRIST
separate us from the *l* . . . . . Rom 8:35
For the *l* compels us . . . . . 2 Cor 5:14
l which passes knowledge . . Eph 3:19

LOVE OF GOD
pass by justice and the *l* . . Luke 11:42
you do not have the *l* . . . . . John 5:42
the *l* has been poured . . . . . Rom 5:5
separate us from the *l* . . . . . Rom 8:39
l is perfected in him . . . . . 1 John 2:5
the *l* abide in him . . . . 1 John 3:17
In this the *l* . . . . 1 John 4:9
For this is the *l* . . . . 1 John 5:3
keep yourselves in the *l* . . . . Jude 21

LOVE ONE ANOTHER
l; as I have loved you . . . . John 13:34
that you *l* as I have . . . . . John 15:12
anything except to *l* . . . . . . Rom 13:8
are taught by God to *l* . . . 1 Thess 4:9
l fervently with a pure . . . . 1 Pet 1:22
that we should *l* . . . . 1 John 3:11
Beloved, let us *l* . . . . 1 John 4:7
the beginning: that we *l* . . . 2 John 5

LOVE THE LORD YOUR GOD
You shall *l* with all your . . . Deut 6:5
to *l* with all your heart . . . Deut 30:6
l, to walk in all His ways . . Josh 22:5
"You shall *l* with . . . . Matt 22:37
l with all your heart . . . . Mark 12:30
l with all your heart . . . . . Luke 10:27

LOVE YOUR ENEMIES
in that you *l* . . . . 2 Sam 19:6
But I say to you, *l* . . . . Matt 5:44
L, do good to those . . . . . . Luke 6:27

LOVE YOUR NEIGHBOR
you shall *l* as yourself . . . . Lev 19:18
l and hate your enemy . . . Matt 5:43
'You shall *l* as yourself . . Matt 19:19
l as yourself . . . . Gal 5:14
"You shall *l* as yourself . . James 2:8

LOVED
Because the Lord has *l* . . . 1 Kin 10:9
L one and friend You . . . . . Ps 88:18
Yet Jacob I have *l* . . . . Mal 1:2
forgiven, for she *l* . . . . Luke 7:47
so *l* the world that . . . . John 3:16
"See how He *l* . . . . John 11:36
whom Jesus *l* . . . . John 13:23
"As the Father *l* . . . . John 15:9
l them as You have . . . . . . John 17:23
"Jacob I have *l* . . . . Rom 9:13
the Son of God, who *l* . . . . Gal 2:20
l the church and gave . . . . Eph 5:25
l righteousness . . . . Heb 1:9
God, but that He *l* . . . . . . 1 John 4:10
Beloved, if God so *l* . . . . . 1 John 4:11
To Him who *l* us and . . . . . . Rev 1:5

LOVELY
l are your tents, O Jacob . . . Num 24:5
of David had a *l* sister . . . . 2 Sam 13:1
The young woman was *l* . . . . Esth 2:7
l is Your tabernacle . . . . Ps 84:1

l woman who lacks . . . . Prov 11:22
I am dark, but *l* . . . . Song 1:5
he is altogether *l* . . . . Song 5:16
whatever things are *l* . . . . Phil 4:8

LOVER
a *l* of what is good . . . . Titus 1:8

LOVERS
the harlot with many *l* . . . . Jer 3:1
your *l* have forgotten you . . . Jer 30:14
"I will go after my *l* . . . . Hos 2:5
Ephraim has hired *l* . . . . Hos 8:9
who were *l* of money . . . . Luke 16:14
For men will be *l* . . . . 2 Tim 3:2

LOVES
l righteousness . . . . Ps 33:5
life, and *l* many days . . . . Ps 34:12
A friend *l* at all . . . . Prov 17:17
He who *l* father or . . . . Matt 10:37
l his life will lose . . . . John 12:25
l Me will be loved . . . . John 14:21
l a cheerful giver . . . . 2 Cor 9:7
who *l* his wife *l* . . . . Eph 5:28
If anyone *l* the world . . . . 1 John 2:15
l God must love his . . . . . . 1 John 4:21
l him who is . . . . 1 John 5:1

LOVESICK
apples, for I am *l* . . . . Song 2:5
you tell him I am *l* . . . . Song 5:8

LOVINGKINDNESS
not concealed Your *l* . . . . . . Ps 40:10
l is better than life . . . . Ps 63:3
to declare Your *l* . . . . Ps 92:2
Who crowns you with *l* . . . . Ps 103:4
l I have drawn . . . . Jer 31:3
You show *l* to thousands . . . Jer 32:18
justice, in *l* and mercy . . . . . Hos 2:19
abundant in *l* . . . . Jon 4:2

LOVINGKINDNESSES
mercies and Your *l* . . . . Ps 25:6
where are Your former *l* . . . . Ps 89:49
the multitude of His *l* . . . . Is 63:7

LOW
He brings *l* and lifts . . . . 1 Sam 2:7
both *l* and high . . . . Ps 49:2
it *l*, He lays it *l* . . . . Is 26:5
and hill brought *l* . . . . Luke 3:5

LOWER
made him a little *l* . . . . Ps 8:5
shall go into the *l* . . . . Ps 63:9
made him a little *l* . . . . Heb 2:7

LOWEST
and sets over it the *l* . . . . . . Dan 4:17

LOWLINESS
with all *l* and . . . . Eph 4:2
or conceit, but in *l* . . . . Phil 2:3

LOWLY
yet He regards the *l* . . . . Ps 138:6
for I am gentle and *l* . . . . . Matt 11:29
He has regarded the *l* . . . . . Luke 1:48
and exalted the *l* . . . . Luke 1:52
in presence am *l* . . . . 2 Cor 10:1
l body that it may be . . . . . . Phil 3:21
l brother glory . . . . James 1:9

LOYAL
be *l* to the LORD our God . . 1 Kin 8:61
truth and with a *l* heart . . . , 2 Kin 20:3
with a *l* heart they . . . . 1 Chr 29:9
faithfully and with a *l* . . . . . 2 Chr 19:9
or else he will be *l* . . . . Matt 6:24

LUCIFER
Name applied to Satan, Is 14:12

LUD
See LYDIA
A people descended from Shem, 1 Chr
1:17

LUKE
"The beloved physician," Col 4:14

Paul's last companion, 2 Tim 4:11
Author of third Gospel, Luke (title)

LUKEWARM
because you are *l* . . . . Rev 3:16

LUMP
from the same *l* . . . . Rom 9:21
you may be a new *l* . . . . 1 Cor 5:7

LUST
Do not *l* after her . . . . Prov 6:25
caught by their *l* . . . . Prov 11:6
looks at a woman to *l* . . . . . Matt 5:28
not fulfill the *l* . . . . Gal 5:16
not in passion of *l* . . . . 1 Thess 4:5
You *l* and do not have . . . . . James 4:2
the *l* of the flesh . . . . 1 John 2:16

LUSTS
to fulfill its *l* . . . . Rom 13:14
l which drown men . . . . 1 Tim 6:9
also youthful *l* . . . . 2 Tim 2:22
and worldly *l* . . . . Titus 2:12
to the former *l* . . . . 1 Pet 1:14
abstain from fleshly *l* . . . . . . 1 Pet 2:11
to their own ungodly *l* . . . . . . Jude 18

LUTE
Awake, *l* and harp . . . . Ps 57:8
l I will praise You . . . . Ps 71:22
harp with the *l* . . . . Ps 81:2
ten strings, on the *l* . . . . Ps 92:3
Awake, *l* and harp . . . . Ps 108:2
Praise Him with the *l* . . . . . . Ps 150:3

LUXURY
l is not fitting . . . . Prov 19:10
l are in kings' courts . . . . . . Luke 7:25
in pleasure and *l* . . . . James 5:5
the abundance of her *l* . . . . . Rev 18:3

LYCAONIA
District of Asia Minor where Paul
preached, Acts 14:6, 11

LYCIA
Province of Asia Minor visited by Paul,
Acts 21:1, 2; 27:5, 6

LYDDA
Aeneas healed at, Acts 9:32–35

LYDIA
Woman of Thyatira; Paul's first Euro-
pean convert, Acts 16:14, 15, 40
—— District of Asia Minor containing
Ephesus, Smyrna, Thyatira, and Sar-
dis, Rev 1:11

LYING
has put a *l* spirit . . . . 1 Kin 22:23
I hate and abhor *l* . . . . Ps 119:163
proud look, a *l* tongue . . . . Prov 6:17
l lips are an . . . . Prov 12:22
righteous man hates *l* . . . . . Prov 13:5
not trust in these *l* . . . . Jer 7:4
a paralytic *l* on a bed . . . . . . Matt 9:2
in swaddling cloths, *l* . . . . . Luke 2:12
the Babe *l* in a manger . . . . Luke 2:16
cloths *l* by themselves . . . Luke 24:12
saw the linen cloths *l* . . . . . John 20:5
putting away *l* . . . . Eph 4:25
signs, and *l* wonders . . . . . 2 Thess 2:9

LYRE
the horn, flute, harp, *l* . . . . Dan 3:15

LYSIAS, CLAUDIUS
See CLAUDIUS LYSIAS

LYSTRA
Paul visits; is worshiped by people of
and stoned by Jews, Acts 14:6–20
Home of Timothy, Acts 16:1, 2

MAACAH (or Maachah)
Small Syrian kingdom near Mt. Hermon, Deut 3:14

Not possessed by Israel, Josh 13:13
—— David's wife; mother of Absalom,
2 Sam 3:3
—— Wife of Rehoboam; mother of King
Abijah, 2 Chr 11:18–21
Makes idol; is deposed as queen
mother, 1 Kin 15:13

MACEDONIA
Paul preaches in, Acts 16:9—17:14
Paul's troubles in, 2 Cor 7:5
Churches of, generous, Rom 15:26;
2 Cor 8:1–5

MACHIR
Manasseh's only son, Gen 50:23
Founder of the family of Machirites,
Num 26:29
Conqueror of Gilead, Num 32:39, 40

MACHPELAH
Field containing a cave; bought by
Abraham, Gen 23:9–18
Sarah and Abraham buried here, Gen
23:19; 25:9, 10
Isaac, Rebekah, Leah, and Jacob bur-
ied here, Gen 49:29–31

MAD
has a demon and is *m* . . . . John 10:20
he said, "I am not *m* . . . . . . Acts 26:25

MADE
m the stars also . . . . Gen 1:16
everything that He had *m* . . . . Gen 1:31
wife the LORD God *m* . . . . . . Gen 3:21
God *m* a wind to pass over . . Gen 8:1
'I have *m* Abram rich' . . . . . Gen 14:23
LORD *m* a covenant with . . . Gen 15:18
I have *m* you a father of . . . Gen 17:5
he *m* him a tunic of many . . Gen 37:3
Joseph *m* himself known . . . Gen 45:1
they *m* their lives bitter . . . . . Ex 1:14
m the sea into dry land . . . . . Ex 14:21
tool, and *m* a molded calf . . . Ex 32:4
He also *m* the mercy seat . . . Ex 37:6
LORD *m* between Himself . . Lev 26:46
Moses *m* a bronze serpent . . Num 21:9
m a covenant . . . . 1 Sam 20:16
has *m* Solomon king . . . . . . 1 Kin 1:43
he *m* the Most Holy Place . . 2 Chr 3:8
had *m* to praise the LORD, . . 2 Chr 7:6
Have You not *m* a hedge . . . . Job 1:10
You have *m* me like clay . . . . Job 10:9
He has *m* me a byword of . . . Job 17:6
For You have *m* him a little . . . . Ps 8:5
You have *m* him to have . . . . . . Ps 8:6
You *m* Me trust while on . . . . . Ps 22:9
by which they have *m* You . . . Ps 45:8
have *m* summer and winter . . Ps 74:17
you have *m* the LORD . . . . Ps 91:9
It is He who has *m* us, and . . Ps 100:3
m known His ways to . . . . Ps 103:7
LORD, who *m* heaven and . . Ps 115:15
the day the LORD has *m* . . . Ps 118:24
by wisdom *m* the heavens . . Ps 136:5
and wonderfully *m* . . . . Ps 139:14
generous soul will be *m* . . . Prov 11:25
m everything beautiful . . . . . . Eccl 3:11
A feast is *m* for laughter . . . Eccl 10:19
hear long ago how I *m* . . . . . . Is 37:26
I have *m* the earth, and . . . . . Is 45:12
things My hand has *m* . . . . Is 66:2
He has *m* the earth by His . . Jer 10:12
I have *m* you a watchman . Ezek 3:17
king *m* a great feast for a . . . . Dan 5:1
your faith has *m* you well . . Matt 9:22
you have *m* it a den of . . . . Matt 21:13
m another five talents . . . . . Matt 25:16
God '*m* them male and . . . . Mark 10:6
temple *m* with hands . . . . Mark 14:58
places shall be *m* straight . . Luke 3:5
she was *m* straight, and . . Luke 13:13
All things were *m* . . . . John 1:3
the water that was *m* wine . . John 2:9

in temples *m* with hands ... Acts 7:48
he *m* havoc of the church, ... Acts 8:3
are heirs, faith is *m* void ... Rom 4:14
m me free from the law of . Rom 8:2
confession is *m* unto ..... Rom 10:10
Has not God *m* foolish .... 1 Cor 1:20
all shall be *m* alive ..... 1 Cor 15:22
m Him who knew no ...... 2 Cor 5:21
strength is *m* perfect ..... 2 Cor 12:9
Seed where the promises *m* .. Gal 3:16
And you He *m* alive, who .... Eph 2:1
and *m* us sit together in ..... Eph 2:6
of God might be *m* .... Eph 3:10
but *m* Himself of no .... Phil 2:7
requests be *m* known to .... Phil 4:6
He has *m* alive together ... Col 2:13
m him a little lower than .... Heb 2:7
are *m* His footstool ...... Heb 10:13
but *m* alive by the Spirit .. 1 Pet 3:18
not been *m* perfect in .... 1 John 4:18
has *m* us kings and priests ... Rev 1:6
m them white in the blood .. Rev 7:14
worship Him who *m* .... Rev 14:7
of the earth were *m* drunk .. Rev 17:2

MADNESS
pretended *m* in .... 1 Sam 21:13
wisdom and to know *m* ..... Eccl 1:17
m is in their hearts .... Eccl 9:3

MAGDALA
City of Galilee, Matt 15:39

MAGDALENE
See MARY

MAGIC
women who sew *m* .... Ezek 13:18
m brought their books .... Acts 19:19

MAGNIFICENCE
m I cannot endure .... Job 31:23

MAGNIFIED
So let Your name be *m* ... 2 Sam 7:26
"Let the LORD be *m* .... Ps 35:27
The LORD be *m* .... Ps 40:16
for You have *m* Your ...... Ps 138:2
The LORD is *m* beyond the.... Mal 1:5
the Lord Jesus was *m* ..... Acts 19:17
also Christ will be *m* ...... Phil 1:20

MAGNIFIES
"My soul *m* the Lord ..... Luke 1:46

MAGNIFY
m the LORD with me .... Ps 34:3
m himself above every .... Dan 11:36

MAGOG
People among Japheth's descendants,
Gen 10:2
Associated with Gog, Ezek 38:2
Representatives of final enemies, Rev
20:8

MAHANAIM
Name given by Jacob to a sacred site,
Gen 32:2
Becomes Ishbosheth's capital, 2 Sam
2:8–29
David flees to, during Absalom's rebel-
lion, 2 Sam 17:24, 27

MAHER-SHALAL-HASH-BAZ
Symbolic name of Isaiah's second son;
prophetic of the fall of Damascus and
Samaria, Is 8:1–4

MAHLON
Husband of Ruth; without child, Ruth
1:2–5

MAIDENS
Both young men and *m* .... Ps 148:12
She has sent out her *m* ..... Prov 9:3

MAIDSERVANT
"I am Ruth, your *m* .... Ruth 3:9
save the son of Your *m* .... Ps 86:16

"Behold the *m* .... Luke 1:38
lowly state of His *m* .... Luke 1:48

MAIDSERVANTS
m shall lead her as .... Nah 2:7
m I will pour out My .... Acts 2:18

MAIMED
to enter into life *m* .... Mark 9:43
the poor and the *m* ...... Luke 14:21

MAINTAIN
and *m* their cause .... 1 Kin 8:45
careful to *m* good works .... Titus 3:8

MAINTAINED
For You have *m* my .... Ps 9:4

MAJESTIC
thunders with His *m* voice .. Job 37:4
which are *m* in pace ...... Prov 30:29
But there the *m* LORD will .... Is 33:21

MAJESTY
Honor and *m* are before .. 1 Chr 16:27
the victory and the *m* .... 1 Chr 29:11
with God is awesome *m* .... Job 37:22
of the LORD is full of *m* .... Ps 29:4
He is clothed with *m* .... Ps 93:1
Honor and *m* are before ...... Ps 96:6
splendor of Your *m* .... Ps 145:5
LORD and the glory of His *m* .. Is 2:10
in the *m* of the name of the ... Mic 5:4
right hand of the *M* .... Heb 1:3
eyewitnesses of His *m* ..... 2 Pet 1:16
wise, be glory and *m* .... Jude 25

MAKE
"Let Us *m* man in Our ..... Gen 1:26
desirable to *m* one wise ..... Gen 3:6
let us *m* a name for .... Gen 11:4
m you a great nation .... Gen 12:2
m My covenant between ..... Gen 17:2
"You shall not *m* .... Ex 20:4
I will *m* of you a great ...... Ex 32:10
m your belly swell and .... Num 5:22
LORD *m* His face shine .... Num 6:25
M a fiery serpent, and ..... Num 21:8
husband may *m* it void ... Num 30:13
m yourself an ark of ...... Deut 10:1
Now *m* us a king to judge . 1 Sam 8:5
m me a small cake from .. 1 Kin 17:13
m confession to the .... Ezra 10:11
I *m* my bed in the .... Job 17:13
LORD, *m* me dwell in safety .... Ps 4:8
M Your face shine upon ..... Ps 31:16
My soul shall *m* its boast in .. Ps 34:2
shall *m* glad the city of God .. Ps 46:4
wings I will *m* my refuge ..... Ps 57:1
m His praise glorious .... Ps 66:2
my mouth will I *m* known .... Ps 89:1
M a joyful shout to the ...... Ps 100:1
I *m* my bed in hell, behold ... Ps 139:8
M haste, my beloved, and .. Song 8:14
m mention that His name .... Is 12:4
m the crooked places .... Is 45:2
I will *m* an everlasting ..... Jer 32:40
writing and *m* known to .... Dan 5:15
m it plain on tablets, that .... Hab 2:2
m me walk on my high ...... Hab 3:19
no one shall *m* them ...... Zeph 3:13
m you fishers of men .... Matt 4:19
till I *m* Your enemies ...... Matt 22:44
let us *m* three tabernacles ... Mark 9:5
there *m* ready for us .... Mark 14:15
M them sit down in .... Luke 9:14
M me like one of your .... Luke 15:19
m haste and come down, .. Luke 19:5
not *m* My Father's house .. John 2:16
the truth shall *m* you free .. John 8:32
m Our home with him .... John 14:23
we then *m* void the law .... Rom 3:31
m no provision for the .... Rom 13:14
m my brother stumble ..... 1 Cor 8:13
m the way of escape .... 1 Cor 10:13
God is able to *m* all grace . 2 Cor 9:8
to *m* known the mystery .... Eph 6:19

Lord *m* you increase .... 1 Thess 3:12
till I *m* Your enemies Your .. Heb 1:13
m you complete in every .. Heb 13:21
diligent to *m* your call .... 2 Pet 1:10
we *m* Him a liar, and ..... 1 John 1:10
will *m* your stomach bitter .. Rev 10:9
Behold, I *m* all things new . Rev 21:5

MAKER
where is God my *M* .... Job 35:10
before the LORD our *M* ...... Ps 95:6
the LORD is the *m* of them .. Prov 22:2
man will look to his *M* .... Is 17:7
who strives with his *M* .... Is 45:9
M is your husband .... Is 54:5
has forgotten his *M* .... Hos 8:14
builder and *m* is God ...... Heb 11:10

MAKES
He *m* nations great, and .... Job 12:23
He *m* my feet like the feet ... Ps 18:33
He *m* me to lie down in ..... Ps 23:2
He *m* wars cease to the end .. Ps 46:9
Who *m* His angels spirits, .. Ps 104:4
son *m* a glad father, ... Prov 10:1
Hope deferred *m* the ...... Prov 13:12
he *m* even his enemies to .. Prov 16:7
He *m* lightnings for the ..... Jer 51:16
for He *m* His sun rise on ... Matt 5:45
m both the deaf to hear ... Mark 7:37
He *m* intercession .... Rom 8:27
m himself an enemy of ... James 4:4

MAKING
is sure, *m* wise the simple .... Ps 19:7
m the word of God of no .. Mark 7:13
m mention of you in my .... Eph 1:16
m melody in your heart to .. Eph 5:19

MAKKEDAH
Canaanite town assigned to Judah,
Josh 15:20, 41

MALACHI
Prophet and writer, Mal 1:1

MALCHISHUA
Son of King Saul, 1 Sam 14:49
Killed at Gilboa, 1 Sam 31:2

MALCHUS
Servant of the high priest, John 18:10

MALE
He created them *m* and ..... Gen 5:2
into the ark to Noah, *m* ...... Gen 7:9
every *m* child in your ..... Gen 17:12
who has borne a *m* or a .... Lev 12:7
lie with a *m* as with a ...... Lev 18:22
utterly destroy every *m* ... Judg 21:11
came, she delivered a *m* .... Is 66:7
beginning 'made them *m* ... Matt 19:4
is neither *m* nor female ..... Gal 3:28
gave birth to the *m* Child .. Rev 12:13

MALICE
in *m* be babes .... 1 Cor 14:20
away from you, with all *m* .. Eph 4:31
wrath, *m*, blasphemy, ... Col 3:8
pleasures, living in *m* ...... Titus 3:3
laying aside all *m* .... 1 Pet 2:1

MALICIOUSNESS
covetousness, *m* .... Rom 1:29

MALIGN
m a servant to his .... Prov 30:10

MALTA
Site of Paul's shipwreck, Acts 28:1–8

MAMMON
cannot serve God and *m* ... Matt 6:24
by unrighteous *m* .... Luke 16:9

MAMRE
Town or district near Hebron, Gen
23:19
Abram dwells by the oaks of, Gen 13:18

MAN
See NEW MAN; OLD MAN; RIGHTEOUS
MAN; SON OF MAN; WISE MAN

"Let Us make *m* ....Gen 1:26
she was taken out of *M* .....Gen 2:23
Therefore a *m* shall leave ...Gen 2:24
were both naked, the *m* .....Gen 2:25
I will destroy *m* whom I .....Gen 6:7
M wrestled with him ......Gen 32:24
God is not He ... that He ...Num 23:19
but *m* lives by every word ...Deut 8:3
No *m* shall be able to .....Deut 11:25
m looks at the outward ...1 Sam 16:7
"You are the *m* ....2 Sam 12:7
and prove yourself a *m* ....1 Kin 2:2
"What is *m* ....Job 7:17
For an empty-headed *m* ....Job 11:12
"Are you the first *m* ....Job 15:7
Blessed is the *m* who ....Ps 1:1
m that You are mindful ....Ps 8:4
The steps of a good *m* are ..Ps 37:23
Blessed is that *m* who .....Ps 40:4
What can *m* do to me ....Ps 118:6
Happy is the *m* who finds ..Prov 3:13
rebuke a wise *m*, and he ....Prov 9:8
A good *m* obtains favor ....Prov 12:2
that seems right to a *m* ...Prov 16:25
The spirit of a *m* is the ....Prov 20:27
Let another *m* praise you, ..Prov 27:2
shall take hold of one *m*, ...Is 4:1
Because I am a *m* of unclean ...Is 6:5
marred more than any *m* ....Is 52:14
M of sorrows and ....Is 53:3
mighty *m* glory in his ......Jer 9:23
Blessed is the *m* who trusts ..Jer 17:7
Son of *m*, can these ......Ezek 37:3
He has shown you, O *m*, ...Mic 6:8
Will a *m* rob God ....Mal 3:8
M shall not live by bread ....Matt 4:4
A good *m* out of the ......Matt 12:35
the mouth defiles a *m* ....Matt 15:11
For this reason a *m* shall ...Matt 19:5
coming of the Son of *M* ...Matt 24:27
first binds the strong *m* ....Mark 3:27
within and defile a *m* .....Mark 7:23
what will it profit a *m* .....Mark 8:36
m had two sons ....Luke 15:11
a certain rich *m* ....Luke 16:19
a *m* named Zacchaeus .....Luke 19:2
can a *m* be born when he ...John 3:4
blind *m* with the clay ....John 9:6
m should die for the ....John 11:50
"Behold the *M* ....John 19:5
name, has made this *m* .....Acts 3:16
a *m* full of faith and the ....Acts 6:5
you are inexcusable, O *m*, ...Rom 2:1
blessed is the *m* to whom ...Rom 4:8
m is not from woman ....1 Cor 11:8
I became a *m*, I put ....1 Cor 13:11
since by *m* came death ...1 Cor 15:21
though our outward *m* ....2 Cor 4:16
for whatever a *m* sows, that ..Gal 6:7
in Himself one new *m* ......Eph 2:15
that the *m* of God may ....2 Tim 3:17
m can tame the tongue .....James 3:8
a righteous *m* avails ......James 5:16
is the number of a *m* ......Rev 13:18

MAN OF GOD

Moses the *m* blessed ....Deut 33:1
"A *m* came to me, and ....Judg 13:6
a *m* came to Eli and said ...1 Sam 2:27
there is in this city a *m* ...1 Sam 9:6
to Shemaiah the *m* ....1 Kin 12:22
a *m* went from Judah to ...1 Kin 13:1
m who was disobedient ...1 Kin 13:26
I to do with you, O *m* ....1 Kin 17:18
a *m* came and spoke to ...1 Kin 20:28
"*M*, the king has said ......2 Kin 1:9
this a holy *m* ....2 Kin 4:9
M, there is death ....2 Kin 4:40
m sent to the king ....2 Kin 6:9
he died, just as the *m* .....2 Kin 7:17
the *m* was angry with ....2 Kin 13:19
"It is the tomb of the *m* ..2 Kin 23:17

for so David the *m* ....2 Chr 8:14
But a *m* came to him .....2 Chr 25:7
Law of Moses the *m* ....Ezra 3:2
command of David the *m* ..Neh 12:24
son of Igdaliah, a *m* ....Jer 35:4
But you, O *m*, flee these ...1 Tim 6:11
m may be complete ....2 Tim 3:17

MAN'S

curse the ground for *m* .....Gen 8:21
every *m* hand against ......Gen 16:12
We are all one *m* sons .....Gen 42:11
each *m* money was in the ..Gen 43:21
The rich *m* wealth is his ...Prov 10:15
When a *m* ways please ....Prov 16:7
A *m* heart plans his way ...Prov 16:9
The rich *m* wealth is his ..Prov 18:11
A *m* gift makes room for ...Prov 18:16
m steps are of the LORD ..Prov 20:24
A *m* pride will bring him ...Prov 29:23
a righteous *m* reward .....Matt 10:41
enter a strong *m* house ...Mark 3:27
from the rich *m* table ....Luke 16:21
one *m* offense many died ...Rom 5:15
on another *m* foundation ..Rom 15:20

MANASSEH

Joseph's firstborn son, Gen 41:50, 51
Adopted by Jacob, Gen 48:5, 6
Loses his birthright to Ephraim, Gen
48:13–20
—— Tribe of:
Numbered, Num 1:34, 35
Half-tribe of, settle east of Jordan, Num
32:33–42; Deut 3:12–15
Help Joshua against Canaanites, Josh
1:12–18
Land assigned to western half-tribe,
Josh 17:1–13
Eastern half-tribe builds altar, Josh
22:9–34
Some of, help David, 1 Chr 12:19–31
—— Wicked king of Judah; son of
Hezekiah, 2 Kin 21:1–18; 2 Chr
33:1–9
Captured and taken to Babylon;
repents and is restored, 2 Chr
33:10–13
Removes idols and altars, 2 Chr
33:14–20

MANGER

Will he bed by your *m* ......Job 39:9
and laid Him in a *m* ....Luke 2:7
the Babe lying in a *m* ......Luke 2:16

MANIFEST

m Myself to him ....John 14:21
is it that You will *m* ......John 14:22
be known of God is *m* in ...Rom 1:19
but now made *m*, and .....Rom 16:26
that I may make it *m*, as I ...Col 4:4
was *m* in these last times ...1 Pet 1:20

MANIFESTATION

But the *m* of the ....1 Cor 12:7
deceitfully, but by *m* ......2 Cor 4:2

MANIFESTED

Galilee, and *m* His glory ...John 2:11
"I have *m* Your name ......John 17:6
God was *m* in the flesh ...1 Tim 3:16
the life was *m* ....1 John 1:2
the Son of God was *m* .....1 John 3:8
the love of God was *m* ....1 John 4:9

MANIFOLD

m are Your works ....Ps 104:24
the *m* wisdom of God ......Eph 3:10
good stewards of the *m* ....1 Pet 4:10

MANKIND

called them *M* in the day ....Gen 5:2
of *m* may seek the LORD ...Acts 15:17
to kill a third of *m* ....Rev 9:15
But the rest of *m*, who .....Rev 9:20

MANNA

of Israel ate *m* ....Ex 16:35

the *m* was like coriander ...Num 11:7
the *m* ceased on the day ...Josh 5:12
Your *m* from their mouth ...Neh 9:20
had rained down *m* ....Ps 78:24
Our fathers ate the *m* .....John 6:31
golden pot that had the *m* ...Heb 9:4
of the hidden *m* ....Rev 2:17

MANNER

in all *m* of workmanship, ...Ex 31:3
Is this the *m* of man ......2 Sam 7:19
In this *m*, therefore, pray ...Matt 6:9
m of life from my youth, ...Acts 26:4
same *m* He also took .....1 Cor 11:25
in an unworthy *m* ....1 Cor 11:27
sorrowed in a godly *m* ....2 Cor 7:11
m of life, purpose, faith, ...2 Tim 3:10
as is the *m* of some ......Heb 10:25
what *m* of persons ....2 Pet 3:11
Behold what *m* of love ....1 John 3:1
m worthy of God ....3 John 6

MANOAH

Danite; father of Samson, Judg
13:1–25

MANSIONS

house are many *m* ....John 14:2

MANTLE

Then he took the *m* ....2 Kin 2:14

MAON

Village in Judah, Josh 15:55
David stays at, 1 Sam 23:24, 25
Nabal's house here, 1 Sam 25:2

MARA

Name chosen by Naomi, Ruth 1:20

MARAH

First Israelite camp after passing
through the Red Sea, Num 33:8, 9

MARCHED

people, when You *m* ....Ps 68:7

MARK (John)

Son of Mary of Jerusalem; travels with
Barnabas and Saul, Acts 12:12, 25
Leaves Paul at Perga, Acts 13:13
Barnabas and Paul separate because
of him, Acts 15:37–40
Later approved by Paul, Col 4:10; 2 Tim
4:11
Companion of Peter, 1 Pet 5:13
Author of the second Gospel, Mark 1:1

MARK

And the LORD set a *m* ....Gen 4:15
M the blameless man ....Ps 37:37
slave, to receive a *m* ......Rev 13:16
whoever receives the *m* ....Rev 14:11

MARKET

is sold in the meat *m* .....1 Cor 10:25

MARRED

so His visage was *m* ....Is 52:14
he made of clay was *m* .....Jer 18:4

MARRIAGE

join in *m* with the people ...Ezra 9:14
were not given in *m* ....Ps 78:63
nor are given in *m* ....Matt 22:30
they were given in *m* .....Luke 17:27
her in *m* does well ....1 Cor 7:38
M is honorable among .....Heb 13:4
the *m* of the Lamb has .....Rev 19:7

MARRIED

and *m* Pharaoh's daughter ..1 Kin 3:1
woman when she is *m* ....Prov 30:23
"for I am *m* to you ....Jer 3:14
first died after he had *m* ...Matt 22:25
said, 'I have *m* a wife .....Luke 14:20
m wives, they were ....Luke 17:27
But he who is *m* ....1 Cor 7:33
But she who is *m* ....1 Cor 7:34

MARRIES

If a man *m* a woman and ...Lev 20:14

MARROW

as a young man *m* a virgin .... Is 62:5
m another, commits .... Matt 19:9
she *m* another man, she ..... Rom 7:3
if a virgin *m*, she has not .. 1 Cor 7:28

MARROW
and of joints and *m* .... Heb 4:12

MARRY
m her, and raise up an ...... Gen 38:8
battle and another man *m* .. Deut 20:7
it is better not to *m* .... Matt 19:10
they neither *m* nor are .... Matt 22:30
The sons of this age *m* .... Luke 20:34
let them *m* .... 1 Cor 7:9
forbidding to *m* .... 1 Tim 4:3
the younger widows *m* .... 1 Tim 5:14

MARRYING
and drinking, *m* .... Matt 24:38

MARTHA
Sister of Mary and Lazarus; loved by
Jesus, John 11:1–5
Affirms her faith, John 11:19–28
Offers hospitality to Jesus, Luke 10:38;
John 12:1, 2
Gently rebuked by Christ, Luke
10:39–42

MARTYR
m Stephen was shed ...... Acts 22:20
was My faithful *m* .... Rev 2:13

MARTYRS
the blood of the *m* .... Rev 17:6

MARVEL
do not *m* at the matter ...... Eccl 5:8
Do not *m* that I said to you .. John 3:7
Do not *m* at this .... John 5:28
Israel, who by you *m* at .... Acts 3:12
I *m* that you are turning ... Gal 1:6
Do not *m*, my brethren ... 1 John 3:13

MARVELED
Jesus heard it, He *m* ...... Matt 8:10
And the multitudes *m* ..... Matt 9:33
these words, they *m* ...... Matt 22:22
the governor *m* greatly .... Matt 27:14
He *m* because of their ..... Mark 6:6
so that Pilate *m* .... Mark 15:5
His mother *m* at those .... Luke 2:33
believe for joy, and *m* .... Luke 24:41
were all amazed and *m* ...... Acts 2:7
And all the world *m* .... Rev 13:3
when I saw her, I *m* .... Rev 17:6

MARVELOUS
Remember His *m* works .. 1 Chr 16:12
m things without number ..... Job 5:9
will tell of all Your *m* works ... Ps 9:1
m things He did .... Ps 78:12
For He has done *m* things .... Ps 98:1
It is *m* in our eyes .... Ps 118:23
M are Your works .... Ps 139:14
I will again do a *m* work .... Is 29:14
LORD has done *m* things ... Joel 2:21
If it is *m* in the eyes of ...... Zech 8:6
Why, this is a *m* thing ..... John 9:30
of darkness into His *m* ..... 1 Pet 2:9
m are Your works, Lord ... Rev 15:3

MARVELS
people I will do *m* .... Ex 34:10

MARY
Mother of Christ, Matt 1:16
Visited by angel, Luke 1:26–38
Visits Elizabeth and offers praise, Luke
1:39–56
Gives birth to Jesus, Luke 2:6–20
Flees to Egypt, Matt 2:13–18
Visits Jerusalem with Jesus, Luke
2:41–52
Entrusted to John's care, John
19:25–27
—— Mother of James and Joses; pres-
ent at crucifixion and burial, Matt
27:55–61

Sees the risen Lord; informs disciples,
Matt 28:1–10
—— Magdalene; delivered from seven
demons; supports Christ's ministry,
Luke 8:2, 3
Present at crucifixion and burial, Matt
27:55–61
First to see the risen Lord, Mark
16:1–10; John 20:1–18
—— Sister of Martha and Lazarus;
loved by Jesus, John 11:1–5
Grieves for Lazarus, John 11:19, 20,
28–33
Anoints Jesus, Matt 26:6–13; John
12:1–8
Commended by Jesus, Luke 10:38–42
—— Mark's mother, Acts 12:12–17

MASSAH AND MERIBAH
First, at Rephidim, Israel just out of
Egypt, Ex 17:1–7
Second, at Kadesh Barnea, 40 years
later, Num 20:1–13

MASTER
of Abraham his *m* .... Gen 24:9
If she does not please her *m* .. Ex 21:8
for your *m* Saul is dead .. 2 Sam 2:7
If only my *m* were with .... 2 Kin 5:3
m! For it was borrowed .... 2 Kin 6:5
no longer call Me 'My *M* .... Hos 2:16
a servant like his *m* .... Matt 10:25
before him, saying, '*M* .... Matt 18:26
servant whom his *m* ...... Matt 24:46
M, M, we are perishing ... Luke 8:24
M, it is good for us to be .. Luke 9:33
m of that servant will ..... Luke 12:46
So the *m* commended the .. Luke 16:8
Jesus, *M*, have mercy .... Luke 17:13
the *m* of the feast called ... John 2:9
is not greater than his *m* ... John 13:16
greater than his *m* .... John 15:20
m builder I have laid ...... 1 Cor 3:10
own *M* also is in heaven ...... Eph 6:9
and useful for the *M* ...... 2 Tim 2:21

MASTERS
look to the hand of their *m* .. Ps 123:2
the soul of his *m* .... Prov 25:13
m besides You have .... Is 26:13
can serve two *m* .... Luke 16:13
her *m* much profit .... Acts 16:16
And you, *m*, do the same ... Eph 6:9
M, give your bondservants ... Col 4:1
who have believing *m* ..... 1 Tim 6:2
be obedient to their own *m* .. Titus 2:9

MATTANIAH
King Zedekiah's original name, 2 Kin
24:17

MATTER
m is found in me .... Job 19:28
He who answers a *m* ..... Prov 18:13

MATTERS
the weightier *m* .... Matt 23:23
judge the smallest *m* ...... 1 Cor 6:2

MATTHEW
Becomes Christ's follower, Matt 9:9
Chosen as one of the Twelve, Matt
10:2, 3
Called Levi, the son of Alphaeus, Mark
2:14
Author of the first Gospel, Matt (title)

MATTHIAS
Chosen by lot to replace Judas, Acts
1:15–26

MATURE
among those who are *m* ... 1 Cor 2:6
understanding be *m* ...... 1 Cor 14:20
us, as many as are *m* ...... Phil 3:15

MEAN
What do you *m* .... Ex 12:26

What does this parable *m* ... Luke 8:9
what these things *m* ...... Acts 17:20
I do not *m* that others ..... 2 Cor 8:13

MEANING
'What is the *m* .... Deut 6:20
if I do not know the *m* .... 1 Cor 14:11

MEANS
or one tittle will by no *m* ... Matt 5:18
you will by no *m* enter ..... Matt 5:20
he shall by no *m* lose his .. Matt 10:42
you will by no *m* enter .... Matt 18:3
words will by no *m* pass .. Matt 24:35
will by no *m* hurt them .. Mark 16:18
shall by any *m* hurt you .. Luke 10:19
to Me I will by no *m* cast .. John 6:37
I must by all *m* keep this .. Acts 18:21
I might by all *m* save ...... 1 Cor 9:22
if, by any *m*, I may attain ... Phil 3:11
godliness is a *m* of gain .... 1 Tim 6:5
by no *m* be put to shame .. 1 Pet 2:6

MEANT
but God *m* it for good ..... Gen 50:20

MEASURE
a perfect and just *m* ...... Deut 25:15
give us a *m* of revival in .... Ezra 9:8
apportion the waters by *m* .. Job 28:25
what is the *m* of my days .... Ps 39:4
and the short *m* .... Mic 6:10
and with the *m* you use, it .. Matt 7:2
good *m*, pressed down, ... Luke 6:38
give the Spirit by *m* ...... John 3:34
to each one a *m* .... Rom 12:3
lest I be exalted above *m* .. 2 Cor 12:7
to the *m* of the stature of .. Eph 4:13
m the temple of God .... Rev 11:1

MEASURED
m heaven with a span ...... Is 40:12
If heaven above can be *m* .. Jer 31:37
nor the sand of the sea *m* ... Jer 33:22
cannot be *m* or numbered .. Hos 1:10
you use, it will be *m* ...... Matt 7:2
it will be *m* back to you .... Luke 6:38
Then he *m* its wall .... Rev 21:17

MEASURES
your house differing *m* .... Deut 25:14
weights and diverse *m* .... Prov 20:10

MEASURING
will make justice the *m* line .. Is 28:17
the man's hand was a *m* ... Ezek 40:5
behold, a man with a *m* .... Zech 2:1
m themselves by .... 2 Cor 10:12
given a reed like a *m* ...... Rev 11:1

MEAT
you *m* to eat in the evening .. Ex 16:8
But while the *m* was still .. Num 11:33
Can He provide *m* .... Ps 78:20
He also rained *m* .... Ps 78:27
good neither to eat *m* ..... Rom 14:21
will never again eat *m* ..... 1 Cor 8:13
is sold in the *m* .... 1 Cor 10:25

MEDDLE
why should you *m* .... 2 Kin 14:10

MEDEBA
Moabite town assigned to Judah, Num
21:29, 30; Josh 13:9, 16

MEDES, MEDIA
Part of Medo-Persian Empire, Esth 1:19
Israel deported to, 2 Kin 17:6
Babylon falls to, Dan 5:30, 31
Daniel rises high in kingdom of, Dan
6:1–28
Cyrus, king of, allows Jews to return,
2 Chr 36:22, 23
Agents in Babylon's fall, Is 13:17–19

MEDIATE
a mediator does not *m* ...... Gal 3:20

MEDIATOR
Nor is there any *m* .... Job 9:33

by the hand of a *m* ....Gal 3:19
is one God and one *M* ......1 Tim 2:5
as He is also *M* ....Heb 8:6
to Jesus the *M* of the ......Heb 12:24

MEDICINE
does good, like *m* ....Prov 17:22

MEDICINES
you will use many *m* ......Jer 46:11

MEDITATE
Isaac went out to *m* ......Gen 24:63
but you shall *m* ....Josh 1:8
M within your heart on ....Ps 4:4
I *m* within my heart ....Ps 77:6
I will *m* on Your ....Ps 119:15
Your heart will *m* ....Is 33:18
m beforehand on what ...Luke 21:14
m on these things ....Phil 4:8

MEDITATES
in His law he *m* ....Ps 1:2

MEDITATION
O Lord, consider my *m* ......Ps 5:1
of my mouth and the *m* .....Ps 19:14
the *m* of my heart shall ....Ps 49:3
m be sweet to Him ....Ps 104:34
It is my *m* all the day ......Ps 119:97

MEDITERRANEAN SEA
Described as:
Sea, Gen 49:13
Great Sea, Josh 1:4; 9:1
Sea of the Philistines, Ex 23:31
Western Sea, Deut 11:24; Joel 2:20;
Zech 14:8

MEDIUM
a woman who is a *m* ......Lev 20:27
a woman who is a *m* ......1 Sam 28:7

MEDIUM'S
shall be like a *m* ....Is 29:4

MEDIUMS
"Seek those who are *m* ....Is 8:19

MEEK
But the *m* shall inherit the ...Ps 37:11
with equity for the *m* ....Is 11:4
all you who of the earth ....Zeph 2:3
Blessed are the *m* ....Matt 5:5

MEEKNESS
with you by the *m* ....2 Cor 10:1
are done in the *m* ....James 3:13
that is in you, with *m* ......1 Pet 3:15

MEET
from the tent door to *m* ...Gen 18:2
For You *m* him with the ......Ps 21:3
mercies come speedily to *m* ..Ps 79:8
prepare to *m* your God ....Amos 4:12
out to *m* the bridegroom ...Matt 25:1
go out to *m* him ....Matt 25:6
a man will *m* you ....Luke 22:10
m the Lord in the air ....1 Thess 4:17

MEETING
In the tabernacle of *m* ......Ex 27:21
burned up all the *m* ....Ps 74:8

MEGIDDO
City of Canaan; scene of battles, Judg
5:19–21; 2 Kin 23:29, 30
Fortified by Solomon, 1 Kin 9:15
Possible site of Armageddon, Rev 16:16

MELCHIZEDEK
Priest and king of Salem, Gen
14:18–20
Type of Christ's eternal priesthood,
Heb 7:1–22

MELODY
make sweet *m* ....Is 23:16
singing and making *m* ......Eph 5:19

MELT
You make his beauty *m* .....Ps 39:11
The mountains *m* like wax ...Ps 97:5

man's heart will *m* ....Is 13:7
mountains will *m* under ......Mic 1:4
the elements will *m* ....2 Pet 3:10

MEMBER
body is not one *m* ....1 Cor 12:14
if they were all one *m* .....1 Cor 12:19
if one *m* suffers, all the ...1 Cor 12:26
tongue is a little *m* ....James 3:5

MEMBERS
you that one of your *m* .....Matt 5:29
do not present your *m* .....Rom 6:13
have many *m* in one body ..Rom 12:4
that your bodies are *m* ....1 Cor 6:15
there are many *m* ....1 Cor 12:20
neighbor, for we are *m* .....Eph 4:25
m that it defiles the ....James 3:6

MEMORIAL
and this is My *m* ....Ex 3:15
day shall be to you a *m* ....Ex 12:14
as a *m* between your eyes, ...Ex 13:9
also be told as a *m* ....Matt 26:13
be told of as a *m* ....Mark 14:9
come up for a *m* before ....Acts 10:4

MEMORY
The *m* of him perishes .....Job 18:17
He may cut off the *m* ......Ps 109:15
The *m* of the righteous .....Prov 10:7

MEMPHIS (or Noph)
Ancient capital of Egypt, Hos 9:6
Prophesied against by Isaiah, Is 19:13
Jews flee to, Jer 44:1
Denounced by the prophets, Jer 46:19

MEN
See WISE MEN
m began to call on the ......Gen 4:26
saw the daughters of *m* ......Gen 6:2
But the *m* of Sodom were ..Gen 13:13
Hebrew *m* were fighting .....Ex 2:13
Send *m* to spy out the .....Num 13:2
So Gideon took ten *m* .....Judg 6:27
with the LORD and *m* .....1 Sam 2:26
reproach of *m*, and despised ..Ps 22:6
All *m* shall fear, and shall ...Ps 64:9
received gifts among *m* ....Ps 68:18
you shall die like *m* ....Ps 82:7
with wise *m* will be wise ..Prov 13:20
are the crown of old *m* .....Prov 17:6
not be envious of evil *m* ...Prov 24:1
m should fear before Him ..Eccl 3:14
the Egyptians are *m* ....Is 31:3
despised and rejected by *m* ...Is 53:3
I see four *m* loose ....Dan 3:25
make you fishers of *m* .....Matt 4:19
light so shine before *m* ....Matt 5:16
forgive *m* their trespasses ..Matt 6:14
confesses Me before *m* ...Matt 10:32
will not be forgiven *m* .....Matt 12:31
every idle word *m* may ...Matt 12:36
was carried by four *m* .....Mark 2:3
Who do *m* say that I am ...Mark 8:27
With *m* it is impossible ...Mark 10:27
goodwill toward *m* ....Luke 2:14
when all *m* speak well of ...Luke 6:26
m always ought to pray ....Luke 18:1
from heaven or from *m* ...Luke 20:4
the life was the light of *m* ...John 1:4
loved the praise of *m* .....John 12:43
old *m* shall dream dreams ..Acts 2:17
have not lied to *m* but to ...Acts 5:4
m everywhere to repent ...Acts 17:30
Likewise also the *m* ....Rom 1:27
in the sight of all *m* ....Rom 12:17
let no one boast in *m* ......1 Cor 3:21
all things to all *m* ....1 Cor 9:22
with the tongues of *m* .....1 Cor 13:1
speak to *m* but to God .....1 Cor 14:2
the Lord, and not to *m* .....Eph 6:7
to the tradition of *m*, ...Col 2:8
between God and *m* ....1 Tim 2:5
rejected indeed by *m* ....1 Pet 2:4

In those days *m* will seek ...Rev 9:6
to scorch *m* with fire ....Rev 16:8

MENAHEM
Cruel king of Israel, 2 Kin 15:14–18

MENSERVANTS
And also on My *m* ....Joel 2:29
And on My *m* and on My ...Acts 2:18

MENTION
I will make *m* of Your ......Ps 71:16
make *m* that His name is ....Is 12:4
by You only we make *m* ....Is 26:13
He has made *m* of My name ..Is 49:1
You who make *m* of the ......Is 62:6
will *m* the lovingkindnesses ..Is 63:7
Make *m* to the nations, ...Jer 4:16
m of you always in my ......Rom 1:9
he was dying, made *m* ......Heb 11:22

MEPHIBOSHETH
Son of King Saul, 2 Sam 21:8
——— Grandson of King Saul; crippled
son of Jonathan, 2 Sam 4:4–6
Sought out and honored by David,
2 Sam 9:1–13
Accused by Ziba, 2 Sam 16:1–4
Later explains himself to David, 2 Sam
19:24–30
Spared by David, 2 Sam 21:7

MERAB
King Saul's eldest daughter, 1 Sam
14:49
Saul promises her to David, but gives
her to Adriel, 1 Sam 18:17–19

MERARI
Third son of Levi, Gen 46:11
——— Descendants of, called Merarites:
Duties in the tabernacle, Num 3:35–37
Cities assigned to, Josh 21:7, 34–40
Duties in the temple, 1 Chr 26:10–19
Assist Ezra after Exile, Ezra 8:18, 19

MERCHANDISE
perceives that her *m* ......Prov 31:18
house a house of *m* ....John 2:16

MERCHANTS
set it in a city of *m* ....Ezek 17:4
have multiplied your *m* .....Nah 3:16
m were the great men .....Rev 18:23

MERCIES
for His *m* are great ......2 Sam 24:14
in Your manifold *m* You ....Neh 9:19
multitude of Your tender *m* ...Ps 51:1
I will sing of the *m* of the .....Ps 89:1
and His tender *m* ....Ps 145:9
give you the sure *m* ......Acts 13:34
brethren, by the *m* of God ..Rom 12:1
the Father of *m* ....2 Cor 1:3
beloved, put on tender *m* ....Col 3:12

MERCIFUL
LORD, the LORD God, *m* ......Ex 34:6
your God is a *m* God.......Deut 4:31
With the *m* You will show ...Ps 18:25
He is ever *m* ....Ps 37:26
God be *m* to us and ....Ps 67:1
for He is gracious and *m* ....Joel 2:13
Blessed are the *m* ....Matt 5:7
Therefore be *m*, just as ....Luke 6:36
saying, 'God be *m* ....Luke 18:13
For I will be *m* ....Heb 8:12
compassionate and *m* ....James 5:11

MERCY
See HAVE MERCY; HIS MERCY ENDURES
FOREVER
but showing *m* to ....Ex 20:6
You shall put the *m* seat ....Ex 26:34
and abundant in *m* ....Num 14:18
m endures forever ....1 Chr 16:34
I have trusted in Your *m* .....Ps 13:5
to Your *m* remember me .....Ps 25:7
I trust in the *m* ....Ps 52:8

shall send forth His *m* . . . . Ps 57:3
You, O Lord, belongs *m* . . . . . Ps 62:12
m ceased forever . . . . Ps 77:8
M and truth have met . . . . Ps 85:10
M shall be built . . . . Ps 89:2
m and truth go before . . . . . . Ps 89:14
m is everlasting . . . . Ps 100:5
I will sing of *m* . . . . Ps 101:1
For Your *m* is great . . . . Ps 108:4
is full of Your *m* . . . . Ps 119:64
the LORD there is *m* . . . . Ps 130:7
to anger and great in *m* . . . . Ps 145:8
Let not *m* and truth . . . . Prov 3:3
who honors Him has *m* . . . Prov 14:31
cruel and have no *m* . . . . Jer 6:23
Lord our God belong *m* . . . . . Dan 9:9
For I desire *m* and not . . . . . . Hos 6:6
do justly, to love *m* . . . . Mic 6:8
'I desire *m* and not . . . . Matt 9:13
And His *m* is on those . . . . . Luke 1:50
"I will have *m* . . . . Rom 9:15
of God who shows *m* . . . . . Rom 9:16
that He might have *m* . . . . Rom 11:32
m has made trustworthy . . . 1 Cor 7:25
as we have received *m* . . . . . 2 Cor 4:1
God, who is rich in *m* . . . . . . Eph 2:4
but I obtained *m* . . . . 1 Tim 1:13
that he may find *m* . . . . 2 Tim 1:18
to His *m* He saved us . . . . . . Titus 3:5
that we may obtain *m* . . . . . Heb 4:16
judgment is without *m* . . . . James 2:13
God, looking for the *m* . . . . . . Jude 21

MERCY SEAT
make a *m* . . . . Ex 25:17
put the *m* on top of the . . . . . Ex 40:20
the veil, before the *m* . . . . . . Lev 16:2
incense may cover the *m* . . Lev 16:13
to him from above the *m* . . . Num 7:89
and the place of the *m* . . . 1 Chr 28:11
glory overshadowing the *m* . . Heb 9:5

MERIB-BAAL
Another name for Mephibosheth, 1 Chr
8:34

MERODACH
Supreme deity of the Babylonians, Jer
50:2
Otherwise called Bel, Is 46:1

MERODACH-BALADAN
Sends ambassadors to Hezekiah, Is
39:1–8
Also called Berodach-Baladan, 2 Kin
20:12

MEROM
Lake on Jordan, Josh 11:5, 7

MEROZ
Town cursed for failing to help the
Lord, Judg 5:23

MERRY
m heart makes a . . . . Prov 15:13
A *m* heart does good . . . . . Prov 17:22
eat, drink, and be *m* . . . . Eccl 8:15
eat, drink, and be *m* . . . . . . Luke 12:19
we should make *m* . . . . Luke 15:32

MESHACH
Babylonian name given to Mishael,
Dan 1:7
Advanced to high position, Dan 2:49
Remains faithful in testing, Dan
3:13–30

MESHECH
Son of Japheth, Gen 10:2
His descendants, mentioned in proph-
ecy, Ezek 27:13; 32:26; 38:2, 3

MESOPOTAMIA
Home of Abraham's relatives, Gen
24:4, 10, 15
Called Padan Aram and Syria, Gen
25:20; 31:20, 24

Israel enslaved to, Judg 3:8–10
Jews from, present at Pentecost, Acts
2:9

MESSAGE
He who sends a *m* by the . . Prov 26:6
I have heard a *m* . . . . Jer 49:14
m was revealed to Daniel . . . Dan 10:1
to it the *m* that I tell you . . . . . Jon 3:2
For the *m* of the cross . . . . . 1 Cor 1:18
is the *m* which we have . . . 1 John 1:5

MESSENGER
Jezebel sent a *m* to Elijah . . 1 Kin 19:2
a *m* came to Job and said, . . . Job 1:14
is a faithful *m* . . . . Prov 25:13
"Behold, I send My *m* . . . . Mal 3:1
'Behold, I send My *m* . . . . . Matt 11:10
a *m* of Satan to buffet me . . 2 Cor 12:7

MESSIAH
until *M* the Prince . . . . Dan 9:25
"We have found the *M* . . . . . John 1:41

MET
the angels of God *m* him . . . . Gen 32:1
and truth have *m* together . . . Ps 85:10
there *m* Him ten men . . . . . Luke 17:12
m Him, but Mary was . . . . John 11:20
coming in, Cornelius *m* . . . Acts 10:25
spirit of divination *m* us . . . Acts 16:16
who *m* Abraham returning . . . Heb 7:1

METHUSELAH
Oldest man on record, Gen 5:27

MICAH
Prophet, contemporary of Isaiah, Is 1:1;
Mic 1:1

MICAIAH (or Michaiah)
Prophet who predicts Ahab's death,
1 Kin 22:8–28
———— Contemporary of Jeremiah, Jer
36:11–13

MICHAEL
Chief prince, Dan 10:13, 21
Disputes with Satan, Jude 9
Fights the dragon, Rev 12:7–9

MICHAL
Daughter of King Saul, 1 Sam 14:49
Loves and marries David, 1 Sam
18:20–28
Saves David from Saul, 1 Sam 19:9–17
Given to Palti, 1 Sam 25:44
David demands her from Abner, 2 Sam
3:13–16
Ridicules David; becomes barren,
2 Sam 6:16–23

MICHMASH
Site of battle with Philistines, 1 Sam
13:5, 11, 16, 23
Scene of Jonathan's victory, 1 Sam
14:1–16

MIDDLE
in the *m* of a wheel . . . . . . Ezek 10:10
boat was in the *m* of the . . Mark 6:47
about the *m* of the feast . . . . John 7:14
broken down the *m* wall . . . . Eph 2:14

MIDIAN
Son of Abraham by Keturah, Gen
25:1–4
———— Region in the Arabian desert occupied by the Midianites, Gen 25:6; Ex
2:15

MIDIANITES
Descendants of Abraham by Keturah,
Gen 25:1, 2
Moses flees to, Ex 2:15
Join Moab in cursing Israel, Num
22:4–7
Intermarriage with incurs God's wrath,
Num 25:1–18
Defeated by Israel, Num 31:1–10

Oppress Israel; defeated by Gideon,
Judg 6; 7

MIDST
God is in the *m* . . . . Ps 46:5
that I am in the *m* . . . . Joel 2:27
I am there in the *m* . . . . . . Matt 18:20

MIGDOL
Israelite encampment, Ex 14:2
Place Jews flee to in Egypt, Jer 44:1

MIGHT
'My power and the *m* . . . . . . Deut 8:17
hand is power and *m* . . . . 1 Chr 29:12
shall speak of the *m* . . . . Ps 145:6
to do, do it with your *m* . . . . Eccl 9:10
the Spirit of counsel and *m* . . Is 11:2
the greatness of His *m* . . . . . Is 40:26
man glory in his *m* . . . . Jer 9:23
their *m* has failed . . . . Jer 51:30
'Not by *m* nor by . . . . Zech 4:6
and power and *m* . . . . Eph 1:21
in the power of His *m* . . . . . Eph 6:10
greater in power and *m* . . . . 2 Pet 2:11
honor and power and *m* . . . . Rev 7:12

MIGHTIER
The LORD on high is *m* . . . . . . Ps 93:4
coming after me is *m* . . . . . Matt 3:11

MIGHTILY
to shake the earth *m* . . . . Is 2:19
sackcloth, and cry *m* to God . . Jon 3:8
word of the Lord grew *m* . . Acts 19:20
which works in me *m* . . . . . . Col 1:29
cried *m* with a loud voice, . . . Rev 18:2

MIGHTY
Those were the *m* men who . . Gen 6:4
He was a *m* hunter . . . . Gen 10:9
and grew exceedingly *m* . . . . . Ex 1:7
son's son the *m* things I . . . . . Ex 10:2
for they are too *m* . . . . Num 22:6
with His *m* power . . . . Deut 4:37
How the *m* have fallen . . . . 2 Sam 1:19
is wise in heart and *m* . . . . Job 9:4
The LORD *m* in battle . . . . Ps 24:8
m man is not delivered by . . Ps 33:16
The *M* One, God the LORD, . . . Ps 50:1
the *m* acts of the LORD . . . . . Ps 106:2
Praise Him for His *m* acts . . Ps 150:2
their Redeemer is *m* . . . . . . Prov 23:11
Woe to men *m* at . . . . Is 5:22
M God, Everlasting Father, ... Is 9:6
Redeemer, the *M* One of . . . . Is 49:26
in righteousness, *m* to save . . Is 63:1
great in counsel and *m* . . . . Jer 32:19
righteousness like a *m* . . . . Amos 5:24
m men are made red . . . . Nah 2:3
For if the *m* works . . . . Matt 11:21
not do many *m* works . . . . Matt 13:58
m has done great . . . . Luke 1:49
He has put down the *m* . . . . Luke 1:52
as of a rushing *m* wind . . . . . Acts 2:2
the flesh, not many *m* . . . . 1 Cor 1:26
m in God for pulling . . . . . . 2 Cor 10:4
the working of His *m* . . . . . . Eph 1:19
from heaven with His *m* . . 2 Thess 1:7
city Babylon, that *m* city . . . Rev 18:10

MILCOM
Ammonite god worshiped by Solomon,
1 Kin 11:5
Altar of, destroyed by Josiah, 2 Kin
23:12, 13

MILETUS
Paul meets Ephesian elders here, Acts
20:15–38
Paul leaves Trophimus here, 2 Tim 4:20

MILK
to a land flowing with *m* . . . . . Ex 3:8
for water, she gave *m* . . . . . Judg 5:25
not pour me out like *m* . . . . Job 10:10
honey and *m* are under . . . . Song 4:11

come, buy wine and *m* . . . . Is 55:1
and whiter than *m* . . . . Lam 4:7
shall flow with *m* . . . . Joel 3:18
have come to need *m* . . . . . Heb 5:12
m is unskilled in the . . . . Heb 5:13
desire the pure *m* . . . . 1 Pet 2:2

MILK AND HONEY
to a land flowing with *m* . . . . . Ex 3:8
It truly flows with *m* . . . . . Num 13:27
land flowing with *m* . . . . Deut 6:3
land flowing with *m* . . . . . . Josh 5:6
land flowing with *m* . . . . Jer 11:5
m, the glory of all . . . . Ezek 20:6

MILL
be grinding at the *m* . . . . . Matt 24:41

MILLO
Fort at Jerusalem, 2 Sam 5:9
Prepared by Solomon, 1 Kin 9:15
Strengthened by Hezekiah, 2 Chr 32:5
Scene of Joash's death, 2 Kin 12:20, 21

MILLSTONE
m were hung around his . . . Matt 18:6
a stone like a great *m* . . . . . Rev 18:21

MIND
the people had a *m* to work . . Neh 4:6
put wisdom in the *m* . . . . . . Job 38:36
perfect peace, whose *m* . . . . . . Is 26:3
and with all your *m* . . . . . . Matt 22:37
and in his right *m* . . . . Mark 5:15
nor have an anxious *m* . . . . Luke 12:29
m I myself serve the . . . . . . Rom 7:25
Because the carnal *m* is . . . . . Rom 8:7
the *m* of the Spirit is . . . . . . Rom 8:27
who has known the *m* . . . . Rom 11:34
renewing of your *m* . . . . . . Rom 12:2
Be of the same *m* . . . . Rom 12:16
convinced in his own *m* . . . . Rom 14:5
have the *m* of Christ . . . . . 1 Cor 2:16
you are out of your *m* . . . . 1 Cor 14:23
Let this *m* be in you . . . . Phil 2:5
Set your *m* on things above, . . Col 3:2
to *m* your own . . . . 1 Thess 4:11
love and of a sound *m* . . . . . 2 Tim 1:7
put My laws in their *m* . . . . . Heb 8:10
the loins of your *m* . . . . . . 1 Pet 1:13

MINDFUL
is man that You are *m* . . . . Ps 8:4
The LORD has been *m* . . . . Ps 115:12
for you are not *m* . . . . Matt 16:23
is man that You are *m* . . . . . . Heb 2:6

MINDS
people change their *m* . . . . . Ex 13:17
put My law in their *m* . . . . . Jer 31:33
I stir up your pure *m* . . . . . . 2 Pet 3:1
He who searches the *m* . . . . . Rev 2:23

MINISTER
to make you a *m* . . . . Acts 26:16
for he is God's *m* . . . . Rom 13:4
you will be a good *m* . . . . . . 1 Tim 4:6
spirits sent forth to *m* for . . . Heb 1:14
a *M* of the sanctuary . . . . Heb 8:2

MINISTERED
But the child *m* . . . . 1 Sam 2:11
a thousand thousands *m* . . . . Dan 7:10
angels came and *m* to . . . . . Matt 4:11
As they *m* to the Lord . . . . . Acts 13:2

MINISTERS
angels spirits, His *m* . . . . . . Ps 104:4
for they are God's *m* . . . . . . Rom 13:6
commend ourselves as *m* . . . 2 Cor 6:4
Are they *m* of Christ . . . . . 2 Cor 11:23
If anyone *m* . . . . 1 Pet 4:11

MINISTRIES
are differences of *m* . . . . . . 1 Cor 12:5

MINISTRY
I magnify my *m* . . . . Rom 11:13
But if the *m* of death . . . . . . 2 Cor 3:7

since we have this *m* . . . . . . 2 Cor 4:1
and has given us the *m* . . . . 2 Cor 5:18
for the work of *m* . . . . Eph 4:12
m which you have . . . . Col 4:17
fulfill your *m* . . . . 2 Tim 4:5
a more excellent *m* . . . . Heb 8:6

MINT
For you pay tithe of *m* . . . . Matt 23:23

MIRACLE
saying, 'Show a *m* . . . . Ex 7:9
no one who works a *m* . . . Mark 9:39
see some *m* done by Him . . Luke 23:8
that a notable *m* . . . . Acts 4:16

MIRACLES
God worked unusual *m* . . . Acts 19:11
the working of *m* . . . . 1 Cor 12:10
Are all workers of *m* . . . . . 1 Cor 12:29
with various *m* . . . . Heb 2:4

MIRIAM
Sister of Aaron and Moses, Num 26:59
Chosen by God; called a prophetess,
Ex 15:20
Punished for rebellion, Num 12:1–16
Buried at Kadesh, Num 20:1

MIRTH
I will test you with *m* . . . . . . Eccl 2:1
is in the house of *m* . . . . Eccl 7:4
joy is darkened, the *m* . . . . . Is 24:11

MISER
eat the bread of a *m* . . . . . . Prov 23:6

MISERIES
m that are coming . . . . James 5:1

MISERY
would forget your *m* . . . . . . Job 11:16
and remember his *m* . . . . . Prov 31:7

MISTREATED
But the Egyptians *m* . . . . . . Deut 26:6
those who are *m* . . . . Heb 13:3

MISTREATS
m his father and . . . . Prov 19:26

MITES
widow putting in two *m* . . . Luke 21:2

MITYLENE
Visited by Paul, Acts 20:13–15

MIZPAH
Site of covenant between Jacob and
Laban, Gen 31:44–53
———— Town of Benjamin; outraged Isra-
elites gather here, Josh 18:21, 26;
Judg 20:1, 3
Samuel gathers Israel, 1 Sam 7:5–16;
10:17–25
Residence of Gedaliah, 2 Kin 25:23, 25

MOAB
Son of Lot, Gen 19:33–37
———— Country of the Moabites, Deut 1:5

MOABITES
Descendants of Lot, Gen 19:36, 37
Join Midian in cursing Israel, Num 22:4
Excluded from Israel, Deut 23:3–6
Kindred of Ruth, Ruth 1:4
Subdued by Israel, 1 Sam 14:47; 2 Sam
8:2; 2 Kin 3:4–27
Women of, lead Solomon astray, 1 Kin
11:1–8
Prophecies concerning, Is 11:14;
15:1–9; Jer 48:1–47; Amos 2:1–3

MOAN
m sadly like doves . . . . Is 59:11

MOCK
I will *m* when your . . . . Prov 1:26
Fools *m* at sin . . . . Prov 14:9
to the Gentiles to *m* . . . . . . Matt 20:19

MOCKED
at noon, that Elijah *m* . . . 1 Kin 18:27

"I am one *m* by his . . . . Job 12:4
knee before Him and *m* . . . Matt 27:29
deceived, God is not *m* . . . . . Gal 6:7

MOCKER
Wine is a *m* . . . . Prov 20:1

MOCKERS
that there would be *m* . . . . . . Jude 18

MOCKINGS
others had trial of *m* . . . . . Heb 11:36

MOCKS
He who *m* the poor . . . . Prov 17:5

MODERATION
with propriety and *m* . . . . . . 1 Tim 2:9

MOLECH
God of the Ammonites; worshiped by
Solomon, 1 Kin 11:7
Human sacrifice made to, Lev 18:21;
2 Kin 23:10

MOMENT
consume them in a *m* . . . . . Num 16:21
In a *m* they die . . . . Job 34:20
For His anger is but for a *m* . . . Ps 30:5
face from you for a *m* . . . . Is 54:8
of the world in a *m* of time . . Luke 4:5
m, in the twinkling . . . . 1 Cor 15:52
which is but for a *m* . . . . . . 2 Cor 4:17

MONEY
man's *m* to his sack . . . . . . Gen 42:25
does not put out his *m* . . . . . . Ps 15:5
m answers every . . . . Eccl 10:19
be redeemed without *m* . . . . . Is 52:3
and you who have no *m* . . . . . Is 55:1
of the *m* changers . . . . Matt 21:12
and hid his lord's *m* . . . . . Matt 25:18
put *m* into the treasury . . . . Mark 12:41
promised to give him *m* . . Mark 14:11
Carry neither *m* . . . . Luke 10:4
I sent you without *m* . . . . . Luke 22:35
the *m* changers doing . . . . . John 2:14
a thief, and had the *m* . . . . John 12:6
be purchased with *m* . . . . . Acts 8:20
not greedy for *m* . . . . 1 Tim 3:3
m is a root of all . . . . 1 Tim 6:10
not greedy for *m* . . . . Titus 1:7

MONSTER
me up like a *m* . . . . Jer 51:34
of Egypt, O great *m* . . . . . Ezek 29:3

MONTH
ark rested in the seventh *m* . Gen 8:4
first *m* of the year to you . . . . Ex 12:2
will bear fruit every *m* . . . Ezek 47:12
latter rain in the first *m* . . . . Joel 2:23
in the sixth *m* the angel . . . Luke 1:26
this is now the sixth *m* . . . . Luke 1:36
yielding its fruit every *m* . . . Rev 22:2

MONTHS
child, she hid him three *m* . . . Ex 2:2
with her about three *m*. . . . Luke 1:56
up three years and six *m* . . Luke 4:25
You observe days and *m* . . . Gal 4:10
to torment them for five *m* . . Rev 9:5
continue for forty-two *m* . . . Rev 13:5

MOON
this time, the sun, the *m* . . . Gen 37:9
and the *m* stopped, till . . . Josh 10:13
of Your fingers, the *m* . . . . . . Ps 8:3
until the *m* is no more . . . . . . Ps 72:7
the *m* for seasons . . . . Ps 104:19
by day, nor the *m* by night . . Ps 121:6
morning, fair as the *m* . . . . Song 6:10
sun and *m* grow dark . . . . . Joel 2:10
the *m* into blood, before . . . Joel 2:31
and *m* will grow dark, and . Joel 3:15
sun and *m* stood still . . . . . Hab 3:11
m will not give its . . . . Mark 13:24
in the sun, in the *m* . . . . . . Luke 21:25
or a new *m* or sabbaths, ... Col 2:16

the *m* became like blood .... Rev 6:12
or of the *m* to shine in it ... Rev 21:23

MORDECAI
Esther's guardian; advises her, Esth
2:5–20
Reveals plot to kill the king, Esth
2:21–23
Refuses homage to Haman, Esth
3:1–6
Honored by the king, Esth 6:1–12
Exalted highly, Esth 8:15; 9:4
Institutes feast of Purim, Esth 9:20–31

MORESHETH GATH
Birthplace of Micah the prophet, Mic
1:14

MORIAH
See MOUNT MORIAH

MORNING
the *m* were the first day ...... Gen 1:5
none of it remain until *m* .... Ex 12:10
they gathered it every *m* .... Ex 16:21
up in the *m* to Mount Sinai ... Ex 34:2
she lay at his feet until *m* .. Ruth 3:14
the eyelids of the *m* .... Job 41:18
You shall hear in the *m* ...... Ps 5:3
but joy comes in the *m* ...... Ps 30:5
Evening and *m* and at ...... Ps 55:17
in the *m* my prayer comes ... Ps 88:13
lovingkindness in the *m* ...... Ps 92:2
the wings of the *m* .... Ps 139:9
looks forth as the *m* ...... Song 6:10
Lucifer, son of the *m* ...... Is 14:12
shall break forth like the *m* .. Is 58:8
They are new every *m* .... Lam 3:23
established as the *m* .... Hos 6:3
in the *m*, 'It will be foul .... Matt 16:3
rooster, or in the *m* ...... Mark 13:35
very early in the *m* .... Luke 24:1
the *m* star rises in your .... 2 Pet 1:19
the Bright and *M* Star ..... Rev 22:16

MORSEL
or eaten my *m* by .... Job 31:17
Better is a dry *m* .... Prov 17:1
Esau, who for one *m* ..... Heb 12:16

MORTAL
sin reign in your *m* .... Rom 6:12
m bodies through His ...... Rom 8:11
and this *m* must put ...... 1 Cor 15:53
Here *m* men receive tithes, ... Heb 7:8

MORTALITY
m may be swallowed .... 2 Cor 5:4

MORTALS
with idolatrous *m* .... Ps 26:4

MOSES
See LAW OF MOSES
Born; hidden by mother; adopted by
Pharaoh's daughter, Ex 2:1–10
Kills Egyptian and flees to Midian, Ex
2:11–22
Receives call from God, Ex 3:1–4:17
Returns to Israelites in Egypt, Ex
4:18–31
Wins Israel's deliverance with plagues,
Ex 5:1–6:13; 6:28–11:10; 12:29–42
Leads Israel out of Egypt and through
the Red Sea, Ex 13:17–14:31
His song of praise, Ex 15:1–18
Provides miraculously for the people,
Ex 15:22—17:7
Appoints judges, Ex 18
Receives the law on Mount Sinai, Ex
19—23
Receives instructions for tabernacle,
Ex 25—31
Intercedes for Israel's sin, Ex 32
Recommissioned and encouraged, Ex
33; 34
Further instructions and building of the
tabernacle, Ex 35—40

Consecrates Aaron, Lev 8:1–36
Takes census, Num 1:1–54
Resumes journey to Canaan, Num
10:11–36
Complains; 70 elders appointed, Num
11:1–35
Intercedes for people when they refuse
to enter Canaan, Num 14:11–25
Puts down Korah's rebellion, Num 16
Sins in anger, Num 20:1–13
Makes bronze serpent, Num 21:4–9
Travels toward Canaan, Num 21:10–20
Takes second census, Num 26
Commissions Joshua as his successor,
Num 27:12–23
Receives further laws, Num 28—30
Commands conquest of Midian, Num
31
Final instructions, Num 32—36
Forbidden to enter Promised Land,
Deut 3:23–28
Gives farewell messages, Deut 32; 33
Sees Promised Land; dies, Deut
34:1–7
Is mourned and extolled, Deut 34:8–12
Appears with Christ at transfiguration,
Matt 17:1–3

MOST
His mouth is *m* sweet ..... Song 5:16
on your *m* holy faith .... Jude 20

MOST HIGH
be Abram of God *M* .... Gen 14:19
the knowledge of the *M* ... Num 24:16
the *M* uttered His voice .. 2 Sam 22:14
praise to Your name, O *M* ..... Ps 9:2
through the mercy of the *M* .. Ps 21:7
the Lord *M* is awesome ...... Ps 47:2
I will cry out to God *M* ...... Ps 57:2
M God their Redeemer ...... Ps 78:35
you are children of the *M* .... Ps 82:6
secret place of the *M* .... Ps 91:1
the counsel of the *M* ...... Ps 107:11
I will be like the *M* .... Is 14:14
from the mouth of the *M* ... Lam 3:38
servants of the *M* God ..... Dan 3:26
M rules in the kingdom of .. Dan 4:17
But the saints of the *M* .... Dan 7:18
Though they call to the *M* .. Hos 11:7
Jesus, Son of the *M* .... Mark 5:7
M does not dwell in .... Acts 7:48
are the servants of the *M* .. Acts 16:17
Salem, priest of the *M* ...... Heb 7:1

MOST HOLY PLACE
m you shall eat it .... Num 18:10
sanctuary, as the *M* .... 1 Kin 6:16
And he made the *M* .... 2 Chr 3:8
to me, "This is the *M* ..... Ezek 41:4
blood He entered the *M* ..... Heb 9:12
high priest enters the *M* .... Heb 9:25

MOTH
m will eat them .... Is 50:9
where *m* and rust .... Matt 6:19

MOTHER
because she was the *m* .... Gen 3:20
your father and your *m* ..... Ex 20:12
your father and your *m* .... Deut 5:16
like a joyful *m* .... Ps 113:9
son is the grief of his *m* ... Prov 10:1
the only one of her *m* ...... Song 6:9
m might have been my .... Jer 20:17
Like *m*, like daughter ..... Ezek 16:44
Child with Mary His *m* .... Matt 2:11
who loves father or *m* .... Matt 10:37
leave his father and *m* ..... Matt 19:5
Who is My *m*, or My ..... Mark 3:33
His *m* marveled at those ... Luke 2:33
but His *m* kept all these ... Luke 2:51
wife's *m* was sick .... Luke 4:38
out, the only son of his *m* .. Luke 7:12
m against daughter .... Luke 12:53

hate his father and *m* ..... Luke 14:26
"Behold your *m* .... John 19:27
free, which is the *m* .... Gal 4:26
without father, without *m* .... Heb 7:3
The *M* of Harlots .... Rev 17:5

MOTHER'S
return each to her *m* house .. Ruth 1:8
Naked I came from my *m* .... Job 1:21
while on My *m* breasts ...... Ps 22:9
who took me out of my *m* ... Ps 71:6
Spirit, even from his *m* .... Luke 1:15
his *m* womb was carried .... Acts 3:2

MOUNT
the *M* of the LORD it shall .. Gen 22:14
come up to *M* Sinai .... Ex 19:23
came down from *M* Sinai ... Ex 34:29
M Zion on the sides of the .... Ps 48:2
Let *M* Zion rejoice, let the ... Ps 48:11
the LORD are like *M* Zion ... Ps 125:1
you like *M* Carmel .... Song 7:5
they shall *m* up with .... Is 40:31
stand on the *M* of Olives .. Zech 14:4
He sat on the *M* of Olives .. Matt 24:3
to the *M* of Olives .... Mark 14:26
for this Hagar is *M* .... Gal 4:25

MOUNT CARMEL
Prophets gather at, 1 Kin 18:19, 20
Elisha journeys to, 2 Kin 2:25
Shunammite woman comes to Elisha
at, 2 Kin 4:25

MOUNT EBAL
Cursed by God, Deut 11:29
Joshua builds an altar on, Josh 8:30

MOUNT GERIZIM
Mount of blessing, Deut 11:29; 27:12
Jotham speaks to people of Shechem
here, Judg 9:7
Samaritans' sacred mountain, John
4:20, 21

MOUNT GILBOA
Men of Israel slain at, 1 Sam 31:1
Saul and his sons slain at, 1 Sam 31:8

MOUNT GILEAD
Gideon divides the people for battle at,
Judg 7:3

MOUNT HOR
Lord speaks to Moses and Aaron on,
Num 20:23
Aaron dies on, Num 20:25–28

MOUNT HOREB
Sons of Israel stripped of ornaments
at, Ex 33:6
The same as Sinai, Ex 3:1

MOUNT MORIAH
Place where Abraham offered Isaac,
Gen 22:2
Elevation where Solomon built the tem-
ple, 1 Chr 3:1

MOUNT NEBO
Place where Moses viewed the
Promised Land, Deut 32:49

MOUNT OF OLIVES
See OLIVES, MOUNT OF

MOUNT SINAI
Lord descends upon, in fire, Ex 19:18
Lord calls Moses to the top of, Ex 19:20
The glory of the Lord rests on, for six
days, Ex 24:16

MOUNT TABOR
Deborah sends Barak there to defeat
Canaanites, Judg 4:6–14

MOUNT ZION
Survivors shall go out from, 2 Kin 19:31

MOUNTAIN
to Horeb, the *m* .... Ex 3:1
Whoever touches the *m* .... Ex 19:12

and a thick cloud on the *m* . . Ex 19:16
Moses was on the *m* forty . . . Ex 24:18
"But as a *m* falls . . . . Job 14:18
You have made my *m* . . . . Ps 30:7
of many peaks is the *m* . . . . . . Ps 68:15
let us go up to the *m* . . . . Is 2:3
be exalted, and every *m* . . . . Is 40:4
image became a great *m* . . . Dan 2:35
an alarm in My holy *m* . . . . . Joel 2:1
Who are you, O great *m* . . . . Zech 4:7
on an exceedingly high *m* . . . Matt 4:8
He went up on a *m* . . . . Matt 5:1
you will say to this *m* . . . . Matt 17:20
came down from the *m* . . . . Mark 9:9
whoever says to this *m* . . Mark 11:23
shall be filled and every *m* . . Luke 3:5
feeding there on the *m* . . . . Luke 8:32
worshiped on this *m* . . . . John 4:20
with Him on the holy *m* . . . 2 Pet 1:18
it is rolled up, and every *m* . . Rev 6:14
to a great and high *m* . . . . . Rev 21:10

MOUNTAINS

tops of the *m* were seen . . . . . Gen 8:5
He removes the *m* . . . . Job 9:5
Surely the *m* yield . . . . Job 40:20
though the *m* be carried . . . . . . Ps 46:2
m will bring peace . . . . Ps 72:3
excellent than the *m* . . . . Ps 76:4
m were brought forth . . . . Ps 90:2
m melt like wax at the . . . . Ps 97:5
m skipped like rams . . . . Ps 114:4
m surround Jerusalem . . . . . . Ps 125:2
forth into singing, you *m* . . . . . Is 44:23
How beautiful upon the *m* . . . . Is 52:7
m shall depart and the . . . . . . Is 54:10
m shook at Your presence . . . Is 64:3
m shall be thrown down . . Ezek 38:20
in Judea flee to the *m* . . . . Matt 24:16
and day, he was in the *m* . . Mark 5:5
begin 'to say to the *m* . . . . Luke 23:30
that I could remove *m* . . . . 1 Cor 13:2
in deserts and *m* . . . . Heb 11:38
m were not found . . . . Rev 16:20

MOURN

and you *m* at last . . . . Prov 5:11
a time to *m* . . . . Eccl 3:4
to comfort all who *m* . . . . Is 61:2
will *m* for Him as one . . . Zech 12:10
are those who *m* . . . . Matt 5:4
m as long as the . . . . Matt 9:15
Lament and *m* and weep . . James 4:9
of the earth will *m* . . . . Rev 1:7

MOURNED

we *m* to you . . . . Matt 11:17
and have not rather *m* . . . . . 1 Cor 5:2

MOURNING

This is a deep *m* . . . . Gen 50:11
for me my *m* into dancing . . . Ps 30:11
m all the day long . . . . Ps 38:6
m shall be ended . . . . Is 60:20
ashes, the oil of joy for *m* . . . . . Is 61:3
men break bread in *m* . . . . . Jer 16:7
I will turn their *m* . . . . Jer 31:13
shall be a great *m* . . . . . . Zech 12:11
be turned to *m* and . . . . James 4:9

MOURNS

heavily, as one who *m* . . . . . Ps 35:14
The earth *m* and fades . . . . Is 24:4
for Him as one *m* . . . . Zech 12:10

MOUTH

"Who has made man's *m* . . . . Ex 4:11
and put the words in his *m* . . Ex 4:15
the earth opened its *m* . . . . Num 16:32
the *m* of the donkey . . . . . Num 22:28
from the *m* of the LORD . . . . . Deut 8:3
near you, in your *m* . . . . Deut 30:14
not depart from your *m* . . . . . Josh 1:8
Out of the *m* of babes . . . . Ps 8:2
Let the words of my *m* and . . Ps 19:14
shall continually be in my *m* . . Ps 34:1

The *m* of the righteous . . . . . Ps 37:30
m shall speak wisdom . . . . Ps 49:3
my *m* shall show forth . . . . . Ps 51:15
with my *m* will I make . . . . Ps 89:1
iniquity stops its *m* . . . . . . Ps 107:42
Then our *m* was filled with . . Ps 126:2
by the words of your *m* . . . . . Prov 6:2
knowledge, but the *m* . . . . Prov 10:14
by the fruit of his *m* . . . . . . Prov 12:14
m preserves his life . . . . Prov 13:3
The *m* of an immoral . . . . . Prov 22:14
and a flattering *m* . . . . Prov 26:28
her *m* with wisdom . . . . . . Prov 31:26
And he touched my *m* with . . . . Is 6:7
yet He opened not His *m* . . . . Is 53:7
not depart from your *m* . . . . . Is 59:21
put My words in your *m* . . . . . Jer 1:9
it was in my *m* like honey . . Ezek 3:3
m speaking pompous . . . . . . Dan 7:8
the doors of your *m* . . . . Mic 7:5
from the *m* of God . . . . Matt 4:4
near to Me with their *m* . . . Matt 15:8
m defiles a man . . . . Matt 15:11
that 'by the *m* of two or . . Matt 18:16
'Out of the *m* of babes . . . Matt 21:16
m I will judge you . . . . Luke 19:22
I will give you a *m* . . . . Luke 21:15
so He opened not His *m* . . . Acts 8:32
is near you, in your *m* . . . . . Rom 10:8
with your *m* the Lord . . . . . Rom 10:9
m confession is made . . . . Rom 10:10
proceed out of your *m*, but . . Eph 4:29
the same *m* proceed . . . . . James 3:10
m great swelling words . . . . . Jude 16
vomit you out of My *m* . . . . Rev 3:16
sweet as honey in your *m* . . . Rev 10:9
m was found no deceit . . . . . Rev 14:5

MOUTHS

gape at Me with their *m* . . . . Ps 22:13
food was still in their *m* . . . . Ps 78:30
have *m*, but they do not . . . . Ps 115:5
near to Me with their *m* . . . . Is 29:13
and shut the lions' *m* . . . . . Dan 6:22

MOVE

and the earth will *m* . . . . Is 13:13
the mountain shall *m* . . . . Zech 14:4
M from here to there,' . . . Matt 17:20
m them with one of their . . Matt 23:4
in Him we live and *m* . . . . Acts 17:28

MOVED

shall never be *m* . . . . Ps 15:5
right hand I shall not be *m* . . Ps 16:8
she shall not be *m* . . . . Ps 46:5
I shall not be greatly *m* . . . . . Ps 62:2
m Him to jealousy with . . . . . Ps 78:58
m with compassion . . . . . . Matt 14:14
all the city was *m* . . . . Matt 21:10
spoke as they were *m* . . . . 2 Pet 1:21

MUCH

m study is wearisome . . . . Eccl 12:12
m better than wine is . . . . . Song 4:10
to whom *m* is given . . . . . Luke 12:48
M more then . . . . Rom 5:9

MULTIPLIED

the more they *m* and grew . . . Ex 1:12
sorrows shall be *m* . . . . Ps 16:4
your days will be *m* . . . . Prov 9:11
When the wicked are *m*, . . Prov 29:16
m before You, and our sins . . Is 59:12
of the disciples *m* . . . . Acts 6:7
Holy Spirit, they were *m* . . . Acts 9:31
word of God grew and *m* . . Acts 12:24
peace, and love be *m* to you . . Jude 2

MULTIPLY

See BE FRUITFUL AND MULTIPLY
"Be fruitful and *m* . . . . Gen 1:22
will greatly *m* your sorrow . . Gen 3:16
m your descendants . . . . . . Gen 16:10
multiplying I will *m* your . . Gen 22:17
m my days as the . . . . Job 29:18

m the descendants . . . . Jer 33:22
m the seed you have . . . . . 2 Cor 9:10

MULTITUDE

stars of heaven in *m* . . . . . . Deut 1:10
m of years should teach . . . . Job 32:7
Your house in the *m* . . . . Ps 5:7
m that kept a pilgrim . . . . . . Ps 42:4
in the *m* of Your mercy, ... Ps 69:13
In the *m* of words sin . . . . Prov 10:19
In a *m* of people is a . . . . . Prov 14:28
bury Gog and all his *m* . . . Ezek 39:11
to the *m* in parables . . . . . Matt 13:34
compassion on the *m* . . . . Matt 15:32
commanded the *m* to sit . . Matt 15:35
a great *m* followed Him . . . Matt 20:29
with the angel a *m* . . . . Luke 2:13
whole *m* sought to touch . . Luke 6:19
because of the *m* of fish . . . John 21:6
stars of the sky in *m* . . . . . Heb 11:12
"love will cover a *m* . . . . . . 1 Pet 4:8
and behold, a great *m* . . . . . Rev 7:9
voice of a great *m* in . . . . . . Rev 19:1

MULTITUDES

M, *m* in the valley of . . . . . Joel 3:14
when the *m* saw it, they . . . . Matt 9:8
all the *m* were amazed . . . Matt 12:23
He commanded the *m* to . . Matt 14:19
taught the *m* from the . . . . . Luke 5:3
m throng and press You . . Luke 8:45
m from sacrificing to . . . . . Acts 14:18

MURDER

"You shall not *m* . . . . Ex 20:13
Will you steal, *m*, commit . . . . Jer 7:9
'You shall not *m* . . . . Matt 5:21
they had committed *m* in . . Mark 15:7
threats and *m* against . . . . . . Acts 9:1
full of envy, *m*, strife . . . . . Rom 1:29
You *m* and covet and . . . . . James 4:2

MURDERED

sons of those who *m* . . . . . Matt 23:31
Jesus whom you *m* . . . . . . Acts 5:30
one and *m* his brother . . . . 1 John 3:12

MURDERER

He was a *m* from the . . . . . . John 8:44
and asked for a *m* . . . . Acts 3:14
of you suffer as a *m* . . . . . . 1 Pet 4:15
his brother is a *m* . . . . 1 John 3:15

MURDERERS

in it, but now *m* . . . . Is 1:21
and profane, for *m* . . . . 1 Tim 1:9
abominable, *m* . . . . Rev 21:8

MURDERS

whoever *m* will be in . . . . . Matt 5:21
evil thoughts, *m* . . . . Matt 15:19
envy, *m*, drunkenness . . . . . Gal 5:21
did not repent of their *m* . . . Rev 9:21

MUSIC

So David played *m* . . . . . 1 Sam 18:10
I will play *m* before the . . 2 Sam 6:21
Israel played *m* before . . . 1 Chr 13:8
whirling and playing *m* . . 1 Chr 15:29
but Asaph made *m* with . . 1 Chr 16:5
the *m* of the LORD, which . . 2 Chr 7:6
m are brought low . . . . Eccl 12:4
the house, he heard *m* . . . Luke 15:25

MUSING

while I was *m*, the fire . . . . . Ps 39:3

MUST

touches the altar *m* be . . . . Ex 29:37
I *m* be regarded as holy . . . . Lev 10:3
m be careful to observe . . . . Deut 8:1
is sleeping and *m* be . . . . 1 Kin 18:27
Him, and you *m* wait for . . . Job 34:14
he *m* restore sevenfold . . . . Prov 6:31
precept *m* be upon precept . . . Is 28:10
that Elijah *m* come first . . . Matt 17:10
offenses *m* come, but woe . . Matt 18:7
Man *m* suffer many . . . . . . Mark 8:31

such things *m* happen ..... Mark 13:7
And the gospel *m* first ... Mark 13:10
m be about My Father's .... Luke 2:49
you, 'You *m* be born again .. John 3:7
He *m* increase, but I .... John 3:30
Him *m* worship in spirit .... John 4:24
I *m* work the works of ...... John 9:4
that He *m* rise again from .. John 20:9
by which we *m* be saved ... Acts 4:12
m suffer for My name's ..... Acts 9:16
you *m* not call common ... Acts 10:15
m put on incorruption, ... 1 Cor 15:53
If I *m* boast, I will .... 2 Cor 11:30
bishop then *m* be .... 1 Tim 3:2
deacons *m* be reverent ..... 1 Tim 3:8
servant of the Lord *m* ..... 2 Tim 2:24
to God *m* believe that He ... Heb 11:6
m love his brother also ... 1 John 4:21
things which *m* shortly ...... Rev 1:1
m be released for a little .... Rev 20:3
m shortly take place .... Rev 22:6

MUSTARD
heaven is like a *m* seed .... Matt 13:31
have faith as a *m* seed .... Matt 17:20

MUTE
Or who makes the *m* .... Ex 4:11
m who does not open .... Ps 38:13
I was *m* with silence .... Ps 39:2
was cast out, the *m* spoke .. Matt 9:33
who has a *m* spirit .... Mark 9:17
But behold, you will be *m* .. Luke 1:20
demon, and it was *m* ..... Luke 11:14

MUTILATION
beware of the *m* .... Phil 3:2

MUTUAL
by the *m* faith both .... Rom 1:12

MUZZLE
"You shall not *m* .... Deut 25:4
"You shall not *m* .... 1 Tim 5:18

MY RIGHT HAND
Because He is at *m* .... Ps 16:8
You hold me by *m* .... Ps 73:23
my Lord, "Sit at *M* .... Ps 110:1
let *m* forget its skill .... Ps 137:5
Look on *m* and see .... Ps 142:4
and *M* has stretched out ..... Is 48:13
but to sit on *M* .... Matt 20:23
to my Lord, "Sit at *M* ..... Matt 22:44
for He is at *m* .... Acts 2:25
Sit at *M*, till I make .... Heb 1:13
stars which you saw in *M* ... Rev 1:20

MYRA
Paul changes ships here, Acts 27:5, 6

MYRRH
perfumed my bed with *m* .. Prov 7:17
my hands dripped with *m* ... Song 5:5
gold, frankincense, and *m* .. Matt 2:11
wine mingled with *m* to .. Mark 15:23

MYSIA
Paul and Silas pass through here, Acts 16:7, 8

MYSTERIES
to you to know the *m* ..... Matt 13:11
and understand all *m* ..... 1 Cor 13:2
the spirit he speaks *m* ..... 1 Cor 14:2

MYSTERIOUS
today is not too *m* .... Deut 30:11

MYSTERY
given to know the *m* ...... Mark 4:11
wisdom of God in a *m* .... 1 Cor 2:7
Behold, I tell you a *m* .... 1 Cor 15:51
made known to us the *m* .... Eph 1:9
This is a great *m* .... Eph 5:32
m which has been .... Col 1:26
the *m* of godliness .... 1 Tim 3:16

NAAMAN
Captain in the Syrian army, 2 Kin 5:1–11
Healed of his leprosy, 2 Kin 5:14–17
Referred to by Christ, Luke 4:27

NABAL
Refuses David's request, 1 Sam 25:2–12
Escapes David's wrath but dies of a stroke, 1 Sam 25:13–39

NABOTH
Murdered for his vineyard by King Ahab, 1 Kin 21:1–16
His murder avenged, 1 Kin 21:17–25

NADAB
Eldest of Aaron's four sons, Ex 6:23
Takes part in affirming covenant, Ex 24:1, 9–12
Becomes priest, Ex 28:1
Consumed by fire, Lev 10:1–7
——— King of Israel, 1 Kin 14:20
Killed by Baasha, 1 Kin 15:25–31

NAHASH
King of Ammon; makes impossible demands, 1 Sam 11:1–15

NAHOR
Grandfather of Abraham, Gen 11:24–26
——— Son of Terah, brother of Abraham, Gen 11:17

NAHUM
Prophet to Judah concerning Nineveh, Nah 1:1

NAILED
n it to the cross .... Col 2:14

NAIN
Village south of Nazareth; Jesus raises widow's son here, Luke 7:11–17

NAIOTH
Prophets' school in Ramah, 1 Sam 19:18, 19, 22, 23

NAKED
And they were both *n* ...... Gen 2:25
knew that they were *n* ...... Gen 3:7
told you that you were *n* .... Gen 3:11
"*N* I came from my .... Job 1:21
Sheol is *n* before Him, and .. Job 26:6
Isaiah has walked *n* .... Is 20:3
I was *n* and you .... Matt 25:36
and fled from them *n* .... Mark 14:52
shall not be found *n* ...... 2 Cor 5:3
but all things are *n* .... Heb 4:13
brother or sister is *n* ..... James 2:15
poor, blind, and *n* .... Rev 3:17

NAKEDNESS
of Canaan, saw the *n* ...... Gen 9:22
The *n* of your father's wife .. Lev 18:8
in hunger, in thirst, in *n* ... Deut 28:48
or famine, or *n* .... Rom 8:35
often, in cold and *n* ...... 2 Cor 11:27
n may not be revealed ...... Rev 3:18

NAME
See CALLED BY MY NAME; HOLY NAME; IN MY NAME
creature, that was its *n* ... Gen 2:19
called his wife's *n* Eve .... Gen 3:20
and make your *n* great .... Gen 12:2
Abram called on the *n* ..... Gen 13:4
your *n* shall be Abraham ... Gen 17:5
but Sarah shall be her *n* ... Gen 17:15
Israel shall be your *n* ..... Gen 35:10
So she called his *n* Moses ... Ex 2:10
This is My *n* forever .... Ex 3:15
My *n* may be declared in .... Ex 9:16
the LORD is His *n* .... Ex 15:3
Israel called its *n* Manna ... Ex 16:31
shall not take the *n* .... Ex 20:7

whose *n* is Jealous, is a ..... Ex 34:14
are called by the *n* .... Deut 28:10
glorious and awesome *n* .. Deut 28:58
by My *n* will humble ...... 2 Chr 7:14
and he has no *n* .... Job 18:17
excellent is Your *n* .... Ps 8:1
n will put their trust .... Ps 9:10
LORD the glory due to His *n* .. Ps 29:2
let us exalt His *n* together .... Ps 34:3
lift up my hands in Your *n* .... Ps 63:4
the clouds, by His *n* YAH .... Ps 68:4
be His glorious *n* .... Ps 72:19
n is great in Israel .... Ps 76:1
do not call on Your *n* .... Ps 79:6
whose *n* alone is the LORD .. Ps 83:18
to Him, and bless His *n* ... Ps 100:4
to Your *n* give glory .... Ps 115:1
above all Your *n* .... Ps 138:2
He calls them all by *n* ..... Ps 147:4
The *n* of the LORD is a .... Prov 18:10
A good *n* is to be .... Prov 22:1
what is His Son's *n* ...... Prov 30:4
And His *n* will be called .... Is 9:6
mention that His *n* is exalted .. Is 12:4
make mention of Your *n* ..... Is 26:13
the LORD, that is My *n* ..... Is 42:8
be to the LORD for a *n* .... Is 55:13
be called by a new *n* .... Is 62:2
Everlasting is Your *n* .... Is 63:16
who calls on Your *n* .... Is 64:7
it shall be to Me a *n* ...... Jer 33:9
and made Yourself a *n* ...... Dan 9:15
we will walk in the *n* ...... Mic 4:5
They will call on My *n* ..... Zech 13:9
n shall be great .... Mal 1:11
to you who fear My *n* ...... Mal 4:2
you shall call His *n* .... Matt 1:21
hallowed be Your *n* .... Matt 6:9
prophesied in Your *n* ...... Matt 7:22
righteous man in the *n* ... Matt 10:41
n Gentiles will trust ...... Matt 12:21
together in My *n* .... Matt 18:20
will come in My *n* .... Matt 24:5
"My *n* is Legion .... Mark 5:9
children in My *n* receives .. Mark 9:37
In My *n* they will cast ..... Mark 16:17
The virgin's *n* was .... Luke 1:27
for me, and holy is His *n* .. Luke 1:49
"His *n* is John .... Luke 1:63
and cast out your *n* .... Luke 6:22
who believe in His *n* .... John 1:12
comes in his own *n* .... John 5:43
his own sheep by *n* .... John 10:3
you ask in My *n* .... John 14:13
Father will send in My *n* .. John 14:26
keep through Your *n* ..... John 17:11
whoever calls on the *n* .... Acts 2:21
through faith in His *n* ..... Acts 3:16
there is no other *n* .... Acts 4:12
suffer shame for His *n* .... Acts 5:41
baptized in the *n* of ...... Acts 10:48
whoever calls on the *n* .... Rom 10:13
every *n* that is named, not .. Eph 1:21
which is above every *n* .... Phil 2:9
at the *n* of Jesus every ..... Phil 2:10
deed, do all in the *n* ...... Col 3:17
a more excellent *n* .... Heb 1:4
giving thanks to His *n* .... Heb 13:15
blaspheme that noble *n* ... James 2:7
with oil in the *n* of the .... James 5:14
reproached for the *n* ...... 1 Pet 4:14
n of the Son of God ...... 1 John 5:13
you hold fast to My *n* ...... Rev 2:13
n that you are alive .... Rev 3:1
and have not denied My *n* ... Rev 3:8
or the *n* of the beast ...... Rev 13:17
having His Father's *n* ...... Rev 14:1
and glorify Your *n* .... Rev 15:4
n written that no one ..... Rev 19:12

NAME'S
by all for My *n* sake ..... Matt 10:22

or lands, for My *n* sake, ... Matt 19:29
saved them for His *n* .... Ps 106:8
forgiven you for His *n* .... 1 John 2:12

NAMED
let my name be *n* .... Gen 48:16
I have *n* you .... Is 45:4
of a young man *n* Saul ..... Acts 7:58
not even *n* among the ..... 1 Cor 5:1
and every name that is *n* .... Eph 1:21

NAMES
So Adam gave *n* to all ...... Gen 2:20
lands after their own *n* ..... Ps 49:11
Now the *n* of the twelve .... Matt 10:2
n are written in heaven ... Luke 10:20
whose *n* are in the Book of .. Phil 4:3
Let everyone who *n* the ... 2 Tim 2:19
whose *n* are not written in .. Rev 17:8
the *n* of the twelve .... Rev 21:12
on them were the *n* of the .. Rev 21:14

NAOMI
Widow of Elimelech, Ruth 1:1–3
Returns to Bethlehem with Ruth, Ruth 1:14–19
Arranges Ruth's marriage to Boaz, Ruth 3; 4

NAPHTALI
Son of Jacob by Bilhah, Gen 30:1–8
Receives Jacob's blessing, Gen 49:21, 28
—— Tribe of:
Numbered, Num 1:42, 43
Territory assigned to, Josh 19:32–39
Joins Gideon's army, Judg 7:23
Attacked by Ben-Hadad and Tiglath-Pileser, 1 Kin 15:20; 2 Kin 15:29
Prophecy of great light in; fulfilled in Christ's ministry, Is 9:1–7; Matt 4:12–16

NARROW
"Enter by the *n* gate .... Matt 7:13
n is the gate and .... Matt 7:14

NATHAN
Son of David, 2 Sam 5:14
Mary's lineage traced through, Zech 12:12
—— Prophet under David and Solomon, 1 Chr 29:29
Reveals God's plan to David, 2 Sam 7:2–29
Rebukes David's sin, 2 Sam 12:1–15
Reveals Adonijah's plot, 1 Kin 1:10–46

NATHANAEL
One of Christ's disciples, John 1:45–51

NATION
make you a great *n* .... Gen 12:2
You slay a righteous *n* ..... Gen 20:4
priests and a holy *n* .... Ex 19:6
Blessed is the *n* whose ..... Ps 33:12
dealt thus with any *n* ...... Ps 147:20
Righteousness exalts a *n* .. Prov 14:34
lift up sword against *n* .... Is 2:4
that the righteous *n* .... Is 26:2
call a *n* you do not know ..... Is 55:5
a small one a strong *n* .... Is 60:22
n that was not called .... Is 65:1
Or shall a *n* be born at once ... Is 66:8
n changed its gods .... Jer 2:11
I will make them one *n* ... Ezek 37:22
since there was a *n* .... Dan 12:1
N shall not lift up sword ..... Mic 4:3
Me, even this whole *n* .... Mal 3:9
n will rise against .... Matt 24:7
for he loves our *n* .... Luke 7:5
N will rise against *n*, ... Luke 21:10
whole *n* should perish ... John 11:50
those who are not a *n* ..... Rom 10:19
royal priesthood, a holy *n* ... 1 Pet 2:9
tribe, tongue, and *n* .... Rev 13:7

NATIONS
Two *n* are in your womb .. Gen 25:23

itself among the *n* .... Num 23:9
shall lend to many *n* ..... Deut 28:12
Why do the *n* rage .... Ps 2:1
I will give You the *n* .... Ps 2:8
be exalted among the *n* .... Ps 46:10
n shall serve Him .... Ps 72:11
n shall call Him .... Ps 72:17
n shall fear the name ..... Ps 102:15
is high above all *n* .... Ps 113:4
All *n* before Him are .... Is 40:17
n who do not know .... Is 55:5
a house of prayer for all *n* ... Is 56:7
the wise men of the *n* ...... Jer 10:7
a reproach to the *n* .... Ezek 22:4
come to the Desire of All *N* .. Hag 2:7
n shall be joined .... Zech 2:11
speak peace to the *n* ...... Zech 9:10
For I will gather all the *n* .. Zech 14:2
disciples of all the *n* ..... Matt 28:19
in His name to all *n* ...... Luke 24:47
the father of many *n* ...... Rom 4:18
In you all the *n* shall be ...... Gal 3:8
who was to rule all *n* ...... Rev 12:5
For all the *n* have drunk of .. Rev 18:3
the healing of the *n* .... Rev 22:2

NATURAL
nor his *n* vigor abated ..... Deut 34:7
women exchanged the *n* ... Rom 1:26
the men, leaving the *n* .... Rom 1:27
did not spare the *n* .... Rom 11:21
n man does not receive .... 1 Cor 2:14
It is sown a *n* body .... 1 Cor 15:44
not first, but the *n* .... 1 Cor 15:46
his *n* face in a mirror ... James 1:23

NATURE
men with the same *n* ..... Acts 14:15
that the Divine *N* is .... Acts 17:29
for what is against *n* ...... Rom 1:26
by *n* do the things in ...... Rom 2:14
n itself teach you .... 1 Cor 11:14
We who are Jews by *n* ..... Gal 2:15
by *n* children of wrath ...... Eph 2:3
on fire the course of *n* .... James 3:6
man with a *n* like ours .. James 5:17
of the divine *n* .... 2 Pet 1:4

NAZARENE
Jesus to be called, Matt 2:23
Descriptive of Jesus' followers, Acts 24:5

NAZARETH
Town in Galilee; considered obscure, John 1:46
City of Jesus' parents, Matt 2:23
Early home of Jesus, Luke 2:39–51
Jesus rejected by, Luke 4:16–30

NEAPOLIS
Seaport of Philippi, Acts 16:11

NEAR
that has God so *n* to it ..... Deut 4:7
But the word is very *n* .... Deut 30:14
The LORD is *n* to all .... Ps 145:18
upon Him while He is *n* ...... Is 55:6
know that it is *n* .... Matt 24:33
kingdom of God is *n* ...... Luke 21:31
"The word is *n* .... Rom 10:8
to those who were *n* .... Eph 2:17
for the time is *n* .... Rev 1:3

NEARER
now our salvation is *n* .... Rom 13:11

NEBO
Babylonian god, Is 46:1
—— Summit of Pisgah; Moses dies here, Deut 32:49; 34:1, 5

NEBUCHADNEZZAR
Monarch of the Neo-Babylonian Empire (605–562 B.C.); carries Jews captive to Babylon, Dan 1:1–3
Crushes Jehoiachin's revolt, 2 Kin 24:10–17

Destroys Jerusalem; captures Zedekiah, Jer 39:5–8
Prophecies concerning, Is 14:4–27; Jer 21:7–10; 25:8, 9; 27:4–11; 32:28–36; 43:10–13; Ezek 26:7–12

NEBUZARADAN
Nebuchadnezzar's captain at siege of Jerusalem, 2 Kin 25:8–20
Protects Jeremiah, Jer 39:11–14

NECESSARY
mouth more than my *n* ..... Job 23:12
and thus it was *n* .... Luke 24:46
n that the word of God .... Acts 13:46
It is *n* to circumcise them, .. Acts 15:5
burden than these *n* ...... Acts 15:28
to be weaker are *n* .... 1 Cor 12:22
Therefore it is *n* that this .... Heb 8:3
Therefore it was *n* that the .. Heb 9:23
I found it *n* to write .... Jude 3

NECESSITIES
have provided for my *n* ... Acts 20:34
and again for my *n* .... Phil 4:16

NECESSITY
n is laid upon me .... 1 Cor 9:16
not grudgingly or of *n* ..... 2 Cor 9:7
there must also of *n* be the .. Heb 9:16

NECK
smooth part of his *n* .... Gen 27:16
wept on his *n* a good ...... Gen 46:29
bind them around your *n*, ... Prov 3:3
and grace to your *n* .... Prov 3:22
and hardens his *n* .... Prov 29:1
Your *n* is like an ivory ..... Song 7:4
and his yoke from your *n* .... Is 10:27
n was an iron sinew .... Is 48:4
were hung around his *n* .... Matt 18:6
ran and fell on his *n* ..... Luke 15:20

NECKS
stiffened their *n* .... Neh 9:29
with outstretched *n* .... Is 3:16
who risked their own *n* .... Rom 16:4

NEED
in nakedness, and in *n* .... Deut 28:48
a prowler, and your *n* ..... Prov 24:34
the things you have *n* ...... Matt 6:8
no *n* of a physician .... Matt 9:12
'The Lord has *n* .... Matt 21:3
did when he was in *n* ..... Mark 2:25
say, 'The Lord has *n* of it .. Mark 11:3
testimony do we *n* .... Luke 22:71
all, as anyone had *n* ...... Acts 2:45
each as anyone had *n* ..... Acts 4:35
hand, "I have no *n* .... 1 Cor 12:21
who ministered to my *n* .... Phil 2:25
to abound and to suffer *n* ... Phil 4:12
supply all your *n* .... Phil 4:19
not *n* to be ashamed ...... 2 Tim 2:15
to help in time of *n* .... Heb 4:16
you *n* someone to teach ... Heb 5:12
do not *n* that anyone .... 1 John 2:27
sees his brother in *n* .... 1 John 3:17
The city had no *n* .... Rev 21:23

NEEDY
your poor and your *n* .... Deut 15:11
They push the *n* .... Job 24:4
n shall not always be ...... Ps 9:18
He will deliver the *n* ...... Ps 72:12
and lifts the *n* .... Ps 113:7
Him has mercy on the *n* .. Prov 14:31
out her hands to the *n* ... Prov 31:20
to rob the *n* of .... Is 10:2
n will lie down in .... Is 14:30
a strength to the *n* .... Is 25:4

NEGLECT
n the gift that is .... 1 Tim 4:14
if we *n* so great a .... Heb 2:3

NEGLECTED
n the weightier .... Matt 23:23
their widows were *n* .... Acts 6:1

NEHEMIAH
Jewish cupbearer to King Artaxerxes; prays for restoration of Jerusalem, Neh 1:4–11

King commissions him to rebuild walls, Neh 2:1–8

Overcomes opposition and accomplishes rebuilding, Neh 4—6

Appointed governor, Neh 5:14

Participates with Ezra in restored worship, Neh 8—10

Registers the people and the priests and Levites, Neh 11:1—12:26

Dedicates the wall, Neh 12:27–43

Returns to Jerusalem after absence and institutes reforms, Neh 13:4–31

NEIGHBOR
See LOVE YOUR NEIGHBOR

every man ask from his *n* .... Ex 11:2
witness against your *n* .... Ex 20:16
you shall love your *n* ...... Lev 19:18
witness against your *n* .... Deut 5:20
secretly slanders his *n* ...... Ps 101:5
Do not say to your, *n*, "Go .. Prov 3:28
He who despises his *n* .... Prov 14:21
against your *n* without .... Prov 24:28
for better is a *n* .... Prov 27:10
every man teach his *n* ...... Jer 31:34
gives drink to his *n* .... Hab 2:15
man the truth to his *n* ..... Zech 8:16
'You shall love your *n* ...... Matt 5:43
love your *n* as yourself .... Matt 22:39
"And who is my *n* .... Luke 10:29
do you think was *n* .... Luke 10:36
"You shall love your *n* ..... Rom 13:9
love your *n* as yourself .... Gal 5:14
of them shall teach his *n* .... Heb 8:11

NEIGHBOR'S
shall not covet your *n* wife .. Ex 20:17
n garment as a pledge ..... Ex 22:26
or anything that is your *n* .. Deut 5:21
remove your *n* landmark .. Deut 19:14
goes in to his *n* wife .... Prov 6:29

NEIGHBORS
from all your *n* .... 2 Kin 4:3
Who speak peace to their *n* .. Ps 28:3
a reproach to our *n* .... Ps 44:13
return to our *n* sevenfold .... Ps 79:12
nor your rich *n* .... Luke 14:12
Therefore the *n* and those ... John 9:8

NEST
As an eagle stirs up its *n* .. Deut 32:11
and make its *n* .... Job 39:27
n is a man who wanders ... Prov 27:8
though you set your *n* .... Obad 4
that he may set his *n* .... Hab 2:9
and *n* in its branches ..... Matt 13:32

NET
me with His *n* .... Job 19:6
pluck my feet out of the *n* ... Ps 25:15
have hidden their *n* .... Ps 35:7
They have prepared a *n* ..... Ps 57:6
an antelope in a *n* .... Is 51:20
catch in their *n* .... Hab 1:15
casting a *n* into the sea .... Matt 4:18
I will let down the *n* .... Luke 5:5
to them, "Cast the *n* .... John 21:6
so many, the *n* was not ... John 21:11

NETHINIM
Servants of the Levites, Ezra 8:20
Possible origins of:
Gibeonites, Josh 9:23–27
Solomon's forced laborers, 1 Kin 9:20, 21
Mentioned, 1 Chr 9:2; Ezra 2:43–54; 7:24; 8:17; Neh 3:31; 7:46–60, 73; 10:28, 29; 11:21

NETS
fall into their own *n* .... Ps 141:10

---

immediately left their *n* .... Matt 4:20
down your *n* for a catch .... Luke 5:4

NEVER
in Me shall *n* thirst .... John 6:35
in Me shall *n* die .... John 11:26
Love *n* fails .... 1 Cor 13:8
n take away sins .... Heb 10:11
"I will *n* leave you .... Heb 13:5
prophecy *n* came by ...... 2 Pet 1:21

NEW
Now there arose a *n* .... Ex 1:8
the LORD creates a *n* ...... Num 16:30
man has taken a *n* wife .... Deut 24:5
They chose *n* gods .... Judg 5:8
him with two *n* ropes .... Judg 15:13
ark of God on a *n* cart .... 2 Sam 6:3
He has put a *n* song in my ... Ps 40:3
sing to the LORD a *n* song..... Ps 96:1
will overflow with *n* wine .. Prov 3:10
and there is nothing *n* ...... Eccl 1:9
Behold, I will do a *n* .... Is 43:19
shall be called by a *n* name ... Is 62:2
For behold, I create *n* ...... Is 65:17
when I will make a *n* ...... Jer 31:31
n every morning .... Lam 3:23
I will give you a *n* heart .. Ezek 36:26
shall overflow with *n* wine .. Joel 2:24
wine into *n* wineskins ..... Matt 9:17
of the *n* covenant .... Matt 26:28
laid it in his *n* tomb ..... Matt 27:60
speak with *n* tongues .... Mark 16:17
n commandment I give ... John 13:34
tell or to hear some *n* ..... Acts 17:21
he is a *n* creation .... 2 Cor 5:17
n man who is renewed ...... Col 3:10
when I will make a *n* .... Heb 8:8
Mediator of the *n* covenant .. Heb 9:15
n heavens and a *n* .... 2 Pet 3:13
n commandment I write ... 1 John 2:8
n name written which ...... Rev 2:17
the N Jerusalem, which .... Rev 3:12
And they sang a *n* .... Rev 5:9
And I saw a *n* heaven ...... Rev 21:1
I make all things *n* .... Rev 21:5

NEW COVENANT
I will make a *n* with .... Jer 31:31
this is My blood of the *n* .. Matt 26:28
"This cup is the *n* in ..... Luke 22:20
"This cup is the *n* .... 1 Cor 11:25
as ministers of the *n* ...... 2 Cor 3:6
"when I will make a *n* ...... Heb 8:8
Mediator of the *n* .... Heb 9:15
the Mediator of the *n* ...... Heb 12:24

NEW MAN
create in Himself one *n* ..... Eph 2:15
that you put on the *n* ...... Eph 4:24
and have put on the *n* ...... Col 3:10

NEWNESS
also should walk in *n* ...... Rom 6:4
should serve in the *n* ...... Rom 7:6

NEWS
heard this bad *n* .... Ex 33:4
Proclaim the good *n* of His ... Ps 96:2
soul, so is good *n* .... Prov 25:25
him who brings good *n* ...... Is 52:7
n of Him went out .... Luke 4:14
good *n* of your faith ...... 1 Thess 3:6

NICANOR
One of the first seven deacons, Acts 6:1–5

NICODEMUS
Pharisee; converses with Jesus, John 3:1–12

Protests unfairness of Christ's trial, John 7:50–52

Brings gifts to anoint Christ's body, John 19:39, 40

NICOLAITANS
Group teaching moral laxity, Rev 2:6–15

NICOLAS
One of the first seven deacons, Acts 6:5

NIGHT
darkness He called N .... Gen 1:5
day and *n* shall not cease .. Gen 8:22
father drink wine that *n* .. Gen 19:33
It is a *n* of solemn .... Ex 12:42
pillar of fire by *n* .... Ex 13:22
strong east wind all that *n* .. Ex 14:21
came to Balaam at *n* ...... Num 22:20
meditate in it day and *n* .... Josh 1:8
and the *n* be ended .... Job 7:4
gives songs in the *n* ...... Job 35:10
law he meditates day and *n* .. Ps 1:2
instructs me in the *n* seasons .. Ps 16:7
n reveals knowledge .... Ps 19:2
Weeping may endure for a *n* .. Ps 30:5
be afraid of the terror by *n* .. Ps 91:5
Your faithfulness every *n* .... Ps 92:2
awake through the *n* ...... Ps 119:148
and stars to rule by *n* ..... Ps 136:9
the *n* shines as the day ..... Ps 139:12
rises while it is yet *n* ..... Prov 31:15
Watchman, what of the *n* ... Is 21:11
desired You in the *n* .... Is 26:9
and perished in a *n* .... Jon 4:10
Child and His mother by *n* .. Matt 2:14
His disciples come by *n* ... Matt 27:64
over their flock by *n* .... Luke 2:8
and continued all *n* .... Luke 6:12
man came to Jesus by *n* .... John 3:2
n is coming when no .... John 9:4
came to Jesus by *n* ...... John 19:39
that *n* Peter was sleeping, .. Acts 12:6
stood by me this *n* .... Acts 27:23
The *n* is far spent .... Rom 13:12
as a thief in the *n* .... 1 Thess 5:2
We are not of the *n* ...... 1 Thess 5:5
they do not rest day or *n* .... Rev 4:8
before our God day and *n* .. Rev 12:10
there shall be no *n* .... Rev 21:25
there shall be no *n* .... Rev 22:5

NIGHTS
earth forty days and forty *n* .. Gen 7:4
forty days and forty *n* ...... Ex 24:18
forty days and forty *n* ...... Matt 4:2
three *n* in the belly of ..... Matt 12:40

NILE
Hebrew children drowned in, Ex 1:22
Moses hidden in, Ex 2:3–10
Water of, turned to blood, Ex 7:14–21
Mentioned in prophecies, Is 19:5–8; 23:3; 27:12; Jer 46:7–9; Amos 9:5

NIMROD
Ham's grandson, Gen 10:6–12

NINE
Adam lived were *n* hundred .. Gen 5:5
of Methuselah were *n* ...... Gen 5:27
where are the *n* .... Luke 17:17

NINETY-NINE
he not leave the *n* .... Matt 18:12
n just persons .... Luke 15:7

NINEVEH
Capital of Assyria, 2 Kin 19:36
Jonah preaches to; people repent, Jon 3:1–10; Matt 12:41
Prophecy against, Nah 2:13—3:19; Zeph 2:13–15

NOAH
Son of Lamech, Gen 5:28–32
Finds favor with God; commissioned to build the ark, Gen 6:8–22
Fills ark and survives flood, Gen 7
Leaves ark; builds altar; receives God's promise, Gen 8
God's covenant with, Gen 9:1–17
Blesses and curses his sons; dies, Gen 9:18–29

NO AMON (or Thebes)
Nineveh compared to, Nah 3:8

NOB
City of priests; David flees to, 1 Sam 21:1–9

Priests of, killed by Saul, 1 Sam 22:9–23

NOBLE
of the king's most *n* princes . Esth 6:9
I had planted you a *n* vine . . . Jer 2:21
heard the word with a *n* . . . Luke 8:15
most *n* Festus, but speak . . Acts 26:25
mighty, not many *n* . . . . . 1 Cor 1:26
whatever things are *n* . . . . . . Phil 4:8
not blaspheme that *n* . . . . . James 2:7

NOBLES
voice of *n* was hushed . . . . . Job 29:10
king is the son of *n* . . . . . . Eccl 10:17
n have sent their lads . . . . Jer 14:3
your *n* rest in the . . . . Nah 3:18

NOD
Place (east of Eden) of Cain's exile, Gen 4:16, 17

NOISE
There is a *n* of war in the . . . Ex 32:17
any *n* with your voice . . . . Josh 6:10
the *n* of a great army . . . . . . 2 Kin 7:6
Than the *n* of many waters . . . Ps 93:4
The *n* of a multitude . . . . Is 13:4
people who make a *n* . . . . Is 17:12
of Egypt, is but a *n* . . . . . . Jer 46:17
They have made a *n* . . . . Lam 2:7
the *n* of many waters . . . . . Ezek 1:24
the *n* of the wheels beside . Ezek 3:13
the *n* of your songs . . . . . . Amos 5:23
n of the day of the . . . . Zeph 1:14
away with a great *n* . . . . . . 2 Pet 3:10

NORTH
Zion on the sides of the *n* . . Ps 48:2
O *n* wind, and come . . . . Song 4:16
I will say to the *n*, 'Give . . . . . Is 43:6
Israel from the land of . . . . . Jer 16:15
Togarmah from the far *n* . . Ezek 38:6
place out of the far *n* . . . . Ezek 38:15
the west, from the *n* . . . . . Luke 13:29

NOSTRILS
n the breath of life . . . . Gen 2:7
breath of God in my *n* . . . . . Job 27:3
breath is in his *n* . . . . Is 2:22

NOTE
urge you, brethren, *n* . . . . . Rom 16:17
n those who so walk . . . . Phil 3:17

NOTHING
For now you are *n* . . . . Job 6:21
rich, yet has *n* . . . . Prov 13:7
"It is good for *n* . . . . Prov 20:14
before Him are as *n* . . . . Is 40:17
their works are *n* . . . . Is 41:29
I can of Myself do *n* . . . . . John 5:30
Me you can do *n* . . . . John 15:5
men, it will come to *n* . . . . . Acts 5:38
bring to *n* the things . . . . . 1 Cor 1:28
For I know of *n* against . . . . . 1 Cor 4:4
have not love, I am *n* . . . . . 1 Cor 13:2
love, it profits me *n* . . . . . . 1 Cor 13:3
Be anxious for *n* . . . . Phil 4:6
For we brought *n* . . . . 1 Tim 6:7
complete, lacking *n* . . . . . . James 1:4
name's sake, taking *n* . . . . . . 3 John 7

NOTORIOUS
n prisoner called . . . . Matt 27:16

NOURISHED
"I have *n* and . . . . Is 1:2
n and knit together . . . . Col 2:19
n in the words of . . . . 1 Tim 4:6

NOURISHES
n and cherishes it . . . . Eph 5:29

NOVICE
not a *n*, lest being . . . . 1 Tim 3:6

NUMBER
if a man could *n* . . . . Gen 13:16
fulfill the *n* of your days . . . . Ex 23:26
that I may know the *n* . . . . 2 Sam 24:2
and moved David to *n* . . . . 1 Chr 21:1
things without *n* . . . . Job 5:9
For now You *n* my steps . . . Job 14:16
n the clouds by wisdom . . . . Job 38:37
teach us to *n* our days . . . . . . Ps 90:12
He counts the *n* . . . . Ps 147:4
Me days without *n* . . . . Jer 2:32
in *n* about five thousand . . . . John 6:10
a great *n* believed and . . . . Acts 11:21
and increased in *n* daily . . . . Acts 16:5
which no one could *n* . . . . Rev 7:9
His *n* is 666 . . . . Rev 13:18

NUMBERED
David *n* the people . . . . . . 2 Sam 18:1
he had *n* the people . . . . . 2 Sam 24:10
are more than can be *n* . . . . . Ps 40:5
death, and He was *n* with . . . Is 53:12
God has *n* your kingdom . . . Dan 5:26
of your head are all *n* . . . . Matt 10:30
n among the twelve . . . . . . Luke 22:3
'And He was *n* with . . . . . . Luke 22:37
was *n* with the eleven . . . . . Acts 1:26

OAKS
Wail, O *o* of Bashan . . . . . Zech 11:2

OARSMEN
o brought you into . . . . . . Ezek 27:26

OATH
two of them swore an *o* . . Gen 21:31
the *o* which He swore to . . . . Deut 7:8
people feared the *o* . . . . . 1 Sam 14:26
Judah rejoiced at the *o* . . 2 Chr 15:15
o to walk in God's Law . . . Neh 10:29
for the sake of your *o* . . . . . Eccl 8:2
I may establish the *o* . . . . . . Jer 11:5
And you shall be an *o* . . . . . Jer 42:18
raised My hand in an *o* . . . Ezek 20:5
the *o* written in the Law . . . . Dan 9:11
he denied with an *o* . . . . . Matt 26:72
o which He swore . . . . Luke 1:73
themselves under an *o* . . . Acts 23:12
made priest without an *o* . . . Heb 7:20
or with any other *o* . . . . . James 5:12

OATHS
shall perform your *o* . . . . . Matt 5:33
because of the *o* . . . . Matt 14:9

OBADIAH
King Ahab's steward, 1 Kin 18:3–16
—— Prophet of Judah, Obad 1

OBED
Son of Boaz and Ruth, Ruth 4:17–22

OBED-EDOM
Philistine from Gath; ark of the Lord left in his house, 2 Sam 6:10–12; 1 Chr 13:13, 14

OBEDIENCE
scorns *o* to his mother . . . . Prov 30:17
and apostleship for *o* . . . . . Rom 1:5
o many will be made . . . . . . Rom 5:19
For your *o* has become . . . . Rom 16:19
glorify God for the *o* of . . . 2 Cor 9:13
captivity to the *o* . . . . 2 Cor 10:5
confidence in your *o* . . . . . Philem 21
yet He learned *o* . . . . Heb 5:8
for *o* and sprinkling . . . . . . 1 Pet 1:2

OBEDIENT
said we will do, and be *o* . . Ex 24:7
you are willing and *o* . . . . . . Is 1:19
of the priests were *o* . . . . . . Acts 6:7
make the Gentiles *o* . . . . . Rom 15:18

OBEY
bondservants, be *o* to . . . . . Eph 6:5
Himself and became *o* . . . . . Phil 2:8
homemakers, good, *o* . . . . . Titus 2:5
as *o* children . . . . 1 Pet 1:14

LORD, that I should *o* . . . . . . Ex 5:2
God and *o* His voice . . . . . Deut 4:30
o the commandments . . . . Deut 11:27
if you diligently *o* the . . . . . Deut 28:1
if you do not *o* the voice . . Deut 28:15
His voice we will *o* . . . . . . Josh 24:24
o is better than . . . . 1 Sam 15:22
they hear of me they *o* . . . . . Ps 18:44
O My voice, and I will be . . . Jer 7:23
O My voice, and do . . . . Jer 11:4
we will *o* the voice of the . . . Jer 42:6
shall serve and *o* Him . . . . . Dan 7:27
if you diligently *o* . . . . Zech 6:15
winds and the sea *o* Him . . Matt 8:27
spirits, and they *o* Him . . . . Mark 1:27
o God rather than men . . . . Acts 5:29
and do not *o* the truth . . . . . Rom 2:8
yourselves slaves to *o* . . . . Rom 6:16
o your parents in all . . . . . . Col 3:20
Bondservants, *o* in all . . . . . Col 3:22
on those who do not *o* . . . 2 Thess 1:8
salvation to all who *o* Him . . Heb 5:9
O those who rule . . . . Heb 13:17
mouths that they may *o* . . . James 3:3
if some do not *o* . . . . 1 Pet 3:1

OBEYED
Abraham *o* My voice . . . . . Gen 26:5
you have not *o* My voice . . . Judg 2:2
bondage anymore, they *o* . . Jer 34:10
of sin, yet you *o* . . . . Rom 6:17
they have not all *o* . . . . . . Rom 10:16
By faith Abraham *o* . . . . Heb 11:8
as Sarah *o* Abraham . . . . . . 1 Pet 3:6

OBEYING
o the truth through . . . . . . 1 Pet 1:22

OBSCURITY
shall see out of *o* . . . . Is 29:18

OBSERVANCE
the LORD, a solemn *o* . . . . . Ex 12:42

OBSERVATION
does not come with *o* . . . . Luke 17:20

OBSERVE
So you shall *o* the Feast of . Ex 12:17
to *o* the Sabbath . . . . Ex 31:16
which I teach you to *o* . . . . Deut 4:1
night, that you may *o* to do . Josh 1:8
man, and *o* the upright . . . . Ps 37:37
is wise will *o* these things . . Ps 107:43
and let your eyes *o* . . . . . . Prov 23:26
o mercy and justice . . . . . Hos 12:6
teaching them to *o* all . . . . Matt 28:20
who does not *o* the day . . . Rom 14:6
o days and months and . . . Gal 4:10
o your chaste conduct . . . . 1 Pet 3:2

OBSERVES
o the wind will not . . . . . . Eccl 11:4
He who *o* the day . . . . Rom 14:6

OBSERVING
o his natural face . . . . James 1:23

OBSESSED
nothing, but is *o* . . . . 1 Tim 6:4

OBSOLETE
Now what is becoming *o* . . . Heb 8:13

OBSTINATE
and made his heart *o* . . . . Deut 2:30
I knew that you were *o* . . . . . Is 48:4

OBTAIN
They shall *o* joy and . . . . . . Is 35:10
for they shall *o* mercy . . . . Matt 5:7
they also may *o* mercy . . . . Rom 11:31
way that you may *o* it . . . . 1 Cor 9:24
o salvation through . . . . . 1 Thess 5:9

o for themselves a good . . . 1 Tim 3:13
that they might o a better . . Heb 11:35
and covet and cannot o . . . . James 4:2

OBTAINED
Esther o favor in the sight . . Esth 2:15
o a part in this . . . . Acts 1:17
yet have now o mercy . . . . Rom 11:30
have o an inheritance . . . . Eph 1:11
He has by inheritance . . . . Heb 1:4
endured, he o the . . . . Heb 6:15
o eternal redemption . . . . . . Heb 9:12
o promises, stopped the . . Heb 11:33
To those who have o . . . . 2 Pet 1:1

OBTAINS
o favor from the LORD . . . . . Prov 8:35

ODED
Prophet of Samaria, 2 Chr 28:9–15

OF THE WORLD
men o who have . . . . Ps 17:14
their words to the end o . . . . . . Ps 19:4
the ends o shall remember . . Ps 22:27
all inhabitants o . . . . Ps 49:1
All inhabitants o . . . . Is 18:3
proclaimed to the end o . . . . Is 62:11
all the kingdoms o . . . . Matt 4:8
You are the light o . . . . Matt 5:14
from the foundation o . . . . Matt 13:35
since the beginning o . . . Matt 24:21
nations o seek after . . . . . . Luke 12:30
takes away the sin o . . . . . . John 1:29
The Christ, the Savior o . . . . John 4:42
give for the life o . . . . John 6:51
"I am the light o . . . . John 8:12
If you were o . . . . John 15:19
have given Me out o . . . . . . John 17:6
he would be the heir o . . . . Rom 4:13
is the reconciling o . . . . . . Rom 11:15
foolish things o to put . . . . . 1 Cor 1:27
not the spirit o . . . . 1 Cor 2:12
made as the filth o . . . . 1 Cor 4:13
cares about the things o . . . 1 Cor 7:33
sorrow o produces death . . 2 Cor 7:10
under the elements o . . . . Gal 4:3
before the foundation o . . . . . Eph 1:4
basic principles o . . . . Col 2:8
wants to be a friend o . . . . James 4:4
escaped the pollutions o . . 2 Pet 2:20
of the Father but is o . . . . . 1 John 2:16
sent the Son as Savior o . . 1 John 4:14
from the foundation o . . . . . . Rev 17:8

OF THIS WORLD
word, and the cares o . . . . . Matt 13:22
o, the deceitfulness . . . . Mark 4:19
sons o are more shrewd . . . Luke 16:8
You are o; I am not o . . . . . . John 8:23
he sees the light o . . . . John 11:9
Now is the judgment o . . . . John 12:31
for the ruler o is coming . . John 14:30
the ruler o is judged . . . . . . John 16:11
"My kingdom is not o . . . . . John 18:36
foolish the wisdom o . . . . . . 1 Cor 1:20
wisdom o is foolishness . . . 1 Cor 3:19
immoral people o . . . . 1 Cor 5:10
form o is passing away . . . . 1 Cor 7:31
according to the course o . . . . Eph 2:2
not chosen the poor o . . . . James 2:5
kingdoms o have become . . Rev 11:15

OFFEND
I will o no more . . . . Job 34:31
that devour him will o . . . . . . Jer 2:3
lest we o them . . . . Matt 17:27
than that he should o . . . . . Luke 17:2
them, "Does this o . . . . John 6:61

OFFENDED
How have I o you, that . . . . Gen 20:9
A brother o is harder . . . . . Prov 18:19
is not o because of Me . . . . Matt 11:6
So they were o at Him . . Matt 13:57
And then many will be o . . Matt 24:10

have I o in anything at all . . Acts 25:8
stumbles or is o . . . . Rom 14:21

OFFENDER
who make a man an o . . . . . . Is 29:21
For if I am an o . . . . Acts 25:11

OFFENSE
and a rock of o . . . . Is 8:14
You are an o to Me . . . . . . Matt 16:23
by whom the o comes . . . . . Matt 18:7
one man's o many died . . . . Rom 5:15
by the one man's o . . . . Rom 5:17
stone and rock of o . . . . Rom 9:33
Give no o, either to . . . . . . 1 Cor 10:32
the o of the cross . . . . Gal 5:11
sincere and without o . . . . . . Phil 1:10
and a rock of o . . . . 1 Pet 2:8

OFFENSES
For o must come . . . . Matt 18:7
impossible that no o . . . . Luke 17:1
up because of our o . . . . Rom 4:25

OFFER
and o him there as a burnt . . Gen 22:2
You shall not o strange . . . . . . Ex 30:9
o for a sweet aroma to the . . Lev 6:21
to o willingly to You . . . . . 1 Chr 29:17
o up for yourselves a burnt . . Job 42:8
Therefore I will o sacrifices . . . Ps 27:6
o to You the sacrifice . . . . . . Ps 116:17
o the blind as a . . . . Mal 1:8
come and o your gift . . . . . . Matt 5:24
one cheek, o the other . . . . . Luke 6:29
egg, will he o him a . . . . . Luke 11:12
to o up sacrifices, first for . . Heb 7:27
which they o continually . . . . Heb 10:1
let us continually o . . . . Heb 13:15
to o up spiritual sacrifices . . . 1 Pet 2:5

OFFERED
Jacob o a sacrifice on . . . Gen 31:54
eaten the same day it is o . . . Lev 7:15
o profane fire before the . . . Lev 10:1
Solomon o a thousand . . . . . 1 Kin 3:4
who willingly o a . . . . Ezra 3:5
he o them money, ... Acts 8:18
from things o to idols . . . . . Acts 15:29
to eat those things o . . . . . . 1 Cor 8:10
"This was o to idols," . . . . 1 Cor 10:28
when He o up Himself . . . . . Heb 7:27
the eternal Spirit o . . . . Heb 9:14
so Christ was o . . . . Heb 9:28
in them" (which are o . . . . . Heb 10:8
o one sacrifice . . . . Heb 10:12
By faith Abel o . . . . Heb 11:4

OFFERING
not respect Cain and his o . . . Gen 4:5
poured a drink o on it . . . . Gen 35:14
a freewill o to the LORD, all . . Ex 35:29
you shall bring your o . . . . . . Lev 1:2
This is the law of the sin o . . Lev 6:25
Do not respect their o . . . . Num 16:15
fifty men who were o . . . . . Num 16:35
he offered the burnt o . . . . 1 Sam 13:9
at the time of the o of . . . . 1 Kin 18:36
the o for the house of our . . Ezra 8:25
of God, with the grain o . . . Neh 13:9
o You did not require . . . . Ps 40:6
You make His soul an o . . . . . Is 53:10
they should present an o . . . Dan 2:46
drink o have been cut off . . . Joel 1:9
I accept an o from your . . . . Mal 1:10
to the LORD an o . . . . Mal 3:3
an o for your cleansing, . . . Luke 5:14
Himself for us, an o . . . . Eph 5:2
out as a drink o . . . . Phil 2:17
o You did not . . . . Heb 10:5
o of the body of Jesus . . . . Heb 10:10
o He has perfected . . . . Heb 10:14
is no longer an o . . . . Heb 10:18

OFFERINGS
and offered burnt o . . . . Gen 8:20
It is most holy of the o . . . . . . Lev 2:3

My food for My o made . . . . Num 28:2
on it burnt o to the LORD . . Josh 8:31
delight in burnt o . . . . 1 Sam 15:22
burnt o and peace o . . . . 2 Sam 24:25
heart brought burnt o . . . 2 Chr 29:31
He remember all your o . . . . . Ps 20:3
freewill o of my mouth . . . . Ps 119:108
enough of burnt o of rams . . . Is 1:11
In burnt o and . . . . Heb 10:6

OFFERS
Whoever o praise glorifies . . Ps 50:23
o sacrifices in the high . . . . Jer 48:35
that he o God service . . . . . John 16:2

OFFICE
He restored me to my o . . . Gen 41:13
let another take his o . . . . . . Ps 109:8
sitting at the tax o . . . . Matt 9:9
Levi, sitting at the tax o . . Luke 5:27
'Let another take his o . . . . . Acts 1:20

OFFICERS
appoint o over the land . . . . Gen 41:34
also make your o . . . . Is 60:17
the o struck Him with . . . . Mark 14:65
o answered, "No man . . . . . John 7:46
o saw Him, they cried . . . . . John 19:6

OFFSCOURING
You have made us an o . . . . Lam 3:45
the o of all things . . . . 1 Cor 4:13

OFFSPRING
You have given me no o . . . . Gen 15:3
also shown me your o . . . . . Gen 48:11
because of the o which . . . . Ruth 4:12
your o like the grass of the . . Job 5:25
My blessing on your o . . . . . . Is 44:3
He seeks godly o . . . . Mal 2:15
wife and raise up o . . . . . . Matt 22:24
had her and left no o . . . . . Mark 12:22
For we are also His o . . . . . Acts 17:28
we are the o of God . . . . . . Acts 17:29
am the Root and the O . . . . Rev 22:16

OFTEN
o I wanted to gather . . . . . . Luke 13:34
as o as you eat this . . . . . . 1 Cor 11:26
in sleeplessness o . . . . 2 Cor 11:27
should offer Himself o . . . . . Heb 9:25

OG
Amorite king of Bashan, Deut 3:1–13
Defeated and killed by Israel, Num
21:32–35

OHOLAH
Symbolic name of Samaria, Ezek 23:4,
5, 36

OIL
for the anointing o . . . . Ex 25:6
o to Me throughout your . . . . Ex 30:31
shall take the anointing o . . . Ex 29:21
anointing o on Aaron's . . . . Lev 8:12
land of olive o and honey . . . Deut 8:8
I cease giving my o . . . . Judg 9:9
a bin, and a little o . . . . . . 1 Kin 17:12
the jar of o run dry . . . . . . 1 Kin 17:16
So the o ceased . . . . 2 Kin 4:6
o to the storehouse . . . . . . Neh 13:12
poured out rivers of o . . . . . Job 29:6
You anoint my head with o . . Ps 23:5
anointed with fresh o . . . . . . Ps 92:10
the heart of man, o . . . . . . Ps 104:15
like the precious o . . . . Ps 133:2
be as excellent o . . . . Ps 141:5
the o of joy for mourning, . . . Is 61:3
and I anointed you with o . . Ezek 16:9
with new wine and o . . . . . . Joel 2:24
thousand rivers of o . . . . Mic 6:7
and took no o with them, . . Matt 25:3
the wise took o in their . . . . Matt 25:4
'Give us some of your o . . . Matt 25:8
very costly fragrant o . . . . . Matt 26:7
o might have been sold . . . Matt 26:9

costly *o* of spikenard ...... Mark 14:3
anoint My head with *o* ... Luke 7:46
wounds, pouring on *o* .... Luke 10:34
Why was this fragrant *o* ... John 12:5
anointing him with *o* ..... James 5:14
and do not harm the *o* .... Rev 6:6

OINTMENT
O and perfume delight ..... Prov 27:9
your name is *o* .... Song 1:3

OLD
was five hundred years *o* ... Gen 5:32
was ninety-nine years *o* ... Gen 17:1
who is ninety years *o* .... Gen 17:17
Remember the days of *o*, ... Deut 32:7
o lion perishes for lack ...... Job 4:11
So Job died, *o* and full of .. Job 42:17
young, and now am *o* ...... Ps 37:25
me off in the time of *o* age .... Ps 71:9
will utter dark sayings of *o* ... Ps 78:2
still bear fruit in *o* age ...... Ps 92:14
are the crown of *o* men .... Prov 17:6
and when he is *o* he will ... Prov 22:6
all manner, new and *o* .... Song 7:13
die one hundred years *o* ... Is 65:20
o men shall dream dreams .. Joel 2:28
was said to those of *o* ...... Matt 5:21
wine into *o* wineskins ...... Matt 9:17
He was twelve years *o* ..... Luke 2:42
man be born when he is *o* .. John 3:4
yet fifty years *o* .... John 8:57
but when you are *o* ...... John 21:18
Your *o* men shall dream .... Acts 2:17
o man was crucified .... Rom 6:6
of the *O* Testament .... 2 Cor 3:14
o things have passed .... 2 Cor 5:17
have put off the *o* man .... Col 3:9
o wives' fables, and .... 1 Tim 4:7
obsolete and growing *o* .... Heb 8:13
that serpent of *o* .... Rev 20:2

OLD MAN
the presence of an *o* .... Lev 19:32
there will not be an *o* ..... 1 Sam 2:31
nor an *o* who has not .... Is 65:20
I am an *o*, and my wife .... Luke 1:18
our *o* was crucified .... Rom 6:6
the *o* which grows corrupt . Eph 4:22
put off the *o* with his .... Col 3:9

OLDER
o shall serve the .... Gen 25:23
o than your father .... Job 15:10
"Now his *o* son was .... Luke 15:25
not rebuke an *o* man .... 1 Tim 5:1
o women as mothers .... 1 Tim 5:2
that the *o* men be sober, ... Titus 2:2
the *o* women likewise, that .. Titus 2:3

OLDEST
beginning with the *o* .... John 8:9

OLIVE
a freshly plucked *o* .... Gen 8:11
o trees which you did not .. Deut 6:11
a land of *o* groves .... 2 Kin 18:32
I am like a green *o* .... Ps 52:8
Your children like *o* plants .. Ps 128:3
of the *o* may fail .... Hab 3:17
the *o* tree have not yielded .. Hag 2:19
and you, being a wild *o* ... Rom 11:17
o tree which is wild ...... Rom 11:24
These are the two *o* trees ... Rev 11:4

OLIVES, MOUNT OF
David flees to, 2 Sam 15:30
Prophecy concerning, Zech 14:4
Christ's triumphal entry from, Matt
   21:1
Prophetic discourse delivered from,
   Matt 24:3
Christ's ascension from, Acts 1:9–12

OMNIPOTENT
For the Lord God *O* .... Rev 19:6

OMRI
Made king of Israel by army, 1 Kin
   16:16, 21, 22
Builds Samaria; reigns wickedly, 1 Kin
   16:23–27

ON
City of Lower Egypt; center of sun wor-
   ship, Gen 41:45, 50
Called Beth Shemesh, Jer 43:13

ONAN
Second son of Judah; slain for failure
   to give his brother an heir, Gen
   38:8–10

ONCE
please come at *o* .... Num 22:6
marched around the city *o* . Josh 6:14
o more with the fleece ..... Judg 6:39
God has spoken, twice I .... Ps 62:11
shall a nation be born at *o* .... Is 66:8
died, He died to sin *o* ...... Rom 6:10
alive *o* without the law ...... Rom 7:9
o I was stoned .... 2 Cor 11:25
o were far off have been .... Eph 2:13
who *o* was unprofitable ...... Philem 11
for this He did *o* for all .... Heb 7:27
Most Holy Place *o* for all ... Heb 9:12
for men to die *o* .... Heb 9:27
so Christ was offered *o* to ... Heb 9:28
who *o* were not a people ... 1 Pet 2:10
also suffered *o* .... 1 Pet 3:18

ONE
See EVIL ONE; HOLY ONE OF ISRAEL;
   LOVE ONE ANOTHER; WITH ONE
   ACCORD
He took *o* of his ribs, and ... Gen 2:21
they shall become *o* flesh .. Gen 2:24
desirable to make *o* wise .... Gen 3:6
o language and *o* speech .... Gen 11:1
our God, the LORD is *o* ...... Deut 6:4
Blessed be the *o* who ...... Ruth 2:19
on a mountain on *o* side .. 1 Sam 17:3
kissed *o* another .... 1 Sam 20:41
in two, and give half to *o* .. 1 Kin 3:25
failed *o* word of all His .... 1 Kin 8:56
I told no *o* what my God .... Neh 2:12
no *o* could withstand them, .. Esth 9:2
o who feared God and .... Job 1:1
o mocked by his friends, ... Job 12:4
find *o* wise man among .... Job 17:10
God may speak in *o* way .... Job 33:14
who does good, no, not *o* .... Ps 53:3
limited the Holy *O* of Israel .. Ps 78:41
Blessed is every *o* who ...... Ps 128:1
there is *o* who withholds .. Prov 11:24
flee when no *o* pursues .... Prov 28:1
Two are better than *o* ...... Eccl 4:9
up, my love, my fair *o* ..... Song 2:10
I will seek the *o* I love ...... Song 3:2
shall take hold of *o* man, ... Is 4:1
open, and no *o* shall shut ..... Is 22:22
you will be gathered *o* ...... Is 27:12
Return now every *o* from ... Jer 18:11
wings touched *o* another .... Ezek 1:9
Each *o* had four faces .... Ezek 10:21
o who is found written .... Dan 12:1
Holy *O* who is faithful ..... Hos 11:12
Has not *o* God created us ... Mal 2:10
deliver us from the evil *o* ... Matt 6:13
whoever causes *o* of .... Matt 18:6
two shall become *o* flesh" ... Matt 19:5
and hour no *o* knows ..... Matt 24:36
watch with Me *o* hour .... Matt 26:40
receives *o* of these .... Mark 9:37
"*O* thing you lack .... Mark 10:21
o on Your right hand .... Mark 10:37
Surely you are *o* of ...... Mark 14:70
The voice of *o* crying in .... Luke 3:4
No *o*, when he has lit a .... Luke 8:16
o thing is needed .... Luke 10:42
o sinner who repents ..... Luke 15:10

You still lack *o* thing ..... Luke 18:22
O sows and another .... John 4:37
Has no *o* condemned you ... John 8:10
I and My Father are *o* .... John 10:30
you love *o* another .... John 13:34
Me, that they may be *o* .... John 17:11
Not of His bones .... John 19:36
Holy *O* to see corruption ... Acts 2:27
o accord in the temple .... Acts 2:46
none righteous, no, not *o* ... Rom 3:10
each *o* a measure of faith .. Rom 12:3
Repay no *o* evil for evil ... Rom 12:17
Owe no *o* anything except . Rom 13:8
that *o* be found faithful ..... 1 Cor 4:2
to *o* is given the word ..... 1 Cor 12:8
body is not *o* member ..... 1 Cor 12:14
if *o* strikes you on the .... 2 Cor 11:20
for you are all *o* .... Gal 3:28
love serve *o* another .... Gal 5:13
Bear *o* another's burdens, ... Gal 6:2
to create in Himself *o* ...... Eph 2:15
o body and *o* Spirit .... Eph 4:4
o Lord, *o* faith, *o* .... Eph 4:5
o God and Father of .... Eph 4:6
but *o* thing I do, forgetting .. Phil 3:13
o Mediator between God ... 1 Tim 2:5
the husband of *o* wife ...... 1 Tim 3:2
Let no *o* despise your ..... 1 Tim 4:12
But each *o* is tempted .... James 1:14
love *o* another fervently ... 1 Pet 1:22
Be hospitable to *o* another .. 1 Pet 4:9
a thousand years as *o* ...... 2 Pet 3:8
and these three are *o* ..... 1 John 5:7
I will give to each *o* of you .. Rev 2:23
Lamb opened *o* of the seals .. Rev 6:1
on the cloud sat *O* like ..... Rev 14:14

ONESIMUS
Slave of Philemon converted by Paul
   in Rome, Philem 10–17
With Tychicus, carries Paul's letters to
   Colosse and to Philemon, Col 4:7–9

ONESIPHORUS
Ephesian Christian commended for his
   service, 2 Tim 1:16–18

ONLY BEGOTTEN SON
The *o*, who is in .... John 1:18
world that He gave His *o* .. John 3:16
offered up his *o* .... Heb 11:17
God has sent His *o* .... 1 John 4:9

OPEN
o his eyes that he may ..... 2 Kin 6:17
o the eyes of these men ... 2 Kin 6:20
o His lips against you .... Job 11:5
His ears are *o* to their cry ... Ps 34:15
You *o* Your hand .... Ps 104:28
O my eyes, that I may see .. Ps 119:18
O rebuke is better than .... Prov 27:5
O your mouth for the ..... Prov 31:8
and no one shall *o* .... Is 22:22
I will *o* your mouth to .... Ezek 29:21
o toward Jerusalem .... Dan 6:10
a lamb in *o* country .... Hos 4:16
o My mouth in parables ... Matt 13:35
Can a demon *o* the eyes ... John 10:21
she did not *o* the gate .... Acts 12:14
our heart is wide *o* .... 2 Cor 6:11
things are naked and *o* ...... Heb 4:13
set before you an *o* door .... Rev 3:8
o the scroll and to .... Rev 5:2

OPENED
eat of it your eyes will be *o* .. Gen 3:5
the earth *o* its mouth ..... Num 16:32
the LORD *o* the mouth .... Num 22:28
the LORD *o* the eyes .... 2 Kin 6:17
Ezra *o* the book in the sight .. Neh 8:5
o not His mouth .... Is 53:7
that the heavens were *o* .... Ezek 1:1
knock, and it will be *o* to .... Matt 7:7
our eyes may be *o* .... Matt 20:33
his ears were *o* .... Mark 7:35

when He had *o* the book ... Luke 4:17
Then their eyes were *o* .. Luke 24:31
o the Scriptures .... Luke 24:32
o their understanding ... Luke 24:45
clay and *o* his eyes .... John 9:14
Lord *o* the prison doors .. Acts 5:19
I see the heavens *o* and .... Acts 7:56
effective door has *o* .... 1 Cor 16:9
when the Lamb *o* .... Rev 6:1
he *o* the bottomless pit, and .. Rev 9:2
Now I saw heaven *o* ..... Rev 19:11
God, and books were *o* ...Rev 20:12

OPENLY
will Himself reward you *o* ... Matt 6:4
to the feast, not *o* .... John 7:10
o among the Jews, ... John 11:54
and showed Him *o* ...... Acts 10:40
They have beaten us *o*, ... Acts 16:37

OPENS
o the ears of men .... Job 33:16
The Lord *o* the eyes of ..... Ps 146:8
him the doorkeeper *o* ..... John 10:3
and shuts and no one *o* .... Rev 3:7
o the door, I will come in ... Rev 3:20

OPHEL
Hill, southeast of Jerusalem, Neh 3:15–27
Fortified by Manasseh, 2 Chr 27:3
Residence of Nethinim, Neh 3:26

OPHIR
Famous for gold, 1 Chr 29:4

OPHRAH
Town in Manasseh; home of Gideon, Judg 6:11, 15
Site of Gideon's burial, Judg 8:32

OPINION
dared not declare my *o* .... Job 32:6
be wise in your own *o* .... Rom 11:25

OPINIONS
falter between two *o* ..... 1 Kin 18:21

OPPORTUNITY
sought *o* to betray Him ... Matt 26:16
o to answer for himself ... Acts 25:16
But sin, taking *o* .... Rom 7:8
but give you *o* to boast .... 2 Cor 5:12
that I may cut off the *o* ... 2 Cor 11:12
liberty as an *o* for the flesh .. Gal 5:13
as we have *o* .... Gal 6:10
but you lacked *o* .... Phil 4:10
no *o* to the adversary ..... 1 Tim 5:14
they would have had *o* .... Heb 11:15

OPPOSES
who *o* and exalts .... 2 Thess 2:4

OPPOSITE
wrote *o* the lampstand on .... Dan 5:5
Go into the village *o* you ... Matt 21:2
Mary, sitting *o* the tomb .. Matt 27:61
Jesus sat *o* the treasury .. Mark 12:41
Gadarenes, which is *o* ..... Luke 8:26

OPPRESS
mistreat a stranger nor *o* ... Ex 22:21
you shall not *o* .... Lev 25:17
You that You should *o* ..... Job 10:3
He does not *o* .... Job 37:23
no more *o* My people ..... Ezek 45:8
he loves to *o* .... Hos 12:7
they *o* a man and his house, .. Mic 2:2
o the widow or the .... Zech 7:10
o them four hundred years .. Acts 7:6
Do not the rich *o* .... James 2:6

OPPRESSED
Whom have I *o* .... 1 Sam 12:3
For he has *o* and .... Job 20:19
fatherless and the *o* .... Ps 10:18
for all who are *o* .... Ps 103:6
The tears of the *o* .... Eccl 4:1
He was *o* and He was .... Is 53:7

her midst, and the *o* .... Amos 3:9
at liberty those who are *o* .. Luke 4:18
healing all who were *o* .... Acts 10:38
Lot, who was *o* by .... 2 Pet 2:7

OPPRESSES
o the poor reproaches ..... Prov 14:31
o the poor to increase ..... Prov 22:16
A poor man who *o* .... Prov 28:3

OPPRESSION
have surely seen the *o* .... Ex 3:7
"For the *o* of the .... Ps 12:5
Do not trust in *o* .... Ps 62:10
their life from *o* .... Ps 72:14
brought low through *o* ..... Ps 107:39
Redeem me from the *o* .. Ps 119:134
considered all the *o* .... Eccl 4:1
o destroys a wise .... Eccl 7:7
justice, but behold, *o* .... Is 5:7
surely seen the *o* .... Acts 7:34

OPPRESSIONS
of *o* they cry out .... Job 35:9

OPPRESSOR
the voice of the *o* .... Job 3:18
Do not envy the *o* .... Prov 3:31
is a great *o* .... Prov 28:16
of the fury of the *o* .... Is 51:13
No more shall an *o* .... Zech 9:8

OPPRESSORS
me from the hand of *o* ...... Job 6:23
not leave me to my *o* ..... Ps 119:121
o there is power .... Eccl 4:1
Lord because of the *o* .... Is 19:20

ORACLES
received the living *o* .... Acts 7:38
were committed the *o* ...... Rom 3:2
principles of the *o* .... Heb 5:12
let him speak as the *o* ..... 1 Pet 4:11

ORDAINED
infants You have *o* .... Ps 8:2
the stars, which You have *o* .. Ps 8:3
o you a prophet .... Jer 1:5
the Man whom He has *o* .. Acts 17:31
God *o* before the ages ...... 1 Cor 2:7

ORDER
in *o* that you may know ...... Ex 8:22
'Set your house in *o* .... 2 Kin 20:1
of the Lord was set in *o* .. 2 Chr 29:35
in *o* to seek the Lord...... Ezra 6:21
set your words in *o* .... Job 33:5
you, and set them in *o* ..... Ps 50:21
to the *o* of Melchizedek ..... Ps 110:4
in *o* to cleanse the land ... Ezek 39:12
swept, and put in *o* ...... Matt 12:44
it swept and put in *o* ..... Luke 11:25
done decently and in *o* ... 1 Cor 14:40
each one in his own *o* ... 1 Cor 15:23
to see your good *o* .... Col 2:5
according to the *o* .... Heb 5:6
in *o* to stir up love .... Heb 10:24

ORDERED
man did as Joseph *o* ...... Gen 43:17
for so the Lord has *o* .... 2 Sam 16:11
for so the king had *o* all ..... Esth 1:8
a good man are *o* by the .... Ps 37:23

ORDERS
o his conduct aright I .... Ps 50:23
as I have given *o* to the .... 1 Cor 16:1

ORDINANCE
the *o* of the Passover .... Ex 12:43
you shall keep My *o* .... Lev 18:30
an *o* forever throughout .... Num 10:8
o for Israel to this day ... 1 Sam 30:25
required by *o* for each day .. Ezra 3:4
forsake the *o* of their God ..... Is 58:2
that we have kept His *o* .... Mal 3:14
resists the *o* of God .... Rom 13:2
yourselves to every *o* ..... 1 Pet 2:13

ORDINANCES
shall you walk in their *o* .... Lev 18:3

o by the hand of Moses ... 2 Chr 33:8
and gave them just *o* ...... Neh 9:13
Do you know the *o* .... Job 38:33
according to Your *o* .... Ps 119:91
"If those *o* depart .... Jer 31:36
not appointed the *o* .... Jer 33:25
gone away from My *o* ...... Mal 3:7
contained in *o* .... Eph 2:15
and fleshly *o* imposed ..... Heb 9:10

ORION
Brilliant constellation, Job 9:9

ORNAMENT
will be a graceful *o* .... Prov 1:9
of gold and an *o* .... Prov 25:12
with them all as an *o* .... Is 49:18

ORNAMENTS
cheeks are lovely with *o* ... Song 1:10
a virgin forget her *o* .... Jer 2:32
I adorned you with *o*, put . Ezek 16:11

ORPAH
Ruth's sister-in-law, Ruth 1:4, 14

ORPHANS
We have become *o* .... Lam 5:3
I will not leave you *o* ..... John 14:18
to visit *o* and widows ..... James 1:27

OSNAPPER
Called "the great and noble," Ezra 4:10

OSTRICHES
o will dwell there .... Is 13:21
is cruel, like *o* .... Lam 4:3
a mourning like the *o* .... Mic 1:8

OTHNIEL
Son of Kenaz, Caleb's youngest brother, Judg 1:13
Captures Kirjath Sepher; receives Caleb's daughter as wife, Josh 15:15–17
First judge of Israel, Judg 3:9–11

OUGHT
what Israel *o* to do .... 1 Chr 12:32
These you *o* to have ...... Matt 23:23
pray for as we *o* .... Rom 8:26
how you *o* to conduct ..... 1 Tim 3:15
which they *o* not .... 1 Tim 5:13
persons *o* you to be .... 2 Pet 3:11

OUTCAST
they called you an *o* .... Jer 30:17
the lame, I will gather the *o* .. Mic 4:6
and the *o* a strong nation ... Mic 4:7

OUTCASTS
gathers together the *o* ...... Ps 147:2
will assemble the *o* .... Is 11:12
hide the *o*, do not betray ..... Is 16:3
Let My *o* dwell with .... Is 16:4

OUTCRY
because the *o* against ..... Gen 19:13
that there be no *o* .... Ps 144:14
Then there arose a loud *o* . Acts 23:9

OUTGOINGS
You make the *o* of the ...... Ps 65:8

OUTRAGE
lewdness and *o* in .... Judg 20:6

OUTRAN
the other disciple *o* .... John 20:4

OUTSIDE
and dish, that the *o* ...... Matt 23:26
Pharisees make the *o* ..... Luke 11:39
toward those who are *o* .... Col 4:5
to Him, *o* the camp .... Heb 13:13
But *o* are dogs and .... Rev 22:15

OUTSTRETCHED
power and by Your *o* arm . Deut 9:29
and with an *o* arm .... Deut 26:8
an *o* arm, Him you shall .. 2 Kin 17:36
against you with an *o* ...... Jer 21:5

OUTWARD
at the o appearance ...... 1 Sam 16:7
Even though our o man .. 2 Cor 4:16
to the o appearance .... 2 Cor 10:7
adornment be merely o ..... 1 Pet 3:3

OUTWARDLY
appear beautiful o .... Matt 23:27
not a Jew who is one o .... Rom 2:28

OUTWIT
The enemy shall not o ...... Ps 89:22

OVEN
make them as a fiery o ..... Ps 21:9
burning like an o .... Mal 4:1
is thrown into the o ...... Matt 6:30

OVERCAME
My throne, as I also o ..... Rev 3:21
And they o him by .... Rev 12:11

OVERCOME
we are well able to o it ... Num 13:30
for they have o me .... Song 6:5
to those who are o with wine .. Is 28:1
good cheer, I have o ..... John 16:33
o when You are judged ..... Rom 3:4
o evil with good .... Rom 12:21
entangled in them and o ... 2 Pet 2:20
because you have o ...... 1 John 2:13
and have o them, ... 1 John 4:4
that has o the world .... 1 John 5:4
and the Lamb will o ...... Rev 17:14

OVERCOMES
of God o the world .... 1 John 5:4
he who o the world ...... 1 John 5:5
o I will give to eat .... Rev 2:7
o shall not be hurt .... Rev 2:11
To him who o I will give ... Rev 2:17
He who o shall be clothed .... Rev 3:5
To him who o I will grant ... Rev 3:21
o shall inherit all .... Rev 21:7

OVERFLOW
Let not the floodwater o .... Ps 69:15
vats will o with new wine .. Prov 3:10
shall o with righteousness ... Is 10:22
rivers, they shall not o you ... Is 43:2
vats shall o with new wine .. Joel 2:24

OVERFLOWING
My heart is o with a .... Ps 45:1
a flood of mighty waters o ... Is 28:2
and shall be an o flood ..... Jer 47:2
But with an o flood He will .. Nah 1:8

OVERSEER
Then he made him o ...... Gen 39:4
having no captain, o .... Prov 6:7
to the Shepherd and O ..... 1 Pet 2:25

OVERSEERS
Spirit has made you o ..... Acts 20:28
you, serving as o .... 1 Pet 5:2

OVERSHADOW
of the Highest will o .... Luke 1:35

OVERTAKE
some evil o me and I die ... Gen 19:19
o you, because you obey ... Deut 28:2
upon you and o you ...... Deut 28:15
and o you, until you are ... Deut 28:45
lest he o us suddenly .... 2 Sam 15:14
does righteousness o ...... Is 59:9
you feared shall o .... Jer 42:16
lest darkness o you ...... John 12:35
and o this chariot .... Acts 8:29
that this Day should o ... 1 Thess 5:4

OVERTAKEN
and anguish have o me ... Ps 119:143
No temptation has o ..... 1 Cor 10:13
if a man is o in any .... Gal 6:1

OVERTHREW
So He o those cities ...... Gen 19:25
will be as when God o ...... Is 13:19

As God o Sodom and ...... Jer 50:40
"I o some of you .... Amos 4:11

OVERTHROW
you shall utterly o .... Ex 23:24
o them in the wilderness ... Ps 106:26
o their descendants .... Ps 106:27
o the righteous in .... Prov 18:5
As in the o of Sodom and ... Jer 49:18
o the throne of .... Hag 2:22
of God, you cannot o it ... Acts 5:39
o the faith of some .... 2 Tim 2:18

OVERTHROWN
Their judges are o .... Ps 141:6
but it is o by the mouth ... Prov 11:11
The wicked are o and are .. Prov 12:7
desolate, as o by strangers ..... Is 1:7
of Sodom, which was o ... Lam 4:6
I will make it o .... Ezek 21:27
and Nineveh shall be o ...... Jon 3:4

OVERTHROWS
and o the mighty .... Job 12:19
o them in the night .... Job 34:25
o the words of the .... Prov 22:12

OVERTURNED
my heart is o within ...... Lam 1:20
o the tables of the .... Matt 21:12
money and o the tables .... John 2:15

OVERWHELM
o the fatherless .... Job 6:27
sends them out, they o ... Job 12:15

OVERWHELMED
when my heart is o .... Ps 61:2
and my spirit was o .... Ps 77:3
o their enemies .... Ps 78:53
waters would have o .... Ps 124:4
my spirit is o within .... Ps 143:4

OVERWORK
Do not o to be rich .... Prov 23:4

OWE
Pay me what you o .... Matt 18:28
'How much do you o ..... Luke 16:5
O no one anything .... Rom 13:8
o me even your own ..... Philem 19

OWED
o him ten thousand ...... Matt 18:24
fellow servants who o .... Matt 18:28
o five hundred denarii .... Luke 7:41

OWN
created man in His o .... Gen 1:27
interpretation of his o ..... Gen 41:11
of his o people as wife ..... Lev 21:14
grasshoppers in our o ... Num 13:33
is right in his o eyes ...... Deut 12:8
each to his o inheritance .. Josh 24:28
a man after His o heart .. 1 Sam 13:14
loved him as his o soul ... 1 Sam 18:1
Your very o people ...... 2 Sam 7:24
Your o we have given .... 1 Chr 29:14
everyone to his o city ...... Ezra 2:1
reproach on their o heads .... Neh 4:4
wise in their o craftiness .... Job 5:13
He who swears to his o hurt .. Ps 15:4
Even my o familiar friend in .. Ps 41:9
on your o understanding .... Prov 3:5
not be wise in your o eyes ... Prov 3:7
troubles his o house ...... Prov 11:29
a fool is right in his o ..... Prov 12:15
a man are pure in his o .... Prov 16:2
wisdom loves his o soul ... Prov 19:8
no rule over his o spirit ... Prov 25:28
forsake your o friend ...... Prov 27:10
her o works praise her ... Prov 31:31
over another to his o hurt .... Eccl 8:9
the work of their o hands ...... Is 2:8
every one from his o fig ..... Is 36:16
dictates of their o heart ..... Jer 9:14
return upon your o head .... Obad 15
idols forsake their o Mercy .. Jon 2:8
men of his o household ..... Mic 7:6

the plank in your o eye ..... Matt 7:3
dead bury their o dead ..... Matt 8:22
and loses his o soul ...... Matt 16:26
honor except in his o ...... Mark 6:4
is known by its o fruit .... Luke 6:44
He came to His o .... John 1:11
not to do My o will .... John 6:38
I do not seek My o glory ... John 8:50
and am known by My o .. John 10:14
having loved His o .... John 13:1
world would love its o .... John 15:19
took her to his o home .... John 19:27
speak in his o language ..... Acts 2:6
by our o power or .... Acts 3:12
His o love toward us .... Rom 5:8
did not spare His o Son .... Rom 8:32
and you are not your o .... 1 Cor 6:19
But each one has his o ...... 1 Cor 7:7
ask their o husbands at .. 1 Cor 14:35
plucked out your o eyes ..... Gal 4:15
submit to your o husbands .. Eph 5:22
ought to love their o wives .. Eph 5:28
work out your o salvation .. Phil 2:12
For all seek their o .... Phil 2:21
who rules his o house ...... 1 Tim 3:4
but with His o blood He ... Heb 9:12
in His o body on the tree .. 1 Pet 2:24
but left their o abode ...... Jude 6
from our sins in His o ...... Rev 1:5

OX
shall not muzzle an o ..... Deut 25:4
"Will the wild o .... Job 39:9
you bind the wild o .... Job 39:10
like a young wild o .... Ps 29:6
exalted like a wild o .... Ps 92:10
o knows its owner .... Is 1:3
had the face of an o ...... Ezek 1:10
Sabbath loose his o ...... Luke 13:15
shall not muzzle an o ...... 1 Cor 9:9

PACE
are majestic in p .... Prov 30:29

PACIFIES
A gift in secret p .... Prov 21:14
for conciliation p .... Eccl 10:4

PADAN ARAM
Same as Mesopotamia, Gen 24:10; see
MESOPOTAMIA
Home of Isaac's wife, Gen 25:20
Jacob flees to, Gen 28:2–7
Jacob returns from, Gen 31:17, 18
People of, called Syrians, Gen 31:24
Language of, called Aramaic, 2 Kin
18:26

PAGAN
have taken p wives from ... Ezra 10:2
by marrying p women ..... Neh 13:27
have begotten p children ... Hos 5:7
priests with the p priests ... Zeph 1:4

PAID
today I have p my vows .... Prov 7:14
p the very last mite .... Luke 12:59
p tithes through Abraham .... Heb 7:9

PAILS
p are full of milk .... Job 21:24

PAIN
p you shall bring .... Gen 3:16
Because I bore him in p .... 1 Chr 4:9
on my affliction and my p ... Ps 25:18
p as a woman in .... Is 13:8
are filled with p .... Is 21:3
before her p came .... Is 66:7
Why is my p perpetual .... Jer 15:18
labor and in p to give birth .. Rev 12:2
shall be no more p .... Rev 21:4

PAINED
My heart is severely p .... Ps 55:4
I am p in my very .... Jer 4:19

PAINFUL
this, it was too p .... Ps 73:16
for the present, but p ... Heb 12:11

PAINS
The p of death .... Ps 116:3
having loosed the p ...... Acts 2:24
upon them, as labor p ... 1 Thess 5:3

PAINT
and she put p on her .... 2 Kin 9:30
your eyes with p .... Jer 4:30

PAINTING
it with cedar and p .... Jer 22:14

PALACE
support from the p .... Ezra 4:14
was taken to the king's p .... Esth 2:8
was great in the king's p .... Esth 9:4
enter the King's p .... Ps 45:15
a p of foreigners .... Is 25:2
to serve in the king's p .... Dan 1:4
the king went to his p ...... Dan 6:18
at the p of the high priest .. Matt 26:3
guards his own p .... Luke 11:21
evident to the whole p ..... Phil 1:13

PALACES
out of the ivory p .... Ps 45:8
God is in her p .... Ps 48:3
has entered our p .... Jer 9:21
has swallowed up all her p .. Lam 2:5
in the p at Ashdod .... Amos 3:9

PALANQUIN
the King made himself a p .. Song 3:9

PALE
his face now grow p .... Is 29:22
and all faces turned p ...... Jer 30:6
behold, a p horse .... Rev 6:8

PALM
of water and seventy p ..... Ex 15:27
p trees, and open flowers .. 1 Kin 6:29
of yours is like a p tree ..... Song 7:7
p branch and bulrush in ...... Is 9:14
p branch or bulrush, may .. Is 19:15
and p trees were carved .. Ezek 41:20
p trees and went out ...... John 12:13
p branches in their .... Rev 7:9

PALMS
you on the p of My hands .... Is 49:16
struck Him with the p .... Matt 26:67

PALTI (or Paltiel)
Man to whom Saul gives Michal, David's wife, in marriage, 1 Sam 25:44;
2 Sam 3:15

PAMPERS
p his servant from .... Prov 29:21

PAMPHYLIA
People from, at Pentecost, Acts 2:10
Paul visits; John Mark returns home
from, Acts 13:13; 15:38
Paul preaches in cities of, Acts 14:24,
25

PANGS
The p of death .... Ps 18:4
P and sorrows will .... Is 13:8
labors with birth p .... Rom 8:22

PANICKED
the men of Benjamin p .... Judg 20:41

PANT
They p after the dust .... Amos 2:7

PANTS
As the deer p for the .... Ps 42:1

PAPHOS
Paul blinds Elymas at, Acts 13:6–13

PAPYRUS
"Can the p grow up .... Job 8:11

PARABLE
open my mouth in a p .... Ps 78:2

speak a p to the house of .. Ezek 17:2
utter a p to the rebellious .. Ezek 24:3
p He did not speak .... Matt 13:34
learn this p from the fig ... Matt 24:32
spoken the p against ...... Mark 12:12
do You speak this p ...... Luke 12:41

PARABLES
'Does he not speak p ..... Ezek 20:49
understand all the p ...... Mark 4:13
rest it is given in p .... Luke 8:10

PARADE
love does not p .... 1 Cor 13:4

PARADISE
will be with Me in P ..... Luke 23:43
was caught up into P ...... 2 Cor 12:4
in the midst of the P .... Rev 2:7

PARALYTIC
then He said to the p ...... Matt 9:6
on which the p was lying .. Mark 2:4

PARALYZED
servant is lying at home p .. Matt 8:6
sick people, blind, lame, p .. John 5:3
who were p and lame ...... Acts 8:7

PARAN
Residence of exiled Ishmael, Gen 21:21
Israelites camp in, Num 10:12
Headquarters of spies, Num 13:3, 26
Site of David's refuge, 1 Sam 25:1

PARCHMENTS
especially the p .... 2 Tim 4:13

PARDON
p your transgressions .... Ex 23:21
You are God, ready to p .... Neh 9:17
not p my transgression ...... Job 7:21
O LORD, p my iniquity ...... Ps 25:11
He will abundantly p .... Is 55:7
p all their iniquities .... Jer 33:8

PARDONED
ended, that her iniquity is p ... Is 40:2

PARDONING
is a God like You, p .... Mic 7:18

PARENTS
will rise up against p ..... Matt 10:21
His p went to Jerusalem ... Luke 2:41
has left house or p .... Luke 18:29
sinned, this man or his p .... John 9:2
disobedient to p .... Rom 1:30
to lay up for the p .... 2 Cor 12:14
obey your p in all things, ... Col 3:20
disobedient to p .... 2 Tim 3:2

PARMENAS
One of the first seven deacons, Acts
6:5

PART
You have no p in the ..... Josh 22:25
has chosen that good p ... Luke 10:42
you, you have no p .... John 13:8
And he kept back p of the ... Acts 5:2
that blindness in p has .... Rom 11:25
to that p which lacks it, .. 1 Cor 12:24
For we know in p .... 1 Cor 13:9
p has a believer .... 2 Cor 6:15
Abraham gave a tenth p ..... Heb 7:2
shall take away his p ..... Rev 22:19

PARTAKE
for we all p of that .... 1 Cor 10:17
you cannot p of the ...... 1 Cor 10:21

PARTAKER
and have been a p .... Ps 50:18
in hope should be p ...... 1 Cor 9:10
Christ, and also a p .... 1 Pet 5:1

PARTAKERS
Gentiles have been p ..... Rom 15:27
of the sacrifices p .... 1 Cor 10:18
know that as you are p ..... 2 Cor 1:7
gospel, you all are p .... Phil 1:7

qualified us to be p .... Col 1:12
For we have become p ...... Heb 3:14

PARTED
them, that He was p ...... Luke 24:51
so sharp that they p .... Acts 15:39

PARTIAL
You shall not be p .... Lev 19:15

PARTIALITY
You shall not show p .... Deut 1:17
unjustly, and show p .... Ps 82:2
is not good to show p ..... Prov 18:5
but have shown p .... Mal 2:9
that God shows no p ..... Acts 10:34
For there is no p .... Rom 2:11
doing nothing with p ..... 1 Tim 5:21
but if you show p .... James 2:9
good fruits, without p .... James 3:17

PARTIES
revelries, drinking p .... 1 Pet 4:3

PARTING
at the p of the road ...... Ezek 21:21

PARTITION
the Testimony, and p .... Ex 40:3

PARTNER
Whoever is a p with a .... Prov 29:24
you count me as a p ...... Philem 17

PARTRIDGE
when one hunts a p ..... 1 Sam 26:20

PARTS
anything but death p ...... Ruth 1:17
in the inward p .... Ps 51:6
uttermost p of the sea ...... Ps 139:9
Shout, you lower p .... Is 44:23
and made four p .... John 19:23
but our presentable p .... 1 Cor 12:24
into the lower p .... Eph 4:9

PASHHUR
Official opposing Jeremiah, Jer 21:1;
38:1–13
—— Priest who puts Jeremiah in jail,
Jer 20:1–6

PASS
I will p over you .... Ex 12:13
of the sea that p .... Ps 8:8
When you p through the ...... Is 43:2
"I will make you p ...... Ezek 20:37
seven times shall p over .... Dan 4:32
I will not p by them .... Amos 7:8
and earth will p .... Matt 24:35
let this cup p from Me .... Matt 26:39
will by no means p .... Mark 13:31
p away with a great noise .. 2 Pet 3:10

PASSED
And behold, the LORD p .. 1 Kin 19:11
and Your waves p over me ... Jon 2:3
p by on the other side .... Luke 10:31
forbearance God had p ..... Rom 3:25
all p through the sea ...... 1 Cor 10:1
old things have p away ... 2 Cor 5:17
High Priest who has p ...... Heb 4:14
By faith they p through ... Heb 11:29
know that we have p ..... 1 John 3:14
former things have p away .. Rev 21:4

PASSES
For the wind p over it ...... Ps 103:16
of Christ which p .... Eph 3:19

PASSING
days are like a p shadow .... Ps 144:4
and p by, to bear His ..... Mark 15:21
Jesus of Nazareth was p .. Luke 18:37
which glory was p away, .. 2 Cor 3:7
the p pleasures of sin ..... Heb 11:25
the darkness is p away .... 1 John 2:8

PASSION
than to burn with p .. 1 Cor 7:9
uncleanness, p, evil .... Col 3:5

PASSIONS
gave them up to vile *p* ..... Rom 1:26

PASSOVER
It is the LORD's *P* .... Ex 12:11
of the Feast of the *P* be left .. Ex 34:25
at twilight the LORD's *P* ... Lev 23:5
the *P* at its appointed time .. Num 9:2
to the rite of the *P* and ..... Num 9:14
sacrifice the *P* at twilight ... Deut 16:6
the *P* on the fourteenth ..... Josh 5:10
of King Josiah this *P* .... 2 Kin 23:23
P in the second month ..... 2 Chr 30:2
of the slaughter of the *P*.. 2 Chr 30:17
Now Josiah kept a *P* to .... 2 Chr 35:1
the *P* lambs for all the ..... Ezra 6:20
you shall observe the *P* ... Ezek 45:21
I will keep the *P* .... Matt 26:18
P with My disciples ..... Mark 14:14
the *P* must be killed ...... Luke 22:7
Now the *P* of the Jews ..... John 2:13
Now the *P*, a feast of the .... John 6:4
P of the Jews was near ... John 11:55
six days before the *P* ..... John 12:1
that they might eat the *P* .. John 18:28
Preparation Day of the *P* . John 19:14
indeed Christ, our *P* .... 1 Cor 5:7
By faith he kept the *P* ..... Heb 11:28

PAST
My days are *p* .... Job 17:11
lo, the winter is *p* .... Song 2:11
harvest is *p*, the summer..... Jer 8:20
and His ways *p* finding .... Rom 11:33
resurrection is already *p* .. 2 Tim 2:18
ways spoke in time *p* .... Heb 1:1
p lifetime in doing .... 1 Pet 4:3

PASTORS
and some *p* and .... Eph 4:11

PASTURE
the sheep of Your *p* .... Ps 74:1
the people of His *p* .... Ps 95:7
feed them in good *p* ..... Ezek 34:14
in and out and find *p* ...... John 10:9

PASTURES
to lie down in green *p* .... Ps 23:2

PATARA
Port of Lycia where Paul changes ships,
Acts 21:1, 2

PATH
You enlarged my *p* .... 2 Sam 22:37
p no bird knows .... Job 28:7
You will show me the *p* ..... Ps 16:11
lead me in a smooth *p* ...... Ps 27:11
comprehend my *p* and my ... Ps 139:3
But the *p* of the just .... Prov 4:18
You weigh the *p* of the just ... Is 26:7
Him in the *p* of justice .... Is 40:14
way in the sea and a *p* ...... Is 43:16

PATHROS
Described as a lowly kingdom, Ezek
29:14–16
Refuge for dispersed Jews, Jer
44:1–15
Jews to be regathered from, Is 11:11

PATHS
He leads me in the *p* .... Ps 23:3
Teach me Your *p* .... Ps 25:4
and all her *p* are .... Prov 3:17
p they have not .... Is 42:16
themselves crooked *p* .... Is 59:8
Make His *p* straight .... Matt 3:3
and make straight *p* ...... Heb 12:13

PATIENCE
'Master, have *p* .... Matt 18:26
and bear fruit with *p* ...... Luke 8:15
p possess your souls ..... Luke 21:19
Now may the God of *p* ..... Rom 15:5
labor of love, and *p* ...... 1 Thess 1:3
faith, love, *p* .... 1 Tim 6:11

and *p* inherit the promises .. Heb 6:12
your faith produces *p* ...... James 1:3
p have its perfect .... James 1:4
of suffering and *p* .... James 5:10
in the kingdom and *p* .... Rev 1:9
Here is the *p* and the ..... Rev 13:10

PATIENT
rejoicing in hope, *p* .... Rom 12:12
uphold the weak, be *p* ... 1 Thess 5:14

PATIENTLY
the LORD, and wait *p* .... Ps 37:7
if you take it *p* .... 1 Pet 2:20

PATMOS
John, banished here, receives the Revelation, Rev 1:9

PATRIARCHS
begot the twelve *p* .... Acts 7:8

PATTERN
p which you were .... Ex 26:30
as you have us for a *p* ...... Phil 3:17
Hold fast the *p* .... 2 Tim 1:13
p shown you on the .... Heb 8:5

PAUL
Roman citizen from Tarsus; studied un-
der Gamaliel, Acts 22:3, 25–28
Originally called Saul; persecutes the
church, Acts 7:58; 8:1, 3; 9:1, 2
Converted on road to Damascus, Acts
9:3–19
Preaches in Damascus; escapes to Jeru-
salem and then to Tarsus, Acts
9:20–30
Ministers in Antioch; sent to Jerusa-
lem, Acts 11:25–30
First missionary journey, Acts 13; 14
Speaks for Gentiles at Jerusalem Coun-
cil, Acts 15:1–5, 12
Second missionary journey, Acts
15:36—18:22
Third missionary journey, Acts
18:23—21:14
Arrested in Jerusalem; defense before
Roman authorities, Acts 21:15—
26:32
Sent to Rome, Acts 27:1—28:31
His epistles, Rom; 1 and 2 Cor; Gal;
Eph; Phil; Col; 1 and 2 Thess; 1 and
2 Tim; Titus; Philem

PAULUS, SERGIUS
Roman proconsul of Cyprus, Acts
13:4, 7

PAVED
a *p* work of sapphire stone .. Ex 24:10

PAVEMENT
that is called The *P* .... John 19:13

PAVILION
shall hide me in His *p* .... Ps 27:5
them secretly in a *p* .... Ps 31:20

PAW
from the *p* of the lion .... 1 Sam 17:37

PAWS
He *p* in the valley .... Job 39:21

PAY
sell the oil and *p* your debt .. 2 Kin 4:7
p attention to my wisdom ... Prov 5:1
with which to *p* .... Prov 22:27
priests teach for *p* .... Mic 3:11
with me, and I will *p* ...... Matt 18:26
p taxes to Caesar .... Matt 22:17
For you *p* tithe of .... Matt 23:23
to *p* taxes to Caesar ..... Mark 12:14

PEACE
"These men are at *p* ...... Gen 34:21
sacrifice of the *p* offering ..... Lev 3:9
I will give *p* in the .... Lev 26:6
you, and give you *p* .... Num 6:26
Joshua made *p* with them .. Josh 9:15

had made *p* with Israel ..... Josh 10:1
'Make *p* with me by a .... 2 Kin 18:31
If you ever return in *p* .... 2 Chr 18:27
field shall be at *p* .... Job 5:23
both lie down in *p* .... Ps 4:8
seek *p* and pursue it .... Ps 34:14
for He will speak *p* .... Ps 85:8
p have those who .... Ps 119:165
I am for *p* .... Ps 120:7
for the *p* of Jerusalem ...... Ps 122:6
P be within your walls ...... Ps 122:7
P be upon Israel .... Ps 125:5
war, and a time of *p* ...... Eccl 3:8
Father, Prince of *P* .... Is 9:6
keep him in perfect *p* .... Is 26:3
p they have not .... Is 59:8
slightly, saying, '*P* .... Jer 6:14
"We looked for *p* .... Jer 8:15
give you assured *p* ...... Jer 14:13
they will seek *p* .... Ezek 7:25
My people, saying, '*P* .... Ezek 13:10
P be multiplied .... Dan 4:1
this One shall be *p* .... Mic 5:5
place I will give *p* .... Hag 2:9
speak *p* to the nations .... Zech 9:10
is worthy, let your *p* ..... Matt 10:13
that I came to bring *p* .... Matt 10:34
and on earth *p* .... Luke 2:14
if a son of *p* is there ...... Luke 10:6
that make for your *p* .... Luke 19:42
I leave with you, My *p* ... John 14:27
in Me you may have *p* ... John 16:33
Grace to you and *p* .... Rom 1:7
by faith, we have *p* .... Rom 5:1
minded is life and *p* .... Rom 8:6
of *p* will crush Satan ...... Rom 16:20
God has called us to *p* ..... 1 Cor 7:15
p will be with you .... 2 Cor 13:11
Spirit is love, joy, *p* .... Gal 5:22
He Himself is our *p* .... Eph 2:14
the Spirit in the bond of *p* ..... Eph 4:3
of the gospel of *p* .... Eph 6:15
and the *p* of God .... Phil 4:7
heaven, having made *p* ...... Col 1:20
And let the *p* of God ...... Col 3:15
Be at *p* among .... 1 Thess 5:13
faith, love, *p* .... 2 Tim 2:22
meaning "king of *p*," .... Heb 7:2
Pursue *p* with all people ... Heb 12:14
is sown in *p* by those ..... James 3:18
p be multiplied .... 2 Pet 1:2
it to take *p* from the earth .... Rev 6:4

PEACEABLE
and *p* life in all .... 1 Tim 2:2
is first pure, then *p* ...... James 3:17

PEACEABLY
Do you come *p* .... 1 Sam 16:4
p?" And he said, "*P*." ..... 1 Kin 2:13
speaks *p* to his neighbor ..... Jer 9:8
He shall enter *p*, even ..... Dan 11:24
on you, live *p* .... Rom 12:18

PEACEFUL
in a *p* habitation .... Is 32:18

PEACEMAKERS
Blessed are the *p* .... Matt 5:9

PEARL
had found one *p* .... Matt 13:46
gate was of one *p* .... Rev 21:21

PEARLS
nor cast your *p* .... Matt 7:6
hair or gold or *p* .... 1 Tim 2:9
gates were twelve *p* ...... Rev 21:21

PEG
wife, took a tent *p* .... Judg 4:21
will fasten him as a *p* ...... Is 22:23

PEKAH
Son of Remaliah; usurps Israel's
throne, 2 Kin 15:25–28
Forms alliance with Rezin of Syria
against Ahaz, Is 7:1–9

PEKAHIAH

Alliance defeated; captives returned,
2 Kin 16:5–9
Territory of, overrun by Tiglath-
Pileser, 2 Kin 15:29
Assassinated by Hoshea, 2 Kin 15:30

PEKAHIAH

Son of Menahem; king of Israel, 2 Kin
15:22–26
Assassinated by Pekah, 2 Kin 15:23–25

PEN

My tongue is the *p* .... Ps 45:1
on it with a man's *p* .... Is 8:1
to write to you with *p* ...... 3 John 13

PENNY

have paid the last *p* .... Matt 5:26

PENTECOST

P had fully come .... Acts 2:1
on the Day of *P* .... Acts 20:16
tarry in Ephesus until *P* ... 1 Cor 16:8

PENUEL

Place east of Jordan; site of Jacob's
wrestling with angel, Gen 32:24–31
Inhabitants of, slain by Gideon, Judg
8:8, 9, 17

PEOPLE

will take you as My *p* ...... Ex 6:7
Who is like you, a *p* ...... Deut 33:29
p shall be my *p* .... Ruth 1:16
p who know the joyful .... Ps 89:15
We are His *p* and the .... Ps 100:3
Happy are the *p* .... Ps 144:15
"Blessed is Egypt My *p* ... Is 19:25
this is a rebellious *p* .... Is 30:9
p who provoke Me .... Is 65:3
and they shall be My *p* ... Jer 24:7
Then they shall be My *p* .. Ezek 37:23
for you are not My *p* .... Hos 1:9
like *p*, like priest .... Hos 4:9
to make ready a *p* .... Luke 1:17
taught the *p* in the .... Luke 20:1
Unless you *p* see signs .... John 4:48
a great multitude of sick *p* .. John 5:3
all the *p* came to Him ...... John 8:2
man should die for the *p* .. John 11:50
favor with all the *p* .... Acts 2:47
were done among the *p* ... Acts 5:12
for they feared the *p*, lest ... Acts 5:26
and signs among the *p* ...... Acts 6:8
the *p* grew and multiplied .. Acts 7:17
of My *p* who are in Egypt .. Acts 7:34
astonished the *p* of .... Acts 8:9
a great many *p* were ...... Acts 11:24
take out of them a *p* ...... Acts 15:14
his defense to the *p* ...... Acts 19:33
of this *p* has grown dull ... Acts 28:27
who were not My *p* .... Rom 9:25
and contrary *p* .... Rom 10:21
His *p* whom He foreknew .. Rom 11:2
and they shall be My *p* ... 2 Cor 6:16
His own special *p* .... Titus 2:14
and they shall be My *p* .... Heb 8:10
Lord will judge His *p* ..... Heb 10:30
His own special *p* .... 1 Pet 2:9
but are now the *p* .... 1 Pet 2:10
tribe and tongue and *p* ..... Rev 5:9
tribe, tongue, and *p* ...... Rev 14:6
they shall be His *p* .... Rev 21:3

PEOPLE OF GOD

in the assembly of the *p* ... Judg 20:2
a thing against the *p* .... 2 Sam 14:13
a rest for the *p* .... Heb 4:9
affliction with the *p* ...... Heb 11:25
people but are now the *p* .. 1 Pet 2:10

PEOPLES

Let *p* serve you .... Gen 27:29
separated you from the *p* .. Lev 20:26
scatter you among all *p* ... Deut 28:64
His deeds among the *p* ... 1 Chr 16:8
The Lord shall judge the *p* .. Ps 7:8

clap your hands, all you *p* .... Ps 47:1
Let all the *p* praise You .... Ps 67:5
of the earth and all *p* ...... Ps 148:11
lift up a banner for the *p* ... Is 62:10
customs of the *p* are futile ... Jer 10:3
to the *p* a pure language, .. Zeph 3:9
sow them among the *p* .... Zech 10:9
heavy stone for all *p* ..... Zech 12:3
will draw all *p* to Myself ... John 12:32

PEOR

Mountain of Moab opposite Jericho,
Num 23:28
Israel's camp seen from, Num 24:2
—— Moabite god called Baal of Peor,
Num 25:3, 5, 18
Israelites punished for worship of, Num
31:16

PERCEIVE

given you a heart to *p* .... Deut 29:4
but I cannot *p* .... Job 23:8
seeing, but do not *p* .... Is 6:9
may see and not *p* ...... Mark 4:12
not yet *p* nor understand .. Mark 8:17
In truth I *p* that God ..... Acts 10:34

PERCEIVED

not heard nor *p* by the ear .... Is 64:4
Jesus *p* their wickedness .. Matt 22:18
when Jesus *p* in His spirit .. Mark 2:8
Jesus *p* their thoughts .... Luke 5:22
for I *p* power going out ... Luke 8:46
p the grace that had been .... Gal 2:9

PERDITION

except the son of *p* .... John 17:12
to them a proof of *p* .... Phil 1:28
revealed, the son of *p* .... 2 Thess 2:3
who draw back to *p* ...... Heb 10:39
day of judgment and *p* .... 2 Pet 3:7

PEREZ

One of Judah's twin sons by Tamar,
Gen 38:24–30

PERFECT

Noah was a just man, *p* .... Gen 6:9
His work is *p* .... Deut 32:4
Give a *p* lot .... 1 Sam 14:41
one who is *p* .... Job 36:4
for God, His way is *p* ...... Ps 18:30
The law of the Lord is *p*, ... Ps 19:7
I hate them with *p* hatred .. Ps 139:22
will keep him in *p* peace ..... Is 26:3
You were *p* in your .... Ezek 28:15
Father in heaven is *p* ..... Matt 5:48
"If you want to be *p* ..... Matt 19:21
they may be made *p* ..... John 17:23
and *p* will of God .... Rom 12:2
when that which is *p* ..... 1 Cor 13:10
is made *p* in weakness .... 2 Cor 12:9
present every man *p* ...... Col 1:28
the law made nothing *p* ... Heb 7:19
more *p* tabernacle .... Heb 9:11
of just men made *p* ...... Heb 12:23
patience have its *p* work ... James 1:4
good gift and every *p* ..... James 1:17
in word, he is a *p* .... James 3:2
p love casts out fear ..... 1 John 4:18

PERFECTED

third day I shall be *p* .... Luke 13:32
or am already *p* .... Phil 3:12
the Son who has been *p* .... Heb 7:28
the love of God is *p* ...... 1 John 2:5

PERFECTION

the *p* of beauty .... Ps 50:2
consummation of all *p* ... Ps 119:96
You were the seal of *p* ... Ezek 28:12
let us go on to *p* .... Heb 6:1

PERFORM

p the duty .... Ruth 3:13
p Your statutes .... Ps 119:112
am ready to *p* My word ..... Jer 1:12
he is obliged to *p* it ...... Matt 23:16

What sign will You *p* ...... John 6:30
how to *p* what is good ..... Rom 7:18

PERFORMED

They *p* His signs .... Ps 105:27
works are *p* by His hands .. Mark 6:2
John *p* no sign .... John 10:41
who *p* the service perfect in .. Heb 9:9

PERFUMER'S

putrefy the *p* ointment ..... Eccl 10:1

PERGA

Visited by Paul, Acts 13:13, 14; 14:25

PERGAMOS

Site of one of the seven churches, Rev
1:11
Special message to, Rev 2:12–17

PERIL

or nakedness, or *p* .... Rom 8:35

PERILOUS

from the *p* pestilence .... Ps 91:3
in the last days *p* .... 2 Tim 3:1

PERILS

journeys often, in *p* ...... 2 Cor 11:26

PERISH

"Surely we die, we *p* ..... Num 17:12
until you *p* from this ..... Josh 23:13
and if I *p*, I *p* .... Esth 4:16
Why did I not *p* .... Job 3:11
All flesh would *p* .... Job 34:15
way of the ungodly shall *p* ... Ps 1:6
He is like the beasts that *p* .. Ps 49:12
they *p* at the rebuke ...... Ps 80:16
very day his plans *p* ...... Ps 146:4
he who speaks lies shall *p* .. Prov 19:9
But those riches *p* through .. Eccl 5:14
they all will *p* together ...... Is 31:3
the remnant in Judah ...... Jer 40:15
so that we may not *p* .... Jon 1:6
one of your members *p* .... Matt 5:29
little ones should *p* ...... Matt 18:14
will *p* by the sword ...... Matt 26:52
will all likewise *p* ...... Luke 13:3
in Him should not *p* ...... John 3:16
they shall never *p* .... John 10:28
whole nation should *p* .... John 11:50
Your money *p* with you, ... Acts 8:20
will also *p* without law ..... Rom 2:12
shall the weak brother *p* ... 1 Cor 8:11
concern things which *p* ..... Col 2:22
among those who *p* ..... 2 Thess 2:10
They will *p*, ... Heb 1:11
that any should *p* .... 2 Pet 3:9

PERISHABLE

do it to obtain a *p* .... 1 Cor 9:25

PERISHED

p being innocent .... Job 4:7
Truth has *p* and has ...... Jer 7:28
The faithful man has *p* ..... Mic 7:2

PERISHES

The old lion *p* for lack of .... Job 4:11
The righteous *p*, ... Is 57:1
for the food which *p* ...... John 6:27
precious than gold that *p* .... 1 Pet 1:7

PERISHING

We are *p* .... Matt 8:25
to those who are *p* .... 2 Cor 4:3

PERIZZITES

One of seven Canaanite nations, Deut
7:1
Possessed Palestine in Abraham's time,
Gen 13:7
Jacob's fear of, Gen 34:30
Many of, slain by Judah, Judg 1:4, 5

PERJURER

p shall be expelled .... Zech 5:3

PERMIT

the Spirit did not *p* .... Acts 16:7
I do not *p* a woman ...... 1 Tim 2:12

PERMITS
you, if the Lord p .... 1 Cor 16:7
we will do if God p .... Heb 6:3

PERMITTED
p no one to do them ...... Ps 105:14

PERPETUAL
p incense before the LORD... Ex 30:8
It shall be a p statute for .. Num 19:21
Why is my pain p .... Jer 15:18
make it a p desolation .... Jer 25:12
saltpits, and a p desolation .. Zeph 2:9

PERPETUATED
Your name shall be p ...... Nah 1:14

PERPLEXED
at one another, p .... John 13:22
we are p .... 2 Cor 4:8

PERSECUTE
p me as God does .... Job 19:22
p me wrongfully .... Ps 119:86
when they revile and p ..... Matt 5:11
Bless those who p .... Rom 12:14

PERSECUTED
p the poor and needy ...... Ps 109:16
p the prophets who .... Matt 5:12
If they p Me............... Jn 15:20
p the church of God ...... 1 Cor 15:9
p, but not forsaken .... 2 Cor 4:9
p us now preaches the ...... Gal 1:23

PERSECUTES
wicked in his pride p .... Ps 10:2

PERSECUTION
p arises because of .... Matt 13:21
At that time a great p ...... Acts 8:1
do I still suffer p .... Gal 5:11

PERSECUTIONS
and lands, with p .... Mark 10:30
in needs, in p .... 2 Cor 12:10
p, afflictions, which .... 2 Tim 3:11

PERSECUTOR
a blasphemer, a p .... 1 Tim 1:13

PERSECUTORS
Deliver me from my p, for ... Ps 142:6
vengeance for me on my p .. Jer 15:15
all her p overtake her in ..... Lam 1:3

PERSEVERANCE
tribulation produces p .... Rom 5:3
to this end will all p ...... Eph 6:18
longsuffering, love, p ..... 2 Tim 3:10
heard of the p of Job ..... James 5:11
to self-control p .... 2 Pet 1:6

PERSEVERE
kept My command to p ..... Rev 3:10

PERSISTENCE
p he will rise and .... Luke 11:8

PERSON
In whose eyes a vile p .... Ps 15:4
p will suffer hunger ...... Prov 19:15
do not regard the p ...... Matt 22:16
One p esteems one day .... Rom 14:5
to eat with such a p .... 1 Cor 5:11
no fornicator, unclean p .... Eph 5:5
that such a p is warped .... Titus 3:11
express image of His p ..... Heb 1:3
let it be the hidden p .... 1 Pet 3:4
by whom a p is overcome .. 2 Pet 2:19

PERSUADE
Who will p Ahab to ..... 1 Kin 22:20
"You almost p me .... Acts 26:28
the Lord, we p men ...... 2 Cor 5:11
For do I now p men .... Gal 1:10

PERSUADED
a ruler is p .... Prov 25:15
neither will they be p .... Luke 16:31
p that He is able .... 2 Tim 1:12

PERSUASIVE
p words of human .... 1 Cor 2:4
you with p words .... Col 2:4

PERTAINING
Priest in things p .... Heb 2:17
for men in things p .... Heb 5:1

PERTURBED
things the earth is p ..... Prov 30:21

PERVERSE
your way is p .... Num 22:32
for the p person is an ..... Prov 3:32
p lips far from you .... Prov 4:24
p heart will be .... Prov 12:8
p man sows strife .... Prov 16:28
but he who is p .... Prov 28:18
from this p generation .... Acts 2:40

PERVERSITY
in oppression and p .... Is 30:12

PERVERT
You shall not p .... Deut 16:19
and p all equity .... Mic 3:9
p the gospel of Christ .... Gal 1:7

PERVERTING
We found this fellow p .... Luke 23:2
will you not cease p ...... Acts 13:10

PERVERTS
p the words of the .... Ex 23:8
p his ways will become .... Prov 10:9

PESTILENCE
from the perilous p .... Ps 91:3
p that walks in .... Ps 91:6
Before Him went p .... Hab 3:5

PESTILENCES
will be famines, p .... Matt 24:7

PETER
Fisherman; called to discipleship, Matt 4:18–20; John 1:40–42
Called as apostle, Matt 10:2–4
Walks on water, Matt 14:28–33
Confesses Christ's deity, Matt 16:13–19
Rebuked by Christ, Matt 16:21–23
Witnesses transfiguration, Matt 17:1–8; 2 Pet 1:16–18
Denies Christ three times, Matt 26:69–75
Commissioned to feed Christ's sheep, John 21:15–17
Leads disciples, Acts 1:15–26
Preaches at Pentecost, Acts 2:1–41
Performs miracles, Acts 3:1–11; 5:14–16; 9:32–43
Called to minister to Gentiles, Acts 10
Defends his visit to Gentiles, Acts 11:1–18
Imprisoned and delivered, Acts 12:3–19
Speaks at Jerusalem Council, Acts 15:7–14
Writes epistles, 1 Pet 1:1; 2 Pet 1:1

PETITION
of Israel grant your p ..... 1 Sam 1:17
What is your p .... Esth 5:6
present your p before Him ... Jer 42:9
makes his p three times .... Dan 6:13

PETITIONS
fulfill all your p .... Ps 20:5
p that we have asked ..... 1 John 5:15

PHARAOH
Kings of Egypt, contemporaries of:
Abraham, Gen 12:15–20
Joseph, Gen 40; 41
Moses in Egypt, Ex 1:8–11
the Exodus, Ex 5—14
Solomon, 1 Kin 3:1; 11:17–20
Other Pharaohs, 1 Kin 14:25, 26; 2 Kin 17:4; 18:21; 19:9; 23:29; Jer 44:30

PHARISEE
"Blind P, first cleanse .... Matt 23:26
P who had invited Him .... Luke 7:39
P asked Him to dine ..... Luke 11:37
temple to pray, one a P .... Luke 18:10
P named Gamaliel ...... Acts 5:34
I am a P, the son of a P .... Acts 23:6
our religion I lived a P .... Acts 26:5
concerning the law, a P ..... Phil 3:5

PHARISEES
See SCRIBES AND PHARISEES
when he saw many of the P . Matt 3:7
when the P saw it, they .... Matt 9:11
we and the P fast often .... Matt 9:14
P said, "He casts out .... Matt 9:34
P saw it, they said to ...... Matt 12:2
P were offended when .... Matt 15:12
of the leaven of the P .... Matt 16:6
P also came to Him .... Matt 19:3
P heard His parables .... Matt 21:45
P went and plotted how .... Matt 22:15
P heard that He had ..... Matt 22:34
P gathered together to .... Matt 27:62
P came out and began to .. Mark 8:11
P and teachers of the law .. Luke 5:17
P and lawyers rejected .... Luke 7:30
you P make the outside ... Luke 11:39
"But woe to you P! For ... Luke 11:42
of the leaven of the P .... Luke 12:1
P came, saying to Him .... Luke 13:31
to the lawyers and P....... Luke 14:3
P and scribes murmured ... Luke 15:2
P, who were lovers of .... Luke 16:14
P when the kingdom of .... Luke 17:20
of the P named Nicodemus .. John 3:1
P heard the crowd .... John 7:32
P therefore said to Him .... John 8:13
P also asked him again .... John 9:15
went away to the P .... John 11:46
P had given a command .. John 11:57
because of the P they ..... John 12:42
of the P who believed .....Acts 15:5
Sadducees and the other P . Acts 23:6

PHILADELPHIA
City of Lydia in Asia Minor; church established here, Rev 1:11

PHILEMON
Christian at Colosse to whom Paul writes, Philem 1
Paul appeals to him to receive Onesimus, Philem 9–21

PHILETUS
False teacher, 2 Tim 2:17, 18

PHILIP
Son of Herod the Great, Matt 14:3
—— One of the twelve apostles, Matt 10:3
Brings Nathanael to Christ, John 1:43–48
Tested by Christ, John 6:5–7
Introduces Greeks to Christ, John 12:20–22
Gently rebuked by Christ, John 14:8–12
—— One of the first seven deacons, Acts 6:5
Called an evangelist, Acts 21:8
Preaches in Samaria, Acts 8:5–13
Leads the Ethiopian eunuch to Christ, Acts 8:26–40

PHILIPPI
City of Macedonia (named after Philip of Macedon); visited by Paul, Acts 16:12; 20:6
Paul writes letter to church of, Phil 1:1

PHILISTIA
The land of the Philistines, Gen 21:32, 34; Josh 13:2; Ps 60:8

PHILISTINES
Not attacked by Joshua, Josh 13:1–3

Left to test Israel, Judg 3:1–4
God delivers Israel to, as punishment,
Judg 10:6, 7
Israel delivered from, by Samson, Judg
13—16
Capture, then return the ark of the
Lord, 1 Sam 4—6
Wars and dealings with Saul and Da-
vid, 1 Sam 13:15—14:23; 17:1–52;
18:25–27; 21:10–15; 27:1—28:6;
29:1–11; 31:1–13; 2 Sam 5:17–25
Originally on the island of Caphtor, Jer
47:4
Prophecies concerning, Is 9:11, 12; Jer
25:15–20; 47:1–7; Ezek 25:15–17;
Zeph 2:4–6

PHILOSOPHERS
p encountered him . . . . Acts 17:18

PHILOSOPHY
cheat you through *p* . . . . Col 2:8

PHINEHAS
Aaron's grandson; executes God's
judgment, Num 25:1–18; Ps 106:30,
31
Settles dispute over memorial altar,
Josh 22:11–32
——— Younger son of Eli; abuses his of-
fice, 1 Sam 1:3; 2:12–17, 22–36
Killed by Philistines, 1 Sam 4:11, 17

PHOENICIA
Mediterranean coastal region includ-
ing the cities of Ptolemais, Tyre,
Zarephath and Sidon; evangelized
by early Christians, Acts 11:19
Jesus preaches here, Matt 15:21

PHRYGIA
Jews from, at Pentecost, Acts 2:1, 10
Visited twice by Paul, Acts 16:6

PHYLACTERIES
They make their *p* . . . . Matt 23:5

PHYSICIAN
Gilead, is there no *p* . . . . Jer 8:22
have no need of a *p* . . . . Matt 9:12
Luke the beloved *p* . . . . Col 4:14

PHYSICIANS
are all worthless *p* . . . . Job 13:4
her livelihood on . . . . Luke 8:43

PI HAHIROTH
Israel camps there before crossing the
Red Sea, Ex 14:2, 9; Num 33:7, 8

PICTURE
what parable shall we *p* . . . Mark 4:30

PIECE
placed each *p* opposite . . . . Gen 15:10
hammered *p* of pure gold . . Ex 25:36
one *p* with the mercy seat . . . . Ex 37:8
two legs or a *p* of an ear . . Amos 3:12
No one puts a *p* . . . . Matt 9:16
bought a *p* of ground . . . . . Luke 14:18
Him a *p* of a broiled fish . . Luke 24:42
from the top in one *p* . . . . . John 19:23

PIECES
for my wages thirty *p* . . . . Zech 11:12
they took the thirty *p* . . . . . Matt 27:9
shall be dashed to *p* . . . . . . Rev 2:27

PIERCE
and his master shall *p* . . . . . . Ex 21:6
a sword will *p* . . . . Luke 2:35

PIERCED
p My hands and My feet . . . . Ps 22:16
Me whom they have *p* . . . . Zech 12:10
of the soldiers *p* . . . . John 19:34
p themselves through . . . . . 1 Tim 6:10
and they also who *p* . . . . Rev 1:7

PIERCING
p even to the division . . . . . . Heb 4:12

PIETY
first learn to show *p* . . . . 1 Tim 5:4

PILATE, PONTIUS
Governor of Judea (A.D. 26–36), Luke
3:1
Questions Jesus and delivers Him to
Jews, Matt 27:2, 11–26; John
18:28—19:16

PILGRIMAGE
heart is set on *p* . . . . Ps 84:5
In the house of my *p* . . . . . Ps 119:54

PILGRIMS
we are aliens and *p* . . . . . 1 Chr 29:15
were strangers and *p* . . . . . Heb 11:13

PILLAR
and she became a *p* . . . . . Gen 19:26
where you anointed the *p* . . Gen 31:13
and by night in a *p* . . . . Ex 13:21
standing by a *p* . . . . 2 Kin 11:14
a *p* to the LORD . . . . Is 19:19
the living God, the *p* . . . . . 1 Tim 3:15
I will make him a *p* in the . . . Rev 3:12

PILLARS
break their sacred *p* . . . . . . Ex 34:13
between the *p* . . . . Judg 16:25
And he cast two *p* . . . . 1 Kin 7:15
bronze *p* that were in . . . . 2 Kin 25:13
I set up its *p* firmly . . . . Ps 75:3
out her seven *p* . . . . Prov 9:1
blood and fire and *p* . . . . . . Joel 2:30
who seemed to be *p* . . . . Gal 2:9
and his feet like *p* . . . . Rev 10:1

PILOT
rudder wherever the *p* . . . . James 3:4

PIM
p for the plowshares . . . . . 1 Sam 13:21

PINE
cypress tree and the *p* . . . . . Is 41:19
for these *p* away . . . . Lam 4:9

PINNACLE
set Him on the *p* . . . . Luke 4:9

PISGAH
Mountain in Moab where Balaam of-
fers sacrifice, Num 23:14
Moses views Promised Land from,
Deut 3:27
Site of Moses' death, Deut 34:1–7

PISHON
One of Eden's four rivers, Gen 2:10,
11

PISIDIA
Twice visited by Paul, Acts 13:13, 14;
14:24

PIT
See BOTTOMLESS PIT
cast him into some *p* . . . . . Gen 37:20
soul draws near the *P* . . . . . Job 33:22
who go down to the *p* . . . . . . Ps 28:1
woman is a deep *p* . . . . Prov 22:14
a harlot is a deep *p* . . . . . . Prov 23:27
fall into his own *p* . . . . Prov 28:10
my life in the *p* . . . . Lam 3:53
who descend into the *P* . . . Ezek 31:16
up my life from the *p* . . . . . . Jon 2:6
from the waterless *p* . . . . . . Zech 9:11
if it falls into a *p* . . . . Matt 12:11
ox that has fallen into a *p* . . Luke 14:5
the key to the bottomless *p* . . Rev 9:1
into the bottomless *p* . . . . . . Rev 20:3

PITCH
inside and outside with *p* . . . Gen 6:14
Israel would *p* their tents . . Num 9:17

PITCHER
her *p* on her shoulder . . . . Gen 24:15
or the *p* shattered at the . . . . Eccl 12:6
carrying a *p* of water . . . . Luke 22:10

PITCHERS
and torches inside the *p* . . . Judg 7:16
the *p* of pure gold . . . . 1 Chr 28:17
the washing of cups, *p* . . . . Mark 7:4

PITHOM
Egyptian city built by Hebrew slaves,
Ex 1:11

PITIABLE
of all men the most *p* . . . . . 1 Cor 15:19

PITS
The proud have dug *p* . . . . . Ps 119:85

PITY
eye shall have no *p* . . . . . . Deut 7:16
"Have *p* on me . . . . Job 19:21
for someone to take *p* . . . . . Ps 69:20
He who has *p* on the . . . . . . Prov 19:17
p He redeemed them . . . . Is 63:9
land, and *p* His people . . . . . Joel 2:18
And should I not *p* . . . . Jon 4:11
just as I had *p* . . . . Matt 18:33

PLACE
See HIGH PLACE; HOLY PLACE;
MOST HOLY PLACE
p know him anymore . . . . Job 7:10
All go to one *p* . . . . Eccl 3:20
return again to My *p* . . . . Hos 5:15
Come, see the *p* . . . . Matt 28:6
My word has no *p* . . . . John 8:37
I go to prepare a *p* . . . . John 14:2
might go to his own *p* . . . . . Acts 1:25

PLACES
See HIGH PLACES
set them in slippery *p* . . . . . Ps 73:18
dark *p* of the earth . . . . Ps 74:20
and the rough *p* . . . . Is 40:4
They love the best *p* . . . . . Matt 23:6
in the heavenly *p* . . . . Eph 1:3

PLAGUE
bring yet one more *p* . . . . . . Ex 11:1
with a very great *p* . . . . Num 11:33
those who died in the *p* . . . Num 25:9
three days' *p* in your . . . . 2 Sam 24:13
p come near your . . . . Ps 91:10
and the *p* was stopped . . . . Ps 106:30
And this shall be the *p* . . . Zech 14:12
because of the *p* of the . . . . Rev 16:21

PLAGUES
I will send all My *p* . . . . Ex 9:14
I will be your *p* . . . . Hos 13:14
p that are written . . . . Rev 22:18

PLAINLY
the Christ, tell us *p* . . . . . . John 10:24
now You are speaking *p* . . . John 16:29
such things declare *p* . . . . . Heb 11:14

PLAN
p evil things in their . . . . Ps 140:2
Let none of you *p* . . . . Zech 7:10
p according to the flesh . . . . 2 Cor 1:17

PLANK
First remove the *p* . . . . Matt 7:5

PLANS
He makes the *p* of the . . . . . Ps 33:10
in that very day his *p* . . . . . Ps 146:4
that devises wicked *p* . . . . . Prov 6:18
A man's heart *p* . . . . Prov 16:9
P are established . . . . Prov 20:18

PLANT
A time to *p* . . . . Eccl 3:2
Him as a tender *p* . . . . Is 53:2
they shall *p* vineyards . . . . . . Is 65:21
p of an alien vine . . . . Jer 2:21
the LORD God prepared a *p* . . Jon 4:6
p which My heavenly . . . . . Matt 15:13

PLANTED
The LORD God *p* a garden . . . Gen 2:8
and he *p* a vineyard . . . . . . Gen 9:20
Abraham *p* a tamarisk . . . . Gen 21:33

shall be like a tree *p* ....Ps 1:3
Your right hand has *p* ....Ps 80:15
p it with the choicest vine ......Is 5:2
shall they be *p* ....Is 40:24
like a tree *p* by the waters ...Is 17:8
by the roots and be *p* ......Luke 17:6
I *p*, Apollos watered ....1 Cor 3:6

PLANTS
our sons may be as *p* ......Ps 144:12
down its choice *p* ....Is 16:8
neither he who *p* ....1 Cor 3:7

PLASTERED
p with untempered ....Ezek 13:14
Her prophets *p* them ......Ezek 22:28

PLATFORM
scribe stood on a *p* ....Neh 8:4

PLATTER
head here on a *p* ....Matt 14:8

PLAY
and rose up to *p* ....Ex 32:6
p skillfully with a ....Ps 33:3
nursing child shall *p* ....Is 11:8
and rose up to *p* ....1 Cor 10:7

PLAYED
So David *p* music with ...1 Sam 18:10
We *p* the flute for you ....Matt 11:17

PLEAD
the one who would *p* ......Judg 6:31
Oh, that one might *p* ....Job 16:21
p my cause against an ....Ps 43:1
p with your friend ....Prov 6:3
Behold, I will *p* ....Jer 2:35
p His case with all ....Jer 25:31

PLEADED
Then Moses *p* with the ......Ex 32:11
this thing I *p* with ....2 Cor 12:8

PLEADING
though God were *p* ....2 Cor 5:20

PLEASANT
food, that it was *p* ....Gen 3:6
fallen to me in *p* places ....Ps 16:6
they despised the *p* ....Ps 106:24
how good and how *p* ......Ps 133:1
and knowledge is *p* ....Prov 2:10
words of the pure are *p* ..Prov 15:26
p words are like a ....Prov 16:24
p places of the ....Jer 23:10
Is he a *p* child ....Jer 31:20
I ate no *p* food ....Dan 10:3

PLEASANTNESS
Her ways are ways of *p* ....Prov 3:17

PLEASE
P say you are my sister, ...Gen 12:13
P, go in to my maid ....Gen 16:2
p let me escape there .....Gen 19:20
P come near, ...Gen 27:21
P hear this dream which I ...Gen 37:6
Now, *p*, forgive the ....Gen 50:17
P, let us go three days' .....Ex 5:3
P inquire of God, ...Judg 18:5
p pardon my sin, ...1 Sam 15:25
yet honor me now, *p*, ...1 Sam 15:30
P bring the ephod here ...1 Sam 30:7
P let my sister Tamar ....2 Sam 13:5
p let my brother ....2 Sam 13:26
When a man's ways *p* .....Prov 16:7
do those things that *p* .....John 8:29
in the flesh cannot *p* ......Rom 8:8
p his neighbor for his .....Rom 15:2
how he may *p* the Lord ...1 Cor 7:32
how he may *p* his wife ...1 Cor 7:33
may *p* her husband ......1 Cor 7:34
Or do I seek to *p* men ....Gal 1:10
is impossible to *p* Him ...Heb 11:6

PLEASED
and she *p* Samson well ...Judg 14:7
Then You shall be *p* ......Ps 51:19

The LORD is well *p*, ...Is 42:21
Yet it *p* the LORD to bruise ...Is 53:10
Would he be *p* with you ....Mal 1:8
in whom I am well *p* .....Matt 3:17
danced before them and *p* ..Matt 14:6
God was not well *p* ......1 Cor 10:5
But when it *p* God, who .....Gal 1:15
testimony, that he *p* ......Heb 11:5
in whom I am well *p* .....2 Pet 1:17

PLEASES
dwell where it *p* you ....Gen 20:15
He does whatever He *p* .....Ps 115:3
Whatever the LORD *p* ....Ps 135:6
who *p* God shall escape ....Eccl 7:26
nor awaken love until it *p* ..Song 2:7

PLEASING
sacrifice, well *p* ....Phil 4:18
for this is well *p* ....Col 3:20
in you what is well *p* ......Heb 13:21

PLEASURE
grown old, shall I have *p* ...Gen 18:12
not a God who takes *p* ....Ps 5:4
has *p* in the prosperity ....Ps 35:27
Do good in Your good *p* ....Ps 51:18
Your servants take *p* ......Ps 102:14
The LORD takes *p* in those ..Ps 147:11
p will be a poor man ......Prov 21:17
for He has no *p* ....Eccl 5:4
shall perform all My *p* ....Is 44:28
your fast you find *p* ....Is 58:3
nor finding your own *p* ......Is 58:13
Do I have any *p* ....Ezek 18:23
I have no *p* in you ....Mal 1:10
your Father's good *p* ....Luke 12:32
to the good *p* of His ....Eph 1:5
to do for His good *p* ......Phil 2:13
fulfill all the good *p* .....2 Thess 1:11
p is dead while ....1 Tim 5:6
for sin You had no *p* ....Heb 10:6
back, My soul has no *p* ...Heb 10:38
p that war in your ....James 4:1
on the earth in *p* ....James 5:5

PLEASURES
Your right hand are *p* ....Ps 16:11
cares, riches, and *p* ......Luke 8:14
to enjoy the passing *p* ....Heb 11:25
may spend it on your *p* ...James 4:3

PLEDGE
give me a *p* till you send ..Gen 38:17
hands in *p* for a stranger ....Prov 6:1
shakes hands in a *p*, and ..Prov 17:18
who shakes hands in a *p* ..Prov 22:26

PLEIADES
Part of God's creation, Job 9:9; Amos 5:8

PLENTIFUL
You, O God, sent a *p* ....Ps 68:9
The harvest truly is *p* ......Matt 9:37

PLENTIFULLY
rich man yielded *p* ....Luke 12:16

PLENTY
p which were in the ....Gen 41:53
LORD will grant you *p* .....Deut 28:11
barns will be filled with *p* ...Prov 3:10
diligent lead surely to *p* ...Prov 21:5
his land will have *p* ....Prov 28:19

PLIGHT
He laughs at the *p* ....Job 9:23

PLOT
in the *p* at Jezreel, so that .2 Kin 9:37
and the people *p* ....Ps 2:1
near the *p* of ground that ...John 4:5
p became known to Saul ...Acts 9:24

PLOTS
The wicked *p* against ....Ps 37:12

PLOTTED
and *p* to take Jesus by ....Matt 26:4
chief priests *p* ....John 12:10

PLOW
lazy man will not *p* ....Prov 20:4
Does one *p* there with ....Amos 6:12
put his hand to the *p* .....Luke 9:62
he who plows should *p* ...1 Cor 9:10

PLOWED
"Zion shall be *p* ....Jer 26:18
You have *p* wickedness ....Hos 10:13
of you Zion shall be *p* ....Mic 3:12

PLOWMAN
p shall overtake the ......Amos 9:13

PLOWSHARES
beat their swords into *p* ......Is 2:4
Beat your *p* into swords ....Joel 3:10
beat their swords into *p* ....Mic 4:3

PLUCK
grain, you may *p* ....Deut 23:25
who pass by the way *p* ....Ps 80:12
obey, I will utterly *p* ......Jer 12:17
p the heads of grain ......Mark 2:23

PLUCKED
p the victim from his ......Job 29:17
cheeks to those who *p* ......Is 50:6
And His disciples *p* ......Luke 6:1
you would have *p* ....Gal 4:15

PLUMB
a *p* line, with a *p* ....Amos 7:7
rejoice to see the *p* ......Zech 4:10

PLUNDER
p the Egyptians ....Ex 3:22
who pass by the way *p* .....Ps 89:41
The *p* of the poor is ....Is 3:14
p you shall become ....Jer 30:16
house and *p* his goods ....Matt 12:29

PLUNDERED
stouthearted were *p* ....Ps 76:5
a people robbed and *p* .....Is 42:22
"And when you are *p* ....Jer 4:30
Because you have *p* ....Hab 2:8

PLUNDERING
me because of the *p* ....Is 22:4
accepted the *p* of your .....Heb 10:34

POETS
some of your own *p* ......Acts 17:28

POINT
obedient to the *p* of death ....Phil 2:8
even to the *p* of chains .....2 Tim 2:9
Now this is the main *p* .....Heb 8:1
yet stumble in one *p* .....James 2:10

POINTS
but was in all *p* tempted ....Heb 4:15

POISON
the *p* of asps is under ....Ps 140:3
"The *p* of asps is ....Rom 3:13
evil, full of deadly *p* .....James 3:8

POISONED
p by bitterness ....Acts 8:23
p their minds against .....Acts 14:2

POLLUTIONS
have escaped the *p* ....2 Pet 2:20

POMEGRANATE
a golden bell and a *p*, a ...Ex 28:34
the *p* tree, the palm tree ....Joel 1:12

POMEGRANATES
you shall make *p* of blue ....Ex 28:33
brought some of the *p* ...Num 13:23
grain or figs or vines or *p* ..Num 20:5
of vines and fig trees and *p* ..Deut 8:8

POMP
multitude and their *p* ....Is 5:14
p is brought down to ....Is 14:11
had come with great *p* ....Acts 25:23

POMPOUS
and a mouth speaking *p* .....Dan 7:8

PONDER
P the path of your . . . . Prov 4:26

PONDERED
p them in her heart . . . . Luke 2:19

PONDERS
p all his paths . . . . Prov 5:21

PONTUS
Jews from, at Pentecost, Acts 2:5, 9
Home of Aquila, Acts 18:2
Christians of, addressed by Peter, 1 Pet 1:1

POOL
the rock into a *p* of water . . . Ps 114:8
the wilderness a *p* . . . . Is 41:18
by the Sheep Gate a *p* . . . . . . John 5:2
at a certain time into the *p* . . . John 5:4
wash in the *p* of Siloam . . . . . John 9:7
'Go to the *p* of Siloam . . . . . John 9:11

POOLS
also covers it with *p* . . . . Ps 84:6
a wilderness into *p* . . . . Ps 107:35
your eyes like the *p* . . . . Song 7:4

POOR
p shall not give less . . . . Ex 30:15
be partial to the *p* . . . . Lev 19:15
p will never cease . . . . Deut 15:11
whether *p* or rich . . . . Ruth 3:10
raises the *p* from the dust . . 1 Sam 2:8
seeing I am a *p* . . . . 1 Sam 18:23
one rich and the other *p* . . 2 Sam 12:1
left some of the *p* . . . . 2 Kin 25:12
and gifts to the *p* . . . . Esth 9:22
So the *p* have hope . . . . Job 5:16
and forsaken the *p* . . . . Job 20:19
I delivered the *p* . . . . Job 29:12
soul grieved for the *p* . . . . . Job 30:25
The expectation of the *p* . . . . Ps 9:18
p shall eat and be . . . . Ps 22:26
p man cried out . . . . Ps 34:6
delivering the *p* from him . . . Ps 35:10
to cast down the *p* . . . . Ps 37:14
But I am *p* and needy . . . . . . Ps 40:17
is he who considers the *p* . . . . Ps 41:1
goodness for the *p* . . . . Ps 68:10
For the LORD hears the *p* . . . . Ps 69:33
and Your *p* with justice . . . . . . Ps 72:2
Let the *p* and needy . . . . Ps 74:21
Defend the *p* and fatherless . . Ps 82:3
yet He sets the *p* . . . . Ps 107:41
at the right hand of the *p* . . Ps 109:31
He has given to the *p* . . . . . . Ps 112:9
He raises the *p* . . . . Ps 113:7
satisfy her *p* with bread . . . Ps 132:15
and justice for the *p* . . . . . . Ps 140:12
a slack hand becomes *p* . . . . Prov 10:4
one who makes himself *p* . . Prov 13:7
p man is hated even . . . . . . Prov 14:20
p reproaches his Maker . . . Prov 17:5
p man uses entreaties . . . . Prov 18:23
Better is the *p* who . . . . Prov 19:1
p will also cry himself . . . . Prov 21:13
p have this in common . . . . Prov 22:2
p man who oppresses . . . . . Prov 28:3
Better is the *p* who . . . . Prov 28:6
the cause of the *p* . . . . Prov 29:7
Or lest I be *p* and steal . . . . Prov 30:9
to devour the *p* from . . . . . Prov 30:14
plead the cause of the *p* . . . Prov 31:9
her hand to the *p* . . . . Prov 31:20
remembered that same *p* . . . Eccl 9:15
He shall judge the *p*, and . . . . Is 11:4
the *p* of His people shall . . . . Is 14:32
a strength to the *p* . . . . Is 25:4
The *p* and needy seek . . . . . . Is 41:17
preach good tidings to the *p* . . Is 61:1
on him who is *p* and of a . . . Is 66:2
delivered the life of the *p* . . Jer 20:13
land of Judah the *p* people . . Jer 39:10
the hand of the *p* . . . . Ezek 16:49

and mistreated the *p* . . . . . Ezek 22:29
by showing mercy to the *p* . . Dan 4:27
for silver, and the *p* . . . . Amos 2:6
you tread down the *p* . . . . . Amos 5:11
the alien or the *p* . . . . Zech 7:10
in particular the *p* . . . . Zech 11:7
"Blessed are the *p* . . . . Matt 5:3
p have the gospel . . . . Matt 11:5
have and give to the *p* . . . . Matt 19:21
For you have the *p* . . . . . . Matt 26:11
one *p* widow came . . . . . . Mark 12:42
the gospel to the *p* . . . . Luke 4:18
Blessed are you *p*, ... Luke 6:20
the *p* have the gospel . . . . . . Luke 7:22
give a feast, invite the *p* . . . Luke 14:13
half of my goods to the *p* . . Luke 19:8
contribution for the *p* . . . . . Rom 15:26
my goods to feed the *p* . . . 1 Cor 13:3
as *p*, yet making many . . . . 2 Cor 6:10
your sakes He became *p* . . . 2 Cor 8:9
He has given to the *p* . . . . . 2 Cor 9:9
should remember the *p* . . . . Gal 2:10
and say to the *p* man . . . . . James 2:3
God not chosen the *p* . . . . . James 2:5
wretched, miserable, *p* . . . . . Rev 3:17
and great, rich and *p* . . . . Rev 13:16

POORLY
we are *p* clothed. . . . . 1 Cor 4:11

POPLAR
himself rods of green *p* . . . Gen 30:37

POPULATED
the whole earth was *p* . . . . . Gen 9:19

POPULOUS
great, mighty, and *p* . . . . . . Deut 26:5

PORCH
p which is called . . . . Acts 3:11

PORCHES
Bethesda, having five *p* . . . . John 5:2

PORCIUS FESTUS
Paul stands trial before, Acts 25:1–22

PORCUPINE
the *p* shall possess it, also . . . . Is 34:11

PORTION
For the LORD's *p* . . . . Deut 32:9
This is the *p* from God . . . . Job 20:29
O LORD, You are the *p* . . . . . . Ps 16:5
heart and my *p* forever . . . . . Ps 73:26
You are my *p* . . . . Ps 119:57
p for her maidservants . . . . Prov 31:15
I will divide Him a *p* . . . . Is 53:12
rejoice in their *p* . . . . Is 61:7
The *P* of Jacob is not . . . . . . Jer 10:16
they have trodden My *p* . . . . Jer 12:10
"The LORD is my *p* . . . . Lam 3:24
p of the king's delicacies . . . . . Dan 1:8
and appoint him his *p* . . . Matt 24:51
to give them their *p* . . . . . Luke 12:42
give me the *p* . . . . Luke 15:12
part nor *p* in this matter . . . Acts 8:21

PORTRAYED
Christ was clearly *p* . . . . Gal 3:1

POSITION
If a man desires the *p* . . . . . 1 Tim 3:1

POSSESS
descendants shall *p* . . . . . . Gen 22:17
which you are going to *p* . . Deut 28:21
land which you go to *p* . . . Deut 28:63
p the land which . . . . Josh 1:11
told them to go in to *p* the . . Neh 9:15
fathers to go in and *p* . . . . . Neh 9:23
may dwell there and *p* it . . . Ps 69:35
tithes of all that I *p* . . . . . . Luke 18:12
By your patience *p* . . . . . . Luke 21:19
as though they did not *p* . . 1 Cor 7:30
p his own vessel . . . . 1 Thess 4:4

POSSESSED
much land yet to be *p* . . . . . Josh 13:1

"The LORD *p* me at . . . . Prov 8:22
of the things he *p* . . . . Acts 4:32
that a certain slave girl *p* . . Acts 16:16

POSSESSING
p knowledge and quick to . . . Dan 1:4
and yet *p* all things . . . . 2 Cor 6:10

POSSESSION
as an everlasting *p* . . . . Gen 17:8
ends of the earth for Your *p* . . . Ps 2:8
the rest of their *p* . . . . Ps 17:14
they did not gain *p* . . . . Ps 44:3
is man's precious *p* . . . . . . Prov 12:27
Sapphira his wife, sold a *p* . . Acts 5:1
to give it to him for a *p* . . . . Acts 7:5
of the purchased *p* . . . . Eph 1:14
and an enduring *p* . . . . Heb 10:34

POSSESSIONS
is full of Your *p* . . . . Ps 104:24
kinds of precious *p* . . . . Prov 1:13
the LORD with your *p* . . . . . . Prov 3:9
Yes, I had greater *p* . . . . Eccl 2:7
for he had great *p* . . . . Mark 10:22
and there wasted his *p* . . . Luke 15:13
and sold their *p* . . . . Acts 2:45

POSSESSOR
P of heaven and earth . . . . . Gen 14:19

POSSESSORS
all who were *p* of lands . . . . Acts 4:34

POSSIBLE
God all things are *p* . . . . . . Matt 19:26
O My Father, if it is *p* . . . . . Matt 26:39
all things are *p* to him . . . . Mark 9:23
God all things are *p* . . . . . Mark 10:27
men are *p* with God . . . . . . Luke 18:27
If it is *p*, as much as . . . . . . Rom 12:18
bear you witness that, if *p* . . . Gal 4:15
p that the blood . . . . Heb 10:4

POSTERITY
to preserve a *p* . . . . Gen 45:7
p shall serve Him . . . . Ps 22:30
p who approve their . . . . Ps 49:13
the *p* of the righteous . . . . . Prov 11:21

POSTPONED
it will no more be *p* . . . . . . Ezek 12:25

POT
to Aaron, "Take a *p* . . . . Ex 16:33
from a boiling *p* . . . . Job 41:20
The refining *p* is for . . . . . . Prov 17:3
p that had the manna . . . . . . Heb 9:4

POTENTATE
the blessed and only *P* . . . . 1 Tim 6:15

POTI-PHERAH
Egyptian priest of On (Heliopolis), Gen 41:45–50
Father of Asenath, Joseph's wife, Gen 46:20

POTIPHAR
High Egyptian officer, Gen 39:1
Puts Joseph in jail, Gen 39:20

POTS
when we sat by the *p* . . . . . . Ex 16:3
also took away the *p* . . . . . Jer 52:18
are regarded as clay *p* . . . . . Lam 4:2

POTSHERD
for himself a *p* . . . . Job 2:8
is dried up like a *p* . . . . Ps 22:15
Let the *p* strive with . . . . Is 45:9

POTTER
Shall the *p* be esteemed as . . Is 29:16
the clay, and You our *p* . . . . . Is 64:8
seemed good to the *p* . . . . . Jer 18:4
Does not the *p* have . . . . . . Rom 9:21

POTTER'S FIELD
Judas's money used for purchase of, Matt 27:7, 8

POUND
Mary took a *p* of very . . . . . John 12:3

POUNDS

about a hundred *p* ....John 19:39

POUR

p out your heart ....Ps 62:8
P out Your wrath ....Ps 79:6
p My Spirit on your ....Is 44:3
and let the skies *p* ....Is 45:8
P out Your fury ....Jer 10:25
that I will *p* out My ....Joel 2:28
"And I will *p* ....Zech 12:10
p out for you such blessing .. Mal 3:10
that I will *p* out of My ......Acts 2:17
My maidservants I will *p* ...Acts 2:18
angels, "Go and *p* ....Rev 16:1

POURED

And now my soul is *p* ......Job 30:16
I am *p* out like water ....Ps 22:14
grace is *p* upon Your ....Ps 45:2
name is ointment *p* ....Song 1:3
visited You, they *p* ....Is 26:16
strong, because He *p* ....Is 53:12
and My fury will be *p* ....Jer 7:20
His fury is *p* out like ....Nah 1:6
broke the flask and *p* .....Mark 14:3
of God has been *p* ....Rom 5:5
if I am being *p* ....Phil 2:17
I am already being *p* ....2 Tim 4:6
whom He *p* out on us ....Titus 3:6

POVERTY

of the poor is their *p* ....Prov 10:15
but it leads to *p* ....Prov 11:24
P and shame will come ...Prov 13:18
leads only to *p* ....Prov 14:23
lest you come to *p* ....Prov 20:13
give me neither *p* ....Prov 30:8
p put in all the ....Luke 21:4
and their deep *p* ....2 Cor 8:2
p might become rich ....2 Cor 8:9
tribulation, and *p* ....Rev 2:9

POWER

that I may show My *p* ......Ex 9:16
become glorious in *p* ....Ex 15:6
for God has *p* to help .....2 Chr 25:8
him who is without *p* ......Job 26:2
p who can understand .....Job 26:14
p belongs to God ....Ps 62:11
p Your enemies shall ....Ps 66:3
gives strength and *p* ....Ps 68:35
when it is in the *p* of your .. Prov 3:27
in the *p* of the tongue .....Prov 18:21
a king is, there is *p* ....Eccl 8:4
No one has *p* over the ......Eccl 8:8
the strength of His *p* ....Is 40:26
bodies the fire had no *p* .....Dan 3:27
truly I am full of *p* ....Mic 3:8
anger and great in *p* ....Nah 1:3
'Not by might nor by *p* .....Zech 4:6
the kingdom and the *p* ....Matt 6:13
the Son of Man has *p* ......Matt 9:6
who had given such *p* ....Matt 9:8
gave them *p* over unclean .. Matt 10:1
Scriptures nor the *p* ......Matt 22:29
the Son of Man has *p* ......Mark 2:10
p to heal sicknesses ....Mark 3:15
that *p* had gone out ....Mark 5:30
Scriptures nor the *p* of ...Mark 12:24
p of the Spirit to Galilee ...Luke 4:14
And the *p* of the Lord .....Luke 5:17
the Son of Man has *p* ......Luke 5:24
p went out from Him ......Luke 6:19
I perceived *p* going out ....Luke 8:46
and gave them *p* ....Luke 9:1
all the *p* of the enemy ....Luke 10:19
and the *p* of darkness ....Luke 22:53
you are endued with *p* ....Luke 24:49
I have *p* to lay it ....John 10:18
not know that I have *p* ....John 19:10
"You could have no *p* ....John 19:11
you shall receive *p* ....Acts 1:8
as though by our own *p* ....Acts 3:12

Stephen, full of faith and *p* ..Acts 6:8
man is the great *p* ....Acts 8:10
"Give me this *p* ....Acts 8:19
Holy Spirit and with *p* ....Acts 10:38
the *p* of Satan to God, ...Acts 26:18
the Son of God with *p* ......Rom 1:4
for it is the *p* ....Rom 1:16
even His eternal *p* ....Rom 1:20
My *p* in you ....Rom 9:17
potter have *p* over the .....Rom 9:21
the *p* of the Holy Spirit ...Rom 15:13
by the *p* of the Spirit of ...Rom 15:19
saved it is the *p* ....1 Cor 1:18
Greeks, Christ the *p* ....1 Cor 1:24
of the Spirit and of *p*, ...1 Cor 2:4
men but in the *p* of God ....1 Cor 2:5
is not in word but in *p* .....1 Cor 4:20
be brought under the *p* ....1 Cor 6:12
and all authority and *p* ...1 Cor 15:24
it is raised in *p* ....1 Cor 15:43
of the *p* may be of God .....2 Cor 4:7
of truth, by the *p* of God ...2 Cor 6:7
that the *p* of Christ ....2 Cor 12:9
He lives by the *p* of God ..2 Cor 13:4
greatness of His *p* ....Eph 1:19
all principality and *p* ....Eph 1:21
prince of the *p* of the air .....Eph 2:2
working of His *p* ....Eph 3:7
to the *p* that works in us ...Eph 3:20
the Lord and in the *p* ......Eph 6:10
the *p* of His resurrection ....Phil 3:10
to His glorious *p* ....Col 1:11
us from the *p* of darkness ...Col 1:13
of all principality and *p* .....Col 2:10
only, but also in *p* ....1 Thess 1:5
the glory of His *p* ....2 Thess 1:9
work of faith with *p* ....2 Thess 1:11
of Satan, with all *p* ....2 Thess 2:9
of fear, but of *p* ....2 Tim 1:7
according to the *p* of God ..2 Tim 1:8
godliness but denying its *p* ..2 Tim 3:5
by the word of His *p* ....Heb 1:3
p of death, that ....Heb 2:14
but according to the *p* .....Heb 7:16
since it has no *p* at all ......Heb 9:17
are kept by the *p* of God ....1 Pet 1:5
as His divine *p* ....2 Pet 1:3
made known to you the *p* ..2 Pet 1:16
who are greater in *p* ....2 Pet 2:11
dominion and *p* ....Jude 25
to him I will give *p* ....Rev 2:26
glory and honor and *p* .....Rev 4:11
honor and glory and *p* .....Rev 5:13
and honor and *p* ....Rev 7:12
and *p* belong to the Lord ...Rev 19:1
the second death has no *p* ..Rev 20:6

POWER OF GOD

the Scriptures nor the *p* ....Matt 22:29
the right hand of the *p* ....Luke 22:69
"This man is the great *p* ....Acts 8:10
it is the *p* to salvation ....Rom 1:16
being saved it is the *p* .....1 Cor 1:18
Christ the *p* and the ......1 Cor 1:24
word of truth, by the *p* ....2 Cor 6:7
yet He lives by the *p* ....2 Cor 13:4
gospel according to the *p* ..2 Tim 1:8
who are kept by the *p* ......1 Pet 1:5

POWERFUL

of the LORD is *p* ....Ps 29:4
of God is living and *p* ......Heb 4:12

POWERS

the *p* of the heavens ......Matt 24:29
nor principalities nor *p*, ...Rom 8:38
p in the heavenly places, ...Eph 3:10
principalities, against *p* ......Eph 6:12
or principalities or *p* ....Col 1:16
principalities and *p* ....Col 2:15
word of God and the *p* ......Heb 6:5
p having been made ....1 Pet 3:22

PRACTICE

to do, that I do not *p* ......Rom 7:15

I will not to do, that I *p* ....Rom 7:19
those who *p* such things .....Gal 5:21
and do not *p* the truth .....1 John 1:6
Whoever does not *p* ....1 John 3:10

PRACTICED

p witchcraft and ....2 Kin 17:17
previously *p* sorcery in .....Acts 8:9
those who had *p* magic ....Acts 19:19
they have *p* deceit ....Rom 3:13
which they have *p* ....2 Cor 12:21

PRACTICES

wrath on him who *p* evil ...Rom 13:4
trained in covetous *p* ......2 Pet 2:14
p righteousness is born ...1 John 2:29
whoever loves and *p* a lie ..Rev 22:15

PRACTICING

For everyone *p* evil hates ...John 3:20
judge those *p* such things ...Rom 2:3

PRAETORIUM

Pilate's palace in Jerusalem, Mark
15:16; John 18:28; Matt 27:27
——— Herod's palace at Caesarea, Acts
23:35

PRAISE

Now I will *p* the LORD ......Gen 29:35
your brothers shall *p* ....Gen 49:8
He is my God, and I will *p* ...Ex 15:2
He is your *p* ....Deut 10:21
which He has made, in *p* ..Deut 26:19
I will sing *p* to the ....Judg 5:3
to *p* the LORD God of ....1 Chr 16:4
to triumph in Your *p* .....1 Chr 16:35
David, "for giving *p*." .....1 Chr 23:5
p the LORD, and ....1 Chr 23:30
and to *p* the LORD..........1 Chr 25:3
p Your glorious name ....1 Chr 29:13
offered *p* by their ministry ..2 Chr 7:6
for their duties (to *p* and ...2 Chr 8:14
"*P* the LORD, for His ....2 Chr 20:21
began to sing and to *p* .....2 Chr 20:22
the Levites to sing *p* ......2 Chr 29:30
to *p* in the gates of the ....2 Chr 31:2
to *p* the LORD, according ...Ezra 3:10
above all blessing and *p* .....Neh 9:5
singers, and songs of *p* ....Neh 12:46
I will *p* You, O LORD ....Ps 9:1
p shall be of You in ....Ps 22:25
For *p* from the upright ......Ps 33:1
p shall continually be ....Ps 34:1
of Your *p* all the day long ...Ps 35:28
the people shall *p* ....Ps 45:17
Whoever offers *p* ....Ps 50:23
P is awaiting You ....Ps 65:1
make His *p* glorious ....Ps 66:2
let all the peoples *p* ....Ps 67:3
Let heaven and earth *p* .....Ps 69:34
p shall be continually ....Ps 71:6
And the heavens will *p* ......Ps 89:5
and into His courts with *p* ..Ps 100:4
silent, O God of my *p* ......Ps 109:1
Seven times a day I *p* .....Ps 119:164
All Your works shall *p* .....Ps 145:10
shall speak the *p* ....Ps 145:21
P the LORD ....Ps 148:1
P Him with high sounding ..Ps 150:5
that has breath *p* ....Ps 150:6
Let another man *p* ....Prov 27:2
let her own works *p* ....Prov 31:31
And your gates *P* ....Is 60:18
the garment of *p* for the ......Is 61:3
He makes Jerusalem a *p* .....Is 62:7
For You are my *p* ....Jer 17:14
Me a name of joy, a *p* ......Jer 33:9
p You, O God of my ....Dan 2:23
Nebuchadnezzar, *p* and ....Dan 4:37
p the name of the LORD ....Joel 2:26
give you fame and *p* ......Zeph 3:20
You have perfected *p* .....Matt 21:16
saw it, gave *p* to God .....Luke 18:43
p God with a loud voice ..Luke 19:37

of men more than the *p* . . . John 12:43
p is not from men but . . . . . . Rom 2:29
will have *p* from the same . . . Rom 13:3
"*P* the LORD, ... Rom 15:11
Then each one's *p* . . . . 1 Cor 4:5
Now I *p* you, brethren . . . . . 1 Cor 11:2
I do not *p* you . . . . 1 Cor 11:22
the brother whose *p* . . . . . . 2 Cor 8:18
to the *p* of the glory of His . . Eph 1:6
should be to the *p* . . . . Eph 1:12
to the *p* of His glory . . . . Eph 1:14
to the glory and *p* . . . . Phil 1:11
I will sing *p* to You . . . . Heb 2:12
the sacrifice of *p* . . . . Heb 13:15
and for the *p* of those . . . . . 1 Pet 2:14
saying, "*P* our God . . . . Rev 19:5

PRAISE THE LORD
and said, "Now I will *p* . . . Gen 29:35
to thank, and to *p* . . . . 1 Chr 16:4
King David had made to *p* . . 2 Chr 7:6
"*P*, for His mercy . . . . 2 Chr 20:21
with cymbals, to *p* . . . . Ezra 3:10
Those who seek Him will *p* . . Ps 22:26
P with the harp . . . . Ps 33:2
yet to be created may *p* . . . Ps 102:18
the Lord, O my soul! *P* . . . . Ps 104:35
P! Oh, give thanks . . . . Ps 106:1
The dead do not *p* . . . . Ps 115:17
p, all you Gentiles . . . . Ps 117:1
while I live I will *p* . . . . Ps 146:2
P! P from the heavens . . . . . . Ps 148:1
that has breath *p* . . . . Ps 150:6
P, call upon His name . . . . Is 12:4
shall eat it, and *p* . . . . Is 62:9
P! For He has delivered . . . . Jer 20:13
P, all you Gentiles . . . . Rom 15:11

PRAISED
who is worthy to be *p* . . . 2 Sam 22:4
and greatly to be *p* . . . . . . 1 Chr 16:25
and *p* the LORD . . . . 1 Chr 16:36
thousand *p* the LORD . . . . . 1 Chr 23:5
music, and *p* the LORD, ... 2 Chr 5:13
and *p* the LORD, saying . . . . . 2 Chr 7:3
the priests *p* the LORD . . . . 2 Chr 30:21
when they *p* the LORD . . . . . Ezra 3:11
and *p* the LORD . . . . Neh 5:13
daily He shall be *p* . . . . Ps 72:15
LORD's name is to be *p* . . . . . Ps 113:3
and greatly to be *p* . . . . Ps 145:3
the LORD, she shall be *p* . . . Prov 31:30
where our fathers *p* . . . . Is 64:11
the Most High and *p* . . . . . . Dan 4:34

PRAISES
in holiness, fearful in *p* . . . . Ex 15:11
sang *p* with gladness, ... 2 Chr 29:30
enthroned in the *p* . . . . Ps 22:3
O LORD, I will sing *p* . . . . . . Ps 101:1
it is good to sing *p* . . . . Ps 147:1
and he *p* her . . . . Prov 31:28
shall proclaim the *p* . . . . Is 60:6
you may proclaim the *p* . . . . 1 Pet 2:9

PRAISEWORTHY
if there is anything *p* . . . . . . Phil 4:8

PRAISING
they sang responsively, *p* . . Ezra 3:11
they will still be *p* . . . . Ps 84:4
of the heavenly host *p* . . . . . Luke 2:13
p God for all the things . . . . Luke 2:20
in the temple *p* . . . . Luke 24:53
p God and having favor . . . . Acts 2:47
leaping, and *p* God . . . . Acts 3:8

PRATING
p fool will fall . . . . Prov 10:8
p against us with . . . . 3 John 10

PRAY
heal her, O God, I *p* . . . . . . Num 12:13
of this people, I *p* . . . . Num 14:19
p to the LORD that He . . . . . . Num 21:7
Strengthen me, I *p* . . . . Judg 16:28

LORD in ceasing to *p* . . . . . 1 Sam 12:23
my God, for to You I will *p* . . . . Ps 5:2
p to You in a time when . . . . . Ps 32:6
at noon I will *p* . . . . Ps 55:17
I *p*, send now prosperity . . . Ps 118:25
who hate you, and *p* . . . . . . Matt 5:44
"And when you *p* . . . . Matt 6:5
But you, when you *p* . . . . Matt 6:6
when you *p*, do not use . . . . . Matt 6:7
manner, therefore, *p* . . . . Matt 6:9
Therefore *p* the Lord of . . . . Matt 9:38
by Himself to *p* . . . . Matt 14:23
hands on them and *p* . . . . . . Matt 19:13
while I go and *p* over . . . . . Matt 26:36
Watch and *p* . . . . Matt 26:41
I cannot now *p* . . . . Matt 26:53
to the mountain to *p* . . . . . . Mark 6:46
you ask when you *p* . . . . . . Mark 11:24
Take heed, watch and *p* . . . Mark 13:33
Sit here while I *p* . . . . Mark 14:32
"Watch and *p*, lest you . . . Mark 14:38
out to the mountain to *p* . . Luke 6:12
p for those who spitefully . . Luke 6:28
up on the mountain to *p* . . . Luke 9:28
"Lord, teach us to *p* . . . . . . Luke 11:1
men always ought to *p* . . . . Luke 18:1
up to the temple to *p* . . . . Luke 18:10
P that you may not . . . . . . Luke 22:40
Rise and *p*, lest you . . . . . . Luke 22:46
And I will *p* . . . . John 14:16
I shall *p* the Father for . . . . John 16:26
I do not *p* for the . . . . John 17:9
I do not *p* that You . . . . . . John 17:15
"I do not *p* for . . . . John 17:20
p God if perhaps the . . . . . . Acts 8:22
P to the Lord for me, that . . Acts 8:24
up on the housetop to *p* . . . . Acts 10:9
know what we should *p* . . . . Rom 8:26
to *p* to God with her . . . . . 1 Cor 11:13
p that he may interpret . . . 1 Cor 14:13
For if I *p* in a tongue . . . . 1 Cor 14:14
I will *p* with the . . . . 1 Cor 14:15
Now I *p* to God . . . . 2 Cor 13:7
And this also we *p* . . . . 2 Cor 13:9
And this I *p*, that your love . . Phil 1:9
do not cease to *p* for you . . . Col 1:9
p without ceasing . . . . 1 Thess 5:17
Brethren, *p* for us . . . . 1 Thess 5:25
we also *p* always . . . . 2 Thess 1:11
p for us, that the word . . . . 2 Thess 3:1
therefore that the men *p* . . . 1 Tim 2:8
P for us, for we are . . . . . . Heb 13:18
Let him *p* . . . . James 5:13
to one another, and *p* . . . . James 5:16
say that he should *p* . . . . . 1 John 5:16
p that you may prosper . . . . 3 John 2

PRAYED
So Abraham *p* to God . . . . . Gen 20:17
So Moses *p* for the people . . Num 21:7
Manoah *p* to the LORD . . . . . Judg 13:8
For this child I *p*, and . . . . 1 Sam 1:27
Then Hezekiah *p* before . . 2 Kin 19:15
times that day, and *p* . . . . . Dan 6:10
Then Jonah *p* to the LORD . . . Jon 2:1
So he *p* to the LORD, ... Jon 4:2
into the wilderness and *p* . . Luke 5:16
Pharisee stood and *p* . . . . Luke 18:11
p more earnestly . . . . Luke 22:44
p earnestly that it . . . . James 5:17

PRAYER
God heeded the *p* . . . . . . 2 Sam 21:14
in heaven their *p* . . . . 1 Kin 8:45
p made in this place . . . . . . 2 Chr 7:15
the thanksgiving with *p* . . . Neh 11:17
fear, and restrain *p* . . . . Job 15:4
And my *p* is pure . . . . Job 16:17
p would return to my . . . . . . Ps 35:13
A *p* to the God of my . . . . Ps 42:8
P also will be made . . . . Ps 72:15
Let my *p* come before . . . . . . Ps 88:2
He shall regard the *p* . . . . . Ps 102:17

but I give myself to *p* . . . . . . Ps 109:4
to the LORD, but the *p* . . . . . . Ps 15:8
hears the *p* of the . . . . Prov 15:29
hear the *p* of Your servant . . Dan 9:17
while I was speaking in *p* . . Dan 9:21
not go out except by *p* . . . Matt 17:21
things you ask in *p* . . . . . . Matt 21:22
out by nothing but *p* . . . . . Mark 9:29
a house of *p* for all . . . . . . Mark 11:17
all night in *p* to God . . . . . Luke 6:12
My house is a house of *p* . Luke 19:46
with one accord in *p* and . . Acts 1:14
the temple at the hour of *p* . . Acts 3:1
continually to *p* . . . . Acts 6:4
your *p* has been heard . . . . Acts 10:31
where *p* was . . . . Acts 16:13
as we went up to *p* . . . . . . Acts 16:16
p to God for Israel is that . . Rom 10:1
steadfastly in *p* . . . . Rom 12:12
to fasting and *p* . . . . 1 Cor 7:5
always with all *p* . . . . Eph 6:18
always in every *p* of mine . . . Phil 1:4
deliverance through your *p* . Phil 1:19
but in everything by *p* . . . . . Phil 4:6
Continue earnestly in *p*, ... Col 4:2
the word of God and *p* . . . . 1 Tim 4:5
And the *p* of faith . . . . James 5:15

PRAYERS
though you make many *p* . . . . Is 1:15
pretense make long *p* . . . . Matt 23:14
fastings and *p* night and . . Luke 2:37
pretense make long *p* . . . . Luke 20:47
of bread, and in *p* . . . . Acts 2:42
Your *p* and your alms . . . . Acts 10:4
always in my *p* . . . . Rom 1:9
me in *p* to God for me . . . Rom 15:30
fervently for you in *p* . . . . . . Col 4:12
that supplications, *p* . . . . . 1 Tim 2:1
and *p* night and day . . . . . 1 Tim 5:5
always in my *p* . . . . Philem 4
when He had offered up *p* . . Heb 5:7
p may not be hindered . . . . . 1 Pet 3:7
are open to their *p* . . . . 1 Pet 3:12
and watchful in your *p* . . . . 1 Pet 4:7
which are the *p* . . . . Rev 5:8

PRAYING
and found Daniel *p* . . . . . . Dan 6:11
whenever you stand *p* . . . . Mark 11:25
Paul and Silas were *p* . . . Acts 16:25
p always with all prayer . . . Eph 6:18
faith, *p* in the Holy Spirit, . . Jude 20

PRAYS
every woman who *p* or . . . 1 Cor 11:5
tongue, my spirit *p* . . . . . 1 Cor 14:14

PREACH
to *p* good tidings . . . . Is 61:1
that great city, and *p* . . . . . . Jon 3:2
time Jesus began to *p* . . . . Matt 4:17
you hear in the ear, *p* . . . Matt 10:27
p the gospel to every . . . . Mark 16:15
P the gospel to the . . . . . Luke 4:18
p the kingdom of God . . . . Luke 9:60
to *p* the word in Asia . . . . . Acts 16:6
ready to *p* the gospel . . . . Rom 1:15
word of faith which we *p*) . . Rom 10:8
And how shall they *p* . . . Rom 10:15
it my aim to *p* the gospel . . Rom 15:20
p Christ crucified . . . . 1 Cor 1:23
is me if I do not *p* . . . . . . 1 Cor 9:16
I or they, so we *p* . . . . . . 1 Cor 15:11
For we do not *p* . . . . 2 Cor 4:5
p any other gospel to you . . Gal 1:8
that I might *p* Him among . . Gal 1:16
gospel which I *p* . . . . Gal 2:2
p Christ even from . . . . Phil 1:15
The former *p* Christ from . . Phil 1:16
P the word . . . . 2 Tim 4:2

PREACH THE GOSPEL
into all the world and *p* . . Mark 16:15
He has anointed Me to *p* . . Luke 4:18

Lord had called us to p : .... Acts 16:10
I am ready to p .... Rom 1:15
the feet of those who p .... Rom 10:15
made it my aim to p , ... Rom 15:20
to baptize, but to p .... 1 Cor 1:17
who p should live from .... 1 Cor 9:14
to p in the regions ...... 2 Cor 10:16

PREACHED
have the gospel p to them .. Matt 11:5
p that people .... Mark 6:12
p to all the nations ...... Mark 13:10
wherever this gospel is p ... Mark 14:9
out and p everywhere .... Mark 16:20
have the gospel p to them .. Luke 7:22
of sins should be p ...... Luke 24:47
p in Jesus the resurrection ... Acts 4:2
p Christ to them .... Acts 8:5
p the word of the Lord, ... Acts 8:25
baptism which John p .... Acts 10:37
through this Man is p .... Acts 13:38
of God was p by Paul .... Acts 17:13
he p to them Jesus .... Acts 17:18
lest, when I have p .... 1 Cor 9:27
whom we have not p .... 2 Cor 11:4
than what we have p .... Gal 1:8
in truth, Christ is p ...... Phil 1:18
was p to every creature .... Col 1:23
might be p fully through .. 2 Tim 4:17
the gospel was p .... Heb 4:2
also He went and p .... 1 Pet 3:19

PREACHER
The words of the P .... Eccl 1:1
they hear without a p .... Rom 10:14
I was appointed a p .... 1 Tim 2:7
I was appointed a p .... 2 Tim 1:11
of eight people, a p .... 2 Pet 2:5

PREACHES
the Jesus whom Paul p .... Acts 19:13
p another Jesus whom .... 2 Cor 11:4
p any other gospel .... Gal 1:9
p the faith which he ...... Gal 1:23

PREACHING
at the p of Jonah .... Matt 12:41
p a baptism of repentance .. Mark 1:4
every city and village, p .... Luke 8:1
p the gospel and healing ... Luke 9:6
p Jesus as the .... Acts 5:42
went everywhere p .... Acts 8:4
to my gospel and the p .... Rom 16:25
p were not with .... 1 Cor 2:4
not risen, then our p ..... 1 Cor 15:14
His word through p .... Titus 1:3

PRECEDE
p those who are asleep .. 1 Thess 4:15

PRECEDING
p them to judgment, ... 1 Tim 5:24

PRECEPT
p must be upon p .... Is 28:10
P upon p, p upon p .... Is 28:13
walked by human p .... Hos 5:11
heart he wrote you this p .. Mark 10:5
p to all the people .... Heb 9:19

PRECEPTS
and commanded them p .... Neh 9:14
all His p are sure .... Ps 111:7
us to keep Your p .... Ps 119:4
Behold, I long for Your p ... Ps 119:40
will meditate on Your p ... Ps 119:78
because I keep Your p .... Ps 119:100
how I love Your p .... Ps 119:159
and kept all his p .... Jer 35:18
by departing from Your p .... Dan 9:5

PRECIOUS
gave p things to her .... Gen 24:53
because my life was p : ... 1 Sam 26:21
with p stones .... 2 Sam 12:30
P in the sight of the .... Ps 116:15
How p also are Your ...... Ps 139:17

She is more p than .... Prov 3:15
rooms are filled with all p .. Prov 24:4
a p cornerstone, a sure ..... Is 28:16
Since you were p .... Is 43:4
p things shall not .... Is 44:9
if you take out the p ...... Jer 15:19
The p sons of Zion .... Lam 4:2
p stones, wood, hay ...... 1 Cor 3:12
farmer waits for the p ..... James 5:7
more p than gold .... 1 Pet 1:7
but with the p blood of .... 1 Pet 1:19
but chosen by God and p .. 1 Pet 2:4
chief cornerstone, elect, p ... 1 Pet 2:6
who believe, He is p .... 1 Pet 2:7
p in the sight of .... 1 Pet 3:4
like p faith with us by the ... 2 Pet 1:1
and p promises, ... 2 Pet 1:4

PREDESTINED
He foreknew, He also p .... Rom 8:29
having p us to .... Eph 1:5
inheritance, being p ...... Eph 1:11

PREEMINENCE
He may have the p .... Col 1:18
loves to have the p .... 3 John 9

PREFERENCE
in honor giving p .... Rom 12:10

PREFERRED
comes after me is p .... John 1:15

PREGNANCY
no birth, no p, and no ...... Hos 9:11

PREGNANT
woe to those who are p ... Matt 24:19
pains upon a p woman ... 1 Thess 5:3

PREJUDICE
these things without p .... 1 Tim 5:21

PREMEDITATE
p what you will .... Mark 13:11

PREPARATION
Now it was the P .... John 19:14
your feet with the p ...... Eph 6:15

PREPARATIONS
p of the heart belong ...... Prov 16:1

PREPARE
P provisions for .... Josh 1:11
'Let us now p to build .... Josh 22:26
p your hearts for the ...... 1 Sam 7:3
p it for myself and my ... 1 Kin 17:12
which I will p for them ..... Esth 5:8
p a table before me in .... Ps 23:5
p mercy and truth .... Ps 61:7
P your outside work, ... Prov 24:27
yet they p their food in .... Prov 30:25
P the way of the Lord .... Is 40:3
P the way for the .... Is 62:10
p the ambushes .... Jer 51:12
P the way of the Lord, ... Matt 3:3
do You want us to p ..... Matt 26:17
P the way of the Lord ..... Mark 1:3
to p for Him .... Luke 9:52
will, and did not p .... Luke 12:47
p the Passover for us ..... Luke 22:8
p a place for you .... John 14:2

PREPARED
place which I have p .... Ex 23:20
You p room for it .... Ps 80:9
When He p the heavens .... Prov 8:27
for the Lord has p .... Zeph 1:7
for whom it is p .... Matt 20:23
fire p for the devil and .... Matt 25:41
which You have p .... Luke 2:31
mercy, which He had p ... Rom 9:23
things which God has p .... 1 Cor 2:9
Now He who has p .... 2 Cor 5:5
p beforehand that we ...... Eph 2:10
p for every good work .... 2 Tim 2:21
God, for He has p .... Heb 11:16
p as a bride adorned for .... Rev 21:2

PRESENCE
themselves from the p ...... Gen 3:8
went out from the p .... Gen 4:16
the p of my mistress Sarai .. Gen 16:8
we die in your p .... Gen 47:15
P will go with you .... Ex 33:14
and honor the p .... Lev 19:32
afraid in any man's p ..... Deut 1:17
am terrified at His p .... Job 23:15
p is fullness of joy .... Ps 16:11
shall dwell in Your p ..... Ps 140:13
not tremble at My p .... Jer 5:22
shall shake at My p ...... Ezek 38:20
fled from the p of the Lord .. Jon 1:10
Be silent in the p .... Zeph 1:7
stands in the p of God .... Luke 1:19
and drank in Your p ...... Luke 13:26
in the p of the people ..... Luke 20:26
full of joy in Your p .... Acts 2:28
to God in the p of them ... Acts 27:35
the p of Him whom he .... Rom 4:17
should glory in His p ..... 1 Cor 1:29
in the p of Christ .... 2 Cor 2:10
who in p am lowly .... 2 Cor 10:1
but his bodily p .... 2 Cor 10:10
obeyed, not as in my p .... Phil 2:12
p of many witnesses ...... 1 Tim 6:12
the P behind the veil .... Heb 6:19
appear in the p of God .... Heb 9:24

PRESENT
a very p help in trouble .... Ps 46:1
we are all p before .... Acts 10:33
not p your members ...... Rom 6:13
for to will is p with me ..... Rom 7:18
evil is p with me .... Rom 7:21
p time are not worthy to ... Rom 8:18
nor things p nor things to .. Rom 8:38
p your bodies a living ..... Rom 12:1
or death, or things p ...... 1 Cor 3:22
absent in body but p ...... 1 Cor 5:3
because of the p distress .. 1 Cor 7:26
p the gospel of Christ .... 1 Cor 9:18
to be p with the Lord .... 2 Cor 5:8
may p you as a chaste ..... 2 Cor 11:2
not only when I am p ...... Gal 4:18
that He might p .... Eph 5:27
to p you holy, ... Col 1:22
to p yourself .... 2 Tim 2:15
and godly in the p age, ... Titus 2:12
established in the p truth .. 2 Pet 1:12
p you faultless .... Jude 24

PRESENTED
p them to Pharaoh .... Gen 47:2
p themselves before God .. Josh 24:1
treasures, they p .... Matt 2:11
And He p him to his ...... Luke 7:15
to whom He also p .... Acts 1:3
they also p Paul to him ... Acts 23:33
For just as you p .... Rom 6:19

PRESENTING
p my supplication before ... Dan 9:20

PRESENTS
kings will bring p .... Ps 68:29

PRESERVE
before you to p life .... Gen 45:5
You shall p me from .... Ps 32:7
O Lord, You p man and ...... Ps 36:6
He shall p your soul .... Ps 121:7
The Lord shall p .... Ps 121:8
discretion will p you ...... Prov 2:11
lips of the wise will p ...... Prov 14:3
the Lord p knowledge ... Prov 22:12
children, I will p .... Jer 49:11
pardon those whom I p .... Jer 50:20
loses his life will p ...... Luke 17:33
every evil work and p ..... 2 Tim 4:18

PRESERVED
and my life is p .... Gen 32:30
p us in all the way that .... Josh 24:17

the LORD *p* David . . . . 2 Sam 8:6
Your care has *p* my spirit . . Job 10:12
soul, and body be *p* . . . . . . 1 Thess 5:23

PRESERVES
For the LORD *p* the . . . . Ps 31:23
p the souls of His . . . . Ps 97:10
The LORD *p* the simple . . . . . Ps 116:6
p the way of His saints . . . . . . Prov 2:8
who guards his mouth *p* . . . Prov 13:3
he who keeps his way *p* . . . Prov 16:17

PRESS
but I *p* on, that I may lay . . . Phil 3:12
I *p* toward the goal . . . . Phil 3:14

PRESSED
p her, virgin bosom . . . . Ezek 23:8
p about Him to touch . . . . . Mark 3:10
the multitude *p* about Him . . Luke 5:1
p down, shaken together, . . Luke 6:38
We are hard *p* on every . . . . 2 Cor 4:8
For I am hard *p* . . . . Phil 1:23

PRESUMPTUOUS
servant also from *p* . . . . Ps 19:13
They are *p*, self-willed . . . . . 2 Pet 2:10

PRETENDED
them, *p* madness . . . . 1 Sam 21:13

PRETENSE
whole heart, but in *p* . . . . Jer 3:10
p make long prayers . . . . . Matt 23:14

PREVAIL
He did not *p* against him . . Gen 32:25
no man shall *p* . . . . 1 Sam 2:9
do not let man *p* . . . . 2 Chr 14:11
our tongue we will *p* . . . . Ps 12:4
He shall *p* against His . . . . . Is 42:13
but they shall not *p* . . . . Jer 1:19
but he will not *p* . . . . Dan 11:12
of Hades shall not *p* . . . . . Matt 16:18
but they did not *p*, ... Rev 12:8

PREVAILED
The waters and greatly . . . Gen 7:18
hand, that Israel *p* . . . . Ex 17:11
Judah *p* over his brothers . . 1 Chr 5:2
with the Angel and *p* . . . . . Hos 12:4
grew mightily and *p* . . . . . Acts 19:20
has *p* to open the scroll and . . Rev 5:5

PREVIOUSLY
who *p* practiced sorcery in . . Acts 8:9

PREY
the mountains of *p* . . . . Ps 76:4
has not given us as *p* . . . . . Ps 124:6
Shall the *p* be taken . . . . Is 49:24
evil makes himself a *p* . . . . Is 59:15
shall no longer be a *p* . . . . Ezek 34:22
when he has no *p* . . . . Amos 3:4

PRICE
be weighed for its *p* . . . . . . Job 28:15
a fool the purchase *p* . . . . . Prov 17:16
one pearl of great *p* . . . . . . Matt 13:46
back part of the *p* . . . . Acts 5:3
you were bought at a *p* . . . . 1 Cor 6:20
You were bought at a *p* . . . . 1 Cor 7:23

PRIDE
p come against me . . . . Ps 36:11
p serves as their necklace . . . . Ps 73:6
p and arrogance and . . . . . . Prov 8:13
By *p* comes nothing . . . . . . Prov 13:10
P goes before . . . . Prov 16:18
p will bring him low . . . . . . Prov 29:23
and her daughter had *p* . . . Ezek 16:49
p He is able to put down . . . . Dan 4:37
was hardened in *p* . . . . Dan 5:20
has sworn by the *p* . . . . Amos 8:7
For the *p* of the . . . . Zech 11:3
evil eye, blasphemy, *p* . . . . Mark 7:22
p he fall into the . . . . 1 Tim 3:6
eyes, and the *p* of life . . . . 1 John 2:16

PRIEST
See HIGH PRIEST

he was the *p* of God . . . . . . Gen 14:18
That son who becomes *p* . . . . Ex 29:30
The sons of Aaron the *p* . . . . . Lev 1:7
the *p* shall burn all on the . . . . Lev 1:9
p shall lay them in order . . . . Lev 1:12
p shall make atonement . . . Lev 19:22
for the *p* is holy to his God . . Lev 21:7
Eleazar the *p* spoke . . . . . . Num 26:3
and Eleazar the *p* . . . . Num 26:63
Eleazar the *p*, Joshua . . . . Josh 19:51
when Phinehas the *p* . . . . . Josh 22:30
The *p* stood at the . . . . Judg 18:17
Eli the *p* was sitting . . . . 1 Sam 1:9
Myself a faithful *p* . . . . 1 Sam 2:35
Eli, the LORD's *p* in . . . . . . 1 Sam 14:3
Saul talked to the *p* . . . . . . 1 Sam 14:19
to Ahimelech the *p* . . . . 1 Sam 21:2
p gave him holy bread . . . . 1 Sam 21:6
Urijah the *p* built an . . . . . . 2 Kin 16:11
Jehoiada the *p* brought . . . 2 Chr 23:14
the *p* found the Book . . . . 2 Chr 34:14
gave Ezra the *p* . . . . Ezra 7:11
p could consult . . . . Neh 7:65
p forever according . . . . Ps 110:4
the *p* and the prophet . . . . Is 28:7
So He shall be a *p* . . . . Zech 6:13
of a *p* should keep . . . . Mal 2:7
show yourself to the *p* . . . . . Matt 8:4
to Caiaphas the high *p* . . . Matt 26:57
And the high *p* arose . . . . Matt 26:62
away to the high *p* . . . . . . Mark 14:53
well as Annas the high *p* . . . Acts 4:6
and faithful High *P* . . . . Heb 2:17
High *P* of our confession, . . . Heb 3:1
we have a great High *P* . . . . Heb 4:14
we do not have a High *P* . . . Heb 4:15
p forever according . . . . Heb 5:6
We have such a High *P*, ... Heb 8:1
high *p* went alone . . . . Heb 9:7
Christ came as High *P* . . . . Heb 9:11

PRIEST'S
the high *p* servant . . . . John 18:10

PRIESTHOOD
be an everlasting *p* . . . . Ex 40:15
have defiled the *p* . . . . Neh 13:29
p being changed . . . . Heb 7:12
has an unchangeable *p* . . . . Heb 7:24
house, a holy *p* . . . . 1 Pet 2:5
generation, a royal *p* . . . . . 1 Pet 2:9

PRIESTS
to Me a kingdom of *p* . . . . . . Ex 19:6
may minister to Me as *p* . . . Ex 28:41
and the *p*, Aaron's sons, ... Lev 1:5
"Command the *p* . . . . Josh 4:16
and let seven *p* bear seven . . Josh 6:6
the *p* blew the trumpets . . . Josh 6:20
had killed the LORD's *p* . . 1 Sam 22:21
removed the idolatrous *p* . . 2 Kin 23:5
Jahaziel the *p* . . . . 1 Chr 16:6
and Benjamin, and the *p* . . . Ezra 1:5
yet told the Jews, the *p* . . . . Neh 2:16
Their *p* fell by the sword, . . . Ps 78:64
Aaron were among His *p* . . . Ps 99:6
Let Your *p* be clothed with . . Ps 132:9
her *p* with salvation . . . . . . Ps 132:16
named the *p* of the LORD . . . . Is 61:6
which the *p* ministered . . . . Jer 52:18
and the iniquities of her *p* . . Lam 4:13
p have violated My law . . . Ezek 22:26
the *p* shall throw salt on . . Ezek 43:24
"Hear this, O *p*! . . . . Hos 5:1
the *p* mourn, who minister . . . Joel 1:9
her *p* teach for pay . . . . Mic 3:11
p in the temple profane . . . Matt 12:5
But when the chief *p* . . . . . Matt 21:15
went to the chief *p* . . . . . . Matt 26:14
of silver to the chief *p* and . . Matt 27:3
the chief *p* stirred up . . . . . Mark 15:11
Caiaphas being high *p* . . . . Luke 3:2
show yourselves to the *p* . . Luke 17:14
Jesus said to the chief *p* . . Luke 22:52

Pilate said to the chief *p* . . . Luke 23:4
But the chief *p* plotted . . . . John 12:10
become *p* without an oath . . Heb 7:21
need daily, as those high *p* . . Heb 7:27
high *p* men who have . . . . . . Heb 7:28
since there are *p* who offer . . Heb 8:4
made us kings and *p* . . . . Rev 1:6
but they shall be *p* . . . . Rev 20:6

PRIESTS'
where the *p* feet stood firm . . Josh 4:3
and the soles of the *p* feet . . Josh 4:18

PRINCE
"Who made you a *p* . . . . Ex 2:14
is the house of the *p* . . . . . . Job 21:28
is the downfall of a *p* . . . . . Prov 14:28
Everlasting Father, *P* . . . . Is 9:6
against the *P* of princes . . . . Dan 8:25
until Messiah the *P* . . . . Dan 9:25
with the *p* of Persia . . . . . . Dan 10:20
except Michael your *p* . . . . Dan 10:21
days without king or *p* . . . . Hos 3:4
p asks for gifts . . . . Mic 7:3
and killed the *P* . . . . Acts 3:15
His right hand to be *P* . . . . Acts 5:31
the *p* of the power . . . . Eph 2:2

PRINCES
He is not partial to *p* . . . . . Job 34:19
to bind his *p* at his . . . . . . Ps 105:22
He may seat him with *p* . . . Ps 113:8
to put confidence in *p* . . . . Ps 118:9
P also sit and speak . . . . . Ps 119:23
p and all judges of . . . . . . Ps 148:11
good, nor to strike *p* . . . . . Prov 17:26
is a child, and your *p* . . . . . Eccl 10:16
of nobles, and your *p* . . . . . Eccl 10:17
children to be their *p* . . . . . . Is 3:4
p will rule with . . . . Is 32:1
He brings the *p* . . . . Is 40:23

PRINCIPAL
Wisdom is the *p* . . . . Prov 4:7

PRINCIPALITIES
nor *p* nor powers . . . . Rom 8:38
and blood, but against *p* . . . Eph 6:12
dominions or *p* or powers . . Col 1:16
disarmed *p* and powers, . . . Col 2:15

PRINCIPALITY
far above all *p* . . . . Eph 1:21
is the head of all *p* . . . . Col 2:10

PRINCIPLES
from the basic *p* . . . . Col 2:20
again the first *p* . . . . Heb 5:12

PRINT
hands the *p* of the nails . . . John 20:25

PRISCILLA (or Prisca)
Wife of Aquila, Acts 18:1–3
With Aquila, instructs Apollos, Acts 18:26
Mentioned by Paul, Rom 16:3; 1 Cor 16:19; 2 Tim 4:19

PRISON
and put him into the *p* . . . . Gen 39:20
Bring my soul out of *p* . . . . . Ps 142:7
in darkness from the *p* . . . . . Is 42:7
the opening of the *p* . . . . . . Is 61:1
should put him in *p* . . . . . . Jer 29:26
John had been put in *p* . . . . Matt 4:12
John had heard in *p* . . . . . . Matt 11:2
had John beheaded in *p* . . . Matt 14:10
I was in *p* and you . . . . . . Matt 25:36
we see You sick, or in *p* . . Matt 25:39
or naked or sick or in *p* . . . Matt 25:44
after John was put in *p* . . . . Mark 1:14
put them in the common *p* . . Acts 5:18
Lord opened the *p* doors . . . Acts 5:19
did not find them in the *p* . . Acts 5:22
was therefore kept in *p* . . . Acts 12:5
of the *p* were shaken . . . . . Acts 16:26
seeing the *p* doors open . . . Acts 16:27

So the keeper of the p .... Acts 16:36
to the spirits in p .... 1 Pet 3:19
a p for every foul spirit, ... Rev 18:2
will be released from his p ... Rev 20:7

PRISONER
the groaning of the p .... Ps 79:11
p called Barabbas .... Matt 27:16
releasing one p to them ... Mark 15:6
reason I, Paul, the p .... Eph 3:1
the p of the Lord, beseech ... Eph 4:1
Lord, nor of me His p .... 2 Tim 1:8
Paul, a p of Christ Jesus, ... Philem 1

PRISONERS
p rest together .... Job 3:18
does not despise His p ...... Ps 69:33
gives freedom to the p ...... Ps 146:7
the stronghold, you p ...... Zech 9:12
the p were listening to .... Acts 16:25
and my fellow p .... Rom 16:7
Remember the p as if .... Heb 13:3

PRISONS
the synagogues and p .... Luke 21:12
p more frequently .... 2 Cor 11:23

PRIVATE
is of any p interpretation .. 2 Pet 1:20

PRIVATELY
disciples came to Jesus .. Matt 17:19
Andrew asked Him p ...... Mark 13:3
aside p into a deserted .... Luke 9:10

PRIZE
life shall be as a p .... Jer 21:9
but one receives the p ..... 1 Cor 9:24
the goal for the p .... Phil 3:14

PROCEED
For they p from evil .... Jer 9:3
heart p evil thoughts .... Matt 15:19
p evil thoughts, adulteries .. Mark 7:21
not permitting us to p .... Acts 27:7
p out of your mouth, ... Eph 4:29
of the same mouth p ..... James 3:10

PROCEEDED
for I p forth .... John 8:42
p from the mouth of Him .. Rev 19:21

PROCEEDINGS
he adjourned the p .... Acts 24:22

PROCEEDS
by every word that p .... Deut 8:3
by every word that p .... Matt 4:4
Spirit of truth who p ..... John 15:26
back part of the p .... Acts 5:2

PROCESS
in the p of time .... 1 Sam 1:20

PROCESSION
They have seen Your p ...... Ps 68:24

PROCHORUS
One of the first seven deacons, Acts
6:5

PROCLAIM
you, and I will p .... Ex 33:19
p the name of the LORD .... Deut 32:3
p it not in the .... 2 Sam 1:20
and they shall p .... Is 60:6
to p liberty to the captives, ... Is 61:1
to p the acceptable year of .... Is 61:2
began to p it freely .... Mark 1:45
knowing, Him I p .... Acts 17:23
drink this cup, you p .... 1 Cor 11:26
that you may p the praises .. 1 Pet 2:9

PROCLAIMED
p the good news .... Ps 40:9
company of those who p ... Ps 68:11
p a fast, and put on .... Jon 3:5
he went his way and p ..... Luke 8:39
inner rooms will be p ..... Luke 12:3

PROCLAIMER
"He seems to be a p ...... Acts 17:18

PROCLAIMS
good news, who p .... Is 52:7

PROCONSUL
seeking to turn the p .... Acts 13:8
When Gallio was p .... Acts 18:12

PRODIGAL
with p living .... Luke 15:13

PRODUCE
land shall yield its p .... Lev 26:4
all kinds of p .... Ps 144:13
p the righteousness of .... James 1:20

PRODUCED
p in me all manner of evil ... Rom 7:8
What diligence it p in ... 2 Cor 7:11

PRODUCES
forcing of wrath p strife ... Prov 30:33
indeed bears fruit and p .. Matt 13:23
if it dies, it p much grain .. John 12:24
tribulation p perseverance .. Rom 5:3
sorrow p repentance ...... 2 Cor 7:10
of your faith p patience .... James 1:3

PRODUCING
p death in me through ..... Rom 7:13

PROFANE
and offered p fire .... Lev 10:1
and priest are p .... Jer 23:11
"But you p it .... Mal 1:12
tried to p the temple ...... Acts 24:6
But reject p and old .... 1 Tim 4:7
p person like Esau .... Heb 12:16

PROFANED
p his crown by casting ...... Ps 89:39
and p My Sabbaths .... Ezek 22:8
p the LORD's holy .... Mal 2:11

PROFANENESS
of Jerusalem p has .... Jer 23:15

PROFANING
p the covenant of the ...... Mal 2:10

PROFESS
They p to know God ...... Titus 1:16

PROFESSING
P to be wise .... Rom 1:22
is proper for women p .... 1 Tim 2:10

PROFIT
p is there in my blood .... Ps 30:9
p has a man from all ...... Eccl 1:3
There was no p under ...... Eccl 2:11
for they will not p .... Is 57:12
words that cannot p .... Jer 7:8
p which you have made .. Ezek 22:13
p is it that we have .... Mal 3:14
For what p is it to .... Matt 16:26
For what will it p .... Mark 8:36
For what p is it to .... Luke 9:25
her masters much p ...... Acts 16:16
hope of p was gone .... Acts 16:19
brought no small p .... Acts 19:24
what is the p of .... Rom 3:1
not seeking my own p ... 1 Cor 10:33
Christ will p you .... Gal 5:2
about words to no p ...... 2 Tim 2:14
them, but He for our p .... Heb 12:10
What does it p .... James 2:14
and sell, and make a p .. James 4:13

PROFITABLE
"Can a man be p .... Job 22:2
It is doubtless not p ..... 2 Cor 12:1
godliness is p for all ...... 1 Tim 4:8
of God, and is p .... 2 Tim 3:16
things are good and p ...... Titus 3:8
to you, but now is p ...... Philem 11

PROFITS
p a man nothing that ...... Job 34:9
from her p she plants a ... Prov 31:16
the flesh p nothing .... John 6:63
have not love, it p .... 1 Cor 13:3
exercise p a little .... 1 Tim 4:8

PROFOUND
with things too p .... Ps 131:1

PROGRESS
your p may be evident .... 1 Tim 4:15

PROLONG
you will not p your .... Deut 4:26
p Your anger to all .... Ps 85:5
nor will he p his days ...... Eccl 8:13

PROLONGED
and his days are p .... Eccl 8:12

PROLONGS
The fear of the LORD p ... Prov 10:27

PROMISE
of all His good p .... 1 Kin 8:56
Has His p failed .... Ps 77:8
remembered His holy p ... Ps 105:42
Behold, I send the P ...... Luke 24:49
but to wait for the P .... Acts 1:4
p of the Holy Spirit, He ... Acts 2:33
For the p is to you .... Acts 2:39
p drew near which God .... Acts 7:17
for the hope of the p ..... Acts 26:6
is made void and the p ... Rom 4:14
p might be sure .... Rom 4:16
p of God through unbelief ... Rom 4:20
For this is the word of p .... Rom 9:9
make the p of no effect .... Gal 3:17
it is no longer of p .... Gal 3:18
heirs according to the p .... Gal 3:29
Isaac was, are children of p .. Gal 4:28
first commandment with p .. Eph 6:2
having p of the life that .... 1 Tim 4:8
Therefore, since a p .... Heb 4:1
endured, he obtained the p .. Heb 6:15
to the heirs of p .... Heb 6:17
did not receive the p ..... Heb 11:39
they p them liberty .... 2 Pet 2:19
not slack concerning His p .. 2 Pet 3:9
p that He has promised ... 1 John 2:25

PROMISED
bless you as He has p ...... Deut 1:11
that what He had p .... Rom 4:21
Him faithful who had p .... Heb 11:11

PROMISES
For all the p of God ...... 2 Cor 1:20
his Seed were the p .... Gal 3:16
patience inherit the p ...... Heb 6:12
having received the p ..... Heb 11:13
great and precious p .... 2 Pet 1:4

PROMOTE
Exalt her, and she will p .... Prov 4:8

PROMOTED
Then the king p Daniel ..... Dan 2:48
Then the king p Shadrach, .. Dan 3:30

PROMOTES
tongue of the wise p ...... Prov 12:18

PROMPTLY
him disciplines him p ..... Prov 13:24

PRONOUNCE
for he could not p it right .. Judg 12:6
P guilty, O God .... Ps 5:10

PROOF
which is to them a p .... Phil 1:28

PROOFS
by many infallible p .... Acts 1:3

PROPER
you, but for what is p ..... 1 Cor 7:35
Is it p for a woman to .... 1 Cor 11:13
but, which is p .... 1 Tim 2:10
are p for sound doctrine .... Titus 2:1

PROPERLY
Let us walk p .... Rom 13:13
that you may walk p ..... 1 Thess 4:12

PROPHECIES
Do not despise p .... 1 Thess 5:20

PROPHECY

if *p*, let us prophesy in ... Rom 12:6
miracles, to another *p* ... 1 Cor 12:10
I have the gift of *p* ...... 1 Cor 13:2
p with the laying on of .... 1 Tim 4:14
for *p* never came by ...... 2 Pet 1:21
is the spirit of *p* .... Rev 19:10
of the book of this *p* ..... Rev 22:19

PROPHESIED

upon them, that they *p* .... Num 11:25
to them, yet they *p* .... Jer 23:21
Lord, have we not *p* ...... Matt 7:22
prophets and the law *p* ... Matt 11:13
virgin daughters who *p* .... Acts 21:9
even more that you *p* ..... 1 Cor 14:5

PROPHESIES

for the prophet who *p* ..... Jer 28:9
woman who prays or *p* ... 1 Cor 11:5
p edifies the church .... 1 Cor 14:4

PROPHESY

prophets, "Do not *p* .... Is 30:10
The prophets *p* falsely ..... Jer 5:31
your daughters shall *p* ..... Joel 2:28
Who can but *p* .... Amos 3:8
saying, "*P* to us .... Matt 26:68
and to say to Him, "*P!*" ... Mark 14:65
your daughters shall *p* ..... Acts 2:17
if prophecy, let us *p* ...... Rom 12:6
know in part and we *p* ... 1 Cor 13:9
that you may *p* .... 1 Cor 14:1
For you can all *p* one .... 1 Cor 14:31
desire earnestly to *p* ..... 1 Cor 14:39

PROPHESYING

he had finished *p* .... 1 Sam 10:13
Every man praying or *p*. .. 1 Cor 11:4
p is not for unbelievers ... 1 Cor 14:22

PROPHET

shall be your *p* .... Ex 7:1
raise up for you a *p* .... Deut 18:15
arisen in Israel a *p* .... Deut 34:10
"I alone am left a *p* ...... 1 Kin 18:22
is no longer any *p* .... Ps 74:9
I ordained you a *p* .... Jer 1:5
p is induced to speak ..... Ezek 14:9
The *p* is a fool .... Hos 9:7
nor was I a son of a *p* .... Amos 7:14
send you Elijah the *p* ...... Mal 4:5
p shall receive a .... Matt 10:41
the sign of the *p* Jonah .... Matt 12:39
p is not without honor .... Matt 13:57
by Daniel the *p* .... Mark 13:14
no *p* is accepted in his .... Luke 4:24
is not a greater *p* .... Luke 7:28
it cannot be that a *p* ..... Luke 13:33
Nazareth, who was a *P* ... Luke 24:19
"Are you the *P* .... John 1:21
"This is truly the *P* .... John 6:14
for no *p* has arisen out of .. John 7:52
p named Agabus .... Acts 21:10
with him the false *p* ...... Rev 19:20

PROPHET'S

shall receive a *p* reward .. Matt 10:41

PROPHETESS

Then Miriam the *p*, ... Ex 15:20
Now Deborah, a *p*, ... Judg 4:4
there was one, Anna, a *p* .. Luke 2:36

PROPHETIC

by the *p* Scriptures ...... Rom 16:26
p word confirmed .... 2 Pet 1:19

PROPHETS

See FALSE PROPHETS; LAW AND THE
PROPHETS

LORD's people were *p* .... Num 11:29
Saul also among the *p* ... 1 Sam 10:12
the mouth of all his *p* ... 1 Kin 22:22
Where now are your *p* ... Jer 37:19
prophesy against the *p* ... Ezek 13:2
Her *p* are insolent .... Zeph 3:4

the Law or the *P* .... Matt 5:17
is the Law and the *P* ..... Matt 7:12
or one of the *p* .... Matt 16:14
the tombs of the *p* .... Matt 23:29
indeed, I send you *p* ..... Matt 23:34
one who kills the *p* ...... Matt 23:37
Then many false *p* .... Matt 24:11
have Moses and the *p* .... Luke 16:29
You are sons of the *p* .... Acts 3:25
p did your fathers not .... Acts 7:52
To Him all the *p* .... Acts 10:43
do you believe the *p* ..... Acts 26:27
before through His *p* ...... Rom 1:2
by the Law and the *P* .... Rom 3:21
have killed Your *p* .... Rom 11:3
p are subject to the ...... 1 Cor 14:32
to be apostles, some *p* .... Eph 4:11
brethren, take the *p* ..... James 5:10
this salvation was *p* .... 1 Pet 1:10
were also false *p* .... 2 Pet 2:1
because many false *p* .... 1 John 4:1
blood of saints and *p* ..... Rev 16:6
found the blood of *p* ..... Rev 18:24
of your brethren the *p* .... Rev 22:9

PROPITIATION

set forth as a *p* .... Rom 3:25
to God, to make *p* .... Heb 2:17
He Himself is the *p* ...... 1 John 2:2
His Son to be the *p* ...... 1 John 4:10

PROPORTION

let us prophesy in *p* ...... Rom 12:6

PROPOSED

And they *p* two .... Acts 1:23

PROPRIETY

modest apparel, with *p* .... 1 Tim 2:9

PROSECUTOR

answer me, that my *P* ..... Job 31:35

PROSELYTE

and sea to win one *p* ..... Matt 23:15
Nicolas, a *p* from Antioch. .. Acts 6:5

PROSELYTES

Rome, both Jews and *p* .... Acts 2:10

PROSPER

made all he did to *p* ...... Gen 39:3
you shall not *p* .... Deut 28:29
LORD, God made him *p* ... 2 Chr 26:5
they *p* who love you ...... Ps 122:6
his sins will not *p* .... Prov 28:13
of the LORD shall *p* .... Is 53:10
against you shall *p* .... Is 54:17
please, and it shall *p* ..... Is 55:11
of the wicked *p* .... Jer 12:1
King shall reign and *p* ..... Jer 23:5
storing up as he may *p* ... 1 Cor 16:2
I pray that you may *p* ..... 3 John 2

PROSPERED

since the LORD has *p* ..... Gen 24:56
he *p* wherever he went ... 2 Kin 18:7
David his father, and *p* .. 1 Chr 29:23
all his heart. So he *p* ... 2 Chr 31:21
Hezekiah *p* in all his .... 2 Chr 32:30
and they *p* through the .... Ezra 6:14
in the LORD will be *p* ..... Prov 28:25
Daniel *p* in the reign .... Dan 6:28
He did all this and *p* ..... Dan 8:12

PROSPERING

His ways are always *p* ..... Ps 10:5

PROSPERITY

p all your days .... Deut 23:6
p exceed the fame .... 1 Kin 10:7
p the destroyer .... Job 15:21
spend their days in *p* ..... Job 36:11
Now in my *p* I said .... Ps 30:6
has pleasure in the *p* ..... Ps 35:27
When I saw the *p* .... Ps 73:3
I pray, send now *p* ...... Ps 118:25
the day of *p* be joyful .... Eccl 7:14
that we have our *p* ...... Acts 19:25

PROSPEROUS

had made his journey *p* ... Gen 24:21
will make your way *p* ...... Josh 1:8

PROSPERS

he turns, he *p* .... Prov 17:8
just as your soul *p* .... 3 John 2

PROSTRATE

of the proud lie *p* .... Job 9:13

PROTECTED

holy man, and he *p* him ... Mark 6:20

PROUD

p waves must stop .... Job 38:11
tongue that speaks *p* .... Ps 12:3
and fully repays the *p* ..... Ps 31:23
does not respect the *p* ..... Ps 40:4
a haughty look and a *p* .... Ps 101:5
p He knows from afar ..... Ps 138:6
the house of the *p* .... Prov 15:25
Everyone *p* in heart ...... Prov 16:5
p heart stirs up .... Prov 28:25
is better than the *p* .... Eccl 7:8
by wine, he is a *p* .... Hab 2:5
He has scattered the *p* .... Luke 1:51
boasters, *p* .... 2 Tim 3:2
"God resists the *p*, but .... James 4:6
"God resists the *p* .... 1 Pet 5:5

PROVE

p yourself a man .... 1 Kin 2:2
does your arguing *p* .... Job 6:25
mind, that you may *p* ..... Rom 12:2

PROVERB

an astonishment, a *p* ..... Deut 28:37
incline my ear to a *p* .... Ps 49:4
that hang limp is a *p* ..... Prov 26:7
of a drunkard is a *p* ..... Prov 26:9
one shall take up a *p* ...... Mic 2:4
to the true *p* .... 2 Pet 2:22

PROVERBS

spoke three thousand *p* ... 1 Kin 4:32
The *p* of Solomon the ...... Prov 1:1
are *p* of Solomon .... Prov 25:1
in order many *p* .... Eccl 12:9

PROVIDE

"My son, God will *p* ...... Gen 22:8
Can He *p* meat for His ..... Ps 78:20
lambs will *p* your .... Prov 27:26
prosperity that I *p* .... Jer 33:9
P neither gold nor .... Matt 10:9
if anyone does not *p* ...... 1 Tim 5:8

PROVIDED

I have *p* Myself a king .... 1 Sam 16:1
p for her from the king's .... Esth 2:9
p from Your godness ..... Ps 68:10
atonement is *p* for iniquity . Prov 16:6
these hands have *p* .... Acts 20:34
p something better .... Heb 11:40

PROVIDES

p food for the raven ...... Job 38:41
p her supplies in the .... Prov 6:8
p food for her household .. Prov 31:15

PROVIDING

p honorable things, ... 2 Cor 8:21

PROVISION

bread of their *p* was dry .... Josh 9:5
Now Solomon's *p* .... 1 Kin 4:22
abundantly bless her *p* .... Ps 132:15
p of the king's delicacies ..... Dan 1:5
no *p* for the flesh .... Rom 13:14

PROVOKE

do not *p* Him .... Ex 23:21
p God are secure .... Job 12:6
Do they *p* Me to .... Jer 7:19
p them to jealousy .... Rom 11:11
you, fathers, do not *p* ...... Eph 6:4
do not *p* your children, lest .. Col 3:21

PROVOKED

How often they *p* .... Ps 78:40

p the Most High .... Ps 78:56
Thus they *p* Him to ...... Ps 106:29
his spirit was *p* .... Acts 17:16
seek its own, is not *p* ...... 1 Cor 13:5

PROVOKING
p one another, envying one .. Gal 5:26

PROWLER
poverty come like a *p* ..... Prov 24:34

PRUDENCE
son, endowed with *p* ...... 2 Chr 2:12
To give *p* to the .... Prov 1:4
wisdom, dwell with *p* ...... Prov 8:12
us in all wisdom and *p* ...... Eph 1:8

PRUDENT
p man covers shame ...... Prov 12:16
A *p* man conceals .... Prov 12:23
The wisdom of the *p* ...... Prov 14:8
p considers well .... Prov 14:15
receives correction is *p* .... Prov 15:5
heart will be called *p* ..... Prov 16:21
p acquires knowledge .... Prov 18:15
p wife is from the .... Prov 19:14
p man foresees evil .... Prov 22:3
perished from the *p* .... Jer 49:7
Therefore the *p* .... Amos 5:13
from the wise and *p* ...... Matt 11:25

PRUDENTLY
Servant shall deal *p* .... Is 52:13

PRUNES
that bears fruit He *p* .... John 15:2

PSALM
and the sound of a *p* .... Ps 98:5
in the second *P* .... Acts 13:33
each of you has a *p* ...... 1 Cor 14:26

PSALMIST
And the sweet *p* .... 2 Sam 23:1

PSALMS
Sing to Him, sing *p* ...... 1 Chr 16:9
to one another in *p* .... Eph 5:19
one another in *p* .... Col 3:16
Let him sing *p* .... James 5:13

PSALTERY
harp, lyre, and *p* .... Dan 3:10

PTOLEMAIS
Seaport city south of Tyre; Paul lands
at, Acts 21:7

PUBLIC
to make her a *p* example ... Matt 1:19

PUBLISHED
to be proclaimed and *p* ...... Jon 3:7

PUBLIUS
Roman official; entertains Paul, Acts
28:7, 8

PUFFED
Now some are *p* up .... 1 Cor 4:18
itself, is not *p* .... 1 Cor 13:4
a novice, lest being *p* ...... 1 Tim 3:6

PUFFS
Knowledge *p* up .... 1 Cor 8:1

PUL
King of Assyria; same as Tiglath-
Pileser, 2 Kin 15:19
—— Country and people in Africa,
Is 66:19

PULL
P me out of the net .... Ps 31:4
I will *p* down my barns ... Luke 12:18

PULLING
for *p* down strongholds .... 2 Cor 10:4

PUNISH
take that man and *p* ...... Deut 22:18
p the righteous is .... Prov 17:26
"I will *p* the world .... Is 13:11
Shall I not *p* them for .... Jer 5:9
p all who oppress them .... Jer 30:20

p your iniquity .... Lam 4:22
So I will *p* them for .... Hos 4:9

PUNISHED
You our God have *p* ...... Ezra 9:13
because He has not *p* ..... Job 35:15
p them often in every ..... Acts 26:11
These shall be *p* .... 2 Thess 1:9

PUNISHES
will you say when He *p* ..... Jer 13:21

PUNISHMENT
p is greater than I .... Gen 4:13
you do in the day of *p* .... Is 10:3
p they shall be cast .... Jer 8:12
p they shall perish .... Jer 10:15
a man for the *p* .... Lam 3:39
The *p* of the iniquity .... Lam 4:6
days of *p* have come .... Hos 9:7
not turn away its *p* .... Amos 1:3
into everlasting *p* .... Matt 25:46
p which was inflicted ...... 2 Cor 2:6
Of how much worse *p* ..... Heb 10:29
sent by him for the *p* ...... 1 Pet 2:14
the unjust under *p* .... 2 Pet 2:9

PUNON
Israelite camp, Num 33:42, 43

PURCHASED
(Now this man *p* a field .... Acts 1:18
of God could be *p* .... Acts 8:20
of the *p* possession .... Eph 1:14

PURE
a mercy seat of *p* gold ...... Ex 25:17
Can a man be more *p* .... Job 4:17
if you were *p* and .... Job 8:6
'My doctrine is *p* .... Job 11:4
that he could be *p* .... Job 15:14
the heavens are not *p* ..... Job 15:15
the stars are not *p* .... Job 25:5
of the LORD are *p* .... Ps 12:6
will show Yourself *p* .... Ps 18:26
To such as are *p* .... Ps 73:1
of the *p* are pleasant ..... Prov 15:26
ways of a man are *p* .... Prov 16:2
my heart clean, I am *p* ..... Prov 20:9
but as for the *p* .... Prov 21:8
a generation that is *p* ..... Prov 30:12
Shall I count *p* .... Mic 6:11
Blessed are the *p* in heart ... Matt 5:8
things indeed are *p* ...... Rom 14:20
whatever things are *p* ...... Phil 4:8
with a *p* conscience .... 1 Tim 3:9
keep yourself *p* .... 1 Tim 5:22
serve with a *p* conscience .. 2 Tim 1:3
p all things are *p* .... Titus 1:15
bodies washed with *p* ..... Heb 10:22
P and undefiled religion .. James 1:27
above is first *p* .... James 3:17
babes, desire the *p* .... 1 Pet 2:2
just as He is *p* .... 1 John 3:3

PURER
p eyes than to behold ...... Hab 1:13

PURGE
P me with hyssop .... Ps 51:7
p them as gold and .... Mal 3:3

PURGED
away, and your sin *p* .... Is 6:7
He had by Himself *p* .... Heb 1:3

PURIFICATION
for the water of *p* .... Num 19:9
with the water of *p* ...... Num 31:23

PURIFIED
earth, *p* seven times .... Ps 12:6
all things are *p* .... Heb 9:22
Since you have *p* .... 1 Pet 1:22

PURIFIES
hope in Him *p* himself ..... 1 John 3:3

PURIFY
p the sons of Levi .... Mal 3:3
and *p* your hearts .... James 4:8

PURIFYING
thus *p* all foods .... Mark 7:19
p their hearts by .... Acts 15:9
sanctifies for the *p* .... Heb 9:13

PURIM
called these days *P* .... Esth 9:26

PURITY
be delivered by the *p* ...... Job 22:30
He who loves *p* of .... Prov 22:11
by *p*, by knowledge .... 2 Cor 6:6
spirit, in faith, in *p* .... 1 Tim 4:12

PURPLE
who was clothed in *p* .... Luke 16:19
they put on Him a *p* ...... John 19:2
She was a seller of *p* ..... Acts 16:14

PURPOSE
and fulfill all your *p* .... Ps 20:4
A time for every *p* .... Eccl 3:1
p that is purposed .... Is 14:26
But for this *p* I came ..... John 12:27
by the determined *p* .... Acts 2:23
them all that with *p* ...... Acts 11:23
called according to His *p* .. Rom 8:28
to the eternal *p* .... Eph 3:11
sent to you for this very *p* .. Eph 6:22
Now the *p* of the .... 1 Tim 1:5
manner of life, *p* .... 2 Tim 3:10
For this *p* the Son of God .. 1 John 3:8
to fulfill His *p* .... Rev 17:17

PURPOSED
For the LORD had *p* ..... 2 Sam 17:14
LORD of hosts has *p* .... Is 23:9
But Daniel *p* in his .... Dan 1:8
Paul *p* in the Spirit ...... Acts 19:21
pleasure which He *p* .... Eph 1:9

PURPOSELY
the bundles fall *p* for her .. Ruth 2:16

PURPOSES
each one give as he *p* ...... 2 Cor 9:7

PURSE
let us all have one *p* .... Prov 1:14

PURSES
p his lips and brings ...... Prov 16:30

PURSUE
And will You *p* dry .... Job 13:25
p my honor as the wind ... Job 30:15
The sword shall *p* .... Jer 48:2
but their hearts *p* .... Ezek 33:31
Let us know, let us *p* .... Hos 6:3
p righteousness........... Rom 9:30
P love, and desire .... 1 Cor 14:1
p what is good .... 1 Thess 5:15
p righteousness .... 1 Tim 6:11
p righteousness, faith ..... 2 Tim 2:22
P peace with all people .... Heb 12:14
him seek peace and *p* ..... 1 Pet 3:11

PURSUES
Evil *p* sinners .... Prov 13:21
flee when no one *p* .... Prov 28:1

PURSUING
but Israel, *p* the law ...... Rom 9:31

PUT
Also He has *p* eternity ..... Eccl 3:11
pride He is able to *p* down .. Dan 4:37
what you will *p* on .... Matt 6:25
p my hand into His .... John 20:25
But *p* on the Lord .... Rom 13:14

PUT OFF
I will *p* my sad face .... Job 9:27
You have *p* my sackcloth .... Ps 30:11
you *p*, concerning your ..... Eph 4:22
you yourselves are to *p* all ... Col 3:8
shortly I must *p* my tent ... 2 Pet 1:14

PUT ON
I *p* righteousness .... Job 29:14

awake, p strength, O arm . . . . . Is 51:9
For He p righteousness . . . . . . Is 59:17
body, what you will p . . . . . . Matt 6:25
they p Him a purple robe . . John 19:2
p the armor of light . . . . Rom 13:12
p the Lord Jesus Christ . . . Rom 13:14
must p incorruption . . . . . . 1 Cor 15:53
into Christ have p Christ . . Gal 3:27
you p the new man . . . . Eph 4:24
P the whole armor of God . . Eph 6:11
having p the breastplate . . . . Eph 6:14
have p the new man . . . . Col 3:10
p tender mercies . . . . Col 3:12
all these things p love . . . . . . Col 3:14
I will p you no other . . . . Rev 2:24

PUTEOLI
Seaport of Italy, Acts 28:13

PUTREFYING
bruises and p sores . . . . Is 1:6

QUAIL
and it brought q . . . . Num 11:31
and He brought q . . . . Ps 105:40

QUAKED
the whole mountain q . . . . . . Ex 19:18
and the earth q . . . . Matt 27:51

QUAKES
The earth q before . . . . Joel 2:10

QUALIFIED
the Father who has q . . . . . . Col 1:12

QUARREL
see how he seeks a q . . . . . 2 Kin 5:7
any fool can start a q . . . . Prov 20:3
He will not q nor cry . . . . . Matt 12:19
of the Lord must not q . . . . 2 Tim 2:24

QUARRELSOME
but gentle, not q . . . . 1 Tim 3:3

QUARTER
in the Second Q . . . . 2 Kin 22:14
from the Second Q . . . . Zeph 1:10

QUARTZ
be made of coral or q . . . . . Job 28:18

QUEEN
Q Vashti also made a . . . . . . Esth 1:9
stands the q in gold . . . . Ps 45:9
burn incense to the q . . . . . . Jer 44:17
The q of the South . . . . Matt 12:42
under Candace the q . . . . . . Acts 8:27
heart, 'I sit as q . . . . Rev 18:7

QUEENS
There are sixty q . . . . Song 6:8
q your nursing mothers . . . . . Is 49:23

QUENCH
Many waters cannot q . . . . . Song 8:7
so that no one can q . . . . Jer 4:4
flax He will not q . . . . Matt 12:20
q all the fiery . . . . Eph 6:16
Do not q the Spirit . . . . . 1 Thess 5:19

QUENCHED
LORD, the fire was q . . . . . . Num 11:2
they were q like a . . . . Ps 118:12
their fire is not q . . . . Is 66:24
that shall never be q . . . . . Mark 9:43
and the fire is not q . . . . . Mark 9:44
q the violence of fire . . . . . Heb 11:34

QUESTIONS
test him with hard q . . . . . . 1 Kin 10:1
and asking them q . . . . Luke 2:46
market, asking no q . . . . . 1 Cor 10:25

QUICK-TEMPERED
q man acts foolishly . . . . . Prov 14:17
not self-willed, not q . . . . . . Titus 1:7

QUICKLY
have turned aside q . . . . Ex 32:8

with your adversary q . . . . . Matt 5:25
"What you do, do q . . . . . . John 13:27
Behold, I am coming q . . . . . Rev 3:11
"Surely I am coming q . . . . Rev 22:20

QUIET
lain still and been q . . . . Job 3:13
'Take heed, and be q . . . . Is 7:4
earth is at rest and q . . . . . . Is 14:7
gladness, He will q . . . . . . Zeph 3:17
warned him to be q . . . . . Mark 10:48
aspire to lead a q . . . . . . 1 Thess 4:11
we may lead a q and . . . . . 1 Tim 2:2
a gentle and q spirit . . . . . . 1 Pet 3:4

QUIETED
calmed and q my soul . . . . . . Ps 131:2
the city clerk had q . . . . . . Acts 19:35

QUIETNESS
will give peace and q . . . . . 1 Chr 22:9
When He gives q . . . . Job 34:29
a handful with q . . . . Eccl 4:6
in q and confidence . . . . . . Is 30:15
of righteousness, q . . . . Is 32:17
that they work in q . . . . . 2 Thess 3:12

QUIETS
q the earth by the . . . . Job 37:17

QUIVER
q rattles against him . . . . . Job 39:23
the man who has his q . . . . . Ps 127:5
q He has hidden Me . . . . . . Is 49:2
Their q is like an . . . . Jer 5:16

RAAMSES
Treasure city built by Hebrew slaves,
Ex 1:11

RABBAH
Capital of Ammon, Amos 1:14
Besieged by Joab; defeated and en-
slaved by David, 2 Sam 12:26–31
Destruction of, foretold, Jer 49:2, 3

RABBI
be called by men, 'R . . . . . Matt 23:7
do not be called 'R . . . . . . Matt 23:8

RABBONI
Mary addresses Christ as, John 20:16

RABMAG
Title applied to Babylonian prince, Jer
39:3, 13

RABSARIS
Title applied to:
Assyrian officials sent by Sen-
nacherib, 2 Kin 18:17
Babylonian prince, Jer 39:3, 13

RABSHAKEH
Sent by king of Assyria to threaten
Hezekiah, 2 Kin 18:17–37; Is 36:2–22
The Lord sends rumor to take him
away, 2 Kin 19:6–8; Is 37:6–8

RACA
to his brother, 'R . . . . Matt 5:22

RACE
man to run its r . . . . Ps 19:5
r is not to the swift . . . . Eccl 9:11
who run in a r all run . . . 1 Cor 9:24
I have finished the r . . . . . . 2 Tim 4:7
with endurance the r . . . . . . Heb 12:1

RACHEL
Laban's younger daughter; Jacob's
favorite wife, Gen 29:28–30
Supports her husband's position, Gen
31:14–16
Mother of Joseph and Benjamin, Gen
30:22–25
Prophecy concerning; quoted, Jer
31:15; Matt 2:18

RADIANT
to Him and were r . . . . Ps 34:5

RAGE
Disperse the r of your . . . . . . Job 40:11
Why do the nations r . . . . Ps 2:1
'Why did the nations r . . . . Acts 4:25

RAGES
he r against all wise . . . . . . Prov 18:1

RAGS
clothe a man with r . . . . . Prov 23:21
are like filthy r . . . . Is 64:6

RAHAB
Prostitute in Jericho; helps Joshua's
spies, Josh 2:1–21
Spared in battle, Josh 6:17–25
Mentioned in the N.T., Matt 1:5; Heb
11:31; James 2:25
——— Used figuratively of Egypt, Ps 87:4

RAIN
had not caused it to r . . . . . . Gen 2:5
And the r was on the . . . . . . Gen 7:12
I will r bread from heaven . . . Ex 16:4
early r and the latter r . . . . Deut 11:14
my teaching drop as the r . . Deut 32:2
be dew nor r these years . . 1 Kin 17:1
sound of abundance of r . . 1 Kin 18:41
He gives r on the . . . . Job 5:10
to the gentle r . . . . Job 37:6
sent a plentiful r . . . . Ps 68:9
clouds, who prepares r . . . . Ps 147:8
snow in summer and r . . . . Prov 26:1
r which leaves no food . . . . Prov 28:3
not return after the r . . . . . . Eccl 12:2
the r is over and gone . . . . Song 2:11
our God, who gives r . . . . Jer 5:24
I will r down on him . . . . Ezek 38:22
given you the former r . . . . . Joel 2:23
there will be no r . . . . Zech 14:17
the good, and sends r . . . . . Matt 5:45
and the r descended . . . . . . Matt 7:25
He did good, gave us r . . . . Acts 14:17
r that often comes . . . . Heb 6:7
the early and latter r . . . . . James 5:7
that it would not r . . . . James 5:17
and the heaven gave r . . . . James 5:18

RAINBOW
I set My r in the . . . . Gen 9:13
the appearance of a r . . . . . Ezek 1:28
and there was a r . . . . Rev 4:3

RAINED
had r down manna on . . . . . . Ps 78:24
r fire and brimstone . . . . . Luke 17:29

RAINS
r righteousness . . . . Hos 10:12

RAISE
shall r up the tabernacle . . . Ex 26:30
that I will r to David a . . . . . Jer 23:5
third day He will r . . . . Hos 6:2
that God is able to r . . . . . . Matt 22:30
in three days I will r . . . . . John 2:19
and I will r him up at . . . . . John 6:40
Lord and will also r . . . . . 1 Cor 6:14
will also r us up with . . . . 2 Cor 4:14
and the Lord will r . . . . . . James 5:15

RAISED
this purpose I have r . . . . . . Ex 9:16
the LORD r up judges . . . . . Judg 2:16
LORD has r up prophets . . . Jer 29:15
be killed, and be r . . . . Matt 16:21
whom God r up . . . . Acts 2:24
just as Christ was r . . . . Rom 6:4
Spirit of Him who r . . . . . . Rom 8:11
And God both r up the . . . 1 Cor 6:14
"How are the dead r . . . . . 1 Cor 15:35
and the dead will be r . . . 1 Cor 15:52
and r us up together . . . . . . Eph 2:6
then you were r . . . . Col 3:1

RAISED FROM THE DEAD
beheaded; he has been r . . . Mark 6:16

whom He had r .... John 12:1
disciples after He was r ... John 21:14
Prince of life, whom God r . Acts 3:15
Christ was r by the glory ... Rom 6:4
been r, dies no more .... Rom 6:9
that He has been r .... 1 Cor 15:12
heaven, whom He r ..... 1 Thess 1:10
r according to my gospel ... 2 Tim 2:8

RAISED HIM FROM THE DEAD
out of his tomb and r ..... John 12:17
But God r .... Acts 13:30
your heart that God has r .. Rom 10:9
God the Father who r ...... Gal 1:1
in Christ when He r .... Eph 1:20
the working of God, who r .. Col 2:12
believe in God, who r ..... 1 Pet 1:21

RAISES
r the poor out of the .... Ps 113:7
r those who are bowed ..... Ps 146:8
For as the Father r .... John 5:21
but in God who r .... 2 Cor 1:9

RAM
r which had two horns ..... Dan 8:3

RAMAH
Fortress built, 1 Kin 15:17–22
Samuel's headquarters, 1 Sam 7:15, 17
David flees to, 1 Sam 19:18–23

RAMOTH GILEAD
City of refuge east of Jordan, Deut 4:43;
Josh 20:8; 1 Chr 6:80
Site of Ahab's fatal conflict with Syr-
ians, 1 Kin 22:1–39

RAMPART
and it stood by the r ..... 2 Sam 20:15
whose r was like the sea, ... Nah 3:8
and set myself on the r ...... Hab 2:1

RAMS
the sweet aroma of r .... Ps 66:15
r of Nebaioth shall .... Is 60:7

RAN
they both r together .... John 20:4
You r well .... Gal 5:7

RANKS
r out of the land of Egypt ... Ex 13:18
war, who could keep r ... 1 Chr 12:38
and they do not break r ..... Joel 2:7

RANSOM
r would not help you ...... Job 36:18
nor give to God a r .... Ps 49:7
The r of a man's life ...... Prov 13:8
"I will r them from .... Hos 13:14
to give His life a r .... Mark 10:45
who gave Himself a r ...... 1 Tim 2:6

RANSOMED
and the r of the LORD .... Is 35:10
redeemed Jacob, and r .... Jer 31:11

RARE
of the LORD was r .... 1 Sam 3:1
make a mortal more r ...... Is 13:12

RASH
Do not be r with your ...... Eccl 5:2

RASHLY
so that he spoke r .... Ps 106:33
and do nothing r .... Acts 19:36

RATS
tumors and five golden r ... 1 Sam 6:4

RAVEN
Then he sent out a r, ... Gen 8:7
food for the r .... Job 38:41
and black as a r .... Song 5:11
and the r shall dwell in it .... Is 34:11

RAVENOUS
inwardly they are r .... Matt 7:15

RAVENS
and to the young r .... Ps 147:9
Consider the r .... Luke 12:24

RAVISHED
You have r my heart ...... Song 4:9
r the women in Zion ...... Lam 5:11

RAYS
He had r flashing from His .. Hab 3:4

RAZOR
no r shall come upon his ... Num 6:5
no r shall come upon his ... Judg 13:5
r has ever come upon .... Judg 16:17
like a sharp r .... Ps 52:2
will shave with a hired r ..... Is 7:20

REACHED
earth, and its top r .... Gen 28:12
For her sins have r .... Rev 18:5

REACHING
r forward to those .... Phil 3:13

READ
saying, "R this, please" ..... Is 29:11
if you can r the writing ..... Dan 5:16
"Have you never r .... Matt 21:42
day, and stood up to r .... Luke 4:16
hearts, known and r ...... 2 Cor 3:2
when Moses is r .... 2 Cor 3:15
when this epistle is r .... Col 4:16
r the scroll, or to look at ..... Rev 5:4

READER
let the r understand ...... Mark 13:14

READINESS
the word with all r .... Acts 17:11
that as there was a r ..... 2 Cor 8:11

READING
r the prophet Isaiah .... Acts 8:30
give attention to r .... 1 Tim 4:13

READS
that he may run who r ...... Hab 2:2
Blessed is he who r .... Rev 1:3

READY
"The LORD was r .... Is 38:20
and those who were r ..... Matt 25:10
"Lord, I am r .... Luke 22:33
and being r to punish ..... 2 Cor 10:6
Be r in season and out ..... 2 Tim 4:2
and always be r .... 1 Pet 3:15

REAFFIRM
r your love to him .... 2 Cor 2:8

REAP
in tears shall r .... Ps 126:5
the clouds will not r ...... Eccl 11:4
r the whirlwind .... Hos 8:7
r in mercy .... Hos 10:12
You shall sow, but not r .... Mic 6:15
they neither sow nor r .... Matt 6:26
you knew that I r .... Matt 25:26
if we r your material ..... 1 Cor 9:11
that he will also r .... Gal 6:7
due season we shall r .... Gal 6:9
in Your sickle and r ...... Rev 14:15

REAPED
wheat but r thorns .... Jer 12:13
you have r iniquity .... Hos 10:13
earth, and the earth was r .. Rev 14:16

REAPER
r does not fill his .... Ps 129:7
shall overtake the r ...... Amos 9:13

REAPERS
I will say to the r .... Matt 13:30
r are the angels .... Matt 13:39

REAPING
r what I did not .... Luke 19:22

REAPS
One sows and another r .... John 4:37

REASON
out wisdom and the r ..... Eccl 7:25
Come now, and let us r ...... Is 1:18

faith, why do you r ...... Matt 16:8
words of truth and r ..... Acts 26:25
who asks you a r .... 1 Pet 3:15

REASONED
for three Sabbaths r .... Acts 17:2
r about righteousness ..... Acts 24:25

REBEKAH
Great-niece of Abraham, Gen 22:20–23
Becomes Isaac's wife, Gen 24:15–67
Mother of Esau and Jacob, Gen
25:21–28
Encourages Jacob to deceive Isaac,
then to flee, Gen 27:1–29, 42–46

REBEL
Only do not r .... Num 14:9
Will you r against the ...... Neh 2:19
There are those who r ..... Job 24:13
and they did not r .... Ps 105:28
if you refuse and r .... Is 1:20

REBELLED
r against You, cast Your .... Neh 9:26
for they have r against You ... Ps 5:10
and they have r against Me ..... Is 1:2
nation that has r against .... Ezek 2:3
have done wickedly and r .... Dan 9:5
For who, having heard, r .... Heb 3:16

REBELLING
more against Him by r ..... Ps 78:17

REBELLION
r is as the sin .... 1 Sam 15:23
For he adds r to his ...... Job 34:37
evil man seeks only r ..... Prov 17:11
you have taught r .... Jer 28:16
hearts as in the r .... Heb 3:8
and perished in the r ...... Jude 11

REBELLIOUS
r exalt themselves .... Ps 66:7
but the r dwell in a .... Ps 68:6
day long to a r people .... Is 65:2
a defiant and r heart ...... Jer 5:23
their princes are r .... Hos 9:15

REBELS
are all stubborn r .... Jer 6:28

REBUILD
God, to r its ruins .... Ezra 9:9
tombs, that I may r .... Neh 2:5
they shall r the old ruins .... Is 61:4
r it as in the days of ...... Amos 9:11
will r the tabernacle of .... Acts 15:16

REBUILDING
we are r the temple that ... Ezra 5:11
heard that we were r the ..... Neh 4:1

REBUILT
be r on its former site ..... Ezra 5:15
heard that I had r the wall ... Neh 6:1
and the ruins shall be r .. Ezek 36:33

REBUKE
He will surely r .... Job 13:10
astonished at His r .... Job 26:11
they perish at the r .... Ps 80:16
At Your r they fled .... Ps 104:7
And let him r me .... Ps 141:5
Turn at my r .... Prov 1:23
r a wise man .... Prov 9:8
R is more effective ...... Prov 17:10
r is better than love ...... Prov 27:5
better to hear the r .... Eccl 7:5
r the oppressor .... Is 1:17
sake I have suffered r .... Jer 15:15
r strong nations .... Mic 4:3
sins against you, r ...... Luke 17:3
r Your disciples .... Luke 19:39
Do not r an older man .... 1 Tim 5:1
who are sinning r .... 1 Tim 5:20
r them sharply .... Titus 1:13
"The Lord r you .... Jude 9
As many as I love, I r .... Rev 3:19

REBUKED
r the winds and the . . . . Matt 8:26
r their unbelief . . . . Mark 16:14
when you are *r* by Him . . . . . Heb 12:5
but he was *r* for his . . . . 2 Pet 2:16

REBUKES
with *r* You correct . . . . Ps 39:11
r a wicked man . . . . Prov 9:7
ear that hears the *r* . . . . Prov 15:31
r a man will find more . . . . Prov 28:23

RECALL
r the former days . . . . Heb 10:32

RECEDED
waters *r* continually from . . . . Gen 8:3
Then the sky *r* as a scroll . . . Rev 6:14

RECEIVE
He shall *r* blessing . . . . Ps 24:5
r us graciously . . . . Hos 14:2
you are willing to *r* . . . . . . Matt 11:14
believing, you will *r* . . . . . . Matt 21:22
and His own did not *r* . . . . . John 1:11
"I do not *r* honor . . . . John 5:41
will come again and *r* . . . . . John 14:3
the world cannot *r* . . . . John 14:17
Ask, and you will *r* . . . . John 16:24
"R the Holy Spirit . . . . John 20:22
"Lord Jesus, *r* . . . . Acts 7:59
r the Holy Spirit . . . . Acts 19:2
R one who is weak . . . . Rom 14:1
that each one may *r* . . . . . 2 Cor 5:10
r the grace of God in . . . . 2 Cor 6:1
r the Spirit by the . . . . Gal 3:2
R him therefore in the . . . . . Phil 2:29
suppose that he will *r* . . . . James 1:7
whatever we ask we *r* . . . 1 John 3:22

RECEIVED
Freely you have *r*, freely . . Matt 10:8
r your consolation . . . . Luke 6:24
in your lifetime you *r* . . . . Luke 16:25
But as many as *r* . . . . John 1:12
and ankle bones *r* strength . . Acts 3:7
for God has *r* him . . . . Rom 14:3
For I *r* from the Lord . . . . . 1 Cor 11:23
I *r* forty stripes minus . . . 2 Cor 11:24
but you *r* me as an angel . . . . Gal 4:14
have *r* Christ Jesus . . . . Col 2:6
tradition which he *r* . . . . . 2 Thess 3:6
r up in glory . . . . 1 Tim 3:16
r the knowledge of the . . . . Heb 10:26
r strength to conceive . . . . . Heb 11:11
who had *r* the promises . . . Heb 11:17
Women *r* their dead . . . . . . Heb 11:35
As each one has *r* a gift. . . 1 Pet 4:10
For He *r* from God the . . . . 2 Pet 1:17
r the mark of the beast . . . . Rev 19:20

RECEIVES
r correction is prudent . . . . . Prov 15:5
r you *r* Me . . . . Matt 10:40
immediately *r* it with joy . . Matt 13:20
r one little child . . . . Matt 18:5
and whoever *r* Me . . . . Mark 9:37
For everyone who asks *r* . . Luke 11:10
This man *r* sinners and . . . . Luke 15:2
run, but one *r* the prize . . . 1 Cor 9:24
who *r* tithes, paid tithes . . . . . Heb 7:9
every son whom He *r* . . . . . Heb 12:6

RECEIVING
r a kingdom which . . . . Heb 12:28

RECHAB
Assassin of Ishbosheth, 2 Sam 4:2, 6
—— Father of Jehonadab, founder of
the Rechabites, 2 Kin 10:15–23
Related to the Kenites, 1 Chr 2:55

RECHABITES
Kenite clan fathered by Rechab, committed to nomadic life, Jer 35:1–19

RECOMPENSE
Vengeance is Mine, and *r* . Deut 32:35

He will accept no *r* . . . . Prov 6:35
not say, "I will *r* . . . . Prov 20:22
the LORD is the God of *r* . . . Jer 51:56
days of *r* have come . . . . Hos 9:7

RECOMPENSED
of my hands He has *r* . . . 2 Sam 22:21
the LORD has *r* me . . . . . . 2 Sam 22:25

RECONCILE
and that He might *r* . . . . . . Eph 2:16
r all things to . . . . Col 1:20

RECONCILED
First be *r* to your . . . . Matt 5:24
were enemies we were *r* . . . Rom 5:10
Christ's behalf, be *r* . . . . . . 2 Cor 5:20

RECONCILIATION
now received the *r* . . . . Rom 5:11
to us the word of *r* . . . . . . 2 Cor 5:19

RECONCILING
cast away is the *r* . . . . Rom 11:15
God was in Christ *r* . . . . . . 2 Cor 5:19

RECORD
r My name I will come . . . . . Ex 20:24

RECOVER
Shall I *r* from this disease . . 2 Kin 8:8
So Jeroboam did not *r* . . . 2 Chr 13:20
sick, and they will *r* . . . . . Mark 16:18

RED
the first came out *r* . . . . . . Gen 25:25
though they are *r* . . . . Is 1:18
Why is Your apparel *r* . . . . . . Is 63:2
for the sky is *r* . . . . Matt 16:2
fiery *r* dragon having . . . . . . Rev 12:3

RED SEA
Divided for Israelites, Ex 14:15–31
Boundary of Promised Land, Ex 23:31

REDEEM
man you shall surely *r* . . . Num 18:15
in our power to *r* them . . . . . Neh 5:5
In famine He shall *r* . . . . . . Job 5:20
R me from the hand of . . . . Job 6:23
can by any means *r* . . . . Ps 49:7
But God will *r* my soul . . . . Ps 49:15
r their life from . . . . Ps 72:14
And He shall *r* Israel . . . . . Ps 130:8
all that it cannot *r* . . . . Is 50:2
I will *r* them from . . . . Hos 13:14
was going to *r* Israel . . . . Luke 24:21
r those who were . . . . Gal 4:5
us, that He might *r* . . . . Titus 2:14

REDEEMED
people whom You have *r* . . . Ex 15:13
r them from the hand . . . . . Ps 106:10
Let the *r* of the LORD . . . . . Ps 107:2
r shall walk there . . . . Is 35:9
sea a road for the *r* . . . . Is 51:10
and you shall be *r* . . . . Is 52:3
and *r* His people . . . . Luke 1:68
Christ has *r* us from . . . . . . Gal 3:13
that you were not *r* . . . . . . 1 Pet 1:18
were slain, and have *r* . . . . . Rev 5:9
These were *r* from . . . . Rev 14:4

REDEEMER
For I know that my *R* . . . . Job 19:25
Most High God their *R* . . . . Ps 78:35
for their *R* is mighty . . . . . Prov 23:11
the LORD and your *R* . . . . . Is 41:14
R will come to Zion . . . . Is 59:20
our *R* from Everlasting . . . . Is 63:16
Their *R* is strong . . . . Jer 50:34

REDEEMING
r the time . . . . Eph 5:16

REDEMPTION
For the *r* of their . . . . Ps 49:8
with Him is abundant *r* . . . Ps 130:7
r is yours to buy it . . . . Jer 32:7
those who looked for *r* . . . Luke 2:38
your *r* draws near . . . . Luke 21:28

grace through the *r* . . . . Rom 3:24
the adoption, the *r* . . . . Rom 8:23
sanctification and *r* . . . . . . 1 Cor 1:30
In Him we have *r* . . . . Eph 1:7
for the day of *r* . . . . Eph 4:30
obtained eternal *r* . . . . Heb 9:12

REED
r He will not break . . . . Is 42:3
r shaken by the wind . . . . . Matt 11:7
A bruised *r* He will not . . . Matt 12:20
on the head with a *r* . . . . . Mark 15:19
sour wine, put it on a *r* . . . Mark 15:36
Then I was given a *r* like a . . Rev 11:1
the city with the *r* . . . . Rev 21:16

REEDS
r flourish without . . . . Job 8:11
the beasts of the *r* . . . . Ps 68:30

REFINED
where gold is *r* . . . . Job 28:1
us as silver is *r* . . . . Ps 66:10
Behold, I have *r* you, but . . . Is 48:10
refine them as silver is *r* . . Zech 13:9
from Me gold *r* in the fire . . Rev 3:18

REFINER
He will sit as a *r* . . . . Mal 3:3

REFINER'S
For He is like a *r* fire . . . . . . Mal 3:2

REFORMATION
until the time of *r* . . . . Heb 9:10

REFRAIN
R from meddling with . . . . 2 Chr 35:21
who have no right to *r* . . . . . 1 Cor 9:6
good days, let him *r* . . . . . . 1 Pet 3:10

REFRESH
bread, that you may *r* . . . . . Gen 18:5
r my heart in the Lord . . . . . Philem 20

REFRESHED
of God, and may be *r* . . . . Rom 15:32
r my spirit and yours . . . . 1 Cor 16:18
his spirit has been *r* . . . . . . 2 Cor 7:13
for he often *r* . . . . 2 Tim 1:16

REFRESHES
r the soul of his . . . . Prov 25:13

REFRESHING
r may come from the . . . . . . Acts 3:19

REFUGE
six cities of *r* . . . . Num 35:6
eternal God is your *r* . . . . Deut 33:27
you have come for *r* . . . . . . Ruth 2:12
but the LORD is his *r* . . . . . . Ps 14:6
God is our *r* and . . . . Ps 46:1
wings I will make my *r* . . . . Ps 57:1
God is a *r* for us . . . . Ps 62:8
You are my strong *r* . . . . . . Ps 71:7
His wings you shall take *r* . . . Ps 91:4
You are my *r*, my . . . . Ps 142:5
the heat, for a place of *r* . . . . . Is 4:6
a *r* from the storm, a shade . . . Is 25:4
who have fled for *r* . . . . Heb 6:18

REFUSE
you *r* to let My people go . . . . Ex 10:4
let my head not *r* it . . . . . . Ps 141:5
but if you *r* and rebel, you . . . Is 1:20
r the evil and choose . . . . Is 7:15
through deceit they *r* . . . . . . Jer 9:6
who *r* to hear My words, . . . Jer 13:10
hear or whether they *r* . . . . Ezek 3:7
r the younger widows . . . . . 1 Tim 5:11
See that you do not *r* . . . . . Heb 12:25

REFUSED
They *r* to obey . . . . Neh 9:17
Queen Vashti *r* to come at . . Esth 1:12
my soul *r* to be comforted . . . Ps 77:2
Inasmuch as these people *r* . . . Is 8:6
because they *r* to repent . . . Hos 11:5
nothing is to be *r* if it is . . . 1 Tim 4:4

REFUSES
My soul r to touch . . . . Job 6:7
he who r correction goes . . Prov 10:17
he who r, let him refuse . . . . Ezek 3:27
And if he r to hear. . . . . Matt 18:17

REGARD
Yet r the prayer of Your . . 1 Kin 8:28
r the rich more than . . . . Job 34:19
r iniquity in my heart . . . . Ps 66:18
r the prayer of the . . . . Ps 102:17
You do not r the person . . . Matt 22:16
did not fear God nor r . . . . . Luke 18:2
we r no one according to . . 2 Cor 5:16

REGARDED
I must be r as holy . . . . Lev 10:3
my hand and no one r . . . . . Prov 1:24
r the lowly state . . . . Luke 1:48

REGARDS
on high, yet He r the lowly . . Ps 138:6
r a rebuke will be . . . . Prov 13:18
He no longer r them . . . . . . Lam 4:16

REGENERATION
to you, that in the r . . . . . . Matt 19:28
the washing of r . . . . Titus 3:5

REGISTERED
So all went to be r . . . . Luke 2:3
firstborn who are r . . . . Heb 12:23

REGRETTED
but afterward he r . . . . Matt 21:29

REGULATIONS
yourselves to r . . . . Col 2:20

REHOBOAM
Son and successor of Solomon; refuses
   reform, 1 Kin 11:43—12:15
Ten tribes revolt against, 1 Kin
   12:16—24
Reigns over Judah 17 years, 1 Kin
   14:21—31; 2 Chr 11:5—23
Apostasizes, then repents, 2 Chr
   12:1—16

REHOBOTH
Name of a well dug by Isaac, Gen 26:22

REIGN
The LORD shall r forever . . . . Ex 15:18
but a king shall r . . . . 1 Sam 12:12
hypocrite should not r . . . . . Job 34:30
so the LORD will r . . . . Mic 4:7
And He will r . . . . Luke 1:33
not have this man to r . . . . Luke 19:14
righteousness will r . . . . Rom 5:17
so grace might r . . . . Rom 5:21
do not let sin r . . . . Rom 6:12
to r over the Gentiles . . . . . Rom 15:12
For He must r till He . . . . 1 Cor 15:25
and we shall r on the . . . . . . Rev 5:10
and He shall r forever . . . . Rev 11:15
of Christ, and shall r . . . . . . Rev 20:6

REIGNED
death r from Adam to . . . . . . Rom 5:14
so that as sin r . . . . Rom 5:21
You have r as kings . . . . 1 Cor 4:8
And they lived and r . . . . . . Rev 20:4

REIGNS
God r over the nations . . . . Ps 47:8
The LORD r . . . . Ps 93:1
to Zion, "Your God r . . . . Is 52:7
Lord God Omnipotent r . . . . . Rev 19:6

REJECT
will these people r . . . . Num 14:11
r all those who stray . . . . . Ps 119:118
"All too well you r . . . . Mark 7:9
R a divisive man . . . . Titus 3:10

REJECTED
r has become the chief . . . . Ps 118:22
He is despised and r . . . . Is 53:3
Israel has r the . . . . Hos 8:3
r has become the chief . . . Matt 21:42

many things and be r . . . . Luke 17:25
This Moses whom they r . . . Acts 7:35
to a living stone, ... 1 Pet 2:4
r has become the chief . . . . . 1 Pet 2:7

REJECTION
you shall know My r . . . . . . Num 14:34

REJECTS
he who r Me r . . . . Luke 10:16
r this does not reject . . . . . 1 Thess 4:8

REJOICE
See BE GLAD AND REJOICE
so the LORD will r . . . . Deut 28:63
let the field r . . . . 1 Chr 16:32
and let Your saints r . . . . . . 2 Chr 6:41
r who put their trust . . . . Ps 5:11
people, let Jacob r . . . . Ps 14:7
R in the LORD . . . . Ps 33:1
mutual confusion who r . . . . Ps 35:26
The righteous shall r . . . . Ps 58:10
of Your wings I will r . . . . Ps 63:7
But the king shall r . . . . Ps 63:11
Let them r before God . . . . Ps 68:3
In Your name they r . . . . Ps 89:16
Let the heavens r . . . . Ps 96:11
Let the earth r . . . . Ps 97:1
righteous see it and r . . . . . Ps 107:42
we will r and be glad . . . . . Ps 118:24
who r in doing evil . . . . Prov 2:14
be blessed, and r . . . . Prov 5:18
she shall r in time to . . . . . Prov 31:25
R, O young man . . . . Eccl 11:9
We will be glad and r . . . . . . Song 1:4
among men shall r . . . . Is 29:19
I will greatly r . . . . Is 61:10
My servants shall r . . . . Is 65:13
your heart shall r . . . . Is 66:14
Yes, I will r . . . . Jer 32:41
Do not r over me . . . . Mic 7:8
He will r over you . . . . Zeph 3:17
do not r in this . . . . Luke 10:20
loved Me, you would r . . . John 14:28
but the world will r . . . . John 16:20
and your heart will r . . . . . John 16:22
R with those who . . . . Rom 12:15
and in this I r . . . . Phil 1:18
faith, I am glad and r . . . . . . Phil 2:17
R in the Lord always . . . . Phil 4:4
R always . . . . 1 Thess 5:16
yet believing, you r . . . . 1 Pet 1:8

REJOICE IN THE LORD
R, O you righteous . . . . Ps 33:1
R, you righteous . . . . Ps 97:12
you shall r, and glory in . . . . . Is 41:16
I will greatly r . . . . Is 61:10
you children of Zion and r . . Joel 2:23
Yet I will r, I will joy . . . . . . Hab 3:18
their heart shall r . . . . Zech 10:7
Finally, my brethren, r . . . . . Phil 3:1
R always. Again I will say . . Phil 4:4

REJOICED
for good as He r . . . . Deut 30:9
for my heart r . . . . Eccl 2:10
and my spirit has r . . . . Luke 1:47
In that hour Jesus r . . . . . . Luke 10:21
Your father Abraham r . . . . John 8:56
But I r in the Lord . . . . Phil 4:10

REJOICES
My heart r in the LORD . . . . 1 Sam 2:1
glad, and my glory r . . . . Ps 16:9
bridegroom r over the bride . . . Is 62:5
r more over that sheep . . . . Matt 18:13
but r in the truth . . . . 1 Cor 13:6

REJOICING
His works with r . . . . Ps 107:22
The voice of r and . . . . Ps 118:15
for they are the r . . . . Ps 119:111
come again with r . . . . Ps 126:6
r in His inhabited . . . . Prov 8:31
he went on his way r . . . . . . Acts 8:39

yet always r . . . . 2 Cor 6:10
or joy, or crown of r . . . . . . 1 Thess 2:19
confidence and the r . . . . Heb 3:6

RELATIVES
r stand afar off . . . . Ps 38:11

RELEASE
shall grant a r of debts . . . . . Deut 15:1
time in the year of r, at . . . Deut 31:10
do you want me to r . . . . . . Matt 27:17
and power to r You . . . . John 19:10
"R the four angels . . . . Rev 9:14

RELEASED
r him, and forgave him . . . Matt 18:27
he r Barabbas to them . . . Matt 27:26
she is r from the law of . . . . Rom 7:2
Satan will be r from his . . . . Rev 20:7

RELEASING
of strife is like r water . . . . Prov 17:14
to r one prisoner to them . . Mark 15:6

RELENT
sworn and will not r . . . . Ps 110:4
and will not r . . . . Jer 4:28
then the LORD will r . . . . . . Jer 26:13
if He will turn and r . . . . Joel 2:14
sworn and will not r . . . . Heb 7:21

RELENTED
So the LORD r from the . . . . Ex 32:14
the LORD looked and r . . . 1 Chr 21:15
and God r from the . . . . Jon 3:10

RELENTING
I am weary of r . . . . Jer 15:6

RELIEF
saw that there was r . . . . Ex 8:15
that I may find r . . . . Job 32:20

RELIEVE
of my lips would r . . . . Job 16:5
r those who are really . . . . . 1 Tim 5:16

RELIEVED
You have r me when I . . . . Ps 4:1

RELIEVES
r the fatherless . . . . Ps 146:9

RELIGION
about their own r . . . . Acts 25:19
in self-imposed r . . . . Col 2:23
heart, this one's r . . . . James 1:26
and undefiled r . . . . James 1:27

RELIGIOUS
things you are very r . . . . . Acts 17:22
you thinks he is r . . . . James 1:26

RELY
name of the LORD and r . . . . Is 50:10
You r on your sword . . . . Ezek 33:26

REMAIN
shall let none of it r . . . . Ex 12:10
r angry forever . . . . Jer 3:5
and this city shall r . . . . Jer 17:25
that if ten men r . . . . Amos 6:9
you, that My joy may r . . . John 15:11
your fruit should r . . . . John 15:16
"If I will that he r . . . . John 21:22
the greater part r . . . . 1 Cor 15:6
Nevertheless to r . . . . Phil 1:24
we who are alive and r . . 1 Thess 4:15
the things which r . . . . Rev 3:2

REMAINDER
with the r of wrath . . . . Ps 76:10
I am deprived of the r . . . . . Is 38:10

REMAINED
Also my wisdom r . . . . Eccl 2:9
And Mary r with her . . . . . . Luke 1:56
like a dove, and He r . . . . . John 1:32

REMAINS
"While the earth r . . . . Gen 8:22
Therefore your sin r . . . . . . John 9:41

There *r* therefore a .... Heb 4:9
sin, for His seed *r* .... 1 John 3:9

REMEMBER
But *r* me when it is .... Gen 40:14
R the Sabbath day .... Ex 20:8
r that you were a .... Deut 5:15
R His marvelous works .. 1 Chr 16:12
but we will *r* the name .... Ps 20:7
r the sins of my youth .... Ps 25:7
r Your name in the .... Ps 119:55
R now your Creator .... Eccl 12:1
r your love more than .... Song 1:4
r the former things .... Is 43:18
"I *r* you, the kindness .... Jer 2:2
and their sin I will *r* ...... Jer 31:34
r the covenant of .... Amos 1:9
in wrath *r* mercy .... Hab 3:2
or *r* the five loaves of the ... Matt 16:9
and to *r* His holy .... Luke 1:72
R Lot's wife .... Luke 17:32
r me when You come .... Luke 23:42
r the words of the .... Acts 20:35
that we should *r* the poor .... Gal 2:10
R my chains .... Col 4:18
R that Jesus Christ .... 2 Tim 2:8
deeds I will *r* no more ..... Heb 8:12
R those who rule .... Heb 13:7
R therefore from where you .. Rev 2:5

REMEMBERED
Then God *r* Noah .... Gen 8:1
r His covenant with .... Ex 2:24
I *r* God, and was .... Ps 77:3
r Your judgments .... Ps 119:52
Who *r* us in our lowly ...... Ps 136:23
yea, we wept when we *r* ..... Ps 137:1
r that same poor man ...... Eccl 9:15
r the days of old .... Is 63:11
And Peter *r* the word ..... Matt 26:75
r the word of the Lord .... Acts 11:16

REMEMBERS
r His covenant forever ..... Ps 105:8
My soul still *r* .... Lam 3:20

REMEMBRANCE
in death there is no *r* .... Ps 6:5
I call to *r* my song .... Ps 77:6
There is no *r* of .... Eccl 1:11
Put Me in *r* .... Is 43:26
do this in *r* of Me .... Luke 22:19
do this in *r* of Me .... 1 Cor 11:24

REMIND
r you always of these ..... 2 Pet 1:12
But I want to *r* you .... Jude 5

REMINDER
there is a *r* of sins .... Heb 10:3
you always have a *r* .... 2 Pet 1:15
pure minds by way of *r* ..... 2 Pet 3:1

REMISSION
repentance for the *r* .... Mark 1:4
Jesus Christ for the *r* ...... Acts 2:38
where there is *r* .... Heb 10:18

REMNANT
Jerusalem shall go a *r* .... 2 Kin 19:31
r of you who have .... 2 Chr 30:6
would be no *r* or survivor .. Ezra 9:14
to us a very small *r* .... Is 1:9
The *r* will return .... Is 10:21
be well with your *r* .... Jer 15:11
I will gather the *r* .... Jer 23:3
and all the *r* of Judah ..... Jer 44:28
Yet I will leave a *r* .... Ezek 6:8
r whom the LORD calls ..... Joel 2:32
I will not treat the *r* ...... Zech 8:11
time there is a *r* .... Rom 11:5

REMORSEFUL
been condemned, was *r* .... Matt 27:3

REMOVE
I will also *r* Judah from .. 2 Kin 23:27
R Your plague from me ..... Ps 39:10
R Your gaze from me ...... Ps 39:13

r your foot from evil .... Prov 4:27
r falsehood and lies .... Prov 30:8
Therefore *r* sorrow .... Eccl 11:10
R violence and .... Ezek 45:9
I will *r* the iniquity of that ... Zech 3:9
let me *r* the speck that .... Luke 6:42
r your lampstand .... Rev 2:5

REMOVED
Though the earth be *r* ...... Ps 46:2
r our transgressions .... Ps 103:12
will never be *r* .... Prov 10:30
and the hills be *r* .... Is 54:10
this mountain, 'Be *r* ...... Matt 21:21

REMOVES
r the mountains .... Job 9:5

REND
So *r* your heart .... Joel 2:13

RENDER
What shall I *r* to the .... Ps 116:12
who will *r* to him the ..... Matt 21:41
"*R* therefore to Caesar .... Matt 22:21
r to each one according .... Rom 2:6
R to her just as she .... Rev 18:6

RENDERS
See that no one *r* evil ... 1 Thess 5:15

RENEW
r a steadfast spirit .... Ps 51:10
r the face of the .... Ps 104:30
on the LORD shall *r* .... Is 40:31

RENEWED
that your youth is *r* .... Ps 103:5
inward man is being *r* .... 2 Cor 4:16
and be *r* in the spirit ...... Eph 4:23
the new man who is *r* ...... Col 3:10

RENEWING
transformed by the *r* ..... Rom 12:2
of regeneration and *r* .... Titus 3:5

RENOUNCE
Why do the wicked *r* .... Ps 10:13

RENOUNCED
r the covenant of Your ...... Ps 89:39
r the hidden things .... 2 Cor 4:2

RENOUNCES
greedy and *r* the LORD .... Ps 10:3

RENOWN
were of old, men of *r* .... Gen 6:4

RENTED
years in his own *r* house .. Acts 28:30

REPAID
done, so God has *r* .... Judg 1:7
And he has *r* me evil .... 1 Sam 25:21
good shall be *r* .... Prov 13:21
Shall evil be *r* .... Jer 18:20

REPAIR
r the house of your .... 2 Chr 24:5
r the ruined cities .... Is 61:4

REPAY
He will *r* him to his .... Deut 7:10
silence, but will *r* .... Is 65:6
He will surely *r* .... Jer 51:56
again, I will *r* .... Luke 10:35
because they cannot *r* .... Luke 14:14
R no one evil for evil ...... Rom 12:17
is Mine, I will *r* .... Rom 12:19
r their parents .... 1 Tim 5:4
I will *r* .... Philem 19

REPAYS
and who *r* him for what .... Job 21:31
r the proud person .... Ps 31:23
shall he be who *r* .... Ps 137:8
the LORD, who fully *r* .... Is 66:6

REPEATS
r a matter separates .... Prov 17:9

REPENT
of man, that He should *r* .. Num 23:19

I abhor myself, and *r* .... Job 42:6
R now everyone of his evil ... Jer 25:5
R, turn away from your .... Ezek 14:6
because they refused to *r* .. Hos 11:5
"*R*, for the kingdom .... Matt 3:2
R, and believe in the ..... Mark 1:15
you *r* you will all .... Luke 13:3
said to them, "*R* .... Acts 2:38
R therefore and be .... Acts 3:19
men everywhere to *r* ...... Acts 17:30
and do the first works, or ... Rev 2:5
be zealous and *r* .... Rev 3:19

REPENTANCE
bear fruits worthy of *r*, ... Matt 3:8
you with water unto *r* ...... Matt 3:11
a baptism of *r* for the .... Mark 1:4
but sinners, to *r* .... Mark 2:17
persons who need no *r* .... Luke 15:7
to the Gentiles *r* to life .... Acts 11:18
of God leads you to *r* ...... Rom 2:4
sorrow produces *r* .... 2 Cor 7:10
will grant them *r* .... 2 Tim 2:25
of *r* from dead works and ... Heb 6:1
renew them again to *r* ..... Heb 6:6
found no place for *r* ...... Heb 12:17
all should come to *r* .... 2 Pet 3:9

REPENTED
No man *r* of his .... Jer 8:6
after my turning, I *r* .... Jer 31:19
it, because they *r* .... Matt 12:41

REPETITIONS
r as the heathen do .... Matt 6:7

REPHAIM
Valley near Jerusalem, 2 Sam 23:13, 14
Scene of Philistine defeats, 2 Sam
   5:18–22

REPHIDIM
Israelite camp, Num 33:12–15
Moses strikes rock at, Ex 17:1–7
Amalek defeated at, Ex 17:8–16

REPORT
circulate a false *r* .... Ex 23:1
For it is not a good *r* ...... 1 Sam 2:24
r makes the bones .... Prov 15:30
Who has believed our *r* ...... Is 53:1
who has believed our *r* .... Rom 10:16
things are of good *r* .... Phil 4:8

REPRIMANDED
And they *r* him sharply .... Judg 8:1

REPROACH
has taken away my *r* ...... Gen 30:23
away the *r* of Egypt from ... Josh 5:9
and bring *r* on all Israel .. 1 Sam 11:2
we may no longer be a *r* .... Neh 2:17
r me as long as I live .... Job 27:6
does he take up a *r* .... Ps 15:3
You make us a *r* .... Ps 44:13
sake I have borne *r* .... Ps 69:7
R has broken my heart ...... Ps 69:20
Remove from me *r* and ..... Ps 119:22
nation, but sin is a *r* .... Prov 14:34
with dishonor comes *r* ..... Prov 18:3
do not fear the *r* .... Is 51:7
not remember the *r* .... Is 54:4
bring an everlasting *r* ...... Jer 23:40
because I bore the *r* .... Jer 31:19
become a desolation, a *r* .... Jer 49:13
you shall bear the *r* .... Mic 6:16
to take away my *r* among .. Luke 1:25
these things You .... Luke 11:45
lest he fall into *r* .... 1 Tim 3:7
esteeming the *r* .... Heb 11:26
the camp, bearing His *r* .... Heb 13:13
and without *r* .... James 1:5

REPROACHED
of those who *r* You fell ..... Rom 15:3
If you are *r* for the .... 1 Pet 4:14

REPROACHES
is not an enemy who *r* ...... Ps 55:12

oppresses the poor *r* ...... Prov 14:31
curse, and Israel to *r* .... Is 43:28
in infirmities, in *r* .... 2 Cor 12:10

REPROACHFULLY
they strike me *r* .... Job 16:10

REPROOF
for doctrine, for *r* .... 2 Tim 3:16

REPROOFS
R of instruction are .... Prov 6:23

REPUTATION
seven men of good *r* .... Acts 6:3
to those who were of *r* .... Gal 2:2
made Himself of no *r* .... Phil 2:7

REQUEST
not withheld the *r* .... Ps 21:2
He gave them their *r* ...... Ps 106:15
the Lord God to make *r* .... Dan 9:3
For Jews *r* a sign .... 1 Cor 1:22
of mine making *r* .... Phil 1:4

REQUESTS
r be made known .... Phil 4:6

REQUIRE
the Lord your God *r* .... Deut 10:12
a foreigner you may *r* ...... Deut 15:3
"You will not *r* .... Ps 10:13
offering You did not *r* ...... Ps 40:6
what does the Lord *r* .... Mic 6:8

REQUIRED
of the world may be *r* ..... Luke 11:50
your soul will be *r* .... Luke 12:20
him much will be *r* ...... Luke 12:48
Moreover it is *r* .... 1 Cor 4:2

REQUIREMENTS
keeps the righteous *r* ...... Rom 2:26
r that was against us .... Col 2:14

RESCUE
R me from their .... Ps 35:17
and no one shall *r* .... Hos 5:14

RESERVE
r the unjust under .... 2 Pet 2:9

RESERVED
Have you not *r* a blessing .. Gen 27:36
I have *r* seven thousand .. 1 Kin 19:18
which I have *r* for the .... Job 38:23
"I have *r* for Myself .... Rom 11:4
r in heaven for you .... 1 Pet 1:4
of darkness, to be *r* .... 2 Pet 2:4
habitation, He has *r* .... Jude 6

RESERVES
He *r* wrath for His enemies .. Nah 1:2

RESIDUE
The *r* of My people .... Zeph 2:9

RESIST
r an evil person .... Matt 5:39
not able to *r* the wisdom .... Acts 6:10
r the Holy Spirit .... Acts 7:51
these also *r* the truth ..... 2 Tim 3:8
R the devil and he .... James 4:7
R him, steadfast in the ...... 1 Pet 5:9

RESISTED
For who has *r* His will ..... Rom 9:19
Jannes and Jambres *r* ...... 2 Tim 3:8
for he has greatly *r* ...... 2 Tim 4:15
You have not yet *r* .... Heb 12:4

RESISTS
"God *r* the proud .... James 4:6
for "God *r* the proud .... 1 Pet 5:5

RESOLVED
I have *r* what to do .... Luke 16:4

RESORT
to which I may *r* .... Ps 71:3

RESOUND
my heart shall *r* .... Is 16:11

RESPECT
Have *r* to the covenant ..... Ps 74:20

his eyes will have *r* .... Is 17:7
saying, 'They will *r* ...... Matt 21:37
of the law held in *r* .... Acts 5:34
and we paid them *r* .... Heb 12:9

RESPECTED
And the Lord *r* Abel....... Gen 4:4
little folly to one *r* .... Eccl 10:1

RESPONSE
in whose mouth is no *r* ..... Ps 38:14

REST
is the Sabbath of *r* .... Ex 31:15
you shall find no *r* .... Deut 28:65
to build a house of *r* ...... 1 Chr 28:2
I would have been at *r* .... Job 3:13
the weary are at *r* .... Job 3:17
My flesh also will *r* in hope ... Ps 16:9
R in the Lord.............. Ps 37:7
fly away and be at *r* .... Ps 55:6
of the Lord shall *r* .... Is 11:2
whole earth is at *r* .... Is 14:7
"This is the *r* .... Is 28:12
sake I will not *r* .... Is 62:1
is the place of My *r* .... Is 66:1
then you will find *r* .... Jer 6:16
and I will give you *r* ..... Matt 11:28
and you will find *r* ...... Matt 11:29
you who are troubled *r* .... 2 Thess 1:7
shall not enter My *r* .... Heb 3:11
remains therefore a *r* ...... Heb 4:9
to enter that *r* .... Heb 4:11
And they do not *r* .... Rev 4:8
that they should *r* .... Rev 6:11
"that they may *r* .... Rev 14:13
But the *r* of the dead ...... Rev 20:5

RESTED
He had done, and He *r* ...... Gen 2:2
glory of the Lord *r* .... Ex 24:16
when the Spirit *r* .... Num 11:25
"And God *r* on the .... Heb 4:4

RESTING
the dove found no *r* place ... Gen 8:9
foot have a *r* place ...... Deut 28:65
do not plunder his *r* ...... Prov 24:15
r place shall be .... Is 11:10
all the earth is *r* .... Zech 1:11
still sleeping and *r* ...... Matt 26:45

RESTLESS
I am *r* in my complaint .... Ps 55:2

RESTORATION
until the times of *r* .... Acts 3:21

RESTORE
R to me the joy .... Ps 51:12
I still must *r* .... Ps 69:4
r your judges as .... Is 1:26
r them to this place .... Jer 27:22
For I will *r* health to ...... Jer 30:17
"So I will *r* to you .... Joel 2:25
declare that I will *r* .... Zech 9:12
and will *r* all things ...... Matt 17:11
I *r* fourfold .... Luke 19:8
You at this time *r* .... Acts 1:6
who are spiritual *r* .... Gal 6:1

RESTORED
it was *r* like his other flesh .... Ex 4:7
whose son he had *r* to life ... 2 Kin 8:1
Lord *r* Job's losses when... Job 42:10
hand was *r* as whole as .... Mark 3:5
that I may be *r* to you the .. Heb 13:19

RESTORER
may he be to you a *r* ...... Ruth 4:15

RESTORES
with joy, for He *r* .... Job 33:26
He *r* my soul .... Ps 23:3

RESTRAIN
now *r* Your hand .... 2 Sam 24:16
Therefore I will not *r* ...... Job 7:11
Will You *r* Yourself .... Is 64:12
no one can *r* His hand ..... Dan 4:35

RESTRAINED
r my feet from every ...... Ps 119:101
Are they *r* .... Is 63:15

RESTRAINS
For nothing *r* the Lord.... 1 Sam 14:6
r his lips is wise .... Prov 10:19
only He who now *r* .... 2 Thess 2:7

RESTRAINT
they have cast off *r* .... Job 30:11
they break all *r* .... Hos 4:2

RESTS
r quietly in the heart ...... Prov 14:33

RESURRECTION
who say there is no *r* .... Matt 22:23
Therefore, in the *r* .... Matt 22:28
of the graves after His *r* ... Matt 27:53
Therefore, in the *r* .... Mark 12:23
repaid at the *r* of the ..... Luke 14:14
being sons of the *r* ...... Luke 20:36
done good, to the *r* .... John 5:29
to her, "I am the *r* .... John 11:25
a witness with us of His *r* .. Acts 1:22
them Jesus and the *r* ...... Acts 17:18
heard of the *r* of the ...... Acts 17:32
that there will be a *r* ...... Acts 24:15
the likeness of His *r* .... Rom 6:5
say that there is no *r* ..... 1 Cor 15:12
and the power of His *r* ..... Phil 3:10
that the *r* is already ...... 2 Tim 2:18
obtain a better *r* .... Heb 11:35
the *r* of Jesus Christ ...... 1 Pet 3:21
This is the first *r* .... Rev 20:5

RETAIN
happy are all who *r* .... Prov 3:18
spirit to *r* the spirit .... Eccl 8:8
r the sins of any .... John 20:23
like to *r* God in their ...... Rom 1:28

RETURN
So the Lord will *r* .... 1 Kin 2:32
and *r* to our neighbors ..... Ps 79:12
R, O Lord .... Ps 90:13
none who go to her *r* ...... Prov 2:19
womb, naked shall he *r* .... Eccl 5:15
the clouds do not *r* .... Eccl 12:2
let him *r* to the Lord ...... Is 55:7
it shall not *r* to Me .... Is 55:11
"If you will *r* .... Jer 4:1
for they shall *r* .... Jer 24:7
me, and I will *r* .... Jer 31:18
say, 'I will go and *r* .... Hos 2:7
help of your God, *r* .... Hos 12:6
"*R* to Me," says the Lord ... Zech 1:3
R to Me, and I will *r* ...... Mal 3:7
he says, 'I will *r* .... Matt 12:44
if not, it will *r* to you ..... Luke 10:6
reviled, did not revile in *r* .. 1 Pet 2:23

RETURNED
and they *r* and sought ..... Ps 78:34
yet you have not *r* .... Amos 4:6
astray, but have now *r* ..... 1 Pet 2:25

RETURNING
"I am *r* to Jerusalem ...... Zech 1:16
r evil for evil or .... 1 Pet 3:9

RETURNS
spirit departs, he *r* .... Ps 146:4
As a dog *r* to his own ..... Prov 26:11
"A dog *r* to his own ...... 2 Pet 2:22

REUBEN
Jacob's eldest son, Gen 29:31, 32
Lies with Bilhah; loses preeminence,
  Gen 35:22; 49:3, 4
Plots to save Joseph, Gen 37:21–30
Offers sons as pledge for Benjamin,
  Gen 42:37
—— Tribe of:
Numbered, Num 1:20, 21; 26:5–11
Settle east of Jordan, Num 32:1–42

Join in war against Canaanites, Josh 1:12–18

Erect memorial altar, Josh 22:10–34

REVEAL
The heavens will r	Job 20:27
I will heal them and r	Jer 33:6
the Son wills to r Him	Matt 11:27
r His Son in me	Gal 1:16
otherwise, God will r	Phil 3:15

REVEALED
things which are r	Deut 29:29
of the LORD shall be r	Is 40:5
righteousness to be r	Is 56:1
Then the secret was r	Dan 2:19
blood has not r this to	Matt 16:17
which will not be r	Mark 4:22
covered that will not be r	Luke 12:2
the Son of Man is r	Luke 17:30
the wrath of God is r	Rom 1:18
glory which shall be r	Rom 8:18
But God has r them to	1 Cor 2:10
secrets of his heart are r	1 Cor 14:25
as it has now been r	Eph 3:5
but now has been r	Col 1:26
the Lord Jesus is r	2 Thess 1:7
lawless one will be r	2 Thess 2:8
ready to be r in the	1 Pet 1:5
when His glory is r	1 Pet 4:13
r what we shall be	1 John 3:2

REVEALER
Lord of kings, and a r	Dan 2:47

REVEALING
waits for the r	Rom 8:19

REVEALS
as a talebearer r	Prov 20:19
r deep and secret	Dan 2:22
r secrets has made	Dan 2:29
r His secret to His	Amos 3:7

REVELATION
was no widespread r	1 Sam 3:1
Where there is no r	Prov 29:18
to bring to the Gentiles	Luke 2:32
the day of wrath and r	Rom 2:5
eagerly waiting for the r	1 Cor 1:7
has a tongue, has a r	1 Cor 14:26
it came through the r	Gal 1:12
And I went up by r, and	Gal 2:2
spirit of wisdom and r	Eph 1:17
r He made known to	Eph 3:3
and glory at the r	1 Pet 1:7
The R of Jesus Christ	Rev 1:1

REVELATIONS
come to visions and r	2 Cor 12:1

REVELRIES
drunkenness, r	Gal 5:21
lusts, drunkenness, r	1 Pet 4:3

REVENGE
and we will take our r	Jer 20:10

REVENUES
than vast r without	Prov 16:8

REVERENCE
and r My sanctuary	Lev 19:30
and to be held in r	Ps 89:7
Master, where is My r	Mal 1:6
submission with all r	1 Tim 3:4
God acceptably with r	Heb 12:28

REVERENT
man who is always r	Prov 28:14
their wives must be r	1 Tim 3:11
older men be sober, r	Titus 2:2

REVILE
are you when they r	Matt 5:11
r God's high priest	Acts 23:4
evildoers, those who r	1 Pet 3:16

REVILED
crucified with Him r	Mark 15:32
who, when He was r	1 Pet 2:23

REVILER
or an idolater, or a r	1 Cor 5:11

REVILERS
nor drunkards, nor r	1 Cor 6:10

REVILING
come envy, strife, r	1 Tim 6:4

REVIVAL
give us a measure of r	Ezra 9:8

REVIVE
troubles, shall r	Ps 71:20
Will You not r us	Ps 85:6
r me according to Your	Ps 119:25
r the spirit of the	Is 57:15
two days He will r	Hos 6:2
r Your work in the	Hab 3:2

REVIVED
they shall be r	Hos 14:7
came, sin r and I died	Rom 7:9

REVOLT
You will r more and	Is 1:5

REVOLTED
Israel have deeply r	Is 31:6
they have r and	Jer 5:23

REVOLTERS
r are deeply involved	Hos 5:2

REWARD
exceedingly great r	Gen 15:1
them there is great r	Ps 19:11
r me evil for good	Ps 35:12
"Surely there is a r	Ps 58:11
look, and see the r	Ps 91:8
will a sure r	Prov 11:18
and the LORD will r	Prov 25:22
and this was my r	Eccl 2:10
behold, His r is with	Is 40:10
r them for their deeds	Hos 4:9
for great is your r	Matt 5:12
you have no r from	Matt 6:1
you, they have their r	Matt 6:2
receive a prophet's r	Matt 10:41
by no means lose his r	Matt 10:42
r will be great	Luke 6:35
we receive the due r	Luke 23:41
will receive his own r	1 Cor 3:8
cheat you of your r	Col 2:18
for he looked to the r	Heb 11:26
may receive a full r	2 John 8
quickly, and My r	Rev 22:12

REWARDED
Thus they have r	Ps 109:5

REWARDER
and that He is a r	Heb 11:6

REWARDS
Whoever r evil for	Prov 17:13
and follows after r	Is 1:23
and give your r	Dan 5:17

REZIN
King of Damascus; joins Pekah against Ahaz, 2 Kin 15:37

Confederacy of, inspires Isaiah's great messianic prophecy, Is 7:1—9:12

REZON
Son of Eliadah; establishes Syrian kingdom, 1 Kin 11:23–25

RHEGIUM
City in Italy where Paul visits, Acts 28:13

RHODA
Servant girl, Acts 12:13–16

RHODES
Island off coast of Asia Minor which Paul passes, Acts 21:1

RIBLAH
Headquarters of:
Pharaoh Necho, 2 Kin 23:31–35

Nebuchadnezzar, 2 Kin 25:6, 20, 21

Zedekiah blinded here, Jer 39:5–7

RICH
Abram was very r	Gen 13:2
makes poor and makes r	1 Sam 2:7
r man will lie down	Job 27:19
the r among the people	Ps 45:12
when one becomes r	Ps 49:16
soul will be made r	Prov 11:25
who makes himself r	Prov 13:7
r has many friends	Prov 14:20
The r and the poor	Prov 22:2
r rules over the poor	Prov 22:7
r man is wise in his	Prov 28:11
do not curse the r	Eccl 10:20
it is hard for a r	Matt 19:23
to you who are r	Luke 6:24
from the r man's table	Luke 16:21
for he was very r	Luke 18:23
Lord over all is r	Rom 10:12
You are already r	1 Cor 4:8
though He was r	2 Cor 8:9
who desire to be r	1 Tim 6:9
but the r in his	James 1:10
So the r man also will	James 1:11
of this world to be r	James 2:5
you say, 'I am r	Rev 3:17

RICHES
Both r and honor come	1 Chr 29:12
He swallows down r	Job 20:15
he heaps up r	Ps 39:6
the abundance of his r	Ps 52:7
if r increase	Ps 62:10
r will be in his house	Ps 112:3
in her left hand r	Prov 3:16
R and honor are	Prov 8:18
R do not profit	Prov 11:4
in his r will fall	Prov 11:28
yet has great r	Prov 13:7
of the wise is their r	Prov 14:24
Houses and r are an	Prov 19:14
of the LORD are r	Prov 22:4
r are not forever	Prov 27:24
r kept for their owner	Eccl 5:13
darkness and hidden r	Is 45:3
you shall eat the r	Is 61:6
so is he who gets r	Jer 17:11
have increased your r	Ezek 28:5
for those who have r	Mark 10:23
do you despise the r	Rom 2:4
might make known the r	Rom 9:23
what are the r	Eph 1:18
show the exceeding r	Eph 2:7
the unsearchable r	Eph 3:8
trust in uncertain r	1 Tim 6:17
r than the treasures	Heb 11:26
r are corrupted	James 5:2
to receive power and r	Rev 5:12

RICHLY
Christ dwell in you r	Col 3:16
God, who gives us r	1 Tim 6:17

RIDDLE
"Let me pose a r	Judg 14:12

RIDDLES
the wise and their r	Prov 1:6

RIDE
wind and cause me to r	Job 30:22
in Your majesty r	Ps 45:4
have caused men to r	Ps 66:12

RIDER
r He has thrown	Ex 15:1
the horse and its r	Job 39:18

RIDES
Behold, the LORD r	Is 19:1

RIDGES
You water its r	Ps 65:10

RIDICULE
those who see Me r Me	Ps 22:7
Whom do you r	Is 57:4

RIDICULED
they r Him .... Matt 9:24

RIGHT
See AT THE RIGHT HAND; HIS RIGHT HAND; MY RIGHT HAND
then I will go to the r .... Gen 13:9
of all the earth do r .... Gen 18:25
tip of the r ear of Aaron ... Ex 29:20
on the thumb of his r hand .. Lev 8:23
you shall do what is r ..... Deut 6:18
the r of the firstborn ..... Deut 21:17
did what was r in his ..... Judg 21:25
my r of redemption .... Ruth 4:6
"Is your heart r .... 2 Kin 10:15
them forth by the r .... Ps 107:7
Lord, "Sit at My r .... Ps 110:1
is a way which seems r ... Prov 14:12
way of a man is r .... Prov 21:2
things that are r .... Is 45:19
until He comes whose r ... Ezek 21:27
of the LORD are r .... Hos 14:9
do not know to do r .... Amos 3:10
If your r eye causes you ... Matt 5:29
slaps you on your r cheek .. Matt 5:39
and whatever is r .... Matt 20:4
Sit at My r hand, till I .... Matt 22:44
sheep on His r hand ..... Matt 25:33
clothed and in his r ...... Mark 5:15
r hand of the Power ..... Mark 14:62
clothed and in his r mind .. Luke 8:35
not judge what is r ...... Luke 12:57
to them He gave the r ..... John 1:12
standing at the r hand of ... Acts 7:55
your heart is not r .... Acts 8:21
Do we have no r .... 1 Cor 9:4
in the Lord, for this is r ..... Eph 6:1
sat down at the r hand of .. Heb 10:12
tabernacle have no r to .... Heb 13:10
seven stars in His r .... Rev 2:1
I saw in the r hand of Him ... Rev 5:1
r hand or on their .... Rev 13:16
the r to the tree of life ..... Rev 22:14

RIGHTEOUS
also destroy the r .... Gen 18:23
Sodom fifty r within the ... Gen 18:26
has been more r than I .... Gen 38:26
not kill the innocent and r ... Ex 23:7
me die the death of the r .. Num 23:10
and they justify the r....... Deut 25:1
"You are more r .... 1 Sam 24:17
down two men more r ..... 1 Kin 2:32
that he could be r .... Job 15:14
r will hold to his way ..... Job 17:9
"The r see it and .... Job 22:19
knows the way of the r ...... Ps 1:6
LORD, will bless the r....... Ps 5:12
r God tests the hearts .... Ps 7:9
what can the r .... Ps 11:3
The r cry out .... Ps 34:17
the LORD upholds the r..... Ps 37:17
r shows mercy and ...... Ps 37:21
I have not seen the r .... Ps 37:25
the r will be in .... Ps 112:6
The LORD is r in all ...... Ps 145:17
the LORD loves the r........ Ps 146:8
will not allow the r .... Prov 10:3
r is a well of life .... Prov 10:11
The labor of the r .... Prov 10:16
r will be gladness .... Prov 10:28
r is delivered from .... Prov 11:8
r will be delivered ...... Prov 11:21
r will flourish .... Prov 11:28
r will be recompensed .... Prov 11:31
r man regards the life .... Prov 12:10
r should choose his ..... Prov 12:26
r there is much .... Prov 15:6
the prayer of the r ...... Prov 15:29
the r run to it and ...... Prov 18:10
r are bold as a lion .... Prov 28:1
When the r are in .... Prov 29:2
r considers the cause ..... Prov 29:7

Do not be overly r .... Eccl 7:16
event happens to the r ...... Eccl 9:2
r that it shall be .... Is 3:10
the gates, that the r .... Is 26:2
with My r right hand ...... Is 41:10
By His knowledge My r .... Is 53:11
The r perishes .... Is 57:1
people shall all be r .... Is 60:21
R are You .... Jer 12:1
your sins by being r ...... Dan 4:27
they sell the r .... Amos 2:6
not come to call the r ..... Matt 9:13
receive a r man's reward .. Matt 10:41
r men desired to see ..... Matt 13:17
r will shine forth as ...... Matt 13:43
the blood of r Abel to .... Matt 23:35
And they were both r ...... Luke 1:6
that they were r .... Luke 18:9
"Certainly this was a r .... Luke 23:47
"There is none r .... Rom 3:10
r man will one die .... Rom 5:7
witness that he was r ...... Heb 11:4
prayer of a r man avails .. James 5:16
If the r one is scarcely .... 1 Pet 4:18
Jesus Christ the r .... 1 John 2:1
just as He is r .... 1 John 3:7
r are Your judgments ..... Rev 16:7
fine linen is the r .... Rev 19:8
who is r, let him be r still .. Rev 22:11

RIGHTEOUS MAN
A little that a r .... Ps 37:16
r walks in his integrity .... Prov 20:7
away justice from the r ...... Is 5:23
if you warn the r .... Ezek 3:21
when a r turns away ..... Ezek 18:24
And he who receives a r .. Matt 10:41
"Certainly this was a r .... Luke 23:47
For scarcely for a r .... Rom 5:7
fervent prayer of a r ..... James 5:16
r, dwelling among them .... 2 Pet 2:8

RIGHTEOUSLY
judge the people r .... Ps 67:4
He who walks r and .... Is 33:15
should live soberly, r ..... Titus 2:12
to Him who judges r ...... 1 Pet 2:23

RIGHTEOUSNESS
it to him for r .... Gen 15:6
In r you shall judge your ... Lev 19:15
Because of my r the LORD ... Deut 9:4
every man for his r ..... 1 Sam 26:23
me according to my r .... 2 Sam 22:21
My r I hold fast .... Job 27:6
I put on r .... Job 29:14
I will ascribe r .... Job 36:3
I call, O God of my r .... Ps 4:1
righteous, He loves r ...... Ps 11:7
from the LORD, and r .... Ps 24:5
shall speak of Your r ..... Ps 35:28
the good news of r .... Ps 40:9
You love r and hate .... Ps 45:7
heavens declare His r ...... Ps 50:6
sing aloud of Your r .... Ps 51:14
r and peace have .... Ps 85:10
R will go before Him ..... Ps 85:13
r they are exalted .... Ps 89:16
will return to r .... Ps 94:15
r and justice are the .... Ps 97:2
and he who does r .... Ps 106:3
r endures forever .... Ps 111:3
r is an everlasting ...... Ps 119:142
r delivers from death ..... Prov 10:2
The r of the blameless .... Prov 11:5
The r of the upright ...... Prov 11:6
r leads to life .... Prov 11:19
the way of r is life ...... Prov 12:28
R guards him whose way .. Prov 13:6
R exalts a nation .... Prov 14:34
found in the way of r ..... Prov 16:31
He who follows r .... Prov 21:21
r lodged in it .... Is 1:21
r He shall judge .... Is 11:4

R shall be the belt .... Is 11:5
he will not learn r .... Is 26:10
and r the plummet .... Is 28:17
r will be peace .... Is 32:17
in the LORD I have r ...... Is 45:24
who are far from r .... Is 46:12
r will be forever .... Is 51:8
I will declare your r ...... Is 57:12
and His own r .... Is 59:16
r as a breastplate .... Is 59:17
be called trees of r .... Is 61:3
r goes forth as .... Is 62:1
The LORD Our R .... Jer 23:6
to David a Branch of r .... Jer 33:15
The Lord Our R .... Jer 33:16
has revealed our r .... Is 51:10
The r of the righteous ... Ezek 18:20
O Lord, r belongs .... Dan 9:7
in everlasting r .... Dan 9:24
who turn many to r .... Dan 12:3
for yourselves r .... Hos 10:12
Seek r, seek humility ...... Zeph 2:3
to fulfill all r .... Matt 3:15
exceeds the r of the ...... Matt 5:20
to you in the way of r .... Matt 21:32
in holiness and r .... Luke 1:75
For in it the r .... Rom 1:17
even the r of God .... Rom 3:22
a seal of the r .... Rom 4:11
accounted to him for r .... Rom 4:22
r will reign in life .... Rom 5:17
might reign through r .... Rom 5:21
is life because of r .... Rom 8:10
who did not pursue r..... Rom 9:30
pursuing the law of r .... Rom 9:31
ignorant of God's r ...... Rom 10:3
we might become the r .... 2 Cor 5:21
the fruits of your r ...... 2 Cor 9:10
r comes through the ...... Gal 2:21
was accounted to him for r .. Gal 3:6
the breastplate of r ...... Eph 6:14
not having my own r ...... Phil 3:9
things and pursue r ..... 1 Tim 6:11
r which we have .... Titus 3:5
r which is according .... Heb 11:7
does not produce the r .... James 1:20
Now the fruit of r is ..... James 3:18
should suffer for r .... 1 Pet 3:14
a preacher of r .... 2 Pet 2:5
a new earth in which r .... 2 Pet 3:13
who practices r .... 1 John 2:29
He who practices r ...... 1 John 3:7
does not practice r ...... 1 John 3:10

RIGHTEOUSNESS OF GOD
r is revealed from faith .... Rom 1:17
demonstrates the r .... Rom 3:5
r through faith .... Rom 3:22
not submitted to the r ..... Rom 10:3
we might become the r .... 2 Cor 5:21
does not produce the r .... James 1:20

RIGHTEOUSNESS'
are persecuted for r sake ... Matt 5:10
should suffer for r sake ... 1 Pet 3:14

RIGHTEOUSNESSES
all our r are like filthy .... Is 64:6

RIGHTLY
wise uses knowledge r .... Prov 15:2
R do they love you .... Song 1:4
"You have answered r ... Luke 10:28
r dividing the word ...... 2 Tim 2:15

RIGHTS
and her marriage r .... Ex 21:10

RING
his signet r from his hand .. Esth 3:10
a r of gold in a swine's .... Prov 11:22
it with his own signet r ... Dan 6:17
and put a r on his hand ... Luke 15:22

RINGLEADER
the world, and a r .... Acts 24:5

RINGS
a man with gold r .... James 2:2

RIPE
figs that are first r .... Jer 24:2

RISE
is vain for you to r .... Ps 127:2
"Now I will r............... Is 33:10
for He makes His sun r .... Matt 5:45
of Nineveh will r .... Matt 12:41
third day He will r ...... Matt 20:19
false prophets will r ..... Matt 24:24
persuaded though one r .. Luke 16:31
third day He will r ...... Luke 18:33
had to suffer and r .... Acts 17:3
be the first to r .... Acts 26:23
fact the dead do not r .... 1 Cor 15:15
in Christ will r .... 1 Thess 4:16

RISEN
of the LORD is r............... Is 60:1
women there has not r .... Matt 11:11
disciples that He is r ..... Matt 28:7
"The Lord is r .... Luke 24:34
furthermore is also r ...... Rom 8:34
then Christ is not r .... 1 Cor 15:13
if Christ is not r .... 1 Cor 15:17
But now Christ is r .... 1 Cor 15:20

RISES
shall I do when God r ...... Job 31:14
every tongue which r .... Is 54:17

RISING
may know from the r .... Is 45:6
questioning what the r .... Mark 9:10
for the fall and r .... Luke 2:34

RIVER
Indeed the r may rage ..... Job 40:23
them drink from the r ...... Ps 36:8
r whose streams shall .... Ps 46:4
the r of God is full .... Ps 65:9
went through the r .... Ps 66:6
peace to her like a r ...... Is 66:12
in the Jordan R .... Mark 1:5
he showed me a pure r ..... Rev 22:1

RIVERS
He turns r into a .... Ps 107:33
R of water run down ...... Ps 119:136
By the r of Babylon .... Ps 137:1
All the r run into the .... Eccl 1:7
us a place of broad r .... Is 33:21
the wilderness and r .... Is 43:19
the sea, I make the r .... Is 50:2
his heart will flow r .... John 7:38

RIZPAH
Saul's concubine taken by Abner,
2 Sam 3:6–8
Sons of, killed, 2 Sam 21:8, 9
Grief-stricken, cares for corpses, 2 Sam
21:10–14

ROAD
I will even make a r .... Is 43:19
depths of the sea a r .... Is 51:10
seen the Lord on the r ...... Acts 9:27

ROAR
Let the sea r .... 1 Chr 16:32
though its waters r .... Ps 46:3
The young lions r .... Ps 104:21
'The LORD will r........... Jer 25:30
He will r like a lion .... Hos 11:10
The LORD also will r .... Joel 3:16
Will a lion r in the .... Amos 3:4

ROARING
wrath is like the r .... Prov 19:12
Like a r lion and a .... Prov 28:15
and the waves r .... Luke 21:25
walks about like a r .... 1 Pet 5:8

ROARS
their voice r like the .... Jer 6:23

"The LORD r from .... Amos 1:2
as when a lion r .... Rev 10:3

ROB
r the poor because he ..... Prov 22:22
r the needy of justice .... Is 10:2
"Will a man r God .... Mal 3:8
do you r temples .... Rom 2:22

ROBBED
r their treasuries .... Is 10:13
But this is a people r .... Is 42:22
Yet you have r Me .... Mal 3:8
r other churches .... 2 Cor 11:8

ROBBER
a son who is a r .... Ezek 18:10
is a thief and a r .... John 10:1
Barabbas was a r .... John 18:40

ROBBERS
and Israel to the r .... Is 42:24
also crucified two r ...... Mark 15:27
Me are thieves and r ...... John 10:8
here who are neither r .... Acts 19:37
waters, in perils of r ..... 2 Cor 11:26

ROBBERY
nor vainly hope in r .... Ps 62:10
I hate r for burnt .... Is 61:8
did not consider it r .... Phil 2:6

ROBE
r of the ephod, the ephod ....Ex 29:5
off a corner of Saul's r ..... 1 Sam 24:4
her r of many colors ...... 2 Sam 13:19
with a r of fine linen. .... 1 Chr 15:27
let a royal r be brought ...... Esth 6:8
justice was like a r .... Job 29:14
instead of a rich r .... Is 3:24
covered me with the r .... Is 61:10
His r became white and .... Luke 9:29
'Bring out the best r ...... Luke 15:22
on Him a purple r .... John 19:2
Then a white r was .... Rev 6:11
with a r dipped in blood. ... Rev 19:13

ROBES
to the King in r .... Ps 45:14
have stained all My r .... Is 63:3
clothe you with rich r ...... Zech 3:4
go around in long r .... Luke 20:46
clothed with white r .... Rev 7:9

ROCK
you shall strike the r .... Ex 17:6
put you in the cleft of the r .. Ex 33:22
and struck the r .... Num 20:11
R who begot you .... Deut 32:18
For their r is not .... Deut 32:31
and fire rose out of the r ... Judg 6:21
nor is there any r .... 1 Sam 2:2
"The LORD is my r........ 2 Sam 22:2
And who is a r .... 2 Sam 22:32
Blessed be my R .... 2 Sam 22:47
away, and as a r .... Job 14:18
set me high upon a r .... Ps 27:5
For You are my r .... Ps 31:3
r that is higher than .... Ps 61:2
and my God the r .... Ps 94:22
who turned the r .... Ps 114:8
been mindful of the R .... Is 17:10
shadow of a great r .... Is 32:2
look to the r from which ...... Is 51:1
that breaks the r in pieces .. Jer 23:29
dwell in the clefts of the r ... Obad 3
his house on the r .... Matt 7:24
r I will build My .... Matt 16:18
Some fell on r .... Luke 8:6
stumbling stone and r ...... Rom 9:33
R that followed them ...... 1 Cor 10:4
and a r of offense .... 1 Pet 2:8

ROCKS
and the r were split ...... Matt 27:51
to the mountains and r ...... Rev 6:16

ROD
And Moses took the r .... Ex 4:20

---

man threw down his r .... Ex 7:12
passes under the r .... Lev 27:32
the rock twice with his r .. Num 20:11
chasten him with the r .... 2 Sam 7:14
break them with a r of iron ... Ps 2:9
Your r and Your staff ...... Ps 23:4
The r and rebuke give .... Prov 29:15
shall come forth a R .... Is 11:1
you pass under the r ..... Ezek 20:37
measuring r six cubits .... Ezek 40:5
I come to you with a r .... 1 Cor 4:21
Aaron's r that budded. ..... Heb 9:4
rule them with a r .... Rev 2:27
rule them with a r of iron .. Rev 19:15

ROLL
ruinous storm they r .... Job 30:14
r away the stone .... Mark 16:3

ROLLED
the heavens shall be r .... Is 34:4
the stone had been r ...... Mark 16:4

ROMAN
Tell me, are you a R ...... Acts 22:27
learned that he was a R ... Acts 23:27

ROME
Jews expelled from. Acts 18:2
Paul:
writes to Christians of. Rom 1:7
desires to go to, Acts 19:21
comes to, Acts 28:14
imprisoned in, Acts 28:16

ROOF
the r he saw a woman .... 2 Sam 11:2
stuck the r of their .... Job 29:10
cling to the r of my mouth ... Ps 137:6
uncovered the r where He .. Mark 2:4

ROOM
See UPPER ROOM
You prepared r for it .... Ps 80:9
until no more r .... Zech 10:10
you a large upper r ...... Mark 14:15
no r for them in the .... Luke 2:7
still there is r .... Luke 14:22
into the upper r .... Acts 1:13

ROOMS
make r in the ark .... Gen 6:14
He is in the inner r ...... Matt 24:26

ROOSTER
him, "Before the r .... Matt 26:75

ROOT
r bearing bitterness .... Deut 29:18
the foolish taking r........... Job 5:3
r may grow old in the ...... Job 14:8
day there shall be a R .... Is 11:10
shall again take r .... Is 37:31
because they had no r ..... Matt 13:6
and if the r is holy .... Rom 11:16
of money is a r .... 1 Tim 6:10
lest any r of .... Heb 12:15
I am the R and the .... Rev 22:16

ROOTED
that you, being r .... Eph 3:17
r and built up in Him .... Col 2:7

ROOTS
because its r reached ...... Ezek 31:7
and lengthen his r .... Hos 14:5
dried up from the r ...... Mark 11:20
pulled up by the r .... Jude 12

ROSE
I am the r of Sharon .... Song 2:1
and blossom as the r .... Is 35:1
end Christ died and r ...... Rom 14:9
buried, and that He r ..... 1 Cor 15:4
that Jesus died and r .... 1 Thess 4:14

ROTTENNESS
is like r in his bones ...... Prov 12:4

ROUGH
and the r places smooth ...... Is 40:4
and the r ways smooth ..... Luke 3:5

ROUGHLY

answered the people r .... 1 Kin 12:13

ROYAL

dwell in the r city with .... 1 Sam 27:5
son was over the r house .. 2 Kin 15:5
and a r house for himself .. 2 Chr 2:1
destroyed all the r heirs .. 2 Chr 22:10
so he set the r crown ...... Esth 2:17
a r diadem in the hand of ..... Is 62:3
to establish a r statute and ... Dan 6:7
the r law according to the . James 2:8
r priesthood, a holy nation .. 1 Pet 2:9

RUBBISH

things, and count them as r . Phil 3:8

RUBIES

of wisdom is above r .... Job 28:18
more precious than r ...... Prov 3:15
is better than r .... Prov 8:11
worth is far above r ...... Prov 31:10
your pinnacles of r .... Is 54:12
ruddy in body than r ...... Lam 4:7

RUDDY

Now he was r .... 1 Sam 16:12
beloved is white and r ..... Song 5:10

RUIN

r those two can bring .... Prov 24:22
flattering mouth works r .. Prov 26:28
have made a city a r .... Is 25:2
I will r the pride of Judah .... Jer 13:9
will not be your r .... Ezek 18:30
And the r of that .... Luke 6:49
to no profit, to the r ...... 2 Tim 2:14

RUINED

shall be utterly r .... Is 60:12
the mighty trees are r ..... Zech 11:2
wineskins will be r .... Luke 5:37

RUINS

rebuild the old r .... Is 61:4
of My house that is in r. .... Hag 1:9
I will rebuild its r, and I ... Acts 15:16

RULE

greater light to r the day .... Gen 1:16
and he shall r .... Gen 3:16
r the raging of the .... Ps 89:9
R in the midst of Your ...... Ps 110:2
A wise servant will r ...... Prov 17:2
Whoever has no r over .... Prov 25:28
Yet he will r over all ...... Eccl 2:19
sit and r on His throne .... Zech 6:13
puts an end to all r .... 1 Cor 15:24
us walk by the same r ..... Phil 3:16
let the peace of God r ..... Col 3:15
Let the elders who r ..... 1 Tim 5:17
Remember those who r ..... Heb 13:7
He shall r them with a rod .. Rev 2:27
He Himself will r them .... Rev 19:15

RULER

the sheep, to be r .... 2 Sam 7:8
down to eat with a r ...... Prov 23:1
bear is a wicked r .... Prov 28:15
r pays attention .... Prov 29:12
to Me the One to be r ...... Mic 5:2
by Beelzebub, the r ...... Matt 12:24
I will make you r .... Matt 25:21
the r of this world ...... John 12:31
because the r of this ..... John 16:11
'Who made you a r .... Acts 7:27
speak evil of a r .... Acts 23:5

RULER OF THE SYNAGOGUE

He said to the r .... Mark 5:36
Jairus, and he was a r .... Luke 8:41
r answered with .... Luke 13:14
r, believed on the Lord ..... Acts 18:8
took Sosthenes, the r ..... Acts 18:17

RULERS

and the r take counsel .... Ps 2:2

r decree justice .... Prov 8:15
"You know that the r .... Matt 20:25
Have any of the r .... John 7:48
r are not a terror .... Rom 13:3
which none of the r ...... 1 Cor 2:8
powers, against the r ...... Eph 6:12
to be subject to r .... Titus 3:1

RULES

'He who r over men ...... 2 Sam 23:3
them know that God r ...... Ps 59:13
He r by His power .... Ps 66:7
r his spirit than he ...... Prov 16:32
that the Most High r ...... Dan 4:17
that the Most High r ...... Dan 4:32
r his own house well ..... 1 Tim 3:4
according to the r .... 2 Tim 2:5

RULING

r their children .... 1 Tim 3:12

RUMOR

r will be upon r .... Ezek 7:26

RUMORS

hear of wars and r .... Matt 24:6
you hear of wars and r .... Mark 13:7

RUN

I will r the course of ..... Ps 119:32
r and not be weary .... Is 40:31
many shall r to and ...... Dan 12:4
Therefore I r thus .... 1 Cor 9:26
I might r, or had r .... Gal 2:2
that I have not r .... Phil 2:16
us, and let us r .... Heb 12:1
that you do not r .... 1 Pet 4:4

RUNNER

are swifter than a r .... Job 9:25
r will run to meet .... Jer 51:31

RUNS

word r very swiftly ...... Ps 147:15
nor of him who r .... Rom 9:16

RUSH

The nations will r .... Is 17:13

RUSHING

like the r of the seas ...... Is 17:12
as of a r mighty wind, and ... Acts 2:2

RUST

r destroy and where ...... Matt 6:19

RUTH

Moabitess, Ruth 1:4
Follows Naomi, Ruth 1:6–18
Marries Boaz, Ruth 4:9–13
Ancestress of Christ, Ruth 4:13, 21, 22

SABAOTH

S had left us a .... Rom 9:29
ears of the Lord of S ..... James 5:4

SABBATH

'Tomorrow is a S .... Ex 16:23
"Remember the S .... Ex 20:8
You shall keep the S ...... Ex 31:14
a S of rest to the LORD ..... Ex 35:2
day is a S of solemn rest .... Lev 23:3
shall keep a s to the LORD .. Lev 25:2
Observe the S day, to ..... Deut 5:12
bear no burden on the S .... Jer 17:21
the grainfields on the S .... Matt 12:1
S was made for man ..... Mark 2:27
is also Lord of the S ...... Mark 2:28
"Is it lawful on the S to do .. Mark 3:4
Is it lawful on the S to do .. Luke 6:9
It is the S; it is not lawful .. John 5:10
not only broke the S ...... John 5:18
circumcise a man on the S . John 7:22
the synagogues every S ... Acts 15:21

SABBATHS

S you shall keep .... Ex 31:13
You shall keep My S ...... Lev 26:2

The New Moons, the S ...... Is 1:13
also gave them My S .... Ezek 20:12
for three S reasoned with ... Acts 17:2
festival or a new moon or s .. Col 2:16

SACKCLOTH

I have sewn s over my ..... Job 16:15
You have put off my s ...... Ps 30:11
and remove the s .... Is 20:2
with fasting, s, and ashes ... Dan 9:3
a fast, and put on s .... Jon 3:5
repented long ago in s .... Matt 11:21

SACRED

have a s assembly .... Num 29:35
iniquity and the s .... Is 1:13
call a s assembly .... Joel 1:14

SACRIFICE

I s to the LORD all males .... Ex 13:15
is a burnt s of the herd .... Lev 1:3
is a s of peace offering ..... Lev 3:1
the law of the s of peace ... Lev 7:11
a s of a peace offering to ... Num 6:17
you shall s the Passover .... Deut 16:2
s to the LORD of hosts ..... 1 Sam 1:3
do you kick at My s ...... 1 Sam 2:29
to s to the LORD your .... 1 Sam 15:15
S and offering You did ..... Ps 40:6
offer to You the s .... Ps 116:17
to the LORD than s .... Prov 21:3
The s of the wicked is ..... Prov 21:27
than to give the s of fools ... Eccl 5:1
in that day, and will make s .. Is 19:21
For the LORD has a s .... Is 34:6
who will bring the s ...... Jer 33:11
I desire mercy and not s .... Hos 6:6
of My offerings they s ..... Hos 8:13
But I will s to You .... Jon 2:9
LORD has prepared a s ..... Zeph 1:7
offer the blind as a s ...... Mal 1:8
desire mercy and not s .... Matt 9:13
'I desire mercy and not s ... Matt 12:7
s will be seasoned .... Mark 9:49
your bodies a living s ..... Rom 12:1
an offering and a s .... Eph 5:2
aroma, an acceptable s .... Phil 4:18
put away sin by the s ...... Heb 9:26
He had offered one s ...... Heb 10:12
no longer remains a s ..... Heb 10:26
God a more excellent s ..... Heb 11:4
offer the s of praise ...... Heb 13:15

SACRIFICED

s their sons and their ..... Ps 106:37
They s to the Baals .... Hos 11:2
our Passover, was s for us .. 1 Cor 5:7
to eat things s .... Rev 2:14

SACRIFICES

He who s to any god .... Ex 22:20
burnt offerings, your s .... Deut 12:6
The s of God are a .... Ps 51:17
the s of thanksgiving ..... Ps 107:22
multitude of your s .... Is 1:11
Bring no more futile s .... Is 1:13
he who s a lamb............ Is 66:3
acceptable, nor your s ..... Jer 6:20
bringing s of praise to the .. Jer 17:26
by him the daily s .... Dan 8:11
burnt offerings and s .... Mark 12:33
priests, to offer up s ...... Heb 7:27
with better s than these .... Heb 9:23
s for sin you had no ...... Heb 10:6
s God is well pleased ..... Heb 13:16
offer up spiritual s .... 1 Pet 2:5

SAD

"Why is your face s .... Neh 2:2
s countenance the .... Eccl 7:3
whom I have not made s .. Ezek 13:22
as you walk and are s .... Luke 24:17

SADDUCEES

Rejected by John, Matt 3:7
Test Jesus, Matt 16:1–12

Silenced by Jesus, Matt 22:23–34
Disturbed by teaching of resurrection,
  Acts 4:1, 2
Oppose apostles, Acts 5:17–40

SAFE
and I shall be s . . . . Ps 119:117
in the LORD shall be s . . . . . Prov 29:25
he has received him s . . . . Luke 15:27

SAFELY
And He led them on s . . . . Ps 78:53
make them lie down s . . . . . . Hos 2:18

SAFETY
sons are far from s . . . . Job 5:4
take your rest in s . . . . Job 11:18
will set him in the s . . . . Ps 12:5
the needy will lie down in s . . Is 14:30
say, "Peace and s . . . . 1 Thess 5:3

SAFETY'S
by you for s sake . . . . Prov 3:29

SAINTS
See ALL THE SAINTS
ten thousands of s . . . . Deut 33:2
the feet of His s . . . . 1 Sam 2:9
puts no trust in His s . . . . . . Job 15:15
s who are on the earth . . . . . . Ps 16:3
does not forsake His s . . . . . . Ps 37:28
"Gather My s . . . . Ps 50:5
the souls of His s . . . . Ps 97:10
is the death of His s . . . . . . Ps 116:15
the way of His s . . . . Prov 2:8
war against the s . . . . Dan 7:21
shall persecute the s . . . . . . Dan 7:25
Jesus, called to be s . . . . . . 1 Cor 1:2
the least of all the s . . . . Eph 3:8
Christ with all His s . . . 1 Thess 3:13
be glorified in His s . . . . 2 Thess 1:10
all delivered to the s . . . . Jude 3
ways, O King of the s . . . . . . Rev 15:3
shed the blood of s . . . . Rev 16:6
the camp of the s . . . . Rev 20:9

SAKE
My servant Abraham's s . . . Gen 26:24
has blessed me for your s . . . Gen 30:27
the Egyptians for Israel's s . . . Ex 18:8
for His great name's s . . . 1 Sam 12:22
kindness for Jonathan's s . . 2 Sam 9:1
for the s of your father . . . 1 Kin 11:12
the s of Your great name . . 2 Chr 6:32
save me for Your mercies' s . . . Ps 6:4
For His name's s . . . . Ps 23:3
Your name's s, O LORD . . . . . Ps 25:11
for Your name's s . . . . Ps 31:3
sins, for Your name's s . . . . . . Ps 79:9
for His name's s . . . . Ps 106:8
me for Your name's s . . . . . . Ps 109:21
LORD, for Your name's s . . . . Ps 143:11
for Your s I have . . . . Jer 15:15
for righteousness' s . . . . . . Matt 5:10
you falsely for My s . . . . Matt 5:11
and kings for My s . . . . . . Matt 10:18
by all for My name's s . . . . Matt 10:22
life for My s will find it . . . Matt 10:39
life for My s will find it . . . Matt 16:25
kingdom of heaven's s . . . . Matt 19:12
lands, for My name's s . . . . Matt 19:29
nations for My name's s . . . . Matt 24:9
elect's s those days will . . . Matt 24:22
loses his life for My s . . . . . Mark 8:35
rulers and kings for My s . . Mark 13:9
men for My name's s . . . . . Mark 13:13
but for the elect's s . . . . . . Mark 13:20
life for My s will save it . . . . Luke 9:24
s of the kingdom of . . . . . Luke 18:29
rulers for My name's s . . . . Luke 21:12
by all for My name's s . . . . Luke 21:17
my life for Your s . . . . John 13:37
down your life for My s . . . John 13:38
to you for My name's s . . . Luke 15:21
suffer for My name's s . . . . Acts 9:16
are fools for Christ's s . . . . 1 Cor 4:10

I do for the gospel's s . . . . . 1 Cor 9:23
s of him who had done . . . . 2 Cor 7:12
for your stomach's s . . . . . . 1 Tim 5:23
suffer for righteousness' s . . 1 Pet 3:14
for His name's s . . . . 1 John 2:12
labored for My name's s . . . . Rev 2:3

SAKES
for their s I sanctify . . . . . . John 17:19
your s He became poor . . . . . 2 Cor 8:9

SALAMIS
Paul preaches here, Acts 13:4, 5

SALEM
Jerusalem's original name, Gen 14:18
Used poetically, Ps 76:2

SALIM
Place near Aenon, John 3:23

SALOME
One of the ministering women, Mark
  15:40, 41
Visits empty tomb, Mark 16:1
——— Herodias' daughter (not named in
  the Bible), Matt 14:6–11

SALT
she became a pillar of s . . . Gen 19:26
shall season with s . . . . Lev 2:13
covenant of s forever . . . . . Num 18:19
city and sowed it with s . . . Judg 9:45
s nor wrapped in . . . . Ezek 16:4
"You are the s . . . . Matt 5:13
s loses its flavor . . . . Mark 9:50
with grace, seasoned with s . . Col 4:6

SALT SEA
O.T. name for the Dead Sea, Gen 14:3;
  Num 34:3, 12

SALVATION
still, and see the s . . . . Ex 14:13
the Rock of my s . . . . . . 2 Sam 22:47
For this is all my s . . . . . . 2 Sam 23:5
the good news of His s . . 1 Chr 16:23
S belongs to the LORD . . . . Ps 3:8
I will rejoice in Your s . . . . . . Ps 9:14
shield and the horn of my s . . Ps 18:2
We will rejoice in your s . . . . Ps 20:5
You are the God of my s . . . . Ps 25:5
is my light and my s . . . . Ps 27:1
to me the joy of Your s . . . . . Ps 51:12
From Him comes my s . . . . . . Ps 62:1
on earth, Your s . . . . Ps 67:2
God is the God of s . . . . Ps 68:20
and Your s all the day . . . . . Ps 71:15
Restore us, O God of our s . . Ps 85:4
Surely His s is near . . . . Ps 85:9
and He has become my s . . Ps 118:14
S is far from the . . . . Ps 119:155
LORD, I hope for Your s . . Ps 119:166
forgotten the God of your s . . Is 17:10
God will appoint s . . . . Is 26:1
with an everlasting s . . . . Is 45:17
for My s is about to . . . . Is 56:1
call your walls S . . . . Is 60:18
s as a lamp that burns . . . . . Is 62:1
LORD our God is the s . . . . . Jer 3:23
joy in the God of my s . . . . . Hab 3:18
is just and having s . . . . . . Zech 9:9
raised up a horn of s . . . . . Luke 1:69
eyes have seen Your s . . . . Luke 2:30
to him, "Today s . . . . Luke 19:9
what we worship, for s . . . . John 4:22
Nor is there in any . . . . Acts 4:12
you should be for s . . . . . . Acts 13:47
the power of God to s . . . . . Rom 1:16
is made unto s . . . . Rom 10:10
s has come to the . . . . Rom 11:11
s is nearer than . . . . Rom 13:11
now is the day of s . . . . 2 Cor 6:2
And take the helmet of s . . . . Eph 6:17
work out your own s . . . . . . Phil 2:12
wrath, but to obtain s . . . 1 Thess 5:9
chose you for s . . . . 2 Thess 2:13

also may obtain the s . . . . . 2 Tim 2:10
of God that brings s . . . . Titus 2:11
neglect so great a s . . . . Heb 2:3
s perfect through . . . . Heb 2:10
s the prophets have . . . . 1 Pet 1:10
"S belongs to our God . . . . . Rev 7:10
S and glory and honor . . . . . Rev 19:1

SAMARIA
Capital of Israel, 1 Kin 16:24–29
Besieged by Ben-Hadad, 1 Kin 20:1–21
Besieged again; miraculously deliv-
  ered, 2 Kin 6:24—7:20
Inhabitants deported by Assyria; re-
  populated with foreigners, 2 Kin
  17:5, 6, 24–41
——— District of Palestine in Christ's
  time, Luke 17:11–19
Disciples forbidden to preach in, Matt
  10:5
Gospel preached there after the ascen-
  sion, Acts 1:8; 9:31; 15:3

SAMARITAN
But a certain S . . . . Luke 10:33
a drink from me, a S . . . . John 4:9

SAMARITANS
People of mixed heredity, 2 Kin
  17:24–41
Christ preaches to, John 4:5–42
Story of "the good Samaritan," Luke
  10:30–37
Converts among, Acts 8:5–25

SAMOS
Paul visits, Acts 20:15

SAMSON
Birth predicted and accomplished,
  Judg 13:2–25
Marries Philistine; avenges betrayal,
  Judg 14
Defeats Philistines singlehandedly,
  Judg 15
Betrayed by Delilah; loses strength,
  Judg 16:4–22
Destroys many in his death, Judg
  16:23–31

SAMUEL
Born in answer to prayer; dedicated
  to God, 1 Sam 1:1–28
Receives revelation; recognized as
  prophet, 1 Sam 3:1–21
Judges Israel, 1 Sam 7:15–17
Warns Israel against a king, 1 Sam
  8:10–18
Anoints Saul, 1 Sam 9:15—10:1
Rebukes Saul, 1 Sam 15:10–35
Anoints David, 1 Sam 16:1–13
Death of, 1 Sam 25:1

SANBALLAT
Influential Samaritan; attempts to
  thwart Nehemiah's plans, Neh 2:10;
  4:7, 8; 6:1–14

SANCTIFICATION
righteousness and s . . . . 1 Cor 1:30
will of God, your s . . . . 1 Thess 4:3
salvation through s . . . . . . 2 Thess 2:13

SANCTIFIED
s it, because in it He rested . . Gen 2:3
s the people, and they . . . . . Ex 19:14
I s to Myself all the . . . . Num 3:13
s this house, that My s . . . . 2 Chr 7:16
I have commanded My s . . . . . Is 13:3
you were born I s . . . . Jer 1:5
Him whom the Father s . . . John 10:36
they also may be s . . . . . . John 17:19
might be acceptable, s . . . . Rom 15:16
to those who are s . . . . 1 Cor 1:2
washed, but you were s . . . . 1 Cor 6:11
husband is s by the . . . . 1 Cor 7:14
for it is s by the . . . . 1 Tim 4:5
those who are being . . . . Heb 2:11

will we have been *s* .... Heb 10:10
who are called, *s* .... Jude 1

SANCTIFIES
or the temple that *s* .... Matt 23:17
For both He who *s* .... Heb 2:11

SANCTIFY
"S yourselves .... Josh 3:5
would send and *s* them ...... Job 1:5
s My great name .... Ezek 36:23
that I, the LORD, *s* .... Ezek 37:28
Myself and *s* Myself ...... Ezek 38:23
S them by Your .... John 17:17
for their sakes I *s* .... John 17:19
that He might *s* .... Eph 5:26
s you completely .... 1 Thess 5:23

SANCTUARY
let them make Me a *s* ...... Ex 25:8
I went into the *s* .... Ps 73:17
set fire to Your *s* .... Ps 74:7
O God, is in the *s* .... Ps 77:13
He will be as a *s* .... Is 8:14
He has abandoned His *s* ..... Lam 2:7
I shall be a little *s* .... Ezek 11:16
to shine on Your *s* .... Dan 9:17
and the earthly *s* .... Heb 9:1
is brought into the *s* ...... Heb 13:11

SAND
descendants as the *s* ...... Gen 32:12
be heavier than the *s* .... Job 6:3
in number than the *s* ..... Ps 139:18
O Israel, be as the *s* .... Is 10:22
innumerable as the *s* ...... Heb 11:12

SANDAL
remove his *s* from his ...... Deut 25:9
So he took off his *s* .... Ruth 4:8
s strap I am not worthy ..... Mark 1:7

SANDALS
Take your *s* off your feet ...... Ex 3:5
beautiful are your feet in *s* .. Song 7:1
whose *s* I am not worthy ... Matt 3:11
bag, knapsack, nor *s* ...... Luke 10:4
tie on your *s* .... Acts 12:8

SANG
s this song to the LORD .... Ex 15:1
worshiped, the singers *s* . 2 Chr 29:28
The singers *s* loudly ...... Neh 12:42
morning stars *s* together .... Job 38:7
They *s* His praise .... Ps 106:12
they *s* a new song, saying ..... Rev 5:9
s as it were a new song ..... Rev 14:3

SAPPHIRA
Wife of Ananias; struck dead for lying.
Acts 5:1–11

SAPPHIRE
shall be a turquoise, a *s* ..... Ex 28:18
was jasper, the second *s* ... Rev 21:19

SAPPHIRES
are the source of *s* .... Job 28:6

SARAH (or Sarai)
Barren wife of Abram, Gen 11:29–31
Represented as Abram's sister, Gen 12:10–20
Gives Abram her maid, Gen 16:1–3
Receives promise of a son, Gen 17:15–21
Gives birth to Isaac, Gen 21:1–8

SARDIS
Site of one of the seven churches, Rev 1:11

SARDONYX
the fifth *s*, the sixth .... Rev 21:20

SASH
tunic, a turban, and a *s* ..... Ex 28:4
get yourself a linen *s* .... Jer 13:1

SASHES
girded them with *s* .... Lev 8:13
s for the merchants .... Prov 31:24

SAT
of Babylon, there we *s* ..... Ps 137:1
I *s* down in his shade ...... Song 2:3
s alone because of .... Jer 15:17
people who *s* in darkness .. Matt 4:16
Now Peter *s* outside in .... Matt 26:69
into heaven, and *s* .... Mark 16:19
s down again, He said .... John 13:12
s down at the right hand .... Heb 1:3
And He who *s* there was .... Rev 4:3
Him who *s* on the horse .... Rev 19:19

SATAN
See DEVIL
S stood up against .... 1 Chr 21:1
before the LORD, and S ...... Job 1:6
And the LORD said to S ..... Zech 3:2
"Away with you, S .... Matt 4:10
"Get behind Me, S .... Matt 16:23
forty days, tempted by S .. Mark 1:13
"How can S cast out ..... Mark 3:23
to them, "I saw S .... Luke 10:18
Then S entered Judas ..... Luke 22:3
S has asked for you ...... Luke 22:31
S filled your heart .... Acts 5:3
S under your feet shortly .. Rom 16:20
such a one to S .... 1 Cor 5:5
For S himself .... 2 Cor 11:14
messenger of S to buffet ... 2 Cor 12:7
to the working of S ...... 2 Thess 2:9
whom I delivered to S .... 1 Tim 1:20
are a synagogue of S ...... Rev 2:9
you, where S dwells ...... Rev 2:13
known the depths of S .... Rev 2:24
called the Devil and S .... Rev 12:9
years have expired, S ..... Rev 20:7

SATIATED
s the weary soul .... Jer 31:25
It shall be *s* and made ...... Jer 46:10

SATISFIED
I shall be *s* when I .... Ps 17:15
his land will be *s* .... Prov 12:11
a good man will be *s* ..... Prov 14:14
s soul loathes the .... Prov 27:7
that are never *s* .... Prov 30:15
silver will not be *s* .... Eccl 5:10
left hand and not be *s* ...... Is 9:20
of His soul, and be *s* ...... Is 53:11
My people shall be *s* ..... Jer 31:14
still were not *s* .... Ezek 16:28
but they were not *s* ...... Amos 4:8
and cannot be *s* .... Hab 2:5

SATISFIES
s your mouth with good ..... Ps 103:5
s the longing soul .... Ps 107:9

SATISFY
s us early with Your .... Ps 90:14
long life I will *s* .... Ps 91:16
s her poor with bread .... Ps 132:15
for what does not *s* .... Is 55:2

SATISFYING
eats to the *s* of his .... Prov 13:25

SAUL
Becomes first king of Israel, 1 Sam 9–11
Sacrifices unlawfully, 1 Sam 13:1–14
Wars with Philistines, 1 Sam 13:15—14:52
Disregards the Lord's command; rejected by God, 1 Sam 15
Suffers from distressing spirits, 1 Sam 16:14–23
Becomes jealous of David; attempts to kill him, 1 Sam 18:5—19:22
Pursues David; twice spared by him, 1 Sam 22—24; 26
Consults medium, 1 Sam 28:7–25
Defeated, commits suicide; buried, 1 Sam 31

—— of Tarsus, apostle to the Gentiles:
see PAUL

SAVE
will *s* Israel by my hand ... Judg 6:37
the LORD does not *s* .... 1 Sam 17:47
there was none to *s* ..... 2 Sam 22:42
s the humble person .... Job 22:29
Oh, *s* me for Your .... Ps 6:4
s me from all those who ..... Ps 7:1
S Your people, and bless ..... Ps 28:9
send from heaven and *s* .... Ps 57:3
Your ear to me, and *s* me .... Ps 71:2
s the children of the .... Ps 72:4
s the souls of the .... Ps 72:13
s me, and I will keep ..... Ps 119:146
LORD, and He will *s* ...... Prov 20:22
He will come and *s* .... Is 35:4
LORD was ready to *s* .... Is 38:20
s your children .... Is 49:25
that it cannot *s* .... Is 59:1
mighty to *s* .... Is 63:1
one who cannot *s* .... Jer 14:9
s you and deliver you ..... Jer 15:20
s me, and I shall be .... Jer 17:14
O LORD, *s* Your people...... Jer 31:7
other, That he may *s* ..... Hos 13:10
Assyria shall not *s* .... Hos 14:3
the Mighty One, will *s* .... Zeph 3:17
JESUS, for He will *s* ...... Matt 1:21
Him, saying, "Lord, *s* us ... Matt 8:25
s his life will lose it ..... Matt 16:25
s that which was .... Matt 18:11
three days, *s* Yourself .... Matt 27:40
s life or to kill .... Mark 3:4
to *s* his life will lose it .... Mark 8:35
s Yourself, and come .... Mark 15:30
to *s* life or to destroy ...... Luke 6:9
life for My sake will *s* it ... Luke 9:24
seeks to *s* his life .... Luke 17:33
let Him *s* Himself if ...... Luke 23:35
You are the Christ, *s* .... Luke 23:39
'Father, *s* Me from .... John 12:27
but to *s* the world .... John 12:47
and *s* some of them ...... Rom 11:14
to *s* those who believe .... 1 Cor 1:21
by all means *s* some ..... 1 Cor 9:22
the world to *s* sinners .... 1 Tim 1:15
doing this you will *s* ..... 1 Tim 4:16
able to *s* Him from death .... Heb 5:7
able to *s* your souls....... James 1:21
Can faith *s* him .... James 2:14
who is able to *s* .... James 4:12
will *s* a soul from death .. James 5:20

SAVED
See WILL BE SAVED
the LORD *s* Israel that day ... Ex 14:30
you will be *s* from your .... Num 10:9
like you, a people *s* ..... Deut 33:29
But You have *s* us from ..... Ps 44:7
blamelessly will be *s* .... Prov 28:18
Look to Me, and be *s* ...... Is 45:22
and we are not *s* .... Jer 8:20
"Who then can be *s* ..... Matt 19:25
to the end shall be *s* ..... Matt 24:13
"He *s* others .... Matt 27:42
"Who then can be *s* .... Mark 10:26
to the end shall be *s* .... Mark 13:13
no flesh would be *s* .... Mark 13:20
"He *s* others .... Mark 15:31
and is baptized will be *s* .. Mark 16:16
That we should be *s* ...... Luke 1:71
"Your faith has *s* .... Luke 7:50
through Him might be *s* .... John 3:17
enters by Me, he will be *s* .. John 10:9
of the LORD shall be *s* .... Acts 2:21
them, saying, "Be *s* ...... Acts 2:40
of Moses, you cannot be *s* .. Acts 15:1
what must I do to be *s* .... Acts 16:30
For we were *s* in this ..... Rom 8:24
is that they may be *s* ..... Rom 10:1
all Israel will be *s* .... Rom 11:26

his spirit may be s .... 1 Cor 5:5
that they may be s ...... 1 Cor 10:33
which also you are s ...... 1 Cor 15:2
those who are being s ..... 2 Cor 2:15
grace you have been s ...... Eph 2:8
that they might be s ..... 2 Thess 2:10
all men to be s .... 1 Tim 2:4
she will be s in .... 1 Tim 2:15
to His mercy He s .... Titus 3:5
eight souls, were s ...... 1 Pet 3:20
of those who are s .... Rev 21:24

SAVES
s the needy from the .... Job 5:15
s such as have a .... Ps 34:18
antitype which now s ...... 1 Pet 3:21

SAVIOR
forgot God their S .... Ps 106:21
He will send them a S ...... Is 19:20
of Israel, your S .... Is 43:3
Me, a just God and a S ...... Is 45:21
I, the LORD, am your S .... Is 60:16
So He became their S .... Is 63:8
his S in time of trouble ...... Jer 14:8
for there is no s .... Hos 13:4
rejoiced in God my S ...... Luke 1:47
the city of David a S ...... Luke 2:11
the Christ, the S .... John 4:42
to be Prince and S .... Acts 5:31
up for Israel a S .... Acts 13:23
and He is the S .... Eph 5:23
of God our S and the ...... 1 Tim 1:1
God, who is the S .... 1 Tim 4:10
of our S Jesus Christ ...... 2 Tim 1:10
God and S Jesus Christ .... Titus 2:13
God our S toward man ...... Titus 3:4
Son as S of the world .... 1 John 4:14
to God our S, who alone is ... Jude 25

SAVIORS
s shall come to Mount ...... Obad 21

SAVOR
days, and I do not s .... Amos 5:21

SAWN
stoned, they were s .... Heb 11:37

SAY
But I s to you that .... Matt 5:22
"But who do you s .... Matt 16:15
s that we have no sin ...... 1 John 1:8

SAYING
disclose my dark s .... Ps 49:4
cannot accept this s ...... Matt 19:11
"This is a hard s .... John 6:60
This is a faithful s .... 1 Tim 1:15

SAYINGS
I will utter dark s .... Ps 78:2
whoever hears these s ..... Matt 7:24

SCALES
You shall have honest s .... Lev 19:36
be weighed on honest s .... Job 31:6
deceitful s are in his .... Hos 12:7
his eyes something like s ... Acts 9:18
on it had a pair of s .... Rev 6:5

SCARLET
midwife took a s thread ... Gen 38:28
s thread, fine linen .... Ex 25:4
s cord in the window ...... Josh 2:18
is clothed with s .... Prov 31:21
are like a strand of s ...... Song 4:3
your sins are like s .... Is 1:18
and put a s robe on Him .. Matt 27:28
s beast which was full ...... Rev 17:3

SCATTER
I will s you among the ..... Lev 26:33
S the peoples who .... Ps 68:30
s the sheep of My .... Jer 23:1
I will s to all winds .... Jer 49:32
s seed on the ground ..... Mark 4:26

SCATTERED
lest we be s abroad .... Gen 11:4

let His enemies be s .... Ps 68:1
of iniquity shall be s .... Ps 92:9
"You have s My flock .... Jer 23:2
s Israel will gather .... Jer 31:10
"Israel is like s sheep ..... Jer 50:17
they were weary and s .... Matt 9:36
where I have not s seed .. Matt 25:26
of the flock will be s ..... Matt 26:31
the sheep will be s ..... Mark 14:27
that you will be s .... John 16:32
tribes which are s abroad .. James 1:1

SCATTERS
s the frost like ashes ...... Ps 147:16
There is one who s .... Prov 11:24
throne of judgment s ...... Prov 20:8
not gather with Me s ..... Matt 12:30

SCEPTER
s shall not depart .... Gen 49:10
S shall rise out of .... Num 24:17
holds out the golden s ...... Esth 4:11
a s of righteousness .... Ps 45:6
a s of righteousness .... Heb 1:8

SCHEME
perfected a shrewd s ...... Ps 64:6

SCHEMER
will be called a s .... Prov 24:8

SCHEMES
who brings wicked s ...... Ps 37:7
sought out many s .... Eccl 7:29

SCHISM
there should be no s .... 1 Cor 12:25

SCHOOL
daily in the s of .... Acts 19:9

SCOFF
They s and speak .... Ps 73:8
They s at kings .... Hab 1:10

SCOFFER
"He who corrects a s ...... Prov 9:7
s does not listen .... Prov 13:1
s seeks wisdom and ...... Prov 14:6
s is an abomination .... Prov 24:9

SCOFFERS
S ensnare a city .... Prov 29:8
s will come in the .... 2 Pet 3:3

SCORCHED
sun was up they were s ... Matt 13:6
And men were s with ...... Rev 16:9

SCORN
My friends s me .... Job 16:20
to our neighbors, a s ...... Ps 44:13
laughed you to s .... Is 37:22

SCORNED
consider, for I am s ...... Lam 1:11
and princes are s .... Hab 1:10

SCORNFUL
nor sits in the seat of the s .... Ps 1:1
the s one is consumed ...... Is 29:20

SCORNS
He s the scornful .... Prov 3:34
s obedience to his .... Prov 30:17

SCORPION
will he offer him a s ...... Luke 11:12

SCORPIONS
and you dwell among s ..... Ezek 2:6
on serpents and s .... Luke 10:19
They had tails like s ..... Rev 9:10

SCOURGE
from the s of the tongue ..... Job 5:21
hosts will stir up a s .... Is 10:26
up to councils and s ...... Matt 10:17
will mock Him, and s .... Mark 10:34
s a man who is a Roman .. Acts 22:25

SCOURGES
will chastise you with s .. 1 Kin 12:11
s every son whom .... Heb 12:6

SCRIBE
a skilled s in the Law ...... Ezra 7:6
"Where is the s .... Is 33:18
the false pen of the s .... Jer 8:8
gave it to Baruch the s ... Jer 36:32
a certain s came and said .. Matt 8:19
s said to Him, "Well .... Mark 12:32
Where is the s? .... 1 Cor 1:20

SCRIBES
and not as the s .... Matt 7:29
"Beware of the s ...... Mark 12:38
s sought how they might .. Mark 14:1

SCRIBES AND PHARISEES
righteousness of the s ...... Matt 5:20
s answered, saying .... Matt 12:38
s who were from .... Matt 15:1
But woe to you, s .... Matt 23:13
the s saw him eating ..... Mark 2:16
s watched Him closely ..... Luke 6:7
Woe to you, s .... Luke 11:44
s brought to him a woman .. John 8:3

SCRIPTURE
what is noted in the S .... Dan 10:21
S was fulfilled which ..... Mark 15:28
"Today this S .... Luke 4:21
S cannot be broken ...... John 10:35
that the S might be ...... John 19:24
place in the S which he ..... Acts 8:32
For what does the S ...... Rom 4:3
S has confined all .... Gal 3:22
All S is given by .... 2 Tim 3:16
that the S says in vain .... James 4:5
that no prophecy of S ..... 2 Pet 1:20

SCRIPTURES
not knowing the S ...... Matt 22:29
S must be fulfilled ...... Mark 14:49
and mighty in the S ..... Acts 18:24
have known the Holy S .. 2 Tim 3:15
also the rest of the S ...... 2 Pet 3:16

SCROLL
in the s of the book .... Ps 40:7
and note it on a s .... Is 30:8
Baruch wrote on a s ...... Jer 36:4
the king had burned the s .. Jer 36:27
eat this s, and go .... Ezek 3:1
saw there a flying s ...... Zech 5:1
on the throne a s .... Rev 5:1
was able to open the s ...... Rev 5:3
the sky receded as a s ..... Rev 6:14

SEA
drowned in the Red S .... Ex 15:4
this great and wide s ..... Ps 104:25
who go down to the s ..... Ps 107:23
to the s its limit .... Prov 8:29
rebuke I dry up the s ...... Is 50:2
the waters cover the s ..... Hab 2:14
and the s obey Him .... Matt 8:27
Him walking on the s ..... Matt 14:26
throne there was a s ...... Rev 4:6
standing on the s .... Rev 15:2
there was no more s ...... Rev 21:1

SEAL
Set me as a s upon .... Song 8:6
the s of perfection ...... Ezek 28:12
therefore s up the vision ... Dan 8:26
has set His s on Him ..... John 6:27
of circumcision, a s ...... Rom 4:11
the s of my apostleship ..... 1 Cor 9:2
stands, having this s ..... 2 Tim 2:19
He opened the second s ..... Rev 6:3
He opened the seventh s ..... Rev 8:1
Do not s the words of the .. Rev 22:10

SEALED
My transgression is s ...... Job 14:17
s till the time of the end ... Dan 12:9
who also has s us and .. 2 Cor 1:22
by whom you were s ..... Eph 4:30
of those who were s .... Rev 7:4

SEALS
sealed with seven s .... Rev 5:1

SEAM
tunic was without s ....John 19:23

SÉANCE
"Please conduct a s ....1 Sam 28:8

SEARCH
"Can you s out the ....Job 11:7
would not God s ....Ps 44:21
glory of kings is to s ....Prov 25:2
found it by secret s ....Jer 2:34
I, the LORD, s the...........Jer 17:10
s the Scriptures ....John 5:39
S and look, for no ....John 7:52

SEARCHED
O LORD, You have s........Ps 139:1
s the Scriptures ....Acts 17:11
and s carefully ....1 Pet 1:10

SEARCHES
for the LORD s all ....1 Chr 28:9
s the hearts knows ....Rom 8:27
For the Spirit s ....1 Cor 2:10
that I am He who s ....Rev 2:23

SEASON
I will give you rain in its s ..Lev 26:4
bring forth its fruit in its s .....Ps 1:3
their food in due s ....Ps 104:27
a word spoken in due s ...Prov 15:23
To everything there is a s ....Eccl 3:1
word in s to him who is ......Is 50:4
give them food in due s ...Matt 24:45
flavor, how will you s it ....Mark 9:50
for in due s we shall reap ....Gal 6:9
Be ready in s and out ......2 Tim 4:2

SEASONED
how shall it be s ....Matt 5:13
"For everyone will be s ....Mark 9:49

SEASONS
let them be for signs and s ..Gen 1:14
appointed the moon for s ...Ps 104:19
the times and the s ....Dan 2:21
for you to know times or s ...Acts 1:7
days and months and s ......Gal 4:10
the times and the s ....1 Thess 5:1

SEAT
See MERCY SEAT
shall make a mercy s .....Ex 25:17
I might come to His s ....Job 23:3
that He may s him with ....Ps 113:8
sit in Moses' s ....Matt 23:2
before the judgment s .....2 Cor 5:10
the mercy s ....Heb 9:5

SEATED
the Ancient of Days was s ...Dan 7:9
s Him at His right hand .....Eph 1:20
who is s at the right hand ....Heb 8:1

SEATS
at feasts, the best s ....Matt 23:6
you love the best s ....Luke 11:43

SECOND
morning were the s day ......Gen 1:8
And the s is like it ....Matt 22:39
Can he enter a s time into ...John 3:4
the s Man is the Lord ....1 Cor 15:47
and behind the s veil, the ....Heb 9:3
He will appear a s time .....Heb 9:28
the s living creature like a ....Rev 4:7
Then the s angel sounded ....Rev 8:8

SECOND DEATH
not be hurt by the s ....Rev 2:11
Over such the s has no .....Rev 20:6
of fire. This is the s ....Rev 20:14
brimstone, which is the s ....Rev 21:8

SECRET
s things belong ....Deut 29:29
The s of the LORD is........Ps 25:14
in the place of His ....Ps 27:5
when I was made in s .....Ps 139:15
do not disclose the s ......Prov 25:9

I have not spoken in s ......Is 45:19
Father who is in the s ....Matt 6:6
s from the foundation of ..Matt 13:35
For nothing is s that will ...Luke 8:17
in s I have said nothing ...John 18:20
s since the world began ...Rom 16:25
are done by them in s ......Eph 5:12

SECRETLY
"Now a word was s........Job 4:12
He lies in wait s ....Ps 10:9
minded to put her away s ..Matt 1:19
a disciple of Jesus, but s ..John 19:38

SECRETS
would show you the s ......Job 11:6
For He knows the s ....Ps 44:21
A talebearer reveals s .....Prov 11:13
heaven who reveals s ......Dan 2:28
God will judge the s ......Rom 2:16
And thus the s of his .....1 Cor 14:25

SECT
him (which is the s ....Acts 5:17
to the strictest s ....Acts 26:5

SECURE
while the camp felt s ......Judg 8:11
dwell safely, and will be s ...Prov 1:33
him as a peg in a s place .....Is 22:23
made s until the third ....Matt 27:64

SECURELY
pleasures, who dwell s ....Is 47:8
nation that dwells s ....Jer 49:31

SECURES
he s it for himself among ....Is 44:14

SECURITY
gives them s, and they .....Job 24:23

SEDUCED
flattering lips she s ....Prov 7:21
because they have s ......Ezek 13:10

SEE
for no man shall s ....Ex 33:20
the LORD does not s.......1 Sam 16:7
in my flesh I shall s ....Job 19:26
s the works of God ....Ps 66:5
lest you s with their ....Is 6:10
for sin, He shall s ....Is 53:10
for they shall s God ....Matt 5:8
seeing they do not s .....Matt 13:13
s greater things than ......John 1:50
rejoiced to s My day ......John 8:56
we wish to s Jesus........John 12:21
and the world will s ......John 14:19
Him, for we shall s ....1 John 3:2
They shall s His face ......Rev 22:4

SEED
s shall be called ....Gen 21:12
s shall be its stump ....Is 6:13
He shall see His s ....Is 53:10
you a noble vine, a s ....Jer 2:21
s is the word of God ......Luke 8:11
had left us a s ....Rom 9:29
to each s its own body ....1 Cor 15:38
S were the promises ....Gal 3:16
you are Abraham's s ....Gal 3:29
of corruptible s ....1 Pet 1:23
not sin, for His s ....1 John 3:9

SEED OF DAVID
Christ comes from the s ....John 7:42
who was born of the s ......Rom 1:3
Jesus Christ, of the s ....2 Tim 2:8

SEEDS
the good s are the ....Matt 13:38
not say, "And to s ....Gal 3:16

SEEK
will find Him if you s ......Deut 4:29
pray and s My face ......2 Chr 7:14
your heart to s God ......2 Chr 19:3
s your God as you do ....Ezra 4:2
may God above not s ....Job 3:4

countenance does not s ......Ps 10:4
LORD, that will I s ....Ps 27:4
You said, "S My face ....Ps 27:8
early will I s You ....Ps 63:1
s me diligently will ....Prov 8:17
s one's own glory ....Prov 25:27
s justice, rebuke ....Is 1:17
Should they s the dead .....Is 8:19
the Gentiles shall s ....Is 11:10
Jacob, 'S Me in vain ....Is 45:19
Yet they s Me daily ....Is 58:2
s great things for ....Jer 45:5
s what was lost ....Ezek 34:16
"S Me and live ....Amos 5:4
and people should s ....Mal 2:7
things the Gentiles s .....Matt 6:32
s, and you will find ....Matt 7:7
of Man has come to s ....Luke 19:10
because I do not s ....John 5:30
You will s Me and ....John 7:34
in doing good s ....Rom 2:7
Because they did not s ....Rom 9:32
Let no one s his own ....1 Cor 10:24
for I do not s yours ......2 Cor 12:14
For all s their own ....Phil 2:21
s those things which ....Col 3:1
s the one to come ....Heb 13:14

SEEK THE LORD
from there you will s ....Deut 4:29
of those rejoice who s ....1 Chr 16:10
heart and your soul to s .1 Chr 22:19
set their heart to s ......2 Chr 11:16
disease he did not s ......2 Chr 16:12
set himself to s ....2 Chr 20:3
of the land in order to s ...Ezra 6:21
who s shall not lack ....Ps 34:10
S and His strength ....Ps 105:4
those who s understand ...Prov 28:5
righteousness, you who s ...Is 51:1
S while He may be found .....Is 55:6
Israel shall return and s ....Hos 3:5
S and live, lest He ....Amos 5:6
S, all you meek ....Zeph 2:3
nations shall come to s ....Zech 8:22
rest of mankind may s ....Acts 15:17
so that they should s .....Acts 17:27

SEEKING
run to and fro, s ....Amos 8:12
and he came s fruit ......Luke 13:6
for the Father is s ....John 4:23
like a roaring lion, s ....1 Pet 5:8

SEEKS
Zion; no one s her ....Jer 30:17
receives, and he who s .....Matt 7:8
There is none who s ....Rom 3:11

SEEMS
There is a way which s ...Prov 14:12
have, even what he s ......Luke 8:18
If anyone among you s ....1 Cor 3:18

SEEN
s God face to face ....Gen 32:30
All this I have s ....Eccl 8:9
s the one I love ....Song 3:3
Who has s such things ......Is 66:8
s strange things today ....Luke 5:26
No one has s God at ......John 1:18
time, nor s His form ....John 5:37
I speak what I have s ......John 8:38
s Me has s the ....John 14:9
things which we have s ....Acts 4:20
Jacob, Jesus Christ our ....1 Cor 9:1
things which are not s ....2 Cor 4:18
whom no man has s ....1 Tim 6:16
heard, which we have s ....1 John 1:1

SEES
here seen Him who s ......Gen 16:13
s all the sons of men .....Ps 33:13
s his brother in need .....1 John 3:17
s his brother sinning .....1 John 5:16

SEIR
Home of Esau, Gen 32:3
Horites of, dispossessed by Esau's
   descendants, Deut 2:12
Desolation of, Ezek 35:15

SEIZE
s the city, for the LORD . . . . . . Josh 8:7
Will not pangs s you, like . . Jer 13:21
also houses, and s them . . . . . . Mic 2:2
s his inheritance . . . . Matt 21:38
you did not s Me . . . . Matt 26:55
further to s Peter also . . . . . . Acts 12:3

SEIZED
pangs have s you like a . . . . . Mic 4:9
For it had often s him . . . . . Luke 8:29
profit was gone, they s . . . Acts 16:19
Jews s me in the temple . . . Acts 26:21

SELF-CONFIDENT
a fool rages and is s . . . . . Prov 14:16

SELF-CONTROL
about righteousness, s . . . . Acts 24:25
because of your lack of s . . . 1 Cor 7:5
they cannot exercise s . . . . . . 1 Cor 7:9
gentleness, s . . . . Gal 5:23
love, and holiness, with s . 1 Tim 2:15
slanderers, without s . . . . 2 Tim 3:3
to knowledge s . . . . 2 Pet 1:6

SELF-CONTROLLED
just, holy, s . . . . Titus 1:8

SELF-SEEKING
envy and s exist . . . . James 3:16

SELFISH
s ambitions, backbitings . . 2 Cor 12:20
s ambitions, dissensions . . . . . Gal 5:20
preach Christ from s . . . . Phil 1:16
s ambition or conceit . . . . Phil 2:3

SELL
said, "S me your . . . . Gen 25:31
s Your people for . . . . Ps 44:12
s the righteous . . . . Amos 2:6
s whatever you have . . . . Mark 10:21
no sword, let him s . . . . . . Luke 22:36
no one may buy or s . . . . . . Rev 13:17

SEND
He shall s from heaven . . . . Ps 57:3
"Whom shall I s . . . . Is 6:8
s them a Savior . . . . Is 19:20
"Behold, I s you out . . . . . . Matt 10:16
The Son of Man will s . . . . Matt 13:41
S the multitudes away . . . . Matt 14:15
He will s His angels . . . . . Matt 24:31
"S us to the swine, that . . . . Mark 5:12
s them out two by two . . . . . . Mark 6:7
S them away, that they . . Mark 6:36
I s you out as lambs . . . . . . Luke 10:3
I will s them prophets . . . . Luke 11:49
s Lazarus that he . . . . . . Luke 16:24
s the Promise of My . . . . . Luke 24:49
God did not s His Son . . . . John 3:17
whom the Father will s . . . John 14:26
has sent Me, I also s . . . . . John 20:21

SENDING
I am s you to Jesse . . . . . . 1 Sam 16:1
God did by s His own Son . . Rom 8:3

SENDS
s rain on the just and . . . . . Matt 5:45
till He s forth justice to . . . Matt 12:20

SENNACHERIB
Assyrian king (705–681 B.C.); son and
   successor of Sargon II, 2 Kin 18:13
Death of, by assassination, 2 Kin 19:36,
   37

SENSELESS
Understand, you s . . . . Ps 94:8

SENSES
of use have their s . . . . Heb 5:14

SENSIBLY
who can answer s . . . . Prov 26:16

SENSUAL
but is earthly, s . . . . James 3:15
These are s persons . . . . Jude 19

SENT
s out the dove . . . . Gen 8:12
'I AM has s me to you . . . . . Ex 3:14
s to spy out the land . . . . Num 13:16
LORD s me to anoint you . . 1 Sam 15:1
and His Spirit have s . . . . . . Is 48:16
s these prophets . . . . Jer 23:21
s this commandment . . . . Mal 2:4
receives Him who s Me . . Matt 10:40
not Me but Him who s . . . Mark 9:37
he s a servant to the . . . . Mark 12:2
He has s Me to heal the . . . Luke 4:18
Baptist has s us to You . . . Luke 7:20
receives Him who s Me . . Luke 9:48
rejects Him who s Me . . . Luke 10:16
a man s from God . . . . John 1:6
the will of Him who s Me . John 6:38
Father who s Me bears . . . John 8:18
is he who is s greater . . . . John 13:16
You s Me into the world . . John 17:18
As the Father has s . . . . . John 20:21
unless they are s . . . . Rom 10:15
Spirit s from heaven . . . . . 1 Pet 1:12
s His Son to be the . . . . . . 1 John 4:10
s His angel to show His . . . . Rev 22:6

SEPARATE
he shall s himself . . . . Num 6:3
s yourselves from the . . . . Ezra 10:11
let not man s . . . . Matt 19:6
Who shall s us from . . . . . Rom 8:35
harmless, undefiled, s . . . . . . Heb 7:26

SEPARATED
but the poor is s . . . . Prov 19:4
"The LORD has utterly s . . . . . . Is 56:3
to be an apostle, s . . . . Rom 1:1
it pleased God, who s . . . . . Gal 1:15

SEPARATES
who repeats a matter s . . . . Prov 17:9

SEPARATION
the middle wall of s . . . . Eph 2:14

SERAPHIM
Above it stood s . . . . Is 6:2

SERGIUS PAULUS
Roman proconsul of Cyprus, converted
   by Paul, Acts 13:7–12

SERIOUS
therefore be s and . . . . 1 Pet 4:7

SERPENT
s was more cunning . . . . Gen 3:1
"The s deceived me . . . . Gen 3:13
"Make a fiery s . . . . Num 21:8
like the poison of a s . . . . . . Ps 58:4
s you shall trample . . . . Ps 91:13
their tongues like a s . . . . . Ps 140:3
air, the way of a s . . . . . . Prov 30:19
s may bite when it is . . . . . Eccl 10:11
be a fiery flying s . . . . Is 14:29
and wounded the s . . . . Is 51:9
will he give him a s . . . . . . Matt 7:10
Moses lifted up the s . . . . . . John 3:14
was cast out, that s . . . . . . Rev 12:9

SERPENTS
is the poison of s . . . . . . Deut 32:33
be wise as s . . . . Matt 10:16
to trample on s . . . . Luke 10:19

SERVANT
a s of servants he . . . . Gen 9:25
take a gift from your s . . . 2 Kin 5:15
the s of the man of God . . 2 Kin 8:4
s who earnestly . . . . Job 7:2
bountifully with Your s . . Ps 119:17
and the fool will be s . . . . Prov 11:29

s will rule over a son . . . . . Prov 17:2
A s will not be . . . . Prov 29:19
Who is blind but My s . . . . . . Is 42:19
"Is Israel a s . . . . Jer 2:14
and a s his master . . . . Mal 1:6
nor a s above his master . . Matt 10:24
My S whom I have . . . . . . Matt 12:18
you, let him be your s . . . Matt 20:26
good and faithful s . . . . . Matt 25:21
'You wicked and lazy s . . Matt 25:26
the unprofitable s . . . . . . Matt 25:30
be last of all and s of all . . . Mark 9:35
you shall be your s . . . . . . Mark 10:43
a s to the vinedressers . . . Mark 12:2
to my s, 'Do this,' . . . . Luke 7:8
that s who knew his . . . . . Luke 12:47
I am, there My s will be . . John 12:26
s does not know what . . . . John 15:15
'A s is not greater than . . . John 15:20
struck the high priest's s . John 18:10
against Your holy S . . . . . . Acts 4:27
Christ has become a s . . . . Rom 15:8

SERVANTS
puts no trust in His s . . . . . . Job 4:18
for all your s . . . . Ps 119:91
on the ground like s . . . . . Eccl 10:7
shall call you the s . . . . Is 61:6
S rule over us . . . . Lam 5:8
Again he sent other s . . . . Matt 21:36
the king said to the s . . . . Matt 22:13
s whom the master . . . . . Luke 12:37
are unprofitable s . . . . . . Luke 17:10
longer do I call you s . . . . John 15:15
My s would fight, so . . . . John 18:36
so consider us, as s . . . . . . 1 Cor 4:1

SERVE
people go, that they may s . . . . Ex 8:1
s you until the Year of . . . . Lev 25:40
LORD your God and s . . . . Deut 6:13
S the LORD . . . . Josh 24:14
land, so you shall s aliens . . . Jer 5:19
s Him with one accord . . . . Zeph 3:9
You cannot s God and . . . Matt 6:24
to be served, but to s . . . . Matt 20:28
to be served, but to s . . . Mark 10:45
the mind I myself s . . . . . . Rom 7:25
but through love s . . . . Gal 5:13
s the living God . . . . Heb 9:14
s Him day and night in . . . Rev 7:15

SERVE THE LORD
men go, that they may s . . . . Ex 10:7
go, s as you have said . . . . Ex 12:31
So you shall s . . . . Ex 23:25
to s your God with all . . . . Deut 10:12
Because you did not s . . . . Deut 28:47
and my house, we will s . . . Josh 24:15
s with all your heart . . . . . 1 Sam 12:20
commanded Judah to s . . 2 Chr 33:16
S with fear, and rejoice . . . . . Ps 2:11
S with gladness . . . . Ps 100:2
the kingdoms, to s . . . . . . Ps 102:22
But they shall s their God . . Jer 30:9
s without distraction . . . . . 1 Cor 7:35
inheritance, for you s . . . . . Col 3:24

SERVED
did not come to be s . . . . Matt 20:28
did not come to be s . . . . Mark 10:45
s the creature rather than . . Rom 1:25

SERVES
If anyone s Me . . . . John 12:26

SERVICE
do you mean by this s . . . . . Ex 12:26
that he offers God s . . . . . John 16:2
is your reasonable s . . . . . Rom 12:1
with goodwill doing s . . . . . . Eph 6:7
your works, love, s . . . . Rev 2:19

SERVING
years I have been s . . . . . Luke 15:29
s the Lord with all . . . . . . Acts 20:19

fervent in spirit, *s* .... Rom 12:11
you, *s* as overseers .... 1 Pet 5:2

SET
"See, I have *s* .... Deut 30:15
s the LORD always .... Ps 16:8
I will *s* him on high .... Ps 91:14
s aside the grace .... Gal 2:21

SET APART
will *s* the land of Goshen ..... Ex 8:22
s to the Lord all that .... Ex 13:12
she shall be *s* seven days ... Lev 15:19
Then Moses *s* three cities . Deut 4:41
as a dog laps, you shall *s* ... Judg 7:5
It was *s* for you .... 1 Sam 9:24
Aaron was *s*, he and his .. 1 Chr 23:13
the Lord has *s* for Himself ..... Ps 4:3
s a district for the Lord ... Ezek 45:1

SETH
Third son of Adam, Gen 4:25
In Christ's ancestry, Luke 3:38

SETTLE
Therefore *s* it in .... Luke 21:14

SETTLED
and my speech *s* .... Job 29:22
O LORD, Your word is *s* .... Ps 119:89
the mountains were *s* ...... Prov 8:25
s accounts with them ..... Matt 25:19

SEVEN
Then *s* priests bearing ..... Josh 6:13
he had *s* hundred wives ... 1 Kin 11:3
the child sneezed *s* times .. 2 Kin 4:35
Joash was *s* years old ..... 2 Chr 24:1
S times a day I praise ..... Ps 119:164
may fall *s* times and rise .. Prov 24:16
there are *s* abominations . Prov 26:25
in that day *s* women shall ..... Is 4:1
Passover, a feast of *s* ..... Ezek 45:21
s times more than it was .... Dan 3:19
let *s* times pass over him ... Dan 4:16
there shall be *s* weeks and . Dan 9:25
He took the *s* loaves ..... Matt 15:36
forgive him? Up to *s* ..... Matt 18:21
wife of the *s* will she be ... Matt 22:28
had come *s* demons .... Luke 8:2
s other spirits more ...... Luke 11:26
s times in a day .... Luke 17:4
out from among you *s* ...... Acts 6:3
s churches which are .... Rev 1:4
I saw *s* golden lampstands .. Rev 1:12
The mystery of the *s* stars .. Rev 1:20
He who holds the *s* stars ..... Rev 2:1
has the *s* Spirits of God ..... Rev 3:1
S lamps of fire were .... Rev 4:5
sealed with *s* seals .... Rev 5:1
saw the *s* angels who stand .. Rev 8:2
s thunders uttered their ..... Rev 10:3
earthquake *s* thousand ..... Rev 11:13
red dragon having *s* heads .. Rev 12:3
of the sea, having *s* heads .. Rev 13:1
s angels having the *s* last .. Rev 15:1
who had the *s* bowls .... Rev 17:1
s last plagues came to me ... Rev 21:9

SEVENFOLD
light of the sun will be *s* ..... Is 30:26

SEVENTH
the *s* day God ended His ..... Gen 2:2
ark rested in the *s* month .... Gen 8:4
on the *s* day there shall ..... Ex 12:16
gather it, but on the *s* day ... Ex 16:26
When He opened the *s* seal .. Rev 8:1
the sounding of the *s* angel .. Rev 10:7
Then the *s* angel sounded .. Rev 11:15
the *s* angel poured out ...... Rev 16:17
s chrysolite, the eighth ..... Rev 21:20

SEVENTY
S weeks are .... Dan 9:24
up to *s* times seven ...... Matt 18:22
Then the *s* returned ...... Luke 10:17

SEVERE
My wound is *s* .... Jer 10:19
not to be too *s* .... 2 Cor 2:5

SEVERITY
the goodness and *s* .... Rom 11:22

SEWS
s a piece of unshrunk ...... Mark 2:21

SEXUAL
s immorality causes her .... Matt 5:32
except for *s* immorality .... Matt 19:9
from *s* immorality, from ... Acts 15:20
s immorality, wickedness .. Rom 1:29
s immorality among you .... 1 Cor 5:1
the body is not for *s* .... 1 Cor 6:13
Flee *s* immorality .... 1 Cor 6:18
commit *s* immorality ...... 1 Cor 10:8
abstain from *s* .... 1 Thess 4:3
to commit *s* immorality ..... Rev 2:14
repent of her *s* immorality .. Rev 2:21

SEXUALLY
company with *s* immoral ... 1 Cor 5:9
s immoral, sorcerers .... Rev 21:8

SHADE
I sat down in his *s* .... Song 2:3
be a tabernacle for *s* .... Is 4:6
may nest under its *s* ...... Mark 4:32

SHADOW
May darkness and the *s* ..... Job 3:5
He flees like a *s* .... Job 14:2
hide me under the *s* .... Ps 17:8
walks about like a *s* .... Ps 39:6
like a passing *s* .... Ps 144:4
he passes like a *s* .... Eccl 6:12
and to trust in the *s* .... Is 30:2
In the *s* of His hand .... Is 49:2
which are a *s* of .... Col 2:17
the law, having a *s* .... Heb 10:1
is no variation or *s* ...... James 1:17

SHADOW OF DEATH
of darkness and the *s* ..... Job 10:21
my eyelids is the *s* .... Job 16:16
seen the doors of the *s* .... Job 38:17
the valley of the *s* .... Ps 23:4
out of darkness and the *s* .. Ps 107:14
s, upon them a light .... Is 9:2
turns the *s* into morning .... Amos 5:8
s light has dawned .... Matt 4:16
in darkness and the *s* ..... Luke 1:79

SHADOWS
my members are like *s* ...... Job 17:7
and the *s* flee away .... Song 2:17

SHADRACH
Hananiah's Babylonian name, Dan 1:3, 7
Cast into the fiery furnace, Dan 3:1–28

SHAKE
Who is he who will *s* .... Job 17:3
their loins *s* continually ..... Ps 69:23
s the earth .... Is 2:19
S yourself from the .... Is 52:2
you *s* your head in scorn ... Jer 48:27
s their heads at the .... Lam 2:15
that the thresholds may *s* .. Amos 9:1
and the knees *s* .... Nah 2:10
hiss and *s* his fist .... Zeph 2:15
little while) I will *s* heaven ... Hag 2:6
I will *s* all nations .... Hag 2:7
s off the dust from your ... Matt 10:14
s off the dust under your .. Mark 6:11
house, and could not *s* it ... Luke 6:48
s not only the earth .... Heb 12:26

SHAKEN
reed is *s* in the water ..... 1 Kin 14:15
quaked and were *s* .... Ps 18:7
he will never be *s* .... Ps 112:6
A reed *s* by the wind ...... Matt 11:7
of the heavens will be *s* ... Matt 24:29

the heavens will be *s* ..... Mark 13:25
s together, and running .... Luke 6:38
together was *s* .... Acts 4:31
of the prison were *s* ...... Acts 16:26
not to be soon *s* .... 2 Thess 2:2
which cannot be *s* .... Heb 12:28

SHAKES
s the earth out of its .... Job 9:6
s the Wilderness .... Ps 29:8
The earth *s* at the noise ..... Jer 49:21

SHALLUM
King of Israel, 2 Kin 15:10–15

SHALMANESER
Assyrian king, 2 Kin 17:3

SHAME
you turn my glory to *s* .... Ps 4:2
let them be put to *s* .... Ps 83:17
s who serve carved .... Ps 97:7
hate Zion be put to *s* .... Ps 129:5
s shall be the .... Prov 3:35
is a son who causes *s* ..... Prov 10:5
hide My face from *s* .... Is 50:6
S has covered our .... Jer 51:51
their glory into *s* .... Hos 4:7
never be put to *s* .... Joel 2:26
Pass by in naked *s*, you ..... Mic 1:11
the unjust knows no *s* ..... Zeph 3:5
worthy to suffer *s* .... Acts 5:41
will not be put to *s* .... Rom 9:33
to put to *s* the wise .... 1 Cor 1:27
I say this to your *s* .... 1 Cor 6:5
glory is in their *s* .... Phil 3:19
put Him to an open *s* .... Heb 6:6
the cross, despising the *s* .. Heb 12:2

SHAMEFUL
committing what is *s* ...... Rom 1:27
for it is *s* for women ..... 1 Cor 14:35
For it is *s* even to .... Eph 5:12

SHAMGAR
Judge of Israel; strikes down 600 Philistines, Judg 3:31

SHAMMAH
Son of Jesse, 1 Sam 16:9
Called Shimea, 1 Chr 2:13
——— One of David's mighty men, 2 Sam 23:11
Also called Shammoth the Harorite, 1 Chr 11:27

SHAPHAN
Scribe under Josiah, 2 Kin 22:3–14

SHARE
a stranger does not *s* ..... Prov 14:10
s in anything done under .... Eccl 9:6
s your bread with the .... Is 58:7
is taught the word *s* .... Gal 6:6
to give, willing to *s* ...... 1 Tim 6:18
to do good and to *s* ...... Heb 13:16
lest you *s* in her sins, and ... Rev 18:4

SHARING
for your liberal *s* .... 2 Cor 9:13

SHARON
Coastal plain between Joppa and Mt. Carmel, 1 Chr 27:29
Famed for roses, Song 2:1
Inhabitants of, turn to the Lord, Acts 9:35

SHARP
destruction, like a *s* razor .... Ps 52:2
S as a two-edged sword ..... Prov 5:4
sledge with *s* teeth .... Is 41:15
My mouth like a *s* sword ..... Is 49:2
son of man, take a *s* sword .. Ezek 5:1
went a *s* two-edged sword .. Rev 1:16
who has the *s* two-edged .... Rev 2:12
and in His hand a *s* sickle .. Rev 14:14

SHARPEN
s their tongue like a .... Ps 64:3
and one does not *s* .... Eccl 10:10

SHARPENS
My adversary s His ....Job 16:9

SHARPNESS
I should use s ....2 Cor 13:10

SHATTERED
at ease, but He has s ....Job 16:12

SHAVE
Then the Nazirite shall s ...Num 6:18
s off the seven locks ......Judg 16:19
will s with a hired razor ......Is 7:20
they may s their heads ....Acts 21:24

SHAVED
s off half of their beards ..2 Sam 10:4
as if her head were s ......1 Cor 11:5

SHEALTIEL
Son of King Jeconiah and father of
Zerubbabel, 1 Chr 3:17

SHEAR-JASHUB
Symbolic name given to Isaiah's son,
Is 7:3

SHEATH
'Return it to its s ....Ezek 21:30
your sword into the s .....John 18:11

SHEAVES
bringing his s ....Ps 126:6
nor he who binds s ....Ps 129:7
gather them like s ....Mic 4:12

SHEBA
Land of, occupied by Sabeans, famous
traders, Job 1:15; Ps 72:10
Queen of, visits Solomon; marvels at
his wisdom, 1 Kin 10:1–13
Mentioned by Christ, Matt 12:42

SHEBAH
Name given to a well and town
(Beersheba), Gen 26:31–33

SHEBNA
Treasurer under Hezekiah, Is 22:15
Demoted to position of scribe, 2 Kin
19:2
Man of pride and luxury, replaced by
Eliakim, Is 22:19–21

SHECHEM
Son of Hamor; rapes Dinah, Jacob's
daughter, Gen 34:1–31
——— Ancient city of Ephraim, Gen 33:18
Joshua's farewell address delivered at,
Josh 24:1–25
Supports Abimelech; destroyed,
Judg 9
Rebuilt by Jeroboam I, 1 Kin 12:25

SHED
s blood without cause ...1 Sam 25:31
s innocent blood ....Ps 106:38
which is s for many ......Matt 26:28
which is s for many ......Mark 14:24
s from the foundation of ..Luke 11:50
blood, which is s for .....Luke 22:20
martyr Stephen was s ,....Acts 22:20
feet are swift to s blood ....Rom 3:15
they have s the blood of ....Rev 16:6
of His servants s by her ....Rev 19:2

SHEDDING
blood, and without s ....Heb 9:22

SHEEP
spared the best of the s ..1 Sam 15:15
as s that have no ......2 Chr 18:16
like s intended for food ....Ps 44:11
as s for the slaughter ....Ps 44:22
s of Your pasture ....Ps 79:13
and the s of His hand ......Ps 95:7
and the s of His pasture ....Ps 100:3
astray like a lost s ......Ps 119:176
All we like s have gone ......Is 53:6
slaughter, and as a s ....Is 53:7

Pull them out like s ....Jer 12:3
scatter the s of My pasture ...Jer 23:1
have been lost s ....Jer 50:6
My s wandered through ...Ezek 34:6
will search for My s ......Ezek 34:11
shall judge between s ....Ezek 34:17
lion among flocks of s .....Mic 5:8
s will be scattered ......Zech 13:7
like s having no shepherd ..Matt 9:36
rather to the lost s ....Matt 10:6
I send you out as s ......Matt 10:16
lost s of the house of .....Matt 15:24
If a man has a hundred s ..Matt 18:12
his s from the goats ......Matt 25:32
And He will set the s ......Matt 25:33
s not having a shepherd ...Mark 6:34
s will be scattered ....Mark 14:27
having a hundred s ....Luke 15:4
plowing or tending ....Luke 17:7
the shepherd of the s ......John 10:2
and he calls his own s .....John 10:3
and I know My s ....John 10:14
s I have which are not ....John 10:16
you are not of My s ....John 10:26
said to him, "Tend My s ....John 21:16
said to him, "Feed My s. ..John 21:17
"He was led as a s ......Acts 8:32
as s for the slaughter ......Rom 8:36
great Shepherd of the s ....Heb 13:20
like s going astray ....1 Pet 2:25

SHEEPFOLDS
lie down among the s ....Ps 68:13

SHEET
object like a great s ....Acts 10:11

SHELTER
I will trust in the s ....Ps 61:4
in You I take s ....Ps 143:9
the LORD will be a s ......Joel 3:16

SHELTERS
s him all the day long ....Deut 33:12
be pastures, with s ....Zeph 2:6

SHEM
Oldest son of Noah, Gen 5:32
Escapes the flood, Gen 7:13
Receives a blessing, Gen 9:23, 26
Ancestor of Semitic people, Gen
10:22–32

SHEMAIAH
Prophet of Judah, 1 Kin 12:22–24
Explains Shishak's invasion as divine
punishment, 2 Chr 12:5–8
Records Rehoboam's reign, 2 Chr 12:15

SHEMER
Sells Omri the hill on which Samaria
is built, 1 Kin 16:23, 24

SHEOL
down to the gates of S .....Job 17:16
not leave my soul in S ......Ps 16:10
S laid hold of me ....Ps 116:3
S cannot thank ....Is 38:18
the belly of S I cried ....Jon 2:2

SHEPHERD
s is an abomination ......Gen 46:34
s My people Israel ....2 Sam 5:2
The LORD is my s ....Ps 23:1
s Jacob His people ....Ps 78:71
His flock like a s ....Is 40:11
of Cyrus, 'He is My s ......Is 44:28
s who follows You ....Jer 17:16
because there was no s ....Ezek 34:5
I will establish one s ......Ezek 34:23
"As a s takes from ....Amos 3:12
to the worthless s ....Zech 11:17
'I will strike the S ......Matt 26:31
"I am the good s ....John 10:11
s the church of God ....Acts 20:28
the dead, that great S .....Heb 13:20
S the flock of God ....1 Pet 5:2

when the Chief S ....1 Pet 5:4
of the throne will s ....Rev 7:17

SHEPHERDS
your sons shall be s ......Num 14:33
And they are s who ....Is 56:11
And I will give you s ......Jer 3:15
s who destroy and ....Jer 23:1
s who feed My people ......Jer 22:3
s have led them astray ....Jer 50:6
s fed themselves ....Ezek 34:8
in the same country s ....Luke 2:8

SHESHACH
Symbolic of Babylon, Jer 25:26

SHESHBAZZAR
Prince of Judah, Ezra 1:8, 11

SHETHAR-BOZNAI
Official of Persia, Ezra 5:3, 6

SHIELD
I am your s ....Gen 15:1
the s of your help and ....Deut 33:29
s of Saul, not anointed ....2 Sam 1:21
whom I trust: my s ...2 Sam 22:3
He is a s to all who ......2 Sam 22:31
gold went into each s .....2 Chr 9:15
are a s for me, my glory ......Ps 3:3
surround him as with a s .....Ps 5:12
my s and the horn of ....Ps 18:2
He is a s to all who trust in ..Ps 18:30
me the s of Your salvation ..Ps 18:35
my strength and my s ....Ps 28:7
He is our help and our s .....Ps 33:20
God is a sun and s ....Ps 84:11
truth shall be your s ....Ps 91:4
He is their help and their s ..Ps 115:9
hiding place and my s ....Ps 119:114
all, taking the s ....Eph 6:16

SHIHOR
Name given to the Nile, Is 23:3
Israel's southwestern border, Josh 13:3

SHILOH
Center of worship, Judg 18:31
Headquarters for division of Promised
Land, Josh 18:1, 10
Benjamites seize women of, Judg
21:19–23
Ark of the covenant taken from, 1 Sam
4:3–11
Punishment given to, Jer 7:12–15
——— Messianic title, Gen 49:10

SHIMEI
Benjamite; insults David, 2 Sam
16:5–13
Pardoned, but confined, 2 Sam
19:16–23
Breaks agreement; executed by Solomon, 1 Kin 2:39–46

SHIMSHAI
Scribe opposing the Jews, Ezra 4:8–24

SHINAR
Tower built at, Gen 11:2–9

SHINE
LORD make His face s ......Num 6:25
even the moon does not s ...Job 25:5
Make Your face s upon .....Ps 31:16
cause His face to s ....Ps 67:1
the cherubim, s ....Ps 80:1
Make Your face s ....Ps 119:135
will not cause its light to s ...Is 13:10
Arise, s; for your light ......Is 60:1
who are wise shall s ....Dan 12:3
your light so s before men ..Matt 5:16
the righteous will s ....Matt 13:43
among whom you s ....Phil 2:15
a third of the day did not s ...Rev 8:12
sun or of the moon to s ....Rev 21:23

SHINED
them a light has s ....Is 9:2

SHINES
But the night s as the day .. Ps 139:12
that s ever brighter unto ... Prov 4:18
And the light s .... John 1:5
light that s in a dark .... 2 Pet 1:19

SHINING
the earth, by clear s ...... 2 Sam 23:4
the just is like the s sun .... Prov 4:18
His clothes became s ...... Mark 9:3
by them in s garments ..... Luke 24:4
light is already s .... 1 John 2:8
was like the sun s .... Rev 1:16

SHIP
the way of a s in the ...... Prov 30:19
found a s going to Tarshish ... Jon 1:3
finding a s sailing over to .. Acts 21:2
some on parts of the s .... Acts 27:44

SHIPHRAH
Hebrew midwife, Ex 1:15

SHIPS
pass by like swift s .... Job 9:26
down to the sea in s .... Ps 107:23
like the merchant s ...... Prov 31:14
Look also at s .... James 3:4

SHIPWRECK
faith have suffered s ...... 1 Tim 1:19

SHONE
the skin of Moses' face s .... Ex 34:35
His face s like the sun ... Matt 17:2
of the Lord s around them .. Luke 2:9
a light s around him .... Acts 9:3
and a light s in the prison .. Acts 12:7

SHOOK
so loudly that the earth s .. 1 Sam 4:5
the earth s and trembled .. 2 Sam 22:8
earth s; the heavens sang .. Ps 68:8
The earth trembled and s .... Ps 77:18
guards s for fear of him .... Matt 28:4
they s off the dust from ... Acts 13:51

SHOOT
they s out the lip .... Ps 22:7
But God shall s .... Ps 64:7

SHORT
of the wicked is s .... Job 20:5
Remember how s my time ... Ps 89:47
for he was of s stature ..... Luke 19:3
have sinned and fall s ...... Rom 3:23
the work and cut it s....... Rom 9:28
fall s of the grace of God .. Heb 12:15
knows that he has a s .... Rev 12:12

SHORTENED
his youth You have s........ Ps 89:45
the wicked will be s ...... Prov 10:27
those days were s .... Matt 24:22
Lord had s those days .... Mark 13:20

SHORTLY
which must s take place ..... Rev 1:1
which must s take place .... Rev 22:6

SHOT
shall be stoned or s .... Heb 12:20

SHOULDER
will be upon His s .... Is 9:6

SHOUT
shall s with a great s .... Josh 6:5
s for joy, all you upright in .. Ps 32:11
skillfully with a s of joy ...... Ps 33:3
s for joy and be glad .... Ps 35:27
S to God with the voice of .... Ps 47:1
Make a joyful s to God, all .. Ps 66:1
Make a joyful s to the God ... Ps 81:1
s joyfully to the Rock ...... Ps 95:1
S joyfully to the LORD .... Ps 98:4
Make a joyful s .... Ps 100:1
from heaven with a s .... 1 Thess 4:16

SHOUTED
So the people s when the ... Josh 6:20
they s, saying, "Crucify ... Luke 23:21

SHOW
a land that I will s .... Gen 12:1
will s Yourself merciful .. 2 Sam 22:26
will s Yourself merciful ..... Ps 18:25
S me Your ways .... Ps 25:4
I will s the salvation of ...... Ps 50:23
mouth shall s forth Your .... Ps 51:15
S us Your mercy, LORD....... Ps 85:7
and s us what will happen ... Is 41:22
s yourselves men .... Is 46:8
s mercy and compassion .... Zech 7:9
s them a sign from .... Matt 16:1
S Me the tax money ...... Matt 22:19
s great signs and .... Matt 24:24
s signs and wonders to ... Mark 13:22
s Him greater works ...... John 5:20
s Yourself to the world ...... John 7:4
s us the Father .... John 14:8
you say, 'S us the Father ... John 14:9
I s you a more excellent .. 1 Cor 12:31
S me your faith without .. James 2:18
I will s you things which ..... Rev 4:1

SHOWBREAD
you shall set the s .... Ex 25:30
s which had been taken ... 1 Sam 21:6
s which was not lawful ..... Matt 12:4

SHOWED
s him mercy, and He ...... Gen 39:21
and the LORD s him a tree ... Ex 15:25
s Him all the kingdoms ..... Matt 4:8
s Him all the kingdoms ..... Luke 4:5
But even Moses s in the .. Luke 20:37
s them His hands and ..... Luke 24:40
s them His hands and .... John 20:20
Jesus s Himself again to ... John 21:1
third day, and s Him .... Acts 10:40
s me the great city, the .... Rev 21:10

SHOWERS
make it soft with s .... Ps 65:10
s have been withheld .... Jer 3:3
can the heavens give s ..... Jer 14:22
from the LORD, like s .... Mic 5:7

SHOWN
You have s Your servant .. Gen 32:10
have s more kindness ..... Ruth 3:10
grace be s to the wicked ... Is 26:10
s you from My Father ... John 10:32

SHOWS
firmament s His handiwork ... Ps 19:1
that God s no partiality ... Acts 10:34
God s personal favoritism .... Gal 2:6

SHREWDLY
because he had dealt s ..... Luke 16:8

SHRINES
who made silver s .... Acts 19:24

SHRIVELED
You have s me up .... Job 16:8

SHUFFLES
with his eyes, he s .... Prov 6:13

SHULAMITE
Beloved of the bridegroom king, Song 6:13

SHUNAMMITE
Abishag, David's nurse, 1 Kin 1:3, 15
—— Woman who cared for Elisha, 2 Kin 4:8–12

SHUNEM
Town of Issachar, Josh 19:18

SHUNNED
feared God and s evil .... Job 1:1

SHUR
Wilderness in south Palestine, Gen 16:7
Israel went from Red Sea to, Ex 15:22
Hagar fled here, Gen. 16:7

SHUSHAN
Residence of Persian monarchs, Esth 1:2

SHUT
s the door behind him ...... Gen 19:6
Let her be s out of the .... Num 12:14
"Or who s in the sea .... Job 38:8
Has He in anger s .... Ps 77:9
For you s up the .... Matt 23:13
came, the doors being s ... John 20:26
door, and no one can s it ..... Rev 3:8
have power to s heaven ..... Rev 11:6

SHUTS
s his ears to the cry .... Prov 21:13
s his eyes from seeing .... Is 33:15
brother in need, and s .... 1 John 3:17
who opens and no one s ..... Rev 3:7

SICK
have made him s .... Hos 7:5
I was s and you .... Matt 25:36
he whom You love is s .... John 11:3
many are weak and s .... 1 Cor 11:30
have left in Miletus s ..... 2 Tim 4:20
faith will save the s ...... James 5:15

SICKLE
Put in the s .... Joel 3:13
"Thrust in Your s .... Rev 14:15

SICKNESS
will sustain him in s ...... Prov 18:14
"This s is not unto......... John 11:4

SICKNESSES
And bore our s .... Matt 8:17

SIDE
two rings shall be on one s .. Ex 25:12
And a cubit on one s .... Ex 26:13
For the south s there shall .... Ex 27:9
this s of the Jordan in the ... Deut 1:1
on this s of the Jordan ..... Josh 1:14
me down on every s .... Job 19:10
wicked prowl on every s .... Ps 12:8
Fear is on every s .... Ps 31:13
hills rejoice on every s ..... Ps 65:12
comfort me on every s ...... Ps 71:21
The LORD is on my s .... Ps 118:6
Lie also on your left s...... Ezek 4:4
gate chambers on one s .. Ezek 40:10
robe sitting on the right s .. Mark 16:5
pierced His s with a ..... John 19:34
His hands and His s ...... John 20:20
put my hand into His s ... John 20:25
the net on the right s ..... John 21:6

SIDON
See TYRE AND SIDON
Canaanite city; inhabitants not expelled, Judg 1:31
Hostile relations with Israel, Judg 10:12; Is 23:12; Joel 3:4–6
Jesus preaches to, Matt 15:21; Luke 6:17

SIFT
s the nations with the .... Is 30:28
s the house of Israel ...... Amos 9:9
for you, that he may s .... Luke 22:31

SIFTS
A wise king s out the ..... Prov 20:26

SIGH
our years like a s .... Ps 90:9
the merry-hearted s .... Is 24:7
of the men who s .... Ezek 9:4

SIGHING
For my s comes before .... Job 3:24
s is not hidden .... Ps 38:9

SIGHT
and see this great s .... Ex 3:3
evil in the s of the LORD.... Judg 2:11
as stupid in your s .... Job 18:3
of human waste in their s .. Ezek 4:12
seemed good in Your s .... Matt 11:26
he received his s .... Mark 10:52
abomination in the s of ... Luke 16:15

SIGN (continued)

washed, and I received *s* ... John 9:11
he marveled at the *s* ... Acts 7:31
three days without *s* ... Acts 9:9
are just in the *s* of God ... Rom 2:13
will be justified in His *s* ... Rom 3:20
by faith, not by *s* ... 2 Cor 5:7
precious in the *s* of God ... 1 Pet 3:4

SIGN

Show me a *s* for good ... Ps 86:17
will give you a *s* ... Is 7:14
for an everlasting *s* ... Is 55:13
we want to see a *s* ... Matt 12:38
seeks after a *s* ... Matt 12:39
And what will be the *s* ... Matt 24:3
s which will be spoken ... Luke 2:34
again is the second *s* ... John 4:54
For Jews request a *s* ... 1 Cor 1:22
Now a great *s* appeared ... Rev 12:1

SIGNS

and let them be for *s* ... Gen 1:14
you not know their *s* ... Job 21:29
They performed His *s* ... Ps 105:27
We are for *s* and ... Is 8:18
How great are His *s* ... Dan 4:3
cannot discern the *s* ... Matt 16:3
the accompanying ... Mark 16:20
s Jesus did in Cana of ... John 2:11
no one can do these *s* ... John 3:2
because you saw the *s* ... John 6:26
is a sinner such *s* ... John 9:16
this Man works many *s* ... John 11:47
Jesus did many other *s* ... John 20:30
demons, performing *s* ... Rev 16:14

SIGNS AND WONDERS

Lord showed *s* ... Deut 6:22
great terror and with *s* ... Deut 26:8
s against Pharaoh ... Neh 9:10
He sent *s* ... Ps 135:9
We are for *s* in Israel ... Is 8:18
good to declare the *s* ... Dan 4:2
He works *s* in heaven ... Dan 6:27
rise and show great *s* ... Matt 24:24
"Unless you people see *s* ... John 4:48
s may be done through ... Acts 4:30
of the apostles many *s* ... Acts 5:12
His grace, granting *s* ... Acts 14:3
mighty *s*, by the power ... Rom 15:19
in *s* and mighty deeds ... 2 Cor 12:12
bearing witness both with *s* ... Heb 2:4

SIHON

Amorite king; defeated by Israel, Num 21:21–32
Territory of, assigned to Reuben and Gad, Num 32:1–38

SILAS (or Silvanus)

Leader in Jerusalem church; sent to Antioch, Acts 15:22–35
Travels with Paul, Acts 15:40, 41
Jailed and released, Acts 16:25–40
Mentioned in epistles, 2 Cor 1:19;
1 Thess 1:1; 2 Thess 1:1; 1 Pet 5:12

SILENCE

that You may *s* ... Ps 8:2
I was mute with *s* ... Ps 39:2
soon have settled in *s* ... Ps 94:17
"Sit in *s* ... Is 47:5
I will not keep *s*, but will ... Is 65:6
in *s* with all submission ... 1 Tim 2:11
s the ignorance of foolish ... 1 Pet 2:15
seal, there was *s* ... Rev 8:1

SILENT

the wicked shall be *s* ... 1 Sam 2:9
Oh, that you would be *s* ... Job 13:5
season, and am not *s* ... Ps 22:2
Do not be *s* to me ... Ps 28:1
praise to You and not be *s* ... Ps 30:12
Let them be *s* in the ... Ps 31:17
come, and shall not keep *s* ... Ps 50:3
before its shearers is *s* ... Is 53:7

Be *s* in the presence ... Zeph 1:7
But Jesus kept *s* ... Matt 26:63
His answer and kept *s* ... Luke 20:26
before its shearer is *s* ... Acts 8:32
Let your women keep *s* ... 1 Cor 14:34

SILK

and covered you with *s* ... Ezek 16:10

SILLY

They are *s* children ... Jer 4:22

SILOAM

Tower of, falls and kills 18 people, Luke 13:4
Blind man washes in pool of, John 9:1–11

SILVER

and your precious *s* ... Job 22:25
Though he heaps up *s* ... Job 27:16
s tried in a furnace ... Ps 12:6
have refined us as *s* ... Ps 66:10
than the profits of *s* ... Prov 3:14
chosen rather than *s* ... Prov 16:16
refining pot is for *s* ... Prov 17:3
He who loves *s* will ... Eccl 5:10
s has become dross ... Is 1:22
call them rejected *s* ... Jer 6:30
may buy the poor for *s* ... Amos 8:6
him thirty pieces of *s* ... Matt 26:15

SIMEON

Son of Jacob by Leah, Gen 29:32, 33
Avenges his sister's dishonor, Gen 34:25–31
Held hostage by Joseph, Gen 42:18–20, 24
Rebuked by Jacob, Gen 49:5–7
—— Tribe of:
Numbered, Num 1:23; 26:12–14
Receive inheritance, Josh 19:1–9
Fight Canaanites with Judah, Judg 1:1–3, 17–20
—— Just man; blesses infant Jesus, Luke 2:25–35

SIMILITUDE

been made in the *s* ... James 3:9

SIMON

Simon Peter: *see* PETER
—— One of the Twelve; called "the Cananite," Matt 10:4
—— One of Jesus' half brothers, Matt 13:55
—— Pharisee, Luke 7:36–40
—— Man of Cyrene, bears Jesus' cross, Matt 27:32
—— Sorcerer, Acts 8:9–24
—— Tanner in Joppa, Acts 9:43

SIMPLE

making wise the *s* ... Ps 19:7
LORD preserves the *s* ... Ps 116:6
understanding to the *s* ... Ps 119:130
s believes every word ... Prov 14:15
the hearts of the *s* ... Rom 16:18

SIMPLICITY

ones, will you love *s* ... Prov 1:22
in the world in *s* ... 2 Cor 1:12
corrupted from the *s* ... 2 Cor 11:3

SIN

not well, *s* lies at the door ... Gen 4:7
because their *s* is very ... Gen 18:20
brothers and their *s* ... Gen 50:17
It is a *s* offering ... Ex 29:14
committed a great *s* ... Ex 32:30
offer to the LORD for his *s* ... Lev 4:3
the *s* which they have ... Lev 4:14
a lamb as his *s* offering ... Lev 4:32
of the goats as a *s* offering ... Lev 5:6
is the law of the *s* offering ... Lev 6:25
They shall bear their *s* ... Lev 20:20
his God shall bear his *s* ... Lev 24:15
any *s* that men commit in ... Num 5:6

If you *s* unintentionally ... Num 15:22
flesh, shall one man *s* ... Num 16:22
he died in his own *s* ... Num 27:3
goats as a *s* offering ... Num 29:5
and be sure your *s* ... Num 32:23
because of all your *s* ... Deut 9:18
it become *s* among you ... Deut 15:9
or any *s* that he commits ... Deut 19:15
you *s* against the LORD ... Deut 20:18
a *s* deserving of death ... Deut 21:22
no *s* deserving of death ... Deut 22:26
to death for his own *s* ... Deut 24:16
forgive the *s* of Your ... 1 Kin 8:34
When they *s* against You ... 1 Kin 8:46
this thing became a *s* ... 1 Kin 12:30
in his *s* by which ... 1 Kin 15:26
and made Israel *s* ... 1 Kin 21:22
to death for his own *s* ... 2 Kin 14:6
made Judah *s* with his ... 2 Kin 21:11
forgive the *s* of Your ... 2 Chr 6:25
and will forgive their *s* ... 2 Chr 7:14
shall die for his own *s* ... 2 Chr 25:4
do not let their *s* be blotted ... Neh 4:5
In all this Job did not *s* nor ... Job 1:22
all this Job did not *s* ... Job 2:10
and search out my *s* ... Job 10:6
he adds rebellion to his *s* ... Job 34:37
Be angry, and do not *s* ... Ps 4:4
whose *s* is covered ... Ps 32:1
I acknowledged my *s* ... Ps 32:5
my bones because of my *s* ... Ps 38:3
my ways, lest I *s* ... Ps 39:1
And cleanse me from my *s* ... Ps 51:2
s is always before me ... Ps 51:3
in *s* my mother ... Ps 51:5
the *s* of their mouth ... Ps 59:12
I might not *s* against You ... Ps 119:11
of the wicked to *s* ... Prov 10:16
Fools mock at *s* ... Prov 14:9
s is a reproach ... Prov 14:34
I am pure from my *s* ... Prov 20:9
mouth cause your flesh to *s* ... Eccl 5:6
good and does not *s* ... Eccl 7:20
away, and your *s* purged ... Is 6:7
soul an offering for *s* ... Is 53:10
And He bore the *s* ... Is 53:12
what is our *s* that we have ... Jer 16:10
your high places of *s* ... Jer 17:3
s I will remember no ... Jer 31:34
he shall die in his *s* ... Ezek 3:20
and confessing my *s* ... Dan 9:20
They eat up the *s* ... Hos 4:8
Now they *s* more and ... Hos 13:2
right eye causes you to *s* ... Matt 5:29
I say to you, every *s* and ... Matt 12:31
who believe in Me to *s* ... Matt 18:6
hand causes you to *s* ... Mark 9:43
who takes away the *s* ... John 1:29
s no more ... John 5:14
"He who is without *s* ... John 8:7
go and *s* no more ... John 8:11
Me, and will die in your *s* ... John 8:21
commits *s* is a slave of *s* ... John 8:34
of you convicts Me of *s* ... John 8:46
you would have no *s* ... John 9:41
convict the world of *s* ... John 16:8
they are all under *s* ... Rom 3:9
law is the knowledge of *s* ... Rom 3:20
LORD shall not impute *s* ... Rom 4:8
s entered the world ... Rom 5:12
s is not imputed ... Rom 5:13
where *s* abounded, grace ... Rom 5:20
s that grace may ... Rom 6:1
that the body of *s* might be ... Rom 6:6
died to *s* once for all ... Rom 6:10
s shall not have ... Rom 6:14
Shall we *s* because we ... Rom 6:15
you were slaves of *s* ... Rom 6:17
been set free from *s* ... Rom 6:22
the wages of *s* is death ... Rom 6:23
Is the law *s*? ... Rom 7:7
s revived and I died ... Rom 7:9

s that dwells in me .... Rom 7:17
me free from the law of s ... Rom 8:2
body is dead because of s .. Rom 8:10
Every s that a man does ... 1 Cor 6:18
you s against Christ .... 1 Cor 8:12
The sting of death is s .... 1 Cor 15:56
Him who knew no s ...... 2 Cor 5:21
man of s is revealed ...... 2 Thess 2:3
we are, yet without s ...... Heb 4:15
appeared to put away s ...... Heb 9:26
longer an offering for s .... Heb 10:18
s willfully after we .... Heb 10:26
it gives birth to s .... James 1:15
partiality, you commit s ... James 2:9
do it, to him it is s .... James 4:17
"Who committed no s ... 1 Pet 2:22
the flesh has ceased from s .. 1 Pet 4:1
that cannot cease from s ... 2 Pet 2:14
cleanses us from all s .... 1 John 1:7
say that we have no s ..... 1 John 1:8
that you may not s .... 1 John 2:1
s is lawlessness .... 1 John 3:4
in Him there is no s ...... 1 John 3:5
and he cannot s .... 1 John 3:9
s which does not lead .... 1 John 5:16
there is s not leading to .. 1 John 5:17

SINAI
Mountain (same as Horeb) where the
law was given, Ex 19:1–25
Used allegorically by Paul, Gal 4:24,
25

SINCERE
Holy Spirit, by s love ...... 2 Cor 6:6
that you may be s .... Phil 1:10
and from s faith .... 1 Tim 1:5
s love of the brethren ...... 1 Pet 1:22

SINCERITY
LORD, serve Him in s ...... Josh 24:14
unleavened bread of s ..... 1 Cor 5:8
simplicity and godly s ..... 2 Cor 1:12
as of s, but as from God, .. 2 Cor 2:17
testing the s of your love ... 2 Cor 8:8
in s of heart, as to Christ .... Eph 6:5
our Lord Jesus Christ in s .. Eph 6:24
men-pleasers, but in s ...... Col 3:22

SINFUL
place, a brood of s men ... Num 32:14
Alas, s nation .... Is 1:4
and s generation .... Mark 8:38
from me, for I am a s ...... Luke 5:8
the hands of s men .... Luke 24:7
become exceedingly s ...... Rom 7:13
likeness of s flesh .... Rom 8:3

SING
"S to the LORD .... Ex 15:21
Awake, awake, s a song ... Judg 5:12
s praises to Your name .. 2 Sam 22:50
S to the LORD, all the..... 1 Chr 16:23
when they began to s .... 2 Chr 20:22
the widow's heart to s ...... Job 29:13
S praises to the LORD, who .. Ps 9:11
I will s to the LORD.......... Ps 13:6
S to Him a new song .... Ps 33:3
my tongue shall s aloud of .. Ps 51:14
shout for joy, they also s .... Ps 65:13
S out the honor .... Ps 66:2
nations be glad and s for ... Ps 67:4
You I will s with the harp ... Ps 71:22
I will s of the mercies of ..... Ps 89:1
s to the LORD a new song .... Ps 98:1
I will s of mercy and .... Ps 101:1
I will s to the LORD as ..... Ps 104:33
S praises to His name ...... Ps 135:3
"S us one of the songs ..... Ps 137:3
they shall s of the ways of .. Ps 138:5
S to the LORD a new song ... Ps 149:1
S to the LORD, for He has ... Is 12:5
up their voice, they shall s .. Is 24:14
S to the LORD a new song .... Is 42:10
My servants shall s .... Is 65:14

she shall s there, as in the .. Hos 2:15
S and rejoice, O daughter .. Zech 2:10
I will s with the .... 1 Cor 14:15
assembly I will s .... Heb 2:12
Let him s psalms .... James 5:13
They s the song of Moses ... Rev 15:3

SINGERS
instruments for s .... 1 Kin 10:12
who bore the ark, the s .. 1 Chr 15:27
instruments for s .... 2 Chr 9:11
s with musical .... 2 Chr 23:13
s sang, and the .... 2 Chr 29:28
The s sang loudly with ... Neh 12:42
The s went before .... Ps 68:25
male and female s .... Eccl 2:8

SINGING
rejoicing and with s ...... 2 Chr 23:18
s to the LORD .... 2 Chr 30:21
with thanksgivings and s .. Neh 12:27
His presence with s .... Ps 100:2
and our tongue with s ...... Ps 126:2
the time of s has come ... Song 2:12
break forth into s .... Is 14:7
even with joy and s .... Is 35:2
come to Zion with s .... Is 35:10
With a voice of s, declare .... Is 48:20
and come to Zion with s .... Is 51:11
and s hymns to God ...... Acts 16:25
and spiritual songs, s ...... Eph 5:19
s with grace in your hearts .. Col 3:16

SINGLENESS
them s of heart to obey .. 2 Chr 30:12

SINISTER
who understands s .... Dan 8:23

SINK
I s in deep mire............ Ps 69:2
to s he cried out .... Matt 14:30

SINNED
had ceased, he s yet more .... Ex 9:34
has s a young bull without ... Lev 4:3
promised, for we have s ... Num 14:40
s against their own souls .. Num 16:38
to the LORD, "We have s .. Judg 10:15
Saul said, "I have s .... 1 Sam 26:21
may be that my sons have s .. Job 1:5
Have I s? What have I ...... Job 7:20
those who have s .... Job 24:19
for I have s against You ...... Ps 41:4
You only, have I s .... Ps 51:4
you say, 'I have not s ...... Jer 2:35
Jerusalem has s .... Lam 1:8
Our fathers s and are ...... Lam 5:7
we have s and committed .... Dan 9:5
the more they s against Me .. Hos 4:7
you have s from the days ... Hos 10:9
"I have s by betraying ..... Matt 27:4
"Father, I have s .... Luke 15:18
"Rabbi, who s .... John 9:2
For as many as have s .... Rom 2:12
for all have s and .... Rom 3:23
marries, she has not s .... 1 Cor 7:28
not spare the angels who s .. 2 Pet 2:4
say that we have not s .... 1 John 1:10
for the devil has s .... 1 John 3:8

SINNED AGAINST THE LORD
"I have s your God .... Ex 10:16
s your God—had made ..... Deut 9:16
"Indeed I have s .... Josh 7:20
said there, "We have s .... 1 Sam 7:6
to Nathan, "I have s .... 2 Sam 12:13
For we have s .... Jer 3:25
because we have s .... Jer 8:14
because you have s .... Jer 44:23
because they have s ...... Zeph 1:17

SINNED AGAINST YOU
saying, "We have s ...... Judg 10:10
I have not s, but you ..... Judg 11:27
I have not s .... 1 Sam 24:11
because they have s ...... 1 Kin 8:33

Your people who have s .. 2 Chr 6:39
Israel which we have s ..... Neh 1:6
heal my soul, for I have s..... Ps 41:4
many, we have s .... Jer 14:7
fathers, because we have s ... Dan 9:8

SINNER
the ungodly and the s ..... Prov 11:31
overthrows the s.......... Prov 13:6
of the s is stored up for ... Prov 13:22
s He gives the work .... Eccl 2:26
s shall be trapped by her ... Eccl 7:26
s does evil a hundred ...... Eccl 8:12
As is the good, so is the s ... Eccl 9:2
s destroys much good ...... Eccl 9:18
the city who was a s ...... Luke 7:37
s who repents than .... Luke 15:7
be merciful to me a s ..... Luke 18:13
can a man who is a s ...... John 9:16
know that this Man is a s .. John 9:24
the ungodly and the s ..... 1 Pet 4:18

SINNERS
See TAX COLLECTORS AND SINNERS
utterly destroy the s ..... 1 Sam 15:18
in the path of s .... Ps 1:1
nor s in the congregation ..... Ps 1:5
therefore He teaches s .... Ps 25:8
soul with s .... Ps 26:9
s be consumed from the .... Ps 104:35
son, if s entice you .... Prov 1:10
Evil pursues s, but to the ... Prov 13:21
not let your heart envy s .. Prov 23:17
The s in Zion are .... Is 33:14
All the s of My people .... Amos 9:10
s came and sat down with .. Matt 9:10
the righteous, but s ...... Matt 9:13
tax collectors and s ...... Matt 11:19
into the hands of s .... Matt 26:45
and s also sat together .... Mark 2:15
into the hands of s ...... Mark 14:41
call the righteous, but s ... Luke 5:32
s love those who love ..... Luke 6:32
of tax collectors and s .... Luke 7:34
Galileans were worse s .... Luke 13:2
man receives s and eats .. Luke 15:2
God does not hear s ...... John 9:31
while we were still s ...... Rom 5:8
many were made s .... Rom 5:19
the ungodly and for s ..... 1 Tim 1:9
the world to save s .... 1 Tim 1:15
separate from s .... Heb 7:26
such hostility from s .... Heb 12:3
things which ungodly s ..... Jude 15

SINS
'If a person s .... Lev 4:2
s unintentionally in regard .. Lev 5:15
of the s of Jeroboam ... 1 Kin 14:16
my iniquities and s .... Job 13:23
from presumptuous s........ Ps 19:13
the s of my youth .... Ps 25:7
pain, and forgive all my s ... Ps 25:18
Hide Your face from my s .... Ps 51:9
s are not hidden from You .... Ps 69:5
atonement for our s .... Ps 79:9
You, our secret s .... Ps 90:8
but he who s against ...... Prov 8:36
but love covers all s ...... Prov 10:12
despises his neighbor s ... Prov 14:21
s against his own life ..... Prov 20:2
s have hidden His face ...... Is 59:2
your s have withheld good ... Jer 5:25
He will uncover your s ..... Lam 4:22
the soul who s shall ...... Ezek 18:4
to make an end of s ...... Dan 9:24
His people from their s .... Matt 1:21
Jordan, confessing their s ... Matt 3:6
power on earth to forgive s .. Matt 9:6
if your brother s .... Matt 18:15
for the remission of s ..... Matt 26:28
for the remission of s ...... Mark 1:4
forgive s but God alone ..... Mark 2:7
for the remission of s ...... Luke 3:3

SION

on earth to forgive s ......Luke 5:24
brother s against you ......Luke 17:3
that you will die in your s ..John 8:24
I take away their s ......Rom 11:27
s according to the ....1 Cor 15:3
are still in your s ....1 Cor 15:17
who gave Himself for our s ...Gal 1:4
the forgiveness of s ....Eph 1:7
blood, the forgiveness of s ...Col 1:14
s are clearly evident ......1 Tim 5:24
by Himself purged our s ....Heb 1:3
once to bear the s ....Heb 9:28
one sacrifice for s forever ..Heb 10:12
cover a multitude of s ....James 5:20
that we, having died to s ...1 Pet 2:24
If we confess our s ....1 John 1:9
propitiation for our s ......1 John 2:2
s are forgiven you ....1 John 2:12
Whoever s has neither ....1 John 3:6
He who s is of the devil ...1 John 3:8
propitiation for our s .....1 John 4:10
you share in her s ....Rev 18:4

SION

See ZION

Name given to all or part of Mt. Hermon. Deut 4:48

SISERA

Canaanite commander of Jabin's army; slain by Jael, Judg 4:2–22

SISTER

Please say you are my s ...Gen 12:13
And he said, "She is my s ..Gen 26:7
of David had a lovely s ...2 Sam 13:1
are my mother and my s ...Job 17:14
fair is your love, my s .....Song 4:10
We have a little s ....Song 8:8
treacherous s Judah saw it ....Jer 3:7
Your elder s is Samaria ...Ezek 16:46
is My brother and s ......Matt 12:50
You not care that my s ...Luke 10:40
loved Martha and her s ....John 11:5
to you Phoebe our s ....Rom 16:1
s is not under bondage ....1 Cor 7:15

SIT

he shall s on my throne ...1 Kin 1:13
Those who s in the ....Ps 69:12
"Come down and s ....Is 47:1
"Why do we s still ....Jer 8:14
but to s on My right ......Matt 20:23
and the Pharisees s ....Matt 23:2
Grant us that we may s ..Mark 10:37
"S at My right hand ....Mark 12:36
those who s in darkness ..Luke 1:79
s down in the lowest .....Luke 14:10
"S at My right hand ....Heb 1:13
say to him, "You s ......James 2:3
I will grant to s ....Rev 3:21
heart, 'I s as queen ....Rev 18:7

SITS

God s on His holy ....Ps 47:8
It is He who s above ....Is 40:22
so that he s as God ....2 Thess 2:4
Him who s on the throne ....Rev 4:9
harlot who s on many ......Rev 17:1
where the harlot s ....Rev 17:15

SITTING

Eli the priest was s on .....1 Sam 1:9
LORD was s on His throne.....1 Kin 22:19
LORD s on His throne ....2 Chr 18:18
You know my s down and ...Ps 139:2
s on a donkey, a colt, the ..Matt 21:5
see the Son of Man s .....Mark 14:62
s on a donkey's colt ....John 12:15
two angels in white s ......John 20:12
where Christ is, s ....Col 3:1
I saw twenty-four elders s ...Rev 4:4
a woman s on a scarlet .....Rev 17:3

SIX

S days you shall gather it, ..Ex 16:26
S days you shall labor ......Ex 20:9

SKIES

thick clouds of the s .....2 Sam 22:12
have you spread out the s ...Job 37:18
the s sent out a sound .....Ps 77:17
and is lifted up to the s .....Jer 51:9

SKILL

hand forget its s ....Ps 137:5
nor favor to men of s .....Eccl 9:11
them knowledge and s ...Dan 1:17
forth to give you s ....Dan 9:22

SKILLFUL

Esau was a s hunter, a ....Gen 25:27
a s player on the harp ...1 Sam 16:16
all types of s men for ....1 Chr 22:15
s work a man is envied .....Eccl 4:4
the hands of a s workman ..Song 7:1
send for s wailing women ...Jer 9:17
who are s to destroy ......Ezek 21:31

SKILLFULNESS

guided them by the s ......Ps 78:72

SKIN

God made tunics of s ......Gen 3:21
s of his face shone while ...Ex 34:29
LORD and said, "S.........Job 2:4
sewn sackcloth over my s ..Job 16:15
have escaped by the s ......Job 19:20
My bones cling to my s ....Ps 102:5
nation tall and smooth of s ....Is 18:2
Ethiopian change his s .....Jer 13:23
s is hot as an oven ....Lam 5:10
who strip the s from My ....Mic 3:2

SKINS

she put the s of the kids ...Gen 27:16

SKIP

He makes them also s ....Ps 29:6

SKIPPING

upon the mountains, s ......Song 2:8

SKULL

to say, Place of a S ....Matt 27:33

SKY

the faithful witness in the s ..Ps 89:37
weather, for the s is red ....Matt 16:2
stars of the s in multitude ..Heb 11:12
s receded as a scroll ....Rev 6:14

SLACK

He will not be s ....Deut 7:10
s hand becomes poor ......Prov 10:4
The Lord is not s ....2 Pet 3:9

SLAIN

s his thousands ....1 Sam 18:7
beauty of Israel is s ....2 Sam 1:19
the dead, like the s ....Ps 88:5
and all who were s ....Prov 7:26
I shall be s in the ....Prov 22:13
s men are not s ....Is 22:2
no more cover her s ....Is 26:21
and the s of the LORD ......Is 66:16
and night for the s ....Jer 9:1
Those s by the sword ......Lam 4:9
the prophets, I have s ......Hos 6:5
is the Lamb who was s .....Rev 5:12

SLANDER

s your own mother's ....Ps 50:20
and whoever spreads s ....Prov 10:18

SLANDERERS

be reverent, not s ....1 Tim 3:11
unforgiving, s ....2 Tim 3:3
in behavior, not s ....Titus 2:3

SLANDEROUSLY

as we are s reported ....Rom 3:8

SLAUGHTER

as sheep for the s ....Ps 44:22
led as a lamb to the s ......Is 53:7
but the Valley of S ....Jer 7:32
lamb brought to the s ......Jer 11:19

"Feed the flock for s ......Zech 11:4
led as a sheep to the s .....Acts 8:32
as sheep for the s ....Rom 8:36

SLAVE

that you were a s ....Deut 15:15
first shall be s of all .....Mark 10:44
commits sin is a s ....John 8:34
you called while a s ......1 Cor 7:21
there is neither s nor free ...Gal 3:28
you are no longer a s ....Gal 4:7
s nor free, but Christ is all ...Col 3:11

SLAVES

here we are, my lord's s ...Gen 44:16
they shall not be sold as s ..Lev 25:42
free his male and female s ...Jer 34:10
should no longer be s ....Rom 6:6
though you were s ....Rom 6:17
your members as s ....Rom 6:19
having become s of God ...Rom 6:22
do not become s ....1 Cor 7:23
whether s or free ....1 Cor 12:13
are s of corruption ....2 Pet 2:19

SLAY

s the righteous ....Gen 18:25
s a righteous nation ....Gen 20:4
Evil shall s the ....Ps 34:21
Oh, that You would s ......Ps 139:19
s them before me ....Luke 19:27

SLEEP

God caused a deep s ....Gen 2:21
Jacob awoke from his s ...Gen 28:16
him to s on her knees ....Judg 16:19
the night, when deep s ......Job 4:13
my eyes, lest I s ....Ps 13:3
Why do You s ....Ps 44:23
have sunk into their s ......Ps 76:5
they are like a s ....Ps 90:5
neither slumber nor s ......Ps 121:4
He gives His beloved s ....Ps 127:2
I will not give s ....Ps 132:4
s will be sweet ....Prov 3:24
For they do not s ....Prov 4:16
A little s ....Prov 6:10
Do not love s ....Prov 20:13
a little s, a little slumber ..Prov 24:33
The s of a laboring ....Eccl 5:12
I s, but my heart is awake ..Song 5:2
the spirit of deep s ....Is 29:10
Also his s went from ......Dan 6:18
I was in a deep s ....Dan 8:18
him were heavy with s ....Luke 9:32
them, "Why do you s ....Luke 22:46
He was overcome by s ....Acts 20:9
time to awake out of s ....Rom 13:11
among you, and many s ...1 Cor 11:30
We shall not all s ....1 Cor 15:51
"Awake, you who s ......Eph 5:14
with Him those who s ...1 Thess 4:14
Therefore let us not s .....1 Thess 5:6

SLEEPERS

gently the lips of s ....Song 7:9

SLEEPING

or perhaps he is s ....1 Kin 18:27
is not dead, but s ....Matt 9:24
"Are you still s ....Matt 26:45
suddenly, he find you s ..Mark 13:36
that night Peter was s ....Acts 12:6

SLEEPLESSNESS

in labors, in s ....2 Cor 6:5
and toil, in s often ....2 Cor 11:27

SLEEPS

wise son; he who s ....Prov 10:5
"Our friend Lazarus s ....John 11:11

SLEPT

I lay down and s ....Ps 3:5
but while men s ....Matt 13:25

SLIGHTED

is the one who is s ....Prov 12:9

SLING
he had. and his s .... 1 Sam 17:40
a stone in a s is he .... Prov 26:8

SLIP
their foot shall s .... Deut 32:35
my footsteps may not s .... Ps 17:5

SLIPPERY
way be dark and s .... Ps 35:6
set them in s places .... Ps 73:18
be to them like s .... Jer 23:12

SLOOPS
all the beautiful s .... Is 2:16

SLOW
but I am s of speech .... Ex 4:10
S to anger, and abounding .. Ps 103:8
He who is s to wrath ..... Prov 14:29
the LORD is s to anger .... Nah 1:3
s of heart to believe in .... Luke 24:25
hear, s to speak, s .... James 1:19

SLOW TO ANGER
s, abundant in kindness .... Neh 9:17
merciful and gracious, s .... Ps 103:8
full of compassion, s .... Ps 145:8
but he who is s allays .... Prov 15:18
gracious and merciful, s ...Joel 2:13
merciful God, s .... Jon 4:2
the Lord is s and great ..... Nah 1:3

SLUGGARD
will you slumber, O s ...... Prov 6:9

SLUMBER
who keeps you will not s .. Ps 121:3
lying down, loving to s ..... Is 56:10
destruction does not s ...... 2 Pet 2:3

SLUMBERED
delayed, they all s .... Matt 25:5

SLUMBERING
upon men, while s .... Job 33:15

SMALL
'The place is too s .... Is 49:20
I will make you s .... Jer 49:15
may stand, for he is s ..... Amos 7:2
I will make you s .... Obad 2
the day of s things .... Zech 4:10
And I saw the dead, s ..... Rev 20:12

SMELL
and he smelled the s ...... Gen 27:27
s there will be a .... Is 3:24

SMELLS
s the battle from afar ...... Job 39:25

SMITTEN
Him stricken, s .... Is 53:4

SMOKE
went up like the s .... Gen 19:28
s is driven away .... Ps 68:2
are consumed like s .... Ps 102:3
like a wineskin in s ...... Ps 119:83
like pillars of s .... Song 3:6
s shall ascend forever ...... Is 34:10
vanish away like s .... Is 51:6
fire and vapor of s .... Acts 2:19
s arose out of the pit .... Rev 9:2
was filled with s .... Rev 15:8
Her s rises up .... Rev 19:3

SMOKING
two stubs of s firebrands .... Is 7:4
s flax He will not quench ..... Is 42:3
s flax He will not quench . Matt 12:20

SMOOTH
speak to us s things .... Is 30:10
And the rough places s ...... Is 40:4
though they speak s .... Jer 12:6
the rough ways s .... Luke 3:5

SMOOTH-SKINNED
man, and I am a s .... Gen 27:11

SMYRNA
Site of one of the seven churches, Rev
1:11

SNAIL
s which melts away as .... Ps 58:8

SNARE
it will surely be a s .... Ex 23:33
It became a s to .... Judg 8:27
that she may be a s .... 1 Sam 18:21
s snatches their .... Job 5:5
and he walks into a s .... Job 18:8
their table become a s ...... Ps 69:22
as a bird from the s .... Ps 124:7
birds caught in a s .... Eccl 9:12
and the pit and the s .... Is 24:17
I have laid a s .... Jer 50:23
s have come upon us ..... Lam 3:47
is a fowler's s .... Hos 9:8
a bird fall into a s .... Amos 3:5
it will come as a s .... Luke 21:35
temptation and a s .... 1 Tim 6:9
and escape the s .... 2 Tim 2:26

SNARED
The wicked is s .... Ps 9:16
and be broken, be s .... Is 8:15
all of them are s .... Is 42:22

SNARES
the s of death .... Ps 18:5
who seek my life lay s ...... Ps 38:12
and built great s .... Eccl 9:14
wait as one who sets s ..... Jer 5:26

SNATCH
s the fatherless .... Job 24:9
neither shall anyone s .... John 10:28

SNATCHES
s away what was .... Matt 13:19

SNEER
and you s at it .... Mal 1:13

SNIFFED
they s at the wind .... Jer 14:6

SNORTING
s strikes terror .... Job 39:20

SNOW
See WHITE AS SNOW
and heat consume the s .... Job 24:19
For He says to the s .... Job 37:6
the treasury of s .... Job 38:22
shall be whiter than s .... Ps 51:7
He gives s like wool ...... Ps 147:16
As s in summer and .... Prov 26:1
She is not afraid of s ..... Prov 31:21
shall be as white as s .... Is 1:18
garment was white as s ..... Dan 7:9
clothing as white as s ..... Matt 28:3
wool, as white as s .... Rev 1:14

SOAKED
their land shall be s .... Is 34:7

SOAP
lye, and use much s .... Jer 2:22

SOBER
of the day be s .... 1 Thess 5:8
the older men be s .... Titus 2:2

SOBERLY
think, but to think s .... Rom 12:3
we should live s .... Titus 2:12

SOCHOH
Town in Judah where David kills Goliath, Josh 15:1, 35; 1 Sam 17:1, 49

SOCKET
touched the s of his hip .... Gen 32:25
arm be torn from the s ..... Job 31:22

SODA
and like vinegar on s ..... Prov 25:20

SODOM
Lot chooses to live there, Gen
13:10–13
Plundered by Chedorlaomer, Gen
14:8–24
Abraham intercedes for, Gen 18:16–33

Destroyed by God, Gen 19:1–29
Cited as example of sin and destruc-
tion, Deut 29:23; 32:32; Is 1:9, 10; 3:9;
Jer 23:14; 49:18; Lam 4:6; Ezek
16:46–63; Matt 11:23, 24; 2 Pet 2:6;
Jude 7

SODOM AND GOMORRAH
and the kings of S .... Gen 14:10
the outcry against S .... Gen 18:20
brimstone and fire on S ... Gen 19:24
like the overthrow of S ... Deut 29:23
As God overthrew S .... Jer 50:40
as God overthrew S ...... Amos 4:11
for the land of S .... Matt 10:15
more tolerable for S ...... Mark 6:11
turning the cities of S ..... 2 Pet 2:6
as S. and the cities ...... Jude 7

SODOMITES
nor homosexuals, nor s ..... 1 Cor 6:9
for fornicators, for s ...... 1 Tim 1:10

SOFT
s answer turns away ...... Prov 15:1
clothed in s garments .... Matt 11:8

SOFTER
his words were s .... Ps 55:21

SOJOURNER
But no s had to lodge ..... Job 31:32

SOJOURNERS
are strangers and s .... Lev 25:23
I beg you as s .... 1 Pet 2:11

SOLD
s his birthright .... Gen 25:33
the house that was s ...... Lev 25:33
their Rock had s .... Deut 32:30
and He s them into the .... Judg 2:14
s themselves to do .... 2 Kin 17:17
Had we been s as male ..... Esth 7:4
who was s as a slave ...... Ps 105:17
s all that he had .... Matt 13:46
they bought, they s ...... Luke 17:28
s their possessions .... Acts 2:45
but I am carnal, s .... Rom 7:14
Eat whatever is s .... 1 Cor 10:25

SOLDIER
hardship as a good s .... 2 Tim 2:3
enlisted him as a s .... 2 Tim 2:4

SOLDIERS
sum of money to the s .... Matt 28:12
The s also mocked .... Luke 23:36
s twisted a crown .... John 19:2

SOLEMN
and very s lamentation .... Gen 50:10
a s observance for all the .... Ex 12:42
a sabbath of s rest for .... Lev 16:31
"Proclaim a s assembly . 2 Kin 10:20
the refuse of your s feasts .... Mal 2:3

SOLEMNLY
saying, "The man s .... Gen 43:3
s testified of the .... Acts 28:23

SOLID
milk and not with s food ... 1 Cor 3:2
the s foundation .... 2 Tim 2:19
need milk and not s food ... Heb 5:12

SOLITARILY
heritage, who dwell s ...... Mic 7:14

SOLITARY
God sets the s in .... Ps 68:6

SOLOMON
David's son by Bathsheba, 2 Sam 12:24
Becomes king, 1 Kin 1:5–53
Receives and carries out David's in-
structions, 1 Kin 2
Prays for and demonstrates wisdom,
1 Kin 3:3–28; 4:29–34
Builds and dedicates temple; builds
palace, 1 Kin 5–8

Lord appears to, 1 Kin 9:1–9
His fame and glory, 1 Kin 9:10—10:29
Falls into idolatry; warned by God,
   1 Kin 11:1–13
Adversaries arise, 1 Kin 11:14–40
Death of, 1 Kin 11:41–43
Writings credited to him, Ps 72; 127;
   Prov 1:1; 10:1; 25:1; Eccl 1:1; Song
   1:1

SOMEBODY
up, claiming to be s .... Acts 5:36

SOMETHING
"Simon, I have s .... Luke 7:40
thinks himself to be s .... Gal 6:3

SON
See BELOVED SON; ONLY BEGOTTEN
   SON
wife shall bear you a s .... Gen 17:19
Abraham a s in his old ..... Gen 21:2
your s, your only s Isaac .... Gen 22:2
the knife to slay his s .... Gen 22:10
he called Esau his older s ... Gen 27:1
"I am your s, your .... Gen 27:32
conceived and bore a s .... Gen 29:32
Joseph my s is still alive ... Gen 45:28
And she bore him a s .... Ex 2:22
a s born to Naomi .... Ruth 4:17
"Send me your s David .. 1 Sam 16:19
she bore a s, and he ..... 2 Sam 12:24
king is grieved for his s ... 2 Sam 19:2
he charged Solomon his s .. 1 Kin 2:1
"My s, as for me, it was ... 1 Chr 22:7
gave his s Solomon ...... 1 Chr 28:11
Me, 'You are My S .... Ps 2:7
Upon the s of man whom .... Ps 80:17
I was my father's s .... Prov 4:3
s makes a glad father ..... Prov 10:1
s is a grief to his .... Prov 17:25
Correct your s, and he .... Prov 29:17
And what, s of my womb ... Prov 31:2
shall conceive and bear a S ... Is 7:14
is born, unto us a S .... Is 9:6
heaven, O Lucifer, s .... Is 14:12
out of Egypt I called My s .. Hos 11:1
He is an unwise s .... Hos 13:13
prophet, nor was I a s .... Amos 7:14
s honors his father .... Mal 1:6
will bring forth a S .... Matt 1:21
"This is My beloved S ..... Matt 3:17
no one knows the S ...... Matt 11:27
not the carpenter's s .... Matt 13:55
are the Christ, the S ..... Matt 16:16
For the S of Man will .... Matt 16:27
of all he sent his s .... Matt 21:37
Whose S is He .... Matt 22:42
'Lord,' how is He his S ... Matt 22:45
as much a s of hell .... Matt 23:15
of the S of Man .... Matt 24:37
'I am the S of God ...... Matt 27:43
of Jesus Christ, the S ...... Mark 1:1
S of Man has power ...... Mark 2:10
"This is My beloved S .... Mark 9:7
'They will respect my s ... Mark 12:6
this Man was the S ..... Mark 15:39
called the S of the .... Luke 1:32
"You are My beloved S ... Luke 3:22
the Christ, the S of God ... Luke 4:41
S of Man has power ..... Luke 5:24
S of Man is also Lord ...... Luke 6:5
out, the only s .... Luke 7:12
S of Man has come ...... Luke 7:34
And if a s of peace .... Luke 10:6
will be divided against s .. Luke 12:53
to be called your s ...... Luke 15:19
because he also is a s ..... Luke 19:9
I will send my beloved s .. Luke 20:13
You then the S of God ... Luke 22:70
The only begotten S ...... John 1:18
gave His only begotten S ... John 3:16
God did not send His S .... John 3:17
the Father loves the S .... John 3:35

S can do nothing .... John 5:19
For the Father loves the S ... John 5:20
everyone who sees the S ... John 6:40
s abides forever .... John 8:35
if the S makes you free .... John 8:36
S of Man must be lifted ... John 12:34
"Woman, behold your s ... John 19:26
S of Encouragement ...... Acts 4:36
Jesus Christ is the S ...... Acts 8:37
in the gospel of His S .... Rom 1:9
by sending His own S .... Rom 8:3
not spare His own S ...... Rom 8:32
S Himself will also be .... 1 Cor 15:28
God sent forth His S .... Gal 4:4
longer a slave but a s .... Gal 4:7
you for my s Onesimus .... Philem 10
"You are My S .... Heb 1:5
but Christ as a S over His .... Heb 3:6
though He was a S .... Heb 5:8
to be called the s .... Heb 11:24
"This is My beloved S ... 2 Pet 1:17
S cleanses us from all sin .. 1 John 1:7
Whoever denies the S .... 1 John 2:23
sent His S to be the ..... 1 John 4:10
Jesus is the S of God ..... 1 John 4:15
God has given of His S ... 1 John 5:10
who has the S has life ... 1 John 5:12

SON OF DAVID
the s had a lovely .... 2 Sam 13:1
Solomon the s king ...... 1 Chr 29:22
proverbs of Solomon the s .. Prov 1:1
of the Preacher, the s .... Eccl 1:1
Jesus Christ, the s .... Matt 1:1
"Joseph, s, do not be ..... Matt 1:20
S, have mercy on us ...... Matt 9:27
"Could this be the S ..... Matt 12:23
on me, O Lord, S .... Matt 15:22
Hosanna to the S .... Matt 21:9
said to Him, "The S ..... Matt 22:42
"Jesus, S, have mercy .... Mark 10:47
that the Christ is the S ... Mark 12:35
son of Nathan, the s ...... Luke 3:31
"Jesus, S, have mercy .... Luke 18:38

SON OF GOD
the fourth is like the S ..... Dan 3:25
"If you are the S .... Matt 4:3
with You, Jesus, You S .... Matt 8:29
"Truly You are the S ..... Matt 14:33
You are the Christ, the S .. Matt 26:63
If You are the S .... Matt 27:40
"Truly this was the S .... Matt 27:54
born will be called the S .. Luke 1:35
of Adam, the s .... Luke 3:38
testified that this is the S... John 1:34
"Rabbi, You are the S .... John 1:49
the only begotten S .... John 3:18
hear the voice of the S .... John 5:25
"Do you believe in the S .. John 9:35
I said, 'I am the S ...... John 10:36
the S may be glorified ..... John 11:4
You are the Christ, the S .. John 11:27
He made Himself the S .... John 19:7
is the Christ, the S ...... John 20:31
declared to be the S .... Rom 1:4
I live by faith in the S ..... Gal 2:20
of the knowledge of the S ... Eph 4:13
heavens, Jesus the S ...... Heb 4:14
again for themselves the S .. Heb 6:6
but made like the S .... Heb 7:3
trampled the S underfoot .. Heb 10:29
For this purpose the S .... 1 John 3:8
that Jesus is the S .... 1 John 5:5
'These things says the S ... Rev 2:18

SON OF MAN
s that You visit him .... Ps 8:4
s, that You are mindful ..... Ps 144:3
in princes, nor in a s ...... Ps 146:3
"S, stand on your feet ..... Ezek 2:1
"S, eat what you find ...... Ezek 3:1
behold One like the s ...... Dan 7:13
the S has nowhere to ..... Matt 8:20

S has power on earth ...... Matt 9:6
Israel before the S .... Matt 10:23
The S came eating and .... Matt 11:19
the S is Lord even .... Matt 12:8
a word against the S ..... Matt 12:32
will the S be three days ... Matt 12:40
the good seed is the S .... Matt 13:37
men say that I, the S .... Matt 16:13
S coming in His .... Matt 16:28
until the S is risen .... Matt 17:9
S is about to be betrayed .. Matt 17:22
S has come to save ...... Matt 18:11
S sits on the throne ...... Matt 19:28
S will be betrayed .... Matt 20:18
S did not come to be ..... Matt 20:28
will the coming of the S ... Matt 24:27
S will be delivered up ..... Matt 26:2
S indeed goes as it is .... Matt 26:24
S must suffer many ...... Mark 8:31
S also will be ashamed ... Mark 8:38
the S also will confess .... Luke 12:8
one of the days of the S .. Luke 17:22
S has come to seek ...... Luke 19:10
to stand before the S .... Luke 21:36
betraying the S with a ... Luke 22:48
descending upon the S .... John 1:51
heaven, that is the S ...... John 3:13
because He is the S .... John 5:27
which the S will give you .. John 6:27
eat the flesh of the S ..... John 6:53
"When you lift up the S ... John 8:28
S should be glorified .... John 12:23
"Now the S is glorified .. John 13:31
heavens opened and the S .. Acts 7:56
S that You take care ...... Heb 2:6
One like the S .... Rev 1:13
cloud sat One like the S ... Rev 14:14

SONG
is my strength and s .... Ex 15:2
Then Israel sang this s .... Num 21:17
Sing to Him a new s .... Ps 33:3
He has put a new s .... Ps 40:3
in the night His s .... Ps 42:8
me, and I am the s .... Ps 69:12
sing to the LORD a new s ... Ps 96:1
LORD is my strength and s .. Ps 118:14
asked of us a s .... Ps 137:3
I will sing a new s .... Ps 144:9
Sing to the LORD a new s .. Ps 149:1
The s of songs, which is ... Song 1:1
to my Well-beloved a s .... Is 5:1
my strength and my s .... Is 12:2
Sing to the LORD a new s .. Is 42:10
their taunting s .... Lam 3:14
I am their taunting s ..... Lam 3:63
as a very lovely s .... Ezek 33:32
They sang a new s .... Rev 5:9
a new s before the throne .. Rev 14:3
And they sing the s .... Rev 15:3

SONGS
my Maker, who gives s .... Job 35:10
surround me with s .... Ps 32:7
have been my s in the ..... Ps 119:54
Sing us one of the s ...... Ps 137:3
is one who sings s ...... Prov 25:20
the noise of your s .... Amos 5:23
and spiritual s .... Eph 5:19

SONS
s of Jacob were twelve .... Gen 35:22
circumcise the s of Israel ... Josh 5:2
the s of Eli were corrupt .. 1 Sam 2:12
the s of the prophets who .. 2 Kin 2:3
s of the prophets cried out .. 2 Kin 4:1
the s of the prophets ..... 2 Kin 4:38
these were the s of David .. 1 Chr 3:1
s come to honor .... Job 14:21
exalted among the s of ..... Ps 12:8
shall be Your s .... Ps 45:16
s of men to do under ..... Eccl 2:3
my beloved among the s .. Song 2:3
Your s shall make haste ... Is 49:17

s shall come from afar ....Is 60:4
"Has Israel no s ....Jer 49:1
The precious s of Zion .....Lam 4:2
eat their s in your midst ...Ezek 5:10
'You are the s ....Hos 1:10
He will purify the s ....Mal 3:3
to him, "Then the s ......Matt 17:26
A man had two s, and ....Matt 21:28
be forgiven the s of men ..Mark 3:28
and you will be s ....Luke 6:35
that you may become s ...John 12:36
You are s of the ....Acts 3:25
called s of the living God ...Rom 9:26
and you shall be My s ....2 Cor 6:18
who are of faith are s ....Gal 3:7
the adoption as s ....Gal 4:5
because you are s ....Gal 4:6
us to adoption as s by Jesus . Eph 1:5
You are all s of light ....1 Thess 5:5
in bringing many s ....Heb 2:10
speaks to you as to s ......Heb 12:5
illegitimate and not s ......Heb 12:8

SONS OF GOD
s saw the daughters of men ..Gen 6:2
s came to present ....Job 1:6
all the s shouted for ....Job 38:7
for they shall be called s ...Matt 5:9
to the angels and are s ...Luke 20:36
Spirit of God, these are s ...Rom 8:14
for the revealing of the s ...Rom 8:19
For you are all s ....Gal 3:26

SOON
for it is s cut off ....Ps 90:10
s forgot His works ....Ps 106:13

SOOTHED
or bound up, or s ....Is 1:6

SOOTHSAYERS
your dreamers, your s, or ....Jer 27:9
A sword is against the s .....Jer 50:36
the s cannot declare to the ..Dan 2:27

SORCERER
omens, or a s ....Deut 18:10
But Elymas the s ....Acts 13:8

SORCERERS
soothsayers, or your s .....Jer 27:9
outside are dogs and s ....Rev 22:15

SORCERESS
shall not permit a s ....Ex 22:18

SORCERY
For there is no s ....Num 23:23
idolatry, s ....Gal 5:20

SORES
and putrefying s ....Is 1:6
Lazarus, full of s ....Luke 16:20

SORROW
multiply your s ....Gen 3:16
s dances before him ....Job 41:22
in my soul, having s ....Ps 13:2
s is continually ....Ps 38:17
I found trouble and s ....Ps 116:3
And He adds no s ....Prov 10:22
the heart may s ....Prov 14:13
S is better than ....Eccl 7:3
Therefore remove s ....Eccl 11:10
and desperate s ....Is 17:11
you shall cry for s ....Is 65:14
to see labor and s ....Jer 20:18
Your s is incurable ....Jer 30:15
added grief to my s ....Jer 45:3
gather those who s ....Zeph 3:18
them sleeping from s .....Luke 22:45
s has filled your ....John 16:6
s will be turned ....John 16:20
that I have great s ....Rom 9:2
s produces repentance ....2 Cor 7:10
lest I should have s ....Phil 2:27
s as others who have ....1 Thess 4:13
no more death, nor s ....Rev 21:4

SORROWFUL
am a woman of s spirit ...1 Sam 1:15
But I am poor and s ....Ps 69:29
For all his days are s .....Eccl 2:23
replenished every s ....Jer 31:25
were exceedingly s ....Matt 17:23
saying, he went away s ....Matt 19:22
soul is exceedingly s .....Matt 26:38
and went away s ....Mark 10:22
and you will be s ....John 16:20
if I make you s ....2 Cor 2:2
and I may be less s ....Phil 2:28

SORROWS
the s of Sheol ....2 Sam 22:6
s God distributes ....Job 21:17
s shall be multiplied ....Ps 16:4
by men, a Man of s ....Is 53:3
are the beginning of s .....Matt 24:8
through with many s ....1 Tim 6:10

SORRY
s that He had made man ....Gen 6:6
who will be s for you ....Is 51:19
And the king was s ....Matt 14:9
For you were made s ....2 Cor 7:9

SOSTHENES
Ruler of the synagogue at Corinth,
    Acts 18:17
——— Paul's Christian brother, 1 Cor 1:1

SOUGHT
I s the LORD ....Ps 34:4
whole heart I have s ......Ps 119:10
s the one I love ....Song 3:1
shall be called S Out ......Is 62:12
So I s for a man ....Ezek 22:30
s what was lost ....Ezek 34:4
s favor from Him ....Hos 12:4
LORD, and have not s .....Zeph 1:6
s it diligently ....Heb 12:17

SOUL
s enter their council ....Gen 49:6
with all your s ....Deut 6:5
was knit to the s ....1 Sam 18:1
your heart and your s ...1 Chr 22:19
"My s loathes my life ......Job 10:1
as you do, if your s ....Job 16:4
s draws near the Pit ......Job 33:22
will not leave my s ....Ps 16:10
converting the s ....Ps 19:7
He restores my s ....Ps 23:3
s shall make its boast ......Ps 34:2
s shall be joyful ....Ps 35:9
you cast down, O my s ....Ps 42:5
s silently waits............Ps 62:1
He has done for my s .....Ps 66:16
Let my s live ....Ps 119:175
s knows very well ......Ps 139:14
No one cares for my s ....Ps 142:4
so destroys his own s .....Prov 6:32
me wrongs his own s ....Prov 8:36
it is not good for a s .....Prov 19:2
A satisfied s loathes ......Prov 27:7
When You make His s .....Is 53:10
s delight itself ....Is 55:2
and your s shall live ....Is 55:3
you have heard, O my s ...Jer 4:19
the s of the father as .....Ezek 18:4
the proud, his s ....Hab 2:4
able to destroy both s .....Matt 10:28
and loses his own s .....Matt 16:26
with all your s ....Matt 22:37
"My s magnifies the Lord ..Luke 1:46
through your own s also ...Luke 2:35
And I will say to my s ....Luke 12:19
Now My s is troubled .....John 12:27
not leave my s in Hades ....Acts 2:27
of one heart and one s ....Acts 4:32
your whole spirit, s .....1 Thess 5:23
to the saving of the s .....Heb 10:39
his way will save a s ....James 5:20
which war against the s ...1 Pet 2:11

his righteous s ....2 Pet 2:8
health, just as your s ......3 John 2

SOULS
See AFFLICT YOUR SOULS
and will save the s ....Ps 72:13
and he who wins s ....Prov 11:30
s shall be like a ....Jer 31:12
who made our very s ......Jer 38:16
will find rest for your s ...Matt 11:29
patience possess your s ...Luke 21:19
unsettling your s ....Acts 15:24
is able to save your s ....James 1:21
the salvation of your s .....1 Pet 1:9
and bodies and s of men ..Rev 18:13
I saw the s of those who ....Rev 20:4

SOUND
He stores up s wisdom .....Prov 2:7
s heart is life ....Prov 14:30
one rises up at the s ......Eccl 12:4
to you at the s of your cry ...Is 30:19
voice was like the s ....Ezek 43:2
s an alarm in My holy ......Joel 2:1
do not s a trumpet ....Matt 6:2
For the trumpet will s ....1 Cor 15:52
is contrary to s doctrine ...1 Tim 1:10
s words which you ....2 Tim 1:13
that they may be s ....Titus 1:13
as the s of many waters ....Rev 1:15
s of their wings was like ....Rev 9:9

SOUNDED
The first angel s ....Rev 8:7

SOUNDNESS
There is no s in my ....Ps 38:3
him this perfect s ....Acts 3:16

SOUNDS
Dreadful s are in his ....Job 15:21
a distinction in the s .....1 Cor 14:7

SOUTH
s comes the whirlwind .....Job 37:9
as the streams in the S .....Ps 126:4
And to the s, 'Do not keep ....Is 43:6
the S shall become strong ..Dan 11:5
The queen of the S will ...Matt 12:42

SOW
s trouble reap ....Job 4:8
then let me s ....Job 31:8
s fields and plant ....Ps 107:37
Those who s in tears ....Ps 126:5
the wind will not s ....Eccl 11:4
Blessed are you who s ....Is 32:20
ground, and do not s ....Jer 4:3
"They s the wind ....Hos 8:7
S for yourselves ....Hos 10:12
You shall s, but not reap ...Mic 6:15
s is not made alive ......1 Cor 15:36
they neither s nor reap ...Luke 12:24

SOWED
s tares among the wheat ..Matt 13:25

SOWER
may give seed to the s ......Is 55:10
"Behold, a s went ....Matt 13:3
a s went out to sow ....Mark 4:3
The s sows the word .....Mark 4:14
A s went out to sow ....Luke 8:5

SOWN
shall they be s ....Is 40:24
a land not s ....Jer 2:2
"You have s much ....Hag 1:6
where you have not s .....Matt 25:24
that was s in their hearts ..Mark 4:15
s spiritual things ....1 Cor 9:11
It is s in weakness ....1 Cor 15:43
of righteousness is s .....James 3:18

SOWS
s righteousness will ....Prov 11:18
s the good seed is the .....Matt 13:37
'One s and another ....John 4:37

s sparingly will .... 2 Cor 9:6
for whatever a man s .... Gal 6:7

SPAN
My life s is gone, taken ...... Is 38:12
measured heaven with a s .. Is 40:12

SPARE
The LORD would not s.... Deut 29:20
hand, but s his life .... Job 2:6
S the poor and needy .... Ps 72:13
I will not pity nor s .... Jer 13:14
say, "S Your people .... Joel 2:17
s them as a man spares .... Mal 3:17
He who did not s .... Rom 8:32
s the natural branches .... Rom 11:21
flesh, but I would s .... 1 Cor 7:28
if God did not s .... 2 Pet 2:4

SPARES
s his rod hates his .... Prov 13:24

SPARK
the work of it as a s .... Is 1:31

SPARKLES
it is red, when it s .... Prov 23:31

SPARKS
to trouble, as the s .... Job 5:7
s you have kindled .... Is 50:11

SPARROW
s has found a home .... Ps 84:3
awake, and am like a s ...... Ps 102:7

SPARROWS
more value than many s .. Matt 10:31

SPAT
Then they s on Him ...... Matt 27:30
in his ears, and He s ...... Mark 7:33

SPEAK
only the word that I s ..... Num 22:35
s just once more .... Judg 6:39
s good words to them ..... 1 Kin 12:7
oh, that God would s .... Job 11:5
Will you s wickedly .... Job 13:7
For God may s in one ..... Job 33:14
Will he s softly to .... Job 41:3
Do not s in the .... Prov 23:9
and a time to s .... Eccl 3:7
If they do not s .... Is 8:20
tongue He will s .... Is 28:11
s anymore in His name ..... Jer 20:9
and s comfort to her .... Hos 2:14
at the end it will s .... Hab 2:3
s each man the truth ...... Zech 8:16
But only s a word, and my .. Matt 8:8
or what you should s ..... Matt 10:19
it is not you who s .... Matt 10:20
to you when all men s ..... Luke 6:26
s what We know and ...... John 3:11
"I who s to you am He ..... John 4:26
s what I have seen .... John 8:38
The words that I s to ..... John 14:10
He hears He will s .... John 16:13
Spirit and began to s .... Acts 2:4
Do all s with tongues ..... 1 Cor 12:30
I s with the tongues .... 1 Cor 13:1
I would rather s .... 1 Cor 14:19
So s and so do as .... James 2:12

SPEAKING
s your own words .... Is 58:13
while they are still s .... Is 65:24
a proof of Christ s .... 2 Cor 13:3
envy, and all evil s .... 1 Pet 2:1

SPEAKS
to face, as a man s .... Ex 33:11
this day that God s .... Deut 5:24
day that I am He who s ..... Is 52:6
the one who s uprightly ... Amos 5:10
He whom God has sent s ... John 3:34
When he s a lie .... John 8:44
he who s with tongues .... 1 Cor 14:5
If anyone s in a tongue ... 1 Cor 14:27
he being dead still s .... Heb 11:4

of sprinkling that s .... Heb 12:24
s evil of a brother .... James 4:11

SPEAR
lay hold on bow and s ...... Jer 6:23
His side with a s .... John 19:34

SPEARS
whose teeth are s .... Ps 57:4
and their s into .... Is 2:4
pruning hooks into s .... Joel 3:10

SPECIAL
you shall be a s treasure ..... Ex 19:5
you to be His s people .... Deut 26:18
Israel for His s treasure ..... Ps 135:4
His own s people .... Titus 2:14
nation, His own s people .... 1 Pet 2:9

SPECK
do you look at the s .... Matt 7:3

SPECTACLE
and make you a s .... Nah 3:6
we have been made a s ..... 1 Cor 4:9
He made a public s .... Col 2:15
you were made a s .... Heb 10:33

SPEECH
one language and one s ..... Gen 11:1
drop as the rain, my s ..... Deut 32:2
s settled on them as ...... Job 29:22
There is no s nor .... Ps 19:3
s is not becoming .... Prov 17:7
your s shall be low .... Is 29:4
a people of obscure s .... Is 33:19
not understand My s ...... John 8:43
s deceive the hearts ...... Rom 16:18
and his s contemptible ... 2 Cor 10:10
I am untrained in s .... 2 Cor 11:6
s always be with grace ...... Col 4:6

SPEECHLESS
your mouth for the s ...... Prov 31:8
And he was s .... Matt 22:12

SPEED
they shall come with s ...... Is 5:26

SPEEDILY
judgment be executed s .... Ezra 7:26
to me, deliver me s .... Ps 31:2
I call, answer me s .... Ps 102:2

SPEND
Why do you s money for ...... Is 55:2
whatever more you s ...... Luke 10:35
I will very gladly s .... 2 Cor 12:15
amiss, that you may s ...... James 4:3

SPENT
strength shall be s .... Lev 26:20
For my life is s .... Ps 31:10
in vain, I have s .... Is 49:4
"But when he had s ...... Luke 15:14

SPICES
s for the anointing oil .... Ex 25:6
s in great quantity ...... 1 Kin 10:10
that its s may flow out .... Song 4:16
and Salome bought s .... Mark 16:1
s which they had .... Luke 24:1
strips of linen with the s .. John 19:40

SPIDER
s skillfully grasps .... Prov 30:28

SPIES
to them, "You are s .... Gen 42:9
men who had been s ...... Josh 6:23
s who pretended .... Luke 20:20

SPIKENARD
fragrant henna with s ..... Song 4:13
of very costly oil of s ..... Mark 14:3

SPIN
neither toil nor s .... Matt 6:28

SPINDLE
her hand holds the s ...... Prov 31:19

SPIRIT
See HOLY SPIRIT; FILLED WITH THE
HOLY SPIRIT; UNCLEAN SPIRIT

S shall not strive .... Gen 6:3
the breath of the s of life .... Gen 7:22
filled with the s of wisdom .. Ex 28:3
and everyone whose s ..... Ex 35:21
S that is upon you .... Num 11:17
And the S rested upon ... Num 11:26
LORD would put His S..... Num 11:29
he has a different s ...... Num 14:24
in whom is the S .... Num 27:18
God sent a s of ill will .... Judg 9:23
portion of your s .... 2 Kin 2:9
I will send a s upon him .. 2 Kin 19:7
there was no more s .... 2 Chr 9:4
s came forward and ..... 2 Chr 18:20
also gave Your good S .... Neh 9:20
against them by Your S .... Neh 9:30
Then a s passed before ...... Job 4:15
care has preserved my s .... Job 10:12
And whose s came from .... Job 26:4
hand I commit my s .... Ps 31:5
Your Holy S from me ...... Ps 51:11
s was not faithful .... Ps 78:8
You send forth Your S .... Ps 104:30
Your S is good .... Ps 143:10
I will pour out my s on ..... Prov 1:23
The s of a man is the .... Prov 20:27
Who knows the s .... Eccl 3:21
s will return to God .... Eccl 12:7
night, yes, by my s .... Is 26:9
out on you the s .... Is 29:10
are flesh, and not s .... Is 31:3
S has gathered them .... Is 34:16
is the life of my s .... Is 38:16
I have put My S .... Is 42:1
and His S have sent Me ..... Is 48:16
s would fail before Me ...... Is 57:16
S entered me when He ..... Ezek 2:2
the S lifted me up .... Ezek 3:12
who follow their own s .... Ezek 13:3
new heart and a new s .... Ezek 18:31
be feeble, every s .... Ezek 21:7
I will put My S .... Ezek 36:27
in him is the S .... Dan 4:8
as an excellent s .... Dan 5:12
walk in a false s .... Mic 2:11
and forms the s .... Zech 12:1
with child of the Holy S .... Matt 1:18
"Blessed are the poor in s ... Matt 5:3
I will put My S .... Matt 12:18
S descending upon Him .... Mark 1:10
Immediately the S .... Mark 1:12
s indeed is willing ...... Mark 14:38
go before Him in the s ..... Luke 1:17
in the power of the S ...... Luke 4:14
manner of s you are of .... Luke 9:55
When an unclean s goes .. Luke 11:24
against the Holy S .... Luke 12:10
hands I commit My s ..... Luke 23:46
they had seen a s .... Luke 24:37
s does not have flesh ..... Luke 24:39
I saw the S descending .... John 1:32
born of water and the S ... John 3:5
God is S .... John 4:24
I speak to you are s .... John 6:63
He groaned in the s...... John 11:33
He was troubled in s ..... John 13:21
all filled with the Holy S.... Acts 2:4
but if a s or an angel ..... Acts 23:9
to the S of holiness, by the .. Rom 1:4
whom I serve with my s ..... Rom 1:9
but according to the S ...... Rom 8:1
according to the S .... Rom 8:5
the flesh but in the S ...... Rom 8:9
s that we are children ..... Rom 8:16
what the mind of the S..... Rom 8:27
to us through His S ...... 1 Cor 2:10
gifts, but the same S....... 1 Cor 12:4
in a tongue, my s ...... 1 Cor 14:14
but the S gives life .... 2 Cor 3:6
Now the Lord is the S..... 2 Cor 3:17
we have the same s ..... 2 Cor 4:13
Having begun in the S ...... Gal 3:3

has sent forth the S ....Gal 4:6
Walk in the S, and you ....Gal 5:16
But if you are led by the S ...Gal 5:18
the fruit of the S is love .....Gal 5:22
If we live in the S, let us .....Gal 5:25
he who sows to the S ....Gal 6:8
with the Holy S ....Eph 1:13
may give to you the s ....Eph 1:17
the unity of the S..........Eph 4:3
is one body and one S ......Eph 4:4
stand fast in one s ....Phil 1:27
yet I am with you in s ......Col 2:5
Do not quench the S ...1 Thess 5:19
and may your whole s ...1 Thess 5:23
sanctification by the S ...2 Thess 2:13
flesh, justified in the S ....1 Tim 3:16
S expressly says that ....1 Tim 4:1
not given us a s of fear .....2 Tim 1:7
division of soul and s ......Heb 4:12
through the eternal S ......Heb 9:14
body without the s is .....James 2:26
S who dwells in us ....James 4:5
S of Christ who was in ...1 Pet 1:11
made alive by the S ....1 Pet 3:18
S whom He has given .....1 John 3:24
do not believe every s .....1 John 4:1
has given us of His S ......1 John 4:13
S who bears witness ......1 John 5:6
not having the S ....Jude 19
I was in the S on the ......Rev 1:10
him hear what the S ....Rev 2:7
Immediately I was in the S ...Rev 4:2
And the S and the ....Rev 22:17

SPIRIT OF GOD
S was hovering over the .....Gen 1:2
a man in whom is the S ...Gen 41:38
filled him with the S ....Ex 31:3
the S came upon him .....Num 24:2
S came upon him ....1 Sam 10:10
the S came upon Saul ....1 Sam 11:6
S came upon the ....1 Sam 19:20
The S has made me ....Job 33:4
in a vision by the S ......Ezek 11:24
that the S is in you ....Dan 5:14
S descending like a dove ..Matt 3:16
out demons by the S ......Matt 12:28
indeed the S dwells in you ..Rom 8:9
by the power of the S .....Rom 15:19
the things of the S ....1 Cor 2:14
the S dwells in you........1 Cor 3:16
I think I also have the S ...1 Cor 7:40
no one speaking by the S ..1 Cor 12:3
By this you know the S ....1 John 4:2

SPIRIT OF THE LORD
The S came upon him ....Judg 3:10
the S came upon Gideon ...Judg 6:34
S came mightily upon .....Judg 14:6
S will come upon you ....1 Sam 10:6
S came upon David .....1 Sam 16:13
S departed from Saul ....1 Sam 16:14
S will carry you ....1 Kin 18:12
S has taken him up ....2 Kin 2:16
The S shall rest upon Him ...Is 11:2
The S GOD is upon Me ....Is 61:1
Then the S fell upon me ...Ezek 11:5
Is the S restricted ....Mic 2:7
am full of power by the S ....Mic 3:8
The S is upon Me ....Luke 4:18
together to test the S ....Acts 5:9
S caught Philip away ......Acts 8:39

SPIRIT OF TRUTH
S, whom the world ....John 14:17
S who proceeds from ....John 15:26
He, the S has come ......John 16:13
By this we know the s .....1 John 4:6

SPIRITS
See UNCLEAN SPIRITS
God, the God of the s .....Num 16:22
who makes His angels s .....Ps 104:4
the LORD weighs the s......Prov 16:2

power over unclean s ......Matt 10:1
discerning of s ....1 Cor 12:10
heed to deceiving s ....1 Tim 4:1
not all ministering s ....Heb 1:14
to the Father of s ....Heb 12:9
and preached to the s .....1 Pet 3:19
spirit, but test the s ....1 John 4:1

SPIRITUAL
the s man is insane ....Hos 9:7
we know that the law is s ..Rom 7:14
s judges all things ....1 Cor 2:15
s people but as to ....1 Cor 3:1
Now concerning s gifts ....1 Cor 12:1
to be a prophet or s ....1 Cor 14:37
However, the s is not .....1 Cor 15:46
s restore such a one ....Gal 6:1
being built up a s house ....1 Pet 2:5

SPIRITUALLY
s minded is life ....Rom 8:6
because they are s ....1 Cor 2:14

SPIT
He had s on his eyes ......Mark 8:23
s on Him, and kill Him ..Mark 10:34
some began to s on Him ..Mark 14:65
insulted and s upon .....Luke 18:32

SPITEFULLY
for those who s ....Matt 5:44

SPITTING
face from shame and s ....Is 50:6

SPLENDOR
with majesty and s ....Job 40:10
Like the s of the meadows ...Ps 37:20
on the glorious s ....Ps 145:5
the s of old men is their ...Prov 20:29
of Zion all her s ....Lam 1:6
wisdom, and defile your s ..Ezek 28:7

SPLIT
ground s apart under .....Num 16:31
pierced his head, she s ....Judg 5:26
the altar shall s apart ....1 Kin 13:3
of Olives shall be s in two ..Zech 14:4
and the rocks were s .....Matt 27:51

SPOIL
hate us have taken s ....Ps 44:10
when they divide the s ....Is 9:3
He shall divide the s ....Is 53:12
Take s of silver ....Nah 2:9
s will be divided ....Zech 14:1

SPOILER
I have created the s ....Is 54:16

SPOKE
God s to Moses and said ......Ex 6:2
s they did not hear ....Is 66:4
who feared the LORD s .....Mal 3:16
"No man ever s ....John 7:46
We know that God s ....John 9:29
I was a child, I s ....1 Cor 13:11
in various ways s ....Heb 1:1
s as they were moved ......2 Pet 1:21

SPOKEN
See LORD HAS SPOKEN
'just as you have s ....Num 14:28
God has s once ....Ps 62:11
I have not s in secret ....Is 45:19
LORD has s against you......Amos 3:1
'What have we s ....Mal 3:13
s this parable against .....Luke 20:19
the prophets have s ......Luke 24:25
why am I evil s ....1 Cor 10:30

SPOKESMAN
So he shall be your s ....Ex 4:16

SPONGE
them ran and took a s ....Matt 27:48

SPOT
and there is no s ....Song 4:7
church, not having s ....Eph 5:27
commandment without s ..1 Tim 6:14

Himself without s ....Heb 9:14
blemish and without s .....1 Pet 1:19

SPOTS
They are s and ....2 Pet 2:13
These are s in your ....Jude 12

SPOUSE
your love, my sister, my s ..Song 4:10
Israel served for a s ......Hos 12:12

SPREAD
fell on my knees and s ......Ezra 9:5
they have s a net by ....Ps 140:5
Then He s it before me ....Ezek 2:10
Then the word of God s ....Acts 6:7
the Lord was being s .....Acts 13:49
their message will s ......2 Tim 2:17

SPREADS
He alone s out the ....Job 9:8
s them out like a tent ....Is 40:22
Zion s out her hands ......Lam 1:17

SPRING
Truth shall s out of ....Ps 85:11
is like a murky s ....Prov 25:26
sister, my spouse, a s ......Song 4:12
s forth I tell you ....Is 42:9
of Israel to s forth ....Ezek 29:21
s shall become dry ....Hos 13:15
s send forth fresh ....James 3:11

SPRINGING
a fountain of water s ......John 4:14
of bitterness s ....Heb 12:15

SPRINGS
"Have you entered the s ...Job 38:16
He sends the s into ....Ps 104:10
and the thirsty land s ....Is 35:7
and the dry land s ....Is 41:18

SPRINKLE
He s many nations ....Is 52:15
Then I will s ....Ezek 36:25

SPRINKLED
s dust on his head ....Job 2:12
and hyssop, and s ....Heb 9:19
having our hearts s ....Heb 10:22

SPRINKLING
s that speaks ....Heb 12:24
for obedience and s ....1 Pet 1:2

SPROUT
down, that it will s ....Job 14:7
and the seed should s .....Mark 4:27

SPY
men to s out the land ......Num 13:2
sent to s out Jericho ....Josh 6:25
to s out the land and ....Judg 18:2
to s out our liberty ....Gal 2:4

SQUARE
the night in the open s .....Gen 19:2
in the open s of the city ...Judg 19:15
took my seat in the open s ..Job 29:7
the city is laid out as a s ..Rev 21:16

SQUARES
voice in the open s ....Prov 1:20
s I will seek the one ....Song 3:2

STABILITY
will be the s of your ....Is 33:6

STAFF
this Jordan with my s ....Gen 32:10
your feet, and your s ......Ex 12:11
the donkey with his s .....Num 22:27
Your rod and Your s ....Ps 23:4
LORD has broken the s ....Is 14:5
'How the strong s ....Jer 48:17
they have been a s ......Ezek 29:6
And I took my s, Beauty ..Zech 11:10
for the journey except a s ..Mark 6:8
on the top of his s ....Heb 11:21

STAG
like a gazelle or a young s ..Song 2:9

STAGGER
and He makes them s ...... Job 12:25
they will drink and s .... Jer 25:16

STAGGERS
as a drunken man s .... Is 19:14

STAKES
s will ever be removed .... Is 33:20

STALLS
be no herd in the s .... Hab 3:17

STAMMERERS
s will be ready .... Is 32:4

STAMMERING
For with s lips and .... Is 28:11
s tongue that you .... Is 33:19

STAMPING
At the noise of the s .... Jer 47:3

STAND
where you s is holy ground ... Ex 3:5
S still, and see the .... Ex 14:13
one shall be able to s ..... Deut 7:24
"Who is able to s .... 1 Sam 6:20
took a s for the covenant ... 2 Kin 23:3
we are not able to s ...... Ezra 10:13
but it does not s .... Job 8:15
lives, and He shall s ...... Job 19:25
ungodly shall not s .... Ps 1:5
Why do You s afar off .... Ps 10:1
Or who may s in His .... Ps 24:3
the world s in awe of Him .... Ps 33:8
Who will s up for me .... Ps 94:16
and let an accuser s .... Ps 109:6
They s fast forever .... Ps 111:8
he will not s before ...... Prov 22:29
Do not take your s .... Eccl 8:3
"It shall not s .... Is 7:7
"S in the ways and .... Jer 6:16
not lack a man to s .... Jer 35:19
whose words will s .... Jer 44:28
s in the gap before Me ... Ezek 22:30
and it shall s .... Dan 2:44
but she shall not s .... Dan 11:17
Who can s before His .... Nah 1:6
s on the Mount of Olives .. Zech 14:4
And who can s when He ..... Mal 3:2
against itself will not s .. Matt 12:25
that kingdom cannot s .... Mark 3:24
how will his kingdom s ... Luke 11:18
why do you s gazing up .... Acts 1:11
you s is holy ground .... Acts 7:33
this grace in which we s .... Rom 5:2
he will be made to s ...... Rom 14:4
Watch, s fast in the ..... 1 Cor 16:13
for by faith you s .... 2 Cor 1:24
S fast therefore in the ..... Gal 5:1
having done all, to s ...... Eph 6:13
S therefore .... Eph 6:14
s fast in the Lord .... Phil 4:1
now we live, if you s .... 1 Thess 3:8
of God in which you s .... 1 Pet 5:12
Behold, I s at the .... Rev 3:20

STANDARD
Lord will lift up a s .... Is 59:19
Set up the s toward .... Jer 4:6

STANDING
the Lord s by the altar .... Amos 9:1
the Lord, and Satan s...... Zech 3:1
they love to pray s .... Matt 6:5
and saw others s idle ..... Matt 20:3
s here who will not taste ... Mark 9:1
the woman s in the midst ... John 8:9
and the Son of Man s ..... Acts 7:56
the Judge is s at the door . James 5:9
Then I saw an angel s .... Rev 19:17

STANDS
Nor s in the path of sinners ... Ps 1:1
counsel of the Lord s...... Ps 33:11
my heart s in awe of .... Ps 119:161
The Lord s up to plead ..... Is 3:13

---

there s One among you .... John 1:26
him who thinks he s ..... 1 Cor 10:12
foundation of God s ...... 2 Tim 2:19

STAR
S shall come out of ...... Num 24:17
For we have seen His s ..... Matt 2:2
for one s differs from .... 1 Cor 15:41
give him the morning s ..... Rev 2:28
And a great s fell .... Rev 8:10
Bright and Morning S .... Rev 22:16

STARS
He made the s also .... Gen 1:16
as the s of the heaven ... Gen 22:17
s bowed down to me ...... Gen 37:9
s are not pure in His ...... Job 25:5
when the morning s .... Job 38:7
the moon and the s .... Ps 8:3
s to rule by night, for His ... Ps 136:9
praise Him, all you s ...... Ps 148:3
the s will diminish their ... Joel 3:15
the s of heaven will fall .. Mark 13:25
born as many as the s .... Heb 11:12
wandering s for whom ..... Jude 13
in His right hand seven s ... Rev 1:16
a garland of twelve s ...... Rev 12:1

STARVED
His strength is s .... Job 18:12

STATE
man at his best s .... Ps 39:5
us in our lowly s .... Ps 136:23
and the last s of that ..... Matt 12:45
learned in whatever s ...... Phil 4:11

STATURE
add one cubit to his s .... Matt 6:27
in wisdom and s .... Luke 2:52
add one cubit to his s .... Luke 12:25
for he was of short s ..... Luke 19:3
the measure of the s ...... Eph 4:13

STATUTE
It shall be a s forever to .... Ex 27:21
be theirs for a perpetual s ... Ex 29:9
shall be a perpetual s ..... Lev 3:17
it shall be a s forever .... Lev 23:14
For this is a s for Israel ..... Ps 81:4
to establish a royal s ...... Dan 6:7

STATUTES
shall therefore keep My s ... Lev 18:5
My ways, to keep My s ... 1 Kin 3:14
not put away His s from .... Ps 18:22
the s of the Lord are .... Ps 19:8
Teach me Your s .... Ps 119:12
s have been my songs ..... Ps 119:54
observe Your s .... Ps 119:117
not walked in My s ...... Ezek 5:6
did not walk in My s .... Ezek 20:21

STAY
her feet would not s ...... Prov 7:11
S here and watch with .... Matt 26:38
for today I must s .... Luke 19:5
the time of your s .... 1 Pet 1:17

STEADFAST
yes, you could be s .... Job 11:15
O God, my heart is s .... Ps 57:7
their heart was not s ...... Ps 78:37
his heart is s .... Ps 112:7
God, and s forever .... Dan 6:26
brethren, be s .... 1 Cor 15:58
faith, grounded and s ...... Col 1:23
angels proved s .... Heb 2:2
of our confidence s .... Heb 3:14
soul, both sure and s ...... Heb 6:19
Resist him, s in the ...... 1 Pet 5:9

STEADFASTLY
s set His face to go ...... Luke 9:51
And they continued s .... Acts 2:42
continuing s in .... Rom 12:12

STEADFASTNESS
good order and the s .... Col 2:5
from your own s .... 2 Pet 3:17

STEADILY
could not look s .... 2 Cor 3:13

STEADY
and his hands were s ...... Ex 17:12

STEAL
"You shall not s .... Ex 20:15
Will you s .... Jer 7:9
s My words every one ..... Jer 23:30
thieves break in and s..... Matt 6:19
night and s Him away .... Matt 27:64
murder, 'Do not s .... Mark 10:19
not come except to s ..... John 10:10
a man should not s .... Rom 2:21
Let him who stole s .... Eph 4:28

STEEP
s places shall fall .... Ezek 38:20
waters poured down a s ..... Mic 1:4
violently down the s ...... Matt 8:32

STEM
forth a Rod from the s ...... Is 11:1

STENCH
there will be a s .... Is 3:24
this time there is a s ..... John 11:39

STEP
there is but a s .... 1 Sam 20:3
s has turned from the ..... Job 31:7

STEPHEN
One of the first seven deacons, Acts 6:1–8

Falsely accused by Jews; gives defense, Acts 6:9—7:53

Becomes first Christian martyr, Acts 7:54–60

STEPS
has held fast to His s ..... Job 23:11
and count all my s .... Job 31:4
and He sees all his s ..... Job 34:21
Uphold my s in Your ...... Ps 17:5
The s of a good man .... Ps 37:23
of his s shall slide .... Ps 37:31
and established my s ...... Ps 40:2
hide, they mark my s ...... Ps 56:6
s had nearly slipped ...... Ps 73:2
Direct my s by Your ..... Ps 119:133
s will not be hindered ..... Prov 4:12
the Lord directs his s ..... Prov 16:9
A man's s are of the ..... Prov 20:24
to direct his own s .... Jer 10:23
should follow His s ...... 1 Pet 2:21

STEWARD
faithful and wise s ...... Luke 12:42
you can no longer be s ... Luke 16:2
commended the unjust s ... Luke 16:8
be blameless, as a s ...... Titus 1:7

STEWARDS
of Christ and s .... 1 Cor 4:1
one another, as good s .... 1 Pet 4:10

STEWARDSHIP
entrusted with a s .... 1 Cor 9:17

STICK
and his bones s .... Job 33:21
and s out the tongue .... Is 57:4
'For Joseph, the s .... Ezek 37:16

STICKS
a man gathering s .... Num 15:32
was there gathering s ... 1 Kin 17:10
And the s on which ..... Ezek 37:20

STIFF
rebellion and your s ..... Deut 31:27
do not speak with a s ...... Ps 75:5

STIFF-NECKED
Now do not be s .... 2 Chr 30:8
"You s and uncircumcised .. Acts 7:51

STILL
on your bed, and be s .... Ps 4:4

s the noise of the . . . . Ps 65:7
earth feared and was s . . . . Ps 76:8
that its waves are s . . . . Ps 107:29
When I awake, I am s . . . . . . Ps 139:18
time, I have been s . . . . Is 42:14
rest and be s . . . . Jer 47:6
sea, "Peace, be s . . . . Mark 4:39
let him be holy s . . . . Rev 22:11

STILLBORN
hidden like a s child . . . . . . Job 3:16
as it goes, like a s . . . . Ps 58:8
burial, I say that a s . . . . Eccl 6:3

STINGS
like a serpent, and s . . . . . Prov 23:32

STIR
that he would dare s . . . . . . Job 41:10
S up Yourself . . . . Ps 35:23
I remind you to s . . . . 2 Tim 1:6
another in order to s . . . . . . Heb 10:24

STIRRED
fulfilled, the LORD s . . 2 Chr 36:22
and my sorrow was s . . . . Ps 39:2
So the LORD s up the . . . . . . Hag 1:14

STIRS
and the innocent s . . . . Job 17:8
it s up the dead for . . . . Is 14:9
on Your name, who s . . . . Is 64:7

STOCKS
put my feet in the s . . . . . . Job 13:27
s that were in the . . . . Jer 20:2

STOIC
and S philosophers . . . . . . Acts 17:18

STOLE
Absalom s the hearts of . . 2 Sam 15:6
s Him away while we . . . . . Matt 28:13
Let him who s steal no . . . . . Eph 4:28

STOLEN
Rachel had the s . . . . Gen 31:19
indeed I was s away . . . . . . Gen 40:15
shall restore what he has s . . Lev 6:4
S water is sweet . . . . Prov 9:17

STOMACH
mouth goes into the s . . . . . Matt 15:17
his heart but his s . . . . Mark 7:19
Foods for the s . . . . 1 Cor 6:13

STOMACH'S
little wine for your s . . . 1 Tim 5:23

STONE
him, a pillar of s . . . . Gen 35:14
to the bottom like a s . . . . . . Ex 15:5
s shall be a witness . . . . . . Josh 24:27
heart is as hard as s . . . . . . Job 41:24
s which the builders . . . . . Ps 118:22
s is heavy and sand is . . . . Prov 27:3
I lay in Zion a s . . . . Is 28:16
take the heart of s . . . . . . Ezek 36:26
You watched while a s . . . . Dan 2:34
s will cry out from . . . . Hab 2:11
to silent s . . . . Hab 2:19
will give him a s . . . . Matt 7:9
s will be broken . . . . Matt 21:44
secure, sealing the s . . . . . Matt 27:66
s which the builders . . . . . Luke 20:17
you, let him throw a s . . . . . John 8:7
those works do you s . . . . John 10:32
Jews sought to s You . . . . . John 11:8
not on tablets of s . . . . 2 Cor 3:3
Him as to a living s . . . . 1 Pet 2:4
give him a white s . . . . Rev 2:17
angel took up a s . . . . Rev 18:21
like a jasper s . . . . Rev 21:11

STONED
s Stephen as he was . . . . . Acts 7:59
once I was s . . . . 2 Cor 11:25
They were s . . . . Heb 11:37

STONES
five smooth s from the . . 1 Sam 17:40

I will lay your s . . . . Is 54:11
Among the smooth s . . . . . . Is 57:6
Abraham from these s . . . . Matt 3:9
command that these s . . . . . Matt 4:3
see what manner of s . . . . . Mark 13:1
also, as living s . . . . 1 Pet 2:5
kinds of precious s . . . . Rev 21:19

STONY
them, and take the s . . . . Ezek 11:19
Some fell on s ground . . . . . Mark 4:5

STOOPED
And again He s down . . . . . . John 8:8

STOP
Please, let us s this usury . . . Neh 5:10
s those who pursue me . . . . . . Ps 35:3

STOPPED
of heaven were also s . . . . Gen 8:2
still, and the moon s . . . . . . Josh 10:13
speak lies shall be s . . . . Ps 63:11
her flow of blood s . . . . Luke 8:44
every mouth may be s . . . . . Rom 3:19
s the mouths of lions . . . . . Heb 11:33

STORE
people s up knowledge . . . . Prov 10:14
no room to s my crops . . . . Luke 12:17

STORED
is s up for the righteous . . . Prov 13:22
his sin is s up . . . . Hos 13:12

STORES
He s up sound wisdom . . . . . Prov 2:7

STORING
s up as he may prosper . . . . 1 Cor 16:2
s up for themselves . . . . 1 Tim 6:19

STORK
s has her home in the . . . . . Ps 104:17
"Even the s in the . . . . Jer 8:7

STORM
from the windy s . . . . Ps 55:8
He calms the s . . . . Ps 107:29
terror comes like a s . . . . . . Prov 1:27
for a shelter from s . . . . Is 4:6
a refuge from the s . . . . Is 25:4
and a destroying s . . . . Is 28:2
coming like a s . . . . Ezek 38:9
whirlwind and in the s . . . . . Nah 1:3

STOUTHEARTED
s were plundered . . . . Ps 76:5

STRAIGHT
make Your way s . . . . Ps 5:8
for who can make s . . . . . . Eccl 7:13
make s in the desert a . . . . . . Is 40:3
Their legs were s . . . . Ezek 1:7
make His paths s . . . . Mark 1:3
LORD; make His paths s . . . . Luke 3:4
s the way of the LORD . . . . . John 1:23
to the street called S . . . . . . Acts 9:11
and make s paths for . . . . . Heb 12:13

STRAIGHTFORWARD
that they were not s . . . . Gal 2:14

STRAIN
Blind guides, who s . . . . . . Matt 23:24

STRAITS
and desperate s . . . . Deut 28:53

STRANGE
were considered a s . . . . Hos 8:12
"We have seen s . . . . Luke 5:26
are bringing some s . . . . . . Acts 17:20
these, they think it s . . . . . . 1 Pet 4:4
s thing happened . . . . 1 Pet 4:12

STRANGER
but he acted as a s . . . . Gen 42:7
"I have been a s . . . . Ex 2:22
neither mistreat a s . . . . Ex 22:21
and loves the s . . . . Deut 10:18
I have become a s . . . . Ps 69:8
s will suffer for it . . . . Prov 11:15

s does not share its . . . . . . Prov 14:10
should You be like a s . . . . . . Jer 14:8
I was a s and you took . . . . Matt 25:35
"Are You the only s . . . . . . Luke 24:18

STRANGERS
descendants will be s . . . Gen 15:13
s plunder his labor . . . . Ps 109:11
watches over the s . . . . Ps 146:9
s devour your land . . . . Is 1:7
S shall stand and feed . . . . . . Is 61:5
know the voice of s . . . . . . John 10:5
of Israel and s . . . . Eph 2:12
you are no longer s . . . . Eph 2:19
if she has lodged s . . . . 1 Tim 5:10
that they were s . . . . Heb 11:13
forget to entertain s . . . . . . Heb 13:2
the brethren and for s . . . . . 3 John 5

STRANGLING
that my soul chooses s . . . . . Job 7:15

STRAP
than I, whose sandal s . . . . . Mark 1:7

STRAW
s to make brick as before . . . . Ex 5:7
They are like s . . . . Job 21:18
lion shall eat s like the ox . . . . Is 11:7
stones, wood, hay, s . . . . . . 1 Cor 3:12

STRAY
the cursed, who s . . . . Ps 119:21
who make my people s . . . . . Mic 3:5

STRAYED
yet I have not s . . . . Ps 119:110
for which some have s . . . . 1 Tim 6:10
who have s concerning . . . 2 Tim 2:18

STREAM
like an overflowing s . . . . . . Is 30:28
of the LORD, like a s . . . . . . Is 30:33
like a flowing s . . . . Is 66:12

STREAMS
He dams up the s . . . . Job 28:11
He also brought s . . . . Ps 78:16
O LORD, as the s . . . . Ps 126:4

STREET
to be heard in the s . . . . Is 42:2
s called Straight . . . . Acts 9:11
And the s of the city . . . . . Rev 21:21
In the middle of its s . . . . . . Rev 22:2

STREETS
the corners of the s . . . . . . Matt 6:5
You taught in our s . . . . . Luke 13:26
out quickly into the s . . . . Luke 14:21

STRENGTH
for by s of hand the . . . . Ex 13:3
just as my s was then . . . . . Josh 14:11
my soul, march on in s . . . . Judg 5:21
a man is, so is his s . . . . . . Judg 8:21
s no man shall . . . . 1 Sam 2:9
the God of my s . . . . 2 Sam 22:3
have armed me with s . . 2 Sam 22:40
the LORD glory and s . . . . 1 Chr 16:28
Is my s the s . . . . Job 6:12
Him are wisdom and s . . . . Job 12:13
him because his s . . . . Job 39:11
You have ordained s . . . . Ps 8:2
love You, O LORD, my s . . . . . Ps 18:1
The LORD is the s . . . . Ps 27:1
The LORD is their s . . . . Ps 28:8
The LORD will give s . . . . Ps 29:11
delivered by great s . . . . . . Ps 33:16
He is their s in the . . . . Ps 37:39
are the God of my s . . . . Ps 43:2
is our refuge and s . . . . Ps 46:1
is He who gives s . . . . Ps 68:35
I will go in the s . . . . Ps 71:16
but God is the s . . . . Ps 73:26
They go from s to . . . . Ps 84:7
the glory of their s . . . . Ps 89:17
s and beauty are in . . . . Ps 96:6
made me bold with s . . . . . Ps 138:3

of the LORD is s.........Prov 10:29
knowledge increases s ....Prov 24:5
S and honor are her ......Prov 31:25
is better than s...........Eccl 9:16
for s and not for ....Eccl 10:17
For You have been a s .....Is 25:4
him take hold of My s .....Is 27:5
of His might and the s ....Is 40:26
might He increases s ......Is 40:29
works it with the s ....Is 44:12
righteousness and s ....Is 45:24
Put on your s ....Is 52:1
O LORD, my s and my ......Jer 16:19
I will destroy the s ......Hag 2:22
He has shown s with .....Luke 1:51
were still without s ....Rom 5:6
s is made perfect ....2 Cor 12:9
you have a little s ....Rev 3:8

STRENGTHEN
and He shall s ....Ps 27:14
S the weak hands ....Is 35:3
"So I will s them in ......Zech 10:12
s your brethren ....Luke 22:32
s the hands ....Heb 12:12
s the things ....Rev 3:2

STRENGTHENED
weak you have not s.......Ezek 34:4
unbelief, but was s........Rom 4:20
of His glory, to be s ......Eph 3:16
stood with me and s .....2 Tim 4:17

STRENGTHENING
s the souls of the ....Acts 14:22

STRENGTHENS
s the wise more than ......Eccl 7:19
through Christ who s ......Phil 4:13

STRETCH
will quickly s out her ......Ps 68:31
said to the man. "S ......Matt 12:13
are old, you will s ....John 21:18

STRETCH OUT MY HAND
I will s and strike Egypt ....Ex 3:20
when I s on Egypt ....Ex 7:5
Lord's anointed, to s .....1 Sam 24:6
forbid that I should s ....1 Sam 26:11
s against the inhabitants ....Jer 6:12
And I will s against you ...Jer 51:25
I will s against them ......Ezek 6:14
I will s against you ....Ezek 25:7
I will s against Judah ....Zeph 1:4

STRETCHED
s himself out on the ......1 Kin 17:21
s himself out on him .....2 Kin 4:35
I have s out my hands........Ps 88:9
but His hand is s out still .....Is 5:25
Who s out the heavens .....Is 51:13
His wisdom, and has s .....Jer 10:12
"All day long I have s .....Rom 10:21

STRETCHED OUT HIS HAND
Abraham s and took the ...Gen 22:10
Aaron s over the waters .....Ex 8:6
Aaron s with his rod ....Ex 8:17
Moses s toward heaven .....Ex 10:22
Moses s over the sea ......Ex 14:21
as soon as he had s ......Josh 8:19
And when the angel s ...2 Sam 24:16
he has s against them ....Is 5:25
He s over the sea ....Is 23:11
And the cherub s..........Ezek 10:7
Jesus s and caught him ...Matt 14:31
Herod the king s to ....Acts 12:1

STRETCHES
For he s out his hand ......Job 15:25

STRICKEN
My heart is s and ....Ps 102:4
yet we esteemed Him s ....Is 53:4
of My people He was s.......Is 53:8
You have s them ....Jer 5:3
He has s, but He will ....Hos 6:1

STRIFE
let there be no s ....Gen 13:8
You have made us a s .....Ps 80:6
at the waters of s ....Ps 106:32
Hatred stirs up s ....Prov 10:12
comes nothing but s ......Prov 13:10
man stirs up s ....Prov 15:18
transgression loves s ......Prov 17:19
borne me, a man of s ......Jer 15:10
and lust, not in s ....Rom 13:13
even from envy and s ......Phil 1:15
which come envy, s ....1 Tim 6:4

STRIKE
said, "S this people ....2 Kin 6:18
The sun shall not s ....Ps 121:6
Let the righteous s ....Ps 141:5
S a scoffer ....Prov 19:25
s your hands ....Ezek 21:14
s the waves of the sea ....Zech 10:11
"S the Shepherd ....Zech 13:7
s the earth with a ....Mal 4:6
'I will s the Shepherd .....Matt 26:31
'I will s the Shepherd ....Mark 14:27
if well, why do you s .....John 18:23
the sun shall not s ....Rev 7:16
s the earth with all ....Rev 11:6

STRIKES
To him who s you on the ..Luke 6:29
if one s you on the face ..2 Cor 11:20
a scorpion when it s ....Rev 9:5

STRINGED
of your s instruments ....Is 14:11
of your s instruments .....Amos 5:23

STRIP
S yourselves ....Is 32:11
s her naked and expose ......Hos 2:3

STRIPES
their iniquity with s ....Ps 89:32
s we are healed ....Is 53:5
be beaten with many s ....Luke 12:47
I received forty s ....2 Cor 11:24
s you were healed ....1 Pet 2:24

STRIVE
"My Spirit shall not s ....Gen 6:3
He will not always s ....Ps 103:9
Do not s with a man ....Prov 3:30
Let the potsherd s ....Is 45:9
"S to enter through ....Luke 13:24
the Lord not to s ....2 Tim 2:14

STRIVING
for a man to stop s ....Prov 20:3

STROKE
with a mighty s ....Jer 14:17

STRONG
with a s hand he will let ....Ex 6:1
Be s and of good courage ..Deut 31:6
be s and very courageous ...Josh 1:7
Be s and conduct ....1 Sam 4:9
indeed He is s ....Job 9:19
The LORD s and mighty.......Ps 24:8
bring me to the s ....Ps 60:9
a s tower from the enemy ...Ps 61:3
s is Your hand ....Ps 89:13
there is s confidence ......Prov 14:26
the LORD is a s tower ......Prov 18:10
A wise man is s ....Prov 24:5
s shall be as tinder ....Is 1:31
"We have a s city ....Is 26:1
She had s branches for ...Ezek 19:11
shall be as s as iron ....Dan 2:40
the weak say, 'I am s ......Joel 3:10
enter a s man's house .....Matt 12:29
one can enter a s man's ...Mark 3:27
When a s man ....Luke 11:21
We then who are s ....Rom 15:1
weak, but you are s ....1 Cor 4:10
I am weak, then I am s ..2 Cor 12:10
are weak and you are s ....2 Cor 13:9

my brethren, be s ....Eph 6:10
weakness were made s ....Heb 11:34
men, because you are s ..1 John 2:14
s is the Lord God ....Rev 18:8

STRONGER
weakness of God is s ......1 Cor 1:25

STRONGHOLD
crag of the rock and the s ..Job 39:28
of my salvation, my s ....Ps 18:2
down the trusted s ....Prov 21:22

STRUCK
s the rock twice ....Num 20:11
the hand of God has s .....Job 19:21
s all my enemies ....Ps 3:7
Behold, He s the rock ......Ps 78:20
I was angry and s ....Is 57:17
in My wrath I s ....Is 60:10
s the head from the ....Hab 3:13
I s you with blight ....Hag 2:17
took the reed and s ......Matt 27:30
the officers s Him with ...Mark 14:65
they s Him on the head ...Mark 15:19
Him, they s Him on the ...Luke 22:64
s Him with their hands ....John 19:3
and s down the Egyptian ...Acts 7:24

STUBBLE
shall bring forth s ....Is 33:11
his sword, as driven s ....Is 41:2
they shall be as s ....Is 47:14
s that passes ....Jer 13:24
do wickedly will be s ....Mal 4:1

STUBBORN
when Pharaoh was s about ..Ex 13:15
If a man has a s ....Deut 21:18
and s children ....Ezek 2:4

STUBBORN-HEARTED
"Listen to Me, you s ....Is 46:12

STUBBORNNESS
do not look on the s ....Deut 9:27

STUDENT
the teacher with the s .....1 Chr 25:8

STUDIED
having never s ....John 7:15

STUMBLE
causes them to s ....Ps 119:165
to make my steps s ....Ps 140:4
your foot will not s ....Prov 3:23
know what makes them s ...Prov 4:19
one will be weary or s ....Is 5:27
among them shall s ....Is 8:15
we s at noonday as at ....Is 59:10
that they might not s ....Is 63:13
before your feet s ....Jer 13:16
they will s and fall ....Jer 46:6
have caused many to s ....Mal 2:8
you will be made to s .....Matt 26:31
if all are made to s ....Matt 26:33
immediately they s ....Mark 4:17
who believe in Me to s ....Mark 9:42
s because of Me this .....Mark 14:27
the day, he does not s .....John 11:9
Who is made to s ....2 Cor 11:29
whole law, and yet s ......James 2:10
For we all s in many ....James 3:2

STUMBLED
and those who s ....1 Sam 2:4
God, for you have s ....Hos 14:1
s that they should ....Rom 11:11

STUMBLES
word, immediately he s ...Matt 13:21

STUMBLING
the deaf, nor put a s ....Lev 19:14
but a stone of s............Is 8:14
Behold, I will lay s ....Jer 6:21
watched for my s ....Jer 20:10
it became their s ....Ezek 7:19
stumbled at that s ....Rom 9:32

I lay in Zion a s .... Rom 9:33
this, not to put a s .... Rom 14:13
to the Jews a s .... 1 Cor 1:23
of yours become a s .... 1 Cor 8:9
and "A stone of s .... 1 Pet 2:8
is no cause for s .... 1 John 2:10
to keep you from s .... Jude 24

STUMBLING BLOCK
s out of the way .... Is 57:14
I lay a s before him .... Ezek 3:20
it became their s .... Ezek 7:19
s and a recompense .... Rom 11:9
not to put a s .... Rom 14:13
to the Jews a s .... 1 Cor 1:23
of yours become a s .... 1 Cor 8:9
taught Balak to put a s .... Rev 2:14

STUMP
whose s remains when it is .... Is 6:13
leave the s and roots ...... Dan 4:15

STUPID
and regarded as s .... Job 18:3
who hates correction is s ... Prov 12:1
Surely I am more s .... Prov 30:2

SUBDUE
s the peoples under us ...... Ps 47:3
shall s three kings .... Dan 7:24
s our iniquities .... Mic 7:19
s all things to .... Phil 3:21

SUBDUED
land was s before them .... Josh 18:1
So the Philistines were s .. 1 Sam 7:13
You have s under me those .. Ps 18:39
through faith s kingdoms .. Heb 11:33

SUBJECT
for it is not s .... Rom 8:7
Let every soul be s .... Rom 13:1
all things are made s ..... 1 Cor 15:28
Remind them to be s .... Titus 3:1
all their lifetime s .... Heb 2:15
having been made s .... 1 Pet 3:22

SUBJECTED
because of Him who s ..... Rom 8:20

SUBJECTION
put all things in s .... Heb 2:8
more readily be in s .... Heb 12:9

SUBMISSION
in silence with all s .... 1 Tim 2:11
his children in s .... 1 Tim 3:4

SUBMISSIVE
Wives, likewise, be s ...... 1 Pet 3:1
Yes, all of you be s .... 1 Pet 5:5

SUBMIT
s yourself under her hand .. Gen 16:9
Your enemies shall s .... Ps 66:3
Wives, s to your own ...... Eph 5:22
s to your own husbands .... Col 3:18
Therefore s to God .... James 4:7
s yourselves to every ...... 1 Pet 2:13
you younger people, s ...... 1 Pet 5:5

SUBSIDED
and the waters s .... Gen 8:1
the king's wrath s .... Esth 7:10

SUBSTANCE
Bless his s .... Deut 33:11
Your eyes saw my s .... Ps 139:16
up all the s of his house .... Prov 6:31
the LORD, and their s....... Mic 4:13
Now faith is the s of .... Heb 11:1

SUCCEED
For this will not s .... Num 14:41
you shall not s .... Jer 32:5

SUCCESS
please give me s .... Gen 24:12
You spoil my s .... Job 30:22
but wisdom brings s ...... Eccl 10:10

SUCCESSFUL
Joseph, and he was a s .... Gen 39:2

SUCCOTH
Place east of the Jordan, Judg 8:4, 5
Jacob's residence here, Gen 33:17
——— Israel's first camp, Ex 12:37

SUDDENLY
whom you seek, will s .... Mal 3:1
s there was with the ...... Luke 2:13

SUE
s you and take away .... Matt 5:40

SUFFER
for a stranger will s .... Prov 11:15
Son of Man must s many .. Mark 8:31
He must s many things .... Mark 9:12
Son of Man must s many .. Luke 9:22
He must s many things ... Luke 17:25
for the Christ to s .... Luke 24:46
that the Christ would s .... Acts 3:18
to s shame for His name .... Acts 5:41
s for My name's sake....... Acts 9:16
that the Christ had to s .... Acts 17:3
that the Christ would s .... Acts 26:23
Christ, if indeed we s ...... Rom 8:17
all the members s .... 1 Cor 12:26
sufferings which we also s .. 2 Cor 1:6
that they may not s .... Gal 6:12
in Him, but also to s .... Phil 1:29
we would s tribulation.... 1 Thess 3:4
s trouble as an .... 2 Tim 2:9
Jesus will s persecution ... 2 Tim 3:12
choosing rather to s ...... Heb 11:25
when you do good and s ... 1 Pet 2:20
even if you should s for .... 1 Pet 3:14
the will of God, to s .... 1 Pet 3:17
s as a murderer .... 1 Pet 4:15
Therefore let those who s .. 1 Pet 4:19
you are about to s .... Rev 2:10

SUFFERED
I have s many things ..... Matt 27:19
s many things from .... Mark 5:26
s these things and to ..... Luke 24:26
Have you s so many .... Gal 3:4
for whom I have s .... Phil 3:8
in that He Himself has s ... Heb 2:18
by the things which He s ... Heb 5:8
with His own blood, s ..... Heb 13:12
because Christ also s ...... 1 Pet 2:21
when He s, He did not ..... 1 Pet 2:23
For Christ also s .... 1 Pet 3:18
since Christ s .... 1 Pet 4:1
after you have s .... 1 Pet 5:10

SUFFERING
My eyes bring s .... Lam 3:51
Himself alive after His s by .. Acts 1:3
for the s of death crowned .. Heb 2:9
as an example of s .... James 5:10
Is anyone among you s ... James 5:13
forth as an example, s .... Jude 7

SUFFERINGS
I consider that the s .... Rom 8:18
share with me in the s..... 2 Tim 1:8
perfect through s .... Heb 2:10
great struggle with s ..... Heb 10:32
beforehand the s .... 1 Pet 1:11

SUFFERS
Love s long and is .... 1 Cor 13:4

SUFFICIENCY
but our s is from God...... 2 Cor 3:5
always having all s .... 2 Cor 9:8

SUFFICIENT
S for the day is its .... Matt 6:34
by the majority is s .... 2 Cor 2:6
Not that we are s .... 2 Cor 3:5

SUITABLE
by the hand of a s .... Lev 16:21

SUM
How great is the s .... Ps 139:17
s I obtained this .... Acts 22:28

SUMMED
commandment, are all s ... Rom 13:9

SUMMER
and heat, winter and s ... Gen 8:22
into the drought of s .... Ps 32:4
You have made s .... Ps 74:17
you know that s .... Matt 24:32

SUMPTUOUSLY
fine linen and fared s ..... Luke 16:19

SUN
So the s stood still ...... Josh 10:13
love Him be like the s ..... Judg 5:31
grows green in the s ...... Job 8:16
a tabernacle for the s ...... Ps 19:4
the LORD God is a s .... Ps 84:11
s shall not strike you ...... Ps 121:6
the s to rule by day ...... Ps 136:8
to behold the s .... Eccl 11:7
while the s and moon ..... Eccl 12:2
moon, clear as the s ...... Song 6:10
s will be sevenfold .... Is 30:26
s returned ten degrees ..... Is 38:8
s shall no longer be .... Is 60:19
s has gone down while ..... Jer 15:9
LORD, who gives the s .... Jer 31:35
the s and moon grow ...... Joel 2:10
s shall be turned .... Joel 2:31
s shall go down on the .... Mic 3:6
The s and moon stood ..... Hab 3:11
for He makes His s .... Matt 5:45
the s was darkened ...... Luke 23:45
is one glory of the s ..... 1 Cor 15:41
do not let the s .... Eph 4:26
s became black as .... Rev 6:12
s shall not strike .... Rev 7:16
had no need of the s ...... Rev 21:23

SUPPER
man gave a great s ...... Luke 14:16
to eat the Lord's S ...... 1 Cor 11:20
took the cup after s ..... 1 Cor 11:25
together for the s .... Rev 19:17

SUPPLICATION
s that you have made ...... 1 Kin 9:3
and make your s .... Job 8:5
LORD has heard my s........ Ps 6:9
to the LORD I made s .... Ps 30:8
Yourself from my s .... Ps 55:1
Let my s come before ..... Ps 119:170
They will make s .... Is 45:14
with all prayer and s ...... Eph 6:18
by prayer and s .... Phil 4:6

SUPPLICATIONS
Will he make many s to ... Job 41:3
of my s when I cry to You .... Ps 28:2
To the voice of my s ...... Ps 130:2
request by prayer and s ..... Dan 9:3
and continues in s and .... 1 Tim 5:5
offered up prayers and s .... Heb 5:7

SUPPLIES
Now may He who s .... 2 Cor 9:10
Therefore He who s .... Gal 3:5
by what every joint s ...... Eph 4:16

SUPPLY
s what was lacking .... Phil 2:30
And my God shall s .... Phil 4:19

SUPPORT
but the LORD was my s .. 2 Sam 22:19
this, that you must s ..... Acts 20:35

SUPPOSE
S there were fifty .... Gen 18:24
"But s they will not believe .... Ex 4:1
s that I came to give ..... Luke 12:51
not drunk, as you s .... Acts 2:15
who s that godliness is a .. 1 Tim 6:5
man s that he will receive .. James 1:7

SUPREME
to the king as s .... 1 Pet 2:13

SURE

s your sin will find .... Num 32:23
build him a s house ...... 1 Sam 2:35
but no man is s .... Job 24:22
testimony of the LORD is s ... Ps 19:7
all His precepts are s .... Ps 111:7
call and election s .... 2 Pet 1:10

SURETY

Be s for Your servant ..... Ps 119:122
one who hates being s .... Prov 11:15
Jesus has become a s ...... Heb 7:22

SURROUND

But you shall s .... 2 Kin 11:8
LORD, mercy shall s .... Ps 32:10

SURROUNDED

the waves of death s ...... 2 Sam 22:5
The pangs of death s .... Ps 18:4
The pains of death s .... Ps 116:3
All nations s me .... Ps 118:10
their own deeds have s ...... Hos 7:2
and the floods s .... Jon 2:3
also, since we are s .... Heb 12:1

SURVIVOR

was no refugee or s .... Lam 2:22

SUSANNA

Believing woman ministering to Christ,
Luke 8:2, 3

SUSPICIONS

reviling, evil s .... 1 Tim 6:4

SUSTAIN

You will s him on his .... Ps 41:3
of a man will s .... Prov 18:14
S me with cakes of .... Song 2:5

SUSTAINED

Forty years You s them ..... Neh 9:21
I awoke, for the LORD s me .... Ps 3:5
and My own fury, it s Me ..... Is 63:5

SWADDLING

thick darkness its s .... Job 38:9
Him in s cloths .... Luke 2:7

SWALLOW

like a flying s .... Prov 26:2
Like a crane or a s .... Is 38:14
s observe the time .... Jer 8:7
great fish to s Jonah .... Jon 1:17
a gnat and s a camel ...... Matt 23:24

SWALLOWED

Aaron's rod s up their rods ... Ex 7:12
the earth s them .... Ex 15:12
s me up like a monster ..... Jer 51:34
He has s up Israel .... Lam 2:5
"Death is s up in victory .. 1 Cor 15:54
s up with too much sorrow .. 2 Cor 2:7

SWEAR

shall I make you s ...... 1 Kin 22:16
in the earth shall s .... Is 65:16
s oaths by the LORD .... Zeph 1:5
'You shall not s .... Matt 5:33
began to curse and s ..... Matt 26:74
because He could s .... Heb 6:13
my brethren, do not s .... James 5:12

SWEARING

By s and lying .... Hos 4:2

SWEARS

he who s to his own .... Ps 15:4
everyone who s by Him ..... Ps 63:11
but whoever s by the ..... Matt 23:18

SWEAT

In the s of your face .... Gen 3:19
Then His s became like ... Luke 22:44

SWEET

it is a s aroma, an offering .. Ex 29:18
a s aroma to the LORD........ Lev 1:9
by fire as a s aroma to ..... Num 28:2
Though evil is s .... Job 20:12
valley shall be s to him .... Job 21:33

s are Your words .... Ps 119:103
my words, for they are s ..... Ps 141:6
his fruit was s to my taste .. Song 2:3
for your voice is s .... Song 2:14
His mouth is most s .... Song 5:16
shall drip with s wine .... Amos 9:13
but it will be as s .... Rev 10:9

SWEETER

"What is s than honey .... Judg 14:18
S also than honey and the ... Ps 19:10
s than honey to my .... Ps 119:103

SWEETNESS

'Should I cease my s ...... Judg 9:11
called prudent, and s ...... Prov 16:21
s of a man's friend gives ... Prov 27:9
mouth like honey in s ...... Ezek 3:3

SWELL

thigh rot and your belly s .. Num 5:21
their feet did not s .... Neh 9:21
your heart shall s with joy .... Is 60:5

SWELLING

they speak great s .... 2 Pet 2:18

SWEPT

his army shall be s away .. Dan 11:26
he finds it empty, s .... Matt 12:44

SWIFT

s as the eagle flies .... Deut 28:49
pass by like s ships .... Job 9:26
handles the bow, the s ..... Amos 2:15
let every man be s .... James 1:19

SWIFTLY

His word runs very s ...... Ps 147:15

SWIM

night I make my bed s .... Ps 6:6

SWINE

the s, though it divides ...... Lev 11:7
cast your pearls before s .... Matt 7:6
went into the herd of s ..... Matt 8:32
the pods that the s ate .... Luke 15:16

SWINE'S

ring of gold in a s snout ... Prov 11:22
in the midst, eating s flesh ... Is 66:17

SWOON

as they s like the .... Lam 2:12

SWORD

See TWO-EDGED SWORD
s which turned every ...... Gen 3:24
but not with your s .... Josh 24:12
the wicked with Your s ..... Ps 17:13
land by their own s .... Ps 44:3
my bow, nor shall my s ..... Ps 44:6
their tongue a sharp s ...... Ps 57:4
shall not lift up s .... Is 2:4
But he shall flee from the s ... Is 31:8
s shall be bathed .... Is 34:5
The s of the LORD is .... Is 34:6
And I will send a s .... Jer 9:16
will die by the s .... Ezek 7:15
'A s, a s is sharpened ..... Ezek 21:9
'A s, a s is drawn .... Ezek 21:28
Bow and s of battle I ...... Hos 2:18
people shall die by the s ... Amos 9:10
not lift up s against nation ... Mic 4:3
"Awake, O s .... Zech 13:7
to bring peace but a s ..... Matt 10:34
for all who take the s ..... Matt 26:52
s will pierce through ...... Luke 2:35
he does not bear the s ..... Rom 13:4
the s of the Spirit .... Eph 6:17
than any two-edged s ...... Heb 4:12
a sharp two-edged s .... Rev 1:16
mouth goes a sharp s ..... Rev 19:15

SWORDS

yet they were drawn s ...... Ps 55:21
shall beat their s .... Is 2:4
beat their s into plowshares .. Mic 4:3
look, here are two s ..... Luke 22:38

SWORE

So I s in My wrath .... Ps 95:11
So I s in My wrath .... Heb 3:11
and s by Him who lives ..... Rev 10:6

SWORN

"By Myself I have s ...... Gen 22:16
The LORD has s in .... Ps 132:11
I have s by Myself .... Is 45:23
"The LORD has s .... Heb 7:21

SYCAMORE

into a s tree to see Him .... Luke 19:4

SYCHAR

Town of Samaria; Jesus talks to
woman at well here, John 4:5–39

SYMBOLIC

which things are s .... Gal 4:24
It was s for the .... Heb 9:9

SYMBOLS

I have given s through ..... Hos 12:10

SYMPATHIZE

Priest who cannot s .... Heb 4:15

SYMPATHY

My s is stirred .... Hos 11:8

SYNAGOGUE

See RULER OF THE SYNAGOGUE
He went into the s .... Luke 4:16
he was a ruler of the s ..... Luke 8:41
in the s every Sabbath ..... Acts 18:4
but are a s of Satan .... Rev 2:9

SYRACUSE

City visited by Paul, Acts 28:12

SYRIANS

Abraham's kindred, Gen 22:20–23;
25:20
Hostile to Israel, 2 Sam 8:11–13;
10:6–19; 1 Kin 20:1–34; 22:1–38;
2 Kin 6:8–7:7
Defeated by Assyria, 2 Kin 16:9
Destruction of, foretold, Is 17:1–3
Gospel preached to, Acts 15:23, 41

SYRO-PHOENICIAN

Daughter of, freed of demon, Mark
7:25–31

TABERAH

Israelite camp; fire destroys many
there, Num 11:1–3

TABERNACLE

that is, the pattern of the t .. Ex 25:9
you shall make the t .... Ex 26:1
called it the t of meeting ..... Ex 33:7
did not depart from the t .... Ex 33:11
covered the t of meeting, ... Ex 40:34
t He shall hide me .... Ps 27:5
I will abide in Your t .... Ps 61:4
In Salem also is His t .... Ps 76:2
How lovely is Your t .... Ps 84:1
Let us go into His t .... Ps 132:7
quiet home, a t .... Is 33:20
has done violence to His t ... Lam 2:6
My t also shall be with t .. Ezek 37:27
You also took up the t ..... Acts 7:43
and will rebuild the t ...... Acts 15:16
the true t which the Lord .... Heb 8:2
and more perfect t .... Heb 9:11
the temple of the t of the .... Rev 15:5
Behold, the t .... Rev 21:3

TABERNACLES

See FEAST OF TABERNACLES
T for seven days to the .... Lev 23:34
Feast of T seven days .... Deut 16:13
us make here three t .... Matt 17:4
Feast of T was at hand ..... John 7:2

TABITHA

See DORCAS

TABLE

shall also make a *t* ....Ex 25:23
prepare a *t* before me ....Ps 23:5
t become a snare ....Ps 69:22
a *t* in the wilderness ......Ps 78:19
head as He sat at the *t* .....Matt 26:7
dogs under the *t* ....Mark 7:28
t in the Pharisee's house ...Luke 7:37
t become a snare ....Rom 11:9
of the Lord's *t* ....1 Cor 10:21

TABLES

t are full of vomit ....Is 28:8
and overturned the *t* ......Matt 21:12
of God and serve *t* ....Acts 6:2

TABLET

write them on the *t* ....Prov 3:3
is engraved on the *t* ....Jer 17:1

TABLETS

I will give you *t* of stone ....Ex 24:12
Cut two *t* of stone like the ...Ex 34:1
wrote on the *t* the words ....Ex 34:28
the two *t* of the Testimony ...Ex 34:29
wrote them on two *t* of ....Deut 4:13
God, not on *t* of stone ......2 Cor 3:3
and the *t* of the covenant ...Heb 9:4

TABOR

Scene of rally against Sisera, Judg 4:6,
12, 14

TADMOR

Trading center near Damascus, 2 Chr
8:4

TAHPANHES (or Tehaphnehes)

City of Egypt; refuge of fleeing Jews,
Jer 2:16; 44:1; Ezek 30:18

TAIL

hand and take it by the *t*" .....Ex 4:4
the head and not the *t* ....Deut 28:13
turned the foxes *t* to *t* ......Judg 15:4
He moves his *t* like a ......Job 40:17
t drew a third of the ....Rev 12:4

TAILS

They had *t* like scorpions, . . Rev 9:10
for their *t* are like serpents . . Rev 9:19

TAKE

You shall *t* with you seven . . . Gen 7:2
T now your son, your only . . Gen 22:2
I will *t* you as My people, ...Ex 6:7
You shall not *t* the name of . . Ex 20:7
I will *t* sickness away ....Ex 23:25
t off your ornaments, that ....Ex 33:5
I will *t* away My hand ......Ex 33:23
t us as Your inheritance ....Ex 34:9
T heed to yourself, lest .....Ex 34:12
shall not *t* vengeance ......Lev 19:18
to *t* the vow of a Nazirite ...Num 6:2
T heed to yourselves, lest ..Deut 4:23
You shall not *t* the name ...Deut 5:11
shall *t* oaths in His name ..Deut 6:13
add to it nor *t* away ....Deut 12:32
T your sandal off your ......Josh 5:15
God does not *t* away ....2 Sam 14:14
How long shall I *t* counsel ....Ps 13:2
t Your Holy Spirit ....Ps 51:11
I will not utterly *t* from .....Ps 89:33
His wings you shall *t* refuge ..Ps 91:4
I will *t* up the cup of ....Ps 116:13
t not the word of ....Ps 119:43
In You I *t* refuge............Ps 141:8
in You I *t* shelter ....Ps 143:9
T firm hold of instruction, . . Prov 4:13
and *t* away all your alloy .....Is 1:25
will *t* the heart of stone ...Ezek 36:26
t words with you ....Hos 14:2
t away your tunic, let him ...Matt 5:40
does not *t* his cross ....Matt 10:38
T My yoke upon ....Matt 11:29
t up his cross, and ....Matt 16:24
T what is yours and ....Matt 20:14

t You in, or naked and ....Matt 25:38
and you did not *t* Me in ...Matt 25:43
T. eat; this is My body ....Matt 26:26
and *t* up his cross ....Mark 8:34
t up the cross, and ....Mark 10:21
T, eat; this is My body ....Mark 14:22
T this cup away ....Mark 14:36
t up his cross daily, and ...Luke 9:23
My life that I may *t* ....John 10:17
I urge you to *t* heart ......Acts 27:22
T, eat; this is My body ....1 Cor 11:24
Therefore *t* up the whole ...Eph 6:13

TAKE HEED

T to yourself and see ....Ex 10:28
'*T* to yourselves that ......Ex 19:12
T to yourself, lest you ......Ex 34:12
t to speak what the Lord ...Num 23:12
t, lest you lift your eyes ....Deut 4:19
your sons *t* to their way ....1 Kin 2:4
T, do not turn to iniquity ...Job 36:21
T, and be quiet ....Is 7:4
t, you peoples from afar ......Is 49:1
Everyone *t* to his neighbor ....Jer 9:4
t to your spirit ....Mal 2:15
T that you do not do ....Matt 6:1
"*T* and beware of the ......Matt 16:6
T that you do not ....Matt 18:10
"*T* that no one deceives ....Matt 24:4
"*T* what you hear ....Mark 4:24
t; see, I have told you ....Mark 13:23
T, watch and pray ......Mark 13:33
t that the light ....Luke 11:35
"*T* and beware ....Luke 12:15
t to yourselves, lest ......Luke 21:34
t how he builds on it ......1 Cor 3:10
stands *t* lest he fall ....1 Cor 10:12
"*T* to the ministry..........Col 4:17
T to yourself and to ......1 Tim 4:16

TAKEN

t from man He made into ...Gen 2:22
because she was *t* out of ....Gen 2:23
for out of it you were *t* ....Gen 3:19
have you *t* us away to die ...Ex 14:11
But the LORD has *t* you....Deut 4:20
t the wife of Uriah ......2 Sam 12:10
and the LORD has *t* away ....Job 1:21
God has *t* away my justice ...Job 34:5
you are *t* by the words ......Prov 6:2
He was *t* from prison ....Is 53:8
righteous is *t* away from ......Is 57:1
of God will be *t* from ......Matt 21:43
one will be *t* and the ......Matt 24:40
what he has will be *t* ......Mark 4:25
He was *t* up ....Acts 1:9
veil is *t* away in Christ ....2 Cor 3:14
until He is *t* out of ....2 Thess 2:7
By faith Enoch was *t* ......Heb 11:5

TAKES

who *t* His name in vain ....Ex 20:7
LORD *t* pleasure in those....Ps 147:11
For the LORD *t* pleasure in . . . Ps 149:4
than he who *t* a city ....Prov 16:32
does not bear fruit He *t* ....John 15:2

TAKING

the fruit of *t* away his sin ....Is 27:9
t Him up on a high ......Luke 4:5
t the shield of faith with ....Eph 6:16
t the form of a bondservant . . Phil 2:7

TALEBEARER

not go about as a *t* ......Lev 19:16
t reveals secrets ....Prov 11:13

TALENT

went and hid your *t* ......Matt 25:25

TALENTS

owed him ten thousand *t* . . Matt 18:24
to one he gave five *t* ......Matt 25:15

TALITHA

T, cumi," which is ....Mark 5:41

TALK

shall *t* of them when ....Deut 6:7

t be vindicated ....Job 11:2
with unprofitable *t* ....Job 15:3
My tongue also shall *t* ......Ps 71:24
entangle Him in His *t* ....Matt 22:15
I will no longer *t* ....John 14:30
turned aside to idle *t* ......1 Tim 1:6

TALKED

within us while He *t* ....Luke 24:32

TALKERS

both idle *t* and ....Titus 1:10

TALL

and *t* as the Anakim ....Deut 2:10
to a nation *t* and ....Is 18:2

TAMAR

Wife of Er and mother of Perez and
Zerah, Gen 38:6–30
—— Absalom's sister, 2 Sam 13:1–32

TAMBOURINE

They sing to the *t* ....Job 21:12
The mirth of the *t* ....Is 24:8

TAME

no man can *t* the tongue ...James 3:8

TANNER

in Joppa with Simon, a *t* ...Acts 9:43

TAPESTRY

She makes *t* for herself ...Prov 31:22

TARES

the *t* also appeared ....Matt 13:26

TARGET

You set me as Your *t* ....Job 7:20
and set me up as a *t* ....Lam 3:12

TARRY

who turns aside to *t* ....Jer 14:8
come and will not *t* ....Heb 10:37

TARSHISH

City at a great distance from Palestine,
Jon 1:3
Ships of, noted in commerce, Ps 48:7

TARSUS

Paul's birthplace, Acts 21:39
Saul sent to, Acts 9:30
Visited by Barnabas, Acts 11:25

TARTAN

Sent to fight against Jerusalem, 2 Kin
18:17

TASK

your *t* in making brick both . . Ex 5:14
this burdensome *t* ....Eccl 1:13

TASKMASTERS

Therefore they set *t* over .....Ex 1:11

TASSELS

Tell them to make *t* on . . . Num 15:38
shall make *t* on the four . . Deut 22:12

TASTE

the *t* of it was like wafers ...Ex 16:31
and its *t* was like the ......Num 11:8
Oh, *t* and see that the ......Ps 34:8
are Your words to my *t* ...Ps 119:103
was sweet to my *t* ....Song 2:3
not *t* death till they see ...Mark 9:1
shall *t* my supper ....Luke 14:24
Do not touch, do not *t* ......Col 2:21
might *t* death for ....Heb 2:9

TASTED

But when He had *t* ......Matt 27:34
t the heavenly gift ....Heb 6:4
t the good word ....Heb 6:5
t that the Lord is ....1 Pet 2:3

TATTENAI

Persian governor opposing the Jews,
Ezra 5:3, 6

TAUGHT

O God, You have *t* ....Ps 71:17
as His counselor has *t* ....Is 40:13

the synagogue and *t* ...... Mark 1:21
He *t* them many things by . Mark 4:2
presence, and You *t* .....Luke 13:26
they shall be all be *t* ......John 6:45
but as My Father *t* ....John 8:28
that they *t* the people and .. Acts 4:2
t accurately the things of .. Acts 18:25
from man, nor was I *t* .....Gal 1:12
and have been *t* by Him . Eph 4:21
the faith, as you have been *t* .. Col 2:7
which you were *t* ......2 Thess 2:15

TAUNT
and a byword, a *t* ....Jer 24:9

TAX
t collectors do the ....Matt 5:46
received the temple *t* .....Matt 17:24
I say to you that *t* ....Matt 21:31
Show Me the *t* ....Matt 22:19

TAX COLLECTOR
Matthew the *t* ....Matt 10:3
like heathen and a *t* .....Matt 18:17
a *t* named Levi ....Luke 5:27
and the other a *t* ....Luke 18:10
who was a chief *t* ....Luke 19:2

TAX COLLECTORS AND SINNERS
your Teacher eat with *t* .. Matt 9:11
He eats and drinks with *t* . Mark 2:16
winebibber, a friend of *t* ... Luke 7:34

TAXES
take customs or *t* ....Matt 17:25
Is it lawful to pay *t* ......Matt 22:17
forbidding to pay *t* ......Luke 23:2
t to whom *t* ....Rom 13:7

TEACH
t them to your children .....Deut 4:9
t them diligently ....Deut 6:7
t Jacob Your judgments ..Deut 33:10
t you the good and the .. 1 Sam 12:23
"Can anyone *t* ....Job 21:22
"I will *t* you about ....Job 27:11
t me what I do not see ....Job 34:32
t me Your paths ....Ps 25:4
T me Your way ....Ps 27:11
t you the fear of the ....Ps 34:11
t You awesome things .....Ps 45:4
t transgressors Your ....Ps 51:13
So *t* us to number our ......Ps 90:12
T me Your statutes ....Ps 119:12
He will *t* us His ways ....Is 2:3
"Whom will he *t* ....Is 28:9
every man *t* his neighbor ...Jer 31:34
a bribe, her priests *t* ....Mic 3:11
t the way of God in ....Matt 22:16
He began to *t* them .....Mark 6:34
t us to pray, as John also .. Luke 11:1
the Holy Spirit will *t* .....Luke 12:12
in My name, He will *t* ....John 14:26
you not to *t* in this name ...Acts 5:28
therefore, who *t* another .. Rom 2:21
even nature itself *t* ......1 Cor 11:14
permit a woman to *t* .....1 Tim 2:12
things command and *t* ....1 Tim 4:11
T and exhort these ....1 Tim 6:2
t you again the first ....Heb 5:12
not need that anyone *t* .. 1 John 2:27

TEACHER
for One is your *T* ....Matt 23:8
T, do You not care that .... Mark 4:38
asked Him, "Good *T* ....Mark 10:17
know that You are a *T* .....John 3:2
T, this woman was caught .. John 8:4
T has come and is ....John 11:28
You call Me *T* ....John 13:13
named Gamaliel, a *t* .....Acts 5:34
a *t* of babes, having ....Rom 2:20
a *t* of the Gentiles in ......1 Tim 2:7

TEACHERS
than all my *t* ....Ps 119:99

t will not be moved ....Is 30:20
prophets, third *t* ....1 Cor 12:28
and some pastors and *t* .....Eph 4:11
desiring to be *t* ....1 Tim 1:7
time you ought to be *t* .....Heb 5:12
of you become *t* ....James 3:1
there will be false *t* ....2 Pet 2:1

TEACHES
therefore He *t* sinners ....Ps 25:8
He who *t* man knowledge ...Ps 94:10
t men so, shall be called ....Matt 5:19
the Holy Spirit *t* ....1 Cor 2:13
If anyone *t* otherwise ......1 Tim 6:3
the same anointing *t* ....1 John 2:27

TEACHING
t them to observe all .....Matt 28:20
were astonished at His *t* ... Mark 1:22
Me, *t* as doctrines the .....Mark 7:7
they did not cease *t* ....Acts 5:42
he who teaches, in *t* ....Rom 12:7
by prophesying, or by *t* ....1 Cor 14:6
t every man in all ....Col 1:28
t things which they ....Titus 1:11
t us that ....Titus 2:12

TEAR
t yourself in anger ....Job 18:4
lest they *t* me like a ....Ps 7:2
I, even I, will *t* ....Hos 5:14
feet, and turn and *t* ....Matt 7:6
will wipe away every *t* ......Rev 21:4

TEARS
I have seen your *t* ....2 Kin 20:5
my couch with my *t* ....Ps 6:6
t have been my food ....Ps 42:3
with the bread of *t* ....Ps 80:5
drench you with my *t* ....Is 16:9
God will wipe away *t* ....Is 25:8
eyes may run with *t* ....Jer 9:18
My eyes fail with *t* ....Lam 2:11
His feet with her *t* ....Luke 7:38
night and day with *t* ......Acts 20:31
mindful of your *t* ....2 Tim 1:4
vehement cries and *t* ......Heb 5:7
it diligently with *t* ....Heb 12:17

TEETH
t whiter than milk ....Gen 49:12
by the skin of my *t* ....Job 19:20
You have broken the *t* ....Ps 3:7
As vinegar to the *t* .....Prov 10:26
you cleanness of *t* ....Amos 4:6
and gnashing of *t* ....Matt 8:12

TEKOA
Home of a wise woman, 2 Sam 14:2,
4, 9
Home of Amos, Amos 1:1

TELL
that you may *t* it to ....Ps 48:13
the message that I *t* ....Jon 3:2
Who can *t* if God ....Jon 3:9
t him his fault ....Matt 18:15
whatever they *t* ....Matt 23:3
He comes, He will *t* ....John 4:25

TEMAN
Tribe in northeast Edom, Gen 36:34
Judgment pronounced against, Amos
1:12
God appears from, Hab 3:3

TEMPERATE
for the prize is *t* in all .....1 Cor 9:25
husband of one wife, *t* .....1 Tim 3:2

TEMPEST
the windy storm and *t* ......Ps 55:8
one, tossed with *t* ....Is 54:11
And suddenly a great *t* .....Matt 8:24

TEMPLE
So Solomon built the *t* ... 1 Kin 6:14
build a *t* for the LORD .....2 Chr 2:12
t for the name of the LORD .. 2 Chr 6:7

of the LORD filled the *t* .....2 Chr 7:1
LORD is in His holy *t* ....Ps 11:4
to inquire in His *t* ....Ps 27:4
The *t* of the LORD ....Jer 7:4
suddenly come to His *t* ......Mal 3:1
One greater than the *t* .....Matt 12:6
murdered between the *t* .. Matt 23:35
veil of the *t* was torn ....Matt 27:51
found Him in the *t* ....Luke 2:46
"Destroy this *t* ....John 2:19
was speaking of the *t* .....John 2:21
one accord in the *t* ....Acts 2:46
the Beautiful Gate of the *t* .. Acts 3:10
that you are the *t* ....1 Cor 3:16
your body is the *t* ....1 Cor 6:19
grows into a holy *t* ....Eph 2:21
sits as God in the *t* ....2 Thess 2:4
Then the *t* of God was .....Rev 11:19
But I saw no *t* in it ....Rev 21:22
and the Lamb are its *t* .....Rev 21:22

TEMPLES
t made with hands ....Acts 7:48

TEMPORARY
which are seen are *t* ......2 Cor 4:18

TEMPT
Why do you *t* the LORD ......Ex 17:2
You shall not *t* the LORD ... Deut 6:16
they even *t* God ....Mal 3:15
t the LORD your God ....Matt 4:7
that Satan does not *t* ......1 Cor 7:5
nor let us *t* Christ ....1 Cor 10:9
nor does He Himself *t* ....James 1:13

TEMPTATION
do not lead us into *t* ....Matt 6:13
lest you enter into *t* ....Matt 26:41
in time of *t* fall away ......Luke 8:13
And do not lead us into *t*, .. Luke 11:4
t has overtaken you ......1 Cor 10:13
to be rich fall into *t* ....1 Tim 6:9
the man who endures *t* ...James 1:12

TEMPTED
because they *t* the LORD .....Ex 17:7
again and again they *t* God .. Ps 78:41
forty days, *t* by Satan .....Mark 1:13
being *t* for forty days by ....Luke 4:2
not allow you to be *t* .....1 Cor 10:13
lest you also be *t* ....Gal 6:1
has suffered, being *t* ....Heb 2:18
in all points *t* ....Heb 4:15
he is *t*, "I am *t* by God" ...James 1:13
But each one is *t* ....James 1:14

TEMPTER
Now when the *t* came ......Matt 4:3

TEN
t should be found ....Gen 18:32
the *T* Commandments ......Ex 34:28
David his *t* thousands .... 1 Sam 18:7
or go backward *t* ....2 Kin 20:9
an instrument of *t* strings ....Ps 92:3
test your servants for *t* ....Dan 1:12
before it, and it had *t* horns .. Dan 7:7
The *t* horns are *t* kings .....Dan 7:24
owed him *t* thousand ....Matt 18:24
him who has *t* talents ....Matt 25:28
there met Him *t* men .....Luke 17:12
t horns, and seven ....Rev 12:3
seven heads and *t* horns ....Rev 13:1
The *t* horns which you .....Rev 17:12

TEND
to him, "*T* My sheep ......John 21:16

TENDER
your heart was *t* ....2 Kin 22:19
t shoots will not ....Job 14:7
Let Your *t* mercies come ....Ps 79:8
Your *t* mercies come to ....Ps 119:77
no more be called *t* ....Is 47:1
through the *t* mercy of ....Luke 1:78
put on *t* mercies ....Col 3:12

TENDERHEARTED
to one another, t .... Eph 4:32
love as brothers, be t ...... 1 Pet 3:8

TENDS
t a flock and does not ..... 1 Cor 9:7

TENT
pitched his t in the .... Gen 26:17
it was, hidden in his t .... Josh 7:22
Israel, every man to his t .... Judg 7:8
shall know that your t ...... Job 5:24
like a shepherd's t .... Is 38:12
the place of your t .... Is 54:2
My t is plundered .... Jer 10:20
earthly house, this t .... 2 Cor 5:1
long as I am in this t ...... 2 Pet 1:13
I must put off my t .... 2 Pet 1:14

TENTH
I will surely give a t to .... Gen 28:22
the t one shall be holy to .. Lev 27:32
to the LORD, a t of the .... Num 18:26
shall bring up a t of ...... Neh 10:38
Abraham gave a t part of .... Heb 7:2

TENTMAKERS
occupation they were t ..... Acts 18:3

TENTS
those who dwell in t .... Gen 4:20
"How lovely are your t .... Num 24:5
The t of robbers .... Job 12:6
than dwell in the t .... Ps 84:10
is in the t of the righteous .. Ps 118:15
I dwell among the t .... Ps 120:5
LORD will save the t ...... Zech 12:7

TERAH
Father of Abram, Gen 11:26
Idolater, Josh 24:2
Dies in Haran, Gen 11:25–32

TEREBINTH
far as the t tree of Moreh ... Gen 12:6
dwelt by the t trees of ..... Gen 13:18
sat under the t tree which .. Judg 6:11
as a t tree or as an oak, ... Is 6:13

TERRESTRIAL
bodies and t bodies ...... 1 Cor 15:40

TERRIBLE
t wilderness .... Deut 1:19
haughtiness of the t .... Is 13:11
is great and very t .... Joel 2:11

TERRIFIED
to you, 'Do not be t .... Deut 1:29
Therefore I am t at His .... Job 23:15
by Your wrath we are t ..... Ps 90:7
But they were t .... Luke 24:37
and not in any way t ...... Phil 1:28

TERRIFIES
and the Almighty t .... Job 23:16

TERRIFY
me with dreams and t ...... Job 7:14
not let dread of Him t ...... Job 9:34
are coming to t them ...... Zech 1:21

TERRIFYING
t was the sight .... Heb 12:21

TERRITORY
smite all your t with frogs .... Ex 8:2
bring locusts into your t ..... Ex 10:4
the t of their inheritance .. Josh 19:41
all the t of Israel .... Judg 19:29
He restored the t of ...... 2 Kin 14:25

TERROR
the t of God was upon the .. Gen 35:5
there shall be t .... Deut 32:25
are nothing, you see t ...... Job 6:21
from God is a t .... Job 31:23
not be afraid of the t ...... Ps 91:5
from the t of the LORD and .... Is 2:10
t to fall on them suddenly ... Jer 15:8
I will make you a t .... Jer 20:4

but a great t fell .... Dan 10:7
the t of the Lord, we ...... 2 Cor 5:11

TERRORS
the t of God are .... Job 6:4
T frighten him on .... Job 18:11
before the king of t .... Job 18:14
T overtake him like a ...... Job 27:20
consumed with t .... Ps 73:19

TERTULLUS
Orator who accuses Paul, Acts 24:1–8

TEST
God has come to t you ..... Ex 20:20
that He might t Israel by .... Judg 3:1
t him with hard .... 1 Kin 10:1
behold, His eyelids t .... Ps 11:4
ask, nor will I t the LORD ... Is 7:12
You who t the righteous, ... Jer 20:12
t them as gold is .... Zech 13:9
said, "Why do you t ...... Matt 22:18
But this He said to t him .... John 6:6
t the Spirit of the .... Acts 5:9
why do you t God by ...... Acts 15:10
and the fire will t .... 1 Cor 3:13
T yourselves .... 2 Cor 13:5
T all things .... 1 Thess 5:21
but t the spirits .... 1 John 4:1
to t those who dwell on .... Rev 3:10

TESTAMENT
where there is a t .... Heb 9:16
For a t is in force .... Heb 9:17

TESTATOR
be the death of the t ...... Heb 9:16

TESTED
that God t Abraham .... Gen 22:1
You have t my heart .... Ps 17:3
And they t God in .... Ps 78:18
t you at the waters of ...... Ps 81:7
When your fathers t .... Ps 95:9
t them ten days .... Dan 1:14
also first be t .... 1 Tim 3:10
Where your fathers t .... Heb 3:9
though it is t by fire ...... 1 Pet 1:7
t those who say they ...... Rev 2:2

TESTIFIED
Yet the LORD t against.... 2 Kin 17:13
who sent Me, has t of Me .. John 5:37
he who has seen has t .... John 19:35
for as you have t .... Acts 23:11
t beforehand the .... 1 Pet 1:11
of God which He has t .... 1 John 5:9
t of the truth that is in you .. 3 John 3

TESTIFIES
and heard, that He t ...... John 3:32
that the Holy Spirit t ..... Acts 20:23

TESTIFY
yes, your own lips t .... Job 15:6
You, and our sins t .... Is 59:12
T against Me .... Mic 6:3
t what We have .... John 3:11
these are they which t ..... John 5:39
to t to the gospel of the ... Acts 20:24
t that the Father .... 1 John 4:14
sent My angel to t .... Rev 22:16

TESTIFYING
was righteous, God t ...... Heb 11:4
t that this is .... 1 Pet 5:12

TESTIMONIES
those who keep His t .... Ps 119:2
for I have kept Your t ...... Ps 119:22
t are my meditation .... Ps 119:99
I love Your t .... Ps 119:119
t are wonderful .... Ps 119:129

TESTIMONY
two tablets of the T .... Ex 31:18
be put to death on the t .... Deut 17:6
For He established a t ...... Ps 78:5
that I may keep the t ...... Ps 119:88

Bind up the t .... Is 8:16
under your feet as a t ..... Mark 6:11
Now this is the t .... John 1:19
no one receives His t ...... John 3:32
who has received His t ..... John 3:33
in your law that the t ...... John 8:17
and we know that his t .... John 21:24
declaring to you the t ..... 1 Cor 2:1
obtained a good t .... Heb 11:2
he had this t .... Heb 11:5
not believed the t .... 1 John 5:10
And this is the t .... 1 John 5:11
for the t which they held .... Rev 6:9
and by the word of their t .. Rev 12:11
For the t of Jesus is ...... Rev 19:10

TESTING
is t you to know whether .. Deut 13:3
t the mind and the heart, ... Jer 11:20
came to Him, t Him ...... Matt 19:3
knowing that the t .... James 1:3

TESTS
the righteous God t .... Ps 7:9
The LORD t the righteous ..... Ps 11:5
gold, but the LORD t ...... Prov 17:3
men, but God who t ..... 1 Thess 2:4

TETRARCH
Herod being t of Galilee ... Luke 3:1
Now Herod the t heard of .. Luke 9:7
with Herod the t .... Acts 13:1

THADDAEUS
One of the Twelve, Mark 3:18

THANK
t offerings into the ...... 2 Chr 29:31
"I t You and praise .... Dan 2:23
"I t You, Father .... Matt 11:25
t that servant because .... Luke 17:9
t You that I am not ...... Luke 18:11
First, I t my God .... Rom 1:8
t God without ceasing .. 1 Thess 2:13
t Christ Jesus our .... 1 Tim 1:12

THANKFUL
Be t to Him.............. Ps 100:4
Him as God, nor were t .... Rom 1:21

THANKFULNESS
Felix, with all t .... Acts 24:3

THANKS
give t to the LORD, for.... 1 Chr 16:34
and giving t to the LORD.... Ezra 3:11
grave who will give You t .... Ps 6:5
give t! For Your wondrous ... Ps 75:1
is good to give t to the LORD .. Ps 92:1
give t to the LORD, for He.... Ps 107:1
give t to the LORD, for He... Ps 136:1
the cup, and gave t ...... Matt 26:27
she gave t to the Lord ..... Luke 2:38
at His feet, giving Him t .. Luke 17:16
t He distributed them .... John 6:11
for he gives God t .... Rom 14:6
when He had given t .... 1 Cor 11:24
But t be to God, who .... 1 Cor 15:57
T be to God for His ...... 2 Cor 9:15
giving t always for .... Eph 5:20
t can we render .... 1 Thess 3:9
in everything give t ..... 1 Thess 5:18
We give You t, O Lord .... Rev 11:17

THANKSGIVING
with the voice of t .... Ps 26:7
Offer to God t .... Ps 50:14
His presence with t .... Ps 95:2
into His gates with t ...... Ps 100:4
the sacrifices of t .... Ps 107:22
supplication, with t .... Phil 4:6
vigilant in it with t .... Col 4:2
to be received with t ..... 1 Tim 4:3
glory and wisdom, t and ... Rev 7:12

THE-LORD-IS-MY-BANNER
and called its name, T ..... Ex 17:15

THE-LORD-IS-PEACE
the LORD, and called it T ... Judg 6:24

THE-LORD-WILL-PROVIDE
the name of the place, T . . . Gen 22:14

THEATER
and rushed into the t . . . . . Acts 19:29

THEOPHILUS
Luke addresses his writings to, Luke
1:3; Acts 1:1

THESSALONICA
Paul preaches in, Acts 17:1–13
Paul writes letters to churches of,
1 Thess 1:1

THICK
T swarms of flies came into . . Ex 8:24
there was t darkness in all . . Ex 10:22
I come to you in the t cloud . . Ex 19:9
cloud, and t darkness . . . . . Deut 4:11
T clouds cover Him, so . . . . . Job 22:14
t darkness its swaddling . . . . Job 38:9
and t clouds of the skies . . . . Ps 18:11
t darkness, like the . . . . Joel 2:2
of clouds and t darkness, . . Zeph 1:15

THIEF
When you saw a t . . . . Ps 50:18
do not despise a t . . . . Prov 6:30
t hates his own life . . . . . . Prov 29:24
t is ashamed when he . . . . . . Jer 2:26
the windows like a t . . . . Joel 2:9
t shall be expelled . . . . Zech 5:3
known what hour the t . . . Matt 24:43
t approaches nor moth . . . Luke 12:33
way, the same is a t . . . . . . John 10:1
because he was a t . . . . John 12:6
Lord will come as a t . . . . . . 2 Pet 3:10
upon you as a t . . . . Rev 3:3
I am coming as a t . . . . . . Rev 16:15

THIEVES
And companions of t . . . . Is 1:23
a den of t in your eyes . . . . . . Jer 7:11
destroy and where t . . . . Matt 6:19
have made it a den of t . . . Matt 21:13
and fell among t . . . . Luke 10:30
before Me and t . . . . John 10:8

THIGH
put your hand under my t . . Gen 24:2
Also the right t you shall . . . . Lev 7:32
LORD makes your t rot . . . Num 5:21
them hip and t with a . . . . . Judg 15:8
Your sword upon Your t . . . . . Ps 45:3
good piece, the t . . . . Ezek 24:4

THINGS
in heaven give good t . . . . . Matt 7:11
evil, speak good t . . . . Matt 12:34
kept all these t . . . . Luke 2:51
Lazarus evil t . . . . Luke 16:25
the Scriptures the t . . . . . . Luke 24:27
share in all good t . . . . Gal 6:6

THINGS OF GOD
search out the deep t . . . . Job 11:7
not mindful of the t . . . . . . Matt 16:23
not mindful of the t . . . . . . Mark 8:33
things, yes, the deep t . . . . . 1 Cor 2:10

THINK
nor does his heart t . . . . Is 10:7
let none of you t evil in . . . . Zech 8:17
Do not t that I came to . . . . Matt 5:17
t that they will be . . . . Matt 6:7
t you have eternal . . . . John 5:39
not to t of himself . . . . Rom 12:3
I t I also have the Spirit . . . 1 Cor 7:40
of ourselves to t . . . . 2 Cor 3:5
let no one t me a fool . . . . 2 Cor 11:16
all that we ask or t . . . . Eph 3:20

THINKS
yet the LORD t upon me . . . . . Ps 40:17
for as he t in his . . . . Prov 23:7
t that he knows . . . . 1 Cor 8:2
t he stands take heed . . . . 1 Cor 10:12

For if anyone t . . . . Gal 6:3
t he is religious . . . . James 1:26

THIRD
morning were the t day . . . Gen 1:13
the end of every t year . . . . Deut 14:28
the t the face of a lion . . . . Ezek 10:14
a t kingdom of bronze, ... Dan 2:39
on the t day He will raise . . . Hos 6:2
and be raised the t day . . . . Matt 16:21
went out about the t hour . . Matt 20:3
again, and prayed the t . . . Matt 26:44
He will rise the t day . . . . . Mark 9:31
the t day He will rise . . . . Mark 10:34
He came the t time . . . . . . Mark 14:41
Now it was the t hour . . . . Mark 15:25
and be raised the t day . . . . Luke 9:22
the t day He will rise . . . . . Luke 18:33
and the t day rise again . . . Luke 24:7
rise from the dead the t . . . Luke 24:46
He said to him the t . . . . . . John 21:17
caught up to the t heaven . 2 Cor 12:2
the t living creature had a . . . Rev 4:7
When He opened the t seal . . Rev 6:5
t of the trees were burned . . Rev 8:7
the t woe is coming . . . . . . Rev 11:14
Then the t angel poured . . . Rev 16:4

THIRD DAY
the morning were the t . . . . Gen 1:13
t the Lord will come down . . Ex 19:11
t must be burned . . . . Lev 7:17
any remains until the t . . . . . Lev 19:6
the unclean on the t . . . . . . Num 19:19
t you shall go up . . . . 2 Kin 20:5
t He will raise us up . . . . Hos 6:2
be raised again the t . . . . . Matt 16:21
t He will be raised up . . . . . Matt 17:23
t He will rise again . . . . . . Matt 20:19
made secure until the t . . . Matt 27:64
He will rise the t . . . . Mark 9:31
t He will rise again . . . . . . Mark 10:34
and be raised the t . . . . Luke 9:22
t I shall be perfected . . . . . Luke 13:32
t He will rise again . . . . . . Luke 18:33
and the t rise again . . . . . . Luke 24:7
today is the t since . . . . . . Luke 24:21
rise from the dead the t . . . Luke 24:46
God raised up on the t . . . . Acts 10:40
He rose again the t . . . . 1 Cor 15:4

THIRST
out of the rock for their t . . . Neh 9:15
tongues fail for t . . . . Is 41:17
those who hunger and t . . . Matt 5:6
give him who will never t . . John 4:14
in Me shall never t . . . . John 6:35
said, "I t!" . . . . John 19:28
we both hunger and t . . . . . 1 Cor 4:11
anymore nor t anymore . . . . Rev 7:16

THIRSTS
My soul t for God . . . . Ps 42:2
saying, "If anyone t . . . . . . John 7:37
freely to him who t . . . . Rev 21:6
And let him who t . . . . Rev 22:17

THIRSTY
and t land where there is . . . . . Ps 63:1
longs for You like a t land . . Ps 143:6
and if he is t . . . . Prov 25:21
as when a t man dreams . . . . . Is 29:8
the drink of the t . . . . Is 32:6
t land springs of . . . . Is 35:7
on him who is t . . . . Is 44:3
but you shall be t . . . . Is 65:13
in a dry and t land . . . . Ezek 19:13
I was t and you gave . . . . . Matt 25:35
we see You hungry or t . . . Matt 25:44
if he is t . . . . Rom 12:20

THIRTY
Joseph was t years old . . . . Gen 41:46
t years old and above . . . . . . Num 4:3
t pieces of silver . . . . Matt 26:15
at about t years of age, ... Luke 3:23

THIS GENERATION
righteous before me in t . . . Gen 7:1
preserve them from t . . . . Ps 12:7
what shall I liken t . . . . . . Matt 11:16
in the judgment with t . . . . Matt 12:41
things will come upon t . . . Matt 23:36
t will by no means pass . . . Matt 24:34
"Why does t seek a sign . . Mark 8:12
Son of Man will be to t . . . Luke 11:30
it shall be required of t . . . Luke 11:51
and be rejected by t . . . . . Luke 17:25
t will by no means . . . . Luke 21:32

THISTLES
t grow instead of . . . . Job 31:40
or figs from t . . . . Matt 7:16

THOMAS
Apostle of Christ, Matt 10:3
Ready to die with Christ, John 11:16
Doubts Christ's resurrection, John
20:24–29

THORN
t that goes into the . . . . Prov 26:9
t shall come up the . . . . Is 55:13
a t in the flesh was . . . . . . 2 Cor 12:7

THORNBUSHES
gather grapes from t . . . . . . Matt 7:16

THORNS
Both t and thistles it . . . . Gen 3:18
T and snares are . . . . Prov 22:5
all overgrown with t . . . . . . Prov 24:31
the crackling of t . . . . Eccl 7:6
Like a lily among t . . . . Song 2:2
and do not sow among t . . . . Jer 4:3
wheat but reaped t . . . . Jer 12:13
And some fell among t . . . . Matt 13:7
twisted a crown of t . . . . . . Matt 27:29
the ones sown among t . . . Mark 4:18
wearing the crown of t . . . . John 19:5

THOUGHT
t is that your houses . . . . Ps 49:11
You t that I was . . . . Ps 50:21
Both the inward t . . . . Ps 64:6
I t about my ways . . . . Ps 119:59
You understand my t . . . . . . Ps 139:2
"Surely, as I have t . . . . Is 14:24
to man what his t . . . . Amos 4:13
perceiving the t . . . . Luke 9:47
And he t within . . . . Luke 12:17
because you t that the gift . . Acts 8:20
t he was seeing a vision . . . . Acts 12:9
I t as a child . . . . 1 Cor 13:11
God, bringing every t . . . . . 2 Cor 10:5
will he be t worthy who . . . Heb 10:29

THOUGHTS
the intent of the t . . . . 1 Chr 28:9
is in none of his t . . . . Ps 10:4
t toward us . . . . Ps 40:5
t are very deep . . . . Ps 92:5
The LORD knows the t . . . . . . Ps 94:11
t will be established . . . . . . Prov 16:3
unrighteous man his t . . . . . . Is 55:7
For My t are not your . . . . Is 55:8
long shall your evil t . . . . . . Jer 4:14
they do not know the t . . . . . Mic 4:12
Jesus, knowing their t . . . . . Matt 9:4
heart proceed evil t . . . . . . Matt 15:19
futile in their t . . . . Rom 1:21
The LORD knows the t . . . . . 1 Cor 3:20
and is a discerner of the t . . . Heb 4:12

THOUSAND
one t from each tribe . . . . . . Num 31:5
two t three hundred days . . . Dan 8:14
one t two hundred . . . . Dan 12:11
eaten were about five t . . . Matt 14:21
who ate were four t men . . . Matt 15:38
loaves were about five t . . . Mark 6:44
eaten were about four t . . . . Mark 8:9
were about five t men . . . . Luke 9:14
one day is as a t years . . . . . 2 Pet 3:8

hundred and forty-four *t* .... Rev 14:1
bound him for a *t* years .... Rev 20:2

THREAT
shall flee at the *t* .... Is 30:17

THREATEN
suffered, He did not *t* ...... 1 Pet 2:23

THREATENING
to them, giving up *t* .... Eph 6:9

THREATS
Lord, look on their *t* .... Acts 4:29
still breathing *t* .... Acts 9:1

THREE
the vine were *t* branches .. Gen 40:10
were *t* white baskets .... Gen 40:16
child, she hid him *t* months ... Ex 2:2
T times you shall keep a .... Ex 23:14
T times in the year all ..... Ex 34:23
T times a year all your .... Deut 16:16
t hundred concubines ..... 1 Kin 11:3
on the child *t* times, and .. 1 Kin 17:21
so he struck *t* times ...... 2 Kin 13:18
either *t* years of famine .. 1 Chr 21:12
Now when Job's *t* friends ... Job 2:11
There are *t* things that .... Prov 30:15
Did we not cast *t* men ..... Dan 3:24
his petition *t* times a day ... Dan 6:13
came up, before which *t* ... Dan 7:20
t more kings will arise in .. Dan 11:2
For *t* transgressions of .... Amos 1:3
Son of Man be *t* days ..... Matt 12:40
make here *t* tabernacles ... Matt 17:4
For where two or *t* are .... Matt 18:20
you will deny Me *t* .... Matt 26:34
temple and build it in *t* ... Matt 27:40
After *t* days I will rise .... Matt 27:63
after *t* days rise again ..... Mark 8:31
will deny Me *t* times .... Mark 14:30
and build it in *t* days ..... Mark 15:29
will deny Me *t* times ..... Luke 22:61
that day about *t* thousand .. Acts 2:41
was *t* days without sight .... Acts 9:9
This was done *t* times ..... Acts 10:16
spoke boldly for *t* months .. Acts 19:8
hope, love, these *t* ...... 1 Cor 13:13
and these *t* are one ...... 1 John 5:7
By these *t* plagues a third .. Rev 9:18
I saw *t* unclean spirits .... Rev 16:13

THRESH
he does not *t* it .... Is 28:28
t the mountains .... Is 41:15
it is time to *t* her .... Jer 51:33
"Arise and *t* .... Mic 4:13

THRESHING
t shall last till the .... Lev 26:5
fleece of wool on the *t* ..... Judg 6:37
went down to the *t* floor .... Ruth 3:6
David bought the *t* floor .. 2 Sam 24:24
like the dust at *t* .... 2 Kin 13:7
t floor of Ornan the ...... 1 Chr 21:18
Oh, my *t* and the grain .... Is 21:10
clean out His *t* floor ...... Matt 3:12

THRESHOLD
with her hands on the *t* ... Judg 19:27
were broken off on the *t* .. 1 Sam 5:4
been, to the *t* of the temple .. Ezek 9:3

THREW
every man *t* down his rod .... Ex 7:12
he *t* stones at David ...... 2 Sam 16:6
t him into the sea, and the .. Jon 1:15
t him into prison till he ... Matt 18:30
he *t* down the pieces ...... Matt 27:5
t their own clothes on .... Luke 19:35
they *t* them into prison, ... Acts 16:23
t it into the great .... Rev 14:19
t it into the sea, saying, ... Rev 18:21

THROAT
t is an open tomb .... Ps 5:9
put a knife to your *t* ...... Prov 23:2

unshod, and your *t* .... Jer 2:25
t is an open tomb .... Rom 3:13

THRONE
LORD sitting on His *t* .... 1 Kin 22:19
He has prepared His *t* .... Ps 9:7
temple, the LORD's *t* .... Ps 11:4
Your *t*, O God, is .... Ps 45:6
has established His *t* ...... Ps 103:19
he upholds his *t* .... Prov 20:28
Lord sitting on a *t* .... Is 6:1
"Heaven is My *t* .... Is 66:1
shall be called The *T* ...... Jer 3:17
do not disgrace the *t* ...... Jer 14:21
A glorious high *t* .... Jer 17:12
t was a fiery flame .... Dan 7:9
sit and rule on His *t* ...... Zech 6:13
for it is God's *t* .... Matt 5:34
will give Him the *t* ...... Luke 1:32
"Your *t*, O God, is .... Heb 1:8
come boldly to the *t* .... Heb 4:16
where Satan's *t* .... Rev 2:13
My Father on His *t* .... Rev 3:21
I saw a great white *t* ...... Rev 20:11

THRONE OF DAVID
set up the *t* over Israel .... 2 Sam 3:10
and set me on the *t* ...... 1 Kin 2:24
t shall be established ..... 1 Kin 2:45
t and over His kingdom .... Is 9:7
princes sitting on the *t* .... Jer 17:25
you who sit on the *t* ...... Jer 22:2
king who sits on the *t* ..... Jer 29:16
no one to sit on the *t* ..... Jer 36:30

THRONE OF GOD
swears by the *t* .... Matt 23:22
right hand of the *t* .... Heb 12:2
they are before the *t* ...... Rev 7:15
without fault before the *t* ... Rev 14:5
proceeding from the *t* ...... Rev 22:1

THRONES
t are set there .... Ps 122:5
also sit on twelve *t* ...... Matt 19:28
mighty from their *t* ...... Luke 1:52
invisible, whether *t* ...... Col 1:16
t I saw twenty-four .... Rev 4:4

THRONG
house of God in the *t* ...... Ps 55:14

THROW
he said, "*T* her down ...... 2 Kin 9:33
keep, and a time to *t* away .. Eccl 3:6
the LORD will *t* you away .... Is 22:17
of your land and *t* .... Mic 5:11
me, "*T* it to the potter" .... Zech 11:13
may build, but I will *t* down .. Mal 1:4
t Yourself down .... Matt 4:6
children's bread and *t* .... Matt 15:26
let him *t* a stone at her .... John 8:7
t them into the fire, and .... John 15:6

THROWN
rider He has *t* into the sea ... Ex 15:1
their slain shall be *t* .... Is 34:3
mountains shall be *t* ..... Ezek 38:20
down and *t* into the fire .... Matt 3:10
neck, and he were *t* ...... Mark 9:42
down and *t* into the fire .... Luke 3:9

THRUST
and rose up and *t* .... Luke 4:29
T in Your sickle and reap .. Rev 14:15

THUMMIM
the Urim and the *T* ...... Ex 28:30
Your *T* and Your Urim .... Deut 33:8
with the Urim and *T* ...... Ezra 2:63
with the Urim and *T* ..... Neh 7:65

THUNDER
But the *t* of His power .... Job 26:14
The voice of Your *t* .... Ps 77:18
the secret place of *t* .... Ps 81:7
t they hastened away ...... Ps 104:7

that is, "Sons of *T*" ...... Mark 3:17
the voice of loud *t* .... Rev 14:2

THUNDERED
"The LORD *t* from ...... 2 Sam 22:14
The LORD *t* .... Ps 18:13

THUNDERINGS
people witnessed the *t* ..... Ex 20:18
the sound of mighty *t* ...... Rev 19:6

THUNDERS
t marvelously with His ..... Job 37:5
The God of glory *t* .... Ps 29:3

THYATIRA
Residence of Lydia, Acts 16:14
Site of one of the seven churches, Rev
2:18–24

TIBERIAS
Sea of Galilee called, John 6:1, 23

TIDINGS
be afraid of evil *t* .... Ps 112:7
you who bring good *t*, lift ..... Is 40:9
brings glad *t* of good things ... Is 52:7
preach good *t* to the poor ..... Is 61:1
of him who brings good *t* ... Nah 1:15
I bring you good *t* .... Luke 2:10
who bring glad *t* .... Rom 10:15

TIGLATH-PILESER
Powerful Assyrian king who invades
Samaria, 2 Kin 15:29

TILL
no man to *t* the ground ..... Gen 2:5

TILLER
but Cain was a *t* .... Gen 4:2

TILLS
t his land will be .... Prov 12:11
t his land will have .... Prov 28:19

TIMBREL
took the *t* in her hand ..... Ex 15:20
Praise Him with the *t* and ... Ps 150:4

TIMBRELS
out to meet him with *t* .... Judg 11:34

TIME
See APPOINTED TIME
in the appointed *t* of the .... Ex 34:18
LORD at its appointed *t* ..... Num 9:13
children ask in *t* to come .... Josh 4:6
t I shall be blameless ...... Judg 15:3
For in the *t* of trouble He ..... Ps 27:5
pray to You in a *t* .... Ps 32:6
ashamed in the evil *t* ...... Ps 37:19
strength in the *t* of trouble ... Ps 37:39
how short my *t* is .... Ps 89:47
t for every purpose under .... Eccl 3:1
A *t* to be born .... Eccl 3:2
but *t* and chance .... Eccl 9:11
LORD, will hasten it in its *t* ... Is 60:22
But in the *t* of their trouble .. Jer 2:27
the *t* of their punishment .... Jer 8:12
you in the *t* of adversity .... Jer 15:11
in the *t* of Your anger ...... Jer 18:23
your *t* was the *t* .... Ezek 16:8
a *t* and times and half a *t* .. Dan 7:25
at that *t* your people shall .. Dan 12:1
The *t* has not come .... Hag 1:2
says, "My *t* is at hand ..... Matt 26:18
A second *t* the rooster .... Mark 14:72
t of temptation fall away .. Luke 8:13
you did not know the *t* .... Luke 19:44
has seen God at any *t* ..... John 1:18
Can he enter a second *t* .... John 3:4
t has not yet come .... John 7:6
the *t* is coming when I .... John 16:25
to him again a second *t* .... John 21:16
I have a convenient *t* ..... Acts 24:25
be revealed in his own *t* .. 2 Thess 2:6
Jesus before *t* began .... 2 Tim 1:9
for the *t* is near .... Rev 1:3
that he has a short *t* ...... Rev 12:12
a *t* and times and half a *t* .. Rev 12:14

TIME OF TROUBLE
I have reserved for the *t* . . . Job 38:23
in the *t* He shall hide me . . . . . Ps 27:5
their strength in the *t* . . . . Ps 37:39
Lord will deliver him in *t* . . . . . Ps 41:1
unfaithful man in *t* . . . . Prov 25:19
salvation also in the *t* . . . . Is 33:2
his Savior in *t* . . . . Jer 14:8
And there shall be a *t* . . . . . . Dan 12:1

TIMES
Three *t* you shall keep a . . . . Ex 23:14
seven *t* in the same . . . . Josh 6:15
in the Jordan seven *t* . . . . . 2 Kin 5:10
understanding of the *t* . . . 1 Chr 12:32
t are not hidden . . . . Job 24:1
t are in Your hand . . . . Ps 31:15
will bless the Lord at all *t* . . . . Ps 34:1
Trust in Him at all *t*, you . . . . Ps 62:8
Seven *t* a day I praise . . . Ps 119:164
A friend loves at all *t* . . . . . Prov 17:17
may fall seven *t* and rise . . Prov 24:16
does evil a hundred *t* . . . . Eccl 8:12
he found them ten *t* better . . Dan 1:20
let seven *t* pass over him . . . Dan 4:16
in those *t* many shall rise . . Dan 11:14
the signs of the *t* . . . . Matt 16:3
up to seventy *t* seven . . . . . Matt 18:22
Gentiles until the *t* . . . . Luke 21:24
not for you to know *t* . . . . Acts 1:7
their preappointed *t* . . . . . Acts 17:26
last days perilous *t* . . . . 2 Tim 3:1
God, who at various *t* . . . . Heb 1:1

TIMON
One of the first seven deacons, Acts
6:1–5

TIMOTHY
Paul's companion, Acts 16:1–3; 18:5;
20:4, 5; 2 Cor 1:19; Phil 1:1; 2 Tim 4:9,
21
Ministers independently, Acts 17:14,
15; 19:22; 1 Cor 4:17; Phil 2:19, 23;
1 Thess 3:1–6; 1 Tim 1:1–3; 4:14

TINGLE
who hears it will *t* . . . . 1 Sam 3:11
hears of it, his ears will *t* . . . . Jer 19:3

TIP
on the *t* of the right ear of . . Ex 29:20
the *t* of his finger in . . . . . . Luke 16:24

TIRZAH
Seat of Jeroboam's rule, 1 Kin 14:17
Capital of Israel until Omri's reign,
1 Kin 16:6–23

TITHE
And he gave him a *t* . . . . . . Gen 14:20
Lord, a tenth of the *t* . . . . . Num 18:26
t of your grain or your . . . . Deut 12:17
"You shall truly *t* . . . . Deut 14:22
shall bring out the *t* . . . . . Deut 14:28
laying aside all the *t* . . . . . Deut 26:12
in abundantly the *t* . . . . . . 2 Chr 31:5
Judah brought the *t* . . . . . . Neh 13:12
For you pay *t* of mint . . . . . Matt 23:23

TITHES
to redeem any of his *t* . . . . . Lev 27:31
t which you receive . . . . . . Num 18:28
and to bring the *t* . . . . Neh 10:37
firstfruits, and the *t* . . . . . . Neh 12:44
the articles, the *t* . . . . Neh 13:5
Bring all the *t* . . . . Mal 3:10
I give *t* of all that I . . . . . . Luke 18:12
to receive *t* from the . . . . Heb 7:5
mortal men receive *t* . . . . Heb 7:8
Levi, who receives *t* . . . . Heb 7:9

TITHING
the year of *t* . . . . Deut 26:12

TITLE
Now Pilate wrote a *t* . . . . . John 19:19

TITTLE
away, one jot or one *t* . . . . . Matt 5:18

TITUS
Ministers in Crete, Titus 1:4, 5
Paul's representative in Corinth, 2 Cor
7:6, 7, 13, 14; 8:6–23

TOBIAH
Ammonite servant; ridicules the Jews,
Neh 2:10

TODAY
Bake what you will bake *t* . . . Ex 16:23
yourselves *t* to the Lord, ... Ex 32:29
for *t* the Lord will appear . . . . Lev 9:4
t shall be in your heart . . . . . Deut 6:6
God makes with you *t* . . . . Deut 29:12
have departed from me *t* . . 1 Sam 10:2
you have *t* rejected . . . . . . 1 Sam 10:19
this day, for *t* the Lord . . 1 Sam 11:13
t I have begotten You . . . . Ps 2:7
of the field, which *t* . . . . Matt 6:30
work *t* in my vineyard . . . . Matt 21:28
T this Scripture is . . . . Luke 4:21
the grass, which *t* . . . . Luke 12:28
T salvation has come to . . . Luke 19:9
t you will be with Me . . . . Luke 23:43
t I have begotten You . . . . . . Heb 1:5
"*T*, if you will hear . . . . Heb 3:7
the same yesterday, *t* . . . . . . Heb 13:8

TOGARMAH
Northern country inhabited by descendants of Gomer, Gen 10:3
Supplied horses to Tyrians and soldiers
to the army of Gog, Ezek 27:14; 38:6

TOIL
t you shall eat of . . . . Gen 3:17
whom do I *t* and deprive . . . . Eccl 4:8
they neither *t* nor . . . . Matt 6:28
our labor and *t* . . . . 1 Thess 2:9

TOILED
I had *t* under the sun . . . . . . Eccl 2:18
"Master, we have *t* . . . . Luke 5:5

TOLD
Behold, I have *t* . . . . Matt 28:7
things which were *t* . . . . Luke 2:18
t me all things that I . . . . John 4:29
t you the truth which . . . . . . John 8:40
so, I would have *t* . . . . John 14:2
"And now I have *t* . . . . John 14:29

TOLERABLE
you, it will be more *t* . . . . . Matt 10:15

TOMB
throat is an open *t* . . . . Ps 5:9
sitting opposite the *t* . . . . . . Matt 27:61
corpse and laid it in a *t* . . . . Mark 6:29
laid Him in a *t* which . . . . . Mark 15:46
rolled away from the *t* . . . . . Luke 24:2
been in the *t* four days . . . . John 11:17
Lazarus out of his *t* . . . . John 12:17
in the garden a new *t* . . . . . John 19:41
Magdalene went to the *t* . . . John 20:1
throat is an open *t* . . . . Rom 3:13

TOMBS
like whitewashed *t* . . . . Matt 23:27
you build the *t* . . . . Matt 23:29
For you build the *t* . . . . Luke 11:47

TOMORROW
yourselves for *t* . . . . Num 11:18
Sanctify yourselves for *t* . . . Josh 7:13
Do not boast about *t*, for . . . Prov 27:1
drink, for *t* we die . . . . Is 22:13
t will be as today . . . . Is 56:12
t is thrown into the . . . . Matt 6:30
do not worry about *t* . . . . . . Matt 6:34
I must journey today, *t* . . . Luke 13:33
drink, for *t* we die . . . . . . 1 Cor 15:32
what will happen *t* . . . . . . James 4:14

TONGUE
of speech and slow of *t* . . . . . Ex 4:10
the scourge of the *t* . . . . Job 5:21
me, and I will hold my *t* . . . . Job 6:24
hides it under his *t* . . . . Job 20:12

the *t* that speaks proud . . . . . . Ps 12:3
Keep your *t* from evil . . . . . . Ps 34:13
t shall speak of Your . . . . Ps 35:28
lest I sin with my *t* . . . . Ps 39:1
t shall sing aloud of Your . . . Ps 51:14
and their *t* a sharp sword . . . . Ps 57:4
to you, you false *t* . . . . Ps 120:3
laughter, and our *t* . . . . Ps 126:2
remember you, let my *t* . . . . Ps 137:6
is not a word on my *t* . . . . . . Ps 139:4
The *t* of the righteous is . . Prov 10:20
but the perverse *t* . . . . Prov 10:31
forever, but a lying *t* . . . . . Prov 12:19
The *t* of the wise uses . . . . . Prov 15:2
A wholesome *t* is a . . . . Prov 15:4
perverse *t* falls into evil . . . Prov 17:20
t keeps his soul . . . . Prov 21:23
t breaks a bone . . . . Prov 25:15
who flatters with the *t* . . . . Prov 28:23
and on her *t* is the law . . . . Prov 31:26
another *t* He will speak to . . . Is 28:11
t shall take an oath . . . . Is 45:23
God has given Me the *t* . . . . . . Is 50:4
of his *t* was loosed . . . . . . Mark 7:35
his *t* loosed, and he . . . . . . Luke 1:64
in water and cool my *t* . . . Luke 16:24
t shall confess to God . . . . . Rom 14:11
he who speaks in a *t* . . . . . 1 Cor 14:2
t should confess that . . . . . . Phil 2:11
does not bridle his *t* . . . . . James 1:26
t is a little member . . . . James 3:5
And the *t* is a fire . . . . James 3:6
no man can tame the *t* . . . . James 3:8
love in word or in *t* . . . . . . 1 John 3:18
every nation, tribe, *t* . . . . . . Rev 14:6

TONGUES
From the strife of *t* . . . . Ps 31:20
speak with new *t* . . . . Mark 16:17
to them divided *t*, as . . . Acts 2:3
speaking in our own *t* . . . . . Acts 2:11
and they spoke with *t* . . . . . Acts 19:6
I speak with the *t* . . . . 1 Cor 13:1
Therefore *t* are for a . . . . 1 Cor 14:22
many peoples, nations, *t*, . . Rev 10:11

TOOK
He *t* one of his ribs, and . . . . Gen 2:21
t of every clean animal . . . . . Gen 8:20
Abram *t* Sarai his wife . . . . . Gen 12:5
they *t* stones and made a . . . Gen 31:46
Then Joseph *t* an oath . . . . . Gen 50:25
Then Moses *t* his wife and . . . Ex 4:20
Moses *t* the rod of God in . . . . Ex 4:20
Then they *t* ashes from the . . . Ex 9:10
t the bones of Joseph . . . . . . Ex 13:19
t outside the camp him . . . . Lev 24:23
Moses *t* the redemption . . . . Num 3:49
t of the Spirit that was . . . Num 11:25
Israel *t* all these cities . . . . Num 21:25
they *t* all the spoil and . . . . Num 31:11
Then I *t* the two tablets . . . . Deut 9:17
Then I *t* your sin, the calf . . Deut 9:21
t up twelve stones from the . . Josh 4:8
Samson *t* hold of the . . . . . Judg 16:29
Tamar *t* the cakes . . . . . . 2 Sam 13:10
he *t* hold of her and . . . . . 2 Sam 13:11
Jehu *t* no heed to walk . . . 2 Kin 10:31
Then David *t* more wives . . 1 Chr 14:3
He *t* away the foreign . . . . 2 Chr 33:15
You are He who *t* me out of . . Ps 71:6
t all the remnant of Judah . . . Jer 43:5
Then the Spirit *t* me up . . . Ezek 11:24
he *t* the young Child and . . . Matt 2:14
Then the devil *t* Him up . . . . Matt 4:5
Himself *t* our infirmities . . . Matt 8:17
He *t* the five loaves and . . . Matt 14:19
they *t* up twelve baskets . . . Matt 14:20
He *t* the seven loaves . . . . Matt 15:36
t up seven large baskets . . Matt 15:37
Then Peter *t* Him aside . . . Matt 16:22
virgins who *t* their lamps . . Matt 25:1
a stranger and you *t* Me . . Matt 25:35

Then He *t* the cup, and ... Matt 26:27
Peter *t* Him aside and ..... Mark 8:32
Then He *t* a little child .... Mark 9:36
He *t* the cup, and gave ... Luke 22:17

TOOTH
eye for eye, *t* .... Ex 21:24
eye for eye, *t* for *t* .... Lev 24:20
t for *t*, hand for hand, ... Deut 19:21
is like a bad *t* .... Prov 25:19
eye for an eye and a *t* ..... Matt 5:38

TOP
a tower whose *t* is in the .... Gen 11:4
consuming fire on the *t* of ..Ex 24:17
mercy seat on *t* of the ark ..Ex 25:21
in two from *t* to bottom ... Matt 27:51
torn in two from *t* to ..... Mark 15:38

TOPHET
See HINNOM, VALLEY OF THE SON OF
T was established .... Is 30:33
the high places of *T* ....Jer 7:31
make this city like *T* ......Jer 19:12
like the place of *T* ....Jer 19:13

TORCH
and a burning *t* that .... Gen 15:17
and like a fiery *t* .... Zech 12:6

TORCHES
When he had set the *t* ..... Judg 15:5
his eyes like *t* .... Dan 10:6
come with flaming *t* .... Nah 2:3

TORE
that he *t* his clothes, and ... Judg 11:35
t his garments and lay ... 2 Sam 13:31
t it into twelve pieces .... 1 Kin 11:30
t down the temple of .... 2 Kin 10:27
temple of Baal, and *t* it ... 2 Chr 23:17
t his robe, and shaved his ... Job 1:20
and each one *t* his robe ..... Job 2:12

TORE HIS CLOTHES
in the pit, and he *t* .... Gen 37:29
Then Jacob *t*, put .... Gen 37:34
Then Joshua *t*, and fell ... Josh 7:6
he *t* and put sackcloth .... 1 Kin 21:27
the letter, that he *t* ...... 2 Kin 5:7
of the Law, that he *t* .... 2 Kin 22:11
of the Law, that he *t* ..... 2 Chr 34:19
he *t* and put on sackcloth .... Esth 4:1
heard it, that he *t* .... Is 37:1
Then the high priest *t* ..... Matt 26:65
Then the high priest *t* ..... Mark 14:63

TORMENT
"How long will you *t* .... Job 19:2
shall lie down in *t* .... Is 50:11
You come here to *t* .... Matt 8:29
to this place of *t* .... Luke 16:28
fear involves *t* .... 1 John 4:18
to *t* them for five months .... Rev 9:5
t ascends forever .... Rev 14:11

TORMENTED
t with unclean spirits ...... Luke 6:18
for I am *t* in this .... Luke 16:24
He shall be *t* with fire ..... Rev 14:10
And they will be *t* .... Rev 20:10

TORMENTS
And being in *t* .... Luke 16:23

TORN
Joseph is *t* to pieces .... Gen 37:33
the altar of Baal, *t* down ... Judg 6:28
has *t* the kingdom .... 1 Sam 15:28
lion, which has *t* him ..... 1 Kin 13:26
aside my ways and *t* ...... Lam 3:11
for He has *t* .... Hos 6:1
of the temple was *t* ...... Matt 27:51
t in two from top to ..... Mark 15:38

TORTURED
Others were *t* .... Heb 11:35

TOSSED
t with tempest .... Is 54:11
t to and fro and .... Eph 4:14

TOTTER
drunkard, and shall *t* .... Is 24:20

TOUCH
eat it, nor shall you *t* it ..... Gen 3:3
the mountain or *t* its base ... Ex 19:12
carcasses you shall not *t* .... Lev 11:8
seven no evil shall *t* .... Job 5:19
t no unclean thing .... Is 52:11
"If only I may *t* .... Matt 9:21
that they might only *t* .... Matt 14:36
If only I may *t* His .... Mark 5:28
and begged Him to *t* him .. Mark 8:22
that He might *t* them .... Luke 18:15
a man not to *t* a woman .... 1 Cor 7:1
Do not *t* what is unclean, .. 2 Cor 6:17
wicked one does not *t* .... 1 John 5:18

TOUCHED
whoever has *t* any slain .. Num 31:19
whose hearts God had *t* ..1 Sam 10:26
t my mouth with it .... Is 6:7
hand and *t* my mouth .... Jer 1:9
but he *t* me, and stood me .. Dan 8:18
said, "Who *t* My clothes .. Mark 5:30
t the open coffin, and ...... Luke 7:14
Jesus said, "Who *t* Me? ... Luke 8:45
mountain that may be *t* ... Heb 12:18

TOUCHES
if a person *t* any unclean ... Lev 5:2
whoever *t* the carcass of .. Lev 11:24
Whoever *t* those things .... Lev 15:27
whoever *t* anything made .. Lev 22:4
He *t* the hills .... Ps 104:32
t you *t* the .... Zech 2:8

TOWEL
His garments, took a *t* ..... John 13:4

TOWER
t whose top is in the .... Gen 11:4
t which the sons of men .... Gen 11:5
the *t* of salvation to ..... 2 Sam 22:51
for me, a strong *t* .... Ps 61:3
my fortress, my high *t* ..... Ps 144:2
like an ivory *t* .... Song 7:4
a watchman in the *t* .... Is 21:5
in it and built a *t* .... Matt 21:33
whom the *t* in Siloam fell .. Luke 13:4
intending to build a *t* .... Luke 14:28

TOWN
Neither go into the *t* ..... Mark 8:26
from the *t* of Bethlehem, ... John 7:42

TOWNS
of Megiddo and its *t* ..... Josh 17:11
as *t* without walls .... Zech 2:4

TRACE
no *t* of them was found ..... Dan 2:35

TRACKED
t our steps so that we ...... Lam 4:18

TRADERS
Then Midianite *t* passed ... Gen 37:28
are princes, whose *t* .... Is 23:8

TRADITION
transgress the *t* .... Matt 15:2
of no effect by your *t* ...... Matt 15:6
holding the *t* of the elders .. Mark 7:3
according to the *t* .... Col 2:8
t which he received ......2 Thess 3:6
conduct received by *t* .... 1 Pet 1:18

TRADITIONS
zealous for the *t* .... Gal 1:14
t which you were ....2 Thess 2:15

TRAIN
T up a child in the .... Prov 22:6
t of His robe filled .... Is 6:1

TRAINED
who is perfectly *t* ....Luke 6:40
those who have been *t* .... Heb 12:11

TRAINING
bring them up in the *t* ....Eph 6:4

TRAITOR
also became a *t* .... Luke 6:16

TRAITORS
t, headstrong .... 2 Tim 3:4

TRAMPLE
Your name we will *t* .... Ps 44:5
serpent you shall *t* .... Ps 91:13
hand, to *t* My courts .... Is 1:12
You shall *t* the wicked ...... Mal 4:3
swine, lest they *t* .... Matt 7:6
you the authority to *t* ...... Lk 10:19

TRAMPLED
wall, and it shall be *t* down ....Is 5:5
as straw is *t* down for the ... Is 25:10
t them in My fury .... Is 63:3
The Lord has *t* underfoot ... Lam 1:15
now she will be *t* .... Mic 7:10
t the nations in anger ...... Hab 3:12
Jerusalem will be *t* ...... Luke 21:24
t the Son of God .... Heb 10:29
the winepress was *t* .... Rev 14:20

TRANCE
he fell into a *t* .... Acts 10:10
t I saw a vision .... Acts 11:5

TRANSFIGURED
and was *t* before them .... Matt 17:2

TRANSFORMED
this world, but be *t* .... Rom 12:2
the Lord, are being *t* ..... 2 Cor 3:18

TRANSFORMING
t themselves into ....2 Cor 11:13

TRANSFORMS
Satan himself *t* himself ... 2 Cor 11:14

TRANSGRESS
t the command of the .... Num 14:41
the LORD's people *t* ..... 1 Sam 2:24
my mouth shall not *t* .... Ps 17:3
his mouth must not *t* ..... Prov 16:10
of bread a man will *t* ..... Prov 28:21
those who *t* against Me .. Ezek 20:38
in which you *t* against ..... Zeph 3:1
do Your disciples *t* .... Matt 15:2

TRANSGRESSED
t My covenant .... Josh 7:11
they had *t* against the .... 2 Chr 12:2
your mediators have *t* ...... Is 43:27
the rulers also *t* .... Jer 2:8
who have *t* My covenant ... Jer 34:18
their fathers have *t* .... Ezek 2:3
Yes, all Israel has *t* .... Dan 9:11
t your commandment .... Luke 15:29

TRANSGRESSES
"Indeed, because he *t* ...... Hab 2:5
Whoever *t* and does not ..... 2 John 9

TRANSGRESSING
God, in *t* His covenant, ... Deut 17:2
t against our God by ...... Neh 13:27

TRANSGRESSION
iniquity and *t* and sin ...... Ex 34:7
Make me know my *t* ...... Job 13:23
t is sealed up in a .... Job 14:17
I am pure, without *t* .... Job 33:9
though I am without *t* ..... Job 34:6
be innocent of great *t* ..... Ps 19:13
is he whose *t* is forgiven .... Ps 32:1
their *t* with the rod .... Ps 89:32
because of their *t* .... Ps 107:17
He who covers a *t* .... Prov 17:9
He who loves *t* loves .... Prov 17:19
By *t* an evil man is .... Prov 29:6
man abounds in *t* .... Prov 29:22
tell My people their *t* .... Is 58:1
and the *t* of desolation ..... Dan 8:13
at Gilgal multiply *t* .... Amos 4:4
my firstborn for my *t* .... Mic 6:7

and passing over the *t* ...... Mic 7:18
no law there is no *t* .... Rom 4:15
deceived, fell into *t* ...... 1 Tim 2:14
steadfast, and every *t* ...... Heb 2:2

TRANSGRESSIONS
He will not pardon your *t* ... Ex 23:21
forgive your *t* nor your .... Josh 24:19
if I have covered my *t* .... Job 31:33
"I will confess my *t* .... Ps 32:5
me from all my *t* .... Ps 39:8
mercies, blot out my *t* ...... Ps 51:1
For I acknowledge my *t* .... Ps 51:3
has He removed our *t* ...... Ps 103:12
who blots out your *t* .... Is 43:25
was wounded for our *t* ...... Is 53:5
for the *t* of My people ...... Is 53:8
for our *t* are with us, and .... Is 59:12
yoke of my *t* was bound .... Lam 1:14
from you all the *t* .... Ezek 18:31
I punish Israel for their *t* .. Amos 3:14
was added because of *t* ..... Gal 3:19
redemption of the *t* .... Heb 9:15

TRANSGRESSOR
and were called a *t* .... Is 48:8
are a *t* of the law .... Rom 2:27
I make myself a *t* .... Gal 2:18
become a *t* of the law ..... James 2:11

TRANSGRESSORS
the *t* shall be destroyed ..... Ps 37:38
Then I will teach *t* .... Ps 51:13
to any wicked *t* .... Ps 59:5
The destruction of *t* and of .... Is 1:28
numbered with the *t* .... Is 53:12
when the *t* have reached ... Dan 8:23
numbered with the *t* ..... Mark 15:28
numbered with the *t* ..... Luke 22:37
convicted by the law as *t* .. James 2:9

TRANSLATED
Immanuel," which is *t* ..... Matt 1:23
cumi," which is *t* .... Mark 5:41
Golgotha, which is *t* ..... Mark 15:22
which is *t*, "My God ..... Mark 15:34
the Messiah" (which is .. John 1:41
Cephas" (which is *t* ...... John 1:42

TRAP
of Israel, as a *t* .... Is 8:14
where there is no *t* .... Amos 3:5
become a snare and a *t* .... Rom 11:9

TRAPS
they have set *t* .... Ps 140:5
for me, and from the *t* ..... Ps 141:9

TRAVEL
For you *t* land and sea .... Matt 23:15
Paul's *t* companions ...... Acts 19:29

TRAVELER
t who turns aside .... Jer 14:8

TRAVELING
lodge, O you *t* companies ... Is 21:13
lie waste, the *t* .... Is 33:8
t in the greatness of His .... Is 63:1
a man *t* to a far country .. Matt 25:14
two of them were *t* that .. Luke 24:13

TRAVERSE
t the way of .... Prov 8:20

TREACHEROUS
the *t* dealer deals .... Is 21:2
The *t* dealers have dealt .... Is 24:16
yet her *t* sister Judah did .... Jer 3:8
an assembly of *t* men ...... Jer 9:2
are insolent, *t* .... Zeph 3:4

TREACHEROUSLY
and you who deal *t* .... Is 33:1
have you dealt *t* with Me .... Jer 3:20
happy who deal so *t* ...... Jer 12:1
even they have dealt *t* ..... Jer 12:6
They have dealt *t* .... Hos 5:7
Why do we deal *t* .... Mal 2:10

that you do not deal *t* .... Mal 2:16
This man dealt *t* .... Acts 7:19

TREAD
t down the wicked in ...... Job 40:12
it is He who shall *t* .... Ps 60:12
You shall *t* upon the ...... Ps 91:13
shout, as those who *t* ..... Jer 25:30
because you *t* down the ... Amos 5:11
will come down and *t* ..... Mic 1:3
And they will *t* .... Rev 11:2

TREADS
like one who *t* in the .... Is 63:2
t the high places .... Amos 4:13
an ox while it *t* .... 1 Tim 5:18
t the winepress .... Rev 19:15

TREASURE
a special *t* above all the .... Deut 7:6
to you His good *t* .... Deut 28:12
one who finds great *t* ..... Ps 119:162
for His special *t* .... Ps 135:4
t my commands within ..... Prov 2:1
there is much *t* .... Prov 15:6
There is desirable *t* ...... Prov 21:20
of the LORD is His *t* .... Is 33:6
For where your *t* .... Matt 6:21
t brings forth evil .... Matt 12:35
is like *t* hidden in a field .. Matt 13:44
t things new and old ...... Matt 13:52
and you will have *t* .... Matt 19:21
will have *t* in heaven ..... Mark 10:21
So is he who lays up *t* .... Luke 12:21
t in the heavens that .... Luke 12:33
For where your *t* is ...... Luke 12:34
will have *t* in heaven .... Luke 18:22
But we have this *t* .... 2 Cor 4:7
You have heaped up *t* ..... James 5:3

TREASURED
t the words of His .... Job 23:12

TREASURER
Erastus, the *t* of the ...... Rom 16:23

TREASURES
sealed up among My *t* .... Deut 32:34
t hidden in the sand ...... Deut 33:19
it more than hidden *t* ...... Job 3:21
her as for hidden *t* .... Prov 2:4
t of wickedness profit ..... Prov 10:2
Getting *t* by a lying ...... Prov 21:6
is no end to their *t* .... Is 2:7
I will give you the *t* .... Is 45:3
in your works and your *t*.... Jer 48:7
Are there yet the *t* .... Mic 6:10
for yourselves *t* .... Matt 6:19
are hidden all the *t* .... Col 2:3
riches than the *t* .... Heb 11:26

TREASURIES
that I may fill their *t* ...... Prov 8:21

TREASURING
t up for yourself wrath in ... Rom 2:5

TREASURY
you entered the *t* of snow .. Job 38:22
who have given to the *t* .. Mark 12:43
their gifts into the *t* ...... Luke 21:1

TREAT
Should he *t* our sister ..... Gen 34:31
not *t* her brutally .... Deut 21:14

TREATED
He *t* Abram well for her ... Gen 12:16
t them spitefully, and ..... Matt 22:6
and be *t* with contempt ... Mark 9:12
were spitefully *t* at .... 1 Thess 2:2

TREATS
Cursed is the one who *t* .. Deut 27:16

TREATY
Now Solomon made a *t* ... 1 Kin 3:1
Let there be a *t* between .. 1 Kin 15:19
So he made a *t* with ..... 1 Kin 20:34
Let there be a *t* between .. 2 Chr 16:3

TREE
LORD God made every *t* .... Gen 2:9
but of the *t* .... Gen 2:17
you eaten from the *t* ...... Gen 3:11
tamarisk *t* in Beersheba ... Gen 21:33
for the *t* of the field is .... Deut 20:19
they said to the olive *t* .... Judg 9:8
the Diviners' Terebinth *T* .. Judg 9:37
the cedar *t* of Lebanon .... 1 Kin 4:33
down under a broom *t* .... 1 Kin 19:4
there is hope for a *t* .... Job 14:7
t planted by the .... Ps 1:3
like a native green *t* ...... Ps 37:35
shall flourish like a palm *t* . Ps 92:12
t falls to the south .... Eccl 11:3
Like an apple *t* .... Song 2:3
the cedar and the acacia *t* ... Is 41:19
for as the days of a *t* ...... Is 65:22
are upright, like a palm *t* ... Jer 10:5
your name, Green Olive *T*.. Jer 11:16
t planted by the .... Jer 17:8
and set it like a willow *t* ... Ezek 17:5
brought down the high *t* .. Ezek 17:24
The *t* that you saw, which .. Dan 4:20
and the fig *t* has withered .. Joel 1:12
t bears good fruit .... Matt 7:17
t is known by its fruit ..... Matt 12:33
And seeing a fig *t* by the .. Matt 21:19
fig *t* which You cursed ... Mark 11:21
For every *t* is known by ... Luke 6:44
a sycamore *t* to see Him .. Luke 19:4
everyone who hangs on a *t* .. Gal 3:13
His own body on the *t* .... 1 Pet 2:24
as a fig *t* drops its late ..... Rev 6:13

TREE OF LIFE
The *t* was also in the midst .. Gen 2:9
and take also of the *t* ..... Gen 3:22
guard the way to the *t* ... Gen 3:24
She is a *t* to those .... Prov 3:18
of the righteous is a *t* .... Prov 11:30
desire comes, it is a *t* ..... Prov 13:12
wholesome tongue is a *t* .. Prov 15:4
to eat from the *t* .... Rev 2:7
t, which bore twelve fruits .. Rev 22:2
have the right to the *t* ..... Rev 22:14

TREES
and the *t* of the field shall .. Lev 26:4
t once went forth .... Judg 9:8
Then all the *t* said to the ... Judg 9:14
Also he spoke of *t* .... 1 Kin 4:33
Then all the *t* of the ...... Ps 96:12
The *t* of the LORD are ..... Ps 104:16
all kinds of fruit *t* .... Eccl 2:5
all the *t* of the field shall ... Is 55:12
they may be called *t* ...... Is 61:3
and on beast, on the *t* .... Jer 7:20
all the *t* of the field shall .. Ezek 17:24
so that all the *t* .... Ezek 31:9
"I see men like *t* .... Mark 8:24
took branches of palm *t* .. John 12:13
late autumn *t* without ..... Jude 12
the sea, or the *t* .... Rev 7:3
third of the *t* were burned ... Rev 8:7

TREMBLE
T before Him .... 1 Chr 16:30
The dead *t*, those under ... Job 26:5
have made the earth *t* ..... Ps 60:2
T before Him, all the earth .. Ps 96:9
let the peoples *t* .... Ps 99:1
T, O earth, at the presence .. Ps 114:7
who made the earth *t* ..... Is 14:16
That the nations may *t* .... Is 64:2
LORD, you who *t* at His ..... Is 66:5
'Will you not *t* .... Jer 5:22
wrath the earth will *t* ..... Jer 10:10
they shall fear and *t* ...... Jer 33:9
my kingdom men must *t* .. Dan 6:26
the inhabitants of the land *t* .. Joel 2:1
before them, the heavens *t* .. Joel 2:10
demons believe—and *t*! ... James 2:19

TREMBLED
the people saw it, they *t* . . . . Ex 20:18
of Edom, the earth *t* . . . . Judg 5:4
for his heart *t* . . . . 1 Sam 4:13
Then everyone who *t* . . . . Ezra 9:4
the earth shook and *t* . . . . Ps 18:7
and indeed they *t* . . . . Jer 4:24
whole land *t* at the sound . . . . Jer 8:16
mountains saw You and *t* . . Hab 3:10
When I heard, my body *t* . . . Hab 3:16

TREMBLES
the earth sees and *t* . . . . Ps 97:4
flesh *t* for fear of You . . . . . Ps 119:120

TREMBLING
t will take hold of them . . . . . Ex 15:15
will give you a *t* heart . . . . Deut 28:65
it was a very great *t* . . . . 1 Sam 14:15
your water with *t* . . . . Ezek 12:18
in fear, and in much *t* . . . . . . 1 Cor 2:3
t you received . . . . 2 Cor 7:15
flesh, with fear and *t* . . . . Eph 6:5
with fear and *t* . . . . Phil 2:12

TRENCH
and he made a *t* . . . . 1 Kin 18:32

TRESPASS
he shall bring his *t* offering . . Lev 5:6
If a person commits a *t*, ... Lev 5:15
commits a *t* against the . . . . . Lev 6:2
this is the law of the *t* . . . . . . Lev 7:1
and offer it as a *t* offering . . Lev 14:12
bring his *t* offering . . . . Lev 19:21
to *t* against the LORD in . . . . Num 31:16
forgive the *t* of your . . . . . 1 Sam 25:28
a man is overtaken in any *t* . . Gal 6:1

TRESPASSED
t against the LORD God . . . . 2 Chr 30:7
We have *t* against our . . . . . Ezra 10:2

TRESPASSES
still goes on in his *t* . . . . Ps 68:21
forgive men their *t* . . . . Matt 6:14
forgive his brother his *t* . . Matt 18:35
forgive you your *t* . . . . . . Mark 11:25
not imputing their *t* . . . . . . 2 Cor 5:19
who were dead in *t* . . . . Eph 2:1
forgiven you all *t* . . . . Col 2:13
Confess your *t* to one . . . . James 5:16

TRIAL
as in the day of *t* . . . . Ps 95:8
in the day of *t* . . . . Heb 3:8
concerning the fiery *t* . . . . . 1 Pet 4:12
t which shall come . . . . Rev 3:10

TRIALS
with Me in My *t* . . . . Luke 22:28
fall into various *t* . . . . James 1:2

TRIBE
a man from every *t* . . . . Num 1:4
Only the *t* of Levi you . . . . . Num 1:49
Do not cut off the *t* of the . . Num 4:18
one thousand from each *t* . . Num 31:6
one leader of every *t* . . . . . Num 34:18
One *t* is cut off from . . . . . . Judg 21:6
of old, the *t* of Your . . . . Ps 74:2
belongs to another *t* . . . . . . Heb 7:13
the Lion of the *t* . . . . Rev 5:5
blood out of every *t* . . . . Rev 5:9
given him over every *t* . . . . . Rev 13:7

TRIBES
See TWELVE TRIBES
are the twelve *t* of Israel . . Gen 49:28
where the *t* go up . . . . Ps 122:4
to raise up the *t* . . . . Is 49:6
the *t* of Your inheritance . . . . Is 63:17
promise our twelve *t* . . . . . Acts 26:7
t which are scattered . . . . . . James 1:1

TRIBULATION
when *t* or persecution . . . . Matt 13:21
there will be great *t* . . . . . . Matt 24:21
t or persecution arises . . . . Mark 4:17

world you will have *t* . . . . John 16:33
Shall *t*, or distress, or . . . . Rom 8:35
in hope, patient in *t* . . . . . Rom 12:12
comforts us in all our *t* . . . . 2 Cor 1:4
joyful in all our *t* . . . . 2 Cor 7:4
that we would suffer *t* . . . 1 Thess 3:4
t those who . . . . 2 Thess 1:6
and you will have *t* . . . . Rev 2:10
with her into great *t* . . . . . . Rev 2:22
out of the great *t* . . . . Rev 7:14

TRIBULATIONS
t enter the kingdom . . . . Acts 14:22
but we also glory in *t* . . . . . Rom 5:3
in much patience, in *t*, in . . 2 Cor 6:4
not lose heart at my *t* . . . . . . Eph 3:13
t that you endure . . . . 2 Thess 1:4

TRICKERY
plotted to take Jesus by *t* . . Matt 26:4
they might take Him by *t* . . Mark 14:1
doctrine, by the *t* of men . . . Eph 4:14

TRIED
like silver *t* in a furnace of . . . Ps 12:6
You have *t* me and have . . . . . Ps 17:3
a *t* stone, a precious . . . . Is 28:16

TRIMMED
and *t* their lamps . . . . Matt 25:7

TRIUMPH
Let not my enemies *t* . . . . . . Ps 25:2
I will *t* in the works . . . . Ps 92:4
how long will the wicked *t* . . Ps 94:3
always leads us in *t* . . . . . . 2 Cor 2:14

TRIUMPHED
the LORD, for He has *t* . . . . . . Ex 15:1

TRIUMPHING
that the *t* of the wicked is . . . Job 20:5
of them, *t* over them in it . . . Col 2:15

TRIUMPHS
Mercy *t* over judgment . . . James 2:13

TROAS
Paul receives vision at, Acts 16:8–11

TRODDEN
t the winepress alone . . . . Is 63:3

TROOP
Then Leah said, "A *t* . . . . . . Gen 30:11
a *t* shall tramp upon him, . . Gen 49:19
I can run against a *t* . . . . . 2 Sam 22:30

TROUBLE
See TIME OF TROUBLE
that they were in *t* . . . . Ex 5:19
The LORD will *t* you this . . . . Josh 7:25
This day is a day of *t* . . . . . . 2 Kin 19:3
no rest, for *t* comes . . . . Job 3:26
yet man is born to *t*, as the . . . Job 5:7
few days and full of *t* . . . . . . Job 14:1
for the time of *t* . . . . Job 38:23
have increased who *t* . . . . Ps 3:1
a refuge in times of *t* . . . . Ps 9:9
under his tongue is *t* . . . . Ps 10:7
from Me, for *t* is near . . . . . . Ps 22:11
t He shall hide me . . . . Ps 27:5
You have considered my *t* . . . Ps 31:7
O LORD, for I am in *t* . . . . Ps 31:9
shall preserve me from *t* . . . . Ps 32:7
strength in the time of *t* . . . . Ps 37:39
Your servant, for I am in *t* . . Ps 69:17
not in *t* as other men . . . . Ps 73:5
will be with him in *t* . . . . Ps 91:15
walk in the midst of *t* . . . . . . Ps 138:7
is delivered from *t* . . . . Prov 11:8
but *t* will come to him . . . Prov 11:27
of the wicked is *t* . . . . Prov 15:6
t is like a bad tooth . . . . . . Prov 25:19
they are a *t* to Me, I am . . . . . Is 1:14
t they have . . . . Is 26:16
also in the time of *t* . . . . Is 33:2
and there was *t* . . . . Jer 8:15
Savior in time of *t* . . . . Jer 14:8

I will hand them over to *t* . . . . Jer 15:4
I will deliver them to *t* . . . . Jer 29:18
there shall be a time of . . . . Dan 12:1
for the day is its own *t* . . . . Matt 6:34
do not *t* Yourself, for I am . . Luke 7:6
such will have *t* . . . . 1 Cor 7:28
there are some who *t* . . . . . . Gal 1:7
and widows in their *t* . . . . James 1:27

TROUBLED
Your face, and I was *t* . . . . . . Ps 30:7
God, and was *t* . . . . Ps 77:3
Your face, they are *t* . . . Ps 104:29
wicked are like the *t* . . . . . . Is 57:20
in distress; my soul is *t* . . . . Lam 1:20
with tears, my heart is *t* . . . . Lam 2:11
heard this, he was *t* . . . . Matt 2:3
on the sea, they were *t*, . . . Matt 14:26
You are worried and *t* . . . Luke 10:41
to give you who are *t* . . . . 2 Thess 1:7
shaken in mind or *t* . . . . . . 2 Thess 2:2

TROUBLES
t shall befall them, so . . . . Deut 31:17
"What *t* the people . . . . . . 1 Sam 11:5
deliver you in six *t* . . . . Job 5:19
The *t* of my heart have . . . . . Ps 25:17
out of all their *t* . . . . Ps 25:22
my soul is full of *t* . . . . Ps 88:3
He who *t* his own house . . Prov 11:29
for gain *t* his own house, . . Prov 15:27
keeps his soul from *t* . . . . . Prov 21:23
because the former *t* . . . . Is 65:16
will be famines and *t* . . . . Mark 13:8
him out of all his *t* . . . . Acts 7:10
but he who *t* you shall . . . . . Gal 5:10

TROUBLING
spirit from God is *t* . . . . . 1 Sam 16:15
wicked cease from *t* . . . . Job 3:17

TRUE
and Your words are *t* . . . . 2 Sam 7:28
let Your word come *t* . . . . 1 Kin 8:26
been without the *t* God . . . . 2 Chr 15:3
t before the LORD his . . . . . 2 Chr 31:20
and *t* laws, good statutes . . . Neh 9:13
it is *t*. Hear it, and know . . . . Job 5:27
judgments of the LORD are *t* . . Ps 19:9
A *t* witness delivers . . . . . . Prov 14:25
But the LORD is the *t* . . . . . . Jer 10:10
"Let the LORD be a *t* . . . . Jer 42:5
executed *t* judgment . . . . . . Ezek 18:8
Execute *t* justice, show . . . . Zech 7:9
we know that You are *t* . . . Matt 22:16
That was the *t* Light . . . . John 1:9
He witnesses of Me is *t* . . . . John 5:32
the *t* bread from heaven . . . John 6:32
One who sent Him is *t* . . . . John 7:18
He who sent Me is *t* . . . . . . John 7:28
judge, My judgment is *t* . . . John 8:16
testimony of two men is *t* . . John 8:17
about this Man were *t* . . . John 10:41
I am the *t* vine, and My . . . . John 15:1
You, the only *t* God . . . . . . John 17:3
Indeed, let God be *t* . . . . Rom 3:4
whatever things are *t* . . . . . . Phil 4:8
which are copies of the *t* . . . Heb 9:24
let us draw near with a *t* . . Heb 10:22
which thing is *t* in Him . . . 1 John 2:8
may know Him who is *t* . . 1 John 5:20
is holy, He who is *t* . . . . Rev 3:7
t are Your ways, O King . . . . Rev 15:3
For *t* and righteous are . . . . . Rev 19:2
"These are the *t* . . . . Rev 19:9
was called Faithful and *T* . . Rev 19:11
for these words are *t* . . . . . . Rev 21:5

TRULY
It *t* flows with milk and . . . Num 13:27
You shall *t* tithe all the . . . Deut 14:22
t my words are not false . . . . Job 36:4
T God is good to Israel, to . . . Ps 73:1
LORD, *t* I am Your servant . . Ps 116:16
T You are God, who hide . . . . Is 45:15

T You are the Son of ..... Matt 14:33
T this was the Son of ..... Matt 27:54
T this Man was the Son .. Mark 15:39
T, I say to you that he ....Luke 12:44
t the Son of Man goes ...Luke 22:22
that this is *t* the Christ .....John 7:26
"*T* this is the Prophet .....John 7:40
that God is *t* among you ...1 Cor 14:25
T the signs of an ....2 Cor 12:12
t righteousness would have ...Gal 3:21
t the love of God is ....1 John 2:5

TRUMPET
When the *t* sounds long, ...Ex 19:13
you hear the sound of the *t* ..Josh 6:5
LORD with the sound of a *t* ...Ps 47:5
Blow the *t* at the time ....Ps 81:3
and when he blows a *t*, you ...Is 18:3
"Blow the *t* in the ....Jer 4:5
Lord GOD will blow the *t*...Zech 9:14
deed, do not sound a *t* ......Matt 6:2
t makes an uncertain ......1 Cor 14:8
For the *t* will sound ......1 Cor 15:52
and with the *t* of God ...1 Thess 4:16
loud voice, as of a *t* ....Rev 1:10
t of the three angels who ...Rev 8:13
sixth angel who had the *t* ...Rev 9:14

TRUMPETS
the priests shall blow the *t* ..Josh 6:4
and their *t* in their hands ....Judg 7:8
With *t* and the sound of a *t* ...Ps 98:6
to them were given seven *t* ..Rev 8:2

TRUST
in whom I will *t* ....2 Sam 22:3
a shield to all who *t* in ...2 Sam 22:31
We *t* in the LORD our .....2 Kin 18:22
they put their *t* in Him ....1 Chr 5:20
t is a spider's web ....Job 8:14
He slay me, yet will I *t* .....Job 13:15
If God puts no *t* ....Job 15:15
and put your *t* in the LORD ....Ps 4:5
who put their *t* in You .....Ps 5:11
strength, in whom I will *t* .....Ps 18:2
shield to all who *t* in Him ...Ps 18:30
you made Me *t* ....Ps 22:9
as for me, I *t* in You, O ...Ps 31:14
T in the LORD...............Ps 37:3
t also in Him, and He shall ...Ps 37:5
I *t* in the mercy of God ....Ps 52:8
In You, O LORD, I put my *t* ...Ps 71:1
You are my *t* from my ....Ps 71:5
my God, in Him I will *t* ....Ps 91:2
It is better to *t* in the LORD ...Ps 118:8
T in the LORD with all ....Prov 3:5
that your *t* may be in .....Prov 22:19
who put their *t* in Him ...Prov 30:5
my salvation, I will *t* ....Is 12:2
T in the LORD forever, for in ...Is 26:4
We *t* in the LORD our God,' ...Is 36:7
Let him *t* in the name ......Is 50:10
But he who puts his *t* in Me ..Is 57:13
Do not *t* in these ....Jer 7:4
My name, in which you *t* ....Jer 7:14
you have put your *t* in Me ...Jer 39:18
Do not *t* in a friend ....Mic 7:5
He knows those who *t* in ....Nah 1:7
name Gentiles will *t* .....Matt 12:21
those who *t* in riches .....Mark 10:24
such *t* through Christ ....2 Cor 3:4
committed to your *t* ....1 Tim 6:20
I will put My *t* in Him ......Heb 2:13

TRUSTED
He *t* in the LORD God of ...2 Kin 18:5
"He *t* in the LORD ....Ps 22:8
Because we have *t* in His .....Ps 33:21
t in the abundance of his .....Ps 52:7
He *t* in God ....Matt 27:43
that we who first *t* ....Eph 1:12
the holy women who *t* ......1 Pet 3:5

TRUSTS
But he who *t* in the ....Ps 32:10

is the man who *t* in Him .....Ps 34:8
whoever *t* in the LORD......Prov 16:20
he who *t* in the LORD.....Prov 28:25
He who *t* in his own .....Prov 28:26
whoever *t* in the LORD .....Prov 29:25
the man who *t* in the LORD ..Jer 17:7

TRUTH
See SPIRIT OF TRUTH; WORD OF TRUTH
led me in the way of *t* .....Gen 24:48
justice, a God of *t* ....Deut 32:4
Him in sincerity and in *t* ...Josh 24:14
serve Him in *t* with all ...1 Sam 12:24
the *t* in the name of the ..2 Chr 18:15
and speaks the *t* ....Ps 15:2
me in Your *t* and teach me ...Ps 25:5
all His work is done in *t* ....Ps 33:4
t continually preserve .....Ps 40:11
Behold, You desire *t* ....Ps 51:6
T shall spring out of ....Ps 85:11
t shall be your shield ....Ps 91:4
And His *t* endures to all .....Ps 100:5
the *t* of the LORD endures....Ps 117:2
t utterly out of my ....Ps 119:43
and Your law is *t* ....Ps 119:142
commandments are *t* .....Ps 119:151
of Your word is *t* ....Ps 119:160
who speaks *t* declares .....Prov 12:17
t belong to those who ....Prov 14:22
t atonement is provided ....Prov 16:6
walked before You in *t* ......Is 38:3
t is fallen in the ....Is 59:14
not valiant for the *t* ....Jer 9:3
cast *t* down to the ground ..Dan 8:12
in the Scripture of *T*.......Dan 10:21
"There is no *t* ....Hos 4:1
called the City of *T* ....Zech 8:3
speak each man the *t* .....Zech 8:16
love *t* and peace ....Zech 8:19
t was in his mouth ....Mal 2:6
t came through Jesus ......John 1:17
worship in spirit and *t* .....John 4:24
you shall know the *t* ....John 8:32
"I am the way, the *t* ....John 14:6
He, the Spirit of *t* ....John 16:13
Your word is *t* ....John 17:17
be sanctified by the *t* .....John 17:19
to Him, "What is *t* ....John 18:38
speak the words of *t* ......Acts 26:25
who suppress the *t* ....Rom 1:18
of sincerity and *t* ....1 Cor 5:8
but rejoices in the *t* ....1 Cor 13:6
but, speaking the *t* ....Eph 4:15
each one speak *t* with his ...Eph 4:25
your waist with *t* ....Eph 6:14
in the word of the *t* ....Col 1:5
the love of the *t* ....2 Thess 2:10
I am speaking the *t* ....1 Tim 2:7
they may know the *t* .....2 Tim 2:25
the knowledge of the *t* ....2 Tim 3:7
in the present *t* ....2 Pet 1:12
way of *t* will be ....2 Pet 2:2
but in deed and in *t* ......1 John 3:18
that we are of the *t* ....1 John 3:19
we know the spirit of *t* ....1 John 4:6
the Spirit is *t* ....1 John 5:6
t that is in you ....3 John 3

TRUTHFUL
The *t* lip shall be ....Prov 12:19

TRUTHFULLY
deal *t* are His delight .....Prov 12:22

TRY
t my mind and my heart ......Ps 26:2
t me, and know my ....Ps 139:23
refine them and *t* them ......Jer 9:7
t Me now in this ....Mal 3:10
which is to *t* you ....1 Pet 4:12

TUBAL
Son of Japheth, Gen 10:2
——— Tribe associated with Javan and
Meshech, Is 66:19

In Gog's army, Ezek 38:2, 3
Punishment of, Ezek 32:26, 27

TUBAL-CAIN
Son of Lamech, Gen 4:19–22

TUMORS
the boils of Egypt, with *t* ..Deut 28:27
and struck them with *t* ...1 Sam 5:6
Five golden *t* and five .....1 Sam 6:4

TUMULT
their waves, and the *t* ....Ps 65:7
Your enemies make a *t* ......Ps 83:2

TUNIC
Also he made him a *t* ......Gen 37:3
and take away your *t* ......Matt 5:40
not withhold your *t* ....Luke 6:29
the *t* was without seam, ..John 19:23

TUNICS
the LORD God made *t*......Gen 3:21
not to put on two *t* ....Mark 6:9
He who has two *t*, let him ..Luke 3:11
weeping, showing the *t* .....Acts 9:39

TURBAN
like a robe and a *t* ....Job 29:14
"Remove the *t* ....Ezek 21:26

TURN
T from Your fierce wrath, ...Ex 32:12
Do not *t* to idols, nor make ..Lev 19:4
you shall not *t* ....Deut 17:11
LORD may *t* away from ....Num 25:4
do not *t* from it to the right ...Josh 1:7
t from their sin because ...1 Kin 8:35
T from your evil ways, ...2 Kin 17:13
do not *t* to iniquity, for .....Job 36:21
t to the LORD, and all the ...Ps 22:27
T Yourself to me, and have ..Ps 25:16
do not *t* Your servant away ..Ps 27:9
Then we will not *t* ....Ps 80:18
but let them not *t* ....Ps 85:8
t to me, and have mercy ....Ps 86:16
yet I do not *t* ....Ps 119:51
T at my rebuke ....Prov 1:23
Do not *t* to the right or ....Prov 4:27
not let your heart *t* ....Prov 7:25
I will *t* My hand against you, ..Is 1:25
every man will *t* to his own ..Is 13:14
'*T* now everyone from ......Jer 35:15
T us back to You, O ....Lam 5:21
"Repent, *t* away from......Ezek 14:6
Repent, and *t* from all ...Ezek 18:30
T, *t* from your evil ways ...Ezek 33:11
T to me with all your ....Joel 2:12
yes, let every one *t* ....Jon 3:8
"*T* now from your evil .....Zech 1:4
those who *t* away an alien ...Mal 3:5
he will *t* the hearts of the ....Mal 4:6
on your right cheek, *t* ....Matt 5:39
t the hearts of the ....Luke 1:17
you that you should *t* .....Acts 14:15
t them from darkness .....Acts 26:18
repent, *t* to God, and do ...Acts 26:20
Let him *t* away from ....1 Pet 3:11
waters to *t* them to blood ..Rev 11:6

TURN ASIDE
t and see this great ....Ex 3:3
t after many to pervert .....Ex 23:2
t and serve other gods ....Deut 11:16
So you shall not *t* ....Deut 28:14
Law of Moses, lest you *t* ..Josh 23:6
they went, and did not *t* ..1 Sam 6:12
t from following the ......1 Sam 12:20
He did not *t* from them ...1 Kin 22:43
did not *t* from it ....2 Chr 20:32
The paths of their way *t* ....Job 6:18
nor such as *t* to lies ....Ps 40:4
I do not *t* from Your law ...Ps 119:51
such as *t* to their crooked ..Ps 125:5
Do not let your heart *t* .....Prov 7:25
to *t* the justice due ....Lam 3:35

did not *t* when they went . . Ezek 1:17
did not *t* when they . . . . . . Ezek 10:11

TURNED
in the river were *t* to blood . . . Ex 7:20
who *t* to the LORD with . . . 2 Kin 23:25
t to the LORD God of . . . . . 2 Chr 15:4
and *t* their backs on . . . . . . 2 Chr 29:6
t me over to the hands of . . Job 16:11
I love have *t* against . . . . Job 19:19
kept His way and not *t* . . . . Job 23:11
The wicked shall be *t* . . . . Ps 9:17
let them be *t* back and . . . . Ps 70:2
t my feet to Your . . . . Ps 119:59
of Israel, they have *t* . . . . Is 1:4
LORD has not *t* back from . . . . . Jer 4:8
shall be *t* into darkness . . . . . Joel 2:31
that they *t* from their evil . . . Jon 3:10
Then He *t* to the woman . . . Luke 7:44
sorrow will be *t* into joy . . . John 16:20
sun shall be *t* into . . . . Acts 2:20
saw him and *t* to the Lord . . Acts 9:35
number believed and *t* . . . . Acts 11:21
and how you *t* to God . . . . 1 Thess 1:9

TURNING
Gentiles who are *t* to . . . . . Acts 15:19
marvel that you are *t* . . . . Gal 1:6
or shadow of *t* . . . . James 1:17
and *t* the cities of Sodom . . . . 2 Pet 2:6

TURNS
of the wicked He *t* . . . . Ps 146:9
A soft answer *t* . . . . Prov 15:1
he *t*, he prospers . . . . Prov 17:8
One who *t* away his ear . . . . Prov 28:9
when a righteous man *t* . . . . Ezek 3:20
But if a wicked man *t* . . . . Ezek 18:21
a wicked man *t* away . . . . . Ezek 18:27
he *t* from his sin and . . . . . Ezek 33:14
t from his wickedness . . . . Ezek 33:19
but no one *t* back . . . . Nah 2:8
that he who *t* . . . . James 5:20

TURTLEDOVE
the life of Your *t* . . . . Ps 74:19
t is heard in our land . . . . . . Song 2:12

TURTLEDOVES
of *t* or young pigeons . . . . Lev 1:14
A pair of *t* or two young . . . Luke 2:24

TUTOR
the law was our *t* . . . . Gal 3:24
no longer under a *t* . . . . Gal 3:25

TWELVE
the sons of Jacob were *t* . . . Gen 35:22
are the *t* tribes of Israel . . . Gen 49:28
were *t* stones according . . . . Ex 39:14
t men, each one . . . . Num 1:44
Joshua set up *t* stones . . . . Josh 4:9
Solomon had *t* governors . . . 1 Kin 4:7
Elijah took *t* stones, ... 1 Kin 18:31
Manasseh was *t* years . . . . . 2 Kin 21:1
called His *t* disciples to . . . . Matt 10:1
These *t* Jesus sent out . . . . . Matt 10:5
they took up *t* baskets . . . . Matt 14:20
more than *t* legions of . . . . Matt 26:53
Then He appointed *t* . . . . . . Mark 3:14
of blood for *t* years . . . . . . Mark 5:25
took up *t* baskets full . . . . Mark 6:43
when He was *t* years old . . . Luke 2:42
He chose *t* whom He . . . . . . Luke 6:13
a flow of blood for *t* . . . . . . Luke 8:43
t baskets of the leftover . . . Luke 9:17
filled *t* baskets with the . . . . John 6:13
I not choose you, the *t* . . . . John 6:70
head a garland of *t* stars . . . Rev 12:1
t gates were *t* pearls . . . . . . Rev 21:21

TWELVE APOSTLES
Now the names of the *t* . . . . Matt 10:2
and the *t* with Him . . . . Luke 22:14
the names of the *t* . . . . Rev 21:14

TWELVE DISCIPLES
when He had called His *t* . . Matt 10:1

commanding His *t* . . . . Matt 11:1
took the *t* aside on the . . . . Matt 20:17
Then He called His *t* . . . . Luke 9:1

TWELVE TRIBES
these are the *t* of Israel . . . . Gen 49:28
pillars according to the *t* . . . . . Ex 24:4
name according to the *t* . . . . . Ex 39:14
inheritance among the *t* . . Ezek 47:13
judging the *t* . . . . Matt 19:28
To this promise our *t* . . . . . . Acts 26:7
the *t* which are scattered . . James 1:1
the names of the *t* . . . . Rev 21:12

TWICE
the rock *t* with his rod . . . . Num 20:11
t as much as he had . . . . Job 42:10
the rooster crows *t* . . . . . . Mark 14:30
the rooster crows *t* . . . . . . Mark 14:72

TWILIGHT
at *t* is the LORD's Passover . . Lev 23:5
sacrifice the Passover at *t* . . Deut 16:6

TWIN
figurehead was the *T* . . . . . Acts 28:11

TWINS
there were *t* in her womb . . Gen 25:24
behold, *t* were in her . . . . . . Gen 38:27
two fawns, *t* of a gazelle . . . . Song 7:3

TWIST
All day they *t* my . . . . Ps 56:5
unstable people *t* to . . . . 2 Pet 3:16

TWO
God made *t* great lights . . . . Gen 1:16
t each of animals that are . . . . Gen 7:2
the ark to Noah, *t* . . . . Gen 7:15
T nations are in your . . . . . Gen 25:23
t rams without blemish, ... Ex 29:1
He gave Moses *t* tablets of . . Ex 31:18
shall be unclean *t* weeks . . . Lev 12:5
t young pigeons . . . . Lev 12:8
t tablets of the covenant . . Deut 9:15
hewed *t* tablets of stone . . . Deut 10:3
by the mouth of *t* or . . . . . Deut 19:15
the *t* middle pillars . . . . . . Judg 16:29
divided the Red Sea in *t* . . . . Ps 136:13
T are better than one . . . . Eccl 4:9
t he covered his . . . . Is 6:2
a ram which had *t* horns . . . . Dan 8:3
saw, having the *t* horns . . . . Dan 8:20
there stood *t* others, one . . . . Dan 12:5
one mile, go with him *t* . . . . Matt 5:41
five loaves and *t* fish . . . . . Matt 14:17
'by the mouth of *t* or . . . . . Matt 18:16
For where *t* or three are . . Matt 18:20
t shall become one . . . . Matt 19:5
A man had *t* sons, and . . . . Matt 21:28
five talents, to another *t* . . Matt 25:15
t robbers were crucified . . Matt 27:38
in *t* from top to bottom . . . Matt 27:51
said, "Five, and *t* fish . . . . . Mark 6:38
t shall become one flesh' . . Mark 10:8
and threw in *t* mites, ... Mark 12:42
also crucified *t* robbers . . . Mark 15:27
in *t* from top to bottom . . . Mark 15:38
t young pigeons . . . . Luke 2:24
t fish, unless we go and . . . . Luke 9:13
certain man had *t* sons . . . . Luke 15:11
servant can serve *t* . . . . Luke 16:13
widow putting in *t* mites . . . Luke 21:2
were also *t* others, ... Luke 23:32
temple was torn in *t* . . . . . Luke 23:45
t of them were traveling . . Luke 24:13
T hundred denarii worth . . . . John 6:7
t small fish, but what are . . . John 6:9

these are the *t* covenants . . . . Gal 4:24
new man from the *t* . . . . Eph 2:15
t shall become one flesh . . . . Eph 5:31
from *t* or three witnesses . . 1 Tim 5:19
was *t* hundred million; I . . . . Rev 9:16
power to my *t* witnesses . . . . Rev 11:3
had *t* horns like a lamb . . . . Rev 13:11

TWO-EDGED SWORD
and a *t* in their hand . . . . . . Ps 149:6
as wormwood, sharp as a *t* . . Prov 5:4
sharper than any *t* . . . . Heb 4:12
His mouth went a sharp *t* . . Rev 1:16
He who has the sharp *t* . . . . Rev 2:12

TYCHICUS
Paul's companion, Acts 20:1, 4
Paul's messenger, Eph 6:21, 22; Col
4:7–9; 2 Tim 4:12

TYPE
of Adam, who is a *t* . . . . Rom 5:14

TYRE
City of Phoenicia noted for its commerce, Josh 19:29; 2 Sam 5:11; Jer
25:22

TYRE AND SIDON
cut off from *T* every helper . . Jer 47:4
you to do with Me, O *T* . . . . . Joel 3:4
had been done in *T* . . . . Matt 11:21
to the region of *T* . . . . Matt 15:21
more tolerable for *T* at . . . . Luke 10:14
with the people of *T* . . . . . . Acts 12:20

UGLY
And the *u* and gaunt cows . . Gen 41:4

ULAI
Scene of Daniel's visions, Dan 8:2–16

UNAFRAID
Do you want to be *u* . . . . Rom 13:3

UNAWARE
I do not want you to be *u* . . Rom 1:13
not want you to be *u* . . . . . 1 Cor 10:11

UNBELIEF
because of their *u* . . . . Matt 13:58
Because of your *u* . . . . Matt 17:20
help my *u* . . . . Mark 9:24
and He rebuked their *u* . . Mark 16:14
promise of God through *u* . . Rom 4:20
did it ignorantly in *u* . . . . . 1 Tim 1:13
you an evil heart of *u* . . . . . . Heb 3:12
enter in because of *u* . . . . . . Heb 3:19

UNBELIEVER
But if the *u* departs, let . . . 1 Cor 7:15
has a believer with an *u* . . 2 Cor 6:15
and is worse than an *u* . . . . . 1 Tim 5:8

UNBELIEVERS
his portion with the *u* . . . . Luke 12:46
who believe but to *u* . . . . . 1 Cor 14:22
are uninformed or *u* . . . . . . 1 Cor 14:23
yoked together with *u* . . . . 2 Cor 6:14

UNBELIEVING
Do not be *u* . . . . John 20:27
u Jews stirred up the . . . . . . Acts 14:2
For the *u* husband is . . . . . . 1 Cor 7:14
u nothing is pure . . . . Titus 1:15
But the cowardly, *u* . . . . Rev 21:8

UNCIRCUMCISED
heed me, for I am of *u* lips . . . Ex 6:12
Behold, I am of *u* lips, and . . . Ex 6:30
For no *u* person shall eat it . . . Ex 12:48
u hearts are humbled . . . . . Lev 26:41
is this *u* Philistine . . . . 1 Sam 17:26
of Israel are *u* in the heart . . . Jer 9:26
u in heart and *u* in flesh . . Ezek 44:7
You stiff-necked and *u* . . . . Acts 7:51
not the physically *u* . . . . . . Rom 2:27
by faith and the *u* . . . . Rom 3:30
only, or upon the *u* also . . . . Rom 4:9

u had been committed . . . . Gal 2:7
nor Jew, circumcised nor *u* . . Col 3:11

UNCIRCUMCISION
has become *u* . . . . Rom 2:25
u is nothing, but keeping . . 1 Cor 7:19
who are called *U* by . . . . Eph 2:11

UNCLEAN
of animals that are *u* . . . . Gen 7:2
person touches any *u* thing . . . Lev 5:2
u thing shall not be eaten . . . Lev 7:19
to the LORD, while he is *u* . . Lev 7:20
who touches any *u* . . . . Lev 7:21
They are *u* to you . . . . Lev 11:8
these you shall become *u* . . Lev 11:24
I am a man of *u* lips . . . . Is 6:5
u shall no longer come . . . . Is 52:1
we are all like an *u* thing . . . . . Is 64:6
I pronounced them *u* . . . . . Ezek 20:26
He commands even the *u* . . Mark 1:27
commands the *u* spirits . . . Luke 4:36
any man common or *u* . . . . Acts 10:28
there is nothing *u* . . . . Rom 14:14
your children would be *u* . . 1 Cor 7:14
Do not touch what is *u* . . . . 2 Cor 6:17
that no fornicator, *u* . . . . Eph 5:5

UNCLEAN SPIRIT
u to depart from the land . . Zech 13:2
u goes out of a man . . . . Matt 12:43
synagogue with an *u* . . . . . . Mark 1:23
u had convulsed him . . . . . . Mark 1:26
"He has an *u* . . . . Mark 3:30
a man with an *u* . . . . Mark 5:2
daughter had an *u* . . . . Mark 7:25
He rebuked the *u* . . . . Mark 9:25
He had commanded the *u* . . Luke 8:29
Jesus rebuked the *u* . . . . . . Luke 9:42
u goes out of a man . . . . . Luke 11:24

UNCLEAN SPIRITS
them power over *u* . . . . Matt 10:1
He commands even the *u* . . Mark 1:27
u, whenever they saw . . . . . Mark 3:11
u went out and entered . . . . Mark 5:13
tormented with *u* . . . . Luke 6:18
who were tormented by *u* . . Acts 5:16
u, crying with a loud . . . . Acts 8:7
three *u* like frogs . . . . Rev 16:13

UNCLEANNESS
of Israel from their *u*, lest . . Lev 15:31
for sin and for *u* . . . . Zech 13:1
men's bones and all *u* . . . . Matt 23:27
also gave them up to *u* . . . . Rom 1:24
members as slaves of *u* . . . . Rom 6:19
adultery, fornication, *u*, ... Gal 5:19
fornication, *u*, passion, evil . . . Col 3:5
did not call us to *u* . . . . . . 1 Thess 4:7
flesh in the lust of *u* . . . . . . 2 Pet 2:10

UNCLEANNESSES
from all your *u* . . . . Ezek 36:29

UNCLOTHED
we want to be *u* . . . . 2 Cor 5:4

UNCOVER
Do not *u* your heads nor . . . Lev 10:6
shall not *u* her nakedness . . . Lev 18:7
u the woman's head, a . . . Num 5:18
the LORD will *u* their secret . . . . Is 3:17
skirt, *u* the thigh . . . . Is 47:2
he will *u* your sins . . . . Lam 4:22

UNCOVERED
and became *u* in his tent . . . Gen 9:21
of the world were *u* . . . 2 Sam 22:16
I have *u* his secret places, . . Jer 49:10
its foundation will be *u* . . . Ezek 13:14
transgressions are *u* . . . . . Ezek 21:24
they *u* the roof where He . . Mark 2:4
head *u* dishonors her . . . . . 1 Cor 11:5
to God with her head *u* . . . 1 Cor 11:13

UNCOVERS
u her nakedness, he has . . . Lev 20:18
u deep things out of . . . . . . Job 12:22

UNDEFILED
Blessed are the *u* . . . . Ps 119:1
all, and the bed *u* . . . . Heb 13:4
u religion before God . . . . James 1:27
incorruptible and *u* . . . . I Pet 1:4

UNDER HIS FEET
And there was *u* . . . . Ex 24:10
down with darkness *u* . . . 2 Sam 22:10
You have put all things *u* . . . . Ps 8:6
has put all enemies *u* . . . 1 Cor 15:25
And He put all things *u* . . . . Eph 1:22
things in subjection *u* . . . . . . Heb 2:8

UNDER THE LAW
to those who are *u* . . . . Rom 3:19
to those who are *u* . . . . . . 1 Cor 9:20
of a woman, born *u* . . . . Gal 4:4
you who desire to be *u* . . . . Gal 4:21
Spirit, you are not *u* . . . . Gal 5:18

UNDERFOOT
Lord has trampled *u* all . . . Lam 1:15
the Son of God *u* . . . . Heb 10:29

UNDERMINE
And you *u* your friend . . . . . . Job 6:27

UNDERSTAND
u one another's speech . . . . Gen 11:7
cause me to *u* wherein I . . . . Job 6:24
of His power who can . . . . Job 26:14
can anyone *u* the . . . . Job 36:29
uttered what I did not . . . . . Job 42:3
if there are any who *u* . . . . . . Ps 14:2
Who can *u* his errors . . . . . . Ps 19:12
in Egypt did not *u* . . . . Ps 106:7
Make me *u* the way of . . . . Ps 119:27
then you will *u* the fear of . . Prov 2:5
you will *u* righteousness . . . Prov 2:9
is to *u* his way . . . . Prov 14:8
Evil men do not *u* . . . . Prov 28:5
hearing, but do not *u* . . . . Is 6:9
so that they cannot *u* . . . . . . Is 44:18
and quick to *u* . . . . Dan 1:4
set your heart to *u* . . . . . . Dan 10:12
u shall instruct many . . . . Dan 11:33
of the wicked shall *u* . . . . . Dan 12:10
people who do not *u* . . . . . Hos 4:14
Let him *u* these things . . . . . Hos 14:9
nor do they *u* His counsel . . Mic 4:12
will hear and shall not *u* . . Matt 13:14
should *u* with their heart . . Matt 13:15
they may hear and not *u* . . Mark 4:12
hearing they may not *u* . . Luke 8:10
Why do you not *u* . . . . . . John 8:43
u with their hearts and . . . John 12:40
I am doing you do not *u* . . . John 13:7
u what you are reading . . . . Acts 8:30
lest they should *u* . . . . . . Acts 28:27
I am doing, I do not *u* . . . . Rom 7:15
have not heard shall *u* . . . Rom 15:21
u all mysteries . . . . 1 Cor 13:2
some things hard to *u* . . . . . 2 Pet 3:16

UNDERSTANDING
of God, in wisdom, in *u*, in . . . Ex 31:3
a woman of good *u* . . . . . . 1 Sam 25:3
asked for yourself *u* . . . . . . 1 Kin 3:11
and exceedingly great *u* . . . 1 Kin 4:29
filled with wisdom and *u* . . . 1 Kin 7:14
He has counsel and *u* . . . . . Job 12:13
He takes away the *u* of . . . . Job 12:24
by His *u* He breaks up . . . . Job 26:12
is the place of *u* . . . . Job 28:12
depart from evil is *u* . . . . . . Job 28:28
Almighty gives him *u* . . . . . . Job 32:8
If you have *u*, hear this . . . . Job 34:16
has given *u* to the heart . . . Job 38:36
not endow her with *u* . . . . . Job 39:17
my heart shall give *u* . . . . Ps 49:3
a good *u* have all those . . . . Ps 111:10
Give me *u* . . . . Ps 119:34
give me *u*, that I may . . . . . Ps 119:73
Your precepts I get *u* . . . . Ps 119:104

give me *u*, that I may . . . . . Ps 119:125
give me *u*, and I shall . . . . Ps 119:144
give me *u* according to . . . . Ps 119:169
His *u* is infinite . . . . Ps 147:5
a man of *u* will attain wise . . Prov 1:5
apply your heart to *u* . . . . . . Prov 2:2
u will keep you . . . . Prov 2:11
lean not on your own *u* . . . . . Prov 3:5
u He established . . . . Prov 3:19
with a woman lacks *u* . . . . . Prov 6:32
As for him who lacks *u*, ... Prov 9:4
and go in the way of *u* . . . . . Prov 9:6
of the Holy One is *u* . . . . . . Prov 9:10
a man of *u* has wisdom . . . Prov 10:23
but a man of *u* holds his . . Prov 11:12
frivolity is devoid of *u* . . . . Prov 12:11
Good *u* gains favor, but . . . Prov 13:15
to wrath has great *u* . . . . . Prov 14:29
him who has *u* seeks . . . . . Prov 15:14
but a man of *u* walks . . . . . Prov 15:21
who heeds rebuke gets *u* . . Prov 15:32
And to get *u* is to be . . . . . Prov 16:16
U is a wellspring . . . . Prov 16:22
A man devoid of *u* . . . . Prov 17:18
A fool has no delight in *u* . . Prov 18:2
u will find good . . . . Prov 19:8
the way of *u* will rest in . . . Prov 21:16
and instruction and *u* . . . . Prov 23:23
but the poor who has *u* . . . Prov 28:2
A ruler who lacks *u* is a . . . Prov 28:16
Spirit of wisdom and *u* . . . . . . Is 11:2
For it is a people of no *u* . . . . Is 27:11
His *u* is unsearchable . . . . . . Is 40:28
the heaven by His *u* . . . . . Jer 51:15
also still without *u* . . . . . . Matt 15:16
heart, with all the *u* . . . . . Mark 12:33
And He opened their *u* . . . Luke 24:45
also pray with the *u* . . . . . 1 Cor 14:15
five words with my *u* . . . . . 1 Cor 14:19
but in *u* be mature . . . . . . 1 Cor 14:20
having their *u* darkened, . . . Eph 4:18
God, which surpasses all *u* . . Phil 4:7
and spiritual *u* . . . . Col 1:9
the Lord give you *u* . . . . . . 2 Tim 2:7
Who is wise and *u* . . . . . . James 3:13
and has given us an *u* . . . 1 John 5:20
him who has *u* calculate . . . Rev 13:18

UNDERSTANDS
God *u* its way, and He . . . . Job 28:23
all plain to him who *u* . . . . . Prov 8:9
is easy to him who *u* . . . . . Prov 14:6
there is none who *u* . . . . . . Rom 3:11

UNDERSTOOD
all Israel *u* that day . . . . 2 Sam 3:37
my ear has heard and *u* it . . Job 13:1
Then I *u* their end . . . . Ps 73:17
My heart has *u* great . . . . . Eccl 1:16
Have you not *u* from . . . . . . Is 40:21
u all these things . . . . Matt 13:51
clearly seen, being *u* . . . . . Rom 1:20
I *u* as a child, I thought . . 1 Cor 13:11

UNDESIRABLE
gather together, O *u* . . . . . . Zeph 2:1

UNDIGNIFIED
I will be even more *u* . . . . 2 Sam 6:22

UNDISCERNING
u, untrustworthy . . . . Rom 1:31

UNDONE
He left nothing *u* of all . . . Josh 11:15
"Woe is me, for I am *u* . . . . . Is 6:5
leaving the others *u* . . . . . Matt 23:23

UNEDUCATED
that they were *u* . . . . Acts 4:13

UNEQUALLY
Do not be *u* yoked . . . . . . 2 Cor 6:14

UNEXPECTEDLY
that Day come on you *u* . . Luke 21:34

UNFAITHFUL
they were *u* to the God .... 1 Chr 5:25
u will be uprooted .... Prov 2:22
but the *u* will be taken by .. Prov 11:6
way of the *u* is hard ...... Prov 13:15
they were *u* to Me ...... Ezek 39:23

UNFAITHFULLY
back and acted *u* .... Ps 78:57

UNFAITHFULNESS
because of their *u* .... 1 Chr 9:1
So Saul died for his *u* .. 1 Chr 10:13
they have persisted in *u*,' .. Ezek 15:8

UNFAMILIAR
to a people of *u* speech ..... Ezek 3:5

UNFORGIVING
unloving, *u* .... Rom 1:31
unloving, *u*, slanderers, ... 2 Tim 3:3

UNFORMED
substance, being yet *u* ..... Ps 139:16

UNFRUITFUL
and it becomes *u* .... Mark 4:19
my understanding is *u* .. 1 Cor 14:14
the *u* works of darkness .... Eph 5:11
that they may not be *u* .... Titus 3:14

UNGODLINESS
u made me afraid .... Ps 18:4
heaven against all *u* ...... Rom 1:18
He will turn away *u* ..... Rom 11:26

UNGODLY
delivered me to the *u* ..... Job 16:11
u shall not stand .... Ps 1:5
of the *u* shall perish .... Ps 1:6
my cause against an *u* ...... Ps 43:1
u man digs up evil .... Prov 16:27
who justifies the *u* .... Rom 4:5
Christ died for the *u* ...... Rom 5:6
and perdition of *u* men ...... 2 Pet 3:7
convict all who are *u* .... Jude 15

UNHOLY
the holy and *u* .... Ezek 22:26
for sinners, for the *u* .... 1 Tim 1:9

UNINFORMED
the place of the *u* .... 1 Cor 14:16

UNINHABITED
shall be *u* forty years ..... Ezek 29:11
and your cities shall be *u* .. Ezek 35:9

UNINTENDED
the LORD, for their *u* sin .. Num 15:25

UNINTENTIONAL
them, for it was *u* .... Num 15:25

UNINTENTIONALLY
If a person sins *u* against ..... Lev 4:2
If you sin *u*, and do not ... Num 15:22
kills his neighbor *u* .... Deut 4:42
sinned *u* or in ignorance .. Ezek 45:20

UNITE
U my heart to fear .... Ps 86:11

UNITY
to dwell together in *u* ...... Ps 133:1
to keep the *u* of the .... Eph 4:3
we all come to the *u* .... Eph 4:13

UNJUST
hope of the *u* perishes ..... Prov 11:7
u knows no shame .... Zeph 3:5
on the just and on the *u* .... Matt 5:45
commended the *u* .... Luke 16:8
he who is *u* in what is .... Luke 16:10
extortioners, *u* .... Luke 18:11
of the just and the *u* .... Acts 24:15
u who inflicts wrath .... Rom 3:5
For God is not *u* .... Heb 6:10
the just for the *u* .... 1 Pet 3:18
let him be *u* still .... Rev 22:11

UNJUSTLY
long will you judge *u* ...... Ps 82:2
he will deal *u* .... Is 26:10

UNKNOWN
not stand before *u* .... Prov 22:29
To The *U* God .... Acts 17:23
And I was *u* by face to ...... Gal 1:22

UNLAWFUL
You know how *u* it is ..... Acts 10:28

UNLEAVENED
See FEAST OF UNLEAVENED BREAD
the Feast of *U* Bread ...... Mark 14:1
since you truly are *u* ...... 1 Cor 5:7

UNLEAVENED BREAD
feast, and baked *u* .... Gen 19:3
roasted in fire, with *u* ...... Ex 12:8
observe the Feast of *U* .... Ex 12:17
u and parched grain .... Josh 5:11
the meat and the *u* ...... Judg 6:20
u among their brethren .... 2 Kin 23:9
to keep the Feast of *U* ... 2 Chr 30:13
they kept the Feast of *U* .... Ezra 6:22
day of the Feast of the *U* .. Matt 26:17
Feast of *U* .... Luke 22:1
during the Days of *U* ...... Acts 12:3
u of sincerity and truth ..... 1 Cor 5:8

UNLOVED
saw that Leah was *u* ...... Gen 29:31
both the loved and the *u*, .. Deut 21:15

UNLOVING
untrustworthy, *u* .... Rom 1:31

UNMARRIED
But I say to the *u* and ...... 1 Cor 7:8

UNMERCIFUL
unforgiving, *u* .... Rom 1:31

UNPREPARED
with me and find you *u* ..... 2 Cor 9:4

UNPRESENTABLE
u parts have greater ...... 1 Cor 12:23

UNPROFITABLE
And cast the *u* .... Matt 25:30
'We are *u* servants ...... Luke 17:10
have together become *u* .... Rom 3:12
who once was *u* to you .... Philem 11
for that would be *u* .... Heb 13:17

UNPROFITABLENESS
of its weakness and *u* .... Heb 7:18

UNPUNISHED
wicked will not go *u* ...... Prov 11:21
witness will not go *u* ...... Prov 19:9
be rich will not go *u* ..... Prov 28:20
You shall not go *u*, but ..... Jer 49:12

UNQUENCHABLE
up the chaff with *u* .... Matt 3:12
He will burn with *u* ...... Luke 3:17

UNRESTRAINED
that the people were *u* ...... Ex 32:25

UNRIGHTEOUS
u man his thoughts .... Is 55:7
been faithful in the *u* ..... Luke 16:11
u will not inherit the ...... 1 Cor 6:9

UNRIGHTEOUSNESS
and there is no *u* .... Ps 92:15
builds his house by *u* ...... Jer 22:13
Him is true, and no *u* ..... John 7:18
all ungodliness and *u* ...... Rom 1:18
the truth, but obey *u* .... Rom 2:8
as instruments of *u* to sin .. Rom 6:13
Is there *u* with God .... Rom 9:14
but had pleasure in *u* .... 2 Thess 2:12
will be merciful to their *u* ... Heb 8:12
receive the wages of *u* ... 2 Pet 2:13
cleanse us from all *u* .... 1 John 1:9
All *u* is sin .... 1 John 5:17

UNRULY
those who are *u* .... 1 Thess 5:14
It is an *u* evil .... James 3:8

UNSEARCHABLE
does great things, and *u* ...... Job 5:9
heart of kings is *u* .... Prov 25:3
u are His judgments ...... Rom 11:33

UNSHRUNK
No one puts a piece of *u* ... Matt 9:16

UNSKILLED
only of milk is *u* .... Heb 5:13

UNSPOTTED
to keep oneself *u* .... James 1:27

UNSTABLE
U as water .... Gen 49:4
man, *u* in all his ways ..... James 1:8
from sin, enticing *u* souls .. 2 Pet 2:14

UNSTOPPED
of the deaf shall be *u* .... Is 35:5

UNTAUGHT
which *u* and unstable ...... 2 Pet 3:16

UNTHANKFUL
disobedient to parents, *u* ... 2 Tim 3:2

UNTRAINED
and *u* men, they marveled .. Acts 4:13
Even though I am *u* in .... 2 Cor 11:6

UNTRUSTWORTHY
undiscerning, *u* .... Rom 1:31

UNUSUAL
to pass His act, His *u* act .... Is 28:21
God worked *u* miracles ... Acts 19:11

UNVEILED
But we all, with *u* face, ... 2 Cor 3:18

UNWASHED
but to eat with *u* hands ... Matt 15:20
eat bread with *u* hands ..... Mark 7:5

UNWISE
He is an *u* son .... Hos 13:13
both to wise and to *u* ...... Rom 1:14
Therefore do not be *u* ..... Eph 5:17

UNWITTINGLY
have *u* entertained angels ... Heb 13:2

UNWORTHY
and judge yourselves *u* .... Acts 13:46
u manner will be .... 1 Cor 11:27

UPHOLD
u the evildoers .... Job 8:20
u me with Your generous .... Ps 51:12
U me according to .... Ps 119:116
you, I will *u* you with My .... Is 41:10
My Servant whom I *u* ...... Is 42:1
there was no one to *u* .... Is 63:5
u the weak, be patient ... 1 Thess 5:14

UPHOLDING
u all things by the .... Heb 1:3

UPHOLDS
the LORD *u* the righteous .... Ps 37:17
Your right hand *u* .... Ps 63:8
LORD *u* all who fall......... Ps 145:14

UPPER ROOM
shut the doors of the *u* ..... Judg 3:23
carried him to the *u* ...... 1 Kin 17:19
the lattice of his *u* .... 2 Kin 1:2
let us make a small *u* .... 2 Kin 4:10
And in his *u* .... Dan 6:10
show you a large *u*...... Mark 14:15
they went up into the *u* ..... Acts 1:13
they laid her in an *u* ...... Acts 9:37
many lamps in the *u* ...... Acts 20:8

UPRIGHT
righteous and *u* is He ..... Deut 32:4
man was blameless and *u* .... Job 1:1
u man, one who fears God .... Job 1:8
where were the *u* .... Job 4:7
Good and *u* is the LORD ...... Ps 25:8
u shall have dominion........ Ps 49:14
declare that the LORD is *u* ... Ps 92:15

u will be blessed ....Ps 112:2
u there arises light ....Ps 112:4
For the *u* will dwell in the . . Prov 2:21
is strength for the *u* ......Prov 10:29
u will guide them ....Prov 11:3
u will deliver them ....Prov 11:6
u will flourish ....Prov 14:11
u is His delight ....Prov 15:8
of the *u* is a highway ......Prov 15:19
Whoever causes the *u* to . . Prov 28:10
that God made man *u* ......Eccl 7:29
and there is no one *u* ....Mic 7:2
his soul is not *u* ....Hab 2:4

UPRIGHT IN HEART
God, Who saves the *u* ....Ps 7:10
shoot secretly at the *u* ......Ps 11:2
shout for joy, all you *u* .....Ps 32:11
righteousness to the *u* ......Ps 36:10
all the *u* shall glory ....Ps 64:10
all the *u* will follow it ....Ps 94:15
gladness for the *u* ....Ps 97:11

UPRIGHTLY
He who walks *u*, and works . . Ps 15:2
from those who walk *u* ......Ps 84:11
shield to those who walk *u* . . Prov 2:7
understanding walks *u* .... Prov 15:21
good to him who walks *u* . . . . Mic 2:7

UPRIGHTNESS
to show man His *u* ....Job 33:23
praise You with *u* of heart . . . Ps 119:7
me in the land of *u* ....Ps 143:10
of *u* to walk in the ways ... Prov 2:13
walks in his *u* fears the .... Prov 14:2
princes for their *u* ....Prov 17:26
of the just is *u* ....Is 26:7
land of *u* he will deal ....Is 26:10

UPROAR
so that the city is in an *u* . . 1 Kin 1:45
be an *u* of the people ......Mark 14:2
After the *u* had ceased, ... Acts 20:1

UPROOT
He will *u* Israel from .... 1 Kin 14:15
then I will *u* ....2 Chr 7:20
u you from the land ....Ps 52:5
u the wheat with ....Matt 13:29

UPROOTED
LORD *u* them from their . . . Deut 29:28
my hope He has *u* like a . . . Job 19:10
unfaithful will be *u* from . . . Prov 2:22

UPWARD
prevailed fifteen cubits *u* .... Gen 7:20
trouble, as the sparks fly *u* . . Job 5:7
winds *u* for the wise ......Prov 15:24
downward, and bear fruit *u* . . Is 37:31
my eyes fail from looking *u* . . . Is 38:14

UR OF THE CHALDEANS
City of Abram's early life, Gen
11:28–31; 15:7
Located in Mesopotamia by Stephen,
Acts 7:2, 4

URGE
I *u* you to take heart, ... Acts 27:22
I *u* you, imitate ....1 Cor 4:16
Therefore I *u* you to ....2 Cor 2:8
I *u* you to become like me . . . Gal 4:12
I *u* you in the sight of ..... 1 Tim 6:13

URGED
the angels *u* Lot to hurry, . . Gen 19:15
His disciples *u* Him ....John 4:31
I strongly *u* him to ....1 Cor 16:12

URIAH
Hittite; one of David's warriors, 2 Sam
23:39
Husband of Bathsheba; condemned to
death by David, 2 Sam 11:1–27

URIJAH
High priest in Ahaz's time, 2 Kin
16:10–16

—— Prophet in Jeremiah's time, Jer
26:20–23

URIM
of judgment of *U* ....Ex 28:30
the judgment of the *U* .... Num 27:21
Thummim and Your *U* .... Deut 33:8
could consult with the *U* . . . Ezra 2:63
could consult with the *U* .... Neh 7:65

US
"God with *u* ....Matt 1:23
who is not against *u* ......Mark 9:40
If God is for *u* ....Rom 8:31
They went out from *u* .... 1 John 2:19

USE
who spitefully *u* you ....Matt 5:44
leaving the natural *u* ......Rom 1:27
u this world as not ....1 Cor 7:31
u liberty as an ....Gal 5:13
u a little wine ....1 Tim 5:23
reason of *u* have their ......Heb 5:14

USEFUL
Is it *u* for any work ....Ezek 15:4
u for the Master ....2 Tim 2:21
you, for he is *u* to me for . . 2 Tim 4:11

USELESS
all of them are *u* ....Is 44:9
are unprofitable and *u* ......Titus 3:9
one's religion is *u* ....James 1:26

USES
if one *u* it lawfully ....1 Tim 1:8

USING
u no figure of speech .....John 16:29
perish with the *u* ....Col 2:22
u liberty as a ....1 Pet 2:16

USURY
Take no *u* or ....Lev 25:36
exacting *u* from his brother . . Neh 5:7
put out his money at *u* .....Ps 15:5

UTTER
u words from their heart ....Job 8:10
nor my tongue *u* deceit .....Job 27:4
u pure knowledge ....Job 33:3
u dark sayings of old ....Ps 78:2
My lips shall *u* praise .....Ps 119:171
a false witness will *u* lies . . . Prov 14:5
heart will *u* perverse ......Prov 23:33
let not your heart *u* ....Eccl 5:2
I will *u* My judgments ......Jer 1:16
lawful for a man to *u* ......2 Cor 12:4

UTTERANCE
the Spirit gave them *u* ......Acts 2:4
u may be given to me ....Eph 6:19

UTTERED
The deep *u* its voice ....Hab 3:10
which cannot be *u* ....Rom 8:26
the seven thunders *u* ......Rev 10:4

UTTERLY
that I will *u* blot out the .....Ex 17:14
they *u* destroyed all that . . . Josh 6:21
lands by *u* destroying .... 2 Kin 19:11
he shall not be *u* cast down . . Ps 37:24
Oh, do not forsake me *u* .....Ps 119:8
it would be *u* despised .....Song 8:7
You have *u* rejected ....Lam 5:22
u destroyed from among . . . Acts 3:23
she will be *u* burned with . . . Rev 18:8

UTTERMOST
upon them to the *u* .....1 Thess 2:16
u those who come ....Heb 7:25

UTTERS
Day unto day *u* speech .....Ps 19:2
u His voice from ....Amos 1:2
and the great man *u* ....Mic 7:3

UZZAH
Son of Abinadab, struck down for
touching the ark of the covenant,
2 Sam 6:3–11

UZZIAH
King of Judah, called Azariah, 2 Kin
14:21; 15:1–7
Reigns righteously, 2 Chr 26:1–15
Usurps priestly function; stricken with
leprosy, 2 Chr 26:16–21
Life of, written by Isaiah, 2 Chr 26:22,
23

VAGABOND
v you shall be on the ....Gen 4:12

VAIN
of the LORD your God in *v* .... Ex 20:7
of the LORD your God in *v* . . Deut 5:11
the people plot a *v* ....Ps 2:1
they labor in *v* who build it . . Ps 127:1
v life which he passes ......Eccl 6:12
'I have labored in *v* ....Is 49:4
And in *v* they worship Me . . Matt 15:9
And in *v* they worship Me, . . Mark 7:7
you believed in *v* ....1 Cor 15:2
labor is not in *v* in the . . . 1 Cor 15:58
law, then Christ died in *v* .... Gal 2:21
run in *v* or labored in *v* ..... Phil 2:16

VALIANT
Only be *v* for me ....1 Sam 18:17
They are not *v* for the ....Jer 9:3
v men swept away ....Jer 46:15

VALIANTLY
while Israel does *v* ......Num 24:18
God we will do *v* ....Ps 60:12
of the LORD does *v* ....Ps 118:15

VALLEY
in the *V* of Megiddo ......2 Chr 35:22
I walk through the *v* ....Ps 23:4
pass through the *V* ....Ps 84:6
the verdure of the *v* ....Song 6:11
v shall be exalted ....Is 40:4
in the midst of the *v* ....Ezek 37:1
in the *v* of decision ....Joel 3:14
v shall be filled ....Luke 3:5

VALLEYS
He is not God of the *v* .... 1 Kin 20:28
and the lily of the *v* ....Song 2:1
the *v* will split like wax ......Mic 1:4

VALOR
a mighty man of *v* ....1 Sam 16:18

VALUE
does not know its *v* ....Job 28:13
of more *v* than they ....Matt 6:26
you are of more *v* than .... Matt 10:31
Of how much more *v* .....Matt 12:12
you are of more *v* than .... Luke 12:7
Of how much more *v* .....Luke 12:24
they counted up the *v* .... Acts 19:19
but are of no *v* against the . . Col 2:23

VALUED
It cannot be *v* in the ....Job 28:16
is *v* by what others say ... Prov 27:21

VANISH
when it is hot, they *v* ....Job 6:17
For the heavens will *v* ....Is 51:6
knowledge, it will *v* ....1 Cor 13:8
old is ready to *v* away ......Heb 8:13

VANISHED
Has their wisdom *v* ....Jer 49:7
and He *v* from their ......Luke 24:31

VANITY
of vanities, all is *v* ....Eccl 1:2
This also is *v* and grasping . . Eccl 6:9
iniquity with cords of *v* ......Is 5:18

VANQUISH
God will *v* him, not man ... Job 32:13

VAPOR
best state is but *v* ....Ps 39:5

surely every man is *v* . . . . . . Ps 39:11
It is even a *v* that . . . . James 4:14

VARIATION
whom there is no *v* . . . . . . James 1:17

VARIETIES
v of tongues . . . . 1 Cor 12:28

VARIOUS
glistening stones of *v* . . 1 Chr 29:2
earthquakes in *v* places . . . . Matt 24:7
were sick with *v* diseases . . Mark 1:34
sins, led away by *v* lusts . . . 2 Tim 3:6
God, who at *v* times and in . . Heb 1:1
when you fall into *v* trials . . James 1:2

VASHTI
Queen of Ahasuerus, deposed and divorced, Esth 1:9–22

VEGETABLES
and let them give us *v* . . . . . . Dan 1:12
is weak eats only *v* . . . . Rom 14:2

VEHEMENT
of fire, a most *v* . . . . Song 8:6

VEIL
she took a *v* and covered . . Gen 24:65
The *v* shall be a divider for . . Ex 26:33
he put a *v* on his face . . . . . . Ex 34:33
temples behind your *v* . . . . . Song 6:7
v of the temple was . . . . Matt 27:51
Moses, who put a *v* . . . . . . 2 Cor 3:13
because the *v* is taken . . . . 2 Cor 3:14
the *v* is taken away . . . . . . 2 Cor 3:16
Presence behind the *v* . . . . . Heb 6:19

VEILED
Give them a *v* heart . . . . Lam 3:65
it is *v* to those who are . . . . 2 Cor 4:3

VEILS
v herself by the flocks of . . . . Song 1:7
I will also tear off your *v* . . Ezek 13:21

VENGEANCE
You shall not take *v* . . . . . . Lev 19:18
V is Mine . . . . Deut 32:35
spare in the day of *v* . . . . . . Prov 6:34
it is the day of the LORD'S *v* . . Is 34:8
God will come with *v* . . . . . . Is 35:4
on the garments of *v* . . . . . . Is 59:17
and the day of *v* of our God . . . Is 61:2
let me see Your *v* . . . . Jer 11:20
for it is the *v* of the LORD . . . Jer 50:15
are the days of *v* . . . . Luke 21:22
written, "V is Mine . . . . . . Rom 12:19
flaming fire taking *v* . . . . 2 Thess 1:8
who said, "V is Mine . . . . . Heb 10:30
suffering the *v* . . . . Jude 7

VENOM
It becomes cobra *v* . . . . Job 20:14

VESSEL
like a potter's *v* . . . . Ps 2:9
v that he made of clay . . . . . Jer 18:4
like a precious *v* . . . . Jer 25:34
been emptied from *v* . . . . . . Jer 48:11
for he is a chosen *v* . . . . . . Acts 9:15
lump to make one *v* . . . . . . Rom 9:21
to possess his own *v* . . . . . 1 Thess 4:4
to the weaker *v* . . . . 1 Pet 3:7

VESSELS
longsuffering the *v* . . . . . . Rom 9:22
treasure in earthen *v* . . . . . . 2 Cor 4:7
like the potter's *v* . . . . Rev 2:27

VEXED
grieved, and I was *v* . . . . . . Ps 73:21

VICE
as a cloak for *v* . . . . 1 Pet 2:16

VICTIM
and plucked the *v* . . . . Job 29:17

VICTORY
brought about a great *v* . . 2 Sam 23:12
is swallowed up in *v* . . . . . 1 Cor 15:54

Hades, where is your *v* . . . 1 Cor 15:55
who gives us the *v* . . . . . . 1 Cor 15:57
v that has overcome . . . . . . 1 John 5:4
have the *v* over the beast . . . Rev 15:2

VIEW
"Go, *v* the land . . . . Josh 2:1

VIGILANT
in prayer, being *v* . . . . Col 4:2
Be sober, be *v* . . . . 1 Pet 5:8

VIGOR
nor his natural *v* . . . . Deut 34:7

VILE
sons made themselves *v* . 1 Sam 3:13
"Behold, I am *v* . . . . Job 40:4
them up to *v* passions . . . . . Rom 1:26

VILLAGES
of Megiddo and its *v* . . . . . . Judg 1:27
they may go into the *v* . . . . Matt 14:15
many *v* of the Samaritans . . Acts 8:25

VINDICATE
V me, O LORD, for I have . . . Ps 26:1
V me, O LORD my God, ... Ps 35:24
V me, O God, And plead . . . . Ps 43:1
And *v* me by Your strength . . . Ps 54:1

VINDICATED
know that I shall be *v* . . . . . Job 13:18

VINDICATES
indeed this *v* you before . . . Gen 20:16

VINDICATION
Let my *v* come from . . . . Ps 17:2

VINE
in my dream a *v* was . . . . . . Gen 40:9
to the choice *v* . . . . Gen 49:11
their *v* is of the *v* . . . . Deut 32:32
You have brought a *v* . . . . . . Ps 80:8
planted you a noble *v* . . . . . Jer 2:21
as a *v* the remnant of Israel . . . Jer 6:9
grapes shall be on the *v* . . . . Jer 8:13
Israel empties his *v* . . . . . . Hos 10:1
shall sit under his *v* . . . . Mic 4:4
the *v* shall give its fruit, . . . Zech 8:12
of this fruit of the *v* . . . . . . Matt 26:29
of the fruit of the *v* . . . . . . Mark 14:25
"I am the true *v* . . . . John 15:1
unless it abides in the *v* . . . . John 15:4
I am the *v*, you are the . . . . . John 15:5

VINEDRESSER
and My Father is the *v* . . . . . John 15:1

VINEDRESSERS
he leased it to *v* and . . . . . . Matt 21:33
leased it to *v* and went . . . . Mark 12:1
a vineyard, leased it to *v* . . . Luke 20:9

VINEGAR
they gave me *v* to drink . . . . . Ps 69:21
As *v* to the teeth and . . . . . Prov 10:26
weather, and like *v* . . . . . . Prov 25:20

VINES
foxes that spoil the *v* . . . . . Song 2:15
nor fruit be on the *v* . . . . Hab 3:17

VINEYARD
and the best of his own *v* . . . . Ex 22:5
shall not glean your *v* . . . . . Lev 19:10
field nor prune your *v* . . . . . Lev 25:4
v which Your right . . . . Ps 80:15
For the *v* of the LORD of . . . . Is 5:7
laborers for his *v* . . . . Matt 20:1
go, work today in my *v* . . . . Matt 21:28
owner of the *v* comes . . . . Matt 21:40
A man planted a *v* and . . . . Mark 12:1
certain man planted a *v* . . . . Luke 20:9
Who plants a *v* and . . . . 1 Cor 9:7

VINEYARDS
which you did not dig, *v* . . . Deut 6:11
in the *v* there will be no . . . . . Is 16:10
wine, a land of bread and . . Is 36:17

nothing, and gave them *v* . . . Jer 39:10
they shall plant *v* and . . . . . Amos 9:14

VIOLENCE
was filled with *v* . . . . Gen 6:11
You save me from *v* . . . . . . 2 Sam 22:3
the one who loves *v* . . . . Ps 11:5
such as breathe out *v* . . . . . . Ps 27:12
from oppression and *v* . . . . . Ps 72:14
v covers the . . . . Prov 10:6
The *v* of the wicked will . . . Prov 21:7
He had done no *v* . . . . Is 53:9
and *v* in the land . . . . Jer 51:46
filled the land with *v* . . . . . . Ezek 8:17
LORD, 'Who store up *v* . . . . . Amos 3:10
cause the seat of *v* . . . . Amos 6:3
For *v* against your . . . . Obad 10
way and from the *v* . . . . Jon 3:8
rich men are full of *v* . . . . . . Mic 6:12
For plundering and *v* . . . . Hab 1:3
have done *v* to the law . . . . . Zeph 3:4
one's garment with *v* . . . . . Mal 2:16
of heaven suffers *v* . . . . . Matt 11:12

VIOLENT
me from the *v* man . . . . Ps 18:48
let evil hunt the *v* . . . . Ps 140:11
A *v* man entices his . . . . . . Prov 16:29
violence, and the *v* . . . . . . Matt 11:12
haters of God, *v* . . . . Rom 1:30
given to wine, not *v* . . . . . . 1 Tim 3:3

VIOLENTLY
The earth is *v* broken, the . . . . Is 24:19
It will fall *v* on the head of . . Jer 23:19
herd ran *v* down the . . . . . . Mark 5:13

VIPER
and stings like a *v* . . . . . Prov 23:32
will come forth a *v* . . . . Is 14:29
which is crushed a *v* . . . . Is 59:5

VIPERS
See BROOD OF VIPERS

VIRGIN
v shall conceive . . . . Is 7:14
O you oppressed *v* . . . . Is 23:12
v daughter of my . . . . Jer 14:17
the *v* daughter of Judah . . . . . Lam 1:15
you, O *v* daughter of Zion . . Lam 2:13
The *v* of Israel has . . . . Amos 5:2
"Behold, the *v* shall . . . . . . Matt 1:23
if a *v* marries, she has . . . 1 Cor 7:28
between a wife and a *v* . . . 1 Cor 7:34
you as a chaste *v* . . . . . . 2 Cor 11:2

VIRGINITY
take a wife in her *v* . . . . . . Lev 21:13
and bewail my *v* . . . . Judg 11:37

VIRGINS
v who took their lamps . . . . Matt 25:1
Now concerning *v*; I . . . . . 1 Cor 7:25
women, for they are *v* . . . . Rev 14:4

VIRTUE
if there is any *v* . . . . Phil 4:8
us by glory and *v* . . . . 2 Pet 1:3
to your faith *v* . . . . 2 Pet 1:5

VIRTUOUS
that you are a *v* woman . . . . Ruth 3:11
Who can find a *v* wife . . . . Prov 31:10

VISAGE
v was marred more than . . . . . Is 52:14

VISIBLE
that are on earth, *v* . . . . Col 1:16
of things which are *v* . . . . . . Heb 11:3

VISION
came to Abram in a *v* . . . . . Gen 15:1
chased away like a *v* . . . . . . Job 20:8
Then You spoke in a *v* . . . . Ps 89:19
the Valley of V . . . . Is 22:1
a dream of a night *v* . . . . Is 29:7
her prophets find no *v* . . . . . Lam 2:9
the fulfillment of every *v* . . Ezek 12:23
v which I saw by the . . . . . . Ezek 43:3

have night without *v* .... Mic 3:6
they had also seen a *v* .... Luke 24:23
in a *v* he has seen a man ... Acts 9:12
in a trance I saw a *v* .... Acts 11:5
v appeared to Paul in .... Acts 16:9
to the heavenly *v* .... Acts 26:19

VISIONS
thoughts from the *v* .... Job 4:13
opened and I saw *v* of God .. Ezek 1:1
These were the *v* of my .... Dan 4:10
young men shall see *v* ...... Joel 2:28
young men shall see *v* ...... Acts 2:17
I will come to *v* .... 2 Cor 12:1

VISIT
but God will surely *v* ...... Gen 50:24
in the day when I *v* .... Ex 32:34
v the earth and water .... Ps 65:9
Oh, *v* me with Your .... Ps 106:4
and you did not *v* Me ..... Matt 25:43
v orphans and widows.... James 1:27

VISITATION
the time of your *v* .... Luke 19:44
God in the day of *v* .... 1 Pet 2:12

VISITED
he will not be *v* .... Prov 19:23
many days you will be *v* ... Ezek 38:8
I was sick and you *v* Me .. Matt 25:36
Israel, for He has *v* .... Luke 1:68
"God has *v* His people ..... Luke 7:16
how God at the first *v* ..... Acts 15:14

VISITING
v the iniquity of the fathers .. Ex 20:5

VISITOR
am a foreigner and a *v* ..... Gen 23:4

VITALITY
v was turned into the .... Ps 32:4

VOICE
"I heard Your *v* .... Gen 3:10
God heard the *v* of the .... Gen 21:17
you have obeyed My *v* .... Gen 22:18
only obey my *v*, and go, ... Gen 27:13
v is Jacob's *v* .... Gen 27:22
I should obey His *v* .... Ex 5:2
God answered him by *v* .... Ex 19:19
your God and obey His *v* ... Deut 4:30
obey the *v* of the LORD .... Deut 30:10
wept with a loud *v* ...... 2 Sam 15:23
heard the *v* of Elijah ..... 1 Kin 17:22
fire a still small *v* .... 1 Kin 19:12
and my flute to the *v* ...... Job 30:31
you thunder with a *v* .... Job 40:9
cried to the LORD with my *v* ... Ps 3:4
with the *v* of thanksgiving .... Ps 26:7
the *v* of my supplications .... Ps 28:6
He uttered His *v* .... Ps 46:6
Hear my *v*, O God, in my .... Ps 64:1
He sends out His *v* .... Ps 68:33
cried out to God with my *v* ... Ps 77:1
have lifted up their *v* .... Ps 93:3
if you will hear His *v* .... Ps 95:7
word, heeding the *v* .... Ps 103:20
for your *v* is sweet .... Song 2:14
their *v* shall be heard as far ... Is 15:4
The *v* of one crying in .... Is 40:3
the *v* of weeping shall .... Is 65:19
A *v* from the temple .... Is 66:6
the *v* of the LORD our God ... Jer 3:25
that does not obey the *v* of ... Jer 7:28
v was heard in Ramah ..... Jer 31:15
the *v* of joy and .... Jer 33:11
I heard a *v* of One .... Ezek 1:28
who has a pleasant *v* .... Ezek 33:32
like the *v* of a multitude .... Dan 10:6
with the *v* of thanksgiving .... Jon 2:9
v was heard in Ramah ..... Matt 2:18
"The *v* of one crying .... Matt 3:3
And suddenly a *v* .... Matt 3:17
will anyone hear His *v* .... Matt 12:19
and suddenly a *v* .... Matt 17:5

cried out with a loud *v* .... Matt 27:46
a loud *v* glorified God, ... Luke 17:15
hear the *v* of the Son of ... John 5:25
for they know his *v* .... John 10:4
v did not come because ... John 12:30
the truth hears My *v* ..... John 18:37
the *v* of an archangel ... 1 Thess 4:16
whose *v* then shook the ... Heb 12:26
glory when such a *v* .... 2 Pet 1:17
If anyone hears My *v* ...... Rev 3:20
I heard a *v* from heaven, ... Rev 14:2

VOICE OF THE LORD
diligently heed the *v* .... Ex 15:26
if we hear the *v* .... Deut 5:25
they did not obey the *v* ..... Josh 5:6
as in obeying the *v* ...... 1 Sam 15:22
you did not obey the *v* ... 1 Sam 28:18
v is over the waters .... Ps 29:3
did not heed the *v* .... Ps 106:25
Also I heard the *v* .... Is 6:8
v, who fully repays .... Is 66:6
they did not obey the *v* ...... Jer 43:7
We have not obeyed the *v* .. Dan 9:10
people, obeyed the *v* ...... Hag 1:12
diligently obey the *v* ..... Zech 6:15
the *v* came to him .... Acts 7:31

VOICES
God of Israel with *v* .... 2 Chr 20:19
shall lift up their *v* .... Is 52:8
demanding with loud *v* ... Luke 23:23
And there were loud *v* ..... Rev 11:15

VOID
was without form, and *v* ..... Gen 1:2
they are a nation *v* .... Deut 32:28
the LORD had made a *v* ... Judg 21:15
regarded Your law as *v* .. Ps 119:126
it shall not return to Me *v* .... Is 55:11
Do we then make *v* .... Rom 3:31
heirs, faith is made *v* ...... Rom 4:14
make my boasting *v* .... 1 Cor 9:15

VOLUME
in the *v* of the book .... Heb 10:7

VOLUNTEERS
Your people shall be *v* ...... Ps 110:3

VOMIT
lest the land *v* .... Lev 18:28
dog returns to his own *v* ... Prov 26:11
man staggers in his *v* .... Is 19:14
returns to his own *v* ...... 2 Pet 2:22
cold nor hot, I will *v* .... Rev 3:16

VOW
Then Jacob made a *v* ..... Gen 28:20
to take the *v* of a Nazirite ... Num 6:2
he carried out his *v* ...... Judg 11:39
v shall be performed .... Ps 65:1
When you make a *v* .... Eccl 5:4
not to *v* than to *v* .... Eccl 5:5
for he had taken a *v* .... Acts 18:18
men who have taken a *v* .. Acts 21:23

VOW TO THE LORD
So Israel made a *v* .... Num 21:2
Or if a woman makes a *v* .. Num 30:3
When you make a *v* ...... Deut 23:21
And Jephthah made a *v* ... Judg 11:30
yes, they will make a *v* ...... Is 19:21

VOWED
If she *v* in her husband's .. Num 30:10
v to the Mighty One of ...... Ps 132:2
Pay what you have *v* .... Eccl 5:4
I will pay what I have *v* ..... Jon 2:9

VOWS
v to the LORD the offering .. Num 6:21
you will pay your *v* .... Job 22:27
I will pay My *v* .... Ps 22:25
V made to You are .... Ps 56:12
Make *v* to the LORD .... Ps 76:11
today I have paid my *v* .... Prov 7:14
to reconsider his *v* .... Prov 20:25

And what, son of my *v* .... Prov 31:2
to the LORD and took *v* ...... Jon 1:16

WAFERS
like *w* made with honey .... Ex 16:31

WAGE
those who exploit *w* ...... Mal 3:5
w the good warfare .... 1 Tim 1:18

WAGES
I will give you your *w* .... Ex 2:9
the *w* of the wicked ...... Prov 10:16
the transgressor his *w* .... Prov 26:10
w will be troubled .... Is 19:10
and he who earns *w* .... Hag 1:6
to you, give me my *w* ..... Zech 11:12
and give them their *w* ..... Matt 20:8
be content with your *w* .... Luke 3:14
is worthy of his *w* .... Luke 10:7
him who works, the *w* ...... Rom 4:4
For the *w* of sin is .... Rom 6:23
is worthy of his *w* .... 1 Tim 5:18
Indeed the *w* of the ...... James 5:4
and will receive the *w* of ... 2 Pet 2:13

WAIL
streets everyone will *w* .... Is 15:3
everyone shall *w* .... Is 16:7
My heart shall *w* .... Jer 48:36
"Son of man, *w* .... Ezek 32:18

WAILING
w is heard from Zion .... Jer 9:19
shall be *w* in all streets ... Amos 5:16
of heart and bitter *w* .... Ezek 27:31
There will be *w* .... Matt 13:42
cried out, weeping and *w* .. Rev 18:19

WAIST
than my father's *w* .... 1 Kin 12:10
Your *w* is a heap of wheat .. Song 7:2
put it around your *w* .... Jer 13:1
the appearance of His *w* ... Ezek 1:27
w was girded with gold .... Dan 10:5
Let your *w* be girded .... Luke 12:35
girded your *w* with truth .... Eph 6:14

WAIT
if he did not lie in *w* .... Ex 21:13
would you *w* for them till .. Ruth 1:13
w until you have .... 1 Sam 1:23
hard service I will *w* .... Job 14:14
If I *w* for the grave .... Job 17:13
w patiently for Him .... Ps 37:7
my eyes fail while I *w* .... Ps 69:3
These all *w* for You .... Ps 104:27
let us lie in *w* to shed ...... Prov 1:11
And I will *w* on the .... Is 8:17
the LORD will *w* .... Is 30:18
not be ashamed who *w* ...... Is 49:23
w quietly for the .... Lam 3:26
I will *w* for the God .... Mic 7:7
Though it tarries, *w* for it ... Hab 2:3
be like men who *w* ...... Luke 12:36
but to *w* for the Promise ..... Acts 1:4
see, we eagerly *w* .... Rom 8:25
w for one another .... 1 Cor 11:33
the Spirit eagerly *w* .... Gal 5:5
we also eagerly *w* .... Phil 3:20
and to *w* for His Son ... 1 Thess 1:10
To those who eagerly *w* .... Heb 9:28

WAIT ON THE LORD
W, be of good courage ...... Ps 27:14
But those who *w* .... Ps 37:9
W, and keep His way .... Ps 37:34
And I will *w* .... Is 8:17
w shall renew their .... Is 40:31

WAITED
w for your salvation .... Gen 49:18
and when I *w* for light ..... Job 30:26
w patiently for the .... Ps 40:1
we have *w* for Him .... Is 25:9

And the people w .... Luke 1:21
day you have w and ...... Acts 27:33
for he w for the city ...... Heb 11:10
Divine longsuffering w ..... 1 Pet 3:20

WAITING
w at the posts of my .... Prov 8:34
who was himself w for ... Mark 15:43
w for the Consolation .... Luke 2:25
who himself was also w .. Luke 23:51
ourselves, eagerly w ...... Rom 8:23
w for the revelation .... 1 Cor 1:7
from that time w .... Heb 10:13

WAITS
of the adulterer w .... Job 24:15
my soul silently w .... Ps 62:1
My soul w for the Lord ...... Ps 130:6
for the one who w .... Is 64:4
the creation eagerly w ..... Rom 8:19

WAKE
us, that whether we w ... 1 Thess 5:10

WALK
w before Me and be .... Gen 17:1
in which they must w ...... Ex 18:20
You shall w in all .... Deut 5:33
Yea, though I w .... Ps 23:4
W about Zion .... Ps 48:12
that Israel would w .... Ps 81:13
I will w within my .... Ps 101:2
I will w before the .... Ps 116:9
Though I w in the .... Ps 138:7
W prudently when you ...... Eccl 5:1
w in the ways of your ..... Eccl 11:9
come and let us w .... Is 2:5
"This is the way, w .... Is 30:21
be weary, they shall w ...... Is 40:31
w in the light of your ...... Is 50:11
people, who w in a way ..... Is 65:2
commit adultery and w .... Jer 23:14
the righteous w .... Hos 14:9
w humbly with your God .. Mic 6:8
take up your bed and w ..... John 5:8
W while you have the .... John 12:35
so we also should w .... Rom 6:4
Let us w properly .... Rom 13:13
For we w by faith .... 2 Cor 5:7
W in the Spirit .... Gal 5:16
that we should w .... Eph 2:10
And w in love .... Eph 5:2
W as children of light ..... Eph 5:8
attained, let us w .... Phil 3:16
note those who so w .... Phil 3:17
that you may w worthy ... Col 1:10
Jesus our Lord, so w .... Col 2:6
us how you ought to w ... 1 Thess 4:1
w just as He .... 1 John 2:6
and they shall w .... Rev 3:4

WALKED
Enoch w with God .... Gen 5:22
by His light I w .... Job 29:3
The people who w .... Is 9:2
He w with Me in peace ..... Mal 2:6
Jesus no longer w .... John 11:54
w according to the .... 2 Cor 10:2
in which you once w .... Eph 2:2
to walk just as He w ..... 1 John 2:6

WALKING
of the Lord God w .... Gen 3:8
see four men loose, w ..... Dan 3:25
before God, w in all ...... Luke 1:6
they saw Jesus w .... John 6:19
And w in the fear of ...... Acts 9:31
you are no longer w ...... Rom 14:15
not w in craftiness .... 2 Cor 4:2
of your children w .... 2 John 4

WALKS
the Lord your God w .... Deut 23:14
is the man who w .... Ps 1:1
He who w uprightly .... Ps 15:2
He who w with .... Prov 10:9

He who w with wise ...... Prov 13:20
w blamelessly will be .... Prov 28:18
w wisely will be .... Prov 28:26
Whoever w the road ...... Is 35:8
Who w in darkness and ..... Is 50:10
it is not in man who w ..... Jer 10:23
do good to him who w ...... Mic 2:7
If anyone w in the day .... John 11:9
he who w in darkness .... John 12:35
adversary the devil w ...... 1 Pet 5:8
is in darkness and w .... 1 John 2:11

WALL
then the w of the city ...... Josh 6:5
his face toward the w ..... 2 Kin 20:2
like a leaning w .... Ps 62:3
and like a high w .... Prov 18:11
If she is a w .... Song 8:9
We grope for the w .... Is 59:10
you, you whitewashed w ... Acts 23:3
a window in the w .... 2 Cor 11:33
down the middle w .... Eph 2:14
Now the w of the city ..... Rev 21:14

WALLS
broken down, without w .. Prov 25:28
salvation for w .... Is 26:1
you shall call your w ...... Is 60:18
By faith the w of .... Heb 11:30

WANDER
and makes them w .... Job 12:24
ones cry to God, and w ... Job 38:41
Indeed, I would w .... Ps 55:7
Oh, let me not w .... Ps 119:10
they have loved to w ...... Jer 14:10

WANDERED
w blind in the streets ...... Lam 4:14
My sheep w through ...... Ezek 34:6
They w in deserts and .... Heb 11:38

WANDERERS
And they shall be w ...... Hos 9:17

WANDERING
learn to be idle, w .... 1 Tim 5:13
w stars for whom is .... Jude 13

WANDERS
He w about for bread ..... Job 15:23
Like a bird that w .... Prov 27:8
if anyone among you w ... James 5:19

WANT
I shall not w .... Ps 23:1
he began to be in w ...... Luke 15:14

WANTING
balances, and found w ..... Dan 5:27

WANTON
necks and w eyes .... Is 3:16
have begun to grow w .... 1 Tim 5:11

WAR
"There is a noise of w ..... Ex 32:17
the Lord for the w .... Num 32:20
my hands to make w .... 2 Sam 22:35
day of battle and w .... Job 38:23
w may rise against .... Ps 27:3
speak, they are for w ...... Ps 120:7
by wise counsel wage .... Prov 20:18
will wage your own w ..... Prov 24:6
shall they learn w .... Is 2:4
from the distress of w ..... Is 21:15
we shall see no w .... Jer 42:14
same horn was making w .. Dan 7:21
men returned from w ...... Mic 2:8
king, going to make w .... Luke 14:31
Who ever goes to w .... 1 Cor 9:7
for pleasure that w ...... James 4:1
You fight and w .... James 4:2
fleshly lusts which w ...... 1 Pet 2:11
w broke out in heaven ..... Rev 12:7
He judges and makes w ... Rev 19:11

WARFARE
to her, that her w .... Is 40:2

w are not carnal .... 2 Cor 10:4
may wage the good w ..... 1 Tim 1:18
w entangles .... 2 Tim 2:4

WARM
but he could not get w ..... 1 Kin 1:1
of the child became w ..... 2 Kin 4:34
they will keep w .... Eccl 4:11
but no one is w .... Hag 1:6

WARMED
w himself at the fire ..... Mark 14:54
Depart in peace, be w ... James 2:16

WARMING
when she saw Peter w ... Mark 14:67

WARMS
w them in the dust .... Job 39:14
He even w himself and ...... Is 44:16

WARN
w the people, lest they ..... Ex 19:21
w the wicked from his ..... Ezek 3:18
w everyone night .... Acts 20:31
beloved children I w ..... 1 Cor 4:14
w those who are .... 1 Thess 5:14

WARNED
"The man solemnly w ... Gen 43:3
them Your servant is w ... Ps 19:11
Then, being divinely w ..... Matt 2:12
Who w you to flee .... Matt 3:7
Noah, being divinely w ..... Heb 11:7

WARNING
he who takes w will save .. Ezek 33:5
w every man and .... Col 1:28

WARPED
such a person is w .... Titus 3:11

WARRING
w against the law of ...... Rom 7:23

WARRIOR
He runs at me like a w .... Job 16:14

WARS
He makes w cease to .... Ps 46:9
And you will hear of w .... Matt 24:6
Where do w and fights .... James 4:1

WASH
w myself with snow .... Job 9:30
I will w my hands in .... Ps 26:6
W me thoroughly .... Ps 51:2
he shall w his feet in ...... Ps 58:10
"W yourselves .... Is 1:16
O Jerusalem, w .... Jer 4:14
head and w your face ..... Matt 6:17
For they do not w .... Matt 15:2
not eat unless they w ...... Mark 7:3
w His feet with her .... Luke 7:38
said to him, "Go, w .... John 9:7
w the disciples' .... John 13:5
"You shall never w .... John 13:8
w one another's .... John 13:14
w away your sins .... Acts 22:16

WASHED
and w my hands in .... Ps 73:13
When the Lord has w ...... Is 4:4
cut, nor were you w ..... Ezek 16:4
w his hands before the .... Matt 27:24
My feet, but she has w ..... Luke 7:44
So when He had w ...... John 13:12
w their stripes .... Acts 16:33
But you were w .... 1 Cor 6:11
if she has w the .... 1 Tim 5:10
Him who loved us and w ... Rev 1:5
w their robes and made ..... Rev 7:14

WASHING
have come up from the w ... Song 4:2
hold, the w of cups ...... Mark 7:4
cleanse her with the w ..... Eph 5:26
us, through the w .... Titus 3:5

WASHINGS
and drinks, various w ..... Heb 9:10

WASTE
who are left shall w ....Lev 26:39
the cities are laid w ....Is 6:11
empty and makes it w ....Is 24:1
w the mountains ....Is 42:15
"Why this w ....Matt 26:8

WASTED
The field is w ....Joel 1:10
this fragrant oil w .....Mark 14:4
w his possessions ....Luke 15:13

WASTELAND
w shall be glad ....Is 35:1

WASTES
His flesh w away from .....Job 33:21
My eye w away because of ....Ps 6:7
cities shall be perpetual w ..Jer 49:13

WASTING
w and destruction are ....Is 59:7
that this man was w ....Luke 16:1

WATCH
Therefore w yourselves ....Deut 2:4
of them we set a w ....Neh 4:9
my steps, but do not w .....Job 14:16
is past, and like a w ....Ps 90:4
keep w over the door ....Ps 141:3
and all who w for ....Is 29:20
W the road ....Nah 2:1
W therefore, for you ......Matt 24:42
"What! Could you not w ...Matt 26:40
W and pray, lest you .....Matt 26:41
W therefore, for you do ...Mark 13:35
Could you not w one .....Mark 14:37
W and pray, lest you .....Mark 14:38
keeping w over their flock ..Luke 2:8
W therefore, and pray ...Luke 21:36
W, stand fast in the ......1 Cor 16:13
submissive, for they w ....Heb 13:17

WATCHED
in the days when God w ....Job 29:2
w while a stone was cut ...Dan 2:34
come, he would have w ...Matt 24:43
Pharisees w Him closely ....Luke 6:7

WATCHER
I done to You, O w of men ..Job 7:20

WATCHES
w the righteous ....Ps 37:32
LORD w over the strangers ...Ps 146:9
She w over the ways of ..Prov 31:27
Blessed is he who w ......Rev 16:15

WATCHFUL
But you be w in all ....2 Tim 4:5
be serious and w ....1 Pet 4:7
Be w, and strengthen the .....Rev 3:2

WATCHING
who listens to me, w .....Prov 8:34
the flock, who were w ....Zech 11:11
he comes, will find w ....Luke 12:37

WATCHMAN
guards the city, the w ......Ps 127:1
W, what of the night ....Is 21:11
I have made you a w ......Ezek 3:17
the day of your w ....Mic 7:4

WATCHMEN
w who go about the ....Song 3:3
w shall lift up their ....Is 52:8
His w are blind ....Is 56:10
I have set w on your ....Is 62:6
Also, I set w over you .....Jer 6:17
strong, set up the w ....Jer 51:12

WATER
Eden to w the garden ....Gen 2:10
Unstable as w ....Gen 49:4
your bread and your w ...Ex 23:25
of affliction and w ....1 Kin 22:27
w disappears from the ....Job 14:11
w wears away stones ......Job 14:19
drinks iniquity like w .....Job 15:16

not given the weary w ......Job 22:7
He binds up the w ....Job 26:8
I am poured out like w .....Ps 22:14
where there is no w ....Ps 63:1
they have shed like w ....Ps 79:3
Drink w from your own ....Prov 5:15
"Stolen w is sweet ....Prov 9:17
the whole supply of w ....Is 3:1
and needy seek w ....Is 41:17
For I will pour w ....Is 44:3
silence and given us w ......Jer 8:14
eye overflows with w ......Lam 1:16
will be as weak as w .....Ezek 7:17
w the land with the ......Ezek 32:6
you gave Me no w ....Luke 7:44
there was much w ....John 3:23
given you living w ....John 4:10
rivers of living w ....John 7:38
blood and w came out ....John 19:34
"Can anyone forbid w ....Acts 10:47
with the washing of w .....Eph 5:26
can yield both salt w .....James 3:12
were saved through w ....1 Pet 3:20
is He who came by w .....1 John 5:6
the Spirit, the w ....1 John 5:8
are clouds without w ......Jude 12

WATER OF LIFE
w freely to him who ....Rev 21:6
a pure river of w ....Rev 22:1
let him take the w ....Rev 22:17

WATERED
w the whole face ....Gen 2:6
that it was well w ....Gen 13:10
I planted, Apollos w ....1 Cor 3:6

WATERPOTS
"Fill four w with water ...1 Kin 18:33
"Fill the w with water .....John 2:7

WATERS
and struck the w ....Ex 7:20
If He withholds the w .....Job 12:15
me beside the still w ....Ps 23:2
though its w roar and ....Ps 46:3
w have come up to my ....Ps 69:1
then the w would have ......Ps 124:4
rich, and he who w ....Prov 11:25
Who has bound the w .....Prov 30:4
your bread upon the w .....Eccl 11:1
a well of living w ....Song 4:15
w cannot quench love .....Song 8:7
of the LORD as the w..........Is 11:9
w will fail from the ....Is 19:5
because I give w ....Is 43:20
have sworn that the w ....Is 54:9
thirsts, come to the w ....Is 55:1
fountain of living w ....Jer 2:13
w flowed over my head ....Lam 3:54
the sound of many w ......Ezek 43:2
w surrounded me ....Jon 2:5
shall be that living w ....Zech 14:8
often, in perils of w .....2 Cor 11:26
living fountains of w ....Rev 7:17
w became wormwood ....Rev 8:11

WAVE
you shall w them as a w ....Ex 29:24
w offering before the LORD ..Lev 7:30
the priest shall w them ....Num 6:20
Its fruit shall w ....Ps 72:16
is like a w of the sea ......James 1:6

WAVER
He did not w at the ....Rom 4:20

WAVERING
of our hope without w .....Heb 10:23

WAVES
and here your proud w ....Job 38:11
all Your w and billows ......Ps 42:7
the noise of their w ....Ps 65:7
the multitude of its w .....Jer 51:42
was covered with the w ....Matt 8:24

sea, tossed by the w .....Matt 14:24
raging w of the sea ....Jude 13

WAX
My heart is like w ....Ps 22:14
w melts before the ....Ps 68:2
mountains melt like w ....Ps 97:5

WAY
and show them the w ......Ex 18:20
day I am going the w ....Josh 23:14
and the right w ....1 Sam 12:23
As for God, His w ......2 Sam 22:31
to a man whose w ....Job 3:23
But He knows the w ....Job 23:10
"Where is the w ....Job 38:19
the LORD knows the w.........Ps 1:6
you perish in the w ....Ps 2:12
Teach me Your w ....Ps 27:11
This is the w of those .....Ps 49:13
w may be known on ....Ps 67:2
Your w was in the sea .....Ps 77:19
where there is no w ....Ps 107:40
I have chosen the w ......Ps 119:30
I hate every false w .....Ps 119:104
in the w everlasting .....Ps 139:24
and preserves the w ....Prov 2:8
The w of the wicked is ....Prov 4:19
instruction are the w .....Prov 6:23
w that seems right ....Prov 14:12
not know what is the w ....Eccl 11:5
of terrors in the w ....Eccl 12:5
The w of the just is ....Is 26:7
"This is the w ....Is 30:21
LORD, who makes a w ....Is 43:16
wicked forsake his w ....Is 55:7
O LORD, I know the w ....Jer 10:23
one heart and one w .....Jer 32:39
Israel, is it not My w .....Ezek 18:25
w which is not fair ......Ezek 33:17
and pervert the w ....Amos 2:7
the LORD has His w ....Nah 1:3
he will prepare the w ......Mal 3:1
and broad is the w ....Matt 7:13
and difficult is the w .....Matt 7:14
will prepare Your w .....Matt 11:10
and teach the w ....Matt 22:16
and the w you know ....John 14:4
to him, "I am the w ....John 14:6
proclaim to us the w .....Acts 16:17
explained to him the w ....Acts 18:26
you a more excellent w ...1 Cor 12:31
w which He consecrated ...Heb 10:20
forsaken the right w .....2 Pet 2:15
to have known the w ......2 Pet 2:21
have gone in the w ....Jude 11

WAY OF THE LORD
that they keep the w ......Gen 18:19
did not walk in the w ...2 Kin 21:22
w is strength for the ....Prov 10:29
Prepare the w, make ....Is 40:3
for they do not know the w ...Jer 5:4
"The w is not fair ......Ezek 18:25
Prepare the w, make His ...Matt 3:3
Prepare the w, make His ...Mark 1:3
Prepare the w, make His ....Luke 3:4
Make straight the w ......John 1:23
instructed in the w ....Acts 18:25

WAYS
for all His w are ....Deut 32:4
they do not know its w .....Job 24:13
is the first of the w ....Job 40:19
Show me Your w ....Ps 25:4
transgressors Your w ......Ps 51:13
would walk in My w ....Ps 81:13
w were directed ....Ps 119:5
I thought about my w .....Ps 119:59
righteous in all His w .....Ps 145:17
For the w of man are .....Prov 5:21
w please the LORD ....Prov 16:7
He will teach us His w ....Is 2:3
nor are your w ....Is 55:8
"Stand in the w ....Jer 6:16

"Amend your w .... Jer 7:3
and examine our w .... Lam 3:40
and owns all your w ...... Dan 5:23
w are everlasting .... Hab 3:6
misery are in their w ...... Rom 3:16
judgments and His w ...... Rom 11:33
unstable in all his w ...... James 1:8
their destructive w .... 2 Pet 2:2
and true are Your w .... Rev 15:3

WEAK
then I shall become w ....Judg 16:7
And I am w today .... 2 Sam 3:39
me, O LORD, for I am w........ Ps 6:2
gives reproof to the w ...... Is 40:29
knee will be as w .... Ezek 7:17
let the w say .... Joel 3:10
not your hands be w ...... Zeph 3:16
but the flesh is w ...... Matt 26:41
And not being w.......... Rom 4:19
Receive one who is w ...... Rom 14:1
God has chosen the w ..... 1 Cor 1:27
We are w, but you are .... 1 Cor 4:10
to the w I became as w .. 1 Cor 9:22
this reason many are w .. 1 Cor 11:30
For when I am w........ 2 Cor 12:10

WEAKENED
w my strength in the ...... Ps 102:23
the ground, you who w ..... Is 14:12

WEAKENS
w the hands of the men ..... Jer 38:4

WEAKER
house of Saul grew w ...... 2 Sam 3:1
the wife, as to the w .... 1 Pet 3:7

WEAKNESS
than men, and the w ...... 1 Cor 1:25
I was with you in w .... 1 Cor 2:3
It is sown in w .... 1 Cor 15:43
is also subject to w .... Heb 5:2
w were made strong....... Heb 11:34

WEAKNESSES
also helps in our w .... Rom 8:26
sympathize with our w ..... Heb 4:15

WEALTH
have gained me this w ..... Deut 8:17
a man of great w .... Ruth 2:1
not asked riches or w ..... 2 Chr 1:11
who trust in their w .... Ps 49:6
W and riches will be in his .. Ps 112:3
w is his strong city .... Prov 10:15
W gained by dishonesty .. Prov 13:11
but the w of the sinner is .. Prov 13:22
The rich man's w is his ... Prov 18:11
W makes many friends .... Prov 19:4
love all the w of his house .. Song 8:7
may bring to you the w .... Is 60:11
shall take away her w ....Ezek 29:19
sea became rich by her w .. Rev 18:19

WEALTHY
w nation that dwells........ Jer 49:31
rich, have become w .... Rev 3:17

WEANED
wait until you have w .... 1 Sam 1:23
w child shall put his .... Is 11:8
Those just w from milk .... Is 28:9

WEAPON
w formed against you ... Is 54:17
with a deadly w .... Ezek 9:1

WEAPONS
is better than w .... Eccl 9:18
the LORD and His w......... Is 13:5
For the w of our .... 2 Cor 10:4

WEAR
garments did not w out ..... Deut 8:4
A woman shall not w ..... Deut 22:5
w an ephod before Me ... 1 Sam 2:28
but the just will w .... Job 27:17
they will not w a robe of .. Zech 13:4

'What shall we w .... Matt 6:31
those who w soft clothing .. Matt 11:8

WEARIED
you have w Me with .... Is 43:24
You are w in the .... Is 57:10
and they have w .... Jer 12:5
You have w the LORD ...... Mal 2:17
therefore, being w .... John 4:6

WEARINESS
say, 'Oh, what a w .... Mal 1:13
in w and toil .... 2 Cor 11:27

WEARING
child, w a linen ephod ... 1 Sam 2:18
David was w a linen ..... 2 Sam 6:14
w the crown of thorns ..... John 19:5
w gold, or putting on .... 1 Pet 3:3

WEARISOME
and much study is w ...... Eccl 12:12

WEARS
As water w away stones ... Job 14:19

WEARY
to Isaac, "I am w.......... Gen 27:46
lest he become w .... Prov 25:17
As cold water to a w ...... Prov 25:25
No one will be w .... Is 5:27
you may cause the w ...... Is 28:12
shall run and not be w ...... Is 40:31
to him who is w .... Is 50:4
I am w of holding it .... Jer 6:11
w themselves to commit ...... Jer 9:5
I was w of holding it .... Jer 20:9
continual coming she w ... Luke 18:5
And let us not grow w ...... Gal 6:9
do not grow w in .... 2 Thess 3:13
lest you become w.......... Heb 12:3

WEATHER
a garment in cold w ...... Prov 25:20
'It will be fair w .... Matt 16:2

WEAVE
You shall skillfully w the ...Ex 28:39
w the seven locks .... Judg 16:13

WEAVER'S
spear was like a w .... 1 Sam 17:7
are swifter than a w shuttle .. Job 7:6

WEDDING
were invited to the w .... Matt 22:3
Come to the w .... Matt 22:4
find, invite to the w .... Matt 22:9
in with him to the w ...... Matt 25:10
day there was a w .... John 2:1

WEEK
Fulfull her w, and we ..... Gen 29:27
with many for one w ...... Dan 9:27
the first day of the w ...... Matt 28:1
I fast twice a w .... Luke 18:12
the first day of the w ...... Acts 20:7
the first day of the w ...... 1 Cor 16:2

WEEKS
See FEAST OF WEEKS
observe the Feast of W .... Ex 34:22
w are determined .... Dan 9:24
w Messiah shall be cut .... Dan 9:26

WEEP
"Hannah, why do you w ... 1 Sam 1:8
a time to w .... Eccl 3:4
you shall w no more .... Is 30:19
it, my soul will w .... Jer 13:17
W not for the dead .... Jer 22:10
to the LORD, w between..... Joel 2:17
this commotion and w ..... Mark 5:39
Blessed are you who w .... Luke 6:21
to her, "Do not w .... Luke 7:13
and you did not w .... Luke 7:32
of Jerusalem, do not w ... Luke 23:28
to the tomb to w there ..... John 11:31
w with those who w .... Rom 12:15
those who w as though .... 1 Cor 7:30

WEEPING
of Israel, who were w ..... Num 25:6
w as they went up .... 2 Sam 15:30
the noise of the w .... Ezra 3:13
face is flushed from w ..... Job 16:16
the voice of my w .... Ps 6:8
my drink with w .... Ps 102:9
of hosts called for w .... Is 22:12
w shall no longer .... Is 65:19
They shall come with w ..... Jer 31:9
w they shall come .... Jer 50:4
were sitting there w ...... Ezek 8:14
with fasting, with w .... Joel 2:12
with tears, with w .... Mal 2:13
There will be w .... Matt 8:12
outside by the tomb w .... John 20:11
why are you w .... John 20:13
do you mean by w .... Acts 21:13

WEIGH
You w out the violence ...... Ps 58:2
O Most Upright, You w ...... Is 26:7

WEIGHED
nor can silver be w .... Job 28:15
W the mountains .... Is 40:12
You have been w .... Dan 5:27
lest your hearts be w ..... Luke 21:34

WEIGHS
eyes, but the LORD w....... Prov 16:2
Where is he who w .... Is 33:18

WEIGHT
a perfect and just w......Deut 25:15
a just w is His delight ...... Prov 11:1
and eternal w of glory ..... 2 Cor 4:17
us lay aside every w ...... Heb 12:1

WEIGHTIER
have neglected the w ..... Matt 23:23

WELFARE
does not seek the w .... Jer 38:4

WELL
If you do w .... Gen 4:7
that it may go w .... Deut 4:40
you when you do w .... Ps 49:18
daughters have done w ... Prov 31:29
know that it will be w ..... Eccl 8:12
wheel broken at the w ..... Eccl 12:6
that it shall be w .... Is 3:10
"Those who are w .... Matt 9:12
said to him, 'W done...... Matt 25:21
faith has made you w ..... Mark 5:34
Now Jacob's w was........ John 4:6
the elders who rule w ..... 1 Tim 5:17

WELL-BEING
them, and their w .... Ps 69:22
each one the other's w ... 1 Cor 10:24

WELL-BELOVED
sing to my W a song .... Is 5:1

WELL KNOWN
we are w to God, and I ... 2 Cor 5:11
as unknown, and yet w .... 2 Cor 6:9

WELLS
draw water from the w ...... Is 12:3
These are w without ...... 2 Pet 2:17

WELLSPRING
w of wisdom is a flowing .. Prov 18:4

WENT
They w out from us ...... 1 John 2:19

WEPT
away from them and w ... Gen 42:24
Joseph w when they ...... Gen 50:17
and behold, the baby w ..... Ex 2:6
voices and w bitterly ...... Judg 21:2
she w and did not .... 1 Sam 1:7
w together, but David .... 1 Sam 20:41
w for the child while .... 2 Sam 12:21
and the man of God w .... 2 Kin 8:11
And Hezekiah w bitterly ... 2 Kin 20:3
for the people w .... Ezra 10:1

that I sat down and w ......Neh 1:4
Have I not w for him......Job 30:25
I w and chastened my soul ..Ps 69:10
down, yea, we w ....Ps 137:1
out and w bitterly ....Matt 26:75
He saw the city and w ....Luke 19:41
Jesus w ....John 11:35
as she w she stooped .....John 20:11
So I w much ....Rev 5:4

WEST
in the w is astonished ....Job 18:20
as the east is from the w ..Ps 103:12
of the LORD from the w ......Is 59:19
male goat came from the w ..Dan 8:5
in two, from east to w ....Zech 14:4
east and flashes to the w ..Matt 24:27
rising out of the w ......Luke 12:54

WET
They are w with the ....Job 24:8
his body was w with ......Dan 4:33

WHEAT
with the finest of w ....Ps 81:16
we may trade w ....Amos 8:5
even sell the bad w ......Amos 8:6
but gather the w ....Matt 13:30
w falls into the ....John 12:24
perhaps w or some ....1 Cor 15:37
oil, fine flour and w ......Rev 18:13

WHEEL
brings the threshing w ....Prov 20:26
the fountain, or the w ......Eccl 12:6
in the middle of a w ......Ezek 1:16

WHEELS
off their chariot w ....Ex 14:25
the rumbling of his w ......Jer 47:3
appearance of the w ......Ezek 1:16
noise of rattling w ....Nah 3:2

WHERE
not knowing w he was .....Heb 11:8

WHIP
A w for the horse ....Prov 26:3
The noise of a w ....Nah 3:2

WHIPS
chastised you with w .....1 Kin 12:11

WHIRLING
saw King David w ....1 Chr 15:29

WHIRLWIND
Elijah went up by a w ....2 Kin 2:11
Job out of the w ....Job 38:1
them away as with a w ......Ps 58:9
w will take them away .....Is 40:24
w shall scatter them ......Is 41:16
w shall be raised ....Jer 25:32
has His way in the w ......Nah 1:3

WHISPER
my ear received a w ....Job 4:12
and wizards, who w ....Is 8:19

WHISPERER
w separates the best ......Prov 16:28

WHISPERERS
they are w ....Rom 1:29

WHISPERINGS
backbitings, w ....2 Cor 12:20

WHISTLE
w for the fly that is in the ....Is 7:18

WHITE
like w coriander seed ......Ex 16:31
leprous, as w as snow ....Num 12:10
My beloved is w ....Song 5:10
they shall be as w as snow ...Is 1:18
and make them w ....Dan 11:35
be purified, made w ......Dan 12:10
red, sorrel, and w ....Zech 1:8
make one hair w or black ..Matt 5:36
his clothing as w as snow ..Matt 28:3
shining, exceedingly w ....Mark 9:3

for they are already w ....John 4:35
saw two angels in w ......John 20:12
by them in w apparel ......Acts 1:10
and hair were w like wool ..Rev 1:14
walk with Me in w ....Rev 3:4
clothed in w garments .....Rev 3:5
behold, a w horse ....Rev 6:2
and made them w ....Rev 7:14
Then I saw a great w .....Rev 20:11

WHITE AS SNOW
became leprous, as w ....Num 12:10
presence leprous, as w ...2 Kin 5:27
they shall be as w ....Is 1:18
His garment was w ....Dan 7:9
his clothing as w ....Matt 28:3
white like wool, as w ......Rev 1:14

WHITEN
launderer on earth can w ..Mark 9:3

WHITER
and I shall be w than snow ...Ps 51:7

WHITEWASHED
you are like w tombs .....Matt 23:27
strike you, you w wall .....Acts 23:3

WHOLE
the face of the w earth ....Gen 11:4
Is not the w land before ....Gen 13:9
w house of Israel, bewail ....Lev 10:6
shall build with w stones ...Deut 27:6
down for about a w day ....Josh 10:13
let the w earth be filled ....Ps 72:19
Who seek Him with the w ...Ps 119:2
my w heart I have sought ..Ps 119:10
observe it with my w ......Ps 119:34
You with my w heart ......Ps 138:1
the w earth is full of His .....Is 6:3
to Me with her w heart ....Jer 3:10
The w earth will rejoice ...Ezek 35:14
on the w house of Israel ..Ezek 39:25
than for your w body to ....Matt 5:29
your w body will be full ....Matt 6:22
if he gains the w world ....Matt 16:26
if he gains the w world ....Mark 8:36
if he gains the w world ....Luke 9:25
the w body will be full ....Luke 11:36
the w creation groans .....Rom 8:22
w body were an eye ......1 Cor 12:17
a debtor to keep the w law ..Gal 5:3
on the w armor of God ....Eph 6:11
may your w spirit, soul ..1 Thess 5:23
also to bridle the w body ...James 3:2
that it defiles the w body ...James 3:6
who deceives the w world ...Rev 12:9

WHOLESOME
w tongue is a tree ....Prov 15:4
not consent to w words .....1 Tim 6:3

WHOLLY
w followed the LORD ....Deut 1:36
I will not leave you w .....Jer 46:28

WICKED
were exceedingly w ......Gen 13:13
the righteous with the w ...Gen 18:25
For I will not justify the w ...Ex 23:7
a w thought in your heart ..Deut 15:9
from every w thing ....Deut 23:9
and condemn the w ......Deut 25:1
w shall be silent ....1 Sam 2:9
proceeds from the w ....1 Sam 24:13
was w in the sight of the ..1 Chr 2:3
turn from their w ways ....2 Chr 7:14
Should you help the w ....2 Chr 19:2
turn from their w works ....Neh 9:35
on the counsel of the w ....Job 10:3
You know that I am not w ..Job 10:7
w man writhes with pain ..Job 15:20
triumphing of the w is ....Job 20:5
Why do the w live and ....Job 21:7
w are reserved for the ....Job 21:30
to nobles, 'You are w ....Job 34:18
of the w come to an end ....Ps 7:9

with the w every day ....Ps 7:11
You have destroyed the w .....Ps 9:5
w is snared in the ....Ps 9:16
w shall be turned ....Ps 9:17
do the w renounce God ....Ps 10:13
w bend their bow ....Ps 11:2
w He will rain coals ....Ps 11:6
the w who oppress me ......Ps 17:9
Evil shall slay the w ....Ps 34:21
w shall be no more ....Ps 37:10
The w watches the ....Ps 37:32
But to the w God says ......Ps 50:16
So let the w perish at the ....Ps 68:2
of the w I will also cut off ...Ps 75:10
how long will the w ....Ps 94:3
nothing w before my eyes ..Ps 101:3
and the w be no more ....Ps 104:35
of the w shall perish ......Ps 112:10
is far from the w ....Ps 119:155
if there is any w ....Ps 139:24
the way of the w He turns ..Ps 146:9
w will be cut off from ......Prov 2:22
The way of the w is like ....Prov 4:19
heart that devises w plans ..Prov 6:18
he who rebukes a w man ...Prov 9:7
the wages of the w to sin ..Prov 10:16
of the w will perish ....Prov 10:28
w will fall by his own ......Prov 11:5
w man does deceptive ....Prov 11:18
w will not go ....Prov 11:21
expectation of the w is ....Prov 11:23
words of the w are, "Lie ...Prov 12:6
mercies of the w are ......Prov 12:10
w covet the catch of evil ..Prov 12:12
The way of the w is an ....Prov 15:9
thoughts of the w are an ..Prov 15:26
LORD is far from the w ....Prov 15:29
He who says to the w ......Prov 24:24
w flee when no one ......Prov 28:1
the righteous and the w ....Eccl 3:17
Do not be overly w ....Eccl 7:17
not be well with the w ......Eccl 8:13
Woe to the w! It shall be ill ...Is 3:11
w forsake his way ....Is 55:7
But the w are like the ......Is 57:20
the way of the w prosper ..Jer 12:1
from the hand of the w ....Jer 15:21
and desperately w ....Jer 17:9
if a w man turns from ....Ezek 18:21
a w man turns away .....Ezek 18:27
if you warn the w to turn ..Ezek 33:9
when the w turns from ....Ezek 33:19
w shall do wickedly ......Dan 12:10
at all acquit the w ....Nah 1:3
the righteous and the w ...Mal 3:18
You shall trample the w ....Mal 4:3
with this w generation ....Matt 12:45
separate the w from .....Matt 13:49
A w and adulterous ....Matt 16:4
fiery darts of the w one ....Eph 6:16
have overcome the w ......1 John 2:14
w one does not touch .....1 John 5:18
the sway of the w ....1 John 5:19

WICKEDLY
brethren, do not do so w ...Gen 19:7
beg you, do not act so w ..Judg 19:23
and I have done w ......2 Sam 24:17
Will you speak w ....Job 13:7
God will never do w ....Job 34:12
iniquity, we have done w ...Ps 106:6
Those who do w ....Dan 11:32
yes, all who do w ....Mal 4:1

WICKEDNESS
LORD saw that the w.......Gen 6:5
can I do this great w ....Gen 39:9
the land become full of w ..Lev 19:29
may be no w among .....Lev 20:14
'W proceeds from the ...1 Sam 24:13
w oppress them ....2 Sam 7:10
if w is found in him, he ....1 Kin 1:52
do w in the sight of the ...1 Kin 21:25

He sees w also .... Job 11:11
Is not your w great .... Job 22:5
be it from God to do w ..... Job 34:10
Oh, let the w of the .... Ps 7:9
righteousness and hate w ..... Ps 45:7
alive into hell, for w .... Ps 55:15
in the tents of w .... Ps 84:10
I will not know w .... Ps 101:4
eat the bread of w .... Prov 4:17
w is an abomination .... Prov 8:7
w overthrows the sinner ... Prov 13:6
w will not deliver .... Eccl 8:8
w burns as the .... Is 9:18
have trusted in your w ..... Is 47:10
w will correct you .... Jer 2:19
wash your heart from w ..... Jer 4:14
wells up with her w .... Jer 6:7
man repented of his w ...... Jer 8:6
the w of your fathers .... Jer 44:9
not turn from his w .... Ezek 3:19
You have plowed w .... Hos 10:13
because of your great w ... Hos 10:15
and cannot look on w ...... Hab 1:13
for those who do w .... Mal 3:15
thefts, covetousness, w ... Mark 7:22
is full of greed and w ..... Luke 11:39
sexual immorality, w ...... Rom 1:29
spiritual hosts of w .... Eph 6:12
and overflow of w .... James 1:21

WIDE
shall open your hand w .... Deut 15:8
opened their mouth w ..... Job 29:23
w his lips shall have ...... Prov 13:3
will build myself a w ...... Jer 22:14
w is the gate and .... Matt 7:13
to you, our heart is w .... 2 Cor 6:11

WIDOW
A w or a divorced woman .. Lev 21:14
w who are among you .... Deut 16:11
does no good for the w .... Job 24:21
They slay the w .... Ps 94:6
and his wife a w .... Ps 109:9
the fatherless and w ...... Ps 146:9
plead for the w .... Is 1:17
How like a w is she .... Lam 1:1
Then one poor w .... Mark 12:42
w putting in two mites .. Luke 21:2
w has children or .... 1 Tim 5:4
Do not let a w under ...... 1 Tim 5:9
sit as queen, and am no w .. Rev 18:7

WIDOW'S
and I caused the w .... Job 29:13

WIDOWS
a defender of w .... Ps 68:5
and let your w trust .... Jer 49:11
w were neglected .... Acts 6:1
Honor w who are really w .. 1 Tim 5:3
that the younger w ...... 1 Tim 5:14
to visit orphans and w .... James 1:27

WIDOWS'
you devour w houses ..... Matt 23:14

WIDTH
all the saints what is the w .. Eph 3:18

WIFE
and be joined to his w ..... Gen 2:24
his w looked back .... Gen 19:26
covet your neighbor's w ... Ex 20:17
becomes jealous of his w .. Num 5:14
Manoah and his w .... Judg 13:19
gives a w to Benjamin ... Judg 21:18
w of Uriah the Hittite .... 2 Sam 11:3
his w said to him, "Do ...... Job 2:9
Your w shall be like a ..... Ps 128:3
an excellent w is the ...... Prov 12:4
w finds a good thing ..... Prov 18:22
but a prudent w .... Prov 19:14
can find a virtuous w ..... Prov 31:10
w whom you love all ...... Eccl 9:9
like a youthful w .... Is 54:6

"Go, take yourself a w ...... Hos 1:2
for a w he tended sheep ... Hos 12:12
with the w of his .... Mal 2:15
take to you Mary your w .. Matt 1:20
or w or children or lands .. Matt 19:29
divorces his w .... Mark 10:11
my w is well advanced in .. Luke 1:18
'I have married a w ...... Luke 14:20
Remember Lot's w .... Luke 17:32
all seven had her as w .... Luke 20:33
w the affection due her ... 1 Cor 7:3
so love his own w .... Eph 5:33
the husband of one w .... 1 Tim 3:2
the husband of one w ...... Titus 1:6
giving honor to the w ..... 1 Pet 3:7
bride, the Lamb's w .... Rev 21:9

WILD
He shall be a w man ...... Gen 16:12
w donkeys quench their ... Ps 104:11
it brought forth w grapes ...... Is 5:2
locusts and w honey ...... Matt 3:4
olive tree which is w ...... Rom 11:24

WILDERNESS
wasteland, a howling w ... Deut 32:10
w yields food for them ..... Job 24:5
coming out of the w ...... Song 3:6
made the world as a w ...... Is 14:17
I will make the w .... Is 41:18
Let the w and its .... Is 42:11
Have I been a w .... Jer 2:31
of one crying in the w ..... Matt 3:3
the serpent in the w ...... John 3:14
congregation in the w .... Acts 7:38

WILES
to stand against the w ..... Eph 6:11

WILL
it of your own free w ...... Lev 22:29
I delight to do Your w ...... Ps 40:8
Teach me to do Your w ... Ps 143:10
w be done on earth as ..... Matt 6:10
but he who does the w .... Matt 7:21
whoever does the w of ... Matt 12:50
of the two did the w ..... Matt 21:31
I drink it, Your w be ..... Matt 26:42
Your w be done on earth ... Luke 11:2
or do according to his w .. Luke 12:47
nevertheless not My w .... Luke 22:42
flesh, nor of the w .... John 1:13
w of Him who sent Me ..... John 4:34
I do not seek My own w ... John 5:30
not to do My own w ...... John 6:38
This is the w .... John 6:39
wills to do His w .... John 7:17
you should know His w ... Acts 22:14
w is present with me ...... Rom 7:18
good pleasure of His w .... Eph 1:5
what the w of the Lord is ... Eph 5:17
works in you both to w .... Phil 2:13
the knowledge of His w .... Col 1:9
according to His own w ..... Heb 2:4
come to do Your w .... Heb 10:9
good work to do His w ..... Heb 13:21

WILL BE SAVED
you w from your enemies .. Num 10:9
walks blamelessly w ..... Prov 28:18
In those days Judah w .... Jer 33:16
endures to the end w ..... Matt 10:22
and is baptized w .... Mark 16:16
enters by Me, he w .... John 10:9
all your household w ...... Acts 11:14
Jesus Christ, and you w .... Acts 16:31
the sea, the remnant w ..... Rom 9:27
from the dead, you w ..... Rom 10:9
And so all Israel w ...... Rom 11:26
but he himself w .... 1 Cor 3:15
she w in childbearing ..... 1 Tim 2:15

WILL OF GOD
For whoever does the w ... Mark 3:35
saints according to the w .. Rom 8:27
acceptable and perfect w ... Rom 12:2

with joy by the w .... Rom 15:32
doing the w from the heart ... Eph 6:6
complete in all the w ...... Col 4:12
For this is the w ...... 1 Thess 4:3
w in Christ Jesus for .... 1 Thess 5:18
you have done the w ...... Heb 10:36
w, that by doing good ..... 1 Pet 2:15
w, to suffer for doing ...... 1 Pet 3:17
of men, but for the w ...... 1 Pet 4:2
suffer according to the w .. 1 Pet 4:19
but he who does the w ... 1 John 2:17

WILLFULLY
For if we sin w .... Heb 10:26
For this they w .... 2 Pet 3:5

WILLING
is of a w heart .... Ex 35:5
then is w to consecrate .... 1 Chr 29:5
If you are w and .... Is 1:19
him, saying, "I am w ...... Matt 8:3
The spirit indeed is w .... Matt 26:41
"If You are w, You can ... Mark 1:40
The spirit indeed is w .... Mark 14:38
"Lord, if You are w ...... Luke 5:12
she is w to live with him ... 1 Cor 7:12
if there is first a w ...... 2 Cor 8:12
w that any should .... 2 Pet 3:9

WILLINGLY
gives it w with his heart ..... Ex 25:2
when the people w offer .... Judg 5:2
w offered himself to the .. 2 Chr 17:16
blessed all the men who w .. Neh 11:2
to futility, not w .... Rom 8:20
For if I do this w .... 1 Cor 9:17
by compulsion but w ...... 1 Pet 5:2

WILLINGNESS
for I know your w .... 2 Cor 9:2

WILLOWS
our harps upon the w ..... Ps 137:2

WILLS
to whom the Son w ...... Matt 11:27
it is not of him who w ..... Rom 9:16
say, "If the Lord w ...... James 4:15

WIN
w one proselyte .... Matt 23:15
to all, that I might w ...... 1 Cor 9:19

WIND
LORD was not in the w.... 1 Kin 19:11
w carries him away .... Job 27:21
the chaff which the w ...... Ps 1:4
He causes His w .... Ps 147:18
will inherit the w .... Prov 11:29
He who observes the w .... Eccl 11:4
is the way of the w .... Eccl 11:5
Awake, O north w .... Song 4:16
the prophets become w .... Jer 5:13
He brings the w .... Jer 51:16
Ephraim feeds on the w .... Hos 12:1
and creates the w .... Amos 4:13
A reed shaken by the w .... Matt 11:7
And the w ceased and ..... Mark 4:39
and rebuked the w .... Luke 8:24
The w blows where .... John 3:8
of a rushing mighty w ..... Acts 2:2
about with every w ...... Eph 4:14

WINDOW
Noah opened the w .... Gen 8:6
by a rope through the w ... Josh 2:15
the scarlet cord in the w ... Josh 2:21
down through a w .... 1 Sam 19:12
in a w sat a certain young .. Acts 20:9
through a w in the wall .. 2 Cor 11:33

WINDOWS
looking through the w ..... Song 2:9
has come through our w ... Jer 9:21
upper room, with his w .... Dan 6:10
not open for you the w .... Mal 3:10

WINDS
from the four w .... Ezek 37:9

be, that even the *w* .... Matt 8:27
holding the four *w* .... Rev 7:1

WINDSTORM
And a great *w* arose ...... Mark 4:37

WINE
Noah awoke from his *w* ... Gen 9:24
Do not drink *w* or .... Lev 10:9
Nazirite may drink *w* ..... Num 6:20
drink *w* or similar drink ... Judg 13:4
I have drunk neither *w* ... 1 Sam 1:15
w for those who are ...... 2 Sam 16:2
king was merry with *w* .... Esth 1:10
drinking *w* in their oldest ... Job 1:13
drink the *w* of confusion ..... Ps 60:3
w that makes glad .... Ps 104:15
W is a mocker .... Prov 20:1
Do not look on the *w* ..... Prov 23:31
w makes merry .... Eccl 10:19
love is better than *w* .... Song 1:2
w goes down smoothly ..... Song 7:9
w inflames them .... Is 5:11
are drunk, but not with *w* ... Is 29:9
Yes, come, buy *w* .... Is 55:1
Take this *w* cup of fury ... Jer 25:15
We will drink no *w*, for ... Jer 35:6
new *w* into old wineskins .. Matt 9:17
they gave Him sour *w* .... Matt 27:34
w nor strong drink .... Luke 1:15
pouring on oil and *w* .... Luke 10:34
when they ran out of *w* .... John 2:3
"They are full of new *w* .... Acts 2:13
do not be drunk with *w* ... Eph 5:18
given to *w*, nor violent ..... 1 Tim 3:3
but use a little *w* .... 1 Tim 5:23
not given to much *w* .... Titus 2:3
not harm the oil and the *w* .. Rev 6:6
the *w* of the wrath of her .. Rev 14:8
her the cup of the *w* ...... Rev 16:19

WINEBIBBER
'Look, a glutton and a *w* .. Luke 7:34

WINEBIBBERS
Do not mix with *w* ..... Prov 23:20

WINEPRESS
"I have trodden the *w* .... Is 63:3
for the *w* is full .... Joel 3:13
into the great *w* .... Rev 14:19
Himself treads the *w* ..... Rev 19:15

WINESKIN
I have become like a *w* ... Ps 119:83

WINESKINS
new wine into old *w* ...... Matt 9:17

WING
maidservant under your *w* .. Ruth 3:9
One *w* of the cherub ...... 1 Kin 6:24
so I spread My *w* .... Ezek 16:8

WINGS
I bore you on eagles' *w* .... Ex 19:4
w you have come .... Ruth 2:12
the shadow of Your *w* ..... Ps 17:8
He flew upon the *w* ...... Ps 18:10
the shadow of Your *w* .... Ps 36:7
w I will make my refuge ... Ps 57:1
If I take the *w* .... Ps 139:9
each one had six *w* .... Is 6:2
up with *w* like eagles ...... Is 40:31
a lion, and had eagle's *w* ... Dan 7:4
with healing in His *w* ...... Mal 4:2
her chicks under her *w* ... Matt 23:37
each having six *w* .... Rev 4:8
woman was given two *w* ... Rev 12:14

WINNOW
You shall *w* them .... Is 41:16

WINNOWING
His *w* fan is in His hand ... Luke 3:17

WINS
w souls is wise .... Prov 11:30

WINTER
have made summer and *w* .. Ps 74:17

For lo, the *w* is past .... Song 2:11
w it shall occur .... Zech 14:8
flight may not be in *w* .... Matt 24:20

WIPE
the Lord GOD will *w* .... Is 25:8
w them with the towel .... John 13:5
w away every tear .... Rev 21:4

WIPED
reproach will not be *w* ..... Prov 6:33
w them with the hair of ... Luke 7:38
w out the handwriting ...... Col 2:14

WIPES
eats and *w* her mouth ..... Prov 30:20

WISDOM
for this is your *w* .... Deut 4:6
God gave Solomon *w* ..... 1 Kin 4:29
w will die with you .... Job 12:2
where can *w* be found .... Job 28:12
fear of the Lord, that is *w* .. Job 28:28
Who has put *w* in the ..... Job 38:36
of the righteous speaks *w* .. Ps 37:30
will make me to know *w* ... Ps 51:6
is the beginning of *w* ..... Ps 111:10
but fools despise *w* and ..... Prov 1:7
For the LORD gives *w* ...... Prov 2:6
is the man who finds *w* .... Prov 3:13
Get *w*! Get understanding! .. Prov 4:5
W is the principal .... Prov 4:7
is the beginning of *w* ..... Prov 9:10
W rests in the heart ...... Prov 14:33
to get *w* than gold .... Prov 16:16
W is in the sight of him ... Prov 17:24
w loves his own soul ...... Prov 19:8
W is too lofty for a .... Prov 24:7
w is much grief .... Eccl 1:18
gives *w* and knowledge ..... Eccl 2:26
W is better than .... Eccl 9:16
W is better than weapons ... Eccl 9:18
He gives *w* to the wise .... Dan 2:21
w is justified by her .... Matt 11:19
Jesus increased in *w* .... Luke 2:52
the *w* of God also .... Luke 11:49
riches both of the *w* ...... Rom 11:33
the gospel, not with *w* ..... 1 Cor 1:17
Greeks seek after *w* .... 1 Cor 1:22
For the *w* of this world .... 1 Cor 3:19
not with fleshly *w* .... 2 Cor 1:12
now the manifold *w* .... Eph 3:10
all the treasures of *w* .... Col 2:3
Walk in *w* toward those ...... Col 4:5
If any of you lacks *w* ...... James 1:5
power and riches and *w* .... Rev 5:12
and glory and *w* .... Rev 7:12

WISE
great nation is a *w* .... Deut 4:6
He catches the *w* .... Job 5:13
God is *w* in heart and ...... Job 9:4
not find one *w* man .... Job 17:10
men are not always *w* ...... Job 32:9
when will you be *w* .... Ps 94:8
w will observe these ...... Ps 107:43
Do not be *w* in your .... Prov 3:7
The *w* in heart will .... Prov 10:8
W people store up .... Prov 10:14
he who wins souls is *w* .... Prov 11:30
w son heeds his father's ... Prov 13:1
The *w* woman builds her ... Prov 14:1
w man fears and departs ... Prov 14:16
The *w* in heart will be ..... Prov 16:21
folly, lest he be *w* .... Prov 26:5
w men turn away wrath ... Prov 29:8
they are exceedingly *w* .... Prov 30:24
The words of the *w* ...... Eccl 12:11
They are *w* to do evil ...... Jer 4:22
is *w*? Let him understand ... Hos 14:9
Therefore be *w* as .... Matt 10:16
five of them were *w* .... Matt 25:2
barbarians, both to *w* ..... Rom 1:14
to God, alone *w* .... Rom 16:27
Where is the *w* .... 1 Cor 1:20

---

sake, but you are *w* ...... 1 Cor 4:10
not as fools but as *w* ...... Eph 5:15
to God who alone is *w* .... 1 Tim 1:17
are able to make you *w* ... 2 Tim 3:15

WISE MAN
select a discerning and *w* .. Gen 41:33
w answer with empty ...... Job 15:2
I shall not find one *w* ..... Job 17:10
A *w* will hear and .... Prov 1:5
rebuke a *w*, and he will ... Prov 9:8
w fears and departs ...... Prov 14:16
w will appease it .... Prov 16:14
w holds them back .... Prov 29:11
what more has the *w* .... Eccl 6:8
found in it a poor *w* .... Eccl 9:15
Let not the *w* glory .... Jer 9:23
w who built his house ..... Matt 7:24
that there is not a *w* ...... 1 Cor 6:5

WISE MEN
Egypt and all its *w* .... Gen 41:8
Pharaoh also called the *w* ... Ex 7:11
the king said to the *w* ..... Esth 1:13
For he sees *w* die .... Ps 49:10
Where are your *w* .... Is 19:12
the wisdom of their *w* ...... Is 29:14
all the *w* of the nations ..... Jer 10:7
to destroy all the *w* ...... Dan 2:12
all the *w* of Babylon ...... Dan 2:48
Now all the king's *w* ...... Dan 5:8
w from the East came ..... Matt 2:1
secretly called the *w* ...... Matt 2:7
he was deceived by the *w* .. Matt 2:16
prophets, *w*, and scribes .. Matt 23:34
I speak as to *w* .... 1 Cor 10:15

WISELY
I will behave *w* .... Ps 101:2
who heeds the word *w* .... Prov 16:20
you do not inquire *w* ...... Eccl 7:10
saw that he answered *w* .. Mark 12:34

WISER
he was *w* than all men .... 1 Kin 4:31
w than the birds .... Job 35:11
w than my enemies ...... Ps 119:98
of God is *w* than men ..... 1 Cor 1:25

WISH
for me to do what I *w* .... Matt 20:15
w it were already .... Luke 12:49
where you do not *w* ...... John 21:18
For I *w* that all men were ... 1 Cor 7:7
I could *w* you were cold or .. Rev 3:15

WISHED
Then he *w* death for .... Jon 4:8
him whatever they *w* ...... Mark 9:13

WISHES
turns it wherever He *w* ... Prov 21:1
wind blows where it *w* ...... John 3:8

WITCHCRAFT
is as the sin of *w* .... 1 Sam 15:23

WITH ALL YOUR HEART
if you seek Him *w* .... Deut 4:29
love the Lord your God *w* ... Deut 6:5
the Lord your God *w* ..... Deut 10:12
and to serve Him *w* ...... Josh 22:5
but serve the Lord *w* .... 1 Sam 12:20
Trust in the Lord *w* .... Prov 3:5
you search for Me *w* ...... Jer 29:13
Lord, "Turn to me *w* ...... Joel 2:12
Be glad and rejoice *w* .... Zeph 3:14
the Lord your God *w* ..... Matt 22:37
the Lord your God *w* ..... Mark 12:30
the Lord your God *w* ..... Luke 10:27
"If you believe *w* .... Acts 8:37

WITH CHILD
you are *w*, and you shall .. Gen 16:11
daughters of Lot were *w* ... Gen 19:36
she is *w* by harlotry." So .. Gen 38:24
fight, and hurt a woman *w* .. Ex 21:22
David, and said, "I am *w* .. 2 Sam 11:5

womb of her who is w ...... Eccl 11:5
As a woman w is in pain ..... Is 26:17
who have not travailed w! ..... Is 54:1
a man is ever in labor w ..... Jer 30:6
women w ripped open ..... Hos 13:16
found w of the Holy Spirit .. Matt 1:18
a virgin shall be w .... Matt 1:23
betrothed wife, who was w .. Luke 2:5
being w, she cried out .... Rev 12:2

WITH ONE ACCORD
words of the prophets w .. 1 Kin 22:13
the Lord, to serve Him w ... Zeph 3:9
w began to make .... Luke 14:18
continued w in prayer ...... Acts 1:14
with w in one place .... Acts 2:1
So continuing daily w ...... Acts 2:46
their voice to God w .... Acts 4:24
w in Solomon's Porch ...... Acts 5:12
multitudes w heeded .... Acts 8:6
being assembled w ..... Acts 15:25

WITHDRAW
God will not w His .... Job 9:13
He does not w His eyes ..... Job 36:7
From such w yourself ...... 1 Tim 6:5

WITHER
also shall not w .... Ps 1:3
w as the green .... Ps 37:2
leaves will not w .... Ezek 47:12
How did the fig tree w .... Matt 21:20

WITHERED
behold, seven heads, w ... Gen 41:23
stricken and w like grass .... Ps 102:4
surely joy has w away ..... Joel 1:12
the plant that it w .... Jon 4:7
man who had a w hand .. Matt 12:10
had no root they w away .. Matt 13:6
the fig tree w away .... Matt 21:19
out as a branch and is w ... John 15:6

WITHERS
The grass w .... Is 40:7
burning heat than it w ... James 1:11
The grass w .... 1 Pet 1:24

WITHHELD
and your sins have w ...... Jer 5:25

WITHHOLD
w Your tender mercies ...... Ps 40:11
good thing will He w ...... Ps 84:11
Do not w good from .... Prov 3:27
your cloak, do not w ..... Luke 6:29

WITHOUT
having no hope and w ..... Eph 2:12
pray w ceasing .... 1 Thess 5:17
w controversy .... 1 Tim 3:16
w works is dead .... James 2:26

WITHSTAND
no one is able to w You ... 2 Chr 20:6
no animal could w him ..... Dan 8:4
was I that I could w ...... Acts 11:17
you may be able to w ...... Eph 6:13

WITHSTOOD
Persia w me twenty-one ... Dan 10:13
I w him to his face .... Gal 2:11

WITNESS
See BEAR WITNESS; FALSE WITNESS
see, God is w between ..... Gen 31:50
Surely even now my w .... Job 16:19
like the faithful w .... Ps 89:37
w does not lie .... Prov 14:5
have given him as a w .... Is 55:4
a true and faithful w ...... Jer 42:5
I will be a swift w .... Mal 3:5
all the world as a w ...... Matt 24:14
This man came for a w .... John 1:7
do not receive Our w ...... John 3:11
"If I bear w of .... John 5:31
is another who bears w .... John 5:32
But I have a greater w .... John 5:36
who was bearing w .... Acts 14:3

For you will be His w ..... Acts 22:15
For God is my w .... Phil 1:8
are three who bear w ..... 1 John 5:7
If we receive the w .... 1 John 5:9
who bore w to the word .... Rev 1:2
Christ, the faithful w .... Rev 1:5
beheaded for their w ...... Rev 20:4

WITNESSED
is revealed, being w .... Rom 3:21
w the good confession .... 1 Tim 6:13

WITNESSES
of two or three w .... Deut 17:6
for Myself faithful w .... Is 8:2
"You are My w .... Is 43:10
the presence of many w ... 1 Tim 6:12
the Holy Spirit also w ..... Heb 10:15
so great a cloud of w ...... Heb 12:1
give power to my two w ..... Rev 11:3

WIVES
two w, one loved .... Deut 21:15
he had seven hundred w .. 1 Kin 11:3
daughters as w for .... Ezra 9:2
you to divorce your w ..... Matt 19:8
W, submit to your own ..... Eph 5:22
Husbands, love your w .... Eph 5:25
Husbands, love your w ...... Col 3:19
w must be reverent ...... 1 Tim 3:11
by the conduct of their w ... 1 Pet 3:1

WIZARDS
who are mediums and w ...... Is 8:19

WOE
W is me, that I dwell in ... Ps 120:5
Who has w? .... Prov 23:29
W to the wicked .... Is 3:11
W to those who call evil ... Is 5:20
W to you, O Jerusalem .... Jer 13:27
"W to the bloody city ..... Ezek 24:9
'W to him who increases .... Hab 2:6
"W to you, Chorazin ...... Matt 11:21
w to that man by whom .... Matt 18:7
But w to you, scribes ..... Matt 23:13
But w to those who are .. Mark 13:17
W to you who are full .... Luke 6:25
w is me if I do not .... 1 Cor 9:16
W, w, w, to the inhabitants .. Rev 8:13
One w is past .... Rev 9:12

WOLF
The w and the lamb .... Is 65:25
the sheep, sees the w ..... John 10:12

WOLVES
they are ravenous w ...... Matt 7:15
out as lambs among w .... Luke 10:3
savage w will come in ... Acts 20:29

WOMAN
she shall be called W ...... Gen 2:23
every w shall ask of her ..... Ex 3:22
A widow or a divorced w .. Lev 21:14
stand the w before the ..... Num 5:18
w shall not wear anything .. Deut 22:5
the w took the two men .. Josh 2:4
that you are a virtuous w .. Ruth 3:11
keep you from the evil w .. Prov 6:24
adultery with a w lacks .... Prov 6:32
A foolish w is clamorous ... Prov 9:13
A gracious w retains ..... Prov 11:16
w builds her house .... Prov 14:1
w who fears the LORD .... Prov 31:30
Can a w forget her nursing .. Is 49:15
w shall encompass a ...... Jer 31:22
whoever looks at a w ..... Matt 5:28
a w of Canaan came ..... Matt 15:22
"O w, great is your faith .. Matt 15:28
if a w divorces .... Mark 10:12
w came having an ...... Mark 14:3
"Do you see this w ...... Luke 7:44
Then the w of Samaria ..... John 4:9
brought to Him a w .... John 8:3
"W, behold your .... John 19:26
w was full of good .... Acts 9:36

Jewish w who believed ..... Acts 16:1
natural use of the w ...... Rom 1:27
a man not to touch a w ..... 1 Cor 7:1
the head of w is man ..... 1 Cor 11:3
For if a w is not covered ... 1 Cor 11:6
w is the glory of man ..... 1 Cor 11:7
but w from man .... 1 Cor 11:8
but w for the man .... 1 Cor 11:9
this reason the w .... 1 Cor 11:10
His Son, born of a w .... Gal 4:4
Let a w learn in .... 1 Tim 2:11
I do not permit a w ...... 1 Tim 2:12
w being deceived .... 1 Tim 2:14
you allow that w Jezebel ... Rev 2:20
w clothed with the sun ..... Rev 12:1
the earth helped the w ..... Rev 12:16
And I saw a w sitting on a .. Rev 17:3
the w whom you saw is .... Rev 17:18

WOMB
nations are in your w ..... Gen 25:23
LORD had closed her w..... 1 Sam 1:5
took Me out of the w .... Ps 22:9
formed you from the w ...... Is 44:2
called Me from the w .... Is 49:1
in the w I knew you .... Jer 1:5
is the fruit of your w ...... Luke 1:42
"Blessed is the w .... Luke 11:27

WOMEN
the Hebrew w are not ...... Ex 1:19
All the w who were gifted .. Ex 35:25
ten w shall bake your ..... Lev 26:26
blessed is she among w .. Judg 5:24
loved many foreign w .... 1 Kin 11:1
pagan w caused .... Neh 13:26
among Your honorable w ... Ps 45:9
O fairest among w ...... Song 1:8
w rule over them .... Is 3:12
new wine the young w ... Zech 9:17
thousand men, besides w .. Matt 14:21
thousand men, besides w .. Matt 15:38
w will be grinding ...... Matt 24:41
w who followed Jesus .... Matt 27:55
are you among w .... Luke 1:28
it just as the w had said .. Luke 24:24
devout and prominent w .. Acts 13:50
not a few of the leading w .. Acts 17:4
w keep silent in the ...... 1 Cor 14:34
the w adorn themselves .... 1 Tim 2:9
which is proper for w ..... 1 Tim 2:10
admonish the young w .... Titus 2:4
times, the holy w .... 1 Pet 3:5
not defiled with w .... Rev 14:4

WONDER
gives you a sign or a w ... Deut 13:1
I have become as a w ...... Ps 71:7
marvelous work and a w ... Is 29:14
they were filled with w ..... Acts 3:10

WONDERFUL
name, seeing it is w ...... Judg 13:18
Your love to me was w ... 2 Sam 1:26
things too w for me .... Job 42:3
Your w works Which You .. Ps 40:5
He has made His w works ... Ps 111:4
Your testimonies are w ... Ps 119:129
things which are too w ... Prov 30:18
name will be called W .... Is 9:6
of hosts, who is w .... Is 28:29
all His w works .... Jer 21:2
and scribes saw the w .... Matt 21:15
our own tongues the w .... Acts 2:11

WONDERFULLY
fearfully and w made ...... Ps 139:14

WONDERS
See SIGNS AND WONDERS
w which I will do .... Ex 3:20
LORD will do w among you .. Josh 3:5
are the God who does w ... Ps 77:14
Shall Your w be known ... Ps 88:12
heavens will praise Your w ... Ps 89:5
who alone does great w .... Ps 136:4

Egypt with signs and *w* .....Jer 32:21
and how mighty His *w* ......Dan 4:3
He works signs and *w* ......Dan 6:27
"And I will show *w* ....Joel 2:30
and done many *w* ....Matt 7:22
w were done among ....Acts 5:12
w God had worked ......Acts 15:12
signs, and lying *w* ......2 Thess 2:9
both with signs and *w* ......Heb 2:4

WONDROUS
the *w* works of God ....Job 37:14
and tell of all Your *w* ......Ps 26:7
I declare Your *w* works .....Ps 71:17
w works declare that ....Ps 75:1
w works in the land of .....Ps 106:22
for they are a *w* ....Zech 3:8

WONDROUSLY
God, who has dealt *w* ....Joel 2:26

WOOD
precious stones, *w* ....1 Cor 3:12

WOODCUTTERS
but let them be *w* ....Josh 9:21

WOODEN IMAGE
any tree, as a *w* ....Deut 16:21
cut down the *w* ....Judg 6:25
And Ahab made a *w* .....1 Kin 16:33
a *w* and worshiped ....2 Kin 17:16
cut down the *w* ....2 Kin 18:4
and burned the *w* ....2 Kin 23:15

WOODEN IMAGES
cut down their *w* ....Ex 34:13
burn their *w* with fire ....Deut 12:3
they have made their *w* ..1 Kin 14:15
w on every high hill ....2 Kin 17:10
you have removed the *w* ..2 Chr 19:3
served *w* and idols ....2 Chr 24:18
the altars and the *w* ....2 Chr 34:7
w nor the incense altars ....Is 17:8
w and incense altars ....Is 27:9
w by the green trees ......Jer 17:2
I will pluck your *w* ....Mic 5:14

WOOL
She seeks *w* and flax .....Prov 31:13
they shall be as *w* ....Is 1:18
head was like pure *w* .....Dan 7:9
hair were white like *w* .....Rev 1:14

WORD
See ACCORDING TO THE WORD OF THE
  LORD
w that proceeds ....Deut 8:3
w is very near you ......Deut 30:14
w of the LORD is proven .....Ps 18:30
For the *w* of the LORD is .....Ps 33:4
w I have hidden ....Ps 119:11
w has given me life ....Ps 119:50
w is a lamp to my feet ....Ps 119:105
w makes it glad ....Prov 12:25
a harsh *w* stirs up anger ...Prov 15:1
w spoken in due season ...Prov 15:23
He who heeds the *w* ......Prov 16:20
w fitly spoken is ....Prov 25:11
The LORD sent a *w* ....Is 9:8
the *w* of our God ....Is 40:8
w has gone out of My .....Is 45:23
w be that goes forth ....Is 55:11
But His *w* was in my ....Jer 20:9
w will be his oracle ......Jer 23:36
w which I speak will .....Ezek 12:28
But only speak a *w* ....Matt 8:8
for every idle *w* ....Matt 12:36
mighty in deed and *w* ....Luke 24:19
beginning was the *W* ....John 1:1
W became flesh and ......John 1:14
if anyone keeps My *w* ....John 8:51
w which you hear is ......John 14:24
Your *w* is truth ....John 17:17
and glorified the *w* ....Acts 13:48
to one is given the *w* .....1 Cor 12:8
of water by the *w* ....Eph 5:26

holding fast the *w* ....Phil 2:16
Let the *w* of Christ ....Col 3:16
come to you in *w* only ....1 Thess 1:5
in every good *w* ....2 Thess 2:17
by the *w* of His power ......Heb 1:3
w which they heard did .....Heb 4:2
the implanted *w* ....James 1:21
does not stumble in *w* .....James 3:2
that by the *w* of God ....2 Pet 3:5
whoever keeps His *w* ......1 John 2:5
let us not love in *w* ......1 John 3:18
the Father, the *W* ....1 John 5:7

WORD OF GOD
announce to you the *w* ....1 Sam 9:27
w came to Nathan ....1 Chr 17:3
Every *w* is pure ....Prov 30:5
the *w* of no effect ....Mark 7:13
the *w* came to John ....Luke 3:2
alone, but by every *w* ......Luke 4:4
about Him to hear the *w* ....Luke 5:1
The seed is the *w* ....Luke 8:11
who hear the *w* and do it ..Luke 8:21
spoke the *w* with boldness ..Acts 4:31
leave the *w* and serve ......Acts 6:2
then the *w* spread ....Acts 6:7
had also received the *w* .....Acts 11:1
necessary that the *w* .....Acts 13:46
that the *w* has taken no ....Rom 9:6
and hearing by the *w* .....Rom 10:17
w come originally ....1 Cor 14:36
peddling the *w* ....2 Cor 2:17
the *w* deceitfully ....2 Cor 4:2
Spirit, which is the *w* ......Eph 6:17
sanctified by the *w* ....1 Tim 4:5
w is not chained ....2 Tim 2:9
w is living and powerful ....Heb 4:12
were framed by the *w* ......Heb 11:3
through the *w* ....1 Pet 1:23
w abides in you ....1 John 2:14
who bore witness to the *w* ....Rev 1:2
had been slain for the *w* ....Rev 6:9
His name is called The *W* ...Rev 19:13
to Jesus and for the *w* ......Rev 20:4

WORD OF TRUTH
And take not the *w* ....Ps 119:43
by the *w*, by the power .....2 Cor 6:7
after you heard the *w* ....Eph 1:13
rightly dividing the *w* .....2 Tim 2:15
us forth by the *w* ....James 1:18

WORDS
I waited for your *w* ....Job 32:11
his *w* are without wisdom ..Job 34:35
Give ear to my *w* ....Ps 5:1
Let the *w* of my mouth .....Ps 19:14
How sweet are Your *w* ....Ps 119:103
I will make my *w* known .....Prov 1:23
pay attention to the *w* ......Prov 7:24
hear the *w* of the wise .....Prov 22:17
The *w* of the wise are .....Eccl 12:11
And I have put My *w* ....Is 51:16
Take with you ....Hos 14:2
Do not My *w* do good to .....Mic 2:7
pass away, but My *w* .....Matt 24:35
at the gracious *w* ....Luke 4:22
w that I speak to you ......John 6:63
You have the *w* of ....John 6:68
My *w* abide in you, you ....John 15:7
And remember the *w* .....Acts 20:35
not with wisdom of *w* .....1 Cor 1:17
those who hear the *w* ....Rev 1:3
is he who keeps the *w* ......Rev 22:7
keep the *w* of this book ....Rev 22:9

WORK
day God ended His *w* ....Gen 2:2
Moses finished the *w* ......Ex 40:33
people had a mind to *w* .....Neh 4:6
You shall desire the *w* .....Job 14:15
for they are all the *w* .....Job 34:19
the *w* of Your fingers ......Ps 8:3
I hate the *w* of those ....Ps 101:3

the heavens are the *w* ......Ps 102:25
Man goes out to his *w* .....Ps 104:23
w is honorable and ....Ps 111:3
man does deceptive *w* ....Prov 11:18
then I saw all the *w* ....Eccl 8:17
for there is no *w* ....Eccl 9:10
God will bring every *w* ....Eccl 12:14
that He may do His *w* ....Is 28:21
and all we are the *w* ....Is 64:8
him nothing for his *w* ......Jer 22:13
and mighty in *w* ....Jer 32:19
For I will *w* a *w* ....Hab 1:5
and said, 'Son, go, *w* .....Matt 21:28
could do no mighty *w* ......Mark 6:5
we do, that we may *w* ......John 6:28
"This is the *w* of God .....John 6:29
I must *w* the works ....John 9:4
w which You have given ...John 17:4
know that all things *w* .....Rom 8:28
He will finish the *w* ....Rom 9:28
w is no longer *w* ....Rom 11:6
Do not destroy the *w* ......Rom 14:20
w will become manifest ....1 Cor 3:13
Are you not my *w* ....1 Cor 9:1
abounding in the *w* ....1 Cor 15:58
without ceasing your *w* ....1 Thess 1:3
good word and *w* ....2 Thess 2:17
If anyone will not *w* .....2 Thess 3:10
but a doer of the *w* ......James 1:25

WORKED
with one hand they *w* ......Neh 4:17
and wonders God had *w* ...Acts 15:12
which He *w* in Christ ....Eph 1:20

WORKER
w is worthy of his ....Matt 10:10
Timothy, my fellow *w* .....Rom 16:21
w who does not need .....2 Tim 2:15

WORKERS
You hate all *w* of ....Ps 5:5
we are God's fellow *w* .....1 Cor 3:9
dogs, beware of evil *w* .....Phil 3:2

WORKERS OF INIQUITY
in company with the *w* ....Job 34:8
You hate all *w* ....Ps 5:5
Depart from me, all you *w* ...Ps 6:8
nor be envious of the *w* .....Ps 37:1
Deliver me from the *w* ......Ps 59:2
when all the *w* flourish ......Ps 92:7
from the traps of the *w* ....Ps 141:9
will come to the *w* ....Prov 10:29
from Me, all you *w* ....Luke 13:27

WORKING
everywhere, the Lord *w* ..Mark 16:20
My Father has been *w* ....John 5:17
according to the *w* ....Eph 1:19
through faith in the *w* ......Col 2:12
manner, not *w* at all .....2 Thess 3:11

WORKMANSHIP
For we are His *w* ....Eph 2:10

WORKS
See GOOD WORKS
the wondrous *w* of God ....Job 37:14
are Your wonderful *w* ......Ps 40:5
Come and see the *w* ....Ps 66:5
how great are Your *w* ......Ps 92:5
manifold are Your *w* ......Ps 104:24
The *w* of the LORD are......Ps 111:2
w shall praise You ....Ps 145:10
and let her own *w* ....Prov 31:31
"For I know their *w* ....Is 66:18
of whose *w* are truth ....Dan 4:37
show Him greater *w* ....John 5:20
w that I do in My ....John 10:25
w that I do he will do ......John 14:12
w righteousness ....Acts 10:35
might stand, not of *w* ......Rom 9:11
let us cast off the *w* ....Rom 13:12
is the same God who *w* ....1 Cor 12:6
Now the *w* of the flesh ......Gal 5:19

the spirit who now *w* .... Eph 2:2
not of *w*, lest anyone .... Eph 2:9
with the unfruitful *w* .... Eph 5:11
for it is God who *w* .... Phil 2:13
w they deny Him .... Titus 1:16
zealous for good *w* .... Titus 2:14
repentance from dead *w* ..... Heb 6:1
but does not have *w* ..... James 2:14
also justified by *w* ...... James 2:25
He might destroy the *w* ... 1 John 3:8
"I know your *w* .... Rev 2:2
their *w* follow them .... Rev 14:13
according to their *w* ...... Rev 20:12

WORKS OF THE LAW
as it were, by the *w* .... Rom 9:32
not justified by the *w* ...... Gal 2:16
the Spirit by the *w* .... Gal 3:2
does He do it by the *w* ...... Gal 3:5
w are under the curse .... Gal 3:10

WORLD
See IN THE WORLD; OF THE WORLD; OF THIS WORLD
He shall judge the *w* .... Ps 9:8
For the *w* is Mine .... Ps 50:12
w is established .... Ps 93:1
The field is the *w* .... Matt 13:38
w are more shrewd .... Luke 16:8
He was in the *w* .... John 1:10
For God so loved the *w* .... John 3:16
His Son into the *w* .... John 3:17
the Savior of the *w* .... John 4:42
w cannot hate you .... John 7:7
You are of this *w* .... John 8:23
Look, the *w* has gone ..... John 12:19
w will see Me no more .... John 14:19
"If the *w* hates you ...... John 15:18
If you were of the *w* ..... John 15:19
I have overcome the *w* .... Jon 16:33
do not pray for the *w* ..... John 17:9
w has not known You .... John 17:25
w may become guilty ...... Rom 3:19
be conformed to this *w* ... Rom 12:2
things of the *w* .... 1 Cor 1:27
w is foolishness .... 1 Cor 3:19
w has been crucified ..... Gal 6:14
without God in the *w* ..... Eph 2:12
loved this present *w* ..... 2 Tim 4:10
He has not put the *w* ...... Heb 2:5
unspotted from the *w* .... James 1:27
w is enmity with God ..... James 4:4
Do not love the *w* ...... 1 John 2:15
all that is in the *w* ...... 1 John 2:16
w is passing away ...... 1 John 2:17
w does not know us ...... 1 John 3:1
They are of the *w* .... 1 John 4:5
so are we in this *w* ...... 1 John 4:17
And all the *w* marveled .... Rev 13:3

WORLDS
also He made the *w* .... Heb 1:2

WORM
w should feed sweetly ..... Job 24:20
But I am a *w* .... Ps 22:6
"Fear not, you *w* .... Is 41:14
their *w* does not die .... Is 66:24
w does not die and the .... Mark 9:44

WORMS
flesh is caked with *w* .... Job 7:5
you, and *w* cover you .... Is 14:11
And he was eaten by *w* .... Acts 12:23

WORMWOOD
end she is bitter as *w* ..... Prov 5:4
who turn justice to *w* ...... Amos 5:7
of the star is *W* .... Rev 8:11

WORRIED
Martha, you are *w* .... Luke 10:41

WORRY
to you, do not *w* .... Matt 6:25
Therefore do not *w* .... Matt 6:31

WORRYING
by *w* can add one cubit .... Matt 6:27

WORSE
w than their fathers .... Jer 7:26

WORSHIP
I will go yonder and *w* ..... Gen 22:5
shall not *w* the LORD ...... Deut 12:31
w the LORD in the .... 1 Chr 16:29
He is your Lord, *w* .... Ps 45:11
Oh come, let us *w* .... Ps 95:6
and have come to *w* Him .... Matt 2:2
will fall down and *w* .... Matt 4:9
"You shall *w* the LORD .... Matt 4:10
And in vain they *w* .... Matt 15:9
w what you do not know .. John 4:22
true worshipers will *w* ..... John 4:23
the One whom you *w* ..... Acts 17:23
w the God of my .... Acts 24:14
false humility and *w* ...... Col 2:18
the angels of God *w* .... Heb 1:6
make them come and *w* .... Rev 3:9
w Him who lives .... Rev 4:10
w Him who made .... Rev 14:7

WORSHIPED
w the LORD, and blessed ... Gen 24:48
w it and sacrificed to it ...... Ex 32:8
w the LORD their God....... Neh 9:3
fell to the ground and *w* ... Job 1:20
w the works of their own ... Jer 1:16
leper came and *w* Him ..... Matt 8:2
she came and *w* Him ..... Matt 15:25
they saw Him, they *w* .... Matt 28:17
w Him, and returned ..... Luke 24:52
Our fathers *w* .... John 4:20
down at his feet and *w* .... Acts 10:25
of God for the lie, and *w* ... Rom 1:25
w Him who lives .... Rev 5:14
on their faces and *w* ...... Rev 11:16
w God who sat on the ...... Rev 19:4

WORSHIPER
if anyone is a *w* .... John 9:31

WORSHIPERS
destroying the *w* of Baal .. 2 Kin 10:19
the true *w* will worship .... John 4:23
with the Gentile *w* .... Acts 17:17

WORTH
and make my speech *w* .... Job 24:25
of the wicked is *w* .... Prov 10:20
her *w* is far above rubies .. Prov 31:10

WORTHLESS
looking at *w* things .... Ps 119:37
A *w* person, a wicked ..... Prov 6:12
Indeed they are all *w* ...... Is 41:29
wooden idol is a *w* doctrine .. Jer 10:8

WORTHLESSNESS
long will you love *w* .... Ps 4:2

WORTHY
I am not *w* of the .... Gen 32:10
LORD, who is *w* to be ..... 2 Sam 22:4
who is *w* to be praised ...... Ps 18:3
sandals I am not *w* ...... Matt 3:11
inquire who in it is *w* ..... Matt 10:11
more than Me is not *w* .... Matt 10:37
invited were not *w* .... Matt 22:8
I am not *w* to stoop down .. Mark 1:7
and I am no longer *w* ..... Luke 15:19
strap I am not *w* to loose .. John 1:27
feet I am not *w* to loose ... Acts 13:25
present time are not *w* .... Rom 8:18
apostles, who am not *w* ... 1 Cor 15:9
to walk *w* of the calling ..... Eph 4:1
w of the gospel of Christ .... Phil 1:27
may walk *w* of the Lord ... Col 1:10
w of God who calls ...... 1 Thess 2:12
w of the kingdom of ..... 2 Thess 1:5
count you of this ...... 2 Thess 1:11
"The laborer is *w* .... 1 Tim 5:18
the world was not *w* ...... Heb 11:38
in a manner *w* of God ...... 3 John 6
white, for they are *w* ...... Rev 3:4

WOUND
I *w* and I heal .... Deut 32:39
My *w* is incurable .... Job 34:6
But God will *w* the .... Ps 68:21
and my *w* incurable .... Jer 15:18
and *w* their weak .... 1 Cor 8:12
and his deadly *w* .... Rev 13:3

WOUNDED
and my heart is *w* .... Ps 109:22
They struck me, they *w* .... Song 5:7
and *w* the serpent .... Is 51:9
But He was *w* for our ...... Is 53:5
there remained only *w* .... Jer 37:10
with which I was *w* ...... Zech 13:6
w him, and departed .... Luke 10:30
house naked and *w* ...... Acts 19:16
to the beast who was *w* .... Rev 13:14

WOUNDING
killed a man for *w* .... Gen 4:23

WOUNDS
He *w*, but His hands make .. Job 5:18
and binds up their *w* ...... Ps 147:3
Faithful are the *w* .... Prov 27:6
For her *w* are incurable ...... Mic 1:9
and bandaged his *w* ..... Luke 10:34

WOVEN
Her clothing is *w* with gold .. Ps 45:13
w from the top in one ..... John 19:23

WRANGLINGS
useless *w* of men of .... 1 Tim 6:5

WRAPPED
weeds were *w* around my .... Jon 2:5
he *w* it in a clean linen .... Matt 27:59
w Him in swaddling cloths .. Luke 2:7
his face was *w* with a ..... John 11:44

WRATH
w has gone out from ..... Num 16:46
provoked the LORD to *w* .... Deut 9:22
Had I not feared the *w* .... Deut 32:27
w kills a foolish .... Job 5:2
speak to them in His *w* ...... Ps 2:5
living and burning *w* .... Ps 58:9
Surely the *w* of man .... Ps 76:10
Your fierce *w* has gone .... Ps 88:16
Will Your *w* burn like ..... Ps 89:46
w we are terrified .... Ps 90:7
So I swore in My *w* .... Ps 95:11
in the day of His *w* .... Ps 110:5
death is the king's *w* .... Prov 16:14
The king's *w* is like ...... Prov 19:12
of great *w* will suffer .... Prov 19:19
w is heavier than .... Prov 27:3
W is cruel and anger a .... Prov 27:4
w I will give him .... Is 10:6
With a little *w* .... Is 54:8
in My *w* I struck you .... Is 60:10
I will pour out my *w* ...... Hos 5:10
w remember mercy .... Hab 3:2
you to flee from the *w* ..... Matt 3:7
see life, but the *w* .... John 3:36
For the *w* of God is .... Rom 1:18
up for yourself *w* .... Rom 2:5
the law brings about *w* .... Rom 4:15
wanting to show His *w* .... Rom 9:22
rather give place to *w* ..... Rom 12:19
not only because of *w* ..... Rom 13:5
outbursts of *w* .... 2 Cor 12:20
nature children of *w* .... Eph 2:3
sun go down on your *w* .... Eph 4:26
Let all bitterness, *w* .... Eph 4:31
delivers us from the *w* .. 1 Thess 1:10
w has come upon them .. 1 Thess 2:16
holy hands, without *w* .... 1 Tim 2:8
So I swore in My *w* .... Heb 3:11
not fearing the *w* .... Heb 11:27

for the *w* of man does .... James 1:20
throne and from the *w* ..... Rev 6:16
to you, having great *w* ..... Rev 12:12
of the wine of the *w* ...... Rev 14:8
winepress of the *w* .... Rev 14:19
for in them the *w* .... Rev 15:1
fierceness of His *w* .... Rev 16:19

WRATH OF GOD
w abides on him .... John 3:36
w is revealed from .... Rom 1:18
w comes upon the sons of .... Eph 5:6
of the wine of the *w* ..... Rev 14:10
great winepress of the *w* ... Rev 14:19
the *w* is complete .... Rev 15:1
the bowls of the *w* .... Rev 16:1

WRATH OF THE LORD
w was aroused against .... Num 11:33
for great is the *w* .... 2 Kin 22:13
w turned from him .... 2 Chr 12:12
fierce *w* is upon you .... 2 Chr 28:11
w fell upon Judah .... 2 Chr 29:8
w did not come upon .... 2 Chr 32:26
w arose against His .... 2 Chr 36:16
w was kindled against ..... Ps 106:40
w of hosts the land .... Is 9:19
w of hosts and in the day ... Is 13:13
in the day of the *w* .... Ezek 7:19

WRATHFUL
w man stirs up strife ...... Prov 15:18

WRESTLE
For we do not *w* .... Eph 6:12

WRESTLED
I have *w* with my sister ..... Gen 30:8
a Man *w* with him until .... Gen 32:24

WRETCHED
w man that I am .... Rom 7:24
know that you are *w* .... Rev 3:17

WRETCHEDNESS
do not let me see my *w* ... Num 11:15

WRINGING
w the nose produces ...... Prov 30:33

WRINKLE
not having spot or *w* .... Eph 5:27

WRITE
I will *w* on these tablets ...... Ex 34:1
"*W* these words .... Ex 34:27
w bitter things .... Job 13:26
w them on the tablet of ..... Prov 3:3
w them on the tablet .... Prov 7:3
'*W* this man down as .... Jer 22:30
and *w* it on their hearts ..... Jer 31:33
w them on their hearts ..... Heb 8:10
their minds I will *w* .... Heb 10:16
w no new commandment .... 1 John 2:7
a new commandment I *w* .. 1 John 2:8
I had many things to *w* .... 3 John 13
W the things which you .... Rev 1:19
w on him My new name .... Rev 3:12

WRITER
is the pen of a ready *w* ...... Ps 45:1

WRITING
the *w* was the *w* .... Ex 32:16
read the *w* to the king ..... Dan 5:17
And the *w* was: Jesus ..... John 19:19

WRITINGS
do not believe his *w* ...... John 5:47

WRITTEN
See AS IT IS WRITTEN; IT IS WRITTEN
which I have *w* .... Ex 24:12
tablets of stone, *w* .... Ex 31:18
tablets were *w* on both ..... Ex 32:15
book which You have *w* .... Ex 32:32
w with the finger of God ... Deut 9:10
law that are *w* in this .... Deut 28:58
w in this Book of the .... Deut 29:21
as it is *w* in the Book of .... Josh 8:31

---

w in the Law of the ...... 1 Chr 16:40
scroll of the Book it is *w* .... Ps 40:7
be *w* with the righteous .... Ps 69:28
book they all were *w* ..... Ps 139:16
Have I not *w* to you ..... Prov 22:20
is found *w* in the book ..... Dan 12:1
thus it is *w* by the prophet ... Matt 2:5
your names are *w* ...... Luke 10:20
are *w* may be fulfilled .... Luke 21:22
"What I have *w* .... John 19:22
as it is *w*, "The just shall ... Rom 1:17
law *w* in their hearts ...... Rom 2:15
it is *w*, "Vengeance is .... Rom 12:19
our epistle *w* in our hearts .. 2 Cor 3:2
ministered by us, *w* ...... 2 Cor 3:3
for it is *w*, "Cursed is .... Gal 3:10
because it is *w*, "Be holy ... 1 Pet 1:16
the stone a new name *w* .... Rev 2:17
names have not been *w* .... Rev 13:8
name *w* on their foreheads ... Rev 14:1
forehead a name was *w* .... Rev 17:5
the plagues that are *w* .... Rev 22:18

WRONG
sinned, we have done *w* ... 2 Chr 6:37
sin nor charge God with *w* ... Job 1:22
I cry out concerning *w* ..... Job 19:7
not charge them with *w* ... Job 24:12
no one to do them *w* ..... Ps 105:14
Do no *w* and do no .... Jer 22:3
I am doing you no *w* .... Matt 20:13
has done nothing *w* ..... Luke 23:41
of them suffer *w* .... Acts 7:24
Jews I have done no *w* .... Acts 25:10
Forgive me this *w* .... 2 Cor 12:13
But he who does *w* .... Col 3:25

WRONGDOING
say if they found any *w* ... Acts 24:20

WRONGED
give it to the one he has *w* ... Num 5:7
have seen how I am *w* ..... Lam 3:59
then that God has *w* .... Job 19:6
We have *w* no one .... 2 Cor 7:2
But if he has *w* .... Philem 18

WRONGFULLY
hate me *w* have multiplied .. Ps 38:19
endures grief, suffering *w* .. 1 Pet 2:19

WRONGS
me *w* his own soul .... Prov 8:36

WROTE
w on the tablets the words .. Ex 34:28
of the hand that *w* .... Dan 5:5
stooped down and *w* ...... John 8:6

WROUGHT
And skillfully *w* .... Ps 139:15

YEAR
first month of the *y* .... Ex 12:2
That fiftieth *y* shall be a .... Lev 25:11
In this *Y* of Jubilee, each ... Lev 25:13
we eat in the seventh *y* .... Lev 25:20
In the *Y* of Jubilee .... Lev 27:24
crown the *y* with Your ...... Ps 65:11
the acceptable *y* .... Is 61:2
be his until the *y* .... Ezek 46:17
to Jerusalem every *y* ...... Luke 2:41
went alone once a *y* .... Heb 9:7
of sins every *y* .... Heb 10:3

YEARS
and for days and *y* .... Gen 1:14
Are Your *y* like the .... Job 10:5
y should teach .... Job 32:7
I will remember the *y* ...... Ps 77:10
For a thousand *y* .... Ps 90:4
lives are seventy *y* .... Ps 90:10
Your *y* are throughout .... Ps 102:24
y will have no end .... Ps 102:27

---

when He was twelve *y* .... Luke 2:42
are not yet fifty *y* .... John 8:57
y will not fail .... Heb 1:12
for a thousand *y* .... Rev 20:2
with Him a thousand *y* ..... Rev 20:6

YES
let your 'Y' be 'Y,' .... Matt 5:37
No, but in Him was Y .... 2 Cor 1:19

YESTERDAY
For we were born *y* .... Job 8:9
Are like *y* when it is past ..... Ps 90:4
Jesus Christ is the same *y* .. Heb 13:8

YIELD
the land will *y* its fruit .... Lev 25:19
y yourselves to the LORD .. 2 Chr 30:8
That they may *y* a fruitful .. Ps 107:37
shall *y* her increase .... Ezek 34:27
But do not *y* to them ...... Acts 23:21
gentle, willing to *y*, full ... James 3:17

YIELDED
y to intense craving .... Num 11:4
y their bodies, that they .... Dan 3:28
good ground and *y* a crop .. Matt 13:8
voice, *y* up His spirit ..... Matt 27:50
rich man *y* plentifully .... Luke 12:16

YIELDS
the herb that *y* seed .... Gen 1:11
of the righteous *y* fruit .... Prov 12:12
it *y* the peaceable .... Heb 12:11

YOKE
you shall break his *y* ...... Gen 27:40
and He will put a *y* ...... Deut 28:48
Your father made our *y* .... 1 Kin 12:4
You have broken the *y* .... Is 9:4
a man to bear the *y* .... Lam 3:27
Take My *y* upon you ..... Matt 11:29
as are under the *y* .... 1 Tim 6:1

YOKED
Do not be unequally *y* .... 2 Cor 6:14

YOU ARE THE CHRIST
answered and said, "Y .... Matt 16:16
God: Tell us if Y .... Matt 26:63
and said to Him, "Y .... Mark 8:29
crying out and saying, "Y... Luke 4:41
If Y, tell us .... Luke 22:67
"If Y, save Yourself .... Luke 23:39
believe and know that Y ... John 6:69
If Y, tell us plainly .... John 10:24
Lord I believe that Y ..... John 11:27

YOUNG
His flesh shall be *y* .... Job 33:25
I have been *y* .... Ps 37:25
she may lay her *y* .... Ps 84:3
How can a *y* man cleanse ... Ps 119:9
The glory of *y* men is ..... Prov 20:29
y ones shall lie .... Is 11:7
dream dreams, your *y* ...... Joel 2:28
y man followed Him .... Mark 14:51
they admonish the *y* ...... Titus 2:4
I write to you, *y* .... 1 John 2:13

YOUNGER
they mock at me, men *y* .... Job 30:1
y son gathered all .... Luke 15:13
let him be as the *y* ...... Luke 22:26
y women as sisters .... 1 Tim 5:2
Likewise you *y* people ..... 1 Pet 5:5

YOURS
all that I have are *y* ...... 1 Kin 20:4
the battle is not *y* ...... 2 Chr 20:15
I am Y, save me .... Ps 119:94
Y is the kingdom .... Matt 6:13
Take what is *y* .... Matt 20:14
y is the kingdom .... Luke 6:20
And all Mine are Y ...... John 17:10
For all things are *y* ...... 1 Cor 3:21
for I do not seek *y* ...... 2 Cor 12:14

YOUTH

for he was only a y ......1 Sam 17:42
the LORD from my y ...... 1 Kin 18:12
the sins of my y .... Ps 25:7
the companion of her y .... Prov 2:17
with the wife of your y .... Prov 5:18
in the days of your y .... Eccl 11:9
and y are vanity .... Eccl 11:10
in the days of your y .... Eccl 12:1
the shame of your y .... Is 54:4
speak, for I am a y .... Jer 1:6
Do not say, 'I am a y,' for ..... Jer 1:7
the kindness of your y .... Jer 2:2
the days of your y .... Ezek 16:22
with the wife of his y .... Mal 2:15
I have kept from my y .... Matt 19:20
I have kept from my y .... Mark 10:20
I have kept from my y .... Luke 18:21
the flower of her y .... 1 Cor 7:36
no one despise your y ..... 1 Tim 4:12

YOUTHFUL

Flee also y lusts .... 2 Tim 2:22

YOUTHS

perceived among the y ...... Prov 7:7
y shall faint and be .... Is 40:30

ZACCHAEUS

Wealthy tax collector converted to
Christ, Luke 19:1–10

ZACHARIAS

Father of John the Baptist, Luke
1:5–17

ZADOK

Co-priest with Abiathar; remains
loyal to David, 2 Sam 15:24–29;
20:25
Rebuked by David, 2 Sam 19:11, 12
Does not follow Adonijah; anoints
Solomon, 1 Kin 1:8–45
Takes Abiathar's place, 1 Kin 2:35

ZALMUNNA

Midianite king, Judg 8:4–21

ZAREPHATH

Town of Sidon where Elijah revives
widow's son, 1 Kin 17:8–24; Luke
4:26

ZEAL

The z of the LORD of ..... 2 Kin 19:31
z has consumed me .... Ps 119:139
He shall stir up His z .... Is 42:13
have spoken it in My z .... Ezek 5:13
for Zion with great z .... Zech 8:2
"Z for Your house has ..... John 2:17
that they have a z .... Rom 10:2
z has stirred up the .... 2 Cor 9:2

ZEALOUS

he was z for his God ..... Num 25:13
"I have been very z ...... 1 Kin 19:10
'I am z for Zion with .... Zech 8:2
they are all z for the law .. Acts 21:20
since you are z .... 1 Cor 14:12
But it is good to be z .... Gal 4:18

z for good works .... Titus 2:14
Therefore be z and repent .. Rev 3:19

ZEBAH

King of Midian killed by Gideon, Judg
8:4–28

ZEBEDEE

Galilean fisherman; father of James
and John, Matt 4:21, 22

ZEBULUN

Sixth son of Jacob and Leah, Gen 30:19,
20
Prophecy concerning, Gen 49:13
—— Tribe of:
Numbered, Num 1:30, 31; 26:27
Territory assigned to, Josh 19:10–16
Joins Gideon in battle, Judg 6:34, 35
Some respond to Hezekiah's reforms,
2 Chr 30:10–18
Christ visits territory of, Matt 4:13–16

ZECHARIAH

King of Israel; last ruler of Jehu's dynasty, 2 Kin 15:8–12
—— Postexilic prophet and priest, Ezra
5:1; Zech 1:1, 7

ZEDEKIAH

Last king of Judah; uncle and successor
of Jehoiachin; reigns wickedly, 2 Kin
24:17–19; 2 Chr 36:10
Rebels against Nebuchadnezzar, 2 Chr
36:11–13
Denounced by Jeremiah, Jer 34:1–22
Consults Jeremiah, Jer 37; 38
Captured and taken to Babylon, 2 Kin
25:1–7; Jer 39:1–7

ZELOPHEHAD

Manassite whose five daughters secure
female rights, Num 27:1–7

ZEPHANIAH

Author of Zephaniah, Zeph 1:1
—— Priest and friend of Jeremiah
during Zedekiah's reign,
Jer 21:1

ZERUBBABEL

Descendant of David, 1 Chr 3:1–19
Leader of Jewish exiles, Neh 7:6, 7; Hag
2:21–23
Rebuilds the temple, Ezra 3:1–10; Zech
4:1–14

ZIBA

Saul's servant, 2 Sam 9:9
Befriends David, 2 Sam 16:1–4
Accused of deception by Mephibo-
sheth, 2 Sam 19:17–30

ZIKLAG

City on the border of Judah, Josh 15:1,
31
Held by David, 1 Sam 27:6
Overthrown by Amalekites, 1 Sam
30:1–31

ZILPAH

Leah's maid, Gen 29:24
Mother of Gad and Asher, Gen
30:9–13

ZIMRI

Simeonite prince slain by Phinehas,
Num 25:6–14
—— King of Israel for seven days, 1 Kin
16:8–20

ZIN

Wilderness through which the Israelites passed, Num 20:1
Border between Judah and Edom, Josh
15:1–3

ZION

Literally, an area in Jerusalem; called
the City of David, 2 Sam 5:6–9; 2 Chr
5:2
Used figuratively of God's kingdom, Ps
125:1; Heb 12:22; Rev 14:1

City of David, which is Z ... 1 Kin 8:1
City of David, which is Z ...2 Chr 5:2
the LORD, who dwells in Z ...Ps 9:11
Is Mount Z on the sides of .... Ps 48:2
in Your good pleasure to Z .. Ps 51:18
God will save Z and build ... Ps 69:35
And of Z it will be said .... Ps 87:5
the LORD shall build up Z .. Ps 102:16
the name of the LORD in Z .. Ps 102:21
back the captivity of Z ...... Ps 126:1
the LORD has chosen Z .... Ps 132:13
when we remembered Z ..... Ps 137:1
Z shall be redeemed with ..... Is 1:27
For out of Z shall go forth ..... Is 2:3
My people, who dwell in Z ... Is 10:24
shout, O Inhabitant of Z ... Is 12:6
hosts will reign on Mount Z .. Is 24:23
I lay in Z a stone for a .... Is 28:16
down to fight for Mount Z .... Is 31:4
come to Z with singing ...... Is 35:10
virgin, the daughter of Z ..... Is 37:22
I will place salvation in Z ... Is 46:13
the LORD will comfort Z....... Is 51:3
come to Z with singing ...... Is 51:11
Redeemer will come to Z .... Is 59:20
Z of the Holy One of Israel .. Is 60:14
Arise, and let us go up to Z .. Jer 31:6
to be forgotten in Z .... Lam 2:6
Blow the trumpet in Z ...... Joel 2:1
for the LORD dwells in Z .... Joel 3:21
on Mount Z there shall be ... Obad 17
For out of Z the law shall .... Mic 4:2
Sing, O daughter of Z .... Zeph 3:14
LORD will gain comfort Z .. Zech 1:17
rejoice, O daughter of Z .... Zech 2:10
Fear not, daughter of Z ... John 12:15
in Z a stumbling stone ..... Rom 9:33
will come out of Z .... Rom 11:26
Behold, I lay in Z a chief .... 1 Pet 2:6

ZIPPORAH

Daughter of Jethro; wife of Moses, Ex
18:1, 2

ZOAR

Ancient city of Canaan originally
named Bela, Gen 14:2, 8
Spared destruction at Lot's request,
Gen 19:20–23

ZOPHAR

Naamathite; friend of Job, Job 2:11

Map 1

THE NATIONS OF GENESIS 10

JAVAN   Descendants of Japheth (Gen. 10:2–5)
PUT   Descendants of Ham (Gen. 10:6–20)
LUD   Descendants of Shem (Gen. 10:21–31)

(Lydia)   Later Biblical name

GOMER

TOGARMAH

HITTITES

ASHKENAZ
(Scythians)

ASSHUR
(Assyria)

MADAI
(Medes)

ARAM
(Syria)

AMORITES

CANAAN

KITTIM
(Cyprus)

PHILISTINES

ELAM
(Persia)

ARPHAXAD

JOKTAN
(Arabia)

LUD
(Lydia)

JAVAN
(Greeks)

PUT

MIZRAIM
(Egypt)

Caspian Sea

Tigris

Euphrates

The Great Sea
(Mediterranean Sea)

Persian Gulf

Red Sea

Nile

Scale of Miles

0   100   200

© Thomas Nelson, Inc. 1983

Map 2

THE EXODUS FROM EGYPT

→ Route of the Exodus

⋯ Alternate routes of Red Sea crossing

→ Unsuccessful invasion of Canaan (Num. 14:39–45)

— Trade routes

? Exact location questionable

Scale of Miles

0   50   100

© Thomas Nelson, Inc. 1983

The Great Sea

Gaza

Hebron

Beersheba

Arad

Baal Zephon

Avaris

Qantir

Pithom

Succoth

Land of Goshen

Memphis

Nile

Way of the Philistines

Way of Shur

Wilderness of Zin

Wilderness of Paran

Route from Egypt to Arabia

Marah?

Elim?

Red Sea

MT. SINAI
HOREB

Kadesh
Barnea

Ezion Geber

Gulf of Aqaba

Arabah

Punon

Zoar

Salt Sea

MT. NEBO

Edom

Moab

Ammon

River Arnon

Brook Zered

Map 3
THE CONQUEST OF CANAAN

△ Philistine cities

▢ Cities of refuge

(1,742) Elevation, in feet

? Exact location questionable

Scale of Miles
0   10   20

4. In a northern thrust, Joshua moved from Gilgal all the way to Hazor (Josh. 11).

2. Joshua made peace with Gibeon, then moved through the Valley of Aijalon and defeated the five Amorite kings (Josh. 9—10).

1. Upon crossing the Jordan, Joshua camped awhile at Gilgal, then moved to take Jericho and Ai. Afterward he returned to Gilgal (Josh. 1—8).

3. From Makkedah, Joshua launched a southern campaign against Lachish, Hebron, Debir, and Gaza. Victorious, he returned to Gilgal (Josh. 10).

Sidon
Damascus
MT. LEBANON (11,000)
MT. HERMON (9,200)
Tyre
Dan
Kedesh
Hazor
Bashan
Acco
Sea of Galilee
Golan? Ashtaroth
Galilee
MT. CARMEL (1,742)
R. Kishon
Jokneam
+ MT. TABOR (1,843)
Dor
En Dor
HILL OF MOREH
Edrei
Megiddo
Shunem
R. Yarmuk
Well of Harod
Ramoth
Ibleam
MT. GILBOA (1,696)
Beth Shean
The Great Sea
Gilead
Tirzah
Zaphon
MT. EBAL (3,080)
Shechem
R. Jabbok
Succoth
MT. GERIZIM (2,890)
Aphek
Tappuah
Shiloh
Ammon
Joppa
Shiloh
River Jordan
Rabbah
Jabneel
Bethel
Ai
Gilgal
Gezer Aijalon Gibeon
Jericho
Ekron Timnah
Kirjath Jearim
Gibeah
Jerusalem
Heshbon
Bezer?
Ashdod
Makkedah
Beth Shemesh
+ MT. NEBO (2,700)
Gath Jarmuth
Bethlehem
Medeba
Ashkelon
Azekah
Philistia
Adullam
Mareshah
Lachish
Hebron
The Salt Sea
Dibon
Aroer
Gaza
Debir
En Gedi
(−1,300)
R. Arnon
Moab
Beersheba

© Thomas Nelson, Inc., 1983

Map 4
THE KINGDOM YEARS

Probable extent of Israelite control during the Kingdom of Solomon, c. 950 B.C.

The Kingdoms of Israel and Judah, c. 860 B.C.

Boundary between Israel and Judah

? Exact location questionable

0   25   50
Scale of Miles

1

Riblah

Zobah

Byblos

2

Sidon
Zarephath
Phoenicia
MT. LEBANON
MT. HERMON
Damascus

Tyre
Dan
Kedesh
Syria

Hazor

3

Acco
Sea of Chinnereth
Ashtaroth
MT. CARMEL
R. Yarmuk
Golan?

The Great Sea
Jokneam
Megiddo
Dor
Jezreel
Ramoth Gilead

Taanach
MT. GILBOA
Jabesh Gilead
Dothan
Tirzah
Zaphon
Samaria
Jordan R.
Succoth
Shechem
R. Jabbok

Aphek
Shiloh
Ammon
Joppa
ISRAEL
Rabbah

4

Mizpah
Bethel
Gezer
Jabneh
Ramah
Heshbon
Philistia
Jerusalem
Beth Shemesh
Bethlehem
Medeba
Ashkelon
Tekoa
Eglon?
Adullam
Dibon
Gaza
Hebron
The Salt Sea
Aroer
Ziklag?
Debir
R. Arnon
Arad
Beersheba
Moab
Kir Hareseth

Zoar
R. Zered

5

JUDAH
Bozrah

Kadesh Barnea
Edom

Brook of Egypt

Teman

6

Note: Other place names significant during the time of the Kingdoms are found on Map 3.

Ezion Geber
Elath

© Thomas Nelson, Inc., 1983

Map 5
JERUSALEM—
FROM DAVID TO CHRIST

Bethesda Place names of Christ's time

Ophel Suggested locations of place names from earlier kingdom period

? Exact location questionable

Suggested extent of the City of David

Suggested extent of Solomon's expansion

Suggested extent of Hezekiah's expansion

Probable extent of Nehemiah's reconstruction

Possible location of walls during Christ's time

Scale

0   250   500 Yards

Christ's Tomb?
Calvary?

Bethesda

Sheep Gate

Gethsemane?

Horse Gate

KIDRON VALLEY

Gate of Benjamin

Temple

Royal Palace

Ophel

Spring of Gihon

Praetorium

Gate of Ephraim

Hezekiah's Tunnel

City of David

Fountain Gate

Christ's Tomb?
Calvary?

Mishneh

Pool of Siloam

Refuse Gate

Caiaphas' House?

Caiaphas' House?

Herod's Palace

Essene Gate

VALLEY OF HINNOM

Map 6
PALESTINE
IN
CHRIST'S TIME

(1,742) Elevation, in feet

? Exact location
   questionable

0   10   20
Scale of Miles

© Thomas Nelson, Inc., 1983

Map 7

**PAUL'S FIRST
AND SECOND JOURNEYS
(Acts 13—14; 15:39—18:22)**

First missionary journey, with Barnabas
and Mark (c. A.D. 46–48)

Second missionary journey, with Silas
(c. A.D. 49–52)

© Thomas Nelson, Inc., 1983

Map 8

**PAUL'S THIRD
AND FOURTH JOURNEYS
(Acts 18:23—21:16; 27—28:16)**

Third missionary journey (c. A.D. 53–57)

Fourth missionary journey (c. A.D. 59–62)

© Thomas Nelson, Inc., 1983

Map 9

THE HOLY LAND
IN MODERN TIMES

Area occupied by Israel
since June, 1967

0   25   50
Scale of Miles

LEBANON

Tripoli

Beirut

BEKAA VALLEY

Damascus

Sidon

LEBANON MTS.

ANTI-LEBANON MTS.

SYRIA

Tyre

Dan

U.N. Buffer Zone
1973 Line

Qiryat
Shemona

Quneitra
1967 Cease-Fire Line

Nahariyya

Safad

Golan
Heights

Akko

Sea of
Galilee

Dera

Haifa

Tiberias

Ramtha

Nazareth

Afula

Mediterranean Sea

Beth Shean

Hadera

Jarash

Netanya

Tulkarm

Jordan River

Nablus

Herzliyya

West
Bank

Tel Aviv
Yafo

Petah
Tiqwa

Amman

Rishon le Zion

Lod

Ramla

Ramalah

Ashdod

Jericho

Jerusalem

Madaba

Ashqelon

Bethlehem

Gaza

Qiryat
Gat

Hebron

Dhiban

En Gedi

Dead
Sea

Beersheba

Al-Arish

Karak

JORDAN

ISRAEL

EGYPT

Negev

Arabah

Sinai

Elat   Aqaba